A KWIC CONCORDANCE
TO LEWIS CARROLL'S
ALICE'S ADVENTURES IN WONDERLAND
AND *THROUGH THE LOOKING-GLASS*

GARLAND REFERENCE LIBRARY
OF THE HUMANITIES
(VOL. 676)

Other Volumes in This Series

A KWIC CONCORDANCE
TO LEWIS CARROLL'S
ALICE'S ADVENTURES IN WONDERLAND
AND *THROUGH THE LOOKING-GLASS*

Michael J. Preston

With a Critical Introduction by
James R. Kincaid

GARLAND PUBLISHING, INC. • NEW YORK & LONDON
1986

This volume is one of a series of Contextual Concordances published by Garland under the general editorship of Michael J. Preston, Director of The Center for Computer Research in the Humanities, University of Colorado at Boulder.

Library of Congress Cataloging-in-Publication Data

Preston, Michael James.
  A KWIC concordance to Lewis Carroll's Alice's adventures in Wonderland and Through the looking-glass.

  (Garland reference library of the humanities ; vol. 676)
  Includes index.
  1. Carroll, Lewis, 1832–1898—Concordances.
2. Carroll, Lewis, 1832–1898. Alice's adventures in Wonderland—Concordances. 3. Carroll, Lewis, 1832–1898. Through the looking-glass—Concordances. 4. Children's stories, English—Concordances. 5. Fantastic fiction, English—Concordances. I. Title. II. Series: Garland reference library of the humanities ; v. 676.
  PR4612.A2 1986   823'.8   86-9965
  ISBN 0-8240-9914-1 (alk. paper)

Printed on acid-free, 250-year-life paper
Manufactured in the United States of America

For
Eugene Floyd Irey (August 6, 1912–December 26, 1985)
and
Stephanie Michele Preston (December 8, 1985–   )

CONTENTS

PREFACE

This concordance is based on Donald J. Gray's edition of Lewis Carroll's *Alice's Adventures in Wonderland* and *Through the Looking-Glass and what Alice found there* (New York: W. W. Norton & Company, Inc., 1971) supplemented by *The Wasp in a Wig: A "Suppressed" Episode of "Through the Looking-Glass and what Alice found there,"* ed. Edward Guiliano (New York: Clarkson N. Potter, Inc., 1977). Although *Wonderland* and *Looking-Glass* are distinct works, they are sufficiently inter-related to suggest inclusion in a concordance together; the Wasp-episode was added because it is additional *Alice* material, important and yet small enough not to clutter up a concordance to Carroll's (Charles Lutwidge Dodgson's) two published classics. This volume is designed to be compatible with my *Concordance to the Verse of Lewis Carroll* (New York: Garland Publishing, Inc., 1985) even though the two concordances are not slavishly identical; prose texts differ formally from verse and require somewhat different treatment. Because of the vast readership of the *Alice* books, it seems best to define what concordances are and then describe what this volume is and some of its special features.

A concordance may generally be conceived of as an alphabetic listing of all the different words in a text, under each of which appear quotations ("contexts") illustrating all occurrences, usually with references back to the original text. Such reference works have a long history, and concordances to the Bible and to the works of Shakespeare are well known (Dodgson owned these and others). Even such medieval writers as William Langland, the author of *Piers Plowman*, seem to have written with a concordance at hand.[1]

Most concordances omit words that few would be interested in, as does this one, but their defining feature is that they illustrate the use of the included words by the quotation of the contexts in which the words occur. This allows one to examine each word in its verbal context and to compare one context to another. Other kinds of reference works are sometimes called concordances—usually word indexes which contain the alphabetic list of words and the references but omit the contexts in which the words occur—but that kind of compilation is very different from a concordance and of less use for the study of complex texts. A word index reveals vocabulary generally, but a concordance is a more broadly useful "research tool" because it is a gross rearrangement of the concorded text itself in that related portions are brought together for study according to the systematic but arbitrary sequence of the alphabet. Although a concordance may be reduced in function by an uninformed user to a word index or even an alphabetized list of words with frequencies, it does provide *all* the evidence of the text itself, brought together according to the specific principles of its composition.[2] The sheer numbers of those who read the *Alice* books argue in favor of there being such a systematic reference work, even though to some that may seem to question certain hierarchical or class-bound assumptions of conventional literary study, assumptions which are often the reasons for making and publishing concordances.[3]

Two sets of appendices appear in this volume. The first set is now traditional and largely the by-product of the use of computers. This includes separate Ranking Frequency Lists for *Alice's Adventures in Wonderland* (26,765 words) and *Through the Looking-Glass* (29,649 words); this includes the titles of chapters because Carroll so obviously considered them a part of his texts, but not the 1,390 words of the Wasp-episode.[4] The frequency lists provide the words of each text arranged by frequency of occurrence, with the percentage of the total words in the text that each word represents. Thus "the" is the most frequently occurring word in *Wonderland* with 1,653 occurrences which represent 6.18% of the total words in the text; "the" is also the most frequently occurring word in *Looking-Glass* with 1,607 occurrences, or 5.42% of the text. The third appendix in the first set is a Reverse Index of the 4,162 different word-forms in the *Alice* books, including the Wasp-episode; this is the product of sorting all the word-forms alphabetically from their ends, thus bringing together related compound words as well as similarly inflected words, such as present participles. The Ranking Frequency Lists, dearly loved by statisticians and casual browsers, are often at least as suggestive as directly useful, but the Reverse Index is usually of considerable practical use in locating related entries in the main concordance. Typical of such computer-generated lists, the Ranking Frequency Lists are insensitive to homographs, etc., while the Reverse Index is sensitive to inflection; whether these are virtues or vices depends upon what the user needs or expects. The second set of appendices is discussed below (pp. xv-xviii).

It might be considered unorthodox to admit to such a practice, but I read only certain texts in standard scholarly editions. I find most definitive editions too bulky to read comfortably or to take with me where I might have occasion to read. This means that relatively inexpensive paper-covered copies get marked up, dog-eared, battered, and toted around, while better editions reside in bookcases and are consulted only on occasion. Although I generally agree with editors of literary texts that one should read what is closest to what an author wrote, in application that seems too narrow a view for such texts as *Wonderland* and *Looking-Glass*. Although these *are* literary classics, they are unlike other classics in that they are commonly read by most of us as we grow up; they are also read by many adults with neither academic interests nor aspirations. My reason for using the "popular" Norton edition rather than the first editions, the last printings which Carroll corrected and emended, or even the Nonesuch edition is that the Norton is a sound text widely read in American universities. If one is concerned with the influence of a text, what an author *wrote* really matters little; it is what readers *read* that is significant.[5] Fortunately, even popular editions of *Wonderland* and *Looking-Glass* are usually only somewhat debased, unlike children's versions of *Gulliver's Travels* which often simplify the first half and omit the second.

In basing this concordance on a text that is essentially sound and widely available at a relatively low cost, I intend to make the concordance convenient for serious readers to use while they are in the process of marking up, dog-earing, and otherwise reading their copies of the *Alice* books; they will not have to go through the too-common process of first having to obtain a less accessible edition to use with the concordance and then transfer what they find from working with the unfamiliar copy and the concordance back to their marked-up texts. The cumbersome nature of that kind of inquiry keeps all but the most determined from using any concordance which is not based on the text that they are reading. On the other hand, I hope that Carroll specialists will understand that I would prefer to put some of them to a minor bother rather than put off the much larger number of occasional readers of Carroll who might become more serious about their reading if barriers were not put in their way; there is, after all, no definitive edition of the Alice books, but rather better or more preferred editions.[6]

This concordance is in the KWIC (Key Word in Context) format and is much like *A KWIC Concordance to the Plays of the Wakefield Master* (New York: Garland Publishing, Inc., 1982) which Jean Pfleiderer and I published to illustrate to students of early English drama the potential of computer-generated concordances. All the different word-forms in the Alice texts appear as "headwords" in alphabetical order on the left of the page—see the example on page xiii—and under each appear references to those texts together with fragments of the text in which the various word-forms appear. The reference is by title and chapter (T5 is the fifth chapter in *Through the Looking-Glass*; A10 is the tenth chapter in *Alice's Adventures in Wonderland*; T8W is the Wasp-episode, cut from the eighth chapter of Looking-Glass) as well as by page-and-line number in the Norton edition (156:35 indicates page 156, line 35); a lower-case *t* indicates further that the context is the title of a chapter, while *I* and *C* signify introductory and concluding verses. Because the chapters are so short, the title-chapter reference may well be sufficient for those who have read the texts repeatedly and prefer other editions.

References to related entries also appear in the alphabetic sequence in "See" and "See also" bracketed comments; entries for word-forms which Carroll did not use are marked by initial hyphens. In inserting these references and cross-references, I assume that one who is looking at the entry for LESSON-BOOK will also consult BOOK, but that few who are looking at the entry for BOOK would think of LESSON-BOOK and MEMORANDUM-BOOK; these are intended primarily to be of convenience for inexperienced concordance-users. An experienced user of concordances would consult the Reverse Index as well.

The contexts of the concordance have been determined by computer, with the concorded word approximately centered; in the main concordance forty-six characters are allowed for preceding context, sixty-two for the concorded word and succeeding context. Word-fragments, which might have been included in the available space, have been suppressed as more often misleading than useful; they are also ugly. For similar reasons, paragraph-boundaries and the beginnings and endings of inset quotations—usually verse—terminate the printed context; white space following a cited context indicates the end of a text-unit, while preceding white space indicates the beginning. Thus, under SCENTED—its frequency of three is given in parentheses—the first context will be seen to end a paragraph while the second context begins one. The text as quoted is intended to represent the Norton edition *verbatim et literatim* with the following exceptions: italics are represented by underscoring; virgules have been inserted to mark verse-line boundaries; the Mouse's tail/tale has, sadly, been reduced to conventional linear text, but the lines from the Looking-glass book, although not printed in proper mirror image, have been printed backwards. (See the entries for 'TWAS, BRILLIG, SLITHY, TOVES, etc.)[7]

Not all word-forms are fully concorded here. In order to keep the volume close to a reasonable size, the contexts for sixty-two word-forms of lesser general interest have been excluded, dangerous as such a selection is for any complex text. These include the articles *a, an,* and *the,* the conjunctions *and, but,* and *however,* certain high-frequency prepositions which also function as adverbs, some interrogatives, and standard forms of pronouns. Non-standard pronouns, because they often reveal stereotypical attitudes—language-based "Irish jokes," for example—are retained as are contractions; "it" is excluded as both a pronoun and a "slot-filler," but "there" is retained because it illustrates as well as "it" Carroll's use of impersonal constructions. Entries for these excluded words appear in their proper alphabetic sequence in the concordance, together with their frequencies of occurrence, but without contexts or references. Excluding these few words reduced the size of the concordance by approximately one-third.

One aspect of the body of the concordance still needs discussion: the sequence in which the contexts appear under the headwords. Those who do not use concordances often perceive of a concordance as a means of finding whether or where certain words or images occur and how often; they may even consider it a means of locating or verifying particular quotations. Although concordances have those simple uses, they can be far more useful—and suggestive—than one would infer from the general habits of the profession. This concordance, although it is intended to meet the needs of conventional concordance-users, is also an attempt to suggest additional uses, both of concordances and of concordances used in conjunction with machine-readable texts and adequate software.

Contexts have traditionally been arranged in the order in which they appear in the concorded text—one can cite the concordance to Chaucer as an example—and this is frequently useful beyond lexicographical inquiry; such a text-ordered concordance allows one to trace a word through a concorded text in a linear fashion. But even hand-made concordances often betray their makers' uneasiness with this arrangement, particularly since it is based on the assumption that the individual word is the primary unit of signification. Bartlett's concordance to Shakespeare, for example, contains many multi-word entries as sub-categories, particularly for words of relatively high frequency such as "full." Bartlett recognized that to reduce a text to the sum of its words was inadequate, and he took some pride in stating in his preface that he had separated out certain word-combinations. Although computer-technology allows one to sort texts various ways if they are properly prepared, *which way* becomes the problem rather than *whether.* No longer need one lament, as did Osgood in his preface to his Spenser concordance, that he would rather have rearranged his entries but that the magnitude of the task prevented him.

In this concordance I have arranged the entries according to the alphabetic sequence of the words which follow the concorded word in order to highlight verbal repetition. Thus an occurrence of a word which has nothing following it—that is, a word which ends a text-unit—appears first and then the various occurrences which

SCENT (1)
    T5   156:35 had begun to fade, and to lose all their scent and beauty, from the very moment that she picked them?
SCENTED (3)
    T5   156:23 at one bunch after another of the darling scented rushes.
    T5   156: 6   "Oh, please! There are some scented rushes!" Alice cried in a sudden transport of delight.
    T5   156:36 very moment that she picked them? Even real scented rushes, you know, last only a very little while--and
SCEPTRE (1)
    T9   199:25 world it was Alice that said / 'I've a sceptre in hand, I've a crown on my head. / Let the
SCHOOL (5) [See also DAY-SCHOOL]
    A10   82:18 thought Alice. "I might just as well be at school at once." However, she got up, and began to repeat it,
    A9   76: 5 the best of educations--in fact, we went to school every day--"
    A9   74:42 sobbing a little now and then, "we went to school in the sea. The master was an old Turtle--we used to
    A9   75: 9   "Yes, we went to school in the sea, though you mayn't believe it--"
    A9   76:13 "Ah! Then yours wasn't a really good school," said the Mock Turtle in a tone of great relief. "Now,
SCHOOLBOYS (1)
    T4   139:13 They looked so exactly like a couple of great schoolboys, that Alice couldn't help pointing her finger at
SCHOOL-ROOM (1)
    A1   8:32 things of this sort in her lessons in the school-room, and though this was not a very good opportunity
SCOLD (1)
    T1   112: 7 in fact, because there'll be no one here to scold me away from the fire. Oh, what fun it'll be, when they
SCOLDED (1)
    A1   12:24 very seldom followed it), and sometimes she scolded herself so severely as to bring tears into her eyes;
SCOLDING (1)
    T9   192: 3 a severe tone (she was always rather fond of scolding herself), "It'll never do for you to be lolling about
-SCOPE [See GYROSCOPE, MICROSCOPE, TELESCOPE]
SCORNFUL (1)
    T6   163:30 use a word," Humpty Dumpty said, in rather a scornful tone, "it means just what I choose it to mean--
SCORNFULLY (1)
    T5   157:10 home with me!" But the Sheep only laughed scornfully, and went on with her knitting.
SCRAMBLE (1)
    T1   108:18 just to see how it would look: this led to a scramble, in which the ball rolled down upon the floor, and
SCRAMBLED (4)
    T5   156:32 cheeks and dripping hair and hands, she scrambled back into her place, and began to arrange her
    T1   108: 3 a voice as she could manage--and then she scrambled back into the arm-chair, taking the kitten and the
    T8   183: 6 "What makes you say that?" he asked, as he scrambled back into the saddle, keeping hold of Alice's hair
    T9   202:26 and three of them (who looked like kangaroos) scrambled into the dish of roast mutton, and began eagerly
SCRAMBLING (3)
    A4   30:41 guess of what sort it was) scratching and scrambling about in the chimney close above her: then, saying
    T4   142:12 All hopping through the frothy waves, / And scrambling to the shore.
    T1   113:22 Lily! My imperial kitten!" and she began scrambling wildly up the side of the fender.
SCRATCHING (1)
    A4   30:41 (she couldn't guess of what sort it was) scratching and scrambling about in the chimney close above her
SCREAM (8)
    T4   146:28 NEW RATTLE!" and his voice rose to a perfect scream.
    T6   168: 1 Humpty Dumpty raised his voice almost to a scream as he repeated this verse, and Alice thought, with a
    T3   132: 3 voice began, when it was drowned by a shrill scream from the engine, and everybody jumped up in alarm,
    A12   97:10 came flying down upon her; she gave a little scream, half of fright and half of anger, and tried to beat
    T5   152:23 "But why don't you scream now?" Alice asked, holding her hands ready to put over
    T8   184:18 than a live horse," Alice said, with a little scream of laughter, in spite of all she could do to prevent it
    A8   65:38 ears--" the Rabbit began. Alice gave a little scream of laughter. "Oh, hush!" the Rabbit whispered in a
    T8W   20: 9   Alice began with a little scream of laughter, which she turned into a cough as well as
SCREAMED (5)
    T9   202:21 drink your health--Queen Alice's health!" she screamed at the top of her voice, and all the guests began
    A10   78:30   "Swim after them!" screamed the Gryphon.
    A5   42:27   "Serpent!" screamed the Pigeon.
    A8   65: 3 "Leave off that!" screamed the Queen. "You make me giddy." And then, turning to
    T9   203: 7 "Take care of yourself!" screamed the White Queen, seizing Alice's hair with both her
SCREAMING (5)
    T5   152:25   "Why, I've done all the screaming already," said the Queen. "What would be the good of
    T1   114: 5 use, and, as the poor little Lily was nearly screaming herself into a fit, she hastily picked up the Queen
    A8   64: 6 at her for a moment like a wild beast, began screaming "Off with her head! Off with--"
    T5   152: 2 a mistake somewhere--," when the Queen began screaming, so loud that she had to leave the sentence
    A8   68:12 she heard the Queen's voice in the distance, screaming with passion. She had already heard her sentence
SCREAMS (1)
    T5   152: 6   Her screams were so exactly like the whistle of a steam-engine,
-SCREW [See CORKSCREW]
SCROLL (1) [See also PARCHMENT-SCROLL]
    A11   86: 6 Rabbit, with a trumpet in one hand, and a scroll of parchment in the other. In the very middle of the
SCRUBBING (1)
    T12 207:30 in my dream--Dinah! Do you know that you're scrubbing a White Queen? Really, it's most disrespectful of
SCURRIED (1)
    A2   15:34 dropped the white kid-gloves and the fan, and scurried away into the darkness as hard as he could go.
SEA (17)
    A9   76:17 said Alice; "living at the bottom of the sea."
    A2   18:19 idea was that she had somehow fallen into the sea, "and in that case I can go back by railway," she said to
    A10   78:29   "--as far out to sea as you can--"
    A10   80: 2 us up and throw us, with the lobsters, out to sea!" / But the snail replied "Too far, too far!", and gave a
    A10   80:25 Turtle: "crumbs would all wash off in the sea. But they have their tails in their mouths; and the reason
    A10   78:31   "Turn a somersault in the sea!" cried the Mock Turtle, capering wildly about.
    A10   78: 8 "You may not have lived much under the sea--" ("I haven't," said Alice)--"and perhaps you were never

are followed by words beginning with *a*, *b*, *c*, and so on. Under SCREAM one finds "scream" ending a text-unit followed by "scream as he repeated." The eight entries of SCREAM end with three occurrences of "scream of laughter," which—suggestively— occur in the eighth chapter of *Wonderland*, the eighth chapter of *Looking-Glass*, and the Wasp episode deleted from the eighth chapter of *Looking-Glass*. Whether or not there is any significance to this pattern, there *is* a definite significance in that "scream of laughter" means something far different from what one normally associates with the word "scream."[8] Thus this arrangement, like Bartlett's, brings multi-word patterns to the foreground which, although useful in themselves in that they reveal a higher level of signification than the sum of the particular words, suggest to the serious reader of Carroll the kinds of linkages identified by Rabinovitz in his recent study of Samuel Beckett's early fiction;[9] certainly no one would assert that "happy summer days" was used twice by accident of language, especially since Carroll places the phrase in quotation marks the second time it appears. It is my belief that this particular ar- rangement of contexts will facilitate both the word-and-phrase-level study of Carroll's use of language and also his larger patterns of internal reference. We should never forget that Carroll's library, as auctioned off after his death,[10] contained many vol- umes of proverbs, idioms, and other multi-word units nor that Carroll lavished an immense amount of care on the *Alice* books. Whatever else they may be about, the *Alice* books are about the ambiguities of language, primarily written, and how that subverts both logic and narrative structure.

But reading the contexts for "scream" reveals more than the pattern "scream of laughter." What we find is that "a little scream of laughter" occurs three times. Thus what precedes a particular word may be as significant as what follows it in a particular entry. Our ingrained habit of reading to the right may obscure the consideration that other rearrangements of text just might be as significant—or even more significant— than sorting what follows a concorded word. Re-reading the "scream" contexts reveals that "little scream" occurs four times, with two of them being a part of the longer phrase "with a little scream" and the other two "gave a little scream." However, "gave a little scream of laughter" differs considerably from "gave a little scream, half of fright and half of anger." Here we have a characteristic playing off of a behavioral aspect of the language of texts: pattern, expectation, frustration or fulfillment. The quasi- formulaic character of these entries suggests that one consider Carroll's frequent reference to fairy-tales and the language-structure of oral formulae and its signifi- cance; it also suggests one consider the less-studied formulae of Victorian language surrounding young girls in popular fiction as well as the discourse of late-nineteenth- century adults about young girls.[11] Some of this is irretrievably lost, but it should be thought about nonetheless. However, from a computer-eye viewpoint, let us think simply about arranging entries according to what precedes a concorded word rather than the more conventional left-to-right sorting. This introduces the second set of appendices.

When one initially confronts the 847 "Alice"'s in the main concordance, one may well be overwhelmed by the number of occurrences because we are so used to working with a few instances from which we abstract significant patterns or, as often, create patterns. This is an interesting contradiction of our belief that frequency is indicative of significance; certainly "Alice" *is* significant of one level of content in the *Alice* books.

But here the KWIC contexts lay out visually in an interesting marriage of computer "data processing" and a kind of computer "graphics" a large number of patterns which one might investigate. First of all, the first occurrences of "Alice" cited have no following context because "Alice" ends a text-unit; these, because there is the same "nothing" to sort on throughout, appear in text-order. Here, upon reflection, one sees that one can trace the ends of things: the paragraphs that end with "Alice."

But because we are generally more concerned with studying things than no-things, early on we encounter "Alice, a little timidly" which occurs in *Wonderland*, chapters 6, 8, and 10, but never in *Looking-Glass*. "Alice asked in a tone of great curiosity" appears word-for-word in A10 and T8 at the end of paragraphs. "Alice thought to herself" occurs three times in *Wonderland*, but nine times in *Looking-glass*. Here are narrated comments begging for analysis. Patterns lie everywhere on the surface, but is there more? Very rarely do such phrases form obvious clusters, and rarely are there large numbers of identical phrases. The surface evidence points towards extreme care having been taken that repetitive phrases not occur very often in proximity. Does this imply that the two occurrences of "Alice was silent" in A7 and T6 require closer scrutiny? Perhaps so, but because this essay introduces a concordance, I leave that question and the others unanswered. What is significant here is that, because the entries are re-arranged on the arbitrary basis of what follows the concorded word, a whole variety of patterns emerge from what would be an otherwise overwhelming, if not boring, "Alice" entry.

What appears in the main concordance suggests another arrangement of text. This becomes the step into the Wonderland of computer applications, beyond, of course, the KWIC form and the extended sort which no reasonable human would produce. But when one has the technology at one's disposal, one can sort entries based on what precedes a key word just as readily as upon what follows. And if what follows Alice—often what Alice did—is of significance, then what precedes Alice— the kind of Alice it was—should also be of significance. (See pp. 555–565.)

Just as Alice ends many text-units, she also begins a good many; these appear in text-order as in the forward-sorted concordance, thus allowing one to see how "Alice" begins text-units. Later on in the reverse-sorted concordance, we find many occurrences of "cried Alice," "exclaimed Alice," and "said Alice," just as in the left-to-right-sorted concordance there were many occurrences of "Alice cried," "Alice explained" (but *not* "exclaimed"), and "Alice said." "Poor Alice" occurs eleven times in *Wonderland*, but just three in *Looking-Glass*. "Pleaded poor Alice" and "thought poor Alice" are obvious sub-categories.

If such phrase-level relationships are suggestive, or of use, then the technology allows a looser level of matching. A Multi-Word KWIC Concordance (pp. 569–574) identifies similar sequences of words, skipping over those supplied—assume here that it was an arbitrary list—which are considered insignificant. This particular appendix contains nothing that is not in the main body of the concordance, but here there is a highlighting of patterns that often take more sifting to locate in a conventional concordance. Certainly the two occurrences of "Alice considered a little" appear together in the body of the concordance, but "frightened at the sudden change" and "frightened by this very sudden change" are not paired up so neatly there.

Text-ordered entries were mentioned earlier as traditional for hand-made concordances (and imitated in early computer-generated concordances), but the text-ordered examples on pp. 577–580 are intended to exaggerate the possibility of plotting a word-form through a text by pulling together the "same" and "related" words.[12] The first entry, RABBIT, includes "rabbit-hole," "rabbit's," and "rabbits" in addition to "rabbit." Just as the extended sorting in a KWIC concordance turned the concordance into a kind of graphic display of textual relationships, so this turns the text-references (with contexts for verification) into a kind of textual analogue to a histogram: one can thus plot the rabbit "in time" through *Wonderland*.

DINAH, the next entry in the text-ordered concordance, introduces some complexities. That word occurs in the first four chapters of *Wonderland* and in the first and twelfth chapters of *Looking-Glass*. All references to Dinah grow out of the manuscript *Alice's Adventures Underground*, and the published version is significant for Carroll's not having elaborated on this. What is even more significant is that *Looking-Glass* uses Dinah only as a part of its frame of reference, a connection between the two books beyond the person of Alice. The pattern of KITTY reinforces that of DINAH in that "kitty" is not used except in the frame for *Looking-Glass*. These linear patterns are reinforced by the theme-word CURIOSITY ("curious," "curiouser," "curiosity," and "curious-looking") which should call to mind such earlier books as *A Puzzle for a Curious Girl* (1803). Although the majority of the occurrences of "curious" appear in *Wonderland*, a sufficient number—fifteen of forty-one—occur in *Looking-Glass*, comprising a repeated, though subdued, theme there.

CROQUET, however, suggests the overt structure Carroll was working from. This "word" (including "croquet-ground," "croqueted," and "croqueting") appears just in *Wonderland*. There is the one reference in chapter one, four anticipatory occurrences in chapter six, the culmination in chapter eight, and one last reference in chapter nine. What seems significant here is that the entire croquet-episode is presented by Carroll as growing out of one "real" reference to croquet. As in a dream, one incident results in an elaborate episode. The other examples in this appendix extend this approach and, at the same time, illustrate the complications inherent in an ambiguous language.

The concordance to italicized words (pp. 583–592) is intended to affirm what most readers of the *Alice* books recognize as they read—that Carroll was playing with spoken language and that he was attempting to "point" his readers with his graphics. Anyone at all acquainted with *The Nursery "Alice"* is aware just how precarious this device—as well as the attitude it signifies—really is. In *Looking-Glass* there is a greater density of italicized control of the reader, and one might speculate that Carroll revealed in this way his increasing loss of rapport with his precious child-friends. But what is significant to the computing context is that a generally-ignored feature of a text may be manipulated to one's advantage in a computer environment. Just as sorting on the nothing that marks the beginnings and endings of text-units revealed certain patterns earlier, here sorting on non-alphabetic somethings reveals yet other patterns; dashes might have been sorted on in order to bring together the various broken structures which abound in the *Alice* books.

The final appendix (pp. 595–628) is a reverse KWIC concordance to particular words; with it we return to the form of the reverse-sorted "Alice" (pp. 555–565). Here, in part because of the selection of the entries, the quasi-formulaic nature of Carroll's language stands out on every page. Words are sometimes words, but more often parts of larger units: "deal" occurs twenty-one times, but of those, ten are "a good deal" and eight are "a great deal." All of the entries, from "anxiously" to "work," illustrate that curious feature of the English language: an uncertainty about whether the primary unit of significance is the word or some other unit.

One of the more astounding structures is revealed by the eighty-four occurrences of "tone." That Carroll should be concerned with this level of qualification in language should surprise no one, particularly in the light of having already examined his use of italics for emphasis. This sensitivity to nuance in language is, in my own personal experience, quite in keeping with a stuttering Dodo-Dodgson: "in [so humble, rather] [a(n), the, his] [very, rather, more] [decided, offended, astonished, low hurried, frightened, pleased, surprised, discontented, subdued, humble, same, severe, plaintive, encouraging, soothing, complaining, wondering, coaxing, pitying, peevish, usual, hopeful, scornful, mournful, respectful, fretful, (slow) thoughtful, sorrowful, sullen, (same) solemn, kinder, louder, calmer, careless, piteous, anxious, triumphant, impatient, deep hollow, sulky, friendly, melancholy, angry] tone." All but two occurrences of "tone" are accounted for in this fashion: "Alice did not at all like the tone" and "she was afraid from the Queen's tone." Preposition + article/pronominal adjective + adverb + adjective + TONE—here is the structure of oral formulae, but also the structure of scientific and academic language, as illustrated so well by the Dodo (A3 22:28–30); the two are formally related. What is significant is the rigidity of the structure in contrast to the variety of what fills the structure. It might seem that the variety of the adjectives would lose much literal signification in the sameness of the structure, not unlike the polysyllabic adjectives in the final line of Edward Lear's limericks, but the emphasis on tone—tone of some kind, tone of *any* kind—makes the reader extremely aware of the modifier. This is one of the two faces of repetition: here it emphasizes rather than negates meaning.

For Dodgson-Carroll, words involve sight and sound and sense and structure, competing senses and competing structures: the illogical logic of language. One of the dangers of concordances is that, after marshalling all the evidence of a kind, one has a tendency to ascribe to this definitive effort an absoluteness which properly applies to the signifier rather than to what is signified. This is reinforced by our tendency to believe that, once a concordance to a particular text has been prepared, that's an end to it—as if all concordances had identical functions. However much one may disagree with Wittgenstein, one of his enduring legacies is the lesson that one should not make equations based on mere similitude. As the Gnat in *Looking-Glass* knows, similitude, so prized in our culture, is as indicative of difference as identity. Alice, called by Daniel F. Kirk[13] a proto-logical positivist, rejects what cannot be verified. She cannot, as can the Gnat, "make a joke on that—something about 'horse' and 'hoarse,' you know." Alice's grasp of language is conventional, often mundane. A word index would be satisfactory for a text as Alice would have it, but more than that is required to illustrate the language of Lewis Carroll and his Gnat. A concordance is a beginning because it is definitive and at the same time suggestive. It is my hope that the variety of appendices will suggest something of the range of what might be produced to aid further study of the Alice books and at the same time serve most immediate needs.

Expressions of thanks come last by convention. I begin with my own "computer mentor," Roy Wisbey, Professor of German, King's College, London, whose greatest help I enjoyed while he was the Director of the Centre for Literary and Linguistic Computing at Cambridge University. I do not forget Professor Lewis Sawin who had established rudimentary facilities here at Colorado before I arrived as a graduate student in 1967, nor Sam Coleman who had taken Wisbey's course and who introduced me to the practical aspects of humanistic computing; Sam remains my programmer and friend even though he has been at the Lawrence Livermore National Laboratory in California for twelve years. I cannot omit Donald Baker, lover of manuscripts and all things literary and humane, for whose instruction I left a reputedly better but more stultified institution in the idealistic madness of the later 1960's, nor John Murphy, always intellectually stimulating, terrifying, and compassionate in the same verbal paragraph. Allies in establishing the Center for Computer Research in the Humanities (CCRH)—especially Ulo Goldsmith, Jacques Barchilon, and L. Michael Bell—will always have special places in my heart.

When I crossed that awkward divide between graduate student and faculty member, friends became students while remaining friends: first Becky Hogan, Lynn Merrill, Michéle Barale, and Jean Pfleiderer, and now Tom Beckwith, Pat McEahern, Kathy Livornesse, and Bobbi Wright. Associates and friends became colleagues here (Jim Kincaid, Gerry Kinneavy, Tom and Anne Lyons, Rubin Rabinovitz, and Ron Brunner) and elsewhere (Michael Taft, Paul Smith, Louis James, Bill Nicolaisen, Herbert Halpert, and John Widdowson). I dare not forget Cathy: wife, lover, student, colleague, teacher, friend, mother-of-our-daughters, and—a significant repetition here!—lover and friend. The catalog could continue because the stresses inherent in computing in the humanities create the best of friends as well as the most bitter of friends-fallen-out (rarely, I am thankful). From all of these I have learned much about the nature of texts and the language of texts, and what may be found to be good in this concordance has sources in these relationships. I do not forget Paul Levitt and Melvin Buxbaum here.

Other thanks are due because few use computer facilities to study texts without incurring obligations. Everly B. Fleischer, Dean of the College of Arts and Sciences, supports CCRH and, indirectly, projects such as this; I owe him thanks as well as a partial apology for my so hard-headedly fighting to keep CCRH afloat, particularly in his first years as Dean. I owe Les Brill, former English department chairman, sincere thanks for his attempts at clarifying to Fleischer what CCRH could possibly be. Except for mainframe computing time, I owe no thanks to other administrators. Those who have moved elsewhere I wish well. I hope that our new generation of administrators will adhere less rigidly to the industrial model of university governance.

Two special debts of gratitude remain to be expressed. The first is my relationship with the various people who are Garland Publishing, Inc.; Gary Kuris, Ralph Carlson, Phyllis Korper, Pam Chergotis, and Julia Johnson (who has moved back to California) are truly special people. The National Endowment for the Humanities also deserves special recognition, not for support of this concordance (support was not sought for this), but for support of the Early English drama project. That has encouraged, and aided, my work with Gerry Kinneavy, Jean Pfleiderer, Don Baker, and—now—Buck McMullen. The particular kind of work that concordances represent may be unintelligible to conventional administrators, but it *is* intelligible to serious humanists. The support of that effort has indirectly encouraged work on this. The Endowment does far more good for the profession than any of us can calculate.

Computing in the humanities at the University of Colorado is a richly rewarding, if complex, activity.

Boulder, Colorado
April Fool's Day, 1986

M.J.P.

Notes

1. See Judson Boyce Allen, "Langland's Reading and Writing: *Detractor* and the Pardon Passus," *Speculum* 59 (1984), 342–362.

2. See T. H. Howard-Hill, *Literary Concordances: A Guide to the Preparation of Manual and Computer Concordances* (New York: Pergamon Press, 1979) and Michael J. Preston and Samuel S. Coleman, "Some Considerations Concerning Encoding and Concording Texts," *Computers and the Humanities* 12 (1978) 3–12.

3. See Leslie A. Fiedler and Houston A. Baker, Jr., eds., *English Literature: Opening up the Canon*, Selected Papers from the English Institute, 1979, New Series, no. 4 (Baltimore: The Johns Hopkins University Press, 1981).

4. Such numbers suggest that the Wasp-episode was deleted by Dodgson because *Looking-Glass* was too long—some complain that it still is too long—to be a "twin" and sequel to *Wonderland*.

5. This is similar to the problem that cultural and oral historians work with: that medieval writers generally *thought* that classic Greeks were liars is of significance, whether they were or not; what we *think* happened in World War II is significant, not what happened. Restricting one's view to "the facts"—whether of texts or of history—is rather often misleading.

6. This is like the problem encountered by folklorists who may speak of such-and-such a ballad, but what they are referring to is a constellation of variants. This carries over into popular printing when there is not the "authority" of an author, whether popular editions of *Gulliver* or chapbook printings of the texts of folklore. See, for example, M. J. Preston, M. G. Smith, and P. S. Smith, *Chapbooks and Traditional Drama, Part I: "Alexander and the King of Egypt" Chapbooks*, CECTAL Bibliographical and Special Series No. 2, University of Sheffield, 1977.

7. Carroll's concern—some have considered it an obsession—with the appearance of his printed text should not be ignored or trivialized; in making this concordance I had similar worries because one cannot separate the form and the appearance from the function and the content. This large problem is too often ignored because of preoccupations with the thematic content of literary works. See my essays, "Xerox-Lore," *Keystone Folklore* XIX (1974), 11–26, and "The English Literal Rebus and the Graphic Riddle Tradition," *Western Folklore* 41 (1982), 104–138, for illustrations of the interplay between "form and content." Dodgson's correspondence is peppered with play with analogous forms.

8. For various approaches to multi-word significance in English, see especially J. R. Firth, "Modes of Meaning," *Papers in Linguistics: 1934–51* (London: Oxford University Press, 1952), pp. 190–215; Judith N. Levi, *The Syntax and Semantics of Complex Nominals* (New York: Academic Press, 1978); Adam Makkai, *Idiom Structure in English* (The Hague: Mouton, 1972); Raoul N. Smith et al., "A

Collocational Model of Information Transfer," *Proceedings of the ASIS Annual Meeting* 19 (1982), unnumbered pages; and Rosemary Courtney, *Longman Dictionary of Phrasal Verbs* (Harlow, Essex: Longman Group Ltd., 1983).

9. Rubin Rabinovitz, *The Development of Samuel Beckett's Fiction* (Chicago and Urbana: University of Illinois Press, 1984).

10. See Jeffrey Stern, ed. *Lewis Carroll's Library*. Carroll Studies No. 5. (The Lewis Carroll Society of North America: Silver Spring, Maryland, 1981).

11. That writing and speech are distinct media of communication has been well documented by Josef Vachek, *Written Language: General Problems of English* (The Hague: Mouton, 1973), but A. B. Lord's *A Singer of Tales* (New York: Atheneum, 1974) has perpetuated a false dichotomy. Rudy S. Spraycar and Lee F. Dunlap, "Formulaic Style in Oral and Literate Epic Poetry," *Perspectives in Computing: Applications in the Academic and Scientific Community*, Vol. 2, No. 4 (1982), 24–33, demonstrated that written texts can be even more formulaic than oral. Carroll attempted to capture speech in print and to illustrate the effects of print on speech, and to play with both.

12. See John B. Smith, "Computer Criticism," *Style* XII (1978), 326–356, as well as his other essays. Although Smith's work is formally reductive in some ways, it *is* stimulating, and this appendix is indebted to him.

13. Daniel F. Kirk, *Charles Dodgson Semeiotician*, University of Florida Monographs No. 11 (Gainsville, Florida, 1962), p. 58.

CRITICAL INTRODUCTION

Bread-and-Butter Flies: Live Concordances and Literary Theory

"What sort of insects do you rejoice in, where *you* come from?" the Gnat inquired.

"I don't *rejoice* in insects at all," Alice explained, "because I'm rather afraid of them—at least the large kinds. But I can tell you the names of some of them."

"Of course they answer to their names?" the Gnat remarked carelessly.

"I never knew them to do it."

"What's the use of their having names," the Gnat said, "if they wo'n't answer to them?"

"No use to *them*," said Alice; "but it's useful to the people that name them, I suppose. If not, why do things have names at all?"

(Through the Looking-Glass, ch. III)

Alice regards names (words) as possessions of the owners/givers, attached to them like the little tags stapled on anaesthetized sea lions and caribou. Words are *useful* in that they provide "to the people that [apply] them" complete power and complete control. They stabilize the world, bringing everything into a tidy orderliness maintained by human zookeepers. So thinks Alice.

But what happens when the anaesthesia wears off, when the wild words go off to pursue a mysterious life of their own? What happens when they disappear? We can, as the Gnat sees, only invite them back—to tea, perhaps. The Gnat is alive himself to a different way of seeing, one that welcomes disorder, play, images of communion. The Gnat's world is not going anywhere in particular; it is open, defenseless, anarchic. Alice's world is controlled, defensive, fiercely regulated by power. Alice, let us say, is now teaching at the University of Chicago: she is the formalist literary critic, regarding texts as fixed objects, language as a medium of exchange, meaning as stable. The Gnat has grown up to be what every parent might dream for: Jacques Derrida. Buzzing and stinging from ear to ear with jokes those humanist Alices cannot understand and regard as violations of true seriousness, true criticism, the true WORD, the Gnat is busy stealing all those identifying tags, mixing them up, teasing us by waving them at us from a point always just beyond our range of vision.

Alice used to love concordances, trudging gamely across campus twice or thrice weekly to sweat down those elephantine volumes from the shelves in order to establish solid textual arguments, prove points. She had published the results in no-nonsense journals with a form of *Philology* in their mastheads. No one could question the fundamental unity of *The Wasteland*, once Alice had shown how the sticky tentacles of vegetation imagery made it all cohere; an even subtler stylistic study of Hardy proved to everyone's satisfaction that our vague sense of Hardy's vagueness, his curious habit of combining "obstinate questioning"* with an equally obstinate refusal to give answers, resulted from his frequent use of the subjunctive and his uncommon fondness for some- (something, somehow, somewhere, and the like) forms. Concordances made all this possible. They also laid the bricks for her lasting edifice, a thorough and exhaustive study of definite and indefinite pronouns (their frequency, position, acceleration or the reverse in the work at hand and in the author's career) found in Restoration drama. Among other things, this labor wiped out forever the uncertainty as to the authorship of *The Wife's Seduction by the Husband, Or, Chastity Begins at Home*. (It also wiped out for good any uncertainty as to Alice's professional standing, leading, as it did, to tenure, two promotions, and a guaranteed annual spot on one or another MLA panel in perpetuity.)

But Alice has become uneasy, downright fidgety, about concordances. She longs for the old, comfy times. The only disturbance then was provided by William Empson and the rumors that he sneered at concordances and their users, that he never used one and never would. "So much is obvious from his work!" Alice would say. No more than a word-worrier, gifted but erratic, Empson never proved anything to Alice's satisfaction, never used *facts*, seemed more interested in raising questions, possibilities (at best, remote possibilities, according to Alice) rather than achieving what Alice longed for most: fulfillment, solid fulfillment, a resounding and unquestionable answer. Alice's was a life devoted to resolutions. She saw them as the goal and justification of the whole critical enterprise and wasn't about to let some slothful ("Doesn't do his homework!") loon like Empson get in the way. But now that Gnat had started his devilish games even with concordances. (It's pure *destruction*! De*con*struction indeed! There's a *con* in it all right, and every young fool I know is buying into this phoney Frog's swindle!) Not much of a joke, even Alice acknowledged. She wasn't used to jokes, distrusted them. As a means of defense they were of little use, being evanescent things, refusing, even while they were around, to stand still and let themselves be properly examined.

She'd like to swat them all, to tell the truth, along with the Gnat and his whining company. Trouble was that the company had become so large, had swollen into a swarm. Bogus journals with words like *Dia*something or *Inquiry* in their titles were popping up and receiving a disgusting amount of attention. Most nauseating, concordance makers themselves were idiotically baring their bodies to this stinging infestation. Alice tried to comfort herself by reading, once again, the OED entry on "concor-

---

*The reference is not to Hardy but to Wordsworth, as Alice well knew. Such establishing of parallels, however, not only enlivened and enriched the study but helped to suggest that the tracing of parallels need by no means be confined to one author. In fact, Alice's next book, *Bone of My Bone: The Adverbial Marriage of Wordsworth and Hardy*, shot forth with a kind of inevitability shortly thereafter.

dance." She loved it, found that it gave her a soothing feeling of well-being. The reassuringly rhinoceros-sized OED pinned things down, left no doubts. "Concordance" was deeply and permanently rooted in "concord," "the fact of agreeing or being concordant; agreement, harmony." The word spread out in an orderly way, honeying all manner of texts and activities with its harmony: political treaties and compacts, musical performances and compositions, citations of parallel passages in a book, especially in the Bible. (This last, Alice knew, was a profound instance of Logocentrism tittered at by the Gnats. Let them titter! The OED and I will outlast them all!) The best the OED saved for last, and it amounted to a vision of the New Jerusalem of scholarship: an alphabetical list of words in a book, "properly *a concordantia*."

But now! All this dissonance and turmoil, with the most sophisticated authors of concordances perversely contributing to the racket! Most of those publishing with Garland, for instance! Alice would love to take some bamboo shoots or a supply of honey and ants and get them for good. Contexts were bad enough, irresistible temptations to these latter-day Empsons she hated so. But these irresponsible, show-offy appendices were really the limit and far beyond. Who wants a reverse index, much less a multi-word KWIC, or a text-ordered KWIC? In the reverse KWIC she found grounds more than sufficient for committing the Garland tribe permanently.

Not that Alice couldn't find plenty of material here to put into her publishable cupcakes. But she regarded such concordances as these as the Gnat's playground. She was right, or so I think. As a most junior gnat myself, I would like to conduct a brief tour of a few of the teeter-totters. Alice will come along and even be allowed too many words on what she takes to be the pilings and structural supports. But she will not be unanswered. Alice has been yapping alone these many years and is getting to be a bit of a bore.

A concordance like this presents itself to us not as a tool but as a text in itself. It is certainly not a harmonious, innocent tome, reflecting another harmonious work, offering itself as a way to harmonious scholarship. It is an infinitely rearrangeable openness, an act of transgression. It has cheerily abandoned its pretense of innocence, having taken several million trips around the block. It openly invites the most kinky associations and dissociations, throwing at us parallels and non-parallels, presences and absences with a wanton lack of discrimination. It plays shamelessly right in plain view of the serious adultness of Alice, mooning her impudently. In place of a neat sequence of words, this concordance horses around with free-floating fragments. After all, don't the oft-quoted Alice books exist really in these quoted fragments, there and in the fragments that float, without sequence or clear reason, into our minds. For a mad book you really need a mad concordance—intended, of course, for mad critics.

"We're all mad here," so we need a time-arresting, gliding concordance. Not, to give Alice a few yips, that we cannot find support here for some of our most obvious and least interesting responses to *Wonderland* and *Looking-Glass*. First of all, these books are, as the concordance indicates, "adventures," that is, entertainments for children. As such, there is a heavy emphasis on the something-new-around-every-corner perspective. Episodes, thus, often seem to have a starting point but no finish: there are 110 "began"s and 5 "started"s, but only 2 "concluded"s, 17 "finished"s and 4 "ended"s. Some might make a great deal of this existential openness and of the unusual way in which it is violated by the main character's central impulse in *Looking-Glass*.

For our critic Alice, however, all this is moonshine, the plethora of unfinished beginnings being simply a matter of the demands of the genre and of the trivial and irresponsible nature of children generally. For once, Alice has something to say: one can, indeed, use some of her hard-nosed skepticism in navigating these concordance waters, as we shall see. More comforting to and safer for traditional thematic critics is the relief in finding that the concordance seems to confirm what they already knew: there are, indeed, many references to curious/curiosity and variants (41). Similarly, the main character is often described in terms of or surrounded by fear (29), loneliness (15), sadness (13); happiness (7) and gladness (21) are overwhelmed. Oddly, forms of "laugh" outnumber those of "cry" 25–17, as long as we omit the 76 instances of "cried," on the grounds that most often "cried" is used as an apparently innocent substitute for "said," as in " 'Ditto, ditto!' cried Tweedledum."

But how innocent are these substitutions of "cried," especially in such numbers, and should they be ignored? Alice would ignore them, on the grounds that they disturb the solidity and clarity of her case. But what effect does this torrent of "cried"s have on a reader attuned to the loneliness and actual crying of the little girl in the story? One might say that the solidity of Alice's case is somewhat wooden or wooden-headed, since it ignores the complexity and subtlety of our response to those words on the page, our willingness to hear echoes of sobs even in a displaced form like "cried."

To be fair, Alice would not be entirely unreceptive to such arguments. Alice has her virtues. Noting, for instance, the large number of references to forms of "eat" (32), Alice would not leap to the conclusion that these books are "oral-aggressive" in character—she would feel justified at this point only in saying, "There seems to be lots of eating going on." She would note that the vast majority of these references are in *Wonderland*, and would record that fact as pointing toward a possible difference between the two books. She would record also the unusual recurrence of references to mouths and teeth (29), finishing in a near dead heat with ears (30) and far outdistancing noses (13). Ah, but there's eye(s) with 74! Whatever one might make of all the eating, then, Alice—who would probably make nothing more of it than that children like to eat and that Carroll was aware of that fact—would insist that the books are visual, not oral, invitations to spectator sports, not banquets or slaughterhouse activities.

Alice is rigorously honest, one must allow her that, and she can be more subtle than we have suggested thus far. Not too subtle, of course, since she is, after all, a firm believer in facts; and the facts, if not quite able to speak through themselves, can certainly speak clearly through Alice's common sense. She has a lot of common sense. Looking at the day/night division and then at the parallel dark/light division, for instance, Alice is as handy as a forest ranger with a compass to those of us prone to get lost in these woods. Here are the facts: 53 references to forms of "day," 16 to forms of "night"; 15 to forms of "dark" and 5 to forms of "light." Seems confusing, seems to demand some unexpected and sophisticated explanation. Why does "day" overwhelm "night" and "dark" overwhelm "light"? Alice is ready to set us all right without any appeals to the highfallutin unexpected and sophisticated. The adventures, first of all, take place in the daytime, so there is less cause to mention the "night" that is never present. (The Gnat whines loudly at this point, but this is Alice's turn at the game.) Further, "day" in English is used in countless English idioms merely to refer to a period of time and not at all to day*light*: "don't take all day about it!"; "I do it every day." The overwhelming majority of the references to "day" in these books are buried metaphors, not to be noticed (Gnat whines); they certainly do not bring up an opposition to "night" (more Gnat whines)—at least in the minds of sane people.

The dark/light problem is absolute mock turtle soup for Alice: since it *is* daylight, there is hardly any point in referring to that light, any light in addition to the sun being superfluous and probably invisible. Alice is not one to slither by problems, though, and she does notice that 9 of the 12 references to "dark" organize themselves in an interesting pattern: in T3 the child worries about getting to the eighth square before it gets dark; in T4 there are four references to the gathering darkness during the Tweedledee-Tweedledum battle; in T5 there are 3 references to the "dark" shop kept by the Sheep and one to "the dark water" on which they later row. Alice recognizes that there is something going on here and that the last reference to "the dark water" looks uncomfortably like a metaphor that won't stay buried. Still, all this is handled with Alice's customary aplomb through a citation from Carroll's Prefatory poem to *Looking-Glass*:

> And, though the shadow of a sigh
>   May tremble through the story,
> For 'happy summer days' gone by,
>   And vanish'd summer glory—
> It shall not touch, with breath of bale,
>   The pleasance of our fairy-tale.

The darkness is simply that "shadow of a sigh" that trembles here but leaves untouched "the pleasance" of the story. Here, after all, is Carroll's own explanation, Carroll's own intentions! (The Gnat is stupefied by this and doesn't bother whining.)

But Alice has a subtlety of her own and some tricks up her sleeve: syntactical and, within limits, metaphorical ones. She points happily to the huge number of "as" and "like" conjunctions, arguing with something approaching a bray that, while the works are undeniably figurative, those figures are predominantly *similes*. ("Well?" says the Gnat.) "Well," explains Alice patiently, "similes are figures of clear connection not disconnection, they refer the unfamiliar to the familiar, they connect the apparent fluidity of Alice's wild and strange experiences to the solidity of her normal world, they are purely REFERENTIAL!" (The Gnat cannot contain himself: "But that's not the way they or any other figures operate!")

Alice smiles and points to the fact that even the unusual number of "un-" words points not to disravelling but to a protection against any threat of disravelling. Words like "un-birthday" or "un-dish-cover" are mere jokes, assuring us that all is safe, sound, and empirically verifiable. ("You're trying to have it both ways—") But Alice is off and pounding down the track: the connective "And" drives the dissociative "But" into the ground by a score of 1,829 to 383, a laugher, while the apparent loss of the affirmative "Yes" (20) to the blocking "No" (164) is, in fact, only apparent, the fact being that "yes" in our language does not have the advantage of the adverbial and adjectival usage, the innocent proliferation of which in terms of "no" accounts for this ratio. To prove it, Alice provides a chart of randomly selected verbs and auxiliaries, cautioning that the odd situation as regards "will" and "wo'n't" in *Alice in Wonderland* is a mere peculiarity and proclaiming that the chart shows clearly the preponderance of the forward-looking, the optimistic, the solid and certain positives! Alice unrolls her parchment-roll clincher of a document like the White Rabbit at the trial and reads as follows:

WILL	20 (T)	WO'N'T	8 (T)
	34 (A)		24 (A)
CAN	70 (T)	CA'N'T	38 (T)
	36 (A)		28 (A)
DID	55 (T)	DIDN'T	37 (T)
	62 (A)		14 (A)
COULD	71 (T)	COULDN'T	38 (T)
	79 (A)		9 (A)
WOULD	91 (T)	WOULDN'T	23 (T)
	83 (A)		13 (A)
WAS	358 (T)	WASN'T	12 (T)
	360 (A)		11 (A)
DO	122 (T)	DON'T	81 (T)
	80 (A)		61 (A)
HAD	135 (T)	HADN'T	17 (T)
	178 (A)		8 (A)
IS	126 (T)	ISN'T	16 (T)
	110 (A)		7 (A)
SHOULD	32 (T)	SHOULDN'T	13 (T)
	28 (A)		5 (A)

"And what do you make of that, you squashed Gnat!"

"I could show you charts in comparison with which that would be a bull-frog!" (But deal with this one!) "Charts make me giddy—they're so ridiculous and orderly." (Evasive!) "Your whole life is a chart. You are charter'd. You disappear into your charts." (Ad hominem! Deal with the issue!) "You mean *your* issues. Look, it's my turn now, my rules, my play. I'm erasing my quotation marks and enclosing you in parentheses, where you'll find it all comfy. Stay there and try to confine yourself to shocked grunts. I won't play long, though I'll be long aplaying—and a paying." (Now, what on earth can that mean!)

Quiet, puffball. I mean what I choose not to mean. But I will, for a moment, play by a couple of your rules, just to show you what I think of your stability and your referentiality. Take another look at what you do with the light/dark problem, one, given your stolid method, you can hardly avoid. You resolve it all, you doubtless think, into a "shadow," one authorized by Carroll himself, a trembling, sighing shadow. Right? (Indisputably the right move.) You think so? This is your referentiality, is it: an evanescent shadow? And what causes that shadow? Which darkness are we discussing? And how can one metaphor ("dark water") be naturalized by another ("dark shadow")? Shame, Alice! (But . . .) And then your treatment of And/But puts you beyond shame. How many times do the "And"s fake real connections, drawing attention to their fakery, pretending to draw together elements so alien that their unconnectability is emphasized? Why, you should know that this is a common Victorian technique, used prominently in such works as *In Memoriam*. (Which happens not to be the text at hand. Besides, I do not recognize the existence of "unconnectability.") Suit yourself on the last point, dearie. As for the first, whose hand are we at, and why won't any text do?

Also, while we're at it, I see you didn't draw attention to what you would doubtless suppose to be a supporting fact: the outranking of "none" (a mere 11) by "All" (a grand 311). A swamper, right? Curious absence there, Alice, in your argument. I wonder if you sensed some shakiness in the organ-toned "All," some wobbling in the whomping cover term that has been used, at least since Wordsworth, as a desperate substitute gesture by poets, fobbed off on us to cover the God that isn't there no more? (I knew we'd get to something like this! Lousy, nihilistic, atheist of an insect!) Yes indeed, Alice, but what exactly does this "all" *mean*, to use your favorite term? Eh? "All" doesn't *mean* anything at all, as all will agree, especially when it is stretched more and more to hide the absence of a meaning-Center. It's like a rubber band, you see: stretch it to a point and it becomes transparent, revealing the emptiness it is supposed to be engulfing, explaining. (Who mentioned rubber bands? Certainly neither I nor Carroll. The insect's mad!)

As for your Yes/No: why consider "No" and not "Know" or "Nose" (which I recall you did mention—Good for you) or "Albino," or "Albumen"? But I am beginning to be fretted by your predictable oppositions and your even more predictable dealings with them. (Grarrg!) Besides, I do not want to hear once again the tiresome charge that I am a parasite, that I need you, Alice. Sorry to break your heart, but I am not a blood-sucker, even assuming you had any to give. I don't bite; I soar, dance, flit. In this case, into those appendices you so abhor. Just one appendix here, so as not to wear you out. No commentary either. Just some samples from the Reverse Index that ought to, but won't, ignite even you, Alice. How do you like this:

> afford
> word
> sword
> absurd

or

> silence
> violence
> insolence
> impertinence
> pence

or

> tipple
> supple
> purple

beetle
gentle

or

chose
those
whose
lose

or

now
know
snow

Last two are a little sad, aren't they? But, then, the pleasantest things always are. (Pervert!)

Let's play with what isn't there, the most interesting parts of this concordance text being revealed in what isn't there, in the terrifying, liberating, and impossible game of "chase the absences." No rules here, you know, and no losers, since there's nothing to catch. (What nonsense!) You sound like you did then, Alice, ineducable as ever, regarding nonsense as some simple inversion of what you call "sense." Why did I ever try to joke with you? (I can't imagine.)

Never mind. I was young then. Back to "after the absences," or whatever the name was—or whatever it was called, and so forth. Let's ask what baggage the little girl does *not* carry with her into Wonderland and behind the Looking-Glass. What isn't there? (A giant tarantula?) Not bad for you, Alice, and you're right. But I'm trying to haunt your old mansion clearly enough so you'll understand. Why I'm doing that I'll never know. But back to our question. The child seems unoriginated, unformed, inorganic. Where are the references to parent(s) (0), mother (0), father (0)? You see some "Fathers," do you, Alice? Look more closely. They are confined to the "Father William" poem, which parodies parental functions, parental being, puts the father to an undignified rout. The "Sister" is confined to the frame, except for slight references in T4 and T9, and the "brother" to the owner of the Latin Grammar in A2. (And the Tweedledum brothers?) Some brothers, and I don't see that they have a sister. Apart from the frames and one reference in Wonderland, there is not even a Nurse. There's only Dinah, the cat: 25 references to "Dinah," 46 to "Cat(s)," 7 to "Cheshire-Cats," 5 to "Purring," and another 50 to "Kittens" and "Kitty." All she has beyond this are "punishments" (11) and "lessons" (16). Why it's downright pathetic, a sort of *Oliver Twist* in fantasy-land.

Or is it? (Certainly not!) Right, but not in the way you think you mean. What is all this absence, all this non-presence? Why, one might say, it is a strategic clearing-away for a filling-up: the bottle is drained of parents and family so that it might be ladled full with a presence. There are 106 references to "Other" in these books, but who is this Other? Why, Carroll of course. (I knew you couldn't avoid something solid, but I never thought you'd land on the author.) But where is this Other? Always around the corner, beckoning sadly, wistfully, hopelessly. He is never there really. He is the great Absence that might have filled the container Alice is, perversely and tragically, holding upside down. He pops in as the Dodo anxious to explain the beautiful non-rules of the deconstructive Caucus Race. She doesn't get the point at all. (Still doesn't, I'm glad to say.) Yes, I know. He pops in again, disguised a little, at the eighth square for one last attempt that is no attempt at all to halt the child's disastrous rush toward adulthood. "And now to be a Queen! How grand it sounds!" Chasing after the source of that grand sound, a solidity she has to pretend is there forever after, she leaves behind the sobbing Knight/Carroll, waving goodbye to all hope, joy, and glamour— for himself and for Alice. With that, Alice cancels the work, erases it, leaves it as the playful, melancholy concordance.

Do you get it, Alice? Do you see? (Not at all.) I feel rotten bad about that, you know. Have you thought about erasing your name, making yourself into an absence?

"That would never do, I'm sure," said Alice: "the governess would never think of excusing me lessons for that. If she couldn't remember my name, she'd call me 'Miss,' as the servants do."

"Well, if she said 'Miss,' and didn't say anything more," the Gnat remarked, "of course you'd miss your lessons. That's a joke. I wish *you* had made it."

"Why do you wish *I* had made it?" Alice asked. "It's a very bad one."

But the Gnat only sighed deeply, while two large tears came rolling down its cheeks.

"You shouldn't make jokes," Alice said, "if it makes you so unhappy."

Then came another of those melancholy little sighs, and this time the poor Gnat really seemed to have sighed itself away, for, when Alice looked up, there was nothing whatever to be seen on the twig, and, as she was getting quite chilly with sitting so long, she got up and walked on.

James R. Kincaid
University of Colorado at Boulder

THE CONCORDANCE

-A-

A (1436) [entries omitted]
ABC (1)
    T9   194:33   "Of course you know your ABC?" said the Red Queen.
ABIDE (1)
    A6   48:32   bother _me_!" said the Duchess. "I never could abide figures!" And with that she began nursing her child
ABLE (7) [See also UNABLE]
    A2   14: 7   for you now, dears? I'm sure I sha'n't be able! I shall be a great deal too far off to trouble myself
    T4   145:25   it all seemed so ridiculous--"I shouldn't be able to cry."
    T9   192: 9   she said as she sat down again, "I shall be able to manage it quite well in time."
    T3   129: 4   as she stood on tiptoe in hopes of being able to see a little further. "Principal rivers--there _are_
    T7   170:18   the King remarked in a fretful tone. "To be able to see Nobody! And at that distance too! Why, it's as
    T2   126:25   doing _that_. She felt as if she would never be able to talk again, she was getting so much out of breath: and
    T3   135:41   she went on, rather surprised at not being able to think of the word. "I mean to get under the--under the
ABOUT (165) [entries omitted]
ABOVE (5)
    A11   89:12   voice, "and I hadn't begun my tea--not above a week or so--and what with the bread-and-butter getting
    A4   30:41   and scrambling about in the chimney close above her: then, saying to herself "This is Bill", she gave
    T5   154:19   a work-box, and was always in the shelf next above the one she was looking at. "And this one is the most
    A7   57:19   'Up above the world you fly, / Like a tea-tray in the sky. /
    T3   133:12   "Look on the branch above your head," said the Gnat, "and there you'll find a
ABSENCE (1)
    A9   72:43   guests had taken advantage of the Queen's absence, and were resting in the shade: however, the moment
ABSURD (2)
    A3   24: 5   Alice thought the whole thing very absurd, but they all looked so grave that she did not dare to
    A6   50:12   a pig, and she felt that it would be quite absurd for her to carry it any further.
ACCENTS (1)
    T8   188:17   His accents mild took up the tale: / He said 'I go my ways, / And
ACCEPTANCE (1)
    A3   24: 2   presented the thimble, saying "We beg your acceptance of this elegant thimble"; and, when it had finished
ACCIDENT (4)
    A12   93:13   very diligently to write out a history of the accident, all except the Lizard, who seemed too much overcome
    A12   92:10   up again as quickly as she could, for the accident of the gold-fish kept running in her head, and she
    T8W   15: 7   While tasting the treacle, they had a sad accident: two of their party were engulphed--"
    T9   196:18   _try_ to remember my name in the middle of an accident! Where would be the use of it?" but she did not say
ACCIDENTALLY (1)
    A12   92: 6   her very much of a globe of gold-fish she had accidentally upset the week before.
ACCOUNT (1)
    A8   67:19   Alice put down her flamingo, and began an account of the game, feeling very glad she had some one to
ACCOUNTING (1)
    A10   84:13   said, in a rather offended tone, "Hm! No accounting for tastes! Sing her 'Turtle Soup,' will you, old
ACCOUNTS (2)
    A7   56:42   "Ah! That accounts for it," said the Hatter. "He wo'n't stand beating.
    T5   152:21   "That accounts for the bleeding, you see," she said to Alice with a
ACCUSATION (1)
    A11   87:13   "Herald, read the accusation!" said the King.
ACCUSTOMED (1)
    A3   22: 5   who wanted leaders, and had been of late much accustomed to usurpation and conquest. Edwin and Morcar, the
ACHE (1) [See also HEADACHE, TOOTHACHE]
    A11   91:28   the next witness. It quite makes my forehead ache!"
ACRES (1)
    T9   195: 1   "How many acres of ground?" said the White Queen. "You mustn't leave out
ACROSS (13)
    T5   153:18   a sudden gust of wind blew the Queen's shawl across a little brook. The Queen spread out her arms again and
    T8   191: 1   as she bounded * * * * * * * * * * * * * * across, and threw herself down to rest on a lawn as soft as
    A1   8: 1   on, Alice started to her feet, for it flashed across her mind that she had never before seen a rabbit with
    A10   78: 2   deeply, and drew the back of one flapper across his eyes. He looked at Alice and tried to speak, but,
    T8   181:14   had a queer-shaped little deal box fastened across his shoulders, upside-down, and with the lid hanging
    T2   125:21   number of tiny little brooks running straight across it from side to side, and the ground between was
    T1   114:23   picked him up very gently, and lifted him across more slowly than she had lifted the Queen, that she
    T7   174:22   eagerly. "There's the White Queen running across the country! She came flying out of the wood over
    A1   8: 3   of it, and burning with curiosity, she ran across the field after it, and was just in time to see it pop
    A8   63:11   moment, Five, who had been anxiously looking across the garden, called out "The Queen! The Queen!" and the
    T7   178: 3   deafened. She started to her feet and sprang across the little brook in her terror, and had just time to
    T4   139:32   make it out) by the branches rubbing one across the other, like fiddles and fiddle-sticks.
    A8   68:20   difficulty was, that her flamingo was gone across the other side of the garden, where Alice could see it
ACT (2)
    A8   66:14   hedgehog had unrolled itself, and was in the act of crawling away: besides all this, there was generally a
    T9   204:26   hold of the little creature in the very act of jumping over a bottle which had just lighted upon the
ACTIVE (1)
    T6   164:31   'lithe and slimy.' 'Lithe' is the same as 'active.' You see it's like a pormanteau--there are two
ACTUALLY (3)
    T5   158:21   How very odd to find trees growing here! And actually here's a little brook! Well, this is the very
    A1   7:16   seemed quite natural); but, when the Rabbit actually took a watch out of its waistcoat-pocket, and looked

ACTUALLY (cont.)
    T2   120:23   and the next moment she found herself actually walking in at the door.
ADA (1)
    A2   16: 4   "I'm sure I'm not Ada," she said, "for her hair goes in such long ringlets, and
ADDED (45)
    T6   165: 8   And a long way beyond it on each side," Alice added.
    T6   159:32   line is much too long for the poetry," she added, almost out loud, forgetting that Humpty Dumpty would
    A7   55:15   riddles--I believe I can guess that," she added aloud.
    T5   149:24   May I put your shawl straight for you?" she added aloud.
    A9   70:37   little chin into Alice's shoulder as she added "and the moral of that is--'Take care of the sense, and
    T5   155: 2   of all--but I'll tell you what--" she added, as a sudden thought struck her. "I'll follow it up to
    T8   190:16   But you'll stay and see me off first?" he added as Alice turned with an eager look in the direction to
    A6   51:13   "--so long as I get somewhere," Alice added as an explanation.
    T6   166:25   only I don't sing it," he added, as an explanation.
    A11   88:24   "I keep them to sell," the Hatter added as an explanation. "I've none of my own. I'm a hatter."
    T9   197: 8   "And now you know the words," she added, as she put her head down on Alice's other shoulder,
    T1   115:13   there, now I think you're tidy enough!" she added, as she smoothed his hair, and set him upon the table
    T8W   13:11   but I'll just ask him what's the matter," she added, checking herself on the very edge. "If I once jump over
    A10   81:38   replied, in an offended tone. And the Gryphon added "Come, let's hear some of your adventures."
    T4   146:17   thing. "Not a rattle-snake, you know," she added hastily, thinking that he was frightened: "only an old
    T6   159:20   And some eggs are very pretty, you know," she added, hoping to turn her remark into a sort of compliment.
    T4   147:45   only you'd better not come very close," he added: "I generally hit every thing I can see--when I get
    T1   110:28   was, "--and if you're not good directly," she added, "I'll put you through into Looking-glass House. How
    T2   124:13   but why did you come out here at all?" she added in a kinder tone. "Curtsey while you're thinking what to
    A4   29: 7   I'll write one--but I'm grown up now," she added in a sorrowful tone: "at least there's no room to grow
    T2   125:27   about somewhere--and so there are!" she added in a tone of delight, and her heart began to beat quick
    A3   24:15   Alice, "and why it is you hate--C and D," she added in a whisper, half afraid that it would be offended
    A12   96:27   "It's a pun!" the King added in an angry tone, and everybody laughed. "Let the jury
    A11   91:26   relief. "Call the next witness." And, he added, in an undertone to the Queen, "Really, my dear, you
    T6   162:18   no, a belt, I mean--I beg your pardon!" she added in dismay, for Humpty Dumpty looked thoroughly offended,
    A12   94:14   He unfolded the paper as he spoke, and added "It isn't a letter, after all: it's a set of verses."
    T2   123:15   "But that's not your fault," the Rose added kindly. "You're beginning to fade, you know--and then
    A7   56: 2   told you butter wouldn't suit the works!" he added, looking angrily at the March Hare.
    T1   108: 1   You ought, Dinah, you know you ought!" she added, looking reproachfully at the old cat, and speaking in
    A7   55:59   "You might just as well say," added the Dormouse, which seemed to be talking in its sleep,
    A9   75: 5   yourself for asking such a simple question," added the Gryphon; and then they both sat silent and looked at
    A9   76: 3   "Hold your tongue!" added the Gryphon, before Alice could speak again. The Mock
    A7   58:30   "And be quick about it," added the Hatter, "or you'll be asleep again before it's done
    A7   55:26   "You might just as well say," added the March Hare, "that 'I like what I get' is the same
    T4   138:13   "Contrariwise," added the one marked 'DEE,' "if you think we're alive, you
    A12   93:40   "Nearly two miles high," added the Queen.
    T8W   16:14   "And it's very good for the conceit," added the Wasp.
    A11   88:18   all three dates on their slates, and then added them up, and reduced the answer to shillings and pence.
    A8   63:41   Majesty," said Alice very politely; but she added, to herself, "Why, they're only a pack of cards, after
    A11   91: 1   just take his head off outside," the Queen added to one of the officers; but the Hatter was out of sight
    A12   95:35   not swim--' you ca'n't swim, can you?" he added, turning to the Knave.
    T4   140: 9   "So much obliged!" added Tweedledee. "You like poetry?"
    T4   145:10   "If that there King was to wake," added Tweedledum, "you'd go out--bang!--just like a candle!"
    T4   147:25   "You know," he added very gravely, "it's one of the most serious things that
    A5   42:30   the Pigeon, but in a more subdued tone, and added, with a kind of sob, "I've tried every way, but nothing
ADDING (1)
    A5   43:22   two, which gave the Pigeon the opportunity of adding "You're looking for eggs, I know that well enough; and
ADDITION (3)
    T9   194:30   The Queen gasped and shut her eyes. "I can do Addition," she said, "if you give me time--but I ca'n't do
    T9   194: 1   "She ca'n't do Addition," the Red Queen interrupted. "Can you do Subtraction?"
    T9   193:24   "Can you do Addition?" the White Queen asked. "What's one and one and one
ADDRESSED (3)
    A5   35: 3   took the hookah out of its mouth, and addressed her in a languid, sleepy voice.
    T6   159:26   her; in fact, his last remark was evidently addressed to a tree--so she stood and softly repeated to
    A6   47:17   but she saw in another moment that it was addressed to the baby, and not to her, so she took courage,
ADDRESSING (4)
    T2   120:30   "O Tiger-lily!" said Alice, addressing herself to one that was waving gracefully about in
    A3   26:23   Dinah here, I know I do!" said Alice aloud, addressing nobody in particular. "She'd soon fetch it back!"
    T12   207: 2   so loud," Alice said, rubbing her eyes, and addressing the kitten, respectfully, yet with some severity.
    T5   149:11   herself. So she began rather timidly: "Am I addressing the White Queen?"
ADJECTIVES (1)
    T6   163:39   particularly verbs: they're the proudest--adjectives you can do anything with, but not verbs--however, I
ADJOURN (1)
    A3   22:29   rising to its feet, "I move that the meeting adjourn, for the immediate adoption of more energetic remedies
ADMIRATION (1)
    T8W   20: 5   looking at her with an expression of admiration: "it's the shape of your head as does it. Your jaws
ADMIRE (1)
    T4   143:18   night is fine,' the Walrus said. / 'Do you admire the view?
ADMIRING (1)
    T8   181:17   "I see you're admiring my little box," the Knight said in a friendly tone.
ADMITTANCE (1)
    T9   198:10   put its head out for a moment and said "No admittance till the week after next!" and shut the door again
ADOPTION (1)
    A3   22:29   that the meeting adjourn, for the immediate adoption of more energetic remedies--"

A-DRESSING (2)
   T5   149:20   at all!" groaned the poor Queen. "I've been a-dressing myself for the last two hours."
   T5   149:13   "Well, yes, if you call that a-dressing," the Queen said. "It isn't my notion of the thing,
ADVANCE (3)
   A10   79:15   how eagerly the lobsters and the turtles all advance! / They are waiting on the shingle--will you come and
   A10   78:20   "--you advance twice--"
   A10   78:22   "Of course," the Mock Turtle said: "advance twice, set to partners--"
ADVANTAGE (4)
   A7   59:41   Hare. The Hatter was the only one who got any advantage from the change; and Alice was a good deal worse off
   T5   150:15   "--but there's one great advantage in it, that one's memory works both ways."
   A9   72:43   The other guests had taken advantage of the Queen's absence, and were resting in the
   A6   48:23   "Which would not be an advantage," said Alice, who felt very glad to get an
ADVENTURES (7)
   A10   81:39   Gryphon added "Come, let's hear some of your adventures."
   T2   120:17   the old room--and there'd be an end of all my adventures!"
   A10   81:40   "I could tell you my adventures--beginning from this morning," said Alice a little
   A10   81:44   "No, no! The adventures first," said the Gryphon in an impatient tone:
   A10   82: 1   So Alice began telling them her adventures from the time when she first saw the White Rabbit.
   A12   98: 8   as she could remember them, all these strange Adventures of hers that you have just been reading about; when
   A12   98:15   of little Alice and all her wonderful Adventures, till she too began dreaming after a fashion, and
ADVERTISEMENTS (1)
   T3   135:32   has got my old name! That's just like the advertisements, you know, when people lose dogs--'answers to
ADVICE (6)
   T6   167:12   I told them twice: / They would not listen to advice.
   T6   162: 7   "I never ask advice about growing," Alice said indignantly.
   T8W   19: 1   But when I followed their advice, / And they had noticed the effect, / They said I did
   A5t   35: 1   ADVICE FROM A CATERPILLAR
   T6   162: 5   sort of age. Now if you'd asked my advice, I'd have said 'Leave off at seven'--but it's too late
   A1   12:23   minute!" She generally gave herself very good advice (though she very seldom followed it), and sometimes she
ADVISABLE (2)
   A3   22:14   patriotic archbishop of Canterbury, found it advisable--'"
   A3   22:22   question, but hurriedly went on, "--found it advisable to go with Edgar Atheling to meet William and offer
ADVISE (2)
   A1   12:22   said Alice to herself rather sharply. "I advise you to leave off this minute!" She generally gave
   T2   123:38   possibly do that," said the Rose: "I should advise you to walk the other way."
AFFAIR (1)
   A12   95:10   or she should chance to be / Involved in this affair, / He trusts to you to set them free, / Exactly as we
AFFECTIONATE (1)
   T4   140:16   Tweedledum replied, giving his brother an affectionate hug.
AFFECTIONATELY (2)
   A9   70: 2   said the Duchess, as she tucked her arm affectionately into Alice's, and they walked off together.
   T7   173:27   you, dear child?" he went on, putting his arm affectionately round Hatta's neck.
AFFORD (1)
   A9   76:18   "I couldn't afford to learn it," said the Mock Turtle with a sigh. "I only
A-FIGHTING (1)
   T8W   20:12   as that," the Wasp persisted. "If you was a-fighting, now--could you get hold of the other one by the
AFORE (1)
   A8   63: 9   know. So you see, Miss, we're doing our best, afore she comes, to--" At this moment, Five, who had been
AFRAID (29)
   T8   186:25   "That wouldn't be very nice, I'm afraid--"
   A1   9: 9   with me! There are no mice in the air, I'm afraid, but you might catch a bat, and that's very like a
   T2   125:16   Alice curtseyed again, as she was afraid from the Queen's tone that she was a little offended:
   T4   144:36   "I'm afraid he'll catch cold with lying on the damp grass," said
   A5   36:31   "I'm afraid I am, Sir," said Alice. "I ca'n't remember things as I
   A5   35:14   "I'm afraid I ca'n't put it more clearly," Alice replied, very
   T6   161:17   "I'm afraid I ca'n't quite remember it," Alice said, very politely.
   A7   58:21   "I'm afraid I don't know one," said Alice, rather alarmed at the
   T6   167: 5   "I'm afraid I don't quite understand," said Alice.
   T3   130: 2   "I'm afraid I haven't got one," Alice said in a frightened tone:
   T4   145:17   help saying "Hush! You'll be waking him, I'm afraid, if you make so much noise."
   T6   166: 1   "And then 'mome raths'?" said Alice. "I'm afraid I'm giving you a great deal of trouble."
   T8   184:37   "so I ca'n't tell for certain--but I'm afraid it would be a little hard."
   T6   161:11   don't know what would happen to his head! I'm afraid it would come off!"
   A2   20:10   dear!" cried Alice in a sorrowful tone. "I'm afraid I've offended it again!" For the Mouse was swimming
   T8W   20:14   "I'm afraid not," said Alice.
   A12   95:24   in the last few minutes that she wasn't a bit afraid of interrupting him,) "I'll give him sixpence. I don't
   A4   29:24   large as the Rabbit, and had no reason to be afraid of it.
   A8   63:42   only a pack of cards, after all. I needn't be afraid of them!"
   T3   132:30   at all," Alice explained, "because I'm rather afraid of them--at least the large kinds. But I can tell you
   A5   41: 2   "Not quite right, I'm afraid," said Alice, timidly: "some of the words have got
   A5   35:11   "I ca'n't explain myself, I'm afraid, Sir," said Alice, "because I'm not myself, you see."
   T8   185:19   time he had kept on very well, and she was afraid that he really was hurt this time. However, though she
   A3   24:16   hate--C and D," she added in a whisper, half afraid that it would be offended again.
   A2   19:28   "Oh, I beg your pardon!" cried Alice hastily, afraid that she had hurt the poor animal's feelings. "I quite
   T9   192: 7   rather stiffly just at first, as she was afraid that the crown might come off: but she comforted
   T8   185: 7   it that Alice did not dare to laugh. "I'm afraid you must have hurt him," she said in a trembling voice,
   T8W   15:17   Alice put down the newspaper. "I'm afraid you're not well," she said in a soothing tone. "Can't I
   T8   183: 3   "I'm afraid you've not had much practice in riding," she ventured
AFRESH (1)
   T6   161:18   "In that case we start afresh," said Humpty Dumpty, "and it's my turn to choose a

```
AFTER (85)
 T4   146:16                    "It's only a rattle," Alice said, after a careful examination of the little white thing. "Not a
A12    98:15    Adventures, till she too began dreaming after a fashion, and this was her dream:--
 A3    21: 6    they had a consultation about this, and after a few minutes it seemed quite natural to Alice to find
 A4    29:17    quite a conversation of it altogether; but after a few minutes she heard a voice outside, and stopped to
 T3   136: 5    didn't help her much, and all she could say, after a great deal of puzzling, was "L, I know it begins with
 T6   159:17    "It's very provoking," Humpty Dumpty said after a long silence, looking away from Alice as he spoke, "to
 T6   163:37    was too much puzzled to say anything; so after a minute Humpty Dumpty began again. "They've a temper,
 A6    52:23    to see it again, but it did not appear, and after a minute or two she walked on in the direction in which
 A4    31:36    had any sense, they'd take the roof off." After a minute or two they began moving about again, and Alice
 T4   144:21                    This was a puzzler. After a pause, Alice began, "Well! They were both very
 T3   129:25    I think I'll go down the other way," she said after a pause; "and perhaps I may visit the elephants later on
 T8   182: 5    "You see," he went on after a pause, "it's as well to be provided for everything.
 A9    71: 6    my arm round your waist," the Duchess said, after a pause: "the reason is, that I'm doubtful about the
 T8   186: 7    of the sort that I ever did," he went on after a pause, "was inventing a new pudding during the
 A2    15:25                    After a time she heard a little pattering of feet in the
 A1    12:13                    After a while, finding that nothing more happened, she decided
 A5    43:32    now and then she had to stop and untwist it. After a while she remembered that she still held the pieces of
 T8   179: 1                    After a while the noise seemed gradually to die away, till all
 T6   159:12    her, she thought he must be a stuffed figure after all.
 T6   162:32    to find that she had chosen a good subject after all.
T11   206: 1    ..--it really was a kitten, after all.
 A2    17:18    tears again as she went on, "I must be Mabel after all, and I shall have to go and live in that poky little
 T3   136: 3    began again. "Then it really has happened, after all! And now, who am I? I will remember, if I can! I'm
 A6    53:17    to herself "Suppose it should be raving mad after all! I almost wish I'd gone to see the Hatter instead!"
 A8    63:42    herself, "Why, they're only a pack of cards, after all. I needn't be afraid of them!"
 A5    36:27    as she had nothing else to do, and perhaps after all it might tell her something worth hearing. For some
A12    94:14    as he spoke, and added "It isn't a letter, after all: it's a set of verses."
A12    95:34    one eye; "I seem to see some meaning in them, after all. '--said I could not swim--' you ca'n't swim, can
 T8   179: 7    to cut the plum-cake, "So I wasn't dreaming, after all," she said to herself, "unless--unless we're all
 T5   149:35    "Come, you look rather better now!" she said, after altering most of the pins. "But really you should have a
 T5   156:22    bright eager eyes she caught at one bunch after another of the darling scented rushes.
 T3   135:39    she said as she stepped under the trees, "after being so hot, to get into the--into the--into what?" she
A11    91:14    the King said with a melancholy air, and, after folding his arms and frowning at the cook till his eyes
 A8    64: 5    The Queen turned crimson with fury, and, after glaring at her for a moment like a wild beast, began
 T2   120: 3    to it--at least, no, it doesn't do that--" (after going a few yards along the path, and turning several
 A6    49:13    out of the room. The cook threw a frying-pan after her as she went, but it just missed her.
 A5    36:18                    "Come back!" the Caterpillar called after her. "I've something important to say!"
 T7   174:25                    "There's some enemy after her, no doubt," the King said, without even looking
 T9   204:21    on the table, merrily running round and round after her own shawl, which was trailing behind her.
 A7    60:33    or twice, half hoping that they would call after her: the last time she saw them, they were trying to put
A11    87: 9    make out at all what had become of it; so, after hunting all about for it, he was obliged to write with
 T3   137:11                    Alice stood looking after it, almost ready to cry with vexation at having lost her
 A3    26:13    back, and finish your story!" Alice called after it. And the others all joined in chorus "Yes, please do!
 T5   153:19    spread out her arms again and went flying after it, and this time she succeeded in catching it herself.
 A1     8: 3    with curiosity, she ran across the field after it, and was just in time to see it pop down a large
 A9    74:14    on!' here," thought Alice, as she went slowly after it: "I never was so ordered about before, in all my life
 A2    20:14                    So she called softly after it, "Mouse dear! Do come back again, and we wo'n't talk
 A1     8: 5                    In another moment down went Alice after it, never once considering how in the world she was to
 T1   107:19    knots and tangles, with the kitten running after its own tail in the middle.
 T2   123:44    A little provoked, she drew back, and, after looking everywhere for the Queen (whom she spied out at
 T9   198:11    moment and said "No admittance till the week after next!" and shut the door again with a bang.
 T5   150: 1        "Oh, things that happened the week after next," the Queen replied in a careless tone. "For
 T7   173: 8    you--be good enough--" Alice panted out, after running a little further, "to stop a minute--just to get
 T5   154:17    here!" she said at last in a plaintive tone, after she had spent a minute or so in vainly pursuing a large
 T3   134: 4    then there's the Butterfly," Alice went on, after she had taken a good look at the insect with its head on
 T9   195: 4    anxiously interrupted. "She'll be feverish after so much thinking." So they set to work and fanned her
 A9    74: 3    to hear his history. I must go back and see after some executions I have ordered;" and she walked off,
 A1     8:23                    "Well!" thought Alice to herself. "After such a fall as this, I shall think nothing of tumbling
 T6   168:17    This was rather sudden, Alice thought: but, after such a very strong hint that she ought to be going, she
 T4   143:15    Oysters cried, / Turning a little blue. / 'After such kindness, that would be / A dismal thing to do!' /
A11    90: 1                    "After that," continued the Hatter, "I cut some more
 A5    36: 4    you will some day, you know--and then after that into a butterfly, I should think you'll feel it a
A11    89:20    the Hatter went on, "and most things twinkled after that--only the March Hare said--"
 T3   131:18                    And after that other voices went on ("What a number of people
 A9    74: 6    be quite as safe to stay with it as to go after that savage Queen: so she waited.
 A3    26:28    think! And oh, I wish you could see her after the birds! Why, she'll eat a little bird as soon as look
 A1    12:10    fancy what the flame of a candle looks like after the candle is blown out, for she could not remember ever
 T4   140:32    the sun / Had got no business to be there / After the day was done--/ 'It's very rude of him,' she said, /
 T8   190:31    off, first on one side and then on the other. After the fourth or fifth tumble he reached the turn, and then
 A8    65:15    for them, and then quietly marched off after the others.
 T5   153:24    politely, as she crossed the little brook after the Queen. * * * * * * * * * * * * *
 A6    53: 6    with the grin, which remained some time after the rest of it had gone.
A10    78:30                    "Swim after them!" screamed the Gryphon.
 A8    63:18    and walked two and two, as the soldiers did. After these came the royal children: there were ten of them,
 T3   132:21    Still, she couldn't feel nervous with it, after they had been talking together so long.
 A7    59: 1    "They lived on treacle," said the Dormouse, after thinking a minute or two.
 T9   192:25    here she broke off with a frown, and, after thinking for a minute, suddenly changed the subject of
 T3   134:20                    After this, Alice was silent for a minute or two, pondering.
 A4    30:13                    There was a long silence after this, and Alice could only hear whispers now and then;
```

```
AFTER (cont.)
   T8   184:21              There was a short silence after this, and then the Knight went on again. "I'm a great
   T8   183:15   could. They went on a little way in silence after this, the Knight with his eyes shut, muttering to
   T2   120: 9   did: wandering up and down, and trying turn after turn, but always coming back to the house, do what she
   A4    29:31        "That you wo'n't!" thought Alice, and after waiting till she fancied she heard the Rabbit just under
   A8    67:11   air: it puzzled her very much at first, but after watching it a minute or two she made it out to be a grin
   T4   143:27   Walrus said, / 'To play them such a trick, / After we've brought them out so far, / And made them trot so
AFTERNOON (4)
   T9   193:15   "I invite you to Alice's dinner-party this afternoon."
   T1   107:12   kitten had been finished with earlier in the afternoon, and so, while Alice was sitting curled up in a
   AI     3: 1                 All in the golden afternoon / Full leisurely we glide; / For both our oars, with
   T6   164:27   there. 'Brillig' means four o'clock in the afternoon--the time when you begin broiling things for dinner
AFTER-TIME (1)
   A12   99: 4   this same little sister of hers would, in the after-time, be herself a grown woman; and how she would keep,
AFTERWARDS (15)
   A12   96:30   no!" said the Queen. "Sentence first--verdict afterwards."
   T7   177:12   remarked. "Hand it round first, and cut it afterwards."
   T9   192:36   think before you speak--and write it down afterwards."
   T4   139:29   This seemed quite natural (she remembered afterwards), and she was not even surprised to hear music
   T5   156:43     come out again (so Alice explained it afterwards), and the consequence was that the handle of it
   T2   120:22   twist and shook itself (as she described it afterwards), and the next moment she found herself actually
   T9   203: 9             And then (as Alice afterwards described it) all sorts of things happened in a
   T2   126:12   could quite make out, in thinking it over afterwards, how it was that they began: all she remembers is,
   A1     7:14   shall be too late!" (when she thought it over afterwards it occurred to her that she ought to have wondered
   T8   187:18   she always remembered most clearly. Years afterwards she could bring the whole scene back again, as if
   T4   147:18             Alice said afterwards she had never seen such a fuss made about anything
   T1   115: 3            She said afterwards that she had never seen in all her life such a face
   T12  207:19   she said, when she was explaining the thing afterwards to her sister: "it turned away its head, and
   T4   139:34   "But it certainly was funny," (Alice said afterwards, when she was telling her sister the history of all
   T9   202:38        ("And they did push so!" she said afterwards, when she was telling her sister the history of her
AGAIN (165)
   A1     8: 6         how in the world she was to get out again.
   A1     9:33   middle, wondering how she was ever to get out again.
   A2    15:19   than ever: she sat down and began to cry again.
   A2    19:45   vulgar things! Don't let me hear the name again!"
   A3    24:16      half afraid that it would be offended again.
   A5    36:21      certainly. Alice turned and came back again.
   A5    37: 8   sure I have none, / Why, I do it again and again."
   A5    41:22   the hookah into its mouth, and began smoking again.
   A6    47:19   not to her, so she took courage, and went on again:--
   A6    52:15   place where it had been, it suddenly appeared again.
   A6    52:21   thought it would," said the Cat, and vanished again.
   A7    56:28    yet?" the Hatter said, turning to Alice again.
   A10   78: 7   tears running down his cheeks, he went on again:--
   A10   83: 1   anything would ever happen in a natural way again.
   A12   94:20   said the King. (The jury all brightened up again.)
   T1   108:20   floor, and yards and yards of it got unwound again.
   T1   116:15   a glass, the words will all go the right way again."
   T2   123:43   found herself walking in at the front-door again.
   T2   128:21   Alice got up and curtseyed, and sat down again.
   T3   136:11   back a little, and then stood looking at her again.
   T4   140:22             Tweedledee smiled gently, and began again:
   T5   149: 6   said, as she helped her to put on her shawl again.
   T5   152:17   clutched wildly at it, and tried to clasp it again.
   T5   152:24   holding her hands ready to put over her ears again.
   T5   152:26   "What would be the good of having it all over again?"
   T5   153:16   things before breakfast. There goes the shawl again!"
   T5   155:26   got fast in it, and would hardly come out again.
   T6   159:31   men / Couldn't put Humpty Dumpty in his place again."
   T6   167:20   said it plain, / 'Then you must wake them up again.'
   T7   172:29    at the top of his voice, "They're at it again!"
   T7   173:10   "to stop a minute--just to get--one's breath again?"
   T7   177:10   slices already, but they always join on again!"
   T8   184:16   in time to save himself from tumbling off again.
   T9   199:41             Then came the chorus again:--
   T9   203: 6   the table, and managed to pull herself down again.
   T8W   18:12   was silent for a few moments, and then began again--
   T8W   19: 8   to do, you know? / My ringlets would not grow again.
   A7    58:16   what happens when you come to the beginning again?" Alice ventured to ask.
   T5   153:21      tone. "Now you shall see me pin it on again, all by myself!"
   A5    37: 8   perfectly sure I have none, / Why, I do it again and again."
   A4    31:38   After a minute or two they began moving about again, and Alice heard the Rabbit say "A barrowful will do, to
   A6    49:31             The baby grunted again, and Alice looked very anxiously into its face to see
   A12   98:35   though she knew she had but to open them again, and all would change to dull reality--the grass would
   A5    44: 5   So she began nibbling at the right-hand bit again, and did not venture to go near the house till she had
   A4    27: 1   It was the White Rabbit, trotting slowly back again, and looking anxiously about as it went, as if it had
   A4    30:16   coward!", and at last she spread out her hand again, and made another snatch in the air. This time there
   T3   137:14   some comfort. Alice--Alice--I won't forget it again. And now, which of these finger-posts ought I to follow,
   A12   93: 7   quite unable to move. She soon got it out again, and put it right; "not that it signifies much," she
   T3   134:22   round and round her head: at last it settled again and remarked "I suppose you don't want to lose your name
```

AGAIN (cont.)

A5	36:29	its arms, took the hookah out of its mouth	again, and said "So you think you're changed, do you?"
A11	88:36	what it was: she was beginning to grow larger	again, and she thought at first she would get up and leave the
A10	78:35	"Back to land	again, and--that's all the first figure," said the Mock Turtle
A2	18:13	door; but, alas! the little door was shut	again, and the little golden key was lying on the glass table
T9	199:35	counting?" In a minute there was silence	again, and the same shrill voice sang another verse:--
A4	32:19	in the wood, "is to grow to my right size	again; and the second thing is to find my way into that lovely
T8	179:25	as the Red Knight had done: then he got on	again, and the two Knights sat and looked at each other for
T1	107:17	it up and down till it had all come undone	again; and there it was, spread over the hearth-rug, all knots
T2	128:22	At the next peg the Queen turned	again, and this time she said "Speak in French when you ca'n't
A2	20:14	softly after it, "Mouse dear! Do come back	again, and we wo'n't talk about cats, or dogs either, if you
A8	68:26	away under her arm, that it might not escape	again, and went back to have a little more conversation with
T5	153:19	a little brook. The Queen spread out her arms	again and went flying after it, and this time she succeeded in
T1	109:13	'Go to sleep, darlings, till the summer comes	again.' And when they wake up in the summer, Kitty, they dress
T8	187:19	she could bring the whole scene back	again, as if it had been only yesterday--the mild blue eyes
A12	92: 9	of great dismay, and began picking them up	again as quickly as she could, for the accident of the
T2	125:16	Alice curtseyed	again, as she was afraid from the Queen's tone that she was a
A2	17:17	poor Alice, and her eyes filled with tears	again as she went on, "I must be Mabel after all, and I shall
T8	179:19	watched him with some anxiety as he mounted	again. As soon as he was comfortably in the saddle, he began
T2	120:16	should have to get through the Looking-glass	again--back into the old room--and there'd be an end of all my
A7	58:31	it," added the Hatter, "or you'll be asleep	again before it's done."
A12	96:16	"Nothing can be clearer than _that_. Then	again--'_before she had this fit_'--you never had _fits_, my dear,
T4	144: 9	a pleasant run! / Shall we be trotting home	again?' / But answer came there none--/ And this was scarcely
T6	168:34	waited a minute to see if he would speak	again, but, as he never opened his eyes or took any further
A7	56: 8	it into his cup of tea, and looked at it	again: but he could think of nothing better to say than his
A6	52:22	waited a little, half expecting to see it	again, but it did not appear, and after a minute or two she
T8	185:10	seriously. "And then he took the helmet off	again--but it took hours and hours to get me out. I was as
T1	108: 5	with her, and began winding up the ball	again. But she didn't get on very fast, as she was talking all
T9	194:39	Here the Red Queen began	again. "Can you answer useful questions?" she said. "How is
A10	85: 1	"Chorus	again!" cried the Gryphon, and the Mock Turtle had just begun
A2	17:22	putting their heads down and saying 'Come up	again, dear!' I shall only look up and say 'Who am I, then?
A1	9: 6	else to do, so Alice soon began talking	again. "Dinah'll miss me very much to-night, I should think!"
T5	153: 9	you?" the Queen said in a pitying tone. "Try	again: draw a long breath, and shut your eyes."
A4	28: 7	does. I do hope it'll make me grow large	again, for really I'm quite tired of being such a tiny little
A3	26:41	any more!" And here poor Alice began to cry	again, for she felt very lonely and low-spirited. In a minute or
A2	20:11	sorrowful tone. "I'm afraid I've offended it	again!" For the Mouse was swimming away from her as hard as it
A2	19:39	mice--oh, I beg your pardon!" cried Alice	again, for this time the Mouse was bristling all over, and she
T8W	14:12	round the tree, but when he got settled down	again he only said, as before, "Worrity, worrity! Can't you
A3	26:42	low-spirited. In a little while, however, she	again heard a little pattering of footsteps in the distance,
A7	59:29	said very humbly. "I wo'n't interrupt you	again. I dare say there may be one."
T9	192: 9	really am a Queen," she said as she sat down	again, "I shall be able to manage it quite well in time."
A1	8:39	Presently she began	again. "I wonder if I shall fall right through the earth! How
T6	168:21	"I shouldn't know you	again if we _did_ meet," Humpty Dumpty replied in a discontented
T7	172:31	and shaking himself. "If you do such a thing	again, I'll have you buttered! It went through and through my
T8	184:22	after this, and then the Knight went on	again. "I'm a great hand at inventing things. Now, I daresay
A6	46:32	"How am I to get in?" asked Alice	again, in a louder tone.
A5	41:23	waited patiently until it chose to speak	again. In a minute or two the Caterpillar took the hookah out
T6	161:14	Humpty Dumpty went on. "They'd pick me up	again in a minute, _they_ would! However, this conversation is
T9	201:17	Bring back the pudding!" and there it was	again in a moment, like a conjuring-trick. It was so large
A3	24:12	it was over at last, and they sat down	again in a ring, and begged the Mouse to tell them something
T2	121: 3	only went on waving about, she spoke	again, in a timid voice--almost in a whisper. "And can _all_ the
T5	158: 1	vanished all in a moment, and she was back	again in the little dark shop.
T1	119:10	and was rather glad to find herself walking	again in the natural way.
A5	43:29	Pigeon in a sulky tone, as it settled down	again into its nest. Alice crouched down among the trees as
T3	136:16	"Think	again," it said: "that wo'n't do."
T6	162:23	for a minute or two. When he _did_ speak	again, it was in a deep growl.
T9	196:11	Here the White Queen began	again. "It was _such_ a thunderstorm, you ca'n't think!" ("She
A8	66:13	had got its head down, and was going to begin	again, it was very provoking to find that the hedgehog had
T9	204: 5	voice from the soup-tureen, and Alice turned	again, just in time to see the Queen's broad good-natured face
A4	33:11	I'd nearly forgotten that I've got to grow up	again! Let me see--how _is_ it to be managed? I suppose I ought
A4	28:26	of chance of her ever getting out of the room	again, no wonder she felt unhappy.
T9	195: 7	"She's all right	again now," said the Red Queen. "Do you know Languages? What's
A6	50: 5	you. Mind now!" The poor little thing sobbed	again (or grunted, it was impossible to say which), and they
A2	19:24	long ago anything had happened.) So she began	again: "Ou est ma chatte?" which was the first sentence in her
T8	184:10	time that Alice was getting him on his feet	again. "Plenty of practice!"
T8	190:27	on his head as usual! However, he gets on	again pretty easily--that comes of having so many things hung
T8W	21:16	the Wasp, and Alice tripped down the hill	again, quite pleased that she had gone back and given a few
A5	42:29	"Serpent, I say	again!" repeated the Pigeon, but in a more subdued tone, and
A7	60:35	"At any rate I'll never go _there_	again!" said Alice, as she picked her way through the wood.
A7	56:22	"The Dormouse is asleep	again," said the Hatter, and he poured a little hot tea upon
T5	153:33	up in wool. Alice rubbed her eyes, and looked	again. She couldn't make out what had happened at all. Was she
A2	18: 4	that?" she thought. "I must be growing small	again." She got up and went to the table to measure herself by
T6	168:20	held out her hand. "Good-bye, till we meet	again!" she said as cheerfully as she could.
T1	116: 4	ready to throw over him, in case he fainted	again), she turned over the leaves, to find some part that she
T7	172:35	earthquake!" thought Alice. "Who are at it	again?" she ventured to ask.
T2	126:25	felt as if she would never be able to talk	again, she was getting so much out of breath: and still the
T2	122:10	down to the daisies, who were just beginning	again, she whispered "If you don't hold your tongues, I'll
A6	48:33	And with that she began nursing her child	again, singing a sort of lullaby to it as she did so, and
A6	52:28	this, she looked up, and there was the Cat	again, sitting on a branch of a tree.
T5	156:42	got fast in the water and _wouldn't_ come out	again (so Alice explained it afterwards), and the consequence

AGAIN (cont.)

A7	60: 3	Alice did not wish to offend the Dormouse	again, so she began very cautiously: "But I don't understand.
A6	49:19	itself up and straightening itself out	again, so that altogether, for the first minute or two, it was
A6	50: 9	when I get it home?" when it grunted	again, so violently, that she looked down into its face in
T5	155:27	"Feather! Feather!" the Sheep cried	again, taking more needles. "You'll be catching a crab
A10	81: 7	their mouths. So they couldn't get them out	again. That's all."
T3	130: 3	a ticket-office where I came from." And	again the chorus of voices went on. "There wasn't room for one
A11	91:24	out, and, by the time they had settled down	again, the cook had disappeared.
A3	23:14	half an hour or so, and were quite dry	again, the Dodo suddenly called out "The race is over!" and
A9	72:23	"Thinking	again?" the Duchess asked, with another dig of her sharp
A9	76: 4	added the Gryphon, before Alice could speak	again. The Mock Turtle went on.
T8	185: 4	the worst of it was, before I could get out	again, the other White Knight came and put it on. He thought
T5	152:14	"When I fasten my shawl	again," the poor Queen groaned out: "the brooch will come
T5	157: 2	she wasn't a bit hurt, and was soon up	again: the Sheep went on with her knitting all the while, just
A12	98:17	she dreamed about little Alice herself: once	again the tiny hands were clasped upon her knee, and the
T3	136: 3	a minute, thinking: then she suddenly began	again. "Then it really has happened, after all! And now, who
A4	32:42	under its feet, ran round the thistle	again: then the puppy began a series of short charges at the
T7	177: 4	know," the Lion growled out as he lay down	again. "There was too much dust to see anything. What a time
A3	21: 5	first question of course was, how to get dry	again: they had a consultation about this, and after a few
T8	180:12	in this way, side by side. When they got up	again, they shook hands, and then the Red Knight mounted and
T6	163:38	so after a minute Humpty Dumpty began	again. "They've a temper, some of them--particularly verbs:
T2	120:27	so there was nothing to be done but start	again. This time she came upon a large flowerbed, with a
T6	167: 7	"I sent to them	again to say / 'It will be better to obey.'
A6	50: 1	she thought, and looked into its eyes	again, to see if there were any tears.
A5	36:10	Which brought them back	again to the beginning of the conversation. Alice felt a
A7	59:22	The Dormouse	again took a minute or two to think about it, and then said
A6	48:30	seemed not to be listening, so she went on	again: "Twenty-four hours, I think; or is it twelve? I--"
A12	96:23	it made no mark; but he now hastily began	again, using the ink, that was trickling down his face, as
A10	79: 1	about like mad things all this time, sat down	again very sadly and quietly, and looked at Alice.
T1	108:22	on, as soon as they were comfortably settled	again, "when I saw all the mischief you had been doing, I was
T8	182:41	fell off in front; and, whenever it went on	again (which it generally did rather suddenly), he fell off
A4	32: 4	and shouted out "You'd better not do that	again!", which produced another dead silence.
T9	198:11	till the week after next!" and shut the door	again with a bang.
A7	60:22	on being pinched by the Hatter, it woke up	again with a little shriek, and went on: "--that begins with
T4	139:17	cried out briskly, and shut his mouth up	again with a snap.
A10	78:33	"Change lobsters	again!" yelled the Gryphon at the top of its voice.
T2	120:14	it was arguing with her. "I'm not going in	again yet. I know I should have to get through the
A9	70: 1	"You ca'n't think how glad I am to see you	again, you dear old thing!" said the Duchess, as she tucked

AGAINST (16)

A4	33: 8	puppy it was!" said Alice, as she leant	against a buttercup to rest herself, and fanned herself with
T8W	13: 6	a wasp) was sitting on the ground, leaning	against a tree, all huddled up together, and shivering as if
T2	127:10	The Queen propped her up	against a tree, and said kindly, "You may rest a little, now
T8	187:25	as, with one hand shading her eyes, she leant	against a tree, watching the strange pair, and listening, in a
A8	65:43	running about in all directions, tumbling up	against each other: however, they got settled down in a minute
A5	42: 1	other bit. Her chin was pressed so closely	against her foot, that there was hardly room to open her mouth
A1	12:27	herself in a game of croquet she was playing	against herself, for this curious child was very fond of
T2	120:12	rather more quickly than usual, she ran	against it before she could stop herself.
A4	29:27	inwards, and Alice's elbow was pressed hard	against it, that attempt proved a failure. Alice heard it say
A6	46:29	it just grazed his nose, and broke to pieces	against one of the trees behind him.
T8	182: 9	"To guard	against the bites of sharks," the Knight replied. "It's an
A4	28:10	half the bottle, she found her head pressing	against the ceiling, and had to stoop to save her neck from
A4	28:18	tried the effect of lying down with one elbow	against the door, and the other arm curled round her head.
A2	15:12	Just at this moment her head struck	against the roof of the hall: in fact she was now rather more
T1	109: 9	"Do you hear the snow	against the window-panes, Kitty? How nice and soft it sounds!
AI	3:12	/ Yet what can one poor voice avail /	Against three tongues together?

AGE (8)

A2	16: 2	the children she knew that were of the same	age as herself, to see if she could have been changed for any
T5	153:14	practice," said the Queen. "When I was your	age, I always did it for half-an-hour a day. Why, sometimes
A5	37: 4	stand on your head--/ Do you think, at your	age, it is right?"
A11	86:26	too, that very few little girls of her	age knew the meaning of it at all. However, "jurymen" would
T6	162: 4	thoughtfully. "An uncomfortable sort of	age. Now if you'd asked my advice, I'd have said 'Leave off at
T6	162:14	(They had had quite enough of the subject of	age, she thought: and, if they really were to take turns in
A3	21:12	as the Lory positively refused to tell its	age, there was no more to be said.
T5	153: 3	things at once, you know. Let's consider your	age to begin with--how old are you?"

AGED (5)

T8	187: 3	the name is called. The name really is 'The	Aged Aged Man.'"
T8	187:33	I can: / There's little to relate. / I saw an	aged aged man, / A-sitting on a gate. / 'Who are you, aged man
T8	187: 3	name is called. The name really is 'The Aged	Aged Man.'"
T8	187:33	/ There's little to relate. / I saw an aged	aged man, / A-sitting on a gate. / 'Who are you, aged man?' I
T8	187:35	man, / A-sitting on a gate. / 'Who are you,	aged man?' I said. / 'And how is it you live?' / And his

AGLOW (1)

| T8 | 190: 4 | like a crow, / With eyes, like cinders, all | aglow, / Who seemed distracted with his woe, / Who rocked his |

AGO (4)

A12	99: 8	even with the dream of Wonderland of long	ago; and how she would feel with all their simple sorrows, and
A2	19:24	Alice had no very clear notion how long	ago anything had happened.) So she began again: "Ou est ma
T8	190:10	like a buffalo--/ That summer evening long	ago, / A-sitting on a gate."
T2	127: 2	repeated. "Why, we passed it ten minutes	ago! Faster!" And they ran on for a time in silence, with the

AGONY (1)

| A6 | 48:17 | cried Alice, jumping up and down in an | agony of terror. "Oh, there goes his precious nose!", as an |

AGREE (3) [See also DISAGREE]
    A9   71:17 it is," said the Duchess, who seemed ready to agree to everything that Alice said: "there's a large
    T4   147: 8   "Of course you agree to have a battle?" Tweedledum said in a calmer tone.
    A9   72: 5   "I quite agree with you," said the Duchess; "and the moral of that is--
AGREED (1)
    T4   138:19   "Tweedledum and Tweedledee / Agreed to have a battle; / For Tweedledum said Tweedledee /
AH (12)
    AI   3: 7   Ah, cruel Three! In such an hour, / Beneath such dreamy
    T8W   13:22 his shoulders, and turned his head away. "Ah, deary me!" he said to himself.
    A3   26:18 the opportunity of saying to her daughter "Ah, my dear! Let this be a lesson to you never to lose your
    A7   56:42   "Ah! That accounts for it," said the Hatter. "He wo'n't stand
    T9   202:14 on the table. / 'Take the dish-cover up!' / Ah, that is so hard that I fear I'm unable!
    A2   15:42 the next question is 'Who in the world am I?' Ah, that's the great puzzle!" And she began thinking over all
    A9   76:13   "Ah! Then yours wasn't a really good school," said the Mock
    A9   70:36   "Ah well! It means much the same thing," said the Duchess,
    T6   160:35   "Ah, well! They may write such things in a book," Humpty Dumpty
    T7   176: 3   "Ah, what is it, now?" the Unicorn cried eagerly. "You'll never
    T6   160:25 fall," he went on, "the King has promised me--ah, you may turn pale, if you like! You didn't think I was
    T6   164: 9   "Ah, you should see 'em come round me of a Saturday night,"
AHEM (1)
    A3   22: 1   "Ahem!" said the Mouse with an important air. "Are you all
AHOY (4)
    T8   179:13 were interrupted by a loud shouting of "Ahoy! Ahoy! Check!" and a Knight, dressed in crimson armour,
    T8   179:21 You're my--" but here another voice broke in "Ahoy! Ahoy! Check!" and Alice looked round in some surprise
    T8   179:13 were interrupted by a loud shouting of "Ahoy! Ahoy! Check!" and a Knight, dressed in crimson armour, came
    T8   179:21 my--" but here another voice broke in "Ahoy! Ahoy! Check!" and Alice looked round in some surprise for the
AIMING (1)
    T2   124: 5 in sight of the hill she had been so long aiming at.
AIN'T [AINT] (3)
    T4   139: 8 it were so, it would be; but as it isn't, it ain't. That's logic."
    T8W   20: 6 the shape of your head as does it. Your jaws aint well shaped, though--I should think you couldn't bite
    T8W   18:10   "It aint what I'm used to," said the Wasp: "however I'll try; wait
AIR (29) [See also NIGHT-AIR]
    A10   78:28 shouted the Gryphon, with a bound into the air.
    T6   162:36 I beg your pardon?" Alice said with a puzzled air.
    A11   91:13 I must," the King said with a melancholy air, and, after folding his arms and frowning at the cook till
    A12   97: 9   At this the whole pack rose up into the air, and came flying down upon her; she gave a little scream,
    T3   132:10 felt the carriage rise straight up into the air, and in her fright she caught at the thing nearest to her
    T3   137: 6 here the Fawn gave a sudden bound into the air, and shook itself free from Alice's arm. "I'm a Fawn!" it
    T1   119: 9 a little giddy with so much floating in the air, and was rather glad to find herself walking again in the
    A3   22: 1 "Ahem!" said the Mouse with an important air. "Are you all ready? This is the driest thing I know.
    T1   115: 4 King made, when he found himself held in the air by an invisible hand, and being dusted: he was far too
    A1   9: 1 curtseying as you're falling through the air! Do you think you could manage it?) "And what an ignorant
    A6   47: 7 There was certainly too much of it in the air. Even the Duchess sneezed occasionally; and as for the
    T1   114: 9 and sat down: the rapid journey through the air had quite taken away her breath, and for a minute or two
    T2   127: 6 that at last they seemed to skim through the air, hardly touching the ground with their feet, till suddenly
    T9   203: 3 side, that they nearly lifted her up into the air. "I rise to return thanks--" Alice began: and she really
    A6   49:25 itself), she carried it out into the open air. "If I don't take this child away with me," thought Alice,
    A1   9: 9 down here with me! There are no mice in the air, I'm afraid, but you might catch a bat, and that's very
    T2   123:34 does it," said the Rose: "wonderfully fine air it is, out here."
    A8   67:10 when she noticed a curious appearance in the air: it puzzled her very much at first, but after watching it
    A12   98:32 of the suppressed guinea-pigs, filled the air, mixed up with the distant sob of the miserable Mock
    A11   91:25   "Never mind!" said the King with an air of great relief. "Call the next witness." And, he added,
    T7   175:16 stood for some time looking at her with an air of the deepest disgust.
    A4   32:35 puppy: whereupon the puppy jumped into the air off all its feet at once, with a yelp of delight, and
    T2   128:29 she was gone. Whether she vanished into the air, or whether she ran quickly into the wood ("and she can
    T7   178: 1 noise came from, she couldn't make out: the air seemed full of it, and it rang through and through her
    T2   122: 8 they all began shouting together, till the air seemed quite full of little shrill voices. "Silence, every
    A4   29:35 spread out her hand, and made a snatch in the air. She did not get hold of anything, but she heard a little
    T2   123:33   "It's the fresh air that does it," said the Rose: "wonderfully fine air it is,
    A4   30:16 hand again, and made another snatch in the air. This time there were two little shrieks, and more sounds
    T6   168:28 two eyes, so--"(marking their places in the air with his thumb) "nose in the middle, mouth under. It's
AIRS (1)
    A5   40: 6 / Said his father. "Don't give yourself airs! / Do you think I can listen all day to such stuff? / Be
ALARM (9)
    T3   132: 4 from the engine, and everybody jumped up in alarm, Alice among the rest.
    T4   148:21 Tweedledum cried out in a shrill voice of alarm; and the two brothers took to their heels and were out
    T4   144:23   " Here she checked herself in some alarm, at hearing something that sounded to her like the
    T3   137: 8 me! you're a human child!" A sudden look of alarm came into its beautiful brown eyes, and in another
    A5   42: 8 in a tone of delight, which changed into alarm in another moment, when she found that her shoulders
    T7   171:16   "You alarm me!" said the King. "I feel faint--Give me a
    T8   179: 2 silence, and Alice lifted up her head in some alarm. There was no one to be seen, and her first thought was
    A6   50:10 that she looked down into its face in some alarm. This time there could be no mistake about it: it was
    T3   134:10 the Gnat (Alice drew her feet back in some alarm), "you may observe a Bread-and-butter-fly. Its wings are
ALARMED (2)
    A7   58:21 afraid I don't know one," said Alice, rather alarmed at the proposal.
    T1   115:16 lay perfectly still; and Alice was a little alarmed at what she had done, and went round the room to see
ALAS (4)
    A1   9:37 belong to one of the doors of the hall; but, alas! either the locks were too large, or the key was too
    A1   12:14   on going into the garden at once; but, alas for poor Alice! when she got to the door, she found she

ALAS (cont.)
A4   28:15   Alas! It was too late to wish that! She went on growing, and
A2   18:13   with all speed back to the little door; but, alas! the little door was shut again, and the little golden
ALICE (847)
A3   23:32   got in your pocket?" it went on, turning to Alice.
A5   42:32   least idea what you're talking about," said Alice.
A6   46:41   "But what am I to do?" said Alice.
A6   51:11   "I don't much care where--" said Alice.
A6   51:25   "How do you know I'm mad?" said Alice.
A6   51:31   "I suppose so," said Alice.
A6   51:35   "I call it purring, not growling," said Alice.
A7   55:18   "Exactly so," said Alice.
A7   56:37   "I don't know what you mean," said Alice.
A7   57:17   "I've heard something like it," said Alice.
A7   58: 7   "How dreadfully savage!" exclaimed Alice.
A7   58:14   "Then you keep moving round, I suppose?" said Alice.
A7   58:29   "Yes, please do!" pleaded Alice.
A7   59:15   "Nobody asked your opinion," said Alice.
A7   60:17   "Why with an M?" said Alice.
A8   65:22   "Yes!" shouted Alice.
A8   65:33   "What for?" said Alice.
A9   71:16   "It's a mineral, I think," said Alice.
A9   72:17   to say it any longer than that," said Alice.
A9   73:15   "I never saw one, or heard of one," said Alice.
A9   74: 9   said the Gryphon, half to itself, half to Alice.
A9   74:10   "What is the fun?" said Alice.
A9   76: 1   "I never said I didn't!" interrupted Alice.
A9   76:20   "What was that?" inquired Alice.
A9   77: 1   "What was that like?" said Alice.
A9   77:14   "What a curious plan!" exclaimed Alice.
A10   79: 1   again very sadly and quietly, and looked at Alice.
A10   79: 4   "Very much indeed," said Alice.
A10   81:36   "Don't you mean 'purpose'?" said Alice.
A10   82:14   he thought it had some kind of authority over Alice.
A11   87: 4   be in, before the trial's over!" thought Alice.
A11   91:33   the top of his shrill little voice, the name "Alice!"
A12   93:17   know about this business?" the King said to Alice.
A12   93:18   "Nothing," said Alice.
A12   93:20   "Nothing whatever," said Alice.
A12   93:37   Everybody looked at Alice.
A12   93:38   "I'm not a mile high," said Alice.
A12   93:44   "Then it ought to be Number One," said Alice.
A12   96:11   on 'they all returned from him to you,'" said Alice.
A12   97: 4   "I wo'n't!" said Alice.
T3   129:11 "just as if it was a regular bee," thought Alice.
T3   130:17 pounds to-night, I know I shall!" thought Alice.
T4   145: 7   "Where I am now, of course," said Alice.
T4   148:13 wish the monstrous crow would come!" thought Alice.
T5   151: 7   "Suppose he never commits the crime?" said Alice.
T5   151:15   "Only for faults," said Alice.
T5   153: 8   "I ca'n't believe that!" said Alice.
T5   157:11   "Are there many crabs here?" said Alice.
T6   162:44   "Three hundred and sixty-five," said Alice.
T6   163:21   "Certainly," said Alice.
T6   166:26   "I see you don't," said Alice.
T6   166:31   "Thank you very much," said Alice.
T6   166:36 "I will, if I can remember it so long," said Alice.
T6   167: 5   "I'm afraid I don't quite understand," said Alice.
T7   170:16   "I see nobody on the road," said Alice.
T7   171: 2   "I beg your pardon?" said Alice.
T7   175:32   "Yes, if you like," said Alice.
T8   181:28 "Can you guess why I did that?" he said to Alice.
T8   181:33 like one--fastened to the saddle," said Alice.
T8   182:12   "It's meant for plum-cake," said Alice.
T8   184:25   "You were a little grave," said Alice.
T9t   192: 1   QUEEN ALICE
T9   194:34   "To be sure I do," said Alice.
T9   199:11 the paint would come off: then he looked at Alice.
T9   202:28 gravy, "just like pigs in a trough!" thought Alice.
T8W   17: 1   "Oh, you mean stiff-neck," said Alice.
T8W   20:14   "I'm afraid not," said Alice.
AI   4: 3   Alice! A childish story take, / And, with a gentle hand, / Lay
A2   18:10   "That was a narrow escape!" said Alice, a good deal frightened at the sudden change, but very
A4   33: 3   This seemed to Alice a good opportunity for making her escape: so she set off
A2   15:20   "You ought to be ashamed of yourself," said Alice, "a great girl like you," (she might well say this), "to
T5   156: 1   This offended Alice a little, so there was no more conversation for a minute
A10   81:41   beginning from this morning," said Alice a little timidly; "but it's no use going back to
A6   47:12   "Please would you tell me," said Alice, a little timidly, for she was not quite sure whether it
A8   63: 3   "Would you tell me, please," said Alice, a little timidly, "why you are painting those roses?"
T6   165: 8   "And a long way beyond it on each side," Alice added.

ALICE (cont.)

A6	51:13	"--so long as I get somewhere," Alice added as an explanation.
T2	120:30	"O Tiger-lily!" said Alice, addressing herself to one that was waving gracefully
A1	8: 5	In another moment down went Alice after it, never once considering how in the world she
T9	203: 9	And then (as Alice afterwards described it) all sorts of things happened in
A7	56:28	the riddle yet?" the Hatter said, turning to Alice again.
A2	19:39	catching mice--oh, I beg your pardon!" cried Alice again, for this time the Mouse was bristling all over,
A6	46:32	"How am I to get in?" asked Alice again, in a louder tone.
T3	137:13	my name now," she said: "that's some comfort. Alice--Alice--I won't forget it again. And now, which of these
T9	201:13	Queen looked sulky, and growled "Pudding----Alice: Alice--Pudding. Remove the pudding!" and the waiters
A5	36: 7	perhaps your feelings may be different," said Alice: "all I know is, it would feel very queer to me."
A8	67:39	"It's a friend of mine--a Cheshire-Cat," said Alice: "allow me to introduce it."
T9	199: 6	Alice almost stamped with irritation at the slow drawl in
A9	74: 4	I have ordered;" and she walked off, leaving Alice alone with the Gryphon. Alice did not quite like the
A3	26:22	wish I had our Dinah here, I know I do!" said Alice aloud, addressing nobody in particular. "She'd soon
A3	26: 6	"A knot!" said Alice, always ready to make herself useful, and looking
T9	192:35	"So you did, you know," the Red Queen said to Alice. "Always speak the truth--think before you speak--and
T3	132: 4	the engine, and everybody jumped up in alarm, Alice among the rest.
A8	68:18	fight with another hedgehog, which seemed to Alice an excellent opportunity for croqueting one of them with
T3	129:38	child!" the Guard went on, looking angrily at Alice. And a great many voices all said together ("like the
A4	29:31	"That you wo'n't!" thought Alice, and after waiting till she fancied she heard the Rabbit
T9	201: 2	got up in the dish and made a little bow to Alice; and Alice returned the bow, not knowing whether to be
A9	72:40	Let's go on with the game," the Queen said to Alice; and Alice was too much frightened to say a word, but
T9	197: 7	the ball--/ Red Queen, and White Queen, and Alice, and all!
A12	98:14	the setting sun, and thinking of little Alice and all her wonderful Adventures, till she too began
T4	145:21	"I am real!" said Alice, and began to cry.
A2	17:16	those are not the right words," said poor Alice, and her eyes filled with tears again as she went on, "I
A6	53: 2	"I said 'pig'," replied Alice; "and I wish you wouldn't keep appearing and vanishing
A1	12:34	marked in currants. "Well, I'll eat it," said Alice, "and if it makes me grow larger, I can reach the key;
A8	67:37	you talking to?" said the King, coming up to Alice, and looking at the Cat's head with great curiosity.
T1	113:15	something began squeaking on the table behind Alice, and made her turn her head just in time to see one of
A10	78: 9	much under the sea--" ("I haven't," said Alice)--"and perhaps you were never even introduced to a
T7	175:26	The Unicorn looked dreamily at Alice, and said "Talk, child."
A8	65:12	"You sha'n't be beheaded!" said Alice, and she put them into a large flower-pot that stood
A9	77:17	This was quite a new idea to Alice, and she thought it over a little before she made her
A12	98: 6	"Oh, I've had such a curious dream!" said Alice. And she told her sister, as well as she could remember
T4	146:10	"Selfish things!" thought Alice, and she was just going to say "Good-night" and leave
A6	51: 6	wider. "Come, it's pleased so far," thought Alice, and she went on. "Would you tell me, please, which way
A3	24:17	and sad tale!" said the Mouse, turning to Alice, and sighing.
T6	164:29	"That'll do very well," said Alice: "and 'slithy'?"
T7	176: 1	"What's this!" he said, blinking lazily at Alice, and speaking in a deep hollow tone that sounded like
T8	190:20	"Of course I'll wait," said Alice: "and thank you very much for coming so far--and for the
T2	126:21	move along with us?" thought poor puzzled Alice. And the Queen seemed to guess her thoughts, for she
T9	198: 5	"I'll wait till the song's over," thought Alice, "and then I'll ring the--the--which bell must I ring?"
T7	173:24	tea when he was sent in," Haigha whispered to Alice: "and they only give them oyster-shells in there--so you
A11	86:21	"And that's the jury-box," thought Alice; "and those twelve creatures," (she was obliged to say
A1	10:16	("which certainly was not here before," said Alice), and tied round the neck of the bottle was a paper
A10	78: 2	of one flapper across his eyes. He looked at Alice and tried to speak, but, for a minute or two, sobs
A5	42:13	"What can all that green stuff be?" said Alice. "And where have my shoulders got to? And oh, my poor
A3	24:14	to tell me your history, you know," said Alice, "and why it is you hate--C and D," she added in a
A7	55: 1	wasn't very civil of you to offer it," said Alice angrily.
A6	52:19	"It turned into a pig," Alice answered very quietly, just as if the Cat had come back
A8	68:33	The moment Alice appeared, she was appealed to by all three to settle the
A8	68:24	sight: "but it doesn't matter much," thought Alice, "as all the arches are gone from this side of the
A12	93: 3	repeated with great emphasis, looking hard at Alice as he said so.
A8	67:45	don't look at me like that!" He got behind Alice as he spoke.
T6	159:18	said after a long silence, looking away from Alice as he spoke, "to be called an egg--very!"
T8W	21: 4	he spoke, and stetched out one claw towards Alice, as if he wished to do the same for her, but she kept
A3	22:25	on now, my dear?" it continued, turning to Alice as it spoke.
T5	158:17	"I wonder why it wouldn't do?" thought Alice, as she groped her way among the tables and chairs, for
A4	33: 7	yet what a dear little puppy it was!" said Alice, as she leant against a buttercup to rest herself, and
A7	60:35	"At any rate I'll never go there again!" said Alice, as she picked her way through the wood. "It's the
T5	158:10	"Then I'll have one, please," said Alice, as she put the money down on the counter. For she
T9	202:30	neat speech," the Red Queen said, frowning at Alice as she spoke.
T3	129: 3	very like learning geography," thought Alice, as she stood on tiptoe in hopes of being able to see a
A8	62:18	things--" when his eye chanced to fall upon Alice, as she stood watching them, and he checked himself
A2	19: 1	"I wish I hadn't cried so much!" said Alice, as she swam about, trying to find her way out. "I shall
T9	196:38	"I haven't got a nightcap with me," said Alice, as she tried to obey the first direction: "and I don't
A4	27:12	Very soon the Rabbit noticed Alice, as she went hunting about, and called out to her, in an
A9	74:13	"Everybody says 'come on!' here," thought Alice, as she went slowly after it: "I never was so ordered
A8	65:20	The soldiers were silent, and looked at Alice, as the question was evidently meant for her.
A7	57: 9	"Is that the way you manage?" Alice asked.
A9	75: 1	did you call him Tortoise, if he wasn't one?" Alice asked.
T2	122: 3	"But what could it do, if any danger came?" Alice asked.
T3	134: 1	"And what does it live on?" Alice asked, as before.
T8	185:24	go on talking so quietly, head downwards?" Alice asked, as she dragged him out by the feet, and laid him
T5	155:36	"Why do you say 'Feather' so often?" Alice asked at last, rather vexed. "I'm not a bird!"
T6	160: 7	"Must a name mean something?" Alice asked doubtfully.
T2	123: 9	"Is she like me?" Alice asked eagerly, for the thought crossed her mind,
T8	186:33	"Is it very long?" Alice asked, for she had heard a good deal of poetry that day.

ALICE (cont.)

T5	152:23	"But why don't you scream now?"	Alice asked, holding her hands ready to put over her ears
T8	186:20	"What did you mean it to be made of?"	Alice asked, hoping to cheer him up, for the poor Knight
A10	81:23	"And what are they made of?"	Alice asked in a tone of great curiosity.
T8	182: 8	"But what are they for?"	Alice asked in a tone of great curiosity.
T9	196: 7	"Is there generally?"	Alice asked in an astonished tone.
T3	135:11	"Why do you wish I had made it?"	Alice asked. "It's a very bad one."
T7	175: 2	"But aren't you going to run and help her?"	Alice asked, very much surprised at his taking it so quietly.
T3	133: 6	"What does it live on?"	Alice asked, with great curiosity.
T2	123:22	"Where does she wear them?"	Alice asked with some curiosity.
T3	137:25	"I do believe," said	Alice at last, "that they live in the same house! I wonder I
T2	124: 9		Alice attended to all these directions, and explained, as well
T4	144:13	"I like the Walrus best," said	Alice: "because he was a little sorry for the poor oysters."
A5	35:11	ca'n't explain myself, I'm afraid, Sir," said	Alice, "because I'm not myself, you see."
T9	201:29	a quantity of poetry repeated to me to-day,"	Alice began, a little frightened at finding that, the moment
T9	203: 4	up into the air. "I rise to return thanks--"	Alice began: and she really did rise as she spoke, several
T3	133: 1	"Well, there's the Horse-fly,"	Alice began, counting off the names on her fingers.
A11	86:33	"Stupid things!"	Alice began in a loud indignant voice; but she stopped herself
A8	67:23	"I don't think they play at all fairly,"	Alice began, in rather a complaining tone, "and they all
A10	82: 1	So	Alice began telling them her adventures from the time when she
A3	26:40	I shall ever see you any more!" And here poor	Alice began to cry again, for she felt very lonely and
A8	67: 3		Alice began to feel very uneasy: to be sure, she had not as
A1	9:11	But do cats eat bats, I wonder?" And here	Alice began to get rather sleepy, and went on saying to
T2	128:32	was no way of guessing, but she was gone, and	Alice began to remember that she was a Pawn, and that it would
A10	78:10	were never even introduced to a lobster--" (	Alice began to say "I once tasted--" but checked herself
T4	144:21	This was a puzzler. After a pause,	Alice began, "Well! They were both very unpleasant characters
T8W	20: 9		Alice began with a little scream of laughter, which she turned
T1	108:11	"Do you know what to-morrow is, Kitty?"	Alice began. "You'd have guessed if you'd been up in the
A12	93:41	"Well, I sha'n't go, at any rate," said	Alice; "besides, that's not a regular rule: you invented it
T6	160: 4	"My name is	Alice, but--"
A6	53: 7	often seen a cat without a grin," thought	Alice; "but a grin without a cat! It's the most curious thing
T6	166:12	"I read it in a book," said	Alice. "But I had some poetry repeated to me much easier than
A6	52: 5	"I should like it very much," said	Alice, "but I haven't been invited yet."
T9	193:17	know I was to have a party at all," said	Alice; "but, if there is to be one, I think I ought to invite
T3	132:37	"No use to them," said	Alice; "but it's useful to the people that name them, I
A4	31:42	"A barrowful of what?" thought	Alice. But she had not long to doubt, for the next moment a
A5	36: 2	perhaps you haven't found it so yet," said	Alice; "but when you have to turn into a chrysalis--you will
A3	26:10	"I didn't mean it!" pleaded poor	Alice. "But you're so easily offended, you know!"
A10	85: 4	"Come on!" cried the Gryphon, and, taking	Alice by the hand, it hurried off, without waiting for the end
A3	26:13	"Please come back, and finish your story!"	Alice called after it. And the others all joined in chorus
A4	31:29	the house down!" said the Rabbit's voice. And	Alice called out, as loud as she could, "If you do, I'll set
T8W	13:17	bones, my old bones!" he was grumbling on as	Alice came up to him.
T5	149:34		Alice carefully released the brush, and did her best to get
T1	107:20	"Oh, you wicked, wicked little thing!" cried	Alice, catching up the kitten, and giving it a little kiss to
A6	49:15		Alice caught the baby with some difficulty, as it was a
A7	56:40	"Perhaps not,"	Alice cautiously replied; "but I know I have to beat time when
A9	71: 9	"He might bite,"	Alice cautiously replied, not feeling at all anxious to have
T8	184:38	He looked so vexed at the idea, that	Alice changed the subject hastily. "What a curious helmet
A4	27:30	the sort of thing that would happen: "'Miss	Alice! Come here directly, and get ready for your walk!'
A7	54: 9	room! No room!" they cried out when they saw	Alice coming. "There's plenty of room!" said Alice indignantly
A7	55:39		Alice considered a little, and then said "The fourth."
T6	162:40		Alice considered a little. "I like birthday presents best,"
T9	194:10		Alice considered. "The bone wouldn't remain, of course, if I
T8	187: 5	have said 'That's what the song is called'?"	Alice corrected herself.
T7	177:22	But before	Alice could answer him, the drums began.
A7	60:29	This piece of rudeness was more than	Alice could bear: she got up in great disgust, and walked off:
A6	49: 3	and the poor little thing howled so, that	Alice could hardly hear the words:--
T1	115:21	in a frightened whisper--so low, that	Alice could hardly hear what they said.
T6	160:23	his lips, and looked so solemn and grand that	Alice could hardly help laughing. "If I did fall," he went on,
A9	74:18	ledge of rock, and, as they came nearer,	Alice could hear him sighing as if his heart would break. She
T7	175:27		Alice could not help her lips curling up into a smile as she
T5	152:40		Alice could not help laughing at this, even in the midst of
T7	173:17	were in such a cloud of dust, that at first	Alice could not make out which was which; but she soon managed
A11	87: 6	had a pencil that squeaked. This, of course,	Alice could not stand, and she went round the court and got
A5	36:15	Here was another puzzling question; and, as	Alice could not think of any good reason, and the Caterpillar
A4	30:13	There was a long silence after this, and	Alice could only hear whispers now and then; such as "Sure, I
T8	186:30		Alice could only look puzzled: she was thinking of the pudding
T7	176: 7	monster!" the Unicorn cried out, before	Alice could reply.
T4	138:15	"I'm sure I'm very sorry," was all	Alice could say; for the words of the old song kept ringing
T9	199:13	it been asking of?" He was so hoarse that	Alice could scarcely hear him.
A11	86:37		Alice could see, as well as if she were looking over their
A8	68:20	across the other side of the garden, where	Alice could see it trying in a helpless sort of way to fly up
A12	93:31	it down "important," and some "unimportant."	Alice could see this, as she was near enough to look over
A9	76: 3	"Hold your tongue!" added the Gryphon, before	Alice could speak again. The Mock Turtle went on.
T8	183:13		Alice could think of nothing better to say than "Indeed?" but
A8	69: 6		Alice could think of nothing else to say but "It belongs to
T7	175:41	carving-knife. How they all came out of it	Alice couldn't guess. It was just like a conjuring-trick, she
T7	170:30	"I love my love with an H,"	Alice couldn't help beginning, "because he is Happy. I hate
T5	150: 1		Alice couldn't help laughing, as she said "I don't want you to
T5	155:10	now working with fourteen pairs at once, and	Alice couldn't help looking at her in great astonishment.

ALICE (cont.)

T4	139:14	like a couple of great schoolboys, that	Alice couldn't help pointing her finger at Tweedledum, and
T4	145:16	He shouted this so loud that	Alice couldn't help saying "Hush! You'll be waking him, I'm
T6	163: 6		Alice couldn't help smiling as she took out her
T9	201:14	and the waiters took it away so quickly that	Alice couldn't return its bow.
T4	144:32		Alice couldn't say honestly that he was. He had a tall red
T3	131:10		Alice couldn't see who was sitting beyond the Beetle, but a
T9	194:41	"I know that!"	Alice cried eagerly. "You take some flour--"
T5	156: 6	"Oh, please! There are some scented rushes!"	Alice cried in a sudden transport of delight. "There really
T12	207:22	"Sit up a little more stiffly, dear!"	Alice cried with a merry laugh. "And curtsey while you're
A5	43:29	tone, as it settled down again into its nest.	Alice crouched down among the trees as well as she could, for
T2	125:16		Alice curtseyed again, as she was afraid from the Queen's tone
A12	98: 4		Alice dear!" said her sister. "Why, what a long sleep you've
A6	46:43	"Oh, there's no use in talking to him," said	Alice desperately: "he's perfectly idiotic!" And she opened
A6	48: 7		Alice did not at all like the tone of this remark, and thought
A10	83:12		Alice did not dare to disobey, though she felt sure it would
T8	185: 6	The Knight looked so solemn about it that	Alice did not dare to laugh. "I'm afraid you must have hurt
A9	76:33		Alice did not feel encouraged to ask any more questions about
T2	127:39		Alice did not know what to say to this, but luckily the Queen
T8W	21:10		Alice did not like having so many personal remarks made on her
T4	139:25		Alice did not like shaking hands with either of them first,
A6	49:35	extremely small for a baby: altogether	Alice did not like the look of the thing at all. "But perhaps
A6	46:35	It was, no doubt: only	Alice did not like to be told so. "It's really dreadful," she
A9	70:25		Alice did not much like her keeping so close to her: first
A7	59:18		Alice did not quite know what to say to this: so she helped
A9	74: 4	off, leaving Alice alone with the Gryphon.	Alice did not quite like the look of the creature, but on the
T7	172:14	"I said there was nothing like it." Which	Alice did not venture to deny.
A7	60: 3		Alice did not wish to offend the Dormouse again, so she began
T2	122:26		Alice did so. "It's very hard," she said; "but I don't see
T7	170: 7	King cried in a tone of delight, on seeing	Alice. "Did you happen to meet any soldiers, my dear, as you
T8W	16:15		Alice didn't catch the word exactly. "Is it a kind of
T2	125: 6		Alice didn't dare to argue the point, but went on: "--and I
T4	140: 2	minute: there was a rather awkward pause, as	Alice didn't know how to begin a conversation with people she
T6	159:24		Alice didn't know what to say to this: it wasn't at all like
T2	125: 4	the Queen, patting her on the head, which	Alice didn't like at all: "though, when you say 'garden'--I've
T2	121:13		Alice didn't like being criticized, so she began asking
T2	123:18		Alice didn't like this idea at all: so, to change the subject,
A6	51:27		Alice didn't think that proved it at all: however, she went on
T6	164:12		(Alice didn't venture to ask what he paid them with; and so you
T6	162: 1		Alice didn't want to begin another argument, so she said
A4	32:36	the stick, and made believe to worry it: then	Alice dodged behind a great thistle, to keep herself from
T3	129:39	("like the chorus of a song," thought	Alice) "Don't keep him waiting, child! Why, his time is worth
A9	76:29	"Yes," said	Alice doubtfully: "it means--to--make--anything--prettier."
T9	199:37	"'O Looking-Glass creatures,' quoth	Alice, 'draw near! / 'Tis an honour to see me, a favour to
T3	134: 9	"Crawling at your feet," said the Gnat	(Alice drew her feet back in some alarm), "you may observe a
T1	110: 1	wind blows--oh, that's very pretty!" cried	Alice, dropping the ball of worsted to clap her hands. "And I
T5	157:14	"To buy!"	Alice echoed in a tone that was half astonished and half
T8	182:28	for keeping the hair from being blown off?"	Alice enquired.
A10	79: 9	they began solemnly dancing round and round	Alice, every now and then treading on her toes when they
T4	145:12	"I shouldn't!"	Alice exclaimed indignantly. "Besides, if I'm only a sort of
T6	161:26	"I thought you meant 'How old are you?'"	Alice explained.
T3	132:29	"I don't rejoice in insects at all,"	Alice explained, "because I'm rather afraid of them--at least
T5	156:42	in the water and wouldn't come out again (so	Alice explained it afterwards), and the consequence was that
T9	194:44	"Well, it isn't picked at all,"	Alice explained: "it's ground--"
T2	128:14	I didn't know I had to make one--just then,"	Alice faltered out.
A10	80:13	it's a very interesting dance to watch," said	Alice, feeling very glad that it was over at last: "and I do
A5	36:11	again to the beginning of the conversation.	Alice felt a little irritated at the Caterpillar's making such
T3	132: 7	Everybody seemed satisfied with this, though	Alice felt a little nervous at the idea of trains jumping at
T3	135:23	it looked much darker than the last wood, and	Alice felt a little timid about going into it. However, on
A11	88:34	Just at this moment	Alice felt a very curious sensation, which puzzled her a good
A7	56:19		Alice felt dreadfully puzzled. The Hatter's remark seemed to
T6	162: 9		Alice felt even more indignant at this suggestion. "I mean,"
T8W	14: 5		Alice felt rather offended at this answer, and was very nearly
T2	126:16	the Queen kept crying "Faster! Faster!" but	Alice felt she could not go faster, though she had no breath
A2	15:31	she be savage if I've kept her waiting!"	Alice felt so desperate that she was ready to ask help of any
T5	149: 9	"Bread-and-butter, bread-and-butter," and	Alice felt that if there was to be any conversation at all,
T6	166:21		Alice felt that in that case she really ought to listen to it;
A6	51:17		Alice felt that this could not be denied, so she tried another
T5	151:10		Alice felt there was no denying that. "Of course it would be
T2	123:30	was her first remark. She had indeed: when	Alice first found her in the ashes, she had been only three
A6	49:11	it a bit, if you like!" the Duchess said to	Alice, flinging the baby at her as she spoke. "I must go and
A5	36:37		Alice folded her hands, and began:--
A8	65:11	execute the unfortunate gardeners, who ran to	Alice for protection.
A7	55: 7	said the Hatter. He had been looking at	Alice for some time with great curiosity, and this was his
T8	186:38	"Or else what?" said	Alice, for the Knight had made a sudden pause.
T2	123:35	"I think I'll go and meet her," said	Alice, for, though the flowers were interesting enough, she
T5	156:19	before breaking them off--and for a while	Alice forgot all about the Sheep and the knitting, as she bent
A8	66: 6	The chief difficulty	Alice found at first was in managing her flamingo: she
A8	65:37	boxed the Queen's ears--" the Rabbit began.	Alice gave a little scream of laughter. "Oh, hush!" the Rabbit
T6	159:19	"I said you looked like an egg, Sir,"	Alice gently explained. "And some eggs are very pretty, you

ALICE (cont.)

T8	181:21	"But the things can get out,"	Alice gently remarked. "Do you know the lid's open?"
A7	59: 3	"They couldn't have done that, you know,"	Alice gently remarked. "They'd have been ill."
T9	200: 8		Alice glanced nervously along the table, as she walked up the
A6	48:28		Alice glanced rather anxiously at the cook, to see if she
T5	157: 4	was a nice crab you caught!" she remarked, as	Alice got back into her place, very much relieved to find
T7	169: 3	that they seemed to fill the whole forest.	Alice got behind a tree, for fear of being run over, and
T8	179:37	away at each other with such fury that	Alice got behind a tree to be out of the way of the blows.
T1	110:23	like her. Now do try, there's a dear!" And	Alice got the Red Queen off the table, and set it up before
T2	128:12	together, and it's all feasting and fun!"	Alice got up and curtseyed, and sat down again.
A12	98:11	run in to your tea: it's getting late." So	Alice got up and ran off, thinking while she ran, as well she
T9	202:32	you, you know," the White Queen whispered, as	Alice got up to do it, very obediently, but a little
A4	27: 6	Where can I have dropped them, I wonder?"	Alice guessed in a moment that it was looking for the fan and
A11	91: 6	She carried the pepper-box in her hand, and	Alice guessed who it was, even before she got into the court,
T2	126:24	Not that	Alice had any idea of doing that. She felt as if she would
A1	9:31	the hall, but they were all locked; and when	Alice had been all the way down one side and up the other,
A7	56:11		Alice had been looking over his shoulder with some curiosity.
T1	110:15	because there were only two of them, and	Alice had been reduced at last to say "Well, you can be one of
A2	18:20	go back by railway," she said to herself. (Alice	had been to the seaside once in her life, and had come
T1	107:16	grand game of romps with the ball of worsted	Alice had been trying to wind up, and had been rolling it up
A1	10:10	things had happened lately, that	Alice had begun to think that very few things indeed were
T1	110:12	her sister only the day before—all because	Alice had begun with "Let's pretend we're kings and queens;"
T9	196:30	pleased she'll be!" But this was more than	Alice had courage to do.
A1	13: 1	generally happens when one eats cake; but	Alice had got so much into the way of expecting nothing but
A1	8:31	miles down, I think—" (for, you see,	Alice had learnt several things of this sort in her lessons in
A11	86:13		Alice had never been in a court of justice before, but she had
A3	23:26		Alice had no idea what to do, and in despair she put her hand
T7	173:14		Alice had no more breath for talking; so they trotted on in
A2	19:23	(For, with all her knowledge of history,	Alice had no very clear notion how long ago anything had
A1	8: 8	then dipped suddenly down, so suddenly that	Alice had not a moment to think about stopping herself before
T5	154: 8	But these, as it happened,	Alice had not got: so she contented herself with turning round
T8	180:10	Another Rule of Battle, that	Alice had not noticed, seemed to be that they always fell on
A1	8:36	what Latitude or Longitude I've got to?" (Alice	had not the slightest idea what Latitude was, or
T12	207: 6	"it is a very inconvenient habit of kittens (Alice	had once made the remark) that, whatever you say to them
T1	115:40	the Queen, looking over the book (in which	Alice had put 'The White Knight is sliding down the poker. He
T7	177: 6		Alice had seated herself on the bank of a little brook, with
T5	152: 7	like the whistle of a steam-engine, that	Alice had to hold both her hands over her ears.
T9	201:14	It spoke in a thick, suety sort of voice, that	Alice hadn't a word to say in reply: she could only sit and
T5	156:38	snow, as they lay in heaps at her feet—but	Alice hardly noticed this, there were so many other curious
A2	19:28	with fright. "Oh, I beg your pardon!" cried	Alice hastily, afraid that she had hurt the poor animal's
A5	43:25	"It matters a good deal to me," said	Alice hastily; "but I'm not looking for eggs, as it happens;
T8W	18: 1	"It isn't that kind,"	Alice hastily explained. "It's to comb hair with—your wig's
T8W	15: 1		Alice hastily ran her eye down the paper and said "No. It says
A7	55:21	"I do,"	Alice hastily replied; "at least—at least I mean what I say—
A5	41: 8	"Oh, I'm not particular as to size,"	Alice hastily replied; "only one doesn't like changing so
T6	166:17	"Oh, it needn't come to that!"	Alice hastily said, hoping to keep him from beginning.
A9	73:10	left off, quite out of breath, and said to	Alice "Have you seen the Mock Turtle yet?"
A7	55:36	day of the month is it?" he said, turning to	Alice: he had taken his watch out of his pocket, and was
T7	175:15	going on, when his eye happened to fall upon	Alice: he turned round instantly, and stood for some time
T9	196: 9	"I know what he came for," said	Alice: "he wanted to punish the fish, because—"
A4	29:27	against it, that attempt proved a failure.	Alice heard it say to itself "Then I'll go round and get in at
A9	73:18	As they walked off together,	Alice heard the King say in a low voice, to the company,
A4	31:38	or two they began moving about again, and	Alice heard the Rabbit say "A barrowful will do, to begin with
T8	182:15	This took a long time to manage, though	Alice held the bag open very carefully, because the Knight was
T2	123:31	and here she was, half a head taller than	Alice herself!
A12	98:17	First, she dreamed about little	Alice herself: once again the tiny hands were clasped upon her
T6	161: 3	fell off the wall in doing so) and offered	Alice his hand. She watched him a little anxiously as she took
A6	46:17	"Please, then," said	Alice, "how am I to get in?"
T12	207:13	So	Alice hunted among the chessmen on the table till she had
A5	36:31	"I'm afraid I am, Sir," said	Alice. "I ca'n't remember things as I used—and I don't keep
A2	19:21	it doesn't understand English," thought	Alice. "I daresay it's a French mouse, come over with William
A9	73:12	"No," said	Alice. "I don't even know what a Mock Turtle is."
A8	65:35	"No, I didn't," said	Alice. "I don't think it's at all a pity. I said 'What for?'"
T9	193:27	"I don't know," said	Alice. "I lost count."
A10	82:18	about, and make one repeat lessons!" thought	Alice. "I might just as well be at school at once." However,
A1	12: 1	"What a curious feeling!" said	Alice. "I must be shutting up like a telescope!"
T9	192: 1	"Well, this is grand!" said	Alice. "I never expected I should be a Queen so soon—and I'll
T5	155:29	"A dear little crab!" thought	Alice. "I should like that."
A4	30:19	of cucumber-frames there must be!" thought	Alice. "I wonder what they'll do next! As for pulling me out
T3	137:14	now," she said: "that's some comfort.	Alice—I won't forget it again. And now, which of these
T5	149:21	have been all the better, as it seemed to	Alice, if she had got some one else to dress her, she was so
A5	43: 5	"But I'm not a serpent, I tell you!" said	Alice. "I'm a—I'm a—"
T6	166: 1	"And then 'mome raths'?" said	Alice. "I'm afraid I'm giving you a great deal of trouble."
A9	72:20	"A cheap sort of present!" thought	Alice. "I'm glad people don't give birthday-presents like
A7	55:13	"Come, we shall have some fun now!" thought	Alice. "I'm glad they've begun asking riddles—I believe I can
T2	127:23	"I'd rather not try, please!" said	Alice. "I'm quite content to stay here—only I am so hot and
T5	152:28	The crow must have flown away, I think," said	Alice: "I'm so glad it's gone. I thought it was the night
A4	32:29	to touch her. "Poor little thing!" said	Alice, in a coaxing tone, and she tried hard to whistle to it;
A2	20: 1	"I wo'n't indeed!" said	Alice, in a great hurry to change the subject of conversation.
A9	77:10	many hours a day did you do lessons?" said	Alice, in a hurry to change the subject.

ALICE (cont.)

```
A3    22:26                        "As wet as ever," said Alice in a melancholy tone: "it doesn't seem to dry me at all
A5    41:18    "But I'm not used to it!" pleaded poor Alice in a piteous tone. And she thought to herself "I wish
A2    19:32                "Well, perhaps not," said Alice in a soothing tone: "don't be angry about it. And yet I
A2    20:10    it kills all the rats and--oh dear!" cried Alice in a sorrowful tone. "I'm afraid I've offended it again!
A5    42: 7        "Come, my head's free at last!" said Alice in a tone of delight, which changed into alarm in
A10   81:32                "Wouldn't it, really?" said Alice, in a tone of great surprise.
T9    198: 2   doorway, over which were the words "QUEEN ALICE" in large letters, and on each side of the arch there
T7    171:12   you with an H," the King said, introducing Alice in the hope of turning off the Messenger's attention
A9    76:12                    "Certainly not!" said Alice indignantly.
A7    54: 9    Alice coming. "There's plenty of room!" said Alice indignantly, and she sat down in a large arm-chair at
A5    42:28            "I'm not a serpent!" said Alice indignantly. "Let me alone!"
T3    131:43            "What kind of insect?" Alice inquired, a little anxiously. What she really wanted to
T6    163:15        "You're holding it upside down!" Alice interrupted.
T6    160:28   "To send all his horses and all his men," Alice interrupted, rather unwisely.
T8    182: 1   wondering what the mouse-trap was for," said Alice. "It isn't very likely there would be any mice on the
A6    51: 1             The Cat only grinned when it saw Alice. It looked good-natured, she thought: still it had very
T5    156:45   of little shrieks of "Oh, oh, oh!" from poor Alice, it swept her straight off the seat, and down among the
A2    15:16                            Poor Alice! It was as much as she could do, lying down on one side,
A1    10: 7    if my head would go through," thought Alice, "it would be of very little use without my shoulders.
A5    44: 2    feet high. "Whoever lives there," thought Alice, "it'll never do to come upon them this size: why, I
T5    150:10        "I don't understand you," said Alice. "It's dreadfully confusing!"
A7    55: 4    "I didn't know it was your table," said Alice: "it's laid for a great many more than three."
A10   81: 8                "Thank you," said Alice, "it's very interesting. I never knew so much about a
A10   80:18                    "Yes," said Alice, "I've often seen them at dinn----" she checked herself
A8    68: 1         "A cat may look at a king," said Alice. "I've read that in some book, but I don't remember
A11   90:16   "I'm glad I've seen that done," thought Alice. "I've so often read in the newspapers, at the end of
A8    65:23    "Come on, then!" roared the Queen, and Alice joined the procession, wondering very much what would
A6    48:16    "Oh, please mind what you're doing!" cried Alice, jumping up and down in an agony of terror. "Oh, there
A3    21:16    a large ring, with the Mouse in the middle. Alice kept her eyes anxiously fixed on it, for she felt sure
A4    29:21    a little pattering of feet on the stairs. Alice knew it was the Rabbit coming to look for her, and she
T4    138: 2   each with an arm round the other's neck, and Alice knew which was which in a moment, because one of them
T9    198:12                        Alice knocked and rang in vain for a long time; but at last a
T4    146:24                        Alice laid her hand upon his arm and said, in a soothing tone,
T4    147:28                        Alice laughed loud: but she managed to turn it into a cough,
A6    46: 5                        Alice laughed so much at this, that she had to run back into
T5    153:11                        Alice laughed. "There's no use trying," she said: "one ca'n't
T4    148: 4                        Alice laughed. "You must hit the trees pretty often, I should
A2    20:24    Eaglet, and several other curious creatures. Alice led the way, and the whole party swam to the shore.
T9    193:22   "Manners are not taught in lessons," said Alice. "Lessons teach you to do sums, and things of that sort
T8    179: 2   to die away, till all was dead silence, and Alice lifted up her head in some alarm. There was no one to be
A1     9:25   There was not a moment to be lost: away went Alice like the wind, and was just in time to hear it say, as
A9    76:16    "You couldn't have wanted it much," said Alice; "living at the bottom of the sea."
A4    33:14    The great question certainly was "What?" Alice looked all round her at the flowers and the blades of
A7    54:14                        Alice looked all round the table, but there was nothing on it
A5    35: 1                The Caterpillar and Alice looked at each other for some time in silence: at last
T8W   17: 9    He untied the handkerchief as he spoke, and Alice looked at his wig in great surprise. It was bright
T8    181:15   upside-down, and with the lid hanging open. Alice looked at it with great curiosity.
A12   93: 4                        Alice looked at the jury-box, and saw that, in her haste, she
T3    133: 8                        Alice looked at the Rocking-horse-fly with great interest, and
A10   81:19                        Alice looked down at them, and considered a little before she
T8    179:26   at each other for some time without speaking. Alice looked from one to the other in some bewilderment.
T1    115:29                        Alice looked on with great interest as the King took an
T2    128: 4    had got all the pegs put in by this time, and Alice looked on with great interest as she returned to the
T8W   16:12                        Alice looked pityingly at him. "Tying up the face is very good
A8    63:13    There was a sound of many footsteps, and Alice looked round, eager to see the Queen.
T2    123:28                        Alice looked round eagerly and found that it was the Red Queen.
T2    127:12                        Alice looked round her in great surprise. "Why, I do believe
T8    179:21    voice broke in "Ahoy! Ahoy! Check!" and Alice looked round in some surprise for the new enemy.
A9    72:31    that was linked into hers began to tremble. Alice looked up, and there stood the Queen in front of them,
T3    135:19   seemed to have sighed itself away, for, when Alice looked up, there was nothing whatever to be seen on the
A6    49:31            The baby grunted again, and Alice looked very anxiously into its face to see what was the
T9    197:12         "What am I to do?" exclaimed Alice, looking about in great perplexity, as first one round
T3    131:31            "Don't tease so," said Alice, looking about in vain to see where the voice came from.
A3    25: 1    "It is a long tail, certainly," said Alice, looking down with wonder at the Mouse's tail; "but why
T8    184:11        "It's too ridiculous!" cried Alice, losing all her patience this time. "You ought to have a
A12   97: 1        "Stuff and nonsense!" said Alice loudly. "The idea of having the sentence first!"
T6    161:22                        Alice made a short calculation, and said "Seven years and six
T2    126:27   and dragged her along. "Are we nearly there?" Alice managed to pant out at last.
T8    181: 6        "Thank you very much," said Alice. "May I help you off with your helmet?" It was evidently
A11   88:43        "Don't talk nonsense," said Alice more boldly: "you know you're growing too."
TC    209:11        Still she haunts me, phantomwise. / Alice moving under skies / Never seen by waking eyes.
T9    200:23   to that leg of mutton," said the Red Queen. "Alice--Mutton: Mutton--Alice." The leg of mutton got up in the
T2    126:12                        Alice never could quite make out, in thinking it over
T2    128:28            How it happened, Alice never knew, but exactly as she came to the last peg, she
A3    23: 2        "What is a Caucus-race?" said Alice; not that she much wanted to know, but the Dodo had
T6    160:11   "Why do you sit out here all alone?" said Alice, not wishing to begin an argument.
A6    45: 7    and large eyes like a frog; and both footmen, Alice noticed, had powdered hair that curled all over their
A4    32: 5                        Alice noticed, with some surprise, that the pebbles were all
A11   90:27   Come, that finishes the guinea-pigs!" thought Alice. "Now we shall get on better."
```

ALICE (cont.)

T5	150: 7	"It must come sometimes to 'jam to-day,'"	Alice objected.
T6	163:28	doesn't mean 'a nice knock-down argument,'"	Alice objected.
T8	185:12	"But that's a different kind of fastness,"	Alice objected.
T9	193: 7	"I don't deny things with my hands,"	Alice objected.
T6	168:32	"It wouldn't look nice,"	Alice objected. But Humpty Dumpty only shut his eyes, and said
T1	116: 1	There was a book lying near	Alice on the table, and while she sat watching the White King
T2	127:37	"No, thank you," said	Alice: "one's quite enough!"
A7	54: 5	Very uncomfortable for the Dormouse," thought	Alice; "only as it's asleep, I suppose it doesn't mind."
A1	10: 1		Alice opened the door and found that it led into a small
A2	15: 1	you can--but I must be kind to them," thought	Alice, "or perhaps they wo'n't walk the way I want to go! Let
T2	122:12	it panted, bending its quivering head towards	Alice, "or they wouldn't dare to do it!"
A10	85: 6	"What trial is it?"	Alice panted as she ran: but the Gryphon only answered "Come
T7	173: 8	"Would you--be good enough--"	Alice panted out, after running a little further, "to stop a
T4	139:18	"Next Boy!" said	Alice, passing on to Tweedledee, though she felt quite certain
T5	157: 7	"Was it? I didn't see it," said	Alice, peeping cautiously over the side of the boat into the
T1	114:23	So	Alice picked him up very gently, and lifted him across more
T5	156:11	I meant--please, may we wait and pick some?"	Alice pleaded. "If you don't mind stopping the boat for a
T9	192:30	"I only said 'if'!" poor	Alice pleaded in a piteous tone.
TC	209: 0		Alice Pleasance Liddell
T9	201:13	looked sulky, and growled "Pudding----Alice:	Alice--Pudding. Remove the pudding!" and the waiters took it
A8	67:19	minute the whole head appeared, and then	Alice put down her flamingo, and began an account of the game,
T8W	15:17		Alice put down the newspaper. "I'm afraid you're not well,"
A7	59:33	"What did they draw?" said	Alice, quite forgetting her promise.
A12	92: 1	"Here!" cried	Alice, quite forgetting in the flurry of the moment how large
A11	86: 8	upon it: they looked so good, that it made	Alice quite hungry to look at them--"I wish they'd get the
A6	47:16	the last word with such sudden violence that	Alice quite jumped; but she saw in another moment that it was
T2	122:35	stupider," a Violet said, so suddenly, that	Alice quite jumped; for it hadn't spoken before.
T6	162:31	"It is really?" said	Alice, quite pleased to find that she had chosen a good
T5	153:31	ended in a long bleat, so like a sheep that	Alice quite started.
T6	159: 9	top of a high wall--such a narrow one that	Alice quite wondered how he could keep his balance--and, as
T4	145:24		Alice ran a little way into the wood, and stopped under a
T8	185:17		Alice ran to the side of the ditch to look for him. She was
A7	58:21	"I'm afraid I don't know one," said	Alice, rather alarmed at the proposal.
A5	43: 9	"I--I'm a little girl," said	Alice, rather doubtfully, as she remembered the number of
A7	59:39	Hare moved into the Dormouse's place, and	Alice rather unwillingly took the place of the March Hare. The
T1	116:16	This was the poem that	Alice read
A8	63:22	mostly Kings and Queens, and among them	Alice recognized the White Rabbit: it was talking in a hurried
A5	41:33		Alice remained looking thoughtfully at the mushroom for a
A6	51:22	"But I don't want to go among mad people,"	Alice remarked.
A9	71:13	"Only mustard isn't a bird,"	Alice remarked.
T8W	17: 4	"Conceit isn't a disease at all,"	Alice remarked.
T5	150:17	"I'm sure mine only works one way,"	Alice remarked. "I ca'n't remember things before they happen
T6	168:24	"The face is what one goes by, generally,"	Alice remarked in a thoughtful tone.
T3	134:18	"But that must happen very often,"	Alice remarked thoughtfully.
T6	164:33	"I see it now,"	Alice remarked thoughtfully: "and what are 'toves'?"
T8W	15:10	"En-gulph-ed,"	Alice repeated, dividing the word into syllables.
T9	200: 5	"Ninety times nine!"	Alice repeated in despair. "Oh, that'll never be done! I'd
T5	150:13	"Living backwards!"	Alice repeated in great astonishment. "I never heard of such a
T8W	16: 5	"Along of the wig?"	Alice repeated, quite pleased to find that he was recovering
T6	164:20	This sounded very hopeful, so	Alice repeated the first verse:--
T7	172:40	run and see them." And they trotted off,	Alice repeating to herself, as she ran, the words of the old
T9	194:20	"Perhaps it would,"	Alice replied cautiously.
A3	26:26		Alice replied eagerly, for she was always ready to talk about
T4	147:33	"Well--yes--a little,"	Alice replied gently.
T9	195: 9	"Fiddle-de-dee's not English,"	Alice replied gravely.
A5	36:35	little busy bee,' but it all came different!"	Alice replied in a very melancholy voice.
A7	59:11	"I've had nothing yet,"	Alice replied in an offended tone: "so I ca'n't take more."
A5	35: 5	an encouraging opening for a conversation.	Alice replied, rather shyly, "I--I hardly know, Sir, just at
A10	84:12	please, if the Mock Turtle would be so kind,"	Alice replied, so eagerly that the Gryphon said, in a rather
A10	80:22	"I believe so,"	Alice replied thoughtfully. "They have their tails in their
A5	35:14	"I'm afraid I ca'n't put it more clearly,"	Alice replied, very politely, "for I ca'n't understand an
A7	56:16	"Of course not,"	Alice replied very readily: "but that's because it stays the
T9	194: 3	"Nine from eight I ca'n't, you know,"	Alice replied very readily: "but--"
A7	56:29	"No, I give it up,"	Alice replied. "What's the answer?"
T9	201: 2	the dish and made a little bow to Alice; and	Alice returned the bow, not knowing whether to be frightened
T5	153:33	to have suddenly wrapped herself up in wool.	Alice rubbed her eyes, and looked again. She couldn't make out
A3	23:33	"Only a thimble," said	Alice sadly.
T6	163:24	"I don't know what you mean by 'glory,'"	Alice said.
T3	134:24	"No, indeed,"	Alice said, a little anxiously.
T8W	15:13	"It's in this newspaper, though,"	Alice said a little timidly.
T4	146:16	"It's only a rattle,"	Alice said, after a careful examination of the little white
T4	147:18		Alice said afterwards she had never seen such a fuss made
T4	139:34	"But it certainly was funny,"	(Alice said afterwards, when she was telling her sister the
T9	194:23		Alice said, as gravely as she could, "They might go different
T5	149:30	you know, if you pin it all on one side,"	Alice said as she gently put it right for her; "and dear me,
T3	136: 9	at all· frightened. "Here then! Here then!"	Alice said, as she held out her hand and tried to stroke it;
T5	149: 5	"I'm very glad I happened to be in the way,"	Alice said, as she helped her to put on her shawl again.
T2	125:25	marked out just like a large chess-board!"	Alice said at last. "There ought to be some men moving about
T1	110:25	the thing didn't succeed, principally,	Alice said, because the kitten wouldn't fold its arms properly

ALICE (cont.)

A10	83: 7	"It's the first position in dancing,"	Alice said; but she was dreadfully puzzled by the whole thing,
T8	181: 1	"I don't know,"	Alice said doubtfully. "I don't want to be anybody's prisoner."
T4	140:10	"Ye-es, pretty well--some poetry,"	Alice said doubtfully. "Would you tell me which road leads out
T5	152:12	"When do you expect to do it?"	Alice said, feeling very much inclined to laugh.
T4	145:24	"If I wasn't real,"	Alice said--half laughing through her tears, it all seemed so
T8W	20: 1	"I'm very sorry for you,"	Alice said heartily: "and I think if your wig fitted a little
T2	122:21	"How is it you can all talk so nicely?"	Alice said, hoping to get it into a better temper by a
T3	135:15	"You shouldn't make jokes,"	Alice said, "if it makes you so unhappy."
T9	199:17	"Nothing!"	Alice said impatiently. "I've been knocking at it!"
T3	130: 2	"I'm afraid I haven't got one,"	Alice said in a frightened tone: "there wasn't a ticket-office
T5	152:33	"Only it is so very lonely here!"	Alice said in a melancholy voice; and, at the thought of her
T2	122:13	"Never mind!"	Alice said in a soothing tone, and, stooping down to the
T5	158: 7	"Then two are cheaper than one?"	Alice said in a surprised tone, taking out her purse.
T6	164: 3	"That's a great deal to make one word mean,"	Alice said in a thoughtful tone.
T1	113: 8	"Here are the Red King and the Red Queen,"	Alice said (in a whisper, for fear of frightening them), "and
T6	162:27	"I know it's very ignorant of me,"	Alice said, in so humble a tone that Humpty Dumpty relented.
T6	162: 7	"I never ask advice about growing,"	Alice said indignantly.
T4	144:18	"That was mean!"	Alice said indignantly. "Then I like the Carpenter best--if he
T2	120:13	"It's no use talking about it,"	Alice said, looking up at the house and pretending it was
T4	145: 3		Alice said "Nobody can guess that."
T3	132:25	"I like them when they can talk,"	Alice said. "None of them ever talk, where I come from."
T2	123: 3	any more people in the garden besides me?"	Alice said, not choosing to notice the Rose's last remark.
T5	155:23	like a remark that needed any answer: so	Alice said nothing, but pulled away. There was something very
A5	41:11		Alice said nothing: she had never been so much contradicted in
A10	82:34		Alice said nothing: she had sat down with her face in her
T8	184:28	"Very much indeed,"	Alice said politely.
T4	139:10	"I was thinking,"	Alice said politely, "which is the best way out of this wood:
T9	201:10	won't be introduced to the pudding, please,"	Alice said rather hastily, "or we shall get no dinner at all.
T3	131:26	"Indeed I sha'n't!"	Alice said rather impatiently. "I don't belong to this railway
T12	207: 1	"Your Red Majesty shouldn't purr so loud,"	Alice said, rubbing her eyes, and addressing the kitten,
T8	182:24	"Only in the usual way,"	Alice said, smiling.
A9	71:18	who seemed ready to agree to everything that	Alice said: "there's a large mustard-mine near here. And the
T8	184:34	I suppose you'd be over when that was done,"	Alice said thoughtfully: "but don't you think it would be
T8W	13:18	"It's rheumatism, I should think,"	Alice said to herself, and she stooped over him, and said very
T8	190:25	wo'n't take long to see him off, I expect,"	Alice said to herself, as she stood watching him. "There he
A6	47: 5	certainly too much pepper in that soup!"	Alice said to herself, as well as she could for sneezing.
T1	119: 4	getting down stairs quickly and easily, as	Alice said to herself. She just kept the tips of her fingers
A4	27:27	"How queer it seems,"	Alice said to herself, "to be going messages for a rabbit! I
T3	137:18	both pointed along it. "I'll settle it,"	Alice said to herself, "when the road divides and they point
A7	60: 9	"But they were in the well,"	Alice said to the Dormouse, not choosing to notice this last
T8	186:42	"Oh, that's the name of the song, is it?"	Alice said, trying to feel interested.
T9	194:28	"Can you do sums?"	Alice said, turning suddenly on the White Queen, for she
T9	195:19	"The cause of lightning,"	Alice said very decidedly, for she felt quite certain about
T5	154: 3	"I don't quite know yet,"	Alice said very gently. "I should like to look all round me
T6	160:34	"I haven't indeed!"	Alice said very gently. "It's in a book."
A7	59:28	"No, please go on!"	Alice said very humbly. "I wo'n't interrupt you again. I dare
T6	161:17	"I'm afraid I ca'n't quite remember it,"	Alice said, very politely.
T9	201:41	"Please do,"	Alice said very politely.
T5	153:23	"Then I hope your finger is better now?"	Alice said very politely, as she crossed the little brook
A6	48: 4	"I don't know of any that do,"	Alice said very politely, feeling quite pleased to have got
A9	72:11	"I think I should understand that better,"	Alice said very politely, "if I had it written down: but I
T8	184:17	"Much more smoothly than a live horse,"	Alice said, with a little scream of laughter, in spite of all
T6	162:36	"I beg your pardon?"	Alice said with a puzzled air.
A7	55: 9	should learn not to make personal remarks,"	Alice said with some severity: "it's very rude."
T8W	14:19		So Alice sat down by him, and spread out the paper on her knees,
T9	200:16	two of them, but the middle one was empty.	Alice sat down in it, rather uncomfortable at the silence, and
T7	177:17	say, this isn't fair!" cried the Unicorn, as	Alice sat with the knife in her hand, very much puzzled how to
T8	187:16	Of all the strange things that	Alice saw in her journey Through The Looking-Glass, this was
T3	131:19	of people there are in the carriage!" thought	Alice), saying "She must go by post, as she's got a head on
A6	50: 4	going to turn into a pig, my dear," said	Alice, seriously, "I'll have nothing more to do with you. Mind
T7	170: 9	"Yes, I did," said	Alice: "several thousand, I should think."
A3	26: 1	"You are not attending!" said the Mouse to	Alice, severely. "What are you thinking of?"
A4	29: 9	"But then," thought	Alice, "shall I never get any older than I am now? That'll be
A9	72:25	"I've a right to think," said	Alice sharply, for she was beginning to feel a little worried
A4	29:13	"Oh, you foolish	Alice!" she answered herself. "How can you learn lessons in
T3	136:14	"I wish I knew!" thought poor	Alice. She answered, rather sadly, "Nothing, just now."
A12	95:23	"If any one of them can explain it," said	Alice, (she had grown so large in the last few minutes that
A12	97: 7	"Who cares for you?" said	Alice (she had grown to her full size by this time). "You're
T8	181:11	his gentle face and large mild eyes to	Alice. She thought she had never seen such a strange-looking
A2	14: 1	"Curiouser and curiouser!" cried	Alice (she was so much surprised, that for the moment she
T6	164: 7	"Oh!" said	Alice. She was too much puzzled to make any other remark.
A8	63:39	tossing her head impatiently; and turning to	Alice, she went on: "What's your name, child?"
A8	67:32	"Not at all," said	Alice: "she's so extremely--" Just then she noticed that the
T8	181:29		Alice shook her head.
T9	195:42		Alice sighed and gave it up. "It's exactly like the riddle
A7	56:32		Alice sighed wearily. "I think you might do something better
T6	161:20	about it just as if it was a game!" thought	Alice.) "So here's a question for you. How old did you say you
A8	63:40	"My name is	Alice, so please your Majesty," said Alice very politely; but
T2	123:40		This sounded nonsense to Alice, so she said nothing, but set off at once towards the

ALICE (cont.)

A1	9: 5	down, down. There was nothing else to do, so	Alice soon began talking again. "Dinah'll miss me very much
A8	66:18	and walking off to other parts of the ground,	Alice soon came to the conclusion that it was a very difficult
T3	129:13	regular bee: in fact, it was an elephant--as	Alice soon found out, though the idea quite took her breath
A1	7:17	and looked at it, and then hurried on,	Alice started to her feet, for it flashed across her mind that
T4	148: 9	"And all about a rattle!" said	Alice, still hoping to make them a little ashamed of fighting
T2	127:16	"Well, in our country," said	Alice, still panting a little, "you'd generally get to
T3	137:11		Alice stood looking after it, almost ready to cry with
T7	174:20	For a minute or two	Alice stood silent, watching him. Suddenly she brightened up.
T2	125:19	For some minutes	Alice stood without speaking, looking out in all directions
T1	118:31	"But oh!" thought	Alice, suddenly jumping up, "if I don't make haste, I shall
T6	162:13	"What a beautiful belt you've got on!"	Alice suddenly remarked. (They had had quite enough of the
T7	172:12	cold water over you would be better,"	Alice suggested: "--or some sal-volatile."
A8	64: 3	"How should I know?" said	Alice, surprised at her own courage. "It's no business of mine
T6	165: 5	grass-plot round a sun-dial, I suppose?" said	Alice, surprised at her own ingenuity.
T2	125:10	"No, I shouldn't," said	Alice, surprised into contradicting her at last: "a hill
A5	36:23	"Is that all?" said	Alice, swallowing down her anger as well as she could.
T9	196:21	must excuse her," the Red Queen said to	Alice, taking one of the White Queen's hands in her own, and
T5	151:19	had done the things I was punished for," said	Alice: "that makes all the difference."
T9	199:24	"To the Looking-Glass world it was	Alice that said / 'I've a sceptre in hand, I've a crown on my
A7	60:12	This answer so confused poor	Alice, that she let the Dormouse go on for some time without
A5	43:21	This was such a new idea to	Alice, that she was quite silent for a minute or two, which
A6	49:29	sneezing by this time). "Don't grunt," said	Alice; "that's not at all a proper way of expressing yourself
T3	135: 5	"That would never do, I'm sure," said	Alice: "the governess would never think of excusing me lessons
T9	201: 1	said the Red Queen. "Alice--Mutton: Mutton--	Alice." The leg of mutton got up in the dish and made a little
A4	28:23	Luckily for	Alice, the little magic bottle had now had its full effect,
A4	32:16	out of a bottle. They all made a rush at	Alice the moment she appeared; but she ran off as hard as she
A6	49:17	directions, "just like a star-fish," thought	Alice. The poor little thing was snorting like a steam-engine
T2	128:31	wood ("and she can run very fast!" thought	Alice), there was no way of guessing, but she was gone, and
A8	63:34	When the procession came opposite to	Alice, they all stopped and looked at her, and the Queen said,
A6	49:26	don't take this child away with me," thought	Alice, "they're sure to kill it in a day or two. Wouldn't it
A1	7:11	nothing so very remarkable in that; nor did	Alice think it so very much out of the way to hear the Rabbit
T4	147:38	"Then you'd better not fight to-day," said	Alice, thinking it a good opportunity to make peace.
A4	32:40	heels in its hurry to get hold of it: then	Alice, thinking it was very like having a game of play with a
T4	147: 7	looking more like a fish than anything else,"	Alice thought.
T8	182:36	It didn't sound a comfortable plan,	Alice thought, and for a few minutes she walked on in silence,
A2	20:17	her: its face was quite pale (with passion,	Alice thought), and it said, in a low trembling voice, "Let us
T6	168:17	This was rather sudden,	Alice thought: but, after such a very strong hint that she
T3	136:17		Alice thought, but nothing came of it. "Please, would you tell
A6	46:22	sky all the time he was speaking, and this	Alice thought decidedly uncivil. "But perhaps he ca'n't help
T5	149:15		Alice thought it would never do to have an argument at the
T2	127:27		Alice thought it would not be civil to say "No," though it
A7	55:33	and the party sat silent for a minute, while	Alice thought over all she could remember about ravens and
A8	66: 1		Alice thought she had never seen such a curious croquet-ground
A5	36:26		Alice thought she might as well wait, as she had nothing else
A8	68:10		Alice thought she might as well go back and see how the game
T9	195:11		Alice thought she saw a way out of the difficulty, this time.
T3	132:21	large Gnat: "about the size of a chicken,"	Alice thought. Still, she couldn't feel nervous with it, after
A3	24: 5		Alice thought the whole thing very absurd, but they all looked
T4	148:18	It was getting dark so suddenly that	Alice thought there must be a thunderstorm coming on. "What a
A8	62: 3	gardeners at it, busily painting them red.	Alice thought this a very curious thing, and she went nearer
A2	19:14	very tired of swimming about here, O Mouse!" (	Alice thought this must be the right way of speaking to a
A9	71: 3	How fond she is of finding morals in things!"	Alice thought to herself.
T9	195:16	"I wish Queens never asked questions,"	Alice thought to herself.
T3	131:13	"It sounds like a horse,"	Alice thought to herself. And an extremely small voice, close
T4	145:28	"I know they're talking nonsense,"	Alice thought to herself: "and it's foolish to cry about it."
T5	149:23	untidy. "Every single thing's crooked,"	Alice thought to herself, "and she's all over pins!--May I put
T1	113: 3	don't keep this room so tidy as the other,"	Alice thought to herself, as she noticed several of the
T9	203:22	directions: "and very like birds they look,"	Alice thought to herself, as well as she could in the dreadful
A9	74:29	sat down, and nobody spoke for some minutes.	Alice thought to herself "I don't see how he can ever finish,
T9	196:17		Alice thought to herself "I never should try to remember my
A4	31:33	There was a dead silence instantly, and	Alice thought to herself "I wonder what they will do next! If
T3	130:10		Alice thought to herself "Then there's no use in speaking."
T9	199:33	followed a confused noise of cheering, and	Alice thought to herself "Thirty times three makes ninety. I
T6	168: 2	to a scream as he repeated this verse, and	Alice thought, with a shudder, "I wouldn't have been the
A7	57: 5	"That would be grand, certainly," said	Alice thoughtfully; "but then--I shouldn't be hungry for it,"
A5	41:15	larger, Sir, if you wouldn't mind," said	Alice: "three inches is such a wretched height to be."
T3	135:35	just fancy calling everything you met 'Alice,'	till one of them answered! Only they wouldn't answer
A10	79: 2	"It must be a very pretty dance," said	Alice timidly.
T6	168:15	"Is that all?"	Alice timidly asked.
A5	41: 2	"Not quite right, I'm afraid," said	Alice, timidly: "some of the words have got altered."
T2	128:25	remember who you are!" She did not wait for	Alice to curtsey, this time, but walked on quickly to the next
A3	21: 7	a few minutes it seemed quite natural to	Alice to find herself talking familiarly with them, as if she
A5	41:29	of what? The other side of what?" thought	Alice to herself.
A1	8:23	"Well!" thought	Alice to herself. "After such a fall as this, I shall think
A4	32:18	"The first thing I've got to do," said	Alice to herself, as she wandered about in the wood, "is to
T2	120: 1	"I should see the garden far better," said	Alice to herself, "if I could get to the top of that hill: and
A1	12: 8	this; "for it might end, you know," said	Alice to herself, "in my going out altogether, like a candle.
A1	12:21	there's no use in crying like that!" said	Alice to herself rather sharply. "I advise you to leave off
A4	30:36	got to come down the chimney, has he?" said	Alice to herself. "Why, they seem to put everything upon Bill!

ALICE (cont.)

T7	175:39	a large cake out of the bag, and gave it to	Alice to hold, while he got out a dish and carving-knife. How
T7	175:20	Haigha replied eagerly, coming in front of	Alice to introduce her, and spreading out both his hands
A1	12:28	people. "But it's no use now," thought poor	Alice, "to pretend to be two people! Why, there's hardly
A2	19:10	"Would it be of any use, now," thought	Alice, "to speak to this mouse? Everything is so
T7	174:15	round trays of white and brown bread.	Alice took a piece to taste, but it was very dry.
A2	15:36		Alice took up the fan and gloves, and, as the hall was very
A7	59: 6		Alice tried a little to fancy to herself what such an
T9	202:37	thing," the Red Queen said very decidedly: so	Alice tried to submit to it with good grace.
T8W	21:15	"Good-bye, and thank-ye," said the Wasp, and	Alice tripped down the hill again, quite pleased that she had
T9	204: 5	am!" cried a voice from the soup-tureen, and	Alice turned again, just in time to see the Queen's broad
A5	36:20	This sounded promising, certainly.	Alice turned and came back again.
T9	199: 2		Alice turned round, ready to find fault with anybody. "Where's
T8	190:16	stay and see me off first?" he added as	Alice turned with an eager look in the direction to which he
T1	110:10	here I wish I could tell you half the things	Alice used to say, beginning with her favourite phrase "Let's
A7	58:17	when you come to the beginning again?"	Alice ventured to ask.
T5	150:21	"What sort of things do you remember best?"	Alice ventured to ask.
T9	195:35	Are five nights warmer than one night, then?"	Alice ventured to ask.
T4	140:19	Here	Alice ventured to interrupt him. "If it's very long," she said
A9	70:21	"Perhaps it hasn't one,"	Alice ventured to remark.
T7	174: 9	soon bring the white bread and the brown?"	Alice ventured to remark.
A9	76:24	"I never heard of 'Uglification,'"	Alice ventured to say. "What is it?"
A1	11: 6	this bottle was not marked "poison," so	Alice ventured to taste it, and, finding it very nice (it had,
T5	149: 4	out wide, as if she were flying, and	Alice very civilly went to meet her with the shawl.
A7	59: 9	"Take some more tea," the March Hare said to	Alice, very earnestly.
A3	26: 3	"I beg your pardon," said	Alice very humbly: "you had got to the fifth bend, I think?"
A8	64: 8	"Nonsense!" said	Alice, very loudly and decidedly, and the Queen was silent.
A11	88:41	"I ca'n't help it," said	Alice very meekly: "I'm growing."
A7	60:26	"Really, now you ask me," said	Alice, very much confused, "I don't think--"
T7	177:13	This sounded nonsense, but	Alice very obediently got up, and carried the dish round, and
A8	63:40	name is Alice, so please your Majesty," said	Alice very politely; but she added, to herself, "Why, they're
A6	52:22		Alice waited a little, half expecting to see it again, but it
T6	168:34		Alice waited a minute to see if he would speak again, but, as
A5	41:23	This time	Alice waited patiently until it chose to speak again.
A8	67:16		Alice waited till the eyes appeared, and then nodded. "It's no
T1	112: 6	warm here as I was in the old room," thought	Alice: "warmer, in fact, because there'll be no one here to
A7	59:41	who got any advantage from the change; and	Alice was a good deal worse off than before, as the March Hare
T1	115:16	on his back, and lay perfectly still; and	Alice was a little alarmed at what she had done, and went
T9	192:38	"I'm sure I didn't mean--"	Alice was beginning, but the Red Queen interrupted her
T9	194: 7	"I suppose--"	Alice was beginning, but the Red Queen answered for her.
A1	7: 1		Alice was beginning to get very tired of sitting by her sister
T5	155:17	but not on land--and not with needles--"	Alice was beginning to say, when suddenly the needles turned
A7	59:24	"There's no such thing!"	Alice was beginning very angrily, but the Hatter and the March
T8	184:10	he went on repeating, all the time that	Alice was getting him on his feet again. "Plenty of practice!"
T2	127: 7	with their feet, till suddenly, just as	Alice was getting quite exhausted, they stopped, and she found
T7	172: 8		Alice was glad to see that it revived him a good deal.
T5	152: 1		Alice was just beginning to say "There's a mistake somewhere--
A6	50: 8		Alice was just beginning to think to herself, "Now, what am I
A5	42:36		Alice was more and more puzzled, but she thought there was no
T8	179:17	Startled as she was,	Alice was more frightened for him than for herself at the
A1	9:21		Alice was not a bit hurt, and she jumped up on to her feet in
A1	10:19	well to say "Drink me," but the wise little	Alice was not going to do that in a hurry. "No, I'll look
A6	52: 9		Alice was not much surprised at this, she was getting so well
A10	84: 7	better leave off," said the Gryphon, and	Alice was only too glad to do so.
T9	195:29		Alice was puzzled. "In our country," she remarked, "there's
T2	122:30	This sounded a very good reason, and	Alice was quite pleased to know it. "I never thought of that
A8	63:28		Alice was rather doubtful whether she ought not to lie down on
A7	60:19		Alice was silent.
T6	166:28	than most," Humpty Dumpty remarked severely.	Alice was silent.
T3	134:20	After this,	Alice was silent for a minute or two, pondering. The Gnat
T1	107:13	with earlier in the afternoon, and so, while	Alice was sitting curled up in a corner of the great arm-chair
T2	121: 1		Alice was so astonished that she couldn't speak for a minute:
A4	27:15	a pair of gloves and a fan! Quick, now!" And	Alice was so much frightened that she ran off at once in the
A3	26:36	On various pretexts they all moved off, and	Alice was soon left alone.
T7	172:27	so as to get close to the King's ear.	Alice was sorry for this, as she wanted to hear the news too.
T7	170:35	idea that he was joining in the game, while	Alice was still hesitating for the name of a town beginning
A10	81:15		Alice was thoroughly puzzled. "Does the boots and shoes!" she
T1	112: 1	In another moment	Alice was through the glass, and had jumped lightly down into
A9	72:40	with the game," the Queen said to Alice; and	Alice was too much frightened to say a word, but slowly
T6	163:37		Alice was too much puzzled to say anything; so after a minute
T1	115:35	for some time without saying anything; but	Alice was too strong for him, and at last he panted out "My
T1	114: 4		Alice was very anxious to be of use, and, as the poor little
A9	70: 4		Alice was very glad to find her in such a pleasant temper, and
T7	170: 3	The confusion got worse every moment, and	Alice was very glad to get out of the wood into an open place,
A9	74:36	constant heavy sobbing of the Mock Turtle.	Alice was very nearly getting up and saying, "Thank you, Sir,
T8	182:44	as he generally did this on the side on which	Alice was walking, she soon found that it was the best plan
T8	183:20	the top of his head exactly in the path where	Alice was walking. She was quite frightened this time, and
T1	114:18		Alice watched the White King as he slowly struggled up from
A11	91:29		Alice watched the White Rabbit as he fumbled over the list,
T8	183:16	with his eyes shut, muttering to himself, and	Alice watching anxiously for the next tumble.

ALICE (cont.)
A9	76:10	"Yes," said Alice: "we learned French and music."
T7	176: 5	The Lion looked at Alice wearily. "Are you animal--or vegetable--or mineral?" he
A4	31:18	squeaking voice ("That's Bill," thought Alice), "Well, I hardly know--No more, thank ye; I'm better
T8	186: 9	to have it cooked for the next course?" said Alice. "Well, that was quick work, certainly!"
T3	134: 4	"And then there's the Butterfly," Alice went on, after she had taken a good look at the insect
T8W	14: 1	"Can I do anything for you?" Alice went on. "Aren't you rather cold here?"
T8W	14:14	Would you like me to read you a bit of this?" Alice went on, as she picked up a newspaper which had been
T1	108:21	"Do you know, I was so angry, Kitty," Alice went on, as soon as they were comfortably settled again,
A9	77:21	"And how did you manage on the twelfth?" Alice went on eagerly.
A2	20: 3	of--of dogs?" The Mouse did not answer, so Alice went on eagerly: "There is such a nice little dog, near
A2	19:35	see her. She is such a dear quiet thing," Alice went on, half to herself, as she swam lazily about in
T6	160:16	you think you'd be safer down on the ground?" Alice went on, not with any idea of making another riddle, but
T8W	15: 5	"In coming back," Alice went on reading, "they found a lake of treacle. The
T10	205: 4	her eyes got large and green: and still, as Alice went on shaking her, she kept on growing shorter--and
A4	27:33	mouse doesn't get out.' Only I don't think," Alice went on, "that they'd let Dinah stop in the house if it
A6	46: 9	Alice went timidly up to the door, and knocked.
A9	73: 9	the players, except the King, the Queen, and Alice, were in custody and under sentence of execution.
T8	184: 7	and stretched out both his arms to show Alice what he meant, and this time he fell flat on his back,
A10	78:13	"No, indeed," said Alice. "What sort of a dance is it?"
T6	163:42	"Would you tell me please," said Alice, "what that means?"
A4	28:27	It was much pleasanter at home," thought poor Alice, "when one wasn't always growing larger and smaller, and
A1	12:14	into the garden at once; but, alas for poor Alice! when she got to the door, she found she had forgotten
A8	65:28	"Very," said Alice. "Where's the Duchess?"
T6	163:33	"The question is," said Alice, "whether you can make words mean so many different
A9	70:34	"Somebody said," Alice whispered, "that it's done by everybody minding their
A11	86:29	very busily on slates. "What are they doing?" Alice whispered to the Gryphon. "They ca'n't have anything to
A7	58:35	"What did they live on?" said Alice, who always took a great interest in questions of eating
T7	172:34	have to be a very tiny earthquake!" thought Alice. "Who are at it again?" she ventured to ask.
A9	75: 6	then they both sat silent and looked at poor Alice, who felt ready to sink into the earth. At last the
T9	196:25	The White Queen looked timidly at Alice, who felt she ought to say something kind, but really
A6	48:23	"Which would not be an advantage," said Alice, who felt very glad to get an opportunity of showing off
A9	72: 3	"Oh, I know!" exclaimed Alice, who had not attended to this last remark. "It's a
T9	200:20	And the waiters set a leg of mutton before Alice, who looked at it rather anxiously, as she had never had
T4	144:37	cold with lying on the damp grass," said Alice, who was a very thoughtful little girl.
A5	43:16	"I have tasted eggs, certainly," said Alice, who was a very truthful child; "but little girls eat
T9	192:20	"But if everybody obeyed that rule," said Alice, who was always ready for a little argument, "and if you
A5	42:41	"I'm very sorry you've been annoyed," said Alice, who was beginning to see its meaning.
T8	187: 8	"Well, what is the song, then?" said Alice, who was by this time completely bewildered.
T7	170:20	All this was lost on Alice, who was still looking intently along the road, shading
A10	81:27	"If I'd been the whiting," said Alice, whose thoughts were still running on the song, "I'd
A10	81:12	"I never thought about it," said Alice. "Why?"
T7	171: 4	"I only meant that I didn't understand," said Alice. "Why one to come and one to go?"
A12	94:30	"It doesn't prove anything of the sort!" said Alice. "Why, you don't even know what they're about!"
T5	152:21	for the bleeding, you see," she said to Alice with a smile. "Now you understand the way things happen
A2	17:25	till I'm somebody else'--but, oh dear!" cried Alice, with a sudden burst of tears, "I do wish they would put
T3	137: 3	So they walked on together through the wood, Alice with her arms clasped lovingly round the soft neck of
T3	136: 7	then a Fawn came wandering by: it looked at Alice with its large gentle eyes, but didn't seem at all
T9	200: 4	and wool with the wine--/ And welcome Queen Alice with ninety-times-nine!"
A3	23:23	she, of course," said the Dodo, pointing to Alice with one finger; and the whole party at once crowded
T9	199:32	and mice in the tea--/ And welcome Queen Alice with thirty-times-three!"
A1	7: 5	it, "and what is the use of a book," thought Alice, "without pictures or conversations?"
T2	124:15	Alice wondered a little at this, but she was too much in awe
T9	204:23	At any other time, Alice would have felt surprised at this, but she was far too
T3	131:35	deeply. It was very unhappy, evidently, and Alice would have said something pitying to comfort it, "if it
A3	21:10	than you, and must know better." And this Alice would not allow, without knowing how old it was, and as
T6	164:14	very clever at explaining words, Sir," said Alice. "Would you kindly tell me the meaning of the poem
T1	108:16	we'll go and see the bonfire to-morrow." Here Alice wound two or three turns of the worsted round the
A9	76: 7	"I've been to a day-school, too," said Alice. "You needn't be so proud as all that."
T5	152:18	"Take care!" cried Alice. "You're holding it all crooked!" And she caught at the
T5	155:32	"Indeed I did," said Alice: "you've said it very often--and very loud. Please,

ALICE'S (34)
A9	70: 3	as she tucked her arm affectionately into Alice's, and they walked off together.
T3	137: 6	into the air, and shook itself free from Alice's arm. "I'm a Fawn!" it cried out in a voice of delight.
T4	147: 3	thing to do, that it quite took off Alice's attention from the angry brother. But he couldn't
T9	204:11	soup ladle was walking up the table towards Alice's chair, and beckoning to her impatiently to get out of
T9	202: 1	White Queen laughed with delight, and stroked Alice's cheek. Then they began:
T9	193:15	saying, to the White Queen, "I invite you to Alice's dinner-party this afternoon."
T9	201:36	and solemnly, putting her mouth close to Alice's ear, "her White Majesty knows a lovely riddle--all in
T2	127: 3	a time in silence, with the wind whistling in Alice's ears, and almost blowing her hair off her head, she
A4	29:26	open it; but, as the door opened inwards, and Alice's elbow was pressed hard against it, that attempt proved
A12t	92: 1	ALICE'S EVIDENCE
A1	9:36	was nothing on it but a tiny golden key, and Alice's first idea was that this might belong to one of the
T8W	13: 9	don't think I can be of any use to him," was Alice's first thought, as she turned to spring over the brook:
T7	172: 1	On which the Messenger, to Alice's great amusement, opened a bag that hung round his neck
A9	72:29	But here, to Alice's great surprise, the Duchess's voice died away, even in
T9	203: 8	yourself!" screamed the White Queen, seizing Alice's hair with both her hands. "Something's going to
T8	183: 7	back into the saddle, keeping hold of Alice's hair with one hand, to save himself from falling over
T4	144:29	the brothers cried, and they each took one of Alice's hands, and led her up to where the King was sleeping.
T4	140: 1	Then they let go of Alice's hands, and stood looking at her for a minute: there

ALICE'S (cont.)

T8W	18: 6	A curious idea came into Alice's head. Almost every one she had met had repeated poetry
A7	58:10	A bright idea came into Alice's head. "Is that the reason so many tea-things are put
T3	134:15	A new difficulty came into Alice's head. "Supposing it couldn't find any?" she suggested
T9	202:20	"Meanwhile, we'll drink your health--Queen Alice's health!" she screamed at the top of her voice, and all
T9	197: 4	"Hush-a-by lady, in Alice's lap! / Till the feast's ready, we've time for a nap. /
A2	15:10	Hearthrug, near the Fender, (with Alice's love).
T9	201:39	to mention it," the White Queen murmured into Alice's other ear, in a voice like the cooing of a pigeon. "It
T9	197: 9	she added, as she put her head down on Alice's other shoulder, "just sing it through to me. I'm
T4	140:13	with great solemn eyes, and not noticing Alice's question.
A2	15: 7	Alice's Right Foot, Esq.
A9	70:27	exactly the right height to rest her chin on Alice's shoulder, and it was an uncomfortably sharp chin.
A9	70:37	Duchess, digging her sharp little chin into Alice's shoulder as she added "and the moral of that is--'Take
T9	196:34	Queen gave a deep sigh, and laid her head on Alice's shoulder. "I am so sleepy!" she moaned.
T8	179:23	time it was a White Knight. He drew up at Alice's side, and tumbled off his horse just as the Red Knight
A9	70:24	it." And she squeezed herself up closer to Alice's side as she spoke.
T1	110:20	But this is taking us away from Alice's speech to the kitten. "Let's pretend that you're the

ALIVE (8)

A8	67: 7	great wonder is, that there's any one left alive!"
T7	175:24	fabulous monsters!" said the Unicorn. "Is it alive?"
T4	138: 6	so still that she quite forgot they were alive, and she was just going round to see if the word
T1	112:13	on the wall next the fire seemed to be all alive, and the very clock on the chimney-piece (you know you
T7	175:29	were fabulous monsters, too? I never saw one alive before!"
A8	67:27	idea how confusing it is all the things being alive: for instance, there's the arch I've got to go through
A12	98:22	to listen, the whole place around her became alive with the strange creatures of her little sister's dream
T4	138:14	the one marked 'DEE,' "if you think we're alive, you ought to speak."

ALL (381)

A3	22:27	tone: "it doesn't seem to dry me at all."
A10	81: 7	So they couldn't get them out again. That's all."
T3	132:38	suppose. If not, why do things have names at all?"
T5	149:14	said. "It isn't my notion of the thing, at all."
T5	150: 6	and of course the crime comes last of all."
T6	159:13	she thought he must be a stuffed figure after all.
T6	162:32	find that she had chosen a good subject after all.
T6	163:36	Humpty Dumpty, "which is to be master--that's all."
T9	197: 7	Red Queen, and White Queen, and Alice, and all!
T11	206: 1	..--it really was a kitten, after all.
A8	65:35	I didn't," said Alice. "I don't think it's at all a pity. I said 'What for?'"
A6	49:30	"Don't grunt," said Alice; "that's not at all a proper way of expressing yourself."
T8	182: 4	do come, I don't choose to have them running all about."
T4	148: 9	"And all about a rattle!" said Alice, still hoping to make them a
A6	45: 9	She felt very curious to know what it was all about, and crept a little way out of the wood to listen.
A10	82:10	"It's all about as curious as it can be," said the Gryphon.
T9	201:37	Majesty knows a lovely riddle--all in poetry--all about fishes. Shall she repeat it?"
T12	208: 1	I had such a quantity of poetry said to me, all about fishes! To-morrow morning you shall have a real
A11	87:10	all what had become of it; so, after hunting all about for it, he was obliged to write with one finger for
T9	201:33	Do you know why they're so fond of fishes, all about here?"
A4	31:14	it, old fellow? What happened to you? Tell us all about it!"
T5	156:19	them off--and for a while Alice forgot all about the Sheep and the knitting, as she bent over the
A10	79:15	See how eagerly the lobsters and the turtles all advance! / They are waiting on the shingle--will you come
T8	190: 4	very like a crow, / With eyes, like cinders, all aglow, / Who seemed distracted with his woe, / Who rocked
T4	138:15	"I'm sure I'm very sorry," was all Alice could say; for the words of the old song kept
T3	132:29	"I don't rejoice in insects at all," Alice explained, "because I'm rather afraid of them--at
T9	194:44	"Well, it isn't picked at all," Alice explained: "it's ground--"
T8W	17: 4	"Conceit isn't a disease at all," Alice remarked.
T6	168:15	"Is that all?" Alice timidly asked.
T1	112:13	on the wall next the fire seemed to be all alive, and the very clock on the chimney-piece (you know
A2	17:27	their heads down! I am so very tired of being all alone here!"
T6	160:11	"Why do you sit out here all alone?" said Alice, not wishing to begin an argument.
T8W	16: 3	"It's all along of the wig," the Wasp said in a much gentler voice.
A2	17:18	again as she went on, "I must be Mabel after all, and I shall have to go and live in that poky little house
A2	16: 5	ringlets, and mine doesn't go in ringlets at all; and I'm sure I ca'n't be Mabel, for I know all sorts of
T3	136: 3	again. "Then it really has happened, after all! And now, who am I? I will remember, if I can! I'm
A9	71: 9	Alice cautiously replied, not feeling at all anxious to have the experiment tried.
T8	191: 5	up to something very heavy, that fitted tight all around her head.
A8	68:14	and she did not like the look of things at all, as the game was in such confusion that she never knew
A4	30:15	as "Sure, I don't like it, yer honour, at all, at all!" "Do as I tell you, you coward!", and at last she
A11	91: 8	way the people near the door began sneezing all at once.
T1	110:12	argument with her sister only the day before--all because Alice had begun with "Let's pretend we're kings
A1	10:23	by wild beasts, and other unpleasant things, all because they would not remember the simple rules their
T3	135:29	when I go in? I shouldn't like to lose it at all--because they'd have to give me another, and it would be
T2	122: 7	that?" cried another Daisy. And here they all began shouting together, till the air seemed quite full of
T2	122:19	are worst of all. When one speaks, they all begin together, and it's enough to make one wither to hear
A12	94:20	else's hand," said the King. (The jury all brightened up again.)
T5	155: 1	at. "And this one is the most provoking of all--but I'll tell you what--" she added, as a sudden thought
A6	49:35	Alice did not like the look of the thing at all. "But perhaps it was only sobbing," she thought, and
T1	110:34	I can see all of it when I get upon a chair--all but the bit just behind the fireplace. Oh! I do so wish I
T5	153:21	tone. "Now you shall see me pin it on again, all by myself!"
A5	36:34	to say 'How doth the little busy bee,' but it all came different!" Alice replied in a very melancholy voice.
A10	82:11	"It all came different!" the Mock Turtle repeated thoughtfully. "I

ALL (cont.)

T7	175:40	he got out a dish and carving-knife. How they	all came out of it Alice couldn't guess. It was just like a
A6	48: 3	"They	all can," said the Duchess; "and most of 'em do."
A3	24: 4	when it had finished this short speech, they	all cheered.
T1	107:17	had been rolling it up and down till it had	all come undone again; and there it was, spread over the
A10	83:12	to disobey, though she felt sure it would	all come wrong, and she went on in a trembling voice:--
A11	86:19	to see how he did it), he did not look at	all comfortable, and it was certainly not becoming.
A10	82: 7	William," to the Caterpillar, and the words	all coming different, and then the Mock Turtle drew a long
T5	152:18	"Take care!" cried Alice. "You're holding it	all crooked!" And she caught at the brooch; but it was too
A3	24: 1	Then they	all crowded round her once more, while the Dodo solemnly
A3	23:15	called out "The race is over!" and they	all crowded round it, panting, and asking "But who has won?"
A7	54: 7	The table was a large one, but the three were	all crowded together at one corner of it. "No room! No room!"
A1	9:22	feet in a moment: she looked up, but it was	all dark overhead: before her was another long passage, and
A9	75: 8	Mock Turtle "Drive on, old fellow! Don't be	all day about it!" and he went on in these words:--
A5	40: 7	yourself airs! / Do you think I can listen	all day to such stuff? / Be off, or I'll kick you down-stairs!
A8	68: 6	The Queen had only one way of settling	all difficulties, great or small. "Off with his head!" she
T9	203:21	with forks for legs, went fluttering about in	all directions: "and very like birds they look," Alice thought
A6	49:16	creature, and held out its arms and legs in	all directions, "just like a star-fish," thought Alice. The
T2	125:20	Alice stood without speaking, looking out in	all directions over the country--and a most curious country it
A8	65:42	of thunder, and people began running about in	all directions, tumbling up against each other: however, they
A4	30:15	Sure, I don't like it, yer honour, at all, at	all!" "Do as I tell you, you coward!", and at last she spread
A3	21: 3	with their fur clinging close to them, and	all dripping wet, cross, and uncomfortable.
A10	82:26	and turns out his toes. / When the sands are	all dry, he is gay as a lark, / And will talk in contemptuous
T4	142: 2	But four young Oysters hurried up, /	All eager for the treat: / Their coats were brushed, their
A10	84:28	Game, or any other dish? / Who would not give	all else for two p / ennyworth only of beautiful Soup? /
A12	93:13	to write out a history of the accident,	all except the Lizard, who seemed too much overcome to do
T9	201:30	opened her lips, there was dead silence, and	all eyes were fixed upon her; "and it's a very curious thing,
A8	67:23	"I don't think they play at	all fairly," Alice began, in rather a complaining tone, "and
T2	128:20	Square we shall be Queens together, and it's	all feasting and fun!" Alice got up and curtseyed, and sat
A10	83:18	as its share of the treat. / When the pie was	all finished, the Owl, as a boon, / Was kindly permitted to
A4	29:15	there's hardly room for you, and no room at	all for any lesson-books!"
T2	128:18	we'll suppose it said--the Seventh Square is	all forest--however, one of the Knights will show you the way
T3	136: 8	its large gentle eyes, but didn't seem at	all frightened. "Here then! Here then!" Alice said, as she
T1	116:15	if I hold it up to a glass, the words will	all go the right way again."
T9	203:12	of things happened in a moment. The candles	all grew up to the ceiling, looking something like a bed of
T5	149:19	"But I don't want it done at	all!" groaned the poor Queen. "I've been a-dressing myself for
A8	63: 8	and, if the Queen was to find out, we should	all have our heads cut off, you know. So you see, Miss, we're
A11	88:30	This did not seem to encourage the witness at	all: he kept shifting from one foot to the other, looking
A12	93: 2	the jurymen are back in their proper places--all," he repeated with great emphasis, looking hard at Alice
A7	55:11	his eyes very wide on hearing this; but	all he said was "Why is a raven like a writing-desk?"
A4	32:32	be very likely to eat her up in spite of	all her coaxing.
A9	74:11	"Why, she," said the Gryphon. "It's	all her fancy that: they never executes nobody, you know. Come
A2	19:13	over with William the Conqueror." (For, with	all her knowledge of history, Alice had no very clear notion
T2	127:30	she had never been so nearly choked in	all her life.
T8	181:12	never seen such a strange-looking soldier in	all her life.
A5	41:12	she had never been so much contradicted in	all her life before, and she felt that she was losing her
A3	21: 8	with them, as if she had known them in	all her life. Indeed, she had quite a long argument with the
T7	169: 5	She thought that in	all her life she had never seen soldiers so uncertain on their
T1	115: 3	said afterwards that she had never seen in	all her life such a face as the King made, when he found
T4	147:19	never seen such a fuss made about anything in	all her life--the way those two bustled about--and the
T10	205: 2	and shook her backwards and forwards with	all her might.
T8	184:11	"It's too ridiculous!" cried Alice, losing	all her patience this time. "You ought to have a wooden horse
A12	99: 5	grown woman; and how she would keep, through	all her riper years, the simple and loving heart of her
A12	98:14	setting sun, and thinking of little Alice and	all her wonderful Adventures, till she too began dreaming
A9	74:21	nearly in the same words as before, "It's	all his fancy, that: he hasn't got no sorrow, you know. Come
T6	160:28	"To send	all his horses and all his men," Alice interrupted, rather
T6	161:13	"Yes,	all his horses and all his men," Humpty Dumpty went on.
T6	160:28	"To send all his horses and	all his men," Alice interrupted, rather unwisely.
T6	161:13	"Yes, all his horses and	all his men," Humpty Dumpty went on. "They'd pick me up again
T4	140:24	sun was shining on the sea, / Shining with	all his might: / He did his very best to make / The billows
T4	142:11	at last, / And more, and more, and more--/	All hopping through the frothy waves, / And scrambling to the
T2	126:19	round them never changed their places at	all: however fast they went, they never seemed to pass
T3	132: 8	nervous at the idea of trains jumping at	all. "However, it'll take us into the Fourth Square, that's
A11	86:26	girls of her age knew the meaning of it at	all. However, "jurymen" would have done just as well.
A6	51:27	Alice didn't think that proved it at	all: however, she went on: "And how do you know that you're
T8W	13: 7	on the ground, leaning against a tree, all	all huddled up together, and shivering as if he were very cold
A6	53:17	"Suppose it should be raving mad after	all! I almost wish I'd gone to see the Hatter instead!"
T8	187:29	she said to herself: "it's 'I give thee	all, I can no more.'" She stood and listened very attentively,
A5	43:20	why, then they're a kind of serpent: that's	all I can say."
A5	36: 7	your feelings may be different," said Alice: "all I know is, it would feel very queer to me."
A4	31:21	but I'm a deal too flustered to tell you--all I know is, something comes at me like a Jack-in-the-box,
A8	63:42	"Why, they're only a pack of cards, after	all. I needn't be afraid of them!"
T3	131:27	"I don't belong to this railway journey at	all--I was in a wood just now--and I wish I could get back
T3	131:37	sigh, that she wouldn't have heard it at	all, if it hadn't come quite close to her ear. The consequence
T3	135:36	them answered! Only they wouldn't answer at	all, if they were wise."
T5	158: 1	and the boat, and the river, had vanished	all in a moment, and she was back again in the little dark
T4	146:14	passion, and his eyes grew large and yellow	all in a moment, as he pointed with a trembling finger at a
A3	26:35	"Come away, my dears! It's high time you were	all in bed!" On various pretexts they all moved off, and Alice
T1	109:14	in the summer, Kitty, they dress themselves	all in green, and dance about--whenever the wind blows--oh,
T9	201:37	"her White Majesty knows a lovely riddle--all in poetry--all about fishes. Shall she repeat it?"

ALL (cont.)

```
T1   116: 5  some  part  that  she could read, "--for it's all in some language I don't know," she said to herself.
AI     3: 1                                                  All in the golden afternoon / Full leisurely we glide; / For
T3   132:23                       "--then you don't like all insects?" the Gnat went on, as quietly as if nothing had
A2    16: 8  she, and I'm I, and--oh dear, how puzzling it all is! I'll try if I know all the things I used to know. Let
A5    36:27  she had nothing else to do, and perhaps after all it might tell her something worth hearing. For some
T5   155: 3  "I'll  follow  it up to the very top shelf of all. It'll puzzle it to go through the ceiling, I expect!"
A12   94:14  he spoke, and added "It isn't a letter, after all: it's a set of verses."
A4    32:35  whereupon  the  puppy jumped into the air off all its feet at once, with a yelp of delight, and rushed at
A3    26:14  story!" Alice called after it. And the others all joined in chorus "Yes, please do!" But the Mouse only
T8   185:21  that  he  was talking on in his usual tone. "All kinds of fastness," he repeated: "but it was careless of
T8   185:13          The Knight shook his head. "It was all kinds of fastness with me, I can assure you!" he said. He
T9   200: 9     that  there  were  about  fifty guests, of all kinds: some were animals, some birds, and there were even
T1   107:18  and there it was, spread over the hearth-rug, all knots and tangles, with the kitten running after its own
A6    51: 4  she  began, rather timidly, as she did not at all know whether it would like the name: however, it only
T3   130:14  confess  that I don't) "Better say nothing at all. Language is worth a thousand pounds a word!"
T6   159:24  didn't know what to say to this: it wasn't at all like conversation, she thought, as he never said anything
A6    48: 7                              Alice did not at all like the tone of this remark, and thought it would be as
A1     9:30  were  doors all round the hall, but they were all locked; and when Alice had been all the way down one side
A12   94:18  the  queerest  thing  about  it." (The jury all looked puzzled.)
A3    24: 5  thought the whole thing very absurd, but they all looked so grave that she did not dare to laugh; and, as
A6    51:23  you  ca'n't  help that," said the Cat: "we're all mad here. I'm mad. You're mad."
A4    32:15  giving  it  something  out  of  a bottle. They all made a rush at Alice the moment she appeared; but she ran
A1     9:34  she  came  upon  a little three-legged table, all made of solid glass: there was nothing on it but a tiny
T5   154:11          The shop seemed to be full of all manner of curious things--but the oddest part of it all
A7    60:16  it was getting very sleepy; "and they drew all manner of things--everything that begins with an M--"
T1   115:38  I ca'n't  manage this one a bit: it writes all manner of things that I don't intend--"
T9   201:11  rather hastily, "or we shall get no dinner at all. May I give you some?"
T1   107: 8  trying  to purr--no doubt feeling that it was all meant for it good.
T1   116:11  emom  eht dnA / ,sevogorob eht erew ysmim llA / :ebaw eht ni elbmig dna eryg diD / sevot yhtils eht dna
T1   116:20  toves  /  Did  gyre and gimble in the wabe: / All mimsy were the borogoves, / And the mome raths outgrabe.
T1   118:23  toves  /  Did  gyre and gimble in the wabe: / All mimsy were the borogoves, / And the mome raths outgrabe.
T6   164:23  toves  /  Did  gyre and gimble in the wabe: / All mimsy were the borogoves, / And the mome raths outgrabe."
A7    59:36  a  clean  cup," interrupted the Hatter: "let's all move one place on."
A3    26:35  were  all  in  bed!" On various pretexts they all moved off, and Alice was soon left alone.
A3    23:21  At last the Dodo said "Everybody has won, and all must have prizes."
T2   120:16  into  the  old room--and there'd be an end of all my adventures!"
T8W   19:10      So  now  that  I  am  old and gray, / And all my hair is nearly gone, / They take my wig from me and say
T1   110:31  Kitty,  and  not talk so much, I'll tell you all my ideas about Looking-glass House. First, there's the
A6    53: 8  It's  the  most  curious  thing I ever saw in all my life!"
A7    60:37  It's the stupidest tea-party I ever was at in all my life!"
A9    74:14  it:  "I never was so ordered about before, in all my life, never!"
A5    38: 6  sage,  as  he shook his grey locks, / "I kept all my limbs very supple / By the use of this ointment--one
T1   109: 1  for Wednesday week--Suppose they had saved up all my punishments?" she went on, talking more to herself than
T5   158:12  she  thought to herself, "They mightn't be at all nice, you know."
T1   110:33  only  the  things go the other way. I can see all of it when I get upon a chair--all but the bit just behind
A8    63: 2  suddenly:  the  others looked round also, and all of them bowed low.
T4   143: 4  /  For  some  of  us are out of breath, / And all of us are fat!' / 'No hurry!' said the Carpenter. / They
A3    21:14  authority  among  them, called out "Sit down, all of you, and listen to me! I'll soon make you dry enough!"
A11   87:17  "The  Queen of Hearts, she made some tarts, / All on a summer day: / The Knave of Hearts, he stole those
T5   149:29  ca'n't  go  straight, you know, if you pin it all on one side," Alice said as she gently put it right for
A8    63:21  along,  hand  in  hand, in couples: they were all ornamented with hearts. Next came the guests, mostly Kings
T5   152:26  Queen.  "What  would be the good of having it all over again?"
A2    19:40  again,  for this time the Mouse was bristling all over, and she felt certain it must be really offended. "We
A10   80:23  have their tails in their mouths--and they're all over crumbs."
T6   159: 6  as certain of it, as if his name were written all over his face!"
T5   149:24      Alice thought to herself, "and she's all over pins!--May I put your shawl straight for you?" she
T2   126: 1  great huge game of chess that's being played--all over the world--if this is the world at all, you know. Oh,
T1   107: 8  then  with  the other paw she rubbed its face all over, the wrong way, beginning at the nose: and just now,
A6    45: 8  Alice  noticed, had powdered hair that curled all over their heads. She felt very curious to know what it
A8    63:17  next the ten courtiers: these were ornamented all over with diamonds, and walked two and two, as the
A2    19:27  leap  out  of the water, and seemed to quiver all over with fright. "Oh, I beg your pardon!" cried Alice
A9    73:19  voice,  to  the  company, generally, "You are all pardoned." "Come, that's a good thing!" she said to
T8   179: 8  she  said  to herself, "unless--unless we're all part of the same dream. Only I do hope it's my dream, and
A12   93:35  and  read out from his book, "Rule Forty-two. All persons more than a mile high to leave the court."
A8    66:20          The players all played at once, without waiting for turns, quarreling all
A8    67:24   in  rather  a complaining tone,  "and they all quarrel so dreadfully one ca'n't hear oneself speak--and
A3    22: 1  the  Mouse  with  an  important air. "Are you all ready? This is the driest thing I know. Silence all round,
T1   116: 3  a  little  anxious about him, and had the ink all ready to throw over him, in case he fainted again), she
A12   96: 9          "But it goes on 'they all returned from him to you,'" said Alice.
A12   95: 7  him  two, / You gave us three or more; / They all returned from him to you, / Though they were mine before.
A8    66: 2  a  curious croquet-ground in her life: it was all ridges and furrows: the croquet balls were live hedgehogs,
T2   121:12  her  petals curled up a little more, she'd be all right."
T9   195: 7                      "She's all right again now," said the Red Queen. "Do you know
A6    53: 4                          "All right," said the Cat; and this time it vanished quite
T3   133: 3                          "All right," said the Gnat. "Half way up that bush, you'll see
A12   95:38                          "All right, so far," said the King; and he went on muttering
A3    23:29  as prizes. There was  exactly one a-piece, all round.
A4    33:14  question certainly was "What?" Alice looked all round her at the flowers and the blades of grass, but she
T2   123:23                      "Why, all round her head, of course," the Rose replied. "I was
```

ALL (cont.)

A3	22: 2	This is the driest thing I know. Silence all round, if you please! 'William the Conqueror, whose cause
A8	69: 3	than no time, she'd have everybody executed, all round. (It was this last remark that had made the whole
T5	154: 4	said very gently. "I should like to look all round me first, if I might."
T6	165:11	bird with its feathers sticking out all round--something like a live mop."
A1	9:30	There were doors all round the hall, but they were all locked; and when Alice
A7	54:14	Alice looked all round the table, but there was nothing on it but tea. "I
T7	176:24	very nervous, and his voice quite quivered. "All round the town?" he said. "That's a good long way. Did you
T7	173: 2	for the crown: / The Lion beat the Unicorn all round the town. / Some gave them white bread, some gave
T7	176:21	"Why, I beat you all round the town, you chicken!" the Lion replied angrily,
T5	154: 6	like," said the Sheep; "but you ca'n't look all round you--unless you've got eyes at the back of your head
T9	193:17	"I didn't know I was to have a party at all," said Alice; "but, if there is to be one, I think I ought
A8	67:32	"Not at all," said Alice: "she's so extremely--" Just then she noticed
A5	36:23	"Is that all?" said Alice, swallowing down her anger as well as she
T6	168:16	"That's all," said Humpty Dumpty. "Good-bye."
A12	95:34	"I seem to see some meaning in them, after all. '--said I could not swim--' you ca'n't swim, can you?" he
A6	46:33	"Are you to get in at all?" said the Footman. "That's the first question, you know
T7	170:26	"Not at all," said the King. "He's an Anglo-Saxon Messenger--and those
A8	67:41	"I don't like the look of it at all," said the King: "however, it may kiss my hand, if it
A12	94:12	"It isn't directed at all," said the White Rabbit: "in fact, there's nothing written
T3	129:38	angrily at Alice. And a great many voices all said together ("like the chorus of a song," thought Alice)
A3	21:15	to me! I'll soon make you dry enough!" They all sat down at once, in a large ring, with the Mouse in
T3	131:24	whispered in her ear, "Never mind what they all say, my dear, but take a return-ticket every time the
A1	7:15	to have wondered at this, but at the time it all seemed quite natural); but, when the Rabbit actually took
T4	145:25	said--half laughing through her tears, it all seemed so ridiculous--"I shouldn't be able to cry."
A8	63:15	came ten soldiers carrying clubs: these were all shaped like the three gardeners, oblong and flat, with
T2	124:13	to me--but why did you come out here at all?" she added in a kinder tone. "Curtsey while you're
T2	126:14	hand, and the Queen went so fast that it was all she could do to keep up with her: and still the Queen kept
T8	184:18	with a little scream of laughter, in spite of all she could do to prevent it.
A7	55:33	silent for a minute, while Alice thought over all she could remember about ravens and writing-desks, which
T3	136: 5	being determined didn't help her much, and all she could say, after a great deal of puzzling, was "L, I
A5	42: 9	that her shoulders were nowhere to be found: all she could see, when she looked down, was an immense length
T5	149:10	that if there was to be any conversation at all, she must manage it herself. So she began rather timidly:
T2	126:13	over afterwards, how it was that they began: all she remembers is, that they were running hand in hand, and
T8	179: 7	the plum-cake, "So I wasn't dreaming, after all," she said to herself, "unless--unless we're all part of
T2	123:18	Alice didn't like this idea at all: so, to change the subject, she asked "Does she ever come
T1	111: 9	Kitty. Let's pretend the glass has got all soft like gauze, so that we can get through. Why, it's
T1	118:27	to herself, that she couldn't make it out at all.) "Somehow it seems to fill my head with ideas--only I
A11	86: 2	with a great crowd assembled about them--all sorts of little birds and beasts, as well as the whole
A2	16: 6	and I'm sure I ca'n't be Mabel, for I know all sorts of things, and she, oh, she knows such a very
T9	203:10	And then (as Alice afterwards described it) all sorts of things happened in a moment. The candles all grew
A2	20: 7	and it'll sit up and beg for its dinner, and all sorts of things--I ca'n't remember half of them--and it
T5	157:12	"Crabs, and all sorts of things," said the Sheep: "plenty of choice, only
A9	70: 8	"I wo'n't have any pepper in my kitchen at all. Soup does very well without--Maybe it's always pepper
T3	131: 8	as the rule seemed to be that they should all speak in turn, he went on with "She'll have to go back
A2	18:12	"And now for the garden!" And she ran with all speed back to the little door; but, alas! the little door
A8	68:35	their arguments to her, though, as they all spoke at once, she found it very hard to make out exactly
A8	63:34	the procession came opposite to Alice, they all stopped and looked at her, and the Queen said, severely,
T2	122:21	"How is it you can all talk so nicely?" Alice said, hoping to get it into a
A8	68:31	the King, and the Queen, who were all talking at once, while all the rest were quite silent, and
A4	30:24	and the sound of a good many voices all talking together: she made out the words: "Where's the
T8W	17:11	was bright yellow like the handkerchief, and all tangled and tumbled about like a heap of sea-weed. "You
A4	30:10	it does, yer honour: but it's an arm for all that."
A9	76: 8	too," said Alice. "You needn't be so proud as all that."
A5	42:13	"What can all that green stuff be?" said Alice. "And where have my
T6	166:10	you'll be quite content. Who's been repeating all that hard stuff to you?"
A10	81: 2	shut his eyes. "Tell her about the reason and all that," he said to the Gryphon.
A10	81:43	"Explain all that," said the Mock Turtle.
A10	84: 3	"What is the use of repeating all that stuff?" the Mock Turtle interrupted, "if you don't
T9	202:24	their heads like extinguishers, and drank all that trickled down their faces--others upset the decanters
A8	68:24	it doesn't matter much," thought Alice, "as all the arches are gone from this side of the ground." So she
T1	115:12	you! And don't keep your mouth so wide open! All the ashes will get into it--there, now I think you're tidy
T5	149:21	It would have been all the better, as it seemed to Alice, if she had got some one
T5	151:16	"And you were all the better for it, I know!" the Queen said triumphantly.
T5	151:11	the better," she said: "but it wouldn't be all the better his being punished."
T5	151:10	was no denying that. "Of course it would be all the better," she said: "but it wouldn't be all the better
T5	151: 8	"That would be all the better, wouldn't it?" the Queen said, as she bound the
A2	16: 1	great puzzle!" And she began thinking over all the children she knew that were of the same age as herself
T9	201:27	said the Red Queen: "it's ridiculous to leave all the conversation to the pudding!"
A6	46:36	dreadful," she muttered to herself, "the way all the creatures argue. It's enough to drive one crazy!"
T5	151:19	I was punished for," said Alice: "that makes all the difference."
A10	78:35	"Back to land again, and--that's all the first figure," said the Mock Turtle, suddenly dropping
T2	121: 4	a timid voice--almost in a whisper. "And can all the flowers talk?"
T9	202:21	she screamed at the top of her voice, and all the guests began drinking it directly, and very queerly
T9	197:16	care of two Queens asleep at once! No, not in all the History of England--it couldn't, you know, because
T7	170:11	said, referring to his book. "I couldn't send all the horses, you know, because two of them are wanted in
A10	78:17	salmon, and so on: then, when you've cleared all the jelly-fish out of the way--"
A11	86:38	she were looking over their shoulders, that all the jurors were writing down "Stupid things!" on their
A12	93: 2	said the King, in a very grave voice, "until all the jurymen are back in their proper places--all," he
A12	92: 4	with the edge of her skirt, upsetting all the jurymen on to the heads of the crowd below, and there

ALL (cont.)

T7	170: 6	"I've sent them **all!**" the King cried in a tone of delight, on seeing Alice.
T6	159:30	a wall: / Humpty Dumpty had a great fall. / **All** the King's horses and all the King's men / Couldn't put
T6	159:30	had a great fall. / All the King's horses and **all** the King's men / Couldn't put Humpty Dumpty in his place
T4	142:17	rested on a rock / Conveniently low: / And **all** the little Oysters stood / And waited in a row.
T9	204:18	Queen, whom she considered as the cause of **all** the mischief--but the Queen was no longer at her side--she
T1	108:22	were comfortably settled again, "when I saw **all** the mischief you had been doing, I was very nearly opening
A12	98:40	of the baby, the shriek of the Gryphon, and **all** the other queer noises, would change (she knew) to the
A3	23: 9	shape doesn't matter," it said,) and then **all** the party were placed along the course, here and there.
T2	128: 4	She had got **all** the pegs put in by this time, and Alice looked on with
A9	73: 8	an hour or so, there were no arches left, and **all** the players, except the King, the Queen, and Alice, were
T6	164:17	hear it," said Humpty Dumpty. "I can explain **all** the poems that ever were invented--and a good many that
A2	20: 9	it's worth a hundred pounds! He says it kills **all** the rats and--oh dear!" cried Alice in a sorrowful tone.
T1	110:16	you can be one of them, then, and I'll be **all** the rest." And once she had really frightened her old
A12	95:19	/ For this must ever be / A secret, kept from **all** the rest, / Between yourself and me."
T6	164: 2	as I suppose you don't mean to stop here **all** the rest of your life."
T1	112:12	was quite common and uninteresting, but that **all** the rest was as different as possible. For instance, the
A8	68:31	Queen, who were all talking at once, while **all** the rest were quite silent, and looked very uncomfortable
A1	8:43	listening, this time, as it didn't sound at **all** the right word) "--but I shall have to ask them what the
T2	122:32	"It's my opinion that you never think at **all,**" the Rose said, in a rather severe tone.
T2	127:20	said the Queen. "Now, here, you see, it takes **all** the running you can do, to keep in the same place. If you
T8	186: 4	to be?" he said. "My mind goes on working **all** the same. In fact, the more head-downwards I am, the more
A2	15:22	this moment, I tell you!" But she went on **all** the same, shedding gallons of tears, until there was a
T5	152:25	"Why, I've done **all** the screaming already," said the Queen. "What would be the
T8	187:16	Of **all** the strange things that Alice saw in her journey Through
T9	202:36	"That wouldn't be at **all** the thing," the Red Queen said very decidedly: so Alice
A8	67:27	them--and you've no idea how confusing it is **all** the things being alive: for instance, there's the arch
A2	16: 8	how puzzling it all is! I'll try if I know **all** the things I used to know. Let me see: four times five is
T2	126:20	never seemed to pass anything. "I wonder if **all** the things move along with us?" thought poor puzzled Alice
T8	181:24	of vexation passing over his face. "Then **all** the things must have fallen out! And the box is no use
T2	124: 8	speak nicely, and don't twiddle your fingers **all** the time."
A4	32:30	to it; but she was terribly frightened **all** the time at the thought that it might be hungry, in which
A6	46:21	you know." He was looking up into the sky **all** the time he was speaking, and this Alice thought decidedly
A2	15:37	hall was very hot, she kept fanning herself **all** the time she went on talking. "Dear, dear! How queer
T1	108: 6	didn't get on very fast, as she was talking **all** the time, sometimes to the kitten, and sometimes to
T8	184: 9	"Plenty of practice!" he went on repeating, **all** the time that Alice was getting him on his feet again.
A9	73: 3	**All** the time they were playing the Queen never left off
T12	208: 2	morning you shall have a real treat. **All** the time you're eating your breakfast, I'll repeat 'The
A8	62:17	down his brush, and had just begun "Well, of **all** the unjust things--" when his eye chanced to fall upon
T6	168:39	comfort to have such a long word to say) "of **all** the unsatisfactory people I ever met--" She never finished
T6	168:38	help saying to herself, as she went, "of **all** the unsatisfactory--" (she repeated this aloud, as it was
A1	9:31	they were all locked; and when Alice had been **all** the way down one side and up the other, trying every door,
T2	124:12	what you mean by your way," said the Queen: "**all** the ways about here belong to me--but why did you come out
A8	66:21	once, without waiting for turns, quarrelling **all** the while, and fighting for the hedgehogs; and in a very
T5	157: 3	up again: the Sheep went on with her knitting **all** the while, just as if nothing had happened. "That was a
T7	172:39	the best of the joke is, that it's my crown **all** the while! Let's run and see them." And they trotted off,
A4	32:44	and a long way back, and barking hoarsely **all** the while, till at last it sat down a good way off,
T5	156:35	the rushes had begun to fade, and to lose **all** their scent and beauty, from the very moment that she
A12	99:10	their simple sorrows, and find a pleasure in **all** their simple joys, remembering her own child-life, and the
A12	99: 9	of long ago; and how she would feel with **all** their simple sorrows, and find a pleasure in all their
A5	43:40	there's half my plan done now! How puzzling **all** these changes are! I'm never sure what I'm going to be,
T2	124: 9	Alice attended to **all** these directions, and explained, as well as she could,
A12	98: 7	sister, as well as she could remember them, **all** these strange Adventures of hers that you have just been
T8	188:23	Macassar-Oil--/ Yet twopence-halfpenny is **all** / They give me for my toil.'
A1	8:24	of tumbling down-stairs! How brave they'll **all** think me at home! Why, I wouldn't say anything about it,
A8	63:26	on a crimson velvet cushion; and, last of **all** this grand procession, came THE KING AND THE QUEEN OF
T2	128:17	"'It's extremely kind of you to tell me **all** this'--however, we'll suppose it said--the Seventh Square
T12	208: 5	let's consider who it was that dreamed it **all.** This is a serious question, my dear, and you should not
T8	187:24	and the black shadows of the forest behind--**all** this she took in like a picture, as, with one hand shading
A8	66:15	and was in the act of crawling away: besides **all** this, there was generally a ridge or a furrow in the way
A7	59:34	said the Dormouse, without considering at **all,** this time.
A10	78:37	who had been jumping about like mad things **all** this time, sat down again very sadly and quietly, and
T3	130:18	**All** this time the Guard was looking at her, first through a
A11	89: 4	**All** this time the Queen had never left off staring at the
T4	147: 1	**All** this time Tweedledee was trying his best to fold up the
T4	139:35	she was telling her sister the history of **all** this), "to find myself singing 'Here we go round the
T7	170:20	**All** this was lost on Alice, who was still looking intently
T8	182: 6	everything. That's the reason the horse has **all** those anklets round his feet."
T2	125: 4	her on the head, which Alice didn't like at **all:** "though, when you say 'garden'--I've seen gardens,
T3	130:12	spoken, but, to her great surprise, they **all** thought in chorus (I hope you understand what thinking in
A11	88:18	to the jury; and the jury eagerly wrote down **all** three dates on their slates, and then added them up, and
A8	68:33	moment Alice appeared, she was appealed to by **all** three to settle the question, and they repeated their
T12	207: 4	dream! And you've been along with me, Kitty--**all** through the Looking-glass world. Did you know it, dear?"
A8	63:31	of a procession," thought she, "if people had **all** to lie down on their faces, so that they couldn't see it?"
A4	32: 5	with some surprise, that the pebbles were **all** turning into little cakes as they lay on the floor, and a
A1	10:19	It was **all** very well to say "Drink me," but the wise little Alice was
T8	179: 1	the noise seemed gradually to die away, till **all** was dead silence, and Alice lifted up her head in some
T5	153:34	She couldn't make out what had happened at **all.** Was she in a shop? And was that really--was it really a
T5	154:12	of curious things--but the oddest part of it **all** was that, whenever she looked hard at any shelf, to make
A10	80:25	crumbs," said the Mock Turtle: "crumbs would **all** wash off in the sea. But they have their tails in their

ALL (cont.)
T2   120:20   till she got to the hill. For a few minutes all went on well, and she was just saying "I really shall do
A11   87: 9   was Bill, the Lizard) could not make out at all what had become of it; so, after hunting all about for it,
T2   127:28   not be civil to say "No," though it wasn't at all what she wanted. She took it, and ate it as well as she
T2   122:18   the Tiger-lily. "The daisies are worst of all. When one speaks, they all begin together, and it's enough
A12   98:36   she knew she had but to open them again, and all would change to dull reality--the grass would be only
A11   86:28   The twelve jurors were all writing very busily on slates. "What are they doing?"
A2   17: 2   is the capital of Rome, and Rome--no, that's all wrong, I'm certain! I must have been changed for Mabel!
A12   95:27   The jury all wrote down, on their slates, "She doesn't believe there's
A11   90:21   "If that's all you know about it, you may stand down," continued the King
T2   126: 2   all over the world--if this is the world at all, you know. Oh, what fun it is! How I wish I was one of
T1   108:27   holding up one finger. "I'm going to tell you all your faults. Number one: you squeaked twice while Dinah
T1   108:39   for any of them yet. You know I'm saving up all your punishments for Wednesday week--Suppose they had
ALLOW (3)
A8   67:39   friend of mine--a Cheshire-Cat," said Alice: "allow me to introduce it."
A5   38: 8   use of this ointment--one shilling the box--/ Allow me to sell you a couple?"
A3   21:11   must know better." And this Alice would not allow, without knowing how old it was, and as the Lory
ALLOWED (1)
T7   174:14   while the King called out "Ten minutes allowed for refreshments!" Haigha and Hatta set to work at
ALMOST (18)
T6   160:10   a name like yours, you might be any shape, almost."
A7   56:44   you only kept on good terms with him, he'd do almost anything you liked with the clock. For instance,
T5   156:26   it certainly did seem a little provoking ("almost as if it happened on purpose," she thought) that,
T2   127: 3   with the wind whistling in Alice's ears, and almost blowing her hair off her head, she fancied.
T3   135:30   have to give me another, and it would be almost certain to be an ugly one. But then the fun would be,
A1   11: 4   much from a bottle marked "poison," it is almost certain to disagree with you, sooner or later.
T8W   18: 6   A curious idea came into Alice's head. Almost every one she had met had repeated poetry to her, and
T6   160:40   you may shake hands with me!" And he grinned almost from ear to ear, as he leant forwards (and as nearly as
T2   121: 4   about, she spoke again, in a timid voice--almost in a whisper. "And can all the flowers talk?"
T5   156:38   and these, being dream-rushes, melted away almost like snow, as they lay in heaps at her feet--but Alice
T6   159:33   is much too long for the poetry," she added, almost out loud, forgetting that Humpty Dumpty would hear her.
A2   14: 5   looked down at her feet, they seemed to be almost out of sight, they were getting so far off). "Oh, my
T3   137:11   Alice stood looking after it, almost ready to cry with vexation at having lost her dear
T9   199: 6   Alice almost stamped with irritation at the slow drawl in which he
A2   15:40   was I the same when I got up this morning? I almost think I can remember feeling a little different. But if
T6   168: 1   Humpty Dumpty raised his voice almost to a scream as he repeated this verse, and Alice
A4   29: 1   being ordered about by mice and rabbits. I almost wish I hadn't gone down that rabbit-hole--and yet--and
A6   53:17   "Suppose it should be raving mad after all! I almost wish I'd gone to see the Hatter instead!"
ALONE (11)
A3   26:36   they all moved off, and Alice was soon left alone.
A5   42:28   a serpent!" said Alice indignantly. "Let me alone!"
T8W   14:13   "Worrity, worrity! Can't you leave a body alone?"
A4   31: 8   of "There goes Bill!" then the Rabbit's voice alone--"Catch him, you by the hedge!" then silence, and then
T8   186:26   "Not very nice alone," he interrupted, quite eagerly: "but you've no idea
T9   199:20   kick with one of his great feet. "You let it alone," he panted out, as he hobbled back to his tree, "and
A2   17:27   heads down! I am so very tired of being all alone here!"
T3   130: 9   man that drives the engine. Why, the smoke alone is worth a thousand pounds a puff!"
T6   160:11   "Why do you sit out here all alone?" said Alice, not wishing to begin an argument.
A9   74: 4   ordered;" and she walked off, leaving Alice alone with the Gryphon. Alice did not quite like the look of
T9   199:21   hobbled back to his tree, "and it'll let you alone, you know."
ALONG (22)
T2   126:27   Queen cried "Faster! Faster!" and dragged her along. "Are we nearly there?" Alice managed to pant out at
T5   155:19   she found they were in a little boat, gliding along between banks: so there was nothing for it but to do her
A8   63:20   and the little dears came jumping merrily along, hand in hand, in couples: they were all ornamented with
A2   15:29   a large fan in the other: he came trotting along in a great hurry, muttering to himself, as he came, "Oh!
T3   137:18   wood, and the two finger-posts both pointed along it. "I'll settle it," Alice said to herself, "when the
T8W   16: 5   "Along of the wig?" Alice repeated, quite pleased to find that
T8W   16: 3   "It's all along of the wig," the Wasp said in a much gentler voice.
T4   141:16   / 'A pleasant walk, a pleasant talk, / Along the briny beach: / We cannot do with more than four, /
A3   23:10   it said,) and then all the party were placed along the course, here and there. There was no "One, two,
T2   123:27   Larkspur. "I hear her footstep, thump, thump, along the gravel-walk!"
A1   10: 2   than a rat-hole: she knelt down and looked along the passage into the loveliest garden you ever saw. How
T2   120: 4   doesn't do that--" (after going a few yards along the path, and turning several sharp corners), "but I
T7   170:14   They're both gone to the town. Just look along the road, and tell me if you can see either of them."
T8   190:30   as she watched the horse walking leisurely along the road, and the Knight tumbling off, first on one side
T8   190:13   up the reins, and turned his horse's head along the road by which they had come. "You've only a few
T7   170:20   lost on Alice, who was still looking intently along the road, shading her eyes with one hand. "I see
A10   78:14   said the Gryphon, "you first form into a line along the sea-shore--"
T9   200: 8   Alice glanced nervously along the table, as she walked up the large hall, and noticed
T7   170:24   down, and wriggling like an eel, as he came along, with his great hands spread out like fans on each side
T12   207: 4   out of oh! such a nice dream! And you've been along with me, Kitty--all through the Looking-glass world. Did
T9   199:40   a privilege high to have dinner and tea / Along with the Red Queen, the White Queen, and me!"
T2   126:21   anything. "I wonder if all the things move along with us?" thought poor puzzled Alice. And the Queen
ALOUD (9)
A6   46:25   --How am I to get in?" she repeated, aloud.
A7   55:15   I believe I can guess that," she added aloud.
T5   149:25   I put your shawl straight for you?" she added aloud.
A3   26:22   had our Dinah here, I know I do!" said Alice aloud, addressing nobody in particular. "She'd soon fetch it
A5   41:32   the Caterpillar, just as if she had asked it aloud; and in another moment it was out of sight.
T6   168:38   all the unsatisfactory--" (she repeated this aloud, as it was a great comfort to have such a long word to

ALOUD (cont.)
  T9   196:19   be the use of it?" but she did not say this aloud, for fear of hurting the poor Queen's feelings.
  A1   8:28   miles I've fallen by this time?" she said aloud. "I must be getting somewhere near the centre of the
  T6   159:14   "And how exactly like an egg he is!" she said aloud, standing with her hands ready to catch him, for she was
ALPHABET (1)
  T3   131: 5   ticket-office, even if she doesn't know her alphabet!"
ALREADY (9)
  T7   177:10   'the Monster'). "I've cut several slices already, but they always join on again!"
  A8   68:12   the distance, screaming with passion. She had already heard her sentence three of the players to be executed
  T9   202:10   it lie in a dish!' / That is easy, because it already is in it.
  T8   182:20   bag." And he hung it to the saddle, which was already loaded with bunches of carrots, and fire-irons, and
  T8   184:31   is with the feet: the head is high enough already.' Now, first I put my head on the top of the gate--
  T5   152:25   "Why, I've done all the screaming already," said the Queen. "What would be the good of having it
  T9   204: 9   There was not a moment to be lost. Already several of the guests were lying down in the dishes,
  T9   200:15   of the table: the Red and White Queens had already taken two of them, but the middle one was empty. Alice
  A6   48:14   hit her; and the baby was howling so much already, that it was quite impossible to say whether the blows
ALSO (4)
  A8   63: 2   himself suddenly: the others looked round also, and all of them bowed low.
  A6   49:34   much more like a snout than a real nose: also its eyes were getting extremely small for a baby:
  T6   164:39   "also they make their nests under sun-dials--also they live on cheese."
  T6   164:38   "They are that," said Humpty Dumpty; "also they make their nests under sun-dials--also they live on
ALTERED (1)
  A5   41: 3   Alice, timidly: "some of the words have got altered."
ALTERING (1)
  T5   149:36   you look rather better now!" she said, after altering most of the pins. "But really you should have a
ALTERNATELY (1)
  A6   47: 9   as for the baby, it was sneezing and howling alternately without a moment's pause. The only two creatures
ALTOGETHER (6)
  A2   18: 9   in time to save herself from shrinking away altogether.
  A6   49:34   eyes were getting extremely small for a baby: altogether Alice did not like the look of the thing at all.
  T3   131: 7   was a very queer carriage-full of passengers altogether), and, as the rule seemed to be that they should
  A4   29:17   other, and making quite a conversation of it altogether; but after a few minutes she heard a voice outside,
  A6   49:19   and straightening itself out again, so that altogether, for the first minute or two, it was as much as she
  A1   12: 8   said Alice to herself, "in my going out altogether, like a candle. I wonder what I should be like then
ALWAYS (43)
  T5   156:28   rushes as the boat glided by, there was always a more lovely one that she couldn't reach.
  T2   122:29   the beds too soft--so that the flowers are always asleep."
  T2   120:10   up and down, and trying turn after turn, but always coming back to the house, do what she would. Indeed,
  T5   153:14   said the Queen. "When I was your age, I always did it for half-an-hour a day. Why, sometimes I've
  T8   179:36   "I always do," said the Red Knight, and they began banging away
  T8   180:11   Alice had not noticed, seemed to be that they always fell on their heads; and the battle ended with their
  T7   169: 7   and whenever one went down, several more always fell over him, so that the ground was soon covered with
  T5   156:30   "The prettiest are always further!" she said at last with a sigh at the obstinacy
  A12   98:21   to keep back the wandering hair that would always get into her eyes--and still as she listened, or seemed
  A8   66:17   to, and, as the doubled-up soldiers were always getting up and walking off to other parts of the ground
  A6   48: 1   "I didn't know that Cheshire-Cats always grinned; in fact, I didn't know that cats could grin."
  A4   28:28   home," thought poor Alice, "when one wasn't always growing larger and smaller, and being ordered about by
  T3   134:19   "It always happens," said the Gnat.
  A2   19:44   if I would talk on such a subject! Our family always hated cats: nasty, low, vulgar things! Don't let me
  T5   154:19   a doll and sometimes like a work-box, and was always in the shelf next above the one she was looking at.
  T7   177:10   "I've cut several slices already, but they always join on again!"
  A8   62: 9   Seven looked up and said "That's right, Five! Always lay the blame on others!"
  T5   150:12   living backwards," the Queen said kindly: "it always makes one a little giddy at first--"
  T6   164: 6   of work like that," said Humpty Dumpty, "I always pay it extra."
  A9   70: 9   all. Soup does very well without--Maybe it's always pepper that makes people hot-tempered," she went on,
  T12 207: 7   remark) that, whatever you say to them, they always purr. "If they would only purr for 'yes,' and mew for
  T5   154:14   what it had on it, that particular shelf was always quite empty, though the others round it were crowded as
  T9   192: 3   she went on, in a severe tone (she was always rather fond of scolding herself), "It'll never do for
  T9   192:20   obeyed that rule," said Alice, who was always ready for a little argument, "and if you only spoke
  A3   26: 6   "A knot!" said Alice, always ready to make herself useful, and looking anxiously
  A3   26:26   Alice replied eagerly, for she was always ready to talk about her pet: "Dinah's our cat. And
  T8   187:17   The Looking-Glass, this was the one that she always remembered most clearly. Years afterwards she could
  T12 207:10   But how can you talk with a person if they always say the same thing?"
  T2   124:20   your mouth a little wider when you speak, and always say 'your Majesty.'"
  A7   58: 9   tone, "he wo'n't do a thing I ask! It's always six o'clock now."
  T9   192:35   did, you know," the Red Queen said to Alice. "Always speak the truth--think before you speak--and write it
  A7   58:12   it," said the Hatter with a sigh: "it's always tea-time, and we've no time to wash the things between
  T6   168:29   thumb) "nose in the middle, mouth under. It's always the same. Now if you had the two eyes on the same side
  T7   175:23   "I always thought they were fabulous monsters!" said the Unicorn.
  T7   175:28   up into a smile as she began: "Do you know, I always thought Unicorns were fabulous monsters, too? I never
  A4   29:11   one way--never to be an old woman--but then--always to have lessons to learn! Oh, I shouldn't like that!"
  A7   58:35   "What did they live on?" said Alice, who always took a great interest in questions of eating and
  T8   185: 1   used to wear it, if I fell off the horse, it always touched the ground directly. So I had a very little way
  T7   169: 6   so uncertain on their feet: they were always tripping over something or other, and whenever one went
  T8   188:11   a plan / To dye one's whiskers green, / And always use so large a fan / That they could not be seen. / So,
  T9   192:22   when you were spoken to, and the other person always waited for you to begin, you see nobody would ever say
  T5   156: 4   than ever), and sometimes under trees, but always with the same tall river-banks frowning over their
  T2   123: 7   the Rose. "I wonder how you do it--" ("You're always wondering," said the Tiger-lily), "but she's more bushy
AM (30)
  T9   192: 9   there was nobody to see her, "and if I really am a Queen," she said as she sat down again, "I shall be able

AM (cont.)
T3   131:42   old friend. And you wo'n't hurt me, though I am an insect."
T6   160: 9   a short laugh: "my name means the shape I am--and a good handsome shape it is, too. With a name like
A4   27:19   surprised he'll be when he finds out who I am! But I'd better take him his fan and gloves--that is, if I
T9   204: 5   leg of mutton sitting in the chair. "Here I am!" cried a voice from the soup-tureen, and Alice turned
T5   149:11   it herself. So she began rather timidly: "Am I addressing the White Queen?"
A2   15:42   same, the next question is 'Who in the world am I?' Ah, that's the great puzzle!" And she began thinking
T3   136: 3   really has happened, after all! And now, who am I? I will remember, if I can! I'm determined to do it!" But
A2   17:23   dear!' I shall only look up and say 'Who am I, then? Tell me that first, and then, if I like being that
T9   197:12   "What am I to do?" exclaimed Alice, looking about in great
A6   46:41   "But what am I to do?" said Alice.
A6   50: 8   beginning to think to herself, "Now, what am I to do with this creature, when I get it home?" when it
A6   46:17   "Please, then," said Alice, "how am I to get in?"
A6   46:32   "How am I to get in?" asked Alice again, in a louder tone.
A6   46:25   at any rate he might answer questions.--How am I to get in?" she repeated, aloud.
T5   156:13   "How am I to stop it?" said the Sheep. "If you leave off rowing,
A4   29: 5   kind of thing never happened, and now here I am in the middle of one! There ought to be a book written
T6   160:38   at me! I'm one that has spoken to a King, I am: mayhap you'll never see such another: and, to show you I'm
T4   145: 7   "Where I am now, of course," said Alice.
A4   29:10   Alice, "shall I never get any older than I am now? That'll be a comfort, one way--never to be an old
T8W   19: 9   So now that I am old and gray, / And all my hair is nearly gone, / They take
T4   145:21   "I am real!" said Alice, and began to cry.
A5   36:31   "I'm afraid I am, Sir," said Alice. "I ca'n't remember things as I used--and
T2   127:24   "I'm quite content to stay here--only I am so hot and thirsty!"
T9   196:35   and laid her head on Alice's shoulder. "I am so sleepy!" she moaned.
A2   17:26   "I do wish they would put their heads down! I am so very tired of being all alone here!"
T8   186: 4   the same. In fact, the more head-downwards I am, the more I keep inventing new things."
T8   191: 3   about it here and there. "Oh, how glad I am to get here! And what is this on my head?" she exclaimed in
A9   70: 1   "You ca'n't think how glad I am to see you again, you dear old thing!" said the Duchess, as
A2   19:14   do you know the way out of this pool? I am very tired of swimming about here, O Mouse!" (Alice thought
AMAZING (1)
T9   196:29   brought up," the Red Queen went on: "but it's amazing how good-tempered she is! Pat her on the head, and see
AMBITION (1)
A9   76:23   then the different branches of Arithmetic--Ambition, Distraction, Uglification, and Derision."
AMONG (28)
T5   156: 3   while the boat glided gently on, sometimes among beds of weeds (which made the oars stick fast in the
A6   51:22   "But I don't want to go among mad people," Alice remarked.
T1   110: 9   that nasty Knight, that came wriggling down among my pieces. Kitty dear, let's pretend--" And here I wish
T1   114:12   to the White King, who was sitting sulkily among the ashes, "Mind the volcano!"
A5   43:30   could, for her neck kept getting entangled among the branches, and every now and then she had to stop and
A7   61: 5   herself at last in the beautiful garden, among the bright flower-beds and the cool fountains.
T12   207:13   So Alice hunted among the chessmen on the table till she had found the Red
T1   113: 5   several of the chessmen down in the hearth among the cinders; but in another moment, with a little "Oh!"
T1   113:21   King, so violently that she knocked him over among the cinders. "My precious Lily! My imperial kitten!" and
A5   42:16   seemed to follow, except a little shaking among the distant green leaves.
T3   129: 9   watching one of them that was bustling about among the flowers, poking its proboscis into them, "just as if
T5   157: 1   it swept her straight off the seat, and down among the heap of rushes.
T8   188:34   He said 'I hunt for haddocks' eyes / Among the heather bright, / And work them into
A5   42:22   a graceful zigzag, and was going to dive in among the leaves, which she found to be nothing but the tops
A3   26:30   This speech caused a remarkable sensation among the party. Some of the birds hurried off at once: one
A1   8:40   the earth! How funny it'll seem to come out among the people that walk with their heads downwards! The
T3   132: 4   and everybody jumped up in alarm, Alice among the rest.
T5   158:18   do?" thought Alice, as she groped her way among the tables and chairs, for the shop was very dark
A4   32:25   and, while she was peering about anxiously among the trees, a little sharp bark just over her head made
A5   43:29   down again into its nest. Alice crouched down among the trees as well as she could, for her neck kept
T4   145:26   "it's far too large to squeeze itself in among the trees. But I wish it wouldn't flap its wings so--it
T5   156:16   stream as it would, till it glided gently in among the waving rushes. And then the little sleeves were
T8   188: 2   He said 'I look for butterflies / That sleep among the wheat: / I make them into mutton-pies, / And sell
A8   63:22   came the guests, mostly Kings and Queens, and among them Alice recognized the White Rabbit: it was talking
A3   21:14   who seemed to be a person of some authority among them, called out "Sit down, all of you, and listen to
T9   200:11   some birds, and there were even a few flowers among them. "I'm glad they've come without waiting to be asked
T3   129:20   shy so suddenly. "It'll never do to go down among them without a good long branch to brush them away--and
A1   10: 4   get out of that dark hall, and wander about among those beds of bright flowers and those cool fountains,
AMUSED (2)
T9   201: 3   bow, not knowing whether to be frightened or amused.
T3   134:21   for a minute or two, pondering. The Gnat amused itself meanwhile by humming round and round her head:
AMUSEMENT (2)
T6   166:20   her remark, "was written entirely for your amusement."
T7   172: 1   On which the Messenger, to Alice's great amusement, opened a bag that hung round his neck, and handed a
AN (116) [entries omitted]
ANCIENT (1)
A9   76:37   off the subjects on his flappers--"Mystery, ancient and modern, with Seaography: then Drawling--the
AND (1829) [entries omitted]
ANGER (2)
A12   97:11   a little scream, half of fright and half of anger, and tried to beat them off, and found herself lying on
A5   36:23   Is that all?" said Alice, swallowing down her anger as well as she could.
ANGLO-SAXON (5)
T7   175:21   out both his hands towards her in an Anglo-Saxon attitude. "We only found it to-day. It's as large
T7   170:27   "He's an Anglo-Saxon Messenger--and those are Anglo-Saxon attitudes. He only does them when he's happy. His
T7   171:13   from himself--but it was of no use--the Anglo-Saxon attitudes only got more extraordinary every moment

ANGLO-SAXON (cont.)
```
  T7   170:26    "Not  at  all,"  said  the  King.  "He's an Anglo-Saxon Messenger--and those are Anglo-Saxon attitudes. He
  T8   179: 5    the  Lion  and  the  Unicorn  and those queer Anglo-Saxon Messengers. However, there was the great dish
```
ANGRILY (13)
```
  A3    26: 5    I had not!" cried the Mouse, sharply and very angrily.
  A7    55: 1    very  civil  of  you to offer it," said Alice angrily.
  T9   199: 4    business it is to answer the door?" she began angrily.
  T3   129:38    ticket,  child!"  the  Guard  went on, looking angrily at Alice. And a great many voices all said together
  A7    56: 2    wouldn't  suit  the  works!"  he added, looking angrily at the March Hare.
  A8    64:12                       The Queen turned angrily away from him, and said to the Knave "Turn them over!
  A7    59:24    no  such  thing!"  Alice  was  beginning very angrily, but the Hatter and the March Hare went "Sh! Sh!" and
  T7   176:22    the  town,  you chicken!" the  Lion  replied angrily, half getting up as he spoke.
  A4    30: 4    "Digging for apples, indeed!" said the Rabbit angrily. "Here! Come help me out of this!" (Sounds of more
  A11   89: 9    "Give  your  evidence,"  the  King repeated angrily, "or I'll have you executed, whether you are nervous
  A9    75: 3    because  he  taught us," said the Mock Turtle angrily. "Really you are very dull!"
  A5    41:16    good  height  indeed!"  said  the Caterpillar angrily, rearing itself upright as it spoke (it was exactly
  T5   155:30    you  hear  me say 'Feather'?" the Sheep cried angrily, taking up quite a bunch of needles.
```
ANGRY (11)
```
  T4   146:25    said,  in a soothing tone, "You needn't be so angry about an old rattle."
  A2    19:33    said Alice in a  soothing  tone: "don't be angry about it. And yet I wish I could show you our cat Dinah.
  A6    51:33    Cat went on, "you see a dog growls when it's angry, and wags its tail when it's pleased. Now I growl when
  T4   147: 3    it quite took off Alice's attention from the angry brother. But he couldn't quite succeed, and it ended in
  T1   108:21                        "Do you know, I was so angry, Kitty," Alice went on, as soon as they were comfortably
  T7   178: 8    * * * * * Unicorn rise to their feet, with angry looks at being interrupted in their feast, before she
  T6   162:22             Evidently Humpty Dumpty was very angry, though he said nothing for a minute or two. When he did
  A12   96:27           "It's a pun!" the King added in an angry tone, and everybody laughed. "Let the jury consider
  A4    27:13    hunting  about,  and called out to her, in an angry tone, "Why, Mary Ann, what are you doing out here? Run
  A4    30: 1                      Next came an angry voice--the Rabbit's--"Pat! Pat! Where are you?" And then
```
ANIMAL (2)
```
  T7   176: 5    The  Lion  looked  at Alice wearily. "Are you animal--or vegetable--or mineral?" he said, yawning at every
  A4    30:40    she could, and waited till she heard a little animal (she couldn't guess of what sort it was) scratching and
```
ANIMAL'S (1)
```
  A2    19:28    hastily,  afraid  that  she had hurt the poor animal's feelings. "I quite forgot you didn't like cats."
```
ANIMALS (5)
```
  A4    32:13    the  house, and found quite a crowd of little animals and birds waiting outside. The poor little Lizard,
  A11   86:23              you see, because some of them were animals, and some were birds,) "I suppose they are the jurors
  T9   200:10    about  fifty  guests, of all kinds: some were animals, some birds, and there were even a few flowers among
  A2    20:22    was  getting quite crowded with the birds and animals that had fallen into it: there was a Duck and a Dodo,
  A3    21: 2    bank--the  birds  with draggled feathers, the animals with their fur clinging close to them, and all
```
ANKLETS (1)
```
  T8   182: 6    That's  the  reason  the  horse has all those anklets round his feet."
```
ANN (4)
```
  A4    27:24    great fear lest she should meet the real Mary Ann, and be turned out of the house before she had found the
  A4    29:19                        "Mary Ann! Mary Ann!" said the voice. "Fetch me my gloves this
  A4    29:19                 "Mary Ann! Mary Ann!" said the voice. "Fetch me my gloves this moment!" Then
  A4    27:13    out  to  her,  in  an  angry tone, "Why, Mary Ann, what are you doing out here? Run home this moment, and
```
ANNOY (1)
```
  A6    48:38    him  when  he  sneezes:  / He only does it to annoy, / Because he knows it teases."
```
ANNOYED (2)
```
  A5    42:41              "I'm very sorry you've been annoyed," said Alice, who was beginning to see its meaning.
  T1   114: 2    by  the  fall.  He had a right to be a little annoyed with the Queen, for he was covered with ashes from
```
ANON (1)
```
  AI     3:19                              Anon, to sudden silence won, / In fancy they pursue / The
```
ANOTHER (56)
```
  T6   160:15    think  I  didn't know the answer to that? Ask another."
  T3   135:30    it  at  all--because  they'd  have to give me another, and it would be almost certain to be an ugly one. But
  T6   160:38    to a King, I am: mayhap you'll never see such another: and, to show you I'm not proud, you may shake hands
  T6   162: 1                  Alice didn't want to begin another argument, so she said nothing.
  T2   127:36    "I  shall  give you your directions--have another biscuit?"
  A4    31:10    you  by  the  hedge!" then silence, and then another confusion of voices--"Hold up his head--Brandy now--
  T2   122: 7            "Didn't you know that?" cried another Daisy. And here they all began shouting together, till
  A4    32: 4    better  not  do  that again!", which produced another dead silence.
  A9    72:23    "Thinking  again?"  the Duchess asked, with another dig of her sharp little chin.
  A10   84: 8                  "Shall we try another figure of the Lobster-Quadrille?" the Gryphon went on.
  A6    45: 6    the  door with his knuckles. It was opened by another footman in livery, with a round face, and large eyes
  T4   142: 8    Four  other  Oysters followed them, / And yet another four; / And thick and fast they came at last, / And
  A8    68:17    The  hedgehog  was  engaged in a fight with another hedgehog, which seemed to Alice an excellent
  A5    43:41    sure  what I'm going to be, from one minute to another! However, I've got back to my right size: the next
  A1    10:13    back  to the table, half hoping she might find another key on it, or at any rate a book of rules for shutting
  T2   123:10    for  the  thought crossed her mind, "There's another little girl in the garden, somewhere!"
  A1     9:23    but  it  was all dark overhead: before her was another long passage, and the White Rabbit was still in sight,
  T8   185:23    repeated:  "but it was careless of him to put another man's helmet on--with the man in it, too."
  A8    67:18    ears  have  come, or at least one of them." In another minute the whole head appeared, and then Alice put
  A4    28:16    very  soon had to kneel down on the floor: in another minute there was not even room for this, and she tried
  T1   112: 1                      In another moment Alice was through the glass, and had jumped
  T9   197:10    through  to me. I'm getting sleepy, too." In another moment both Queens were fast asleep, and snoring loud
  A1     8: 5                      In another moment down went Alice after it, never once
  T3   137: 9    came  into its beautiful brown eyes, and in another moment it had darted away at full speed.
  A5    41:32    just  as  if  she had asked it aloud; and in another moment it was out of sight.
```

ANOTHER (cont.)
T3	132: 9	that's some comfort!" she said to herself. In another moment she felt the carriage rise straight up into the
T3	137:32	that she could not help starting back, but in another moment she recovered herself, feeling sure that they
A2	18:17	she said these words her foot slipped, and in another moment, splash! she was up to her chin in saltwater.
A6	47:17	that Alice quite jumped; but she saw in another moment that it was addressed to the baby, and not to
T5	149: 2	she spoke, and looked about for the owner: in another moment the White Queen came running wildly through the
A5	42: 8	tone of delight, which changed into alarm in another moment, when she found that her shoulders were nowhere
T1	113: 5	down in the hearth among the cinders; but in another moment, with a little "Oh!" of surprise, she was down
T5	156:22	eager eyes she caught at one bunch after another of the darling scented rushes.
A12	94:15	they in the prisoner's handwriting?" asked another of the jurymen.
T3	135:17	Then came another of those melancholy little sighs, and this time the
T3	137: 5	neck of the Fawn, till they came out into another open field, and here the Fawn gave a sudden bound into
T5	155:21	"Feather!" cried the Sheep, as she took up another pair of needles.
T5	155: 8	a teetotum?" the Sheep said, as she took up another pair of needles. "You'll make me giddy soon, if you go
T8	179: 9	not the Red King's! I don't like belonging to another person's dream," she went on in a rather complaining
T6	165:10	'mimsy' is 'flimsy and miserable' (there's another portmanteau for you). And a 'borogove' is a thin
A5	36:15	Here was another puzzling question; and, as Alice could not think of
A6	51:17	that this could not be denied, so she tried another question. "What sort of people live about here?"
T6	160:17	Alice went on, not with any idea of making another riddle, but simply in her good-natured anxiety for the
T8	180:10	Another Rule of Battle, that Alice had not noticed, seemed to
T8	180: 5	if he misses, he tumbles off himself--and another Rule seems to be that they hold their clubs with their
A4	32:38	appeared on the other side, the puppy made another rush at the stick, and tumbled head over heels in its
T7	172: 4	"Another sandwich!" said the King.
A10	80: 8	we go?" his scaly friend replied. / "There is another shore, you know, upon the other side. / The further
T4	143:22	/ The Carpenter said nothing but / 'Cut us another slice. / I wish you were not quite so deaf--/ I've had
A4	30:16	last she spread out her hand again, and made another snatch in the air. This time there were two little
A10	84:10	Or would you like the Mock Turtle to sing you another song?"
T9	194: 8	for her. "Bread-and-butter, of course. Try another Subtraction sum. Take a bone from a dog: what remains
T8	187: 6	"No, you oughtn't: that's quite another thing! The song is called 'Ways and Means': but that's
T8W	14:21	"Latest News. The Exploring Party have made another tour in the Pantry, and have found five new lumps of
T9	199:36	silence again, and the same shrill voice sang another verse:--
T8	179:20	he began once more "You're my--" but here another voice broke in "Ahoy! Ahoy! Check!" and Alice looked

ANSWER (32)
A7	56:29	No, I give it up," Alice replied. "What's the answer?"
T9	194:14	"I think that's the answer."
T8W	14: 5	Alice felt rather offended at this answer, and was very nearly walking on and leaving him, but
T3	137:16	It was not a very difficult question to answer, as there was only one road through the wood, and the
T3	135:35	till one of them answered! Only they wouldn't answer at all, if they were wise."
T6	167: 2	The little fishes of the sea, / They sent an answer back to me.
T9	197:19	on in an impatient tone; but there was no answer but a gentle snoring.
T2	128: 1	but luckily the Queen did not wait for an answer, but went on. "At the end of three yards I shall repeat
T4	144:10	/ Shall we be trotting home again?' / But answer came there none--/ And this was scarcely odd, because /
A1	9:14	bats eat cats?" for, you see, as she couldn't answer either question, it didn't much matter which way she
T7	177:22	But before Alice could answer him, the drums began.
T2	124:18	"It's time for you to answer now," the Queen said looking at her watch: "open your
A6	46:24	the top of his head. But at any rate he might answer questions.--How am I to get in?" she repeated, aloud.
T9	195:43	it up. "It's exactly like the riddle with no answer!" she thought.
T5	155:23	didn't sound like a remark that needed any answer: so Alice said nothing, but pulled away. There was
A2	20: 8	are you fond--of--of dogs?" The Mouse did not answer, so Alice went on eagerly: "There is such a nice little
A7	60:12	This answer so confused poor Alice, that she let the Dormouse go on
T9	199:12	"To answer the door?" he said. "What's it been asking of?" He was
T9	199: 3	"Where's the servant whose business it is to answer the door?" she began angrily.
A10	81:20	and considered a little before she gave her answer. "They're done with blacking, I believe."
A7	55:16	you mean that you think you can find out the answer to it?" said the March Hare.
A11	88:19	and then added them up, and reduced the answer to shillings and pence.
T9	194: 6	Divide a loaf by a knife--what's the answer to that?"
T6	160:14	Dumpty. "Did you think I didn't know the answer to that? Ask another."
T3	132:32	"Of course they answer to their names?" the Gnat remarked carelessly.
T3	132:36	having names," the Gnat said, "if they wo'n't answer to them?"
T6	168:36	said "Good-bye!" once more, and, getting no answer to this, she quietly walked away: but she couldn't help
T8	187:37	I said. / 'And how is it you live?' / And his answer trickled through my head, / Like water through a sieve.
T9	194:39	Here the Red Queen began again. "Can you answer useful questions?" she said. "How is bread made?"
T9	201:34	She spoke to the Red Queen, whose answer was a little wide of the mark. "As to fishes," she said
T6	167: 3	The little fishes' answer was / 'We cannot do it, Sir, because--'
A3	23:17	This question the Dodo could not answer without a great deal of thought, and it stood for a

ANSWERED (10)
A10	85: 7	Alice panted as she ran: but the Gryphon only answered "Come on!" and ran the faster, while more and more
T9	194: 8	Alice was beginning, but the Red Queen answered for her. "Bread-and-butter, of course. Try another
A4	29:13	"Oh, you foolish Alice!" she answered herself. "How can you learn lessons in here? Why,
T3	135:35	everything you met 'Alice,' till one of them answered! Only they wouldn't answer at all, if they were wise
T3	136:14	"I wish I knew!" thought poor Alice. She answered, rather sadly, "Nothing, just now."
A5	40: 5	"I have answered three questions, and that is enough," / Said his
A9	74:20	she asked the Gryphon. And the Gryphon answered, very nearly in the same words as before, "It's all
A6	52:19	"It turned into a pig," Alice answered very quietly, just as if the Cat had come back in a
T6	167: 9	The fishes answered, with a grin, / 'Why, what a temper you are in!'
T8	186:23	"It began with blotting-paper," the Knight answered with a groan.

ANSWERS (2)
| A7 | 56:34 | wasting it in asking riddles that have no answers." |
| T3 | 135:33 | you know, when people lose dogs--'answers to the name of "Dash": had on a brass collar'--just |

ANTIPATHIES (1)
    A1   8:41 that walk with their heads downwards! The antipathies, I think--" (she was rather glad there <u>was</u> no one
ANXIETY (2)
    T8   179:18 at the moment, and watched him with some anxiety as he mounted again. As soon as he was comfortably in
    T6   160:18   riddle, but simply in her good-natured anxiety for the queer creature. "That wall is so <u>very</u> narrow!
ANXIOUS (10)
    A8   69: 5 had made the whole party look so grave and anxious.)
    T1   116: 2 the White King (for she was still a little anxious about him, and had the ink all ready to throw over him
    A11   90:29 finish my tea," said the Hatter, with an anxious look at the Queen, who was reading the list of singers
    T8W   13:15 Wasp--rather unwillingly, for she was <u>very</u> anxious to be a Queen.
    T1   114: 4   Alice was very anxious to be of use, and, as the poor little Lily was nearly
    T3   131:32 see where the voice came from. "If you're so anxious to have a joke made, why don't you make one yourself?"
    A9   71:10 Alice cautiously replied, not feeling at all anxious to have the experiment tried.
    T8   184: 1 quite frightened this time, and said in an anxious tone, as she picked him up, "I hope no bones are
    T8   186:31   "You are sad," the Knight said in an anxious tone: "let me sing you a song to comfort you."
    T9   195:17 let us quarrel," the White Queen said in an anxious tone. "What is the cause of lightning?"
ANXIOUSLY (23)
    A9   76: 9 With extras?" asked the Mock Turtle, a little anxiously.
    T3   134:24   "No, indeed," Alice said, a little anxiously.
    A4   27: 2   trotting slowly back again, and looking anxiously about as it went, as if it had lost something; and
    A3   26: 7 ready to make herself useful, and looking anxiously about her. "Oh, do let me help to undo it!"
    A4   32:24 about it; and, while she was peering about anxiously among the trees, a little sharp bark just over her
    T9   200:20 mutton before Alice, who looked at it rather anxiously, as she had never had to carve a joint before.
    T6   161: 4 Alice his hand. She watched him a little anxiously as she took it. "If he smiled much more the ends of
    A6   48:28   Alice glanced rather anxiously at the cook, to see if she meant to take the hint;
    A11   91:11   The King looked anxiously at the White Rabbit, who said, in a low voice, "Your
    T8W   13: 4 <u>very</u> unhappy there," she thought, looking anxiously back to see what was the matter. Something like a
    A3   21:16 the Mouse in the middle. Alice kept her eyes anxiously fixed on it, for she felt sure she would catch a bad
    T8   183:16 muttering to himself, and Alice watching anxiously for the next tumble.
    T9   195: 3   "Fan her head!" the Red Queen anxiously interrupted. "She'll be feverish after so much
    A8   65:26 walking by the White Rabbit, who was peeping anxiously into her face.
    A6   49:31 The baby grunted again, and Alice looked very anxiously into its face to see what was the matter with it.
    T1   114:13 "What volcano?" said the King, looking up anxiously into the fire, as if he thought that was the most
    A8   63:10 to--" At this moment, Five, who had been anxiously looking across the garden, called out "The Queen!
    A8   65:30 the Rabbit in a low hurried tone. He looked anxiously over his shoulder as he spoke, and then raised
    A11   86:36 and the King put on his spectacles and looked anxiously round, to make out who was talking.
    A11   89:26 Dormouse said--" the Hatter went on, looking anxiously round to see if he would deny it too; but the
    A1   12:38   She ate a little bit, and said anxiously to herself "Which way? Which way?", holding her hand
    T3   131:43 kind of insect?" Alice inquired, a little anxiously. What she really wanted to know was, whether it
    T8   182:25   "That's hardly enough," he said, anxiously. "You see the wind is so <u>very</u> strong here. It's as
ANY (82)
    A7   59:41 Hare. The Hatter was the only one who got any advantage from the change; and Alice was a good deal worse
    A12   95:31 trouble, you know, as we needn't try to find any. And yet I don't know," he went on, spreading out the
    T5   155:23 This didn't sound like a remark that needed any answer: so Alice said nothing, but pulled away. There was
    T8W   14:24   "Any brown sugar?" the Wasp interrupted.
    T9   194:31 me time--but I ca'n't do Subtraction under <u>any</u> circumstances!"
    T5   149:10   and Alice felt that if there was to be any conversation at all, she must manage it herself. So she
    T2   122: 3   "But what could it do, if any danger came?" Alice asked.
    A5   42:20 find that her neck would bend about easily in any direction, like a serpent. She had just succeeded in
    A8   67: 4 uneasy: to be sure, she had not as yet had any dispute with the Queen, but she knew that it might happen
    T4   142: 6 was <u>odd</u>, <u>because</u>, <u>you</u> <u>know</u>, / <u>They</u> hadn't <u>any</u> feet.
    A6   50:13 it would be quite absurd for her to carry it any further.
    T6   168:35 but, as he never opened his eyes or took any further notice of her, she said "Good-bye!" once more, and
    A1   12: 7 few minutes to see if she was going to shrink any further: she felt a little nervous about this; "for it
    A5   36:16 question; and, as Alice could not think of any good reason, and the Caterpillar seemed to be in a <u>very</u>
    T1   107: 5   so you see that it <u>couldn't</u> have had any hand in the mischief.
    T2   126:24   Not that Alice had any idea of doing <u>that</u>. She felt as if she would never be able
    T6   160:17 down on the ground?" Alice went on, not with any idea of making another riddle, but simply in her
    A4   29:15 hardly room for <u>you</u>, and no room at all for any lesson-books!"
    T4   144:25 more likely to be a wild beast. "Are there any lions or tigers about here?" she asked timidly.
    A4   30:21 <u>could</u>! I'm sure I don't want to stay in here any longer!"
    T9   204:13   "I ca'n't stand this any longer!" she cried, as she jumped up and seized the
    A9   72:16   "Pray don't trouble yourself to say it any longer than that," said Alice.
    T9   193: 3 do you suppose is the use of a child without any meaning? Even a joke should have some meaning--and a
    T8   182: 2 Alice. "It isn't very likely there would be any mice on the horse's back."
    A8   67: 5 the Queen, but she knew that it might happen any minute, "and then," thought she, "what would become of me?
    A3   26:40 dear Dinah! I wonder if I shall ever see you any more!" And here poor Alice began to cry again, for she
    A4   28:13 "That's quite enough--I hope I sha'n't grow any more--As it is, I ca'n't get out at the door--I do wish I
    T1   108:32 up, it wouldn't have happened. Now don't make any more excuses, but listen! Number two: you pulled Snowdrop
    A4   29: 8 tone: "at least there's no room to grow up any more <u>here</u>."
    A2   19:41 be really offended. "We wo'n't talk about her any more, <u>if</u> you'd rather not."
    T2   123: 3   "Are there any more people in the garden besides me?" Alice said, not
    A9   76:33   Alice did not feel encouraged to ask any more questions about it: so she turned to the Mock Turtle,
    T7   174:17   "I don't think they'll fight any more to-day," the King said to Hatta: "go and order the
    T3   135: 3 have to leave off, because there wouldn't be any name for her to call, and of course you wouldn't have to
    T3   129: 6 on the only one, but I don't think it's got any name. Principal towns--why, what <u>are</u> those creatures,
    A2   16: 3 to see if she could have been changed for any of them.
    A1   9:38 too small, but at any rate it would not open any of them. However, on the second time round, she came upon
    T1   108:38   Kitty, and you've not been punished for any of them yet. You know I'm saving up all your punishments
    A4   29: 9 "But then," thought Alice, "shall I <u>never</u> get any older than I am now? That'll be a comfort, one way--never

ANY (cont.)

T9   197:15 "I don't think it ever happened before, that any one had to take care of two Queens asleep at once! No, not
A8   67: 7 here: the great wonder is, that there's any one left alive!"
A12   95:23   "If any one of them can explain it," said Alice, (she had grown so
A2   15:32 desperate that she was ready to ask help of any one: so, when the Rabbit came near her, she began, in a
T9   201: 7 very decidedly: "it isn't etiquette to cut any one you've been introduced to. Remove the joint!" And the
T9   199:34 "Thirty times three makes ninety. I wonder if any one's counting?" In a minute there was silence again, and
T5   150: 9 "It's jam every other day: to-day isn't any other day, you know."
A10   84:27   Soup! Who cares for fish, / Game, or any other dish? / Who would not give all else for two p /
T6   164: 7 said Alice. She was too much puzzled to make any other remark.
T9   204:23   At any other time, Alice would have felt surprised at this, but
A9   70: 8 a very hopeful tone, though), "I wo'n't have any pepper in my kitchen at all. Soup does very well without--
T8   182:14 Knight said. "It'll come in handy if we find any plum-cake. Help me to get it into this bag."
T1   118:29 somebody killed something: that's clear, at any rate--"
T5   150: 4   "Well, I don't want any to-day, at any rate."
A1   10:14 she might find another key on it, or at any rate a book of rules for shutting people up like
A4   30:11 "Well, it's got no business there, at any rate: go and take it away!"
A6   46:24 so very nearly at the top of his head. But at any rate he might answer questions.--How am I to get in?" she
T4   146: 1 and went on, as cheerfully as she could, "At any rate, I'd better be getting out of the wood, for really
A7   60:35   "At any rate I'll never go there again!" said Alice, as she picked
A1   9:38 too large, or the key was too small, but at any rate it would not open any of them. However, on the second
T3   135:38 it looked very cool and shady. "Well, at any rate it's a great comfort," she said as she stepped under
A12   93:41   "Well, I sha'n't go, at any rate," said Alice; "besides, that's not a regular rule:
T5   151:13 "You're wrong there, at any rate," said the Queen. "Were you ever punished?"
A11   89:25   "Well, at any rate, the Dormouse said--" the Hatter went on, looking
A2   19:12 I should think very likely it can talk: at any rate, there's no harm in trying." So she began: "O Mouse,
T12   207: 8 only purr for 'yes,' and mew for 'no,' or any rule of that sort," she had said, "so that one could keep
A8   67:25 oneself speak--and they don't seem to have any rules in particular: at least, if there are, nobody
A7   54:16   "There isn't any," said the March Hare.
A4   31:35 "I wonder what they will do next! If they had any sense, they'd take the roof off." After a minute or two
T6   160:10 is, too. With a name like yours, you might be any shape, almost."
T3   134:16 Alice's head. "Supposing it couldn't find any?" she suggested.
T5   154:12 it all was that, whenever she looked hard at any shelf, to make out exactly what it had on it, that
A10   81:26 the Gryphon replied, rather impatiently: "any shrimp could have told you that."
T7   170: 7 on seeing Alice. "Did you happen to meet any soldiers, my dear, as you came through the wood?"
T9   197: 1 obey the first direction: "and I don't know any soothing lullabies."
A6   50: 2 into its eyes again, to see if there were any tears.
A6   48: 4   "I don't know of any that do," Alice said very politely, feeling quite pleased
T5   150: 4   "Well, I don't want any to-day, at any rate."
A2   19:10   "Would it be of any use, now," thought Alice, "to speak to this mouse?
T8W   13: 9   "I don't think I can be of any use to him," was Alice's first thought, as she turned to
T1   115:17 went round the room to see if she could find any water to throw over him. However, she could find nothing
T1   115:24 To which the Queen replied "You haven't got any whiskers."
A7   54:15 there was nothing on it but tea. "I don't see any wine," she remarked.

ANYBODY (5)

T6   159: 5 it was HUMPTY DUMPTY himself. "It ca'n't be anybody else!" she said to herself. "I'm as certain of it, as
T2   122:34   "I never saw anybody that looked stupider," a Violet said, so suddenly,
T9   199: 2 Alice turned round, ready to find fault with anybody. "Where's the servant whose business it is to answer
T2   120:32 can talk," said the Tiger-lily, "when there's anybody worth talking to."
T2   122:37 cried the Tiger-lily. "As if you ever saw anybody! You keep your head under the leaves, and snore away

ANYBODY'S (1)

T8   181: 1 Alice said doubtfully. "I don't want to be anybody's prisoner. I want to be a Queen."

ANYHOW (1)

T7   177:20   "She's kept none for herself, anyhow," said the Lion. "Do you like plum-cake, Monster?"

ANYTHING (42)

A3   23: 4 speak, and no one else seemed inclined to say anything.
T6   168: 3 "I wouldn't have been the messenger for anything!"
A1   8:25 all think me at home! Why, I wouldn't say anything about it, even if I fell off the top of the house!"
T9   196:26 something kind, but really couldn't think of anything at the moment.
T3   129:12   However, this was anything but a regular bee: in fact, it was an elephant--as
T1   115:35 with the pencil for some time without saying anything; but Alice was too strong for him, and at last he
A4   29:36 a snatch in the air. She did not get hold of anything, but she heard a little shriek and a fall, and a
A12   93:14 Lizard, who seemed too much overcome to do anything but sit with its mouth open, gazing up into the roof
A4   34:11 taking not the smallest notice of her or of anything else.
T4   147: 7 large eyes--"looking more like a fish than anything else," Alice thought.
T4   147:22 be more like bundles of old clothes than anything else, by the time they're ready!" she said to herself
T9   200: 2 up the glasses with treacle and ink, / Or anything else that is pleasant to drink: / Mix sand with the
T8W   16: 1 she said in a soothing tone. "Can't I do anything for you?"
T8W   14: 1   "Can I do anything for you?" Alice went on. "Aren't you rather cold here
A2   19:24 Alice had no very clear notion how long ago anything had happened.) So she began again: "Ou est ma chatte
T8W   20:11 last she managed to say gravely, "I can bite anything I want."
T2   126:20 fast they went, they never seemed to pass anything. "I wonder if all the things move along with us?"
T4   147:19 she had never seen such a fuss made about anything in all her life--the way those two bustled about--and
A4   30:22 She waited for some time without hearing anything more: at last came a rumbling of little cart-wheels,
T3   135: 8 "Well, if she said 'Miss,' and didn't say anything more," the Gnat remarked, "of course you'd miss your
A5   42:37 but she thought there was no use in saying anything more till the Pigeon had finished.
A5   43:37   It was so long since she had been anything near the right size, that it felt quite strange at
T9   204:24 was far too much excited to be surprised at anything now. "As for you," she repeated, catching hold of the
A12   94:30   "It doesn't prove anything of the sort!" said Alice. "Why, you don't even know
T5   152:39 to-day. Consider what o'clock it is. Consider anything, only don't cry!"

ANYTHING (cont.)
  A9   76:29   said Alice doubtfully: "it means--to--make--anything--prettier."
  T6   163:37   Alice was too much puzzled to say anything; so after a minute Humpty Dumpty began again.
  A4   28: 6   she said to herself, "whenever I eat or drink anything: so I'll just see what this bottle does. I do hope
  T9   192:23   you to begin, you see nobody would ever say anything, so that--"
  A8   68:41   The King's argument was that anything that had a head could be beheaded, and that you
  A4   34: 2   the blades of grass, but she could not see anything that looked like the right thing to eat or drink
  A1   8:14   she was coming to, but it was too dark to see anything: then she looked at the sides of the well, and
  T6   159:25   conversation, she thought, as he never said anything to her; in fact, his last remark was evidently
  A11   86:30   whispered to the Gryphon. "They ca'n't have anything to put down yet, before the trial's begun."
  A3   24: 7   dare to laugh; and, as she could not think of anything to say, she simply bowed, and took the thimble,
  T4   141: 3   Were walking close at hand: / They wept like anything to see / Such quantities of sand: / 'If this were
  A5   39: 2   the youth, "and your jaws are too weak / For anything tougher than suet; / Yet you finished the goose, with
  T7   177: 4   down again. "There was too much dust to see anything. What a time the Monster is, cutting up that cake!"
  T6   163:40   they're the proudest--adjectives you can do anything with, but not verbs--however, I can manage the whole
  A10   83: 1   down with her face in her hands, wondering if anything would ever happen in a natural way again.
  A6   46:42   "Anything you like," said the Footman, and began whistling.
  A7   56:44   kept on good terms with him, he'd do almost anything you liked with the clock. For instance, suppose it
ANYWHERE (1)
  A10   81:31   the Mock Turtle said. "No wise fish would go anywhere without a porpoise."
A-PIECE (1)
  A3   23:29   them round as prizes. There was exactly one a-piece, all round.
APPEALED (1)
  A8   68:33   The moment Alice appeared, she was appealed to by all three to settle the question, and they
APPEAR (3)
  A6   52:23   expecting to see it again, but it did not appear, and after a minute or two she walked on in the
  T8W   19:13   And still, whenever I appear, / They hoot at me and call me 'Pig!' / And that is why
  A9   72: 8   not to be otherwise than what it might appear to others that what you were or might have been was not
APPEARANCE (1)
  A8   67:10   being seen, when she noticed a curious appearance in the air: it puzzled her very much at first, but
APPEARED (9) [See also DISAPPEARED]
  A8   67:22   enough of it now in sight, and no more of it appeared.
  T9   200: 7   and there was a dead silence the moment she appeared.
  A6   52:14   at the place where it had been, it suddenly appeared again.
  A8   67:18   of them." In another minute the whole head appeared, and then Alice put down her flamingo, and began an
  A8   67:16   Alice waited till the eyes appeared, and then nodded. "It's no use speaking to it," she
  A4   32:16   They all made a rush at Alice the moment she appeared; but she ran off as hard as she could, and soon found
  A4   32:38   from being run over; and, the moment she appeared on the other side, the puppy made another rush at the
  A8   68:33   The moment Alice appeared, she was appealed to by all three to settle the
  A9   72:10   otherwise than what you had been would have appeared to them to be otherwise.'"
APPEARING (1)
  A6   53: 3   replied Alice; "and I wish you wouldn't keep appearing and vanishing so suddenly; you make one quite giddy!
APPLAUSE (1)
  A11   90:18   the end of trials, 'There was some attempt at applause, which was immediately suppressed by the officers of
APPLES (2)
  A4   30: 4   "Digging for apples, indeed!" said the Rabbit angrily. "Here! Come help me
  A4   30: 3   before, "Sure then I'm here! Digging for apples, yer honour!"
ARCH (2)
  A8   67:28   things being alive: for instance, there's the arch I've got to go through next walking about at the other
  T9   198: 3   in large letters, and on each side of the arch there was a bell-handle; one was marked "Visitors' Bell,"
ARCHBISHOP (2)
  A3   22:20   or a worm. The question is, what did the archbishop find?"
  A3   22:13   for him; and even Stigand, the patriotic archbishop of Canterbury, found it advisable--'"
ARCHED (1)
  T9   198: 1   She was standing before an arched doorway, over which were the words "QUEEN ALICE" in
ARCHES (4)
  A8   66: 5   stand on their hands and feet, to make the arches.
  A8   68:24   matter much," thought Alice, "as all the arches are gone from this side of the ground." So she tucked
  A9   73: 8   the end of half an hour or so, there were no arches left, and all the players, except the King, the Queen,
  A9   73: 6   who of course had to leave off being arches to do this, so that, by the end of half an hour or so,
ARE (135)
  T2   123: 8   Tiger-lily), "but she's more bushy than you are."
  T3   131:41   "I know you are a friend," the little voice went on: "a dear friend, and
  T9   192:27   "What do you mean by 'If you really are a Queen'? What right have you to call yourself so? You
  A9   76:32   on, "if you don't know what to uglify is, you are a simpleton."
  A10   82:26   and turns out his toes. / When the sands are all dry, he is gay as a lark, / And will talk in
  A9   73:19   a low voice, to the company, generally, "You are all pardoned." "Come, that's a good thing!" she said to
  T2   122:29   make the beds too soft--so that the flowers are always asleep."
  T5   156:30   "The prettiest are always further!" she said at last with a sigh at the
  T9   195:40   cold--just as I'm five times as rich as you are, and five times as clever!"
  T5   156: 7   a sudden transport of delight. "There really are--and such beauties!"
  T7   170:27   "He's an Anglo-Saxon Messenger--and those are Anglo-Saxon attitudes. He only does them when he's happy.
  A10   82:28   Shark: / But, when the tide rises and sharks are around, / His voice has a timid and tremulous sound."
  T7   172:35   a very tiny earthquake!" thought Alice. "Who are at it again?" she ventured to ask.
  A12   93: 2   in a very grave voice, "until all the jurymen are back in their proper places--all," he repeated with great
  T8   184: 2   tone, as she picked him up, "I hope no bones are broken?"
  T6   166:34   In autumn, when the leaves are brown, / Take pen and ink, and write it down."
  TI   103:23   to unwelcome bed / A melancholy maiden! / We are but older children, dear, / Who fret to find our bedtime
  T2   122: 6   cried a Daisy. "That's why its branches are called boughs!"
  T5   158: 7   "Then two are cheaper than one?" Alice said in a surprised tone, taking

ARE (cont.)

T5	152:37	in despair. "Consider what a great girl you are. Consider what a long way you've come to-day. Consider
A10	81:22	sea," the Gryphon went on in a deep voice, "are done with whiting. Now you know."
T4	143: 4	some of us are out of breath, / And all of us are fat!' / 'No hurry!' said the Carpenter. / They thanked him
A4	27: 5	She'll get me executed, as sure as ferrets are ferrets! Where can I have dropped them, I wonder?" Alice
A5	36:13	"I think you ought to tell me who you are, first."
T9	195:35	"Are five nights warmer than one night, then?" Alice ventured
T1	110: 3	look sleepy in the autumn, when the leaves are getting brown.
T6	166:29	"In spring, when woods are getting green, / I'll try and tell you what I mean:"
A8	68:24	much," thought Alice, "as all the arches are gone from this side of the ground." So she tucked it away
A8	65:17	"Their heads are gone, if it please your Majesty!" the soldiers shouted in
TI	103: 4	/ Though time be fleet, and I and thou / Are half a life asunder, / Thy loving smile will surely hail /
T8	184:33	then I stand on my head--then the feet are high enough, you see--then I'm over, you see."
T1	118:29	ideas--only I don't exactly know what they are! However, somebody killed something: that's clear, at any
A5	43:40	plan done now! How puzzling all these changes are! I'm never sure what I'm going to be, from one minute to
T6	167:10	with a grin, / 'Why, what a temper you are in!'
T6	167:18	one came to me and said / 'The little fishes are in bed.'
T3	131:19	went on ("What a number of people there are in the carriage!" thought Alice), saying "She must go by
T6	166:32	"In summer, when the days are long, / Perhaps you'll understand the song:
A7	60:24	memory, and muchness--you know you say things are 'much of a muchness'--did you ever see such a thing as a
A11	89:10	"or I'll have you executed, whether you are nervous or not."
A1	9: 9	I wish you were down here with me! There are no mice in the air, I'm afraid, but you might catch a bat,
A8	67:26	any rules in particular: at least, if there are, nobody attends to them--and you've no idea how confusing
T3	129: 4	a little further. "Principal rivers--there are none. Principal mountains--I'm on the only one, but I
A3	26: 1	"You are not attending!" said the Mouse to Alice, severely. "What
T9	193:22	"Manners are not taught in lessons," said Alice. "Lessons teach you to
A2	17:16	"I'm sure those are not the right words," said poor Alice, and her eyes filled
A5	36:36	"Repeat 'You are old, Father William,'" said the Caterpillar.
A5	37: 1	"You are old, Father William," the young man said, / "And your hair
A10	82: 6	she got to the part about her repeating "You are old, Father William," to the Caterpillar, and the words
A5	39: 1	"You are old," said the youth, "and your jaws are too weak / For
A5	38: 1	"You are old," said the youth, "as I mentioned before, / And have
A5	40: 1	"You are old," said the youth, "one would hardly suppose / That
T4	143: 3	/ 'Before we have our chat; / For some of us are out of breath, / And all of us are fat!' / 'No hurry!'
A8	63: 4	said Alice, a little timidly, "why you are painting those roses?"
T6	164:26	with," Humpty Dumpty interrupted: "there are plenty of hard words there. 'Brillig' means four o'clock
AI	3: 4	our oars, with little skill, / By little arms are plied, / While little hands make vain pretence / Our
A7	58:11	head. "Is that the reason so many tea-things are put out here?" she asked.
T4	145:26	"I hope you don't suppose those are real tears?" Tweedledum interrupted in a tone of great
T8	186:31	"You are sad," the Knight said in an anxious tone: "let me sing you
A12	93:39	"You are," said the King.
A12	96:12	"Why, there they are!" said the King triumphantly, pointing to the tarts on the
T5	155:38	"You are," said the Sheep: "you're a little goose."
A6	46:12	I'm on the same side of the door as you are: secondly, because they're making such a noise inside, no
T2	125:27	some men moving about somewhere--and so there are!" she added in a tone of delight, and her heart began to
T2	128:25	your toes as you walk--and remember who you are!" She did not wait for Alice to curtsey, this time, but
T8	180: 1	"I wonder, now, what the Rules of Battle are," she said to herself, as she watched the fight, timidly
T2	123:12	Rose said: "but she's redder--and her petals are shorter, I think."
T3	134: 6	"I wonder if that's the reason insects are so fond of flying into candles--because they want to turn
T8	182:19	he said, as they got it in at last; "there are so many candlesticks in the bag." And he hung it to the
A6	46:23	help it," she said to herself; "his eyes are so very nearly at the top of his head. But at any rate he
T5	156: 6	"Oh, please! There are some scented rushes!" Alice cried in a sudden transport of
T6	164:35	"Well 'toves' are something like badgers--they're something like lizards--
T1	110:39	as if they had a fire. Well then, the books are something like our books, only the words go the wrong way:
T9	194:25	to herself "What dreadful nonsense we are talking!"
A11	91:15	out of sight, he said, in a deep voice, "What are tarts made of?"
T6	164:38	"They are that," said Humpty Dumpty; "also they make their nests
T5	155:33	it very often--and very loud. Please, where are the crabs?"
A11	86:23	and some were birds,) "I suppose they are the jurors." She said this last word two or three times
T1	113: 8	"Here are the Red King and the Red Queen," Alice said (in a whisper,
T1	113: 9	for fear of frightening them), "and there are the White King and the White Queen sitting on the edge of
A8	65:16	"Are their heads off?" shouted the Queen.
T4	144:25	it was more likely to be a wild beast. "Are there any lions or tigers about here?" she asked timidly.
T2	123: 3	"Are there any more people in the garden besides me?" Alice
T6	162:43	about!" cried Humpty Dumpty. "How many days are there in a year?"
T5	157:11	"Are there many crabs here?" said Alice.
A8	63:43	"And who are these?" said the Queen, pointing to the three gardeners
A11	86:29	were all writing very busily on slates. "What are they doing?" Alice whispered to the Gryphon. "They ca'n't
T8	182: 8	"But what are they for?" Alice asked in a tone of great curiosity.
T7	174: 3	"Speak, wo'n't you!" cried the King. "How are they getting on with the fight?"
A12	94:15	"Are they in the prisoner's handwriting?" asked another of the
T8	180: 8	into the fender! And how quiet the horses are! They let them get on and off them just as if they were
A10	81:23	"And what are they made of?" Alice asked in a tone of great curiosity.
T3	134:11	may observe a Bread-and-butter-fly. Its wings are thin slices of bread-and-butter, its body is a crust, and
T3	129: 6	it's got any name. Principal towns--why, what are those creatures, making honey down there? They ca'n't be
T6	163:19	just now--and that shows that there are three hundred and sixty-four days when you might get
T8W	21: 1	"Well, that's because your jaws are too short," the Wasp went on: "but the top of your head is
A5	39: 1	"You are old," said the youth, "and your jaws are too weak / For anything tougher than suet; / Yet you
T6	164:33	now," Alice remarked thoughtfully: "and what are 'toves'?"
AI	4: 5	hand, / Lay it where Childhood's dreams are twined / In Memory's mystic band. / Like pilgrim's

ARE (cont.)

T1	113:11	sitting on the edge of the shovel--and here are two Castles walking arm in arm--I don't think they can
T6	164:31	You see it's like a pormanteau--there are two meanings packed up into one word."
A9	75: 3	said the Mock Turtle angrily. "Really you are very dull!"
T4	143:10	chiefly need: / Pepper and vinegar besides / Are very good indeed--/ Now, if you're ready, Oysters dear, /
T4	143:20	'It was so kind of you to come! / And you are very nice!' / The Carpenter said nothing but / 'Cut us
T6	159:20	Sir," Alice gently explained. "And some eggs are very pretty, you know," she added, hoping to turn her
A10	79:16	lobsters and the turtles all advance! / They are waiting on the shingle--will you come and join the dance?
T7	170:12	all the horses, you know, because two of them are wanted in the game. And I haven't sent the two Messengers,
T2	126:27	"Faster! Faster!" and dragged her along. "Are we nearly there?" Alice managed to pant out at last.
T6	166:23	"In winter, when the fields are white, / I sing this song for your delight--
A2	18:14	on the glass table as before, "and things are worse than ever," thought the poor child, "for I never was
T2	122:18	right!" said the Tiger-lily. "The daisies are worst of all. When one speaks, they all begin together,
A5	36: 9	said the Caterpillar contemptuously. "Who are you?"
T5	153: 3	consider your age to begin with--how old are you?"
T5	155: 7	"Are you a child or a teetotum?" the Sheep said, as she took up
T8	187:35	aged aged man, / A-sitting on a gate. / 'Who are you, aged man?' I said. / 'And how is it you live?' / And
T6	161:26	"I thought you meant 'How old are you?'" Alice explained.
A3	22: 1	Ahem!" said the Mouse with an important air. "Are you all ready? This is the driest thing I know. Silence
A4	30: 1	angry voice--the Rabbit's--"Pat! Pat! Where are you?" And then a voice she had never heard before, "Sure
T7	176: 5	The Lion looked at Alice wearily. "Are you animal--or vegetable--or mineral?" he said, yawning at
A2	20: 2	hurry to change the subject of conversation. "Are you--are you fond--of--of dogs?" The Mouse did not answer,
A5	41:13	"Are you content now?" said the Caterpillar.
T9	199:15	English, doesn't I?" the Frog went on. "Or are you deaf? What did it ask you?"
T7	173:26	so you see he's very hungry and thirsty. How are you, dear child?" he went on, putting his arm
A4	27:14	her, in an angry tone, "Why, Mary Ann, what are you doing out here? Run home this moment, and fetch me a
A2	20: 2	change the subject of conversation. "Are you--are you fond--of--of dogs?" The Mouse did not answer, so Alice
A3	22:24	But the insolence of his Normans--' How are you getting on now, my dear?" it continued, turning to
A8	67:14	"How are you getting on?" said the Cat, as soon as there was mouth
T2	124: 7	come from?" said the Red Queen. "And where are you going? Look up, speak nicely, and don't twiddle your
T4	145:13	I'm only a sort of thing in his dream, what are you, I should like to know?"
A5	35: 4	"Who are you?" said the Caterpillar.
A5	43: 7	"Well! What are you?" said the Pigeon. "I can see you're trying to invent
A8	67:37	"Who are you talking to?" said the King, coming up to Alice, and
T8W	17:14	"What, you're a Bee, are you?" the Wasp said, looking at her with more interest.
A3	26: 2	said the Mouse to Alice, severely. "What are you thinking of?"
A6	46:33	"Are you to get in at all?" said the Footman. "That's the first
A10	81:17	"Why, what are your shoes done with?" said the Gryphon. "I mean, what

AREN'T (3)

T7	175: 2	"But aren't you going to run and help her?" Alice asked, very much
T8W	14: 1	"Can I do anything for you?" Alice went on. "Aren't you rather cold here?"
T2	121:14	criticized, so she began asking questions. "Aren't you sometimes frightened at being planted out here,

ARGUE (2)

A6	46:37	to herself, "the way all the creatures argue. It's enough to drive one crazy!"
T2	125: 6	Alice didn't dare to argue the point, but went on: "--and I thought I'd try and

ARGUED (2)

A5	39: 6	said his father, "I took to the law, / And argued each case with my wife; / And the muscular strength,
T1	110:14	her sister, who liked being very exact, had argued that they couldn't, because there were only two of them

ARGUING (1)

T2	120:14	looking up at the house and pretending it was arguing with her. "I'm not going in again yet. I know I should

ARGUMENT (11)

T6	160:12	alone?" said Alice, not wishing to begin an argument.
T6	163:28	"But 'glory' doesn't mean 'a nice knock-down argument,'" Alice objected.
T9	192:21	said Alice, who was always ready for a little argument, "and if you only spoke when you were spoken to, and
T5	149:15	Alice thought it would never do to have an argument at the very beginning of their conversation, so she
T6	163:26	tell you. I meant 'there's a nice knock-down argument for you!'"
T6	162: 1	Alice didn't want to begin another argument, so she said nothing.
A8	68:41	The King's argument was that anything that had a head could be beheaded,
A8	69: 2	The Queen's argument was that, if something wasn't done about it in less
A8	68:37	The executioner's argument was, that you couldn't cut off a head unless there
T1	110:12	"Let's pretend." She had had quite a long argument with her sister only the day before--all because
A3	21: 8	all her life. Indeed, she had quite a long argument with the Lory, who at last turned sulky, and would

ARGUMENTS (1)

A8	68:34	settle the question, and they repeated their arguments to her, though, as they all spoke at once, she found

ARITHMETIC (1)

A9	76:22	replied; "and then the different branches of Arithmetic--Ambition, Distraction, Uglification, and Derision

ARM (21)

A6	45:11	began by producing from under his arm a great letter, nearly as large as himself, and this he
A9	70: 2	thing!" said the Duchess, as she tucked her arm affectionately into Alice's, and they walked off together
T7	173:26	are you, dear child?" he went on, putting his arm affectionately round Hatta's neck.
T4	146:24	Alice laid her hand upon his arm and said, in a soothing tone, "You needn't be so angry
A8	64:10	The King laid his hand upon her arm, and timidly said "Consider, my dear: she is only a child!
T8	183:18	began in a loud voice, waving his right arm as he spoke, "is to keep--" Here the sentence ended as
A4	28:18	one elbow against the door, and the other arm curled round her head. Still she went on growing, and, as
A4	30:10	"Sure, it does, yer honour: but it's an arm for all that."
T1	113:11	and here are two Castles walking arm in arm--I don't think they can hear me," she went on, as she put
T3	137: 6	the air, and shook itself free from Alice's arm. "I'm a Fawn!" it cried out in a voice of delight. "And,
T1	113:11	the shovel--and here are two Castles walking arm in arm--I don't think they can hear me," she went on, as
A11	88:13	Hare, who had followed him into the court, arm-in-arm with the Dormouse. "Fourteenth of March, I think it
A4	28:20	growing, and, as a last resource, she put one arm out of the window, and one foot up the chimney, and said

ARM (cont.)
T4   138: 1   They were standing under a tree, each with an arm round the other's neck, and Alice knew which was which in
A9   71: 5   dare say you're wondering why I don't put my arm round your waist," the Duchess said, after a pause: "the
A8   68:26   the ground." So she tucked it away under her arm, that it might not escape again, and went back to have a
A9   72:30   middle of her favourite word "moral", and the arm that was linked into hers began to tremble. Alice looked
A8   66: 8   tucked away, comfortably enough, under her arm, with its legs hanging down, but generally, just as she
A11   88:13   who had followed him into the court, arm-in-arm with the Dormouse. "Fourteenth of March, I think it was,"
A4   30: 7   "Sure, it's an arm, yer honour!" (He pronounced it "arrum.")
A4   30: 8   "An arm, you goose! Who ever saw one that size? Why, it fills the

ARM-CHAIR (4)
A7   54:10   indignantly, and she sat down in a large arm-chair at one end of the table.
T1   107:14   sitting curled up in a corner of the great arm-chair, half talking to herself and half asleep, the kitten
T5   153:39   to her was an old Sheep, sitting in an arm-chair, knitting, and every now and then leaving off to
T1   108: 3   manage--and then she scrambled back into the arm-chair, taking the kitten and the worsted with her, and

ARMOUR (3)
T8   179:14   Check!" and a Knight, dressed in crimson armour, came galloping down upon her, brandishing a great club
T8   187:21   gleaming through his hair, and shining on his armour in a blaze of light that quite dazzled her--the horse
T8   181:13   He was dressed in tin armour, which seemed to fit him very badly, and he had a

ARMS (19)
T5   153:19   a little brook. The Queen spread out her arms again and went flying after it, and this time she
A11   91:14   with a melancholy air, and, after folding his arms and frowning at the cook till his eyes were nearly out of
A6   49:16   little creature, and held out its arms and legs in all directions, "just like a star-fish,"
T8W   14:11   The Wasp took her arms, and let her help him round the tree, but when he got
AI   3: 4   both our oars, with little skill, / By little arms are plied, / While little hands make vain pretence / Our
T8   180: 6   to be that they hold their clubs with their arms, as if they were Punch and Judy--What a noise they make
T3   137: 4   on together through the wood, Alice with her arms clasped lovingly round the soft neck of the Fawn, till
A9   72:32   stood the Queen in front of them, with her arms folded, frowning like a thunderstorm.
A4   34: 9   that was sitting on the top, with its arms folded, quietly smoking a long hookah, and taking not the
T4   147:13   the wood, and returned in a minute with their arms full of things--such as bolsters, blankets, hearth-rugs,
T1   118:18   hast thou slain the Jabberwock? / Come to my arms, my beamish boy! / O frabjous day! Callooh! Callay!" / He
T1   110:26   said, because the kitten wouldn't fold its arms properly. So, to punish it, she held it up to the
A5   41:36   question. However, at last she stretched her arms round it as far as they would go, and broke off a bit of
T8   184:15   in a tone of great interest, clasping her arms round the horse's neck as he spoke, just in time to save
T5   149: 3   running wildly through the wood, with both arms stretched out wide, as if she were flying, and Alice very
T8   184: 6   let go the bridle, and stretched out both his arms to show Alice what he meant, and this time he fell flat
A5   36:29   without speaking; but at last it unfolded its arms, took the hookah out of its mouth again, and said "So you
T5   156:17   were carefully rolled up, and the little arms were plunged in elbow-deep, to get hold of the rushes a
T1   110:22   know, I think if you sat up and folded your arms, you'd look exactly like her. Now do try, there's a dear!

AROUND (4)
A12   98:22   or seemed to listen, the whole place around her became alive with the strange creatures of her
T8   191: 5   something very heavy, that fitted tight all around her head.
A10   82:28   / But, when the tide rises and sharks are around, / His voice has a timid and tremulous sound."
A12   98:30   knee, while plates and dishes crashed around it--once more the shriek of the Gryphon, the squeaking

ARRANGE (1)
T5   156:33   scrambled back into her place, and began to arrange her new-found treasures.

ARRANGED (2)
T4   147:23   they're ready!" she said to herself, as she arranged a bolster round the neck of Tweedledee, "to keep his
A4   32:23   plan, no doubt, and very neatly and simply arranged: the only difficulty was, that she had not the

ARRIVED (2)
T7   171: 8   At this moment the Messenger arrived: he was far too much out of breath to say a word, and
A11   86: 2   Hearts were seated on their throne when they arrived, with a great crowd assembled about them--all sorts of

ARROW (1)
A8   69: 9   here." And the executioner went off like an arrow.

ARRUM (1)
A4   30: 7   it's an arm, yer honour!" (He pronounced it "arrum.")

ART (2)
T8   184: 4   breaking two or three of them. "The great art of riding, as I was saying is--to keep your balance
T8   183:17   "The great art of riding," the Knight suddenly began in a loud voice,

AS (594)
A10   83:18   / When the pie was all finished, the Owl, as a boon, / Was kindly permitted to pocket the spoon: / While
A7   54: 4   fast asleep, and the other two were using it as a cushion, resting their elbows on it, and talking over its
T2   125:15   compared with which that would be as sensible as a dictionary!"
A7   60:25   of a muchness'--did you ever see such a thing as a drawing of a muchness!"
A10   82:24   baked me too brown, I must sugar my hair.' / As a duck with his eyelids, so he with his nose / Trims his
T9   196:24   but she ca'n't help saying foolish things as a general rule."
A10   82:23   toes. / When the sands are all dry, he is gay as a lark, / And will talk in contemptuous tones of the Shark:
A4   28:19   her head. Still she went on growing, and, as a last resource, she put one arm out of the window, and one
T3   131:20   she's got a head on her--" "She must be sent as a message by the telegraph--" "She must draw the train
T1   110:24   the table, and set it up before the kitten as a model for it to imitate: however, the thing didn't
A10   78:21   "Each with a lobster as a partner!" cried the Gryphon.
T5   155: 2   of all--but I'll tell you what--" she added, as a sudden thought struck her. "I'll follow it up to the very
T4   139: 2   then flew down a monstrous crow, / As black as a tar-barrel; / Which frightened both the heroes so, / They
T6   164:30   means 'lithe and slimy.' 'Lithe' is the same as 'active.' You see it's like a portmanteau--there are two
T9   203: 9   And then (as Alice afterwards described it) all sorts of things happened
T8W   13:17   old bones, my old bones!" he was grumbling on as Alice came up to him.
A5   36:15   Here was another puzzling question; and, as Alice could not think of any good reason, and the
T4   140: 2   a minute: there was a rather awkward pause, as Alice didn't know how to begin a conversation with people
T5   157: 4   was a nice crab you caught!" she remarked, as Alice got back into her place, very much relieved to find
T9   202:32   you, you know," the White Queen whispered, as Alice got up to do it, very obediently, but a little
T1   119: 4   for getting down stairs quickly and easily, as Alice said to herself. She just kept the tips of her

AS (cont.)

```
T7   177:17  "I say, this isn't fair!" cried the Unicorn, as Alice sat with the knife in her hand, very much puzzled how
T3   129:13  a regular bee: in fact, it was an elephant--as Alice soon found out, though the idea quite took her breath
T8   190:16  you'll stay and see me off first?" he added as Alice turned with an eager look in the direction to which
T2   127: 7  ground with their feet, till suddenly, just as Alice was getting quite exhausted, they stopped, and she
T10  205: 4  and her eyes got large and green: and still, as Alice went on shaking her, she kept on growing shorter--and
A9    76: 8  too," said Alice. "You needn't be so proud as all that."
A8    68:24  "but it doesn't matter much," thought Alice, "as all the arches are gone from this side of the ground." So
T9   201:16  should be the only one to give orders; so, as an experiment, she called out "Waiter! Bring back the
A6    51:13  "--so long as I get somewhere," Alice added as an explanation.
T6   166:25         only I don't sing it," he added, as an explanation.
A11   88:24  "I keep them to sell," the Hatter added as an explanation. "I've none of my own. I'm a hatter."
A6    48:18  terror. "Oh, there goes his precious nose!", as an unusually large saucepan flew close by it, and very
T8   185:11  hours and hours to get me out. I was as fast as--as lightning, you know."
T8W   16:11  a yellow handkerchief. And I ties up my face--as at the present."
T3   134: 1  "And what does it live on?" Alice asked, as before.
A2    18:14  golden key was lying on the glass table as before, "and things are worse than ever," thought the poor
A9    74:21  answered, very nearly in the same words as before, "It's all his fancy, that: he hasn't got no sorrow,
T8   186:15  "Well, not the next day," the Knight repeated as before: "not the next day. In fact," he went on, holding
T8W   14:13  when he got settled down again he only said, as before, "Worrity, worrity! Can't you leave a body alone?"
T4   139: 2  Just then flew down a monstrous crow, / As black as a tar-barrel; / Which frightened both the heroes
T4   147:13  a minute with their arms full of things--such as bolsters, blankets, hearth-rugs, table-cloths, dish-covers,
T1   112: 4  find that there was a real one, blazing away as brightly as the one she had left behind. "So I shall be as
T6   159: 5  be anybody else!" she said to herself. "I'm as certain of it, as if his name were written all over his
T6   168:20  "Good-bye, till we meet again!" she said as cheerfully as she could.
T4   146: 1  So she brushed away her tears, and went on, as cheerfully as she could, "At any rate, I'd better be
T9   195:41  five times as rich as you are, and five times as clever!"
T9   195:38         "But they should be five times as cold, by the same rule--"
T9   195:40  Queen. "Five times as warm, and five times as cold--just as I'm five times as rich as you are, and five
T1   108: 2  reproachfully at the old cat, and speaking in as cross a voice as she could manage--and then she scrambled
A10   82:10             "It's all about as curious as it can be," said the Gryphon.
T4   148:16  sharp. Only we must begin quick. It's getting as dark as it can."
T1   112:12  and uninteresting, but that all the rest was as different as possible. For instance, the pictures on the
T8W   20: 6  of admiration: "it's the shape of your head as does it. Your jaws aint well shaped, though--I should think
T4   140:36  was wet as wet could be, / The sands were dry as dry. / You could not see a cloud, because / No cloud was in
A3    22:26                     "As wet as ever," said Alice in a melancholy tone: "it doesn't seem to
A5    40: 2  hardly suppose / That your eye was as steady as ever; / Yet you balanced an eel on the end of your nose--/
T5   155:25  very queer about the water, she thought, as every now and then the oars got fast in it, and would
T6   168:27  said Humpty Dumpty. "Your face is the same as everybody has--the two eyes, so--"(marking their places in
T5   158:27  on, wondering more and more at every step, as everything turned into a tree the moment she came up to it,
A5    41:36  at last she stretched her arms round it as far as they would go, and broke off a bit of the edge with
T1   111: 4  wide open: and it's very like our passage as far as you can see, only you know it may be quite different
A4    30:39             She drew her foot as far down the chimney as she could, and waited till she
A10   78:29              "--as far out to sea as you can--"
T8   185:11  it took hours and hours to get me out. I was as fast as--as lightning, you know."
T2   127:21  somewhere else, you must run at least twice as fast as that!"
A4    27: 5  and whiskers! She'll get me executed, as sure as ferrets are ferrets! Where can I have dropped them, I
T9   197:13  Alice, looking about in great perplexity, as first one round head, and then the other, rolled down from
T9   195:33  and sometimes in the winter we take as many as five nights together--for warmth, you know."
A11   87:15  then unrolled the parchment-scroll, and read as follows:--
A4    30:19    Alice. "I wonder what they'll do next! As for pulling me out of the window, I only wish they could!
T8   185:18  for him. She was rather startled by the fall, as for some time he had kept on very well, and she was afraid
A6    47: 8  Even the Duchess sneezed occasionally; and as for the baby, it was sneezing and howling alternately
T9   204:24  excited to be surprised at anything now. "As for you," she repeated, catching hold of the little
T9   204:17              "And as for you," she went on, turning fiercely upon the Red Queen,
T5   154:15  though the others round it were crowded as full as they could hold.
T9   194:23         Alice said, as gravely as she could, "They might go different ways." But
T8   186:28  it makes, mixing it with other things--such as gunpowder and sealing-wax. And here I must leave you." They
A2    15:35  the fan, and scurried away into the darkness as hard as he could go.
A2    20:11  For the Mouse was swimming away from her as hard as it could go, and making quite a commotion in the
A4    32:16  the moment she appeared; but she ran off as hard as she could, and soon found herself safe in a thick
T7   170:24  up and down, and wriggling like an eel, as he came along, with his great hands spread out like fans on
A2    15:29  along in a great hurry, muttering to himself, as he came, "Oh! The Duchess, the Duchess! Oh! Wo'n't she be
T8   180:15  victory, wasn't it?" said the White Knight, as he came up panting.
T4   144:20             "But he ate as many as he could get," said Tweedledum.
A2    15:35  and scurried away into the darkness as hard as he could go.
T4   147:10  "I suppose so," the other sulkily replied, as he crawled out of the umbrella: "only she must help us to
T6   162:33  it me," Humpty Dumpty continued thoughtfully, as he crossed one knee over the other and clasped his hands
A12   96:22  off writing on his slate with one finger, as he found it made no mark; but he now hastily began again,
A11   91:29          Alice watched the White Rabbit as he fumbled over the list, feeling very curious to see what
T8   182:44  of now and then falling off sideways; and, as he generally did this on the side on which Alice was
T9   199:20  feet. "You let it alone," he panted out, as he hobbled back to his tree, "and it'll let you alone, you
T7   177: 3  "I'm sure I don't know," the Lion growled out as he lay down again. "There was too much dust to see anything
T6   160:40  me!" And he grinned almost from ear to ear, as he leant forwards (and as nearly as possible fell off the
T8   179:18  the moment, and watched him with some anxiety as he mounted again. As soon as he was comfortably in the
T7   172: 9  hay when you're faint," he remarked to her, as he munched away.
T6   168:34  a minute to see if he would speak again, but, as he never opened his eyes or took any further notice of her,
T6   159:25  wasn't at all like conversation, she thought, as he never said anything to her; in fact, his last remark was
T7   175: 7  creature," he repeated softly to himself, as he opened his memorandum-book. "Do you spell 'creature'
T7   175:11  he said to the King, just glancing at him as he passed.
```

AS (cont.)

T4	146:14	eyes grew large and yellow all in a moment, as	he pointed with a trembling finger at a small white thing
T8	179:15	down upon her, brandishing a great club. Just as	he reached her, the horse stopped suddenly: "You're my
T6	168: 1	Dumpty raised his voice almost to a scream as	he repeated this verse, and Alice thought, with a shudder,
T4	147:24	"to keep his head from being cut off," as	he said.
A12	93: 3	with great emphasis, looking hard at Alice as	he said so.
T8	185:15	said. He raised his hands in some excitement as	he said this, and instantly rolled out of the saddle, and
T8	183: 6	remark. "What makes you say that?" he asked, as	he scrambled back into the saddle, keeping hold of Alice's
A5	38: 5	"In my youth," said the sage, as	he shook his grey locks, / "I kept all my limbs very supple
T1	114:18	Alice watched the White King as	he slowly struggled up from bar to bar, till at last she
A8	67:45	look at me like that!" He got behind Alice as	he spoke.
A12	93:25	tone, but frowning and making faces at him as	he spoke.
T7	176:22	the Lion replied angrily, half getting up as	he spoke.
A12	94:13	on the outside." He unfolded the paper as	he spoke, and added "It isn't a letter, after all: it's a
T8W	17: 9	He untied the handkerchief as	he spoke, and Alice looked at his wig in great surprise. It
T8W	21: 3	is nice and round." He took off his own wig as	he spoke, and stetched out one claw towards Alice, as if he
A7	59:38	He moved on as	he spoke, and the Dormouse followed him: the March Hare
A8	65:30	tone. He looked anxiously over his shoulder as	he spoke, and then raised himself upon tiptoe, put his
T8	181:25	box is no use without them." He unfastened it as	he spoke, and was just going to throw it into the bushes,
T8	183:18	began in a loud voice, waving his right arm as	he spoke, "is to keep--" Here the sentence ended as
T8	184:15	clasping his arms round the horse's neck as	he spoke, just in time to save himself from tumbling off
T6	159:18	after a long silence, looking away from Alice as	he spoke, "to be called an egg--very!"
A8	65: 7	in a very humble tone, going down on one knee as	he spoke, "we were trying--"
T8	179:31	fight for her, then," said the Red Knight, as	he took up his helmet (which hung from the saddle, and was
T8	179:16	"You're my prisoner!" the Knight cried, as	he tumbled off his horse.
T8	179:19	some anxiety as he mounted again. As soon as	he was comfortably in the saddle, he began once more
A11	86:17	The judge, by the way, was the King; and, as	he wore his crown over the wig (look at the frontispiece if
T8	183:14	better to say than "Indeed?" but she said it as	heartily as she could. They went on a little way in silence
T5	155:35	sticking some of the needles into her hair, as	her hands were full. "Feather, I say!"
A4	34: 4	growing near her, about the same height as	herself; and, when she had looked under it, and on both
A2	16: 2	children she knew that were of the same age as	herself, to see if she could have been changed for any of
A6	45:12	under his arm a great letter, nearly as large as	himself, and this he handed over to the other, saying, in a
T6	159:10	wondered how he could keep his balance--and, as	his eyes were steadily fixed in the opposite direction, and
T5	149:17	me the right way to begin, I'll do it as well as	I can."
T7	170:19	And at that distance too! Why, it's as much as	I can do to see real people, by this light!"
A7	56:35	"If you knew Time as well as	I do," said the Hatter, "you wouldn't talk about wasting it
A7	55:24	say that 'I see what I eat' is the same thing as	'I eat what I see'!"
A6	51:13	"--so long as	I get somewhere," Alice added as an explanation.
A7	55:27	"that 'I like what I get' is the same thing as	'I get what I like'!"
T1	108:34	you pulled Snowdrop away by the tail just as	I had put down the saucer of milk before her! What, you
A5	38: 1	"You are old," said the youth, "as	I mentioned before, / And have grown most uncommonly fat; /
T1	107: 9	way, beginning at the nose: and just now, as	I said, she was hard at work on the white kitten, which was
A7	55:30	'I breathe when I sleep' is the same thing as	'I sleep when I breathe'!"
T6	164: 1	if you'd mention what you mean to do next, as	I suppose you don't mean to stop here all the rest of your
A4	30:15	like it, yer honour, at all, at all!" "Do as	I tell you, you coward!", and at last she spread out her
T8	190:23	said doubtfully: "but you didn't cry so much as	I thought you would."
A5	36:31	Sir," said Alice. "I ca'n't remember things as	I used--and I don't keep the same size for ten minutes
T1	112: 6	had left behind. "So I shall be as warm here as	I was in the old room," thought Alice: "warmer, in fact,
T8	184: 4	or three of them. "The great art of riding, as	I was saying is--to keep your balance properly. Like this,
T6	163:17	for him. "I thought it looked a little queer. As	I was saying, that seems to be done right--though I haven't
A5	43: 2	raising its voice to a shriek, "and just as	I was thinking I should be free of them at last, they must
A5	43: 1	"And just as	I'd taken the highest tree in the wood," continued the
A6	46:15	and every now and then a great crash, as	if a dish or kettle had been broken to pieces.
T12	208: 7	should not go on licking your paw like that--as	if Dinah hadn't washed you this morning! You see, Kitty, it
T8	184: 3	"None to speak of," the Knight said, as	if he didn't mind breaking two or three of them. "The great
T8	187:14	smile lighting up his gentle foolish face, as	if he enjoyed the music of his song, he began.
A10	78: 3	a minute or two, sobs choked his voice. "Same as	if he had a bone in his throat," said the Gryphon; and it
A10	82:13	Tell her to begin." He looked at the Gryphon as	if he thought it had some kind of authority over Alice.
T1	114:14	the King, looking up anxiously into the fire, as	if he thought that was the most likely place to find one.
T9	199: 9	he went nearer and rubbed it with his thumb, as	if he were trying whether the paint would come off: then he
A12	93:28	unimportant--unimportant--important--" as	if he were trying which word sounded best.
T8W	13: 7	tree, all huddled up together, and shivering as	if he were very cold.
T8W	21: 4	and stetched out one claw towards Alice, as	if he wished to do the same for her, but she kept out of
A9	74:18	came nearer, Alice could hear him sighing as	if his heart would break. She pitied him deeply. "What is
T8	190: 8	and fro, / And muttered mumblingly and low, / As	if his mouth were full of dough, / Who snorted like a
T6	159: 5	she said to herself. "I'm as certain of it, as	if his name were written all over his face!"
T1	113:13	sure they ca'n't see me. I feel somehow as	if I was getting invisible--"
A2	19:43	was trembling down to the end of its tail. "As	if I would talk on such a subject! Our family always hated
T4	139:37	know when I began it, but somehow I felt as	if I'd been singing it a long long time!"
T8	187:19	she could bring the whole scene back again, as	if it had been only yesterday--the mild blue eyes and
A4	27: 2	and looking anxiously about as it went, as	if it had lost something; and she heard it muttering to
T5	156:26	did seem a little provoking ("almost as	if it happened on purpose," she thought) that, though she
A3	23: 3	much wanted to know, but the Dodo had paused as	if it thought that somebody ought to speak, and no one else
T6	161:19	choose a subject--" ("He talks about it just as	if it was a game!" thought Alice.) "So here's a question
T3	129:10	poking its proboscis into them, "just as	if it was a regular bee," thought Alice.
A5	42:38	"As if it wasn't trouble enough hatching the eggs," said the
T5	155: 6	through the ceiling as quietly as possible, as	if it were quite used to it.
T1	108: 9	out one paw and gently touching the ball, as	if it would be glad to help if it might.
A6	46:31	Footman continued in the same tone, exactly as	if nothing had happened.
T3	132:24	all insects?" the Gnat went on, as quietly as	if nothing had happened.

AS (cont.)

T5	157: 3	went on with her knitting all the while, just as	if nothing had happened. "That was a nice crab you caught!"
A5	41:31	"Of the mushroom," said the Caterpillar, just as	if she had asked it aloud; and in another moment it was out
A3	21: 7	to find herself talking familiarly with them, as	if she had known them all her life. Indeed, she had quite a
T5	152: 4	shouted the Queen, shaking her hand about as	if she wanted to shake it off. "My finger's bleeding! Oh,
T5	149: 3	the wood, with both arms stretched out wide, as	if she were flying, and Alice very civilly went to meet her
A11	86:37	Alice could see, as well as	if she were looking over their shoulders, that all the
A2	17: 4	and she crossed her hands on her lap as	if she were saying lessons, and began to repeat it, but her
T9	196: 1	the White Queen went on in a low voice, more as	if she were talking to herself. "He came to the door with a
T2	126:24	Alice had any idea of doing that. She felt as	if she would never be able to talk again, she was getting
A6	52:19	a pig," Alice answered very quietly, just as	if the Cat had come back in a natural way.
T1	110:38	may be only pretence, just to make it look as	if they had a fire. Well then, the books are something like
T8	180: 6	that they hold their clubs with their arms, as	if they were Punch and Judy--What a noise they make when
T8	180: 9	are! They let them get on and off them just as	if they were tables!"
T2	122:36	"Hold _your_ tongue!" cried the Tiger-lily. "As	if _you_ ever saw anybody! You keep your head under the
T1	110: 6	we were playing just now, you watched just as	if you understood it: and when I said 'Check!' you purred!
T7	174:10	'em now," said Hatta; "this is a bit of it as	I'm eating."
T9	195:40	times as warm, _and_ five times as cold--just as	I'm five times as rich as you are, _and_ five times as
T1	118: 9	And, as	in uffish thought he stood, / The Jabberwock, with eyes of
T1	118:12	through the tulgey wood, / And burbled as	it came!
T4	148:16	we must begin quick. It's getting as dark as	it can."
A10	82:10	"It's all about as curious as	it can be," said the Gryphon.
A4	32: 8	sure to make _some_ change in my size; and, as	it ca'n't possibly make me larger, it must make me smaller,
A2	20:12	the Mouse was swimming away from her as hard as	it could go, and making quite a commotion in the pool as it
A1	8:42	glad there _was_ no one listening, this time, as	it didn't sound at all the right word) "--but I shall have
T8	183:19	keep--" Here the sentence ended as suddenly as	it had begun, as the Knight fell heavily on the top of his
T5	154: 8	But these, as	it happened, Alice had _not_ got: so she contented herself
T9	196: 5	he was looking for a hippopotamus. Now, as	it happened, there wasn't such a thing in the house, that
A5	43:26	Alice hastily; "but I'm not looking for eggs, as	it happens; and, if I was, I shouldn't want _yours_: I don't
A11	90:23	lower," said the Hatter: "I'm on the floor, as	it is."
A4	28:13	quite enough--I hope I sha'n't grow any more--As	it is, I ca'n't get out at the door--I do wish I hadn't
T4	139: 8	might be; and if it were so, it would be; but as	it isn't, it ain't. That's logic."
A12	96:24	that was trickling down his face, as long as	it lasted.)
A11	87:11	of the day; and this was of very little use, as	it left no mark on the slate.
T9	202:25	upset the decanters, and drank the wine as	it ran off the edges of the table--and three of them (who
T5	149:21	It would have been all the better, as	it seemed to Alice, if she had got some one else to dress
A5	43:28	off, then!" said the Pigeon in a sulky tone, as	it settled down again into its nest. Alice crouched down
A3	22:25	now, my dear?" it continued, turning to Alice as	it spoke.
A5	41:17	Caterpillar angrily, rearing itself upright as	it spoke (it was exactly three inches high).
A1	9:25	wind, and was just in time to hear it say, as	it turned a corner, "Oh my ears and whiskers, how late it's
T2	127:13	this tree the whole time! Everything's just as	it was!"
T6	168:38	unsatisfactory--" (she repeated this aloud, as	it was a great comfort to have such a long word to say) "of
A6	49:15	Alice caught the baby with some difficulty, as	it was a queer-shaped little creature, and held out its
A6	52:37	it wo'n't be raving mad--at least not so mad as	it was in March." As she said this, she looked up, and
A5	41:34	make out which were the two sides of it; and, as	it was perfectly round, she found this a very difficult
A3	26:16	it wouldn't stay!" sighed the Lory, as soon as	it was quite out of sight. And an old Crab took the
A2	20:12	go, and making quite a commotion in the pool as	it went.
A4	27: 2	back again, and looking anxiously about as	it went, as if it had lost something; and she heard it
A5	41:27	away into the grass, merely remarking, as	it went, "One side will make you grow taller, and the other
T5	156:15	So the boat was left to drift down the stream as	it would, till it glided gently in among the waving rushes.
A7	54: 6	for the Dormouse," thought Alice; "only as	it's asleep, I suppose it doesn't mind."
A10	83:17	gravy, _and_ meat, / While the Owl had the dish as	its share of the treat. / When the pie was _all_ finished,
A6	45:12	from under his arm a great letter, nearly as	large as himself, and this he handed over to the other,
T7	175:21	attitude. "We only found it to-day. It's as	large as life, and twice as natural!"
A4	29:23	that she was now about a thousand times as	large as the Rabbit, and had no reason to be afraid of it.
T7	175:22	"We only found it to-day. It's as large as	life, and twice as natural!"
T8	185:11	and hours to get me out. I was as fast as--as	lightning, you know."
T2	126: 8	can be the White Queen's Pawn, if you like, as	Lily's too young to play: and you're in the Second Square
A12	96:24	the ink, that was trickling down his face, as	long as it lasted.)
A11	88:38	thoughts she decided to remain where she was as	long as there was room for her.
A7	57: 8	"but you could keep it to half-past one as	long as you liked."
A3	26:29	birds! Why, she'll eat a little bird as soon as	look at it!"
A4	31:29	the Rabbit's voice. And Alice called out, as	loud as she could, "If you do, I'll set Dinah at you!"
T3	131: 9	on with "She'll have to go back from here as	luggage!"
T9	195:33	a time, and sometimes in the winter we take as	many as five nights together--for warmth, you know."
T4	144:20	"But he ate as much as he could get," said Tweedledum.	
T5	153:15	a day. Why, sometimes I've believed as	many as six impossible things before breakfast. There goes
T7	177:19	"The Monster has given the Lion twice as much as	me!"
T8	191: 1	threw herself down to rest on a lawn as soft as	moss, with little flowerbeds dotted about it here and there
A7	60:23	and went on: "--that begins with an M, such as	mouse-traps, and the moon, and memory, and muchness--you
T7	170:19	Nobody! And at that distance too! Why, it's as	much as _I_ can do to see real people, by this light!"
T7	177:19	begin. "The Monster has given the Lion twice as	much as me!"
A5	43:17	child; "but little girls eat eggs quite as	much as serpents do, you know."
A2	15:16	Poor Alice! It was as	much as she could do, lying down on one side, to look
A6	49:20	for the first minute or two, it was as much as	she could do to hold it.
A9	72:27	"Just about as	much right," said the Duchess, "as pigs have to fly; and
A12	93: 8	to herself; "I should think it would be _quite_ as	much use in the trial one way up as the other."
T7	175:22	it to-day. It's as large as life, and twice as	natural!"
T6	160:40	from ear to ear, as he leant forwards (and as	nearly as possible fell off the wall in doing so) and
A2	18: 5	to measure herself by it, and found that, as	nearly as she could guess, she was now about two feet high,

AS (cont.)

T6	166:15	his great hands, "I can repeat poetry as well as other folk, if it comes to that--"
T1	110:32	see through the glass--that's just the same as our drawing-room, only the things go the other way. I can
A6	50:18	children she knew, who might do very well as pigs, and was just saying to herself "if one only knew the
A9	72:27	Just about as much right," said the Duchess, "as pigs have to fly; and the m----"
A7	56:21	"I don't quite understand you," she said, as politely as she could.
T4	140:20	interrupt him. "If it's very long," she said, as politely as she could, "would you please tell me first
T5	155: 6	'thing' went through the ceiling as quietly as possible, as if it were quite used to it.
T6	161: 1	to ear, as he leant forwards (and as nearly as possible fell off the wall in doing so) and offered Alice
T1	112:12	but that all the rest was as different as possible. For instance, the pictures on the wall next the
A3	23:28	had not got into it), and handed them round as prizes. There was exactly one a-piece, all round.
T9	199:29	"Then fill up the glasses as quick as you can, / And sprinkle the table with buttons and
A12	92: 9	great dismay, and began picking them up again as quickly as she could, for the accident of the gold-fish
T3	132:23	don't like all insects?" the Gnat went on, as quietly as if nothing had happened.
T5	155: 5	failed: the 'thing' went through the ceiling as quietly as possible, as if it were quite used to it.
T9	195:40	five times as cold--just as I'm five times as rich as you are, and five times as clever!"
A9	74: 5	on the whole she thought it would be quite as safe to stay with it as to go after that savage Queen: so
T2	125:15	nonsense, compared with which that would be as sensible as a dictionary!"
A5	43:17	"but little girls eat eggs quite as much as serpents do, you know."
T4	148:15	"but you can have the umbrella--it's quite as sharp. Only we must begin quick. It's getting as dark as it
A9	70:37	her sharp little chin into Alice's shoulder as she added "and the moral of that is--'Take care of the
T4	147:23	the time they're ready!" she said to herself, as she arranged a bolster round the neck of Tweedledee, "to
T7	175:27	not help her lips curling up into a smile as she began: "Do you know, I always thought Unicorns were
T5	156:20	forgot all about the Sheep and the knitting, as she bent over the side of the boat, with just the ends of
T5	151: 8	all the better, wouldn't it?" the Queen said, as she bound the plaster round her finger with a bit of ribbon
T8	190:37	brook. "The Eighth Square at last!" she cried as she bounded * * * * * * * * * * * * * * across, and threw
T2	128:28	it happened, Alice never knew, but exactly as she came to the last peg, she was gone. Whether she
T5	154: 9	with turning round, looking at the shelves as she came to them.
A8	62: 4	and she went nearer to watch them, and, just as she came up to them, she heard one of them say "Look out
A3	24: 8	and took the thimble, looking as solemn as she could.
A5	36:23	said Alice, swallowing down her anger as well as she could.
A7	56:21	quite understand you," she said, as politely as she could.
A9	70:29	not like to be rude: so she bore it as well as she could.
T6	168:20	till we meet again!" she said as cheerfully as she could.
T2	127:28	she wanted. She took it, and ate it as well as she could: and it was very dry: and she thought she had
A4	32:16	moment she appeared; but she ran off as hard as she could, and soon found herself safe in a thick wood.
A4	30:39	She drew her foot as far down the chimney as she could, and waited till she heard a little animal (she
T4	146: 1	away her tears, and went on, as cheerfully as she could, "At any rate, I'd better be getting out of the
T8W	20:10	which she turned into a cough as well as she could. At last she managed to say gravely, "I can bite
A2	15:16	Poor Alice! It was as much as she could do, lying down on one side, to look through into
A6	49:20	for the first minute or two, it was as much as she could do to hold it.
A5	43:30	Alice crouched down among the trees as well as she could, for her neck kept getting entangled among the
A6	47: 6	in that soup!" Alice said to herself, as well as she could for sneezing.
A12	92: 9	and began picking them up again as quickly as she could, for the accident of the gold-fish kept running
A1	7: 6	she was considering, in her own mind (as well as she could, for the hot day made her feel very sleepy and
T7	173: 6	that wins--get the crown?" she asked, as well as she could, for the run was putting her quite out of breath
A2	18: 5	herself by it, and found that, as nearly as she could guess, she was now about two feet high, and was
A4	31:30	Rabbit's voice. And Alice called out, as loud as she could, "If you do, I'll set Dinah at you!"
T9	204: 1	they look," Alice thought to herself, as well as she could in the dreadful confusion that was beginning.
T4	139:31	they were dancing, and it was done (as well as she could make it out) by the branches rubbing one across
T1	108: 3	the old cat, and speaking in as cross a voice as she could manage--and then she scrambled back into the
A3	24: 6	so grave that she did not dare to laugh; and, as she could not think of anything to say, she simply bowed,
A12	98: 7	said Alice. And she told her sister, as well as she could remember them, all these strange Adventures of
T2	124: 9	all these directions, and explained, as well as she could, that she had lost her way.
T9	194:23	Alice said, as gravely as she could, "They might go different ways." But she couldn't
T8	183:14	than "Indeed?" but she said it as heartily as she could. They went on a little way in silence after this,
T4	140:20	"If it's very long," she said, as politely as she could, "would you please tell me first which road--"
A1	9:14	sometimes "Do bats eat cats?" for, you see, as she couldn't answer either question, it didn't much matter
T5	153:24	is better now?" Alice said very politely, as she crossed the little brook after the Queen. * * * * * * *
T2	120:22	path gave a sudden twist and shook itself (as she described it afterwards), and the next moment she found
A6	51: 4	"Cheshire-Puss," she began, rather timidly, as she did not at all know whether it would like the name:
A6	48:34	child again, singing a sort of lullaby to it as she did so, and giving it a violent shake at the end of
T7	177:15	and the cake divided itself into three pieces as she did so. "Now cut it up," said the Lion, as she returned
T8	185:25	so quietly, head downwards?" Alice asked, as she dragged him out by the feet, and laid him in a heap on
A1	8:21	managed to put it into one of the cupboards as she fell past it.
T5	149:30	if you pin it all on one side," Alice said as she gently put it right for her; "and dear me, what a state
T5	158:17	"I wonder why it wouldn't do?" thought Alice, as she groped her way among the tables and chairs, for the
T9	201:19	couldn't help feeling a little shy with it, as she had been with the mutton; however, she conquered her
A8	66: 9	its legs hanging down, but generally, just as she had got its neck nicely straightened out, and was going
A4	27:37	room with a table in the window, and on it (as she had hoped) a fan and two or three pairs of tiny white
A6	49:22	As soon as she had made out the proper way of nursing it (which was to
T9	200:20	Alice, who looked at it rather anxiously, as she had never had to carve a joint before.
A5	36:26	Alice thought she might as well wait, as she had nothing else to do, and perhaps after all it might
T1	114:10	but hug the little Lily in silence. As soon as she had recovered her breath a little, she called out to
T3	130:11	The voices didn't join in, this time, as she hadn't spoken, but, to her great surprise, they all
A8	68:11	go back and see how the game was going on, as she heard the Queen's voice in the distance, screaming with
T3	136: 9	"Here then! Here then!" Alice said, as she held out her hand and tried to stroke it; but it only
T5	149: 5	I happened to be in the way," Alice said, as she helped her to put on her shawl again.
T9	204:13	"I ca'n't stand this any longer!" she cried, as she jumped up and seized the tablecloth with both hands:
A4	33: 7	what a dear little puppy it was!" said Alice, as she leant against a buttercup to rest herself, and fanned

AS (cont.)

A12	98:13	But her sister sat still just as	she left her, leaning her head on her hand, watching the
T8	191: 7	without my knowing it?" she said to herself, as	she lifted it off, and set it on her lap to make out what
A12	98:21	would always get into her eyes--and still as	she listened, or seemed to listen, the whole place around
T1	113: 4	tidy as the other," Alice thought to herself, as	she noticed several of the chessmen down in the hearth
A1	8:18	She took down a jar from one of the shelves as	she passed: it was labeled "ORANGE MARMALADE," but to her
A7	60:35	rate I'll never go there again!" said Alice, as	she picked her way through the wood. "It's the stupidest
T8	184: 2	this time, and said in an anxious tone, as	she picked him up, "I hope no bones are broken?"
T8W	14:15	me to read you a bit of this?" Alice went on, as	she picked up a newspaper which had been lying at his feet
T8	191: 4	my head?" she exclaimed in a tone of dismay, as	she put her hands up to something very heavy, that fitted
T1	113:12	I don't think they can hear me," she went on, as	she put her head closer down, "and I'm nearly sure they
T9	197: 8	"And now you know the words," she added, as	she put her head down on Alice's other shoulder, "just sing
T5	158:10	"Then I'll have one, please," said Alice, as	she put the money down on the counter. For she thought to
A10	85: 6	"What trial is it?" Alice panted as	she ran: but the Gryphon only answered "Come on!" and ran
A4	27:18	me for his housemaid," she said to herself as	she ran. "How surprised he'll be when he finds out who I
T7	172:40	they trotted off, Alice repeating to herself, as	she ran, "the words of the old song:--
A5	43: 9	little girl," said Alice, rather doubtfully, as	she remembered the number of changes she had gone through,
T7	177:15	she did so. "Now cut it up," said the Lion, as	she returned to her place with the empty dish.
T2	128: 5	time, and Alice looked on with great interest as	she returned to the tree, and then began slowly walking
T1	113:19	of my child!" the White Queen cried out, as	she rushed past the King, so violently that she knocked him
T5	150: 1	Alice couldn't help laughing, as	she said "I don't want you to hire me--and I don't care for
T5	152:15	brooch will come undone directly. Oh, oh!" As	she said the words the brooch flew open, and the Queen
A2	18:17	As	she said these words her foot slipped, and in another
T2	126: 6	She glanced rather shyly at the real Queen as	she said this, but her companion only smiled pleasantly,
A5	43:43	garden--how is that to be done, I wonder?" As	she said this, she came suddenly upon an open place, with a
A4	27:20	fan and gloves--that is, if I can find them." As	she said this, she came upon a neat little house, on the
A2	18: 1	As	she said this she looked down at her hands, and was
A6	52:27	mad--at least not so mad as it was in March." As	she said this, she looked up, and there was the Cat again,
A7	60:38	Just as	she said this, she noticed that one of the trees had a door
T9	192: 9	her, "and if I really am a Queen," she said as	she sat down again, "I shall be able to manage it quite
T12	207:32	Dinah turn to, I wonder?" she prattled on, as	she settled comfortably down, with one elbow on the rug,
T1	115:13	now I think you're tidy enough!" she added, as	she smoothed his hair, and set him upon the table near the
A9	70:24	squeezed herself up closer to Alice's side as	she spoke.
T5	155:15	asked, handing her a pair of knitting-needles as	she spoke.
T9	202:30	the Red Queen said, frowning at Alice as	she spoke.
T5	153:17	The brooch had come undone as	she spoke, and a sudden gust of wind blew the Queen's shawl
T5	149: 1	She caught the shawl as	she spoke, and looked about for the owner: in another
T10	205: 1	She took her off the table as	she spoke, and shook her backwards and forwards with all
A5	42:15	I ca'n't see you?" She was moving them about, as	she spoke, but no result seemed to follow, except a little
A9	72:37	shouted the Queen, stamping on the ground as	she spoke; "either you or your head must be off, and that
A1	8:45	Or Australia?" (and she tried to curtsey as	she spoke--fancy, curtseying as you're falling through the
A6	49:11	said to Alice, flinging the baby at her as	she spoke. "I must go and get ready to play croquet with
T9	203: 4	Alice began: and she really did rise as	she spoke, several inches; but she got hold of the edge of
A12	96:21	furiously, throwing an inkstand at the Lizard as	she spoke. (The unfortunate little Bill had left off
T5	150: 3	a large piece of plaster on her finger as	she spoke, "there's the King's Messenger. He's in prison
T3	135:39	at any rate it's a great comfort," she said as	she stepped under the trees, "after being so hot, to get
T3	129: 3	very like learning geography," thought Alice, as	she stood on tiptoe in hopes of being able to see a little
T8	190:26	him off, I expect," Alice said to herself, as	she stood watching him. "There he goes! Right on his head
A8	62:18	when his eye chanced to fall upon Alice, as	she stood watching them, and he checked himself suddenly:
A2	19: 1	"I wish I hadn't cried so much!" said Alice, as	she swam about, trying to find her way out. "I shall be
A2	19:35	quiet thing," Alice went on, half to herself, as	she swam lazily about in the pool, "and she sits purring so
T6	161: 5	his hand. She watched him a little anxiously as	she took it. "If he smiled much more the ends of his mouth
T6	163: 6	Alice couldn't help smiling as	she took out her memorandum-book, and worked the sum for
T5	155: 7	you a child or a teetotum?" the Sheep said, as	she took up another pair of needles. "You'll make me giddy
T5	155:21	"Feather!" cried the Sheep, as	she took up another pair of needles.
T3	132:16	But the beard seemed to melt away as	she touched it, and she found herself sitting quietly under
T9	196:38	haven't got a nightcap with me," said Alice, as	she tried to obey the first direction: "and I don't know
A9	70: 2	again, you dear old thing!" said the Duchess, as	she tucked her arm affectionately into Alice's, and they
T6	163:16	"To be sure I was!" Humpty Dumpty said gaily as	she turned it round for him. "I thought it looked a little
T8	190:34	"I hope it encouraged him," she said, as	she turned to run down the hill: "and now for the last
T8W	13:10	any use to him," was Alice's first thought, as	she turned to spring over the brook:--but I'll just ask him
T9	200: 8	Alice glanced nervously along the table, as	she walked up the large hall, and noticed that there were
A4	32:18	thing I've got to do," said Alice to herself, as	she wandered about in the wood, "is to grow to my right
T7	172:27	to the King's ear. Alice was sorry for this, as	she wanted to hear the news too. However, instead of
T2	125:16	Alice curtseyed again, as	she was afraid from the Queen's tone that she was a little
T9	192: 6	walked about--rather stiffly just at first, as	she was afraid that the crown might come off: but she
T8	179:17	Startled as	she was, Alice was more frightened for him than for herself
T3	129:18	just yet," she went on, checking herself just as	she was beginning to run down the hill, and trying to find
T3	135:20	nothing whatever to be seen on the twig, and, as	she was getting quite chilly with sitting still so long,
T8	183: 4	practice in riding," she ventured to say, as	she was helping him up from his fifth tumble.
A12	93:31	and some "unimportant." Alice could see this, as	she was near enough to look over their slates; "but it
A5	41:42	she felt that there was no time to be lost, as	she was shrinking rapidly: so she set to work at once to
A4	32:11	that she began shrinking directly. As soon as	she was small enough to get through the door, she ran out
T1	108: 5	ball again. But she didn't get on very fast, as	she was talking all the time, sometimes to the kitten, and
T8	180: 2	Rules of Battle are," she said to herself, as	she watched the fight, timidly peeping out from her
T8	190:29	horse--" So she went on talking to herself, as	she watched the horse walking leisurely along the road, and
A6	49:13	room. The cook threw a frying-pan after her as	she went, but it just missed her.
A1	8:12	fell very slowly, for she had plenty of time as	she went down to look about her, and to wonder what was
A4	27:12	Very soon the Rabbit noticed Alice, as	she went hunting about, and called out to her, in an angry
T6	168:37	but she couldn't help saying to herself, as	she went, "of all the unsatisfactory--" (she repeated this

AS (cont.)

A10	82: 5	mouths so very wide; but she gained courage as she went on. Her listeners were perfectly quiet till she
A2	17:17	Alice, and her eyes filled with tears again as she went on, "I must be Mabel after all, and I shall have
T2	125:28	her heart began to beat quick with excitement as she went on. "It's a great huge game of chess that's being
T5	153:29	the Queen, her voice rising into a squeak as she went on. "Much be-etter! Be-etter! Be-e-e-etter!
A9	74:13	says 'come on!' here," thought Alice, as she went slowly after it: "I never was so ordered about
T3	137:29	dark!" So she wandered on, talking to herself as she went, till, on turning a sharp corner, she came upon
T5	153:36	sitting on the other side of the counter? Rub as she would, she could make nothing more of it: she was in a
T3	131:20	thought Alice), saying "She must go by post, as she's got a head on her--" "She must be sent as a message
T5	153:15	a day. Why, sometimes I've believed as many as six impossible things before breakfast. There goes the
T8W	20:11	"Not with a mouth as small as that," the Wasp persisted. "If you was a-fighting,
T8	191: 1	and threw herself down to rest on a lawn as soft as moss, with little flowerbeds dotted about it here
A3	24: 8	simply bowed, and took the thimble, looking as solemn as she could.
T8	179:19	him with some anxiety as he mounted again. As soon as he was comfortably in the saddle, he began once
A3	26:16	a pity it wouldn't stay!" sighed the Lory, as soon as it was quite out of sight. And an old Crab took the
A3	26:29	the birds! Why, she'll eat a little bird as soon as look at it!"
A6	49:22	As soon as she had made out the proper way of nursing it
T1	114:10	nothing but hug the little Lily in silence. As soon as she had recovered her breath a little, she called
A4	32:11	to find that she began shrinking directly. As soon as she was small enough to get through the door, she
A12	93:10	As soon as the jury had a little recovered from the shock of
T5	152: 8	"What is the matter?" she said, as soon as there was a chance of making herself heard. "Have
A8	67:14	"How are you getting on?" said the Cat, as soon as there was mouth enough for it to speak with.
T1	108:21	know, I was so angry, Kitty," Alice went on, as soon as they were comfortably settled again, "when I saw
T8	182:26	wind is so very strong here. It's as strong as soup."
A5	40: 2	"one would hardly suppose / That your eye was as steady as ever; / Yet you balanced an eel on the end of
T8	182:26	You see the wind is so very strong here. It's as strong as soup."
T8	183:19	spoke, "is to keep--" Here the sentence ended as suddenly as it had begun, as the Knight fell heavily on the
T4	139:41	panted out, and they left off dancing as suddenly as they had begun: the music stopped at the same
A4	27: 4	my fur and whiskers! She'll get me executed, as sure as ferrets are ferrets! Where can I have dropped them,
A4	30:14	could only hear whispers now and then; such as "Sure, I don't like it, yer honour, at all, at all!" "Do as
T2	127:22	else, you must run at least twice as fast as that!"
A1	11: 1	rules their friends had taught them: such as, that a red-hot poker will burn you if you hold it too long
A11	90:12	suppressed by the officers of the court. (As that is rather a hard word, I will just explain to you how
A5	43:13	in my time, but never one with such a neck as that! No, no! You're a serpent; and there's no use denying
T8W	20:11	"Not with a mouth as small as that," the Wasp persisted. "If you was a-fighting, now--
T4	139:26	fear of hurting the other one's feelings; so, as the best way out of the difficulty, she took hold of both
T5	156:28	managed to pick plenty of beautiful rushes as the boat glided by, there was always a more lovely one that
T9	204:18	upon the Red Queen, whom she considered as the cause of all the mischief--but the Queen was no longer
TC	209:17	In a Wonderland they lie, / Dreaming as the days go by, / Dreaming as the summers die:
A4	29:26	up to the door, and tried to open it; but, as the door opened inwards, and Alice's elbow was pressed hard
A11	89: 5	left off staring at the Hatter, and, just as the Dormouse crossed the court, she said, to one of the
A8	66:17	she wanted to send the hedgehog to, and, as the doubled-up soldiers were always getting up and walking
A8	68:14	she did not like the look of things at all, as the game was in such confusion that she never knew whether
A2	15:36	Alice took up the fan and gloves, and, as the hall was very hot, she kept fanning herself all the
A12	93:10	As soon as the jury had a little recovered from the shock of being
T1	115: 4	had never seen in all her life such a face as the King made, when he found himself held in the air by an
T1	115:29	Alice looked on with great interest as the King took an enormous memorandum-book out of his pocket
T8	183:19	sentence ended as suddenly as it had begun, as the Knight fell heavily on the top of his head exactly in
T8	190:12	As the Knight sang the last words of the ballad, he gathered
A3	24:10	this caused some noise and confusion, as the large birds complained that they could not taste theirs
A3	21:11	allow, without knowing how old it was, and as the Lory positively refused to tell its age, there was no
A12	98:26	she could hear the rattle of the teacups as the March Hare and his friends shared their never-ending
A7	60: 1	Alice was a good deal worse off than before, as the March Hare had just upset the milk-jug into his plate.
T1	112: 5	was a real one, blazing away as brightly as the one she had left behind. "So I shall be as warm here as
A12	93: 9	be quite as much use in the trial one way up as the other."
T1	113: 3	"They don't keep this room so tidy as the other," Alice thought to herself, as she noticed
T3	129:35	out a ticket: they were about the same size as the people, and quite seemed to fill the carriage.
T1	114: 4	Alice was very anxious to be of use, and, as the poor little Lily was nearly screaming herself into a
A8	65:20	soldiers were silent, and looked at Alice, as the question was evidently meant for her.
A4	29:23	she was now about a thousand times as large as the Rabbit, and had no reason to be afraid of it.
T8	179:24	Alice's side, and tumbled off his horse just as the Red Knight had done: then he got on again, and the two
A8	64: 1	and the pattern on their backs was the same as the rest of the pack, she could not tell whether they were
T3	131: 7	carriage-full of passengers altogether), and, as the rule seemed to be that they should all speak in turn,
T3	135: 7	remember my name, she'd call me 'Miss,' as the servants do."
A8	63:18	over with diamonds, and walked two and two, as the soldiers did. After these came the royal children:
AI	3:25	And ever, as the story drained / The wells of fancy dry, / And faintly
TC	209:18	lie, / Dreaming as the days go by, / Dreaming as the summers die:
A7	58:15	"Exactly so," said the Hatter: "as the things get used up."
T2	121: 2	seemed to take her breath away. At length, as the Tiger-lily only went on waving about, she spoke again,
T4	144:19	the Carpenter best--if he didn't eat so many as the Walrus."
T8W	21:11	so many personal remarks made on her, and as the Wasp had quite recovered his spirits, and was getting
A12	98:24	The long grass rustled at her feet as the White Rabbit hurried by--the frightened Mouse splashed
A11	86: 3	all sorts of little birds and beasts, as well as the whole pack of cards: the Knave was standing before them
A5	42:18	As there seemed to be no chance of getting her hands up to her
A4	28:25	larger: still it was very uncomfortable, and, as there seemed to be no sort of chance of her ever getting
T5	152: 8	"What is the matter?" she said, as soon as there was a chance of making herself heard. "Have you
A8	67:14	are you getting on?" said the Cat, as soon as there was mouth enough for it to speak with.
A1	8:33	opportunity for showing off her knowledge, as there was no one to listen to her, still it was good
T3	137:16	was not a very difficult question to answer, as there was only one road through the wood, and the two
A11	88:38	she decided to remain where she was as long as there was room for her.

AS (cont.)

A8	68:35	they repeated their arguments to her, though, as they all spoke at once, she found it very hard to make out
A9	74:17	and lonely on a little ledge of rock, and, as they came nearer, Alice could hear him sighing as if his
T5	154:15	the others round it were crowded as full as they could hold.
T8	182:18	"It's rather a tight fit, you see," he said, as they got it in at last; "there are so many candlesticks in
T4	139:41	out, and they left off dancing as suddenly as they had begun: the music stopped at the same moment.
T8W	19: 4	effect, / They said I did not look so nice / As they had ventured to expect.
T5	156:38	dream-rushes, melted away almost like snow, as they lay in heaps at her feet--but Alice hardly noticed
A4	32: 6	pebbles were all turning into little cakes as they lay on the floor, and a bright idea came into her head
T8	182:22	your hair well fastened on?" he continued, as they set off.
A2	17: 6	strange, and the words did not come the same as they used to do:--
A9	73:18	As they walked off together, Alice heard the King say in a low
T1	108:21	was so angry, Kitty," Alice went on, as soon as they were comfortably settled again, "when I saw all the
A8	63:44	were lying round the rose-tree; for, you see, as they were lying on their faces, and the pattern on their
A5	41:36	last she stretched her arms round it as far as they would go, and broke off a bit of the edge with each
A2	18:16	the poor child, "for I never was so small as this before, never! And I declare it's too bad, that it is!
A1	8:23	thought Alice to herself. "After such a fall as this, I shall think nothing of tumbling down-stairs! How
A6	52:26	be much the most interesting, and perhaps, as this is May, it wo'n't be raving mad--at least not so mad
A1	12:24	and sometimes she scolded herself so severely as to bring tears into her eyes; and once she remembered
T9	201:35	whose answer was a little wide of the mark. "As to fishes," she said, very slowly and solemnly, putting her
T7	172:26	in the shape of a trumpet and stooping so as to get close to the King's ear. Alice was sorry for this,
A9	74: 6	it would be quite as safe to stay with it as to go after that savage Queen: so she waited.
T6	166:14	"As to poetry, you know," said Humpty Dumpty, stretching out
A6	49:24	tight hold of its right ear and left foot, so as to prevent its undoing itself), she carried it out into the
T7	170:28	His name is Haigha." (He pronounced it so as to rhyme with 'mayor.')
A5	41: 8	"Oh, I'm not particular as to size," Alice hastily replied; "only one doesn't like
T9	203:16	a bed of rushes with fireworks at the top. As to the bottles, they each took a pair of plates, which they
A10	80:16	"Oh, as to the whiting," said the Mock Turtle, "they--you've seen
T4	144:35	snoring loud--"fit to snore his head off!" as Tweedledum remarked.
T8W	21: 8	front, no doubt. One would have done as well as two, if you must have them so close--"
A5	43:39	a few minutes, and began talking to herself, as usual, "Come, there's half my plan done now! How puzzling
T6	159:22	said Humpty Dumpty, looking away from her, as usual, "have no more sense than a baby!"
T8	190:27	him. "There he goes! Right on his head as usual! However, he gets on again pretty easily--that comes
A2	15:39	is to-day! And yesterday things went on just as usual. I wonder if I've changed in the night? Let me think:
A9	71:14	"Right, as usual," said the Duchess: "what a clear way you have of
T9	194:15	"Wrong, as usual," said the Red Queen: "the dog's temper would remain
T9	195:39	"Just so!" cried the Red Queen. "Five times as warm, and five times as cold--just as I'm five times as
T1	112: 5	the one she had left behind. "So I shall be as warm here as I was in the old room," thought Alice: "warmer
T9	195:37	"Five times as warm, of course."
A12	95:31	"that saves a world of trouble, you know, as we needn't try to find any. And yet I don't know," he went
A12	95:12	He trusts to you to set them free, / Exactly as we were.
A11	86:27	all. However, "jurymen" would have done just as well.
T5	149:17	tell me the right way to begin, I'll do it as well as I can."
A7	56:35	"If you knew Time as well as I do," said the Hatter, "you wouldn't talk about
A11	86:37	Alice could see, as well as if she were looking over their shoulders, that all
T6	166:15	one of his great hands, "I can repeat poetry as well as other folk, if it comes to that--"
A5	36:23	all?" said Alice, swallowing down her anger as well as she could.
A9	70:29	she did not like to be rude: so she bore it as well as she could.
T2	127:28	all what she wanted. She took it, and ate it as well as she could: and it was very dry: and she thought she
T8W	20:10	of laughter, which she turned into a cough as well as she could. At last she managed to say gravely, "I
A5	43:29	its nest. Alice crouched down among the trees as well as she could, for her neck kept getting entangled
A6	47: 6	pepper in that soup!" Alice said to herself, as well as she could for sneezing.
A1	7: 6	So she was considering, in her own mind (as well as she could, for the hot day made her feel very
T7	173: 6	one--that wins--get the crown?" she asked, as well as she could, for the run was putting her quite out of
T9	203:23	birds they look," Alice thought to herself, as well as she could in the dreadful confusion that was
T4	139:31	which they were dancing, and it was done (as well as she could make it out) by the branches rubbing one
A12	98: 7	dream!" said Alice. And she told her sister, as well as she could remember them, all these strange
T2	124: 9	to all these directions, and explained, as well as she could, that she had lost her way.
A11	86: 3	them--all sorts of little birds and beasts, as well as the whole pack of cards: the Knave was standing
T8W	21: 8	much in front, no doubt. One would have done as well as two, if you must have them so close--"
T2	121: 5	"As well as you can," said the Tiger-lily. "And a great deal
A10	82:18	repeat lessons!" thought Alice. "I might just as well be at school at once." However, she got up, and began
T1	115: 2	put him on the table, she thought she might as well dust him a little, he was so covered with ashes.
A8	68:10	Alice thought she might as well go back and see how the game was going on, as she
A7	60:40	everything's curious to-day. I think I may as well go in at once." And in she went.
T6	163:45	enough of that subject, and it would be just as well if you'd mention what you mean to do next, as I
A4	34: 6	behind it, it occurred to her that she might as well look and see what was on top of it.
A7	55:28	"You might just as well say," added the Dormouse, which seemed to be talking
A7	55:26	"You might just as well say," added the March Hare, "that 'I like what I get'
A7	55:24	a bit!" said the Hatter. "Why, you might just as well say that 'I see what I eat' is the same thing as 'I
A12	98:11	got up and ran off, thinking while she ran, as well she might, what a wonderful dream it had been.
A7	56: 5	"Yes, but some crumbs must have got in as well," the Hatter grumbled: "you shouldn't have put it in
T8	182: 5	"You see," he went on after a pause, "it's as well to be provided for everything. That's the reason the
A6	48: 8	tone of this remark, and thought it would be as well to introduce some other subject of conversation. While
T7	175: 5	King. "She runs so fearfully quick. You might as well try to catch a Bandersnatch! But I'll make a
T7	173:12	minute goes by so fearfully quick. You might as well try to stop a Bandersnatch!"
A5	36:26	Alice thought she might as well wait, as she had nothing else to do, and perhaps after
A3	22:26	"As wet as ever," said Alice in a melancholy tone: "it doesn't
T4	140:35	The sea was wet as wet could be, / The sands were dry as dry. / You could not
T2	127:18	else--if you ran very fast for a long time as we've been doing."

AS (cont.)

T9	203:19	pair of plates, which they hastily fitted on as wings, and so, with forks for legs, went fluttering about
T5	156:31	of the rushes in growing so far off, as, with flushed cheeks and dripping hair and hands, she
T8	187:24	behind--all this she took in like a picture, as, with one hand shading her eyes, she leant against a tree,
A9	72:19	"I make you a present of everything I've said as yet."
A8	67: 3	to feel very uneasy: to be sure, she had not as yet had any dispute with the Queen, but she knew that it
T9	195:40	times as cold--just as I'm five times as rich as you are, and five times as clever!"
A6	46:12	because I'm on the same side of the door as you are: secondly, because they're making such a noise
T7	170: 7	Did you happen to meet any soldiers, my dear, as you came through the wood?"
A10	78:29	"--as far out to sea as you can--"
T9	199:29	"Then fill up the glasses as quick as you can, / And sprinkle the table with buttons and bran: /
T2	121: 5	"As well as you can," said the Tiger-lily. "And a great deal louder."
T1	111: 4	open: and it's very like our passage as far as you can see, only you know it may be quite different on
A10	84: 4	Turtle interrupted, "if you don't explain it as you go on? It's by far the most confusing thing that I ever
A7	57: 8	you could keep it to half-past one as long as you liked."
A3	23: 6	best way to explain it is to do it." (And, as you might like to try the thing yourself some winter-day, I
A9	72:12	it written down: but I ca'n't quite follow it as you say it."
T6	162:29	"It's a cravat, child, and a beautiful one, as you say. It's a present from the White King and Queen.
T2	123:11	"Well, she has the same awkward shape as you," the Rose said: "but she's redder--and her petals are
T2	128:24	the English for a thing--turn out your toes as you walk--and remember who you are!" She did not wait for
A1	9: 1	to curtsey as she spoke--fancy, curtseying as you're falling through the air! Do you think you could

ASHAMED (4)

T4	148:10	Alice, still hoping to make them a little ashamed of fighting for such a trifle.
T12	207:20	not to see it: but it looked a little ashamed of itself, so I think it must have been the Red Queen
A9	75: 4	"You ought to be ashamed of yourself for asking such a simple question," added
A2	15:20	"You ought to be ashamed of yourself," said Alice, "a great girl like you,"

ASHES (5)

T1	115: 2	dust him a little, he was so covered with ashes.
T1	114: 3	with the Queen, for he was covered with ashes from head to foot.
T1	114:12	White King, who was sitting sulkily among the ashes, "Mind the volcano!"
T2	123:30	had indeed: when Alice first found her in the ashes, she had been only three inches high--and here she was,
T1	115:12	don't keep your mouth so wide open! All the ashes will get into it--there, now I think you're tidy enough!

A-SITTING (3)

T8	190:11	a buffalo--/ That summer evening long ago, / A-sitting on a gate."
T8	187:11	that," the Knight said. "The song really is 'A-sitting On A Gate': and the tune's my own invention."
T8	187:34	little to relate. / I saw an aged aged man, / A-sitting on a gate. / 'Who are you, aged man?' I said. / 'And

ASK (25)

A6	52:18	baby?" said the Cat. "I'd nearly forgotten to ask."
A7	58:17	to the beginning again?" Alice ventured to ask.
T3	132: 1	this wouldn't be quite a civil question to ask.
T5	150:22	do you remember best?" Alice ventured to ask.
T7	172:35	Alice. "Who are at it again?" she ventured to ask.
T9	195:36	than one night, then?" Alice ventured to ask.
T6	162: 7	"I never ask advice about growing," Alice said indignantly.
T6	160:14	you think I didn't know the answer to that? Ask another."
A9	76:33	Alice did not feel encouraged to ask any more questions about it: so she turned to the Mock
A2	15:31	Alice felt so desperate that she was ready to ask help of any one: so, when the Rabbit came near her, she
A8	69: 7	but "It belongs to the Duchess: you'd better ask her about it."
T8W	13:11	to spring over the brook:--but I'll just ask him what's the matter," she added, checking herself on the
A11	87: 2	how to spell "stupid," and that he had to ask his neighbour to tell him. "A nice muddle their slates'll
T6	160:20	"What tremendously easy riddles you ask!" Humpty Dumpty growled out. "Of course I don't think so!
A7	58: 9	in a mournful tone, "he wo'n't do a thing I ask! It's always six o'clock now."
T3	129:21	them away--and what fun it'll be when they ask me how I liked my walk. I shall say 'Oh, I liked it well
A7	60:26	"Really, now you ask me," said Alice, very much confused, "I don't think--"
A1	9: 3	think me for asking! No, it'll never do to ask: perhaps I shall see it written up somewhere."
A3	26:24	"And who is Dinah, if I might venture to ask the question?" said the Lory.
T9	192:14	each side: she would have liked very much to ask them how they came there, but she feared it would not be
T3	137:27	I'll just call and say 'How d'ye do?' and ask them the way out of the wood. If I could only get to the
A1	8:43	at all the right word) "--but I shall have to ask them what the name of the country is, you know. Please,
T6	164:12	(Alice didn't venture to ask what he paid them with; and so you see I ca'n't tell you
T9	199:16	Frog went on. "Or are you deaf? What did it ask you?"
T4	143:24	you were not quite so deaf--/ I've had to ask you twice!'

ASKANCE (1)

A10	80: 3	replied "Too far, too far!", and gave a look askance--/ Said he thanked the whiting kindly, but he would

ASKED (47)

A3	23:22	to give the prizes?" quite a chorus of voices asked.
A5	41: 7	"What size do you want to be?" it asked.
A7	57: 9	"Is that the way you manage?" Alice asked.
A7	58:11	so many tea-things are put out here?" she asked.
A9	75: 1	call him Tortoise, if he wasn't one?" Alice asked.
A11	90: 3	what did the Dormouse say?" one of the jury asked.
A12	94:34	Where shall I begin, please your Majesty?" he asked.
T2	122: 3	what could it do, if any danger came?" Alice asked.
T5	152:42	keep from crying by considering things?" she asked.
T6	168:15	"Is that all?" Alice timidly asked.
T8W	16:16	exactly. "Is it a kind of toothache?" she asked.
A6	46:32	"How am I to get in?" asked Alice again, in a louder tone.
A12	94:15	"Are they in the prisoner's handwriting?" asked another of the jurymen.
T3	134: 1	"And what does it live on?" Alice asked, as before.
T8	183: 6	at the remark. "What makes you say that?" he asked, as he scrambled back into the saddle, keeping hold of

ASKED (cont.)
```
T8   185:25  on talking so quietly, head downwards?" Alice asked, as she dragged him out by the feet, and laid him in a
T7   173: 5  Does--the one--that wins--get the crown?" she asked, as well as she could, for the run was putting her quite
T5   155:36  "Why do you say 'Feather' so often?" Alice asked at last, rather vexed. "I'm not a bird!"
T2   123:19  idea at all: so, to change the subject, she asked "Does she ever come out here?"
T6   160: 7      "Must a name mean something?" Alice asked doubtfully.
T2   123: 9          "Is she like me?" Alice asked eagerly, for the thought crossed her mind, "There's
T8   186:33          "Is it very long?" Alice asked, for she had heard a good deal of poetry that day.
T5   155:14          "Can you row?" the Sheep asked, handing her a pair of knitting-needles as she spoke.
T5   152:23    "But why don't you scream now?" Alice asked, holding her hands ready to put over her ears again.
T8   186:20  "What did you mean it to be made of?" Alice asked, hoping to cheer him up, for the poor Knight seemed
T9   194:42  do you pick the flower?" the White Queen asked: "In a garden or in the hedges?"
A10   81:23          "And what are they made of?" Alice asked in a tone of great curiosity.
T8   182: 8          "But what are they for?" Alice asked in a tone of great curiosity.
T8   184:14  "Does that kind go smoothly?" the Knight asked in a tone of great interest, clasping his arms round the
T8W   15: 9          "Were what?" the Wasp asked in a very cross voice.
T9   196: 7          "Is there generally?" Alice asked in an astonished tone.
A5    41:31  said the Caterpillar, just as if she had asked it aloud; and in another moment it was out of sight.
T3   135:11    "Why do you wish I had made it?" Alice asked. "It's a very bad one."
T6   162: 4  "An uncomfortable sort of age. Now if you'd asked my advice, I'd have said 'Leave off at seven'--but it's
T9   195:16          "I wish Queens never asked questions," Alice thought to herself.
T9   200:12  "I'm glad they've come without waiting to be asked," she thought: "I should never have known who were the
A9    74:20  pitied him deeply. "What is his sorrow?" she asked the Gryphon. And the Gryphon answered, very nearly in
A9    76: 9          "With extras?" asked the Mock Turtle, a little anxiously.
T4   144:26  there any lions or tigers about here?" she asked timidly.
A7    59:16  making personal remarks now?" the Hatter asked triumphantly.
T7   175: 2  aren't you going to run and help her?" Alice asked, very much surprised at his taking it so quietly.
T8W   18: 9  too. "Would you mind saying it in rhyme?" she asked very politely.
T9   193:24    "Can you do Addition?" the White Queen asked. "What's one and one and one and one and one and one and
A9    72:23          "Thinking again?" the Duchess asked, with another dig of her sharp little chin.
T3   133: 6    "What does it live on?" Alice asked, with great curiosity.
T2   123:22    "Where does she wear them?" Alice asked with some curiosity.
A7    59:15          "Nobody asked your opinion," said Alice.
```
ASKING (10)
```
A3    23:15  and they all crowded round it, panting, and asking "But who has won?"
T9   192:16    there would be no harm, she thought, in asking if the game was over. "Please, would you tell me--" she
T1   110: 5  play chess? Now, don't smile, my dear. I'm asking it seriously. Because, when we were playing just now,
A1    9: 3  an ignorant little girl she'll think me for asking! No, it'll never do to ask: perhaps I shall see it
T9   199:12  To answer the door?" he said. "What's it been asking of?" He was so hoarse that Alice could scarcely hear
T2   121:13  didn't like being criticized, so she began asking questions. "Aren't you sometimes frightened at being
A7    55:14  now!" thought Alice. "I'm glad they've begun asking riddles--I believe I can guess that," she added aloud.
A7    56:33  with the time," she said, "than wasting it in asking riddles that have no answers."
T4   140: 7      "Nohow. And thank you very much for asking," said Tweedledum.
A9    75: 4  "You ought to be ashamed of yourself for asking such a simple question," added the Gryphon; and then
```
ASLEEP (12)
```
A11   89:27  but the Dormouse denied nothing, being fast asleep.
T2   122:29  beds too soft--so that the flowers are always asleep."
A7    58:30  about it," added the Hatter, "or you'll be asleep again before it's done."
A7    56:22          "The Dormouse is asleep again," said the Hatter, and he poured a little hot tea
T9   197:11  too." In another moment both Queens were fast asleep, and snoring loud.
A7    54: 3  it: a Dormouse was sitting between them, fast asleep, and the other two were using it as a cushion, resting
T9   197:16  that any one had to take care of two Queens asleep at once! No, not in all the History of England--it
A7    54: 6  the Dormouse," thought Alice; "only as it's asleep, I suppose it doesn't mind."
A9    73:22  very soon came upon a Gryphon, lying fast asleep in the sun. (If you don't know what a Gryphon is, look
A7    60:30  disgust, and walked off: the Dormouse fell asleep instantly, and neither of the others took the least
A7    58:25  Dormouse slowly opened its eyes. "I wasn't asleep," it said in a hoarse, feeble voice, "I heard every
T1   107:14  arm-chair, half talking to herself and half asleep, the kitten had been having a grand game of romps with
```
ASSEMBLED (2)
```
A11   86: 2  throne when they arrived, with a great crowd assembled about them--all sorts of little birds and beasts, as
A3    21: 1  They were indeed a queer-looking party that assembled on the bank--the birds with draggled feathers, the
```
ASSISTANCE (1)
```
T6   162:12  said Humpty Dumpty; "but two can. With proper assistance, you might have left off at seven."
```
ASSURE (2)
```
T8   185:14  "It was all kinds of fastness with me, I can assure you!" he said. He raised his hands in some excitement
T1   115:22          The King was saying "I assure you, my dear, I turned cold to the very ends of my
```
ASTONISHED (4)
```
T5   157:14  To buy!" Alice echoed in a tone that was half astonished and half frightened--for the oars, and the boat,
T2   121: 1          Alice was so astonished that she couldn't speak for a minute: it quite
T1   115: 5  hand, and being dusted: he was far too much astonished to cry out, but his eyes and his mouth went on
T9   196: 7  "Is there generally?" Alice asked in an astonished tone.
```
ASTONISHMENT (2)
```
T5   155:10  Alice couldn't help looking at her in great astonishment.
T5   150:13  "Living backwards!" Alice repeated in great astonishment. "I never heard of such a thing!"
```
ASUNDER (1)
```
TI   103: 4  be fleet, and I and thou / Are half a life asunder, / Thy loving smile will surely hail / The love-gift
```
AT (456) [entries omitted]
ATE (4)
```
A1    12:38          She ate a little bit, and said anxiously to herself "Which way?
T4   144:20          "But he ate as many as he could get," said Tweedledum.
T2   127:28  at all what she wanted. She took it, and ate it as well as she could: and it was very dry: and she
```

ATE (cont.)
T4   144:15   "He ate more than the Carpenter, though," said Tweedledee. "You
ATHELING (1)
A3   22:22   on, "--found it advisable to go with Edgar Atheling to meet William and offer him the crown. William's
ATOM (2)
A12   95:26   give him sixpence. I don't believe there's an atom of meaning in it."
A12   95:28   their slates, "She doesn't believe there's an atom of meaning in it," but none of them attempted to explain
ATTEMPT (2)
A11   90:18   at the end of trials, 'There was some attempt at applause, which was immediately suppressed by the
A4   29:27   elbow was pressed hard against it, that attempt proved a failure. Alice heard it say to itself "Then
ATTEMPTED (1)
A12   95:28   an atom of meaning in it," but none of them attempted to explain the paper.
ATTEND (1)
T1   110:30   "Now, if you'll only attend, Kitty, and not talk so much, I'll tell you all my
ATTENDED (2)
T2   124: 9   Alice attended to all these directions, and explained, as well as
A9   72: 3   "Oh, I know!" exclaimed Alice, who had not attended to this last remark. "It's a vegetable. It doesn't
ATTENDING (3)
A3   26: 1   "You are not attending!" said the Mouse to Alice, severely. "What are you
A5   42:34   tried hedges," the Pigeon went on, without attending to her; "but those serpents! There's no pleasing
A6   46:19   your knocking," the Footman went on, without attending to her, "if we had the door between us. For instance
ATTENDS (1)
A8   67:26   in particular: at least, if there are, nobody attends to them--and you've no idea how confusing it is all
ATTENTION (2)
T7   171:12   in the hope of turning off the Messenger's attention from himself--but it was of no use--the Anglo-Saxon
T4   147: 3   thing to do, that it quite took off Alice's attention from the angry brother. But he couldn't quite
ATTENTIVELY (1)
T8   187:30   I can no more.'" She stood and listened very attentively, but no tears came into her eyes.
ATTITUDE (1)
T7   175:21   both his hands towards her in an Anglo-Saxon attitude. "We only found it to-day. It's as large as life, and
ATTITUDES (3)
T7   170:23   But he's coming very slowly--and what curious attitudes he goes into!" (For the Messenger kept skipping up
T7   170:27   Messenger--and those are Anglo-Saxon attitudes. He only does them when he's happy. His name is
T7   171:13   but it was of no use--the Anglo-Saxon attitudes only got more extraordinary every moment, while the
AUDIBLY (1)
A3   22:34   a smile: some of the other birds tittered audibly.
AUSTRALIA (1)
A1   8:45   know. Please, Ma'am, is this New Zealand? Or Australia?" (and she tried to curtsey as she spoke--fancy,
AUTHORITY (2)
A3   21:13   the Mouse, who seemed to be a person of some authority among them, called out "Sit down, all of you, and
A10   82:14   Gryphon as if he thought it had some kind of authority over Alice.
AUTUMN (3)
TC   209: 9   sunny sky: / Echoes fade and memories die: / Autumn frosts have slain July.
T6   166:34   In autumn, when the leaves are brown, / Take pen and ink, and
T1   110: 3   true! I'm sure the woods look sleepy in the autumn, when the leaves are getting brown.
AVAIL (1)
AI   3:11   feather! / Yet what can one poor voice avail / Against three tongues together?
AWAY (64)
A4   30:12   business there, at any rate: go and take it away!"
A5   36:17   a very unpleasant state of mind, she turned away.
A11   87:19   he stole those tarts / And took them quite away!"
T4   145:28   the wood--here's somebody's shawl being blown away!"
T5   156:10   put 'em there, and I'm not going to take 'em away."
T7   172:10   faint," he remarked to her, as he munched away.
T8W   13:22   only shook his shoulders, and turned his head away. "Ah, deary me!" he said to himself.
T5   156:38   while--and these, being dream-rushes, melted away almost like snow, as they lay in heaps at her feet--but
A2   18: 9   just in time to save herself from shrinking away altogether.
T7   174: 2   cried impatiently. But Hatta only munched away, and drank some more tea.
T3   129:21   them without a good long branch to brush them away--and what fun it'll be when they ask me how I liked my
T1   112: 4   to find that there was a real one, blazing away as brightly as the one she had left behind. "So I shall
T3   132:16   But the beard seemed to melt away as she touched it, and she found herself sitting quietly
T8   179:37   said the Red Knight, and they began banging away at each other with such fury that Alice got behind a tree
T3   129:14   out, though the idea quite took her breath away at first. "And what enormous flowers they must be!" was
T3   137: 9   eyes, and in another moment it had darted away at full speed.
T2   121: 2   a minute: it quite seemed to take her breath away. At length, as the Tiger-lily only went on waving about,
A8   66:15   itself, and was in the act of crawling away: besides all this, there was generally a ridge or a
T1   115: 1   the Queen, that she mightn't take his breath away; but, before she put him on the table, she thought she
T6   168:37   getting no answer to this, she quietly walked away: but she couldn't help saying to herself, as she went,
A3   23:11   and there. There was no "One, two, three, and away!", but they began running when they liked, and left off
T1   108:33   but listen! Number two: you pulled Snowdrop away by the tail just as I had put down the saucer of milk
A8   66: 7   she succeeded in getting its body tucked away, comfortably enough, under her arm, with its legs hanging
T7   177: 7   the great dish on her knees, and was sawing away diligently with the knife. "It's very provoking!" she
A9   72:29   great surprise, the Duchess's voice died away, even in the middle of her favourite word "moral", and
T3   135:18   poor Gnat really seemed to have sighed itself away, for, when Alice looked up, there was nothing whatever to
T6   159:18   Dumpty said after a long silence, looking away from Alice as he spoke, "to be called an egg--very!"
T1   110:20   But this is taking us away from Alice's speech to the kitten. "Let's pretend that
A2   20:11   it again!" For the Mouse was swimming away from her as hard as it could go, and making quite a
T6   159:22   "Some people," said Humpty Dumpty, looking away from her as usual, "have no more sense than a baby!"
A8   64:12   The Queen turned angrily away from him, and said to the Knave "Turn them over!"
T1   112: 7   because there'll be no one here to scold me away from the fire. Oh, what fun it'll be, when they see me

AWAY (cont.)
    T1   114: 9 rapid journey through the air had quite taken away her breath, and for a minute or two she could do nothing
    T4   145:29 it's foolish to cry about it." So she brushed away her tears, and went on, as cheerfully as she could, "At
    T8W   15:16   stop there!" said the Wasp, fretfully turning away his head.
    T5   152:28 was getting light. "The crow must have flown away, I think," said Alice: "I'm so glad it's gone. I thought
    T5   158:13   The Sheep took the money, and put it away in a box: then she said "I never put things into people's
    A2   15:35   white kid-gloves and the fan, and scurried away into the darkness as hard as he could go.
    T8   190:24 shook hands, and then the Knight rode slowly away into the forest. "It wo'n't take long to see him off, I
    A5   41:26   it got down off the mushroom, and crawled away into the grass, merely remarking, as it went, "One side
    T12   207:19 thing afterwards to her sister: "it turned away its head, and pretended not to see it: but it looked a
    T9   194:21   "Then if the dog went away, its temper would remain!" the Queen exclaimed
    T1   111:13 And certainly the glass was beginning to melt away, just like a bright silvery mist.
    T7   174:19 the drums to begin." And Hatta went bounding away like a grasshopper.
    A3   26:34   in a trembling voice, to its children, "Come away, my dears! It's high time you were all in bed!" On
    A6   50:15   down, and felt quite relieved to see it trot away quietly into the wood. "If it had grown up," she said to
    A11   87: 7   very soon found an opportunity of taking it away. She did it so quickly that the poor little juror (it was
    T9   201:14 Remove the pudding!" and the waiters took it away so quickly that Alice couldn't return its bow.
    T3   130:21 wrong way," and shut up the window, and went away. "So young a child," said the gentleman sitting opposite
    A12   98: 2   lap of her sister, who was gently brushing away some dead leaves that had fluttered down from the trees
    A8   69:10   The Cat's head began fading away the moment he was gone, and, by the time he had come back
    T5   158:19 the end. "The egg seems to get further away the more I walk towards it. Let me see, is this a chair?
    A11   86:12   began looking at everything about her to pass away the time.
    T2   122:37 keep your head under the leaves, and snore away there, till you know no more what's going on in the world
    T5   155:24 any answer: so Alice said nothing, but pulled away. There was something very queer about the water, she
    T4   141: 5   of sand: / 'If this were only cleared away,' / They said, 'it would be grand!'
    T8   179: 1   a while the noise seemed gradually to die away, till all was dead silence, and Alice lifted up her head
    A8   68:25   this side of the ground." So she tucked it away under her arm, that it might not escape again, and went
    A1   9:24   down it. There was not a moment to be lost: away went Alice like the wind, and was just in time to hear it
    A8   67:30   the Queen's hedgehog just now, only it ran away when it saw mine coming!"
    A6   49:26   the open air. "If I don't take this child away with me," thought Alice, "they're sure to kill it in a
    A8   67: 9   escape, and wondering whether she could get away without being seen, when she noticed a curious appearance
    A5   36:28   worth hearing. For some minutes it puffed away without speaking; but at last it unfolded its arms, took
    A3   26: 9   sort," said the Mouse, getting up and walking away. "You insult me by talking such nonsense!"
AWE (1)
    T2   124:15 a little at this, but she was too much in awe of the Queen to disbelieve it. "I'll try it when I go home
AWFULLY (1)
    A5   40: 4   on the end of your nose--/ What made you so awfully clever?"
AWHILE (1)
    T1   118: 8   So rested he by the Tumtum tree, / And stood awhile in thought.
AWKWARD (3)
    T8   182:16 carefully, because the Knight was so very awkward in putting in the dish: the first two or three times
    T4   140: 2   at her for a minute: there was a rather awkward pause, as Alice didn't know how to begin a
    T2   123:11   "Well, she has the same awkward shape as you," the Rose said: "but she's redder--and
AXES (1)
    A6   48:27   "Talking of axes," said the Duchess, "chop off her head!"
AXIS (1)
    A6   48:26   takes twenty-four hours to turn round on its axis--"

-B-

BABY (15) [See also PIG-BABY]
```
   T6    159:23  from her as usual, "have no more sense than a baby!"
   A6     49:34  its eyes were getting extremely small for a baby: altogether Alice did not like the look of the thing at
   A6     47:18  another moment that it was addressed to the baby, and not to her, so she took courage, and went on again:
   A6     49:11  the Duchess said to Alice, flinging the baby at her as she spoke. "I must go and get ready to play
   A6     49:31                                        The baby grunted again, and Alice looked very anxiously into its
   T9    202: 4  the fish must be caught.' / That is easy: a baby, I think, could have caught it. / 'Next, the fish must be
   A6     47: 8  Duchess sneezed occasionally; and as for the baby, it was sneezing and howling alternately without a
   A6     48:41            CHORUS (in which the cook and the baby joined):--
   A6     52:17        "By-the-bye, what became of the baby?" said the Cat. "I'd nearly forgotten to ask."
   A6     47: 2  a three-legged stool in the middle, nursing a baby: the cook was leaning over the fire, stirring a large
   A6     48:11  within her reach at the Duchess and the baby--the fire-irons came first; then followed a shower of
   A12    98:40  of the shepherd-boy--and the sneeze of the baby, the shriek of the Gryphon, and all the other queer
   A6     49: 2  verse of the song, she kept tossing the baby violently up and down, and the poor little thing howled
   A6     48:14  of them even when they hit her; and the baby was howling so much already, that it was quite impossible
   A6     49:15                              Alice caught the baby with some difficulty, as it was a queer-shaped little
```
BACK (78)
```
   A3     26:23  nobody in particular. "She'd soon fetch it back!"
   T1    118:16  dead, and with its head / He went galumphing back.
   T8    182: 2  likely there would be any mice on the horse's back."
   T8W    14:23  sugar, large and in fine condition. In coming back--"
   T3    136:10  and tried to stroke it; but it only started back a little, and then stood looking at her again.
   A5     36:20  promising, certainly. Alice turned and came back again.
   A4     27: 1  It was the White Rabbit, trotting slowly back again, and looking anxiously about as it went, as if it
   A2     20:14  called softly after it, "Mouse dear! Do come back again, and we wo'n't talk about cats, or dogs either, if
   T8    187:18  afterwards she could bring the whole scene back again, as if it had been only yesterday--the mild blue
   T5    158: 1  had vanished all in a moment, and she was back again in the little dark shop.
   A5     36:10          Which brought them back again to the beginning of the conversation. Alice felt a
   T8W    15: 5                      "In coming back," Alice went on reading, "they found a lake of treacle.
   T2    123:44        A little provoked, she drew back, and, after looking everywhere for the Queen (whom she
   A4     32:44  little way forwards each time and a long way back, and barking hoarsely all the while, till at last it sat
   A3     26:13        "Please come back, and finish your story!" Alice called after it. And the
   T8W    21:17  hill again, quite pleased that she had gone back and given a few minutes to making the poor old creature
   T1    115:15  The King immediately fell flat on his back, and lay perfectly still; and Alice was a little alarmed
   A9     74: 2  Turtle, and to hear his history. I must go back and see after some executions I have ordered;" and she
   A8     68:10        Alice thought she might as well go back and see how the game was going on, as she heard the
   A4     27:32  got to watch this mouse-hole till Dinah comes back, and see that the mouse doesn't get out.' Only I don't
   A10    78: 5  to work shaking him and punching him in the back. At last the Mock Turtle recovered his voice, and, with
   T3    137:31  so suddenly that she could not help starting back, but in another moment she recovered herself, feeling
   A2     18:20  into the sea, "and in that case I can go back by railway," she said to herself. (Alice had been to the
   T3    131: 9  in turn, he went on with "She'll have to go back from here as luggage!"
   T8    181:10  more easily," said the Knight, putting back his shaggy hair with both hands, and turning his gentle
   A3     24:12  small ones choked and had to be patted on the back. However, it was over at last, and they sat down again in
   A5     42:24  wandering, when a sharp hiss made her draw back in a hurry: a large pigeon had flown into her face, and
   A6     52:20  very quietly, just as if the Cat had come back in a natural way.
   T3    134: 9  feet," said the Gnat (Alice drew her feet back in some alarm), "you may observe a Bread-and-butter-fly.
   A12    93: 2  very grave voice, "until all the jurymen are back in their proper places--all," he repeated with great
   T5    156:32  and dripping hair and hands, she scrambled back into her place, and began to arrange her new-found
   T5    157: 5  crab you caught!" she remarked, as Alice got back into her place, very much relieved to find herself still
   T1    108: 3  as she could manage--and then she scrambled back into the arm-chair, taking the kitten and the worsted
   A12    92:12  that they must be collected at once and put back into the jury-box, or they would die.
   T2    120:16  have to get through the Looking-glass again--back into the old room--and there'd be an end of all my
   T8    183: 7  you say that?" he asked, as he scrambled back into the saddle, keeping hold of Alice's hair with one
   A6     46: 5  laughed so much at this, that she had to run back into the wood for fear of their hearing her; and, when
   T4    138: 8  see if the word 'TWEEDLE' was written at the back of each collar, when she was startled by a voice coming
   T1    112:14  chimney-piece (you know you can only see the back of it in the Looking-glass) had got the face of a little
   A10    78: 1  The Mock Turtle sighed deeply, and drew the back of one flapper across his eyes. He looked at Alice and
   T4    138: 5  "I suppose they've got 'TWEEDLE' round at the back of the collar," she said to herself.
   T8W    20:13  could you get hold of the other one by the back of the neck?"
   T5    154: 7  all round you--unless you've got eyes at the back of your head."
   A7     60:32  least notice of her going, though she looked back once or twice, half hoping that they would call after her
   A10    81:28  song, "I'd have said to the porpoise 'Keep back, please! We don't want you with us!'"
   T8    184: 7  he meant, and this time he fell flat on his back, right under the horse's feet.
   T3    135:25  her mind to go on: "for I certainly won't go back," she thought to herself, and this was the only way to
   A5     36:18                    "Come back!" the Caterpillar called after her. "I've something
   A8     68:22  she had caught the flamingo and brought it back, the fight was over, and both the hedgehogs were out of
   T9    201:17  an experiment, she called out "Waiter! Bring back the pudding!" and there it was again in a moment, like a
   A12    98:20  that queer little toss of her head to keep back the wandering hair that would always get into her eyes--
   T3    131:28  in a wood just now--and I wish I could get back there!"
   T1    118:32  "if I don't make haste, I shall have to go back through the Looking-glass, before I've seen what the rest
   A3     26:44  Mouse had changed his mind, and was coming back to finish his story.
   A8     68:26  arm, that it might not escape again, and went back to have a little more conversation with her friend.
   A2     20:17  heard this, it turned round and swam slowly back to her: its face was quite pale (with passion, Alice
```

BACK (cont.)
T9   199:21 let _it_ alone," he panted out, as he hobbled back to his tree, "and it'll let _you_ alone, you know."
A10   78:35   "Back to land again, and--that's all the first figure," said
T6   167: 2 fishes of the sea, / They sent an answer back to me.
A5   43:42 from one minute to another! However, I've got back to my right size: the next thing is, to get into that
T8W   13: 4   there," she thought, looking anxiously back to see what was the matter. Something like a very old man
A8   68:28   When she got back to the Cheshire-Cat, she was surprised to find quite a
A9   72:42 to say a word, but slowly followed her back to the croquet-ground.
A8   69:13 for it, while the rest of the party went back to the game.
A9   73: 1   the moment they saw her, they hurried back to the game, the Queen merely remarking that a moment's
T2   120:10 and trying turn after turn, but always coming back to the house, do what she would. Indeed, once, when she
T2   120: 7 I suppose--no, it doesn't! This goes straight back to the house! Well then, I'll try it the other way."
T6   161:15 is going on a little too fast: let's go back to the last remark but one."
A2   18:12 for the garden!" And she ran with all speed back to the little door; but, alas! the little door was shut
A1   12:16 the little golden key, and when she went back to the table for it, she found she could not possibly
A1   10:13 in waiting by the little door, so she went back to the table, half hoping she might find another key on
T8W   13:14   So she went back to the Wasp--rather unwillingly, for she was _very_ anxious
A12   93:12 slates and pencils had been found and handed back to them, they set to work very diligently to write out a
A10   81:41 a little timidly; "but it's no use going back to yesterday, because I was a different person then."
T2   120:18 So, resolutely turning her back upon the house, she set out once more down the
T1   115:19 nothing but a bottle of ink, and when she got back with it she found he had recovered, and he and the Queen
A8   69:11 he was gone, and, by the time he had come back with the Duchess, it had entirely disappeared: so the
T8   181: 5 to the end of the wood--and then I must go back, you know. That's the end of my move."
BACKS (1)
A8   63:45 on their faces, and the pattern on their backs was the same as the rest of the pack, she could not tell
BACK-SOMERSAULT (1)
A5   38: 3 grown most uncommonly fat; / Yet you turned a back-somersault in at the door--/ Pray, what is the reason of
BACKWARDS (4)
T5   150:13   "Living backwards!" Alice repeated in great astonishment. "I never
T10   205: 1 her off the table as she spoke, and shook her backwards and forwards with all her might.
T5   150:19 "It's a poor sort of memory that only works backwards," the Queen remarked.
T5   150:11   "That's the effect of living backwards," the Queen said kindly: "it always makes one a
BAD (5)
A3   21:17 on it, for she felt sure she would catch a bad cold if she did not get dry very soon.
T6   160:30   "Now I declare that's too bad!" Humpty Dumpty cried, breaking into a sudden passion.
T3   135:11 I had made it?" Alice asked. "It's a very bad one."
T2   120:24   "Oh, it's too bad!" she cried. "I never saw such a house for getting in the
A2   18:16 as this before, never! And I declare it's too bad, that it is!"
BADGERS (1)
T6   164:35   "Well 'toves' are something like badgers--they're something like lizards--and they're something
BADLY (2)
T8   181:14 in tin armour, which seemed to fit him very badly, and he had a queer-shaped little deal box fastened
T1   115:41 is sliding down the poker. He balances very badly'). "That's not a memorandum of _your_ feelings!"
BAG (8)
T7   172: 6 now," the Messenger said, peeping into the bag.
T8   182:14 any plum-cake. Help me to get it into this bag."
T7   175:39 Haigha took a large cake out of the bag, and gave it to Alice to hold, while he got out a dish and
T8   182:19 last; "there are so many candlesticks in the bag." And he hung it to the saddle, which was already loaded
T7   175:37 muttered, and beckoned to Haigha. "Open the bag!" he whispered. "Quick! Not that one--that's full of hay!
T8   182:15 a long time to manage, though Alice held the bag open very carefully, because the Knight was so _very_
T7   172: 2   to Alice's great amusement, opened a bag that hung round his neck, and handed a sandwich to the
A11   90:14 you how it was done. They had a large canvas bag, which tied up at the mouth with strings: into this they
BAKED (1)
A10   82:23 the Lobster: I heard him declare / 'You have baked me too brown, I must sugar my hair.' / As a duck with
BALANCE (2)
T6   159:10 Alice quite wondered how he could keep his balance--and, as his eyes were steadily fixed in the opposite
T8   184: 5 of riding, as I was saying is--to keep your balance properly. Like this, you know--"
BALANCED (1)
A5   40: 3 your eye was as steady as ever; / Yet you balanced an eel on the end of your nose--/ What made you so
BALANCES (1)
T1   115:41 White Knight is sliding down the poker. He balances very badly'). "That's not a memorandum of your
BALANCING (1)
T3   132:18 was the insect she had been talking to) was balancing itself on a twig just over her head, and fanning her
BALE (1)
TI   103:35 glory--/ It shall not touch, with breath of bale, / The pleasance of our fairy-tale.
BALL (6)
T1   108: 5 worsted with her, and began winding up the ball again. But she didn't get on very fast, as she was
T1   108: 9 putting out one paw and gently touching the ball, as if it would be glad to help if it might.
T1   107:15 been having a grand game of romps with the ball of worsted Alice had been trying to wind up, and had been
T1   110: 1 very pretty!" cried Alice, dropping the ball of worsted to clap her hands. "And I do so _wish_ it was
T9   197: 6 nap. / When the feast's over, we'll go to the ball--/ Red Queen, and White Queen, and Alice, and all!
T1   108:18 look: this led to a scramble, in which the ball rolled down upon the floor, and yards and yards of it got
BALLAD (1)
T8   190:12 As the Knight sang the last words of the ballad, he gathered up the reins, and turned his horse's head
BALLS (1)
A8   66: 2 it was all ridges and furrows: the croquet balls were live hedgehogs, and the mallets live flamingoes,
BAND (1)
AI   4: 6 dreams are twined / In Memory's mystic band. / Like pilgrim's wither'd wreath of flowers / Pluck'd in
BANDERSNATCH (3)
T1   118: 4 the Jubjub bird, and shun / The frumious Bandersnatch!"

BANDERSNATCH (cont.)
    T7   173:13   quick. You might as well try to stop a Bandersnatch!"
    T7   175: 5   quick. You might as well try to catch a Bandersnatch! But I'll make a memorandum about her, if you
BANG (2)
    T9   198:11   after next!" and shut the door again with a bang.
    T4   145:11   to wake," added Tweedledum, "you'd go out--bang!--just like a candle!"
BANGING (1)
    T8   179:36   do," said the Red Knight, and they began banging away at each other with such fury that Alice got
BANK (5)
    T8   186: 1   by the feet, and laid him in a heap on the bank.
    A1   7: 2   very tired of sitting by her sister on the bank and of having nothing to do: once or twice she had peeped
    T7   177: 6   Alice had seated herself on the bank of a little brook, with the great dish on her knees, and
    A3   21: 2   a queer-looking party that assembled on the bank--the birds with draggled feathers, the animals with their
    A12   98: 1   beat them off, and found herself lying on the bank, with her head in the lap of her sister, who was gently
BANKS (3) [See also RIVER-BANKS]
    A5   42:33   I've tried the roots of trees, and I've tried banks, and I've tried hedges," the Pigeon went on, without
    T8W   15: 6   reading, "they found a lake of treacle. The banks of the lake were blue and white, and looked like china.
    T5   155:19   were in a little boat, gliding along between banks: so there was nothing for it but to do her best.
BANQUET (1)
    A10   84: 2   and fork with a growl, / And concluded the banquet by--"
BAR (2)
    T1   114:19   King as he slowly struggled up from bar to bar, till at last she said "Why, you'll be hours and hours
    T1   114:19   the White King as he slowly struggled up from bar to bar, till at last she said "Why, you'll be hours and
BARGAIN (1)
    T7   175:31   believe in me, I'll believe in you. Is that a bargain?"
BARGAINS (1)
    T9   195:15   rather stiffly, and said "Queens never make bargains."
BARK (3)
    A4   32:25   anxiously among the trees, a little sharp bark just over her head made her look up in a great hurry.
    T2   122: 4   "It could bark," said the Rose.
    A4   33: 5   tired and out of breath, and till the puppy's bark sounded quite faint in the distance.
BARKING (1)
    A4   32:44   forwards each time and a long way back, and barking hoarsely all the while, till at last it sat down a
BARLEY-SUGAR (1)
    A9   70:12   and camomile that makes them bitter--and--and barley-sugar and such things that make children sweet-tempered
-BARREL [See TAR-BARREL]
BARROWFUL (2)
    A4   31:41   "A barrowful of what?" thought Alice. But she had not long to
    A4   31:39   again, and Alice heard the Rabbit say "A barrowful will do, to begin with."
BAT (3)
    A1   9:10   in the air, I'm afraid, but you might catch a bat, and that's very like a mouse, you know. But do cats eat
    A7   57:14   'Twinkle, twinkle, little bat! / How I wonder what you're at!'
    A1   9:18   Dinah, tell me the truth: did you ever eat a bat?" when suddenly, thump! thump! down she came upon a heap
BATHING-MACHINES (1)
    A2   18:23   to on the English coast, you find a number of bathing-machines in the sea, some children digging in the sand
BATS (4)
    A1   9:13   sort of way, "Do cats eat bats? Do cats eat bats?" and sometimes "Do bats eat cats?" for, you see, as she
    A1   9:13   in a dreamy sort of way, "Do cats eat bats? Do cats eat bats?" and sometimes "Do bats eat cats?" for
    A1   9:13   bats? Do cats eat bats?" and sometimes "Do bats eat cats?" for, you see, as she couldn't answer either
    A1   9:11   very like a mouse, you know. But do cats eat bats, I wonder?" And here Alice began to get rather sleepy,
BATTER (1)
    T8   188:26   I was thinking of a way / To feed oneself on batter, / And so go on from day to day / Getting a little
BATTLE (7)
    T8   180: 1   "I wonder, now, what the Rules of Battle are," she said to herself, as she watched the fight,
    T8   180:11   that they always fell on their heads; and the battle ended with their both falling off in this way, side by
    T4   138:19   "Tweedledum and Tweedledee / Agreed to have a battle; / For Tweedledum said Tweedledee / Had spoiled his
    T8   179:34   "You will observe the Rules of Battle, of course?" the White Knight remarked, putting on his
    T8   180:10   Another Rule of Battle, that Alice had not noticed, seemed to be that they
    T4   147:26   things that can possibly happen to one in a battle--to get one's head cut off."
    T4   147: 8   "Of course you agree to have a battle?" Tweedledum said in a calmer tone.
BAWLED (1)
    A7   58: 5   verse," said the Hatter, "when the Queen bawled out 'He's murdering the time! Off with his head!'"
BE (311)
    A5   41:15   "three inches is such a wretched height to be."
    T4   145: 6   about you, where do you suppose you'd be?"
    T8   191: 8   on her lap to make out what it could possibly be.
    A4   29: 5   I am in the middle of one! There ought to be a book written about me, that there ought! And when I grow
    A3   23: 1   "was that the best thing to get us dry would be a Caucus-race."
    A4   29:10   I never get any older than I am now? That'll be a comfort, one way--never to be an old woman--but then--
    T4   143:15   blue. / 'After such kindness, that would be / A dismal thing to do!' / 'The night is fine,' the Walrus
    A6   45: 3   out of the wood--(she considered him to be a footman because he was in livery: otherwise, judging by
    A2   14: 7   dears? I'm sure I sha'n't be able! I shall be a great deal too far off to trouble myself about you: you
    A8   67:11   it a minute or two she made it out to be a grin, and she said to herself "It's the Cheshire-Cat: now
    A3   26:18   saying to her daughter "Ah, my dear! Let this be a lesson to you never to lose your temper!" "Hold your
    A12   94: 8   yet," said the White Rabbit; "but it seems to be a letter, written by the prisoner to--to somebody."
    T1   114: 2   had been hurt by the fall. He had a right to be a little annoyed with the Queen, for he was covered with
    T8   184:37   tell for certain--but I'm afraid it would be a little hard."
    A5   41:14   "Well, I should like to be a little larger, Sir, if you wouldn't mind," said Alice:
    A3   21:13   At last the Mouse, who seemed to be a person of some authority among them, called out "Sit down
    T8   181: 2   want to be anybody's prisoner. I want to be a Queen."

BE (cont.)

```
T8W   13:15   unwillingly, for she was very anxious to be a Queen.
T2    126: 4  might join--though of course I should like to be a Queen, best."
T8    190:15  and over that little brook, and then you'll be a Queen--But you'll stay and see me off first?" he added as
T8    190:35  the hill: "and now for the last brook, and to be a Queen! How grand it sounds!" A very few steps brought her
T2    126:10  when you get to the Eighth Square you'll be a Queen--"Just at this moment, somehow or other, they began
T9    192: 1   said Alice. "I never expected I should be a Queen so soon--and I'll tell you what it is, your Majesty
T9    192:28  have you to call yourself so? You ca'n't be a Queen, you know, till you've passed the proper
A2    19: 3   by being drowned in my own tears! That will be a queer thing, to be sure! However, everything is queer
T7    170: 1   they stumbled now and then; and it seemed to be a regular rule that, whenever a horse stumbled, the rider
A12   95:18   she liked them best, / For this must ever be / A secret, kept from all the rest, / Between yourself and
T6    159:12  the least notice of her, she thought he must be a stuffed figure after all.
T4    148:18  so suddenly that Alice thought there must be a thunderstorm coming on. "What a thick black cloud that
T4    148: 7  smile. "I don't suppose," he said, "there'll be a tree left standing, for ever so far round, by the time
T2    125:11  contradicting her at last: "a hill ca'n't be a valley, you know. That would be nonsense--"
A1    8:10    she found herself falling down what seemed to be a very deep well.
A10   79: 2                    "It must be a very pretty dance," said Alice timidly.
T7    172:34              "It would have to be a very tiny earthquake!" thought Alice. "Who are at it
A2    19: 7   out what it was: at first she thought it must be a walrus or hippopotamus, but then she remembered how small
T4    144:25  them, though she feared it was more likely to be a wild beast. "Are there any lions or tigers about here?"
T2    125: 5  seen gardens, compared with which this would be a wilderness."
A2    14: 7    for you now, dears? I'm sure I sha'n't be able! I shall be a great deal too far off to trouble myself
T4    145:25  it all seemed so ridiculous--"I shouldn't be able to cry."
T9    192: 9  she said as she sat down again, "I shall be able to manage it quite well in time."
T7    170:18  the King remarked in a fretful tone. "To be able to see Nobody! And at that distance too! Why, it's as
T2    126:25  of doing that. She felt as if she would never be able to talk again, she was getting so much out of breath:
A4    29:24   as large as the Rabbit, and had no reason to be afraid of it.
A8    63:42   only a pack of cards, after all. I needn't be afraid of them!"
T1    112:13  pictures on the wall next the fire seemed to be all alive, and the very clock on the chimney-piece (you
A9    75: 8   the Mock Turtle "Drive on, old fellow! Don't be all day about it!" and he went on in these words:--
T2    121:12  her petals curled up a little more, she'd be all right."
T5    151:11  all the better," she said: "but it wouldn't be all the better his being punished."
T5    151:10  was no denying that. "Of course it would be all the better," she said: "but it wouldn't be all the
T5    151: 8            "That would be all the better, wouldn't it?" the Queen said, as she bound
T1    110:16  "Well, you can be one of them, then, and I'll be all the rest." And once she had really frightened her old
T3    135:30  they'd have to give me another, and it would be almost certain to be an ugly one. But then the fun would be
A2    14: 5   she looked down at her feet, they seemed to be almost out of sight, they were getting so far off). "Oh, my
A6    48:23              "Which would not be an advantage," said Alice, who felt very glad to get an
T2    120:16  again--back into the old room--and there'd be an end of all my adventures!"
A4    29:10   now? That'll be a comfort, one way--never to be an old woman--but then--always to have lessons to learn! Oh
T3    135:31  me another, and it would be almost certain to be an ugly one. But then the fun would be, trying to find the
T4    139: 8  continued Tweedledee, "if it was so, it might be; and if it were so, it would be; but as it isn't, it ain't.
A2    19:32   not," said Alice in a soothing tone: "don't be angry about it. And yet I wish I could show you our cat
T5    149:10   and Alice felt that if there was to be any conversation at all, she must manage it herself. So she
T8    182: 2  said Alice. "It isn't very likely there would be any mice on the horse's back."
T3    135: 3  have to leave off, because there wouldn't be any name for her to call, and of course you wouldn't have
T6    160:10  it is, too. With a name like yours, you might be any shape, almost."
T6    159: 5  that it was HUMPTY DUMPTY himself. "It ca'n't be anybody else!" she said to herself. "I'm as certain of it,
T8    181: 1   Alice said doubtfully. "I don't want to be anybody's prisoner. I want to be a Queen."
T2    125:15  nonsense, compared with which that would be as sensible as a dictionary!"
T1    112: 5  as the one she had left behind. "So I shall be as warm here as I was in the old room," thought Alice:
A6    48: 8   the tone of this remark, and thought it would be as well to introduce some other subject of conversation.
A9    75: 4              "You ought to be ashamed of yourself for asking such a simple question,"
A2    15:20   "You ought to be ashamed of yourself," said Alice, "a great girl like you,"
T9    200:11  "I'm glad they've come without waiting to be asked," she thought: "I should never have known who were
A7    58:30   quick about it," added the Hatter, "or you'll be asleep again before it's done."
T5    158:12  For she thought to herself, "They mightn't be at all nice, you know."
T9    202:36            "That wouldn't be at all the thing," the Red Queen said very decidedly: so
A10   82:18   thought Alice. "I might just as well be at school at once." However, she got up, and began to
T3    129: 7   making honey down there? They ca'n't be bees--nobody ever saw bees a mile off, you know--" and for
A8    62:12   the Queen say only yesterday you deserved to be beheaded."
A8    68:41   was that anything that had a head could be beheaded, and that you weren't to talk nonsense.
A8    65:12              "You sha'n't be beheaded!" said Alice, and she put them into a large
T7    172:11  think throwing cold water over you would be better," Alice suggested: "--or some sal-volatile."
T6    167: 8  "I sent to them again to say / 'It will be better to obey.'
T9    202: 5  could have caught it. / 'Next, the fish must be bought.' / That is easy: a penny, I think, could have
T4    139: 8  so, it might be; and if it were so, it would be; but as it isn't, it ain't. That's logic."
T9    196:30  her on the head, and see how pleased she'll be!" But this was more than Alice had courage to do.
T6    159:18  looking away from Alice as he spoke, "to be called an egg--very!"
T5    155:28  cried again, taking more needles. "You'll be catching a crab directly."
T9    202: 3   "'First, the fish must be caught.' / That is easy: a baby, I think, could have caught
T2    127:27            Alice thought it would not be civil to say "No," though it wasn't at all what she wanted.
T6    168:19  to be going, she felt that it would hardly be civil to stay. So she got up, and held out her hand.
A7    59:26   the Dormouse sulkily remarked "If you ca'n't be civil, you'd better finish the story for yourself."
A12   96:15   to the tarts on the table. "Nothing can be clearer than that. Then again--'before she had this fit'--
A12   92:11   she had a vague sort of idea that they must be collected at once and put back into the jury-box, or they
T9    199:26  the Looking-Glass creatures, whatever they be, / Come and dine with the Red Queen, the White Queen, and
T8    186:18  fact, I don't believe that pudding ever will be cooked! And yet it was a very clever pudding to invent."
T8W   16: 7              "You'd be cross too, if you'd a wig like mine," the Wasp went on.
A6    51:17       Alice felt that this could not be denied, so she tried another question. "What sort of people
```

BE (cont.)

A5	36: 7	"Well, perhaps <u>your</u> feelings may be different," said Alice: "all I know is, it would feel very
T9	192: 5	about on the grass like that! Queens have to be dignified, you know!"
T9	194:37	one letter! Isn't <u>that</u> grand? However, don't be discouraged. You'll come to it in time."
T2	120:27	hill full in sight, so there was nothing to be done but start again. This time she came upon a large
A5	43:43	into that beautiful garden--how <u>is</u> that to be done, I wonder?" As she said this, she came suddenly upon
T9	200: 6	Alice repeated in despair. "Oh, that'll never be done! I'd better go in at once--" and in she went, and
T6	163:14	and looked at it carefully. "That seems to be done right--" he began.
T6	163:18	little queer. As I was saying, that <u>seems</u> to be done right--though I haven't time to look it over
T1	111:10	into a sort of mist now, I declare! It'll be easy enough to get through--" She was up on the
A8	68:13	heard her sentence three of the players to be executed for having missed their turns, and she did not
T2	123:36	interesting enough, she felt that it would be far grander to have a talk with a real Queen.
T9	195: 4	the Red Queen anxiously interrupted. "She'll be feverish after so much thinking." So they set to work and
T9	195:38	"But they should be five times as <u>cold</u>, by the same rule--"
TI	103: 3	/ And <u>dreaming eyes of wonder</u>! / <u>Though time</u> be <u>fleet</u>, <u>and I and thou</u> / <u>Are half a life asunder</u>, / <u>Thy</u>
A5	42: 9	she found that her shoulders were nowhere to be found: all she could see, when she looked down, was an
A1	8:30	centre of the earth. Let me see: that would be four thousand miles down, I think--" (for, you see, Alice
A5	43: 3	shriek, "and just as I was thinking I should be free of them at last, they must needs come wriggling down
T9	201: 2	returned the bow, not knowing whether to be frightened or amused.
A5	43:41	changes are! I'm never sure what I'm going to be, from one minute to another! However, I've got back to my
T5	154:11	The shop seemed to be full of all manner of curious things--but the oddest part
A6	47: 3	stirring a large cauldron which seemed to be full of soup.
A3	26:32	up very carefully, remarking "I really must be getting home: the night-air doesn't suit my throat!" And a
T4	146: 1	as she could, "At any rate, I'd better be getting out of the wood, for really it's coming on very
A1	8:29	fallen by this time?" she said aloud. "I must be getting somewhere near the centre of the earth. Let me see:
T5	152:30	"I wish <u>I</u> could manage to be glad!" the Queen said. "Only I never can remember the rule.
T1	108: 9	and gently touching the ball, as if it would be glad to help if it might.
A4	27:27	queer it seems," Alice said to herself, "to be going messages for a rabbit! I suppose Dinah'll be sending
T8W	21:13	she might safely leave him. "I think I must be going now," she said. "Good-bye."
T6	168:18	such a <u>very</u> strong hint that she ought to be going, she felt that it would be hardly be civil to stay. So
T1	109: 5	let me see--suppose each punishment was to be going without a dinner: then, when the miserable day came,
T7	173: 8	"Would you--be good enough--" Alice panted out, after running a little
T4	141: 6	<u>only cleared away</u>,' / <u>They said</u>, '<u>it</u> would <u>be grand</u>!'
A7	57: 5	"That would be grand, certainly," said Alice thoughtfully; "but then--I
A2	18: 4	<u>can</u> I have done that?" she thought. "I must be growing small again." She got up and went to the table to
T8	186: 3	"What does it matter where my body happens to be?" he said. "My mind goes on working all the same. In fact,
A12	99: 4	sister of hers would, in the after-time, be herself a grown woman; and how she would keep, through all
T1	114:19	to bar, till at last she said "Why, you'll be hours and hours getting to the table, at that rate. I'd far
A7	57: 6	Alice thoughtfully; "but then--I shouldn't be hungry for it, you know."
A4	32:31	all the time at the thought that it might be hungry, in which case it would be very likely to eat her up
T1	111: 5	on beyond. Oh, Kitty, how nice it would be if we could only get through into Looking-glass House! I'm
T3	134:26	tone: "only think how convenient it would be if you could manage to go home without it! For instance, if
A8	67:44	"Don't be impertinent," said the King, "and don't look at me like
A5	36:16	good reason, and the Caterpillar seemed to be in a <u>very</u> unpleasant state of mind, she turned away.
A11	87: 3	to tell him. "A nice muddle their slates'll be in, before the trial's over!" thought Alice.
A4	30:37	seem to put everything upon Bill! I wouldn't be in Bill's place for a good deal: this fireplace is narrow,
T5	149: 5	"I'm very glad I happened to be in the way," Alice said, as she helped her to put on her
T9	201:10	"I won't be introduced to the pudding, please," Alice said rather
A12	95: 9	If <u>I or she should chance to be</u> / <u>Involved in this affair</u>, / <u>He trusts to you to set them</u>
A5	41: 7	"What size do you want to be?" it asked.
A3	25:35	or judge, would be wasting our breath. 'I'll be judge, I'll be jury, said cunning old Fury: 'I'll try the
A3	25:37	be wasting our breath. 'I'll be judge, I'll be jury, said cunning old Fury: 'I'll try the whole cause, and
T6	163:45	had enough of that subject, and it would be just as well if you'd mention what you mean to do next, as
A2	14: 9	must manage the best way you can--but I must be kind to them," thought Alice, "or perhaps they wo'n't walk
T3	131:16	gentle voice in the distance said, "She must be labeled 'Lass, with care,' you know--"
A7	59: 7	such an extraordinary way of living would be like, but it puzzled her too much: so she went on: "But why
A11	91:30	curious to see what the next witness would be like, "--for they haven't got much evidence <u>yet</u>," she said
A1	12: 9	like a candle. I wonder what I should be like then?" And she tried to fancy what the flame of a
A6	48:30	busily stirring the soup, and seemed not to be listening, so she went on again: "Twenty-four hours, I
T9	192: 4	scolding herself), "It'll never do for you to be lolling about on the grass like that! Queens have to be
T8	190:17	the direction to which he pointed. "I sha'n't be long. You'll wait and wave your handkerchief when I get to
T4	138:11	to pay, you know. Wax-works weren't made to be looked at for nothing. Nohow!"
T9	204: 9	There was not a moment to be lost. Already several of the guests were lying down in the
A5	41:42	but she felt that there was no time to be lost, as she was shrinking rapidly: so she set to work at
A1	9:24	hurrying down it. There was not a moment to be lost: away went Alice like the wind, and was just in time
A2	17:17	with tears again as she went on, "I must be Mabel after all, and I shall have to go and live in that
A2	16: 6	go in ringlets at all; and I'm sure I ca'n't be Mabel, for I know all sorts of things, and she, oh, she
T8	186:20	"What did you mean it to be made of?" Alice asked, hoping to cheer him up, for the poor
A4	33:11	to grow up again! Let me see--how <u>is</u> it to be managed? I suppose I ought to eat or drink something or
T6	163:35	is," said Humpty Dumpty, "which is to be master--that's all."
T4	147:21	and fastening buttons--"Really they'll be more like bundles of old clothes than anything else, by the
A9	74:38	but she could not help thinking there <u>must</u> be more to come, so she sat still and said nothing.
A6	52:25	she said to herself: "the March Hare <u>will</u> be much the most interesting, and perhaps, as this is May, it
A6	49:27	sure to kill it in a day or two. Wouldn't it be murder to leave it behind?" She said the last words out
A11	88:28	your evidence," said the King: "and don't be nervous, or I'll have you executed on the spot."
A5	42:18	As there seemed to be no chance of getting her hands up to her head, she tried to
A11	86:10	round the refreshments!" But there seemed to be no chance of this; so she began looking at everything about
A6	49:32	see what was the matter with it. There could be no doubt that it had a <u>very</u> turn-up nose, much more like a
T9	192:15	not be quite civil. However, there would be no harm, she thought, in asking if the game was over.
A6	50:11	its face in some alarm. This time there could be <u>no</u> mistake about it: it was neither more nor less than a

BE (cont.)

T1	112: 7	Alice: "warmer, in fact, because there'll be no one here to scold me away from the fire. Oh, what fun
A4	28:25	very uncomfortable, and, as there seemed to be no sort of chance of her ever getting out of the room again
A1	10:12	There seemed to be no use in waiting by the little door, so she went back to
A2	17:21	it: if I'm Mabel, I'll stay down here. It'll be no use their putting their heads down and saying 'Come up
T2	125:11	hill ca'n't be a valley, you know. That would be nonsense--"
AI	3:16	In gentler tones Secunda hopes / "There will be nonsense in it!" / While Tertia interrupts the tale / Not
A5	42:23	dive in among the leaves, which she found to be nothing but the tops of the trees under which she had been
T4	145: 8	Tweedledee retorted contemptuously. "You'd be nowhere. Why, you're only a sort of thing in his dream!"
A12	93:44	"Then it ought to be Number One," said Alice.
A2	19:10	"Would it be of any use, now," thought Alice, "to speak to this mouse?
T8W	13: 9	"I don't think I can be of any use to him," was Alice's first thought, as she
T1	114: 4	Alice was very anxious to be of use, and, as the poor little Lily was nearly screaming
A1	10: 7	go through," thought poor Alice, "it would be of very little use without my shoulders. Oh, how I wish I
A9	72:37	as she spoke; "either you or your head must be off, and that in about half no time! Take your choice!"
A5	40: 8	think I can listen all day to such stuff? / Be off, or I'll kick you down-stairs!"
A5	43:28	"Well, be off, then!" said the Pigeon in a sulky tone, as it settled
A3	24:16	added in a whisper, half afraid that it would be offended again.
A5	42:39	the eggs," said the Pigeon; "but I must be on the look-out for serpents, night and day! Why, I haven't
A7	59:29	interrupt you again. I dare say there may be one."
T9	193:18	at all," said Alice; "but, if there is to be one, I think I ought to invite the guests."
T9	198: 8	and I'm not a servant. There ought to be one marked 'Queen,' you know--"
T1	110:16	been reduced at last to say "Well, you can be one of them, then, and I'll be all the rest." And once she
T1	110:38	smoke comes up in that room too--but that may be only pretence, just to make it look as if they had a fire.
A12	98:36	would change to dull reality--the grass would be only rustling in the wind, and the pool rippling to the
A9	72: 6	moral of that is--'Be what you would seem to be'--or, if you'd like it put more simply--'Never imagine
A9	72:10	you had been would have appeared to them to be otherwise.'"
A9	72: 7	more simply--'Never imagine yourself not to be otherwise than what it might appear to others that what you
T8W	14:10	me help you round to the other side? You'll be out of the cold wind there."
T8	179:38	such fury that Alice got behind a tree to be out of the way of the blows.
T8	184:34	"Yes, I suppose you'd be over when that was done," Alice said thoughtfully: "but
A4	30:28	enough yet--Oh, they'll do well enough. Don't be particular--Here, Bill! Catch hold of this rope--Will the
A3	24:11	theirs, and the small ones choked and had to be patted on the back. However, it was over at last, and they
T8	182: 5	he went on after a pause, "it's as well to be provided for everything. That's the reason the horse has
A2	19: 2	about, trying to find her way out. "I shall be punished for it now, I suppose, by being drowned in my own
T2	128:20	the way--and in the Eighth Square we shall be Queens together, and it's all feasting and fun!" Alice got
A7	58:30	"And be quick about it," added the Hatter, "or you'll be asleep
T3	132: 1	sting or not, but she thought this wouldn't be quite a civil question to ask.
A6	50:12	less than a pig, and she felt that it would be quite absurd for her to carry it any further.
A12	93: 8	she said to herself; "I should think it would be quite as much use in the trial one way up as the other."
A9	74: 5	but on the whole she thought it would be quite as safe to stay with it as to go after that savage
T9	192:14	they came there, but she feared it would not be quite civil. However, there would be no harm, she thought,
T6	166:10	and, when you've once heard it, you'll be quite content. Who's been repeating all that hard stuff to
T1	111: 5	as far as you can see, only you know it may be quite different on beyond. Oh, Kitty, how nice it would be
T8	184:35	thoughtfully: "but don't you think it would be rather hard?"
A6	53:17	timidly, saying to herself "Suppose it should be raving mad after all! I almost wish I'd gone to see the
A6	52:26	and perhaps, as this is May, it wo'n't be raving mad--at least not so mad as it was in March." As she
A2	19:40	all over, and she felt certain it must be really offended. "We wo'n't talk about her any more, if
A8	68: 3	"Well, it must be removed," said the King very decidedly; and he called to
A9	70:28	sharp chin. However, she did not like to be rude: so she bore it as well as she could.
T6	160:16	"Don't you think you'd be safer down on the ground?" Alice went on, not with any idea
A3	21:12	refused to tell its age, there was no more to be said.
A5	42:13	"What can all that green stuff be?" said Alice. "And where have my shoulders got to? And oh,
A6	51:26	"You must be," said the Cat, "or you wouldn't have come here."
A10	82:10	"It's all about as curious as it can be," said the Gryphon.
A10	80:20	"I don't know where Dinn may be," said the Mock Turtle; "but, if you've seen them so often,
A2	15:30	"Oh! The Duchess, the Duchess! Oh! Wo'n't she be savage if I've kept her waiting!" Alice felt so desperate
T8	179: 3	her head in some alarm. There was no one to be seen, and her first thought was that she must have been
A4	27: 8	about for them, but they were nowhere to be seen--everything seemed to have changed since her swim in
T1	112:10	looking about, and noticed that what could be seen from the old room was quite common and uninteresting,
T3	135:19	looked up, there was nothing whatever to be seen on the twig, and, as she was getting quite chilly with
A1	9:28	the corner, but the Rabbit was no longer to be seen: she found herself in a long, low hall, which was lit
T8	188:12	use so large a fan / That they could not be seen. / So, having no reply to give / To what the old man
A4	27:28	messages for a rabbit! I suppose Dinah'll be sending me on messages next!" And she began fancying the
T3	131:20	post, as she's got a head on her--" "She must be sent as a message by the telegraph--" "She must draw the
T1	109: 3	would they do at the end of a year? I should be sent to prison, I suppose, when the day came. Or--let me
T8W	18:15	on my head: / And then they said 'You should be shaved, / And wear a yellow wig instead.'
A1	12: 1	"What a curious feeling!" said Alice. "I must be shutting up like a telescope!"
T4	146:25	and said, in a soothing tone, "You needn't be so angry about an old rattle."
A5	41:19	to herself "I wish the creatures wouldn't be so easily offended!"
A10	84:11	"Oh, a song, please, if the Mock Turtle would be so kind," Alice replied, so eagerly that the Gryphon said,
A9	76: 7	a day-school, too," said Alice. "You needn't be so proud as all that."
A9	70:14	wish people knew that: then they wouldn't be so stingy about it, you know--"
T6	168:31	instance--or the mouth at the top--that would be some help."
T2	125:26	Alice said at last. "There ought to be some men moving about somewhere--and so there are!" she
A6	46:18	"There might be some sense in your knocking," the Footman went on, without
T9	201:40	voice like the cooing of a pigeon. "It would be such a treat! May I?"
A4	30:38	for a good deal: this fireplace is narrow, to be sure; but I think I can kick a little!"
A2	19: 4	my own tears! That will be a queer thing, to be sure! However, everything is queer to-day."
T9	194:34	"To be sure I do," said Alice.

BE (cont.)
```
T6    163:16                                            "To be sure I was!" Humpty Dumpty said gaily as she turned it
T3    136: 1    I  do  believe  it's  got  no  name--why, to be sure it hasn't!"
T7    172:38                                  "Yes, to be sure," said the King: "and the best of the joke is, that
A8    67: 3         Alice  began  to  feel  very  uneasy: to be sure, she had not as yet had any dispute with the Queen,
T8    185: 3    there  was  the danger of falling into it, to be sure. That happened to me once--and the worst of it was,
A1    12:41    to  find  that she remained the same size. To be sure, this is what generally happens when one eats cake;
T9    204:24    at  this, but she was far too much excited to be surprised at anything now. "As for you," she repeated,
A7    55:29    say," added  the  Dormouse, which seemed to be talking in its sleep, "that 'I breathe when I sleep' is the
A5    43:14    there's  no  use denying it. I suppose you'll be telling me next that you never tasted an egg!"
T8    180: 3    out  from  her  hiding-place. "One Rule seems to be, that if one Knight hits the other, he knocks him off his
T8    180:10    Battle, that Alice had not noticed, seemed to be that they always fell on their heads; and the battle ended
T8    180: 5        off  himself--and another Rule seems to be that they hold their clubs with their arms, as if they were
T3    131: 7    altogether),  and, as  the rule seemed to be that they should all speak in turn, he went on with "She'll
A4    32:21    into  that lovely garden. I think that will be the best plan."
T3    132:12    thing nearest to her hand, which happened to be the Goat's beard. * * * * * * * * * * * * *
T5    152:26        already," said  the  Queen. "What would be the good of having it all over again?"
T8    186:13                    "Then it would have to be the next day. I suppose you wouldn't have two
T9    201:15    she  didn't  see  why  the  Red Queen should be the only one to give orders; so, as an experiment, she
A12   96: 2    'If  she should push the matter on'--that must be the Queen--'What would become of you?'--What, indeed!--'I
T12   207:29    with  your White Majesty, I wonder? That must be the reason you were so untidy in my dream--Dinah! Do you
A6    53:11    house  of the March Hare: she thought it must be the right house, because the chimneys were shaped like ears
A2    19:15    here, O Mouse!" (Alice thought this must be the right way of speaking to a mouse: she had never done
T4    140:35                The sea was wet as wet could be, / The sands were dry as dry. / You could not see a cloud,
A8    63:31    rule  at processions; "and besides, what would be the use of a procession," thought she, "if people had all
T9    196:18    in  the  middle  of  an accident! Where would be the use of it?" but she did not say this aloud, for fear of
T2    126: 8    and  said "That's easily managed. You can be the White Queen's Pawn, if you like, as Lily's too young to
T3    135:27                        "This must be the wood," she said thoughtfully to herself, "where things
T4    140:31    she  thought the sun / Had got no business to be there / After the day was done--/ 'It's very rude of him,'
A4    30:18    "What  a number of cucumber-frames there must be!" thought Alice. "I wonder what they'll do next! As for
T2    128:33    that  she was a Pawn, and that it would soon be time for her to move.
A6    46:35    It  was, no doubt: only Alice did not like to be told so. "It's really dreadful," she muttered to herself,
A1    7:13    say  to itself "Oh dear! Oh dear! I shall be too late!" (when she thought it over afterwards it occurred
A4    32:41    a  cart-horse, and expecting every moment to be trampled under its feet, ran round the thistle again: then
A6    51: 3    many  teeth,  so  she  felt that it ought to be treated with respect.
T4    144: 9    /  'You've  had  a  pleasant  run! / Shall we be trotting home again?' / But answer came there none--/ And
A12   95: 2    them  word  I  had  not gone / (We know it to be true): / If she should push the matter on, / What would
A12   95:39    over  the  verses to himself: "'We know it to be true'--that's the jury, of course--'If she should push the
T3    135:31    to  be  an ugly one. But then the fun would be, trying to find the creature that has got my old name!
A4    27:25    lest  she  should meet the real Mary Ann, and be turned out of the house before she had found the fan and
T3    137:33        herself, feeling sure that they must be TWEEDLEDUM AND TWEEDLEDEE
T3    137:21    wherever the road divided, there were sure to be two finger-posts pointing the same way, one marked "TO
A1    12:28    curious  child was very fond of pretending to be two people. "But it's no use now," thought poor Alice, "to
A1    12:29    use  now," thought poor Alice, "to pretend to be two people! Why, there's hardly enough of me left to make
T6    164:37                    "They must be very curious-looking creatures."
T5    152:31    "Only I never can remember the rule. You must be very happy, living in this wood, and being glad whenever
A4    32:31    it  might  be  hungry, in which case it would be very likely to eat her up in spite of all her coaxing.
T8    186:25                    "That wouldn't be very nice, I'm afraid--"
T4    145:17    that  Alice couldn't help saying "Hush! You'll be waking him, I'm afraid, if you make so much noise."
T3    129:14    first.  "And  what enormous flowers they must be!" was her next idea. "Something like cottages with the
A3    25:32    trial, dear sir, With no jury or judge, would be wasting our breath. 'I'll be judge, I'll be jury, said
A12   96: 6    her  one, they gave him two'--why, that must be what he did with the tarts, you know--"
A9    72: 6    said  the  Duchess; "and the moral of that is--'Be what you would seem to be'--or, if you'd like it put more
A4    27:19    to  herself  as she ran. "How surprised he'll be when he finds out who I am! But I'd better take him his fan
T3    129:21    branch  to brush them away--and what fun it'll be when they ask me how I liked my walk. I shall say 'Oh, I
T1    112: 8    me  away  from the fire. Oh, what fun it'll be, when they see me through the glass in here, and ca'n't get
A10   80: 1    really  have no notion how delightful it will be / When they take us up and throw us, with the lobsters, out
A1    7: 8    the  pleasure  of making a daisy-chain would be worth the trouble of getting up and picking the daisies,
```
BEACH (1)
```
T4    141:16    walk,  a  pleasant  talk, / Along the briny beach: / We cannot do with more than four, / To give a hand to
```
BEAK (2)
```
A5    39: 3    finished  the  goose,  with the bones and the beak--/ Pray, how did you manage to do it?"
T9    198:10    a  little  way,  and  a creature with a long beak put its head out for a moment and said "No admittance
```
BEAMISH (1)
```
T1    118:18    slain  the  Jabberwock? / Come to my arms, my beamish boy! / O frabjous day! Callooh! Callay!" / He chortled
```
BEAR (2)
```
A4    30:29    Bill!  Catch hold of this rope--Will the roof bear?--Mind that loose slate--Oh, it's coming down! Heads
A7    60:29    piece  of  rudeness was more than Alice could bear: she got up in great disgust, and walked off: the
```
BEARD (2)
```
T3    132:12    to  her hand, which happened to be the Goat's beard. * * * * * * * * * * * * *
T3    132:16                    But the beard seemed to melt away as she touched it, and she found
```
BEARING (1)
```
T1    107: 4    old  cat for the last quarter of an hour (and bearing it pretty well, considering): so you see that it
```
BEAST (3)
```
AI    3:23    wild  and  new, / In friendly chat with bird or beast--/ And half believe it true.
T4    144:25    she  feared  it  was  more likely to be a wild beast. "Are there any lions or tigers about here?" she asked
A8    64: 6    after  glaring at her for a moment like a wild beast, began screaming "Off with her head! Off with--"
```
BEASTS (2)
```
A1    10:23    who  had  got burnt, and eaten up by wild beasts, and other unpleasant things, all because they would
A11   86: 3    about  them--all  sorts  of little birds and beasts, as well as the whole pack of cards: the Knave was
```

BEAT (7)
A6   49: 5   "I speak severely to my boy, / I beat him when he sneezes; / For he can thoroughly enjoy / The
A6   48:37   "Speak roughly to your little boy, / And beat him when he sneezes: / He only does it to annoy, /
T2   125:28   in a tone of delight, and her heart began to beat quick with excitement as she went on. "It's a great huge
T7   173: 2   were fighting for the crown: / The Lion beat the Unicorn all round the town. / Some gave them white
A12   97:11   of fright and half of anger, and tried to beat them off, and found herself lying on the bank, with her
A7   56:41   cautiously replied; "but I know I have to beat time when I learn music."
T7   176:21   "Why, I beat you all round the town, you chicken!" the Lion replied
BEATING (3)
A5   42:25   large pigeon had flown into her face, and was beating her violently with its wings.
A7   56:43   for it," said the Hatter. "He wo'n't stand beating. Now, if you only kept on good terms with him, he'd do
T8   187:13   let the reins fall on its neck: then, slowly beating time with one hand, and with a faint smile lighting up
BEAUTIES (1)
T5   156: 7   of delight. "There really are--and such beauties!"
BEAUTIFUL (25)
A10   84:25   Soo--oop! / Soo--oop of the e--e--evening, / Beautiful, beautiful Soup!
A10   84:34   Soo--oop! / Soo--oop of the e--e--evening, / Beautiful, beauti--FUL SOUP!"
A10   85:11   "Soo--oop of the e--e--evening, / Beautiful, beautiful Soup!"
T6   162:13   "What a beautiful belt you've got on!" Alice suddenly remarked. (They
T3   137: 8   child!" A sudden look of alarm came into its beautiful brown eyes, and in another moment it had darted away
T6   162:17   she corrected herself on second thoughts, "a beautiful cravat, I should have said--no, a belt, I mean--I
T8   186:35   long," said the Knight, "but it's very, very beautiful. Everybody that hears me sing it--either it brings
A7   61: 5   and then--she found herself at last in the beautiful garden, among the bright flower-beds and the cool
A5   43:43   size: the next thing is, to get into that beautiful garden--how is that to be done, I wonder?" As she
T6   162:29   "It's a cravat, child, and a beautiful one, as you say. It's a present from the White King
T5   156:28   that, though she managed to pick plenty of beautiful rushes as the boat glided by, there was always a
A10   84:25   / Soo--oop of the e--e--evening, / Beautiful, beautiful Soup!
A10   84:34   / Soo--oop of the e--e--evening, / Beautiful, beauti--FUL SOUP!"
A10   85:11   "Soo--oop of the e--e--evening, / Beautiful, beautiful Soup!"
A10   84:21   beautiful Soup! / Soup of the evening, beautiful Soup! / Beau--ootiful Soo--oop! / Beau--ootiful
A10   84:30   only of beautiful Soup? / Pennyworth only of beautiful soup. / Beau--ootiful Soo--oop! / Beau--ootiful
A10   84:22   / Soup of the evening, beautiful Soup! / Beau--ootiful Soo--oop! / Beau--ootiful Soo--oop! / Soo--oop
A10   84:31   Soup? / Pennyworth only of beautiful soup. / Beau--ootiful Soo--oop! / Beau--ootiful Soo--oop! / Soo--oop
A10   84:29   give all else for two p / ennyworth only of beautiful Soup? / Pennyworth only of beautiful soup. /
A10   84:17   "Beautiful Soup, so rich and green, / Waiting in a hot tureen!
A10   84:20   would not stoop? / Soup of the evening, beautiful Soup! / Soup of the evening, beautiful Soup! /
A10   84:23   beautiful Soup! / Beau--ootiful Soo--oop! / Beau--ootiful Soo--oop! / Soo--oop of the e--e--evening, /
A10   84:32   beautiful soup. / Beau--ootiful Soo--oop! / Beau--ootiful Soo--oop! / Soo--oop of the e--e--evening, /
A10   84:26   "Beautiful Soup! Who cares for fish, / Game, or any other dish?
T1   111: 7   House! I'm sure it's got, oh! such beautiful things in it! Let's pretend there's a way of getting
BEAUTIFULLY (3)
A1   12:33   small cake, on which the words "EAT ME" were beautifully marked in currants. "Well, I'll eat it," said
A1   10:17   was a paper label, with the words "DRINK ME" beautifully printed on it in large letters.
T2   124: 3   It succeeded beautifully. She had not been walking a minute before she
BEAUTIFY (1)
A9   76:27   uglifying!" it exclaimed. "You know what to beautify is, I suppose?"
BEAUTY (1)
T5   156:35   to fade, and to lose all their scent and beauty, from the very moment that she picked them? Even real
BECAME (2)
A12   98:22   seemed to listen, the whole place around her became alive with the strange creatures of her little sister's
A6   52:16   "By-the-bye, what became of the baby?" said the Cat. "I'd nearly forgotten to
BECAUSE (47)
T6   167: 4   fishes' answer was / 'We cannot do it, Sir, because--'"
T9   196:10   said Alice: "he wanted to punish the fish, because--"
T1   110:12   with her sister only the day before--all because Alice had begun with "Let's pretend we're kings and
T7   170:31   with an H," Alice couldn't help beginning, "because he is Happy. I hate him with an H, because he is
T7   170:31   "because he is Happy. I hate him with an H, because he is Hideous. I fed him with--with--with
A6   48:39   he sneezes: / He only does it to annoy, / Because he knows it teases."
A9   75: 2   "We called him Tortoise because he taught us," said the Mock Turtle angrily. "Really
T4   144:13   "I like the Walrus best," said Alice: "because he was a little sorry for the poor oysters."
A6   45: 3   the wood--(she considered him to be a footman because he was in livery: otherwise, judging by his face only,
T9   196: 5   he would come in," the White Queen went on, "because he was looking for a hippopotamus. Now, as it happened
A10   81:42   "but it's no use going back to yesterday, because I was a different person then."
T8W   19:16   'Pig!' / And that is why they do it, dear, / Because I wear a yellow wig."
A5   35:11   myself, I'm afraid, Sir," said Alice, "because I'm not myself, you see."
A6   46:11   Footman, "and that for two reasons. First, because I'm on the same side of the door as you are: secondly,
T3   132:29   rejoice in insects at all," Alice explained, "because I'm rather afraid of them--at least the large kinds.
T9   202:10   / 'Let it lie in a dish!' / That is easy, because it already is in it.
T6   165: 6   Of course it is. It's called 'wabe' you know, because it goes a long way before it, and a long way behind it
T8   182:34   fruit-tree. Now the reason hair falls off is because it hangs down--things never fall upwards, you know.
A7   56:16   not," Alice replied very readily: "but that's because it stays the same year for such a long time together
T4   140:27   smooth and bright--/ And this was odd, because it was / The middle of the night.
T1   110:40   only the words go the wrong way: I know that, because I've held up one of our books to the glass, and then
T4   140:37   were dry as dry. / You could not see a cloud, because / No cloud was in the sky: / No birds were flying
A11   86:16   "That's the judge," she said to herself, "because of his great wig."
T4   138: 3   and Alice knew which was which in a moment, because one of them had 'DUM' embroidered on his collar, and
T8   183: 9   "Because people don't fall off quite so often, when they've had
T4   140:30   The moon was shining sulkily, / Because she thought the sun / Had got no business to be there
A9   70:26   the Duchess was very ugly; and secondly, because she was exactly the right height to rest her chin on
A11   86:22   (she was obliged to say "creatures," you see, because some of them were animals, and some were birds,) "I

BECAUSE (cont.)

A6	53:12	Hare: she thought it must be the right house, because the chimneys were shaped like ears and the roof was
A9	70:25	much like her keeping so close to her: first because the Duchess was <u>very</u> ugly; and secondly, because she
T1	110:26	didn't succeed, principally, Alice said, because the kitten wouldn't fold its arms properly. So, to
T8	182:16	Alice held the bag open very carefully, because the Knight was so <u>very</u> awkward in putting in the dish:
T9	197:17	History of England--it couldn't, you know, because there never was more than one Queen at a time. Do wake
T1	110:14	very exact, had argued that they couldn't, because there were only two of them, and Alice had been
T3	135: 3	and there she would have to leave off, because there wouldn't be any name for her to call, and of
T1	112: 6	old room," thought Alice: "warmer, in fact, because there'll be no one here to scold me away from the fire
T6	160:13	"Why, because there's nobody with me!" cried Humpty Dumpty. "Did you
A9	77:16	called lessons," the Gryphon remarked: "because they lessen from day to day."
T3	134: 7	insects are so fond of flying into candles--because they want to turn into Snap-dragon-flies!"
A1	10:23	wild beasts, and other unpleasant things, all because they <u>would</u> not remember the simple rules their friends
T4	144:11	<u>came there none</u>--/ And <u>this was scarcely odd</u>, <u>because</u> / They'd <u>eaten every one</u>."
T3	135:29	I go in? I shouldn't like to lose it at all--because they'd have to give me another, and it would be almost
A6	46:12	same side of the door as you are: secondly, because they're making such a noise inside, no one could
T7	170:12	"I couldn't send all the horses, you know, because two of them are wanted in the game. And I haven't sent
T1	110: 5	smile, my dear. I'm asking it seriously. Because, when we were playing just now, you watched just as if
T4	142: 5	were <u>clean and neat</u>--/ And <u>this was odd</u>, <u>because</u>, <u>you know</u>, / They <u>hadn't any feet</u>.
T8W	21: 1	"Well, that's because your jaws are too short," the Wasp went on: "but the

BECKONED (1)

| T7 | 175:36 | Certainly--certainly!" the King muttered, and beckoned to Haigha. "Open the bag!" he whispered. "Quick! Not |

BECKONING (1)

| T9 | 204:11 | up the table towards Alice's chair, and beckoning to her impatiently to get out of its way. |

BECOME (7)

A11	87: 9	Lizard) could not make out at all what had become of it; so, after hunting all about for it, he was
A4	28:22	I can do no more, whatever happens. What <u>will</u> become of me?"
A8	67: 5	minute, "and then," thought she, "what would become of me? They're dreadfully fond of beheading people here
T3	135:28	"where things have no names. I wonder what'll become of <u>my</u> name when I go in? I shouldn't like to lose it at
A12	95: 4	she <u>should push the matter on</u>, / What <u>would become of you</u>?
A12	96: 3	<u>on</u>"--that must be the Queen--'What <u>would become of you</u>?'--What, indeed!--'<u>I gave her one</u>, <u>they gave him</u>
A5	37: 2	the <u>young man said</u>, / "And <u>your hair has become very white</u>; / And <u>yet you incessantly stand on your</u>

BECOMING (1)

| A11 | 86:20 | at all comfortable, and it was certainly not becoming. |

BED (4) [See also FLOWERBED, OYSTER-BED]

T6	167:18	to <u>me and said</u> / 'The <u>little fishes are in</u> bed.'
TI	103:21	<u>tidings laden</u>, / <u>Shall summon to unwelcome</u> bed / A <u>melancholy maiden</u>! / <u>We are but older children, dear</u>,
T9	203:14	up to the ceiling, looking something like a bed of rushes with fireworks at the top. As to the bottles,
A3	26:35	my dears! It's high time you were all in bed!" On various pretexts they all moved off, and Alice was

BEDS (3) [See also FLOWER-BEDS]

A1	10: 4	that dark hall, and wander about among those beds of bright flowers and those cool fountains, but she could
T5	156: 3	the boat glided gently on, sometimes among beds of weeds (which made the oars stick fast in the water,
T2	122:28	gardens," the Tiger-lily said, "they make the beds too soft--so that the flowers are always asleep."

BEDTIME (1)

| TI | 103:24 | <u>older children, dear</u>, / Who <u>fret to find our</u> bedtime <u>near</u>. |

BEE (5)

T8W	17:14	"What, you're a Bee, are you?" the Wasp said, looking at her with more
A5	36:34	I've tried to say 'How <u>doth the little busy bee</u>,' but it all came different!" Alice replied in a very
T8	181:35	tone, "one of the best kind. But not a single bee has come near it yet. And the other thing is a mouse-trap.
T3	129:12	However, this was anything but a regular bee: in fact, it was an elephant--as Alice soon found out,
T3	129:10	into them, "just as if it was a regular bee," thought Alice.

BE-E-EHH (1)

| T5 | 153:30 | on. "Much be-etter! Be-etter! Be-e-e-etter! Be-e-ehh!" The last word ended in a long bleat, so like a |

BEE-HIVE (2)

T8	181:32	"But you've got a bee-hive--or something like one--fastened to the saddle," said
T8	181:34	"Yes, it's a very good bee-hive," the Knight said in a discontented tone, "one of the

BEEN (83)

A12	98:12	well she might, what a wonderful dream it had been.
A9	77:19	next remark. "Then the eleventh day must have been a holiday?"
T4	148:12	it so much," said Tweedledum, "if it hadn't been a new one."
T12	207:25	little kiss, "just in honour of its having been a Red Queen."
A8	63: 7	is, you see, Miss, this here ought to have been a <u>red</u> rose-tree, and we put a white one in by mistake;
T5	149:20	done at all!" groaned the poor Queen. "I've been a-dressing myself for the last two hours."
T5	149:21	It would have been all the better, as it seemed to Alice, if she had got
A1	9:31	but they were all locked; and when Alice had been all the way down one side and up the other, trying every
T12	207: 4	me out of oh! such a nice dream! And you've been along with me, Kitty--all through the Looking-glass world
A5	42:41	"I'm very sorry you've been annoyed," said Alice, who was beginning to see its
A8	63:10	comes, to--" At this moment, Five, who had been anxiously looking across the garden, called out "The
A5	43:37	It was so long since she had been anything near the right size, that it felt quite strange
T9	199:12	"To answer the door?" he said. "What's it been asking of?" He was so hoarse that Alice could scarcely
A12	95:13	My <u>notion was that you had</u> been / (Before <u>she had this fit</u>) / An <u>obstacle that came</u>
T5	151:21	done them," the Queen said, "that would have been better still; better, and better, and better!" Her voice
A6	46:16	a great crash, as if a dish or kettle had been broken to pieces.
A2	16: 2	same age as herself, to see if she could have been changed for any of them.
A2	17: 3	<u>that's</u> all wrong, I'm certain! I must have been changed for Mabel! I'll try and say '<u>How doth the little</u>
A5	35: 8	got up this morning, but I think I must have been changed several times since then."
T4	140: 3	begin a conversation with people she had just been dancing with. "It would never do to say 'How d'ye do?'
T2	127:18	if you ran very fast for a long time as we've been doing."
A8	65: 5	to the rose-tree, she went on "What <u>have</u> you been doing here?"
T1	108:23	again, "when I saw all the mischief you had been doing, I was very nearly opening the window, and putting

BEEN (cont.)
```
  T7    174: 7  he said in a choking voice: "each of them has been down about eighty-seven times."
  T8    179: 4  and her first thought was that she must have been dreaming about the Lion and the Unicorn and those queer
  T12   208: 8  this morning! You see, Kitty, it must have been either me or the Red King. He was part of my dream, of
  A8     65: 8  "I see!" said the Queen, who had meanwhile been examining the roses. "Off with their heads!" and the
  T1    107:12           But the black kitten had been finished with earlier in the afternoon, and so, while
  A12    93:33           At this moment the King, who had been for some time busily writing in his note-book, called out
  T1    110: 8  and really I might have won, if it hadn't been for that nasty Knight, that came wriggling down among my
  A12    93:11  being upset, and their slates and pencils had been found and handed back to them, they set to work very
  T1    107:15  to herself and half asleep, the kitten had been having a grand game of romps with the ball of worsted
  T1    107: 3  fault entirely. For the white kitten had been having its face washed by the old cat for the last
  T7    172:22  do that," said the King, "or else he'd have been here first. However, now you've got your breath, you may
  T1    114: 2  said the King, rubbing his nose, which had been hurt by the fall. He had a right to be a little annoyed
  A7     59: 4  know," Alice gently remarked. "They'd have been ill."
  A11    86:13            Alice had never been in a court of justice before, but she had read about them
  T2    122:22  into a better temper by a compliment. "I've been in many gardens before, but none of the flowers could
  T9    201: 7  "it isn't etiquette to cut any one you've been introduced to. Remove the joint!" And the waiters carried
  T6    164:19  were invented--and a good many that haven't been invented just yet."
  A6     52: 5  it very much," said Alice, "but I haven't been invited yet."
  A6     52:14  was still looking at the place where it had been, it suddenly appeared again.
  A10    78:37  his voice; and the two creatures, who had been jumping about like mad things all this time, sat down
  T3    133: 9   and made up her mind that it must have been just repainted, it looked so bright and sticky; and then
  T9    199:17  "Nothing!" Alice said impatiently. "I've been knocking at it!"
  T6    160:31   breaking into a sudden passion. "You've been listening at doors--and behind trees--and down chimneys--
  A7     55: 6  hair wants cutting," said the Hatter. He had been looking at Alice for some time with great curiosity, and
  A7     56:11            Alice had been looking over his shoulder with some curiosity. "What a
  T8W    14:15  on, as she picked up a newspaper which had been lying at his feet.
  A3     22: 5  by the English, who wanted leaders, and had been of late much accustomed to usurpation and conquest. Edwin
  T2    123:30  Alice first found her in the ashes, she had been only three inches high--and here she was, half a head
  T8    187:19  the whole scene back again, as if it had been only yesterday--the mild blue eyes and kindly smile of
  A12    94: 5  up in a great hurry: "this paper has just been picked up."
  T1    108:38  "That's three faults, Kitty, and you've not been punished for any of them yet. You know I'm saving up all
  A12    98: 8  strange Adventures of hers that you have just been reading about; when she had finished, her sister kissed
  T12   207:37            "By the way, Kitty, if only you'd been really with me in my dream, there was one thing you would
  T1    110:15  there were only two of them, and Alice had been reduced at last to say "Well, you can be one of them,
  T6    166:10  once heard it, you'll be quite content. Who's been repeating all that hard stuff to you?"
  T1    107:16  Alice had been trying to wind up, and had been rolling it up and down till it had all come undone again;
  A3     23:13  the race was over. However, when they had been running half an hour or so, and were quite dry again, the
  T4    139:37  when I began it, but somehow I felt as if I'd been singing it a long long time!"
  T2    124: 5  Queen, and full in sight of the hill she had been so long aiming at.
  A5     41:11            Alice said nothing: she had never been so much contradicted in all her life before, and she felt
  T2    127:29  was very dry: and she thought she had never been so nearly choked in all her life.
  T3    132:18  the Gnat (for that was the insect she had been talking to) was balancing itself on a twig just over her
  T3    132:22  couldn't feel nervous with it, after they had been talking together so long.
  A12    94: 9            "It must have been that," said the King, "unless it was written to nobody,
  T6    168: 3  thought, with a shudder, "I wouldn't have been the messenger for anything!"
  T12   207:21  ashamed of itself, so I think it must have been the Red Queen.")
  A4     33:10  teaching it tricks very much, if--if I'd only been the right size to do it! Oh dear! I'd nearly forgotten
  A10    81:27            "If I'd been the whiting," said Alice, whose thoughts were still
  A9     76: 7            "I've been to a day-school, too," said Alice. "You needn't be so
  A12    94:39            "They told me you had been to her, / And mentioned me to him: / She gave me a good
  A2     18:20  by railway," she said to herself. (Alice had been to the seaside once in her life, and had come to the
  T1    107:16  of romps with the ball of worsted Alice had been trying to wind up, and had been rolling it up and down
  T2    127:13  in great surprise. "Why, I do believe we've been under this tree the whole time! Everything's just as it
  T1    108:12  Alice began. "You'd have guessed if you'd been up in the window with me--only Dinah was making you tidy,
  T2    124: 3    It succeeded beautifully. She had not been walking a minute before she found herself face to face
  A5     42:23  but the tops of the trees under which she had been wandering, when a sharp hiss made her draw back in a
  A9     72: 7  to others that what you were or might have been was not otherwise than what you had been would have
  T9    201:19  help feeling a little shy with it, as she had been with the mutton; however, she conquered her shyness by a
  A9     72: 9  have been was not otherwise than what you had been would have appeared to them to be otherwise.'"
  T6    159: 7            It might have been written a hundred times, easily, on that enormous face.
```
BEES (5)
```
  T3    129: 8  there? They ca'n't be bees--nobody ever saw bees a mile off, you know--" and for some time she stood
  T8    181:37  I suppose the mice keep the bees out--or the bees keep the mice out, I don't know which."
  T8    181:30            "In hopes some bees may make a nest in it--then I should get the honey."
  T3    129: 7   making honey down there? They ca'n't be bees--nobody ever saw bees a mile off, you know--" and for
  T8    181:37  is a mouse-trap. I suppose the mice keep the bees out--or the bees keep the mice out, I don't know which."
```
BEETLE (2)
```
  T3    131:10  Alice couldn't see who was sitting beyond the Beetle, but a hoarse voice spoke next. "Change engines--" it
  T3    131: 6            There was a Beetle sitting next the Goat (it was a very queer
```
BEFORE (72)
```
  A10    81: 9    I never knew so much about a whiting before."
  A12    92: 7  gold-fish she had accidentally upset the week before.
  A12    95: 8  from him to you, / Though they were mine before.
  T2    122:35  that Alice quite jumped; for it hadn't spoken before.
  T3    134: 1  "And what does it live on?" Alice asked, as before.
  T7    175:29  fabulous monsters, too? I never saw one alive before!"
  T9    200:21    as she had never had to carve a joint before.
  T7    177:22            But before Alice could answer him, the drums began.
  T7    176: 7  a fabulous monster!" the Unicorn cried out, before Alice could reply.
```

BEFORE (cont.)

A9	76: 3	"Hold your tongue!" added the Gryphon,	before Alice could speak again. The Mock Turtle went on.
T9	200:20	joint!" And the waiters set a leg of mutton	before Alice, who looked at it rather anxiously, as she had
T1	110:12	a long argument with her sister only the day	before--all because Alice had begun with "Let's pretend we're
T9	198: 1	She was standing	before an arched doorway, over which were the words "QUEEN
A1	9:40	came upon a low curtain she had not noticed	before, and behind it was a little door about fifteen inches
A5	38: 1	You are old," said the youth, "as I mentioned	before, / And have grown most uncommonly fat; / Yet you turned
A8	68:39	that he had never had to do such a thing	before, and he wasn't going to begin at his time of life.
A5	41:12	been so much contradicted in all her life	before, and she felt that she was losing her temper.
A2	18:14	golden key was lying on the glass table as	before, "and things are worse than ever," thought the poor
A7	60: 1	and Alice was a good deal worse off than	before, as the March Hare had just upset the milk-jug into his
T5	153:15	believed as many as six impossible things	before breakfast. There goes the shawl again!"
T5	156:18	get hold of the rushes a good long way down	before breaking them off--and for a while Alice forgot all
T3	137:26	same house! I wonder I never thought of that	before--But I ca'n't stay there long. I'll just call and say
T2	122:23	by a compliment. "I've been in many gardens	before, but none of the flowers could talk."
A11	86:13	Alice had never been in a court of justice	before, but she had read about them in books, and she was
A2	19:16	to a mouse: she had never done such a thing	before, but she remembered having seen, in her brother's Latin
A7	57:11	he replied. "We quarreled last March--just	before he went mad, you know--" (pointing his teaspoon at the
A1	9:22	she looked up, but it was all dark overhead:	before her was another long passage, and the White Rabbit was
T1	108:34	just as I had put down the saucer of milk	before her! What, you were thirsty, were you? How do you know
T4	144: 6	size, / Holding his pocket-handkerchief /	Before his streaming eyes.
T8	185: 4	happened to me once--and the worst of it was,	before I could get out again, the other White Knight came and
A9	74:14	after it: "I never was so ordered about	before, in all my life, never!"
T6	165: 7	'wabe' you know, because it goes a long way	before it, and a long way behind it--"
T3	137:29	If I could only get to the Eighth Square	before it gets dark!" So she wandered on, talking to herself
A9	74:21	answered, very nearly in the same words as	before, "It's all his fancy, that: he hasn't got no sorrow,
A7	58:31	added the Hatter, "or you'll be asleep again	before it's done."
T1	118:32	have to go back through the Looking-glass,	before I've seen what the rest of the house is like! Let's
A2	18:16	poor child, "for I never was so small as this	before, never! And I declare it's too bad, that it is!"
T8	186:15	not the next day," the Knight repeated as	before: "not the next day. In fact," he went on, holding his
A1	10:16	bottle on it ("which certainly was not here	before," said Alice), and tied round the neck of the bottle
A10	82:32	"Well, I never heard it	before," said the Mock Turtle; "but it sounds uncommon
A1	8: 1	it flashed across her mind that she had never	before seen a rabbit with either a waistcoat-pocket, or a
A6	53:10	She had not gone much farther	before she came in sight of the house of the March Hare: she
T2	120:12	more quickly than usual, she ran against it	before she could stop herself.
T9	204: 7	her for a moment over the edge of the tureen,	before she disappeared into the soup.
T7	178: 9	looks at being interrupted in their feast,	before she dropped to her knees, and put her hands over her
T2	124: 4	She had not been walking a minute	before she found herself face to face with the Red Queen, and
A1	8: 9	not a moment to think about stopping herself	before she found herself falling down what seemed to be a very
A10	81:19	looked down at them, and considered a little	before she gave her answer. "They're done with blacking, I
A11	91: 6	her hand, and Alice guessed who it was, even	before she got into the court, by the way the people near the
A4	28: 9	and much sooner than she had expected:	before she had drunk half the bottle, she found her head
A4	27:25	real Mary Ann, and be turned out of the house	before she had found the fan and gloves.
A12	95:14	My notion was that you had been /	(Before she had this fit) / An obstacle that came between / Him
A12	96:16	can be clearer than that. Then again--'	before she had this fit'--you never had fits, my dear, I think
A9	77:18	to Alice, and she thought it over a little	before she made her next remark. "Then the eleventh day must
T1	115: 1	that she mightn't take his breath away; but,	before she put him on the table, she thought she might as well
T2	122:31	pleased to know it. "I never thought of that	before!" she said.
A6	52:24	Hare was said to live. "I've seen hatters	before," she said to herself: "the March Hare will be much the
A4	30: 2	you?" And then a voice she had never heard	before, "Sure then I'm here! Digging for apples, yer honour!"
A11	88: 3	interrupted. "There's a great deal to come	before that!"
T9	197:15	in her lap. "I don't think it ever happened	before, that any one had to take care of two Queens asleep at
T5	156:41	They hadn't gone much farther	before the blade of one of the oars got fast in the water and
A11	86:32	in reply, "for fear they should forget them	before the end of the trial."
T1	110:24	the Red Queen off the table, and set it up	before the kitten as a model for it to imitate: however, the
A11	91: 2	the officers; but the Hatter was out of sight	before the officer could get to the door.
A11	86:30	"They ca'n't have anything to put down yet,	before the trial's begun."
A11	87: 3	him. "A nice muddle their slates'll be in,	before the trial's over!" thought Alice.
A11	86: 4	whole pack of cards: the Knave was standing	before them, in chains, with a soldier on each side to guard
T5	150:18	Alice remarked. "I ca'n't remember things	before they happen."
A9	74:16	They had not gone far	before they saw the Mock Turtle in the distance, sitting sad
T4	143: 2	'But wait a bit,' the Oysters cried, /	'Before we have our chat; / For some of us are out of breath, /
T8W	14:13	he got settled down again he only said, as	before, "Worrity, worrity! Can't you leave a body alone?"
T9	192:36	said to Alice. "Always speak the truth--think	before you speak--and write it down afterwards."

BEG (14)

AI	3: 9	an hour, / Beneath such dreamy weather, / To	beg a tale of breath too weak / To stir the tiniest feather! /
A2	20: 7	when you throw them, and it'll sit up and	beg for its dinner, and all sorts of things--I ca'n't remember
A11	88: 7	a piece of bread-and-butter in the other. "I	beg pardon, your Majesty," he began, "for bringing these in;
T7	171: 3	"It isn't respectable to	beg," said the King.
T9	195: 5	her with bunches of leaves, till she had to	beg them to leave off, it blew her hair about so.
A3	24: 2	solemnly presented the thimble, saying "We	beg your acceptance of this elegant thimble"; and, when it had
T6	162:36		"I beg your pardon?" Alice said with a puzzled air.
A2	19:39	such a capital one for catching mice--oh, I	beg your pardon!" cried Alice again, for this time the Mouse
A2	19:27	seemed to quiver all over with fright. "Oh, I	beg your pardon!" cried Alice hastily, afraid that she had
T7	171: 2		"I beg your pardon?" said Alice.
A3	26: 3		"I beg your pardon," said Alice very humbly: "you had got to the
A3	22: 8		"I beg your pardon!" said the Mouse, frowning, but very politely.
T6	162:17	I should have said--no, a belt, I mean--I	beg your pardon!" she added in dismay, for Humpty Dumpty
A12	92: 8		"Oh, I beg your pardon!" she exclaimed in a tone of great dismay, and

BEGAN (110)
```
A5     36:37                    Alice folded her hands, and began:--
A8     65:44    settled down in a minute or two, and the game began.
A11    90: 9    one knee. "I'm a poor man, your Majesty," he began.
T6    163:14    carefully. "That seems to be done right--" he began.
T7    177:22    But before Alice could answer him, the drums began.
T8    187:15    as if he enjoyed the music of his song, he began.
T9    197: 3    it myself, then," said the Red Queen, and she began:--
T9    202: 2    delight, and stroked Alice's cheek. Then she began:
T9    201:29    of poetry repeated to me to-day," Alice began, a little frightened at finding that, the moment she
A4     32:42    ran round the thistle again: then the puppy began a series of short charges at the stick, running a very
T4    140:22                    Tweedledee smiled gently, and began again:
T8W    18:12    He was silent for a few moments, and then began again--
T9    194:39                    Here the Red Queen began again. "Can you answer useful questions?" she said. "How
A1      8:39                    Presently she began again. "I wonder if I shall fall right through the
T9    196:11                    Here the White Queen began again. "It was such a thunderstorm, you ca'n't think!"
A2     19:24    how long ago anything had happened.) So she began again: "Ou est ma chatte?" which was the first sentence
T3    136: 2    for a minute, thinking: then she suddenly began again. "Then it really has happened, after all! And now,
T6    163:38    say anything; so after a minute Humpty Dumpty began again. "They've a temper, some of them--particularly
A12    96:23    he found it made no mark; but he now hastily began again, using the ink, that was trickling down his face,
A8     65:37    "She boxed the Queen's ears--" the Rabbit began. Alice gave a little scream of laughter. "Oh, hush!" the
T2    126:13    it over afterwards, how it was that they began: all she remembers is, that they were running hand in
A8     67:19    and then Alice put down her flamingo, and began an account of the game, feeling very glad she had some
T9    203: 4    the air. "I rise to return thanks--" Alice began: and she really did rise as she spoke, several inches;
T9    199: 3    whose business it is to answer the door?" she began angrily.
T2    121:13    Alice didn't like being criticized, so she began asking questions. "Aren't you sometimes frightened at
T8    179:36    "I always do," said the Red Knight, and they began banging away at each other with such fury that Alice got
A8     65: 1    the three gardeners instantly jumped up, and began bowing to the King, the Queen, the royal children, and
A6     45:11                    The Fish-Footman began by producing from under his arm a great letter, nearly
A7     61: 1    better this time," she said to herself, and began by taking the little golden key, and unlocking the door
T3    133: 1    "Well, there's the Horse-fly," Alice began, counting off the names on her fingers.
T7    175:28    help her lips curling up into a smile as she began: "Do you know, I always thought Unicorns were fabulous
A12    98:15    all her wonderful Adventures, till she too began dreaming after a fashion, and this was her dream:--
T9    202:22    at the top of her voice, and all the guests began drinking it directly, and very queerly they managed it:
T9    202:27    scrambled into the dish of roast mutton, and began eagerly lapping up the gravy, "just like pigs in a
A8     69:10                    The Cat's head began fading away the moment he was gone, and, by the time he
A4     27:29    be sending me on messages next!" And she began fancying the sort of thing that would happen: "'Miss
A11    88: 8    the other. "I beg pardon, your Majesty," he began, "for bringing these in; but I hadn't quite finished my
A4     27: 7    white kid-gloves, and she very good-naturedly began hunting about for them, but they were nowhere to be seen
A7     58:33    were three little sisters," the Dormouse began in a great hurry; "and their names were Elsie, Lacie,
A11    86:33                    "Stupid things!" Alice began in a loud indignant voice; but she stopped herself
T8    183:17    The great art of riding," the Knight suddenly began in a loud voice, waving his right arm as he spoke, "is
A2     15:32    one: so, when the Rabbit came near her, she began, in a low, timid voice, "If you please, Sir--" The
A8     63: 5    Seven said nothing, but looked at Two. Two began, in a low voice, "Why, the fact is, you see, Miss, this
A9     72:34    "A fine day, your Majesty!" the Duchess began in a low, weak voice.
A11    89:11    "I'm a poor man, your Majesty," the Hatter began, in a trembling voice, "and I hadn't begun my tea--not
A10    84:15                    The Mock Turtle sighed deeply, and began, in a voice choked with sobs, to sing this:--
A8     67:23    I don't think they play at all fairly," Alice began, in rather a complaining tone, "and they all quarrel so
T4    140:17                    Tweedledee began instantly:
T4    139:37    round the mulberry bush.' I don't know when I began it, but somehow I felt as if I'd been singing it a long
T8W    14:20    and spread out the paper on her knees, and began. "Latest News. The Exploring Party have made another
T1    112:10                    Then she began looking about, and noticed that what could be seen from
A11    86:11    there seemed to be no chance of this; so she began looking at everything about her to pass away the time.
T9    192:17    was over. "Please, would you tell me--" she began, looking timidly at the Red Queen.
T2    127:33    out of her pocket, marked in inches, and began measuring the ground, and sticking little pegs in here
A4     31:37    the roof off." After a minute or two they began moving about again, and Alice heard the Rabbit say "A
A5     44: 4    frighten them out of their wits!" So she began nibbling at the right-hand bit again, and did not
A6     48:33    never could abide figures!" And with that she began nursing her child again, singing a sort of lullaby to it
A2     19:13    any rate, there's no harm in trying." So she began: "O Mouse, do you know the way out of this pool? I am
T12   208:12    paw can wait!" But the provoking kitten only began on the other paw, and pretended it hadn't heard the
T8    179:20    soon as he was comfortably in the saddle, he began once more "You're my--" but here another voice broke in
A4     27:34    that they'd let Dinah stop in the house if it began ordering people about like that!"
A12    92: 9    she exclaimed in a tone of great dismay, and began picking them up again as quickly as she could, for the
T5    149:11    at all, she must manage it herself. So she began rather timidly: "Am I addressing the White Queen?"
A6     51: 4                    "Cheshire-Puss," she began, rather timidly, as she did not at all know whether it
A8     65:42    the Queen in a voice of thunder, and people began running about in all directions, tumbling up against
A3     23:11    was no "One, two, three, and away!", but they began running when they liked, and left off when they liked,
T1    113:22    precious Lily! My imperial kitten!" and she began scrambling wildly up the side of the fender.
A8     64: 6    at her for a moment like a wild beast, began screaming "Off with her head! Off with--"
T5    152: 2    a mistake somewhere--," when the Queen began screaming, so loud that she had to leave the sentence
T2    122: 8    that?" cried another Daisy. And here they all began shouting together, till the air seemed quite full of
A4     32:11    the cakes, and was delighted to find that she began shrinking directly. As soon as she was small enough to
A7     58: 1                    Here the Dormouse shook itself, and began singing in its sleep "Twinkle, twinkle, twinkle, twinkle
T2    128: 5    as she returned to the tree, and then began slowly walking down the row.
A5     41:22    and it put the hookah into its mouth, and began smoking again.
A11    91: 7    court, by the way the people near the door began sneezing all at once.
A10    79: 9                    So they began solemnly dancing round and round Alice, every now and
T1    113:15                    Here something began squeaking on the table behind Alice, and made her turn
A11    88:26    Here the Queen put on her spectacles, and began staring hard at the Hatter, who turned pale and fidgeted
A1      9: 6    There was nothing else to do, so Alice soon began talking again. "Dinah'll miss me very much to-night, I
```

```
BEGAN (cont.)
  A5    43:39   but  she got used to it in a few minutes, and began talking to herself, as usual, "Come, there's half my
  A10   82: 1                           So Alice began telling them her adventures from the time when she first
  A2    16: 1   am  I?' Ah, that's the great puzzle!" And she began thinking over all the children she knew that were of the
  A6    50:17   rather  a handsome pig,  I think." And she began thinking over other children she knew, who might do very
  T5   156:33   hands, she scrambled back into her place, and began to arrange her new-found treasures.
  T2   125:28   she added in a tone of delight, and her heart began to beat quick with excitement as she went on. "It's a
  T4   145:21               "I am real!" said Alice, and began to cry.
  A2    15:18   was more hopeless than ever: she sat down and began to cry again.
  A3    26:40   ever  see  you any more!" And here poor Alice began to cry again, for she felt very lonely and low-spirited.
  A8    67: 3                              Alice began to feel very uneasy: to be sure, she had not as yet had
  A1     9:11   do cats eat bats, I wonder?" And here Alice began to get rather sleepy, and went on saying to herself, in
  T2   128:32   way of guessing, but she was gone, and Alice began to remember that she was a Pawn, and that it would soon
  A10   82:19   at  school at once." However, she got up, and began to repeat it, but her head was so full of the
  A2    17: 5   on her lap as if she were saying lessons, and began to repeat it, but her voice sounded hoarse and strange,
  T2   126:11   "Just  at this moment, somehow or other, they began to run.
  A10   78:10   never  even introduced to a lobster--" (Alice began to say "I once tasted--" but checked herself hastily,
  A9    72:31   moral", and the arm that was linked into hers began to tremble. Alice looked up, and there stood the Queen
  T6   162:19   Dumpty looked thoroughly offended, and she began to wish she hadn't chosen that subject. "If only I knew
  A7    60: 3   not wish to offend the Dormouse again, so she began very cautiously: "But I don't understand. Where did they
  T4   144:21   This  was a puzzler. After a pause, Alice began, "Well! They were both very unpleasant characters--"
  T3   132: 2   "What,  then  you don't--" the little voice began, when it was drowned by a shrill scream from the engine,
  A6    46:42   "Anything  you  like," said the Footman, and began whistling.
  T1   108: 4   the  kitten  and  the  worsted  with her, and began winding up the ball again. But she didn't get on very
  T8W   20: 9                        Alice began with a little scream of laughter, which she turned into
  T8   186:23                    "It began with blotting-paper," the Knight answered with a groan.
  A11   89:16                    "It began with the tea," the Hatter replied.
  A3    26:31   the birds hurried off at once: one old Magpie began wrapping itself up very carefully, remarking "I really
  T1   115:30   memorandum-book  out  of  his pocket,  and began writing. A sudden thought struck her, and she took hold
  T1   115:32   which  came  some  way over his shoulder, and began writing for him.
  T1   108:11   "Do you know what to-morrow is, Kitty?" Alice began. "You'd have guessed if you'd been up in the window with
  T9   200:18               At last the Red Queen began. "You've missed the soup and fish," she said. "Put on
BEGGED (1)
  A3    24:13   last,  and they sat down again in a ring, and begged the Mouse to tell them something more.
BEGIN (32)
  A11   88:11   have  finished," said the King. "When did you begin?"
  T4   140: 7   awkward  pause,  as Alice didn't know how to begin a conversation with people she had just been dancing
  A8    66:13   she  had  got its head down, and was going to begin again, it was very provoking to find that the hedgehog
  T6   160:12   here  all  alone?" said Alice, not wishing to begin an argument.
  T7   174:18   said to Hatta: "go and order the drums to begin." And Hatta went bounding away like a grasshopper.
  T6   162: 1                 Alice didn't want to begin another argument, so she said nothing.
  A8    68:39   such  a  thing before, and he wasn't going to begin at his time of life.
  A12   94:35                        "Begin at the beginning," the King said, very gravely, "and go
  T6   164:27   o'clock  in  the afternoon--the time when you begin broiling things for dinner."
  A9    74:31   see  how  he can ever finish, if he doesn't begin." But she waited patiently.
  A1    10: 9   I  think I could,  if  I only knew how to begin." For, you see, so many out-of-the-way things had
  A10   82:13   her try and repeat something now. Tell her to begin." He looked at the Gryphon as if he thought it had some
  T5   149:17   Majesty  will  only  tell  me the right way to begin, I'll do it as well as I can."
  AI     3:14   Imperious Prima flashes forth / Her edict "to begin it": / In gentler tones Secunda hopes / "There will be
  T9   192:29   the  proper  examination.  And the sooner we begin it, the better."
  T1   113:17   to  see  one of the White Pawns roll over and begin kicking: she watched it with great curiosity to see what
  A7    56:45   nine  o'clock  in  the  morning, just time to begin lessons: you'd only have to whisper a hint to Time, and
  A12   94:33   Rabbit  put on his spectacles. "Where shall I begin, please your Majesty?" he asked.
  T4   148:16   umbrella--it's  quite  as sharp. Only we must begin quick. It's getting as dark as it can."
  T7   177:18   knife  in her hand, very much puzzled how to begin. "The Monster has given the Lion twice as much as me!"
  T5   150: 5   being  punished:  and  the trial doesn't even begin till next Wednesday: and of course the crime comes last
  T4   143:12   Now,  if you're ready, Oysters dear, / We can begin to feed.'
  T2   122:19   are  worst  of all. When one speaks, they all begin together, and it's enough to make one wither to hear the
  A4    31:40   heard the Rabbit say "A barrowful will do, to begin with."
  A5    35:15   "for  I ca'n't understand it myself, to begin with; and being so many different sizes in a day is very
  T5   153: 3   at  once, you know. Let's consider your age to begin with--how old are you?"
  T6   164:25                "That's enough to begin with," Humpty Dumpty interrupted: "there are plenty of
  A6    51:29                        "To begin with," said the Cat, "a dog's not mad. You grant that?"
  A9    76:21   "Reeling  and  Writhing,  of  course, to begin with," the Mock Turtle replied; "and then the different
  T2   126: 9   to  play: and you're in the Second Square to begin with: when you get to the Eighth Square you'll be a
  T2   121: 7                "It isn't manners for us to begin, you know," said the Rose, "and I really was wondering
  T9   192:22   and the other person always waited for you to begin, you see nobody would ever say anything, so that--"
BEGINNING (30)
  T6   166:18   Alice  hastily  said, hoping to keep him from beginning.
  T9   204: 1   she  could  in the dreadful confusion that was beginning.
  A7    58:16   "But  what  happens  when  you  come to the beginning again?" Alice ventured to ask.
  T2   122:14   stooping  down  to the daisies, who were just beginning again, she whispered "If you don't hold your tongues
  T1   107: 8   she  rubbed its face all over, the wrong way, beginning at the nose: and just now, as I said, she was hard
  T7   170:30   love  my  love with an H," Alice couldn't help beginning, "because he is Happy. I hate him with an H, because
  T9   194: 7   "I  suppose--" Alice was beginning, but the Red Queen answered for her.
  T9   192:38   "I'm  sure  I  didn't mean--" Alice was beginning, but the Red Queen interrupted her impatiently.
  A10   81:40   "I  could tell you my adventures--beginning from this morning," said Alice a little timidly;
  A5    36:10   Which  brought  them  back  again  to the beginning of the conversation. Alice felt a little irritated
  T5   149:16   never  do  to  have  an  argument at the very beginning of their conversation, so she smiled and said "If
  A12   94:35                        "Begin at the beginning," the King said, very gravely, "and go on till you
```

BEGINNING (cont.)
```
 A5    41: 4                        "It is wrong from beginning to end," said the Caterpillar, decidedly; and there
 T2   123:16    your  fault," the Rose added kindly. "You're beginning to fade, you know--and then one ca'n't help one's
 A9    72:25    to  think," said Alice sharply, for she was beginning to feel a little worried.
 A1     7: 1                           Alice was beginning to get very tired of sitting by her sister on the
 A11   88:36    deal until she made out what it was: she was beginning to grow larger again, and she thought at first she
 T1   111:13    had got there. And certainly the glass was beginning to melt away, just like a bright silvery mist.
 T3   129:18    she went on, checking herself just as she was beginning to run down the hill, and trying to find some excuse
 T5   152: 1                        Alice was just beginning to say "There's a mistake somewhere--," when the
 T5   155:17    on  land--and  not  with  needles--" Alice was beginning to say, when suddenly the needles turned into oars
 A5    42:41    you've been annoyed," said Alice, who was beginning to see its meaning.
 T4   146:20          "I knew it was!" cried Tweedledum, beginning to stamp about wildly and tear his hair. "It's
 A6    50: 8                        Alice was just beginning to think to herself, "Now, what am I to do with this
 A12   93:22    said, turning to the jury. They were just beginning to write this down on their slates, when the White
 A7    59:24            "There's no such thing!" Alice was beginning very angrily, but the Hatter and the March Hare went
 A10   85: 2    to repeat it, when a cry of "The trial's beginning!" was heard in the distance.
 T7   170:36    was still hesitating for the name of a town beginning with H. "The other Messenger's called Hatta. I must
 T1   110:10    tell you half the things Alice used to say, beginning with her favourite phrase "Let's pretend." She had
 A6    53: 5    Cat; and this time it vanished quite slowly, beginning with the end of the tail, and ending with the grin,
```
BEGINS (5)
```
 A10   83:10    the  next verse," the Gryphon repeated: "it begins 'I passed by his garden.'"
 A11   89:17              "Of course twinkling begins with a T!" said the King sharply. "Do you take me for a
 A7    60:16    drew all manner of things--everything that begins with an M--"
 A7    60:22    with a little shriek, and went on: "--that begins with an M, such as mouse-traps, and the moon, and
 T3   136: 6    a great deal of puzzling, was "L, I know it begins with L!"
```
BEGUN (13)
```
 A11   86:30    anything to put down yet, before the trial's begun."
 T8   183:19    Here the sentence ended as suddenly as it had begun, as the Knight fell heavily on the top of his head
 A7    55:14    fun now!" thought Alice. "I'm glad they've begun asking riddles--I believe I can guess that," she added
 TI   103:13                        A tale begun in other days, / When summer suns were glowing--/ A
 A11   89:12    began, in a trembling voice, "and I hadn't begun my tea--not above a week or so--and what with the
 T4   139:41    they left off dancing as suddenly as they had begun: the music stopped at the same moment.
 A1     9:16    felt that she was dozing off, and had just begun to dream that she was walking hand in hand with Dinah,
 T5   156:34    it to her just then that the rushes had begun to fade, and to lose all their scent and beauty, from
 A10   85: 2    the Gryphon, and the Mock Turtle had just begun to repeat it, when a cry of "The trial's beginning!" was
 A1    10:11    things had happened lately, that Alice had begun to think that very few things indeed were really
 A8    62:17    Seven flung down his brush, and had just begun "Well, of all the unjust things--" when his eye chanced
 T1   110:13    only the day before--all because Alice had begun with "Let's pretend we're kings and queens;" and her
 T4   139:21                        "You've begun wrong!" cried Tweedledum. "The first thing in a visit is
```
BEHEAD (1)
```
 A11   91:19    that Dormouse!" the Queen shrieked out. "Behead that Dormouse! Turn that Dormouse out of court!
```
BEHEADED (3)
```
 A8    62:12    Queen say only yesterday you deserved to be beheaded."
 A8    69: 1    was that anything that had a head could be beheaded, and that you weren't to talk nonsense.
 A8    65:12              "You sha'n't be beheaded!" said Alice, and she put them into a large
```
BEHEADING (1)
```
 A8    67: 6    become of me? They're dreadfully fond of beheading people here: the great wonder is, that there's any
```
BEHIND (25)
```
 A4    32:36    made believe to worry it: then Alice dodged behind a great thistle, to keep herself from being run over;
 T7   169: 4    seemed to fill the whole forest. Alice got behind a tree, for fear of being run over, and watched them go
 T8   179:37    at each other with such fury that Alice got behind a tree to be out of the way of the blows.
 T1   113:15    Here something began squeaking on the table behind Alice, and made her turn her head just in time to see
 A8    67:45    "and don't look at me like that!" He got behind Alice as he spoke.
 T8   187:24    her feet--and the black shadows of the forest behind--all this she took in like a picture, as, with one hand
 A11   91:18              "Treacle," said a sleepy voice behind her.
 T9   204:22    round after her own shawl, which was trailing behind her.
 T8W   13: 2    deep sigh, which seemed to come from the wood behind her.
 A8    67:33    then she noticed that the Queen was close behind her, listening: so she went on "--likely to win, that
 A6    46:29    and broke to pieces against one of the trees behind him.
 A11   87: 7    stand, and she went round the court and got behind him, and very soon found an opportunity of taking it
 T6   165: 7    it goes a long way before it, and a long way behind it--"
 A4    34: 5    looked under it, and on both sides of it, and behind it, it occurred to her that she might as well look and
 A1     9:40    a low curtain she had not noticed before, and behind it was a little door about fifteen inches high: she
 A1     9:27    how late it's getting!" She was close behind it when she turned the corner, but the Rabbit was no
 T8   182:42    generally did rather suddenly), he fell off behind. Otherwise he kept on pretty well, except that he had a
 A6    49:27    day or two. Wouldn't it be murder to leave it behind?" She said the last words out loud, and the little
 T6   161: 7    much more the ends of his mouth might meet behind," she thought. "And then I don't know what would happen
 T1   112: 5    away as brightly as the one she had left behind. "So I shall be as warm here as I was in the old room,"
 T1   110:34    when I get upon a chair--all but the bit just behind the fireplace. Oh! I do so wish I could see that bit! I
 A2    18:24    spades, then a row of lodging-houses, and behind them a railway station.) However, she soon made out
 A8    65:10    moved on, three of the soldiers remaining behind to execute the unfortunate gardeners, who ran to Alice
 T6   160:32    passion. "You've been listening at doors--and behind trees--and down chimneys--or you couldn't have known
 A10   79:14    to a snail, / "There's a porpoise close behind us, and he's treading on my tail. / See how eagerly the
```
BEING (41)
```
 T2   126: 3    How I wish I was one of them! I wouldn't mind being a Pawn, if only I might join--though of course I should
 T3   129: 4    Alice, as she stood on tiptoe in hopes of being able to see a little further. "Principal rivers--there
 T3   135:41    what?" she went on, rather surprised at not being able to think of the word. "I mean to get under the--
 A8    67:27    no idea how confusing it is all the things being alive: for instance, there's the arch I've got to go
 A2    17:27    put their heads down! I am so very tired of being all alone here!"
 A9    73: 6    the soldiers, who of course had to leave off being arches to do this, so that, by the end of half an hour
```

BEING (cont.)
T4	145:28	in the wood--here's somebody's shawl being blown away!"
T8	182:27	you invented a plan for keeping the hair from being blown off?" Alice enquired.
A4	28:11	and had to stoop to save her neck from being broken. She hastily put down the bottle, saying to
T7	177: 9	to the Lion (she was getting quite used to being called 'the Monster'). "I've cut several slices already,
T2	121:13	Alice didn't like being criticized, so she began asking questions. "Aren't you
T4	147:24	neck of Tweedledee, "to keep his head from being cut off," as he said.
T3	136: 4	if I can! I'm determined to do it!" But being determined didn't help her much, and all she could say,
T5	156:37	last only a very little while--and these, being dream-rushes, melted away almost like snow, as they lay
A2	19: 3	I shall be punished for it now, I suppose, by being drowned in my own tears! That will be a queer thing, to
T1	115: 5	held in the air by an invisible hand, and being dusted: he was far too much astonished to cry out, but
A11	89:27	deny it too; but the Dormouse denied nothing, being fast asleep.
T9	194:29	on the White Queen, for she didn't like being found fault with so much.
T5	152:32	must be very happy, living in this wood, and being glad whenever you like!"
A4	32:14	poor little Lizard, Bill, was in the middle, being held up by two guinea-pigs, who were giving it something
T7	178: 8	rise to their feet, with angry looks at being interrupted in their feast, before she dropped to her
A7	55: 2	wasn't very civil of you to sit down without being invited," said the March Hare.
A12	95:37	it?" he said. (Which he certainly did not, being made entirely of cardboard.)
T8	185: 8	hurt him," she said in a trembling voice, "being on the top of his head."
A4	28:28	wasn't always growing larger and smaller, and being ordered about by mice and rabbits. I almost wish I
A7	60:21	time, and was going off into a doze; but, on being pinched by the Hatter, it woke up again with a little
T2	121:14	"Aren't you sometimes frightened at being planted out here, with nobody to take care of you?"
T2	126: 1	on. "It's a great huge game of chess that's being played--all over the world--if this is the world at all,
T5	151:11	said: "but it wouldn't be all the better his being punished."
T5	150: 4	the King's Messenger. He's in prison now, being punished: and the trial doesn't even begin till next
A12	93: 6	waving its tail about in a melancholy way, being quite unable to move. She soon got it out again, and put
A11	86:25	last word two or three times over to herself, being rather proud of it: for she thought, and rightly too,
A4	32:37	behind a great thistle, to keep herself from being run over; and, the moment she appeared on the other side
T7	169: 4	forest. Alice got behind a tree, for fear of being run over, and watched them go by.
A8	67: 9	wondering whether she could get away without being seen, when she noticed a curious appearance in the air:
T3	135:39	said as she stepped under the trees, "after being so hot, to get into the--into the--into what?" she went
A5	35:15	understand it myself, to begin with; and being so many different sizes in a day is very confusing."
A4	28: 7	large again, for really I'm quite tired of being such a tiny little thing!"
A2	17:23	then? Tell me that first, and then, if I like being that person, I'll come up: if not, I'll stay down here
A12	93:10	jury had a little recovered from the shock of being upset, and their slates and pencils had been found and
T1	110:14	kings and queens;" and her sister, who liked being very exact, had argued that they couldn't, because there

BELIEVE (23) [See also DISBELIEVE]
A10	81:20	her answer. "They're done with blacking, I believe."
A7	55:14	"I'm glad they've begun asking riddles--I believe I can guess that," she added aloud.
T5	153: 6	without that. Now I'll give you something to believe. I'm just one hundred and one, five months and a day
T5	153:12	There's no use trying," she said: "one ca'n't believe impossible things."
T7	175:31	each other," said the Unicorn, "if you'll believe in me, I'll believe in you. Is that a bargain?"
T7	175:31	the Unicorn, "if you'll believe in me, I'll believe in you. Is that a bargain?"
A9	75: 9	went to school in the sea, though you mayn't believe it--"
A5	43:19	"I don't believe it," said the Pigeon; "but if they do, why, then
AI	3:24	friendly chat with bird or beast--/ And half believe it true.
T5	153: 5	say 'exactly,'" the Queen remarked. "I can believe it without that. Now I'll give you something to
T3	135:43	"What does it call itself, I wonder? I do believe it's got no name--why, to be sure it hasn't!"
T4	148:20	she said. "And how fast it comes! Why, I do believe it's got wings!"
T12	208: 4	the Carpenter' to you; and then you can make believe it's oysters, dear!
T3	137:25	"I do believe," said Alice at last, "that they live in the same
A10	80:22	"I believe so," Alice replied thoughtfully. "They have their
T8	186:17	his voice getting lower and lower, "I don't believe that pudding ever was cooked! In fact, I don't believe
T8	186:18	pudding ever was cooked! In fact, I don't believe that pudding ever will be cooked! And yet it was a
T5	153: 8	"I ca'n't believe that!" said Alice.
A12	95:25	him,) "I'll give him sixpence. I don't believe there's an atom of meaning in it."
A12	95:27	all wrote down, on their slates, "She doesn't believe there's an atom of meaning in it," but none of them
A4	32:36	of delight, and rushed at the stick, and made believe to worry it: then Alice dodged behind a great thistle,
T2	127:12	round her in great surprise. "Why, I do believe we've been under this tree the whole time!
A3	22:32	those long words, and, what's more, I don't believe you do either!" And the Eaglet bent down its head to

BELIEVED (2)
| T5 | 153:15 | for half-an-hour a day. Why, sometimes I've believed as many as six impossible things before breakfast. |
| A12 | 98:34 | So she sat on, with closed eyes, and half believed herself in Wonderland, though she knew she had but to |

BELL (4)
T7	176: 2	tone that sounded like the tolling of a great bell.
T9	198: 4	"Visitors' Bell," and the other "Servants' Bell."
T9	198: 3	was a bell-handle; one was marked "Visitors' Bell," and the other "Servants' Bell."
T9	198: 6	Alice, "and then I'll ring the--the--which bell must I ring?" she went on, very much puzzled by the names

BELL-HANDLE (1)
| T9 | 198: 3 | and on each side of the arch there was a bell-handle; one was marked "Visitors' Bell," and the other |

BELLOWING (1)
| T6 | 166: 7 | "Well, 'outgribing' is something between bellowing and whistling, with a kind of sneeze in the middle: |

-BELLS [See SHEEP-BELLS]

BELONG (3)
T2	124:12	said the Queen: "all the ways about here belong to me--but why did you come out here at all?" she added
A1	9:36	and Alice's first idea was that this might belong to one of the doors of the hall; but, alas! either the
T3	131:26	Alice said rather impatiently. "I don't belong to this railway journey at all--I was in a wood just

BELONGING (1)
| T8 | 179: 9 | dream, and not the Red King's! I don't like belonging to another person's dream," she went on in a rather |

BELONGS (4)
A2   20: 8   I ca'n't remember half of them--and it belongs to a farmer, you know, and he says it's so useful,
T2   128:12   the Fifth is mostly water--the Sixth belongs to Humpty Dumpty--But you make no remark?"
A8   69: 6   could think of nothing else to say but "It belongs to the Duchess: you'd better ask her about it."
T2   128:11   Fourth Square in no time. Well, that square belongs to Tweedledum and Tweedledee--the Fifth is mostly
BELOVED (1)
A10   80:10   nearer is to France. / Then turn not pale, beloved snail, but come and join the dance. / Will you, wo'n't
BELOW (3)
A4   30:30   that loose slate--Oh, it's coming down! Heads below!" (a loud crash)--"Now, who did that?--It was Bill, I
A12   92: 5   all the jurymen on to the heads of the crowd below, and there they lay sprawling about, reminding her very
A5   42:12   out of a sea of green leaves that lay far below her.
BELT (4)
T6   162:26   "when a person doesn't know a cravat from a belt!"
A10   82:25   his eyelids, so he with his nose / Trims his belt and his buttons, and turns out his toes. / When the sands
T6   162:17   a beautiful cravat, I should have said--no, a belt, I mean--I beg your pardon!" she added in dismay, for
T6   162:13   "What a beautiful belt you've got on!" Alice suddenly remarked. (They had had
BEND (2)
A5   42:20   and was delighted to find that her neck would bend about easily in any direction, like a serpent. She had
A3   26: 4   Alice very humbly: "you had got to the fifth bend, I think?"
BENDING (2)
T2   122:11   "They know I ca'n't get at them!" it panted, bending its quivering head towards Alice, "or they wouldn't
T8W   16:18   "it's when you hold up your head--so--without bending your neck."
BENEATH (3)
TC   209: 1   A boat, beneath a sunny sky / Lingering onward dreamily / In an
AI   3: 8   Ah, cruel Three! In such an hour, / Beneath such dreamy weather, / To beg a tale of breath too
AI   4: 2   is done, / And home we steer, a merry crew, / Beneath the setting sun.
BENT (2)
A3   22:33   don't believe you do either!" And the Eaglet bent down its head to hide a smile: some of the other birds
T5   156:20   all about the Sheep and the knitting, as she bent over the side of the boat, with just the ends of her
-BERRY [See MULBERRY]
BESEECH (1)
T4   141:14   come and walk with us!' / The Walrus did beseech. / 'A pleasant walk, a pleasant talk, / Along the
BESIDES (8)
A8   66:15   itself, and was in the act of crawling away: besides all this, there was generally a ridge or a furrow in
T4   143: 9   what we chiefly need: / Pepper and vinegar besides / Are very good indeed--/ Now, if you're ready,
T3   129:26   perhaps I may visit the elephants later on. Besides, I do so want to get into the Third Square!"
T4   145:12   "I shouldn't!" Alice exclaimed indignantly. "Besides, if I'm only a sort of thing in his dream, what are
T2   123: 3   "Are there any more people in the garden besides me?" Alice said, not choosing to notice the Rose's
A2   16: 7   and she, oh, she knows such a very little! Besides, she's she, and I'm I, and--oh dear, how puzzling it
A12   93:41   I sha'n't go, at any rate," said Alice; "besides, that's not a regular rule: you invented it just now."
A8   63:30   heard of such a rule at processions; "and besides, what would be the use of a procession," thought she,
BEST (29)
A12   93:29   as if he were trying which word sounded best.
T2   126: 5   though of course I should like to be a Queen, best."
T5   155:20   so there was nothing for it but to do her best.
A8   63: 9   you know. So you see, Miss, we're doing our best, afore she comes, to--" At this moment, Five, who had
T5   150:21   "What sort of things do you remember best?" Alice ventured to ask.
A7   56: 4   "It was the best butter," the March Hare meekly replied.
A7   56:10   to say than his first remark, "It was the best butter, you know."
A3   26:39   like her, down here, and I'm sure she's the best cat in the world! Oh, my dear Dinah! I wonder if I shall
A12   95:17   Don't let him know she liked them best, / For this must ever be / A secret, kept from all the
T4   144:19   said indignantly. "Then I like the Carpenter best--if he didn't eat so many as the Walrus."
T8   181:35   said in a discontented tone, "one of the best kind. But not a single bee has come near it yet. And the
A9   76: 5   "We had the best of educations--in fact, we went to school every day--"
T7   175:10   with his hands in his pockets. "I had the best of it this time?" he said to the King, just glancing at
T7   172:38   "Yes, to be sure," said the King: "and the best of the joke is, that it's my crown all the while! Let's
A4   32:21   that lovely garden. I think that will be the best plan."
T8   183: 1   was walking, she soon found that it was the best plan not to walk quite close to the horse.
T4   144:13   "I like the Walrus best," said Alice: "because he was a little sorry for the poor
T6   162:40   a little. "I like birthday presents best," she said at last.
T7   172:20   "I do my best," the Messenger said in a sullen tone. "I'm sure nobody
A3   23: 1   the Dodo in an offended tone, "was that the best thing to get us dry would be a Caucus-race."
A1   12:18   plainly through the glass, and she tried her best to climb up one of the legs of the table, but it was too
T4   147: 1   All this time Tweedledee was trying his best to fold up the umbrella, with himself in it: which was
T5   149:34   carefully released the brush, and did her best to get the hair into order. "Come, you look rather better
T4   140:25   Shining with all his might: / He did his very best to make / The billows smooth and bright--/ And this was
T7   177: 1   old bridge, or the market-place? You get the best view by the old bridge."
T4   139:26   hurting the other one's feelings; so, as the best way out of the difficulty, she took hold of both hands at
T4   139:10   thinking," Alice said politely, "which is the best way out of this wood: it's getting so dark. Would you
A3   23: 5   "Why," said the Dodo, "the best way to explain it is to do it." (And, as you might like
A2   14: 9   trouble myself about you: you must manage the best way you can--but I must be kind to them," thought Alice,
BETTER (49)
A11   90:28   thought Alice. "Now we shall get on better."
T9   192:29   examination. And the sooner we begin it, the better."
A9   72:11   "I think I should understand that better," Alice said very politely, "if I had it written down:
T7   172:11   think throwing cold water over you would be better," Alice suggested: "--or some sal-volatile."
T5   151:21   said, "that would have been better still; better, and better, and better!" Her voice went higher with
T5   151:21   would have been better still; better, and better, and better!" Her voice went higher with each "better,"
A3   21:10   only say, "I'm older than you, and must know better." And this Alice would not allow, without knowing how
T5   149:21   It would have been all the better, as it seemed to Alice, if she had got some one else to

BETTER (cont.)
```
A8     69: 7   to  say  but  "It belongs to the Duchess: you'd better ask her about it."
T4    146: 1   as cheerfully as she could, "At any rate, I'd better be getting out of the wood, for really it's coming on
T5    153:29  as  she  went  on.  "Much be-etter! Be-etter! Be-e-e-etter! Be-e-ehh!" The last word ended in a long bleat,
T5    153:29  into a squeak as she went on. "Much be-etter! Be-etter! Be-e-e-etter! Be-e-ehh!" The last word ended in a
T5    153:29  rising  into  a  squeak  as she went on. "Much be-etter! Be-etter! Be-e-e-etter! Be-e-ehh!" The last word
T5    153:28            "Oh, much better!" cried the Queen, her voice rising into a squeak as
A7     59:26  remarked  "If  you  ca'n't  be  civil, you'd better finish the story for yourself."
T5    151:16           "And you were all the better for it, I know!" the Queen said triumphantly.
T9    200: 6   in despair. "Oh, that'll never be done! I'd better go in at once--" and in she went, and there was a dead
T1    114:20  getting  to  the  table, at that rate. I'd far better help you, hadn't I?" But the King took no notice of the
T5    151:21  been better still; better, and better, and better!" Her voice went higher with each "better," till it got
T5    151:11       she  said:  "but  it  wouldn't  be all the better his being punished."
A10    84: 6                    Yes, I think you'd better leave off," said the Gryphon, and Alice was only too
T1    107:22  "Really,  Dinah  ought  to  have  taught you better manners! You ought, Dinah, you know you ought!" she
T4    147:45  sadly:  "and  she  can  watch us--only you'd better not come very close," he added: "I generally hit every
A4     32: 4   she  said  to  herself, and shouted out "You'd better not do that again!", which produced another dead
T4    147:38             "Then you'd better not fight to-day," said Alice, thinking it a good
T12   207:35  Dumpty?  I  think  you  did--however, you'd better not mention it to your friends just yet, for I'm not
A8     62:11                     "You'd better not talk!" said Five. "I heard the Queen say only
T5    153:23       "Then I hope your finger is better now?" Alice said very politely, as she crossed the
A4     31:20  "Well,  I  hardly  know--No more, thank ye; I'm better now--but I'm a deal too flustered to tell you--all I
T5    149:35  the  hair  into  order. "Come, you look rather better now!" she said, after altering most of the pins. "But
A9     70:30          "The game's going on rather better now," she said, by way of keeping up the conversation a
T8    184:42  saddle. "Yes," he said; "but I've invented a better one than that--like a sugar-loaf. When I used to wear
T2    120: 1        "I should see the garden far better," said Alice to herself, "if I could get to the top of
T3    130:14  means--for  I  must  confess  that  I  don't) "Better say nothing at all. Language is worth a thousand pounds
T5    151:11  denying  that.  "Of course it would be all the better," she said: "but it wouldn't be all the better his
T5    151:21  them,"  the  Queen  said, "that would have been better still; better, and better, and better!" Her voice went
A4     27:20  he'll  be when he finds out who I am! But I'd better take him his fan and gloves--that is, if I can find
T8    182:13              "We'd better take it with us," the Knight said. "It'll come in handy
T2    122:22  nicely?" Alice said, hoping to get it into a better temper by a compliment. "I've been in many gardens
T7    169:11       Having  four  feet,  these  managed rather better than the foot-soldiers; but even they stumbled now and
T7    172:13        "I didn't say there was nothing better," the King replied. "I said there was nothing like it."
T8W    20: 2   "and  I  think  if  your  wig fitted a little better, they wouldn't tease you quite so much."
A7     60:43  to  the  little glass table. "Now, I'll manage better this time," she said to herself, and began by taking
T5    151:22  and better!" Her voice went higher with each "better," till it got quite to a squeak at last.
T6    167: 8   "I  sent  to  them again to say / 'It will be better to obey.'
A7     56: 9   at  it  again:  but he could think of nothing better to say than his first remark, "It was the best butter,
T8    183:13           Alice could think of nothing better to say than "Indeed?" but she said it as heartily as
A7     56:32  wearily.  "I  think  you  might  do  something better with the time," she said, "than wasting it in asking
T5    151: 8        "That would be all the better, wouldn't it?" the Queen said, as she bound the plaster
```
BETWEEN (10)
```
T5    155:19  they  were  in  a  little boat, gliding along between banks: so there was nothing for it but to do her best
T6    166: 7          "Well, 'outgribing' is something between bellowing and whistling, with a kind of sneeze in the
A12    95:15  she  had  this  fit)  / An obstacle that came between / Him, and ourselves, and it.
A8     68:30     round it: there was a dispute going on between the executioner, the King, and the Queen, who were all
T7    176:14  very  uncomfortable  at  having  to  sit down between the two great creatures; but there was no other place
A7     54: 3   were having tea at it: a Dormouse was sitting between them, fast asleep, and the other two were using it as
A6     46:19  without attending to her, "if we had the door between us. For instance, if you were inside, you might knock,
T2    125:22  across  it  from side to side, and the ground between was divided up into squares by a number of little
A7     58:13       and we've no time to wash the things between whiles."
A12    95:20  ever  be  / A secret, kept from all the rest, / Between yourself and me."
```
BEWARE (2)
```
T1    118: 1                    "Beware the Jabberwock, my son! / The jaws that bite, the claws
T1    118: 3   / The jaws that bite, the claws that catch! / Beware the Jubjub bird, and shun / The frumious Bandersnatch!"
```
BEWILDERED (1)
```
T8    187: 9   said  Alice, who was by this time completely bewildered.
```
BEWILDERMENT (1)
```
T8    179:27  Alice  looked  from  one to the other in some bewilderment.
```
BEYOND (4)
```
T6    165: 8                "And a long way beyond it on each side," Alice added.
T1    111: 5   only  you  know  it may be quite different on beyond. Oh, Kitty, how nice it would be if we could only get
T4    140: 5   she  said  to  herself:  "we seem to have got beyond that, somehow!"
T3    131:10           Alice couldn't see who was sitting beyond the Beetle, but a hoarse voice spoke next. "Change
```
BILL (13)
```
A4t    27: 1                THE RABBIT SENDS IN A LITTLE BILL
A4     30:29  do  well  enough.  Don't be particular--Here, Bill! Catch hold of this rope--Will the roof bear?--Mind that
A4     30:26   to  bring  but  one.  Bill's got the other--Bill! Fetch it here, lad!--Here, put 'em up at this corner--No
A9     76:15  "Now,  at  ours,  they had, at the end of the bill, 'French, music, and washing--extra.'"
A12    96:21  Lizard as she spoke. (The unfortunate little Bill had left off writing on his slate with one finger, as he
A4     30:31  (a  loud  crash)--"Now, who did that?--It was Bill, I fancy--Who's to go down the chimney?--Nay, I sha'n't!
A4     30:36     "Why,  they  seem  to  put  everything upon Bill! I wouldn't be in Bill's place for a good deal: this
A4     31: 2   above  her:  then, saying to herself "This is Bill", she gave one sharp kick, and waited to see what would
A11    87: 8   so quickly that the poor little juror (it was Bill, the Lizard) could not make out at all what had become of
A4     30:33  I  wo'n't,  then!--Bill's got to go down--Here, Bill! The master says you've got to go down the chimney!"
A4     31: 7   she heard was a general chorus of "There goes Bill!" then the Rabbit's voice alone--"Catch him, you by the
A4     31:17  a  little  feeble,  squeaking voice ("That's Bill," thought Alice), "Well, I hardly know--No more, thank ye
A4     32:14  waiting  outside.  The  poor little Lizard, Bill, was in the middle, being held up by two guinea-pigs, who
```

BILLOWS (1)
    T4   140:26   might: / He did his very best to make / The billows smooth and bright--/ And this was odd, because it was
BILL'S (4)
    A4   30:26   ladder?--Why, I hadn't to bring but one. Bill's got the other--Bill! Fetch it here, lad!--Here, put 'em
    A4   30:35   "Oh! So Bill's got to come down the chimney, has he?" said Alice to
    A4   30:33   I sha'n't! You do it!--That I wo'n't, then!--Bill's got to go down--Here, Bill! The master says you've got
    A4   30:37   to put everything upon Bill! I wouldn't be in Bill's place for a good deal: this fireplace is narrow, to be
BIRD (6)
    T5   155:37   Alice asked at last, rather vexed. "I'm not a bird!"
    A9   71:13   "Only mustard isn't a bird," Alice remarked.
    T1   118: 3   the claws that catch! / Beware the Jubjub bird, and shun / The frumious Bandersnatch!"
    A3   26:29   her after the birds! Why, she'll eat a little bird as soon as look at it!"
    AI   3:23   wonders wild and new, / In friendly chat with bird or beast--/ And half believe it true.
    T6   165:11   And a 'borogove' is a thin shabby-looking bird with its feathers sticking out all round--something like
BIRDS (14)
    A2   20:22   the pool was getting quite crowded with the birds and animals that had fallen into it: there was a Duck
    A11   86: 3   assembled about them--all sorts of little birds and beasts, as well as the whole pack of cards: the
    T9   200:10   guests, of all kinds: some were animals, some birds, and there were even a few flowers among them. "I'm glad
    A3   24:10   caused some noise and confusion, as the large birds complained that they could not taste theirs, and the
    A3   26:31   sensation among the party. Some of the birds hurried off at once: one old Magpie began wrapping
    A11   86:23   some of them were animals, and some were birds,) "I suppose they are the jurors." She said this last
    A9   71:12   mustard both bite. And the moral of that is--'Birds of a feather flock together.'"
    T9   203:22   about in all directions: "and very like birds they look," Alice thought to herself, as well as she
    A3   22:34   its head to hide a smile: some of the other birds tittered audibly.
    T4   140:40   birds were flying overhead--/ There were no birds to fly.
    A4   32:13   and found quite a crowd of little animals and birds waiting outside. The poor little Lizard, Bill, was in
    T4   140:39   because / No cloud was in the sky: / No birds were flying overhead--/ There were no birds to fly.
    A3   26:29   And oh, I wish you could see her after the birds! Why, she'll eat a little bird as soon as look at it!"
    A3   21: 2   party that assembled on the bank--the birds with draggled feathers, the animals with their fur
BIRTHDAY (4) [See also UNBIRTHDAY]
    T6   162:39   "A present given when it isn't your birthday, of course."
    T6   162:40   Alice considered a little. "I like birthday presents best," she said at last.
    A9   72:21   thought Alice. "I'm glad people don't give birthday-presents like that!" But she did not venture to say
    T6   163:22   "And only one for birthday presents, you know. There's glory for you!"
BIRTHDAYS (1)
    T6   162:45   "And how many birthdays have you?"
BISCUIT (2)
    T2   127:26   a little box out of her pocket. "Have a biscuit?"
    T2   127:36   shall give you your directions--have another biscuit?"
-BISHOP [See ARCHBISHOP]
BIT (30)
    A5   42: 3   managed to swallow a morsel of the left-hand bit. * * * * * * * * * * * * * *
    A9   70:20   of that is, but I shall remember it in a bit."
    A11   88:32   at the Queen, and in his confusion he bit a large piece out of his teacup instead of the
    A12   95:24   in the last few minutes that she wasn't a bit afraid of interrupting him,) "I'll give him sixpence. I
    A5   44: 4   So she began nibbling at the right-hand bit again, and did not venture to go near the house till she
    AI   12:38   She ate a little bit, and said anxiously to herself "Which way? Which way?",
    T8W   18:11   to," said the Wasp: "however I'll try; wait a bit." He was silent for a few moments, and then began again--
    A5   41:43   set to work at once to eat some of the other bit. Her chin was pressed so closely against her foot, that
    AI   9:21   Alice was not a bit hurt, and she jumped up on to her feet in a moment: she
    T5   157: 2   However, she wasn't a bit hurt, and was soon up again: the Sheep went on with her
    T1   110:35   fireplace. Oh! I do so wish I could see that bit! I want so much to know whether they've a fire in the
    A6   49:10   "Here! You may nurse it a bit, if you like!" the Duchess said to Alice, flinging the
    T1   115:37   a thinner pencil. I ca'n't manage this one a bit: it writes all manner of things that I don't intend--"
    T1   110:34   of it when I get upon a chair--all but the bit just behind the fireplace. Oh! I do so wish I could see
    T4   147:40   "We must have a bit of a fight, but I don't care about going on long," said
    T7   174:10   waiting for 'em now," said Hatta, "this is a bit of it as I'm eating."
    A6   53:14   she had nibbled some more of the left-hand bit of mushroom, and raised herself to about two feet high:
    T5   151: 9   she bound the plaster round her finger with a bit of ribbon.
    A4   32:33   knowing what she did, she picked up a little bit of stick, and held it out to the puppy: whereupon the
    A5   41:37   it as far as they would go, and broke off a bit of the edge with each hand.
    T1   108:36   too? Now for number three: you unwound every bit of the worsted while I wasn't looking!
    T8W   14:14   "Would you like me to read you a bit of this?" Alice went on, as she picked up a newspaper
    T4   145:22   "You wo'n't make yourself a bit realler by crying," Tweedledee remarked: "there's nothing
    A5   36: 6   "Not a bit," said the Caterpillar.
    A7   55:23   "Not the same thing a bit!" said the Hatter. "Why, you might just as well say that
    A12   93:32   over their slates; "but it doesn't matter a bit," she thought to herself.
    T9   192:11   was happening so oddly that she didn't feel a bit surprised at finding the Red Queen and the White Queen
    T4   143: 1   'But wait a bit,' the Oysters cried, / 'Before we have our chat; / For
    T9   194:26   "She ca'n't do sums a bit!" the Queens said together, with great emphasis.
    A5   41:39   and nibbled a little of the right-hand bit to try the effect. The next moment she felt a violent blow
BITE (6)
    A9   71: 9   "He might bite," Alice cautiously replied, not feeling at all anxious to
    A9   71:12   the Duchess: "flamingoes and mustard both bite. And the moral of that is--'Birds of a feather flock
    T8W   20:11   At last she managed to say gravely, "I can bite anything I want."
    T9   194:11   and the dog wouldn't remain: it would come to bite me--and I'm sure I shouldn't remain!"
    T1   118: 2   the Jabberwock, my son! / The jaws that bite, the claws that catch! / Beware the Jubjub bird, and shun
    T8W   20: 7   shaped, though--I should think you couldn't bite well?"
BITES (1)
    T8   182: 9   "To guard against the bites of sharks," the Knight replied. "It's an invention of my

BITTER (3)
    A9   70:12   makes them sour--and camomile that makes them bitter--and--and barley-sugar and such things that make
    T4   141:12   doubt it,' said the Carpenter, / And shed a bitter tear.
    TI   103:20   hearken then, ere voice of dread, / With bitter tidings laden, / Shall summon to unwelcome bed / A
BLACK (5)
    T4   139: 2   Just then flew down a monstrous crow, / As black as a tar-barrel; / Which frightened both the heroes so,
    T4   148:19   be a thunderstorm coming on. "What a thick black cloud that is!" she said. "And how fast it comes! Why, I
    T1   107:12   But the black kitten had been finished with earlier in the afternoon,
    T1   107: 2   had had nothing to do with it--it was the black kitten's fault entirely. For the white kitten had been
    T8   187:23   neck, cropping the grass at her feet--and the black shadows of the forest behind--all this she took in like
BLACKING (1)
    A10   81:20   she gave her answer. "They're done with blacking, I believe."
BLADE (2)
    T5   156:41   They hadn't gone much farther before the blade of one of the oars got fast in the water and wouldn't
    T1   118:14   two! And through and through / The vorpal blade went snicker-snack! / He left it dead, and with its head
BLADES (1)
    A4   34: 1   looked all round her at the flowers and the blades of grass, but she could not see anything that looked
BLAME (1)
    A8   62:10   and said "That's right, Five! Always lay the blame on others!"
BLANKETS (1)
    T4   147:14   their arms full of things--such as bolsters, blankets, hearth-rugs, table-cloths, dish-covers, and
BLAST (1)
    TI   103:30   thee fast: / Thou shalt not heed the raving blast.
BLASTS (2)
    A11   88: 5   the King; and the White Rabbit blew three blasts on the trumpet, and called out "First witness!"
    A11   87:14   On this the White Rabbit blew three blasts on the trumpet, and then unrolled the parchment-scroll,
BLAZE (2)
    T8   188:20   when I find a mountain-rill, / I set it in a blaze; / And thence they make a stuff they call / Rowland's
    T8   187:21   his hair, and shining on his armour in a blaze of light that quite dazzled her--the horse quietly
BLAZING (1)
    T1   112: 4   pleased to find that there was a real one, blazing away as brightly as the one she had left behind. "So I
BLEAT (1)
    T5   153:30   Be-e-ehh!" The last word ended in a long bleat, so like a sheep that Alice quite started.
BLEEDING (2)
    T5   152: 5   if she wanted to shake it off. "My finger's bleeding! Oh, oh, oh, oh!"
    T5   152:21   "That accounts for the bleeding, you see," she said to Alice with a smile. "Now you
BLEEDS (1)
    A1   11: 3   finger very deeply with a knife, it usually bleeds; and she had never forgotten that, if you drink much
BLEW (5)
    T9   195: 6   till she had to beg them to leave off, it blew her hair about so.
    T1   114:15   "Blew--me--up," panted the Queen, who was still a little out of
    T5   153:18   as she spoke, and a sudden gust of wind blew the Queen's shawl across a little brook. The Queen spread
    A11   87:14   On this the White Rabbit blew three blasts on the trumpet, and then unrolled the
    A11   88: 5   witness," said the King; and the White Rabbit blew three blasts on the trumpet, and called out "First
BLINDING (1)
    TI   103:25   Without, the frost, the blinding snow, / The storm-wind's moody madness--/ Within, the
BLINKING (1)
    T7   176: 1   eyes were half shut. "What's this!" he said, blinking lazily at Alice, and speaking in a deep hollow tone
BLOTTING-PAPER (1)
    T8   186:23   "It began with blotting-paper," the Knight answered with a groan.
BLOW (2)
    A5   41:40   effect. The next moment she felt a violent blow underneath her chin: it had struck her foot!
    A8   66:10   out, and was going to give the hedgehog a blow with its head, it would twist itself round and look up in
BLOWING (1)
    T2   127: 3   wind whistling in Alice's ears, and almost blowing her hair off her head, she fancied.
BLOWN (4)
    T4   145:28   in the wood--here's somebody's shawl being blown away!"
    T8   182:28   a plan for keeping the hair from being blown off?" Alice enquired.
    A1   12:11   of a candle looks like after the candle is blown out, for she could not remember ever having seen such a
    T1   114:16   "Mind you come up--the regular way--don't get blown up!"
BLOWS (3)
    T8   179:38   got behind a tree to be out of the way of the blows.
    A6   48:15   it was quite impossible to say whether the blows hurt it or not.
    T1   109:15   in green, and dance about--whenever the wind blows--oh, that's very pretty!" cried Alice, dropping the ball
BLUE (5)
    T4   143:14   on us!' the Oysters cried, / Turning a little blue. / 'After such kindness, that would be / A dismal thing
    T8W   15: 6   a lake of treacle. The banks of the lake were blue and white, and looked like china. While tasting the
    A4   34: 8   and her eyes immediately met those of a large blue caterpillar, that was sitting on the top, with its arms
    T8   188:30   well from side to side, / Until his face was blue: / 'Come, tell me how you live,' I cried, / 'And what it
    T8   187:19   as if it had been only yesterday--the mild blue eyes and kindly smile of the Knight--the setting sun
-BOARD [See CARDBOARD, CHESS-BOARD]
-BOARDS [See CUPBOARDS]
BOAT (11)
    T5   157: 6   much relieved to find herself still in the boat.
    T5   157:15   and half frightened--for the oars, and the boat, and the river, had vanished all in a moment, and she was
    TC   209: 1   A boat, beneath a sunny sky / Lingering onward dreamily / In an
    T5   156:12   pleaded. "If you don't mind stopping the boat for a minute."
    T5   156:28   to pick plenty of beautiful rushes as the boat glided by, there was always a more lovely one that she
    T5   156: 2   conversation for a minute or two, while the boat glided gently on, sometimes among beds of weeds (which
    T5   155:18   hands, and she found they were in a little boat, gliding along between banks: so there was nothing for it

BOAT (cont.)
T5   157: 8   peeping cautiously over the side of the boat into the dark water. "I wish it hadn't let go--I should
T5   156:15   So the boat was left to drift down the stream as it would, till it
T5   156:20   knitting, as she bent over the side of the boat, with just the ends of her tangled hair dipping into the
T5   156:24   "I only hope the boat wo'n't tipple over!" she said to herself. "Oh, what a
BODY (7) [See also ANYBODY, EVERYBODY, etc.]
T8W 14:13   before, "Worrity, worrity! Can't you leave a body alone?"
T8   186: 3   the question. "What does it matter where my body happens to be?" he said. "My mind goes on working all the
T3   134:11   are thin slices of bread-and-butter, its body is a crust, and its head is a lump of sugar."
T3   133:13   "and there you'll find a Snap-dragon-fly. Its body is made of plum-pudding, its wings of holly-leaves, and
T8   190: 6   distracted with his woe, / Who rocked his body to and fro, / And muttered mumblingly and low, / As if
A8   68:38   couldn't cut off a head unless there was a body to cut it off from: that he had never had to do such a
A8   66: 7   her flamingo: she succeeded in getting its body tucked away, comfortably enough, under her arm, with its
-BODY'S [See ANYBODY'S, etc.]
BOILING (2)
T4   142:23   Of cabbages--and kings--/ And why the sea is boiling hot--/ And whether pigs have wings.'
T8   189:10   / To keep the Menai bridge from rust / By boiling it in wine. / I thanked him much for telling me / The
BOLDLY (1)
A11 88:43   "Don't talk nonsense," said Alice more boldly: "you know you're growing too."
BOLSTER (1)
T4   147:23   she said to herself, as she arranged a bolster round the neck of Tweedledee, "to keep his head from
BOLSTERS (1)
T4   147:13   with their arms full of things--such as bolsters, blankets, hearth-rugs, table-cloths, dish-covers,
BONE (4)
T1   110:19   pretend that I'm a hungry hyaena and you're a bone!"
T9   194: 9   course. Try another Subtraction sum. Take a bone from a dog: what remains?"
A10 78: 4   sobs choked his voice. "Same as if he had a bone in his throat," said the Gryphon; and it set to work
T9   194:10   Alice considered. "The bone wouldn't remain, of course, if I took it--and the dog
BONES (4)
A5   39: 3   suet; / Yet you finished the goose, with the bones and the beak--/ Pray, how did you manage to do it?"
T8   184: 2   tone, as she picked him up, "I hope no bones are broken?"
T8W 13:16   "Oh, my old bones, my old bones!" he was grumbling on as Alice came up to him.
T8W 13:16   "Oh, my old bones, my old bones!" he was grumbling on as Alice came up to
BONFIRE (2)
T1   108:14   watching the boys getting in sticks for the bonfire--and it wants plenty of sticks, Kitty! Only it got so
T1   108:16   leave off. Never mind, we'll go and see the bonfire to-morrow." Here Alice wound two or three turns of the
BOOK (15) [See also LESSON-BOOK, MEMORANDUM-BOOK, etc.]
T6   160:34   indeed!" Alice said very gently. "It's in a book."
T6   163:13   Humpty Dumpty took the book and looked at it carefully. "That seems to be done right
A8   68: 2   a king," said Alice. "I've read that in some book, but I don't remember where."
A1   7: 3   to do: once or twice she had peeped into the book her sister was reading, but it had no pictures or
T6   160:35   "Ah, well! They may write such things in a book," Humpty Dumpty said in a calmer tone. "That's what you
T7   170:11   number," the King said, referring to his book. "I couldn't send all the horses, you know, because two
T1   115:40   of things?" said the Queen, looking over the book (in which Alice had put 'The White Knight is sliding down
T1   116: 1   There was a book lying near Alice on the table, and while she sat watching
T1   116:14   struck her. "Why, it's a Looking-glass book, of course! And, if I hold it up to a glass, the words
A1   10:14   find another key on it, or at any rate a book of rules for shutting people up like telescopes: this
A12 93:35   called out "Silence!", and read out from his book, "Rule Forty-two. All persons more than a mile high to
T6   166:12   "I read it in a book," said Alice. "But I had some poetry repeated to me much
A12 93:43   "It's the oldest rule in the book," said the King.
A1   7: 4   in it, "and what is the use of a book," thought Alice, "without pictures or conversations?"
A4   29: 6   am in the middle of one! There ought to be a book written about me, that there ought! And when I grow up,
BOOKS (4) [See also LESSON-BOOKS]
A11 86:14   before, but she had read about them in books, and she was quite pleased to find that she knew the
T1   110:39   it look as if they had a fire. Well then, the books are something like our books, only the words go the
T1   110:39   Well then, the books are something like our books, only the words go the wrong way: I know that, because
T1   110:41   I know that, because I've held up one of our books to the glass, and then they hold up one in the other
BOOK-SHELVES (1)
A1   8:16   that they were filled with cupboards and book-shelves: here and there she saw maps and pictures hung
BOON (1)
A10 83:18   When the pie was all finished, the Owl, as a boon, / Was kindly permitted to pocket the spoon: / While the
BOOTS (5)
A10 81:15   Alice was thoroughly puzzled. "Does the boots and shoes!" she repeated in a wondering tone.
A10 81:13   "It does the boots and shoes," the Gryphon replied very solemnly.
A10 81:21   "Boots and shoes under the sea," the Gryphon went on in a deep
A2   15: 2   go! Let me see. I'll give them a new pair of boots every Christmas."
T9   198:15   dressed in bright yellow, and had enormous boots on.
BORDER (1)
T2   120:28   time she came upon a large flowerbed, with a border of daisies, and a willow-tree growing in the middle.
BORE (1)
A9   70:29   However, she did not like to be rude: so she bore it as well as she could.
BOROGOVE (1)
T6   165:10   (there's another portmanteau for you). And a 'borogove' is a thin shabby-looking bird with its feathers
BOROGOVES (4)
T1   116:11   .ebargtuo shtar emom eht dnA / ,sevogorob eht erew ysmim llA / :ebaw eht ni elbmig dna eryg diD / sevot
T1   116:20   and gimble in the wabe: / All mimsy were the borogoves, / And the mome raths outgrabe.
T1   118:23   and gimble in the wabe: / All mimsy were the borogoves, / And the mome raths outgrabe.
T6   164:23   and gimble in the wabe: / All mimsy were the borogoves, / And the mome raths outgrabe."

BOTH (34)
  T5   149: 3   came running wildly through the wood, with both arms stretched out wide, as if she were flying, and Alice
  A9   71:11   said   the   Duchess: "flamingoes and mustard both bite. And the moral of that is--'Birds of a feather flock
  A6   46: 4   Then they both bowed, and their curls got entangled together.
  A9   77: 9   said the Gryphon, sighing in his turn; and both creatures hid their faces in their paws.
  A7   58:23   "Then the Dormouse shall!" they both cried. "Wake up, Dormouse!" And they pinched it on both
  T8 180:12   their heads; and the battle ended with their both falling off in this way, side by side. When they got up
  A6   45: 7   a round face, and large eyes like a frog; and both footmen, Alice noticed, had powdered hair that curled all
  A3   25: 9   to a mouse, That he met in the house, 'Let us both go to law: I will prosecute you.--Come, I'll take no
  T7 170:14   sent the two Messengers, either. They're both gone to the town. Just look along the road, and tell me
  T9 193: 6   couldn't deny that, even if you tried with both hands."
  T8 181:10   the Knight, putting back his shaggy hair with both hands, and turning his gentle face and large mild eyes to
  T4 139:27   way out of the difficulty, she took hold of both hands at once: the next moment they were dancing round in
  T9 204:14   she jumped up and seized the tablecloth with both hands: one good pull, and plates, dishes, guests, and
  T5 152: 7   of a steam-engine, that Alice had to hold both her hands over her ears.
  T9 203: 8   the White Queen, seizing Alice's hair with both her hands. "Something's going to happen!"
  T8 184: 6   He let go the bridle, and stretched out both his arms to show Alice what he meant, and this time he
  T7 175:20   of Alice to introduce her, and spreading out both his hands towards her in an Anglo-Saxon attitude. "We
 A11   89: 8   Hatter trembled so, that he shook off both his shoes.
  T5 158: 9   "Only you must eat them both, if you buy two," said the Sheep.
  A9   76:26   The Gryphon lifted up both its paws in surprise. "Never heard of uglifying!" it
  A6   51:21   a March Hare. Visit either you like: they're both mad."
  A9   74:28   Turtle in a deep, hollow tone. "Sit down, both of you, and don't speak a word till I've finished."
  T7 176:10   putting his chin on his paws. "And sit down, both of you," (to the King and the Unicorn): "fair play with
  AI   3: 3   afternoon / Full leisurely we glide; / For both our oars, with little skill, / By little arms are plied,
  T3 137:17   through the wood, and the two finger-posts both pointed along it. "I'll settle it," Alice said to herself
  T9 197:10   I'm getting sleepy, too." In another moment both Queens were fast asleep, and snoring loud.
  A9   75: 5   question," added the Gryphon; and then they both sat silent and looked at poor Alice, who felt ready to
  A7   58:24   "Wake up, Dormouse!" And they pinched it on both sides at once.
  T5 154: 5   "You may look in front of you, and on both sides, if you like," said the Sheep; "but you ca'n't look
  A4   34: 5   and, when she had looked under it, and on both sides of it, and behind it, it occurred to her that she
  A8   68:23   and brought it back, the fight was over, and both the hedgehogs were out of sight: "but it doesn't matter
  T4 139: 3   As black as a tar-barrel; / Which frightened both the heroes so, / They quite forgot their quarrel."
  T4 144:22   After a pause, Alice began, "Well! They were both very unpleasant characters--" Here she checked herself in
  T5 150:16   advantage in it, that one's memory works both ways."
BOTHER (1)
  A6   48:32   "Oh, don't bother me!" said the Duchess. "I never could abide figures!"
BOTTLE (12)
  A4   28: 6   or drink anything: so I'll just see what this bottle does. I do hope it'll make me grow large again, for
  A4   28:23   Luckily for Alice, the little magic bottle had now had its full effect, and she grew no larger:
  A1   11: 4   forgotten that, if you drink much from a bottle marked "poison," it is almost certain to disagree with
  T1 115:18   him. However, she could find nothing but a bottle of ink, and when she got back with it she found he had
  A1   10:15   like telescopes: this time she found a little bottle on it ("which certainly was not here before," said
  A4   28:12   from being broken. She hastily put down the bottle, saying to herself "That's quite enough--I hope I
  A4   28:10   had expected: before she had drunk half the bottle, she found her head pressing against the ceiling, and
  A4   28: 2   the room, when her eye fell upon a little bottle that stood near the looking-glass. There was no label
  A4   32:15   who were giving it something out of a bottle. They all made a rush at Alice the moment she appeared;
  A1   10:17   said Alice), and tied round the neck of the bottle was a paper label, with the words "DRINK ME"
  A1   11: 6   However, this bottle was not marked "poison," so Alice ventured to taste it,
  T9 204:26   creature in the very act of jumping over a bottle which had just lighted upon the table, "I'll shake you
BOTTLES (1)
  T9 203:16   rushes with fireworks at the top. As to the bottles, they each took a pair of plates, which they hastily
BOTTOM (4)
  A7   58:34   Lacie, and Tillie; and they lived at the bottom of a well--"
  A7   59: 8   so she went on: "But why did they live at the bottom of a well?"
  A7   59:21   her question. "Why did they live at the bottom of a well?"
  A9   76:17   wanted it much," said Alice; "living at the bottom of the sea."
BOUGH (1)
  A6   50:21   by seeing the Cheshire-Cat sitting on a bough of a tree a few yards off.
BOUGHS (1)
  T2 122: 6   a Daisy. "That's why its branches are called boughs!"
BOUGHT (4)
  T9 202: 6   / That is easy: a penny, I think, could have bought it.
  T4 146:27   fury than ever. "It's new, I tell you--I bought it yesterday--my nice NEW RATTLE!" and his voice rose
  T3 130: 6   excuses," said the Guard: "you should have bought one from the engine-driver." And once more the chorus
  T9 202: 5   have caught it. / 'Next, the fish must be bought.' / That is easy: a penny, I think, could have bought
BOUGHWOUGH (1)
  T2 122: 5   "It says 'Boughwough!'" cried a Daisy. "That's why its branches are
BOUND (3)
 A10   78:28   "The lobsters!" shouted the Gryphon, with a bound into the air.
  T3 137: 6   open field, and here the Fawn gave a sudden bound into the air, and shook itself free from Alice's arm.
  T5 151: 9   better, wouldn't it?" the Queen said, as she bound the plaster round her finger with a bit of ribbon.
BOUNDED (1)
  T8 190:37   "The Eighth Square at last!" she cried as she bounded * * * * * * * * * * * * * * across, and threw herself
BOUNDING (1)
  T7 174:18   and order the drums to begin." And Hatta went bounding away like a grasshopper.
BOW (3)
  T9 201:14   so quickly that Alice couldn't return its bow.
  T9 201: 2   a little bow to Alice; and Alice returned the bow, not knowing whether to be frightened or amused.

BOW (cont.)
T9   201: 1 mutton got up in the dish and made a little bow to Alice; and Alice returned the bow, not knowing whether
BOWED (4)
A8   63:36 She said it to the Knave of Hearts, who only bowed and smiled in reply.
A6   46: 4   Then they both bowed, and their curls got entangled together.
A3   24: 7 not think of anything to say, she simply bowed, and took the thimble, looking as solemn as she could.
A8   63: 2 the others looked round also, and all of them bowed low.
BOWING (1)
A8   65: 1 gardeners instantly jumped up, and began bowing to the King, the Queen, the royal children, and
BOX (9) [See also CHRISTMAS-BOX, JACK-IN-THE-BOX, etc.]
A5   38: 7 By the use of this ointment--one shilling the box--/ Allow me to sell you a couple?"
T8   181:14 badly, and he had a queer-shaped little deal box fastened across his shoulders, upside-down, and with the
A1   12:25 her eyes; and once she remembered trying to box her own ears for having cheated herself in a game of
T8   181:25 all the things must have fallen out! And the box is no use without them." He unfastened it as he spoke, and
A3   23:27 put her hand in her pocket, and pulled out a box of comfits (luckily the saltwater had not got into it),
T2   127:26 Queen said good-naturedly, taking a little box out of her pocket. "Have a biscuit?"
A1   12:31   Soon her eye fell on a little glass box that was lying under the table: she opened it, and found
T8   181:17   "I see you're admiring my little box," the Knight said in a friendly tone. "It's my own
T5   158:13 Sheep took the money, and put it away in a box: then she said "I never put things into people's hands--
BOXED (1)
A8   65:37   "She boxed the Queen's ears--" the Rabbit began. Alice gave a
BOY (5) [See also SHEPHERD-BOY]
T4   139:15 her finger at Tweedledum, and saying "First Boy!"
A6   48:36   "Speak roughly to your little boy, / And beat him when he sneezes: / He only does it to
A6   49: 4   "I speak severely to my boy, / I beat him when he sneezes; / For he can thoroughly
T1   118:18 the Jabberwock? / Come to my arms, my beamish boy! / O frabjous day! Callooh! Callay!" / He chortled in his
T4   139:18   "Next Boy!" said Alice, passing on to Tweedledee, though she felt
BOYS (1) [See also SCHOOLBOYS]
T1   108:13 you tidy, so you couldn't. I was watching the boys getting in sticks for the bonfire--and it wants plenty of
BRAIN (1)
A5   37: 6 to his son, / "I feared it might injure the brain; / But, now that I'm perfectly sure I have none, / Why,
BRAN (1)
T9   199:30 / And sprinkle the table with buttons and bran: / Put cats in the coffee, and mice in the tea--/ And
BRANCH (5)
T3   133: 5 gets about by swinging itself from branch to branch."
T3   133:12   "Look on the branch above your head," said the Gnat, "and there you'll find
A6   52:28 up, and there was the Cat again, sitting on a branch of a tree.
T3   133: 5 wood, and gets about by swinging itself from branch to branch."
T3   129:21 do to go down among them without a good long branch to brush them away--and what fun it'll be when they ask
BRANCHES (5)
A5   43:31 for her neck kept getting entangled among the branches, and every now and then she had to stop and untwist
T2   122: 5 'Boughwough!'" cried a Daisy. "That's why its branches are called boughs!"
T5   158:20 Let me see, is this a chair? Why, it's got branches, I declare! How very odd to find trees growing here!
A9   76:22 Mock Turtle replied; "and then the different branches of Arithmetic--Ambition, Distraction, Uglification,
T4   139:32 (as well as she could make it out) by the branches rubbing one across the other, like fiddles and
BRANDISHING (1)
T8   179:14 crimson armour, came galloping down upon her, brandishing a great club. Just as he reached her, the horse
BRANDY (2)
T3   133:15   and its head is a raisin burning in brandy."
A4   31:11 confusion of voices--"Hold up his head--Brandy now--Don't choke him--How was it, old fellow? What
BRASS (2)
T3   135:34 'answers to the name of "Dash": had on a brass collar'--just fancy calling everything you met 'Alice,'
A4   27:22 house, on the door of which was a bright brass plate with the name "W. RABBIT" engraved upon it. She
BRAVE (2)
T4   147:34   "I'm very brave, generally," he went on in a low voice: "only to-day I
A1   8:24 think nothing of tumbling down-stairs! How brave they'll all think me at home! Why, I wouldn't say
BREAD (7)
T8   188: 7 on stormy seas; / And that's the way I get my bread--/ A trifle, if you please.'
T7   174:15 once, carrying round trays of white and brown bread. Alice took a piece to taste, but it was very dry.
T7   174: 8 "Then I suppose they'll soon bring the white bread and the brown?" Alice ventured to remark.
T7   175:34 from her to the King. "None of your brown bread for me!"
T9   194:40 answer useful questions?" she said. "How is bread made?"
T7   173: 3 all round the town. / Some gave them white bread, some gave them brown: / Some gave them plum-cake and
T4   143: 7   'A loaf of bread,' the Walrus said, / 'Is what we chiefly need: / Pepper
BREAD-AND-BUTTER (13)
A11   88:33 large piece out of his teacup instead of the bread-and-butter.
A11   90: 1 that," continued the Hatter, "I cut some more bread-and-butter--"
T7   173:28 looked round and nodded, and went on with his bread-and-butter.
T5   149: 9 herself that sounded like "Bread-and-butter, bread-and-butter," and Alice felt that if there was to be any
A7   59:19 this: so she helped herself to some tea and bread-and-butter, and then turned to the Dormouse, and
A11   90: 7 The miserable Hatter dropped his teacup and bread-and-butter and went down on one knee. "I'm a poor man,
T5   149: 9 in a whisper to herself that sounded like "Bread-and-butter, bread-and-butter," and Alice felt that if
A11   89:13 not above a week or so--and what with the bread-and-butter getting so thin--and the twinkling of the tea
T7   173:22 with a cup of tea in one hand and a piece of bread-and-butter in the other.
A11   88: 7 in with a teacup in one hand and a piece of bread-and-butter in the other. "I beg pardon, your Majesty,"
T3   134:11   Its wings are thin slices of bread-and-butter, its body is a crust, and its head is a lump
T9   194: 8   but the Red Queen answered for her. "Bread-and-butter, of course. Try another Subtraction sum. Take
T7   174: 6 effort, and swallowed a large piece of bread-and-butter. "They're getting on very well," he said in a
BREAD-AND-BUTTER-FLY (1)
T3   134:10 feet back in some alarm), "you may observe a Bread-and-butter-fly. Its wings are thin slices of

BREAD-KNIFE (1)
  A7   56: 6   "you shouldn't have put it in with the bread-knife."
BREAK (2)
  A9   74:19   could hear him sighing as if his heart would break. She pitied him deeply. "What is his sorrow?" she asked
  A7   55:35   The Hatter was the first to break the silence. "What day of the month is it?" he said,
BREAKFAST (2)
  T12 208: 3   a real treat. All the time you're eating your breakfast, I'll repeat 'The Walrus and the Carpenter' to you;
  T5 153:16   as many as six impossible things before breakfast. There goes the shawl again!"
BREAKING (3)
  T6 160:30 declare that's too bad!" Humpty Dumpty cried, breaking into a sudden passion. "You've been listening at
  T5 156:19 of the rushes a good long way down before breaking them off--and for a while Alice forgot all about the
  T8 184: 3 of," the Knight said, as if he didn't mind breaking two or three of them. "The great art of riding, as I
BREATH (22)
  T7 173: 6 for the run was putting her quite out of breath.
  T1 114:11 in silence. As soon as she had recovered her breath a little, she called out to the White King, who was
  T7 173:10   "to stop a minute--just to get--one's breath again?"
  T4 143: 3 we have our chat; / For some of us are out of breath, / And all of us are fat!' / 'No hurry!' said the
  T1 114: 9 through the air had quite taken away her breath, and for a minute or two she could do nothing but hug
  A10 82: 8   and then the Mock Turtle drew a long breath, and said "That's very curious!"
  A9 73:10   Then the Queen left off, quite out of breath, and said to Alice "Have you seen the Mock Turtle yet
  T5 153:10 in a pitying tone. "Try again: draw a long breath, and shut your eyes."
  T2 126:26 to talk again, she was getting so much out of breath: and still the Queen cried "Faster! Faster!" and
  A4 33: 5 and ran till she was quite tired and out of breath, and till the puppy's bark sounded quite faint in the
  T3 129:14 found out, though the idea quite took her breath away at first. "And what enormous flowers they must be!
  T2 121: 2 for a minute: it quite seemed to take her breath away. At length, as the Tiger-lily only went on waving
  T1 115: 1 lifted the Queen, that she mightn't take his breath away; but, before she put him on the table, she thought
  T7 173:14   Alice had no more breath for talking; so they trotted on in silence, till they
  T4 139:39 two dancers were fat, and very soon out of breath. "Four times round is enough for one dance," Tweedledum
  A3 25:34 With no jury or judge, would be wasting our breath. 'I'll be judge, I'll be jury, said cunning old Fury:
  T2 126:17 she could not go faster, though she had no breath left to say so.
  T1 114:16 the Queen, who was still a little out of breath. "Mind you come up--the regular way--don't get blown
  TI 103:35 summer glory--/ It shall not touch, with breath of bale, / The pleasance of our fairy-tale.
  T7 171: 9 Messenger arrived: he was far too much out of breath to say a word, and could only wave his hands about, and
  AI   3: 9   such dreamy weather, / To beg a tale of breath too weak / To stir the tiniest feather! / Yet what can
  T7 172:23 been here first. However, now you've got your breath, you may tell us what's happened in the town."
BREATHE (4)
  A7 55:30 I sleep' is the same thing as 'I sleep when I breathe'!"
  A11 88:40 who was sitting next to her. "I can hardly breathe."
  T8 181: 9   "Now one can breathe more easily," said the Knight, putting back his shaggy
  A7 55:29 seemed to be talking in its sleep, "that 'I breathe when I sleep' is the same thing as 'I sleep when I
BREATHLESS (1)
  T2 127: 9 and she found herself sitting on the ground, breathless and giddy.
BREEZE (1)
  A10 85: 8 more and more faintly came, carried on the breeze that followed them, the melancholy words:--
BRIDGE (3)
  T7 177: 2   You get the best view by the old bridge."
  T8 189: 9 / Completed my design / To keep the Menai bridge from rust / By boiling it in wine. / I thanked him much
  T7 177: 1 That's a good long way. Did you go by the old bridge, or the market-place? You get the best view by the old
BRIDLE (1)
  T8 184: 6   He let go the bridle, and stretched out both his arms to show Alice what he
BRIGHT (16)
  A12 99: 7 other little children, and make their eyes bright and eager with many a strange tale, perhaps even with
  T3 133:10 must have been just repainted, it looked so bright and sticky; and then she went on.
  T4 140:26 very best to make / The billows smooth and bright--/ And this was odd, because it was / The middle of the
  T8 188:34 hunt for haddocks' eyes / Among the heather bright, / And work them into waistcoat-buttons / In the silent
  A4 27:22 neat little house, on the door of which was a bright brass plate with the name "W. RABBIT" engraved upon it.
  T5 156:22 hair dipping into the water--while with bright eager eyes she caught at one bunch after another of the
  A12 98:18 hands were clasped upon her knee, and the bright eager eyes were looking up into hers--she could hear
  A7 61: 6 at last in the beautiful garden, among the bright flower-beds and the cool fountains.
  A1 10: 5 hall, and wander about among those beds of bright flowers and those cool fountains, but she could not
  A7 58:10   A bright idea came into Alice's head. "Is that the reason so
  A4 32: 6 little cakes as they lay on the floor, and a bright idea came into her head. "If I eat one of these cakes,"
  T1 111:13 glass was beginning to melt away, just like a bright silvery mist.
  T5 154:17 a minute or so in vainly pursuing a large bright thing that looked sometimes like a doll and sometimes
  T1 116:13   over this for some time, but at last a bright thought struck her. "Why, it's a Looking-glass book, of
  T9 198:14 hobbled slowly towards her: he was dressed in bright yellow, and had enormous boots on.
  T8W 17:10 looked at his wig in great surprise. It was bright yellow like the handkerchief, and all tangled and
BRIGHTENED (3)
  A12 94:20 else's hand," said the King. (The jury all brightened up again.)
  A1 12: 4 was now only ten inches high, and her face brightened up at the thought that she was now the right size
  T7 174:21 stood silent, watching him. Suddenly she brightened up. "Look, look!" she cried, pointing eagerly.
BRIGHT-EYED (1)
  A2 20: 5 house, I should like to show you! A little bright-eyed terrier, you know, with oh, such long curly brown
BRIGHTLY (1)
  T1 112: 5 that there was a real one, blazing away as brightly as the one she had left behind. "So I shall be as
BRILLIG (5)
  T1 116: 9 dna eryg diD / sevot yhtils eht dna ,gillirb sawT'
  T1 116:18   'Twas brillig, and the slithy toves / Did gyre and gimble in the
  T1 118:21   'Twas brillig, and the slithy toves / Did gyre and gimble in the
  T6 164:21   "'Twas brillig, and the slithy toves / Did gyre and gimble in the

BRILLIG (cont.)
T6   164:26   "there are plenty of hard words there. 'Brillig' means four o'clock in the afternoon--the time when
BRING (7)
T9   201:17   so, as an experiment, she called out "Waiter! Bring back the pudding!" and there it was again in a moment,
A4   30:25   "Where's the other ladder?--Why, I hadn't to bring but one. Bill's got the other--Bill! Fetch it here, lad!
T9   202:11   'Bring it here! Let me sup!' / It is easy to set such a dish on
A11   89: 6   said, to one of the officers of the court, "Bring me the list of the singers in the last concert!" on
A1   12:24   she scolded herself so severely as to bring tears into her eyes; and once she remembered trying to
T7   174: 8   "Then I suppose they'll soon bring the white bread and the brown?" Alice ventured to remark
T8   187:18   most clearly. Years afterwards she could bring the whole scene back again, as if it had been only
BRINGING (3)
A5   43:35   sometimes shorter, until she had succeeded in bringing herself down to her usual height.
A8   62:16   said Five. "And I'll tell him--it was for bringing the cook tulip-roots instead of onions."
A11   88: 8   "I beg pardon, your Majesty," he began, "for bringing these in; but I hadn't quite finished my tea when I
BRINGS (1)
T8   186:36   Everybody that hears me sing it--either it brings the tears into their eyes, or else--"
BRINY (1)
T4   141:16   pleasant walk, a pleasant talk, / Along the briny beach: / We cannot do with more than four, / To give a
BRISKLY (1)
T4   139:16   "Nohow!" Tweedledum cried out briskly, and shut his mouth up again with a snap.
BRISTLING (1)
A2   19:40   Alice again, for this time the Mouse was bristling all over, and she felt certain it must be really
BROAD (1)
T9   204: 6   turned again, just in time to see the Queen's broad good-natured face grinning at her for a moment over the
BROILING (1)
T6   164:27   in the afternoon--the time when you begin broiling things for dinner."
BROKE (5)
T8   179:20   more "You're my--" but here another voice broke in "Ahoy! Ahoy! Check!" and Alice looked round in some
A5   41:37   arms round it as far as they would go, and broke off a bit of the edge with each hand.
T9   192:25   Queen. "Why, don't you see, child--" here she broke off with a frown, and, after thinking for a minute,
T9   193:14   The Red Queen broke the silence by saying, to the White Queen, "I invite you
A6   46:29   Footman's head: it just grazed his nose, and broke to pieces against one of the trees behind him.
BROKEN (8)
T4   146:19   "only an old rattle--quite old and broken."
T8   184: 2   as she picked him up, "I hope no bones are broken?"
A4   30: 5   Come help me out of this!" (Sounds of more broken glass.)
A4   29:38   a little shriek and a fall, and a crash of broken glass, from which she concluded that it was just
A4   30:17   were two little shrieks, and more sounds of broken glass. "What a number of cucumber-frames there must be!
A9   74:34   words were followed by a very long silence, broken only by an occasional exclamation of "Hjckrrh!" from
A4   28:11   and had to stoop to save her neck from being broken. She hastily put down the bottle, saying to herself
A6   46:16   great crash, as if a dish or kettle had been broken to pieces.
BROOCH (4)
T5   152:19   it all crooked!" And she caught at the brooch; but it was too late: the pin had slipped, and the
T5   152:16   directly. Oh, oh!" As she said the words the brooch flew open, and the Queen clutched wildly at it, and
T5   153:17   The brooch had come undone as she spoke, and a sudden gust of wind
T5   152:15   again," the poor Queen groaned out: "the brooch will come undone directly. Oh, oh!" As she said the
BROOK (13)
T2   125:24   green hedges, that reached from brook to brook.
T5   153:24   said very politely, as she crossed the little brook after the Queen. * * * * * * * * * * * * *
T8   190:15   he said, "down the hill and over that little brook, and then you'll be a Queen--But you'll stay and see me
T8   190:35   to run down the hill: "and now for the last brook, and to be a Queen! How grand it sounds!" A very few
T8W   13:10   thought, as she turned to spring over the brook:--but I'll just ask him what's the matter," she added,
T7   178: 4   to her feet and sprang across the little brook in her terror, and had just time to see the Lion and the
T8   181: 3   "So you will, when you've crossed the next brook," said the White Knight. "I'll see you safe to the end
T8   190:37   very few steps brought her to the edge of the brook. "The Eighth Square at last!" she cried as she bounded *
T5   153:16   wind blew the Queen's shawl across a little brook. The Queen spread out her arms again and went flying
T2   125:23   of little green hedges, that reached from brook to brook.
T3   132: 6   quietly drew it in and said "It's only a brook we have to jump over." Everybody seemed satisfied with
T5   158:22   growing here! And actually here's a little brook! Well, this is the very queerest shop I ever saw!" * * *
T7   177: 6   had seated herself on the bank of a little brook, with the great dish on her knees, and was sawing away
BROOKS (2)
T3   129:29   and jumped over the first of the six little brooks. * * * * * * * * * * * * * *
T2   125:21   it was. There were a number of tiny little brooks running straight across it from side to side, and the
BROTHER (4)
T4   140:16   the longest," Tweedledum replied, giving his brother an affectionate hug.
T4   146: 5   spread a large umbrella over himself and his brother, and looked up into it. "No, I don't think it is," he
T4   147: 4   took off Alice's attention from the angry brother. But he couldn't quite succeed, and it ended in his
T4   148:15   one sword, you know," Tweedledum said to his brother: "but you can have the umbrella--it's quite as sharp.
BROTHER'S (1)
A2   19:17   but she remembered having seen, in her brother's Latin Grammar, "A mouse--of a mouse--to a mouse--a
BROTHERS (4)
T4   144:28   "Come and look at him!" the brothers cried, and they each took one of Alice's hands, and
T4   139:23   d'ye do?' and shake hands!" And here the two brothers gave each other a hug, and then they held out the two
T4   148:22   out in a shrill voice of alarm; and the two brothers took to their heels and were out of sight in a moment
T4   147:12   So the two brothers went off hand-in-hand into the wood, and returned in
BROUGHT (7)
T9   201: 8   joint!" And the waiters carried it off, and brought a large plum-pudding in its place.
T8   190:36   Queen! How grand it sounds!" A very few steps brought her to the edge of the brook. "The Eighth Square at
A5   44: 6   not venture to go near the house till she had brought herself down to nine inches high.
A8   68:22   By the time she had caught the flamingo and brought it back, the fight was over, and both the hedgehogs

BROUGHT (cont.)
A5   36:10   Which brought them back again to the beginning of the conversation.
T4   143:27   / 'To play them such a trick, / After we've brought them out so far, / And made them trot so quick!' / The
T9   196:28   "She never was really well brought up," the Red Queen went on: "but it's amazing how
BROW (1)
TI   103: 1   Child of the pure unclouded brow / And dreaming eyes of wonder! / Though time be fleet,
BROWN (12)
T1   110: 3   in the autumn, when the leaves are getting brown.
T8W   15: 2   the paper and said "No. It says nothing about brown."
T7   174: 9   they'll soon bring the white bread and the brown?" Alice ventured to remark.
T7   174:15   at once, carrying round trays of white and brown bread. Alice took a piece to taste, but it was very dry.
T7   175:34   turning from her to the King. "None of your brown bread for me!"
T3   137: 9   sudden look of alarm came into its beautiful brown eyes, and in another moment it had darted away at full
A2   20: 5   terrier, you know, with oh, such long curly brown hair! And it'll fetch things when you throw them, and
A10   82:23   I heard him declare / 'You have baked me too brown, I must sugar my hair.' / As a duck with his eyelids, so
T7   173: 3   / Some gave them white bread, some gave them brown: / Some gave them plum-cake and drummed them out of town
T8W   15: 3   "No brown sugar!" grumbled the Wasp. "A nice exploring party!"
T8W   14:24   "Any brown sugar?" the Wasp interrupted.
T6   166:34   In autumn, when the leaves are brown, / Take pen and ink, and write it down."
BRUSH (4)
T5   149:34   Alice carefully released the brush, and did her best to get the hair into order. "Come, you
A8   62:17   Seven flung down his brush, and had just begun "Well, of all the unjust things--"
T5   149:32   "The brush has got entangled in it!" the Queen said with a sigh.
T3   129:21   down among them without a good long branch to brush them away--and what fun it'll be when they ask me how I
BRUSHED (2)
T4   145:29   "and it's foolish to cry about it." So she brushed away her tears, and went on, as cheerfully as she
T4   142: 3   / All eager for the treat: / Their coats were brushed, their faces washed, / Their shoes were clean and neat
BRUSHING (1)
A12   98: 1   head in the lap of her sister, who was gently brushing away some dead leaves that had fluttered down from
BUD (1)
T2   123: 2   going on in the world, than if you were a bud!"
BUFFALO (1)
T8   190: 9   were full of dough, / Who snorted like a buffalo--/ That summer evening long ago, / A-sitting on a gate
BUNCH (2)
T5   156:22   with bright eager eyes she caught at one bunch after another of the darling scented rushes.
T5   155:31   the Sheep cried angrily, taking up quite a bunch of needles.
BUNCHES (2)
T8   182:20   to the saddle, which was already loaded with bunches of carrots, and fire-irons, and many other things.
T9   195: 5   So they set to work and fanned her with bunches of leaves, till she had to beg them to leave off, it
BUNDLES (1)
T4   147:22   buttons--"Really they'll be more like bundles of old clothes than anything else, by the time they're
BUNDLING (1)
T4   147: 5   succeed, and it ended in his rolling over, bundling up in the umbrella, with only his head out: and there
BURBLED (1)
T1   118:12   Came whiffling through the tulgey wood, / And burbled as it came!
BURN (2)
A4   31:27   "We must burn the house down!" said the Rabbit's voice. And Alice
A1   11: 1   them: such as, that a red-hot poker will burn you if you hold it too long; and that, if you cut your
BURNING (2)
T3   133:14   of holly-leaves, and its head is a raisin burning in brandy."
A1   8: 3   or a watch to take out of it, and burning with curiosity, she ran across the field after it, and
BURNT (1)
A1   10:22   little stories about children who had got burnt, and eaten up by wild beasts, and other unpleasant
BURST (1)
A2   17:25   but, oh dear!" cried Alice, with a sudden burst of tears, "I do wish they would put their heads down! I
BURSTING (1)
A8   66:12   a puzzled expression that she could not help bursting out laughing; and, when she had got its head down,
BUSH (2)
T4   139:36   myself singing 'Here we go round the mulberry bush.' I don't know when I began it, but somehow I felt as if
T3   133: 3   "All right," said the Gnat. "Half way up that bush, you'll see a Rocking-horse-fly, if you look. It's made
BUSHES (1)
T8   181:26   and was just going to throw it into the bushes, when a sudden thought seemed to strike him, and he
BUSHY (1)
T2   123: 7   said the Tiger-lily), "but she's more bushy than you are."
BUSILY (5)
A11   86:28   The twelve jurors were all writing very busily on slates. "What are they doing?" Alice whispered to
A8   62: 3   white, but there were three gardeners at it, busily painting them red. Alice thought this a very curious
A6   48:29   she meant to take the hint; but the cook was busily stirring the soup, and seemed not to be listening, so
T7   170: 5   found the White King seated on the ground, busily writing in his memorandum-book.
A12   93:33   moment the King, who had been for some time busily writing in his note-book, called out "Silence!", and
BUSINESS (10)
A9   70:35   that it's done by everybody minding their own business!"
T6   160: 3   first time, "but tell me your name and your business."
T9   199: 3   with anybody. "Where's the servant whose business it is to answer the door?" she began angrily.
A8   64: 4   Alice, surprised at her own courage. "It's no business of mine."
A8   62:15   "Yes, it is his business!" said Five. "And I'll tell him--it was for bringing
A6   48:20   "If everybody minded their own business," the Duchess said, in a hoarse growl, "the world
A12   93:16   "What do you know about this business?" the King said to Alice.
A4   30:11   "Well, it's got no business there, at any rate: go and take it away!"
T4   140:31   / Because she thought the sun / Had got no business to be there / After the day was done--/ 'It's very

BUSINESS (cont.)
```
 A8    62:14                              "That's none of your business, Two!" said Seven.
```
BUSTLED (1)
```
 T4   147:19  anything  in  all her life--the way those two bustled about--and the quantity of things they put on--and the
```
BUSTLING (1)
```
 T3   129: 9  stood  silent,  watching one of them that was bustling about among the flowers, poking its proboscis into
```
BUSY (2)
```
 A5    36:34  "Well, I've tried to say 'How doth the little busy bee,' but it all came different!" Alice replied in a very
 A12   99: 1  (she  knew)  to  the  confused clamour of the busy farm-yard--while the lowing of the cattle in the distance
```
BUT (383) [entries omitted]
BUTTER (3) [See also BREAD-AND-BUTTER(-FLY)]
```
 A7    56: 4                              "It was the best butter," the March Hare meekly replied.
 A7    56: 1  days  wrong!" sighed the Hatter. "I told you butter wouldn't suit the works!" he added, looking angrily at
 A7    56:10  say  than  his first remark, "It was the best butter, you know."
```
BUTTERCUP (1)
```
 A4    33: 8  it  was!"  said Alice, as she leant against a buttercup to rest herself, and fanned herself with one of the
```
BUTTERED (3)
```
 T7   172:32  "If  you do such a thing again, I'll have you buttered! It went through and through my head like an
 T8   188:41                      'I sometimes dig for buttered rolls, / Or set limed twigs for crabs: / I sometimes
 A1    11: 9  pine-apple,  roast  turkey,  toffy,  and  hot buttered toast), she very soon finished it off. * * * * * * *
```
BUTTERFLIES (1)
```
 T8   188: 1                      He said 'I look for butterflies / That sleep among the wheat: / I make them into
```
BUTTERFLY (2)
```
 T3   134: 4                              "And then there's the Butterfly," Alice went on, after she had taken a good look at
 A5    36: 4  day,  you  know--and  then  after that into a butterfly, I should think you'll feel it a little queer,
```
BUTTER'S (1)
```
 T4   143:30    /  The  Carpenter  said  nothing  but  / 'The butter's spread too thick!'
```
BUTTONS (3) [See also WAISTCOAT-BUTTONS]
```
 T9   199:30  as  you  can,  /  And sprinkle the table with buttons and bran: / Put cats in the coffee, and mice in the
 A10   82:25  so  he with his nose / Trims his belt and his buttons, and turns out his toes. / When the sands are all dry,
 T4   147:21  they  gave her in tying strings and fastening buttons--"Really they'll be more like bundles of old clothes
```
BUY (5)
```
 T5   157:13  make  up  your mind. Now, what do you want to buy?"
 T5   157:14                              "To buy!" Alice echoed in a tone that was half astonished and half
 T5   158: 3                      "I should like to buy an egg, please," she said timidly. "How do you sell them?"
 T5   154: 1                      "What is it you want to buy?" the Sheep said at last, looking up for a moment from her
 T5   158: 9  "Only  you  must  eat  them  both, if you buy two," said the Sheep.
```
BY (123) [entries omitted]
BY-THE-BYE (1)
```
 A6    52:16                              "By-the-bye, what became of the baby?" said the Cat. "I'd
```

-C-

C (1)
    A3   24:15   know," said Alice, "and why it is you hate--C and D," she added in a whisper, half afraid that it would be
CABBAGES (1)
    T4   142:22   / Of shoes--and ships--and sealing wax--/ Of cabbages--and kings--/ And why the sea is boiling hot--/ And
-CABS [See HANSOM-CABS]
CAKE (7) [See also PLUM-CAKE]
    A1   13: 5   set to work, and very soon finished off the cake. * * * * * * * * * *
    T7   177: 5   What a time the Monster is, cutting up that cake!"
    A1   13: 1   this is what generally happens when one eats cake; but Alice had got so much into the way of expecting
    T7   177:14   got up, and carried the dish round, and the cake divided itself into three pieces as she did so. "Now cut
    A1   12:32   she opened it, and found in it a very small cake, on which the words "EAT ME" were beautifully marked in
    T7   175:39   Haigha took a large cake out of the bag, and gave it to Alice to hold, while he
    T7   176:11   King and the Unicorn): "fair play with the cake, you know!"
CAKES (4)
    A4   32:10   So she swallowed one of the cakes, and was delighted to find that she began shrinking
    A4   32: 6   that the pebbles were all turning into little cakes as they lay on the floor, and a bright idea came into
    A4   32: 7   came into her head. "If I eat one of these cakes," she thought, "it's sure to make some change in my size
    T7   177:11   "You don't know how to manage Looking-glass cakes," the Unicorn remarked. "Hand it round first, and cut it
CALCULATION (1)
    T6   161:22   Alice made a short calculation, and said "Seven years and six months."
CALL (25)
    T6   160:36   said in a calmer tone. "That's what you call a History of England, that is. Now, take a good look at
    A7   60:33   once or twice, half hoping that they would call after her: the last time she saw them, they were trying
    T3   135: 4   because there wouldn't be any name for her to call, and of course you wouldn't have to go, you know."
    T3   137:27   But I ca'n't stay there long. I'll just call and say 'How d'ye do?' and ask them the way out of the
    A9   74:42   sea. The master was an old Turtle--we used to call him Tortoise--"
    A9   75: 1   "Why did you call him Tortoise, if he wasn't one?" Alice asked.
    T2   125:13   The Red Queen shook her head. "You may call it 'nonsense' if you like," she said, "but I've heard
    A6   51:35   "I call it purring, not growling," said Alice.
    A3   25: 2   wonder at the Mouse's tail; but why do you call it sad?" And she kept on puzzling about it while the
    A6   52: 1   "Call it what you like," said the Cat. "Do you play croquet
    T3   135:43   hand on the trunk of the tree. "What does it call itself, I wonder? I do believe it's got no name--why, to
    T3   135: 7   that. If she couldn't remember my name, she'd call me 'Miss,' as the servants do."
    T8W   19:14   whenever I appear, / They hoot at me and call me 'Pig!' / And that is why they do it, dear, / Because I
    T3   135: 2   wanted to call you to your lessons, she would call out 'Come here--,' and there she would have to leave off,
    T8   188:21   a blaze; / And thence they make a stuff they call / Rowland's Macassar-Oil--/ Yet twopence-halfpenny is all
    T2   125: 9   you hills, in comparison with which you'd call that a valley."
    T7   172:30   "Do you call that a whisper?" cried the poor King, jumping up and
    T5   149:13   "Well, yes, if you call that a-dressing," the Queen said. "It isn't my notion of
    A11   88: 4   "Call the first witness," said the King; and the White Rabbit
    A11   91:25   said the King with an air of great relief. "Call the next witness." And, he added, in an undertone to the
    A11   91: 4   "Call the next witness!" said the King.
    T3   135: 1   it! For instance, if the governess wanted to call you to your lessons, she would call out 'Come here--,'
    T3   136:18   of it. "Please, would you tell me what you call yourself?" she said timidly. "I think that might help a
    T9   192:27   really are a Queen'? What right have you to call yourself so? You ca'n't be a Queen, you know, till you've
    T3   136:12   "What do you call yourself?" the Fawn said at last. Such a soft sweet voice
CALLAY (1)
    T1   118:19   my beamish boy! / O frabjous day! Callooh! Callay!" / He chortled in his joy.
CALLED (32)
    A10   81:11   said the Gryphon. "Do you know why it's called a whiting?"
    A5   36:18   "Come back!" the Caterpillar called after her. "I've something important to say!"
    A3   26:13   come back, and finish your story!" Alice called after it. And the others all joined in chorus "Yes,
    T8   187: 4   I ought to have said 'That's what the song is called'?" Alice corrected herself.
    T6   159:18   looking away from Alice as he spoke, "to be called an egg--very!"
    T2   122: 6   cried a Daisy. "That's why its branches are called boughs!"
    T8   186:40   it doesn't, you know. The name of the song is called 'Haddocks' Eyes.'"
    T7   170:37   town beginning with H. "The other Messenger's called Hatta. I must have two, you know--to come and go. One
    A6   45: 5   judging by his face only, she would have called him a fish)--and rapped loudly at the door with his
    A9   75: 2   "We called him Tortoise because he taught us," said the Mock
    T4   147:31   coming up to have his helmet tied on. (He called it a helmet, though it certainly looked much more like
    T8W   17: 2   Wasp said "That's a new-fangled name. They called it conceit in my time."
    T6   164:15   you kindly tell me the meaning of the poem called 'Jabberwocky'?"
    A9   77:15   "That's the reason they're called lessons," the Gryphon remarked: "because they lessen
    A4   31:29   down!" said the Rabbit's voice. And Alice called out, as loud as she could, "If you do, I'll set Dinah
    A11   88: 5   Rabbit blew three blasts on the trumpet, and called out "First witness!"
    A3   26:33   doesn't suit my throat!" And a Canary called out in a trembling voice, to its children, "Come away,
    A12   93:34   some time busily writing in his note-book, called out "Silence!", and read out from his book, "Rule
    A3   21:14   to be a person of some authority among them, called out "Sit down, all of you, and listen to me! I'll soon
    T7   174:13   the Unicorn sat down, panting, while the King called out "Ten minutes allowed for refreshments!" Haigha and
    A8   63:11   had been anxiously looking across the garden, called out "The Queen! The Queen!" and the three gardeners
    A3   23:14   and were quite dry again, the Dodo suddenly called out "The race is over!" and they all crowded round it,
    A4   27:13   noticed Alice, as she went hunting about, and called out to her, in an angry tone, "Why, Mary Ann, what are
    T1   114:11   as she had recovered her breath a little, she called out to the White King, who was sitting sulkily among

CALLED (cont.)
T9   201:16   one to give orders; so, as an experiment, she called out "Waiter! Bring back the pudding!" and there it was
A2   20:14   So she called softly after it, "Mouse dear! Do come back again, and
T7   177: 9   the Lion (she was getting quite used to being called 'the Monster'). "I've cut several slices already, but
T8   187: 2   a little vexed. "That's what the name is called. The name really is 'The Aged Aged Man.'"
A8   68: 4   said the King very decidedly; and he called to the Queen, who was passing at the moment, "My dear!
T6   165: 6   "Of course it is. It's called 'wabe' you know, because it goes a long way before it,
T8   187: 6   that's quite another thing! The song is called 'Ways and Means': but that's only what it's called, you
T8   187: 7   'Ways and Means': but that's only what it's called, you know!"

CALLING (2)
T3   135:34   of "Dash": had on a brass collar'--just fancy calling everything you met 'Alice,' till one of them answered!
A3   23:24   the whole party at once crowded round her, calling out, in a confused way, "Prizes! Prizes!"

CALLOOH (1)
T1   118:19   to my arms, my beamish boy! / O frabjous day! Callooh! Callay!" / He chortled in his joy.

CALMER (2)
T4   147: 9   agree to have a battle?" Tweedledum said in a calmer tone.
T6   160:36   things in a book," Humpty Dumpty said in a calmer tone. "That's what you call a History of England, that

CALMLY (1)
A9   74:41   the Mock Turtle went on at last, more calmly, though still sobbing a little now and then, "we went

CAME (92)
T1   118:12   through the tulgey wood, / And burbled as it came!
A4   31:16   Last came a little feeble, squeaking voice ("That's Bill," thought
A4   29:20   voice. "Fetch me my gloves this moment!" Then came a little pattering of feet on the stairs. Alice knew it
A4   30:23   time without hearing anything more: at last came a rumbling of little cart-wheels, and the sound of a good
T2   122: 3   "But what could it do, if any danger came?" Alice asked.
T7   170:24   up and down, and wriggling like an eel, as he came along, with his great hands spread out like fans on each
A4   30: 1   Next came an angry voice--the Rabbit's--"Pat! Pat! Where are you?"
T8   185: 4   I could get out again, the other White Knight came and put it on. He thought it was his own helmet."
T8   179:29   "Yes, but then I came and rescued her!" the White Knight replied.
T3   135:17   Then came another of those melancholy little sighs, and this time
T4   142: 9   yet another four; / And thick and fast they came at last, / And more, and more, and more--/ All hopping
A5   36:20   promising, certainly. Alice turned and came back again.
A12   95:15   (Before she had this fit) / An obstacle that came between / Him, and ourselves, and it.
A10   85: 8   ran the faster, while more and more faintly came, carried on the breeze that followed them, the melancholy
T9   204:15   pull, and plates, dishes, guests, and candles came crashing down together in a heap on the floor.
A5   36:35   'How doth the little busy bee,' but it all came different!" Alice replied in a very melancholy voice.
A10   82:11   "It all came different!" the Mock Turtle repeated thoughtfully. "I
A6   48:11   at the Duchess and the baby--the fire-irons came first; then followed a shower of saucepans, plates, and
A12   97: 9   this the whole pack rose up into the air, and came flying down upon her; she gave a little scream, half of
T7   174:22   White Queen running across the country! She came flying out of the wood over yonder--How fast those Queens
T9   196: 9   "I know what he came for," said Alice: "he wanted to punish the fish, because
T3   130: 3   tone: "there wasn't a ticket-office where I came from." And again the chorus of voices went on. "There
T3   131:32   looking about in vain to see where the voice came from. "If you're so anxious to have a joke made, why
T7   178: 1   Where the noise came from, she couldn't make out: the air seemed full of it,
T3   130: 5   went on. "There wasn't room for one where she came from. The land there is worth a thousand pounds an inch!"
T8   179:14   and a Knight, dressed in crimson armour, came galloping down upon her, brandishing a great club. Just
T1   109: 6   a dinner: then, when the miserable day came, I should have to go without fifty dinners at once! Well,
A6   53:10   She had not gone much farther before she came in sight of the house of the March Hare: she thought it
A11   88: 6   The first witness was the Hatter. He came in with a teacup in one hand and a piece of
T8W   18: 6   A curious idea came into Alice's head. Almost every one she had met had
A7   58:10   A bright idea came into Alice's head. "Is that the reason so many tea-things
T3   134:15   A new difficulty came into Alice's head. "Supposing it couldn't find any?" she
T8   187:30   and listened very attentively, but no tears came into her eyes.
A4   32: 6   as they lay on the floor, and a bright idea came into her head. "If I eat one of these cakes," she thought
T3   137: 8   you're a human child!" A sudden look of alarm came into its beautiful brown eyes, and in another moment it
T7   173:15   so they trotted on in silence, till they came into sight of a great crowd, in the middle of which the
A8   63:20   there were ten of them, and the little dears came jumping merrily along, hand in hand, in couples: they
A2   15:32   to ask help of any one: so, when the Rabbit came near her, she began, in a low, timid voice, "If you
A9   74:18   on a little ledge of rock, and, as they came nearer, Alice could hear him sighing as if his heart
T3   136:17   Alice thought, but nothing came of it. "Please, would you tell me what you call yourself
T9   196:13   said the Red Queen.) "And part of the roof came off, and ever so much thunder got in--and it went rolling
A2   15:29   in a great hurry, muttering to himself, as he came, "Oh! The Duchess, the Duchess! Oh! Wo'n't she be savage
A8   63:34   When the procession came opposite to Alice, they all stopped and looked at her,
T1   109: 4   be sent to prison, I suppose, when the day came. Or--let me see--suppose each punishment was to be going
T3   137: 5   round the soft neck of the Fawn, till they came out into another open field, and here the Fawn gave a
T7   175:40   out a dish and carving-knife. How they all came out of it Alice couldn't guess. It was just like a
A8   65:39   tone. "The Queen will hear you! You see she came rather late, and the Queen said--"
A4   32: 1   the next moment a shower of little pebbles came rattling in at the window, and some of them hit her in
T5   152:34   thought of her loneliness, two large tears came rolling down her cheeks.
T3   135:13   Gnat only sighed deeply while two large tears came rolling down its cheeks.
A6   45: 2   to do next, when suddenly a footman in livery came running out of the wood--(she considered him to be a
T7   169: 1   The next moment soldiers came running through the wood, at first in twos and threes,
T5   149: 2   the owner: in another moment the White Queen came running wildly through the wood, with both arms stretched
A6   46:28   door of the house opened, and a large plate came skimming out, straight at the Footman's head: it just
T1   115:32   she took hold of the end of the pencil, which came some way over his shoulder, and began writing for him.
A5   44: 1   to be done, I wonder?" As she said this, she came suddenly upon an open place, with a little house in it
A8   63:15   First came ten soldiers carrying clubs: these were all shaped like
T9   199:41   Then came the chorus again:--
T3   129:23   say 'Oh, I liked it well enough--' (here came the favourite little toss of the head), 'only it was so
A8   63:21   they were all ornamented with hearts. Next came the guests, mostly Kings and Queens, and among them Alice

CAME (cont.)
```
T7    169:10                                    Then came the horses. Having four feet, these managed rather better
A8     63:26    and,  last  of  all  this  grand procession, came THE KING AND THE QUEEN OF HEARTS.
A8     63:19    two and two, as the soldiers did. After these came the royal children: there were ten of them, and the
T9    192:14    have  liked  very  much  to ask them how they came there, but she feared it would not be quite civil.
T4    144:10    we be trotting home again?' / But answer came there none--/ And this was scarcely odd, because / They'd
T7    170: 8    happen  to meet any soldiers, my dear, as you came through the wood?"
T3    135:22                          She very soon came to an open field, with a wood on the other side of it: it
T6    167:17                    Then some one came to me and said / 'The little fishes are in bed.'
A10    81:33    not," said the Mock Turtle. "Why, if a fish came to me, and told me he was going a journey, I should say
A8     66:18    off  to other parts of the ground, Alice came to the conclusion that it was a very difficult game
T9    196: 1    more as  if she were talking to herself. "He came to the door with a corkscrew in his hand--"
T2    128:28      Alice  never  knew,  but  exactly as she came to the last peg, she was gone. Whether she vanished into
T5    154: 9    turning  round, looking at the shelves as she came to them.
T8    184:29                     "I'll tell you how I came to think of it," said the Knight. "You see, I said to
T8W    18: 3                     "I'll tell you how I came to wear it," the Wasp said. "When I was young, you know,
A2     15:28    in  one hand and a large fan in the other: he came trotting along in a great hurry, muttering to himself, as
T8    180:16    wasn't it?" said the White Knight, as he came up panting.
T8W    13:17    my old bones!" he was grumbling on as Alice came up to him.
T5    158:28    everything  turned into a tree the moment she came up to it, and she quite expected the egg to do the same.
A4     29:25                    Presently the Rabbit came up to the door, and tried to open it; but, as the door
A8     62: 4    went  nearer  to watch them, and, just as she came up to them, she heard one of them say "Look out now,
A9     73:22              They very soon came upon a Gryphon, lying fast asleep in the sun. (If you
A1      9:19    a bat?" when suddenly, thump! thump! down she came upon a heap of sticks and dry leaves, and the fall was
T2    120:27    to  be  done  but  start again. This time she came upon a large flowerbed, with a border of daisies, and a
A1      9:34              Suddenly she came upon a little three-legged table, all made of solid glass
A1      9:39    them.  However, on the second time round, she came upon a low curtain she had not noticed before, and behind
A4     27:21    if  I  can  find them." As she said this, she came upon a neat little house, on the door of which was a
T3    137:30    went,  till,  on  turning a sharp corner, she came upon two fat little men, so suddenly that she could not
A10    82:21    knew  what  she  was  saying;  and the words came very queer indeed:--
T3    136: 7                    Just then a Fawn came wandering by: it looked at Alice with its large gentle
T1    118:11    / The Jabberwock, with eyes of flame, / Came whiffling through the tulgey wood, / And burbled as it
T1    110: 8    if it hadn't been for that nasty Knight, that came wriggling down among my pieces. Kitty dear, let's pretend
```
CAMOMILE (1)
```
A9     70:12    rule,  "and vinegar that makes them sour--and camomile that makes them bitter--and--and barley-sugar and
```
CAN (110)
```
A10    78:29                "--as far out to sea as you can--"
T4    148:16    must  begin quick. It's getting as dark as it can."
T5    149:18    right  way  to begin, I'll do it as well as I can."
T2    122:21                    "How is it you can all talk so nicely?" Alice said, hoping to get it into a
A5     42:13                    "What can all that green stuff be?" said Alice. "And where have my
T2    121: 4    in  a  timid voice--almost in a whisper. "And can all the flowers talk?"
T9    199:29    "Then fill up the glasses as quick as you can, / And sprinkle the table with buttons and bran: / Put
T8    185:14    "It  was all  kinds of  fastness with me, I can assure you!" he said. He raised his hands in some
A12    96:15    pointing  to the tarts on the table. "Nothing can be clearer than that. Then again--'before she had this
T8W    13: 9                "I don't think I can be of any use to him," was Alice's first thought, as she
T1    110:16    had  been  reduced  at last to say "Well, you can be one of them, then, and I'll be all the rest." And once
A10    82:10          "It's all about as curious as it can be," said the Gryphon.
T2    126: 8      and said "That's easily managed. You can be the White Queen's Pawn, if you like, as Lily's too
T4    143:12    Now, if you're ready, Oysters dear, / We can begin to feed.'
T5    153: 5    say 'exactly,'" the Queen remarked. "I can believe it without that. Now I'll give you something to
T8W    20:11    could. At last she managed to say gravely, "I can bite anything I want."
T8    181: 9                "Now one can breathe more easily," said the Knight, putting back his
A2     14: 9    about  you:  you must manage the best way you can--but I must be kind to them," thought Alice, "or perhaps
A1     12:35    the  key;  and if it makes me grow smaller, I can creep under the door: so either way I'll get into the
T9    194:30    The  Queen gasped and  shut her eyes. "I can do Addition," she said, "if you give me time--but I ca'n't
T6    163:39    verbs:  they're  the proudest--adjectives you can do anything with, but not verbs--however, I can manage the
A10    79: 6    said the Mock Turtle to the Gryphon. "We can do it without lobsters, you know. Which shall sing?"
A4     28:21    up  the chimney,  and said to herself "Now I can do no more, whatever happens. What will become of me?"
T9    202:34    very  much," she  whispered in reply, "but I can do quite well without."
T2    127:20    here,  you  see, it takes all the running you can do, to keep in the same place. If you want to get
T7    170:19    at  that distance too! Why, it's as much as I can do to see real people, by this light!"
T5    153: 2    the  Queen said with great decision: "nobody can do two things at once, you know. Let's consider your age
A7     60: 6                    "You can draw water out of a water-well," said the Hatter; "so I
A9     74:30    Alice  thought to herself "I don't see how he can ever finish, if he doesn't begin." But she waited
T6    164:17    "Let's  hear  it," said Humpty Dumpty. "I can explain all the poems that ever were invented--and a good
A12    95:23            "If any one of them can explain it," said Alice, (she had grown so large in the
A9     70:23    "Everything's  got  a  moral, if only you can find it." And she squeezed herself up closer to Alice's
A7     55:16          "Do you mean that you think you can find out the answer to it?" said the March Hare.
A4     27:20    take  him his fan and gloves--that is, if I can find them." As she said this, she came upon a neat little
T8    181:21                "But the things can get out," Alice gently remarked. "Do you know the lid's
T1    111: 9    glass has got all soft like gauze, so that we can get through. Why, it's turning into a sort of mist now, I
A2     18:20    fallen  into the sea, "and in that case I can go back by railway," she said to herself. (Alice had been
T4    145: 3                    Alice said "Nobody can guess that."
A7     55:14    they've  begun asking riddles--I believe I can guess that," she added aloud.
A11    88:40    the Dormouse, who was sitting next to her. "I can hardly breathe."
T1    115:11    hear  her. "You make me laugh so that I can hardly hold you! And don't keep your mouth so wide open!
A4     29: 3    you know, this sort of life! I do wonder what can have happened to me! When I used to read fairy tales, I
A10    78:11    hastily,  and said "No never") "--so you can have no idea what a delightful thing a Lobster-Quadrille
T4    148:15    Tweedledum  said to his brother: "but you can have the umbrella--it's quite as sharp. Only we must begin
```

CAN (cont.)
```
T1    113:11    walking  arm  in  arm--I  don't  think  they can hear me," she went on, as she put her head closer down,
T8W    14: 1                                                 "Can I do anything for you?" Alice went on. "Aren't you rather
A2     18: 3    white  kid-gloves  while  she  was  talking. "How can I have done that?" she thought. "I must be growing small
A4     27: 5      as  sure  as  ferrets  are  ferrets! Where can I have dropped them, I wonder?" Alice guessed in a moment
T3    136: 4    all! And now, who am I? I will remember, if I can! I'm determined to do it!" But being determined didn't
T8    191: 6                          "But how can it have got there without my knowing it?" she said
T1    111: 2    oh, Kitty! now we come to the passage. You can just see a little peep of the passage in Looking-glass
A4     30:38          is  narrow,  to  be  sure;  but  I think I can kick a little!"
A5     40: 7    "Don't  give  yourself  airs! / Do you think I can listen all day to such stuff? / Be off, or I'll kick you
T12   208: 4    and  the  Carpenter'  to you; and then you can make believe it's oysters, dear!
T6    163:33    "The  question  is," said Alice, "whether you can make words mean so many different things."
T6    163:40    do  anything  with, but not verbs--however, I can manage the whole lot of them! Impenetrability! That's what
T2    123: 5    "There's  one other flower in the garden that can move about like you," said the Rose. "I wonder how you do
T4    145:25    the  wood,  and stopped under a large tree. "It can never get at me here," she thought: "it's far too large to
T8    187:29    said  to  herself:  "it's 'I give the all, I can no more.'" She stood and listened very attentively, but no
AI     3:11    /  To  stir  the  tiniest  feather! / Yet what can one poor voice avail / Against three tongues together?
T1    112:14    very clock on the chimney-piece (you know you can only see the back of it in the Looking-glass) had got the
T4    147:26    "it's  one  of  the  most serious things that can possibly happen to one in a battle--to get one's head cut
A1     12:34    Alice,  "and  if  it  makes me grow larger, I can reach the key; and if it makes me grow smaller, I can
T9    194:36    together,  dear. And I'll tell you a secret--I can read words of one letter! Isn't that grand? However, don't
A10    80: 1                          "You can really have no notion how delightful it will be / When
A2     15:41    when  I got up this morning? I almost think I can remember feeling a little different. But if I'm not the
T6    166:36                          "I will, if I can remember it so long," said Alice.
T5    152:31    to  be  glad!"  the Queen said. "Only I never can remember the rule. You must be very happy, living in this
T6    166:15    stretching  out  one  of  his great hands, "I can repeat poetry as well as other folk, if it comes to that--
T7    174:23    the  wood  over yonder--How fast those Queens can run!"
T2    128:30    she  ran  quickly  into  the  wood ("and she can run very fast!" thought Alice), there was no way of
A6     48: 3                    "They all can," said the Duchess; "and most of 'em do."
T2    121: 5                    "As well as you can," said the Tiger-lily. "And a great deal louder."
A5     43:20    then  they're a kind of serpent: that's all I can say."
T1    110:33          only  the  things  go  the  other way. I can see all of it when I get upon a chair--all but the bit
T7    170:15    Just  look along the road, and tell me if you can see either of them."
T4    148: 3    within  reach,"  cried Tweedledum, "whether I can see it or not!"
T1    111: 4    and  it's very like our passage as far as you can see, only you know it may be quite different on beyond. Oh
T1    110:32          House. First, there's the room you can see through the glass--that's just the same as our
T4    148: 1    he  added:  "I  generally  hit  every thing I can see--when I get really excited."
T6    166:27                    "If you can see whether I'm singing or not, you've sharper eyes than
A5     43: 7    "Well!  What  are  you?" said the Pigeon. "I can see you're trying to invent something!"
T5    155:12                    "How can she knit with so many?" the puzzled child thought to
T3    132:25          "I like them when they can talk," Alice said. "None of them ever talk, where I come
A2     19:12    down  here, that I should think very likely it can talk: at any rate, there's no harm in trying." So she
T7    175:25                    "It can talk," said Haigha solemnly.
T2    120:32                    "We can talk," said the Tiger-lily, "when there's anybody worth
T1    110:36    they've  a  fire  in  the  winter: you never can tell, you know, unless our fire smokes, and then smoke
A10    81:10                          "I can tell you more than that, if you like," said the Gryphon.
T3    132:30    of  them--at  least  the  large  kinds. But I can tell you the names of some of them."
T8    187:31          "I'll tell thee everything I can: / There's little to relate. / I saw an aged aged man, /
A6     49: 6    boy,  /  I beat him when he sneezes; / For he can thoroughly enjoy / The pepper when he pleases!"
T12   208:12    do  help  to  settle  it! I'm sure your paw can wait!" But the provoking kitten only began on the other
T4    147:44    well,"  the  other said, rather sadly: "and she can watch us--only you'd better not come very close," he added
T6    162:11          perhaps,"  said  Humpty  Dumpty; "but two can. With proper assistance, you might have left off at seven
T9    194:39                    Here the Red Queen began again. "Can you answer useful questions?" she said. "How is bread made
T9    193:24                          "Can you do Addition?" the White Queen asked. "What's one and
T9    194: 5    do  Subtraction,"  said  the  White Queen. "Can you do Division? Divide a loaf by a knife--what's the
T9    194: 1    do  Addition,"  the  Red  Queen interrupted. "Can you do Subtraction? Take nine from eight."
T9    194:28                          "Can you do sums?" Alice said, turning suddenly on the White
T8    185:24                    "How can you go on talking so quietly, head downwards?" Alice asked
T8    181:27    him,  and  he  hung  it carefully on a tree. "Can you guess why I did that?" he said to Alice.
A12    95:34    '--said I could not swim--' you ca'n't swim, can you?" he added, turning to the Knave.
T5    152:41    at  this,  even  in  the  midst of her tears. "Can you keep from crying by considering things?" she asked.
A4     29:13    foolish  Alice!"  she  answered herself. "How can you learn lessons in here? Why, there's hardly room for
T1    110: 4                    "Kitty, can you play chess? Now, don't smile, my dear. I'm asking it
A8     65:19          "That's  right!"  shouted  the  Queen. "Can you play croquet?"
T8W    19:12    /  They  take  my  wig from me and say / 'How can you put such rubbish on?'
T5    155:14                    "Can you row?" the Sheep asked, handing her a pair of
T12   207:10    one  could  keep  up  a conversation! But how can you talk with a person if they always say the same thing
```
CANARY (1)
```
A3     26:33    the  night-air doesn't suit my throat!" And a Canary called out in a trembling voice, to its children, "Come
```
CANDLE (4)
```
T4    145:11    Tweedledum,  "you'd go out--bang!--just like a candle!"
A1     12: 9    herself,  "in my going out altogether, like a candle. I wonder what I should be like then?" And she tried to
A1     12:10    the  flame  of  a candle looks like after the candle is blown out, for she could not remember ever having
A1     12:10    And  she  tried  to fancy what the flame of a candle looks like after the candle is blown out, for she could
```
CANDLES (3)
```
T9    203:12    all  sorts of things happened in a moment. The candles all grew up to the ceiling, looking something like a
T3    134: 7    the  reason insects are so fond of flying into candles--because they want to turn into Snap-dragon-flies!"
T9    204:15    good  pull,  and  plates, dishes, guests, and candles came crashing down together in a heap on the floor.
```
CANDLESTICKS (1)
```
T8    182:19    as  they got it in at last; "there are so many candlesticks in the bag." And he hung it to the saddle, which
```

```
CANNOT (3)
 T6   167: 4              The little fishes' answer was / 'We cannot do it, Sir, because--'"
 T4   141:17  pleasant talk, / Along the briny beach: / We cannot do with more than four, / To give a hand to each.'
 A12   93: 1                           "The trial cannot proceed," said the King, in a very grave voice, "until
CA'N'T [CAN'T] (69)
 T9   192:28  What right have you to call yourself so? You ca'n't be a Queen, you know, till you've passed the proper
 T2   125:11  into contradicting her at last: "a hill ca'n't be a valley, you know. That would be nonsense--"
 T6   159: 5     that it was HUMPTY DUMPTY himself. "It ca'n't be anybody else!" she said to herself. "I'm as certain
 T3   129: 7  creatures, making honey down there? They ca'n't be bees--nobody ever saw bees a mile off, you know--"
 A7   59:26  and the Dormouse sulkily remarked "If you ca'n't be civil, you'd better finish the story for yourself."
 A2   16: 5  doesn't go in ringlets at all; and I'm sure I ca'n't be Mabel, for I know all sorts of things, and she, oh,
 T5   153:11     "There's no use trying," she said: "one ca'n't believe impossible things."
 T5   153: 8                            "I ca'n't believe that!" said Alice.
 T1   108:28  was washing your face this morning. Now you ca'n't deny it, Kitty: I heard you! What's that you say?"
 T9   194: 1                       "She ca'n't do Addition," the Red Queen interrupted. "Can you do
 T9   194: 5                       "She ca'n't do Subtraction," said the White Queen. "Can you do
 T9   194:31    she said, "if you give me time--but I ca'n't do Subtraction under any circumstances!"
 T9   194:26                       "She ca'n't do sums a bit!" the Queens said together, with great
 T7   172:22                      "He ca'n't do that," said the King, "or else he'd have been here
 A10   83: 3                     "She ca'n't explain it," said the Gryphon hastily. "Go on with the
 A5   35:11                       "I ca'n't explain myself, I'm afraid, Sir," said Alice, "because
 T1   112: 8  they see me through the glass in here, and ca'n't get at me!"
 T2   122:11  and trembling with excitement. "They know I ca'n't get at them!" it panted, bending its quivering head
 T8   181:19  see I carry it upside-down, so that the rain ca'n't get in."
 A4   28:13  I hope I sha'n't grow any more--As it is, I ca'n't get out at the door--I do wish I hadn't drunk quite so
 A11   90:23                       "I ca'n't go no lower," said the Hatter: "I'm on the floor, as it
 T5   149:29             "It ca'n't go straight, you know, if you pin it all on one side,"
 A11   86:29  doing?" Alice whispered to the Gryphon. "They ca'n't have anything to put down yet, before the trial's begun
 A8   67:24  tone, "and they all quarrel so dreadfully one ca'n't hear oneself speak--and they don't seem to have any
 T6   162:10  suggestion. "I mean," she said, "that one ca'n't help growing older."
 T8W   13:13  jump over, everything will change, and then I can't help him."
 A11   88:41                       "I ca'n't help it," said Alice very meekly: "I'm growing."
 A6   46:23  thought decidedly uncivil. "But perhaps he ca'n't help it," she said to herself; "his eyes are so very
 T2   123:16  beginning to fade, you know--and then one ca'n't help one's petals getting a little untidy--"
 T9   196:23  gently stroking it: "she means well, but she ca'n't help saying foolish things as a general rule."
 A6   51:23           "Oh, you ca'n't help that," said the Cat: "we're all mad here. I'm mad.
 T8W   16: 1  not well," she said in a soothing tone. "Can't I do anything for you?"
 T5   154: 6  sides, if you like," said the Sheep; "but you ca'n't look all round you--unless you've got eyes at the back
 T1   115:37  dear! I really must get a thinner pencil. I ca'n't manage this one a bit: it writes all manner of things
 T6   162:11                     "One ca'n't, perhaps," said Humpty Dumpty; "but two can. With
 T2   123:38                     "You ca'n't possibly do that," said the Rose: "I should advise you
 A4   32: 8  to make some change in my size; and, as it ca'n't possibly make me larger, it must make me smaller, I
 A12   94:22  said the Knave, "I didn't write it, and they ca'n't prove that I did: there's no name signed at the end."
 A5   35:14                       "I'm afraid I ca'n't put it more clearly," Alice replied, very politely,
 A9   72:12  politely, "if I had it written down: but I ca'n't quite follow it as you say it."
 T6   161:17                      "I'm afraid I ca'n't quite remember it," Alice said, very politely.
 A2   20: 7  for its dinner, and all sorts of things--but I ca'n't remember half of them--and it belongs to a farmer, you
 T3   137: 2  come a little further on," the Fawn said. "I ca'n't remember here."
 A11   90: 4                       "That I ca'n't remember," said the Hatter.
 A5   36:31     "I'm afraid I am, Sir," said Alice. "I ca'n't remember things as I used--and I don't keep the same
 T5   150:17  mine only works one way," Alice remarked. "I ca'n't remember things before they happen."
 A5   36:33                       "Ca'n't remember what things?" said the Caterpillar.
 T5   150: 8               "No, it ca'n't," said the Queen. "It's jam every other day: to-day
 T3   132:39               "I ca'n't say," the Gnat replied. "Further on, in the wood down
 T1   113:13  head closer down, "and I'm nearly sure they ca'n't see me. I feel somehow as if I was getting invisible--
 A5   42:14  got to? And oh, my poor hands, how is it I ca'n't see you?" She was moving them about, as she spoke, but
 A9   77: 2                "Well, I ca'n't show it you, myself," the Mock Turtle said: "I'm too
 T9   204:13                "I ca'n't stand this any longer!" she cried, as she jumped up and
 T3   137:26  wonder I never thought of that before--But I ca'n't stay there long. I'll just call and say 'How d'ye do?'
 A12   95:34  after all. '--said I could not swim--' you ca'n't swim, can you?" he added, turning to the Knave.
 A7   59:13                "You mean you ca'n't take less," said the Hatter: "it's very easy to take
 A7   59:12  Alice replied in an offended tone: "so I ca'n't take more."
 T8   184:36  it yet," the Knight said, gravely; "so I ca'n't tell for certain--but I'm afraid it would be a little
 T6   164:13  ask what he paid them with; and so you see I ca'n't tell you.)
 A9   70:19  my dear, and that makes you forget to talk. I ca'n't tell you just now what the moral of that is, but I
 A3   26:28  such a capital one for catching mice, you ca'n't think! And oh, I wish you could see her after the
 A9   70: 1                "You ca'n't think how glad I am to see you again, you dear old
 T2   128:23  this time she said "Speak in French when you ca'n't think of the English for a thing--turn out your toes as
 T9   196:12  began again. "It was such a thunderstorm, you ca'n't think!" ("She never could, you know," said the Red
 A5   35:15        Alice replied, very politely, "for I ca'n't understand it myself, to begin with; and being so many
 T7   174: 1              "Speak, ca'n't you!" Haigha cried impatiently. But Hatta only munched
 T9   194: 3           "Nine from eight I ca'n't, you know," Alice replied very readily: "but--"
 T8W   14:13  he only said, as before, "Worrity, worrity! Can't you leave a body alone?"
 T5   153: 9                        "Ca'n't you?" the Queen said in a pitying tone. "Try again:
CANTERBURY (1)
 A3   22:13  and even Stigand, the patriotic archbishop of Canterbury, found it advisable--'"
CANVAS (1)
 A11   90:13  to you how it was done. They had a large canvas bag, which tied up at the mouth with strings: into this
```

-CAP [See NIGHT-CAP]
CAPERING (1)
    A10   78:31   in the sea!" cried the Mock Turtle, capering wildly about.
CAPITAL (4)
    A2   17: 1   signify: let's try Geography. London is the capital of Paris, and Paris is the capital of Rome, and Rome--
    A2   17: 1   is the capital of Paris, and Paris is the capital of Rome, and Rome--no, that's all wrong, I'm certain!
    A2   19:38   a nice soft thing to nurse--and she's such a capital one for catching mice--oh, I beg your pardon!" cried
    A3   26:27   her pet: "Dinah's our cat. And she's such a capital one for catching mice, you ca'n't think! And oh, I
CARDBOARD (1)
    A12   95:37   he certainly did not, being made entirely of cardboard.)
CARDS (3)
    A12   97: 8   by this time). "You're nothing but a pack of cards!"
    A8   63:42   to herself, "Why, they're only a pack of cards, after all. I needn't be afraid of them!"
    A11   86: 3   and beasts, as well as the whole pack of cards: the Knave was standing before them, in chains, with a
CARE (12)
    T4   147:40   "We must have a bit of a fight, but I don't care about going on long," said Tweedledum. "What's the time
    T2   121:11   "I don't care about the colour," the Tiger-lily remarked. "If only her
    T5   152:18   "Take care!" cried Alice. "You're holding it all crooked!" And she
    T5   150: 2   "I don't want you to hire me--and I don't care for jam."
    A9   71: 1   as she added "and the moral of that is--'Take care of the sense, and the sounds will take care of themselves
    A9   71: 2   care of the sense, and the sounds will take care of themselves.'"
    T9   197:15   happened before, that any one had to take care of two Queens asleep at once! No, not in all the History
    T2   121:15   being planted out here, with nobody to take care of you?"
    T9   203: 7   "Take care of yourself!" screamed the White Queen, seizing Alice's
    A6   51:11   "I don't much care where--" said Alice.
    A1   12:36   way I'll get into the garden, and I don't care which happens!"
    T3   131:17   said, "She must be labeled 'Lass, with care,' you know--"
CAREFUL (1)
    T4   146:16   "It's only a rattle," Alice said, after a careful examination of the little white thing. "Not a
CAREFULLY (8)
    T8   182:16   manage, though Alice held the bag open very carefully, because the Knight was so very awkward in putting
    A5   43:33   in her hands, and she set to work very carefully, nibbling first at one and then at the other, and
    T8   181:27   thought seemed to strike him, and he hung it carefully on a tree. "Can you guess why I did that?" he said
    T5   149:34   Alice carefully released the brush, and did her best to get the hair
    A3   26:32   one old Magpie began wrapping itself up very carefully, remarking "I really must be getting home: the
    T5   156:17   rushes. And then the little sleeves were carefully rolled up, and the little arms were plunged in
    T6   163:13   Humpty Dumpty took the book and looked at it carefully. "That seems to be done right--" he began.
    A8   64:14   The Knave did so, very carefully, with one foot.
CARELESS (3)
    T8   185:22   kinds of fastness," he repeated: "but it was careless of him to put another man's helmet on--with the man
    T5   150: 2   the week after next," the Queen replied in a careless tone. "For instance, now," she went on, sticking a
    T3   134:25   "And yet I don't know," the Gnat went on in a careless tone: "only think how convenient it would be if you
CARELESSLY (2)
    T3   132:33   answer to their names?" the Gnat remarked carelessly.
    T7   175:14   "It didn't hurt him," the Unicorn said carelessly, and he was going on, when his eye happened to fall
CARES (2)
    A10   84:26   "Beautiful Soup! Who cares for fish, / Game, or any other dish? / Who would not
    A12   97: 7   "Who cares for you?" said Alice (she had grown to her full size by
CARPENTER (12)
    T4   141:11   could get it clear?' / 'I doubt it,' said the Carpenter, / And shed a bitter tear.
    T4   144:18   Alice said indignantly. "Then I like the Carpenter best--if he didn't eat so many as the Walrus."
    T4   144:16   held his handkerchief in front, so that the Carpenter couldn't count how many he took: contrariwise."
    T4   140:15   "'The Walrus and the Carpenter' is the longest," Tweedledum replied, giving his
    T4   143:21   you to come! / And you are very nice!' / The Carpenter said nothing but / 'Cut us another slice. / I wish
    T4   143:29   so far, / And made them trot so quick!' / The Carpenter said nothing but / 'The butter's spread too thick!'
    T4   143: 5   all of us are fat!' / 'No hurry!' said the Carpenter. / They thanked him much for that.
    T4   144:15   "He ate more than the Carpenter, though," said Tweedledee. "You see he held his
    T12   208: 3   breakfast, I'll repeat 'The Walrus and the Carpenter' to you; and then you can make believe it's oysters,
    T4   142:13   The Walrus and the Carpenter / Walked on a mile or so, / And then they rested on
    T4   141: 1   The Walrus and the Carpenter / Were walking close at hand: / They wept like
    T4   144: 7   'O Oysters,' said the Carpenter, / 'You've had a pleasant run! / Shall we be
CARRIAGE (3)
    T3   129:36   as the people, and quite seemed to fill the carriage.
    T3   132:10   to herself. In another moment she felt the carriage rise straight up into the air, and in her fright she
    T3   131:19   on ("What a number of people there are in the carriage!" thought Alice), saying "She must go by post, as
CARRIAGE-FULL (1)
    T3   131: 6   sitting next the Goat (it was a very queer carriage-full of passengers altogether), and, as the rule
CARRIED (6)
    A6   48:19   saucepan flew close by it, and very nearly carried it off.
    T9   201: 8   to. Remove the joint!" And the waiters carried it off, and brought a large plum-pudding in its place
    A6   49:25   so as to prevent its undoing itself), she carried it out into the open air. "If I don't take this child
    A10   85: 8   the faster, while more and more faintly came, carried on the breeze that followed them, the melancholy words
    T7   177:14   but Alice very obediently got up, and carried the dish round, and the cake divided itself into three
    A11   91: 5   The next witness was the Duchess's cook. She carried the pepper-box in her hand, and Alice guessed who it
CARRIER (1)
    A2   15: 4   how she would manage it. "They must go by the carrier," she thought; "and how funny it'll seem, sending
CARROTS (1)
    T8   182:21   which was already loaded with bunches of carrots, and fire-irons, and many other things.
CARRY (4)
    T7   171: 7   to fetch and carry. One to fetch, and one to carry."

CARRY (cont.)
```
 A6   50:13  felt that it would be quite absurd for her to carry it any further.
 T8  181:19  to keep clothes and sandwiches in. You see I carry it upside-down, so that the rain ca'n't get in."
 T7  171: 7  impatiently. "I must have two--to fetch and carry. One to fetch, and one to carry."
```
CARRYING (3)
```
 A8   63:15                 First came ten soldiers carrying clubs: these were all shaped like the three gardeners
 T7  174:15     Haigha and Hatta set to work at once, carrying round trays of white and brown bread. Alice took a
 A8   63:25  her. Then followed the Knave of Hearts, carrying the King's crown on a crimson velvet cushion; and,
```
CART-HORSE (1)
```
 A4   32:41  it was very like having a game of play with a cart-horse, and expecting every moment to be trampled under
```
CART-WHEELS (1)
```
 A4   30:23  more: at last came a rumbling of little cart-wheels, and the sound of a good many voices all talking
```
CARVE (1)
```
 T9  200:21  it rather anxiously, as she had never had to carve a joint before.
```
CARVING-KNIFE (1)
```
 T7  175:40  to Alice to hold, while he got out a dish and carving-knife. How they all came out of it Alice couldn't
```
CASE (8)
```
 T1  116: 3  had the ink all ready to throw over him, in case he fainted again), she turned over the leaves, to find
 A2   18:19  had somehow fallen into the sea, "and in that case I can go back by railway," she said to herself. (Alice
 A4   32:31  the thought that it might be hungry, in which case it would be very likely to eat her up in spite of all her
 A3   22:28                           "In that case," said the Dodo solemnly, rising to its feet, "I move
 T6  166:21         Alice felt that in that case she really ought to listen to it; so she sat down, and
 T6  161:18                "In that case we start afresh," said Humpty Dumpty, "and it's my turn
 A7   56:18       "Which is just the case with mine," said the Hatter.
 A5   39: 6  father, "I took to the law, / And argued each case with my wife; / And the muscular strength, which it gave
```
CASTLES (1)
```
 T1  113:11  on the edge of the shovel--and here are two Castles walking arm in arm--I don't think they can hear me,"
```
CAT (33) [See also CHESHIRE-CAT]
```
 A6   51:10  deal on where you want to get to," said the Cat.
 A6   51:12  it doesn't matter which way you go," said the Cat.
 A6   53: 1  "Did you say 'pig', or 'fig'?" said the Cat.
 A6   51:29              "To begin with," said the Cat, "a dog's not mad. You grant that?"
 A6   52:28  said this, she looked up, and there was the Cat again, sitting on a branch of a tree.
 A3   26:27  ready to talk about her pet: "Dinah's our cat. And she's such a capital one for catching mice, you
 T1  108: 2  she added, looking reproachfully at the old cat, and speaking in as cross a voice as she could manage--and
 A6   53: 4              "All right," said the Cat; and this time it vanished quite slowly, beginning with
 A6   52: 8          "You'll see me there," said the Cat, and vanished.
 A6   52:21  "I thought it would," said the Cat, and vanished again.
 A8   67:14  "How are you getting on?" said the Cat, as soon as there was mouth enough for it to speak with.
 A2   19:33  about it. And yet I wish I could show you our cat Dinah. I think you'd take a fancy to cats, if you could
 A6   52: 2          "Call it what you like," said the Cat. "Do you play croquet with the Queen to-day?"
 T1  107: 3  had been having its face washed by the old cat for the last quarter of an hour (and bearing it pretty
 A6   47:14  manners for her to speak first, "why your cat grins like that?"
 A6   52:20  Alice answered very quietly, just as if the Cat had come back in a natural way.
 A1    9: 7  to-night, I should think!" (Dinah was the cat.) "I hope they'll remember her saucer of milk at tea-time.
 A6   52:17      what became of the baby?" said the Cat. "I'd nearly forgotten to ask."
 A6   51:15  "Oh, you're sure to do that," said the Cat, "if you only walk long enough."
 A8   67:31  "How do you like the Queen?" said the Cat in a low voice.
 A3   26:39  her, down here, and I'm sure she's the best cat in the world! Oh, my dear Dinah! I wonder if I shall ever
 A6   53: 8  a grin," thought Alice; "but a grin without a cat! It's the most curious thing I ever saw in all my life!"
 A8   68: 1                      "A cat may look at a king," said Alice. "I've read that in some
 A6   51: 1              The Cat only grinned when it saw Alice. It looked good-natured,
 A6   51:26      "You must be," said the Cat, "or you wouldn't have come here."
 A8   67:43          "I'd rather not," the Cat remarked.
 A8   68: 5  moment, "My dear! I wish you would have this cat removed!"
 A6   51:19      "In that direction," the Cat said, waving its right paw round, "lives a Hatter: and in
 A8   67:20  glad she had some one to listen to her. The Cat seemed to think that there was enough of it now in sight,
 A6   51:32          "Well, then," the Cat went on, "you see a dog growls when it's angry, and wags
 A6   51:23  "Oh, you ca'n't help that," said the Cat: "we're all mad here. I'm mad. You're mad."
 A6   47:10  did not sneeze, were the cook, and a large cat, which was lying on the hearth and grinning from ear to
 A6   53: 7          "Well! I've often seen a cat without a grin," thought Alice; "but a grin without a cat!
```
CATCH (9)
```
 A3   21:17  fixed on it, for she felt sure she would catch a bad cold if she did not get dry very soon.
 T7  175: 5  so fearfully quick. You might as well try to catch a Bandersnatch! But I'll make a memorandum about her, if
 A1    9:10  no mice in the air, I'm afraid, but you might catch a bat, and that's very like a mouse, you know. But do
 T1  118: 2  my son! / The jaws that bite, the claws that catch! / Beware the Jubjub bird, and shun / The frumious
 T4  144:36          "I'm afraid he'll catch cold with lying on the damp grass," said Alice, who was
 T6  159:15  said aloud, standing with her hands ready to catch him, for she was every moment expecting him to fall.
 A4   31: 8  goes Bill!" then the Rabbit's voice alone--"Catch him, you by the hedge!" then silence, and then another
 A4   30:29  well enough. Don't be particular--Here, Bill! Catch hold of this rope--Will the roof bear?--Mind that loose
 T8W  16:15              Alice didn't catch the word exactly. "Is it a kind of toothache?" she asked
```
CATCHES (1)
```
 T8W  17: 6  have it, and then you'll know. And when you catches it, just try tying a yellow handkerchief round your
```
CATCHING (6)
```
 T5  155:28  cried again, taking more needles. "You'll be catching a crab directly."
 T9  204:25  at anything now. "As for you," she repeated, catching hold of the little creature in the very act of
 T5  153:20  after it, and this time she succeeded in catching it herself. "I've got it!" she cried in a triumphant
 A2   19:38  to nurse--and she's such a capital one for catching mice--oh, I beg your pardon!" cried Alice again, for
 A3   26:27  our cat. And she's such a capital one for catching mice, you ca'n't think! And oh, I wish you could see
 T1  107:20  wicked, wicked little thing!" cried Alice, catching up the kitten, and giving it a little kiss to make it
```

CATERPILLAR (27)
```
A5t    35: 1                              ADVICE FROM A CATERPILLAR
A5     35: 4                     "Who are you?" said the Caterpillar.
A5     35:13                     "I don't see," said the Caterpillar.
A5     36: 1                      "It isn't," said the Caterpillar.
A5     36: 6                     "Not a bit," said the Caterpillar.
A5     36:14                        "Why?" said the Caterpillar.
A5     36:22              "Keep your temper," said the Caterpillar.
A5     36:25                         "No," said the Caterpillar.
A5     36:33        "Ca'n't remember what things?" said the Caterpillar.
A5     36:36     'You are old, Father William,'" said the Caterpillar.
A5     41: 1              "That is not said right," said the Caterpillar.
A5     41:10              "I don't know," said the Caterpillar.
A5     41:13             "Are you content now?" said the Caterpillar.
A5     35: 1                         The Caterpillar and Alice looked at each other for some time in
A5     41:21     "You'll get used to it in time," said the Caterpillar; and it put the hookah into its mouth, and began
A10    82: 7      "You are old, Father William," to the Caterpillar, and the words all coming different, and then the
A5     41:16     "It is a very good height indeed!" said the Caterpillar angrily, rearing itself upright as it spoke (it
A5     36:18                       "Come back!" the Caterpillar called after her. "I've something important to
A5     36: 9                          "You!" said the Caterpillar contemptuously. "Who are you?"
A5     41: 4     "It is wrong from beginning to end," said the Caterpillar, decidedly; and there was silence for some minutes
A5     41:31               "Of the mushroom," said the Caterpillar, just as if she had asked it aloud; and in another
A5     36:16     could not think of any good reason, and the Caterpillar seemed to be in a very unpleasant state of mind,
A5     35: 9        "What do you mean by that?" said the Caterpillar, sternly. "Explain yourself!"
A4     34: 9     eyes immediately met those of a large blue caterpillar, that was sitting on the top, with its arms folded
A5     35: 2     other for some time in silence: at last the Caterpillar took the hookah out of its mouth, and addressed
A5     41:24     chose to speak again. In a minute or two the Caterpillar took the hookah out of its mouth, and yawned once
A5     41: 6                            The Caterpillar was the first to speak.
```
CATERPILLAR'S (1)
```
A5     36:11     Alice felt a little irritated at the Caterpillar's making such very short remarks, and she drew
```
CAT'S (2)
```
A8     69:10                              The Cat's head began fading away the moment he was gone, and, by
A8     67:38     King, coming up to Alice, and looking at the Cat's head with great curiosity.
```
CATS (13) [See also CHESHIRE-CATS]
```
A2     19:29     feelings. "I quite forgot you didn't like cats."
A2     20:20      and you'll understand why it is I hate cats and dogs."
A6     48: 2     always grinned; in fact, I didn't know that cats could grin."
A2     19:30                          "Not like cats!" cried the Mouse in a shrill passionate voice. "Would
A1      9:13     a dreamy sort of way, "Do cats eat bats? Do cats eat bats?" and sometimes "Do bats eat cats?" for, you see
A1      9:13     to herself, in a dreamy sort of way, "Do cats eat bats? Do cats eat bats?" and sometimes "Do bats eat
A1      9:11     that's very like a mouse, you know. But do cats eat bats, I wonder?" And here Alice began to get rather
A1      9:14     Do cats eat bats?" and sometimes "Do bats eat cats?" for, you see, as she couldn't answer either question,
A2     19:34     our cat Dinah. I think you'd take a fancy to cats, if you could only see her. She is such a dear quiet
A2     19:31     in a shrill passionate voice. "Would you like cats, if you were me?"
T9    199:31     the table with buttons and bran: / Put cats in the coffee, and mice in the tea--/ And welcome Queen
A2     19:44     on such a subject! Our family always hated cats: nasty, low, vulgar things! Don't let me hear the name
A2     20:15     Do come back again, and we wo'n't talk about cats, or dogs either, if you don't like them!" When the Mouse
```
CATTLE (1)
```
A12    99: 1     the busy farm-yard--while the lowing of the cattle in the distance would take the place of the Mock
```
CAUCUS-RACE (3)
```
A3     23: 1     that the best thing to get us dry would be a Caucus-race."
A3t    21: 1                              A CAUCUS-RACE AND A LONG TALE
A3     23: 2                     "What is a Caucus-race?" said Alice; not that she much wanted to know,
```
CAUGHT (13)
```
T5    156:22     the water--while with bright eager eyes she caught at one bunch after another of the darling scented
T5    152:19     "You're holding it all crooked!" And she caught at the brooch; but it was too late: the pin had slipped
T3    132:11     up into the air, and in her fright she caught at the thing nearest to her hand, which happened to be
T5    156:44     and the consequence was that the handle of it caught her under the chin, and, in spite of a series of little
T1    119: 8     at the door in the same way, if she hadn't caught hold of the door-post. She was getting a little giddy
A6     49:18     was snorting like a steam-engine when she caught it, and kept doubling itself up and straightening
T9    202: 4     / That is easy: a baby, I think, could have caught it. / 'Next, the fish must be bought.' / That is easy:
T12   207:24     to purr. It saves time, remember!" And she caught it up and gave it one little kiss, "just in honour of
T5    157: 4     had happened. "That was a nice crab you caught!" she remarked, as Alice got back into her place, very
T9    202: 3                     "'First, the fish must be caught.' / That is easy: a baby, I think, could have caught it
A6     49:15                              Alice caught the baby with some difficulty, as it was a queer-shaped
A8     68:22                     By the time she had caught the flamingo and brought it back, the fight was over,
T5    149: 1                              She caught the shawl as she spoke, and looked about for the owner:
```
CAULDRON (2)
```
A6     48: 9     was trying to fix on one, the cook took the cauldron of soup off the fire, and at once set to work
A6     47: 3     was leaning over the fire, stirring a large cauldron which seemed to be full of soup.
```
CAUSE (6) [See also BECAUSE]
```
A3     25:48     said cunning old Fury: 'I'll try the whole cause, and condemn you to death.
T9    204:18     the Red Queen, whom she considered as the cause of all the mischief--but the Queen was no longer at her
T9    195:18     Queen said in an anxious tone. "What is the cause of lightning?"
T9    195:19     "The cause of lightning," Alice said very decidedly, for she felt
A2     18: 7     rapidly: she soon found out that the cause of this was the fan she was holding, and she dropped it
A3     22: 3     if you please! 'William the Conqueror, whose cause was favoured by the pope, was soon submitted to by the
```
CAUSED (2)
```
A3     26:30                              This speech caused a remarkable sensation among the party. Some of the
A3     24: 9     The next thing was to eat the comfits: this caused some noise and confusion, as the large birds complained
```

```
CAUTIOUSLY (5)
  T9   194:20                    "Perhaps it would," Alice replied cautiously.
  A7    60: 4  offend the Dormouse again, so she began very cautiously: "But I don't understand. Where did they draw the
  T5   157: 7  Was it? I didn't see it," said Alice, peeping cautiously over the side of the boat into the dark water. "I
  A7    56:40                    "Perhaps not," Alice cautiously replied; "but I know I have to beat time when I
  A9    71: 9                    "He might bite," Alice cautiously replied, not feeling at all anxious to have the
CEILING (4)
  A4    28:11  she found her head pressing against the ceiling, and had to stoop to save her neck from being broken.
  T5   155: 5  plan failed: the 'thing' went through the ceiling as quietly as possible, as if it were quite used to it
  T5   155: 4  of all. It'll puzzle it to go through the ceiling, I expect!"
  T9   203:13  in a moment. The candles all grew up to the ceiling, looking something like a bed of rushes with fireworks
CENTRE (1)
  A1     8:29  aloud. "I must be getting somewhere near the centre of the earth. Let me see: that would be four thousand
CERTAIN (10) [See also UNCERTAIN]
  T6   166: 3  is a sort of green pig: but 'mome' I'm not certain about. I think it's short for 'from home'--meaning
  T9   195:20  Alice said very decidedly, for she felt quite certain about this, "is the thunder--no, no!" she hastily
  T8   184:37  Knight said, gravely; "so I ca'n't tell for certain--but I'm afraid it would be a little hard."
  T4   139:19  on to Tweedledee, though she felt quite certain he would only shout out "Contrariwise!" and so he did.
  A2    17: 2  of Rome, and Rome--no, that's all wrong, I'm certain! I must have been changed for Mabel! I'll try and say
  A2    19:40  Mouse was bristling all over, and she felt certain it must be really offended. "We wo'n't talk about her
  T6   159: 5  anybody else!" she said to herself. "I'm as certain of it, as if his name were written all over his face!
  T1   107: 1                    One thing was certain, that the white kitten had had nothing to do with it--
  T3   135:30  to give me another, and it would be almost certain to be an ugly one. But then the fun would be, trying
  A1    11: 4  from a bottle marked "poison," it is almost certain to disagree with you, sooner or later.
CERTAINLY (27)
  T8   186:10  said Alice. "Well, that was quick work, certainly!"
  A5    36:20                    This sounded promising, certainly. Alice turned and came back again.
  A12   98:10  her, and said "It was a curious dream, dear, certainly; but now run in to your tea: it's getting late." So
  T7   175:36                    "Certainly--certainly!" the King muttered, and beckoned to
  A12   95:37  "Do I look like it?" he said. (Which he certainly did not, being made entirely of cardboard.)
  T5   156:25  one! Only I couldn't quite reach it." And it certainly did seem a little provoking ("almost as if it
  A7    56:20  have no sort of meaning in it, and yet it was certainly English. "I don't quite understand you," she said,
  T4   147:31  tied on. (He called it a helmet, though it certainly looked much more like a saucepan.)
  A11   86:19  did not look at all comfortable, and it was certainly not becoming.
  A9    76:12                    "Certainly not!" said Alice indignantly.
  T8   186:12  the Knight said in slow thoughtful tone: "no, certainly not the next course."
  T9   201: 6                    "Certainly not," the Red Queen said, very decidedly: "it isn't
  T6   163:21                    "Certainly," said Alice.
  A3    25: 1            "It is a long tail, certainly," said Alice, looking down with wonder at the
  A7    57: 5            "That would be grand, certainly," said Alice thoughtfully; "but then--I shouldn't be
  A5    43:16            "I have tasted eggs, certainly," said Alice, who was a very truthful child; "but
  T1   111:12  she hardly knew how she had got there. And certainly the glass was beginning to melt away, just like a
  T7   175:36                    "Certainly--certainly!" the King muttered, and beckoned to Haigha. "Open
  A6    46:13  inside, no one could possibly hear you." And certainly there was a most extraordinary noise going on within
  A6    47: 7                    There was certainly too much of it in the air. Even the Duchess sneezed
  A6    47: 5            "There's certainly too much pepper in that soup!" Alice said to herself
  T3   132:20            It certainly was a very large Gnat: "about the size of a chicken
  T4   139:34            "But it certainly was funny," (Alice said afterwards, when she was
  T8   182:38  then stopping to help the poor Knight, who certainly was not a good rider.
  A1    10:15  time she found a little bottle on it ("which certainly was not here before," said Alice), and tied round
  A4    33:14            The great question certainly was "What?" Alice looked all round her at the
  T3   135:25          she made up her mind to go on: "for I certainly won't go back," she thought to herself, and this was
-CHAIN [See DAISY-CHAIN]
CHAINS (1)
  A11   86: 4  cards: the Knave was standing before them, in chains, with a soldier on each side to guard him; and near the
CHAIR (4) [See also ARM-CHAIR]
  T1   110:34  way. I can see all of it when I get upon a chair--all but the bit just behind the fireplace. Oh! I do so
  T9   204:11  was walking up the table towards Alice's chair, and beckoning to her impatiently to get out of its way
  T9   204: 4  there was the leg of mutton sitting in the chair. "Here I am!" cried a voice from the soup-tureen, and
  T5   158:20  more I walk towards it. Let me see, is this a chair? Why, it's got branches, I declare! How very odd to find
CHAIRS (2)
  T9   200:14                    There were three chairs at the head of the table: the Red and White Queens had
  T5   158:18  as she groped her way among the tables and chairs, for the shop was very dark towards the end. "The egg
CHANCE (7)
  T8   189:15            And now, if e'er by chance I put / My fingers into glue, / Or madly squeeze a
  T6   160:22  Why, if ever I did fáll óff--which there's no chance of--but if I did--" Here he pursed up his lips, and
  A5    42:18            As there seemed to be no chance of getting her hands up to her head, she tried to get
  A4    28:25    and, as there seemed to be no sort of chance of her ever getting out of the room again, no wonder
  T5   152: 8  the matter?" she said, as soon as there was a chance of making herself heard. "Have you pricked your finger
  A11   86:11  the refreshments!" But there seemed to be no chance of this; so she began looking at everything about her
  A12   95: 9            If I or she should chance to be / Involved in this affair, / He trusts to you to
CHANCED (1)
  A8    62:18  of all the unjust things--" when his eye chanced to fall upon Alice, as she stood watching them, and he
CHANGE (17)
  A7    59:41  the only one who got any advantage from the change; and Alice was a good deal worse off than before, as
  T8W   13:13  edge. "If I once jump over, everything will change, and then I can't help him."
  A5    41:41  a good deal frightened by this very sudden change, but she felt that there was no time to be lost, as she
  A2    18:11  Alice, a good deal frightened at the sudden change, but very glad to find herself still in existence. "And
  T3   131:11  the Beetle, but a hoarse voice spoke next. "Change engines--" it said, and there it choked and was obliged
  A4    32: 8  cakes," she thought, "it's sure to make some change in my size; and, as it ca'n't possibly make me larger,
```

CHANGE (cont.)
A10	78:33	"Change lobsters again!" yelled the Gryphon at the top of its
A10	78:24	"--change lobsters, and retire in same order," continued the
A12	98:41	and all the other queer noises, would change (she knew) to the confused clamour of the busy
A9	77:11	you do lessons?" said Alice, in a hurry to change the subject.
A10	83: 8	puzzled by the whole thing, and longed to change the subject.
A2	20: 1	indeed!" said Alice, in a great hurry to change the subject of conversation. "Are you--are you fond--of
T2	123:18	Alice didn't like this idea at all: so, to change the subject, she asked "Does she ever come out here?"
A7	58:18	"Suppose we change the subject," the March Hare interrupted, yawning. "I'm
A6	50:19	to herself "if one only knew the right way to change them--" when she was a little startled by seeing the
A12	98:36	she had but to open them again, and all would change to dull reality--the grass would be only rustling in
A12	98:38	of the reeds--the rattling teacups would change to tinkling sheep-bells, and the Queen's shrill cries

CHANGED (11)
A5	36:30	mouth again, and said "So you think you're changed, do you?"
A2	16: 3	age as herself, to see if she could have been changed for any of them.
A2	17: 3	all wrong, I'm certain! I must have been changed for Mabel! I'll try and say 'How doth the little--',"
A3	26:44	up eagerly, half hoping that the Mouse had changed his mind, and was coming back to finish his story.
A2	15:39	went on just as usual. I wonder if I've changed in the night? Let me think: was I the same when I got
A5	42: 8	last!" said Alice in a tone of delight, which changed into alarm in another moment, when she found that her
A5	35: 8	up this morning, but I think I must have been changed several times since then."
A4	27: 9	nowhere to be seen--everything seemed to have changed since her swim in the pool; and the great hall, with
T8	184:38	He looked so vexed at the idea, that Alice changed the subject hastily. "What a curious helmet you've
T9	192:26	and, after thinking for a minute, suddenly changed the subject of the conversation. "What do you mean by
T2	126:19	trees and the other things round them never changed their places at all: however fast they went, they

CHANGES (2)
| A5 | 43:40 | half my plan done now! How puzzling all these changes are! I'm never sure what I'm going to be, from one |
| A5 | 43:10 | doubtfully, as she remembered the number of changes she had gone through, that day. |

CHANGING (2)
| A5 | 41: 9 | Alice hastily replied; "only one doesn't like changing so often, you know." |
| A6 | 46: 1 | repeated, in the same solemn tone, only changing the order of the words a little, "From the Queen. An |

CHARACTER (1)
| A12 | 94:41 | And mentioned me to him: / She gave me a good character, / But said I could not swim. |

CHARACTERS (1)
| T4 | 144:22 | began, "Well! They were both very unpleasant characters--" Here she checked herself in some alarm, at |

CHARGES (1)
| A4 | 32:43 | again: then the puppy began a series of short charges at the stick, running a very little way forwards each |

CHAT (2)
| T4 | 143: 2 | the Oysters cried, / 'Before we have our chat; / For some of us are out of breath, / And all of us are |
| AI | 3:23 | land / Of wonders wild and new, / In friendly chat with bird or beast--/ And half believe it true. |

CHATTE (1)
| A2 | 19:25 | had happened.) So she began again: "Ou est ma chatte?" which was the first sentence in her French |

CHATTERING (1)
| T6 | 160: 1 | "Don't stand chattering to yourself like that," Humpty Dumpty said, looking |

CHEAP (1)
| A9 | 72:20 | "A cheap sort of present!" thought Alice. "I'm glad people don't |

CHEAPER (1)
| T5 | 158: 7 | "Then two are cheaper than one?" Alice said in a surprised tone, taking out |

CHEATED (1)
| A1 | 12:26 | trying to box her own ears for having cheated herself in a game of croquet she was playing against |

CHECK (4)
T8	179:13	by a loud shouting of "Ahoy! Ahoy! Check!" and a Knight, dressed in crimson armour, came
T8	179:21	but here another voice broke in "Ahoy! Ahoy! Check!" and Alice looked round in some surprise for the new
T1	110: 7	said 'Check!' you purred! Well, it was a nice check, Kitty, and really I might have won, if it hadn't been
T1	110: 6	as if you understood it: and when I said 'Check!' you purred! Well, it was a nice check, Kitty, and

CHECKED (4)
A10	80:19	Alice, "I've often seen them at dinn----" she checked herself hastily.
A10	78:10	(Alice began to say "I once tasted--" but checked herself hastily, and said "No never") "--so you can
T4	144:22	both very unpleasant characters--" Here she checked herself in some alarm, at hearing something that
A8	63: 1	Alice, as she stood watching them, and he checked himself suddenly: the others looked round also, and

CHECKING (2)
| T3 | 129:18 | and--no, I wo'n't go just yet," she went on, checking herself just as she was beginning to run down the |
| T8W | 13:11 | just ask him what's the matter," she added, checking herself on the very edge. "If I once jump over, |

CHEEK (2)
| T7 | 173:32 | and this time a tear or two trickled down his cheek; but not a word would he say. |
| T9 | 202: 2 | laughed with delight, and stroked Alice's cheek. Then she began: |

CHEEKS (4)
T3	135:14	while two large tears came rolling down its cheeks.
T5	152:35	two large tears came rolling down her cheeks.
T5	156:32	in growing so far off, as, with flushed cheeks and dripping hair and hands, she scrambled back into
A10	78: 6	his voice, and, with tears running down his cheeks, he went on again:--

CHEER (1)
| T8 | 186:21 | it to be made of?" Alice asked, hoping to cheer him up, for the poor Knight seemed quite low-spirited |

CHEERED (3)
A3	24: 4	it had finished this short speech, they all cheered.
A11	90:11	Here one of the guinea-pigs cheered, and was immediately suppressed by the officers of the
A11	90:26	Here the other guinea-pig cheered, and was suppressed.

CHEERFULLY (4)
T6	168:20	"Good-bye, till we meet again!" she said as cheerfully as she could.
T4	146: 1	she brushed away her tears, and went on, as cheerfully as she could, "At any rate, I'd better be getting
A2	17:12	"How cheerfully he seems to grin, / How neatly spreads his claws, /

CHEERFULLY (cont.)
```
   T8   184:39  "What  a curious helmet you've got!" she said cheerfully. "Is that your invention too?"
```
CHEERING (1)
```
   T9   199:33           Then followed a confused noise of cheering, and Alice thought to herself "Thirty times three
```
CHEESE (1)
```
   T6   164:39  nests  under  sun-dials--also  they  live  on cheese."
```
CHERRY-TART (1)
```
   A1    11: 8  (it had, in fact, a sort of mixed flavour of cherry-tart, custard, pine-apple, roast turkey, toffy, and hot
```
CHESHIRE-CAT (5)
```
   A8    67:12  be  a grin, and she said to herself "It's the Cheshire-Cat: now I shall have somebody to talk to."
   A8    67:39              "It's a friend of mine--a Cheshire-Cat," said Alice: "allow me to introduce it."
   A6    47:15                "It's a Cheshire-Cat," said the Duchess, "and that's why. Pig!"
   A8    68:28      When she got back to the Cheshire-Cat, she was surprised to find quite a large crowd
   A6    50:20  when  she was a little startled by seeing the Cheshire-Cat sitting on a bough of a tree a few yards off.
```
CHESHIRE-CATS (1)
```
   A6    48: 1      "I didn't know that Cheshire-Cats always grinned; in fact, I didn't know that cats
```
CHESHIRE-PUSS (1)
```
   A6    51: 4            "Cheshire-Puss," she began, rather timidly, as she did not at
```
CHESS (2)
```
   T1   110: 4        "Kitty, can you play chess? Now, don't smile, my dear. I'm asking it seriously.
   T2   126: 1  as  she  went  on. "It's a great huge game of chess that's being played--all over the world--if this is the
```
CHESS-BOARD (1)
```
   T2   125:25  "I declare it's marked out just like a large chess-board!" Alice said at last. "There ought to be some men
```
CHESSMEN (3)
```
   T1   113: 4  to  herself, as  she  noticed several of the chessmen down in the hearth among the cinders; but in another
   T12  207:13           So Alice hunted among the chessmen on the table till she had found the Red Queen: then
   T1   113: 7  on her  hands  and  knees watching them. The chessmen were walking about, two and two!
```
CHICKEN (2)
```
   T3   132:20  was a very large Gnat: "about the size of a chicken," Alice thought. Still, she couldn't feel nervous with
   T7   176:21  "Why, I beat  you  all  round the town, you chicken!" the Lion replied angrily, half getting up as he
```
CHIEF (1)
```
   A8    66: 6              The chief difficulty Alice found at first was in managing her
```
CHIEFLY (2)
```
   T8   189:13  telling me / The way he got his wealth, / But chiefly for his wish that he / Might drink my noble health.
   T4   143: 8  of  bread,' the Walrus said, / 'Is what we chiefly need: / Pepper and vinegar besides / Are very good
```
CHILD (27) [See also DREAM-CHILD]
```
   A8    63:39  to Alice, she went on: "What's your name, child?"
   A8    64:11      said "Consider, my dear: she  is only a child!"
   T7   175:26  looked dreamily at Alice, and said "Talk, child."
   T8W   14: 4  "Worrity, worrity! There  never  was such a child!"
   T3   137: 8  of  delight. "And, dear me! you're a human child!" A sudden look of alarm came into its beautiful brown
   A6    48:33  figures!" And with that she began nursing her child again, singing a sort of lullaby to it as she did so,
   T6   162:29      "It's a cravat, child, and a beautiful one, as you say. It's a present from
   A6    49:26  out  into the open air. "If I don't take this child away with me," thought Alice, "they're sure to kill it
   A6    50:16    "it  would  have  made  a  dreadfully ugly child: but it makes rather a handsome pig, I think." And she
   A5    43:17      said Alice, who was  a  very truthful child; "but little girls eat eggs quite as much as serpents do
   A2    18:15  things are worse than ever," thought the poor child, "for I never was so small as this before, never! And I
   T7   175:19              "This is a child!" Haigha replied eagerly, coming in front of Alice to
   T7   173:26  very hungry  and  thirsty. How are you, dear child?" he went on, putting his arm affectionately round
   T9   192:24    cried the Queen. "Why, don't you see, child--" here she broke off with a frown, and, after thinking
   TI   103: 1              Child of the pure unclouded brow / And dreaming eyes of
   T5   155: 7              "Are you a child or a teetotum?" the Sheep said, as she took up another
   T7   173:30      "Were you happy in prison, dear child?" said Haigha.
   T6   163:43      "Now you talk like a reasonable child," said Humpty Dumpty, looking very much pleased. "I
   A9    70:22              "Tut, tut, child!" said the Duchess. "Everything's got a moral, if only
   T3   130:21  up  the  window, and  went away. "So young a child," said the gentleman sitting opposite to her, (he was
   A10   82:30      from  what  I  used to say when I was a child," said the Gryphon.
   T3   129:37      "Now then! Show your ticket, child!" the Guard went on, looking angrily at Alice. And a
   T1   113:19      "It is the voice of my child!" the White Queen cried out, as she rushed past the King
   T5   155:12  "How  can she knit with so many?" the puzzled child thought to herself. "She gets more and more like a
   A1    12:27  was playing against herself, for this curious child was very fond of pretending to be two people. "But it's
   T3   130: 1  thought  Alice) "Don't  keep  him  waiting, child! Why, his time is worth a thousand pounds a minute!"
   T9   193: 3  meant! What  do  you suppose is the use of a child without any meaning? Even a joke should have some
```
CHILDHOOD (1)
```
   A12   99: 6  years,  the  simple  and  loving heart of her childhood; and how she would gather about her other little
```
CHILDHOOD'S (2)
```
   AI    4: 5  / And, with a gentle hand, / Lay it where Childhood's dreams are twined / In Memory's mystic band. /
   TI   103:28  Within,  the  firelight's ruddy glow, / And childhood's nest of gladness. / The magic words shall hold
```
CHILDISH (1)
```
   AI    4: 3              Alice! A childish story take, / And, with a gentle hand, / Lay it where
```
CHILD-LIFE (1)
```
   A12   99:10  in all their simple joys, remembering her own child-life, and the happy summer days.
```
CHILDREN (13)
```
   A8    64: 2  soldiers,  or  courtiers, or three of her own children.
   A8    65: 2  bowing  to  the  King, the  Queen, the royal children, and everybody else.
   A12   99: 7  how  she  would gather about her other little children, and make their eyes bright and eager with many a
   A3    26:34    called out in a trembling voice, to its children, "Come away, my dears! It's high time you were all in
   TI   103:23  bed / A melancholy maiden! / We are but older children, dear, / Who fret to find our bedtime near.
   A2    18:23  a number of bathing-machines in the sea, some children digging in the sand with wooden spades, then a row of
   A2    16: 1  puzzle!" And she began thinking over all the children she knew that were of the same age as herself, to see
```

CHILDREN (cont.)
A6   50:18 I think." And she began thinking over other children she knew, who might do very well as pigs, and was
A9   70:13 and barley-sugar and such things that make children sweet-tempered. I only wish people knew that: then
A8   63:19 the soldiers did. After these came the royal children: there were ten of them, and the little dears came
TC   209: 4 Children three that nestle near, / Eager eye and willing ear,
A1   10:22 had read several nice little stories about children who had got burnt, and eaten up by wild beasts, and
TC   209:13 Children yet, the tale to hear, / Eager eye and willing ear, /
CHILDREN'S (1)
T1   107: 6 The way Dinah washed her children's faces was this: first she held the poor thing down
CHILD'S (1)
T9   193: 4 Even a joke should have some meaning--and a child's more important than a joke, I hope. You couldn't deny
CHILLY (1)
T3   135:20 on the twig, and, as she was getting quite chilly with sitting still so long, she got up and walked on.
CHIME (1)
TI   103:15 / When summer suns were glowing--/ A simple chime, that served to time / The rhythm of our rowing--/ Whose
CHIMNEY (6)
A4   30:34 The master says you've got to go down the chimney!"
A4   28:21 arm out of the window, and one foot up the chimney, and said to herself "Now I can do no more, whatever
A4   30:39 She drew her foot as far down the chimney as she could, and waited till she heard a little
A4   30:41 was) scratching and scrambling about in the chimney close above her: then, saying to herself "This is Bill
A4   30:35 "Oh! So Bill's got to come down the chimney, has he?" said Alice to herself. "Why, they seem to
A4   30:32 --It was Bill, I fancy--Who's to go down the chimney?--Nay, I sha'n't! You do it!--That I wo'n't, then!--
CHIMNEY-PIECE (2)
T1   111:11 enough to get through--" She was up on the chimney-piece while she said this, though she hardly knew how
T1   112:14 to be all alive, and the very clock on the chimney-piece (you know you can only see the back of it in the
CHIMNEYS (2)
T6   160:32 at doors--and behind trees--and down chimneys--or you couldn't have known it!"
A6   53:12 it must be the right house, because the chimneys were shaped like ears and the roof was thatched with
CHIN (10)
A9   72:24 asked, with another dig of her sharp little chin.
T5   156:44 that the handle of it caught her under the chin, and, in spite of a series of little shrieks of "Oh, oh,
A9   70:28 shoulder, and it was an uncomfortably sharp chin. However, she did not like to be rude: so she bore it as
T12 207:33 down, with one elbow on the rug, and her chin in her hand, to watch the kittens. "Tell me, Dinah, did
A2   18:18 in another moment, splash! she was up to her chin in saltwater. Her first idea was that she had somehow
A9   70:37 said the Duchess, digging her sharp little chin into Alice's shoulder as she added "and the moral of that
A5   41:40 moment she felt a violent blow underneath her chin: it had struck her foot!
A9   70:27 she was exactly the right height to rest her chin on Alice's shoulder, and it was an uncomfortably sharp
T7   176:10 the Lion said, lying down and putting his chin on his paws. "And sit down, both of you," (to the King
A5   42: 1 at once to eat some of the other bit. Her chin was pressed so closely against her foot, that there was
CHINA (1)
T8W   15: 7 the lake were blue and white, and looked like china. While tasting the treacle, they had a sad accident: two
CHOICE (3)
A9   72:38 and that in about half no time! Take your choice!"
A9   72:39 The Duchess took her choice, and was gone in a moment.
T5   157:13 sorts of things," said the Sheep: "plenty of choice, only make up your mind. Now, what do you want to buy
CHOKE (1)
A4   31:12 voices--"Hold up his head--Brandy now--Don't choke him--How was it, old fellow? What happened to you? Tell
CHOKED (5)
A3   24:11 could not taste theirs, and the small ones choked and had to be patted on the back. However, it was over
T3   131:12 "Change engines--" it said, and there it choked and was obliged to leave off.
A10   78: 3 to speak, but, for a minute or two, sobs choked his voice. "Same as if he had a bone in his throat,"
T2   127:30 and she thought she had never been so nearly choked in all her life.
A10   84:15 Turtle sighed deeply, and began, in a voice choked with sobs, to sing this:--
CHOKING (3)
A12   98:32 of the Lizard's slate-pencil, and the choking of the suppressed guinea-pigs, filled the air, mixed
T7   174: 6 "They're getting on very well," he said in a choking voice: "each of them has been down about eighty-seven
T4   146:13 "Do you see that?" he said, in a voice choking with passion, and his eyes grew large and yellow all
CHOOSE (4)
T6   161:19 said Humpty Dumpty, "and it's my turn to choose a subject--" ("He talks about it just as if it was a
T6   163:31 rather a scornful tone, "it means just what I choose it to mean--neither more nor less."
T8   182: 4 the Knight; "but, if they do come, I don't choose to have them running all about."
T4   140:23 his heavy head--/ Meaning to say he did not choose / To leave the oyster-bed.
CHOOSES (1)
T4   146: 8 "It may--if it chooses," said Tweedledee: "we've no objection. Contrariwise."
CHOOSING (3)
T6   162:15 and, if they really were to take turns in choosing subjects, it was her turn now.) "At least," she
T2   123: 4 in the garden besides me?" Alice said, not choosing to notice the Rose's last remark.
A7   60:10 in the well," Alice said to the Dormouse, not choosing to notice this last remark.
CHOP (1)
A6   48:27 "Talking of axes," said the Duchess, "chop off her head!"
CHORTLED (1)
T1   118:20 boy! / O frabjous day! Callooh! Callay!" / He chortled in his joy.
CHORUS (13)
A6   49: 8 CHORUS
T9   199:28 And hundreds of voices joined in the chorus:--
T9   199:41 Then came the chorus again:--
A10   85: 1 "Chorus again!" cried the Gryphon, and the Mock Turtle had just
T3   130:12 to her great surprise, they all thought in chorus (I hope you understand what thinking in chorus means--
A6   48:40 CHORUS (in which the cook and the baby joined):--
T3   130:13 (I hope you understand what thinking in chorus means--for I must confess that I don't) "Better say

CHORUS (cont.)
T3   129:39   many voices all said together ("like the chorus of a song," thought Alice) "Don't keep him waiting,
A4   31: 6   The first thing she heard was a general chorus of "There goes Bill!" then the Rabbit's voice alone--
A3   23:22   "But who is to give the prizes?" quite a chorus of voices asked.
T3   130: 4   where I came from." And again the chorus of voices went on. "There wasn't room for one where she
T3   130: 7   from the engine-driver." And once more the chorus of voices went on with "The man that drives the engine.
A3   26:14   called after it. And the others all joined in chorus "Yes, please do!" But the Mouse only shook its head
CHOSE (2)
A9   72:14   "That's nothing to what I could say if I chose," the Duchess replied, in a pleased tone.
A5   41:23   This time Alice waited patiently until it chose to speak again. In a minute or two the Caterpillar took
CHOSEN (2)
T6   162:32   Alice, quite pleased to find that she had chosen a good subject after all.
T6   162:19   offended, and she began to wish she hadn't chosen that subject. "If only I knew," she thought to herself,
CHRISTMAS (1)
A2   15: 2   see. I'll give them a new pair of boots every Christmas."
CHRISTMAS-BOX (1)
T3   134: 3   the Gnat replied; "and it makes its nest in a Christmas-box."
CHRYSALIS (1)
A5   36: 3   said Alice; "but when you have to turn into a chrysalis--you will some day, you know--and then after that
CHUCKLED (1)
A9   74: 8   the Queen till she was out of sight: then it chuckled. "What fun!" said the Gryphon, half to itself, half
CIDER (1)
T9   200: 3   is pleasant to drink: / Mix sand with the cider, and wool with the wine--/ And welcome Queen Alice with
CINDERS (3)
T8   190: 4   face was very like a crow, / With eyes, like cinders, all aglow, / Who seemed distracted with his woe, /
T1   113: 5   of the chessmen down in the hearth among the cinders; but in another moment, with a little "Oh!" of
T1   113:21   violently that she knocked him over among the cinders. "My precious Lily! My imperial kitten!" and she began
CIRCLE (1)
A3   23: 8   it marked out a race-course, in a sort of circle, ("the exact shape doesn't matter," it said,) and then
CIRCUMSTANCES (2)
T9   194:32   time--but I ca'n't do Subtraction under any circumstances!"
A4   34: 3   the right thing to eat or drink under the circumstances. There was a large mushroom growing near her,
CIVIL (7) [See also UNCIVIL]
T9   192:15   there, but she feared it would not be quite civil. However, there would be no harm, she thought, in asking
A7   55: 1   "Then it wasn't very civil of you to offer it," said Alice angrily.
A7   55: 2   "It wasn't very civil of you to sit down without being invited," said the
T3   132: 1   not, but she thought this wouldn't be quite a civil question to ask.
T2   127:27   Alice thought it would not be civil to say "No," though it wasn't at all what she wanted.
T6   168:19   to be going, she felt that it would hardly be civil to stay. So she got up, and held out her hand. "Good-bye
A7   59:26   Dormouse sulkily remarked "If you ca'n't be civil, you'd better finish the story for yourself."
CIVILLY (1)
T5   149: 4   wide, as if she were flying, and Alice very civilly went to meet her with the shawl.
CLAMOUR (1)
A12   98:41   would change (she knew) to the confused clamour of the busy farm-yard--while the lowing of the cattle
CLAP (1)
T1   110: 1   cried Alice, dropping the ball of worsted to clap her hands. "And I do so wish it was true! I'm sure the
CLAPPING (3)
T12   207:16   look at each other. "Now Kitty!" she cried, clapping her hands triumphantly. "Confess that was what you
T4   145: 4   "Why, about you!" Tweedledee exclaimed, clapping his hands triumphantly. "And if he left off dreaming
A12   94:26   There was a general clapping of hands at this: it was the first really clever
CLASP (1)
T5   152:17   the Queen clutched wildly at it, and tried to clasp it again.
CLASPED (3)
T6   162:34   as he crossed one knee over the other and clasped his hands round it, "they gave it me--for an
T3   137: 4   through the wood, Alice with her arms clasped lovingly round the soft neck of the Fawn, till they
A12   98:18   Alice herself: once again the tiny hands were clasped upon her knee, and the bright eager eyes were looking
CLASPING (2) [See also UNCLASPING]
T9   195:26   White Queen said, looking down and nervously clasping and unclasping her hands, "we had such a thunderstorm
T8   184:15   the Knight asked in a tone of great interest, clasping his arms round the horse's neck as he spoke, just in
CLASSICAL (1)
A9   77: 4   time," said the Gryphon: "I went to the Classical master, though. He was an old crab, he was."
CLAW (1)
T8W   21: 4   his own wig as he spoke, and stetched out one claw towards Alice, as if he wished to do the same for her,
CLAWS (3)
A6   51: 2   she thought: still it had very long claws and a great many teeth, so she felt that it ought to be
A2   17:13   he seems to grin, / How neatly spreads his claws, / And welcomes little fishes in, / With gently smiling
T1   118: 2   Jabberwock, my son! / The jaws that bite, the claws that catch! / Beware the Jubjub bird, and shun / The
CLEAN (2)
T4   142: 4   their faces washed, / Their shoes were clean and neat--/ And this was odd, because, you know, / They
A7   59:36   "I want a clean cup," interrupted the Hatter: "let's all move one place
CLEAR (6)
T1   118:29   However, somebody killed something: that's clear, at any rate--"
T4   141:10   the Walrus said, / 'That they could get it clear?' / 'I doubt it,' said the Carpenter, / And shed a
T6   167:21   I said it very loud and clear: / I went and shouted in his ear."
A2   19:23   her knowledge of history, Alice had no very clear notion how long ago anything had happened.) So she began
T1   114:21   took no notice of the question: it was quite clear that he could neither hear her nor see her.
A9   71:14   "Right, as usual," said the Duchess: "what a clear way you have of putting things!"
CLEARED (2)
A10   78:17   turtles, salmon, and so on: then, when you've cleared all the jelly-fish out of the way--"
T4   141: 5   Such quantities of sand: / 'If this were only cleared away,' / They said, 'it would be grand!'

CLEARER (1)
A12   96:15   to the tarts on the table. "Nothing can be clearer than _that_. Then again--'_before she had this fit_'--you
CLEARLY (3)
A5   35:14   "I'm afraid I ca'n't put it more clearly," Alice replied, very politely, "for I ca'n't
T6   159: 4   and, when she had come close to it, she saw clearly that it was HUMPTY DUMPTY himself. "It ca'n't be
T8   187:18   was the one that she always remembered most clearly. Years afterwards she could bring the whole scene back
CLEVER (6)
A5   40: 4   _end of your nose_--/ _What made you so awfully clever?_"
T9   195:41   times as rich as you are, _and five times as clever!_"
T6   164:14   "You seem very clever at explaining words, Sir," said Alice. "Would you
T2   121: 9   has got _some_ sense in it, though it's not a clever one!' Still, you're the right colour, and that goes a
T8   186:19   ever _will_ be cooked! And yet it was a very clever pudding to invent."
A12   94:27   of hands at this: it was the first really clever thing the King had said that day.
CLEVEREST (1)
T8   186: 6   "Now the cleverest thing of the sort that I ever did," he went on after
CLIMB (1)
A1   12:18   through the glass, and she tried her best to climb up one of the legs of the table, but it was too slippery
CLINGING (1)
A3   21: 3   draggled feathers, the animals with their fur clinging close to them, and all dripping wet, cross, and
CLOCK (4) [See also O'CLOCK]
T4   138:17   through her head like the ticking of a clock, and she could hardly help saying them out loud:--
A7   56:44   he'd do almost anything you liked with the clock. For instance, suppose it were nine o'clock in the
A7   57: 1   to whisper a hint to Time, and round goes the clock in a twinkling! Half-past one, time for dinner!"
T1   112:14   the fire seemed to be all alive, and the very clock on the chimney-piece (you know you can only see the back
CLOSE (26)
T8W   21: 9   done as well as two, if you _must_ have them so close--"
A4   30:41   and scrambling about in the chimney close above her: then, saying to herself "This is Bill", she
A10   79:10   treading on her toes when they passed too close, and waving their fore-paws to mark the time, while the
T4   141: 2   _The Walrus and the Carpenter / Were walking close at hand: / They wept like anything to see / Such_
A8   67:33   Just then she noticed that the Queen was close behind her, listening: so she went on "--likely to win,
A1   9:27   and whiskers, how late it's getting!" She was close behind it when she turned the corner, but the Rabbit was
A10   79:14   _a whiting to a snail, / "There's a porpoise close behind us, and he's treading on my tail. / See how_
A1   7:10   suddenly a White Rabbit with pink eyes ran close by her.
A6   48:18   nose!", as an unusually large saucepan flew close by it, and very nearly carried it off.
T4   147:45   can watch us--only you'd better not come _very_ close," he added: "I generally hit every thing I can see--when
T2   123:13   "They're done up close, like a dahlia," said the Tiger-lily: "not tumbled about
T9   201:36   very slowly and solemnly, putting her mouth close to Alice's ear, "her White Majesty knows a lovely riddle
A8   65:31   raised himself upon tiptoe, put his mouth close to her ear, and whispered "She's under sentence of
T3   131:14   to herself. And an extremely small voice, close to her ear, said "You might make a joke on that--
T3   131:29   make a joke on _that_," said the little voice close to her ear: "something about '_you would if you could_,'
T3   131:38   have heard it at _all_, if it hadn't come _quite_ close to her ear. The consequence of this _was_ that it tickled
A9   70:17   a little startled when she heard her voice close to her ear. "You're thinking about something, my dear,
A9   70:25   Alice did not much like her keeping so close to her: first because the Duchess was _very_ ugly; and
A10   82: 3   it, just at first, the two creatures got so close to her, one on each side, and opened their eyes and
T9   192:13   the Red Queen and the White Queen sitting close to her, one on each side: she would have liked very much
T6   159: 3   a nose and a mouth; and, when she had come close to it, she saw clearly that it was HUMPTY DUMPTY himself
T8   183: 2   that it was the best plan not to walk _quite_ close to the horse.
T7   172:26   shape of a trumpet and stooping so as to get close to the King's ear. Alice was sorry for this, as she
A7   60:42   more she found herself in the long hall, and close to the little glass table. "Now, I'll manage better this
A3   21: 3   feathers, the animals with their fur clinging close to them, and all dripping wet, cross, and uncomfortable
T7   173:20   They placed themselves close to where Hatta, the other Messenger, was standing
CLOSED (2)
A12   98:34   So she sat on, with closed eyes, and half believed herself in Wonderland, though
A7   60:20   The Dormouse had closed its eyes by this time, and was going off into a doze;
CLOSELY (1)
A5   42: 1   of the other bit. Her chin was pressed so closely against her foot, that there was hardly room to open
CLOSER (2)
T1   113:12   hear me," she went on, as she put her head closer down, "and I'm nearly sure they ca'n't see me. I feel
A9   70:23   you can find it." And she squeezed herself up closer to Alice's side as she spoke.
-CLOTH [See TABLECLOTH]
CLOTHES (2)
T8   181:18   tone. "It's my own invention--to keep clothes and sandwiches in. You see I carry it upside-down, so
T4   147:22   "Really they'll be more like bundles of old clothes than anything else, by the time they're ready!" she
-CLOTHS [See TABLECLOTHS]
CLOUD (4)
T4   140:37   _sands were dry as dry. / You could not see a cloud, because / No cloud was in the sky: / No birds were_
T7   173:17   Unicorn were fighting. They were in such a cloud of dust, that at first Alice could not make out which
T4   148:19   a thunderstorm coming on. "What a thick black cloud that is!" she said. "And how fast it comes! Why, I do
T4   140:38   _/ You could not see a cloud, because / No cloud was in the sky: / No birds were flying overhead--/ There_
-CLOUDED [See UNCLOUDED]
CLUB (1)
T8   179:14   galloping down upon her, brandishing a great club. Just as he reached her, the horse stopped suddenly:
CLUBS (2)
A8   63:15   First came ten soldiers carrying clubs: these were all shaped like the three gardeners, oblong
T8   180: 5   another Rule seems to be that they hold their clubs with their arms, as if they were Punch and Judy--What a
CLUTCHED (1)
T5   152:16   the words the brooch flew open, and the Queen clutched wildly at it, and tried to clasp it again.
COAL-SCUTTLES (1)
T4   147:14   hearth-rugs, table-cloths, dish-covers, and coal-scuttles. "I hope you're a good hand at pinning and tying

COAST (1)
A2   18:22   that wherever you go to on the English coast, you find a number of bathing-machines in the sea, some
COATS (1)
T4   142: 3   up, / All eager for the treat: / Their coats were brushed, their faces washed, / Their shoes were
COAXING (2)
A4   32:32   very likely to eat her up in spite of all her coaxing.
A4   32:29   her. "Poor little thing!" said Alice, in a coaxing tone, and she tried hard to whistle to it; but she was
COFFEE (1)
T9   199:31   with buttons and bran: / Put cats in the coffee, and mice in the tea--/ And welcome Queen Alice with
COILS (1)
A9   76:40   us Drawling, Stretching, and Fainting in Coils."
COIN (1)
T8   188:38   / And these I do not sell for gold / Or coin of silvery shine, / But for a copper halfpenny, / And
COLD (11)
T8W   13: 8   up together, and shivering as if he were very cold.
T8W   16: 9   one. And then I gets cross. And I gets cold. And I gets under a tree. And I gets a yellow
T1   108:15   wants plenty of sticks, Kitty! Only it got so cold, and it snowed so, they had to leave off. Never mind,
T9   195:38   "But they should be five times as cold, by the same rule--"
T8W   14: 2   for you?" Alice went on. "Aren't you rather cold here?"
A3   21:17   it, for she felt sure she would catch a bad cold if she did not get dry very soon.
T9   195:40   Queen. "Five times as warm, and five times as cold--just as I'm five times as rich as you are, and five
T1   115:22   was saying "I assure you, my dear, I turned cold to the very ends of my whiskers!"
T7   172:11   "I should think throwing cold water over you would be better," Alice suggested: "--or
T8W   14:10   round to the other side? You'll be out of the cold wind there."
T4   144:36   "I'm afraid he'll catch cold with lying on the damp grass," said Alice, who was a very
COLLAR (5)
T4   138: 3   one of them had 'DUM' embroidered on his collar, and the other 'DEE.' "I suppose they've got 'TWEEDLE'
T3   135:34   to the name of "Dash": had on a brass collar'--just fancy calling everything you met 'Alice,' till
T4   138: 5   got 'TWEEDLE' round at the back of the collar," she said to herself.
A11   91:19   "Collar that Dormouse!" the Queen shrieked out. "Behead that
T4   138: 8   'TWEEDLE' was written at the back of each collar, when she was startled by a voice coming from the one
COLLECTED (2)
A12   92:11   had a vague sort of idea that they must be collected at once and put back into the jury-box, or they
A8   68:29   she was surprised to find quite a large crowd collected round it: there was a dispute going on between the
COLOUR (2)
T2   121:10   not a clever one!' Still, you're the right colour, and that goes a long way."
T2   121:11   "I don't care about the colour," the Tiger-lily remarked. "If only her petals curled
COMB (4)
T8W   17:13   much neater," she said, "if only you had a comb."
T8W   18: 2   that kind," Alice hastily explained. "It's to comb hair with--your wig's so very rough, you know."
T8W   17:15   at her with more interest. "And you've got a comb. Much honey?"
T5   149:33   the Queen said with a sigh. "And I lost the comb yesterday."
COME (98)
T3   137: 1   "I'll tell you, if you'll come a little further on," the Fawn said. "I ca'n't remember
T9   199:27   Looking-Glass creatures, whatever they be, / Come and dine with the Red Queen, the White Queen, and me!'"
T7   170:37   called Hatta. I must have two, you know--to come and go. One to come, and one to go."
A10   79:16   / They are waiting on the shingle--will you come and join the dance? / Will you, wo'n't you, will you,
A10   80:10   / Then turn not pale, beloved snail, but come and join the dance. / Will you, wo'n't you, will you,
T4   144:28   "Come and look at him!" the brothers cried, and they each took
T7   171: 1   have two, you know--to come and go. One to come, and one to go."
T7   171: 5   I didn't understand," said Alice. "Why one to come and one to go?"
T4   140:34   'It's very rude of him,' she said, / 'To come and spoil the fun!'
T4   141:13   'O Oysters, come and walk with us!' / The Walrus did beseech. / 'A
T4   143:19   'It was so kind of you to come! / And you are very nice!' / The Carpenter said nothing
A3   26:34   out in a trembling voice, to its children, "Come away, my dears! It's high time you were all in bed!" On
A2   20:14   she called softly after it, "Mouse dear! Do come back again, and we wo'n't talk about cats, or dogs either
A3   26:13   "Please come back, and finish your story!" Alice called after it. And
A6   52:20   answered very quietly, just as if the Cat had come back in a natural way.
A5   36:18   "Come back!" the Caterpillar called after her. "I've something
A8   69:11   moment he was gone, and, by the time he had come back with the Duchess, it had entirely disappeared: so
A11   88: 3   hastily interrupted. "There's a great deal to come before that!"
T6   159: 3   and a nose and a mouth; and, when she had come close to it, she saw clearly that it was HUMPTY DUMPTY
A4   30:35   "Oh! So Bill's got to come down the chimney, has he?" said Alice to herself. "Why,
T7   175:33   "Come, fetch out the plum-cake, old man!" the Unicorn went on,
T3   132:26   Alice said. "None of them ever talk, where I come from."
T2   124: 6   "Where do you come from?" said the Red Queen. "And where are you going? Look
T3   132:27   sort of insects do you rejoice in, where you come from?" the Gnat inquired.
T4   139:30   surprised to hear music playing: it seemed to come from the tree under which they were dancing, and it was
T8W   13: 2   when she heard a deep sigh, which seemed to come from the wood behind her.
TI   103:19   Come, hearken then, ere voice of dread, / With bitter tidings
A4   30: 5   indeed!" said the Rabbit angrily. "Here! Come help me out of this!" (Sounds of more broken glass.)
A6   51:26   must be," said the Cat, "or you wouldn't have come here."
T3   135: 2   call you to your lessons, she would call out 'Come here--,' and there she would have to leave off, because
A4   27:30   of thing that would happen: "'Miss Alice! Come here directly, and get ready for your walk!' 'Coming in a
T8   182: 4   perhaps," said the Knight; "but, if they do come, I don't choose to have them running all about."
A3   25:13   us both go to law: I will prosecute you.--Come, I'll take no denial: We must have the trial; For really
T8   182:13   take it with us," the Knight said. "It'll come in handy if we find any plum-cake. Help me to get it into
T9   196: 4   "He said he would come in," the White Queen went on, "because he was looking for
A6   51: 6   however, it only grinned a little wider. "Come, it's pleased so far," thought Alice, and she went on.
A10   81:38   in an offended tone. And the Gryphon added "Come, let's hear some of your adventures."

COME (cont.)

A10	79: 5	"Come, let's try the first figure!" said the Mock Turtle to the
A5	42: 7	"Come, my head's free at last!" said Alice in a tone of delight
T8	181:35	of the best kind. But not a single bee has come near it yet. And the other thing is a mouse-trap. I
T6	161:11	would happen to his head! I'm afraid it would come off!"
T9	192: 7	first, as she was afraid that the crown might come off: but she comforted herself with the thought that
T9	199:10	as if he were trying whether the paint would come off: then he looked at Alice.
A9	74:12	that: they never executes nobody, you know. Come on!"
A9	74:22	that: he hasn't got no sorrow, you know. Come on!"
A10	85: 7	as she ran: but the Gryphon only answered "Come on!" and ran the faster, while more and more faintly came
A10	85: 4	"Come on!" cried the Gryphon, and, taking Alice by the hand, it
A9	74:13	"Everybody says 'come on!' here," thought Alice, as she went slowly after it:
A8	65:23	"Come on, then!" roared the Queen, and Alice joined the
A9	73:16	"Come on, then," said the Queen, "and he shall tell you his
A9	76:39	was an old conger-eel, that used to come once a week: he taught us Drawling, Stretching, and
A8	67:17	to it," she thought, "till its ears have come, or at least one of them." In another minute the whole
T5	155:26	the oars got fast in it, and would hardly come out again.
T5	156:42	the oars got fast in the water and wouldn't come out again (so Alice explained it afterwards), and the
A1	8:40	through the earth! How funny it'll seem to come out among the people that walk with their heads
T2	123:19	change the subject, she asked "Does she ever come out here?"
T2	124:12	ways about here belong to me--but why did you come out here at all?" she added in a kinder tone. "Curtsey
A2	19:22	Alice. "I daresay it's a French mouse, come over with William the Conqueror." (For, with all her
T3	131:38	wouldn't have heard it at all, if it hadn't come quite close to her ear. The consequence of this was that
T6	164: 9	"Ah, you should see 'em come round me of a Saturday night," Humpty Dumpty went on,
A9	74:39	could not help thinking there must be more to come, so she sat still and said nothing.
T5	150: 7	"It must come sometimes to 'jam to-day,'" Alice objected.
T8	188:15	give / To what the old man said, / I cried 'Come, tell me how you live!' / And thumped him on the head.
T8	188:31	side to side, / Until his face was blue: / 'Come, tell me how you live,' I cried, / 'And what it is you
A11	90:27	"Come, that finishes the guinea-pigs!" thought Alice. "Now we
A9	73:19	company, generally, "You are all pardoned." "Come, that's a good thing!" she said to herself, for she had
A2	17: 6	hoarse and strange, and the words did not come the same as they used to do:--
T4	142:19	'The time has come,' the Walrus said, / 'To talk of many things: / Of shoes
A5	43:39	and began talking to herself, as usual, "Come, there's half my plan done now! How puzzling all these
A1	12:21	"Come, there's no use in crying like that!" said Alice to
T4	148:13	"I wish the monstrous crow would come!" thought Alice.
A1	8:27	Down, down, down. Would the fall never come to an end? "I wonder how many miles I've fallen by this
T9	194:11	it--and the dog wouldn't remain: it would come to bite me--and I'm sure I shouldn't remain!"
T9	194:38	grand? However, don't be discouraged. You'll come to it in time.
T1	118:18	"And, hast thou slain the Jabberwock? / Come to my arms, my beamish boy! / O frabjous day! Callooh!
T6	166:17	"Oh, it needn't come to that!" Alice hastily said, hoping to keep him from
A7	58:16	"But what happens when you come to the beginning again?" Alice ventured to ask.
T8	186:29	And here I must leave you." They had just come to the end of the wood.
A12	94:36	King said, very gravely, "and go on till you come to the end: then stop."
A2	18:21	been to the seaside once in her life, and had come to the general conclusion that wherever you go to on the
T1	111: 1	isn't good to drink--but oh, Kitty! now we come to the passage. You can just see a little peep of the
T5	152:38	girl you are. Consider what a long way you've come to-day. Consider what o'clock it is. Consider anything,
T1	107:17	been rolling it up and down till it had all come undone again; and there it was, spread over the
T5	153:17	The brooch had come undone as she spoke, and a sudden gust of wind blew the
T5	152:15	the poor Queen groaned out: "the brooch will come undone directly. Oh, oh!" As she said the words the
A2	17:22	their putting their heads down and saying 'Come up again, dear!' I shall only look up and say 'Who am I,
A2	17:24	and then, if I like being that person, I'll come up: if not, I'll stay down here till I'm somebody else'--
T1	114:16	was still a little out of breath. "Mind you come up--the regular way--don't get blown up!"
A5	44: 3	there," thought Alice, "it'll never do to come upon them this size: why, I should frighten them out of
T4	147:45	"and she can watch us--only you'd better not come very close," he added: "I generally hit every thing I can
A7	55:13	"Come, we shall have some fun now!" thought Alice. "I'm glad
T6	159: 2	larger, and more and more human: when she had come within a few yards of it, she saw that it had eyes and a
T9	200:11	a few flowers among them. "I'm glad they've come without waiting to be asked," she thought: "I should
A5	43: 3	be free of them at last, they must needs come wriggling down from the sky! Ugh, Serpent!"
A10	83:13	to disobey, though she felt sure it would all come wrong, and she went on in a trembling voice:--
A12	94: 3	"There's more evidence to come yet, please your Majesty," said the White Rabbit, jumping
T5	149:35	and did her best to get the hair into order. "Come, you look rather better now!" she said, after altering
T8	190:14	horse's head along the road by which they had come. "You've only a few yards to go," he said, "down the hill

COMES (9)

T1	109:13	says 'Go to sleep, darlings, till the summer comes again.' And when they wake up in the summer, Kitty, they
A4	31:22	to tell you--all I know is, something comes at me like a Jack-in-the-box, and up I goes like a
A4	27:32	I've got to watch this mouse-hole till Dinah comes back, and see that the mouse doesn't get out.' Only I
T5	150: 6	till next Wednesday: and of course the crime comes last of all."
T8	190:27	However, he gets on again pretty easily--that comes of having so many things hung round the horse--" So she
A8	63:10	see, Miss, we're doing our best, afore she comes, to--" At this moment, Five, who had been anxiously
T6	166:16	repeat poetry as well as other folk, if it comes to that--"
T1	110:37	know, unless our fire smokes, and then smoke comes up in that room too--but that may be only pretence, just
T4	148:20	cloud that is!" she said. "And how fast it comes! Why, I do believe it's got wings!"

COMFITS (2)

A3	23:27	hand in her pocket, and pulled out a box of comfits (luckily the saltwater had not got into it), and
A3	24: 9	The next thing was to eat the comfits: this caused some noise and confusion, as the large

COMFORT (7)

T3	137:13	I know my name now," she said: "that's some comfort. Alice--Alice--I won't forget it again. And now, which
T3	131:35	Alice would have said something pitying to comfort it, "if it would only sigh like other people!" she
A4	29:10	get any older than I am now? That'll be a comfort, one way--never to be an old woman--but then--always
T3	135:38	and shady. "Well, at any rate it's a great comfort," she said as she stepped under the trees, "after

COMFORT (cont.)
    T3   132: 9 take us into the Fourth Square, that's some comfort!" she said to herself. In another moment she felt the
    T6   168:39 (she repeated this aloud, as it was a great comfort to have such a long word to say) "of all the
    T8   186:32 an anxious tone: "let me sing you a song to comfort you."
COMFORTABLE (3) [See also UNCOMFORTABLE]
    T8W   21:18   a few minutes to making the poor old creature comfortable.
    A11   86:19   to see how he did it), he did not look at all comfortable, and it was certainly not becoming.
    T8   182:36   It didn't sound a comfortable plan, Alice thought, and for a few minutes she
COMFORTABLY (4) [See also UNCOMFORTABLY]
    T12   207:33 I wonder?" she prattled on, as she settled comfortably down, with one elbow on the rug, and her chin in
    A8   66: 7   succeeded in getting its body tucked away, comfortably enough, under her arm, with its legs hanging down,
    T8   179:19   as he mounted again. As soon as he was comfortably in the saddle, he began once more "You're my--"
    T1   108:22 Kitty," Alice went on, as soon as they were comfortably settled again, "when I saw all the mischief you
COMFORTED (1)
    T9   192: 7 afraid that the crown might come off: but she comforted herself with the thought that there was nobody to
COMING (23)
    A8   67:30   just now, only it ran away when it saw mine coming!"
    T8W   14:22   white sugar, large and in fine condition. In coming back--"
    T8W   15: 5   "In coming back," Alice went on reading, "they found a lake of
    A3   26:44   that the Mouse had changed his mind, and was coming back to finish his story.
    T2   120:10 down, and trying turn after turn, but always coming back to the house, do what she would. Indeed, once,
    T2   123:26   "She's coming!" cried the Larkspur. "I hear her footstep, thump,
    A10   82: 7   to the Caterpillar, and the words all coming different, and then the Mock Turtle drew a long breath,
    A4   30:30   roof bear?--Mind that loose slate--Oh, it's coming down! Heads below!" (a loud crash)--"Now, who did that?
    T4   138: 6 each collar, when she was startled by a voice coming from the one marked 'DUM.'
    A4   27:31   here directly, and get ready for your walk!' 'Coming in a minute, nurse! But I've got to watch this
    T7   175:19 "This is a child!" Haigha replied eagerly, coming in front of Alice to introduce her, and spreading out
    A2   15:26   she hastily dried her eyes to see what was coming. It was the White Rabbit returning, splendidly dressed,
    T5   152:29 so glad it's gone. I thought it was the night coming on."
    T4   146: 2 be getting out of the wood, for really it's coming on very dark. Do you think it's going to rain?"
    T4   148:19 Alice thought there must be a thunderstorm coming on. "What a thick black cloud that is!" she said. "And
    T8   190:21 said Alice: "and thank you very much for coming so far--and for the song--I liked it very much."
    A7   54: 9   No room!" they cried out when they saw Alice coming. "There's plenty of room!" said Alice indignantly, and
    A1   8:14   tried to look down and make out what she was coming to, but it was too dark to see anything: then she
    A4   29:21   on the stairs. Alice knew it was the Rabbit coming to look for her, and she trembled till she shook the
    T8   187:10   "I was coming to that," the Knight said. "The song really is
    A8   67:37 "Who are you talking to?" said the King, coming up to Alice, and looking at the Cat's head with great
    T4   147:30 "Do I look very pale?" said Tweedledum, coming up to have his helmet tied on. (He called it a helmet,
    T7   170:22   now!" she exclaimed at last. "But he's coming very slowly--and what curious attitudes he goes into!"
COMMITS (1)
    T5   151: 7   "Suppose he never commits the crime?" said Alice.
COMMON (2) [See also UNCOMMON]
    T1   112:11 could be seen from the old room was quite common and uninteresting, but that all the rest was as
    A1   13: 3   dull and stupid for life to go on in the common way.
-COMMONLY [See UNCOMMONLY]
COMMOTION (1)
    A2   20:12   as hard as it could go, and making quite a commotion in the pool as it went.
COMPANION (1)
    T2   126: 7   at the real Queen as she said this, but her companion only smiled pleasantly, and said "That's easily
COMPANY (1)
    A9   73:19   heard the King say in a low voice, to the company, generally, "You are all pardoned." "Come, that's a
COMPARED (2)
    T2   125:14 like," she said, "but I've heard nonsense, compared with which that would be as sensible as a dictionary!
    T2   125: 5 when you say 'garden'--I've seen gardens, compared with which this would be a wilderness."
COMPARISON (1)
    T2   125: 9 interrupted, "I could show you hills, in comparison with which you'd call that a valley."
COMPLAIN (2)
    T6   168:26   "That's just what I complain of," said Humpty Dumpty. "Your face is the same as
    T9   193: 2   "That's just what I complain of! You should have meant! What do you suppose is the
COMPLAINED (1)
    A3   24:10   some noise and confusion, as the large birds complained that they could not taste theirs, and the small
COMPLAINING (2)
    A8   67:24   play at all fairly," Alice began, in rather a complaining tone, "and they all quarrel so dreadfully one
    T8   179:10 person's dream," she went on in a rather complaining tone: "I've a great mind to go and wake him, and
COMPLETED (1)
    T8   189: 8   I heard him then, for I had just / Completed my design / To keep the Menai bridge from rust / By
COMPLETELY (2)
    A4   27:10   glass table and the little door, had vanished completely.
    T8   187: 9 song, then?" said Alice, who was by this time completely bewildered.
COMPLIMENT (2)
    T6   159:21 hoping to turn her remark into a sort of compliment.
    T2   122:22 hoping to get it into a better temper by a compliment. "I've been in many gardens before, but none of the
CONCEIT (3)
    T8W   16:14   "And it's very good for the conceit," added the Wasp.
    T8W   17: 3 "That's a new-fangled name. They called it conceit in my time."
    T8W   17: 4   "Conceit isn't a disease at all," Alice remarked.
CONCERT (2)
    A7   57:13   at the March Hare,) "--it was at the great concert given by the Queen of Hearts, and I had to sing
    A11   89: 7 "Bring me the list of the singers in the last concert!" on which the wretched Hatter trembled so, that he

CONCLUDED (2)
    A4   29:39   and a crash of broken glass, from which she concluded that it was just possible it had fallen into a
    A10   84: 2   received knife and fork with a growl, / And concluded the banquet by--"
CONCLUSION (2)
    A8   66:18   parts of the ground, Alice soon came to the conclusion that it was a very difficult game indeed.
    A2   18:21   once in her life, and had come to the general conclusion that wherever you go to on the English coast, you
CONDEMN (1)
    A3   25:50   old Fury: 'I'll try the whole cause, and condemn you to death.
CONDITION (1)
    T8W   14:22   new lumps of white sugar, large and in fine condition. In coming back--"
CONDUCT (1)
    A3   22:23   William and offer him the crown. William's conduct at first was moderate. But the insolence of his
CONFESS (3)
    T1   118:26   to understand!" (You see she didn't like to confess, even to herself, that she couldn't make it out at all
    T3   130:13   what thinking in chorus means--for I must confess that I don't) "Better say nothing at all. Language is
    T12   207:16   she cried, clapping her hands triumphantly. "Confess that was what you turned into!"
CONFUSED (5)
    A12   98:41   queer noises, would change (she knew) to the confused clamour of the busy farm-yard--while the lowing of
    A7   60:26   now you ask me," said Alice, very much confused, "I don't think--"
    T9   199:33   Then followed a confused noise of cheering, and Alice thought to herself
    A7   60:12   This answer so confused poor Alice, that she let the Dormouse go on for some
    A3   23:25   at once crowded round her, calling out, in a confused way, "Prizes! Prizes!"
CONFUSING (4)
    A5   35:16   so many different sizes in a day is very confusing."
    T5   150:10   understand you," said Alice. "It's dreadfully confusing!"
    A8   67:27   attends to them--and you've no idea how confusing it is all the things being alive: for instance,
    A10   84: 5   explain it as you go on? It's by far the most confusing thing that I ever heard!"
CONFUSION (7)
    A3   24:10   eat the comfits: this caused some noise and confusion, as the large birds complained that they could not
    A11   91:22   For some minutes the whole court was in confusion, getting the Dormouse turned out, and, by the time
    T7   170: 2   stumbled, the rider fell off instantly. The confusion got worse every moment, and Alice was very glad to
    A11   88:32   looking uneasily at the Queen, and in his confusion he bit a large piece out of his teacup instead of
    A4   31:10   by the hedge!" then silence, and then another confusion of voices--"Hold up his head--Brandy now--Don't
    A8   68:14   of things at all, as the game was in such confusion that she never knew whether it was her turn or not.
    T9   204: 1   herself, as well as she could in the dreadful confusion that was beginning.
CONGER-EEL (1)
    A9   76:39   then Drawling--the Drawling-master was an old conger-eel, that used to come once a week: he taught us
CONJURING-TRICK (2)
    T9   201:18   and there it was again in a moment, like a conjuring-trick. It was so large that she couldn't help
    T7   175:41   it Alice couldn't guess. It was just like a conjuring-trick, she thought.
CONQUERED (1)
    T9   201:20   as she had been with the mutton; however, she conquered her shyness by a great effort, and cut a slice and
CONQUEROR (2)
    A2   19:22   a French mouse, come over with William the Conqueror." (For, with all her knowledge of history, Alice had
    A3   22: 3   all round, if you please! 'William the Conqueror, whose cause was favoured by the pope, was soon
CONQUEST (1)
    A3   22: 5   of late much accustomed to usurpation and conquest. Edwin and Morcar, the earls of Mercia and
CONSENTED (1)
    A7   59:31   said the Dormouse indignantly. However, he consented to go on. "And so these three little sisters--they
CONSEQUENCE (2)
    T3   131:38   if it hadn't come quite close to her ear. The consequence of this was that it tickled her ear very much, and
    T5   156:43   (so Alice explained it afterwards), and the consequence was that the handle of it caught her under the
CONSEQUENCES (1)
    T9   195:23   a thing, that fixes it, and you must take the consequences."
CONSIDER (10)
    T5   152:39   come to-day. Consider what o'clock it is. Consider anything, only don't cry!"
    A8   64:10   laid his hand upon her arm, and timidly said "Consider, my dear: she is only a child!"
    A12   96:28   tone, and everybody laughed. "Let the jury consider their verdict," the King said, for about the
    T5   152:37   poor Queen, wringing her hands in despair. "Consider what a great girl you are. Consider what a long way
    T5   152:37   despair. "Consider what a great girl you are. Consider what a long way you've come to-day. Consider what
    T5   152:38   Consider what a long way you've come to-day. Consider what o'clock it is. Consider anything, only don't
    T12   208: 5   "Now, Kitty, let's consider who it was that dreamed it all. This is a serious
    T5   153: 2   can do two things at once, you know. Let's consider your age to begin with--how old are you?"
    A12   94: 1   turned pale, and shut his note-book hastily. "Consider your verdict," he said to the jury, in a low
    A11   88: 1   "Consider your verdict," the King said to the jury.
CONSIDERED (7)
    A7   55:39   Alice considered a little, and then said "The fourth."
    A10   81:19   Alice looked down at them, and considered a little before she gave her answer. "They're done
    T6   162:40   Alice considered a little. "I like birthday presents best," she said
    T8W   16:17   The Wasp considered a little. "Well, no," he said: "it's when you hold
    T9   204:18   turning fiercely upon the Red Queen, whom she considered as the cause of all the mischief--but the Queen was
    A6   45: 3   in livery came running out of the wood--(she considered him to be a footman because he was in livery:
    T9   194:10   Alice considered. "The bone wouldn't remain, of course, if I took it
CONSIDERING (5)
    A7   59:34   "Treacle," said the Dormouse, without considering at all, this time.
    A1   8: 5   moment down went Alice after it, never once considering how in the world she was to get out again.
    A1   7: 6   So she was considering, in her own mind (as well as she could, for the
    T1   107: 4   of an hour (and bearing it pretty well, considering): so you see that it couldn't have had any hand in
    T5   152:41   of her tears. "Can you keep from crying by considering things?" she asked.

CONSTANT (2)
   A9   74:36   of "Hjckrrh!" from the Gryphon, and the constant heavy sobbing of the Mock Turtle. Alice was very
   A6   46:14   a most extraordinary noise going on within--a constant howling and sneezing, and every now and then a great
CONSULTATION (1)
   A3   21: 6   course was, how to get dry again: they had a consultation about this, and after a few minutes it seemed
CONTEMPT (2)
   T4   145:27   Tweedledum interrupted in a tone of great contempt.
   A5   43:12   said the Pigeon, in a tone of the deepest contempt. "I've seen a good many little girls in my time, but
CONTEMPTUOUS (1)
   A10   82:27   dry, he is gay as a lark, / And will talk in contemptuous tones of the Shark: / But, when the tide rises
CONTEMPTUOUSLY (4)
   A7   56:38   you don't!" the Hatter said, tossing his head contemptuously. "I dare say you never even spoke to Time!"
   T6   163:25   Humpty Dumpty smiled contemptuously. "Of course you don't--till I tell you. I meant
   A5   36: 9   "You!" said the Caterpillar contemptuously. "Who are you?"
   T4   145: 8   "Not you!" Tweedledee retorted contemptuously. "You'd be nowhere. Why, you're only a sort of
CONTENT (3)
   A5   41:13   "Are you content now?" said the Caterpillar.
   T2   127:23   not try, please!" said Alice. "I'm quite content to stay here--only I am so hot and thirsty!"
   T6   166:10   when you've once heard it, you'll be quite content. Who's been repeating all that hard stuff to you?"
CONTENTED (1)
   T5   154: 8   as it happened, Alice had not got: so she contented herself with turning round, looking at the shelves
CONTINUED (10) [See also DISCONTINUED]
   T8   182:22   you've got your hair well fastened on?" he continued, as they set off.
   A6   46:30   "--or next day, maybe," the Footman continued in the same tone, exactly as if nothing had happened
   A7   57:18   "It goes on, you know," the Hatter continued, "in this way:--
   A10   78:24   --change lobsters, and retire in same order," continued the Gryphon.
   A11   90: 1   "After that," continued the Hatter, "I cut some more bread-and-butter--"
   A11   90:21   all you know about it, you may stand down," continued the King.
   A5   43: 1   as I'd taken the highest tree in the wood," continued the Pigeon, raising its voice to a shriek, "and just
   T6   162:33   "They gave it me," Humpty Dumpty continued thoughtfully as he crossed one knee over the other
   A3   22:25   How are you getting on now, my dear?" it continued, turning to Alice as it spoke.
   T4   139: 7   "Contrariwise," continued Tweedledee, "if it was so, it might be; and if it
CONTRADICTED (1)
   A5   41:11   said nothing: she had never been so much contradicted in all her life before, and she felt that she was
CONTRADICTING (1)
   T2   125:10   "No, I shouldn't," said Alice, surprised into contradicting her at last: "a hill ca'n't be a valley, you
CONTRARIWISE (5)
   T4   144:17   Carpenter couldn't count how many he took: contrariwise."
   T4   146: 9   said Tweedledee: "we've no objection. Contrariwise."
   T4   138:13   "Contrariwise," added the one marked 'DEE,' "if you think we're
   T4   139:19   felt quite certain he would only shout out "Contrariwise!" and so he did.
   T4   139: 7   "Contrariwise," continued Tweedledee, "if it was so, it might
CONVENIENT (1) [See also INCONVENIENT]
   T3   134:26   went on in a careless tone: "only think how convenient it would be if you could manage to go home without
CONVENIENTLY (1)
   T4   142:16   or so, / And then they rested on a rock / Conveniently low: / And all the little Oysters stood / And
CONVERSATION (18)
   A6   48: 5   feeling quite pleased to have got into a conversation.
   A9   70:31   now," she said, by way of keeping up the conversation a little.
   A5   36:10   them back again to the beginning of the conversation. Alice felt a little irritated at the
   A5   35: 5   This was not an encouraging opening for a conversation. Alice replied, rather shyly, "I--I hardly know,
   A2   20: 2   in a great hurry to change the subject of conversation. "Are you--are you fond--of--of dogs?" The Mouse
   T5   149:10   and Alice felt that if there was to be any conversation at all, she must manage it herself. So she began
   T12 207: 9   she had said, "so that one could keep up a conversation! But how can you talk with a person if they
   A7   55:32   with you," said the Hatter, and here the conversation dropped, and the party sat silent for a minute,
   T5   156: 1   offended Alice a little, so there was no more conversation for a minute or two, while the boat glided gently
   T6   161:15   again in a minute, they would! However, this conversation is going on a little too fast: let's go back to
   A4   29:17   side and then the other, and making quite a conversation of it altogether; but after a few minutes she
   T6   159:24   what to say to this: it wasn't at all like conversation, she thought, as he never said anything to her;
   T5   149:16   an argument at the very beginning of their conversation, so she smiled and said "If your Majesty will
   T9   201:27   Red Queen: "it's ridiculous to leave all the conversation to the pudding!"
   T9   192:26   a minute, suddenly changed the subject of the conversation. "What do you mean by 'If you really are a Queen'
   A6   48: 8   be as well to introduce some other subject of conversation. While she was trying to fix on one, the cook
   A8   68:27   again, and went back to have a little more conversation with her friend.
   T4   140: 3   pause, as Alice didn't know how to begin a conversation with people she had just been dancing with. "It
CONVERSATIONS (2)
   A1   7: 5   a book," thought Alice, "without pictures or conversations?"
   A1   7: 4   sister was reading, but it had no pictures or conversations in it, "and what is the use of a book," thought
COOING (1)
   T9   201:39   into Alice's other ear, in a voice like the cooing of a pigeon. "It would be such a treat! May I?"
COOK (14)
   A11   91:10   "Sha'n't," said the cook.
   A11   91:17   "Pepper, mostly," said the cook.
   A6   47:10   in the kitchen, that did not sneeze, were the cook, and a large cat, which was lying on the hearth and
   A6   48:41   CHORUS (in which the cook and the baby joined):--
   A11   91:24   by the time they had settled down again, the cook had disappeared.
   T9   202: 7   'Now cook me the fish!' / That is easy, and will not take more than
   A11   91: 5   The next witness was the Duchess's cook. She carried the pepper-box in her hand, and Alice
   A6   49:13   Queen," and she hurried out of the room. The cook threw a frying-pan after her as she went, but it just
   A11   91:14   after folding his arms and frowning at the cook till his eyes were nearly out of sight, he said, in a

COOK (cont.)
A6   48:28   Alice glanced rather anxiously at the cook, to see if she meant to take the hint; but the cook was
A6   48: 9   While she was trying to fix on one, the cook took the cauldron of soup off the fire, and at once set
A8   62:16   "And I'll tell him--it was for bringing the cook tulip-roots instead of onions."
A6   48:29   to see if she meant to take the hint; but the cook was busily stirring the soup, and seemed not to be
A6   47: 2   stool in the middle, nursing a baby: the cook was leaning over the fire, stirring a large cauldron
COOKED (3)
T8   186:19   I don't believe that pudding ever will be cooked! And yet it was a very clever pudding to invent."
T8   186: 9   "In time to have it cooked for the next course?" said Alice. "Well, that was quick
T8   186:18   lower, "I don't believe that pudding ever was cooked! In fact, I don't believe that pudding ever will be
COOL (3)
T3   135:38   way when she reached the wood: it looked very cool and shady. "Well, at any rate it's a great comfort," she
A7   61: 6   garden, among the bright flower-beds and the cool fountains.
A1   10: 5   among those beds of bright flowers and those cool fountains, but she could not even get her head through
COPPER (1)
T8   188:39   gold / Or coin of silvery shine, / But for a copper halfpenny, / And that will purchase nine.
-CORKED [See UNCORKED]
CORKSCREW (3)
T6   168: 8   I took a corkscrew from the shelf: / I went to wake them up myself.
T9   196: 2   to herself. "He came to the door with a corkscrew in his hand--"
T2   120: 6   But how curiously it twists! It's more like a corkscrew than a path! Well this turn goes to the hill, I
CORKSCREWS (1)
T6   164:36   like lizards--and they're something like corkscrews."
CORNER (7)
A1   9:27   She was close behind it when she turned the corner, but the Rabbit was no longer to be seen: she found
A4   30:27   Fetch it here, lad!--Here, put 'em up at this corner--No, tie 'em together first--they don't reach half high
A7   54: 8   the three were all crowded together at one corner of it. "No room! No room!" they cried out when they saw
T1   107:13   so, while Alice was sitting curled up in a corner of the great arm-chair, half talking to herself and
A1   9:26   just in time to hear it say, as it turned a corner, "Oh my ears and whiskers, how late it's getting!" She
T2   120:11   she would. Indeed, once, when she turned a corner rather more quickly than usual, she ran against it
T3   137:30   herself as she went, till, on turning a sharp corner, she came upon two fat little men, so suddenly that she
CORNERS (2)
T2   120: 4   along the path, and turning several sharp corners), "but I suppose it will at last. But how curiously it
A8   63:17   and flat, with their hands and feet at the corners: next the ten courtiers: these were ornamented all
CORRECT (1)
T9   195:22   "It's too late to correct it," said the Red Queen: "when you've once said a
CORRECTED (3)
T8   187: 5   said 'That's what the song is called'?" Alice corrected herself.
T9   195:20   this, "is the thunder--no, no!" she hastily corrected herself. "I meant the other way."
T6   162:16   it was her turn now.) "At least," she corrected herself on second thoughts, "a beautiful cravat, I
COST (1)
A9   73: 2   merely remarking that a moment's delay would cost them their lives.
COTTAGES (1)
T3   129:15   must be!" was her next idea. "Something like cottages with the roofs taken off, and stalks put to them--and
COUGH (2)
T8W   20:10   scream of laughter, which she turned into a cough as well as she could. At last she managed to say gravely
T4   147:28   loud: but she managed to turn it into a cough, for fear of hurting his feelings.
COULD (153)
A3   24: 8   took the thimble, looking as solemn as she could.
A5   36:24   swallowing down her anger as well as she could.
A7   56:21   understand you," she said, as politely as she could.
A9   70:29   to be rude: so she bore it as well as she could.
T6   168:20   we meet again!" she said as cheerfully as she could.
A6   48:32   don't bother me!" said the Duchess. "I never could abide figures!" And with that she began nursing her
T2   127:28   She took it, and ate it as well as she could: and it was very dry: and she thought she had never been
A4   32:17   she appeared; but she ran off as hard as she could, and soon found herself safe in a thick wood.
A4   30:39   drew her foot as far down the chimney as she could, and waited till she heard a little animal (she couldn't
T7   177:22   But before Alice could answer him, the drums began.
T4   146: 1   her tears, and went on, as cheerfully as she could, "At any rate, I'd better be getting out of the wood,
T8W   20:10   which she turned into a cough as well as she could. At last she managed to say gravely, "I can bite
T2   122: 4   "It could bark," said the Rose.
A8   68:41   argument was that anything that had a head could be beheaded, and that you weren't to talk nonsense.
A6   49:32   to see what was the matter with it. There could be no doubt that it had a very turn-up nose, much more
A6   50:11   into its face in some alarm. This time there could be no mistake about it: it was neither more nor less
T1   112:10   began looking about, and noticed that what could be seen from the old room was quite common and
T4   140:35   The sea was wet as wet could be, / The sands were dry as dry. / You could not see a
A7   60:29   This piece of rudeness was more than Alice could bear: she got up in great disgust, and walked off: the
T8   187:18   remembered most clearly. Years afterwards she could bring the whole scene back again, as if it had been only
A2   15:16   Poor Alice! It was as much as she could do, lying down on one side, to look through into the
T1   114:10   away her breath, and for a minute or two she could do nothing but hug the little Lily in silence. As soon
A6   49:20   first minute or two, it was as much as she could do to hold it.
T2   126:15   the Queen went so fast that it was all she could do to keep up with her: and still the Queen kept crying
T8   184:18   scream of laughter, in spite of all she could do to prevent it.
A7   60: 7   said the Hatter; "so I should think you could draw treacle out of a treacle-well--eh, stupid?"
A11   87: 1   "Stupid things!" on their slates, and she could even make out that one of them didn't know how to spell
T9   197:21   and sounded more like a tune: at last she could even make out words, and she listened so eagerly that,
T1   115:17   done, and went round the room to see if she could find any water to throw over him. However, she could
T1   115:18   any water to throw over him. However, she could find nothing but a bottle of ink, and when she got back
A5   43:30   crouched down among the trees as well as she could, for her neck kept getting entangled among the branches,
A6   47: 6   soup!" Alice said to herself, as well as she could for sneezing.

COULD (cont.)

A12	92: 9	began picking them up again as quickly as she could, for the accident of the gold-fish kept running in her
A1	7: 6	considering, in her own mind (as well as she could, for the hot day made her feel very sleepy and stupid),
T7	173: 6	get the crown?" she asked, as well as she could, for the run was putting her quite out of breath.
A8	67: 9	some way of escape, and wondering whether she could get away without being seen, when she noticed a curious
T3	131:28	all--I was in a wood just now--and I wish I could get back there!"
T4	141:10	you suppose,' the Walrus said, / 'That they could get it clear?' / 'I doubt it,' said the Carpenter, / And
T8	185: 4	to me once--and the worst of it was, before I could get out again, the other White Knight came and put it on
T4	144:20	"But he ate as many as he could get," said Tweedledum.
A11	91: 3	Hatter was out of sight before the officer could get to the door.
T2	120: 2	far better," said Alice to herself, "if I could get to the top of that hill: and here's a path that
A2	15:35	scurried away into the darkness as hard as he could go.
A2	20:12	was swimming away from her as hard as it could go, and making quite a commotion in the pool as it went
A6	48: 2	grinned; in fact, I didn't know that cats could grin."
A2	18: 6	by it, and found that, as nearly as she could guess, she was now about two feet high, and was going on
A6	49: 3	the poor little thing howled so, that Alice could hardly hear the words:--
T1	115:21	in a frightened whisper--so low, that Alice could hardly hear what they said.
T6	160:23	and looked so solemn and grand that Alice could hardly help laughing. "If I did fall," he went on, "the
T4	138:17	her head like the ticking of a clock, and she could hardly help saying them out loud:--
A2	16: 2	of the same age as herself, to see if she could have been changed for any of them.
T9	202: 6	be bought.' / That is easy: a penny, I think, could have bought it.
T9	202: 4	be caught.' / That is easy: a baby, I think, could have caught it. / 'Next, the fish must be bought.' /
A10	81:26	replied, rather impatiently: "any shrimp could have told you that."
A10	83: 5	his toes?" the Mock Turtle persisted. "How could he turn them out with his nose, you know?"
A9	74:18	of rock, and, as they came nearer, Alice could hear him sighing as if his heart would break. She pitied
A12	98:26	his way through the neighbouring pool--she could hear the rattle of the teacups as the March Hare and his
A12	98:19	eager eyes were looking up into hers--she could hear the very tones of her voice, and see that queer
T5	154:15	others round it were crowded as full as they could hold.
A1	10: 9	I could shut up like a telescope! I think I could, if I only knew how to begin." For, you see, so many
A4	31:30	voice. And Alice called out, as loud as she could, "If you do, I'll set Dinah at you!"
A4	30:20	me out of the window, I only wish they could! I'm sure I don't want to stay in here any longer!"
T9	204: 1	Alice thought to herself, as well as she could in the dreadful confusion that was beginning.
T2	122: 3	"But what could it do, if any danger came?" Alice asked.
T6	159:10	a narrow one that Alice quite wondered how he could keep his balance--and, as his eyes were steadily fixed
A7	57: 7	at first, perhaps," said the Hatter: "but you could keep it to half-past one as long as you liked."
T12	207: 9	of that sort," she had said, "so that one could keep up a conversation! But how can you talk with a
A6	46:20	if you were inside, you might knock, and I could let you out, you know." He was looking up into the sky
T4	139:31	were dancing, and it was done (as well as she could make it out) by the branches rubbing one across the
T5	153:36	side of the counter? Rub as she would, she could make nothing more of it: she was in a little dark shop,
T8W	17:12	tumbled about like a heap of sea-weed. "You could make your wig much neater," she said, "if only you had a
T1	108: 3	cat, and speaking in as cross a voice as she could manage--and then she scrambled back into the arm-chair,
T8	181: 7	your helmet?" It was evidently more than he could manage by himself: however, she managed to shake him out
A1	9: 2	falling through the air! Do you think you could manage it?) "And what an ignorant little girl she'll
T5	152:30	"I wish I could manage to be glad!" the Queen said. "Only I never can
T3	134:26	"only think how convenient it would be if you could manage to go home without it! For instance, if the
T1	114:22	of the question: it was quite clear that he could neither hear her nor see her.
A3	23:17	This question the Dodo could not answer without a great deal of thought, and it stood
A6	51:17	Alice felt that this could not be denied, so she tried another question. "What sort
T8	188:12	/ And always use so large a fan / That they could not be seen. / So, having no reply to give / To what the
A10	80: 5	the dance. / Would not, could not, would not, could not, could not join the dance. / Would not, could not,
A10	80: 6	the dance. / Would not, could not, would not, could not, could not join the dance.
A1	10: 5	flowers and those cool fountains, but she could not even get her head through the doorway; "and even if
T2	126:16	crying "Faster! Faster!" but Alice felt she could not go faster, though she had no breath left to say so.
A8	66:12	face, with such a puzzled expression that she could not help bursting out laughing; and, when she had got
T7	175:27	Alice could not help her lips curling up into a smile as she began:
T5	152:40	Alice could not help laughing at this, even in the midst of her
T3	137:31	upon two fat little men, so suddenly that she could not help starting back, but in another moment she
A9	74:38	Sir, for your interesting story," but she could not help thinking there must be more to come, so she sat
A10	80: 6	/ Would not, could not, would not, could not, could not join the dance.
A10	80: 5	/ Would not, could not, would not, could not, could not join the dance. / Would not, could not, would not,
A11	87: 9	poor little juror (it was Bill, the Lizard) could not make out at all what had become of it; so, after
T7	173:17	in such a cloud of dust, that at first Alice could not make out which was which; but she soon managed to
A1	12:16	went back to the table for it, she found she could not possibly reach it: she could see it quite plainly
A1	12:11	like after the candle is blown out, for she could not remember ever having seen such a thing.
A8	63:29	on her face like the three gardeners, but she could not remember ever having heard of such a rule at
T4	140:37	could be, / The sands were dry as dry. / You could not see a cloud, because / No cloud was in the sky: / No
A4	34: 1	the flowers and the blades of grass, but she could not see anything that looked like the right thing to eat
A11	87: 6	pencil that squeaked. This, of course, Alice could not stand, and she went round the court and got behind
A12	94:42	/ She gave me a good character, / But said I could not swim.
A12	95:34	some meaning in them, after all. '--said I could not swim--' you ca'n't swim, can you?" he added, turning
A3	24:10	as the large birds complained that they could not taste theirs, and the small ones choked and had to
A8	64: 1	was the same as the rest of the pack, she could not tell whether they were gardeners, or soldiers, or
A5	36:15	was another puzzling question; and, as Alice could not think of any good reason, and the Caterpillar seemed
A3	24: 6	that she did not dare to laugh; and, as she could not think of anything to say, she simply bowed, and took
A10	80: 5	but he would not join the dance. / Would not, could not, would not, could not, could not join the dance. /
A10	80: 6	not, could not join the dance. / Would not, could not, would not, could not, could not join the dance.
T1	111: 6	beyond. Oh, Kitty, how nice it would be if we could only get through into Looking-glass House! I'm sure it's
T3	137:28	and ask them the way out of the wood. If I could only get to the Eighth Square before it gets dark!" So
A4	30:13	was a long silence after this, and Alice could only hear whispers now and then; such as "Sure, I don't
T8	186:30	Alice could only look puzzled: she was thinking of the pudding.

COULD (cont.)

A2	19:34	I think you'd take a fancy to cats, if you could only see her. She is such a dear quiet thing," Alice
T9	201:25	and Alice hadn't a word to say in reply: she could only sit and look at it and gasp.
T7	171: 9	far too much out of breath to say a word, and could only wave his hands about, and make the most fearful
T8	191: 8	and set it on her lap to make out what it could possibly be.
A6	46:13	they're making such a noise inside, no one could possibly hear you." And certainly there was a most
T2	126:12	Alice never could quite make out, in thinking it over afterwards, how it
T1	116: 5	over the leaves, to find some part that she could read, "--for it's all in some language I don't know,"
A7	55:33	a minute, while Alice thought over all she could remember about ravens and writing-desks, which wasn't
A12	98: 7	And she told her sister, as well as she could remember them, all these strange Adventures of hers that
T7	176: 8	monster!" the Unicorn cried out, before Alice could reply.
T3	136: 5	determined didn't help her much, and all she could say, after a great deal of puzzling, was "L, I know it
T4	138:15	"I'm sure I'm very sorry," was all Alice could say; for the words of the old song kept ringing through
A9	72:14	"That's nothing to what I could say if I chose," the Duchess replied, in a pleased tone
T9	199:13	been asking of?" He was so hoarse that Alice could scarcely hear him.
A11	86:37	Alice could see, as well as if she were looking over their shoulders
A3	26:28	mice, you ca'n't think! And oh, I wish you could see her after the birds! Why, she'll eat a little bird
A1	12:17	found she could not possibly reach it: she could see it quite plainly through the glass, and she tried
A8	68:20	the other side of the garden, where Alice could see it trying in a helpless sort of way to fly up into a
T8	185:20	was hurt this time. However, though she could see nothing but the soles of his feet, she was much
T1	110:35	just behind the fireplace. Oh! I do so wish I could see that bit! I want so much to know whether they've a
A12	93:31	"important," and some "unimportant." Alice could see this, as she was near enough to look over their
A5	42: 9	shoulders were nowhere to be found: all she could see, when she looked down, was an immense length of neck
T2	125: 8	you say 'hill'," the Queen interrupted, "I could show you hills, in comparison with which you'd call that
A2	19:33	"don't be angry about it. And yet I wish I could show you our cat Dinah. I think you'd take a fancy to
A1	10: 8	use without my shoulders. Oh, how I wish I could shut up like a telescope! I think I could, if I only
A9	76: 3	your tongue!" added the Gryphon, before Alice could speak again. The Mock Turtle went on.
T3	131:44	she really wanted to know was, whether it could sting or not, but she thought this wouldn't be quite a
T2	120:12	than usual, she ran against it before she could stop herself.
T2	120:31	gracefully about in the wind, "I wish you could talk!"
T2	122:23	many gardens before, but none of the flowers could talk."
T1	110:10	dear, let's pretend--" And here I wish I could tell you half the things Alice used to say, beginning
A10	81:40	"I could tell you my adventures--beginning from this morning,"
T2	124:10	directions, and explained, as well as she could, that she had lost her way.
T9	194:23	Alice said, as gravely as she could, "They might go different ways." But she couldn't help
T8	183:14	"Indeed?" but she said it as heartily as she could. They went on a little way in silence after this, the
A7	56: 9	cup of tea, and looked at it again: but he could think of nothing better to say than his first remark,
T8	183:13	Alice could think of nothing better to say than "Indeed?" but she
A8	69: 6	Alice could think of nothing else to say but "It belongs to the
T4	140:20	it's very long," she said, as politely as she could, "would you please tell me first which road--"
T8W	20:12	Wasp persisted. "If you was a-fighting, now--could you get hold of the other one by the back of the neck?"
T3	131:30	her ear: "something about 'you would if you could,' you know."
T9	196:12	thunderstorm, you ca'n't think!" ("She never could, you know," said the Red Queen.) "And part of the roof

COULDN'T (49)

T7	176: 4	Unicorn cried eagerly. "You'll never guess! I couldn't."
A9	76:18	"I couldn't afford to learn it," said the Mock Turtle with a sigh
A1	9:14	"Do bats eat cats?" for, you see, as she couldn't answer either question, it didn't much matter which
T1	110:14	liked being very exact, had argued that they couldn't, because there were only two of them, and Alice had
T8W	20: 7	aint well shaped, though--I should think you couldn't bite well?"
T4	144:17	handkerchief in front, so that the Carpenter couldn't count how many he took: contrariwise."
A8	68:37	The executioner's argument was, that you couldn't cut off a head unless there was a body to cut it off
T9	193: 5	more important than a joke, I hope. You couldn't deny that, even if you tried with both hands."
T8W	18: 8	and she thought she would try if the Wasp couldn't do it too. "Would you mind saying it in rhyme?" she
T3	132:21	size of a chicken," Alice thought. Still, she couldn't feel nervous with it, after they had been talking
T3	134:15	came into Alice's head. "Supposing it couldn't find any?" she suggested.
A10	81: 7	got their tails fast in their mouths. So they couldn't get them out again. That's all."
T7	175:41	How they all came out of it Alice couldn't guess. It was just like a conjuring-trick, she
A4	30:40	waited till she heard a little animal (she couldn't guess of what sort it was) scratching and scrambling
A7	59: 3	"They couldn't have done that, you know," Alice gently remarked.
T1	107: 5	pretty well, considering): so you see that it couldn't have had any hand in the mischief.
T5	150: 5	"You couldn't have it if you did want it," the Queen said. "The
T6	160:32	and behind trees--and down chimneys--or you couldn't have known it!"
A9	76:16	"You couldn't have wanted it much," said Alice; "living at the
T1	115:10	she cried out, quite forgetting that the King couldn't hear her. "You make me laugh so that I can hardly
T7	170:30	"I love my love with an H," Alice couldn't help beginning, "because he is Happy. I hate him with
T9	201:18	a conjuring-trick. It was so large that she couldn't help feeling a little shy with it, as she had been
A8	62: 7	"I couldn't help it," said Five, in a sulky tone. "Seven jogged
T5	150: 1	Alice couldn't help laughing, as she said "I don't want you to hire
T5	155:10	with fourteen pairs at once, and Alice couldn't help looking at her in great astonishment.
T4	139:14	like a couple of great schoolboys, that Alice couldn't help pointing her finger at Tweedledum, and saying
T4	145:16	He shouted this so loud that Alice couldn't help saying "Hush! You'll be waking him, I'm afraid,
T6	168:37	to this, she quietly walked away: but she couldn't help saying to herself, as she went, "of all the
T6	163: 6	Alice couldn't help smiling as she took out her memorandum-book, and
T9	194:24	"They might go different ways." But she couldn't help thinking to herself "What dreadful nonsense we
T1	108:13	me--only Dinah was making you tidy, so you couldn't. I was watching the boys getting in sticks for the
T9	193: 9	you did," said the Red Queen. "I said you couldn't if you tried."
T1	118:27	like to confess, even to herself, that she couldn't make it out at all.) "Somehow it seems to fill my
T7	178: 1	Where the noise came from, she couldn't make out: the air seemed full of it, and it rang
T5	153:34	Alice rubbed her eyes, and looked again. She couldn't make out what had happened at all. Was she in a shop?
T6	159:31	the King's horses and all the King's men / Couldn't put Humpty Dumpty in his place again."

COULDN'T (cont.)
```
T5   156:25   to  herself.  "Oh,  what  a  lovely  one!  Only  I  couldn't  quite  reach  it."  And  it  certainly  did  seem  a  little
T4   147: 4   attention  from  the  angry  brother.  But  he  couldn't  quite  succeed,  and  it  ended  in  his  rolling  over,
T5   156:29   there  was  always  a  more  lovely  one  that  she  couldn't  reach.
T3   135: 6   think  of  excusing  me  lessons  for  that.  If  she  couldn't  remember  my  name,  she'd  call  me  'Miss,'  as  the
T9   196:16    and  things--till  I  was  so  frightened,  I  couldn't  remember  my  own  name!"
T9   201:14   waiters  took  it  away  so  quickly  that  Alice  couldn't  return  its  bow.
T4   144:32                              Alice  couldn't  say  honestly  that  he  was.  He  had  a  tall  red  night-cap
A8    63:32   all  to  lie  down  on  their  faces,  so  that  they  couldn't  see  it?"  So  she  stood  where  she  was,  and  waited.
T3   131:10                              Alice  couldn't  see  who  was  sitting  beyond  the  Beetle,  but  a  hoarse
T7   170:11   the  King  said,  referring  to  his  book.  "I  couldn't  send  all  the  horses,  you  know,  because  two  of  them
T2   121: 1         Alice  was  so  astonished  that  she  couldn't  speak  for  a  minute:  it  quite  seemed  to  take  her
T9   196:26   she  ought  to  say  something  kind,  but  really  couldn't  think  of  anything  at  the  moment.
T9   197:17   No,  not  in  all  the  History  of  England--it  couldn't,  you  know,  because  there  never  was  more  than  one
```
COUNT (2)
```
T9   193:27       "I  don't  know,"  said  Alice.  "I  lost  count."
T4   144:17   in  front,  so  that  the  Carpenter  couldn't  count  how  many  he  took:  contrariwise."
```
COUNTER (3)
```
T5   153:38   dark  shop,  leaning  with  her  elbows  on  the  counter,  and  opposite  to  her  was  an  old  Sheep,  sitting  in  an
T5   158:11   said  Alice,  as  she  put  the  money  down  on  the  counter.  For  she  thought  to  herself,  "They  mightn't  be  at  all
T5   153:36   that  was  sitting  on  the  other  side  of  the  counter?  Rub  as  she  would,  she  could  make  nothing  more  of  it:
```
COUNTING (3)
```
T9   199:35   three  makes  ninety.  I  wonder  if  any  one's  counting?"  In  a  minute  there  was  silence  again,  and  the  same
T3   133: 1   "Well,  there's  the  Horse-fly,"  Alice  began,  counting  off  the  names  on  her  fingers.
A9    76:36   there  was  Mystery,"  the  Mock  Turtle  replied,  counting  off  the  subjects  on  his  flappers--"Mystery,  ancient
```
COUNTRY (8)
```
T2   125:20    looking  out  in  all  directions  over  the  country--and  a  most  curious  country  it  was.  There  were  a
A1     8:44   I  shall  have  to  ask  them  what  the  name  of  the  country  is,  you  know.  Please,  Ma'am,  is  this  New  Zealand?  Or
T2   125:20         over  the  country--and  a  most  curious  country  it  was.  There  were  a  number  of  tiny  little  brooks
T2   127:16                     "Well,  in  our  country,"  said  Alice,  still  panting  a  little,  "you'd  generally
T2   127:19                  "A  slow  sort  of  country!"  said  the  Queen.  "Now,  here,  you  see,  it  takes  all
T7   174:22   "There's  the  White  Queen  running  across  the  country!  She  came  flying  out  of  the  wood  over  yonder--How  fast
T9   195:29               Alice  was  puzzled.  "In  our  country,"  she  remarked,  "there's  only  one  day  at  a  time."
T3   129: 2   thing  to  do  was  to  make  a  grand  survey  of  the  country  she  was  going  to  travel  through.  "It's  something  very
```
COUPLE (2)
```
A5    38: 8   shilling  the  box--/  Allow  me  to  sell  you  a  couple?"
T4   139:13                  They  looked  so  exactly  like  a  couple  of  great  schoolboys,  that  Alice  couldn't  help  pointing
```
COUPLES (1)
```
A8    63:20   came  jumping  merrily  along,  hand  in  hand,  in  couples:  they  were  all  ornamented  with  hearts.  Next  came  the
```
COURAGE (4)
```
A6    47:18   to  the  baby,  and  not  to  her,  so  she  took  courage,  and  went  on  again:--
A10   82: 5   eyes  and  mouths  so  very  wide;  but  she  gained  courage  as  she  went  on.  Her  listeners  were  perfectly  quiet
A8    64: 3   I  know?"  said  Alice,  surprised  at  her  own  courage.  "It's  no  business  of  mine."
T9   196:31   she'll  be!"  But  this  was  more  than  Alice  had  courage  to  do.
```
COURSE (61) [See also MEAT-COURSE, RACE-COURSE]
```
A9    76:19   Turtle  with  a  sigh.  "I  only  took  the  regular  course."
A10   80:17   the  Mock  Turtle,  "they--you've  seen  them,  of  course?"
T3   134:17                "Then  it  would  die,  of  course."
T6   162:39   present  given  when  it  isn't  your  birthday,  of  course."
T6   163: 3                "Three  hundred  and  sixty-four,  of  course."
T8   186:12   thoughtful  tone:  "no,  certainly  not  the  next  course."
T9   195:37                "Five  times  as  warm,  of  course."
T9   199: 7   slow  drawl  in  which  he  spoke.  "This  door,  of  course!"
A11   87: 5   jurors  had  a  pencil  that  squeaked.  This,  of  course,  Alice  could  not  stand,  and  she  went  round  the  court
T1   116:14   her.  "Why,  it's  a  Looking-glass  book,  of  course!  And,  if  I  hold  it  up  to  a  glass,  the  words  will  all  go
T12  208: 9   or  the  Red  King.  He  was  part  of  my  dream,  of  course--but  then  I  was  part  of  his  dream,  too!  Was  it  the  Red
A9    73: 6   taken  into  custody  by  the  soldiers,  who  of  course  had  to  leave  off  being  arches  to  do  this,  so  that,  by
A12   93:24       "Unimportant,  your  Majesty  means,  of  course,"  he  said,  in  a  very  respectful  tone,  but  frowning  and
A3    23:10   and  then  all  the  party  were  placed  along  the  course,  here  and  there.  There  was  no  "One,  two,  three,  and
T4   146:21   wildly  and  tear  his  hair.  "It's  spoilt,  of  course!"  Here  he  looked  at  Tweedledee,  who  immediately  sat
T6   160:21   you  ask!"  Humpty  Dumpty  growled  out.  "Of  course  I  don't  think  so!  Why,  if  ever  I  did  fall  off--which
A12   93:26                "Unimportant,  of  course,  I  meant,"  the  King  hastily  said,  and  went  on  to
T2   126: 4   being  a  Pawn,  if  only  I  might  join--though  of  course  I  should  like  to  be  a  Queen,  best."
T9   194:10   considered.  "The  bone  wouldn't  remain,  of  course,  if  I  took  it--and  the  dog  wouldn't  remain:  it  would
A12   96: 1   "'We  know  it  to  be  true'--that's  the  jury,  of  course--'If  she  should  push  the  matter  on'--that  must  be  the
T8   190:20                     "Of  course  I'll  wait,"  said  Alice:  "and  thank  you  very  much  for
T6   165: 6                     "Of  course  it  is.  It's  called  'wabe'  you  know,  because  it  goes  a
A9    71:17                     "Of  course  it  is,"  said  the  Duchess,  who  seemed  ready  to  agree  to
T2   127:15                     "Of  course  it  is,"  said  the  Queen.  "What  would  you  have  it?"
T6   160: 8                     "Of  course  it  must,"  Humpty  Dumpty  said  with  a  short  laugh:  "my
A9    77:20                     "Of  course  it  was,"  said  the  Mock  Turtle.
T5   151:10   Alice  felt  there  was  no  denying  that.  "Of  course  it  would  be  all  the  better,"  she  said:  "but  it  wouldn't
A7    56:25   without  opening  its  eyes,  "Of  course,  of  course:  just  what  I  was  going  to  remark  myself."
T7   172:19   the  King:  "this  young  lady  saw  him  too.  So  of  course  Nobody  walks  slower  than  you."
A7    56:16                     "Of  course  not,"  Alice  replied  very  readily:  "but  that's  because
A10   81:33                     "Of  course  not,"  said  the  Mock  Turtle.  "Why,  if  a  fish  came  to  me,
A7    56:25   and  said,  without  opening  its  eyes,  "Of  course,  of  course:  just  what  I  was  going  to  remark  myself."
T4   145: 7              "Where  I  am  now,  of  course,"  said  Alice.
T8   186: 9   "In  time  to  have  it  cooked  for  the  next  course?"  said  Alice.  "Well,  that  was  quick  work,  certainly!"
A3    23:23                "Why,  she,  of  course,"  said  the  Dodo;  pointing  to  Alice  with  one  finger;  and
```

COURSE (cont.)
```
T7    172:36              "Why the Lion and the Unicorn, of course," said the King.
A12    94:28              "That proves his guilt, of course," said the Queen, "so, off with--"
T5    155:34              "In the water, of course!" said the Sheep, sticking some of the needles into her
T5    150: 5    even  begin  till  next  Wednesday:  and of course the crime comes last of all."
A3     23:31                     "Of course," the Dodo replied very gravely. "What else have you
T3    129: 1                     Of course the first thing to do was to make a grand survey of the
A10    81:25              "Soles and eels, of course," the Gryphon replied, rather impatiently: "any shrimp
T8    186:11              "Well, not the next course," the Knight said in slow thoughtful tone: "no,
T8    185: 9              "I had to kick him, of course," the Knight said, very seriously. "And then he took
A10    78:22                     "Of course," the Mock Turtle said: "advance twice, set to partners
T2    123:23              "Why, all round her head, of course," the Rose replied. "I was wondering you hadn't got
T8    179:34  "You  will  observe  the  Rules of Battle, of course?" the White Knight remarked, putting on his helmet too
T3    132:32                     "Of course they answer to their names?" the Gnat remarked
A7     60:11                     "Of course they were," said the Dormouse: "well in."
A9     76:21              "Reeling and Writhing, of course, to begin with," the Mock Turtle replied; "and then the
T9    194: 8    Queen answered for her. "Bread-and-butter, of course. Try another Subtraction sum. Take a bone from a dog:
A11    89:17                     "Of course twinkling begins with a T!" said the King sharply. "Do
A3     21: 5              The first question of course was, how to get dry again: they had a consultation
T4    147: 8                     "Of course you agree to have a battle?" Tweedledum said in a
A7     56:38                     "Of course you don't!" the Hatter said, tossing his head
T6    163:25    Humpty  Dumpty  smiled  contemptuously.  "Of course you don't--till I tell you. I meant 'there's a nice
A3     22:16    it," the  Mouse  replied rather crossly: "of course you know what 'it' means."
A10    80:21    "but,  if  you've  seen  them  so often, of course you know what they're like?"
T9    194:33                     "Of course you know your ABC?" said the Red Queen.
T3    135: 4    wouldn't  be any name for her to call, and of course you wouldn't have to go, you know."
T3    135: 9    say  anything  more," the Gnat remarked, "of course you'd miss your lessons. That's a joke. I wish you had
```
-COURSES [See PUDDING-COURSES]
COURT (19)
```
A11    89: 3    and  crossed  over  to  the  other side of the court.
A12    93:15    mouth  open,  gazing  up  into the roof of the court.
A12    93:36    persons more than a mile high to leave the court."
A11    87: 6    Alice could not stand, and she went round the court and got behind him, and very soon found an opportunity
A11    90:19    immediately suppressed by the officers of the court,' and I never understood what it meant till now."
A11    86:35    the  White  Rabbit  cried out "Silence in the court!", and the King put on his spectacles and looked
A11    88:13    the March Hare, who had followed him into the court, arm-in-arm with the Dormouse. "Fourteenth of March, I
A11    90:12    immediately suppressed by the officers of the court. (As that is rather a hard word, I will just explain to
A11    89: 6    she  said,  to  one  of  the officers of the court, "Bring me the list of the singers in the last concert!"
A11    88:37    at  first  she  would  get  up and leave the court; but on second thoughts she decided to remain where she
A11    91: 7    who  it  was,  even  before  she got into the court, by the way the people near the door began sneezing all
A11    86:13              Alice had never been in a court of justice before, but she had read about them in books,
A11    89: 5    Hatter, and, just as the Dormouse crossed the court, she said, to one of the officers of the court, "Bring
A11    91:20    that  Dormouse! Turn that Dormouse out of court! Suppress him! Pinch him! Off with his whiskers!"
A11    86: 7    in  the  other.  In  the  very middle of the court was a table, with a large dish of tarts upon it: they
A11    91:22              For some minutes the whole court was in confusion, getting the Dormouse turned out, and,
A12    94:37              There was dead silence in the court, whilst the White Rabbit read out these verses:--
A12    96:26    fit  you," said  the  King looking round the court with a smile. There was a dead silence.
A11    90:32    the  King,  and the Hatter hurriedly left the court, without even waiting to put his shoes on.
```
COURTIERS (2)
```
A8     64: 2    whether  they were gardeners, or soldiers, or courtiers, or three of her own children.
A8     63:17    hands  and  feet at the corners: next the ten courtiers: these were ornamented all over with diamonds, and
```
-COVER [See DISH-COVER, UN-DISH-COVER]
COVERED (3)
```
T1    115: 2    might  as  well  dust  him  a little, he was so covered with ashes.
T1    114: 3    a  little  annoyed with the Queen, for he was covered with ashes from head to foot.
T7    169: 8    fell  over  him,  so that the ground was soon covered with little heaps of men.
```
COVERS (1) [See also DISH-COVERS]
```
T1    109:11    that  it  kisses  them so gently? And then it covers them up snug, you know, with a white quilt; and perhaps
```
COWARD (1)
```
A4     30:15    at  all,  at  all!" "Do as I tell you, you coward!", and at last she spread out her hand again, and made
```
CRAB (7)
```
A3     26:20    "Hold  your  tongue,  Ma!"  said  the young Crab, a little snappishly. "You're enough to try the patience
T5    155:28    taking  more  needles. "You'll be catching a crab directly."
A9     77: 5    the  Classical  master, though. He was an old crab, he was."
T5    155:29                     "A dear little crab!" thought Alice. "I should like that."
T5    157: 9    it  hadn't  let  go--I should so like a little crab to take home with me!" But the Sheep only laughed
A3     26:17    soon  as it was quite out of sight. And an old Crab took the opportunity of saying to her daughter "Ah, my
T5    157: 4    as  if nothing had happened. "That was a nice crab you caught!" she remarked, as Alice got back into her
```
CRABS (4)
```
T5    155:33    often--and  very  loud. Please, where are the crabs?"
T5    157:12                     "Crabs, and all sorts of things," said the Sheep: "plenty of
T5    157:11                     "Are there many crabs here?" said Alice.
T8    188:42    for  buttered rolls, / Or set limed twigs for crabs: / I sometimes search for grassy knolls / For wheels of
```
CRASH (4)
```
A6     46:15    and  sneezing, and every now and then a great crash, as if a dish or kettle had been broken to pieces.
A4     30:31    Oh,  it's  coming down! Heads below!" (a loud crash)--"Now, who did that?--It was Bill, I fancy--Who's to go
A4     29:38    she  heard  a little shriek and a fall, and a crash of broken glass, from which she concluded that it was
T6    168:41    the  sentence,  for  at  this  moment a heavy crash shook the forest from end to end.
```
CRASHED (1)
```
A12    98:30    the  Duchess's  knee, while plates and dishes crashed around it--once more the shriek of the Gryphon, the
```

```
CRASHING (1)
  T9    204:15   and plates, dishes, guests, and candles came crashing down together in a heap on the floor.
CRAVAT (3)
  T6    162:29                                       "It's a cravat, child, and a beautiful one, as you say. It's a present
  T6    162:26   said at last, "when a person doesn't know a cravat from a belt!"
  T6    162:17   herself on second thoughts, "a beautiful cravat, I should have said--no, a belt, I mean--I beg your
CRAWLED (2)
  A5     41:26        Then it got down off the mushroom, and crawled away into the grass, merely remarking, as it went,
  T4    147:10   suppose so," the other sulkily replied, as he crawled out of the umbrella: "only she must help us to dress
CRAWLING (2)
  T3    134: 9                                      "Crawling at your feet," said the Gnat (Alice drew her feet
  A8     66:15   had unrolled itself, and was in the act of crawling away: besides all this, there was generally a ridge
CRAZY (1)
  A6     46:37   the creatures argue. It's enough to drive one crazy!"
CREAM (1)
  T3    134:14                     "Weak tea with cream in it."
CREATURE (13)
  T3    131:40    from the unhappiness of the poor little creature.
  T9    201:23   it, if I were to cut a slice out of you, you creature!"
  A6     49:16   difficulty, as it was a queer-shaped little creature, and held out its arms and legs in all directions,
  A9     74: 5   Alice did not quite like the look of the creature, but on the whole she thought it would be quite as
  T8W    21:17   given a few minutes to making the poor old creature comfortable.
  A6     50:14                  So she set the little creature down, and felt quite relieved to see it trot away
  T7    175: 6   about her, if you like--She's a dear good creature," he repeated softly to himself, as he opened his
  T9    204:25   she repeated, catching hold of the little creature in the very act of jumping over a bottle which had
  T3    135:31   But then the fun would be, trying to find the creature that has got my old name! That's just like the
  T6    160:18   in her good-natured anxiety for the queer creature. "That wall is so very narrow!"
  A6     50: 9   to herself, "Now, what am I to do with this creature, when I get it home?" when it grunted again, so
  T7    175: 8   he opened his memorandum-book. "Do you spell 'creature' with a double 'e'?"
  T9    198: 9   Just then the door opened a little way, and a creature with a long beak put its head out for a moment and
CREATURES (16)
  T6    164:37               "They must be very curious-looking creatures."
  A2     20:24   Lory and an Eaglet, and several other curious creatures. Alice led the way, and the whole party swam to the
  A6     46:36   she muttered to herself, "the way all the creatures argue. It's enough to drive one crazy!"
  T7    176:14   at having to sit down between the two great creatures; but there was no other place for him.
  A10    82: 3   nervous about it, just at first, the two creatures got so close to her, one on each side, and opened
  A9     77: 9   the Gryphon, sighing in his turn; and both creatures hid their faces in their paws.
  A6     47: 9     without a moment's pause. The only two creatures in the kitchen, that did not sneeze, were the cook,
  T3    129: 6   name. Principal towns--why, what are those creatures, making honey down there? They ca'n't be bees--
  A12    98:23   around her became alive with the strange creatures of her little sister's dream.
  A10    82:17                  "How the creatures order one about, and make one repeat lessons!"
  T9    199:37               "'O Looking-Glass creatures,' quoth Alice, 'draw near! / 'Tis an honour to see
  A11    86:21   jury-box," thought Alice; "and those twelve creatures," (she was obliged to say "creatures," you see,
  T9    199:26   a crown on my head. / Let the Looking-Glass creatures, whatever they be, / Come and dine with the Red
  A10    78:36   suddenly dropping his voice; and the two creatures, who had been jumping about like mad things all this
  A5     41:19   tone. And she thought to herself "I wish the creatures wouldn't be so easily offended!"
  A11    86:22   twelve creatures," (she was obliged to say "creatures," you see, because some of them were animals, and
CREEP (2)
  A1     12:35   key; and if it makes me grow smaller, I can creep under the door: so either way I'll get into the garden,
  T8    182:33   said the Knight. "Then you make your hair creep up it, like a fruit-tree. Now the reason hair falls off
CREPT (1)
  A6     45: 9   curious to know what it was all about, and crept a little way out of the wood to listen.
CREW (1)
  AI      4: 1   tale is done, / And home we steer, a merry crew, / Beneath the setting sun.
CRIED (76)
  A1     12:20   trying, the poor little thing sat down and cried.
  T2    122: 5                       "It says 'Boughwough!'" cried a Daisy. "That's why its branches are called boughs!"
  T9    204: 5   of mutton sitting in the chair. "Here I am!" cried a voice from the soup-tureen, and Alice turned again,
  T5    155:27                  "Feather! Feather!" the Sheep cried again, taking more needles. "You'll be catching a crab
  A2     19:39   for catching mice--oh, I beg your pardon!" cried Alice again, for this time the Mouse was bristling all
  T1    107:20   "Oh, you wicked, wicked little thing!" cried Alice, catching up the kitten, and giving it a little
  T1    110: 1   the wind blows--oh, that's very pretty!" cried Alice, dropping the ball of worsted to clap her hands.
  A2     19:28   over with fright. "Oh, I beg your pardon!" cried Alice hastily, afraid that she had hurt the poor
  A2     20:10   He says it kills all the rats and--oh dear!" cried Alice in a sorrowful tone. "I'm afraid I've offended it
  A6     48:16      "Oh, please mind what you're doing!" cried Alice, jumping up and down in an agony of terror. "Oh,
  T8    184:11                  "It's too ridiculous!" cried Alice, losing all her patience this time. "You ought to
  A12    92: 1                                "Here!" cried Alice, quite forgetting in the flurry of the moment how
  A2     14: 1               "Curiouser and curiouser!" cried Alice (she was so much surprised, that for the moment
  A2     17:25   here till I'm somebody else'--but, oh dear!" cried Alice, with a sudden burst of tears, "I do wish they
  T5    152:18                       "Take care!" cried Alice. "You're holding it all crooked!" And she caught
  T4    144:28        "Come and look at him!" the brothers cried, and they each took one of Alice's hands, and led her up
  T8    188:31   was blue: / 'Come, tell me how you live,' I cried, / 'And what it is you do!'
  T5    155:30   "Didn't you hear me say 'Feather'?" the Sheep cried angrily, taking up quite a bunch of needles.
  T2    122: 7               "Didn't you know that?" cried another Daisy. And here they all began shouting together
  T8    179:16   suddenly: "You're my prisoner!" the Knight cried, as he tumbled off his horse.
  T8    190:37   the brook. "The Eighth Square at last!" she cried as she bounded * * * * * * * * * * * * * * * across, and
  T9    204:13   "I ca'n't stand this any longer!" she cried, as she jumped up and seized the tablecloth with both
  T4    143: 1               'But wait a bit,' the Oysters cried, / 'Before we have our chat; / For some of us are out of
  T6    160:30   "Now I declare that's too bad!" Humpty Dumpty cried, breaking into a sudden passion. "You've been listening
  T12   207:16   Queen to look at each other. "Now Kitty!" she cried, clapping her hands triumphantly. "Confess that was what
```

CRIED (cont.)
T8   188:15   reply to give / To what the old man said, / I cried 'Come, tell me how you live!' / And thumped him on the
T9   194:41   "I know that!" Alice cried eagerly. "You take some flour--"
T7   176: 3   "Ah, what is it, now?" the Unicorn cried eagerly. "You'll never guess! I couldn't."
T2   126:22   Queen seemed to guess her thoughts, for she cried "Faster! Don't try to talk!"
T2   126:26   so much out of breath: and still the Queen cried "Faster! Faster!" and dragged her along. "Are we nearly
T6   160:13   "Why, because there's nobody with me!" cried Humpty Dumpty. "Did you think I didn't know the answer
T6   162:42   "You don't know what you're talking about!" cried Humpty Dumpty. "How many days are there in a year?"
T2   120:24   "Oh, it's too bad!" she cried. "I never saw such a house for getting in the way!
T7   174: 1   "Speak, ca'n't you!" Haigha cried impatiently. But Hatta only munched away, and drank some
T4   146:26   "But it isn't old!" Tweedledum cried, in a greater fury than ever. "It's new, I tell you--I
T5   156: 6   please! There are some scented rushes!" Alice cried in a sudden transport of delight. "There really are--and
T7   170: 6   "I've sent them all!" the King cried in a tone of delight, on seeing Alice. "Did you happen
T5   153:20   in catching it herself. "I've got it!" she cried in a triumphant tone. "Now you shall see me pin it on
T1   113:19   It is the voice of my child!" the White Queen cried out, as she rushed past the King, so violently that she
T7   176: 7   "It's a fabulous monster!" the Unicorn cried out, before Alice could reply.
T4   139:16   "Nohow!" Tweedledum cried out briskly, and shut his mouth up again with a snap.
T4   148:21   "It's the crow!" Tweedledum cried out in a shrill voice of alarm; and the two brothers
T3   137: 7   free from Alice's arm. "I'm a Fawn!" it cried out in a voice of delight. "And, dear me! you're a human
T1   115: 9   please don't make such faces, my dear!" she cried out, quite forgetting that the King couldn't hear her.
A11 86:34   stopped herself hastily, for the White Rabbit cried out "Silence in the court!", and the King put on his
A7   54: 8   at one corner of it. "No room! No room!" they cried out when they saw Alice coming. "There's plenty of room!
T7   174:21   Suddenly she brightened up. "Look, look!" she cried, pointing eagerly. "There's the White Queen running
A2   19: 1   "I wish I hadn't cried so much!" said Alice, as she swam about, trying to find
T9   194:18   "Why, look here!" the Red Queen cried. "The dog would lose its temper, wouldn't it?"
A10 78:21   "Each with a lobster as a partner!" cried the Gryphon.
A10 85: 4   "Come on!" cried the Gryphon, and, taking Alice by the hand, it hurried
A10 85: 1   "Chorus again!" cried the Gryphon, and the Mock Turtle had just begun to
T7   174: 3   "Speak, wo'n't you!" cried the King. "How are they getting on with the fight?"
T2   123:26   "She's coming!" cried the Larkspur. "I hear her footstep, thump, thump, along
A10 78:31   "Turn a somersault in the sea!" cried the Mock Turtle, capering wildly about.
A10 78:16   "Two lines!" cried the Mock Turtle. "Seals, turtles, salmon, and so on:
A2   19:30   "Not like cats!" cried the Mouse in a shrill passionate voice. "Would you like
A3   26: 5   "I had not!" cried the Mouse, sharply and very angrily.
A2   19:42   "We, indeed!" cried the Mouse, who was trembling down to the end of its tail
T7   172:30   "Do you call that a whisper?" cried the poor King, jumping up and shaking himself. "If you
T5   152:36   "Oh, don't go on like that!" cried the poor Queen, wringing her hands in despair. "Consider
T2   127: 5   "Now! Now!" cried the Queen. "Faster! Faster!" And they went so fast that
T5   153:28   "Oh, much better!" cried the Queen, her voice rising into a squeak as she went on
T9   192:24   "Ridiculous!" cried the Queen. "Why, don't you see, child--" here she broke
T9   195:39   "Just so!" cried the Red Queen. "Five times as warm, and five times as
T5   155:21   "Feather!" cried the Sheep, as she took up another pair of needles.
T2   122:36   "Hold your tongue!" cried the Tiger-lily. "As if you ever saw anybody! You keep
T2   122: 9   shrill voices. "Silence, every one of you!" cried the Tiger-lily, waving itself passionately from side to
T7   177:17   "I say, this isn't fair!" cried the Unicorn, as Alice sat with the knife in her hand,
T4   143:13   'But not on us!' the Oysters cried, / Turning a little blue. / 'After such kindness, that
T4   145:15   "Ditto, ditto!" cried Tweedledee.
T4   146:20   "I knew it was!" cried Tweedledum, beginning to stamp about wildly and tear his
T4   139:21   "You've begun wrong!" cried Tweedledum. "The first thing in a visit is to say 'How
T4   148: 2   "And I hit every thing within reach," cried Tweedledum, "whether I can see it or not!"
A7   58:23   "Then the Dormouse shall!" they both cried. "Wake up, Dormouse!" And they pinched it on both sides
T12 207:22   "Sit up a little more stiffly, dear!" Alice cried with a merry laugh. "And curtsey while you're thinking
CRIES (1)
A12 98:39   tinkling sheep-bells, and the Queen's shrill cries to the voice of the shepherd-boy--and the sneeze of the
CRIME (2)
T5   150: 5   begin till next Wednesday: and of course the crime comes last of all."
T5   151: 7   "Suppose he never commits the crime?" said Alice.
CRIMSON (3)
T8   179:13   "Ahoy! Ahoy! Check!" and a Knight, dressed in crimson armour, came galloping down upon her, brandishing a
A8   63:25   of Hearts, carrying the King's crown on a crimson velvet cushion; and, last of all this grand procession
A8   64: 5   The Queen turned crimson with fury, and, after glaring at her for a moment like
CRINKLED (1)
T8W 18:14   was young, my ringlets waved / And curled and crinkled on my head: / And then they said 'You should be
CRITICISMS (1)
T8W 21: 6   not take the hint. So he went on with his criticisms.
CRITICIZED (1)
T2   121:13   Alice didn't like being criticized, so she began asking questions. "Aren't you
CROCODILE (1)
A2   17: 8   "How doth the little crocodile / Improve his shining tail, / And pour the waters of
CROOKED (2)
T5   149:23   so dreadfully untidy. "Every single thing's crooked," Alice thought to herself, "and she's all over pins!
T5   152:18   care!" cried Alice. "You're holding it all crooked!" And she caught at the brooch; but it was too late:
CROPPING (1)
T8   187:23   with the reins hanging loose on his neck, cropping the grass at her feet--and the black shadows of the
CROQUET (7)
A6   46: 3   Queen. An invitation for the Duchess to play croquet."
A8   65:19   right!" shouted the Queen. "Can you play croquet?"
A8   66: 2   her life: it was all ridges and furrows: the croquet balls were live hedgehogs, and the mallets live
A1   12:26   ears for having cheated herself in a game of croquet she was playing against herself, for this curious
A6   45:14   Duchess. An invitation from the Queen to play croquet." The Frog-Footman repeated, in the same solemn tone,

CROQUET (cont.)
```
  A6   49:12   she  spoke.  "I must go and get ready to play croquet with the Queen," and she hurried out of the room. The
  A6   52: 2   it what you like," said the Cat. "Do you play croquet with the Queen to-day?"
```
CROQUETED (1)
```
  A8   67:29   other  end  of  the ground--and I should have croqueted the Queen's hedgehog just now, only it ran away when
```
CROQUET-GROUND (3)
```
  A8t  62: 1                           THE QUEEN'S CROQUET-GROUND
  A9   72:42   a  word,  but slowly followed her back to the croquet-ground.
  A8   66: 1   thought  she  had  never  seen such a curious croquet-ground in her life: it was all ridges and furrows: the
```
CROQUETING (1)
```
  A8   68:18   seemed  to Alice an excellent opportunity for croqueting one of them with the other: the only difficulty was
```
CROSS (6)
```
  T1  108: 2              at the old cat, and speaking in as cross a voice as she could manage--and then she scrambled back
  T8W  16: 9   at one. And they worrits one. And then I gets cross. And I gets cold. And I gets under a tree. And I gets a
  A3   21: 3   clinging close to them, and all dripping wet, cross, and uncomfortable.
  T8W  14: 7   "Perhaps  it's  only  pain  that makes him so cross." So she tried once more.
  T8W  16: 7                        "You'd be cross too, if you'd a wig like mine," the Wasp went on. "They
  T8W  15: 9     "Were what?" the Wasp asked in a very cross voice.
```
CROSSED (8)
```
  A2   17: 4   try and say 'How doth the little--'," and she crossed her hands on her lap as if she were saying lessons,
  T2  123: 9   me?" Alice asked eagerly, for the thought crossed her mind, "There's another little girl in the garden,
  T6  159: 8   Humpty  Dumpty  was  sitting,  with his legs crossed like a Turk, on the top of a high wall--such a narrow
  T6  162:34   Humpty  Dumpty  continued  thoughtfully as he crossed one knee over the other and clasped his hands round it
  A11  89: 2   fashion." And he got up very sulkily and crossed over to the other side of the court.
  A11  89: 5   at the Hatter, and, just as the Dormouse crossed the court, she said, to one of the officers of the
  T5  153:24   better now?" Alice said very politely, as she crossed the little brook after the Queen. * * * * * * * * * *
  T8  181: 3                "So you will, when you've crossed the next brook," said the White Knight. "I'll see you
```
CROSS-EXAMINE (2)
```
  A11  91:27   to  the Queen, "Really, my dear, you must cross-examine the next witness. It quite makes my forehead
  A11  91:12   who  said, in a low voice, "Your Majesty must cross-examine this witness."
```
CROSSLY (1)
```
  A3   22:16     "Found it," the Mouse replied rather crossly: "of course you know what 'it' means."
```
CROUCHED (1)
```
  A5   43:29   as it settled down again into its nest. Alice crouched down among the trees as well as she could, for her
```
CROW (5)
```
  T4  139: 1             Just then flew down a monstrous crow, / As black as a tar-barrel; / Which frightened both the
  T5  152:27   By  this  time  it  was  getting light. "The crow must have flown away, I think," said Alice: "I'm so glad
  T4  148:21                    "It's the crow!" Tweedledum cried out in a shrill voice of alarm; and
  T8  190: 3   than  the  snow, / Whose face was very like a crow, / With eyes, like cinders, all aglow, / Who seemed
  T4  148:13             "I wish the monstrous crow would come!" thought Alice.
```
CROWD (5)
```
  A11  86: 2   their  throne when they arrived, with a great crowd assembled about them--all sorts of little birds and
  A12  92: 4      all  the  jurymen  on  to the heads of the crowd below, and there they lay sprawling about, reminding her
  A8   68:29   she  was  surprised to find quite a large crowd collected round it: there was a dispute going on between
  T7  173:15   silence, till they came into sight of a great crowd, in the middle of which the Lion and Unicorn were
  A4   32:13   she  ran  out of the house, and found quite a crowd of little animals and birds waiting outside. The poor
```
CROWDED (6)
```
  T5  154:14   quite  empty, though the others round it were crowded as full as they could hold.
  A3   23:24   with  one finger; and the whole party at once crowded round her, calling out, in a confused way, "Prizes!
  A3   24: 1                Then they all crowded round her once more, while the Dodo solemnly presented
  A3   23:15   called  out  "The race is over!" and they all crowded round it, panting, and asking "But who has won?"
  A7   54: 7   table was a large one, but the three were all crowded together at one corner of it. "No room! No room!" they
  A2   20:21   time  to  go,  for the pool was getting quite crowded with the birds and animals that had fallen into it:
```
CROWDS (1)
```
  T7  169: 3   ten  or  twenty together, and at last in such crowds that they seemed to fill the whole forest. Alice got
```
CROWN (12)
```
  T7  172:37                       "Fighting for the crown?"
  T8  191: 9                     It was a golden crown.
  T7  172:39   "and  the  best  of  the joke is, that it's my crown all the while! Let's run and see them." And they trotted
  T9  192: 7   just  at  first,  as she was afraid that the crown might come off: but she comforted herself with the
  T7  176:16      "What  a  fight  we might have for the crown now!" the Unicorn said, looking slyly up at the crown,
  A8   63:25   the  Knave  of  Hearts,  carrying the King's crown on a crimson velvet cushion; and, last of all this grand
  T9  199:25   that  said  / 'I've a sceptre in hand, I've a crown on my head. / Let the Looking-Glass creatures, whatever
  A11  86:17   by  the  way, was the King; and, as he wore his crown over the wig (look at the frontispiece if you want to
  T7  173: 5          "Does--the one--that wins--get the crown?" she asked, as well as she could, for the run was
  T7  173: 1   Lion  and  the  Unicorn were fighting for the crown: / The Lion beat the Unicorn all round the town. / Some
  T7  176:17   the  Unicorn  said,  looking slyly up at the crown, which the poor King was nearly shaking off his head, he
  A3   22:23   Atheling  to meet William and offer him the crown. William's conduct at first was moderate. But the
```
CRUEL (1)
```
  AI   3: 7                      Ah, cruel Three! In such an hour, / Beneath such dreamy weather, /
```
CRUMBS (4)
```
  A10  80:23   tails  in  their mouths--and they're all over crumbs."
  A7   56: 5              "Yes, but some crumbs must have got in as well," the Hatter grumbled: "you
  A10  80:24            "You're wrong about the crumbs," said the Mock Turtle: "crumbs would all wash off in
  A10  80:25   about  the  crumbs,"  said the Mock Turtle: "crumbs would all wash off in the sea. But they have their
```
CRUMPLED (1)
```
  T4  144:33   night-cap on, with a tassel, and he was lying crumpled up into a sort of untidy heap, and snoring loud--"fit
```
CRUST (1) [See also PIE-CRUST]
```
  T3  134:11   slices  of  bread-and-butter,  its  body is a crust, and its head is a lump of sugar."
```

CRY (12)
    AI   3:30   time--" "It is next time!" / The happy voices cry.
    T4   145:21   "I am real!" said Alice, and began to cry.
    T4   145:25   seemed so ridiculous--"I shouldn't be able to cry."
    T5   152:39   o'clock it is. Consider anything, only don't cry!"
    T4   145:23   Tweedledee remarked: "there's nothing to cry about."
    T4   145:29   thought to herself: "and it's foolish to cry about it." So she brushed away her tears, and went on, as
    A2   15:19   hopeless than ever: she sat down and began to cry again.
    A3   26:40   you any more!" And here poor Alice began to cry again, for she felt very lonely and low-spirited. In a
    A10   85: 2   Turtle had just begun to repeat it, when a cry of "The trial's beginning!" was heard in the distance.
    T1   115: 6   dusted: he was far too much astonished to cry out, but his eyes and his mouth went on getting larger and
    T8   190:22   the Knight said doubtfully: "but you didn't cry so much as I thought you would."
    T3   137:11   Alice stood looking after it, almost ready to cry with vexation at having lost her dear little
CRYING (5)
    T5   152:41   in the midst of her tears. "Can you keep from crying by considering things?" she asked.
    T2   126:15   to keep up with her: and still the Queen kept crying "Faster! Faster!" but Alice felt she could not go
    A2   15:21   you," (she might well say this), "to go on crying in this way! Stop this moment, I tell you!" But she
    A1   12:21   "Come, there's no use in crying like that!" said Alice to herself rather sharply. "I
    T4   145:22   "You wo'n't make yourself a bit realler by crying," Tweedledee remarked: "there's nothing to cry about."
CUCUMBER-FRAME (1)
    A4   29:41   it was just possible it had fallen into a cucumber-frame, or something of the sort.
CUCUMBER-FRAMES (1)
    A4   30:18   sounds of broken glass. "What a number of cucumber-frames there must be!" thought Alice. "I wonder what
CUNNING (1)
    A3   25:40   breath. 'I'll be judge, I'll be jury, said cunning old Fury: 'I'll try the whole cause, and condemn you
CUP (3) [See also BUTTERCUP, TEACUP]
    A7   59:36   "I want a clean cup," interrupted the Hatter: "let's all move one place on."
    A7   56: 8   at it gloomily: then he dipped it into his cup of tea, and looked at it again: but he could think of
    T7   173:21   was standing watching the fight, with a cup of tea in one hand and a piece of bread-and-butter in the
CUPBOARDS (2)
    A1   8:16   well, and noticed that they were filled with cupboards and book-shelves: here and there she saw maps and
    A1   8:21   so managed to put it into one of the cupboards as she fell past it.
-CUPS [See TEACUPS]
CUR (1)
    A3   25:25   I've nothing to do.' Said the mouse to the cur, Such a trial, dear sir, With no jury or judge, would be
CURE (1)
    T8W   17: 7   a yellow handkerchief round your face. It'll cure you in no time!"
CURIOSITY (10)
    A8   67:38   and looking at the Cat's head with great curiosity.
    A10   81:24   they made of?" Alice asked in a tone of great curiosity.
    T2   123:22   does she wear them?" Alice asked with some curiosity.
    T3   133: 6   does it live on?" Alice asked, with great curiosity.
    T8   181:16   hanging open. Alice looked at it with great curiosity.
    T8   182: 8   are they for?" Alice asked in a tone of great curiosity.
    A7   55: 7   looking at Alice for some time with great curiosity, and this was his first speech.
    A1   8: 3   a watch to take out of it, and burning with curiosity, she ran across the field after it, and was just in
    T1   113:17   and begin kicking: she watched it with great curiosity to see what would happen next.
    A7   56:11   had been looking over his shoulder with some curiosity. "What a funny watch!" she remarked. "It tells the
CURIOUS (27)
    A10   82: 9   drew a long breath, and said "That's very curious!"
    A8   67:10   away without being seen, when she noticed a curious appearance in the air: it puzzled her very much at
    A10   82:10   last. "It's all about as curious as it can be," said the Gryphon.
    T7   170:23   last. "But he's coming very slowly--and what curious attitudes he goes into!" (For the Messenger kept
    A1   12:27   she was playing against herself, for this curious child was very fond of pretending to be two people.
    T2   125:20   all directions over the country--and a most curious country it was. There were a number of tiny little
    A2   20:23   Dodo, a Lory and an Eaglet, and several other curious creatures. Alice led the way, and the whole party swam
    A8   66: 1   Alice thought she had never seen such a curious croquet-ground in her life: it was all ridges and
    A12   98: 9   her sister kissed her, and said "It was a curious dream, dear, certainly; but now run in to your tea."
    A12   98: 6   "Oh, I've had such a curious dream!" said Alice. And she told her sister, as well
    A1   12: 1   "What a curious feeling!" said Alice. "I must be shutting up like a
    T8   184:39   Alice changed the subject hastily. "What a curious helmet you've got!" she said cheerfully. "Is that your
    T8W   18: 6   A curious idea came into Alice's head. Almost every one she had
    T2   126:18   The most curious part of the thing was, that the trees and the other
    A9   77:14   "What a curious plan!" exclaimed Alice.
    A11   88:34   Just at this moment Alice felt a very curious sensation, which puzzled her a good deal until she
    A7   60:39   a door leading right into it. "That's very curious!" she thought. "But everything's curious to-day. I
    A10   80:15   it was over at last: "and I do so like that curious song about the whiting!"
    A8   62: 3   painting them red. Alice thought this a very curious thing, and she went nearer to watch them, and, just as
    A6   53: 8   "but a grin without a cat! It's the most curious thing I ever saw in all my life!"
    T9   201:31   eyes were fixed upon her; "and it's a very curious thing, I think--every poem was about fishes in some
    T5   154:11   The shop seemed to be full of all manner of curious things--but the oddest part of it all was that,
    T5   156:39   hardly noticed this, there were so many other curious things to think about.
    A6   45: 8   curled all over their heads. She felt very curious to know what it was all about, and crept a little way
    A11   91:30   as he fumbled over the list, feeling very curious to see what the next witness would be like, "--for
    A7   60:40   very curious!" she thought. "But everything's curious to-day. I think I may as well go in at once." And in
    A4   29: 2   rabbit-hole--and yet--and yet--it's rather curious, you know, this sort of life! I do wonder what can
CURIOUSER (2)
    A2   14: 1   "Curiouser and curiouser!" cried Alice (she was so much
    A2   14: 1   "Curiouser and curiouser!" cried Alice (she was so much surprised, that for

CURIOUS-LOOKING (1)
T6   164:37   "They must be very curious-looking creatures."
CURIOUSLY (1)
T2   120: 5   "but I suppose it will at last. But how curiously it twists! It's more like a corkscrew than a path!
CURLED (5)
A6   45: 8   Alice noticed, had powdered hair that curled all over their heads. She felt very curious to know
T8W   18:14   "When I was young, my ringlets waved / And curled and crinkled on my head: / And then they said 'You
A4   28:19   one elbow against the door, and the other arm curled round her head. Still she went on growing, and, as a
T2   121:12   the Tiger-lily remarked. "If only her petals curled up a little more, she'd be all right."
T1   107:13   afternoon, and so, while Alice was sitting curled up in a corner of the great arm-chair, half talking to
CURLING (1)
T7   175:27   Alice could not help her lips curling up into a smile as she began: "Do you know, I always
CURLS (1)
A6   46: 4   Then they both bowed, and their curls got entangled together.
CURLY (1)
A2   20: 5   terrier, you know, with oh, such long curly brown hair! And it'll fetch things when you throw them,
CURRANTS (1)
A1   12:33   the words "EAT ME" were beautifully marked in currants. "Well, I'll eat it," said Alice, "and if it makes me
CURTAIN (1)
A1   9:39   on the second time round, she came upon a low curtain she had not noticed before, and behind it was a little
CURTSEY (4)
A1   8:45   New Zealand? Or Australia?" (and she tried to curtsey as she spoke--fancy, curtseying as you're falling
T2   128:25   who you are!" She did not wait for Alice to curtsey, this time, but walked on quickly to the next peg,
T2   124:13   here at all?" she added in a kinder tone. "Curtsey while you're thinking what to say. It saves time."
T12   207:23   dear!" Alice cried with a merry laugh. "And curtsey while you're thinking what to--what to purr. It saves
CURTSEYED (2)
T2   125:16   Alice curtseyed again, as she was afraid from the Queen's tone that
T2   128:21   it's all feasting and fun!" Alice got up and curtseyed, and sat down again.
CURTSEYING (1)
A1   9: 1   she tried to curtsey as she spoke--fancy, curtseying as you're falling through the air! Do you think you
CURVING (1)
A5   42:21   like a serpent. She had just succeeded in curving it down into a graceful zigzag, and was going to dive
CUSHION (2)
A8   63:26   carrying the King's crown on a crimson velvet cushion; and, last of all this grand procession, came THE KING
A7   54: 4   asleep, and the other two were using it as a cushion, resting their elbows on it, and talking over its head
CUSTARD (1)
A1   11: 8   fact, a sort of mixed flavour of cherry-tart, custard, pine-apple, roast turkey, toffy, and hot buttered
CUSTODY (2)
A9   73: 9   the King, the Queen, and Alice, were in custody and under sentence of execution.
A9   73: 6   Those whom she sentenced were taken into custody by the soldiers, who of course had to leave off being
CUT (15)
T9   201:20   conquered her shyness by a great effort, and cut a slice and handed it to the Red Queen.
T9   201:23   "I wonder how you'd like it, if I were to cut a slice out of you, you creature!"
T9   201: 7   said, very decidedly: "it isn't etiquette to cut any one you've been introduced to. Remove the joint!" And
T7   177:12   Unicorn remarked. "Hand it round first, and cut it afterwards."
A8   68:38   cut off a head unless there was a body to cut it off from: that he had never had to do such a thing
T7   177:15   itself into three pieces as she did so. "Now cut it up," said the Lion, as she returned to her place with
T4   147:27   happen to one in a battle--to get one's head cut off."
A8   68:37   executioner's argument was, that you couldn't cut off a head unless there was a body to cut it off from:
T4   147:24   of Tweedledee, "to keep his head from being cut off," as he said.
A8   63: 9   was to find out, we should all have our heads cut off, you know. So you see, Miss, we're doing our best,
T7   177: 9   used to being called 'the Monster'). "I've cut several slices already, but they always join on again!"
A11   90: 1   "After that," continued the Hatter, "I cut some more bread-and-butter--"
T8   179: 6   lying at her feet, on which she had tried to cut the plum-cake, "So I wasn't dreaming, after all," she said
T4   143:22   nice!' / The Carpenter said nothing but / 'Cut us another slice. / I wish you were not quite so deaf--/
A1   11: 2   you if you hold it too long; and that, if you cut your finger very deeply with a knife, it usually bleeds;
CUTTING (2)
A7   55: 6   "Your hair wants cutting," said the Hatter. He had been looking at Alice for
T7   177: 5   to see anything. What a time the Monster is, cutting up that cake!"

-D-

D (1)
  A3   24:15   said Alice, "and why it is you hate--C and D," she added in a whisper, half afraid that it would be
DAHLIA (1)
  T2   123:13   "They're done up close, like a dahlia," said the Tiger-lily: "not tumbled about, like yours
DAINTIES (1)
  A10   84:19   / Waiting in a hot tureen! / Who for such dainties would not stoop? / Soup of the evening, beautiful
DAISIES (5)
  T2   120:28   came upon a large flowerbed, with a border of daisies, and a willow-tree growing in the middle.
  T2   122:18   "That's right!" said the Tiger-lily. "The daisies are worst of all. When one speaks, they all begin
  T2   122:16   silence in a moment, and several of the pink daisies turned white.
  A1   7: 9   the trouble of getting up and picking the daisies, when suddenly a White Rabbit with pink eyes ran close
  T2   122:14   in a soothing tone, and, stooping down to the daisies, who were just beginning again, she whispered "If you
DAISY (2)
  T2   122: 7   "Didn't you know that?" cried another Daisy. And here they all began shouting together, till the air
  T2   122: 5   "It says 'Boughwough!'" cried a Daisy. "That's why its branches are called boughs!"
DAISY-CHAIN (1)
  A1   7: 8   and stupid), whether the pleasure of making a daisy-chain would be worth the trouble of getting up and
DAMP (1)
  T4   144:36   I'm afraid he'll catch cold with lying on the damp grass," said Alice, who was a very thoughtful little girl
DANCE (15)
  A10   79:18   will you, wo'n't you, wo'n't you join the dance?
  A10   80: 6   not, would not, could not, could not join the dance.
  A10   80:12   will you, wo'n't you, wo'n't you join the dance?"
  T1   109:15   they dress themselves all in green, and dance about--whenever the wind blows--oh, that's very pretty!"
  A10   78:13   "No, indeed," said Alice. "What sort of a dance is it?"
  A10   79: 2   "It must be a very pretty dance," said Alice timidly.
  A10   81: 5   "that they would go with the lobsters to the dance. So they got thrown out to sea. So they had to fall a
  A10   80:13   "Thank you, it's a very interesting dance to watch," said Alice, feeling very glad that it was
  T4   139:40   breath. "Four times round is enough for one dance," Tweedledum panted out, and they left off dancing as
  A10   79:16   on the shingle--will you come and join the dance? / Will you, wo'n't you, will you, wo'n't you, will you
  A10   79:17   you, will you, wo'n't you, will you join the dance? / Will you, wo'n't you, will you, wo'n't you, wo'n't
  A10   80:10   pale, beloved snail, but come and join the dance. / Will you, wo'n't you, will you, wo'n't you, will you
  A10   80:11   you, will you, wo'n't you, will you join the dance? / Will you, wo'n't you, will you, wo'n't you, will you
  A10   80: 4   the whiting kindly, but he would not join the dance. / Would not, could not, would not, could not, could not
  A10   80: 5   not, would not, could not, could not join the dance. / Would not, could not, would not, could not, could not
DANCERS (1)
  T4   139:39   The other two dancers were fat, and very soon out of breath. "Four times
DANCING (6)
  A10   83: 7   "It's the first position in dancing," Alice said; but she was dreadfully puzzled by the
  T4   139:31   to come from the tree under which they were dancing, and it was done (as well as she could make it out) by
  T4   139:41   Tweedledum panted out, and they left off dancing as suddenly as they had begun: the music stopped at
  A10   79: 9   So they began solemnly dancing round and round Alice, every now and then treading on
  T4   139:28   both hands at once: the next moment they were dancing round in a ring. This seemed quite natural (she
  T4   140: 3   a conversation with people she had just been dancing with. "It would never do to say 'How d'ye do?' now,"
DANGER (2)
  T2   122: 3   "But what could it do, if any danger came?" Alice asked.
  T8   185: 2   way to fall, you see--But there was the danger of falling into it, to be sure. That happened to me
DARE (13)
  A2   19:21   understand English," thought Alice. "I daresay it's a French mouse, come over with William the
  A7   59:29   very humbly. "I wo'n't interrupt you again. I dare say there may be one."
  T5   153:13   "I daresay you haven't had much practice," said the Queen. "When
  A7   56:39   said, tossing his head contemptuously. "I dare say you never even spoke to Time!"
  T8   184:22   "I'm a great hand at inventing things. Now, I daresay you noticed, the last time you picked me up, that I
  T2   123:20   "I daresay you'll see her soon," said the Rose. "She's one of the
  A9   71: 5   "I dare say you're wondering why I don't put my arm round your
  T9   193:20   of doing it," the Red Queen remarked: "but I daresay you've not had many lessons in manners yet."
  T2   125: 6   Alice didn't dare to argue the point, but went on: "--and I thought I'd try
  A10   83:12   Alice did not dare to disobey, though she felt sure it would all come wrong,
  T2   122:12   head towards Alice, "or they wouldn't dare to do it!"
  A3   24: 6   but they all looked so grave that she did not dare to laugh; and, as she could not think of anything to say,
  T8   185: 6   looked so solemn about it that Alice did not dare to laugh. "I'm afraid you must have hurt him," she said
DARK (12)
  T4   148:16   Only we must begin quick. It's getting as dark as it can."
  T4   146: 2   of the wood, for really it's coming on very dark. Do you think it's going to rain?"
  A1   10: 4   ever saw. How she longed to get out of that dark hall, and wander about among those beds of bright flowers
  A1   9:22   in a moment: she looked up, but it was all dark overhead: before her was another long passage, and the
  T5   158: 1   moment, and she was back again in the little dark shop.
  T5   153:37   make nothing more of it: she was in a little dark shop, leaning with her elbows on the counter, and
  T3   137:29   only get to the Eighth Square before it gets dark!" So she wandered on, talking to herself as she went,
  T4   148:18   It was getting dark so suddenly that Alice thought there must be a
  A1   8:14   out what she was coming to, but it was too dark to see anything: then she looked at the sides of the well
  T5   158:18   the tables and chairs, for the shop was very dark towards the end. "The egg seems to get further away the
  T5   157: 8   cautiously over the side of the boat into the dark water. "I wish it hadn't let go--I should so like a

DARK (cont.)
T4   139:11   best way out of this wood: it's getting so dark. Would you tell me, please?"
DARKER (2)
T4   148:17   "And darker," said Tweedledee.
T3   135:23   wood on the other side of it: it looked much darker than the last wood, and Alice felt a little timid about
DARKNESS (1)
A2   15:35   and the fan, and scurried away into the darkness as hard as he could go.
DARLING (2)
T5   156:22   she caught at one bunch after another of the darling scented rushes.
T1   108:25   have deserved it, you little mischievous darling! What have you got to say for yourself? Now don't
DARLINGS (1)
T1   109:13   quilt; and perhaps it says 'Go to sleep, darlings, till the summer comes again.' And when they wake up
DARTED (1)
T3   137: 9   brown eyes, and in another moment it had darted away at full speed.
DASH (1)
T3   135:34   people lose dogs--'answers to the name of "Dash": had on a brass collar'--just fancy calling everything
DATES (1)
A11 88:18   and the jury eagerly wrote down all three dates on their slates, and then added them up, and reduced the
DAUGHTER (2)
T1   114: 7   on the table by the side of her noisy little daughter.
A3   26:18   Crab took the opportunity of saying to her daughter "Ah, my dear! Let this be a lesson to you never to
DAY (41) [See also BIRTHDAY, HOLIDAY, etc.]
A5   43:10   number of changes she had gone through, that day.
A9   76: 6   educations--in fact, we went to school every day--"
A9   77:16   remarked: "because they lessen from day to day."
A12 94:27   really clever thing the King had said that day.
A12 96:29   King said, for about the twentieth time that day.
T5   149:39   said. "Two pence a week, and jam every other day."
T5   153: 7   just one hundred and one, five months and a day."
T8   186:34   for she had heard a good deal of poetry that day.
A9   75: 8   Turtle "Drive on, old fellow! Don't be all day about it!" and he went on in these words:--
A6   48:25   "Just think what work it would make with the day and night! You see the earth takes twenty-four hours to
A11 87:11   to write with one finger for the rest of the day; and this was of very little use, as it left no mark on
T9   195:30   our country," she remarked, "there's only one day at a time."
T1   110:12   a long argument with her sister only the day before--all because Alice had begun with "Let's pretend
T1   118:19   Come to my arms, my beamish boy! / O frabjous day! Callooh! Callay!" / He chortled in his joy.
T1   109: 6   without a dinner: then, when the miserable day came, I should have to go without fifty dinners at once!
T1   109: 4   should be sent to prison, I suppose, when the day came. Or--let me see--suppose each punishment was to be
A9   77:10   "And how many hours a day did you do lessons?" said Alice, in a hurry to change the
T8   188:27   oneself on batter, / And so go on from day to day / Getting a little fatter. / I shook him well from side to
T8   186:13   "Then it would have to be the next day. I suppose you wouldn't have two pudding-courses in one
T8   186:16   the Knight repeated as before: "not the next day. In fact," he went on, holding his head down, and his
A5   35:16   with; and being so many different sizes in a day is very confusing."
A1   7: 7   own mind (as well as she could, for the hot day made her feel very sleepy and stupid), whether the
A6   46:30   "--or next day, maybe," the Footman continued in the same tone, exactly
A9   77:18   she made her next remark. "Then the eleventh day must have been a holiday?"
A7   56:12   a funny watch!" she remarked. "It tells the day of the month, and doesn't tell what o'clock it is!"
A7   55:35   was the first to break the silence. "What day of the month is it?" he said, turning to Alice: he had
A6   49:26   thought Alice, "they're sure to kill it in a day or two. Wouldn't it be murder to leave it behind?" She
A8   65:25   "It's--it's a very fine day!" said a timid voice at her side. She was walking by the
A9   77:12   "Ten hours the first day," said the Mock Turtle: "nine the next, and so on."
A11 87:17   she made some tarts, / All on a summer day: / The Knave of Hearts, he stole those tarts / And took
T8   186:15   "Well, not the next day," the Knight repeated as before: "not the next day. In
A9   77:16   Gryphon remarked: "because they lessen from day to day."
T8   188:27   feed oneself on batter, / And so go on from day to day / Getting a little fatter. / I shook him well from
A5   40: 7   airs! / Do you think I can listen all day to such stuff? / Be off, or I'll kick you down-stairs!"
T5   150: 9   said the Queen. "It's jam every other day: to-day isn't any other day, you know."
T4   140:32   / Had got no business to be there / After the day was done--' 'It's very rude of him,' she said, / 'To come
A5   42:39   be on the look-out for serpents, night and day! Why, I haven't had a wink of sleep these three weeks!"
T5   153:14   your age, I always did it for half-an-hour a day. Why, sometimes I've believed as many as six impossible
T5   150: 9   jam every other day: to-day isn't any other day, you know.
A5   36: 3   have to turn into a chrysalis--you will some day, you know--and then after that into a butterfly, I should
A9   72:34   "A fine day, your Majesty!" the Duchess began in a low, weak voice.
DAYS (11) [See also BIRTHDAYS, THURSDAYS, etc.]
A6   46:40   sit here," he said, "on and off, for days and days."
A12 99:11   her own child-life, and the happy summer days.
A6   46:40   "I shall sit here," he said, "on and off, for days and days."
T9   195:32   way of doing things. Now here, we mostly have days and nights two or three at a time, and sometimes in the
T6   166:32   "In summer, when the days are long, / Perhaps you'll understand the song:
T6   162:43   about!" cried Humpty Dumpty. "How many days are there in a year?"
TC   209:17   In a Wonderland they lie, / Dreaming as the days go by, / Dreaming as the summers die:
TI   103:33   through the story, / For "happy summer days" gone by, / And vanish'd summer glory--/ It shall not
TI   103:13   A tale begun in other days, / When summer suns were glowing--/ A simple chime, that
T6   163:20   that there are three hundred and sixty-four days when you might get un-birthday presents--"
A7   56: 1   "Two days wrong!" sighed the Hatter. "I told you butter wouldn't
DAY-SCHOOL (1)
A9   76: 7   "I've been to a day-school, too," said Alice. "You needn't be so proud as all
DAZZLED (1)
T8   187:21   on his armour in a blaze of light that quite dazzled her--the horse quietly moving about, with the reins

DEAD (9)
T1	118:15	vorpal blade went snicker-snack! / He left it dead, and with its head / He went galumphing back.
A12	98: 2	her sister, who was gently brushing away some dead leaves that had fluttered down from the trees upon her
A4	32: 4	not do that again!", which produced another dead silence.
A12	96:26	round the court with a smile. There was a dead silence.
T8	179: 2	seemed gradually to die away, till all was dead silence, and Alice lifted up her head in some alarm.
T9	201:30	the moment she opened her lips, there was dead silence, and all eyes were fixed upon her; "and it's a
A12	94:37	There was dead silence in the court, whilst the White Rabbit read out
A4	31:32	There was a dead silence instantly, and Alice thought to herself "I wonder
T9	200: 7	at once--" and in she went, and there was a dead silence the moment she appeared.

DEAF (2)
T4	143:23	another slice. / I wish you were not quite so deaf--/ I've had to ask you twice!'
T9	199:16	doesn't I?" the Frog went on. "Or are you deaf? What did it ask you?"

DEAFENED (1)
T7	178: 3	and through her head till she felt quite deafened. She started to her feet and sprang across the little

DEAL (21)
T8	181:14	very badly, and he had a queer-shaped little deal box fastened across his shoulders, upside-down, and with
A6	48:21	a hoarse growl, "the world would go round a deal faster than it does."
A2	18:10	That was a narrow escape!" said Alice, a good deal frightened at the sudden change, but very glad to find
A5	41:41	She was a good deal frightened by this very sudden change, but she felt that
T2	121: 5	you can," said the Tiger-lily. "And a great deal louder."
T9	192:33	"But she said a great deal more than that!" the White Queen moaned, wringing her
T8	186:33	long?" Alice asked, for she had heard a good deal of poetry that day.
T3	136: 6	much, and all she could say, after a great deal of puzzling, was "L, I know it begins with L!"
A3	23:17	the Dodo could not answer without a great deal of thought, and it stood for a long time with one finger
T6	166: 2	Alice. "I'm afraid I'm giving you a great deal of trouble."
A6	51: 9	"That depends a good deal on where you want to get to," said the Cat.
T7	172: 8	was glad to see that it revived him a good deal. "There's nothing like eating hay when you're faint," he
A4	30:37	I wouldn't be in Bill's place for a good deal: this fireplace is narrow, to be sure; but I think I can
A11	88: 3	Rabbit hastily interrupted. "There's a great deal to come before that!"
T6	164: 3	"That's a great deal to make one word mean," Alice said in a thoughtful tone.
A5	43:25	"It matters a good deal to me," said Alice hastily; "but I'm not looking for eggs
A2	14: 8	sure I sha'n't be able! I shall be a great deal too far off to trouble myself about you: you must manage
A4	31:20	No more, thank ye; I'm better now--but I'm a deal too flustered to tell you--all I know is, something comes
A11	88:35	curious sensation, which puzzled her a good deal until she made out what it was: she was beginning to grow
T2	123:29	it was the Red Queen. "She's grown a good deal!" was her first remark. She had indeed: when Alice first
A7	60: 1	from the change; and Alice was a good deal worse off than before, as the March Hare had just upset

DEAR (55)
T12	207: 5	the Looking-glass world. Did you know it, dear?"
T12	208: 4	and then you can make believe it's oysters, dear!
T12	207:22	"Sit up a little more stiffly, dear!" Alice cried with a merry laugh. "And curtsey while
T1	110:23	look exactly like her. Now do try, there's a dear!" And Alice got the Red Queen off the table, and set it
T9	194:36	whispered: "we'll often say it over together, dear. And I'll tell you a secret--I can read words of one
A9	70:18	her ear. "You're thinking about something, my dear, and that makes you forget to talk. I ca'n't tell you
T12	208: 6	it all. This is a serious question, my dear, and you should not go on licking your paw like that--as
T7	170: 7	"Did you happen to meet any soldiers, my dear, as you came through the wood?"
T8W	19:15	call me 'Pig!' / And that is why they do it, dear, / Because I wear a yellow wig."
T3	131:24	in her ear, "Never mind what they all say, my dear, but take a return-ticket every time the train stops."
A12	98:10	kissed her, and said "It was a curious dream, dear, certainly; but now run in to your tea: it's getting late
T7	173:26	he's very hungry and thirsty. How are you, dear child?" he went on, putting his arm affectionately round
T7	173:30	"Were you happy in prison, dear child?" said Haigha.
A2	20:10	pounds! He says it kills all the rats and--oh dear!" cried Alice in a sorrowful tone. "I'm afraid I've
A2	17:25	down here till I'm somebody else'--but, oh dear!" cried Alice, with a sudden burst of tears, "I do wish
A2	15:37	herself all the time she went on talking. "Dear, dear! How queer everything is to-day! And yesterday
A3	26:39	sure she's the best cat in the world! Oh, my dear Dinah! I wonder if I shall ever see you any more!" And
A2	20:14	So she called softly after it, "Mouse dear! Do come back again, and we wo'n't talk about cats, or
T3	131:41	are a friend," the little voice went on: "a dear friend, and an old friend. And you wo'n't hurt me, though
T7	175: 6	a memorandum about her, if you like--She's a dear good creature," he repeated softly to himself, as he
A2	16: 7	Besides, she's she, and I'm I, and--oh dear, how puzzling it all is! I'll try if I know all the
A2	15:38	all the time she went on talking. "Dear, dear! How queer everything is to-day! And yesterday things
T1	115:36	strong for him, and at last he panted out "My dear! I really must get a thinner pencil. I ca'n't manage this
A1	7:13	to hear the Rabbit say to itself "Oh dear! Oh dear! I shall be too late!" (when she thought it over
A2	16:10	six is thirteen, and four times seven is--oh dear! I shall never get to twenty at that rate! However, the
A2	17:22	their heads down and saying 'Come up again, dear!' I shall only look up and say 'Who am I, then? Tell me
A12	96:18	she had this fit'--you never had fits, my dear, I think?" he said to the Queen.
T1	115:22	The King was saying "I assure you, my dear, I turned cold to the very ends of my whiskers!"
A1	9: 8	her saucer of milk at tea-time. Dinah my dear! I wish you were down here with me! There are no mice in
A8	68: 4	the Queen, who was passing at the moment, "My dear! I wish you would have this cat removed!"
A4	33:10	if I'd only been the right size to do it! Oh dear! I'd nearly forgotten that I've got to grow up again! Let
T1	110: 4	can you play chess? Now, don't smile, my dear. I'm asking it seriously. Because, when we were playing
A3	22:25	his Normans--' How are you getting on now, my dear?" it continued, turning to Alice as it spoke.
A3	26:18	opportunity of saying to her daughter "Ah, my dear! Let this be a lesson to you never to lose your temper!"
T1	110: 9	came wriggling down among my pieces. Kitty dear, let's pretend--" And here I wish I could tell you half
T5	155:29	"A dear little crab!" thought Alice. "I should like that."
T3	137:12	ready to cry with vexation at having lost her dear little fellow-traveler so suddenly. "However, I know my
A4	33: 7	"And yet what a dear little puppy it was!" said Alice, as she leant against a
T7	173: 7	"Dear me, no!" said the King. "What an idea!"
T5	149:30	said as she gently put it right for her; "and dear me, what a state your hair is in!"
T3	137: 7	it cried out in a voice of delight. "And, dear me! you're a human child!" A sudden look of alarm came
A1	7:13	the way to hear the Rabbit say to itself "Oh dear! Oh dear! I shall be too late!" (when she thought it over

DEAR (cont.)
A9   70: 1   think how glad I am to see you again, you dear old thing!" said the Duchess, as she tucked her arm
A4   27: 4   to itself, "The Duchess! The Duchess! Oh my dear paws! Oh my fur and whiskers! She'll get me executed, as
A2   19:35   if you could only see her. She is such a dear quiet thing," Alice went on, half to herself, as she swam
A6   50: 4   "If you're going to turn into a pig, my dear," said Alice, seriously, "I'll have nothing more to do
A12   98: 4   "Wake up, Alice dear!" said her sister. "Why, what a long sleep you've had!"
T1   115: 9   "Oh! please don't make such faces, my dear!" she cried out, quite forgetting that the King couldn't
A8   64:11   upon her arm, and timidly said "Consider, my dear: she is only a child!"
A3   25:27   do.' Said the mouse to the cur, Such a trial, dear sir, With no jury or judge, would be wasting our breath.
T12   208:10 it the Red King, Kitty? You were his wife, my dear, so you ought to know--Oh, Kitty, do help to settle it!
T4   143:11 good indeed--/ Now, if you're ready, Oysters dear, / We can begin to feed.'
A2   15:11   Oh dear, what nonsense I'm talking!"
TI   103:23   maiden! / We are but older children, dear, / Who fret to find our bedtime near.
A11   91:27   in an undertone to the Queen, "Really, my dear, you must cross-examine the next witness. It quite makes
DEARS (3)
A8   63:20   there were ten of them, and the little dears came jumping merrily along, hand in hand, in couples:
A2   14: 7   put on your shoes and stockings for you now, dears? I'm sure I sha'n't be able! I shall be a great deal too
A3   26:34   voice, to its children, "Come away, my dears! It's high time you were all in bed!" On various
DEARY (1)
T8W   13:22   his shoulders, and turned his head away. "Ah, deary me!" he said to himself.
DEATH (1)
A3   25:53   'I'll try the whole cause, and condemn you to death.
DECANTERS (1)
T9   202:24 trickled down their faces--others upset the decanters, and drank the wine as it ran off the edges of the
DECIDED (3)
A1   12:13   finding that nothing more happened, she decided on going into the garden at once; but, alas for poor
A11   88:37   leave the court; but on second thoughts she decided to remain where she was as long as there was room for
A9   77:24   lessons," the Gryphon interrupted in a very decided tone. "Tell her something about the games now."
DECIDEDLY (7)
A8   68: 3   Well, it must be removed," said the King very decidedly; and he called to the Queen, who was passing at the
A8   64: 8   "Nonsense!" said Alice, very loudly and decidedly, and the Queen was silent.
A5   41: 5   from beginning to end," said the Caterpillar, decidedly; and there was silence for some minutes.
T9   195:19 "The cause of lightning," Alice said very decidedly, for she felt quite certain about this, "is the
T9   201: 6   "Certainly not," the Red Queen said, very decidedly: "it isn't etiquette to cut any one you've been
T9   202:37 be at all the thing," the Red Queen said very decidedly: so Alice tried to submit to it with good grace.
A6   46:22   time he was speaking, and this Alice thought decidedly uncivil. "But perhaps he ca'n't help it," she said
DECISION (1)
T5   153: 1   the way it's done," the Queen said with great decision: "nobody can do two things at once, you know. Let's
DECLARE (6)
T5   158:21 is this a chair? Why, it's got branches, I declare! How very odd to find trees growing here! And actually
T1   111:10 Why, it's turning into a sort of mist now, I declare! It'll be easy enough to get through--" She was up on
T2   125:25   "I declare it's marked out just like a large chess-board!" Alice
A2   18:16   was so small as this before, never! And I declare it's too bad, that it is!"
T6   160:30   "Now I declare that's too bad!" Humpty Dumpty cried, breaking into a
A10   82:22   "'Tis the voice of the Lobster: I heard him declare / 'You have baked me too brown, I must sugar my hair.'
DECLARED (1)
A3   22:12   Morcar, the earls of Mercia and Northumbria, declared for him; and even Stigand, the patriotic archbishop
DEE (2)
T4   138: 4   embroidered on his collar, and the other 'DEE.' "I suppose they've got 'TWEEDLE' round at the back of
T4   138:13   "Contrariwise," added the one marked 'DEE,' "if you think we're alive, you ought to speak."
DEED (1)
T6   167:14 I took a kettle large and new, / Fit for the deed I had to do.
DEEP (13) [See also ELBOW-DEEP]
A2   15:24   was a large pool round her, about four inches deep, and reaching half down the hall.
T8   185:16 out of the saddle, and fell headlong into a deep ditch.
T6   162:23 or two. When he did speak again, it was in a deep growl.
T9   199: 1   "What is it, now?" the Frog said in a deep hoarse whisper.
A9   74:27   "I'll tell it her," said the Mock Turtle in a deep, hollow tone. "Sit down, both of you, and don't speak a
T7   176: 1   blinking lazily at Alice, and speaking in a deep hollow tone that sounded like the tolling of a great bell
A1   8:11   Either the well was very deep, or she fell very slowly, for she had plenty of time as
T9   196:34   The White Queen gave a deep sigh, and laid her head on Alice's shoulder. "I am so
A9   74:32   "Once," said the Mock Turtle at last, with a deep sigh, "I was a real Turtle."
T8W   13: 2   just going to spring over, when she heard a deep sigh, which seemed to come from the wood behind her.
A10   81:22   under the sea," the Gryphon went on in a deep voice, "are done with whiting. Now you know."
A11   91:15   eyes were nearly out of sight, he said, in a deep voice, "What are tarts made of?"
A1   8:10   herself falling down what seemed to be a very deep well.
DEEPEST (2)
A5   43:11   indeed!" said the Pigeon, in a tone of the deepest contempt. "I've seen a good many little girls in my
T7   175:17 some time looking at her with an air of the deepest disgust.
DEEPLY (7)
A10   84:15   The Mock Turtle sighed deeply, and began, in a voice choked with sobs, to sing this:
A10   78: 1   The Mock Turtle sighed deeply, and drew the back of one flapper across his eyes. He
T3   131:34   The little voice sighed deeply. It was very unhappy, evidently, and Alice would have
T4   144: 2   'I weep for you,' the Walrus said: / 'I deeply sympathize.' / With sobs and tears he sorted out /
A9   74:19   as if his heart would break. She pitied him deeply. "What is his sorrow?" she asked the Gryphon. And the
T3   135:13   But the Gnat only sighed deeply while two large tears came rolling down its cheeks.
A1   11: 2   long; and that, if you cut your finger very deeply with a knife, it usually bleeds; and she had never
DELAY (1)
A9   73: 2   the Queen merely remarking that a moment's delay would cost them their lives.

DELIGHT (9)
T6   166:24   fields are white, / I sing this song for your delight--
T3   137: 7   arm. "I'm a Fawn!" it cried out in a voice of delight. "And, dear me! you're a human child!" A sudden look
T2   125:27   and so there are!" she added in a tone of delight, and her heart began to beat quick with excitement as
A4   32:35   air off all its feet at once, with a yelp of delight, and rushed at the stick, and made believe to worry it
T9   202: 1   The White Queen laughed with delight, and stroked Alice's cheek. Then she began:
A1   9:42   golden key in the lock, and to her great delight it fitted!
T7   170: 6   sent them all!" the King cried in a tone of delight, on seeing Alice. "Did you happen to meet any soldiers
T5   156: 7   rushes!" Alice cried in a sudden transport of delight. "There really are--and such beauties!"
A5   42: 7   head's free at last!" said Alice in a tone of delight, which changed into alarm in another moment, when she
DELIGHTED (2)
A5   42:19   tried to get her head down to them, and was delighted to find that her neck would bend about easily in any
A4   32:10   So she swallowed one of the cakes, and was delighted to find that she began shrinking directly. As soon
DELIGHTFUL (2)
A10   80: 1   "You can really have no notion how delightful it will be / When they take us up and throw us,
A10   78:12   "No never") "--so you can have no idea what a delightful thing a Lobster-Quadrille is!"
DEMURELY (1)
T1   108: 7   and sometimes to herself. Kitty sat very demurely on her knee, pretending to watch the progress of the
DENIAL (1)
A3   25:14   I will prosecute you.--Come, I'll take no denial: We must have the trial; For really this morning I've
DENIED (2)
A11   89:27   see if he would deny it too; but the Dormouse denied nothing, being fast asleep.
A6   51:17   Alice felt that this could not be denied, so she tried another question. "What sort of people
DENIES (1)
A11   89:24   "He denies it," said the King: "leave out that part."
DENY (8)
T7   172:14   like it." Which Alice did not venture to deny.
T9   193:11   deny something--only she doesn't know what to deny!"
T1   108:29   your face this morning. Now you ca'n't deny it, Kitty: I heard you! What's that you say?" (pretending
A11   89:23   "I deny it!" said the March Hare.
A11   89:26   looking anxiously round to see if he would deny it too; but the Dormouse denied nothing, being fast
T9   193:11   said the White Queen, "that she wants to deny something--only she doesn't know what to deny!"
T9   193: 5   important than a joke, I hope. You couldn't deny that, even if you tried with both hands."
T9   193: 7   "I don't deny things with my hands," Alice objected.
DENYING (2)
A5   43:14   No, no! You're a serpent; and there's no use denying it. I suppose you'll be telling me next that you never
T5   151:10   Alice felt there was no denying that. "Of course it would be all the better," she said
DEPENDS (1)
A6   51: 9   "That depends a good deal on where you want to get to," said the Cat
DERISION (1)
A9   76:23   Ambition, Distraction, Uglification, and Derision."
DESCRIBED (2)
T2   120:22   gave a sudden twist and shook itself (as she described it afterwards), and the next moment she found
T9   203:10   And then (as Alice afterwards described it) all sorts of things happened in a moment. The
DESERVED (2)
T1   108:24   putting you out into the snow! And you'd have deserved it, you little mischievous darling! What have you got
A8   62:12   "I heard the Queen say only yesterday you deserved to be beheaded."
DESIGN (1)
T8   189: 8   heard him then, for I had just / Completed my design / To keep the Menai bridge from rust / By boiling it in
-DESK [See WRITING-DESK]
-DESKS [See WRITING-DESKS]
DESPAIR (3)
T5   152:37   cried the poor Queen, wringing her hands in despair. "Consider what a great girl you are. Consider what a
T9   200: 5   "Ninety times nine!" Alice repeated in despair. "Oh, that'll never be done! I'd better go in at once
A3   23:26   Alice had no idea what to do, and in despair she put her hand in her pocket, and pulled out a box
DESPERATE (2)
T7   174: 5   Hatta made a desperate effort, and swallowed a large piece of
A2   15:31   if I've kept her waiting!" Alice felt so desperate that she was ready to ask help of any one: so, when
DESPERATELY (1)
A6   46:43   there's no use in talking to him," said Alice desperately: "he's perfectly idiotic!" And she opened the door
DETERMINED (3)
T3   136: 5   if I can! I'm determined to do it!" But being determined didn't help her much, and all she could say, after
T3   136: 4   now, who am I? I will remember, if I can! I'm determined to do it!" But being determined didn't help her
T2   120:19   house, she set out once more down the path, determined to keep straight on till she got to the hill. For a
DEVOURED (1)
T7   172: 3   neck, and handed a sandwich to the King, who devoured it greedily.
-DIAL [See SUN-DIAL]
-DIALS [See SUN-DIALS]
DIAMONDS (1)
A8   63:18   these were ornamented all over with diamonds, and walked two and two, as the soldiers did. After
DICTIONARY (1)
T2   125:15   with which that would be as sensible as a dictionary!"
DID (120)
T4   139:20   only shout out "Contrariwise!" and so he did.
A8   63:18   and walked two and two, as the soldiers did. After these came the royal children: there were ten of
A1   7:11   was nothing so very remarkable in that; nor did Alice think it so very much out of the way to hear the
T4   141:14   Oysters, come and walk with us!' / The Walrus did beseech. / 'A pleasant walk, a pleasant talk, / Along the
T12   207:32   "And what did Dinah turn to, I wonder?" she prattled on, as she settled
T6   160:24   that Alice could hardly help laughing. "If I did fall," he went on, "the King has promised me--ah, you may
T6   160:21   "Of course I don't think so! Why, if ever I did fall off--which there's no chance of--but if I did--" Here

DID (cont.)

T1	116:10	ysmim llA / :ebaw eht ni elbmig dna eryg diD / sevot yhtils eht dna ,gillirb sawT'
T1	116:19	'Twas brillig, and the slithy toves / Did gyre and gimble in the wabe: / All mimsy were the
T1	118:22	'Twas brillig, and the slithy toves / Did gyre and gimble in the wabe: / All mimsy were the
T6	164:22	"'Twas brillig, and the slithy toves / Did gyre and gimble in the wabe: / All mimsy were the
T9	196: 3	"What did he want?" said the Red Queen.
T8	186: 6	the cleverest thing of the sort that I ever did," he went on after a pause, "was inventing a new pudding
T5	149:34	Alice carefully released the brush, and did her best to get the hair into order. "Come, you look
T6	160:22	off--which there's no chance of--but if I did--" Here he pursed up his lips, and looked so solemn and
T4	140:25	the sea, / Shining with all his might: / He did his very best to make / The billows smooth and bright--/
T12	207:35	did you turn to Humpty Dumpty? I think you did--however, you'd better not mention it to your friends just
T9	199:16	I?" the Frog went on. "Or are you deaf? What did it ask you?"
A5	42: 2	was hardly room to open her mouth; but she did it at last, and managed to swallow a morsel of the
T5	153:14	the Queen. "When I was your age, I always did it for half-an-hour a day. Why, sometimes I've believed as
A11	86:18	at the frontispiece if you want to see how he did it), he did not look at all comfortable, and it was
A11	87: 8	found an opportunity of taking it away. She did it so quickly that the poor little juror (it was Bill, the
T6	168:21	"I shouldn't know you again if we did meet," Humpty Dumpty replied in a discontented tone,
A2	20: 3	you--are you fond--of--of dogs?" The Mouse did not answer, so Alice went on eagerly: "There is such a
A6	52:22	half expecting to see it again, but it did not appear, and after a minute or two she walked on in the
A6	51: 4	she began, rather timidly, as she did not at all know whether it would like the name: however,
A6	48: 7	Alice did not at all like the tone of this remark, and thought it
A12	95:37	I look like it?" he said. (Which he certainly did not, being made entirely of cardboard.)
T4	140:23	And shook his heavy head--/ Meaning to say he did not choose / To leave the oyster-bed.
A2	17: 6	sounded hoarse and strange, and the words did not come the same as they used to do:--
A10	83:12	Alice did not dare to disobey, though she felt sure it would all
A3	24: 6	absurd, but they all looked so grave that she did not dare to laugh; and, as she could not think of anything
T8	185: 6	Knight looked so solemn about it that Alice did not dare to laugh. "I'm afraid you must have hurt him,"
A9	76:33	Alice did not feel encouraged to ask any more questions about it: so
T8W	19: 5	They said it did not fit, and so / It made me look extremely plain: / But
A3	21:17	felt sure she would catch a bad cold if she did not get dry very soon.
A4	29:36	her hand, and made a snatch in the air. She did not get hold of anything, but she heard a little shriek
T2	127:39	Alice did not know what to say to this, but luckily the Queen did
T8W	21:10	Alice did not like having so many personal remarks made on her, and
T4	139:25	Alice did not like shaking hands with either of them first, for fear
A6	49:35	extremely small for a baby: altogether Alice did not like the look of the thing at all. "But perhaps it was
A8	68:14	for having missed their turns, and she did not like the look of things at all, as the game was in
A9	70:28	was an uncomfortably sharp chin. However, she did not like to be rude: so she bore it as well as she could.
A6	46:35	It was, no doubt: only Alice did not like to be told so. "It's really dreadful," she
A1	8:20	to her great disappointment it was empty: she did not like to drop the jar, for fear of killing somebody
A6	53:13	with fur. It was so large a house, that she did not like to go nearer till she had nibbled some more of
A11	86:19	if you want to see how he did it), he did not look at all comfortable, and it was certainly not
T8W	19: 3	they had noticed the effect, / They said I did not look so nice / As they had ventured to expect.
A9	70:25	Alice did not much like her keeping so close to her: first because
A3	22:21	The Mouse did not notice this question, but hurriedly went on, "--found
A7	59:18	Alice did not quite know what to say to this: so she helped herself
A9	74: 4	leaving Alice alone with the Gryphon. Alice did not quite like the look of the creature, but on the whole
T9	196:19	Where would be the use of it?" but she did not say this aloud, for fear of hurting the poor Queen's
T3	137:20	But this did not seem likely to happen. She went on and on, a long way,
A11	88:30	This did not seem to encourage the witness at all: he kept shifting
A6	47:10	The only two creatures in the kitchen, that did not sneeze, were the cook, and a large cat, which was
T7	172:14	said there was nothing like it." Which Alice did not venture to deny.
A5	44: 5	nibbling at the right-hand bit again, and did not venture to go near the house till she had brought
A9	72:21	give birthday-presents like that!" But she did not venture to say it out loud.
T2	128:25	as you walk--and remember who you are!" She did not wait for Alice to curtsey, this time, but walked on
T2	128: 1	what to say to this, but luckily the Queen did not wait for an answer, but went on. "At the end of three
A7	60: 3	Alice did not wish to offend the Dormouse again, so she began very
A4	31:25	"So you did, old fellow!" said the others.
T9	202:38	("And they did push so!" she said afterwards, when she was telling her
T8	182:41	whenever it went on again (which it generally did rather suddenly), he fell off behind. Otherwise he kept on
T9	203: 4	return thanks--" Alice began: and she really did rise as she spoke, several inches; but she got hold of the
T7	170: 9	"Yes, I did," said Alice: "several thousand, I should think."
T5	155:32	"Indeed I did," said Alice: "you've said it very often--and very loud.
A9	77: 8	"So he did, so he did," said the Gryphon, sighing in his turn; and both
A11	89:22	"You did!" said the Hatter.
A9	76: 2	"You did," said the Mock Turtle.
A3	22:11	"I thought you did," said the Mouse. "I proceed. 'Edwin and Morcar, the earls
T9	193: 8	"Nobody said you did," said the Red Queen. "I said you couldn't if you tried."
T5	156:26	I couldn't quite reach it." And it certainly did seem a little provoking ("almost as if it happened on
A4	32:33	Hardly knowing what she did, she picked up a little bit of stick, and held it out to
A6	48:34	again, singing a sort of lullaby to it as she did so, and giving it a violent shake at the end of every line
A9	77: 8	"So he did, so he did," said the Gryphon, sighing in his turn; and
A4	28: 9	It did so indeed, and much sooner than she had expected: before
T2	122:26	Alice did so. "It's very hard," she said; "but I don't see what that
T7	177:15	cake divided itself into three pieces as she did so. "Now cut it up," said the Lion, as she returned to her
A8	64:14	The Knave did so, very carefully, with one foot.
T6	162:23	he said nothing for a minute or two. When he did speak again, it was in a deep growl.
T3	129:24	it was so dusty and hot, and the elephants did tease so!'"
T8	181:28	it carefully on a tree. "Can you guess why I did that?" he said to Alice.
A4	30:31	down! Heads below!" (a loud crash)--"Now, who did that?--It was Bill, I fancy--Who's to go down the chimney?
A3	22:20	a frog, or a worm. The question is, what did the archbishop find?"

DID (cont.)
```
A11    90: 3                                      "But what did the Dormouse say?" one of the jury asked.
A12    94:22    didn't write it, and they ca'n't prove that I did: there's no name signed at the end."
A7     59:33                              "What did they draw?" said Alice, quite forgetting her promise.
A7     60: 4    cautiously: "But I don't understand. Where did they draw the treacle from?"
A7     59: 8      her too much: so she went on: "But why did they live at the bottom of a well?"
A7     59:20    the Dormouse, and repeated her question. "Why did they live at the bottom of a well?"
A7     58:35                                  "What did they live on?" said Alice, who always took a great
T8    182:44    falling off sideways; and, as he generally did this on the side on which Alice was walking, she soon
T8    182:40        Whenever the horse stopped (which it did very often), he fell off in front; and, whenever it went
T2    120: 9                                      And so she did: wandering up and down, and trying turn after turn, but
T5    150: 5          "You couldn't have it if you did want it," the Queen said. "The rule is, jam to-morrow and
T1    112: 3    Looking-glass room. The very first thing she did was to look whether there was a fire in the fireplace, and
A12    96: 7    they gave him two'--why, that must be what he did with the tarts, you know--"
A11    88:10    ought to have finished," said the King. "When did you begin?"
A9     75: 1                                      "Why did you call him Tortoise, if he wasn't one?" Alice asked.
T2    124:12    all the ways about here belong to me--but why did you come out here at all?" she added in a kinder tone.
A9     77:10                    "And how many hours a day did you do lessons?" said Alice, in a hurry to change the
A1      9:18    earnestly, "Now, Dinah, tell me the truth: did you ever eat a bat?" when suddenly, thump! thump! down she
A7     60:24    know you say things as 'much of a muchness'--did you ever see such a thing as a drawing of a' muchness!"
T7    176:25    the town?" he said. "That's a good long way. Did you go by the old bridge, or the market-place? You get the
T7    170: 7    cried in a tone of delight, on seeing Alice. "Did you happen to meet any soldiers, my dear, as you came
T12   207: 5    Kitty--all through the Looking-glass world. Did you know it, dear?"
T9    192:35                          "So you did, you know," the Red Queen said to Alice. "Always speak the
A9     77:21                  "And how did you manage on the twelfth?" Alice went on eagerly.
A5     39: 4    with the bones and the beak--/ Pray, how did you manage to do it?"
T8    186:20                      "What did you mean it to be made of?" Alice asked, hoping to cheer
T7    172:15                          "Who did you pass on the road?" the King went on, holding out his
A6     53: 1                          "Did you say 'pig', or 'fig'?" said the Cat.
A8     65:34                          "Did you say 'What a pity!'?" the Rabbit said.
T6    161:21      "So here's a question for you. How old did you say you were?"
A3     22: 9    said the Mouse, frowning, but very politely. "Did you speak?"
T6    160:26    You didn't think I was going to say that, did you? The King has promised me--with his very own mouth--to
T6    160:40      nobody with me!" cried Humpty Dumpty. "Did you think I didn't know the answer to that? Ask another."
T12   207:34    hand, to watch the kittens. "Tell me, Dinah, did you turn to Humpty Dumpty? I think you did--however, you'd
```
DIDN'T (52)
```
T8W    16:15                              Alice didn't catch the word exactly. "Is it a kind of toothache?"
T8    190:22    so," the Knight said doubtfully: "but you didn't cry so much as I thought you would."
T2    125: 6                              Alice didn't dare to argue the point, but went on: "--and I thought
T4    144:19      "Then I like the Carpenter best--if he didn't eat so many as the Walrus."
T9    192:11    Everything was happening so oddly that she didn't feel a bit surprised at finding the Red Queen and the
T1    108: 5    and began winding up the ball again. But she didn't get on very fast, as she was talking all the time,
T3    136: 5    determined to do it!" But being determined didn't help her much, and all she could say, after a great
T7    175:14                              "It didn't hurt him," the Unicorn said carelessly, and he was
A9     76: 1              "I never said I didn't!" interrupted Alice.
T3    130:11    "Then there's no use in speaking." The voices didn't join in, this time, as she hadn't spoken, but, to her
T4    140: 2    there was a rather awkward pause, as Alice didn't know how to begin a conversation with people she had
A11    87: 1    and she could even make out that one of them didn't know how to spell "stupid," and that he had to ask his
T2    128:14                          "I--I didn't know I had to make one--just then," Alice faltered out.
T9    193:17                          "I didn't know I was to have a party at all," said Alice; "but,
T8    181:23                          "I didn't know it," the Knight said, a shade of vexation passing
A7     55: 4                          "I didn't know it was your table," said Alice: "it's laid for a
A6     48: 2    that Cheshire-Cats always grinned; in fact, I didn't know that cats could grin."
A6     48: 1                          "I didn't know that Cheshire-Cats always grinned; in fact, I
T6    160:14    me!" cried Humpty Dumpty. "Did you think I didn't know the answer to that? Ask another."
T6    159:24                              Alice didn't know what to say to this: it wasn't at all like
T2    125: 4    Queen, patting her on the head, which Alice didn't like at all: "though, when you say 'garden'--I've seen
T2    121:13                              Alice didn't like being criticized, so she began asking questions.
T9    194:29    turning suddenly on the White Queen, for she didn't like being found fault with so much.
A2     19:29    poor animal's feelings. "I quite forgot you didn't like cats."
T2    123:18                              Alice didn't like this idea at all: so, to change the subject, she
T1    118:26    it's rather hard to understand!" (You see she didn't like to confess, even to herself, that she couldn't
T9    192:38                          "I'm sure I didn't mean--" Alice was beginning, but the Red Queen
A3     26:10                          "I didn't mean it!" pleaded poor Alice. "But you're so easily
T8    184: 3    "None to speak of," the Knight said, as if he didn't mind breaking two or three of them. "The great art of
A1      9:14    as she couldn't answer either question, it didn't much matter which way she put it. She felt that she was
T5    156: 9    without looking up from her knitting: "I didn't put 'em there, and I'm not going to take 'em away."
A8     65:35                          "No, I didn't," said Alice. "I don't think it's at all a pity. I said
T3    135: 8      "Well, if she said 'Miss,' and didn't say anything more," the Gnat remarked, "of course you'd
T7    172:13                          "I didn't say there was nothing better," the King replied. "I
T5    157: 7              "Was it? I didn't see it," said Alice, peeping cautiously over the side
T9    201:15                          However, she didn't see why the Red Queen should be the only one to give
T3    136: 8    at Alice with its large gentle eyes, but didn't seem at all frightened. "Here then! Here then!" Alice
A12    94:23                          "If you didn't sign it," said the King, "that only makes the matter
T8    182:36                          It didn't sound a comfortable plan, Alice thought, and for a few
A1      8:42    there was no one listening, this time, as it didn't sound at all the right word) "--but I shall have to ask
T5    155:23                          This didn't sound like a remark that needed any answer: so Alice
T1    110:25    a model for it to imitate: however, the thing didn't succeed, principally, Alice said, because the kitten
T6    159:11      fixed in the opposite direction, and he didn't take the least notice of her, she thought he must be a
A11    89:21                          "I didn't!" the March Hare interrupted in a great hurry.
```

DIDN'T (cont.)
T6   160:25 me--ah, you may turn pale, if you like! You didn't think I was going to say that, did you? The King has
A6   51:27   Alice didn't think that proved it at all: however, she went on: "And
T7   171: 4   "I only meant that I didn't understand," said Alice. "Why one to come and one to go
T6   164:12   (Alice didn't venture to ask what he paid them with; and so you see I
T6   162: 1   Alice didn't want to begin another argument, so she said nothing.
A12   94:21 "Please, your Majesty," said the Knave, "I didn't write it, and they ca'n't prove that I did: there's no
T5   155:30   "Didn't you hear me say 'Feather'?" the Sheep cried angrily,
T2   122: 7   "Didn't you know that?" cried another Daisy. And here they all
DIE (5)
A12   92:12 and put back into the jury-box, or they would die.
TC   209:18 as the days go by, / Dreaming as the summers die:
TC   209: 8 that sunny sky: / Echoes fade and memories die: / Autumn frosts have slain July.
T8   179: 1 After a while the noise seemed gradually to die away, till all was dead silence, and Alice lifted up her
T3   134:17   "Then it would die, of course."
DIED (1)
A9   72:29 Alice's great surprise, the Duchess's voice died away, even in the middle of her favourite word "moral",
DIFFERENCE (2)
T5   151:19   for," said Alice: "that makes all the difference."
T8   186:27 quite eagerly: "but you've no idea what a difference it makes, mixing it with other things--such as
DIFFERENT (15)
A5   36:35 doth the little busy bee,' but it all came different!" Alice replied in a very melancholy voice.
A10   82: 7 to the Caterpillar, and the words all coming different, and then the Mock Turtle drew a long breath, and
T1   112:12 uninteresting, but that all the rest was as different as possible. For instance, the pictures on the wall
A9   76:22 with," the Mock Turtle replied; "and then the different branches of Arithmetic--Ambition, Distraction,
A2   15:41 almost think I can remember feeling a little different. But if I'm not the same, the next question is 'Who
A10   82:30   "That's different from what I used to say when I was a child," said
T8   185:12   "But that's a different kind of fastness," Alice objected.
T1   111: 5 as you can see, only you know it may be quite different on beyond. Oh, Kitty, how nice it would be if we
A10   81:42 use going back to yesterday, because I was a different person then."
A5   36: 7   "Well, perhaps your feelings may be different," said Alice: "all I know is, it would feel very
A5   35:16 it myself, to begin with; and being so many different sizes in a day is very confusing."
A10   82:11   "It all came different!" the Mock Turtle repeated thoughtfully. "I should
T6   163:34 "whether you can make words mean so many different things."
T3   137:19   "when the road divides and they point different ways."
T9   194:23 said, as gravely as she could, "They might go different ways." But she couldn't help thinking to herself
DIFFICULT (4)
T9   203: 1   In fact it was rather difficult for her to keep in her place while she made her
A8   66:19 came to the conclusion that it was a very difficult game indeed.
A5   41:35 it was perfectly round, she found this a very difficult question. However, at last she stretched her arms
T3   137:16   It was not a very difficult question to answer, as there was only one road
DIFFICULTIES (1)
A8   68: 6 The Queen had only one way of settling all difficulties, great or small. "Off with his head!" she said
DIFFICULTY (8)
A8   66: 6   The chief difficulty Alice found at first was in managing her flamingo:
A6   49:15   Alice caught the baby with some difficulty, as it was a queer-shaped little creature, and held
T3   134:15   A new difficulty came into Alice's head. "Supposing it couldn't find
T8   184:30 Knight. "You see, I said to myself 'The only difficulty is with the feet: the head is high enough already.'
T4   139:27 feelings; so, as the best way out of the difficulty, she took hold of both hands at once: the next
T9   195:11   Alice thought she saw a way out of the difficulty, this time. "If you'll tell me what language
A8   68:19 one of them with the other: the only difficulty was, that her flamingo was gone across the other
A4   32:23 and very neatly and simply arranged: the only difficulty was, that she had not the smallest idea how to set
DIG (2)
T8   188:41   'I sometimes dig for buttered rolls, / Or set limed twigs for crabs: / I
A9   72:23 again?" the Duchess asked, with another dig of her sharp little chin.
DIGGING (4)
A4   30: 4   "Digging for apples, indeed!" said the Rabbit angrily. "Here!
A4   30: 3 had never heard before, "Sure then I'm here! Digging for apples, yer honour!"
A9   70:37 means much the same thing," said the Duchess, digging her sharp little chin into Alice's shoulder as she
A2   18:23 of bathing-machines in the sea, some children digging in the sand with wooden spades, then a row of
DIGNIFIED (1)
T9   192: 5 on the grass like that! Queens have to be dignified, you know!"
DILIGENTLY (2)
A12   93:12 handed back to them, they set to work very diligently to write out a history of the accident, all except
T7   177: 7 great dish on her knees, and was sawing away diligently with the knife. "It's very provoking!" she said, in
DINAH (22)
A1   9:17 dream that she was walking hand in hand with Dinah, and was saying to her, very earnestly, "Now, Dinah,
A4   31:31 as loud as she could, "If you do, I'll set Dinah at you!"
A4   27:32 But I've got to watch this mouse-hole till Dinah comes back, and see that the mouse doesn't get out.'
T12 207:34 in her hand, to watch the kittens. "Tell me, Dinah, did you turn to Humpty Dumpty? I think you did--however
T12 207:30 be the reason you were so untidy in my dream--Dinah! Do you know that you're scrubbing a White Queen? Really
T12 208: 7 not go on licking your paw like that--as if Dinah hadn't washed you this morning! You see, Kitty, it must
T12 207:28 patiently undergoing its toilet, "when will Dinah have finished with your White Majesty, I wonder? That
A3   26:22   "I wish I had our Dinah here, I know I do!" said Alice aloud, addressing nobody
A2   19:33 it. And yet I wish I could show you our cat Dinah. I think you'd take a fancy to cats, if you could only
A3   26:39 she's the best cat in the world! Oh, my dear Dinah! I wonder if I shall ever see you any more!" And here
A3   26:24   "And who is Dinah, if I might venture to ask the question?" said the Lory.
A1   9: 8 remember her saucer of milk at tea-time. Dinah, my dear! I wish you were down here with me! There are
T1   107:22 understand that it was in disgrace. "Really, Dinah ought to have taught you better manners! You ought,
A3   26:37   "I wish I hadn't mentioned Dinah!" she said to herself in a melancholy tone. "Nobody

DINAH (cont.)
    A4   27:34   don't think," Alice went on, "that they'd let Dinah stop in the house if it began ordering people about like
    A1   9:17   and was saying to her, very earnestly, "Now, Dinah, tell me the truth: did you ever eat a bat?" when
    T12 207:32   "And what did Dinah turn to, I wonder?" she prattled on, as she settled
    T1   108:12   if you'd been up in the window with me--only Dinah was making you tidy, so you couldn't. I was watching the
    A1   9: 7   miss me very much to-night, I should think!" (Dinah was the cat.) "I hope they'll remember her saucer of
    T1   108:28   faults. Number one: you squeaked twice while Dinah was washing your face this morning. Now you ca'n't deny
    T1   107: 6   The way Dinah washed her children's faces was this: first she held the
    T1   108: 1   to have taught you better manners! You ought, Dinah, you know you ought!" she added, looking reproachfully
DINAH'LL (2)
    A4   27:28   "to be going messages for a rabbit! I suppose Dinah'll be sending me on messages next!" And she began
    A1   9: 6   to do, so Alice soon began talking again. "Dinah'll miss me very much to-night, I should think!" (Dinah
DINAH'S (1)
    A3   26:27   she was always ready to talk about her pet: "Dinah's our cat. And she's such a capital one for catching
DINE (1)
    T9   199:27   creatures, whatever they be, / Come and dine with the Red Queen, the White Queen, and me!'"
DINN (1)
    A10   80:20   "I don't know where Dinn may be," said the Mock Turtle; "but, if you've seen them
DINN-- (1)
    A10   80:18   "Yes," said Alice, "I've often seen them at dinn----" she checked herself hastily.
DINNER (9)
    A7   57: 2   clock in a twinkling! Half-past one, time for dinner!"
    T2   124:17   herself, "the next time I'm a little late for dinner."
    T6   164:28   the time when you begin broiling things for dinner."
    T8   186:14   you wouldn't have two pudding-courses in one dinner?"
    A2   20: 7   throw them, and it'll sit up and beg for its dinner, and all sorts of things--I ca'n't remember half of
    T9   199:39   to hear: / 'Tis a privilege high to have dinner and tea / Along with the Red Queen, the White Queen,
    T9   201:11   said rather hastily, "or we shall get no dinner at all. May I give you some?"
    T4   147:43   "Let's fight till six, and then have dinner," said Tweedledum.
    T1   109: 5   each punishment was to be going without a dinner: then, when the miserable day came, I should have to go
DINNER-PARTY (1)
    T9   193:15   to the White Queen, "I invite you to Alice's dinner-party this afternoon."
DINNERS (1)
    T1   109: 6   day came, I should have to go without fifty dinners at once! Well, I shouldn't mind that much! I'd far
DIPPED (2)
    A7   56: 8   the watch and looked at it gloomily: then he dipped it into his cup of tea, and looked at it again: but he
    A1   8: 8   on like a tunnel for some way, and then dipped suddenly down, so suddenly that Alice had not a moment
DIPPING (1)
    T5   156:21   boat, with just the ends of her tangled hair dipping into the water--while with bright eager eyes she
DIRECTED (2)
    A12   94:12   "It isn't directed at all," said the White Rabbit: "in fact, there's
    A12   94:11   "Who is it directed to?" said one of the jurymen.
DIRECTION (9)
    T2   124: 2   plan, this time, of walking in the opposite direction.
    T6   159:11   his eyes were steadily fixed in the opposite direction, and he didn't take the least notice of her, she
    T9   197: 1   said Alice, as she tried to obey the first direction: "and I don't know any soothing lullabies."
    A6   52:23   after a minute or two she walked on in the direction in which the March Hare was said to live. "I've seen
    A4   27:16   frightened that she ran off at once in the direction it pointed to, without trying to explain the mistake
    A5   42:20   that her neck would bend about easily in any direction, like a serpent. She had just succeeded in curving
    A6   51:19   "In that direction," the Cat said, waving its right paw round, "lives a
    T8   190:17   as Alice turned with an eager look in the direction to which he pointed. "I sha'n't be long. You'll wait
    A6   51:20   right paw round, "lives a Hatter: and in that direction," waving the other paw, "lives a March Hare. Visit
DIRECTIONS (7)
    T2   124: 9   Alice attended to all these directions, and explained, as well as she could, that she had
    T9   203:21   forks for legs, went fluttering about in all directions: "and very like birds they look," Alice thought to
    T2   127:36   to mark the distance, "I shall give you your directions--have another biscuit?"
    A6   49:16   and held out its arms and legs in all directions, "just like a star-fish," thought Alice. The poor
    T2   125:20   stood without speaking, looking out in all directions over the country--and a most curious country it was
    A8   65:42   and people began running about in all directions, tumbling up against each other: however, they got
    A2   15: 5   presents to one's own feet! And how odd the directions will look!
DIRECTLY (7)
    T5   155:28   more needles. "You'll be catching a crab directly."
    A4   27:30   that would happen: "'Miss Alice! Come here directly, and get ready for your walk!' 'Coming in a minute,
    T9   202:22   voice, and all the guests began drinking it directly, and very queerly they managed it: some of them put
    A4   32:11   delighted to find that she began shrinking directly. As soon as she was small enough to get through the
    T5   152:15   groaned out: "the brooch will come undone directly. Oh, oh!" As she said the words the brooch flew open,
    T1   110:28   how sulky it was, "--and if you're not good directly," she added, "I'll put you through into Looking-glass
    T8   185: 1   off the horse, it always touched the ground directly. So I had a very little way to fall, you see--But
DISAGREE (1)
    A1   11: 4   marked "poison," it is almost certain to disagree with you, sooner or later.
DISAPPEARED (3)
    A11   91:24   they had settled down again, the cook had disappeared.
    T9   204: 7   over the edge of the tureen, before she disappeared into the soup.
    A8   69:12   come back with the Duchess, it had entirely disappeared: so the King and the executioner ran wildly up and
DISAPPOINTMENT (1)
    A1   8:19   labeled "ORANGE MARMALADE," but to her great disappointment it was empty: she did not like to drop the jar,
DISBELIEVE (1)
    T2   124:16   but she was too much in awe of the Queen to disbelieve it. "I'll try it when I go home," she thought to
DISCONTENTED (2)
    T6   168:22   if we did meet," Humpty Dumpty replied in a discontented tone, giving her one of his fingers to shake:

DISCONTENTED (cont.)
   T8   181:34 a very good bee-hive," the Knight said in a discontented tone, "one of the best kind. But not a single bee
DISCOURAGED (1)
   T9   194:37 letter! Isn't _that_ grand? However, don't be discouraged. You'll come to it in time."
DISEASE (1)
   T8W   17: 4   "Conceit isn't a disease at all," Alice remarked.
DISGRACE (1)
   T1   107:22 kiss to make it understand that it was in disgrace. "Really, Dinah ought to have taught you better
DISGUST (2)
   T7   175:17 looking at her with an air of the deepest disgust.
   A7   60:30 than Alice could bear: she got up in great disgust, and walked off: the Dormouse fell asleep instantly,
DISH (16)
   T7   177:16 as she returned to her place with the empty dish.
   T7   175:40 gave it to Alice to hold, while he got out a dish and carving-knife. How they all came out of it Alice
   T9   201: 1   Alice." The leg of mutton got up in the dish and made a little bow to Alice; and Alice returned the
   A10   83:17 and gravy, _and meat, / While the Owl had the dish as its share of the treat. / When the pie was all_
   T8   182:11 with you to the end of the wood--What's that dish for?"
   T9   202:26 looked like kangaroos) scrambled into the dish of roast mutton, and began eagerly lapping up the gravy,
   A11   86: 7 middle of the court was a table, with a large dish of tarts upon it: they looked so good, that it made Alice
   T7   177: 7 on the bank of a little brook, with the great dish on her knees, and was sawing away diligently with the
   T9   202:12 here! _Let me sup!' / It is easy to set such a dish on the table. / 'Take the dish-cover up!' / Ah, that is_
   A6   46:15 and every now and then a great crash, as if a dish or kettle had been broken to pieces.
   T7   177:14 Alice very obediently got up, and carried the dish round, and the cake divided itself into three pieces as
   T8   179: 5 Messengers. However, there was the great dish still lying at her feet, on which she had tried to cut
   T9   202: 9 take more than a minute. / _Let it lie in a dish!' / That is easy, because it already is in it._
   T8   182:17 Knight was so _very awkward in putting in the dish: the first two or three times that he tried he fell in_
   T9   202:16 _it holds it like glue--/ Holds the lid to the dish, while it lies in the middle: / Which is easiest to do, /_
   A10   84:27 _Who cares for fish, / Game, or any other dish? / Who would not give all else for two p / ennyworth only_
DISH-COVER (2) [See also UN-DISH-COVER]
   T9   202:18 _easiest to do, / Un-dish-cover the fish, or dishcover the riddle?"_
   T9   202:13 _to set such a dish on the table. / 'Take the dish-cover up!' / Ah, that is so hard that I fear I'm unable!_
DISH-COVERS (1)
   T4   147:14   blankets, hearth-rugs, table-cloths, dish-covers, and coal-scuttles. "I hope you're a good hand at
DISHES (4)
   T9   204:10 several of the guests were lying down in the dishes, and the soup ladle was walking up the table towards
   A12   98:30   on the Duchess's knee, while plates and dishes crashed around it--once more the shriek of the Gryphon,
   T9   204:15 with both hands: one good pull, and plates, dishes, guests, and candles came crashing down together in a
   A6   48:12 followed a shower of saucepans, plates, and dishes. The Duchess took no notice of them even when they hit
DISMAL (1)
   T4   143:16 / _'After such kindness, that would be / A dismal thing to do!' / 'The night is fine,' the Walrus said. /_
DISMAY (3)
   A12   92: 9 pardon!" she exclaimed in a tone of great dismay, and began picking them up again as quickly as she
   T8   191: 4 this on my head?" she exclaimed in a tone of dismay, as she put her hands up to something very heavy, that
   T6   162:18 I mean--I beg your pardon!" she added in dismay, for Humpty Dumpty looked thoroughly offended, and she
DISOBEY (1)
   A10   83:12   Alice did not dare to disobey, though she felt sure it would all come wrong, and she
DISPUTE (2)
   A8   68:29 a large crowd collected round it: there was a dispute going on between the executioner, the King, and the
   A8   67: 4   to be sure, she had not as yet had any dispute with the Queen, but she knew that it might happen any
DISRESPECTFUL (1)
   T12 207:31 scrubbing a White Queen? Really, it's most disrespectful of you!
DISTANCE (11)
   A4   33: 5 the puppy's bark sounded quite faint in the distance.
   A10   85: 3 of "The trial's beginning!" was heard in the distance.
   A2   15:25 she heard a little pattering of feet in the distance, and she hastily dried her eyes to see what was
   A3   26:42 heard a little pattering of footsteps in the distance, and she looked up eagerly, half hoping that the
   A1   8:35 say it over) "--yes, that's about the right distance--but then I wonder what Latitude or Longitude I've
   T2   127:36 she said, putting in a peg to mark the distance, "I shall give you your directions--have another
   T3   131:16   Then a very gentle voice in the distance said, "She must be labeled 'Lass, with care,' you
   A8   68:11 on, as she heard the Queen's voice in the distance, screaming with passion. She had already heard her
   A9   74:17 far before they saw the Mock Turtle in the distance, sitting sad and lonely on a little ledge of rock,
   T7   170:18 tone. "To be able to see Nobody! And at that distance too! Why, it's as much as _I_ can do to see real people
   A12   99: 2   while the lowing of the cattle in the distance would take the place of the Mock Turtle's heavy sobs
DISTANT (2)
   A5   42:16 to follow, except a little shaking among the distant green leaves.
   A12   98:33   filled the air, mixed up with the distant sob of the miserable Mock Turtle.
DISTINCT (1)
   T9   197:20   The snoring got more distinct every minute, and sounded more like a tune: at last
DISTINGUISH (1)
   T7   173:18 out which was which; but she soon managed to distinguish the Unicorn by his horn.
DISTRACTED (1)
   T8   190: 5 _eyes, like cinders, all aglow, / Who seemed distracted with his woe, / Who rocked his body to and fro, /_
DISTRACTION (1)
   A9   76:23 different branches of Arithmetic--Ambition, Distraction, Uglification, and Derision."
DITCH (2)
   T8   185:16 of the saddle, and fell headlong into a deep ditch.
   T8   185:17   Alice ran to the side of the ditch to look for him. She was rather startled by the fall, as
DITTO (3)
   T4   145:15   "Ditto, ditto!" cried Tweedledee.
   T4   145:15   "Ditto, ditto!" cried Tweedledee.

```
DITTO (cont.)
  T4    145:14                                              "Ditto," said Tweedledum.
DIVE (1)
  A5     42:22   down into a graceful zigzag, and was going to dive in among the leaves, which she found to be nothing but
DIVIDE (1)
  T9    194: 6   said  the  White Queen. "Can you do Division? Divide a loaf by a knife--what's the answer to that?"
DIVIDED (3)
  T7    177:14   up,  and carried the dish round, and the cake divided itself into three pieces as she did so. "Now cut it up
  T3    137:21   on and on, a long way, but wherever the road divided, there were sure to be two finger-posts pointing the
  T2    125:22   from side to side, and the ground between was divided up into squares by a number of little green hedges,
DIVIDES (1)
  T3    137:19   it," Alice  said  to herself, "when the road divides and they point different ways."
DIVIDING (1)
  T8W    15:10                         "En-gulph-ed," Alice repeated, dividing the word into syllables.
DIVISION (1)
  T9    194: 6                    said the White Queen. "Can you do Division? Divide a loaf by a knife--what's the answer to that
DO (208) [See also UNDO]
  A2     17: 7   words did  not come the same as they used to do:--
  A6     48: 3   all  can," said the Duchess; "and most of 'em do."
  A9     74:26   "she wants for  to  know your history, she do."
  T3    135: 7   name, she'd call me 'Miss,' as the servants do."
  T3    136:16        "Think  again,"  it  said: "that wo'n't do."
  T6    167:14   large  and  new, / Fit for the deed I had to do.
  T7    172:21   "I'm  sure nobody walks  much faster than I do!"
  T8    188:32   how you live,' I cried, / 'And what it is you do!'
  T9    196:31   But  this  was more than Alice had courage to do.
  T6    164: 5          "When I make a word do a lot of work like that," said Humpty Dumpty, "I always pay
  A7     58: 9   Hatter went on in a mournful tone, "he wo'n't do a thing I ask! It's always six o'clock now."
  T9    194:30   The  Queen  gasped  and shut her eyes. "I can do Addition," she said, "if you give me time--but I ca'n't do
  T9    194: 1               "She ca'n't do Addition," the Red Queen interrupted. "Can you do
  T9    193:24                 "Can you do Addition?" the White Queen asked. "What's one and one and
  A7     55:21            "I do," Alice hastily replied; "at least--at least I mean what I
  T9    201:41                 "Please do," Alice said very politely.
  A6     48: 4           "I don't know of any that do," Alice said very politely, feeling quite pleased to have
  A7     56:43   if you only kept on good terms with him, he'd do almost anything you liked with the clock. For instance,
  T3    137:27   there  long.  I'll just call and say 'How d'ye do?' and ask them the way out of the wood. If I could only get
  A3     23:26            Alice had no idea what to do, and in despair she put her hand in her pocket, and pulled
  A5     36:27   as  well  wait,  as  she  had nothing else to do, and perhaps after all it might tell her something worth
  T4    139:22   first  thing  in a visit is to say 'How d'ye do?' and shake hands!" And here the two brothers gave each
  A12    93:14   the  Lizard,  who seemed too much overcome to do anything but sit with its mouth open, gazing up into the
  T8W    16: 1   well,"  she  said in a soothing tone. "Can't I do anything for you?"
  T8W    14: 1               "Can I do anything for you?" Alice went on. "Aren't you rather cold
  T6    163:40    they're the  proudest--adjectives  you  can do anything with, but not verbs--however, I can manage the
  A4     30:15   don't  like  it, yer honour, at all, at all!" "Do as I tell you, you coward!", and at last she spread out her
  T1    109: 3   to  herself  than the kitten. "What would they do at the end of a year? I should be sent to prison, I suppose
  A1      9:13   eat bats? Do cats eat bats?" and sometimes "Do bats eat cats?" for, you see, as she couldn't answer either
  T3    135:43   tree. "What does it call itself, I wonder? I do believe it's got no name--why, to be sure it hasn't!"
  T4    148:20   is!" she said. "And how fast it comes! Why, I do believe it's got wings!"
  T3    137:25               "I do believe," said Alice at last, "that they live in the same
  T2    127:12   looked  round her in great surprise. "Why, I do believe we've been under this tree the whole time!
  A3     26:14   the  others all joined in chorus "Yes, please do!" But the Mouse only shook its head impatiently, and walked
  A1      9:13   in  a  dreamy sort of way, "Do cats eat bats? Do cats eat bats?" and sometimes "Do bats eat cats?" for, you
  A1      9:12   saying  to herself, in a dreamy sort of way, "Do cats eat bats? Do cats eat bats?" and sometimes "Do bats
  A1      9:11   and  that's  very like a mouse, you know. But do cats eat bats, I wonder?" And here Alice began to get
  A2     20:14   So  she  called softly after it, "Mouse dear! Do come back again, and we wo'n't talk about cats, or dogs
  T8    182: 3   perhaps," said the Knight; "but, if they do come, I don't choose to have them running all about."
  T9    194: 6   Subtraction,"  said the White Queen. "Can you do Division? Divide a loaf by a knife--what's the answer to
  A3     22:32   words,  and, what's more, I don't believe you do either!" And the Eaglet bent down its head to hide a smile:
  T9    197:12               "What am I to do?" exclaimed Alice, looking about in great perplexity, as
  T9    192: 4   fond  of  scolding herself), "It'll  never  do for you to be lolling about on the grass like that! Queens
  T12   208:11   my dear,  so  you  ought to know--Oh, Kitty, do help to settle it! I'm sure your paw can wait!" But the
  T5    155:19   banks:  so  there  was  nothing for it but to do her best.
  A4     28: 6   so  I'll  just  see  what this bottle does. I do hope it'll make me grow large again, for really I'm quite
  T8    179: 8   we're  all  part  of  the same dream. Only I do hope it's my dream, and not the Red King's! I don't like
  A12    95:36          The Knave shook his head sadly. "Do I look like it?" he said. (Which he certainly did not,
  T4    147:30               "Do I look very pale?" said Tweedledum, coming up to have his
  T9    194:35               "So do I," the White Queen whispered: "we'll often say it over
  T2    122: 3           "But what could it do, if any danger came?" Alice asked.
  A4     31:30   called  out,  as  loud  as she could, "If you do, I'll set Dinah at you!"
  T3    135: 5           "That would never do, I'm sure," said Alice: "the governess would never think of
  A5     39: 4   and  the  beak--/ Pray, how did you manage to do it?"
  T2    122:12   head towards Alice, "or they wouldn't dare to do it!"
  T3    132:34               "I never knew them do it."
  A5     37: 8   that I'm perfectly sure I have none, / Why, I do it again and again."
  T5    152:12               "When do you expect to do it?" Alice said, feeling very much inclined to laugh.
  A3     23: 5   the  Dodo,  "the best way to explain it is to do it." (And, as you might like to try the thing yourself some
  T5    149:17   only  tell me  the  right way to begin, I'll do it as well as I can."
  T3    136: 4   I  will remember, if I can! I'm determined to do it!" But being determined didn't help her much, and all she
  T8W    19:15   me  and call me 'Pig!' / And that is why they do it, dear, / Because I wear a yellow wig."
  T9    197: 2               "I must do it myself, then," said the Red Queen, and she began:--
```

DO (cont.)

A4	33:10	much, if--if I'd only been the right size to do it! Oh dear! I'd nearly forgotten that I've got to grow up
T6	167: 4	The little fishes' answer was / 'We cannot do it, Sir, because--'"
A4	30:32	to go down the chimney?--Nay, I sha'n't! You do it!--That I wo'n't, then!--Bill's got to go down--Here,
T2	120:21	well, and she was just saying "I really shall do it this time--" when the path gave a sudden twist and shook
T8W	18: 8	thought she would try if the Wasp couldn't do it too. "Would you mind saying it in rhyme?" she asked very
T9	202:32	the White Queen whispered, as Alice got up to do it, very obediently, but a little frightened.
A10	79: 6	said the Mock Turtle to the Gryphon. "We can do it without lobsters, you know. Which shall sing?"
T2	123: 6	like you," said the Rose. "I wonder how you do it--" ("You're always wondering," said the Tiger-lily),
A9	77:10	"And how many hours a day did you do lessons?" said Alice, in a hurry to change the subject.
A3	26: 7	useful, and looking anxiously about her. "Oh, do let me help to undo it!"
T1	110:18	by shouting suddenly in her ear, "Nurse! Do let's pretend that I'm a hungry hyaena and you're a bone!"
A2	15:16	Poor Alice! It was as much as she could do, lying down on one side, to look through into the garden
T7	172:20	"I do my best," the Messenger said in a sullen tone. "I'm sure
A4	30:19	be!" thought Alice. "I wonder what they'll do next! As for pulling me out of the window, I only wish they
T6	164: 1	as well if you'd mention what you mean to do next, as I suppose you don't mean to stop here all the rest
A4	31:35	thought to herself "I wonder what they will do next! If they had any sense, they'd take the roof off."
A6	45: 2	looking at the house, and wondering what to do next, when suddenly a footman in livery came running out of
A4	28:21	the chimney, and said to herself "Now I can do no more, whatever happens. What will become of me?"
T8	188:37	/ In the silent night. / And these I do not sell for gold / Or coin of silvery shine, / But for a
T1	114:10	her breath, and for a minute or two she could do nothing but hug the little Lily in silence. As soon as she
A3	26: 8	"I shall do nothing of the sort," said the Mouse, getting up and
T4	140: 4	with. "It would never do to say 'How d'ye do?' now," she said to herself: "we seem to have got beyond
A1	7: 2	sister on the bank and of having nothing to do: once or twice she had peeped into the book her sister was
A7	58:29	"Yes, please do!" pleaded Alice.
A6	46:41	"But what am I to do?" said Alice.
T9	194:34	"To be sure I do," said Alice.
A3	26:22	"I wish I had our Dinah here, I know I do!" said Alice aloud, addressing nobody in particular. "She'd
A4	32:18	"The first thing I've got to do," said Alice to herself, as she wandered about in the wood,
A7	56:35	"If you knew Time as well as I do," said the Hatter, "you wouldn't talk about wasting it.
A3	25:22	For really this morning I've nothing to do.' Said the mouse to the cur, Such a trial, dear sir, With
T8	179:36	"I always do," said the Red Knight, and they began banging away at each
A10	84: 7	the Gryphon, and Alice was only too glad to do so.
A1	9: 5	Down, down, down. There was nothing else to do, so Alice soon began talking again. "Dinah'll miss me very
A10	80:14	very glad that it was over at last: "and I do so like that curious song about the whiting!"
T3	129:26	may visit the elephants later on. Besides, I do so want to get into the Third Square!"
T1	110:35	but the bit just behind the fireplace. Oh! I do so wish I could see that bit! I want so much to know
T1	110: 2	the ball of worsted to clap her hands. "And I do so wish it was true! I'm sure the woods look sleepy in the
A7	56:32	Alice sighed wearily. "I think you might do something better with the time," she said, "than wasting it
T9	194: 5	"She ca'n't do Subtraction," said the White Queen. "Can you do Division?
T9	194: 2	the Red Queen interrupted. "Can you do Subtraction? Take nine from eight."
T9	194:31	she said, "if you give me time--but I ca'n't do Subtraction under any circumstances!"
T7	172:31	King, jumping up and shaking himself. "If you do such a thing again, I'll have you buttered! It went through
A8	68:39	to cut it off from: that he had never had to do such a thing before, and he wasn't going to begin at his
T9	194:26	"She ca'n't do sums a bit!" the Queens said together, with great emphasis.
T9	194:28	"Can you do sums?" Alice said, turning suddenly on the White Queen, for
T9	193:23	lessons," said Alice. "Lessons teach you to do sums, and things of that sort."
T2	120: 3	straight to it--at least, no, it doesn't do that--" (after going a few yards along the path, and
A4	32: 4	to herself, and shouted out "You'd better not do that again!", which produced another dead silence.
A1	10:20	but the wise little Alice was not going to do that in a hurry. "No, I'll look first," she said, "and see
T4	147: 3	it: which was such an extraordinary thing to do, that it quite took off Alice's attention from the angry
A6	51:15	"Oh, you're sure to do that," said the Cat, "if you only walk long enough."
T7	172:22	"He ca'n't do that," said the King, "or else he'd have been here first.
T2	123:38	"You ca'n't possibly do that," said the Rose: "I should advise you to walk the
T9	199:18	"Shouldn't do that--shouldn't do that--" the Frog muttered. "Wexes it,
T9	199:18	"Shouldn't do that--shouldn't do that--" the Frog muttered. "Wexes it, you know." Then he
T4	143:16	kindness, that would be / A dismal thing to do!' / 'The night is fine,' the Walrus said. / 'Do you admire
T5	158:29	up to it, and she quite expected the egg to do the same.
T8W	21: 4	one claw towards Alice, as if he wished to do the same for her, but she kept out of reach, and would not
T3	132:38	people that name them, I suppose. If not, why do things have names at all?"
A9	73: 7	of course had to leave off being arches to do this, so that, by the end of half an hour or so, there were
T5	158:17	"I wonder why it wouldn't do?" thought Alice, as she groped her way among the tables and
A1	9: 3	she'll think me for asking! No, it'll never do to ask: perhaps I shall see it written up somewhere."
A4	31:40	Alice heard the Rabbit say "A barrowful will do, to begin with."
A5	44: 3	lives there," thought Alice, "it'll never do to come upon them this size: why, I should frighten them
T3	129:20	for turning shy so suddenly. "It'll never do to go down among them without a good long branch to brush
T5	149:15	Alice thought it would never do to have an argument at the very beginning of their
A6	49:20	minute or two, it was as much as she could do to hold it.
T2	127:20	you see, it takes all the running you can do, to keep in the same place. If you want to get somewhere
T2	126:15	Queen went so fast that it was all she could do to keep up with her: and still the Queen kept crying
T8	184:18	scream of laughter, in spite of all she could do to prevent it.
T4	140: 4	had just been dancing with. "It would never do to say 'How d'ye do?' now," she said to herself: "we seem
T7	170:19	that distance too! Why, it's as much as I can do to see real people, by this light!"
T1	110:23	your arms, you'd look exactly like her. Now do try, there's a dear!" And Alice got the Red Queen off the
T5	153: 2	Queen said with great decision: "nobody can do two things at once, you know. Let's consider your age to
T9	202:17	it lies in the middle: / Which is easiest to do, / Un-dish-cover the fish, or dishcover the riddle?"
A6	50:18	over other children she knew, who might do very well as pigs, and was just saying to herself "if one
T6	164:29	"That'll do very well," said Alice: "and 'slithy'?"
T9	197:18	never was more than one Queen at a time. Do wake up, you heavy things!" she went on in an impatient

DO (cont.)

T3	129: 1	Of course the first thing to do was to make a grand survey of the country she was going to
A4	30:28	don't reach half high enough yet--Oh, they'll do well enough. Don't be particular--Here, Bill! Catch hold of
T2	120:10	turn, but always coming back to the house, do what she would. Indeed, once, when she turned a corner
A5	43:19	believe it," said the Pigeon; "but if they do, why, then they're a kind of serpent: that's all I can say
A4	28:14	As it is, I ca'n't get out at the door--I do wish I hadn't drunk quite so much!"
A2	17:26	cried Alice, with a sudden burst of tears, "I do wish they would put their heads down! I am so very tired of
T2	122:27	she said; "but I don't see what that has to do with it."
T1	107: 2	that the white kitten had had nothing to do with it--it was the black kitten's fault entirely. For the
T4	141:17	talk, / Along the briny beach: / We cannot do with more than four, / To give a hand to each.'
A6	50: 9	to think to herself, "Now, what am I to do with this creature, when I get it home?" when it grunted
A6	50: 4	Alice, seriously, "I'll have nothing more to do with you. Mind now!" The poor little thing sobbed again (or
A4	29: 3	curious, you know, this sort of life! I do wonder what can have happened to me! When I used to read
T9	196:32	and putting her hair in papers--would do wonders with her--"
A5	36:30	again, and said "So you think you're changed, do you?"
T4	143:18	/ 'The night is fine,' the Walrus said. / 'Do you admire the view?
A3	25: 2	with wonder at the Mouse's tail; "but why do you call it sad?" And she kept on puzzling about it while
T7	172:30	"Do you call that a whisper?" cried the poor King, jumping up
T3	136:12	"What do you call yourself?" the Fawn said at last. Such a soft
T2	124: 6	"Where do you come from?" said the Red Queen. "And where are you
T5	152:12	"When do you expect to do it?" Alice said, feeling very much
T1	109: 9	"Do you hear the snow against the window-panes, Kitty? How nice
A5	43:17	girls eat eggs quite as much as serpents do, you know."
A12	93:16	"What do you know about this business?" the King said to Alice.
T7	175:28	lips curling up into a smile as she began: "Do you know, I always thought Unicorns were fabulous monsters,
T1	110:21	pretend that you're the Red Queen, Kitty! Do you know, I think if you sat up and folded your arms, you'd
T1	108:21	"Do you know, I was so angry, Kitty," Alice went on, as soon as
A6	51:25	"How do you know I'm mad?" said Alice.
T9	201:28	"Do you know, I've had such a quantity of poetry repeated to me
T9	195: 7	all right again now," said the Red Queen. "Do you know Languages? What's the French for fiddle-de-dee?"
T8W	19: 7	me look extremely plain: / But what was I to do, you know? / My ringlets would not grow again.
T1	108:35	her! What, you were thirsty, were you? How do you know she wasn't thirsty too? Now for number three: you
A6	51:28	it at all: however, she went on: "And how do you know that you're mad?"
T12	207:30	reason you were so untidy in my dream--Dinah? Do you know that you're scrubbing a White Queen? Really, it's
T8	181:21	things can get out," Alice gently remarked. "Do you know the lid's open?"
A2	19:13	no harm in trying." So she began: "O Mouse, do you know the way out of this pool? I am very tired of
T1	108:11	"Do you know what to-morrow is, Kitty?" Alice began. "You'd
A10	81:19	than that, if you like," said the Gryphon. "Do you know why it's called a whiting?"
T9	201:32	every poem was about fishes in some way. Do you know why they're so fond of fishes, all about here?"
T7	177:20	none for herself, anyhow," said the Lion. "Do you like plum-cake, Monster?"
A8	67:31	"How do you like the Queen?" said the Cat in a low voice.
T9	192:26	the subject of the conversation. "What do you mean by 'If you really are a Queen'? What right have
A5	35: 9	"What do you mean by that?" said the Caterpillar, sternly. "Explain
A7	55:16	"Do you mean that you think you can find out the answer to it?"
T5	158:15	things into people's hands--that would never do--you must get it for yourself." And so saying, she went off
T9	194:42	"Where do you pick the flower?" the White Queen asked: "In a garden
A6	52: 2	"Call it what you like," said the Cat. "Do you play croquet with the Queen to-day?"
T3	132:27	"What sort of insects do you rejoice in, where you come from?" the Gnat inquired.
T5	150:21	"What sort of things do you remember best?" Alice ventured to ask.
T5	155:36	"Why do you say 'Feather' so often?" Alice asked at last, rather
T4	146:13	"Do you see that?" he said, in a voice choking with passion,
T5	158: 3	buy an egg, please," she said timidly. "How do you sell them?"
T6	160:11	"Why do you sit out here all alone?" said Alice, not wishing to
T7	175: 8	himself, as he opened his memorandum-book. "Do you spell 'creature' with a double 'e'?"
T9	193: 3	I complain of! You should have meant! What do you suppose is the use of a child without any meaning? Even
T4	141: 9	with seven mops / Swept it for half a year, / Do you suppose,' the Walrus said, / 'That they could get it
T4	145: 5	"And if he left off dreaming about you, where do you suppose you'd be?"
A11	89:18	begins with a T!" said the King sharply. "Do you take me for a dunce? Go on!"
A5	37: 4	And yet you incessantly stand on your head--/ Do you think, at your age, it is right?"
T4	145: 1	dreaming now," said Tweedledee: "and what do you think he's dreaming about?"
A5	40: 7	Said his father. "Don't give yourself airs! / Do you think I can listen all day to such stuff? / Be off, or
T12	208:14	Which do you think it was?
T4	146: 2	wood, for really it's coming on very dark. Do you think it's going to rain?"
A1	9: 1	curtseying as you're falling through the air! Do you think you could manage it?) "And what an ignorant
A5	41: 7	"What size do you want to be?" it asked.
T5	157:13	of choice, only make up your mind. Now, what do you want to buy?"
T3	135:11	"Why do you wish I had made it?" Alice asked. "It's a very bad one

DODGED (1)

A4	32:36	and made believe to worry it: then Alice dodged behind a great thistle, to keep herself from being run

DODO (13)

A3	23:34	"Hand it over here," said the Dodo.
A2	20:23	had fallen into it: there was a Duck and a Dodo, a Lory and an Eaglet, and several other curious
A3	23:17	This question the Dodo could not answer without a great deal of thought, and it
A3	23: 3	not that she much wanted to know, but the Dodo had paused as if it thought that somebody ought to speak,
A3	22:35	"What I was going to say," said the Dodo in an offended tone, "was that the best thing to get us
A3	23: 7	some winter-day, I will tell you how the Dodo managed it.)
A3	23:23	"Why, she, of course," said the Dodo, pointing to Alice with one finger; and the whole party
A3	23:31	"Of course," the Dodo replied very gravely. "What else have you got in your
A3	23:21	while the rest waited in silence. At last the Dodo said "Everybody has won, and all must have prizes."
A3	24: 1	all crowded round her once more, while the Dodo solemnly presented the thimble, saying "We beg your

DODO (cont.)
A3   22:28   "In that case," said the Dodo solemnly, rising to its feet, "I move that the meeting
A3   23:14   an hour or so, and were quite dry again, the Dodo suddenly called out "The race is over!" and they all
A3   23: 5   "Why," said the Dodo, "the best way to explain it is to do it." (And, as you
DOES (23)
A6   48:22   world would go round a deal faster than it does."
A4   28: 6   anything: so I'll just see what this bottle does. I do hope it'll make me grow large again, for really I'm
T3   135:43   her hand on the trunk of the tree. "What does it call itself, I wonder? I do believe it's got no name--
T3   134:13   "And what does it live on?"
T3   134: 1   "And what does it live on?" Alice asked, as before.
T3   133: 6   "What does it live on?" Alice asked, with great curiosity.
A5   43:23   for eggs, I know that well enough; and what does it matter to me whether you're a little girl or a serpent
T8   186: 2   looked surprised at the question. "What does it matter where my body happens to be?" he said. "My mind
T6   160: 6   Humpty Dumpty interrupted impatiently. "What does it mean?"
T2   123:33   "It's the fresh air that does it," said the Rose: "wonderfully fine air it is, out here
A6   48:38   / And beat him when he sneezes: / He only does it to annoy, / Because he knows it teases."
T8W   20: 6   admiration: "it's the shape of your head as does it. Your jaws aint well shaped, though--I should think
T6   166: 6   "And what does 'outgrabe' mean?"
T2   123:19   at all: so, to change the subject, she asked "Does she ever come out here?"
T2   123:22   "Where does she wear them?" Alice asked with some curiosity.
T8   184:14   "Does that kind go smoothly?" the Knight asked in a tone of
A10   81:15   Alice was thoroughly puzzled. "Does the boots and shoes!" she repeated in a wondering tone.
A10   81:13   "It does the boots and shoes," the Gryphon replied very solemnly.
T7   173: 5   "Does--the one--that wins--get the crown?" she asked, as well
T7   170:27   and those are Anglo-Saxon attitudes. He only does them when he's happy. His name is Haigha." (He pronounced
A9   70: 9   have any pepper in my kitchen at all. Soup does very well without--Maybe it's always pepper that makes
A4   30:10   "Sure, it does, yer honour: but it's an arm for all that."
A7   56:14   "Why should it?" muttered the Hatter. "Does your watch tell you what year it is?"
DOESN'T (28)
A9   74:30   "I don't see how he can ever finish, if he doesn't begin." But she waited patiently.
A12   95:27   jury all wrote down, on their slates, "She doesn't believe there's an atom of meaning in it," but none of
T2   120: 3   that leads straight to it--at least, no, it doesn't do that--" (after going a few yards along the path,
T7   178:11   "If that doesn't 'drum them out of town,'" she thought to herself,
T5   150: 5   in prison now, being punished: and the trial doesn't even begin till next Wednesday: and of course the
A4   27:32   till Dinah comes back, and see that the mouse doesn't get out.' Only I don't think," Alice went on, "that
A2   16: 5   her hair goes in such long ringlets, and mine doesn't go in ringlets at all; and I'm sure I ca'n't be Mabel,
T9   199:15   "I speaks English, doesn't I?" the Frog went on. "Or are you deaf? What did it
T6   162:26   thing," he said at last, "when a person doesn't know a cravat from a belt!"
T3   131: 5   her way to the ticket-office, even if she doesn't know her alphabet!"
T3   131: 1   to know which way she's going, even if she doesn't know her own name!"
T9   193:11   "that she wants to deny something--only she doesn't know what to deny!"
A5   41: 9   as to size," Alice hastily replied; "only one doesn't like changing so often, you know."
A9   72: 4   to this last remark. "It's a vegetable. It doesn't look like one, but it is."
A12   93:32   enough to look over their slates; "but it doesn't matter a bit," she thought to herself.
A3   23: 9   in a sort of circle, ("the exact shape doesn't matter," it said,) and then all the party were placed
A8   68:24   both the hedgehogs were out of sight: "but it doesn't matter much," thought Alice, "as all the arches are
A6   51:12   "Then it doesn't matter which way you go," said the Cat.
T6   163:28   "But 'glory' doesn't mean 'a nice knock-down argument,'" Alice objected.
A7   54: 6   Alice; "only as it's asleep, I suppose it doesn't mind."
A12   94:30   "It doesn't prove anything of the sort!" said Alice. "Why, you
A3   22:26   ever," said Alice in a melancholy tone: "it doesn't seem to dry me at all."
A2   16:11   that rate! However, the Multiplication-Table doesn't signify: let's try Geography. London is the capital of
A3   26:33   "I really must be getting home: the night-air doesn't suit my throat!" And a Canary called out in a
A7   56:13   remarked. "It tells the day of the month, and doesn't tell what o'clock it is!"
T2   120: 7   this turn goes to the hill, I suppose--no, it doesn't! This goes straight back to the house! Well then, I'll
A2   19:21   "Perhaps it doesn't understand English," thought Alice. "I daresay it's a
T8   186:40   "Or else it doesn't, you know. The name of the song is called 'Haddocks'
DOG (6)
A6   51:32   "Well, then," the Cat went on, "you see a dog growls when it's angry, and wags its tail when it's
A2   20: 4   went on eagerly: "There is such a nice little dog, near our house, I should like to show you! A little
T9   194:21   "Then if the dog went away, its temper would remain!" the Queen exclaimed
T9   194: 9   another Subtraction sum. Take a bone from a dog: what remains?"
T9   194:18   "Why, look here!" the Red Queen cried. "The dog would lose its temper, wouldn't it?"
T9   194:11   remain, of course, if I took it--and the dog wouldn't remain: it would come to bite me--and I'm sure I
DOG'S (2)
A6   51:29   "To begin with," said the Cat, "a dog's not mad. You grant that?"
T9   194:15   "Wrong, as usual," said the Red Queen: "the dog's temper would remain."
DOGS (4)
A2   20:20   you'll understand why it is I hate cats and dogs."
T3   135:33   advertisements, you know, when people lose dogs--'answers to the name of "Dash": had on a brass collar'--
A2   20:15   back again, and we wo'n't talk about cats, or dogs either, if you don't like them!" When the Mouse heard
A2   20: 2   conversation. "Are you--are you fond--of--of dogs?" The Mouse did not answer, so Alice went on eagerly:
DOING (11) [See also UNDOING]
T2   127:18   ran very fast for a long time as we've been doing."
A11   86:29   writing very busily on slates. "What are they doing?" Alice whispered to the Gryphon. "They ca'n't have
A6   48:16   "Oh, please mind what you're doing!" cried Alice, jumping up and down in an agony of terror
A8   65: 5   rose-tree, she went on "What have you been doing here?"
T1   108:23   "when I saw all the mischief you had been doing, I was very nearly opening the window, and putting you
T9   193:19   "We gave you the opportunity of doing it," the Red Queen remarked: "but I daresay you've not
A8   63: 9   cut off, you know. So you see, Miss, we're doing our best, afore she comes, to--" At this moment, Five,

DOING (cont.)
```
A4     27:14   an  angry  tone, "Why, Mary Ann, what are you doing out here? Run home this moment, and fetch me a pair of
T6    161: 2   as  nearly  as  possible fell off the wall in doing so) and offered Alice his hand. She watched him a little
T2    126:24              Not that Alice had any idea of doing that. She felt as if she would never be able to talk
T9    195:31   The Red Queen said "That's a poor thin way of doing things. Now here, we mostly have days and nights two or
```
DOLL (2)
```
T5    154:18   bright  thing  that  looked  sometimes like a doll and sometimes like a work-box, and was always in the
T9    204:20      dwindled  down  to  the  size  of a little doll, and was now on the table, merrily running round and
```
DONE (34) [See also UNDONE]
```
A7     58:31   "or you'll be asleep  again  before it's done."
A8     69: 2   argument  was that, if something wasn't done about it in less than no time, she'd have everybody
T8    184:34   "Yes, I  suppose you'd be over when that was done," Alice said thoughtfully: "but don't you think it would
T5    152:25                  "Why, I've done all the screaming already," said the Queen. "What would
AI     3:34   were hammered out--/ And now the tale is done, / And home we steer, a merry crew, / Beneath the setting
T1    115:16   Alice was a little alarmed at what she had done, and went round the room to see if she could find any
T4    139:31   under  which  they  were  dancing, and it was done (as well as she could make it out) by the branches
T8W    21: 8   too  much  in front, no doubt. One would have done as well as two, if you must have them so close--"
T5    149:19                  "But I don't want it done at all!" groaned the poor Queen. "I've been a-dressing
T2    120:27   full  in  sight,  so  there was nothing to be done but start again. This time she came upon a large
A9     70:34   "Somebody  said,"  Alice whispered, "that it's done by everybody minding their own business!"
A5     43:43   into that beautiful garden--how is that to be done, I wonder?" As she said this, she came suddenly upon an
T9    200: 6   repeated  in  despair. "Oh, that'll never be done! I'd better go in at once--" and in she went, and there
T4    140:32   no  business  to be there / After the day was done--/ 'It's very rude of him,' she said, / 'To come and
A11    86:27   of it at all. However, "jurymen" would have done just as well.
T6    166: 9   sneeze in the middle: however, you'll hear it done, maybe--down in the wood yonder--and, when you've once
A5     43:40      as  usual,  "Come,  there's half  my plan done now! How puzzling all these changes are! I'm never sure
T6    163: 4   Dumpty  looked doubtful. "I'd rather see that done on paper," he said.
T6    163:14   and looked at it carefully. "That seems to be done right--" he began.
T6    163:18   queer. As I  was  saying,  that seems to be done right--though I haven't time to look it over thoroughly
A11    86: 9   to look at them--"I wish they'd get the trial done," she thought, "and hand round the refreshments!" But
A2     19:16   way  of  speaking  to  a mouse: she had never done such a thing before, but she remembered having seen, in
A2     18: 3      while  she  was  talking.  "How can I have done that?" she thought. "I must be growing small again." She
A7     59: 3                  "They couldn't have done that, you know," Alice gently remarked. "They'd have been
T5    153: 1                  "That's the way it's done," the Queen said with great decision: "nobody can do two
T5    151:18                  "Yes, but then I had done the things I was punished for," said Alice: "that makes
T5    151:20                  "But if you hadn't done them," the Queen said, "that would have been better still
T8    179:24   off  his  horse  just  as  the Red Knight had done: then he got on again, and the two Knights sat and looked
A11    90:13   word,  I  will just explain to you how it was done. They had a large canvas bag, which tied up at the mouth
A11    90:16                  "I'm glad I've seen that done," thought Alice. "I've so often read in the newspapers,
T2    123:13                  "They're done up close, like a dahlia," said the Tiger-lily: "not
A10    81:20   a little before she gave her answer. "They're done with blacking, I believe."
A10    81:17                  "Why, what are your shoes done with?" said the Gryphon. "I mean, what makes them so
A10    81:22   the  Gryphon  went  on  in a deep voice, "are done with whiting. Now you know."
```
DON'T (143)
```
A9     75: 7   to the Mock Turtle "Drive on, old fellow! Don't be all day about it!" and he went on in these words:--
A2     19:32   perhaps not," said Alice in a soothing tone: "don't be angry about it. And yet I wish I could show you our
T9    194:37   of  one  letter!  Isn't that grand? However, don't be discouraged. You'll come to it in time."
A8     67:44                  "Don't be impertinent," said the King, "and don't look at me
A11    88:28   "Give your evidence," said  the King: "and don't be nervous, or I'll have you executed on the spot."
A4     30:28   high  enough  yet--Oh, they'll do well enough. Don't be particular--Here, Bill! Catch hold of this rope--Will
A5     43:19                  "I don't believe it," said the Pigeon; "but if they do, why, then
T8    186:17   and his voice getting lower and lower, "I don't believe that pudding ever was cooked! In fact, I don't
T8    186:18   that pudding ever was cooked! In fact, I don't believe that pudding ever will be cooked! And yet it was
A12    95:25   interrupting him,) "I'll give him sixpence. I don't believe there's an atom of meaning in it."
A3     22:32   of half those long words, and, what's more, I don't believe you do either!" And the Eaglet bent down its
T3    131:26   I sha'n't!" Alice said rather impatiently. "I don't belong to this railway journey at all--I was in a wood
T3    130:13   in  chorus  means--for I must confess that I don't) "Better say nothing at all. Language is worth a
A6     48:32                  "Oh, don't bother me!" said the Duchess. "I never could abide
T4    147:40   "We must  have  a  bit  of a fight, but I don't care about going on long," said Tweedledum. "What's the
T2    121:11                  "I don't care about the colour," the Tiger-lily remarked. "If
T5    150: 2   she  said "I don't want you to hire me--and I don't care for jam."
A1     12:36   so either way I'll get into the garden, and I don't care which happens!"
A4     31:12   of voices--"Hold  up  his  head--Brandy now--Don't choke him--How was it, old fellow? What happened to you?
T8    182: 4   said  the  Knight;  "but, if they do come, I don't choose to have them running all about."
T5    152:39   what o'clock it is. Consider anything, only don't cry!"
T9    193: 7                  "I don't deny things with my hands," Alice objected.
A9     73:12                  "No," said Alice. "I don't even know what a Mock Turtle is."
A12    94:31   anything of the sort!" said Alice. "Why, you don't even know what they're about!"
T1    118:28   it  seems  to fill my head with ideas--only I don't exactly know what they are! However, somebody killed
A10    84: 4   stuff?"  the Mock Turtle interrupted, "if you don't explain it as you go on? It's by far the most confusing
T8    183: 9                  "Because people don't fall off quite so often, when they've had much practice
A12    96:25                  "Then the words don't fit you," said the King looking round the court with a
T1    114:16   breath.  "Mind  you come up--the regular way--don't get blown up!"
A9     72:20   of  present!" thought Alice. "I'm glad people don't give birthday-presents like that!" But she did not
A5     40: 6   and  that  is  enough,"  / Said his father. "Don't give yourself airs! / Do you think I can listen all day
T5    152:36                  "Oh, don't go on like that!" cried the poor Queen, wringing her
A8     62: 5   heard  one  of  them  say "Look out now, Five! Don't go splashing paint over me like that!"
A6     49:29   (it  had  left  off  sneezing by this time). "Don't grunt," said Alice; "that's not at all a proper way of
T2    122:15   just  beginning  again, she whispered "If you don't hold your tongues, I'll pick you!"
T7    171: 6                  "Don't I tell you?" the King repeated impatiently. "I must have
```

DON'T (cont.)

T1	115:38	a bit: it writes all manner of things that I don't intend--"
T1	108:26	What have you got to say for yourself? Now don't interrupt me!" she went on, holding up one finger. "I'm
T3	129:39	("like the chorus of a song," thought Alice) "Don't keep him waiting, child! Why, his time is worth a
A5	36:32	"I ca'n't remember things as I used--and I don't keep the same size for ten minutes together!"
T1	113: 3	"They don't keep this room so tidy as the other," Alice thought to
T1	115:11	me laugh so that I can hardly hold you! And don't keep your mouth so wide open! All the ashes will get
T8	181: 1	"I don't know," Alice said doubtfully. "I don't want to be
T9	197: 1	she tried to obey the first direction: "and I don't know any soothing lullabies."
A12	95:31	as we needn't try to find any. And yet I don't know," he went on, spreading out the verses on his knee,
T7	177:11	"You don't know how to manage Looking-glass cakes," the Unicorn
A6	48: 6	"You don't know much," said the Duchess; "and that's a fact."
A6	48: 4	"I don't know of any that do," Alice said very politely, feeling
A7	58:21	"I'm afraid I don't know one," said Alice, rather alarmed at the proposal.
T9	193:27	"I don't know," said Alice. "I lost count."
A5	41:10	"I don't know," said the Caterpillar.
T1	116: 5	read, "--for it's all in some language I don't know," she said to herself.
T3	134:25	"And yet I don't know," the Gnat went on in a careless tone: "only think
T7	177: 3	"I'm sure I don't know," the Lion growled out as he lay down again. "There
A3	22:31	"Speak English!" said the Eaglet. "I don't know the meaning of half those long words, and, what's
A9	73:23	lying fast asleep in the sun. (If you don't know what a Gryphon is, look at the picture.) "Up, lazy
A9	76:31	"Well, then," the Gryphon went on, "if you don't know what to uglify is, you are a simpleton."
T6	161: 9	might meet behind," she thought: "And then I don't know what would happen to his head! I'm afraid it would
T6	163:24	"I don't know what you mean by 'glory,'" Alice said.
T2	124:11	"I don't know what you mean by your way," said the Queen: "all
A7	56:37	"I don't know what you mean," said Alice.
T9	199:14	"I don't know what you mean," she said.
T6	162:42	"You don't know what you're talking about!" cried Humpty Dumpty.
T5	149:26	"I don't know what's the matter with it!" the Queen said, in a
T4	139:36	'Here we go round the mulberry bush.' I don't know when I began it, but somehow I felt as if I'd been
A10	80:20	"I don't know where Dinn may be," said the Mock Turtle; "but, if
T8	181:37	bees out--or the bees keep the mice out, I don't know which."
A12	95:17	Don't let him know she liked them best, / For this must ever
A2	19:44	always hated cats: nasty, low, vulgar things! Don't let me hear the name again!"
T9	195:17	"Don't let us quarrel," the White Queen said in an anxious tone
T3	132:23	"--then you don't like all insects?" the Gnat went on, as quietly as if
T8	179: 9	hope it's my dream, and not the Red King's! I don't like belonging to another person's dream," she went on
A4	30:14	hear whispers now and then; such as "Sure, I don't like it, yer honour, at all, at all!" "Do as I tell you,
A8	67:41	"I don't like the look of it at all," said the King: "however, it
A5	43:27	and, if I was, I shouldn't want yours: I don't like them raw."
A2	20:15	talk about cats, or dogs either, if you don't like them!" When the Mouse heard this, it turned round
A8	67:44	"Don't be impertinent," said the King, "and don't look at me like that!" He got behind Alice as he spoke.
T1	115:27	"You will, though," the Queen said, "if you don't make a memorandum of it."
T1	108:32	them tight up, it wouldn't have happened. Now don't make any more excuses, but listen! Number two: you
T3	130: 6	"Don't make excuses," said the Guard: "you should have bought
T1	118:31	thought Alice, suddenly jumping up, "if I don't make haste, I shall have to go back through the
T1	115: 9	"Oh! please don't make such faces, my dear!" she cried out, quite
T6	164: 1	what you mean to do next, as I suppose you don't mean to stop here all the rest of your life."
T5	156:12	wait and pick some?" Alice pleaded. "If you don't mind stopping the boat for a minute."
A6	51:11	"I don't much care where--" said Alice.
A9	71: 5	"I dare say you're wondering why I don't put my arm round your waist," the Duchess said, after a
T5	154: 3	"I don't quite know yet," Alice said very gently. "I should like
T6	167: 5	"I'm afraid I don't quite understand," said Alice.
A7	56:21	in it, and yet it was certainly English. "I don't quite understand you," she said, as politely as she
A4	30:27	this corner--No, tie 'em together first--they don't reach half high enough yet--Oh, they'll do well enough.
T3	132:29	"I don't rejoice in insects at all," Alice explained, "because
A8	68: 2	Alice. "I've read that in some book, but I don't remember where."
T6	166:26	"I see you don't," said Alice.
A7	54:15	but there was nothing on it but tea. "I don't see any wine," she remarked.
T9	194:17	"But I don't see how--"
A9	74:30	for some minutes. Alice thought to herself "I don't see how he can ever finish, if he doesn't begin." But
A5	35:13	"I don't see," said the Caterpillar.
T2	122:26	did so. "It's very hard," she said; "but I don't see what that has to do with it."
A8	67:25	one ca'n't hear oneself speak--and they don't seem to have any rules in particular: at least, if there
T6	166:25	only I don't sing it," he added, as an explanation.
T1	110: 4	"Kitty, can you play chess? Now, don't smile, my dear. I'm asking it seriously. Because, when
A9	74:28	hollow tone. "Sit down, both of you, and don't speak a word till I've finished."
T6	160: 1	"Don't stand chattering to yourself like that," Humpty Dumpty
T4	148: 6	looked round him with a satisfied smile. "I don't suppose," he said, "there'll be a tree left standing,"
T4	145:26	"I hope you don't suppose those are real tears?" Tweedledum interrupted in
A6	49:25	she carried it out into the open air. "If I don't take this child away with me," thought Alice, "they're
A9	72:18	"Oh, don't talk about trouble!" said the Duchess. "I make you a
A11	88:43	"Don't talk nonsense," said Alice more boldly: "you know you're
T3	131:31	"Don't tease so," said Alice, looking about in vain to see
A7	56:38	"Of course you don't!" the Hatter said, tossing his head contemptuously. "I
T3	132: 2	"What, then you don't--" the little voice began, when it was drowned by a
A7	60:27	ask me," said Alice, very much confused, "I don't think--"
A4	27:33	see that the mouse doesn't get out.' Only I don't think," Alice went on, "that they'd let Dinah stop in
T8W	13: 9	"I don't think I can be of any use to him," was Alice's first
T9	197:14	and lay like a heavy lump in her lap. "I don't think it ever happened before, that any one had to take

DON'T (cont.)

T4	146: 5	his brother, and looked up into it. "No, I don't think it is," he said: "at least--not under here. Nohow
A8	65:35	"No, I didn't," said Alice. "I don't think it's at all a pity. I said 'What for?'"
T3	129: 5	mountains--I'm on the only one, but I don't think it's got any name. Principal towns--why, what are
T6	160:21	ask!" Humpty Dumpty growled out. "Of course I don't think so! Why, if ever I did fall off--which there's no
T1	113:11	here are two Castles walking arm in arm--I don't think they can hear me," she went on, as she put her
A8	67:23	"I don't think they play at all fairly," Alice began, in rather a
T7	174:17	"I don't think they'll fight any more to-day," the King said to
T6	163:26	Dumpty smiled contemptuously. "Of course you don't--till I tell you. I meant 'there's a nice knock-down
A9	72:16	"Pray don't trouble yourself to say it any longer than that," said
T2	126:23	to guess her thoughts, for she cried "Faster! Don't try to talk!"
T2	124: 7	are you going? Look up, speak nicely, and don't twiddle your fingers all the time."
T8	187: 1	"No, you don't understand," the Knight said, looking a little vexed.
A7	60: 4	again, so she began very cautiously: "But I don't understand. Where did they draw the treacle from?"
T5	150:10	"I don't understand you," said Alice. "It's dreadfully confusing!
T5	150: 4	"Well, I don't want any to-day, at any rate."
T5	149:19	"But I don't want it done at all!" groaned the poor Queen. "I've been
T8	181: 1	"I don't know," Alice said doubtfully. "I don't want to be anybody's prisoner. I want to be a Queen."
A6	51:22	"But I don't want to go among mad people," Alice remarked.
T3	134:22	it settled again and remarked "I suppose you don't want to lose your name?"
A4	30:20	window, I only wish they could! I'm sure I don't want to stay in here any longer!"
T5	150: 1	Alice couldn't help laughing, as she said "I don't want you to hire me--and I don't care for jam."
A10	81:29	said to the porpoise 'Keep back, please! We don't want you with us!'"
T3	131:33	If you're so anxious to have a joke made, why don't you make one yourself?"
A10	81:36	"Don't you mean 'purpose'?" said Alice.
T5	152:23	"But why don't you scream now?" Alice asked, holding her hands ready to
T9	192:24	"Ridiculous!" cried the Queen. "Why, don't you see, child--" here she broke off with a frown, and,
T8	184:35	that was done," Alice said thoughtfully: "but don't you think it would be rather hard?"
T6	160:16	"Don't you think you'd be safer down on the ground?" Alice went

DOOR (45) [See also FRONT-DOOR]

A2	15:15	golden key and hurried off to the garden door.
A11	91: 3	of sight before the officer could get to the door.
T2	120:23	she found herself actually walking in at the door.
T9	199:19	it, you know." Then he went up and gave the door a kick with one of his great feet. "You let it alone," he
A1	9:40	noticed before, and behind it was a little door about fifteen inches high: she tried the little golden
T9	198:11	till the week after next!" and shut the door again with a bang.
A1	10: 1	Alice opened the door and found that it led into a small passage, not much
A6	46: 9	Alice went timidly up to the door, and knocked.
A4	28:18	of lying down with one elbow against the door, and the other arm curled round her head. Still she went
A4	29:25	Presently the Rabbit came up to the door, and tried to open it; but, as the door opened inwards,
A6	46:44	"he's perfectly idiotic!" And she opened the door and went in.
A6	46:12	First, because I'm on the same side of the door as you are: secondly, because they're making such a noise
A11	91: 7	the court, by the way the people near the door began sneezing all at once.
A6	46:19	on, without attending to her, "if we had the door between us. For instance, if you were inside, you might
A2	18:13	And she ran with all speed back to the little door; but, alas! the little door was shut again, and the
A4	27:10	hall, with the glass table and the little door, had vanished completely.
T9	199:12	"To answer the door?" he said. "What's it been asking of?" He was so hoarse
A4	28:14	any more--As it is, I ca'n't get out at the door--I do wish I hadn't drunk quite so much!"
T1	119: 8	hall, and would have gone straight out at the door in the same way, if she hadn't caught hold of the
A1	12: 5	the right size for going through the little door into that lovely garden. First, however, she waited for a
A7	60:38	this, she noticed that one of the trees had a door leading right into it. "That's very curious!" she thought
A6	46:45	The door led right into a large kitchen, which was full of smoke
T9	199: 7	at the slow drawl in which he spoke. "This door, of course!"
T1	111: 3	in Looking-glass House, if you leave the door of our drawing-room wide open: and it's very like our
A6	46:27	At this moment the door of the house opened, and a large plate came skimming out,
A4	27:21	she came upon a neat little house, on the door of which was a bright brass plate with the name "W.
T9	198: 9	Just then the door opened a little way, and a creature with a long beak put
A4	29:26	the door, and tried to open it; but, as the door opened inwards, and Alice's elbow was pressed hard
A5	38: 3	/ Yet you turned a back-somersault in at the door--/ Pray, what is the reason of that?
T9	199: 5	"Which door?" said the Frog.
T9	199: 3	servant whose business it is to answer the door?" she began angrily.
A1	12:15	but, alas for poor Alice! when she got to the door, she found she had forgotten the little golden key, and
A4	32:12	as she was small enough to get through the door, she ran out of the house, and found quite a crowd of
A1	9:32	down one side and up the other, trying every door, she walked sadly down the middle, wondering how she was
A1	12:36	makes me grow smaller, I can creep under the door: so either way I'll get into the garden, and I don't care
A1	10:12	seemed to be no use in waiting by the little door, so she went back to the table, half hoping she might
A6	46: 8	the other was sitting on the ground near the door, staring stupidly up into the sky.
A7	61: 2	the little golden key, and unlocking the door that led into the garden. Then she set to work nibbling
T9	199:22	At this moment the door was flung open, and a shrill voice was heard singing:--
T6	168:10	And when I found the door was locked, / I pulled and pushed and kicked and knocked
A2	18:13	to the little door; but, alas! the little door was shut again, and the little golden key was lying on
T6	168:12	And when I found the door was shut, / I tried to turn the handle, but--"
T9	196: 2	she were talking to herself. "He came to the door with a corkscrew in his hand--"
A6	45: 5	called him a fish)--and rapped loudly at the door with his knuckles. It was opened by another footman in
T9	199: 8	The Frog looked at the door with his large dull eyes for a minute: then he went

DOOR-POST (1)

T1	119: 8	same way, if she hadn't caught hold of the door-post. She was getting a little giddy with so much

DOORS (3)

A1	9:30	There were doors all round the hall, but they were all locked; and when
T6	160:31	a sudden passion. "You've been listening at doors--and behind trees--and down chimneys--or you couldn't

```
DOORS (cont.)
  A1     9:36   idea was that this might belong to one of the doors of the hall; but, alas! either the locks were too large,
DOORWAY (2)
  A1    10: 6   she  could  not even get her head through the doorway; "and even if my head would go through," thought poor
  T9   198: 1            She was standing before an arched doorway, over which were the words "QUEEN ALICE" in large
DORMOUSE (39)
  A11   88:16                        "Sixteenth," said the Dormouse.
  A11   88:42   "You've  no  right  to  grow  here," said the Dormouse.
  A7    59: 1            "They lived on treacle," said the Dormouse, after thinking a minute or two.
  A7    60: 3            Alice did not wish to offend the Dormouse again, so she began very cautiously: "But I don't
  A7    59:22                        The Dormouse again took a minute or two to think about it, and
  A7    59:19   and  bread-and-butter, and then turned to the Dormouse, and repeated her question. "Why did they live at the
  A7    58:23   Dormouse shall!" they both cried. "Wake up, Dormouse!" And they pinched it on both sides at once.
  A7    58:32   a  time there were three little sisters," the Dormouse began in a great hurry; "and their names were Elsie,
  A11   89: 5   off  staring at the Hatter, and, just as the Dormouse crossed the court, she said, to one of the officers
  A11   89:27   round to see if he would deny it too; but the Dormouse denied nothing, being fast asleep.
  A7    60:30   got  up in great disgust, and walked off: the Dormouse fell asleep instantly, and neither of the others took
  A7    59:38            He moved on as he spoke, and the Dormouse followed him: the March Hare moved into the
  A11   88:13    him into the court, arm-in-arm with the Dormouse. "Fourteenth of March, I think it was," he said.
  A7    60:12   so  confused poor Alice, that she let the Dormouse go on for some time without interrupting it.
  A7    60:20                        The Dormouse had closed its eyes by this time, and was going off
  A7    59:30            "One, indeed!" said the Dormouse indignantly. However, he consented to go on. "And so
  A7    60:34   she  saw them,  they  were trying to put the Dormouse into the teapot.
  A7    56:22                        "The Dormouse is asleep again," said the Hatter, and he poured a
  A7    60: 9   But they were in the well," Alice said to the Dormouse, not choosing to notice this last remark.
  A11   89: 1   but  I  grow  at a reasonable pace," said the Dormouse: "not in that ridiculous fashion." And he got up very
  A11   91:20       out. "Behead that Dormouse! Turn that Dormouse out of court! Suppress him! Pinch him! Off with his
  A11   89:25            "Well, at any rate, the Dormouse said--" the Hatter went on, looking anxiously round
  A11   90: 3            "But what did the Dormouse say?" one of the jury asked.
  A7    58:23                        "Then the Dormouse shall!" they both cried. "Wake up, Dormouse!" And
  A7    56:24            "The Dormouse shook its head impatiently, and said, without opening
  A7    58: 1            Here the Dormouse shook itself, and began singing in its sleep "Twinkle
  A7    58:25            The Dormouse slowly opened its eyes. "I wasn't asleep," it said in
  A7    59:25   and  the  March Hare went "Sh! Sh!" and the Dormouse sulkily remarked "If you ca'n't be civil, you'd
  A11   91:19            "Collar that Dormouse!" the Queen shrieked out. "Behead that Dormouse! Turn
  A7    54: 5   over  its head. "Very uncomfortable for the Dormouse," thought Alice; "only as it's asleep, I suppose it
  A11   91:20       the  Queen shrieked out. "Behead that Dormouse! Turn that Dormouse out of court! Suppress him! Pinch
  A11   91:23   the whole court was in confusion, getting the Dormouse turned out, and, by the time they had settled down
  A7    59: 5            "So they were," said the Dormouse; "very ill."
  A7    54: 2   Hare  and the Hatter were having tea at it: a Dormouse was sitting between them, fast asleep, and the other
  A7    60:11            "Of course they were," said the Dormouse: "well in."
  A7    60:14            "They were learning to draw," the Dormouse went on, yawning and rubbing its eyes, for it was
  A7    55:28   "You  might  just  as  well say," added the Dormouse, which seemed to be talking in its sleep, "that 'I
  A11   88:39   "I  wish  you  wouldn't squeeze so," said the Dormouse, who was sitting next to her. "I can hardly breathe
  A7    59:34            "Treacle," said the Dormouse, without considering at all, this time.
DORMOUSE'S (1)
  A7    59:39   followed  him:  the March Hare moved into the Dormouse's place, and Alice rather unwillingly took the place
DOTH (3)
  A2    17: 3   been changed for Mabel! I'll try and say 'How doth the little--',"  and she crossed her hands on her lap as
  A5    36:34            "Well, I've tried to say 'How doth the little busy bee,' but it all came different!" Alice
  A2    17: 8                        "How doth the little crocodile / Improve his shining tail, / And
DOTTED (1)
  T8   191: 2   lawn  as soft as moss, with little flowerbeds dotted about it here and there. "Oh, how glad I am to get
DOUBLE (2)
  T7   175: 8            "Do you spell 'creature' with a double 'e'?"
  A8    66: 4   live  flamingoes,  and  the  soldiers  had  to double themselves up and stand on their hands and feet, to
DOUBLED-UP (1)
  A8    66:17   wanted  to  send the hedgehog to, and, as the doubled-up soldiers were always getting up and walking off to
DOUBLING (1)
  A6    49:18   a  steam-engine  when she caught it, and kept doubling itself up and straightening itself out again, so that
DOUBT (8)
  A4    32:22            It sounded an excellent plan, no doubt, and very neatly and simply arranged: the only
  T1   107:11   was  lying quite still and trying to purr--no doubt feeling that it was all meant for its good.
  A4    32: 1   what?" thought Alice. But she had not long to doubt, for the next moment a shower of little pebbles came
  T4   141:11   said,  / 'That they could get it clear?' / 'I doubt it,' said the Carpenter, / And shed a bitter tear.
  T8W   21: 7   Then your eyes--they're too much in front, no doubt. One would have done as well as two, if you must have
  A6    46:35            It was, no doubt: only Alice did not like to be told so. "It's really
  A6    49:32   was  the  matter  with  it. There could be no doubt that it had a very turn-up nose, much more like a snout
  T7   174:25            "There's some enemy after her, no doubt," the King said, without even looking round. "That
DOUBTFUL (3)
  A9    71: 7   said, after a pause: "the reason is, that I'm doubtful about the temper of your flamingo. Shall I try the
  T6   163: 4            Humpty Dumpty looked doubtful. "I'd rather see that done on paper," he said.
  A8    63:28            Alice was rather doubtful whether she ought not to lie down on her face like
DOUBTFULLY (6)
  T6   160: 7   "Must  a  name  mean  something?" Alice asked doubtfully.
  A5    43: 9   "I--I'm  a  little  girl," said Alice, rather doubtfully, as she remembered the number of changes she had
  T8   190:22            "I hope so," the Knight said doubtfully: "but you didn't cry so much as I thought you would
  T8   181: 1            "I don't know," Alice said doubtfully. "I don't want to be anybody's prisoner. I want to
  A9    76:29            "Yes," said Alice doubtfully: "it means--to--make--anything--prettier."
  T4   140:10   "Ye-es, pretty well--some poetry," Alice said doubtfully. "Would you tell me which road leads out of the
```

DOUGH (1)
```
T8    190: 8  and  low,  /  As  if  his  mouth  were  full  of  dough,  /  Who  snorted  like  a  buffalo--/  That  summer  evening
```
DOWN (178) [See also KNOCK-DOWN, UPSIDE-DOWN]
```
T6    166:35  are  brown,  /  Take  pen  and  ink,  and  write  it  down."
A4     33: 1  hoarsely  all  the  while,  till  at  last  it  sat  down  a  good  way  off,  panting,  with  its  tongue  hanging  out  of
A1      8:17  maps  and  pictures  hung  upon  pegs.  She  took  down  a  jar  from  one  of  the  shelves  as  she  passed:  it  was
A1      8: 4  after  it,  and  was  just  in  time  to  see  it  pop  down  a  large  rabbit-hole  under  the  hedge.
T4    139: 1                    Just  then  flew  down  a  monstrous  crow,  /  As  black  as  a  tar-barrel;  /  Which
T7    174: 7  in  a  choking  voice:  "each  of  them  has  been  down  about  eighty-seven  times."
T9    192:36  truth--think  before  you  speak--and  write  it  down  afterwards."
T2    128:21  and  fun!"  Alice  got  up  and  curtseyed,  and  sat  down  again.
T9    203: 6  of  the  table,  and  managed  to  pull  herself  down  again.
T8W    14:12  him  round  the  tree,  but  when  he  got  settled  down  again  he  only  said,  as  before,  "Worrity,  worrity!  Can't
T9    192: 9  if  I  really  am  a  Queen,"  she  said  as  she  sat  down  again,  "I  shall  be  able  to  manage  it  quite  well  in  time
A3     24:12  However,  it  was  over  at  last,  and  they  sat  down  again  in  a  ring,  and  begged  the  Mouse  to  tell  them
A5     43:29  the  Pigeon  in  a  sulky  tone,  as  it  settled  down  again  into  its  nest.  Alice  crouched  down  among  the  trees
A11    91:23  turned  out,  and,  by  the  time  they  had  settled  down  again,  the  cook  had  disappeared.
T7    177: 3  I  don't  know,"  the  Lion  growled  out  as  he  lay  down  again.  "There  was  too  much  dust  to  see  anything.  What  a
A10    79: 1  about  like  mad  things  all  this  time,  sat  down  again  very  sadly  and  quietly,  and  looked  at  Alice.
T6    163:15            "You're  holding  it  upside  down!"  Alice  interrupted.
A3     21:14  of  some  authority  among  them,  called  out  "Sit  down,  all  of  you,  and  listen  to  me!  I'll  soon  make  you  dry
A11    88:18  said  to  the  jury;  and  the  jury  eagerly  wrote  down  all  three  dates  on  their  slates,  and  then  added  them  up,
T1    110: 9  for  that  nasty  Knight,  that  came  wriggling  down  among  my  pieces.  Kitty  dear,  let's  pretend--"  And  here  I
T5    157: 1  it  swept  her  straight  off  the  seat,  and  down  among  the  heap  of  rushes.
A5     43:29  down  again  into  its  nest.  Alice  crouched  down  among  the  trees  as  well  as  she  could,  for  her  neck  kept
T3    129:20     shy  so  suddenly.  "It'll  never  do  to  go  down  among  them  without  a  good  long  branch  to  brush  them  away
A2     15:18  through  was  more  hopeless  than  ever:  she  sat  down  and  began  to  cry  again.
A1     12:20  out  with  trying,  the  poor  little  thing  sat  down  and  cried.
T2    122:24                    "Put  your  hand  down,  and  feel  the  ground,"  said  the  Tiger-lily.  "Then  you'll
A6     50:14         So  she  set  the  little  creature  down,  and  felt  quite  relieved  to  see  it  trot  away  quietly  into
T8    186:16  day.  In  fact,"  he  went  on,  holding  his  head  down,  and  his  voice  getting  lower  and  lower,  "I  don't  believe
T1    113:12  me,"  she  went  on,  as  she  put  her  head  closer  down,  "and  I'm  nearly  sure  they  ca'n't  see  me.  I  feel  somehow
A1     10: 2  not  much  larger  than  a  rat-hole:  she  knelt  down  and  looked  along  the  passage  into  the  loveliest  garden
A1      8:13  to  happen  next.  First,  she  tried  to  look  down  and  make  out  what  she  was  coming  to,  but  it  was  too  dark
T9    195:25  reminds  me--"  the  White  Queen  said,  looking  down  and  nervously  clasping  and  unclasping  her  hands,  "we  had
T3    129:17  of  honey  they  must  make!  I  think  I'll  go  down  and--no,  I  wo'n't  go  just  yet,"  she  went  on,  checking
A9     74:29            So  they  sat  down,  and  nobody  spoke  for  some  minutes.  Alice  thought  to
T7    176:10  the  plum-cake,  Monster,"  the  Lion  said,  lying  down  and  putting  his  chin  on  his  paws.  "And  sit  down,  both  of
T6    166:22  she  really  ought  to  listen  to  it;  so  she  sat  down,  and  said  "Thank  you"  rather  sadly,
A2     17:21  It'll  be  no  use  their  putting  their  heads  down  and  saying  'Come  up  again,  dear!'  I  shall  only  look  up
A6     49: 2  she  kept  tossing  the  baby  violently  up  and  down,  and  the  poor  little  thing  howled  so,  that  Alice  could
T2    120: 9            And  so  she  did:  wandering  up  and  down,  and  trying  turn  after  turn,  but  always  coming  back  to
A8     66:13  out  laughing;  and,  when  she  had  got  its  head  down,  and  was  going  to  begin  again,  it  was  very  provoking  to
T7    170:24  (For  the  Messenger  kept  skipping  up  and  down,  and  wriggling  like  an  eel,  as  he  came  along,  with  his
A2     14: 4  was!  Good-bye,  feet!"  (for  when  she  looked  down  at  her  feet,  they  seemed  to  be  almost  out  of  sight,  they
A2     18: 1            As  she  said  this  she  looked  down  at  her  hands,  and  was  surprised  to  see  that  she  had  put
A4     32:27            An  enormous  puppy  was  looking  down  at  her  with  large  round  eyes,  and  feebly  stretching  out
A3     21:15  I'll  soon  make  you  dry  enough!"  They  all  sat  down  at  once,  in  a  large  ring,  with  the  Mouse  in  the  middle.
A10    81:19            Alice  looked  down  at  them,  and  considered  a  little  before  she  gave  her
T5    156:18  to  get  hold  of  the  rushes  a  good  long  way  down  before  breaking  them  off--and  for  a  while  Alice  forgot
T7    176:14  evidently  very  uncomfortable  at  having  to  sit  down  between  the  two  great  creatures;  but  there  was  no  other
A9     74:28  the  Mock  Turtle  in  a  deep,  hollow  tone.  "Sit  down,  both  of  you,  and  don't  speak  a  word  till  I've  finished
T7    176:10  and  putting  his  chin  on  his  paws.  "And  sit  down,  both  of  you,"  (to  the  King  and  the  Unicorn):  "fair  play
A8     66: 8  enough,  under  her  arm,  with  its  legs  hanging  down,  but  generally,  just  as  she  had  got  its  neck  nicely
A9     72:12  said  very  politely,  "if  I  had  it  written  down:  but  I  ca'n't  quite  follow  it  as  you  say  it."
T8W    14:19            So  Alice  sat  down  by  him,  and  spread  out  the  paper  on  her  knees,  and  began.
T1    107: 7  faces  was  this:  first  she  held  the  poor  thing  down  by  its  ear  with  one  paw,  and  then  with  the  other  paw  she
T6    160:32  listening  at  doors--and  behind  trees--and  down  chimneys--or  you  couldn't  have  known  it!"
A11    90:21  that's  all  you  know  about  it,  you  may  stand  down,"  continued  the  King.
A1      9: 5                    Down,  down,  down.  There  was  nothing  else  to  do,  so  Alice  soon
A1      8:27                    Down,  down,  down.  Would  the  fall  never  come  to  an  end?  "I
A1      9: 5            Down,  down,  down.  There  was  nothing  else  to  do,  so  Alice  soon  began
A1      8:27            Down,  down,  down.  Would  the  fall  never  come  to  an  end?  "I  wonder  how
T9    197:13  one  round  head,  and  then  the  other,  rolled  down  from  her  shoulder,  and  lay  like  a  heavy  lump  in  her  lap.
A5     43: 4  them  at  last,  they  must  needs  come  wriggling  down  from  the  sky!  Ugh,  Serpent!"
A12    98: 2  away  some  dead  leaves  that  had  fluttered  down  from  the  trees  upon  her  face.
A4     30:30  bear?--Mind  that  loose  slate--Oh,  it's  coming  down!  Heads  below!"  (a  loud  crash)--"Now,  who  did  that?--It
A5     36:23  "Is  that  all?"  said  Alice,  swallowing  down  her  anger  as  well  as  she  could.
T5    152:35  her  loneliness,  two  large  tears  came  rolling  down  her  cheeks.
A8     67:19  the  whole  head  appeared,  and  then  Alice  put  down  her  flamingo,  and  began  an  account  of  the  game,  feeling
A3     26:38  a  melancholy  tone.  "Nobody  seems  to  like  her,  down  here,  and  I'm  sure  she's  the  best  cat  in  the  world!  Oh,
A4     30:33  it!--That  I  wo'n't,  then!--Bill's  got  to  go  down--Here,  Bill!  The  master  says  you've  got  to  go  down  the
A2     17:21  up  my  mind  about  it:  if  I'm  Mabel,  I'll  stay  down  here.  It'll  be  no  use  their  putting  their  heads  down  and
A2     19:11  this  mouse?  Everything  is  so  out-of-the-way  down  here,  that  I  should  think  very  likely  it  can  talk:  at  any
A2     17:24  that  person,  I'll  come  up:  if  not,  I'll  stay  down  here  till  I'm  somebody  else'--but,  oh  dear!"  cried  Alice,
A1      9: 9  at  tea-time.  Dinah,  my  dear!  I  wish  you  were  down  here  with  me!  There  are  no  mice  in  the  air,  I'm  afraid,
A8     62:17            Seven  flung  down  his  brush,  and  had  just  begun  "Well,  of  all  the  unjust
T7    173:32  more,  and  this  time  a  tear  or  two  trickled  down  his  cheek;  but  not  a  word  would  he  say.
A10    78: 6  recovered  his  voice,  and,  with  tears  running  down  his  cheeks,  he  went  on  again:--
A12    96:23  again,  using  the  ink,  that  was  trickling  down  his  face,  as  long  as  it  lasted.)
```

DOWN (cont.)

A2	17:26	tears, "I do wish they <u>would</u> put their heads down! I am so <u>very</u> tired of being all alone here!"
A1	8:30	Let me see: that would be <u>four</u> thousand miles down, I think--" (for, you see, Alice had learnt several
A12	93:30	Some of the jury wrote it down "important," and some "unimportant." Alice could see this
A7	54:10	of room!" said Alice indignantly, and she sat down in a large arm-chair at one end of the table.
A8	65:43	against each other: however, they got settled down in a minute or two, and the game began.
A6	48:17	you're doing!" cried Alice, jumping up and down in an agony of terror. "Oh, there goes his <u>precious</u> nose!
T9	200:16	them, but the middle one was empty. Alice sat down in it, rather uncomfortable at the silence, and longing
T9	204:10	Already several of the guests were lying down in the dishes, and the soup ladle was walking up the
T1	113: 4	as she noticed several of the chessmen down in the hearth among the cinders; but in another moment,
T6	166: 9	middle: however, you'll hear it done, maybe--down in the wood yonder--and, when you've once heard it,
A5	42:21	serpent. She had just succeeded in curving it down into a graceful zigzag, and was going to dive in among
A6	50:10	grunted again, so violently, that she looked down into its face in some alarm. This time there could be <u>no</u>
T1	112: 2	was through the glass, and had jumped lightly down into the Looking-glass room. The very first thing she did
A1	9:24	the White Rabbit was still in sight, hurrying down it. There was not a moment to be lost: away went Alice
T3	135:14	deeply while two large tears came rolling down its cheeks.
A3	22:33	believe you do either!" And the Eaglet bent down its head to hide a smile: some of the other birds
A8	69:13	King and the executioner ran wildly up and down, looking for it, while the rest of the party went back to
A5	41:25	once or twice, and shook itself. Then it got down off the mushroom, and crawled away into the grass, merely
T9	197: 9	the words," she added, as she put her head down on Alice's other shoulder, "just sing it through to <u>me</u>.
A8	63:28	rather doubtful whether she ought not to lie down on her face like the three gardeners, but she could not
T1	113: 6	with a little "Oh!" of surprise, she was down on her hands and knees watching them. The chessmen were
T12	207:14	she had found the Red Queen: then she went down on her knees on the hearth-rug, and put the kitten and
A8	65: 7	said Two, in a very humble tone, going down on one knee as he spoke, "we were trying--"
A11	90: 8	his teacup and bread-and-butter and went down on one knee. "I'm a poor man, your Majesty," he began.
A2	15:16	Alice! It was as much as she could do, lying down on one side, to look through into the garden with one eye
T5	158:11	please," said Alice, as she put the money down on the counter. For she thought to herself, "They
A4	28:16	and growing, and very soon had to kneel down on the floor: in another minute there was not even room
T6	160:16	"Don't you think you'd be safer down on the ground?" Alice went on, not with any idea of
T4	146:22	he looked at Tweedledee, who immediately sat down on the ground, and tried to hide himself under the
A8	63:32	thought she, "if people had all to lie down on their faces, so that they couldn't see it?" So she
A12	95:27	The jury all wrote down, on their slates, "<u>She</u> doesn't believe there's an atom of
A12	93:22	jury. They were just beginning to write this down on their slates, when the White Rabbit interrupted:
A1	9:31	locked; and when Alice had been all the way down one side and up the other, trying every door, she walked
T7	174:13	just then, and the Lion and the Unicorn sat down, panting, while the King called out "Ten minutes allowed
T8	184:41	The Knight looked down proudly at his helmet, which hung from the saddle. "Yes,"
A4	31:28	"We must burn the house down!" said the Rabbit's voice. And Alice called out, as loud
T7	169: 7	something or other, and whenever one went down, several more always fell over him, so that the ground
A1	9:19	ever eat a bat?" when suddenly, thump! thump! down she came upon a heap of sticks and dry leaves, and the
A1	8: 8	tunnel for some way, and then dipped suddenly down, so suddenly that Alice had not a moment to think about
A5	40: 8	<u>day</u> to <u>such</u> <u>stuff</u>? / <u>Be</u> <u>off</u>, or <u>I'll</u> <u>kick</u> <u>you</u> down-stairs!"
A1	8:24	as this, I shall think nothing of tumbling down-stairs! How brave they'll all think me at home! Why, I
T1	119: 2	She was out of the room in a moment, and ran down stairs--or, at least, it wasn't exactly running, but a
T1	119: 4	running, but a new invention for getting down stairs quickly and easily, as Alice said to herself. She
A11	86:38	shoulders, that all the jurors were writing down "Stupid things!" on their slates, and she could even make
A4	29: 1	mice and rabbits. I almost wish I hadn't gone down that rabbit-hole--and yet--and yet--it's rather curious,
A4	28:12	her neck from being broken. She hastily put down the bottle, saying to herself "That's quite enough--I
A4	30:34	Here, Bill! The master says you've got to go down the chimney!"
A4	30:39	She drew her foot as far down the chimney as she could, and waited till she heard a
A4	30:35	"Oh! So Bill's got to come down the chimney, has he?" said Alice to herself. "Why, they
A4	30:32	did that?--It was Bill, I fancy--Who's to go down the chimney?--Nay, I sha'n't! <u>You</u> do it!--<u>That</u> I wo'n't,
A2	15:24	about four inches deep, and reaching half down the hall.
T8W	21:16	thank-ye," said the Wasp, and Alice tripped down the hill again, quite pleased that she had gone back and
T3	129:28	So, with this excuse, she ran down the hill, and jumped over the first of the six little
T8	190:34	him," she said, as she turned to run down the hill: "and now for the last brook, and to be a Queen!
T8	190:14	"You've only a few yards to go," he said, "down the hill and over that little brook, and then you'll be a
T3	129:18	herself just as she was beginning to run down the hill, and trying to find some excuse for turning shy
A11	90:25	"Then you may <u>sit</u> down," the King replied.
A11	88:17	"Write that down," the King said to the jury; and the jury eagerly wrote
A7	61: 4	she was about a foot high; then she walked down the little passage: and <u>then</u>--she found herself at last
A1	9:32	other, trying every door, she walked sadly down the middle, wondering how she was ever to get out again.
T8W	15:17	Alice put down the newspaper. "I'm afraid you're not well," she said in
T3	129:25	"I think I'll go down the other way," she said after a pause; "and perhaps I
T8W	15: 1	Alice hastily ran her eye down the paper and said "No. It says nothing about brown."
T2	120:19	back upon the house, she set out once more down the path, determined to keep straight on till she got to
T1	115:40	Alice had put '<u>The</u> <u>White</u> <u>Knight</u> <u>is</u> <u>sliding</u> down the poker. He balances <u>very</u> <u>badly</u>'). "That's not a
A1t	7: 1	DOWN THE RABBIT-HOLE
T1	114: 8	The Queen gasped, and sat down: the rapid journey through the air had quite taken away
T2	128: 6	to the tree, and then began slowly walking down the row.
T1	108:34	Snowdrop away by the tail just as I had put down the saucer of milk before her! What, you were thirsty,
T5	156:15	So the boat was left to drift down the stream as it would, till it glided gently in among
TC	209:19	Ever <u>drifting</u> down the stream--/ Lingering in the golden gleam--/ Life, what
T9	202:24	extinguishers, and drank all that trickled down their faces--others upset the decanters, and drank the
A11	86:31	"They're putting down their names," the Gryphon whispered in reply, "for fear
T3	129: 7	why, what <u>are</u> those creatures, making honey down there? They ca'n't be bees--nobody ever saw bees a mile
T3	132:39	the Gnat replied. "Further on, in the wood down there, they've got no names--however, go on with your
A1	9: 5	Down, down, down. There was nothing else to do, so Alice soon began
T8	182:34	the reason hair falls off is because it hangs <u>down</u>--things never fall <u>upwards</u>, you know. It's a plan of my
T1	107:17	to wind up, and had been rolling it up and down till it had all come undone again; and there it was,
A5	43:36	until she had succeeded in bringing herself down to her usual height.

DOWN (cont.)
A1	8:12	for she had plenty of time as she went down to look about her, and to wonder what was going to happen
A5	44: 6	near the house till she had brought herself down to nine inches high.
T8	191: 1	* * * * * * * * * * across, and threw herself down to rest on a lawn as soft as moss, with little flowerbeds
T2	122:13	Alice said in a soothing tone, and, stooping down to the daisies, who were just beginning again, she
A2	19:42	indeed!" cried the Mouse, who was trembling down to the end of its tail. "As if I would talk on such a
T9	204:20	longer at her side--she had suddenly dwindled down to the size of a little doll, and was now on the table,
A5	42:19	up to her head, she tried to get her head down to them, and was delighted to find that her neck would
T9	204:15	dishes, guests, and candles came crashing down together in a heap on the floor.
T8	179:14	dressed in crimson armour, came galloping down upon her, brandishing a great club. Just as he reached
A12	97:10	pack rose up into the air, and came flying down upon her; she gave a little scream, half of fright and
T1	108:19	led to a scramble, in which the ball rolled down upon the floor, and yards and yards of it got unwound
A5	42:10	be found: all she could see, when she looked down, was an immense length of neck, which seemed to rise like
A1	8: 5	In another moment down went Alice after it, never once considering how in the
A1	8:10	herself before she found herself falling down what seemed to be a very deep well.
A10	82:34	Alice said nothing: she had sat down with her face in her hands, wondering if anything would
A4	28:18	for this, and she tried the effect of lying down with one elbow against the door, and the other arm curled
T12	207:33	she prattled on, as she settled comfortably down, with one elbow on the rug, and her chin in her hand, to
A3	25: 1	a long tail, certainly," said Alice, looking down with wonder at the Mouse's tail; "but why do you call it
A7	55: 2	"It wasn't very civil of you to sit down without being invited," said the March Hare.
T1	119: 6	fingers on the hand-rail, and floated gently down without even touching the stairs with her feet: then she
A1	8:27	Down, down, down. Would the fall never come to an end? "I wonder how many
A11	86:30	Gryphon. "They ca'n't have anything to put down yet, before the trial's begun."

DOWNWARDS (4)
T8	185:24	"How can you go on talking so quietly, head downwards?" Alice asked, as she dragged him out by the feet,
A12	93: 5	in her haste, she had put the Lizard in head downwards, and the poor little thing was waving its tail about
T8	186: 4	working all the same. In fact, the more head-downwards I am, the more I keep inventing new things."
A1	8:41	among the people that walk with their heads downwards! The antipathies, I think--" (she was rather glad

DOZE (1)
A7	60:21	eyes by this time, and was going off into a doze; but, on being pinched by the Hatter, it woke up again

DOZING (1)
A1	9:15	which way she put it. She felt that she was dozing off, and had just begun to dream that she was walking

DRAGGED (2)
T2	126:26	still the Queen cried "Faster! Faster!" and dragged her along. "Are we nearly there?" Alice managed to
T8	185:25	quietly, head downwards?" Alice asked, as she dragged him out by the feet, and laid him in a heap on the

DRAGGLED (1)
A3	21: 2	that assembled on the bank--the birds with draggled feathers, the animals with their fur clinging close

-DRAGON-FLIES [See SNAP-DRAGON-FLIES]
DRAGON-FLY (1) [See also SNAP-DRAGON-FLY]
T3	133:11	"And there's the Dragon-fly."

DRAINED (1)
AI	3:25	And ever, as the story drained / The wells of fancy dry, / And faintly strove that

DRANK (3)
T9	202:24	upon their heads like extinguishers, and drank all that trickled down their faces--others upset the
T7	174: 2	impatiently. But Hatta only munched away, and drank some more tea.
T9	202:25	their faces--others upset the decanters, and drank the wine as it ran off the edges of the table--and three

DRAW (10)
T5	153:10	the Queen said in a pitying tone. "Try again: draw a long breath, and shut your eyes."
A5	42:24	been wandering, when a sharp hiss made her draw back in a hurry: a large pigeon had flown into her face,
T9	199:37	"'O Looking-Glass creatures,' quoth Alice, 'draw near! / 'Tis an honour to see me, a favour to hear: /
A7	59:33	"What did they draw?" said Alice, quite forgetting her promise.
A7	60:14	"They were learning to draw," the Dormouse went on, yawning and rubbing its eyes, for
T3	131:21	as a message by the telegraph--" "She must draw the train herself the rest of the way--," and so on.
A7	60: 4	"But I don't understand. Where did they draw the treacle from?"
A7	60: 7	said the Hatter; "so I should think you could draw treacle out of a treacle-well--eh, stupid?"
A7	60: 6	"You can draw water out of a water-well," said the Hatter; "so I should
A7	59:32	three little sisters--they were learning to draw, you know--"

DRAWING (1)
A7	60:25	muchness'--did you ever see such a thing as a drawing of a muchness!"

DRAWING-ROOM (2)
T1	110:33	the glass--that's just the same as our drawing-room, only the things go the other way. I can see all
T1	111: 3	House, if you leave the door of our drawing-room wide open: and it's very like our passage as far

DRAWL (1)
T9	199: 6	almost stamped with irritation at the slow drawl in which he spoke. "This door, of course!"

DRAWLING (2)
A9	76:39	that used to come once a week: he taught us Drawling, Stretching, and Fainting in Coils."
A9	76:38	ancient and modern, with Seaography: then Drawling--the Drawling-master was an old conger-eel, that used

DRAWLING-MASTER (1)
A9	76:38	modern, with Seaography: then Drawling--the Drawling-master was an old conger-eel, that used to come once

DREAD (1)
TI	103:19	Come, hearken then, ere voice of dread, / With bitter tidings laden, / Shall summon to

DREADFUL (5)
T9	204: 1	to herself, as well as she could in the dreadful confusion that was beginning.
T9	194:24	she couldn't help thinking to herself "What dreadful nonsense we are talking!"
A6	46:36	did not like to be told so. "It's really dreadful," she muttered to herself, "the way all the creatures
A10	81:45	an impatient tone: "explanations take such a dreadful time."
T7	178:10	over her ears, vainly trying to shut out the dreadful uproar.

DREADFULLY (8)
T5	150:10	"I don't understand you," said Alice. "It's dreadfully confusing!"
A8	67: 6	she, "what would become of me? They're dreadfully fond of beheading people here: the great wonder is,

DREADFULLY (cont.)

A8   67:24 a complaining tone, "and they all quarrel so dreadfully one ca'n't hear oneself speak--and they don't seem

A10   83: 7 position in dancing," Alice said; but she was dreadfully puzzled by the whole thing, and longed to change

A7   56:19   Alice felt dreadfully puzzled. The Hatter's remark seemed to her to have

A7   58: 7   "How dreadfully savage!" exclaimed Alice.

A6   50:16 she said to herself, "it would have made a dreadfully ugly child: but it makes rather a handsome pig, I

T5   149:22 got some one else to dress her, she was so dreadfully untidy. "Every single thing's crooked," Alice

DREAM (20) [See also HALF-DREAM]

A12   98:16 dreaming after a fashion, and this was her dream:--

A12   98:23 the strange creatures of her little sister's dream.

T4   145: 9 Why, you're only a sort of thing in his dream!"

TC   209:21 in the golden gleam--/ Life, what is it but a dream?

T3   130:16   "I shall dream about a thousand pounds to-night, I know I shall!"

T8   179: 8 of the same dream. Only I do hope it's my dream, and not the Red King's! I don't like belonging to

T12 207: 3 severity. "You woke me out of oh! such a nice dream! And you've been along with me, Kitty--all through the

A12   98:10 sister kissed her, and said "It was a curious dream, dear, certainly; but now run in to your tea: it's

T12 207:30 must be the reason you were so untidy in my dream--Dinah! Do you know that you're scrubbing a White Queen?

A12   98:12 she ran, as well she might, what a wonderful dream it had been.

T12 208: 9 either me or the Red King. He was part of my dream, of course--but then I was part of his dream, too! Was

A12   99: 8 many a strange tale, perhaps even with the dream of Wonderland of long ago; and how she would feel with

T8   179: 8 "unless--unless we're all part of the same dream. Only I do hope it's my dream, and not the Red King's! I

A12   98: 6   "Oh, I've had such a curious dream!" said Alice. And she told her sister, as well as she

T8   179:10 I don't like belonging to another person's dream," she went on in a rather complaining tone: "I've a

A1   9:16 she was dozing off, and had just begun to dream that she was walking hand in hand with Dinah, and was

T12 207:38 if only you'd been really with me in my dream, there was one thing you would have enjoyed--I had such

T12 208: 9 dream, of course--but then I was part of his dream, too! Was it the Red King, Kitty? You were his wife, my

T4   145:13 "Besides, if I'm only a sort of thing in his dream, what are you, I should like to know?"

T4   145:19 "when you're only one of the things in his dream. You know very well you're not real."

DREAM-CHILD (1)

AI   3:21 silence won, / In fancy they pursue / The dream-child moving through a land / Of wonders wild and new, /

DREAMED (3)

A12   98:17   First, she dreamed about little Alice herself: once again the tiny hands

T12t 207: 1   WHICH DREAMED IT?

T12 208: 5 "Now, Kitty, let's consider who it was that dreamed it all. This is a serious question, my dear, and you

DREAMILY (2)

T7   175:26   The Unicorn looked dreamily at Alice, and said "Talk, child."

TC   209: 2 boat, beneath a sunny sky / Lingering onward dreamily / In an evening of July--

DREAMING (9)

T4   145: 2 said Tweedledee: "and what do you think he's dreaming about?"

T8   179: 4 her first thought was that she must have been dreaming about the Lion and the Unicorn and those queer

T4   145: 5 his hands triumphantly. "And if he left off dreaming about you, where do you suppose you'd be?"

A12   98:15 her wonderful Adventures, till she too began dreaming after a fashion, and this was her dream:--

T8   179: 7 had tried to cut the plum-cake, "So I wasn't dreaming, after all," she said to herself, "unless--unless

TC   209:17   In a Wonderland they lie, / Dreaming as the days go by, / Dreaming as the summers die:

TC   209:18 they lie, / Dreaming as the days go by, / Dreaming as the summers die:

TI   103: 2 Child of the pure unclouded brow / And dreaming eyes of wonder! / Though time be fleet, and I and

T4   145: 1   "He's dreaming now," said Tweedledee: "and what do you think he's

DREAM-RUSHES (1)

T5   156:37 only a very little while--and these, being dream-rushes, melted away almost like snow, as they lay in

DREAMS (1)

AI   4: 5 a gentle hand, / Lay it where Childhood's dreams are twined / In Memory's mystic band. / Like pilgrim's

DREAMY (2)

A1   9:12 sleepy, and went on saying to herself, in a dreamy sort of way, "Do cats eat bats? Do cats eat bats?" and

AI   3: 8 cruel Three! In such an hour, / Beneath such dreamy weather, / To beg a tale of breath too weak / To stir

DRESS (3)

T5   149:22 to Alice, if she had got some one else to dress her, she was so dreadfully untidy. "Every single thing's

T1   109:14 when they wake up in the summer, Kitty, they dress themselves all in green, and dance about--whenever the

T4   147:11 of the umbrella: "only she must help us to dress up, you know."

DRESSED (6)

T9   198:14 got up and hobbled slowly towards her: he was dressed in bright yellow, and had enormous boots on.

T8   179:13   of "Ahoy! Ahoy! Check!" and a Knight, dressed in crimson armour, came galloping down upon her,

T8   181:13   He was dressed in tin armour, which seemed to fit him very badly, and

T3   131:23   But the gentleman dressed in white paper leaned forwards and whispered in her

T3   130:22 gentleman sitting opposite to her, (he was dressed in white paper), "ought to know which way she's going,

A2   15:27 It was the White Rabbit returning, splendidly dressed, with a pair of white kid-gloves in one hand and a

-DRESSING [See A-DRESSING]

DREW (10)

A10   82: 8 coming different, and then the Mock Turtle drew a long breath, and said "That's very curious!"

A7   60:15 for it was getting very sleepy; "and they drew all manner of things--everything that begins with an M--

T2   123:44   A little provoked, she drew back, and, after looking everywhere for the Queen (whom

T3   134: 9 "Crawling at your feet," said the Gnat (Alice drew her feet back in some alarm), "you may observe a

A4   30:39   She drew her foot as far down the chimney as she could, and waited

A5   36:12 making such very short remarks, and she drew herself up and said, very gravely, "I think you ought to

T9   195:14   But the Red Queen drew herself up rather stiffly, and said "Queens never make

T3   132: 6 had put his head out of the window, quietly drew it in and said "It's only a brook we have to jump over."

A10   78: 1   The Mock Turtle sighed deeply, and drew the back of one flapper across his eyes. He looked at

T8   179:23 This time it was a White Knight. He drew up at Alice's side, and tumbled off his horse just as the

DRIED (1)

A2   15:26 of feet in the distance, and she hastily dried her eyes to see what was coming. It was the White Rabbit

DRIEST (1)
A3   22: 2   air. "Are you all ready? This is the driest thing I know. Silence all round, if you please!
DRIFT (1)
T5   156:15   So the boat was left to drift down the stream as it would, till it glided gently in
DRIFTING (1)
TC   209:19   Ever drifting down the stream--/ Lingering in the golden gleam--/
DRINK (12)
A4   28: 6   she said to herself, "whenever I eat or drink anything: so I'll just see what this bottle does. I do
T1   111: 1   Perhaps Looking-glass milk isn't good to drink--but oh, Kitty! now we come to the passage. You can just
A1   10:17   the bottle was a paper label, with the words "DRINK ME" beautifully printed on it in large letters.
A4   28: 3   There was no label this time with the words "DRINK ME," but nevertheless she uncorked it and put it to her
A1   10:19   It was all very well to say "Drink me," but the wise little Alice was not going to do that
T9   200: 2   ink, / Or anything else that is pleasant to drink: / Mix sand with the cider, and wool with the wine--/
A1   11: 3   and she had never forgotten that, if you drink much from a bottle marked "poison," it is almost certain
T8   189:14   / But chiefly for his wish that he / Might drink my noble health.
A4   33:12   it to be managed? I suppose I ought to eat or drink something or other; but the great question is 'What'?"
A4   34: 2   that looked like the right thing to eat or drink under the circumstances. There was a large mushroom
T9   202:20   guess," said the Red Queen. "Meanwhile, we'll drink your health--Queen Alice's health!" she screamed at the
T8   189: 5   I get my wealth--/ And very gladly will I drink / Your Honour's noble health.'
DRINKING (2)
A7   58:36   a great interest in questions of eating and drinking.
T9   202:22   top of her voice, and all the guests began drinking it directly, and very queerly they managed it: some
DRIPPING (2)
T5   156:32   so far off, as, with flushed cheeks and dripping hair and hands, she scrambled back into her place,
A3   21: 3   their fur clinging close to them, and all dripping wet, cross, and uncomfortable.
DRIVE (2)
A9   75: 7   At last the Gryphon said to the Mock Turtle "Drive on, old fellow! Don't be all day about it!" and he went
A6   46:37   way all the creatures argue. It's enough to drive one crazy!"
-DRIVER [See ENGINE-DRIVER]
DRIVES (1)
T3   130: 8   chorus of voices went on with "The man that drives the engine. Why, the smoke alone is worth a thousand
DROP (3) [See also SNOWDROP]
A1   8:20   it was empty: she did not like to drop the jar, for fear of killing somebody underneath, so
T8   189:19   foot / Into a left-hand shoe, / Or if I drop upon my toe / A very heavy weight, / I weep, for it
T1   115: 8   so with laughter that she nearly let him drop upon the floor.
DROPPED (6)
A7   55:32   said the Hatter, and here the conversation dropped, and the party sat silent for a minute, while Alice
A11   90: 7   The miserable Hatter dropped his teacup and bread-and-butter and went down on one
A2   18: 8   of this was the fan she was holding, and she dropped it hastily, just in time to save herself from
A2   15:34   please, Sir--" The Rabbit started violently, dropped the white kid-gloves and the fan, and scurried away
A4   27: 5   sure as ferrets are ferrets! Where can I have dropped them, I wonder?" Alice guessed in a moment that it was
T7   178: 9   being interrupted in their feast, before she dropped to her knees, and put her hands over her ears, vainly
DROPPING (2)
A10   78:36   first figure," said the Mock Turtle, suddenly dropping his voice; and the two creatures, who had been
T1   110: 1   blows--oh, that's very pretty!" cried Alice, dropping the ball of worsted to clap her hands. "And I do so
DROWNED (2)
T3   132: 2   don't--" the little voice began, when it was drowned by a shrill scream from the engine, and everybody
A2   19: 3   be punished for it now, I suppose, by being drowned in my own tears! That will be a queer thing, to be
DRUM (1)
T7   178:11   "If that doesn't 'drum them out of town,'" she thought to herself, "nothing ever
DRUMMED (1)
T7   173: 4   them brown: / Some gave them plum-cake and drummed them out of town."
DRUMS (2)
T7   177:22   But before Alice could answer him, the drums began.
T7   174:18   the King said to Hatta: "go and order the drums to begin." And Hatta went bounding away like a
DRUNK (2)
A4   28:10   sooner than she had expected: before she had drunk half the bottle, she found her head pressing against the
A4   28:14   get out at the door--I do wish I hadn't drunk quite so much!"
DRY (13)
T7   174:16   Alice took a piece to taste, but it was very dry.
A3   23:14   running half an hour or so, and were quite dry again, the Dodo suddenly called out "The race is over!"
A3   21: 5   The first question of course was, how to get dry again: they had a consultation about this, and after a few
AI   3:26   as the story drained / The wells of fancy dry, / And faintly strove that weary one / To put the subject
T2   127:29   ate it as well as she could: and it was very dry: and she thought she had never been so nearly choked in
T4   140:36   sea was wet as wet could be, / The sands were dry as dry. / You could not see a cloud, because / No cloud
A3   21:15   of you, and listen to me! I'll soon make you dry enough!" They all sat down at once, in a large ring, with
A10   82:26   turns out his toes. / When the sands are all dry, he is gay as a lark, / And will talk in contemptuous
A1   9:19   down she came upon a heap of sticks and dry leaves, and the fall was over.
A3   22:27   in a melancholy tone: "it doesn't seem to dry me at all."
A3   21:18   she would catch a bad cold if she did not get dry very soon.
A3   23: 1   tone, "was that the best thing to get us dry would be a Caucus-race."
T4   140:36   wet as wet could be, / The sands were dry as dry. / You could not see a cloud, because / No cloud was in
DUCHESS (39)
A8   65:28   "Very," said Alice. "Where's the Duchess?"
A6   45:13   the other, saying, in a solemn tone, "For the Duchess. An invitation from the Queen to play croquet." The
A6   48: 3   "They all can," said the Duchess; "and most of 'em do."
A6   48: 6   "You don't know much," said the Duchess; "and that's a fact."
A6   47:15   "It's a Cheshire-Cat," said the Duchess, "and that's why. Pig!"
A6   48:11   throwing everything within her reach at the Duchess and the baby--the fire-irons came first; then followed
A9   70:32   "'Tis so," said the Duchess: "and the moral of that is--'Oh, 'tis love, 'tis love,

DUCHESS (cont.)

A9	72: 5	"I quite agree with you," said the Duchess; "and the moral of that is--'Be what you would seem to
A9	72:27	"Just about as much right," said the Duchess, "as pigs have to fly; and the m----"
A9	70: 2	see you again, you dear old thing!" said the Duchess, as she tucked her arm affectionately into Alice's,
A9	72:23	"Thinking again?" the Duchess asked, with another dig of her sharp little chin.
A9	72:34	"A fine day, your Majesty!" the Duchess began in a low, weak voice.
A9	70:16	She had quite forgotten the Duchess by this time, and was a little startled when she heard
A6	48:27	"Talking of axes," said the Duchess, "chop off her head!"
A9	70:36	well! It means much the same thing," said the Duchess, digging her sharp little chin into Alice's shoulder
A9	70:22	"Tut, tut, child!" said the Duchess. "Everything's got a moral, if only you can find it."
A9	71:11	"Very true," said the Duchess: "flamingoes and mustard both bite. And the moral of
A9	72:18	"Oh, don't talk about trouble!" said the Duchess. "I make you a present of everything I've said as yet
A6	48:32	"Oh, don't bother me!" said the Duchess. "I never could abide figures!" And with that she
A8	69:11	and, by the time he had come back with the Duchess, it had entirely disappeared: so the King and the
A4	27: 3	it muttering to itself, "The Duchess! The Duchess! Oh my dear paws! Oh my fur and whiskers! She'll get
A2	15:30	to himself, as he came, "Oh! The Duchess, the Duchess! Oh! Wo'n't she be savage if I've kept her waiting!"
A9	72:14	nothing to what I could say if I chose," the Duchess replied, in a pleased tone.
A9	71: 6	why I don't put my arm round your waist," the Duchess said, after a pause: "the reason is, that I'm doubtful
A6	48:20	"If everybody minded their own business," the Duchess said, in a hoarse growl, "the world would go round a
A6	49:10	You may nurse it a bit, if you like!" the Duchess said to Alice, flinging the baby at her as she spoke.
A6	49: 1	While the Duchess sang the second verse of the song, she kept tossing
A9	70: 7	"When I'm a Duchess," she said to herself (not in a very hopeful tone,
A6	47: 7	certainly too much of it in the air. Even the Duchess sneezed occasionally; and as for the baby, it was
A4	27: 3	and she heard it muttering to itself, "The Duchess! The Duchess! Oh my dear paws! Oh my fur and whiskers!
A2	15:30	muttering to himself, as he came, "Oh! The Duchess, the Duchess! Oh! Wo'n't she be savage if I've kept
A6	46: 2	"From the Queen. An invitation for the Duchess to play croquet."
A9	72:39	The Duchess took her choice, and was gone in a moment.
A6	48:13	shower of saucepans, plates, and dishes. The Duchess took no notice of them even when they hit her; and the
A6	47: 1	full of smoke from one end to the other: the Duchess was sitting on a three-legged stool in the middle,
A9	70:26	keeping so close to her: first because the Duchess was very ugly; and secondly, because she was exactly
A9	71:14	"Right, as usual," said the Duchess: "what a clear way you have of putting things!"
A9	71:17	"Of course it is," said the Duchess, who seemed ready to agree to everything that Alice
A8	69: 7	of nothing else to say but "It belongs to the Duchess: you'd better ask her about it."

DUCHESS'S (3)

A11	91: 5	The next witness was the Duchess's cook. She carried the pepper-box in her hand, and
A12	98:29	once more the pig-baby was sneezing on the Duchess's knee, while plates and dishes crashed around it--
A9	72:29	But here, to Alice's great surprise, the Duchess's voice died away, even in the middle of her favourite

DUCK (4)

A3	22:15	"Found what?" said the Duck.
A2	20:23	animals that had fallen into it: there was a Duck and a Dodo, a Lory and an Eaglet, and several other
A3	22:19	well enough, when I find a thing," said the Duck: "it's generally a frog, or a worm. The question is, what
A10	82:24	me too brown, I must sugar my hair.' / As a duck with his eyelids, so he with his nose / Trims his belt

DULL (4)

A9	75: 3	the Mock Turtle angrily. "Really you are very dull!"
A1	13: 3	things to happen, that it seemed quite dull and stupid for life to go on in the common way.
T9	199: 8	The Frog looked at the door with his large dull eyes for a minute: then he went nearer and rubbed it with
A12	98:36	to open them again, and all would change to dull reality--the grass would be only rustling in the wind,

DUM (2)

T4	138: 9	by a voice coming from the one marked 'DUM.'
T4	138: 3	which in a moment, because one of them had 'DUM' embroidered on his collar, and the other 'DEE.' "I

DUNCE (1)

A11	89:18	said the King sharply. "Do you take me for a dunce? Go on!"

DURING (1)

T8	186: 7	after a pause, "was inventing a new pudding during the meat-course."

DUST (3) [See also SAWDUST]

T1	115: 2	on the table, she thought she might as well dust him a little, he was so covered with ashes.
T7	173:17	were fighting. They were in such a cloud of dust, that at first Alice could not make out which was which;
T7	177: 4	out as he lay down again. "There was too much dust to see anything. What a time the Monster is, cutting up

DUSTED (1)

T1	115: 5	in the air by an invisible hand, and being dusted: he was far too much astonished to cry out, but his

DUSTY (1)

T3	129:24	little toss of the head), 'only it was so dusty and hot, and the elephants did tease so!'"

DWINDLED (1)

T9	204:19	was no longer at her side--she had suddenly dwindled down to the size of a little doll, and was now on the

D'YE (3)

T3	137:27	stay there long. I'll just call and say 'How d'ye do?' and ask them the way out of the wood. If I could
T4	139:22	"The first thing in a visit is to say 'How d'ye do?' and shake hands!" And here the two brothers gave
T4	140: 4	dancing with. "It would never do to say 'How d'ye do?' now," she said to herself: "we seem to have got

DYE (1)

T8	188:10	But I was thinking of a plan / To dye one's whiskers green, / And always use so large a fan /

-E-

E (1)
T7   175: 8   "Do you spell 'creature' with a double 'e'?"
EACH (28)
T4   141:18   do with more than four, / To give a hand to each.'
T5   151:22   and better!" Her voice went higher with each "better," till it got quite to a squeak at last.
A5   39: 6   his father, "I took to the law, / And argued each case with my wife, / And the muscular strength, which it
T4   138: 8   the word 'TWEEDLE' was written at the back of each collar, when she was startled by a voice coming from the
A5   41:37   go, and broke off a bit of the edge with each hand.
T7   174: 7   on very well," he said in a choking voice: "each of them has been down about eighty-seven times."
T4   139:23   shake hands!" And here the two brothers gave each other a hug, and then they held out the two hands that
T4   139:12   But the fat little men only looked at each other and grinned.
T9   192:31   The two Queens looked at each other, and the Red Queen remarked, with a little shudder,
A5   35: 1   The Caterpillar and Alice looked at each other for some time in silence: at last the Caterpillar
T8   179:25   again, and the two Knights sat and looked at each other for some time without speaking. Alice looked from
A8   65:43   about in all directions, tumbling up against each other: however, they got settled down in a minute or two,
T12   207:15   and put the kitten and the Queen to look at each other. "Now Kitty!" she cried, clapping her hands
T7   175:30   "Well, now that we have seen each other," said the Unicorn, "if you'll believe in me, I'll
T8   179:37   Red Knight, and they began banging away at each other with such fury that Alice got behind a tree to be
T1   109: 5   when the day came. Or--let me see--suppose each punishment was to be going without a dinner: then, when
T7   170:25   with his great hands spread out like fans on each side.)
T6   165: 8   "And a long way beyond it on each side," Alice added.
A10   82: 3   the two creatures got so close to her, one on each side, and opened their eyes and mouths so very wide; but
T9   198: 2   words "QUEEN ALICE" in large letters, and on each side of the arch there was a bell-handle; one was marked
T9   192:13   the White Queen sitting close to her, one on each side: she would have liked very much to ask them how they
T9   203: 2   speech: the two Queens pushed her so, one on each side, that they nearly lifted her up into the air. "I
A11   86: 4   before them, in chains, with a soldier on each side to guard him; and near the King was the White Rabbit
A4   32:43   the stick, running a very little way forwards each time and a long way back, and barking hoarsely all the
T9   203:17   fireworks at the top. As to the bottles, they each took a pair of plates, which they hastily fitted on as
T4   144:28   look at him!" the brothers cried, and they each took one of Alice's hands, and led her up to where the
A10   78:21   "Each with a lobster as a partner!" cried the Gryphon.
T4   138: 1   They were standing under a tree, each with an arm round the other's neck, and Alice knew which
EAGER (8)
TC   209:14   Children yet, the tale to hear, / Eager eye and willing ear, / Lovingly shall nestle near.
TC   209: 5   Children three that nestle near, / Eager eye and willing ear, / Pleased a simple tale to hear--
T5   156:22   dipping into the water--while with bright eager eyes she caught at one bunch after another of the
A12   98:18   were clasped upon her knee, and the bright eager eyes were looking up into hers--she could hear the very
T4   142: 2   But four young Oysters hurried up, / All eager for the treat: / Their coats were brushed, their faces
T8   190:17   off first?" he added as Alice turned with an eager look in the direction to which he pointed. "I sha'n't be
A8   63:14   of many footsteps, and Alice looked round, eager to see the Queen.
A12   99: 7   children, and make their eyes bright and eager with many a strange tale, perhaps even with the dream of
EAGERLY (17)
A9   77:22   did you manage on the twelfth?" Alice went on eagerly.
T2   123:28   Alice looked round eagerly and found that it was the Red Queen. "She's grown a
A8   68: 8   fetch the executioner myself," said the King eagerly, and he hurried off.
T8   186:26   "Not very nice alone," he interrupted, quite eagerly: "but you've no idea what a difference it makes,
T7   175:19   "This is a child!" Haigha replied eagerly, coming in front of Alice to introduce her, and
A3   26:26   Alice replied eagerly, for she was always ready to talk about her pet:
T2   123: 9   "Is she like me?" Alice asked eagerly, for the thought crossed her mind, "There's another
A3   26:43   footsteps in the distance, and she looked up eagerly, half hoping that the Mouse had changed his mind, and
T9   202:27   into the dish of roast mutton, and began eagerly lapping up the gravy, "just like pigs in a trough!"
A10   84:12   Turtle would be so kind," Alice replied, so eagerly that the Gryphon said, in a rather offended tone, "Hm!
T9   197:22   even make out words, and she listened so eagerly that, when the two great heads suddenly vanished from
A10   79:15   us, and he's treading on my tail. / See how eagerly the lobsters and the turtles all advance! / They are
A2   20: 3   The Mouse did not answer, so Alice went on eagerly: "There is such a nice little dog, near our house, I
T7   174:21   up. "Look, look!" she cried, pointing eagerly. "There's the White Queen running across the country!"
A11   88:18   the King said to the jury; and the jury eagerly wrote down all three dates on their slates, and then
T9   194:41   "I know that!" Alice cried eagerly. "You take some flour--"
T7   176: 3   "Ah, what is it, now?" the Unicorn cried eagerly. "You'll never guess! I couldn't."
EAGLET (3)
A2   20:23   there was a Duck and a Dodo, a Lory and an Eaglet, and several other curious creatures. Alice led the way
A3   22:33   more, I don't believe you do either!" And the Eaglet bent down its head to hide a smile: some of the other
A3   22:31   "Speak English!" said the Eaglet. "I don't know the meaning of half those long words,
EAR (21)
A6   47:11   lying on the hearth and grinning from ear to ear.
A7   55:38   it every now and then, and holding it to his ear.
T6   167:22   loud and clear: / I went and shouted in his ear."
T7   172:27   and stooping so as to get close to the King's ear. Alice was sorry for this, as she wanted to hear the news
A6   49:24   knot, and then keep tight hold of its right ear and left foot, so as to prevent its undoing itself), she
A8   65:31   upon tiptoe, put his mouth close to her ear, and whispered "She's under sentence of execution."
T6   160:40   with me!" And he grinned almost from ear to ear, as he leant forwards (and as nearly as possible fell off
T9   201:36   solemnly, putting her mouth close to Alice's ear, "her White Majesty knows a lovely riddle--all in poetry--
T9   201:39   the White Queen murmured into Alice's other ear, in a voice like the cooing of a pigeon. "It would be such
TC   209:14   the tale to hear, / Eager eye and willing ear, / Lovingly shall nestle near.

EAR (cont.)
T3	131:24	paper leaned forwards and whispered in her ear, "Never mind what they all say, my dear, but take a
T1	110:18	her old nurse by shouting suddenly in her ear, "Nurse! Do let's pretend that I'm a hungry hyaena and
TC	209: 5	that nestle near, / Eager eye and willing ear, / Pleased a simple tale to hear--
T3	131:14	And an extremely small voice, close to her ear, said "You might make a joke on that--something about
T3	131:30	on that," said the little voice close to her ear: "something about 'you would if you could,' you know."
T3	131:38	at all, if it hadn't come quite close to her ear. The consequence of this was that it tickled her ear very
A6	47:11	was lying on the hearth and grinning from ear to ear.
T6	160:40	hands with me!" And he grinned almost from ear to ear, as he leant forwards (and as nearly as possible
T3	131:39	consequence of this was that it tickled her ear very much, and quite took off her thoughts from the
T1	107: 7	first she held the poor thing down by its ear with one paw, and then with the other paw she rubbed its
A9	70:17	when she heard her voice close to her ear. "You're thinking about something, my dear, and that makes

EARLIER (1)
| T1 | 107:12 | But the black kitten had been finished with earlier in the afternoon, and so, while Alice was sitting |

EARLS (2)
| A3 | 22: 6 | and conquest. Edwin and Morcar, the earls of Mercia and Northumbria--'" |
| A3 | 22:12 | the Mouse. "I proceed. 'Edwin and Morcar, the earls of Mercia and Northumbria, declared for him; and even |

EARNESTLY (2)
| A7 | 59: 9 | more tea," the March Hare said to Alice, very earnestly. |
| A1 | 9:17 | hand with Dinah, and was saying to her, very earnestly, "Now, Dinah, tell me the truth: did you ever eat a |

EARS (9)
T5	152: 7	Alice had to hold both her hands over her ears.
T5	152:24	holding her hands ready to put over her ears again.
T2	127: 3	silence, with the wind whistling in Alice's ears, and almost blowing her hair off her head, she fancied.
A6	53:12	house, because the chimneys were shaped like ears and the roof was thatched with fur. It was so large a
A1	9:26	to hear it say, as it turned a corner, "Oh my ears and whiskers, how late it's getting!" She was close
A1	12:25	and once she remembered trying to box her own ears for having cheated herself in a game of croquet she was
A8	67:17	use speaking to it," she thought, "till its ears have come, or at least one of them." In another minute
A8	65:37	"She boxed the Queen's ears--" the Rabbit began. Alice gave a little scream of
T7	178:10	to her knees, and put her hands over her ears, vainly trying to shut out the dreadful uproar.

EARTH (4)
A9	75: 6	poor Alice, who felt ready to sink into the earth. At last the Gryphon said to the Mock Turtle "Drive on,
A1	8:40	"I wonder if I shall fall right through the earth! How funny it'll seem to come out among the people that
A1	8:29	be getting somewhere near the centre of the earth. Let me see: that would be four thousand miles down, I
A6	48:26	make with the day and night! You see the earth takes twenty-four hours to turn round on its axis--"

EARTHQUAKE (2)
| T7 | 172:32 | It went through and through my head like an earthquake!" |
| T7 | 172:34 | "It would have to be a very tiny earthquake!" thought Alice. "Who are at it again?" she |

EASIER (2)
| T6 | 167: 6 | "It gets easier further on," Humpty Dumpty replied. |
| T6 | 166:13 | "But I had some poetry repeated to me much easier than that, by--Tweedledee, I think it was." |

EASIEST (1)
| T9 | 202:17 | dish, while it lies in the middle: / Which is easiest to do, / Un-dish-cover the fish, or dishcover the |

EASILY (8) [See also UNEASILY]
T1	119: 4	invention for getting down stairs quickly and easily, as Alice said to herself. She just kept the tips of
A5	42:20	to find that her neck would bend about easily in any direction, like a serpent. She had just
T2	126: 7	only smiled pleasantly, and said "That's easily managed. You can be the White Queen's Pawn, if you like
A5	41:20	herself "I wish the creatures wouldn't be so easily offended!"
A3	26:10	mean it!" pleaded poor Alice. "But you're so easily offended, you know!"
T6	159: 7	It might have been written a hundred times, easily, on that enormous face. Humpty Dumpty was sitting, with
T8	181: 9	"Now one can breathe more easily," said the Knight, putting back his shaggy hair with
T8	190:27	as usual! However, he gets on again pretty easily--that comes of having so many things hung round the

EASY (10) [See also UNEASY]
T9	202: 4	"'First, the fish must be caught.' / That is easy: a baby, I think, could have caught it. / 'Next, the fish
T9	202: 6	/ 'Next, the fish must be bought.' / That is easy: a penny, I think, could have bought it.
T9	202: 8	'Now cook me the fish!' / That is easy, and will not take more than a minute. / 'Let it lie in a
T9	202:10	a minute. / 'Let it lie in a dish!' / That is easy, because it already is in it.
T1	111:10	into a sort of mist now, I declare! It'll be easy enough to get through--" She was up on the chimney-piece
T6	160:20	"What tremendously easy riddles you ask!" Humpty Dumpty growled out. "Of course I
T7	176:19	"I should win easy," said the Lion.
A3	23:12	left off when they liked, so that it was not easy to know when the race was over. However, when they had
T9	202:12	'Bring it here! Let me sup!' / It is easy to set such a dish on the table. / 'Take the dish-cover
A7	59:13	take less," said the Hatter: "it's very easy to take more than nothing."

EAT (21)
A1	9:18	"Now, Dinah, tell me the truth: did you ever eat a bat?" when suddenly, thump! thump! down she came upon a
A3	26:29	could see her after the birds! Why, she'll eat a little bird as soon as look at it!"
A1	9:13	sort of way, "Do cats eat bats? Do cats eat bats?" and sometimes "Do bats eat cats?" for, you see, as
A1	9:13	to herself, in a dreamy sort of way, "Do cats eat bats? Do cats eat bats?" and sometimes "Do bats eat cats?"
A1	9:11	very like a mouse, you know. But do cats eat bats, I wonder?" And here Alice began to get rather sleepy
A1	9:13	Do cats eat bats?" and sometimes "Do bats eat cats?" for, you see, as she couldn't answer either
A5	43:17	was a very truthful child; "but little girls eat eggs quite as much as serpents do, you know."
A4	32:32	in which case it would be very likely to eat her up in spite of all her coaxing.
A7	55:24	you might just as well say that 'I see what I eat' is the same thing as 'I eat what I see'!"
A1	12:34	beautifully marked in currants. "Well, I'll eat it," said Alice, "and if it makes me grow larger, I can
A1	12:33	in it a very small cake, on which the words "EAT ME" were beautifully marked in currants. "Well, I'll eat
A4	32: 7	and a bright idea came into her head. "If I eat one of these cakes," she thought, "it's sure to make some
A4	28: 5	to happen," she said to herself, "whenever I eat or drink anything: so I'll just see what this bottle does.
A4	33:12	how is it to be managed? I suppose I ought to eat or drink something or other; but the great question is
A4	34: 2	anything that looked like the right thing to eat or drink under the circumstances. There was a large
T4	144:19	"Then I like the Carpenter best--if he didn't eat so many as the Walrus."

EAT (cont.)
```
    A5    41:43   rapidly: so  she  set  to  work at once to eat some of the other bit. Her chin was pressed so closely
    A3    24: 9                       The next thing was to eat the comfits: this caused some noise and confusion, as the
    T1   109: 8   much! I'd  far  rather  go without them than eat them!
    T5   158: 9                    "Only you must eat them both, if you buy two," said the Sheep.
    A7    55:24   'I see what  I eat' is the same thing as 'I eat what I see'!"
```
EATEN (2)
```
    T4   144:12   And this was scarcely odd, because / They'd eaten every one."
    A1    10:22   stories about children who had got burnt, and eaten up by wild beasts, and other unpleasant things, all
```
EATING (4)
```
    T7   174:11   now," said Hatta; "this is a bit of it as I'm eating."
    A7    58:36   always  took a great interest in questions of eating and drinking.
    T7   172: 9    him a good deal. "There's nothing like eating hay when you're faint," he remarked to her, as he
    T12  208: 2   shall  have a real treat. All the time you're eating your breakfast, I'll repeat 'The Walrus and the
```
EATS (1)
```
    A1    13: 1   sure, this is what generally happens when one eats cake; but Alice had got so much into the way of expecting
```
ECHOED (1)
```
    T5   157:14                       "To buy!" Alice echoed in a tone that was half astonished and half frightened
```
ECHOES (2)
```
    TC   209: 8           Long has paled that sunny sky: / Echoes fade and memories die: / Autumn frosts have slain July
    TI   103:17   to  time / The rhythm of our rowing--/ Whose echoes live in memory yet, / Though envious years would say
```
EDGAR (1)
```
    A3    22:22   went on, "--found  it  advisable to go with Edgar Atheling to meet William and offer him the crown.
```
EDGE (8)
```
    T8W   13:12    she  added,  checking  herself  on  the  very edge. "If I once jump over, everything will change, and then I
    A12   92: 3   that  she  tipped  over  the  jury-box with the edge of her skirt, upsetting all the jurymen on to the heads
    T8   190:36   sounds!" A very few steps brought her to the edge of the brook. "The Eighth Square at last!" she cried as
    A4    34: 7   herself  up  on  tiptoe,  and peeped over the edge of the mushroom, and her eyes immediately met those of a
    T1   113:10   White King and the White Queen sitting on the edge of the shovel--and here are two Castles walking arm in
    T9   203: 5    several  inches;  but she got hold of the edge of the table, and managed to pull herself down again.
    T9   204: 7   face grinning at her for a moment over the edge of the tureen, before she disappeared into the soup.
    A5    41:37   as  they would go, and broke off a bit of the edge with each hand.
```
EDGES (1)
```
    T9   202:25      and  drank  the  wine  as  it ran off the edges of the table--and three of them (who looked like
```
EDICT (1)
```
    AI     3:14       Imperious Prima flashes forth / Her edict "to begin it": / In gentler tones Secunda hopes / "There
```
EDUCATIONS (1)
```
    A9    76: 5                    "We had the best of educations--in fact, we went to school every day--"
```
EDWIN (2)
```
    A3    22: 6   much accustomed  to usurpation and conquest. Edwin and Morcar, the earls of Mercia and Northumbria--'"
    A3    22:11    you did," said the Mouse. "I proceed. 'Edwin and Morcar, the earls of Mercia and Northumbria,
```
EEL (2) [See also CONGER-EEL]
```
    T7   170:24   skipping  up  and down, and wriggling like an eel, as he came along, with his great hands spread out like
    A5    40: 3   was  as steady as ever; / Yet you balanced an eel on the end of your nose--/ What made you so awfully clever
```
EELS (1)
```
    A10   81:25                    "Soles and eels, of course," the Gryphon replied, rather impatiently:
```
E'ER (1)
```
    T8   189:15                    And now, if e'er by chance I put / My fingers into glue, / Or madly
```
EFFECT (5)
```
    A4    28:24   the  little magic bottle had now had its full effect, and she grew no larger: still it was very
    T5   150:11                    "That's the effect of living backwards," the Queen said kindly: "it always
    A4    28:17   was not even room for this, and she tried the effect of lying down with one elbow against the door, and the
    A5    41:39   a little of  the  right-hand bit to try the effect. The next moment she felt a violent blow underneath her
    T8W   19: 2   their  advice,  /  And  they  had noticed the effect, / They said I did not look so nice / As they had
```
EFFORT (2)
```
    T9   201:20   however, she conquered her shyness by a great effort, and cut a slice and handed it to the Red Queen.
    T7   174: 5                    Hatta made a desperate effort, and swallowed a large piece of bread-and-butter.
```
EGG (9)
```
    A5    43:15   be telling me next that you never tasted an egg!"
    T6   159:14                    "And how exactly like an egg he is!" she said aloud, standing with her hands ready to
    T6   159: 1                    However, the egg only got larger and larger, and more and more human: when
    T5   158: 3                    "I should like to buy an egg, please," she said timidly. "How do you sell them?"
    T5   158:19   the shop was very dark towards the end. "The egg seems to get further away the more I walk towards it. Let
    T6   159:19                    "I said you looked like an egg, Sir," Alice gently explained. "And some eggs are very
    T5   158:29   she came up to it, and she quite expected the egg to do the same.
    T5   158:16   off to the other end of the shop, and set the egg upright on a shelf.
    T6   159:18   away from Alice as he spoke, "to be called an egg--very!"
```
EGGS (6)
```
    T6   159:20   egg, Sir," Alice gently explained. "And some eggs are very pretty, you know," she added, hoping to turn her
    A5    43:26   said Alice hastily; "but I'm not looking for eggs, as it happens; and, if I was, I shouldn't want yours: I
    A5    43:16                    "I have tasted eggs, certainly," said Alice, who was a very truthful child;
    A5    43:23   the opportunity of adding "You're looking for eggs, I know that well enough; and what does it matter to me
    A5    43:17   a very truthful child; "but little girls eat eggs quite as much as serpents do, you know."
    A5    42:38   "As if it wasn't trouble enough hatching the eggs," said the Pigeon; "but I must be on the look-out for
```
EH (1)
```
    A7    60: 7   you could draw treacle out of a treacle-well--eh, stupid?"
```
EIGHT (2)
```
    T9   194: 2   "Can you do Subtraction? Take nine from eight."
    T9   194: 3                    "Nine from eight I ca'n't, you know," Alice replied very readily: "but--"
```

EIGHTH (5)
    T3   135:26   to herself, and this was the only way to the Eighth Square.
    T8   190:37   brought her to the edge of the brook. "The Eighth Square at last!" she cried as she bounded * * * * * * *
    T3   137:28   out of the wood. If I could only get to the Eighth Square before it gets dark!" So she wandered on,
    T2   128:19   the Knights will show you the way--and in the Eighth Square we shall be Queens together, and it's all
    T2   126:10   Square to begin with: when you get to the Eighth Square you'll be a Queen--"Just at this moment, somehow
EIGHTY-SEVEN (1)
    T7   174: 7   voice: "each of them has been down about eighty-seven times."
EITHER (15)
    A1   8: 2   that she had never before seen a rabbit with either a waistcoat-pocket, or a watch to take out of it, and
    A3   22:33   and, what's more, I don't believe you do either!" And the Eaglet bent down its head to hide a smile:
    A1   8:37   idea what Latitude was, or Longitude either, but she thought they were nice grand words to say.)
    A2   20:15   again, and we wo'n't talk about cats, or dogs either, if you don't like them!" When the Mouse heard this, it
    T8 186:36   beautiful. Everybody that hears me sing it--either it brings the tears into their eyes, or else--"
    T12 208: 8   morning! You see, Kitty, it must have been either me or the Red King. He was part of my dream, of course
    T7 170:15   along the road, and tell me if you can see either of them."
    T4 139:25   Alice did not like shaking hands with either of them first, for fear of hurting the other one's
    A1   9:14   cats?" for, you see, as she couldn't answer either question, it didn't much matter which way she put it.
    A1   9:37   to one of the doors of the hall; but, alas! either the locks were too large, or the key was too small, but
    A1   8:11   Either the well was very deep, or she fell very slowly, for
    T7 170:13   game. And I haven't sent the two Messengers, either. They're both gone to the town. Just look along the
    A1   12:36   grow smaller, I can creep under the door: so either way I'll get into the garden, and I don't care which
    A6   51:21   the other paw, "lives a March Hare. Visit either you like: they're both mad."
    A9   72:37   Queen, stamping on the ground as she spoke; "either you or your head must be off, and that in about half no
ELBOW (4)
    A8   62: 8   said Five, in a sulky tone. "Seven jogged my elbow."
    A4   28:18   she tried the effect of lying down with one elbow against the door, and the other arm curled round her
    T12 207:33   on, as she settled comfortably down, with one elbow on the rug, and her chin in her hand, to watch the
    A4   29:26   but, as the door opened inwards, and Alice's elbow was pressed hard against it, that attempt proved a
ELBOW-DEEP (1)
    T5 156:18   up, and the little arms were plunged in elbow-deep, to get hold of the rushes a good long way down
ELBOWS (2)
    A7   54: 4   two were using it as a cushion, resting their elbows on it, and talking over its head. "Very uncomfortable
    T5 153:38   was in a little dark shop, leaning with her elbows on the counter, and opposite to her was an old Sheep,
ELDEST (2)
    T4 140:19   The eldest Oyster looked at him, / But never a word he said: / The
    T4 140:21   at him, / But never a word he said: / The eldest Oyster winked his eye, / And shook his heavy head--/
ELEGANT (1)
    A3   24: 3   saying "We beg your acceptance of this elegant thimble"; and, when it had finished this short speech,
ELEPHANT (1)
    T3 129:13   but a regular bee: in fact, it was an elephant--as Alice soon found out, though the idea quite took
ELEPHANTS (2)
    T3 129:24   head), 'only it was so dusty and hot, and the elephants did tease so!'"
    T3 129:26   after a pause; "and perhaps I may visit the elephants later on. Besides, I do so want to get into the
ELEVENTH (1)
    A9   77:18   before she made her next remark. "Then the eleventh day must have been a holiday?"
ELSE (23)
    A4   34:11   not the smallest notice of her or of anything else.
    A8   65: 2   the Queen, the royal children, and everybody else.
    T8 186:37   it brings the tears into their eyes, or else--"
    T4 147: 7   eyes--"looking more like a fish than anything else," Alice thought.
    A2   17:25   if not, I'll stay down here till I'm somebody else'--but, oh dear!" cried Alice, with a sudden burst of
    T4 147:22   like bundles of old clothes than anything else, by the time they're ready!" she said to herself, as she
    A10 84:28   or any other dish? / Who would not give all else for two p / ennyworth only of beautiful Soup? /
    A9   76:34   she turned to the Mock Turtle, and said "What else had you to learn?"
    A3   23:31   course," the Dodo replied very gravely. "What else have you got in your pocket?" it went on, turning to
    T7 172:22   "He ca'n't do that," said the King, "or else he'd have been here first. However, now you've got your
    T2 127:17   a little, "you'd generally get to somewhere else--if you ran very fast for a long time as we've been doing
    T2 122: 1   the tree in the middle," said the Rose. "What else is it good for?"
    T8 186:40   "Or else it doesn't, you know. The name of the song is called
    A3   23: 4   that somebody ought to speak, and no one else seemed inclined to say anything.
    T6 159: 5   HUMPTY DUMPTY himself. "It ca'n't be anybody else!" he said to herself. "I'm as certain of it, as if his
    T9 200: 2   glasses with treacle and ink, / Or anything else that is pleasant to drink: / Mix sand with the cider, and
    A5   36:26   she might as well wait, as she had nothing else to do, and perhaps after all it might tell her something
    A1   9: 5   Down, down, down. There was nothing else to do, so Alice soon began talking again. "Dinah'll miss
    T5 149:22   it seemed to Alice, if she had got some one else to dress her, she was so dreadfully untidy. "Every single
    A8   69: 6   Alice could think of nothing else to say but "It belongs to the Duchess: you'd better ask
    T8 186:38   "Or else what?" said Alice, for the Knight had made a sudden pause
    T2 127:21   the same place. If you want to get somewhere else, you must run at least twice as fast as that!"
    A12 94:24   worse. You must have meant some mischief, or else you'd have signed your name like an honest man."
ELSE'S (1)
    A12 94:19   "He must have imitated somebody else's hand," said the King. (The jury all brightened up again
ELSIE (1)
    A7   58:33   began in a great hurry; "and their names were Elsie, Lacie, and Tillie; and they lived at the bottom of a
'EM (8)
    T5 156:10   put 'em there, and I'm not going to take 'em away."
    T6 164: 9   "Ah, you should see 'em come round me of a Saturday night," Humpty Dumpty went on,
    A6   48: 3   They all can," said the Duchess; "and most of 'em do."
    T7 174:10   "It's waiting for 'em now," said Hatta; "this is a bit of it as I'm eating."
    T5 156: 8   "You needn't say 'please' to me about 'em," the Sheep said, without looking up from her knitting: "I

'EM (cont.)
```
  T5   156: 9  looking up from her knitting: "I didn't put 'em there, and I'm not going to take 'em away."
  A4    30:27  Here, put 'em up at this corner--No, tie 'em together first--they don't reach half high enough yet--Oh,
  A4    30:26  other--Bill! Fetch it here, lad!--Here, put 'em up at this corner--No, tie 'em together first--they don't
```
EMBROIDERED (1)
```
  T4   138: 3  in a moment, because one of them had 'DUM' embroidered on his collar, and the other 'DEE.' "I suppose
```
EMPHASIS (2)
```
  T9   194:27  a bit!" the Queens said together, with great emphasis.
  A12   93: 3  proper places--all," he repeated with great emphasis, looking hard at Alice as he said so.
```
EMPTY (4)
```
  T9   200:16  taken two of them, but the middle one was empty. Alice sat down in it, rather uncomfortable at the
  T7   177:16  Lion, as she returned to her place with the empty dish.
  A1     8:19  but to her great disappointment it was empty: she did not like to drop the jar, for fear of killing
  T5   154:14  on it, that particular shelf was always quite empty, though the others round it were crowded as full as they
```
ENCOURAGE (2)
```
  T8   190:19  I get to that turn in the road? I think it'll encourage me, you see."
  A11   88:30          This did not seem to encourage the witness at all: he kept shifting from one foot
```
ENCOURAGED (2)
```
  T8   190:34               "I hope it encouraged him," she said, as she turned to run down the hill:
  A9    76:33       Alice did not feel encouraged to ask any more questions about it: so she turned
```
ENCOURAGING (2)
```
  A5    35: 5              This was not an encouraging opening for a conversation. Alice replied, rather
  A7    54:12  "Have some wine," the March Hare said in an encouraging tone.
```
END (32)
```
  A12   94:22  that I did: there's no name signed at the end."
  T6   168:41  a heavy crash shook the forest from end to end.
  A1     8:27  down, down. Would the fall never come to an end? "I wonder how many miles I've fallen by this time?" she
  T1   109: 3  than the kitten. "What would they do at the end of a year? I should be sent to prison, I suppose, when the
  T2   120:16  back into the old room--and there'd be an end of all my adventures!"
  A6    48:35  did so, and giving it a violent shake at the end of every line:--
  T2   128: 3  end of four, I shall say good-bye. And at the end of five, I shall go!"
  T2   128: 2  for fear of your forgetting them. At the end of four, I shall say good-bye. And at the end of five, I
  A9    73: 7  off being arches to do this, so that, by the end of half an hour or so, there were no arches left, and all
  A2    19:43  the Mouse, who was trembling down to the end of its tail. "As if I would talk on such a subject! Our
  T8   181: 5  and then I must go back, you know. That's the end of my move."
  A9    76:15  great relief. "Now, at ours, they had, at the end of the bill, 'French, music, and washing--extra.'"
  A8    67:28  to go through next walking about at the other end of the ground--and I should have croqueted the Queen's
  T1   115:31  thought struck her, and she took hold of the end of the pencil, which came some way over his shoulder, and
  T5   158:16  And so saying, she went off to the other end of the shop, and set the egg upright on a shelf.
  A10   85: 5  hand, it hurried off, without waiting for the end of the song.
  A7    54:10  and she sat down in a large arm-chair at one end of the table.
  A6    53: 5  it vanished quite slowly, beginning with the end of the tail, and ending with the grin, which remained some
  A11   86:32  "for fear they should forget them before the end of the trial."
  T8   186:29  I must leave you." They had just come to the end of the wood.
  T8   181: 4  the White Knight. "I'll see you safe to the end of the wood--and then I must go back, you know. That's the
  T8   182:11  And now help me on. I'll go with you to the end of the wood--What's that dish for?"
  T2   128: 1  not wait for an answer, but went on. "At the end of three yards I shall repeat them--for fear of your
  A11   90:17  "I've so often read in the newspapers, at the end of trials, 'There was some attempt at applause, which was
  T2   127:35               "At the end of two yards," she said, putting in a peg to mark the
  A5    40: 3  as ever; / Yet you balanced an eel on the end of your nose--/ What made you so awfully clever?"
  A5    41: 4               "It is wrong from beginning to end," said the Caterpillar, decidedly; and there was silence
  T5   158:19  for the shop was very dark towards the end. "The egg seems to get further away the more I walk
  A12   94:36  very gravely, "and go on till you come to the end: then stop."
  T6   168:41  moment a heavy crash shook the forest from end to end.
  A6    47: 1  kitchen, which was full of smoke from one end to the other: the Duchess was sitting on a three-legged
  A1    12: 7  a little nervous about this; "for it might end, you know," said Alice to herself, "in my going out
```
ENDED (4)
```
  T8   183:19  as he spoke, "is to keep--" Here the sentence ended as suddenly as it had begun, as the Knight fell heavily
  T5   153:30  Be-e-e-etter! Be-e-ehh!" The last word ended in a long bleat, so like a sheep that Alice quite
  T4   147: 4  But he couldn't quite succeed, and it ended in his rolling over, bundling up in the umbrella, with
  T8   180:11  always fell on their heads; and the battle ended with their both falling off in this way, side by side.
```
ENDING (1) [See also NEVER-ENDING]
```
  A6    53: 5  beginning with the end of the tail, and ending with the grin, which remained some time after the rest
```
ENDS (3)
```
  T5   156:21  bent over the side of the boat, with just the ends of her tangled hair dipping into the water--while with
  T6   161: 6  as she took it. "If he smiled much more the ends of his mouth might meet behind," she thought: "And then I
  T1   115:23  you, my dear, I turned cold to the very ends of my whiskers!"
```
ENEMY (2)
```
  T8   179:22  looked round in some surprise for the new enemy.
  T7   174:25               "There's some enemy after her, no doubt," the King said, without even
```
ENERGETIC (1)
```
  A3    22:30  adjourn, for the immediate adoption of more energetic remedies--"
```
ENGAGED (1)
```
  A8    68:17               The hedgehog was engaged in a fight with another hedgehog, which seemed to
```
ENGINE (2) [See also STEAM-ENGINE]
```
  T3   132: 3  it was drowned by a shrill scream from the engine, and everybody jumped up in alarm, Alice among the rest
  T3   130: 8  voices went on with "The man that drives the engine. Why, the smoke alone is worth a thousand pounds a
```
ENGINE-DRIVER (1)
```
  T3   130: 7  Guard: "you should have bought one from the engine-driver." And once more the chorus of voices went on
```

ENGINES (1)
T3   131:11   but a hoarse voice spoke next. "Change engines--" it said, and there it choked and was obliged to
ENGLAND (3)
T9   197:16   asleep at once! No, not in all the History of England--it couldn't, you know, because there never was more
T6   160:37   tone. "That's what you call a History of England, that is. Now, take a good look at me! I'm one that
A10   80: 9   upon the other side. / The further off from England the nearer is to France. / Then turn not pale, beloved
ENGLISH (9)
T9   195: 9   "Fiddle-de-dee's not English," Alice replied gravely.
A2   18:22   conclusion that wherever you go to on the English coast, you find a number of bathing-machines in the
T9   199:15   "I speaks English, doesn't I?" the Frog went on. "Or are you deaf? What
T2   128:23   "Speak in French when you ca'n't think of the English for a thing--turn out your toes as you walk--and
A7   56:20   of meaning in it, and yet it was certainly English. "I don't quite understand you," she said, as politely
A2   14: 3   the moment she quite forgot how to speak good English). "Now I'm opening out like the largest telescope that
A3   22:31   "Speak English!" said the Eaglet. "I don't know the meaning of half
A2   19:21   "Perhaps it doesn't understand English," thought Alice. "I daresay it's a French mouse, come
A3   22: 4   by the pope, was soon submitted to by the English, who wanted leaders, and had been of late much
ENGRAVED (1)
A4   27:23   bright brass plate with the name "W. RABBIT" engraved upon it. She went in without knocking, and hurried
EN-GULPH-ED [ENGULPHED] (2)
T8W   15: 8   had a sad accident: two of their party were engulphed--"
T8W   15:10   "En-gulph-ed," Alice repeated, dividing the word into syllables
ENJOY (1)
A6   49: 6   him when he sneezes; / For he can thoroughly enjoy / The pepper when he pleases!"
ENJOYED (2)
T12   207:38   my dream, there was one thing you would have enjoyed--I had such a quantity of poetry said to me, all about
T8   187:14   lighting up his gentle foolish face, as if he enjoyed the music of his song, he began.
ENORMOUS (5)
T9   198:14   her: he was dressed in bright yellow, and had enormous boots on.
T6   159: 7   been written a hundred times, easily, on that enormous face. Humpty Dumpty was sitting, with his legs
T3   129:14   took her breath away at first. "And what enormous flowers they must be!" was her next idea. "Something
T1   115:29   on with great interest as the King took an enormous memorandum-book out of his pocket, and began writing.
A4   32:27   An enormous puppy was looking down at her with large round eyes,
ENOUGH (37)
A6   51:16   that," said the Cat, "if you only walk long enough."
T2   127:37   "No, thank you," said Alice: "one's quite enough!"
A9   77:23   "That's enough about lessons," the Gryphon interrupted in a very
T7   173: 8   "Would you--be good enough--" Alice panted out, after running a little further,
T8   184:31   difficulty is with the feet: the head is high enough already.' Now, first I put my head on the top of the
A5   43:23   "You're looking for eggs, I know that well enough; and what does it matter to me whether you're a little
A4   30:28   half high enough yet--Oh, they'll do well enough. Don't be particular--Here, Bill! Catch hold of this
A8   67:15   on?" said the Cat, as soon as there was mouth enough for it to speak with.
T4   139:40   very soon out of breath. "Four times round is enough for one dance," Tweedledum panted out, and they left
A5   42:38   "As if it wasn't trouble enough hatching the eggs," said the Pigeon; "but I must be on
T8   182:25   "That's hardly enough," he said, anxiously. "You see the wind is so very
T3   129:23   my walk. I shall say 'Oh, I liked it well enough--' (here came the favourite little toss of the head),
T6   160: 5   "It's a stupid name enough!" Humpty Dumpty interrupted impatiently. "What does it
A4   28:13   the bottle, saying to herself "That's quite enough--I hope I sha'n't grow any more--As it is, I ca'n't get
A8   67:21   her. The Cat seemed to think that there was enough of it now in sight, and no more of it appeared.
A1   12:29   pretend to be two people! Why, there's hardly enough of me left to make one respectable person!"
T6   163:45   "I meant by 'impenetrability' that we've had enough of that subject, and it would be just as well if you'd
T6   162:14   Alice suddenly remarked. (They had had quite enough of the subject of age, she thought: and, if they really
A5   40: 5   "I have answered three questions, and that is enough," / Said his father. "Don't give yourself airs! / Do
T1   115:13   get into it--there, now I think you're tidy enough!" she added, as she smoothed his hair, and set him upon
T2   123:36   for, though the flowers were interesting enough, she felt that it would be far grander to have a talk
TI   103:11   a place / In thy young life's hereafter--/ Enough that now thou wilt not fail / To listen to my
T7   173:11   "I'm good enough," the King said, "only I'm not strong enough. You see,
T8   184:32   on the top of the gate--then the head's high enough--then I stand on my head--then the feet are high enough
A3   21:15   you, and listen to me! I'll soon make you dry enough!" They all sat down at once, in a large ring, with the
T6   164:25   "That's enough to begin with," Humpty Dumpty interrupted: "there are
A6   46:37   "the way all the creatures argue. It's enough to drive one crazy!"
T1   111:10   a sort of mist now, I declare! It'll be easy enough to get through--" She was up on the chimney-piece while
A4   32:11   shrinking directly. As soon as she was small enough to get through the door, she ran out of the house, and
A12   93:31   Alice could see this, as she was near enough to look over their slates; "but it doesn't matter a bit
T2   122:19   one speaks, they all begin together, and it's enough to make one wither to hear the way they go on!"
A3   26:20   the young Crab, a little snappishly. "You're enough to try the patience of an oyster!"
A8   66: 8   in getting its body tucked away, comfortably enough, under her arm, with its legs hanging down, but
A3   22:18   "I know what 'it' means well enough, when I find a thing," said the Duck: "it's generally a
A4   30:28   together first--they don't reach half high enough yet--Oh, they'll do well enough. Don't be particular--
T7   173:11   enough," the King said, "only I'm not strong enough. You see, a minute goes by so fearfully quick. You
T8   184:33   I stand on my head--then the feet are high enough, you see--then I'm over, you see."
ENQUIRED (2)
T6   162: 8   "Too proud?" the other enquired.
T8   182:28   keeping the hair from being blown off?" Alice enquired.
ENTANGLED (3)
A5   43:30   well as she could, for her neck kept getting entangled among the branches, and every now and then she had
T5   149:32   "The brush has got entangled in it!" the Queen said with a sigh. "And I lost the
A6   46: 4   Then they both bowed, and their curls got entangled together.
ENTIRELY (5)
A8   69:11   he had come back with the Duchess, it had entirely disappeared: so the King and the executioner ran
T1   107: 2   do with it--it was the black kitten's fault entirely. For the white kitten had been having its face washed

ENTIRELY (cont.)

T6   166:20 on without noticing her remark, "was written entirely for your amusement."

A12   95:37 said. (Which he certainly did <u>not</u>, being made entirely of cardboard.)

T3   133: 4 a Rocking-horse-fly, if you <u>look</u>. It's made entirely of wood, and gets about by swinging itself from

ENTRANCE (1)

A8   62: 1   A large rose-tree stood near the entrance of the garden: the roses growing on it were white,

ENVIOUS (1)

TI   103:18 Whose <u>echoes</u> <u>live</u> <u>in</u> <u>memory</u> <u>yet</u>, / <u>Though</u> <u>envious</u> <u>years</u> <u>would</u> <u>say</u> "<u>forget</u>."

ERE (1)

TI   103:19   <u>Come</u>, <u>hearken</u> <u>then</u>, <u>ere</u> <u>voice</u> <u>of</u> <u>dread</u>, / <u>With</u> <u>bitter</u> <u>tidings</u> <u>laden</u>, / <u>Shall</u>

ESCAPE (4)

A8   68:26 it away under her arm, that it might not escape again, and went back to have a little more conversation

A8   67: 8   She was looking about for some way of escape, and wondering whether she could get away without being

A2   18:10   "That <u>was</u> a narrow escape!" said Alice, a good deal frightened at the sudden

A4   33: 3 to Alice a good opportunity for making her escape: so she set off at once, and ran till she was quite

ESQ. (1)

A2   15: 7   <u>Alice's</u> <u>Right</u> <u>Foot</u>, <u>Esq</u>.

EST (1)

A2   19:25 had happened.) So she began again: "Ou est ma chatte?" which was the first sentence in her French

ETIQUETTE (1)

T9   201: 7 the Red Queen said, very decidedly: "it isn't etiquette to cut any one you've been introduced to. Remove the

EVEN (34)

T9   200:10 some were animals, some birds, and there were even a few flowers among them. "I'm glad they've come without

T9   193: 3 is the use of a child without any meaning? Even a joke should have some meaning--and a child's more

A11   91: 6 in her hand, and Alice guessed who it was, even before she got into the court, by the way the people near

T5   150: 5 now, being punished: and the trial doesn't even begin till next Wednesday: and of course the crime comes

A1   10: 5 and those cool fountains, but she could not even get her head through the doorway; "and even if my head

A1   8:25 home! Why, I wouldn't say anything about it, even if I fell off the top of the house!" (Which was very

A1   10: 6 even get her head through the doorway; "and even if my head <u>would</u> go through," thought poor Alice, "it

T3   131: 5 ought to know her way to the ticket-office, even if she doesn't know her alphabet!"

T3   131: 1 paper), "ought to know which way she's going, even if she doesn't know her own name!"

T9   193: 5 than a joke, I hope. You couldn't deny that, even if you tried with both hands."

A9   72:30 surprise, the Duchess's voice died away, even in the middle of her favourite word "moral", and the arm

T5   152:40   Alice could not help laughing at this, even in the midst of her tears. "Can <u>you</u> keep from crying by

A10   78: 9 said Alice)--"and perhaps you were never even introduced to a lobster--" (Alice began to say "I once

A9   73:12   "No," said Alice. "I don't even know what a Mock Turtle is."

A12   94:31 of the sort!" said Alice. "Why, you don't even know what they're about!"

A8   68: 7 small. "Off with his head!" she said without even looking round.

T7   175: 1 after her, no doubt," the King said, without even looking round. "That wood's full of them."

A11   87: 1 things!" on their slates, and she could even make out that one of them didn't know how to spell

T9   197:21 sounded more like a tune: at last she could even make out words, and she listened so eagerly that, when

T6   162: 9   Alice felt even more indignant at this suggestion. "I mean," she said,

T5   156:36 from the very moment that she picked them? Even real scented rushes, you know, last only a very little

A4   28:17 on the floor: in another minute there was not even room for this, and she tried the effect of lying down

A7   56:39 head, contemptuously. "I dare say you never even spoke to Time!"

A3   22:13 Mercia and Northumbria, declared for him; and even Stigand, the patriotic archbishop of Canterbury, found it

T4   139:29 (she remembered afterwards), and she was not even surprised to hear music playing: it seemed to come from

A6   47: 7 was certainly too much of it in the <u>air</u>. Even the Duchess sneezed occasionally; and as for the baby, it

A6   53:15 and raised herself to about two feet <u>high</u>: even then she walked up towards it rather timidly, saying to

T7   169:11 rather better than the foot-soldiers; but even <u>they</u> stumbled now and then; and it seemed to be a regular

T5   155: 5   But even this plan failed: the 'thing' went through the ceiling as

T1   118:27   (You see she didn't like to confess, even to herself, that she couldn't make it out at all.)

T1   119: 6 hand-rail, and floated gently down without even touching the stairs with her feet: then she floated on

A11   90:32 the Hatter hurriedly left the court, without even waiting to put his shoes on.

A6   48:13 dishes. The Duchess took no notice of them even when they hit her; and the baby was howling so much

A12   99: 8 and eager with many a strange tale, perhaps even with the dream of Wonderland of long ago; and how she

EVENING (7)

A10   84:24 / <u>Beau--ootiful</u> <u>Soo--oop</u>! / <u>Soo--oop</u> <u>of</u> <u>the</u> <u>e--e--evening</u>, / <u>Beautiful</u>, beautiful Soup!

A10   84:33 / <u>Beau--ootiful</u> <u>Soo--oop</u>! / <u>Soo--oop</u> <u>of</u> <u>the</u> <u>e--e--evening</u>, / <u>Beautiful</u>, beauti--FUL SOUP!"

A10   85:10   "<u>Soo--oop</u> <u>of</u> <u>the</u> <u>e--e--evening</u>, / <u>Beautiful</u>, <u>beautiful</u> Soup!"

A10   84:21 of the evening, beautiful Soup! / Soup of the evening, beautiful Soup! / Beau--ootiful Soo--oop! /

A10   84:20 such dainties would not stoop? / Soup of the evening, beautiful Soup! / Soup of the evening, beautiful

T8   190:10 / <u>Who</u> <u>snorted</u> <u>like</u> <u>a</u> <u>buffalo</u>--/ <u>That</u> <u>summer</u> evening long ago, / <u>A-sitting</u> <u>on</u> <u>a</u> <u>gate</u>."

TC   209: 3 <u>sunny</u> <u>sky</u> / <u>Lingering</u> <u>onward</u> <u>dreamily</u> / <u>In</u> <u>an</u> <u>evening</u> <u>of</u> <u>July</u>--

EVENTS (1)

AI   3:33 / <u>Thus</u> <u>slowly</u>, <u>one</u> <u>by</u> <u>one</u>, / <u>Its</u> <u>quaint</u> events were <u>hammered</u> <u>out</u>--/ <u>And</u> <u>now</u> <u>the</u> <u>tale</u> <u>is</u> <u>done</u>, / <u>And</u>

EVER (45)

T5   156: 4 the oars stick fast in the water, worse than ever), and sometimes under trees, but always with the same

AI   3:25   And ever, <u>as</u> <u>the</u> <u>story</u> <u>drained</u> / <u>The</u> <u>wells</u> <u>of</u> <u>fancy</u> <u>dry</u>, / <u>And</u>

A12   95:18 <u>him</u> <u>know</u> <u>she</u> <u>liked</u> <u>them</u> <u>best</u>, / <u>For</u> <u>this</u> <u>must</u> ever be / <u>A</u> <u>secret</u>, <u>kept</u> <u>from</u> <u>all</u> <u>the</u> <u>rest</u>, / <u>Between</u> <u>yourself</u>

T2   123:19 to change the subject, she asked "Does she ever come out here?"

T8   186: 6 "Now the cleverest thing of the sort that I ever did," he went on after a pause, "was inventing a new

TC   209:19   <u>Ever</u> <u>drifting</u> <u>down</u> <u>the</u> <u>stream</u>--/ <u>Lingering</u> <u>in</u> <u>the</u> <u>golden</u> <u>gleam</u>

A1   9:18   "Now, Dinah, tell me the truth: did you ever eat a bat?" when suddenly, thump! thump! down she came

A9   74:30 thought to herself "I don't see how he can ever finish, if he doesn't begin." But she waited patiently.

A4   28:25 there seemed to be no sort of chance of her ever getting out of the room again, no wonder she felt unhappy

A10   83: 1 in her hands, wondering if anything would <u>ever</u> happen in a natural way again.

T9   197:15 a heavy lump in her lap. "I don't think it <u>ever</u> happened before, that any one had to take care of two

A8   63:29 three gardeners, but she could not remember ever having heard of such a rule at processions; "and besides,

A1   12:11 is blown out, for she could not remember ever having seen such a thing.

EVER (cont.)

A10	84: 5	It's by far the most confusing thing that I ever heard!"
T6	160:21	out. "Of course I don't think so! Why, if ever I did fall off--which there's no chance of--but if I did
T4	146:27	Tweedledum cried, in a greater fury than ever. "It's new, I tell you--I bought it yesterday--my nice
T6	168:40	to say) "of all the unsatisfactory people I ever met--" She never finished the sentence, for at this
T5	151:14	at any rate," said the Queen. "Were you ever punished?"
A3	22:26	"As wet as ever," said Alice in a melancholy tone: "it doesn't seem to
T9	195:10	"Who ever said it was?" said the Red Queen.
T2	122:36	tongue!" cried the Tiger-lily. "As if you ever saw anybody! You keep your head under the leaves, and
T3	129: 7	honey down there? They ca'n't be bees--nobody ever saw bees a mile off, you know--" and for some time she
A1	10: 3	the passage into the loveliest garden you ever saw. How she longed to get out of that dark hall, and
A6	53: 8	without a cat! It's the most curious thing I ever saw in all my life!"
A4	30: 8	"An arm, you goose! Who ever saw one that size? Why, it fills the whole window!"
T5	158:22	brook! Well, this is the very queerest shop I ever saw!" * * * * * * * * * * * * * * * So she went on,
T9	192:23	waited for you to begin, you see nobody would ever say anything, so that--"
A7	60:25	say things are 'much of a muchness'--did you ever see such a thing as a drawing of a muchness!"
A3	26:40	world! Oh, my dear Dinah! I wonder if I shall ever see you any more!" And here poor Alice began to cry again
A2	15:18	but to get through was more hopeless than ever: she sat down and began to cry again.
A7	58: 8	"And ever since that," the Hatter went on in a mournful tone, "he
T4	148: 7	said, "there'll be a tree left standing, for ever so far round, by the time we've finished!"
A2	17:19	have next to no toys to play with, and oh, ever so many lessons to learn! No, I've made up my mind about
T9	192:34	White Queen moaned, wringing her hands. "Oh, ever so much more than that!"
T9	196:13	Queen.) "And part of the roof came off, and ever so much thunder got in--and it went rolling round the
T3	132:26	they can talk," Alice said. "None of them ever talk, where I come from."
A2	18:15	table as before, "and things are worse than ever," thought the poor child, "for I never was so small as
A1	9:33	sadly down the middle, wondering how she was ever to get out again.
A7	60:36	the wood. "It's the stupidest tea-party I ever was at in all my life!"
T8	186:17	and lower, "I don't believe that pudding ever was cooked! In fact, I don't believe that pudding ever
A2	14: 3	opening out like the largest telescope that ever was! Good-bye, feet!" (for when she looked down at her
T6	164:18	Dumpty. "I can explain all the poems that ever were invented--and a good many that haven't been invented
T7	178:12	of town,'" she thought to herself, "nothing ever will!"
T8	186:18	cooked! In fact, I don't believe that pudding ever will be cooked! And yet it was a very clever pudding to
A5	40: 2	suppose / That your eye was as steady as ever; / Yet you balanced an eel on the end of your nose--/

EVERY (34)

T1	108:36	too? Now for number three: you unwound every bit of the worsted while I wasn't looking!
A2	15: 2	me see. I'll give them a new pair of boots every Christmas."
A9	76: 6	of educations--in fact, we went to school every day--"
A1	9:32	way down one side and up the other, trying every door, she walked sadly down the middle, wondering how
A2	17:11	tail, / And pour the waters of the Nile / On every golden scale!
A6	48:35	and giving it a violent shake at the end of every line:--
T5	155:13	"She gets more and more like a porcupine every minute!"
T9	197:20	The snoring got more distinct every minute, and sounded more like a tune: at last she could
T7	170: 2	fell off instantly. The confusion got worse every moment, and Alice was very glad to get out of the wood
T6	159:15	her hands ready to catch him, for she was every moment expecting him to fall.
A4	32:41	game of play with a cart-horse, and expecting every moment to be trampled under its feet, ran round the
T7	171:14	attitudes only got more extraordinary every moment, while the great eyes rolled wildly from side to
A6	46:15	within--a constant howling and sneezing, and every now and then a great crash, as if a dish or kettle had
A7	55:37	and was looking at it uneasily, shaking it every now and then, and holding it to his ear.
T5	153:39	Sheep, sitting in an arm-chair, knitting, and every now and then leaving off to look at her through a great
A5	43:31	getting entangled among the branches, and every now and then she had to stop and untwist it. After a
T8	182:37	on in silence, puzzling over the idea, and every now and then stopping to help the poor Knight, who
T5	155:25	very queer about the water, she thought, as every now and then the oars got fast in it, and would hardly
A10	79: 9	began solemnly dancing round and round Alice, every now and then treading on her toes when they passed too
T4	144:12	this was scarcely odd, because / They'd eaten every one."
T4	147:16	and tying strings?" Tweedledum remarked. "Every one of these things has got to go on, somehow or other
T2	122: 9	quite full of little shrill voices. "Silence, every one of you!" cried the Tiger-lily, waving itself
T8W	18: 6	A curious idea came into Alice's head. Almost every one she had met had repeated poetry to her, and she
T5	149:39	the Queen said. "Two pence a week, and jam every other day."
T5	150: 8	"No, it ca'n't," said the Queen. "It's jam every other day: to-day isn't any other day, you know."
T7	176: 6	vegetable--or mineral?" he said, yawning at every other word.
T9	201:31	her; "and it's a very curious thing, I think--every poem was about fishes in some way. Do you know why
T5	149:23	to dress her, she was so dreadfully untidy. "Every single thing's crooked," Alice thought to herself, "and
T5	158:27	* So she went on, wondering more and more at every step, as everything turned into a tree the moment she
T4	148: 1	come very close," he added: "I generally hit every thing I can see--when I get really excited."
T4	148: 2	"And I hit every thing within reach," cried Tweedledum, "whether I can
T3	131:25	all say, my dear, but take a return-ticket every time the train stops."
A5	42:30	and added, with a kind of sob, "I've tried every way, but nothing seems to suit them!"
A7	58:26	it said in a hoarse, feeble voice, "I heard every word you fellows were saying."

EVERYBODY (14)

A8	65: 2	the King, the Queen, the royal children, and everybody else.
A8	69: 3	about it in less than no time, she'd have everybody executed, all round. (It was this last remark that
T6	168:27	said Humpty Dumpty. "Your face is the same as everybody has--the two eyes, so--"(marking their places in the
A3	23:21	waited in silence. At last the Dodo said "Everybody has won, and all must have prizes."
T3	132: 3	by a shrill scream from the engine, and everybody jumped up in alarm, Alice among the rest.
A12	96:27	a pun!" the King added in an angry tone, and everybody laughed. "Let the jury consider their verdict," the
A12	93:37	Everybody looked at Alice.
A6	48:20	"If everybody minded their own business," the Duchess said, in a
A9	70:34	said," Alice whispered, "that it's done by everybody minding their own business!"
T9	192:20	"But if everybody obeyed that rule," said Alice, who was always ready
A9	74:13	"Everybody says 'come on!' here," thought Alice, as she went

EVERYBODY (cont.)
T3   132: 6 "It's only a brook we have to jump over." Everybody seemed satisfied with this, though Alice felt a
T8   186:35 the Knight, "but it's very, very beautiful. Everybody that hears me sing it--either it brings the tears
T3   129:34   his head in at the window. In a moment everybody was holding out a ticket: they were about the same
EVERYTHING (18)
A11   86:11 be no chance of this; so she began looking at everything about her to pass away the time.
T8   187:31   "I'll tell thee everything I can: / There's little to relate. / I saw an aged
A2   19: 4 will be a queer thing, to be sure! However, everything is queer to-day."
A2   19:11 now," thought Alice, "to speak to this mouse? Everything is so out-of-the-way down here, that I should think
A2   15:38 she went on talking. "Dear, dear! How queer everything is to-day! And yesterday things went on just as
A9   72:19 said the Duchess. "I make you a present of everything I've said as yet."
A4   27: 8 for them, but they were nowhere to be seen--everything seemed to have changed since her swim in the pool;
A9   71:18 the Duchess, who seemed ready to agree to everything that Alice said: "there's a large mustard-mine near
A7   60:16 sleepy; "and they drew all manner of things--everything that begins with an M--"
A8   63:24 in a hurried nervous manner, smiling at everything that was said, and went by without noticing her.
T8   182: 6 a pause, "it's as well to be provided for everything. That's the reason the horse has all those anklets
A11   86:15 to find that she knew the name of nearly everything there. "That's the judge," she said to herself,
T5   158:27 on, wondering more and more at every step, as everything turned into a tree the moment she came up to it,
A4   30:36 said Alice to herself. "Why, they seem to put everything upon Bill! I wouldn't be in Bill's place for a good
T9   192:11   Everything was happening so oddly that she didn't feel a bit
T8W   13:12 on the very edge. "If I once jump over, everything will change, and then I can't help him."
A6   48:10 the fire, and at once set to work throwing everything within her reach at the Duchess and the baby--the
T3   135:34 had on a brass collar'--just fancy calling everything you met 'Alice,' till one of them answered! Only
EVERYTHING'S (3)
A7   60:40 it. "That's very curious!" she thought. "But everything's curious to-day. I think I may as well go in at
A9   70:22   "Tut, tut, child!" said the Duchess. "Everything's got a moral, if only you can find it." And she
T2   127:13 we've been under this tree the whole time! Everything's just as it was!"
EVERYWHERE (1)
T2   123:44 provoked, she drew back, and, after looking everywhere for the Queen (whom she spied out at last, a long
EVIDENCE (7)
A12t 92: 1   ALICE'S EVIDENCE
A11   91: 9   "Give your evidence," said the King.
A11   88:28   "Give your evidence," said the King: "and don't be nervous, or I'll have
A11   89: 9   "Give your evidence," the King repeated angrily, "or I'll have you
A12   94: 3   "There's more evidence to come yet, please your Majesty," said the White
A12   95:21   "That's the most important piece of evidence we've heard yet," said the King, rubbing his hands;
A11   91:31 would be like, "--for they haven't got much evidence yet," she said to herself. Imagine her surprise, when
EVIDENTLY (6)
T6   159:26 anything to her; in fact, his last remark was evidently addressed to a tree--so she stood and softly
T3   131:34 voice sighed deeply. It was very unhappy, evidently, and Alice would have said something pitying to
T6   162:22   Evidently Humpty Dumpty was very angry, though he said nothing
A8   65:21 and looked at Alice, as the question was evidently meant for her.
T8   181: 7 "May I help you off with your helmet?" It was evidently more than he could manage by himself: however, she
T7   176:13   The King was evidently very uncomfortable at having to sit down between the
EXACT (3)
T1   110:14 queens;" and her sister, who liked being very exact, had argued that they couldn't, because there were only
T7   170:10 thousand two hundred and seven, that's the exact number," the King said, referring to his book. "I
A3   23: 8 out a race-course, in a sort of circle, ("the exact shape doesn't matter," it said,) and then all the party
EXACTLY (23)
T5   153: 4   "I'm seven and a half, exactly."
A6   46:31 the Footman continued in the same tone, exactly as if nothing had happened.
T2   128:28   How it happened, Alice never knew, but exactly as she came to the last peg, she was gone. Whether she
A12   95:12   / He trusts to you to set them free, / Exactly as we were.
T8   183:20 Knight fell heavily on the top of his head exactly in the path where Alice was walking. She was quite
T8W   16:15   Alice didn't catch the word exactly. "Is it a kind of toothache?" she asked.
T1   118:28 to fill my head with ideas--only I don't exactly know what they are! However, somebody killed something
T4   139:13   They looked so exactly like a couple of great schoolboys, that Alice couldn't
T6   159:14   "And how exactly like an egg he is!" she said aloud, standing with her
T1   110:22 you sat up and folded your arms, you'd look exactly like her. Now do try, there's a dear!" And Alice got
T6   168:23 her one of his fingers to shake: "you're so exactly like other people."
T9   195:42   Alice sighed and gave it up. "It's exactly like the riddle with no answer!" she thought.
T5   152: 6   Her screams were so exactly like the whistle of a steam-engine, that Alice had to
A3   23:29 and handed them round as prizes. There was exactly one a-piece, all round.
T1   119: 3 and ran down stairs--or, at least, it wasn't exactly running, but a new invention for getting down stairs
A7   55:18   "Exactly so," said Alice.
A7   58:15   "Exactly so," said the Hatter: "as the things get used up."
T6   165: 9   "Exactly so. Well then, 'mimsy' is 'flimsy and miserable'
T5   153: 5   "You needn't say 'exactly,'" the Queen remarked. "I can believe it without that.
A9   70:26 was very ugly; and secondly, because she was exactly the right height to rest her chin on Alice's shoulder,
A5   41:17 rearing itself upright as it spoke (it was exactly three inches high).
T5   154:13 she looked hard at any shelf, to make out exactly what it had on it, that particular shelf was always
A8   68:36 at once, she found it very hard to make out exactly what they said.
EXAMINATION (2)
T9   192:29 you know, till you've passed the proper examination. And the sooner we begin it, the better."
T4   146:16 only a rattle," Alice said, after a careful examination of the little white thing. "Not a rattle-snake,
-EXAMINE [See CROSS-EXAMINE]
EXAMINING (1)
A8   65: 8 see!" said the Queen, who had meanwhile been examining the roses. "Off with their heads!" and the
EXCELLENT (2)
A8   68:18 another hedgehog, which seemed to Alice an excellent opportunity for croqueting one of them with the

EXCELLENT (cont.)
A4   32:22   It sounded an excellent plan, no doubt, and very neatly and simply arranged:
EXCEPT (4)
A5   42:16   as she spoke, but no result seemed to follow, except a little shaking among the distant green leaves.
T8   182:43   off behind. Otherwise he kept on pretty well, except that he had a habit of now and then falling off
A9   73: 8   were no arches left, and all the players, except the King, the Queen, and Alice, were in custody and
A12   93:13   to write out a history of the accident, all except the Lizard, who seemed too much overcome to do anything
EXCITED (2)
T4   148: 1   hit every thing I can see--when I get really excited."
T9   204:24   surprised at this, but she was far too much excited to be surprised at anything now. "As for you," she
EXCITEMENT (3)
T8   185:14   you!" he said. He raised his hands in some excitement as he said this, and instantly rolled out of the
T2   125:28   and her heart began to beat quick with excitement as she went on. "It's a great huge game of chess
T2   122:10   from side to side, and trembling with excitement. "They know I ca'n't get at them!" it panted,
EXCLAIMED (14)
A7   58: 7   "How dreadfully savage!" exclaimed Alice.
A9   77:14   "What a curious plan!" exclaimed Alice.
T9   197:12   "What am I to do?" exclaimed Alice, looking about in great perplexity, as first
A9   72: 3   "Oh, I know!" exclaimed Alice, who had not attended to this last remark.
T7   170:22   eyes with one hand. "I see somebody now!" she exclaimed at last. "But he's coming very slowly--and what
T4   145: 4   "Why, about you!" Tweedledee exclaimed, clapping his hands triumphantly. "And if he left
T8   191: 3   get here! And what is this on my head?" she exclaimed in a tone of dismay, as she put her hands up to
A12   92: 8   "Oh, I beg your pardon!" she exclaimed in a tone of great dismay, and began picking them up
T4   145:12   "I shouldn't!" Alice exclaimed indignantly. "Besides, if I'm only a sort of thing
T9   194:22   away, its temper would remain!" the Queen exclaimed triumphantly.
T9   195:13   is, I'll tell you the French for it!" she exclaimed triumphantly.
T6   161:24   "Wrong!" Humpty Dumpty exclaimed triumphantly. "You never said a word like it!"
A11   88:22   "Stolen!" the King exclaimed, turning to the jury, who instantly made a
A9   76:27   in surprise. "Never heard of uglifying!" it exclaimed. "You know what to beautify is, I suppose?"
EXCLAMATION (1)
A9   74:35   long silence, broken only by an occasional exclamation of "Hjckrrh!" from the Gryphon, and the constant
EXCUSE (3)
T3   129:19   to run down the hill, and trying to find some excuse for turning shy so suddenly. "It'll never do to go down
T9   196:21   "Your Majesty must excuse her," the Red Queen said to Alice, taking one of the
T3   129:28   So, with this excuse, she ran down the hill, and jumped over the first of
EXCUSES (2)
T1   108:33   have happened. Now don't make any more excuses, but listen! Number two: you pulled Snowdrop away by
T3   130: 6   "Don't make excuses," said the Guard: "you should have bought one from the
EXCUSING (1)
T3   135: 6   Alice: "the governess would never think of excusing me lessons for that. If she couldn't remember my name
EXECUTE (1)
A8   65:10   on, three of the soldiers remaining behind to execute the unfortunate gardeners, who ran to Alice for
EXECUTED (6)
A11   90: 6   remarked the King, "or I'll have you executed."
A8   69: 3   it in less than no time, she'd have everybody executed, all round. (It was this last remark that had made
A4   27: 4   paws! Oh my fur and whiskers! She'll get me executed, as sure as ferrets are ferrets! Where can I have
A8   68:13   heard her sentence three of the players to be executed for having missed their turns, and she did not like
A11   88:29   King: "and don't be nervous, or I'll have you executed on the spot."
A11   89:10   the King repeated angrily, "or I'll have you executed, whether you are nervous or not."
EXECUTES (1)
A9   74:12   Gryphon. "It's all her fancy that: they never executes nobody, you know. Come on!"
EXECUTION (3)
A8   65:32   ear, and whispered "She's under sentence of execution."
A9   73: 9   Alice, were in custody and under sentence of execution.
A12   98:28   Queen ordering off her unfortunate guests to execution--once more the pig-baby was sneezing on the
EXECUTIONER (5)
A8   69: 8   "She's in prison," the Queen said to the executioner: "fetch her here." And the executioner went off
A8   68: 8   "I'll fetch the executioner myself," said the King eagerly, and he hurried off
A8   69:12   had entirely disappeared: so the King and the executioner ran wildly up and down, looking for it, while the
A8   68:30   it: there was a dispute going on between the executioner, the King, and the Queen, who were all talking at
A8   69: 9   to the executioner: "fetch her here." And the executioner went off like an arrow.
EXECUTIONER'S (1)
A8   68:37   The executioner's argument was, that you couldn't cut off a head
EXECUTIONS (2)
A9   74: 3   history. I must go back and see after some executions I have ordered;" and she walked off, leaving Alice
A9   73:21   she had felt quite unhappy at the number of executions the Queen had ordered.
EXHAUSTED (1)
T2   127: 8   suddenly, just as Alice was getting quite exhausted, they stopped, and she found herself sitting on the
EXISTENCE (1)
A2   18:11   but very glad to find herself still in existence. "And now for the garden!" And she ran with all
EXPECT (4)
T5   155: 4   It'll puzzle it to go through the ceiling, I expect!"
T8W   19: 4   not look so nice / As they had ventured to expect.
T8   190:25   "It wo'n't take long to see him off, I expect," Alice said to herself, as she stood watching him.
T5   152:12   "When do you expect to do it?" Alice said, feeling very much inclined to
EXPECTED (3)
A4   28: 9   did so indeed, and much sooner than she had expected: before she had drunk half the bottle, she found her
T9   192: 1   "Well, this is grand!" said Alice. "I never expected I should be a Queen so soon--and I'll tell you what
T5   158:29   the moment she came up to it, and she quite expected the egg to do the same.

EXPECTING (4)
  A4   32:41 having a game of play with a cart-horse, and expecting every moment to be trampled under its feet, ran
  T6 159:16 ready to catch him, for she was every moment expecting him to fall.
  A1   13: 2 but Alice had got so much into the way of expecting nothing but out-of-the-way things to happen, that it
  A6   52:22   Alice waited a little, half expecting to see it again, but it did not appear, and after a
EXPERIMENT (3)
  A9   71: 7 the temper of your flamingo. Shall I try the experiment'"
  T9 201:16 be the only one to give orders; so, as an experiment, she called out "Waiter! Bring back the pudding!"
  A9   71:10   not feeling at all anxious to have the experiment tried.
EXPLAIN (11)
  A10 81:43   "Explain all that," said the Mock Turtle.
  T6 164:17 "Let's hear it," said Humpty Dumpty. "I can explain all the poems that ever were invented--and a good many
  A10 84: 4 the Mock Turtle interrupted, "if you don't explain it as you go on? It's by far the most confusing thing
  A3   23: 5   "Why," said the Dodo, "the best way to explain it is to do it." (And, as you might like to try the
  A12 95:23   "If any one of them can explain it," said Alice, (she had grown so large in the last
  A10 83: 3   "She ca'n't explain it," said the Gryphon hastily. "Go on with the next
  A5   35:11   "I ca'n't explain _myself_, I'm afraid, Sir," said Alice, "because I'm not
  A4   27:17 direction it pointed to, without trying to explain the mistake that it had made.
  A12 95:29 meaning in it," but none of them attempted to explain the paper.
  A11 90:13 (As that is rather a hard word, I will just explain to you how it was done. They had a large canvas bag,
  A5   35:10 by that?" said the Caterpillar, sternly. "Explain yourself!"
EXPLAINED (8)
  T6 161:26 I thought you meant 'How old _are_ you?'" Alice explained.
  T6 159:19 you _looked_ like an egg, Sir," Alice gently explained. "And some eggs are very pretty, you know," she
  T2 124: 9 Alice attended to all these directions, and explained, as well as she could, that she had lost her way.
  T3 132:29 "I don't _rejoice_ in insects at all," Alice explained, "because I'm rather afraid of them--at least the
  T5 156:43 water and _wouldn't_ come out again (so Alice explained it afterwards), and the consequence was that the
  T9 194:44   "Well, it _isn't_ picked at all," Alice explained: "it's ground--"
  T8W 18: 1   "It isn't that _kind_," Alice hastily explained. "It's to comb hair with--your wig's so _very_ rough,
  A10 83: 2   "I should like to have it explained," said the Mock Turtle.
EXPLAINING (2)
  T12 207:18 wouldn't look at it," she said, when she was explaining the thing afterwards to her sister: "it turned away
  T6 164:14   "You seem very clever at explaining words, Sir," said Alice. "Would you kindly tell me
EXPLANATION (3)
  A6   51:13 long as I get _somewhere_," Alice added as an explanation.
  T6 166:25   only I don't _sing_ it," he added, as an explanation.
  A11 88:24 "I keep them to sell," the Hatter added as an explanation. "I've none of my own. I'm a hatter."
EXPLANATIONS (1)
  A10 81:45   said the Gryphon in an impatient tone: "explanations take such a dreadful time."
EXPLORING (2)
  T8W 15: 3 "No brown sugar!" grumbled the Wasp. "A nice exploring party!"
  T8W 14:20 on her knees, and began. "_Latest News. The Exploring Party have made another tour in the Pantry, and have_
EXPRESSING (1)
  A6   49:30 Alice; "that's not at all a proper way of expressing yourself."
EXPRESSION (2)
  T8W 20: 5 the Wasp murmured, looking at her with an expression of admiration: "it's the shape of your head as does
  A8   66:11 and look up in her face, with such a puzzled expression that she could not help bursting out laughing; and,
EXTINGUISHERS (1)
  T9 202:23 them put their glasses upon their heads like extinguishers, and drank all that trickled down their faces--
EXTRA (2)
  A9   76:15 end of the bill, 'French, music, _and washing--extra._'"
  T6 164: 6 that," said Humpty Dumpty, "I _always_ pay it extra."
EXTRAORDINARY (4)
  T7 171:14 use--the Anglo-Saxon attitudes only got more extraordinary every moment, while the great eyes rolled wildly
  A6   46:14 hear you." And certainly there _was_ a most extraordinary noise going on within--a constant howling and
  T4 147: 2   with himself in it: which was such an extraordinary thing to do, that it quite took off Alice's
  A7   59: 6 a little to fancy to herself what such an extraordinary way of living would be like, but it puzzled her
EXTRAS (1)
  A9   76: 9   "With extras?" asked the Mock Turtle, a little anxiously.
EXTREMELY (5)
  A8   67:32   "Not at all," said Alice: "she's so extremely--" Just then she noticed that the Queen was close
  T2 128:17 went on in a tone of grave reproof, "'It's extremely kind of you to tell me all this'--however, we'll
  T8W 19: 6 said it did _not_ fit, and so / It made me look extremely plain: / But what was I to do, you know? / My
  A6   49:34 than a real nose: also its eyes were getting extremely small for a baby: altogether Alice did not like the
  T3 131:14 a horse," Alice thought to herself. And an extremely small voice, close to her ear, said "You might make
EYE (13)
  T4 140:21 word he said: / The eldest Oyster winked his eye, / And shook his heavy head--/ Meaning to say he _did_ not
  TC 209:14 _Children yet, the tale to hear, / Eager eye and willing ear, / Lovingly shall nestle near._
  TC 209: 5 _Children three that nestle near, / Eager eye and willing ear, / Pleased a simple tale to hear--_
  A2   15:17 to look through into the garden with one eye; but to get through was more hopeless than ever: she sat
  A8   62:18 "Well, of all the unjust things--" when his eye chanced to fall upon Alice, as she stood watching them,
  T8W 15: 1   Alice hastily ran her eye down the paper and said "No. It says nothing about brown
  A1   12:31   Soon her eye fell on a little glass box that was lying under the table:
  A4   28: 2 was just going to leave the room, when her eye fell upon a little bottle that stood near the
  T7 175:15 carelessly, and he was going on, when his eye happened to fall upon Alice: he turned round instantly,
  A10 83:14 "I _passed by his garden, and marked, with one eye, / How the Owl and the Panther were sharing a pie:_ / The
  A12 95:33 on his knee, and looking at them with one eye; "I seem to see some meaning in them, after all. '--said I
  A5   40: 2 youth, "_one would hardly suppose / That your eye was as steady as ever; / Yet you balanced an eel on the_
  T1 108:30 kitten was speaking). "Her paw went into your eye? Well, that's _your_ fault, for keeping your eyes open--if

-EYED [See BRIGHT-EYED]
EYELIDS (1)
```
  A10   82:24   I must sugar my hair.' / As a duck with his eyelids, so he with his nose / Trims his belt and his buttons,
```
EYES (71)
```
  T4   144: 6   pocket-handkerchief / Before his streaming eyes.
  T5   153:10   "Try again: draw a long breath, and shut your eyes."
  T8   186:41   The name of the song is called 'Haddocks' Eyes.'"
  T8   187:30   very attentively, but no tears came into her eyes.
  TC   209:12   moving under skies / Never seen by waking eyes.
  A6    50: 1   sobbing," she thought, and looked into its eyes again, to see if there were any tears.
  T8   188:33          He said 'I hunt for haddocks' eyes / Among the heather bright, / And work them into
  T6   159: 3   within a few yards of it, she saw that it had eyes and a nose and a mouth; and, when she had come close to
  T12  207: 2      purr so loud," Alice said, rubbing her eyes, and addressing the kitten, respectfully, yet with some
  A4    32:28   was looking down at her with large round eyes, and feebly stretching out one paw, trying to touch her.
  A12   98:34          So she sat on, with closed eyes, and half believed herself in Wonderland, though she knew
  T1   115: 6   far too much astonished to cry out, but his eyes and his mouth went on getting larger and larger, and
  T3   137: 9   look of alarm came into its beautiful brown eyes, and in another moment it had darted away at full speed.
  T8   187:19   if it had been only yesterday--the mild blue eyes and kindly smile of the Knight--the setting sun gleaming
  T5   153:33   wrapped herself up in wool. Alice rubbed her eyes, and looked again. She couldn't make out what had
  A10   82: 4   to her, one on each side, and opened their eyes and mouths so very wide; but she gained courage as she
  T4   140:13   looking round at Tweedledum with great solemn eyes, and not noticing Alice's question.
  A1    12:25      so severely as to bring tears into her eyes; and once she remembered trying to box her own ears for
  T3   131: 4   next to the gentleman in white, shut his eyes and said in a loud voice, "She ought to know her way to
  T6   168:33   objected. But Humpty Dumpty only shut his eyes, and said "Wait till you've tried."
  A12   98:21   wandering hair that would always get into her eyes--and still as she listened, or seemed to listen, the
  A3    21:16   with the Mouse in the middle. Alice kept her eyes anxiously fixed on it, for she felt sure she would catch
  A8    67:16          Alice waited till the eyes appeared, and then nodded. "It's no use speaking to it,"
  A6    46:23   he ca'n't help it," she said to herself; "his eyes are so very nearly at the top of his head. But at any
  T5   154: 7   ca'n't look all round you--unless you've got eyes at the back of your head."
  A12   99: 7   her other little children, and make their eyes bright and eager with many a strange tale, perhaps even
  T3   136: 8   by: it looked at Alice with its large gentle eyes, but didn't seem at all frightened. "Here then! Here
  A2    19:19   seemed to her to wink with one of its little eyes, but it said nothing.
  A7    60:20          The Dormouse had closed its eyes by this time, and was going off into a doze; but, on
  A2    17:17   the right words," said poor Alice, and her eyes filled with tears again as she went on, "I must be Mabel
  T9   199: 8   Frog looked at the door with his large dull eyes for a minute: then he went nearer and rubbed it with his
  A7    60:15   the Dormouse went on, yawning and rubbing its eyes, for it was getting very sleepy; "and they drew all
  A9    74:24   Mock Turtle, who looked at them with large eyes full of tears, but said nothing.
  T10  205: 4      only her face grew very small, and her eyes got large and green: and still, as Alice went on shaking
  T4   146:14   in a voice choking with passion, and his eyes grew large and yellow all in a moment, as he pointed with
  A4    33: 2   hanging out of its mouth, and its great eyes half shut.
  A10   78: 2   and drew the back of one flapper across his eyes. He looked at Alice and tried to speak, but, for a minute
  T9   194:30          The Queen gasped and shut her eyes. "I can do Addition," she said, "if you give me time--but
  A7    58:25          The Dormouse slowly opened its eyes. "I wasn't asleep," it said in a hoarse, feeble voice, "I
  A4    34: 8   peeped over the edge of the mushroom, and her eyes immediately met those of a large blue caterpillar, that
  A6    45: 7   in livery, with a round face, and large eyes like a frog; and both footmen, Alice noticed, had
  T8   190: 4   / Whose face was very like a crow, / With eyes, like cinders, all aglow, / Who seemed distracted with
  T4   147: 6   opening and shutting his mouth and his large eyes--"looking more like a fish than anything else," Alice
  A7    56:25   impatiently, and said, without opening its eyes, "Of course, of course: just what I was going to remark
  T1   118:10   thought he stood, / The Jabberwock, with eyes of flame, / Came whiffling through the tulgey wood, / And
  TI   103: 2   of the pure unclouded brow / And dreaming eyes of wonder! / Though time be fleet, and I and thou / Are
  T6   168:29   It's always the same. Now if you had the two eyes on the same side of the nose, for instance--or the mouth
  T1   108:31   Well, that's your fault, for keeping your eyes open--if you'd shut them tight up, it wouldn't have
  T8   186:37   it--either it brings the tears into their eyes, or else--"
  T6   168:35   speak again, but, as he never opened his eyes or took any further notice of her, she said "Good-bye!"
  A1     7:10      when suddenly a White Rabbit with pink eyes ran close by her.
  T7   171:11   extraordinary every moment, while the great eyes rolled wildly from side to side.
  T5   156:22   into the water--while with bright eager eyes she caught at one bunch after another of the darling
  T8   187:25   like a picture, as, with one hand shading her eyes, she leant against a tree, watching the strange pair, and
  T8   183:15   in silence after this, the Knight with his eyes shut, muttering to himself, and Alice watching anxiously
  T6   168:27   face is the same as everybody has--the two eyes, so--"(marking their places in the air with his thumb)
  A10   81: 2   here the Mock Turtle yawned and shut his eyes. "Tell her about the reason and all that," he said to the
  T6   166:27   whether I'm singing or not, you've sharper eyes than most," Humpty Dumpty remarked severely. Alice was
  T7   170:17          "I only wish I had such eyes," the King remarked in a fretful tone. "To be able to see
  A9    74: 7          The Gryphon sat up and rubbed its eyes: then it watched the Queen till she was out of sight:
  T8W   21: 7          "Then your eyes--they're too much in front, no doubt. One would have done
  T8   181:11   and turning his gentle face and large mild eyes to Alice. She thought she had never seen such a
  A2    15:26   in the distance, and she hastily dried her eyes to see what was coming. It was the White Rabbit returning
  A7    55:11          The Hatter opened his eyes very wide on hearing this; but all he said was "Why is a
  T9   201:30   her lips, there was dead silence, and all eyes were fixed upon her; "and it's a very curious thing, I
  A6    49:34   more like a snout than a real nose: also its eyes were getting extremely small for a baby: altogether Alice
  T7   175:44   on: he looked very tired and sleepy, and his eyes were half shut. "What's this!" he said, blinking lazily
  A12   98:18   clasped upon her knee, and the bright eager eyes were looking up into hers--she could hear the very tones
  A11   91:14   his arms and frowning at the cook till his eyes were nearly out of sight, he said, in a deep voice, "What
  T6   159:10   how he could keep his balance--and, as his eyes were steadily fixed in the opposite direction, and he
  T7   170:21   looking intently along the road, shading her eyes with one hand. "I see somebody now!" she exclaimed at
```

-F-

FABULOUS (3)
T7   176: 7   "It's a fabulous monster!" the Unicorn cried out, before Alice could
T7   175:23   "I always thought they were fabulous monsters!" said the Unicorn. "Is it alive?"
T7   175:28   "Do you know, I always thought Unicorns were fabulous monsters, too? I never saw one alive before!"
FACE (39)
A8   65:27   Rabbit, who was peeping anxiously into her face.
A12   98: 3   had fluttered down from the trees upon her face.
T6   159: 6   it, as if his name were written all over his face!"
T1   107: 8   and then with the other paw she rubbed its face all over, the wrong way, beginning at the nose: and just
A6   45: 6   by another footman in livery, with a round face, and large eyes like a frog; and both footmen, Alice
T8   181:10   hair with both hands, and turning his gentle face and large mild eyes to Alice. She thought she had never
A2   19:37   by the fire, licking her paws and washing her face--and she is such a nice soft thing to nurse--and she's
A5   42:25   in a hurry: a large pigeon had flown into her face, and was beating her violently with its wings.
T8W   16:10   gets a yellow handkerchief. And I ties up my face--as at the present."
T8   187:14   a faint smile lighting up his gentle foolish face, as if he enjoyed the music of his song, he began.
A12   96:24   using the ink, that was trickling down his face, as long as it lasted.)
T1   115: 4   she had never seen in all her life such a face as the King made, when he found himself held in the air
A1   12: 4   she was now only ten inches high, and her face brightened up at the thought that she was now the right
T10   205: 3   Queen made no resistance whatever: only her face grew very small, and her eyes got large and green: and
T9   204: 6   in time to see the Queen's broad good-natured face grinning at her for a moment over the edge of the tureen,
T2   121: 9   when you'd speak! Said I to myself, 'Her face has got some sense in it, though it's not a clever one!'
T6   159: 8   a hundred times, easily, on that enormous face. Humpty Dumpty was sitting, with his legs crossed like a
A4   32: 2   the window, and some of them hit her in the face. "I'll put a stop to this," she said to herself, and
A10   82:34   Alice said nothing: she had sat down with her face in her hands, wondering if anything would ever happen in
A6   50:10   so violently, that she looked down into its face in some alarm. This time there could be no mistake about
T6   168:27   I complain of," said Humpty Dumpty. "Your face is the same as everybody has--the two eyes, so--"(marking
T8W   16:12   Alice looked pityingly at him. "Tying up the face is very good for the toothache," she said.
T6   168:24   "The face is what one goes by, generally," Alice remarked in a
T8W   17: 7   try tying a yellow handkerchief round your face. It'll cure you in no time!"
A8   63:29   whether she ought not to lie down on her face like the three gardeners, but she could not remember ever
TI   103: 7   I have not seen thy sunny face, / Nor heard thy silver laughter: / No thought of me
T1   113: 1   back of it in the Looking-glass) had got the face of a little old man, and grinned at her.
A6   45: 4   he was in livery: otherwise, judging by his face only, she would have called him a fish)--and rapped
T8   181:24   said, a shade of vexation passing over his face. "Then all the things must have fallen out! And the box
T1   108:28   squeaked twice while Dinah was washing your face this morning. Now you ca'n't deny it, Kitty: I heard you!
T2   124: 4   walking a minute before she found herself face to face with the Red Queen, and full in sight of the hill
A6   49:32   and Alice looked very anxiously into its face to see what was the matter with it. There could be no
T8   188:30   shook him well from side to side, / Until his face was blue: / 'Come, tell me how you live,' I cried, / 'And
T8W   13: 5   Something like a very old man (only that his face was more like a wasp) was sitting on the ground, leaning
A2   20:17   turned round and swam slowly back to her: its face was quite pale (with passion, Alice thought), and it said
T8   190: 3   Whose hair was whiter than the snow, / Whose face was very like a crow, / With eyes, like cinders, all
T1   107: 3   For the white kitten had been having its face washed by the old cat for the last quarter of an hour
A8   66:11   would twist itself round and look up in her face, with such a puzzled expression that she could not help
T2   124: 4   a minute before she found herself face to face with the Red Queen, and full in sight of the hill she had
FACED (1)
T2   128: 7   At the two-yard peg she faced round, and said "A pawn goes two squares in its first
FACES (10)
A8   63:45   for, you see, as they were lying on their faces, and the pattern on their backs was the same as the rest
A12   93:25   very respectful tone, but frowning and making faces at him as he spoke.
T7   171:10   his hands about, and make the most fearful faces at the poor King.
A9   77: 9   in his turn; and both creatures hid their faces in their paws.
T1   115: 9   "Oh! please don't make such faces, my dear!" she cried out, quite forgetting that the King
T9   202:24   and drank all that trickled down their faces--others upset the decanters, and drank the wine as it
A8   63:32   she, "if people had all to lie down on their faces, so that they couldn't see it?" So she stood where she
A8   63:12   instantly threw themselves flat upon their faces. There was a sound of many footsteps, and Alice looked
T1   107: 6   The way Dinah washed her children's faces was this: first she held the poor thing down by its ear
T4   142: 3   the treat: / Their coats were brushed, their faces washed, / Their shoes were clean and neat--/ And this
FACT (15)
A6   48: 6   know much," said the Duchess; "and that's a fact."
A11   88:23   jury, who instantly made a memorandum of the fact.
A1   11: 7   it, and, finding it very nice (it had, in fact, a sort of mixed flavour of cherry-tart, custard,
T1   112: 6   in the old room," thought Alice: "warmer, in fact, because there'll be no one here to scold me away from
T8   186:16   repeated as before: "not the next day. In fact," he went on, holding his head down, and his voice
T6   159:25   thought, as he never said anything to her; in fact, his last remark was evidently addressed to a tree--so
A6   48: 1   know that Cheshire-Cats always grinned; in fact, I didn't know that cats could grin."
T8   186:18   believe that pudding ever was cooked! In fact, I don't believe that pudding ever will be cooked! And
A8   63: 6   at Two. Two began, in a low voice, "Why, the fact is, you see, Miss, this here ought to have been a red
T3   129:12   this was anything but a regular bee: in fact, it was an elephant--as Alice soon found out, though the
T9   203: 1   In fact it was rather difficult for her to keep in her place
A2   15:13   head struck against the roof of the hall: in fact she was now rather more than nine feet high, and she at
T8   186: 4   "My mind goes on working all the same. In fact, the more head-downwards I am, the more I keep inventing
A12   94:12   directed at all," said the White Rabbit: "in fact, there's nothing written on the outside." He unfolded the
A9   76: 5   "We had the best of educations--in fact, we went to school every day--"

FADE (3)
TC   209: 8   Long has paled that sunny sky: / Echoes fade and memories die: / Autumn frosts have slain July.
T5   156:35   to her just then that the rushes had begun to fade, and to lose all their scent and beauty, from the very
T2   123:16   the Rose added kindly. "You're beginning to fade, you know--and then one ca'n't help one's petals getting
FADING (1)
A8   69:10   The Cat's head began fading away the moment he was gone, and, by the time he had
FAIL (1)
TI   103:11   hereafter--/ Enough that now thou wilt not fail / To listen to my fairy-tale.
FAILED (1)
T5   155: 5   But even this plan failed: the 'thing' went through the ceiling as quietly as
FAILURE (1)
A4   29:27   hard against it, that attempt proved a failure. Alice heard it say to itself "Then I'll go round and
FAINT (5)
T7   171:16   "You alarm me!" said the King. "I feel faint--Give me a ham-sandwich!"
T7   172: 9   "There's nothing like eating hay when you're faint," he remarked to her, as he munched away.
A4   33: 5   and till the puppy's bark sounded quite faint in the distance.
T8   187:13   slowly beating time with one hand, and with a faint smile lighting up his gentle foolish face, as if he
T7   172: 7   "Hay, then," the King murmured in a faint whisper.
FAINTED (1)
T1   116: 4   ink all ready to throw over him, in case he fainted again), she turned over the leaves, to find some part
FAINTING (1)
A9   76:40   week: he taught us Drawling, Stretching, and Fainting in Coils."
FAINTLY (2)
A10   85: 8   on!" and ran the faster, while more and more faintly came, carried on the breeze that followed them, the
AI   3:27   story drained / The wells of fancy dry, / And faintly strove that weary one / To put the subject by, / "The
FAIR (3)
T7   177:17   "I say, this isn't fair!" cried the Unicorn, as Alice sat with the knife in her
T7   176:11   both of you," (to the King and the Unicorn): "fair play with the cake, you know!"
A9   72:36   "Now, I give you fair warning," shouted the Queen, stamping on the ground as
FAIRLY (1)
A8   67:23   "I don't think they play at all fairly," Alice began, in rather a complaining tone, "and they
FAIRY (4)
TI   103: 6   smile will surely hail / The love-gift of a fairy-tale.
TI   103:12   that now thou wilt not fail / To listen to my fairy-tale.
TI   103:36   with breath of bale, / The pleasance of our fairy-tale.
A4   29: 4   can have happened to me! When I used to read fairy tales, I fancied that kind of thing never happened, and
FALL (18)
T6   159:16   for she was every moment expecting him to fall.
A10   81: 6   So they got thrown out to sea. So they had to fall a long way. So they got their tails fast in their mouths.
T6   159:29   sat on a wall: / Humpty Dumpty had a great fall. / All the King's horses and all the King's men /
A4   29:38   anything, but she heard a little shriek and a fall, and a crash of broken glass, from which she concluded
T8   185:18   look for him. She was rather startled by the fall, as for some time he had kept on very well, and she was
A1   8:23   thought Alice to herself. "After such a fall as this, I shall think nothing of tumbling down-stairs!
T1   114: 2   rubbing his nose, which had been hurt by the fall. He had a right to be a little annoyed with the Queen,
T6   160:24   Alice could hardly help laughing. "If I did fall," he went on, "the King has promised me--ah, you may turn
A1   8:27   Down, down, down. Would the fall never come to an end? "I wonder how many miles I've
T8   183: 9   "Because people don't fall off quite so often, when they've had much practice."
T6   160:21   course I don't think so! Why, if ever I did fall off--which there's no chance of--but if I did--" Here he
T8   187:12   he stopped his horse and let the reins fall on its neck: then, slowly beating time with one hand, and
A1   8:39   she began again. "I wonder if I shall fall right through the earth! How funny it'll seem to come out
A8   62:18   the unjust things--" when his eye chanced to fall upon Alice, as she stood watching them, and he checked
T7   175:15   and he was going on, when his eye happened to fall upon Alice: he turned round instantly, and stood for some
T8   182:34   off is because it hangs down--things never fall upwards, you know. It's a plan of my own invention. You
A1   9:20   upon a heap of sticks and dry leaves, and the fall was over.
T8   185: 2   directly. So I had a very little way to fall, you see--But there was the danger of falling into it, to
FALLEN (5)
A1   8:28   come to an end? "I wonder how many miles I've fallen by this time?" she said aloud. "I must be getting
A4   29:41   concluded that it was just possible it had fallen into a cucumber-frame, or something of the sort.
A2   20:22   crowded with the birds and animals that had fallen into it: there was a Duck and a Dodo, a Lory and an
A2   18:19   Her first idea was that she had somehow fallen into the sea, "and in that case I can go back by
T8   181:24   over his face. "Then all the things must have fallen out! And the box is no use without them." He unfastened
FALLING (8)
A1   8:10   stopping herself before she found herself falling down what seemed to be a very deep well.
T8   185: 2   to fall, you see--But there was the danger of falling into it, to be sure. That happened to me once--and the
T8   180: 7   tumble! Just like a whole set of fire-irons falling into the fender! And how quiet the horses are! They
T8   182:30   "But I've got a plan for keeping it from falling off."
T8   180:12   heads; and the battle ended with their both falling off in this way, side by side. When they got up again,
T8   182:43   except that he had a habit of now and then falling off sideways; and, as he generally did this on the
T8   183: 8   hair with one hand, to save himself from falling over on the other side.
A1   9: 1   as she spoke--fancy, curtseying as you're falling through the air! Do you think you could manage it?)
FALLS (1)
T8   182:34   up it, like a fruit-tree. Now the reason hair falls off is because it hangs down--things never fall upwards,
FALTERED (1)
T2   128:14   know I had to make one--just then," Alice faltered out.
FAMILIARLY (1)
A3   21: 7   natural to Alice to find herself talking familiarly with them, as if she had known them all her life.
FAMILY (1)
A2   19:43   "As if I would talk on such a subject! Our family always hated cats: nasty, low, vulgar things! Don't let
FAN (12)
A4   27:38   of tiny white kid-gloves: she took up the fan and a pair of the gloves, and was just going to leave the

FAN (cont.)
    A4   27:25   out   of   the   house   before   she   had   found   the   fan   and   gloves.
    A2   15:36   Alice took up the fan and gloves, and, as the hall was very hot, she kept
    A4   27:20   out who I am! But I'd better take him his fan and gloves--that is, if I can find them." As she said this
    A2   15:34   dropped   the   white   kid-gloves   and   the   fan,   and   scurried away into the darkness as hard as he could
    A4   27: 6   in   a   moment   that   it   was   looking   for   the   fan   and the pair of white kid-gloves, and she very
    A4   27:37   in the window, and on it (as she had hoped) a fan and two or three pairs of tiny white kid-gloves: she took
    T9   195: 3   "Fan her head!" the Red Queen anxiously interrupted. "She'll be
    A2   15:28   of   white   kid-gloves   in   one   hand   and   a   large   fan in the other: he came trotting along in a great hurry,
    A4   27:15   moment,   and   fetch me a pair of gloves and a fan! Quick, now!" And Alice was so much frightened that she
    A2   18: 8   soon found out that the cause of this was the fan she was holding, and she dropped it hastily, just in time
    T8   188:11   whiskers green, / And always use so large a fan / That they could not be seen. / So, having no reply to
FANCIED (3)
    T2   127: 4   and almost blowing her hair off her head, she fancied.
    A4   29:32   thought   Alice,   and   after   waiting   till   she   fancied she heard the Rabbit just under the window, she
    A4   29: 4   to me! When I used to read fairy tales, I fancied that kind of thing never happened, and now here I am
FANCY (10)
    T3   135:34   name of "Dash": had on a brass collar'--just fancy calling everything you met 'Alice,' till one of them
    A1   9: 1   (and   she   tried   to   curtsey   as   she   spoke--fancy, curtseying as you're falling through the air! Do you
    AI   3:26   And ever, as the story drained / The wells of fancy dry, / And faintly strove that weary one / To put the
    A9   74:21   in   the   same   words   as   before,   "It's all his fancy, that: he hasn't got no sorrow, you know. Come on!"
    A9   74:11   "Why,   she,"   said   the   Gryphon.   "It's all her fancy that: they never executes nobody, you know. Come on!"
    AI   3:20   Anon, to sudden silence won, / In fancy they pursue / The dream-child moving through a land / Of
    A2   19:34   show you our cat Dinah. I think you'd take a fancy to cats, if you could only see her. She is such a dear
    A7   59: 6   Alice tried a little to fancy to herself what such an extraordinary way of living
    A1   12:10   what I should be like then?" And she tried to fancy what the flame of a candle looks like after the candle
    A4   30:31   crash)--"Now,   who   did   that?--It was Bill, I fancy--Who's to go down the chimney?--Nay, I sha'n't! You do
FANCYING (1)
    A4   27:29   sending   me   on   messages   next!" And she began fancying the sort of thing that would happen: "'Miss Alice!
FANNED (2)
    T9   195: 5   so   much   thinking."   So they set to work and fanned her with bunches of leaves, till she had to beg them to
    A4   33: 8   against   a   buttercup   to   rest   herself,   and fanned herself with one of the leaves. "I should have liked
FANNING (2)
    T3   132:19   itself   on   a   twig   just   over   her   head,   and fanning her with its wings.
    A2   15:37   and,   as   the   hall   was   very   hot,   she   kept fanning herself all the time she went on talking. "Dear, dear!
FANS (1)
    T7   170:25   along,   with   his   great   hands   spread   out   like fans on each side.)
FAR (27)
    T8   190:21   Alice: "and thank you very much for coming so far--and for the song--I liked it very much."
    A10   80: 3   sea!"   /   But the snail replied "Too far, too far!", and gave a look askance--/ Said he thanked the whiting
    T4   143:27   a   trick,   /   After we've brought them out so far, / And made them trot so quick!' / The Carpenter said
    A5   41:36   at   last   she   stretched   her   arms   round   it   as far as they would go, and broke off a bit of the edge with
    T1   111: 4   wide   open: and   it's   very   like   our   passage   as far as you can see, only you know it may be quite different on
    A9   74:16   They had not gone far before they saw the Mock Turtle in the distance, sitting
    A5   42:11   a stalk out of a sea of green leaves that lay far below her.
    T1   114:20   hours getting to the table, at that rate. I'd far better help you, hadn't I?" But the King took no notice of
    T2   120: 1   "I should see the garden far better," said Alice to herself, "if I could get to the top
    A4   30:39   She drew her foot as far down the chimney as she could, and waited till she heard a
    T2   123:36   interesting   enough,   she   felt   that   it   would   be far grander to have a talk with a real Queen.
    T5   156:31   at   the   obstinacy   of   the   rushes   in   growing   so far off, as, with flushed cheeks and dripping hair and hands,
    A2   14: 5   be   almost   out   of   sight,   they   were   getting   so far off). "Oh, my poor little feet, I wonder who will put on
    A2   14: 8   sha'n't   be   able!   I   shall be a great deal too far off to trouble myself about you: you must manage the best
    A10   78:29   "--as far out to sea as you can--"
    T1   109: 7   once!   Well,   I   shouldn't   mind   that   much!   I'd far rather go without them than eat them!
    T4   148: 7   there'll be a tree left standing, for ever so far round, by the time we've finished!"
    A12   95:38   "All right, so far," said the King; and he went on muttering over the verses
    A10   84: 4   if you don't explain it as you go on? It's by far the most confusing thing that I ever heard!"
    A6   51: 6   a   little   wider.   "Come,   it's   pleased   so   far," thought Alice, and she went on. "Would you tell me,
    A10   80: 3   out to sea!" / But the snail replied "Too far, too far!", and gave a look askance--/ Said he thanked the
    T4   145:25   can never get at me here," she thought: "it's far too large to squeeze itself in among the trees. But I wish
    T1   115: 5   an   invisible   hand,   and   being   dusted: he   was far too much astonished to cry out, but his eyes and his mouth
    T9   204:24   have   felt   surprised   at   this,   but   she   was far too much excited to be surprised at anything now. "As for
    T7   171: 8   At   this   moment   the   Messenger   arrived: he   was far too much out of breath to say a word, and could only wave
    A10   80: 7   "What matters it how far we go?" his scaly friend replied. / "There is another
    T4   147:37   who had overheard the remark. "I'm far worse than you!"
FARMER (1)
    A2   20: 8   remember   half   of   them--and it belongs to a farmer, you know, and he says it's so useful, it's worth a
FARM-YARD (1)
    A12   99: 1   knew)   to   the   confused   clamour   of   the   busy farm-yard--while the lowing of the cattle in the distance
FAR-OFF (1)
    AI   4: 8   wither'd   wreath   of   flowers   /   Pluck'd in a far-off land.
FARTHER (2)
    A6   53:10   She had not gone much farther before she came in sight of the house of the March
    T5   156:41   They hadn't gone much farther before the blade of one of the oars got fast in the
FARTHING (1)
    T5   158: 5   "Fivepence farthing for one--twopence for two," the Sheep replied.
FASHION (2)
    A11   89: 2   said   the   Dormouse: "not in that ridiculous fashion." And he got up very sulkily and crossed over to the
    A12   98:15   till   she   too   began   dreaming   after   a   fashion, and this was her dream:--

FAST (21) [See also BREAKFAST]

T8	185:11	took hours and hours to get me out. I was as fast as--as lightning, you know."
T1	108: 5	up the ball again. But she didn't get on very fast, as she was talking all the time, sometimes to the kitten
T2	127:21	else, you must run at least twice as fast as that!"
A11	89:27	too; but the Dormouse denied nothing, being fast asleep.
T9	197:10	too." In another moment both Queens were fast asleep, and snoring loud.
A7	54: 3	at it: a Dormouse was sitting between them, fast asleep, and the other two were using it as a cushion,
A9	73:22	They very soon came upon a Gryphon, lying fast asleep in the sun. (If you don't know what a Gryphon is,
T2	127:17	get to somewhere else--if you ran very fast for a long time as we've been doing."
T5	155:26	thought, as every now and then the oars got fast in it, and would hardly come out again.
T5	156:42	before the blade of one of the oars got fast in the water and wouldn't come out again (so Alice
T5	156: 3	beds of weeds (which made the oars stick fast in the water, worse than ever), and sometimes under trees
A10	81: 6	to fall a long way. So they got their tails fast in their mouths. So they couldn't get them out again.
T4	148:20	black cloud that is!" she said. "And how fast it comes! Why, I do believe it's got wings!"
T6	161:15	this conversation is going on a little too fast: let's go back to the last remark but one."
T2	127: 6	the Queen. "Faster! Faster!" And they went so fast that at last they seemed to skim through the air, hardly
T2	126:14	running hand in hand, and the Queen went so fast that it was all she could do to keep up with her: and
T4	142: 9	them, / And yet another four; / And thick and fast they came at last, / And more, and more, and more--/ All
T2	126:20	never changed their places at all: however fast they went, they never seemed to pass anything. "I wonder
T7	174:23	came flying out of the wood over yonder--How fast those Queens can run!"
TI	103:29	gladness. / The magic words shall hold thee fast: / Thou shalt not heed the raving blast.
T2	128:31	quickly into the wood ("and she can run very fast!" thought Alice), there was no way of guessing, but she

FASTEN (1)

| T5 | 152:14 | "When I fasten my shawl again," the poor Queen groaned out: "the |

FASTENED (3) [See also UNFASTENED]

T8	181:14	and he had a queer-shaped little deal box fastened across his shoulders, upside-down, and with the lid
T8	182:22	"I hope you've got your hair well fastened on?" he continued, as they set off.
T8	181:32	you've got a bee-hive--or something like one--fastened to the saddle," said Alice.

FASTENING (1)

| T4 | 147:21 | trouble they gave her in tying strings and fastening buttons--"Really they'll be more like bundles of old |

FASTER (13)

T2	126:26	of breath: and still the Queen cried "Faster! Faster!" and dragged her along. "Are we nearly there?" Alice
T2	127: 2	repeated. "Why, we passed it ten minutes ago! Faster!" And they ran on for a time in silence, with the wind
T2	127: 5	"Now! Now!" cried the Queen. "Faster! Faster!" And they went so fast that at last they seemed to
T2	126:16	her: and still the Queen kept crying "Faster! Faster!" but Alice felt she could not go faster, though she
T2	126:22	seemed to guess her thoughts, for she cried "Faster! Don't try to talk!"
T2	126:26	out of breath: and still the Queen cried "Faster! Faster!" and dragged her along. "Are we nearly there?"
T2	127: 5	"Now! Now!" cried the Queen. "Faster! Faster!" And they went so fast that at last they
T2	126:16	up with her: and still the Queen kept crying "Faster! Faster!" but Alice felt she could not go faster,
A10	79:13	"Will you walk a little faster?" said a whiting to a snail, / "There's a porpoise
T7	172:21	in a sullen tone. "I'm sure nobody walks much faster than I do!"
A6	48:21	growl, "the world would go round a deal faster than it does."
T2	126:16	Faster!" but Alice felt she could not go faster, though she had no breath left to say so.
A10	85: 7	Gryphon only answered "Come on!" and ran the faster, while more and more faintly came, carried on the

FASTNESS (3)

T8	185:12	"But that's a different kind of fastness," Alice objected.
T8	185:22	talking on in his usual tone. "All kinds of fastness," he repeated: "but it was careless of him to put
T8	185:13	Knight shook his head. "It was all kinds of fastness with me, I can assure you!" he said. He raised his

FAT (5)

T4	139:39	The other two dancers were fat, and very soon out of breath. "Four times round is enough
T4	139:12	But the fat little men only looked at each other and grinned.
T3	137:30	on turning a sharp corner, she came upon two fat little men, so suddenly that she could not help starting
T4	143: 4	of us are out of breath, / And all of us are fat!' / 'No hurry!' said the Carpenter. / They thanked him
A5	38: 2	before, / And have grown most uncommonly fat; / Yet you turned a back-somersault in at the door--/ Pray

FATHER (6)

A5	40: 6	questions, and that is enough," / Said his father. "Don't give yourself airs! / Do you think I can listen
A5	39: 5	"In my youth," said his father, "I took to the law, / And argued each case with my
A5	37: 5	"In my youth," Father William replied to his son, / "I feared it might injure
A5	36:36	"Repeat 'You are old, Father William,'" said the Caterpillar.
A5	37: 1	"You are old, Father William," the young man said, / "And your hair has
A10	82: 6	to the part about her repeating "You are old, Father William," to the Caterpillar, and the words all coming

FATTER (2)

| T10 | 205: 5 | shaking her, she kept on growing shorter--and fatter--and softer--and rounder--and-- |
| T8 | 188:28 | so go on from day to day / Getting a little fatter. / I shook him well from side to side, / Until his face |

FAULT (5)

T1	107: 2	to do with it--it was the black kitten's fault entirely. For the white kitten had been having its face
T1	108:31	Her paw went into your eye? Well, that's your fault, for keeping your eyes open--if you'd shut them tight up
T2	123:15	"But that's not your fault," the Rose added kindly. "You're beginning to fade, you
T9	199: 2	Alice turned round, ready to find fault with anybody. "Where's the servant whose business it is
T9	194:29	White Queen, for she didn't like being found fault with so much.

FAULTS (3)

T1	108:38	"That's three faults, Kitty, and you've not been punished for any of them
T1	108:27	one finger. "I'm going to tell you all your faults. Number one: you squeaked twice while Dinah was washing
T5	151:15	"Only for faults," said Alice.

FAVOUR (1)

| T9 | 199:38 | 'draw near! / 'Tis an honour to see me, a favour to hear: / 'Tis a privilege high to have dinner and tea |

FAVOURED (1)

| A3 | 22: 3 | 'William the Conqueror, whose cause was favoured by the pope, was soon submitted to by the English, |

FAVOURITE (3)

| T3 | 129:23 | 'Oh, I liked it well enough--' (here came the favourite little toss of the head), 'only it was so dusty and |

FAVOURITE (cont.)
    T1   110:11 things Alice used to say, beginning with her favourite phrase "Let's pretend." She had had quite a long
    A9   72:30 voice died away, even in the middle of her favourite word "moral", and the arm that was linked into hers
FAWN (6)
    T3   136: 7   Just then a Fawn came wandering by: it looked at Alice with its large
    T3   137: 5 out into another open field, and here the Fawn gave a sudden bound into the air, and shook itself free
    T3   137: 7 shook itself free from Alice's arm. "I'm a Fawn!" it cried out in a voice of delight. "And, dear me!
    T3   136:12   "What do you call yourself?" the Fawn said at last. Such a soft sweet voice it had!
    T3   137: 1 you, if you'll come a little further on," the Fawn said. "I ca'n't remember here."
    T3   137: 4 clasped lovingly round the soft neck of the Fawn, till they came out into another open field, and here the
FEAR (11)
    T9   202:14 dish-cover up!' / Ah, that is so hard that I fear I'm unable!
    A4   27:24 knocking, and hurried upstairs, in great fear lest she should meet the real Mary Ann, and be turned out
    T7   169: 4 whole forest. Alice got behind a tree, for fear of being run over, and watched them go by.
    T1   113: 9 the Red Queen," Alice said (in a whisper, for fear of frightening them), "and there are the White King and
    T4   147:29 but she managed to turn it into a cough, for fear of hurting his feelings.
    T4   139:26 shaking hands with either of them first, for fear of hurting the other one's feelings; so, as the best way
    T9   196:19 of it?" but she did not say this aloud, for fear of hurting the poor Queen's feelings.
    A1   8:20 empty: she did not like to drop the jar, for fear of killing somebody underneath, so managed to put it into
    A6   46: 6 that she had to run back into the wood for fear of their hearing her; and, when she next peeped out, the
    T2   128: 2 end of three yards I shall repeat them--for fear of your forgetting them. At the end of four, I shall say
    A11   86:32 names," the Gryphon whispered in reply, "for fear they should forget them before the end of the trial."
FEARED (3)
    A5   37: 6 Father William replied to his son, / "I feared it might injure the brain; / But, now that I'm
    T4   144:25   in the wood near them, though she feared it was more likely to be a wild beast. "Are there any
    T9   192:14 much to ask them how they came there, but she feared it would not be quite civil. However, there would be no
FEARFUL (1)
    T7   171:10 only wave his hands about, and make the most fearful faces at the poor King.
FEARFULLY (2)
    T7   173:12 strong enough. You see, a minute goes by so fearfully quick. You might as well try to stop a Bandersnatch!
    T7   175: 4 "No use, no use!" said the King. "She runs so fearfully quick. You might as well try to catch a
FEAST (2)
    T7   178: 9 angry looks at being interrupted in their feast, before she dropped to her knees, and put her hands over
    T9   202:39 she was telling her sister the history of her feast. "You would have thought they wanted to squeeze me flat!
FEASTING (1)
    T2   128:20 we shall be Queens together, and it's all feasting and fun!" Alice got up and curtseyed, and sat down
FEAST'S (2)
    T9   197: 6 ready, we've time for a nap. / When the feast's over, we'll go to the ball--/ Red Queen, and White
    T9   197: 5 "Hush-a-by lady, in Alice's lap! / Till the feast's ready, we've time for a nap. / When the feast's over,
FEATHER (8)
    T5   155:21   "Feather!" cried the Sheep, as she took up another pair of
    T5   155:27   "Feather! Feather!" the Sheep cried again, taking more needles.
    A9   71:12 bite. And the moral of that is--'Birds of a feather flock together.'"
    T5   155:35 into her hair, as her hands were full. "Feather, I say!"
    T5   155:36   "Why do you say 'Feather' so often?" Alice asked at last, rather vexed. "I'm
    T5   155:27   "Feather! Feather!" the Sheep cried again, taking more needles. "You'll
    T5   155:30   "Didn't you hear me say 'Feather'?" the Sheep cried angrily, taking up quite a bunch of
    AI   3:10 tale of breath too weak / To stir the tiniest feather! / Yet what can one poor voice avail / Against three
FEATHERS (2)
    T6   165:11 is a thin shabby-looking bird with its feathers sticking out all round--something like a live mop."
    A3   21: 2 on the bank--the birds with draggled feathers, the animals with their fur clinging close to them,
FED (1)
    T7   170:32 hate him with an H, because he is Hideous. I fed him with--with--with Ham-sandwiches and Hay. His name is
FEEBLE (2)
    A4   31:16   Last came a little feeble, squeaking voice ("That's Bill," thought Alice), "Well,
    A7   58:26 eyes. "I wasn't asleep," it said in a hoarse, feeble voice, "I heard every word you fellows were saying."
FEEBLY (2)
    T9   193:16   The White Queen smiled feebly, and said "And I invite you."
    A4   32:28 down at her with large round eyes, and feebly stretching out one paw, trying to touch her. "Poor
FEED (2)
    T4   143:12 you're ready, Oysters dear, / We can begin to feed.'
    T8   188:26   But I was thinking of a way / To feed oneself on batter, / And so go on from day to day /
FEEL (14)
    T9   192:11 was happening so oddly that she didn't feel a bit surprised at finding the Red Queen and the White
    A9   72:26 said Alice sharply, for she was beginning to feel a little worried.
    A9   76:33   Alice did not feel encouraged to ask any more questions about it: so she
    T7   171:16 "You alarm me!" said the King. "I feel faint--Give me a ham-sandwich!"
    T8   186:43 of the song, is it?" Alice said, trying to feel interested.
    A5   36: 5 that into a butterfly, I should think you'll feel it a little queer, wo'n't you?"
    T3   132:21 chicken," Alice thought. Still, she couldn't feel nervous with it, after they had been talking together so
    T1   113:13 "and I'm nearly sure they ca'n't see me. I feel somehow as if I was getting invisible--"
    T2   122:24   "Put your hand down, and feel the ground," said the Tiger-lily. "Then you'll know why."
    A5   36: 8 said Alice: "all I know is, it would feel very queer to me."
    A1   7: 7 well as she could, for the hot day made her feel very sleepy and stupid), whether the pleasure of making a
    A8   67: 3   Alice began to feel very uneasy: to be sure, she had not as yet had any
    A1   12:39 holding her hand on the top of her head to feel which way it was growing; and she was quite surprised to
    A12   99: 9 of Wonderland of long ago; and how she would feel with all their simple sorrows, and find a pleasure in all
FEELING (11)
    A2   15:41 this morning? I almost think I can remember feeling a little different. But if I'm not the same, the next
    T9   201:18 It was so large that she couldn't help feeling a little shy with it, as she had been with the mutton;

FEELING (cont.)
A9   71: 9   He might bite," Alice cautiously replied, not feeling at all anxious to have the experiment tried.
A6   48: 4   of any that do," Alice said very politely, feeling quite pleased to have got into a conversation.
A1   12: 1   "What a curious feeling!" said Alice. "I must be shutting up like a telescope!
T3   137:32   but in another moment she recovered herself, feeling sure that they must be TWEEDLEDUM AND TWEEDLEDEE
T1   107:11   quite still and trying to purr--no doubt feeling that it was all meant for it good.
A11   91:30   the White Rabbit as he fumbled over the list, feeling very curious to see what the next witness would be
A8   67:20   flamingo, and began an account of the game, feeling very glad she had some one to listen to her. The Cat
A10   80:14   very interesting dance to watch," said Alice, feeling very glad that it was over at last: "and I do so like
T5   152:12   "When do you expect to do it?" Alice said, feeling very much inclined to laugh.
FEELINGS (6)
T1   115:42   badly'). "That's not a memorandum of your feelings!"
T4   147:29   turn it into a cough, for fear of hurting his feelings.
T9   196:20   aloud, for fear of hurting the poor Queen's feelings.
A2   19:28   afraid that she had hurt the poor animal's feelings. "I quite forgot you didn't like cats."
A5   36: 7   "Well, perhaps your feelings may be different," said Alice: "all I know is, it
T4   139:26   first, for fear of hurting the other one's feelings; so, as the best way out of the difficulty, she took
FEET (40)
T4   142: 6   was odd, because, you know, / They hadn't any feet.
T8   182: 7   the horse has all those anklets round his feet."
T8   184: 8   flat on his back, right under the horse's feet.
T8W   14:16   up a newspaper which had been lying at his feet.
T8   184:10   the time that Alice was getting him on his feet again. "Plenty of practice!"
A2   15: 5   it'll seem, sending presents to one's own feet! And how odd the directions will look!
T8   185:25   Alice asked, as she dragged him out by the feet, and laid him in a heap on the bank.
T7   178: 3   she felt quite deafened. She started to her feet and sprang across the little brook in her terror, and had
T8   187:23   loose on his neck, cropping the grass at her feet--and the black shadows of the forest behind--all this she
T8   184:33   enough--then I stand on my head--then the feet are high enough, you see--then I'm over, you see."
A12   98:24   The long grass rustled at her feet as the White Rabbit hurried by--the frightened Mouse
A4   32:35   the puppy jumped into the air off all its feet at once, with a yelp of delight, and rushed at the stick,
A8   63:16   oblong and flat, with their hands and feet at the corners: next the ten courtiers: these were
T3   134: 9   at your feet," said the Gnat (Alice drew her feet back in some alarm), "you may observe a
T5   156:38   almost like snow, as they lay in heaps at her feet--but Alice hardly noticed this, there were so many other
A1   7:17   it, and then hurried on, Alice started to her feet, for it flashed across her mind that she had never before
A2   14: 4   largest telescope that ever was! Good-bye, feet!" (for when she looked down at her feet, they seemed to
A2   18:26   of tears which she had wept when she was nine feet high.
A2   15:13   in fact she was now rather more than nine feet high, and she at once took up the little golden key and
A2   18: 6   as she could guess, she was now about two feet high, and was going on shrinking rapidly: she soon found
A6   53:15   of mushroom, and raised herself to about two feet high: even then she walked up towards it rather timidly,
A5   44: 2   place, with a little house in it about four feet high. "Whoever lives there," thought Alice, "it'll never
A3   22:28   case," said the Dodo solemnly, rising to its feet, "I move that the meeting adjourn, for the immediate
A2   14: 6   were getting so far off). "Oh, my poor little feet, I wonder who will put on your shoes and stockings for
A1   9:21   not a bit hurt, and she jumped up on to her feet in a moment: she looked up, but it was all dark overhead:
A2   15:25   After a time she heard a little pattering of feet in the distance, and she hastily dried her eyes to see
A4   29:20   this moment!" Then came a little pattering of feet on the stairs. Alice knew it was the Rabbit coming to
T8   179: 6   there was the great dish still lying at her feet, on which she had tried to cut the plum-cake, "So I
A4   32:42   every moment to be trampled under its feet, ran round the thistle again: then the puppy began a
T3   134: 9   "Crawling at your feet," said the Gnat (Alice drew her feet back in some alarm),
T8   185:20   she could see nothing but the soles of his feet, she was much relieved to hear that he was talking on in
T8   184:30   to myself 'The only difficulty is with the feet: the head is high enough already.' Now, first I put my
T1   119: 6   without even touching the stairs with her feet: then she floated on through the hall, and would have
T7   169:10   Then came the horses. Having four feet, these managed rather better than the foot-soldiers; but
A2   14: 4   feet!" (for when she looked down at her feet, they seemed to be almost out of sight, they were getting
T7   169: 6   had never seen soldiers so uncertain on their feet: they were always tripping over something or other, and
T2   127: 7   air, hardly touching the ground with their feet, till suddenly, just as Alice was getting quite exhausted
A8   66: 4   themselves up and stand on their hands and feet, to make the arches.
T7   178: 8   * * * * * * * * * * * Unicorn rise to their feet, with angry looks at being interrupted in their feast,
T9   199:20   gave the door a kick with one of his great feet. "You let it alone," he panted out, as he hobbled back to
FELL (18)
A7   60:30   great disgust, and walked off: the Dormouse fell asleep instantly, and neither of the others took the
T1   115:15   The King immediately fell flat on his back, and lay perfectly still; and Alice was
T8   184: 7   to show Alice what he meant, and this time he fell flat on his back, right under the horse's feet.
T8   185:15   and instantly rolled out of the saddle, and fell headlong into a deep ditch.
T8   183:19   as suddenly as it had begun, as the Knight fell heavily on the top of his head exactly in the path where
T8   182:17   the first two or three times that he tried he fell in himself instead. "It's rather a tight fit, you see,"
T8   182:42   (which it generally did rather suddenly), he fell off behind. Otherwise he kept on pretty well, except that
T8   182:40   horse stopped (which it did very often), he fell off in front; and, whenever it went on again (which it
T7   170: 2   that, whenever a horse stumbled, the rider fell off instantly. The confusion got worse every moment, and
T8   184:43   a sugar-loaf. When I used to wear it, if I fell off the horse, it always touched the ground directly. So
A1   8:26   I wouldn't say anything about it, even if I fell off the top of the house!" (Which was very likely true.)
T6   161: 1   he leant forwards (and as nearly as possible fell off the wall in doing so) and offered Alice his hand. She
A1   12:31   Soon her eye fell on a little glass box that was lying under the table: she
T8   180:11   not noticed, seemed to be that they always fell on their heads; and the battle ended with their both
T7   169: 7   whenever one went down, several more always fell over him, so that the ground was soon covered with little
A1   8:21   to put it into one of the cupboards as she fell past it.
A4   28: 2   just going to leave the room, when her eye fell upon a little bottle that stood near the looking-glass.
A1   8:11   Either the well was very deep, or she fell very slowly, for she had plenty of time as she went down
FELLOW (4)
A10   84:14   tastes! Sing her 'Turtle Soup,' will you, old fellow?"
A9   75: 7   said to the Mock Turtle "Drive on, old fellow! Don't be all day about it!" and he went on in these

FELLOW (cont.)
A4   31:25   "So you did, old fellow!" said the others.
A4   31:13   Brandy now--Don't choke him--How was it, old fellow? What happened to you? Tell us all about it!"
FELLOWS (1)
A7   58:26   hoarse, feeble voice, "I heard every word you fellows were saying."
FELLOW-TRAVELER (1)
T3   137:12   with vexation at having lost her dear little fellow-traveler so suddenly. "However, I know my name now,"
FELT (41)
A5   36:11   to the beginning of the conversation. Alice felt a little irritated at the Caterpillar's making such very
A1   12: 7   if she was going to shrink any further: she felt a little nervous about this; "for it might end, you know
T3   132: 7   seemed satisfied with this, though Alice felt a little nervous at the idea of trains jumping at all.
T3   135:23   much darker than the last wood, and Alice felt a little timid about going into it. However, on second
A11   88:34   Just at this moment Alice felt a very curious sensation, which puzzled her a good deal
A5   41:40   bit to try the effect. The next moment she felt a violent blow underneath her chin: it had struck her
T4   139:37   I don't know when I began it, but somehow I felt as if I'd been singing it a long long time!"
T2   126:24   that Alice had any idea of doing that. She felt as if she would never be able to talk again, she was
A2   19:40   the Mouse was bristling all over, and she felt certain it must be really offended. "We wo'n't talk about
A7   56:19   Alice felt dreadfully puzzled. The Hatter's remark seemed to her to
T6   162: 9   Alice felt even more indignant at this suggestion. "I mean," she
T9   195:19   Alice said very decidedly, for she felt quite certain about this, "is the thunder--no, no!" she
T4   139:19   Alice, passing on to Tweedledee, though she felt quite certain he would only shout out "Contrariwise!" and
T7   178: 3   it rang through and through her head till she felt quite deafened. She started to her feet and sprang across
A6   50:14   So she set the little creature down, and felt quite relieved to see it trot away quietly into the wood.
A5   43:38   been anything near the right size, that it felt quite strange at first; but she got used to it in a few
A9   73:20   good thing!" she said to herself, for she had felt quite unhappy at the number of executions the Queen had
T8W   14: 5   Alice felt rather offended at this answer, and was very nearly
A9   75: 6   both sat silent and looked at poor Alice, who felt ready to sink into the earth. At last the Gryphon said to
T2   126:16   Queen kept crying "Faster! Faster!" but Alice felt she could not go faster, though she had no breath left to
T9   196:25   The White Queen looked timidly at Alice, who felt she ought to say something kind, but really couldn't
A2   15:31   be savage if I've kept her waiting!" Alice felt so desperate that she was ready to ask help of any one:
A10   83:12   Alice did not dare to disobey, though she felt sure it would all come wrong, and she went on in a
A3   21:17   kept her eyes anxiously fixed on it, for she felt sure she would catch a bad cold if she did not get dry
T9   204:23   At any other time, Alice would have felt surprised at this, but she was far too much excited to
T5   149:10   bread-and-butter," and Alice felt that if there was to be any conversation at all, she must
T6   166:21   Alice felt that in that case she really ought to listen to it; so
A6   51: 3   long claws and a great many teeth, so she felt that it ought to be treated with respect.
T2   123:36   the flowers were interesting enough, she felt that it would be far grander to have a talk with a real
A6   50:12   was neither more nor less than a pig, and she felt that it would be quite absurd for her to carry it any
T6   168:18   strong hint that she ought to be going, she felt that it would hardly be civil to stay. So she got up, and
A1   9:15   didn't much matter which way she put it. She felt that she was dozing off, and had just begun to dream that
A5   41:12   contradicted in all her life before, and she felt that she was losing her temper.
A5   41:42   by this very sudden change, but she felt that there was no time to be lost, as she was shrinking
A6   51:17   Alice felt that this could not be denied, so she tried another
T3   132:10   she said to herself. In another moment she felt the carriage rise straight up into the air, and in her
T5   151:10   Alice felt there was no denying that. "Of course it would be all the
A4   28:26   getting out of the room again, no wonder she felt unhappy.
A6   45: 8   hair that curled all over their heads. She felt very curious to know what it was all about, and crept a
A6   48:23   would not be an advantage," said Alice, who felt very glad to get an opportunity of showing off a little
A3   26:41   here poor Alice began to cry again, for she felt very lonely and low-spirited. In a little while, however,
FENDER (3)
T1   113:22   began scrambling wildly up the side of the fender.
T8   180: 8   a whole set of fire-irons falling into the fender! And how quiet the horses are! They let them get on and
A2   15: 9   Hearthrug, near the Fender, (with Alice's love).
FERRETS (2)
A4   27: 5   whiskers! She'll get me executed, as sure as ferrets are ferrets! Where can I have dropped them, I wonder?"
A4   27: 5   get me executed, as sure as ferrets are ferrets! Where can I have dropped them, I wonder?" Alice
FETCH (10)
T7   171: 7   repeated impatiently. "I must have two--to fetch and carry. One to fetch, and one to carry."
T7   171: 7   "I must have two--to fetch and carry. One to fetch, and one to carry."
A8   69: 8   prison," the Queen said to the executioner: "fetch her here." And the executioner went off like an arrow.
A3   26:23   addressing nobody in particular. "She'd soon fetch it back!"
A4   30:26   to bring but one. Bill's got the other--Bill! Fetch it here, lad!--Here, put 'em up at this corner--No, tie
A4   27:14   you doing out here? Run home this moment, and fetch me a pair of gloves and a fan! Quick, now!" And Alice
A4   29:19   "Mary Ann! Mary Ann!" said the voice. "Fetch me my gloves this moment!" Then came a little pattering
T7   175:33   "Come, fetch out the plum-cake, old man!" the Unicorn went on,
A8   68: 8   "I'll fetch the executioner myself," said the King eagerly, and he
A2   20: 6   oh, such long curly brown hair! And it'll fetch things when you throw them, and it'll sit up and beg for
FEVERISH (1)
T9   195: 4   Red Queen anxiously interrupted. "She'll be feverish after so much thinking." So they set to work and
FEW (18)
T9   200:10   animals, some birds, and there were even a few flowers among them. "I'm glad they've come without waiting
A11   86:26   for she thought, and rightly too, that very few little girls of her age knew the meaning of it at all.
T2   120:20   straight on till she got to the hill. For a few minutes all went on well, and she was just saying "I
A5   43:38   strange at first; but she got used to it in a few minutes, and began talking to herself, as usual, "Come,
A12   92: 2   moment how large she had grown in the last few minutes, and she jumped up in such a hurry that she tipped
A3   21: 6   had a consultation about this, and after a few minutes it seemed quite natural to Alice to find herself
A4   29:17   a conversation of it altogether; but after a few minutes she heard a voice outside, and stopped to listen.
T8   182:36   a comfortable plan, Alice thought, and for a few minutes she walked on in silence, puzzling over the idea,
A12   95:24   Alice, (she had grown so large in the last few minutes that she wasn't a bit afraid of interrupting him,)
T8W   21:17   pleased that she had gone back and given a few minutes to making the poor old creature comfortable.

FEW (cont.)
```
  A1    12: 6  garden. First, however, she waited for a few minutes to see if she was going to shrink any further: she
  T8W   18:11  I'll try; wait a bit." He was silent for a few moments, and then began again--
  T8   190:36  to be a Queen! How grand it sounds!" A very few steps brought her to the edge of the brook. "The Eighth
  A1    10:11  that Alice had begun to think that very few things indeed were really impossible.
  T2   120: 4  no, it doesn't do that--" (after going a few yards along the path, and turning several sharp corners),
  T6   159: 2  and more human: when she had come within a few yards of it, she saw that it had eyes and a nose and a
  A6    50:21  Cheshire-Cat sitting on a bough of a tree a few yards off.
  T8   190:14  road by which they had come. "You've only a few yards to go," he said, "down the hill and over that little
```
FIDDLE-DE-DEE (2)
```
  T9   195: 8  "Do you know Languages? What's the French for fiddle-de-dee?"
  T9   195:12  this time. "If you'll tell me what language 'fiddle-de-dee' is, I'll tell you the French for it!" she
```
FIDDLE-DE-DEE'S (1)
```
  T9   195: 9                            "Fiddle-de-dee's not English," Alice replied gravely.
```
FIDDLES (1)
```
  T4   139:33  branches rubbing one across the other, like fiddles and fiddle-sticks.
```
FIDDLESTICK (1)
```
  T1   114: 1                      "Imperial fiddlestick!" said the King, rubbing his nose, which had been
```
FIDDLE-STICKS (1)
```
  T4   139:33  one across the other, like fiddles and fiddle-sticks.
```
FIDGETED (1)
```
  A11   88:27  hard at the Hatter, who turned pale and fidgeted.
```
FIELD (3)
```
  A1     8: 3  burning with curiosity, she ran across the field after it, and was just in time to see it pop down a
  T3   137: 5  Fawn, till they came out into another open field, and here the Fawn gave a sudden bound into the air, and
  T3   135:22            She very soon came to an open field, with a wood on the other side of it: it looked much
```
FIELDS (2)
```
  T6   166:23            "In winter, when the fields are white, / I sing this song for your delight--
  T1   109:11  I wonder if the snow loves the trees and fields, that it kisses them so gently? And then it covers them
```
FIERCELY (1)
```
  T9   204:17  "And as for you," she went on, turning fiercely upon the Red Queen, whom she considered as the cause
```
FIFTEEN (1)
```
  A1     9:40  before, and behind it was a little door about fifteen inches high: she tried the little golden key in the
```
FIFTEENTH (1)
```
  A11   88:15                            "Fifteenth," said the March Hare.
```
FIFTH (4)
```
  A3    26: 4  said Alice very humbly: "you had got to the fifth bend, I think?"
  T2   128:11  belongs to Tweedledum and Tweedledee--the Fifth is mostly water--the Sixth belongs to Humpty Dumpty--But
  T8   183: 4  to say, as she was helping him up from his fifth tumble.
  T8   190:31  and then on the other. After the fourth or fifth tumble he reached the turn, and then she waved her
```
FIFTY (2)
```
  T1   109: 6  day came, I should have to go without fifty dinners at once! Well, I shouldn't mind that much! I'd
  T9   200: 9  large hall, and noticed that there were about fifty guests, of all kinds: some were animals, some birds, and
```
FIG (1)
```
  A6    53: 1                      "Did you say 'pig', or 'fig'?" said the Cat.
```
FIGHT (12)
```
  T7   174: 4  the King. "How are they getting on with the fight?"
  T7   174:17            "I don't think they'll fight any more to-day," the King said to Hatta: "go and order
  T4   147:40            "We must have a bit of a fight, but I don't care about going on long," said Tweedledum.
  T8   179:31            "Well, we must fight for her, then," said the Red Knight, as he took up his
  T7   174:12            There was a pause in the fight just then, and the Lion and the Unicorn sat down,
  T4   147:43            "Let's fight till six, and then have dinner," said Tweedledum.
  T8   180: 2  are," she said to herself, as she watched the fight, timidly peeping out from her hiding-place. "One Rule
  T4   147:38            "Then you'd better not fight to-day," said Alice, thinking it a good opportunity to
  A8    68:23  caught the flamingo and brought it back, the fight was over, and both the hedgehogs were out of sight: "but
  T7   176:16            "What a fight we might have for the crown now!" the Unicorn said,
  T7   173:21  other Messenger, was standing watching the fight, with a cup of tea in one hand and a piece of
  A8    68:17            The hedgehog was engaged in a fight with another hedgehog, which seemed to Alice an
```
FIGHTING (5) [See also A-FIGHTING]
```
  T4   148:10  still hoping to make them a little ashamed of fighting for such a trifle.
  T7   172:37                            "Fighting for the crown?"
  T7   173: 1            "The Lion and the Unicorn were fighting for the crown: / The Lion beat the Unicorn all round
  A8    66:21  for turns, quarreling all the while, and fighting for the hedgehogs; and in a very short time the Queen
  T7   173:16  the middle of which the Lion and Unicorn were fighting. They were in such a cloud of dust, that at first
```
FIGURE (4)
```
  T6   159:12  of her, she thought he must be a stuffed figure after all.
  A10   84: 8            "Shall we try another figure of the Lobster-Quadrille?" the Gryphon went on. "Or
  A10   78:35  Back to land again, and--that's all the first figure," said the Mock Turtle, suddenly dropping his voice;
  A10   79: 5            "Come, let's try the first figure!" said the Mock Turtle to the Gryphon. "We can do it
```
FIGURES (1)
```
  A6    48:33  me!" said the Duchess. "I never could abide figures!" And with that she began nursing her child again,
```
FILL (5)
```
  T1   118:28  make it out at all.) "Somehow it seems to fill my head with ideas--only I don't exactly know what they
  T3   129:35  same size as the people, and quite seemed to fill the carriage.
  T7   169: 3  at last in such crowds that they seemed to fill the whole forest. Alice got behind a tree, for fear of
  T9   199:29                      "Then fill up the glasses as quick as you can, / And sprinkle the
  T9   200: 1                      "Then fill up the glasses with treacle and ink, / Or anything else
```
FILLED (4)
```
  A12   98:32  the choking of the suppressed guinea-pigs, filled the air, mixed up with the distant sob of the miserable
  T6   167:16  My heart went hop, my heart went thump: / I filled the kettle at the pump.
```

FILLED (cont.)
A1   8:16   sides of the well, and noticed that they were filled with cupboards and book-shelves: here and there she saw
A2   17:17   right words," said poor Alice, and her eyes filled with tears again as she went on, "I must be Mabel after
FILLS (1)
A4   30: 8   goose! Who ever saw one that size? Why, it fills the whole window!"
FIND (43)
A3   22:20   The question is, what did the archbishop find?"
T8   188:19   tale: / He said 'I go my ways, / And when I find a mountain-rill, / I set it in a blaze; / And thence they
A2   18:22   wherever you go to on the English coast, you find a number of bathing-machines in the sea, some children
TI   103: 9   thy silver laughter: / No thought of me shall find a place / In thy young life's hereafter--/ Enough that
A12   99: 9   would feel with all their simple sorrows, and find a pleasure in all their simple joys, remembering her own
T3   133:13   your head," said the Gnat, "and there you'll find a Snap-dragon-fly. Its body is made of plum-pudding, its
A3   22:18   "I know what 'it' means well enough, when I find a thing," said the Duck: "it's generally a frog, or a
A1   10:13   went back to the table, half hoping she might find another key on it, or at any rate a book of rules for
A12   95:31   of trouble, you know, as we needn't try to find any. And yet I don't know," he went on, spreading out the
T8   182:14   the Knight said. "It'll come in handy if we find any plum-cake. Help me to get it into this bag."
T3   134:16   into Alice's head. "Supposing it couldn't find any?" she suggested.
T1   115:17   and went round the room to see if she could find any water to throw over him. However, she could find
T9   199: 2   Alice turned round, ready to find fault with anybody. "Where's the servant whose business
A9   70: 4   Alice was very glad to find her in such a pleasant temper, and thought to herself
A2   19: 2   said Alice, as she swam about, trying to find her way out. "I shall be punished for it now, I suppose,
A2   18:11   at the sudden change, but very glad to find herself still in existence. "And now for the garden!" And
T5   157: 5   back into her place, very much relieved to find herself still in the boat.
A3   21: 7   minutes it seemed quite natural to Alice to find herself talking familiarly with them, as if she had known
T1   119:10   floating in the air, and was rather glad to find herself walking again in the natural way.
A9   70:23   "Everything's got a moral, if only you can find it." And she squeezed herself up closer to Alice's side
A4   32:20   right size again; and the second thing is to find my way into that lovely garden. I think that will be the
T2   125: 7   but went on: "--and I thought I'd try and find my way to the top of that hill--"
T4   139:35   her sister the history of all this), "to find myself singing 'Here we go round the mulberry bush.' I
T1   115:18   water to throw over him. However, she could find nothing but a bottle of ink, and when she got back with
T1   114:14   he thought that was the most likely place to find one.
TI   103:24   are but older children, dear, / Who fret to find our bedtime near.
A7   55:16   "Do you mean that you think you can find out the answer to it?" said the March Hare.
A8   63: 8   one in by mistake; and, if the Queen was to find out, we should all have our heads cut off, you know. So
A8   68:29   to the Cheshire-Cat, she was surprised to find quite a large crowd collected round it: there was a
T3   129:19   beginning to run down the hill, and trying to find some excuse for turning shy so suddenly. "It'll never do
T1   116: 4   again), she turned over the leaves, to find some part that she could read, "--for it's all in some
T8W   16: 6   of the wig?" Alice repeated, quite pleased to find that he was recovering his temper.
A5   42:20   her head down to them, and was delighted to find that her neck would bend about easily in any direction,
A4   32:10   one of the cakes, and was delighted to find that she began shrinking directly. As soon as she was
T6   162:31   "It is really?" said Alice, quite pleased to find that she had chosen a good subject after all.
A11   86:14   them in books, and she was quite pleased to find that she knew the name of nearly everything there.
A1   12:40   was growing; and she was quite surprised to find that she remained the same size. To be sure, this is what
A8   66:14   to begin again, it was very provoking to find that the hedgehog had unrolled itself, and was in the act
T1   112: 4   the fireplace, and she was quite pleased to find that there was a real one, blazing away as brightly as
T3   135:31   one. But then the fun would be, trying to find the creature that has got my old name! That's just like
A4   27:20   him his fan and gloves--that is, if I can find them." As she said this, she came upon a neat little
T5   158:21   it's got branches, I declare! How very odd to find trees growing here! And actually here's a little brook!
T2   128:10   by railway, I should think--and you'll find yourself in the Fourth Square in no time. Well, that
FINDING (5)
A1   11: 7   "poison," so Alice ventured to taste it, and, finding it very nice (it had, in fact, a sort of mixed flavour
A9   71: 3   "How fond she is of finding morals in things!" Alice thought to herself.
A1   12:13   After a while, finding that nothing more happened, she decided on going into
T9   201:29   to-day," Alice began, a little frightened at finding that, the moment she opened her lips, there was dead
T9   192:12   oddly that she didn't feel a bit surprised at finding the Red Queen and the White Queen sitting close to her
FINDS (1)
A4   27:19   as she ran. "How surprised he'll be when he finds out who I am! But I'd better take him his fan and gloves
FINE (5)
T2   123:33   that does it," said the Rose: "wonderfully fine air it is, out here."
T8W   14:22   five new lumps of white sugar, large and in fine condition. In coming back--"
A8   65:25   "It's--it's a very fine day!" said a timid voice at her side. She was walking by
A9   72:34   "A fine day, your Majesty!" the Duchess began in a low, weak
T4   143:17   be / A dismal thing to do!' / 'The night is fine,' the Walrus said. / 'Do you admire the view?
FINGER (13)
T5   152: 9   making herself heard. "Have you pricked your finger?"
T5   152:20   had slipped, and the Queen had pricked her finger.
A3   23:24   said the Dodo, pointing to Alice with one finger; and the whole party at once crowded round her, calling
A12   96:22   had left off writing on his slate with one finger, as he found it made no mark; but he now hastily began
T5   150: 3   on, sticking a large piece of plaster on her finger as she spoke, "there's the King's Messenger. He's in
T4   146:15   in a moment, as he pointed with a trembling finger at a small white thing lying under the tree.
T4   139:14   that Alice couldn't help pointing her finger at Tweedledum, and saying "First Boy!"
A11   87:10   for it, he was obliged to write with one finger for the rest of the day; and this was of very little
T1   108:26   interrupt me!" she went on, holding up one finger. "I'm going to tell you all your faults. Number one:
T5   153:23   "Then I hope your finger is better now?" Alice said very politely, as she
A3   23:18   and it stood for a long time with one finger pressed upon its forehead (the position in which you
A1   11: 2   hold it too long; and that, if you cut your finger very deeply with a knife, it usually bleeds; and she
T5   151: 9   said, as she bound the plaster round her finger with a bit of ribbon.
FINGER-POSTS (3)
T3   137:17   only one road through the wood, and the two finger-posts both pointed along it. "I'll settle it," Alice
T3   137:14   forget it again. And now, which of these finger-posts ought I to follow, I wonder?"

FINGER-POSTS (cont.)
  T3   137:22 the road divided, there were sure to be two finger-posts pointing the same way, one marked "TO
FINGER'S (1)
  T5   152: 5 about as if she wanted to shake it off. "My finger's bleeding! Oh, oh, oh, oh!"
FINGERS (5)
  T3   133: 2 Alice began, counting off the names on her fingers.
  T2   124: 8 Look up, speak nicely, and don't twiddle your fingers all the time."
  T8   189:16   And now, if e'er by chance I put / My fingers into glue, / Or madly squeeze a right-hand foot / Into
  T1   119: 5 to herself. She just kept the tips of her fingers on the hand-rail, and floated gently down without even
  T6   168:22 in a discontented tone, giving her one of his fingers to shake: "you're so exactly like other people."
FINISH (5)
  A3   26:44 had changed his mind, and was coming back to finish his story.
  A9   74:30 to herself "I don't see how he can ever finish, if he doesn't begin." But she waited patiently.
  A11 90:29   "I'd rather finish my tea," said the Hatter, with an anxious look at the
  A7   59:26   "If you ca'n't be civil, you'd better finish the story for yourself."
  A3   26:13   "Please come back, and finish your story!" Alice called after it. And the others all
FINISHED (17) [See also UNFINISHED]
  A5   42:37 in saying anything more till the Pigeon had finished.
  A9   74:28 both of you, and don't speak a word till I've finished."
  T4   148: 8 for ever so far round, by the time we've finished!"
  A12 98: 9 have just been reading about; when she had finished, her sister kissed her, and said "It was a curious
  T7   173:23 "He's only just out of prison, and he hadn't finished his tea when he was sent in," Haigha whispered to
  T1   118:25 "It seems very pretty," she said when she had finished it, "but it's rather hard to understand!" (You see
  A1   11: 9 toffy, and hot buttered toast), she very soon finished it off. * * * * * * * * * * *
  A11 88: 9 "for bringing these in; but I hadn't quite finished my tea when I was sent for."
  A1   13: 5   So she set to work, and very soon finished off the cake. * * * * * * * * * * *
  A11 88:10   "You ought to have finished," said the King. "When did you begin?"
  A7   58: 4   "Well, I'd hardly finished the first verse," said the Hatter, "when the Queen
  A5   39: 3 / For anything tougher than suet; / Yet you finished the goose, with the bones and the beak--/ Pray, how
  A10 83:18 share of the treat. / When the pie was all finished, the Owl, as a boon, / Was kindly permitted to pocket
  T6   168:40 unsatisfactory people I ever met--" She never finished the sentence, for at this moment a heavy crash shook
  A3   24: 3 of this elegant thimble"; and, when it had finished this short speech, they all cheered.
  T1   107:12   But the black kitten had been finished with earlier in the afternoon, and so, while Alice
  T12 207:28 undergoing its toilet, "when will Dinah have finished with your White Majesty, I wonder? That must be the
FINISHES (1)
  A11 90:27   "Come, that finishes the guinea-pigs!" thought Alice. "Now we shall get on
FINISHING (1)
  A8   67:34 --likely to win, that it's hardly worth while finishing the game."
FIRE (11) [See also BONFIRE]
  A6   48:10 the cook took the cauldron of soup off the fire, and at once set to work throwing everything within her
  T3   134: 5 a good look at the insect with its head on fire, and had thought to herself, "I wonder if that's the
  T1   114:14 said the King, looking up anxiously into the fire, as if he thought that was the most likely place to find
  T1   112: 3 thing she did was to look whether there was a fire in the fireplace, and she was quite pleased to find that
  T1   110:36 bit! I want so much to know whether they've a fire in the winter: you never can tell, you know, unless our
  A2   19:37 pool, "and she sits purring so nicely by the fire, licking her paws and washing her face--and she is such a
  T1   112: 7 be no one here to scold me away from the fire. Oh, what fun it'll be, when they see me through the
  T1   112:13 instance, the pictures on the wall next the fire seemed to be all alive, and the very clock on the
  T1   110:37 you never can tell, you know, unless our fire smokes, and then smoke comes up in that room too--but
  A6   47: 3 nursing a baby: the cook was leaning over the fire, stirring a large cauldron which seemed to be full of
  T1   110:39 just to make it look as if they had a fire. Well then, the books are something like our books, only
FIRE-IRONS (3)
  T8   182:21 already loaded with bunches of carrots, and fire-irons, and many other things.
  A6   48:11 her reach at the Duchess and the baby--the fire-irons came first; then followed a shower of saucepans,
  T8   180: 7 when they tumble! Just like a whole set of fire-irons falling into the fender! And how quiet the horses
FIRELIGHT'S (1)
  TI   103:27 The storm-wind's moody madness--/ Within, the firelight's ruddy glow, / And childhood's nest of gladness. /
FIREPLACE (3)
  T1   112: 3 was to look whether there was a fire in the fireplace, and she was quite pleased to find that there was a
  A4   30:37 be in Bill's place for a good deal: this fireplace is narrow, to be sure; but I think I can kick a
  T1   110:34 upon a chair--all but the bit just behind the fireplace. Oh! I do so wish I could see that bit! I want so
FIREWORKS (1)
  T9   203:15 looking something like a bed of rushes with fireworks at the top. As to the bottles, they each took a pair
FIRST (85)
  A5   36:13 "I think you ought to tell me who you are, first."
  A8   62:13 "What for?" said the one who had spoken first.
  A12 97: 2 loudly. "The idea of having the sentence first!"
  T5   150:12 "it always makes one a little giddy at first--"
  T7   173:17 They were in such a cloud of dust, that at first Alice could not make out which was which; but she soon
  T7   177:12 cakes," the Unicorn remarked. "Hand it round first, and cut it afterwards."
  A2   17:23 look up and say 'Who am I, then? Tell me that first, and then, if I like being that person, I'll come up: if
  A11 90:15 into this they slipped the guinea-pig, head first, and then sat upon it.)
  T3   129:14 though the idea quite took her breath away at first. "And what enormous flowers they must be!" was her next
  T9   192: 6 up and walked about--rather stiffly just at first, as she was afraid that the crown might come off: but
  A5   43:34 and she set to work very carefully, nibbling first at one and then at the other, and growing sometimes
  A6   46:11 said the Footman, "and that for two reasons. First, because I'm on the same side of the door as you are:
  A9   70:25 not much like her keeping so close to her: first because the Duchess was very ugly; and secondly, because
  T4   139:15 her finger at Tweedledum, and saying "First Boy!"
  A8   67:10 in the air: it puzzled her very much at first, but after watching it a minute or two she made it out
  A5   43:38 the right size, that it felt quite strange at first; but she got used to it in a few minutes, and began
  A8   63:15   First came ten soldiers carrying clubs: these were all shaped

FIRST (cont.)

A9	77:12	"Ten hours the first day," said the Mock Turtle: "nine the next, and so on."
T9	197: 1	me," said Alice, as she tried to obey the first direction: "and I don't know any soothing lullabies."
A10	78:35	"Back to land again, and--that's all the first figure," said the Mock Turtle, suddenly dropping his
A10	79: 5	"Come, let's try the first figure!" said the Mock Turtle to the Gryphon. "We can do
T4	139:25	not like shaking hands with either of them first, for fear of hurting the other one's feelings; so, as
A10	78:14	"Why," said the Gryphon, "you first form into a line along the sea-shore--"
T2	123:30	her first remark. She had indeed: when Alice first found her in the ashes, she had been only three inches
T8	190:16	be a Queen--But you'll stay and see me off first?" he added as Alice turned with an eager look in the
T7	172:23	said the King, "or else he'd have been here first. However, now you've got your breath, you may tell us
A1	12: 5	the little door into that lovely garden. First, however, she waited for a few minutes to see if she was
T8	184:31	feet: the head is high enough already.' Now, first I put my head on the top of the gate--then the head's
A2	18:18	she was up to her chin in saltwater. Her first idea was that she had somehow fallen into the sea, "and
A1	9:36	on it but a tiny golden key, and Alice's first idea was that this might belong to one of the doors of
T5	154: 4	gently. "I should like to look all round me first, if I might."
T7	169: 2	soldiers came running through the wood, at first in twos and threes, then ten or twenty together, and at
A3	23: 8	First it marked out a race-course, in a sort of circle, ("the
A6	49:20	itself out again, so that altogether, for the first minute or two, it was as much as she could do to hold it
T2	128: 8	and said "A pawn goes two squares in its first move, you know. So you'll go very quickly through the
T3	129:29	she ran down the hill, and jumped over the first of the six little brooks. * * * * * * * * * * * * * *
T8	190:30	along the road, and the Knight tumbling off, first on one side and then on the other. After the fourth or
T9	197:13	Alice, looking about in great perplexity, as first one round head, and then the other, rolled down from her
A4	29:16	And so she went on, taking first one side and then the other, and making quite a
A7	57: 7	"Not at first, perhaps," said the Hatter: "but you could keep it to
A10	83: 7	"It's the first position in dancing," Alice said; but she was dreadfully
A3	21: 5	The first question of course was, how to get dry again: they had a
A6	46:33	get in at all?" said the Footman. "That's the first question, you know."
A12	94:26	general clapping of hands at this: it was the first really clever thing the King had said that day.
A7	56: 9	could think of nothing better to say than his first remark, "It was the best butter, you know."
T2	123:29	Red Queen. "She's grown a good deal!" was her first remark. She had indeed: when Alice first found her in
A10	81:44	"No, no! The adventures first," said the Gryphon in an impatient tone: "explanations
A10	82: 2	them her adventures from the time when she first saw the White Rabbit. She was a little nervous about it,
A2	19:25	again: "Ou est ma chatte?" which was the first sentence in her French lesson-book. The Mouse gave a
A12	98:17	First, she dreamed about little Alice herself: once again the
T1	107: 6	Dinah washed her children's faces was this: first she held the poor thing down by its ear with one paw,
A1	10:20	going to do that in a hurry. "No, I'll look first," she said, "and see whether it's marked 'poison' or not
A2	19: 6	she swam nearer to make out what it was: at first she thought it must be a walrus or hippopotamus, but
A1	8:13	and to wonder what was going to happen next. First, she tried to look down and make out what she was coming
T1	119: 2	is like! Let's have a look at the garden first!" She was out of the room in a moment, and ran down
A11	88:36	to grow larger again, and she thought at first she would get up and leave the court; but on second
A7	55: 7	time with great curiosity, and this was his first speech.
T9	202: 3	"'First, the fish must be caught.' / That is easy: a baby, I
A10	82: 3	She was a little nervous about it, just at first, the two creatures got so close to her, one on each side
A6	48:12	the Duchess and the baby--the fire-irons came first; then followed a shower of saucepans, plates, and dishes
T1	110:31	you all my ideas about Looking-glass House. First, there's the room you can see through the glass--that's
A4	30:27	'em up at this corner--No, tie 'em together first--they don't reach half high enough yet--Oh, they'll do
T4	139:21	"You've begun wrong!" cried Tweedledum. "The first thing in a visit is to say 'How d'ye do?' and shake
A4	32:18	"The first thing I've got to do," said Alice to herself, as she
T1	112: 2	down into the Looking-glass room. The very first thing she did was to look whether there was a fire in
A4	31: 5	The first thing she heard was a general chorus of "There goes
T3	129: 1	Of course the first thing to do was to make a grand survey of the country
T8W	13:10	I can be of any use to him," was Alice's first thought, as she turned to spring over the brook:--but
T8	179: 3	alarm. There was no one to be seen, and her first thought was that she must have been dreaming about the
T3	130:18	All this time the Guard was looking at her, first through a telescope, then through a microscope, and then
T6	160: 2	Humpty Dumpty said, looking at her for the first time, "but tell me your name and your business."
A7	55:35	The Hatter was the first to break the silence. "What day of the month is it?" he
A5	41: 6	The Caterpillar was the first to speak.
T8	182:17	so very awkward in putting in the dish: the first two or three times that he tried he fell in himself
A12	96:30	"No, no!" said the Queen. "Sentence first--verdict afterwards."
T6	164:20	sounded very hopeful, so Alice repeated the first verse:--
A7	58: 4	"Well, I'd hardly finished the first verse," said the Hatter, "when the Queen bawled out
A8	66: 6	The chief difficulty Alice found at first was in managing her flamingo: she succeeded in getting
A3	22:23	and offer him the crown. William's conduct at first was moderate. But the insolence of his Normans--' How
T4	140:20	as she could, "would you please tell me first which road--"
A6	47:14	whether it was good manners for her to speak first, "why your cat grins like that?"
A11	88: 5	three blasts on the trumpet, and called out "First witness!"
A11	88: 4	"Call the first witness," said the King; and the White Rabbit blew three
A11	88: 6	The first witness was the Hatter. He came in with a teacup in one
T8	182:32	"First you take an upright stick," said the Knight. "Then you

FISH (12) [See also GOLD-FISH, JELLY-FISH, STAR-FISH]

A6	45: 5	by his face only, she would have called him a fish)--and rapped loudly at the door with his knuckles. It was
T9	196:10	for," said Alice: "he wanted to punish the fish, because--"
A10	81:33	course not," said the Mock Turtle. "Why, if a fish came to me, and told me he was going a journey, I should
A10	84:26	"Beautiful Soup! Who cares for fish, / Game, or any other dish? / Who would not give all else
T6	166:39	"I sent a message to the fish: / I told them 'This is what I wish.'
T9	202: 5	I think, could have caught it.' / 'Next, the fish must be bought.' / That is easy: a penny, I think, could
T9	202: 3	"'First, the fish must be caught.' / That is easy: a baby, I think, could
T9	202:18	/ Which is easiest to do, / Un-dish-cover the fish, or dishcover the riddle?"
T9	200:19	Red Queen began. "You've missed the soup and fish," she said. "Put on the joint!" And the waiters set a leg
T4	147: 7	and his large eyes--"looking more like a fish than anything else," Alice thought.

FISH (cont.)
T9   202: 7   'Now cook me the fish!' / That is easy, and will not take more than a minute. /
A10   81:31 with them," the Mock Turtle said. "No wise fish would go anywhere without a porpoise."
FISHES (9)
T9   201:33 some way. Do you know why they're so fond of fishes, all about here?"
T6   167: 9   The fishes answered, with a grin, / 'Why, what a temper you are
T6   167:18 some one came to me and said / 'The little fishes are in bed.'
T9   201:32 curious thing, I think--every poem was about fishes in some way. Do you know why they're so fond of fishes,
A2   17:14 spreads his claws, / And welcomes little fishes in, / With gently smiling jaws!
T6   167: 1   The little fishes of the sea, / They sent an answer back to me.
T9   201:37 a lovely riddle--all in poetry--all about fishes. Shall she repeat it?"
T9   201:35 answer was a little wide of the mark. "As to fishes," she said, very slowly and solemnly, putting her mouth
T12   208: 1 a quantity of poetry said to me, all about fishes! To-morrow morning you shall have a real treat. All the
FISHES' (1)
T6   167: 3   The little fishes' answer was / 'We cannot do it, Sir, because--'"
FISH-FOOTMAN (2)
A6   45:11   The Fish-Footman began by producing from under his arm a great
A6   46: 7 her; and, when she next peeped out, the Fish-Footman was gone, and the other was sitting on the ground
FIT (9)
A12   95:14 was that you had been / (Before she had this fit) / An obstacle that came between / Him, and ourselves, and
T8W   19: 5   They said it did not fit, and so / It made me look extremely plain: / But what was
T6   167:14   I took a kettle large and new, / Fit for the deed I had to do.
T8   181:13 He was dressed in tin armour, which seemed to fit him very badly, and he had a queer-shaped little deal box
T1   114: 5 Lily was nearly screaming herself into a fit, she hastily picked up the Queen and set her on the table
T4   144:34 a sort of untidy heap, and snoring loud--"fit to snore his head off!" as Tweedledum remarked.
A12   96:17 than that. Then again--'before she had this fit'--you never had fits, my dear, I think?" he said to the
A12   96:25   "Then the words don't fit you," said the King looking round the court with a smile.
T8   182:18 fell in himself instead. "It's rather a tight fit, you see," he said, as they got it in at last; "there are
FITS (2)
A12   96:17 'before she had this fit'--you never had fits, my dear, I think?" he said to the Queen.
T8W   20: 4   "Your wig fits very well," the Wasp murmured, looking at her with an
FITTED (4)
A1   9:42 key in the lock, and to her great delight it fitted!
T8W   20: 2 Alice said heartily: "and I think if your wig fitted a little better, they wouldn't tease you quite so much
T9   203:18 took a pair of plates, which they hastily fitted on as wings, and so, with forks for legs, went
T8   191: 5 her hands up to something very heavy, that fitted tight all around her head.
FIVE (19)
A8   62: 9 which Seven looked up and said "That's right, Five! Always lay the blame on others!"
A8   62:15   "Yes, it is his business!" said Five. "And I'll tell him--it was for bringing the cook
A8   63: 5   Five and Seven said nothing, but looked at Two. Two began, in
A8   62: 5 she heard one of them say "Look out now, Five! Don't go splashing paint over me like that!"
A8   62:11   "You'd better not talk!" said Five. "I heard the Queen say only yesterday you deserved to be
T2   128: 3 four, I shall say good-bye. And at the end of five, I shall go!"
A8   62: 7   "I couldn't help it," said Five, in a sulky tone. "Seven jogged my elbow."
A2   16: 9 things I used to know. Let me see: four times five is twelve, and four times six is thirteen, and four times
T5   153: 7 to believe. I'm just one hundred and one, five months and a day."
T8W   14:21 another tour in the Pantry, and have found five new lumps of white sugar, large and in fine condition. In
T9   195:33 sometimes in the winter we take as many as five nights together--for warmth, you know."
T9   195:35   "Are five nights warmer than one night, then?" Alice ventured to
T9   195:40 as I'm five times as rich as you are, and five times as clever!"
T9   195:38   "But they should be five times as cold, by the same rule--"
T9   195:33 cried the Red Queen. "Five times as warm, and five times as cold--just as I'm five times as rich as you are,
T9   195:40 as warm, and five times as cold--just as I'm five times as rich as you are, and five times as clever!"
T9   195:39   "Just so!" cried the Red Queen. "Five times as warm, and five times as cold--just as I'm five
T9   195:37   "Five times as warm, of course."
A8   63:10 best, afore she comes, to--" At this moment, Five, who had been anxiously looking across the garden, called
FIVEPENCE (1)
T5   158: 5   "Fivepence farthing for one--twopence for two," the Sheep
FIX (1)
A6   48: 9 of conversation. While she was trying to fix on one, the cook took the cauldron of soup off the fire,
FIXED (3)
T6   159:11 his balance--and, as his eyes were steadily fixed in the opposite direction, and he didn't take the least
A3   21:17 in the middle. Alice kept her eyes anxiously fixed on it, for she felt sure she would catch a bad cold if
T9   201:31 there was dead silence, and all eyes were fixed upon her; "and it's a very curious thing, I think--every
FIXES (1)
T9   195:23 Queen: "when you've once said a thing, that fixes it, and you must take the consequences."
FLAME (2)
T1   118:10 he stood, / The Jabberwock, with eyes of flame, / Came whiffling through the tulgey wood, / And burbled
A1   12:10 like then?" And she tried to fancy what the flame of a candle looks like after the candle is blown out,
FLAMINGO (5)
A8   67:19 head appeared, and then Alice put down her flamingo, and began an account of the game, feeling very glad
A8   68:22   By the time she had caught the flamingo and brought it back, the fight was over, and both the
A9   71: 7 that I'm doubtful about the temper of your flamingo. Shall I try the experiment'"
A8   66: 6 Alice found at first was in managing her flamingo: she succeeded in getting its body tucked away,
A8   68:19 the other: the only difficulty was, that her flamingo was gone across the other side of the garden, where
FLAMINGOES (2)
A9   71:11   "Very true," said the Duchess: "flamingoes and mustard both bite. And the moral of that is--
A8   66: 3 were live hedgehogs, and the mallets live flamingoes, and the soldiers had to double themselves up and
FLAP (1)
T4   145:26 in among the trees. But I wish it wouldn't flap its wings so--it makes quite a hurricane in the wood--

FLAPPER (1)
    A10   78: 2   sighed   deeply,   and   drew   the   back of one flapper across his eyes. He looked at Alice and tried to speak
FLAPPERS (1)
    A9   76:37   replied,   counting   off   the   subjects on his flappers--"Mystery, ancient and modern, with Seaography: then
FLASHED (1)
    A1   8: 1   hurried on, Alice started to her feet, for it flashed across her mind that she had never before seen a
FLASHES (1)
    AI   3:13   Imperious Prima flashes forth / Her edict "to begin it": / In gentler tones
FLAT (5)
    T9   202:40   would   have thought they wanted to squeeze me flat!")
    T1   115:15   The King immediately fell flat on his back, and lay perfectly still; and Alice was a
    T8   184: 7   Alice   what   he   meant, and this time he fell flat on his back, right under the horse's feet.
    A8   63:12   three   gardeners   instantly   threw themselves flat upon their faces. There was a sound of many footsteps,
    A8   63:16   shaped   like   the   three gardeners, oblong and flat, with their hands and feet at the corners: next the ten
FLAVOUR (1)
    A1   11: 8   very   nice   (it had, in fact, a sort of mixed flavour of cherry-tart, custard, pine-apple, roast turkey,
FLEET (1)
    TI   103: 3   And dreaming eyes of wonder! / Though time be fleet, and I and thou / Are half a life asunder, / Thy loving
FLEW (3)
    A6   48:18   nose!",   as   an   unusually   large saucepan flew close by it, and very nearly carried it off.
    T4   139: 1   Just then flew down a monstrous crow, / As black as a tar-barrel; /
    T5   152:16   Oh, oh!" As she said the words the brooch flew open, and the Queen clutched wildly at it, and tried to
-FLIES [See BUTTERFLIES, SNAP-DRAGON-FLIES]
FLIMSY (1)
    T6   165: 9   "Exactly so. Well then, 'mimsy' is 'flimsy and miserable' (there's another portmanteau for you).
FLINGING (1)
    A6   49:11   bit, if you like!" the Duchess said to Alice, flinging the baby at her as she spoke. "I must go and get
FLOATED (2)
    T1   119: 5   the tips of her fingers on the hand-rail, and floated gently down without even touching the stairs with her
    T1   119: 7   touching   the   stairs   with her feet: then she floated on through the hall, and would have gone straight out
FLOATING (1)
    T1   119: 9   She   was   getting a little giddy with so much floating in the air, and was rather glad to find herself
FLOCK (1)
    A9   71:12   And the moral of that is--'Birds of a feather flock together.'"
FLOOR (6)
    T1   115: 8   that   she   nearly   let   him   drop upon the floor.
    T9   204:16   came   crashing down together in a heap on the floor.
    A4   32: 6   turning   into little cakes as they lay on the floor, and a bright idea came into her head. "If I eat one of
    T1   108:19   in   which   the   ball   rolled   down upon the floor, and yards and yards of it got unwound again.
    A11   90:23   go   no   lower," said the Hatter: "I'm on the floor, as it is."
    A4   28:16   and   very   soon   had   to   kneel down on the floor: in another minute there was not even room for this, and
FLOUR (1)
    T9   194:41   that!"   Alice   cried   eagerly. "You take some flour--"
FLOW (1)
    T5   154:16   "Things flow about so here!" she said at last in a plaintive tone,
FLOWER (2)
    T2   123: 5   "There's one other flower in the garden that can move about like you," said the
    T9   194:42   "Where do you pick the flower?" the White Queen asked: "In a garden or in the hedges
FLOWERBED (1)
    T2   120:27   start   again. This time she came upon a large flowerbed, with a border of daisies, and a willow-tree growing
FLOWER-BEDS [FLOWERBEDS] (2)
    A7   61: 6   in   the   beautiful   garden,   among the bright flower-beds and the cool fountains.
    T8   191: 2   rest   on   a lawn as soft as moss, with little flowerbeds dotted about it here and there. "Oh, how glad I am
FLOWER-POT (1)
    A8   65:13   said   Alice,   and   she   put them into a large flower-pot that stood near. The three soldiers wandered about
FLOWERS (11)
    T2t   120: 1   THE GARDEN OF LIVE FLOWERS
    T9   200:11   some   birds,   and   there   were   even a few flowers among them. "I'm glad they've come without waiting to
    A4   34: 1   was "What?" Alice looked all round her at the flowers and the blades of grass, but she could not see
    A1   10: 5   and   wander   about among those beds of bright flowers and those cool fountains, but she could not even get
    T2   122:29   "they   make   the   beds   too soft--so that the flowers are always asleep."
    T2   122:23   been   in many gardens before, but none of the flowers could talk."
    AI   4: 7   band. / Like pilgrim's wither'd wreath of flowers / Pluck'd in a far-off land.
    T3   129: 9   one of them that was bustling about among the flowers, poking its proboscis into them, "just as if it was a
    T2   121: 4   voice--almost   in a whisper. "And can all the flowers talk?"
    T3   129:14   her   breath away at first. "And what enormous flowers they must be!" was her next idea. "Something like
    T2   123:35   go and meet her," said Alice, for, though the flowers were interesting enough, she felt that it would be far
FLOWN (2)
    T5   152:27   it   was   getting light. "The crow must have flown away, I think," said Alice: "I'm so glad it's gone. I
    A5   42:25   her   draw back in a hurry: a large pigeon had flown into her face, and was beating her violently with its
FLUNG (2)
    A8   62:17   Seven flung down his brush, and had just begun "Well, of all the
    T9   199:22   At this moment the door was flung open, and a shrill voice was heard singing:--
FLURRY (1)
    A12   92: 1   "Here!"   cried Alice, quite forgetting in the flurry of the moment how large she had grown in the last few
FLUSHED (1)
    T5   156:31   of the rushes in growing so far off, as, with flushed cheeks and dripping hair and hands, she scrambled back
FLUSTERED (1)
    A4   31:21   thank ye; I'm better now--but I'm a deal too flustered to tell you--all I know is, something comes at me

FLUTTERED (1)
    A12   98: 2   brushing   away   some   dead   leaves   that   had fluttered down from the trees upon her face.
FLUTTERING (1)
    T9   203:20   as wings,   and so, with forks for legs, went fluttering about in all directions: "and very like birds they
FLY (4) [See also BREAD-AND-BUTTER-FLY, DRAGON-FLY, etc.]
    T4   140:40   flying overhead--/ There were no birds to fly.
    A9   72:28   right,"   said   the   Duchess, "as pigs have to fly; and the m----"
    A7   57:19   'Up above the world you fly, / Like a tea-tray in the sky. / Twinkle, twinkle--'"
    A8   68:21   see it   trying in a helpless sort of way to fly up into a tree.
FLYING (6)
    T5   153:19   The Queen spread out her arms again and went flying after it, and this time she succeeded in catching it
    T5   149: 4   both   arms stretched out wide, as if she were flying, and Alice very civilly went to meet her with the shawl
    A12   97: 9   the whole pack rose up into the air, and came flying down upon her; she gave a little scream, half of fright
    T3   134: 7   if that's the reason insects are so fond of flying into candles--because they want to turn into
    T7   174:23   Queen   running across the country! She came flying out of the wood over yonder--How fast those Queens can
    T4   140:39   / No cloud was in the sky: / No birds were flying overhead--/ There were no birds to fly.
FOE (1)
    T1   118: 6   vorpal sword in hand: / Long time the manxome foe he sought--/ So rested he by the Tumtum tree, / And stood
FOLD (2)
    T1   110:26   Alice   said, because the kitten wouldn't fold its arms properly. So, to punish it, she held it up to
    T4   147: 1   this time Tweedledee was trying his best to fold up the umbrella, with himself in it: which was such an
FOLDED (4) [See also UNFOLDED]
    A9   72:32   the   Queen   in front of them, with her arms folded, frowning like a thunderstorm.
    A5   36:37   Alice folded her hands, and began:--
    A4   34: 9   that was sitting on the top, with its arms folded, quietly smoking a long hookah, and taking not the
    T1   110:22   Kitty! Do you know, I think if you sat up and folded your arms, you'd look exactly like her. Now do try,
FOLDING (1)
    A11   91:14   King said with a melancholy air, and, after folding his arms and frowning at the cook till his eyes were
FOLK (1)
    T6   166:15   hands, "I can repeat poetry as well as other folk, if it comes to that--"
FOLLOW (4)
    A5   42:16   about, as she spoke, but no result seemed to follow, except a little shaking among the distant green leaves
    T3   137:15   now,   which of these finger-posts ought I to follow, I wonder?"
    A9   72:12   "if I had it written down: but I ca'n't quite follow it as you say it."
    T5   155: 3   added, as a sudden thought struck her. "I'll follow it up to the very top shelf of all. It'll puzzle it to
FOLLOWED (11)
    T9   199:33   Then followed a confused noise of cheering, and Alice thought to
    A6   48:12   and the baby--the fire-irons came first; then followed a shower of saucepans, plates, and dishes. The
    A9   74:34   These words were followed by a very long silence, broken only by an occasional
    A9   72:41   too much frightened to say a word, but slowly followed her back to the croquet-ground.
    A11   88:12   The Hatter looked at the March Hare, who had followed him into the court, arm-in-arm with the Dormouse.
    A7   59:38   He moved on as he spoke, and the Dormouse followed him: the March Hare moved into the Dormouse's place,
    A1   12:23   very   good   advice (though she very seldom followed it), and sometimes she scolded herself so severely as
    A8   63:25   said,   and went by without noticing her. Then followed the Knave of Hearts, carrying the King's crown on a
    T8W   19: 1   But when I followed their advice, / And they had noticed the effect, /
    T4   142: 7   Four other Oysters followed them, / And yet another four; / And thick and fast
    A10   85: 8   more faintly came, carried on the breeze that followed them, the melancholy words:--
FOLLOWS (1)
    A11   87:15   unrolled the parchment-scroll, and read as follows:--
FOND (7)
    A8   67: 6   "what would become of me? They're dreadfully fond of beheading people here: the great wonder is, that
    T9   201:33   in some way. Do you know why they're so fond of fishes, all about here?"
    T3   134: 7   "I wonder if that's the reason insects are so fond of flying into candles--because they want to turn into
    A2   20: 2   subject of conversation. "Are you--are you fond--of--of dogs?" The Mouse did not answer, so Alice went on
    A1   12:27   herself,   for this curious child was very fond of pretending to be two people. "But it's no use now,"
    T9   192: 3   on, in a severe tone (she was always rather fond of scolding herself), "It'll never do for you to be
    A9   71: 3   "How fond she is of finding morals in things!" Alice thought to
FOOLISH (4)
    A4   29:13   "Oh, you foolish Alice!" she answered herself. "How can you learn
    T8   187:14   and with a faint smile lighting up his gentle foolish face, as if he enjoyed the music of his song, he began
    T9   196:23   "she means well, but she ca'n't help saying foolish things as a general rule."
    T4   145:29   Alice thought to herself: "and it's foolish to cry about it." So she brushed away her tears, and
FOOT (12)
    A5   41:40   blow underneath her chin: it had struck her foot!
    A8   64:14   The Knave did so, very carefully, with one foot.
    T1   114: 3   for he was covered with ashes from head to foot.
    A4   30:39   She drew her foot as far down the chimney as she could, and waited till she
    A2   15: 7   Alice's Right Foot, Esq.
    A7   61: 4   of it in her pocket) till she was about a foot high; then she walked down the little passage: and then--
    T8   189:17   into glue, / Or madly squeeze a right-hand foot / Into a left-hand shoe, / Or if I drop upon my toe / A
    A2   18:17   As she said these words her foot slipped, and in another moment, splash! she was up to her
    A6   49:24   keep tight hold of its right ear and left foot, so as to prevent its undoing itself), she carried it out
    A5   42: 1   Her chin was pressed so closely against her foot, that there was hardly room to open her mouth; but she
    A11   88:31   the witness at all: he kept shifting from one foot to the other, looking uneasily at the Queen, and in his
    A4   28:20   she put one arm out of the window, and one foot up the chimney, and said to herself "Now I can do no more
FOOTMAN (10) [See also FISH-FOOTMAN, FROG-FOOTMAN]
    A6   46:42   "Anything you like," said the Footman, and began whistling.
    A6   46:10   There's no sort of use in knocking," said the Footman, "and that for two reasons. First, because I'm on the
    A6   45: 3   out of the wood--(she considered him to be a footman because he was in livery: otherwise, judging by his
    A6   46:30   "--or next day, maybe," the Footman continued in the same tone, exactly as if nothing had

FOOTMAN (cont.)
A6   45: 2 wondering what to do next, when suddenly a footman in livery came running out of the wood--(she
A6   45: 6 with his knuckles. It was opened by another footman in livery, with a round face, and large eyes like a
A6   46:26   "I shall sit here," the Footman remarked, "till to-morrow--"
A6   46:38   The Footman seemed to think this a good opportunity for repeating
A6   46:33   "Are you to get in at all?" said the Footman. "That's the first question, you know."
A6   46:18 might be some sense in your knocking," the Footman went on, without attending to her, "if we had the door
FOOTMAN'S (1)
A6   46:28 plate came skimming out, straight at the Footman's head: it just grazed his nose, and broke to pieces
FOOTMEN (1)
A6   45: 7 face, and large eyes like a frog; and both footmen, Alice noticed, had powdered hair that curled all over
FOOT-SOLDIERS (1)
T7   169:11 feet, these managed rather better than the foot-soldiers; but even they stumbled now and then; and it
FOOTSTEP (1)
T2   123:26 coming!" cried the Larkspur. "I hear her footstep, thump, thump, along the gravel-walk!"
FOOTSTEPS (2)
A8   63:13 upon their faces. There was a sound of many footsteps, and Alice looked round, eager to see the Queen.
A3   26:42   she again heard a little pattering of footsteps in the distance, and she looked up eagerly, half
FOR (361) [entries omitted]
FOREHEAD (2)
A11   91:28   the next witness. It quite makes my forehead ache!"
A3   23:19 a long time with one finger pressed upon its forehead (the position in which you usually see Shakespeare,
FORE-PAWS (1)
A10   79:11 when they passed too close, and waving their fore-paws to mark the time, while the Mock Turtle sang this,
FOREST (5)
T7   169: 3 crowds that they seemed to fill the whole forest. Alice got behind a tree, for fear of being run over,
T8   187:24 at her feet--and the black shadows of the forest behind--all this she took in like a picture, as, with
T6   168:41 for at this moment a heavy crash shook the forest from end to end.
T2   128:18 suppose it said--the Seventh Square is all forest--however, one of the Knights will show you the way--and
T8   190:25 and then the Knight rode slowly away into the forest. "It wo'n't take long to see him off, I expect," Alice
FORGET (5)
TI   103:18 memory yet, / Though envious years would say "forget."
T1   115:26 the King went on, "I shall never, never forget!"
T3   137:14 "that's some comfort. Alice--Alice--I won't forget it again. And now, which of these finger-posts ought I
A11   86:32 whispered in reply, "for fear they should forget them before the end of the trial."
A9   70:18 about something, my dear, and that makes you forget to talk. I ca'n't tell you just now what the moral of
FORGETTING (6)
A7   59:33 "What did they draw?" said Alice, quite forgetting her promise.
A12   92: 1   "Here!" cried Alice, quite forgetting in the flurry of the moment how large she had grown
T6   159:33 for the poetry," she added, almost out loud, forgetting that Humpty Dumpty would hear her.
A4   29:22 she trembled till she shook the house, quite forgetting that she was now about a thousand times as large as
T1   115:10 such faces, my dear!" she cried out, quite forgetting that the King couldn't hear her. "You make me laugh
T2   128: 2 yards I shall repeat them--for fear of your forgetting them. At the end of four, I shall say good-bye. And
FORGOT (5)
T5   156:19 breaking them off--and for a while Alice forgot all about the Sheep and the knitting, as she bent over
A2   14: 2 much surprised, that for the moment she quite forgot how to speak good English). "Now I'm opening out like
T4   139: 4 frightened both the heroes so, / They quite forgot their quarrel."
T4   138: 6   They stood so still that she quite forgot they were alive, and she was just going round to see if
A2   19:29 had hurt the poor animal's feelings. "I quite forgot you didn't like cats."
FORGOTTEN (6)
A1   11: 3 a knife, it usually bleeds; and she had never forgotten that, if you drink much from a bottle marked "poison
A4   33:10 the right size to do it! Oh dear! I'd nearly forgotten that I've got to grow up again! Let me see--how is
A9   70:16   She had quite forgotten the Duchess by this time, and was a little startled
A1   12:15 when she got to the door, she found she had forgotten the little golden key, and when she went back to the
A10   79: 8 "Oh, you sing," said the Gryphon. "I've forgotten the words."
A6   52:18 of the baby?" said the Cat. "I'd nearly forgotten to ask."
FORK (2)
T9   201: 4 a slice?" she said, taking up the knife and fork, and looking from one Queen to the other.
A10   84: 1 spoon: / While the Panther received knife and fork with a growl, / And concluded the banquet by--"
FORKS (1)
T9   203:19 they hastily fitted on as wings, and so, with forks for legs, went fluttering about in all directions: "and
FORM (1)
A10   78:14   "Why," said the Gryphon, "you first form into a line along the sea-shore--"
FORTH (1)
AI   3:13   Imperious Prima flashes forth / Her edict "to begin it": / In gentler tones Secunda
-FORTUNATE [See UNFORTUNATE]
FORTY-TWO (1)
A12   93:35 "Silence!", and read out from his book, "Rule Forty-two. All persons more than a mile high to leave the
FORWARDS (4)
T6   160:40 grinned almost from ear to ear, as he leant forwards (and as nearly as possible fell off the wall in doing
T3   131:23 the gentleman dressed in white paper leaned forwards and whispered in her ear, "Never mind what they all
A4   32:43 at the stick, running a very little way forwards each time and a long way back, and barking hoarsely
T10 205: 2 as she spoke, and shook her backwards and forwards with all her might.
FOUND (52) [See also NEW-FOUND]
T8W   15: 5 In coming back," Alice went on reading, "they found a lake of treacle. The banks of the lake were blue and
A1   10:15 people up like telescopes: this time she found a little bottle on it ("which certainly was not here
A5   42: 9 found that her shoulders were nowhere to be found: all she could see, when she looked down, was an immense
A11   87: 7 the court and got behind him, and very soon found an opportunity of taking it away. She did it so quickly
A12   93:11 upset, and their slates and pencils had been found and handed back to them, they set to work very
A8   66: 6   The chief difficulty Alice found at first was in managing her flamingo: she succeeded in

FOUND (cont.)
```
T9    194:29  on the White Queen, for she didn't like being found fault with so much.
T8W    14:21  made another tour in the Pantry, and have found five new lumps of white sugar, large and in fine
T1    115:19  of ink, and when she got back with it she found he had recovered, and he and the Queen were talking
A4     28:10  before she had drunk half the bottle, she found her head pressing against the ceiling, and had to stoop
T2    123:30  remark. She had indeed: when Alice first found her in the ashes, she had been only three inches high--
A4     27:36              By this time she had found her way into a tidy little room with a table in the
T2    120:23  it afterwards), and the next moment she found herself actually walking in at the door.
A7     61: 5  walked down the little passage: and then--she found herself at last in the beautiful garden, among the
T2    124: 4  She had not been walking a minute before she found herself face to face with the Red Queen, and full in
A1     8: 9   to think about stopping herself before she found herself falling down what seemed to be a very deep well
A1     9:28   but the Rabbit was no longer to be seen: she found herself in a long, low hall, which was lit up by a row
A7     60:42              Once more she found herself in the long hall, and close to the little glass
A12    97:11  of anger, and tried to beat them off, and found herself lying on the bank, with her head in the lap of
A4     32:17  she ran off as hard as she could, and soon found herself safe in a thick wood.
T2    127: 8  quite exhausted, they stopped, and she found herself sitting on the ground, breathless and giddy.
T3    132:17  to melt away as she touched it, and she found herself sitting quietly under a tree--while the Gnat
T2    123:42  she lost sight of her in a moment, and found herself walking in at the front-door again.
T1    115: 4  life such a face as the King made, when he found himself held in the air by an invisible hand, and being
A1     12:32  was lying under the table: she opened it, and found in it a very small cake, on which the words "EAT ME"
A3     22:13  the patriotic archbishop of Canterbury, found it advisable--'
A3     22:22  this question, but hurriedly went on, "--found it advisable to go with Edgar Atheling to meet William
A12    96:22  writing on his slate with one finger, as he found it made no mark; but he now hastily began again, using
A5     36: 2  "Well, perhaps you haven't found it so yet," said Alice; "but when you have to turn into
A3     22:16              "Found it," the Mouse replied rather crossly: "of course you
T7    175:21  her in an Anglo-Saxon attitude. "We only found it to-day. It's as large as life, and twice as natural!
A8     68:35  her, though, as they all spoke at once, she found it very hard to make out exactly what they said.
A9     70:11  she went on, very much pleased at having found out a new kind of rule, "and vinegar that makes them
A2     18: 7  and was going on shrinking rapidly: she soon found out that the cause of this was the fan she was holding,
T3    129:13  in fact, it was an elephant--as Alice soon found out, though the idea quite took her breath away at first
A4     32:12  the door, she ran out of the house, and found quite a crowd of little animals and birds waiting
A1     12:16  when she went back to the table for it, she found she could not possibly reach it: she could see it quite
A1     12:15  for poor Alice! when she got to the door, she found she had forgotten the little golden key, and when she
A2     18: 5  to the table to measure herself by it, and found that, as nearly as she could guess, she was now about
A5     42: 8  into alarm in another moment, when she found that her shoulders were nowhere to be found: all she
A1     10: 1              Alice opened the door and found that it led into a small passage, not much larger than a
T8    183: 1  the side on which Alice was walking, she soon found that it was the best plan not to walk quite close to the
T2    123:28              Alice looked round eagerly and found that it was the Red Queen. "She's grown a good deal!"
T6    168:10              And when I found the door was locked, / I pulled and pushed and kicked
T6    168:12              And when I found the door was shut, / I tried to turn the handle, but--"
A4     27:25  and be turned out of the house before she had found the fan and gloves.
T12   207:14  among the chessmen on the table till she had found the Red Queen: then she went down on her knees on the
T7    170: 4  out of the wood into an open place, where she found the White King seated on the ground, busily writing in
T5    155:18  turned into oars in her hands, and she found they were in a little boat, gliding along between banks:
A5     41:35  of it; and, as it was perfectly round, she found this a very difficult question. However, at last she
A5     42:22  going to dive in among the leaves, which she found to be nothing but the tops of the trees under which she
A3     22:15              "Found what?" said the Duck.
```
FOUNTAINS (2)
```
A7     61: 6  among the bright flower-beds and the cool fountains.
A1     10: 5  those beds of bright flowers and those cool fountains, but she could not even get her head through the
```
FOUR (16)
```
T4    147:42  looked at his watch, and said "Half-past four."
T4    142: 8  Oysters followed them, / And yet another four; / And thick and fast they came at last, / And more, and
A5     44: 2  open place, with a little house in it about four feet high. "Whoever lives there," thought Alice, "it'll
T7    169:10              Then came the horses. Having four feet, these managed rather better than the foot-soldiers;
T2    128: 3  fear of your forgetting them. At the end of four, I shall say good-bye. And at the end of five, I shall
A2     15:24  until there was a large pool round her, about four inches deep, and reaching half down the hall.
T6    164:26  plenty of hard words there. 'Brillig' means four o'clock in the afternoon--the time when you begin
T4    142: 7              Four other Oysters followed them, / And yet another four; /
A1     8:30   of the earth. Let me see: that would be four thousand miles down, I think--" (for, you see, Alice had
T7    170:10              "Four thousand two hundred and seven, that's the exact number,"
A2     16: 9  all the things I used to know. Let me see: four times five is twelve, and four times six is thirteen, and
T4    139:40  were fat, and very soon out of breath. "Four times round is enough for one dance," Tweedledum panted
A2     16:10  twelve, and four times six is thirteen, and four times seven is--oh dear! I shall never get to twenty at
A2     16: 9  Let me see: four times five is twelve, and four times six is thirteen, and four times seven is--oh dear!
T4    141:17  briny beach: / We cannot do with more than four, / To give a hand to each.'
T4    142: 1              But four young Oysters hurried up, / All eager for the treat: /
```
FOURTEEN (1)
```
T5    155: 9  round like that." She was now working with fourteen pairs at once, and Alice couldn't help looking at her
```
FOURTEENTH (1)
```
A11    88:13  the court, arm-in-arm with the Dormouse. "Fourteenth of March, I think it was," he said.
```
FOURTH (4)
```
A7     55:39  Alice considered a little, and then said "The fourth."
T8    190:31  on one side and then on the other. After the fourth or fifth tumble he reached the turn, and then she waved
T2    128:10  should think--and you'll find yourself in the Fourth Square in no time. Well, that square belongs to
T3    132: 9  at all. "However, it'll take us into the Fourth Square, that's some comfort!" she said to herself. In
```
FRABJOUS (1)
```
T1    118:19  / Come to my arms, my beamish boy! / O frabjous day! Callooh! Callay!" / He chortled in his joy.
```

-FRAME [See CUCUMBER-FRAME]
FRANCE (1)
    A10   80: 9   The further off from England the nearer is to France. / Then turn not pale, beloved snail, but come and join
FREE (5)
    A5   42: 7   "Come, my head's free at last!" said Alice in a tone of delight, which changed
    A12   95:11   this affair, / He trusts to you to set them free, / Exactly as we were.
    T3   137: 6 a sudden bound into the air, and shook itself free from Alice's arm. "I'm a Fawn!" it cried out in a voice
    A5   43: 3   "and just as I was thinking I should be free of them at last, they must needs come wriggling down from
    T4   139:24 then they held out the two hands that were free, to shake hands with her.
FRENCH (7)
    A9   76:10   "Yes," said Alice: "we learned French and music."
    T9   195: 8 Red Queen. "Do you know Languages? What's the French for fiddle-de-dee?"
    T9   195:13   'fiddle-de-dee' is, I'll tell you the French for it!" she exclaimed triumphantly.
    A2   19:25   chatte?" which was the first sentence in her French lesson-book. The Mouse gave a sudden leap out of the
    A2   19:22   English," thought Alice. "I daresay it's a French mouse, come over with William the Conqueror." (For,
    A9   76:15   at ours, they had, at the end of the bill, 'French, music, and washing--extra.'"
    T2   128:23 again, and this time she said "Speak in French when you ca'n't think of the English for a thing--turn
FRESH (1) [See also AFRESH]
    T2   123:33   "It's the fresh air that does it," said the Rose: "wonderfully fine air
-FRESHING [See REFRESHING]
-FRESHMENTS [See REFRESHMENTS]
FRET (1)
    TI   103:24 / We are but older children, dear, / Who fret to find our bedtime near.
FRETFUL (1)
    T7   170:17 wish I had such eyes," the King remarked in a fretful tone. "To be able to see Nobody! And at that distance
FRETFULLY (1)
    T8W   15:15   "Let it stop there!" said the Wasp, fretfully turning away his head.
FRIEND (6)
    A8   68:27   to have a little more conversation with her friend.
    T3   131:41 a friend," the little voice went on: "a dear friend, and an old friend. And you wo'n't hurt me, though I am
    T3   131:42 voice went on: "a dear friend, and an old friend. And you wo'n't hurt me, though I am an insect."
    A8   67:39   "It's a friend of mine--a Cheshire-Cat," said Alice: "allow me to
    A10   80: 7   "What matters it how far we go?" his scaly friend replied. / "There is another shore, you know, upon the
    T3   131:41   "I know you are a friend," the little voice went on: "a dear friend, and an old
FRIENDLY (2)
    AI   3:23   a land / Of wonders wild and new, / In friendly chat with bird or beast--/ And half believe it true.
    T8   181:18 admiring my little box," the Knight said in a friendly tone. "It's my own invention--to keep clothes and
FRIENDS (3)
    A1   10:24   would not remember the simple rules their friends had taught them: such as, that a red-hot poker will
    T12   207:36 however, you'd better not mention it to your friends just yet, for I'm not sure.
    A12   98:27   of the teacups as the March Hare and his friends shared their never-ending meal, and the shrill voice
FRIGHT (3)
    A12   97:10   upon her; she gave a little scream, half of fright and half of anger, and tried to beat them off, and
    A2   19:27   the water, and seemed to quiver all over with fright. "Oh, I beg your pardon!" cried Alice hastily, afraid
    T3   132:11 rise straight up into the air, and in her fright she caught at the thing nearest to her hand, which
FRIGHTEN (1)
    A5   44: 3   do to come upon them this size: why, I should frighten them out of their wits!" So she began nibbling at the
FRIGHTENED (22)
    T9   202:32 up to do it, very obediently, but a little frightened.
    A4   32:30   hard to whistle to it; but she was terribly frightened all the time at the thought that it might be hungry
    T2   121:14 began asking questions. "Aren't you sometimes frightened at being planted out here, with nobody to take care
    T9   201:29 repeated to me to-day," Alice began, a little frightened at finding that, the moment she opened her lips,
    A2   18:10   was a narrow escape!" said Alice, a good deal frightened at the sudden change, but very glad to find herself
    T4   139: 3 crow, / As black as a tar-barrel; / Which frightened both the heroes so, / They quite forgot their
    A5   41:41   She was a good deal frightened by this very sudden change, but she felt that there
    T8   179:17   Startled as she was, Alice was more frightened for him than for herself at the moment, and watched
    T5   157:15 in a tone that was half astonished and half frightened--for the oars, and the boat, and the river, had
    T1   110:17 be all the rest." And once she had really frightened her old nurse by shouting suddenly in her ear,
    T3   136: 8 its large gentle eyes, but didn't seem at all frightened. "Here then! Here then!" Alice said, as she held
    T9   196:16 over the tables and things--till I was so frightened, I couldn't remember my own name!"
    A12   98:25   her feet as the White Rabbit hurried by--the frightened Mouse splashed his way through the neighbouring
    T4   146:18 she added hastily, thinking that he was frightened: "only an old rattle--quite old and broken."
    T9   201: 3 returned the bow, not knowing whether to be frightened or amused.
    T5   149: 7 White Queen only looked at her in a helpless frightened sort of way, and kept repeating something in a
    A4   27:16   and a fan! Quick, now!" And Alice was so much frightened that she ran off at once in the direction it
    T8   184: 1 path where Alice was walking. She was quite frightened this time, and said in an anxious tone, as she
    A9   72:41   Queen said and Alice was too much frightened to say a word, but slowly followed her back to the
    A8   65:39   "Oh, hush!" the Rabbit whispered in a frightened tone. "The Queen will hear you! You see she came
    T3   130: 2 afraid I haven't got one," Alice said in a frightened tone: "there wasn't a ticket-office where I came
    T1   115:20 he and the Queen were talking together in a frightened whisper--so low, that Alice could hardly hear what
FRIGHTENING (1)
    T1   113: 9 Queen," Alice said (in a whisper, for fear of frightening them), "and there are the White King and the White
FRO (1)
    T8   190: 6 with his woe, / Who rocked his body to and fro, / And muttered mumblingly and low, / As if his mouth were
FROG (8)
    T9   199: 5   "Which door?" said the Frog.
    A6   45: 7   with a round face, and large eyes like a frog; and both footmen, Alice noticed, had powdered hair that
    T9   199: 8   The Frog looked at the door with his large dull eyes for a minute:
    T9   199:18 "Shouldn't do that--shouldn't do that--" the Frog muttered. "Wexes it, you know." Then he went up and gave
    A3   22:19   a thing," said the Duck: "it's generally a frog, or a worm. The question is, what did the archbishop find

FROG (cont.)
T9   199: 1   "What is it, now?" the Frog said in a deep hoarse whisper.
T9   199:15   "I speaks English, doesn't I?" the Frog went on. "Or are you deaf? What did it ask you?"
T9   198:13   vain for a long time; but at last a very old Frog, who was sitting under a tree, got up and hobbled slowly
FROG-FOOTMAN (1)
A6   45:14   from the Queen to play croquet." The Frog-Footman repeated, in the same solemn tone, only changing
FROM (104) [entries omitted]
FRONT (7)
T8   182:41   (which it did very often), he fell off in front; and, whenever it went on again (which it generally did
T8W   21: 7   "Then your eyes--they're too much in front, no doubt. One would have done as well as two, if you
T7   175:19   a child!" Haigha replied eagerly, coming in front of Alice to introduce her, and spreading out both his
A7   54: 1   There was a table set out under a tree in front of the house, and the March Hare and the Hatter were
A9   72:32   Alice looked up, and there stood the Queen in front of them, with her arms folded, frowning like a
T5   154: 5   "You may look in front of you, and on both sides, if you like," said the Sheep,
T4   144:16   "You see he held his handkerchief in front, so that the Carpenter couldn't count how many he took:
FRONT-DOOR (1)
T2   123:42   a moment, and found herself walking in at the front-door again.
FRONTISPIECE (1)
A11   86:18   he wore his crown over the wig (look at the frontispiece if you want to see how he did it), he did not
FROST (1)
TI   103:25   Without, the frost, the blinding snow, / The storm-wind's moody madness--/
FROSTS (1)
TC   209: 9   sky: / Echoes fade and memories die: / Autumn frosts have slain July.
FROTHY (1)
T4   142:11   and more, and more--/ All hopping through the frothy waves, / And scrambling to the shore.
FROWN (1)
T9   192:25   you see, child--" here she broke off with a frown, and, after thinking for a minute, suddenly changed the
FROWNING (6)
A12   93:24   he said, in a very respectful tone, but frowning and making faces at him as he spoke.
T9   202:30   thanks in a neat speech," the Red Queen said, frowning at Alice as she spoke.
A11   91:14   air, and, after folding his arms and frowning at the cook till his eyes were nearly out of sight,
A3   22: 8   "I beg your pardon!" said the Mouse, frowning, but very politely. "Did you speak?"
A9   72:32   Queen in front of them, with her arms folded, frowning like a thunderstorm.
T5   156: 5   but always with the same tall river-banks frowning over their heads.
FRUIT-TREE (1)
T8   182:33   "Then you make your hair creep up it, like a fruit-tree. Now the reason hair falls off is because it hangs
FRUMENTY (1)
T3   134: 2   "Frumenty and mince-pie," the Gnat replied; "and it makes its
FRUMIOUS (1)
T1   118: 4   / Beware the Jubjub bird, and shun / The frumious Bandersnatch!"
FRYING-PAN (1)
A6   49:13   she hurried out of the room. The cook threw a frying-pan after her as she went, but it just missed her.
FULL (19)
T5   154:15   though the others round it were crowded as full as they could hold.
A4   28:23   the little magic bottle had now had its full effect, and she grew no larger: still it was very
T5   155:35   the needles into her hair, as her hands were full. "Feather, I say!"
T2   124: 4   herself face to face with the Red Queen, and full in sight of the hill she had been so long aiming at.
T2   120:26   However, there was the hill full in sight, so there was nothing to be done but start again
AI   3: 2   All in the golden afternoon / Full leisurely we glide; / For both our oars, with little
T5   154:11   The shop seemed to be full of all manner of curious things--but the oddest part of
T8   190: 8   mumblingly and low, / As if his mouth were full of dough, / Who snorted like a buffalo--/ That summer
T7   175:38   he whispered. "Quick! Not that one--that's full of hay!"
T7   178: 2   from, she couldn't make out: the air seemed full of it, and it rang through and through her head till she
T2   122: 8   shouting together, till the air seemed quite full of little shrill voices. "Silence, every one of you!"
A6   46:45   led right into a large kitchen, which was full of smoke from one end to the other: the Duchess was
A6   47: 3   stirring a large cauldron which seemed to be full of soup.
A9   74:24   Turtle, who looked at them with large eyes full of tears, but said nothing.
A10   82:20   and began to repeat it, but her head was so full of the Lobster-Quadrille, that she hardly knew what she
T7   175: 1   without even looking round. "That wood's full of them."
T4   147:13   and returned in a minute with their arms full of things--such as bolsters, blankets, hearth-rugs,
A12   97: 7   for you?" said Alice (she had grown to her full size by this time). "You're nothing but a pack of cards!"
T3   137: 9   and in another moment it had darted away at full speed.
FUMBLED (1)
A11   91:29   Alice watched the White Rabbit as he fumbled over the list, feeling very curious to see what the
FUN (9)
T4   140:34   of him,' she said, / 'To come and spoil the fun!'
T2   128:20   be Queens together, and it's all feasting and fun!" Alice got up and curtseyed, and sat down again.
T2   126: 2   this is the world at all, you know. Oh, what fun it is! How I wish I was one of them! I wouldn't mind being
T3   129:21   good long branch to brush them away--and what fun it'll be when they ask me how I liked my walk. I shall say
T1   112: 8   here to scold me away from the fire. Oh, what fun it'll be, when they see me through the glass in here, and
A7   55:13   "Come, we shall have some fun now!" thought Alice. "I'm glad they've begun asking
A9   74:10   "What is the fun?" said Alice.
A9   74: 8   she was out of sight: then it chuckled. "What fun!" said the Gryphon, half to itself, half to Alice.
T3   135:31   certain to be an ugly one. But then the fun would be, trying to find the creature that has got my old
FUNNY (4)
T4   139:34   "But it certainly was funny," (Alice said afterwards, when she was telling her
A2   15: 4   go by the carrier," she thought; "and how funny it'll seem, sending presents to one's own feet! And how
A1   8:40   if I shall fall right through the earth! How funny it'll seem to come out among the people that walk with
A7   56:12   his shoulder with some curiosity. "What a funny watch!" she remarked. "It tells the day of the month,

FUR (3)
   A4   27: 4   Duchess! The Duchess! Oh my dear paws! Oh my fur and whiskers! She'll get me executed, as sure as ferrets
   A3   21: 2   draggled feathers, the animals with their fur clinging close to them, and all dripping wet, cross, and
   A6   53:13   like ears and the roof was thatched with fur. It was so large a house, that she did not like to go
FURIOUS (1)
   A8   66:22   and in a very short time the Queen was in a furious passion, and went stamping about, and shouting "Off
FURIOUSLY (1)
   A12   96:20   "Never!" said the Queen, furiously, throwing an inkstand at the Lizard as she spoke.
FURROW (1)
   A8   66:16   all this, there was generally a ridge or a furrow in the way wherever she wanted to send the hedgehog to,
FURROWS (1)
   A8   66: 2   in her life: it was all ridges and furrows: the croquet balls were live hedgehogs, and the
FURTHER (11)
   A6   50:13   would be quite absurd for her to carry it any further.
   T5   158:19   dark towards the end. "The egg seems to get further away the more I walk towards it. Let me see, is this a
   T6   168:35   but, as he never opened his eyes or took any further notice of her, she said "Good-bye!" once more, and,
   A10   80: 9   shore, you know, upon the other side. / The further off from England the nearer is to France. / Then turn
   T6   167: 6   "It gets easier further on," Humpty Dumpty replied.
   T3   132:39   "I ca'n't say," the Gnat replied. "Further on, in the wood down there, they've got no names--
   T3   137: 1   "I'll tell you, if you'll come a little further on," the Fawn said. "I ca'n't remember here."
   T3   129: 4   tiptoe in hopes of being able to see a little further. "Principal rivers--there are none. Principal
   A1   12: 7   minutes to see if she was going to shrink any further: she felt a little nervous about this; "for it might
   T5   156:30   "The prettiest are always further!" she said at last with a sigh at the obstinacy of the
   T7   173: 9   Alice panted out, after running a little further, "to stop a minute--just to get--one's breath again?"
FURY (5)
   A8   64: 5   The Queen turned crimson with fury, and, after glaring at her for a moment like a wild beast
   A3   25:43   be judge, I'll be jury, said cunning old Fury: 'I'll try the whole cause, and condemn you to death.
   A3   25: 5   "Fury said to a mouse, That he met in the house, 'Let us both
   T4   146:26   it isn't old!" Tweedledum cried, in a greater fury than ever. "It's new, I tell you--I bought it yesterday--
   T8   179:37   began banging away at each other with such fury that Alice got behind a tree to be out of the way of the
FUSS (1)
   T4   147:18   said afterwards she had never seen such a fuss made about anything in all her life--the way those two

-G-

GAILY (1)
 T6   163:16   "To be sure I was!" Humpty Dumpty said gaily as she turned it round for him. "I thought it looked a
GAINED (1)
 A10   82: 4   their eyes and mouths so very wide; but she gained courage as she went on. Her listeners were perfectly
GALLONS (1)
 A2   15:23   you!" But she went on all the same, shedding gallons of tears, until there was a large pool round her,
GALLOPED (1)
 T8   180:13   hands, and then the Red Knight mounted and galloped off.
GALLOPING (1)
 T8   179:14   and a Knight, dressed in crimson armour, came galloping down upon her, brandishing a great club. Just as he
GALUMPHING (1)
 T1   118:16   He left it dead, and with its head / He went galumphing back.
GAME (18)
 A8   67:35   that it's hardly worth while finishing the game."
 A8   69:14   while the rest of the party went back to the game.
 T7   170:13   know, because two of them are wanted in the game. And I haven't sent the two Messengers, either. They're
 A8   65:44   got settled down in a minute or two, and the game began.
 A8   67:20   her flamingo, and began an account of the game, feeling very glad she had some one to listen to her. The
 A8   66:19   the conclusion that it was a very difficult game indeed.
 T2   126: 1   excitement as she went on. "It's a great huge game of chess that's being played--all over the world--if this
 A1   12:26   her own ears for having cheated herself in a game of croquet she was playing against herself, for this
 A4   32:40   Alice, thinking it was very like having a game of play with a cart-horse, and expecting every moment to
 T1   107:15   asleep, the kitten had been having a grand game of romps with the ball of worsted Alice had been trying
 A10   84:27   "Beautiful Soup! Who cares for fish, / Game, or any other dish? / Who would not give all else for two
 A9   73: 1   moment they saw her, they hurried back to the game, the Queen merely remarking that a moment's delay would
 A9   72:40   "Let's go on with the game," the Queen said to Alice; and Alice was too much
 T6   161:20   ("He talks about it just as if it was a game!" thought Alice.) "So here's a question for you. How old
 A8   68:10   she might as well go back and see how the game was going on, as she heard the Queen's voice in the
 A8   68:14   not like the look of things at all, as the game was in such confusion that she never knew whether it was
 T9   192:16   be no harm, she thought, in asking if the game was over. "Please, would you tell me--" she began,
 T7   170:35   the least idea that he was joining in the game, while Alice was still hesitating for the name of a town
GAME'S (1)
 A9   70:30   "The game's going on rather better now," she said, by way of
GAMES (1)
 A9   77:24   decided tone. "Tell her something about the games now."
GARDEN (25)
 A10   83:11   Gryphon repeated: "it begins 'I passed by his garden.'"
 A7   61: 5   she found herself at last in the beautiful garden, among the bright flower-beds and the cool fountains.
 A1   12:36   the door: so either way I'll get into the garden, and I don't care which happens!"
 A10   83:14   "I passed by his garden, and marked, with one eye, / How the Owl and the
 A2   18:12   herself still in existence. "And now for the garden!" And she ran with all speed back to the little door;
 A1   12:14   more happened, she decided on going into the garden at once; but, alas for poor Alice! when she got to the
 T2   123: 3   "Are there any more people in the garden besides me?" Alice said, not choosing to notice the
 A8   63:11   who had been anxiously looking across the garden, called out "The Queen! The Queen!" and the three
 A2   15:14   the little golden key and hurried off to the garden door.
 T2   120: 1   "I should see the garden far better," said Alice to herself, "if I could get to
 A1   12: 5   through the little door into that lovely garden. First, however, she waited for a few minutes to see if
 T1   119: 2   the house is like! Let's have a look at the garden first!" She was out of the room in a moment, and ran
 A5   43:43   the next thing is, to get into that beautiful garden--how is that to be done, I wonder?" As she said this,
 A4   32:20   thing is to find my way into that lovely garden. I think that will be the best plan."
 T2   125: 4   didn't like at all: "though, when you say 'garden'--I've seen gardens, compared with which this would be
 T2t   120: 1   THE GARDEN OF LIVE FLOWERS
 T9   194:43   the flower?" the White Queen asked: "In a garden or in the hedges?"
 T2   123:10   her mind, "There's another little girl in the garden, somewhere!"
 T2   123: 5   "There's one other flower in the garden that can move about like you," said the Rose. "I wonder
 A8   62: 1   rose-tree stood near the entrance of the garden: the roses growing on it were white, but there were
 A7   61: 2   key, and unlocking the door that led into the garden. Then she set to work nibbling at the mushroom (she had
 T2   125: 1   "I only wanted to see what the garden was like, your Majesty--"
 A8   68:20   was gone across the other side of the garden, where Alice could see it trying in a helpless sort of
 A2   15:17   down on one side, to look through into the garden with one eye; but to get through was more hopeless than
 A1   10: 3   looked along the passage into the loveliest garden you ever saw. How she longed to get out of that dark
GARDENERS (8)
 A8   62: 2   on it were white, but there were three gardeners at it, busily painting them red. Alice thought this
 A8   63:29   not to lie down on her face like the three gardeners, but she could not remember ever having heard of
 A8   65: 1   Queen in a shrill, loud voice, and the three gardeners instantly jumped up, and began bowing to the King,
 A8   63:12   out "The Queen! The Queen!" and the three gardeners instantly threw themselves flat upon their faces.
 A8   63:16   clubs: these were all shaped like the three gardeners, oblong and flat, with their hands and feet at the
 A8   64: 2   pack, she could not tell whether they were gardeners, or soldiers, or courtiers, or three of her own
 A8   65:10   remaining behind to execute the unfortunate gardeners, who ran to Alice for protection.
 A8   63:43   these?" said the Queen, pointing to the three gardeners who were lying round the rose-tree; for, you see, as
GARDENS (3)
 T2   122:22   temper by a compliment. "I've been in many gardens before, but none of the flowers could talk."
 T2   125: 5   "though, when you say 'garden'--I've seen gardens, compared with which this would be a wilderness."

GARDENS (cont.)
T2   122:28   "In most gardens," the Tiger-lily said, "they make the beds too soft--
GASP (1)
T9   201:25   reply: she could only sit and look at it and gasp.
GASPED (2)
T1   114: 8   The Queen gasped, and sat down: the rapid journey through the air had
T9   194:30   The Queen gasped and shut her eyes. "I can do Addition," she said, "if
GATE (5)
T8   190:11   summer evening long ago, / A-sitting on a gate."
T8   187:11   said. "The song really is 'A-sitting On A Gate': and the tune's my own invention."
T8   184:32   Now, first I put my head on the top of the gate--then the head's high enough--then I stand on my head--
T8   187:34   / I saw an aged aged man, / A-sitting on a gate. / 'Who are you, aged man?' I said. / 'And how is it you
T8   184:27   I was inventing a new way of getting over a gate--would you like to hear it?"
GATHER (1)
A12   99: 6   heart of her childhood; and how she would gather about her other little children, and make their eyes
GATHERED (1)
T8   190:12   Knight sang the last words of the ballad, he gathered up the reins, and turned his horse's head along the
GAUZE (1)
T1   111: 9   Let's pretend the glass has got all soft like gauze, so that we can get through. Why, it's turning into a
GAVE (31)
T9   196:34   The White Queen gave a deep sigh, and laid her head on Alice's shoulder. "I am
A12   97:10   the air, and came flying down upon her; she gave a little scream, half of fright and half of anger, and
A8   65:37   the Queen's ears--" the Rabbit began. Alice gave a little scream of laughter. "Oh, hush!" the Rabbit
A10   80: 3   the snail replied "Too far, too far!", and gave a look askance--/ Said he thanked the whiting kindly, but
T3   137: 5   into another open field, and here the Fawn gave a sudden bound into the air, and shook itself free from
A2   19:26   sentence in her French lesson-book. The Mouse gave a sudden leap out of the water, and seemed to quiver all
T2   120:21   really shall do it this time--" when the path gave a sudden twist and shook itself (as she described it
T8   189: 3   of Hansom-cabs. / And that's the way' (he gave a wink) / 'By which I get my wealth--/ And very gladly
T4   139:23   and shake hands!" And here the two brothers gave each other a hug, and then they held out the two hands
A10   81:20   at them, and considered a little before she gave her answer. "They're done with blacking, I believe."
T4   147:20   of things they put on--and the trouble they gave her in tying strings and fastening buttons--"Really
A12   95: 5   I gave her one, they gave him two, / You gave us three or more;
A12   96: 5   would become of you?'--What, indeed!--'I gave her one, they gave him two'--why, that must be what he
A1   12:23   you to leave off this minute!" She generally gave herself very good advice (though she very seldom followed
A12   96: 5   you?'--What, indeed!--'I gave her one, they gave him two'--why, that must be what he did with the tarts,
A12   95: 5   I gave her one, they gave him two, / You gave us three or more; / They all returned
T6   162:35   other and clasped his hands round it, "they gave it me--for an un-birthday present."
T6   162:33   "They gave it me," Humpty Dumpty continued thoughtfully as he
T12   207:24   time, remember!" And she caught it up and gave it one little kiss, "just in honour of its having been a
T7   175:39   Haigha took a large cake out of the bag, and gave it to Alice to hold, while he got out a dish and
T9   195:42   Alice sighed and gave it up. "It's exactly like the riddle with no answer!" she
A12   94:41   been to her, / And mentioned me to him: / She gave me a good character, / But said I could not swim.
A4   31: 2   then, saying to herself "This is Bill", she gave one sharp kick, and waited to see what would happen next.
T9   199:19   "Wexes it, you know." Then he went up and gave the door a kick with one of his great feet. "You let it
A5   43:22   was quite silent for a minute or two, which gave the Pigeon the opportunity of adding "You're looking for
T7   173: 3   the town. / Some gave them white bread, some gave them brown: / Some gave them plum-cake and drummed them
T7   173: 4   white bread, some gave them brown: / Some gave them plum-cake and drummed them out of town."
T7   173: 3   beat the Unicorn all round the town. / Some gave them white bread, some gave them brown: / Some gave them
A5   39: 7   wife; / And the muscular strength, which it gave to my jaw / Has lasted the rest of my life."
A12   95: 6   I gave her one, they gave him two, / You gave us three or more; / They all returned from him to you, /
T9   193:19   "We gave you the opportunity of doing it," the Red Queen remarked:
GAY (1)
A10   82:26   his toes. / When the sands are all dry, he is gay as a lark, / And will talk in contemptuous tones of the
GAZING (1)
A12   93:14   to do anything but sit with its mouth open, gazing up into the roof of the court.
GENERAL (4)
A4   31: 6   The first thing she heard was a general chorus of "There goes Bill!" then the Rabbit's voice
A12   94:26   There was a general clapping of hands at this: it was the first really
A2   18:21   seaside once in her life, and had come to the general conclusion that wherever you go to on the English
T9   196:24   she can't help saying foolish things as a general rule."
GENERALLY (14)
A3   22:19   when I find a thing," said the Duck: "it's generally a frog, or a worm. The question is, what did the
A8   66:15   of crawling away: besides all this, there was generally a ridge or a furrow in the way wherever she wanted
T9   196: 7   "Is there generally?" Alice asked in an astonished tone.
T6   168:24   "The face is what one goes by, generally," Alice remarked in a thoughtful tone.
T8   182:41   and, whenever it went on again (which it generally did rather suddenly), he fell off behind. Otherwise
T8   182:44   now and then falling off sideways; and, as he generally did this on the side on which Alice was walking, she
A1   12:22   "I advise you to leave off this minute!" She generally gave herself very good advice (though she very
T2   127:17   said Alice, still panting a little, "you'd generally get to somewhere else--if you ran very fast for a
A1   12:41   the same size. To be sure, this is what generally happens when one eats cake; but Alice had got so
T4   147:34   "I'm very brave, generally," he went on in a low voice: "only to-day I happen
T4   147:45   better not come very close," he added: "I generally hit every thing I can see--when I get really excited
A8   66: 8   her arm, with its legs hanging down, but generally, just as she had got its neck nicely straightened
A10   78:19   "That generally takes some time," interrupted the Gryphon.
A9   73:19   the King say in a low voice, to the company, generally, "You are all pardoned." "Come, that's a good thing!
GENTLE (6)
T3   136: 8   by: it looked at Alice with its large gentle eyes, but didn't seem at all frightened. "Here then!
T8   181:10   shaggy hair with both hands, and turning his gentle face and large mild eyes to Alice. She thought she had
T8   187:14   hand, and with a faint smile lighting up his gentle foolish face, as if he enjoyed the music of his song,
AI   4: 4   Alice! A childish story take, / And, with a gentle hand, / Lay it where Childhood's dreams are twined / In

GENTLE (cont.)
T9   197:19   impatient tone; but there was no answer but a gentle snoring.
T3   131:16   Then a very gentle voice in the distance said, "She must be labeled 'Lass,
GENTLEMAN (3)
T3   131:23   But the gentleman dressed in white paper leaned forwards and whispered
T3   131: 3   A Goat, that was sitting next to the gentleman in white, shut his eyes and said in a loud voice,
T3   130:21   and went away. "So young a child," said the gentleman sitting opposite to her, (he was dressed in white
GENTLER (2)
AI   3:15   flashes forth / Her edict "to begin it": / In gentler tones Secunda hopes / "There will be nonsense in it!"
T8W   16: 4   along of the wig," the Wasp said in a much gentler voice.
GENTLY (17)
T4   147:33   "Well--yes--a little," Alice replied gently.
T4   140:22   Tweedledee smiled gently, and began again:
T1   114:23   So Alice picked him up very gently, and lifted him across more slowly than she had lifted
T1   109:11   the trees and fields, that it kisses them so gently? And then it covers them up snug, you know, with a
A12   98: 1   her head in the lap of her sister, who was gently brushing away some dead leaves that had fluttered down
T1   119: 6   of her fingers on the hand-rail, and floated gently down without even touching the stairs with her feet:
T6   159:19   "I said you looked like an egg, Sir," Alice gently explained. "And some eggs are very pretty, you know,"
T5   154: 3   "I don't quite know yet," Alice said very gently. "I should like to look all round me first, if I might
T5   156:16   down the stream as it would, till it glided gently in among the waving rushes. And then the little sleeves
T6   160:34   "I haven't indeed!" Alice said very gently. "It's in a book."
T5   156: 2   for a minute or two, while the boat glided gently on, sometimes among beds of weeds (which made the oars
T5   149:30   pin it all on one side," Alice said as she gently put it right for her; "and dear me, what a state your
T8   181:21   "But the things can get out," Alice gently remarked. "Do you know the lid's open?"
A7   59: 3   couldn't have done that, you know," Alice gently remarked. "They'd have been ill."
A2   17:15   / And welcomes little fishes in, / With gently smiling jaws!
T9   196:22   of the White Queen's hands in her own, and gently stroking it: "she means well, but she ca'n't help
T1   108: 9   and now and then putting out one paw and gently touching the ball, as if it would be glad to help if it
GEOGRAPHY (2)
A2   17: 1   doesn't signify: let's try Geography. London is the capital of Paris, and Paris is the
T3   129: 3   through. "It's something very like learning geography," thought Alice, as she stood on tiptoe in hopes of
GET (98)
T1   115:37   at last he panted out "My dear! I really must get a thinner pencil. I ca'n't manage this one a bit: it
A6   48:24   advantage," said Alice, who felt very glad to get an opportunity of showing off a little of her knowledge.
A4   29: 9   "But then," thought Alice, "shall I never get any older than I am now? That'll be a comfort, one way--
T1   112: 9   see me through the glass in here, and ca'n't get at me!"
T4   145:25   and stopped under a large tree. "It can never get at me here," she thought: "it's far too large to squeeze
T2   122:11   with excitement. "They know I ca'n't get at them!" it panted, bending its quivering head towards
A8   67: 9   of escape, and wondering whether she could get away without being seen, when she noticed a curious
T3   131:28   I was in a wood just now--and I wish I could get back there!"
T1   114:16   "Mind you come up--the regular way--don't get blown up!"
T7   172:26   the shape of a trumpet and stooping so as to get close to the King's ear. Alice was sorry for this, as she
A3   21: 5   The first question of course was, how to get dry again: they had a consultation about this, and after a
A3   21:18   she would catch a bad cold if she did not get dry very soon.
T5   158:19   very dark towards the end. "The egg seems to get further away the more I walk towards it. Let me see, is
A5   42:19   her hands up to her head, she tried to get her head down to them, and was delighted to find that her
A1   10: 5   those cool fountains, but she could not even get her head through the doorway; "and even if my head would
T8   191: 3   it here and there. "Oh, how glad I am to get here! And what is this on my head?" she exclaimed in a
A4   29:36   and made a snatch in the air. She did not get hold of anything, but she heard a little shriek and a fall
A4   32:39   and tumbled head over heels in its hurry to get hold of it: then Alice, thinking it was very like having a
T8W   20:12   "If you was a-fighting, now--could you get hold of the other one by the back of the neck?"
T5   156:18   little arms were plunged in elbow-deep, to get hold of the rushes a good long way down before breaking
A6   46:17   "Please, then," said Alice, "how am I to get in?"
T8   181:19   carry it upside-down, so that the rain ca'n't get in."
A6   46:32   "How am I to get in?" asked Alice again, in a louder tone.
A6   46:33   "Are you to get in at all?" said the Footman. "That's the first question,
A4   29:28   it say to itself "Then I'll go round and get in at the window."
A6   46:25   rate he might answer questions.--How am I to get in?" she repeated, aloud.
A12   98:21   back the wandering hair that would always get into her eyes--and still as she listened, or seemed to
T1   115:12   your mouth so wide open! All the ashes will get into it--there, now I think you're tidy enough!" she added
A5   43:42   back to my right size: the next thing is, to get into that beautiful garden--how is that to be done, I
A1   12:36   can creep under the door: so either way I'll get into the garden, and I don't care which happens!"
T3   135:40   under the trees, "after being so hot, to get into the--into the--into what?" she went on, rather
T3   129:27   elephants later on. Besides, I do want to get into the Third Square!"
A7   55:27   added the March Hare, "that 'I like what I get' is the same thing as 'I get what I like'!"
T4   141:10   suppose,' the Walrus said, or 'That they could get it clear?' / 'I doubt it,' said the Carpenter, / And shed
T5   158:15   people's hands--that would never do--you must get it for yourself." And so saying, she went off to the other
A6   50: 9   what am I to do with this creature, when I get it home?" when it grunted again, so violently, that she
T2   122:21   all talk so nicely?" Alice said, hoping to get it into a better temper by a compliment. "I've been in
T8   182:14   in handy if we find any plum-cake. Help me to get it into this bag."
A4   27: 4   my dear paws! Oh my fur and whiskers! She'll get me executed, as sure as ferrets are ferrets! Where can I
T8   185:11   off again--but it took hours and hours to get me out. I was as fast as--as lightning, you know."
T8   188: 7   sail on stormy seas; / And that's the way I get my bread--/ A trifle, if you please.'
T8   189: 4   the way' (he gave a wink) / 'By which I get my wealth--/ And very gladly will I drink / Your Honour's
T9   201:11   Alice said rather hastily, "or we shall get no dinner at all. May I give you some?"
T8   180: 9   And how quiet the horses are! They let them get on and off them just as if they were tables!"
A11   90:28   guinea-pigs!" thought Alice. "Now we shall get on better."
T1   108: 5   winding up the ball again. But she didn't get on very fast, as she was talking all the time, sometimes
T8   184:19   "I'll get one," the Knight said thoughtfully to himself. "One or two
T7   173: 9   a little further, "to stop a minute--just to get--one's breath again?"

GET (cont.)

T4	147:26	can possibly happen to one in a battle--to get one's head cut off."
A1	8: 6	once considering how in the world she was to get out again.
A1	9:33	the middle, wondering how she was ever to get out again.
T8	185: 4	once--and the worst of it was, before I could get out again, the other White Knight came and put it on. He
T8	181:21	"But the things can get out," Alice gently remarked. "Do you know the lid's open?"
A4	28:13	I sha'n't grow any more--As it is, I ca'n't get out at the door--I do wish I hadn't drunk quite so much!"
T9	204:12	chair, and beckoning to her impatiently to get out of its way.
A1	10: 4	garden you ever saw. How she longed to get out of that dark hall, and wander about among those beds
T7	170: 3	every moment, and Alice was very glad to get out of the wood into an open place, where she found the
A4	27:33	comes back, and see that the mouse doesn't get out.' Only I don't think," Alice went on, "that they'd let
A1	9:11	eat bats, I wonder?" And here Alice began to get rather sleepy, and went on saying to herself, in a dreamy
A4	27:30	happen: "'Miss Alice! Come here directly, and get ready for your walk!' 'Coming in a minute, nurse! But I've
A6	49:11	the baby at her as she spoke. "I must go and get ready to play croquet with the Queen," and she hurried out
T4	148: 1	I generally hit every thing I can see--when I get really excited."
T4	144:20	"But he ate as many as he could get," said Tweedledum.
A6	51:13	"--so long as I get somewhere," Alice added as an explanation.
T2	127:21	do, to keep in the same place. If you want to get somewhere else, you must run at least twice as fast as
T7	177: 1	by the old bridge, or the market-place? You get the best view by the old bridge."
T7	173: 5	"Does--the one--that wins--get the crown?" she asked, as well as she could, for the run
T5	149:34	released the brush, and did her best to get the hair into order. "Come, you look rather better now!"
T8	181:30	bees may make a nest in it--then I should get the honey."
A11	86: 9	quite hungry to look at them--"I wish they'd get the trial done," she thought, "and hand round the
T6	164:11	his head gravely from side to side, "for to get their wages, you know."
A10	81: 7	tails fast in their mouths. So they couldn't get them out again. That's all."
T1	111: 6	Kitty, how nice it would be if we could only get through into Looking-glass House! I'm sure it's got, oh!
T1	111:10	mist now, I declare! It'll be easy enough to get through--" She was up on the chimney-piece while she said
A4	32:12	directly. As soon as she was small enough to get through the door, she ran out of the house, and found
T2	120:15	going in again yet. I know I should have to get through the Looking-glass again--back into the old room--
A2	15:17	through into the garden with one eye; but to get through was more hopeless than ever: she sat down and
T1	111: 9	has got all soft like gauze, so that we can get through. Why, it's turning into a sort of mist now, I
A6	51: 9	That depends a good deal on where you want to get to," said the Cat.
T2	127:17	still panting a little, "you'd generally get to somewhere else--if you ran very fast for a long time as
T8	190:18	You'll wait and wave your handkerchief when I get to that turn in the road? I think it'll encourage me, you
A11	91: 3	was out of sight before the officer could get to the door.
T3	137:28	them the way out of the wood. If I could only get to the Eighth Square before it gets dark!" So she wandered
T2	126:10	in the Second Square to begin with: when you get to the Eighth Square you'll be a Queen--"Just at this
A2	20:18	it said, in a low trembling voice, "Let us get to the shore, and then I'll tell you my history, and
T2	120: 2	better," said Alice to herself, "if I could get to the top of that hill: and here's a path that leads
A2	16:10	four times seven is--oh dear! I shall never get to twenty at that rate! However, the Multiplication-Table
A8	65:41	"Get to your places!" shouted the Queen in a voice of thunder,
T6	163:20	hundred and sixty-four days when you might get un-birthday presents--"
T3	135:41	being able to think of the word. "I mean to get under the--under the--under this, you know!" putting her
A11	88:37	again, and she thought at first she would get up and leave the court; but on second thoughts she decided
A8	64:15	"Get up!" said the Queen in a shrill, loud voice, and the three
T1	110:34	go the other way. I can see all of it when I get upon a chair--all but the bit just behind the fireplace.
A3	23: 1	an offended tone, "was that the best thing to get us dry would be a Caucus-race."
A5	41:21	"You'll get used to it in time," said the Caterpillar; and it put the
A7	58:15	"Exactly so," said the Hatter: "as the things get used up."
A1	7: 1	Alice was beginning to get very tired of sitting by her sister on the bank and of
A7	55:27	'I like what I get' is the same thing as 'I get what I like'!"

GETS (9)

T8W	16:10	I gets cold. And I gets under a tree. And I gets a yellow handkerchief. And I ties up my face--as at the
T3	133: 4	if you look. It's made entirely of wood, and gets about by swinging itself from branch to branch."
T8W	16: 9	worrits one. And then I gets cross. And I gets cold. And I gets under a tree. And I gets a yellow
T8W	16: 9	at one. And they worrits one. And then I gets cross. And I gets cold. And I gets under a tree. And I
T3	137:29	could only get to the Eighth Square before it gets dark!" So she wandered on, talking to herself as she went
T6	167: 6	"It gets easier further on," Humpty Dumpty replied.
T5	155:13	the puzzled child thought to herself. "She gets more and more like a porcupine every minute!"
T8	190:27	goes! Right on his head as usual! However, he gets on again pretty easily--that comes of having so many
T8W	16: 9	And then I gets cross. And I gets cold. And I gets under a tree. And I gets a yellow handkerchief. And I

GETTING (52)

T8	188:28	on batter, / And so go on from day to day / Getting a little fatter. / I shook him well from side to side,
T1	119: 9	hadn't caught hold of the door-post. She was getting a little giddy with so much floating in the air, and
T2	123:17	know--and then one ca'n't help one's petals getting a little untidy."
T4	148:16	as sharp. Only we must begin quick. It's getting as dark as it can."
T1	110: 3	sleepy in the autumn, when the leaves are getting brown.
T4	148:18	It was getting dark so suddenly that Alice thought there must be a
T1	119: 4	exactly running, but a new invention for getting down stairs quickly and easily, as Alice said to
A5	43:30	trees as well as she could, for her neck kept getting entangled among the branches, and every now and then
A6	49:34	a snout than a real nose: also its eyes were getting extremely small for a baby: altogether Alice did not
T6	166:29	"In spring, when woods are getting green, / I'll try and tell you what I mean:"
A5	42:18	As there seemed to be no chance of getting her hands up to her head, she tried to get her head
T8	184:10	on repeating, all the time that Alice was getting him on his feet again. "Plenty of practice!"
A3	26:32	very carefully, remarking "I really must be getting home: the night-air doesn't suit my throat!" And a
T1	108:13	so you couldn't. I was watching the boys getting in sticks for the bonfire--and it wants plenty of
T2	120:24	she cried. "I never saw such a house for getting in the way! Never!"
T1	113:13	ca'n't see me. I feel somehow as if I was getting invisible--"
A8	66: 7	in managing her flamingo: she succeeded in getting its body tucked away, comfortably enough, under her
T1	115: 6	cry out, but his eyes and his mouth went on getting larger and larger, and rounder and rounder, till her

GETTING (cont.)
```
 A12    98:10   certainly;  but  now run in to your tea: it's getting late." So Alice got up and ran off, thinking while she
 T5    152:27                      By this time it was getting light. "The crow must have flown away, I think," said
 T8    186:17   went on, holding his head down, and his voice getting lower and lower, "I don't believe that pudding ever
 T6    168:36   of her, she said "Good-bye!" once more, and, getting no answer to this, she quietly walked away: but she
 A3     22:24   the  insolence  of his Normans--' How are you getting on now, my dear?" it continued, turning to Alice as it
 A8     67:14                        "How are you getting on?" said the Cat, as soon as there was mouth enough
 T7    174: 6   a  large  piece of bread-and-butter. "They're getting on very well," he said in a choking voice: "each of
 T7    174: 3   wo'n't you!"  cried  the King. "How are they getting on with the fight?"
 A4     28:25   seemed  to  be  no sort of chance of her ever getting out of the room again, no wonder she felt unhappy.
 T4    146: 2   as she could, "At any rate, I'd better be getting out of the wood, for really it's coming on very dark.
 T8    184:26   "Well, just then I was inventing a new way of getting over a gate--would you like to hear it?"
 T3    135:20    to be seen on the twig, and, as she was getting quite chilly with sitting still so long, she got up
 A2     20:21   It was high time to go, for the pool was getting quite crowded with the birds and animals that had
 T2    127: 8   their feet, till suddenly, just as Alice was getting quite exhausted, they stopped, and she found herself
 T7    177: 9   she said, in reply to the Lion (she was getting quite used to being called 'the Monster'). "I've cut
 A1      9:26   "Oh my ears and whiskers, how late it's getting!" She was close behind it when she turned the corner,
 T9    197:10   shoulder,  "just  sing  it through to me. I'm getting sleepy, too." In another moment both Queens were fast
 T4    139:11   "which is the best way out of this wood: it's getting so dark. Would you tell me, please?"
 A2     14: 5   seemed  to be almost out of sight, they were getting so far off). "Oh, my poor little feet, I wonder who
 T2    126:25   would  never  be  able to talk again, she was getting so much out of breath: and still the Queen cried
 A11    89:13   or so--and what with the bread-and-butter getting so thin--and the twinkling of the tea--"
 A6     52:10   Alice was not much surprised at this, she was getting so well used to queer things happening. While she was
 A1      8:29   by  this  time?" she said aloud. "I must be getting somewhere near the centre of the earth. Let me see:
 A11    91:22   minutes  the  whole court was in confusion, getting the Dormouse turned out, and, by the time they had
 T1    111: 8   things  in it! Let's pretend there's a way of getting through into it, somehow, Kitty. Let's pretend
 A7     58:19   the  March  Hare  interrupted, yawning. "I'm getting tired of this. I vote the young lady tells us a story
 T1    114:19   last she said "Why, you'll be hours and hours getting to the table, at that rate. I'd far better help you,
 A1      7: 8   a  daisy-chain would be worth the trouble of getting up and picking the daisies, when suddenly a White
 A9     74:37   of  the  Mock Turtle. Alice was very nearly getting up and saying, "Thank you, Sir, for your interesting
 A3     26: 8   do nothing of the sort," said the Mouse, getting up and walking away. "You insult me by talking such
 A8     66:17   and,  as  the doubled-up soldiers were always getting up and walking off to other parts of the ground, Alice
 T7    176:22   you  chicken!" the Lion replied angrily, half getting up as he spoke.
 A7     60:15   on,  yawning and rubbing its eyes, for it was getting very sleepy; "and they drew all manner of things--
 T8W    21:12   Wasp had quite recovered his spirits, and was getting very talkative, she thought she might safely leave him
```
GIDDY (6)
```
 A6     53: 3   and vanishing so suddenly; you make one quite giddy!"
 T2    127: 9   herself sitting on the ground, breathless and giddy.
 A8     65: 3   off  that!"  screamed the Queen. "You make me giddy." And then, turning to the rose-tree, she went on "What
 T5    150:12   said  kindly:  "it  always makes one a little giddy at first--"
 T5    155: 8   up another pair of needles. "You'll make me giddy soon, if you go on turning round like that." She was now
 T1    119: 9   of  the  door-post. She was getting a little giddy with so much floating in the air, and was rather glad to
```
-GIFT [See LOVE-GIFT]
GIMBLE (6)
```
 T6    165: 1              "And what's to 'gyre' and to 'gimble'?"
 T1    116:10   eht erew ysmim 11A / :ebaw eht ni elbmig dna eryg diD / sevot yhtils eht dna ,gillirb sawT'
 T1    116:19   brillig,  and the slithy toves / Did gyre and gimble in the wabe: / All mimsy were the borogoves, / And the
 T1    118:22   brillig,  and  the  slithy toves / Did gyre and gimble in the wabe: / All mimsy were the borogoves, / And the
 T6    164:22   brillig,  and  the  slithy toves / Did gyre and gimble in the wabe: / All mimsy were the borogoves, / And the
 T6    165: 2   to go  round and round like a gyroscope. To 'gimble' is to make holes like a gimlet."
```
GIMLET (1)
```
 T6    165: 3      To 'gimble' is to make holes like a gimlet."
```
GIRL (7)
```
 T4    144:37   said Alice, who was a very thoughtful little girl.
 T2    123:10   crossed  her  mind, "There's another little girl in the garden, somewhere!"
 A2     15:20   be ashamed of yourself," said Alice, "a great girl like you," (she might well say this), "to go on crying in
 A5     43:24   does  it matter to me whether you're a little girl or a serpent?"
 A5     43: 9                    "I--I'm a little girl," said Alice, rather doubtfully, as she remembered the
 A1      9: 2   manage  it?) "And  what an ignorant little girl she'll think me for asking! No, it'll never do to ask:
 T5    152:37   her  hands in despair. "Consider what a great girl you are. Consider what a long way you've come to-day.
```
GIRLS (3)
```
 A5     43:17   who was a very truthful child; "but little girls eat eggs quite as much as serpents do, you know."
 A5     43:12   contempt.  "I've  seen  a good many little girls in my time, but never one with such a neck as that! No,
 A11    86:26      and  rightly too, that very few little girls of her age knew the meaning of it at all. However,
```
GIVE (26)
```
 T4    141:18   / We cannot do with more than four, / To give a hand to each.'
 A10    84:28   / Game, or any other dish? / Who would not give all else for two p / ennyworth only of beautiful Soup? /
 A9     72:21   thought  Alice.  "I'm glad people don't give birthday-presents like that!" But she did not venture to
 A12    95:25   a bit afraid of interrupting him,) "I'll give him sixpence. I don't believe there's an atom of meaning
 A7     56:29                    "No, I give it up," Alice replied. "What's the answer?"
 T7    171:16   "You alarm me!" said the King. "I feel faint--Give me a ham-sandwich!"
 T3    135:30   to  lose it at all--because they'd have to give me another, and it would be almost certain to be an ugly
 T8    188:24      Yet twopence-halfpenny is all / They give me for my toil.'
 T9    194:31   eyes.  "I can do Addition," she said, "if you give me time--but I ca'n't do Subtraction under any
 T9    201:16   why  the  Red Queen should be the only one to give orders; so, as an experiment, she called out "Waiter!
 A8     66:10   nicely  straightened  out, and  was going to give the hedgehog a blow with its head, it would twist itself
 A3     23:22                 "But who is to give the prizes?" quite a chorus of voices asked.
 T8    187:29   own invention," she said to herself: "it's 'I give thee all, I can no more.'" She stood and listened very
 A2     15: 2   walk  the  way I want to go! Let me see. I'll give them a new pair of boots every Christmas."
 T7    173:25   Haigha whispered to Alice: "and they only give them oyster-shells in there--so you see he's very hungry
```

GIVE (cont.)
T8   188:13   could not be seen. / So, having no reply to give / To what the old man said, / I cried 'Come, tell me how
T9   201: 4   "May I give you a slice?" she said, taking up the knife and fork, and
A9   72:36   "Now, I give you fair warning," shouted the Queen, stamping on the
T1   110:44   House, Kitty? I wonder if they'd give you milk in there? Perhaps Looking-glass milk isn't good
T9   201:11   "or we shall get no dinner at all. May I give you some?"
T5   153: 6   "I can believe it without that. Now I'll give you something to believe. I'm just one hundred and one,
T2   127:36   in a peg to mark the distance, "I shall give you your directions--have another biscuit?"
A11   88:28   "Give your evidence," said the King: "and don't be nervous, or
A11   91: 9   "Give your evidence," said the King.
A11   89: 9   "Give your evidence," the King repeated angrily, "or I'll have
A5   40: 6   that is enough," / Said his father. "Don't give yourself airs! / Do you think I can listen all day to
GIVEN (4)
T8W   21:17   quite pleased that she had gone back and given a few minutes to making the poor old creature
A7   57:13   March Hare,) "--it was at the great concert given by the Queen of Hearts, and I had to sing
T7   177:19   much puzzled how to begin. "The Monster has given the Lion twice as much as me!"
T6   162:39   "A present given when it isn't your birthday, of course."
GIVING (6)
T6   168:22   Humpty Dumpty replied in a discontented tone, giving her one of his fingers to shake: "you're so exactly
T4   140:16   is the longest," Tweedledum replied, giving his brother an affectionate hug.
T1   107:21   cried Alice, catching up the kitten, and giving it a little kiss to make it understand that it was in
A6   48:34   a sort of lullaby to it as she did so, and giving it a violent shake at the end of every line:--
A4   32:15   being held up by two guinea-pigs, who were giving it something out of a bottle. They all made a rush at
T6   166: 1   'mome raths'?" said Alice. "I'm afraid I'm giving you a great deal of trouble."
GLAD (21)
T8   191: 3   dotted about it here and there. "Oh, how glad I am to get here! And what is this on my head?" she
A9   70: 1   "You ca'n't think how glad I am to see you again, you dear old thing!" said the
T5   149: 5   "I'm very glad I happened to be in the way," Alice said, as she helped
T5   152:28   flown away, I think," said Alice: "I'm so glad it's gone. I thought it was the night coming on."
A11   90:16   "I'm glad I've seen that done," thought Alice. "I've so often read
A9   72:20   A cheap sort of present!" thought Alice. "I'm glad people don't give birthday-presents like that!" But she
A8   67:20   began an account of the game, feeling very glad she had some one to listen to her. The Cat seemed to
A10   80:14   dance to watch," said Alice, feeling very glad that it was over at last: "and I do so like that curious
T5   152:30   "I wish I could manage to be glad!" the Queen said. "Only I never can remember the rule.
A1   8:42   The antipathies, I think--" (she was rather glad there was no one listening, this time, as it didn't sound
A7   55:13   shall have some fun now!" thought Alice. "I'm glad they've begun asking riddles--I believe I can guess that
T9   200:11   were even a few flowers among them. "I'm glad they've come without waiting to be asked," she thought:
A10   84: 7   said the Gryphon, and Alice was only too glad to do so.
A9   70: 4   Alice was very glad to find her in such a pleasant temper, and thought to
A2   18:11   frightened at the sudden change, but very glad to find herself still in existence. "And now for the
T1   119:10   so much floating in the air, and was rather glad to find herself walking again in the natural way.
A6   48:24   be an advantage," said Alice, who felt very glad to get an opportunity of showing off a little of her
T7   170: 3   got worse every moment, and Alice was very glad to get out of the wood into an open place, where she
T1   108: 9   gently touching the ball, as if it would be glad to help if it might.
T7   172: 8   Alice was glad to see that it revived him a good deal. "There's nothing
T5   152:32   be very happy, living in this wood, and being glad whenever you like!"
GLADLY (1)
T8   189: 5   wink) / 'By which I get my wealth--/ And very gladly will I drink / Your Honour's noble health.'
GLADNESS (1)
TI   103:28   ruddy glow, / And childhood's nest of gladness. / The magic words shall hold thee fast: / Thou shalt
GLANCED (3)
T9   200: 8   Alice glanced nervously along the table, as she walked up the large
A6   48:28   Alice glanced rather anxiously at the cook, to see if she meant to
T2   126: 6   She glanced rather shyly at the real Queen as she said this, but
GLANCING (1)
T7   175:11   of it this time?" he said to the King, just glancing at him as he passed.
GLARING (1)
A8   64: 5   Queen turned crimson with fury, and, after glaring at her for a moment like a wild beast, began screaming
GLASS (16) [See also LOOKING-GLASS, OPERA-GLASS]
A4   30: 5   help me out of this!" (Sounds of more broken glass.)
T1   112: 1   In another moment Alice was through the glass, and had jumped lightly down into the Looking-glass room
A1   12:18   she could see it quite plainly through the glass, and she tried her best to climb up one of the legs of
T1   110:41   because I've held up one of our books to the glass, and then they hold up one in the other room.
A1   12:31   Soon her eye fell on a little glass box that was lying under the table: she opened it, and
A4   29:39   shriek and a fall, and a crash of broken glass, from which she concluded that it was just possible it
T1   111: 8   into it, somehow, Kitty. Let's pretend the glass has got all soft like gauze, so that we can get through.
T1   112: 8   fun it'll be, when they see me through the glass in here, and ca'n't get at me!"
A4   27:10   in the pool; and the great hall, with the glass table and the little door, had vanished completely.
A2   18:14   and the little golden key was lying on the glass table as before, "and things are worse than ever,"
A7   60:43   in the long hall, and close to the little glass table. "Now, I'll manage better this time," she said to
T1   110:32   there's the room you can see through the glass--that's just the same as our drawing-room, only the
T1   116:15   book, of course! And, if I hold it up to a glass, the words will all go the right way again."
A1   9:35   little three-legged table, all made of solid glass: there was nothing on it but a tiny golden key, and
T1   111:13   knew how she had got there. And certainly the glass was beginning to melt away, just like a bright silvery
A4   30:17   two little shrieks, and more sounds of broken glass. "What a number of cucumber-frames there must be!"
GLASSES (3)
T9   199:29   "Then fill up the glasses as quick as you can, / And sprinkle the table with
T9   202:23   they managed it: some of them put their glasses upon their heads like extinguishers, and drank all
T9   200: 1   "Then fill up the glasses with treacle and ink, / Or anything else that is

GLEAM (1)
TC   209:20   down the stream--/ Lingering in the golden gleam--/ Life, what is it but a dream?
GLEAMING (1)
T8   187:20   kindly smile of the Knight--the setting sun gleaming through his hair, and shining on his armour in a
GLIDE (1)
AI   3: 2   in the golden afternoon / Full leisurely we glide; / For both our oars, with little skill, / By little
GLIDED (3)
T5   156:28   pick plenty of beautiful rushes as the boat glided by, there was always a more lovely one that she
T5   156:16   to drift down the stream as it would, till it glided gently in among the waving rushes. And then the little
T5   156: 2   for a minute or two, while the boat glided gently on, sometimes among beds of weeds (which made
GLIDING (1)
T5   155:18   and she found they were in a little boat, gliding along between banks: so there was nothing for it but
GLOBE (1)
A12   92: 6   sprawling about, reminding her very much of a globe of gold-fish she had accidentally upset the week before
GLOOMILY (1)
A7   56: 7   March Hare took the watch and looked at it gloomily: then he dipped it into his cup of tea, and looked at
GLORIOUS (1)
T8   180:15   "It was a glorious victory, wasn't it?" said the White Knight, as he
GLORY (4)
T6   163:24   "I don't know what you mean by 'glory,'" Alice said.
T6   163:28   "But 'glory' doesn't mean 'a nice knock-down argument,'" Alice
T6   163:22   one for birthday presents, you know. There's glory for you!"
TI   103:34   summer days" gone by, / And vanish'd summer glory--/ It shall not touch, with breath of bale, / The
GLOVES (6) [See also KID-GLOVES]
A4   27:26   of the house before she had found the fan and gloves.
A4   27:15   Run home this moment, and fetch me a pair of gloves and a fan! Quick, now!" And Alice was so much
A2   15:36   Alice took up the fan and gloves, and, as the hall was very hot, she kept fanning
A4   28: 1   she took up the fan and a pair of the gloves, and was just going to leave the room, when her eye
A4   27:20   who I am! But I'd better take him his fan and gloves--that is, if I can find them." As she said this, she
A4   29:19   Ann! Mary Ann!" said the voice. "Fetch me my gloves this moment!" Then came a little pattering of feet on
GLOW (1) [See also AGLOW]
TI   103:27   madness--/ Within, the firelight's ruddy glow, / And childhood's nest of gladness. / The magic words
GLOWING (1)
TI   103:14   begun in other days, / When summer suns were glowing--/ A simple chime, that served to time / The rhythm of
GLUE (2)
T9   202:15   For it holds it like glue--/ Holds the lid to the dish, while it lies in the middle
T8   189:16   if e'er by chance I put / My fingers into glue, / Or madly squeeze a right-hand foot / Into a left-hand
GNAT (18)
T3   134:19   "It always happens," said the Gnat.
T3   132:20   It certainly was a very large Gnat: "about the size of a chicken," Alice thought. Still, she
T3   134: 9   "Crawling at your feet," said the Gnat (Alice drew her feet back in some alarm), "you may
T3   134:21   silent for a minute or two, pondering. The Gnat amused itself meanwhile by humming round and round her
T3   133:12   Look on the branch above your head," said the Gnat, "and there you'll find a Snap-dragon-fly. Its body is
T3   132:17   sitting quietly under a tree--while the Gnat (for that was the insect she had been talking to) was
T3   133: 7   "Sap and sawdust," said the Gnat. "Go on with the list."
T3   133: 3   "All right," said the Gnat. "Half way up that bush, you'll see a Rocking-horse-fly,
T3   132:28   do you rejoice in, where you come from?" the Gnat inquired.
T3   135:13   But the Gnat only sighed deeply while two large tears came rolling
T3   135:18   little sighs, and this time the poor Gnat really seemed to have sighed itself away, for, when Alice
T3   132:32   "Of course they answer to their names?" the Gnat remarked carelessly.
T3   135: 9   'Miss,' and didn't say anything more," the Gnat remarked, "of course you'd miss your lessons. That's a
T3   134: 2   "Frumenty and mince-pie," the Gnat replied; "and it makes its nest in a Christmas-box."
T3   132:39   "I ca'n't say," the Gnat replied. "Further on, in the wood down there, they've got
T3   132:35   "What's the use of their having names," the Gnat said, "if they wo'n't answer to them?"
T3   132:23   "--then you don't like all insects?" the Gnat went on, as quietly as if nothing had happened.
T3   134:25   "And yet I don't know," the Gnat went on in a careless tone: "only think how convenient it
GO (111)
A2   15:35   away into the darkness as hard as he could go.
T2   128: 3   say good-bye. And at the end of five, I shall go!"
T7   171: 1   know--to come and go. One to come, and one to go."
T7   171: 5   said Alice. "Why one to come and one to go?"
A9   74: 6   would be quite as safe to stay with it as to go after that savage Queen: so she waited.
A6   51:22   "But I don't want to go among mad people," Alice remarked.
A5   41:37   her arms round it as far as they would go, and broke off a bit of the edge with each hand.
A6   49:11   the baby at her as she spoke. "I must go and get ready to play croquet with the Queen," and she
A2   17:18   must be Mabel after all, and I shall have to go and live in that poky little house, and have next to no
A2   20:12   swimming away from her as hard as it could go, and making quite a commotion in the pool as it went.
T2   123:35   "I think I'll go and meet her," said Alice, for, though the flowers were
T7   174:18   any more to-day," the King said to Hatta: "go and order the drums to begin." And Hatta went bounding away
T1   108:16   so, they had to leave off. Never mind, we'll go and see the bonfire to-morrow." Here Alice wound two or
A4   30:11   it's got no business there, at any rate: go and take it away!"
T8   179:11   complaining tone: "I've a great mind to go and wake him, and see what happens!"
T6   168: 7   he was very proud and stiff: / He said 'I'd go and wake them, if--'
A10   81:31   the Mock Turtle said. "No wise fish would go anywhere without a porpoise."
A12   93:41   "Well, I sha'n't go, at any rate," said Alice; "besides, that's not a regular
A9   74: 2   Mock Turtle, and to hear his history. I must go back and see after some executions I have ordered;" and she
A8   68:10   Alice thought she might as well go back and see how the game was going on, as she heard the
A2   18:20   fallen into the sea, "and in that case I can go back by railway," she said to herself. (Alice had been to
T3   131: 9   in turn, he went on with "She'll have to go back from here as luggage!"
T3   135:25   up her mind to go on: "for I certainly won't go back," she thought to herself, and this was the only way to

GO (cont.)

T1	118:32	up, "if I don't make haste, I shall have to	go back through the Looking-glass, before I've seen what the
T6	161:15	is going on a little too fast: let's	go back to the last remark but one."
T8	181: 5	safe to the end of the wood--and then I must	go back, you know. That's the end of my move."
T7	169: 4	for fear of being run over, and watched them	go by.
TC	209:17	a Wonderland they lie, / Dreaming as the days	go by, / Dreaming as the summers die:
T3	131:19	carriage!" thought Alice), saying "She must	go by post, as she's got a head on her--" "She must be sent as
A2	15: 4	herself how she would manage it. "They must	go by the carrier," she thought; "and how funny it'll seem,
T7	176:25	he said. "That's a good long way. Did you	go by the old bridge, or the market-place? You get the best
T9	194:23	said, as gravely as she could, "They might	go different ways." But she couldn't help thinking to herself
T3	129:20	turning shy so suddenly. "It'll never do to	go down among them without a good long branch to brush them
T3	129:17	of honey they must make! I think I'll	go down and--no, I wo'n't go just yet," she went on, checking
A4	30:33	do it!--That I wo'n't, then!--Bill's got to	go down--Here, Bill! The master says you've got to go down the
A4	30:34	Here, Bill! The master says you've got to	go down the chimney!"
A4	30:31	who did that?--It was Bill, I fancy--Who's to	go down the chimney?--Nay, I sha'n't! You do it!--That I
T3	129:25	"I think I'll	go down the other way," she said after a pause; "and perhaps I
T2	126:16	Faster! Faster!" but Alice felt she could not	go faster, though she had no breath left to say so.
A2	20:21	It was high time to	go, for the pool was getting quite crowded with the birds and
A6	51: 7	you tell me, please, which way I ought to	go from here?"
T8	190:14	they had come. "You've only a few yards to	go," he said, "down the hill and over that little brook, and
A10	80: 7	"What matters it how far we	go?" his scaly friend replied. / "There is another shore, you
T2	124:16	Queen to disbelieve it. "I'll try it when I	go home," she thought to herself, "the next time I'm a little
T3	134:28	convenient it would be if you could manage to	go home without it! For instance, if the governess wanted to
T5	157: 8	into the dark water. "I wish it hadn't let	go--I should so like a little crab to take home with me!" But
A7	60:40	curious to-day. I think I may as well	go in at once." And in she went.
T9	200: 6	"Oh, that'll never be done! I'd better	go in at once--" and in she went, and there was a dead silence
T3	135:29	I wonder what'll become of my name when I	go in? I shouldn't like to lose it at all--because they'd have
A2	16: 5	goes in such long ringlets, and mine doesn't	go in ringlets at all; and I'm sure I ca'n't be Mabel, for I
T3	129:17	make! I think I'll go down and--no, I wo'n't	go just yet," she went on, checking herself just as she was
A2	15: 1	or perhaps they wo'n't walk the way I want to	go! Let me see. I'll give them a new pair of boots every
T8	188:18	accents mild took up the tale: / He said 'I	go my ways, / And when I find a mountain-rill, / I set it in a
A5	44: 5	right-hand bit again, and did not venture to	go near the house till she had brought herself down to nine
A6	53:14	so large a house, that she did not like to	go nearer till she had nibbled some more of the left-hand bit
A11	90:23	"I ca'n't	go no lower," said the Hatter: "I'm on the floor, as it is."
T4	140: 1	Then they let	go of Alice's hands, and stood looking at her for a minute:
A11	89:18	King sharply. "Do you take me for a dunce? Go on!"
T2	122:20	to make one wither to hear the way they	go on!"
A7	59:28	"No, please	go on!" Alice said very humbly. "I wo'n't interrupt you again.
A7	59:31	indignantly. However, he consented to	go on. "And so these three little sisters--they were learning
A2	15:21	like you," (she might well say this), "to	go on crying in this way! Stop this moment, I tell you!" But
T3	135:25	on second thoughts, she made up her mind to	go on: "for I certainly won't go back," she thought to herself
A7	60:13	poor Alice, that she let the Dormouse	go on for some time without interrupting it.
T8	188:27	a way / To feed oneself on batter, / And so	go on from day to day / Getting a little fatter. / I shook him
A1	13: 3	it seemed quite dull and stupid for life to	go on in the common way.
A10	84: 4	interrupted, "if you don't explain it as you	go on? It's by far the most confusing thing that I ever heard!
T12	208: 6	serious question, my dear, and you should not	go on licking your paw like that--as if Dinah hadn't washed
T5	152:36	"Oh, don't	go on like that!" cried the poor Queen, wringing her hands in
T6	166:37	"You needn't	go on making remarks like that," Humpty Dumpty said: "they're
T4	147:16	"Every one of these things has got to	go on, somehow or other."
T8	185:24	"How can you	go on talking so quietly, head downwards?" Alice asked, as she
T8W	14: 3	"How you	go on!" the Wasp said in a peevish tone. "Worrity, worrity!
A12	94:35	beginning," the King said, very gravely, "and	go on till you come to the end: then stop."
T5	155: 8	needles. "You'll make me giddy soon, if you	go on turning round like that." She was now working with
A9	72:40	"Let's	go on with the game," the Queen said to Alice; and Alice was
T3	133: 7	"Sap and sawdust," said the Gnat. "Go on with the list."
A10	83: 3	explain it," said the Gryphon hastily. "Go on with the next verse."
A10	83:10	"Go on with the next verse," the Gryphon repeated: "it begins
T3	132:40	down there, they've got no names--however,	go on with your list of insects: you're wasting time."
T7	170:37	Hatta. I must have two, you know--to come and	go. One to come, and one to go."
T4	145:10	King was to wake," added Tweedledum, "you'd	go out--bang!--just like a candle!"
A9	70:33	'tis love, 'tis love, that makes the world	go round!'"
A6	48:21	said, in a hoarse growl, "the world would	go round a deal faster than it does."
A4	29:28	Alice heard it say to itself "Then I'll	go round and get in at the window."
T6	165: 2	"To 'gyre' is to	go round and round like a gyroscope. To 'gimble' is to make
T4	139:36	all this), "to find myself singing 'Here we	go round the mulberry bush.' I don't know when I began it, but
A6	51:12	"Then it doesn't matter which way you	go," said the Cat.
A11	90:31	"You may	go," said the King, and the Hatter hurriedly left the court,
T8	184:14	"Does that kind	go smoothly?" the Knight asked in a tone of great interest,
A8	62: 5	one of them say "Look out now, Five! Don't	go splashing paint over me like that!"
T5	149:29	"It ca'n't	go straight, you know, if you pin it all on one side," Alice
T8	184: 6	He let	go the bridle, and stretched out both his arms to show Alice
T1	110:33	the same as our drawing-room, only the things	go the other way. I can see all of it when I get upon a chair
T1	116:15	I hold it up to a glass, the words will all	go the right way again."
T1	110:40	are something like our books, only the words	go the wrong way: I know that, because I've held up one of our
A7	60:35	"At any rate I'll never	go there again!" said Alice, as she picked her way through the
A8	67:28	for instance, there's the arch I've got to	go through next walking about at the other end of the ground--
T5	155: 3	the very top shelf of all. It'll puzzle it to	go through the ceiling, I expect!"
A1	10: 6	the doorway; "and even if my head would	go through," thought poor Alice, "it would be of very little
A3	25: 9	mouse, That he met in the house, 'Let us both	go to law: I will prosecute you.--Come, I'll take no denial:
A2	18:22	to the general conclusion that wherever you	go to on the English coast, you find a number of

GO (cont.)
```
T1   109:12  with  a  white  quilt;  and  perhaps it says 'Go to sleep, darlings, till the summer comes again.' And when
T9   197: 6  for  a  nap.  /  When the feast's over, we'll go to the ball--/ Red Queen, and White Queen, and Alice, and
T2   128: 8  in  its  first  move,  you  know. So you'll go very quickly through the Third Square--by railway, I should
A3    22:22  hurriedly went on, "--found it advisable to go with Edgar Atheling to meet William and offer him the crown
A10   81: 4  is," said the Gryphon, "that they would go with the lobsters to the dance. So they got thrown out to
T8   182:10  invention of my own. And now help me on. I'll go with you to the end of the wood--What's that dish for?"
T1   109: 6  when the miserable day came, I should have to go without fifty dinners at once! Well, I shouldn't mind that
T1   109: 7  I  shouldn't  mind  that much! I'd far rather go without them than eat them!
T3   135: 4  to  call,  and of course you wouldn't have to go, you know."
```
GOAT (2)
```
T3   131: 6         There  was  a  Beetle  sitting  next the Goat (it was a very queer carriage-full of passengers
T3   131: 3                              A Goat, that was sitting next to the gentleman in white, shut
```
GOAT'S (1)
```
T3   132:12  nearest to her hand, which happened to be the Goat's beard. * * * * * * * * * * * * * *
```
GOES (18)
```
T2   121:10  Still,  you're  the  right  colour,  and that goes a long way."
T6   165: 6  is.  It's  called 'wabe' you know, because it goes a long way before it, and a long way behind it--"
A4    31: 6  she  heard  was  a  general  chorus of "There goes Bill!" then the Rabbit's voice alone--"Catch him, you by
T6   168:24                "The face is what one goes by, generally," Alice remarked in a thoughtful tone,
T7   173:12  only I'm not strong enough. You see, a minute goes by so fearfully quick. You might as well try to stop a
A6    48:17  up and down in an agony of terror. "Oh, there goes his precious nose!", as an unusually large saucepan flew
A2    16: 4  sure  I'm  not  Ada," she said, "for her hair goes in such long ringlets, and mine doesn't go in ringlets at
T7   170:23  very  slowly--and  what  curious attitudes he goes into!" (For the Messenger kept skipping up and down, and
A4    31:23  comes  at me like a Jack-in-the-box, and up I goes like a sky-rocket!"
A12   96: 9                    "But it goes on 'they all returned from him to you,'" said Alice.
T8   186: 3  my  body  happens  to  be?" he said. "My mind goes on working all the same. In fact, the more head-downwards
A7    57:18              "It goes on, you know," the Hatter continued, "in this way:--
T8   190:26  herself, as she stood watching him. "There he goes! Right on his head as usual! However, he gets on again
T2   120: 7  to  the  hill, I suppose--no, it doesn't! This goes straight back to the house! Well then, I'll try it the
A7    57: 1  have  to  whisper  a  hint to Time, and round goes the clock in a twinkling! Half-past one, time for dinner!
T5   153:16  six impossible things before breakfast. There goes the shawl again!"
T2   120: 6  like  a  corkscrew than a path! Well this turn goes to the hill, I suppose--no, it doesn't! This goes
T2   128: 7       peg she faced round, and said "A pawn goes two squares in its first move, you know. So you'll go
```
GOING (52) [See also UNDERGOING]
```
T2   120: 3  at  least,  no,  it  doesn't do that--" (after going a few yards along the path, and turning several sharp
A10   81:34  Why, if a fish came to me, and told me he was going a journey, I should say 'With what porpoise?'"
A10   81:41  said  Alice  a  little  timidly; "but it's no use going back to yesterday, because I was a different person then
A8    65: 7  Majesty,"  said  Two,  in a very humble tone, going down on one knee as he spoke, "we were trying--"
T3   131: 1  white  paper),  "ought to know which way she's going, even if she doesn't know her own name!"
T2   120:14  pretending it was arguing with her. "I'm not going in again yet. I know I should have to get through the
T3   135:24  wood,  and  Alice  felt a little timid about going into it. However, on second thoughts, she made up her
A1    12:14  that  nothing  more  happened, she decided on going into the garden at once; but, alas for poor Alice! when
T2   124: 7  from?"  said  the Red Queen. "And where are you going? Look up, speak nicely, and don't twiddle your fingers
A4    27:27  it  seems,"  Alice  said  to  herself, "to be going messages for a rabbit! I suppose Dinah'll be sending me
A7    60:20  had  closed  its  eyes  by this time, and was going off into a doze; but, on being pinched by the Hatter, it
T6   161:15  they  would!  However,  this conversation is going on a little too fast: let's go back to the last remark
A8    68:11  as  well  go  back  and see how the game was going on, as she heard the Queen's voice in the distance,
A8    68:30  crowd collected round it: there was a dispute going on between the executioner, the King, and the Queen, who
T7   175:43   The  Lion  had  joined  them while this was going on: he looked very tired and sleepy, and his eyes were
T7   176:23  the  King  interrupted, to prevent the quarrel going on: he was very nervous, and his voice quite quivered.
T2   123: 1  away  there,  till you know no more what's going on in the world, than if you were a bud!"
T4   147:40  have a bit of a fight, but I don't care about going on long," said Tweedledum. "What's the time now?"
T8W   21:13  might  safely  leave  him. "I think I must be going on now," she said. "Good-bye."
A9    70:30                "The game's going on rather better now," she said, by way of keeping up
A2    18: 6  she  was  now  about  two feet high, and was going on shrinking rapidly: she soon found out that the cause
T7   175:15  him,"  the  Unicorn  said carelessly, and he was going on, when his eye happened to fall upon Alice: he turned
A6    46:14        there  was  a  most  extraordinary  noise going on within--a constant howling and sneezing, and every
A1    12: 8  end,  you  know," said Alice to herself, "in my going out altogether, like a candle. I wonder what I should be
T4   138: 7  forgot  they  were  alive,  and she was just going round to see if the word 'TWEEDLE' was written at the
T6   168:18  such  a  very  strong  hint that she ought to be going, she felt that it would hardly be civil to stay. So she
A7    60:32  of  the  others  took the least notice of her going, though she looked back once or twice, half hoping that
A1    12: 5  thought  that  she  was now the right size for going through the little door into that lovely garden. First,
A5    43:41  these  changes  are!  I'm never sure what I'm going to be, from one minute to another! However, I've got
A8    66:13  and,  when she had got its head down, and was going to begin again, it was very provoking to find that the
A8    68:39  had  to  do  such a thing before, and he wasn't going to begin at his time of life."
A5    42:22  it  down  into  a  graceful zigzag, and was going to dive in among the leaves, which she found to be
A1    10:20  "Drink  me,"  but the wise little Alice was not going to do that in a hurry. "No, I'll look first," she said,
A8    66: 9  got its neck nicely straightened out, and was going to give the hedgehog a blow with its head, it would
T9   203: 8      hair  with  both  her hands. "Something's going to happen!"
A1     8:13  to  look  about  her,  and to wonder what was going to happen next. First, she tried to look down and make
A4    28: 1  fan and a pair of the gloves, and was just going to leave the room, when her eye fell upon a little
T4   146: 3  it's  coming  on very dark. Do you think it's going to rain?"
A7    56:25  eyes,  "Of course, of course: just what I was going to remark myself."
T6   166:19            "The piece I'm going to repeat," he went on without noticing her remark, "was
T7   175: 2        "But aren't you going to run and help her?" Alice asked, very much surprised
T4   146:10  things!"  thought  Alice,  and  she was just going to say "Good-night" and leave them, when Tweedledum
A3    22:35        "What I was going to say," said the Dodo in an offended tone, "was that
T6   160:26  pale,  if  you  like! You didn't think I was going to say that, did you? The King has promised me--with his
A1    12: 6  waited  for  a  few  minutes to see if she was going to shrink any further: she felt a little nervous about
```

GOING (cont.)

T8W	13: 1	...and she was just going to spring over, when she heard a deep sigh, which seemed
T5	156:10	"I didn't put 'em there, and I'm not going to take 'em away."
T1	108:27	me!" she went on, holding up one finger. "I'm going to tell you all your faults. Number one: you squeaked
T8	181:26	He unfastened it as he spoke, and was just going to throw it into the bushes, when a sudden thought
T3	129: 2	to make a grand survey of the country she was going to travel through. "It's something very like learning
A6	50: 3	No, there were no tears. "If you're going to turn into a pig, my dear," said Alice, seriously,
T1	109: 5	let me see--suppose each punishment was to be going without a dinner: then, when the miserable day came, I

GOLD (1)

T8	188:37	silent night. / And these I do not sell for gold / Or coin of silvery shine, / But for a copper halfpenny,

GOLDEN (10)

AI	3: 1	All in the golden afternoon / Full leisurely we glide; / For both our
T8	191: 9	It was a golden crown.
TC	209:20	drifting down the stream--/ Lingering in the golden gleam--/ Life, what is it but a dream?
A1	9:35	glass: there was nothing on it but a tiny golden key, and Alice's first idea was that this might belong
A2	15:14	feet high, and she at once took up the little golden key and hurried off to the garden door.
A7	61: 1	to herself, and began by taking the little golden key, and unlocking the door that led into the garden.
A1	12:15	door, she found she had forgotten the little golden key, and when she went back to the table for it, she
A1	9:41	fifteen inches high: she tried the little golden key in the lock, and to her great delight it fitted!
A2	18:14	little door was shut again, and the little golden key was lying on the glass table as before, "and things
A2	17:11	/ And pour the waters of the Nile / On every golden scale!

GOLD-FISH (2)

A12	92:10	quickly as she could, for the accident of the gold-fish kept running in her head, and she had a vague sort
A12	92: 6	about, reminding her very much of a globe of gold-fish she had accidentally upset the week before.

GONE (22)

A6	53: 6	remained some time after the rest of it had gone.
A8	68:20	only difficulty was, that her flamingo was gone across the other side of the garden, where Alice could
T2	128:32	there was no way of guessing, but she was gone, and Alice began to remember that she was a Pawn, and
A8	69:10	head began fading away the moment he was gone, and, by the time he had come back with the Duchess, it
A6	46: 7	she next peeped out, the Fish-Footman was gone, and the other was sitting on the ground near the door,
T8W	21:16	the hill again, quite pleased that she had gone back and given a few minutes to making the poor old
TI	103:33	through the story, / For "happy summer days" gone by, / And vanish'd summer glory--/ It shall not touch,
A4	29: 1	by mice and rabbits. I almost wish I hadn't gone down that rabbit-hole--and yet--and yet--it's rather
A9	74:16	They had not gone far before they saw the Mock Turtle in the distance,
A8	68:24	much," thought Alice, "as all the arches are gone from this side of the ground." So she tucked it away
T5	152:28	away, I think," said Alice: "I'm so glad it's gone. I thought it was the night coming on."
A8	65:17	"Their heads are gone, if it please your Majesty!" the soldiers shouted in
A9	72:39	The Duchess took her choice, and was gone in a moment.
A6	53:10	She had not gone much farther before she came in sight of the house of the
T5	156:41	They hadn't gone much farther before the blade of one of the oars got fast
T1	119: 7	floated on through the hall, and would have gone straight out at the door in the same way, if she hadn't
T8W	19:10	am old and gray, / And all my hair is nearly gone, / They take my wig from me and say / 'How can you put
A5	43:10	she remembered the number of changes she had gone through, that day.
A6	53:17	be raving mad after all! I almost wish I'd gone to see the Hatter instead!"
T7	170:14	sent the two Messengers, either. They're both gone to the town. Just look along the road, and tell me if you
A12	95: 1	He sent them word I had not gone / (We know it to be true): / If she should push the
T2	128:29	exactly as she came to the last peg, she was gone. Whether she vanished into the air, or whether she ran

GOOD (54)

T1	107:11	doubt feeling that it was all meant for its good.
A1	12:23	this minute!" She generally gave herself very good advice (though she very seldom followed it), and
T8	181:34	"Yes, it's a very good bee-hive," the Knight said in a discontented tone, "one
A12	94:41	/ And mentioned me to him: / She gave me a good character, / But said I could not swim.
T7	175: 6	about her, if you like--She's a dear good creature," he repeated softly to himself, as he opened
A2	18:10	"That was a narrow escape!" said Alice, a good deal frightened at the sudden change, but very glad to
A5	41:41	She was a good deal frightened by this very sudden change, but she felt
T8	186:33	very long?" Alice asked, for she had heard a good deal of poetry that day.
A6	51: 9	"That depends a good deal on where you want to get to," said the Cat.
T7	172: 8	Alice was glad to see that it revived him a good deal. "There's nothing like eating hay when you're faint
A4	30:37	Bill! I wouldn't be in Bill's place for a good deal: this fireplace is narrow, to be sure; but I think I
A5	43:25	"It matters a good deal to me," said Alice hastily; "but I'm not looking for
A11	88:35	a very curious sensation, which puzzled her a good deal until she made out what it was: she was beginning to
T2	123:29	that it was the Red Queen. "She's grown a good deal!" was her first remark. She had indeed: when Alice
A7	60: 1	advantage from the change; and Alice was a good deal worse off than before, as the March Hare had just
T1	110:28	see how sulky it was, "--and if you're not good directly," she added, "I'll put you through into
A2	14: 2	for the moment she quite forgot how to speak good English!" Now I'm opening out like the largest telescope
T7	173: 8	"Would you--be good enough--" Alice panted out, after running a little
T7	173:11	"I'm good enough," the King said, "only I'm not strong enough. You
T2	122: 2	the middle," said the Rose. "What else is it good for?"
T8W	16:14	"And it's very good for the conceit," added the Wasp.
T8W	16:13	pityingly at him. "Tying up the face is very good for the toothache," she said.
T9	202:37	so Alice tried to submit to it with good grace.
T4	147:15	and coal-scuttles. "I hope you're a good hand at pinning and tying strings?" Tweedledum remarked.
T6	160: 9	laugh: "my name means the shape I am--and a good handsome shape it is, too. With a name like yours, you
A5	41:16	"It is a very good height indeed!" said the Caterpillar angrily, rearing
T4	143:10	need: / Pepper and vinegar besides / Are very good indeed--/ Now, if you're ready, Oysters dear, / We can
T5	150: 3	"It's very good jam," said the Queen.
T3	129:20	never do to go down among them without a good long branch to brush them away--and what fun it'll be
T7	176:25	"All round the town?" he said. "That's a good long way. Did you go by the old bridge, or the
T5	156:18	in elbow-deep, to get hold of the rushes a good long way down before breaking them off--and for a while
T6	160:37	a History of England, that is. Now, take a good look at me! I'm one that has spoken to a King, I am:

```
GOOD (cont.)
  T3   134: 5      Alice went on, after she had taken a good look at the insect with its head on fire, and had thought
  A6    47:13  for she was not quite sure whether it was good manners for her to speak first, "why your cat grins like
  A5    43:12  a tone of the deepest contempt. "I've seen a good many little girls in my time, but never one with such a
  T6   164:18  all the poems that ever were invented--and a good many that haven't been invented just yet."
  A4    30:23  of little cart-wheels, and the sound of a good many voices all talking together: she made out the words:
  T5   152:26  already," said the Queen. "What would be the good of having it all over again?"
  A4    33: 3             This seemed to Alice a good opportunity for making her escape: so she set off at once
  A6    46:38     The Footman seemed to think this a good opportunity for repeating his remark, with variations. "I
  A1     8:32  school-room, and though this was not a very good opportunity for showing off her knowledge, as there was
  T4   147:39  not fight to-day," said Alice, thinking it a good opportunity to make peace.
  A1     8:34  was no one to listen to her, still it was good practice to say it over) "--yes, that's about the right
  T9   204:14  seized the tablecloth with both hands: one good pull, and plates, dishes, guests, and candles came
  T2   122:30            This sounded a very good reason, and Alice was quite pleased to know it. "I never
  A5    36:16      and, as Alice could not think of any good reason, and the Caterpillar seemed to be in a very
  T8   182:39  help the poor Knight, who certainly was not a good rider.
  A9    76:13         "Ah! Then yours wasn't a really good school," said the Mock Turtle in a tone of great relief.
  T6   162:32  quite pleased to find that she had chosen a good subject after all.
  A7    56:43  stand beating. Now, if you only kept on good terms with him, he'd do almost anything you liked with
  A11   86: 8  a large dish of tarts upon it: they looked so good, that it made Alice quite hungry to look at them--"I wish
  A9    73:20  "You are all pardoned." "Come, that's a good thing!" she said to herself, for she had felt quite
  T1   111: 1  in there? Perhaps Looking-glass milk isn't good to drink--but oh, Kitty! now we come to the passage. You
  A4    33: 1  all the while, till at last it sat down a good way off, panting, with its tongue hanging out of its
GOOD-BYE (8)
  T6   168:16             "That's all," said Humpty Dumpty. "Good-bye."
  T8W   21:14  "I think I must be going on now," she said. "Good-bye."
  T2   128: 3  them. At the end of four, I shall say good-bye. And at the end of five, I shall go!"
  T8W   21:15               "Good-bye, and thank-ye," said the Wasp, and Alice tripped down
  T2   128:27  peg, where she turned for a moment to say "Good-bye," and then hurried on to the last.
  A2    14: 4  out like the largest telescope that ever was! Good-bye, feet!" (for when she looked down at her feet, they
  T6   168:36  or took any further notice of her, she said "Good-bye!" once more, and, getting no answer to this, she
  T6   168:19  stay. So she got up, and held out her hand. "Good-bye, till we meet again!" she said as cheerfully as she
GOOD-NATURED (3)
  T6   160:18  of making another riddle, but simply in her good-natured anxiety for the queer creature. "That wall is so
  T9   204: 6  again, just in time to see the Queen's broad good-natured face grinning at her for a moment over the edge
  A6    51: 1  Cat only grinned when it saw Alice. It looked good-natured, she thought: still it had very long claws and a
GOOD-NATUREDLY (2)
  A4    27: 7  the pair of white kid-gloves, and she very good-naturedly began hunting about for them, but they were
  T2   127:25  "I know what you'd like!" the Queen said good-naturedly, taking a little box out of her pocket. "Have a
GOOD-NIGHT (1)
  T4   146:11  thought Alice, and she was just going to say "Good-night" and leave them, when Tweedledum sprang out from
GOOD-TEMPERED (1)
  T9   196:29  the Red Queen went on: "but it's amazing how good-tempered she is! Pat her on the head, and see how pleased
GOOSE (3)
  T5   155:38  "You are," said the Sheep: "you're a little goose."
  A4    30: 8               "An arm, you goose! Who ever saw one that size? Why, it fills the whole
  A5    39: 3  tougher than suet; / Yet you finished the goose, with the bones and the beak--/ Pray, how did you manage
GOT (116)
  T8   181:32               "But you've got a bee-hive--or something like one--fastened to the saddle
  T8W   17:15  at her with more interest. "And you've got a comb. Much honey?"
  T3   131:20  Alice), saying "She must go by post, as she's got a head on her--" "She must be sent as a message by the
  A9    70:22  tut, child!" said the Duchess. "Everything's got a moral, if only you can find it." And she squeezed
  T9   196:38            "I haven't got a nightcap with me," said Alice, as she tried to obey the
  T8   182:29  "Not yet," said the Knight. "But I've got a plan for keeping it from falling off."
  T4   147:36               "And I've got a toothache!" said Tweedledee, who had overheard the
  T1   111: 9  somehow, Kitty. Let's pretend the glass has got all soft like gauze, so that we can get through. Why, it's
  T2   128: 4               She had got all the pegs put in by this time, and Alice looked on with
  A5    41: 3  said Alice, timidly: "some of the words have got altered."
  A7    59:41  March Hare. The Hatter was the only one who got any advantage from the change; and Alice was a good deal
  T3   129: 6  I'm on the only one, but I don't think it's got any name. Principal towns--why, what are those creatures,
  T1   115:24  To which the Queen replied "You haven't got any whiskers."
  T5   157: 5  nice crab you caught!" she remarked, as Alice got back into her place, very much relieved to find herself
  A5    43:42  be, from one minute to another! However, I've got back to my right size: the next thing is, to get into that
  A8    68:28               When she got back to the Cheshire-Cat, she was surprised to find quite
  T1   115:19  nothing but a bottle of ink, and when she got back with it she found he had recovered, and he and the
  T7   169: 3  they seemed to fill the whole forest. Alice got behind a tree, for fear of being run over, and watched
  T8   179:37  away at each other with such fury that Alice got behind a tree to be out of the way of the blows.
  A8    67:45  King, "and don't look at me like that!" He got behind Alice as he spoke.
  A11   87: 6  not stand, and she went round the court and got behind him, and very soon found an opportunity of taking
  T4   140: 7  now," she said to herself: "we seem to have got beyond that, somehow!"
  T5   158:20  it. Let me see, is this a chair? Why, it's got branches, I declare! How very odd to find trees growing
  A1    10:22  nice little stories about children who had got burnt, and eaten up by wild beasts, and other unpleasant
  A5    41:25  once or twice, and shook itself. Then it got down off the mushroom, and crawled away into the grass,
  T5   149:32               "The brush has got entangled in it!" the Queen said with a sigh. "And I lost
  A6    46: 4  you ca'n't look all round you--unless you've got entangled together.
  T5   154: 7  you ca'n't look all round you--unless you've got eyes at the back of your head."
  T5   155:25  she thought, as every now and then the oars got fast in it, and would hardly come out again.
  T5   156:42  farther before the blade of one of the oars got fast in the water and wouldn't come out again (so Alice
  T8   189:12  thanked him much for telling me / The way he got his wealth, / But chiefly for his wish that he / Might
  T9   203: 5  rise as she spoke, several inches; but she got hold of the edge of the table, and managed to pull herself
```

GOT (cont.)

T9	196:14	the roof came off, and ever so much thunder	got in--and it went rolling round the room in great lumps--and
A7	56: 5	"Yes, but some crumbs must have	got in as well," the Hatter grumbled: "you shouldn't have put
A3	23:32	replied very gravely. "What else have you	got in your pocket?" it went on, turning to Alice.
A6	48: 5	very politely, feeling quite pleased to have	got into a conversation.
A3	23:28	box of comfits (luckily the saltwater had not	got into it), and handed them round as prizes. There was
A11	91: 7	and Alice guessed who it was, even before she	got into the court, by the way the people near the door began
T8	182:19	a tight fit, you see," he said, as they	got it in at last; "there are so many candlesticks in the bag
A12	93: 7	way, being quite unable to move. She soon	got it out again, and put it right; "not that it signifies
T5	153:20	she succeeded in catching it herself. "I've	got it!" she cried in a triumphant tone. "Now you shall see me
A8	66:12	help bursting out laughing; and, when she had	got its head down, and was going to begin again, it was very
A8	66: 9	hanging down, but generally, just as she had	got its neck nicely straightened out, and was going to give
T10	205: 4	only her face grew very small, and her eyes	got large and green: and still, as Alice went on shaking her,
T6	159: 1	However, the egg only	got larger and larger, and more and more human: when she had
T9	197:20	The snoring	got more distinct every minute, and sounded more like a tune:
T7	171:13	was of no use--the Anglo-Saxon attitudes only	got more extraordinary every moment, while the great eyes
A11	91:31	witness would be like, "--for they haven't	got much evidence yet," she said to herself. Imagine her
T3	135:32	be, trying to find the creature that has	got my old name! That's just like the advertisements, you know
A4	30:11	"Well, it's	got no business there, at any rate: go and take it away!"
T4	140:31	sulkily, / Because she thought the sun / Had	got no business to be there / After the day was done--/ 'It's
T3	136: 1	it call itself, I wonder? I do believe it's	got no name--why, to be sure it hasn't!"
T3	132:40	"Further on, in the wood down there, they've	got no names--however, go on with your list of insects: you're
A9	74:21	before, "It's all his fancy, that: he hasn't	got no sorrow, you know. Come on!"
T1	111: 7	into Looking-glass House! I'm sure it's	got, oh! such beautiful things in it! Let's pretend there's a
T8	179:25	just as the Red Knight had done: then he	got on again, and the two Knights sat and looked at each other
T6	162:13	"What a beautiful belt you've	got on!" Alice suddenly remarked. (They had had quite enough
T3	130: 2	"I'm afraid I haven't	got one," Alice said in a frightened tone: "there wasn't a
T7	175:40	bag, and gave it to Alice to hold, while he	got out a dish and carving-knife. How they all came out of it
T5	151:22	voice went higher with each "better," till it	got quite to a squeak at last.
T8W	14:12	let her help him round the tree, but when he	got settled down again he only said, as before, "Worrity,
A8	65:43	tumbling up against each other: however, they	got settled down in a minute or two, and the game began.
T8	184:39	hastily. "What a curious helmet you've	got!" she said cheerfully. "Is that your invention too?"
A10	82: 3	about it, just at first, the two creatures	got so close to her, one on each side, and opened their eyes
T1	108:15	and it wants plenty of sticks, Kitty! Only it	got so cold, and it snowed so, they had to leave off. Never
A1	13: 1	happens when one eats cake; but Alice had	got so much into the way of expecting nothing but
T5	154: 8	But these, as it happened, Alice had not	got: so she contented herself with turning round, looking at
T5	149:22	the better, as it seemed to Alice, if she had	got some one else to dress her, she was so dreadfully untidy.
T2	121: 9	you'd speak! Said I to myself, 'Her face has	got some sense in it, though it's not a clever one!' Still,
T2	123:24	the Rose replied. "I was wondering you hadn't	got some too. I thought it was the regular rule."
T1	113: 1	see the back of it in the Looking-glass) had	got the face of a little old man, and grinned at her.
A4	30:26	--Why, I hadn't to bring but one. Bill's	got the other--Bill! Fetch it here, lad!--Here, put 'em up at
T1	110:23	her. Now do try, there's a dear!" And Alice	got the Red Queen off the table, and set it up before the
A10	81: 6	sea. So they had to fall a long way. So they	got their tails fast in their mouths. So they couldn't get
T1	111:12	said this, though she hardly knew how she had	got there. And certainly the glass was beginning to melt away,
T8	191: 6	"But how can it have	got there without my knowing it?" she said to herself, as she
A10	81: 5	go with the lobsters to the dance. So they	got thrown out to sea. So they had to fall a long way. So they
A1	8:36	then I wonder what Latitude or Longitude I've	got to?" (Alice had not the slightest idea what Latitude was,
A5	42:14	be?" said Alice. "And where have my shoulders	got to? And oh, my poor hands, how is it I ca'n't see you?"
A4	30:35	"Oh! So Bill's	got to come down the chimney, has he?" said Alice to herself.
A4	32:18	"The first thing I've	got to do," said Alice to herself, as she wandered about in
A4	30:33	You do it!--That I wo'n't, then!--Bill's	got to go down--Here, Bill! The master says you've got to go
A4	30:34	go down--Here, Bill! The master says you've	got to go down the chimney!"
T4	147:16	remarked. "Every one of these things has	got to go on, somehow or other."
A8	67:28	alive: for instance, there's the arch I've	got to go through next walking about at the other end of the
A4	33:11	it! Oh dear! I'd nearly forgotten that I've	got to grow up again! Let me see--how is it to be managed? I
T1	108:25	you little mischievous darling! What have you	got to say for yourself? Now don't interrupt me!" she went on,
A1	12:15	at once; but, alas for poor Alice! when she	got to the door, she found she had forgotten the little golden
A3	26: 3	pardon," said Alice very humbly: "you had	got to the fifth bend, I think?"
T2	120:19	path, determined to keep straight on till she	got to the hill. For a few minutes all went on well, and she
A10	82: 6	Her listeners were perfectly quiet till she	got to the part about her repeating "You are old, Father
T2	125:18	and they walked on in silence till they	got to the top of the little hill.
A4	27:31	walk!' 'Coming in a minute, nurse! But I've	got to watch this mouse-hole till Dinah comes back, and see
T4	138: 4	and the other 'DEE.' "I suppose they've	got 'TWEEDLE' round at the back of the collar," she said to
T1	108:19	upon the floor, and yards and yards of it	got unwound again.
T8	180:12	off in this way, side by side. When they	got up again, they shook hands, and then the Red Knight
A10	82:19	as well be at school at once." However, she	got up, and began to repeat it, but her head was so full of
T7	177:13	sounded nonsense, but Alice very obediently	got up, and carried the dish round, and the cake divided
T2	128:21	and it's all feasting and fun!" Alice	got up and curtseyed, and sat down again.
T6	168:19	that it would hardly be civil to stay. So she	got up, and held out her hand. "Good-bye, till we meet again!"
T9	198:13	very old Frog, who was sitting under a tree,	got up and hobbled slowly towards her: he was dressed in
A12	98:11	in to your tea: it's getting late." So Alice	got up and ran off, thinking while she ran, as well she might,
T9	192: 6	So she	got up and walked about--rather stiffly just at first, as she
T3	135:21	quite chilly with sitting still so long, she	got up and walked on.
A2	18: 4	thought. "I must be growing small again." She	got up and went to the table to measure herself by it, and
A7	60:29	rudeness was more than Alice could bear: she	got up in great disgust, and walked off: the Dormouse fell
T9	201: 1	Mutton: Mutton--Alice." The leg of mutton	got up in the dish and made a little bow to Alice; and Alice
A5	35: 1	at present--at least I know who I was when I	got up this morning, but I think I must have been changed
A2	15:40	night? Let me think: was I the same when I	got up this morning? I almost think I can remember feeling a
T9	202:32	know," the White Queen whispered, as Alice	got up to do it, very obediently, but a little frightened.
A11	89: 2	"not in that ridiculous fashion." And he	got up very sulkily and crossed over to the other side of the

GOT (cont.)
A5   43:38 that it felt quite strange at first; but she got used to it in a few minutes, and began talking to herself,
T4   148:20 And how fast it comes! Why, I do believe it's got wings!"
T7   170: 2 the rider fell off instantly. The confusion got worse every moment, and Alice was very glad to get out of
T7   172:23 have been here first. However, now you've got your breath, you may tell us what's happened in the town
T8   182:22   "I hope you've got your hair well fastened on?" he continued, as they set off
GOVERNESS (2)
T3   135: 1 to go home without it! For instance, if the governess wanted to call you to your lessons, she would call
T3   135: 5 would never do, I'm sure," said Alice: "the governess would never think of excusing me lessons for that.
GRACE (1)
T9   202:37 so Alice tried to submit to it with good grace.
GRACEFUL (1)
A5   42:21 had just succeeded in curving it down into a graceful zigzag, and was going to dive in among the leaves,
GRACEFULLY (1)
T2   120:31 addressing herself to one that was waving gracefully about in the wind, "I wish you could talk!"
GRADUALLY (1)
T8   179: 1   After a while the noise seemed gradually to die away, till all was dead silence, and Alice
GRAMMAR (1)
A2   19:17   having seen, in her brother's Latin Grammar, "A mouse--of a mouse--to a mouse--a mouse--O mouse!")
GRAND (10)
T4   141: 6 only cleared away,' / They said, 'it would be grand!'
A7   57: 5   "That would be grand, certainly," said Alice thoughtfully; "but then--I
T1   107:15 and half asleep, the kitten had been having a grand game of romps with the ball of worsted Alice had been
T9   194:37 I can read words of one letter! Isn't that grand? However, don't be discouraged. You'll come to it in
T8   190:36 for the last brook, and to be a Queen! How grand it sounds!" A very few steps brought her to the edge of
A8   63:26 crimson velvet cushion; and, last of all this grand procession, came THE KING AND THE QUEEN OF HEARTS.
T9   192: 1   "Well, this is grand!" said Alice. "I never expected I should be a Queen so
T3   129: 1 Of course the first thing to do was to make a grand survey of the country she was going to travel through.
T6   160:23 pursed up his lips, and looked so solemn and grand that Alice could hardly help laughing. "If I did fall,"
A1   8:37   either, but she thought they were nice grand words to say.)
GRANDER (1)
T2   123:36   enough, she felt that it would be far grander to have a talk with a real Queen.
GRANT (1)
A6   51:29 with," said the Cat, "a dog's not mad. You grant that?"
GRASS (7)
T8   187:23 reins hanging loose on his neck, cropping the grass at her feet--and the black shadows of the forest behind
A4   34: 1 round her at the flowers and the blades of grass, but she could not see anything that looked like the
T9   192: 4 never do for you to be lolling about on the grass like that! Queens have to be dignified, you know!"
A5   41:26 off the mushroom, and crawled away into the grass, merely remarking, as it went, "One side will make you
A12   98:24   The long grass rustled at her feet as the White Rabbit hurried by--the
T4   144:36 he'll catch cold with lying on the damp grass," said Alice, who was a very thoughtful little girl.
A12   98:36 and all would change to dull reality--the grass would be only rustling in the wind, and the pool
GRASSHOPPER (1)
T7   174:19 begin." And Hatta went bounding away like a grasshopper.
GRASS-PLOT (1)
T6   165: 4   "And 'the wabe' is the grass-plot round a sun-dial, I suppose?" said Alice, surprised
GRASSY (1)
T8   189: 1 twigs for crabs: / I sometimes search for grassy knolls / For wheels of Hansom-cabs. / And that's the
GRAVE (5)
A8   69: 5 remark that had made the whole party look so grave and anxious.)
T2   128:16 have said," the Queen went on in a tone of grave reproof, "'It's extremely kind of you to tell me all
T8   184:25   "You were a little grave," said Alice.
A3   24: 6 thing very absurd, but they all looked so grave that she did not dare to laugh; and, as she could not
A12   93: 1 cannot proceed," said the King, in a very grave voice, "until all the jurymen are back in their proper
GRAVEL-WALK (1)
T2   123:27 "I hear her footstep, thump, thump, along the gravel-walk!"
GRAVELY (10)
T9   195: 9 "Fiddle-de-dee's not English," Alice replied gravely.
A12   94:35 "Begin at the beginning," the King said, very gravely, "and go on till you come to the end: then stop."
T9   194:23   Alice said, as gravely as she could, "They might go different ways." But she
T6   164:10 Humpty Dumpty went on, wagging his head gravely from side to side, "for to get their wages, you know
T8W   20:11 well as she could. At last she managed to say gravely, "I can bite anything I want."
A5   36:12   and she drew herself up and said, very gravely, "I think you ought to tell me who you are, first."
T4   147:25   "You know," he added very gravely, "it's one of the most serious things that can
T8   183:11 had plenty of practice," the Knight said very gravely: "plenty of practice!"
T8   184:36 "I haven't tried it yet," the Knight said, gravely; "so I ca'n't tell for certain--but I'm afraid it
A3   23:31   "Of course," the Dodo replied very gravely. "What else have you got in your pocket?" it went on,
GRAVY (2)
A10   83:16 a pie: / The Panther took pie-crust, and gravy, and meat, / While the Owl had the dish as its share of
T9   202:27 mutton, and began eagerly lapping up the gravy, "just like pigs in a trough!" thought Alice.
GRAY (1)
T8W   19: 9   So now that I am old and gray, / And all my hair is nearly gone, / They take my wig
GRAZED (1)
A6   46:28 out, straight at the Footman's head: it just grazed his nose, and broke to pieces against one of the trees
GREAT (90)
T5   150:15   "--but there's one great advantage in it, that one's memory works both ways."
T7   172: 1   On which the Messenger, to Alice's great amusement, opened a bag that hung round his neck, and
T1   107:14 was sitting curled up in a corner of the great arm-chair, half talking to herself and half asleep, the
T8   184: 4 mind breaking two or three of them. "The great art of riding, as I was saying is--to keep your balance
T8   183:17   "The great art of riding," the Knight suddenly began in a loud

GREAT (cont.)

T5	155:10	and Alice couldn't help looking at her in great astonishment.
T5	150:13	"Living backwards!" Alice repeated in great astonishment. "I never heard of such a thing!"
T7	176: 2	tone that sounded like the tolling of a great bell.
T8	179:14	came galloping down upon her, brandishing a great club. Just as he reached her, the horse stopped suddenly
T3	135:38	cool and shady. "Well, at any rate it's a great comfort," she said as she stepped under the trees,
T6	168:39	(she repeated this aloud, as it was a great comfort to have such a long word to say) "of all the
A7	57:13	teaspoon at the March Hare,) "--it was at the great concert given by the Queen of Hearts, and I had to sing
T4	145:27	tears?" Tweedledum interrupted in a tone of great contempt.
A6	46:15	and sneezing, and every now and then a great crash, as if a dish or kettle had been broken to pieces
T7	176:14	at having to sit down between the two great creatures; but there was no other place for him.
A11	86: 2	on their throne when they arrived, with a great crowd assembled about them--all sorts of little birds
T7	173:15	on in silence, till they came into sight of a great crowd, in the middle of which the Lion and Unicorn were
A8	67:38	to Alice, and looking at the Cat's head with great curiosity.
A10	81:23	are they made of?" Alice asked in a tone of great curiosity.
T3	133: 6	"What does it live on?" Alice asked, with great curiosity.
T8	181:16	the lid hanging open. Alice looked at it with great curiosity.
T8	182: 8	what are they for?" Alice asked in a tone of great curiosity.
A7	55: 7	had been looking at Alice for some time with great curiosity, and this was his first speech.
T1	113:17	over and begin kicking: she watched it with great curiosity to see what would happen next.
T2	121: 5	well as you can," said the Tiger-lily. "And a great deal louder."
T9	192:33	"But she said a great deal more than that!" the White Queen moaned, wringing
T3	136: 6	help her much, and all she could say, after a great deal of puzzling, was "L, I know it begins with L!"
A3	23:17	question the Dodo could not answer without a great deal of thought, and it stood for a long time with one
T6	166: 2	said Alice. "I'm afraid I'm giving you a great deal of trouble."
A11	88: 3	the Rabbit hastily interrupted. "There's a great deal to come before that!"
T6	164: 3	"That's a great deal to make one word mean," Alice said in a thoughtful
A2	14: 8	I'm sure I sha'n't be able! I shall be a great deal too far off to trouble myself about you: you must
T5	153: 1	the way it's done," the Queen said with great decision: "nobody can do two things at once, you know.
A1	9:42	the little golden key in the lock, and to her great delight it fitted!
A1	8:19	it was labeled "ORANGE MARMALADE," but to her great disappointment it was empty: she did not like to drop
A7	60:30	was more than Alice could bear: she got up in great disgust, and walked off: the Dormouse fell asleep
T7	177: 7	on the bank of a little brook, with the great dish on her knees, and was sawing away diligently with
T8	179: 5	Messengers. However, there was the great dish still lying at her feet, on which she had tried to
A12	92: 8	beg your pardon!" she exclaimed in a tone of great dismay, and began picking them up again as quickly as
T9	201:20	however, she conquered her shyness by a great effort, and cut a slice and handed it to the Red Queen.
T9	194:26	sums a bit!" the Queens said together, with great emphasis.
A12	93: 3	their proper places--all," he repeated with great emphasis, looking hard at Alice as he said so.
A4	33: 2	its tongue hanging out of its mouth, and its great eyes half shut.
T7	171:14	more extraordinary every moment, while the great eyes rolled wildly from side to side.
T6	159:29	Dumpty sat on a wall: / Humpty Dumpty had a great fall. / All the King's horses and all the King's men /
A4	27:24	in without knocking, and hurried upstairs, in great fear lest she should meet the real Mary Ann, and be
T9	199:20	up and gave the door a kick with one of his great feet. "You let it alone," he panted out, as he hobbled
A2	15:20	to be ashamed of yourself," said Alice, "a great girl like you," (she might well say this), "to go on
T5	152:37	her hands in despair. "Consider what a great girl you are. Consider what a long way you've come
A4	27: 9	changed since her swim in the pool; and the great hall, with the glass table and the little door, had
T8	184:22	and then the Knight went on again. "I'm a great hand at inventing things. Now, I daresay you noticed,
T6	166:15	said Humpty Dumpty, stretching out one of his great hands, "I can repeat poetry as well as other folk, if it
T7	170:25	like an eel, as he came along, with his great hands spread out like fans on each side.)
T9	197:22	she listened so eagerly that, when the two great heads suddenly vanished from her lap, she hardly missed
T2	126: 1	quick with excitement as she went on. "It's a great huge game of chess that's being played--all over the
A4	32:26	bark just over her head made her look up in a great hurry.
A11	89:21	"I didn't!" the March Hare interrupted in a great hurry.
A7	58:33	little sisters," the Dormouse began in a great hurry; "and their names were Elsie, Lacie, and Tillie;
A2	15:29	fan in the other: he came trotting along in a great hurry, muttering to himself, as he came, "Oh! The
A12	94: 4	said the White Rabbit, jumping up in a great hurry: "this paper has just been picked up."
A2	20: 1	"I wo'n't indeed!" said Alice, in a great hurry to change the subject of conversation. "Are you--
T3	133: 8	Alice looked at the Rocking-horse-fly with great interest, and made up her mind that it must have been
T2	128: 5	put in by this time, and Alice looked on with great interest as she returned to the tree, and then began
T1	115:29	Alice looked on with great interest as the King took an enormous memorandum-book
T8	184:15	go smoothly?" the Knight asked in a tone of great interest, clasping his arms round the horse's neck as he
A7	58:35	they live on?" said Alice, who always took a great interest in questions of eating and drinking.
A6	45:12	began by producing from under his arm a great letter, nearly as large as himself, and this he handed
T9	196:14	got in--and it went rolling round the room in great lumps--and knocking over the tables and things--till I
A7	55: 5	was your table," said Alice: "it's laid for a great many more than three."
A6	51: 2	thought: still it had very long claws and a great many teeth, so she felt that it ought to be treated with
T3	129:38	went on, looking angrily at Alice. And a great many voices all said together ("like the chorus of a
T8	179:10	went on in a rather complaining tone: "I've a great mind to go and wake him, and see what happens!"
A8	68: 6	only one way of settling all difficulties, great or small. "Off with his head!" she said without even
T5	153:40	and then leaving off to look at her through a great pair of spectacles.
T9	197:12	I to do?" exclaimed Alice, looking about in great perplexity, as first one round head, and then the other,
A2	15:42	is 'Who in the world am I?' Ah, that's the great puzzle!" And she began thinking over all the children
A4	33:14	The great question certainly was "What?" Alice looked all round
A4	33:13	to eat or drink something or other; but the great question is 'What'?"
A11	91:25	"Never mind!" said the King with an air of great relief. "Call the next witness." And, he added, in an
A9	76:14	school," said the Mock Turtle in a tone of great relief. "Now, at ours, they had, at the end of the bill,
T4	139:13	They looked so exactly like a couple of great schoolboys, that Alice couldn't help pointing her finger
T4	140:13	Tweedledee, looking round at Tweedledum with great solemn eyes, and not noticing Alice's question.
A10	81:32	it, really?" said Alice, in a tone of great surprise.
T8W	17:10	as he spoke, and Alice looked at his wig in great surprise. It was bright yellow like the handkerchief,

GREAT (cont.)
A9   72:29   But here, to Alice's great surprise, the Duchess's voice died away, even in the
T3   130:12   this time, as she hadn't spoken, but, to her great surprise, they all thought in chorus (I hope you
T2   127:12   Alice looked round her in great surprise. "Why, I do believe we've been under this tree
A4   32:37 to worry it: then Alice dodged behind a great thistle, to keep herself from being run over; and, the
A11   86:16 judge," she said to herself, "because of his great wig."
A8   67: 6 dreadfully fond of beheading people here: the great wonder is, that there's any one left alive!"

GREATER (1)
T4   146:26 "But it isn't old!" Tweedledum cried, in a greater fury than ever. "It's new, I tell you--I bought it

GREEDILY (1)
T7   172: 3 a sandwich to the King, who devoured it greedily.

GREEN (10)
T8   188:10 thinking of a plan / To dye one's whiskers green, / And always use so large a fan / That they could not
T1   109:14 summer, Kitty, they dress themselves all in green, and dance about--whenever the wind blows--oh, that's
T10 205: 4 grew very small, and her eyes got large and green: and still, as Alice went on shaking her, she kept on
T2   125:23 divided up into squares by a number of little green hedges, that reached from brook to brook.
T6   166:29   "In spring, when woods are getting green, / I'll try and tell you what I mean:"
A5   42:16 except a little shaking among the distant green leaves.
A5   42:11 seemed to rise like a stalk out of a sea of green leaves that lay far below her.
T6   166: 3   "Well, a 'rath' is a sort of green pig: but 'mome' I'm not certain about. I think it's
A5   42:13   "What can all that green stuff be?" said Alice. "And where have my shoulders got
A10 84:17   "Beautiful Soup, so rich and green, / Waiting in a hot tureen! / Who for such dainties

GREW (5)
T4   146:14 in a voice choking with passion, and his eyes grew large and yellow all in a moment, as he pointed with a
A4   28:24 bottle had now had its full effect, and she grew no larger: still it was very uncomfortable, and, as there
AI   3:31   Thus grew the tale of Wonderland / Thus slowly, one by one, / Its
T9   203:12 things happened in a moment. The candles all grew up to the ceiling, looking something like a bed of rushes
T10 205: 3 made no resistance whatever: only her face grew very small, and her eyes got large and green: and still,

GREY (1)
A5   38: 5 "In my youth," said the sage, as he shook his grey locks, / "I kept all my limbs very supple / By the use of

GRIEF (1)
A9   77: 7 said with a sigh. "He taught Laughing and Grief, they used to say."

GRIN (7)
A6   48: 2   in fact, I didn't know that cats could grin."
A8   67:11 it a minute or two she made it out to be a grin, and she said to herself "It's the Cheshire-Cat: now I
A2   17:12   "How cheerfully he seems to grin, / How neatly spreads his claws, / And welcomes little
A6   53: 7   "Well! I've often seen a cat without a grin," thought Alice; "but a grin without a cat! It's the most
A6   53: 5 with the end of the tail, and ending with the grin, which remained some time after the rest of it had gone.
T6   167: 9   The fishes answered, with a grin, / 'Why, what a temper you are in!'
A6   53: 8 a cat without a grin," thought Alice; "but a grin without a cat! It's the most curious thing I ever saw in

GRINNED (6)
T4   139:12 fat little men only looked at each other and grinned.
A6   51: 5 it would like the name: however, it only grinned a little wider. "Come, it's pleased so far," thought
T6   160:40 proud, you may shake hands with me!" And he grinned almost from ear to ear, as he leant forwards (and as
T1   113: 2 had got the face of a little old man, and grinned at her.
A6   48: 1 "I didn't know that Cheshire-Cats always grinned; in fact, I didn't know that cats could grin."
A6   51: 1   The Cat only grinned when it saw Alice. It looked good-natured, she thought

GRINNING (2)
T9   204: 6 to see the Queen's broad good-natured face grinning at her for a moment over the edge of the tureen,
A6   47:11 large cat, which was lying on the hearth and grinning from ear to ear.

GRINS (1)
A6   47:14 manners for her to speak first, "why your cat grins like that?"

GROAN (1)
T8   186:24 blotting-paper," the Knight answered with a groan.

GROANED (2)
T5   152:14 When I fasten my shawl again," the poor Queen groaned out: "the brooch will come undone directly. Oh, oh!"
T5   149:19   "But I don't want it done at all!" groaned the poor Queen. "I've been a-dressing myself for the

GROPED (1)
T5   158:17 why it wouldn't do?" thought Alice, as she groped her way among the tables and chairs, for the shop was

GROUND (18) [See also CROQUET-GROUND]
T9   194:44 isn't picked at all," Alice explained: "it's ground--"
A8   66:18 up and walking off to other parts of the ground, Alice soon came to the conclusion that it was a very
T6   160:16 "Don't you think you'd be safer down on the ground?" Alice went on, not with any idea of making another
A8   67:29 next walking about at the other end of the ground--and I should have croqueted the Queen's hedgehog just
T2   127:33 marked in inches, and began measuring the ground, and sticking little pegs in here and there.
T4   146:22 Tweedledee, who immediately sat down on the ground, and tried to hide himself under the umbrella.
A9   72:37 warning," shouted the Queen, stamping on the ground as she spoke; "either you or your head must be off, and
T2   125:22 straight across it from side to side, and the ground between was divided up into squares by a number of
T2   127: 9 stopped, and she found herself sitting on the ground, breathless and giddy.
T7   170: 4 where she found the White King seated on the ground, busily writing in his memorandum-book.
T8   185: 1 I fell off the horse, it always touched the ground directly. So I had a very little way to fall, you see--
T8W   13: 6 face was more like a wasp) was sitting on the ground, leaning against a tree, all huddled up together, and
A6   46: 8 was gone, and the other was sitting on the ground near the door, staring stupidly up into the sky.
T2   122:24   "Put your hand down, and feel the ground," said the Tiger-lily. "Then you'll know why."
T9   195: 1   "How many acres of ground?" said the White Queen. "You mustn't leave out so many
A8   68:25 all the arches are gone from this side of the ground." So she tucked it away under her arm, that it might
T7   169: 8 more always fell over him, so that the ground was soon covered with little heaps of men.
T2   127: 7 to skim through the air, hardly touching the ground with their feet, till suddenly, just as Alice was

GROW (14)
T8W   19: 8 I to do, you know? / My ringlets would not grow again.

GROW (cont.)
A4   28:13   "That's quite enough--I hope I sha'n't grow any more--As it is, I ca'n't get out at the door--I do
A11   89: 1   "Yes, but I grow at a reasonable pace," said the Dormouse: "not in that
A11   88:42   "You've no right to grow here," said the Dormouse.
A4   28: 7   this bottle does. I do hope it'll make me grow large again, for really I'm quite tired of being such a
A11   88:36   made out what it was: she was beginning to grow larger again, and she thought at first she would get up
A1   12:34   I'll eat it," said Alice, "and if it makes me grow larger, I can reach the key; and if it makes me grow
A5   41:28   grow taller, and the other side will make you grow shorter."
A1   12:35   I can reach the key; and if it makes me grow smaller, I can creep under the door: so either way I'll
A5   41:27   as it went, "One side will make you grow taller, and the other side will make you grow shorter."
A4   32:19   as she wandered about in the wood, "is to grow to my right size again; and the second thing is to find
A4   33:11   dear! I'd nearly forgotten that I've got to grow up again! Let me see--how is it to be managed? I suppose
A4   29: 8   sorrowful tone: "at least there's no room to grow up any more here."
A4   29: 6   about me, that there ought! And when I grow up, I'll write one--but I'm grown up now," she added in a
GROWING (17)
A11   88:41   ca'n't help it," said Alice very meekly: "I'm growing."
T6   162: 7   "I never ask advice about growing," Alice said indignantly.
A4   28:19   arm curled round her head. Still she went on growing, and, as a last resource, she put one arm out of the
A4   28:15   It was too late to wish that! She went on growing, and growing, and very soon had to kneel down on the
A1   12:40   the top of her head to feel which way it was growing; and she was quite surprised to find that she remained
A4   28:16   late to wish that! She went on growing, and growing, and very soon had to kneel down on the floor: in
T5   158:21   I declare! How very odd to find trees growing here! And actually here's a little brook! Well, this
T2   120:28   with a border of daisies, and a willow-tree growing in the middle.
A4   28:28   thought poor Alice, "when one wasn't always growing larger and smaller, and being ordered about by mice
A4   34: 3   the circumstances. There was a large mushroom growing near her, about the same height as herself; and, when
T6   162:10   "I mean," she said, "that one ca'n't help growing older."
A8   62: 2   near the entrance of the garden: the roses growing on it were white, but there were three gardeners at it
T10 205: 5   as Alice went on shaking her, she kept on growing shorter--and fatter--and softer--and rounder--and--
A2   18: 4   I have done that?" she thought. "I must be growing small again." She got up and went to the table to
T5   156:31   with a sigh at the obstinacy of the rushes in growing so far off, as, with flushed cheeks and dripping hair
A5   43:34   first at one and then at the other, and growing sometimes taller, and sometimes shorter, until she had
A11   88:44   said Alice more boldly: "you know you're growing too."
GROWL (4)
T6   162:24   When he did speak again, it was in a deep growl.
A10   84: 1   the Panther received knife and fork with a growl, / And concluded the banquet by--"
A6   48:21   own business," the Duchess said, in a hoarse growl, "the world would go round a deal faster than it does."
A6   51:33   and wags its tail when it's pleased. Now I growl when I'm pleased, and wag my tail when I'm angry.
GROWLED (4)
A3   26:12   The Mouse only growled in reply.
T7   177: 3   "I'm sure I don't know," the Lion growled out as he lay down again. "There was too much dust to
T6   160:21   easy riddles you ask!" Humpty Dumpty growled out. "Of course I don't think so! Why, if ever I did
T9   201:12   But the Red Queen looked sulky, and growled "Pudding----Alice: Alice--Pudding. Remove the pudding!
GROWLING (1)
A6   51:35   "I call it purring, not growling," said Alice.
GROWLS (1)
A6   51:32   "Well, then," the Cat went on, "you see a dog growls when it's angry, and wags its tail when it's pleased.
GROWN (8)
T2   123:29   and found that it was the Red Queen. "She's grown a good deal!" was her first remark. She had indeed: when
A12   92: 2   in the flurry of the moment how large she had grown in the last few minutes, and she jumped up in such a
A5   38: 2   the youth, "as I mentioned before, / And have grown most uncommonly fat; / Yet you turned a back-somersault
A12   95:23   of them can explain it," said Alice, (she had grown so large in the last few minutes that she wasn't a bit
A12   97: 7   "Who cares for you?" said Alice (she had grown to her full size by this time). "You're nothing but a
A4   29: 7   And when I grow up, I'll write one--but I'm grown up now," she added in a sorrowful tone: "at least
A6   50:15   trot away quietly into the wood. "If it had grown up," she said to herself, "it would have made a
A12   99: 4   hers would, in the after-time, be herself a grown woman; and how she would keep, through all her riper
GRUMBLED (2)
T8W   15: 3   "No brown sugar!" grumbled the Wasp. "A nice exploring party!"
A7   56: 6   crumbs must have got in as well," the Hatter grumbled: "you shouldn't have put it in with the bread-knife
GRUMBLING (1)
T8W   13:16   "Oh, my old bones, my old bones!" he was grumbling on as Alice came up to him.
GRUNT (1)
A6   49:29   had left off sneezing by this time). "Don't grunt," said Alice; "that's not at all a proper way of
GRUNTED (4)
A6   49:31   The baby grunted again, and Alice looked very anxiously into its face
A6   50: 9   this creature, when I get it home?" when it grunted again, so violently, that she looked down into its
A6   49:28   the last words out loud, and the little thing grunted in reply (it had left off sneezing by this time).
A6   50: 5   now!" The poor little thing sobbed again (or grunted, it was impossible to say which), and they went on for
GRYPHON (55)
A10   78:19   generally takes some time," interrupted the Gryphon.
A10   78:21   "Each with a lobster as a partner!" cried the Gryphon.
A10   78:25   and retire in same order," continued the Gryphon.
A10   78:30   "Swim after them!" screamed the Gryphon.
A10   81: 3   the reason and all that," he said to the Gryphon.
A10   82:10   all about as curious as it can be," said the Gryphon.
A10   82:16   "'Tis the voice of the sluggard,'" said the Gryphon.
A10   82:31   I used to say when I was a child," said the Gryphon.
A10   81:38   Turtle replied, in an offended tone. And the Gryphon added "Come, let's hear some of your adventures."
A9   74: 4   she walked off, leaving Alice alone with the Gryphon. Alice did not quite like the look of the creature,
A10   84: 6   I think you'd better leave off," said the Gryphon, and Alice was only too glad to do so.
A12   98:40   and the sneeze of the baby, the shriek of the Gryphon, and all the other queer noises, would change (she

GRYPHON (cont.)
```
  A10   78: 4  as if he had a bone in his throat," said the Gryphon; and it set to work shaking him and punching him in
  A10   85: 4              "Come on!" cried the Gryphon, and, taking Alice by the hand, it hurried off,
   A9   74:35  occasional exclamation of "Hjckrrh!" from the Gryphon, and the constant heavy sobbing of the Mock Turtle.
   A9   74:20  deeply. "What is his sorrow?" she asked the Gryphon. And the Gryphon answered, very nearly in the same
  A10   85: 1           "Chorus again!" cried the Gryphon, and the Mock Turtle had just begun to repeat it, when
   A9   75: 5  for asking such a simple question," added the Gryphon; and then they both sat silent and looked at poor
   A9   74:20  his  sorrow?"  she asked the Gryphon. And the Gryphon answered, very nearly in the same words as before,
  A10   82:13  now. Tell her to begin." He looked at the Gryphon as if he thought it had some kind of authority over
  A10   78:33        "Change lobsters again!" yelled the Gryphon at the top of its voice.
   A9   76: 3         "Hold your tongue!" added the Gryphon, before Alice could speak again. The Mock Turtle went
  A10   81:10  you more than that, if you like," said the Gryphon. "Do you know why it's called a whiting?"
   A9   74: 9  sight: then it chuckled. "What fun!" said to itself, half to Alice.
  A10   83: 3           "She ca'n't explain it," said the Gryphon hastily. "Go on with the next verse."
  A10   81:17  Why, what are your shoes done with?" said the Gryphon. "I mean, what makes them so shiny?"
   A9   77: 4            "Hadn't time," said the Gryphon: "I went to the Classical master, though. He was an
  A10   81:44  "No, no! The adventures first," said the Gryphon in an impatient tone: "explanations take such a
   A9   77:23      "That's enough about lessons," the Gryphon interrupted in a very decided tone. "Tell her
   A9   73:23  asleep in the sun. (If you don't know what a Gryphon is, look at the picture.) "Up, lazy thing!" said the
   A9   74:11           "Why, she," said the Gryphon. "It's all her fancy that: they never executes nobody,
  A10   79: 8       "Oh, you sing," said the Gryphon. "I've forgotten the words."
   A9   76:26               The Gryphon lifted up both its paws in surprise. "Never heard of
   A9   73:22          They very soon came upon a Gryphon, lying fast asleep in the sun. (If you don't know what
   A9   77: 3  the Mock Turtle said: "I'm too stiff. And the Gryphon never learnt it."
  A10   85: 6  is it?" Alice panted as she ran: but the Gryphon only answered "Come on!" and ran the faster, while
   A9   77:15   the reason they're called lessons," the Gryphon remarked: "because they lessen from day to day."
  A10   83:10       "Go on with the next verse," the Gryphon repeated: "it begins 'I passed by his garden.'"
  A10   81:25      "Soles and eels, of course," the Gryphon replied, rather impatiently: "any shrimp could have
  A10   81:13      "It does the boots and shoes," the Gryphon replied very solemnly.
  A10   84:12  so kind," Alice replied, so eagerly that the Gryphon said, in a rather offended tone, "Hm! No accounting
   A9   75: 7  ready to sink into the earth. At last the Gryphon said to the Mock Turtle "Drive on, old fellow! Don't
   A9   74: 7              The Gryphon sat up and rubbed its eyes: then it watched the Queen
   A9   74:25      "This here young lady," said the Gryphon, "she wants for to know your history, she do."
   A9   77: 8      "So he did, so he did," said the Gryphon, sighing in his turn; and both creatures hid their
  A10   81: 4          "The reason is," said the Gryphon, "that they would go with the lobsters to the dance.
  A12   98:31     around it--once more the shriek of the Gryphon, the squeaking of the Lizard's slate-pencil, and the
  A11   86:29  "What are they doing?" Alice whispered to the Gryphon. "They ca'n't have anything to put down yet, before
  A10   79: 6  first figure!" said the Mock Turtle to the Gryphon. "We can do it without lobsters, you know. Which shall
   A9   76:31          "Well, then," the Gryphon went on, "if you don't know what to uglify is, you are
  A10   81:21      "Boots and shoes under the sea," the Gryphon went on in a deep voice, "are done with whiting. Now
  A10   84: 9  another figure of the Lobster-Quadrille?" the Gryphon went on. "Or would you like the Mock Turtle to sing
  A11   86:31  "They're putting down their names," the Gryphon whispered in reply, "for fear they should forget them
  A10   78:28      "The lobsters!" shouted the Gryphon, with a bound into the air.
  A10   78:14       "Why," said the Gryphon, "you first form into a line along the sea-shore--"
```
GUARD (6)
```
   T8  182: 9                           "To guard against the bites of sharks," the Knight replied. "It's
  A11   86: 5  in chains, with a soldier on each side to guard him; and near the King was the White Rabbit, with a
   T3  129:33       "Tickets, please!" said the Guard, putting his head in at the window. In a moment
   T3  130:18            All this time the Guard was looking at her, first through a telescope, then
   T3  129:37  "Now then! Show your ticket, child!" the Guard went on, looking angrily at Alice. And a great many
   T3  130: 6      "Don't make excuses," said the Guard: "you should have bought one from the engine-driver."
```
GUESS (10)
```
   T2  126:22  poor puzzled Alice. And the Queen seemed to guess her thoughts, for she cried "Faster! Don't try to talk!
   T7  176: 4  the Unicorn cried eagerly. "You'll never guess! I couldn't."
   T7  175:41  How they all came out of it Alice couldn't guess. It was just like a conjuring-trick, she thought.
   A4   30:40  till she heard a little animal (she couldn't guess of what sort it was) scratching and scrambling about in
   T9  202:19  "Take a minute to think about it, and then guess," said the Red Queen. "Meanwhile, we'll drink your
   A2   18: 6  by it, and found that, as nearly as she could guess, she was now about two feet high, and was going on
   T4  145: 3              Alice said "Nobody can guess that."
   A7   55:14  they've begun asking riddles--I believe I can guess that," she added aloud.
  T12  207:12  kitten only purred: and it was impossible to guess whether it meant "yes" or "no."
   T8  181:28  and he hung it carefully on a tree. "Can you guess why I did that?" he said to Alice.
```
GUESSED (4)
```
   T1  108:12       is, Kitty?" Alice began. "You'd have guessed if you'd been up in the window with me--only Dinah was
   A4   27: 6  can I have dropped them, I wonder?" Alice guessed in a moment that it was looking for the fan and the
   A7   56:27              "Have you guessed the riddle yet?" the Hatter said, turning to Alice
  A11   91: 6  carried the pepper-box in her hand, and Alice guessed who it was, even before she got into the court, by the
```
GUESSING (1)
```
   T2  128:31  fast!" thought Alice), there was no way of guessing, but she was gone, and Alice began to remember that
```
GUESTS (8)
```
   T9  193:18  is to be one, I think I ought to invite the guests."
   T9  204:15  hands: one good pull, and plates, dishes, guests, and candles came crashing down together in a heap on
   T9  202:21  screamed at the top of her voice, and all the guests began drinking it directly, and very queerly they
   A9   72:43               The other guests had taken advantage of the Queen's absence, and were
   A8   63:21  all ornamented with hearts. Next came the guests, mostly Kings and Queens, and among them Alice
   T9  200: 9  hall, and noticed that there were about fifty guests, of all kinds: some were animals, some birds, and there
  A12   98:28  of the Queen ordering off her unfortunate guests to execution--once more the pig-baby was sneezing on
   T9  204: 9  a moment to be lost. Already several of the guests were lying down in the dishes, and the soup ladle was
```
GUIDE (1)
```
   AI   3: 6  hands make vain pretence / Our wanderings to guide.
```

GUILT (1)
    A12   94:28   "That _proves_ his guilt, of course," said the Queen, "so, off with--"
GUINEA-PIG (2)
    A11   90:26   Here the other guinea-pig cheered, and was suppressed.
    A11   90:15 with strings: into this they slipped the guinea-pig, head first, and then sat upon it.)
GUINEA-PIGS (4)
    A11   90:11   Here one of the guinea-pigs cheered, and was immediately suppressed by the
    A12   98:32   and the choking of the suppressed guinea-pigs, filled the air, mixed up with the distant sob of
    A11   90:27   "Come, that finishes the guinea-pigs!" thought Alice. "Now we shall get on better."
    A4   32:14 Bill, was in the middle, being held up by two guinea-pigs, who were giving it something out of a bottle.
GUNPOWDER (1)
    T8   186:28 makes, mixing it with other things--such as gunpowder and sealing-wax. And here I must leave you." They
GUST (1)
    T5   153:17 had   come   undone as she spoke, and a sudden gust of wind blew the Queen's shawl across a little brook. The
GYRE (6)
    T1   116:10 _erew ysmim 11A_ / :ebaw eht ni elbmig dna _eryg_ diD / sevot yhtils eht dna ,gillirb sawT'
    T1   116:19 'Twas brillig, and the slithy toves / Did _gyre_ and gimble in the wabe: / _All mimsy were the borogoves_, /
    T1   118:22 'Twas brillig, and the slithy toves / Did _gyre_ and gimble in the wabe: / _All mimsy were the borogoves_, /
    T6   164:22 "'Twas brillig, and the slithy toves / Did _gyre_ and gimble in the wabe: / _All mimsy were the borogoves_, /
    T6   165: 1   "And what's to '_gyre_' and to '_gimble_'?"
    T6   165: 2   "To '_gyre_' is to go round and round like a gyroscope. To '_gimble_'
GYROSCOPE (1)
    T6   165: 2 "To '_gyre_' is to go round and round like a gyroscope. To '_gimble_' is to make holes like a gimlet."

-H-

H (4)

T7	170:30	"I love my love with an H," Alice couldn't help beginning, "because he is Happy. I
T7	170:31	"because he is Happy. I hate him with an H, because he is Hideous. I fed him with--with--with
T7	171:11	"This young lady loves you with an H," the King said, introducing Alice in the hope of turning
T7	170:36	for the name of a town beginning with H. "The other Messenger's called Hatta. I must have two, you

HABIT (2)

| T12 | 207: 6 | "it is a very inconvenient habit of kittens (Alice had once made the remark) that, |
| T8 | 182:43 | he kept on pretty well, except that he had a habit of now and then falling off sideways; and, as he |

HAD (322)

A12	98: 5	her sister. "Why, what a long sleep you've had!"
T3	136:13	Fawn said at last. Such a soft sweet voice it had!
A10	78: 3	or two, sobs choked his voice. "Same as if he had a bone in his throat," said the Gryphon; and it set to
T8W	17:13	your wig much neater," she said, "if only you had a comb."
A3	21: 5	of course was, how to get dry again: they had a consultation about this, and after a few minutes it
A7	60:38	said this, she noticed that one of the trees had a door leading right into it. "That's very curious!" she
T1	110:39	pretence, just to make it look as if they had a fire. Well then, the books are something like our books,
T6	159:29	"Humpty Dumpty sat on a wall: / Humpty Dumpty had a great fall. / All the King's horses and all the King's
T8	182:43	he kept on pretty well, except that he had a habit of now and then falling off sideways; and, as he
A8	68:41	The King's argument was that anything that had a head could be beheaded, and that you weren't to talk
A11	90:13	just explain to you how it was done. They had a large canvas bag, which tied up at the mouth with
A12	93:10	As soon as the jury had a little recovered from the shock of being upset, and
A11	87: 5	One of the jurors had a pencil that squeaked. This, of course, Alice could not
T4	144: 8	'O Oysters,' said the Carpenter, / 'You've had a pleasant run! / Shall we be trotting home again?' / But
T8	181:14	which seemed to fit him very badly, and he had a queer-shaped little deal box fastened across his
T1	114: 2	his nose, which had been hurt by the fall. He had a right to be a little annoyed with the Queen, for he was
T8W	15: 7	like china. While tasting the treacle, they had a sad accident: two of their party were engulphed--"
T4	144:32	Alice couldn't say honestly that he was. He had a tall red night-cap on, with a tassel, and he was lying
A12	92:11	gold-fish kept running in her head, and she had a vague sort of idea that they must be collected at once
T8	185: 1	it always touched the ground directly. So I had a very little way to fall, you see--But there was the
A6	49:33	with it. There could be no doubt that it had a very turn-up nose, much more like a snout than a real
A5	42:40	for serpents, night and day! Why, I haven't had a wink of sleep these three weeks!"
A12	92: 6	her very much of a globe of gold-fish she had accidentally upset the week before.
T1	107:17	and had been rolling it up and down till it had all come undone again; and there it was, spread over the
A8	63:31	use of a procession," thought she, "if people had all to lie down on their faces, so that they couldn't see
A8	68:12	in the distance, screaming with passion. She had already heard her sentence three of the players to be
T9	200:15	head of the table: the Red and White Queens had already taken two of them, but the middle one was empty.
A8	67: 4	very uneasy: to be sure, she had not as yet had any dispute with the Queen, but she knew that it might
T1	107: 5	so you see that it couldn't have had any hand in the mischief.
T2	126:24	Not that Alice had any idea of doing that. She felt as if she would never be
A4	31:35	"I wonder what they will do next! If they had any sense, they'd take the roof off." After a minute or
T1	110:14	and her sister, who liked being very exact, had argued that they couldn't, because there were only two of
A5	41:31	said the Caterpillar, just as if she had asked it aloud; and in another moment it was out of sight
A9	76:14	a tone of great relief. "Now, at ours, they had, at the end of the bill, 'French, music, and washing--
A11	87: 9	the Lizard) could not make out at all what had become of it; so, after hunting all about for it, he was
A12	98:12	as well she might, what a wonderful dream it had been.
A1	9:31	but they were all locked; and when Alice had been all the way down one side and up the other, trying
A8	63:10	she comes, to--" At this moment, Five, who had been anxiously looking across the garden, called out "The
A5	43:37	It was so long since she had been anything near the right size, that it felt quite
A12	95:13	My notion was that you had been / (Before she had this fit) / An obstacle that came
A6	46:16	then a great crash, as if a dish or kettle had been broken to pieces.
T1	108:23	again, "when I saw all the mischief you had been doing, I was very nearly opening the window, and
T1	107:12	But the black kitten had been finished with earlier in the afternoon, and so, while
A12	93:33	At this moment the King, who had been for some time busily writing in his note-book, called
A12	93:11	of being upset, and their slates and pencils had been found and handed back to them, they set to work very
T1	107:15	to herself and half asleep, the kitten had been having a grand game of romps with the ball of worsted
T1	107: 3	kitten's fault entirely. For the white kitten had been having its face washed by the old cat for the last
T1	114: 2	said the King, rubbing his nose, which had been hurt by the fall. He had a right to be a little
A6	52:14	she was still looking at the place where it had been, it suddenly appeared again.
A10	78:37	his voice; and the two creatures, who had been jumping about like mad things all this time, sat down
A7	55: 6	Your hair wants cutting," said the Hatter. He had been looking at Alice for some time with great curiosity,
A7	56:11	Alice had been looking over his shoulder with some curiosity. "What
T8W	14:15	went on, as she picked up a newspaper which had been lying at his feet.
A3	22: 5	to by the English, who wanted leaders, and had been of late much accustomed to usurpation and conquest.
T2	123:30	when Alice first found her in the ashes, she had been only three inches high--and here she was, half a head
T8	187:19	bring the whole scene back again, as if it had been only yesterday--the mild blue eyes and kindly smile
T1	110:15	there were only two of them, and Alice had been reduced at last to say "Well, you can be one of them,
T1	107:16	worsted Alice had been trying to wind up, and had been rolling it up and down till it had all come undone
A3	23:13	when the race was over. However, when they had been running half an hour or so, and were quite dry again,
T2	124: 5	Red Queen, and full in sight of the hill she had been so long aiming at.
T3	132:18	while the Gnat (for that was the insect she had been talking to) was balancing itself on a twig just over
T3	132:22	she couldn't feel nervous with it, after they had been talking together so long.
A12	94:39	"They told me you had been to her, / And mentioned me to him: / She gave me a
A2	18:20	back by railway," she said to herself. (Alice had been to the seaside once in her life, and had come to the

HAD (cont.)

T1	107:16	game of romps with the ball of worsted Alice had	been trying to wind up, and had been rolling it up and
A5	42:23	but the tops of the trees under which she had	been wandering, when a sharp hiss made her draw back in a
T9	201:19	help feeling a little shy with it, as she had	been with the mutton; however, she conquered her shyness
A9	72: 9	have been was not otherwise than what you had	been would have appeared to them to be otherwise.'"
T8	183:19	Here the sentence ended as suddenly as it had	begun, as the Knight fell heavily on the top of his head.
T4	139:41	and they left off dancing as suddenly as they had	begun: the music stopped at the same moment.
T5	156:34	mattered it to her just then that the rushes had	begun to fade, and to lose all their scent and beauty,
A1	10:10	things had happened lately, that Alice had	begun to think that very few things indeed were really
T1	110:12	sister only the day before--all because Alice had	begun with "Let's pretend we're kings and queens;" and her
A5	44: 5	did not venture to go near the house till she had	brought herself down to nine inches high.
A12	98:35	herself in Wonderland, though she knew she had	but to open them again, and all would change to dull
A8	68:22	By the time she had	caught the flamingo and brought it back, the fight was
A3	26:43	looked up eagerly, half hoping that the Mouse had	changed his mind, and was coming back to finish his story.
T6	162:31	said Alice, quite pleased to find that she had	chosen a good subject after all.
A7	60:20	The Dormouse had	closed its eyes by this time, and was going off into a
A6	52:20	answered very quietly, just as if the Cat had	come back in a natural way.
A8	69:11	the moment he was gone, and, by the time he had	come back with the Duchess, it had entirely disappeared:
T6	159: 3	eyes and a nose and a mouth; and, when she had	come close to it, she saw clearly that it was HUMPTY
A2	18:21	had been to the seaside once in her life, and had	come to the general conclusion that wherever you go to on
T5	153:17	The brooch had	come undone as she spoke, and a sudden gust of wind blew
T6	159: 2	and larger, and more and more human: when she had	come within a few yards of it, she saw that it had eyes
T8	190:14	his horse's head along the road by which they had	come. "You've only a few yards to go," he said, "down the
T9	196:31	she'll be!" But this was more than Alice had	courage to do.
T3	137: 9	brown eyes, and in another moment it had	darted away at full speed.
A11	91:24	time they had settled down again, the cook had	disappeared.
T1	115:16	and Alice was a little alarmed at what she had	done, and went round the room to see if she could find any
T5	151:18	"Yes, but then I had	done the things I was punished for," said Alice: "that
T8	179:24	tumbled off his horse just as the Red Knight had	done: then he got on again, and the two Knights sat and
A4	28:10	much sooner than she had expected: before she had	drunk half the bottle, she found her head pressing against
T4	138: 3	was which in a moment, because one of them had	'DUM' embroidered on his collar, and the other 'DEE.' "I
T9	198:14	her: he was dressed in bright yellow, and had	enormous boots on.
T6	163:45	"I meant by 'impenetrability' that we've had	enough of that subject, and it would be just as well if
A8	69:11	time he had come back with the Duchess, it had	entirely disappeared: so the King and the executioner ran
A4	28: 9	It did so indeed, and much sooner than she had	expected: before she had drunk half the bottle, she found
T6	159: 3	within a few yards of it, she saw that it had	eyes and a nose and a mouth; and, when she had come close
A4	29:40	she concluded that it was just possible it had	fallen into a cucumber-frame, or something of the sort.
A2	20:22	quite crowded with the birds and animals that had	fallen into it: there was a Duck and a Dodo, a Lory and an
A9	73:20	a good thing!" she said to herself, for she had	felt quite unhappy at the number of executions the Queen
A5	42:37	use in saying anything more till the Pigeon had	finished.
A12	98: 9	you have just been reading about; when she had	finished, her sister kissed her, and said "It was a
T1	118:25	"It seems very pretty," she said when she had	finished it, "but it's rather hard to understand!" (You
A3	24: 3	of this elegant thimble"; and, when it had	finished this short speech, they all cheered.
A12	96:17	again--'before she had this fit'--you never had	fits, my dear, I think?" he said to the Queen.
A5	42:25	made her draw back in a hurry: a large pigeon had	flown into her face, and was beating her violently with
A12	98: 2	gently brushing away some dead leaves that had	fluttered down from the trees upon her face.
A11	88:12	The Hatter looked at the March Hare, who had	followed him into the court, arm-in-arm with the Dormouse.
A1	12:15	when she got to the door, she found she had	forgotten the little golden key, and when she went back to
A4	27:36	By this time she had	found her way into a tidy little room with a table in the
A4	27:25	and be turned out of the house before she had	found the fan and gloves.
T12	207:13	among the chessmen on the table till she had	found the Red Queen: then she went down on her knees on
A6	53: 6	which remained some time after the rest of it had	gone.
T8W	21:16	down the hill again, quite pleased that she had	gone back and given a few minutes to making the poor old
A5	43:10	as she remembered the number of changes she had	gone through, that day.
T2	128: 4	She had	got all the pegs put in by this time, and Alice looked on
A1	10:22	nice little stories about children who had	got burnt, and eaten up by wild beasts, and other
A8	66:12	not help bursting out laughing; and, when she had	got its head down, and was going to begin again, it was
A8	66: 9	legs hanging down, but generally, just as she had	got its neck nicely straightened out, and was going to
T4	140:31	sulkily, / Because she thought the sun / Had	got no business to be there / After the day was done--/
A1	13: 1	happens when one eats cake; but Alice had	got so much into the way of expecting nothing but
T5	149:22	all the better, as it seemed to Alice, if she had	got some one else to dress her, she was so dreadfully
T1	113: 1	only see the back of it in the Looking-glass) had	got the face of a little old man, and grinned at her.
T1	111:12	she said this, though she hardly knew how she had	got there. And certainly the glass was beginning to melt
A3	26: 3	your pardon," said Alice very humbly: "you had	got to the fifth bend, I think?"
A12	92: 2	in the flurry of the moment how large she had	grown in the last few minutes, and she jumped up in such a
A12	95:23	one of them can explain it," said Alice, (she had	grown so large in the last few minutes that she wasn't a
A12	97: 7	"Who cares for you?" said Alice (she had	grown to her full size by this time). "You're nothing but
A6	50:15	it trot away quietly into the wood. "If it had	grown up," she said to herself, "it would have made a
T1	107: 1	One thing was certain, that the white kitten had	had nothing to do with it--it was the black kitten's fault
T1	110:11	her favourite phrase "Let's pretend." She had	had quite a long argument with her sister only the day
T6	162:14	got on!" Alice suddenly remarked. (They had	had quite enough of the subject of age, she thought: and,
A6	46:31	in the same tone, exactly as if nothing had	happened.
T3	132:24	the Gnat went on, as quietly as if nothing had	happened.
T5	153:34	and looked again. She couldn't make out what had	happened at all. Was she in a shop? And was that really--
A1	10:10	For, you see, so many out-of-the-way things had	happened lately, that Alice had begun to think that very
A2	19:24	no very clear notion how long ago anything had	happened.) So she began again: "Où est ma chatte?" which
T5	157: 3	knitting all the while, just as if nothing had	happened. "That was a nice crab you caught!" she remarked,
T8	186:33	"Is it very long?" Alice asked, for she had	heard a good deal of poetry that day.
A4	27:37	with a table in the window, and on it (as she had	hoped) a fan and two or three pairs of tiny white
A2	19:28	pardon!" cried Alice hastily, afraid that she had	hurt the poor animal's feelings. "I quite forgot you

HAD (cont.)

A1	11: 7	to taste it, and, finding it very nice (it had, in fact, a sort of mixed flavour of cherry-tart, custard,
T2	123:29	grown a good deal!" was her first remark. She had indeed: when Alice first found her in the ashes, she had
A9	72:12	that better," Alice said very politely, "if I had it written down: but I ca'n't quite follow it as you say
A4	28:23	for Alice, the little magic bottle had now had its full effect, and she grew no larger: still it was very
T7	175:43	The Lion had joined them while this was going on: he looked very tired
T1	112: 1	moment Alice was through the glass, and had jumped lightly down into the Looking-glass room. The very
T4	140: 3	how to begin a conversation with people she had just been dancing with. "It would never do to say 'How
A1	9:16	put it. She felt that she was dozing off, and had just begun to dream that she was walking hand in hand with
A10	85: 1	cried the Gryphon, and the Mock Turtle had just begun to repeat it, when a cry of "The trial's
A8	62:17	Seven flung down his brush, and had just begun "Well, of all the unjust things--" when his eye
T8	186:29	sealing-wax. And here I must leave you." They had just come to the end of the wood.
T8	189: 7	I heard him then, for I had just / Completed my design / To keep the Menai bridge from
T9	204:26	the very act of jumping over a bottle which had just lighted upon the table, "I'll shake you into a kitten
A5	42:21	easily in any direction, like a serpent. She had just succeeded in curving it down into a graceful zigzag,
T7	178: 4	across the little brook in her terror, and had just time to see the Lion and the * * * * * * * * * * *
A7	60: 1	deal worse off than before, as the March Hare had just upset the milk-jug into his plate.
A7	61: 3	she set to work nibbling at the mushroom (she had kept a piece of it in her pocket) till she was about a
T8	185:18	startled by the fall, as for some time he had kept on very well, and she was afraid that he really was
A3	21: 8	talking familiarly with them, as if she had known them all her life. Indeed, she had quite a long
A1	8:31	miles down, I think--" (for, you see, Alice had learnt several things of this sort in her lessons in the
T1	112: 5	one, blazing away as brightly as the one she had left behind. "So I shall be as warm here as I was in the
A6	49:28	and the little thing grunted in reply (it had left off sneezing by this time). "Don't grunt," said Alice
A12	96:21	as she spoke. (The unfortunate little Bill had left off writing on his slate with one finger, as he found
T1	114:24	and lifted him across more slowly than she had lifted the Queen, that she mightn't take his breath away;
A4	34: 4	the same height as herself; and, when she had looked under it, and on both sides of it, and behind it,
T2	124:10	and explained, as well as she could, that she had lost her way.
A4	27: 2	looking anxiously about as it went, as if it had lost something; and she heard it muttering to itself, "The
A4	27:17	without trying to explain the mistake that it had made.
T8	186:38	"Or else what?" said Alice, for the Knight had made a sudden pause.
A9	70: 5	that perhaps it was only the pepper that had made her so savage when they met in the kitchen.
T3	135:10	miss your lessons. That's a joke. I wish you had made it."
T3	135:11	"Why do you wish I had made it?" Alice asked. "It's a very bad one."
A6	49:22	As soon as she had made out the proper way of nursing it (which was to twist
A8	69: 4	all round. (It was this last remark that had made the whole party look so grave and anxious.)
T9	193:20	Red Queen remarked: "but I daresay you've not had many lessons in manners yet."
A8	65: 8	"I see!" said the Queen, who had meanwhile been examining the roses. "Off with their heads!
T8W	18: 7	came into Alice's head. Almost every one had met had repeated poetry to her, and she thought she would
T8	183: 9	don't fall off quite so often, when they've had much practice."
T8	183: 3	"I'm afraid you've not had much practice in riding," she ventured to say, as she was
T5	153:13	"I daresay you haven't had much practice," said the Queen. "When I was your age, I
A11	86:13	Alice had never been in a court of justice before, but she had read
A5	41:11	Alice said nothing: she had never been so much contradicted in all her life before,
T2	127:29	and it was very dry: and she thought she had never been so nearly choked in all her life.
A1	8: 1	feet, for it flashed across her mind that she had never before seen a rabbit with either a waistcoat-pocket,
A2	19:15	be the right way of speaking to a mouse: she had never done such a thing before, but she remembered having
A1	11: 3	with a knife, it usually bleeds; and she had never forgotten that, if you drink much from a bottle
T9	200:20	who looked at it rather anxiously, as she had never had to carve a joint before.
A8	68:38	there was a body to cut it off from: that he had never had to do such a thing before, and he wasn't going
A4	30: 2	Pat! Where are you?" And then a voice she had never heard before, "Sure then I'm here! Digging for
A11	89: 4	All this time the Queen had never left off staring at the Hatter, and, just as the
T1	115: 3	She said afterwards that she had never seen in all her life such a face as the King made,
T7	169: 5	She thought that in all her life she had never seen soldiers so uncertain on their feet: they were
A8	66: 1	Alice thought she had never seen such a curious croquet-ground in her life: it
T4	147:18	Alice said afterwards she had never seen such a fuss made about anything in all her life
T8	181:11	and large mild eyes to Alice. She thought she had never seen such a strange-looking soldier in all her life
A6	53:14	that she did not like to go nearer till she had nibbled some more of the left-hand bit of mushroom, and
T2	126:17	felt she could not go faster, though she had no breath left to say so.
A3	23:26	Alice had no idea what to do, and in despair she put her hand in her
T7	173:14	Alice had no more breath for talking; so they trotted on in silence,
A1	7: 3	into the book her sister was reading, but it had no pictures or conversations in it, "and what is the use
A4	29:23	a thousand times as large as the Rabbit, and had no reason to be afraid of it.
A2	19:23	with all her knowledge of history, Alice had no very clear notion how long ago anything had happened.)
A1	8: 8	dipped suddenly down, so suddenly that Alice had not a moment to think about stopping herself before she
A8	67: 3	began to feel very uneasy: to be sure, she had not as yet had any dispute with the Queen, but she knew
A9	72: 3	"Oh, I know!" exclaimed Alice, who had not attended to this last remark. "It's a vegetable. It
T2	124: 3	It succeeded beautifully. She had not been walking a minute before she found herself face to
A3	26: 5	"I had not!" cried the Mouse, sharply and very angrily.
A9	74:16	They had not gone far before they saw the Mock Turtle in the
A6	53:10	She had not gone much farther before she came in sight of the
A12	95: 1	He sent them word I had not gone / (We know it to be true): / If she should push
A3	23:28	out a box of comfits (luckily the saltwater had not got into it), and handed them round as prizes. There
T5	154: 8	But these, as it happened, Alice had not got: so she contented herself with turning round,
A4	31:42	"A barrowful of what?" thought Alice. But she had not long to doubt, for the next moment a shower of little
A1	9:39	time round, she came upon a low curtain she had not noticed before, and behind it was a little door about
T8	180:10	Another Rule of Battle, that Alice had not noticed, seemed to be that they always fell on their
A1	8:36	Latitude or Longitude I've got to?" (Alice had not the slightest idea what Latitude was, or Longitude
A4	32:23	arranged: the only difficulty was, that she had not the smallest idea how to set about it; and, while she
A5	36:26	Alice thought she might as well wait, as she had nothing else to do, and perhaps after all it might tell
T1	107: 1	thing was certain, that the white kitten had had nothing to do with it--it was the black kitten's fault

HAD (cont.)

A7	59:11		"I've had nothing yet," Alice replied in an offended tone: "so I
T8W	19: 2	But when I followed their advice, / And they had	noticed the effect, / They said I did not look so nice /
A4	28:23	Luckily for Alice, the little magic bottle had	now had its full effect, and she grew no larger: still it
T3	135:34	lose dogs--'answers to the name of "Dash": had	on a brass collar'--just fancy calling everything you met
T5	154:13	at any shelf, to make out exactly what it had	on it, that particular shelf was always quite empty,
T12	207: 6	a very inconvenient habit of kittens (Alice had	once made the remark) that, whatever you say to them, they
A8	68: 6	The Queen had	only one way of settling all difficulties, great or small.
A9	73:21	unhappy at the number of executions the Queen had	ordered.
A3	26:22	"I wish I had	our Dinah here, I know I do!" said Alice aloud, addressing
T4	147:36	I've got a toothache!" said Tweedledee, who had	overheard the remark. "I'm far worse than you!"
A3	23: 3	that she much wanted to know, but the Dodo had	paused as if it thought that somebody ought to speak, and
A1	7: 2	of having nothing to do: once or twice she had	peeped into the book her sister was reading, but it had no
T8	183:11	"I've had	plenty of practice," the Knight said very gravely: "plenty
A1	8:11	very deep, or she fell very slowly, for she had	plenty of time as she went down to look about her, and to
A6	45: 7	like a frog; and both footmen, Alice noticed, had	powdered hair that curled all over their heads. She felt
T5	152:20	too late: the pin had slipped, and the Queen had	pricked her finger.
T1	108:34	pulled Snowdrop away by the tail just as I had	put down the saucer of milk before her! What, you were
T3	132: 5	The Horse, who had	put his head out of the window, quietly drew it in and
A2	18: 2	her hands, and was surprised to see that she had	put on one of the Rabbit's little white kid-gloves while
A12	93: 4	the jury-box, and saw that, in her haste, she had	put the Lizard in head downwards, and the poor little
T1	115:40	Queen, looking over the book (in which Alice had	put 'The White Knight is sliding down the poker. He
A3	21: 8	she had known them all her life. Indeed, she had	quite a long argument with the Lory, who at last turned
T1	110:11	her favourite phrase "Let's pretend." She had	quite a long argument with her sister only the day before
T6	162:14	got on!" Alice suddenly remarked. (They had	quite enough of the subject of age, she thought: and, if
A9	70:16	She had	quite forgotten the Duchess by this time, and was a little
T8W	21:11	personal remarks made on her, and as the Wasp had	quite recovered his spirits, and was getting very
T1	114: 9	sat down: the rapid journey through the air had	quite taken away her breath, and for a minute or two she
A11	86:13	been in a court of justice before, but she had	read about them in books, and she was quite pleased to
A1	10:21	whether it's marked 'poison' or not"; for she had	read several nice little stories about children who had
T1	110:17	then, and I'll be all the rest." And once she had	really frightened her old nurse by shouting suddenly in
T1	115:19	and when she got back with it she found he had	recovered, and he and the Queen were talking together in a
T1	114:11	the little Lily in silence. As soon as she had	recovered her breath a little, she called out to the White
T8W	18: 7	Alice's head. Almost every one she had met had	repeated poetry to her, and she thought she would try if
T12	207: 9	mew for 'no,' or any rule of that sort," she had	said, "so that one could keep up a conversation! But how
A12	94:27	it was the first really clever thing the King had	said that day.
A10	82:34	Alice said nothing: she had	sat down with her face in her hands, wondering if anything
T1	109: 1	punishments for Wednesday week--Suppose they had	saved up all my punishments?" she went on, talking more to
T7	177: 6	Alice had	seated herself on the bank of a little brook, with the
A11	91:23	Dormouse turned out, and, by the time they had	settled down again, the cook had disappeared.
T5	152:19	at the brooch; but it was too late: the pin had	slipped, and the Queen had pricked her finger.
A2	19: 9	soon made out that it was only a mouse, that had	slipped in like herself.
A10	82:14	He looked at the Gryphon as if he thought it had	some kind of authority over Alice.
A8	67:20	an account of the game, feeling very glad she had	some one to listen to her. The Cat seemed to think that
T6	166:12	"I read it in a book," said Alice. "But I had	some poetry repeated to me much easier than that, by--
A2	18:19	in saltwater. Her first idea was that she had	somehow fallen into the sea, "and in that case I can go
T5	154:17	said at last in a plaintive tone, after she had	spent a minute or so in vainly pursuing a large bright
T4	138:21	a battle; / For Tweedledum said Tweedledee / Had	spoiled his nice new rattle.
A8	62:13	"What for?" said the one who had	spoken first.
A5	41:40	felt a violent blow underneath her chin: it had	struck her foot!
A5	43:35	taller, and sometimes shorter, until she had	succeeded in bringing herself down to her usual height.
A12	98: 6	"Oh, I've had	such a curious dream!" said Alice. And she told her sister
T9	201:28	"Do you know, I've had	such a quantity of poetry repeated to me to-day," Alice
T12	207:38	there was one thing you would have enjoyed--I had	such a quantity of poetry said to me, all about fishes!
T9	195:26	clasping and unclasping her hands, "we had	such a thunderstorm last Tuesday--I mean one of the last
T7	170:17	"I only wish I had	such eyes," the King remarked in a fretful tone. "To be
T9	204:19	but the Queen was no longer at her side--she had	suddenly dwindled down to the size of a little doll, and
T3	134: 4	the Butterfly," Alice went on, after she had	taken a good look at the insect with its head on fire, and
A9	72:43	The other guests had	taken advantage of the Queen's absence, and were resting
A7	55:36	month is it?" he said, turning to Alice: he had	taken his watch out of his pocket, and was looking at it
A1	10:24	not remember the simple rules their friends had	taught them: such as, that a red-hot poker will burn you
A9	76: 5	"We had	the best of educations--in fact, we went to school every
T7	175:10	by them, with his hands in his pockets. "I had	the best of it this time?" he said to the King, just
A10	83:17	and gravy, and meat, / While the Owl had	the dish as its share of the treat. / When the pie was all
A6	46:19	went on, without attending to her, "if we had	the door between us. For instance, if you were inside, you
T1	116: 3	she was still a little anxious about him, and had	the ink all ready to throw over him, in case he fainted
T6	168:29	mouth under. It's always the same. Now if you had	the two eyes on the same side of the nose, for instance--
A12	95:14	My notion was that you had been / (Before she had	this fit) / An obstacle that came between / Him, and
A12	96:16	be clearer than that. Then again--'before she had	this fit'--you never had fits, my dear, I think?" he said
T3	134: 5	look at the insect with its head on fire, and had	thought to herself, "I wonder if that's the reason insects
A1	12:19	table, but it was too slippery; and when she had	tired herself out with trying, the poor little thing sat
A11	87: 2	know how to spell "stupid," and that he had	to ask his neighbour to tell him. "A nice muddle their
T4	143:24	/ I wish you were not quite so deaf-- / I've had	to ask you twice!'
A3	24:11	taste theirs, and the small ones choked and had	to be patted on the back. However, it was over at last,
T9	195: 5	fanned her with bunches of leaves, till she had	to beg them to leave off, it blew her hair about so.
T9	200:21	at it rather anxiously, as she had never had	to carve a joint before.
T6	167:14	a kettle large and new, / Fit for the deed I had	to do.
A8	68:38	a body to cut it off from: that he had never had	to do such a thing before, and he wasn't going to begin at
A8	66: 3	the mallets live flamingoes, and the soldiers had	to double themselves up and stand on their hands and feet,
A10	81: 5	dance. So they got thrown out to sea. So they had	to fall a long way. So they got their tails fast in their

HAD (cont.)

T5	152: 7	the whistle of a steam-engine, that Alice had to hold both her hands over her ears.
T8	185: 9	"I had to kick him, of course," the Knight said, very seriously.
A4	28:16	went on growing, and growing, and very soon had to kneel down on the floor: in another minute there was
A9	73: 6	into custody by the soldiers, who of course had to leave off being arches to do this, so that, by the end
T1	108:15	Only it got so cold, and it snowed so, they had to leave off. Never mind, we'll go and see the bonfire
T5	152: 3	the Queen began screaming, so loud that she had to leave the sentence unfinished. "Oh, oh, oh!" shouted
T2	128:14	"I--I didn't know I had to make one--just then," Alice faltered out.
A7	58: 3	twinkle--" and went on so long that they had to pinch it to make it stop.
A6	46: 5	Alice laughed so much at this, that she had to run back into the wood for fear of their hearing her;
A7	57:13	concert given by the Queen of Hearts, and I had to sing
A4	28:11	her head pressing against the ceiling, and had to stoop to save her neck from being broken. She hastily
A5	43:31	the branches, and every now and then she had to stop and untwist it. After a while she remembered that
T9	197:15	think it ever happened before, that any one had to take care of two Queens asleep at once! No, not in all
T8	179: 6	dish still lying at her feet, on which she had tried to cut the plum-cake, "So I wasn't dreaming, after
A8	66:14	was very provoking to find that the hedgehog had unrolled itself, and was in the act of crawling away:
T5	157:15	for the oars, and the boat, and the river, had vanished all in a moment, and she was back again in the
A4	27:10	with the glass table and the little door, had vanished completely.
T8W	19: 4	/ They said I did not look so nice / As they had ventured to expect.
A6	51: 2	It looked good-natured, she thought: still it had very long claws and a great many teeth, so she felt that
A2	18:26	that she was in the pool of tears which she had wept when she was nine feet high.
A9	76:34	to the Mock Turtle, and said "What else had you to learn?"

HADDOCKS' (2)

T8	186:41	you know. The name of the song is called 'Haddocks' Eyes.'"
T8	188:33	He said 'I hunt for haddocks' eyes / Among the heather bright, / And work them

HADN'T (25)

T9	201:24	in a thick, suety sort of voice, and Alice hadn't a word to say in reply: she could only sit and look at
T4	142: 6	And this was odd, because, you know, / They hadn't any feet.
T4	148:12	minded it so much," said Tweedledum, "if it hadn't been a new one."
T1	110: 8	Kitty, and really I might have won, if it hadn't been for that nasty Knight, that came wriggling down
A11	89:12	Hatter began, in a trembling voice, "and I hadn't begun my tea--not above a week or so--and what with the
T1	119: 8	out at the door in the same way, if she hadn't caught hold of the door-post. She was getting a little
T6	162:19	offended, and she began to wish she hadn't chosen that subject. "If only I knew," she thought to
T3	131:38	that she wouldn't have heard it at all, if it hadn't come quite close to her ear. The consequence of this
A2	19: 1	"I wish I hadn't cried so much!" said Alice, as she swam about, trying
T5	151:20	"But if you hadn't done them," the Queen said, "that would have been
A4	28:14	is, I ca'n't get out at the door--I do wish I hadn't drunk quite so much!"
T7	173:23	"He's only just out of prison, and he hadn't finished his tea when he was sent in," Haigha whispered
A4	29: 1	about by mice and rabbits. I almost wish I hadn't gone down that rabbit-hole--and yet--and yet--it's
T5	156:41	They hadn't gone much farther before the blade of one of the oars
T2	123:24	the Rose replied. "I was wondering you hadn't got some too. I thought it was the regular rule."
T12	208:13	only began on the other paw, and pretended it hadn't heard the question.
T1	114:20	table, at that rate. I'd far better help you, hadn't I?" But the King took no notice of the question: it was
T5	157: 8	of the boat into the dark water. "I wish I hadn't let go--I should so like a little crab to take home
A3	26:37	"I wish I hadn't mentioned Dinah!" she said to herself in a melancholy
A11	88: 8	he began, "for bringing these in; but I hadn't quite finished my tea when I was sent for."
T2	122:35	so suddenly, that Alice quite jumped; for it hadn't spoken before.
T3	130:11	The voices didn't join in, this time, as she hadn't spoken, but, to her great surprise, they all thought in
A9	77: 4	"Hadn't time," said the Gryphon: "I went to the Classical
A4	30:25	the words: "Where's the other ladder?--Why, I hadn't to bring but one. Bill's got the other--Bill! Fetch it
T12	208: 7	go on licking your paw like that--as if Dinah hadn't washed you this morning! You see, Kitty, it must have

HAIGHA (10)

T7	173:30	"Were you happy in prison, dear child?" said Haigha.
T7	174:14	out "Ten minutes allowed for refreshments!" Haigha and Hatta set to work at once, carrying round trays of
T7	170:33	with Ham-sandwiches and Hay. His name is Haigha, and he lives--"
T7	174: 1	"Speak, ca'n't you!" Haigha cried impatiently. But Hatta only munched away, and
T7	170:28	only does them when he's happy. His name is Haigha." (He pronounced it so as to rhyme with 'mayor.')
T7	175:37	the King muttered, and beckoned to Haigha. "Open the bag!" he whispered. "Quick! Not that one--
T7	175:19	"This is a child!" Haigha replied eagerly, coming in front of Alice to introduce
T7	175:25	"It can talk," said Haigha solemnly.
T7	175:39	Haigha took a large cake out of the bag, and gave it to Alice
T7	173:24	hadn't finished his tea when he was sent in," Haigha whispered to Alice: "and they only give them

HAIL (1)

TI	103: 5	life asunder, / Thy loving smile will surely hail / The love-gift of a fairy-tale.

HAIR (29)

T9	195: 6	she had to beg them to leave off, it blew her hair about so.
T5	156:32	far off, as, with flushed cheeks and dripping hair and hands, she scrambled back into her place, and began
A2	20: 5	you know, with oh, such long curly brown hair! And it'll fetch things when you throw them, and it'll
T1	115:13	tidy enough!" she added, as she smoothed his hair, and set him upon the table near the Queen.
T8	187:21	Knight--the setting sun gleaming through his hair, and shining on his armour in a blaze of light that quite
A10	82:23	'You have baked me too brown, I must sugar my hair.' / As a duck with his eyelids, so he with his nose /
T5	155:35	Sheep, sticking some of the needles into her hair, as her hands were full. "Feather, I say!"
T8	182:33	stick," said the Knight. "Then you make your hair creep up it, like a fruit-tree. Now the reason hair falls
T5	156:21	the boat, with just the ends of her tangled hair dipping into the water--while with bright eager eyes she
T8	182:33	up it, like a fruit-tree. Now the reason hair falls off is because it hangs down--things never fall
T8	182:27	"Have you invented a plan for keeping the hair from being blown off?" Alice enquired.
A2	16: 4	"I'm sure I'm not Ada," she said, "for her hair goes in such long ringlets, and mine doesn't go in
A5	37: 2	William," the young man said, / "And your hair has become very white; / And yet you incessantly stand on
T9	196:32	"A little kindness--and putting her hair in papers--would do wonders with her--"
T5	149:35	the brush, and did her best to get the hair into order. "Come, you look rather better now!" she said,

HAIR (cont.)
T5   149:31 for her; "and dear me, what a state your hair is in!"
T8W   19:10 So now that I am old and gray, / And all my hair is nearly gone, / They take my wig from me and say / 'How
T4   146:21 beginning to stamp about wildly and tear his hair. "It's spoilt, of course!" Here he looked at Tweedledee,
T9   196:37 poor thing!" said the Red Queen. "Smoothe her hair--lend her your nightcap--and sing her a soothing lullaby
T2   127: 3 in Alice's ears, and almost blowing her hair off her head, she fancied.
A6   45: 8 and both footmen, Alice noticed, had powdered hair that curled all over their heads. She felt very curious
A12   98:21 toss of her head to keep back the wandering hair that would always get into her eyes--and still as she
A7   55: 6   "Your hair wants cutting," said the Hatter. He had been looking at
T8   190: 2 look was mild, whose speech was slow, / Whose hair was whiter than the snow, / Whose face was very like a
T8   182:22   "I hope you've got your hair well fastened on?" he continued, as they set off.
T8   181:10 said the Knight, putting back his shaggy hair with both hands, and turning his gentle face and large
T9   203: 8 screamed the White Queen, seizing Alice's hair with both her hands. "Something's going to happen!"
T8   183: 7 back into the saddle, keeping hold of Alice's hair with one hand, to save himself from falling over on the
T8W   18: 2 kind," Alice hastily explained. "It's to comb hair with--your wig's so very rough, you know."
HALF (36)
T2   123:31 only three inches high--and here she was, half a head taller than Alice herself!
TI   103: 4 / Though time be fleet, and I and thou / Are half a life asunder, / Thy loving smile will surely hail / The
T4   141: 8 seven maids with seven mops / Swept it for half a year, / Do you suppose,' the Walrus said, / 'That they
A3   24:15 you hate--C and D," she added in a whisper, half afraid that it would be offended again.
T5   153:14 "When I was your age, I always did it for half-an-hour a day. Why, sometimes I've believed as many as
A3   23:13 was over. However, when they had been running half an hour or so, and were quite dry again, the Dodo
A9   73: 7 arches to do this, so that, by the end of half an hour or so, there were no arches left, and all the
T1   107:14 great arm-chair, half talking to herself and half asleep, the kitten had been having a grand game of romps
T5   157:14 "To buy!" Alice echoed in a tone that was half astonished and half frightened--for the oars, and the
AI   3:24 / In friendly chat with bird or beast--/ And half believe it true.
A12   98:34   So she sat on, with closed eyes, and half believed herself in Wonderland, though she knew she had
A2   15:24 her, about four inches deep, and reaching half down the hall.
T5   153: 4   "I'm seven and a half, exactly."
A6   52:22   Alice waited a little, half expecting to see it again, but it did not appear, and
T5   157:15 echoed in a tone that was half astonished and half frightened--for the oars, and the boat, and the river,
T7   176:22 town, you chicken!" the Lion replied angrily, half getting up as he spoke.
A4   30:27 No, tie 'em together first--they don't reach half high enough yet--Oh, they'll do well enough. Don't be
A1   10:13 little door, so she went back to the table, half hoping she might find another key on it, or at any rate a
A3   26:43 in the distance, and she looked up eagerly, half hoping that the Mouse had changed his mind, and was
A7   60:32 going, though she looked back once or twice, half hoping that they would call after her: the last time she
T4   145:24   "If I wasn't real," Alice said--half laughing through her tears, it all seemed so ridiculous--
A5   43:39 talking to herself, as usual, "Come, there's half my plan done now! How puzzling all these changes are! I'm
A9   72:38 or your head must be off, and that in about half no time! Take your choice!"
A12   97:10 she gave a little scream, half of fright and half of anger, and tried to beat them off, and found herself
A12   97:10 down upon her; she gave a little scream, half of fright and half of anger, and tried to beat them off,
A2   20: 7 and all sorts of things--I ca'n't remember half of them--and it belongs to a farmer, you know, and he
A4   33: 2 hanging out of its mouth, and its great eyes half shut.
T7   175:44 very tired and sleepy, and his eyes were half shut. "What's this!" he said, blinking lazily at Alice,
T1   107:14 curled up in a corner of the great arm-chair, half talking to herself and half asleep, the kitten had been
A4   28:10 than she had expected: before she had drunk half the bottle, she found her head pressing against the
T1   110:10 pretend--" And here I wish I could tell you half the things Alice used to say, beginning with her
A3   22:32 said the Eaglet. "I don't know the meaning of half those long words, and, what's more, I don't believe you
A9   74: 9 "What fun!" said the Gryphon, half to itself, half to Alice.
A2   19:35 is such a dear quiet thing," Alice went on, half to herself, as she swam lazily about in the pool, "and
A9   74: 9 it chuckled. "What fun!" said the Gryphon, half to itself, half to Alice.
T3   133: 3   "All right," said the Gnat. "Half way up that bush, you'll see a Rocking-horse-fly, if you
HALF-DREAM (1)
T8   187:26   the strange pair, and listening, in a half-dream, to the melancholy music of the song.
HALF-PAST (3)
T4   147:42 Tweedledee looked at his watch, and said "Half-past four."
A7   57: 8 said the Hatter: "but you could keep it to half-past one as long as you liked."
A7   57: 2 and round goes the clock in a twinkling! Half-past one, time for dinner!"
HALFPENNY (1) [See also TWOPENCE-HALFPENNY]
T8   188:39 Or coin of silvery shine, / But for a copper halfpenny, / And that will purchase nine.
HALL (11)
A2   15:24 four inches deep, and reaching half down the hall.
A7   60:42 Once more she found herself in the long hall, and close to the little glass table. "Now, I'll manage
T9   200: 9 along the table, as she walked up the large hall, and noticed that there were about fifty guests, of all
A1   10: 4 saw. How she longed to get out of that dark hall, and wander about among those beds of bright flowers and
T1   119: 7 her feet: then she floated on through the hall, and would have gone straight out at the door in the same
A1   9:37 this might belong to one of the doors of the hall; but, alas! either the locks were too large, or the key
A1   9:30   There were doors all round the hall, but they were all locked; and when Alice had been all
A2   15:12 her head struck against the roof of the hall: in fact she was now rather more than nine feet high, and
A2   15:36 Alice took up the fan and gloves and, as the hall was very hot, she kept fanning herself all the time she
A1   9:28 to be seen: she found herself in a long, low hall, which was lit up by a row of lamps hanging from the roof
A4   27:10 since her swim in the pool; and the great hall, with the glass table and the little door, had vanished
HAMMERED (1)
AI   3:33 slowly, one by one, / Its quaint events were hammered out--/ And now the tale is done, / And home we steer,
HAM-SANDWICH (1)
T7   171:16 me!" said the King. "I feel faint--Give me a ham-sandwich!"
HAM-SANDWICHES (1)
T7   170:32 he is Hideous. I fed him with--with--with Ham-sandwiches and Hay. His name is Haigha, and he lives--"
HAND (53) [See also LEFT-HAND, RIGHT-HAND]
A5   41:37 go, and broke off a bit of the edge with each hand.

HAND (cont.)
```
T9    196: 2   "He  came to the door with a corkscrew in his hand--"
T5    152: 4   "Oh,  oh, oh!" shouted the Queen, shaking her hand about as if she wanted to shake it off. "My finger's
A4    30:16   you  coward!", and at last she spread out her hand again, and made another snatch in the air. This time
A2    15:28    with  a  pair  of  white  kid-gloves in one hand and a large fan in the other: he came trotting along in a
A11   88: 7   the  Hatter. He came in with a teacup in one hand and a piece of bread-and-butter in the other. "I beg
T7    173:22  watching  the fight, with a cup of tea in one hand and a piece of bread-and-butter in the other.
A11   86: 6   was  the  White Rabbit, with a trumpet in one hand, and a scroll of parchment in the other. In the very
A11   91: 6    cook.  She  carried  the  pepper-box  in her hand, and Alice guessed who it was, even before she got into
T1    115: 5   found  himself held in the air by an invisible hand, and being dusted: he was far too much astonished to cry
A4    29:34   under  the window, she suddenly spread out her hand, and made a snatch in the air. She did not get hold of
T2    126:14  remembers  is, that they were running hand in hand, and the Queen went so fast that it was all she could do
T3    136: 9   Here  then!" Alice said, as she held out her hand and tried to stroke it; but it only started back a little
T8    187:13  its  neck: then, slowly beating time with one hand, and with a faint smile lighting up his gentle foolish
T8    184:22  then  the Knight went on again. "I'm a great hand at inventing things. Now, I daresay you noticed, the last
T4    147:15  and  coal-scuttles. "I hope you're a good hand at pinning and tying strings?" Tweedledum remarked.
T2    122:24              "Put your hand down, and feel the ground," said the Tiger-lily. "Then
T6    168:19  to  stay.  So  she  got  up, and held out her hand. "Good-bye, till we meet again!" she said as cheerfully
T7    170:21  along  the  road,  shading  her  eyes with one hand. "I see somebody now!" she exclaimed at last. "But he's
A8    67:42   all,"  said the King: "however, it may kiss my hand, if it likes."
A8    63:20   dears  came  jumping  merrily  along, hand in hand, in couples: they were all ornamented with hearts. Next
T2    126:14  all  she remembers is, that they were running hand in hand, and the Queen went so fast that it was all she
A8    63:20   the  little dears came jumping merrily along, hand in hand, in couples: they were all ornamented with hearts
T4    147:12              So the two brothers went off hand-in-hand into the wood, and returned in a minute with
A1     9:16   had  just begun to dream that she was walking hand in hand with Dinah, and was saying to her, very earnestly
A3    23:26   idea  what to do, and in despair she put her hand in her pocket, and pulled out a box of comfits (luckily
T1    107: 5   so  you see that it couldn't have had any hand in the mischief.
T4    147:12              So the two brothers went off hand-in-hand into the wood, and returned in a minute with their arms
A10   85: 4   cried  the  Gryphon, and, taking Alice by the hand, it hurried off, without waiting for the end of the song
A3    23:34              "Hand it over here," said the Dodo.
T7    177:12  Looking-glass  cakes," the Unicorn remarked. "Hand it round first, and cut it afterwards."
T9    199:25  it  was  Alice that said / 'I've a sceptre in hand, I've a crown on my head. / Let the Looking-Glass
AI     4: 4   A  childish  story take, / And, with a gentle hand, / Lay it where Childhood's dreams are twined / In
T1    118: 5              He took his vorpal sword in hand: / Long time the manxome foe he sought--/ So rested he by
A1    12:39   herself  "Which way? Which way?", holding her hand on the top of her head to feel which way it was growing;
T3    135:42  under  the--under this, you know!" putting her hand on the trunk of the tree. "What does it call itself, I
T7    176: 9              "Then hand round the plum-cake, Monster," the Lion said, lying down
A11   86:10   they'd  get the trial done," she thought, "and hand round the refreshments!" But there seemed to be no chance
A12   94:19   "He  must have imitated somebody else's hand," said the King. (The jury all brightened up again.)
T8    187:25  this  she took in like a picture, as, with one hand shading her eyes, she leant against a tree, watching the
T6    161: 3   the  wall  in doing so) and offered Alice his hand. She watched him a little anxiously as she took it. "If
T1    115: 7   and  larger, and rounder and rounder, till her hand shook so with laughter that she nearly let him drop upon
T4    141: 2   and  the  Carpenter  /  Were walking close at hand: / They wept like anything to see / Such quantities of
T4    141:18  We  cannot  do with more than four, / To give a hand to each.'
T8    183: 8   saddle,  keeping hold of Alice's hair with one hand, to save himself from falling over on the other side.
T7    172:16  the  road?" the King went on, holding out his hand to the Messenger for some hay.
T12   207:34  one  elbow  on  the  rug, and her chin in her hand, to watch the kittens. "Tell me, Dinah, did you turn to
A8    64:10              The King laid his hand upon her arm, and timidly said "Consider, my dear: she is
T4    146:24              Alice laid her hand upon his arm and said, in a soothing tone, "You needn't
T7    177:18  Unicorn,  as  Alice sat with the knife in her hand, very much puzzled how to begin. "The Monster has given
A12   98:14   just  as she left her, leaning her head on her hand, watching the setting sun, and thinking of little Alice
T3    132:11  fright  she caught at the thing nearest to her hand, which happened to be the Goat's beard. * * * * * * * * *
A1     9:16   begun  to  dream that she was walking hand in hand with Dinah, and was saying to her, very earnestly, "Now,
```
HANDED (5)
```
T7    172: 2   opened  a  bag  that hung round his neck, and handed a sandwich to the King, who devoured it greedily.
A12   93:11   their  slates  and pencils had been found and handed back to them, they set to work very diligently to write
T9    201:20   by  a  great  effort,  and  cut a slice and handed it to the Red Queen.
A6    45:12   nearly  as  large  as  himself,  and this he handed over to the other, saying, in a solemn tone, "For the
A3    23:28   the  saltwater  had  not  got  into it), and handed them round as prizes. There was exactly one a-piece,
```
HANDING (1)
```
T5    155:14              "Can you row?" the Sheep asked, handing her a pair of knitting-needles as she spoke.
```
HANDKERCHIEF (7) [See also POCKET-HANDKERCHIEF]
```
T8W   17:11   great  surprise. It was bright yellow like the handkerchief, and all tangled and tumbled about like a heap of
T8W   16:10   And  I gets under a tree. And I gets a yellow handkerchief. And I ties up my face--as at the present."
T8W   17: 9              He untied the handkerchief as he spoke, and Alice looked at his wig in great
T4    144:16   said  Tweedledee. "You  see he  held his handkerchief in front, so that the Carpenter couldn't count
T8W   17: 7   when  you catches it, just try tying a yellow handkerchief round your face. It'll cure you in no time!"
T8    190:32  he  reached  the turn, and then she waved her handkerchief to him, and waited till he was out of sight.
T8    190:18  "I  sha'n't be long. You'll wait and wave your handkerchief when I get to that turn in the road? I think
```
HANDLE (2) [See also BELL-HANDLE]
```
T6    168:13  the  door  was  shut,  /  I tried to turn the handle, but--"
T5    156:43  afterwards),  and  the  consequence was that the handle of it caught her under the chin, and, in spite of a
```
HAND-RAIL (1)
```
T1    119: 5   She  just kept the tips of her fingers on the hand-rail, and floated gently down without even touching the
```
HANDS (53)
```
T9    193: 6   deny  that,  even  if  you  tried with both hands."
T7    171: 9   breath  to say a word, and could only wave his hands about, and make the most fearful faces at the poor King
T9    193: 7              "I don't deny things with my hands," Alice objected.
A5    36:37              Alice folded her hands, and began:--
A8    63:16   three  gardeners, oblong and flat, with their hands and feet at the corners: next the ten courtiers: these
```

HANDS (cont.)

A8	66: 4	to double themselves up and stand on their hands and feet, to make the arches.
T4	139:22	in a visit is to say 'How d'ye do?' and shake hands!" And here the two brothers gave each other a hug, and
T1	110: 1	dropping the ball of worsted to clap her hands. "And I do so wish it was true! I'm sure the woods look
T1	113: 6	little "Oh!" of surprise, she was down on her hands and knees watching them. The chessmen were walking about
T4	144:29	cried, and they each took one of Alice's hands, and led her up to where the King was sleeping.
T5	155:18	suddenly the needles turned into oars in her hands, and she found they were in a little boat, gliding along
A5	43:33	she still held the pieces of mushroom in her hands, and she set to work very carefully, nibbling first at
T4	140: 1	Then they let go of Alice's hands, and stood looking at her for a minute: there was a
T8	190:24	So they shook hands, and then the Knight rode slowly away into the forest.
T8	180:13	by side. When they got up again, they shook hands, and then the Red Knight mounted and galloped off.
T8	181:10	putting back his shaggy hair with both hands, and turning his gentle face and large mild eyes to
A2	18: 1	As she said this she looked down at her hands, and was surprised to see that she had put on one of the
T4	139:27	out of the difficulty, she took hold of both hands at once: the next moment they were dancing round in a
A12	94:26	There was a general clapping of hands at this: it was the first really clever thing the King
A5	42:14	have my shoulders got to? And oh, my poor hands, how is it I ca'n't see you?" She was moving them about,
T6	166:15	Dumpty, stretching out one of his great hands, "I can repeat poetry as well as other folk, if it comes
T5	152:37	that!" cried the poor Queen, wringing her hands in despair. "Consider what a great girl you are.
T9	196:22	to Alice, taking one of the White Queen's hands in her own, and gently stroking it: "she means well, but
T7	175: 9	the Unicorn sauntered by them, with his hands in his pockets. "I had the best of it this time?" he
T8	185:14	me, I can assure you!" he said. He raised his hands in some excitement as he said this, and instantly rolled
AI	3: 5	/ By little arms are plied, / While little hands make vain pretence / Our wanderings to guide.
T9	192:34	that!" the White Queen moaned, wringing her hands. "Oh, ever so much more than that!"
A2	17: 4	'How doth the little--'," and she crossed her hands on her lap as if she were saying lessons, and began to
T9	204:14	jumped up and seized the tablecloth with both hands: one good pull, and plates, dishes, guests, and candles
T5	152: 7	steam-engine, that Alice had to hold both her hands over her ears.
T7	178: 9	before she dropped to her knees, and put her hands over her ears, vainly trying to shut out the dreadful
T6	159:15	egg he is!" she said aloud, standing with her hands ready to catch him, for she was every moment expecting
T5	152:24	you scream now?" Alice asked, holding her hands ready to put over her ears again.
T6	162:34	one knee over the other and clasped his hands round it, "they gave it me--for an un-birthday present."
T5	156:32	as, with flushed cheeks and dripping hair and hands, she scrambled back into her place, and began to arrange
A12	95:22	we've heard yet," said the King, rubbing his hands; "so now let the jury--"
T9	203: 8	Queen, seizing Alice's hair with both her hands. "Something's going to happen!"
T7	170:25	like an eel, as he came along, with his great hands spread out like fans on each side.)
T4	139:24	other a hug, and then they held out the two hands that were free, to shake hands with her.
T5	158:14	she said "I never put things into people's hands--that would never do--you must get it for yourself." And
T7	172:25	whisper it," said the Messenger, putting his hands to his mouth in the shape of a trumpet and stooping so
T7	175:20	to introduce her, and spreading out both his hands towards her in an Anglo-Saxon attitude. "We only found
T4	145: 4	you!" Tweedledee exclaimed, clapping his hands triumphantly. "And if he left off dreaming about you,
T12	207:16	other. "Now Kitty!" she cried, clapping her hands triumphantly. "Confess that was what you turned into!"
A5	42:18	there seemed to be no chance of getting her hands up to her head, she tried to get her head down to them,
T8	191: 4	exclaimed in a tone of dismay, as she put her hands up to something very heavy, that fitted tight all around
T9	195:26	and nervously clasping and unclasping her hands, "we had such a thunderstorm last Tuesday--I mean one of
A12	98:14	little Alice herself: once again the tiny hands were clasped upon her knee, and the bright eager eyes
T5	155:35	some of the needles into her hair, as her hands were full. "Feather, I say!"
T4	139:25	Alice did not like shaking hands with either of them first, for fear of hurting the other
T4	139:24	out the two hands that were free, to shake hands with her.
T6	160:39	and, to show you I'm not proud, you may shake hands with me!" And he grinned almost from ear to ear, as he
A10	82:34	she had sat down with her face in her hands, wondering if anything would ever happen in a natural

HANDSOME (2)

| A6 | 50:17 | dreadfully ugly child: but it makes rather a handsome pig, I think." And she began thinking over other |
| T6 | 160: 9 | "my name means the shape I am--and a good handsome shape it is, too. With a name like yours, you might |

HANDWRITING (1)

| A12 | 94:15 | "Are they in the prisoner's handwriting?" asked another of the jurymen. |

HANDY (1)

| T8 | 182:14 | it with us," the Knight said. "It'll come in handy if we find any plum-cake. Help me to get it into this |

HANGING (5)

A8	66: 8	enough, under her arm, with its legs hanging down, but generally, just as she had got its neck
A1	9:29	low hall, which was lit up by a row of lamps hanging from the roof.
T8	187:22	horse quietly moving about, with the reins hanging loose on his neck, cropping the grass at her feet--and
T8	181:15	his shoulders, upside-down, and with the lid hanging open. Alice looked at it with great curiosity.
A4	33: 1	down a good way off, panting, with its tongue hanging out of its mouth, and its great eyes half shut.

HANGS (1)

| T8 | 182:34 | Now the reason hair falls off is because it hangs down--things never fall upwards, you know. It's a plan |

HANSOM-CABS (1)

| T8 | 189: 2 | search for grassy knolls / For wheels of Hansom-cabs. / And that's the way' (he gave a wink) / 'By |

HAPPEN (18)

T5	150:18	"I ca'n't remember things before they happen."
T9	203: 8	with both her hands. "Something's going to happen!"
A8	67: 5	with the Queen, but she knew that it might happen any minute, "and then," thought she, "what would become
T5	152:22	a smile. "Now you understand the way things happen here."
A10	83: 1	her hands, wondering if anything would ever happen in a natural way again.
A4	27:30	began fancying the sort of thing that would happen: "'Miss Alice! Come here directly, and get ready for
A4	31: 4	one sharp kick, and waited to see what would happen next.
A8	65:24	procession, wondering very much what would happen next.
T1	113:18	it with great curiosity to see what would happen next.
A1	8:13	about her, and to wonder what was going to happen next. First, she tried to look down and make out what
A4	28: 5	"I know something interesting is sure to happen," she said to herself, "whenever I eat or drink
T3	137:20	But this did not seem likely to happen. She went on and on, a long way, but wherever the road
A1	13: 2	nothing but out-of-the-way things to happen, that it seemed quite dull and stupid for life to go on

HAPPEN (cont.)
```
  T4    147:35  he  went  on  in  a  low  voice:  "only to-day I happen to have a headache."
  T6    161:10  thought:  "And  then  I don't know what would happen to his head! I'm afraid it would come off!"
  T7    170: 7  a  tone  of  delight,  on  seeing Alice. "Did you happen to meet any soldiers, my dear, as you came through the
  T4    147:26  of  the  most  serious  things that can possibly happen to one in a battle--to get one's head cut off."
  T3    134:18                      "But that must happen very often," Alice remarked thoughtfully.
```
HAPPENED (24)
```
  A6     46:31  in  the  same  tone,  exactly as if nothing had happened.
  T3    132:24  Gnat  went  on,  as  quietly as if nothing had happened.
  T3    136: 3  she  suddenly  began  again.  "Then it really has happened, after all! And now, who am I? I will remember, if I
  T5    154: 8              But these, as it happened, Alice had not got: so she contented herself with
  T2    128:28              How it happened, Alice never knew, but exactly as she came to the
  A4     29: 4  tales,  I  fancied  that  kind of thing never happened, and now here I am in the middle of one! There ought
  T5    153:34  looked  again.  She  couldn't make out what had happened at all. Was she in a shop? And was that really--was
  T9    197:15  heavy  lump  in  her  lap. "I don't think it ever happened before, that any one had to take care of two Queens
  T9    203:11  afterwards  described  it)  all sorts of things happened in a moment. The candles all grew up to the ceiling,
  T7    172:24  got  your  breath,  you  may tell us what's happened in the town."
  A1     10:10  you  see,  so  many  out-of-the-way things had happened lately, that Alice had begun to think that very few
  T1    108:32  if  you'd  shut  them tight up, it wouldn't have happened. Now don't make any more excuses, but listen! Number
  T5    156:26  did  seem  a  little  provoking ("almost as if it happened on purpose," she thought) that, though she managed to
  A1     12:13  After  a  while,  finding  that nothing more happened, she decided on going into the garden at once; but,
  A2     19:24  very  clear  notion  how  long ago anything had happened.) So she began again: "Ou est ma chatte?" which was
  T5    157: 3      all  the  while,  just  as  if nothing had happened. "That was a nice crab you caught!" she remarked, as
  T5    150: 1              "Oh, things that happened the week after next," the Queen replied in a careless
  T9    196: 5  he  was  looking  for  a hippopotamus. Now, as it happened, there wasn't such a thing in the house, that morning
  T5    149: 5              "I'm very glad I happened to be in the way," Alice said, as she helped her to
  T3    132:11  at  the  thing  nearest  to  her hand, which happened to be the Goat's beard. * * * * * * * * * * * * * *
  T7    175:15  carelessly,  and  he  was going on, when his eye happened to fall upon Alice: he turned round instantly, and
  T8    185: 3  danger  of  falling into it, to be sure. That happened to me once--and the worst of it was, before I could
  A4     29: 3  this  sort  of  life!  I do wonder what can have happened to me! When I used to read fairy tales, I fancied
  A4     31:13  Don't  choke  him--How  was it, old fellow? What happened to you? Tell us all about it!"
```
HAPPENING (2)
```
  T9    192:11                  Everything was happening so oddly that she didn't feel a bit surprised at
  A6     52:11  she  was  getting  so  well used to queer things happening. While she was still looking at the place where it
```
HAPPENS (8)
```
  A1     12:37  get  into  the  garden,  and I don't care which happens!"
  T8    179:11  a  great  mind  to  go and wake him, and see what happens!"
  A5     43:26  hastily;  "but  I'm  not  looking for eggs, as it happens; and, if I was, I shouldn't want yours: I don't like
  T3    134:19              "It always happens," said the Gnat.
  T8    186: 3  question.  "What  does  it  matter where my body happens to be?" he said. "My mind goes on working all the same
  A4     28:22  to  herself  "Now  I  can do no more, whatever happens. What will become of me?"
  A1     13: 1  same  size.  To  be  sure, this is what generally happens when one eats cake; but Alice had got so much into the
  A7     58:16              "But what happens when you come to the beginning again?" Alice ventured
```
-HAPPINESS [See UNHAPPINESS]
HAPPY (7) [See also UNHAPPY]
```
  T7    170:28      attitudes.  He  only  does  them  when he's happy. His name is Haigha." (He pronounced it so as to rhyme
  T7    170:31  Alice  couldn't  help  beginning, "because he is Happy. I hate him with an H, because he is Hideous. I fed him
  T7    173:30              "Were you happy in prison, dear child?" said Haigha.
  T5    152:31  never  can  remember  the rule. You must be very happy, living in this wood, and being glad whenever you like!
  A12    99:11  joys,  remembering  her  own child-life, and the happy summer days.
  TI    103:33  sigh / May tremble through the story, / For "happy summer days" gone by, / And vanish'd summer glory--/ It
  AI      3:30  rest next time--" "It is next time!" / The happy voices cry.
```
HARD (18)
```
  T8    184:35  "but  don't  you  think  it  would be rather hard?"
  T8    184:37  certain--but  I'm  afraid  it  would be a little hard."
  A4     29:26  opened  inwards,  and  Alice's elbow was pressed hard against it, that attempt proved a failure. Alice heard it
  A2     15:35  fan,  and  scurried  away  into the darkness as hard as he could go.
  A2     20:12  For  the  Mouse  was  swimming away from her as hard as it could go, and making quite a commotion in the pool
  A4     32:16  the  moment  she  appeared; but she ran off as hard as she could, and soon found herself safe in a thick wood
  A12    93: 3  he  repeated  with  great  emphasis,  looking hard at Alice as he said so.
  T5    154:12  part  of  it  all  was that, whenever she looked hard at any shelf, to make out exactly what it had on it, that
  A11    88:26  put  on  her  spectacles,  and  began staring hard at the Hatter, who turned pale and fidgeted.
  T1    107: 9  at  the  nose:  and  just now, as I said, she was hard at work on the white kitten, which was lying quite still
  T2    122:26          Alice did so. "It's very hard," she said; "but I don't see what that has to do with it
  T6    166:11  quite  content.  Who's  been repeating all that hard stuff to you?"
  T9    202:14  /  'Take the dish-cover up!' / Ah, that is so hard that I fear I'm unable!
  A8     68:35  as  they  all  spoke at once, she found it very hard to make out exactly what they said.
  T1    118:11  when  she  had  finished it, "but it's rather hard to understand!" (You see she didn't like to confess, even
  A4     32:29  said  Alice,  in  a coaxing tone, and she tried hard to whistle to it; but she was terribly frightened all the
  A11    90:12  officers  of  the  court. (As that is rather a hard word, I will just explain to you how it was done. They
  T6    164:26  Dumpty  interrupted:  "there  are  plenty of hard words there. 'Brillig' means four o'clock in the
```
HARDLY (23)
```
  T6    168:18  she  ought  to  be going, she felt that it would hardly be civil to stay. So she got up, and held out her hand.
  A11    88:40  Dormouse,  who  was  sitting next to her. "I can hardly breathe."
  T5    155:26  and  then  the  oars got fast in it, and would hardly come out again.
  T8    182:25              "That's hardly enough," he said, anxiously. "You see the wind is so
  A1     12:29  "to  pretend  to  be  two people! Why, there's hardly enough of me left to make one respectable person!"
  A7     58: 4              "Well, I'd hardly finished the first verse," said the Hatter, "when the
  A6     49: 3  poor  little  thing  howled so, that Alice could hardly hear the words:--
  T1    115:21  frightened  whisper--so  low,  that Alice could hardly hear what they said.
```

HARDLY (cont.)
```
T6   160:24  looked  so  solemn and grand that Alice could hardly help laughing. "If I did fall," he went on, "the King
T4   138:17  like  the  ticking of a clock, and she could hardly help saying them out loud:--
T1   115:11  hear her.  "You  make me laugh so that I can hardly hold you! And don't keep your mouth so wide open! All
T1   111:12  chimney-piece while she said this, though she hardly knew how she had got there. And certainly the glass was
A10   82:20  so  full  of the Lobster-Quadrille, that she hardly knew what she was saying; and the words came very queer
A4    31:18  ("That's Bill," thought Alice), "Well, I hardly know--No more, thank ye; I'm better now--but I'm a deal
A5    35: 6          Alice replied, rather shyly, "I--I hardly know, Sir, just at present--at least I know who I was
A4    32:33                                            Hardly knowing what she did, she picked up a little bit of
T9   197:23  heads suddenly vanished from her lap, she hardly missed them.
T5   156:39  as  they  lay in heaps at her feet--but Alice hardly noticed this, there were so many other curious things
A4    29:14  can  you  learn lessons in here? Why, there's hardly room for you, and no room at all for any lesson-books!"
A5    42: 1  so  closely  against her foot, that there was hardly room to open her mouth; but she did it at last, and
A5    40: 1  "You are old," said the youth, "one would hardly suppose / That your eye was as steady as ever; / Yet
T2   127: 6  at  last they seemed to skim through the air, hardly touching the ground with their feet, till suddenly,
A8    67:34  so  she went on "--likely to win, that it's hardly worth while finishing the game."
```
HARE (31)
```
A7    54:16                "There isn't any," said the March Hare.
A7    55: 3  down  without  being invited," said the March Hare.
A7    55:17  find  out  the  answer to it?" said the March Hare.
A7    56: 3  he  added,  looking angrily at the March Hare.
A7    56:31                        "Nor I," said the March Hare.
A7    58:28            "Tell us a story!" said the March Hare.
A7    60:18               "Why not?" said the March Hare.
A11   88:15            "Fifteenth," said the March Hare.
A11   89:23            "I deny it!" said the March Hare.
A12   98:27  hear the  rattle of the teacups as the March Hare and his friends shared their never-ending meal, and the
A7    54: 2  a  tree in front of the house, and the March Hare and the Hatter were having tea at it: a Dormouse was
A7    60: 1  good deal worse off than before, as the March Hare had just upset the milk-jug into his plate.
A11   89:21                "I didn't!" the March Hare interrupted in a great hurry.
A7    58:18  "Suppose  we  change the subject," the March Hare interrupted, yawning. "I'm getting tired of this. I vote
A7    57:12  know--"  (pointing  his teaspoon at the March Hare,) "--it was at the great concert given by the Queen of
A7    56: 4        "It  was the  best butter," the March Hare meekly replied.
A7    59:39  and  the Dormouse followed him:  the March Hare moved into the Dormouse's place, and Alice rather
A11   89:20  things twinkled after that--only the March Hare said--
A7    54:12                    "Have some wine," the March Hare said in an encouraging tone.
A7    59: 9          "Take some more tea," the March Hare said to Alice, very earnestly.
A7    57: 3        ("I only wish it was," the March Hare said to itself in a whisper.)
A6    53:11  she  came  in sight of the house of the March Hare: she thought it must be the right house, because the
A7    55:26  "You might just as well say," added the March Hare, "that 'I like what I get' is the same thing as 'I get
A7    59:40  unwillingly  took  the  place  of the March Hare. The Hatter was the only one who got any advantage from
A7    56: 7                        The March Hare took the watch and looked at it gloomily: then he dipped
A6    51:21  waving  the  other  paw,  "lives a March Hare. Visit either you like: they're both mad."
A6    52:24  walked on in the direction in which the March Hare was said to live. "I've seen hatters before," she said to
A7    55:19  Then you should say what you mean," the March Hare went on.
A7    59:25  very  angrily,  but the Hatter and the March Hare went "Sh! Sh!" and the Dormouse sulkily remarked "If you
A11   88:12          The Hatter looked at the March Hare, who had followed him into the court, arm-in-arm with the
A6    52:25  before,"  she  said to herself:  "the March Hare will be much the most interesting, and perhaps, as this
```
HARM (2)
```
A2    19:12  likely  it  can talk: at any rate, there's no harm in trying." So she began: "O Mouse, do you know the way
T9   192:15  be  quite  civil.  However, there would be no harm, she thought, in asking if the game was over. "Please,
```
HAS (26)
```
A10   82:29  tide rises and sharks are around, / His voice has a timid and tremulous sound."
T8   182: 6  for  everything. That's the reason the horse has all those anklets round his feet."
A5    37: 2        the  young  man  said,  / "And your hair has become very white; / And yet you incessantly stand on your
T7   174: 7  he  said  in a  choking voice: "each of them has been down about eighty-seven times."
T8   181:35  "one  of  the best kind. But not a single bee has come near it yet. And the other thing is a mouse-trap. I
T4   142:19                          'The time has come,' the Walrus said, / 'To talk of many things: / Of
T7   177:19  very  much puzzled how to begin. "The Monster has given the Lion twice as much as me!"
T1   111: 8  it,  somehow, Kitty. Let's pretend the glass has got all soft like gauze, so that we can get through. Why,
T5   149:32                        "The brush has got entangled in it!" the Queen said with a sigh. "And I
T3   135:32  would  be,  trying  to find the creature that has got my old name! That's just like the advertisements, you
T2   121: 9  when you'd speak! Said I to myself, 'Her face has got some sense in it, though it's not a clever one!' Still
T4   147:16        remarked. "Every  one  of  these  things has got to go on, somehow or other."
T3   136: 3  she  suddenly  began again. "Then it really has happened, after all! And now, who am I? I will remember,
A4    30:35  "Oh!  So Bill's got to come down the chimney, has he?" said Alice to herself. "Why, they seem to put
A12   94: 4  jumping  up in a  great hurry: "this paper has just been picked up."
A5    39: 8  muscular  strength, which it gave to my jaw / Has lasted the rest of my life."
T2   123:21  said  the  Rose.  "She's one of the kind that has nine spikes, you know."
TC   209: 7                            Long has paled that sunny sky: / Echoes fade and memories die: /
T6   160:24  "If  I  did  fall," he  went on, "the King has promised me--ah, you may turn pale, if you like! You
T6   160:26  I  was  going to say that, did you? The King has promised me--with his very own mouth--to--to--"
T6   160:37  is. Now, take a good look at me! I'm one that has spoken to a King, I am: mayhap you'll never see such
T2   123:11                    "Well, she has the same awkward shape as you," the Rose said: "but she's
T6   168:27  Dumpty. "Your  face is the same as everybody has--the two eyes, so--"(marking their places in the air with
T2   122:27  hard,"  she  said; "but I don't see what that has to do with it."
A3    23:16  round  it,  panting,  and asking "But who has won?"
A3    23:21  in  silence. At last the Dodo said "Everybody has won, and all must have prizes."
```
HASN'T (3)
```
T3   136: 1  believe  it's got no name--why, to be sure it hasn't!"
```

HASN'T (cont.)
A9   74:21   as before, "It's all his fancy, that: he hasn't got no sorrow, you know. Come on!"
A9   70:21   "Perhaps it hasn't one," Alice ventured to remark.
HAST (1)
T1   118:17   "And, hast thou slain the Jabberwock? / Come to my arms, my beamish
HASTE (2)
T1   118:32   Alice, suddenly jumping up, "if I don't make haste, I shall have to go back through the Looking-glass,
A12   93: 4   looked at the jury-box, and saw that, in her haste, she had put the Lizard in head downwards, and the poor
HASTILY (25)
A3   22:10   "Not I!" said the Lory, hastily.
A10   80:19   seen them at dinn----" she checked herself hastily.
A2   19:28   fright. "Oh, I beg your pardon!" cried Alice hastily, afraid that she had hurt the poor animal's feelings.
A10   78:11   to say "I once tasted--" but checked herself hastily, and said "No never") "--so you can have no idea what
A12   96:23   as he found it made no mark; but he now hastily began again, using the ink, that was trickling down
A5   43:25   "It matters a good deal to me," said Alice hastily; "but I'm not looking for eggs, as it happens; and, if
A12   94: 1   The King turned pale, and shut his note-book hastily. "Consider your verdict," he said to the jury, in a
T9   195:20   about this, "is the thunder--no, no!" she hastily corrected herself. "I meant the other way."
A2   15:26   pattering of feet in the distance, and she hastily dried her eyes to see what was coming. It was the
T8W   18: 1   "It isn't that kind," Alice hastily explained. "It's to comb hair with--your wig's so very
T9   203:18   they each took a pair of plates, which they hastily fitted on as wings, and so, with forks for legs, went
A11   86:34   loud indignant voice; but she stopped herself hastily, for the White Rabbit cried out "Silence in the court!
A10   83: 3   "She ca'n't explain it," said the Gryphon hastily. "Go on with the next verse."
A11   88: 2   "Not yet, not yet!" the Rabbit hastily interrupted. "There's a great deal to come before
A2   18: 8   the fan she was holding, and she dropped it hastily, just in time to save herself from shrinking away
T9   201:11   to the pudding, please," Alice said rather hastily, "or we shall get no dinner at all. May I give you
T1   114: 5   was nearly screaming herself into a fit, she hastily picked up the Queen and set her on the table by the
A4   28:12   stoop to save her neck from being broken. She hastily put down the bottle, saying to herself "That's quite
T8W   15: 1   Alice hastily ran her eye down the paper and said "No. It says
A7   55:21   "I do," said Alice hastily replied; "at least--at least I mean what I say--that's
A5   41: 8   "Oh, I'm not particular as to size," Alice hastily replied; "only one doesn't like changing so often, you
A12   93:26   "Unimportant, of course, I meant," the King hastily said, and went on to himself in an undertone,
T6   166:17   "Oh, it needn't come to that!" Alice hastily said, hoping to keep him from beginning.
T4   146:17   "Not a rattle-snake, you know," she added hastily, thinking that he was frightened: "only an old rattle
T8   184:39   at the idea, that Alice changed the subject hastily. "What a curious helmet you've got!" she said
HAT (1)
A11   88:20   "Take off your hat," the King said to the Hatter.
HATCHING (1)
A5   42:38   "As if it wasn't trouble enough hatching the eggs," said the Pigeon; "but I must be on the
HATE (3)
A3   24:15   you know," said Alice, "and why it is you hate--C and D," she added in a whisper, half afraid that it
A2   20:20   my history, and you'll understand why it is I hate cats and dogs."
T7   170:31   help beginning, "because he is Happy. I hate him with an H, because he is Hideous. I fed him with--
HATED (1)
A2   19:44   talk on such a subject! Our family always hated cats: nasty, low, vulgar things! Don't let me hear the
HATTA (10)
T7   174:18   fight any more to-day," the King said to Hatta: "go and order the drums to begin." And Hatta went
T7   170:37   with H. "The other Messenger's called Hatta. I must have two, you know--to come and go. One to come,
T7   173:28   Hatta looked round and nodded, and went on with his
T7   173:31   Hatta looked round once more, and this time a tear or two
T7   174: 5   Hatta made a desperate effort, and swallowed a large piece of
T7   174: 1   ca'n't you!" Haigha cried impatiently. But Hatta only munched away, and drank some more tea.
T7   174:14   minutes allowed for refreshments!" Haigha and Hatta set to work at once, carrying round trays of white and
T7   173:20   They placed themselves close to where Hatta, the other Messenger, was standing watching the fight,
T7   174:10   "It's waiting for 'em now," said Hatta; "this is a bit of it as I'm eating."
T7   174:18   Hatta: "go and order the drums to begin." And Hatta went bounding away like a grasshopper.
HATTA'S (1)
T7   173:27   went on, putting his arm affectionately round Hatta's neck.
HATTER (55)
A7   56:18   "Which is just the case with mine," said the Hatter.
A7   56:30   "I haven't the slightest idea," said the Hatter.
A7   60:28   "Then you shouldn't talk," said the Hatter.
A11   88:20   "Take off your hat," the King said to the Hatter.
A11   88:21   "It isn't mine," said the Hatter.
A11   88:25   an explanation. "I've none of my own. I'm a hatter."
A11   89:22   "You did!" said the Hatter.
A11   90: 4   "That I ca'n't remember," said the Hatter.
A11   88:24   "I keep them to sell," the Hatter added as an explanation. "I've none of my own. I'm a
A7   56:22   "The Dormouse is asleep again," said the Hatter, and he poured a little hot tea upon its nose.
A7   55:31   "It is the same thing with you," said the Hatter, and here the conversation dropped, and the party sat
A6   51:20   said, waving its right paw round, "lives a Hatter: and in that direction," waving the other paw, "lives a
A11   89: 4   the Queen had never left off staring at the Hatter, and, just as the Dormouse crossed the court, she said,
A7   59:25   Alice was beginning very angrily, but the Hatter and the March Hare went "Sh! Sh!" and the Dormouse
A7   58:15   "Exactly so," said the Hatter: "as the things get used up."
A7   59:16   "Who's making personal remarks now?" the Hatter asked triumphantly.
A11   89:11   "I'm a poor man, your Majesty," the Hatter began, in a trembling voice, "and I hadn't begun my tea
A7   57: 7   "Not at first, perhaps," said the Hatter: "but you could keep it to half-past one as long as you
A7   57:18   "It goes on, you know," the Hatter continued, "in this way:--
A7   56:14   "Why should it?" muttered the Hatter. "Does your watch tell you what year it is?"
A11   90: 7   The miserable Hatter dropped his teacup and bread-and-butter and went down
A7   56: 5   some crumbs must have got in as well," the Hatter grumbled: "you shouldn't have put it in with the

HATTER (cont.)
A11   88: 6   The first witness was the Hatter. He came in with a teacup in one hand and a piece of
A7   55: 6   "Your hair wants cutting," said the Hatter. He had been looking at Alice for some time with great
A7   56:42   "Ah! That accounts for it," said the Hatter. "He wo'n't stand beating. Now, if you only kept on
A11   90:31   "You may go," said the King, and the Hatter hurriedly left the court, without even waiting to put
A11   90: 1   "After that," continued the Hatter, "I cut some more bread-and-butter--"
A7   56: 1   "Two days wrong!" sighed the Hatter. "I told you butter wouldn't suit the works!" he added,
A11   90:23   "I ca'n't go no lower," said the Hatter: "I'm on the floor, as it is."
A6   53:18   after all! I almost wish I'd gone to see the Hatter instead!"
A7   60:21   off into a doze; but, on being pinched by the Hatter, it woke up again with a little shriek, and went on:
A7   59:13   "You mean you ca'n't take less," said the Hatter: "it's very easy to take more than nothing."
A7   59:36   "I want a clean cup," interrupted the Hatter: "let's all move one place on."
A11   88:12   The Hatter looked at the March Hare, who had followed him into the
A7   55:11   The Hatter opened his eyes very wide on hearing this; but all he
A7   58:30   "And be quick about it," added the Hatter, "or you'll be asleep again before it's done."
A11   89:16   "It began with the tea," the Hatter replied.
A7   56:38   "Of course you don't!" the Hatter said, tossing his head contemptuously. "I dare say you
A7   56:27   "Have you guessed the riddle yet?" the Hatter said, turning to Alice again.
A7   57:10   The Hatter shook his head mournfully. "Not I!" he replied. "We
A7   60: 6   can draw water out of a water-well," said the Hatter; "so I should think you could draw treacle out of a
A11   89: 7   in the last concert!" on which the wretched Hatter trembled so, that he shook off both his shoes.
A11   91: 2   Queen added to one of the officers; but the Hatter was out of sight before the officer could get to the
A7   55:35   The Hatter was the first to break the silence. "What day of the
A7   59:40   took the place of the March Hare. The Hatter was the only one who got any advantage from the change;
A11   89:19   "I'm a poor man," the Hatter went on, "and most things twinkled after that--only the
A7   58: 8   "And ever since that," the Hatter went on in a mournful tone, "he wo'n't do a thing I
A11   89:25   "Well, at any rate, the Dormouse said--" the Hatter went on, looking anxiously round to see if he would
A7   54: 2   of the house, and the March Hare and the Hatter were having tea at it: a Dormouse was sitting between
A7   58: 4   hardly finished the first verse," said the Hatter, "when the Queen bawled out 'He's murdering the time!
A11   88:27   her spectacles, and began staring hard at the Hatter, who turned pale and fidgeted.
A7   55:23   "Not the same thing a bit!" said the Hatter. "Why, you might just as well say that 'I see what I
A7   58:12   "Yes, that's it," said the Hatter with a sigh: "it's always tea-time, and we've no time
A11   90:29   "I'd rather finish my tea," said the Hatter, with an anxious look at the Queen, who was reading the
A7   56:35   "If you knew Time as well as I do," said the Hatter, "you wouldn't talk about wasting it. It's him."
HATTER'S (1)
A7   56:19   Alice felt dreadfully puzzled. The Hatter's remark seemed to her to have no sort of meaning in it
HATTERS (1)
A6   52:24   the March Hare was said to live. "I've seen hatters before," she said to herself: "the March Hare will be
HAUNTS (1)
TC   209:10   Still she haunts me, phantomwise. / Alice moving under skies / Never
HAVE (185)
T4   138:19   "Tweedledum and Tweedledee / Agreed to have a battle; / For Tweedledum said Tweedledee / Had spoiled
T4   147: 8   "Of course you agree to have a battle?" Tweedledum said in a calmer tone.
T2   127:26   taking a little box out of her pocket. "Have a biscuit?"
T4   147:40   "We must have a bit of a fight, but I don't care about going on long,"
T4   147:35   on in a low voice: "only to-day I happen to have a headache."
T3   131:32   the voice came from. "If you're so anxious to have a joke made, why don't you make one yourself?"
T5   149:36   most of the pins. "But really you should have a lady's maid!"
A8   68:26   it might not escape again, and went back to have a little more conversation with her friend.
T1   119: 1   what the rest of the house is like! Let's have a look at the garden first!" She was out of the room in a
T9   193:17   "I didn't know I was to have a party at all," said Alice; "but, if there is to be one,
A3   23:30   "But she must have a prize herself, you know," said the Mouse.
T12 208: 2   all about fishes! To-morrow morning you shall have a real treat. All the time you're eating your breakfast,
T2   123:37   she felt that it would be far grander to have a talk with a real Queen.
T8   184:12   all her patience this time. "You ought to have a wooden horse on wheels, that you ought!"
T5   149:15   Alice thought it would never do to have an argument at the very beginning of their conversation,
T2   127:36   distance, "I shall give you your directions--have another biscuit?"
A5   40: 5   "I have answered three questions, and that is enough," / Said his
A9   70: 8   in a very hopeful tone, though), "I wo'n't have any pepper in my kitchen at all. Soup does very well
A8   67:25   hear oneself speak--and they don't seem to have any rules in particular: at least, if there are, nobody
A11   86:30   Alice whispered to the Gryphon. "They ca'n't have anything to put down yet, before the trial's begun."
A9   72: 9   not otherwise than what you had been would have appeared to them to be otherwise.'"
A10   82:23   of the Lobster: I heard him declare / 'You have baked me too brown, I must sugar my hair.' / As a duck
A9   77:19   her next remark. "Then the eleventh day must have been a holiday?"
A8   63: 7   fact is, you see, Miss, this here ought to have been a red rose-tree, and we put a white one in by
T5   149:21   It would have been all the better, as it seemed to Alice, if she had
T5   151:21   done them," the Queen said, "that would have been better still; better, and better, and better!" Her
A2   16: 2   the same age as herself, to see if she could have been changed for any of them.
A2   17: 3   no, that's all wrong, I'm certain! I must have been changed for Mabel! I'll try and say 'How doth the
A5   35: 8   I got up this morning, but I think I must have been changed several times since then."
T8   179: 3   seen, and her first thought was that she must have been dreaming about the Lion and the Unicorn and those
T12 208: 8   you this morning! You see, Kitty, it must have been either me or the Red King. He was part of my dream,
T7   172:22   ca'n't do that," said the King, "or else he'd have been here first. However, now you've got your breath, you
A7   59: 1   you know," Alice gently remarked. "They'd have been ill."
T3   133: 9   interest, and made up her mind that it must have been just repainted, it looked so bright and sticky; and
A12   94: 9   "It must have been that," said the King, "unless it was written to
T6   168: 3   Alice thought, with a shudder, "I wouldn't have been the messenger for anything!"
T12 207:21   little ashamed of itself, so I think it must have been the Red Queen.")
A9   72: 8   appear to others that what you were or might have been was not otherwise than what you had been would have
T6   159: 7   It might have been written a hundred times, easily, on that enormous

HAVE (cont.)

T9	202: 6	/ That is easy: a penny, I think, could have bought it.
T3	130: 6	make excuses," said the Guard: "you should have bought one from the engine-driver." And once more the
A6	45: 4	judging by his face only, she would have called him a fish)--and rapped loudly at the door with
T9	202: 4	/ That is easy: a baby, I think, could have caught it. / 'Next, the fish must be bought.' / That is
A4	27: 9	were nowhere to be seen--everything seemed to have changed since her swim in the pool; and the great hall,
A6	51:26	"You must be," said the Cat, "or you wouldn't have come here."
A8	67:17	speaking to it," she thought, "till its ears have come, or at least one of them." In another minute the
A8	67:29	at the other end of the ground--and I should have croqueted the Queen's hedgehog just now, only it ran away
T9	195:32	thin way of doing things. Now here, we mostly have days and nights two or three at a time, and sometimes in
T1	108:24	and putting you out into the snow! And you'd have deserved it, you little mischievous darling! What have
T9	199:39	a favour to hear: / 'Tis a privilege high to have dinner and tea / Along with the Red Queen, the White
T4	147:43	"Let's fight till six, and then have dinner," said Tweedledum.
T8W	21: 8	too much in front, no doubt. One would have done as well as two, if you must have them so close--"
A11	86:27	of it at all. However, "jurymen" would have done just as well.
A2	18: 3	kid-gloves while she was talking. "How can I have done that?" she thought. "I must be growing small again."
A7	59: 3	"They couldn't have done that, you know," Alice gently remarked. "They'd have
A4	27: 5	as sure as ferrets are ferrets. Where can I have dropped them, I wonder?" Alice guessed in a moment that
T12	207:38	me in my dream, there was one thing you would have enjoyed--I had such a quantity of poetry said to me, all
A8	69: 3	done about it in less than no time, she'd have everybody executed, all round. (It was this last remark
T8	181:24	over his face. "Then all the things must have fallen out! And the box is no use without them." He
T9	204:23	At any other time, Alice would have felt surprised at this, but she was far too much excited
A11	88:10	"You ought to have finished," said the King. "When did you begin?"
T12	207:28	undergoing its toilet, "when will Dinah have finished with your White Majesty, I wonder? That must be
T5	152:27	time it was getting light. "The crow must have flown away, I think," said Alice: "I'm so glad it's gone.
T7	176:16	"What a fight we might have for the crown now!" the Unicorn said, looking slyly up at
T8W	14:21	have made another tour in the Pantry, and have found five new lumps of white sugar, large and in fine
T1	119: 7	she floated on through the hall, and would have gone straight out at the door in the same way, if she
A5	41: 3	said Alice, timidly: "some of the words have got altered."
T4	140: 5	do?' now," she said to herself: "we seem to have got beyond that, somehow!"
A7	56: 5	"Yes, but some crumbs must have got in as well," the Hatter grumbled: "you shouldn't have
A6	48: 5	said very politely, feeling quite pleased to have got into a conversation.
T8	191: 6	"But how can it have got there without my knowing it?" she said to herself, as
A5	38: 2	said the youth, "as I mentioned before, / And have grown most uncommonly fat; / Yet you turned a
T1	108:12	to-morrow is, Kitty?" Alice began. "You'd have guessed if you'd been up in the window with me--only
T1	107: 5	considering): so you see that it couldn't have had any hand in the mischief.
T1	108:32	if you'd shut them tight up, it wouldn't have happened. Now don't make any more excuses, but listen!
A4	29: 3	know, this sort of life! I do wonder what can have happened to me! When I used to read fairy tales, I
T3	131:37	a wonderfully small sigh, that she wouldn't have heard it at all, if it hadn't come quite close to her ear
A10	81:30	"They were obliged to have him with them," the Mock Turtle said. "No wise fish would
T4	147:30	very pale?" said Tweedledum, coming up to have his helmet tied on. (He called it a helmet, though it
T8	185: 7	did not dare to laugh. "I'm afraid you must have hurt him," she said in a trembling voice, "being on the
A12	94:19	"He must have imitated somebody else's hand," said the King. (The jury
T2	127:15	it is," said the Queen. "What would you have it?"
T8W	17: 5	It is, though," said the Wasp: "wait till you have it, and then you'll know. And when you catches it, just
T8	186: 9	"In time to have it cooked for the next course?" said Alice. "Well, that
A10	83: 2	"I should like to have it explained," said the Mock Turtle.
T5	150: 5	"You couldn't have it if you did want it," the Queen said. "The rule is, jam
A12	98: 8	all these strange Adventures of hers that you have just been reading about; when she had finished, her
T6	160:32	trees--and down chimneys--or you couldn't have known it!"
T9	200:12	to be asked," she thought: "I should never have known who were the right people to invite!"
T6	162:12	two can. With proper assistance, you might have left off at seven."
A4	29:11	never to be an old woman--but then--always to have lessons to learn! Oh, I shouldn't like that!"
A4	33: 9	herself with one of the leaves. "I should have liked teaching it tricks very much, if--if I'd only been
T9	192:13	close to her, one on each side: she would have liked very much to ask them how they came there, but she
A10	78: 8	"You may not have lived much under the sea--" ("I haven't," said Alice)--
A6	50:16	had grown up," she said to herself, "it would have made a dreadfully ugly child: but it makes rather a
T8W	14:21	and began. "Latest News. The Exploring Party have made another tour in the Pantry, and have found five new
A12	94:24	"that only makes the matter worse. You must have meant some mischief, or else you'd have signed your name
T9	193: 2	"That's just what I complain of! You should have meant! What do you suppose is the use of a child without
T4	148:11	"I shouldn't have minded it so much," said Tweedledum, "if it hadn't been a
A5	42:13	that green stuff be?" said Alice. "And where have my shoulders got to? And oh, my poor hands, how is it I
T3	132:38	name them, I suppose. If not, why do things have names at all?"
A2	17:19	to go and live in that poky little house, and have next to no toys to play with, and oh, ever so many
A7	56:34	said, "than wasting it in asking riddles that have no answers."
A10	78:11	hastily, and said "No never") "--so you can have no idea what a delightful thing a Lobster-Quadrille is!"
T6	159:23	Dumpty, looking away from her as usual, "have no more sense than a baby!"
T3	135:28	said thoughtfully to herself, "where things have no names. I wonder what'll become of my name when I go in
A10	80: 1	"You can really have no notion how delightful it will be / When they take us
A7	56:20	puzzled. The Hatter's remark seemed to her to have no sort of meaning in it, and yet it was certainly
A5	37: 7	brain; / But, now that I'm perfectly sure I have none, / Why, I do it again and again."
TI	103: 7	I have not seen thy sunny face, / Nor heard thy silver laughter:
A6	50: 4	a pig, my dear," said Alice, seriously, "I'll have nothing more to do with you. Mind now!" The poor little
A9	71:14	said the Duchess: "what a clear way you have of putting things!"
T5	158:10	"Then I'll have one, please," said Alice, as she put the money down on
A9	74: 3	must go back and see after some executions I have ordered;" and she walked off, leaving Alice alone with
T4	143: 2	wait a bit,' the Oysters cried, / 'Before we have our chat; / For some of us are out of breath, / And all
A8	63: 8	if the Queen was to find out, we should all have our heads cut off, you know. So you see, Miss, we're
A3	23:21	Dodo said "Everybody has won, and all must have prizes."
A7	56: 6	as well," the Hatter grumbled: "you shouldn't have put it in with the bread-knife."

HAVE (cont.)
```
T7    175:13   replied, rather nervously. "You shouldn't have run him through with your horn, you know."
T6    161:27                     "If I'd meant that, I'd have said it," said Humpty Dumpty.
T6    162: 5   of age. Now if you'd asked my advice, I'd have said 'Leave off at seven'--but it's too late now."
T6    162:17   thoughts, "a beautiful cravat, I should have said--no, a belt, I mean--I beg your pardon!" she added
T3    131:35   was very unhappy, evidently, and Alice would have said something pitying to comfort it, "if it would only
T8    187: 4                 "Then I ought to have said 'That's what the song is called'?" Alice corrected
T2    128:16               "You should have said," the Queen went on in a tone of grave reproof,
A10    81:28   thoughts were still running on the song, "I'd have said to the porpoise 'Keep back, please! We don't want
T7    175:30             "Well, now that we have seen each other," said the Unicorn, "if you'll believe in
T3    135:18   and this time the poor Gnat really seemed to have sighed itself away, for, when Alice looked up, there was
A12    94:25   must have meant some mischief, or else you'd have signed your name like an honest man."
TC    209: 9   Echoes fade and memories die: / Autumn frosts have slain July.
A7     55:13                 "Come, we shall have some fun now!" thought Alice. "I'm glad they've begun
T9    193: 4   child without any meaning? Even a joke should have some meaning--and a child's more important than a joke, I
A7     54:12               "Have some wine," the March Hare said in an encouraging tone.
A8     67:12   herself "It's the Cheshire-Cat: now I shall have somebody to talk to."
T6    168:39   this aloud, as it was a great comfort to have such a long word to say) "of all the unsatisfactory
T5    153:32   She looked at the Queen, who seemed to have suddenly wrapped herself up in wool. Alice rubbed her
A5     43:16               "I have tasted eggs, certainly," said Alice, who was a very
T1    107:22   it was in disgrace. "Really, Dinah ought to have taught you better manners! You ought, Dinah, you know you
A9     71:10   replied, not feeling at all anxious to have the experiment tried.
A3     25:16   you.--Come, I'll take no denial: We must have the trial; For really this morning I've nothing to do.'
T4    148:15   Tweedledum said to his brother: "but you can have the umbrella--it's quite as sharp. Only we must begin
A10    80:22   so," Alice replied thoughtfully. "They have their tails in their mouths--and they're all over crumbs
A10    80:25   would all wash off in the sea. But they have their tails in their mouths; and the reason is--" here
T8    182: 4   "but, if they do come, I don't choose to have them running all about."
T8W    21: 8   would have done as well as two, if you must have them so close--"
A8     68: 5   at the moment, "My dear! I wish you would have this cat removed!"
T9    202:39   sister the history of her feast. "You would have thought they wanted to squeeze me flat!")
A1      8:43   sound at all the right word) "--but I shall have to ask them what the name of the country is, you know.
T7    172:34               "It would have to be a very tiny earthquake!" thought Alice. "Who are at
T9    192: 5   lolling about on the grass like that! Queens have to be dignified, you know!"
T8    186:13               "Then it would have to be the next day. I suppose you wouldn't have two
A7     56:40   not," Alice cautiously replied; "but I know I have to beat time when I learn music."
A9     72:27   as much right," said the Duchess, "as pigs have to fly; and the m----"
T2    120:15   "I'm not going in again yet. I know I should have to get through the Looking-glass again--back into the old
T3    135:30   like to lose it at all--because they'd have to give me another, and it would be almost certain to be
A2     17:18   on, "I must be Mabel after all, and I shall have to go and live in that poky little house, and have next
T3    131: 8   all speak in turn, he went on with "She'll have to go back from here as luggage!"
T1    118:32   jumping up, "if I don't make haste, I shall have to go back through the Looking-glass, before I've seen
T1    109: 6   then, when the miserable day came, I should have to go without fifty dinners at once! Well, I shouldn't
T3    135: 4   for her to call, and of course you wouldn't have to go, you know."
T3    132: 6   drew it in and said "It's only a brook we have to jump over." Everybody seemed satisfied with this,
T3    135: 3   call out 'Come here--,' and there she would have to leave off, because there wouldn't be any name for her
A5     36: 3   found it so yet," said Alice; "but when you have to turn into a chrysalis--you will some day, you know--
A7     57: 1   just time to begin lessons: you'd only have to whisper a hint to Time, and round goes the clock in a
A10    81:26   rather impatiently: "any shrimp could have told you that."
T8    186:14   to be the next day. I suppose you wouldn't have two pudding-courses in one dinner?"
T7    171: 6   you?" the King repeated impatiently. "I must have two--to fetch and carry. One to fetch, and one to carry
T7    170:37   "The other Messenger's called Hatta. I must have two, you know--to come and go. One to come, and one to go
A9     76:16               "You couldn't have wanted it much," said Alice; "living at the bottom of the
T4    142:24   the sea is boiling hot--/ And whether pigs have wings.'
T1    110: 7   was a nice check, Kitty, and really I might have won, if it hadn't been for that nasty Knight, that came
A1      7:14   it occurred to her that she ought to have wondered at this, but at the time it all seemed quite
T6    162:45               "And how many birthdays have you?"
A8     65: 4   turning to the rose-tree, she went on "What have you been doing here?"
T7    172:31   himself. "If you do such a thing again, I'll have you buttered! It went through and through my head like an
A11    90: 5   must remember," remarked the King, "or I'll have you executed."
A11    88:29   said the King: "and don't be nervous, or I'll have you executed on the spot."
A11    89: 9   the King repeated angrily, "or I'll have you executed, whether you are nervous or not."
A3     23:31   the Dodo replied very gravely. "What else have you got in your pocket?" it went on, turning to Alice.
T1    108:25   it, you little mischievous darling! What have you got to say for yourself? Now don't interrupt me!" she
A7     56:27               "Have you guessed the riddle yet?" the Hatter said, turning to
T8    182:27               "Have you invented a plan for keeping the hair from being blown
T5    152: 9   there was a chance of making herself heard. "Have you pricked your finger?"
A9     73:11   off, quite out of breath, and said to Alice "Have you seen the Mock Turtle yet?"
T9    192: 5   by 'If you really are a Queen'? What right have you to call yourself so? You ca'n't be a Queen, you know,
```
HAVEN'T (18)
```
T6    164:18   that ever were invented--and a good many that haven't been invented just yet."
A6     52: 5   should like it very much," said Alice, "but I haven't been invited yet."
A5     36: 2   "Well, perhaps you haven't found it so yet," said Alice; "but when you have to
T9    196:38               "I haven't got a nightcap with me," said Alice, as she tried to
T1    115:24   To which the Queen replied "You haven't got any whiskers."
A11    91:31   the next witness would be like, "--for they haven't got much evidence yet," she said to herself. Imagine
T3    130: 2               "I'm afraid I haven't got one," Alice said in a frightened tone: "there
A5     42:40   look-out for serpents, night and day! Why, I haven't had a wink of sleep these three weeks!"
T5    153:13               "I daresay you haven't had much practice," said the Queen. "When I was your
T6    160:34               "I haven't indeed!" Alice said very gently. "It's in a book."
A12    94: 7               "I haven't opened it yet," said the White Rabbit; "but it seems
```

HAVEN'T (cont.)
T5	152:10	"I haven't pricked it <u>yet</u>," the Queen said, "but I soon shall--oh
A10	78: 8	may not have lived much under the sea--" ("I haven't," said Alice)--"and perhaps you were never even
T7	170:13	two of them are wanted in the game. And I haven't sent the two Messengers, either. They're both gone to
A5	42:32	"I haven't the least idea what you're talking about," said Alice.
A7	56:30	"I haven't the slightest idea," said the Hatter.
T6	163:18	saying, that <u>seems</u> to be done right--though I haven't time to look it over thoroughly just now--and that
T8	184:36	"I haven't tried it yet," the Knight said, gravely; "so I ca'n't

HAVING (21)
A4	32:40	of it: then Alice, thinking it was very like having a game of play with a cart-horse, and expecting every
T1	107:15	herself and half asleep, the kitten had been having a grand game of romps with the ball of worsted Alice
T12	207:25	it one little kiss, "just in honour of its having been a Red Queen."
A1	12:26	she remembered trying to box her own ears for having cheated herself in a game of croquet she was playing
A9	70:10	she went on, very much pleased at having found out a new kind of rule, "and vinegar that makes
T7	169:10	Then came the horses. Having four feet, these managed rather better than the
A8	63:30	gardeners, but she could not remember ever having heard of such a rule at processions; "and besides, what
T5	152:26	said the Queen. "What would be the good of having it all over again?"
T1	107: 3	fault entirely. For the white kitten had been having its face washed by the old cat for the last quarter of
T3	137:12	it, almost ready to cry with vexation at having lost her dear little fellow-traveler so suddenly.
A8	68:13	three of the players to be executed for having missed their turns, and she did not like the look of
T3	132:35	"What's the use of their having names," the Gnat said, "if they wo'n't answer to them
T8	188:13	<u>a fan / That they</u> could <u>not be seen. / So</u>, <u>having</u> <u>no</u> <u>reply</u> <u>to</u> <u>give</u> <u>/</u> <u>To</u> <u>what</u> <u>the</u> <u>old</u> <u>man</u> <u>said</u>, / <u>I</u> <u>cried</u>
A1	7: 2	of sitting by her sister on the bank and of having nothing to do: once or twice she had peeped into the
A2	19:16	done such a thing before, but she remembered having seen, in her brother's Latin Grammar, "A mouse--of a
A1	12:11	is blown out, for she could not remember ever having seen such a thing.
T8W	21:10	Alice did not like having so many personal remarks made on her, and as the Wasp
T8	190:28	he gets on again pretty easily--that comes of having so many things hung round the horse--" So she went on
A7	54: 2	house, and the March Hare and the Hatter were having tea at it: a Dormouse was sitting between them, fast
A12	97: 1	nonsense!" said Alice loudly. "The idea of having the sentence first!"
T7	176:13	The King was evidently very uncomfortable at having to sit down between the two great creatures; but there

HAY (6)
T7	172:16	out his hand to the Messenger for some hay.
T7	175:38	"Quick! Not that one--that's full of hay!"
T7	170:32	I fed him with--with--with Ham-sandwiches and Hay. His name is Haigha, and he lives--"
T7	172: 5	"There's nothing but hay left now," the Messenger said, peeping into the bag.
T7	172: 7	"Hay, then," the King murmured in a faint whisper.
T7	172: 9	him a good deal. "There's nothing like eating hay when you're faint," he remarked to her, as he munched away

HE (345) [entries omitted]

HEAD (118) [See also BEHEAD, FOREHEAD, OVERHEAD]
A6	48:27	of axes," said the Duchess, "chop off her head!"
A7	58: 6	out 'He's murdering the time! Off with his head!'"
T5	154: 7	unless you've got eyes at the back of your head."
T8	181:29	Alice shook her head.
T8	185: 8	a trembling voice, "being on the top of his head."
T8	188:16	<u>me</u> <u>how</u> <u>you</u> <u>live</u>!' / <u>And</u> <u>thumped</u> <u>him</u> <u>on</u> <u>the</u> <u>head</u>.
T8	191: 5	very heavy, that fitted tight all around her head.
T8W	15:16	said the Wasp, fretfully turning away his head.
A8	67: 1	"Off with his head!" or "Off with her head!" about once in a minute.
T8W	18: 6	A curious idea came into Alice's head. Almost every one she had met had repeated poetry to her,
T8	190:13	gathered up the reins, and turned his horse's head along the road by which they had come. "You've only a few
T3	132:19	was balancing itself on a twig just over her head, and fanning her with its wings.
T12	207:19	afterwards to her sister: "it turned away its head, and pretended not to see it: but it looked a <u>little</u>
T8	179:33	and was something the shape of a horse's head) and put it on.
T9	196:30	how good-tempered she is! Pat her on the head, and see how pleased she'll be!" But this was more than
A12	92:10	accident of the gold-fish kept running in her head, and she had a vague sort of idea that they must be
T9	197:13	about in great perplexity, as first one round head, and then the other, rolled down from her shoulder, and
T8W	18:14	<u>waved</u> <u>/</u> <u>And</u> <u>curled</u> <u>and</u> <u>crinkled</u> <u>on</u> <u>my</u> <u>head</u>: / <u>And</u> <u>then</u> <u>they</u> <u>said</u> 'You <u>should</u> <u>be</u> <u>shaved</u>, / <u>And</u> <u>wear</u> <u>a</u>
A8	67:18	one of them." In another minute the whole head appeared, and then Alice put down her flamingo, and began
T8W	20: 6	of admiration: "it's the shape of your head as does it. Your jaws aint well shaped, though--I should
T8	190:27	watching him. "There he goes! Right on his head as usual! However, he gets on again pretty easily--that
T3	134:22	meanwhile by humming round and round her head: at last it settled again and remarked "I suppose you
T8W	13:22	Wasp only shook his shoulders, and turned his head away. "Ah, deary me!" he said to himself.
A8	69:10	The Cat's head began fading away the moment he was gone, and, by the
A4	31:11	another confusion of voices--"Hold up his head--Brandy now--Don't choke him--How was it, old fellow?
A6	46:24	his eyes are so <u>very</u> nearly at the top of his head. But at any rate he might answer questions.--How am I to
T1	113:12	can hear me," she went on, as she put her head closer down, "and I'm nearly sure they ca'n't see me. I
A7	56:38	you don't!" the Hatter said, tossing his head contemptuously. "I dare say you never even spoke to Time!
A8	68:41	King's argument was that anything that had a head could be beheaded, and that you weren't to talk nonsense
T4	147:27	happen to one in a battle--to get one's head cut off."
A5	37: 3	/ And <u>yet</u> <u>you</u> <u>incessantly</u> <u>stand</u> <u>on</u> <u>your</u> head--/ <u>Do</u> <u>you</u> think, <u>at</u> <u>your</u> <u>age</u>, <u>it</u> <u>is</u> <u>right</u>?"
T8	186:16	next day. In fact," he went on, holding his head down, and his voice getting lower and lower, "I don't
A8	66:13	out laughing; and, when she had got its head down, and was going to begin again, it was very provoking
T9	197: 9	know the words," she added, as she put her head down on Alice's other shoulder, "just sing it through to
A5	42:19	hands up to her head, she tried to get her head down to <u>them</u>, and was delighted to find that her neck
T8	185:24	"How <u>can</u> you go on talking so quietly, head downwards?" Alice asked, as she dragged him out by the
A12	93: 5	that, in her haste, she had put the Lizard in head downwards, and the poor little thing was waving its tail
T8	186: 4	on working all the same. In fact, the more head-downwards I am, the more I keep inventing new things."
T8	183:20	as the Knight fell heavily on the top of his head exactly in the path where Alice was walking. She was
A11	90:15	into this they slipped the guinea-pig, head first, and then sat upon it.)
T4	147:24	round the neck of Tweedledee, "to keep his head from being cut off," as he said.

HEAD (cont.)

T6	164:10	night," Humpty Dumpty went on, wagging his head gravely from side to side, "for to get their wages, you
T7	176:18	the poor King was nearly shaking off his head, he trembled so much.
T1	118:15	/ He left it dead, and with its head / He went galumphing back.
A4	32: 7	on the floor, and a bright idea came into her head. "If I eat one of these cakes," she thought, "it's sure
T6	161:10	then I don't know what would happen to his head! I'm afraid it would come off!"
A7	56:24	"The Dormouse shook its head impatiently, and said, without opening its eyes, "Of
A8	63:38	"Idiot!" said the Queen, tossing her head impatiently; and turning to Alice, she went on: "What's
A3	26:15	Yes, please do!" But the Mouse only shook its head impatiently, and walked a little quicker.
T3	129:33	Tickets, please!" said the Guard, putting his head in at the window. In a moment everybody was holding out a
T8	179: 2	all was dead silence, and Alice lifted up her head in some alarm. There was no one to be seen, and her first
A12	98: 1	and found herself lying on the bank, with her head in the lap of her sister, who was gently brushing away
T3	134:11	its body is a crust, and its head is a lump of sugar."
T3	133:14	its wings of holly-leaves, and its head is a raisin burning in brandy."
T8	184:30	'The only difficulty is with the feet: the head is high enough already.' Now, first I put my head on the
T8W	21: 2	the Wasp went on: "but the top of your head is nice and round." He took off his own wig as he spoke,
A7	58:10	A bright idea came into Alice's head. "Is that the reason so many tea-things are put out here
A6	46:28	came skimming out, straight at the Footman's head: it just grazed his nose, and broke to pieces against one
T8	185:13	The Knight shook his head. "It was all kinds of fastness with me, I can assure you!
A8	66:10	going to give the hedgehog a blow with its head, it would twist itself round and look up in her face,
T1	113:16	the table behind Alice, and made her turn her head just in time to see one of the White Pawns roll over and
T9	199:25	/ 'I've a sceptre in hand, I've a crown on my head. / Let the Looking-Glass creatures, whatever they be, /
T7	172:32	you buttered! It went through and through my head like an earthquake!"
T4	138:16	of the old song kept ringing through her head like the ticking of a clock, and she could hardly help
T8	187:37	live?' / And his answer trickled through my head, / Like water through a sieve.
A4	32:25	the trees, a little sharp bark just over her head made her look up in a great hurry.
T4	140:22	Oyster winked his eye, / And shook his heavy head--/ Meaning to say he did not choose / To leave the
A7	57:10	The Hatter shook his head mournfully. "Not I!" he replied. "We quarrelled last March
A9	72:37	the ground as she spoke; "either you or your head must be off, and that in about half no time! Take your
T2	123:23	"Why, all round her head, of course," the Rose replied. "I was wondering you
T9	200:14	There were three chairs at the head of the table: the Red and White Queens had already taken
T4	144:34	heap, and snoring loud--"fit to snore his head off!" as Tweedledum remarked.
A11	91: 1	"--and just take his head off outside," the Queen added to one of the officers; but
A8	64: 7	a wild beast, began screaming "Off with her head! Off with--"
T9	196:34	White Queen gave a deep sigh, and laid her head on Alice's shoulder. "I am so sleepy!" she moaned.
T3	134: 5	had taken a good look at the insect with its head on fire, and had thought to herself, "I wonder if that's
A12	98:13	sat still just as she left her, leaning her head on her hand, watching the setting sun, and thinking of
T3	131:20	saying "She must go by post, as she's got a head on her--" "She must be sent as a message by the telegraph
T8	184:31	is high enough already.' Now, first I put my head on the top of the gate--then the head's high enough--then
T3	129:23	(here came the favourite little toss of the head), 'only it was so dusty and hot, and the elephants did
A8	67: 1	stamping about, and shouting "Off with his head!" or "Off with her head!" about once in a minute.
A9	73: 4	the other players, and shouting "Off with his head!" or "Off with her head!" Those whom she sentenced were
T4	147: 5	bundling up in the umbrella, with only his head out: and there he lay, opening and shutting his mouth and
T9	198:10	way, and a creature with a long beak put its head out for a moment and said "No admittance till the week
T3	132: 5	The Horse, who had put his head out of the window, quietly drew it in and said "It's only
A4	32:39	made another rush at the stick, and tumbled head over heels in its hurry to get hold of it: then Alice,
A4	28:10	she had drunk half the bottle, she found her head pressing against the ceiling, and had to stoop to save
A12	95:36	The Knave shook his head sadly. "Do I look like it?" he said. (Which he certainly
T3	133:12	"Look on the branch above your head," said the Gnat, "and there you'll find a Snap-dragon-fly
T8	191: 3	glad I am to get here! And what is this on my head?" she exclaimed in a tone of dismay, as she put her hands
T2	127: 4	ears, and almost blowing her hair off her head, she fancied.
A8	68: 7	difficulties, great or small. "Off with his head!" she said without even looking round.
A5	42:19	be no chance of getting her hands up to her head, she tried to get her head down to them, and was
T8W	16:18	no," he said: "it's when you hold up your head--so--without bending your neck."
A4	28:19	the door, and the other arm curled round her head. Still she went on growing, and, as a last resource, she
A2	15:12	Just at this moment her head struck against the roof of the hall: in fact she was now
T3	134:15	A new difficulty came into Alice's head. "Supposing it couldn't find any?" she suggested.
T2	123:31	three inches high--and here she was, half a head taller than Alice herself!
A12	97: 5	"Off with her head!" the Queen shouted at the top of her voice. Nobody moved
T9	195: 3	"Fan her head!" the Red Queen anxiously interrupted. "She'll be
T8	184:32	the head's high enough--then I stand on my head--then the feet are high enough, you see--then I'm over,
A9	73: 5	"Off with his head!" or "Off with her head!" Those whom she sentenced were taken into custody by the
A1	10: 6	fountains, but she could not even get her head through the doorway; "and even if my head would go
T7	178: 2	of it, and it rang through and through her head till she felt quite deafened. She started to her feet and
A1	12:39	way?", holding her hand on the top of her head to feel which way it was growing; and she was quite
T1	114: 3	the Queen, for he was covered with ashes from head to foot.
A3	22:33	you do either!" And the Eaglet bent down its head to hide a smile: some of the other birds tittered audibly
A12	98:20	voice, and see that queer little toss of her head to keep back the wandering hair that would always get
T2	122:12	at them!" it panted, bending its quivering head towards Alice, "or they wouldn't dare to do it!"
T2	122:37	"As if you ever saw anybody! You keep your head under the leaves, and snore away there, till you know no
A8	68:37	argument was, that you couldn't cut off a head unless there was a body to cut it off from: that he had
A7	54: 5	their elbows on it, and talking over its head. "Very uncomfortable for the Dormouse," thought Alice;
A10	82:19	she got up, and began to repeat it, but her head was so full of the Lobster-Quadrille, that she hardly
T2	125: 3	right," said the Queen, patting her on the head, which Alice didn't like at all: "though, when you say
A8	67:38	coming up to Alice, and looking at the Cat's head with great curiosity.
T1	118:28	it out at all.) "Somehow it seems to fill my head with ideas--only I don't exactly know what they are!
A1	10: 6	her head through the doorway; "and even if my head would go through," thought poor Alice, "it would be of
T2	125:13	The Red Queen shook her head. "You may call it 'nonsense' if you like," she said, "but

HEADACHE (1)

T4	147:35	a low voice: "only to-day I happen to have a headache."

```
-HEADED [See BEHEADED]
-HEADING [See BEHEADING]
HEADLONG (1)
    T8   185:16   instantly rolled out of the saddle, and fell headlong into a deep ditch.
HEAD'S (2)
    A5    42: 7                              "Come, my head's free at last!" said Alice in a tone of delight, which
    T8   184:32   put my head on the top of the gate--then the head's high enough--then I stand on my head--then the feet are
HEADS (14)
    T5   156: 5   the same tall river-banks frowning over their heads.
    T8   180:11   seemed to be that they always fell on their heads; and the battle ended with their both falling off in
    A8    65: 9   been examining the roses. "Off with their heads!" and the procession moved on, three of the soldiers
    A8    65:17                               "Their heads are gone, if it please your Majesty!" the soldiers
    A4    30:30   Mind that loose slate--Oh, it's coming down! Heads below!" (a loud crash)--"Now, who did that?--It was Bill
    A8    63: 8   Queen was to find out, we should all have our heads cut off, you know. So you see, Miss, we're doing our
    A2    17:21   here. It'll be no use their putting their heads down and saying 'Come up again, dear!' I shall only look
    A2    17:26   of tears, "I do wish they would put their heads down! I am so very tired of being all alone here!"
    A1     8:41   out among the people that walk with their heads downwards! The antipathies, I think--" (she was rather
    T9   202:23   it: some of them put their glasses upon their heads like extinguishers, and drank all that trickled down
    A12   92: 4   skirt, upsetting all the jurymen on to the heads of the crowd below, and there they lay sprawling about,
    A8    65:16                               "Are their heads off?" shouted the Queen.
    A6    45: 8   had powdered hair that curled all over their heads. She felt very curious to know what it was all about,
    T9   197:22   listened so eagerly that, when the two great heads suddenly vanished from her lap, she hardly missed them.
HEALTH (4)
    T8   189: 6   gladly will I drink / Your Honour's noble health.'
    T8   189:14   for his wish that he / Might drink my noble health.
    T9   202:20   the Red Queen. "Meanwhile, we'll drink your health--Queen Alice's health!" she screamed at the top of her
    T9   202:21   we'll drink your health--Queen Alice's health!" she screamed at the top of her voice, and all the
HEAP (6)
    T4   144:34   was lying crumpled up into a sort of untidy heap, and snoring loud--"fit to snore his head off!" as
    T5   157: 1   her straight off the seat, and down among the heap of rushes.
    T8W   17:12   and all tangled and tumbled about like a heap of sea-weed. "You could make your wig much neater," she
    A1     9:19   suddenly, thump! thump! down she came upon a heap of sticks and dry leaves, and the fall was over.
    T8   185:25   him out by the feet, and laid him in a heap on the bank.
    T9   204:15   and candles came crashing down together in a heap on the floor.
HEAPS (2)
    T5   156:38   melted away almost like snow, as they lay in heaps at her feet--but Alice hardly noticed this, there were
    T7   169: 8   that the ground was soon covered with little heaps of men.
HEAR (34)
    TC   209: 6   and willing ear, / Pleased a simple tale to hear--
    TC   209:13              Children yet, the tale to hear, / Eager eye and willing ear, / Lovingly shall nestle
    T6   159:33   out loud, forgetting that Humpty Dumpty would hear her.
    T2   123:26   "She's coming!" cried the Larkspur. "I hear her footstep, thump, thump, along the gravel-walk!"
    T1   114:22   it was quite clear that he could neither hear her nor see her.
    A10   82:12   repeated thoughtfully. "I should like to hear her try and repeat something now. Tell her to begin." He
    T1   115:10   out, quite forgetting that the King couldn't hear her. "You make me laugh so that I can hardly hold you!
    T9   199:13   He was so hoarse that Alice could scarcely hear him.
    A9    74:18   rock, and, as they came nearer, Alice could hear him sighing as if his heart would break. She pitied him
    A9    74: 2   young lady to see the Mock Turtle, and to hear his history. I must go back and see after some executions
    T8   184:27   way of getting over a gate--would you like to hear it?"
    T6   166: 8   kind of sneeze in the middle: however, you'll hear it done, maybe--down in the wood yonder--and, when you've
    T6   164:17                              "Let's hear it," said Humpty Dumpty. "I can explain all the poems
    A1     9:25   Alice like the wind, and was just in time to hear it say, as it turned a corner, "Oh my ears and whiskers,
    T8   182:31                    "I should like to hear it, very much."
    T5   155:30                    "Didn't you hear me say 'Feather'?" the Sheep cried angrily, taking up
    T1   113:12   walking arm in arm--I don't think they can hear me," she went on, as she put her head closer down, "and
    T4   139:30            and she was not even surprised to hear music playing: it seemed to come from the tree under
    A8    67:24   and they all quarrel so dreadfully one ca'n't hear oneself speak--and they don't seem to have any rules in
    A10   81:38   tone. And the Gryphon added "Come, let's hear some of your adventures."
    T8   185:21   soles of his feet, she was much relieved to hear that he was talking on in his usual tone. "All kinds of
    A2    19:44   cats: nasty, low, vulgar things! Don't let me hear the name again!"
    T7   172:27   Alice was sorry for this, as she wanted to hear the news too. However, instead of whispering, he simply
    A1     7:12   Alice think it so very much out of the way to hear the Rabbit say to itself "Oh dear! Oh dear! I shall be
    A12   98:26   way through the neighbouring pool--she could hear the rattle of the teacups as the March Hare and his
    T1   109: 9                    "Do you hear the snow against the window-panes, Kitty? How nice and
    A12   98:19   eyes were looking up into hers--she could hear the very tones of her voice, and see that queer little
    T2   122:20   and it's enough to make one wither to hear the way they go on!"
    A6    49: 3   thing howled so, that Alice could hardly hear the words:--
    T9   199:38   near! / 'Tis an honour to see me, a favour to hear: / 'Tis a privilege high to have dinner and tea / Along
    T1   115:21   whisper--so low, that Alice could hardly hear what they said.
    A4    30:13   long silence after this, and Alice could only hear whispers now and then; such as "Sure, I don't like it,
    A6    46:13   such a noise inside, no one could possibly hear you." And certainly there was a most extraordinary noise
    A8    65:39   in a frightened tone. "The Queen will hear you! You see she came rather late, and the Queen said--"
HEARD (43) [See also OVERHEARD]
    A10   84: 5   by far the most confusing thing that I ever heard!"
    T8W   13: 1   she was just going to spring over, when she heard a deep sigh, which seemed to come from the wood behind
    T8   186:33   "Is it very long?" Alice asked, for she had heard a good deal of poetry that day.
    T9   204: 2                    At this moment she heard a hoarse laugh at her side, and turned to see what was
    A4    30:40   the chimney as she could, and waited till she heard a little animal (she couldn't guess of what sort it was)
    A2    15:25              After a time she heard a little pattering of feet in the distance, and she
    A3    26:42   In a little while, however, she again heard a little pattering of footsteps in the distance, and she
```

HEARD (cont.)

A4	29:37	She did not get hold of anything, but she heard a little shriek and a fall, and a crash of broken glass,
A4	29:18	of it altogether; but after a few minutes she heard a voice outside, and stopped to listen.
A4	30: 2	are you?" And then a voice she had never heard before, "Sure then I'm here! Digging for apples, yer
A7	58:26	it said in a hoarse, feeble voice, "I heard every word you fellows were saying."
T5	152: 9	soon as there was a chance of making herself heard. "Have you pricked your finger?"
A8	68:12	screaming with passion. She had already heard her sentence three of the players to be executed for
A9	70:17	this time, and was a little startled when she heard her voice close to her ear. "You're thinking about
A10	82:22	"'Tis the voice of the Lobster: I heard him declare / 'You have baked me too brown, I must sugar
T8	189: 7	I heard him then, for I had just / Completed my design / To keep
A10	85: 3	when a cry of "The trial's beginning!" was heard in the distance.
T3	131:37	small sigh, that she wouldn't have heard it at all, if it hadn't come quite close to her ear. The
A10	82:32	"Well, I never heard it before," said the Mock Turtle; "but it sounds
A4	27: 3	it went, as if it had lost something; and she heard it muttering to itself, "The Duchess! The Duchess! Oh my
A4	29:27	it, that attempt proved a failure. Alice heard it say to itself "Then I'll go round and get in at the
T6	166:10	in the wood yonder--and, when you've once heard it, you'll be quite content. Who's been repeating all
T2	125:14	'nonsense' if you like," she said, "but I've heard nonsense, compared with which that would be as sensible
A9	73:15	"I never saw one, or heard of one," said Alice.
A8	63:30	but she could not remember ever having heard of such a rule at processions; "and besides, what would
T5	150:14	repeated in great astonishment. "I never heard of such a thing!"
A9	76:24	"I never heard of 'Uglification,'" Alice ventured to say. "What is it?"
A9	76:26	lifted up both its paws in surprise. "Never heard of uglifying!" it exclaimed. "You know what to beautify
A8	62: 5	them, and, just as she came up to them, she heard one of them say "Look out now, Five! Don't go splashing
T9	199:23	door was flung open, and a shrill voice was heard singing:--
A7	57:17	"I've heard something like it," said Alice.
A2	19: 5	Just then she heard something splashing about in the pool a little way off,
A9	73:18	As they walked off together, Alice heard the King say in a low voice, to the company, generally,
A8	62:11	"You'd better not talk!" said Five. "I heard the Queen say only yesterday you deserved to be beheaded
A8	68:11	and see how the game was going on, as she heard the Queen's voice in the distance, screaming with
T12	208:13	on the other paw, and pretended it hadn't heard the question.
A4	29:32	Alice, and after waiting till she fancied she heard the Rabbit just under the window, she suddenly spread
A4	31:39	two they began moving about again, and Alice heard the Rabbit say "A barrowful will do, to begin with."
A2	20:16	if you don't like them!" When the Mouse heard this, it turned round and swam slowly back to her: its
TI	103: 8	I have not seen thy sunny face, / Nor heard thy silver laughter: / No thought of me shall find a
A4	31: 5	The first thing she heard was a general chorus of "There goes Bill!" then the
A12	95:21	the most important piece of evidence we've heard yet," said the King, rubbing his hands; "so now let the
T1	108:29	morning. Now you ca'n't deny it, Kitty: I heard you! What's that you say?" (pretending that the kitten

HEARING (5)

A4	30:22	She waited for some time without hearing anything more: at last came a rumbling of little
A5	36:27	after all it might tell her something worth hearing. For some minutes it puffed away without speaking; but
A6	46: 6	to run back into the wood for fear of their hearing her; and, when she next peeped out, the Fish-Footman
T4	144:23	Here she checked herself in some alarm, at hearing something that sounded to her like the puffing of a
A7	55:11	The Hatter opened his eyes very wide on hearing this; but all he said was "Why is a raven like a

HEARKEN (1)

TI	103:19	Come, hearken then, ere voice of dread, / With bitter tidings laden,

HEARS (1)

T8	186:36	but it's very, very beautiful. Everybody that hears me sing it--either it brings the tears into their eyes,

HEART (5)

T2	125:28	are!" she added in a tone of delight, and her heart began to beat quick with excitement as she went on.
A12	99: 5	all her riper years, the simple and loving heart of her childhood; and how she would gather about her
T6	167:15	My heart went hop, my heart went thump: / I filled the kettle at
T6	167:15	My heart went hop, my heart went thump: / I filled the kettle at the pump.
A9	74:18	Alice could hear him sighing as if his heart would break. She pitied him deeply. "What is his sorrow

HEARTH (2)

T1	113: 5	noticed several of the chessmen down in the hearth among the cinders; but in another moment, with a little
A6	47:11	cook, and a large cat, which was lying on the hearth and grinning from ear to ear.

HEARTH-RUG [HEARTHRUG] (3)

T1	107:18	again; and there it was, spread over the hearth-rug, all knots and tangles, with the kitten running
T12	207:15	Queen: then she went down on her knees on the hearth-rug, and put the kitten and the Queen to look at each
A2	15: 8	Hearthrug, near the Fender, (with Alice's love).

HEARTH-RUGS (1)

T4	147:14	full of things--such as bolsters, blankets, hearth-rugs, table-cloths, dish-covers, and coal-scuttles. "I

HEARTILY (2)

T8W	20: 1	"I'm very sorry for you," Alice said heartily: "and I think if your wig fitted a little better,
T8	183:14	to say than "Indeed?" but she said it as heartily as she could. They went on a little way in silence

HEARTS (8)

A8	63:27	procession, came THE KING AND THE QUEEN OF HEARTS.
A7	57:13	at the great concert given by the Queen of Hearts, and I had to sing
A8	63:25	noticing her. Then followed the Knave of Hearts, carrying the King's crown on a crimson velvet cushion;
A11	87:18	tarts, / All on a summer day: / The Knave of Hearts, he stole those tarts / And took them quite away!"
A8	63:21	in couples: they were all ornamented with hearts. Next came the guests, mostly Kings and Queens, and
A11	87:16	"The Queen of Hearts, she made some tarts, / All on a summer day: / The
A11	86: 1	The King and Queen of Hearts were seated on their throne when they arrived, with a
A8	63:36	"Who is this?" She said it to the Knave of Hearts, who only bowed and smiled in reply.

HEATHER (1)

T8	188:34	said 'I hunt for haddocks' eyes / Among the heather bright, / And work them into waistcoat-buttons / In

HEAVILY (1)

T8	183:20	suddenly as it had begun, as the Knight fell heavily on the top of his head exactly in the path where Alice

HEAVY (8)

T6	168:41	finished the sentence, for at this moment a heavy crash shook the forest from end to end.

HEAVY (cont.)
T4   140:22   eldest Oyster winked his eye, / And shook his heavy head--/ Meaning to say he did not choose / To leave the
T9   197:14   rolled down from her shoulder, and lay like a heavy lump in her lap. "I don't think it ever happened before,
A9   74:36   "Hjckrrh!" from the Gryphon, and the constant heavy sobbing of the Mock Turtle. Alice was very nearly
A12   99: 2   would take the place of the Mock Turtle's heavy sobs.
T8   191: 5   as she put her hands up to something very heavy, that fitted tight all around her head.
T9   197:18   than one Queen at a time. Do wake up, you heavy things!" she went on in an impatient tone; but there was
T8   189:20   shoe, / Or if I drop upon my toe / A very heavy weight, / I weep, for it reminds me so / Of that old man

HE'D (2)
A7   56:43   Now, if you only kept on good terms with him, he'd do almost anything you liked with the clock. For instance
T7   172:22   "He ca'n't do that," said the King, "or else he'd have been here first. However, now you've got your breath

HEDGE (2)
A1   8: 4   see it pop down a large rabbit-hole under the hedge.
A4   31: 9   Rabbit's voice alone--"Catch him, you by the hedge!" then silence, and then another confusion of voices--

HEDGEHOG (7)
A8   68:16   turn or not. So she went off in search of her hedgehog.
A8   66:10   straightened out, and was going to give the hedgehog a blow with its head, it would twist itself round and
A8   66:14   again, it was very provoking to find that the hedgehog had unrolled itself, and was in the act of crawling
A8   67:29   and I should have croqueted the Queen's hedgehog just now, only it ran away when it saw mine coming!"
A8   66:16   in the way wherever she wanted to send the hedgehog to, and, as the doubled-up soldiers were always
A8   68:17   The hedgehog was engaged in a fight with another hedgehog, which
A8   68:17   hedgehog was engaged in a fight with another hedgehog, which seemed to Alice an excellent opportunity for

HEDGEHOGS (3)
A8   66:21   all the while, and fighting for the hedgehogs; and in a very short time the Queen was in a furious
A8   66: 3   and furrows: the croquet balls were live hedgehogs, and the mallets live flamingoes, and the soldiers
A8   68:23   it back, the fight was over, and both the hedgehogs were out of sight: "but it doesn't matter much,"

HEDGES (3)
T9   194:43   the White Queen asked: "In a garden or in the hedges?"
T2   125:23   up into squares by a number of little green hedges, that reached from brook to brook.
A5   42:34   trees, and I've tried banks, and I've tried hedges," the Pigeon went on, without attending to her; "but

HEED (1)
TI   103:30   words shall hold thee fast: / Thou shalt not heed the raving blast.

HEELS (2)
T4   148:22   of alarm; and the two brothers took to their heels and were out of sight in a moment.
A4   32:39   rush at the stick, and tumbled head over heels in its hurry to get hold of it: then Alice, thinking it

HEIGHT (5)
A5   43:36   in bringing herself down to her usual height.
A4   34: 4   mushroom growing near her, about the same height as herself; and, when she had looked under it, and on
A5   41:16   "It is a very good height indeed!" said the Caterpillar angrily, rearing itself
A5   41:15   said Alice: "three inches is such a wretched height to be."
A9   70:27   secondly, because she was exactly the right height to rest her chin on Alice's shoulder, and it was an

HELD (13)
T4   144:16   though," said Tweedledee. "You see he held his handkerchief in front, so that the Carpenter couldn't
T1   115: 4   face as the King made, when he found himself held in the air by an invisible hand, and being dusted: he was
A4   32:34   did, she picked up a little bit of stick, and held it out to the puppy: whereupon the puppy jumped into the
T1   110:27   fold its arms properly. So, to punish it, she held it up to the Looking-glass, that it might see how sulky
T3   136: 9   "Here then! Here then!" Alice said, as she held out her hand and tried to stroke it; but it only started
T6   168:19   hardly be civil to stay. So she got up, and held out her hand. "Good-bye, till we meet again!" she said as
A6   49:16   as it was a queer-shaped little creature, and held out its arms and legs in all directions, "just like a
T4   139:23   brothers gave each other a hug, and then they held out the two hands that were free, to shake hands with her
T8   182:15   This took a long time to manage, though Alice held the bag open very carefully, because the Knight was so
A5   43:32   After a while she remembered that she still held the pieces of mushroom in her hands, and she set to work
T1   107: 7   her children's faces was this: first she held the poor thing down by its ear with one paw, and then
A4   32:14   little Lizard, Bill, was in the middle, being held up by two guinea-pigs, who were giving it something out
T1   110:40   go the wrong way: I know that, because I've held up one of our books to the glass, and then they hold up

HE'LL (2)
A4   27:19   said to herself as she ran. "How surprised he'll be when he finds out who I am! But I'd better take him
T4   144:36   "I'm afraid he'll catch cold with lying on the damp grass," said Alice,

HELMET (10)
T8   185: 5   came and put it on. He thought it was his own helmet."
T8   181: 7   said Alice. "May I help you off with your helmet?" It was evidently more than he could manage by himself
T8   185:10   said, very seriously. "And then he took the helmet off again--but it took hours and hours to get me out. I
T8   185:23   it was careless of him to put another man's helmet on--with the man in it, too."
T4   147:31   to have his helmet tied on. (He called it a helmet, though it certainly looked much more like a saucepan
T4   147:31   pale?" said Tweedledum, coming up to have his helmet tied on. (He called it a helmet, though it certainly
T8   179:35   the White Knight remarked, putting on his helmet too.
T8   179:32   then," said the Red Knight, as he took up his helmet (which hung from the saddle, and was something the
T8   184:41   The Knight looked down proudly at his helmet, which hung from the saddle. "Yes," he said; "but I've
T8   184:39   changed the subject hastily. "What a curious helmet you've got!" she said cheerfully. "Is that your

HELP (41)
T6   168:31   or the mouth at the top--that would be some help."
T3   136:19   she said timidly. "I think that might help a little."
T7   170:30   "I love my love with an H," Alice couldn't help beginning, "because he is Happy. I hate him with an H,
A8   66:12   such a puzzled expression that she could not help bursting out laughing; and, when she had got its head
T9   201:18   It was so large that she couldn't help feeling a little shy with it, as she had been with the
T6   162:10   "I mean," she said, "that one ca'n't help growing older."
T7   175: 2   "But aren't you going to run and help her?" Alice asked, very much surprised at his taking it
T7   175:27   Alice could not help her lips curling up into a smile as she began: "Do you
T3   136: 5   to do it!" But being determined didn't help her much, and all she could say, after a great deal of
T8W   13:13   everything will change, and then I can't help him."

HELP (cont.)
```
T8W    14:11        The Wasp took her arms, and let her help him round the tree, but when he got settled down again he
T1    108: 9   touching the ball, as if it would be glad to help if it might.
A11   88:41                             "I ca'n't help it," said Alice very meekly: "I'm growing."
A8    62: 7                            "I couldn't help it," said Five, in a sulky tone. "Seven jogged my elbow."
A6    46:23   decidedly uncivil. "But perhaps he ca'n't help it," she said to herself; "his eyes are so very nearly at
T5   150: 1                        Alice couldn't help laughing, as she said "I don't want you to hire me--and I
T5   152:40                      Alice could not help laughing at this, even in the midst of her tears. "Can
T6   160:24   so solemn and grand that Alice could hardly help laughing. "If I did fall," he went on, "the King has
T5   155:10   fourteen pairs at once, and Alice couldn't help looking at her in great astonishment.
T8   182:10     "It's an invention of my own. And now help me on. I'll go with you to the end of the wood--What's
A4    30: 5   indeed!" said the Rabbit angrily. "Here! Come help me out of this!" (Sounds of more broken glass.)
T8   182:14   It'll come in handy if we find any plum-cake. Help me to get it into this bag."
A2    15:31   felt so desperate that she was ready to ask help of any one: so, when the Rabbit came near her, she began,
T2   123:16     to fade, you know--and then one ca'n't help one's petals getting a little untidy."
T4   139:14   of great schoolboys, that Alice couldn't help pointing her finger at Tweedledum, and saying "First Boy!"
T9   196:23   stroking it: "she means well, but she ca'n't help saying foolish things as a general rule."
T4   145:16   He shouted this so loud that Alice couldn't help saying "Hush! You'll be waking him, I'm afraid, if you
T4   138:17   the ticking of a clock, and she could hardly help saying them out loud:--
T6   168:37   she quietly walked away: but she couldn't help saying to herself, as she went, "of all the
T6   163: 6                        Alice couldn't help smiling as she took out her memorandum-book, and worked
T3   137:31   little men, so suddenly that she could not help starting back, but in another moment she recovered
A6    51:23              "Oh, you ca'n't help that," said the Cat: "we're all mad here. I'm mad. You're
T8   182:38   the idea, and every now and then stopping to help the poor Knight, who certainly was not a good rider.
A9    74:38   your interesting story," but she could not help thinking there must be more to come, so she sat still and
T9   194:24   might go different ways." But she couldn't help thinking to herself "What dreadful nonsense we are
T12  208:11   my dear, so you ought to know--Oh, Kitty, do help to settle it! I'm sure your paw can wait!" But the
A3    26: 7   looking anxiously about her. "Oh, do let me help to undo it!"
T4   147:11   crawled out of the umbrella: "only she must help us to dress up, you know."
T1   114:20   to the table, at that rate. I'd far better help you, hadn't I?" But the King took no notice of the
T8   181: 6   "Thank you very much," said Alice. "May I help you off with your helmet?" It was evidently more than he
T8W    14: 9                    "Won't you let me help you round to the other side? You'll be out of the cold
```
HELPED (2)
```
T5   149: 6     to be in the way," Alice said, as she helped her to put on her shawl again.
A7    59:18   not quite know what to say to this: so she helped herself to some tea and bread-and-butter, and then
```
HELPING (1)
```
T8   183: 4   in riding," she ventured to say, as she was helping him up from his fifth tumble.
```
HELPLESS (2)
```
T5   149: 7   The White Queen only looked at her in a helpless frightened sort of way, and kept repeating something
A8    68:21   garden, where Alice could see it trying in a helpless sort of way to fly up into a tree.
```
HER (534) [entries omitted]
HERALD (1)
```
A11   87:13                             "Herald, read the accusation!" said the King.
```
HERE (110)
```
A2    17:27   down! I am so very tired of being all alone here!"
A4    29: 8   "at least there's no room to grow up any more here."
A6    51: 8   tell me, please, which way I ought to go from here?"
A6    51:18   question. "What sort of people live about here?"
A6    51:26   be," said the Cat, "or you wouldn't have come here."
A8    65: 5     she went on "What have you been doing here?"
T2   123:19   subject, she asked "Does she ever come out here?"
T2   123:34   the Rose: "wonderfully fine air it is, out here."
T3   137: 2     on," the Fawn said. "I ca'n't remember here."
T5   152:22   "Now you understand the way things happen here."
T9   201:33   know why they're so fond of fishes, all about here?"
T8W    14: 2   you?" Alice went on. "Aren't you rather cold here?"
A1     9:11   know. But do cats eat bats, I wonder?" And here Alice began to get rather sleepy, and went on saying to
T5   152:33           "Only it is so very lonely here!" Alice said in a melancholy voice; and, at the thought
T4   140:19                       Here Alice ventured to interrupt him. "If it's very long," she
T1   108:16   we'll go and see the bonfire to-morrow." Here Alice wound two or three turns of the worsted round the
T6   160:11   "Why do you sit out here all alone?" said Alice, not wishing to begin an argument.
T6   164: 2   do next, as I suppose you don't mean to stop here all the rest of your life."
T5   158:21   I declare! How very odd to find trees growing here! And actually here's a little brook! Well, this is the
T1   112: 8   be, when they see me through the glass in here, and ca'n't get at me!"
A3    26:38   tone. "Nobody seems to like her, down here, and I'm sure she's the best cat in the world! Oh, my
T5   149:27   "It's out of temper, I think. I've pinned it here, and I've pinned it there, but there's no pleasing it!"
A8    69: 9   the Queen said to the executioner: "fetch her here." And the executioner went off like an arrow.
A9    71:18   said: "there's a large mustard-mine near here. And the moral of that is--'The more there is of mine,
T2   127:34     the ground, and sticking little pegs in here and there.
T8   191: 2   moss, with little flowerbeds dotted about it here and there. "Oh, how glad I am to get here! And what is
A1     8:16   were filled with cupboards and book-shelves: here and there she saw maps and pictures hung upon pegs. She
T3   135: 2   you to your lessons, she would call out 'Come here--,' and there she would have to leave off, because there
A3    23:10   all the party were placed along the course, here and there. There was no "One, two, three, and away!", but
T8   191: 3   it here and there. "Oh, how glad I am to get here! And what is this on my head?" she exclaimed in a tone of
T8   179:20   saddle, he began once more "You're my--" but here another voice broke in "Ahoy! Ahoy! Check!" and Alice
A4    30:21   they could! I'm sure I don't want to stay in here any longer!"
T1   113: 8                       "Here are the Red King and the Red Queen," Alice said (in a
T1   113:11   Queen sitting on the edge of the shovel--and here are two Castles walking arm in arm--I don't think they
T1   112: 5   she had left behind. "So I shall be as warm here as I was in the old room," thought Alice: "warmer, in
T3   131: 9   he went on with "She'll have to go back from here as luggage!"
```

```
HERE (cont.)
  T2  124:13  here belong to me--but why did you come out here at all?" she added in a kinder tone. "Curtsey while
  A1   10:16  little bottle on it ("which certainly was not here before," said Alice), and tied round the neck of the
  T2  124:12  way," said the Queen: "all the ways about here belong to me--but why did you come out here at all?" she
  A4   30:29  they'll do well enough. Don't be particular--Here, Bill! Catch hold of this rope--Will the roof bear?--Mind
  A4   30:33  That I wo'n't, then!--Bill's got to go down--Here, Bill! The master says you've got to go down the chimney!
  T3  129:23  I shall say 'Oh, I liked it well enough--' (here came the favourite little toss of the head), 'only it was
  A4   30: 4  apples, indeed!" said the Rabbit angrily. "Here! Come help me out of this!" (Sounds of more broken glass
  A12  92: 1                                          "Here!" cried Alice, quite forgetting in the flurry of the
  A4   30: 3  she had never heard before, "Sure then I'm here! Digging for apples, yer honour!"
  A4   27:30  thing that would happen: "'Miss Alice! Come here directly, and get ready for your walk!' 'Coming in a
  T7  172:22  that," said the King, "or else he'd have been here first. However, now you've got your breath, you may tell
  T4  146:21  and tear his hair. "It's spoilt, of course!" Here he looked at Tweedledee, who immediately sat down on the
  T6  160:22  which there's no chance of--but if I did--" Here he pursed up his lips, and looked so solemn and grand
  A6   46:39  his remark, with variations. "I shall sit here," he said, "on and off, for days and days."
  T9  204: 4  was the leg of mutton sitting in the chair. "Here I am!" cried a voice from the soup-tureen, and Alice
  A4   29: 5  that kind of thing never happened, and now here I am in the middle of one! There ought to be a book
  A3   26:22              "I wish I had our Dinah here, I know I do!" said Alice aloud, addressing nobody in
  T8  186:28  such as gunpowder and sealing-wax. And here I must leave you." They had just come to the end of the
  T1  110: 9  my pieces. Kitty dear, let's pretend--" And here I wish I could tell you half the things Alice used to say
  A6   51:23  help that," said the Cat: "we're all mad here. I'm mad. You're mad."
  A2   17:21  mind about it: if I'm Mabel, I'll stay down here. It'll be no use their putting their heads down and
  T8  182:26      "You see the wind is so very strong here. It's as strong as soup."
  A4   30:26  but one. Bill's got the other--Bill! Fetch it here, lad!--Here, put 'em up at this corner--No, tie 'em
  T9  202:11                              'Bring it here! Let me sup!' / It is easy to set such a dish on the
  T4  146: 6  think it is," he said: "at least--not under here. Nohow."
  A2   19:14  this pool? I am very tired of swimming about here, O Mouse!" (Alice thought this must be the right way of
  A11  90:11                                          Here one of the guinea-pigs cheered, and was immediately
  T2  127:24      said Alice. "I'm quite content to stay here--only I am so hot and thirsty!"
  A8   63: 6  voice, "Why, the fact is, you see, Miss, this here ought to have been a red rose-tree, and we put a white
  A3   26:40  wonder if I shall ever see you any more!" And here poor Alice began to cry again, for she felt very lonely
  A4   30:26  got the other--Bill! Fetch it here, lad!--Here, put 'em up at this corner--No, tie 'em together first--
  A4   27:14  tone, "Why, Mary Ann, what are you doing out here? Run home this moment, and fetch me a pair of gloves and
  T5  157:11              "Are there many crabs here?" said Alice.
  A3   23:34              "Hand it over here," said the Dodo.
  A11  88:42      "You've no right to grow here," said the Dormouse.
  A7   58:11  the reason so many tea-things are put out here?" she asked.
  T4  144:26  beast. "Are there any lions or tigers about here?" she asked timidly.
  T9  192:25  the Queen. "Why, don't you see, child--" here she broke off with a frown, and, after thinking for a
  T4  144:22  They were both very unpleasant characters--" Here she checked herself in some alarm, at hearing something
  T5  154:16              "Things flow about so here!" she said at last in a plaintive tone, after she had
  T4  145:25  under a large tree. "It can never get at me here," she thought: "it's far too large to squeeze itself in
  T2  123:31  she had been only three inches high--and here she was, half a head taller than Alice herself!
  T1  113:15                                          Here something began squeaking on the table behind Alice, and
  A2   19:11  mouse? Everything is so out-of-the-way down here, that I should think very likely it can talk: at any rate
  A7   55:31  same thing with you," said the Hatter, and here the conversation dropped, and the party sat silent for a
  A7   58: 1                                          here the Dormouse shook itself, and began singing in its sleep
  T3  137: 5  they came out into another open field, and here the Fawn gave a sudden bound into the air, and shook
  A6   46:26              "I shall sit here," the Footman remarked, "till to-morrow--"
  A8   67: 6  They're dreadfully fond of beheading people here: the great wonder is, that there's any one left alive!"
  T7  176:23                                          Here the King interrupted, to prevent the quarrel going on: he
  A10  81: 1  tails in their mouths; and the reason is--" here the Mock Turtle yawned and shut his eyes. "Tell her about
  A11  90:26                                          Here the other guinea-pig cheered, and was suppressed.
  A11  88:26                                          Here the Queen put on her spectacles, and began staring hard
  T9  194:39                                          Here the Red Queen began again. "Can you answer useful
  T9  194:18                              "Why, look here!" the Red Queen cried. "The dog would lose its temper,
  T8  183:18  his right arm as he spoke, "is to keep--" Here the sentence ended as suddenly as it had begun, as the
  T4  139:22  to say 'How d'ye do?' and shake hands!" And here the two brothers gave each other a hug, and then they
  T9  196:11                                          Here the White Queen began again. "It was such a thunderstorm,
  T3  136: 9  didn't seem at all frightened. "Here then! Here then!" Alice said, as she held out her hand and tried to
  T3  136: 8  eyes, but didn't seem at all frightened. "Here then! Here then!" Alice said, as she held out her hand
  T2  122: 7  you know that?" cried another Daisy. And here they all began shouting together, till the air seemed
  A9   74:13      "Everybody says 'come on!' here," thought Alice, as she went slowly after it: "I never
  A2   17:24  person, I'll come up: if not, I'll stay down here till I'm somebody else'--but, oh dear!" cried Alice, with
  A9   72:29                              But here, to Alice's great surprise, the Duchess's voice died away
  T1  112: 7  "warmer, in fact, because there'll be no one here to scold me away from the fire. Oh, what fun it'll be,
  A5   36:15                                          Here was another puzzling question; and, as Alice could not
  T4  139:36  of all this), "to find myself singing 'Here we go round the mulberry bush.' I don't know when I began
  T9  195:32  "That's a poor thin way of doing things. Now here, we mostly have days and nights two or three at a time,
  A4   29:14  herself. "How can you learn lessons in here? Why, there's hardly room for you, and no room at all for
  A1   9: 9      Dinah, my dear! I wish you were down here with me! There are no mice in the air, I'm afraid, but
  T2  121:14  you sometimes frightened at being planted out here, with nobody to take care of you?"
  A6   49:10                      "Here! You may nurse it a bit, if you like!" the Duchess said
  T2  127:19  slow sort of country!" said the Queen. "Now, here, you see, it takes all the running you can do, to keep in
  A9   74:25      "This here young lady," said the Gryphon, "she wants for to know
HEREAFTER (1)
  TI  103:10  me shall find a place / In thy young life's hereafter--/ Enough that now thou wilt not fail / To listen to
HERE'S (4)
  T5  158:22  odd to find trees growing here! And actually here's a little brook! Well, this is the very queerest shop I
  T2  120: 2  "if I could get to the top of that hill: and here's a path that leads straight to it--at least, no, it
```

HERE'S (cont.)
    T6   161:20   as if it was a game!" thought Alice.) "So here's a question for you. How old did you say you were?"
    T4   145:27   so--it makes quite a hurricane in the wood--here's somebody's shawl being blown away!"
HEROES (1)
    T4   139: 3   as a tar-barrel; / Which frightened both the heroes so, / They quite forgot their quarrel."
HERS (4) [entries omitted]
HERSELF (163) [entries omitted]
HE'S (11)
    T7   170:26   "Not at all," said the King. "He's an Anglo-Saxon Messenger--and those are Anglo-Saxon
    T7   170:22   somebody now!" she exclaimed at last. "But he's coming very slowly--and what curious attitudes he goes
    T4   145: 2   now," said Tweedledee: "and what do you think he's dreaming about?"
    T4   145: 1   "He's dreaming now," said Tweedledee: "and what do you think
    T7   170:28   Anglo-Saxon attitudes. He only does them when he's happy. His name is Haigha." (He pronounced it so as to
    T5   150: 4   as she spoke, "there's the King's Messenger. He's in prison now, being punished: and the trial doesn't even
    A7   58: 5   said the Hatter, "when the Queen bawled out 'He's murdering the time! Off with his head!'"
    T7   173:23   "He's only just out of prison, and he hadn't quite finished his tea
    A6   46:44   in talking to him," said Alice desperately: "he's perfectly idiotic!" And she opened the door and went in.
    A10   79:14   / "There's a porpoise close behind us, and he's treading on my tail. / See how eagerly the lobsters and
    T7   173:25   give them oyster-shells in there--so you see he's very hungry and thirsty. How are you, dear child?" he
HESITATING (1)
    T7   170:35   joining in the game, while Alice was still hesitating for the name of a town beginning with H. "The other
HID (1)
    A9   77: 9   sighing in his turn; and both creatures hid their faces in their paws.
HIDE (2)
    A3   22:33   either!" And the Eaglet bent down its head to hide a smile: some of the other birds tittered audibly.
    T4   146:23   sat down on the ground, and tried to hide himself under the umbrella.
HIDEOUS (1)
    T7   170:32   is Happy. I hate him with an H, because he is Hideous. I fed him with--with--with Ham-sandwiches and Hay.
HIDING-PLACE (1)
    T8   180: 3   the fight, timidly peeping out from her hiding-place. "One Rule seems to be, that if one Knight hits
HIGH (22)
    A2   18:27   which she had wept when she was nine feet high.
    A5   41:17   as it spoke (it was exactly three inches high).
    A5   44: 6   she had brought herself down to nine inches high.
    A12   93:40   "Nearly two miles high," added the Queen.
    A1   12: 3   so it was indeed: she was now only ten inches high, and her face brightened up at the thought that she was
    T2   123:31   in the ashes, she had been only three inches high--and here she was, half a head taller than Alice
    A2   15:13   fact she was now rather more than nine feet high, and she at once took up the little golden key and
    A2   18: 6   she could guess, she was now about two feet high, and was going on shrinking rapidly: she soon found out
    T8   184:31   only difficulty is with the feet: the head is high enough already.' Now, first I put my head on the top of
    T8   184:32   head on the top of the gate--then the head's high enough--then I stand on my head--then the feet are high
    A4   30:27   tie 'em together first--they don't reach half high enough yet--Oh, they'll do well enough. Don't be
    T8   184:33   then I stand on my head--then the feet are high enough, you see--then I'm over, you see."
    A6   53:15   and raised herself to about two feet high: even then she walked up towards it rather timidly,
    A12   93:38   "I'm not a mile high," said Alice.
    A1   9:41   it was a little door about fifteen inches high: she tried the little golden key in the lock, and to her
    A7   61: 4   it in her pocket) till she was about a foot high; then she walked down the little passage: and then--she
    A2   20:21   It was high time to go, for the pool was getting quite crowded with
    A3   26:35   to its children, "Come away, my dears! It's high time you were all in bed!" On various pretexts they all
    T9   199:39   see me, a favour to hear: / 'Tis a privilege high to have dinner and tea / Along with the Red Queen, the
    A12   93:35   "Rule Forty-two. All persons more than a mile high to leave the court."
    T6   159: 9   his legs crossed like a Turk, on the top of a high wall--such a narrow one that Alice quite wondered how he
    A5   44: 2   with a little house in it about four feet high. "Whoever lives there," thought Alice, "it'll never do to
HIGHER (1)
    T5   151:22   and better, and better!" Her voice went higher with each "better," till it got quite to a squeak at
HIGHEST (1)
    A5   43: 1   "And just as I'd taken the highest tree in the wood," continued the Pigeon, raising its
HILL (15)
    T2   125: 7   I'd try and find my way to the top of that hill--"
    T2   125:18   till they got to the top of the little hill.
    T8W   21:16   said the Wasp, and Alice tripped down the hill again, quite pleased that she had gone back and given a
    T2   120: 2   herself, "if I could get to the top of that hill: and here's a path that leads straight to it--at least,
    T3   129:28   So, with this excuse, she ran down the hill, and jumped over the first of the six little brooks. * *
    T8   190:35   him," she said, as she turned to run down the hill: "and now for the last brook, and to be a Queen! How
    T8   190:14   only a few yards to go," he said, "down the hill and over that little brook, and then you'll be a Queen--
    T3   129:19   just as she was beginning to run down the hill, and trying to find some excuse for turning shy so
    T2   125:11   surprised into contradicting her at last: "a hill ca'n't be a valley, you know. That would be nonsense--"
    T2   120:20   to keep straight on till she got to the hill. For a few minutes all went on well, and she was just
    T2   120:26   However, there was the hill full in sight, so there was nothing to be done but start
    T2   120: 6   than a path! Well this turn goes to the hill, I suppose--no, it doesn't! This goes straight back to
    T2   124: 5   with the Red Queen, and full in sight of the hill she had been so long aiming at.
    T7   170:34   "He lives on the Hill," the King remarked simply, without the least idea that
    T2   125: 8   "When you say 'hill'," the Queen interrupted, "I could show you hills, in
HILLS (1)
    T2   125: 9   the Queen interrupted, "I could show you hills, in comparison with which you'd call that a valley."
HIM (119) [entries omitted]
HIMSELF (22) [entries omitted]
HINDERING (1)
    T8W   14:18   to," the Wasp said, rather sulkily. "Nobody's hindering you, that I know of."

HINT (4)
     A6   48:29 at the cook, to see if she meant to take the hint; but the cook was busily stirring the soup, and seemed
     T8W   21: 5 she kept out of reach, and would not take the hint. So he went on with his criticisms.
     T6   168:18 Alice thought: but, after such a very strong hint that she ought to be going, she felt that it would hardly
     A7   57: 1 begin lessons: you'd only have to whisper a hint to Time, and round goes the clock in a twinkling!
HIPPOPOTAMUS (2)
     A2   19: 7 at first she thought it must be a walrus or hippopotamus, but then she remembered how small she was now,
     T9   196: 5 Queen went on, "because he was looking for a hippopotamus. Now, as it happened, there wasn't such a thing
HIRE (1)
     T5   150: 2 laughing, as she said "I don't want you to hire me--and I don't care for jam."
HIS (253) [entries omitted]
HISS (1)
     A5   42:24 which she had been wandering, when a sharp hiss made her draw back in a hurry: a large pigeon had flown
HISTORY (11)
     A9   73:16 said the Queen, "and he shall tell you his history."
     A2   19:23 Conqueror." (For, with all her knowledge of history, Alice had no very clear notion how long ago anything
     A2   20:19 get to the shore, and then I'll tell you my history, and you'll understand why it is I hate cats and dogs
     A9   74: 2 lady to see the Mock Turtle, and to hear his history. I must go back and see after some executions I have
     T4   139:35   when she was telling her sister the history of all this), "to find myself singing 'Here we go
     T9   197:16 two Queens asleep at once! No, not in all the History of England--it couldn't, you know, because there never
     T6   160:36 in a calmer tone. "That's what you call a History of England, that is. Now, take a good look at me! I'm
     T9   202:39   when she was telling her sister the history of her feast. "You would have thought they wanted to
     A12   93:12 set to work very diligently to write out a history of the accident, all except the Lizard, who seemed too
     A9   74:26 said the Gryphon, "she wants for to know your history, she do."
     A3   24:14   "You promised to tell me your history, you know," said Alice, "and why it is you hate--C and
HIT (5)
     T4   148: 1 not come very close," he added: "I generally hit every thing I can see--when I get really excited."
     T4   148: 2   "And I hit every thing within reach," cried Tweedledum, "whether I
     A6   48:13 Duchess took no notice of them even when they hit her; and the baby was howling so much already, that it was
     A4   32: 2 rattling in at the window, and some of them hit her in the face. "I'll put a stop to this," she said to
     T4   148: 4   Alice laughed. "You must hit the trees pretty often, I should think," she said.
HITS (1)
     T8   180: 3 "One Rule seems to be, that if one Knight hits the other, he knocks him off his horse; and, if he misses
HJCKRRH (1)
     A9   74:35 broken only by an occasional exclamation of "Hjckrrh!" from the Gryphon, and the constant heavy sobbing of
HM (1)
     A10   84:13 the Gryphon said, in a rather offended tone, "Hm! No accounting for tastes! Sing her 'Turtle Soup,' will you
HOARSE (8)
     A2   17: 5 and began to repeat it, but her voice sounded hoarse and strange, and the words did not come the same as
     A7   58:26 its eyes. "I wasn't asleep," it said in a hoarse, feeble voice, "I heard every word you fellows were
     A6   48:21 their own business," the Duchess said, in a hoarse growl, "the world would go round a deal faster than it
     T9   204: 2   At this moment she heard a hoarse laugh at her side, and turned to see what was the
     T9   199:13 said. "What's it been asking of?" He was so hoarse that Alice could scarcely hear him.
     T3   131:11 see who was sitting beyond the Beetle, but a hoarse voice spoke next. "Change engines--" it said, and there
     T9   199: 1 "What is it, now?" the Frog said in a deep hoarse whisper.
     T3   131:15 a joke on that--something about 'horse' and 'hoarse,' you know."
HOARSELY (1)
     A4   32:44 each time and a long way back, and barking hoarsely all the while, till at last it sat down a good way
HOBBLED (2)
     T9   199:21 "You let it alone," he panted out, as he hobbled back to his tree, "and it'll let you alone, you know
     T9   198:13 who was sitting under a tree, got up and hobbled slowly towards her: he was dressed in bright yellow,
HOLD (29)
     T5   154:15 round it were crowded as full as they could hold.
     T5   152: 7 whistle of a steam-engine, that Alice had to hold both her hands over her ears.
     A6   49:20 or two, it was as much as she could do to hold it.
     A1   11: 1 as, that a red-hot poker will burn you if you hold it too long; and that, if you cut your finger very deeply
     T1   116:15 a Looking-glass book, of course! And, if I hold it up to a glass, the words will all go the right way
     T8   183: 7 as he scrambled back into the saddle, keeping hold of Alice's hair with one hand, to save himself from
     A4   29:36 and made a snatch in the air. She did not get hold of anything, but she heard a little shriek and a fall,
     T4   139:27 the best way out of the difficulty, she took hold of both hands at once: the next moment they were dancing
     A4   32:39 tumbled head over heels in its hurry to get hold of it: then Alice, thinking it was very like having a
     A6   49:24 up into a sort of knot, and then keep tight hold of its right ear and left foot, so as to prevent its
     T1   119: 8 door in the same way, if she hadn't caught hold of the door-post. She was getting a little giddy with so
     T9   203: 5 as she spoke, several inches; but she got hold of the edge of the table, and managed to pull herself
     T1   115:31 A sudden thought struck her, and she took hold of the end of the pencil, which came some way over his
     T9   204:25 now. "As for you," she repeated, catching hold of the little creature in the very act of jumping over a
     T8W   20:12 "If you was a-fighting, now--could you get hold of the other one by the back of the neck?"
     T5   156:18 arms were plunged in elbow-deep, to get hold of the rushes a good long way down before breaking them
     A4   30:29   Don't be particular--Here, Bill! Catch hold of this rope--Will the roof bear?--Mind that loose slate
     TI   103:29 nest of gladness. / The magic words shall hold thee fast: / Thou shalt not heed the raving blast.
     T8   180: 5 and another Rule seems to be that they hold their clubs with their arms, as if they were Punch and
     A4   31:11 and another confusion of voices--"Hold his head--Brandy now--Don't choke him--How was it, old
     T1   110:41 one of our books to the glass, and then they hold up one in the other room.
     T8W   16:18 a little. "Well, no," he said: "it's when you hold up your head--so--without bending your neck."
     T7   175:40 cake out of the bag, and gave it to Alice to hold, while he got out a dish and carving-knife. How they all
     T1   115:11 her. "You make me laugh so that I can hardly hold you! And don't keep your mouth so wide open! All the
     A9   76: 3   "Hold your tongue!" added the Gryphon, before Alice could speak
     T2   122:36   "Hold your tongue!" cried the Tiger-lily. "As if you ever saw
     A3   26:19 a lesson to you never to lose your temper!" "Hold your tongue, Ma!" said the young Crab, a little
     A12   97: 3   "Hold your tongue!" said the Queen, turning purple.

HOLD (cont.)
T2   122:15   beginning again, she whispered "If you don't hold your tongues, I'll pick you!"
HOLDING (11)
A2   18: 8   that the cause of this was the fan she was holding, and she dropped it hastily, just in time to save
A1   12:39   anxiously to herself "Which way? Which way?", holding her hand on the top of her head to feel which way it
T5   152:23   "But why don't you scream now?" Alice asked, holding her hands ready to put over her ears again.
T8   186:16   "not the next day. In fact," he went on, holding his head down, and his voice getting lower and lower,
T4   144: 5   he sorted out / Those of the largest size, / Holding his pocket-handkerchief / Before his streaming eyes.
T5   152:18   "Take care!" cried Alice. "You're holding it all crooked!" And she caught at the brooch; but it
A7   55:38   uneasily, shaking it every now and then, and holding it to his ear.
T6   163:15   "You're holding it upside down!" Alice interrupted.
T3   129:34   in at the window. In a moment everybody was holding out a ticket: they were about the same size as the
T7   172:15   did you pass on the road?" the King went on, holding out his hand to the Messenger for some hay.
T1   108:26   Now don't interrupt me!" she went on, holding up one finger. "I'm going to tell you all your faults.
HOLDS (2)
T9   202:15   For it holds it like glue--/ Holds the lid to the dish, while it lies
T9   202:16   For it holds it like glue--/ Holds the lid to the dish, while it lies in the middle: /
-HOLE [See MOUSE-HOLE, RABBIT-HOLE, RAT-HOLE]
HOLES (1)
T6   165: 3   like a gyroscope. To 'gimble' is to make holes like a gimlet."
HOLIDAY (1)
A9   77:19   "Then the eleventh day must have been a holiday?"
HOLLOW (2)
A9   74:27   tell it her," said the Mock Turtle in a deep, hollow tone. "Sit down, both of you, and don't speak a word
T7   176: 1   lazily at Alice, and speaking in a deep hollow tone that sounded like the tolling of a great bell.
HOLLY-LEAVES (1)
T3   133:14   body is made of plum-pudding, its wings of holly-leaves, and its head is a raisin burning in brandy."
HOME (11)
T4   144: 9   had a pleasant run! / Shall we be trotting home again?' / But answer came there none--/ And this was
T6   166: 4   certain about. I think it's short for 'from home'--meaning that they'd lost their way, you know."
T2   124:16   to disbelieve it. "I'll try it when I go home," she thought to herself, "the next time I'm a little
A3   26:33   remarking "I really must be getting home: the night-air doesn't suit my throat!" And a Canary
A4   27:14   Mary Ann, what are you doing out here? Run home this moment, and fetch me a pair of gloves and a fan!
A4   28:27   "It was much pleasanter at home," thought poor Alice, "when one wasn't always growing
AI   4: 1   out--/ And now the tale is done, / And home we steer, a merry crew, / Beneath the setting sun.
A6   50: 9   am I to do with this creature, when I get it home?" when it grunted again, so violently, that she looked
A1   8:25   How brave they'll all think me at home! Why, I wouldn't say anything about it, even if I fell
T5   157: 9   go--I should so like a little crab to take home with me!" But the Sheep only laughed scornfully, and went
T3   135: 1   it would be if you could manage to go home without it! For instance, if the governess wanted to call
HONEST (1)
A12   94:25   or else you'd have signed your name like an honest man."
HONESTLY (1)
T4   144:32   Alice couldn't say honestly that he was. He had a tall red night-cap on, with a
HONEY (4)
T8   181:31   may make a nest in it--then I should get the honey."
T8W   17:16   more interest. "And you've got a comb. Much honey?"
T3   129: 7   towns--why, what are those creatures, making honey down there? They ca'n't be bees--nobody ever saw bees a
T3   129:16   stalks put to them--and what quantities of honey they must make! I think I'll go down and--no, I wo'n't
HONOUR (6)
A4   30: 3   "Sure then I'm here! Digging for apples, yer honour!"
A4   30:14   and then; such as "Sure, I don't like it, yer honour, at all, at all!" "Do as I tell you, you coward!", and
A4   30:10   "Sure, it does, yer honour: but it's an arm for all that."
A4   30: 7   "Sure, it's an arm, yer honour!" (He pronounced it "arrum.")
T12 207:25   it up and gave it one little kiss, "just in honour of its having been a Red Queen."
T9   199:38   quoth Alice, 'draw near! / 'Tis an honour to see me, a favour to hear: / 'Tis a privilege high to
HONOUR'S (1)
T8   189: 6   wealth--/ And very gladly will I drink / Your Honour's noble health.'
HOOKAH (5)
A4   34:10   with its arms folded, quietly smoking a long hookah, and taking not the smallest notice of her or of
A5   41:22   time," said the Caterpillar; and it put the hookah into its mouth, and began smoking again.
A5   36:29   but at last it unfolded its arms, took the hookah out of its mouth again, and said "So you think you're
A5   35: 2   in silence: at last the Caterpillar took the hookah out of its mouth, and addressed her in a languid
A5   41:24   In a minute or two the Caterpillar took the hookah out of its mouth, and yawned once or twice, and shook
HOOT (1)
T8W   19:14   And still, whenever I appear, / They hoot at me and call me 'Pig!' / And that is why they do it,
HOP (1)
T6   167:15   My heart went hop, my heart went thump: / I filled the kettle at the pump.
HOPE (18)
A4   28:13   saying to herself "That's quite enough--I hope I sha'n't grow any more--As it is, I ca'n't get out at
T8   190:34   "I hope it encouraged him," she said, as she turned to run down
A4   28: 6   so I'll just see what this bottle does. I do hope it'll make me grow large again, for really I'm quite
T8   179: 8   we're all part of the same dream. Only I do hope it's my dream, and not the Red King's! I don't like
T8   184: 2   in an anxious tone, as she picked him up, "I hope no bones are broken?"
T7   171:12   H," the King said, introducing Alice in the hope of turning off the Messenger's attention from himself--
T2   127:38   "Thirst quenched, I hope?" said the Queen.
T8   190:22   "I hope so," the Knight said doubtfully: "but you didn't cry so
T5   156:24   "I only hope the boat wo'n't tipple over!" she said to herself. "Oh,
A1   9: 7   I should think!" (Dinah was the cat.) "I hope they'll remember her saucer of milk at tea-time. Dinah,
T9   193: 5   and a child's more important than a joke, I hope. You couldn't deny that, even if you tried with both
T4   145:26   "I hope you don't suppose those are real tears?" Tweedledum

```
HOPE (cont.)
 T3    130:12   great surprise, they all thought in chorus (I hope you understand what thinking in chorus means--for I must
 T5    153:23                               "Then I hope your finger is better now?" Alice said very politely, as
 T4    147:15          dish-covers, and coal-scuttles. "I hope you're a good hand at pinning and tying strings?"
 T8W   13:19   stooped over him, and said very kindly, "I hope you're not in much pain?"
 T4    140: 6                               "I hope you're not much tired?" she said at last.
 T8    182:22                               "I hope you've got your hair well fastened on?" he continued, as
HOPED (1)
 A4    27:37   a table in the window, and on it (as she had hoped) a fan and two or three pairs of tiny white kid-gloves:
HOPEFUL (2)
 T6    164:20                     This sounded very hopeful, so Alice repeated the first verse:--
 A9    70: 7   Duchess," she said to herself (not in a very hopeful tone, though), "I wo'n't have any pepper in my kitchen
HOPELESS (1)
 A2    15:18   with one eye; but to get through was more hopeless than ever: she sat down and began to cry again.
HOPES (3)
 T3    129: 3   thought Alice, as she stood on tiptoe in hopes of being able to see a little further. "Principal rivers
 T8    181:30                               "In hopes some bees may make a nest in it--then I should get the
 AI     3:15   "to begin it": / In gentler tones Secunda hopes / "There will be nonsense in it!" / While Tertia
HOPING (8)
 A1    10:13   door, so she went back to the table, half hoping she might find another key on it, or at any rate a book
 A3    26:43   the distance, and she looked up eagerly, half hoping that the Mouse had changed his mind, and was coming
 A7    60:32   though she looked back once or twice, half hoping that they would call after her: the last time she saw
 T8    186:20   did you mean it to be made of?" Alice asked, hoping to cheer him up, for the poor Knight seemed quite
 T2    122:21   it you can all talk so nicely?" Alice said, hoping to get it into a better temper by a compliment. "I've
 T6    166:17   it needn't come to that!" Alice hastily said, hoping to keep him from beginning.
 T4    148: 9   "And all about a rattle!" said Alice, still hoping to make them a little ashamed of fighting for such a
 T6    159:20   eggs are very pretty, you know," she added, hoping to turn her remark into a sort of compliment.
-HOPPER [See GRASSHOPPER]
HOPPING (1)
 T4    142:11   last, / And more, and more, and more--/ All hopping through the frothy waves, / And scrambling to the
HORN (2)
 T7    173:19   managed to distinguish the Unicorn by his horn.
 T7    175:13   "You shouldn't have run him through with your horn, you know."
HORROR (1)
 T1    115:25                               "The horror of that moment," the King went on, "I shall never,
HORSE (18) [See also CART-HORSE]
 T8    179:16   the Knight cried, as he tumbled off his horse.
 T8    183: 2   the best plan not to walk quite close to the horse.
 T8    184:17   "Much more smoothly than a live horse," Alice said, with a little scream of laughter, in spite
 T3    131:13                   "It sounds like a horse," Alice thought to herself. And an extremely small voice
 T3    131:15   might make a joke on that--something about 'horse' and 'hoarse,' you know."
 T8    180: 4   Knight hits the other, he knocks him off his horse; and, if he misses, he tumbles off himself--and another
 T8    187:12                 So saying, he stopped his horse and let the reins fall on its neck: then, slowly beating
 T8    182: 6   for everything. That's the reason the horse has all those anklets round his feet."
 T8    185: 1   When I used to wear it, if I fell off the horse, it always touched the ground directly. So I had a very
 T8    179:24   drew up at Alice's side, and tumbled off his horse just as the Red Knight had done: then he got on again,
 T8    184:12   this time. "You ought to have a wooden horse on wheels, that you ought!"
 T8    187:22   a blaze of light that quite dazzled her--the horse quietly moving about, with the reins hanging loose on
 T8    190:28   comes of having so many things hung round the horse--" So she went on talking to herself, as she watched the
 T8    179:15   a great club. Just as he reached her, the horse stopped suddenly: "You're my prisoner!" the Knight cried
 T8    182:40   Whenever the horse stopped (which it did very often), he fell off in front;
 T7    170: 1   seemed to be a regular rule that, whenever a horse stumbled, the rider fell off instantly. The confusion
 T8    190:29   on talking to herself, as she watched the horse walking leisurely along the road, and the Knight
 T3    132: 5                   The Horse, who had put his head out of the window, quietly drew it
HORSE-FLY (1) [See also ROCKING-HORSE-FLY]
 T3    133: 1                   "Well, there's the Horse-fly," Alice began, counting off the names on her fingers
HORSE'S (5)
 T8    182: 2   very likely there would be any mice on the horse's back."
 T8    184: 8   he fell flat on his back, right under the horse's feet.
 T8    190:13   he gathered up the reins, and turned his horse's head along the road by which they had come. "You've
 T8    179:33   the saddle, and was something the shape of a horse's head) and put it on.
 T8    184:15   great interest, clasping his arms round the horse's neck as he spoke, just in time to save himself from
HORSES (6)
 T6    160:28                 "To send all his horses and all his men," Alice interrupted, rather unwisely.
 T6    161:13                 "Yes, all his horses and all his men," Humpty Dumpty went on. "They'd pick
 T6    159:30   Dumpty had a great fall. / All the King's horses and all the King's men / Couldn't put Humpty Dumpty in
 T8    180: 8   falling into the fender! And how quiet the horses are! They let them get on and off them just as if they
 T7    169:10                 Then came the horses. Having four feet, these managed rather better than the
 T7    170:12   to his book. "I couldn't send all the horses, you know, because two of them are wanted in the game.
HOT (9) [See also RED-HOT]
 T3    129:24   toss of the head), 'only it was so dusty and hot, and the elephants did tease so!'"
 T2    127:24   "I'm quite content to stay here--only I am so hot and thirsty!"
 T4    142:23   and kings--/ And why the sea is boiling hot--/ And whether pigs have wings.'
 A1    11: 9   custard, pine-apple, roast turkey, toffy, and hot buttered toast), she very soon finished it off. * * * * *
 A1     7: 7   her own mind (as well as she could, for the hot day made her feel very sleepy and stupid), whether the
 A2    15:36   the fan and gloves, and, as the hall was very hot, she kept fanning herself all the time she went on talking
 A7    56:23   said the Hatter, and he poured a little hot tea upon its nose.
 T3    135:39   she stepped under the trees, "after being so hot, to get into the--into the--into what?" she went on,
 A10   84:18   Soup, so rich and green, / Waiting in a hot tureen! / Who for such dainties would not stoop? / Soup of
```

HOT-TEMPERED (1)
A9   70:10 Maybe it's always pepper that makes people hot-tempered," she went on, very much pleased at having found
HOUR (5)
T5   153:14 I was your age, I always did it for half-an-hour a day. Why, sometimes I've believed as many as six
T1   107: 4 by the old cat for the last quarter of an hour (and bearing it pretty well, considering): so you see
AI   3: 7   Ah, cruel Three! In such an hour, / Beneath such dreamy weather, / To beg a tale of breath
A3   23:13 However, when they had been running half an hour or so, and were quite dry again, the Dodo suddenly called
A9   73: 7 to do this, so that, by the end of half an hour or so, there were no arches left, and all the players,
HOURS (9)
T5   149:20 "I've been a-dressing myself for the last two hours."
A9   77:10   "And how many hours a day did you do lessons?" said Alice, in a hurry to
T1   114:19 to bar, till at last she said "Why, you'll be hours and hours getting to the table, at that rate. I'd far
T8   185:10 he took the helmet off again--but it took hours and hours to get me out. I was as fast as--as lightning,
T1   114:19 at last she said "Why, you'll be hours and hours getting to the table, at that rate. I'd far better help
A6   48:30 listening, so she went on again: "Twenty-four hours, I think; or is it twelve? I--"
A9   77:12   "Ten hours the first day," said the Mock Turtle: "nine the next,
T8   185:11 the helmet off again--but it took hours and hours to get me out. I was as fast as--as lightning, you know
A6   48:26 night! You see the earth takes twenty-four hours to turn round on its axis--"
HOUSE (34)
T1t 107: 1   LOOKING-GLASS HOUSE
A4   32:12 to get through the door, she ran out of the house, and found quite a crowd of little animals and birds
A2   17:18 shall have to go and live in that poky little house, and have next to no toys to play with, and oh, ever so
T2   120:13 about it," Alice said, looking up at the house and pretending it was arguing with her. "I'm not going
A7   54: 1 a table set out under a tree in front of the house, and the March Hare and the Hatter were having tea at it
T3   137:23 the same way, one marked "TO TWEEDLEDUM'S HOUSE," and the other "TO THE HOUSE OF TWEEDLEDEE."
A6   45: 1 For a minute or two she stood looking at the house, and wondering what to do next, when suddenly a footman
A6   53:11 March Hare: she thought it must be the right house, because the chimneys were shaped like ears and the roof
A4   27:25 the real Mary Ann, and be turned out of the house before she had found the fan and gloves.
T2   120:10 after turn, but always coming back to the house, do what she would. Indeed, once, when she turned a
A4   31:27   "We must burn the house down!" said the Rabbit's voice. And Alice called out, as
T1   110:31 tell you all my ideas about Looking-glass House. First, there's the room you can see through the glass--
T2   120:24 it's too bad!" she cried. "I never saw such a house for getting in the way! Never!"
T1   110:29 "I'll put you through into Looking-glass House. How would you like that?
A2   20: 4 "There is such a nice little dog, near our house, I should like to show you! A little bright-eyed terrier
T3   137:26 Alice at last, "that they live in the same house! I wonder I never thought of that before--But I ca'n't
A4   27:34 went on, "that they'd let Dinah stop in the house if it began ordering people about like that!"
T1   111: 3 a little peep of the passage in Looking-glass House, if you leave the door of our drawing-room wide open:
T1   111: 6 we could only get through into Looking-glass House! I'm sure it's got, oh! such beautiful things in it!
A5   44: 1 suddenly upon an open place, with a little house in it about four feet high. "Whoever lives there,"
T1   119: 1   before I've seen what the rest of the house is like! Let's have a look at the garden first!" She was
T1   110:43 "How would you like to live in Looking-glass House, Kitty? I wonder if they'd give you milk in there?
A3   25: 8 "Fury said to a mouse, That he met in the house, 'Let us both go to law: I will prosecute you.--Come,
A6   53:11 much farther before she came in sight of the March Hare: she thought it must be the right
T3   137:23 TO TWEEDLEDUM'S HOUSE," and the other "TO THE HOUSE OF TWEEDLEDEE."
A4   27:21 As she said this, she came upon a neat little house, on the door of which was a bright brass plate with the
A6   46:27   At this moment the door of the house opened, and a large plate came skimming out, straight at
A4   29:22 for her, and she trembled till she shook the house, quite forgetting that she was now about a thousand
T2   120:18 So, resolutely turning her back upon the house, she set out once more down the path, determined to keep
T9   196: 6 it happened, there wasn't such a thing in the house, that morning."
A6   53:13 roof was thatched with fur. It was so large a house, that she did not like to go nearer till she had nibbled
A5   44: 5 bit again, and did not venture to go near the house till she had brought herself down to nine inches high.
T2   120: 7 it doesn't! This goes straight back to the house! Well then, I'll try it the other way."
A1   8:26 about it, even if I fell off the top of the house!" (Which was very likely true.)
HOUSEMAID (1)
A4   27:18   "He took me for his housemaid," she said to herself as she ran. "How surprised
-HOUSES (1) [See LODGING-HOUSES]
HOW (127) [See also ANYHOW, NOHOW, etc.]
T9   194:17   "But I don't see how--"
A6   46:17   "Please, then," said Alice, "how am I to get in?"
A6   46:32   "How am I to get in?" asked Alice again, in a louder tone.
A6   46:25 But at any rate he might answer questions.--How am I to get in?" she repeated, aloud.
T5   156:13   "How am I to stop it?" said the Sheep. "If you leave off rowing
T7   174: 3 "Speak, wo'n't you!" cried the King. "How are they getting on with the fight?"
T7   173:26 so you see he's very hungry and thirsty. How are you, dear child?" he went on, putting his arm
A3   22:24 moderate. But the insolence of his Normans--' How are you getting on now, my dear?" it continued, turning to
A8   67:14   "How are you getting on?" said the Cat, as soon as there was
A1   8:24 shall think nothing of tumbling down-stairs! How brave they'll all think me at home! Why, I wouldn't say
A2   18: 3 white kid-gloves while she was talking. "How can I have done that?" she thought. "I must be growing
T8   191: 6   "But how can it have got there without my knowing it?" she said to
T5   155:12   "How can she knit with so many?" the puzzled child thought to
T8   185:24   "How can you go on talking so quietly, head downwards?" Alice
A4   29:13 you foolish Alice!" she answered herself. "How can you learn lessons in here? Why, there's hardly room
T8W   19:12 gone, / They take my wig from me and say / 'How can you put such rubbish on?'
T12 207:10 so that one could keep up a conversation! But how can you talk with a person if they always say the same
A2   17:12   "How cheerfully he seems to grin, / How neatly spreads his
A8   67:27 nobody attends to them--and you've no idea how confusing it is all the things being alive: for instance,
T3   134:26 Gnat went on in a careless tone: "only think how convenient it would be if you could manage to go home
A10 83: 5 about his toes?" the Mock Turtle persisted. "How could he turn them out with his nose, you know?"
T2   120: 5 corners), "but I suppose it will at last. But how curiously it twists! It's more like a corkscrew than a
A10 80: 1   "You can really have no notion how delightful it will be / When they take us up and throw us,

HOW (cont.)

A9	77:21	"And how did you manage on the twelfth?" Alice went on eagerly.
A5	39: 4	goose, with the bones and the beak--/ Pray, how did you manage to do it?"
A6	51:25	"How do you know I'm mad?" said Alice.
T1	108:35	before her! What, you were thirsty, were you? How do you know she wasn't thirsty too? Now for number three:
A6	51:28	proved it at all: however, she went on: "And how do you know that you're mad?"
A8	67:31	"How do you like the Queen?" said the Cat in a low voice.
T5	158: 3	to buy an egg, please," she said timidly. "How do you sell them?"
A2	17: 3	been changed for Mabel! I'll try and say 'How doth the little--'," and she crossed her hands on her lap
A5	36:34	"Well, I've tried to say 'How doth the little busy bee,' but it all came different!"
A2	17: 8	"How doth the little crocodile / Improve his shining tail, /
A7	58: 7	"How dreadfully savage!" exclaimed Alice.
T3	137:27	stay there long. I'll just call and say 'How d'ye do?' and ask them the way out of the wood. If I could
T4	139:22	"The first thing in a visit is to say 'How d'ye do?' and shake hands!" And here the two brothers gave
T4	140: 4	been dancing with. "It would never do to say 'How d'ye do?' now," she said to herself: "we seem to have got
A10	79:15	us, and he's treading on my tail. / See how eagerly the lobsters and the turtles all advance! / They
T6	159:14	"And how exactly like an egg he is!" she said aloud, standing with
A10	80: 7	"What matters it how far we go?" his scaly friend replied. / There is another
T4	148:20	a thick black cloud that is!" she said. "And how fast it comes! Why, I do believe it's got wings!"
T7	174:23	She came flying out of the wood over yonder--How fast those Queens can run!"
A9	71: 3	"How fond she is of finding morals in things!" Alice thought to
A2	15: 4	must go by the carrier," she thought; "and how funny it'll seem, sending presents to one's own feet! And
A1	8:40	if I shall fall right through the earth! How funny it'll seem to come out among the people that walk
T8	191: 2	dotted about it here and there. "Oh, how glad I am to get here! And what is this on my head?" she
A9	70: 1	"You ca'n't think how glad I am to see you again, you dear old thing!" said
T9	196:29	up," the Red Queen went on: "but it's amazing how good-tempered she is! Pat her on the head, and see how
T8	190:35	now for the last brook, and to be a Queen! How grand it sounds!" A very few steps brought her to the edge
A9	74:30	Alice thought to herself "I don't see how he can ever finish, if he doesn't begin." But she waited
T6	159:10	such a narrow one that Alice quite wondered how he could keep his balance--and, as his eyes were steadily
A11	86:18	(look at the frontispiece if you want to see how he did it), he did not look at all comfortable, and it was
T8	184:29	"I'll tell you how I came to think of it," said the Knight. "You see, I said
T8W	18: 3	"I'll tell you how I came to wear it," the Wasp said. "When I was young, you
T3	129:22	away--and what fun it'll be when they ask me how I liked my walk. I shall say 'Oh, I liked it well enough--
A1	10: 8	of very little use without my shoulders. Oh, how I wish I could shut up like a telescope! I think I could,
T2	126: 3	world at all, you know. Oh, what fun it is! How I wish I was one of them! I wouldn't mind being a Pawn, if
A7	57:15	'Twinkle, twinkle, little bat! / How I wonder what you're at!'
A1	8: 6	went Alice after it, never once considering how in the world she was to get out again.
T9	194:40	"Can you answer useful questions?" she said. "How is bread made?"
A5	42:14	my shoulders got to? And oh, my poor hands, how is it I ca'n't see you?" She was moving them about, as she
A4	33:11	that I've got to grow up again! Let me see--how is it to be managed? I suppose I ought to eat or drink
T2	122:21	"How is it you can all talk so nicely?" Alice said, hoping to
T8	187:36	/ 'Who are you, aged man?' I said. / 'And how is it you live?' / And his answer trickled through my head
A5	43:43	thing is, to get into that beautiful garden--how is that to be done, I wonder?" As she said this, she came
T2	128:22	How it happened, Alice never knew, but exactly as she came to
A11	90:13	a hard word, I will just explain to you how it was done. They had a large canvas bag, which tied up at
T2	126:13	make out, in thinking it over afterwards, how it was that they began: all she remembers is, that they
T1	108:18	worsted round the kitten's neck, just to see how it would look: this led to a scramble, in which the ball
A12	92: 2	quite forgetting in the flurry of the moment how large she had grown in the last few minutes, and she
A1	9:26	it turned a corner, "Oh my ears and whiskers, how late it's getting!" She was close behind it when she
A2	19:24	of history, Alice had no very clear notion how long ago anything had happened.) So she began again: "Ou
T9	195: 1	"How many acres of ground?" said the White Queen. "You mustn't
T6	162:45	"And how many birthdays have you?"
T6	162:43	you're talking about!" cried Humpty Dumpty. "How many days are there in a year?"
T4	144:17	front, so that the Carpenter couldn't count how many he took: contrariwise."
A9	77:10	"And how many hours a day did you do lessons?" said Alice, in a
A1	8:28	the fall never come to an end? "I wonder how many miles I've fallen by this time?" she said aloud. "I
A2	17:13	"How cheerfully he seems to grin, / How neatly spreads his claws, / And welcomes little fishes in,
T1	109: 9	the snow against the window-panes, Kitty? How nice and soft it sounds! I wonder if the snow loves the
T1	111: 5	may be quite different on beyond. Oh, Kitty, how nice it would be if we could only get through into
A2	15: 5	seem, sending presents to one's own feet! And how odd the directions will look!
T5	153: 3	know. Let's consider your age to begin with--how old are you?"
T6	161:26	"I thought you meant 'How old are you?'" Alice explained.
T6	161:20	Alice.) "So here's a question for you. How old did you say you were?"
A3	21:11	this Alice would not allow, without knowing how old it was, and as the Lory positively refused to tell its
T9	196:30	she is! Pat her on the head, and see how pleased she'll be!" But this was more than Alice had
A5	43:40	usual, "Come, there's half my plan done now! How puzzling all these changes are! I'm never sure what I'm
A2	16: 7	Besides, she's she, and I'm I, and--oh dear, how puzzling it all is! I'll try if I know all the things I
A2	15:38	the time she went on talking. "Dear, dear! How queer everything is to-day! And yesterday things went on
A4	27:27	"How queer it seems," Alice said to herself, "to be going
T8	180: 8	of fire-irons falling into the fender! And how quiet the horses are! They let them get on and off them
T1	111:12	while she said this, though she hardly knew how she had got there. And certainly the glass was beginning
A1	10: 3	into the loveliest garden you ever saw. How she longed to get out of that dark hall, and wander about
A1	9:33	she walked sadly down the middle, wondering how she was ever to get out again.
A12	99: 9	with the dream of Wonderland of long ago; and how she would feel with all their simple sorrows, and find a
A12	99: 6	simple and loving heart of her childhood; and how she would gather about her other little children, and make
A12	99: 4	the after-time, be herself a grown woman; and how she would keep, through all her riper years, the simple
A2	15: 3	And she went on planning to herself how she would manage it. "They must go by the carrier," she
A8	64: 3	"How should I know?" said Alice, surprised at her own courage.
A2	19: 8	or hippopotamus, but then she remembered how small she was now, and she soon made out that it was only
T1	110:27	it up to the Looking-glass, that it might see how sulky it was, "--and if you're not good directly," she

HOW (cont.)

A4	27:19	housemaid," she said to herself as she ran.	"How surprised he'll be when he finds out who I am! But I'd
A10	82:17		"How the creatures order one about, and make one repeat
A3	23: 7	yourself some winter-day, I will tell you	how the Dodo managed it.)
A8	68:10	thought she might as well go back and see	how the game was going on, as she heard the Queen's voice in
A10	83:15	by his garden, and marked, with one eye, /	How the Owl and the Panther were sharing a pie: / The Panther
T7	175:40	while he got out a dish and carving-knife.	How they all came out of it Alice couldn't guess. It was just
T9	192:14	she would have liked very much to ask them	how they came there, but she feared it would not be quite
A12	99: 3	Lastly, she pictured to herself	how this same little sister of hers would, in the after-time,
T4	140: 3	a rather awkward pause, as Alice didn't know	how to begin a conversation with people she had just been
A1	10: 9	a telescope! I think I could, if I only knew	how to begin." For, you see, so many out-of-the-way things had
T7	177:18	with the knife in her hand, very much puzzled	how to begin. "The Monster has given the Lion twice as much as
A3	21: 5	The first question of course was,	how to get dry again: they had a consultation about this, and
T7	177:11		"You don't know how to manage Looking-glass cakes," the Unicorn remarked.
A4	32:24	was, that she had not the smallest idea	how to set about it; and, while she was peering about
A2	14: 2	that for the moment she quite forgot	how to speak good English). "Now I'm opening out like the
A11	87: 2	even make out that one of them didn't know	how to spell "stupid," and that he had to ask his neighbour to
T5	158:21	a chair? Why, it's got branches, I declare!	How very odd to find trees growing here! And actually here's a
A4	31:12	up his head--Brandy now--Don't choke him--How	was it, old fellow? What happened to you? Tell us all
T1	110:29	put you through into Looking-glass House. How	would you like that?
T1	110:43		"How would you like to live in Looking-glass House, Kitty? I
T2	123: 6	about like you," said the Rose. "I wonder	how you do it--" ("You're always wondering," said the
T8W	14: 3		"How you go on!" the Wasp said in a peevish tone. "Worrity,
T8	188:15	the old man said, / I cried 'Come, tell me	how you live!' / And thumped him on the head.
T8	188:31	/ Until his face was blue: / 'Come, tell me	how you live,' I cried, / 'And what it is you do!'
T9	201:22	impertinence!" said the Pudding. "I wonder	how you'd like it, if I were to cut a slice out of you, you

HOWEVER (49) [entries omitted]

HOWLED (1)

A6	49: 3	up and down, and the poor little thing	howled so, that Alice could hardly hear the words:--

HOWLING (3)

A6	47: 8	and as for the baby, it was sneezing and	howling alternately without a moment's pause. The only two
A6	46:14	noise going on within--a constant	howling and sneezing, and every now and then a great crash, as
A6	48:14	them even when they hit her; and the baby was	howling so much already, that it was quite impossible to say

HUDDLED (1)

T8W	13: 7	on the ground, leaning against a tree, all	huddled up together, and shivering as if he were very cold.

HUG (3)

T4	140:16	replied, giving his brother an affectionate	hug.
T4	139:23	And here the two brothers gave each other a	hug, and then they held out the two hands that were free, to
T1	114:10	for a minute or two she could do nothing but	hug the little Lily in silence. As soon as she had recovered

HUGE (1)

T2	126: 1	with excitement as she went on. "It's a great	huge game of chess that's being played--all over the world--if

HUMAN (2)

T3	137: 8	a voice of delight. "And, dear me! you're a	human child!" A sudden look of alarm came into its beautiful
T6	159: 2	only got larger and larger, and more and more	human: when she had come within a few yards of it, she saw

HUMBLE (2)

T6	162:27	it's very ignorant of me," Alice said, in so	humble a tone that Humpty Dumpty relented.
A8	65: 6	it please your Majesty," said Two, in a very	humble tone, going down on one knee as he spoke, "we were

HUMBLY (2)

A7	59:28	"No, please go on!" Alice said very	humbly. "I wo'n't interrupt you again. I dare say there may be
A3	26: 3	"I beg your pardon," said Alice very	humbly: "you had got to the fifth bend, I think?"

HUMMING (1)

T3	134:21	The Gnat amused itself meanwhile by	humming round and round her head: at last it settled again and

HUMPTY DUMPTY (53)

T6t	159: 1		HUMPTY DUMPTY
T6	161:27	"If I'd meant that, I'd have said it," said	Humpty Dumpty.
T6	162:37	"I'm not offended," said	Humpty Dumpty.
T6	164:38	"They are that," said	Humpty Dumpty; "also they make their nests under sun-dials--
T6	161:18	"In that case we start afresh," said	Humpty Dumpty, "and it's my turn to choose a subject--" ("He
T6	163:38	puzzled to say anything; so after a minute	Humpty Dumpty began again. "They've a temper, some of them--
T6	162:11	"One ca'n't, perhaps," said	Humpty Dumpty; "but two can. With proper assistance, you might
T2	128:12	Fifth is mostly water--the Sixth belongs to	Humpty Dumpty--But you make no remark?"
T6	162:33	"They gave it me,"	Humpty Dumpty continued thoughtfully as he crossed one knee
T6	160:30	"Now I declare that's too bad!"	Humpty Dumpty cried, breaking into a sudden passion. "You've
T6	160:13	"Why, because there's nobody with me!" cried	Humpty Dumpty. "Did you think I didn't know the answer to that
T6	161:24	"Wrong!"	Humpty Dumpty exclaimed triumphantly. "You never said a word
T6	168:16	"That's all," said	Humpty Dumpty. "Good-bye."
T6	160:20	"What tremendously easy riddles you ask!"	Humpty Dumpty growled out. "Of course I don't think so! Why,
T6	159:29	"Humpty Dumpty sat on a wall: /	Humpty Dumpty had a great fall. / All the King's horses and
T6	159: 4	come close to it, she saw clearly that it was	HUMPTY DUMPTY himself. "It ca'n't be anybody else!" she said
T6	162:42	don't know what you're talking about!" cried	Humpty Dumpty. "How many days are there in a year?"
T6	164: 5	make a word do a lot of work like that," said	Humpty Dumpty, "I always pay it extra."
T6	164:17	"Let's hear it," said	Humpty Dumpty. "I can explain all the poems that ever were
T12	207:35	the kittens. "Tell me, Dinah, did you turn to	Humpty Dumpty? I think you did--however, you'd better not
T6	159:31	horses and all the King's men / Couldn't put	Humpty Dumpty in his place again."
T6	160: 5	"It's a stupid name enough!"	Humpty Dumpty interrupted impatiently. "What does it mean?"
T6	164:25	"That's enough to begin with,"	Humpty Dumpty interrupted: "there are plenty of hard words
T6	163: 4		Humpty Dumpty looked doubtful. "I'd rather see that done on
T6	162:18	I beg your pardon!" she added in dismay, for	Humpty Dumpty looked thoroughly offended, and she began to
T6	159:22	"Some people," said	Humpty Dumpty, looking away from her as usual, "have no more
T6	163:43	"Now you talk like a reasonable child," said	Humpty Dumpty, looking very much pleased. "I meant by

HUMPTY (cont.)
T6 168:32 "It wouldn't look nice," Alice objected. But Humpty Dumpty only shut his eyes, and said "Wait till you've
T6 168: 1   Humpty Dumpty raised his voice almost to a scream as he
T6 162:28 of me," Alice said, in so humble a tone that Humpty Dumpty relented.
T6 166:28 or not, you've sharper eyes than most," Humpty Dumpty remarked severely. Alice was silent.
T6 162: 3   "Seven years and six months!" Humpty Dumpty repeated thoughtfully. "An uncomfortable sort of
T6 167: 6   "It gets easier further on," Humpty Dumpty replied.
T6 168:21 "I shouldn't know you again if we did meet," Humpty Dumpty replied in a discontented tone, giving her one
T6 159:17   "It's very provoking," Humpty Dumpty said after a long silence, looking away from
T6 163:16   "To be sure I was!" Humpty Dumpty said gaily as she turned it round for him. "I
T6 160:35 well! They may write such things in a book," Humpty Dumpty said in a calmer tone. "That's what you call a
T6 163:30   "When I use a word," Humpty Dumpty said, in rather a scornful tone, "it means just
T6 160: 1 stand chattering to yourself like that," Humpty Dumpty said, looking at her for the first time, "but
T6 166:37 "You needn't go on making remarks like that," Humpty Dumpty said: "they're not sensible, and they put me out
T6 160: 8   "Of course it must," Humpty Dumpty said with a short laugh: "my name means the
T6 159:28   "Humpty Dumpty sat on a wall: / Humpty Dumpty had a great fall.
T9 195:44   "Humpty Dumpty saw it too," the White Queen went on in a low
T6 163:25   Humpty Dumpty smiled contemptuously. "Of course you don't--
T6 166:14   "As to poetry, you know," said Humpty Dumpty, stretching out one of his great hands, "I can
T6 163:13   Humpty Dumpty took the book and looked at it carefully. "That
T6 159: 8 hundred times, easily, on that enormous face. Humpty Dumpty was sitting, with his legs crossed like a Turk,
T6 162:22   Evidently Humpty Dumpty was very angry, though he said nothing for a
T6 161:13 "Yes, all his horses and all his men," Humpty Dumpty went on. "They'd pick me up again in a minute,
T6 164:10 see 'em come round me of a Saturday night," Humpty Dumpty went on, wagging his head gravely from side to
T6 163:35   "The question is," said Humpty Dumpty, "which is to be master--that's all."
T6 159:33 she added, almost out loud, forgetting that Humpty Dumpty would hear her.
T6 168:26 "That's just what I complain of," said Humpty Dumpty. "Your face is the same as everybody has--the
HUNDRED (8)
T5 153: 7 give you something to believe. I'm just one hundred and one, five months and a day."
T7 170:10   "Four thousand two hundred and seven, that's the exact number," the King said,
T6 162:44   "Three hundred and sixty-five," said Alice.
T6 163: 1   "And if you take one from three hundred and sixty-five what remains?"
T6 163:19 just now--and that shows that there are three hundred and sixty-four days when you might get un-birthday
T6 163: 3   "Three hundred and sixty-four, of course."
A2   20: 9 and he says it's so useful, it's worth a hundred pounds! He says it kills all the rats and--oh dear!"
T6 159: 7   It might have been written a hundred times, easily, on that enormous face. Humpty Dumpty
HUNDREDS (1)
T9 199:28   And hundreds of voices joined in the chorus:--
HUNG (7)
T8 179:32 Red Knight, as he took up his helmet (which hung from the saddle, and was something the shape of a horse's
T8 184:41 looked down proudly at his helmet, which hung from the saddle. "Yes," he said; "but I've invented a
T8 181:27 a sudden thought seemed to strike him, and he hung it carefully on a tree. "Can you guess why I did that?"
T8 182:20 are so many candlesticks in the bag." And he hung it to the saddle, which was already loaded with bunches
T7 172: 2 to Alice's great amusement, opened a bag that hung round his neck, and handed a sandwich to the King, who
T8 190:28 easily--that comes of having so many things hung round the horse--" So she went on talking to herself, as
A1   8:17 here and there she saw maps and pictures hung upon pegs. She took down a jar from one of the shelves as
HUNGRY (5)
T7 173:25 oyster-shells in there--so you see he's very hungry and thirsty. How are you, dear child?" he went on,
A7   57: 6 Alice thoughtfully; "but then--I shouldn't be hungry for it, you know."
T1 110:18 her ear, "Nurse! Do let's pretend that I'm a hungry hyaena and you're a bone!"
A4   32:31 all the time at the thought that it might be hungry, in which case it would be very likely to eat her up in
A11 86: 8 they looked so good, that it made Alice quite hungry to look at them--"I wish they'd get the trial done,"
HUNT (1)
T8 188:33   He said 'I hunt for haddocks' eyes / Among the heather bright, / And work
HUNTED (1)
T12 207:13   So Alice hunted among the chessmen on the table till she had found the
HUNTING (3)
A4   27:12 soon the Rabbit noticed Alice, as she went hunting about, and called out to her, in an angry tone, "Why,
A4   27: 7 kid-gloves, and she very good-naturedly began hunting about for them, but they were nowhere to be seen--
A11 87:10 out at all what had become of it; so, after hunting all about for it, he was obliged to write with one
HURRICANE (1)
T4 145:27 wouldn't flap its wings so--it makes quite a hurricane in the wood--here's somebody's shawl being blown
HURRIED (13)
A9   73: 1 shade: however, the moment they saw her, they hurried back to the game, the Queen merely remarking that a
A12 98:24 grass rustled at her feet as the White Rabbit hurried by--the frightened Mouse splashed his way through the
A8   63:23 the White Rabbit: it was talking in a hurried nervous manner, smiling at everything that was said,
A8   68: 9 myself," said the King eagerly, and he hurried off.
A3   26:31 sensation among the party. Some of the birds hurried off at once: one old Magpie began wrapping itself up
A2   15:14 she at once took up the little golden key and hurried off to the garden door.
A10 85: 5 Gryphon, and, taking Alice by the hand, it hurried off, without waiting for the end of the song.
A1   7:17 waistcoat-pocket, and looked at it, and then hurried on, Alice started to her feet, for it flashed across
T2 128:27 for a moment to say "Good-bye," and then hurried on to the last.
A6   49:12 to play croquet with the Queen," and she hurried out of the room. The cook threw a frying-pan after her
A8   65:29 "Hush! Hush!" said the Rabbit in a low hurried tone. He looked anxiously over his shoulder as he
T4 142: 1   But four young Oysters hurried up, / All eager for the treat: / Their coats were
A4   27:23 upon it. She went in without knocking, and hurried upstairs, in great fear lest she should meet the real
HURRIEDLY (2)
A11 90:31 "You may go," said the King, and the Hatter hurriedly left the court, without even waiting to put his
A3   22:21 The Mouse did not notice this question, but hurriedly went on, "--found it advisable to go with Edgar

HURRY (12)
```
A4    32:26   over  her  head  made  her  look  up  in  a  great  hurry.
A11   89:21       the  March  Hare  interrupted  in  a  great  hurry.
A5    42:24   when  a  sharp  hiss  made  her  draw  back  in  a  hurry:  a  large  pigeon  had  flown  into  her  face,  and  was  beating
A7    58:33   sisters,"  the  Dormouse  began  in  a  great  hurry;  "and  their  names  were  Elsie,  Lacie,  and  Tillie;  and
A2    15:29   the  other:  he  came  trotting  along  in  a  great  hurry,  muttering  to  himself,  as  he  came,  "Oh!  The  Duchess,  the
A1    10:20   little  Alice  was  not  going  to  do  that  in  a  hurry.  "No,  I'll  look  first,"  she  said,  "and  see  whether  it's
T4   143: 5   of  breath,  /  And  all  of  us  are  fat!'  /  'No  hurry!'  said  the  Carpenter.  /  They  thanked  him  much  for  that.
A12   92: 3   last  few  minutes,  and  she  jumped  up  in  such  a  hurry  that  she  tipped  over  the  jury-box  with  the  edge  of  her
A12   94: 4   said  the  White  Rabbit,  jumping  up  in  a  great  hurry:  "this  paper  has  just  been  picked  up."
A9    77:11   a  day  did  you  do  lessons?"  said  Alice,  in  a  hurry  to  change  the  subject.
A2    20: 1   "I  wo'n't  indeed!"  said  Alice,  in  a  great  hurry  to  change  the  subject  of  conversation.  "Are  you--are  you
A4    32:39   the  stick,  and  tumbled  head  over  heels  in  its  hurry  to  get  hold  of  it:  then  Alice,  thinking  it  was  very  like
```
HURRYING (1)
```
A1     9:24   and  the  White  Rabbit  was  still  in  sight,  hurrying  down  it.  There  was  not  a  moment  to  be  lost:  away  went
```
HURT (9)
```
A1     9:21                             Alice  was  not  a  bit  hurt,  and  she  jumped  up  on  to  her  feet  in  a  moment:  she  looked
T5   157: 2             However,  she  wasn't  a  bit  hurt,  and  was  soon  up  again:  the  Sheep  went  on  with  her
T1   114: 2   the  King,  rubbing  his  nose,  which  had  been  hurt  by  the  fall.  He  had  a  right  to  be  a  little  annoyed  with
T8   185: 7   not  dare  to  laugh.  "I'm  afraid  you  must  have  hurt  him,"  she  said  in  a  trembling  voice,  "being  on  the  top  of
T7   175:14                             "It  didn't  hurt  him,"  the  Unicorn  said  carelessly,  and  he  was  going  on,
A6    48:15   was  quite  impossible  to  say  whether  the  blows  hurt  it  or  not.
T3   131:42   friend,  and  an  old  friend.  And  you  wo'n't  hurt  me,  though  I  am  an  insect."
A2    19:28   cried  Alice  hastily,  afraid  that  she  had  hurt  the  poor  animal's  feelings.  "I  quite  forgot  you  didn't
T8   185:19   well,  and  she  was  afraid  that  he  really  was  hurt  this  time.  However,  though  she  could  see  nothing  but  the
```
HURTING (3)
```
T4   147:29   managed  to  turn  it  into  a  cough,  for  fear  of  hurting  his  feelings.
T4   139:26   hands  with  either  of  them  first,  for  fear  of  hurting  the  other  one's  feelings;  so,  as  the  best  way  out  of
T9   196:19   but  she  did  not  say  this  aloud,  for  fear  of  hurting  the  poor  Queen's  feelings.
```
HUSH (4)
```
A8    65:29                                     "Hush!  Hush!"  said  the  Rabbit  in  a  low  hurried  tone.  He  looked
A8    65:29                                     "Hush!  Hush!"  said  the  Rabbit  in  a  low  hurried  tone.  He  looked
A8    65:38   Alice  gave  a  little  scream  of  laughter.  "Oh,  hush!"  the  Rabbit  whispered  in  a  frightened  tone.  "The  Queen
T4   145:16   this  so  loud  that  Alice  couldn't  help  saying  "Hush!  You'll  be  waking  him,  I'm  afraid,  if  you  make  so  much
```
HUSH-A-BY (1)
```
T9   197: 4                                     "Hush-a-by  lady,  in  Alice's  lap!  /  Till  the  feast's  ready,
```
HYAENA (1)
```
T1   110:19   "Nurse!  Do  let's  pretend  that  I'm  a  hungry  hyaena  and  you're  a  bone!"
```

-I-

I (961) [entries omitted]
I'D (23)
```
    T4     139:37   when  I  began  it,  but somehow I felt as if I'd been singing it a long long time!"
    A10     81:27                                "If I'd been the whiting," said Alice, whose thoughts were still
    T4     146: 1   on, as cheerfully as she could, "At any rate, I'd better be getting out of the wood, for really it's coming
    T9     200: 6    in despair. "Oh, that'll never be done! I'd better go in at once--" and in she went, and there was a
    A4      27:19   he'll be when he finds out who I am! But I'd better take him his fan and gloves--that is, if I can find
    T1     114:20   and hours getting to the table, at that rate. I'd far better help you, hadn't I?" But the King took no
    T1     109: 7   at once! Well, I shouldn't mind that much! I'd far rather go without them than eat them!
    T6     168: 7   And  he  was  very  proud  and  stiff: / He said 'I'd go and wake them, if--'
    A6      53:17   should be raving mad after all! I almost wish I'd gone to see the Hatter instead!"
    A7      58: 4                                    "Well, I'd hardly finished the first verse," said the Hatter, "when
    T6     161:27                                    "If I'd meant that, I'd have said it," said Humpty Dumpty.
    T6     162: 5   sort of age. Now if you'd asked my advice, I'd have said 'Leave off at seven'--but it's too late now."
    A10     81:28   thoughts were still running on the song, "I'd have said to the porpoise 'Keep back, please! We don't
    T6     161:27                                    "If I'd meant that, I'd have said it," said Humpty Dumpty.
    A4      33:10   only been the right size to do it! Oh dear! I'd nearly forgotten that I've got to grow up again! Let me
    A6      52:17   what became of the baby?" said the Cat. "I'd nearly forgotten to ask."
    A4      33:10   liked teaching it tricks very much, if--if I'd only been the right size to do it! Oh dear! I'd nearly
    A11     90:29                                    "I'd rather finish my tea," said the Hatter, with an anxious
    A8      67:43                                    "I'd rather not," the Cat remarked.
    T2     127:23                                    "I'd rather not try, please!" said Alice. "I'm quite content to
    T6     163: 4   Humpty Dumpty looked doubtful. "I'd rather see that done on paper," he said.
    A5      43: 1                                "And just as I'd taken the highest tree in the wood," continued the Pigeon,
    T2     125: 7   the point, but went on: "--and I thought I'd try and find my way to the top of that hill--"
```
IDEA (28)
```
    T7     173: 7      "Dear me, no!" said the King. "What an idea!"
    T8     182:37   she walked  on in silence, puzzling over the idea, and every now and then stopping to help the poor Knight,
    T2     123:18             Alice didn't like this idea at all: so, to change the subject, she asked "Does she
    T8W     18: 6                     A curious idea came into Alice's head. Almost every one she had met had
    A7      58:10                     A bright idea came into Alice's head. "Is that the reason so many
    A4      32: 6   cakes  as they lay on the floor, and a bright idea came into her head. "If I eat one of these cakes," she
    A8      67:26   are, nobody attends to them--and you've no idea how confusing it is all the things being alive: for
    A4      32:24   difficulty was, that she had not the smallest idea how to set about it; and, while she was peering about
    T2     126:24             Not that Alice had any idea of doing that. She felt as if she would never be able to
    A12     97: 1   "Stuff and nonsense!" said Alice loudly. "The idea of having the sentence first!"
    T6     160:17   on the ground?" Alice went on, not with any idea of making another riddle, but simply in her good-natured
    A3      25: 4   it while the mouse was speaking, so that her idea of the tale was something like this:--
    T3     132: 8   though Alice felt a little nervous at the idea of trains jumping at all. "However, it'll take us into
    T3     129:13   elephant--as Alice soon found out, though the idea quite took her breath away at first. "And what enormous
    A7      56:30         "I haven't the slightest idea," said the Hatter.
    T3     129:15   enormous  flowers they must be!" was her next idea. "Something like cottages with the roofs taken off, and
    T8     184:38             He looked so vexed at the idea, that Alice changed the subject hastily. "What a curious
    T7     170:35   the King remarked simply, without the least idea that he was joining in the game, while Alice was still
    A12     92:11   in her head, and she had a vague sort of idea that they must be collected at once and put back into the
    A9      77:17             This was quite a new idea to Alice, and she thought it over a little before she
    A5      43:21             This was such a new idea to Alice, that she was quite silent for a minute or two,
    A2      18:18   was up to her chin in saltwater. Her first idea was that she had somehow fallen into the sea, "and in
    A1       9:36   it but a tiny golden key, and Alice's first idea was that this might belong to one of the doors of the
    A10     78:11   and said "No never") "--so you can have no idea what a delightful thing a Lobster-Quadrille is!"
    T8     186:27   he interrupted, quite eagerly: "but you've no idea what a difference it makes, mixing it with other things--
    A1       8:36   I've got to?" (Alice had not the slightest idea what Latitude was, or Longitude either, but she thought
    A3      23:26             Alice had no idea what to do, and in despair she put her hand in her pocket
    A5      42:32         "I haven't the least idea what you're talking about," said Alice.
```
IDEAS (2)
```
    T1     110:31   and not talk so much, I'll tell you all my ideas about Looking-glass House. First, there's the room you
    T1     118:28   all.) "Somehow it seems to fill my head with ideas--only I don't exactly know what they are! However,
```
IDIOT (1)
```
    A8      63:38                                    "Idiot!" said the Queen, tossing her head impatiently; and
```
IDIOTIC (1)
```
    A6      46:44   him," said Alice desperately: "he's perfectly idiotic!" And she opened the door and went in.
```
IF (262)
```
    T6     168: 7   and  stiff: / He said 'I'd go and wake them, if--'
    T9     192:32   a  little  shudder,  "She says she only said 'if'--"
    A6      46:15   and every now and then a great crash, as if a dish or kettle had been broken to pieces.
    A10     81:33   "Of course not," said the Mock Turtle. "Why, if a fish came to me, and told me he was going a journey, I
    T2     126:20   they never seemed to pass anything. "I wonder if all the things move along with us?" thought poor puzzled
    T2     122: 3             "But what could it do, if any danger came?" Alice asked.
    A12     95:23             "If any one of them can explain it," said Alice, (she had grown
    T9     199:34   "Thirty times three makes ninety. I wonder if any one's counting?" In a minute there was silence again,
    A10     83: 1   down with her face in her hands, wondering if anything would ever happen in a natural way again.
    T12    208: 7   not go on licking your paw like that--as if Dinah hadn't washed you this morning! You see, Kitty, it
    T8     189:15                     And now, if e'er by chance I put / My fingers into glue, / Or madly
```

IF (cont.)

```
T6    160:21    out.  "Of  course  I  don't  think  so! Why, if ever I did fall off--which there's no chance of--but if I
A6     48:20                                          "If everybody minded their own business," the Duchess said, in
T9    192:20                                      "But if everybody obeyed that rule," said Alice, who was always
T4    144:19    indignantly. "Then I like the Carpenter best--if he didn't eat so many as the Walrus."
T8    184: 3    "None to speak of," the Knight said, as if he didn't mind breaking two or three of them. "The great
A9     74:30    herself  "I don't see how he can ever finish, if he doesn't begin." But she waited patiently.
T8    187:14    smile lighting up his gentle foolish face, as if he enjoyed the music of his song, he began.
A10    78: 3    or  two,  sobs  choked  his  voice. "Same as if he had a bone in his throat," said the Gryphon; and it set
T4    145: 5         clapping his hands triumphantly. "And if he left off dreaming about you, where do you suppose you'd
T8    180: 4    the  other, he knocks him off his horse; and, if he misses, he tumbles off himself--and another Rule seems
T6    161: 5    him  a  little  anxiously  as  she took it. "If he smiled much more the ends of his mouth might meet behind
A10    82:13    her  to  begin."  He looked at the Gryphon as if he thought it had some kind of authority over Alice.
T1    114:14    King,  looking up anxiously into the fire, as if he thought that was the most likely place to find one.
A9     75: 1              "Why did you call him Tortoise, if he wasn't one?" Alice asked.
T9    199: 9    went  nearer and rubbed it with his thumb, as if he were trying whether the paint would come off: then he
A12    93:28       unimportant--unimportant--important--"  as if he were trying which word sounded best.
T8W    13: 7    all  huddled  up  together,  and shivering as if he were very cold.
T8W    21: 4    and  stetched  out one claw towards Alice, as if he wished to do the same for her, but she kept out of reach
A11    89:26    went  on,  looking  anxiously  round to see if he would deny it too; but the Dormouse denied nothing,
T6    168:34              Alice waited a minute to see if he would speak again, but, as he never opened his eyes or
A9     74:18    came  nearer, Alice could hear him sighing as if his heart would break. She pitied him deeply. "What is his
T8    190: 8    fro,  / And muttered mumblingly and low, / As if his mouth were full of dough, / Who snorted like a buffalo
T6    159: 6    said  to  herself. "I'm as certain of it, as if his name were written all over his face!"
A4     27:20    better  take him his fan and gloves--that is, if I can find them." As she said this, she came upon a neat
T3    136: 4    all!  And  now,  who  am  I? I will remember, if I can! I'm determined to do it!" But being determined
T6    166:36                          "I will, if I can remember it so long," said Alice.
A9     72:14    "That's  nothing  to  what  I  could say if I chose," the Duchess replied, in a pleased tone.
T2    120: 1    garden  far  better," said Alice to herself, "if I could get to the top of that hill: and here's a path that
T3    137:28    do?'  and  ask  them the way out of the wood. "If I could only get to the Eighth Square before it gets dark!"
T6    160:24    grand  that Alice could hardly help laughing. "If I did fall," he went on, "the King has promised me--ah, you
T6    160:22    did  fall  off--which there's no chance of--but if I did--" Here he pursed up his lips, and looked so solemn
T1    118:31    But  oh!"  thought Alice, suddenly jumping up, "if I don't make haste, I shall have to go back through the
A6     49:25    she  carried  it  out  into the open air. "If I don't take this child away with me," thought Alice,
T8    189:19    right-hand foot / Into a left-hand shoe, / Or if I drop upon my toe / A very heavy weight, / I weep, for it
A4     32: 7    floor, and a bright idea came into her head. "If I eat one of these cakes," she thought, "it's sure to make
T8    184:43    like  a  sugar-loaf. When I used to wear it, if I fell off the horse, it always touched the ground directly
A1      8:25    Why,  I  wouldn't say anything about it, even if I fell off the top of the house!" (Which was very likely
A9     72:12    that  better," Alice said very politely, "if I had it written down: but I ca'n't quite follow it as you
T1    116:14    it's  a  Looking-glass book, of course! And, if I hold it up to a glass, the words will all go the right
A2     16: 8    oh  dear,  how  puzzling  it all is! I'll try if I know all the things I used to know. Let me see: four
A2     17:23    am  I, then? Tell  me that first, and then, if I like being that person, I'll come up: if not, I'll stay
T5    154: 4    "I  should  like  to  look all round me first, if I might."
A3     26:24              "And who is Dinah, if I might venture to ask the question?" said the Lory.
A11    91:13                    "Well, if I must, I must," the King said with a melancholy air, and,
T8W    13:12    added,  checking  herself on the very edge. "If I once jump over, everything will change, and then I can't
A1     10: 9    shut  up  like  a telescope! I think I could, if I only knew how to begin." For, you see, so many
A12    95: 9                          If I or she should chance to be / Involved in this affair, /
T9    192: 8    that  there  was nobody to see her, "and if I really am a Queen," she said as she sat down again, "I
A3     26:39    cat  in the world! Oh, my dear Dinah! I wonder if I shall ever see you any more!" And here poor Alice began
A1      8:39         Presently she began again. "I wonder if I shall fall right through the earth! How funny it'll seem
T9    194:10    "The  bone  wouldn't remain, of course, if I took it--and the dog wouldn't remain: it would come to
T1    113:13    sure  they  ca'n't  see me. I feel somehow as if I was getting invisible--"
A5     43:26    I'm  not looking for eggs, as it happens; and, if I was, I shouldn't want yours: I don't like them raw."
T4    145:24                                      "If I wasn't real," Alice said--half laughing through her tears
T9    201:23    the  Pudding. "I wonder how you'd like it, if I were to cut a slice out of you, you creature!"
A2     19:43    trembling  down  to  the end of its tail. "As if I would talk on such a subject! Our family always hated
T4    139:37    know  when  I began it, but somehow I felt as if I'd been singing it a long long time!"
A10    81:27                                      "If I'd been the whiting," said Alice, whose thoughts were
T6    161:27                                      "If I'd meant that, I'd have said it," said Humpty Dumpty.
A4     33:10    have  liked teaching it tricks very much, if--if I'd only been the right size to do it! Oh dear! I'd nearly
A4     33:10    have  liked  teaching  it  tricks  very much, if--if I'd only been the right size to do it! Oh dear! I'd
A2     17:20    to  learn! No, I've made up my mind about it: if I'm Mabel, I'll stay down here. It'll be no use their
A2     15:41    can  remember feeling a little different. But if I'm not the same, the next question is 'Who in the world am
T4    145:12        Alice exclaimed indignantly. "Besides, if I'm only a sort of thing in his dream, what are you, I
A4     27:34    on,  "that they'd let Dinah stop in the house if it began ordering people about like that!"
T4    146: 8                          "It may--if it chooses," said Tweedledee: "we've no objection.
T6    166:15    "I  can  repeat poetry as well as other folk, if it comes to that--"
T8    187:19    could  bring  the  whole scene back again, as if it had been only yesterday--the mild blue eyes and kindly
A6     50:15    to  see  it trot away quietly into the wood. "If it had grown up," she said to herself, "it would have made
A4     27: 2    and  looking  anxiously about as it went, as if it had lost something; and she heard it muttering to itself
T4    148:11    have  minded  it  so much," said Tweedledum, "if it hadn't been a new one."
T1    110: 8    check,  Kitty, and  really I might have won, if it hadn't been for that nasty Knight, that came wriggling
T3    131:37    sigh,  that she wouldn't have heard it at all, if it hadn't come quite close to her ear. The consequence of
T5    156:26    did  seem  a  little  provoking ("almost as if it happened on purpose," she thought) that, though she
A8     67:42    said  the King: "however, it may kiss my hand, if it likes."
A1     12:34    "Well,  I'll  eat  it,"  said Alice, "and if it makes me grow larger, I can reach the key; and if it
A1     12:35    me  grow  larger,  I  can  reach the key; and if it makes me grow smaller, I can creep under the door: so
T3    135:15    "You  shouldn't  make  jokes," Alice  said, "if it makes you so unhappy."
T1    108: 9    the  ball,  as  if  it  would be glad to help if it might.
```

IF (cont.)

A8	65:17		"Their heads are gone, if	it please your Majesty!" the soldiers shouted in reply.

A8   65:17   "Their heads are gone, if it please your Majesty!" the soldiers shouted in reply.
A3   23: 3   wanted to know, but the Dodo had paused as if it thought that somebody ought to speak, and no one else
T6   161:19   a subject--" ("He talks about it just as if it was a game!" thought Alice.) "So here's a question for
T3   129:10   poking its proboscis into them, "just as if it was a regular bee," thought Alice.
T4   139: 7   "Contrariwise," continued Tweedledee, "if it was so, it might be; and if it were so, it would be; but
A5   42:38   "As if it wasn't trouble enough hatching the eggs," said the
T5   155: 6   the ceiling as quietly as possible, as if it were quite used to it.
T4   139: 8   Tweedledee, "if it was so, it might be; and if it were so, it would be; but as it isn't, it ain't. That's
T1   108: 9   out one paw and gently touching the ball, as if it would be glad to help if it might.
T3   131:35   have said something pitying to comfort it, "if it would only sigh like other people!" she thought. But
T4   140:19   Here Alice ventured to interrupt him. "If it's very long," she said, as politely as she could, "would
A2   15:39   things went on just as usual. I wonder if I've changed in the night? Let me think: was I the same
A2   15:30   the Duchess! Oh! Wo'n't she be savage if I've kept her waiting!" Alice felt so desperate that she
A1   10: 6   get her head through the doorway; "and even if my head would go through," thought poor Alice, "it would be
A2   17:24   if I like being that person, I'll come up: if not, I'll stay down here till I'm somebody else'--but, oh
T3   132:38   to the people that name them, I suppose: if not, why do things have names at all?"
A6   46:31   continued in the same tone, exactly as if nothing had happened.
T3   132:24   all insects?" the Gnat went on, as quietly as if nothing had happened.
T5   157: 3   on with her knitting all the while, just as if nothing had happened. "That was a nice crab you caught!"
T8   180: 3   her hiding-place. "One Rule seems to be, that if one Knight hits the other, he knocks him off his horse; and
A6   50:19   well as pigs, and was just saying to herself "if one only knew the right way to change them--" when she was
T2   121:11   about the colour," the Tiger-lily remarked. "If only her petals curled up a little more, she'd be all right
T6   162:20   to wish she hadn't chosen that subject. "If only I knew," she thought to herself, "which was neck and
T2   126: 3   one of them! I wouldn't mind being a Pawn, if only I might join--though of course I should like to be a
A9   70:23   said the Duchess. "Everything's got a moral, if only you can find it." And she squeezed herself up closer
T8W   17:13   could make your wig much neater," she said, "if only you had a comb."
T12 207:37   "By the way, Kitty, if only you'd been really with me in my dream, there was one
A8   63:31   be the use of a procession," thought she, "if people had all to lie down on their faces, so that they
T9   192:30   "I only said 'if'!" poor Alice pleaded in a piteous tone.
T4   141: 7   'If seven maids with seven mops / Swept it for half a year, /
T1   115:17   she had done, and went round the room to see if she could find any water to throw over him. However, she
A2   16: 2   that were of the same age as herself, to see if she could have been changed for any of them.
T3   135: 6   never think of excusing me lessons for that. If she couldn't remember my name, she'd call me 'Miss,' as the
A3   21:17   for she felt sure she would catch a bad cold if she did not get dry very soon.
T3   131: 5   to know her way to the ticket-office, even if she doesn't know her alphabet!"
T3   131: 1   "ought to know which way she's going, even if she doesn't know her own name!"
A5   41:31   the mushroom," said the Caterpillar, just as if she had asked it aloud; and in another moment it was out of
T5   149:21   been all the better, as it seemed to Alice, if she had got some one else to dress her, she was so
A3   21: 7   find herself talking familiarly with them, as if she had known them all her life. Indeed, she had quite a
T1   119: 8   straight out at the door in the same way, if she hadn't caught hold of the door-post. She was getting a
A6   48:28   glanced rather anxiously at the cook, to see if she meant to take the hint; but the cook was busily
T3   135: 8   "Well, she said 'Miss,' and didn't say anything more," the Gnat
A12   95: 3   I had not gone / (We know it to be true): / If she should push the matter on, / What would become of you?
A12   96: 1   it to be true'--that's the jury, of course--'If she should push the matter on'--that must be the Queen--
T5   152: 4   shouted the Queen, shaking her hand about as if she wanted to shake it off. "My finger's bleeding! Oh, oh,
A1   12: 6   however, she waited for a few minutes to see if she was going to shrink any further: she felt a little
T5   149: 3   wood, with both arms stretched out wide, as if she were flying, and Alice very civilly went to meet her
A11   86:37   Alice could see, as well as if she were looking over their shoulders, that all the jurors
A2   17: 4   and she crossed her hands on her lap as if she were saying lessons, and began to repeat it, but her
T9   196: 1   White Queen went on in a low voice, more as if she were talking to herself. "He came to the door with a
T2   126:24   Alice had any idea of doing that. She felt as if she would never be able to talk again, she was getting so
A8   69: 2   The Queen's argument was that, if something wasn't done about it in less than no time, she'd
T7   178:11   "If that doesn't 'drum them out of town,'" she thought to
T4   145:10   "If that there King was to wake," added Tweedledum, "you'd go
A11   90:21   "If that's all you know about it, you may stand down,"
T3   134: 6   fire, and had thought to herself, "I wonder if that's the reason insects are so fond of flying into
A6   52:19   a pig," Alice answered very quietly, just as if the Cat had come back in a natural way.
T9   194:21   "Then if the dog went away, its temper would remain!" the Queen
T9   192:16   would be no harm, she thought, in asking if the game was over. "Please, would you tell me--" she began,
T3   135: 1   manage to go home without it! For instance, if the governess wanted to call you to your lessons, she would
A10   84:11   "Oh, a song, please, if the Mock Turtle would be so kind," Alice replied, so
A8   63: 8   and we put a white one in by mistake; and, if the Queen was to find out, we should all have our heads cut
T1   109:10   Kitty? How nice and soft it sounds! I wonder if the snow loves the trees and fields, that it kisses them so
T8W   18: 8   poetry to her, and she thought she would try if the Wasp couldn't do it too. "Would you mind saying it in
T4   138: 7   alive, and she was just going round to see if the word 'TWEEDLE' was written at the back of each collar,
A8   67:26   to have any rules in particular: at least, if there are, nobody attends to them--and you've no idea how
T9   193:17   to have a party at all," said Alice; "but, if there is to be one, I think I ought to invite the guests."
T5   149:10   bread-and-butter," and Alice felt that if there was to be any conversation at all, she must manage it
A6   50: 2   and looked into its eyes again, to see if there were any tears.
A12   95:30   "If there's no meaning in it," said the King, "that saves a
T12 207:10   But how can you talk with a person if they always say the same thing?"
T8   182: 3   very likely, perhaps," said the Knight; "but, if they do come, I don't choose to have them running all about
A5   43:19   "I don't believe it," said the Pigeon; "but if they do, why, then they're a kind of serpent: that's all I
T1   110:38   may be only pretence, just to make it look as if they had a fire. Well then, the books are something like
A4   31:35   to herself "I wonder what they will do next! If they had any sense, they'd take the roof off." After a
T6   162:15   of the subject of age, she thought: and, if they really were to take turns in choosing subjects, it was
T8   180: 6   they hold their clubs with their arms, as if they were Punch and Judy--What a noise they make when they
T8   180: 9   They let them get on and off them just as if they were tables!"
T3   135:36   answered! Only they wouldn't answer at all, if they were wise."

IF (cont.)

T3	132:35	use of their having names," the Gnat said, "if	they wo'n't answer to them?"
T12	207: 7	whatever you say to them, they always purr. "If	they would only purr for 'yes,' and mew for 'no,' or any
T1	110:44	live in Looking-glass House, Kitty? I wonder if	they'd give you milk in there? Perhaps Looking-glass milk
T2	126: 2	that's being played--all over the world--if	this is the world at all, you know. Oh, what fun it is! How
T4	141: 5	anything to see / Such quantities of sand! / 'If	this were only cleared away,' / They said, 'it would be
T1	111: 6	on beyond. Oh, Kitty, how nice it would be if	we could only get through into Looking-glass House! I'm
T6	168:21	"I shouldn't know you again if	we did meet," Humpty Dumpty replied in a discontented tone,
T8	182:14	us," the Knight said. "It'll come in handy if	we find any plum-cake. Help me to get it into this bag."
A6	46:19	Footman went on, without attending to her, "if	we had the door between us. For instance, if you were
T5	158: 9	"Only you must eat them both, if	you buy two," said the Sheep.
T5	149:13	"Well, yes, if	you call that a-dressing," the Queen said. "It isn't my
T7	170:14	town. Just look along the road, and tell me if	you can see either of them."
T6	166:27	"If	you can see whether I'm singing or not, you've sharper eyes
A7	59:26	"Sh! Sh!" and the Dormouse sulkily remarked "If	you ca'n't be civil, you'd better finish the story for
T3	134:26	tone: "only think how convenient it would be "If	you could manage to go home without it! For instance, if
A2	19:34	Dinah. I think you'd take a fancy to cats, if	you could only see her. She is such a dear quiet thing,"
T3	131:30	close to her ear: "something about 'you would if	you could,' you know."
A1	11: 2	burn you if you hold it too long; and that, if	you cut your finger very deeply with a knife, it usually
T5	150: 5	"You couldn't have it if	you did want it," the Queen said. "The rule is, jam
A12	94:23	"If	you didn't sign it," said the King, "that only makes the
A4	31:30	And Alice called out, as loud as she could, "If	you do, I'll set Dinah at you!"
T7	172:31	poor King, jumping up and shaking himself. "If	you do such a thing again, I'll have you buttered! It went
A10	84: 4	that stuff?" the Mock Turtle interrupted, "if	you don't explain it as you go on? It's by far the most
T2	122:14	who were just beginning again, she whispered "If	you don't hold your tongues, I'll pick you!"
A9	73:23	a Gryphon, lying fast asleep in the sun. (If	you don't know what a Gryphon is, look at the picture.) "Up
A9	76:31	"Well, then," the Gryphon went on, "if	you don't know what to uglify is, you are a simpleton."
A2	20:15	we wo'n't talk about cats, or dogs either, if	you don't like them!" When the Mouse heard this, it turned
T1	115:27	"You will, though," the Queen said, "if	you don't make a memorandum of it."
T5	156:12	may we wait and pick some?" Alice pleaded. "If	you don't mind stopping the boat for a minute."
A1	11: 3	bleeds; and she had never forgotten that, if	you drink much from a bottle marked "poison," it is almost
T2	122:36	"Hold your tongue!" cried the Tiger-lily. "As if	you ever saw anybody! You keep your head under the leaves,
T9	194:31	her eyes. "I can do Addition," she said, "if	you give me time--but I ca'n't do Subtraction under any
T5	155: 8	pair of needles. "You'll make me giddy soon, if	you go on turning round like that." She was now working
T6	168:29	mouth under. It's always the same. Now if	you had the two eyes on the same side of the nose, for
T5	151:20	"But if	you hadn't done them," the Queen said, "that would have
A1	11: 1	such as, that a red-hot poker will burn you if	you hold it too long; and that, if you cut your finger very
A7	56:35	"If	you knew Time as well as I do," said the Hatter, "you
T5	156:13	"How am I to stop it?" said the Sheep. "If	you leave off rowing, it'll stop of itself."
T1	111: 3	peep of the passage in Looking-glass House, if	you leave the door of our drawing-room wide open: and it's
T8	182:35	a plan of my own invention. You may try it if	you like."
T2	126: 8	managed. You can be the White Queen's Pawn, if	you like, as Lily's too young to play: and you're in the
T7	175:32	"Yes, if	you like," said Alice.
A10	81:10	"I can tell you more than that, if	you like," said the Gryphon. "Do you know why it's called a
T5	154: 5	may look in front of you, and on both sides, if	you like," said the Sheep; "but you ca'n't look all round
T2	125:13	shook her head. "You may call it 'nonsense' if	you like," she said, "but I've heard nonsense, compared
T7	175: 6	But I'll make a memorandum about her, if	you like--She's a dear good creature," he repeated softly
A6	49:10	"Here! You may nurse it a bit, if	you like!" the Duchess said to Alice, flinging the baby at
T6	160:25	King has promised me--ah, you may turn pale, if	you like! You didn't think I was going to say that, did you
T3	133: 4	up that bush, you'll see a Rocking-horse-fly, if	you look. It's made entirely of wood, and gets about by
T4	145:17	"Hush! You'll be waking him, I'm afraid, if	you make so much noise."
T8W	21: 8	no doubt. One would have done as well as two, if	you must have them so close--"
A7	56:43	the Hatter. "He wo'n't stand beating. Now, if	you only kept on good terms with him, he'd do almost
T9	192:21	was always ready for a little argument, "and if	you only spoke when you were spoken to, and the other
A6	51:15	"Oh, you're sure to do that," said the Cat, "if	you only walk long enough."
T5	149:29	"It ca'n't go straight, you know, if	you pin it all on one side," Alice said as she gently put
T8	188: 8	that's the way I get my bread--/ A trifle, if	you please.'
A2	15:33	near her, she began, in a low, timid voice, "If	you please, Sir--" The Rabbit started violently, dropped
A3	22: 2	the driest thing I know. Silence all round, if	you please! 'William the Conqueror, whose cause was
T2	127:17	"you'd generally get to somewhere else--if	you ran very fast for a long time as we've been doing."
T9	192:27	of the conversation. "What do you mean by 'If	you really are a Queen'? What right have you to call
T1	110:22	the Red Queen, Kitty! Do you know, I think if	you sat up and folded your arms, you'd look exactly like
T6	163: 1	"And if	you take one from three hundred and sixty-five what remains
T4	138:13	"Contrariwise," added the one marked 'DEE,' "if	you think we're alive, you ought to speak."
T4	138:10	"If	you think we're wax-works," he said, "you ought to pay, you
T9	193: 9	said the Red Queen. "I said you couldn't if	you tried."
T9	193: 5	a joke, I hope. You couldn't deny that, even if	you tried with both hands."
T1	110: 6	we were playing just now, you watched just as if	you understood it: and when I said 'Check!' you purred!
T2	127:20	you can do, to keep in the same place. If	you want to get somewhere else, you must run at least twice
A11	86:18	crown over the wig (look at the frontispiece if	you want to see how he did it), he did not look at all
T8W	20:12	mouth as small as that," the Wasp persisted. "If	you was a-fighting, now--could you get hold of the other
T2	123: 1	no more what's going on in the world, than if	you were a bud!"
A6	46:20	"if we had the door between us. For instance, if	you were inside, you might knock, and I could let you out,
A2	19:31	passionate voice. "Would you like cats, if	you were me?"
A5	41:14	I should like to be a little larger, Sir, if	you wouldn't mind," said Alice: "three inches is such a
T8W	16: 7	"You'd be cross too, if	you'd a wig like mine," the Wasp went on. "They jokes at
T6	162: 4	"An uncomfortable sort of age. Now if	you'd asked my advice, I'd have said 'Leave off at seven'--
T1	108:12	is, Kitty?" Alice began. "You'd have guessed if	you'd been up in the window with me--only Dinah was making
A9	72: 6	that is--'Be what you would seem to be'--or, if	you'd like it put more simply--'Never imagine yourself not
T6	163:45	of that subject, and it would be just as well if	you'd mention what you mean to do next, as I suppose you

IF (cont.)
A2   19:41   offended. "We wo'n't talk about her any more, if you'd rather not."
T1   108:31   your fault, for keeping your eyes open--if you'd shut them tight up, it wouldn't have happened. Now
T7   175:30   we have seen each other," said the Unicorn, "if you'll believe in me, I'll believe in you. Is that a
T3   137: 1   "I'll tell you, if you'll come a little further on," the Fawn said. "I ca'n't
T1   110:30   "Now, I'll only attend, Kitty, and not talk so much, I'll tell
T9   195:11   saw a way out of the difficulty, this time. "If you'll tell me what language 'fiddle-de-dee' is, I'll tell
T5   149:16   their conversation, so she smiled and said "If your Majesty will only tell me the right way to begin, I'll
T8W   20: 2   for you," Alice said heartily: "and I think if your wig fitted a little better, they wouldn't tease you
A6   50: 3   No, there were no tears. "If you're going to turn into a pig, my dear," said Alice,
T1   110:28   that it might see how sulky it was, "--and if you're not good directly," she added, "I'll put you through
T4   143:11   besides / Are very good indeed--/ Now, if you're ready, Oysters dear, / We can begin to feed.'
T3   131:32   in vain to see where the voice came from. "If you're so anxious to have a joke made, why don't you make
T8W   14:17   "You may read it if you've a mind to," the Wasp said, rather sulkily. "Nobody's
A10   80:21   Dinn may be," said the Mock Turtle; "but, if you've seen them so often, of course you know what they're
IGNORANT (2)
A1   9: 2   you think you could manage it?) "And what an ignorant little girl she'll think me for asking! No, it'll
T6   162:27   "I know it's very ignorant of me," Alice said, in so humble a tone that Humpty
I'LL (71)
T1   110:16   say "Well, you can be one of them, then, and I'll be all the rest." And once she had really frightened her
A3   25:35   jury or judge, would be wasting our breath. 'I'll be judge, I'll be jury, said cunning old Fury: 'I'll try
A3   25:37   would be wasting our breath. 'I'll be judge, I'll be jury, said cunning old Fury: 'I'll try the whole cause
T7   175:31   said the Unicorn, "if you'll believe in me, I'll believe in you. Is that a bargain?"
A2   17:24   first, and then, if I like being that person, I'll come up: if not, I'll stay down here till I'm somebody
T5   149:16   will only tell me the right way to begin, I'll do it as well as I can."
A1   12:34   were beautifully marked in currants. "Well, I'll eat it," said Alice, "and if it makes me grow larger, I
A8   68: 8   "I'll fetch the executioner myself," said the King eagerly, and
T5   155: 2   she added, as a sudden thought struck her. "I'll follow it up to the very top shelf of all. It'll puzzle
A1   12:36   I can creep under the door: so either way I'll get into the garden, and I don't care which happens!"
T8   184:19   "I'll get one," the Knight said thoughtfully to himself. "One
A12   95:25   wasn't a bit afraid of interrupting him,) "I'll give him sixpence. I don't believe there's an atom of
A2   15: 2   wo'n't walk the way I want to go! Let me see. I'll give them a new pair of boots every Christmas."
T5   153: 6   remarked. "I can believe it without that. Now I'll give you something to believe. I'm just one hundred and
T2   123:35   "I think I'll go and meet her," said Alice, for, though the flowers
T3   129:17   quantities of honey they must make! I think I'll go down and--no, I wo'n't go just yet," she went on,
T3   129:25   "I think I'll go down the other way," she said after a pause; "and
A4   29:28   a failure. Alice heard it say to itself "Then I'll go round and get in at the window."
T8   182:10   an invention of my own. And now help me on. I'll go with you to the end of the wood--What's that dish for
A6   50: 4   into a pig, my dear," said Alice, seriously, "I'll have nothing more to do with you. Mind now!" The poor
T5   158:10   "Then I'll have one, please," said Alice, as she put the money down
T7   172:31   himself. "If you do such a thing again, I'll have you buttered! It went through and through my head
A11   90: 5   "You must remember," remarked the King, "or I'll have you executed."
A11   88:29   said the King: "and don't be nervous, or I'll have you executed on the spot."
A11   89: 9   evidence," the King repeated angrily, "or I'll have you executed, whether you are nervous or not."
T8W   13:11   as she turned to spring over the brook:--but I'll just ask him what's the matter," she added, checking
T3   137:27   of that before--But I ca'n't stay there long. I'll just call and say 'How d'ye do?' and ask them the way out
A4   28: 6   "whenever I eat or drink anything: so I'll just see what this bottle does. I do hope it'll make me
T2   127:31   you're refreshing yourself," said the Queen, "I'll just take the measurements." And she took a ribbon out of
A5   40: 8   listen all day to such stuff? / Be off, or I'll kick you down-stairs!"
A1   10:20   was not going to do that in a hurry. "No, I'll look first," she said, "and see whether it's marked
T7   175: 5   as well try to catch a Bandersnatch! But I'll make a memorandum about her, if you like--She's a dear
A7   60:43   and close to the little glass table. "Now, I'll manage better this time," she said to herself, and began
A7   60:35   "At any rate I'll never go there again!" said Alice, as she picked her way
T2   122:15   whispered "If you don't hold your tongues, I'll pick you!"
A4   32: 3   and some of them hit her in the face. "I'll put a stop to this," she said to herself, and shouted out
T1   110:28   and if you're not good directly," she added, "I'll put you through into Looking-glass House. How would you
T12   208: 3   All the time you're eating your breakfast, I'll repeat 'The Walrus and the Carpenter' to you; and then
T9   198: 5   the song's over," thought Alice, "and then I'll ring the--the--which bell must I ring?" she went on, very
T8   181: 4   the next brook," said the White Knight. "I'll see you safe to the end of the wood--and then I must go
A4   31:30   called out, as loud as she could, "If you do, I'll set Dinah at you!"
T3   137:18   the two finger-posts both pointed along it. "I'll settle it," Alice said to herself, "when the road divides
T9   204:27   which had just lighted upon the table, "I'll shake you into a kitten, that I will!"
A3   21:14   out "Sit down, all of you, and listen to me! I'll soon make you dry enough!" They all sat down at once, in
A2   17:20   I've made up my mind about it: if I'm Mabel, I'll stay down here. It'll be no use their putting their heads
A2   17:24   like being that person, I'll come up: if not, I'll stay down here till I'm somebody else'--but, oh dear!"
A3   25:13   both go to law: I will prosecute you.--Come, I'll take no denial: We must have the trial; For really this
T5   149:38   "I'm sure I'll take you with pleasure!" the Queen said. "Two pence a
A8   62:15   "Yes, it is his business!" said Five. "And I'll tell him--it was for bringing the cook tulip-roots
A9   74:27   "I'll tell it her," said the Mock Turtle in a deep, hollow tone
T8   187:31   "I'll tell thee everything I can: / There's little to relate. /
T9   194:36   "we'll often say it over together, dear. And I'll tell you a secret--I can read words of one letter! Isn't
T1   110:30   only attend, Kitty, and not talk so much, I'll tell you all my ideas about Looking-glass House. First,
T8   184:29   "I'll tell you how I came to think of it," said the Knight.
T8W   18: 3   "I'll tell you how I came to wear it," the Wasp said. "When I
T3   137: 1   "I'll tell you, if you'll come a little further on," the Fawn
A2   20:19   voice, "Let us get to the shore, and then I'll tell you my history, and you'll understand why it is I
T9   195:12   tell me what language 'fiddle-de-dee' is, I'll tell you the French for it!" she exclaimed triumphantly.
T9   192: 2   expected I should be a Queen so soon--and I'll tell you what it is, your Majesty," she went on, in a
T5   155: 1   this one is the most provoking of all--but I'll tell you what--" she added, as a sudden thought struck
A2   17: 3   certain! I must have been changed for Mabel! I'll try and say 'How doth the little--'," and she crossed her

I'LL (cont.)

T6	166:30	"In spring, when woods are getting green, / I'll try and tell you what I mean:"
A2	16: 8	I'm I, and--oh dear, how puzzling it all is! I'll try if I know all the things I used to know. Let me see:
T2	120: 8	goes straight back to the house! Well then, I'll try it the other way."
T2	124:16	much in awe of the Queen to disbelieve it. "I'll try it when I go home," she thought to herself, "the next
A3	25:44	judge, I'll be jury, said cunning old Fury: 'I'll try the whole cause, and condemn you to death.
T8W	18:11	what I'm used to," said the Wasp: "however I'll try; wait a bit." He was silent for a few moments, and
T8	190:20	"Of course I'll wait," said Alice: "and thank you very much for coming so
T9	198: 5	"I'll wait till the song's over," thought Alice, "and then I'll
T7	172:25	"I'll whisper it," said the Messenger, putting his hands to his
A4	29: 7	me, that there ought! And when I grow up, I'll write one--but I'm grown up now," she added in a

ILL (2)

A7	59: 4	Alice gently remarked. "They'd have been ill."
A7	59: 5	"So they were," said the Dormouse; "very ill."

I'M (129)

A5	43: 5	a serpent, I tell you!" said Alice. "I'm a--I'm a--"
A4	31:20	know--No more, thank ye; I'm better now--but I'm a deal too flustered to tell you--all I know is, something
A9	70: 7	"When I'm a Duchess," she said to herself (not in a very hopeful
T3	137: 6	air, and shook itself free from Alice's arm. "I'm a Fawn!" it cried out in a voice of delight. "And, dear
T8	184:22	this, and then the Knight went on again. "I'm a great hand at inventing things. Now, I daresay you
A11	88:25	as an explanation. "I've none of my own. I'm a hatter."
T1	110:18	in her ear, "Nurse! Do let's pretend that I'm a hungry hyaena and you're a bone!"
A5	43: 5	I'm not a serpent, I tell you!" said Alice. "I'm a--I'm a--"
A5	43: 9	"I--I'm a little girl," said Alice, rather doubtfully, as she
T2	124:17	home," she thought to herself, "the next time I'm a little late for dinner."
A11	89:19	"I'm a poor man," the Hatter went on, "and most things twinkled
A11	90: 8	bread-and-butter and went down on one knee. "I'm a poor man, your Majesty," he began.
A11	89:11	"I'm a poor man, your Majesty," the Hatter began, in a
T8	186:25	"That wouldn't be very nice, I'm afraid--"
A1	9: 9	here with me! There are no mice in the air, I'm afraid, but you might catch a bat, and that's very like a
T4	144:36	"I'm afraid he'll catch cold with lying on the damp grass,"
A5	36:31	"I'm afraid I am, Sir," said Alice. "I ca'n't remember things
A5	35:14	"I'm afraid I ca'n't put it more clearly," Alice replied, very
T6	161:17	"I'm afraid I ca'n't quite remember it," Alice said, very
A7	58:21	"I'm afraid I don't know one," said Alice, rather alarmed at
T6	167: 5	"I'm afraid I don't quite understand," said Alice.
T3	130: 2	"I'm afraid I haven't got one," Alice said in a frightened tone
T4	145:17	help saying "Hush! You'll be waking him, I'm afraid, if you make so much noise."
T6	166: 1	"And then 'mome raths'?" said Alice. "I'm afraid I'm giving you a great deal of trouble."
T8	184:37	gravely; "so I ca'n't tell for certain--but I'm afraid it would be a little hard."
T6	161:11	I don't know what would happen to his head! I'm afraid it would come off!"
A2	20:10	oh dear!" cried Alice in a sorrowful tone. "I'm afraid I've offended it again!" For the Mouse was swimming
T8W	20:14	"I'm afraid not," said Alice.
A5	41: 2	"Not quite right, I'm afraid," said Alice, timidly: "some of the words have got
A5	35:11	"I ca'n't explain myself, I'm afraid, Sir," said Alice, "because I'm not myself, you see
T8	185: 7	about it that Alice did not dare to laugh. "I'm afraid you must have hurt him," she said in a trembling
T8W	15:17	Alice put down the newspaper. "I'm afraid you're not well," she said in a soothing tone.
T8	183: 3	"I'm afraid you've not had much practice in riding," she
A6	51:34	growl when I'm pleased, and wag my tail when I'm angry. Therefore I'm mad."
T6	159: 5	be anybody else!" she said to herself. "I'm as certain of it, as if his name were written all over his
T1	110: 4	you play chess? Now, don't smile, my dear. I'm asking it seriously. Because, when we were playing just
A4	31:19	"Well, I hardly know--No more, thank ye; I'm better now--but I'm a deal too flustered to tell you--all
A2	17: 2	of Rome, and Rome--no, that's all wrong, I'm certain! I must have been changed for Mabel! I'll try and
T3	136: 4	And now, who am I? I will remember, if I can! I'm determined to do it!" But being determined didn't help her
A9	71: 6	said, after a pause: "the reason is, that I'm doubtful about the temper of your flamingo. Shall I try
T7	174:10	'em now," said Hatta; "this is a bit of it as I'm eating."
T4	147:37	Tweedledee, who had overheard the remark. "I'm far worse than you!"
T9	195:40	as warm, and five times as cold--just as I'm five times as rich as you are, and five times as clever!"
T9	197: 9	other shoulder, "just sing it through to me. I'm getting sleepy, too." In another moment both Queens were
A7	58:19	the March Hare interrupted, yawning. "I'm getting tired of this. I vote the young lady tells us a
T6	166: 1	then 'mome raths'?" said Alice. "I'm afraid I'm giving you a great deal of trouble."
A11	90:16	"I'm glad I've seen that done," thought Alice. "I've so often
A9	72:20	"A cheap sort of present!" thought Alice. "I'm glad people don't give birthday-presents like that!" But
A7	55:13	we shall have some fun now!" thought Alice. "I'm glad they've begun asking riddles--I believe I can guess
T9	200:11	there were even a few flowers among them. "I'm glad they've come without waiting to be asked," she
A5	43:41	all these changes are! I'm never sure what I'm going to be, from one minute to another! However, I've got
T6	166:19	"The piece I'm going to repeat," he went on without noticing her remark,
T1	108:26	me!" she went on, holding up one finger. "I'm going to tell you all your faults. Number one: you
T7	173:11	"I'm good enough," the King said, "only I'm not strong enough.
A11	88:41	"I ca'n't help it," said Alice very meekly: "I'm growing."
A4	29: 7	And when I grow up, I'll write one--but I'm grown up now," she added in a sorrowful tone: "at least
A4	30: 2	voice she had never heard before, "Sure then I'm here! Digging for apples, yer honour!"
A2	16: 7	such a very little! Besides, she's she, and I'm I, and--oh dear, how puzzling it all is! I'll try if I
T5	153: 6	that. Now I'll give you something to believe. I'm just one hundred and one, five months and a day."
A2	17:20	learn! No, I've made up my mind about it: if I'm Mabel, I'll stay down here. It'll be no use their putting
A6	51:34	and wag my tail when I'm angry. Therefore I'm mad."
A6	51:25	"How do you know I'm mad?" said Alice.
A6	51:24	that," said the Cat: "we're all mad here. I'm mad. You're mad."
T1	113:12	on, as she put her head closer down, "and I'm nearly sure they ca'n't see me. I feel somehow as if I was
A5	43:40	done now! How puzzling all these changes are! I'm never sure what I'm going to be, from one minute to

I'M (cont.)
```
T5    155:37   often?" Alice  asked at last, rather vexed. "I'm not a bird!"
A12    93:38                                               "I'm not a mile high," said Alice.
A5     43: 5                                  "But I'm not a serpent, I tell you!" said Alice. "I'm a--I'm a--"
A5     42:28                                       "I'm not a serpent!" said Alice indignantly. "Let me alone!"
T9    198: 7   puzzled by the names. "I'm not a visitor, and I'm not a servant. There ought to be one marked 'Queen,' you
T9    198: 7   she went on, very much puzzled by the names. "I'm not a visitor, and I'm not a servant. There ought to be
A2     16: 4                                 "I'm sure I'm not Ada," she said, "for her hair goes in such long
T6    166: 3   a 'rath' is a sort of green pig: but 'mome' I'm not certain about. I think it's short for 'from home'--
T2    120:14   and pretending it was arguing with her. "I'm not going in again yet. I know I should have to get
T5    156:10   her knitting: "I didn't put 'em there, and I'm not going to take 'em away."
A5     43:25   a good deal to me," said Alice hastily; "but I'm not looking for eggs, as it happens; and, if I was, I
A5     35:11     I'm afraid, Sir," said Alice, "because I'm not myself, you see."
T6    162:37                                         "I'm not offended," said Humpty Dumpty.
A5     41: 8                             "Oh, I'm not particular as to size," Alice hastily replied; "only
T6    160:39   never see such another: and, to show you I'm not proud, you may shake hands with me!" And he grinned
T7    176:20                                        "I'm not so sure of that," said the Unicorn.
T7    173:11    "I'm good enough," the King said, "only I'm not strong enough. You see, a minute goes by so fearfully
T12   207:36   not mention it to your friends just yet, for I'm not sure.
A2     15:41   remember feeling a little different. But if I'm not the same, the next question is 'Who in the world am I
A5     41:18                                 "But I'm not used to it!" pleaded poor Alice in a piteous tone. And
A3     21:10   at last turned sulky, and would only say, "I'm older than you, and must know better." And this Alice
A11    90:23   "I can't go no lower," said the Hatter: "I'm on the floor, as it is."
T3    129: 5   rivers--there are none. Principal mountains--I'm on the only one, but I don't think it's got any name.
A6     46:11   "and that for two reasons. First, because I'm on the same side of the door as you are: secondly, because
T6    160:37       that is. Now, take a good look at me! I'm one that has spoken to a King, I am: mayhap you'll never
T4    145:12   Alice exclaimed indignantly. "Besides, if I'm only a sort of thing in his dream, what are you, I should
A2     14: 3   quite forgot how to speak good English). "Now I'm opening out like the largest telescope that ever was!
T8    184:33   then the feet are high enough, you see--then I'm over, you see."
A5     37: 7   it might injure the brain; / But, now that I'm perfectly sure I have none, / Why, I do it again and again
A6     51:33   its tail when it's pleased. Now I growl when I'm pleased, and wag my tail when I'm angry. Therefore I'm mad
T2    127:23   "I'd rather not try, please!" said Alice. "I'm quite content to stay here--only I am so hot and thirsty!"
A4     28: 7   it'll make me grow large again, for really I'm quite tired of being such a tiny little thing!"
T3    132:29   in insects at all," Alice explained, "because I'm rather afraid of them--at least the large kinds. But I can
T1    108:39   been punished for any of them yet. You know I'm saving up all your punishments for Wednesday week--Suppose
T5    153: 4                                        "I'm seven and a half, exactly."
T6    166:27          "If you can see whether I'm singing or not, you've sharper eyes than most," Humpty
T5    152:28   must have flown away, I think," said Alice: "I'm so glad it's gone. I thought it was the night coming on."
A2     17:24   come up: if not, I'll stay down here till I'm somebody else'--but, oh dear!" cried Alice, with a sudden
A2     16: 5   and mine doesn't go in ringlets at all; and I'm sure I ca'n't be Mabel, for I know all sorts of things,
T9    192:38                                        "I'm sure I didn't mean--" Alice was beginning, but the Red
T7    177: 3                                        "I'm sure I don't know," the Lion growled out as he lay down
A4     30:20   me out of the window, I only wish they could! I'm sure I don't want to stay in here any longer!"
A2     14: 7   your shoes and stockings for you now, dears? I'm sure I sha'n't be able! I shall be a great deal too far
T9    194:12      remain: it would come to bite me--and I'm sure I shouldn't remain!"
T5    149:38                                        "I'm sure I'll take you with pleasure!" the Queen said. "Two
A2     16: 4                                        "I'm sure I'm not Ada," she said, "for her hair goes in such
T4    138:15                                        "I'm sure I'm very sorry," was all Alice could say; for the
T1    111: 6   only get through into Looking-glass House! I'm sure it's got, oh! such beautiful things in it! Let's
T5    150:17                                        "I'm sure mine only works one way," Alice remarked. "I ca'n't
T7    172:20   best," the Messenger said in a sullen tone. "I'm sure nobody walks much faster than I do!"
T3    135: 5                       "That would never do, I'm sure," said Alice: "the governess would never think of
A3     26:38   "Nobody seems to like her, down here, and I'm sure she's the best cat in the world! Oh, my dear Dinah! I
T1    110: 2   her hands. "And I do so wish it was true! I'm sure the woods look sleepy in the autumn, when the leaves
A2     17:16                                        "I'm sure those are not the right words," said poor Alice, and
T12   208:11   to know--Oh, Kitty, do help to settle it! I'm sure your paw can wait!" But the provoking kitten only
A2     15:11                          Oh dear, what nonsense I'm talking!
A9     77: 2   show it you, myself," the Mock Turtle said: "I'm too stiff. And the Gryphon never learnt it."
T9    202:14      up!' / Ah, that is so hard that I fear I'm unable!
T8W    18:10                                 "It aint what I'm used to," said the Wasp: "however I'll try; wait a bit."
T4    147:34   "I'm very brave, generally," he went on in a low voice: "only
T5    149: 5   "I'm very glad I happened to be in the way," Alice said, as she
T8W    20: 1   "I'm very sorry for you," Alice said heartily: "and I think if
T4    138:15                               "I'm sure I'm very sorry," was all Alice could say; for the words of the
A5     42:41                               "I'm very sorry you've been annoyed," said Alice, who was
```
IMAGINE (2)
```
A11    91:32   got much evidence yet," she said to herself. Imagine her surprise, when the White Rabbit read out, at the
A9     72: 7   or, if you'd like it put more simply--'Never imagine yourself not to be otherwise than what it might appear
```
IMITATE (1)
```
T1    110:24   it up before the kitten as a model for it to imitate: however, the thing didn't succeed, principally, Alice
```
IMITATED (1)
```
A12    94:19                              "He must have imitated somebody else's hand," said the King. (The jury all
```
IMMEDIATE (1)
```
A3     22:29   "I move that the meeting adjourn, for the immediate adoption of more energetic remedies--"
```
IMMEDIATELY (5)
```
T1    115:15                              The King immediately fell flat on his back, and lay perfectly still;
A4     34: 8   over the edge of the mushroom, and her eyes immediately met those of a large blue caterpillar, that was
T4    146:22   of course!" Here he looked at Tweedledee, who immediately sat down on the ground, and tried to hide himself
A11    90:11   Here one of the guinea-pigs cheered, and was immediately suppressed by the officers of the court. (As that
A11    90:18   was some attempt at applause, which was immediately suppressed by the officers of the court,' and I
```

IMMENSE (1)
  A5   42:10 she could see, when she looked down, was an immense length of neck, which seemed to rise like a stalk out
IMPATIENT (2)
  T9   197:18 wake up, you heavy things!" she went on in an impatient tone; but there was no answer but a gentle snoring.
  A10   81:44 The adventures first," said the Gryphon in an impatient tone: "explanations take such a dreadful time."
IMPATIENTLY (11)
  T9   193: 1 beginning, but the Red Queen interrupted her impatiently.
  A7   56:24   "The Dormouse shook its head impatiently, and said, without opening its eyes, "Of course,
  A8   63:38 "Idiot!" said the Queen, tossing her head impatiently; and turning to Alice, she went on: "What's your
  A3   26:15 please do!" But the Mouse only shook its head impatiently, and walked a little quicker.
  A10   81:25 eels, of course," the Gryphon replied, rather impatiently: "any shrimp could have told you that."
  T7   174: 1   "Speak, ca'n't you!" Haigha cried impatiently. But Hatta only munched away, and drank some more
  T3   131:26   "Indeed I sha'n't!" Alice said rather impatiently. "I don't belong to this railway journey at all--I
  T7   171: 6   "Don't I tell you?" the King repeated impatiently. "I must have two--to fetch and carry. One to
  T9   199:17   "Nothing!" Alice said impatiently. "I've been knocking at it!"
  T9   204:11 towards Alice's chair, and beckoning to her impatiently to get out of its way.
  T6   160: 6   name enough!" Humpty Dumpty interrupted impatiently. "What does it mean?"
IMPENETRABILITY (2)
  T6   163:44 looking very much pleased. "I meant by 'impenetrability' that we've had enough of that subject, and it
  T6   163:41 however, I can manage the whole lot of them! Impenetrability! That's what I say!"
IMPERIAL (2)
  T1   114: 1   "Imperial fiddlestick!" said the King, rubbing his nose, which
  T1   113:21 over among the cinders. "My precious Lily! My imperial kitten!" and she began scrambling wildly up the side
IMPERIOUS (1)
  AI   3:13   Imperious Prima flashes forth / Her edict "to begin it": / In
IMPERTINENCE (1)
  T9   201:22   "What impertinence!" said the Pudding. "I wonder how you'd like it,
IMPERTINENT (1)
  A8   67:44   "Don't be impertinent," said the King, "and don't look at me like that!"
IMPORTANT (8)
  A3   22: 1   "Ahem!" said the Mouse with an important air. "Are you all ready? This is the driest thing I
  A12   93:30   Some of the jury wrote it down "important," and some "unimportant." Alice could see this, as
  A12   93:28   "important--unimportant--unimportant--important--" as if he were trying which word sounded best.
  A12   95:21   "That's the most important piece of evidence we've heard yet," said the King,
  T9   193: 4 should have some meaning--and a child's more important than a joke, I hope. You couldn't deny that, even if
  A12   93:21   "That's very important," the King said, turning to the jury. They were just
  A5   36:19 Caterpillar called after her. "I've something important to say!"
  A12   93:27 and went on to himself in an undertone, "important--unimportant--unimportant--important--" as if he
IMPOSSIBLE (6)
  A1   10:11 think that very few things indeed were really impossible.
  T5   153:12 no use trying," she said: "one ca'n't believe impossible things."
  T5   153:15 Why, sometimes I've believed as many as six impossible things before breakfast. There goes the shawl
  T12   207:11 occasion the kitten only purred: and it was impossible to guess whether it meant "yes" or "no."
  A6   48:14 howling so much already, that it was quite impossible to say whether the blows hurt it or not.
  A6   50: 6 little thing sobbed again (or grunted, it was impossible to say which), and they went on for some while in
IMPROVE (1)
  A2   17: 9   "How doth the little crocodile / Improve his shining tail, / And pour the waters of the Nile /
IN (801) [entries omitted]
INCESSANTLY (1)
  A5   37: 3 hair has become very white; / And yet you incessantly stand on your head--/ Do you think, at your age,
INCH (1)
  T3   130: 5 The land there is worth a thousand pounds an inch!"
INCHES (9)
  T2   127:33 took a ribbon out of her pocket, marked in inches, and began measuring the ground, and sticking little
  T9   203: 5 and she really did rise as she spoke, several inches; but she got hold of the edge of the table, and managed
  A2   15:24 there was a large pool round her, about four inches deep, and reaching half down the hall.
  A5   41:17 upright as it spoke (it was exactly three inches high).
  A5   44: 6 till she had brought herself down to nine inches high.
  A1   12: 3 And so it was indeed: she was now only ten inches high, and her face brightened up at the thought that
  T2   123:31 her in the ashes, she had been only three inches high--and here she was, half a head taller than Alice
  A1   9:41 and behind it was a little door about fifteen inches high: she tried the little golden key in the lock, and
  A5   41:15 if you wouldn't mind," said Alice: "three inches is such a wretched height to be."
INCLINED (2)
  T5   152:13 to do it?" Alice said, feeling very much inclined to laugh.
  A3   23: 4 ought to speak, and no one else seemed inclined to say anything.
INCONVENIENT (1)
  T12   207: 6   "it is a very inconvenient habit of kittens (Alice had once made the remark)
INDEED (25)
  A8   66:19 conclusion that it was a very difficult game indeed.
  A10   82:21 she was saying; and the words came very queer indeed:--
  A3   21: 1   They were indeed a queer-looking party that assembled on the bank--the
  T3   134:24   "No, indeed," Alice said, a little anxiously.
  T8   184:28   "Very much indeed," Alice said politely.
  T6   160:34   "I haven't indeed!" Alice said very gently. "It's in a book."
  A4   28: 9   It did so indeed, and much sooner than she had expected: before she had
  T8   183:13 could think of nothing better to say than "Indeed?" but she said it as heartily as she could. They went
  A2   19:42   "We, indeed!" cried the Mouse, who was trembling down to the end of
  T5   155:32   "Indeed I did," said Alice: "you've said it very often--and
  A12   96: 4 the Queen--'What would become of you?'--What, indeed!--'I gave her one, they gave him two'--why, that must
  T3   131:26   "Indeed I sha'n't!" Alice said rather impatiently. "I don't

INDEED (cont.)
```
T4   143:10  / Pepper and vinegar besides / Are very good indeed--/ Now, if you're ready, Oysters dear, / We can begin
T2   120:11  coming back to the house, do what she would. Indeed, once, when she turned a corner rather more quickly
A10   79: 4                                    "Very much indeed," said Alice.
A2    20: 1                                  "I wo'n't indeed!" said Alice, in a great hurry to change the subject of
A10   78:13                                       "No, indeed," said Alice. "What sort of a dance is it?"
A5    41:16            "It is a very good height indeed!" said the Caterpillar angrily, rearing itself upright
A7    59:30                              "One, indeed!" said the Dormouse indignantly. However, he consented
A5    43:11                     "A likely story indeed!" said the Pigeon, in a tone of the deepest contempt.
A4    30: 4                   "Digging for apples, indeed!" said the Rabbit angrily. "Here! Come help me out of
A3    21: 8  them, as if she had known them all her life. Indeed, she had quite a long argument with the Lory, who at
A1    12: 3                                    And so it was indeed: she was now only ten inches high, and her face
A1    10:11  Alice had begun to think that very few things indeed were really impossible.
T2   123:30  a good deal!" was her first remark. She had indeed: when Alice first found her in the ashes, she had been
```
INDIGNANT (2)
```
T6   162: 9                      Alice felt even more indignant at this suggestion. "I mean," she said, "that one
A11   86:33  "Stupid things!" Alice began in a loud indignant voice; but she stopped herself hastily, for the
```
INDIGNANTLY (7)
```
A9    76:12                        "Certainly not!" said Alice indignantly.
T6   162: 7  I never ask advice about growing," Alice said indignantly.
A7    54:10  coming. "There's plenty of room!" said Alice indignantly, and she sat down in a large arm-chair at one end
T4   145:12              "I shouldn't!" Alice exclaimed indignantly. "Besides, if I'm only a sort of thing in his
A7    59:30  "One, indeed!" said the Dormouse indignantly. However, he consented to go on. "And so these
A5    42:28            "I'm not a serpent!" said Alice indignantly. "Let me alone!"
T4   144:18            "That was mean!" Alice said indignantly. "Then I like the Carpenter best--if he didn't eat
```
INGENUITY (1)
```
T6   165: 5  I suppose?" said Alice, surprised at her own ingenuity.
```
INJURE (1)
```
A5    37: 6  replied to his son, / "I feared it might injure the brain; / But, now that I'm perfectly sure I have
```
INK (5)
```
T1   116: 3  still a little anxious about him, and had the ink all ready to throw over him, in case he fainted again),
T1   115:18    she could find nothing but a bottle of ink, and when she got back with it she found he had recovered,
T6   166:35  when the leaves are brown, / Take pen and ink, and write it down."
T9   200: 1  "Then fill up the glasses with treacle and ink, / Or anything else that is pleasant to drink: / Mix sand
A12   96:23  but he now hastily began again, using the ink, that was trickling down his face, as long as it lasted.)
```
INKSTAND (1)
```
A12   96:20  said the Queen, furiously, throwing an inkstand at the Lizard as she spoke. (The unfortunate little
```
INQUIRED (3)
```
T3   132:28  rejoice in, where you come from?" the Gnat inquired.
T3   131:43            "What kind of insect?" Alice inquired, a little anxiously. What she really wanted to know
A9    76:20                  "What was that?" inquired Alice.
```
INQUISITIVELY (1)
```
A2    19:18  O mouse!") The mouse looked at her rather inquisitively, and seemed to her to wink with one of its
```
INSECT (4)
```
T3   131:42    And you wo'n't hurt me, though I am an insect."
T3   131:43                  "What kind of insect?" Alice inquired, a little anxiously. What she really
T3   132:18  a tree--while the Gnat (for that was the insect she had been talking to) was balancing itself on a twig
T3   134: 5  on, after she had taken a good look at the insect with its head on fire, and had thought to herself, "I
```
INSECTS (6)
```
T3t  129: 1                      LOOKING-GLASS INSECTS
T3   134: 6  to herself, "I wonder if that's the reason insects are so fond of flying into candles--because they want
T3   132:29              "I don't rejoice in insects at all," Alice explained, "because I'm rather afraid
T3   132:27            "What sort of insects do you rejoice in, where you come from?" the Gnat
T3   132:23      "--then you don't like all insects?" the Gnat went on, as quietly as if nothing had
T3   132:41  no names--however, go on with your list of insects: you're wasting time."
```
INSIDE (2)
```
A6    46:13  secondly, because they're making such a noise inside, no one could possibly hear you." And certainly there
A6    46:20  door between us. For instance, if you were inside, you might knock, and I could let you out, you know."
```
INSOLENCE (1)
```
A3    22:24  conduct at first was moderate. But the insolence of his Normans--' How are you getting on now, my
```
INSTANCE (7)
```
T3   135: 1  you could manage to go home without it! For instance, if the governess wanted to call you to your lessons,
A6    46:20  to her, "if we had the door between us. For instance, if you were inside, you might knock, and I could let
T5   150: 2  the Queen replied in a careless tone. "For instance, now," she went on, sticking a large piece of plaster
T6   168:30  two eyes on the same side of the nose, for instance--or the mouth at the top--that would be some help."
A7    56:44  almost anything you liked with the clock. For instance, suppose it were nine o'clock in the morning, just
T1   112:12  the rest was as different as possible. For instance, the pictures on the wall next the fire seemed to be
A8    67:27    it is all the things being alive: for instance, there's the arch I've got to go through next walking
```
INSTANTLY (9)
```
T4   140:17                      Tweedledee began instantly:
A4    31:32          There was a dead silence instantly, and Alice thought to herself "I wonder what they
A7    60:31  and walked off: the Dormouse fell asleep instantly, and neither of the others took the least notice of
T7   175:16  happened to fall upon Alice: he turned round instantly, and stood for some time looking at her with an air
A8    65: 1  a shrill, loud voice, and the three gardeners instantly jumped up, and began bowing to the King, the Queen,
A11   88:22  the King exclaimed, turning to the jury, who instantly made a memorandum of the fact.
T8   185:15  hands in some excitement as he said this, and instantly rolled out of the saddle, and fell headlong into a
T7   170: 2  whenever a horse stumbled, the rider fell off instantly. The confusion got worse every moment, and Alice was
A8    63:12  Queen! The Queen!" and the three gardeners instantly threw themselves flat upon their faces. There was a
```
INSTEAD (7)
```
A6    53:18  all! I almost wish I'd gone to see the Hatter instead!"
```

INSTEAD (cont.)
T8W   18:16   should be shaved, / And wear a yellow wig instead.'
T8   182:18   three times that he tried he fell in himself instead. "It's rather a tight fit, you see," he said, as they
A8   62:16   him--it was for bringing the cook tulip-roots instead of onions."
A11   88:32   he bit a large piece out of his teacup instead of the bread-and-butter.
T9   204: 3   was the matter with the White Queen; but, instead of the Queen, there was the leg of mutton sitting in
T7   172:28   as she wanted to hear the news too. However, instead of whispering, he simply shouted, at the top of his
INSULT (1)
A3   26: 9   the Mouse, getting up and walking away. "You insult me by talking such nonsense!"
INTEND (1)
T1   115:38   it writes all manner of things that I don't intend--"
INTENTLY (1)
T7   170:20   this was lost on Alice, who was still looking intently along the road, shading her eyes with one hand. "I
INTEREST (6)
T3   133: 8   looked at the Rocking-horse-fly with great interest, and made up her mind that it must have been just
T8W   17:15   you?" the Wasp said, looking at her with more interest. "And you've got a comb. Much honey?"
T2   128: 5   by this time, and Alice looked on with great interest as she returned to the tree, and then began slowly
T1   115:29   Alice looked on with great interest as the King took an enormous memorandum-book out of
T8   184:15   the Knight asked in a tone of great interest, clasping his arms round the horse's neck as he spoke
A7   58:36   live on?" said Alice, who always took a great interest in questions of eating and drinking.
INTERESTED (1)
T8   186:43   the song, is it?" Alice said, trying to feel interested.
INTERESTING (6) [See also UNINTERESTING]
A6   52:25   "the March Hare will be much the most interesting, and perhaps, as this is May, it wo'n't be raving
A10   80:13   "Thank you, it's a very interesting dance to watch," said Alice, feeling very glad
T2   123:36   said Alice, for, though the flowers were interesting enough, she felt that it would be far grander to
A10   81: 8   "Thank you," said Alice, "it's very interesting. I never knew so much about a whiting before."
A4   28: 5   it and put it to her lips. "I know something interesting is sure to happen," she said to herself, "whenever
A9   74:37   up and saying, "Thank you, Sir, for your interesting story," but she could not help thinking there must
INTERRUPT (3)
T4   140:19   Here Alice ventured to interrupt him. "If it's very long," she said, as politely as
T1   108:26   have you got to say for yourself? Now don't interrupt me!" she went on, holding up one finger. "I'm going
A7   59:28   go on!" Alice said very humbly. "I wo'n't interrupt you again. I dare say there may be one."
INTERRUPTED (24)
T6   163:15   "You're holding it upside down!" Alice interrupted.
T8W   14:24   "Any brown sugar?" the Wasp interrupted.
A9   76: 1   "I never said I didn't!" interrupted Alice.
T8   179:12   At this moment her thoughts were interrupted by a loud shouting of "Ahoy! Ahoy! Check!" and a
T9   194: 1   "She ca'n't do Addition," the Red Queen interrupted. "Can you do Subtraction? Take nine from eight."
T9   192:18   when you're spoken to!" the Queen sharply interrupted her.
T9   193: 1   Alice was beginning, but the Red Queen interrupted her impatiently.
T2   125: 8   "When you say 'hill'," the Queen interrupted, "I could show you hills, in comparison with which
A10   84: 4   of repeating all that stuff?" the Mock Turtle interrupted, "if you don't explain it as you go on? It's by
T6   160: 5   "It's a stupid name enough!" Humpty Dumpty interrupted impatiently. "What does it mean?"
A11   89:21   "I didn't!" the March Hare interrupted in a great hurry.
T4   145:27   suppose those are real tears?" Tweedledum interrupted in a tone of great contempt.
A9   77:23   "That's enough about lessons," the Gryphon interrupted in a very decided tone. "Tell her something about
T7   178: 8   rise to their feet, with angry looks at being interrupted in their feast, before she dropped to her knees,
T8   186:26   "Not very nice alone," he interrupted, quite eagerly: "but you've no idea what a
T6   160:28   send all his horses and all his men," Alice interrupted, rather unwisely.
T9   195: 3   "Fan her head!" the Red Queen anxiously interrupted. "She'll be feverish after so much thinking." So
A10   78:19   "That generally takes some time," interrupted the Gryphon.
A7   59:36   "I want a clean cup," interrupted the Hatter: "let's all move one place on."
T6   164:25   "That's enough to begin with," Humpty Dumpty interrupted: "there are plenty of hard words there. 'Brillig'
A11   88: 2   "Not yet, not yet!" the Rabbit hastily interrupted. "There's a great deal to come before that!"
T7   176:23   Here the King interrupted, to prevent the quarrel going on: he was very
A12   93:23   down on their slates, when the White Rabbit interrupted: "Unimportant, your Majesty means, of course," he
A7   58:18   we change the subject," the March Hare interrupted, yawning. "I'm getting tired of this. I vote the
INTERRUPTING (2)
A12   95:24   few minutes that she wasn't a bit afraid of interrupting him,) "I'll give him sixpence. I don't believe
A7   60:13   let the Dormouse go on for some time without interrupting it.
INTERRUPTS (1)
AI   3:17   There will be nonsense in it!" / While Tertia interrupts the tale / Not more than once a minute.
INTO (145) [entries omitted]
INTRODUCE (4)
T7   175:20   replied eagerly, coming in front of Alice to introduce her, and spreading out both his hands towards her in
A8   67:40   a Cheshire-Cat," said Alice: "allow me to introduce it."
A6   48: 8   remark, and thought it would be as well to introduce some other subject of conversation. While she was
T9   200:22   "You look a little shy: let me introduce you to that leg of mutton," said the Red Queen.
INTRODUCED (3)
A10   78: 9   said Alice)--"and perhaps you were never even introduced to a lobster--" (Alice began to say "I once tasted
T9   201: 7   it isn't etiquette to cut any one you've been introduced to. Remove the joint!" And the waiters carried it
T9   201:10   "I won't be introduced to the pudding, please," Alice said rather hastily,
INTRODUCING (1)
T7   171:11   lady loves you with an H," the King said, introducing Alice in the hope of turning off the Messenger's
INVENT (2)
T8   186:19   And yet it was a very clever pudding to invent."
A5   43: 8   said the Pigeon. "I can see you're trying to invent something!"
INVENTED (5)
T8   184:42   from the saddle. "Yes," he said; "but I've invented a better one than that--like a sugar-loaf. When I

INVENTED (cont.)
```
T8    182:27                           "Have you invented a plan for keeping the hair from being blown off?"
T6    164:18   "I  can  explain  all  the  poems  that  ever  were  invented--and a good many that haven't been invented just yet
A12    93:42   "besides,  that's  not  a  regular  rule:  you  invented it just now."
T6    164:19   invented--and  a  good  many  that  haven't  been  invented just yet."
```
INVENTING (4)
```
T8    186: 7   I  ever  did,"  he  went  on  after  a  pause,  "was  inventing a new pudding during the meat-course."
T8    184:26              "Well,  just  then  I  was  inventing a new way of getting over a gate--would you like to
T8    186: 5   the  more  head-downwards  I  am,  the  more  I  keep  inventing new things."
T8    184:22   Knight  went  on  again.  "I'm a great hand at  inventing things. Now, I daresay you noticed, the last time
```
INVENTION (8)
```
T8t   179: 1                           "IT'S MY OWN INVENTION"
T8    187:11   'A-sitting  On  A  Gate':  and  the  tune's  my  own  invention."
T1    119: 3   least,  it  wasn't  exactly  running,  but  a  new  invention for getting down stairs quickly and easily, as Alice
T8    182:10   of  sharks,"  the  Knight  replied.  "It's an  invention of my own. And now help me on. I'll go with you to
T8    187:28              "But  the  tune  isn't  his  own  invention," she said to herself: "it's 'I give thee all, I can
T8    181:18   Knight  said  in  a  friendly  tone.  "It's my own  invention--to keep clothes and sandwiches in. You see I carry
T8    184:40   got!"  she  said  cheerfully.  "Is that your  invention too?"
T8    182:35   fall  upwards,  you  know.  It's a plan of my own  invention. You may try it if you like."
```
INVISIBLE (2)
```
T1    113:14   see  me.  I  feel  somehow  as  if  I  was  getting  invisible--"
T1    115: 5   when  he  found  himself  held  in  the  air  by  an  invisible hand, and being dusted: he was far too much
```
INVITATION (2)
```
A6     46: 2   of  the  words  a  little,  "From  the  Queen.  An  invitation for the Duchess to play croquet."
A6     45:13    in  a  solemn  tone,  "For  the  Duchess.  An  invitation from the Queen to play croquet." The Frog-Footman
```
INVITE (4)
```
T9    200:13   never  have  known  who  were  the  right  people  to  invite!"
T9    193:18   if  there  is  to  be  one,  I  think  I  ought  to  invite the guests."
T9    193:16   White  Queen  smiled  feebly,  and  said  "And  I  invite you."
T9    193:15   the  silence  by  saying,  to  the  White  Queen,  "I  invite you to Alice's dinner-party this afternoon."
```
INVITED (2)
```
A7     55: 2   very  civil  of  you  to  sit  down  without  being  invited," said the March Hare.
A6     52: 6   very  much,"  said  Alice,  "but  I  haven't  been  invited yet."
```
INVOLVED (1)
```
A12    95:10          If I or she should chance to be / Involved in this affair, / He trusts to you to set them free,
```
INWARDS (1)
```
A4     29:26   and  tried  to  open  it;  but,  as  the  door  opened  inwards, and Alice's elbow was pressed hard against it, that
```
-IRONS [See FIRE-IRONS]
IRRITATED (1)
```
A5     36:11   of  the  conversation.  Alice  felt  a  little  irritated at the Caterpillar's making such very short remarks,
```
IRRITATION (1)
```
T9    199: 6              Alice almost stamped with  irritation at the slow drawl in which he spoke. "This door, of
```
IS (242)
```
A2     18:16   never!  And  I  declare  it's  too  bad,  that  it  is!"
A7     56:13   the  month,  and  doesn't  tell  what  o'clock  it  is!"
A7     56:15    "Does  your  watch  tell  you  what  year  it  is?"
A9     72: 4   a  vegetable.  It  doesn't  look  like  one,  but  it  is."
A9     73:12   Alice.  "I  don't  even  know  what  a  Mock  Turtle  is."
A10    78:12   what  a  delightful  thing  a  Lobster-Quadrille  is!"
A11    90:24   said  the  Hatter:  "I'm  on  the  floor,  as  it  is."
T7    174:10   "It's  waiting  for  'em  now,"  said  Hatta;  "this  is a bit of it as I'm eating."
A3     23: 2                           "What is a Caucus-race?" said Alice; not that she much wanted to
T7    175:19              "This  is a child!" Haigha replied eagerly, coming in front of Alice
T3    134:11   are  thin  slices  of  bread-and-butter,  its  body  is a crust, and its head is a lump of sugar."
A3     24:17              "Mine  is a long and sad tale!" said the Mouse, turning to Alice, and
A3     25: 1              "It  is a long tail, certainly," said Alice, looking down with
T3    134:12          its  body  is  a  crust,  and  its  head  is a lump of sugar."
T6    162:25              "It  is a--most--provoking--thing," he said at last, "when a person
T8    181:36   bee  has  come  near  it  yet.  And  the  other  thing  is a mouse-trap. I suppose the mice keep the bees out--or the
T3    133:14   its  wings  of  holly-leaves,  and  its  head  is a raisin burning in brandy."
A7     55:12   on  hearing  this;  but  all  he  said  was  "Why  is a raven like a writing-desk?"
T12   208: 6   consider  who  it  was  that  dreamed  it  all.  This  is a serious question, my dear, and you should not go on
T6    166: 3              "Well,  a  'rath'  is a sort of green pig: but 'mome' I'm not certain about. I
T6    165:10    portmanteau  for  you).  And  a  'borogove'  is a thin shabby-looking bird with its feathers sticking out
A5     41:16              "It  is a very good height indeed!" said the Caterpillar angrily,
T12   207: 6              "it  is a very inconvenient habit of kittens (Alice had once made
T6    160: 4              "My  name  is Alice, but--"
A8     63:40              "My  name  is Alice, so please your Majesty," said Alice very politely;
T2    128:18   we'll  suppose  it  said--the  Seventh  Square  is all forest--however, one of the Knights will show you the
A8     67:27   to  them--and  you've  no  idea  how  confusing  it  is all the things being alive: for instance, there's the arch
T8    188:23   Macassar-Oil--/  Yet  twopence-halfpenny  is all / They give me for my toil.'
A1     11: 4   drink  much  from  a  bottle  marked  "poison,"  it  is almost certain to disagree with you, sooner or later.
T6    162:38              "I  mean,  what  is an un-birthday present?"
A10    80: 8   we  go?"  his  scaly  friend  replied.  / "There  is another shore, you know, upon the other side. / The further
T8    187:10   to  that,"  the  Knight  said.  "The  song  really  is 'A-sitting On A Gate': and the tune's my own invention."
A7     56:22              "The  Dormouse  is asleep again," said the Hatter, and he poured a little hot
A9     72: 6   said  the  Duchess;  "and  the  moral  of  that  is--'Be what you would seem to be'--or, if you'd like it put
T8    182:34   a  fruit-tree.  Now  the  reason  hair  falls  off  is because it hangs down--things never fall upwards, you know.
T5    153:23              "Then  I  hope  your  finger  is better now?" Alice said very politely, as she crossed the
A4     31: 2   above  her:  then,  saying  to  herself  "This  is Bill", she gave one sharp kick, and waited to see what
```

IS (cont.)
```
A9    71:12   and mustard both bite. And the moral of that is--'Birds of a feather flock together.'"
A1    12:10   flame of a candle looks like after the candle is blown out, for she could not remember ever having seen such
T4   142:23   Of cabbages--and kings--/ And why the sea is boiling hot--/ And whether pigs have wings.'
T9   194:40   you answer useful questions?" she said. "How is bread made?"
A9    70:19   tell you just now what the moral of that is, but I shall remember it in a bit."
T8   187: 4   I ought to have said 'That's what the song is called'?" Alice corrected herself.
T8   186:40   it doesn't, you know. The name of the song is called 'Haddocks' Eyes.'"
T8   187: 2   looking a little vexed. "That's what the name is called. The name really is 'The Aged Aged Man.'"
T8   187: 6   that's quite another thing! The song is called 'Ways and Means': but that's only what it's called,
T5   152:38   you've come to-day. Consider what o'clock it is. Consider anything, only don't cry!"
T7   177: 5   dust to see anything. What a time the Monster is, cutting up that cake!"
A3    26:24                          "And who is Dinah, if I might venture to ask the question?" said the
AI     3:34   events were hammered out--/ And now the tale is done, / And home we steer, a merry crew, / Beneath the
T9   202:17   dish, while it lies in the middle: / Which is easiest to do, / Un-dish-cover the fish, or dishcover the
T9   202: 4   "'First, the fish must be caught.' / That is easy: a baby, I think, could have caught it. / 'Next, the
T9   202: 6   it.' / 'Next, the fish must be bought.' / That is easy: a penny, I think, could have bought it.
T9   202: 8   'Now cook me the fish!' / That is easy, and will not take more than a minute. / 'Let it lie
T9   202:10   a minute. / 'Let it lie in a dish!' / That is easy, because it already is in it.
T9   202:12   'Bring it here! Let me sup!' / It is easy to set such a dish on the table. / 'Take the
T4   139:40   very soon out of breath. "Four times round is enough for one dance," Tweedledum panted out, and they left
A5    40: 5   "I have answered three questions, and that is enough," / Said his father. "Don't give yourself airs! / Do
T4   143:17   be / A dismal thing to do!' / 'The night is fine,' the Walrus said. / 'Do you admire the view?
T6   165: 9            "Exactly so. Well then, 'mimsy' is 'flimsy and miserable' (there's another portmanteau for
A10   82:26   his toes. / When the sands are all dry, he is gay as a lark, / And will talk in contemptuous tones of the
T6   161:15   they would! However, this conversation is going on a little too fast: let's go back to the last
T9   192: 1                        "Well, this is grand!" said Alice. "I never expected I should be a Queen
T7   170:33   with--with Ham-sandwiches and Hay. His name is Haigha, and he lives--"
T7   170:28   He only does them when he's happy. His name is Haigha." (He pronounced it so as to rhyme with 'mayor.')
T7   170:31   Alice couldn't help beginning, "because he is Happy. I hate him with an H, because he is Hideous. I fed
T4   146: 5   and looked up into it. "No, I don't think it is," he said: "at least--not under here. Nohow."
A10   81: 1   their tails in their mouths; and the reason is--" here the Mock Turtle yawned and shut his eyes. "Tell her
T7   170:31   he is Happy. I hate him with an H, because he is Hideous. I fed him with--with--with Ham-sandwiches and Hay.
T8   184:31   only difficulty is with the feet: the head is high enough already.' Now, first I put my head on the top
A8    62:15                "Yes, it is his business!" said Five. "And I'll tell him--it was for
A9    74:19   would break. She pitied him deeply. "What is his sorrow?" she asked the Gryphon. And the Gryphon
T2   126: 2   the world at all, you know. Oh, what fun it is! How I wish I was one of them! I wouldn't mind being a Pawn
A4    28:13   enough--I hope I sha'n't grow any more--As it is, I ca'n't get out at the door--I do wish I hadn't drunk
A2    20:20   you my history, and you'll understand why it is I hate cats and dogs."
A9    76:27   it exclaimed. "You know what to beautify is, I suppose?"
A4    27:20   I'd better take him his fan and gloves--that is, if I can find them." As she said this, she came upon a
T9   195:12   you'll tell me what language 'fiddle-de-dee' is, I'll tell you the French for it!" she exclaimed
A2    16: 8   and I'm I, and--oh dear, how puzzling it all is! I'll try if I know all the things I used to know. Let me
T5   149:31   for her; "and dear me, what a state your hair is in!"
T9   202:10   a dish!' / That is easy, because it already is in it.
A9    76:25   'Uglification,'" Alice ventured to say. "What is it?"
A10   78:13   indeed," said Alice. "What sort of a dance is it?"
T8W   16:15   Alice didn't catch the word exactly. "Is it a kind of toothache?" she asked.
A10   85: 6                "What trial is it?" Alice panted as she ran: but the Gryphon only answered
T8   186:42   "Oh, that's the name of the song, is it?" Alice said, trying to feel interested.
T7   175:24   were fabulous monsters!" said the Unicorn. "Is it alive?"
TC   209:21   Lingering in the golden gleam--/ Life, what is it but a dream?
A12   94:11               "Who is it directed to?" said one of the jurymen.
T2   122: 1   in the middle," said the Rose. "What else is it good for?"
A7    55:36   to break the silence. "What day of the month is it?" he said, turning to Alice: he had taken his watch out
A5    42:14   shoulders got to? And oh, my poor hands, how is it I ca'n't see you?" She was moving them about, as she
T9   199: 1                "What is it, now?" the Frog said in a deep hoarse whisper.
T7   176: 3        "Ah, what is it, now?" the Unicorn cried eagerly. "You'll never guess! I
A4    33:11   I've got to grow up again! Let me see--how is it to be managed? I suppose I ought to eat or drink
A6    48:31   on again: "Twenty-four hours, I think; or is it twelve? I--"
T8   186:33                      "Is it very long?" Alice asked, for she had heard a good deal
A5    36: 8   may be different," said Alice: "all I know is, it would feel very queer to me."
T2   122:21                "How is it you can all talk so nicely?" Alice said, hoping to get
T8   187:36   / 'Who are you, aged man?' I said. / 'And how is it you live?' / And his answer trickled through my head, /
T5   154: 1                "What is it you want to buy?" the Sheep said at last, looking up for
T6   165: 6             "Of course it is. It's called 'wabe' you know, because it goes a long way
T5   150: 6   you did want it," the Queen said. "The rule is, jam to-morrow and jam yesterday--but never jam to-day."
A7    56:18              "Which is the case with mine," said the Hatter.
T1   108:11           "Do you know what to-morrow is, Kitty?" Alice began. "You'd have guessed if you'd been up
T1   119: 1   before I've seen what the rest of the house is like! Let's have a look at the garden first!" She was out
A9    73:23   in the sun. (If you don't know what a Gryphon is, look at the picture.) "Up, lazy thing!" said the Queen,
A9    73:13   "It's the thing Mock Turtle Soup is made from," said the Queen.
T3   133:13   there you'll find a Snap-dragon-fly. Its body is made of plum-pudding, its wings of holly-leaves, and its
A6    52:26   the most interesting, and perhaps, as this is May, it wo'n't be raving mad--at least not so mad as it was
T2   128:11   to Tweedledum and Tweedledee--the Fifth is mostly water--the Sixth belongs to Humpty Dumpty--But you
T6   159:32            "That last line is much too long for the poetry," she added, almost out loud,
A4    30:37   Bill's place for a good deal: this fireplace is narrow, to be sure; but I think I can kick a little!"
T8W   19:10   now that I am old and gray, / And all my hair is nearly gone, / They take my wig from me and say / 'How can
AI     3:29   the subject by, / "The rest next time--" "It is next time!" / The happy voices cry.
T8W   21: 2   the Wasp went on: "but the top of your head is nice and round." He took off his own wig as he spoke, and
```

IS (cont.)

T8	181:25	the things must have fallen out! And the box is no use without them." He unfastened it as he spoke, and was
A5	41: 1	"That is not said right," said the Caterpillar.
T6	160:37	what you call a History of England, that is. Now, take a good look at me! I'm one that has spoken to a
A9	71: 3	"How fond she is of finding morals in things!" Alice thought to herself.
A9	72: 1	And the moral of that is--'The more there is of mine, the less there is of yours.'"
A9	72: 2	'The more there is of mine, the less there is of yours.'"
A2	16:10	times six is thirteen, and four times seven is--oh dear! I shall never get to twenty at that rate! However
A9	70:32	so," said the Duchess: "and the moral of that is--'Oh, 'tis love, 'tis love, that makes the world go round!'
A8	64:11	arm, and timidly said "Consider, my dear: she is only a child!"
T2	123:34	it," said the Rose: "wonderfully fine air it is, out here."
A3	23:15	again, the Dodo suddenly called out "The race is over!" and they all crowded round it, panting, and asking
T9	196:29	on: "but it's amazing how good-tempered she is! Pat her on the head, and see how pleased she'll be!" But
T9	200: 2	with treacle and ink, / Or anything else that is pleasant to drink: / Mix sand with the cider, and wool with
A2	19: 4	queer thing, to be sure! However, everything is queer to-day."
A11	90:12	by the officers of the court. (As that is rather a hard word, I will just explain to you how it was
T6	162:31	"It is really?" said Alice, quite pleased to find that she had
A5	37: 4	on your head--/ Do you think, at your age, it is right?"
T6	163:33	"The question is," said Alice, "whether you can make words mean so many
T6	163:35	"The question is," said Humpty Dumpty, "which is to be master--that's all."
A9	71:17	"Of course it is," said the Duchess, who seemed ready to agree to everything
A10	81: 4	"The reason is," said the Gryphon, "that they would go with the lobsters
T2	127:15	"Of course it is," said the Queen. "What would you have it?"
T2	123: 9	"Is she like me?" Alice asked eagerly, for the thought crossed
T6	159:14	"And how exactly like an egg he is!" she said aloud, standing with her hands ready to catch
T4	148:19	coming on. "What a thick black cloud that is!" she said. "And how fast it comes! Why, I do believe it's
T1	115:40	(in which Alice had put 'The White Knight is sliding down the poker. He balances very badly'). "That's
T9	202:14	table. / 'Take the dish-cover up!' / Ah, that is so hard that I fear I'm unable!
A2	19:11	Alice, "to speak to this mouse? Everything is so out-of-the-way down here, that I should think very
T5	152:33	"Only it is so very lonely here!" Alice said in a melancholy voice; and
T6	160:18	anxiety for the queer creature. "That wall is so very narrow!"
T8	182:25	he said, anxiously. "You see the wind is so very strong here. It's as strong as soup."
T6	166: 7	"Well, 'outgribing' is something between bellowing and whistling, with a kind of
A4	31:22	a deal too flustered to tell you--all I know is, something comes at me like a Jack-in-the-box, and up I
A2	19:34	fancy to cats, if you could only see her. She is such a dear quiet thing," Alice went on, half to herself,
A2	20: 3	not answer, so Alice went on eagerly: "There is such a nice little dog, near our house, I should like to
A2	19:37	her paws and washing her face--and she is such a nice soft thing to nurse--and she's such a capital
A5	41:15	you wouldn't mind," said Alice: "three inches is such a wretched height to be."
A4	28: 5	it to her lips. "I know something interesting is sure to happen," she said to herself, "whenever I eat or
A9	71: 1	shoulder as she added "and the moral of that is--'Take care of the sense, and the sounds will take care of
T1	110:20	But this is taking us away from Alice's speech to the kitten. "Let's
T7	175:31	if you'll believe in me, I'll believe in you. Is that a bargain?"
T6	168:15	"Is that all?" Alice timidly asked.
A5	36:23	"Is that all?" said Alice, swallowing down her anger as well as
A9	71: 6	the Duchess said, after a pause: "the reason is, that I'm doubtful about the temper of your flamingo. Shall
T7	172:38	said the King: "and the best of the joke is, that it's my crown all the while! Let's run and see them."
A7	58:10	A bright idea came into Alice's head. "Is that the reason so many tea-things are put out here?" she
A7	57: 9	"Is that the way you manage?" Alice asked.
A8	67: 7	of beheading people here: the great wonder is, that there's any one left alive!"
T2	126:13	how it was that they began: all she remembers is, that they were running hand in hand, and the Queen went so
A5	43:43	is, to get into that beautiful garden--how is that to be done, I wonder?" As she said this, she came
T8	184:40	helmet you've got!" she said cheerfully. "Is that your invention too?"
T8	187: 2	what the name is called. The name really is 'The Aged Aged Man.'"
T4	139:10	"I was thinking," Alice said politely, "which is the best way out of this wood: it's getting so dark. Would
A2	17: 1	doesn't signify: let's try Geography. London is the capital of Paris, and Paris is the capital of Rome, and
A2	17: 1	London is the capital of Paris, and Paris is the capital of Rome, and Rome--no, that's all wrong, I'm
T9	195:18	White Queen said in an anxious tone. "What is the cause of lightning?"
A3	22: 3	an important air. "Are you all ready? This is the driest thing I know. Silence all round, if you please!
A9	74:10	"What is the fun?" said Alice.
T6	165: 4	"And 'the wabe' is the grass-plot round a sun-dial, I suppose?" said Alice,
T4	140:15	"'The Walrus and the Carpenter' is the longest," Tweedledum replied, giving his brother an
T5	152: 8	"What is the matter?" she said, as soon as there was a chance of
A9	72: 1	mustard-mine near here. And the moral of that is--'The more there is of mine, the less there is of yours.'"
T5	155: 1	the one she was looking at. "And this one is the most provoking of all--but I'll tell you what--" she
A5	38: 4	back-somersault in at the door--/ Pray, what is the reason of that?
T6	164:29	'slithy' means 'lithe and slimy.' 'Lithe' is the same as 'active.' You see it's like a pormanteau--there
T6	168:27	complain of," said Humpty Dumpty. "Your face is the same as everybody has--the two eyes, so--"(marking
A7	55:24	just as well say that 'I see what I eat' is the same thing as 'I eat what I see'!"
A7	55:27	the March Hare, "that 'I like what I get' is the same thing as 'I get what I like'!"
A7	55:29	in its sleep, "that 'I breathe when I sleep' is the same thing as 'I sleep when I breathe'!"
A7	55:31	"It is the same thing with you," said the Hatter, and here the
T8	187: 8	"Well, what is the song, then?" said Alice, who was by this time
T9	195:20	for she felt quite certain about this, "is the thunder--no, no!" she hastily corrected herself. "I
A1	7: 4	no pictures or conversations in it, "and what is the use of a book," thought Alice, "without pictures or
T9	193: 3	You should have meant! What do you suppose is the use of a child without any meaning? Even a joke should
A10	84: 3	"What is the use of repeating all that stuff?" the Mock Turtle
T5	158:22	actually here's a little brook! Well, this is the very queerest shop I ever saw!" * * * * * * * * * * * *
T1	113:19	"It is the voice of my child!" the White Queen cried out, as she
T2	126: 2	being played--all over the world--if this is the world at all, you know. Oh, what fun it is! How I wish
T9	196: 7	"Is there generally?" Alice asked in an astonished tone.

IS (cont.)

A2	16: 9	four times five is twelve, and four times six is thirteen, and four times seven is--oh dear! I shall never
T5	158:20	away the more I walk towards it. Let me see, is this a chair? Why, it's got branches, I declare! How very
T7	175:18	"What--is--this?" he said at last.
A1	8:44	of the country is, you know. Please, Ma'am, is this New Zealand? Or Australia?" (and she tried to curtsey
T8	191: 3	"Oh, how glad I am to get here! And what is this on my head?" she exclaimed in a tone of dismay, as she
A8	63:35	at her, and the Queen said, severely, "Who is this?" She said it to the Knave of Hearts, who only bowed
T8W	17: 5	"It is, though," said the Wasp: "wait till you have it, and then
T9	199: 3	"Where's the servant whose business it is to answer the door?" she began angrily.
T6	163:35	"The question is," said Humpty Dumpty, "which is to be master--that's all."
T9	193:18	a party at all," said Alice; "but, if there is to be one, I think I ought to invite the guests."
A3	23: 5	said the Dodo, "the best way to explain it is to do it." (And, as you might like to try the thing
A4	32:20	to my right size again; and the second thing is to find my way into that lovely garden. I think that will
A10	80: 9	/ The further off from England the nearer is to France. / Then turn not pale, beloved snail, but come
A5	43:42	got back to my right size: the next thing is, to get into that beautiful garden--how is that to be done,
A3	23:22	"But who is to give the prizes?" quite a chorus of voices asked.
T6	165: 2	"To 'gyre' is to go round and round like a gyroscope. To 'gimble' is to
A4	32:19	herself, as she wandered about in the wood, "is to grow to my right size again; and the second thing is to
T8	183:18	voice, waving his right arm as he spoke, "is to keep--" Here the sentence ended as suddenly as it had
T8	184: 5	"The great art of riding, as I was saying is--to keep your balance properly. Like this, you know--"
T6	165: 3	round and round like a gyroscope. To 'gimble' is to make holes like a gimlet."
T4	139:22	cried Tweedledum. "The first thing in a visit is to say 'How d'ye do?' and shake hands!" And here the two
A2	15:38	on talking. "Dear, dear! How queer everything is to-day! And yesterday things went on just as usual. I
T6	160:10	the shape I am--and a good handsome shape it is, too. With a name like yours, you might be any shape,
A2	16: 9	I used to know. Let me see: four times five is twelve, and four times six is thirteen, and four times
A5	35:16	and being so many different sizes in a day is very confusing."
T8W	16:12	looked pityingly at him. "Tying up the face is very good for the toothache," she said.
A4	33:13	something or other; but the great question is 'What'?"
A3	22:19	generally a frog, or a worm. The question is, what did the archbishop find?"
A1	12:41	she remained the same size. To be sure, this is what generally happens when one eats cake; but Alice had
T6	166:40	a message to the fish: / I told them 'This is what I wish.'
T6	168:24	"The face is what one goes by, generally," Alice remarked in a
T4	143: 8	'A loaf of bread,' the Walrus said, / 'Is what we chiefly need: / Pepper and vinegar besides / Are
A5	41:38	"And now which is which?" she said to herself, and nibbled a little of the
A2	15:42	But if I'm not the same, the next question is 'Who in the world am I?' Ah, that's the great puzzle!" And
T8W	19:15	They hoot at me and call me 'Pig!' / And that is why they do it, dear, / Because I wear a yellow wig."
T8	184:30	see, I said to myself 'The only difficulty is with the feet: the head is high enough already.' Now, first
T3	130: 1	"Don't keep him waiting, child! Why, his time is worth a thousand pounds a minute!"
T3	130: 9	that drives the engine. Why, the smoke alone is worth a thousand pounds a puff!"
T3	130:14	I don't) "Better say nothing at all. Language is worth a thousand pounds a word!"
T3	130: 5	for one where she came from. The land there is worth a thousand pounds an inch!"
A5	41: 4	"It is wrong from beginning to end," said the Caterpillar,
A9	76:32	went on, "if you don't know what to uglify is, you are a simpleton."
T8	188:32	me how you live,' I cried, / 'And what it is you do!'
A3	24:15	history, you know," said Alice, "and why it is you hate--C and D," she added in a whisper, half afraid
A1	8:44	have to ask them what the name of the country is, you know. Please, Ma'am, is this New Zealand? Or Australia
A8	63: 6	Two began, in a low voice, "Why, the fact is, you see, Miss, this here ought to have been a red
T9	192: 2	be a Queen so soon--and I'll tell you what it is, your Majesty," she went on, in a severe tone (she was

ISN'T (25)

A9	71:13	"Only mustard isn't a bird," Alice remarked.
T8W	17: 4	"Conceit isn't a disease at all," Alice remarked.
A12	94:14	unfolded the paper as he spoke, and added "It isn't a letter, after all: it's a set of verses."
T5	150: 9	the Queen. "It's jam every other day: to-day isn't any other day, you know."
A7	54:16	"There isn't any," said the March Hare.
A12	94:12	"It isn't directed at all," said the White Rabbit: "in fact,
T9	201: 6	not," the Red Queen said, very decidedly: "it isn't etiquette to cut any one you've been introduced to."
T7	177:17	"I say, this isn't fair!" cried the Unicorn, as Alice sat with the knife in
T1	111: 1	you milk in there? Perhaps Looking-glass milk isn't good to drink--but oh, Kitty! now we come to the passage
T4	144:31	"Isn't he a lovely sight?" said Tweedledum.
T8	187:28	"But the tune isn't his own invention," she said to herself: "it's 'I give
T4	139: 8	be; and if it were so, it would be; but as it isn't, it ain't. That's logic."
T2	121: 7	"It isn't manners for us to begin, you know," said the Rose, "and
A11	88:21	"It isn't mine," said the Hatter.
T5	149:13	call that a-dressing," the Queen said. "It isn't my notion of the thing, at all."
T4	146:26	"But it isn't old!" Tweedledum cried, in a greater fury than ever.
T9	194:44	"Well, it isn't picked at all," Alice explained: "it's ground--"
T7	171: 3	"It isn't respectable to beg," said the King.
A5	36: 1	"It isn't," said the Caterpillar.
T4	139: 6	thinking about," said Tweedledum; "but it isn't so, nohow."
T9	194:37	you a secret--I can read words of one letter! Isn't that grand? However, don't be discouraged. You'll come
T8W	18: 1	"It isn't that kind," Alice hastily explained. "It's to comb hair
A12	94:10	King, "unless it was written to nobody, which isn't usual, you know."
T8	182: 2	what the mouse-trap was for," said Alice. "It isn't very likely there would be any mice on the horse's back
T6	162:39	"A present given when it isn't your birthday, of course."

IT (1119) [entries omitted]

IT'LL (20)

T1	111:10	turning into a sort of mist now, I declare! It'll be easy enough to get through--" She was up on the
A2	17:21	about it: if I'm Mabel, I'll stay down here. It'll be no use their putting their heads down and saying
T3	129:21	long branch to brush them away--and what fun it'll be when they ask me how I liked my walk. I shall say 'Oh
T1	112: 8	to scold me away from the fire. Oh, what fun it'll be, when they see me through the glass in here, and

IT'LL (cont.)

T8	182:13	better take it with us," the Knight said. "It'll come in handy if we find any plum-cake. Help me to get
T8W	17: 7	tying a yellow handkerchief round your face. It'll cure you in no time!"
T8	190:19	when I get to that turn in the road? I think it'll encourage me, you see."
A2	20: 6	with oh, such long curly brown hair! And it'll fetch things when you throw them, and it'll sit up and
T9	199:21	out, as he hobbled back to his tree, "and it'll let you alone, you know."
A4	28: 7	just see what this bottle does. I do hope it'll make me grow large again, for really I'm quite tired of
T9	192: 4	was always rather fond of scolding herself), "It'll never do for you to be lolling about on the grass like
A1	9: 3	little girl she'll think me for asking! No, it'll never do to ask: perhaps I shall see it written up
A5	44: 2	high. "Whoever lives there," thought Alice, "it'll never do to come upon them this size: why, I should
T3	129:20	some excuse for turning shy so suddenly. "It'll never do to go down among them without a good long
T5	155: 3	follow it up to the very top shelf of all. It'll puzzle it to go through the ceiling, I expect!"
A2	15: 4	by the carrier," she thought; "and how funny it'll seem, sending presents to one's own feet! And how odd
A1	8:40	shall fall right through the earth! How funny it'll seem to come out among the people that walk with their
A2	20: 6	it'll fetch things when you throw them, and it'll sit up and beg for its dinner, and all sorts of things--
T5	156:14	said the Sheep. "If you leave off rowing, it'll stop of itself."
T3	132: 8	the idea of trains jumping at all. "However, it'll take us into the Fourth Square, that's some comfort!"

IT'S (158)

A6	47:15	"It's a Cheshire-Cat," said the Duchess, "and that's why. Pig!"
T6	162:29	"It's a cravat, child, and a beautiful one, as you say. It's a
T7	176: 7	"It's a fabulous monster!" the Unicorn cried out, before Alice
A2	19:22	English," thought Alice. "I daresay it's a French mouse, come over with William the Conqueror."
A8	67:39	"It's a friend of mine--a Cheshire-Cat," said Alice: "allow me
T3	135:38	very cool and shady. "Well, at any rate it's a great comfort," she said as she stepped under the trees
T2	125:28	beat quick with excitement as she went on. "It's a great huge game of chess that's being played--all over
T1	116:14	at last a bright thought struck her. "Why, it's a Looking-glass book, of course! And, if I hold it up to
A9	71:16	"It's a mineral, I think," said Alice.
T8	182:35	down--things never fall upwards, you know. It's a plan of my own invention. You may try it if you like."
T5	150:19	"It's a poor sort of memory that only works backwards," the
T6	162:29	child, and a beautiful one, as you say. It's a present from the White King and Queen. There now!"
A12	96:27	"It's a pun!" the King added in an angry tone, and everybody
A12	94:14	and added "It isn't a letter, after all: it's a set of verses."
T6	160: 5	"It's a stupid name enough!" Humpty Dumpty interrupted
A9	72: 4	who had not attended to this last remark. "It's a vegetable. It doesn't look like one, but it is."
T3	135:11	Why do you wish I had made it?" Alice asked. "It's a very bad one."
T9	201:31	and all eyes were fixed upon her; "and it's a very curious thing, I think--every poem was about
A8	65:25	"It's--it's a very fine day!" said a timid voice at her side. She was
T8	181:34	"Yes, it's a very good bee-hive," the Knight said in a discontented
A10	80:13	"Thank you, it's a very interesting dance to watch," said Alice, feeling
A10	82:10	"It's all about as curious as it can be," said the Gryphon.
T8W	16: 3	"It's all along of the wig," the Wasp said in a much gentler
T2	128:29	Square we shall be Queens together, and it's all feasting and fun!" Alice got up and curtseyed, and
A9	74:11	"Why, she," said the Gryphon. "It's all her fancy that: they never executes nobody, you know.
A9	74:21	very nearly in the same words as before, "It's all his fancy, that: he hasn't got no sorrow, you know.
T1	116: 5	to find some part that she could read, "--for it's all in some language I don't know," she said to herself.
A9	70: 9	at all. Soup does very well without--Maybe it's always pepper that makes people hot-tempered," she went
A7	58: 9	a mournful tone, "he wo'n't do a thing I ask! It's always six o'clock now."
A7	58:12	that's it," said the Hatter with a sigh: "it's always tea-time, and we've no time to wash the things
T6	168:29	his thumb) "nose in the middle, mouth under. It's always the same. Now if you had the two eyes on the same
T9	196:29	well brought up," the Red Queen went on: "but it's amazing how good-tempered she is! Pat her on the head,
A4	30:10	"Sure, it does, yer honour: but it's an arm for all that."
A4	30: 7	"Sure, it's an arm, yer honour!" (He pronounced it "arrum.")
T8	182: 9	the bites of sharks," the Knight replied. "It's an invention of my own. And now help me on. I'll go with
A6	51:32	the Cat went on, "you see a dog growls when it's angry, and wags its tail when it's pleased. Now I growl
T7	175:21	attitude. "We only found it to-day. It's as large as life, and twice as natural!"
T7	170:19	to see Nobody! And at that distance too! Why, it's as much as I can do to see real people, by this light!"
T8	182:26	"You see the wind is so very strong here. It's as strong as soup."
T8	182: 5	"You see," he went on after a pause, "it's as well to be provided for everything. That's the reason
A7	54: 6	for the Dormouse," thought Alice; "only as it's asleep, I suppose it doesn't mind."
A8	65:35	"No, I didn't," said Alice. "I don't think it's at all a pity. I said 'What for?'"
A10	84: 4	"if you don't explain it as you go on? It's by far the most confusing thing that I ever heard!"
A10	81:11	you like," said the Gryphon. "Do you know why it's called a whiting?"
T6	165: 6	"Of course it is. It's called 'wabe' you know, because it goes a long way before
T8	187: 7	called 'Ways and Means': but that's only what it's called, you know!"
A4	30:30	the roof bear?--Mind that loose slate--Oh, it's coming down! Heads below!" (a loud crash)--"Now, who did
T4	146: 2	better be getting out of the wood, for really it's coming on very dark. Do you think it's going to rain?"
A7	58:31	the Hatter, "or you'll be asleep again before it's done."
A9	70:34	"Somebody said," Alice whispered, "that it's done by everybody minding their own business!"
T5	153: 1	"That's the way it's done," the Queen said with great decision: "nobody can do
T5	150:10	"I don't understand you," said Alice. "It's dreadfully confusing!"
A6	46:37	to herself, "the way all the creatures argue. It's enough to drive one crazy!"
T2	122:19	When one speaks, they all begin together, and it's enough to make one wither to hear the way they go on!"
T9	195:42	Alice sighed and gave it up. "It's exactly like the riddle with no answer!" she thought.
T2	128:17	Queen went on in a tone of grave reproof, "'It's extremely kind of you to tell me all this'--however,
T4	145:25	"It can never get at me here," she thought: "it's far too large to squeeze itself in among the trees. But I
T4	145:29	nonsense," Alice thought to herself: "and it's foolish to cry about it." So she brushed away her tears,
A3	22:19	enough, when I find a thing," said the Duck: "it's generally a frog, or a worm. The question is, what did
T4	148:16	quite as sharp. Only we must begin quick. It's getting as dark as it can."
A12	98:10	dear, certainly; but now run in to your tea: it's getting late." So Alice got up and ran off, thinking
A1	9:26	a corner, "Oh my ears and whiskers, how late it's getting!" She was close behind it when she turned the

IT'S (cont.)

T4	139:11	"which is the best way out of this wood: it's getting so dark. Would you tell me, please?"
T4	146: 3	really it's coming on very dark. Do you think it's going to rain?"
T5	152:28	away, I think," said Alice: "I'm so glad it's gone. I thought it was the night coming on."
T3	129: 6	I'm on the only one, but I don't think it's got any name. Principal towns--why, what <u>are</u> those
T5	158:20	towards it. Let me see, is this a chair? Why, it's got branches, I declare! How very odd to <u>find</u> trees
A4	30:11	"Well, it's got no business there, at any rate: go and take it away!"
T3	136: 1	<u>does</u> it call itself, I wonder? I do believe it's got no name--why, to be sure it hasn't!"
T1	111: 6	through into Looking-glass House! I'm sure it's got, oh! such beautiful things in it! Let's pretend
T4	148:20	"And how fast it comes! Why, I do believe it's got wings!"
T9	194:44	it isn't <u>picked</u> at all," Alice explained: "it's <u>ground</u>--"
A8	67:34	so she went on "--likely to win, that it's <u>hardly</u> worth while finishing the game."
A3	26:35	voice, to its children, "Come away, my dears! It's high time you were all in bed!" On various pretexts they
A7	56:36	Hatter, "you wouldn't talk about wasting <u>it</u>. It's <u>him</u>."
T8	187:28	his own invention," she said to herself: "it's <u>'I give thee all</u>, I <u>can no more</u>.'" She stood and listened
T6	160:34	"I haven't indeed!" Alice said very gently. "It's in a book."
T8W	15:13	"It's in this newspaper, though," Alice said a little timidly.
A8	65:25	"It's--it's a very fine day!" said a timid voice at her side.
T5	150: 8	"No, it ca'n't," said the Queen. "It's jam every <u>other</u> day: to-day isn't any other day, you know
A7	55: 4	didn't know it was <u>your</u> table," said Alice: "it's laid for a <u>great</u> many more than three."
T6	164:31	'Lithe' is the same as 'active.' You see it's like a portmanteau--there are two meanings packed up into
T8	186:35	"It's long," said the Knight, "but it's very, <u>very</u> beautiful.
T3	133: 4	you'll see a Rocking-horse-fly, if you look. It's made entirely of wood, and gets about by swinging itself
T2	125:25	"I declare it's marked out just like a large chess-board!" Alice said at
A1	10:21	I'll look first," she said, "and see whether it's marked '<u>poison</u>' or not"; for she had read several nice
T8	182:12	"It's meant for plum-cake," said Alice.
T2	120: 5	it will at last. But how curiously it twists! It's more like a corkscrew than a path! Well <u>this</u> turn goes to
T12	207:31	that you're scrubbing a White Queen? Really, it's most disrespectful of you!
T7	172:39	the King: "and the best of the joke is, that it's <u>my</u> crown all the while! Let's run and see them." And they
T8	179: 8	all part of the same dream. Only I do hope it's <u>my</u> dream, and not the Red King's! I don't like belonging
T2	122:32	"It's <u>my</u> opinion that you never think <u>at all</u>," the Rose said,
T8t	179: 1	"IT'S MY OWN INVENTION"
T8	181:18	box," the Knight said in a friendly tone. "It's my own invention--to keep clothes and sandwiches in. You
T6	161:18	we start afresh," said Humpty Dumpty, "and it's my turn to choose a subject--" ("He talks about it just
T4	146:27	cried, in a greater fury than ever. "It's <u>new</u>, I tell you--I bought it yesterday--my nice NEW
A8	64: 4	said Alice, surprised at her own courage. "It's <u>no</u> business of <u>mine</u>."
A10	81:41	morning," said Alice a little timidly; "but it's no use going back to yesterday, because I was a different
A1	12:28	fond of pretending to be two people. "But it's no use now," thought poor Alice, "to pretend to be two
A8	67:16	till the eyes appeared, and then nodded. "It's no use speaking to it," she thought, "till its ears have
T2	120:13	"It's no use talking about it," Alice said, looking up at the
T4	145:18	"Well, it's no use <u>your</u> talking about waking him," said Tweedledum,
T2	121: 9	'Her face has got <u>some</u> sense in it, though it's not a clever one!' Still, you're the right colour, and
T4	147:25	"You know," he added very gravely, "it's one of the most serious things that can possibly happen
T3	132: 6	of the window, quietly drew it in and said "It's only a brook we have to jump over." Everybody seemed
T4	146:16	"It's only a rattle," Alice said, after a careful examination
T8W	14: 7	him, but she thought to herself "Perhaps it's only pain that makes him so cross." So she tried once
T4	144:27	"It's only the Red King snoring," said Tweedledee.
T5	149:27	it!" the Queen said, in a melancholy voice. "It's out of temper, I think. I've pinned it here, and I've
T12	208: 4	to you; and then you can make believe it's oysters, dear!
A6	51:33	when it's angry, and wags its tail when it's pleased. Now <u>I</u> growl when I'm pleased, and wag my tail
A6	51: 6	it only grinned a little wider. "Come, it's pleased so far," thought Alice, and she went on. "Would
T4	148:15	his brother: "but <u>you</u> can have the umbrella--it's quite as sharp. Only we must begin quick. It's getting as
T8	182:18	that he tried he <u>fell</u> in himself instead. "It's rather a tight fit, you see," he said, as they got it in
A4	29: 2	gone down that rabbit-hole--and yet--and yet--it's rather curious, you know, this sort of life! I do wonder
T1	118:26	she said when she had finished it, "but it's <u>rather</u> hard to understand!" (You see she didn't like to
A6	46:35	only Alice did not like to be told so. "It's <u>really</u> dreadful," she muttered to herself, "the way all
T8W	13:18	"It's rheumatism, I should think," Alice said to herself, and
T9	201:26	"Make a remark," said the Red Queen: "it's ridiculous to leave all the conversation to the pudding!
T6	166: 4	but '<u>mome</u>' I'm not certain about. I think it's short for 'from home'--meaning that they'd lost their way
A2	20: 8	it belongs to a farmer, you know, and he says it's so useful, it's worth a hundred pounds! He says it kills
T3	129: 2	the country she was going to travel through. "It's something very like learning geography," thought Alice,
T4	146:21	to stamp about wildly and tear his hair. "It's spoilt, of course!" Here he looked at Tweedledee, who
A4	32: 7	"If I eat one of these cakes," she thought, "it's sure to make <u>some</u> change in my size; and, as it ca'n't
A8	67:12	it out to be a grin, and she said to herself "It's the Cheshire-Cat: now I shall have somebody to talk to."
T4	148:21	"It's the crow!" Tweedledum cried out in a shrill voice of
A10	83: 7	"It's the first position in dancing," Alice said; but she was
T2	123:33	"It's the fresh air that does it," said the Rose: "wonderfully
A6	53: 8	thought Alice; "but a grin without a cat! It's the most curious thing I ever saw in all my life!"
A12	93:43	"It's the oldest rule in the book," said the King.
T8W	20: 5	at her with an expression of admiration: "it's the shape of your head as does it. Your jaws aint well
A7	60:36	as she picked her way through the wood. "It's the stupidest tea-party I ever was at in all my life!"
A9	73:13	"It's the thing Mock Turtle Soup is made from," said the Queen.
T2	124:18	"It's time for you to answer now," the Queen said looking at
T8W	18: 1	isn't that kind," Alice hastily explained. "It's to comb hair with--your wig's so <u>very</u> rough, you know."
T2	120:24	"Oh, it's too bad!" she cried. "I never saw <u>such</u> a house for
A2	18:16	so small as this before, never! And I declare it's too bad, that it is!"
T6	162: 5	I'd have said 'Leave off at seven'--but it's too late now."
T9	195:22	"It's too late to correct it," said the Red Queen: "when you've
T8	184:11	"It's too ridiculous!" cried Alice, losing all her patience
T1	111: 9	like gauze, so that we can get through. Why, it's turning into a sort of mist now, I declare! It'll be easy

IT'S (cont.)
```
T3    132:37              "No use to them," said Alice; "but it's useful to the people that name them, I suppose. If not,
A7     59:13  mean you ca'n't take less," said the Hatter: "it's very easy to take more than nothing."
T8W    16:14                              "And it's very good for the conceit," added the Wasp.
T5    150: 3                              "It's very good jam," said the Queen.
T2    122:26                 Alice did so. "It's very hard," she said; "but I don't see what that has to
T6    162:27               "I know it's very ignorant of me," Alice said, in so humble a tone
A10    81: 8       "Thank you," said Alice, "it's very interesting. I never knew so much about a whiting
T1    111: 4  the door of our drawing-room wide open: and it's very like our passage as far as you can see, only you
T4    140:19  Here Alice ventured to interrupt him. "If it's very long," she said, as politely as she could, "would
T6    159:17                              "It's very provoking," Humpty Dumpty said after a long silence,
T7    177: 8  was sawing away diligently with the knife. "It's very provoking!" she said, in reply to the Lion (she was
A7     55:10  remarks," Alice said with some severity: "it's very rude."
T4    140:33  to be there / After the day was done--/ 'It's very rude of him,' she said, / 'To come and spoil the
T8    186:35              "It's long," said the Knight, "but it's very, very beautiful. Everybody that hears me sing it--
T7    174:10                              "It's waiting for 'em now," said Hatta; "this is a bit of it as
T8W    16:17  considered a little. "Well, no," he said: "it's when you hold up your head--so--without bending your neck
A2     20: 9  farmer, you know, and he says it's so useful, it's worth a hundred pounds! He says it kills all the rats and
```
ITS (95) [entries omitted]
ITSELF (26) [entries omitted]
I'VE (57)
```
T9    199:25  Alice that said / 'I've a sceptre in hand, I've a crown on my head. / Let the Looking-Glass creatures,
T8    179:10  she went on in a rather complaining tone: "I've a great mind to go and wake him, and see what happens!"
A9     72:25                              "I've a right to think," said Alice sharply, for she was
T9    199:25  Looking-Glass world it was Alice that said / 'I've a sceptre in hand, I've a crown on my head. / Let the
T5    149:19  it done at all!" groaned the poor Queen. "I've been a-dressing myself for the last two hours."
T2    122:22  get it into a better temper by a compliment. "I've been in many gardens before, but none of the flowers
T9    199:17              "Nothing!" Alice said impatiently. "I've been knocking at it!"
A9     76: 7                              "I've been to a day-school, too," said Alice. "You needn't be
T5    153:15  did it for half-an-hour a day. Why, sometimes I've believed as many as six impossible things before
A2     15:39  things went on just as usual. I wonder if I've changed in the night? Let me think: was I the same when I
T7    177: 9  quite used to being called 'the Monster'). "I've cut several slices already, but they always join on
T5    152:25              "Why, I've done all the screaming already," said the Queen. "What
A1     8:28  come to an end? "I wonder how many miles I've fallen by this time?" she said aloud. "I must be getting
A9     74:28  both of you, and don't speak a word till I've finished."
A10    79: 8       "Oh, you sing," said the Gryphon. "I've forgotten the words."
T8    182:29       "Not yet," said the Knight. "But I've got a plan for keeping it from falling off."
T4    147:36              "And I've got a toothache!" said Tweedledee, who had overheard the
A5     43:42  to be, from one minute to another! However, I've got back to my right size: the next thing is, to get into
T5    153:20  time she succeeded in catching it herself. "I've got it!" she cried in a triumphant tone. "Now you shall
A1     8:35  but then I wonder what Latitude or Longitude I've got to?" (Alice had not the slightest idea what Latitude
A4     32:18              "The first thing I've got to do," said Alice to herself, as she wandered about
A8     67:28  being alive: for instance, there's the arch I've got to go through next walking about at the other end of
A4     33:11  to do it! Oh dear! I'd nearly forgotten that I've got to grow up again! Let me see--how is it to be managed
A4     27:31  your walk!' 'Coming in a minute, nurse! But I've got to watch this mouse-hole till Dinah comes back, and
A7     59:11                              "I've had nothing yet," Alice replied in an offended tone: "so
T8    183:11                              "I've had plenty of practice," the Knight said very gravely:
A12    98: 6              "Oh, I've had such a curious dream!" said Alice. And she told her
T9    201:28              "Do you know, I've had such a quantity of poetry repeated to me to-day,"
T4    143:24  slice. / I wish you were not quite so deaf--/ I've had to ask you twice!'
T2    125:14  it 'nonsense' if you like," she said, "but I've heard nonsense, compared with which that would be as
A7     57:17                              "I've heard something like it," said Alice.
T1    110:40  words go the wrong way: I know that, because I've held up one of our books to the glass, and then they hold
T8    184:42  hung from the saddle. "Yes," he said; "but I've invented a better one than that--like a sugar-loaf. When
A2     15:30  the Duchess! Oh! Wo'n't she be savage if I've kept her waiting!" Alice felt so desperate that she was
A2     17:20  and oh, ever so many lessons to learn! No, I've made up my mind about it: if I'm Mabel, I'll stay down
A11    88:24  sell," the Hatter added as an explanation. "I've none of my own. I'm a hatter."
A3     25:20  must have the trial; For really this morning I've nothing to do.' Said the mouse to the cur, Such a trial,
A2     20:10  cried Alice in a sorrowful tone. "I'm afraid I've offended it again!" For the Mouse was swimming away from
A6     53: 7                              "Well! I've often seen a cat without a grin," thought Alice; "but a
A10    80:18       "Yes," said Alice, "I've often seen them at dinn----" she checked herself hastily
T5    149:27       voice. "It's out of temper, I think. I've pinned it here, and I've pinned it there, but there's no
T5    149:28  of temper, I think. I've pinned it here, and I've pinned it there, but there's no pleasing it!"
A8     68: 1  "A cat may look at a king," said Alice. "I've read that in some book, but I don't remember where."
A9     72:19  Duchess. "I make you a present of everything I've said as yet."
A5     43:12  Pigeon, in a tone of the deepest contempt. "I've seen a good many little girls in my time, but never one
T2    125: 4  like at all: "though, when you say 'garden'--I've seen gardens, compared with which this would be a
A6     52:24  in which the March Hare was said to live. "I've seen hatters before," she said to herself: "the March
A11    90:16              "I'm glad I've seen that done," thought Alice. "I've so often read in
T1    118:32  to go back through the Looking-glass, before I've seen what the rest of the house is like! Let's have a
T7    170: 6                              "I've sent them all!" the King cried in a tone of delight, on
A11    90:16  glad I've seen that done," thought Alice. "I've so often read in the newspapers, at the end of trials,
A5     36:18  back!" the Caterpillar called after her. "I've something important to say!"
A5     42:33       "I've tried the roots of trees, and I've tried banks, and I've tried hedges," the Pigeon went on,
A5     42:30  subdued tone, and added, with a kind of sob, "I've tried every way, but nothing seems to suit them!"
A5     42:33  the roots of trees, and I've tried banks, and I've tried hedges," the Pigeon went on, without attending to
A5     42:33              "I've tried the roots of trees, and I've tried banks, and I've
A5     36:34              "Well, I've tried to say 'How doth the little busy bee,' but it all
```

-J-

JABBERWOCK (3)
T1   118:17   "And, hast thou slain the Jabberwock? / Come to my arms, my beamish boy! / O frabjous
T1   118: 1   "Beware the Jabberwock, my son! / The jaws that bite, the claws that
T1   118:10   And, as in uffish thought he stood, / The Jabberwock, with eyes of flame, / Came whiffling through the
JABBERWOCKY (3)
T1   116: 8   YKCOWREBBAJ
T1   116:17   JABBERWOCKY
T6   164:16   tell me the meaning of the poem called 'Jabberwocky'?"
JACK-IN-THE-BOX (1)
A4   31:23   all I know is, something comes at me like a Jack-in-the-box, and up I goes like a sky-rocket!"
JAM (8)
T5   150: 2   want you to hire me--and I don't care for jam."
T5   149:39   the Queen said. "Two pence a week, and jam every other day."
T5   150: 8   "No, it ca'n't," said the Queen. "It's jam every other day: to-day isn't any other day, you know."
T5   150: 3   "It's very good jam," said the Queen.
T5   150: 6   jam to-morrow and jam yesterday--but never jam to-day."
T5   150: 7   "It must come sometimes to 'jam to-day,'" Alice objected.
T5   150: 6   did want it," the Queen said. "The rule is, jam to-morrow and jam yesterday--but never jam to-day."
T5   150: 6   Queen said. "The rule is, jam to-morrow and jam yesterday--but never jam to-day."
JAR (2)
A1   8:20   it was empty: she did not like to drop the jar, for fear of killing somebody underneath, so managed to
A1   8:17   and pictures hung upon pegs. She took down a jar from one of the shelves as she passed: it was labeled
JAW (1)
A5   39: 7   the muscular strength, which it gave to my jaw / Has lasted the rest of my life."
JAWS (5)
A2   17:15   little fishes in, / With gently smiling jaws!
T8W   20: 6   "it's the shape of your head as does it. Your jaws aint well shaped, though--I should think you couldn't
T8W   21: 1   "Well, that's because your jaws are too short," the Wasp went on: "but the top of your
A5   39: 1   "You are old," said the youth, "and your jaws are too weak / For anything tougher than suet; / Yet you
T1   118: 2   "Beware the Jabberwock, my son! / The jaws that bite, the claws that catch! / Beware the Jubjub bird
JELLY-FISH (1)
A10   78:17   and so on: then, when you've cleared all the jelly-fish out of the way--"
JOGGED (1)
A8   62: 7   help it," said Five, in a sulky tone. "Seven jogged my elbow."
JOIN (12)
T3   130:11   no use in speaking." The voices didn't join in, this time, as she hadn't spoken, but, to her great
T7   177:10   cut several slices already, but they always join on again!"
A10   79:18   wo'n't you, will you, wo'n't you, wo'n't you join the dance?
A10   80: 6   could not, would not, could not, could not join the dance.
A10   80:12   wo'n't you, will you, wo'n't you, wo'n't you join the dance?"
A10   79:16   are waiting on the shingle--will you come and join the dance? / Will you, wo'n't you, will you, wo'n't you,
A10   79:17   wo'n't you, will you, wo'n't you, will you join the dance? / Will you, wo'n't you, will you, wo'n't you,
A10   80:10   turn not pale, beloved snail, but come and join the dance. / Will you, wo'n't you, will you, wo'n't you,
A10   80:11   wo'n't you, will you, wo'n't you, will you join the dance? / Will you, wo'n't you, will you, wo'n't you,
A10   80: 4   thanked the whiting kindly, but he would not join the dance. / Would not, could not, would not, could not,
A10   80: 5   could not, would not, could not, could not join the dance. / Would not, could not, would not, could not,
T2   126: 4   I wouldn't mind being a Pawn, if only I might join--though of course I should like to be a Queen, best."
JOINED (5)
A6   48:41   CHORUS (in which the cook and the baby joined):--
A3   26:14   Alice called after it. And the others all joined in chorus "Yes, please do!" But the Mouse only shook
T9   199:28   And hundreds of voices joined in the chorus:--
A8   65:23   "Come on, then!" roared the Queen, and Alice joined the procession, wondering very much what would happen
T7   175:43   The Lion had joined them while this was going on: he looked very tired and
JOINING (1)
T7   170:35   simply, without the least idea that he was joining in the game, while Alice was still hesitating for the
JOINT (3)
T9   201: 8   any one you've been introduced to. Remove the joint!" And the waiters carried it off, and brought a large
T9   200:19   the soup and fish," she said. "Put on the joint!" And the waiters set a leg of mutton before Alice, who
T9   200:21   anxiously, as she had never had to carve a joint before.
JOKE (7)
T9   193: 5   meaning--and a child's more important than a joke, I hope. You couldn't deny that, even if you tried with
T3   135: 9   "of course you'd miss your lessons. That's a joke. I wish you had made it."
T7   172:38   be sure," said the King: "and the best of the joke is, that it's my crown all the while! Let's run and see
T3   131:32   came from. "If you're so anxious to have a joke made, why don't you make one yourself?"
T3   131:29   "You might make a joke on that," said the little voice close to her ear:
T3   131:14   close to her ear, said "You might make a joke on that--something about 'horse' and 'hoarse,' you know
T9   193: 4   use of a child without any meaning? Even a joke should have some meaning--and a child's more important
JOKES (2)
T3   135:15   "You shouldn't make jokes," Alice said, "if it makes you so unhappy."
T8W   16: 8   a wig like mine," the Wasp went on. "They jokes at one. And they worrits one. And then I gets cross. And
JOURNEY (4)
T3   131:27   impatiently. "I don't belong to this railway journey at all--I was in a wood just now--and I wish I could
A10   81:34   a fish came to me, and told me he was going a journey, I should say 'With what porpoise?'"

JOURNEY (cont.)
```
  T1   114: 8   The  Queen  gasped,  and  sat  down: the rapid journey through the air had quite taken away her breath, and
  T8   187:16   all  the  strange  things  that Alice saw in her journey Through The Looking-Glass, this was the one that she
```
JOY (1) [See also ENJOY]
```
  T1   118:20   day!  Callooh!  Callay!" / He chortled in his joy.
```
-JOYED [See ENJOYED]
JOYS (1)
```
  A12   99:10   and  find  a  pleasure  in  all their simple joys, remembering her own child-life, and the happy summer
```
JUBJUB (1)
```
  T1   118: 3   that bite, the claws that catch! / Beware the Jubjub bird, and shun / The frumious Bandersnatch!"
```
JUDGE (4)
```
  A11   86:17                                       The judge, by the way, was the King; and, as he wore his crown
  A3   25:36   judge,  would be wasting our breath. 'I'll be judge, I'll be jury, said cunning old Fury: 'I'll try the
  A11   86:15   name  of nearly everything there. "That's the judge," she said to herself, "because of his great wig."
  A3   25:30   cur,  Such a trial, dear sir, With no jury or judge, would be wasting our breath. 'I'll be judge, I'll be
```
JUDGING (1)
```
  A6   45: 4   footman  because he was in livery: otherwise, judging by his face only, she would have called him a fish)--
```
JUDY (1)
```
  T8   180: 6   with  their  arms,  as if they were Punch and Judy--What a noise they make when they tumble! Just like a
```
-JUG [See MILK-JUG]
JULY (2)
```
  TC   209: 3   Lingering onward dreamily / In an evening of July--
  TC   209: 9   and  memories die: / Autumn frosts have slain July.
```
JUMP (2)
```
  T3   132: 6   it in and said "It's only a brook we have to jump over." Everybody seemed satisfied with this, though Alice
  T8W   13:12   checking herself on the very edge. "If I once jump over, everything will change, and then I can't help him
```
JUMPED (10)
```
  A6   47:17   with  such  sudden  violence that Alice quite jumped; but she saw in another moment that it was addressed to
  T2   122:35   a  Violet said, so suddenly, that Alice quite jumped; for it hadn't spoken before.
  A4   32:34   held it out to the puppy: whereupon the puppy jumped into the air off all its feet at once, with a yelp of
  T1   112: 1   moment Alice was through the glass, and had jumped lightly down into the Looking-glass room. The very
  T3   129:28   with  this excuse, she ran down the hill, and jumped over the first of the six little brooks. * * * * * *
  A8   65: 1   loud voice, and the three gardeners instantly jumped up, and began bowing to the King, the Queen, the royal
  T9   204:13   stand  this  any  longer!" she cried, as she jumped up and seized the tablecloth with both hands: one good
  T3   132: 3   shrill  scream from the engine, and everybody jumped up in alarm, Alice among the rest.
  A12   92: 2   had grown in the last few minutes, and she jumped up in such a hurry that she tipped over the jury-box
  A1    9:21            Alice was not a bit hurt, and she jumped up on to her feet in a moment: she looked up, but it
```
JUMPING (8)
```
  A10   78:37   voice;  and  the  two creatures, who had been jumping about like mad things all this time, sat down again
  T3   132: 8   felt  a  little nervous at the idea of trains jumping at all. "However, it'll take us into the Fourth Square
  A8   63:20   were  ten  of them, and the little dears came jumping merrily along, hand in hand, in couples: they were all
  T9   204:26   of  the  little  creature in the very act of jumping over a bottle which had just lighted upon the table,
  A6   48:16   please  mind what you're doing!" cried Alice, jumping up and down in an agony of terror. "Oh, there goes his
  T7   172:30   call  that  a  whisper?" cried the poor King, jumping up and shaking himself. "If you do such a thing again,
  T1   118:31          "But oh!" thought Alice, suddenly jumping up, "if I don't make haste, I shall have to go back
  A12   94: 4   please  your Majesty," said the White Rabbit, jumping up in a great hurry: "this paper has just been picked
```
JUROR (1)
```
  A11   87: 8   She did it so quickly that the poor little juror (it was Bill, the Lizard) could not make out at all what
```
JURORS (4)
```
  A11   87: 5                         One of the jurors had a pencil that squeaked. This, of course, Alice
  A11   86:24   and some were birds,) "I suppose they are the jurors." She said this last word two or three times over to
  A11   86:28                          The twelve jurors were all writing very busily on slates. "What are they
  A11   86:38   looking  over  their  shoulders, that all the jurors were writing down "Stupid things!" on their slates, and
```
JURY (17)
```
  A11   88: 1   "Consider your verdict," the King said to the jury.
  A12   95:22   the  King, rubbing his hands; "so now let the jury--"
  A12   94:20   somebody  else's  hand," said the King. (The jury all brightened up again.)
  A12   94:18   and  that's the queerest thing about it." (The jury all looked puzzled.)
  A12   95:27                     The jury all wrote down, on their slates, "She doesn't believe
  A11   88:17   "Write  that  down,"  the King said to the jury; and the jury eagerly wrote down all three dates on their
  A11   90: 3   "But  what  did the Dormouse say?" one of the jury asked.
  A12   96:28   angry  tone,  and everybody laughed. "Let the jury consider their verdict," the King said, for about the
  A11   88:17   down,"  the  King said to the jury; and the jury eagerly wrote down all three dates on their slates, and
  A12   93:10                     As soon as the jury had a little recovered from the shock of being upset, and
  A12   94: 2   "Consider  your  verdict," he said to the jury, in a low trembling voice.
  A12   95:39   himself: "'We know it to be true'--that's the jury, of course--'If she should push the matter on'--that must
  A3   25:29   to  the  cur,  Such a trial, dear sir, With no jury or judge, would be wasting our breath. 'I'll be judge,
  A3   25:38   wasting  our  breath. 'I'll be judge, I'll be jury, said cunning old Fury: 'I'll try the whole cause, and
  A12   93:21   important,"  the  King said,  turning to the jury. They were just beginning to write this down on their
  A11   88:22   "Stolen!"  the  King exclaimed, turning to the jury, who instantly made a memorandum of the fact.
  A12   93:30                         Some of the jury wrote it down "important," and some "unimportant." Alice
```
JURY-BOX (4)
```
  A12   93: 4                     Alice looked at the jury-box, and saw that, in her haste, she had put the Lizard
  A12   92:12   be  collected  at once and put back into the jury-box, or they would die.
  A11   86:21                  "And that's the jury-box," thought Alice; "and those twelve creatures," (she
  A12   92: 3   up  in  such a hurry that she tipped over the jury-box with the edge of her skirt, upsetting all the jurymen
```
JURYMEN (5)
```
  A12   94:11   "Who  is  it  directed  to?" said one of the jurymen.
  A12   94:16   prisoner's  handwriting?" asked another of the jurymen.
  A12   93: 2   King,  in  a very grave voice, "until all the jurymen are back in their proper places--all," he repeated
```

JURYMEN (cont.)
A12   92: 4 with the edge of her skirt, upsetting all the jurymen on to the heads of the crowd below, and there they lay
A11   86:27 age knew the meaning of it at all. However, "jurymen" would have done just as well.
JUST (130) [See also UNJUST]
A9   72:27   "Just about as much right," said the Duchess, "as pigs have to
T2   127: 7 the ground with their feet, till suddenly, just as Alice was getting quite exhausted, they stopped, and
T8   179:15 down upon her, brandishing a great club. Just as he reached her, the horse stopped suddenly: "You're my
T1   108:34 two: you pulled Snowdrop away by the tail just as I had put down the saucer of milk before her! What,
A5   43: 2 Pigeon, raising its voice to a shriek, "and just as I was thinking I should be free of them at last, they
A5   43: 1   "And just as I'd taken the highest tree in the wood," continued the
T6   161:19 to choose a subject--" ("He talks about it just as if it was a game!" thought Alice.) "So here's a
T3   129:10 the flowers, poking its proboscis into them, "just as if it was a regular bee," thought Alice.
T5   157: 3 went on with her knitting all the while, just as if nothing had happened. "That was a nice crab you
A5   41:31 "Of the mushroom," said the Caterpillar, just as if she had asked it aloud; and in another moment it
A6   52:19 into a pig," Alice answered very quietly, just as if the Cat had come back in a natural way.
T8   180: 9 horses are! They let them get on and off them just as if they were tables!"
T1   110: 6 when we were playing just now, you watched just as if you understood it: and when I said 'Check!' you
T9   195:40 "Five times as warm, and five times as cold--just as I'm five times as rich as you are, and five times as
T2   127:13 under this tree the whole time! Everything's just as it was!"
A8   62: 4 and she went nearer to watch them, and, just as she came up to them, she heard one of them say "Look
A8   66: 9 with its legs hanging down, but generally, just as she had got its neck nicely straightened out, and was
A12   98:13   But her sister sat still just as she left her, leaning her head on her hand, watching
A7   60:38   Just as she said this, she noticed that one of the trees had a
T3   129:18 go just yet," she went on, checking herself just as she was beginning to run down the hill, and trying to
A11   89: 5 never left off staring at the Hatter, and, just as the Dormouse crossed the court, she said, to one of
T8   179:24 up at Alice's side, and tumbled off his horse just as the Red Knight had done: then he got on again, and the
A2   15:39 is to-day! And yesterday things went on just as usual. I wonder if I've changed in the night? Let me
A11   86:27 it at all. However, "jurymen" would have done just as well.
A10   82:18 one repeat lessons!" thought Alice. "I might just as well be at school at once." However, she got up, and
T6   163:45 had enough of that subject, and it would be just as well if you'd mention what you mean to do next, as I
A7   55:28   "You might just as well say," added the Dormouse, which seemed to be
A7   55:26   "You might just as well say," added the March Hare, "that 'I like what I
A7   55:24 a bit!" said the Hatter. "Why, you might just as well say that 'I see what I eat' is the same thing as
T8W   13:11 turned to spring over the brook:--but I'll just ask him what's the matter," she added, checking herself
T9   192: 6 she got up and walked about--rather stiffly just at first, as she was afraid that the crown might come off
A10   82: 3 Rabbit. She was a little nervous about it, just at first, the two creatures got so close to her, one on
A5   35: 6   rather shyly, "I--I hardly know, Sir, just at present--at least I know who I was when I got up this
A11   88:34   Just at this moment Alice felt a very curious sensation, which
A2   15:12   Just at this moment her head struck against the roof of the
T2   126:10 get to the Eighth Square you'll be a Queen--"Just at this moment, somehow or other, they began to run.
T4   140: 3 to begin a conversation with people she had just been dancing with. "It would never do to say 'How d'ye do
A12   94: 5 jumping up in a great hurry: "this paper has just been picked up."
A12   98: 8 strange Adventures of hers that you have just been reading about; when she had finished, her sister
A7   57:11 Not I!" he replied. "We quarrelled last March--just before he went mad, you know--" (pointing his teaspoon at
T2   122:14 and, stooping down to the daisies, who were just beginning again, she whispered "If you don't hold your
T5   152: 1   Alice was just beginning to say "There's a mistake somewhere--," when
A6   50: 8   Alice was just beginning to think to herself, "Now, what am I to do with
A12   93:22 the King said, turning to the jury. They were just beginning to write this down on their slates, when the
A1   9:16 it. She felt that she was dozing off, and had just begun to dream that she was walking hand in hand with
A10   85: 2 cried the Gryphon, and the Mock Turtle had just begun to repeat it, when a cry of "The trial's beginning!"
A8   62:17   Seven flung down his brush, and had just begun "Well, of all the unjust things--" when his eye
T1   110:34 it when I get upon a chair--all but the bit just behind the fireplace. Oh! I do so wish I could see that
T3   137:27 before--But I ca'n't stay there long. I'll just call and say 'How d'ye do?' and ask them the way out of
T8   186:29   And here I must leave you." They had just come to the end of the wood.
T8   189: 7   I heard him then, for I had just / Completed my design / To keep the Menai bridge from
A11   90:13 court. (As that is rather a hard word, I will just explain to you how it was done. They had a large canvas
T3   135:34 the name of "Dash": had on a brass collar'--just fancy calling everything you met 'Alice,' till one of
T7   175:11 best of it this time?" he said to the King, just glancing at him as he passed.
T4   138: 7 she quite forgot they were alive, and she was just going round to see if the word 'TWEEDLE' was written at
A4   28: 1 up the fan and a pair of the gloves, and was just going to leave the room, when her eye fell upon a little
T4   146:10 "Selfish things!" thought Alice, and she was just going to say "Good-night" and leave them, when Tweedledum
T8W   13: 1   ...and she was just going to spring over, when she heard a deep sigh, which
T8   181:26 them." He unfastened it as he spoke, and was just going to throw it into the bushes, when a sudden thought
A6   46:28 out, straight at the Footman's head: it just grazed his nose, and broke to pieces against one of the
T12 207:25 caught it up and gave it one little kiss, "just in honour of its having been a Red Queen."
A1   9:25 lost: away went Alice like the wind, and was just in time to hear it say, as it turned a corner, "Oh my
A2   18: 8 she was holding, and she dropped it hastily, just in time to save herself from shrinking away altogether.
T8   184:16 his arms round the horse's neck as he spoke, just in time to save himself from tumbling off again.
A1   8: 3 she ran across the field after it, and was just in time to see it pop down a large rabbit-hole under the
T1   113:16 behind Alice, and made her turn her head just in time to see one of the White Pawns roll over and begin
T9   204: 6 from the soup-tureen, and Alice turned again, just in time to see the Queen's broad good-natured face
T1   119: 5 and easily, as Alice said to herself. She just kept the tips of her fingers on the hand-rail, and
T9   204:26 very act of jumping over a bottle which had just lighted upon the table, "I'll shake you into a kitten,
T1   111:13   the glass was beginning to melt away, just like a bright silvery mist.
T4   145:11 added Tweedledum, "you'd go out--bang!--just like a candle!"
T7   175:41 came out of it Alice couldn't guess. It was just like a conjuring-trick, she thought.
T2   125:25   "I declare it's marked out just like a large chess-board!" Alice said at last. "There
A6   49:17 out its arms and legs in all directions, "just like a star-fish," thought Alice. The poor little thing
T8   180: 7 What a noise they make when they tumble! Just like a whole set of fire-irons falling into the fender!
T9   202:27 and began eagerly lapping up the gravy, "just like pigs in a trough!" thought Alice.

JUST (cont.)

T3	135:32	the creature that has got my old name! That's just like the advertisements, you know, when people lose dogs
T7	170:14	either. They're both gone to the town. Just look along the road, and tell me if you can see either of
A6	49:13	a frying-pan after her as she went, but it just missed her.
A12	93:42	that's not a regular rule: you invented it just now."
T3	136:15	Alice. She answered, rather sadly, "Nothing, just now."
T3	131:27	this railway journey at all--I was in a wood just now--and I wish I could get back there!"
T6	163:19	I haven't time to look it over thoroughly just now--and that shows that there are three hundred and
T1	107: 9	the wrong way, beginning at the nose: and just now, as I said, she was hard at work on the white kitten,
A8	67:30	I should have croqueted the Queen's hedgehog just now, only it ran away when it saw mine coming!"
A9	70:19	makes you forget to talk. I ca'n't tell you just now what the moral of that is, but I shall remember it in
T1	110: 5	it seriously. Because, when we were playing just now, you watched just as if you understood it: and when I
T5	153: 6	Now I'll give you something to believe. I'm just one hundred and one, five months and a day."
T7	173:23	"He's only just out of prison, and he hadn't finished his tea when he was
T3	132:19	talking to) was balancing itself on a twig just over her head, and fanning her with its wings.
A4	32:25	among the trees, a little sharp bark just over her head made her look up in a great hurry.
A4	29:40	glass, from which she concluded that it was just possible it had fallen into a cucumber-frame, or
T3	133: 9	and made up her mind that it must have been just repainted, it looked so bright and sticky; and then she
T2	120:20	a few minutes all went on well, and she was just saying "I really shall do it this time--" when the path
A6	50:19	knew, who might do very well as pigs, and was just saying to herself "if one only knew the right way to
T1	111: 2	Kitty! now we come to the passage. You can just see a little peep of the passage in Looking-glass House,
A4	28: 6	"whenever I eat or drink anything: so I'll just see what this bottle does. I do hope it'll make me grow
T9	197: 9	put her head down on Alice's other shoulder, "just sing it through to me. I'm getting sleepy, too." In
T9	195:39	"Just so!" cried the Red Queen. "Five times as warm, and five
A5	42:21	in any direction, like a serpent. She had just succeeded in curving it down into a graceful zigzag, and
A11	91: 1	"--and just take his head off outside," the Queen added to one of the
T2	127:31	refreshing yourself," said the Queen, "I'll just take the measurements." And she took a ribbon out of her
A7	56:18	"Which is just the case with mine," said the Hatter.
T5	156:20	as she bent over the side of the boat, with just the ends of her tangled hair dipping into the water--
T1	110:32	room you can see through the glass--that's just the same as our drawing-room, only the things go the
T3	136: 7	Just then a Fawn came wandering by: it looked at Alice with
T2	128:14	"I--I didn't know I had to make one--just then," Alice faltered out.
T7	174:12	There was a pause in the fight just then, and the Lion and the Unicorn sat down, panting,
T4	139: 1	Just then flew down a monstrous crow, / As black as a
T8	184:26	"Well, just then I was inventing a new way of getting over a gate--
A2	19: 5	Just then she heard something splashing about in the pool a
A8	67:32	at all," said Alice: "she's so extremely--" Just then she noticed that the Queen was close behind her,
T5	156:34	What mattered it to her just then that the rushes had begun to fade, and to lose all
T9	198: 9	Just then the door opened a little way, and a creature with a
A6	48:25	of showing off a little of her knowledge. "Just think what work it would make with the day and night! You
A7	56:45	suppose it were nine o'clock in the morning, just time to begin lessons: you'd only have to whisper a hint
T7	178: 4	the little brook in her terror, and just time to see the Lion and the * * * * * * * * * * * * * *
T7	173: 9	running a little further, "to stop a minute--just to get--one's breath again?"
T1	110:38	that room too--but that may be only pretence, just to make it look as if they had a fire. Well then, the
T1	108:17	turns of the worsted round the kitten's neck, just to see how it would look: this led to a scramble, in
T8W	17: 6	then you'll know. And when you catches it, just try tying a yellow handkerchief round your face. It'll
A4	29:33	waiting till she fancied she heard the Rabbit just under the window, she suddenly spread out her hand, and
A7	60: 1	worse off than before, as the March Hare had just upset the milk-jug into his plate.
T6	163:31	said, in rather a scornful tone, "it means just what I choose it to mean--neither more nor less."
T6	168:26	"That's just what I complain of," said Humpty Dumpty. "Your face is
T9	193: 2	"That's just what I complain of! You should have meant! What do you
A7	56:25	opening its eyes, "Of course, of course: just what I was going to remark myself."
T6	164:19	and a good many that haven't been invented just yet."
T12	207:36	you'd better not mention it to your friends just yet, for I'm not sure.
T3	129:17	I think I'll go down and--no, I wo'n't go just yet," she went on, checking herself just as she was

JUSTICE (1)

A11	86:13	Alice had never been in a court of justice before, but she had read about them in books, and she

-K-

KANGAROOS (1)
    T9   202:26   the table--and three of them (who looked like kangaroos) scrambled into the dish of roast mutton, and began
KEEP (31)
    A6   53: 2   replied Alice; "and I wish you wouldn't keep appearing and vanishing so suddenly; you make one quite
    A10   81:28   on the song, "I'd have said to the porpoise 'Keep back, please! We don't want you with us!'"
    A12   98:20   and see that queer little toss of her head to keep back the wandering hair that would always get into her
    T8   181:18   a friendly tone. "It's my own invention--to keep clothes and sandwiches in. You see I carry it upside-down
    T5   152:41   even in the midst of her tears. "Can you keep from crying by considering things?" she asked.
    T8   183:18   waving his right arm as he spoke, "is to keep--" Here the sentence ended as suddenly as it had begun,
    A4   32:37   then Alice dodged behind a great thistle, to keep herself from being run over; and, the moment she appeared
    T6   166:17   come to that!" Alice hastily said, hoping to keep him from beginning.
    T3   129:39   the chorus of a song," thought Alice) "Don't keep him waiting, child! Why, his time is worth a thousand
    T6   159:10   one that Alice quite wondered how he could keep his balance--and, as his eyes were steadily fixed in the
    T4   147:24   a bolster round the neck of Tweedledee, "to keep his head from being cut off," as he said.
    T9   203: 1   In fact it was rather difficult for her to keep in her place while she made her speech: the two Queens
    T2   127:20   see, it takes all the running you can do, to keep in the same place. If you want to get somewhere else, you
    T8   186: 5   the more head-downwards I am, the more I keep inventing new things."
    A7   57: 7   perhaps," said the Hatter: "but you could keep it to half-past one as long as you liked."
    A7   58:14   "Then you keep moving round, I suppose?" said Alice.
    T2   120:19   out once more down the path, determined to keep straight on till she got to the hill. For a few minutes
    T8   181:37   thing is a mouse-trap. I suppose the mice keep the bees out--or the bees keep the mice out, I don't know
    T8   189: 9   for I had just / Completed my design / To keep the Menai bridge from rust / By boiling it in wine. / I
    T8   181:37   the mice keep the bees out--or the bees keep the mice out, I don't know which."
    A5   36:32   ca'n't remember things as I used--and I don't keep the same size for ten minutes together!"
    A11   88:24   "I keep them to sell," the Hatter added as an explanation. "I've
    T1   113: 3   "They don't keep this room so tidy as the other," Alice thought to herself
    A12   99: 5   be herself a grown woman; and how she would keep, through all her riper years, the simple and loving heart
    A6   49:23   to twist it up into a sort of knot, and then keep tight hold of its right ear and left foot, so as to
    T12   207: 9   that sort," she had said, "so that one could keep up a conversation! But how can you talk with a person if
    T2   126:15   went so fast that it was all she could do to keep up with her: and still the Queen kept crying "Faster!
    T8   184: 5   great art of riding, as I was saying is--to keep your balance properly. Like this, you know--"
    T2   122:37   Tiger-lily. "As if you ever saw anybody! You keep your head under the leaves, and snore away there, till
    T1   115:11   so that I can hardly hold you! And don't keep your mouth so wide open! All the ashes will get into it--
    A5   36:22   "Keep your temper," said the Caterpillar.
KEEPING (6)
    T8   183: 7   asked, as he scrambled back into the saddle, keeping hold of Alice's hair with one hand, to save himself
    T8   182:29   said the Knight. "But I've got a plan for keeping it from falling off."
    A9   70:25   Alice did not much like her keeping so close to her: first because the Duchess was very
    T8   182:27   "Have you invented a plan for keeping the hair from being blown off?" Alice enquired.
    A9   70:31   on rather better now," she said, by way of keeping up the conversation a little.
    T1   108:31   into your eye? Well, that's your fault, for keeping your eyes open--if you'd shut them tight up, it
KEPT (23)
    A7   61: 3   set to work nibbling at the mushroom (she had kept a piece of it in her pocket) till she was about a foot
    A5   38: 6   the sage, as he shook his grey locks, / "I kept all my limbs very supple / By the use of this ointment--
    T2   126:15   do to keep up with her: and still the Queen kept crying "Faster! Faster!" but Alice felt she could not go
    A6   49:18   like a steam-engine when she caught it, and kept doubling itself up and straightening itself out again, so
    A2   15:37   gloves, and, as the hall was very hot, she kept fanning herself all the time she went on talking. "Dear,
    A12   95:19   best, / For this must ever be / A secret, kept from all the rest, / Between yourself and me."
    A5   43:30   the trees as well as she could, for her neck kept getting entangled among the branches, and every now and
    A3   21:16   ring, with the Mouse in the middle. Alice kept her eyes anxiously fixed on it, for she felt sure she
    A2   15:30   the Duchess! Oh! Wo'n't she be savage if I've kept her waiting!" Alice felt so desperate that she was ready
    T7   177:20   "She's kept none for herself, anyhow," said the Lion. "Do you like
    A7   56:43   "He wo'n't stand beating. Now, if you only kept on good terms with him, he'd do almost anything you liked
    T10   205: 5   and still, as Alice went on shaking her, she kept on growing shorter--and fatter--and softer--and rounder--
    T8   182:42   suddenly), he fell off behind. Otherwise he kept on pretty well, except that he had a habit of now and
    A3   25: 3   tail; "but why do you call it sad?" And she kept on puzzling about it while the mouse was speaking, so
    T8   185:18   startled by the fall, as for some time he had kept on very well, and she was afraid that he really was hurt
    T8W   21: 5   if he wished to do the same for her, but she kept out of reach, and would not take the hint. So he went on
    T5   149: 8   her in a helpless frightened sort of way, and kept repeating something in a whisper to herself that sounded
    T4   138:16   could say; for the words of the old song kept ringing through her head like the ticking of a clock, and
    A12   92:10   she could, for the accident of the gold-fish kept running in her head, and she had a vague sort of idea
    A11   88:30   not seem to encourage the witness at all: he kept shifting from one foot to the other, looking uneasily at
    T7   170:23   attitudes he goes into!" (For the Messenger kept skipping up and down, and wriggling like an eel, as he
    T1   119: 5   easily, as Alice said to herself. She just kept the tips of her fingers on the hand-rail, and floated
    A6   49: 1   sang the second verse of the song, she kept tossing the baby violently up and down, and the poor
KETTLE (3)
    T6   167:16   went hop, my heart went thump: / I filled the kettle at the pump.
    A6   46:16   now and then a great crash, as if a dish or kettle had been broken to pieces.
    T6   167:13   I took a kettle large and new, / Fit for the deed I had to do.
KEY (9)
    A1   9:35   there was nothing on it but a tiny golden key, and Alice's first idea was that this might belong to one
    A2   15:14   and she at once took up the little golden key and hurried off to the garden door.
    A1   12:35   if it makes me grow larger, I can reach the key; and if it makes me grow smaller, I can creep under the

KEY (cont.)
```
   A7   61: 1    and began by taking the  little golden key, and unlocking the door that led into the garden. Then she
   A1   12:15    she found she had forgotten the little golden key, and when she went back to the table for it, she found she
   A1    9:41    inches high: she  tried  the  little golden key in the lock, and to her great delight it fitted!
   A1   10:13    the table, half hoping she might find another key on it, or at any rate a book of rules for shutting people
   A2   18:14    door was shut again, and the little golden key was lying on the glass table as before, "and things are
   A1    9:37    alas! either the locks were too large, or the key was too small, but at any rate it would not open any of
```
KICK (5)
```
   A4   30:38    is narrow, to be sure; but I think I can kick a little!"
   A4   31: 3    to herself "This is Bill", she gave one sharp kick, and waited to see what would happen next.
   T8  185: 9                              "I had to kick him, of course," the Knight said, very seriously. "And
   T9  199:19    know." Then he went up and gave the door a kick with one of his great feet. "You let it alone," he panted
   A5   40: 8    all day to such stuff? / Be off, or I'll kick you down-stairs!"
```
KICKED (1)
```
   T6  168:11    door was locked, / I pulled and pushed and kicked and knocked.
```
KICKING (1)
```
   T1  113:17    one of the White Pawns roll over and begin kicking: she watched it with great curiosity to see what would
```
KID-GLOVES (5)
```
   A4   27: 7    was looking for the fan and the pair of white kid-gloves, and she very good-naturedly began hunting about
   A2   15:34    Rabbit started violently, dropped the white kid-gloves and the fan, and scurried away into the darkness as
   A2   15:28    splendidly dressed, with a pair of white kid-gloves in one hand and a large fan in the other: he came
   A4   27:38    a fan and two or three pairs of tiny white kid-gloves: she took up the fan and a pair of the gloves, and
   A2   18: 2    had put on one of the Rabbit's little white kid-gloves while she was talking. "How can I have done that?"
```
KILL (1)
```
   A6   49:26    with me," thought Alice, "they're sure to kill it in a day or two. Wouldn't it be murder to leave it
```
KILLED (1)
```
   T1  118:29    exactly know what they are! However, somebody killed something: that's clear, at any rate--"
```
KILLING (1)
```
   A1    8:20    she did not like to drop the jar, for fear of killing somebody underneath, so managed to put it into one of
```
KILLS (1)
```
   A2   20: 9    it's worth a hundred pounds! He says it kills all the rats and--oh dear!" cried Alice in a sorrowful
```
KIND (19)
```
  T8W   18: 1                              "It isn't that kind," Alice hastily explained. "It's to comb hair with--your
  A10   84:11    song, please, if the Mock Turtle would be so kind," Alice replied, so eagerly that the Gryphon said, in a
   T8  181:35    said in a discontented tone, "one of the best kind. But not a single bee has come near it yet. And the other
   T9  196:26    at Alice, who felt she ought to say something kind, but really couldn't think of anything at the moment.
   T8  184:14                              "Does that kind go smoothly?" the Knight asked in a tone of great
  A10   82:14    at the Gryphon as if he thought it had some kind of authority over Alice.
   T8  185:12                    "But that's a different kind of fastness," Alice objected.
   T3  131:43                    "What kind of insect?" Alice inquired, a little anxiously. What she
   A9   70:11    very much pleased at having found out a new kind of rule, "and vinegar that makes them sour--and camomile
   A5   43:20    Pigeon; "but if they do, why, then they're a kind of serpent: that's all I can say."
   T6  166: 8    between bellowing and whistling, with a kind of sneeze in the middle: however, you'll hear it done,
   A5   42:30    but in a more subdued tone, and added, with a kind of sob, "I've tried every way, but nothing seems to suit
   A4   29: 4    I used to read fairy tales, I fancied that kind of thing never happened, and now here I am in the middle
  T8W   16:15    Alice didn't catch the word exactly. "Is it a kind of toothache?" she asked.
   T4  143:19                    'It was so kind of you to come! / And you are very nice!' / The Carpenter
   T2  128:17    in a tone of grave reproof, "'It's extremely kind of you to tell me all this'--however, we'll suppose it
   T2  123:21    her soon," said the Rose. "She's one of the kind that has nine spikes, you know."
   T9  201:38                    "Her Red Majesty's very kind to mention it," the White Queen murmured into Alice's
   A2   14: 9    manage the best way you can--but I must be kind to them," thought Alice, "or perhaps they wo'n't walk the
```
KINDER (1)
```
   T2  124:13    did you come out here at all?" she added in a kinder tone. "Curtsey while you're thinking what to say. It
```
KINDLY (8)
```
  A10   80: 4    a look askance--/ Said he thanked the whiting kindly, but he would not join the dance. / Would not, could
  T8W   13:19    and she stooped over him, and said very kindly, "I hope you're not in much pain?"
   T5  150:11    effect of living backwards," the Queen said kindly: "it always makes one a little giddy at first--"
  A10   83:19    was all finished, the Owl, as a boon, / Was kindly permitted to pocket the spoon: / While the Panther
   T8  187:20    been only yesterday--the mild blue eyes and kindly smile of the Knight--the setting sun gleaming through
   T6  164:15    words, Sir," said Alice. "Would you kindly tell me the meaning of the poem called 'Jabberwocky'?"
   T2  127:10    Queen propped her up against a tree, and said kindly, "You may rest a little, now."
   T2  123:15    "But that's not your fault," the Rose added kindly. "You're beginning to fade, you know--and then one
```
KINDNESS (2)
```
   T9  196:32                    "A little kindness--and putting her hair in papers--would do wonders
   T4  143:15    cried, / Turning a little blue. / 'After such kindness, that would be / A dismal thing to do!' / 'The night
```
KINDS (4)
```
   T3  132:30    I'm rather afraid of them--at least the large kinds. But I can tell you the names of some of them."
   T8  185:21    he was talking on in his usual tone. "All kinds of fastness," he repeated: "but it was careless of him
   T8  185:13    The Knight shook his head. "It was all kinds of fastness with me, I can assure you!" he said. He
   T9  200:10    that there were about fifty guests, of all kinds: some were animals, some birds, and there were even a
```
KING (122)
```
  A11   87:13    "Herald, read the accusation!" said the King.
  A11   89:15                    "The twinkling of what?" said the King.
  A11   90:10    "You're a very poor speaker," said the King.
  A11   90:22    about it, you may stand down," continued the King.
  A11   91: 4                    "Call the next witness!" said the King.
  A11   91: 9                    "Give your evidence," said the King.
  A12   93:19                    "Nothing whatever?" persisted the King.
  A12   93:39                    "You are," said the King.
  A12   93:43    "It's the oldest rule in the book," said the King.
```

KING (cont.)

A12	94:32	"Read them," said the King.
T7	171: 3	"It isn't respectable to beg," said the King.
T7	171:10	and make the most fearful faces at the poor King.
T7	172: 4	"Another sandwich!" said the King.
T7	172:36	Lion and the Unicorn, of course," said the King.
A12	96:27	"It's a pun!" the King added in an angry tone, and everybody laughed. "Let the
A11	86:17	The judge, by the way, was the King; and, as he wore his crown over the wig (look at the
A11	88:28	"Give your evidence," said the King: "and don't be nervous, or I'll have you executed on the
A8	67:44	"Don't be impertinent," said the King, "and don't look at me like that!" He got behind Alice as
A12	95:38	"All right, so far," said the King; and he went on muttering over the verses to himself:
A11	86: 1	The King and Queen of Hearts were seated on their throne when they
T6	162:30	as you say. It's a present from the White King and Queen. There now!"
T7	172:38	"Yes, to be sure," said the King: "and the best of the joke is, that it's my crown all the
A8	69:12	Duchess, it had entirely disappeared: so the King and the executioner ran wildly up and down, looking for
A11	90:31	"You may go," said the King, and the Hatter hurriedly left the court, without even
A8	63:27	last of all this grand procession, came THE KING AND THE QUEEN OF HEARTS.
A8	68:30	dispute going on between the executioner, the King, and the Queen, who were all talking at once, while all
T1	113: 8	"Here are the Red King and the Red Queen," Alice said (in a whisper, for fear of
T7	176:11	paws. "And sit down, both of you," (to the King and the Unicorn): "fair play with the cake, you know!"
T1	113:10	frightening them), "and there are the White King and the White Queen sitting on the edge of the shovel--
A11	88: 4	"Call the first witness," said the King; and the White Rabbit blew three blasts on the trumpet,
T1	114:18	Alice watched the White King as he slowly struggled up from bar to bar, till at last
T7	174:13	and the Unicorn sat down, panting, while the King called out "Ten minutes allowed for refreshments!" Haigha
A8	67:37	"Who are you talking to?" said the King, coming up to Alice, and looking at the Cat's head with
T1	115:10	she cried out, quite forgetting that the King couldn't hear her. "You make me laugh so that I can
T7	170: 6	"I've sent them all!" the King cried in a tone of delight, on seeing Alice. "Did you
A8	68: 8	"I'll fetch the executioner myself," said the King eagerly, and he hurried off.
A11	88:22	"Stolen!" the King exclaimed, turning to the jury, who instantly made a
T1	116: 2	table, and while she sat watching the White King (for she was still a little anxious about him, and had
A12	94:27	it was the first really clever thing the King had said that day.
T6	160:24	laughing. "If I did fall," he went on, "the King has promised me--ah, you may turn pale, if you like! You
T6	160:26	think I was going to say that, did you? The King has promised me--with his very own mouth--to--to--"
A12	93:26	"Unimportant, of course, I meant," the King hastily said, and went on to himself in an undertone,
T12	208: 8	Kitty, it must have been either me or the Red King. He was part of my dream, of course--but then I was part
T7	170:26	"Not at all," said the King. "He's an Anglo-Saxon Messenger--and those are
T7	174: 3	"Speak, wo'n't you!" cried the King. "How are they getting on with the fight?"
A8	67:41	I don't like the look of it at all," said the King: "however, it may kiss my hand, if it likes."
T6	160:38	good look at me! I'm one that has spoken to a King, I am: mayhap you'll never see such another: and, to show
T7	171:16	"You alarm me!" said the King. "I feel faint--Give me a ham-sandwich!"
T1	115:15	The King immediately fell flat on his back, and lay perfectly
A12	93: 1	"The trial cannot proceed," said the King, in a very grave voice, "until all the jurymen are back
T7	176:23	Here the King interrupted, to prevent the quarrel going on: he was very
T7	172:30	"Do you call that a whisper?" cried the poor King, jumping up and shaking himself. "If you do such a thing
T7	175:11	had the best of it this time?" he said to the King, just glancing at him as he passed.
T12	208:10	I was part of his dream, too! Was it the Red King, Kitty? You were his wife, my dear, so you ought to know
A8	64:10	The King laid his hand upon her arm, and timidly said "Consider,
A11	89:24	"He denies it," said the King: "leave out that part."
A11	91:11	The King looked anxiously at the White Rabbit, who said, in a low
T1	115:34	The poor King looked puzzled and unhappy, and struggled with the pencil
A12	96:25	"Then the words don't fit you," said the King looking round the court with a smile. There was a dead
T1	114:13	"What volcano?" said the King, looking up anxiously into the fire, as if he thought
T1	115: 4	never seen in all her life such a face as the King made, when he found himself held in the air by an
T7	172: 7	"Hay, then," the King murmured in a faint whisper.
T7	175:36	"Certainly--certainly!" the King muttered, and beckoned to Haigha. "Open the bag!" he
T7	175:34	the Unicorn went on, turning from her to the King. "None of your brown bread for me!"
T7	172:22	"He ca'n't do that," said the King, "or else he'd have been here first. However, now you've
A11	90: 5	"You must remember," remarked the King, "or I'll have you executed."
A11	86:35	cried out "Silence in the court!", and the King put on his spectacles and looked anxiously round, to make
T7	170:17	"I only wish I had such eyes," the King remarked in a fretful tone. "To be able to see Nobody!
T7	170:34	"He lives on the Hill," the King remarked simply, without the least idea that he was
A11	89: 9	"Give your evidence," the King repeated angrily, "or I'll have you executed, whether you
T7	171: 6	"Don't I tell you?" the King repeated impatiently. "I must have two--to fetch and
A11	90:25	"Then you may sit down," the King replied.
T7	172:13	"I didn't say there was nothing better," the King replied. "I said there was nothing like it." Which Alice
T7	175:12	"A little--a little," the King replied, rather nervously. "You shouldn't have run him
A12	95:22	piece of evidence we've heard yet," said the King, rubbing his hands; "so now let the jury--"
T1	114: 1	"Imperial fiddlestick!" said the King, rubbing his nose, which had been hurt by the fall. He
A8	68: 1	"A cat may look at a king," said Alice. "I've read that in some book, but I don't
A12	96:28	"Let the jury consider their verdict," the King said, for about the twentieth time that day.
T7	171:11	"This young lady loves you with an H," the King said, introducing Alice in the hope of turning off the
T7	173:11	"I'm good enough," the King said, "only I'm not strong enough. You see, a minute goes
T7	170:11	and seven, that's the exact number," the King said, referring to his book. "I couldn't send all the
A12	93:16	"What do you know about this business?" the King said to Alice.
T7	174:17	think they'll fight any more to-day," the King said to Hatta: "go and order the drums to begin." And
A11	88:20	"Take off your hat," the King said to the Hatter.
A11	88: 1	"Consider your verdict," the King said to the jury.
A11	88:17	"Write that down," the King said to the jury; and the jury eagerly wrote down all
A12	93:21	"That's very important," the King said, turning to the jury. They were just beginning to
A12	94:35	"Begin at the beginning," the King said, very gravely, "and go on till you come to the end:

KING (cont.)
```
A11    91:13              "Well, if I must, I must," the King said with a melancholy air, and, after folding his arms
T7    174:25    "There's some enemy after her, no doubt," the King said, without even looking round. "That wood's full of
A9     73:18    As  they walked off together, Alice heard the King say in a low voice, to the company, generally, "You are
T7     170: 4    into an open place, where she found the White King seated on the ground, busily writing in his
A11    89:17    course twinkling begins with a T!" said the King sharply. "Do you take me for a dunce? Go on!"
T7     175: 4              "No use, no use!" said the King. "She runs so fearfully quick. You might as well try to
T4    144:27                "It's only the Red King snoring," said Tweedledee.
T1    113:20    White Queen cried out, as she rushed past the King, so violently that she knocked him over among the cinders
A12    94:23          "If you didn't sign it," said the King, "that only makes the matter worse. You must have meant
A12    95:30    "If  there's no meaning in it," said the King, "that saves a world of trouble, you know, as we needn't
A12    94:19    have imitated somebody else's hand," said the King. (The jury all brightened up again.)
A9     73: 8    arches  left, and all the players, except the King, the Queen, and Alice, were in custody and under sentence
A8     65: 1    instantly  jumped up, and began bowing to the King, the Queen, the royal children, and everybody else.
T7    172:18              "Quite right," said the King: "this young lady saw him too. So of course Nobody walks
T1    115:29    Alice looked on with great interest as the King took an enormous memorandum-book out of his pocket, and
T1    114:21    I'd  far  better help you, hadn't I?" But the King took no notice of the question: it was quite clear that
A12    96:13            "Why, there they are!" said the King triumphantly, pointing to the tarts on the table.
A12    94: 1                                    The King turned pale, and shut his note-book hastily. "Consider
A12    94: 9        "It must have been that," said the King, "unless it was written to nobody, which isn't usual, you
A8     68: 3      "Well,  it  must  be  removed,"  said the King very decidedly; and he called to the Queen, who was
T7    176:13                                    The King was evidently very uncomfortable at having to sit down
T7    176:17    looking slyly up at the crown, which the poor King was nearly shaking off his head, he trembled so much.
T1    115:22                                    The King was saying "I assure you, my dear, I turned cold to the
T4    144:29    of Alice's hands, and led her up to where the King was sleeping.
A11    86: 5      on each side to guard him; and near the King was the White Rabbit, with a trumpet in one hand, and a
T4    145:10                    "If that there King was to wake," added Tweedledum, "you'd go out--bang!--
T7    172:15      "Who  did  you  pass  on  the road?" the King went on, holding out his hand to the Messenger for some
T1    115:25          "The horror of that moment," the King went on, "I shall never, never forget!"
T7    173: 7            "Dear me, no!" said the King. "What an idea!"
A11    88:10      "You  ought  to  have  finished,"  said the King. "When did you begin?"
T7    172: 2    round  his neck, and handed a sandwich to the King, who devoured it greedily.
A12    93:33                    At this moment the King, who had been for some time busily writing in his
T1    114:11    breath  a  little, she called out to the White King, who was sitting sulkily among the ashes, "Mind the
A11    91:25              "Never mind!" said the King with an air of great relief. "Call the next witness." And
```
KING'S (7)
```
A8     68:41                                    The King's argument was that anything that had a head could be
A8     63:25    followed the Knave of Hearts, carrying the King's crown on a crimson velvet cushion; and, last of all
T7    172:27      and stooping so as to get close to the King's ear. Alice was sorry for this, as she wanted to hear
T6    159:30    / Humpty Dumpty had a great fall. / All the King's horses and all the King's men / Couldn't put Humpty
T8    179: 9    Only I do hope it's my dream, and not the Red King's! I don't like belonging to another person's dream," she
T6    159:30    fall. / All the King's horses and all the King's men / Couldn't put Humpty Dumpty in his place again."
T5    150: 4    on her finger as she spoke, "there's the King's Messenger. He's in prison now, being punished: and the
```
KINGS (3)
```
A8     63:22    with hearts. Next came the guests, mostly Kings and Queens, and among them Alice recognized the White
T1    110:13    Alice had begun with "Let's pretend we're kings and queens;" and her sister, who liked being very exact,
T4    142:22    ships--and sealing wax--/ Of cabbages--and kings--/ And why the sea is boiling hot--/ And whether pigs
```
KISS (3)
```
T12   207:24    And she caught it up and gave it one little kiss, "just in honour of its having been a Red Queen."
A8     67:42    it  at  all," said the King: "however, it may kiss my hand, if it likes."
T1    107:21      up the kitten, and giving it a little kiss to make it understand that it was in disgrace. "Really,
```
KISSED (1)
```
A12    98: 9    about; when she had finished, her sister kissed her, and said "It was a curious dream, dear, certainly;
```
KISSES (1)
```
T1    109:11    the snow loves the trees and fields, that it kisses them so gently? And then it covers them up snug, you
```
KITCHEN (4)
```
A9     70: 6    had made her so savage when they met in the kitchen.
A9     70: 8    though), "I wo'n't have any pepper in my kitchen at all. Soup does very well without--Maybe it's always
A6     47:10    moment's pause. The only two creatures in the kitchen, that did not sneeze, were the cook, and a large cat,
A6     46:45              The door led right into a large kitchen, which was full of smoke from one end to the other:
```
KITTEN (22)
```
T11   206: 1                  ..--it really was a kitten, after all.
T1    107:21    little  thing!"  cried Alice, catching up the kitten, and giving it a little kiss to make it understand that
T1    113:21    the cinders. "My precious Lily! My imperial kitten!" and she began scrambling wildly up the side of the
T1    108: 6    was  talking  all  the  time, sometimes to the kitten, and sometimes to herself. Kitty sat very demurely on
T12   207:15    on  her knees on the hearth-rug, and put the kitten and the Queen to look at each other. "Now Kitty!" she
T1    108: 4    scrambled back into the arm-chair, taking the kitten and the worsted with her, and began winding up the ball
T1    110:24    Queen off the table, and set it up before the kitten as a model for it to imitate: however, the thing didn't
T1    107:12                    But the black kitten had been finished with earlier in the afternoon, and so
T1    107:14    half  talking to herself and half asleep, the kitten had been having a grand game of romps with the ball of
T1    107: 3    black  kitten's fault entirely. For the white kitten had been having its face washed by the old cat for the
T1    107: 1      One thing was certain, that the white kitten had had nothing to do with it--it was the black
T1    110:20    is  taking us away from Alice's speech to the kitten. "Let's pretend that you're the Red Queen, Kitty! Do
T12   208:12    sure  your  paw  can wait!" But the provoking kitten only began on the other paw, and pretended it hadn't
T12   207:11              On this occasion the kitten only purred: and it was impossible to guess whether it
T12   207: 2    said, rubbing her eyes, and addressing the kitten, respectfully, yet with some severity. "You woke me out
T1    107:18    hearth-rug,  all  knots and tangles, with the kitten running after its own tail in the middle.
T9    204:27      upon the table, "I'll shake you into a kitten, that I will!"
T1    108:30    What's  that  you  say?" (pretending that the kitten was speaking). "Her paw went into your eye? Well,
T1    109: 2    she went on, talking more to herself than the kitten. "What would they do at the end of a year? I should be
```

KITTEN (cont.)
T1   107:10   as I said, she was hard at work on the white kitten, which was lying quite still and trying to purr--no
T12   207:27   on, looking over her shoulder at the White Kitten, which was still patiently undergoing its toilet, "when
T1   110:26   succeed, principally, Alice said, because the kitten wouldn't fold its arms properly. So, to punish it, she
KITTEN'S (2)
T1   107: 2   had nothing to do with it--it was the black kitten's fault entirely. For the white kitten had been having
T1   108:17   two or three turns of the worsted round the kitten's neck, just to see how it would look: this led to a
KITTENS (2)
T12   207: 6   "it is a very inconvenient habit of kittens (Alice had once made the remark) that, whatever you
T12   207:34   rug, and her chin in her hand, to watch the kittens. "Tell me, Dinah, did you turn to Humpty Dumpty? I
KITTY (24)
T1   108:11   "Do you know what to-morrow is, Kitty?" Alice began. "You'd have guessed if you'd been up in
T1   108:21   "Do you know, I was so angry, Kitty," Alice went on, as soon as they were comfortably
T12   207: 4   a nice dream! And you've been along with me, Kitty--all through the Looking-glass world. Did you know it,
T1   110:30   "Now, if you'll only attend, Kitty, and not talk so much, I'll tell you all my ideas about
T1   110: 7   you purred! Well, it was a nice check, Kitty, and really I might have won, if it hadn't been for that
T1   108:38   "That's three faults, Kitty, and you've not been punished for any of them yet. You
T1   110: 4   "Kitty, can you play chess? Now, don't smile, my dear. I'm
T1   110: 9   that came wriggling down among my pieces. Kitty dear, let's pretend--" And here I wish I could tell you
T12   208:11   his wife, my dear, so you ought to know--Oh, Kitty, do help to settle it! I'm sure your paw can wait!" But
T1   110:21   "Let's pretend that you're the Red Queen, Kitty! Do you know, I think if you sat up and folded your arms
T1   109: 9   you hear the snow against the window-panes, Kitty? How nice and soft it sounds! I wonder if the snow loves
T1   111: 5   know it may be quite different on beyond. Oh, Kitty, how nice it would be if we could only get through into
T1   108:29   face this morning. Now you ca'n't deny it, Kitty: I heard you! What's that you say?" (pretending that the
T1   110:43   you like to live in Looking-glass House, Kitty? I wonder if they'd give you milk in there? Perhaps
T12   207:37   "By the way, Kitty, if only you'd been really with me in my dream, there
T12   208: 8   hadn't washed you this morning! You see, Kitty, it must have been either me or the Red King. He was
T12   208: 5   "Now, Kitty, let's consider who it was that dreamed it all. This is
T1   111: 8   a way of getting through into it, somehow, Kitty. Let's pretend the glass has got all soft like gauze, so
T1   111: 1   milk isn't good to drink--but oh, Kitty! now we come to the passage. You can just see a little
T1   108:14   the bonfire--and it wants plenty of sticks, Kitty! Only it got so cold, and it snowed so, they had to
T1   108: 7   to the kitten, and sometimes to herself. Kitty sat very demurely on her knee, pretending to watch the
T12   207:16   and the Queen to look at each other. "Now Kitty!" she cried, clapping her hands triumphantly. "Confess
T1   109:14   again.' And when they wake up in the summer, Kitty, they dress themselves all in green, and dance about--
T12   208:10   part of his dream, too! Was it the Red King, Kitty? You were his wife, my dear, so you ought to know--Oh,
KNAVE (9)
A12   95:35   swim, can you?" he added, turning to the Knave.
A8   64:14   The Knave did so, very carefully, with one foot.
A12   94:21   "Please, your Majesty," said the Knave, "I didn't write it, and they ca'n't prove that I did:
A8   63:25   by without noticing her. Then followed the Knave of Hearts, carrying the King's crown on a crimson velvet
A11   87:18   made some tarts, / All on a summer day: / The Knave of Hearts, he stole those tarts / And took them quite
A8   63:36   severely, "Who is this?" She said it to the Knave of Hearts, who only bowed and smiled in reply.
A12   95:36   The Knave shook his head sadly. "Do I look like it?" he said.
A8   64:12   turned angrily away from him, and said to the Knave "Turn them over!"
A11   86: 4   as well as the whole pack of cards: the Knave was standing before them, in chains, with a soldier on
KNEE (7)
A12   95:32   he went on, spreading out the verses on his knee, and looking at them with one eye; "I seem to see some
A12   98:18   again the tiny hands were clasped upon her knee, and the bright eager eyes were looking up into hers--she
A8   65: 7   Two, in a very humble tone, going down on one knee as he spoke, "we were trying--"
A11   90: 8   and bread-and-butter and went down on one knee. "I'm a poor man, your Majesty," he began.
T6   162:34   continued thoughtfully as he crossed one knee over the other and clasped his hands round it, "they gave
T1   108: 7   to herself. Kitty sat very demurely on her knee, pretending to watch the progress of the winding, and now
A12   98:29   the pig-baby was sneezing on the Duchess's knee, while plates and dishes crashed around it--once more the
KNEEL (1)
A4   28:16   on growing, and growing, and very soon had to kneel down on the floor: in another minute there was not even
KNEES (5)
T8W   14:20   down by him, and spread out the paper on her knees, and began. "Latest News. The Exploring Party have made
T7   178: 9   in their feast, before she dropped to her knees, and put her hands over her ears, vainly trying to shut
T7   177: 7   of a little brook, with the great dish on her knees, and was sawing away diligently with the knife. "It's
T12   207:14   the Red Queen: then she went down on her knees on the hearth-rug, and put the kitten and the Queen to
T1   113: 6   of surprise, she was down on her hands and knees watching them. The chessmen were walking about, two and
KNELT (1)
A1   10: 2   passage, not much larger than a rat-hole: she knelt down and looked along the passage into the loveliest
KNEW (22)
T2   128:28   How it happened, Alice never knew, but exactly as she came to the last peg, she was gone.
T1   111:12   while she said this, though she hardly knew how she had got there. And certainly the glass was
A1   10: 9   like a telescope! I think I could, if I only knew how to begin." For, you see, so many out-of-the-way
T4   146:20   "I knew it was!" cried Tweedledum, beginning to stamp about
A4   29:21   little pattering of feet on the stairs. Alice knew it was the Rabbit coming to look for her, and she
A12   98:35   believed herself in Wonderland, though she knew she had but to open them again, and all would change to
T6   162:20   she hadn't chosen that subject. "If only I knew," she thought to herself, "which was neck and which was
A10   81: 8   said Alice, "it's very interesting. I never knew so much about a whiting before."
A8   67: 4   yet had any dispute with the Queen, but she knew that it might happen any minute, "and then," thought she,
A9   70:14   children sweet-tempered. I only wish people knew that: then they wouldn't be so stingy about it, you know
A2   16: 1   she began thinking over all the children she knew that were of the same age as herself, to see if she could
A11   86:26   too, that very few little girls of her age knew the meaning of it at all. However, "jurymen" would have
A11   86:15   and she was quite pleased to find that she knew the name of nearly everything there. "That's the judge,"
A6   50:19   and was just saying to herself "if one only knew the right way to change them--" when she was a little
T3   132:34   "I never knew them do it."
T3   136:14   "I wish I knew!" thought poor Alice. She answered, rather sadly,

KNEW (cont.)
```
A7     56:35                                          "If you knew Time as well as I do," said the Hatter, "you wouldn't
A12    98:41  all the other queer noises, would change (she knew) to the confused clamour of the busy farm-yard--while the
A10    82:20  of  the  Lobster-Quadrille,  that  she hardly knew what she was saying; and the words came very queer indeed
A8     68:15  the game was in such confusion that she never knew whether it was her turn or not. So she went off in search
T4    138: 2  with an arm round the other's neck, and Alice knew which was which in a moment, because one of them had
A6     50:18  she began thinking over other children she knew, who might do very well as pigs, and was just saying to
```
KNIFE (6) [See also BREAD-KNIFE, CARVING-KNIFE]
```
T9    201: 4  I give you a slice?" she said, taking up the knife and fork, and looking from one Queen to the other.
A10    84: 1  the  spoon: / While  the  Panther received knife and fork with a growl, / And concluded the banquet by--
T7    177:18  cried  the  Unicorn,  as  Alice sat with the knife in her hand, very much puzzled how to begin. "The
A1     11: 2  if  you  cut  your  finger very deeply with a knife, it usually bleeds; and she had never forgotten that, if
T7    177: 8  and was sawing away diligently with the knife. "It's very provoking!" she said, in reply to the Lion
T9    194: 6  "Can  you  do Division? Divide  a loaf by a knife--what's the answer to that?"
```
KNIGHT (57)
```
T8    179:36                            "I always do," said the Red Knight, and they began banging away at each other with such
T8    186:23                "It began with blotting-paper," the Knight answered with a groan.
T8    180:15  glorious  victory, wasn't it?" said the White Knight, as he came up panting.
T8    179:31  we  must  fight  for  her, then," said the Red Knight, as he took up his helmet (which hung from the saddle,
T8    184:14                "Does that kind go smoothly?" the Knight asked in a tone of great interest, clasping his arms
T8    182: 3  "Not  very  likely,  perhaps," said the Knight; "but, if they do come, I don't choose to have them
T8    186:35                  "It's long," said the Knight, "but it's very, very beautiful. Everybody that hears
T8    182:29                "Not yet," said the Knight. "But I've got a plan for keeping it from falling off."
T8    185: 4  before I could get out again, the other White Knight came and put it on. He thought it was his own helmet."
T8    179:16  stopped suddenly: "You're my prisoner!" the Knight cried, as he tumbled off his horse.
T8    179:13  a loud shouting of "Ahoy! Ahoy! Check!" and a Knight, dressed in crimson armour, came galloping down upon
T8    183:19  ended  as  suddenly  as  it had begun, as the Knight fell heavily on the top of his head exactly in the path
T8    179:24  and  tumbled  off  his  horse just as the Red Knight had done: then he got on again, and the two Knights sat
T8    186:38          "Or  else  what?"  said Alice,  for the Knight had made a sudden pause.
T8    179:23                  This time it was a White Knight. He drew up at Alice's side, and tumbled off his horse
T8    180: 3        "One Rule seems to be, that if one Knight hits the other, he knocks him off his horse; and, if he
T8    181: 4  crossed  the  next  brook," said  the  White Knight. "I'll see you safe to the end of the wood--and then I
T1    115:40  the  book  (in which Alice had put 'The White Knight is sliding down the poker. He balances very badly').
T8    184:41                                          The Knight looked down proudly at his helmet, which hung from the
T8    185: 6                                          The Knight looked so solemn about it that Alice did not dare to
T8    186: 2                                          The Knight looked surprised at the question. "What does it matter
T8    183: 5                                          The Knight looked very much surprised, and a little offended at
T8    180:13  up  again, they shook hands, and then the Red Knight mounted and galloped off.
T8    181: 9  "Now  one  can breathe more easily," said the Knight, putting back his shaggy hair with both hands, and
T8    179:35  the  Rules  of  Battle, of  course?" the White Knight remarked, putting on his helmet too.
T8    186:15            "Well, not the next day," the Knight repeated as before: "not the next day. In fact," he
T8    179:29  but  then  I came and rescued her!" the White Knight replied.
T8    182: 9  "To  guard  against the bites of sharks," the Knight replied. "It's an invention of my own. And now help me
T8    190:24            So they shook hands, and then the Knight rode slowly away into the forest. "It wo'n't take long
T8    181:23              "I didn't know it," the Knight said, a shade of vexation passing over his face. "Then
T8    184: 3            "None to speak of," the Knight said, as if he didn't mind breaking two or three of
T8    179:28  "She's my  prisoner,  you  know!"  the Red Knight said at last.
T8    190:22                  "I hope so," the Knight said doubtfully: "but you didn't cry so much as I
T8    184:36            "I haven't tried it yet," the Knight said, gravely; "so I ca'n't tell for certain--but I'm
T8    181:34      "Yes,  it's  a  very  good  bee-hive," the Knight said in a discontented tone, "one of the best kind. But
T8    181:17  "I  see  you're  admiring my little box," the Knight said in a friendly tone. "It's my own invention--to
T8    186:31              "You are sad," the Knight said in an anxious tone: "let me sing you a song to
T8    186:11        "Well, not the next course," the Knight said in slow thoughtful tone: "no, certainly not the
T8    182:13  "We'd better take it with us," the Knight said. "It'll come in handy if we find any plum-cake.
T8    187: 1    "No, you don't understand," the Knight said, looking a little vexed. "That's what the name is
T8    187:10          "I was coming to that," the Knight said. "The song really is 'A-sitting On A Gate': and
T8    184:19      "I'll get one," the Knight said thoughtfully to himself. "One or two--several."
T8    183:11        "I've had plenty of practice," the Knight said very gravely: "plenty of practice!"
T8    185: 9    "I  had  to  kick  him, of course," the Knight said, very seriously. "And then he took the helmet off
T8    190:12                              As the Knight sang the last words of the ballad, he gathered up the
T8    186:21  asked,  hoping  to cheer him up, for the poor Knight seemed quite low-spirited about it.
T8    185:13                                  The Knight shook his head. "It was all kinds of fastness with me,
T8    183:17          "The great art of riding," the Knight suddenly began in a loud voice, waving his right arm as
T1    110: 8  have  won,  if  it hadn't been for that nasty Knight, that came wriggling down among my pieces. Kitty dear,
T8    187:20  the  mild  blue  eyes and kindly smile of the Knight--the setting sun gleaming through his hair, and shining
T8    182:32  "First  you take an upright stick," said the Knight. "Then you make your hair creep up it, like a
T8    190:30  walking  leisurely  along  the  road, and the Knight tumbling off, first on one side and then on the other.
T8    182:16  held  the bag open very carefully, because the Knight was so very awkward in putting in the dish: the first
T8    184:21  was  a  short  silence after this, and then the Knight went on again. "I'm a great hand at inventing things.
T8    182:38  every  now  and  then stopping to help the poor Knight, who certainly was not a good rider.
T8    183:15  on  a  little  way in silence after this, the Knight with his eyes shut, muttering to himself, and Alice
T8    184:29  tell you how I came to think of it," said the Knight. "You see, I said to myself 'The only difficulty is
```
KNIGHTS (2)
```
T8    179:25  had  done: then he got on again, and the two Knights sat and looked at each other for some time without
T2    128:19  Square  is  all  forest--however,  one of the Knights will show you the way--and in the Eighth Square we
```
KNIT (1)
```
T5    155:12                        "How can she knit with so many?" the puzzled child thought to herself. "She
```
KNITTING (6)
```
T5    154: 2  at  last,  looking  up  for a moment from her knitting.
T5    157:10  only laughed scornfully, and went on with her knitting.
```

KNITTING (cont.)
T5   157: 3   was soon up again: the Sheep went on with her knitting all the while, just as if nothing had happened. "That
T5   153:39   was an old Sheep, sitting in an arm-chair, knitting, and every now and then leaving off to look at her
T5   156:20   Alice forgot all about the Sheep and the knitting, as she bent over the side of the boat, with just the
T5   156: 9   the Sheep said, without looking up from her knitting: "I didn't put 'em there, and I'm not going to take
KNITTING-NEEDLES (1)
T5   155:14   row?" the Sheep asked, handing her a pair of knitting-needles as she spoke.
KNOCK (1)
A6   46:20   For instance, if you were inside, you might knock, and I could let you out, you know." He was looking up
KNOCK-DOWN (2)
T6   163:28   "But 'glory' doesn't mean 'a nice knock-down argument,'" Alice objected.
T6   163:26   till I tell you. I meant 'there's a nice knock-down argument for you!'"
KNOCKED (4)
A6   46: 9   Alice went timidly up to the door, and knocked.
T6   168:11   locked, / I pulled and pushed and kicked and knocked.
T9   198:12   Alice knocked and rang in vain for a long time; but at last a very
T1   113:20   rushed past the King, so violently that she knocked him over among the cinders. "My precious Lily! My
KNOCKING (5)
A4   27:23   RABBIT" engraved upon it. She went in without knocking, and hurried upstairs, in great fear lest she should
T9   199:17   "Nothing!" Alice said impatiently. "I've been knocking at it!"
T9   196:15   rolling round the room in great lumps--and knocking over the tables and things--till I was so frightened,
A6   46:10   "There's no sort of use in knocking," said the Footman, "and that for two reasons. First,
A6   46:18   "There might be some sense in your knocking," the Footman went on, without attending to her, "if
KNOCKS (1)
T8   180: 4   to be, that if one Knight hits the other, he knocks him off his horse; and, if he misses, he tumbles off
KNOLLS (1)
T8   189: 1   for crabs: / I sometimes search for grassy knolls / For wheels of Hansom-cabs. / And that's the way' (he
KNOT (2)
A6   49:23   it (which was to twist it up into a sort of knot, and then keep tight hold of its right ear and left foot,
A3   26: 6   "A knot!" said Alice, always ready to make herself useful, and
KNOTS (1)
T1   107:18   there it was, spread over the hearth-rug, all knots and tangles, with the kitten running after its own tail
KNOW (219)
A3   26:11   Alice. "But you're so easily offended, you know!"
A5   41: 9   "only one doesn't like changing so often, you know."
A5   43:18   eat eggs quite as much as serpents do, you know."
A6   46:34   the Footman. "That's the first question, you know."
A7   55:22   I mean what I say--that's the same thing, you know."
A7   56:10   first remark, "It was the best butter, you know."
A7   57: 6   "but then--I shouldn't be hungry for it, you know."
A7   59:32   sisters--they were learning to draw, you know--"
A9   70:15   then they wouldn't be so stingy about it, you know--"
A10 81:22   a deep voice, "are done with whiting. Now you know."
A10 83: 6   How could he turn them out with his nose, you know?"
A12 94:10   was written to nobody, which isn't usual, you know."
A12 96: 8   that must be what he did with the tarts, you know--"
T2   123:21   one of the kind that has nine spikes, you know."
T3   131:15   something about 'horse' and 'hoarse,' you know."
T3   131:17   "She must be labeled 'Lass, with care,' you know--"
T3   131:30   something about 'you would if you could,' you know."
T3   135: 4   and of course you wouldn't have to go, you know."
T4   145:13   in his dream, what are you, I should like to know?"
T4   147:11   "only she must help us to dress up, you know."
T5   150: 9   other day: to-day isn't any other day, you know."
T5   158:12   herself, "They mightn't be at all nice, you know."
T6   164:11   side to side, "for to get their wages, you know."
T6   166: 5   meaning that they'd lost their way, you know."
T7   175:13   have run him through with your horn, you know."
T7   176:12   the Unicorn): "fair play with the cake, you know!"
T8   184: 5   to keep your balance properly. Like this, you know--"
T8   185:11   me out. I was as fast as--as lightning, you know."
T8   187: 7   Means': but that's only what it's called, you know!"
T9   192: 5   like that! Queens have to be dignified, you know!"
T9   195:28   I mean one of the last set of Tuesdays, you know."
T9   195:34   many as five nights together--for warmth, you know."
T9   198: 8   There ought to be one marked 'Queen,' you know--"
T9   199:21   to his tree, "and it'll let you alone, you know."
T8W 18: 2   comb hair with--your wig's so very rough, you know."
T6   162:26   he said at last, "when a person doesn't know a cravat from a belt!"
A11 90:21   "If that's all you know about it, you may stand down," continued the King.
A12 93:16   "What do you know about this business?" the King said to Alice.
A7   59: 3   "They couldn't have done that, you know," Alice gently remarked. "They'd have been ill."
T9   194: 3   "Nine from eight I ca'n't, you know," Alice replied very readily: "but--"
T8   181: 1   "I don't know," Alice said doubtfully. "I don't want to be anybody's
A2   16: 6   at all; and I'm sure I ca'n't be Mabel, for I know all sorts of things, and she, oh, she knows such a very
A2   16: 8   dear, how puzzling it all is! I'll try if I know all the things I used to know. Let me see: four times
T3   129: 8   be bees--nobody ever saw bees a mile off, you know--" and for some time she stood silent, watching one of
A2   20: 8   half of them--and it belongs to a farmer, you know, and he says it's so useful, it's worth a hundred pounds!
A5   36: 4   turn into a chrysalis--you will some day, you know--and then after that into a butterfly, I should think
T2   123:16   added kindly. "You're beginning to fade, you know--and then one ca'n't help one's petals getting a little

KNOW (cont.)

T8W	17: 6	Wasp: "wait till you have it, and then you'll know. And when you catches it, just try tying a yellow
T9	197: 1	to obey the first direction: "and I don't know any soothing lullabies."
A12	95:31	the King, "that saves a world of trouble, you know, as we needn't try to find any. And yet I don't know," he
T6	165: 6	"Of course it is. It's called 'wabe' you know, because it goes a long way before it, and a long way
T9	197:17	all the History of England--it couldn't, you know, because there never was more than one Queen at a time.
T7	170:12	book. "I couldn't send all the horses, you know, because two of them are wanted in the game. And I
A3	21:10	would only say, "I'm older than you, and must know better." And this Alice would not allow, without knowing
A1	9:10	a bat, and that's very like a mouse, you know. But do cats eat bats, I wonder?" And here Alice began to
A3	23: 3	said Alice; not that she much wanted to know, but the Dodo had paused as if it thought that somebody
A9	74:12	fancy that: they never executes nobody, you know. Come on!"
A9	74:22	his fancy, that: he hasn't got no sorrow, you know. Come on!"
A9	72: 3	"Oh, I know!" exclaimed Alice, who had not attended to this last
T4	147:25	"You know," he added very gravely, "it's one of the most serious
A6	46:21	you might knock, and I could let you out, you know." He was looking up into the sky all the time he was
A12	95:32	we needn't try to find any. And yet I don't know," he went on, spreading out the verses on his knee, and
T3	131: 5	way to the ticket-office, even if she doesn't know her alphabet!"
T3	131: 1	which way she's going, even if she doesn't know her own name!"
T3	131: 4	eyes and said in a loud voice, "She ought to know her way to the ticket-office, even if she doesn't know
T4	140: 2	was a rather awkward pause, as Alice didn't know how to begin a conversation with people she had just been
T7	177:11	"You don't know how to manage Looking-glass cakes," the Unicorn remarked.
A11	87: 2	could even make out that one of them didn't know how to spell "stupid," and that he had to ask his
T7	175:28	curling up into a smile as she began: "Do you know, I always thought Unicorns were fabulous monsters, too? I
T2	122:11	to side, and trembling with excitement. "They know I ca'n't get at them!" it panted, bending its quivering
A3	26:22	"I wish I had our Dinah here, I know I do!" said Alice aloud, addressing nobody in particular.
T2	128:14	"I--I don't know I had to make one--just then," Alice faltered out.
A7	56:40	not," Alice cautiously replied; "but I know I have to beat time when I learn music."
T3	130:16	dream about a thousand pounds to-night, I know I shall!" thought Alice.
T2	120:15	with her. "I'm not going in again yet. I know I should have to get through the Looking-glass again--
T1	110:21	that you're the Red Queen, Kitty! Do you know, I think if you sat up and folded your arms, you'd look
T1	108:21	"Do you know, I was so angry, Kitty," Alice went on, as soon as they
T9	193:17	"I didn't know I was to have a party at all," said Alice; "but, if there
T5	149:29	"It ca'n't go straight, you know, if you pin it all on one side," Alice said as she gently
A6	51:25	"How do you know I'm mad?" said Alice.
T1	108:39	not been punished for any of them yet. You know I'm saving up all your punishments for Wednesday week--
A5	36: 8	may be different," said Alice: "all I know is, it would feel very queer to me."
A4	31:21	I'm a deal too flustered to tell you--all I know is, something comes at me like a Jack-in-the-box, and up
T3	136: 6	after a great deal of puzzling, was "L, I know it begins with L!"
T12	207: 5	all through the Looking-glass world. Did you know it, dear?"
T2	122:31	good reason, and Alice was quite pleased to know it. "I never thought of that before!" she said.
T1	111: 4	our passage as far as you can see, only you know it may be quite different on beyond. Oh, Kitty, how nice
T8	181:23	"I didn't know it," the Knight said, a shade of vexation passing over
A12	95: 2	He sent them word I had not gone / (We know it to be true): / If she should push the matter on, /
A12	95:39	on muttering over the verses to himself: "'We know it to be true'--that's the jury, of course--'If she
A7	55: 4	"I didn't know it was your table," said Alice: "it's laid for a great
T8	182:35	it hangs down--things never fall upwards, you know. It's a plan of my own invention. You may try it if you
T6	162:27	"I know it's very ignorant of me," Alice said, in so humble a
T9	201:28	"Do you know, I've had such a quantity of poetry repeated to me to-day
T9	195: 7	right again now," said the Red Queen. "Do you know Languages? What's the French for fiddle-de-dee?"
T5	156:36	picked them? Even real scented rushes, you know, last only a very little while--and these, being
A2	16: 8	I'll try if I know all the things I used to know. Let me see: four times five is twelve, and four times
T5	153: 2	"nobody can do two things at once, you know. Let's consider your age to begin with--how old are you
A6	48: 6	"You don't know much," said the Duchess; "and that's a fact."
T3	137:13	fellow-traveler so suddenly. "However, I know my name now," she said: "that's some comfort. Alice--
T8W	18: 4	it," the Wasp said. "When I was young, you know, my ringlets used to wave--"
T8W	19: 7	extremely plain: / But what was I to do, you know? / My ringlets would not grow again.
A4	31:19	That's Bill," thought Alice), "Well, I hardly know--No more, thank ye; I'm better now--but I'm a deal too
T2	123: 1	the leaves, and snore away there, till you know no more what's going on in the world, than if you were a
T8W	14:18	sulkily. "Nobody's hindering you, that I know of."
A6	48: 4	"I don't know of any that do," Alice said very politely, feeling quite
T12	208:11	You were his wife, my dear, so you ought to know--Oh, Kitty, do help to settle it! I'm sure your paw can
T2	126: 2	the world--if this is the world at all, you know. Oh, what fun it is! How I wish I was one of them! I
A7	58:21	"I'm afraid I don't know one," said Alice, rather alarmed at the proposal.
A1	8:44	ask them what the name of the country is, you know. Please, Ma'am, is this New Zealand? Or Australia?" (and
A7	57:11	last March--just before he went mad, you know--" (pointing his teaspoon at the March Hare,) "--it was
T3	135:42	to get under the--under the--under this, you know!" putting her hand on the trunk of the tree. "What does
A3	24:14	"You promised to tell me your history, you know," said Alice, "and why it is you hate--C and D," she
T9	193:27	"I don't know," said Alice. "I lost count."
A8	64: 3	"How should I know?" said Alice, surprised at her own courage. "It's no
A1	12: 8	nervous about this; "for it might end, you know," said Alice to herself, "in my going out altogether,
T6	166:14	"As to poetry, you know," said Humpty Dumpty, stretching out one of his great
A5	41:10	"I don't know," said the Caterpillar.
A3	23:30	"But she must have a prize herself, you know," said the Mouse.
T9	196:12	you ca'n't think!" ("She never could, you know," said the Red Queen.) "And part of the roof came off,
T2	121: 7	"It isn't manners for us to begin, you know," said the Rose, "and I really was wondering when you'd
T4	146:17	little white thing. "Not a rattle-snake, you know," she added hastily, thinking that he was frightened:
T6	159:20	"And some eggs are very pretty, you know," she added, hoping to turn her remark into a sort of
A12	95:17	Don't let him know she liked them best, / For this must ever be / A secret,
T1	116: 5	"--for it's all in some language I don't know," she said to herself.
T1	108:35	What, you were thirsty, were you? How do you know she wasn't thirsty too? Now for number three: you unwound

KNOW (cont.)

A3	22: 2	Are you all ready? This is the driest thing I know. Silence all round, if you please! 'William the Conqueror
A5	35: 6	Alice replied, rather shyly, "I--I hardly know, Sir, just at present--at least I know who I <u>was</u> when I
A8	63: 9	we should all have our heads cut off, you know. So you see, Miss, we're doing our best, afore she comes,
T2	128: 8	pawn goes two squares in its first move, you know. So you'll go <u>very</u> quickly through the Third Square--by
A4	28: 4	she uncorked it and put it to her lips. "I know something interesting is sure to happen," she said to
T9	194:41	"I know <u>that</u>!" Alice cried eagerly. "You take some flour--"
T1	110:40	our books, only the words go the wrong way: I know <u>that</u>, because I've held up one of our books to the glass,
A6	48: 2	always grinned; in fact, I didn't know that cats <u>could</u> grin."
A6	48: 1	"I didn't know that Cheshire-Cats always grinned; in fact, I didn't know
T2	122: 7	"Didn't you know <u>that</u>?" cried another Daisy. And here they all began
A5	43:23	of adding "You're looking for eggs, I know <u>that</u> well enough; and what does it matter to me whether
T2	125:11	her at last: "a hill <u>ca'n't</u> be a valley, you know. That would be nonsense--"
A6	51:28	at all: however, she went on: "And how do you know that you're mad?"
T12	207:30	you were so untidy in my dream--Dinah! Do you know that you're scrubbing a White Queen? Really, it's most
T8	181: 5	end of the wood--and then I must go back, you know. That's the end of my move."
T6	160:14	cried Humpty Dumpty. "Did you think I didn't know the answer to <u>that</u>? Ask another."
T3	134:25	"And yet I don't know," the Gnat went on in a careless tone: "only think how
A7	57:18	"It goes on, you know," the Hatter continued, "in this way:--
T8	181:22	can get <u>out</u>," Alice gently remarked. "Do you know the lid's open?"
T7	177: 3	"I'm sure I don't know," the Lion growled out as he lay down again. "There was
A3	22:31	"Speak English!" said the Eaglet. "I don't know the meaning of half those long words, and, what's more, I
A10	78:26	"Then, you know," the Mock Turtle went on, "you throw the--"
T8	186:40	"Or else it doesn't, you know. The name of the song is called '<u>Haddocks' Eyes</u>.'"
T5	151:16	"And you were all the better for it, I know!" the Queen said triumphantly.
T8	179:28	"She's <u>my</u> prisoner, you know!" the Red Knight said at last.
T9	192:35	"So you did, you know," the Red Queen said to Alice. "Always speak the truth--
A7	57:16	You know the song, perhaps?"-
A2	19:13	in trying." So she began: "O Mouse, do you know the way out of this pool? I am very tired of swimming
T9	202:31	"We must support you, you know," the White Queen whispered, as Alice got up to do it,
T9	197: 8	"And now you know the words," she added, as she put her head down on
T9	199:19	do that--" the Frog muttered. "Wexes it, you know." Then he went up and gave the door a kick with one of
T6	163:22	"And only <u>one</u> for birthday presents, you know. There's glory for you!"
T4	142: 5	and neat--/ And <u>this</u> was odd, because, <u>you</u> know, / They hadn't <u>any</u> feet.
T4	145:28	"I know they're talking nonsense," Alice thought to herself: "and
A4	29: 2	and yet--and yet--it's rather curious, you know, this sort of life! I do wonder what <u>can</u> have happened to
T9	192:28	call yourself so? You ca'n't be a Queen, you know, till you've passed the proper examination. And the
T7	170:37	called Hatta. I must have <u>two</u>, you know--to come and go. One to come, and one to go."
T4	148:14	"There's only one sword, you know," Tweedledum said to his brother: "but <u>you</u> can have the
T1	110:36	a fire in the winter: you never <u>can</u> tell, you know, unless our fire smokes, and then smoke comes up in that
A10	80: 8	replied. / "<u>There</u> is <u>another</u> shore, <u>you</u> know, <u>upon</u> the <u>other</u> side. / The <u>further</u> off <u>from</u> <u>England</u> the
T4	145:19	only one of the things in his dream. You know very well you're not real."
T3	131:44	a little anxiously. What she really wanted to know, was, whether it could sting or not, but she thought this
T4	138:11	wax-works," he said, "you ought to pay, you know. Wax-works weren't made to be looked at for nothing.
A9	73:23	lying fast asleep in the sun. (If you don't know what a Gryphon is, look at the picture.) "Up, lazy thing!
A9	73:12	"No," said Alice. "I don't even know what a Mock Turtle is."
T9	196: 9	"I know what he came for," said Alice: "he wanted to punish the
A3	22:17	Mouse replied rather crossly: "of course you know what 'it' means."
A3	22:18	"I know what 'it' means well enough, when <u>I</u> find a thing," said
A6	45: 9	over their heads. She felt very curious to know what it was all about, and crept a little way out of the
T1	118:28	fill my head with ideas--only I don't exactly know what they are! However, <u>somebody</u> killed <u>something</u>: that's
A12	94:31	the sort!" said Alice. "Why, you don't even know what they're about!"
A10	80:21	if you've seen them so often, of course you know what they're like?"
A9	76:27	Never heard of uglifying!" it exclaimed. "You know what to beautify is, I suppose?"
T9	193:11	she wants to deny <u>something</u>--only she doesn't know what to deny!"
T2	127:39	Alice did not know what to say to this, but luckily the Queen did not wait
T6	159:24	Alice didn't know what to say to this: it wasn't at all like conversation,
A7	59:18	Alice did not quite know what to say to this: so she helped herself to some tea
A9	76:31	then," the Gryphon went on, "if you don't know what to uglify is, you <u>are</u> a simpleton."
T1	108:11	"Do you know what to-morrow is, Kitty?" Alice began. "You'd have
T6	161: 9	meet behind," she thought: "And then I don't know <u>what</u> would happen to his head! I'm afraid it would come
T6	163:24	"I don't know what you mean by 'glory,'" Alice said.
T2	124:11	"I don't know what you mean by <u>your</u> way," said the Queen: "all the ways
A7	56:37	"I don't know what you mean," said Alice.
T9	199:14	"I don't know what you mean," she said.
T2	127:25	"I know what <u>you'd</u> like!" the Queen said good-naturedly, taking a
T6	162:42	"You don't know what you're talking about!" cried Humpty Dumpty. "How
T4	139: 5	"I know what you're thinking about," said Tweedledum; "but it
T5	149:26	"I don't know what's the matter with it!" the Queen said, in a
T4	139:36	'<u>Here</u> we go <u>round</u> the <u>mulberry</u> bush.' I don't know when I began it, but somehow I felt as if I'd been
T3	135:33	That's just like the advertisements, you know, when people lose dogs--'<u>answers</u> to the <u>name</u> of "Dash":
A3	23:12	when they liked, so that it was not easy to know when the race was over. However, when they had been
A10	80:20	"I don't know where Dinn may be," said the Mock Turtle; "but, if you've
A6	51: 5	began, rather timidly, as she did not at all know whether it would like the name: however, it only grinned
T1	110:35	wish I could see <u>that</u> bit! I want so much to know whether they've a fire in the winter: you never <u>can</u> tell,
T8	181:37	out--or the bees keep the mice out, I don't know which."
A10	79: 6	Gryphon. "We can do it without lobsters, you know. Which shall sing?"
T3	131: 1	(he was dressed in white paper), "ought to know which way she's going, even if she doesn't know her own
A5	35: 7	hardly know, Sir, just at present--at least I know who I <u>was</u> when I got up this morning, but I think I must
T8	189:22	<u>it</u> reminds <u>me</u> so / Of that <u>old</u> <u>man</u> I used to know--/ Whose <u>look</u> was <u>mild</u>, whose <u>speech</u> was <u>slow</u>, / Whose

KNOW (cont.)

T2	122:25	ground," said the Tiger-lily. "Then you'll know why."
A10	81:11	that, if you like," said the Gryphon. "Do you know why it's called a whiting?"
T9	201:32	poem was about fishes in some way. Do you know why they're so fond of fishes, all about here?"
T1	109:12	gently? And then it covers them up snug, you know, with a white quilt; and perhaps it says 'Go to sleep,
A2	20: 5	show you! A little bright-eyed terrier, you know, with oh, such long curly brown hair! And it'll fetch
T5	154: 3	"I don't quite know yet," Alice said very gently. "I should like to look all
T6	168:21	"I shouldn't know you again if we did meet," Humpty Dumpty replied in a
T3	131:41	"I know you are a friend," the little voice went on: "a dear
T1	112:14	and the very clock on the chimney-piece (you know you can only see the back of it in the Looking-glass) had
T1	108: 1	you better manners! You ought, Dinah, you know you ought!" she said, looking reproachfully at the old
A7	60:24	and the moon, and memory, and muchness--you know you say things are 'much of a muchness'--did you ever see
T9	194:33	"Of course you know your ABC?" said the Red Queen.
A9	74:26	lady," said the Gryphon, "she wants for to know your history, she do."
A11	88:43	talk nonsense," said Alice more boldly: "you know you're growing too."

KNOWING (4)

A3	21:11	And this Alice would not allow, without knowing how old it was, and as the Lory positively refused to
T8	191: 6	"But how can it have got there without my knowing it?" she said to herself, as she lifted it off, and
A4	32:33	Hardly knowing what she did, she picked up a little bit of stick, and
T9	201: 2	bow to Alice; and Alice returned the bow, not knowing whether to be frightened or amused.

KNOWLEDGE (3)

A1	8:33	a very good opportunity for showing off her knowledge, as there was no one to listen to her, still it was
A6	48:24	an opportunity of showing off a little of her knowledge. "Just think what work it would make with the day
A2	19:23	William the Conqueror." (For, with all her knowledge of history, Alice had no very clear notion how long

KNOWN (3)

T6	160:32	and down chimneys--or you couldn't have known it!"
A3	21: 8	talking familiarly with them, as if she had known them all her life. Indeed, she had quite a long argument
T9	200:12	be asked," she thought: "I should never have known who were the right people to invite!"

KNOWS (3)

T9	201:36	close to Alice's ear, "her White Majesty knows a lovely riddle--all in poetry--all about fishes. Shall
A6	48:39	/ He only does it to annoy, / Because he knows it teases."
A2	16: 6	I know all sorts of things, and she, oh, she knows such a very little! Besides, she's she, and I'm I, and--

KNUCKLES (1)

A6	45: 5	fish)--and rapped loudly at the door with his knuckles. It was opened by another footman in livery, with a

-L-

L (2)
  T3   136: 6   of puzzling, was "L, I know it begins with L!"
  T3   136: 6   say, after a great deal of puzzling, was "L, I know it begins with L!"
LABEL (2)
  A4   28: 3   stood near the looking-glass. There was no label this time with the words "DRINK ME," but nevertheless
  A1   10:17   tied round the neck of the bottle was a paper label, with the words "DRINK ME" beautifully printed on it in
LABELED (2)
  T3   131:17   voice in the distance said, "She must be labeled 'Lass, with care,' you know--"
  A1   8:18   from one of the shelves as she passed: it was labeled "ORANGE MARMALADE," but to her great disappointment it
LACIE (1)
  A7   58:33   a great hurry; "and their names were Elsie, Lacie, and Tillie; and they lived at the bottom of a well--"
LAD (1)
  A4   30:26   Bill's got the other--Bill! Fetch it here, lad!--Here, put 'em up at this corner--No, tie 'em together
LADDER (1)
  A4   30:25   she made out the words: "Where's the other ladder?--Why, I hadn't to bring but one. Bill's got the other
LADEN (1)
  TI   103:20   ere voice of dread, / With bitter tidings laden, / Shall summon to unwelcome bed / A melancholy maiden!
LADLE (1)
  T9   204:10   were lying down in the dishes, and the soup ladle was walking up the table towards Alice's chair, and
LADY (6)
  T9   197: 4   "Hush-a-by lady, in Alice's lap! / Till the feast's ready, we've time for
  T7   171:11   "This young lady loves you with an H," the King said, introducing Alice in
  A9   74:25   "This here young lady," said the Gryphon, "she wants for to know your history,
  T7   172:18   "Quite right," said the King: "this young lady saw him too. So of course Nobody walks slower than you."
  A7   58:19   "I'm getting tired of this. I vote the young lady tells us a story."
  A9   74: 1   thing!" said the Queen, "and take this young lady to see the Mock Turtle, and to hear his history. I must
LADY'S (1)
  T5   149:36   of the pins. "But really you should have a lady's maid!"
LAID (5)
  A7   55: 4   know it was your table," said Alice: "it's laid for a great many more than three."
  T4   146:24   Alice laid her hand upon his arm and said, in a soothing tone, "You
  T9   196:34   The White Queen gave a deep sigh, and laid her head on Alice's shoulder. "I am so sleepy!" she
  T8   185:25   as she dragged him out by the feet, and laid him in a heap on the bank.
  A8   64:10   The King laid his hand upon her arm, and timidly said "Consider, my
LAKE (2)
  T8W   15: 5   back," Alice went on reading, "they found a lake of treacle. The banks of the lake were blue and white,
  T8W   15: 6   found a lake of treacle. The banks of the lake were blue and white, and looked like china. While tasting
LAMPS (1)
  A1   9:29   long, low hall, which was lit up by a row of lamps hanging from the roof.
LAND (5) [See also WONDERLAND]
  AI   4: 8   wreath of flowers / Pluck'd in a far-off land.
  A10   78:35   "Back to land again, and--that's all the first figure," said the Mock
  T5   155:16   "Yes, a little--but not on land--and not with needles--" Alice was beginning to say, when
  AI   3:21   pursue / The dream-child moving through a land / Of wonders wild and new, / In friendly chat with bird
  T3   130: 5   wasn't room for one where she came from. The land there is worth a thousand pounds an inch!"
LANGUAGE (4)
  T9   195:12   this time. "If you'll tell me what language 'fiddle-de-dee' is, I'll tell you the French for it!"
  T1   116: 5   that she could read, "--for it's all in some language I don't know," she said to herself.
  T3   130:14   that I don't) "Better say nothing at all. Language is worth a thousand pounds a word!"
  T8W   15:12   "There's no such word in the language!" said the Wasp.
LANGUAGES (1)
  T9   195: 8   again now," said the Red Queen. "Do you know Languages? What's the French for fiddle-de-dee?"
LANGUID (1)
  A5   35: 3   out of its mouth, and addressed her in a languid, sleepy voice.
LAP (6)
  A2   17: 4   little--'," and she crossed her hands on her lap as if she were saying lessons, and began to repeat it, but
  T9   197:14   shoulder, and lay like a heavy lump in her lap. "I don't think it ever happened before, that any one had
  A12   98: 1   lying on the bank, with her head in the lap of her sister, who was gently brushing away some dead
  T9   197:23   two great heads suddenly vanished from her lap, she hardly missed them.
  T9   197: 4   "Hush-a-by lady, in Alice's lap! / Till the feast's ready, we've time for a nap. / When
  T8   191: 7   as she lifted it off, and set it on her lap to make out what it could possibly be.
LAPPING (1)
  T9   202:27   the dish of roast mutton, and began eagerly lapping up the gravy, "just like pigs in a trough!" thought
LARGE (61)
  T8   188:11   dye one's whiskers green, / And always use so large a fan / That they could not be seen. / So, having no
  A6   53:13   and the roof was thatched with fur. It was so large a house, that she did not like to go nearer till she had
  A4   28: 7   bottle does. I do hope it'll make me grow large again, for really I'm quite tired of being such a tiny
  T10   205: 4   her face grew very small, and her eyes got large and green: and still, as Alice went on shaking her, she
  T8W   14:22   and have found five new lumps of white sugar, large and in fine condition. In coming back--"
  T6   167:13   I took a kettle large and new, / Fit for the deed I had to do.
  T4   146:14   voice choking with passion, and his eyes grew large and yellow all in a moment, as he pointed with a
  A7   54:10   said Alice indignantly, and she sat down in a large arm-chair at one end of the table.
  A6   45:12   from under his arm a great letter, nearly as large as himself, and this he handed over to the other, saying

LARGE (cont.)

T7	175:22	attitude. "We only found it to-day. It's as	large as life, and twice as natural!"
A4	29:23	that she was now about a thousand times as	large as the Rabbit, and had no reason to be afraid of it.
A3	24:10	this caused some noise and confusion, as the	large birds complained that they could not taste theirs, and
A4	34: 8	and her eyes immediately met those of a	large blue caterpillar, that was sitting on the top, with its
T5	154:17	had spent a minute or so in vainly pursuing a	large bright thing that looked sometimes like a doll and
T7	175:39	Haigha took a	large cake out of the bag, and gave it to Alice to hold, while
A11	90:13	explain to you how it was done. They had a	large canvas bag, which tied up at the mouth with strings:
A6	47:10	that did not sneeze, were the cook, and a	large cat, which was lying on the hearth and grinning from ear
A6	47: 3	cook was leaning over the fire, stirring a	large cauldron which seemed to be full of soup.
T2	125:25	"I declare it's marked out just like a	large chess-board!" Alice said at last. "There ought to be
A8	68:29	she was surprised to find quite a	large crowd collected round it: there was a dispute going on
A11	86: 7	very middle of the court was a table, with a	large dish of tarts upon it: they looked so good, that it made
T9	199: 8	The Frog looked at the door with his	large dull eyes for a minute: then he went nearer and rubbed
A9	74:24	to the Mock Turtle, who looked at them with	large eyes full of tears, but said nothing.
A6	45: 7	footman in livery, with a round face, and	large eyes like a frog; and both footmen, Alice noticed, had
T4	147: 6	lay, opening and shutting his mouth and his	large eyes--"looking more like a fish than anything else,"
A2	15:28	a pair of white kid-gloves in one hand and a	large fan in the other: he came trotting along in a great
T2	120:27	but start again. This time she came upon a	large flowerbed, with a border of daisies, and a willow-tree
A8	65:13	said Alice, and she put them into a	large flower-pot that stood near. The three soldiers wandered
T3	136: 8	wandering by: it looked at Alice with its	large gentle eyes, but didn't seem at all frightened. "Here
T3	132:20	It certainly was a very	large Gnat: "about the size of a chicken," Alice thought.
T9	200: 9	along the table, as she walked up the	large hall, and noticed that there were about fifty guests, of
A12	95:24	explain it," said Alice, (she had grown so	large in the last few minutes that she wasn't a bit afraid of
T3	132:30	I'm rather afraid of them--at least the	large kinds. But I can tell you the names of some of them."
A6	46:45	The door led right into a	large kitchen, which was full of smoke from one end to the
A1	10:18	words "DRINK ME" beautifully printed on it in	large letters.
T9	198: 2	over which were the words "QUEEN ALICE" in	large letters, and on each side of the arch there was a
T8	181:11	both hands, and turning his gentle face and	large mild eyes to Alice. She thought she had never seen such
A4	34: 3	or drink under the circumstances. There was a	large mushroom growing near her, about the same height as
A9	71:18	to everything that Alice said: "there's a	large mustard-mine near here. And the moral of that is--'The
A7	54: 7	The table was a	large one, but the three were all crowded together at one
A1	9:37	hall; but, alas! either the locks were too	large, or the key was too small, but at any rate it would not
T7	174: 5	made a desperate effort, and swallowed a	large piece of bread-and-butter. "They're getting on very well
T5	150: 3	"For instance, now," she went on, sticking a	large piece of plaster on her finger as she spoke, "there's
A11	88:32	at the Queen, and in his confusion he bit a	large piece out of his teacup instead of the bread-and-butter
A5	42:25	a sharp hiss made her draw back in a hurry: a	large pigeon had flown into her face, and was beating her
A6	46:27	moment the door of the house opened, and a	large plate came skimming out, straight at the Footman's head:
T9	201: 8	And the waiters carried it off, and brought a	large plum-pudding in its place.
A2	15:23	shedding gallons of tears, until there was a	large pool round her, about four inches deep, and reaching
A1	8: 4	it, and was just in time to see it pop down a	large rabbit-hole under the hedge.
A3	21:15	dry enough!" They all sat down at once, in a	large ring, with the Mouse in the middle. Alice kept her eyes
A8	62: 1	A	large rose-tree stood near the entrance of the garden: the
A4	32:27	enormous puppy was looking down at her with	large round eyes, and feebly stretching out one paw, trying to
A6	48:18	goes his precious nose!", as an unusually	large saucepan flew close by it, and very nearly carried it
A12	92: 2	forgetting in the flurry of the moment how	large she had grown in the last few minutes, and she jumped up
T4	144:24	that sounded to her like the puffing of a	large steam-engine in the wood near them, though she feared it
T3	135:13	But the Gnat only sighed deeply while two	large tears came rolling down its cheeks.
T5	152:34	and, at the thought of her loneliness, two	large tears came rolling down her cheeks.
T9	201:18	a moment, like a conjuring-trick. It was so	large that she couldn't help feeling a little shy with it, as
T4	145:25	get at me here," she thought: "it's far too	large to squeeze itself in among the trees. But I wish it
T4	145:24	little way into the wood, and stopped under a	large tree. "It can never get at me here," she thought: "it's
T4	146: 4	Tweedledum spread a	large umbrella over himself and his brother, and looked up

LARGER (11)

A11	88:36	out what it was: she was beginning to grow	larger again, and she thought at first she would get up and
T6	159: 1	However, the egg only got	larger and larger, and more and more human: when she had come
T1	115: 6	but his eyes and his mouth went on getting	larger and larger, and rounder and rounder, till her hand
T6	159: 1	However, the egg only got larger and	larger, and more and more human: when she had come within a
T1	115: 7	eyes and his mouth went on getting larger and	larger, and rounder and rounder, till her hand shook so with
A4	28:28	poor Alice, "when one wasn't always growing	larger and smaller, and being ordered about by mice and
A1	12:34	eat it," said Alice, "and if it makes me grow	larger, I can reach the key; and if it makes me grow smaller,
A4	32: 9	my size; and, as it ca'n't possibly make me	larger, it must make me smaller, I suppose."
A5	41:14	"Well, I should like to be a little	larger, Sir, if you wouldn't mind," said Alice: "three inches
A4	28:24	had now had its full effect, and she grew no	larger: still it was very uncomfortable, and, as there seemed
A1	10: 2	that it led into a small passage, not much	larger than a rat-hole: she knelt down and looked along the

LARGEST (2)

T4	144: 4	sobs and tears he sorted out / Those of the	largest size, / Holding his pocket-handkerchief / Before his
A2	14: 3	good English). "Now I'm opening out like the	largest telescope that ever was! Good-bye, feet!" (for when

LARK (1)

A10	82:26	/ When the sands are all dry, he is gay as a	lark, / And will talk in contemptuous tones of the Shark: /

LARKSPUR (1)

T2	123:26	"She's coming!" cried the Larkspur. "I hear her footstep, thump, thump, along the	

LASS (1)

T3	131:17	in the distance said, "She must be labeled 'Lass, with care,' you know--"	

LAST (84)

T2	126:27	nearly there?" Alice managed to pant out at	last.
T2	128:27	to say "Good-bye," and then hurried on to the	last.
T4	140: 6	"I hope you're not much tired?" she said at	last.
T5	151:22	"better," till it got quite to a squeak at	last.
T6	162:41	"I like birthday presents best," she said at	last.

LAST (cont.)

T7	175:18		"What--is--this?" he said at last.
T8	179:28	prisoner, you know!" the Red Knight said at last.	
T8	181: 8	she managed to shake him out of it at last.	
T1	116:13	She puzzled over this for some time, but at	last a bright thought struck her. "Why, it's a Looking-glass
T2	125:11	Alice, surprised into contradicting her at	last: "a hill ca'n't be a valley, you know. That would be
T2	123:45	for the Queen (whom she spied out at	last, a long way off), she thought she would try the plan,
T9	198:12	and rang in vain for a long time; but at	last a very old Frog, who was sitting under a tree, got up and
A10	80:14	Alice, feeling very glad that it was over at	last: "and I do so like that curious song about the whiting!"
A5	42: 2	room to open her mouth; but she did it at	last, and managed to swallow a morsel of the left-hand bit. *
T4	142: 9	four; / And thick and fast they came at	last, / And more, and more, and more--/ All hopping through
A3	24:12	patted on the back. However, it was over at	last, and they sat down again in a ring, and begged the Mouse
T8	190:35	turned to run down the hill: "and now for the	last brook, and to be a Queen! How grand it sounds!" A very
T7	170:22	hand. "I see somebody now!" she exclaimed at	last. "But he's coming very slowly--and what curious attitudes
T2	120: 5	sharp corners), "but I suppose it will at	last. But how curiously it twists! It's more like a corkscrew
A4	31:16		Last came a little feeble, squeaking voice ("That's Bill,"
A4	30:22	some time without hearing anything more: at	last came a rumbling of little cart-wheels, and the sound of a
A11	89: 6	"Bring me the list of the singers in the	last concert!" on which the wretched Hatter trembled so, that
A12	92: 2	of the moment how large she had grown in the	last few minutes, and she jumped up in such a hurry that she
A12	95:24	said Alice, (she had grown so large in the	last few minutes that she wasn't a bit afraid of interrupting
T1	115:36	but Alice was too strong for him, and at	last he panted out "My dear! I really must get a thinner
T3	130:20	and then through an opera-glass. At	last he said "You're traveling the wrong way," and shut up the
T5	154:16	"Things flow about so here!" she said at	last in a plaintive tone, after she had spent a minute or so
T7	169: 2	threes, then ten or twenty together, and at	last in such crowds that they seemed to fill the whole forest.
A7	61: 5	passage: and then--she found herself at	last in the beautiful garden, among the bright flower-beds and
A4	33: 1	and barking hoarsely all the while, till at	last it sat down a good way off, panting, with its tongue
T3	134:22	by humming round and round her head: at	last it settled again and remarked "I suppose you don't want
A5	36:28	it puffed away without speaking; but at	last it unfolded its arms, took the hookah out of its mouth
T6	159:32		"That last line is much too long for the poetry," she added, almost
T5	154: 1	is it you want to buy?" the Sheep said at	last, looking up for a moment from her knitting.
A7	57:11	"Not I!" he replied. "We quarreled	last March--just before he went mad, you know--" (pointing his
A9	74:40	still little," the Mock Turtle went on at	last, more calmly, though still sobbing a little now and then,
T5	150: 6	next Wednesday: and of course the crime comes	last of all."
A8	63:26	crown on a crimson velvet cushion; and,	last of all this grand procession, came THE KING AND THE QUEEN
T5	156:36	them? Even real scented rushes, you know,	last only a very little while--and these, being dream-rushes,
T2	128:29	never knew, but exactly as she came to the	last peg, she was gone. Whether she vanished into the air, or
T1	107: 3	having its face washed by the old cat for the	last quarter of an hour (and bearing it pretty well,
T5	155:36	you say 'Feather' so often?" Alice asked at	last, rather vexed. "I'm not a bird!"
A7	60:10	to the Dormouse, not choosing to notice this	last remark.
T2	123: 4	Alice said, not choosing to notice the Rose's	last remark.
T6	161:15	on a little too fast: let's go back to the	last remark but one."
A9	72: 4	exclaimed Alice, who had not attended to this	last remark. "It's a vegetable. It doesn't look like one, but
A8	69: 4	everybody executed, all round. (It was this	last remark that had made the whole party look so grave and
T6	159:26	he never said anything to her; in fact, his	last remark was evidently addressed to a tree--so she stood
A4	28:19	head. Still she went on growing, and, as a	last resource, she put one arm out of the window, and one foot
A5	42: 7	"Come, my head's free at	last!" said Alice in a tone of delight, which changed into
T9	195:27	thunderstorm last Tuesday--I mean one of the	last set of Tuesdays, you know."
T9	197:21	minute, and sounded more like a tune: at	last she could even make out words, and she listened so
T8	190:37	the edge of the brook. "The Eighth Square at	last!" she cried as she bounded * * * * * * * * * * * * *
T8W	20:10	turned into a cough as well as she could. At	last she managed to say gravely, "I can bite anything I want
T1	114:19	slowly struggled up from bar to bar, till at	last she said "Why, you'll be hours and hours getting to the
A4	30:15	all!" "Do as I tell you, you coward!", and at	last she spread out her hand again, and made another snatch in
A5	41:36	this a very difficult question. However, at	last she stretched her arms round it as far as they would go,
T3	136:12	"What do you call yourself?" the Fawn said at	last. Such a soft sweet voice it had!
T3	137:25	"I do believe," said Alice at	last, "that they live in the same house! I wonder I never
A5	35: 2	at each other for some time in silence: at	last the Caterpillar took the hookah out of its mouth, and
A3	23:20	of him), while the rest waited in silence. At	last the Dodo said "Everybody has won, and all must have
A9	75: 6	who felt ready to sink into the earth. At	last the Gryphon said to the Mock Turtle "Drive on, old
A10	78: 5	shaking him and punching him in the back. At	last the Mock Turtle recovered his voice, and, with tears
A3	21:13		At last the Mouse, who seemed to be a person of some authority
T9	200:18		At last the Red Queen began. "You've missed the soup and fish,"
T8	182:19	fit, you see," he said, as they got it in at	last; "there are so many candlesticks in the bag." And he hung
T2	125:26	just like a large chess-board!" Alice said at	last. "There ought to be some men moving about somewhere--and
A5	43: 3	as I was thinking I should be free of them at	last, they must needs come wriggling down from the sky! Ugh,
T2	127: 6	Faster!" And they went so fast that at	last they seemed to skim through the air, hardly touching the
A7	60:33	hoping that they would call after her: the	last time she saw them, they were trying to put the Dormouse
T8	184:23	things. Now, I daresay you noticed the	last time you picked me up, that I was looking rather
T1	110:15	two of them, and Alice had been reduced at	last to say "Well, you can be one of them, then, and I'll be
T9	195:27	her hands, "we had such a thunderstorm	last Tuesday--I mean one of the last set of Tuesdays, you know
A3	21: 9	quite a long argument with the Lory, who at	last turned sulky, and would only say, "I'm older than you,
T5	149:20	Queen. "I've been a-dressing myself for the	last two hours."
T6	162:25	"It is a--most--provoking--thing," he said at	last, "when a person doesn't know a cravat from a belt!"
A9	74:32	"Once," said the Mock Turtle at	last, with a deep sigh, "I was a real Turtle."
T5	156:30	prettiest are always further!" she said at	last with a sigh at the obstinacy of the rushes in growing so
T3	135:23	side of it: it looked much darker than the	last wood, and Alice felt a little timid about going into it.
T5	153:30	Be-etter! Be-e-e-etter! Be-e-ehh!" The	last word ended in a long bleat, so like a sheep that Alice
A11	86:24	I suppose they are the jurors." She said this	last word two or three times over to herself, being rather
A6	47:16		She said the last word with such sudden violence that Alice quite jumped;
T8	190:12		As the Knight sang the last words of the ballad, he gathered up the reins, and turned
A6	49:28	be murder to leave it behind?" She said the	last words out loud, and the little thing grunted in reply (it

LASTED (2)
A12   96:24 was trickling down his face, as long as it lasted.)
A5   39: 8 strength, which it gave to my jaw / Has lasted the rest of my life."
LASTLY (1)
A12   99: 3   Lastly, she pictured to herself how this same little sister of
LATE (10)
A8   65:40 Queen will hear you! You see she came rather late, and the Queen said--"
T2   124:17 to herself, "the next time I'm a little late for dinner."
A1   9:26 a corner, "Oh my ears and whiskers, how late it's getting!" She was close behind it when she turned
A3   22: 5 English, who wanted leaders, and had been of late much accustomed to usurpation and conquest. Edwin and
T6   162: 5 have said 'Leave off at seven'--but it's too late now."
A12   98:11 but now run in to your tea: it's getting late." So Alice got up and ran off, thinking while she ran, as
T5   152:19 And she caught at the brooch; but it was too late: the pin had slipped, and the Queen had pricked her
T9   195:22   "It's too late to correct it," said the Red Queen: "when you've once
A4   28:15   Alas! It was too late to wish that! She went on growing, and growing, and very
A1   7:13 to itself "Oh dear! Oh dear! I shall be too late!" (when she thought it over afterwards it occurred to her
LATELY (1)
A1   10:10 so many out-of-the-way things had happened lately, that Alice had begun to think that very few things
LATER (2)
A1   11: 5 certain to disagree with you, sooner or later.
T3 129:26 pause; "and perhaps I may visit the elephants later on. Besides, I do so want to get into the Third Square!
LATEST (1)
T8W 14:20 out the paper on her knees, and began. "Latest News. The Exploring Party have made another tour in the
LATIN (1)
A2   19:17 she remembered having seen, in her brother's Latin Grammar, "A mouse--of a mouse--to a mouse--a mouse--O
LATITUDE (2)
A1   8:35 the right distance--but then I wonder what Latitude or Longitude I've got to?" (Alice had not the
A1   8:36 to?" (Alice had not the slightest idea what Latitude was, or Longitude either, but she thought they were
LAUGH (7)
T5 152:13 Alice said, feeling very much inclined to laugh.
A3   24: 6 all looked so grave that she did not dare to laugh; and, as she could not think of anything to say, she
T12 207:22 more stiffly, dear!" Alice cried with a merry laugh. "And curtsey while you're thinking what to--what to
T9 204: 2   At this moment she heard a hoarse laugh at her side, and turned to see what was the matter with
T8 185: 7 so solemn about it that Alice did not dare to laugh. "I'm afraid you must have hurt him," she said in a
T6 160: 8 it must," Humpty Dumpty said with a short laugh: "my name means the shape I am--and a good handsome
T1 115:11 that the King couldn't hear her. "You make me laugh so that I can hardly hold you! And don't keep your mouth
LAUGHED (7)
A12   96:28 King added in an angry tone, and everybody laughed. "Let the jury consider their verdict," the King said,
T4 147:28   Alice laughed loud: but she managed to turn it into a cough, for
T5 157:10 to take home with me!" But the Sheep only laughed scornfully, and went on with her knitting.
A6   46: 5   Alice laughed so much at this, that she had to run back into the
T5 153:11   Alice laughed. "There's no use trying," she said: "one ca'n't
T9 202: 1   The White Queen laughed with delight, and stroked Alice's cheek. Then she
T4 148: 4   Alice laughed. "You must hit the trees pretty often, I should think
LAUGHING (6)
A9   77: 7 the Mock Turtle said with a sigh. "He taught Laughing and Grief, they used to say."
A8   66:12 that she could not help bursting out laughing; and, when she had got its head down, and was going
T5 150: 1   Alice couldn't help laughing, as she said "I don't want you to hire me--and I
T5 152:40   Alice could not help laughing at this, even in the midst of her tears. "Can you
T6 160:24 solemn and grand that Alice could hardly help laughing. "If I did fall," he went on, "the King has promised
T4 145:24 "If I wasn't real," Alice said--half laughing through her tears, it all seemed so ridiculous--"I
LAUGHTER (5)
T8 184:18 horse," Alice said, with a little scream of laughter, in spite of all she could do to prevent it.
TI 103: 8 seen thy sunny face, / Nor heard thy silver laughter: / No thought of me shall find a place / In thy young
A8   65:38 Rabbit began. Alice gave a little scream of laughter. "Oh, hush!" the Rabbit whispered in a frightened
T1 115: 7 and rounder, till her hand shook so with laughter that she nearly let him drop upon the floor.
T8W 20: 9   Alice began with a little scream of laughter, which she turned into a cough as well as she could.
LAW (2)
A5   39: 5 In my youth," said his father, "I took to the law, / And argued each case with my wife; / And the muscular
A3   25:10 That he met in the house, 'Let us both go to law: I will prosecute you.--Come, I'll take no denial: We must
LAWN (1)
T8 191: 1 * across, and threw herself down to rest on a lawn as soft as moss, with little flowerbeds dotted about it
LAY (11)
T7 177: 3 I don't know," the Lion growled out as he lay down again. "There was too much dust to see anything. What
A5   42:11 a stalk out of a sea of green leaves that lay far below her.
T5 156:38   melted away almost like snow, as they lay in heaps at her feet--but Alice hardly noticed this, there
AI   4: 5 story take, / And, with a gentle hand, / Lay it where Childhood's dreams are twined / In Memory's
T9 197:14 the other, rolled down from her shoulder, and lay like a heavy lump in her lap. "I don't think it ever
A4   32: 6 were all turning into little cakes as they lay on the floor, and a bright idea came into her head. "If I
T4 147: 6 with only his head out: and there he lay, opening and shutting his mouth and his large eyes--
T1 115:15 King immediately fell flat on his back, and lay perfectly still; and Alice was a little alarmed at what
A12   92: 5 the heads of the crowd below, and there they lay sprawling about, reminding her very much of a globe of
A8   62:10 up and said "That's right, Five! Always lay the blame on others!"
LAZILY (2)
A2   19:36 Alice went on, half to herself, as she swam lazily about in the pool, "and she sits purring so nicely by
T7 176: 1 half shut. "What's this!" he said, blinking lazily at Alice, and speaking in a deep hollow tone that
LAZY (1)
A9   74: 1 what a Gryphon is, look at the picture.) "Up, lazy thing!" said the Queen, "and take this young lady to see
LEADERS (1)
A3   22: 4 soon submitted to by the English, who wanted leaders, and had been of late much accustomed to usurpation

LEADING (1)
  A7   60:39 she noticed that one of the trees had a door leading right into it. "That's very curious!" she thought.
LEADS (2)
  T4 140:11 doubtfully. "Would you tell me which road leads out of the wood?"
  T2 120: 2 the top of that hill: and here's a path that leads straight to it--at least, no, it doesn't do that--"
LEANED (1)
  T3 131:23 But the gentleman dressed in white paper leaned forwards and whispered in her ear, "Never mind what
LEANING (4)
  T8W 13: 6 more like a wasp) was sitting on the ground, leaning against a tree, all huddled up together, and shivering
  A12 98:13 her sister sat still just as she left her, leaning her head on her hand, watching the setting sun, and
  A6   47: 2 in the middle, nursing a baby: the cook was leaning over the fire, stirring a large cauldron which seemed
  T5 153:37 more of it: she was in a little dark shop, leaning with her elbows on the counter, and opposite to her
LEANT (3)
  A4   33: 8 dear little puppy it was!" said Alice, as she leant against a buttercup to rest herself, and fanned herself
  T8 187:25 as, with one hand shading her eyes, she leant against a tree, watching the strange pair, and listening
  T6 160:40 And he grinned almost from ear to ear, as he leant forwards (and as nearly as possible fell off the wall in
LEAP (1)
  A2   19:26 French lesson-book. The Mouse gave a sudden leap out of the water, and seemed to quiver all over with
LEARN (7)
  A9   76:35 Mock Turtle, and said "What else had you to learn?"
  A9   76:18   "I couldn't afford to learn it," said the Mock Turtle with a sigh. "I only took the
  A4   29:14 Alice!" she answered herself. "How can you learn lessons in here? Why, there's hardly room for you, and
  A7   56:41   "but I know I have to beat time when I learn music."
  A2   17:20 to play with, and oh, ever so many lessons to learn! No, I've made up my mind about it: if I'm Mabel, I'll
  A7   55: 9   "You should learn not to make personal remarks," Alice said with some
  A4   29:11 woman--but then--always to have lessons to learn! Oh, I shouldn't like that!"
LEARNED (1)
  A9   76:10   "Yes," said Alice: "we learned French and music."
LEARNING (3)
  T3 129: 3 to travel through. "It's something very like learning geography," thought Alice, as she stood on tiptoe in
  A7   60:14   "They were learning to draw," the Dormouse went on, yawning and rubbing
  A7   59:32 "And so these three little sisters--they were learning to draw, you know--"
LEARNT (2)
  A9   77: 3 said: "I'm too stiff. And the Gryphon never learnt it."
  A1   8:31 down, I think--" (for, you see, Alice had learnt several things of this sort in her lessons in the
LEAST (17)
  A7   55:21   "I do," Alice hastily replied; "at least--at least I mean what I say--that's the same thing, you
  A5   35: 7 "I--I hardly know, Sir, just at present--at least I know who I was when I got up this morning, but I think
  A7   55:21 "I do," Alice hastily replied; "at least--at least I mean what I say--that's the same thing, you know.
  T7 170:35 Hill," the King remarked simply, without the least idea that he was joining in the game, while Alice was
  A5   42:32   "I haven't the least idea what you're talking about," said Alice.
  A8   67:26 seem to have any rules in particular: at least, if there are, nobody attends to them--and you've no
  T1 119: 3 room in a moment, and ran down stairs--or, at least, it wasn't exactly running, but a new invention for
  T2 120: 3 here's a path that leads straight to it--at least, no, it doesn't do that--" (after going a few yards
  A6   52:27 as this is May, it wo'n't be raving mad--at least not so mad as it was in March." As she said this, she
  T4 146: 6 it. "No, I don't think it is," he said: "at least--not under here. Nohow."
  A7   60:31 instantly, and neither of the others took the least notice of her going, though she looked back once or
  T6 159:12 opposite direction, and he didn't take the least notice of her, she thought he must be a stuffed figure
  A8   67:17 she thought, "till its ears have come, or at least one of them." In another minute the whole head appeared,
  T6 162:16 choosing subjects, it was her turn now.) "At least," she corrected herself on second thoughts, "a beautiful
  T3 132:30   "because I'm rather afraid of them--at least the large kinds. But I can tell you the names of some of
  A4   29: 8 up now," she added in a sorrowful tone: "at least there's no room to grow up any more here."
  T2 127:21 want to get somewhere else, you must run at least twice as fast as that!"
LEAVE (24)
  T8W 14:13 said, as before, "Worrity, worrity! Can't you leave a body alone?"
  T9 201:26 said the Red Queen: "it's ridiculous to leave all the conversation to the pudding!"
  T8W 21:13 very talkative, she thought she might safely leave him. "I think I must be going on now," she said.
  A6   49:27 it in a day or two. Wouldn't it be murder to leave it behind?" She said the last words out loud, and the
  T3 131:12 said, and there it choked and was obliged to leave off.
  T6 162: 5 Now if you'd asked my advice, I'd have said 'Leave off at seven'--but it's too late now."
  T3 135: 3 'Come here--,' and there would have to leave off, because there wouldn't be any name for her to call,
  A9   73: 6 custody by the soldiers, who of course had to leave off being arches to do this, so that, by the end of half
  T9 195: 5 of leaves, till she had to beg them to leave off, it blew her hair about so.
  T1 108:15 it got so cold, and it snowed so, they had to leave off. Never mind, we'll go and see the bonfire to-morrow
  T5 156:13 How am I to stop it?" said the Sheep. "If you leave off rowing, it'll stop of itself."
  A10 84: 6   Yes, I think you'd better leave off," said the Gryphon, and Alice was only too glad to
  A8   65: 3   "Leave off that!" screamed the Queen. "You make me giddy." And
  A1   12:22 to herself rather sharply. "I advise you to leave off this minute!" She generally gave herself very good
  T9 195: 2 ground?" said the White Queen. "You mustn't leave out so many things."
  A11 89:24   "He denies it," said the King: "leave out that part."
  A12 93:36   All persons more than a mile high to leave the court."
  A11 88:37 and she thought at first she would get up and leave the court; but on second thoughts she decided to remain
  T1 111: 3 of the passage in Looking-glass House, if you leave the door of our drawing-room wide open: and it's very
  T4 140:24 head--/ Meaning to say he did not choose / To leave the oyster-bed.
  A4   28: 1 a pair of the gloves, and was just going to leave the room, when her eye fell upon a little bottle that
  T5 152: 3 began screaming, so loud that she had to leave the sentence unfinished. "Oh, oh, oh!" shouted the Queen.
  T4 146:11 she was just going to say "Good-night" and leave them, when Tweedledum sprang out from under the umbrella
  T8 186:28 as gunpowder and sealing-wax. And here I must leave you." They had just come to the end of the wood.
LEAVES (11) [See also HOLLY-LEAVES]
  A5   42:17 a little shaking among the distant green leaves.

LEAVES (cont.)
T2 122:37 saw anybody! You keep your head under the leaves, and snore away there, till you know no more what's
A1   9:19   down she came upon a heap of sticks and dry leaves, and the fall was over.
T6 166:34   In autumn, when the leaves are brown, / Take pen and ink, and write it down."
T1 110: 3 the woods look sleepy in the autumn, when the leaves are getting brown.
A4   33: 9 herself, and fanned herself with one of the leaves. "I should have liked teaching it tricks very much, if
A12 98: 2 who was gently brushing away some dead leaves that had fluttered down from the trees upon her face.
A5   42:11 to rise like a stalk out of a sea of green leaves that lay far below her.
T9 195: 5 set to work and fanned her with bunches of leaves, till she had to beg them to leave off, it blew her
T1 116: 4 case he fainted again), she turned over the leaves, to find some part that she could read, "--for it's all
A5   42:22 zigzag, and was going to dive in among the leaves, which she found to be nothing but the tops of the
LEAVING (3)
A9   74: 3   I have ordered;" and she walked off, leaving Alice alone with the Gryphon. Alice did not quite like
T8W 14: 6 answer, and was very nearly walking on and leaving him, but she thought to herself "Perhaps it's only
T5 153:39 arm-chair, knitting, and every now and then leaving off to look at her through a great pair of spectacles.
LED (6)
T4 144:29 and they each took one of Alice's hands, and led her up to where the King was sleeping.
A1   10: 1   Alice opened the door and found that it led into a small passage, not much larger than a rat-hole: she
A7   61: 2   golden key, and unlocking the door that led into the garden. Then she set to work nibbling at the
A6   46:45   The door led right into a large kitchen, which was full of smoke from
A2   20:24 and several other curious creatures. Alice led the way, and the whole party swam to the shore.
T1 108:18 neck, just to see how it would look: this led to a scramble, in which the ball rolled down upon the
LEDGE (1)
A9   74:17 distance, sitting sad and lonely on a little ledge of rock, and, as they came nearer, Alice could hear him
LEFT (23)
A8   67: 7 the great wonder is, that there's any one left alive!"
A3   26:36   they all moved off, and Alice was soon left alone.
A9   73: 8 of half an hour or so, there were no arches left, and all the players, except the King, the Queen, and
T1 112: 5 blazing away as brightly as the one she had left behind. "So I shall be as warm here as I was in the old
A6   49:24 and then keep tight hold of its right ear and left foot, so as to prevent its undoing itself), she carried
A12 98:13 But her sister sat still just as she left her, leaning her head on her hand, watching the setting
T1 118:15 / The vorpal blade went snicker-snack! / He left it dead, and with its head / He went galumphing back.
A11 87:11 day; and this was of very little use, as it left no mark on the slate.
T7 172: 5   "There's nothing but hay left now," the Messenger said, peeping into the bag.
T6 162:12 can. With proper assistance, you might have left off at seven."
T4 139:41 one dance," Tweedledum panted out, and they left off dancing as suddenly as they had begun: the music
T4 145: 5 clapping his hands triumphantly. "And if he left off dreaming about you, where do you suppose you'd be?"
A9   73: 3 the time they were playing the Queen never left off quarreling with the other players, and shouting "Off
A9   73:10   Then the Queen left off, quite out of breath, and said to Alice "Have you
A6   49:29 and the little thing grunted in reply (it had left off sneezing by this time). "Don't grunt," said Alice;
A11 89: 4   All this time the Queen had never left off staring at the Hatter, and, just as the Dormouse
A3   23:11 but they began running when they liked, and left off when they liked, so that it was not easy to know when
A12 96:21 she spoke. (The unfortunate little Bill had left off writing on his slate with one finger, as he found it
T4 148: 7 don't suppose," he said, "there'll be a tree left standing, for ever so far round, by the time we've
A11 90:31 go," said the King, and the Hatter hurriedly left the court, without even waiting to put his shoes on.
T5 156:15   So the boat was left to drift down the stream as it would, till it glided
A1   12:29 two people! Why, there's hardly enough of me left to make one respectable person!"
T2 126:17 could not go faster, though she had no breath left to say so.
LEFT-HAND (3)
A5   42: 3 last, and managed to swallow a morsel of the left-hand bit. * * * * * * * * * * * * * *
A6   53:14 nearer till she had nibbled some more of the left-hand bit of mushroom, and raised herself to about two
T8 189:18 / Or madly squeeze a right-hand foot / Into a left-hand shoe, / Or if I drop upon my toe / A very heavy
LEG (4)
T9 200:19 "Put on the joint!" And the waiters set a leg of mutton before Alice, who looked at it rather anxiously,
T9 201: 1 Queen. "Alice--Mutton: Mutton--Alice." The leg of mutton got up in the dish and made a little bow to
T9 200:22 a little shy: let me introduce you to that leg of mutton," said the Red Queen. "Alice--Mutton: Mutton--
T9 204: 4 but, instead of the Queen, there was the leg of mutton sitting in the chair. "Here I am!" cried a voice
-LEGGED [See THREE-LEGGED]
LEGS (5)
T6 159: 8 face. Humpty Dumpty was sitting, with his legs crossed like a Turk, on the top of a high wall--such a
A8   66: 8 comfortably enough, under her arm, with its legs hanging down, but generally, just as she had got its neck
A6   49:16 little creature, and held out its arms and legs in all directions, "just like a star-fish," thought Alice
A1   12:18 and she tried her best to climb up one of the legs of the table, but it was too slippery; and when she had
T9 203:20 fitted on as wings, and so, with forks for legs, went fluttering about in all directions: "and very like
LEISURELY (2)
T8 190:29 to herself, as she watched the horse walking leisurely along the road, and the Knight tumbling off, first
AI   3: 2   All in the golden afternoon / Full leisurely we glide; / For both our oars, with little skill, /
LEND (1)
T9 196:37 said the Red Queen. "Smoothe her hair--lend her your nightcap--and sing her a soothing lullaby."
LENGTH (2)
T2 121: 2 it quite seemed to take her breath away. At length, as the Tiger-lily only went on waving about, she spoke
A5   42:10 see, when she looked down, was an immense length of neck, which seemed to rise like a stalk out of a sea
LESS (5)
T6 163:32 what I choose it to mean--neither more nor less."
A7   59:13   "You mean you ca'n't take less," said the Hatter: "it's very easy to take more than
A6   50:12 no mistake about it: it was neither more nor less than a pig, and she felt that it would be quite absurd
A8   69: 3 that, if something wasn't done about it in less than no time, she'd have everybody executed, all round.
A9   72: 1 of that is--'The more there is of mine, the less there is of yours.'"
LESSEN (1)
A9   77:16 lessons," the Gryphon remarked: "because they lessen from day to day."

LESSON (1)
```
A3    26:18  to her daughter "Ah, my dear! Let this be a lesson to you never to lose your temper!" "Hold your tongue,
```
LESSON-BOOK (1)
```
A2    19:25  which was the first sentence in her French lesson-book. The Mouse gave a sudden leap out of the water,
```
LESSON-BOOKS (1)
```
A4    29:15  room for you, and no room at all for any lesson-books!"
```
LESSONS (16)
```
A2    17: 5  her hands on her lap as if she were saying lessons, and began to repeat it, but her voice sounded hoarse
T3   135: 6  governess would never think of excusing me lessons for that. If she couldn't remember my name, she'd call
A4    29:14  she answered herself. "How can you learn lessons in here? Why, there's hardly room for you, and no room
T9   193:20  remarked: "but I daresay you've not had many lessons in manners yet."
A1     8:31  had learnt several things of this sort in her lessons in the school-room, and though this was not a very
A9    77:10  "And how many hours a day did you do lessons?" said Alice, in a hurry to change the subject.
T9   193:22  "Manners are not taught in lessons," said Alice. "Lessons teach you to do sums, and
T3   135: 2  if the governess wanted to call you to your lessons, she would call out 'Come here--,' and there she would
T9   193:22  are not taught in lessons," said Alice. "Lessons teach you to do sums, and things of that sort."
T3   135: 9  the Gnat remarked, "of course you'd miss your lessons. That's a joke. I wish you had made it."
A9    77:23  "That's enough about lessons," the Gryphon interrupted in a very decided tone.
A9    77:15  "That's the reason they're called lessons," the Gryphon remarked: "because they lessen from day
A10   82:17  order one about, and make one repeat lessons!" thought Alice. "I might just as well be at school at
A2    17:19  to no toys to play with, and oh, ever so many lessons to learn! No, I've made up my mind about it: if I'm
A4    29:11  to be an old woman--but then--always to have lessons to learn! Oh, I shouldn't like that!"
A7    56:45  o'clock in the morning, just time to begin lessons: you'd only have to whisper a hint to Time, and round
```
LEST (1)
```
A4    27:24  knocking, and hurried upstairs, in great fear lest she should meet the real Mary Ann, and be turned out of
```
LET (36)
```
A4    27:33  I don't think," Alice went on, "that they'd let Dinah stop in the house if it began ordering people about
T5   157: 8  boat into the dark water. "I wish it hadn't let go--I should so like a little crab to take home with me!"
T4   140: 1  Then they let go of Alice's hands, and stood looking at her for a minute
T8   184: 6  He let go the bridle, and stretched out both his arms to show
T8W   14:11  The Wasp took her arms, and let her help him round the tree, but when he got settled down
T1   115: 8  hand shook so with laughter that she nearly let him drop upon the floor.
A12   95:17  Don't let him know she liked them best, / For this must ever be / A
T9   199:20  door a kick with one of his great feet. "You let it alone," he panted out, as he hobbled back to his tree,
T9   202: 9  and will not take more than a minute. / 'Let it lie in a dish!' / That is easy, because it already is
T8W   15:15  "Let it stop there!" said the Wasp, fretfully turning away his
A5    42:28  "I'm not a serpent!" said Alice indignantly. "Let me alone!"
A2    19:44  hated cats: nasty, low, vulgar things! Don't let me hear the name again!"
A3    26: 7  and looking anxiously about her. "Oh, do let me help to undo it!"
T8W   14: 9  "Won't you let me help you round to the other side? You'll be out of the
T9   200:22  "You look a little shy: let me introduce you to that leg of mutton," said the Red
A2    16: 9  try if I know all the things I used to know. Let me see: four times five is twelve, and four times six is
A4    33:11  forgotten that I've got to grow up again! Let me see--how is it to be managed? I suppose I ought to eat
A2    15: 2  they wo'n't walk the way I want to go! Let me see. I'll give them a new pair of boots every Christmas
T5   158:20  get further away the more I walk towards it. Let me see, is this a chair? Why, it's got branches, I
T1   109: 4  to prison, I suppose, when the day came. Or--let me see--suppose each punishment was to be going without a
A1     8:29  somewhere near the centre of the earth. Let me see: that would be four thousand miles down, I think--"
T8   186:31  sad," the Knight said in an anxious tone: "let me sing you a song to comfort you."
T9   202:11  'Bring it here! Let me sup!' / It is easy to set such a dish on the table. /
A2    15:39  usual. I wonder if I've changed in the night? Let me think: was I the same when I got up this morning? I
A7    60:12  This answer so confused poor Alice, that she let the Dormouse go on for some time without interrupting it.
A12   95:21  said the King, rubbing his hands; "so now let the jury--"
A12   96:28  in an angry tone, and everybody laughed. "Let the jury consider their verdict," the King said, for about
T9   199:26  a sceptre in hand, I've a crown on my head. / Let the Looking-Glass creatures, whatever they be, / Come and
T8   187:12  So saying, he stopped his horse and let the reins fall on its neck: then, slowly beating time with
T8   180: 8  fender! And how quiet the horses are! They let them get on and off them just as if they were tables!"
A3    26:18  of saying to her daughter "Ah, my dear! Let this be a lesson to you never to lose your temper!" "Hold
A3    25: 8  said to a mouse, That he met in the house, 'Let us both go to law: I will prosecute you.--Come, I'll take
A2    20:18  and it said, in a low trembling voice, "Let us get to the shore, and then I'll tell you my history,
T9   195:17  "Don't let us quarrel," the White Queen said in an anxious tone.
T9   199:21  as he hobbled back to his tree, "and it'll let you alone, you know."
A6    46:20  you were inside, you might knock, and I could let you out, you know." He was looking up into the sky all the
```
LET'S (19)
```
A7    59:36  I want a clean cup," interrupted the Hatter: "let's all move one place on."
T12  208: 5  "Now, Kitty, let's consider who it was that dreamed it all. This is a
T5   153: 2  "nobody can do two things at once, you know. Let's consider your age to begin with--how old are you?"
T4   147:43  "Let's fight till six, and then have dinner," said Tweedledum.
T6   161:15  conversation is going on a little too fast: let's go back to the last remark but one."
A9    72:40  "Let's go on with the game," the Queen said to Alice; and Alice
T1   119: 1  I've seen what the rest of the house is like! Let's have a look at the garden first!" She was out of the
T6   164:17  "Let's hear it," said Humpty Dumpty. "I can explain all the
A10   81:38  offended tone. And the Gryphon added "Come, let's hear some of your adventures."
T1   110: 9  wriggling down among my pieces. Kitty dear, let's pretend--" And here I wish I could tell you half the
T1   110:11  to say, beginning with her favourite phrase "Let's pretend." She had had quite a long argument with her
T1   110:18  by shouting suddenly in her ear, "Nurse! Do let's pretend that I'm a hungry hyaena and you're a bone!"
T1   110:21  us away from Alice's speech to the kitten. "Let's pretend that you're the Red Queen, Kitty! Do you know, I
T1   111: 8  of getting through into it, somehow, Kitty. Let's pretend the glass has got all soft like gauze, so that
T1   111: 7  it's got, oh! such beautiful things in it! Let's pretend there's a way of getting through into it,
T1   110:13  day before--all because Alice had begun with "Let's pretend we're kings and queens;" and her sister, who
T7   172:39  joke is, that it's my crown all the while! Let's run and see them." And they trotted off, Alice repeating
```

LET'S (cont.)
A2	16:11	the Multiplication-Table doesn't signify: let's try Geography. London is the capital of Paris, and Paris
A10	79: 5	"Come, let's try the first figure!" said the Mock Turtle to the

LETTER (4)
A12	94:14	the paper as he spoke, and added "It isn't a letter, after all: it's a set of verses."
T9	194:37	tell you a secret--I can read words of one letter! Isn't that grand? However, don't be discouraged.
A6	45:12	began by producing from under his arm a great letter, nearly as large as himself, and this he handed over to
A12	94: 8	said the White Rabbit; "but it seems to be a letter, written by the prisoner to--to somebody."

LETTERS (2)
A1	10:18	"DRINK ME" beautifully printed on it in large letters.
T9	198: 2	which were the words "QUEEN ALICE" in large letters, and on each side of the arch there was a bell-handle;

LICKING (2)
A2	19:37	"and she sits purring so nicely by the fire, licking her paws and washing her face--and she is such a nice
T12	208: 6	question, my dear, and you should not go on licking your paw like that--as if Dinah hadn't washed you this

LID (2)
T8	181:15	his shoulders, upside-down, and with the lid hanging open. Alice looked at it with great curiosity.
T9	202:16	For it holds it like glue--/ Holds the lid to the dish, while it lies in the middle: / Which is

LIDDELL (1)
TC	209: 0	Alice Pleasance Liddell

LID'S (1)
T8	181:22	out," Alice gently remarked. "Do you know the lid's open?"

-LIDS [See EYELIDS]

LIE (4)
A8	63:28	was rather doubtful whether she ought not to lie down on her face like the three gardeners, but she could
A8	63:32	thought she, "if people had all to lie down on their faces, so that they couldn't see it?" So she
TC	209:16	In a Wonderland they lie, / Dreaming as the days go by, / Dreaming as the summers
T9	202: 9	will not take more than a minute. / 'Let it lie in a dish!' / That is easy, because it already is in it.

LIES (1)
T9	202:16	glue--/ Holds the lid to the dish, while it lies in the middle: / Which is easiest to do, / Un-dish-cover

LIFE (20) [See also CHILD-LIFE]
A5	39: 8	it gave to my jaw / Has lasted the rest of my life."
A6	53: 9	the most curious thing I ever saw in all my life!"
A7	60:37	stupidest tea-party I ever was at in all my life!"
A8	68:40	and he wasn't going to begin at his time of life.
T2	127:30	had never been so nearly choked in all her life.
T6	164: 2	don't mean to stop here all the rest of your life."
T8	181:12	such a strange-looking soldier in all her life.
A2	18:21	(Alice had been to the seaside once in her life, and had come to the general conclusion that wherever you
T7	175:22	"We only found it to-day. It's as large as life, and twice as natural!"
TI	103: 4	time be fleet, and I and thou / Are half a life asunder, / Thy loving smile will surely hail / The
A5	41:12	never been so much contradicted in all her life before, and she felt that she was losing her temper.
A4	29: 3	it's rather curious, you know, this sort of life! I do wonder what can have happened to me! When I used to
A3	21: 8	with them, as if she had known them all her life. Indeed, she had quite a long argument with the Lory, who
A8	66: 2	seen such a curious croquet-ground in her life: it was all ridges and furrows: the croquet balls were
A9	74:14	never was so ordered about before, in all my life, never!"
T7	169: 5	She thought that in all her life she had never seen soldiers so uncertain on their feet:
T1	115: 3	afterwards that she had never seen in all her life such a face as the King made, when he found himself held
T4	147:19	such a fuss made about anything in all her life--the way those two bustled about--and the quantity of
A1	13: 3	that it seemed quite dull and stupid for life to go on in the common way.
TC	209:21	stream--/ Lingering in the golden gleam--/ Life, what is it but a dream?

LIFE'S (1)
TI	103:10	of me shall find a place / In thy young life's hereafter--/ Enough that now thou wilt not fail / To

LIFTED (6)
T9	203: 3	her so, one on each side, that they nearly lifted her up into the air. "I rise to return thanks--" Alice
T1	114:23	So Alice picked him up very gently, and lifted him across more slowly than she had lifted the Queen,
T8	191: 7	my knowing it?" she said to herself, as she lifted it off, and set it on her lap to make out what it could
T1	114:24	lifted him across more slowly than she had lifted the Queen, that she mightn't take his breath away; but,
A9	76:26	The Gryphon lifted up both its paws in surprise. "Never heard of
T8	179: 2	away, till all was dead silence, and Alice lifted up her head in some alarm. There was no one to be seen,

LIGHT (3)
T7	170:19	much as I can do to see real people, by this light!"
T8	187:21	hair, and shining on his armour in a blaze of light that quite dazzled her--the horse quietly moving about,
T5	152:27	By this time it was getting light. "The crow must have flown away, I think," said Alice:

LIGHTED (1)
T9	204:26	act of jumping over a bottle which had just lighted upon the table, "I'll shake you into a kitten, that I

LIGHTING (1)
T8	187:14	time with one hand, and with a faint smile lighting up his gentle foolish face, as if he enjoyed the

LIGHTLY (1)
T1	112: 2	Alice was through the glass, and had jumped lightly down into the Looking-glass room. The very first thing

LIGHTNING (3)
T9	195:18	in an anxious tone. "What is the cause of lightning?"
T9	195:19	"The cause of lightning," Alice said very decidedly, for she felt quite
T8	185:11	and hours to get me out. I was as fast as--as lightning, you know."

-LIGHT'S [See FIRELIGHT'S]

LIKE (217)
A7	55:27	I get' is the same thing as 'I get what I like'!"
A10	80:21	so often, of course you know what they're like?"
T5	152:32	in this wood, and being glad whenever you like!"
T8	182:35	of my own invention. You may try it if you like."
T9	203:14	all grew up to the ceiling, looking something like a bed of rushes with fireworks at the top. As to the

LIKE (cont.)

T1	111:13	the glass was beginning to melt away, just like a bright silvery mist.
T8	190: 9	his mouth were full of dough, / Who snorted like a buffalo--/ That summer evening long ago, / A-sitting on
T4	145:11	added Tweedledum, "you'd go out--bang!--just like a candle!"
A1	12: 8	to herself, "in my going out altogether, like a candle. I wonder what I should be like then?" And she
T9	201:17	pudding!" and there it was again in a moment, like a conjuring-trick. It was so large that she couldn't help
T7	175:41	out of it Alice couldn't guess. It was just like a conjuring-trick, she thought.
T2	120: 5	last. But how curiously it twists! It's more like a corkscrew than a path! Well this turn goes to the hill,
T4	139:13	They looked so exactly like a couple of great schoolboys, that Alice couldn't help
T8	190: 3	whiter than the snow, / Whose face was very like a crow, / With eyes, like cinders, all aglow, / Who
T2	123:13	"They're done up close, like a dahlia," said the Tiger-lily: "not tumbled about, like
T5	154:18	a large bright thing that looked sometimes like a doll and sometimes like a work-box, and was always in
T4	147: 7	his mouth and his large eyes--"looking more like a fish than anything else," Alice thought.
A6	45: 7	in livery, with a round face, and large eyes like a frog; and both footmen, Alice noticed, had powdered
T8	182:33	Knight. "Then you make your hair creep up it, like a fruit-tree. Now the reason hair falls off is because it
T6	165: 3	a gyroscope. To 'gimble' is to make holes like a gimlet.
T7	174:19	drums to begin." And Hatta went bounding away like a grasshopper.
T6	165: 2	"To 'gyre' is to go round and round like a gyroscope. To 'gimble' is to make holes like a gimlet
T8W	17:11	and all tangled and tumbled about like a heap of sea-weed. "You could make your wig much neater
T9	197:14	other, rolled down from her shoulder, and lay like a heavy lump in her lap. "I don't think it ever happened
T3	131:13	"It sounds like a horse," Alice thought to herself. And an extremely
A4	31:22	you--all I know is, something comes at me like a Jack-in-the-box, and up I goes like a sky-rocket!"
T2	125:25	"I declare it's marked out just like a large chess-board!" Alice said at last. "There ought to
T5	157: 9	water. "I wish it hadn't let go--I should so like a little crab to take home with me!" But the Sheep only
T6	165:12	feathers sticking out all round--something like a live mop."
A1	9:10	but you might catch a bat, and that's very like a mouse, you know. But do cats eat bats, I wonder?" And
T8	187:24	of the forest behind--all this she took in like a picture, as, with one hand shading her eyes, she leant
T5	155:13	thought to herself. "She gets more and more like a porcupine every minute!"
T6	164:31	'Lithe' is the same as 'active.' You see it's like a pormanteau--there are two meanings packed up into one
T6	163:43	"Now you talk like a reasonable child," said Humpty Dumpty, looking very
T5	155:23	This didn't sound like a remark that needed any answer: so Alice said nothing,
T4	147:32	helmet, though it certainly looked much more like a saucepan.)
A5	42:20	would bend about easily in any direction, like a serpent. She had just succeeded in curving it down into
T5	153:30	The last word ended in a long bleat, so like a sheep that Alice quite started.
A4	31:24	at me like a Jack-in-the-box, and up I goes like a sky-rocket!"
A6	49:33	that it had a very turn-up nose, much more like a snout than a real nose: also its eyes were getting
A5	42:11	immense length of neck, which seemed to rise like a stalk out of a sea of green leaves that lay far below
A6	49:17	its arms and legs in all directions, "just like a star-fish," thought Alice. The poor little thing was
A6	49:18	Alice. The poor little thing was snorting like a steam-engine when she caught it, and kept doubling
T8	184:43	"but I've invented a better one than that--like a sugar-loaf. When I used to wear it, if I fell off the
A7	57:20	'Up above the world you fly, / Like a tea-tray in the sky. / Twinkle, twinkle--'"
A1	12: 2	feeling!" said Alice. "I must be shutting up like a telescope!"
A1	10: 8	my shoulders. Oh, how I wish I could shut up like a telescope! I think I could, if I only knew how to begin
A9	72:33	front of them, with her arms folded, frowning like a thunderstorm.
T9	197:21	more distinct every minute, and sounded more like a tune: at last she could even make out words, and she
A1	8: 7	The rabbit-hole went straight on like a tunnel for some way, and then dipped suddenly down, so
T6	159: 8	Dumpty was sitting, with his legs crossed like a Turk, on the top of a high wall--such a narrow one that
T8W	13: 5	back to see what was the matter. Something like a very old man (only that his face was more like a wasp)
T8W	13: 5	a very old man (only that his face was more like a wasp) was sitting on the ground, leaning against a tree
T8	180: 7	What a noise they make when they tumble! Just like a whole set of fire-irons falling into the fender! And
A8	64: 6	fury, and, after glaring at her for a moment like a wild beast, began screaming "Off with her head! Off
T5	154:18	looked sometimes like a doll and sometimes like a work-box, and was always in the shelf next above the
A7	55:12	this; but all he said was "Why is a raven like a writing-desk?"
A1	12:10	to fancy what the flame of a candle looks like after the candle is blown out, for she could not remember
T3	132:23	"--then you don't like all insects?" the Gnat went on, as quietly as if nothing
A8	69: 9	fetch her here." And the executioner went off like an arrow.
T7	172:32	buttered! It went through and through my head like an earthquake!"
T7	170:24	kept skipping up and down, and wriggling like an eel, as he came along, with his great hands spread out
T6	159:14	"And how exactly like an egg he is!" she said aloud, standing with her hands
T6	159:19	"I said you looked like an egg, Sir," Alice gently explained. "And some eggs are
A12	94:25	mischief, or else you'd have signed your name like an honest man."
T4	141: 3	/ Were walking close at hand: / They wept like anything to see / Such quantities of sand: / 'If this
T2	126: 8	You can be the White Queen's Pawn, if you like, as Lily's too young to play: and you're in the Second
T2	125: 4	patting her on the head, which Alice didn't like at all: "though, when you say 'garden'--I've seen gardens
T6	164:35	"Well 'toves' are something like badgers--they're something like lizards--and they're
T2	121:13	Alice didn't like being criticized, so she began asking questions. "Aren't
T9	194:29	suddenly on the White Queen, for she didn't like being found fault with so much.
A2	17:23	I, then? Tell me that first, and then, if I like being that person, I'll come up: if not, I'll stay down
T8	179: 9	my dream, and not the Red King's! I don't like belonging to another person's dream," she went on in a
T9	203:22	fluttering about in all directions: "and very like birds they look," Alice thought to herself, as well as
T6	162:40	Alice considered a little. "I like birthday presents best," she said at last.
T5	149: 9	in a whisper to herself that sounded like "Bread-and-butter, bread-and-butter," and Alice felt that
T4	147:21	fastening buttons--"Really they'll be more like bundles of old clothes than anything else, by the time
A7	59: 7	such an extraordinary way of living would be like, but it puzzled her too much: so she went on: "But why
A2	19:29	animal's feelings. "I quite forgot you didn't like cats."
A2	19:30	"Not like cats!" cried the Mouse in a shrill passionate voice.
A2	19:31	in a shrill passionate voice. "Would you like cats, if you were me?"
A5	41: 9	Alice hastily replied; "only one doesn't like changing so often, you know."
T8W	15: 7	of the lake were blue and white, and looked like china. While tasting the treacle, they had a sad accident
T8	190: 4	Whose face was very like a crow, / With eyes, like cinders, all aglow, / Who seemed distracted with his woe,

LIKE (cont.)

T6	159:24	know what to say to this: it wasn't at all like conversation, she thought, as he never said anything to
T6	164:36	something like lizards--and they're something like corkscrews."
T3	129:15	they must be!" was her next idea. "Something like cottages with the roofs taken off, and stalks put to them
A6	53:12	right house, because the chimneys were shaped like ears and the roof was thatched with fur. It was so large
T7	172: 9	it revived him a good deal. "There's nothing like eating hay when you're faint," he remarked to her, as he
T9	202:23	of them put their glasses upon their heads like extinguishers, and drank all that trickled down their
T7	170:25	came along, with his great hands spread out like fans on each side.)
T4	139:32	by the branches rubbing one across the other, like fiddles and fiddle-sticks.
A11	91:30	curious to see what the next witness would be like, "--for they haven't got much evidence yet," she said to
T1	111: 9	Let's pretend the glass has got all soft like gauze, so that we can get through. Why, it's turning into
T9	202:15	For it holds it like glue--/ Holds the lid to the dish, while it lies in the
A4	32:40	hold of it: then Alice, thinking it was very like having a game of play with a cart-horse, and expecting
T8W	21:10	Alice did not like having so many personal remarks made on her, and as the
A3	26:38	in a melancholy tone. "Nobody seems to like her, down here, and I'm sure she's the best cat in the
A9	70:25	Alice did not much like her keeping so close to her: first because the Duchess
T1	110:22	up and folded your arms, you'd look exactly like her. Now do try, there's a dear!" And Alice got the Red
A2	19: 9	that it was only a mouse, that had slipped in like herself.
T6	161:25	triumphantly. "You never said a word like it!"
A12	95:36	The Knave shook his head sadly. "Do I look like it?" he said. (Which he certainly did not, being made
T9	201:23	said the Pudding. "I wonder how you'd like it, if I were to cut a slice out of you, you creature!"
A9	72: 6	'Be what you would seem to be'--or, if you'd like it put more simply--'Never imagine yourself not to be
A7	57:17	"I've heard something like it," said Alice.
A6	52: 4	"I should like it very much," said Alice, "but I haven't been invited
T7	172:14	the King replied. "I said there was nothing like it." Which Alice did not venture to deny.
A4	30:14	whispers now and then; such as "Sure, I don't like it, yer honour, at all, at all!" "Do as I tell you, you
T9	202:26	of the table--and three of them (who looked like kangaroos) scrambled into the dish of roast mutton, and
T3	129: 2	going to travel through. "It's something very like learning geography," thought Alice, as she stood on
T1	119: 1	I've seen what the rest of the house is like! Let's have a look at the garden first!" She was out of
T6	164:36	are something like badgers--they're something like lizards--and they're something like corkscrews."
A10	78:37	the two creatures, who had been jumping about like mad things all this time, sat down again very sadly and
T2	123: 9	"Is she like me?" Alice asked eagerly, for the thought crossed her
T8W	14:14	"Would you like me to read you a bit of this?" Alice went on, as she
T8W	16: 7	"You'd be cross too, if you'd a wig like mine," the Wasp went on. "They jokes at one. And they
A9	72: 4	remark. "It's a vegetable. It doesn't look like one, but it is."
T8	181:32	"But you've got a bee-hive--or something like one--fastened to the saddle," said Alice.
T6	168:23	of his fingers to shake: "you're so exactly like other people."
T3	131:36	pitying to comfort it, "if it would only sigh like other people!" she thought. But this was such a
T1	110:39	a fire. Well then, the books are something like our books, only the words go the wrong way: I know that,
T1	111: 4	of our drawing-room wide open: and it's very like our passage as far as you can see, only you know it may
T9	202:27	and began eagerly lapping up the gravy, "just like pigs in a trough!" thought Alice.
AI	4: 7	are twined / In Memory's mystic band. / Like pilgrim's wither'd wreath of flowers / Pluck'd in a
T7	177:21	for herself, anyhow," said the Lion. "Do you like plum-cake, Monster?"
T4	140: 9	"So much obliged!" added Tweedledee. "You like poetry?"
A9	77: 1	"What was that like?" said Alice.
T7	175:32	"Yes, if you like," said Alice.
A6	52: 1	"Call it what you like," said the Cat. "Do you play croquet with the Queen
A6	46:42	"Anything you like," said the Footman, and began whistling.
A10	81:10	"I can tell you more than that, if you like," said the Gryphon. "Do you know why it's called a
T5	154: 5	in front of you, and on both sides, if you like," said the Sheep; "but you ca'n't look all round you--
T4	139:25	Alice did not like shaking hands with either of them first, for fear of
T2	125:14	her head. "You may call it 'nonsense' if you like," she said, "but I've heard nonsense, compared with which
T7	175: 6	But I'll make a memorandum about her, if you like--She's a dear good creature," he repeated softly to
T5	156:38	these, being dream-rushes, melted away almost like snow, as they lay in heaps at her feet--but Alice hardly
A1	10:14	rate a book of rules for shutting people up like telescopes: this time she found a little bottle on it
A4	27:34	the house if it began ordering people about like that!"
A4	29:11	to have lessons to learn! Oh, I shouldn't like that!"
A6	47:14	for her to speak first, "why your cat grins like that?"
A8	62: 6	now, Five! Don't go splashing paint over me like that!"
T1	110:29	into Looking-glass House. How would you like that?
T5	155:29	A dear little crab!" thought Alice. "I should like that.
T12	208: 7	and you should not go on licking your paw like that--as if Dinah hadn't washed you this morning! You see
A9	72:21	"I'm glad people don't give birthday-presents like that!" But she did not venture to say it out loud.
T5	152:36	"Oh, don't go on like that!" cried the poor Queen, wringing her hands in
A10	80:14	glad that it was over at last: "and I do so like that curious song about the whiting!"
A8	67:45	said the King, "and don't look at me like that!" He got behind Alice as he spoke.
T6	160: 1	"Don't stand chattering to yourself like that," Humpty Dumpty said, looking at her for the first
T6	166:37	"You needn't go on making remarks like that," Humpty Dumpty said: "they're not sensible, and
T9	192: 4	do for you to be lolling about on the grass like that! Queens have to be dignified, you know!"
A1	12:21	"Come, there's no use in crying like that!" said Alice to herself rather sharply. "I advise
T6	164: 5	"When I make a word do a lot of work like that," said Humpty Dumpty, "I always pay it extra."
T5	155: 9	me giddy soon, if you go on turning round like that." She was now working with fourteen pairs at once,
T3	135:32	that has got my old name! That's just like the advertisements, you know, when people lose dogs--
T4	144:18	was mean!" Alice said indignantly. "Then I like the Carpenter best--if he didn't eat so many as the
T3	129:39	And a great many voices all said together ("like the chorus of a song," thought Alice) "Don't keep him
T9	201:31	murmured into Alice's other ear, in a voice like the cooing of a pigeon. "It would be such a treat! May I
A6	49:10	"Here! You may nurse it a bit, if you like!" the Duchess said to Alice, flinging the baby at her as
T8W	17:10	wig in great surprise. It was bright yellow like the handkerchief, and all tangled and tumbled about like
A2	14: 3	to speak good English). "Now I'm opening out like the largest telescope that ever was! Good-bye, feet!"
A8	67:41	"I don't like the look of it at all," said the King: "however, it may

LIKE (cont.)
```
A9    74: 4  alone  with  the  Gryphon. Alice did not quite like the look of the creature, but on the whole she thought it
A6    49:35  small  for  a  baby: altogether Alice did not like the look of the thing at all. "But perhaps it was only
A8    68:14  having  missed  their  turns, and she did not like the look of things at all, as the game was in such
A10   84: 9          the Gryphon went on. "Or would you like the Mock Turtle to sing you another song?"
A6    51: 5  as  she  did not at all know whether it would like the name: however, it only grinned a little wider. "Come,
T4   144:23  at  hearing  something  that  sounded  to her like the puffing of a large steam-engine in the wood near them
T2   127:25                    "I know what you'd like!" the Queen said good-naturedly, taking a little box out
A8    67:31                  "How do you like the Queen?" said the Cat in a low voice.
T9   195:42  Alice sighed and  gave it up. "It's exactly like the riddle with no answer!" she thought.
A4    34: 2  but  she  could  not see anything that looked like the right thing to eat or drink under the circumstances.
A8    63:29  whether she ought not to lie down on her face like the three gardeners, but she could not remember ever
A8    63:15        carrying clubs: these  were  all  shaped like the three gardeners, oblong and flat, with their hands
T4   138:16  of the old song kept ringing through her head like the ticking of a clock, and she could hardly help saying
T7   176: 2  speaking in  a  deep hollow tone that sounded like the tolling of a great bell.
A6    48: 7            Alice did not at all like the tone of this remark, and thought it would be as well
T4   144:13                    "I like the Walrus best," said Alice: "because he was a little
T5   152: 6            Her screams were so exactly like the whistle of a steam-engine, that Alice had to hold
A1     9:25  was  not a moment to be lost: away went Alice like the wind, and was just in time to hear it say, as it
A5    43:27  if  I  was,  I  shouldn't want yours: I don't like them raw."
A2    20:15  talk about cats, or dogs either, if you don't like them!" When the Mouse heard this, it turned round and
T3   132:25                    "I like them when they can talk," Alice said. "None of them ever
A1    12: 9  like  a  candle. I  wonder  what I should be like then?" And she tried to fancy what the flame of a candle
A6    51:21  paw,  "lives  a  March Hare. Visit either you like: they're both mad."
A3    25: 4  so that  her  idea of the tale was something like this:--
T1   116: 7                    It was like this.
T2   123:18            Alice didn't like this idea at all: so, to change the subject, she asked
T8   184: 5  was saying is--to keep your balance properly. Like this, you know--"
A5    41:14            "Well, I should like to be a little larger, Sir, if you wouldn't mind," said
T2   126: 4  only  I might join--though of course I should like to be a Queen, best."
A9    70:28        sharp chin. However, she did not like to be rude: so she bore it as well as she could.
A6    46:35    It  was,  no  doubt: only Alice did not like to be told so. "It's really dreadful," she muttered to
T5   158: 3                  "I should like to buy an egg, please," she said timidly. "How do you
T1   118:26  hard  to  understand!" (You  see  she didn't like to confess, even to herself, that she couldn't make it
A1     8:20  disappointment  it  was  empty: she did not like to drop the jar, for fear of killing somebody underneath,
A6    53:13  It  was so  large a house, that she did not like to go nearer till she had nibbled some more of the
A10   83: 2                  "I should like to have it explained," said the Mock Turtle.
A10   82:12  Mock Turtle repeated thoughtfully. "I should like to hear her try and repeat something now. Tell her to
T8   184:27  a  new  way of getting over a gate--would you like to hear it?"
T8   182:31                  "I should like to hear it, very much."
T4   145:13  of thing in his dream, what are you, I should like to know?"
T1   110:43            "How would you like to live in Looking-glass House, Kitty? I wonder if they'd
T5   154: 3  know  yet," Alice said very gently. "I should like to look all round me first, if I might."
T3   135:29  become  of  my name when I go in? I shouldn't like to lose it all--because they'd have to give me another
A10   79: 3                  "Would you like to see a little of it?" said the Mock Turtle.
A2    20: 4  a  nice  little dog, near our house, I should like to show you! A little bright-eyed terrier, you know, with
A3    23: 6  explain  it  is to do it." (And, as you might like to try the thing yourself some winter-day, I will tell
T8   187:38  /  And his answer trickled through my head, / Like water through a sieve.
A7    55:27  as  well say," added the March Hare, "that 'I like what I get' is the same thing as 'I get what I like'!"
T6   160:25  promised  me--ah,  you  may turn pale, if you like! You didn't think I was going to say that, did you? The
T2   123: 5  flower  in  the  garden that  can move about like you," said the Rose. "I wonder how you do it--" ("You're
A2    15:21  of  yourself," said  Alice, "a great girl like you," (she might well say this), "to go on crying in this
T2   125: 1  "I  only  wanted  to  see what the garden was like, your Majesty--"
T2   123:14  said the Tiger-lily: "not  tumbled  about, like yours."
T6   160:10  a good handsome shape it is, too. With a name like yours, you might be any shape, almost."
```
LIKED (11)
```
A7    57: 8  could keep it to half-past one as long as you liked."
A3    23:11  and  away!", but they began running when they liked, and left off when they liked, so that it was not easy
T1   110:14  we're  kings and queens;" and her sister, who liked being very exact, had argued that they couldn't, because
T8   190:21  much  for  coming so far--and for the song--I liked it very much."
T3   129:22  me  how  I  liked my walk. I shall say 'Oh, I liked it well enough--' (here came the favourite little toss
T3   129:22  and  what fun it'll be when they ask me how I liked my walk. I shall say 'Oh, I liked it well enough--'
A3    23:12    when  they  liked,  and  left off when they liked, so that it was not easy to know when the race was over.
A4    33: 9      with  one  of  the  leaves. "I should have liked teaching it tricks very much, if--if I'd only been the
A12   95:17              Don't let him know she liked them best, / For this must ever be / A secret, kept from
T9   192:13  to  her,  one on  each  side: she would have liked very much to ask them how they came there, but she
A7    56:44  terms  with  him, he'd do almost anything you liked with the clock. For instance, suppose it were nine
```
LIKELY (10)
```
A2    19:12      down  here, that I should think very likely it can talk: at any rate, there's no harm in trying."
T8   182: 3                  "Not very likely, perhaps," said the Knight; "but, if they do come, I
T1   114:14  the  fire, as if he thought that was the most likely place to find one.
A5    43:11                  "A likely story indeed!" said the Pigeon, in a tone of the
T8   182: 2      was  for," said  Alice. "It  isn't very likely there would be any mice on the horse's back."
T4   144:25  wood near them, though she feared it was more likely to be a wild beast. "Are there any lions or tigers
A4    32:32  be  hungry, in  which case it would be very likely to eat her up in spite of all her coaxing.
T3   137:20            But this did not seem likely to happen. She went on and on, a long way, but wherever
A8    67:34  behind  her,  listening: so  she  went on "--likely to win, that it's hardly worth while finishing the game
A1     8:26  off  the  top  of the house!" (Which was very likely true.)
```
LIKES (1)
```
A8    67:42  King: "however, it  may kiss my hand, if it likes."
```

```
LILY (3) [See also TIGER-LILY]
  T1   114:10  two  she  could do nothing but hug the little Lily in silence. As soon as she had recovered her breath a
  T1   113:21  him  over  among  the  cinders. "My precious Lily! My imperial kitten!" and she began scrambling wildly up
  T1   114: 4  anxious to be of use, and, as the poor little Lily was nearly screaming herself into a fit, she hastily
LILY'S (1)
  T2   126: 8  be  the  White  Queen's Pawn, if you like, as Lily's too young to play: and you're in the Second Square to
LIMBS (1)
  A5    38: 6  as  he  shook  his  grey  locks, / "I kept all my limbs very supple / By the use of this ointment--one shilling
LIMED (1)
  T8   188:42  'I  sometimes  dig  for  buttered  rolls, / Or set limed twigs for crabs: / I sometimes search for grassy knolls
LINE (3)
  A6    48:35  giving it a violent shake at the end of every line:--
  A10   78:14  said  the  Gryphon, "you first   form into a line along the sea-shore--"
  T6   159:32                              "That last line is much too long for the poetry," she added, almost out
LINES (1)
  A10   78:16                          "Two lines!" cried the Mock Turtle. "Seals, turtles, salmon, and so
LINGERING (2)
  TC   209:20         Ever drifting down the stream--/ Lingering in the golden gleam--/ Life, what is it but a dream?
  TC   209: 2           A boat, beneath a sunny sky / Lingering onward dreamily / In an evening of July--
LINKED (1)
  A9    72:31  favourite  word "moral", and the arm that was linked into hers began to tremble. Alice looked up, and there
LION (18)
  T7   176:19            "I should win easy," said the Lion.
  T7t  169: 1                     THE LION AND THE UNICORN
  T8   179: 4  that  she  must  have  been  dreaming about the Lion and the Unicorn and those queer Anglo-Saxon Messengers.
  T7   172:36                   "Why the Lion and the Unicorn, of course," said the King.
  T7   178: 4  in  her  terror, and had just time to see the Lion and the * * * * * * * * * * * * * Unicorn rise to their
  T7   174:12  was  a  pause in the fight just then, and the Lion and the Unicorn sat down, panting, while the King called
  T7   173: 1              "The Lion and the Unicorn were fighting for the crown: / The Lion
  T7   173:16  of  a great crowd, in the middle of which the Lion and Unicorn were fighting. They were in such a cloud of
  T7   173: 2  Unicorn were fighting for the crown: / The Lion beat the Unicorn all round the town. / Some gave them
  T7   177:20  kept  none  for  herself, anyhow," said the Lion. "Do you like plum-cake, Monster?"
  T7   177: 3            "I'm sure I don't know," the Lion growled out as he lay down again. "There was too much
  T7   175:43                   The Lion had joined them while this was going on: he looked very
  T7   176: 5                   The Lion looked at Alice wearily. "Are you animal--or vegetable--
  T7   176:21  you  all  round  the  town, you chicken!" the Lion replied angrily, half getting up as he spoke.
  T7   176: 9  "Then hand round the plum-cake, Monster," the Lion said, lying down and putting his chin on his paws. "And
  T7   177: 8  very  provoking!"  she  said, in reply to the Lion (she was getting quite used to being called 'the
  T7   177:19  how  to begin. "The Monster  has given the Lion twice as much as me!"
LIONS (1)
  T4   144:25  likely  to  be  a  wild beast. "Are there any lions or tigers about here?" she asked timidly.
LIPS (4)
  T6   160:23  of--but  if  I  did--" Here he pursed up his lips, and looked so solemn and grand that Alice could hardly
  T7   175:27            Alice could not help her lips curling up into a smile as she began: "Do you know, I
  A4    28: 4             she uncorked it and put it to her lips. "I know something interesting is sure to happen," she
  T9   201:30  at  finding that, the moment she opened her lips, there was dead silence, and all eyes were fixed upon her
LIST (5)
  T3   133: 7  and  sawdust," said the Gnat. "Go on with the list."
  A11   91:29  the  White  Rabbit as he fumbled over the list, feeling very curious to see what the next witness would
  T3   132:40  got  no  names--however, go  on  with your list of insects: you're wasting time."
  A11   90:30  look  at  the  Queen, who was reading the list of singers.
  A11   89: 6  of  the  officers of the court, "Bring me the list of the singers in the last concert!" on which the
LISTEN (11)
  A4    29:18  she  heard  a  voice  outside, and stopped to listen.
  A6    45:10  and  crept  a  little  way out of the wood to listen.
  A5    40: 7  give  yourself  airs! / Do you think I can listen all day to such stuff? / Be off, or I'll kick you
  T1   108:33        Now don't make any more excuses, but listen! Number two: you pulled Snowdrop away by the tail just
  A12   98:22  eyes--and still as she listened, or seemed to listen, the whole place around her became alive with the
  T6   167:12  once,  I  told  them twice: / They would not listen to advice.
  A1     8:33  off  her  knowledge, as there was no one to listen to her, still it was good practice to say it over)
  A8    67:20  game,  feeling  very glad she had some one to listen to her. The Cat seemed to think that there was enough
  T6   166:21  felt  that  in  that case she really ought to listen to it; so she sat down, and said "Thank you" rather
  A3    21:14  them,  called  out "Sit down, all of you, and listen to me! I'll soon make you dry enough!" They all sat
  TI   103:12  Enough that now thou wilt not fail / To listen to my fairy-tale.
LISTENED (3)
  A12   98:21  always  get  into her eyes--and still as she listened, or seemed to listen, the whole place around her
  T9   197:21  last  she  could even make out words, and she listened so eagerly that, when the two great heads suddenly
  T8   187:29  give  thee  all,  I can no more.'" She stood and listened very attentively, but no tears came into her eyes.
LISTENERS (1)
  A10   82: 5  but  she  gained  courage as she went on. Her listeners were perfectly quiet till she got to the part about
LISTENING
  T6   160:31  breaking  into a sudden passion. "You've been listening at doors--and behind trees--and down chimneys--or
  T8   187:26  a  tree,  watching  the strange pair, and listening, in a half-dream, to the melancholy music of the
  A6    48:30  stirring  the  soup,  and  seemed not to be listening, so she went on again: "Twenty-four hours, I think;
  A8    67:33  noticed  that the Queen was close behind her, listening: so she went on "--likely to win, that it's hardly
  A1     8:42  (she  was  rather  glad  there was no one listening, this time, as it didn't sound at all the right
LIT (1)
  A1     9:29  found  herself  in a long, low hall, which was lit up by a row of lamps hanging from the roof.
```

LITHE (2)
```
T6    164:30                              "Well, 'slithy' means 'lithe and slimy.' 'Lithe' is the same as 'active.' You see
T6    164:30     "Well,  'slithy'  means  'lithe  and slimy.' 'Lithe' is the same as 'active.' You see it's like a pormanteau
```
LITTLE (253)
```
A4     30:38   narrow,  to be sure; but I think I can kick a little!"
A9     70:31   said, by way of keeping up the conversation a little.
T3    136:19   she  said timidly. "I think that might help a little."
T7    175:12                              "A little--a little," the King replied, rather nervously. "You
T1    115:16   and lay perfectly still; and Alice was a little alarmed at what she had done, and went round the room
A12    98:14   watching  the  setting  sun,  and thinking of little Alice and all her wonderful Adventures, till she too
A12    98:17                   First, she dreamed about little Alice herself: once again the tiny hands were clasped
T4    147:33                    "Well--yes--a little," Alice replied gently.
A1     10:19   all very well to say "Drink me," but the wise little Alice was not going to do that in a hurry. "No, I'll
A2     17: 4   for Mabel! I'll try and say 'How doth the little--'," and she crossed her hands on her lap as if she
A7     55:39                  Alice considered a little, and then said "The fourth."
T3    136:10   to stroke it;  but  it  only started back a little, and then stood looking at her again.
A4     30:40   as  she  could,  and  waited till she heard a little animal (she couldn't guess of what sort it was)
A4     32:13   out  of the house, and found quite a crowd of little animals and birds waiting outside. The poor little
T1    114: 2   been hurt by the fall. He had a right to be a little annoyed with the Queen, for he was covered with ashes
T1    116: 2   watching  the White King (for she was still a little anxious about him, and had the ink all ready to throw
A9     76: 9   "With extras?"  asked  the  Mock Turtle, a little anxiously.
T3    134:24                "No, indeed," Alice said, a little anxiously.
T6    161: 4   and offered Alice his hand. She watched him a little anxiously as she took it. "If he smiled much more the
T3    131:43   "What  kind  of  insect?" Alice inquired, a little anxiously. What she really wanted to know was, whether
T9    192:21   rule," said Alice, who was always ready for a little argument, "and if you only spoke when you were spoken
AI      3: 4   / For both our oars, with little skill, / By little arms are plied, / While little hands make vain pretence
T5    156:17   sleeves  were  carefully  rolled  up, and the little arms were plunged in elbow-deep, to get hold of the
T4    148:10   said Alice, still hoping to make them a little ashamed of fighting for such a trifle.
T12   207:20   and  pretended not to see it: but it looked a little ashamed of itself, so I think it must have been the Red
T2    124:15                  Alice wondered a little at this, but she was too much in awe of the Queen to
A7     57:14                  'Twinkle, twinkle, little bat! / How I wonder what you're at!'
A10    81:19   Alice  looked  down at them, and considered a little before she gave her answer. "They're done with blacking
A9     77:18   new  idea to Alice, and she thought it over a little before she made her next remark. "Then the eleventh day
A2     16: 7   of things, and she, oh, she knows such a very little! Besides, she's she, and I'm I, and--oh dear, how
T8W    20: 2   heartily:  "and  I think if your wig fitted a little better, they wouldn't tease you quite so much."
A4t    27: 1                    THE RABBIT SENDS IN A LITTLE BILL
A12    96:21   at  the Lizard as she spoke. (The unfortunate little Bill had left off writing on his slate with one finger,
A3     26:29   see  her  after  the birds! Why, she'll eat a little bird as soon as look at it!"
A11    86: 3   crowd  assembled  about  them--all  sorts  of little birds and beasts, as well as the whole pack of cards:
A1     12:38                  She ate a little bit, and said anxiously to herself "Which way? Which
A4     32:33   Hardly  knowing what she did, she picked up a little bit of stick, and held it out to the puppy: whereupon
T4    143:14   not on us!'  the Oysters cried, / Turning a little blue. / 'After such kindness, that would be / A dismal
T5    155:18   in  her  hands,  and she found they were in a little boat, gliding along between banks: so there was nothing
A1     10:15   up  like telescopes:  this  time she found a little bottle on it ("which certainly was not here before,"
A4     28: 2   to  leave  the  room, when her eye fell upon a little bottle that stood near the looking-glass. There was no
T9    201: 1   leg  of mutton got up in the dish and made a little bow to Alice; and Alice returned the bow, not knowing
T2    127:26   the  Queen  said  good-naturedly,  taking a little box out of her pocket. "Have a biscuit?"
T8    181:17               "I see you're admiring my little box," the Knight said in a friendly tone. "It's my own
A6     48:36                  "Speak roughly to your little boy, / And beat him when he sneezes: / He only does it
A2     20: 4   near our house, I should like to show you! A little bright-eyed terrier, you know, with oh, such long curly
T5    153:24   Alice  said very politely, as she crossed the little brook after the Queen. * * * * * * * * * * * * *
T8    190:15   to go," he said, "down the hill and over that little brook, and then you'll be a Queen--But you'll stay and
T7    178: 4   She started on her feet and sprang across the little brook in her terror, and had just time to see the Lion
T5    153:18   gust  of wind blew the Queen's shawl across a little brook. The Queen spread out her arms again and went
T5    158:22   trees  growing  here! And actually here's a little brook! Well, this is the very queerest shop I ever saw!
T7    177: 6   Alice  had  seated  herself on the bank of a little brook, with the great dish on her knees, and was sawing
T3    129:29   hill,  and  jumped  over the first of the six little brooks. * * * * * * * * * * * * *
T2    125:21   country it was. There were a number of tiny little brooks running straight across it from side to side,
A5     36:34                  "Well,  I've  tried  to say 'How doth the little busy bee,' but it all came different!" Alice replied in
T5    155:16                  "Yes, a little--but not on land--and not with needles--" Alice was
A4     32: 6   that the pebbles were all turning into little cakes as they lay on the floor, and a bright idea came
A4     30:23   anything  more:  at  last came a rumbling of little cart-wheels, and the sound of a good many voices all
A12    99: 6   and  how  she  would  gather  about her other little children, and make their eyes bright and eager with
A9     72:24   Duchess  asked, with another dig of her sharp little chin.
A9     70:37   thing," said the Duchess, digging her sharp little chin into Alice's shoulder as she added "and the moral
T5    155:29                  "A dear little crab!" thought Alice. "I should like that."
T5    157: 9   "I wish it hadn't let go--I should so like a little crab to take home with me!" But the Sheep only laughed
T3    131:40   her thoughts from the unhappiness of the poor little creature.
A6     49:16   some difficulty, as it was a queer-shaped little creature, and held out its arms and legs in all
A6     50:14                  So she set the little creature down, and felt quite relieved to see it trot
T9    204:25   for you," she repeated, catching hold of the little creature in the very act of jumping over a bottle which
A2     17: 8                  "How doth the little crocodile / Improve his shining tail, / And pour the
T5    158: 1   in  a  moment,  and she was back again in the little dark shop.
T5    153:37   could  make  nothing more of it: she was in a little dark shop, leaning with her elbows on the counter, and
T1    114: 6   set her on the table by the side of her noisy little daughter.
T8    181:14   fit him very badly, and he had a queer-shaped little deal box fastened across his shoulders, upside-down,
A8     63:20   children:  there  were ten of them, and the little dears came jumping merrily along, hand in hand, in
A2     15:41   I  almost  think  I can remember feeling a little different. But if I'm not the same, the next question
A2     20: 4   Alice  went on eagerly: "There is such a nice little dog, near our house, I should like to show you! A
T9    204:20   had  suddenly  dwindled  down to the size of a little doll, and was now on the table, merrily running round
```

LITTLE (cont.)

A1	9:40	had not noticed before, and behind it was a	little	door about fifteen inches high: she tried the little
A2	18:13	And she ran with all speed back to the	little	door; but, alas! the little door was shut again, and
A4	27:10	the great hall, with the glass table and the	little	door, had vanished completely.
A1	12: 5	was now the right size for going through the	little	door into that lovely garden. First, however, she
A1	10:12	There seemed to be no use in waiting by the	little	door, so she went back to the table, half hoping she
A2	18:13	speed back to the little door; but, alas! the	little	door was shut again, and the little golden key was
A2	19:19	and seemed to her to wink with one of its	little	eyes, but it said nothing.
A10	79:13	"Will you walk a	little	faster?" said a whiting to a snail, / "There's a
T8	188:28	/ And so go on from day to day / Getting a	little	fatter. / I shook him well from side to side, / Until
A4	31:16	Last came a little feeble, squeaking voice ("That's Bill," thought Alice),
A2	14: 6	they were getting so far off). "Oh, my poor	little	feet, I wonder who will put on your shoes and stockings
T3	137:12	to cry with vexation at having lost her dear	little	fellow-traveler so suddenly. "However, I know my name
T6	167: 3	The	little	fishes' answer was / 'We cannot do it, Sir, because--'"
T6	167:18	Then some one came to me and said / 'The	little	fishes are in bed.'
A2	17:14	How neatly spreads his claws, / And welcomes	little	fishes in, / With gently smiling jaws!
T6	167: 1	The	little	fishes of the sea, / They sent an answer back to me.
T8	191: 2	down to rest on a lawn as soft as moss, with	little	flowerbeds dotted about it here and there. "Oh, how
T9	202:32	Alice got up to do it, very obediently, but a	little	frightened.
T9	201:29	poetry repeated to me to-day," Alice began, a	little	frightened at finding that, the moment she opened her
A6	46: 2	tone, only changing the order of the words a	little	, "From the Queen. An invitation for the Duchess to play
T3	137: 1	"I'll tell you, if you'll come a	little	further on," the Fawn said. "I ca'n't remember here."
T3	129: 4	on tiptoe in hopes of being able to see a	little	further. "Principal rivers--there are none. Principal
T7	173: 9	enough--" Alice panted out, after running a	little	further, "to stop a minute--just to get--one's breath
T5	150:12	the Queen said kindly: "it always makes one a	little	giddy at first--"
T1	119: 9	hold of the door-post. She was getting a	little	giddy with so much floating in the air, and was rather
T4	144:37	grass," said Alice, who was a very thoughtful	little	girl.
T2	123:10	thought crossed her mind, "There's another	little	girl in the garden, somewhere!"
A5	43:24	what does it matter to me whether you're a	little	girl or a serpent?"
A5	43: 9	"I--I'm a	little	girl," said Alice, rather doubtfully, as she remembered
A1	9: 2	you could manage it?) "And what an ignorant	little	girl she'll think me for asking! No, it'll never do to
A5	43:17	Alice, who was a very truthful child; "but	little	girls eat eggs quite as much as serpents do, you know
A5	43:12	the deepest contempt. "I've seen a good many	little	girls in my time, but never one with such a neck as
A11	86:26	she thought, and rightly too, that very few	little	girls of her age knew the meaning of it at all. However
A1	12:31	Soon her eye fell on a	little	glass box that was lying under the table: she opened it
A7	60:43	herself in the long hall, and close to the	little	glass table. "Now, I'll manage better this time," she
A2	15:14	nine feet high, and she at once took up the	little	golden key and hurried off to the garden door.
A7	61: 1	she said to herself, and began by taking the	little	golden key, and unlocking the door that led into the
A1	12:15	to the door, she found she had forgotten the	little	golden key, and when she went back to the table for it,
A1	9:41	door about fifteen inches high: she tried the	little	golden key in the lock, and to her great delight it
A2	18:13	alas! the little door was shut again, and the	little	golden key was lying on the glass table as before, "and
T5	155:38	"You are," said the Sheep: "you're a	little	goose."
T8	184:25	"You were a	little	grave," said Alice.
T2	125:23	was divided up into squares by a number of	little	green hedges, that reached from brook to brook.
A6	52:22	Alice waited a	little	, half expecting to see it again, but it did not appear,
AI	3: 5	skill, / By little arms are plied, / While	little	hands make vain pretence / Our wanderings to guide.
T8	184:37	for certain--but I'm afraid it would be a	little	hard."
T1	115: 2	she thought she might as well dust him a	little	, he was so covered with ashes.
T7	169: 8	him, so that the ground was soon covered with	little	heaps of men.
T2	125:18	on in silence till they got to the top of the	little	hill.
A7	56:23	again," said the Hatter, and he poured a	little	hot tea upon its nose.
A2	17:18	and I shall have to go and live in that poky	little	house, and have next to no toys to play with, and oh,
A5	44: 1	she came suddenly upon an open place, with a	little	house in it about four feet high. "Whoever lives there
A4	27:21	them." As she said this, she came upon a neat	little	house, on the door of which was a bright brass plate
T6	162:40	Alice considered a	little	. "I like birthday presents best," she said at last.
A5	36:11	beginning of the conversation. Alice felt a	little	irritated at the Caterpillar's making such very short
A11	87: 8	it away. She did it so quickly that the poor	little	juror (it was Bill, the Lizard) could not make out at
T9	196:32	"A	little	kindness--and putting her hair in papers--would do
T12	207:24	And she caught it up and gave it one	little	kiss, "just in honour of its having been a Red Queen."
T1	107:21	catching up the kitten, and giving it a	little	kiss to make it understand that it was in disgrace.
A5	41:14	"Well, I should like to be a	little	larger, Sir, if you wouldn't mind," said Alice: "three
T2	124:17	she thought to herself, "the next time I'm a	little	late for dinner."
A9	74:17	in the distance, sitting sad and lonely on a	little	ledge of rock, and, as they came nearer, Alice could
T1	114:10	or two she could do nothing but hug the	little	Lily in silence. As soon as she had recovered her
T1	114: 4	very anxious to be of use, and, as the poor	little	Lily was nearly screaming herself into a fit, she
A4	32:13	animals and birds waiting outside. The poor	little	Lizard, Bill, was in the middle, being held up by two
A4	28:23	Luckily for Alice, the	little	magic bottle had now had its full effect, and she grew
T4	139:12	But the fat	little	men only looked at each other and grinned.
T3	137:30	turning a sharp corner, she came upon two fat	little	men, so suddenly that she could not help starting back,
T1	108:25	the snow! And you'd have deserved it, you	little	mischievous darling! What have you got to say for
A8	68:26	not escape again, and went back to have a	little	more conversation with her friend.
T2	121:12	remarked. "If only her petals curled up a	little	more, she'd be all right."
T12	207:22	"Sit up a	little	more stiffly, dear!" Alice cried with a merry laugh.
A10	82: 2	she first saw the White Rabbit. She was a	little	nervous about it, just at first, the two creatures got
A1	12: 7	was going to shrink any further: she felt a	little	nervous about this; "for it might end, you know," said
T3	132: 7	satisfied with this, though Alice felt a	little	nervous at the idea of trains jumping at all. "However,
T2	127:11	a tree, and said kindly, "You may rest a	little	, now."
A9	74:41	at last, more calmly, though still sobbing a	little	now and then, "we went to school in the sea. The master
A6	48:24	glad to get an opportunity of showing off a	little	of her knowledge. "Just think what work it would make
A10	79: 3	"Would you like to see a	little	of it?" said the Mock Turtle.

LITTLE (cont.)

A5	41:39	is which?" she said to herself, and nibbled a little of the right-hand bit to try the effect. The next
T2	125:17	afraid from the Queen's tone that she was a little offended: and they walked on in silence till they got
T8	183: 5	The Knight looked very much surprised, and a little offended at the remark. "What makes you say that?" he
T1	113: 5	the cinders; but in another moment, with a little "Oh!" of surprise, she was down on her hands and knees
T1	113: 1	in the Looking-glass) had got the face of a little old man, and grinned at her.
T1	114:15	me--up," panted the Queen, who was still a little out of breath. "Mind you come up--the regular way--
T4	142:17	on a rock / Conveniently low: / And all the little Oysters stood / And waited in a row.
A7	61: 4	about a foot high; then she walked down the little passage: and then--she found herself at last in the
A2	15:25	After a time she heard a little pattering of feet in the distance, and she hastily
A4	29:20	"Fetch me my gloves this moment!" Then came a little pattering of feet on the stairs. Alice knew it was the
A3	26:42	In a little while, however, she again heard a little pattering of footsteps in the distance, and she looked
A4	32: 1	to doubt, for the next moment a shower of little pebbles came rattling in at the window, and some of
T1	111: 2	we come to the passage. You can just see a little peep of the passage in Looking-glass House, if you
T2	127:34	and began measuring the ground, and sticking little pegs in here and there.
T2	123:44	A little provoked, she drew back, and, after looking everywhere
T5	156:26	quite reach it." And it certainly did seem a little provoking ("almost as if it happened on purpose," she
A4	33: 7	"And yet what a dear little puppy it was!" said Alice, as she leant against a
T6	163:17	it round for him. "I thought it looked a little queer. As I was saying, that seems to be done right--
A5	36: 5	a butterfly, I should think you'll feel it a little queer, wo'n't you?"
A3	26:15	only shook its head impatiently, and walked a little quicker.
A12	93:10	As soon as the jury had a little recovered from the shock of being upset, and their
A4	27:36	this time she had found her way into a tidy little room with a table in the window, and on it (as she had
A12	97:10	and came flying down upon her; she gave a little scream, half of fright and half of anger, and tried to
T8	184:17	than a live horse," Alice said, with a little scream of laughter, in spite of all she could do to
A8	65:38	ears--" the Rabbit began. Alice gave a little scream of laughter. "Oh, hush!" the Rabbit whispered in
T8W	20: 9	Alice began with a little scream of laughter, which she turned into a cough as
A5	42:16	but no result seemed to follow, except a little shaking among the distant green leaves.
A4	32:25	peering about anxiously among the trees, a little sharp bark just over her head made her look up in a
T1	114:11	As soon as she had recovered her breath a little, she called out to the White King, who was sitting
A4	29:37	did not get hold of anything, but she heard a little shriek and a fall, and a crash of broken glass, from
A7	60:22	by the Hatter, it woke up again with a little shriek, and went on: "--that begins with an M, such as
A4	30:17	snatch in the air. This time there were two little shrieks, and more sounds of broken glass. "What a
T5	156:44	under the chin, and, in spite of a series of little shrieks of "Oh, oh, oh!" from poor Alice, it swept her
T2	122: 8	together, till the air seemed quite full of little shrill voices. "Silence, every one of you!" cried the
T9	192:32	other, and the Red Queen remarked, with a little shudder, "She says she only said 'if'--"
T9	200:22	"You look a little shy: let me introduce you to that leg of mutton," said
T9	201:19	was so large that she couldn't help feeling a little shy with it, as she had been with the mutton; however,
T3	135:17	Then came another of those melancholy little sighs, and this time the poor Gnat really seemed to
A12	99: 3	Lastly, she pictured to herself how this same little sister of hers would, in the after-time, be herself a
A12	98:23	alive with the strange creatures of her little sister's dream.
A7	58:32	"Once upon a time there were three little sisters," the Dormouse began in a great hurry; "and
A7	59:31	he consented to go on. "And so these three little sisters--they were learning to draw, you know--
AI	3: 3	leisurely we glide; / For both our oars, with little skill, / By little arms are plied, / While little hands
T5	156:16	in among the waving rushes. And then the little sleeves were carefully rolled up, and the little arms
A3	26:20	Hold your tongue, Ma!" said the young Crab, a little snappishly. "You're enough to try the patience of an
T5	156: 1	This offended Alice a little, so there was no more conversation for a minute or two,
T4	144:13	Walrus best," said Alice: "because he was a little sorry for the poor oysters."
A6	50:20	right way to change them--" when she was a little startled by seeing the Cheshire-Cat sitting on a bough
A9	70:17	forgotten the Duchess by this time, and was a little startled when she heard her voice close to her ear.
A1	10:22	or not"; for she had read several nice little stories about children who had got burnt, and eaten up
T7	175:12	"A little--a little," the King replied, rather nervously. "You shouldn't
A9	74:40	"When we were still little," the Mock Turtle went on at last, more calmly, though
A4	28: 8	really I'm quite tired of being such a tiny little thing!"
T1	107:20	"Oh, you wicked, wicked little thing!" cried Alice, catching up the kitten, and giving
A6	49:28	She said the last words out loud, and the little thing grunted in reply (it had left off sneezing by
A6	49: 2	the baby violently up and down, and the poor little thing howled so, that Alice could hardly hear the words
A4	32:29	out one paw, trying to touch her. "Poor little thing!" said Alice, in a coaxing tone, and she tried
A1	12:20	had tired herself out with trying, the poor little thing sat down and cried.
A6	50: 5	more to do with you. Mind now!" The poor little thing sobbed again (or grunted, it was impossible to
A6	49:17	like a star-fish," thought Alice. The poor little thing was snorting like a steam-engine when she caught
A12	93: 5	the Lizard in head downwards, and the poor little thing was waving its tail about in a melancholy way,
A1	9:34	Suddenly she came upon a little three-legged table, all made of solid glass: there was
T3	135:24	darker than the last wood, and Alice felt a little timid about going into it. However, on second thoughts,
T8W	15:13	It's in this newspaper, though," Alice said a little timidly.
A10	81:41	beginning from this morning," said Alice a little timidly; "but it's no use going back to yesterday,
A6	47:12	"Please would you tell me," said Alice, a little timidly, for she was not quite sure whether it was good
A8	63: 3	"Would you tell me, please," said Alice, a little timidly, "why you are painting those roses?"
A7	59: 6	Alice tried a little to fancy to herself what such an extraordinary way of
T8	187:32	"I'll tell thee everything I can: / There's little to relate. / I saw an aged aged man, / A-sitting on a
T6	161:15	However, this conversation is going on a little too fast: let's go back to the last remark but one."
A12	98:20	very tones of her voice, and see that queer little toss of her head to keep back the wandering hair that
T3	129:23	it well enough--' (here came the favourite little toss of the head), 'only it was so dusty and hot, and
T2	123:17	then one ca'n't help one's petals getting a little untidy."
A11	87:11	for the rest of the day; and this was of very little use, as it left no mark on the slate.
A1	10: 7	thought poor Alice, "it would be of very little use without my shoulders. Oh, how I wish I could shut
T8	187: 1	don't understand," the Knight said, looking a little vexed. "That's what the name is called. The name really
T3	132: 2	"What, then you don't--" the little voice began, when it was drowned by a shrill scream
T3	131:29	"You might make a joke on that," said the little voice close to her ear: "something about 'you would if
T3	131:34	The little voice sighed deeply. It was very unhappy, evidently,

LITTLE (cont.)
```
 A11    91:33  Rabbit  read  out,  at  the  top  of  his  shrill  little  voice, the name "Alice!"
 T3    131:41           "I know you are a friend," the  little  voice went on: "a dear friend, and an old friend. And
 T9    198: 9           Just then the door opened a  little  way, and a creature with a long beak put its head out
 A4     32:43  of short charges at the stick, running a very  little  way forwards each time and a long way back, and barking
 T8    183:14  it  as  heartily as she could. They went on a  little  way in silence after this, the Knight with his eyes
 T4    145:24                            Alice ran a  little  way into the wood, and stopped under a large tree. "It
 A2     19: 6  heard something splashing about in the pool a  little  way off, and she swam nearer to make out what it was:
 A6     45: 9  to  know  what  it was all about, and crept a  little  way out of the wood to listen.
 T8    185: 2  touched  the ground directly. So I had a very  little  way to fall, you see--But there was the danger of
 T8W    16:17               The Wasp considered a  little.  "Well, no," he said: "it's when you hold up your head
 T5    156:37  scented  rushes,  you  know, last only a very  little  while--and these, being dream-rushes, melted away
 A3     26:41  she  felt  very  lonely and low-spirited. In a  little  while, however, she again heard a little pattering of
 A2     18: 2  see  that  she had put on one of the Rabbit's  little  white kid-gloves while she was talking. "How can I have
 T4    146:17  said,  after  a  careful  examination of the  little  white thing. "Not a rattle-snake, you know," she added
 T9    201:34  spoke  to  the  Red Queen, whose answer was a  little  wide of the mark. "As to fishes," she said, very slowly
 A6     51: 6  like  the  name:  however,  it only grinned a  little  wider. "Come, it's pleased so far," thought Alice, and
 T2    124:19  said looking at her watch: "open your mouth a  little  wider when you speak, and always say 'your Majesty.'"
 A9     72:26  sharply,  for  she  was  beginning to feel a  little  worried.
 T2    127:16  in  our country," said Alice, still panting a  little,  "you'd generally get to somewhere else--if you ran
```
LIVE (21) [See also ALIVE]
```
 A6     51:18  tried  another question. "What sort of people  live  about here?"
 T8    187:36  you,  aged man?' I said. / 'And how is it you  live?' / And his answer trickled through my head, / Like water
 T8    188:15  man  said,  /  I  cried 'Come, tell me how you  live!' / And thumped him on the head.
 A7     59: 8  too  much:  so she went on: "But why did they  live  at the bottom of a well?"
 A7     59:20  and  repeated her question. "Why did they  live  at the bottom of a well?"
 A8     66: 3  balls  were  live  hedgehogs, and the mallets  live  flamingoes, and the soldiers had to double themselves up
 T2t   120: 1                    THE GARDEN OF  LIVE  FLOWERS
 A8     66: 2  ridges  and  furrows:  the croquet balls were  live  hedgehogs, and the mallets live flamingoes, and the
 T8    184:17           "Much more smoothly than a  live  horse," Alice said, with a little scream of laughter, in
 T8    188:31  his  face  was blue: / 'Come, tell me how you  live,' I cried, / 'And what it is you do!'
 T1    110:43           "How would you like to  live  in Looking-glass House, Kitty? I wonder if they'd give
 TI    103:17  /  The  rhythm of our rowing--/ Whose echoes  live  in memory yet, / Though envious years would say "forget
 A2     17:18  Mabel  after  all,  and I shall have to go and  live  in that poky little house, and have next to no toys to
 T3    137:25  I do believe," said Alice at last, "that they  live  in the same house! I wonder I never thought of that
 A6     52:24  direction in which the March Hare was said to  live.  "I've seen hatters before," she said to herself: "the
 T6    165:12  sticking  out  all  round--something  like  a  live  mop."
 T3    134:13                  "And what does it  live  on?"
 T3    134: 1           "And what does it  live  on?" Alice asked, as before.
 T3    133: 6           "What does it  live  on?" Alice asked, with great curiosity.
 T6    164:39  make  their  nests under sun-dials--also they  live  on cheese."
 A7     58:35                "What did they  live  on?" said Alice, who always took a great interest in
```
LIVED (3)
```
 A7     58:34  names were Elsie, Lacie, and Tillie; and they  lived  at the bottom of a well--"
 A10    78: 8           "You may not have  lived  much under the sea--" ("I haven't," said Alice)--"and
 A7     59: 1                    "They  lived  on treacle," said the Dormouse, after thinking a minute
```
LIVERY (3)
```
 A6     45: 2  what  to  do next, when suddenly a footman in  livery  came running out of the wood--(she considered him to be
 A6     45: 4      him  to  be  a  footman because he was in  livery:  otherwise, judging by his face only, she would have
 A6     45: 6  knuckles. It was opened by another footman in  livery,  with a round face, and large eyes like a frog; and
```
LIVES (6)
```
 A9     73: 2  that  a  moment's delay would cost them their  lives.
 T7    170:33        and  Hay.  His  name  is  Haigha, and he  lives--"
 A6     51:20  the  Cat  said,  waving its right paw round, "  lives  a Hatter: and in that direction," waving the other paw,
 A6     51:21  in  that  direction," waving the other paw, "  lives  a March Hare. Visit either you like: they're both mad."
 T7    170:34                    "He  lives  on the Hill," the King remarked simply, without the
 A5     44: 2  house  in  it  about four feet high. "Whoever  lives  there," thought Alice, "it'll never do to come upon them
```
LIVING (5)
```
 A9     76:16  couldn't  have  wanted it much," said Alice; "  living  at the bottom of the sea."
 T5    150:13                    "Living  backwards!" Alice repeated in great astonishment. "I
 T5    150:11           "That's the effect of  living  backwards," the Queen said kindly: "it always makes one
 T5    152:31  remember  the rule. You must be very happy,  living  in this wood, and being glad whenever you like!"
 A7     59: 7  to  herself what such an extraordinary way of  living  would be like, but it puzzled her too much: so she went
```
LIZARD (5)
```
 A12    96:21  Queen,  furiously, throwing an inkstand at the  Lizard  as she spoke. (The unfortunate little Bill had left off
 A4     32:14  and  birds  waiting  outside. The poor little  Lizard,  Bill, was in the middle, being held up by two
 A11    87: 9  that  the  poor little juror (it was Bill, the  Lizard)  could not make out at all what had become of it; so,
 A12    93: 5  and  saw  that, in her haste, she had put the  Lizard  in head downwards, and the poor little thing was waving
 A12    93:13  out  a history of the accident, all except the  Lizard,  who seemed too much overcome to do anything but sit
```
LIZARD'S (1)
```
 A12    98:31  shriek  of  the Gryphon, the squeaking of the  Lizard's  slate-pencil, and the choking of the suppressed
```
LIZARDS (1)
```
 T6    164:36           like badgers--they're something like  lizards--and they're something like corkscrews."
```
LOADED (1)
```
 T8    182:20  he  hung  it to the saddle, which was already  loaded  with bunches of carrots, and fire-irons, and many other
```
LOAF (2) [See also SUGAR-LOAF]
```
 T9    194: 6  White  Queen. "Can you do Division? Divide a  loaf  by a knife--what's the answer to that?"
 T4    143: 7                'A  loaf  of bread,' the Walrus said, / 'Is what we chiefly need: /
```
LOBSTER (3)
```
 A10    78:10  perhaps  you  were never even introduced to a  lobster--" (Alice began to say "I once tasted--" but checked
```

LOBSTER (cont.)
A10 78:21   "Each with a lobster as a partner!" cried the Gryphon.
A10 82:22   "'Tis the voice of the Lobster: I heard him declare / 'You have baked me too brown, I
LOBSTER-QUADRILLE (4)
A10t 78: 1   THE LOBSTER-QUADRILLE
A10 78:12 can have no idea what a delightful thing a Lobster-Quadrille is!"
A10 82:20 to repeat it, but her head was so full of the Lobster-Quadrille, that she hardly knew what she was saying;
A10 84: 8   "Shall we try another figure of the Lobster-Quadrille?" the Gryphon went on. "Or would you like
LOBSTERS (7)
A10 78:33   "Change lobsters again!" yelled the Gryphon at the top of its voice.
A10 78:24   "--change lobsters, and retire in same order," continued the Gryphon.
A10 79:15 treading on my tail. / See how eagerly the lobsters and the turtles all advance! / They are waiting on
A10 80: 2 / When they take us up and throw us, with the lobsters, out to sea!" / But the snail replied "Too far, too
A10 78:28   "The lobsters!" shouted the Gryphon, with a bound into the air.
A10 81: 5 the Gryphon, "that they would go with the lobsters to the dance. So they got thrown out to sea. So they
A10 79: 6 Turtle to the Gryphon. "We can do it without lobsters, you know. Which shall sing?"
LOCK (1)
A1   9:41 high: she tried the little golden key in the lock, and to her great delight it fitted!
LOCKED (2)
A1   9:30 doors all round the hall, but they were all locked; and when Alice had been all the way down one side and
T6   168:10   And when I found the door was locked, / I pulled and pushed and kicked and knocked.
-LOCKING [See UNLOCKING]
LOCKS (2)
A5   38: 5 youth," said the sage, as he shook his grey locks, / "I kept all my limbs very supple / By the use of this
A1   9:37 the doors of the hall; but, alas! either the locks were too large, or the key was too small, but at any
LODGING-HOUSES (1)
A2   18:24 in the sand with wooden spades, then a row of lodging-houses, and behind them a railway station.) However,
LOGIC (1)
T4   139: 9 would be; but as it isn't, it ain't. That's logic."
LOLLING (1)
T9   192: 4 herself), "It'll never do for you to be lolling about on the grass like that! Queens have to be
LONDON (1)
A2   17: 1   doesn't signify: let's try Geography. London is the capital of Paris, and Paris is the capital of
LONELINESS (1)
T5   152:34 melancholy voice; and, at the thought of her loneliness, two large tears came rolling down her cheeks.
LONELY (3)
A3   26:41 Alice began to cry again, for she felt very lonely and low-spirited. In a little while, however, she again
T5   152:33   "Only it is so very lonely here!" Alice said in a melancholy voice; and, at the
A9   74:17 Mock Turtle in the distance, sitting sad and lonely on a little ledge of rock, and, as they came nearer,
LONG (70)
T3   132:22 it, after they had been talking together so long.
A12 99: 8 perhaps even with the dream of Wonderland of long ago; and how she would feel with all their simple sorrows
A2   19:24 history, Alice had no very clear notion how long ago anything had happened.) So she began again: "Ou est
T8   190:10 snorted like a buffalo--/ That summer evening long ago, / A-sitting on a gate."
T2   124: 5 and full in sight of the hill she had been so long aiming at.
T8   186:33   "Is it very long?" Alice asked, for she had heard a good deal of poetry
A3   24:17   "Mine is a long and sad tale!" said the Mouse, turning to Alice, and
A1   11: 2   poker will burn you if you hold it too long; and that, if you cut your finger very deeply with a
T1   110:11 phrase "Let's pretend." She had had quite a long argument with her sister only the day before--all because
A3   21: 8 them all her life. Indeed, she had quite a long argument with the Lory, who at last turned sulky, and
A6   51:13   "--so long as I get somewhere," Alice added as an explanation.
A12 96:24 the ink, that was trickling down his face, as long as it lasted.)
A11 88:38   she decided to remain where she was as long as there was room for her.
A7   57: 8 "but you could keep it to half-past one as long as you liked."
T9   198:10 opened a little way, and a creature with a long beak put its head out for a moment and said "No
T5   153:30   Be-e-ehh!" The last word ended in a long bleat, so like a sheep that Alice quite started.
T3   129:20 never do to go down among them without a good long branch to brush them away--and what fun it'll be when
A10 82: 8 different, and then the Mock Turtle drew a long breath, and said "That's very curious!"
T5   153:10 said in a pitying tone. "Try again: draw a long breath, and shut your eyes."
A6   51: 2 good-natured, she thought: still it had very long claws and a great many teeth, so she felt that it ought
A2   20: 5 bright-eyed terrier, you know, with oh, such long curly brown hair! And it'll fetch things when you throw
A6   51:16 to do that," said the Cat, "if you only walk long enough."
T6   159:32   "That last line is much too long for the poetry," she added, almost out loud, forgetting
A12 98:24   The long grass rustled at her feet as the White Rabbit hurried by
A7   60:42   Once more she found herself in the long hall, and close to the little glass table. "Now, I'll
TC   209: 7   Long has paled that sunny sky: / Echoes fade and memories die:
A4   34:10 top, with its arms folded, quietly smoking a long hookah, and taking not the smallest notice of her or of
T3   137:27 of that before--But I ca'n't stay there long. I'll just call and say 'How d'ye do?' and ask them the
T4   139:37 somehow I felt as if I'd been singing it a long long time!"
A1   9:28 no longer to be seen: she found herself in a long, low hall, which was lit up by a row of lamps hanging
A1   9:23 was all dark overhead: before her was another long passage, and the White Rabbit was still in sight,
T6   168:14   There was a long pause.
T6   166:32   "In summer, when the days are long, / Perhaps you'll understand the song:
A2   16: 4 Ada," she said, "for her hair goes in such long ringlets, and mine doesn't go in ringlets at all; and I'm
T6   166:36   "I will, if I can remember it so long," said Alice.
T8   186:35   "It's long," said the Knight, "but it's very, very beautiful.
T4   147:41 of a fight, but I don't care about going on long," said Tweedledum. "What's the time now?"
T3   135:21 getting quite chilly with sitting still so long, she got up and walked on.
T4   140:19 ventured to interrupt him. "If it's very long," she said, as politely as she could, "would you please
A4   30:13   There was a long silence after this, and Alice could only hear whispers

LONG (cont.)

A9	74:34	These words were followed by a very long silence, broken only by an occasional exclamation of
T6	159:17	very provoking," Humpty Dumpty said after a long silence, looking away from Alice as he spoke, "to be
A5	43:37	It was so long since she had been anything near the right size, that it
A12	98: 4	Alice dear!" said her sister. "Why, what a long sleep you've had!"
A3	25: 1	"It is a long tail, certainly," said Alice, looking down with wonder at
A3t	21: 1	A CAUCUS-RACE AND A LONG TALE
A7	58: 2	twinkle, twinkle, twinkle--" and went on so long that they had to pinch it to make it stop.
T4	139:37	I felt as if I'd been singing it a long long time!"
T2	127:17	to somewhere else--if you ran very fast for a long time as we've been doing."
T9	198:12	Alice knocked and rang in vain for a long time; but at last a very old Frog, who was sitting under
T1	118: 6	He took his vorpal sword in hand: / Long time the manxome foe he sought--/ So rested he by the
T8	182:15	This took a long time to manage, though Alice held the bag open very
A7	56:17	because it stays the same year for such a long time together."
A3	23:18	a great deal of thought, and it stood for a long time with one finger pressed upon its forehead (the
A4	32: 1	of what?" thought Alice. But she had not long to doubt, for the next moment a shower of little pebbles
T8	190:25	slowly away into the forest. "It wo'n't take long to see him off, I expect," Alice said to herself, as she
T2	121:10	you're the right colour, and that goes a long way."
A4	32:44	a very little way forwards each time and a long way back, and barking hoarsely all the while, till at
T6	165: 7	called 'wabe' you know, because it goes a long way before it, and a long way behind it--"
T6	165: 7	because it goes a long way before it, and a long way behind it--"
T6	165: 8	"And a long way beyond it on each side," Alice added.
T3	137:21	seem likely to happen. She went on and on, a long way, but wherever the road divided, there were sure to be
T7	176:25	"All round the town?" he said. "That's a good long way. Did you go by the old bridge, or the market-place?
T5	156:18	elbow-deep, to get hold of the rushes a good long way down before breaking them off--and for a while Alice
T2	123:45	for the Queen (whom she spied out at last, a long way off), she thought she would try the plan, this time,
A10	81: 6	got thrown out to sea. So they had to fall a long way. So they got their tails fast in their mouths. So
T5	152:38	what a great girl you are. Consider what a long way you've come to-day. Consider what o'clock it is.
T6	168:39	as it was a great comfort to have such a long word to say) "of all the unsatisfactory people I ever met
A3	22:32	"I don't know the meaning of half those long words, and, what's more, I don't believe you do either!"
T8	190:17	direction to which he pointed. "I sha'n't be long. You'll wait and wave your handkerchief when I get to

LONGED (2)

A10	83: 8	dreadfully puzzled by the whole thing, and longed to change the subject.
A1	10: 3	the loveliest garden you ever saw. How she longed to get out of that dark hall, and wander about among

LONGER (5)

A4	30:21	I'm sure I don't want to stay in here any longer!"
T9	204:19	of all the mischief--but the Queen was no longer at her side--she had suddenly dwindled down to the size
T9	204:13	"I ca'n't stand this any longer!" she cried, as she jumped up and seized the tablecloth
A9	72:16	"Pray don't trouble yourself to say it any longer than that," said Alice.
A1	9:28	she turned the corner, but the Rabbit was no longer to be seen: she found herself in a long, low hall,

LONGEST (1)

T4	140:15	"'The Walrus and the Carpenter' is the longest," Tweedledum replied, giving his brother an

LONGING (1)

T9	200:17	it, rather uncomfortable at the silence, and longing for some one to speak.

LONGITUDE (2)

A1	8:37	not the slightest idea what Latitude was, or Longitude either, but she thought they were nice grand words
A1	8:35	distance--but then I wonder what Latitude or Longitude I've got to?" (Alice had not the slightest idea what

LOOK (65)

A2	15: 6	own feet! And how odd the directions will look!
T9	200:22	"You look a little shy: let me introduce you to that leg of mutton
A1	8:12	she had plenty of time as she went down to look about her, and to wonder what was going to happen next.
T9	203:22	in all directions: "and very like birds they look," Alice thought to herself, as well as she could in the
T5	154: 4	Alice said very gently. "I should like to look all round me first, if I might."
T5	154: 6	if you like," said the Sheep; "but you ca'n't look all round you--unless you've got eyes at the back of your
T7	170:14	either. They're both gone to the town. Just look along the road, and tell me if you can see either of them
A4	34: 6	it, it occurred to her that she might as well look and see what was on top of it.
T1	110:38	that may be only pretence, just to make it look as if they had a fire. Well then, the books are something
A10	80: 3	snail replied "Too far, too far!", and gave a look askance--/ Said he thanked the whiting kindly, but he
A8	68: 1	"A cat may look at a king," said Alice. "I've read that in some book, but
A11	86:19	if you want to see how he did it), he did not look at all comfortable, and it was certainly not becoming.
T12	207:15	and put the kitten and the Queen to look at each other. "Now Kitty!" she cried, clapping her hands
T5	153:40	and every now and then leaving off to look at her through a great pair of spectacles.
T4	144:28	"Come and look at him!" the brothers cried, and they each took one of
A3	26:29	Why, she'll eat a little bird as soon as look at it!"
T9	201:25	word to say in reply: she could only sit and look at it and gasp.
T12	207:18	("But it wouldn't look at it," she said, when she was explaining the thing
T6	160:37	History of England, that is. Now, take a good look at me! I'm one that has spoken to a King, I am: mayhap
A8	67:44	be impertinent," said the King, "and don't look at me like that!" He got behind Alice as he spoke.
A11	86:18	King; and, as he wore his crown over the wig (look at the frontispiece if you want to see how he did it), he
T1	119: 1	the rest of the house is like! Let's have a look at the garden first!" She was out of the room in a moment
T3	134: 5	Alice went on, after she had taken a good look at the insect with its head on fire, and had thought to
A9	73:23	sun. (If you don't know what a Gryphon is, look at the picture.) "Up, lazy thing!" said the Queen, "and
A11	90:29	my tea," said the Hatter, with an anxious look at the Queen, who was reading the list of singers.
A11	86: 9	so good, that it made Alice quite hungry to look at them--"I wish they'd get the trial done," she thought,
A1	8:13	was going to happen next. First, she tried to look down and make out what she was coming to, but it was too
T1	110:22	if you sat up and folded your arms, you'd look exactly like her. Now do try, there's a dear!" And Alice
T8W	19: 6	They said it did not fit, and so / It made me look extremely plain: / But what was I to do, you know? / My
A1	10:20	not going to do that in a hurry. "No, I'll look first," she said, "and see whether it's marked 'poison'
T8	188: 1	He said 'I look for butterflies / That sleep among the wheat: / I make
A4	29:21	Alice knew it was the Rabbit coming to look for her, and she trembled till she shook the house, quite

LOOK (cont.)

T8	185:17	Alice ran to the side of the ditch to look for him. She was rather startled by the fall, as for some
T9	194:18	"Why, look here!" the Red Queen cried. "The dog would lose its
T5	154: 5	"You may look in front of you, and on both sides, if you like," said
T8	190:17	he added as Alice turned with an eager look in the direction to which he pointed. "I sha'n't be long.
T6	163:18	to be done right--though I haven't time to look it over thoroughly just now--and that shows that there
T3	133: 4	bush, you'll see a Rocking-horse-fly, if you look. It's made entirely of wood, and gets about by swinging
A12	95:36	The Knave shook his head sadly. "Do I look like it?" he said. (Which he certainly did not, being
A9	72: 4	last remark. "It's a vegetable. It doesn't look like one, but it is."
T7	174:21	watching him. Suddenly she brightened up. "Look, look!" she cried, pointing eagerly. "There's the White
T6	168:32	"It wouldn't look nice," Alice objected. But Humpty Dumpty only shut his
T3	137: 8	And, dear me! you're a human child!" A sudden look of alarm came into its beautiful brown eyes, and in
A8	67:41	"I don't like the look of it at all," said the King: "however, it may kiss my
A9	74: 4	the Gryphon. Alice did not quite like the look of the creature, but on the whole she thought it would be
A6	49:35	for a baby: altogether Alice did not like the look of the thing at all. "But perhaps it was only sobbing,"
A8	68:14	missed their turns, and she did not like the look of things at all, as the game was in such confusion that
T3	133:12	"Look on the branch above your head," said the Gnat, "and there
A8	62: 5	came up to them, she heard one of them say "Look out now, Five! Don't go splashing paint over me like
A12	93:31	could see this, as she was near enough to look over their slates; "but it doesn't matter a bit," she
T8	186:30	Alice could only look puzzled: she was thinking of the pudding.
T5	149:35	best to get the hair into order. "Come, you look rather better now!" she said, after altering most of the
T7	174:21	him. Suddenly she brightened up. "Look, look!" she cried, pointing eagerly. "There's the White Queen
T1	110: 2	I do so wish it was true! I'm sure the woods look sleepy in the autumn, when the leaves are getting brown.
A8	69: 4	last remark that had made the whole party look so grave and anxious.)
T8W	19: 3	had noticed the effect, / They said I did not look so nice / As they had ventured to expect.
T1	108:18	the kitten's neck, just to see how it would look: this led to a scramble, in which the ball rolled down
A2	15:17	as she could do, lying down on one side, to look through into the garden with one eye; but to get through
A2	17:22	saying 'Come up again, dear!' I shall only look up and say 'Who am I, then? Tell me that first, and then,
A4	32:26	little sharp bark just over her head made her look up in a great hurry.
A8	66:11	its head, it would twist itself round and look up in her face, with such a puzzled expression that she
T2	124: 7	said the Red Queen. "And where are you going? Look up, speak nicely, and don't twiddle your fingers all the
T4	147:30	"Do I look very pale?" said Tweedledum, coming up to have his helmet
T8	190: 1	so / Of that old man I used to know--/ Whose look was mild, whose speech was slow, / Whose hair was whiter
T1	112: 3	room. The very first thing she did was to look whether there was a fire in the fireplace, and she was

LOOKED (103)

T12	207:20	its head, and pretended not to see it: but it looked a little ashamed of itself, so I think it must have
T6	163:17	as she turned it round for him. "I thought it looked a little queer. As I was saying, that seems to be done
T5	149: 1	She caught the shawl as she spoke, and looked about for the owner: in another moment the White Queen
T5	153:33	up in wool. Alice rubbed her eyes, and looked again. She couldn't make out what had happened at all.
A4	33:14	great question certainly was "What?" Alice looked all round her at the flowers and the blades of grass,
A7	54:14	Alice looked all round the table, but there was nothing on it but
A1	10: 2	larger than a rat-hole: she knelt down and looked along the passage into the loveliest garden you ever
A11	91:11	The King looked anxiously at the White Rabbit, who said, in a low voice
A8	65:29	said the Rabbit in a low hurried tone. He looked anxiously over his shoulder as he spoke, and then
A11	86:35	and the King put on his spectacles and looked anxiously round, to make out who was talking.
A10	79: 1	sat down again very sadly and quietly, and looked at Alice.
A12	93:37	Everybody looked at Alice.
T9	199:10	whether the paint would come off: then he looked at Alice.
A10	78: 2	the back of one flapper across his eyes. He looked at Alice and tried to speak, but, for a minute or two,
A8	65:20	The soldiers were silent, and looked at Alice, as the question was evidently meant for her.
T7	176: 5	The Lion looked at Alice wearily. "Are you animal--or vegetable--or
T3	136: 7	Just then a Fawn came wandering by: it looked at Alice with its large gentle eyes, but didn't seem at
T4	139:12	But the fat little men only looked at each other and grinned.
T9	192:31	The two Queens looked at each other, and the Red Queen remarked, with a
A5	35: 1	The Caterpillar and Alice looked at each other for some time in silence: at last the
T8	179:25	he got on again, and the two Knights sat and looked at each other for some time without speaking. Alice
T4	138:11	pay, you know. Wax-works weren't made to be looked at for nothing. Nohow!"
A8	63:35	came opposite to Alice, they all stopped and looked at her, and the Queen said, severely, "Who is this?"
T5	149: 7	The White Queen only looked at her in a helpless frightened sort of way, and kept
A2	19:18	to a mouse--a mouse--O mouse!") The mouse looked at her rather inquisitively, and seemed to her to wink
T4	140:19	The eldest Oyster looked at him, / But never a word he said: / The eldest Oyster
T4	147:42	Tweedledee looked at his watch, and said "Half-past four."
T8W	17: 9	the handkerchief as he spoke, and Alice looked at his wig in great surprise. It was bright yellow like
A7	56: 8	then he dipped it into his cup of tea, and looked at it again: but he could think of nothing better to
A1	7:17	took a watch out of its waistcoat-pocket, and looked at it, and then hurried on, Alice started to her feet,
T6	163:13	Humpty Dumpty took the book and looked at it carefully. "That seems to be done right--" he
A7	56: 7	The March Hare took the watch and looked at it gloomily: then he dipped it into his cup of tea,
T9	200:20	waiters set a leg of mutton before Alice, who looked at it rather anxiously, as she had never had to carve a
T8	181:16	and with the lid hanging open. Alice looked at it with great curiosity.
A9	75: 6	Gryphon; and then they both sat silent and looked at poor Alice, who felt ready to sink into the earth.
T9	199: 8	The Frog looked at the door with his large dull eyes for a minute: then
A10	82:13	repeat something now. Tell her to begin." He looked at the Gryphon as if he thought it had some kind of
A12	93: 4	Alice looked at the jury-box, and saw that, in her haste, she had
A11	88:12	The Hatter looked at the March Hare, who had followed him into the court,
T5	153:32	She looked at the Queen, who seemed to have suddenly wrapped
T3	133: 8	Alice looked at the Rocking-horse-fly with great interest, and made
A1	8:15	but it was too dark to see anything: then she looked at the sides of the well, and noticed that they were
A9	74:23	So they went up to the Mock Turtle, who looked at them with large eyes full of tears, but said nothing
T4	146:21	his hair. "It's spoilt, of course!" Here he looked at Tweedledee, who immediately sat down on the ground,
A8	63: 5	Five and Seven said nothing, but looked at Two. Two began, in a low voice, "Why, the fact is,

LOOKED (cont.)

A7	60:32	the least notice of her going, though she looked back once or twice, half hoping that they would call
T6	163: 4	Humpty Dumpty looked doubtful. "I'd rather see that done on paper," he said.
A2	14: 4	that ever was! Good-bye, feet!" (for when she looked down at her feet, they seemed to be almost out of sight
A2	18: 1	As she said this she looked down at her hands, and was surprised to see that she
A10	81:19	Alice looked down at them, and considered a little before she gave
A6	50:10	when it grunted again, so violently, that she looked down into its face in some alarm. This time there could
T8	184:41	The Knight looked down proudly at his helmet, which hung from the saddle.
A5	42:10	to be found: all she could see, when she looked down, was an immense length of neck, which seemed to
T7	175:26	The Unicorn looked dreamily at Alice, and said "Talk, child."
T8	179:26	other for some time without speaking. Alice looked from one to the other in some bewilderment.
A6	51: 1	The Cat only grinned when it saw Alice. It looked good-natured, she thought: still it had _very_ long claws
T5	154:12	oddest part of it all was that, whenever she looked hard at any shelf, to make out exactly what it had on
A6	50: 1	it was only sobbing," she thought, looked into its eyes again, to see if there were any tears.
T6	159:19	"I said you looked like an egg, Sir," Alice gently explained. "And some
T8W	15: 6	banks of the lake were blue and white, and looked like china. While tasting the treacle, they had a sad
T9	202:26	edges of the table--and three of them (who looked like kangaroos) scrambled into the dish of roast mutton
A4	34: 2	of grass, but she could not see anything that looked like the right thing to eat or drink under the
T3	135:23	with a wood on the other side of it: it looked much darker than the last wood, and Alice felt a little
T4	147:31	(He _called_ it a helmet, though it certainly looked much more like a saucepan.)
T1	115:29	Alice looked on with great interest as the King took an enormous
T2	128: 4	all the pegs put in by this time, and Alice looked on with great interest as she returned to the tree, and
T8W	16:12	Alice looked pityingly at him. "Tying up the face is very good for
A12	94:18	the queerest thing about it." (The jury all looked puzzled.)
T1	115:34	The poor King looked puzzled and unhappy, and struggled with the pencil for
A8	63: 2	and he checked himself suddenly: the others looked round also, and all of them bowed low.
T7	173:28	Hatta looked round and nodded, and went on with his bread-and-butter
A8	63:13	was a sound of many footsteps, and Alice looked round, eager to see the Queen.
T2	123:28	Alice looked round eagerly and found that it was the Red Queen.
T2	127:12	Alice looked round her in great surprise. "Why, I do believe we've
T4	148: 6	Tweedledum looked round him with a satisfied smile. "I don't suppose," he
T8	179:21	voice broke in "Ahoy! Ahoy! Check!" and Alice looked round in some surprise for the new enemy.
T7	173:31	Hatta looked round once more, and this time a tear or two trickled
T3	133: 9	that it must have been just repainted, it looked so bright and sticky; and then she went on.
T4	139:13	They looked so exactly like a couple of great schoolboys, that
A11	86: 8	with a large dish of tarts upon it: they looked so good, that it made Alice quite hungry to look at
A3	24: 5	the whole thing very absurd, but they all looked so grave that she did not dare to laugh; and, as she
T8	185: 6	The Knight looked so solemn about it that Alice did not dare to laugh.
T6	160:23	if I did--" Here he pursed up his lips, and looked so solemn and grand that Alice could hardly help
T8	184:38	He looked so vexed at the idea, that Alice changed the subject
T5	154:18	in vainly pursuing a large bright thing that looked sometimes like a doll and sometimes like a work-box,
T2	122:34	"I never saw anybody that looked stupider," a Violet said, so suddenly, that Alice quite
T9	201:12	But the Red Queen looked sulky, and growled "Pudding----Alice: Alice--Pudding.
T8	186: 2	The Knight looked surprised at the question. "What does it matter where
T6	162:18	she added in dismay, for Humpty Dumpty looked thoroughly offended, and she began to wish she hadn't
T9	196:25	The White Queen looked timidly at Alice, who felt she _ought_ to say something
A4	34: 4	the same height as herself; and, when she had looked under it, and on both sides of it, and behind it, it
A8	62: 9	On which Seven looked up and said "That's right, Five! Always lay the blame
A9	72:31	was linked into hers began to tremble. Alice looked up, and there stood the Queen in front of them, with
A6	52:27	as it was in March." As she said this, she looked up, and there was the Cat again, sitting on a branch of
A1	9:22	she jumped up on to her feet in a moment: she looked up, but it was all dark overhead: before her was
A3	26:43	of footsteps in the distance, and she looked up eagerly, half hoping that the Mouse had changed his
T4	146: 5	umbrella over himself and his brother, and looked up into it. "No, I don't think it is," he said: "at
T3	135:19	to have sighed itself away, for, when Alice looked up, there was nothing whatever to be seen on the twig,
A6	49:31	The baby grunted again, and Alice looked very anxiously into its face to see what was the matter
T3	135:38	on in this way when she reached the wood: it looked very cool and shady. "Well, at any rate it's a great
T8	183: 5	The Knight looked very much surprised, and a little offended at the
T7	175:43	had joined them while this was going on: he looked very tired and sleepy, and his eyes were half shut.
A8	68:32	while all the rest were quite silent, and looked very uncomfortable.

LOOKING (72) [See CURIOUS-LOOKING, QUEER-LOOKING, etc.]

T1	108:37	every bit of the worsted while I wasn't looking!
T8	187: 1	"No, you don't understand," the Knight said, looking a little vexed. "That's what the name is called. The
T1	112:10	Then she began looking about, and noticed that what could be seen from the
A8	67: 8	She was looking about for some way of escape, and wondering whether
T9	197:12	"What _am_ I to do?" exclaimed Alice, looking about in great perplexity, as first one round head,
T3	131:31	"Don't tease so," said Alice, looking about in vain to see where the voice came from. "If
A8	63:10	At this moment, Five, who had been anxiously looking across the garden, called out "The Queen! The Queen!"
T3	137:11	Alice stood looking after it, almost ready to cry with vexation at having
T3	129:37	Show your ticket, child!" the Guard went on, looking angrily at Alice. And a great many voices all said
A7	56: 2	butter wouldn't suit the works!" he added, looking angrily at the March Hare.
A4	27: 1	White Rabbit, trotting slowly back again, and looking anxiously about as it went, as if it had lost
A3	26: 7	always ready to make herself useful, and looking anxiously about her. "Oh, do let me help to undo it!"
T8W	13: 4	somebody _very_ unhappy there," she thought, looking anxiously back to see what was the matter. Something
A11	89:26	the Dormouse said--" the Hatter went on, looking anxiously round to see if he would deny it too; but
A3	24: 7	say, she simply bowed, and took the thimble, looking as solemn as she could.
A7	55: 6	wants cutting," said the Hatter. He had been looking at Alice for some time with great curiosity, and this
T5	155: 1	in the shelf next above the one she was looking at. "And this one is the most provoking of all--but
A11	86:11	seemed to be no chance of this; so she began looking at everything about her to pass away the time.
T3	136:10	it only started back a little, and then stood looking at her again.
T3	130:18	All this time the Guard was looking at her, first through a telescope, then through a

LOOKING (cont.)

T4	140: 1	Then they let go of Alice's hands, and stood	looking at her for a minute: there was a rather awkward pause,
T6	160: 2	to yourself like that," Humpty Dumpty said,	looking at her for the first time, "but tell me your name and
T5	155:10	pairs at once, and Alice couldn't help	looking at her in great astonishment.
T2	124:18	time for you to answer now," the Queen said	looking at her watch: "open your mouth a _little_ wider when you
T7	175:16	round instantly, and stood for some time	looking at her with an air of the deepest disgust.
T8W	20: 4	"Your wig fits very well," the Wasp murmured,	looking at her with an expression of admiration: "it's the
T8W	17:14	"What, you're a Bee, are you?" the Wasp said,	looking at her with more interest. "And you've got a comb.
A7	55:37	taken his watch out of his pocket, and was	looking at it uneasily, shaking it every now and then, and
A8	67:38	to?" said the King, coming up to Alice, and	looking at the Cat's head with great curiosity.
A6	45: 1	For a minute or two she stood	looking at the house, and wondering what to do next, when
A6	52:13	queer things happening. While she was still	looking at the place where it had been, it suddenly appeared
T5	154: 9	so she contented herself with turning round,	looking at the shelves as she came to them.
A12	95:32	on, spreading out the verses on his knee, and	looking at them with one eye; "I seem to see some meaning in
T6	159:18	Humpty Dumpty said after a long silence,	looking away from Alice as he spoke, "to be called an egg--
T6	159:22	"Some people," said Humpty Dumpty,	looking away from her as usual, "have no more sense than a
T9	195:25	"Which reminds me--" the White Queen said,	looking down and nervously clasping and unclasping her hands,
A4	32:27	An enormous puppy was	looking down at her with large round eyes, and feebly
A3	25: 1	"It _is_ a long tail, certainly," said Alice,	looking down with wonder at the Mouse's tail; "but why do you
T2	123:44	A little provoked, she drew back, and, after	looking everywhere for the Queen (whom she spied out at last,
T9	196: 5	in," the White Queen went on, "because he was	looking for a hippopotamus. Now, as it happened, there wasn't
A5	43:26	deal to _me_," said Alice hastily; "but I'm not	looking for eggs, as it happens; and, if I was, I shouldn't
A5	43:23	the Pigeon the opportunity of adding "You're	looking for eggs, I know _that_ well enough; and what does it
A8	69:13	and the executioner ran wildly up and down,	looking for it, while the rest of the party went back to the
A4	27: 6	Alice guessed in a moment that it was	looking for the fan and the pair of white kid-gloves, and she
A8	65:14	soldiers wandered about for a minute or two,	looking for them, and then quietly marched off after the
T9	201: 5	she said, taking up the knife and fork, and	looking from one Queen to the other.
A12	93: 3	all," he repeated with great emphasis,	looking hard at Alice as he said so.
T7	170:20	All this was lost on Alice, who was still	looking intently along the road, shading her eyes with one
T4	147: 7	and shutting his mouth and his large eyes--"	looking more like a fish than anything else," Alice thought.
T2	125:19	some minutes Alice stood without speaking,	looking out in all directions over the country--and a most
T12	207:26	"Snowdrop, my pet!" she went on,	looking over her shoulder at the White Kitten, which was still
A7	56:11	Alice had been	looking over his shoulder with some curiosity. "What a funny
T1	115:39	"What manner of things?" said the Queen,	looking over the book (in which Alice had put 'The White
A11	86:37	Alice could see, as well as if she were	looking over their shoulders, that all the jurors were writing
T8	184:23	the last time you picked me up, that I was	looking rather thoughtful?"
T1	108: 2	ought, Dinah, you know you ought!" she added,	looking reproachfully at the old cat, and speaking in as cross
A8	68: 7	"Off with his head!" she said without even	looking round.
T4	140:12	What shall I repeat to her?" said Tweedledee,	looking round at Tweedledum with great solemn eyes, and not
T7	175: 1	her, no doubt," the King said, without even	looking round. "That wood's full of them."
A12	96:25	"Then the words don't _fit_ you," said the King	looking round the court with a smile. There was a dead silence
T7	176:17	have for the crown _now_!" the Unicorn said,	looking slyly up at the crown, which the poor King was nearly
T9	203:13	The candles all grew up to the ceiling,	looking something like a bed of rushes with fireworks at the
A5	41:33	Alice remained	looking thoughtfully at the mushroom for a minute, trying to
T9	192:17	"Please, would you tell me--" she began,	looking timidly at the Red Queen.
A11	88:31	he kept shifting from one foot to the other,	looking uneasily at the Queen, and in his confusion he bit a
T1	114:13	"What volcano?" said the King,	looking anxiously into the fire, as if he thought that was
T2	120:13	"It's no use talking about it," Alice said,	looking up at the house and pretending it was arguing with her
T5	154: 1	it you want to buy?" the Sheep said at last,	looking up for a moment from her knitting.
T5	156: 9	to _me_ about 'em," the Sheep said, without	looking up from her knitting: "I didn't put 'em there, and I'm
A12	98:19	upon her knee, and the bright eager eyes were	looking up into hers--she could hear the very tones of her
A6	46:21	and I could let you out, you know." He was	looking up into the sky all the time he was speaking, and this
T6	163:44	like a reasonable child," said Humpty Dumpty,	looking very much pleased. "I meant by 'impenetrability' that

LOOKING-GLASS (21)

T2	120:15	yet. I know I should have to get through the	Looking-glass again--back into the old room--and there'd be an
T1	118:32	haste, I shall have to go back through the	Looking-glass, before I've seen what the rest of the house is
T1	116:14	a bright thought struck her. "Why, it's a	Looking-glass book, of course! And, if I hold it up to a glass
T7	177:11	"You don't know how to manage	Looking-glass cakes," the Unicorn remarked. "Hand it round
T9	199:37	"'O	Looking-Glass creatures,' quoth Alice, 'draw near! / 'Tis an
T9	199:26	in hand, I've a crown on my head. / Let the	Looking-Glass creatures, whatever they be, / Come and dine
T1	113: 1	know you can only see the back of it in the	Looking-glass) had got the face of a little old man, and
T1t	107: 1		LOOKING-GLASS HOUSE
T1	110:31	so much, I'll tell you all my ideas about	Looking-glass House. First, there's the room you can see
T1	110:29	she added, "I'll put you through into	Looking-glass House. How would you like _that_?
T1	111: 2	can just see a little peep of the passage in	Looking-glass House, if you leave the door of our drawing-room
T1	111: 6	it would be if we could only get through into	Looking-glass House! I'm sure it's got, oh! such beautiful
T1	110:43	"How would you like to live in	Looking-glass House, Kitty? I wonder if they'd give you milk
T3t	129: 1		LOOKING-GLASS INSECTS
T1	110:44	if they'd give you milk in there? Perhaps	Looking-glass milk isn't good to drink--but oh, Kitty! now we
T1	112: 2	glass, and had jumped lightly down into the	Looking-glass room. The very first thing she did was to look
T1	110:27	So, to punish it, she held it up to the	Looking-glass, that it might see how sulky it was, "--and if
A4	28: 2	fell upon a little bottle that stood near the	looking-glass. There was no label this time with the words
T8	187:17	that Alice saw in her journey Through The	Looking-Glass, this was the one that she always remembered
T12	207: 4	been along with me, Kitty--all through the	Looking-glass world. Did you know it, dear?"
T9	199:24	"To the	Looking-Glass world it was Alice that said / 'I've a sceptre

LOOK-OUT (1)

A5	42:39	eggs," said the Pigeon; "but I must be on the	look-out for serpents, night and day! Why, I haven't had a

LOOKS (2)

T7	178: 8	* * * Unicorn rise to their feet, with angry	looks at being interrupted in their feast, before she dropped
A1	12:10	she tried to fancy what the flame of a candle	looks like after the candle is blown out, for she could not

LOOSE (2)
T8   187:23   quietly moving about, with the reins hanging loose on his neck, cropping the grass at her feet--and the
A4   30:30   of this rope--Will the roof bear?--Mind that loose slate--Oh, it's coming down! Heads below!" (a loud

LORY (7)
A3   26:25   might venture to ask the question?" said the Lory.
A2   20:23   into it: there was a Duck and a Dodo, a Lory and an Eaglet, and several other curious creatures. Alice
A3   26:16   "What a pity it wouldn't stay!" sighed the Lory, as soon as it was quite out of sight. And an old Crab
A3   22:10   "Not I!" said the Lory, hastily.
A3   21:11   without knowing how old it was, and as the Lory positively refused to tell its age, there was no more to
A3   21: 9   she had quite a long argument with the Lory, who at last turned sulky, and would only say, "I'm older
A3   22: 7   "Ugh!" said the Lory, with a shiver.

LOSE (6)
T5   156:35   that the rushes had begun to fade, and to lose all their scent and beauty, from the very moment that she
T3   135:33   the advertisements, you know, when people lose dogs--'answers to the name of "Dash": had on a brass
T3   135:29   of my name when I go in? I shouldn't like to lose it at all--because they'd have to give me another, and it
T9   194:18   here!" the Red Queen cried. "The dog would lose its temper, wouldn't it?"
T3   134:23   and remarked "I suppose you don't want to lose your name?"
A3   26:19   my dear! Let this be a lesson to you never to lose your temper!" "Hold your tongue, Ma!" said the young Crab

LOSING (2)
T8   184:11   "It's too ridiculous!" cried Alice, losing all her patience this time. "You ought to have a wooden
A5   41:12   her life before, and she felt that she was losing her temper.

LOST (11)
T9   204: 9   There was not a moment to be lost. Already several of the guests were lying down in the
A5   41:42   but she felt that there was no time to be lost, as she was shrinking rapidly: so she set to work at once
A1   9:24   down it. There was no moment to be lost: away went Alice like the wind, and was just in time to
T9   193:27   "I don't know," said Alice. "I lost count."
T3   137:12   almost ready to cry with vexation at having lost her dear little fellow-traveler so suddenly. "However, I
T2   124:10   explained, as well as she could, that she had lost her way.
T7   170:20   All this was lost on Alice, who was still looking intently along the road,
T2   123:41   towards the Red Queen. To her surprise she lost sight of her in a moment, and found herself walking in at
A4   27: 2   anxiously about as it went, as if it had lost something; and she heard it muttering to itself, "The
T5   149:33   in it!" the Queen said with a sigh. "And I lost the comb yesterday."
T6   166: 4   short for 'from home'--meaning that they'd lost their way, you know."

LOT (2)
T6   163:41   not verbs--however, I can manage the whole lot of them! Impenetrability! That's what I say!"
T6   164: 5   "When I make a word do a lot of work like that," said Humpty Dumpty, "I always pay it

LOUD (20) [See also ALOUD]
A9   72:22   that!" But she did not venture to say it out loud.
T4   138:17   and she could hardly help saying them out loud:--
T6   168: 5   and proud: / He said, 'You needn't shout so loud!'
T9   197:11   both Queens were fast asleep, and snoring loud.
T12   207: 1   "Your Red Majesty shouldn't purr so loud," Alice said, rubbing her eyes, and addressing the kitten
T6   167:21   I said it very loud and clear: / I went and shouted in his ear."
A6   49:28   leave it behind?" She said the last words out loud, and the little thing grunted in reply (it had left off
A4   31:29   the Rabbit's voice. And Alice called out, as loud as she could, "If you do, I'll set Dinah at you!"
T4   147:28   Alice laughed loud: but she managed to turn it into a cough, for fear of
A4   30:30   slate--Oh, it's coming down! Heads below!" (a loud crash)--"Now, who did that?--It was Bill, I fancy--Who's
T4   144:54   up into a sort of untidy heap, and snoring loud--"fit to snore his head off!" as Tweedledum remarked.
T6   159:33   long for the poetry," she added, almost out loud, forgetting that Humpty Dumpty would hear her.
A11   86:33   "Stupid things!" Alice began in a loud indignant voice; but she stopped herself hastily, for the
T5   155:33   Alice: "you've said it very often--and very loud. Please, where are the crabs?"
T8   179:12   moment her thoughts were interrupted by a loud shouting of "Ahoy! Ahoy! Check!" and a Knight, dressed in
T4   145:16   He shouted this so loud that Alice couldn't help saying "Hush! You'll be waking
T5   152: 2   when the Queen began screaming, so loud that she had to leave the sentence unfinished. "Oh, oh,
A8   64:15   "Get up!" said the Queen in a shrill, loud voice, and the three gardeners instantly jumped up, and
T3   131: 4   in white, shut his eyes and said in a loud voice, "She ought to know her way to the ticket-office,
T8   183:17   of riding," the Knight suddenly began in a loud voice, waving his right arm as he spoke, "is to keep--"

LOUDER (2)
T2   121: 6   can," said the Tiger-lily. "And a great deal louder."
A6   46:32   "How am I to get in?" asked Alice again, in a louder tone.

LOUDLY (3)
A8   64: 8   "Nonsense!" said Alice, very loudly and decidedly, and the Queen was silent.
A6   45: 5   she would have called him a fish)--and rapped loudly at the door with his knuckles. It was opened by another
A12   97: 1   "Stuff and nonsense!" said Alice loudly. "The idea of having the sentence first!"

LOVE (5)
A2   15:10   Hearthrug, near the Fender, (with Alice's love).
T7   170:30   "I love my love with an H," Alice couldn't help beginning,
A9   70:33   the moral of that is--'Oh, 'tis love, 'tis love, that makes the world go round!'"
A9   70:33   Duchess: "and the moral of that is--'Oh, 'tis love, 'tis love, that makes the world go round!'"
T7   170:30   "I love my love with an H," Alice couldn't help beginning, "because he is

-LOVED [See BELOVED]

LOVE-GIFT (1)
TI   103: 6   / Thy loving smile will surely hail / The love-gift of a fairy-tale.

LOVELIEST (1)
A1   10: 3   down and looked along the passage into the loveliest garden you ever saw. How she longed to get out of

LOVELY
A1   12: 5   for going through the little door into that lovely garden. First, however, she waited for a few minutes to
A4   32:20   the second thing is to find my way into that lovely garden. I think that will be the best plan."
T5   156:25   over!" she said to herself. "Oh, what a lovely one! Only I couldn't quite reach it." And it certainly
T5   156:29   the boat glided by, there was always a more lovely one that she couldn't reach.

LOVELY (cont.)
  T9   201:37   to Alice's ear, "her White Majesty knows a lovely riddle--all in poetry--all about fishes. Shall she
  T4   144:31   "Isn't he a lovely sight?" said Tweedledum.
LOVES (2)
  T1   109:10   nice and soft it sounds! I wonder if the snow loves the trees and fields, that it kisses them so gently? And
  T7   171:11   "This young lady loves you with an H," the King said, introducing Alice in the
LOVING (2)
  A12   99: 5   through all her riper years, the simple and loving heart of her childhood; and how she would gather about
  TI   103: 5   I and thou / Are half a life asunder, / Thy loving smile will surely hail / The love-gift of a fairy-tale
LOVINGLY (2)
  T3   137: 4   through the wood, Alice with her arms clasped lovingly round the soft neck of the Fawn, till they came out
  TC   209:15   tale to hear, / Eager eye and willing ear, / Lovingly shall nestle near.
LOW (18) [See BELOW]
  A8   63: 2   looked round also, and all of them bowed low.
  T4   142:16   And then they rested on a rock / Conveniently low: / And all the little Oysters stood / And waited in a row.
  T8   190: 7   to and fro, / And muttered mumblingly and low, / As if his mouth were full of dough, / Who snorted like
  A1   9:39   on the second time round, she came upon a low curtain she had not noticed before, and behind it was a
  A1   9:28   to be seen: she found herself in a long, low hall, which was lit up by a row of lamps hanging from the
  A8   65:29   "Hush! Hush!" said the Rabbit in a low hurried tone. He looked anxiously over his shoulder as he
  T1   115:20   talking together in a frightened whisper--so low, that Alice could hardly hear what they said.
  A2   15:33   the Rabbit came near her, she began, in a low, timid voice, "If you please, Sir--" The Rabbit started
  A12   94: 2   your verdict," he said to the jury, in a low trembling voice.
  A2   20:18   passion, Alice thought), and it said, in a low trembling voice, "Let us get to the shore, and then I'll
  A8   67:31   How do you like the Queen?" said the Cat in a low voice.
  T9   196: 1   saw it too," the White Queen went on in a low voice, more as if she were talking to herself. "He came to
  T4   147:34   "I'm very brave, generally," he went on in a low voice: "only to-day I happen to have a headache."
  A9   73:18   off together, Alice heard the King say in a low voice, to the company, generally, "You are all pardoned."
  A8   63: 6   nothing, but looked at Two. Two began, in a low voice, "Why, the fact is, you see, Miss, this here ought
  A11   91:12   anxiously at the White Rabbit, who said, in a low voice, "Your Majesty must cross-examine this witness."
  A2   19:44   subject! Our family always hated cats: nasty, low, vulgar things! Don't let me hear the name again!"
  A9   72:34   day, your Majesty!" the Duchess began in a low, weak voice.
LOWER (3)
  T8   186:17   holding his head down, and his voice getting lower and lower, "I don't believe that pudding ever was
  T8   186:17   head down, and his voice getting lower and lower, "I don't believe that pudding ever was cooked! In fact,
  A11   90:23   "I ca'n't go no lower," said the Hatter: "I'm on the floor, as it is."
LOWING (1)
  A12   99: 1   clamour of the busy farm-yard--while the lowing of the cattle in the distance would take the place of
LOW-SPIRITED (2)
  T8   186:21   him up, for the poor Knight seemed quite low-spirited about it.
  A3   26:41   to cry again, for she felt very lonely and low-spirited. In a little while, however, she again heard a
LUCKILY (3)
  A4   28:23   Luckily for Alice, the little magic bottle had now had its
  T2   127:39   Alice did not know what to say to this, but luckily the Queen did not wait for an answer, but went on. "At
  A3   23:27   her pocket, and pulled out a box of comfits (luckily the saltwater had not got into it), and handed them
LUGGAGE (1)
  T3   131: 9   on with "She'll have to go back from here as luggage!"
LULLABIES (1)
  T9   197: 1   direction: "and I don't know any soothing lullabies."
LULLABY (2)
  T9   196:37   her your nightcap--and sing her a soothing lullaby."
  A6   48:34   nursing her child again, singing a sort of lullaby to it as she did so, and giving it a violent shake at
LUMP (2)
  T9   197:14   down from her shoulder, and lay like a heavy lump in her lap. "I don't think it ever happened before, that
  T3   134:12   its body is a crust, and its head is a lump of sugar."
LUMPS (2)
  T9   196:15   and it went rolling round the room in great lumps--and knocking over the tables and things--till I was so
  T8W   14:22   tour in the Pantry, and have found five new lumps of white sugar, large and in fine condition. In coming
LYING (18)
  T8   179: 6   However, there was the great dish still lying at her feet, on which she had tried to cut the plum-cake
  T8W   14:16   as she picked up a newspaper which had been lying at his feet.
  T4   144:33   red night-cap on, with a tassel, and he was lying crumpled up into a sort of untidy heap, and snoring loud
  T7   176:10   round the plum-cake, Monster," the Lion said, lying down and putting his chin on his paws. "And sit down,
  T9   204:10   be lost. Already several of the guests were lying down in the dishes, and the soup ladle was walking up
  A2   15:16   Poor Alice! It was as much as she could do, lying down on one side, to look through into the garden with
  A4   28:18   room for this, and she tried the effect of lying down with one elbow against the door, and the other arm
  A9   73:22   They very soon came upon a Gryphon, lying fast asleep in the sun. (If you don't know what a
  T1   116: 1   There was a book lying near Alice on the table, and while she sat watching the
  A12   97:11   and tried to beat them off, and found herself lying on the bank, with her head in the lap of her sister, who
  T4   144:36   "I'm afraid he'll catch cold with lying on the damp grass," said Alice, who was a very
  A2   18:14   was shut again, and the little golden key was lying on the glass table as before, "and things are worse than
  A6   47:11   were the cook, and a large cat, which was lying on the hearth and grinning from ear to ear.
  A8   63:45   the rose-tree; for, you see, as they were lying on their faces, and the pattern on their backs was the
  T1   107:10   hard at work on the white kitten, which was lying quite still and trying to purr--no doubt feeling that it
  A8   63:44   pointing to the three gardeners who were lying round the rose-tree; for, you see, as they were lying on
  A1   12:31   her eye fell on a little glass box that was lying under the table: she opened it, and found in it a very
  T4   146:15   a trembling finger at a small white thing lying under the tree.

-M-

M (3)
    A7   60:16   of things--everything that begins with an M--"
    A7   60:17   "Why with an M?" said Alice
    A7   60:23   shriek, and went on: "--that begins with an M, such as mouse-traps, and the moon, and memory, and muchness
M-- (1)
    A9   72:28   the Duchess, "as pigs have to fly; and the m----"
MA (2)
    A2   19:25   had happened.) So she began again: "Ou est ma chatte?" which was the first sentence in her French
    A3   26:19   to lose your temper!" "Hold your tongue, Ma!" said the young Crab, a little snappishly. "You're enough
MA'AM (1)
    A1   8:44   the name of the country is, you know. Please, Ma'am, is this New Zealand? Or Australia?" (and she tried to
MABEL (4)
    A2   17:17   with tears again as she went on, "I must be Mabel after all, and I shall have to go and live in that poky
    A2   16: 6   in ringlets at all; and I'm sure I ca'n't be Mabel, for I know all sorts of things, and she, oh, she knows
    A2   17:20   No, I've made up my mind about it: if I'm Mabel, I'll stay down here. It'll be no use their putting
    A2   17: 3   I'm certain! I must have been changed for Mabel! I'll try and say 'How doth the little--'," and she
MACASSAR-OIL (1)
    T8   188:22   they make a stuff they call / Rowland's Macassar-Oil--/ Yet twopence-halfpenny is all / They give me
-MACHINES [See BATHING-MACHINES]
MAD (15)
    A6   51:21   Hare. Visit either you like: they're both mad."
    A6   51:24   the Cat: "we're all mad here. I'm mad. You're mad."
    A6   51:28   she went on: "And how do you know that you're mad?"
    A6   51:34   and wag my tail when I'm angry. Therefore I'm mad."
    A6   53:17   to herself "Suppose it should be raving mad after all! I almost wish I'd gone to see the Hatter
    A6   52:27   May, it wo'n't be raving mad--at least not so mad as it was in March." As she said this, she looked up, and
    A6   52:26   perhaps, as this is May, it wo'n't be raving mad--at least not so mad as it was in March." As she said this
    A6   51:23   ca'n't help that," said the Cat: "we're all mad here. I'm mad. You're mad."
    A6   51:22   "But I don't want to go among mad people," Alice remarked.
    A6   51:25   "How do you know I'm mad?" said Alice.
    A7t   54: 1   A MAD TEA-PARTY
    A10   78:37   creatures, who had been jumping about like mad things all this time, sat down again very sadly and
    A6   51:29   "To begin with," said the Cat, "a dog's not mad. You grant that?"
    A7   57:11   "We quarreled last March--just before he went mad, you know--" (pointing his teaspoon at the March Hare,)
    A6   51:24   that," said the Cat: "we're all mad here. I'm mad. You're mad."
MADE (55)
    A4   27:17   trying to explain the mistake that it had made.
    T9   194:40   useful questions?" she said. "How is bread made?"
    T7   174: 5   Hatta made a desperate effort, and swallowed a large piece of
    A6   50:16   up," she said to herself, "it would have made a dreadfully ugly child: but it makes rather a handsome
    T9   201: 1   The leg of mutton got up in the dish and made a little bow to Alice; and Alice returned the bow, not
    A11   88:23   exclaimed, turning to the jury, who instantly made a memorandum of the fact.
    A4   32:15   giving it something out of a bottle. They all made a rush at Alice the moment she appeared; but she ran off
    T6   161:22   Alice made a short calculation, and said "Seven years and six months
    A4   29:35   window, she suddenly spread out her hand, and made a snatch in the air. She did not get hold of anything,
    T8   186:38   Or else what?" said Alice, for the Knight had made a sudden pause.
    T4   147:18   afterwards she had never seen such a fuss made about anything in all her life--the way those two bustled
    A11   86: 8   tarts upon it: they looked so good, that it made Alice quite hungry to look at them--"I wish they'd get
    A4   32:38   she appeared on the other side, the puppy made another rush at the stick, and tumbled head over heels in
    A4   30:16   at last she spread out her hand again, and made another snatch in the air. This time there were two
    T8W   14:21   began. "Latest News. The Exploring Party have made another tour in the Pantry, and have found five new lumps
    A4   32:36   yelp of delight, and rushed at the stick, and made believe to worry it: then Alice dodged behind a great
    A12   95:37   he said. (Which he certainly did not, being made entirely of cardboard.)
    T3   133: 4   see a Rocking-horse-fly, if you look. It's made entirely of wood, and gets about by swinging itself from
    A9   73:13   "It's the thing Mock Turtle Soup is made from," said the Queen.
    A5   42:24   she had been wandering, when a sharp hiss made her draw back in a hurry: a large pigeon had flown into
    A1   7: 7   mind (as well as she could, for the hot day made her feel very sleepy and stupid), whether the pleasure of
    A4   32:25   trees, a little sharp bark just over her head made her look up in a great hurry.
    A9   77:18   and she thought it over a little before she made her next remark. "Then the eleventh day must have been a
    A9   70: 6   that perhaps it was only the pepper that had made her so savage when they met in the kitchen.
    T9   203: 2   for her to keep in her place while she made her speech: the two Queens pushed her so, one on each
    T1   113:16   squeaking on the table behind Alice, and made her turn her head just in time to see one of the White
    T3   135:10   your lessons. That's a joke. I wish you had made it."
    T3   135:11   "Why do you wish I had made it?" Alice asked. "It's a very bad one."
    A8   67:11   but after watching it a minute or two she made it out to be a grin, and she said to herself "It's the
    T8W   19: 6   They said it did not fit, and so / It made me look extremely plain: / But what was I to do, you know
    A12   96:22   on his slate with one finger, as he found it made no mark; but he now hastily began again, using the ink,
    T10 205: 3   The Red Queen made no resistance whatever: only her face grew very small,
    A11   91:16   he said, in a deep voice, "What are tarts made of?"
    T8   186:20   "What did you mean it to be made of?" Alice asked, hoping to cheer him up, for the poor
    A10   81:23   "And what are they made of?" Alice asked in a tone of great curiosity.
    T3   133:13   you'll find a Snap-dragon-fly. Its body is made of plum-pudding, its wings of holly-leaves, and its head
    A1   9:34   came upon a little three-legged table, all made of solid glass: there was nothing on it but a tiny golden

MADE (cont.)
```
T8W   21:11  did  not like having so many personal remarks made on her, and as the Wasp had quite recovered his spirits,
A2    19: 8        how  small  she  was  now,  and she soon made out that it was only a mouse, that had slipped in like
A2    18:25  them  a  railway  station.)  However, she soon made out that she was in the pool of tears which she had wept
A6    49:22              As soon as she had made out the proper way of nursing it (which was to twist it
A4    30:24  a  good many voices all talking together: she made out the words: "Where's the other ladder?--Why, I hadn't
A11   88:35  which  puzzled  her  a  good  deal until she made out what it was: she was beginning to grow larger again,
A11   87:16      "The Queen of Hearts, she made some tarts, / All on a summer day: / The Knave of Hearts,
T5   156: 3  on, sometimes among beds of weeds (which made the oars stick fast in the water, worse than ever), and
T12  207: 6  inconvenient habit of kittens (Alice had once made the remark) that, whatever you say to them, they always
A8    69: 4  all  round.  (It was this last remark that had made the whole party look so grave and anxious.)
T4   143:28  / After we've brought them out so far, / And made them trot so quick!' / The Carpenter said nothing but /
T4   138:11  you ought to pay, you know. Wax-works weren't made to be looked at for nothing. Nohow!"
T3   133: 9  Rocking-horse-fly with great interest, and made up her mind that it must have been just repainted, it
T3   135:25  into  it.  However,  on  second thoughts, she made up her mind to go on: "for I certainly won't go back,"
A2    17:20  oh,  ever  so many lessons to learn! No, I've made up my mind about it: if I'm Mabel, I'll stay down here.
T1   115: 4  seen  in all her life such a face as the King made, when he found himself held in the air by an invisible
T3   131:32  from. "If you're so anxious to have a joke made, why don't you make one yourself?"
A5    40: 4  an  eel  on  the  end  of  your nose--/ What made you so awfully clever?"
```
MADLY (1)
```
T8   189:17  by  chance  I  put  /  My  fingers  into glue, / Or madly squeeze a right-hand foot / Into a left-hand shoe, / Or
```
MADNESS (1)
```
TI   103:26  the  blinding  snow,  /  The storm-wind's moody madness--/ Within, the firelight's ruddy glow, / And
```
MAGIC (2)
```
A4    28:23              Luckily for Alice, the little magic bottle had now had its full effect, and she grew no
TI   103:29  /  And  childhood's  nest  of  gladness.  /  The magic words shall hold thee fast: / Thou shalt not heed the
```
MAGPIE (1)
```
A3    26:31  of  the  birds  hurried  off at once: one old Magpie began wrapping itself up very carefully, remarking "I
```
MAID (1) [See also HOUSEMAID]
```
T5   149:37  pins. "But  really  you should have a lady's maid!"
```
MAIDEN (1)
```
TI   103:22  Shall summon to unwelcome bed / A melancholy maiden! / We are but older children, dear, / Who fret to find
```
MAIDS (1)
```
T4   141: 7                          'If seven maids with seven mops / Swept it for half a year, / Do you
```
MAJESTY (20)
```
T2   124:20  wider  when  you  speak, and always say 'your Majesty.'"
T2   125: 2  wanted  to  see  what  the garden was like, your Majesty--"
A12   94:34  spectacles. "Where shall I begin, please your Majesty?" he asked.
A11   90: 8  went  down  on one knee. "I'm a poor man, your Majesty," he began.
A11   88: 8          in the other. "I beg pardon, your Majesty," he began, "for bringing these in; but I hadn't quite
T12  207:28  when will Dinah have finished with your White Majesty, I wonder? That must be the reason you were so untidy
T9   201:36  her  mouth  close  to Alice's ear, "her White Majesty knows a lovely riddle--all in poetry--all about fishes
A12   93:23  White  Rabbit interrupted: "Unimportant, your Majesty means, of course," he said, in a very respectful tone,
A11   91:12  White Rabbit, who said, in a low voice, "Your Majesty must cross-examine this witness."
T9   196:21              "Your Majesty must excuse her," the Red Queen said to Alice, taking
A8    63:40      "My name is Alice, so please your Majesty," said Alice very politely; but she added, to herself,
A12   94:21      "Please, your Majesty," said the Knave, "I didn't write it, and they ca'n't
A12   94: 3  more  evidence  to  come  yet,  please your Majesty," said the White Rabbit, jumping up in a great hurry:
A8    65: 6          "May it please your Majesty," said Two, in a very humble tone, going down on one
T9   192: 2  so  soon--and  I'll tell you what it is, your Majesty," she went on, in a severe tone (she was always rather
T12  207: 1          "Your Red Majesty shouldn't purr so loud," Alice said, rubbing her eyes,
A9    72:34      "A fine day, your Majesty!" the Duchess began in a low, weak voice.
A11   89:11      "I'm a poor man, your Majesty," the Hatter began, in a trembling voice, "and I
A8    65:17  "Their  heads  are  gone,  if it please your Majesty!" the soldiers shouted in reply.
T5   149:17  conversation, so she smiled and said "If your Majesty will only tell me the right way to begin, I'll do it
```
MAJESTY'S (1)
```
T9   201:38          "Her Red Majesty's very kind to mention it," the White Queen murmured
```
MAKE (80)
```
T3   129: 1  Of  course  the  first  thing  to do was to make a grand survey of the country she was going to travel
T3   131:29          "You might make a joke on that," said the little voice close to her ear:
T3   131:14  voice,  close  to  her  ear,  said "You might make a joke on that--something about 'horse' and 'hoarse,' you
T7   175: 5  as well try to catch a Bandersnatch! But I'll make a memorandum about her, if you like--She's a dear good
T1   115:27  will,  though,"  the Queen said, "if you don't make a memorandum of it."
T8   181:30      "In hopes some bees may make a nest in it--then I should get the honey."
T9   201:26          "Make a remark," said the Red Queen: "it's ridiculous to leave
T8   188:21  / I set it in a blaze; / And thence they make a stuff they call / Rowland's Macassar-Oil--/ Yet
T6   164: 5          "When I make a word do a lot of work like that," said Humpty Dumpty,
T1   108:32  up,  it  wouldn't have happened. Now don't make any more excuses, but listen! Number two: you pulled
T6   164: 7  "Oh!" said Alice. She was too much puzzled to make any other remark.
A9    76:29  "Yes," said Alice doubtfully: "it means--to--make--anything--prettier."
T9   195:15  up  rather  stiffly,  and said "Queens never make bargains."
T12  208: 4  and  the  Carpenter'  to you; and then you can make believe it's oysters, dear!
A9    70:13  and--and  barley-sugar  and  such things that make children sweet-tempered. I only wish people knew that:
T3   130: 6          "Don't make excuses," said the Guard: "you should have bought one
T1   118:31  Alice,  suddenly  jumping  up,  "if I don't make haste, I shall have to go back through the Looking-glass,
A3    26: 6  "A knot!" said Alice, always ready to make herself useful, and looking anxiously about her. "Oh, do
T6   165: 3  and round like a gyroscope. To 'gimble' is to make holes like a gimlet."
T3   129:17  them--and  what quantities of honey they must make! I think I'll go down and--no, I wo'n't go just yet," she
T1   110:38  too--but  that  may be only pretence, just to make it look as if they had a fire. Well then, the books are
T1   118:27  confess,  even  to herself, that she couldn't make it out at all.) "Somehow it seems to fill my head with
```

MAKE (cont.)

T4	139:32	and it was done (as well as she could make it out) by the branches rubbing one across the other,
A7	58: 3	went on so long that they had to pinch it to make it stop.
T1	107:21	up the kitten, and giving it a little kiss to make it understand that it was in disgrace. "Really, Dinah
T3	135:15	"You shouldn't make jokes," Alice said, "if it makes you so unhappy."
A8	65: 3	"Leave off that!" screamed the Queen. "You make me giddy." And then, turning to the rose-tree, she went
T5	155: 8	she took up another pair of needles. "You'll make me giddy soon, if you go on turning round like that." She
A4	28: 7	see what this bottle does. I do hope it'll make me grow large again, for really I'm quite tired of being
A4	32: 8	change in my size; and, as it ca'n't possibly make me larger, it must make me smaller, I suppose."
T1	115:10	that the King couldn't hear her. "You make me laugh so that I can hardly hold you! And don't keep
A4	32: 9	as it ca'n't possibly make me larger, it must make me smaller, I suppose."
T2	128:12	the Sixth belongs to Humpty Dumpty--But you make no remark?"
T5	153:36	of the counter? Rub as she would, she could make nothing more of it: she was in a little dark shop,
T2	128:14	"I--I didn't know I had to make one--just then," Alice faltered out.
A6	53: 3	keep appearing and vanishing so suddenly; you make one quite giddy!"
A10	82:17	"How the creatures order one about, and make one repeat lessons!" thought Alice. "I might just as well
A1	12:30	Why, there's hardly enough of me left to make one respectable person!"
T2	122:19	they all begin together, and it's enough to make one wither to hear the way they go on!"
T6	164: 3	"That's a great deal to make one word mean," Alice said in a thoughtful tone.
T3	131:33	so anxious to have a joke made, why don't you make one yourself?"
A11	87: 9	juror (it was Bill, the Lizard) could not make out at all what had become of it; so, after hunting all
T5	154:13	whenever she looked hard at any shelf, to make out exactly what it had on it, that particular shelf was
A8	68:35	all spoke at once, she found it very hard to make out exactly what they said.
T2	126:12	Alice never could quite make out, in thinking it over afterwards, how it was that they
A11	87: 1	things!" on their slates, and she could even make out that one of them didn't know how to spell "stupid,"
T7	178: 1	Where the noise came from, she couldn't make out: the air seemed full of it, and it rang through and
T5	153:34	her eyes, and looked again. She couldn't make out what had happened at all. Was she in a shop? And was
T8	191: 7	she lifted it off, and set it on her lap to make out what it could possibly be.
A2	19: 6	pool a little way off, and she swam nearer to make out what it was: at first she thought it must be a walrus
A1	8:14	next. First, she tried to look down and make out what she was coming to, but it was too dark to see
T7	173:17	cloud of dust, that at first Alice could not make out which was which; but she soon managed to distinguish
A5	41:34	at the mushroom for a minute, trying to make out which were the two sides of it; and, as it was
A11	86:36	his spectacles and looked anxiously round, to make out who was talking.
T9	197:21	more like a tune: at last she could even make out words, and she listened so eagerly that, when the two
T4	147:39	said Alice, thinking it a good opportunity to make peace.
A7	55: 9	"You should learn not to make personal remarks," Alice said with some severity: "it's
T4	145:17	You'll be waking him, I'm afraid, if you make so much noise."
A4	32: 8	of these cakes," she thought, "it's sure to make some change in my size; and, as it ca'n't possibly make
T1	115: 9	"Oh! please don't make such faces, my dear!" she cried out, quite forgetting
A8	66: 4	up and stand on their hands and feet, to make the arches.
T2	122:28	"In most gardens," the Tiger-lily said, "they make the beds too soft--so that the flowers are always asleep
T4	140:25	with all his might: / He did his very best to make / The billows smooth and bright--/ And this was odd,
T7	171:10	and could only wave his hands about, and make the most fearful faces at the poor King.
A12	99: 7	gather about her other little children, and make their eyes bright and eager with many a strange tale,
T6	164:38	are that," said Humpty Dumpty; "also they make their nests under sun-dials--also they live on cheese."
T4	148: 9	about a rattle!" said Alice, still hoping to make them a little ashamed of fighting for such a trifle.
T8	188: 3	butterflies / That sleep among the wheat: / I make them into mutton-pies, / And sell them in the street. / I
T5	157:13	said the Sheep: "plenty of choice, only make up your mind. Now, what do you want to buy?"
AI	3: 5	little arms are plied, / While little hands make vain pretence / Our wanderings to guide.
T8	180: 7	they were Punch and Judy--What a noise they make when they tumble! Just like a whole set of fire-irons
A6	48:25	her knowledge. "Just think what work it would make with the day and night! You see the earth takes
T6	163:33	question is," said Alice, "whether you can make words mean so many different things."
A9	72:18	talk about trouble!" said the Duchess. "I make you a present of everything I've said as yet."
A3	21:15	down, all of you, and listen to me! I'll soon make you dry enough!" They all sat down at once, in a large
A5	41:28	make you grow taller, and the other side will make you grow shorter."
A5	41:27	merely remarking, as it went, "One side will make you grow taller, and the other side will make you grow
T8	182:33	an upright stick," said the Knight. "Then you make your hair creep up it, like a fruit-tree. Now the reason
T8W	17:12	about like a heap of sea-weed. "You could make your wig much neater," she said, "if only you had a comb
T4	145:22	"You wo'n't make yourself a bit realler by crying," Tweedledee remarked:

MAKES (20)

T5	151:19	things I was punished for," said Alice: "that makes all the difference."
T8W	14: 7	to herself "Perhaps it's only pain that makes him so cross." So she tried once more.
T3	134: 2	and mince-pie," the Gnat replied; "and it makes its nest in a Christmas-box."
A1	12:34	"Well, I'll eat it," said Alice, "and if it makes me grow larger, I can reach the key; and if it makes me
A1	12:35	grow larger, I can reach the key; and if it makes me grow smaller, I can creep under the door: so either
T8	186:27	"but you've no idea what a difference it makes, mixing it with other things--such as gunpowder and
A11	91:28	must cross-examine the next witness. It quite makes my forehead ache!"
T9	199:34	Alice thought to herself "Thirty times three makes ninety. I wonder if any one's counting?" In a minute
T5	150:12	backwards," the Queen said kindly: "it always makes one a little giddy at first--"
A9	70: 9	well without--Maybe it's always pepper that makes people hot-tempered," she went on, very much pleased at
T4	145:27	But I wish it wouldn't flap its wings so--it makes quite a hurricane in the wood--here's somebody's shawl
A6	50:17	have made a dreadfully ugly child: but it makes rather a handsome pig, I think." And she began thinking
A12	94:23	didn't sign it," said the King, "that only makes the matter worse. You must have meant some mischief, or
A9	70:33	of that is--'Oh, 'tis love, 'tis love, that makes the world go round!'"
A9	70:12	that makes them sour--and camomile that makes them bitter--and--and barley-sugar and such things that
A10	81:18	done with?" said the Gryphon. "I mean, what makes them so shiny?"
A9	70:11	out a new kind of rule, "and vinegar that makes them sour--and camomile that makes them bitter--and--and
A9	70:18	thinking about something, my dear, and that makes you forget to talk. I ca'n't tell you just now what the
T8	183: 6	and a little offended at the remark. "What makes you say that?" he asked, as he scrambled back into the
T3	135:15	You shouldn't make jokes," Alice said, "if it makes you so unhappy."

MAKING (14)
A1   7: 8   sleepy and stupid), whether the pleasure of making a daisy-chain would be worth the trouble of getting up
T6   160:17   ground?" Alice went on, not with any idea of making another riddle, but simply in her good-natured anxiety
A12   93:25   in a very respectful tone, but frowning and making faces at him as he spoke.
A4   33: 3   This seemed to Alice a good opportunity for making her escape: so she set off at once, and ran till she
T5   152: 9   she said, as soon as there was a chance of making herself heard. "Have you pricked your finger?"
T3   129: 7   towns--why, what are those creatures, making honey down there? They ca'n't be bees--nobody ever saw
A7   59:16   "Who's making personal remarks now?" the Hatter asked triumphantly.
A2   20:12   away from her as hard as it could go, and making quite a commotion in the pool as it went.
A4   29:17   taking first one side and then the other, and making quite a conversation of it altogether; but after a few
T6   166:37   "You needn't go on making remarks like that," Humpty Dumpty said: "they're not
A6   46:12   door as you are: secondly, because they're making such a noise inside, no one could possibly hear you."
A5   36:11   felt a little irritated at the Caterpillar's making such very short remarks, and she drew herself up and
T8W   21:17   she had gone back and given a few minutes to making the poor old creature comfortable.
T1   108:13   been up in the window with me--only Dinah was making you tidy, so you couldn't. I was watching the boys
MALLETS (1)
A8   66: 3   croquet balls were live hedgehogs, and the mallets live flamingoes, and the soldiers had to double
MAN (15)
A12   94:25   you'd have signed your name like an honest man."
T8   187: 3   is called. The name really is 'The Aged Aged Man.'"
T1   113: 1   had got the face of a little old man, and grinned at her.
T8   187:33   little to relate. / I saw an aged aged man, / A-sitting on a gate. / 'Who are you, aged man?' I said.
T8   187:35   / A-sitting on a gate. / 'Who are you, aged man?' I said. / 'And how is it you live?' / And his answer
T8   189:22   / I weep, for it reminds me so / Of that old man I used to know--/ Whose look was mild, whose speech was
T8   185:23   him to put another man's helmet on--with the man in it, too."
T8W   13: 5   was the matter. Something like a very old man (only that his face was more like a wasp) was sitting on
A5   37: 1   "You are old, Father William," the young man said, / "And your hair has become very white; / And yet
T8   188:14   So, having no reply to give / To what the old man said, / I cried 'Come, tell me how you live!' / And
T3   130: 8   more the chorus of voices went on with "The man that drives the engine. Why, the smoke alone is worth a
A11   89:19   "I'm a poor man," the Hatter went on, "and most things twinkled after that
T7   175:33   "Come, fetch out the plum-cake, old man!" the Unicorn went on, turning from her to the King. "None
A11   90: 8   and went down on one knee. "I'm a poor man, your Majesty," he began.
A11   89:11   "I'm a poor man, your Majesty," the Hatter began, in a trembling voice,
MANAGE (17)
A7   57: 9   "Is that the way you manage?" Alice asked.
T1   108: 3   and speaking in as cross a voice as she could manage--and then she scrambled back into the arm-chair, taking
A7   60:43   close to the little glass table. "Now, I'll manage better this time," she said to herself, and began by
T8   181: 7   helmet?" It was evidently more than he could manage by himself: however, she managed to shake him out of it
A1   9: 2   through the air! Do you think you could manage it?) "And what an ignorant little girl she'll think me
T5   149:11   was to be any conversation at all, she must manage it herself. So she began rather timidly: "Am I
T9   192:10   as she sat down again, "I shall be able to manage it quite well in time."
A2   15: 3   she went on planning to herself how she would manage it. "They must go by the carrier," she thought; "and
T7   177:11   "You don't know how to manage Looking-glass cakes," the Unicorn remarked. "Hand it
A9   77:21   "And how did you manage on the twelfth?" Alice went on eagerly.
A2   14: 9   far off to trouble myself about you: you must manage the best way you can--but I must be kind to them,"
T6   163:40   anything with, but not verbs--however, I can manage the whole lot of them! Impenetrability! That's what I
T1   115:37   I really must get a thinner pencil. I ca'n't manage this one a bit: it writes all manner of things that I
T8   182:15   This took a long time to manage, though Alice held the bag open very carefully, because
T5   152:30   "I wish I could manage to be glad!" the Queen said. "Only I never can remember
A5   39: 4   the bones and the beak--/ Pray, how did you manage to do it?"
T3   134:26   think how convenient it would be if you could manage to go home without it! For instance, if the governess
MANAGED (14)
A4   33:12   to grow up again! Let me see--how is it to be managed? I suppose I ought to eat or drink something or other;
A3   23: 7   some winter-day, I will tell you how the Dodo managed it.)
T9   202:22   drinking it directly, and very queerly they managed it: some of them put their glasses upon their heads
T7   169:10   Then came the horses. Having four feet, these managed rather better than the foot-soldiers; but even they
T7   173:18   not make out which was which; but she soon managed to distinguish the Unicorn by his horn.
T2   126:27   her along. "Are we nearly there?" Alice managed to pant out at last.
T5   156:27   on purpose," she thought) that, though she managed to pick plenty of beautiful rushes as the boat glided
T9   203: 5   she got hold of the edge of the table, and managed to pull herself down again.
A1   8:21   for fear of killing somebody underneath, so managed to put it into one of the cupboards as she fell past
T8W   20:11   a cough as well as she could. At last she managed to say gravely, "I can bite anything I want."
T8   181: 8   than he could manage by himself: however, she managed to shake him out of it at last.
A5   42: 2   open her mouth; but she did it at last, and managed to swallow a morsel of the left-hand bit. * * * * *
T4   147:28   Alice laughed loud: but she managed to turn it into a cough, for fear of hurting his
T2   126: 7   smiled pleasantly, and said "That's easily managed. You can be the White Queen's Pawn, if you like, as
MANAGING (1)
A8   66: 6   chief difficulty Alice found at first was in managing her flamingo: she succeeded in getting its body
MANNER (5)
T5   154:11   The shop seemed to be full of all manner of curious things--but the oddest part of it all was
A7   60:16   was getting very sleepy; "and they drew all manner of things--everything that begins with an M--"
T1   115:39   "What manner of things?" said the Queen, looking over the book (in
T1   115:38   I ca'n't manage this one a bit: it writes all manner of things that I don't intend--"
A8   63:23   Rabbit: it was talking in a hurried nervous manner, smiling at everything that was said, and went by
MANNERS (5)
T9   193:22   "Manners are not taught in lessons," said Alice. "Lessons teach
A6   47:13   she was not quite sure whether it was good manners for her to speak first, "why your cat grins like that
T2   121: 7   "It isn't manners for us to begin, you know," said the Rose, "and I
T9   193:20   "but I daresay you've not had many lessons in manners yet."
T1   108: 1   Really, Dinah ought to have taught you better manners! You ought, Dinah, you know you ought!" she added,

MAN'S (1)
T8   185:23   "but it was careless of him to put another man's helmet on--with the man in it, too."
MANXOME (1)
T1   118: 6   his vorpal sword in hand: / Long time the manxome foe he sought--/ So rested he by the Tumtum tree, /
MANY (34)
A12   99: 7   and make their eyes bright and eager with many a strange tale, perhaps even with the dream of Wonderland
T9   195: 1   "How many acres of ground?" said the White Queen. "You mustn't
T9   195:33   time, and sometimes in the winter we take as many as five nights together--for warmth, you know."
T4   144:20   "But he ate as many as he could get," said Tweedledum.
T5   153:15   a day. Why, sometimes I've believed as many as six impossible things before breakfast. There goes the
T4   144:19   like the Carpenter best--if he didn't eat so many as the Walrus."
T6   162:45   "And how many birthdays have you?"
T8   182:19   as they got it in at last; "there are so many candlesticks in the bag." And he hung it to the saddle,
T5   157:11   "Are there many crabs here?" said Alice.
T6   162:43   talking about!" cried Humpty Dumpty. "How many days are there in a year?"
A5   35:16   it myself, to begin with; and being so many different sizes in a day is very confusing."
T6   163:34   Alice, "whether you can make words mean so many different things."
A8   63:13   flat upon their faces. There was a sound of many footsteps, and Alice looked round, eager to see the Queen
T2   122:22   better temper by a compliment. "I've been in many gardens before, but none of the flowers could talk."
T4   144:21   so that the Carpenter couldn't count how many he took: contrariwise."
A9   77:10   "And how many hours a day did you do lessons?" said Alice, in a hurry
T9   193:20   Queen remarked: "but I daresay you've not had many lessons in manners yet."
A2   17:19   next to no toys to play with, and oh, ever so many lessons to learn! No, I've made up my mind about it: if
A5   43:12   of the deepest contempt. "I've seen a good many little girls in my time, but never one with such a neck
A1   8:28   the fall never come to an end? "I wonder how many miles I've fallen by this time?" she said aloud. "I must
A7   55: 5   table," said Alice: "it's laid for a great many more than three."
T5   156:39   but Alice hardly noticed this, there were so many other curious things to think about.
T8   182:21   with bunches of carrots, and fire-irons, and many other things.
A1   10:10   I only knew how to begin." For, you see, so many out-of-the-way things had happened lately, that Alice had
T8W   21:10   Alice did not like having so many personal remarks made on her, and as the Wasp had quite
A7   58:11   into Alice's head. "Is that the reason so many tea-things are put out here?" she asked.
A6   51: 2   still it had very long claws and a great many teeth, so she felt that it ought to be treated with
T6   164:18   the poems that ever were invented--and a good many that haven't been invented just yet."
T5   155:12   "How can she knit with so many?" the puzzled child thought to herself. "She gets more
T9   195: 2   the White Queen. "You mustn't leave out so many things."
T8   190:28   again pretty easily--that comes of having so many things hung round the horse--" So she went on talking to
T4   142:20   has come,' the Walrus said, / 'To talk of many things: / Of shoes--and ships--and sealing wax--/ Of
T3   129:38   on, looking angrily at Alice. And a great many voices all said together ("like the chorus of a song,"
A4   30:24   little cart-wheels, and the sound of a good many voices all talking together: she made out the words:
MAPS (1)
A1   8:17   and book-shelves: here and there she saw maps and pictures hung upon pegs. She took down a jar from one
MARCH (34)
A6   52:27   raving mad--at least not so mad as it was in March." As she said this, she looked up, and there was the Cat
A7   54:16   "There isn't any," said the March Hare.
A7   55: 3   to sit down without being invited," said the March Hare.
A7   55:17   you can find out the answer to it?" said the March Hare.
A7   56: 2   the works!" he added, looking angrily at the March Hare.
A7   56:31   "Nor I," said the March Hare.
A7   58:28   "Tell us a story!" said the March Hare.
A7   60:18   "Why not?" said the March Hare.
A11   88:15   "Fifteenth," said the March Hare.
A11   89:23   "I deny it!" said the March Hare.
A12   98:26   could hear the rattle of the teacups as the March Hare and his friends shared their never-ending meal, and
A7   54: 2   under a tree in front of the house, and the March Hare and the Hatter were having tea at it: a Dormouse
A7   60: 1   was a good deal worse off than before, as the March Hare had just upset the milk-jug into his plate.
A11   89:21   "I didn't!" the March Hare interrupted in a great hurry.
A7   58:18   "Suppose we change the subject," the March Hare interrupted, yawning. "I'm getting tired of this. I
A7   57:12   you know--" (pointing his teaspoon at the March Hare,) "--it was at the great concert given by the Queen
A7   56: 4   "It was the best butter," the March Hare meekly replied.
A7   59:39   he spoke, and the Dormouse followed him: the March Hare moved into the Dormouse's place, and Alice rather
A11   89:20   and most things twinkled after that--only the March Hare said--"
A7   54:12   "Have some wine," the March Hare said in an encouraging tone.
A7   59: 9   "Take some more tea," the March Hare said to Alice, very earnestly.
A7   57: 3   ("I only wish it was," the March Hare said to itself in a whisper.)
A6   53:11   before she came in sight of the house of the March Hare: she thought it must be the right house, because
A7   55:26   "You might just as well say," added the March Hare, "that 'I like what I get' is the same thing as 'I
A7   59:40   rather unwillingly took the place of the March Hare. The Hatter was the only one who got any advantage
A7   56: 7   The March Hare took the watch and looked at it gloomily: then he
A6   51:21   direction," waving the other paw, "lives a March Hare. Visit either you like: they're both mad."
A6   52:24   she walked on in the direction in which the March Hare was said to live. "I've seen hatters before," she
A7   55:19   "Then you should say what you mean," the March Hare went on.
A7   59:25   very angrily, but the Hatter and the March Hare went "Sh! Sh!" and the Dormouse sulkily remarked
A11   88:12   The Hatter looked at the March Hare, who had followed him into the court, arm-in-arm
A6   52:25   hatters before," she said to herself: "the March Hare will be much the most interesting, and perhaps, as
A11   88:14   arm-in-arm with the Dormouse. "Fourteenth of March, I think it was," he said.
A7   57:11   "Not I!" he replied. "We quarreled last March--just before he went mad, you know--" (pointing his
MARCHED (1)
A8   65:14   or two, looking for them, and then quietly marched off after the others.
MARK (5)
T9   201:35   Queen, whose answer was a little wide of the mark. "As to fishes," she said, very slowly and solemnly,

MARK (cont.)
A12   96:22   slate with one finger, as he found it made no mark; but he now hastily began again, using the ink, that was
A11   87:11   this was of very little use, as it left no mark on the slate.
T2   127:35   of two yards," she said, putting in a peg to mark the distance, "I shall give you your directions--have
A10   79:11   too close, and waving their fore-paws to mark the time, while the Mock Turtle sang this, very slowly
MARKED (13)
T4   138:13   "Contrariwise," added the one marked 'DEE,' "if you think we're alive, you ought to speak."
T4   138: 9   was startled by a voice coming from the one marked 'DUM.'
A1   12:33   on which the words "EAT ME" were beautifully marked in currants. "Well, I'll eat it," said Alice, "and if
T2   127:33   And she took a ribbon out of her pocket, marked in inches, and began measuring the ground, and sticking
A3   23: 8   First it marked out a race-course, in a sort of circle, ("the exact
T2   125:25   "I declare it's marked out just like a large chess-board!" Alice said at last.
A1   11: 4   that, if you drink much from a bottle marked "poison," it is almost certain to disagree with you,
A1   10:21   look first," she said, "and see whether it's marked 'poison' or not"; for she had read several nice little
A1   11: 6   However, this bottle was not marked "poison," so Alice ventured to taste it, and, finding
T9   198: 8   and I'm not a servant. There ought to be one marked 'Queen,' you know--"
T3   137:22   two finger-posts pointing the same way, one marked "TO TWEEDLEDUM'S HOUSE," and the other "TO THE HOUSE OF
T9   198: 3   of the arch there was a bell-handle; one was marked "Visitors' Bell," and the other "Servants' Bell."
A10   83:14   "I passed by his garden, and marked, with one eye, / How the Owl and the Panther were
MARKET-PLACE (1)
T7   177: 1   way. Did you go by the old bridge, or the market-place? You get the best view by the old bridge."
MARKING (1)
T6   168:27   same as everybody has--the two eyes, so--"(marking their places in the air with his thumb) "nose in the
MARMALADE (1)
A1   8:19   shelves as she passed: it was labeled "ORANGE MARMALADE," but to her great disappointment it was empty: she
MARY ANN (4)
A4   27:24   in great fear lest she should meet the real Mary Ann, and be turned out of the house before she had found
A4   29:19   "Mary Ann! Mary Ann!" said the voice. "Fetch me my gloves this
A4   29:19   "Mary Ann! Mary Ann!" said the voice. "Fetch me my gloves this moment!"
A4   27:13   called out to her, in an angry tone, "Why, Mary Ann, what are you doing out here? Run home this moment,
MASTER (4) [See also DRAWLING-MASTER]
A4   30:33   then!--Bill's got to go down--Here, Bill! The master says you've got to go down the chimney!"
T6   163:35   is," said Humpty Dumpty, "which is to be master--that's all."
A9   77: 5   said the Gryphon: "I went to the Classical master, though. He was an old crab, he was."
A9   74:42   and then, "we went to school in the sea. The master was an old Turtle--we used to call him Tortoise--"
MATTER (16)
A12   93:32   to look over their slates; "but it doesn't matter a bit," she thought to herself.
A3   23: 9   a sort of circle, ("the exact shape doesn't matter," it said,) and then all the party were placed along
A8   68:24   hedgehogs were out of sight: "but it doesn't matter much," thought Alice, "as all the arches are gone from
A12   96: 8   the jury, of course--'If she should push the matter on'--that must be the Queen--'What would become of you
A12   95: 3   know it to be true): / If she should push the matter on, / What would become of you?
T8W   13:11   the brook:--but I'll just ask him what's the matter," she added, checking herself on the very edge. "If I
T5   152: 8   "What is the matter?" she said, as soon as there was a chance of making
T8W   13: 4   looking anxiously back to see what was the matter. Something like a very old man (only that his face was
A5   43:24   I know that well enough; and what does it matter to me whether you're a little girl or a serpent?"
T8   186: 3   surprised at the question. "What does it matter where my body happens to be?" he said. "My mind goes on
A1   9:15   answer either question, it didn't much matter which way she put it. She felt that she was dozing off,
A6   51:12   "Then it doesn't matter which way you go," said the Cat.
T5   149:26   "I don't know what's the matter with it!" the Queen said, in a melancholy voice. "It's
A6   49:32   anxiously into its face to see what was the matter with it. There could be no doubt that it had a very
T9   204: 3   at her side, and turned to see what was the matter with the White Queen; but, instead of the Queen, there
A12   94:24   sign it," said the King, "that only makes the matter worse. You must have meant some mischief, or else you'd
MATTERED (1)
T5   156:34   What mattered it to her just then that the rushes had begun to fade
MATTERS (2)
A5   43:25   "It matters a good deal to me," said Alice hastily; "but I'm not
A10   80: 7   "What matters it how far we go?" his scaly friend replied. / "There
MAY (36)
A7   60:40   "But everything's curious to-day. I think I may as well go in at once." And in she went.
A5   36: 7   "Well, perhaps your feelings may be different," said Alice: "all I know is, it would feel
A7   59:29   wo'n't interrupt you again. I dare say there may be one.--"
T1   110:38   smoke comes up in that room too--but that may be only pretence, just to make it look as if they had a
T1   111: 5   as far as you can see, only you know it may be quite different on beyond. Oh, Kitty, how nice it would
A10   80:20   "I don't know where Dinn may be," said the Mock Turtle; "but, if you've seen them so
T2   125:13   The Red Queen shook her head. "You may call it 'nonsense' if you like," she said, "but I've heard
A11   90:31   "You may go," said the King, and the Hatter hurriedly left the
T9   201:40   of a pigeon. "It would be such a treat! May I?"
T9   201: 4   "May I give you a slice?" she said, taking up the knife and
T9   201:11   hastily, "or we shall get no dinner at all. May I give you some?"
T8   181: 6   "Thank you very much," said Alice. "May I help you off with your helmet?" It was evidently more
T5   149:24   to herself, "and she's all over pins!--May I put your shawl straight for you?" she added aloud.
T4   146: 8   "It may--if it chooses," said Tweedledee: "we've no objection.
A8   65: 6   "May it please your Majesty," said Two, in a very humble tone,
A6   52:26   the most interesting, and perhaps, as this is May, it wo'n't be raving mad--at least not so mad as it was in
A8   67:42   of it at all," said the King: "however, it may kiss my hand, if it likes."
A8   68: 1   "A cat may look at a king," said Alice. "I've read that in some book,
T5   154: 5   "You may look in front of you, and on both sides, if you like,"
T8   181:30   "In hopes some bees may make a nest in it--then I should get the honey."
A10   78: 8   "You may not have lived much under the sea--" ("I haven't," said
A6   49:10   "Here! You may nurse it a bit, if you like!" the Duchess said to Alice,

MAY (cont.)
```
  T3    134:10  drew  her  feet  back  in  some alarm), "you may observe a Bread-and-butter-fly. Its wings are thin slices
  T4    146: 7                                  "But it may rain outside?"
  T8W    14:17                       "You may read it if you've a mind to," the Wasp said, rather
  T2    127:11  her up against a tree, and said kindly, "You may rest a little, now."
  T6    160:39  another: and, to show you I'm not proud, you may shake hands with me!" And he grinned almost from ear to
  A11    90:25                               "Then you may sit down," the King replied.
  A11    90:21     "If that's all you know about it, you may stand down," continued the King.
  T7    172:23  However, now you've got your breath, you may tell us what's happened in the town."
  TI    103:32            And, though the shadow of a sigh / May tremble through the story, / For "happy summer days" gone
  T8    182:35  know. It's a plan of my own invention. You may try it if you like."
  T6    160:25  went on, "the King has promised me--ah, you may turn pale, if you like! You didn't think I was going to
  T3    129:26  way," she said after a pause; "and perhaps I may visit the elephants later on. Besides, I do so want to get
  T5    156:11         "No, but I meant--please, may we wait and pick some?" Alice pleaded. "If you don't mind
  T6    160:35            "Ah, well! They may write such things in a book," Humpty Dumpty said in a
```
MAYBE (3)
```
  T6    166: 9  in the middle: however, you'll hear it done, maybe--down in the wood yonder--and, when you've once heard it
  A9     70: 9  kitchen at all. Soup does very well without--Maybe it's always pepper that makes people hot-tempered," she
  A6     46:30                         "--or next day, maybe," the Footman continued in the same tone, exactly as if
```
MAYHAP (1)
```
  T6    160:38  me! I'm one that has spoken to a King, I am: mayhap you'll never see such another: and, to show you I'm not
```
MAYN'T (1)
```
  A9     75: 9  Yes, we went to school in the sea, though you mayn't believe it--"
```
MAYOR (1)
```
  T7    170:29  (He pronounced it so as to rhyme with 'mayor.')
```
ME (172) [entries omitted]
MEAL (1)
```
  A12    98:27  and his friends shared their never-ending meal, and the shrill voice of the Queen ordering off her
```
MEAN (33)
```
  T6    160: 6  Dumpty interrupted impatiently. "What does it mean?"
  T6    166: 6                        "And what does 'outgrabe' mean?"
  T6    166:30  getting green, / I'll try and tell you what I mean:"
  T6    163:28         "But 'glory' doesn't mean 'a nice knock-down argument,'" Alice objected.
  T6    164: 3    "That's a great deal to make one word mean," Alice said in a thoughtful tone.
  T4    144:18                "That was mean!" Alice said indignantly. "Then I like the Carpenter best
  T9    192:38         "I'm sure I didn't mean--" Alice was beginning, but the Red Queen interrupted her
  T6    163:24         "I don't know what you mean by 'glory,'" Alice said.
  T9    192:27  the subject of the conversation. "What do you mean by 'If you really are a Queen'? What right have you to
  A5     35: 9               "What do you mean by that?" said the Caterpillar, sternly. "Explain
  T2    124:11        "I don't know what you mean by your way," said the Queen: "all the ways about here
  T6    162:17  cravat, I should have said--no, a belt, I mean--I beg your pardon!" she added in dismay, for Humpty
  A3     26:10                "I didn't mean it!" pleaded poor Alice. "But you're so easily offended,
  T8    186:20         "What did you mean it to be made of?" Alice asked, hoping to cheer him up,
  T6    163:31  tone, "it means just what I choose it to mean--neither more nor less."
  T9    195:27  "we had such a thunderstorm last Tuesday--I mean one of the last set of Tuesdays, you know."
  A10    81:36                    "Don't you mean 'purpose'?" said Alice.
  A7     56:37               "I don't know what you mean," said Alice.
  T9    199:14               "I don't know what you mean," she said.
  T6    162: 9  even more indignant at this suggestion. "I mean," she said, "that one ca'n't help growing older."
  T6    163:34  is," said Alice, "whether you can make words mean so many different things."
  T6    160: 7                   "Must a name mean something?" Alice asked doubtfully.
  T8W    17: 1               "Oh, you mean stiff-neck," said Alice.
  A7     55:16  "Do you mean that you think you can find out the answer to it?" said
  A7     55:19     "Then you should say what you mean," the March Hare went on.
  T6    164: 1  be just as well if you'd mention what you mean to do next, as I suppose you don't mean to stop here all
  T3    135:41  at not being able to think of the word. "I mean to get under the--under the--under this, you know!"
  T6    164: 2  you mean to do next, as I suppose you don't mean to stop here all the rest of your life."
  A7     55:21  Alice hastily replied; "at least--at least I mean what I say--that's the same thing, you know."
  A10    81:37                    "I mean what I say," the Mock Turtle replied, in an offended tone
  T6    162:38               "I mean, what is an un-birthday present?"
  A10    81:18  your shoes done with?" said the Gryphon. "I mean, what makes them so shiny?"
  A7     59:13              "You mean you ca'n't take less," said the Hatter: "it's very easy
```
MEANING (13)
```
  A5     42:42  said Alice, who was beginning to see its meaning.
  T9    193: 4  any meaning? Even a joke should have some meaning--and a child's more important than a joke, I hope. You
  T9    193: 3  you suppose is the use of a child without any meaning? Even a joke should have some meaning--and a child's
  A12    95:26  sixpence. I don't believe there's an atom of meaning in it."
  A7     56:20  remark seemed to her to have no sort of meaning in it, and yet it was certainly English. "I don't
  A12    95:28  "She doesn't believe there's an atom of meaning in it," but none of them attempted to explain the
  A12    95:30            "If there's no meaning in it," said the King, "that saves a world of trouble,
  A12    95:33  at them with one eye; "I seem to see some meaning in them, after all. '--said I could not swim--' you
  A3     22:31  English!" said the Eaglet. "I don't know the meaning of half those long words, and, what's more, I don't
  A11    86:26  very few little girls of her age knew the meaning of it at all. However, "jurymen" would have done just
  T6    164:15  said Alice. "Would you kindly tell me the meaning of the poem called 'Jabberwocky'?"
  T6    166: 4  about. I think it's short for 'from home'--meaning that they'd lost their way, you know."
  T4    140:23  winked his eye, / And shook his heavy head--/ Meaning to say he did not choose / To leave the oyster-bed.
```
MEANINGS (1)
```
  T6    164:31  You see it's like a portmanteau--there are two meanings packed up into one word."
```
MEANS (13)
```
  A3     22:17  rather crossly: "of course you know what 'it' means."
```

MEANS (cont.)
```
T6    163:42  you  tell  me please," said Alice, "what that means?"
T8    187: 7  another  thing!  The song is called 'Ways and Means': but that's only what it's called, you know!"
T3    130:13  hope  you  understand what thinking in chorus means--for I must confess that I don't) "Better say nothing at
T6    164:26  are  plenty  of  hard  words there. 'Brillig' means four o'clock in the afternoon--the time when you begin
T6    163:31  Dumpty  said,  in rather a scornful tone, "it means just what I choose it to mean--neither more nor less."
T6    164:30                   "Well, 'slithy' means 'lithe and slimy.' 'Lithe' is the same as 'active.' You
A9    70:36               "Ah well! It means much the same thing," said the Duchess, digging her
A12   93:23    interrupted: "Unimportant, your Majesty means, of course," he said, in a very respectful tone, but
T6    160: 9  Dumpty  said with  a  short  laugh: "my name means the shape I am--and a good handsome shape it is, too.
A9    76:29          "Yes," said Alice doubtfully: "it means--to--make--anything--prettier."
T9    196:23  in  her  own,  and  gently  stroking it: "she means well, but she ca'n't help saying foolish things as a
A3    22:18               "I know what 'it' means well enough, when I find a thing," said the Duck: "it's
```
MEANT (17)
```
T8    184: 7  out  both his  arms  to  show Alice what he meant, and this time he fell flat on his back, right under the
T6    163:44  Humpty  Dumpty, looking very much pleased. "I meant by 'impenetrability' that we've had enough of that
A8    65:21  at  Alice,  as  the  question  was evidently meant for her.
T1    107:11  to  purr--no  doubt  feeling  that it was all meant for its good.
T8    182:12                   "It's meant for plum-cake," said Alice.
T6    161:26          "I thought you meant 'How old are you?'" Alice explained.
T5    156:11          "No, but I meant--please, may we wait and pick some?" Alice pleaded. "If
A12   94:24  only  makes  the  matter worse. You must have meant some mischief, or else you'd have signed your name like
T7    171: 4          "I only meant that I didn't understand," said Alice. "Why one to come
T6    161:27          "If I'd meant that, I'd have said it," said Humpty Dumpty.
A12   93:26          "Unimportant, of course, I meant," the King hastily said, and went on to himself in an
T9    195:21  no,  no!" she  hastily corrected herself. "I meant the other way."
T6    163:26  "Of  course  you  don't--till  I  tell you. I meant 'there's a nice knock-down argument for you!'"
A11   90:19  of  the court,' and I never understood what it meant till now."
A6    48:28  rather  anxiously  at the cook, to see if she meant to take the hint; but the cook was busily stirring the
T9    193: 2  just  what  I  complain of! You should have meant! What do you suppose is the use of a child without any
T12   207:12  and  it  was  impossible to guess whether it meant "yes" or "no."
```
MEANWHILE (3)
```
A8    65: 8             "I see!" said the Queen, who had meanwhile been examining the roses. "Off with their heads!"
T3    134:21  or  two,  pondering.  The Gnat amused itself meanwhile by humming round and round her head: at last it
T9    202:20  it,  and  then  guess,"  said the Red Queen. "Meanwhile, we'll drink your health--Queen Alice's health!" she
```
MEASURE (1)
```
A2    18: 5  again." She got up and went to the table to measure herself by it, and found that, as nearly as she could
```
MEASUREMENTS (1)
```
T2    127:32     said  the  Queen,  "I'll  just  take the measurements." And she took a ribbon out of her pocket, marked
```
MEASURING (1)
```
T2    127:33  of  her  pocket,  marked in inches, and began measuring the ground, and sticking little pegs in here and
```
MEAT (1)
```
A10   83:16  / The Panther took pie-crust, and gravy, and meat, / While the Owl had the dish as its share of the treat.
```
MEAT-COURSE (1)
```
T8    186: 7  "was  inventing  a  new  pudding  during the meat-course."
```
MEEKLY (2)
```
A11   88:41     "I ca'n't  help  it,"  said  Alice very meekly: "I'm growing."
A7    56: 4  "It  was  the  best  butter,"  the March Hare meekly replied.
```
MEET (8)
```
T6    168:20  up, and held out her hand. "Good-bye, till we meet again!" she said as cheerfully as she could.
T7    170: 7  delight,  on seeing Alice. "Did you happen to meet any soldiers, my dear, as you came through the wood?"
T6    161: 7  smiled  much more the ends of his mouth might meet behind," she thought: "And then I don't know what would
T2    123:35              "I think I'll go and meet her," said Alice, for, though the flowers were
T5    149: 4  were  flying,  and Alice very civilly went to meet her with the shawl.
T6    168:21    "I  shouldn't  know  you  again  if we did meet," Humpty Dumpty replied in a discontented tone, giving
A4    27:24  upstairs,  in  great  fear  lest  she should meet the real Mary Ann, and be turned out of the house before
A3    22:22  it  advisable  to  go  with Edgar Atheling to meet William and offer him the crown. William's conduct at
```
MEETING (1)
```
A3    22:29     rising  to  its  feet, "I move that the meeting adjourn, for the immediate adoption of more energetic
```
MELANCHOLY (11)
```
A11   91:13  if  I  must,  I  must," the King said with a melancholy air, and, after folding his arms and frowning at
T3    135:17           Then came another of those melancholy little sighs, and this time the poor Gnat really
TI    103:22  laden,  / Shall  summon to unwelcome bed / A melancholy maiden! / We are but older children, dear, / Who
T8    187:26  pair,  and listening, in a half-dream, to the melancholy music of the song.
A3    22:26          "As wet as ever," said Alice in a melancholy tone: "it doesn't seem to dry me at all."
A3    26:37  mentioned  Dinah!"  she said to herself in a melancholy tone. "Nobody seems to like her, down here, and I'm
A5    36:35  all  came different!" Alice replied in a very melancholy voice.
T5    152:33  it is so very lonely here!" Alice said in a melancholy voice; and, at the thought of her loneliness, two
T5    149:27  the  matter  with  it!" the Queen said, in a melancholy voice. "It's out of temper, I think. I've pinned it
A12   93: 6  little  thing  was waving its tail about in a melancholy way, being quite unable to move. She soon got it
A10   85: 9  carried  on  the breeze that followed them, the melancholy words:--
```
MELT (2)
```
T3    132:16              But the beard seemed to melt away as she touched it, and she found herself sitting
T1    111:13  And  certainly  the glass was beginning to melt away, just like a bright silvery mist.
```
MELTED (1)
```
T5    156:37  little  while--and these, being dream-rushes, melted away almost like snow, as they lay in heaps at her feet
```
MEMORANDUM (4)
```
T7    175: 6  try  to  catch a Bandersnatch! But I'll make a memorandum about her, if you like--She's a dear good creature
T1    115:28  though," the Queen said, "if you don't make a memorandum of it."
A11   88:23  turning  to  the  jury,  who instantly made a memorandum of the fact.
```

MEMORANDUM (cont.)
T1   115:41   He balances very badly'). "That's not a memorandum of your feelings!"
MEMORANDUM-BOOK (4)
T7   170: 5   seated on the ground, busily writing in his memorandum-book.
T6   163: 6   couldn't help smiling as she took out her memorandum-book, and worked the sum for him:
T7   175: 7   repeated softly to himself, as he opened his memorandum-book. "Do you spell 'creature' with a double 'e'?"
T1   115:30   great interest as the King took an enormous memorandum-book out of his pocket, and began writing. A sudden
MEMORIES (1)
TC   209: 8   has paled that sunny sky: / Echoes fade and memories die: / Autumn frosts have slain July.
MEMORY (4)
A7   60:23   an M, such as mouse-traps, and the moon, and memory, and muchness--you know you say things are 'much of a
T5   150:19   "It's a poor sort of memory that only works backwards," the Queen remarked.
T5   150:15   there's one great advantage in it, that one's memory works both ways."
TI   103:17   rhythm of our rowing--/ Whose echoes live in memory yet, / Though envious years would say "forget."
MEMORY'S (1)
AI   4: 6   it where Childhood's dreams are twined / In Memory's mystic band. / Like pilgrim's wither'd wreath of
MEN (8)
T7   169: 9   ground was soon covered with little heaps of men.
T6   160:28   "To send all his horses and all his men," Alice interrupted, rather unwisely.
T6   159:30   / All the King's horses and all the King's men / Couldn't put Humpty Dumpty in his place again."
T8   188: 5   sell them in the street. / I sell them unto men,' he said, / 'Who sail on stormy seas; / And that's the
T6   161:13   "Yes, all his horses and all his men," Humpty Dumpty went on. "They'd pick me up again in a
T2   125:26   Alice said at last. "There ought to be some men moving about somewhere--and so there are!" she added in a
T4   139:12   But the fat little men only looked at each other and grinned.
T3   137:31   a sharp corner, she came upon two fat little men, so suddenly that she could not help starting back, but in
MENAI (1)
T8   189: 9   had just / Completed my design / To keep the Menai bridge from rust / By boiling it in wine. / I thanked
MENTION (3)
T9   201:38   "Her Red Majesty's very kind to mention it," the White Queen murmured into Alice's other ear,
T12 207:36   I think you did--however, you'd better not mention it to your friends just yet, for I'm not sure.
T6   164: 1   and it would be just as well if you'd mention what you mean to do next, as I suppose you don't mean
MENTIONED (3)
A5   38: 1   "You are old," said the youth, "as I mentioned before, / And have grown most uncommonly fat; / Yet
A3   26:37   "I wish I hadn't mentioned Dinah!" she said to herself in a melancholy tone.
A12   94:40   "They told me you had been to her, / And mentioned me to him: / She gave me a good character, / But
MERCIA (2)
A3   22: 6   and conquest. Edwin and Morcar, the earls of Mercia and Northumbria--'"
A3   22:12   "I proceed. 'Edwin and Morcar, the earls of Mercia and Northumbria, declared for him; and even Stigand,
MERELY (2)
A5   41:26   mushroom, and crawled away into the grass, merely remarking, as it went, "One side will make you grow
A9   73: 1   her, they hurried back to the game, the Queen merely remarking that a moment's delay would cost them their
MERRILY (2)
A8   63:20   of them, and the little dears came jumping merrily along, hand in hand, in couples: they were all
T9   204:20   of a little doll, and was now on the table, merrily running round and round after her own shawl, which was
MERRY (2)
AI   4: 1   now the tale is done, / And home we steer, a merry crew, / Beneath the setting sun.
T12 207:22   more stiffly, dear!" Alice cried with a merry laugh. "And curtsey while you're thinking what to--what
MESSAGE (2)
T3   131:20   got a head on her--" "She must be sent as a message by the telegraph--" "She must draw the train herself
T6   166:39   "I sent a message to the fish: / I told them 'This is what I wish.'
MESSAGES (2)
A4   27:27   seems," Alice said to herself, "to be going messages for a rabbit! I suppose Dinah'll be sending me on
A4   27:28   a rabbit! I suppose Dinah'll be sending me on messages next!" And she began fancying the sort of thing that
MESSENGER (12)
T7   172:17   "Nobody," said the Messenger.
T7   170:26   at all," said the King. "He's an Anglo-Saxon Messenger--and those are Anglo-Saxon attitudes. He only does
T7   171: 8   At this moment the Messenger arrived: he was far too much out of breath to say a
T6   168: 3   with a shudder, "I wouldn't have been the messenger for anything!"
T7   172:16   the King went on, holding out his hand to the Messenger for some hay.
T5   150: 4   her finger as she spoke, "there's the King's Messenger. He's in prison now, being punished: and the trial
T7   170:23   curious attitudes he goes into!" (For the Messenger kept skipping up and down, and wriggling like an eel
T7   172:25   "I'll whisper it," said the Messenger, putting his hands to his mouth in the shape of a
T7   172:20   "I do my best," the Messenger said in a sullen tone. "I'm sure nobody walks much
T7   172: 5   "There's nothing but hay left now," the Messenger said, peeping into the bag.
T7   172: 1   On which the Messenger, to Alice's great amusement, opened a bag that hung
T7   173:20   themselves close to where Hatta, the other Messenger, was standing watching the fight, with a cup of tea
MESSENGER'S (2)
T7   171:12   Alice in the hope of turning off the Messenger's attention from himself--but it was of no use--the
T7   170:36   name of a town beginning with H. "The other Messenger's called Hatta. I must have two, you know--to come
MESSENGERS (2)
T7   170:13   in the game. And I haven't sent the two Messengers, either. They're both gone to the town. Just look
T8   179: 5   and the Unicorn and those queer Anglo-Saxon Messengers. However, there was the great dish still lying at
MET (6)
T3   135:35   collar'--just fancy calling everything you met 'Alice,' till one of them answered! Only they wouldn't
T8W   18: 7   into Alice's head. Almost every one she had met had repeated poetry to her, and she thought she would try
A3   25: 7   "Fury said to a mouse, That he met in the house, 'Let us both go to law: I will prosecute you
A9   70: 6   pepper that had made her so savage when they met in the kitchen.
T6   168:40   say) "of all the unsatisfactory people I ever met--" She never finished the sentence, for at this moment a
A4   34: 8   of the mushroom, and her eyes immediately met those of a large blue caterpillar, that was sitting on the

MEW (1)
 T12 207: 8 purr. "If they would only purr for 'yes,' and mew for 'no,' or any rule of that sort," she had said, "so
MICE (8)
 A4   29: 1   and smaller, and being ordered about by mice and rabbits. I almost wish I hadn't gone down that
 A1   9: 9   wish you were down here with me! There are no mice in the air, I'm afraid, but you might catch a bat, and
 T9   199:31 and bran: / Put cats in the coffee, and mice in the tea--/ And welcome Queen Alice with
 T8   181:36 other thing is a mouse-trap. I suppose the mice keep the bees out--or the bees keep the mice out, I don't
 A2   19:39   and she's such a capital one for catching mice--oh, I beg your pardon!" cried Alice again, for this time
 T8   182: 2   "It isn't very likely there would be any mice on the horse's back."
 T8   181:37 mice keep the bees out--or the bees keep the mice out, I don't know which."
 A3   26:28   And she's such a capital one for catching mice, you ca'n't think! And oh, I wish you could see her after
MICROSCOPE (1)
 T3   130:19 first through a telescope, then through a microscope, and then through an opera-glass. At last he said
MIDDLE (17)
 T1   107:19 the kitten running after its own tail in the middle.
 T2   120:29 of daisies, and a willow-tree growing in the middle.
 A3   21:16   once, in a large ring, with the Mouse in the middle. Alice kept her eyes anxiously fixed on it, for she
 A4   32:14   The poor little Lizard, Bill, was in the middle, being held up by two guinea-pigs, who were giving it
 T6   166: 8   and whistling, with a kind of sneeze in the middle: however, you'll hear it done, maybe--down in the wood
 T6   168:28   in the air with his thumb) "nose in the middle, mouth under. It's always the same. Now if you had the
 A6   47: 2   was sitting on a three-legged stool in the middle, nursing a baby: the cook was leaning over the fire,
 T9   196:18 I never should try to remember my name in the middle of an accident! Where would be the use of it?" but she
 A9   72:30   the Duchess's voice died away, even in the middle of her favourite word "moral", and the arm that was
 A4   29: 5   never happened, and now here I am in the middle of one! There ought to be a book written about me, that
 A11 86: 7   scroll of parchment in the other. In the very middle of the court was a table, with a large dish of tarts
 T4   140:28   And this was odd, because it was / The middle of the night.
 T7   173:15 they came into sight of a great crowd, in the middle of which the Lion and Unicorn were fighting. They were
 T9   200:15 Queens had already taken two of them, but the middle one was empty. Alice sat down in it, rather
 T2   122: 1   "There's the tree in the middle," said the Rose. "What else is it good for?"
 T9   202:16 the lid to the dish, while it lies in the middle: / Which is easiest to do, / Un-dish-cover the fish, or
 A1   9:32   trying every door, she walked sadly down the middle, wondering how she was ever to get out again.
MIDST (1)
 T5   152:40 could not help laughing at this, even in the midst of her tears. "Can you keep from crying by considering
MIGHT (52)
 T1   108:10 ball, as if it would be glad to help if it might.
 T5   154: 4   should like to look all round me first, if I might."
 T10 205: 2   shook her backwards and forwards with all her might.
 A6   46:24   at the top of his head. But at any rate he might answer questions.--How am I to get in?" she repeated,
 A9   72: 7   yourself not to be otherwise than what it might appear to others that what you were or might have been
 T1   115: 2   she put him on the table, she thought she might as well dust him a little, he was so covered with ashes.
 A8   68:10   Alice thought she might as well go back and see how the game was going on, as
 A4   34: 6   and behind it, it occurred to her that she might as well look and see what was on top of it.
 T7   175: 5   the King. "She runs so fearfully quick. You might as well try to catch a Bandersnatch! But I'll make a
 T7   173:12 see, a minute goes by so fearfully quick. You might as well try to stop a Bandersnatch!"
 A5   36:26   Alice thought she might as well wait, as she had nothing else to do, and perhaps
 T4   139: 7   continued Tweedledee, "if it was so, it might be; and if it were so, it would be; but as it isn't, it
 T6   160:10 shape it is, too. With a name like yours, you might be any shape, almost."
 A4   32:31   all the time at the thought that it might be hungry, in which case it would be very likely to eat
 A6   46:18   "There might be some sense in your knocking," the Footman went on,
 A1   9:36   key, and Alice's first idea was that this might belong to one of the doors of the hall; but, alas!
 A9   71: 9   "He might bite," Alice cautiously replied, not feeling at all
 A1   9:10   are no mice in the air, I'm afraid, but you might catch a bat, and that's very like a mouse, you know. But
 T9   192: 7   at first, as she was afraid that the crown might come off: but she comforted herself with the thought
 A7   56:32   Alice sighed wearily. "I think you might do something better with the time," she said, "than
 A6   50:18   thinking over other children she knew, who might do very well as pigs, and was just saying to herself "if
 T8   189:14 wealth, / But chiefly for his wish that he / Might drink my noble health.
 A1   12: 7   she felt a little nervous about this; "for it might end, you know," said Alice to herself, "in my going out
 A1   10:13   she went back to the table, half hoping she might find another key on it, or at any rate a book of rules
 T6   163:20 three hundred and sixty-four days when you might get un-birthday presents--"
 T9   194:23 Alice said, as gravely as she could, "They might go different ways." But she couldn't help thinking to
 A8   67: 4   dispute with the Queen, but she knew that it might happen any minute, "and then," thought she, "what would
 A9   72: 8   might appear to others that what you were or might have been was not otherwise than what you had been would
 T6   159: 7   It might have been written a hundred times, easily, on that
 T7   176:16   "What a fight we might have for the crown now!" the Unicorn said, looking slyly
 T6   162:12 "but two can. With proper assistance, you might have left off at seven."
 T1   110: 7   it was a nice check, Kitty, and really I might have won, if it hadn't been for that nasty Knight, that
 T4   140:24 shining on the sea, / Shining with all his might: / He did his very best to make / The billows smooth and
 T3   136:18 yourself?" she said timidly. "I think that might help a little."
 A5   37: 6   William replied to his son, / "I feared it might injure the brain; / But, now that I'm perfectly sure I
 T2   126: 4   them! I wouldn't mind being a Pawn, if only I might join--though of course I should like to be a Queen, best
 A10 82:18   make one repeat lessons!" thought Alice. "I might just as well be at school at once." However, she got up,
 A7   55:26   "You might just as well say," added the March Hare, "that 'I like
 A7   55:28   "You might just as well say," added the Dormouse, which seemed to
 A7   55:23   same thing a bit!" said the Hatter. "Why, you might just as well say that 'I see what I eat' is the same
 A6   46:20   us. For instance, if you were inside, you might knock, and I could let you out, you know." He was
 A3   23: 6   way to explain it is to do it." (And, as you might like to try the thing yourself some winter-day, I will
 T3   131:29   "You might make a joke on that," said the little voice close to her
 T3   131:14 small voice, close to her ear, said "You might make a joke on that--something about 'horse' and 'hoarse
 T6   161: 7   "If he smiled much more the ends of his mouth might meet behind," she thought: "And then I don't know what
 A8   68:26   So she tucked it away under her arm, that it might not escape again, and went back to have a little more

MIGHT (cont.)
```
 T8W   21:12   was  getting  very talkative, she thought she might safely leave him. "I think I must be going on now," she
 T1   110:27   she held it up to the Looking-glass, that it might see how sulky it was, "--and if you're not good directly
 A5    36:27   nothing  else  to  do,  and perhaps after all it might tell her something worth hearing. For some minutes it
 A3    26:24              "And who is Dinah, if I might venture to ask the question?" said the Lory.
 A2    15:21   said  Alice,  "a  great  girl like you," (she might well say this), "to go on crying in this way! Stop this
 A12   98:12   ran  off, thinking while she ran, as well she might, what a wonderful dream it had been.
```
MIGHTN'T (2)
```
 T5   158:11   counter.  For  she  thought to herself, "They mightn't be at all nice, you know."
 T1   114:24    than  she  had  lifted  the  Queen, that she mightn't take his breath away; but, before she put him on the
```
MILD (4)
```
 T8   187:19   again,  as if it had been only yesterday--the mild blue eyes and kindly smile of the Knight--the setting sun
 T8   181:11   hands,  and turning his gentle face and large mild eyes to Alice. She thought she had never seen such a
 T8   188:17               His accents mild took up the tale: / He said 'I go my ways, / And when I
 T8   190: 1   that old man I used to know--/ Whose look was mild, whose speech was slow, / Whose hair was whiter than the
```
MILE (4)
```
 A12   93:38                "I'm not a mile high," said Alice.
 A12   93:35   "Rule Forty-two. All persons more than a mile high to leave the court."
 T3   129: 8   They ca'n't be bees--nobody ever saw bees a mile off, you know--" and for some time she stood silent,
 T4   142:14   The  Walrus  and  the Carpenter / Walked on a mile or so, / And then they rested on a rock / Conveniently
```
MILES (3)
```
 A1    8:30   Let  me  see:  that  would  be four thousand miles down, I think--" (for, you see, Alice had learnt several
 A12   93:40                "Nearly two miles high," added the Queen.
 A1    8:28   fall never come to an end? "I wonder how many miles I've fallen by this time?" she said aloud. "I must be
```
MILK (4)
```
 A1    9: 8   cat.) "I hope they'll remember her saucer of milk at tea-time. Dinah, my dear! I wish you were down here
 T1   108:34   the tail just as I had put down the saucer of milk before her! What, you were thirsty, were you? How do you
 T1   110:44   House, Kitty? I  wonder  if they'd give you milk in there? Perhaps Looking-glass milk isn't good to drink
 T1   110:44   give you milk in there? Perhaps Looking-glass milk isn't good to drink--but oh, Kitty! now we come to the
```
MILK-JUG (1)
```
 A7    60: 2   before,  as the March Hare had just upset the milk-jug into his plate.
```
MIMSY (5)
```
 T6   165: 9               "Exactly so. Well then, 'mimsy' is 'flimsy and miserable' (there's another portmanteau
 T1   116:11   emom  eht  dnA  /  ,sevogorob  eht erew ysmim llA / :ebaw eht ni elbmig dna eryg diD / sevot yhtils eht dna
 T1   116:20   / Did  gyre  and  gimble  in the wabe: / All mimsy were the borogoves, / And the mome raths outgrabe.
 T1   118:23   / Did  gyre  and  gimble  in the wabe: / All mimsy were the borogoves, / And the mome raths outgrabe.
 T6   164:23   / Did  gyre  and  gimble  in the wabe: / All mimsy were the borogoves, / And the mome raths outgrabe."
```
MINCE-PIE (1)
```
 T3   134: 2               "Frumenty and mince-pie," the Gnat replied; "and it makes its nest in a
```
MIND (29)
```
 A7    54: 6   "only  as  it's  asleep,  I suppose it doesn't mind."
 A2    17:20   so many lessons to learn! No, I've made up my mind about it: if I'm Mabel, I'll stay down here. It'll be no
 T2   122:13                "Never mind!" Alice said in a soothing tone, and, stooping down to
 A3    26:44   half  hoping  that  the Mouse had changed his mind, and was coming back to finish his story.
 A1    7: 6          So she was considering, in her own mind (as well as she could, for the hot day made her feel very
 T2   126: 3   is! How I wish I was one of them! I wouldn't mind being a Pawn, if only I might join--though of course I
 T8   184: 3   speak of," the Knight said, as if he didn't mind breaking two or three of them. "The great art of riding,
 T8   186: 3   where my body happens to be?" he said. "My mind goes on working all the same. In fact, the more
 A6    50: 5   "I'll  have  nothing  more  to  do with you. Mind now!" The poor little thing sobbed again (or grunted, it
 T5   157:13   Sheep: "plenty of choice, only make up your mind. Now, what do you want to buy?"
 A5    41:15   to  be  a little larger, Sir, if you wouldn't mind," said Alice: "three inches is such a wretched height to
 A11   91:25                "Never mind!" said the King with an air of great relief. "Call the
 T9   193:10               "She's in that state of mind," said the White Queen, "that she wants to deny something
 T8W   18: 9   if the Wasp couldn't do it too. "Would you mind saying it in rhyme?" she asked very politely.
 A5    36:17   seemed  to  be  in a very unpleasant state of mind, she turned away.
 T5   156:12   and  pick some?" Alice pleaded. "If you don't mind stopping the boat for a minute."
 T3   133: 9   with great interest, and made up her mind that it must have been just repainted, it looked so
 A4    30:29   Catch hold of this rope--Will the roof bear?--Mind that loose slate--Oh, it's coming down! Heads below!" (a
 T1   109: 7   fifty dinners at once! Well, I shouldn't mind that much! I'd far rather go without them than eat them!
 A1    8: 1    to her feet, for it flashed across her mind that she had never before seen a rabbit with either a
 T1   114:12   who was sitting sulkily among the ashes, "Mind the volcano!"
 T2   123:10   asked eagerly, for the thought crossed her mind, "There's another little girl in the garden, somewhere!"
 T8   179:11   in  a  rather complaining tone: "I've a great mind to go and wake him, and see what happens!"
 T3   135:25   However, on second thoughts, she made up her mind to go on: "for I certainly won't go back," she thought to
 T8W   14:17               "You may read it if you've a mind to," the Wasp said, rather sulkily. "Nobody's hindering
 T1   108:16   it  snowed so, they had to leave off. Never mind, we'll go and see the bonfire to-morrow." Here Alice
 T3   131:24   forwards  and  whispered  in  her ear, "Never mind what they all say, my dear, but take a return-ticket
 A6    48:16               "Oh, please mind what you're doing!" cried Alice, jumping up and down in
 T1   114:16   Queen, who was still a little out of breath. "Mind you come up--the regular way--don't get blown up!"
```
MINDED (2)
```
 T4   148:11               "I shouldn't have minded it so much," said Tweedledum, "if it hadn't been a new
 A6    48:20               "If everybody minded their own business," the Duchess said, in a hoarse
```
MINDING (1)
```
 A9    70:35   Alice whispered, "that it's done by everybody minding their own business!"
```
MINE (11) [entries omitted]

-MINE [See MUSTARD-MINE]

MINERAL (2)
```
 T7   176: 6   wearily. "Are  you  animal--or vegetable--or mineral?" he said, yawning at every other word.
 A9    71:16               "It's a mineral, I think," said Alice.
```

MINUTE (48)
AI	3:18	interrupts the tale / Not more than once a minute.
A8	67: 2	or "Off with her head!" about once in a minute.
T3	130: 1	Why, his time is worth a thousand pounds a minute!"
T5	155:13	She gets more and more like a porcupine every minute!"
T5	156:12	"If you don't mind stopping the boat for a minute."
T9	197:20	The snoring got more distinct every minute, and sounded more like a tune: at last she could even
A8	67: 5	Queen, but she knew that it might happen any minute, "and then," thought she, "what would become of me?
T2	124: 3	beautifully. She had not been walking a minute before she found herself face to face with the Red
T7	173:12	said, "only I'm not strong enough. You see, a minute goes by so fearfully quick. You might as well try to
T6	163:37	too much puzzled to say anything; so after a minute Humpty Dumpty began again. "They've a temper, some of
T2	121: 1	so astonished that she couldn't speak for a minute: it quite seemed to take her breath away. At length, as
T7	173: 9	after running a little further, "to stop a minute--just to get--one's breath again?"
T9	202: 8	/ That is easy, and will not take more than a minute. / 'Let it lie in a dish!' / That is easy, because it
A4	27:31	and get ready for your walk!' 'Coming in a minute, nurse! But I've got to watch this mouse-hole till
T5	154:17	in a plaintive tone, after she had spent a minute or so in vainly pursuing a large bright thing that
A7	59: 2	treacle," said the Dormouse, after thinking a minute or two.
T9	193:13	then there was an uncomfortable silence for a minute or two.
T7	174:20	For a minute or two Alice stood silent, watching him. Suddenly she
A8	65:43	other: however, they got settled down in a minute or two, and the game began.
A6	49:20	out again, so that altogether, for the first minute or two, it was as much as she could do to hold it.
A8	65:14	near. The three soldiers wandered about for a minute or two, looking for them, and then quietly marched off
T3	134:20	After this, Alice was silent for a minute or two, pondering. The Gnat amused itself meanwhile by
T1	114: 9	had quite taken away her breath, and for a minute or two she could do nothing but hug the little Lily in
A8	67:11	very much at first, but after watching it a minute or two she made it out to be a grin, and she said to
A6	45: 1	For a minute or two she stood looking at the house, and wondering
A6	52:23	it again, but it did not appear, and after a minute or two she walked on in the direction in which the
A10	78: 3	at Alice and tried to speak, but, for a minute or two, sobs choked his voice. "Same as if he had a
A5	41:24	patiently until it chose to speak again. In a minute or two the Caterpillar took the hookah out of its mouth
A4	31:37	any sense, they'd take the roof off." After a minute or two they began moving about again, and Alice heard
A7	59:22	The Dormouse again took a minute or two to think about it, and then said "It was a
T6	162:23	was very angry, though he said nothing for a minute or two. When he did speak again, it was in a deep growl
A5	43:22	to Alice, that she was quite silent for a minute or two, which gave the Pigeon the opportunity of adding
T5	156: 2	so there was no more conversation for a minute or two, while the boat glided gently on, sometimes
A1	12:22	sharply. "I advise you to leave off this minute!" She generally gave herself very good advice (though
T9	192:25	off with a frown, and, after thinking for a minute, suddenly changed the subject of the conversation.
A8	67:18	come, or at least one of them." In another minute the whole head appeared, and then Alice put down her
T9	199: 9	at the door with his large dull eyes for a minute: then he went nearer and rubbed it with his thumb, as
T4	140: 2	Alice's hands, and stood looking at her for a minute: there was a rather awkward pause, as Alice didn't know
A4	28:17	had to kneel down on the floor: in another minute there was not even room for this, and she tried the
T9	199:35	ninety. I wonder if any one's counting?" In a minute there was silence again, and the same shrill voice sang
T6	161:14	Dumpty went on. "They'd pick me up again in a minute, they would! However, this conversation is going on a
T3	136: 2	She stood silent for a minute, thinking: then she suddenly began again. "Then it
A5	43:41	I'm never sure what I'm going to be, from one minute to another! However, I've got back to my right size:
T6	168:34	Alice waited a minute to see if he would speak again, but, as he never opened
T9	202:19	"Take a minute to think about it, and then guess," said the Red Queen.
A5	41:34	looking thoughtfully at the mushroom for a minute, trying to make out which were the two sides of it; and
A7	55:32	dropped, and the party sat silent for a minute, while Alice thought over all she could remember about
T4	147:13	hand-in-hand into the wood, and returned in a minute with their arms full of things--such as bolsters,

MINUTES (17)
A5	41: 5	decidedly; and there was silence for some minutes.
T2	127: 2	the Queen repeated. "Why, we passed it ten minutes ago! Faster!" And they ran on for a time in silence,
T2	125:19	For some minutes Alice stood without speaking, looking out in all
A9	74:29	So they sat down, and nobody spoke for some minutes. Alice thought to herself "I don't see how he can ever
T2	120:20	on till she got to the hill. For a few minutes all went on well, and she was just saying "I really
T7	174:13	down, panting, while the King called out "Ten minutes allowed for refreshments!" Haigha and Hatta set to
A5	43:39	at first; but she got used to it in a few minutes, and began talking to herself, as usual, "Come,
A12	92: 2	how large she had grown in the last few minutes, and she jumped up in such a hurry that she tipped
A5	36:28	tell her something worth hearing. For some minutes it puffed away without speaking; but at last it
A3	21: 6	a consultation about this, and after a few minutes it seemed quite natural to Alice to find herself
A4	29:17	of it altogether; but after a few minutes she heard a voice outside, and stopped to listen.
T8	182:37	plan, Alice thought, and for a few minutes she walked on in silence, puzzling over the idea, and
A12	95:24	(she had grown so large in the last few minutes that she wasn't a bit afraid of interrupting him,)
A11	91:22	For some minutes the whole court was in confusion, getting the Dormouse
T8W	21:17	that she had gone back and given a few minutes to making the poor old creature comfortable.
A1	12: 6	garden. First, however, she waited for a few minutes to see if she was going to shrink any further: she
A5	36:32	used--and I don't keep the same size for ten minutes together!"

MISCHIEF (4)
T1	107: 5	see that it couldn't have had any hand in the mischief.
T9	204:18	whom she considered as the cause of all the mischief--but the Queen was no longer at her side--she had
A12	94:24	the matter worse. You must have meant some mischief, or else you'd have signed your name like an honest
T1	108:22	settled again, "when I saw all the mischief you had been doing, I was very nearly opening the

MISCHIEVOUS (1)
| T1 | 108:25 | snow! And you'd have deserved it, you little mischievous darling! What have you got to say for yourself? |

MISERABLE (4)
T1	109: 6	to be going without a dinner: then, when the miserable day came, I should have to go without fifty dinners
A11	90: 7	The miserable Hatter dropped his teacup and bread-and-butter and
A12	98:33	the air, mixed up with the distant sob of the miserable Mock Turtle.
T6	165: 9	Exactly so. Well then, 'mimsy' is 'flimsy and miserable' (there's another portmanteau for you). And a

MISS (7)
A4   27:30   the sort of thing that would happen: "'Miss Alice! Come here directly, and get ready for your walk!'
T3   135: 8   "Well, if she said 'Miss,' and didn't say anything more," the Gnat remarked, "of
T3   135: 7   she couldn't remember my name, she'd call me 'Miss,' as the servants do."
A1   9: 6   so Alice soon began talking again. "Dinah'll miss me very much to-night, I should think!" (Dinah was the
A8   63: 6   in a low voice, "Why, the fact is, you see, Miss, this here ought to have been a red rose-tree, and we put
A8   63: 9   have our heads cut off, you know. So you see, Miss, we're doing our best, afore she comes, to--" At this
T3   135: 9   more," the Gnat remarked, "of course you'd miss your lessons. That's a joke. I wish you had made it."
MISSED (4)
A6   49:14   frying-pan after her as she went, but it just missed her.
T9   200:18   At last the Red Queen began. "You've missed the soup and fish," she said. "Put on the joint!" And
A8   68:13   of the players to be executed for having missed their turns, and she did not like the look of things at
T9   197:23   suddenly vanished from her lap, she hardly missed them.
MISSES (1)
T8   180: 4   he knocks him off his horse; and, if he misses, he tumbles off himself--and another Rule seems to be
MIST (2)
T1   111:13   to melt away, just like a bright silvery mist.
T1   111:10   get through. Why, it's turning into a sort of mist now, I declare! It'll be easy enough to get through--"
MISTAKE (4)
A6   50:11   in some alarm. This time there could be no mistake about it: it was neither more nor less than a pig, and
A8   63: 7   a red rose-tree, and we put a white one in by mistake; and, if the Queen was to find out, we should all have
T5   152: 1   Alice was just beginning to say "There's a mistake somewhere--," when the Queen began screaming, so loud
A4   27:17   it pointed to, without trying to explain the mistake that it had made.
MIX (1)
T9   200: 3   Or anything else that is pleasant to drink: / Mix sand with the cider, and wool with the wine--/ And welcome
MIXED (2)
A1   11: 7   it very nice (it had, in fact, a sort of mixed flavour of cherry-tart, custard, pine-apple, roast
A12   98:32   the suppressed guinea-pigs, filled the air, mixed up with the distant sob of the miserable Mock Turtle.
MIXING (1)
T8   186:27   you've no idea what a difference it makes, mixing it with other things--such as gunpowder and sealing-wax
MOANED (2)
T9   196:35   on Alice's shoulder. "I am so sleepy!" she moaned.
T9   192:34   a great deal more than that!" the White Queen moaned, wringing her hands. "Oh, ever so much more than that!"
MOCK TURTLE (56)
A9   76: 2   "You did," said the Mock Turtle.
A9   76:11   "And washing?" said the Mock Turtle.
A9   77:20   "Of course it was," said the Mock Turtle.
A10   79: 3   you like to see a little of it?" said the Mock Turtle.
A10   81:43   "Explain all that," said the Mock Turtle.
A10   83: 2   I should like to have it explained," said the Mock Turtle.
A12   98:33   up with the distant sob of the miserable Mock Turtle.
A9   76: 9   "With extras?" asked the Mock Turtle, a little anxiously.
A9   74:36   and the constant heavy sobbing of the Mock Turtle. Alice was very nearly getting up and saying,
A9   76:34   more questions about it: so she turned to the Mock Turtle, and said "What else had you to learn?"
A9   74: 2   Queen, "and take this young lady to see the Mock Turtle, and to hear his history. I must go back and see
A9   75: 2   him Tortoise because he taught us," said the Mock Turtle angrily. "Really you are very dull!"
A9   74:32   "Once," said the Mock Turtle at last, with a deep sigh, "I was a real Turtle."
A10   80:20   "I don't know where Dinn may be," said the Mock Turtle; "but, if you've seen them so often, of course you
A10   82:32   "Well, I never heard it before," said the Mock Turtle; "but it sounds uncommon nonsense."
A10   78:31   "Turn a somersault in the sea!" cried the Mock Turtle, capering wildly about.
A10   80:24   "You're wrong about the crumbs," said the Mock Turtle: "crumbs would all wash off in the sea. But they
A10   82: 8   the words all coming different, and then the Mock Turtle drew a long breath, and said "That's very curious!
A9   75: 7   the earth. At last the Gryphon said to the Mock Turtle "Drive on, old fellow! Don't be all day about it!"
A10   85: 1   "Chorus again!" cried the Gryphon, and the Mock Turtle had just begun to repeat it, when a cry of "The
A9   74:27   "I'll tell it her," said the Mock Turtle in a deep, hollow tone. "Sit down, both of you,
A9   76:13   yours wasn't a really good school," said the Mock Turtle in a tone of great relief. "Now, at ours, they had
A9   74:16   They had not gone far before they saw the Mock Turtle in the distance, sitting sad and lonely on a
A10   84: 3   is the use of repeating all that stuff?" the Mock Turtle interrupted, "if you don't explain it as you go on
A9   73:12   "No," said Alice. "I don't even know what a Mock Turtle is."
A9   77:12   "Ten hours the first day," said the Mock Turtle: "nine the next, and so on."
A10   83: 5   "But about his toes?" the Mock Turtle persisted. "How could he turn them out with his
A10   78: 5   him and punching him in the back. At last the Mock Turtle recovered his voice, and, with tears running down
A10   82:11   "It all came different!" the Mock Turtle repeated thoughtfully. "I should like to hear her
A9   76:21   and Writhing, of course, to begin with," the Mock Turtle replied; "and then the different branches of
A9   76:36   "Well, there was Mystery," the Mock Turtle replied, counting off the subjects on his flappers
A10   81:37   "I mean what I say," the Mock Turtle replied, in an offended tone. And the Gryphon
A10   78:22   "Of course," the Mock Turtle said: "advance twice, set to partners--"
A9   77: 2   "Well, I ca'n't show it you, myself," the Mock Turtle said: "I'm too stiff. And the Gryphon never learnt
A10   81:30   They were obliged to have him with them," the Mock Turtle said. "No wise fish would go anywhere without a
A9   77: 6   "I never went to him," the Mock Turtle said with a sigh. "He taught Laughing and Grief,
A10   79:11   their fore-paws to mark the time, while the Mock Turtle sang this, very slowly and sadly:--
A10   78:16   "Two lines!" cried the Mock Turtle. "Seals, turtles, salmon, and so on: then, when
A10   78: 1   The Mock Turtle sighed deeply, and drew the back of one flapper
A10   84:15   The Mock Turtle sighed deeply, and began, in a voice choked with
A9   73:13   "It's the thing Mock Turtle Soup is made from," said the Queen.
A10   78:36   and--that's all the first figure," said the Mock Turtle, suddenly dropping his voice; and the two
A10   80:16   "Oh, as to the whiting," said the Mock Turtle, "they--you've seen them, of course?"
A10   84: 9   the Gryphon went on. "Or would you like the Mock Turtle to sing you another song?"
A10   79: 5   "Come, let's try the first figure!" said the Mock Turtle to the Gryphon. "We can do it without lobsters,
A9   76: 4   Gryphon, before Alice could speak again. The Mock Turtle went on.

MOCK (cont.)
```
A9    74:40   "When we were still little," the Mock Turtle went on at last, more calmly, though still sobbing
A10   78:26             "Then, you know," the Mock Turtle went on, "you throw the--"
A9    74:23         So they went up to the Mock Turtle, who looked at them with large eyes full of tears,
A10   81:33   "Of course not," said the Mock Turtle. "Why, if a fish came to me, and told me he was
A9    76:18   "I couldn't afford to learn it," said the Mock Turtle with a sigh. "I only took the regular course."
A10   84:11      "Oh, a song, please, if the Mock Turtle would be so kind," Alice replied, so eagerly that
A10   81: 1   their mouths; and the reason is--" here the Mock Turtle yawned and shut his eyes. "Tell her about the
A9    73:11   breath, and said to Alice "Have you seen the Mock Turtle yet?"
A12   99: 2   in the distance would take the place of the Mock Turtle's heavy sobs.
A9t   70: 1                          THE MOCK TURTLE'S STORY
```
MODEL (1)
```
T1   110:24   table, and set it up before the kitten as a model for it to imitate: however, the thing didn't succeed,
```
MODERATE (1)
```
A3    22:23   him the crown. William's conduct at first was moderate. But the insolence of his Normans--' How are you
```
MODERN (1)
```
A9    76:37      on his flappers--"Mystery, ancient and modern, with Seaography: then Drawling--the Drawling-master
```
MOME (6)
```
T6   166: 3   "Well, a 'rath' is a sort of green pig: but 'mome' I'm not certain about. I think it's short for 'from
T1   116:12             .ebargtuo shtar emom eht dnA / ,sevogorob eht erew ysmim llA / :ebaw eht ni elbmig
T1   116:21   / All mimsy were the borogoves, / And the mome raths outgrabe.
T1   118:24   / All mimsy were the borogoves, / And the mome raths outgrabe.
T6   164:24   / All mimsy were the borogoves, / And the mome raths outgrabe."
T6   166: 1                          "And then 'mome raths'?" said Alice. "I'm afraid I'm giving you a great
```
MOMENT (73)
```
A9    72:39   Duchess took her choice, and was gone in a moment.
T4   139:42   they had begun: the music stopped at the same moment.
T4   148:23   to their heels and were out of sight in a moment.
T9   196:27   but really couldn't think of anything at the moment.
T6   168:41   She never finished the sentence, for at this moment a heavy crash shook the forest from end to end.
A4    32: 1   But she had not long to doubt, for the next moment a shower of little pebbles came rattling in at the
A8    68:33                          The moment Alice appeared, she was appealed to by all three to
A11   88:34             Just at this moment Alice felt a very curious sensation, which puzzled her
T1   112: 1             In another moment Alice was through the glass, and had jumped lightly
T7   170: 3   off instantly. The confusion got worse every moment, and Alice was very glad to get out of the wood into an
A4    27:14   what are you doing out here? Run home this moment, and fetch me a pair of gloves and a fan! Quick, now!"
T2   123:42   To her surprise she lost sight of her in a moment, and found herself walking in at the front-door again.
T1   119: 2   garden first!" She was out of the room in a moment, and ran down stairs--or, at least, it wasn't exactly
T9   198:10    with a long beak put its head out for a moment and said "No admittance till the week after next!" and
T2   122:16             There was silence in a moment, and several of the pink daisies turned white.
T5   158: 1   boat, and the river, had vanished all in a moment, and she was back again in the little dark shop.
T8   179:18   frightened for him than for herself at the moment, and watched him with some anxiety as he mounted again.
T4   146:14   and his eyes grew large and yellow all in a moment, as he pointed with a trembling finger at a small white
T4   138: 2   neck, and Alice knew which was which in a moment, because one of them had 'DUM' embroidered on his
T9   197:10   to me. I'm getting sleepy, too." In another moment both Queens were fast asleep, and snoring loud.
A1     8: 5             In another moment down went Alice after it, never once considering how in
T3   129:34    putting his head in at the window. In a moment everybody was holding out a ticket: they were about the
T6   159:15   hands ready to catch him, for she was every moment expecting him to fall.
A8    63:10   our best, afore she comes, to--" At this moment, Five, who had been anxiously looking across the garden
T5   154: 2   the Sheep said at last, looking up for a moment from her knitting.
A8    69:10      The Cat's head began fading away the moment he was gone, and, by the time he had come back with the
A2    15:12             Just at this moment her head struck against the roof of the hall: in fact
T8   179:12             At this moment her thoughts were interrupted by a loud shouting of
A12   92: 1   Alice, quite forgetting in the flurry of the moment how large she had grown in the last few minutes, and
A2    15:22   "to go on crying in this way! Stop this moment, I tell you!" But she went on all the same, shedding
T3   137: 9   into its beautiful brown eyes, and in another moment it had darted away at full speed.
A5    41:32   as if she had asked it aloud; and in another moment it was out of sight.
T9   201:17   the pudding!" and there it was again in a moment, like a conjuring-trick. It was so large that she
A8    64: 6   with fury, and, after glaring at her for a moment like a wild beast, began screaming "Off with her head!
A8    68: 4   called to the Queen, who was passing at the moment, "My dear! I wish you would have this cat removed!"
T9   204: 7   broad good-natured face grinning at her for a moment over the edge of the tureen, before she disappeared
T9   200: 7   in she went, and there was a dead silence the moment she appeared.
A4    32:16   a bottle. They all made a rush at Alice the moment she appeared; but she ran off as hard as she could, and
A4    32:37   to keep herself from being run over; and, the moment she appeared on the other side, the puppy made another
T5   158:28   step, as everything turned into a tree the moment she came up to it, and she quite expected the egg to do
A5    41:39   right-hand bit to try the effect. The next moment she felt a violent blow underneath her chin: it had
T3   132:10   comfort!" she said to herself. In another moment she felt the carriage rise straight up into the air,
T2   120:23   she described it afterwards), and the next moment she found herself actually walking in at the door.
T9   204: 2             At this moment she heard a hoarse laugh at her side, and turned to see
A1     9:22   hurt, and she jumped up on to her feet in a moment: she looked up, but it was all dark overhead: before
T9   201:30   a little frightened at finding that, the moment she opened her lips, there was dead silence, and all
A2    14: 2   (she was so much surprised, that for the moment she quite forgot how to speak good English). "Now I'm
T3   137:32   could not help starting back, but in another moment she recovered herself, feeling sure that they must be
T7   169: 1             The next moment soldiers came running through the wood, at first in
T2   126:11   Square you'll be a Queen--"Just at this moment, somehow or other, they began to run.
A2    18:18   these words her foot slipped, and in another moment, splash! she was up to her chin in saltwater. Her first
A6    47:17   Alice quite jumped; but she saw in another moment that it was addressed to the baby, and not to her, so
A4    27: 6   dropped them, I wonder?" Alice guessed in a moment that it was looking for the fan and the pair of white
T5   156:35   all their scent and beauty, from the very moment that she picked them? Even real scented rushes, you
T9   203:11    it) all sorts of things happened in a moment. The candles all grew up to the ceiling, looking
```

MOMENT (cont.)
A6   46:27   At this moment the door of the house opened, and a large plate came
T9   199:22   At this moment the door was flung open, and a shrill voice was heard
T1   115:25   "The horror of that moment," the King went on, "I shall never, never forget!"
A12   93:33   At this moment the King, who had been for some time busily writing in
T7   171: 8   At this moment the Messenger arrived: he was far too much out of
T7   175: 9   At this moment the Unicorn sauntered by them, with his hands in his
T5   149: 2   and   looked   about   for the owner: in another moment the White Queen came running wildly through the wood,
A4   29:20   said the voice. "Fetch me my gloves this moment!" Then came a little pattering of feet on the stairs.
A9   72:44   and   were   resting   in the shade: however, the moment they saw her, they hurried back to the game, the Queen
T4   139:28   she took hold of both hands at once: the next moment they were dancing round in a ring. This seemed quite
T9   204: 9   There was not a moment to be lost. Already several of the guests were lying
A1   9:24   in sight, hurrying down it. There was not a moment to be lost: away went Alice like the wind, and was just
A4   32:41   play with a cart-horse, and expecting every moment to be trampled under its feet, ran round the thistle
T2   128:26   to the next peg, where she turned for a moment to say "Good-bye," and then hurried on to the last.
A1   8: 9   down, so suddenly that Alice had not a moment to think about stopping herself before she found
A5   42: 8   delight, which changed into alarm in another moment, when she found that her shoulders were nowhere to be
T7   171:14   attitudes only got more extraordinary every moment, while the great eyes rolled wildly from side to side.
T1   113: 5   the hearth among the cinders; but in another moment, with a little "Oh!" of surprise, she was down on her
MOMENT'S (2)
A9   73: 2   the game, the Queen merely remarking that a moment's delay would cost them their lives.
A6   47: 9   sneezing and howling alternately without a moment's pause. The only two creatures in the kitchen, that
MOMENTS (1)
T8W   18:11   try; wait a bit." He was silent for a few moments, and then began again--
MONEY (2)
T5   158:13   The Sheep took the money, and put it away in a box: then she said "I never put
T5   158:10   have one, please," said Alice, as she put the money down on the counter. For she thought to herself, "They
MONSTER (6)
T7   177:21   said the Lion. "Do you like plum-cake, Monster?"
T7   177:18   hand, very much puzzled how to begin. "The Monster has given the Lion twice as much as me!"
T7   177: 5   much dust to see anything. What a time the Monster is, cutting up that cake!"
T7   177: 9   was getting quite used to being called 'the Monster'). "I've cut several slices already, but they always
T7   176: 9   "Then hand round the plum-cake, Monster," the Lion said, lying down and putting his chin on
T7   176: 7   "It's a fabulous monster!" the Unicorn cried out, before Alice could reply.
MONSTERS (2)
T7   175:23   "I always thought they were fabulous monsters!" said the Unicorn. "Is it alive?"
T7   175:29   know, I always thought Unicorns were fabulous monsters, too? I never saw one alive before!"
MONSTROUS (2)
T4   139: 1   Just then flew down a monstrous crow, / As black as a tar-barrel; / Which frightened
T4   148:13   "I wish the monstrous crow would come!" thought Alice.
MONTH (2)
A7   56:13   she remarked. "It tells the day of the month, and doesn't tell what o'clock it is!"
A7   55:36   first to break the silence. "What day of the month is it?" he said, turning to Alice: he had taken his
MONTHS (3)
T6   161:23   calculation, and said "Seven years and six months."
T5   153: 7   believe. I'm just one hundred and one, five months and a day."
T6   162: 3   "Seven years and six months!" Humpty Dumpty repeated thoughtfully. "An
MOODY (1)
TI   103:26   frost, the blinding snow, / The storm-wind's moody madness--/ Within, the firelight's ruddy glow, / And
MOON (2)
A7   60:23   with an M, such as mouse-traps, and the moon, and memory, and muchness--you know you say things are
T4   140:29   The moon was shining sulkily, / Because she thought the sun / Had
MOP (1)
T6   165:12   sticking out all round--something like a live mop."
MOPS (1)
T4   141: 7   'If seven maids with seven mops / Swept it for half a year, / Do you suppose,' the Walrus
MORAL (8) [See also M--]
A9   72:30   even in the middle of her favourite word "moral", and the arm that was linked into hers began to tremble
A9   70:22   child!" said the Duchess. "Everything's got a moral, if only you can find it." And she squeezed herself up
A9   72: 5   agree with you," said the Duchess; "and the moral of that is--'Be what you would seem to be'--or, if you'd
A9   71:12   "flamingoes and mustard both bite. And the moral of that is--'Birds of a feather flock together.'"
A9   70:19   to talk. I ca'n't tell you just now what the moral of that is, but I shall remember it in a bit."
A9   70:32   "'Tis so," said the Duchess: "and the moral of that is--'Oh, 'tis love, 'tis love, that makes the
A9   71: 1   into Alice's shoulder as she added "and the moral of that is--'Take care of the sense, and the sounds will
A9   72: 1   a large mustard-mine near here. And the moral of that is--'The more there is of mine, the less there
MORALS (1)
A9   71: 3   "How fond she is of finding morals in things!" Alice thought to herself.
MORCAR (2)
A3   22: 6   to usurpation and conquest. Edwin and Morcar, the earls of Mercia and Northumbria--'"
A3   22:12   did," said the Mouse. "I proceed. 'Edwin and Morcar, the earls of Mercia and Northumbria, declared for him;
MORE (114)
A3   24:13   and begged the Mouse to tell them something more.
A7   59:12   in an offended tone: "so I ca'n't take more."
T8W   14: 8   that makes him so cross." So she tried once more.
T4   142:10   they came at last, / And more, and more, and more--/ All hopping through the frothy waves, / And scrambling
T7   169: 7   or other, and whenever one went down, several more always fell over him, so that the ground was soon covered
T6   168:36   notice of her, she said "Good-bye!" once more, and, getting no answer to this, she quietly walked away:
A3   26:40   Dinah! I wonder if I shall ever see you any more!" And here poor Alice began to cry again, for she felt
T4   142:10   and fast they came at last, / And more, and more, and more--/ All hopping through the frothy waves, / And
T4   142:10   / And thick and fast they came at last, / And more, and more, and more--/ All hopping through the frothy

MORE (cont.)

T5	158:27	* * * * * * * * * * So she went on, wondering more and more at every step, as everything turned into a tree
A10	85: 7	answered "Come on!" and ran the faster, while more and more faintly came, carried on the breeze that
T6	159: 1	the egg only got larger and larger, and more and more human: when she had come within a few yards of
T5	155:13	puzzled child thought to herself. "She gets more and more like a porcupine every minute!"
A5	42:36	Alice was more and more puzzled, but she thought there was no use in
T7	173:31	Hatta looked round once more, and this time a tear or two trickled down his cheek; but
T9	196: 1	too," the White Queen went on in a low voice, more as if she were talking to herself. "He came to the door
A4	28:13	quite enough--I hope I sha'n't grow any more--As it is, I ca'n't get out at the door--I do wish I
T5	158:27	* * * * * So she went on, wondering more and. more at every step, as everything turned into a tree the
A4	30:22	waited for some time without hearing anything more: at last came a rumbling of little cart-wheels, and the
A11	88:43	"Don't talk nonsense," said Alice more boldly: "you know you're growing too."
A11	90: 1	that," continued the Hatter, "I cut some more bread-and-butter--"
T7	173:14	Alice had no more breath for talking; so they trotted on in silence, till
A4	30: 5	"Here! Come help me out of this!" (Sounds of more broken glass.)
T2	123: 7	wondering," said the Tiger-lily), "but she's more bushy than you are."
A9	74:41	little," the Mock Turtle went on at last, more calmly, though still sobbing a little now and then, "we
A5	35:14	"I'm afraid I ca'n't put it more clearly," Alice replied, very politely, "for I ca'n't
T5	156: 1	This offended Alice a little, so there was no more conversation for a minute or two, while the boat glided
A8	68:27	escape again, and went back to have a little more conversation with her friend.
T9	197:20	The snoring got more distinct every minute, and sounded more like a tune: at
T2	120:19	her back upon the house, she set out once more down the path, determined to keep straight on till she
T8	181: 9	"Now one can breathe more easily," said the Knight, putting back his shaggy hair
A3	22:30	adjourn, for the immediate adoption of more energetic remedies--"
A12	94: 3	"There's more evidence to come yet, please your Majesty," said the
T1	108:32	it wouldn't have happened. Now don't make any more excuses, but listen! Number two: you pulled Snowdrop away
T7	171:14	of no use--the Anglo-Saxon attitudes only got more extraordinary every moment, while the great eyes rolled
A10	85: 8	"Come on!" and ran the faster, while more and more faintly came, carried on the breeze that followed them,
T8	179:17	Startled as she was, Alice was more frightened for him than for herself at the moment, and
A1	12:13	After a while, finding that nothing more happened, she decided on going into the garden at once;
T8	186: 4	goes on working all the same. In fact, the more head-downwards I am, the more I keep inventing new things
A4	29: 8	"at least there's no room to grow up any more here."
A2	15:18	garden with one eye; but to get through was more hopeless than ever: she sat down and began to cry again.
T6	159: 1	egg only got larger and larger, and more and more human: when she had come within a few yards of it, she
A3	22:32	meaning of half those long words, and, what's more, I don't believe you do either!" And the Eaglet bent down
T8	186: 5	In fact, the more head-downwards I am, the more I keep inventing new things."
T5	158:19	end. "The egg seems to get further away the more I walk towards it. Let me see, is this a chair? Why, it's
A2	19:41	offended. "We wo'n't talk about her any more, if you'd rather not."
T9	193: 4	joke should have some meaning--and a child's more important than a joke, I hope. You couldn't deny that,
T6	162: 9	Alice felt even more indignant at this suggestion. "I mean," she said, "that
T8W	17:15	are you?" the Wasp said, looking at her with more interest. "And you've got a comb. Much honey?"
T2	120: 5	at last. But how curiously it twists! It's more like a corkscrew than a path! Well this turn goes to the
T4	147: 7	his mouth and his large eyes--"looking more like a fish than anything else," Alice thought.
T5	155:13	child thought to herself. "She gets more and more like a porcupine every minute!"
T4	147:32	it a helmet, though it certainly looked much more like a saucepan.)
A6	49:33	doubt that it had a very turn-up nose, much more like a snout than a real nose: also its eyes were getting
T9	197:20	got more distinct every minute, and sounded more like a tune: at last she could even make out words, and
T8W	13: 5	like a very old man (only that his face was more like a wasp) was sitting on the ground, leaning against a
T4	147:21	and fastening buttons--"Really they'll be more like bundles of old clothes than anything else, by the
T4	144:25	the wood near them, though she feared it was more likely to be a wild beast. "Are there any lions or tigers
T5	156:28	as the boat glided by, there was always a more lovely one that she couldn't reach.
T5	155:27	Feather!" the Sheep cried again, taking more needles. "You'll be catching a crab directly."
T6	163:31	means just what I choose it to mean--neither more nor less."
A6	50:11	could be no mistake about it: it was neither more nor less than a pig, and she felt that it would be quite
A8	67:22	there was enough of it now in sight, and no more of it appeared.
T5	153:37	Rub as she would, she could make nothing more of it: she was in a little dark shop, leaning with her
A6	53:14	like to go nearer till she had nibbled some more of the left-hand bit of mushroom, and raised herself to
T2	123: 3	"Are there any more people in the garden besides me?" Alice said, not
A5	42:36	Alice was more and more puzzled, but she thought there was no use in saying
A9	76:33	Alice did not feel encouraged to ask any more questions about it: so she turned to the Mock Turtle, and
T2	120:11	Indeed, once, when she turned a corner rather more quickly than usual, she ran against it before she could
T6	159:23	looking away from her as usual, "have no more sense than a baby!"
A7	60:42	Once more she found herself in the long hall, and close to the
T8	187:29	to herself: "it's 'I give thee all, I can no more.'" She stood and listened very attentively, but no tears
T2	121:12	"If only her petals curled up a little more, she'd be all right."
A9	72: 7	would seem to be'--or, if you'd like it put more simply--'Never imagine yourself not to be otherwise than
T1	114:23	him up very gently, and lifted him across more slowly than she had lifted the Queen, that she mightn't
T8	184:17	"Much more smoothly than a live horse," Alice said, with a little
A4	30:17	This time there were two little shrieks, and more sounds of broken glass. "What a number of cucumber-frames
T12	207:22	"Sit up a little more stiffly, dear!" Alice cried with a merry laugh. "And
A5	42:29	I say again!" repeated the Pigeon, but in a more subdued tone, and added, with a kind of sob, "I've tried
T7	174: 2	But Hatta only munched away, and drank some more tea.
A7	59: 9	"Take some more tea," the March Hare said to Alice, very earnestly.
A12	93:35	from his book, "Rule Forty-two. All persons more than a mile high to leave the court."
T9	202: 8	the fish!' / That is easy, and will not take more than a minute. / 'Let it lie in a dish!' / That is easy,
A7	60:29	This piece of rudeness was more than Alice could bear: she got up in great disgust, and
T9	196:30	and see how pleased she'll be!" But this was more than Alice had courage to do.
T4	141:17	/ Along the briny beach: / We cannot do with more than four, / To give a hand to each.'
T8	181: 7	you off with your helmet?" It was evidently more than he could manage by himself: however, she managed to
A2	15:13	roof of the hall: in fact she was now rather more than nine feet high, and she at once took up the little

MORE (cont.)
```
 A7    59:14  said  the  Hatter:  "it's  very  easy  to  take  more  than  nothing."
 AI     3:18  it!"  /  While  Tertia  interrupts  the  tale  /  Not  more  than  once  a  minute.
 T9   197:17  couldn't,  you  know,  because  there  never  was  more  than  one  Queen  at  a  time.  Do  wake  up,  you  heavy  things!"
 T9   192:34  moaned,  wringing  her  hands.  "Oh,  ever  so  much  more  than  that!"
 A10   81:10                          "I  can  tell  you  more  than  that,  if  you  like,"  said  the  Gryphon.  "Do  you  know
 T9   192:33           "But  she  said  a  great  deal  more  than  that!"  the  White  Queen  moaned,  wringing  her  hands.
 T4   144:15                    "He  ate  more  than  the  Carpenter,  though,"  said  Tweedledee.  "You  see  he
 A7    55: 5  said  Alice:  "it's  laid  for  a  great  many  more  than  three."
 A4    31:19  thought  Alice),  "Well,  I  hardly  know--No  more,  thank  ye;  I'm  better  now--but  I'm  a  deal  too  flustered
 T3   130: 7  bought  one  from  the  engine-driver."  And  once  more  the  chorus  of  voices  went  on  with  "The  man  that  drives
 T6   161: 6  anxiously  as  she  took  it.  "If  he  smiled  much  more  the  ends  of  his  mouth  might  meet  behind,"  she  thought:
 T3   135: 8  if  she  said  'Miss,'  and  didn't  say  anything  more,"  the  Gnat  remarked,  "of  course  you'd  miss  your  lessons.
 A12   98:29  off  her  unfortunate  guests  to  execution--once  more  the  pig-baby  was  sneezing  on  the  Duchess's  knee,  while
 A12   98:30  plates  and  dishes  crashed  around  it--once  more  the  shriek  of  the  Gryphon,  the  squeaking  of  the  Lizard's
 A9    72: 1  near  here.  And  the  moral  of  that  is--'The  more  there  is  of  mine,  the  less  there  is  of  yours.'"
 A12   95: 6  they  gave  him  two,  /  You  gave  us  three  or  more;  /  They  all  returned  from  him  to  you,  /  Though  they  were
 A5    42:37  thought  there  was  no  use  in  saying  anything  more  till  the  Pigeon  had  finished.
 A3    21:12     refused  to  tell  its  age,  there  was  no  more  to  be  said.
 A9    74:38  but  she  could  not  help  thinking  there  must  be  more  to  come,  so  she  sat  still  and  said  nothing.
 A6    50: 4  said  Alice,  seriously,  "I'll  have  nothing  more  to  do  with  you.  Mind  now!"  The  poor  little  thing  sobbed
 T1   109: 2  up  all  my  punishments?"  she  went  on,  talking  more  to  herself  than  the  kitten.  "What  would  they  do  at  the
 T7   174:17          "I  don't  think  they'll  fight  any  more  to-day,"  the  King  said  to  Hatta:  "go  and  order  the  drums
 A4    28:21  chimney,  and  said  to  herself  "Now  I  can  do  no  more,  whatever  happens.  What  will  become  of  me?"
 T2   123: 1  and  snore  away  there,  till  you  know  no  more  what's  going  on  in  the  world,  than  if  you  were  a  bud!"
 A3    24: 1       Then  they  all  crowded  round  her  once  more,  while  the  Dodo  solemnly  presented  the  thimble,  saying
 T8   179:20  was  comfortably  in  the  saddle,  he  began  once  more  "You're  my--"  but  here  another  voice  broke  in  "Ahoy!
```
MORNING (9)
```
 T9   196: 6  there  wasn't  such  a  thing  in  the  house,  that  morning."
 A5    35: 7  at  least  I  know  who  I  was  when  I  got  up  this  morning,  but  I  think  I  must  have  been  changed  several  times
 A2    15:40  me  think:  was  I  the  same  when  I  got  up  this  morning?  I  almost  think  I  can  remember  feeling  a  little
 A3    25:19   We  must  have  the  trial;  For  really  this  morning  I've  nothing  to  do.'  Said  the  mouse  to  the  cur,  Such  a
 A7    56:45  instance,  suppose  it  were  nine  o'clock  in  the  morning,  just  time  to  begin  lessons:  you'd  only  have  to
 T1   108:28  twice  while  Dinah  was  washing  your  face  this  morning.  Now  you  ca'n't  deny  it,  Kitty:  I  heard  you!  What's
 A10   81:40  tell  you  my  adventures--beginning  from  this  morning,"  said  Alice  a  little  timidly;  "but  it's  no  use  going
 T12  208: 7  like  that--as  if  Dinah  hadn't  washed  you  this  morning!  You  see,  Kitty,  it  must  have  been  either  me  or  the
 T12  208: 1  said  to  me,  all  about  fishes!  To-morrow  morning  you  shall  have  a  real  treat.  All  the  time  you're
```
MORSEL (1)
```
 A5    42: 3  she  did  it  at  last,  and  managed  to  swallow  a  morsel  of  the  left-hand  bit.  * * * * * * * * * * * * * *
```
MOSS (1)
```
 T8   191: 1  herself  down  to  rest  on  a  lawn  as  soft  as  moss,  with  little  flowerbeds  dotted  about  it  here  and  there.
```
MOST (20)
```
 T8   187:18  this  was  the  one  that  she  always  remembered  most  clearly.  Years  afterwards  she  could  bring  the  whole  scene
 A10   84: 5  explain  it  as  you  go  on?  It's  by  far  the  most  confusing  thing  that  I  ever  heard!"
 T2   125:20  out  in  all  directions  over  the  country--and  a  most  curious  country  it  was.  There  were  a  number  of  tiny
 T2   126:18                    The  most  curious  part  of  the  thing  was,  that  the  trees  and  the
 A6    53: 8  Alice;  "but  a  grin  without  a  cat!  It's  the  most  curious  thing  I  ever  saw  in  all  my  life!"
 T12  207:31  you're  scrubbing  a  White  Queen?  Really,  it's  most  disrespectful  of  you!
 A6    46:14  possibly  hear  you."  And  certainly  there  was  a  most  extraordinary  noise  going  on  within--a  constant  howling
 T7   171:10  could  only  wave  his  hands  about,  and  make  the  most  fearful  faces  at  the  poor  King.
 T2   122:28                    "In  most  gardens,"  the  Tiger-lily  said,  "they  make  the  beds  too
 T6   166:28  I'm  singing  or  not,  you've  sharper  eyes  than  most,"  Humpty  Dumpty  remarked  severely.  Alice  was  silent.
 A12   95:21                "That's  the  most  important  piece  of  evidence  we've  heard  yet,"  said  the
 A6    52:25  to  herself:  "the  March  Hare  will  be  much  the  most  interesting,  and  perhaps,  as  this  is  May,  it  wo'n't  be
 T1   114:14  into  the  fire,  as  if  he  thought  that  was  the  most  likely  place  to  find  one.
 A6    48: 3   "They  all  can,"  said  the  Duchess;  "and  most  of  'em  do."
 T5   149:36  rather  better  now!"  she  said,  after  altering  most  of  the  pins.  "But  really  you  should  have  a  lady's  maid!"
 T5   155: 1  one  she  was  looking  at.  "And  this  one  is  the  most  provoking  of  all--but  I'll  tell  you  what--"  she  added,  as
 T6   162:25              "It  is  a--most--provoking--thing,"  he  said  at  last,  "when  a  person
 T4   147:25  he  added  very  gravely,  "it's  one  of  the  most  serious  things  that  can  possibly  happen  to  one  in  a
 A11   89:19  "I'm  a  poor  man,"  the  Hatter  went  on,  "and  most  things  twinkled  after  that--only  the  March  Hare  said--"
 A5    38: 2  "as  I  mentioned  before,  /  And  have  grown  most  uncommonly  fat;  /  Yet  you  turned  a  back-somersault  in  at
```
MOSTLY (4)
```
 T9   195:32  a  poor  thin  way  of  doing  things.  Now  here,  we  mostly  have  days  and  nights  two  or  three  at  a  time,  and
 A8    63:21  ornamented  with  hearts.  Next  came  the  guests,  mostly  Kings  and  Queens,  and  among  them  Alice  recognized  the
 A11   91:17                    "Pepper,  mostly,"  said  the  cook.
 T2   128:11  to  Tweedledum  and  Tweedledee--the  Fifth  is  mostly  water--the  Sixth  belongs  to  Humpty  Dumpty--But  you  make
```
MOUNTAIN-RILL (1)
```
 T8   188:19  /  He  said  'I  go  my  ways,  /  And  when  I  find  a  mountain-rill,  /  I  set  it  in  a  blaze;  /  And  thence  they  make  a
```
MOUNTAINS (1)
```
 T3   129: 5  "Principal  rivers--there  are  none.  Principal  mountains--I'm  on  the  only  one,  but  I  don't  think  it's  got  any
```
MOUNTED (2)
```
 T8   179:19  and  watched  him  with  some  anxiety  as  he  mounted  again.  As  soon  as  he  was  comfortably  in  the  saddle,  he
 T8   180:13  they  shook  hands,  and  then  the  Red  Knight  mounted  and  galloped  off.
```
MOURNFUL (1)
```
 A7    58: 8  And  ever  since  that,"  the  Hatter  went  on  in  a  mournful  tone,  "he  wo'n't  do  a  thing  I  ask!  It's  always  six
```
MOURNFULLY (1)
```
 A7    57:10              The  Hatter  shook  his  head  mournfully.  "Not  I!"  he  replied.  "We  quarreled  last  March--
```
MOUSE (42)
```
 A3    23:30  have  a  prize  herself,  you  know,"  said  the  Mouse.
```

MOUSE (cont.)
A2   19:17 Latin Grammar, "A mouse--of a mouse--to a mouse--a mouse--O mouse!") The mouse looked at her rather
A2   19:14 I am very tired of swimming about here, O Mouse!" (Alice thought this must be the right way of speaking
A2   19:22   thought Alice. "I daresay it's a French mouse, come over with William the Conqueror." (For, with all
A2   20:14   So she called softly after it, "Mouse dear! Do come back again, and we wo'n't talk about cats,
A2   20: 3 "Are you--are you fond--of--of dogs?" The Mouse did not answer, so Alice went on eagerly: "There is such
A3   22:21   The Mouse did not notice this question, but hurriedly went on,
A2   19:13 there's no harm in trying." So she began: "O Mouse, do you know the way out of this pool? I am very tired
A4   27:32   till Dinah comes back, and see that the mouse doesn't get out.' Only I don't think," Alice went on,
A2   19:11 use, now," thought Alice, "to speak to this mouse? Everything is so out-of-the-way down here, that I
A3   22: 8   "I beg your pardon!" said the Mouse, frowning, but very politely. "Did you speak?"
A2   19:26 first sentence in her French lesson-book. The Mouse gave a sudden leap out of the water, and seemed to
A3   26: 8 "I shall do nothing of the sort," said the Mouse, getting up and walking away. "You insult me by talking
A3   26:43 she looked up eagerly, half hoping that the Mouse had changed his mind, and was coming back to finish his
A2   20:16 either, if you don't like them!" When the Mouse heard this, it turned round and swam slowly back to her:
A3   22:11   "I thought you did," said the Mouse. "I proceed. 'Edwin and Morcar, the earls of Mercia and
A2   19:30   "Not like cats!" cried the Mouse in a shrill passionate voice. "Would you like cats, if
A3   21:16 sat down at once, in a large ring, with the Mouse in the middle. Alice kept her eyes anxiously fixed on it
A2   19:18 a mouse--to a mouse--a mouse--O mouse!") The mouse looked at her rather inquisitively, and seemed to her to
A2   19:18 Grammar, "A mouse--of a mouse--to a mouse--a mouse--O mouse!") The mouse looked at her rather inquisitively
A2   19:17 seen, in her brother's Latin Grammar, "A mouse--of a mouse--to a mouse--a mouse--O mouse!") The mouse
A3   26:12   The Mouse only growled in reply.
A3   26:15 joined in chorus "Yes, please do!" But the Mouse only shook its head impatiently, and walked a little
A3   22:16   "Found it," the Mouse replied rather crossly: "of course you know what 'it'
A3   26: 5   "I had not!" cried the Mouse, sharply and very angrily.
A2   19:15 this must be the right way of speaking to a mouse: she had never done such a thing before, but she
A12   98:25 the White Rabbit hurried by--the frightened Mouse splashed his way through the neighbouring pool--she
A2   19: 9 now, and she soon made out that it was only a mouse, that had slipped in like herself.
A3   25: 6   "Fury said to a mouse, That he met in the house, 'Let us both go to law: I
A2   19:18 "A mouse--of a mouse--to a mouse--a mouse--O mouse!") The mouse looked at her rather inquisitively, and
A2   19:17 her brother's Latin Grammar, "A mouse--of a mouse--to a mouse--a mouse--O mouse!") The mouse looked at her
A3   26: 1   "You are not attending!" said the Mouse to Alice, severely. "What are you thinking of?"
A3   24:13 they sat down again in a ring, and begged the Mouse to tell them something more.
A3   25:24 this morning I've nothing to do.' Said the mouse to the cur, Such a trial, dear sir, With no jury or
A3   24:17 "Mine is a long and sad tale!" said the Mouse, turning to Alice, and sighing.
A2   19:40 pardon!" cried Alice again, for this time the Mouse was bristling all over, and she felt certain it must be
A3   25: 3 And she kept on puzzling about it while the mouse was speaking, so that her idea of the tale was something
A2   20:11 "I'm afraid I've offended it again!" For the Mouse was swimming away from her as hard as it could go, and
A3   21:13   At last the Mouse, who seemed to be a person of some authority among them,
A2   19:42   "We, indeed!" cried the Mouse, who was trembling down to the end of its tail. "As if I
A3   22: 1   "Ahem!" said the Mouse with an important air. "Are you all ready? This is the
A1   9:10 you might catch a bat, and that's very like a mouse, you know. But do cats eat bats, I wonder?" And here
MOUSE-HOLE (1)
A4   27:32 a minute, nurse! But I've got to watch this mouse-hole till Dinah comes back, and see that the mouse
MOUSE'S (1)
A3   25: 2 said Alice, looking down with wonder at the Mouse's tail; "but why do you call it sad?" And she kept on
MOUSE-TRAP (2)
T8   181:36 come near it yet. And the other thing is a mouse-trap. I suppose the mice keep the bees out--or the bees
T8   182: 1   "I was wondering what the mouse-trap was for," said Alice. "It isn't very likely there
MOUSE-TRAPS (1)
A7   60:23 went on: "--that begins with an M, such as mouse-traps, and the moon, and memory, and muchness--you know
MOUTH (24)
T2   124:19 Queen said looking at her watch: "open your mouth a little wider when you speak, and always say 'your
A5   36:29 unfolded its arms, took the hookah out of its mouth again, and said "So you think you're changed, do you?"
A5   35: 2 the Caterpillar took the hookah out of its mouth, and addressed her in a languid, sleepy voice.
A5   41:22 Caterpillar; and it put the hookah into its mouth, and began smoking again.
T4   147: 6 and there he lay, opening and shutting his mouth and his large eyes--"looking more like a fish than
A4   33: 2 panting, with its tongue hanging out of its mouth, and its great eyes half shut.
T6   159: 3 it, she saw that it had eyes and a nose and a mouth; and, when she had come close to it, she saw clearly
A5   41:24 the Caterpillar took the hookah out of its mouth, and yawned once or twice, and shook itself. Then it got
T8W   20:11   "Not with a mouth as small as that," the Wasp persisted. "If you was
T6   168:30 same side of the nose, for instance--or the mouth at the top--that would be some help."
A5   42: 2 foot, that there was hardly room to open her mouth; but she did it at last, and managed to swallow a morsel
T9   201:36 said, very slowly and solemnly, putting her mouth close to Alice's ear, "her White Majesty knows a lovely
A8   65:31 and then raised himself upon tiptoe, put his mouth close to her ear, and whispered "She's under sentence of
A8   67:15 on?" said the Cat, as soon as there was mouth enough for it to speak with.
T7   172:26 said the Messenger, putting his hands to his mouth in the shape of a trumpet and stooping so as to get
T6   161: 7 it. "If he smiled much more the ends of his mouth might meet behind," she thought: "And then I don't know
A12   93:14 much overcome to do anything but sit with its mouth open, gazing up into the roof of the court.
T1   115:11 I can hardly hold you! And don't keep your mouth so wide open! All the ashes will get into it--there, now
T6   160:27 The King has promised me--with his very own mouth--to--to--"
T6   168:28 the air with his thumb) "nose in the middle, mouth under. It's always the same. Now if you had the two eyes
T4   139:16 Tweedledum cried out briskly, and shut his mouth up again with a snap.
T1   115: 6 astonished to cry out, but his eyes and his mouth went on getting larger and larger, and rounder and
T8   190: 8 And muttered mumblingly and low, / As if his mouth were full of dough, / Who snorted like a buffalo--/ That
A11   90:14 had a large canvas bag, which tied up at the mouth with strings: into this they slipped the guinea-pig,
MOUTHS (4)
A10   81: 1 the sea. But they have their tails in their mouths; and the reason is--" here the Mock Turtle yawned and
A10   80:23 thoughtfully. "They have their tails in their mouths--and they're all over crumbs."
A10   81: 6 way. So they got their tails fast in their mouths. So they couldn't get them out again. That's all."

MOUTHS (cont.)
A10   82: 4 one on each side, and opened their eyes and mouths so very wide; but she gained courage as she went on.
MOVE (8) [See also REMOVE]
T2   128:33 and that it would soon be time for her to move.
T8   181: 5 must go back, you know. That's the end of my move."
T2   123: 5 one other flower in the garden that can move about like you," said the Rose. "I wonder how you do it--
T2   126:21 to pass anything. "I wonder if all the things move along with us?" thought poor puzzled Alice. And the Queen
A7   59:36 cup," interrupted the Hatter: "let's all move one place on."
A12   93: 7 in a melancholy way, being quite unable to move. She soon got it out again, and put it right; "not that
A3   22:29 the Dodo solemnly, rising to its feet, "I move that the meeting adjourn, for the immediate adoption of
T2   128: 8 said "A pawn goes two squares in its first move, you know. So you'll go very quickly through the Third
MOVED (5) [See also REMOVED]
A12   97: 6 Queen shouted at the top of her voice. Nobody moved.
A7   59:39 and the Dormouse followed him: the March Hare moved into the Dormouse's place, and Alice rather unwillingly
A3   26:36 all in bed!" On various pretexts they all moved off, and Alice was soon left alone.
A7   59:38 He moved on as he spoke, and the Dormouse followed him: the March
A8   65: 9 "Off with their heads!" and the procession moved on, three of the soldiers remaining behind to execute
MOVING (7)
A4   31:38 roof off." After a minute or two they began moving about again, and Alice heard the Rabbit say "A
T2   125:26 said at last. "There ought to be some men moving about somewhere--and so there are!" she added in a tone
T8   187:22 that quite dazzled her--the horse quietly moving about, with the reins hanging loose on his neck,
A7   58:14 "Then you keep moving round, I suppose?" said Alice.
A5   42:15 hands, how is it I ca'n't see you?" She was moving them about, as she spoke, but no result seemed to
AI   3:21 won, / In fancy they pursue / The dream-child moving through a land / Of wonders wild and new, / In friendly
TC   209:11 Still she haunts me, phantomwise. / Alice moving under skies / Never seen by waking eyes.
MUCH (115)
A4   28:14 the door--I do wish I hadn't drunk quite so much!"
A7   55:34 about ravens and writing-desks, which wasn't much.
T7   176:18 nearly shaking off his head, he trembled so much.
T8   182:31 "I should like to hear it, very much."
T8   190:21 so far--and for the song--I liked it very much."
T9   194:29 for she didn't like being found fault with so much.
T8W   20: 3 better, they wouldn't tease you quite so much."
A10   81: 9 "it's very interesting. I never knew so much about a whiting before."
A3   22: 5 who wanted leaders, and had been of late much accustomed to usurpation and conquest. Edwin and Morcar,
A6   48:14 they hit her; and the baby was howling so much already, that it was quite impossible to say whether the
T3   136: 5 do it!" But being determined didn't help her much, and all she could say, after a great deal of puzzling,
T3   131:39 of this was that it tickled her ear very much, and quite took off her thoughts from the unhappiness of
T7   170:19 And at that distance too! Why, it's as much as I can do to see real people, by this light!"
T8   190:23 said doubtfully: "but you didn't cry so much as I thought you would."
T7   177:19 "The Monster has given the Lion twice as much as me!"
A5   43:17 child; "but little girls eat eggs quite as much as serpents do, you know."
A2   15:16 Poor Alice! It was as much as she could do, lying down on one side, to look through
A6   49:20 for the first minute or two, it was as much as she could do to hold it.
T1   115: 5 hand, and being dusted: he was far too much astonished to cry out, but his eyes and his mouth went on
A8   67:10 appearance in the air: it puzzled her very much at first, but after watching it a minute or two she made
A6   46: 5 Alice laughed so much at this, that she had to run back into the wood for fear
T5   153:29 voice rising into a squeak as she went on. "Much be-etter! Be-etter! Be-e-e-etter! Be-e-ehh!" The last
T5   153:28 "Oh, much better!" cried the Queen, her voice rising into a squeak
A6   51:11 "I don't much care where--" said Alice.
A7   60:26 "Really, now you ask me," said Alice, very much confused, "I don't think--"
A5   41:11 Alice said nothing: she had never been so much contradicted in all her life before, and she felt that
T3   135:23 a wood on the other side of it: it looked much darker than the last wood, and Alice felt a little timid
T7   177: 4 out as he lay down again. "There was too much dust to see anything. What a time the Monster is, cutting
T6   166:13 Alice. "But I had some poetry repeated to me much easier than that, by--Tweedledee, I think it was."
A11   91:31 would be like, "--for they haven't got much evidence yet," she said to herself. Imagine her surprise,
T9   204:24 felt surprised at this, but she was far too much excited to be surprised at anything now. "As for you,"
A6   53:10 She had not gone much farther before she came in sight of the house of the
T5   156:41 They hadn't gone much farther before the blade of one of the oars got fast in
T7   172:21 said in a sullen tone. "I'm sure nobody walks much faster than I do!"
T1   119: 9 She was getting a little giddy with so much floating in the air, and was rather glad to find herself
T4   140: 7 "Nohow. And thank you very much for asking," said Tweedledum.
T8   190:20 I'll wait," said Alice: "and thank you very much for coming so far--and for the song--I liked it very much
T8   189:11 rust / By boiling it in wine. / I thanked him much for telling me / The way he got his wealth, / But chiefly
T4   143: 6 said the Carpenter. / They thanked him much for that.
A4   27:15 and a fan! Quick, now!" And Alice was so much frightened that she ran off at once in the direction it
A9   72:41 the Queen said to Alice; and Alice was too much frightened to say a word, but slowly followed her back to
A1   11: 4 she had never forgotten that, if you drink much from a bottle marked "poison," it is almost certain to
T8W   16: 3 all along of the wig," the Wasp said in a much gentler voice.
T8W   17:16 with more interest. "And you've got a comb. Much honey?"
T1   109: 7 dinners at once! Well, I shouldn't mind that much! I'd far rather go without them than eat them!
A4   33: 9 "I should have liked teaching it tricks very much, if--if I'd only been the right size to do it! Oh dear!
T1   110:30 if you'll only attend, Kitty, and not talk so much, I'll tell you all my ideas about Looking-glass House.
T2   124:15 wondered a little at this, but she was too much in awe of the Queen to disbelieve it. "I'll try it when I
T8W   21: 7 "Then your eyes--they're too much in front, no doubt. One would have done as well as two,
T5   152:12 expect to do it?" Alice said, feeling very much inclined to laugh.
T8   184:28 "Very much indeed," Alice said politely.
A10   79: 4 "Very much indeed," said Alice.
A1   13: 1 when one eats cake; but Alice had got so much into the way of expecting nothing but out-of-the-way
A1   10: 2 found that it led into a small passage, not much larger than a rat-hole: she knelt down and looked along

MUCH (cont.)
A9	70:25	Alice did not much like her keeping so close to her: first because the
A1	9:15	couldn't answer either question, it didn't much matter which way she put it. She felt that she was dozing
T4	147:32	it a helmet, though it certainly looked much more like a saucepan.)
A6	49:33	be no doubt that it had a very turn-up nose, much more like a snout than a real nose: also its eyes were
T8	184:17	"Much more smoothly than a live horse," Alice said, with a
T9	192:34	moaned, wringing her hands. "Oh, ever so much more than that!"
T6	161: 6	anxiously as she took it. "If he smiled much more the ends of his mouth might meet behind," she
T8W	17:12	a heap of sea-weed. "You could make your wig much neater," she said, "if only you had a comb."
T4	145:17	be waking him, I'm afraid, if you make so much noise."
T4	140: 9	"So much obliged!" added Tweedledee. "You like poetry?"
A12	92: 6	they lay sprawling about, reminding her very much of a globe of gold-fish she had accidentally upset the
A7	60:24	and muchness—you know you say things are 'much of a muchness'—did you ever see such a thing as a
A6	47: 7	There was certainly too much of it in the air. Even the Duchess sneezed occasionally;
T2	126:25	be able to talk again, she was getting so much out of breath: and still the Queen cried "Faster! Faster!
T7	171: 8	moment the Messenger arrived: he was far too much out of breath to say a word, and could only wave his
A1	7:12	in that; nor did Alice think it so very much out of the way to hear the Rabbit say to itself "Oh dear!
A12	93:13	all except the Lizard, who seemed too much overcome to do anything but sit with its mouth open,
T8W	13:20	and said very kindly, "I hope you're not in much pain?"
A6	47: 5	"There's certainly too much pepper in that soup!" Alice said to herself, as well as
A4	28:27	"It was much pleasanter at home," thought poor Alice, "when one wasn't
A9	70:10	makes people hot-tempered," she went on, very much pleased at having found out a new kind of rule, "and
T6	163:44	child," said Humpty Dumpty, looking very much pleased. "I meant by 'impenetrability' that we've had
T8	183:10	fall off quite so often, when they've had much practice."
T8	183: 3	"I'm afraid you've not had much practice in riding," she ventured to say, as she was
T5	153:13	"I daresay you haven't had much practice," said the Queen. "When I was your age, I always
T9	198: 6	which bell must I ring?" she went on, very much puzzled by the names. "I'm not a visitor, and I'm not a
T7	177:18	as Alice sat with the knife in her hand, very much puzzled how to begin. "The Monster has given the Lion
T6	164: 7	"Oh!" said Alice. She was too much puzzled to make any other remark.
T6	163:37	Alice was too much puzzled to say anything; so after a minute Humpty Dumpty
T5	157: 5	as Alice got back into her place, very much relieved to find herself still in the boat.
T8	185:20	nothing but the soles of his feet, she was much relieved to hear that he was talking on in his usual tone
A9	72:27	"Just about as much right," said the Duchess, "as pigs have to fly; and the
T6	166:31	"Thank you very much," said Alice.
A2	19: 1	"I wish I hadn't cried so much!" said Alice, as she swam about, trying to find her way
A6	52: 4	"I should like it very much," said Alice, "but I haven't been invited yet."
A9	76:16	"You couldn't have wanted it much," said Alice; "living at the bottom of the sea."
T8	181: 6	"Thank you very much," said Alice. "May I help you off with your helmet?" It
A6	48: 6	"You don't know much," said the Duchess; "and that's a fact."
T4	148:11	"I shouldn't have minded it so much," said Tweedledum, "if it hadn't been a new one."
A12	93: 8	and put it right; "not that it signifies much," she said to herself; "I should think it would be quite
T9	202:34	"Thank you very much," she whispered in reply, "but I can do quite well
A7	59: 7	living would be like, but it puzzled her too much: so she went on: "But why did they live at the bottom of
A4	28: 9	It did so indeed, and much sooner than she had expected: before she had drunk half
T8	183: 5	The Knight looked very much surprised, and a little offended at the remark. "What
T7	175: 3	going to run and help her?" Alice asked, very much surprised at his taking it so quietly.
A6	52: 9	Alice was not much surprised at this, she was getting so well used to queer
A2	14: 1	and curiouser!" cried Alice (she was so much surprised, that for the moment she quite forgot how to
A6	52:25	she said to herself: "the March Hare will be much the most interesting, and perhaps, as this is May, it
A9	70:36	"Ah well! It means much the same thing," said the Duchess, digging her sharp
T9	195: 4	interrupted. "She'll be feverish after so much thinking." So they set to work and fanned her with
A8	68:24	were out of sight: "but it doesn't matter much," thought Alice, "as all the arches are gone from this
T9	196:13	"And part of the roof came off, and ever so much thunder got in—and it went rolling round the room in
T4	140: 6	"I hope you're not much tired?" she said at last.
T9	192:13	one on each side: she would have liked very much to ask them how they came there, but she feared it would
T1	110:35	I do so wish I could see that bit! I want so much to know whether they've a fire in the winter: you never
A1	9: 6	began talking again. "Dinah'll miss me very much to-night, I should think!" (Dinah was the cat.) "I hope
T6	159:32	"That last line is much too long for the poetry," she added, almost out loud,
A10	78: 8	"You may not have lived much under the sea—" ("I haven't," said Alice)—"and perhaps
A12	93: 9	herself; "I should think it would be quite as much use in the trial one way up as the other."
A3	23: 2	is a Caucus-race?" said Alice; not that she much wanted to know, but the Dodo had paused as if it thought
A8	65:24	Alice joined the procession, wondering very much what would happen next.

MUCHNESS (3)
A7	60:25	you ever see such a thing as a drawing of a muchness!"
A7	60:24	you know you say things are 'much of a muchness'—did you ever see such a thing as a drawing of a
A7	60:23	as mouse-traps, and the moon, and memory, and muchness—you know you say things are 'much of a muchness'—

MUDDLE (1)
| A11 | 87: 3 | had to ask his neighbour to tell him. "A nice muddle their slates'll be in, before the trial's over!" |

MULBERRY (1)
| T4 | 139:36 | "to find myself singing 'Here we go round the mulberry bush.' I don't know when I began it, but somehow I |

MULTIPLICATION-TABLE (1)
| A2 | 16:11 | get to twenty at that rate! However, the Multiplication-Table doesn't signify: let's try Geography. |

MUMBLINGLY (1)
| T8 | 190: 7 | rocked his body to and fro, / And muttered mumblingly and low, / As if his mouth were full of dough, / |

MUNCHED (2)
| T7 | 172:10 | when you're faint," he remarked to her, as he munched away. |
| T7 | 174: 2 | Haigha cried impatiently. But Hatta only munched away, and drank some more tea. |

MURDER (1)
| A6 | 49:27 | to kill it in a day or two. Wouldn't it be murder to leave it behind?" She said the last words out loud, |

MURDERING (1)
A7   58: 5   the Hatter, "when the Queen bawled out 'He's murdering the time! Off with his head!'"
MURMURED (3)
T7   172: 7   "Hay, then," the King murmured in a faint whisper.
T9   201:39   very kind to mention it," the White Queen murmured into Alice's other ear, in a voice like the cooing of
T8W   20: 4   "Your wig fits very well," the Wasp murmured, looking at her with an expression of admiration:
MUSCULAR (1)
A5   39: 7   And argued each case with my wife; / And the muscular strength, which it gave to my jaw / Has lasted the
MUSHROOM (8)
A5   41:26   and shook itself. Then it got down off the mushroom, and crawled away into the grass, merely remarking,
A4   34: 8   up on tiptoe, and peeped over the edge of the mushroom, and her eyes immediately met those of a large blue
A6   53:15   had nibbled some more of the left-hand bit of mushroom, and raised herself to about two feet high: even then
A5   41:33   Alice remained looking thoughtfully at the mushroom for a minute, trying to make out which were the two
A4   34: 3   under the circumstances. There was a large mushroom growing near her, about the same height as herself;
A5   43:33   remembered that she still held the pieces of mushroom in her hands, and she set to work very carefully,
A5   41:31   "Of the mushroom," said the Caterpillar, just as if she had asked it
A7   61: 3   garden. Then she set to work nibbling at the mushroom (she had kept a piece of it in her pocket) till she
MUSIC (7)
A7   56:41   "but I know I have to beat time when I learn music."
A9   76:10   "Yes," said Alice: "we learned French and music."
A9   76:15   they had, at the end of the bill, 'French, music, and washing--extra.'"
T8   187:14   his gentle foolish face, as if he enjoyed the music of his song, he began.
T8   187:27   listening, in a half-dream, to the melancholy music of the song.
T4   139:30   and she was not even surprised to hear music playing: it seemed to come from the tree under which
T4   139:42   dancing as suddenly as they had begun: the music stopped at the same moment.
MUST (94)
T6   160: 7   "Must a name mean something?" Alice asked doubtfully.
T6   159:12   take the least notice of her, she thought he must be a stuffed figure after all.
T4   148:18   dark so suddenly that Alice thought there must be a thunderstorm coming on. "What a thick black cloud
A10   79: 2   "It must be a very pretty dance," said Alice timidly.
A2   19: 7   make out what it was: at first she thought it must be a walrus or hippopotamus, but then she remembered how
T9   202: 5   could have caught it. / 'Next, the fish must be bought.' / That is easy: a penny, I think, could have
T9   202: 3   "'First, the fish must be caught.' / That is easy: a baby, I think, could have
A12   92:11   and she had a vague sort of idea that they must be collected at once and put back into the jury-box, or
A3   26:32   itself up very carefully, remarking "I really must be getting home: the night-air doesn't suit my throat!"
A1   8:29   I've fallen by this time?" she said aloud. "I must be getting somewhere near the centre of the earth. Let me
T8W   21:13   she might safely leave him. "I think I must be going on now," she said. "Good-bye."
A2   18: 4   "How can I have done that?" she thought. "I must be growing small again." She got up and went to the table
A2   14: 9   you must manage the best way you can--but I must be kind to them," thought Alice, "or perhaps they wo'n't
T3   131:16   very gentle voice in the distance said, "She must be labeled 'Lass, with care,' you know--"
A2   17:17   filled with tears again as she went on, "I must be Mabel after all, and I shall have to go and live in
A9   74:38   story," but she could not help thinking there must be more to come, so she sat still and said nothing.
A9   72:37   ground as she spoke; "either you or your head must be off, and that in about half no time! Take your choice!
A5   42:39   hatching the eggs," said the Pigeon; "but I must be on the look-out for serpents, night and day! Why, I
A2   19:40   bristling all over, and she felt certain it must be really offended. "We wo'n't talk about her any more,
A8   68: 3   "Well, it must be removed," said the King very decidedly; and he called
A6   51:26   "You must be," said the Cat, "or you wouldn't have come here."
T3   131:20   by post, as she's got a head on her--" "She must be sent as a message by the telegraph--" "She must draw
A1   12: 1   "What a curious feeling!" said Alice. "I must be shutting up like a telescope!"
A12   96: 2   'If she should push the matter on'--that must be the Queen--'What would become of you?'--What, indeed!
T12   207:29   with your White Majesty, I wonder? That must be the reason you were so untidy in my dream--Dinah! Do
A6   53:11   the house of the March Hare: she thought it must be the right house, because the chimneys were shaped like
A2   19:15   about here, O Mouse!" (Alice thought this must be the right way of speaking to a mouse: she had never
T3   135:27   "This must be the wood," she said thoughtfully to herself, "where
A4   30:18   "What a number of cucumber-frames there must be!" thought Alice. "I wonder what they'll do next! As
T3   137:32   she recovered herself, feeling sure that they must be TWEEDLEDUM AND TWEEDLEDEE
T6   164:37   "They must be very curious-looking creatures."
T5   152:31   "Only I never can remember the rule. You must be very happy, living in this wood, and being glad
T3   129:14   at first. "And what enormous flowers they must be!" was her next idea. "Something like cottages with the
A12   96: 6   gave her one, they gave him two'--why, that must be what he did with the tarts, you know--"
T4   148:16   the umbrella--it's quite as sharp. Only we must begin quick. It's getting as dark as it can."
A4   31:27   "We must burn the house down!" said the Rabbit's voice. And Alice
T5   150: 7   "It must come sometimes to 'jam to-day,'" Alice objected.
T3   130:13   what thinking in chorus means--for I must confess that I don't) "Better say nothing at all.
A11   91:27   undertone to the Queen, "Really, my dear, you must cross-examine the next witness. It quite makes my
A11   91:12   who said, in a low voice, "Your Majesty must cross-examine this witness."
T9   197: 2   "I must do it myself, then," said the Red Queen, and she began:--
T3   131:21   be sent as a message by the telegraph--" "She must draw the train herself the rest of the way--," and so on
T5   158: 9   "Only you must eat them both, if you buy two," said the Sheep.
A12   95:18   let him know she liked them best, / For this must ever be / A secret, kept from all the rest, / Between
T9   196:21   "Your Majesty must excuse her," the Red Queen said to Alice, taking one of
T8   179:31   "Well, we must fight for her, then," said the Red Knight, as he took up
T1   115:37   and at last he panted out "My dear! I really must get a thinner pencil. I ca'n't manage this one a bit: it
T5   158:15   into people's hands--that would never do--you must get it for yourself." And so saying, she went off to the
A6   49:11   flinging the baby at her as she spoke. "I must go and get ready to play croquet with the Queen," and she
A9   74: 2   the Mock Turtle, and to hear his history. I must go back and see after some executions I have ordered;"
T8   181: 5   you safe to the end of the wood--and then I must go back, you know. That's the end of my move."
T3   131:19   in the carriage!" thought Alice), saying "She must go by post, as she's got a head on her--" "She must be
A2   15: 4   to herself how she would manage it. "They must go by the carrier," she thought; "and how funny it'll
T3   134:18   "But that must happen very often," Alice remarked thoughtfully.

MUST (cont.)
```
T4    147:40                                    "We must have a bit of a fight, but I don't care about going on
A3     23:30                                    "But she must have a prize herself, you know," said the Mouse.
A9     77:19  made her next remark. "Then the eleventh day must have been a holiday?"
A2     17: 2  Rome--no, that's all wrong, I'm certain! I must have been changed for Mabel! I'll try and say 'How doth
A5     35: 8  was when I got up this morning, but I think I must have been changed several times since then."
T8    179: 3  be seen, and her first thought was that she must have been dreaming about the Lion and the Unicorn and
T12   208: 8  washed you this morning! You see, Kitty, it must have been either me or the Red King. He was part of my
T3    133: 9  great interest, and made up her mind that it must have been just repainted, it looked so bright and sticky;
A12    94: 9                                    "It must have been that," said the King, "unless it was written to
T12   207:21  a little ashamed of itself, so I think it must have been the Red Queen.")
T8    181:24  passing over his face. "Then all the things must have fallen out! And the box is no use without them." He
T5    152:27  By this time it was getting light. "The crow must have flown away, I think," said Alice: "I'm so glad it's
A7     56: 5                                    "Yes, but some crumbs must have got in as well," the Hatter grumbled: "you shouldn't
T8    185: 7  Alice did not dare to laugh. "I'm afraid you must have hurt him," she said in a trembling voice, "being on
A12    94:19                                    "He must have imitated somebody else's hand," said the King. (The
A12    94:24  King, "that only makes the matter worse. You must have meant some mischief, or else you'd have signed your
A3     23:21  the Dodo said "Everybody has won, and all must have prizes."
A3     25:16  prosecute you.--Come, I'll take no denial: We must have the trial; For really this morning I've nothing to
T8W    21: 8  One would have done as well as two, if you must have them so close--"
T7    171: 6  tell you?" the King repeated impatiently. "I must have two--to fetch and carry. One to fetch, and one to
T7    170:37  H. "The other Messenger's called Hatta. I must have two, you know--to come and go. One to come, and one
T4    147:11  as he crawled out of the umbrella: "only she must help us to dress up, you know."
T4    148: 4                          Alice laughed. "You must hit the trees pretty often, I should think," she said.
T6    160: 8                          "Of course it must," Humpty Dumpty said with a short laugh: "my name means
A11    91:13                          "Well, if I must, I must," the King said with a melancholy air, and, after
T9    198: 6  "and then I'll ring the--the--which bell must I ring?" she went on, very much puzzled by the names.
A3     21:10  and would only say, "I'm older than you, and must know better." And this Alice would not allow, without
T8    186:28  such as gunpowder and sealing-wax. And here I must leave you." They had just come to the end of the wood.
T3    129:17  to them--and what quantities of honey they must make! I think I'll go down and--no, I wo'n't go just yet
A4     32: 9  and, as it ca'n't possibly make me larger, it must make me smaller, I suppose."
T5    149:10  there was to be any conversation at all, she must manage it herself. So she began rather timidly: "Am I
A2     14: 8  too far off to trouble myself about you: you must manage the best way you can--but I must be kind to them,"
A5     43: 3   I should be free of them at last, they must needs come wriggling down from the sky! Ugh, Serpent!"
A11    90: 5                                    "You must remember," remarked the King, "or I'll have you executed
T2    127:21  place. If you want to get somewhere else, you must run at least twice as fast as that!"
A10    82:23  him declare / 'You have baked me too brown, I must sugar my hair.' / As a duck with his eyelids, so he with
T9    202:31                                    "We must support you, you know," the White Queen whispered, as
T9    195:23  once said a thing, that fixes it, and you must take the consequences."
A11    91:13                          "Well, if I must, I must," the King said with a melancholy air, and, after folding
T6    167:20  I said to him, I said it plain, / 'Then you must wake them up again.'
```
MUSTARD (2)
```
A9     71:11  Very true," said the Duchess: "flamingoes and mustard both bite. And the moral of that is--'Birds of a
A9     71:13                                    "Only mustard isn't a bird," Alice remarked.
```
MUSTARD-MINE (1)
```
A9     71:18  everything that Alice said: "there's a large mustard-mine near here. And the moral of that is--'The more
```
MUSTN'T (1)
```
T9    195: 2  acres of ground?" said the White Queen. "You mustn't leave out so many things."
```
MUTTERED (5)
```
T7    175:36                          "Certainly--certainly!" the King muttered, and beckoned to Haigha. "Open the bag!" he whispered
T8    190: 7  woe, / Who rocked his body to and fro, / And muttered mumblingly and low, / As if his mouth were full of
A7     56:14                          "Why should it?" muttered the Hatter. "Does your watch tell you what year it is
A6     46:36  to be told so. "It's really dreadful," she muttered to herself, "the way all the creatures argue. It's
T9    199:18   do that--shouldn't do that--" the Frog muttered. "Wexes it, you know." Then he went up and gave the
```
MUTTERING (4)
```
A12    95:38  right, so far," said the King; and he went on muttering over the verses to himself: "'We know it to be true'
T8    183:15  after this, the Knight with his eyes shut, muttering to himself, and Alice watching anxiously for the
A2     15:29  he came trotting along in a great hurry, muttering to himself, as he came, "Oh! The Duchess, the
A4     27: 3  as if it had lost something; and she heard it muttering to itself, "The Duchess! The Duchess! Oh my dear
```
MUTTON (8)
```
T9    200:23  mutton," said the Red Queen. "Alice--Mutton: Mutton--Alice." The leg of mutton got up in the dish and made
T9    202:27  kangaroos) scrambled into the dish of roast mutton, and began eagerly lapping up the gravy, "just like
T9    200:20  on the joint!" And the waiters set a leg of mutton before Alice, who looked at it rather anxiously, as she
T9    201: 1  "Alice--Mutton: Mutton--Alice." The leg of mutton got up in the dish and made a little bow to Alice; and
T9    201:19  little shy with it, as she had been with the mutton; however, she conquered her shyness by a great effort,
T9    200:23  leg of mutton," said the Red Queen. "Alice--Mutton: Mutton--Alice." The leg of mutton got up in the dish
T9    200:23  shy: let me introduce you to that leg of mutton," said the Red Queen. "Alice--Mutton: Mutton--Alice."
T9    204: 4  instead of the Queen, there was the leg of mutton sitting in the chair. "Here I am!" cried a voice from
```
MUTTON-PIES (1)
```
T8    188: 3  sleep among the wheat: / I make them into mutton-pies, / And sell them in the street. / I sell them unto
```
MY (144) [entries omitted]
MYSELF (14) [entries omitted]
MYSTERY (2)
```
A9     76:37  counting off the subjects on his flappers--"Mystery, ancient and modern, with Seaography: then Drawling--
A9     76:36                          "Well, there was Mystery," the Mock Turtle replied, counting off the subjects
```
MYSTIC (1)
```
AI     4: 6  Childhood's dreams are twined / In Memory's mystic band. / Like pilgrim's wither'd wreath of flowers /
```

-N-

NAME (38)
    T3   131: 2   she's going, even if she doesn't know her own name!"
    T3   134:23   "I suppose you don't want to lose your name?"
    T9   196:16   was so frightened, I couldn't remember my own name!"
    A2   19:45   low, vulgar things! Don't let me hear the name again!"
    A11   91:33   at the top of his shrill little voice, the name "Alice!"
    T6   160: 2   at her for the first time, "but tell me your name and your business."
    A8   63:39   turning to Alice, she went on: "What's your name, child?"
    T6   160: 5   "It's a stupid name enough!" Humpty Dumpty interrupted impatiently. "What
    T3   135: 3   to leave off, because there wouldn't be any name for her to call, and of course you wouldn't have to go,
    A6   51: 5   did not at all know whether it would like the name: however, it only grinned a little wider. "Come, it's
    T9   196:18   to herself "I never should try to remember my name in the middle of an accident! Where would be the use of
    T6   160: 4   "My name is Alice, but--"
    A8   63:40   "My name is Alice, so please your Majesty," said Alice very
    T8   187: 2   looking a little vexed. "That's what the name is called. The name really is 'The Aged Aged Man.'"
    T7   170:33   with--with--with Ham-sandwiches and Hay. His name is Haigha, and he lives--"
    T7   170:28   He only does them when he's happy. His name is Haigha." (He pronounced it so as to rhyme with 'mayor
    A12   94:25   some mischief, or else you'd have signed your name like an honest man."
    T6   160:10   and a good handsome shape it is, too. With a name like yours, you might be any shape, almost."
    T6   160: 7   "Must a name mean something?" Alice asked doubtfully.
    T6   160: 9   Humpty Dumpty said with a short laugh: "my name means the shape I am--and a good handsome shape it is,
    T3   137:13   so suddenly. "However, I know my name now," she said: "that's some comfort. Alice--Alice--I
    T7   170:36   while Alice was still hesitating for the name of a town beginning with H. "The other Messenger's called
    T3   135:33   know, when people lose dogs--'answers to the name of "Dash": had on a brass collar'--just fancy calling
    A11   86:15   was quite pleased to find that she knew the name of nearly everything there. "That's the judge," she said
    A1   8:44   "--but I shall have to ask them what the name of the country is, you know. Please, Ma'am, is this New
    T8   186:40   "Or else it doesn't, you know. The name of the song is called 'Haddocks' Eyes.'"
    T8   186:42   "Oh, that's the name of the song, is it?" Alice said, trying to feel
    T3   129: 6   the only one, but I don't think it's got any name. Principal towns--why, what are those creatures, making
    T8   187: 2   vexed. "That's what the name is called. The name really is 'The Aged Aged Man.'"
    T3   135: 7   lessons for that. If she couldn't remember my name, she'd call me 'Miss,' as the servants do."
    A12   94:22   and they ca'n't prove that I did: there's no name signed at the end."
    T3   135:32   to find the creature that has got my old name! That's just like the advertisements, you know, when
    T3   132:38   Alice; "but it's useful to the people that name them, I suppose. If not, why do things have names at all
    T8W   17: 2   The Wasp said "That's a new-fangled name. They called it conceit in my time."
    A4   27:22   of which was a bright brass plate with the name "W. RABBIT" engraved upon it. She went in without
    T6   159: 6   to herself. "I'm as certain of it, as if his name were written all over his face!"
    T3   135:29   have no names. I wonder what'll become of my name when I go in? I shouldn't like to lose it at all--because
    T3   136: 1   itself, I wonder? I do believe it's got no name--why, to be sure it hasn't!"
NAMES (10)
    T3   132:38   them, I suppose. If not, why do things have names at all?"
    T3   132:40   on, in the wood down there, they've got no names--however, go on with your list of insects: you're
    T3   135:28   to herself, "where things have no names. I wonder what'll become of my name when I go in? I
    T9   198: 7   ring?" she went on, very much puzzled by the names. "I'm not a visitor, and I'm not a servant. There ought
    T3   132:31   least the large kinds. But I can tell you the names of some of them."
    T3   133: 2   the Horse-fly," Alice began, counting off the names on her fingers.
    T3   132:32   "Of course they answer to their names?" the Gnat remarked carelessly.
    T3   132:35   "What's the use of their having names," the Gnat said, "if they wo'n't answer to them?"
    A11   86:31   "They're putting down their names," the Gryphon whispered in reply, "for fear they should
    A7   58:33   Dormouse began in a great hurry; "and their names were Elsie, Lacie, and Tillie; and they lived at the
NAP (1)
    T9   197: 5   / Till the feast's ready, we've time for a nap. / When the feast's over, we'll go to the ball--/ Red
NARROW (4)
    T6   160:19   for the queer creature. "That wall is so very narrow!"
    A2   18:10   "That was a narrow escape!" said Alice, a good deal frightened at the
    T6   159: 9   a Turk, on the top of a high wall--such a narrow one that Alice quite wondered how he could keep his
    A4   30:37   place for a good deal: this fireplace is narrow, to be sure; but I think I can kick a little!"
NASTY (3)
    T1   110: 8   I might have won, if it hadn't been for that nasty Knight, that came wriggling down among my pieces. Kitty
    A2   19:44   such a subject! Our family always hated cats: nasty, low, vulgar things! Don't let me hear the name again!"
    T9   193:12   "A nasty, vicious temper," the Red Queen remarked; and then there
NATURAL (7)
    T7   175:22   to-day. It's as large as life, and twice as natural!"
    A1   7:15   at this, but at the time it all seemed quite natural); but, when the Rabbit actually took a watch out of
    T4   139:28   dancing round in a ring. This seemed quite natural (she remembered afterwards), and she was not even
    A3   21: 7   this, and after a few minutes it seemed quite natural to Alice to find herself talking familiarly with them,
    A6   52:20   just as if the Cat had come back in a natural way.
    T1   119:10   glad to find herself walking again in the natural way.
    A10   83: 1   wondering if anything would ever happen in a natural way again.
-NATURED [See GOOD-NATURED]
NAY (1)
    A4   30:32   Bill, I fancy--Who's to go down the chimney?--Nay, I sha'n't! You do it!--That I wo'n't, then!--Bill's got

NEAR (23)
```
TI    103:24         dear, / Who fret to find our bedtime near.
TC    209:15  eye and willing ear, / Lovingly shall nestle near.
T1    116: 1            There was a book lying near Alice on the table, and while she sat watching the White
TC    209: 4            Children three that nestle near, / Eager eye and willing ear, / Pleased a simple tale to
A12    93:31        Alice could see this, as she was near enough to look over their slates; "but it doesn't matter
A4     34: 3         There was a large mushroom growing near her, about the same height as herself; and, when she had
A2     15:32  ask help of any one: so, when the Rabbit came near her, she began, in a low, timid voice, "If you please,
A9     71:18  Alice said: "there's a large mustard-mine near here. And the moral of that is--'The more there is of
T8    181:36  the best kind. But not a single bee has come near it yet. And the other thing is a mouse-trap. I suppose
A2     20: 4  on eagerly: "There is such a nice little dog, near our house, I should like to show you! A little
A1      8:29  she said aloud. "I must be getting somewhere near the centre of the earth. Let me see: that would be four
A11    91: 7  she got into the court, by the way the people near the door began sneezing all at once.
A6     46: 8  gone, and the other was sitting on the ground near the door, staring stupidly up into the sky.
A8     62: 1           A large rose-tree stood near the entrance of the garden: the roses growing on it were
A2     15: 9            Hearthrug, near the Fender, (with Alice's love).
A5     44: 5     bit again, and did not venture to go near the house till she had brought herself down to nine
A11    86: 5  with a soldier on each side to guard him; and near the King was the White Rabbit, with a trumpet in one hand
A4     28: 2  her eye fell upon a little bottle that stood near the looking-glass. There was no label this time with the
T1    115:14  smoothed his hair, and set him upon the table near the Queen.
A5     43:37  It was so long since she had been anything near the right size, that it felt quite strange at first; but
A8     65:13  put them into a large flower-pot that stood near. The three soldiers wandered about for a minute or two,
T4    144:24  puffing of a large steam-engine in the wood near them, though she feared it was more likely to be a wild
T9    199:37  Looking-Glass creatures,' quoth Alice, 'draw near! / 'Tis an honour to see me, a favour to hear: / 'Tis a
```
NEARER (6)
```
A9     74:18  on a little ledge of rock, and, as they came nearer, Alice could hear him sighing as if his heart would
T9    199: 9  large dull eyes for a minute: then he went nearer and rubbed it with his thumb, as if he were trying
A10    80: 9  side. / The further off from England the nearer is to France. / Then turn not pale, beloved snail, but
A6     53:14  so large a house, that she did not like to go nearer till she had nibbled some more of the left-hand bit of
A2     19: 6  in the pool a little way off, and she swam nearer to make out what it was: at first she thought it must
A8     62: 4    this a very curious thing, and she went nearer to watch them, and, just as she came up to them, she
```
NEAREST (1)
```
T3    132:11  and in her fright she caught at the thing nearest to her hand, which happened to be the Goat's beard. *
```
NEARLY (23)
```
A6     45:12  producing from under his arm a great letter, nearly as large as himself, and this he handed over to the
T6    161: 1  from ear to ear, as he leant forwards (and as nearly as possible fell off the wall in doing so) and offered
A2     18: 5  to measure herself by it, and found that, as nearly as she could guess, she was now about two feet high,
A6     46:24  she said to herself; "his eyes are so very nearly at the top of his head. But at any rate he might answer
A6     48:19  large saucepan flew close by it, and very nearly carried it off.
T2    127:29  dry: and she thought she had never been so nearly choked in all her life.
A11    86:15  pleased to find that she knew the name of nearly everything there. "That's the judge," she said to
A4     33:10  been the right size to do it! Oh dear! I'd nearly forgotten that I've got to grow up again! Let me see--
A6     52:18  what became of the baby?" said the Cat. "I'd nearly forgotten to ask."
A9     74:37  sobbing of the Mock Turtle. Alice was very nearly getting up and saying, "Thank you, Sir, for your
T8W    19:10  that I am old and gray, / And all my hair is nearly gone, / They take my wig from me and say / 'How can you
A9     74:20  the Gryphon. And the Gryphon answered, very nearly in the same words as before, "It's all his fancy, that:
T1    115: 8  till her hand shook so with laughter that she nearly let him drop upon the floor.
T9    203: 3  pushed her so, one on each side, that they nearly lifted her up into the air. "I rise to return thanks--"
T1    108:23  the mischief you had been doing, I was very nearly opening the window, and putting you out into the snow!
A11    91:15  and frowning at the cook till his eyes were nearly out of sight, he said, in a deep voice, "What are tarts
T1    114: 5  be of use, and, as the poor little Lily was nearly screaming herself into a fit, she hastily picked up the
T7    176:17  up at the crown, which the poor King was nearly shaking off his head, he trembled so much.
T1    113:13  on, as she put her head closer down, "and I'm nearly sure they ca'n't see me. I feel somehow as if I was
T2    126:27  Faster!" and dragged her along. "Are we nearly there?" Alice managed to pant out at last.
T2    127: 1                       "Nearly there!" the Queen repeated. "Why, we passed it ten
A12    93:40                       "Nearly two miles high," added the Queen.
T8W    14: 6  rather offended at this answer, and was very nearly walking on and leaving him, but she thought to herself
```
NEAT (3)
```
T4    142: 4  faces washed, / Their shoes were clean and neat--/ And this was odd, because, you know, / They hadn't any
A4     27:21  find them." As she said this, she came upon a neat little house, on the door of which was a bright brass
T9    202:29            "You ought to return thanks in a neat speech," the Red Queen said, frowning at Alice as she
```
NEATER (1)
```
T8W    17:12  of sea-weed. "You could make your wig much neater," she said, "if only you had a comb."
```
NEATLY (2)
```
A4     32:22  sounded an excellent plan, no doubt, and very neatly and simply arranged: the only difficulty was, that she
A2     17:13  "How cheerfully he seems to grin, / How neatly spreads his claws, / And welcomes little fishes in, /
```
NECK (19) [See also STIFF-NECK]
```
T7    173:27  putting his arm affectionately round Hatta's neck.
T8W    16:19  hold up your head--so--without bending your neck."
T8W    20:13  get hold of the other one by the back of the neck?"
T4    138: 2  a tree, each with an arm round the other's neck, and Alice knew which was which in a moment, because one
T7    172: 2  amusement, opened a bag that hung round his neck, and handed a sandwich to the King, who devoured it
T6    162:20  I knew," she thought to herself, "which was neck and which was waist!"
T8    184:15  interest, clasping his arms round the horse's neck as he spoke, just in time to save himself from tumbling
A5     43:13  girls in my time, but never one with such a neck as that! No, no! You're a serpent; and there's no use
T8    187:23  about, with the reins hanging loose on his neck, cropping the grass at her feet--and the black shadows of
A4     28:11  the ceiling, and had to stoop to save her neck from being broken. She hastily put down the bottle,
T1    108:17  three turns of the worsted round the kitten's neck, just to see how it would look: this led to a scramble,
A5     43:30  among the trees as well as she could, for her neck kept getting entangled among the branches, and every now
A8     66: 9  down, but generally, just as she had got its neck nicely straightened out, and was going to give the
```

NECK (cont.)
A1   10:16   here before," said Alice), and tied round the neck of the bottle was a paper label, with the words "DRINK ME
T3   137: 4   with her arms clasped lovingly round the soft neck of the Fawn, till they came out into another open field,
T4   147:23   herself, as she arranged a bolster round the neck of Tweedledee, "to keep his head from being cut off," as
T8   187:12   his horse and let the reins fall on its neck: then, slowly beating time with one hand, and with a
A5   42:10   she looked down, was an immense length of neck, which seemed to rise like a stalk out of a sea of green
A5   42:20   to them, and was delighted to find that her neck would bend about easily in any direction, like a serpent.
NEED (1)
T4   143: 8   the Walrus said, / 'Is what we chiefly need: / Pepper and vinegar besides / Are very good indeed--/
NEEDED (1)
T5   155:23   This didn't sound like a remark that needed any answer: so Alice said nothing, but pulled away.
NEEDLES (7) [See also KNITTING-NEEDLES]
T5   155:21   the Sheep, as she took up another pair of needles.
T5   155:31   cried angrily, taking up quite a bunch of needles.
T5   155:16   "Yes, a little--but not on land--and not with needles--" Alice was beginning to say, when suddenly the
T5   155:35   course!" said the Sheep, sticking some of the needles into her hair, as her hands were full. "Feather, I
T5   155:17   Alice was beginning to say, when suddenly the needles turned into oars in her hands, and she found they were
T5   155:27   Feather!" the Sheep cried again, taking more needles. "You'll be catching a crab directly."
T5   155: 8   Sheep said, as she took up another pair of needles. "You'll make me giddy soon, if you go on turning
NEEDN'T (9)
A8   63:42   they're only a pack of cards, after all. I needn't be afraid of them!"
T4   146:25   his arm and said, in a soothing tone, "You needn't be so angry about an old rattle."
A9   76: 7   been to a day-school, too," said Alice. "You needn't be so proud as all that."
T6   166:17   "Oh, it needn't come to that!" Alice hastily said, hoping to keep him
T6   166:37   "You needn't go on making remarks like that," Humpty Dumpty said:
T5   153: 5   "You needn't say 'exactly,'" the Queen remarked. "I can believe it
T5   156: 8   "You needn't say 'please' to me about 'em," the Sheep said, without
T6   168: 5   he was very stiff and proud: / He said, 'You needn't shout so loud!'
A12   95:31   saves a world of trouble, you know, as we needn't try to find any. And yet I don't know," he went on,
NEEDS (1)
A5   43: 3   I should be free of them at last, they must needs come wriggling down from the sky! Ugh, Serpent!"
NEIGHBOUR (1)
A11   87: 2   to spell "stupid," and that he had to ask his neighbour to tell him. "A nice muddle their slates'll be in,
NEIGHBOURING (1)
A12   98:25   frightened Mouse splashed his way through the neighbouring pool--she could hear the rattle of the teacups as
NEITHER (4)
T1   114:22   question: it was quite clear that he could neither hear her nor see her.
T6   163:31   "it means just what I choose it to mean--neither more nor less."
A6   50:11   there could be no mistake about it: it was neither more nor less than a pig, and she felt that it would
A7   60:31   off: the Dormouse fell asleep instantly, and neither of the others took the least notice of her going,
NERVOUS (8)
A10   82: 2   first saw the White Rabbit. She was a little nervous about it, just at first, the two creatures got so
A1   12: 7   to shrink any further: she felt a little nervous about this; "for it might end, you know," said Alice
T7   176:24   to prevent the quarrel going on: he was very nervous, and his voice quite quivered. "All round the town?"
T3   132: 7   with this, though Alice felt a little nervous at the idea of trains jumping at all. "However, it'll
A8   63:23   the White Rabbit: it was talking in a hurried nervous manner, smiling at everything that was said, and went
A11   88:28   your evidence," said the King: "and don't be nervous, or I'll have you executed on the spot."
A11   89:10   "or I'll have you executed, whether you are nervous or not."
T3   132:21   Alice thought. Still, she couldn't feel nervous with it, after they had been talking together so long.
NERVOUSLY (3)
T9   200: 8   Alice glanced nervously along the table, as she walked up the large hall,
T9   195:26   me--" the White Queen said, looking down and nervously clasping and unclasping her hands, "we had such a
T7   175:12   A little--a little," the King replied, rather nervously. "You shouldn't have run him through with your horn,
NEST (4)
A5   43:29   sulky tone, as it settled down again into its nest. Alice crouched down among the trees as well as she could
T3   134: 3   the Gnat replied; "and it makes its nest in a Christmas-box."
T8   181:30   "In hopes some bees may make a nest in it--then I should get the honey."
TI   103:28   the firelight's ruddy glow, / And childhood's nest of gladness. / The magic words shall hold thee fast: /
NESTLE (2)
TC   209:15   / Eager eye and willing ear, / Lovingly shall nestle near.
TC   209: 4   Children three that nestle near, / Eager eye and willing ear, / Pleased a simple
NESTS (1)
T6   164:39   said Humpty Dumpty; "also they make their nests under sun-dials--also they live on cheese."
NEVER (105)
A9   74:15   was so ordered about before, in all my life, never!"
T2   120:25   saw such a house for getting in the way! Never!"
T4   140:20   The eldest Oyster looked at him, / But never a word he said: / The eldest Oyster winked his eye, /
A2   18:16   "for I never was so small as this before, never! And I declare it's too bad, that it is!"
T6   162: 7   "I never ask advice about growing," Alice said indignantly.
T9   195:16   "I wish Queens never asked questions," Alice thought to herself.
T2   126:25   idea of doing that. She felt as if she would never be able to talk again, she was getting so much out of
T9   200: 6   Alice repeated in despair. "Oh, that'll never be done! I'd better go in at once--" and in she went,
A11   86:13   Alice had never been in a court of justice before, but she had read
A5   41:11   Alice said nothing: she had never been so much contradicted in all her life before, and
T2   127:29   and it was very dry: and she thought she had never been so nearly choked in all her life.
A1   8: 1   for it flashed across her mind that she had never before seen a rabbit with either a waistcoat-pocket, or
T5   152:31   manage to be glad!" the Queen said. "Only I never can remember the rule. You must be very happy, living in
T1   110:36   whether they've a fire in the winter: you never can tell, you know, unless our fire smokes, and then
T2   126:19   the trees and the other things round them never changed their places at all: however fast they went,
A1   8:27   Down, down, down. Would the fall never come to an end? "I wonder how many miles I've fallen by

NEVER (cont.)

T5	151: 7	"Suppose he never commits the crime?" said Alice.
A6	48:32	"Oh, don't bother me!" said the Duchess. "I never could abide figures!" And with that she began nursing
T2	126:12	Alice never could quite make out, in thinking it over afterwards,
T9	196:12	such a thunderstorm, you ca'n't think!" ("She never could, you know," said the Red Queen.) "And part of the
T9	192: 4	rather fond of scolding herself), "It'll never do for you to be lolling about on the grass like that!
T3	135: 5	"That would never do, I'm sure," said Alice: "the governess would never
A1	9: 3	girl she'll think me for asking! No, it'll never do to ask: perhaps I shall see it written up somewhere
A5	44: 3	"Whoever lives there," thought Alice, "it'll never do to come upon them this size: why, I should frighten
T3	129:20	excuse for turning shy so suddenly. "It'll never do to go down among them without a good long branch to
T5	149:15	Alice thought it would never do to have an argument at the very beginning of their
T4	140: 4	she had just been dancing with. "It would never do to say 'How d'ye do?' now," she said to herself: "we
T5	158:14	put things into people's hands--that would never do--you must get it for yourself." And so saying, she
A2	19:15	the right way of speaking to a mouse: she had never done such a thing before, but she remembered having seen
A10	78: 9	haven't," said Alice)--"and perhaps you were never even introduced to a lobster--" (Alice began to say "I
A7	56:39	his head contemptuously. "I dare say you never even spoke to Time!"
A9	74:12	the Gryphon. "It's all her fancy that: they never executes nobody, you know. Come on!"
T9	192: 1	"Well, this is grand!" said Alice. "I never expected I should be a Queen so soon--and I'll tell you
T8	182:34	falls off is because it hangs down--things never fall upwards, you know. It's a plan of my own invention.
T6	168:40	the unsatisfactory people I ever met--" She never finished the sentence, for at this moment a heavy crash
T1	115:26	moment," the King went on, "I shall never, never forget!"
A1	11: 3	with a knife, it usually bleeds; and she had never forgotten that, if you drink much from a bottle marked
A4	29: 9	"But then," thought Alice, "shall I never get any older than I am now? That'll be a comfort, one
T4	145:25	wood, and stopped under a large tree. "It can never get at me here," she thought: "it's far too large to
A2	16:10	and four times seven is--oh dear! I shall never get to twenty at that rate! However, the
A7	60:35	"At any rate I'll never go there again!" said Alice, as she picked her way
T7	176: 3	it, now?" the Unicorn cried eagerly. "You'll never guess! I couldn't."
A12	96:17	Then again--'before she had this fit'--you never had fits, my dear, I think?" he said to the Queen.
T9	200:21	who looked at it rather anxiously, as she had never had to carve a joint before.
A8	68:38	was a body to cut it off from: that he had never had to do such a thing before, and he wasn't going to
A4	29: 4	fairy tales, I fancied that kind of thing never happened, and now here I am in the middle of one! There
T9	200:12	waiting to be asked," she thought: "I should never have known who were the right people to invite!"
A4	30: 2	Pat! Where are you?" And then a voice she had never heard before, "Sure then I'm here! Digging for apples,
A10	82:32	"Well, I never heard it before," said the Mock Turtle; "but it sounds
T5	150:14	Alice repeated in great astonishment. "I never heard of such a thing!"
A9	76:24	"I never heard of 'Uglification,'" Alice ventured to say. "What
A9	76:26	Gryphon lifted up both its paws in surprise. "Never heard of uglifying!" it exclaimed. "You know what to
A9	72: 7	be'--or, if you'd like it put more simply--'Never imagine yourself not to be otherwise than what it might
T5	150: 6	rule is, jam to-morrow and jam yesterday--but never jam to-day."
T2	128:28	How it happened, Alice never knew, but exactly as she came to the last peg, she was
A10	81: 8	you," said Alice, "it's very interesting. I never knew so much about a whiting before."
T3	132:34	"I never knew them do it."
A8	68:15	as the game was in such confusion that she never knew whether it was her turn or not. So she went off in
A9	77: 3	Turtle said: "I'm too stiff. And the Gryphon never learnt it."
A9	73: 3	All the time they were playing the Queen never left off quarreling with the other players, and shouting
A11	89: 4	All this time the Queen had never left off staring at the Hatter, and, just as the
T9	195:15	herself up rather stiffly, and said "Queens never make bargains."
T2	122:13	"Never mind!" Alice said in a soothing tone, and, stooping down
A11	91:25	"Never mind!" said the King with an air of great relief. "Call
T1	108:15	and it snowed so, they had to leave off. Never mind, we'll go and see the bonfire to-morrow." Here
T3	131:24	leaned forwards and whispered in her ear, "Never mind what they all say, my dear, but take a
T1	115:25	of that moment," the King went on, "I shall never, never forget!"
A1	8: 5	In another moment down went Alice after it, never once considering how in the world she was to get out
A5	43:12	seen a good many little girls in my time, but never one with such a neck as that! No, no! You're a serpent;
T6	168:35	to see if he would speak again, but, as he never opened his eyes or took any further notice of her, she
T5	158:14	and put it away in a box: then she said "I never put things into people's hands--that would never do--you
T6	161:25	Humpty Dumpty exclaimed triumphantly. "You never said a word like it!"
T6	159:25	at all like conversation, she thought, as he never said anything to her; in fact, his last remark was
A9	76: 1	"I never said I didn't!" interrupted Alice.
A12	96:20	"Never!" said the Queen, furiously, throwing an inkstand at the
T2	122:34	"I never saw anybody that looked stupider," a Violet said, so
T7	175:29	Unicorns were fabulous monsters, too? I never saw one alive before!"
A9	73:15	"I never saw one, or heard of one," said Alice.
T2	120:24	"Oh, it's too bad!" she cried. "I never saw such a house for getting in the way! Never!"
T6	160:38	has spoken to a King, I am: mayhap you'll never see such another: and, to show you I'm not proud, you
T2	126:20	places at all: however fast they went, they never seemed to pass anything. "I wonder if all the things
TC	209:12	me, phantomwise. / Alice moving under skies / Never seen by waking eyes.
T1	115: 3	She said afterwards that she had never seen in all her life such a face as the King made, when
T7	169: 5	She thought that in all her life she had never seen soldiers so uncertain on their feet: they were
A8	66: 1	Alice thought she had never seen such a curious croquet-ground in her life: it was
T4	147:18	Alice said afterwards she had never seen such a fuss made about anything in all her life--
T8	181:11	large mild eyes to Alice. She thought she had never seen such a strange-looking soldier in all her life.
T9	196:17	Alice thought to herself "I never should try to remember my name in the middle of an
A10	78:11	but checked herself hastily, and said "No never") "--so you can have no idea what a delightful thing a
A5	43:40	now! How puzzling all these changes are! I'm never sure what I'm going to be, from one minute to another!
A5	43:15	I suppose you'll be telling me next that you never tasted an egg!"
T2	122:32	"It's my opinion that you never think at all," the Rose said, in a rather severe tone.
T3	135: 6	I'm sure," said Alice: "the governess would never think of excusing me lessons for that. If she couldn't
A10	81:12	"I never thought about it," said Alice. "Why?"
T3	137:26	"that they live in the same house! I wonder I never thought of that before--But I ca'n't stay there long.

NEVER (cont.)
 T2   122:31   and Alice was quite pleased to know it. "I never thought of that before!" she said.
 A4   29:10   than I am now? That'll be a comfort, one way--never to be an old woman--but then--always to have lessons to
 A3   26:19   "Ah, my dear! Let this be a lesson to you never to lose your temper!" "Hold your tongue, Ma!" said the
 A11   90:19   by the officers of the court,' and I never understood what it meant till now."
 T9   197:17   England--it couldn't, you know, because there never was more than one Queen at a time. Do wake up, you heavy
 T9   196:28   "She never was really well brought up," the Red Queen went on: "but
 A9   74:14   Alice, as she went slowly after it: "I never was so ordered about before, in all my life, never!"
 A2   18:15   than ever," thought the poor child, "for I never was so small as this before, never! And I declare it's
 T8W   14: 4   in a peevish tone. "Worrity, worrity! There never was such a child!"
 A9   77: 6   "I never went to him," the Mock Turtle said with a sigh. "He
NEVER-ENDING (1)
 A12   98:27   the March Hare and his friends shared their never-ending meal, and the shrill voice of the Queen ordering
NEVERTHELESS (1)
 A4   28: 3   this time with the words "DRINK ME," but nevertheless she uncorked it and put it to her lips. "I know
NEW (18)
 T3   134:15   A new difficulty came into Alice's head. "Supposing it couldn't
 T8   179:22   Alice looked round in some surprise for the new enemy.
 T6   167:13   I took a kettle large and new, / Fit for the deed I had to do.
 T4   146:27   cried, in a greater fury than ever. "It's new, I tell you--I bought it yesterday--my nice NEW RATTLE!"
 A9   77:17   This was quite a new idea to Alice, and she thought it over a little before she
 A5   43:21   This was such a new idea to Alice, that she was quite silent for a minute or
 AI   3:22   moving through a land / Of wonders wild and new, / In friendly chat with bird or beast--/ And half believe
 T1   119: 3   at least, it wasn't exactly running, but a new invention for getting down stairs quickly and easily, as
 A9   70:11   on, very much pleased at having found out a new kind of rule, "and vinegar that makes them sour--and
 T8W   14:21   tour in the Pantry, and have found five new lumps of white sugar, large and in fine condition. In
 T4   148:12   much," said Tweedledum, "if it hadn't been a new one."
 A2   15: 2   I want to go! Let me see. I'll give them a new pair of boots every Christmas."
 T8   186: 7   he went on after a pause, "was inventing a new pudding during the meat-course."
 T4   138:21   said Tweedledee / Had spoiled his nice new rattle.
 T4   146:27   I tell you--I bought it yesterday--my nice NEW RATTLE!" and his voice rose to a perfect scream.
 T8   186: 5   I am, the more I keep inventing new things."
 T8   184:26   "Well, just then I was inventing a new way of getting over a gate--would you like to hear it?"
 A1   8:44   country is, you know. Please, Ma'am, is this New Zealand? Or Australia?" (and she tried to curtsey as she
NEW-FANGLED (1)
 T8W   17: 2   The Wasp said "That's a new-fangled name. They called it conceit in my time."
NEW-FOUND (1)
 T5   156:33   back into her place, and began to arrange her new-found treasures.
NEWS (2)
 T8W   14:20   the paper on her knees, and began. "Latest News. The Exploring Party have made another tour in the Pantry
 T7   172:28   was sorry for this, as she wanted to hear the news too. However, instead of whispering, he simply shouted,
NEWSPAPER (3)
 T8W   15:17   Alice put down the newspaper. "I'm afraid you're not well," she said in a
 T8W   15:13   "It's in this newspaper, though," Alice said a little timidly.
 T8W   14:15   of this?" Alice went on, as she picked up a newspaper which had been lying at his feet.
NEWSPAPERS (1)
 A11   90:17   thought Alice. "I've so often read in the newspapers, at the end of trials, 'There was some attempt at
NEXT (59)
 A4   31: 4   kick, and waited to see what would happen next.
 A8   65:24   wondering very much what would happen next.
 T1   113:18   with great curiosity to see what would happen next.
 T5   154:19   like a work-box, and was always in the shelf next above the one she was looking at. "And this one is the
 A4   27:29   I suppose Dinah'll be sending me on messages next!" And she began fancying the sort of thing that would
 T9   198:11   and said "No admittance till the week after next!" and shut the door again with a bang.
 A9   77:12   first day," said the Mock Turtle: "nine the next, and so on."
 A4   30:19   be!" thought Alice. "I wonder what they'll do next! As for pulling me out of the window, I only wish they
 T6   164: 1   as well if you'd mention what you mean to do next, as I suppose you don't mean to stop here all the rest of
 T4   139:18   "Next Boy!" said Alice, passing on to Tweedledee, though she
 T8   181: 3   "So you will, when you've crossed the next brook," said the White Knight. "I'll see you safe to the
 A4   30: 1   Next came an angry voice--the Rabbit's--"Pat! Pat! Where are
 A8   63:21   they were all ornamented with hearts. Next came the guests, mostly Kings and Queens, and among them
 T3   131:11   beyond the Beetle, but a hoarse voice spoke next. "Change engines--" it said, and there it choked and was
 T8   186:12   slow thoughtful tone: "no, certainly not the next course."
 T8   186: 9   "In time to have it cooked for the next course?" said Alice. "Well, that was quick work,
 T8   186:11   "Well, not the next course," the Knight said in slow thoughtful tone: "no,
 T8   186:13   "Then it would have to be the next day. I suppose you wouldn't have two pudding-courses in
 T8   186:16   day," the Knight repeated as before: "not the next day. In fact," he went on, holding his head down, and his
 A6   46:30   "--or next day, maybe," the Footman continued in the same tone,
 T8   186:15   "Well, not the next day," the Knight repeated as before: "not the next day.
 A1   8:13   her, and to wonder what was going to happen next. First, she tried to look down and make out what she was
 T3   129:15   what enormous flowers they must be!" was her next idea. "Something like cottages with the roofs taken off,
 A4   31:35   to herself "I wonder what they will do next! If they had any sense, they'd take the roof off." After
 A4   32: 1   Alice. But she had not long to doubt, for the next moment a shower of little pebbles came rattling in at the
 A5   41:39   of the right-hand bit to try the effect. The next moment she felt a violent blow underneath her chin: it
 T2   120:23   (as she described it afterwards), and the next moment she found herself actually walking in at the door
 T7   169: 1   The next moment soldiers came running through the wood, at first
 T4   139:27   she took hold of both hands at once: the next moment they were dancing round in a ring. This seemed
 A6   46: 6   for fear of their hearing her; and, when she next peeped out, the Fish-Footman was gone, and the other was
 T2   128:22   At the next peg the Queen turned again, and this time she said "Speak
 T2   128:26   this time, but walked on quickly to the next peg, where she turned for a moment to say "Good-bye," and

NEXT (cont.)
```
A2      15:42   different. But if I'm not the same, the next question is 'Who in the world am I?' Ah, that's the great
A9      77:18   thought it over a little before she made her next remark. "Then the eleventh day must have been a holiday
A5      43:14   denying it. I suppose you'll be telling me next that you never tasted an egg!"
T1     112:13   For instance, the pictures on the wall next the fire seemed to be all alive, and the very clock on
T9     202: 5   a baby, I think, could have caught it. / 'Next, the fish must be bought.' / That is easy: a penny, I
T3     131: 6                      There was a Beetle sitting next the Goat (it was a very queer carriage-full of passengers
T5     150: 1   "Oh, things that happened the week after next," the Queen replied in a careless tone. "For instance,
A8      63:17   with their hands and feet at the corners: next the ten courtiers: these were ornamented all over with
A5      43:42   However, I've got back to my right size: the next thing is, to get into that beautiful garden--how is that
A3      24: 9                          The next thing was to eat the comfits: this caused some noise and
T2     124:17   when I go home," she thought to herself, "the next time I'm a little late for dinner."
AI       3:29   one / To put the subject by, / "The rest next time--" "It is next time!" / The happy voices cry.
AI       3:29   subject by, / "The rest next time--" "It is next time!" / The happy voices cry.
A11     88:40   so," said the Dormouse, who was sitting next to her. "I can hardly breathe."
A2      17:19   and live in that poky little house, and have next to no toys to play with, and oh, ever so many lessons to
T3     131: 3              A Goat, that was sitting next to the gentleman in white, shut his eyes and said in a
T8     183:16   himself, and Alice watching anxiously for the next tumble.
A10     83: 4   said the Gryphon hastily. "Go on with the next verse."
A10     83:10             "Go on with the next verse," the Gryphon repeated: "it begins 'I passed by his
A8      67:28   there's the arch I've got to go through next walking about at the other end of the ground--and I
T5     150: 5   and the trial doesn't even begin till next Wednesday: and of course the crime comes last of all."
A6      45: 2   at the house, and wondering what to do next, when suddenly a footman in livery came running out of
A11     91:26   King with an air of great relief. "Call the next witness." And, he added, in an undertone to the Queen,
A11     91:27   "Really, my dear, you must cross-examine the next witness. It quite makes my forehead ache!"
A11     91: 4                  "Call the next witness!" said the King.
A11     91: 5              The next witness was the Duchess's cook. She carried the
A11     91:30   list, feeling very curious to see what the next witness would be like, "--for they haven't got much
```
NIBBLED (2)
```
A5      41:38   now which is which?" she said to herself, and nibbled a little of the right-hand bit to try the effect. The
A6      53:14   she did not like to go nearer till she had nibbled some more of the left-hand bit of mushroom, and raised
```
NIBBLING (3)
```
A7      61: 2   led into the garden. Then she set to work nibbling at the mushroom (she had kept a piece of it in her
A5      44: 4   them out of their wits!" So she began nibbling at the right-hand bit again, and did not venture to
A5      43:33   hands, and she set to work very carefully, nibbling first at one and then at the other, and growing
```
NICE (23)
```
T6     168:32               "It wouldn't look nice," Alice objected. But Humpty Dumpty only shut his eyes,
T8     186:26              "Not very nice alone," he interrupted, quite eagerly: "but you've no
T8W     21: 2   Wasp went on: "but the top of your head is nice and round." He took off his own wig as he spoke, and
T1     109:10   the snow against the window-panes, Kitty? How nice and soft it sounds! I wonder if the snow loves the trees
T8W     19: 3   the effect, / They said I did not look so nice / As they had ventured to expect.
T1     110: 7   I said 'Check!' you purred! Well, it was a nice check, Kitty, and really I might have won, if it hadn't
T5     157: 1   just as if nothing had happened. "That was a nice crab you caught!" she remarked, as Alice got back into
T12    207: 3   some severity. "You woke me out of oh! such a nice dream! And you've been along with me, Kitty--all through
T8W     15: 3   "No brown sugar!" grumbled the Wasp. "A nice exploring party!"
A1       8:37   Longitude either, but she thought they were nice grand words to say.)
T8     186:25              "That wouldn't be very nice, I'm afraid--"
A1      11: 7   ventured to taste it, and, finding it very nice (it had, in fact, a sort of mixed flavour of cherry-tart,
T1     111: 5   be quite different on beyond. Oh, Kitty, how nice it would be if we could only get through into
T6     163:28              "But 'glory' doesn't mean 'a nice knock-down argument,'" Alice objected.
T6     163:26   don't--till I tell you. I meant 'there's a nice knock-down argument for you!'"
A2      20: 4   so Alice went on eagerly: "There is such a nice little dog, near our house, I should like to show you! A
A1      10:22   'poison' or not"; for she had read several nice little stories about children who had got burnt, and
A11     87: 3   he had to ask his neighbour to tell him. "A nice muddle their slates'll be in, before the trial's over!"
T4     138:21   Tweedledum said Tweedledee / Had spoiled his nice new rattle.
T4     146:27   new, I tell you--I bought it yesterday--my nice NEW RATTLE!" and his voice rose to a perfect scream.
A2      19:38   paws and washing her face--and she is such a nice soft thing to nurse--and she's such a capital one for
T4     143:20   so kind of you to come! / And you are very nice!' / The Carpenter said nothing but / 'Cut us another
T5     158:12   thought to herself, "They mightn't be at all nice, you know."
```
NICELY (4)
```
T2     122:21             "How is it you can all talk so nicely?" Alice said, hoping to get it into a better temper by
T2     124: 7   "And where are you going? Look up, speak nicely, and don't twiddle your fingers all the time."
A2      19:36   about in the pool, "and she sits purring so nicely by the fire, licking her paws and washing her face--and
A8      66: 9   but generally, just as she had got its neck nicely straightened out, and was going to give the hedgehog a
```
NIGHT (9) [See also GOOD-NIGHT, TO-NIGHT]
```
T4     140:28   was odd, because it was / The middle of the night.
A5      42:39   "but I must be on the look-out for serpents, night and day! Why, I haven't had a wink of sleep these three
T8     188:36   them into waistcoat-buttons / In the silent night. / And these I do not sell for gold / Or coin of silvery
T5     152:29   "I'm so glad it's gone. I thought it was the night coming on."
T6     164: 9   should see 'em come round me of a Saturday night," Humpty Dumpty went on, wagging his head gravely from
T4     143:17   that would be / A dismal thing to do!' / 'The night is fine,' the Walrus said. / 'Do you admire the view?
A2      15:39   as usual. I wonder if I've changed in the night? Let me think: was I the same when I got up this morning
T9     195:35              "Are five nights warmer than one night, then?" Alice ventured to ask.
A6      48:25   what work it would make with the day and night! You see the earth takes twenty-four hours to turn round
```
NIGHT-AIR (1)
```
A3      26:33   remarking "I really must be getting home: the night-air doesn't suit my throat!" And a Canary called out in
```
NIGHTCAP [NIGHT-CAP] (3)
```
T9     196:37   Red Queen. "Smoothe her hair--lend her your nightcap--and sing her a soothing lullaby."
T4     144:33   say honestly that he was. He had a tall red night-cap on, with a tassel, and he was lying crumpled up into
T9     196:38              "I haven't got a nightcap with me," said Alice, as she tried to obey the first
```

NIGHTS (3)
T9   195:33   in the winter we take as many as five nights together--for warmth, you know."
T9   195:32   things. Now here, we mostly have days and nights two or three at a time, and sometimes in the winter we
T9   195:35   "Are five nights warmer than one night, then?" Alice ventured to ask.
NILE (1)
A2   17:10   shining tail, / And pour the waters of the Nile / On every golden scale!
NINE (11)
T8   188:40   a copper halfpenny, / And that will purchase nine.
T9   200: 4   And welcome Queen Alice with ninety-times-nine!"
T9   200: 5   "Ninety times nine!" Alice repeated in despair. "Oh, that'll never be done!
A2   18:26   pool of tears which she had wept when she was nine feet high.
A2   15:13   hall: in fact she was now rather more than nine feet high, and she at once took up the little golden key
T9   194: 2   interrupted. "Can you do Subtraction? Take nine from eight."
T9   194: 3   "Nine from eight I ca'n't, you know," Alice replied very
A5   44: 6   house till she had brought herself down to nine inches high.
A7   56:45   with the clock. For instance, suppose it were nine o'clock in the morning, just time to begin lessons: you'd
T2   123:21   the Rose. "She's one of the kind that has nine spikes, you know."
A9   77:12   hours the first day," said the Mock Turtle: "nine the next, and so on."
NINETY (3)
T9   200: 4   with the wine--/ And welcome Queen Alice with ninety-times-nine!"
T9   199:34   thought to herself "Thirty times three makes ninety. I wonder if any one's counting?" In a minute there was
T9   200: 5   "Ninety times nine!" Alice repeated in despair. "Oh, that'll
NO (164)
T12   207:12   to guess whether it meant "yes" or "no."
T6   162:17   "a beautiful cravat, I should have said--no, a belt, I mean--I beg your pardon!" she added in dismay,
A10   84:13   Gryphon said, in a rather offended tone, "Hm! No accounting for tastes! Sing her 'Turtle Soup,' will you,
T9   198:10   beak put its head out for a moment and said "No admittance till the week after next!" and shut the door
T9   197:19   went on in an impatient tone; but there was no answer but a gentle snoring.
T9   195:42   it up. "It's exactly like the riddle with no answer!" she thought.
T6   168:36   she said "Good-bye!" once more, and, getting no answer to this, she quietly walked away: but she couldn't
A7   56:34   "than wasting it in asking riddles that have no answers."
A9   73: 7   by the end of half an hour or so, there were no arches left, and all the players, except the King, the
T4   140:40   / No birds were flying overhead--/ There were no birds to fly.
T4   140:39   a cloud, because / No cloud was in the sky: / No birds were flying overhead--/ There were no birds to fly.
T8   184: 2   anxious tone, as she picked him up, "I hope no bones are broken?"
T2   126:17   felt she could not go faster, though she had no breath left to say so.
T8W   15: 3   "No brown sugar!" grumbled the Wasp. "A nice exploring party!"
A8   64: 4   Alice, surprised at her own courage. "It's no business of mine."
A4   30:11   "Well, it's got no business there, at any rate: go and take it away!"
T4   140:31   / Because she thought the sun / Had got no business to be there / After the day was done--/ 'It's very
T5   156:11   "No, but I meant--please, may we wait and pick some?" Alice
T8   186:12   the Knight said in slow thoughtful tone: "no, certainly not the next course."
T6   160:22   Why, if ever I did fall off--which there's no chance of--but if I did--" Here he pursed up his lips, and
A5   42:18   As there seemed to be no chance of getting her hands up to her head, she tried to
A11   86:10   the refreshments!" But there seemed to be no chance of this; so she began looking at everything about
T4   140:38   dry. / You could not see a cloud, because / No cloud was in the sky: / No birds were flying overhead--/
A3   25:14   law: I will prosecute you.--Come, I'll take no denial: We must have the trial; For really this morning
T5   151:10   Alice felt there was no denying that. "Of course it would be all the better," she
T9   201:11   Alice said rather hastily, "or we shall get no dinner at all. May I give you some?"
A4   32:22   It sounded an excellent plan, no doubt, and very neatly and simply arranged: the only
T1   107:10   was lying quite still and trying to purr--no doubt feeling that it was all meant for its good.
T8W   21: 7   "Then your eyes--they're too much in front, no doubt. One would have done as well as two, if you must have
A6   46:35   It was, no doubt: only Alice did not like to be told so. "It's really
A6   49:32   what was the matter with it. There could be no doubt that it had a very turn-up nose, much more like a
T7   174:25   "There's some enemy after her, no doubt," the King said, without even looking round. "That
A2   19:12   very likely it can talk: at any rate, there's no harm in trying." So she began: "O Mouse, do you know the
T9   192:15   not be quite civil. However, there would be no harm, she thought, in asking if the game was over. "Please,
T8W   16:17   The Wasp considered a little. "Well, no," he said: "it's when you hold up your head--so--without
T4   143: 5   out of breath, / And all of us are fat!' / 'No hurry!' said the Carpenter. / They thanked him much for
A8   65:35   "No, I didn't," said Alice. "I don't think it's at all a pity.
T4   146: 5   and his brother, and looked up into it. "No, I don't think it is," he said: "at least--not under here.
A7   56:29   "No, I give it up," Alice replied. "What's the answer?"
T2   125:10   "No, I shouldn't," said Alice, surprised into contradicting her
T3   129:17   they must make! I think I'll go down and--no, I wo'n't go just yet," she went on, checking herself just
A8   67:26   there are, nobody attends to them--and you've no idea how confusing it is all the things being alive: for
A10   78:11   and said "No never") "--so you can have no idea what a delightful thing a Lobster-Quadrille is!"
T8   186:27   he interrupted, quite eagerly: "but you've no idea what a difference it makes, mixing it with other
A3   23:26   Alice had no idea what to do, and in despair she put her hand in her
A1   10:20   Alice was not going to do that in a hurry. "No, I'll look first," she said, "and see whether it's marked
T3   134:24   "No, indeed," Alice said, a little anxiously.
A10   78:13   "No, indeed," said Alice. "What sort of a dance is it?"
T5   150: 8   "No, it ca'n't," said the Queen. "It's jam every other day:
T2   120: 3   a path that leads straight to it--at least, no, it doesn't do that--" (after going a few yards along the
T2   120: 7   Well this turn goes to the hill, I suppose--no, it doesn't! This goes straight back to the house! Well
T8W   15: 1   hastily ran her eye down the paper and said "No. It says nothing about brown."
A1   9: 3   little girl she'll think me for asking! No, it'll never do to ask: perhaps I shall see it written up
A2   17:20   with, and oh, ever so many lessons to learn! No, I've made up my mind about it: if I'm Mabel, I'll stay
A3   25:29   to the cur, Such a trial, dear sir, With no jury or judge, would be wasting our breath. 'I'll be judge,
A4   28: 3   that stood near the looking-glass. There was no label this time with the words "DRINK ME," but nevertheless
A4   28:24   had now had its full effect, and she grew no larger: still it was very uncomfortable, and, as there

NO (cont.)

T9	204:19	cause of all the mischief--but the Queen was no longer at her side--she had suddenly dwindled down to the
A1	9:27	she turned the corner, but the Rabbit was no longer to be seen: she found herself in a long, low hall,
A11	90:23	"I ca'n't go no lower," said the Hatter: "I'm on the floor, as it is."
A12	96:22	slate with one finger, as he found it made no mark; but he now hastily began again, using the ink, that
A11	87:11	and this was of very little use, as it left no mark on the slate.
A12	95:30	"If there's no meaning in it," said the King, "that saves a world of
A1	9: 9	I wish you were down here with me! There are no mice in the air, I'm afraid, but you might catch a bat, and
A6	50:11	face in some alarm. This time there could be no mistake about it: it was neither more nor less than a pig,
T7	173:14	Alice had no more breath for talking; so they trotted on in silence,
T5	156: 1	This offended Alice a little, so there was no more conversation for a minute or two, while the boat
A8	67:21	that there was enough of it now in sight, and no more of it appeared.
T6	159:23	Dumpty, looking away from her as usual, "have no more sense than a baby!"
T8	187:29	to herself: "it's 'I give thee all, I can no more.'" She stood and listened very attentively, but no
A4	31:19	Bill," thought Alice), "Well, I hardly know--No more, thank ye; I'm better now--but I'm a deal too
A3	21:12	positively refused to tell its age, there was no more to be said.
A4	28:21	chimney, and said to herself "Now I can do no more, whatever happens. What will become of me?"
T2	123: 1	leaves, and snore away there, till you know no more what's going on in the world, than if you were a bud!"
A12	94:22	it, and they ca'n't prove that I did: there's no name signed at the end."
T3	136: 1	call itself, I wonder? I do believe it's got no name--why, to be sure it hasn't!"
T3	132:40	on, in the wood down there, they've got no names--however, go on with your list of insects: you're
T3	135:28	thoughtfully to herself, "where things have no names. I wonder what'll become of my name when I go in? I
A10	78:11	but checked herself hastily, and said "No never") "--so you can have no idea what a delightful thing
A12	96:30	"No, no!" said the Queen. "Sentence first--verdict afterwards."
T9	195:20	quite certain about this, "is the thunder--no, no!" she hastily corrected herself. "I meant the other way
A10	81:44	"No, no! The adventures first," said the Gryphon in an
A5	43:13	time, but never one with such a neck as that! No, no! You're a serpent; and there's no use denying it. I
T9	197:16	to take care of two Queens asleep at once! No, not in all the History of England--it couldn't, you know,
T1	114:21	better help you, hadn't I?" But the King took no notice of the question: it was quite clear that he could
A6	48:13	plates, and dishes. The Duchess took no notice of them even when they hit her; and the baby was
A10	80: 1	"You can really have no notion how delightful it will be / When they take us up and
T4	146: 8	may--if it chooses," said Tweedledee: "we've no objection. Contrariwise."
A6	46:13	because they're making such a noise inside, no one could possibly hear you." And certainly there was a
A3	23: 4	it thought that somebody ought to speak, and no one else seemed inclined to say anything.
T1	112: 7	Alice: "warmer, in fact, because there'll be no one here to scold me away from the fire. Oh, what fun it'll
A1	8:42	I think--" (she was rather glad there was no one listening, this time, as it didn't sound at all the
T8	179: 3	lifted up her head in some alarm. There was no one to be seen, and her first thought was that she must
A1	8:33	for showing off her knowledge, as there was no one to listen to her, still it was good practice to say it
A3	23:10	along the course, here and there. There was no "One, two, three, and away!", but they began running when
T12	207: 8	they would only purr for 'yes,' and mew for 'no,' or any rule of that sort," she had said, "so that one
T7	176:14	the two great creatures; but there was no other place for him.
A1	7: 3	the book her sister was reading, but it had no pictures or conversations in it, "and what is the use of a
A7	59:28	"No, please go on!" Alice said very humbly. "I wo'n't interrupt
T5	149:28	here, and I've pinned it there, but there's no pleasing it!"
A5	42:35	to her; "but those serpents! There's no pleasing them!"
A4	29:23	times as large as the Rabbit, and had no reason to be afraid of it.
T2	128:12	Sixth belongs to Humpty Dumpty--But you make no remark?"
T8	188:13	/ That they could not be seen. / So, having no reply to give / To what the old man said, / I cried 'Come,
T10	205: 3	The Red Queen made no resistance whatever: only her face grew very small, and her
A5	42:15	She was moving them about, as she spoke, but no result seemed to follow, except a little shaking among the
A11	88:42	"You've no right to grow here," said the Dormouse.
A4	29:14	here? Why, there's hardly room for you, and no room at all for any lesson-books!"
A7	54: 8	all crowded together at one corner of it. "No room! No room!" they cried out when they saw Alice coming.
A7	54: 8	together at one corner of it. "No room! No room!" they cried out when they saw Alice coming. "There's
A4	29: 8	added in a sorrowful tone: "at least there's no room to grow up any more here."
A9	73:12	"No," said Alice. "I don't even know what a Mock Turtle is."
A5	36:25	"No," said the Caterpillar.
T7	173: 7	"Dear me, no!" said the King. "What an idea!"
A12	96:30	"No, no!" said the Queen. "Sentence first--verdict afterwards."
T9	195:20	certain about this, "is the thunder--no, no!" she hastily corrected herself. "I meant the other way."
A9	74:21	"It's all his fancy, that: he hasn't got no sorrow, you know. Come on!"
A4	28:25	uncomfortable, and, as there seemed to be no sort of chance of her ever getting out of the room again,
A7	56:20	The Hatter's remark seemed to her to have no sort of meaning in it, and yet it was certainly English. "I
A6	46:10	"There's no sort of use in knocking," said the Footman, "and that for
A7	59:24	"There's no such thing!" Alice was beginning very angrily, but the
T8W	15:12	"There's no such word in the language!" said the Wasp.
T8	187:30	She stood and listened very attentively, but no tears came into her eyes.
A6	50: 3	No, there were no tears. "If you're going to turn into a pig, my dear," said
T2	127:37	"No, thank you," said Alice: "one's quite enough!"
A2	17: 2	and Paris is the capital of Rome, and Rome--no, that's all wrong, I'm certain! I must have been changed
A10	81:44	"No, no! The adventures first," said the Gryphon in an impatient
A6	50: 3	No, there were no tears. "If you're going to turn into a pig,
A12	94:17	"No, they're not," said the White Rabbit, "and that's the
T2	127:27	Alice thought it would not be civil to say "No," though it wasn't at all what she wanted. She took it, and
TI	103: 9	face, / Nor heard thy silver laughter: / No thought of me shall find a place / In thy young life's
A4	30:27	here, lad!--Here, put 'em up at this corner--No, tie 'em together first--they don't reach half high enough
T8W	17: 8	round your face. It'll cure you in no time!"
A8	69: 3	something wasn't done about it in less than no time, she'd have everybody executed, all round. (It was
A9	72:38	your head must be off, and that in about half no time! Take your choice!"
A5	41:42	sudden change, but she felt that there was no time to be lost, as she was shrinking rapidly: so she set

NO (cont.)
```
A7    58:13  with a sigh: "it's always tea-time, and we've no time to wash the things between whiles."
T2   128:10  you'll find yourself in the Fourth Square in no time. Well, that square belongs to Tweedledum and
A2    17:19  in that poky little house, and have next to no toys to play with, and oh, ever so many lessons to learn!
A5    43:14  that! No, no! You're a serpent; and there's no use denying it. I suppose you'll be telling me next that
A10   81:41    said Alice a little timidly; "but it's no use going back to yesterday, because I was a different
A1    12:21           "Come, there's no use in crying like that!" said Alice to herself rather
A5    42:36  and more puzzled, but she thought there was no use in saying anything more till the Pigeon had finished.
T3   130:10  Alice thought to herself "Then there's no use in speaking." The voices didn't join in, this time, as
A6    46:43           "Oh, there's no use in talking to him," said Alice desperately: "he's
A1    10:12     There seemed to be no use in waiting by the little door, so she went back to the
T7   175: 4              "No use, no use!" said the King. "She runs so fearfully quick.
A1    12:28  of pretending to be two people. "But it's no use now," thought poor Alice, "to pretend to be two people!
T7   175: 4              "No use, no use!" said the King. "She runs so fearfully quick. You
A8    67:16  the eyes appeared, and then nodded. "It's no use speaking to it," she thought, "till its ears have come,
T2   120:13           "It's no use talking about it," Alice said, looking up at the house
T7   171:13  attention from himself--but it was of no use--the Anglo-Saxon attitudes only got more extraordinary
A2    17:21  if I'm Mabel, I'll stay down here. It'll be no use their putting their heads down and saying 'Come up
T3   132:37           "No use to them," said Alice; "but it's useful to the people
T5   153:11  Alice laughed. "There's no use trying," she said: "one ca'n't believe impossible
T8   181:25  things must have fallen out! And the box is no use without them." He unfastened it as he spoke, and was
T4   145:18           "Well, it's no use your talking about waking him," said Tweedledum, "when
A2    19:23  with all her knowledge of history, Alice had no very clear notion how long ago anything had happened.) So
T2   128:31  can run very fast!" thought Alice), there was no way of guessing, but she was gone, and Alice began to
A10   81:31  have him with them," the Mock Turtle said. "No wise fish would go anywhere without a porpoise."
A4    28:26  of her ever getting out of the room again, no wonder she felt unhappy.
T8   187: 1           "No, you don't understand," the Knight said, looking a little
T8   187: 6           "No, you oughtn't: that's quite another thing! The song is
A5    43:13  but never one with such a neck as that! No, no! You're a serpent; and there's no use denying it. I suppose
```
NOBLE (2)
```
T8   189: 6  And very gladly will I drink / Your Honour's noble health.'
T8   189:14  chiefly for his wish that he / Might drink my noble health.
```
NOBODY (21)
```
T7   170:18  in a fretful tone. "To be able to see Nobody! And at that distance too! Why, it's as much as I can
A7    59:15           "Nobody asked your opinion," said Alice.
A8    67:26  rules in particular: at least, if there are, nobody attends to them--and you've no idea how confusing it is
T5   153: 2  done," the Queen said with great decision: "nobody can do two things at once, you know. Let's consider
T4   145: 3           Alice said "Nobody can guess that."
T3   129: 7  making honey down there? They ca'n't be bees--nobody ever saw bees a mile off, you know--" and for some time
A3    26:23  I know I do!" said Alice aloud, addressing nobody in particular. "She'd soon fetch it back!"
A12   97: 6  the Queen shouted at the top of her voice. Nobody moved.
T7   170:16           "I see nobody on the road," said Alice.
T7   172:17           "Nobody," said the Messenger.
T9   193: 8           "Nobody said you did," said the Red Queen. "I said you couldn't
A3    26:38  she said to herself in a melancholy tone. "Nobody seems to like her, down here, and I'm sure she's the
A9    74:29     So they sat down, and nobody spoke for some minutes. Alice thought to herself "I
T9   192: 8  herself with the thought that there was nobody to see her, "and if I really am a Queen," she said as
T2   121:15  frightened at being planted out here, with nobody to take care of you?"
T7   172:21  Messenger said in a sullen tone. "I'm sure nobody walks much faster than I do!"
T7   172:19  "this young lady saw him too. So of course Nobody walks slower than you."
A12   94:10  said the King, "unless it was written to nobody, which isn't usual, you know."
T6   160:13           "Why, because there's nobody with me!" cried Humpty Dumpty. "Did you think I didn't
T9   192:23  always waited for you to begin, you see nobody would ever say anything, so that--"
A9    74:12  "It's all her fancy that: they never executes nobody, you know. Come on!"
```
NOBODY'S (1)
```
T8W   14:18  a mind to," the Wasp said, rather sulkily. "Nobody's hindering you, that I know of."
```
NODDED (2)
```
T7   173:28           Hatta looked round and nodded, and went on with his bread-and-butter.
A8    67:16  Alice waited till the eyes appeared, and then nodded. "It's no use speaking to it," she thought, "till its
```
NOHOW (5)
```
T4   138:12  weren't made to be looked at for nothing. Nohow!"
T4   139: 6  about," said Tweedledum; "but it isn't so, nohow."
T4   146: 6  it is," he said: "at least--not under here. Nohow."
T4   140: 7           "Nohow. And thank you very much for asking," said Tweedledum.
T4   139:16           "Nohow!" Tweedledum cried out briskly, and shut his mouth up
```
NOISE (8)
```
T4   145:17  waking him, I'm afraid, if you make so much noise."
A3    24: 9  was to eat the comfits: this caused some noise and confusion, as the large birds complained that they
T7   178: 1           Where the noise came from, she couldn't make out: the air seemed full of
A6    46:14  And certainly there was a most extraordinary noise going on within--a constant howling and sneezing, and
A6    46:12  are: secondly, because they're making such a noise inside, no one could possibly hear you." And certainly
T9   199:33     Then followed a confused noise of cheering, and Alice thought to herself "Thirty times
T8   179: 1     After a while the noise seemed gradually to die away, till all was dead silence,
T8   180: 6  arms, as if they were Punch and Judy--What a noise they make when they tumble! Just like a whole set of
```
NOISES (1)
```
A12   98:41  of the Gryphon, and all the other queer noises, would change (she knew) to the confused clamour of the
```
NOISY (1)
```
T1   114: 6  and set her on the table by the side of her noisy little daughter.
```
NONE (11)
```
T4   144:10  trotting home again?' / But answer came there none--/ And this was scarcely odd, because / They'd eaten
```

NONE (cont.)
```
T7    177:20                              "She's kept none for herself, anyhow," said the Lion. "Do you like
A11    88:25   the Hatter added as an explanation. "I've none of my own. I'm a hatter."
T2    122:23    "I've been in many gardens before, but none of the flowers could talk."
A12    95:28    there's an atom of meaning in it," but none of them attempted to explain the paper.
T3    132:25   I like them when they can talk," Alice said. "None of them ever talk, where I come from."
T7    175:34   went on, turning from her to the King. "None of your brown bread for me!"
A8     62:14                              "That's none of your business, Two!" said Seven.
T3    129: 5   little further. "Principal rivers--there are none. Principal mountains--I'm on the only one, but I don't
T8    184: 3                              "None to speak of," the Knight said, as if he didn't mind
A5     37: 7   / But, now that I'm perfectly sure I have none, / Why, I do it again and again."
```
NONSENSE (15)
```
A3     26: 9   walking away. "You insult me by talking such nonsense!"
A8     69: 1   be beheaded, and that you weren't to talk nonsense.
A10    82:33   said the Mock Turtle; "but it sounds uncommon nonsense."
T2    125:11   ca'n't be a valley, you know. That would be nonsense--"
T4    145:28                              "I know they're talking nonsense," Alice thought to herself: "and it's foolish to cry
T7    177:13                              This sounded nonsense, but Alice very obediently got up, and carried the
T2    125:14   if you like," she said, "but I've heard nonsense, compared with which that would be as sensible as a
T2    125:13   Red Queen shook her head. "You may call it 'nonsense' if you like," she said, "but I've heard nonsense,
A2     15:11                              Oh dear, what nonsense I'm talking!
AI     3:16   gentler tones Secunda hopes / "There will be nonsense in it!" / While Tertia interrupts the tale / Not more
A12    97: 1                              "Stuff and nonsense!" said Alice loudly. "The idea of having the sentence
A11    88:43                              "Don't talk nonsense," said Alice more boldly: "you know you're growing
A8     64: 8                              "Nonsense!" said Alice, very loudly and decidedly, and the
T2    123:40                              This sounded nonsense to Alice, so she said nothing, but set off at once
T9    194:25   help thinking to herself "What dreadful nonsense we are talking!"
```
-NOON [See AFTERNOON]
NOR (6)
```
A1     7:11   There was nothing so very remarkable in that; nor did Alice think it so very much out of the way to hear the
TI    103: 8           I have not seen thy sunny face, / Nor heard thy silver laughter: / No thought of me shall find a
A7     56:31                              "Nor I," said the March Hare.
T6    163:32   just what I choose it to mean--neither more nor less."
A6     50:11   be no mistake about it: it was neither more nor less than a pig, and she felt that it would be quite
T1    114:22   quite clear that he could neither hear her nor see her.
```
NORMANS (1)
```
A3     22:24   first was moderate. But the insolence of his Normans--' How are you getting on now, my dear?" it continued,
```
NORTHUMBRIA (2)
```
A3     22: 6   Edwin and Morcar, the earls of Mercia and Northumbria--'"
A3     22:12   'Edwin and Morcar, the earls of Mercia and Northumbria, declared for him; and even Stigand, the patriotic
```
NOSE (13)
```
A7     56:23    and he poured a little hot tea upon its nose.
A6     49:34   nose, much more like a snout than a real nose: also its eyes were getting extremely small for a baby:
T6    159: 3   yards of it, she saw that it had eyes and a nose and a mouth; and, when she had come close to it, she saw
A6     46:29   at the Footman's head: it just grazed his nose, and broke to pieces against one of the trees behind him
T1    107: 9   all over, the wrong way, beginning at the nose: and just now, as I said, she was hard at work on the
A6     48:18   agony of terror. "Oh, there goes his precious nose!", as an unusually large saucepan flew close by it, and
T6    168:30   you had the two eyes on the same side of the nose, for instance--or the mouth at the top--that would be
T6    168:28   their places in the air with his thumb) "nose in the middle, mouth under. It's always the same. Now if
A6     49:33   could be no doubt that it had a very turn-up nose, much more like a snout than a real nose: also its eyes
A10    82:24   / As a duck with his eyelids, so he with his nose / Trims his belt and his buttons, and turns out his toes.
A5     40: 3   / Yet you balanced an eel on the end of your nose--/ What made you so awfully clever?"
T1    114: 1   fiddlestick!" said the King, rubbing his nose, which had been hurt by the fall. He had a right to be a
A10    83: 6    "How could he turn them out with his nose, you know?"
```
NOT (253)
```
A2     19:41   talk about her any more, if you'd rather not."
A6     48:15    to say whether the blows hurt it or not.
A11    89:10   have you executed, whether you are nervous or not."
T4    148: 3   cried Tweedledum, "whether I can see it or not!"
T5    155:37   Alice asked at last, rather vexed. "I'm not a bird!"
A1     9:21                              Alice was not a bit hurt, and she jumped up on to her feet in a moment:
A5     36: 6                              "Not a bit," said the Caterpillar.
T2    121: 9   face has got some sense in it, though it's not a clever one!' Still, you're the right colour, and that
T8    182:39   to help the poor Knight, who certainly was not a good rider.
T1    115:41   the poker. He balances very badly'). "That's not a memorandum of your feelings!"
A12    93:38                              "I'm not a mile high," said Alice.
T9    204: 9                              There was not a moment to be lost. Already several of the guests were
A1     9:24   still in sight, hurrying down it. There was not a moment to be lost: away went Alice like the wind, and
A1     8: 8   suddenly down, so suddenly that Alice had not a moment to think about stopping herself before she found
T4    146:17   examination of the little white thing. "Not a rattle-snake, you know," she added hastily, thinking
A12    93:41   at any rate," said Alice; "besides, that's not a regular rule: you invented it just now."
A5     43: 5                              "But I'm not a serpent, I tell you!" said Alice. "I'm a--I'm a--"
A5     42:28                              "I'm not a serpent!" said Alice indignantly. "Let me alone!"
T9    198: 7   by the names. "I'm not a visitor, and I'm not a servant. There ought to be one marked 'Queen,' you know
T8    181:35   discontented tone, "one of the best kind. But not a single bee has come near it yet. And the other thing is
T3    137:16                              It was not a very difficult question to answer, as there was only one
A1     8:32   in the school-room, and though this was not a very good opportunity for showing off her knowledge, as
T9    198: 7   went on, very much puzzled by the names. "I'm not a visitor, and I'm not a servant. There ought to be one
T7    173:32   a tear or two trickled down his cheek; but not a word would he say.
A11    89:12   trembling voice, "and I hadn't begun my tea--not above a week or so--and what with the bread-and-butter
```

NOT (cont.)

A2	16: 4	"I'm sure I'm not Ada," she said, "for her hair goes in such long ringlets,
A7	56:40	"Perhaps not," Alice cautiously replied; "but I know I have to beat
A7	56:16	"Of course not," Alice replied very readily: "but that's because it stays
A3	21:11	and must know better." And this Alice would not allow, without knowing how old it was, and as the Lory
A5	35: 5	This was not an encouraging opening for a conversation. Alice replied,
A2	20: 3	are you fond--of--of dogs?" The Mouse did not answer, so Alice went on eagerly: "There is such a nice
A3	23:17	This question the Dodo could not answer without a great deal of thought, and it stood for a
A6	52:22	half expecting to see it again, but it did not appear, and after a minute or two she walked on in the
A8	67: 3	to feel very uneasy: to be sure, she had not as yet had any dispute with the Queen, but she knew that
A6	49:30	time). "Don't grunt," said Alice; "that's not at all a proper way of expressing yourself."
A6	51: 4	she began, rather timidly, as she did not at all know whether it would like the name: however, it
A6	48: 7	Alice did not at all like the tone of this remark, and thought it would
A8	67:32	"Not at all," said Alice: "she's so extremely--" Just then she
T7	170:26	"Not at all," said the King. "He's an Anglo-Saxon Messenger--
A7	57: 7	"Not at first, perhaps," said the Hatter: "but you could keep
A9	72: 3	"Oh, I know!" exclaimed Alice, who had not attended to this last remark. "It's a vegetable. It
A3	26: 1	"You are not attending!" said the Mouse to Alice, severely. "What are
A6	48:23	"Which would not be an advantage," said Alice, who felt very glad to get an
T2	127:27	Alice thought it would not be civil to say "No," though it wasn't at all what she
A6	51:17	Alice felt that this could not be denied, so she tried another question. "What sort of
T9	192:14	how they came there, but she feared it would not be quite civil. However, there would be no harm, she
T8	188:12	always use so large a fan / That they could not be seen. / So, having no reply to give / To what the old
A11	86:19	look at all comfortable, and it was certainly not becoming.
T1	108:38	"That's three faults, Kitty, and you've not been punished for any of them yet. You know I'm saving up
T2	124: 3	It succeeded beautifully. She had not been walking a minute before she found herself face to
T3	135:41	into what?" she went on, rather surprised at not being able to think of the word. "I mean to get under the
A12	95:37	like it?" he said. (Which he certainly did not, being made entirely of cardboard.)
T3	131:44	wanted to know was, whether it could sing or not, but she thought this wouldn't be quite a civil question
T6	166: 3	'rath' is a sort of green pig: but 'mome' I'm not certain about. I think it's short for 'from home'--meaning
T4	140:23	shook his heavy head--/ Meaning to say he did not choose / To leave the oyster-bed.
T2	123: 4	people in the garden besides me?" Alice said, not choosing to notice the Rose's last remark.
A7	60: 9	in the well," Alice said to the Dormouse, not choosing to notice this last remark.
A2	17: 6	sounded hoarse and strange, and the words did not come the same as they used to do:--
T4	147:45	"and she can watch us--only you'd better not come very close," he added: "I generally hit every thing I
A10	80: 5	join the dance. / Would not, could not, would not, could not, could not join the dance. / Would not, could
A10	80: 6	join the dance. / Would not, could not, would not, could not, could not join the dance.
A10	80: 6	/ Would not, could not, would not, could not, could not join the dance.
A10	80: 5	/ Would not, could not, would not, could not, could not join the dance. / Would not, could not, would
A10	80: 5	but he would not join the dance. / Would not, could not, would not, could not, could not join the dance
A10	80: 6	could not, could not join the dance. / Would not, could not, would not, could not, could not join the dance
A3	26: 5	"I had not!" cried the Mouse, sharply and very angrily.
A10	83:12	Alice did not dare to disobey, though she felt sure it would all come
A3	24: 6	but they all looked so grave that she did not dare to laugh; and, as she could not think of anything to
T8	185: 6	looked so solemn about it that Alice did not dare to laugh. "I'm afraid you must have hurt him," she
A4	32: 4	to herself, and shouted out "You'd better not do that again!", which produced another dead silence.
A3	23:12	and left off when they liked, so that it was not easy to know when the race was over. However, when they
T9	195: 9	"Fiddle-de-dee's not English," Alice replied gravely.
A8	68:26	tucked it away under her arm, that it might not escape again, and went back to have a little more
A1	10: 5	and those cool fountains, but she could not even get her head through the doorway; "and even if my
A4	28:17	on the floor: in another minute there was not even room for this, and she tried the effect of lying down
T4	139:29	(she remembered afterwards), and she was not even surprised to hear music playing: it seemed to come
TI	103:11	life's hereafter--/ Enough that now thou wilt not fail / To listen to my fairy-tale.
A9	76:33	Alice did not feel encouraged to ask any more questions about it: so she
A9	71: 9	"He might bite," Alice cautiously replied, not feeling at all anxious to have the experiment tried.
T4	147:38	"Then you'd better not fight to-day," said Alice, thinking it a good opportunity
T8W	19: 5	They said it did not fit, and so / It made me look extremely plain: / But what
A1	10:21	"and see whether it's marked 'poison' or not"; for she had read several nice little stories about
A3	21:18	sure she would catch a bad cold if she did not get dry very soon.
A4	29:36	hand, and made a snatch in the air. She did not get hold of anything, but she heard a little shriek and a
A10	84:28	fish, / Game, or any other dish? / Who would not give all else for two p / ennyworth only of beautiful Soup
T2	126:16	"Faster! Faster!" but Alice felt she could not go faster, though she had no breath left to say so.
T12	208: 6	a serious question, my dear, and you should not go on licking your paw like that--as if Dinah hadn't
T2	120:14	and pretending it was arguing with her. "I'm not going in again yet. I know I should have to get through
A1	10:20	say "Drink me," but the wise little Alice was not going to do that in a hurry. "No, I'll look first," she
T5	156:10	knitting: "I didn't put 'em there, and I'm not going to take 'em away."
A9	74:16	They had not gone far before they saw the Mock Turtle in the distance,
A6	53:10	She had not gone much farther before she came in sight of the house of
A12	95: 1	He sent them word I had not gone / (We know it to be true): / If she should push the
T1	110:28	might see how sulky it was, "--and if you're not good directly," she added, "I'll put you through into
A3	23:28	a box of comfits (luckily the saltwater had not got into it), and handed them round as prizes. There was
T5	154: 8	But these, as it happened, Alice had not got: so she contented herself with turning round, looking
T8W	19: 8	was I to do, you know? / My ringlets would not grow again.
A6	51:35	"I call it purring, not growling," said Alice.
T9	193:20	the Red Queen remarked: "but I daresay you've not had many lessons in manners yet."
T8	183: 3	"I'm afraid you've not had much practice in riding," she ventured to say, as she
A10	78: 8	"You may not have lived much under the sea--" ("I haven't," said Alice)
TI	103:30	words shall hold thee fast: / Thou shalt not heed the raving blast.
A8	66:12	with such a puzzled expression that she could not help bursting out laughing; and, when she had got its head
T7	175:27	Alice could not help her lips curling up into a smile as she began: "Do

NOT (cont.)

T5	152:40	Alice could not help laughing at this, even in the midst of her tears.
T3	137:31	fat little men, so suddenly that she could not help starting back, but in another moment she recovered
A9	74:38	for your interesting story," but she could not help thinking there <u>must</u> be more to come, so she sat still
A1	10:16	a little bottle on it ("which certainly was not here before," said Alice), and tied round the neck of the
A7	57:10	The Hatter shook his head mournfully. "Not I!" he replied. "We quarrelled last March--just before <u>he</u>
A3	22:10	"Not I!" said the Lory, hastily.
A2	17:24	if I like being that person, I'll come up: if not, I'll stay down here till I'm somebody else'--but, oh
A9	70: 7	"When <u>I'm</u> a Duchess," she said to herself (not in a very hopeful tone, though), "I wo'n't have any pepper
T9	197:16	take care of two Queens asleep at once! No, not in all the History of England--it couldn't, you know,
T8W	13:20	him, and said very kindly, "I hope you're not in much pain?"
A11	89: 1	at a reasonable pace," said the Dormouse: "not in that ridiculous fashion." And he got up very sulkily
A10	80: 6	<u>not</u>, <u>could</u> <u>not</u>, <u>would</u> <u>not</u>, <u>could</u> <u>not</u>, <u>could</u> <u>not</u> <u>join</u> <u>the</u> <u>dance</u>.
A10	80: 4	<u>he</u> <u>thanked</u> <u>the</u> <u>whiting</u> <u>kindly</u>, <u>but</u> <u>he</u> <u>would</u> <u>not</u> <u>join</u> <u>the</u> <u>dance</u>. / <u>Would</u> <u>not</u>, <u>could</u> <u>not</u>, <u>would</u> <u>not</u>, <u>could</u>
A10	80: 5	<u>not</u>, <u>could</u> <u>not</u>, <u>would</u> <u>not</u>, <u>could</u> <u>not</u>, <u>could</u> <u>not</u> <u>join</u> <u>the</u> <u>dance</u>. / <u>Would</u> <u>not</u>, <u>could</u> <u>not</u>, <u>would</u> <u>not</u>, <u>could</u>
T2	127:39	Alice did not know what to say to this, but luckily the Queen did not
T9	201: 2	bow to Alice; and Alice returned the bow, not knowing whether to be frightened or amused.
A2	19:30	"Not like cats!" cried the Mouse in a shrill passionate voice.
T8W	21:10	Alice did not like having so many personal remarks made on her, and as
T4	139:25	Alice did not like shaking hands with either of them first, for fear of
A6	49:35	small for a baby: altogether Alice did not like the look of the thing at all. "But perhaps it was
A8	68:14	for having missed their turns, and she did not like the look of things at all, as the game was in such
A9	70:28	an uncomfortably sharp chin. However, she did not like to be rude: so she bore it as well as she could.
A6	46:35	It was, no doubt: only Alice did not like to be told so. "It's really dreadful," she muttered
A1	8:20	great disappointment it was empty: she did not like to drop the jar, for fear of killing somebody
A6	53:13	fur. It was so large a house, that she did not like to go nearer till she had nibbled some more of the
T6	167:12	<u>them</u> <u>once</u>, I <u>told</u> <u>them</u> <u>twice</u>: / <u>They</u> <u>would</u> <u>not</u> <u>listen</u> <u>to</u> <u>advice</u>.
A4	31:42	of <u>what</u>?" thought Alice. But she had not long to doubt, for the next moment a shower of little
A11	86:19	if you <u>want</u> to see how he did it), he did not look at all comfortable, and it was certainly not becoming
T8W	19: 3	<u>had</u> <u>noticed</u> <u>the</u> <u>effect</u>, / <u>They</u> <u>said</u> <u>I</u> <u>did</u> <u>not</u> <u>look</u> <u>so</u> <u>nice</u> / <u>As</u> <u>they</u> <u>had</u> <u>ventured</u> <u>to</u> <u>expect</u>.
A5	43:25	deal to me," said Alice hastily; "but I'm not looking for eggs, as it happens; and, if I was, I
A6	51:29	"To begin with," said the Cat, "a dog's not mad. You grant that?"
A11	87: 9	little juror (it was Bill, the Lizard) could not make out at all what had become of it; so, after hunting
T7	173:17	a cloud of dust, that at first Alice could not make out which was which; but she soon managed to
A1	11: 6	However, this bottle was <u>not</u> marked "poison," so Alice ventured to taste it, and,
T12	207:35	I <u>think</u> you did--however, you'd better not mention it to your friends just yet, for I'm not sure.
AI	3:18	in <u>it</u>!" / While <u>Tertia</u> <u>interrupts</u> <u>the</u> <u>tale</u> / <u>Not</u> more <u>than</u> <u>once</u> a <u>minute</u>.
A1	10: 2	and found that it led into a small passage, not much larger than a rat-hole: she knelt down and looked
A9	70:25	Alice did not much like her keeping so close to her: first because the
A6	52: 9	Alice was not much surprised at this, she was getting so well used to
T4	140: 6	"I hope you're not much tired?" she said at last.
A5	35:12	I'm afraid, Sir," said Alice, "because I'm not myself, you see."
A3	22:21	The Mouse did not notice this question, but hurriedly went on, "--found it
A1	9:40	round, she came upon a low curtain she had not noticed before, and behind it was a little door about
T8	180:10	Another Rule of Battle, that Alice had not noticed, seemed to be that they always fell on their heads
T4	140:13	at Tweedledum with great solemn eyes, and not noticing Alice's question.
T6	162:37	"I'm not offended," said Humpty Dumpty.
T5	155:16	"Yes, a little--but not on land--and not with needles--" Alice was beginning to
T4	143:13	'But <u>not</u> on us!' the <u>Oysters</u> <u>cried</u>, / <u>Turning</u> a <u>little</u> <u>blue</u>. /
A1	9:38	key was too small, but at any rate it would not open any of them. However, on the second time round, she
A9	72: 9	that what you are or might have been was not otherwise than what you had been would have appeared to
A10	80:10	<u>England</u> <u>the</u> <u>nearer</u> <u>is</u> <u>to</u> <u>France</u>. / <u>Then</u> <u>turn</u> <u>not</u> <u>pale</u>, <u>beloved</u> <u>snail</u>, <u>but</u> <u>come</u> <u>and</u> <u>join</u> <u>the</u> <u>dance</u>. / <u>Will</u>
A5	41: 8	"Oh, I'm not particular as to size," Alice hastily replied; "only one
A1	12:17	back to the table for it, she found she could not possibly reach it: she could see it quite plainly through
T6	160:39	never see such another: and, to show you I'm not proud, you may shake hands with me!" And he grinned almost
A7	59:18	Alice did not quite know what to say to this: so she helped herself to
A9	74: 4	Alice alone with the Gryphon. Alice did not quite like the look of the creature, but on the whole she
A5	41: 2	"Not <u>quite</u> right, I'm afraid," said Alice, timidly: "some of
T4	143:23	/ 'Cut <u>us</u> <u>another</u> <u>slice</u>. / <u>I</u> <u>wish</u> <u>you</u> <u>were</u> <u>not</u> <u>quite</u> <u>so</u> <u>deaf</u>--/ <u>I've</u> <u>had</u> <u>to</u> <u>ask</u> <u>you</u> <u>twice</u>!'
A6	47:13	said Alice, a little timidly, for she was not quite sure whether it was good manners for her to speak
T4	145:20	in his dream. You know very well you're not real."
A8	63:29	face like the three gardeners, but she could not remember ever having heard of such a rule at processions;
A1	12:11	after the candle is blown out, for she could not remember ever having seen such a thing.
A1	10:24	unpleasant things, all because they <u>would</u> not remember the simple rules their friends had taught them:
T8W	20:14	"I'm afraid not," said Alice.
A2	19:32	"Well, perhaps not," said Alice in a soothing tone: "don't be angry about it."
A9	76:12	"Certainly not!" said Alice indignantly.
A5	41: 1	"That is not said right," said the Caterpillar.
A7	60:18	"Why not?" said the March Hare.
A10	81:33	"Of course not," said the Mock Turtle. "Why, if a fish came to <u>me</u>, and
A12	94:17	"No, they're not," said the White Rabbit, "and that's the queerest thing
T9	196:19	Where would be the use of it?" but she did not say this aloud, for fear of hurting the poor Queen's
T4	140:37	be, / <u>The</u> <u>sands</u> <u>were</u> <u>dry</u> <u>as</u> <u>dry</u>. / <u>You</u> <u>could</u> <u>not</u> <u>see</u> <u>a</u> <u>cloud</u>, <u>because</u> / <u>No</u> <u>cloud</u> <u>was</u> <u>in</u> <u>the</u> <u>sky</u>: / <u>No</u> <u>birds</u>
A4	34: 1	and the blades of grass, but she could not see anything that looked like the right thing to eat or
T3	137:20	But this did not seem likely to happen. She went on and on, a long way, but
A11	88:30	This did not seem to encourage the witness at all: he kept shifting
TI	103: 7	<u>I</u> <u>have</u> <u>not</u> <u>seen</u> <u>thy</u> <u>sunny</u> <u>face</u>, / <u>Nor</u> <u>heard</u> <u>thy</u> <u>silver</u> <u>laughter</u>: / <u>No</u>
T8	188:37	/ <u>In</u> <u>the</u> <u>silent</u> <u>night</u>. / <u>And</u> <u>these</u> <u>I</u> <u>do</u> <u>not</u> <u>sell</u> <u>for</u> <u>gold</u> / <u>Or</u> <u>coin</u> <u>of</u> <u>silvery</u> <u>shine</u>, / <u>But</u> <u>for</u> <u>a</u>
T6	166:38	like that," Humpty Dumpty said: "they're not sensible, and they put me out."
A6	47:10	only two creatures in the kitchen, that did <u>not</u> sneeze, were the cook, and a large cat, which was lying on

NOT (cont.)
```
A6    52:27   is May, it wo'n't be raving mad--at least not so mad as it was in March." As she said this, she looked
A8    68:15   she never knew whether it was her turn or not. So she went off in search of her hedgehog.
T7   176:20                                    "I'm not so sure of that," said the Unicorn.
A11   87: 6   that squeaked. This, of course, Alice could not stand, and she went round the court and got behind him,
A10   84:19   a hot tureen! / Who for such dainties would not stoop? / Soup of the evening, beautiful Soup! / Soup of
T7   173:11   "I'm good enough," the King said, "only I'm not strong enough. You see, a minute goes by so fearfully
T12  207:36   mention it to your friends just yet, for I'm not sure.
A12   94:42   gave me a good character, / But said I could not swim.
A12   95:34   meaning in them, after all. '--said I could not swim--' you ca'n't swim, can you?" he added, turning to
T9   202: 8   cook me the fish!' / That is easy, and will not take more than a minute. / 'Let it lie in a dish!' / That
T8W   21: 5   for her, but she kept out of reach, and would not take the hint. So he went on with his criticisms.
A8    62:11                                    "You'd better not talk!" said Five. "I heard the Queen say only yesterday
T1   110:30   "Now, if you'll only attend, Kitty, and not talk so much, I'll tell you all my ideas about
A3    24:10   as the large birds complained that they could not taste theirs, and the small ones choked and had to be
T9   193:22                                    "Manners are not taught in lessons," said Alice. "Lessons teach you to do
A8    64: 1   the same as the rest of the pack, she could not tell whether they were gardeners, or soldiers, or
T2   126:24                                    Not that Alice had any idea of doing that. She felt as if she
A12   93: 7   She soon got it out again, and put it right; "not that it signifies much," she said to herself; "I should
T7   175:37   Haigha. "Open the bag!" he whispered. "Quick! Not that one--that's full of hay!"
A3    23: 2   "What is a Caucus-race?" said Alice; not that she much wanted to know, but the Dodo had paused as
A8    67:43                                    "I'd rather not," the Cat remarked.
T8   186:12   said in slow thoughtful tone: "no, certainly not the next course."
T8   186:11   "Well, not the next course," the Knight said in slow thoughtful tone:
T8   186:15   next day," the Knight repeated as before: "not the next day. In fact," he went on, holding his head down,
T8   186:15   "Well, not the next day," the Knight repeated as before: "not the
T8   179: 9   same dream. Only I do hope it's my dream, and not the Red King's! I don't like belonging to another person's
T9   201: 6   "Certainly not," the Red Queen said, very decidedly: "it isn't etiquette
A2    17:16   "I'm sure those are not the right words," said poor Alice, and her eyes filled
A2    15:41   feeling a little different. But if I'm not the same, the next question is 'Who in the world am I?' Ah
A7    55:23                                    "Not the same thing a bit!" said the Hatter. "Why, you might
A1     8:36   or Longitude I've got to?" (Alice had not the slightest idea what Latitude was, or Longitude either,
A4    32:23   the only difficulty was, that she had not the smallest idea how to set about it; and, while she was
A4    34:10   quietly smoking a long hookah, and taking not the smallest notice of her or of anything else.
A5    36:15   puzzling question; and, as Alice could not think of any good reason, and the Caterpillar seemed to be
A3    24: 6   she did not dare to laugh; and, as she could not think of anything to say, she simply bowed, and took the
A6    48:30   cook was busily stirring the soup, and seemed not to be listening, so she went on again: "Twenty-four hours,
A9    72: 7   it put more simply--'Never imagine yourself not to be otherwise than what it might appear to others that
A6    47:18   moment that it was addressed to the baby, and not to her, so she took courage, and went on again:--
A8    63:28   Alice was rather doubtful whether she ought not to lie down on her face like the three gardeners, but she
A7    55: 9   "You should learn not to make personal remarks," Alice said with some severity:
T12  207:20   "it turned away its head, and pretended not to see it: but it looked a little ashamed of itself, so I
T8   183: 1   she soon found that it was the best plan not to walk quite close to the horse.
TI   103:35   by, / And vanish'd summer glory--/ It shall not touch, with breath of bale, / The pleasance of our
T2   127:23                                    "I'd rather not try, please!" said Alice. "I'm quite content to stay here
T2   123:13   close, like a dahlia," said the Tiger-lily: "not tumbled about, like yours."
T4   146: 6   No, I don't think it is," he said: "at least--not under here. Nohow."
A5    41:18                                    "But I'm not used to it!" pleaded poor Alice in a piteous tone. And she
T7   172:14   there was nothing like it." Which Alice did not venture to deny.
A5    44: 5   nibbling at the right-hand bit again, and did not venture to go near the house till she had brought herself
A9    72:21   birthday-presents like that!" But she did not venture to say it out loud.
T6   163:40   adjectives you can do anything with, but not verbs--however, I can manage the whole lot of them!
T8   182: 3                                    "Not very likely, perhaps," said the Knight; "but, if they do
T8   186:26                                    "Not very nice alone," he interrupted, quite eagerly: "but
T2   128:25   you walk--and remember who you are!" She did not wait for Alice to curtsey, this time, but walked on
T2   128: 1   to say to this, but luckily the Queen did not wait for an answer, but went on. "At the end of three
T8W   15:17   put down the newspaper. "I'm afraid you're not well," she said in a soothing tone. "Can't I do anything
T3   132:38   to the people that name them, I suppose. If not, why do things have names at all?"
A7    60: 3                                    Alice did not wish to offend the Dormouse again, so she began very
T6   160:11   do you sit out here all alone?" said Alice, not wishing to begin an argument.
T8W   20:11                                    "Not with a mouth as small as that," the Wasp persisted. "If
T6   160:17   be safer down on the ground?" Alice went on, not with any idea of making another riddle, but simply in her
T5   155:16   "Yes, a little--but not on land--and not with needles--" Alice was beginning to say, when suddenly
A10   80: 5   would not join the dance. / Would not, could not, would not, could not, could not join the dance. / Would
A10   80: 6   could not join the dance. / Would not, could not, would not, could not, could not join the dance.
A11   88: 2                                    "Not yet, not yet!" the Rabbit hastily interrupted. "There's a
T8   182:29                                    "Not yet," said the Knight. "But I've got a plan for keeping it
A11   88: 2                                    "Not yet, not yet!" the Rabbit hastily interrupted. "There's a great
T4   145: 8                                    "Not you!" Tweedledee retorted contemptuously. "You'd be
T2   123:15                                    "But that's not your fault," the Rose added kindly. "You're beginning to
T6   166:27   "If you can see whether I'm singing or not, you've sharper eyes than most," Humpty Dumpty remarked
```
NOTE-BOOK (2)
```
A12   93:34   had been for some time busily writing in his note-book, called out "Silence!", and read out from his book,
A12   94: 1   The King turned pale, and shut his note-book hastily. "Consider your verdict," he said to the
```
NOTHING (63)
```
A2    19:20   wink with one of its little eyes, but it said nothing.
A7    59:14   the Hatter: "it's very easy to take more than nothing."
A9    74:24   them with large eyes full of tears, but said nothing.
A9    74:39   be more to come, so she sat still and said nothing.
T6   162: 1   want to begin another argument, so she said nothing.
```

NOTHING (cont.)
```
T8W    15: 2  her  eye down the paper and said "No. It says nothing about brown."
T9    199:17                                    "Nothing!" Alice said impatiently. "I've been knocking at it!"
T3    130:14  for I must confess that I don't) "Better say nothing at all. Language is worth a thousand pounds a word!"
A11    89:27  he would deny it too; but the Dormouse denied nothing, being fast asleep.
T7    172:13              "I didn't say there was nothing better," the King replied. "I said there was nothing
A7     56: 9  and looked at it again: but he could think of nothing better to say than his first remark, "It was the best
T8    183:13              Alice could think of nothing better to say than "Indeed?" but she said it as
T1    115:18  to throw over him. However, she could find nothing but a bottle of ink, and when she got back with it she
A12    97: 8  grown to her full size by this time). "You're nothing but a pack of cards!"
T4    143:21  And you are very nice!' / The Carpenter said nothing but / 'Cut us another slice. / I wish you were not
T7    172: 5              "There's nothing but hay left now," the Messenger said, peeping into
T1    114:10  breath, and for a minute or two she could do nothing but hug the little Lily in silence. As soon as she had
A8     63: 5              Five and Seven said nothing, but looked at Two. Two began, in a low voice, "Why,
A1     13: 2  had got so much into the way of expecting nothing but out-of-the-way things to happen, that it seemed
T5    155:24  remark that needed any answer: so Alice said nothing, but pulled away. There was something very queer about
T2    123:40  This sounded nonsense to Alice, so she said nothing, but set off at once towards the Red Queen. To her
T4    143:29  them trot so quick!' / The Carpenter said nothing but / 'The butter's spread too thick!'
T8    185:20  hurt this time. However, though she could see nothing but the soles of his feet, she was much relieved to
A5     42:23  in among the leaves, which she found to be nothing but the tops of the trees under which she had been
T3    136:17              Alice thought, but nothing came of it. "Please, would you tell me what you call
A12    96:14      pointing to the tarts on the table. "Nothing can be clearer than that. Then again--'before she had
A5     36:26  thought she might as well wait, as she had nothing else to do, and perhaps after all it might tell her
A1      9: 5              Down, down, down. There was nothing else to do, so Alice soon began talking again.
A8     69: 6              Alice could think of nothing else to say but "It belongs to the Duchess: you'd
T7    178:12  them out of town,'" she thought to herself, "nothing ever will!"
T6    162:22  Humpty Dumpty was very angry, though he said nothing for a minute or two. When he did speak again, it was
T5    155:19  gliding along between banks: so there was nothing for it but to do her best.
A6     46:31  continued in the same tone, exactly as if nothing had happened.
T3    132:24  insects?" the Gnat went on, as quietly as if nothing had happened.
T5    157: 3  with her knitting all the while, just as if nothing had happened. "That was a nice crab you caught!" she
T3    136:15  poor Alice. She answered, rather sadly, "Nothing, just now."
T7    172: 9  see that it revived him a good deal. "There's nothing like eating hay when you're faint," he remarked to her
T7    172: 4  better," the King replied. "I said there was nothing like it." Which Alice did not venture to deny.
A1     12:13              After a while, finding that nothing more happened, she decided on going into the garden at
T5    153:36  the counter? Rub as she would, she could make nothing more of it: she was in a little dark shop, leaning
A6     50: 4  my dear," said Alice, seriously, "I'll have nothing more to do with you. Mind now!" The poor little thing
T4    138:11  Wax-works weren't made to be looked at for nothing. Nohow!"
A3     26: 8              "I shall do nothing of the sort," said the Mouse, getting up and walking
A1      8:24  "After such a fall as this, I shall think nothing of tumbling down-stairs! How brave they'll all think
A1      9:35  table, all made of solid glass: there was nothing on it but a tiny golden key, and Alice's first idea
A7     54:14  looked all round the table, but there was nothing on it but tea. "I don't see any wine," she remarked.
A12    93:18              "Nothing," said Alice.
A5     42:31  a kind of sob, "I've tried every way, but nothing seems to suit them!"
A5     41:11              Alice said nothing: she had never been so much contradicted in all her
A10    82:34              Alice said nothing: she had sat down with her face in her hands,
A1      7:11              There was nothing so very remarkable in that; nor did Alice think it so
T2    120:26  was the hill full in sight, so there was nothing to be done but start again. This time she came upon a
T4    145:23  by crying," Tweedledee remarked: "there's nothing to cry about."
A1      7: 2  by her sister on the bank and of having nothing to do: once or twice she had peeped into the book her
A3     25:21  have the trial; For really this morning I've nothing to do.' Said the mouse to the cur, Such a trial, dear
T1    107: 1  was certain, that the white kitten had had nothing to do with it--it was the black kitten's fault
A9     72:14              "That's nothing to what I could say if I chose," the Duchess replied,
A12    93:19              "Nothing whatever?" persisted the King.
A12    93:20              "Nothing whatever," said Alice.
T3    135:19  away, for, when Alice looked up, there was nothing whatever to be seen on the twig, and, as she was
T9    194:13              "Then you think nothing would remain?" said the Red Queen.
A12    94:13  said the White Rabbit: "in fact, there's nothing written on the outside." He unfolded the paper as he
A7     59:11              "I've had nothing yet," Alice replied in an offended tone: "so I ca'n't
```
NOTICE (9)
```
A7     60:31  and neither of the others took the least notice of her going, though she looked back once or twice,
A4     34:10  a long hookah, and taking not the smallest notice of her or of anything else.
T6    168:35  he never opened his eyes or took any further notice of her, she said "Good-bye!" once more, and, getting no
T6    159:12  direction, and he didn't take the least notice of her, she thought he must be a stuffed figure after
T1    114:21  help you, hadn't I?" But the King took no notice of the question: it was quite clear that he could
A6     48:13  plates, and dishes. The Duchess took no notice of them even when they hit her; and the baby was
T2    123: 4  besides me?" Alice said, not choosing to notice the Rose's last remark.
A7     60:10  Alice said to the Dormouse, not choosing to notice this last remark.
A3     22:21              The Mouse did not notice this question, but hurriedly went on, "--found it
```
NOTICED (15)
```
A8     67: 9  could get away without being seen, when she noticed a curious appearance in the air: it puzzled her very
A4     27:12              Very soon the Rabbit noticed Alice, as she went hunting about, and called out to
A1      9:40  she came upon a low curtain she had not noticed before, and behind it was a little door about fifteen
A6     45: 7  eyes like a frog; and both footmen, Alice noticed, had powdered hair that curled all over their heads.
T8    180:10  Another Rule of Battle, that Alice had not noticed, seemed to be that they always fell on their heads;
T1    113: 4  the other," Alice thought to herself, as she noticed several of the chessmen down in the hearth among the
A7     60:38              Just as she said this, she noticed that one of the trees had a door leading right into it
A8     67:33  Alice: "she's so extremely--" Just then she noticed that the Queen was close behind her, listening: so she
T9    200: 9  table, as she walked up the large hall, and noticed that there were about fifty guests, of all kinds: some
A1      8:15  then she looked at the sides of the well, and noticed that they were filled with cupboards and book-shelves:
```

NOTICED (cont.)
T1   112:10   Then she began looking about, and noticed that what could be seen from the old room was quite
T8W   19: 2   when I followed their advice, / And they had noticed the effect, / They said I did not look so nice / As
T8   184:23 hand at inventing things. Now, I daresay you noticed, the last time you picked me up, that I was looking
T5   156:39 lay in heaps at her feet--but Alice hardly noticed this, there were so many other curious things to think
A4   32: 5   Alice noticed, with some surprise, that the pebbles were all turning
NOTICING (3)
T4   140:13 at Tweedledum with great solemn eyes, and not noticing Alice's question.
T6   166:19 I'm going to repeat," he went on without noticing her remark, "was written entirely for your amusement
A8   63:24 everything that was said, and went by without noticing her. Then followed the Knave of Hearts, carrying the
NOTION (4)
A10   80: 1   "You can really have no notion how delightful it will be / When they take us up and
A2   19:24 knowledge of history, Alice had no very clear notion how long ago anything had happened.) So she began again
T5   149:14 a-dressing," the Queen said. "It isn't my notion of the thing, at all."
A12   95:13   My notion was that you had been / (Before she had this fit) / An
NOW (146)
A7   58: 9   do a thing I ask! It's always six o'clock now."
A9   77:24   tone. "Tell her something about the games now."
A11   90:20   and I never understood what it meant till now."
A12   93:42   not a regular rule: you invented it just now."
T2   127:11 and said kindly, "You may rest a little, now."
T3   136:15 She answered, rather sadly, "Nothing, just now."
T4   147:41 on long," said Tweedledum. "What's the time now?"
T6   162: 6   said 'Leave off at seven'--but it's too late now."
T6   162:30 present from the White King and Queen. There now!"
A4   29:22   the house, quite forgetting that she was now about a thousand times as large as the Rabbit, and had no
A2   18: 6   that, as nearly as she could guess, she was now about two feet high, and was going on shrinking rapidly:
T5   152:23   "But why don't you scream now?" Alice asked, holding her hands ready to put over her
T6   164:33   "I see it now," Alice remarked thoughtfully: "and what are 'toves'?"
T5   153:23   "Then I hope your finger is better now?" Alice said very politely, as she crossed the little
A4   27:15   fetch me a pair of gloves and a fan! Quick, now!" And Alice was so much frightened that she ran off at
T3   131:27 railway journey at all--I was in a wood just now--and I wish I could get back there!"
A2   19: 8   but then she remembered how small she was now, and she soon made out that it was only a mouse, that had
T6   163:19 haven't time to look it over thoroughly just now--and that shows that there are three hundred and
A6   46:15   a constant howling and sneezing, and every now and then a great crash, as if a dish or kettle had been
A7   55:37   was looking at it uneasily, shaking it every now and then, and holding it to his ear.
T7   169:11 the foot-soldiers; but even they stumbled now and then; and it seemed to be a regular rule that,
T8   182:43 on pretty well, except that he had a habit of now and then falling off sideways; and, as he generally did
T5   153:39 sitting in an arm-chair, knitting, and every now and then leaving off to look at her through a great pair
T1   108: 8   to watch the progress of the winding, and now and then putting out one paw and gently touching the ball,
A5   43:31   entangled among the branches, and every now and then she had to stop and untwist it. After a while she
T8   182:38 in silence, puzzling over the idea, and every now and then stopping to help the poor Knight, who certainly
A4   30:14   this, and Alice could only hear whispers now and then; such as "Sure, I don't like it, yer honour," at
T5   155:25 queer about the water, she thought, as every now and then the oars got fast in it, and would hardly come
A10   79:10 solemnly dancing round and round Alice, every now and then treading on her toes when they passed too close,
A9   74:41   more calmly, though still sobbing a little now and then, "we went to school in the sea. The master was an
T9   204:24 too much excited to be surprised at anything now. "As for you," she repeated, catching hold of the little
T1   107: 9   wrong way, beginning at the nose: and just now, as I said, she was hard at work on the white kitten,
T9   196: 5   "because he was looking for a hippopotamus. Now, as it happened, there wasn't such a thing in the house,
T6   162:16 turns in choosing subjects, it was her turn now.) "At least," she corrected herself on second thoughts, "a
A9   76:14   the Mock Turtle in a tone of great relief. "Now, at ours, they had, at the end of the bill, 'French, music
T5   150: 4   "there's the King's Messenger. He's in prison now, being punished: and the trial doesn't even begin till
A4   31:20   I hardly know--No more, thank ye; I'm better now--but I'm a deal too flustered to tell you--all I know is,
T9   202: 7   'Now cook me the fish!' / That is easy, and will not take more
T8W   20:12   the Wasp persisted. "If you was a-fighting, now--could you get hold of the other one by the back of the
T2   127: 5   "Now! Now!" cried the Queen. "Faster! Faster!" And they went so fast
T7   177:15 itself into three pieces as she did so. "Now cut it up," said the Lion, as she returned to her place
A2   14: 7   will put on your shoes and stockings for you now, dears? I'm sure I sha'n't be able! I shall be a great
A1   9:17   and was saying to her, very earnestly, "Now, Dinah, tell me the truth: did you ever eat a bat?" when
T1   110:23 your arms, you'd look exactly like her. Now do try, there's a dear!" And Alice got the Red Queen off
A4   31:12   of voices--"Hold up his head--Brandy now--Don't choke him--How was it, old fellow? What happened to
T1   108:26 What have you got to say for yourself? Now don't interrupt me!" she went on, holding up one finger.
T1   108:32 them tight up, it wouldn't have happened. Now don't make any more excuses, but listen! Number two: you
T1   110: 4   "Kitty, can you play chess? Now, don't smile, my dear. I'm asking it seriously. Because,
T8   184:31 the feet: the head is high enough already.' Now, first I put my head on the top of the gate--then the
A8   62: 5   to them, she heard one of them say "Look out now, Five! Don't go splashing paint over me like that!"
T1   108:36 you? How do you know she wasn't thirsty too? Now for number three: you unwound every bit of the worsted
A2   18:12   glad to find herself still in existence. "And now for the garden!" And she ran with all speed back to the
T8   190:35 as she turned to run down the hill: "and now for the last brook, and to be a Queen! How grand it
A4   28:23   for Alice, the little magic bottle had now had its full effect, and she grew no larger: still it was
A12   96:23   finger, as he found it made no mark; but he now hastily began again, using the ink, that was trickling
T8   182:10 replied. "It's an invention of my own. And now help me on. I'll go with you to the end of the wood--
A4   29: 5   that kind of thing never happened, and now here I am in the middle of one! There ought to be a book
T9   195:32 said "That's a poor thin way of doing things. Now here, we mostly have days and nights two or three at a
T2   127:19 "A slow sort of country!" said the Queen. "Now, here, you see, it takes all the running you can do, to
A5   43:40   as usual, "Come, there's half my plan done now! How puzzling all these changes are! I'm never sure what
A4   28:21   one foot up the chimney, and said to herself "Now I can do no more, whatever happens. What will become of me
T8   184:22 again. "I'm a great hand at inventing things. Now, I daresay you noticed, the last time you picked me up,
T1   111:10   Why, it's turning into a sort of mist now, I declare! It'll be easy enough to get through--" She was
T6   160:30   "Now I declare that's too bad!" Humpty Dumpty cried, breaking

NOW (cont.)

A9	72:36	"Now, I give you fair warning," shouted the Queen, stamping on
A6	51:33	angry, and wags its tail when it's pleased. Now I growl when I'm pleased, and wag my tail when I'm angry.
A8	67:12	she said to herself "It's the Cheshire-Cat: now I shall have somebody to talk to."
A2	19: 2	find her way out. "I shall be punished for it now, I suppose, by being drowned in my own tears! That will be
T1	115:12	open! All the ashes will get into it--there, now I think you're tidy enough!" she added, as she smoothed
T8	189:15	And now, if e'er by chance I put / My fingers into glue, / Or
T6	168:29	middle, mouth under. It's always the same. Now if you had the two eyes on the same side of the nose, for
A7	56:43	said the Hatter. "He wo'n't stand beating. Now, if you only kept on good terms with him, he'd do almost
T6	162: 4	thoughtfully. "An uncomfortable sort of age. Now if you'd asked my advice, I'd have said 'Leave off at
T1	110:30	"Now, if you'll only attend, Kitty, and not talk so much, I'll
T4	143:11	and vinegar besides / Are very good indeed--/ Now if you're ready, Oysters dear, / We can begin to feed.'
T5	153: 6	remarked. "I can believe it without that. Now I'll give you something to believe. I'm just one hundred
A7	60:43	hall, and close to the little glass table. "Now, I'll manage better this time," she said to herself, and
A2	14: 3	she quite forgot how to speak good English). "Now I'm opening out like the largest telescope that ever was!
A8	67:21	seemed to think that there was enough of it now in sight, and no more of it appeared.
T12	208: 5	"Now, Kitty, let's consider who it was that dreamed it all.
T12	207:16	kitten and the Queen to look at each other. "Now Kitty!" she cried, clapping her hands triumphantly.
A12	95:22	yet," said the King, rubbing his hands; "so now let the jury--"
A3	22:25	of his Normans--' How are you getting on now, my dear?" it continued, turning to Alice as it spoke.
T2	127: 5	"Now! Now!" cried the Queen. "Faster! Faster!" And they went so
T4	145: 7	"Where I am now, of course," said Alice.
T9	204:20	down to the size of a little doll, and was now on the table, merrily running round and round after her
T8	181: 9	"Now one can breathe more easily," said the Knight, putting
A8	67:30	have croqueted the Queen's hedgehog just now, only it ran away when it saw mine coming!"
A1	12: 3	And so it was indeed: she was now only ten inches high, and her face brightened up at the
A2	15:13	against the roof of the hall: in fact she was now rather more than nine feet high, and she at once took up
A12	98:10	"It was a curious dream, dear, certainly; but now run in to your tea: it's getting late." So Alice got up
T7	174:10	"It's waiting for 'em now," said Hatta; "this is a bit of it as I'm eating."
A5	41:13	"Are you content now?" said the Caterpillar.
T9	195: 7	"She's all right again now," said the Red Queen. "Do you know Languages? What's the
T4	145: 1	"He's dreaming now," said Tweedledee: "and what do you think he's dreaming
A4	29: 7	I grow up, I'll write one--but I'm grown up now," she added in a sorrowful tone: "at least there's no room
T7	170:21	her eyes with one hand. "I see somebody now!" she exclaimed at last. "But he's coming very slowly--and
T5	149:35	into order. "Come, you look rather better now!" she said, after altering most of the pins. "But really
A9	70:30	"The game's going on rather better now," she said, by way of keeping up the conversation a little
T8W	21:13	safely leave him. "I think I must be going on now," she said. "Good-bye."
T3	137:13	so suddenly. "However, I know my name now," she said: "that's some comfort. Alice--Alice--I won't
T4	140: 4	"It would never do to say 'How d'ye do?' now," she said to herself: "we seem to have got beyond that,
T5	150: 2	replied in a careless tone. "For instance, now," she went on, sticking a large piece of plaster on her
T6	160:37	what you call a History of England, that is. Now, take a good look at me! I'm one that has spoken to a King
A10	82:12	like to hear her try and repeat something now. Tell her to begin." He looked at the Gryphon as if he
A4	30: 6	"Now tell me, Pat, what's that in the window?"
T8W	19: 9	So now that I am old and gray, / And all my hair is nearly gone,
A5	37: 7	/ "I feared it might injure the brain; / But, now that I'm perfectly sure I have none, / Why, I do it again
T7	175:30	"Well, now that we have seen each other," said the Unicorn, "if
A4	29:10	Alice, "shall I never get any older than I am now? That'll be a comfort, one way--never to be an old woman--
T8	186: 6	"Now the cleverest thing of the sort that I ever did," he went
T9	199: 1	"What is it, now?" the Frog said in a deep hoarse whisper.
A7	59:16	"Who's making personal remarks now?" the Hatter asked triumphantly.
T7	172: 5	"There's nothing but hay left now," the Messenger said, peeping into the bag.
A6	50: 5	"I'll have nothing more to do with you. Mind now!" The poor little thing sobbed again (or grunted, it was
T2	124:18	"It's time for you to answer now," the Queen said looking at her watch: "open your mouth a
T8	182:33	your hair creep up it, like a fruit-tree. Now the reason hair falls off is because it hangs down--things
A1	12: 4	brightened up at the thought that she was now the right size for going through the little door into that
AI	3:34	/ Its quaint events were hammered out--/ And now the tale is done, / And home we steer, a merry crew, /
T7	176: 3	"Ah, what is it, now?" the Unicorn cried eagerly. "You'll never guess! I
T7	176:16	"What a fight we might have for the crown now!" the Unicorn said, looking slyly up at the crown, which
T3	129:37	"Now then! Show your ticket, child!" the Guard went on, looking
TI	103:11	In thy young life's hereafter--/ Enough that now thou wilt not fail / To listen to my fairy-tale.
A7	55:13	"Come, we shall have some fun now!" thought Alice. "I'm glad they've begun asking riddles--I
A2	19:10	"Would it be of any use, now," thought Alice, "to speak to this mouse? Everything is so
A1	12:28	pretending to be two people. "But it's no use now," thought poor Alice, "to pretend to be two people! Why,
T1	111: 1	milk isn't good to drink--but oh, Kitty! now we come to the passage. You can just see a little peep of
A11	90:27	finishes the guinea-pigs!" thought Alice. "Now we shall get on better."
A6	50: 8	was just beginning to think to herself, "Now, what am I to do with this creature, when I get it home?"
T5	157:13	"plenty of choice, only make up your mind. Now, what do you want to buy?"
A9	70:19	you forget to talk. I ca'n't tell you just now what the moral of that is, but I shall remember it in a
T8	180: 1	"I wonder, now, what the Rules of Battle are," she said to herself, as
A5	41:38	"And now which is which?" she said to herself, and nibbled a little
T3	137:14	Alice--Alice--I won't forget it again. And now, which of these finger-posts ought I to follow, I wonder
T3	136: 3	"Then it really has happened, after all! And now, who am I? I will remember, if I can! I'm determined to do
A4	30:31	coming down! Heads below!" (a loud crash)--"Now, who did that?--It was Bill, I fancy--Who's to go down the
T5	155: 9	you go on turning round like that." She was now working with fourteen pairs at once, and Alice couldn't
A7	60:26	"Really, now you ask me," said Alice, very much confused, "I don't
T1	108:28	Dinah was washing your face this morning. Now you ca'n't deny it, Kitty: I heard you! What's that you
A10	81:22	on in a deep voice, "are done with whiting. Now you know."
T9	197: 8	"And now you know the words," she added, as she put her head down
T5	153:21	got it!" she cried in a triumphant tone. "Now you shall see me pin it on again, all by myself!"
T6	163:43	"Now you talk like a reasonable child," said Humpty Dumpty,

NOW (cont.)
```
  T5   152:22  you see," she said to Alice with a smile. "Now you understand the way things happen here."
  T1   110: 5  seriously. Because, when we were playing just now, you watched just as if you understood it: and when I said
  T7   172:23  "or else he'd have been here first. However, now you've got your breath, you may tell us what's happened in
```
NOWHERE (3)
```
  A5    42: 9    when she found that her shoulders were nowhere to be found: all she could see, when she looked down,
  A4    27: 8  began hunting about for them, but they were nowhere to be seen--everything seemed to have changed since
  T4   145: 9  Tweedledee retorted contemptuously. "You'd be nowhere. Why, you're only a sort of thing in his dream!"
```
NUMBER (12)
```
  A2    18:22  you go to on the English coast, you find a number of bathing-machines in the sea, some children digging
  A5    43:10  rather doubtfully, as she remembered the number of changes she had gone through, that day.
  A4    30:18  and more sounds of broken glass. "What a number of cucumber-frames there must be!" thought Alice. "I
  A9    73:21    for she had felt quite unhappy at the number of executions the Queen had ordered.
  T2   125:23  between was divided up into squares by a number of little green hedges, that reached from brook to
  T3   131:18  And after that other voices went on ("What a number of people there are in the carriage!" thought Alice),
  T2   125:21  a most curious country it was. There were a number of tiny little brooks running straight across it from
  A12   93:44                 "Then it ought to be Number One," said Alice.
  T1   108:27  "I'm going to tell you all your faults. Number one: you squeaked twice while Dinah was washing your
  T7   170:11  two hundred and seven, that's the exact number," the King said, referring to his book. "I couldn't
  T1   108:36  do you know she wasn't thirsty too? Now for number three: you unwound every bit of the worsted while I
  T1   108:33  Now don't make any more excuses, but listen! Number two: you pulled Snowdrop away by the tail just as I had
```
NURSE (5)
```
  A2    19:38  face--and she is such a nice soft thing to nurse--and she's such a capital one for catching mice--oh, I
  A4    27:31  ready for your walk!' 'Coming in a minute, nurse! But I've got to watch this mouse-hole till Dinah comes
  T1   110:17  And once she had really frightened her old nurse by shouting suddenly in her ear, "Nurse! Do let's
  T1   110:18  old nurse by shouting suddenly in her ear, "Nurse! Do let's pretend that I'm a hungry hyaena and you're a
  A6    49:10                   "Here! You may nurse it a bit, if you like!" the Duchess said to Alice,
```
NURSING (3)
```
  A6    47: 2    on a three-legged stool in the middle, nursing a baby: the cook was leaning over the fire, stirring a
  A6    48:33  could abide figures!" And with that she began nursing her child again, singing a sort of lullaby to it as
  A6    49:22  As soon as she had made out the proper way of nursing it (which was to twist it up into a sort of knot, and
```

-O-

O (8)
```
  T1    118:19        /  Come  to  my  arms,  my beamish boy! / O frabjous day! Callooh! Callay!" / He chortled in his joy.
  T9    199:37                                  "'O Looking-Glass creatures,' quoth Alice, 'draw near! / 'Tis an
  A2     19:14    pool? I am very tired of swimming about here, O Mouse!" (Alice thought this must be the right way of
  A2     19:13    there's no harm in trying." So she began: "O Mouse, do you know the way out of this pool? I am very tired
  A2     19:18    "A mouse--of a mouse--to a mouse--a mouse--O mouse!") The mouse looked at her rather inquisitively, and
  T4    141:13                                  'O Oysters, come and walk with us!' / The Walrus did beseech. /
  T4    144: 7                                  'O Oysters,' said the Carpenter, / 'You've had a pleasant run!
  T2    120:30                        "O Tiger-lily!" said Alice, addressing herself to one that was
```
OARS (6)
```
  T5    157:15    half astonished and half frightened--for the oars, and the boat, and the river, had vanished all in a
  T5    155:25    water, she thought, as every now and then the oars got fast in it, and would hardly come out again.
  T5    156:42    much farther before the blade of one of the oars got fast in the water and wouldn't come out again (so
  T5    155:18    to say, when suddenly the needles turned into oars in her hands, and she found they were in a little boat,
  T5    156: 3    sometimes among beds of weeds (which made the oars stick fast in the water, worse than ever), and sometimes
  AI      3: 3    / Full leisurely we glide; / For both our oars, with little skill, / By little arms are plied, / While
```
OBEDIENTLY (2)
```
  T9    202:32    whispered, as Alice got up to do it, very obediently, but a little frightened.
  T7    177:13        This sounded nonsense, but Alice very obediently got up, and carried the dish round, and the cake
```
OBEY (2) [See also DISOBEY]
```
  T6    167: 8    to them again to say / 'It will be better to obey.'
  T9    197: 1    with me," said Alice, as she tried to obey the first direction: "and I don't know any soothing
```
OBEYED (1)
```
  T9    192:20              "But if everybody obeyed that rule," said Alice, who was always ready for a
```
OBJECTED (5)
```
  T5    150: 7    must come sometimes to 'jam to-day,'" Alice objected.
  T6    163:29    mean 'a nice knock-down argument,'" Alice objected.
  T8    185:12    that's a different kind of fastness," Alice objected.
  T9    193: 7    "I don't deny things with my hands," Alice objected.
  T6    168:32            "It wouldn't look nice," Alice objected. But Humpty Dumpty only shut his eyes, and said "Wait
```
OBJECTION (1)
```
  T4    146: 8    if it chooses," said Tweedledee: "we've no objection. Contrariwise."
```
OBLIGED (5)
```
  T4    140: 9                    "So much obliged!" added Tweedledee. "You like poetry?"
  A10    81:30                    "They were obliged to have him with them," the Mock Turtle said. "No wise
  T3    131:12        it said, and there it choked and was obliged to leave off.
  A11    86:22    Alice; "and those twelve creatures," (she was obliged to say "creatures," you see, because some of them were
  A11    87:10    so, after hunting all about for it, he was obliged to write with one finger for the rest of the day; and
```
OBLONG (1)
```
  A8     63:16    were all shaped like the three gardeners, oblong and flat, with their hands and feet at the corners:
```
OBSERVE (2)
```
  T3    134:10    drew her feet back in some alarm), "you may observe a Bread-and-butter-fly. Its wings are thin slices of
  T8    179:34                    "You will observe the Rules of Battle, of course?" the White Knight
```
OBSTACLE (1)
```
  A12    95:15    you had been / (Before she had this fit) / An obstacle that came between / Him, and ourselves, and it.
```
OBSTINACY (1)
```
  T5    156:31    further!" she said at last with a sigh at the obstinacy of the rushes in growing so far off, as, with
```
OCCASION (1)
```
  T12   207:11                    On this occasion the kitten only purred: and it was impossible to
```
OCCASIONAL (1)
```
  A9     74:35    by a very long silence, broken only by an occasional exclamation of "Hjckrrh!" from the Gryphon, and the
```
OCCASIONALLY (1)
```
  A6     47: 8    of it in the air. Even the Duchess sneezed occasionally; and as for the baby, it was sneezing and howling
```
OCCURRED (2)
```
  A4     34: 5    and on both sides of it, and behind it, it occurred to her that she might as well look and see what was
  A1      7:14    (when she thought it over afterwards it occurred to her that she ought to have wondered at this, but
```
O'CLOCK (5)
```
  T6    164:26    of hard words there. 'Brillig' means four o'clock in the afternoon--the time when you begin broiling
  A7     56:45    the clock. For instance, suppose it were nine o'clock in the morning, just time to begin lessons: you'd only
  A7     56:13    the day of the month, and doesn't tell what o'clock it is!"
  T5    152:38    a long way you've come to-day. Consider what o'clock it is. Consider anything, only don't cry!"
  A7     58: 9    "he wo'n't do a thing I ask! It's always six o'clock now."
```
ODD (5)
```
  T4    140:27    The billows smooth and bright--/ And this was odd, because it was / The middle of the night.
  T4    144:11    came there none--/ And this was scarcely odd, because / They'd eaten every one."
  T4    142: 5    shoes were clean and neat--/ And this was odd, because, you know, / They hadn't any feet.
  A2     15: 5    sending presents to one's own feet! And how odd the directions will look!
  T5    158:21    Why, it's got branches, I declare! How very odd to find trees growing here! And actually here's a little
```
ODDEST (1)
```
  T5    154:12    full of all manner of curious things--but the oddest part of it all was that, whenever she looked hard at
```
ODDLY (1)
```
  T9    192:11                    Everything was happening so oddly that she didn't feel a bit surprised at finding the Red
```

OF (1031) [entries omitted]
OFF (141) [entries omitted]
OFFEND (1)
```
   A7    60: 3                           Alice did not wish to offend the Dormouse again, so she began very cautiously: "But
```
OFFENDED (15)
```
   A5    41:20   "I wish the creatures wouldn't be so easily offended!"
   A3    24:16   in a whisper, half afraid that it would be offended again.
   T5   156: 1                          This offended Alice a little, so there was no more conversation for
   T6   162:19   dismay, for Humpty Dumpty looked thoroughly offended, and she began to wish she hadn't chosen that subject
   T2   125:17   from the Queen's tone that she was a little offended: and they walked on in silence till they got to the
   T8   183: 5   looked very much surprised, and a little offended at the remark. "What makes you say that?" he asked,
   T8W   14: 5           Alice felt rather offended at this answer, and was very nearly walking on and
   A2    20:11   Alice in a sorrowful tone. "I'm afraid I've offended it again!" For the Mouse was swimming away from her
   T6   162:37                          "I'm not offended," said Humpty Dumpty.
   A10   81:37   what I say," the Mock Turtle replied, in an offended tone. And the Gryphon added "Come, let's hear some of
   A10   84:13   so eagerly that the Gryphon said, in a rather offended tone, "Hm! No accounting for tastes! Sing her 'Turtle
   A7    59:11   "I've had nothing yet," Alice replied in an offended tone: "so I ca'n't take more."
   A3    22:35   What I was going to say," said the Dodo in an offended tone, "was that the best thing to get us dry would be
   A2    19:41   over, and she felt certain it must be really offended. "We wo'n't talk about her any more, if you'd rather
   A3    26:11   pleaded poor Alice. "But you're so easily offended, you know!"
```
OFFER (2)
```
   A3    22:23   to go with Edgar Atheling to meet William and offer him the crown. William's conduct at first was moderate.
   A7    55: 1           "Then it wasn't very civil of you to offer it," said Alice angrily.
```
OFFERED (1)
```
   T6   161: 2   possible fell off the wall in doing so) and offered Alice his hand. She watched him a little anxiously as
```
-OFFICE [See TICKET-OFFICE]
OFFICER (1)
```
   A11   91: 3   but the Hatter was out of sight before the officer could get to the door.
```
OFFICERS (4)
```
   A11   91: 2   off outside," the Queen added to one of the officers; but the Hatter was out of sight before the officer
   A11   90:19   which was immediately suppressed by the officers of the court,' and I never understood what it meant
   A11   90:12   and was immediately suppressed by the officers of the court. (As that is rather a hard word, I will
   A11   89: 6   crossed the court, she said, to one of the officers of the court, "Bring me the list of the singers in
```
OFTEN (12)
```
   T5   155:36                  "Why do you say 'Feather' so often?" Alice asked at last, rather vexed. "I'm not a bird!"
   T3   134:18                  "But that must happen very often," Alice remarked thoughtfully.
   T5   155:32   I did," said Alice: "you've said it very often--and very loud. Please, where are the crabs?"
   T8   182:40   Whenever the horse stopped (which it did very often), he fell off in front; and, whenever it went on again
   T4   148: 4   Alice laughed. "You must hit the trees pretty often, I should think," she said.
   A10   80:21   the Mock Turtle; "but, if you've seen them so often, of course you know what they're like?"
   A11   90:16   I've seen that done," thought Alice. "I've so often read in the newspapers, at the end of trials, 'There was
   T9   194:35   "So do I," the White Queen whispered: "we'll often say it over together, dear. And I'll tell you a secret--
   A6    53: 7                  "Well! I've often seen a cat without a grin," thought Alice; "but a grin
   A10   80:18                  "Yes," said Alice, "I've often seen them at dinn----" she checked herself hastily.
   T8   183: 9   "Because people don't fall off quite so often, when they've had much practice."
   A5    41: 9   replied; "only one doesn't like changing so often, you know."
```
OH (88)
```
   T5   152: 5   it off. "My finger's bleeding! Oh, oh, oh, oh!"
   T5   152:11   the Queen said, "but I soon shall--oh, oh, oh!"
   A10   84:11                  "Oh, a song, please, if the Mock Turtle would be so kind,"
   T5   152:15   "the brooch will come undone directly. Oh, oh!" As she said the words the brooch flew open, and the Queen
   A10   80:16                  "Oh, as to the whiting," said the Mock Turtle, "they--you've
   A2    20:10   pounds! He says it kills all the rats and--oh dear!" cried Alice in a sorrowful tone. "I'm afraid I've
   A2    17:25   stay down here till I'm somebody else'--but, oh dear!" cried Alice, with a sudden burst of tears, "I do
   A2    16: 7   little! Besides, she's she, and I'm I, and--oh dear, how puzzling it all is! I'll try if I know all the
   A1     7:13   to hear the Rabbit say to itself "Oh dear! Oh dear! I shall be too late!" (when she thought it over
   A2    16:10   six is thirteen, and four times seven is--oh dear! I shall never get to twenty at that rate! However,
   A4    33:10   if--if I'd only been the right size to do it! Oh dear! I'd nearly forgotten that I've got to grow up again!
   A1     7:13   of the way to hear the Rabbit say to itself "Oh dear! Oh dear! I shall be too late!" (when she thought it
   A2    15:11                  Oh dear, what nonsense I'm talking!"
   A3    26: 7   useful, and looking anxiously about her. "Oh, do let me help to undo it!"
   A6    48:32                  "Oh, don't bother me!" said the Duchess. "I never could abide
   T5   152:36                  "Oh, don't go on like that!" cried the poor Queen, wringing her
   A9    72:18                  "Oh, don't talk about trouble!" said the Duchess. "I make you a
   A2    17:19   and have next to no toys to play with, and oh, ever so many lessons to learn! No, I've made up my mind
   T9   192:34   the White Queen moaned, wringing her hands. "Oh, ever so much more than that!"
   T5   156:45   of a series of little shrieks of "Oh, oh, oh!" from poor Alice, it swept her straight off the seat, and
   T8   191: 2   flowerbeds dotted about it here and there. "Oh, how glad I am to get here! And what is this on my head?"
   A1    10: 8   be of very little use without my shoulders. Oh, how I wish I could shut up like a telescope! I think I
   A8    65:38   Alice gave a little scream of laughter. "Oh, hush!" the Rabbit whispered in a frightened tone. "The
   A2    19:27   and seemed to quiver all over with fright. "Oh, I beg your pardon!" cried Alice hastily, afraid that she
   A2    19:39   she's such a capital one for catching mice--oh, I beg your pardon!" cried Alice again, for this time the
   A12   92: 8                  "Oh, I beg your pardon!" she exclaimed in a tone of great
   T1   110:35   all but the bit just behind the fireplace. Oh! I do so wish I could see that bit! I want so much to know
   A9    72: 3                  "Oh, I know!" exclaimed Alice, who had not attended to this
   T3   129:22   they ask me how I liked my walk. I shall say 'Oh, I liked it well enough--' (here came the favourite little
   A4    29:11   but then--always to have lessons to learn! Oh, I shouldn't like that!"
   A3    26:28   one for catching mice, you ca'n't think! And oh, I wish you could see her after the birds! Why, she'll eat
   A5    41: 8                  "Oh, I'm not particular as to size," Alice hastily replied;
   T6   166:17                  "Oh, it needn't come to that!" Alice hastily said, hoping to
```

OH (cont.)
```
A4     30:30   Will  the  roof bear?--Mind that loose slate--Oh, it's coming down! Heads below!" (a loud crash)--"Now, who
T2    120:24                                                "Oh, it's too bad!" she cried. "I never saw such a house for
A12    98: 6                                                "Oh, I've had such a curious dream!" said Alice. And she told
T12   208:11   were his wife, my dear, so you ought to know--Oh, Kitty, do help to settle it! I'm sure your paw can wait!"
T1    111: 5   you know it may be quite different on beyond. Oh, Kitty, how nice it would be if we could only get through
T1    111: 1   Looking-glass milk isn't good to drink--but oh, Kitty! now we come to the passage. You can just see a
T5    153:28                                                "Oh, much better!" cried the Queen, her voice rising into a
A3     26:39   and I'm sure she's the best cat in the world! Oh, my dear Dinah! I wonder if I shall ever see you any more!"
A4     27: 3     to itself, "The Duchess! The Duchess! Oh my dear paws! Oh my fur and whiskers! She'll get me
A1      9:26   time  to hear it say, as it turned a corner, "Oh my ears and whiskers, how late it's getting!" She was close
A4     27: 4   "The Duchess! The Duchess! Oh my dear paws! Oh my fur and whiskers! She'll get me executed, as sure as
T8W    13:16                                                "Oh, my old bones, my old bones!" he was grumbling on as Alice
A5     42:14   "And where have my  shoulders  got to? And oh, my poor hands, how is it I ca'n't see you?" She was moving
A2     14: 6   out of sight, they were getting so far off). "Oh, my poor little feet, I wonder who will put on your shoes
T1    113: 6   but  in another moment, with  a little "Oh!" of surprise, she was down on her hands and knees watching
T5    152: 5   shake  it off. "My finger's bleeding! Oh, oh, oh, oh!"
T5    152:11   yet," the Queen said, "but I soon shall--oh, oh, oh!"
T5    152:15   out: "the  brooch will come undone directly. Oh, oh!" As she said the words the brooch flew open, and the
T5    156:45   spite  of a series of little shrieks of "Oh, oh, oh!" from poor Alice, it swept her straight off the seat,
T5    152: 5   to  shake  it off. "My finger's bleeding! Oh, oh, oh!"
T5    152:11   it  yet," the Queen said, "but I soon shall--oh, oh, oh!"
T5    156:45   in  spite  of a series of little shrieks of "Oh, oh, oh!" from poor Alice, it swept her straight off the
T5    152: 5    to  shake  it off. "My finger's bleeding! Oh, oh, oh, oh!"
T5    152: 3   she had to leave the sentence unfinished. "Oh, oh, oh!" shouted the Queen, shaking her hand about as if
T5    152: 3   had  to leave the sentence unfinished. "Oh, oh, oh!" shouted the Queen, shaking her hand about as if she
T1    115: 9                                                "Oh! please don't make such faces, my dear!" she cried out,
A6     48:16                                                "Oh, please mind what you're doing!" cried Alice, jumping up
T5    156: 6                                                "Oh, please! There are some scented rushes!" Alice cried in a
T6    164: 7                                                "Oh!" said Alice. She was too much puzzled to make any other
A2     16: 6   for I know all  sorts of things, and she, oh, she knows such a very little! Besides, she's she, and I'm
T5    152: 3   to leave the sentence unfinished. "Oh, oh, oh!" shouted the Queen, shaking her hand about as if she
A4     30:35                                                "Oh! So Bill's got to come down the chimney, has he?" said
T12   207: 3   yet with some severity. "You woke me out of oh! such a nice dream! And you've been along with me, Kitty--
T1    111: 7   into  Looking-glass House! I'm sure it's got, oh! such beautiful things in it! Let's pretend there's a way
A2     20: 5   A little bright-eyed terrier, you know, with oh, such long curly brown hair! And it'll fetch things when
T9    200: 5   times nine!" Alice repeated in  despair. "Oh, that'll never be done! I'd better go in at once--" and in
T8    186:42                                                "Oh, that's the name of the song, is it?" Alice said, trying to
T1    109:15   and  dance about--whenever the wind blows--oh, that's very pretty!" cried Alice, dropping the ball of
A2     15:29   hurry,  muttering to himself, as he came, "Oh! The Duchess, the Duchess! Oh! Wo'n't she be savage if I've
A6     48:17   jumping  up  and down in an agony of terror. "Oh, there goes his precious nose!", as an unusually large
A6     46:43                                                "Oh, there's no use in talking to him," said Alice desperately:
A4     30:28   first--they don't reach half high enough yet--Oh, they'll do well enough. Don't be particular--Here, Bill!
T5    150: 1                                                "Oh, things that happened the week after next," the Queen
T1    118:31                                          "But oh!" thought Alice, suddenly jumping up, "if I don't make
A9     70:32   said the Duchess: "and the moral of that is--'Oh, 'tis love, 'tis love, that makes the world go round!'"
T5    156:25   wo'n't tipple over!" she said to herself. "Oh, what a lovely one! Only I couldn't quite reach it." And it
T2    126: 2   world--if this is the world at all, you know. Oh, what fun it is! How I wish I was one of them! I wouldn't
T1    112: 7   no  one  here to scold me away from the fire. Oh, what fun it'll be, when they see me through the glass in
A2     15:30   as  he  came,  "Oh! The Duchess, the Duchess! Oh! Wo'n't she be savage if I've kept her waiting!" Alice felt
A6     51:23                                                "Oh, you ca'n't help that," said the Cat: "we're all mad here.
A4     29:13                                                "Oh, you foolish Alice!" she answered herself. "How can you
T8W    17: 1                                                "Oh, you mean stiff-neck," said Alice.
A10    79: 8                                                "Oh, you sing," said the Gryphon. "I've forgotten the words."
T1    107:20                                                "Oh, you wicked, wicked little thing!" cried Alice, catching up
A6     51:15                                                "Oh, you're sure to do that," said the Cat, "if you only walk
```
-OIL [See MACASSAR-OIL]
OINTMENT (1)
```
A5     38: 7   all my limbs very supple / By the use of this ointment--one shilling the box--/ Allow me to sell you a
```
OLD (50)
```
T4    146:18   he was frightened: "only an old rattle--quite old and broken."
T8W    19: 9                          So now that I am old and gray, / And all my hair is nearly gone, / They take my
T5    153: 3   Let's  consider  your  age to begin with--how old are you?"
T6    161:26                          "I thought you meant 'How old are you?'" Alice explained.
T8W    13:16                  "Oh, my old bones, my old bones!" he was grumbling on as Alice came up to him.
T8W    13:16                          "Oh, my old bones, my old bones!" he was grumbling on as Alice came up
T7    177: 1   market-place? You get the best view by the old bridge."
T7    176:25   "That's a good  long way. Did you go by the old bridge, or the market-place? You get the best view by the
T1    108: 2   she added, looking reproachfully at  the old cat, and speaking in as cross a voice as she could manage
T1    107: 3   kitten had been having its face washed by the old cat for the last quarter of an hour (and bearing it pretty
T4    147:22   "Really they'll be  more  like bundles of old clothes than anything else, by the time they're ready!"
A9     76:38   then Drawling--the Drawling-master was an old conger-eel, that used to come once a week: he taught us
A9     77: 5   to  the Classical master, though. He was an old crab, he was."
A3     26:17   as  soon as it was quite out of sight. And an old Crab took the opportunity of saying to her daughter "Ah,
T8W    21:17   and  given a  few minutes to making the poor old creature comfortable.
T6    161:21   Alice.) "So here's  a question for you. How old did you say you were?"
A5     36:36                          "Repeat You are old, Father William,'" said the Caterpillar.
A5     37: 1                          "You are old, Father William," the young man said, / "And your hair has
A10    82: 6   got  to the part about her repeating "You are old, Father William," to the Caterpillar, and the words all
A10    84:14   for tastes! Sing her 'Turtle Soup,' will you, old fellow?"
```

OLD (cont.)
```
  A9    75: 7   Gryphon  said  to  the Mock Turtle "Drive on, old fellow! Don't be all day about it!" and he went on in
  A4    31:25                                          "So you did, old fellow!" said the others.
  A4    31:13   Brandy  now--Don't  choke  him--How  was  it, old fellow? What happened to you? Tell us all about it!"
  T3   131:42   little  voice went on: "a dear friend, and an old friend. And you wo'n't hurt me, though I am an insect."
  T9   198:13   in vain for a long time; but at last a very old Frog, who was sitting under a tree, got up and hobbled
  A3    25:42   'I'll be judge, I'll be jury, said cunning old Fury: 'I'll try the whole cause, and condemn you to death.
  A3    21:11   Alice  would  not  allow,  without knowing how old it was, and as the Lory positively refused to tell its age
  A3    26:31   Some  of  the  birds hurried off at once: one old Magpie began wrapping itself up very carefully, remarking
  T1   113: 1   Looking-glass)  had  got  the  face of a little old man, and grinned at her.
  T8   189:22   /  I  weep,  for  it  reminds me so / Of that old man I used to know--/ Whose look was mild, whose speech
  T8W   13: 5   what  was  the  matter. Something like a very old man (only that his face was more like a wasp) was sitting
  T8   188:14   /  So,  having no reply to give / To what the old man said, / I cried 'Come, tell me how you live!' / And
  T7   175:33                "Come, fetch out the plum-cake, old man!" the Unicorn went on, turning from her to the King.
  T3   135:32   trying  to  find the creature that has got my old name! That's just like the advertisements, you know, when
  T1   110:17   rest." And once she had really frightened her old nurse by shouting suddenly in her ear, "Nurse! Do let's
  T4   146:25   tone,  "You  needn't  be  so  angry about an old rattle."
  T4   146:18   thinking  that  he  was  frightened: "only an old rattle--quite old and broken."
  T2   120:16        the  Looking-glass  again--back  into  the old room--and there'd be an end of all my adventures!"
  T1   112: 6   "So I shall be as warm here as I was in the old room," thought Alice: "warmer, in fact, because there'll
  T1   112:11   and  noticed that what could be seen from the old room was quite common and uninteresting, but that all the
  A5    39: 1                                    "You are old," said the youth, "and your jaws are too weak / For
  A5    38: 1                                    "You are old," said the youth, "as I mentioned before, / And have grown
  A5    40: 1                                    "You are old," said the youth, "one would hardly suppose / That your
  T5   153:38   on  the  counter,  and opposite to her was an old Sheep, sitting in an arm-chair, knitting, and every now
  T7   172:41   to  herself,  as  she  ran,  the words of the old song:--
  T4   138:16   was all Alice could say; for the words of the old song kept ringing through her head like the ticking of a
  A9    70: 1   how  glad  I  am  to see you again, you dear old thing!" said the Duchess, as she tucked her arm
  A9    74:42   went  to school in the sea. The master was an old Turtle--we used to call him Tortoise--"
  T4   146:26   That'll be a comfort, one way--never to be an old woman--but then--always to have lessons to learn! Oh, I
  A4    29:10                                              "But it isn't old!" Tweedledum cried, in a greater fury than ever. "It's new
```
OLDER (4)
```
  T6   162:10   she  said,  "that one ca'n't help growing older."
  TI   103:23   bed  /  A  melancholy  maiden!  / We are but older children, dear, / Who fret to find our bedtime near.
  A4    29: 9   then,"  thought Alice, "shall I never get any older than I am now? That'll be a comfort, one way--never to
  A3    21:10   last turned sulky, and would only say, "I'm older than you, and must know better." And this Alice would
```
OLDEST (1)
```
  A12   93:43                                   "It's the oldest rule in the book," said the King.
```
ON (463) [entries omitted]
ONCE (57)
```
  A7    58:24        And  they  pinched  it  on  both sides at once.
  A11   91: 8   people  near  the  door began sneezing all at once.
  AI     3:18   Tertia  interrupts  the  tale  / Not more than once a minute.
  A9    76:39   was  an old conger-eel, that used to come once a week: he taught us Drawling, Stretching, and Fainting
  A12   98:17   she  dreamed  about  little Alice herself: once again the tiny hands were clasped upon her knee, and the
  T5   155:10   She  was  now  working with fourteen pairs at once, and Alice couldn't help looking at her in great
  A7    60:40   to-day. I think I may as well go in at once." And in she went.
  T9   200: 6   that'll  never  be  done! I'd better go in at once--" and in she went, and there was a dead silence the
  A12   92:11   sort  of  idea  that they must be collected at once and put back into the jury-box, or they would die.
  A4    33: 4   for  making her escape: so she set off at once, and ran till she was quite tired and out of breath, and
  T8   185: 3   into  it,  to  be  sure. That happened to me once--and the worst of it was, before I could get out again,
  A1    12:14   she  decided  on  going  into the garden at once; but, alas for poor Alice! when she got to the door, she
  T7   174:15             Haigha and Hatta set to work at once, carrying round trays of white and brown bread. Alice
  A1     8: 5   moment  down  went  Alice after it, never once considering how in the world she was to get out again.
  A3    23:24   Alice with one finger; and the whole party at once crowded round her, calling out, in a confused way,
  T6   166: 9   down  in  the  wood  yonder--and, when you've once heard it, you'll be quite content. Who's been repeating
  A10   82:18   Alice. "I might just as well be at school at once." However, she got up, and began to repeat it, but her
  T6   167:11                              I told them once, I told them twice: / They would not listen to advice.
  A3    21:15   make  you  dry  enough!" They all sat down at once, in a large ring, with the Mouse in the middle. Alice
  A8    67: 2   with his head!" or "Off with her head!" about once in a minute.
  A2    18:21   to  herself.  (Alice had been to the seaside once in her life, and had come to the general conclusion that
  A4    27:16   was  so  much  frightened that she ran off at once in the direction it pointed to, without trying to explain
  T8W   13:12   checking  herself  on  the  very  edge.  "If I once jump over, everything will change, and then I can't help
  T12  207: 6   very inconvenient habit of kittens (Alice had once made the remark) that, whatever you say to them, they
  T8W   14: 8   pain  that  makes  him so cross." So she tried once more.
  T6   168:36   further  notice  of  her, she said "Good-bye!" once more, and, getting no answer to this, she quietly walked
  T7   173:31                          Hatta looked round once more, and this time a tear or two trickled down his cheek
  T2   120:18   turning  her  back upon the house, she set out once more down the path, determined to keep straight on till
  A7    60:42                            Once more she found herself in the long hall, and close to the
  T3   130: 7   have  bought one from the engine-driver." And once more the chorus of voices went on with "The man that
  A12   98:29   off  her  unfortunate guests to execution--once more the pig-baby was sneezing on the Duchess's knee,
  A12   98:30   while  plates  and  dishes crashed around it--once more the shriek of the Gryphon, the squeaking of the
  A3    24: 1   the  party.  Some of the birds hurried off at once: one old Magpie began wrapping itself up very carefully,
  T8   179:20   as he was comfortably in the saddle, he began once more "You're my--" but here another voice broke in "Ahoy!
  T9   197:16   one  had  to  take care of two Queens asleep at once! No, not in all the History of England--it couldn't, you
  A3    26:31   the  party.  Some of the birds hurried off at once: one old Magpie began wrapping itself up very carefully,
  A5    41:25   took  the  hookah out of its mouth, and yawned once or twice, and shook itself. Then it got down off the
  A7    60:32   notice  of  her  going, though she looked back once or twice, half hoping that they would call after her: the
  A1     7: 2   on  the  bank  and of having nothing to do: once or twice she had peeped into the book her sister was
  T9   195:23   correct it," said the Red Queen: "when you've once said a thing, that fixes it, and you must take the
```

ONCE (cont.)
```
A9    74:32                                                "Once," said the Mock Turtle at last, with a deep sigh, "I was
A6    48:10   the  cauldron  of  soup  off  the  fire, and at once set to work throwing everything within her reach at the
A8    68:35        to  her,  though,  as  they  all spoke at once, she found it very hard to make out exactly what they
T1   110:17   of them, then, and I'll be all the rest." And once she had really frightened her old nurse by shouting
A1    12:25   severely as to bring tears into her eyes; and once she remembered trying to box her own ears for having
A10   78:10   to  a  lobster--" (Alice began to say "I once tasted--" but checked herself hastily, and said "No never
T4   139:27   difficulty, she took hold of both hands at once: the next moment they were dancing round in a ring. This
A5    41:43   was  shrinking rapidly: so she set to work at once to eat some of the other bit. Her chin was pressed so
A2    15:14   rather  more  than nine feet high, and she at once took up the little golden key and hurried off to the
T2   123:41   to Alice, so she said nothing, but set off at once towards the Red Queen. To her surprise she lost sight of
A7    58:32                                                "Once upon a time there were three little sisters," the
T1   109: 7   I  should have to go without fifty dinners at once! Well, I shouldn't mind that much! I'd far rather go
T2   120:11   back to the house, do what she would. Indeed, once, when she turned a corner rather more quickly than usual,
A8    68:31   King,  and the Queen, who were all talking at once, while all the rest were quite silent, and looked very
A4    32:35   puppy jumped into the air off all its feet at once, with a yelp of delight, and rushed at the stick, and
A8    66:20              The players all played at once, without waiting for turns, quarrelling all the while, and
T5   153: 2   great  decision: "nobody can do two things at once, you know. Let's consider your age to begin with--how old
```
ONE (260) [See also ALONE]
```
A7    59:29   interrupt  you again. I dare say there may be one."
T1   114:14      that  was  the  most  likely  place to find one.
T3   135:12   I had made it?" Alice asked. "It's a very bad one."
T4   144:12   scarcely  odd,  because  / They'd eaten every one."
T4   148:12   said Tweedledum, "if it hadn't been a new one."
T6   161:16   fast:  let's  go  back to the last remark but one."
T6   162:46                                                "One."
T9   193:26   and  one and one and one and one and one and one?"
T1   115:37   get  a  thinner pencil. I ca'n't manage this one a bit: it writes all manner of things that I don't intend
T5   150:12   the  Queen  said  kindly: "it  always  makes one a little giddy at first--"
A10   82:17              "How the creatures order one about, and make one repeat lessons!" thought Alice. "I
T4   139:32   could  make  it  out" by the branches rubbing one across the other, like fiddles and fiddle-sticks.
A9    75: 1   "Why  did  you call him Tortoise, if he wasn't one?" Alice asked.
T3   130: 2              "I'm afraid I haven't got one," Alice said in a frightened tone: "there wasn't a
T5   158: 7         "Then two are cheaper than one?" Alice said in a surprised tone, taking out her purse.
A9    70:21         "Perhaps it hasn't one," Alice ventured to remark.
T7   175:29   were  fabulous monsters, too? I  never saw one alive before!"
T9   193:26   and  one   and one and one and one and one and one and one?"
T9   193:25   and  one   and one and one and one and one and one and one?"
T9   193:25   and  one   and one and one and one and one and one and one?"
T9   193:24   do  Addition?" the White Queen asked. "What's one and one and one and one and one and one and one and one
T9   193:25      the  White  Queen  asked. "What's  one and one and one and one and one and one and one and one
T9   193:25   White  Queen  asked. "What's  one and one and one and one and one and one and one and one and one?"
T9   193:25   Queen  asked. "What's  one and one and one and one and one and one and one and one and one?"
T9   193:25   "What's  one  and  one  and  one  and  one and one and one and one and one and one?"
T9   193:25   one  and  one  and  one  and  one and one and one and one and one and one and one?"
A5    43:34   set to work very carefully, nibbling first at one and then at the other, and growing sometimes taller, and
T8W   16: 8   went on. "They jokes at one. And they worrits one. And then I gets cross. And I gets cold. And I gets under
T8W   16: 8   like  mine," the Wasp went on. "They jokes at one. And they worrits one. And then I gets cross. And I gets
A3    23:29   them  round as prizes. There was exactly one a-piece, all round.
A4    28:20   on  growing, and, as a last resource, she put one arm out of the window, and one foot up the chimney, and
A7    57: 8   Hatter:  "but  you could keep it to half-past one as long as you liked."
T6   162:29     "It's  a cravat, child, and a beautiful one, as you say. It's a present from the White King and Queen.
A4    30:25   the other ladder?--Why, I hadn't to bring but one. Bill's got the other--Bill! Fetch it here, lad!--Here,
T1   112: 4   quite  pleased to find that there was a real one, blazing away as brightly as the one she had left behind.
T5   156:22   while  with  bright  eager eyes she caught at one bunch after another of the darling scented rushes.
T3   129: 5   none.  Principal mountains--I'm on the only one, but I don't think it's got any name. Principal towns--why
A4    29: 7   there  ought! And when I grow up, I'll write one--but I'm grown up now," she added in a sorrowful tone: "at
A9    72: 4   "It's  a  vegetable.  It doesn't look like one, but it is."
A7    54: 7              The table was a large one, but the three were all crowded together at one corner of
T3   135:31   and  it would be almost certain to be an ugly one. But then the fun would be, trying to find the creature
AI     3:32   grew  the  tale  of Wonderland: / Thus slowly, one by one, / Its quaint events were hammered out--/ And now
T8W   20:13      now--could  you  get  hold  of  the other one by the back of the neck?"
T6   167:17                        Then some one came to me and said / 'The little fishes are in bed.'
T8   181: 9                        "Now one can breathe more easily," said the Knight, putting back
T5   153:11   laughed. "There's no use trying," she said: "one ca'n't believe impossible things."
A8    67:24   tone,  "and  they  all  quarrel so dreadfully one ca'n't hear oneself speak--and they don't seem to have any
T6   162:10   at this suggestion. "I mean," she said, "that one ca'n't help growing older."
T2   123:16   "You're beginning to fade, you know--and then one ca'n't help one's petals getting a little untidy."
T6   162:11              "One ca'n't, perhaps," said Humpty Dumpty; "but two can. With
T8W   21: 3   off his own wig as he spoke, and stetched out one claw towards Alice, as if he wished to do the same for her
A7    54: 8   but  the  three  were all crowded together at one corner of it. "No room! No room!" they cried out when they
T12  207: 9   rule  of  that sort," she had said, "so that one could keep up a conversation! But how can you talk with a
A6    46:13      they're  making  such  a  noise  inside, no one could possibly hear you." And certainly there was a most
A6    46:37   all the creatures argue. It's enough to drive one crazy!"
T4   139:40   of  breath.  "Four  times round is enough for one dance," Tweedledum panted out, and they left off dancing
T9   195:30   "In  our  country," she remarked, "there's only one day at a time."
T8   186:14   you  wouldn't  have two pudding-courses in one dinner?"
A5    41: 9   as  to  size," Alice hastily replied; "only one doesn't like changing so often, you know."
A1    13: 1   be  sure, this is what generally happens when one eats cake; but Alice had got so much into the way of
A4    28:18   and  she  tried the effect of lying down with one elbow against the door, and the other arm curled round her
```

ONE (cont.)

T12	207:33	on, as she settled comfortably down, with one elbow on the rug, and her chin in her hand, to watch the
A3	23: 4	thought that somebody ought to speak, and no one else seemed inclined to say anything.
T5	149:22	as it seemed to Alice, if she had got some one else to dress her, she was so dreadfully untidy. "Every
A7	54:10	and she sat down in a large arm-chair at one end of the table.
A6	47: 1	a large kitchen, which was full of smoke from one end to the other: the Duchess was sitting on a
A2	15:17	side, to look through into the garden with one eye; but to get through was more hopeless than ever: she
A10	83:14	"I passed by his garden, and marked, with one eye, / How the Owl and the Panther were sharing a pie: /
A12	95:33	verses on his knee, and looking at them with one eye; "I seem to see some meaning in them, after all.
T8	181:32	"But you've got a bee-hive--or something like one--fastened to the saddle," said Alice.
A3	23:24	said the Dodo, pointing to Alice with one finger; and the whole party at once crowded round her,
A12	96:22	Bill had left off writing on his slate with one finger, as he found it made no mark; but he now hastily
A11	87:10	about for it, he was obliged to write with one finger for the rest of the day; and this was of very
T1	108:26	don't interrupt me!" she went on, holding up one finger. "I'm going to tell you all your faults. Number one
A3	23:18	of thought, and it stood for a long time with one finger pressed upon its forehead (the position in which
T5	153: 7	to believe. I'm just one hundred and one, five months and a day."
A10	78: 1	Turtle sighed deeply, and drew the back of one flapper across his eyes. He looked at Alice and tried to
A8	64:14	The Knave did so, very carefully, with one foot.
A11	88:31	the witness at all: he kept shifting from one foot to the other, looking uneasily at the Queen, and in
A4	28:20	she put one arm out of the window, and one foot up the chimney, and said to herself "Now I can do no
T6	163:22	"And only one for birthday presents, you know. There's glory for you!"
A2	19:38	soft thing to nurse--and she's such a capital one for catching mice--oh, I beg your pardon!" cried Alice
A3	26:27	"Dinah's our cat. And she's such a capital one for catching mice, you ca'n't think! And oh, I wish you
T3	130: 7	said the Guard: "you should have bought one from the engine-driver." And once more the chorus of
T6	163: 1	"And if you take one from three hundred and sixty-five what remains?"
T6	168:24	"The face is what one goes by, generally," Alice remarked in a thoughtful tone.
T9	204:14	up and seized the tablecloth with both hands: one good pull, and plates, dishes, guests, and candles came
T5	150:15	"--but there's one great advantage in it, that one's memory works both ways."
T9	197:15	don't think it ever happened before, that any one had to take care of two Queens asleep at once! No, not in
A2	15:28	dressed, with a pair of white kid-gloves in one hand and a large fan in the other: he came trotting along
A11	88: 6	was the Hatter. He came in with a teacup in one hand and a piece of bread-and-butter in the other. "I beg
T7	173:21	watching the fight, with a cup of tea in one hand and a piece of bread-and-butter in the other.
A11	86: 6	King was the White Rabbit, with a trumpet in one hand, and a scroll of parchment in the other. In the very
T8	187:13	on its neck: then, slowly beating time with one hand, and with a faint smile lighting up his gentle
T7	170:21	along the road, shading her eyes with one hand. "I see somebody now!" she exclaimed at last. "But
T8	187:25	all this she took in like a picture, as, with one hand shading her eyes, she leant against a tree, watching
T8	183: 7	the saddle, keeping hold of Alice's hair with one hand, to save himself from falling over on the other side
T1	112: 7	"warmer, in fact, because there'll be no one here to scold me away from the fire. Oh, what fun it'll be
T5	153: 7	I'll give you something to believe. I'm just one hundred and one, five months and a day."
T9	193:18	at all," said Alice; "but, if there is to be one, I think I ought to invite the guests."
T4	147:26	serious things that can possibly happen to one in a battle--to get one's head cut off."
A8	63: 7	have been a red rose-tree, and we put a white one in by mistake; and, if the Queen was to find out, we
T1	110:41	our books to the glass, and then they hold up one in the other room.
A7	59:30	"One, indeed!" said the Dormouse indignantly. However, he
T5	155: 1	above the one she was looking at. "And this one is the most provoking of all--but I'll tell you what--"
AI	3:32	the tale of Wonderland: / Thus slowly, one by one, / Its quaint events were hammered out--/ And now the tale
T2	128:14	"I--I didn't know I had to make one--just then," Alice faltered out.
A8	65: 7	Two, in a very humble tone, going down on one knee as he spoke, "we were trying--"
A11	90: 8	teacup and bread-and-butter and went down on one knee. "I'm a poor man, your Majesty," he began.
T6	162:34	Dumpty continued thoughtfully as he crossed one knee over the other and clasped his hands round it, "they
T8	180: 3	hiding-place. "One Rule seems to be, that if one Knight hits the other, he knocks him off his horse; and,
A8	67: 7	here: the great wonder is, that there's any one left alive!"
T9	194:36	I'll tell you a secret--I can read words of one letter! Isn't that grand? However, don't be discouraged.
A1	8:42	I think--" (she was rather glad there was no one listening, this time, as it didn't sound at all the right
T12	207:24	remember!" And she caught it up and gave it one little kiss, "just in honour of its having been a Red
T4	138:13	"Contrariwise," added the one marked 'DEE,' "if you think we're alive, you ought to
T4	138: 9	she was startled by a voice coming from the one marked 'DUM.'
T9	198: 8	and I'm not a servant. There ought to be one marked 'Queen,' you know--"
T3	137:22	to be two finger-posts pointing the same way, one marked "TO TWEEDLEDUM'S HOUSE," and the other "TO THE
A5	43:41	I'm never sure what I'm going to be, from one minute to another! However, I've got back to my right size
T9	195:35	"Are five nights warmer than one night, then?" Alice ventured to ask.
T4	144:29	him!" the brothers cried, and they each took one of Alice's hands, and led her up to where the King was
T6	168:22	replied in a discontented tone, giving her one of his fingers to shake: "you're so exactly like other
T9	199:20	Then he went up and gave the door a kick with one of his great feet. "You let it alone," he panted out, as
T6	166:15	you know," said Humpty Dumpty, stretching out one of his great hands, "I can repeat poetry as well as other
A2	19:19	inquisitively, and seemed to her to wink with one of its little eyes, but it said nothing.
T1	110:40	wrong way: I know that, because I've held up one of our books to the glass, and then they hold up one in
T8	181:35	the Knight said in a discontented tone, "one of the best kind. But not a single bee has come near it
A4	32:10	So she swallowed one of the cakes, and was delighted to find that she began
A1	8:21	underneath, so managed to put it into one of the cupboards as she fell past it.
A1	9:36	first idea was that this might belong to one of the doors of the hall; but, alas! either the locks were
A11	90:11	Here one of the guinea-pigs cheered, and was immediately suppressed
A11	87: 5	One of the jurors had a pencil that squeaked. This, of course,
A11	90: 3	"But what did the Dormouse say?" one of the jury asked.
A12	94:11	"Who is it directed to?" said one of the jurymen.
T2	123:20	you'll see her soon," said the Rose. "She's one of the kind that has nine spikes, you know."
T2	128:19	the Seventh Square is all forest--however, one of the Knights will show you the way--and in the Eighth
T9	195:27	had such a thunderstorm last Tuesday--I mean one of the last set of Tuesdays, you know."
A4	33: 9	to rest herself, and fanned herself with one of the leaves. "I should have liked teaching it tricks
A1	12:18	the glass, and she tried her best to climb up one of the legs of the table, but it was too slippery; and

ONE (cont.)

```
T4    147:25  "You know," he added  very  gravely, "it's one of the most serious things that can possibly happen to one
T5    156:41  hadn't  gone much farther before the blade of one of the oars got fast in the water and wouldn't come out
A11    91: 2  his  head  off  outside,"  the Queen added to one of the officers; but the Hatter was out of sight before
A11    89: 5  the  Dormouse crossed the court, she said, to one of the officers of the court, "Bring me the list of the
A2     18: 2  and  was surprised to see that she had put on one of the Rabbit's little white kid-gloves while she was
A1      8:18  hung  upon pegs.  She  took  down a jar from one of the shelves as she passed: it was labeled "ORANGE
T4    145:19  him,"  said  Tweedledum,  "when you're  only one of the things in his dream. You know very well you're not
A6     46:29  grazed  his nose, and broke to pieces against one of the trees behind him.
A7     60:38   Just  as she  said this, she noticed that one of the trees had a door leading right into it. "That's
T1    113:16  made  her  turn  her head  just in time to see one of the White Pawns roll over and begin kicking: she
T9    196:22  her,"  the  Red Queen said to Alice, taking one of the White Queen's hands in her own, and gently stroking
T3    135:35  calling  everything  you  met  'Alice,' till one of them answered! Only they wouldn't answer at all, if
A12    95:23                      "If any  of  them can explain it," said Alice, (she had grown so
A11    87: 1  slates,  and  she  could  even make out that one of them didn't know how to spell "stupid," and that he had
T4    138: 3  knew  which  was  which  in a moment, because one of them had 'DUM' embroidered on his collar, and the other
T2    126: 3  know.  Oh,  what  fun it is! How I wish I was one of them! I wouldn't mind being a Pawn, if only I might
A8     67:18      "till  its  ears have come,  or at least one of them." In another minute the whole head appeared, and
A8     62: 5  and,  just  as she came up to her, she heard one of them say "Look out now, Five! Don't go splashing paint
T3    129: 9  and  for  some time she stood silent, watching one of them that was bustling about among the flowers, poking
T1    110:16  been  reduced at last to say "Well, you can be one of them, then, and I'll be all the rest." And once she had
A8     68:18  Alice  an excellent opportunity for croqueting one of them with the other: the only difficulty was, that her
A4     32: 7  a  bright  idea came into her head. "If I eat one of these cakes," she thought, "it's sure to make some
T4    147:16  tying  strings?"  Tweedledum remarked. "Every one of these things has got to go on, somehow or other."
T2    122: 9  full  of  little shrill voices. "Silence, every one of you!" cried the Tiger-lily, waving itself passionately
A3     26:31  party.  Some of the birds hurried off at once: one old Magpie began wrapping itself up very carefully,
A10    82: 3  first,  the two creatures got so close to her, one on each side, and opened their eyes and mouths so very
T9    192:13  and  the  White  Queen sitting close to her, one on each side: she would have liked very much to ask them
T9    203: 2  her  speech:  the  two Queens pushed her so, one on each side, that they nearly lifted her up into the air.
T5    156:25  she  said  to herself.  "Oh, what a lovely one! Only I couldn't quite reach it." And it certainly did
A6     50:19  as  pigs,  and was just saying to herself "if one only knew the right way to change them--" when she was a
A9     73:15                       "I never saw one, or heard of one," said Alice.
T8    184:19  the  Knight  said  thoughtfully  to himself. "One or two--several."
T2    123: 5                       "There's other flower in the garden that can move about like you,"
T1    108: 8  of  the winding, and now and then putting out one paw and gently touching the ball, as if it would be glad
T1    107: 7  she  held the poor thing down by its ear with one paw, and then with the other paw she rubbed its face all
A4     32:28  large  round  eyes, and feebly stretching out one paw, trying to touch her. "Poor little thing!" said Alice,
A7     59:36  cup,"  interrupted the  Hatter: "let's all move one place on."
T5    158:10                        "Then I'll have one, please," said Alice, as she put the money down on the
AI      3:11  /  To  stir  the tiniest feather! / Yet what can one poor voice avail / Against three tongues together?
T9    197:17  you  know,  because there never was more than one Queen at a time. Do wake up, you heavy things!" she went
T9    201: 5  up  the  knife  and  fork, and looking from one Queen to the other.
A6     53: 3  appearing  and vanishing so suddenly; you make one quite giddy!"
A10    82:17  "How  the creatures order one about, and make one repeat lessons!" thought Alice. "I might just as well be
A1     12:30  Why,  there's hardly enough of me left to make one respectable person!"
T3    137:17      question  to answer, as  there  was only one road through the wood, and the two finger-posts both
T9    197:13  looking  about  in great perplexity, as first one round head, and then the other, rolled down from her
T8    180: 3  timidly  peeping  out  from her hiding-place. "One Rule seems to be, that if one Knight hits the other, he
A9     73:15                       "I never saw one, or heard of one," said Alice.
A12    93:44                      "Then it ought to be Number One," said Alice.
A7     58:21                      "I'm afraid I don't know one," said Alice, rather alarmed at the proposal.
A4     31: 2  saying  to  herself  "This is Bill", she gave one sharp kick, and waited to see what would happen next.
T1    112: 5  a  real one, blazing away as brightly as the one she had left behind. "So I shall be as warm here as I was
T8W    18: 7  idea  came  into  Alice's head. Almost every one she had met had repeated poetry to her, and she thought
T5    154:19  and  was  always  in the shelf next above the one she was looking at. "And this one is the most provoking of
A5     38: 7  very  supple  /  By the use of this ointment--one shilling the box--/ Allow me to sell you a couple?"
T5    149:29  go  straight,  you  know, if you pin it all on one side," Alice said as she gently put it right for her; "and
T8    190:30  road,  and  the  Knight tumbling off, first on one side and then on the other. After the fourth or fifth
A4     29:16                       And so she went on, taking first one side and then the other, and making quite a conversation
A1      9:31  and  when  Alice  had  been  all the way down one side and up the other, trying every door, she walked sadly
A5     41:29                       "One side of what? The other side of what?" thought Alice to
A2     15:16  It  was as much as she could do, lying down on one side, to look through into the garden with one eye; but to
A5     41:27  the  grass,  merely  remarking,  as it went, "One side will make you grow taller, and the other side will
A2     15:32      that  she  was  ready  to  ask help of any one: so, when the Rabbit came near her, she began, in a low,
T2    122:19  "The  daisies  are  worst  of  all.  When one speaks, they all begin together, and it's enough to make
T2    121: 9  some  sense  in  it, though it's not a clever one!' Still, you're the right colour, and that goes a long way
T4    148:14                       "There's only one sword, you know," Tweedledum said to his brother: "but you
T8    184:42  "Yes,"  he  said; "but I've invented a better one than that--like a sugar-loaf. When I used to wear it, if I
T6    159: 9  on  the  top  of  a  high wall--such a narrow one that Alice quite wondered how he could keep his balance--
T6    160:37  that  is.  Now,  take a good look at me! I'm one that has spoken to a King, I am: mayhap you'll never see
T8    187:17   Through  The  Looking-Glass,  this  was  the one that she always remembered most clearly. Years afterwards
T5    156:29  glided  by,  there  was  always a more lovely one that she couldn't reach.
A4     30: 8                       "An arm, you goose! Who ever saw one that size? Why, it fills the whole window!"
T2    120:30                       said Alice, addressing herself to one that was waving gracefully about in the wind, "I wish you
T7    173: 5                       "Does--the one--that wins--get the crown?" she asked, as well as she
T7    175:37  Open  the bag!" he whispered. "Quick! Not that one--that's full of hay!"
A6     48: 9  conversation.  While she was trying to fix on one, the cook took the cauldron of soup off the fire, and at
T8    184:19                        "I'll get one," the Knight said thoughtfully to himself. "One or two--
A4     29: 5  happened,  and now here I am in the middle of one! There ought to be a book written about me, that there
A12    96: 5  become  of  you?'--What, indeed!--'I gave her one, they gave him two'--why, that must be what he did with
```

ONE (cont.)
```
A12    95: 5                                              I gave her one, they gave him two, / You gave us three or more; / They
T1    107: 1                                              One thing was certain, that the white kitten had had nothing
T12   207:38   been really with me in my dream, there was one thing you would have enjoyed--I had such a quantity of
A7     57: 2   goes the clock in a twinkling! Half-past one, time for dinner!"
T8    179: 3   up her head in some alarm. There was no one to be seen, and her first thought was that she must have
T7    171: 7   two--to fetch and carry. One to fetch, and one to carry."
T7    171: 1   I must have two, you know--to come and go. One to come, and one to go."
T7    171: 4   that I didn't understand," said Alice. "Why one to come and one to go?"
T7    171: 7   "I must have two--to fetch and carry. One to fetch, and one to carry."
T9    201:16   see why the Red Queen should be the only one to give orders; so, as an experiment, she called out
T7    171: 1   you know--to come and go. One to come, and one to go."
T7    171: 5   understand," said Alice. "Why one to come and one to go?"
A1      8:33   showing off her knowledge, as there was no one to listen to her, still it was good practice to say it
A8     67:20   of the game, feeling very glad she had some one to listen to her. The Cat seemed to think that there was
AI      3:27   of fancy dry, / And faintly strove that weary one / To put the subject by, / "The rest next time--" It is
T9    200:17   at the silence, and longing for some one to speak.
T8    179:26   some time without speaking. Alice looked from one to the other in some bewilderment.
T1    118:13                                              One, two! One, two! And through and through / The vorpal blade went
T1    118:13                                              One, two! One, two! And through and through / The vorpal blade
A3     23:10   the course, here and there. There was no "One, two, three, and away!", but they began running when they
T5    158: 5   "Fivepence farthing for one--twopence for two," the Sheep replied.
T9    200:15   had already taken two of them, but the middle one was empty. Alice sat down in it, rather uncomfortable at
T9    198: 3   side of the arch there was a bell-handle; one was marked "Visitors' Bell," and the other "Servants' Bell
A4     28:28   at home," thought poor Alice, "when one wasn't always growing larger and smaller, and being
T5    150:17   "I'm sure mine only works one way," Alice remarked. "I ca'n't remember things before
A4     29:10   older than I am now? That'll be a comfort, one way--never to be an old woman--but then--always to have
A8     68: 6   The Queen had only one way of settling all difficulties, great or small. "Off
A12    93: 9   it would be quite as much use in the trial one way up as the other."
T7    169: 7   over something or other, and whenever one went down, several more always fell over him, so that the
T3    130: 4   of voices went on. "There wasn't room for one where she came from. The land there is worth a thousand
A7     59:41   of the March Hare. The Hatter was the only one who got any advantage from the change; and Alice was a
A8     62:13   "What for?" said the one who had spoken first.
A5     43:13   good many little girls in my time, but never one with such a neck as that! No, no! You're a serpent; and
T2    122:20   all begin together, and it's enough to make one wither to hear the way they go on!"
T6    164:32   there are two meanings packed up into one word."
T6    164: 3   "That's a great deal to make one word mean," Alice said in a thoughtful tone.
A5     40: 1   "You are old," said the youth, "one would hardly suppose / That your eye was as steady as ever
T8W    21: 8   eyes--they're too much in front, no doubt. One would have done as well as two, if you must have them so
T1    108:27   I'm going to tell you all your faults. Number one: you squeaked twice while Dinah was washing your face this
T3    131:33   to have a joke made, why don't you make one yourself?"
T9    201: 7   decidedly: "it isn't etiquette to cut any one you've been introduced to. Remove the joint!" And the
```
ONE'S (9)
```
T7    173: 9   further, "to stop a minute--just to get--one's breath again?"
T9    199:34   times three makes ninety. I wonder if any one's counting?" In a minute there was silence again, and the
T4    139:26   of them first, for fear of hurting the other one's feelings; so, as the best way out of the difficulty, she
T4    147:26   possibly happen to one in a battle--to get one's head cut off."
T5    150:15   --but there's one great advantage in it, that one's memory works both ways."
A2     15: 5   and how funny it'll seem, sending presents to one's own feet! And how odd the directions will look!
T2    123:16   to fade, you know--and then one ca'n't help one's petals getting a little untidy."
T2    127:37   "No, thank you," said Alice: "one's quite enough!"
T8    188:10   But I was thinking of a plan / To dye one's whiskers green, / And always use so large a fan / That
```
ONES (1)
```
A3     24:11   they could not taste theirs, and the small ones choked and had to be patted on the back. However, it was
```
ONESELF (2)
```
T8    188:26   But I was thinking of a way / To feed oneself on batter, / And so go on from day to day / Getting a
A8     67:25   all quarrel so dreadfully one ca'n't hear oneself speak--and they don't seem to have any rules in
```
ONIONS (1)
```
A8     62:16   for bringing the cook tulip-roots instead of onions."
```
ONLY (149)
```
T3    132: 6   the window, quietly drew it in and said "It's only a brook we have to jump over." Everybody seemed satisfied
A8     64:11   and timidly said "Consider, my dear: she is only a child!"
T8    190:14   the road by which they had come. "You've only a few yards to go," he said, "down the hill and over that
A2     19: 9   was now, and she soon made out that it was only a mouse, that had slipped in like herself.
A8     63:41   but she added, to herself, "Why, they're only a pack of cards, after all. I needn't be afraid of them!"
T4    146:16   "It's only a rattle," Alice said, after a careful examination of the
T4    145: 9   "You'd be nowhere. Why, you're only a sort of thing in his dream!"
T4    145:12   Alice exclaimed indignantly. "Besides, if I'm only a sort of thing in his dream, what are you, I should like
A3     23:33   "Only a thimble," said Alice sadly.
T5    156:37   Even real scented rushes, you know, last only a very little while--and these, being dream-rushes,
A6     46:35   It was, no doubt: only Alice did not like to be told so. "It's really dreadful,"
T4    146:18   hastily, thinking that he was frightened: "only an old rattle--quite old and broken."
A10    85: 7   it?" Alice panted as she ran: but the Gryphon only answered "Come on!" and ran the faster, while more and
A7     54: 6   for the Dormouse," thought Alice; "only as it's asleep, I suppose it doesn't mind."
T1    110:30   "Now, if you'll only attend, Kitty, and not talk so much, I'll tell you all my
A4     33:10   teaching it tricks very much, if--if I'd only been the right size to do it! Oh dear! I'd nearly
T12   208:12   your paw can wait!" But the provoking kitten only began on the other paw, and pretended it hadn't heard the
A8     63:36   She said it to the Knave of Hearts, who only bowed and smiled in reply.
A9     74:34   were followed by a very long silence, broken only by an occasional exclamation of "Hjckrrh!" from the
A6     46: 1   repeated, in the same solemn tone, only changing the order of the words a little, "From the Queen
```

ONLY (cont.)

T4	141: 5	/ Such quantities of sand: / 'If this were only cleared away,' / They said, 'it would be grand!'
T8	184:30	the Knight. "You see, I said to myself 'The only difficulty is with the feet: the head is high enough
A8	68:19	croqueting one of them with the other: the only difficulty was, that her flamingo was gone across the
A4	32:23	and very neatly and simply arranged: the only difficulty was, that she had not the smallest idea how to
T1	108:12	if you'd been up in the window with me--only Dinah was making you tidy, so you couldn't. I was
A6	48:38	boy, / And beat him when he sneezes: / He only does it to annoy, / Because he knows it teases."
T7	170:27	and those are Anglo-Saxon attitudes. He only does them when he's happy. His name is Haigha." (He
T5	152:39	what o'clock it is. Consider anything, only don't cry!"
T5	151:15	"Only for faults," said Alice.
T7	175:21	towards her in an Anglo-Saxon attitude. "We only found it to-day. It's as large as life, and twice as
T1	111: 6	Oh, Kitty, how nice it would be if we could only get through into Looking-glass House! I'm sure it's got,
T3	137:28	ask them the way out of the wood. If I could only get to the Eighth Square before it gets dark!" So she
T7	173:24	in," Haigha whispered to Alice: "and they only give them oyster-shells in there--so you see he's very
T6	159: 1	However, the egg only got larger and larger, and more and more human: when she
T7	171:13	it was of no use--the Anglo-Saxon attitudes only got more extraordinary every moment, while the great eyes
A6	51: 5	whether it would like the name: however, it only grinned a little wider. "Come, it's pleased so far,"
A6	51: 1	The Cat only grinned when it saw Alice. It looked good-natured, she
A3	26:12	The Mouse only growled in reply.
A7	57: 1	morning, just time to begin lessons: you'd only have to whisper a hint to Time, and round goes the clock
A4	30:13	a long silence after this, and Alice could only hear whispers now and then; such as "Sure, I don't like
T10	205: 3	The Red Queen made no resistance whatever: only her face grew very small, and her eyes got large and
T2	121:11	the colour," the Tiger-lily remarked. "If only her petals curled up a little more, she'd be all right."
T4	147: 5	over, bundling up in the umbrella, with only his head out: and there he lay, opening and shutting his
T5	156:24	"I hope the boat wo'n't tipple over!" she said to herself.
T2	127:24	said Alice. "I'm quite content to stay here--only I am so hot and thirsty!"
T5	156:25	she said to herself. "Oh, what a lovely one! Only I couldn't quite reach it." And it certainly did seem a
T8	179: 8	unless we're all part of the same dream. Only I do hope it's my dream, and not the Red King's! I don't
T1	118:28	"Somehow it seems to fill my head with ideas--only I don't exactly know what they are! However, somebody
T6	166:25	only I don't sing it," he added, as an explanation.
A4	27:33	and see that the mouse doesn't get out.' Only I don't think," Alice went on, "that they'd let Dinah
T6	162:20	to wish she hadn't chosen that subject. "If only I knew," she thought to herself, "which was neck and
T2	126: 4	one of them! I wouldn't mind being a Pawn, if only I might join--though of course I should like to be a
T5	152:30	I could manage to be glad!" the Queen said. "Only I never can remember the rule. You must be very happy,
T7	173:11	"I'm good enough," the King said, "only I'm not strong enough. You see, a minute goes by so
T8	182:24	"Only in the usual way," Alice said, smiling.
T1	108:15	and it wants plenty of sticks, Kitty! Only it got so cold, and it snowed so, they had to leave off.
T5	152:33	"Only it is so very lonely here!" Alice said in a melancholy
A8	67:30	have croqueted the Queen's hedgehog just now, only it ran away when it saw mine coming!"
T3	129:23	came the favourite little toss of the head), 'only it was so dusty and hot, and the elephants did tease so!'
T7	173:23	"He's only just out of prison, and he hadn't finished his tea when
A7	56:43	Hatter. "He wo'n't stand beating. Now, if you only kept on good terms with him, he'd do almost anything you
A1	10: 9	up like a telescope! I think I could, if I only knew how to begin." For, you see, so many out-of-the-way
A6	50:19	pigs, and was just saying to herself "if one only knew the right way to change them--" when she was a
T5	157:10	crab to take home with me!" But the Sheep only laughed scornfully, and went on with her knitting.
T8	186:30	Alice could only look puzzled: she was thinking of the pudding.
A2	17:22	and saying 'Come up again, dear!' I shall only look up and say 'Who am I, then? Tell me that first, and
T4	139:12	But the fat little men only looked at each other and grinned.
T5	149: 7	The White Queen only looked at her in a helpless frightened sort of way, and
T5	157:13	things," said the Sheep: "plenty of choice, only make up your mind. Now, what do you want to buy?"
A12	94:23	"If you didn't sign it," said the King, "that only makes the matter worse. You must have meant some mischief
T7	171: 4	"I only meant that I didn't understand," said Alice. "Why one to
T7	174: 1	you!" Haigha cried impatiently. But Hatta only munched away, and drank some more tea.
A9	71:13	"Only mustard isn't a bird," Alice remarked.
A10	84:30	only of beautiful Soup? / Pennyworth only of beautiful soup. / Beau--ootiful Soo--oop! /
A10	84:29	would not give all else for two p / ennyworth only of beautiful Soup? / Pennyworth only of beautiful soup. /
T9	196: 8	"Well, only on Thursdays," said the Queen.
T3	129: 5	are none. Principal mountains--I'm on the only one, but I don't think it's got any name. Principal towns
T9	195:29	"In our country," she remarked, "there's only one day at a time."
A5	41: 8	as to size," Alice hastily replied; "only one doesn't like changing so often, you know."
T6	163:22	"And only one for birthday presents, you know. There's glory for
T4	145:19	waking him," said Tweedledum, "when you're only one of the things in his dream. You know very well you're
T3	137:16	difficult question to answer, as there was only one road through the wood, and the two finger-posts both
T4	148:14	"There's only one sword, you know," Tweedledum said to his brother:
T9	201:15	didn't see why the Red Queen should be the only one to give orders; so, as an experiment, she called out
A8	68: 6	The Queen had only one way of settling all difficulties, great or small.
A7	59:41	place of the March Hare. The Hatter was the only one who got any advantage from the change; and Alice was
T8W	14: 7	him, but she thought to herself "Perhaps it's only pain that makes him so cross." So she tried once more.
T1	110:38	comes up in that room too--but that may be only pretence, just to make it look as if they had a fire.
T12	207: 8	say to them, they always purr. "If they would only purr for 'yes,' and mew for 'no,' or any rule of that
T12	207:11	On this occasion the kitten only purred: and it was impossible to guess whether it meant
A12	98:36	change to dull reality--the grass would be only rustling in the wind, and the pool rippling to the waving
T8W	14:12	tree, but when he got settled down again he only said, as before, "Worrity, worrity! Can't you leave a
T9	192:32	with a little shudder, "She says she only said 'if'--"
T9	192:30	"I only said 'if'!" poor Alice pleaded in a piteous tone.
A3	21: 9	the Lory, who at last turned sulky, and would only say, "I'm older than you, and must know better." And this
A2	19:34	you'd take a fancy to cats, if you could only see her. She is such a dear quiet thing," Alice went on,
T1	112:14	clock on the chimney-piece (you know you can only see the back of it in the Looking-glass) had got the face
T9	193:11	Queen, "that she wants to deny something--only she doesn't know what to deny!"
T4	147:11	replied, as he crawled out of the umbrella: "only she must help us to dress up, you know."

ONLY (cont.)
A6	45: 4	was in livery: otherwise, judging by his face only, she would have called him a fish)--and rapped loudly at
T8W	13:21	The Wasp only shook his shoulders, and turned his head away. "Ah, deary
A3	26:15	in chorus "Yes, please do!" But the Mouse only shook its head impatiently, and walked a little quicker.
T4	139:19	though she felt quite certain he would only shout out "Contrariwise!" and so he did.
T6	168:33	look nice," Alice objected. But Humpty Dumpty only shut his eyes, and said "Wait till you've tried."
T3	131:36	something pitying to comfort it, "if it would only sigh like other people!" she thought. But this was such a
T3	135:13	But the Gnat only sighed deeply while two large tears came rolling down its
T9	201:25	hadn't a word to say in reply: she could only sit and look at it and gasp.
T2	126: 7	Queen as she said this, but her companion only smiled pleasantly, and said "That's easily managed. You
A6	50: 1	look of the thing at all. "But perhaps it was only sobbing," she thought, and looked into its eyes again, to
T9	192:21	ready for a little argument, "and if you only spoke when you were spoken to, and the other person
T3	136:10	out her hand and tried to stroke it; but it only started back a little, and then stood looking at her
T5	149:17	so she smiled and said "If your Majesty will only tell me the right way to begin, I'll do it as well as I
A1	12: 3	And so it was indeed: she was now only ten inches high, and her face brightened up at the
T8W	13: 5	the matter. Something like a very old man (only that his face was more like a wasp) was sitting on the
T1	110:12	had had quite a long argument with her sister only the day before--all because Alice had begun with "Let's
A11	89:20	on, "and most things twinkled after that--only the March Hare said--"
A9	70: 5	and thought to herself that perhaps it was only the pepper that had made her so savage when they met in
T4	144:27	"It's only the Red King snoring," said Tweedledee.
T1	110:33	that's just the same as our drawing-room, only the things go the other way. I can see all of it when I
T1	110:39	then, the books are something like our books, only the words go the wrong way: I know that, because I've
T3	135:35	you met 'Alice,' till one of them answered! Only they wouldn't answer at all, if they were wise."
T3	134:26	know," the Gnat went on in a careless tone: "only think how convenient it would be if you could manage to
T2	123:30	first found her in the ashes, she had been only three inches high--and here she was, half a head taller
T4	147:34	generally," he went on in a low voice: "only to-day I happen to have a headache."
A10	84: 7	leave off," said the Gryphon, and Alice was only too glad to do so.
A9	76:19	it," said the Mock Turtle with a sigh. "I only took the regular course."
A6	47: 9	alternately without a moment's pause. The only two creatures in the kitchen, that did not sneeze, were
T1	110:15	argued that they couldn't, because there were only two of them, and Alice had been reduced at last to say
A6	51:15	sure to do that," said the Cat, "if you only walk long enough."
T2	125: 1	"I only wanted to see what the garden was like, your Majesty--"
T7	171: 9	much out of breath to say a word, and could only wave his hands about, and make the most fearful faces at
T3	135:26	she thought to herself, and this was the only way to the Eighth Square.
T4	148:15	can have the umbrella--it's quite as sharp. Only we must begin quick. It's getting as dark as it can."
T2	121: 3	her breath away. At length, as the Tiger-lily only went on waving about, she spoke again, in a timid voice--
T8	187: 7	song is called 'Ways and Means': but that's only what it's called, you know!"
T7	170:17	"I only wish I had such eyes," the King remarked in a fretful
A7	57: 3	("I only wish it was," the March Hare said to itself in a whisper
A9	70:13	things that make children sweet-tempered. I only wish people knew that: then they wouldn't be so stingy
A4	30:20	next! As for pulling me out of the window, I only wish they could! I'm sure I don't want to stay in here
T5	150:19	"It's a poor sort of memory that only works backwards," the Queen remarked.
T5	150:17	"I'm sure mine only works one way," Alice remarked. "I ca'n't remember things
T8	187:19	the whole scene back again, as if it had been only yesterday--the mild blue eyes and kindly smile of the
A8	62:11	not talk!" said Five. "I heard the Queen say only yesterday you deserved to be beheaded."
A9	70:23	the Duchess. "Everything's got a moral, if only you can find it." And she squeezed herself up closer to
T8W	17:13	make your wig much neater," she said, "if only you had a comb."
T1	111: 4	very like our passage as far as you can see, only you know it may be quite different on beyond. Oh, Kitty,
T5	158: 9	"Only you must eat them both, if you buy two," said the Sheep.
T12	207:37	"By the way, Kitty, if only you'd been really with me in my dream, there was one
T4	147:45	said, rather sadly: "and she can watch us--only you'd better not come very close," he added: "I generally

ONWARD (1)
| TC | 209: 2 | A boat, beneath a sunny sky / Lingering onward dreamily / In an evening of July-- |

OPEN (20)
T8	181:22	Alice gently remarked. "Do you know the lid's open?"
A6	49:25	undoing itself), she carried it out into the open air. "If I don't take this child away with me," thought
T8	181:15	upside-down, and with the lid hanging open. Alice looked at it with great curiosity.
T1	115:12	hold you! And don't keep your mouth so wide open! All the ashes will get into it--there, now I think
T9	199:22	At this moment the door was flung open, and a shrill voice was heard singing:--
T1	111: 3	you leave the door of our drawing-room wide open: and it's very like our passage as far as you can see,
T5	152:16	oh!" As she said the words the brooch flew open, and the Queen clutched wildly at it, and tried to clasp
A1	9:38	was too small, but at any rate it would not open any of them. However, on the second time round, she came
T3	137: 5	of the Fawn, till they came out into another open field, and here the Fawn gave a sudden bound into the air
T3	135:22	She very soon came to an open field, with a wood on the other side of it: it looked
A12	93:14	to do anything but sit with its mouth open, gazing up into the roof of the court.
A5	42: 2	her foot, that there was hardly room to open her mouth; but she did it at last, and managed to swallow
T1	108:31	that's your fault, for keeping your eyes open--if you'd shut them tight up, it wouldn't have happened.
A4	29:25	the Rabbit came up to the door, and tried to open it; but, as the door opened inwards, and Alice's elbow
T7	170: 4	was very glad to get out of the wood into an open place, where she found the White King seated on the
A5	44: 1	As she said this, she came suddenly upon an open place, with a little house in it about four feet high.
T7	175:37	the King muttered, and beckoned to Haigha. "Open the bag!" he whispered. "Quick! Not that one--that's full
A12	98:35	in Wonderland, though she knew she had but to open them again, and all would change to dull reality--the
T8	182:16	time to manage, though Alice held the bag open very carefully, because the Knight was so very awkward in
T2	124:19	now," the Queen said looking at her watch: "open your mouth a little wider when you speak, and always say

OPENED (15)
T7	172: 1	the Messenger, to Alice's great amusement, opened a bag that hung round his neck, and handed a sandwich
T9	198: 9	Just then the door opened a little way, and a creature with a long beak put its
A6	46:27	At this moment the door of the house opened, and a large plate came skimming out, straight at the
A6	45: 6	loudly at the door with his knuckles. It was opened by another footman in livery, with a round face, and
T9	201:30	frightened at finding that, the moment she opened her lips, there was dead silence, and all eyes were

OPENED (cont.)
```
  T6   168:35   see if he would speak again, but, as he never opened his eyes or took any further notice of her, she said
  A7    55:11                         The Hatter opened his eyes very wide on hearing this; but all he said was
  T7   175: 7      he repeated softly to himself, as he opened his memorandum-book. "Do you spell 'creature' with a
  A4    29:26   door, and tried to open it; but, as the door opened inwards, and Alice's elbow was pressed hard against it,
  A1    12:32   glass box that was lying under the table: she opened it, and found in it a very small cake, on which the
  A12   94: 7                          "I haven't opened it yet," said the White Rabbit; "but it seems to be a
  A7    58:25              The Dormouse slowly opened its eyes. "I wasn't asleep," it said in a hoarse,
  A1    10: 1                              Alice opened the door and found that it led into a small passage,
  A6    46:44         "he's perfectly idiotic!" And she opened the door and went in.
  A10   82: 4   got so close to her, one on each side, and opened their eyes and mouths so very wide; but she gained
```
OPENING (5)
```
  T4   147: 6   with only his head out: and there he lay, opening and shutting his mouth and his large eyes--"looking
  A5    35: 5              This was not an encouraging opening for a conversation. Alice replied, rather shyly, "I--I
  A7    56:25   shook its head impatiently, and said, without opening its eyes, "Of course, of course: just what I was going
  A2    14: 3   forgot how to speak good English). "Now I'm opening out like the largest telescope that ever was! Good-bye
  T1   108:23      you had been doing, I was very nearly opening the window, and putting you out into the snow! And
```
OPERA-GLASS (1)
```
  T3   130:19   through a microscope, and then through an opera-glass. At last he said "You're traveling the wrong way,"
```
OPINION (2)
```
  A7    59:15                  "Nobody asked your opinion," said Alice.
  T2   122:32              "It's my opinion that you never think at all," the Rose said, in a
```
OPPORTUNITY (10)
```
  A8    68:18   hedgehog, which seemed to Alice an excellent opportunity for croqueting one of them with the other: the
  A4    33: 3                  This seemed to Alice a good opportunity for making her escape: so she set off at once, and
  A6    46:38   The Footman seemed to think this a good opportunity for repeating his remark, with variations. "I
  A1     8:32         and though this was not a very good opportunity for showing off her knowledge, as there was no one
  A5    43:22   a minute or two, which gave the Pigeon the opportunity of adding "You're looking for eggs, I know that
  T9   193:19                 "We gave you the opportunity of doing it," the Red Queen remarked: "but I
  A3    26:17   quite out of sight. And an old Crab took the opportunity of saying to her daughter "Ah, my dear! Let this
  A6    48:24   said Alice, who felt very glad to get an opportunity of showing off a little of her knowledge. "Just
  A11   87: 7   and got behind him, and very soon found an opportunity of taking it away. She did it so quickly that the
  T4   147:39   fight to-day," said Alice, thinking it a good opportunity to make peace.
```
OPPOSITE (5)
```
  T2   124: 1   try the plan, this time, of walking in the opposite direction.
  T6   159:11   and, as his eyes were steadily fixed in the opposite direction, and he didn't take the least notice of her
  A8    63:34              When the procession came opposite to Alice, they all stopped and looked at her, and the
  T3   130:22   So young a child," said the gentleman sitting opposite to her, (he was dressed in white paper), "ought to
  T5   153:38   leaning with her elbows on the counter, and opposite to her was an old Sheep, sitting in an arm-chair,
```
OR (132)
```
  A8    66:15   besides all this, there was generally a ridge or a furrow in the way wherever she wanted to send the
  A5    43:24   it matter to me whether you're a little girl or a serpent?"
  T5   155: 7                  "Are you a child or a teetotum?" the Sheep said, as she took up another pair of
  A1     8: 2   seen a rabbit with either a waistcoat-pocket, or a watch to take out of it, and burning with curiosity, she
  A3    22:19      said the Duck: "it's generally a frog, or a worm. The question is, what did the archbishop find?"
  T9   201: 3   the bow, not knowing whether to be frightened or amused.
  A10   84:27   "Beautiful Soup! Who cares for fish, / Game, or any other dish? / Who would not give all else for two p /
  T12  207: 8   would only purr for 'yes,' and mew for 'no,' or any rule of that sort," she had said, "so that one could
  T9   200: 2   fill up the glasses with treacle and ink, / Or anything else that is pleasant to drink: / Mix sand with
  T9   199:15   English, doesn't I?" the Frog went on. "Or are you deaf? What did it ask you?"
  A1    10:14   half hoping she might find another key on it, or at any rate a book of rules for shutting people up like
  T1   119: 3   of the room in a moment, and ran down stairs--or, at least, it wasn't exactly running, but a new invention
  A8    67:17   it," she thought, "till its ears have come, or at least one of them." In another minute the whole head
  A1     8:45   you know. Please, Ma'am, is this New Zealand? Or Australia?" (and she tried to curtsey as she spoke--fancy,
  AI     3:23   wild and new, / In friendly chat with bird or beast--/ And half believe it true.
  T8   188:38   night. / And these I do not sell for gold / Or coin of silvery shine, / But for a copper halfpenny, / And
  A1     7: 5   of a book," thought Alice, "without pictures or conversations?"
  A1     7: 4   sister was reading, but it had no pictures or conversations in it, "and what is the use of a book,"
  A8    64: 2   whether they were gardeners, or soldiers, or courtiers, or three of her own children.
  T9   202:18   is easiest to do, / Un-dish-cover the fish, or dishcover the riddle?"
  A2    20:15   back again, and we wo'n't talk about cats, or dogs either, if you don't like them!" When the Mouse heard
  A4    28: 6   happen," she said to herself, "whenever I eat or drink anything: so I'll just see what this bottle does. I
  A4    33:12   is it to be managed? I suppose I ought to eat or drink something or other; but the great question is 'What'
  A4    34: 2   that looked like the right thing to eat or drink under the circumstances. There was a large mushroom
  T8   186:37   either it brings the tears into their eyes, or else--"
  T7   172:22      "He ca'n't do that," said the King, "or else he'd have been here first. However, now you've got
  T8   186:40                  "Or else it doesn't, you know. The name of the song is called
  T8   186:38                  "Or else what?" said Alice, for the Knight had made a sudden
  A12   94:24   worse. You must have meant some mischief, or else you'd have signed your name like an honest man."
  T8   190:31   side and then on the other. After the fourth or fifth tumble he reached the turn, and then she waved her
  A6    53: 1                  "Did you say 'pig', or 'fig'?" said the Cat.
  A6    50: 5   now!" The poor little thing sobbed again (or grunted, it was impossible to say which), and they went on
  A9    73:15                  "I never saw one, or heard of one," said Alice.
  A2    19: 7   was: at first she thought it must be a walrus or hippopotamus, but then she remembered how small she was now
  T8   189:19   a right-hand foot / Into a left-hand shoe, / Or if I drop upon my toe / A very heavy weight, / I weep, for
  A9    72: 6   of that is--'Be what you would seem to be'--or, if you'd like it put more simply--'Never imagine yourself
  A11   90: 5   "You must remember," remarked the King, "or I'll have you executed."
  A11   88:28      said the King: "and don't be nervous, or I'll have you executed on the spot."
  A11   89: 9   your evidence," the King repeated angrily, "or I'll have you executed, whether you are nervous or not."
  A5    40: 8   I can listen all day to such stuff? / Be off, or I'll kick you down-stairs!"
```

OR (cont.)
```
T9    194:43  flower?" the White Queen asked: "In a garden or in the hedges?"
A6     48:31  went on  again: "Twenty-four hours, I think; or is it twelve? I--"
A3     25:30  the cur, Such a trial, dear sir, With no jury or judge, would be wasting our breath. 'I'll be judge, I'll be
A6     46:15  now and  then a great crash, as if a dish or kettle had been broken to pieces.
A1     11: 5  almost certain to disagree with you, sooner or later.
T1    109: 4  sent to prison, I suppose, when the day came. Or--let me see--suppose each punishment was to be going
A1      8:36  had not the slightest idea what Latitude was, or Longitude either, but she thought they were nice grand
A1      8:35  distance--but then I  wonder  what Latitude or Longitude I've got to?" (Alice had not the slightest idea
T8    189:17  by chance I put / My fingers into glue, / Or madly squeeze a right-hand foot / Into a left-hand shoe, /
A9     72: 8  it might appear to others that what you were or might have been was not otherwise than what you had been
T7    176: 6  Alice wearily. "Are you animal--or vegetable--or mineral?" he said, yawning at every other word.
A12    95: 6  one, they gave him two, / You gave us three or more; / They all returned from him to you, / Though they
A6     46:30                                            "--or next day, maybe," the Footman continued in the same tone,
T12   207:12  impossible to guess whether it meant "yes" or "no."
A6     48:15  impossible to say whether the blows hurt it or not.
A11    89:10  have you executed, whether you are nervous or not."
T4    148: 3  cried Tweedledum, "whether I can see it or not!"
T3    131:44  wanted to know was, whether it could sting or not, but she thought this wouldn't be quite a civil
A1     10:21  said, "and see whether it's marked 'poison' or not"; for she had read several nice little stories about
A8     68:15  that she never knew whether it was her turn or not. So she went off in search of her hedgehog.
T6    166:27   "If you can see whether I'm singing or not, you've sharper eyes than most," Humpty Dumpty remarked
A4     34:11  and taking not the smallest notice of her or of anything else.
A8     67: 1  about, and shouting "Off with his head!" or "Off with her head!" about once in a minute.
A9     73: 4  players, and shouting "Off with his head!" or "Off with her head!" Those whom she sentenced were taken
T4    147:17  one of these things has got to go on, somehow or other."
T7    169: 7  they were always tripping over something or other, and whenever one went down, several more always fell
A4     33:12  I suppose I ought to eat or drink something or other; but the great question is 'What'?"
T2    126:11  be a Queen--"Just at this moment, somehow or other, they began to run.
A2     15: 1  but I must be kind to them," thought Alice, "or perhaps they wo'n't walk the way I want to go! Let me see.
A12    98:22  get into her eyes--and still as she listened, or seemed to listen, the whole place around her became alive
T8    188:42  'I sometimes dig for buttered rolls, / Or set limed twigs for crabs: / I sometimes search for grassy
A1      8:11           Either the well was very deep, or she fell very slowly, for she had plenty of time as she
A12    95: 9                     If I or she should chance to be / Involved in this affair, / He
A8     68: 6  one way of settling all difficulties, great or small. "Off with his head!" she said without even looking
T4    142:14  Walrus and the Carpenter / Walked on a mile or so, / And then they rested on a rock / Conveniently low: /
A3     23:13  when they had  been running half an hour or so, and were quite dry again, the Dodo suddenly called out
A11    89:12  "and I hadn't begun my tea--not above a week or so--and what with the bread-and-butter getting so thin--and
T5    154:17  plaintive tone, after she had spent a minute or so in vainly pursuing a large bright thing that looked
A9     73: 7  do this, so that, by the end of half an hour or so, there were no arches left, and all the players, except
A8     64: 2  could not tell whether they were gardeners, or soldiers, or courtiers, or three of her own children.
T7    172:12  you would be better," Alice suggested: "--or some sal-volatile."
T8    181:32              "But you've got a bee-hive--or something like one--fastened to the saddle," said Alice.
A4     29:42  possible it had fallen into a cucumber-frame, or something of the sort.
T8    181:37  I suppose the mice keep the bees out--or the bees keep the mice out, I don't know which."
A1      9:37  but, alas! either the locks were too large, or the key was too small, but at any rate it would not open
T7    177: 1  good long way. Did you go by the old bridge, or the market-place? You get the best view by the old bridge
T6    168:30  on the same side of the nose, for instance--or the mouth at the top--that would be some help."
T12   208: 8  You see, Kitty, it must have been either me or the Red King. He was part of my dream, of course--but then
A12    92:12  at once and put back into the jury-box, or they would die.
T2    122:12  bending its quivering head towards Alice, "or they wouldn't dare to do it!"
T9    195:32  Now here, we mostly have days and nights two or three at a time, and sometimes in the winter we take as
A8     64: 2  were gardeners, or soldiers, or courtiers, or three of her own children.
T8    184: 4  said, as if he didn't mind breaking two or three of them. "The great art of riding, as I was saying is
A4     27:38  and on it (as she had hoped) a fan and two or three pairs of tiny white kid-gloves: she took up the fan
A11    86:24  are the jurors." She said this last word two or three times over to herself, being rather proud of it: for
T8    182:17  awkward in putting in the dish: the first two or three times that he tried he fell in himself instead. "It's
T1    108:17  the bonfire to-morrow." Here Alice wound two or three turns of the worsted round the kitten's neck, just to
T4    144:26  to be a wild beast. "Are there any lions or tigers about here?" she asked timidly.
T6    168:35  speak again, but, as he never opened his eyes or took any further notice of her, she said "Good-bye!" once
T7    169: 2  wood, at first in twos and threes, then ten or twenty together, and at last in such crowds that they
A5     41:25  the hookah out of its mouth, and yawned once or twice, and shook itself. Then it got down off the mushroom,
A7     60: 3  of her going, though she looked back once or twice, half hoping that they would call after her: the last
A1      7: 2  on the bank and of having nothing to do: once or twice she had peeped into the book her sister was reading,
A7     59: 2  said the Dormouse, after thinking a minute or two.
T9    193:13  was an uncomfortable silence for a minute or two.
T7    174:20                  For a minute or two Alice stood silent, watching him. Suddenly she
A8     65:43  however, they got settled down in a minute or two, and the game began.
A6     49:20  so that altogether, for the first minute or two, it was as much as she could do to hold it.
A8     65:14  three soldiers wandered about for a minute or two, looking for them, and then quietly marched off after
T3    134:20  After this, Alice was silent for a minute or two, pondering. The Gnat amused itself meanwhile by humming
T8    184:19  the Knight said thoughtfully to himself. "One or two--several."
T1    114: 9  quite taken away her breath, and for a minute or two she could do nothing but hug the little Lily in silence
A8     67:11  much at first, but after watching it a minute or two she made it out to be a grin, and she said to herself
A6     45: 1                          For a minute or two she stood looking at the house, and wondering what to
A6     52:23  but it did not appear, and after a minute or two she walked on in the direction in which the March Hare
A10    78: 3  Alice and tried to speak, but, for a minute or two, sobs choked his voice. "Same as if he had a bone in
A5     41:24  until it chose to speak again. In a minute or two the Caterpillar took the hookah out of its mouth, and
A4     31:37  they'd take the roof off." After a minute or two they began moving about again, and Alice heard the
A7     59:22          The Dormouse again took a minute or two to think about it, and then said "It was a treacle-well
```

OR (cont.)
```
T7    173:31   looked   round once more, and this time a tear or two trickled down his cheek; but not a word would he say.
T6    162:23   angry,   though   he   said nothing for a minute or two. When he did speak again, it was in a deep growl.
A5     43:22   Alice, that she was quite silent for a minute or two, which gave the Pigeon the opportunity of adding
T5    156: 2   there   was   no more conversation for a minute or two, while the boat glided gently on, sometimes among beds
A6     49:27   Alice,   "they're   sure   to   kill   it in a day or two. Wouldn't it be murder to leave it behind?" She said
T7    176: 5   looked at Alice wearily. "Are you animal--or vegetable--or mineral?" he said, yawning at every other
T9    201:11   pudding, please," Alice said rather hastily, "or we shall get no dinner at all. May I give you some?"
T2    128:29   was   gone. Whether she vanished into the air, or whether she ran quickly into the wood ("and she can run
A10    84: 9   the Lobster-Quadrille?" the Gryphon went on. "Or would you like the Mock Turtle to sing you another song?"
T6    160:32   doors--and behind trees--and down chimneys--or you couldn't have known it!"
A6     51:26                   "You must be," said the Cat, "or you wouldn't have come here."
A7     58:30   "And   quick about it," added the Hatter, "or you'll be asleep again before it's done."
A9     72:37   on   the   ground   as she spoke; "either you or your head must be off, and that in about half no time! Take
```
ORANGE (1)
```
A1     8:18   of the shelves as she passed: it was labeled "ORANGE MARMALADE," but to her great disappointment it was
```
ORDER (5)
```
T5    149:35   brush,   and did her best to get the hair into order. "Come, you look rather better now!" she said, after
A10    78:24   "--change   lobsters,   and   retire   in   same order," continued the Gryphon.
A6     46: 1   in   the   same   solemn tone, only changing the order of the words a little, "From the Queen. An invitation
A10    82:17                       "How the creatures order one about, and make one repeat lessons!" thought Alice.
T7    174:18   more to-day," the King said to Hatta: "go and order the drums to begin." And Hatta went bounding away like a
```
ORDERED (4)
```
A9     73:21   at   the   number   of   executions the Queen had ordered.
A9     74:14   as she went slowly after it: "I never was so ordered about before, in all my life, never!"
A4     28:28   always   growing larger and smaller, and being ordered about by mice and rabbits. I almost wish I hadn't gone
A9     74: 3   go   back and see after some executions I have ordered;" and she walked off, leaving Alice alone with the
```
ORDERING (2)
```
A12    98:28   meal,   and   the   shrill   voice   of the Queen ordering off her unfortunate guests to execution--once more
A4     27:34   let   Dinah   stop   in   the   house if it began ordering people about like that!"
```
ORDERS (1)
```
T9    201:16   the   Red Queen should be the only one to give orders; so, as an experiment, she called out "Waiter! Bring
```
-ORDINARY [See EXTRAORDINARY]
ORNAMENTED (2)
```
A8     63:17   corners:   next   the ten courtiers: these were ornamented all over with diamonds, and walked two and two, as
A8     63:21   hand   in   hand,   in   couples:   they were all ornamented with hearts. Next came the guests, mostly Kings and
```
OTHER (106)
```
A12    93: 9   as   much   use   in the trial one way up as the other."
T4    147:17   of   these things has got to go on, somehow or other."
T7    173:22   hand   and   a piece of bread-and-butter in the other.
T9    201: 5   and   fork, and looking from one Queen to the other.
T4    139:23   hands!"   And here the two brothers gave each other a hug, and then they held out the two hands that were
T8    190:31   off,   first   on   one side and then on the other. After the fourth or fifth tumble he reached the turn,
T1    113: 3   "They   don't   keep   this room so tidy as the other," Alice thought to herself, as she noticed several of
T6    162:34   thoughtfully   as he crossed one knee over the other and clasped his hands round it, "they gave it me--for an
T4    139:12   But   the   fat   little men only looked at each other and grinned.
A5     43:34     nibbling first   at   one   and   then at the other, and growing sometimes taller, and sometimes shorter,
A4     29:16   went   on,   taking first one side and then the other, and making quite a conversation of it altogether; but
T9    192:31             The two Queens looked at each other, and the Red Queen remarked, with a little shudder, "She
T7    169: 7   they   were   always   tripping over something or other, and whenever one went down, several more always fell
A4     28:18   down with one elbow against the door, and the other arm curled round her head. Still she went on growing,
A4     30:26   I   hadn't   to   bring   one. Bill's got the other--Bill! Fetch it here, lad!--Here, put 'em up at this
A3     22:34   down   its   head   to hide a smile: some of the other birds tittered audibly.
A5     41:43   so she set to work at once to eat some of the other bit. Her chin was pressed so closely against her foot,
A4     33:12   suppose   I ought to eat or drink something or other; but the great question is 'What'?"
A6     50:18   pig,   I   think."   And she began thinking over other children she knew, who might do very well as pigs, and
A2     20:23   and a Dodo, a Lory and an Eaglet, and several other curious creatures. Alice led the way, and the whole
T5    156:39   Alice hardly noticed this, there were so many other curious things to think about.
T5    149:39   Queen   said. "Two pence a week, and jam every other day."
T5    150: 8   it   ca'n't,"   said the Queen. "It's jam every other day: to-day isn't any other day, you know."
T5    150: 9   "It's   jam   every other day: to-day isn't any other day, you know."
TI    103:13                     A tale begun in other days, / When summer suns were glowing--/ A simple chime,
T4    138: 4   had   'DUM' embroidered on his collar, and the other 'DEE.' "I suppose they've got 'TWEEDLE' round at the
A10    84:27   Soup! Who cares for fish, / Game, or any other dish? / Who would not give all else for two p /
T9    201:39   it,"   the   White Queen murmured into Alice's other ear, in a voice like the cooing of a pigeon. "It would
A8     67:28   got   to   go through next walking about at the other end of the ground--and I should have croqueted the
T5    158:16   yourself." And so saying, she went off to the other end of the shop, and set the egg upright on a shelf.
T6    162: 8                       "Too proud?" the other enquired.
T2    123: 5                   "There's one other flower in the garden that can move about like you," said
T6    166:15   great   hands, "I can repeat poetry as well as other folk, if it comes to that--"
A5     35: 1   The Caterpillar and Alice looked at each other for some time in silence: at last the Caterpillar took
T8    179:25   and   the   two Knights sat and looked at each other for some time without speaking. Alice looked from one to
A9     72:43                       The other guests had taken advantage of the Queen's absence, and
A11    90:26                   Here the other guinea-pig cheered, and was suppressed.
A2     15:28   kid-gloves in one hand and a large fan in the other: he came trotting along in a great hurry, muttering to
T8    180: 4   Rule seems to be, that if one Knight hits the other, he knocks him off his horse; and, if he misses, he
A8     65:43   in all   directions, tumbling up against each other: however, they got settled down in a minute or two, and
A11    88: 7   hand   and a piece of bread-and-butter in the other. "I beg pardon, your Majesty," he began, "for bringing
T8    179:26   speaking.   Alice looked from one to the other in some bewilderment.
A11    86: 6   in one hand, and a scroll of parchment in the other. In the very middle of the court was a table, with a
```

OTHER (cont.)
A4	30:25	she made out the words: "Where's the other ladder?--Why, I hadn't to bring but one. Bill's got the
T4	139:32	out) by the branches rubbing one across the other, like fiddles and fiddle-sticks.
A12	99: 6	childhood; and how she would gather about her other little children, and make their eyes bright and eager
A11	88:31	at all: he kept shifting from one foot to the other, looking uneasily at the Queen, and in his confusion he
T7	173:20	placed themselves close to where Hatta, the other Messenger, was standing watching the fight, with a cup
T7	170:36	for the name of a town beginning with H. "The other Messenger's called Hatta. I must have two, you know--to
T12	207:15	put the kitten and the Queen to look at each other. "Now Kitty!" she cried, clapping her hands triumphantly
T8W	20:13	a-fighting, now--could you get hold of the other one by the back of the neck?"
T4	139:26	either of them first, for fear of hurting the other one's feelings; so, as the best way out of the
T4	142: 7	Four other Oysters followed them, / And yet another four; / And
A8	66:18	were always getting up and walking off to other parts of the ground, Alice soon came to the conclusion
T12	208:13	But the provoking kitten only began on the other paw, and pretended it hadn't heard the question.
A6	51:20	a Hatter: and in that direction," waving the other paw, "lives a March Hare. Visit either you like: they're
T1	107: 8	by its ear with one paw, and then with the other paw she rubbed its face all over, the wrong way,
T6	168:23	his fingers to shake: "you're so exactly like other people."
T3	131:36	to comfort it, "if it would only sigh like other people!" she thought. But this was such a wonderfully
T9	192:22	only spoke when you were spoken to, and the other person always waited for you to begin, you see nobody
T7	176:14	the two great creatures; but there was no other place for him.
A9	73: 4	the Queen never left off quarreling with the other players, and shouting "Off with his head!" or "Off with
A12	98:41	baby, the shriek of the Gryphon, and all the other queer noises, would change (she knew) to the confused
T6	164: 7	Alice. She was too much puzzled to make any other remark.
T9	197:13	as first one round head, and then the other, rolled down from her shoulder, and lay like a heavy
T1	110:41	the glass, and then they hold up one in the other room.
T4	147:44	"Very well," the other said, rather sadly: "and she can watch us--only you'd
T7	175:30	"Well, now that we have seen each other," said the Unicorn, "if you'll believe in me, I'll
A6	45:13	as himself, and this he handed over to the other, saying, in a solemn tone, "For the Duchess. An
T9	198: 4	one was marked "Visitors' Bell," and the other "Servants' Bell."
T9	197: 9	added, as she put her head down on Alice's other shoulder, "just sing it through to me. I'm getting
T8	183: 8	to save himself from falling over on the other side.
T3	135:22	came to an open field, with a wood on the other side of it: it looked much darker than the last wood,
T5	153:36	was it really a sheep that was sitting on the other side of the counter? Rub as she would, she could make
A11	89: 3	got up very sulkily and crossed over to the other side of the court.
A8	68:20	was, that her flamingo was gone across the other side of the garden, where Alice could see it trying in a
A5	41:29	"One side of what? The other side of what?" thought Alice to herself.
A10	80: 8	/ "There is another shore, you know, upon the other side. / The further off from England the nearer is to
A4	32:38	run over; and, the moment she appeared on the other side, the puppy made another rush at the stick, and
A5	41:27	"One side will make you grow taller, and the other side will make you grow shorter."
T8W	14: 9	"Won't you let me help you round to the other side? You'll be out of the cold wind there."
A6	48: 8	thought it would be as well to introduce some other subject of conversation. While she was trying to fix on
T4	147:10	"I suppose so," the other sulkily replied, as he crawled out of the umbrella:
A6	47: 1	which was full of smoke from one end to the other: the Duchess was sitting on a three-legged stool in the
A8	68:19	for croqueting one of them with the other: the only difficulty was, that her flamingo was gone
T2	126:11	be a Queen--"Just at this moment, somehow or other, they began to run.
T8	181:36	a single bee has come near it yet. And the other thing is a mouse-trap. I suppose the mice keep the bees
T8	182:21	bunches of carrots, and fire-irons, and many other things.
T2	126:19	part of the thing was, that the trees and the other things round them never changed their places at all:
T8	186:27	what a difference it makes, mixing it with other things--such as gunpowder and sealing-wax. And here I
T9	204:23	At any other time, Alice would have felt surprised at this, but she
T3	137:23	one marked "TO TWEEDLEDUM'S HOUSE," and the other "TO THE HOUSE OF TWEEDLEDEE."
A1	9:32	had been all the way down one side and up the other, trying every door, she walked sadly down the middle,
T4	139:39	The other two dancers were fat, and very soon out of breath. "Four
A7	54: 1	sitting between them, fast asleep, and the other two were using it as a cushion, resting their elbows on
A1	10:23	got burnt, and eaten up by wild beasts, and other unpleasant things, all because they would not remember
T3	131:18	And after that other voices went on ("What a number of people there are in
A6	46: 7	out, the Fish-Footman was gone, and the other was sitting on the ground near the door, staring
T2	120: 8	back to the house! Well then, I'll try it the other way."
T2	123:39	the Rose: "I should advise you to walk the other way."
T9	195:21	she hastily corrected herself. "I meant the other way."
T1	110:33	as our drawing-room, only the things go the other way. I can see all of it when I get upon a chair--all
T3	129:25	"I think I'll go down the other way," she said after a pause; "and perhaps I may visit
T8	185: 4	of it was, before I could get out again, the other White Knight came and put it on. He thought it was his
T8	179:37	Knight, and they began banging away at each other with such fury that Alice got behind a tree to be out of
T7	176: 6	or mineral?" he said, yawning at every other word.

OTHER'S (1)
| T4 | 138: 2 | under a tree, each with an arm round the other's neck, and Alice knew which was which in a moment, |

OTHERS (9)
A4	31:26	"So you did, old fellow!" said the others.
A8	62:10	"That's right, Five! Always lay the blame on others!"
A8	65:15	them, and then quietly marched off after the others.
A3	26:14	your story!" Alice called after it. And the others all joined in chorus "Yes, please do!" But the Mouse
A8	63: 2	them, and he checked himself suddenly: the others looked round also, and all of them bowed low.
T5	154:14	shelf was always quite empty, though the others round it were crowded as full as they could hold.
A9	72: 8	to be otherwise than what it might appear to others that what you were or might have been was not otherwise
A7	60:31	fell asleep instantly, and neither of the others took the least notice of her going, though she looked
T9	202:24	and drank all that trickled down their faces--others upset the decanters, and drank the wine as it ran off

OTHERWISE (5)
A9	72:10	had been would have appeared to them to be otherwise.'"
T8	182:42	did rather suddenly), he fell off behind. Otherwise he kept on pretty well, except that he had a habit
A6	45: 4	him to be a footman because he was in livery: otherwise, judging by his face only, she would have called him

OTHERWISE (cont.)
A9   72: 7 simply--'Never imagine yourself not to be otherwise than what it might appear to others that what you
A9   72: 9 that what you were or might have been was not otherwise than what you had been would have appeared to them
OU (1)
A2   19:25 anything had happened.) So she began again: "Ou est ma chatte?" which was the first sentence in her French
OUGHT (33)
T8   184:13 to have a wooden horse on wheels, that you ought!"
A4   29: 6 to be a book written about me, that there ought! And when I grow up, I'll write one--but I'm grown up
T1   108: 1 ought to have taught you better manners! You ought, Dinah, you know you ought!" she added, looking
T3   137:15 again. And now, which of these finger-posts ought I to follow, I wonder?"
A8   63:28 Alice was rather doubtful whether she ought not to lie down on her face like the three gardeners,
T1   108: 1 manners! You ought, Dinah, you know you ought!" she added, looking reproachfully at the old cat, and
A4   29: 5 and now here I am in the middle of one! There ought to be a book written about me, that there ought! And
A2   15:20   "You ought to be ashamed of yourself," said Alice, "a great girl
A9   75: 4   "You ought to be ashamed of yourself for asking such a simple
T6   168:18 but, after such a very strong hint that she ought to be going, she felt that it would hardly be civil to
A12   93:44   "Then it ought to be Number One," said Alice.
T9   198: 8 not a visitor, and I'm not a servant. There ought to be one marked 'Queen,' you know--"
T2   125:26 chess-board!" Alice said at last. "There ought to be some men moving about somewhere--and so there are!
A6   51: 3 and a great many teeth, so she felt that it ought to be treated with respect.
A4   33:12 me see--how is it to be managed? I suppose I ought to eat or drink something or other; but the great
A6   51: 7 on. "Would you tell me, please, which way I ought to go from here?"
T8   184:12 losing all her patience this time. "You ought to have a wooden horse on wheels, that you ought!"
A8   63: 6 "Why, the fact is, you see, Miss, this here ought to have been a red rose-tree, and we put a white one in
A11   88:10   "You ought to have finished," said the King. "When did you begin?"
T8   187: 4   "Then I ought to have said 'That's what the song is called'?" Alice
T1   107:22 that it was in disgrace. "Really, Dinah ought to have taught you better manners! You ought, Dinah, you
A1   7:14 over afterwards it occurred to her that she ought to have wondered at this, but at the time it all seemed
T9   193:18 Alice; "but, if there is to be one, I think I ought to invite the guests."
T3   131: 4 shut his eyes and said in a loud voice, "She ought to know her way to the ticket-office, even if she
T12 208:11 Kitty? You were his wife, my dear, so you ought to know--Oh, Kitty, do help to settle it! I'm sure your
T3   130:22 to her, (he was dressed in white paper), "ought to know which way she's going, even if she doesn't know
T6   166:21 Alice felt that in that case she really ought to listen to it; so she sat down, and said "Thank you"
T4   138:10 "If you think we're wax-works," he said, "you ought to pay, you know. Wax-works weren't made to be looked at
T9   202:29   "You ought to return thanks in a neat speech," the Red Queen said,
T9   196:25 Queen looked timidly at Alice, who felt she ought to say something kind, but really couldn't think of
T4   138:14 marked 'DEE,' "if you think we're alive, you ought to speak."
A3   23: 4 had paused as if it thought that somebody ought to speak, and no one else seemed inclined to say
A5   36:13 up and said, very gravely, "I think you ought to tell me who you are, first."
OUGHTN'T (1)
T8   187: 6   "No, you oughtn't: that's quite another thing! The song is called 'Ways
OUR (22) [entries omitted]
OURS (1) [entry omitted]
OURSELVES (1) [entry omitted]
OUT (234) [entries omitted]
OUTGRABE (5)
T1   116:12   .ebargtuo shtar emom eht dnA / ,sevogorob eht erew ysmim llA / :ebaw eht
T1   116:21 were the borogoves, / And the mome raths outgrabe.
T1   118:24 were the borogoves, / And the mome raths outgrabe.
T6   164:24 were the borogoves, / And the mome raths outgrabe."
T6   166: 6   "And what does 'outgrabe' mean?"
OUTGRIBING (1)
T6   166: 7   "Well, 'outgribing' is something between bellowing and whistling, with
OUT-OF-THE-WAY (3)
A2   19:11 "to speak to this mouse? Everything is so out-of-the-way down here, that I should think very likely it
A1   10:10 knew how to begin." For, you see, so many out-of-the-way things had happened lately, that Alice had
A1   13: 2 so much into the way of expecting nothing but out-of-the-way things to happen, that it seemed quite dull and
OUTSIDE (5)
T4   146: 7   "But it may rain outside?"
A4   29:18 but after a few minutes she heard a voice outside, and stopped to listen.
A12   94:13 "in fact, there's nothing written on the outside." He unfolded the paper as he spoke, and added "It
A4   32:13 a crowd of little animals and birds waiting outside. The poor little Lizard, Bill, was in the middle,
A11   91: 1   "--and just take his head off outside," the Queen added to one of the officers; but the
OVER (95)
A1   9:20 of sticks and dry leaves, and the fall was over.
A8   64:13 from him, and said to the Knave "Turn them over!"
T9   204:26 little creature in the very act of jumping over a bottle which had just lighted upon the table, "I'll
T8   184:26 then I was inventing a new way of getting over a gate--would you like to hear it?"
A9   77:17 quite a new idea to Alice, and she thought it over a little before she made her next remark. "Then the
T2   126:22 never could quite make out, in thinking it over afterwards, how it was that they began: all she remembers
A1   7:14 I shall be too late!" (when she thought it over afterwards it occurred to her that she ought to have
T5   152:26 "What would be the good of having it all over again?"
A10   82:14 if he thought it had some kind of authority over Alice.
A7   55:33 sat silent for a minute, while Alice thought over all she could remember about ravens and writing-desks,
A2   16: 1 the great puzzle!" And she began thinking over all the children she knew that were of the same age as
T1   113:20 the King, so violently that she knocked him over among the cinders. "My precious Lily! My imperial kitten!
T1   113:17 in time to see one of the White Pawns roll over and begin kicking: she watched it with great curiosity to
A8   68:23 flamingo and brought it back, the fight was over, and both the hedgehogs were out of sight: "but it
A2   19:40 for this time the Mouse was bristling all over, and she felt certain it must be really offended. "We
A4   32:37 great thistle, to keep herself from being run over; and, the moment she appeared on the other side, the

OVER (cont.)

A3	23:15	the Dodo suddenly called out "The race is over!" and they all crowded round it, panting, and asking "But
T7	169: 4	got behind a tree, for fear of being run over, and watched them go by.
A10	80:14	said Alice, feeling very glad that it was over at last: "and I do so like that curious song about the
A3	24:12	had to be patted on the back. However, it was over at last, and they sat down again in a ring, and begged
T4	147: 5	quite succeed, and it ended in his rolling over, bundling up in the umbrella, with only his head out: and
A10	80:23	their tails in their mouths--and they're all over crumbs."
T3	132: 6	and said "It's only a brook we have to jump over." Everybody seemed satisfied with this, though Alice felt
T8W	13:12	herself on the very edge. "If I once jump over, everything will change, and then I can't help him."
A4	32:39	another rush at the stick, and tumbled head over heels in its hurry to get hold of it: then Alice,
T5	152: 7	that Alice had to hold both her hands over her ears.
T5	152:24	Alice asked, holding her hands ready to put over her ears again.
T7	178: 9	she dropped to her knees, and put her hands over her ears, vainly trying to shut out the dreadful uproar.
T3	132:19	to) was balancing itself on a twig just over her head, and fanning her with its wings.
A4	32:25	among the trees, a little sharp bark just over her head made her look up in a great hurry.
T12	207:26	"Snowdrop, my pet!" she went on, looking over her shoulder at the White Kitten, which was still
A3	23:34	"Hand it over here," said the Dodo.
T8W	13:19	Alice said to herself, and she stooped over him, and said very kindly, "I hope you're not in much
T1	115:17	to see if she could find any water to throw over him. However, she could find nothing but a bottle of ink,
T1	116: 3	about him, and had the ink all ready to throw over him, in case he fainted again), she turned over the
T7	169: 8	one went down, several more always fell over him, so that the ground was soon covered with little
T4	146: 4	Tweedledum spread a large umbrella over himself and his brother, and looked up into it. "No, I
T6	159: 6	of it, as if his name were written all over his face!"
T8	181:24	the Knight said, a shade of vexation passing over his face. "Then all the things must have fallen out! And
T1	115:32	of the end of the pencil, which came some way over his shoulder, and began writing for him.
A8	65:30	in a low hurried tone. He looked anxiously over his shoulder as he spoke, and then raised himself upon
A7	56:11	Alice had been looking over his shoulder with some curiosity. "What a funny watch!"
A3	23:13	it was not easy to know when the race was over. However, when they had been running half an hour or so,
A7	54: 4	resting their elbows on it, and talking over its head. "Very uncomfortable for the Dormouse," thought
A8	62: 6	"Look out now, Five! Don't go splashing paint over me like that!"
T8	183: 8	with one hand, to save himself from falling over on the other side.
A6	50:18	pig, I think." And she began thinking over other children she knew, who might do very well as pigs,
T5	149:24	Alice thought to herself, "and she's all over pins!--May I put your shawl straight for you?" she added
T9	192:16	harm, she thought, in asking if the game was over. "Please, would you tell me--" she began, looking timidly
T5	156:24	"I only hope the boat wo'n't tipple over!" she said to herself. "Oh, what a lovely one! Only I
T7	169: 6	on their feet: they were always tripping over something or other, and whenever one went down, several
T8	190:15	few yards to go," he said, "down the hill and over that little brook, and then you'll be a Queen--But you'll
T1	115:39	manner of things?" said the Queen, looking over the book (in which Alice had put 'The White Knight is
T8W	13:10	first thought, as she turned to spring over the brook:--but I'll just ask him what's the matter," she
T2	125:20	speaking, looking out in all directions over the country--and a most curious country it was. There
A4	34: 7	stretched herself up on tiptoe, and peeped over the edge of the mushroom, and her eyes immediately met
T9	204: 7	face grinning at her for a moment over the edge of the tureen, before she disappeared into the
A6	47: 3	middle, nursing a baby: the cook was leaning over the fire, stirring a large cauldron which seemed to be
T3	129:28	excuse, she ran down the hill, and jumped over the first of the six little brooks. * * * * * * * * * *
T1	107:18	come undone again; and there it was, spread over the hearth-rug, all knots and tangles, with the kitten
T8	182:37	minutes she walked on in silence, puzzling over the idea, and every now and then stopping to help the
A12	92: 3	she jumped up in such a hurry that she tipped over the jury-box with the edge of her skirt, upsetting all
T1	116: 4	him, in case he fainted again), she turned over the leaves, to find some part that she could read, "--for
A11	91:29	Alice watched the White Rabbit as he fumbled over the list, feeling very curious to see what the next
T6	162:34	continued thoughtfully as he crossed one knee over the other and clasped his hands round it, "they gave it
T5	157: 7	see it," said Alice, peeping cautiously over the side of the boat into the dark water. "I wish it
T5	156:20	about the Sheep and the knitting, as she bent over the side of the boat, with just the ends of her tangled
T9	196:15	round the room in great lumps--and knocking over the tables and things--till I was so frightened, I
A12	95:38	far," said the King; and he went on muttering over the verses to himself: "'We know it to be true'--that's
A11	86:18	way, was the King; and, as he wore his crown over the wig (look at the frontispiece if you want to see how
T2	126: 1	huge game of chess that's being played--all over the world--if this is the world at all, you know. Oh,
T1	107: 8	with the other paw she rubbed its face all over, the wrong way, beginning at the nose: and just now, as I
T5	156: 5	with the same tall river-banks frowning over their heads.
A6	45: 8	noticed, had powdered hair that curled all over their heads. She felt very curious to know what it was
A11	86:37	could see, as well as if she were looking over their shoulders, that all the jurors were writing down
A12	93:31	see this, as she was near enough to look over their slates; "but it doesn't matter a bit," she thought
T1	116:13	She puzzled over this for some time, but at last a bright thought struck
T6	163:18	done right--though I haven't time to look it over thoroughly just now--and that shows that there are three
A11	87: 4	their slates'll be in, before the trial's over!" thought Alice.
T9	198: 5	"I'll wait till the song's over," thought Alice, "and then I'll ring the--the--which bell
A11	86:24	She said this last word two or three times over to herself, being rather proud of it: for she thought,
A6	45:12	as large as himself, and this he handed over to the other, saying, in a solemn tone, "For the Duchess.
A11	89: 3	And he got up very sulkily and crossed over to the other side of the court.
T9	194:35	White Queen whispered: "we'll often say it over together, dear. And I'll tell you a secret--I can read
T9	197: 6	we've time for a nap. / When the feast's over, we'll go to the ball--/ Red Queen, and White Queen, and
T8W	13: 1	...and she was just going to spring over, when she heard a deep sigh, which seemed to come from
T8	184:34	"Yes, I suppose you'd be over when that was done," Alice said thoughtfully: "but don't
T9	198: 1	She was standing before an arched doorway, over which were the words "QUEEN ALICE" in large letters, and
A8	63:17	the ten courtiers: these were ornamented all over with diamonds, and walked two and two, as the soldiers
A2	19:27	out of the water, and seemed to quiver all over with fright. "Oh, I beg your pardon!" cried Alice hastily
A2	19:22	Alice. "I daresay it's a French mouse, come over with William the Conqueror." (For, with all her knowledge
A1	8:34	to her, still it was good practice to say it over) "--yes, that's about the right distance--but then I
T7	174:23	the country! She came flying out of the wood over yonder--How fast those Queens can run!"
T8	184:33	the feet are high enough, you see--then I'm over, you see."
T7	172:11	"I should think throwing cold water over you would be better," Alice suggested: "--or some

OVERCOME (1)
   A12   93:13   all   except   the   Lizard, who seemed too much overcome to do anything but sit with its mouth open, gazing up
OVERHEAD (2)
   A1   9:22   a moment: she looked up, but it was all dark overhead: before her was another long passage, and the White
   T4   140:39   cloud was in the sky: / No birds were flying overhead--/ There were no birds to fly.
OVERHEARD (1)
   T4   147:36   got a toothache!" said Tweedledee, who had overheard the remark. "I'm far worse than you!"
OWL (3)
   A10   83:15   garden, and marked, with one eye, / How the Owl and the Panther were sharing a pie: / The Panther took
   A10   83:18   treat. / When the pie was all finished, the Owl, as a boon, / Was kindly permitted to pocket the spoon: /
   A10   83:17   pie-crust, and gravy, and meat, / While the Owl had the dish as its share of the treat. / When the pie was
OWN (25)
   T9   196:22   taking one of the White Queen's hands in her own, and gently stroking it: "she means well, but she ca'n't
   T8   182:10   the Knight replied. "It's an invention of my own. And now help me on. I'll go with you to the end of the
   A9   70:35   "that it's done by everybody minding their own business!"
   A6   48:20   "If everybody minded their own business," the Duchess said, in a hoarse growl, "the world
   A12   99:10   in all their simple joys, remembering her own child-life, and the happy summer days.
   A8   64: 2   or soldiers, or courtiers, or three of her own children.
   A8   64: 3   should I know?" said Alice, surprised at her own courage. "It's no business of mine."
   A1   12:25   and once she remembered trying to box her own ears for having cheated herself in a game of croquet she
   A2   15: 5   funny it'll seem, sending presents to one's own feet! And how odd the directions will look!
   T8   185: 5   came and put it on. He thought it was his own helmet."
   A11   88:25   added as an explanation. "I've none of my own. I'm a hatter."
   T6   165: 5   I suppose?" said Alice, surprised at her own ingenuity.
   T8t   179: 1   "IT'S MY OWN INVENTION"
   T8   187:11   is 'A-sitting On A Gate': and the tune's my own invention."
   T8   187:28   "But the tune isn't his own invention," she said to herself: "it's 'I give thee all, I
   T8   181:18   the Knight said in a friendly tone. "It's my own invention--to keep clothes and sandwiches in. You see I
   T8   182:35   fall upwards, you know. It's a plan of my own invention. You may try it if you like."
   A1   7: 6   So she was considering, in her own mind (as well as she could, for the hot day made her feel
   T6   160:27   you? The King has promised me--with his very own mouth--to--to--"
   T3   131: 1   way she's going, even if she doesn't know her own name!"
   T9   196:16   I was so frightened, I couldn't remember my own name!"
   T9   204:21   merrily running round and round after her own shawl, which was trailing behind her.
   T1   107:19   tangles, with the kitten running after its own tail in the middle.
   A2   19: 3   for it now, I suppose, by being drowned in my own tears! That will be a queer thing, to be sure! However,
   T8W   21: 3   your head is nice and round." He took off his own wig as he spoke, and stetched out one claw towards Alice,
OWNER (1)
   T5   149: 2   shawl as she spoke, and looked about for the owner: in another moment the White Queen came running wildly
OYSTER (4)
   A3   26:21   "You're enough to try the patience of an oyster!"
   T9   202: 0   An oyster.
   T4   140:19   The eldest Oyster looked at him, / But never a word he said: / The eldest
   T4   140:21   him, / But never a word he said: / The eldest Oyster winked his eye, / And shook his heavy head--/ Meaning
OYSTER-BED (1)
   T4   140:24   to say he did not choose / To leave the oyster-bed.
OYSTERS (10)
   T4   144:14   "because he was a little sorry for the poor oysters."
   T4   141:13   'O Oysters, come and walk with us!' / The Walrus did beseech. /
   T4   143: 1   'But wait a bit,' the Oysters cried, / 'Before we have our chat; / For some of us
   T4   143:13   'But not on us!' the Oysters cried, / Turning a little blue. / 'After such kindness
   T12   208: 4   to you; and then you can make believe it's oysters, dear!
   T4   143:11   Are very good indeed--/ Now, if you're ready, Oysters dear, / We can begin to feed.'
   T4   142: 7   Four other Oysters followed them, / And yet another four; / And thick and
   T4   142: 1   But four young Oysters hurried up, / All eager for the treat: / Their coats
   T4   144: 7   'O Oysters,' said the Carpenter, / 'You've had a pleasant run! /
   T4   142:17   rock / Conveniently low: / And all the little Oysters stood / And waited in a row.
OYSTER-SHELLS (1)
   T7   173:25   whispered to Alice: "and they only give them oyster-shells in there--so you see he's very hungry and

-P-

PACE (1)
  A11   89: 1   "Yes, but I grow at a reasonable pace," said the Dormouse: "not in that ridiculous fashion."
PACK (5)
  A12   97: 8   size by this time). "You're nothing but a pack of cards!"
  A8   63:41   she added, to herself, "Why, they're only a pack of cards, after all. I needn't be afraid of them!"
  A11   86: 3   little birds and beasts, as well as the whole pack of cards: the Knave was standing before them in chains,
  A12   97: 9   At this the whole pack rose up into the air, and came flying down upon her; she
  A8   64: 1   their backs was the same as the rest of the pack, she could not tell whether they were gardeners, or
PACKED (1)
  T6   164:32   like a portmanteau--there are two meanings packed up into one word."
PAID (1)
  T6   164:12   (Alice didn't venture to ask what he paid them with; and so you see I ca'n't tell you.)
PAIN (2)
  T8W   13:20   said very kindly, "I hope you're not in much pain?"
  T8W   14: 7   but she thought to herself "Perhaps it's only pain that makes him so cross." So she tried once more.
PAINT (2)
  A8   62: 6   say "Look out now, Five! Don't go splashing paint over me like that!"
  T9   199:10   his thumb, as if he were trying whether the paint would come off: then he looked at Alice.
-PAINTED [See REPAINTED]
PAINTING (2)
  A8   62: 3   but there were three gardeners at it, busily painting them red. Alice thought this a very curious thing,
  A8   63: 4   said Alice, a little timidly, "why you are painting those roses?"
PAIR (11)
  T8   187:26   leant against a tree, watching the strange pair, and listening, in a half-dream, to the melancholy music
  A2   15: 2   want to go! Let me see. I'll give them a new pair of boots every Christmas."
  A4   27:15   here? Run home this moment, and fetch me a pair of gloves and a fan! Quick, now!" And Alice was so much
  T5   155:14   "Can you row?" the Sheep asked, handing her a pair of knitting-needles as she spoke.
  T5   155:21   cried the Sheep, as she took up another pair of needles.
  T5   155: 8   the Sheep said, as she took up another pair of needles. "You'll make me giddy soon, if you go on
  T9   203:17   the top. As to the bottles, they each took a pair of plates, which they hastily fitted on as wings, and so,
  T5   153:40   leaving off to look at her through a great pair of spectacles.
  A4   28: 1   white kid-gloves: she took up the fan and a pair of the gloves, and was just going to leave the room, when
  A4   27: 7   that it was looking for the fan and the pair of white kid-gloves, and she very good-naturedly began
  A2   15:27   Rabbit returning, splendidly dressed, with a pair of white kid-gloves in one hand and a large fan in the
PAIRS (2)
  T5   155: 9   like that." She was now working with fourteen pairs at once, and Alice couldn't help looking at her in great
  A4   27:38   it (as she had hoped) a fan and two or three pairs of tiny white kid-gloves: she took up the fan and a pair
PALE (6)
  A11   88:27   began staring hard at the Hatter, who turned pale and fidgeted.
  A12   94: 1   The King turned pale, and shut his note-book hastily. "Consider your verdict,"
  A10   80:10   the nearer is to France. / Then turn not pale, beloved snail, but come and join the dance. / Will you,
  T6   160:25   "the King has promised me--ah, you may turn pale, if you like! You didn't think I was going to say that,
  T4   147:30   "Do I look very pale?" said Tweedledum, coming up to have his helmet tied on.
  A2   20:17   swam slowly back to her: its face was quite pale (with passion, Alice thought), and it said, in a low
PALED (1)
  TC   209: 7   Long has paled that sunny sky: / Echoes fade and memories die: / Autumn
-PAN [See FRYING-PAN, SAUCEPAN]
-PANE [See WINDOW-PANES]
-PANS [See SAUCEPANS]
PANT (1)
  T2   126:27   "Are we nearly there?" Alice managed to pant out at last.
PANTED (7)
  A10   85: 6   "What trial is it?" Alice panted as she ran: but the Gryphon only answered "Come on!"
  T2   122:11   "They know I ca'n't get at them!" it panted, bending its quivering head towards Alice, "or they
  T7   173: 8   "Would you--be good enough--" Alice panted out, after running a little further, "to stop a minute
  T4   139:40   round is enough for one dance," Tweedledum panted out, and they left off dancing as suddenly as they had
  T9   199:20   one of his great feet. "You let it alone," he panted out, as he hobbled back to his tree, "and it'll let you
  T1   115:36   Alice was too strong for him, and at last he panted out "My dear! I really must get a thinner pencil. I
  T1   114:15   "Blew--me--up," panted the Queen, who was still a little out of breath. "Mind
PANTHER (3)
  A10   84: 1   permitted to pocket the spoon: / While the Panther received knife and fork with a growl, / And concluded
  A10   83:16   Owl and the Panther were sharing a pie: / The Panther took pie-crust, and gravy, and meat, / While the Owl
  A10   83:15   marked, with one eye, / How the Owl and the Panther were sharing a pie: / The Panther took pie-crust, and
PANTING (5)
  T8   180:16   it?" said the White Knight, as he came up panting.
  T2   127:16   "Well, in our country," said Alice, still panting a little, "you'd generally get to somewhere else--if
  A3   23:15   race is over!" and they all crowded round it, panting, and asking "But who has won?"
  T7   174:13   then, and the Lion and the Unicorn sat down, panting, while the King called out "Ten minutes allowed for
  A4   33: 1   till at last it sat down a good way off, panting, with its tongue hanging out of its mouth, and its
PANTRY (1)
  T8W   14:21   Exploring Party have made another tour in the Pantry, and have found five new lumps of white sugar, large
PAPER (9) [See also BLOTTING-PAPER, NEWSPAPER]
  A12   95:29   but none of them attempted to explain the paper.

PAPER (cont.)
T8W   15: 1   Alice hastily ran her eye down the paper and said "No. It says nothing about brown."
A12   94:13   written on the outside." He unfolded the paper as he spoke, and added "It isn't a letter, after all:
A12   94: 4   Rabbit, jumping up in a great hurry: "this paper has just been picked up."
T6   163: 5   looked doubtful. "I'd rather see that done on paper," he said.
A1   10:17   and tied round the neck of the bottle was a paper label, with the words "DRINK ME" beautifully printed on
T3   131:23   But the gentleman dressed in white paper leaned forwards and whispered in her ear, "Never mind
T8W   14:19   So Alice sat down by him, and spread out the paper on her knees, and began. "Latest News. The Exploring
T3   130:22   opposite to her, (he was dressed in white paper), "ought to know which way she's going, even if she
PAPERS (1) [See also NEWSPAPERS]
T9   196:32   "A little kindness--and putting her hair in papers--would do wonders with her--"
PARCHMENT (1)
A11   86: 6   with a trumpet in one hand, and a scroll of parchment in the other. In the very middle of the court was a
PARCHMENT-SCROLL (1)
A11   87:15   blasts on the trumpet, and then unrolled the parchment-scroll, and read as follows:--
PARDON (9)
T6   162:36   "I beg your pardon?" Alice said with a puzzled air.
A2   19:39   capital one for catching mice--oh, I beg your pardon!" cried Alice again, for this time the Mouse was
A2   19:27   quiver all over with fright. "Oh, I beg your pardon!" cried Alice hastily, afraid that she had hurt the
T7   171: 2   "I beg your pardon?" said Alice.
A3   26: 3   "I beg your pardon," said Alice very humbly: "you had got to the fifth
A3   22: 8   "I beg your pardon!" said the Mouse, frowning, but very politely. "Did you
T6   162:18   have said--no, a belt, I mean--I beg your pardon!" she added in dismay, for Humpty Dumpty looked
A12   92: 8   "Oh, I beg your pardon!" she exclaimed in a tone of great dismay, and began
A11   88: 7   of bread-and-butter in the other. "I beg pardon, your Majesty," he began, "for bringing these in; but I
PARDONED (1)
A9   73:19   to the company, generally, "You are all pardoned." "Come, that's a good thing!" she said to herself,
PARIS (2)
A2   17: 1   let's try Geography. London is the capital of Paris, and Paris is the capital of Rome, and Rome--no, that's
A2   17: 1   London is the capital of Paris, and Paris is the capital of Rome, and Rome--no, that's all wrong,
PART (9)
A11   89:24   He denies it," said the King: "leave out that part."
A10   82: 6   were perfectly quiet till she got to the part about her repeating "You are old, Father William," to the
T12   208: 9   part of my dream, of course--but then I was part of his dream, too! Was it the Red King, Kitty? You were
T5   154:12   all manner of curious things--but the oddest part of it all was that, whenever she looked hard at any shelf
T12   208: 9   have been either me or the Red King. He was part of my dream, of course--but then I was part of his dream,
T9   196:13   could, you know," said the Red Queen.) "And part of the roof came off, and ever so much thunder got in--
T8   179: 8   said to herself, "unless--unless we're all part of the same dream. Only I do hope it's my dream, and not
T2   126:18   The most curious part of the thing was, that the trees and the other things
T1   116: 4   she turned over the leaves, to find some part that she could read, "--for it's all in some language I
PARTICULAR (5)
A5   41: 8   "Oh, I'm not particular as to size," Alice hastily replied; "only one
A8   67:25   and they don't seem to have any rules in particular: at least, if there are, nobody attends to them--
A4   30:28   yet--Oh, they'll do well enough. Don't be particular--Here, Bill! Catch hold of this rope--Will the roof
A3   26:23   I do!" said Alice aloud, addressing nobody in particular. "She'd soon fetch it back!"
T5   154:13   to make out exactly what it had on it, that particular shelf was always quite empty, though the others
PARTICULARLY (1)
T6   163:39   began again. "They've a temper, some of them--particularly verbs: they're the proudest--adjectives you can
PARTNER (1)
A10   78:21   "Each with a lobster as a partner!" cried the Gryphon.
PARTNERS (1)
A10   78:22   the Mock Turtle said: "advance twice, set to partners--"
PARTS (1)
A8   66:18   always getting up and walking off to other parts of the ground, Alice soon came to the conclusion that it
PARTY (12) [See also DINNER-PARTY, TEA-PARTY]
T8W   15: 4   sugar!" grumbled the Wasp. "A nice exploring party!"
T9   193:17   "I didn't know I was to have a party at all," said Alice; "but, if there is to be one, I
A3   23:24   to Alice with one finger; and the whole party at once crowded round her, calling out, in a confused
T8W   14:20   knees, and began. "Latest News. The Exploring Party have made another tour in the Pantry, and have found
A8   69: 4   was this last remark that had made the whole party look so grave and anxious.)
A7   55:32   and here the conversation dropped, and the party sat silent for a minute, while Alice thought over all
A3   26:30   caused a remarkable sensation among the party. Some of the birds hurried off at once: one old Magpie
A2   20:24   creatures. Alice led the way, and the whole party swam to the shore.
A3   21: 1   They were indeed a queer-looking party that assembled on the bank--the birds with draggled
A8   69:13   down, looking for it, while the rest of the party went back to the game.
T8W   15: 8   they had a sad accident: two of their party were engulphed--"
A3   23: 9   doesn't matter," it said,) and then all the party were placed along the course, here and there. There was
PASS (3)
T2   126:20   however fast they went, they never seemed to pass anything. "I wonder if all the things move along with us
A11   86:12   she began looking at everything about her to pass away the time.
T7   172:15   "Who did you pass on the road?" the King went on, holding out his hand to
PASSAGE (7)
A1   9:23   dark overhead: before her was another long passage, and the White Rabbit was still in sight, hurrying
A7   61: 4   a foot high; then she walked down the little passage: and then--she found herself at last in the beautiful
T1   111: 4   wide open: and it's very like our passage as far as you can see, only you know it may be quite
T1   111: 2   You can just see a little peep of the passage in Looking-glass House, if you leave the door of our
A1   10: 3   rat-hole: she knelt down and looked along the passage into the loveliest garden you ever saw. How she longed
A1   10: 1   the door and found that it led into a small passage, not much larger than a rat-hole: she knelt down and
T1   111: 1   to drink--but oh, Kitty! now we come to the passage. You can just see a little peep of the passage in

PASSED (8)
  T7   175:11 said to the King, just glancing at him as he passed.
  A10   83:11 verse," the Gryphon repeated: "it begins 'I passed by his garden.'"
  A10   83:14   "I passed by his garden, and marked, with one eye, / How the Owl
  T2   127: 1 "Nearly there!" the Queen repeated. "Why, we passed it ten minutes ago! Faster!" And they ran on for a time
  A1   8:18 down a jar from one of the shelves as she passed: it was labeled "ORANGE MARMALADE," but to her great
  A8   67:36   The Queen smiled and passed on.
  T9   192:28 You ca'n't be a Queen, you know, till you've passed the proper examination. And the sooner we begin it, the
  A10   79:10 now and then treading on her toes when they passed too close, and waving their fore-paws to mark the time,
PASSENGERS (1)
  T3   131: 7 Goat (it was a very queer carriage-full of passengers altogether), and, as the rule seemed to be that
PASSING (3)
  A8   68: 4   and he called to the Queen, who was passing at the moment, "My dear! I wish you would have this
  T4   139:18   "Next Boy!" said Alice, passing on to Tweedledee, though she felt quite certain he
  T8   181:23 it," the Knight said, a shade of vexation passing over his face. "Then all the things must have fallen
PASSION (5)
  A2   20:17 back to her: its face was quite pale (with passion, Alice thought), and it said, in a low trembling voice
  T4   146:13 see that?" he said, in a voice choking with passion, and his eyes grew large and yellow all in a moment,
  A8   66:22 a very short time the Queen was in a furious passion, and went stamping about, and shouting "Off with his
  A8   68:12 Queen's voice in the distance, screaming with passion. She had already heard her sentence three of the
  T6   160:31 Humpty Dumpty cried, breaking into a sudden passion. "You've been listening at doors--and behind trees--
PASSIONATE (1)
  A2   19:30 "Not like cats!" cried the Mouse in a shrill passionate voice. "Would you like cats, if you were me?"
PASSIONATELY (1)
  T2   122:10 of you!" cried the Tiger-lily, waving itself passionately from side to side, and trembling with excitement.
PAST (2) [See also HALF-PAST]
  A1   8:22 put it into one of the cupboards as she fell past it.
  T1   113:20 the White Queen cried out, as she rushed past the King, so violently that she knocked him over among
PAT (4)
  T9   196:29 "but it's amazing how good-tempered she is! Pat her on the head, and see how pleased she'll be!" But this
  A4   30: 1 Next came an angry voice--the Rabbit's--"Pat! Pat! Where are you?" And then a voice she had never heard
  A4   30: 6   "Now tell me, Pat, what's that in the window?"
  A4   30: 1 Next came an angry voice--the Rabbit's--"Pat! Pat! Where are you?" And then a voice she had never heard
PATH (6)
  T2   120: 4 do that--" (after going a few yards along the path, and turning several sharp corners), "but I suppose it
  T2   120:19 the house, she set out once more down the path, determined to keep straight on till she got to the hill.
  T2   120:21 "I really shall do it this time--" when the path gave a sudden twist and shook itself (as she described it
  T2   120: 2 get to the top of that hill: and here's a path that leads straight to it--at least, no, it doesn't do
  T2   120: 6 it twists! It's more like a corkscrew than a path! Well this turn goes to the hill, I suppose--no, it
  T8   183:20 heavily on the top of his head exactly in the path where Alice was walking. She was quite frightened this
PATIENCE (2)
  A3   26:20 little snappishly. "You're enough to try the patience of an oyster!"
  T8   184:11 too ridiculous!" cried Alice, losing all her patience this time. "You ought to have a wooden horse on
-PATIENT [See IMPATIENT]
PATIENTLY (3) [See also IMPATIENTLY]
  A9   74:31 finish, if he doesn't begin." But she waited patiently.
  T12   207:27 shoulder at the White Kitten, which was still patiently undergoing its toilet, "when will Dinah have
  A5   41:23   This time Alice waited patiently until it chose to speak again. In a minute or two
PATRIOTIC (1)
  A3   22:13 declared for him; and even Stigand, the patriotic archbishop of Canterbury, found it advisable--'"
PATTED (1)
  A3   24:11 and the small ones choked and had to be patted on the back. However, it was over at last, and they sat
PATTERING (3)
  A2   15:25   After a time she heard a little pattering of feet in the distance, and she hastily dried her
  A4   29:20 me my gloves this moment!" Then came a little pattering of feet on the stairs. Alice knew it was the Rabbit
  A3   26:42 while, however, she again heard a little pattering of footsteps in the distance, and she looked up
PATTERN (1)
  A8   63:45 as they were lying on their faces, and the pattern on their backs was the same as the rest of the pack,
PATTING (1)
  T2   125: 3   "That's right," said the Queen, patting her on the head, which Alice didn't like at all:
PAUSE (10)
  T6   168:14   There was a long pause.
  T8   186:39 said Alice, for the Knight had made a sudden pause.
  T4   144:21   This was a puzzler. After a pause, Alice began, "Well! They were both very unpleasant
  T3   129:25 I'll go down the other way," she said after a pause; "and perhaps I may visit the elephants later on.
  T4   140: 2 her for a minute: there was a rather awkward pause, as Alice didn't know how to begin a conversation with
  T7   174:12   There was a pause in the fight just then, and the Lion and the Unicorn sat
  T8   182: 5   "You see," he went on after a pause, "it's as well to be provided for everything. That's the
  A6   47: 9 and howling alternately without a moment's pause. The only two creatures in the kitchen, that did not
  A9   71: 6 round your waist," the Duchess said, after a pause: "the reason is, that I'm doubtful about the temper of
  T8   186: 7 the sort that I ever did," he went on after a pause, "was inventing a new pudding during the meat-course."
PAUSED (1)
  A3   23: 3 she much wanted to know, but the Dodo had paused as if it thought that somebody ought to speak, and no
PAW (10)
  T1   108: 8 the winding, and now and then putting out one paw and gently touching the ball, as if it would be glad to
  T12   208:13 the provoking kitten only began on the other paw, and pretended it hadn't heard the question.
  T1   107: 7 held the poor thing down by its ear with one paw, and then with the other paw she rubbed its face all over,
  T12   208:12 Kitty, do help to settle it! I'm sure your paw can wait!" But the provoking kitten only began on the
  T12   208: 7 dear, and you should not go on licking your paw like that--as if Dinah hadn't washed you this morning! You
  A6   51:20 and in that direction," waving the other paw, "lives a March Hare. Visit either you like: they're both

PAW (cont.)
A6   51:19   direction," the Cat said, waving its right paw round, "lives a Hatter: and in that direction," waving the
T1   107: 8   its ear with one paw, and then with the other paw she rubbed its face all over, the wrong way, beginning at
A4   32:28   round eyes, and feebly stretching out one paw, trying to touch her. "Poor little thing!" said Alice, in
T1   108:30   that the kitten was speaking). "Her paw went into your eye? Well, that's your fault, for keeping
PAWN (4)
T2   128:32   and Alice began to remember that she was a Pawn, and that it would soon be time for her to move.
T2   128: 7   the two-yard peg she faced round, and said "A pawn goes two squares in its first move, you know. So you'll
T2   126: 3   I was one of them! I wouldn't mind being a Pawn, if only I might join--though of course I should like to
T2   126: 8   easily managed. You can be the White Queen's Pawn, if you like, as Lily's too young to play: and you're in
PAWNS (1)
T1   113:16   her head just in time to see one of the White Pawns roll over and begin kicking: she watched it with great
PAWS (5) [See also FORE-PAWS]
A9   77: 9   and both creatures hid their faces in their paws.
T7   176:10   said, lying down and putting his chin on his paws. "And sit down, both of you," (to the King and the
A2   19:37   purring so nicely by the fire, licking her paws and washing her face--and she is such a nice soft thing
A9   76:26   The Gryphon lifted up both its paws in surprise. "Never heard of uglifying!" it exclaimed.
A4   27: 4   itself, "The Duchess! The Duchess! Oh my dear paws! Oh my fur and whiskers! She'll get me executed, as sure
PAY (2)
T6   164: 6   like that," said Humpty Dumpty, "I always pay it extra."
T4   138:10   we're wax-works," he said, "you ought to pay, you know. Wax-works weren't made to be looked at for
PEACE (1)
T4   147:39   Alice, thinking it a good opportunity to make peace.
PEBBLES (2)
A4   32: 1   doubt, for the next moment a shower of little pebbles came rattling in at the window, and some of them hit
A4   32: 5   Alice noticed, with some surprise, that the pebbles were all turning into little cakes as they lay on the
PEEP (1)
T1   111: 2   to the passage. You can just see a little peep of the passage in Looking-glass House, if you leave the
PEEPED (3)
A1   7: 3   having nothing to do: once or twice she had peeped into the book her sister was reading, but it had no
A6   46: 6   fear of their hearing her; and, when she next peeped out, the Fish-Footman was gone, and the other was
A4   34: 7   She stretched herself up on tiptoe, and peeped over the edge of the mushroom, and her eyes immediately
PEEPING (4)
A8   65:26   She was walking by the White Rabbit, who was peeping anxiously into her face.
T5   157: 7   "Was it? I didn't see it," said Alice, peeping cautiously over the side of the boat into the dark
T7   172: 5   but hay left now," the Messenger said, peeping into the bag.
T8   180: 2   to herself, as she watched the fight, timidly peeping out from her hiding-place. "One Rule seems to be, that
PEERING (1)
A4   32:24   idea how to set about it; and, while she was peering about anxiously among the trees, a little sharp bark
PEEVISH (1)
T8W   14: 3   "How you go on!" the Wasp said in a peevish tone. "Worrity, worrity! There never was such a child!
PEG (5)
T2   128: 7   At the two-yard peg she faced round, and said "A pawn goes two squares in its
T2   128:29   knew, but exactly as she came to the last peg, she was gone. Whether she vanished into the air, or
T2   128:22   At the next peg the Queen turned again, and this time she said "Speak in
T2   127:35   the end of two yards," she said, putting in a peg to mark the distance, "I shall give you your directions--
T2   128:26   this time, but walked on quickly to the next peg, where she turned for a moment to say "Good-bye," and then
PEGS (3)
T2   127:34   measuring the ground, and sticking little pegs in here and there.
T2   128: 4   She had got all the pegs put in by this time, and Alice looked on with great
A1   8:17   and there she saw maps and pictures hung upon pegs. She took down a jar from one of the shelves as she
PEN (1)
T6   166:35   In autumn, when the leaves are brown, / Take pen and ink, and write it down."
PENCE (2) [See also TWOPENCE-HALFPENNY, fivepence, etc.]
A11   88:19   up, and reduced the answer to shillings and pence.
T5   149:39   take you with pleasure!" the Queen said. "Two pence a week, and jam every other day."
PENCIL (4) [See also SLATE-PENCIL]
T1   115:35   puzzled and unhappy, and struggled with the pencil for some time without saying anything; but Alice was
T1   115:37   out "My dear! I really must get a thinner pencil. I ca'n't manage this one a bit: it writes all manner
A11   87: 5   One of the jurors had a pencil that squeaked. This, of course, Alice could not stand,
T1   115:31   her, and she took hold of the end of the pencil, which came some way over his shoulder, and began
PENCILS (1)
A12   93:11   shock of being upset, and their slates and pencils had been found and handed back to them, they set to
PENNY (1) [See also TWOPENCE-HALFPENNY, HALFPENNY]
T9   202: 6   the fish must be bought.' / That is easy: a penny, I think, could have bought it.
PENNYWORTH (2)
A10   84:28   dish? / Who would not give all else for two p / ennyworth only of beautiful Soup? / Pennyworth only of
A10   84:30   two p / ennyworth only of beautiful Soup? / Pennyworth only of beautiful soup. / Beau--ootiful Soo--oop! /
PEOPLE (27)
T6   168:23   to shake: "you're so exactly like other people."
A4   27:34   Dinah stop in the house if it began ordering people about like that!"
A6   51:22   "But I don't want to go among mad people," Alice remarked.
T3   129:35   ticket: they were about the same size as the people, and quite seemed to fill the carriage.
A8   65:42   shouted the Queen in a voice of thunder, and people began running about in all directions, tumbling up
A1   12:28   child was very fond of pretending to be two people. "But it's no use now," thought poor Alice, "to pretend
T7   170:19   Why, it's as much as I can do to see real people, by this light!"
T8   183: 9   "Because people don't fall off quite so often, when they've had much
A9   72:20   sort of present!" thought Alice. "I'm glad people don't give birthday-presents like that!" But she did
A8   63:31   be the use of a procession," thought she, "if people had all to lie down on their faces, so that they
A8   67: 6   of me? They're dreadfully fond of beheading people here: the great wonder is, that there's any one left

PEOPLE (cont.)
```
A9     70:10   without--Maybe it's always pepper that makes people hot-tempered," she went on, very much pleased at having
T6    168:40   long  word  to say) "of all the unsatisfactory people I ever met--" She never finished the sentence, for at
T2    123: 3                        "Are there any more people in the garden besides me?" Alice said, not choosing to
A9     70:14   make  children  sweet-tempered.  I only wish people knew that: then they wouldn't be so stingy about it,
A6     51:18   so  she tried another question. "What sort of people live about here?"
T3    135:33   just  like the advertisements, you know, when people lose dogs--'answers to the name of "Dash": had on a
A11    91: 7   before she got into the court, by the way the people near the door began sneezing all at once.
T6    159:22                            "Some people," said Humpty Dumpty, looking away from her as usual,
T4    140: 3   didn't  know how to begin a conversation with people she had just been dancing with. "It would never do to
T3    131:36   comfort it, "if it would only sigh like other people!" she thought. But this was such a wonderfully small
T3    132:37   to them," said Alice; "but it's useful to the people that name them, I suppose. If not, why do things have
A1      8:40   How  funny it'll seem to come out among the people that walk with their heads downwards! The antipathies,
T3    131:18   that  other voices went on ("What a number of people there are in the carriage!" thought Alice), saying "She
T9    200:13   "I should never have known who were the right people to invite!"
A1     10:14   or  at  any rate a book of rules for shutting people up like telescopes: this time she found a little bottle
A1     12:29   thought  poor Alice, "to  pretend to be two people! Why, there's hardly enough of me left to make one
```
PEOPLE'S (1)
```
T5    158:14   a box: then she said "I never put things into people's hands--that would never do--you must get it for
```
PEPPER (8)
```
A6t    45: 1                          PIG AND PEPPER
T4    143: 9   Walrus said, / 'Is what we chiefly need: / Pepper and vinegar besides / Are very good indeed--/ Now, if
A9     70: 8   hopeful  tone,  though), "I wo'n't have any pepper in my kitchen at all. Soup does very well without--
A6     47: 5       "There's certainly too much pepper in that soup!" Alice said to herself, as well as she
A11    91:17                            "Pepper, mostly," said the cook.
A9     70: 5    to herself that perhaps it was only the pepper that had made her so savage when they met in the
A9     70: 9   does very well without--Maybe it's always pepper that makes people hot-tempered," she went on, very much
A6     49: 7   sneezes; / For he can thoroughly enjoy / The pepper when he pleases!"
```
PEPPER-BOX (1)
```
A11    91: 5   was  the  Duchess's  cook.  She  carried the pepper-box in her hand, and Alice guessed who it was, even
```
PERFECT (1)
```
T4    146:28   my  nice NEW RATTLE!" and his voice rose to a perfect scream.
```
PERFECTLY (5)
```
A6     46:44       to him," said Alice desperately: "he's perfectly idiotic!" And she opened the door and went in.
A10    82: 5   courage  as  she went on. Her listeners were perfectly quiet till she got to the part about her repeating
A5     41:35   were  the  two  sides  of  it; and, as it was perfectly round, she found this a very difficult question.
T1    115:15   immediately  fell  flat  on his back, and lay perfectly still; and Alice was a little alarmed at what she
A5     37: 7   might  injure  the  brain; / But, now that I'm perfectly sure I have none, / Why, I do it again and again."
```
PERHAPS (25)
```
A7     57:16                       You know the song, perhaps?"
A5     36:27   well wait, as she had nothing else to do, and perhaps after all it might tell her something worth hearing.
A6     52:26   Hare  will  be much the most interesting, and perhaps, as this is May, it wo'n't be raving mad--at least not
A12    99: 8   bright  and  eager  with many a strange tale, perhaps even with the dream of Wonderland of long ago; and how
A6     46:22   this  Alice  thought  decidedly uncivil. "But perhaps he ca'n't help it," she said to herself; "his eyes are
T3    129:26   the  other way," she said after a pause; "and perhaps I may visit the elephants later on. Besides, I do so
A1      9: 3   me  for  asking! No,  it'll never do to ask: perhaps I shall see it written up somewhere."
A2     19:21                       "Perhaps it doesn't understand English," thought Alice. "I
A9     70:21                       "Perhaps it hasn't one," Alice ventured to remark.
T1    109:12   up  snug,  you  know, with a white quilt; and perhaps it says 'Go to sleep, darlings, till the summer comes
A6     49:35   not  like  the  look of the thing at all. "But perhaps it was only sobbing," she thought, and looked into its
A9     70: 5   pleasant  temper, and thought to herself that perhaps it was only the pepper that had made her so savage
T9    194:20                       "Perhaps it would," Alice replied cautiously.
T8W    14: 7   and  leaving him, but she thought to herself "Perhaps it's only pain that makes him so cross." So she tried
T1    110:44   I  wonder  if  they'd give you milk in there? Perhaps Looking-glass milk isn't good to drink--but oh, Kitty!
A7     56:40                       "Perhaps not," Alice cautiously replied; "but I know I have to
A2     19:32                       "Well, perhaps not," said Alice in a soothing tone: "don't be angry
T6    162:11                     "One ca'n't, perhaps," said Humpty Dumpty; "but two can. With proper
A7     57: 7                   "Not at first, perhaps," said the Hatter: "but you could keep it to half-past
T8    182: 3               "Not very likely, perhaps," said the Knight; "but, if they do come, I don't
A2     15: 1   I  must  be kind to them," thought Alice, "or perhaps they wo'n't walk the way I want to go! Let me see.
A5     36: 2                       "Well, perhaps you haven't found it so yet," said Alice; "but when
A10    78: 9   the  sea--" ("I  haven't," said Alice)--"and perhaps you were never even introduced to a lobster--" (Alice
T6    166:33   "In  summer,  when  the  days  are long, / Perhaps you'll understand the song:
A5     36: 7                       "Well, perhaps your feelings may be different," said Alice: "all I
```
PERMITTED (1)
```
A10    83:19   finished,  the  Owl,  as a boon, / Was kindly permitted to pocket the spoon: / While the Panther received
```
PERPLEXITY (1)
```
T9    197:12   do?" exclaimed Alice, looking about in great perplexity, as first one round head, and then the other,
```
PERSISTED (3)
```
A10    83: 5       "But about his toes?" the Mock Turtle persisted. "How could he turn them out with his nose, you know
T8W    20:11   "Not with a mouth as small as that," the Wasp persisted. "If you was a-fighting, now--could you get hold of
A12    93:19                   "Nothing whatever?" persisted the King.
```
PERSON (7)
```
A1     12:30   enough  of me left to make one respectable person!"
T9    192:22   spoke  when you were spoken to, and the other person always waited for you to begin, you see nobody would
T6    162:26   provoking--thing," he said at last, "when a person doesn't know a cravat from a belt!"
T12   207:10   a  conversation! But how can you talk with a person if they always say the same thing?"
A2     17:23   me that first, and then, if I like being that person, I'll come up: if not, I'll stay down here till I'm
A3     21:13       At  last the Mouse, who seemed to be a person of some authority among them, called out "Sit down, all
A10    81:42   back  to yesterday, because I was a different person then."
```

PERSONAL (3)
 A7 55: 9   "You should learn not to make personal remarks," Alice said with some severity: "it's very
 T8W 21:10   Alice did not like having so many personal remarks made on her, and as the Wasp had quite
 A7 59:16   "Who's making personal remarks now?" the Hatter asked triumphantly.
PERSON'S (1)
 T8 179: 9 Red King's! I don't like belonging to another person's dream," she went on in a rather complaining tone:
PERSONS (1)
 A12 93:35 read out from his book, "Rule Forty-two. All persons more than a mile high to leave the court."
PET (2)
 A3 26:27 for she was always ready to talk about her pet: "Dinah's our cat. And she's such a capital one for
 T12 207:26   "Snowdrop, my pet!" she went on, looking over her shoulder at the White
PETALS (3)
 T2 123:12 the Rose said: "but she's redder--and her petals are shorter, I think."
 T2 121:12   the Tiger-lily remarked. "If only her petals curled up a little more, she'd be all right."
 T2 123:16 you know--and then one ca'n't help one's petals getting a little untidy."
PHANTOMWISE (1)
 TC 209:10   Still she haunts me, phantomwise. / Alice moving under skies / Never seen by waking
PHRASE (1)
 T1 110:11 used to say, beginning with her favourite phrase "Let's pretend." She had had quite a long argument with
PICK (5)
 T6 161:14 all his men," Humpty Dumpty went on. "They'd pick me up again in a minute, they would! However, this
 T5 156:27 she thought) that, though she managed to pick plenty of beautiful rushes as the boat glided by, there
 T5 156:11 "No, but I meant--please, may we wait and pick some?" Alice pleaded. "If you don't mind stopping the
 T9 194:42   "Where do you pick the flower?" the White Queen asked: "In a garden or in
 T2 122:15   "If you don't hold your tongues, I'll pick you!"
PICKED (10)
 T9 194:44   "Well, it isn't picked at all," Alice explained: "it's ground--"
 A7 60:35 never go there again!" said Alice, as she picked her way through the wood. "It's the stupidest tea-party
 T8 184: 2 time, and said in an anxious tone, as she picked him up, "I hope no bones are broken?"
 T1 114:23   So Alice picked him up very gently, and lifted him across more slowly
 T8 184:23 Now, I daresay you noticed, the last time you picked me up, that I was looking rather thoughtful?"
 T5 156:36 and beauty, from the very moment that she picked them? Even real scented rushes, you know, last only a
 A12 94: 5 in a great hurry: "this paper has just been picked up."
 A4 32:33   Hardly knowing what she did, she picked up a little bit of stick, and held it out to the puppy:
 T8W 14:15 you a bit of this?" Alice went on, as she picked up a newspaper which had been lying at his feet.
 T1 114: 5 screaming herself into a fit, she hastily picked up the Queen and set her on the table by the side of
PICKING (2)
 A1 7: 9 would be worth the trouble of getting up and picking the daisies, when suddenly a White Rabbit with pink
 A12 92: 9   in a tone of great dismay, and began picking them up again as quickly as she could, for the
PICTURE (2)
 T8 187:24 forest behind--all this she took in like a picture, as, with one hand shading her eyes, she leant against
 A9 73:23 you don't know what a Gryphon is, look at the picture.) "Up, lazy thing!" said the Queen, "and take this
PICTURED (1)
 A12 99: 3   Lastly, she pictured to herself how this same little sister of hers would,
PICTURES (5)
 A1 8:17 book-shelves: here and there she saw maps and pictures hung upon pegs. She took down a jar from one of the
 A3 23:20 in which you usually see Shakespeare, in the pictures of him), while the rest waited in silence. At last
 T1 112:12 as different as possible. For instance, the pictures on the wall next the fire seemed to be all alive, and
 A1 7: 5 the use of a book," thought Alice, "without pictures or conversations next?"
 A1 7: 3 book her sister was reading, but it had no pictures or conversations in it, "and what is the use of a
PIE (2) [See also MINCE-PIE]
 A10 83:15 / How the Owl and the Panther were sharing a pie: / The Panther took pie-crust, and gravy, and meat, /
 A10 83:18 dish as its share of the treat. / When the pie was all finished, the Owl, as a boon, / Was kindly
PIECE (10) [See also A-PIECE, CHIMNEY-PIECE, etc.]
 T6 166:19   "The piece I'm going to repeat," he went on without noticing her
 A11 88: 7 He came in with a teacup in one hand and a piece of bread-and-butter in the other. "I beg pardon, your
 T7 173:22 fight, with a cup of tea in one hand and a piece of bread-and-butter. "They're getting on very well," he
 T7 174: 5 a desperate effort, and swallowed a large piece of bread-and-butter. "They're getting on very well," he
 A12 95:21   "That's the most important piece of evidence we've heard yet," said the King, rubbing his
 A7 61: 3 work nibbling at the mushroom (she had kept a piece of it in her pocket) till she was about a foot high;
 T5 150: 3 instance, now," she went on, sticking a large piece of plaster on her finger as she spoke, "there's the
 A7 60:29   This piece of rudeness was more than Alice could bear: she got up
 A11 88:32 Queen, and in his confusion he bit a large piece out of his teacup instead of the bread-and-butter.
 T7 174:16 trays of white and brown bread. Alice took a piece to taste, but it was very dry.
PIECES (5)
 A6 46:16 as if a dish or kettle had been broken to pieces.
 A6 46:29 head: it just grazed his nose, and broke to pieces against one of the trees behind him.
 T7 177:14 round, and the cake divided itself into three pieces as she did so. "Now cut it up," said the Lion, as she
 T1 110: 9 Knight, that came wriggling down among my pieces. Kitty dear, let's pretend--" And here I wish I could
 A5 43:32 while she remembered that she still held the pieces of mushroom in her hands, and she set to work very
PIE-CRUST (1)
 A10 83:16 were sharing a pie: / The Panther took pie-crust, and gravy, and meat, / While the Owl had the dish
-PIES [See MUTTON-PIES]
PIG (10)
 A6 47:15   said the Duchess, "and that's why. Pig!"
 A6 52:19   "It turned into a pig," Alice answered very quietly, just as if the Cat had come
 A6t 45: 1   PIG AND PEPPER
 A6 50:12 about it: it was neither more nor less than a pig, and she felt that it would be quite absurd for her to
 T8W 19:14 I appear, / They hoot at me and call me 'Pig!' / And that is why they do it, dear, / Because I wear a
 T6 166: 3   "Well, a 'rath' is a sort of green pig: but 'mome' I'm not certain about. I think it's short for

```
PIG (cont.)
  A6    50:17  ugly  child:  but  it makes rather a handsome pig, I think." And she began thinking over other children she
  A6    50: 3  no  tears.  "If  you're  going  to turn into a pig, my dear," said Alice, seriously, "I'll have nothing more
  A6    53: 1                                              "Did you say 'pig', or 'fig'?" said the Cat.
  A6    53: 2                                "I said 'pig'," replied Alice; "and I wish you wouldn't keep appearing
PIG-BABY (1)
  A12   98:29        guests to execution--once more the pig-baby was sneezing on the Duchess's knee, while plates and
PIGEON (13)
  A5    42:27                              "Serpent!" screamed the Pigeon.
  A5    42:39  trouble  enough  hatching the eggs," said the Pigeon; "but I must be on the look-out for serpents, night and
  A5    43:19              "I don't believe it," said the Pigeon; "but if they do, why, then they're a kind of serpent:
  A5    42:29     "Serpent, I say again!" repeated the Pigeon, but in a more subdued tone, and added, with a kind of
  A5    42:37  was  no  use in saying anything more till the Pigeon had finished.
  A5    42:25  hiss made  her draw back in a hurry: a large pigeon had flown into her face, and was beating her violently
  A5    43: 7              "Well! What are you?" said the Pigeon. "I can see you're trying to invent something!"
  A5    43:28         "Well, be off, then!" said the Pigeon in a sulky tone, as it settled down again into its nest
  A5    43:11        "A likely story indeed!" said the Pigeon, in a tone of the deepest contempt. "I've seen a good
  T9   201:40  other ear, in a voice like the cooing of a pigeon. "It would be such a treat! May I?"
  A5    43: 2  the  highest tree in the wood," continued the Pigeon, raising its voice to a shriek, "and just as I was
  A5    43:22  silent  for  a minute or two, which gave the Pigeon the opportunity of adding "You're looking for eggs, I
  A5    42:34  I've  tried banks, and I've tried hedges," the Pigeon went on, without attending to her; "but those serpents!
PIGS (4)
  A6    50:18  children she knew, who might do very well as pigs, and was just saying to herself "if one only knew the
  A9    72:27  about  as  much right," said the Duchess, "as pigs have to fly; and the m----"
  T4   142:24  And why the sea is boiling hot--/ And whether pigs have wings.'
  T9   202:28  eagerly  lapping  up  the gravy, "just like pigs in a trough!" thought Alice.
PILGRIM'S (1)
  AI     4: 7  are  twined / In Memory's mystic band. / Like pilgrim's wither'd wreath of flowers / Pluck'd in a far-off
PIN (3)
  T5   152:19  at  the brooch; but it was too late: the pin had slipped, and the Queen had pricked her finger.
  T5   149:29  "It  ca'n't  go straight, you know, if you pin it all on one side," Alice said as she gently put it right
  T5   153:21  in  a  triumphant tone. "Now you shall see me pin it on again, all by myself!"
PINCH (2)
  A11   91:20  that Dormouse out of court! Suppress him! Pinch him! Off with his whiskers!"
  A7    58: 3        and went on so long that they had to pinch it to make it stop.
PINCHED (2)
  A7    60:21  and  was going off into a doze; but, on being pinched by the Hatter, it woke up again with a little shriek,
  A7    58:24  both  cried. "Wake up, Dormouse!" And they pinched it on both sides at once.
PINE-APPLE (1)
  A1    11: 8  of  mixed flavour of cherry-tart, custard, pine-apple, roast turkey, toffy and hot buttered toast), she
PINK (2)
  T2   122:16  was  silence  in a moment, and several of the pink daisies turned white.
  A1     7:10  daisies,  when  suddenly a White Rabbit with pink eyes ran close by her.
PINNED (2)
  T5   149:27  voice. "It's out of temper, I think. I've pinned it here, and I've pinned it there, but there's no
  T5   149:28   I think. I've pinned it here, and I've pinned it there, but there's no pleasing it!"
PINNING (1)
  T4   147:15  coal-scuttles. "I hope you're a good hand at pinning and tying strings?" Tweedledum remarked. "Every one of
PINS (2)
  T5   149:36  now!" she said, after altering most of the pins. "But really you should have a lady's maid!"
  T5   149:24  Alice thought to herself, "and she's all over pins!--May I put your shawl straight for you?" she added aloud
PITEOUS (2)
  T9   192:30  "I  only  said 'if'!" poor Alice pleaded in a piteous tone.
  A5    41:18  I'm  not used to it!" pleaded poor Alice in a piteous tone. And she thought to herself "I wish the creatures
PITIED (1)
  A9    74:19  him  sighing as if his heart would break. She pitied him deeply. "What is his sorrow?" she asked the Gryphon
PITY (3)
  A8    65:35  said  Alice. "I don't think it's at all a pity. I said 'What for?'"
  A3    26:16                           "What a pity it wouldn't stay!" sighed the Lory, as soon as it was
  A8    65:34                   "Did you say 'What a pity!'?" the Rabbit said.
PITYING (2)
  T3   131:35        and Alice would have said something pitying to comfort it, "if it would only sigh like other
  T5   153: 9         "Ca'n't you?" the Queen said in a pitying tone. "Try again: draw a long breath, and shut your
PITYINGLY (1)
  T8W   16:12                    Alice looked pityingly at him. "Tying up the face is very good for the
PLACE (19) [See also FIREPLACE, HIDING-PLACE, etc.]
  T9   201: 9  off,  and brought a large plum-pudding in its place.
  T6   159:31  men / Couldn't put Humpty Dumpty in his place again."
  A7    59:39  him: the March Hare moved into the Dormouse's place, and Alice rather unwillingly took the place of the
  T5   156:33  hair  and  hands, she scrambled back into her place, and began to arrange her new-found treasures.
  A12   98:22  she  listened,  or seemed to listen, the whole place around her became alive with the strange creatures of
  A4    30:37  everything upon Bill! I wouldn't be in Bill's place for a good deal: this fireplace is narrow, to be sure;
  T7   176:14  two  great  creatures; but there was no other place for him.
  T2   127:20  the  running  you can do, to keep in the same place. If you want to get somewhere else, you must run at
  TI   103: 9  laughter: / No thought of me shall find a place / In thy young life's hereafter--/ Enough that now thou
  A7    59:40  place,  and Alice rather unwillingly took the place of the March Hare. The Hatter was the only one who got
  A12   99: 2  of  the cattle in the distance would take the place of the Mock Turtle's heavy sobs.
  A7    59:37  interrupted  the Hatter: "let's all move one place on."
  T1   114:14  as  if  he thought that was the most likely place to find one.
  T5   157: 5  she  remarked,  as Alice got back into her place, very much relieved to find herself still in the boat.
```

PLEADED (cont.)
A3   26:10   "I didn't mean it!" pleaded poor Alice. "But you're so easily offended, you know!
A5   41:18   "But I'm not used to it!" pleaded poor Alice in a piteous tone. And she thought to
PLEASANCE (2)
TC   209: 0   Alice Pleasance Liddell
TI   103:36 shall not touch, with breath of bale, / The pleasance of our fairy-tale.
PLEASANT (5) [See also UNPLEASANT]
T4   144: 8 Oysters,' said the Carpenter, / 'You've had a pleasant run! / Shall we be trotting home again?' / But answer
T4   141:15 The Walrus did beseech. / 'A pleasant walk, a pleasant talk, / Along the briny beach: / We cannot do with
A9   70: 4 Alice was very glad to find her in such a pleasant temper, and thought to herself that perhaps it was
T9   200: 2 treacle and ink, / Or anything else that is pleasant to drink: / Mix sand with the cider, and wool with
T4   141:15 walk with us!' / The Walrus did beseech. / 'A pleasant walk, a pleasant talk, / Along the briny beach: / We
PLEASANTER (1)
A4   28:27   "It was much pleasanter at home," thought poor Alice, "when one wasn't
PLEASANTLY (1)
T2   126: 7 she said this, but her companion only smiled pleasantly, and said "That's easily managed. You can be the
PLEASE (37)
T4   139:11 it's getting so dark. Would you tell me, please?"
T8   188: 8 the way I get my bread--/ A trifle, if you please.'
T9   201:10 "I won't be introduced to the pudding, please," Alice said rather hastily, "or we shall get no dinner
A3   26:13   "Please come back, and finish your story!" Alice called after
T9   201:41   "Please do," Alice said very politely.
A3   26:14 it. And the others all joined in chorus "Yes, please do!" But the Mouse only shook its head impatiently, and
A7   58:29   "Yes, please do!" pleaded Alice.
T1   115: 9   "Oh! please don't make such faces, my dear!" she cried out, quite
A7   59:28   "No, please go on!" Alice said very humbly. "I wo'n't interrupt you
A10   84:11   "Oh, a song, please, if the Mock Turtle would be so kind," Alice replied,
A1   8:44 what the name of the country is, you know. Please, Ma'am, is this New Zealand? Or Australia?" (and she
T5   156:11   "No, but I meant--please, may we wait and pick some?" Alice pleaded. "If you
A6   48:16   "Oh, please mind what you're doing!" cried Alice, jumping up and
A8   63: 3   "Would you tell me, please," said Alice, a little timidly, "why you are painting
T5   158:10   "Then I'll have one, please," said Alice, as she put the money down on the counter.
T2   127:23   "I'd rather not try, please!" said Alice. "I'm quite content to stay here--only I
T6   163:42   "Would you tell me please," said Alice, "what that means?"
T3   129:33   "Tickets, please!" said the Guard, putting his head in at the window. In
T5   158: 3   "I should like to buy an egg, please," she said timidly. "How do you sell them?"
A2   15:33 she began, in a low, timid voice, "If you please, Sir--" The Rabbit started violently, dropped the white
T4   140:20 said, as politely as she could, "would you please tell me first which road--"
A6   46:17   "Please, then," said Alice, "how am I to get in?"
T5   156: 6   "Oh, please! There are some scented rushes!" Alice cried in a
T5   156: 8   "You needn't say 'please' to me about 'em," the Sheep said, without looking up
A10   81:29 "I'd have said to the porpoise 'Keep back, please! We don't want you with us!'"
T5   155:33 "you've said it very often--and very loud. Please, where are the crabs?"
A6   51: 7 Alice, and she went on. "Would you tell me, please, which way I ought to go from here?"
A3   22: 3 thing I know. Silence all round, if you please! 'William the Conqueror, whose cause was favoured by
A6   47:12   "Please would you tell me," said Alice, a little timidly, for
T9   192:16 she thought, in asking if the game was over. "Please, would you tell me--" she began, looking timidly at the
T3   136:17 Alice thought, but nothing came of it. "Please, would you tell me what you call yourself?" she said
A12   94:34 put on his spectacles. "Where shall I begin, please your Majesty?" he asked.
A8   63:40   "My name is Alice, so please your Majesty," said Alice very politely; but she added,
A12   94:21   "Please, your Majesty," said the Knave, "I didn't write it, and
A12   94: 3 "There's more evidence to come yet, please your Majesty," said the White Rabbit, jumping up in a
A8   65: 6   "May it please your Majesty," said Two, in a very humble tone, going
A8   65:17 "Their heads are gone, if it please your Majesty!" the soldiers shouted in reply.
PLEASED (15)
TC   209: 6 nestle near, / Eager eye and willing ear, / Pleased a simple tale to hear--
A6   51:34 tail when it's pleased. Now I growl when I'm pleased, and wag my tail when I'm angry. Therefore I'm mad."
A9   70:10 people hot-tempered," she went on, very much pleased at having found out a new kind of rule, "and vinegar
T6   163:44 child," said Humpty Dumpty, looking very much pleased. "I meant by 'impenetrability' that we've had enough
A6   51:33 when it's angry, and wags its tail when it's pleased. Now I growl when I'm pleased, and wag my tail when
T9   196:30 she is! Pat her on the head, and see how pleased she'll be!" But this was more than Alice had courage
A6   51: 6 it only grinned a little wider. "Come, it's pleased so far," thought Alice, and she went on. "Would you
T8W   21:16 and Alice tripped down the hill again, quite pleased that she had gone back and given a few minutes to
T8W   16: 5 "Along of the wig?" Alice repeated, quite pleased to find that he was recovering his temper.
T6   162:31   "It is really?" said Alice, quite pleased to find that she had chosen a good subject after all.
A11   86:14 read about them in books, and she was quite pleased to find that she knew the name of nearly everything
T1   112: 4 a fire in the fireplace, and she was quite pleased to find that there was a real one, blazing away as
A6   48: 5 do," Alice said very politely, feeling quite pleased to have got into a conversation.
T2   122:30 a very good reason, and Alice was quite pleased to know it. "I never thought of that before!" she said
A9   72:15 say if I chose," the Duchess replied, in a pleased tone.
PLEASES (1)
A6   49: 7 he can thoroughly enjoy / The pepper when he pleases!"
PLEASING (2)
T5   149:28 and I've pinned it there, but there's no pleasing it!"
A5   42:35 to her; "but those serpents! There's no pleasing them!"
PLEASURE (3)
A12   99: 9 with all their simple sorrows, and find a pleasure in all their simple joys, remembering her own
A1   7: 8 her feel very sleepy and stupid), whether the pleasure of making a daisy-chain would be worth the trouble of
T5   149:38   "I'm sure I'll take you with pleasure!" the Queen said. "Two pence a week, and jam every

PLENTY (10)
    T5   156:27   she thought) that, though she managed to pick plenty of beautiful rushes as the boat glided by, there was
    T5   157:12   and all sorts of things," said the Sheep: "plenty of choice, only make up your mind. Now, what do you
    T6   164:26   with," Humpty Dumpty interrupted: "there are plenty of hard words there. 'Brillig' means four o'clock in
    T8   183:12   of practice," the Knight said very gravely: "plenty of practice!"
    T8   184:10   Alice was getting him on his feet again. "Plenty of practice!"
    T8   184: 9   "Plenty of practice!" he went on repeating, all the time that
    T8   183:11   "I've had plenty of practice," the Knight said very gravely: "plenty of
    A7   54: 9   out when they saw Alice coming. "There's plenty of room!" said Alice indignantly, and she sat down in a
    T1   108:14   in sticks for the bonfire--and it wants plenty of sticks, Kitty! Only it got so cold, and it snowed so
    A1   8:12   deep, or she fell very slowly, for she had plenty of time as she went down to look about her, and to
PLIED (1)
    AI   3: 4   oars, with little skill, / By little arms are plied, / While little hands make vain pretence / Our
-PLOT [See GRASS-PLOT]
PLUCK'D (1)
    AI   4: 8   / Like pilgrim's wither'd wreath of flowers / Pluck'd in a far-off land.
PLUM-CAKE (7)
    T7   173: 4   bread, some gave them brown: / Some gave them plum-cake and drummed them out of town."
    T8   182:14   said. "It'll come in handy if we find any plum-cake. Help me to get it into this bag."
    T7   177:21   herself, anyhow," said the Lion. "Do you like plum-cake, Monster?"
    T7   176: 9   "Then hand round the plum-cake, Monster," the Lion said, lying down and putting his
    T7   175:33   "Come, fetch out the plum-cake, old man!" the Unicorn went on, turning from her to
    T8   182:12   "It's meant for plum-cake," said Alice.
    T8   179: 6   her feet, on which she had tried to cut the plum-cake, "So I wasn't dreaming, after all," she said to
PLUM-PUDDING (2)
    T9   201: 8   waiters carried it off, and brought a large plum-pudding in its place.
    T3   133:13   find a Snap-dragon-fly. Its body is made of plum-pudding, its wings of holly-leaves, and its head is a
PLUNGED (1)
    T5   156:17   carefully rolled up, and the little arms were plunged in elbow-deep, to get hold of the rushes a good long
POCKET (8) [See also WAISTCOAT-POCKET]
    T1   115:30   took an enormous memorandum-book out of his pocket, and began writing. A sudden thought struck her, and
    A3   23:27   to do, and in despair she put her hand in her pocket, and pulled out a box of comfits (luckily the saltwater
    A7   55:37   to Alice: he had taken his watch out of his pocket, and was looking at it uneasily, shaking it every now
    T2   127:26   taking a little box out of her pocket. "Have a biscuit?"
    A3   23:32   very gravely. "What else have you got in your pocket?" it went on, turning to Alice.
    T2   127:32   And she took a ribbon out of her pocket, marked in inches, and began measuring the ground, and
    A10   83:19   the Owl, as a boon, / Was kindly permitted to pocket the spoon: / While the Panther received knife and fork
    A7   61: 3   mushroom (she had kept a piece of it in her pocket) till she was about a foot high; then she walked down
POCKET-HANDKERCHIEF (1)
    T4   144: 5   / Those of the largest size, / Holding his pocket-handkerchief / Before his streaming eyes.
POCKETS (1)
    T7   175:10   sauntered by them, with his hands in his pockets. "I had the best of it this time?" he said to the King
POEM (3)
    T6   164:15   "Would you kindly tell me the meaning of the poem called 'Jabberwocky'?"
    T1   116:16   This was the poem that Alice read
    T9   201:32   and it's a very curious thing, I think--every poem was about fishes in some way. Do you know why they're so
POEMS (1)
    T6   164:18   said Humpty Dumpty. "I can explain all the poems that ever were invented--and a good many that haven't
POETRY (11)
    T4   140: 9   So much obliged!" added Tweedledee. "You like poetry?"
    T4   140:10   "Ye-es, pretty well--some poetry," Alice said doubtfully. "Would you tell me which road
    T9   201:37   White Majesty knows a lovely riddle--all in poetry--all about fishes. Shall she repeat it?"
    T6   166:15   out one of his great hands, "I can repeat poetry as well as other folk, if it comes to that--"
    T6   166:12   it in a book," said Alice. "But I had some poetry repeated to me much easier than that, by--Tweedledee, I
    T9   201:28   "Do you know, I've had such a quantity of poetry repeated to me to-day," Alice began, a little
    T12   208: 1   would have enjoyed--I had such a quantity of poetry said to me, all about fishes! To-morrow morning you
    T6   159:32   "That last line is much too long for the poetry," she added, almost out loud, forgetting that Humpty
    T8   186:34   Alice asked, for she had heard a good deal of poetry that day.
    T8W   18: 7   Almost every one she had met had repeated poetry to her, and she thought she would try if the Wasp
    T6   166:14   "As to poetry, you know," said Humpty Dumpty, stretching out one of
POINT (2)
    T2   125: 6   Alice didn't dare to argue the point, but went on: "--and I thought I'd try and find my way
    T3   137:19   to herself, "when the road divides and they point different ways."
POINTED (4)
    T3   137:17   the wood, and the two finger-posts both pointed along it. "I'll settle it," Alice said to herself,
    T8   190:17   an eager look in the direction to which he pointed. "I sha'n't be long. You'll wait and wave your
    A4   27:16   that she ran off at once in the direction it pointed to, without trying to explain the mistake that it had
    T4   146:14   grew large and yellow all in a moment, as he pointed with a trembling finger at a small white thing lying
POINTING (7)
    T7   174:21   she brightened up. "Look, look!" she cried, pointing eagerly. "There's the White Queen running across the
    T4   139:14   of great schoolboys, that Alice couldn't help pointing her finger at Tweedledum, and saying "First Boy!"
    A7   57:12   March--just before he went mad, you know--" (pointing his teaspoon at the March Hare,) "--it was at the
    T3   137:22   there were sure to be two finger-posts pointing the same way, one marked "TO TWEEDLEDUM'S HOUSE," and
    A3   23:23   "Why, she, of course," said the Dodo, pointing to Alice with one finger; and the whole party at once
    A12   96:13   there they are!" said the King triumphantly, pointing to the tarts on the table. "Nothing can be clearer
    A8   63:43   "And who are these?" said the Queen, pointing to the three gardeners who were lying round the
POISON (3)
    A1   11: 4   that, if you drink much from a bottle marked "poison," it is almost certain to disagree with you, sooner or
    A1   10:21   she said, "and see whether it's marked 'poison' or not"; for she had read several nice little stories
    A1   11: 6   However, this bottle was not marked "poison," so Alice ventured to taste it, and, finding it very

POKER (2)
T1   115:41   had put 'The White Knight is sliding down the poker. He balances very badly'). "That's not a memorandum of
A1   11: 1   had taught them: such as, that a red-hot poker will burn you if you hold it too long; and that, if you
POKING (1)
T3   129:10   that was bustling about among the flowers, poking its proboscis into them, "just as if it was a regular
POKY (1)
A2   17:18   all, and I shall have to go and live in that poky little house, and have next to no toys to play with, and
POLITELY (13)
T6   161:17   I ca'n't quite remember it," Alice said, very politely.
T8   184:28   "Very much indeed," Alice said politely.
T9   201:41   "Please do," Alice said very politely.
T8W   18: 9   you mind saying it in rhyme?" she asked very politely.
A7   56:21   "I don't quite understand you," she said, as politely as she could.
T4   140:20   him. "If it's very long," she said, as politely as she could, "would you please tell me first which
T5   153:23   your finger is better now?" Alice said very politely, as she crossed the little brook after the Queen. * *
A8   63:40   so please your Majesty," said Alice very politely; but she added, to herself, "Why, they're only a pack
A3   22: 8   pardon!" said the Mouse, frowning, but very politely. "Did you speak?"
A6   48: 4   I don't know of any that do," Alice said very politely, feeling quite pleased to have got into a
A5   35:14   put it more clearly," Alice replied, very politely, "for I ca'n't understand it myself, to begin with;
A9   72:11   understand that better," Alice said very politely, "if I had it written down: but I ca'n't quite follow
T4   139:10   "I was thinking," Alice said politely, "which is the best way out of this wood: it's
PONDERING (1)
T3   134:20   this, Alice was silent for a minute or two, pondering. The Gnat amused itself meanwhile by humming round
POOL (11)
A2   19: 5   she heard something splashing about in the pool a little way off, and she swam nearer to make out what it
A2   19:36   to herself, as she swam lazily about in the pool, "and she sits purring so nicely by the fire, licking her
A4   27: 9   seemed to have changed since her swim in the pool; and the great hall, with the glass table and the little
A2   20:12   could go, and making quite a commotion in the pool as it went.
A2t   14: 1   "O Mouse, do you know the way out of this pool? I am very tired of swimming about here, O Mouse!" (Alice
A2   19:13   THE POOL OF TEARS
A2   18:26   she soon made out that she was in the pool of tears which she had wept when she was nine feet high.
A12   98:37   would be only rustling in the wind, and the pool rippling to the waving of the reeds--the rattling teacups
A2   15:23   gallons of tears, until there was a large pool round her, about four inches deep, and reaching half down
A12   98:26   splashed his way through the neighbouring pool--she could hear the rattle of the teacups as the March
A2   20:21   It was high time to go, for the pool was getting quite crowded with the birds and animals that
POOR (51)
A2   17:16   I'm sure those are not the right words," said poor Alice, and her eyes filled with tears again as she went
A3   26:40   if I shall ever see you any more!" And here poor Alice began to cry again, for she felt very lonely and
A3   26:10   "I didn't mean it!" pleaded poor Alice. "But you're so easily offended, you know!"
A5   41:18   "But I'm not used to it!" pleaded poor Alice in a piteous tone. And she thought to herself "I
T5   156:45   of little shrieks of "Oh, oh, oh!" from poor Alice, it swept her straight off the seat, and down among
A2   15:16   Poor Alice! It was as much as she could do, lying down on one
A1   10: 7   even if my head would go through," thought poor Alice, "it would be of very little use without my
T9   192:30   "I only said 'if'!" poor Alice pleaded in a piteous tone.
T3   136:14   "I wish I knew!" thought poor Alice. She answered, rather sadly, "Nothing, just now."
A7   60:12   This answer so confused poor Alice, that she let the Dormouse go on for some time
A1   12:28   be two people. "But it's no use now," thought poor Alice, "to pretend to be two people! Why, there's hardly
A4   28:27   "It was much pleasanter at home," thought poor Alice, "when one wasn't always growing larger and smaller
A1   12:14   going into the garden at once; but, alas for poor Alice! when she got to the door, she found she had
A9   75: 6   and then they both sat silent and looked at poor Alice, who felt ready to sink into the earth. At last the
A2   19:28   Alice hastily, afraid that she had hurt the poor animal's feelings. "I quite forgot you didn't like cats
A2   18:15   "and things are worse than ever," thought the poor child, "for I never was so small as this before, never!
T3   135:18   melancholy little sighs, and this time the poor Gnat really seemed to have sighed itself away, for, when
A5   42:14   where have my shoulders got to? And oh, my poor hands, how is it I ca'n't see you?" She was moving them
T7   171:10   about, and make the most fearful faces at the poor King.
T7   172:30   "Do you call that a whisper?" cried the poor King, jumping up and shaking himself. "If you do such a
T1   115:34   The poor King looked puzzled and unhappy, and struggled with the
T7   176:17   looking slyly up at the crown, which the poor King was nearly shaking off his head, he trembled so much
T8   186:21   Alice asked, hoping to cheer him up, for the poor Knight seemed quite low-spirited about it.
T8   182:38   and every now and then stopping to help the poor Knight, who certainly was not a good rider.
T3   131:40   off her thoughts from the unhappiness of the poor little creature.
A2   14: 6   sight, they were getting so far off). "Oh, my poor little feet, I wonder who will put on your shoes and
A11   87: 8   it away. She did it so quickly that the poor little juror (it was Bill, the Lizard) could not make out
T1   114: 4   was very anxious to be of use, and, as the poor little Lily was nearly screaming herself into a fit, she
A4   32:13   little animals and birds waiting outside. The poor little Lizard, Bill, was in the middle, being held up by
A6   49: 2   the baby violently up and down, and the poor little thing howled so, that Alice could hardly hear the
A4   32:28   stretching out one paw, trying to touch her. "Poor little thing!" said Alice, in a coaxing tone, and she
A1   12:20   she had tired herself out with trying, the poor little thing sat down and cried.
A6   50: 5   nothing more to do with you. Mind now!" The poor little thing sobbed again (or grunted, it was impossible
A6   49:17   "just like a star-fish," thought Alice. The poor little thing was snorting like a steam-engine when she
A12   93: 5   had put the Lizard in head downwards, and the poor little thing was waving its tail about in a melancholy
A11   89:19   "I'm a poor man," the Hatter went on, "and most things twinkled after
A11   90: 8   and went down on one knee. "I'm a poor man, your Majesty," he began.
A11   89:11   "I'm a poor man, your Majesty," the Hatter began, in a trembling
T8W   21:17   back and given a few minutes to making the poor old creature comfortable.
T4   144:14   Alice: "because he was a little sorry for the poor oysters."
T2   126:21   all the things move along with us?" thought poor puzzled Alice. And the Queen seemed to guess her thoughts
T5   152:14   "When I fasten my shawl again," the poor Queen groaned out: "the brooch will come undone directly.
T5   149:19   But I don't want it done at all!" groaned the poor Queen. "I've been a-dressing myself for the last two
T5   152:36   "Oh, don't go on like that!" cried the poor Queen, wringing her hands in despair. "Consider what a

POOR (cont.)
T9   196:19 not say this aloud, for fear of hurting the poor Queen's feelings.
T5   150:19   "It's a poor sort of memory that only works backwards," the Queen
A11   90:10   "You're a very poor speaker," said the King.
T9   195:31   The Red Queen said "That's a poor thin way of doing things. Now here, we mostly have days
T1   107: 7 children's faces was this: first she held the poor thing down by its ear with one paw, and then with the
T9   196:36   "She's tired, poor thing!" said the Red Queen. "Smoothe her hair--lend her
AI   3:11   stir the tiniest feather! / Yet what can one poor voice avail / Against three tongues together?
POP (1)
A1   8: 4   after it, and was just in time to see it pop down a large rabbit-hole under the hedge.
POPE (1)
A3   22: 4   Conqueror, whose cause was favoured by the pope, was soon submitted to by the English, who wanted leaders
PORCUPINE (1)
T5   155:13 to herself. "She gets more and more like a porcupine every minute!"
PORPOISE (4)
A10   81:31 "No wise fish would go anywhere without a porpoise."
A10   81:35 was going a journey, I should say 'With what porpoise?'"
A10   79:14 said a whiting to a snail, / "There's a porpoise close behind us, and he's treading on my tail. / See
A10   81:28 running on the song, "I'd have said to the porpoise 'Keep back, please! We don't want you with us!'"
PORTMANTEAU (2)
T6   165:10 is 'flimsy and miserable' (there's another portmanteau for you). And a 'borogove' is a thin
T6   164:31 is the same as 'active.' You see it's like a portmanteau--there are two meanings packed up into one word."
POSITION (2)
A10   83: 7   "It's the first position in dancing," Alice said; but she was dreadfully
A3   23:19 one finger pressed upon its forehead (the position in which you usually see Shakespeare, in the pictures
POSITIVELY (1)
A3   21:11 knowing how old it was, and as the Lory positively refused to tell its age, there was no more to be
POSSIBLE (4) [See also IMPOSSIBLE]
T5   155: 6 went through the ceiling as quietly as possible, as if it were quite used to it.
T6   161: 1 ear, as he leant forwards (and as nearly as possible fell off the wall in doing so) and offered Alice his
T1   112:12 but that all the rest was as different as possible. For instance, the pictures on the wall next the fire
A4   29:40 from which she concluded that it was just possible it had fallen into a cucumber-frame, or something of
POSSIBLY (6)
T8   191: 8 set it on her lap to make out what it could possibly be.
T2   123:38   "You ca'n't possibly do that," said the Rose: "I should advise you to walk
T4   147:26 "it's one of the most serious things that can possibly happen to one in a battle--to get one's head cut off
A6   46:13 making such a noise inside, no one could possibly hear you." And certainly there was a most
A4   32: 8 some change in my size; and, as it ca'n't possibly make me larger, it must make me smaller, I suppose."
A1   12:17 to the table for it, she found she could not possibly reach it: she could see it quite plainly through the
POST (1) [See also DOOR-POST]
T3   131:20   thought Alice), saying "She must go by post, as she's got a head on her--" "She must be sent as a
-POSTS [See FINGER-POSTS]
-POT [See FLOWER-POT, TEAPOT]
POUNDS (6)
T3   130: 1 child! Why, his time is worth a thousand pounds a minute!"
T3   130: 9 Why, the smoke alone is worth a thousand pounds a puff!"
T3   130:14 nothing at all. Language is worth a thousand pounds a word!"
T3   130: 5 came from. The land there is worth a thousand pounds an inch!"
A2   20: 9 he says it's so useful, it's worth a hundred pounds! He says it kills all the rats and--oh dear!" cried
T3   130:16   "I shall dream about a thousand pounds to-night, I know I shall!" thought Alice.
POUR (1)
A2   17:10 crocodile / Improve his shining tail, / And pour the waters of the Nile / On every golden scale!
POURED (1)
A7   56:22 is asleep again," said the Hatter, and he poured a little hot tea upon its nose.
-POWDER [See GUNPOWDER]
POWDERED (1)
A6   45: 8 a frog; and both footmen, Alice noticed, had powdered hair that curled all over their heads. She felt very
PRACTICE (8)
T8   183:10 off quite so often, when they've had much practice."
T8   183:12 the Knight said very gravely: "plenty of practice!"
T8   184:10 was getting him on his feet again. "Plenty of practice!"
T8   184: 9   "Plenty of practice!" he went on repeating, all the time that Alice was
T8   183: 3   "I'm afraid you've not had much practice in riding," she ventured to say, as she was helping
T5   153:13   "I daresay you haven't had much practice," said the Queen. "When I was your age, I always did
T8   183:11   "I've had plenty of practice," the Knight said very gravely: "plenty of practice!
A1   8:34   no one to listen to her, still it was good practice to say it over) "--yes, that's about the right
PRATTLED (1)
T12   207:32 "And what did Dinah turn to, I wonder?" she prattled on, as she settled comfortably down, with one elbow
PRAY (3)
A9   72:16   "Pray don't trouble yourself to say it any longer than that,"
A5   39: 4 the goose, with the bones and the beak--/ Pray, how did you manage to do it?"
A5   38: 4 turned a back-somersault in at the door--/ Pray, what is the reason of that?
PRECIOUS (2)
T1   113:21 she knocked him over among the cinders. "My precious Lily! My imperial kitten!" and she began scrambling
A6   48:17 in an agony of terror. "Oh, there goes his precious nose!", as an unusually large saucepan flew close by
PRESENT (8)
T6   162:35 it, "they gave it me--for an un-birthday present."
T6   162:38   "I mean, what is an un-birthday present?"
T8W   16:11   And I ties up my face--as at the present."
A5   35: 6 rather shyly, "I--I hardly know, Sir, just at present--at least. I know who I was when I got up this morning,

PRESENT (cont.)
T6   162:29   and a beautiful one, as you say. It's a present from the White King and Queen. There now!"
T6   162:39   "A present given when it isn't your birthday, of course."
A9   72:19   trouble!" said the Duchess. "I make you a present of everything I've said as yet."
A9   72:20   "A cheap sort of present!" thought Alice. "I'm glad people don't give
PRESENTED (1)
A3   24: 2   round her once more, while the Dodo solemnly presented the thimble, saying "We beg your acceptance of this
PRESENTLY (2)
A1   8:39   Presently she began again. "I wonder if I shall fall right
A4   29:25   Presently the Rabbit came up to the door, and tried to open it
PRESENTS (5)
T6   163:20   days when you might get un-birthday presents--"
T6   162:40   Alice considered a little. "I like birthday presents best," she said at last.
A9   72:21   Alice. "I'm glad people don't give birthday-presents like that!" But she did not venture to say it out
A2   15: 5   thought; "and how funny it'll seem, sending presents to one's own feet! And how odd the directions will
T6   163:22   "And only one for birthday presents, you know. There's glory for you!"
PRESSED (3)
A4   29:26   door opened inwards, and Alice's elbow was pressed hard against it, that attempt proved a failure. Alice
A5   42: 1   to eat some of the other bit. Her chin was pressed so closely against her foot, that there was hardly
A3   23:18   and it stood for a long time with one finger pressed upon its forehead (the position in which you usually
PRESSING (1)
A4   28:10   had drunk half the bottle, she found her head pressing against the ceiling, and had to stoop to save her
PRETENCE (2)
T1   110:38   up in that room too--but that may be only pretence, just to make it look as if they had a fire. Well
AI   3: 5   are plied, / While little hands make vain pretence / Our wanderings to guide.
PRETEND (8)
T1   110: 9   down among my pieces. Kitty dear, let's pretend--" And here I wish I could tell you half the things
T1   110:11   beginning with her favourite phrase "Let's pretend." She had had quite a long argument with her sister
T1   110:18   suddenly in her ear, "Nurse! Do let's pretend that I'm a hungry hyaena and you're a bone!"
T1   110:21   from Alice's speech to the kitten. "Let's pretend that you're the Red Queen, Kitty! Do you know, I think
T1   111: 8   through into it, somehow, Kitty. Let's pretend the glass has got all soft like gauze, so that we can
T1   111: 7   got, oh! such beautiful things in it! Let's pretend there's a way of getting through into it, somehow,
A1   12:28   But it's no use now," thought poor Alice, "to pretend to be two people! Why, there's hardly enough of me
T1   110:13   all because Alice had begun with "Let's pretend we're kings and queens;" and her sister, who liked
PRETENDED (2)
T12   208:13   kitten only began on the other paw, and pretended it hadn't heard the question.
T12   207:20   to her sister: "it turned away its head, and pretended not to see it: but it looked a little ashamed of
PRETENDING (4)
T2   120:14   it," Alice said, looking up at the house and pretending it was arguing with her. "I'm not going in again
T1   108:29   Kitty: I heard you! What's that you say?" (pretending that the kitten was speaking). "Her paw went into
A1   12:27   for this curious child was very fond of pretending to be two people. "But it's no use now," thought
T1   108: 7   herself. Kitty sat very demurely on her knee, pretending to watch the progress of the winding, and now and
PRETEXTS (1)
A3   26:35   high time you were all in bed!" On various pretexts they all moved off, and Alice was soon left alone.
PRETTIER (1)
A9   76:30   doubtfully: "it means--to--make--anything--prettier."
PRETTIEST (1)
T5   156:30   "The prettiest are always further!" she said at last with a sigh at
PRETTY (9)
T1   109:15   whenever the wind blows--oh, that's very pretty!" cried Alice, dropping the ball of worsted to clap her
A10   79: 2   "It must be a very pretty dance," said Alice timidly.
T8   190:27   his head as usual! However, he gets on again pretty easily--that comes of having so many things hung round
T4   148: 4   Alice laughed. "You must hit the trees pretty often, I should think," she said.
T1   118:25   "It seems very pretty," she said when she had finished it, "but it's rather
T1   107: 4   the last quarter of an hour (and bearing it pretty well, considering): so you see that it couldn't have
T8   182:42   he fell off behind. Otherwise he kept on pretty well, except that he had a habit of now and then
T4   140:10   "Ye-es, pretty well--some poetry," Alice said doubtfully. "Would you
T6   159:20   gently explained. "And some eggs are very pretty, you know," she added, hoping to turn her remark into a
PREVENT (3)
T8   184:18   of laughter, in spite of all she could do to prevent it.
A6   49:24   hold of its right ear and left foot, so as to prevent its undoing itself), she carried it out into the open
T7   176:23   Here the King interrupted, to prevent the quarrel going on: he was very nervous, and his
PRICKED (3)
T5   152:20   late: the pin had slipped, and the Queen had pricked her finger.
T5   152:10   "I haven't pricked it yet," the Queen said, "but I soon shall--oh, oh,
T5   152: 9   a chance of making herself heard. "Have you pricked your finger?"
PRIMA (1)
AI   3:13   Imperious Prima flashes forth / Her edict "to begin it": / In gentler
PRINCIPAL (3)
T3   129: 5   further. "Principal rivers--there are none. Principal mountains--I'm on the only one, but I don't think
T3   129: 4   hopes of being able to see a little further. "Principal rivers--there are none. Principal mountains--I'm on
T3   129: 6   one, but I don't think it's got any name. Principal towns--why, what are those creatures, making honey
PRINCIPALLY (1)
T1   110:25   imitate: however, the thing didn't succeed, principally, Alice said, because the kitten wouldn't fold its
PRINTED (1)
A1   10:18   label, with the words "DRINK ME" beautifully printed on it in large letters.
PRISON (5)
T7   173:23   "He's only just out of prison, and he hadn't finished his tea when he was sent in,"
T7   173:30   "Were you happy in prison, dear child?" said Haigha.
T1   109: 4   do at the end of a year? I should be sent to prison, I suppose, when the day came. Or--let me see--suppose

PRISON (cont.)
T5   150: 4   spoke, "there's the King's Messenger. He's in prison now, being punished: and the trial doesn't even begin
A8   69: 8   "She's in prison," the Queen said to the executioner: "fetch her here."
PRISONER (4)
T8   181: 2   doubtfully. "I don't want to be anybody's prisoner. I want to be a Queen."
T8   179:16   her, the horse stopped suddenly: "You're my prisoner!" the Knight cried, as he tumbled off his horse.
A12   94: 8   "but it seems to be a letter, written by the prisoner to--to somebody."
T8   179:28   "She's _my_ prisoner, you know!" the Red Knight said at last.
PRISONER'S (1)
A12   94:15   "Are they in the prisoner's handwriting?" asked another of the jurymen.
PRIVILEGE (1)
T9   199:39   honour to see me, a favour to hear: / 'Tis a privilege high to have dinner and tea / Along with the Red
PRIZE (1)
A3   23:30   "But she must have a prize herself, you know," said the Mouse.
PRIZES (5)
A3   23:21   said "Everybody has won, and all must have prizes."
A3   23:25   her, calling out, in a confused way, "Prizes! Prizes!"
A3   23:25   round her, calling out, in a confused way, "Prizes! Prizes!"
A3   23:22   "But who is to give the prizes?" quite a chorus of voices asked.
A3   23:28   not got into it), and handed them round as prizes. There was exactly one a-piece, all round.
PROBOSCIS (1)
T3   129:10   bustling about among the flowers, poking its proboscis into them, "just as if it was a regular bee,"
PROCEED (2)
A3   22:11   "I thought you did," said the Mouse. "I proceed. 'Edwin and Morcar, the earls of Mercia and
A12   93: 1   "The trial cannot proceed," said the King, in a very grave voice, "until all the
PROCESSION (5)
A8   63:34   When the procession came opposite to Alice, they all stopped and looked
A8   63:26   velvet cushion; and, last of all this grand procession, came THE KING AND THE QUEEN OF HEARTS.
A8   65: 9   the roses. "Off with their heads!" and the procession moved on, three of the soldiers remaining behind to
A8   63:31   "and besides, what would be the use of a procession," thought she, "if people had all to lie down on
A8   65:24   then!" roared the Queen, and Alice joined the procession, wondering very much what would happen next.
PROCESSIONS (1)
A8   63:30   remember ever having heard of such a rule at processions; "and besides, what would be the use of a
PRODUCED (1)
A4   32: 4   out "You'd better not do that again!", which produced another dead silence.
PRODUCING (1)
A6   45:11   The Fish-Footman began by producing from under his arm a great letter, nearly as large
PROGRESS (1)
T1   108: 8   demurely on her knee, pretending to watch the progress of the winding, and now and then putting out one paw
PROMISE (1)
A7   59:33   they draw?" said Alice, quite forgetting her promise.
PROMISED (3)
T6   160:25   "If I _did_ fall," he went on, "the King has promised me--ah, you may turn pale, if you like! You didn't
T6   160:26   was going to say that, did you? The King has promised me--with his very own mouth--to--to--"
A3   24:14   "You promised to tell me your history, you know," said Alice, "and
PROMISING (1)
A5   36:20   This sounded promising, certainly. Alice turned and came back again.
PRONOUNCED (2)
A4   30: 7   "Sure, it's an arm, yer honour!" (He pronounced it "arrum.")
T7   170:28   when he's happy. His name is Haigha." (He pronounced it so as to rhyme with 'mayor.')
PROPER (5)
T6   162:12   said Humpty Dumpty; "but two can. With proper assistance, you might have left off at seven."
T9   192:29   be a Queen, you know, till you've passed the proper examination. And the sooner we begin it, the better."
A12   93: 2   "until all the jurymen are back in their proper places--all," he repeated with great emphasis, looking
A6   49:30   grunt," said Alice; "that's not at all a proper way of expressing yourself."
A6   49:22   As soon as she had made out the proper way of nursing it (which was to twist it up into a sort
PROPERLY (2)
T8   184: 5   as I was saying is--to keep your balance properly. Like this, you know--"
T1   110:26   because the kitten wouldn't fold its arms properly. So, to punish it, she held it up to the
PROPOSAL (1)
A7   58:22   know one," said Alice, rather alarmed at the proposal.
PROPPED (1)
T2   127:10   The Queen propped her up against a tree, and said kindly, "You may rest
PROSECUTE (1)
A3   25:11   in the house, 'Let us both go to law: I will prosecute you.--Come, I'll take no denial: We must have the
PROTECTION (1)
A8   65:11   unfortunate gardeners, who ran to Alice for protection.
PROUD (6)
T6   168: 6   And he was very proud and stiff: / He said 'I'd go and wake them, if--'
A9   76: 8   too," said Alice. "You needn't be so proud as all that."
T6   168: 4   "But he was very stiff and proud: / He said, 'You needn't shout so loud!'
A11   86:25   or three times over to herself, being rather proud of it: for she thought, and rightly too, that very few
T6   162: 8   "Too proud?" the other enquired.
T6   160:39   see such another: and, to show you I'm not proud, you may shake hands with me!" And he grinned almost
PROUDEST (1)
T6   163:39   some of them--particularly verbs: they're the proudest--adjectives you can do anything with, but not verbs--
PROUDLY (1)
T8   184:41   The Knight looked down proudly at his helmet, which hung from the saddle. "Yes," he
PROVE (2)
A12   94:30   "It doesn't prove anything of the sort!" said Alice. "Why, you don't even

PROVE (cont.)
A12   94:22 Knave, "I didn't write it, and they ca'n't prove that I did: there's no name signed at the end."
PROVED (2)
A4   29:27 was pressed hard against it, that attempt proved a failure. Alice heard it say to itself "Then I'll go
A6   51:27   Alice didn't think that proved it at all: however, she went on: "And how do you know
PROVES (1)
A12   94:28   "That proves his guilt, of course," said the Queen, "so, off with--"
PROVIDED (1)
T8   182: 5 he went on after a pause, "it's as well to be provided for everything. That's the reason the horse has all
PROVOKED (1)
T2   123:44   A little provoked, she drew back, and, after looking everywhere for the
PROVOKING (7)
T5   156:26 reach it." And it certainly did seem a little provoking ("almost as if it happened on purpose," she thought)
T6   159:17   "It's very provoking," Humpty Dumpty said after a long silence, looking
T12 208:12 it! I'm sure your paw can wait!" But the provoking kitten only began on the other paw, and pretended it
T5   155: 1 she was looking at. "And this one is the most provoking of all--but I'll tell you what--" she added, as a
T7   177: 8 away diligently with the knife. "It's very provoking!" she said, in reply to the Lion (she was getting
T6   162:25   "It is a--most--provoking--thing," he said at last, "when a person doesn't
A8   66:13 and was going to begin again, it was very provoking to find that the hedgehog had unrolled itself, and
PUDDING (12) [See also PLUM-PUDDING]
T8   186:30 only look puzzled: she was thinking of the pudding.
T9   201:27   to leave all the conversation to the pudding!"
T9   201:12 But the Red Queen looked sulky, and growled "Pudding----Alice: Alice--Pudding. Remove the pudding!" and the
T9   201:13 "Pudding----Alice: Alice--Pudding. Remove the pudding!" and the waiters took it away so quickly that Alice
T9   201: 7 she called out "Waiter! Bring back the pudding!" and there it was again in a moment, like a
T8   186: 7 went on after a pause, "was inventing a new pudding during the meat-course."
T8   186:17 lower and lower, "I don't believe that pudding ever was cooked! In fact, I don't believe that pudding
T8   186:18 was cooked! In fact, I don't believe that pudding ever will be cooked! And yet it was a very clever
T9   201:22   "What impertinence!" said the Pudding. "I wonder how you'd like it, if I were to cut a slice
T9   201:10   "I won't be introduced to the pudding, please," Alice said rather hastily, "or we shall get
T9   201:13 sulky, and growled "Pudding----Alice: Alice--Pudding. Remove the pudding!" and the waiters took it away so
T8   186:19 will be cooked! And yet it was a very clever pudding to invent."
PUDDING-COURSES (1)
T8   186:14 the next day. I suppose you wouldn't have two pudding-courses in one dinner?"
PUFF (1)
T3   130: 9 the smoke alone is worth a thousand pounds a puff!"
PUFFED (1)
A5   36:28 something worth hearing. For some minutes it puffed away without speaking; but at last it unfolded its arms
PUFFING (1)
T4   144:24 something that sounded to her like the puffing of a large steam-engine in the wood near them, though
PULL (2)
T9   204:14 the tablecloth with both hands: one good pull, and plates, dishes, guests, and candles came crashing
T9   203: 6 hold of the edge of the table, and managed to pull herself down again.
PULLED (4)
T6   168:11 And when I found the door was locked, / I pulled and pushed and kicked and knocked.
T5   155:24 needed any answer: so Alice said nothing, but pulled away. There was something very queer about the water,
A3   23:27 despair she put her hand in her pocket, and pulled out a box of comfits (luckily the saltwater had not got
T1   108:33 any more excuses, but listen! Number two: you pulled Snowdrop away by the tail just as I had put down the
PULLING (1)
A4   30:19 Alice. "I wonder what they'll do next! As for pulling me out of the window, I only wish they could! I'm sure
PUMP (1)
T6   167:16 went thump: / I filled the kettle at the pump.
PUN (1)
A12   96:27   "It's a pun!" the King added in an angry tone, and everybody laughed.
PUNCH (1)
T8   180: 6 their clubs with their arms, as if they were Punch and Judy--What a noise they make when they tumble! Just
PUNCHING (1)
A10   78: 5 Gryphon; and it set to work shaking him and punching him in the back. At last the Mock Turtle recovered
PUNISH (2)
T1   110:26 wouldn't fold its arms properly. So, to punish it, she held it up to the Looking-glass, that it might
T9   196: 9 what he came for," said Alice: "he wanted to punish the fish, because--"
PUNISHED (6)
T5   151:12 "but it wouldn't be all the better his being punished."
T5   151:14 at any rate," said the Queen. "Were you ever punished?"
T5   150: 4 King's Messenger. He's in prison now, being punished: and the trial doesn't even begin till next Wednesday
T1   108:38 three faults, Kitty, and you've not been punished for any of them yet. You know I'm saving up all your
A2   19: 2 trying to find her way out. "I shall be punished for it now, I suppose, by being drowned in my own
T5   151:18 "Yes, but then I had done the things I was punished for," said Alice: "that makes all the difference."
PUNISHMENT (1)
T1   109: 5 the day came. Or--let me see--suppose each punishment was to be going without a dinner: then, when the
PUNISHMENTS (2)
T1   108:39 of them yet. You know I'm saving up all your punishments for Wednesday week--Suppose they had saved up all
T1   109: 1 week--Suppose they had saved up all my punishments?" she went on, talking more to herself than the
PUPPY (6)
A4   32:42 feet, ran round the thistle again: then the puppy began a series of short charges at the stick, running a
A4   33: 7   "And yet what a dear little puppy it was!" said Alice, as she leant against a buttercup to
A4   32:34 and held it out to the puppy: whereupon the puppy jumped into the air off all its feet at once, with a
A4   32:38 moment she appeared on the other side, the puppy made another rush at the stick, and tumbled head over
A4   32:27   An enormous puppy was looking down at her with large round eyes, and
A4   32:34 a little bit of stick, and held it out to the puppy: whereupon the puppy jumped into the air off all its

PUPPY'S (1)
    A4   33: 5   quite tired and out of breath, and till the puppy's bark sounded quite faint in the distance.
PURCHASE (1)
    T8   188:40   / But for a copper halfpenny, / And that will purchase nine.
PURE (1)
    TI   103: 1   Child of the pure unclouded brow / And dreaming eyes of wonder! / Though
PURPLE (1)
    A12   97: 3   "Hold your tongue!" said the Queen, turning purple.
PURPOSE (2)
    A10   81:36   "Don't you mean 'purpose'?" said Alice.
    T5   156:27   provoking ("almost as if it happened on purpose," she thought) that, though she managed to pick plenty
PURR (5)
    T12 207: 8   them, they always purr. "If they would only purr for 'yes,' and mew for 'no,' or any rule of that sort,"
    T12 207: 7   that, whatever you say to them, they always purr. "If they would only purr for 'yes,' and mew for 'no,' or
    T12 207:23   while you're thinking what to--what to purr. It saves time, remember!" And she caught it up and gave
    T1   107:10   which was lying quite still and trying to purr--no doubt feeling that it was all meant for its good.
    T12 207: 1   "Your Red Majesty shouldn't purr so loud," Alice said, rubbing her eyes, and addressing
PURRED (2)
    T12 207:11   On this occasion the kitten only purred: and it was impossible to guess whether it meant "yes"
    T1   110: 7   understood it: and when I said 'Check!' you purred! Well, it was a nice check, Kitty, and really I might
PURRING (2)
    A6   51:35   "I call it purring, not growling," said Alice.
    A2   19:36   swam lazily about in the pool, "and she sits purring so nicely by the fire, licking her paws and washing
PURSE (1)
    T5   158: 8   said in a surprised tone, taking out her purse.
PURSED (1)
    T6   160:23   there's no chance of--but if I did--" Here he pursed up his lips, and looked so solemn and grand that Alice
PURSUE (1)
    AI   3:20   Anon, to sudden silence won, / In fancy they pursue / The dream-child moving through a land / Of wonders
PURSUING (1)
    T5   154:17   after she had spent a minute or so in vainly pursuing a large bright thing that looked sometimes like a
PUSH (3)
    T9   202:38   ("And they did push so!" she said afterwards, when she was telling her sister
    A12   96: 1   that's the jury, of course--'If she should push the matter on'--that must be the Queen--'What would
    A12   95: 3   / (We know it to be true): / If she should push the matter on, / What would become of you?
PUSHED (2)
    T6   168:11   I found the door was locked, / I pulled and pushed and kicked and knocked.
    T9   203: 2   while she made her speech: the two Queens pushed her so, one on each side, that they nearly lifted her
-PUSS [See CHESHIRE-PUSS]
PUT (67)
    A4   32: 3   and some of them hit her in the face. "I'll put a stop to this," she said to herself, and shouted out
    A8   63: 7   ought to have been a red rose-tree, and we put a white one in by mistake; and, if the Queen was to find
    T8   185:22   he repeated: "but it was careless of him to put another man's helmet on--with the man in it, too."
    A12   92:12   idea that they must be collected at once and put back into the jury-box, or they would die.
    T9   199:31   sprinkle the table with buttons and bran: / Put cats in the coffee, and mice in the tea--/ And welcome
    A8   67:19   the whole head appeared, and then Alice put down her flamingo, and began an account of the game,
    A4   28:12   save her neck from being broken. She hastily put down the bottle, saying to herself "That's quite enough--I
    T8W   15:17   Alice put down the newspaper. "I'm afraid you're not well," she said
    T1   108:34   Snowdrop away by the tail just as I had put down the saucer of milk before her! What, you were thirsty
    A11   86:30   to the Gryphon. "They ca'n't have anything to put down yet, before the trial's begun."
    T5   156: 9   looking up from her knitting: "I didn't put 'em there, and I'm not going to take 'em away."
    A4   30:26   the other--Bill! Fetch it here, lad!--Here, put 'em up at this corner--No, tie 'em together first--they
    A4   30:36   said Alice to herself. "Why, they seem to put everything upon Bill! I wouldn't be in Bill's place for a
    A3   23:26   had no idea what to do, and in despair she put her hand in her pocket, and pulled out a box of comfits
    T7   178: 9   feast, before she dropped to her knees, and put her hands over her ears, vainly trying to shut out the
    T8   191: 4   she exclaimed in a tone of dismay, as she put her hands up to something very heavy, that fitted tight
    T1   113:12   think they can hear me," she went on, as she put her head closer down, "and I'm nearly sure they ca'n't see
    T9   197: 8   now you know the words," she added, as she put her head down on Alice's other shoulder, "just sing it
    T1   115: 1   take his breath away; but, before she put him on the table, she thought she might as well dust him a
    T3   132: 5   The Horse, who had put his head out of the window, quietly drew it in and said
    A8   65:31   spoke, and then raised himself upon tiptoe, put his mouth close to her ear, and whispered "She's under
    A11   90:32   left the court, without even waiting to put his shoes on.
    T6   159:31   horses and all the King's men / Couldn't put Humpty Dumpty in his place again."
    T2   128: 4   She had got all the pegs put in by this time, and Alice looked on with great interest
    T5   158:13   The Sheep took the money, and put it away in a box: then she said "I never put things into
    A7   56: 6   the Hatter grumbled: "you shouldn't have put it in with the bread-knife."
    A1   8:21   of killing somebody underneath, so managed to put it into one of the cupboards as she fell past it.
    A5   35:14   "I'm afraid I ca'n't put it more clearly," Alice replied, very politely, "for I
    T8   179:33   something the shape of a horse's head) and put it on.
    T8   185: 4   out again, the other White Knight came and put it on. He thought it was his own helmet."
    T5   149:30   it all on one side," Alice said as she gently put it right for her; "and dear me, what a state your hair is
    A12   93: 7   to move. She soon got it out again, and put it right; "not that it signifies much," she said to
    A1   9:15   question, it didn't much matter which way she put it. She felt that she was dozing off, and had just begun
    A4   28: 4   ME," but nevertheless she uncorked it and put it to her lips. "I know something interesting is sure to
    T9   198:10   a little way, and a creature with a long beak put its head out for a moment and said "No admittance till the
    T6   166:38   Dumpty said: "they're not sensible, and they put me out."
    A9   72: 6   you would seem to be'--or, if you'd like it put more simply--'Never imagine yourself not to be otherwise
    A9   71: 5   "I dare say you're wondering why I don't put my arm round your waist," the Duchess said, after a pause:
    T8   189:15   And now, if e'er by chance I put / My fingers into glue, / Or madly squeeze a right-hand
    T8   184:31   head is high enough already.' Now, first I put my head on the top of the gate--then the head's high

PUT (cont.)

T4	147:20	about--and the quantity of things they put on--and the trouble they gave her in tying strings and
T5	149: 6	in the way," Alice said, as she helped her to put on her shawl again.
A11	88:26	Here the Queen put on her spectacles, and began staring hard at the Hatter,
A11	86:35	out "Silence in the court!", and the King put on his spectacles and looked anxiously round, to make out
A12	94:33	The White Rabbit put on his spectacles. "Where shall I begin, please your
A2	18: 2	hands, and was surprised to see that she had put on one of the Rabbit's little white kid-gloves while she
T9	200:19	"You've missed the soup and fish," she said. "Put on the joint!" And the waiters set a leg of mutton before
A2	14: 6	"Oh, my poor little feet, I wonder who will put on your shoes and stockings for you now, dears? I'm sure I
A4	28:20	went on growing, and, as a last resource, she put one arm out of the window, and one foot up the chimney,
A7	58:11	"Is that the reason so many tea-things are put out here?" she asked.
T5	152:24	now?" Alice asked, holding her hands ready to put over her ears again.
T8W	19:12	take my wig from me and say / 'How can you put such rubbish on?'
A7	60:34	last time she saw them, they were trying to put the Dormouse into the teapot.
A5	41:21	to it in time," said the Caterpillar; and it put the hookah into its mouth, and began smoking again.
T12	207:15	went down on her knees on the hearth-rug, and put the kitten and the Queen to look at each other. "Now
A12	93: 5	jury-box, and saw that, in her haste, she had put the Lizard in head downwards, and the poor little thing
T5	158:10	I'll have one, please," said Alice, as she put the money down on the counter. For she thought to herself,
AI	3:28	dry, / And faintly strove that weary one / To put the subject by, / "The rest next time--" "It is next time!
T1	115:40	looking over the book (in which Alice had put 'The White Knight is sliding down the poker. He balances
T9	202:23	very queerly they managed it: some of them put their glasses upon their heads like extinguishers, and
A2	17:26	sudden burst of tears, "I do wish they would put their heads down! I am so very tired of being all alone
A8	65:12	You sha'n't be beheaded!" said Alice, and she put them into a large flower-pot that stood near. The three
T5	158:14	put it away in a box: then she said "I never put things into people's hands--that would never do--you must
T3	129:16	cottages with the roofs taken off, and stalks put to them--and what quantities of honey they must make! I
T1	110:28	you're not good directly," she added, "I'll put you through into Looking-glass House. How would you like
T2	122:24	"Put your hand down, and feel the ground," said the Tiger-lily.
T5	149:24	to herself, "and she's all over pins!--May I put your shawl straight for you?" she added aloud.

PUTTING (17)

T8	181: 9	can breathe more easily," said the Knight, putting back his shaggy hair with both hands, and turning his
A11	86:31	"They're putting down their names," the Gryphon whispered in reply,
T9	196:32	"A little kindness--and putting her hair in papers--would do wonders with her--"
T3	135:42	under the--under the--under this, you know!" putting her hand on the trunk of the tree. "What does it call
T9	201:35	fishes," she said, very slowly and solemnly, putting her mouth close to Alice's ear, "her White Majesty
T7	173: 6	asked, as well as she could, for the run was putting her quite out of breath.
T7	173:26	How are you, dear child?" he went on, putting his arm affectionately round Hatta's neck.
T7	176:10	Monster," the Lion said, lying down and putting his chin on his paws. "And sit down, both of you," (to
T7	172:25	"I'll whisper it," said the Messenger, putting his hands to his mouth in the shape of a trumpet and
T3	129:33	"Tickets, please!" said the Guard, putting his head in at the window. In a moment everybody was
T2	127:35	"At the end of two yards," she said, putting in a peg to mark the distance, "I shall give you your
T8	182:16	because the Knight was so very awkward in putting in the dish: the first two or three times that he
T8	179:35	of course?" the White Knight remarked, putting on his helmet too.
T1	108: 8	the progress of the winding, and now and then putting out one paw and gently touching the ball, as if it
A2	17:21	I'll stay down here. It'll be no use their putting their heads down and saying 'Come up again, dear!' I
A9	71:15	the Duchess: "what a clear way you have of putting things!"
T1	108:24	I was very nearly opening the window, and putting you out into the snow! And you'd have deserved it, you

PUZZLE (2)

| A2 | 16: 1 | 'Who in the world am I?' Ah, that's the great puzzle!" And she began thinking over all the children she knew |
| T5 | 155: 3 | it up to the very top shelf of all. It'll puzzle it to go through the ceiling, I expect!" |

PUZZLED (20)

A12	94:18	thing about it." (The jury all looked puzzled.)
T6	162:36	"I beg your pardon?" Alice said with a puzzled air.
T2	126:21	the things move along with us?" thought poor puzzled Alice. And the Queen seemed to guess her thoughts, for
T1	115:34	The poor King looked puzzled and unhappy, and struggled with the pencil for some
A5	42:36	Alice was more and more puzzled, but she thought there was no use in saying anything
T9	198: 6	bell must I ring?" she went on, very much puzzled by the names. "I'm not a visitor, and I'm not a
A10	83: 8	dancing," Alice said; but she was dreadfully puzzled by the whole thing, and longed to change the subject.
T5	155:12	"How can she knit with so many?" the puzzled child thought to herself. "She gets more and more like
A10	81:15	Alice was thoroughly puzzled. "Does the boots and shoes!" she repeated in a
A8	66:11	round and look up in her face, with such a puzzled expression that she could not help bursting out
A11	88:35	Alice felt a very curious sensation, which puzzled her a good deal until she made out what it was: she
A7	59: 7	way of living would be like, but it puzzled her too much: so she went on: "But why did they live
A8	67:10	noticed a curious appearance in the air: it puzzled her very much at first, but after watching it a minute
T7	177:18	sat with the knife in her hand, very much puzzled how to begin. "The Monster has given the Lion twice as
T9	195:29	Alice was puzzled. "In our country," she remarked, "there's only one day
T1	116:13	She puzzled over this for some time, but at last a bright thought
T8	186:30	Alice could only look puzzled: she was thinking of the pudding.
A7	56:19	Alice felt dreadfully puzzled. The Hatter's remark seemed to her to have no sort of
T6	164: 7	"Oh!" said Alice. She was too much puzzled to make any other remark.
T6	163:37	Alice was too much puzzled to say anything; so after a minute Humpty Dumpty began

PUZZLER (1)

| T4 | 144:21 | This was a puzzler. After a pause, Alice began, "Well! They were both |

PUZZLING (6)

A3	25: 3	"but why do you call it sad?" And she kept on puzzling about it while the mouse was speaking, so that her
A5	43:40	"Come, there's half my plan done now! How puzzling all these changes are! I'm never sure what I'm going
A2	16: 8	she's she, and I'm I, and--oh dear, how puzzling it all is! I'll try if I know all the things I used
T8	182:37	for a few minutes she walked on in silence, puzzling over the idea, and every now and then stopping to
A5	36:15	Here was another puzzling question; and, as Alice could not think of any good
T3	136: 6	and all she could say, after a great deal of puzzling, was "L, I know it begins with L!"

-Q-

-QUADRILLE [See LOBSTER-QUADRILLE]
QUAINT (1)
   AI   3:33 <u>Wonderland</u>: / <u>Thus</u> <u>slowly</u>, <u>one</u> <u>by</u> <u>one</u>, / <u>Its</u> <u>quaint</u> <u>events</u> <u>were</u> <u>hammered</u> <u>out</u>--/ <u>And</u> <u>now</u> <u>the</u> <u>tale</u> <u>is</u> <u>done</u>, /
-QUAKE [See EARTHQUAKE]
QUANTITIES (2)
   T3 129:16 taken off, and stalks put to them--and what quantities of honey they must make! I think I'll go down and--
   T4 141: 4 hand: / <u>They</u> <u>wept</u> <u>like</u> <u>anything</u> <u>to</u> see / Such quantities of sand: / 'If <u>this</u> <u>were</u> <u>only</u> <u>cleared</u> <u>away</u>,' / <u>They</u>
QUANTITY (3)
   T9 201:28   "Do you know, I've had such a quantity of poetry repeated to me to-day," Alice began, a
  T12 208: 1 thing you would have enjoyed--I had such a quantity of poetry said to me, all about fishes! To-morrow
   T4 147:20 the way those two bustled about--and the quantity of things they put on--and the trouble they gave her
QUARREL (4)
   T4 139: 4 <u>both</u> <u>the</u> <u>heroes</u> <u>so</u>, / <u>They</u> <u>quite</u> <u>forgot</u> <u>their</u> <u>quarrel</u>."
   T7 176:23 Here the King interrupted, to prevent the quarrel going on: he was very nervous, and his voice quite
   A8 67:24 in rather a complaining tone, "and they all quarrel so dreadfully one ca'n't hear oneself speak--and they
   T9 195:17   "Don't let us quarrel," the White Queen said in an anxious tone. "What is
QUARRELED (1)
   A7 57:11 his head mournfully. "Not I!" he replied. "We quarreled last March--just before <u>he</u> went mad, you know--"
QUARRELING (2)
   A8 66:20 played at once, without waiting for turns, quarreling all the while, and fighting for the hedgehogs; and
   A9 73: 3 they were playing the Queen never left off quarreling with the other players, and shouting "Off with his
QUARTER (1)
   T1 107: 4 its face washed by the old cat for the last quarter of an hour (and bearing it pretty well, considering):
QUEEN (250)
   A8 63:14 and Alice looked round, eager to see the Queen.
   A8 65:16   "Are their heads off?" shouted the Queen.
   A9 73:14 Mock Turtle Soup is made from," said the Queen.
  A12 93:40   "Nearly two miles high," added the Queen.
  A12 94: 6   "What's in it?" said the Queen.
  A12 96:19 had <u>fits</u>, my dear, I think?" he said to the Queen.
   T1 115:14 his hair, and set him upon the table near the Queen.
   T2 123:37 be far grander to have a talk with a real Queen.
   T2 127:38   "Thirst quenched, I hope?" said the Queen.
   T5 149:12 rather timidly: "Am I addressing the White Queen?"
   T5 150: 3   "It's very good jam," said the Queen.
   T5 153:24 as she crossed the little brook after the Queen. * * * * * * * * * * * * *
   T8 181: 2 want to be anybody's prisoner. I want to be a Queen."
   T9 192:17 me--" she began, looking timidly at the Red Queen.
   T9 194:13 you think nothing would remain?" said the Red Queen.
   T9 194:33 "Of course you know your ABC?" said the Red Queen.
   T9 195:10   "Who ever said it was?" said the Red Queen.
   T9 196: 3   "What did he want?" said the Red Queen.
   T9 196: 8   "Well, only on Thursdays," said the Queen.
   T9 201:21 and cut a slice and handed it to the Red Queen.
  T12 207:21 itself, so I think it <u>must</u> have been the Red Queen.")
  T12 207:25 "just in honour of <u>its</u> having been a Red Queen."
  T8W 13:15 unwillingly, for she was <u>very</u> anxious to be a Queen.
  A11 91: 1 "--and just take his head off outside," the Queen added to one of the officers; but the Hatter was out of
  T9t 192: 1   QUEEN ALICE
   T9 198: 2 an arched doorway, over which were the words "QUEEN ALICE" in large letters, and on each side of the arch
   T9 200:23 you to that leg of mutton," said the Red Queen. "Alice--Mutton: Mutton--Alice." The leg of mutton got
   T1 113: 8   "Here are the Red King and the Red Queen," Alice said (in a whisper, for fear of frightening
   T9 200: 4 <u>cider</u>, <u>and</u> <u>wool</u> <u>with</u> <u>the</u> <u>wine</u>--/ <u>And</u> <u>welcome</u> <u>Queen</u> <u>Alice</u> <u>with</u> <u>ninety-times-nine</u>!"
   T9 199:32 <u>coffee</u>, <u>and</u> <u>mice</u> <u>in</u> <u>the</u> <u>tea</u>--/ <u>And</u> <u>welcome</u> <u>Queen</u> <u>Alice</u> <u>with</u> <u>thirty-times-three</u>!"
   T9 202:20 Queen. "Meanwhile, we'll drink your health--Queen Alice's health!" she screamed at the top of her voice,
   T2 124:11 know what you mean by <u>your</u> way," said the Queen: "all the ways about here belong to <u>me</u>--but <u>why</u> did you
   A6 46: 2 the order of the words a little, "From the Queen. An invitation for the Duchess to play croquet."
   T9 197: 7 <u>we'll</u> <u>go</u> <u>to</u> <u>the</u> <u>ball</u>--/ <u>Red</u> <u>Queen</u>, <u>and</u> <u>White</u> <u>Queen</u>, <u>and</u> <u>Alice</u>, <u>and</u> <u>all</u>!
   A8 65:23   "Come on, then!" roared the Queen, and Alice joined the procession, wondering very much
   A9 73: 8 and all the players, except the King, the Queen, and Alice, were in custody and under sentence of
   T2 124: 4 she found herself face to face with the Red Queen, and full in sight of the hill she had been so long
   A9 73:16   "Come on, then," said the Queen, "and he shall tell you his history."
  A11 88:31 foot to the other, looking uneasily at the Queen, and in his confusion he bit a large piece out of his
   T9 199:27 / <u>Come</u> <u>and</u> <u>dine</u> <u>with</u> <u>the</u> <u>Red</u> <u>Queen</u>, <u>the</u> <u>White</u> <u>Queen</u>, <u>and</u> <u>me</u>!'"
   T9 199:40 <u>and</u> <u>tea</u> / <u>Along</u> <u>with</u> <u>the</u> <u>Red</u> <u>Queen</u>, <u>the</u> <u>White</u> <u>Queen</u>, <u>and</u> <u>me</u>!"
   T9 196:13 ("She <u>never</u> <u>could</u>, you know," said the Red Queen.) "And part of the roof came off, and ever so much
   T1 114: 6 herself into a fit, she hastily picked up the Queen and set her on the table by the side of her noisy little
   T9 197: 2 "I must do it myself, then," said the Red Queen, and she began:--
   A6 49:12 go and get ready to play croquet with the Queen," and she hurried out of the room. The cook threw a
   A9 74: 1 at the picture.) "Up, lazy thing!" said the Queen, "and take this young lady to see the Mock Turtle, and
   A8 63:11 across the garden, called out "The Queen! The Queen!" and the three gardeners instantly threw themselves
   T9 192:12 feel a bit surprised at finding the Red Queen and the White Queen sitting close to her, one on each
   T2 124: 6   "Where do you come from?" said the Red Queen. "And where are you going? Look up, speak nicely, and

QUEEN (cont.)

T9	197: 7	the feast's over, we'll go to the ball--/ Red Queen, and White Queen, and Alice, and all!
T9	194: 7	I suppose--" Alice was beginning, but the Red Queen answered for her. "Bread-and-butter, of course. Try
T9	195: 3	"Fan her head!" the Red Queen anxiously interrupted. "She'll be feverish after so much
T2	126: 6	She glanced rather shyly at the real Queen as she said this, but her companion only smiled
T9	194:42	"Where do you pick the flower?" the White Queen asked: "In a garden or in the hedges?"
T9	193:24	"Can you do Addition?" the White Queen asked. "What's one and one and one and one and
T9	197:17	know, because there never was more than one Queen at a time. Do wake up, you heavy things!" she went on in
A7	58: 5	the first verse," said the Hatter, "when the Queen bawled out 'He's murdering the time! Off with his head!'
T9	194:39	Here the Red Queen began again. "Can you answer useful questions?" she said
T9	196:11	Here the White Queen began again. "It was such a thunderstorm, you ca'n't
T5	152: 2	say "There's a mistake somewhere--," when the Queen began screaming, so loud that she had to leave the
T9	200:18	At last the Red Queen began. "You've missed the soup and fish," she said. "Put
T2	126: 4	join--though of course I should like to be a Queen, best."
T9	193:14	The Red Queen broke the silence by saying, to the White Queen, "I
T9	204: 3	to see what was the matter with the White Queen; but, instead of the Queen, there was the leg of mutton
A8	67: 4	she had not as yet had any dispute with the Queen, but she knew that it might happen any minute, "and then
T8	190:15	over that little brook, and then you'll be a Queen--But you'll stay and see me off first?" he added as
T5	149: 2	for the owner: in another moment the White Queen came running wildly through the wood, with both arms
T9	194: 5	"She ca'n't do Subtraction," said the White Queen. "Can you do Division? Divide a loaf by a knife--what's
A8	65:19	"That's right!" shouted the Queen. "Can you play croquet?"
T5	152:16	said the words the brooch flew open, and the Queen clutched wildly at it, and tried to clasp it again.
T2	126:26	getting so much out of breath: and still the Queen cried "Faster! Faster!" and dragged her along. "Are we
T1	113:19	"It is the voice of my child!" the White Queen cried out, as she rushed past the King, so violently
T9	194:18	"Why, look here!" the Red Queen cried. "The dog would lose its temper, wouldn't it?"
T2	127:39	not know what to say to this, but luckily the Queen did not wait for an answer, but went on. "At the end of
T9	195: 7	"She's all right again now," said the Red Queen. "Do you know Languages? What's the French for
T9	195:14	But the Red Queen drew herself up rather stiffly, and said "Queens never
T9	194:22	dog went away, its temper would remain!" the Queen exclaimed triumphantly.
T2	127: 5	"Now! Now!" cried the Queen. "Faster! Faster!" And they went so fast that at last
T9	195:39	"Just so!" cried the Red Queen. "Five times as warm, and five times as cold--just as
T1	114: 3	had a right to be a little annoyed with the Queen, for he was covered with ashes from head to foot.
T9	194:29	Alice said, turning suddenly on the White Queen, for she didn't like being found fault with so much.
A12	96:20	"Never!" said the Queen, furiously, throwing an inkstand at the Lizard as she
T1	114: 8	The Queen gasped, and sat down: the rapid journey through the air
T9	194:30	The Queen gasped and shut her eyes. "I can do Addition," she said,
T9	196:34	The White Queen gave a deep sigh, and laid her head on Alice's shoulder.
T5	152:14	"When I fasten my shawl again," the poor Queen groaned out: "the brooch will come undone directly. Oh,
A11	89: 4	All this time the Queen had never left off staring at the Hatter, and, just as
A8	68: 6	The Queen had only one way of settling all difficulties, great or
A9	73:21	quite unhappy at the number of executions the Queen had ordered.
T5	152:20	it was too late: the pin had slipped, and the Queen had pricked her finger.
T5	153:28	"Oh, much better!" cried the Queen, her voice rising into a squeak as she went on. "Much
T8	190:35	"and now for the last brook, and to be a Queen! How grand it sounds!" A very few steps brought her to
T9	193:15	broke the silence by saying, to the White Queen, "I invite you to Alice's dinner-party this afternoon."
T9	193: 8	"Nobody said you did," said the Red Queen. "I said you couldn't if you tried."
T2	127:31	"While you're refreshing yourself," said the Queen, "I'll just take the measurements." And she took a
A8	64:15	"Get up!" said the Queen in a shrill, loud voice, and the three gardeners
A8	65:41	"Get to your places!" shouted the Queen in a voice of thunder, and people began running about in
A9	72:32	tremble. Alice looked up, and there stood the Queen in front of them, with her arms folded, frowning like a
T9	194: 1	"She ca'n't do Addition," the Red Queen interrupted. "Can you do Subtraction? Take nine from
T9	193: 1	mean--" Alice was beginning, but the Red Queen interrupted her impatiently.
T2	125: 8	"When you say 'hill'," the Queen interrupted, "I could show you hills, in comparison with
T5	150: 8	"No, it ca'n't," said the Queen. "It's jam every other day: to-day isn't any other day,
T9	201:26	"Make a remark," said the Red Queen: "it's ridiculous to leave all the conversation to the
T5	149:19	don't want it done at all!" groaned the poor Queen. "I've been a-dressing myself for the last two hours."
T2	126:10	when you get to the Eighth Square you'll be a Queen--"Just at this moment, somehow or other, they began to
T2	126:15	could do to keep up with her: and still the Queen kept crying "Faster! Faster!" but Alice felt she could
T1	110:21	kitten. "Let's pretend that you're the Red Queen, Kitty! Do you know, I think if you sat up and folded
T9	202: 1	The White Queen laughed with delight, and stroked Alice's cheek. Then
A9	73:10	Then the Queen left off, quite out of breath, and said to Alice "Have
T9	201:12	But the Red Queen looked sulky, and growled "Pudding----Alice: Alice--
T9	196:25	The White Queen looked timidly at Alice, who felt she ought to say
T1	115:39	"What manner of things?" said the Queen, looking over the book (in which Alice had put 'The
T10	205: 3	The Red Queen made no resistance whatever: only her face grew very
T9	202:20	think about it, and then guess," said the Red Queen. "Meanwhile, we'll drink your health--Queen Alice's
A9	73: 1	saw her, they hurried back to the game, the Queen merely remarking that a moment's delay would cost them
T9	192:33	said a great deal more than that!" the White Queen moaned, wringing her hands. "Oh, ever so much more than
T9	201:38	Majesty's very kind to mention it," the White Queen murmured into Alice's other ear, in a voice like the
A9	73: 3	All the time they were playing the Queen never left off quarreling with the other players, and
T2	127:19	"A slow sort of country!" said the Queen. "Now, here, you see, it takes all the running you can
A8	63:27	this grand procession, came THE KING AND THE QUEEN OF HEARTS.
A7	57:13	"--it was at the great concert given by the Queen of Hearts, and I had to sing
A11	87:16	"The Queen of Hearts, she made some tarts, / All on a summer day: /
A11	86: 1	The King and Queen of Hearts were seated on their throne when they arrived,
T1	110:23	try, there's a dear!" And Alice got the Red Queen off the table, and set it up before the kitten as a
T5	149: 7	The White Queen only looked at her in a helpless frightened sort of way,
A12	98:28	meal, and the shrill voice of the Queen ordering off her unfortunate guests to execution--once
T2	125: 3	"That's right," said the Queen, patting her on the head, which Alice didn't like at all
A8	63:43	"And who are these?" said the Queen, pointing to the three gardeners who were lying round

QUEEN (cont.)

T2	127:10	The Queen propped her up against a tree, and said kindly, "You may
A11	88:26	Here the Queen put on her spectacles, and began staring hard at the
T12	207:31	Do you know that you're scrubbing a White Queen? Really, it's most disrespectful of you!
A11	91:26	And, he added, in an undertone to the Queen, "Really, my dear, you must cross-examine the next
T5	150:20	of memory that only works backwards," the Queen remarked.
T9	193:12	"A nasty, vicious temper," the Red Queen remarked; and then there was an uncomfortable silence
T9	193:19	you the opportunity of doing it," the Red Queen remarked: "but I daresay you've not had many lessons in
T5	153: 5	"You needn't say 'exactly,'" the Queen remarked. "I can believe it without that. Now I'll give
T9	192:31	two Queens looked at each other, and the Red Queen remarked, with a little shudder, "She says she only said
T2	127: 1	"Nearly there!" the Queen repeated. "Why, we passed it ten minutes ago! Faster!"
T5	150: 1	that happened the week after next," the Queen replied in a careless tone. "For instance, now," she
T1	115:24	To which the Queen replied "You haven't got any whiskers."
T7	174:22	cried, pointing eagerly. "There's the White Queen running across the country! She came flying out of the
A8	65:40	you! You see she came rather late, and the Queen said--"
T5	151: 8	would be all the better, wouldn't it?" the Queen said, as she bound the plaster round her finger with a
T5	152:10	"I haven't pricked it yet," the Queen said, "but I soon shall--oh, oh, oh!"
T9	202:29	to return thanks in a neat speech," the Red Queen said, frowning at Alice as she spoke.
T2	127:25	"I know what you'd like!" the Queen said good-naturedly, taking a little box out of her
T1	115:27	"You will, though," the Queen said, "if you don't make a memorandum of it."
T5	149:26	"I don't know what's the matter with it!" the Queen said, in a melancholy voice. "It's out of temper, I
T5	153: 9	"Ca'n't you?" the Queen said in a pitying tone. "Try again: draw a long breath,
T9	195:17	"Don't let us quarrel," the White Queen said in an anxious tone. "What is the cause of lightning
T5	149:13	"Well, yes, if you call that a-dressing," the Queen said. "It isn't my notion of the thing, at all."
T5	150:11	"That's the effect of living backwards," the Queen said kindly: "it always makes one a little giddy at
T2	124:18	"It's time for you to answer now," the Queen said looking at her watch: "open your mouth a little
T9	195:25	"Which reminds me--" the White Queen said, looking down and nervously clasping and unclasping
T5	152:30	"I wish I could manage to be glad!" the Queen said. "Only I never can remember the rule. You must be
A8	63:35	they all stopped and looked at her, and the Queen said, severely, "Who is this?" She said it to the Knave
T5	151:20	"But if you hadn't done them," the Queen said, "that would have been better still; better, and
T9	195:31	The Red Queen said "That's a poor thin way of doing things. Now here,
A8	67:31	"How do you like the Queen?" said the Cat in a low voice.
T5	150: 5	You couldn't have it if you did want it," the Queen said. "The rule is, jam to-morrow and jam yesterday--but
T9	192:35	"So you did, you know," the Red Queen said to Alice. "Always speak the truth--think before you
A9	72:40	"Let's go on with the game," the Queen said to Alice; and Alice was too much frightened to say
T9	196:21	"Your Majesty must excuse her," the Red Queen said to Alice, taking one of the White Queen's hands in
A8	69: 8	"She's in prison," the Queen said to the executioner: "fetch her here." And the
T5	151:16	you were all the better for it, I know!" the Queen said triumphantly.
T5	149:38	"I'm sure I'll take you with pleasure!" the Queen said. "Two pence a week, and jam every other day."
T9	201: 6	"Certainly not," the Red Queen said, very decidedly: "it isn't etiquette to cut any one
T9	202:36	"That wouldn't be at all the thing," the Red Queen said very decidedly: so Alice tried to submit to it with
T5	149:32	"The brush has got entangled in it!" the Queen said with a sigh. "And I lost the comb yesterday."
T5	153: 1	"That's the way it's done," the Queen said with great decision: "nobody can do two things at
A8	62:11	better not talk!" said Five. "I heard the Queen say only yesterday you deserved to be beheaded."
T2	126:22	with us?" thought poor puzzled Alice. And the Queen seemed to guess her thoughts, for she cried "Faster!
T9	203: 7	"Take care of yourself!" screamed the White Queen, seizing Alice's hair with both her hands. "Something's
A12	96:30	"No, no!" said the Queen. "Sentence first--verdict afterwards."
T5	152: 4	unfinished. "Oh, oh, oh!" shouted the Queen, shaking her hand about as if she wanted to shake it off
T9	192:18	"Speak when you're spoken to!" the Queen sharply interrupted her.
T9	192: 9	was nobody to see her, "and if I really am a Queen," she said as she sat down again, "I shall be able to
T2	123:29	round eagerly and found that it was the Red Queen. "She's grown a good deal!" was her first remark. She
T2	125:13	The Red Queen shook her head. "You may call it 'nonsense' if you like
T9	201:15	However, she didn't see why the Red Queen should be the only one to give orders; so, as an
A12	97: 5	"Off with her head!" the Queen shouted at the top of her voice. Nobody moved.
A11	91:19	"Collar that Dormouse!" the Queen shrieked out. "Behead that Dormouse! Turn that Dormouse
T9	192:12	at finding the Red Queen and the White Queen sitting close to her, one on each side: she would have
T1	113:10	"and there are the White King and the White Queen sitting on the edge of the shovel--and here are two
A8	67:36	The Queen smiled and passed on.
T9	193:16	The White Queen smiled feebly, and said "And I invite you."
T9	196:36	"She's tired, poor thing!" said the Red Queen. "Smoothe her hair--lend her your nightcap--and sing her
A12	94:28	"That proves his guilt, of course," said the Queen, "so, off with--"
A9	74: 6	to stay with it as to go after that savage Queen: so she waited.
T9	192: 2	said Alice. "I never expected I should be a Queen so soon--and I'll tell you what it is, your Majesty,"
T5	153:18	the Queen's shawl across a little brook. The Queen spread out her arms again and went flying after it, and
A9	72:36	"Now, I give you fair warning," shouted the Queen, stamping on the ground as she spoke; "either you or
T1	114:24	across more slowly than she had lifted the Queen, that she mightn't take his breath away; but, before she
T9	193:10	"She's in that state of mind," said the White Queen, "that she wants to deny something--only she doesn't
T9	194:15	"Wrong, as usual," said the Red Queen: "the dog's temper would remain."
A8	63:11	looking across the garden, called out "The Queen! The Queen!" and the three gardeners instantly threw
A8	65: 2	jumped up, and began bowing to the King, the Queen, the royal children, and everybody else.
T9	199:27	they be, / Come and dine with the Red Queen, the White Queen, and me!'"
T9	199:40	to have dinner and tea / Along with the Red Queen, the White Queen, and me!"
T12	207:14	on the table till she had found the Red Queen: then she went down on her knees on the hearth-rug, and
T6	162:30	say. It's a present from the White King and Queen. There now!"
T9	204: 4	with the White Queen; but, instead of the Queen, there was the leg of mutton sitting in the chair. "Here
A9	74: 8	up and rubbed its eyes: then it watched the Queen till she was out of sight: then it chuckled. "What fun!"
T2	124:16	at this, but she was too much in awe of the Queen to disbelieve it. "I'll try it when I go home," she
T2	123:41	nothing, but set off at once towards the Red Queen. To her surprise she lost sight of her in a moment, and
T12	207:15	on the hearth-rug, and put the kitten and the Queen to look at each other. "Now Kitty!" she cried, clapping
A6	45:14	"For the Duchess. An invitation from the Queen to play croquet." The Frog-Footman repeated, in the same

```
QUEEN (cont.)
T9   201: 5   up  the  knife and fork, and looking from one Queen to the other.
A6    52: 3   said   the  Cat.  "Do you play croquet with the Queen to-day?"
A8    63:38                       "Idiot!" said the Queen, tossing her head impatiently; and turning to Alice, she
T2   128:22              At the next peg the Queen turned again, and this time she said "Speak in French
A8    64:12                            The Queen turned angrily away from him, and said to the Knave
A8    64: 5                            The Queen turned crimson with fury, and, after glaring at her for
A12   97: 3           "Hold your tongue!" said the Queen, turning purple.
A8    67:33   extremely--"  Just  then she noticed that the Queen was close behind her, listening: so she went on
A8    66:22   the  hedgehogs; and in a very short time the Queen was in a furious passion, and went stamping about, and
T9   204:19   as  the  cause  of  all the mischief--but the Queen was no longer at her side--she had suddenly dwindled
A8    64: 9   Alice,  very  loudly  and  decidedly, and the Queen was silent.
A8    63: 8   we put a white one in by mistake; and, if the Queen was to find out, we should all have our heads cut off,
T9   196: 4   "He said he would come in," the White Queen went on, "because he was looking for a hippopotamus. Now
T9   196:28   never was really well brought up," the Red Queen went on: "but it's amazing how good-tempered she is! Pat
T9   195:44   "Humpty  Dumpty  saw  it  too,"  the White Queen went on in a low voice, more as if she were talking to
T2   128:16             "You should have said," the Queen went on in a tone of grave reproof, "'It's extremely
T2   126:14   that  they were running hand in hand, and the Queen went so fast that it was all she could do to keep up
T1   115:20   it she found he had recovered, and he and the Queen were talking together in a frightened whisper--so low,
T5   151:13   "You're  wrong  there, at any rate," said the Queen. "Were you ever punished?"
T9   192:27   "What do you mean by 'If you really are a Queen'? What right have you to call yourself so? You ca'n't be
T5   152:25   done  all  the  screaming  already," said the Queen. "What would be the good of having it all over again?"
A12   96: 3   should  push the matter on'--that must be the Queen--'What would become of you?'--What, indeed!--'I gave her
T2   127:15   "Of course it is," said the Queen. "What would you have it?"
T5   153:13   you haven't had much practice,"  said the Queen. "When I was your age, I always did it for half-an-hour
T9   195:22   "It's  too  late to correct it," said the Red Queen: "when you've once said a thing, that fixes it, and you
T9   202:31   "We  must  support  you, you know," the White Queen whispered, as Alice got up to do it, very obediently,
T9   194:35          "So do I," the White Queen whispered: "we'll often say it over together, dear. And
A8    65: 8              "I see!" said the Queen, who had meanwhile been examining the roses. "Off with
T5   153:32              She looked at the Queen, who seemed to have suddenly wrapped herself up in wool.
A8    68: 4   the King very decidedly; and he called to the Queen, who was passing at the moment, "My dear! I wish you
A11   90:30   said  the Hatter, with an anxious look at the Queen, who was reading the list of singers.
T1   114:15         "Blew--me--up," panted the Queen, who was still a little out of breath. "Mind you come up
A8    68:30   on between the executioner, the King, and the Queen, who were all talking at once, while all the rest were
T9   204:18   she  went on,  turning fiercely upon the Red Queen, whom she considered as the cause of all the mischief--
T2   123:45   back,  and,  after looking everywhere for the Queen (whom she spied out at last, a long way off), she
T9   201:34              She spoke to the Red Queen, whose answer was a little wide of the mark. "As to
T9   192:24            "Ridiculous!" cried the Queen. "Why, don't you see, child--" here she broke off with a
A8    65:39   Rabbit  whispered  in a frightened tone. "The Queen will hear you! You see she came rather late, and the
T5   152:36   "Oh,  don't  go on like that!" cried the poor Queen, wringing her hands in despair. "Consider what a great
T9   198: 8   not  a servant. There ought to be one marked 'Queen,' you know--"
T9   192:28   have  you to call yourself so? You ca'n't be a Queen, you know, till you've passed the proper examination.
A8    65: 3           "Leave off that!" screamed the Queen. "You make me giddy." And then, turning to the rose-tree
T9   195: 1   "How  many  acres of ground?" said the White Queen. "You mustn't leave out so many things."
QUEEN'S (13)
A9    72:43   The  other  guests had taken advantage of the Queen's absence, and were resting in the shade: however, the
A8    69: 2                    The Queen's argument was that, if something wasn't done about it
T9   204: 6   Alice  turned  again,  just in time to see the Queen's broad good-natured face grinning at her for a moment
A8t   62: 1                       THE QUEEN'S CROQUET-GROUND
A8    65:37         "She boxed the Queen's ears--" the Rabbit began. Alice gave a little scream
T9   196:20   say  this aloud, for fear of hurting the poor Queen's feelings.
T9   196:22   Queen said to Alice, taking one of the White Queen's hands in her own, and gently stroking it: "she means
A8    67:29   the ground--and I should have croqueted the Queen's hedgehog just now, only it ran away when it saw mine
T2   126: 8   "That's  easily managed. You can be the White Queen's Pawn, if you like, as Lily's too young to play: and
T5   153:18   she spoke, and a sudden gust of wind blew the Queen's shawl across a little brook. The Queen spread out her
A12   98:39   would  change to tinkling sheep-bells, and the Queen's shrill cries to the voice of the shepherd-boy--and she
T2   125:16   curtseyed  again,  as she was afraid from the Queen's tone that she was a little offended: and they walked
A8    68:11   how  the  game was going on, as she heard the Queen's voice in the distance, screaming with passion. She had
QUEENS (13)
A8    63:22   Next  came the  guests,  mostly  Kings and Queens, and among them Alice recognized the White Rabbit: it
T1   110:13   had begun with "Let's pretend we're kings and queens;" and her sister, who liked being very exact, had
T9   197:16   before,  that any one had to take care of two Queens asleep at once! No, not in all the History of England--
T7   174:23   out  of  the wood over yonder--How fast those Queens can run!"
T9   200:15   at  the  head of the table: the Red and White Queens had already taken two of them, but the middle one was
T9   192: 5   to  be  lolling about on the grass like that! Queens have to be dignified, you know!"
T9   192:31                   The two Queens looked at each other, and the Red Queen remarked, with
T9   195:16              "I wish Queens never asked questions," Alice thought to herself.
T9   195:15   drew  herself  up rather  stiffly, and said "Queens never make bargains."
T9   203: 2   her  place while she made her speech: the two Queens pushed her so, one on each side, that they nearly
T9   194:26           "She ca'n't do sums a bit!" the two Queens said together, with great emphasis.
T2   128:20   the  way--and in the Eighth Square we shall be Queens together, and it's all feasting and fun!" Alice got up
T9   197:10   getting  sleepy, too." In another moment both Queens were fast asleep, and snoring loud.
QUEER (15)
T5   155:24   but  pulled  away. There  was something very queer about the water, she thought, as every now and then the
T8   179: 4   about  the  Lion and  the  Unicorn and those queer Anglo-Saxon Messengers. However, there was the great
T6   163:17   round  for him. "I thought it looked a little queer. As I was saying, that seems to be done right--though I
T3   131: 6   a Beetle sitting next the Goat (it was a very queer carriage-full of passengers altogether), and, as the
T6   160:18   simply  in  her  good-natured anxiety for the queer creature. "That wall is so very narrow!"
A2    15:38   time  she  went on talking. "Dear, dear! How queer everything is to-day! And yesterday things went on just
A10   82:21   what  she was saying; and the words came very queer indeed:--
```

QUEER (cont.)
  A4   27:27   "How queer it seems," Alice said to herself, "to be going messages
  A12   98:20   the   very   tones   of   her voice,. and see that queer little toss of her head to keep back the wandering hair
  A12   98:41   the   shriek of the Gryphon, and all the other queer noises, would change (she knew) to the confused clamour
  A2   19: 3   being drowned in my own tears! That will be a queer thing, to be sure! However, everything is queer to-day
  A6   52:11   at this, she was getting so well used to queer things happening. While she was still looking at the
  A5   36: 8   Alice: "all   I   know   is, it would feel very queer to me."
  A2   19: 4   thing, to be sure! However, everything is queer to-day."
  A5   36: 5   I should think you'll feel it a little queer, wo'n't you?"
QUEEREST (2)
  T5   158:22 here's a little brook! Well, this is the very queerest shop I ever saw!" * * * * * * * * * * * * * * So she
  A12   94:17   not," said the White Rabbit, "and that's the queerest thing about it." (The jury all looked puzzled.)
QUEER-LOOKING (1)
  A3   21: 1   They were indeed a queer-looking party that assembled on the bank--the birds with
QUEERLY (1)
  T9   202:22 guests began drinking it directly, and very queerly they managed it: some of them put their glasses upon
QUEER-SHAPED (2)
  A6   49:15   the baby with some difficulty, as it was a queer-shaped little creature, and held out its arms and legs
  T8   181:14 seemed to fit him very badly, and he had a queer-shaped little deal box fastened across his shoulders,
QUENCHED (1)
  T2   127:38   "Thirst quenched, I hope?" said the Queen.
QUESTION (27)
  T4   140:13 great   solemn   eyes, and not noticing Alice's question.
  T12   208:13 other paw, and pretended it hadn't heard the question.
  A9   75: 5   ashamed of yourself for asking such a simple question," added the Gryphon; and then they both sat silent
  A5   36:15   Here was another puzzling question; and, as Alice could not think of any good reason,
  A8   68:34 was appealed to by all three to settle the question, and they repeated their arguments to her, though, as
  A3   22:21   The Mouse did not notice this question, but hurriedly went on, "--found it advisable to go
  A4   33:14   The great question certainly was "What?" Alice looked all round her at
  T6   161:20 it was a game!" thought Alice.) "So here's a question for you. How old did you say you were?"
  A5   41:35   round, she found this a very difficult question. However, at last she stretched her arms round it as
  T6   163:33   "The question is," said Alice, "whether you can make words mean so
  T6   163:35   "The question is," said Humpty Dumpty, "which is to be master--
  A4   33:13   or drink something or other; but the great question is 'What'?"
  A3   22:19 Duck: "it's generally a frog, or a worm. The question is, what did the archbishop find?"
  A2   15:42 different. But if I'm not the same, the next question is 'Who in the world am I?' Ah, that's the great
  A1   9:14 for, you see, as she couldn't answer either question, it didn't much matter which way she put it. She felt
  T1   114:21 hadn't I?" But the King took no notice of the question: it was quite clear that he could neither hear her
  T12   208: 6 it was that dreamed it all. This is a serious question, my dear, and you should not go on licking your paw
  A3   21: 5   The first question of course was, how to get dry again: they had a
  A3   26:24 who is Dinah, if I might venture to ask the question?" said the Lory.
  A3   23:17   This question the Dodo could not answer without a great deal of
  T3   137:16   It was not a very difficult question to answer, as there was only one road through the
  T3   132: 1 she thought this wouldn't be quite a civil question to ask.
  A8   65:20 were silent, and looked at Alice, as the question was evidently meant for her.
  T8   186: 2   The Knight looked surprised at the question. "What does it matter where my body happens to be?"
  A6   51:18 could not be denied, so she tried another question. "What sort of people live about here?"
  A7   59:20 then turned to the Dormouse, and repeated her question. "Why did they live at the bottom of a well?"
  A6   46:34 at all?" said the Footman. "That's the first question, you know."
QUESTIONS (7)
  A9   76:33 Alice did not feel encouraged to ask any more questions about it: so she turned to the Mock Turtle, and said
  T9   195:16   "I wish Queens never asked questions," Alice thought to herself.
  A5   40: 5   "I have answered three questions, and that is enough," / Said his father. "Don't give
  T2   121:13 like being criticized, so she began asking questions. "Aren't you sometimes frightened at being planted
  A6   46:24 of his head. But at any rate he might answer questions.--How am I to get in?" she repeated, aloud.
  A7   58:36 Alice, who always took a great interest in questions of eating and drinking.
  T9   194:39 Red Queen began again. "Can you answer useful questions?" she said. "How is bread made?"
QUICK (10)
  A7   58:30   "And be quick about it," added the Hatter, "or you'll be asleep again
  T9   199:29   "Then fill up the glasses as quick as you can, / And sprinkle the table with buttons and
  T4   148:16   it's quite as sharp. Only we must begin quick. It's getting as dark as it can."
  T7   175:37 to Haigha. "Open the bag!" he whispered. "Quick! Not that one--that's full of hay!"
  A4   27:15 and fetch me a pair of gloves and a fan! Quick, now!" And Alice was so much frightened that she ran off
  T4   143:28 them   out   so   far,   /   And made them trot so quick!' / The Carpenter said nothing but / 'The butter's
  T2   125:28 tone of delight, and her heart began to beat quick with excitement as she went on. "It's a great huge game
  T8   186:10 the next course?" said Alice. "Well, that was quick work, certainly!"
  T7   173:12   You see, a minute goes by so fearfully quick. You might as well try to stop a Bandersnatch!"
  T7   175: 4 use!" said the King. "She runs so fearfully quick. You might as well try to catch a Bandersnatch! But I'll
QUICKER (1)
  A3   26:15 its head impatiently, and walked a little quicker.
QUICKLY (8)
  T1   119: 4 but a new invention for getting down stairs quickly and easily, as Alice said to herself. She just kept
  A12   92: 9 dismay, and began picking them up again as quickly as she could, for the accident of the gold-fish kept
  T2   128:30 she vanished into the air, or whether she ran quickly into the wood ("and she can run very fast!" thought
  T2   120:11 once, when she turned a corner rather more quickly than usual, she ran past it before she could stop
  T9   201:14 the pudding!" and the waiters took it away so quickly that Alice couldn't return its bow.
  A11   87: 8 opportunity of taking it away. She did it so quickly that the poor little juror (it was Bill, the Lizard)
  T2   128: 8 its first move, you know. So you'll go very quickly through the Third Square--by railway, I should think--
  T2   128:26 Alice to curtsey, this time, but walked on quickly to the next peg, where she turned for a moment to say

QUIET (3)
T8   180: 8   fire-irons falling into the fender! And how quiet the horses are! They let them get on and off them just
A2   19:35   if you could only see her. She is such a dear quiet thing," Alice went on, half to herself, as she swam
A10   82: 5   as she went on. Her listeners were perfectly quiet till she got to the part about her repeating "You are

QUIETLY (13)
T7   175: 3   very much surprised at his taking it so quietly.
A10   79: 1   all this time, sat down again very sadly and quietly, and looked at Alice.
T3   132:23   don't like all insects?" the Gnat went on, as quietly as if nothing had happened.
T5   155: 6   the 'thing' went through the ceiling as quietly as possible, as if it were quite used to it.
T3   132: 5   who had put his head out of the window, quietly drew it in and said "It's only a brook we have to jump
T8   185:24   "How can you go on talking so quietly, head downwards?" Alice asked, as she dragged him out
A6   50:15   and felt quite relieved to see it trot away quietly into the wood. "If it had grown up," she said to
A6   52:19   "It turned into a pig," Alice answered very quietly, just as if the Cat had come back in a natural way.
A8   65:14   a minute or two, looking for them, and then quietly marched off after the others.
T8   187:22   of light that quite dazzled her--the horse quietly moving about, with the reins hanging loose on his neck
A4   34: 9   was sitting on the top, with its arms folded, quietly smoking a long hookah, and taking not the smallest
T3   132:17   she touched it, and she found herself sitting quietly under a tree--while the Gnat (for that was the insect
T6   168:36   more, and, getting no answer to this, she quietly walked away: but she couldn't help saying to herself,

QUILT (1)
T1   109:12   covers them up snug, you know, with a white quilt; and perhaps it says 'Go to sleep, darlings, till the

QUITE (121)
T5   155:31   the Sheep cried angrily, taking up quite a bunch of needles.
A3   23:22   "But who is to give the prizes?" quite a chorus of voices asked.
T3   132: 1   or not, but she thought this wouldn't be quite a civil question to ask.
A2   20:12   from her as hard as it could go, and making quite a commotion in the pool as it went.
A4   29:17   first one side and then the other, and making quite a conversation of it altogether; but after a few minutes
A4   32:12   the door, she ran out of the house, and found quite a crowd of little animals and birds waiting outside. The
T4   145:27   wish it wouldn't flap its wings so--it makes quite a hurricane in the wood--here's somebody's shawl being
A8   68:29   the Cheshire-Cat, she was surprised to find quite a large crowd collected round it: there was a dispute
T1   110:11   favourite phrase "Let's pretend." She had had quite a long argument with her sister only the day before--all
A3   21: 8   had known them all her life. Indeed, she had quite a long argument with the Lory, who at last turned sulky,
A9   77:17   This was quite a new idea to Alice, and she thought it over a little
A6   50:12   than a pig, and she felt that it would be quite absurd for her to carry it any further.
A9   72: 5   "I quite agree with you," said the Duchess; "and the moral of
T8   187: 6   "No, you oughtn't: that's quite another thing! The song is called 'Ways and Means': but
A5   43:17   truthful child; "but little girls eat eggs quite as much as serpents do, you know."
A12   93: 8   said to herself, "I should think it would be quite as much use in the trial one way up as the other."
A9   74: 5   but on the whole she thought it would be quite as safe to stay with it as to go after that savage Queen
T4   148:15   brother: "but you can have the umbrella--it's quite as sharp. Only we must begin quick. It's getting as dark
A11   87:19   Hearts, he stole those tarts / And took them quite away!"
T9   195:20   Alice said very decidedly, for she felt quite certain about this, "is the thunder--no, no!" she
T4   139:19   passing on to Tweedledee, though she felt quite certain he would only shout out "Contrariwise!" and so
T3   135:20   be seen on the twig, and, as she was getting quite chilly with sitting still so long, she got up and walked
T9   192:15   came there, but she feared it would not be quite civil. However, there would be no harm, she thought, in
T1   114:21   King took no notice of the question: it was quite clear that he could neither hear her nor see her.
T3   131:38   have heard it at all, if it hadn't come quite close to her ear. The consequence of this was that it
T8   183: 2   found that it was the best plan not to walk quite close to the horse.
T1   112:11   that what could be seen from the old room was quite common and uninteresting, but that all the rest was as
T2   127:23   I'd rather not try, please!" said Alice. "I'm quite content to stay here--only I am so hot and thirsty!"
T6   166:10   and, when you've once heard it, you'll be quite content. Who's been repeating all that hard stuff to you
A2   20:21   was high time to go, for the pool was getting quite crowded with the birds and animals that had fallen into
T8   187:21   on his armour in a blaze of light that quite dazzled her--the horse quietly moving about, with the
T7   178: 3   through and through her head till she felt quite deafened. She started to her feet and sprang across the
T1   111: 5   far as you can see, only you know it may be quite different on beyond. Oh, Kitty, how nice it would be if
A3   23:14   had been running half an hour or so, and were quite dry again, the Dodo suddenly called out "The race is
A1   13: 3   things to happen, that it seemed quite dull and stupid for life to go on in the common way.
T8   186:26   "Not very nice alone," he interrupted, quite eagerly: "but you've no idea what a difference it makes,
T5   154:14   had on it, that particular shelf was always quite empty, though the others round it were crowded as full
T2   127:37   "No, thank you," said Alice: "one's quite enough!"
A4   28:12   down the bottle, saying to herself "That's quite enough--I hope I sha'n't grow any more--As it is, I
T6   162:14   on!" Alice suddenly remarked. (They had had quite enough of the subject of age, she thought: and, if they
T2   127: 8   till suddenly, just as Alice was getting quite exhausted, they stopped, and she found herself sitting
T5   158:29   a tree the moment she came up to it, and she quite expected the egg to do the same.
A4   33: 5   of breath, and till the puppy's bark sounded quite faint in the distance.
A11   88: 8   began, "for bringing these in; but I hadn't quite finished my tea when I was sent for."
A9   72:12   "if I had it written down: but I ca'n't quite follow it as you say it."
A7   59:33   "What did they draw?" said Alice, quite forgetting her promise.
A12   92: 1   "Here!" cried Alice, quite forgetting in the flurry of the moment how large she had
A4   29:22   and she trembled till she shook the house, quite forgetting that she was now about a thousand times as
T1   115:10   make such faces, my dear!" she cried out, quite forgetting that the King couldn't hear her. "You make me
A2   14: 2   so much surprised, that for the moment she quite forgot how to speak good English). "Now I'm opening out
T4   139: 4   / Which frightened both the heroes so, / They quite forgot their quarrel."
T4   138: 6   They stood so still that she quite forgot they were alive, and she was just going round to
A2   19:29   she had hurt the poor animal's feelings. "I quite forgot you didn't like cats."
A9   70:16   She had quite forgotten the Duchess by this time, and was a little
T8   184: 1   in the path where Alice was walking. She was quite frightened this time, and said in an anxious tone, as
T2   122: 8   began shouting together, till the air seemed quite full of little shrill voices. "Silence, every one of
A6   53: 3   and vanishing so suddenly; you make one quite giddy!"
A11   86: 8   it: they looked so good, that it made Alice quite hungry to look at them--"I wish they'd get the trial
A6   48:14   baby was howling so much already, that it was quite impossible to say whether the blows hurt it or not.

QUITE (cont.)

A6	47:16	word with such sudden violence that Alice quite jumped; but she saw in another moment that it was
T2	122:35	a Violet said, so suddenly, that Alice quite jumped; for it hadn't spoken before.
A7	59:18	Alice did not quite know what to say to this: so she helped herself to some
T5	154: 3	"I don't quite know yet," Alice said very gently. "I should like to
A9	74: 4	Alice alone with the Gryphon. Alice did not quite like the look of the creature, but on the whole she
T8	186:21	to cheer him up, for the poor Knight seemed quite low-spirited about it.
T2	126:12	Alice never could quite make out, in thinking it over afterwards, how it was
A11	91:27	you must cross-examine the next witness. It quite makes my forehead ache!"
A1	7:15	at this, but at the time it all seemed quite natural); but, when the Rabbit actually took a watch out
T4	139:28	were dancing round in a ring. This seemed quite natural (she remembered afterwards), and she was not
A3	21: 6	about this, and after a few minutes it seemed quite natural to Alice to find herself talking familiarly with
T4	146:18	that he was frightened: "only an old rattle--quite old and broken."
T7	173: 6	as she could, for the run was putting her quite out of breath.
A9	73:10	Then the Queen left off, quite out of breath, and said to Alice "Have you seen the Mock
A3	26:17	stay!" sighed the Lory, as soon as it was quite out of sight. And an old Crab took the opportunity of
A2	20:17	and swam slowly back to her: its face was quite pale (with passion, Alice thought), and it said, in a
A1	12:17	could not possibly reach it: she could see it quite plainly through the glass, and she tried her best to
T8W	21:16	Wasp, and Alice tripped down the hill again, quite pleased that she had gone back and given a few minutes
T8W	16: 5	"Along of the wig?" Alice repeated, quite pleased to find that he was recovering his temper.
A11	86:14	she had read about them in books, and she was quite pleased to find that she knew the name of nearly
T6	162:31	"It is really?" said Alice, quite pleased to find that she had chosen a good subject after
T1	112: 4	was a fire in the fireplace, and she was quite pleased to find that there was a real one, blazing away
A6	48: 5	that do," Alice said very politely, feeling quite pleased to have got into a conversation.
T2	122:30	sounded a very good reason, and Alice was quite pleased to know it. "I never thought of that before!"
T7	176:24	going on: he was very nervous, and his voice quite quivered. "All round the town?" he said. "That's a good
T5	156:25	"Oh, what a lovely one! Only I couldn't quite reach it." And it certainly did seem a little provoking
T8W	21:11	remarks made on her, and as the Wasp had quite recovered his spirits, and was getting very talkative,
A6	50:14	So she set the little creature down, and felt quite relieved to see it trot away quietly into the wood. "If
T6	161:17	"I'm afraid I ca'n't quite remember it," Alice said, very politely.
A5	41: 2	"Not quite right, I'm afraid," said Alice, timidly: "some of the
T7	172:18	"Quite right," said the King: "this young lady saw him too. So
T3	129:35	were about the same size as the people, and quite seemed to fill the carriage.
T2	121: 2	that she couldn't speak for a minute: it quite seemed to take her breath away. At length, as the
A8	68:31	all talking at once, while all the rest were quite silent, and looked very uncomfortable.
A5	43:21	was such a new idea to Alice, that she was quite silent for a minute or two, which gave the Pigeon the
A6	53: 4	said the Cat; and this time it vanished quite slowly, beginning with the end of the tail, and ending
T4	143:23	'Cut us another slice. / I wish you were not quite so deaf--/ I've had to ask you twice!'
A4	28:14	get out at the door--I do wish I hadn't drunk quite so much!"
T8W	20: 3	a little better, they wouldn't tease you quite so much."
T8	183: 9	"Because people don't fall off quite so often, when they've had much practice."
T5	153:31	in a long bleat, so like a sheep that Alice quite started.
T1	107:10	at work on the white kitten, which was lying quite still and trying to purr--no doubt feeling that it was
A5	43:38	anything near the right size, that it felt quite strange at first; but she got used to it in a few
T4	147: 4	from the angry brother. But he couldn't quite succeed, and it ended in his rolling over, bundling up
A6	47:13	said Alice, a little timidly, for she was not quite sure whether it was good manners for her to speak first,
A1	12:40	to feel which way it was growing; and she was quite surprised to find that she remained the same size. To be
T1	114: 9	down: the rapid journey through the air had quite taken away her breath, and for a minute or two she could
A4	33: 4	so she set off at once, and ran till she was quite tired and out of breath, and till the puppy's bark
A4	28: 7	make me grow large again, for really I'm quite tired of being such a tiny little thing!"
T5	151:22	went higher with each "better," till it got quite to a squeak at last.
T3	129:14	as Alice soon found out, though the idea quite took her breath away at first. "And what enormous
T4	147: 3	such an extraordinary thing to do, that it quite took off Alice's attention from the angry brother. But
T3	131:39	was that it tickled her ear very much, and quite took off her thoughts from the unhappiness of the poor
A12	93: 6	its tail about in a melancholy way, being quite unable to move. She soon got it out again, and put it
T6	167: 5	"I'm afraid I don't quite understand," said Alice.
A7	56:21	and yet it was certainly English. "I don't quite understand you," she said, as politely as she could.
A9	73:20	thing!" she said to herself, for she had felt quite unhappy at the number of executions the Queen had
T7	177: 9	said, in reply to the Lion (she was getting quite used to being called 'the Monster'). "I've cut several
T5	155: 6	ceiling as quietly as possible, as if it were quite used to it.
T9	192:10	sat down again, "I shall be able to manage it quite well in time."
T9	202:35	much," she whispered in reply, "but I can do quite well without."
T6	159:10	of a high wall--such a narrow one that Alice quite wondered how he could keep his balance--and, as his eyes

QUIVER (1)

A2	19:27	a sudden leap out of the water, and seemed to quiver all over with fright. "Oh, I beg your pardon!" cried

QUIVERED (1)

T7	176:24	on: he was very nervous, and his voice quite quivered. "All round the town?" he said. "That's a good long

QUIVERING (1)

T2	122:11	I ca'n't get at them!" it panted, bending its quivering head towards Alice, "or they wouldn't dare to do it!

QUOTH (1)

T9	199:37	"'O Looking-Glass creatures,' quoth Alice, 'draw near! / 'Tis an honour to see me, a favour

-R-

RABBIT (43)
A1   7:16   it all seemed quite natural); but, when the Rabbit actually took a watch out of its waistcoat-pocket, and
A4   29:23   now about a thousand times as large as the Rabbit, and had no reason to be afraid of it.
A12   94:17   "No, they're not," said the White Rabbit, "and that's the queerest thing about it." (The jury
A4   30: 4   "Digging for apples, indeed!" said the Rabbit angrily. "Here! Come help me out of this!" (Sounds of
A11   91:29   Alice watched the White Rabbit as he fumbled over the list, feeling very curious to
A8   65:37   "She boxed the Queen's ears--" the Rabbit began. Alice gave a little scream of laughter. "Oh,
A11   87:14   On this the White Rabbit blew three blasts on the trumpet, and then unrolled the
A11   88: 4   first witness," said the King; and the White Rabbit blew three blasts on the trumpet, and called out "First
A12   94: 7   "I haven't opened it yet," said the White Rabbit; "but it seems to be a letter, written by the prisoner
A2   15:32   ready to ask help of any one: so, when the Rabbit came near her, she began, in a low, timid voice, "If
A4   29:25   Presently the Rabbit came up to the door, and tried to open it; but, as the
A4   29:21   of feet on the stairs. Alice knew it was the Rabbit coming to look for her, and she trembled till she shook
A11   86:34   she stopped herself hastily, for the White Rabbit cried out "Silence in the court!", and the King put on
A4   27:22   was a bright brass plate with the name "W. RABBIT" engraved upon it. She went in without knocking, and
A11   88: 2   "Not yet, not yet!" the Rabbit hastily interrupted. "There's a great deal to come
A12   98:24   long grass rustled at her feet as the White Rabbit hurried by--the frightened Mouse splashed his way
A4   27:28   said to herself, "to be going messages for a rabbit! I suppose Dinah'll be sending me on messages next!"
A8   65:29   "Hush! Hush!" said the Rabbit in a low hurried tone. He looked anxiously over his
A12   94:12   "It isn't directed at all," said the White Rabbit: "in fact, there's nothing written on the outside." He
A12   93:23   this down on their slates, when the White Rabbit interrupted: "Unimportant, your Majesty means, of
A8   63:23   and among them Alice recognized the White Rabbit: it was talking in a hurried nervous manner, smiling at
A12   94: 4   yet, please your Majesty," said the White Rabbit, jumping up in a great hurry: "this paper has just been
A4   29:32   after waiting till she fancied she heard the Rabbit just under the window, she suddenly spread out her hand
A4   27:12   Very soon the Rabbit noticed Alice, as she went hunting about, and called
A12   94:33   The White Rabbit put on his spectacles. "Where shall I begin, please
A11   91:32   herself. Imagine her surprise, when the White Rabbit read out, at the top of his shrill little voice, the
A12   94:37   dead silence in the court, whilst the White Rabbit read out these verses:--
A2   15:27   eyes to see what was coming. It was the White Rabbit returning, splendidly dressed, with a pair of white
A8   65:34   "Did you say 'What a pity!'?" the Rabbit said.
A4   31:39   began moving about again, and Alice heard the Rabbit say "A barrowful will do, to begin with."
A1   7:12   it so very much out of the way to hear the Rabbit say to itself "Oh dear! Oh dear! I shall be too late!"
A4t   27: 1   THE RABBIT SENDS IN A LITTLE BILL
A10   82: 2   from the time when she first saw the White Rabbit. She was a little nervous about it, just at first, the
A2   15:33   low, timid voice, "If you please, Sir--" The Rabbit started violently, dropped the white kid-gloves and the
A4   27: 1   It was the White Rabbit, trotting slowly back again, and looking anxiously
A1   9:27   behind it when she turned the corner, but the Rabbit was no longer to be seen: she found herself in a long,
A1   9:23   her was another long passage, and the White Rabbit was still in sight, hurrying down it. There was not a
A8   65:38   a little scream of laughter. "Oh, hush!" the Rabbit whispered in a frightened tone. "The Queen will hear
A11   91:11   The King looked anxiously at the White Rabbit, who said, in a low voice, "Your Majesty must
A8   65:26   at her side. She was walking by the White Rabbit, who was peeping anxiously into her face.
A11   86: 5   to guard him; and near the King was the White Rabbit, with a trumpet in one hand, and a scroll of parchment
A1   8: 1   her mind that she had never before seen a rabbit with either a waistcoat-pocket, or a watch to take out
A1   7: 9   picking the daisies, when suddenly a White Rabbit with pink eyes ran close by her.
RABBIT-HOLE (4)
A1t   7: 1   DOWN THE RABBIT-HOLE
A4   29: 2   I almost wish I hadn't gone down that rabbit-hole--and yet--and yet--it's rather curious, you know,
A1   8: 4   was just in time to see it pop down a large rabbit-hole under the hedge.
A1   8: 7   The rabbit-hole went straight on like a tunnel for some way, and
RABBIT'S (4)
A2   18: 2   to see that she had put on one of the Rabbit's little white kid-gloves while she was talking. "How
A4   30: 1   Next came an angry voice--the Rabbit's--"Pat! Pat! Where are you?" And then a voice she had
A4   31: 7   general chorus of "There goes Bill!" then the Rabbit's voice alone--"Catch him, you by the hedge!" then
A4   31:28   "We must burn the house down!" said the Rabbit's voice. And Alice called out, as loud as she could,
RABBITS (1)
A4   29: 1   smaller, and being ordered about by mice and rabbits. I almost wish I hadn't gone down that rabbit-hole--
RACE (2) [See also CAUCUS-RACE]
A3   23:14   dry again, the Dodo suddenly called out "The race is over!" and they all crowded round it, panting, and
A3   23:12   so that it was not easy to know when the race was over. However, when they had been running half an
RACE-COURSE (1)
A3   23: 8   First it marked out a race-course, in a sort of circle, ("the exact shape doesn't
-RAIL [See HAND-RAIL]
RAILWAY (4)
T2   128: 9   go very quickly through the Third Square--by railway, I should think--and you'll find yourself in the
T3   131:27   rather impatiently. "I don't belong to this railway journey at all--I was in a wood just now--and I wish I
A2   18:20   the sea, "and in that case I can go back by railway," she said to herself. (Alice had been to the seaside
A2   18:25   a row of lodging-houses, and behind them a railway station.) However, she soon made out that she was in
RAIN (3)
T4   146: 3   on very dark. Do you think it's going to rain?"
T8   181:19   You see I carry it upside-down, so that the rain ca'n't get in."
T4   146: 7   "But it may rain outside?"
RAISED (4)
A6   53:15   more of the left-hand bit of mushroom, and raised herself to about two feet high: even then she walked up

RAISED (cont.)
A8   65:30   over his shoulder as he spoke, and then raised himself upon tiptoe, put his mouth close to her ear,
T8   185:14   with me, I can assure you!" he said. He raised his hands in some excitement as he said this, and
T6   168: 1   Humpty Dumpty raised his voice almost to a scream as he repeated this verse,
RAISIN (1)
T3   133:14   its wings of holly-leaves, and its head is a raisin burning in brandy."
RAISING (1)
A5   43: 2   tree in the wood," continued the Pigeon, raising its voice to a shriek, "and just as I was thinking I
RAMBLING (1)
T3   135:37   She was rambling on in this way when she reached the wood: it looked
RAN (27)
T4   145:24   Alice ran a little way into the wood, and stopped under a large tree
A1   8: 3   out of it, and burning with curiosity, she ran across the field after it, and was just in time to see it
T2   120:12   a corner rather more quickly than usual, she ran against it before she could stop herself.
A12   98:11   Alice got up and ran off, thinking while she ran, as well she might, what a wonderful dream it had been.
A8   67:30   the Queen's hedgehog just now, only it ran away when it saw mine coming!"
A10   85: 6   "What trial is it?" Alice panted as she ran: but the Gryphon only answered "Come on!" and ran the
A1   7:10   when suddenly a White Rabbit with pink eyes ran close by her.
T1   119: 2   She was out of the room in a moment, and ran down stairs--or, at least, it wasn't exactly running, but
T3   129:28   So, with this excuse, she ran down the hill, and jumped over the first of the six little
T8W   15: 1   Alice hastily ran her eye down the paper and said "No. It says nothing about
A4   27:18   his housemaid," she said to herself as she ran. "How surprised he'll be when he finds out who I am! But
A4   32:16   at Alice the moment she appeared; but she ran off as hard as she could, and soon found herself safe in a
A4   27:16   And Alice was so much frightened that she ran off at once in the direction it pointed to, without trying
T9   202:25   upset the decanters, and drank the wine as it ran off the edges of the table--and three of them (who looked
A12   98:11   tea: it's getting late." So Alice got up and ran off, thinking while she ran, as well she might, what a
T2   127: 2   passed it ten minutes ago! Faster!" And they ran on for a time in silence, with the wind whistling in
A4   32:12   was small enough to get through the door, she ran out of the house, and found quite a crowd of little
T2   128:30   she vanished into the air, or whether she ran quickly into the wood ("and she can run very fast!"
A4   32:42   every moment to be trampled under its feet, ran round the thistle again: then the puppy began a series of
A10   85: 7   but the Gryphon only answered "Come on!" and ran the faster, while more and more faintly came, carried on
T7   172:40   off, Alice repeating to herself, as she ran, the words of the old song:--
A4   33: 4   her escape: so she set off at once, and ran till she was quite tired and out of breath, and till the
A8   65:11   to execute the unfortunate gardeners, who ran to Alice for protection.
T8   185:17   Alice ran to the side of the ditch to look for him. She was rather
T2   127:17   you'd generally get to somewhere else--if you ran very fast for a long time as we've been doing."
A8   69:12   disappeared: so the King and the executioner ran wildly up and down, looking for it, while the rest of the
A2   18:12   existence. "And now for the garden!" And she ran with all speed back to the little door; but, alas! the
RANG (2)
T9   198:12   Alice knocked and rang in vain for a long time; but at last a very old Frog, who
T7   178: 2   make out: the air seemed full of it, and it rang through and through her head till she felt quite deafened
RAPID (1)
T1   114: 8   The Queen gasped, and sat down: the rapid journey through the air had quite taken away her breath,
RAPIDLY (2)
A2   18: 7   two feet high, and was going on shrinking rapidly: she soon found out that the cause of this was the fan
A5   41:42   was no time to be lost, as she was shrinking rapidly: so she set to work at once to eat some of the other
RAPPED (1)
A6   45: 5   only, she would have called him a fish)--and rapped loudly at the door with his knuckles. It was opened by
RATE (15)
T1   118:30   killed something: that's clear, at any rate--"
T5   150: 4   "Well, I don't want any to-day, at any rate."
A1   10:14   she might find another key on it, or at any rate a book of rules for shutting people up like telescopes:
A4   30:11   "Well, it's got no business there, at any rate: go and take it away!"
A6   46:24   nearly at the top of his head. But at any rate he might answer questions.--How am I to get in?" she
A2   16:11   oh dear! I shall never get to twenty at that rate! However, the Multiplication-Table doesn't signify: let's
T4   146: 1   went on, as cheerfully as she could, "At any rate, I'd better be getting out of the wood, for really it's
T1   114:20   hours and hours getting to the table, at that rate. I'd far better help you, hadn't I?" But the King took no
A7   60:35   "At any rate I'll never go there again!" said Alice, as she picked her
A1   9:38   large, or the key was too small, but at any rate it would not open any of them. However, on the second
T3   135:38   it looked very cool and shady. "Well, at any rate it's a great comfort," she said as she stepped under the
A12   93:41   "Well, I sha'n't go, at any rate," said Alice; "besides, that's not a regular rule: you
T5   151:13   "You're wrong there, at any rate," said the Queen. "Were you ever punished?"
A11   89:25   "Well, at any rate, the Dormouse said--" the Hatter went on, looking
A2   19:12   should think very likely it can talk: at any rate, there's no harm in trying." So she began: "O Mouse, do
RATH (1)
T6   166: 3   "Well, a 'rath' is a sort of green pig: but 'mome' I'm not certain about
RATHER (66)
A8   67:23   they play at all fairly," Alice began, in rather a complaining tone, "and they all quarrel so dreadfully
A6   50:17   made a dreadfully ugly child: but it makes rather a handsome pig, I think." And she began thinking over
A11   90:12   by the officers of the court. (As that is rather a hard word, I will just explain to you how it was done
T6   163:30   "When I use a word," Humpty Dumpty said, in rather a scornful tone, "it means just what I choose it to
T8   182:18   he tried he fell in himself instead. "It's rather a tight fit, you see," he said, as they got it in at
T3   132:30   at all," Alice explained, "because I'm rather afraid of them--at least the large kinds. But I can
A7   58:21   "I'm afraid I don't know one," said Alice, rather alarmed at the proposal.
T9   200:20   leg of mutton before Alice, who looked at it rather anxiously, as she had never had to carve a joint before
A6   48:28   Alice glanced rather anxiously at the cook, to see if she meant to take the
T4   140: 2   looking at her for a minute: there was a rather awkward pause, as Alice didn't know how to begin a
T5   149:35   to get the hair into order. "Come, you look rather better now!" she said, after altering most of the pins.
A9   70:30   "The game's going on rather better now," she said, by way of keeping up the
T7   169:10   the horses. Having four feet, these managed rather better than the foot-soldiers; but even they stumbled

RATHER (cont.)
T8W	14: 2	anything for you?" Alice went on. "Aren't you rather cold here?"
T8	179:10	to another person's dream," she went on in a rather complaining tone: "I've a great mind to go and wake him
A3	22:16	"Found it," the Mouse replied rather crossly: "of course you know what 'it' means."
A4	29: 2	down that rabbit-hole--and yet--and yet--it's rather curious, you know, this sort of life! I do wonder what
T9	203: 1	In fact it was rather difficult for her to keep in her place while she made
A8	63:28	Alice was rather doubtful whether she ought not to lie down on her face
A5	43: 9	"I--I'm a little girl," said Alice, rather doubtfully, as she remembered the number of changes she
A11	90:29	"I'd rather finish my tea," said the Hatter, with an anxious look
T9	192: 3	she went on, in a severe tone (she was always rather fond of scolding herself), "It'll never do for you to
A1	8:42	The antipathies, I think--" (she was rather glad there was no one listening, this time, as it
T1	119:10	with so much floating in the air, and was rather glad to find herself walking again in the natural way.
T1	109: 7	Well, I shouldn't mind that much! I'd far rather go without them than eat them!
T8	184:35	"but don't you think it would be rather hard?"
T1	118:26	she said when she had finished it, "but it's rather hard to understand!" (You see she didn't like to
T9	201:10	to the pudding, please," Alice said rather hastily, "or we shall get no dinner at all. May I give
A10	81:25	and eels, of course," the Gryphon replied, rather impatiently: "any shrimp could have told you that."
T3	131:26	"Indeed I sha'n't!" Alice said rather impatiently. "I don't belong to this railway journey at
A2	19:18	a mouse--O mouse!") The mouse looked at her rather inquisitively, and seemed to her to wink with one of
A8	65:40	"The Queen will hear you! You see she came rather late, and the Queen said--"
T2	120:11	would. Indeed, once, when she turned a corner rather more quickly than usual, she ran against it before she
A2	15:13	the roof of the hall: in fact she was now rather more than nine feet high, and she at once took up the
T7	175:12	"A little--a little," the King replied, rather nervously. "You shouldn't have run him through with
A2	19:41	"We wo'n't talk about her any more, if you'd rather not."
A8	67:43	"I'd rather not," the Cat remarked.
T2	127:23	"I'd rather not try, please!" said Alice. "I'm quite content to
T8W	14: 5	Alice felt rather offended at this answer, and was very nearly walking on
A10	84:12	so eagerly that the Gryphon said, in a rather offended tone, "Hm! No accounting for tastes! Sing her
A11	86:25	two or three times over to herself, being rather proud of it: for she thought, and rightly too, that
T6	166:22	to it; so she sat down, and said "Thank you" rather sadly,
T4	147:44	"Very well," the other said, rather sadly: "and she can watch us--only you'd better not
T3	136:14	I knew!" thought poor Alice. She answered, rather sadly, "Nothing, just now."
T6	163: 4	Humpty Dumpty looked doubtful. "I'd rather see that done on paper," he said.
T2	122:33	you never think at all," the Rose said, in a rather severe tone.
A1	12:22	in crying like that!" said Alice to herself rather sharply. "I advise you to leave off this minute!" She
T2	126: 6	She glanced rather shyly at the real Queen as she said this, but her
A5	35: 6	opening for a conversation. Alice replied, rather shyly, "I--I hardly know, Sir, just at present--at
A1	9:11	bats, I wonder?" And here Alice began to get rather sleepy, and went on saying to herself, in a dreamy sort
T8	185:17	side of the ditch to look for him. She was rather startled by the fall, as for some time he had kept on
T9	195:14	But the Red Queen drew herself up rather stiffly, and said "Queens never make bargains."
T9	192: 6	So she got up and walked about--rather stiffly just at first, as she was afraid that the crown
T6	168:17	This was rather sudden, Alice thought: but, after such a very strong
T8	182:42	it went on again (which it generally did rather suddenly), he fell off behind. Otherwise he kept on
T8W	14:18	read it if you've a mind to," the Wasp said, rather sulkily. "Nobody's hindering you, that I know of."
T3	135:40	into the--into the--into what?" she went on, rather surprised at not being able to think of the word. "I
T8	184:24	time you picked me up, that I was looking rather thoughtful?"
T5	149:11	all, she must manage it herself. So she began rather timidly: "Am I addressing the White Queen?"
A6	51: 4	"Cheshire-Puss," she began, rather timidly, as she did not at all know whether it would
A6	53:16	feet high: even then she walked up towards it rather timidly, saying to herself "Suppose it should be raving
T9	200:16	middle one was empty. Alice sat down in it, rather uncomfortable at the silence, and longing for some one
T8W	13:14	So she went back to the Wasp--rather unwillingly, for she was very anxious to be a Queen.
A7	59:39	moved into the Dormouse's place, and Alice rather unwillingly took the place of the March Hare. The
T6	160:29	horses and all his men," Alice interrupted, rather unwisely.
T5	155:36	say 'Feather' so often?" Alice asked at last, rather vexed. "I'm not a bird!"

RAT-HOLE (1)
A1	10: 2	into a small passage, not much larger than a rat-hole: she knelt down and looked along the passage into the

RATHS (5)
T1	116:12	.ebargtuo shtar emom eht dnA / ,sevogorob eht erew ysmim llA / :ebaw eht ni
T1	116:21	All mimsy were the borogoves, / And the mome raths outgrabe.
T1	118:24	All mimsy were the borogoves, / And the mome raths outgrabe.
T6	164:24	All mimsy were the borogoves, / And the mome raths outgrabe."
T6	166: 1	"And then 'mome raths'?" said Alice. "I'm afraid I'm giving you a great deal

RATS (1)
A2	20: 9	a hundred pounds! He says it kills all the rats and--oh dear!" cried Alice in a sorrowful tone. "I'm

RATTLE (7)
T4	138:21	said Tweedledee / Had spoiled his nice new rattle.
T4	146:25	tone, "You needn't be so angry about an old rattle."
T4	146:16	"It's only a rattle," Alice said, after a careful examination of the little
T4	146:28	tell you--I bought it yesterday--my nice NEW RATTLE!" and his voice rose to a perfect scream.
A12	98:26	the neighbouring pool--she could hear the rattle of the teacups as the March Hare and his friends shared
T4	146:18	thinking that he was frightened: "only an old rattle--quite old and broken."
T4	148: 9	"And all about a rattle!" said Alice, still hoping to make them a little

RATTLE-SNAKE (1)
T4	146:17	examination of the little white thing. "Not a rattle-snake, you know," she added hastily, thinking that he

RATTLING (2)
A4	32: 2	next moment a shower of little pebbles came rattling in at the window, and some of them hit her in the
A12	98:38	pool rippling to the waving of the reeds--the rattling teacups would change to tinkling sheep-bells, and the

RAVEN (1)
A7	55:12	hearing this; but all he said was "Why is a raven like a writing-desk?"

RAVENS (1)
    A7   55:33   thought over all she could remember about ravens and writing-desks, which wasn't much.
RAVING (3)
    TI   103:30   hold thee fast: / Thou shalt not heed the raving blast.
    A6   53:17   saying to herself "Suppose it should be raving mad after all! I almost wish I'd gone to see the Hatter
    A6   52:26   and perhaps, as this is May, it wo'n't be raving mad--at least not so mad as it was in March." As she
RAW (1)
    A5   43:27   I shouldn't want yours: I don't like them raw."
REACH (8)
    T5   156:29   always a more lovely one that she couldn't reach.
    T8W   21: 5   to do the same for her, but she kept out of reach, and would not take the hint. So he went on with his
    A6   48:11   set to work throwing everything within her reach at the Duchess and the baby--the fire-irons came first;
    T4   148: 2   "And I hit every thing within reach," cried Tweedledum, "whether I can see it or not!"
    A4   30:27   No, tie 'em together first--they don't reach half high enough yet--Oh, they'll do well enough. Don't
    T5   156:25   "Oh, what a lovely one! Only I couldn't quite reach it." And it certainly did seem a little provoking
    A1   12:17   for it, she found she could not possibly reach it: she could see it quite plainly through the glass,
    A1   12:34   Alice, "and if it makes me grow larger, I can reach the key; and if it makes me grow smaller, I can creep
REACHED (4)
    T2   125:23   by a number of little green hedges, that reached from brook to brook.
    T8   179:15   her, brandishing a great club. Just as he reached her, the horse stopped suddenly: "You're my prisoner!"
    T8   190:31   other. After the fourth or fifth tumble he reached the turn, and then she waved her handkerchief to him,
    T3   135:37   She was rambling on in this way when she reached the wood: it looked very cool and shady. "Well, at any
REACHING (1)
    A2   15:24   pool round her, about four inches deep, and reaching half down the hall.
READ (17)
    T1   116:16   This was the poem that Alice read
    A11   86:14   in a court of justice before, but she had read about them in books, and she was quite pleased to find
    A11   87:15   and then unrolled the parchment-scroll, and read as follows:--
    A4   29: 4   what can have happened to me! When I used to read fairy tales, I fancied that kind of thing never happened,
    T1   116: 5   the leaves, to find some part that she could read, "--for it's all in some language I don't know," she said
    A11   90:17   that done," thought Alice. "I've so often read in the newspapers, at the end of trials, 'There was some
    T8W   14:17   "You may read it if you've a mind to," the Wasp said, rather sulkily.
    T6   166:12   "I read it in a book," said Alice. "But I had some poetry
    A11   91:32   Imagine her surprise, when the White Rabbit read out, at the top of his shrill little voice, the name
    A12   93:34   in his note-book, called out "Silence!", and read out from his book, "Rule Forty-two. All persons more than
    A12   94:38   silence in the court, whilst the White Rabbit read out these verses:--
    A1   10:21   it's marked 'poison' or not"; for she had read several nice little stories about children who had got
    A8   68: 1   "A cat may look at a king," said Alice. "I've read that in some book, but I don't remember where."
    A11   87:13   "Herald, read the accusation!" said the King.
    A12   94:32   "Read them," said the King.
    T9   194:36   dear. And I'll tell you a secret--I can read words of one letter! Isn't that grand? However, don't be
    T8W   14:14   "Would you like me to read you a bit of this?" Alice went on, as she picked up a
READILY (2)
    T9   194: 3   eight I ca'n't, you know," Alice replied very readily: "but--"
    A7   56:16   "Of course not," Alice replied very readily: "but that's because it stays the same year for such a
READING (4)
    A12   98: 8   Adventures of hers that you have just been reading about; when she had finished, her sister kissed her,
    A1   7: 3   she had peeped into the book her sister was reading, but it had no pictures or conversations in it, "and
    A11   90:30   with an anxious look at the Queen, who was reading the list of singers.
    T8W   15: 5   "In coming back," Alice went on reading, "they found a lake of treacle. The banks of the lake
READY (17) [See also ALREADY]
    T9   192:21   obeyed that rule," said Alice, who was always ready for a little argument, "and if you only spoke when you
    A4   27:30   "'Miss Alice! Come here directly, and get ready for your walk!' 'Coming in a minute, nurse! But I've got
    T4   143:11   / Are very good indeed--/ Now, if you're ready, Oysters dear, / We can begin to feed.'
    T4   147:23   than anything else, by the time they're ready!" she said to herself, as she arranged a bolster round
    A3   22: 2   the Mouse with an important air. "Are you all ready? This is the driest thing I know. Silence all round, if
    A9   71:17   course it is," said the Duchess, who seemed ready to agree to everything that Alice said: "there's a large
    A2   15:31   Alice felt so desperate that she was ready to ask help of any one: so, when the Rabbit came near
    T6   159:15   is!" she said aloud, standing with her hands ready to catch him, for she was every moment expecting him to
    T3   137:11   Alice stood looking after it, almost ready to cry with vexation at having lost her dear little
    T9   199: 2   Alice turned round, ready to find fault with anybody. "Where's the servant whose
    A3   26: 6   "A knot!" said Alice, always ready to make herself useful, and looking anxiously about her.
    A6   49:12   baby at her as she spoke. "I must go and get ready to play croquet with the Queen," and she hurried out of
    T5   152:24   scream now?" Alice asked, holding her hands ready to put over her ears again.
    A9   75: 6   sat silent and looked at poor Alice, who felt ready to sink into the earth. At last the Gryphon said to the
    A3   26:26   Alice replied eagerly, for she was always ready to talk about her pet: "Dinah's our cat. And she's such
    T1   116: 3   little anxious about him, and had the ink all ready to throw over him, in case he fainted again), she turned
    T9   197: 5   lady, in Alice's lap! / Till the feast's ready, we've time for a nap. / When the feast's over, we'll go
REAL (13)
    T4   145:20   in his dream. You know very well you're not real."
    T4   145:24   "If I wasn't real," Alice said--half laughing through her tears, it all
    A4   27:24   in great fear lest she should meet the real Mary Ann, and be turned out of the house before she had
    A6   49:33   turn-up nose, much more like a snout than a real nose: also its eyes were getting extremely small for a
    T1   112: 4   was quite pleased to find that there was a real one, blazing away as brightly as the one she had left
    T7   170:19   too! Why, it's as much as I can do to see real people, by this light!"
    T2   123:37   it would be far grander to have a talk with a real Queen as she said this, but her companion only smiled
    T2   126: 6   She glanced rather shyly at the real Queen as she said this, but her companion only smiled
    T4   145:21   "I am real!" said Alice, and began to cry.
    T5   156:36   the very moment that she picked them? Even real scented rushes, you know, last only a very little while--
    T4   145:26   "I hope you don't suppose those are real tears?" Tweedledum interrupted in a tone of great

REAL (cont.)
T12 208: 2 fishes! To-morrow morning you shall have a real treat. All the time you're eating your breakfast, I'll
A9   74:33 Turtle at last, with a deep sigh, "I was a real Turtle."
REALITY (1)
A12 98:36 open them again, and all would change to dull reality--the grass would be only rustling in the wind, and the
REALLER (1)
T4 145:22   "You wo'n't make yourself a bit realler by crying," Tweedledee remarked: "there's nothing to
REALLY (43)
T5 153:35 she in a shop? And was that really--was it really a sheep that was sitting on the other side of the
T9 192: 9 that there was nobody to see her, "and if I really am a Queen," she said as she sat down again, "I shall
T9 192:27 conversation. "What do you mean by 'If you really are a Queen'? What right have you to call yourself so?
T5 156: 7 in a sudden transport of delight. "There really are--and such beauties!"
A12 94:27 clapping of hands at this: it was the first really clever thing the King had said that day.
T9 196:26 who felt she ought to say something kind, but really couldn't think of anything at the moment.
T9 203: 4 rise to return thanks--" Alice began: and she really did rise as she spoke, several inches; but she got hold
T1 107:22 make it understand that it was in disgrace. "Really, Dinah ought to have taught you better manners! You
A6   46:36 only Alice did not like to be told so. "It's really dreadful," she muttered to herself, "the way all the
T4 148: 1   hit every thing I can see--when I get really excited."
T1 110:17 and I'll be all the rest." And once she had really frightened her old nurse by shouting suddenly in her
A9   76:13   "Ah! Then yours wasn't a really good school," said the Mock Turtle in a tone of great
T3 136: 3 then she suddenly began again. "Then it really has happened, after all! And now, who am I? I will
A10 80: 1   "You can really have no notion how delightful it will be / When they
T1 110: 7 purred! Well, it was a nice check, Kitty, and really I might have won, if it hadn't been for that nasty
A4   28: 7 I do hope it'll make me grow large again, for really I'm quite tired of being such a tiny little thing!"
A1   10:11 to think that very few things indeed were really impossible.
T8 187:10 coming to that," the Knight said. "The song really is 'A-sitting On A Gate': and the tune's my own
T8 187: 2 "That's what the name is called. The name really is 'The Aged Aged Man.'"
T4 146: 2 I'd better be getting out of the wood, for really it's coming on very dark. Do you think it's going to
T12 207:31 you know that you're scrubbing a White Queen? Really, it's most disrespectful of you!
A3   26:42 itself up very carefully, remarking "I really must be getting home: the night-air doesn't suit my
T1 115:36 him, and at last he panted out "My dear! I really must get a thinner pencil. I ca'n't manage this one a
A11 91:27 And, he added, in an undertone to the Queen, "Really, my dear, you must cross-examine the next witness. It
A7   60:26   "Really, now you ask me," said Alice, very much confused, "I
A2   19:40 all over, and she felt certain it must be really offended. "We wo'n't talk about her any more, if you'd
T6 166:21   Alice felt that in that case she really ought to listen to it; so she sat down, and said "Thank
A10 81:32   "Wouldn't it, really?" said Alice, in a tone of great surprise.
T6 162:31   "It is really?" said Alice, quite pleased to find that she had chosen
T3 135:18 little sighs, and this time the poor Gnat really seemed to have sighed itself away, for, when Alice
T2 120:21 all went on very well, and she was just saying "I really shall do it this time--" when the path gave a sudden
T4 147:21 her in tying strings and fastening buttons--"Really they'll be more like bundles of old clothes than
A3   25:18 take no denial: We must have the trial; For really this morning I've nothing to do.' Said the mouse to the
T3 131:44 Alice inquired, a little anxiously. What she really wanted to know was, whether it could sting or not, but
T11 206: 1   ..--it really was a kitten, after all.
T8 185:19 kept on very well, and she was afraid that it really was hurt this time. However, though she could see
T5 153:35 at all. Was she in a shop? And was that really--was it really a sheep that was sitting on the other
T2 121: 8 us to begin, you know," said the Rose, "and I really was wondering when you'd speak! Said I to myself, 'Her
T9 196:28   "She never was really well brought up," the Red Queen went on: "but it's
T6 162:15 the subject of age, she thought: and, if they really were to take turns in choosing subjects, it was her
T12 207:37 "By the way, Kitty, if only you'd been really with me in my dream, there was one thing you would have
A9   75: 3 he taught us," said the Mock Turtle angrily. "Really you are very dull!"
T5 149:36 said, after altering most of the pins. "But really you should have a lady's maid!"
REARING (1)
A5   41:17 height indeed!" said the Caterpillar angrily, rearing itself upright as it spoke (it was exactly three
REASON (14)
T2 122:30   This sounded a very good reason, and Alice was quite pleased to know it. "I never
A10 81: 2 yawned and shut his eyes. "Tell her about the reason and all that," he said to the Gryphon.
A5   36:16 and, as Alice could not think of any good reason, and the Caterpillar seemed to be in a very unpleasant
T8 182:33 hair creep up it, like a fruit-tree. Now the reason hair falls off is because it hangs down--things never
T3 134: 6 thought to herself, "I wonder if that's the reason insects are so fond of flying into candles--because
A10 81: 1 have their tails in their mouths; and the reason is--" here the Mock Turtle yawned and shut his eyes.
A10 81: 4   "The reason is," said the Gryphon, "that they would go with the
A9   71: 6 waist," the Duchess said, after a pause: "the reason is, that I'm doubtful about the temper of your flamingo
A5   38: 4   in at the door--/ Pray, what is the reason of that?
A7   58:10 idea came into Alice's head. "Is that the reason so many tea-things are put out here?" she asked.
T8 182: 6 to be provided for everything. That's the reason the horse has all those anklets round his feet."
A9   77:15   "That's the reason they're called lessons," the Gryphon remarked: "because
A4   29:23 times as large as the Rabbit, and had no reason to be afraid of it.
T12 207:29 White Majesty, I wonder? That must be the reason you were so untidy in my dream--Dinah! Do you know that
REASONABLE (2)
T6 163:43   "Now you talk like a reasonable child," said Humpty Dumpty, looking very much
A11 89: 1   "Yes, but I grow at a reasonable pace," said the Dormouse: "not in that ridiculous
REASONS (1)
A6   46:11   said the Footman, "and that for two reasons. First, because I'm on the same side of the door as
RECEIVED (1)
A10 84: 1 to pocket the spoon: / While the Panther received knife and fork with a growl, / And concluded the
RECOGNIZED (1)
A8   63:22 mostly Kings and Queens, and among them Alice recognized the White Rabbit: it was talking in a hurried
RECOVERED (6)
T1 115:19 when she got back with it she found he had recovered, and he and the Queen were talking together in a
A12 93:10   As soon as the jury had a little recovered from the shock of being upset, and their slates and

RECOVERED (cont.)
T1	114:11	little Lily in silence. As soon as she had recovered her breath a little, she called out to the White
T3	137:32	help starting back, but in another moment she recovered herself, feeling sure that they must be TWEEDLEDUM
T8W	21:11	made on her, and as the Wasp had quite recovered his spirits, and was getting very talkative, she
A10	78: 5	him in the back. At last the Mock Turtle recovered his voice, and, with tears running down his cheeks,

RECOVERING (1)
| T8W | 16: 6 | repeated, quite pleased to find that he was recovering his temper. |

RED (72)
A8	62: 3	three gardeners at it, busily painting them red. Alice thought this a very curious thing, and she went
T9	200:14	three chairs at the head of the table: the Red and White Queens had already taken two of them, but the
T1	113: 8	"Here are the Red King and the Red Queen," Alice said (in a whisper, for
T12	208: 8	Kitty, it _must_ have been either me or the Red King. He was part of my dream, of course--but then I was
T12	208:10	then I was _part_ of his dream, too! _Was_ it the Red King, Kitty? You were his wife, my dear, so you ought to
T4	144:27	"It's only the Red King snoring," said Tweedledee.
T8	179: 9	Only I do hope it's _my_ dream, and not the Red King's! I don't like belonging to another person's dream,"
T8	179:36	"I always do," said the Red Knight, and they began banging away at each other with
T8	179:31	"Well, we must fight for her, then," said the Red Knight, as he took up his helmet (which hung from the
T8	179:24	side, and tumbled off his horse just as the Red Knight had done: then he got on again, and the two Knights
T8	180:13	got up again, they shook hands, and then the Red Knight mounted and galloped off.
T8	179:28	"She's _my_ prisoner, you know!" the Red Knight said at last.
T12	207: 1	"Your Red Majesty shouldn't purr so loud," Alice said, rubbing her
T9	201:38	"Her Red Majesty's very kind to mention it," the White Queen
T4	144:32	say honestly that he was. He had a tall red night-cap on, with a tassel, and he was lying crumpled up
T9	192:17	tell me--" she began, looking timidly at the Red Queen.
T9	194:13	you think nothing would remain?" said the Red Queen.
T9	194:33	"Of course you know your ABC?" said the Red Queen.
T9	195:10	"Who ever said it was?" said the Red Queen.
T9	196: 3	"What did he want?" said the Red Queen.
T9	201:21	effort, and cut a slice and handed it to the Red Queen.
T12	207:21	of itself, so I think it _must_ have been the Red Queen.")
T12	207:25	kiss, "just in honour of _its_ having been a Red Queen."
T9	200:23	you to that leg of mutton," said the Red Queen. "Alice--Mutton: Mutton--Alice." The leg of mutton
T1	113: 8	"Here are the Red King and the Red Queen," Alice said (in a whisper, for fear of frightening
T2	124: 4	she found herself face to face with the Red Queen, and full in sight of the hill she had been so long
T9	196:13	("She _never_ could, you know," said the Red Queen.) "And part of the roof came off, and ever so much
T9	197: 2	"I must do it myself, then," said the Red Queen, and she began:--
T9	192:12	didn't feel a bit surprised at finding the Red Queen and the White Queen sitting close to her, one on
T2	124: 6	"Where do you come from?" said the Red Queen. "And where are you going? Look up, speak nicely,
T9	197: 7	the _feast's_ over, we'll go to the ball--/ Red Queen, and White Queen, and Alice, and all!
T9	194: 7	"I suppose--" Alice was beginning, but the Red Queen answered for her. "Bread-and-butter, of course. Try
T9	195: 3	"Fan her head!" the Red Queen anxiously interrupted. "She'll be feverish after so
T9	194:39	Here the Red Queen began again. "Can you answer useful questions?" she
T9	200:18	At last the Red Queen began. "You've missed the soup and fish," she said.
T9	193:14	The Red Queen broke the silence by saying, to the White Queen, "I
T9	194:18	"Why, look here!" the Red Queen cried. "The dog would lose its temper, wouldn't it
T9	195: 7	"She's all right again now," said the Red Queen. "Do you know Languages? What's the French for
T9	195:14	But the Red Queen drew herself up rather stiffly, and said "Queens
T9	195:39	"Just so!" cried the Red Queen. "Five times as warm, _and_ five times as cold--just
T9	193: 8	"Nobody said you did," said the Red Queen. "I said you couldn't _if_ you tried."
T9	194: 1	"She ca'n't do Addition," the Red Queen interrupted. "Can you do Subtraction? Take nine from
T9	192:38	I didn't mean--" Alice was beginning, but the Red Queen interrupted her impatiently.
T9	201:26	"Make a remark," said the Red Queen: "it's ridiculous to leave all the conversation to
T1	110:21	to the kitten. "Let's pretend that you're the Red Queen, Kitty! Do you know, I think if you sat up and
T9	201:12	But the Red Queen looked sulky, and growled "Pudding----Alice: Alice--
T10	205: 3	The Red Queen made no resistance whatever: only her face grew very
T9	202:19	to think about it, and then guess," said the Red Queen. "Meanwhile, we'll drink your health--Queen Alice's
T1	110:23	do try, there's a dear!" And Alice got the Red Queen off the table, and set it up before the kitten as a
T9	193:12	"A nasty, vicious temper," the Red Queen remarked; and then there was an uncomfortable
T9	193:19	We gave you the opportunity of doing it," the Red Queen remarked: "but I daresay you've not had many lessons
T9	192:31	The two Queens looked at each other, and the Red Queen remarked, with a little shudder, "She _says_ she only
T9	202:29	ought to return thanks in a neat speech," the Red Queen said, frowning at Alice as she spoke.
T9	195:31	The Red Queen said "That's a poor thin way of doing things. Now
T9	192:35	"So you did, you know," the Red Queen said to Alice. "Always speak the truth--think before
T9	196:21	"Your Majesty must excuse her," the Red Queen said to Alice, taking one of the White Queen's hands
T9	201: 6	"Certainly not," the Red Queen said, very decidedly: "it isn't etiquette to cut any
T9	202:36	"That wouldn't be at all the thing," the Red Queen said very decidedly: so Alice tried to submit to it
T2	123:28	round eagerly and found that it was the Red Queen. "She's grown a good deal!" was her first remark.
T2	125:13	The Red Queen shook her head. "You may call it 'nonsense' if you
T9	201:15	However, she didn't see why the Red Queen should be the only one to give orders; so, as an
T9	196:36	"She's tired, poor thing!" said the Red Queen. "Smoothe her hair--lend her your nightcap--and sing
T9	194:15	"Wrong, as usual," said the Red Queen: "the dog's temper would remain."
T9	199:27	whatever they be, / Come and dine with the Red Queen, the White Queen, and me!'"
T9	199:40	high to have dinner and tea / Along with the Red Queen, the White Queen, and me!"
T12	207:14	chessmen on the table till she had found the Red Queen: then she went down on her knees on the hearth-rug,
T2	123:41	said nothing, but set off at once towards the Red Queen. To her surprise she lost sight of her in a moment,
T9	196:28	"She never was really well brought up," the Red Queen went on: "but it's amazing how good-tempered she is!
T9	195:22	"It's too late to correct it," said the Red Queen: "when you've once said a thing, that fixes it, and
T9	204:17	you," she went on, turning fiercely upon the Red Queen, whom she considered as the cause of all the
T9	201:34	She spoke to the Red Queen, whose answer was a little wide of the mark. "As to
A8	63: 7	you see, Miss, this here ought to have been a red rose-tree, and we put a white one in by mistake; and, if

REDDER (1)
T2 123:12 shape as you," the Rose said: "but she's redder--and her petals are shorter, I think."
RED-HOT (1)
A1   11: 1 friends had taught them: such as, that a red-hot poker will burn you if you hold it too long; and that,
REDUCED (2)
T1 110:15 were only two of them, and Alice had been reduced at last to say "Well, you can be one of them, then,
A11 88:19 on their slates, and then added them up, and reduced the answer to shillings and pence.
REEDS (1)
A12 98:38 and the pool rippling to the waving of the reeds--the rattling teacups would change to tinkling
REELING (1)
A9   76:21   "Reeling and Writhing, of course, to begin with," the Mock
REFERRING (1)
T7 170:11 that's the exact number," the King said, referring to his book. "I couldn't send all the horses, you
REFRESHING (1)
T2 127:31   "While you're refreshing yourself," said the Queen, "I'll just take the
REFRESHMENTS (2)
A11 86:10 trial done," she thought, "and hand round the refreshments!" But there seemed to be no chance of this; so
T7 174:14 the King called out "Ten minutes allowed for refreshments!" Haigha and Hatta set to work at once, carrying
REFUSED (1)
A3   21:12 how old it was, and as the Lory positively refused to tell its age, there was no more to be said.
REGULAR (7)
T3 129:12   However, this was anything but a regular bee: in fact, it was an elephant--as Alice soon found
T3 129:10 its proboscis into them, "just as if it was a regular bee," thought Alice.
A9   76:19 the Mock Turtle with a sigh. "I only took the regular course."
T2 123:24 you hadn't got some too. I thought it was the regular rule."
T7 170: 1 stumbled now and then; and it seemed to be a regular rule that, whenever a horse stumbled, the rider fell
A12 93:42 any rate," said Alice; "besides, that's not a regular rule: you invented it just now."
T1 114:16 little out of breath. "Mind you come up--the regular way--don't get blown up!"
REINS (3)
T8 190:13 last words of the ballad, he gathered up the reins, and turned his horse's head along the road by which
T8 187:12 So saying, he stopped his horse and let the reins fall on its neck: then, slowly beating time with one
T8 187:22 her--the horse quietly moving about, with the reins hanging loose on his neck, cropping the grass at her
REJOICE (2)
T3 132:29   "I don't rejoice in insects at all," Alice explained, "because I'm
T3 132:27   "What sort of insects do you rejoice in, where you come from?" the Gnat inquired.
RELATE (1)
T8 187:32 thee everything I can: / There's little to relate. / I saw an aged aged man, / A-sitting on a gate. /
RELEASED (1)
T5 149:34   Alice carefully released the brush, and did her best to get the hair into
RELENTED (1)
T6 162:28 said, in so humble a tone that Humpty Dumpty relented.
RELIEF (2)
A11 91:25 mind!" said the King with an air of great relief. "Call the next witness." And, he added, in an
A9   76:14 said the Mock Turtle in a tone of great relief. "Now, at ours, they had, at the end of the bill,
RELIEVED (3)
T5 157: 5 as Alice got back into her place, very much relieved to find herself still in the boat.
T8 185:21 but the soles of his feet, she was much relieved to hear that he was talking on in his usual tone.
A6   50:14 set the little creature down, and felt quite relieved to see it trot away quietly into the wood. "If it had
REMAIN (7)
T9 194:12 come to bite me--and I'm sure I shouldn't remain!"
T9 194:16 said the Red Queen: "the dog's temper would remain."
T9 194:11 of course, if I took it--and the dog wouldn't remain: it would come to bite me--and I'm sure I shouldn't
T9 194:10   Alice considered. "The bone wouldn't remain, of course, if I took it--and the dog wouldn't remain:
T9 194:13   "Then you think nothing would remain?" said the Red Queen.
T9 194:21 "Then if the dog went away, its temper would remain!" the Queen exclaimed triumphantly.
A11 88:38 court; but on second thoughts she decided to remain where she was as long as there was room for her.
REMAINED (3)
A5   41:33   Alice remained looking thoughtfully at the mushroom for a minute,
A6   53: 6 of the tail, and ending with the grin, which remained some time after the rest of it had gone.
A1   12:41 and she was quite surprised to find that she remained the same size. To be sure, this is what generally
REMAINING (1)
A8   65:10 procession moved on, three of the soldiers remaining behind to execute the unfortunate gardeners, who ran
REMAINS (2)
T6 163: 2 one from three hundred and sixty-five what remains?"
T9 194: 9 Subtraction sum. Take a bone from a dog: what remains?"
REMARK (24)
A7   60:10 Dormouse, not choosing to notice this last remark.
A9   70:21 "Perhaps it hasn't one," Alice ventured to remark.
T2 123: 4 said, not choosing to notice the Rose's last remark.
T2 128:13 belongs to Humpty Dumpty--But you make no remark?"
T6 164: 8 She was too much puzzled to make any other remark.
T7 174: 9 white bread and the brown?" Alice ventured to remark.
A6   48: 7 Alice did not at all like the tone of this remark, and thought it would be as well to introduce some
T6 161:16 a little too fast: let's go back to the last remark but one."
T4 147:37 said Tweedledee, who had overheard the remark. "I'm far worse than you!"
T6 159:21 you know," she added, hoping to turn her remark into a sort of compliment.
A7   56: 9 think of nothing better to say than his first remark, "It was the best butter, you know."
A9   72: 4 Alice, who had not attended to this last remark. "It's a vegetable. It doesn't look like one, but it is
A7   56:26 course, of course: just what I was going to remark myself."
T9 201:26   "Make a remark," said the Red Queen: "it's ridiculous to leave all the

REMARK (cont.)
A7   56:19   Alice felt dreadfully puzzled. The Hatter's remark seemed to her to have no sort of meaning in it, and yet
T2   123:29   "She's grown a good deal!" was her first remark. She had indeed: when Alice first found her in the
A8   69: 4   executed, all round. (It was this last remark that had made the whole party look so grave and anxious
T5   155:23   This didn't sound like a remark that needed any answer: so Alice said nothing, but
T12 207: 7   habit of kittens (Alice had once made the remark) that, whatever you say to them, they always purr. "If
A9   77:18   it over a little before she made her next remark. "Then the eleventh day must have been a holiday?"
T6   159:26   never said anything to her; in fact, his last remark was evidently addressed to a tree--so she stood and
T6   166:20   to repeat," he went on without noticing her remark, "was written entirely for your amusement."
T8   183: 6   much surprised, and a little offended at the remark. "What makes you say that?" he asked, as he scrambled
A6   46:39   this a good opportunity for repeating his remark, with variations. "I shall sit here," he said, "on and
REMARKABLE (2)
A1   7:11   There was nothing so very remarkable in that; nor did Alice think it so very much out of
A3   26:30   This speech caused a remarkable sensation among the party. Some of the birds
REMARKED (37)
A6   51:22   I don't want to go among mad people," Alice remarked.
A7   54:15   on it but tea. "I don't see any wine," she remarked.
A8   67:43   "I'd rather not," the Cat remarked.
A9   71:13   "Only mustard isn't a bird," Alice remarked.
T4   144:35   "fit to snore his head off!" as Tweedledum remarked.
T5   150:20   memory that only works backwards," the Queen remarked.
T8W   17: 4   "Conceit isn't a disease at all," Alice remarked.
T9   193:12   "A nasty, vicious temper," the Red Queen remarked; and then there was an uncomfortable silence for a
T5   157: 4   "That was a nice crab you caught!" she remarked, as Alice got back into her place, very much relieved
A9   77:16   reason they're called lessons," the Gryphon remarked: "because they lessen from day to day."
T9   193:20   the opportunity of doing it," the Red Queen remarked: "but I daresay you've not had many lessons in
T3   132:32   course they answer to their names?" the Gnat remarked carelessly.
T8   181:21   "But the things can get out," Alice gently remarked. "Do you know the lid's open?"
T4   147:16   at pinning and tying strings?" Tweedledum remarked. "Every one of these things has got to go on, somehow
T7   177:12   to manage Looking-glass cakes," the Unicorn remarked. "Hand it round first, and cut it afterwards."
T5   153: 5   "You needn't say 'exactly,'" the Queen remarked. "I can believe it without that. Now I'll give you
T5   150:17   "I'm sure mine only works one way," Alice remarked. "I ca'n't remember things before they happen."
T3   134:22   round her head: at last it settled again and remarked "I suppose you don't want to lose your name?"
T2   121:11   don't care about the colour," the Tiger-lily remarked. "If only her petals curled up a little more, she'd
A7   59:26   Hare went "Sh! Sh!" and the Dormouse sulkily remarked "If you ca'n't be civil, you'd better finish the
T7   170:17   "I only wish I had such eyes," the King remarked in a fretful tone. "To be able to see Nobody! And at
T6   168:24   face is what one goes by, generally," Alice remarked in a thoughtful tone.
A7   56:12   some curiosity. "What a funny watch!" she remarked. "It tells the day of the month, and doesn't tell
T3   135: 9   and didn't say anything more," the Gnat remarked, "of course you'd miss your lessons. That's a joke. I
T8   179:35   Rules of Battle, of course?" the White Knight remarked, putting on his helmet too.
T6   166:28   you've sharper eyes than most," Humpty Dumpty remarked severely. Alice was silent.
T7   170:34   "He lives on the Hill," the King remarked simply, without the least idea that he was joining in
A11   90: 5   "You must remember," remarked the King, "or I'll have you executed."
T4   145:23   yourself a bit realler by crying," Tweedledee remarked: "there's nothing to cry about."
T9   195:29   Alice was puzzled. "In our country," she remarked, "there's only one day at a time."
T6   162:13   beautiful belt you've got on!" Alice suddenly remarked. (They had had quite enough of the subject of age,
A7   59: 4   have done that, you know," Alice gently remarked. "They'd have been ill."
T3   134:18   "But that must happen very often," Alice remarked thoughtfully.
T6   164:33   "I see it now," Alice remarked thoughtfully: "and what are 'toves'?"
A6   46:26   "I shall sit here," the Footman remarked, "till to-morrow--"
T7   172: 9   like eating hay when you're faint," he remarked to her, as he munched away.
T9   192:32   looked at each other, and the Red Queen remarked, with a little shudder, "She says she only said 'if'
REMARKING (3)
A5   41:26   and crawled away into the grass, merely remarking, as it went, "One side will make you grow taller,
A3   26:32   began wrapping itself up very carefully, remarking "I really must be getting home: the night-air
A9   73: 1   hurried back to the game, the Queen merely remarking that a moment's delay would cost them their lives.
REMARKS (5)
A7   55: 9   "You should learn not to make personal remarks," Alice said with some severity: "it's very rude."
A5   36:12   at the Caterpillar's making such very short remarks, and she drew herself up and said, very gravely, "I
T6   166:37   "You needn't go on making remarks like that," Humpty Dumpty said: "they're not sensible,
T8W   21:10   Alice did not like having so many personal remarks made on her, and as the Wasp had quite recovered his
A7   59:16   "Who's making personal remarks now?" the Hatter asked triumphantly.
REMEDIES (1)
A3   22:30   for the immediate adoption of more energetic remedies--"
REMEMBER (27)
A7   55:33   while Alice thought over all she could remember about ravens and writing-desks, which wasn't much.
T12 207:24   what to--what to purr. It saves time, remember!" And she caught it up and gave it one little kiss,
T5   150:21   "What sort of things do you remember best?" Alice ventured to ask.
A8   63:29   like the three gardeners, but she could not remember ever having heard of such a rule at processions; "and
A1   12:11   the candle is blown out, for she could not remember ever having seen such a thing.
A2   15:41   I got up this morning? I almost think I can remember feeling a little different. But if I'm not the same,
A2   20: 7   its dinner, and all sorts of things--I ca'n't remember half of them--and it belongs to a farmer, you know,
A1   9: 7   think!" (Dinah was the cat.) "I hope they'll remember her saucer of milk at tea-time. Dinah, my dear! I
T3   137: 2   little further on," the Fawn said. "I ca'n't remember here."
T3   136: 4   after all! And now, who am I? I will remember, if I can! I'm determined to do it!" But being
T6   161:17   "I'm afraid I ca'n't quite remember it," Alice said, very politely.
A9   70:20   now what the moral of that is, but I shall remember it in a bit."
T6   166:36   "I will, if I can remember it so long," said Alice.
T9   196:17   thought to herself "I never should try to remember my name in the middle of an accident! Where would be
T3   135: 7   excusing me lessons for that. If she couldn't remember my name, she'd call me 'Miss,' as the servants do."

REMEMBER (cont.)
```
T9    196:16   things--till  I was so frightened, I couldn't remember my own name!"
A11   90: 5                                   "You must remember," remarked the King, "or I'll have you executed."
A11   90: 4                             "That I ca'n't remember," said the Hatter.
T2    128:32   but she was  gone,  and  Alice began to remember that she was a Pawn, and that it would soon be time
T5    152:31   be  glad!"  the Queen said. "Only I never can remember the rule. You must be very happy, living in this wood
A1    10:24    unpleasant things, all because they would not remember the simple rules their friends had taught them: such
A12   98: 7    And she told her sister, as well as she could remember them, all these strange Adventures of hers that you
A5    36:31    "I'm afraid I am, Sir," said Alice. "I ca'n't remember things as I used--and I don't keep the same size for
T5    150:18   works  one  way,"  Alice remarked. "I ca'n't remember things before they happen."
A5    36:33                            "Ca'n't remember what things?" said the Caterpillar.
A8    68: 2    "I've  read  that  in  some book, but I don't remember where."
T2    128:24   a  thing--turn out your toes as you walk--and remember who you are!" She did not wait for Alice to curtsey,
```
REMEMBERED (7)
```
T4    139:29   in a ring. This  seemed quite natural (she remembered afterwards), and she was not even surprised to hear
A2    19:16    had  never  done such a thing before, but she remembered having seen, in her brother's Latin Grammar, "A
A2    19: 8    be a  walrus  or  hippopotamus, but then she remembered how small she was now, and she soon made out that
T8    187:17              this was the one that she always remembered most clearly. Years afterwards she could bring the
A5    43:32    had to stop and untwist it. After a while she remembered that she still held the pieces of mushroom in her
A5    43: 9    girl,"  said Alice, rather doubtfully, as she remembered the number of changes she had gone through, that
A1    12:25    as to bring tears into her eyes; and once she remembered trying to box her own ears for having cheated
```
REMEMBERING (1)
```
A12   99:10    and find a pleasure in all their simple joys, remembering her own child-life, and the happy summer days.
```
REMEMBERS (1)
```
T2    126:13       how it was  that  they  began: all she remembers is, that they were running hand in hand, and the
```
REMINDING (1)
```
A12   92: 5    below,  and  there  they lay sprawling about, reminding her very much of a globe of gold-fish she had
```
REMINDS (2)
```
T8    189:21   toe / A very heavy weight, / I weep, for it reminds me so / Of that old man I used to know--/ Whose look
T9    195:25                         "Which reminds me--" the White Queen said, looking down and nervously
```
REMOVE (2)
```
T9    201: 7    to cut  any  one  you've been introduced to. Remove the joint!" And the waiters carried it off, and brought
T9    201:13   growled  "Pudding----Alice: Alice--Pudding. Remove the pudding!" and the waiters took it away so quickly
```
REMOVED (2)
```
A8    68: 5    "My  dear! I  wish  you  would have this cat removed!"
A8    68: 3                  "Well, it must be removed," said the King very decidedly; and he called to the
```
REPAINTED (1)
```
T3    133: 9    made  up her mind that it must have been just repainted, it looked so bright and sticky; and then she went
```
REPEAT (13)
```
T6    166:19                "The piece I'm going to repeat," he went on without noticing her remark, "was written
T9    201:37   all  in  poetry--all  about fishes. Shall she repeat it?"
A10   82:19    at  once." However, she got up, and began to repeat it, but her head was so full of the Lobster-Quadrille,
A2    17: 5    as  if  she were saying lessons, and began to repeat it, but her voice sounded hoarse and strange, and the
A10   85: 2    and  the  Mock Turtle had  just begun to repeat it, when a cry of "The trial's beginning!" was heard in
A10   82:17    the  creatures  order one about, and make one repeat lessons!" thought Alice. "I might just as well be at
T6    166:15   stretching out one of his great hands, "I can repeat poetry as well as other folk, if it comes to that--"
A10   82:12    "I should like to hear her try and repeat something now. Tell her to begin." He looked at the
T12   208: 3    the  time  you're eating your breakfast, I'll repeat 'The Walrus and the Carpenter' to you; and then you can
T2    128: 2    went on.  "At the end of three yards I shall repeat them--for fear of your forgetting them. At the end of
A10   82:15                        "Stand up and repeat ''Tis the voice of the sluggard,'" said the Gryphon.
T4    140:12                "What shall I repeat to her?" said Tweedledee, looking round at Tweedledum
A5    36:36                  "Repeat 'You are old, Father William,'" said the Caterpillar.
```
REPEATED (28)
```
A6    46:25    answer questions.--How am I to get in?" she repeated, aloud.
A11   89: 9        "Give your evidence," the King repeated angrily, "or I'll have you executed, whether you are
T8    186:15    "Well,  not  the  next  day," the Knight repeated as before: "not the next day. In fact," he went on,
T8    185:22   his  usual  tone. "All kinds of fastness," he repeated: "but it was careless of him to put another man's
T9    204:25   surprised at anything now. "As for you," she repeated, catching hold of the little creature in the very act
T8W   15:10                   "En-gulph-ed," Alice repeated, dividing the word into syllables.
A7    59:20    and  then turned to the  Dormouse, and repeated her question. "Why did they live at the bottom of a
T7    171: 6    "Don't I tell you?" the King repeated impatiently. "I must have two--to fetch and carry.
A10   81:16    puzzled. "Does  the  boots and  shoes!" she repeated in a wondering tone.
T9    200: 5        "Ninety times nine!" Alice repeated in despair. "Oh, that'll never be done! I'd better go
T5    150:13       "Living backwards!" Alice repeated in great astonishment. "I never heard of such a
A6    46: 1    the  Queen to play croquet." The Frog-Footman repeated, in the same solemn tone, only changing the order of
A10   83:10    "Go on  with the  next verse," the Gryphon repeated: "it begins 'I passed by his garden.'"
T8W   18: 7    head. Almost  every  one she had met had repeated poetry to her, and she thought she would try if the
T8W   16: 5                  "Along of the wig?" Alice repeated, quite pleased to find that he was recovering his
T7    175: 7    if  you like--She's a dear good creature," he repeated softly to himself, as he opened his memorandum-book.
T6    164:20       This  sounded very hopeful,  so Alice repeated the first verse:--
A5    42:29           "Serpent, I say again!" repeated the Pigeon, but in a more subdued tone, and added,
A8    68:34    by all three to settle the question, and they repeated their arguments to her, though, as they all spoke at
T6    168:38    she went, "of all the unsatisfactory--" (she repeated this aloud, as it was a great comfort to have such a
T6    168: 2    raised his  voice almost  to a scream as he repeated this verse, and Alice thought, with a shudder, "I
T6    162: 3    "Seven  years  and six months!" Humpty Dumpty repeated thoughtfully. "An uncomfortable sort of age. Now if
A10   82:11    "It  all  came different!" the Mock Turtle repeated thoughtfully. "I should like to hear her try and
T6    159:27    addressed  to a tree--so she stood and softly repeated to herself:--
T6    166:12    a  book,"  said Alice. "But I had some poetry repeated to me much easier than that, by--Tweedledee, I think
T9    201:28    you  know, I've had such a quantity of poetry repeated to me to-day," Alice began, a little frightened at
T2    127: 1                "Nearly there!" the Queen repeated. "Why, we passed it ten minutes ago! Faster!" And
```

REPEATED (cont.)
 A12   93: 3 are back in their proper places--all," he repeated with great emphasis, looking hard at Alice as he said
REPEATING (7)
 T6   166:10 heard it, you'll be quite content. Who's been repeating all that hard stuff to you?"
 A10   84: 3   "What is the use of repeating all that stuff?" the Mock Turtle interrupted, "if
 T8   184: 9   "Plenty of practice!" he went on repeating, all the time that Alice was getting him on his feet
 A6   46:39 seemed to think this a good opportunity for repeating his remark, with variations. "I shall sit here," he
 T5   149: 8 a helpless frightened sort of way, and kept repeating something in a whisper to herself that sounded like
 T7   172:40 and see them." And they trotted off, Alice repeating to herself, as she ran, the words of the old song:--
 A10   82: 6 quiet till she got to the part about her repeating "You are old, Father William," to the Caterpillar,
REPLIED (49)
 A7   56: 4 was the best butter," the March Hare meekly replied.
 A11   89:16   "It began with the tea," the Hatter replied.
 A11   90:25   "Then you may sit down," the King replied.
 T5   158: 6   for one--twopence for two," the Sheep replied.
 T6   167: 6 "It gets easier further on," Humpty Dumpty replied.
 T8   179:30 I came and rescued her!" the White Knight replied.
 A6   53: 2   "I said 'pig'," replied Alice; "and I wish you wouldn't keep appearing and
 T3   134: 2   "Frumenty and mince-pie," the Gnat replied; "and it makes its nest in a Christmas-box."
 A9   76:22 of course, to begin with," the Mock Turtle replied; "and then the different branches of Arithmetic--
 T7   176:22 all round the town, you chicken!" the Lion replied angrily, half getting up as he spoke.
 T4   147:10   "I suppose so," the other sulkily replied, as he crawled out of the umbrella: "only she must
 A7   55:21   "I do," Alice hastily replied; "at least--at least I mean what I say--that's the
 A7   56:40   "Perhaps not," Alice cautiously replied; "but I know I have to beat time when I learn music."
 T9   194:20   "Perhaps it would," Alice replied cautiously.
 A9   76:36 "Well, there was Mystery," the Mock Turtle replied, counting off the subjects on his flappers--"Mystery,
 T7   175:19   "This is a child!" Haigha replied eagerly, coming in front of Alice to introduce her,
 A3   26:26   Alice replied eagerly, for she was always ready to talk about her
 T3   132:39   "I ca'n't say," the Gnat replied. "Further on, in the wood down there, they've got no
 T4   147:33   "Well--yes--a little," Alice replied gently.
 T4   140:16 the Carpenter' is the longest," Tweedledum replied, giving his brother an affectionate hug.
 T9   195: 9   "Fiddle-de-dee's not English," Alice replied gravely.
 T7   172:13 say there was nothing better," the King replied. "I said there was nothing like it." Which Alice did
 T2   123:23 Why, all round her head, of course," the Rose replied. "I was wondering you hadn't got some too. I thought
 T5   150: 2 that happened the week after next," the Queen replied in a careless tone. "For instance, now," she went on,
 T6   168:22 know you again if we did meet," Humpty Dumpty replied in a discontented tone, giving her one of his fingers,
 A9   72:15 to what I could say if I chose," the Duchess replied, in a pleased tone.
 A5   36:35 busy bee,' but it all came different!" Alice replied in a very melancholy voice.
 A10   81:37   "I mean what I say," the Mock Turtle replied, in an offended tone. And the Gryphon added "Come,
 A7   59:11   "I've had nothing yet," Alice replied in an offended tone: "so I ca'n't take more."
 T8   182: 9 against the bites of sharks," the Knight replied. "It's an invention of my own. And now help me on.
 A9   71: 9   "He might bite," Alice cautiously replied, not feeling at all anxious to have the experiment
 A5   41: 8 I'm not particular as to size," Alice hastily replied; "only one doesn't like changing so often, you know."
 A3   22:16   "Found it," the Mouse replied rather crossly: "of course you know what 'it' means."
 A10   81:25 "Soles and eels, of course," the Gryphon replied, rather impatiently: "any shrimp could have told you
 T7   175:12   "A little--a little," the King replied, rather nervously. "You shouldn't have run him through
 A5   35: 6 encouraging opening for a conversation. Alice replied, rather shyly, "I--I hardly know, Sir, just at present
 A10   84:12 if the Mock Turtle would be so kind," Alice replied, so eagerly that the Gryphon said, in a rather
 A10   80: 7 matters it how far we go?" his scaly friend replied. / "There is another shore, you know, upon the other
 A10   80:22   "I believe so," Alice replied thoughtfully. "They have their tails in their mouths--
 A5   37: 5   "In my youth," Father William replied to his son, / "I feared it might injure the brain; /
 A10   80: 3 the lobsters, out to sea!" / But the snail replied "Too far, too far!", and gave a look askance--/ Said
 A3   23:31   "Of course," the Dodo replied very gravely. "What else have you got in your pocket?"
 A5   35:14 afraid I ca'n't put it more clearly," Alice replied, very politely, "for I ca'n't understand it myself, to
 T9   194: 3 "Nine from eight I ca'n't, you know," Alice replied very readily: "but--"
 A7   56:16   "Of course not," Alice replied very readily: "but that's because it stays the same
 A10   81:13 "It does the boots and shoes," the Gryphon replied very solemnly.
 A7   57:10 Hatter shook his head mournfully. "Not I!" he replied. "We quarrelled last March--just before he went mad,
 A7   56:29   "No, I give it up," Alice replied. "What's the answer?"
 T1   115:24   To which the Queen replied "You haven't got any whiskers."
REPLY (10)
 A3   26:12   The Mouse only growled in reply.
 A8   63:37 Knave of Hearts, who only bowed and smiled in reply.
 A8   65:18 please your Majesty!" the soldiers shouted in reply.
 T7   176: 8 the Unicorn cried out, before Alice could reply.
 T9   202:34 "Thank you very much," she whispered in reply, "but I can do quite well without."
 A11   86:32 down their names," the Gryphon whispered in reply, "for fear they should forget them before the end of the
 A6   49:28 out loud, and the little thing grunted in reply (it had left off sneezing by this time). "Don't grunt,"
 T9   201:25 of voice, and Alice hadn't a word to say in reply: she could only sit and look at it and gasp.
 T8   188:13 That they could not be seen. / So, having no reply to give / To what the old man said, / I cried 'Come,
 T7   177: 8 knife. "It's very provoking!" she said, in reply to the Lion (she was getting quite used to being called
REPROACHFULLY (1)
 T1   108: 2 you know you ought!" she added, looking reproachfully at the old cat, and speaking in as cross a voice
REPROOF (1)
 T2   128:17 said," the Queen went on in a tone of grave reproof, "'It's extremely kind of you to tell me all this'--
RESCUED (1)
 T8   179:29   "Yes, but then I came and rescued her!" the White Knight replied.
RESISTANCE (1)
 T10 205: 3   The Red Queen made no resistance whatever: only her face grew very small, and her

```
RESOLUTELY (1)
  T2   120:18                                      So, resolutely turning her back upon the house, she set out once
RESOURCE (1)
  A4    28:20  Still  she  went  on  growing, and, as a last resource, she put one arm out of the window, and one foot up
RESPECT (1)
  A6    51: 3  so she felt that it ought to be treated with respect.
RESPECTABLE (2)
  A1    12:30  there's  hardly enough of me left to make one respectable person!"
  T7   171: 3                                      "It isn't respectable to beg," said the King.
RESPECTFUL (1) [See also DISRESPECTFUL]
  A12   93:24  Majesty means, of course," he said, in a very respectful tone, but frowning and making faces at him as he
RESPECTFULLY (1)
  T12  207: 2  rubbing  her eyes, and addressing the kitten, respectfully, yet with some severity. "You woke me out of oh!
REST (19)
  T3   132: 4  everybody jumped up in alarm, Alice among the rest.
  T2   127:11  up  against a tree, and said kindly, "You may rest a little, now."
  T1   110:16  can be one of them, then, and I'll be all the rest." And once she had really frightened her old nurse by
  A12   95:19  must  ever  be  / A secret, kept from all the rest, / Between yourself and me."
  A9    70:27  because  she  was exactly the right height to rest her chin on Alice's shoulder, and it was an uncomfortably
  A4    33: 8  Alice,  as  she  leant against a buttercup to rest herself, and fanned herself with one of the leaves. "I
  AI     3:29  weary  one  /  To put the subject by, / The rest next time--" "It is next time!" / The happy voices cry.
  A6    53: 6  the  grin, which remained some time after the rest of it had gone.
  A5    39: 8  which  it  gave  to  my jaw / Has lasted the rest of my life."
  A11   87:11  was  obliged  to write with one finger for the rest of the day; and this was of very little use, as it left
  T1   119: 1  the  Looking-glass, before I've seen what the rest of the house is like! Let's have a look at the garden
  A8    64: 1  pattern  on  their  backs was the same as the rest of the pack, she could not tell whether they were
  A8    69:13  wildly  up and down, looking for it, while the rest of the party went back to the game.
  T3   131:22      "She  must  draw  the  train herself the rest of the way--," and so on.
  T6   164: 2  I suppose you don't mean to stop here all the rest of your life."
  T8   191: 1  * * * * * * across, and threw herself down to rest on a lawn as soft as moss, with little flowerbeds dotted
  A3    23:20             in the pictures of him), while the rest waited in silence. At last the Dodo said "Everybody has
  T1   112:12  common  and  uninteresting,  but that all the rest was as different as possible. For instance, the pictures
  A8    68:31  who  were  all talking at once, while all the rest were quite silent, and looked very uncomfortable.
RESTED (2)
  T1   118: 7  /  Long  time  the manxome foe he sought--/ So rested he by the Tumtum tree, / And stood awhile in thought.
  T4   142:15  /  Walked  on  a  mile or so, / And then they rested on a rock / Conveniently low: / And all the little
RESTING (2)
  A9    72:44  advantage  of  the  Queen's absence, and were resting in the shade: however, the moment they saw her, they
  A7    54: 4  and the other two were using it as a cushion, resting their elbows on it, and talking over its head. "Very
RESULT (1)
  A5    42:15  was  moving  them about, as she spoke, but no result seemed to follow, except a little shaking among the
RETIRE (1)
  A10   78:24               "--change lobsters, and retire in same order," continued the Gryphon.
RETORTED (1)
  T4   145: 8            "Not you!" Tweedledee retorted contemptuously. "You'd be nowhere. Why, you're only a
RETURN (3)
  T9   201:14  took  it  away so quickly that Alice couldn't return its bow.
  T9   203: 3  nearly lifted her up into the air. "I rise to return thanks--" Alice began: and she really did rise as she
  T9   202:29                           "You ought to return thanks in a neat speech," the Red Queen said, frowning
RETURNED (6)
  A12   96: 9             "But it goes on 'they all returned from him to you,'" said Alice.
  A12   95: 7  two,  / You gave us three or more; / They all returned from him to you, / Though they were mine before.
  T4   147:13  went  off  hand-in-hand  into  the  wood, and returned in a minute with their arms full of things--such as
  T9   201: 2  and  made  a  little  bow to Alice; and Alice returned the bow, not knowing whether to be frightened or
  T7   177:15  so.  "Now  cut  it  up," said the Lion, as she returned to her place with the empty dish.
  T2   128: 5  Alice  looked  on  with great interest as she returned to the tree, and then began slowly walking down the
RETURNING (1)
  A2    15:27  see  what was coming. It was the White Rabbit returning, splendidly dressed, with a pair of white kid-gloves
RETURN-TICKET (1)
  T3   131:25  mind  what  they all say, my dear, but take a return-ticket every time the train stops."
REVIVED (1)
  T7   172: 8             Alice was glad to see that it revived him a good deal. "There's nothing like eating hay when
RHEUMATISM (1)
  T8W   13:18                          "It's rheumatism, I should think," Alice said to herself, and she
RHYME (2)
  T8W   18: 9  do  it  too.  "Would  you  mind saying it in rhyme?" she asked very politely.
  T7   170:29  name  is  Haigha." (He pronounced it so as to rhyme with 'mayor.')
RHYTHM (1)
  TI   103:16  A  simple  chime,  that served to time / The rhythm of our rowing--/ Whose echoes live in memory yet, /
RIBBON (2)
  T5   151: 9  the  plaster  round  her finger with a bit of ribbon.
  T2   127:32  just  take  the measurements." And she took a ribbon out of her pocket, marked in inches, and began
RICH (2)
  A10   84:17                  "Beautiful Soup, so rich and green, / Waiting in a hot tureen! / Who for such
  T9   195:40  five times as cold--just as I'm five times as rich as you are, and five times as clever!"
RIDDLE (5)
  T9   202:18  /  Un-dish-cover  the  fish, or dishcover the riddle?"
  T9   201:37  ear,  "her  White  Majesty  knows a lovely riddle--all in poetry--all about fishes. Shall she repeat it
  T6   160:17  went  on, not with any idea of making another riddle, but simply in her good-natured anxiety for the queer
  T9   195:42  sighed and gave it up. "It's exactly like the riddle with no answer!" she thought.
```

RIDDLE (cont.)
A7   56:27   "Have you guessed the riddle yet?" the Hatter said, turning to Alice again.
RIDDLES (3)
A7   55:14   thought Alice. "I'm glad they've begun asking riddles--I believe I can guess that," she added aloud.
A7   56:33   time," she said, "than wasting it in asking riddles that have no answers."
T6   160:20   "What tremendously easy riddles you ask!" Humpty Dumpty growled out. "Of course I
RIDER (2)
T8   182:39   the poor Knight, who certainly was not a good rider.
T7   170: 2   rule that, whenever a horse stumbled, the rider fell off instantly. The confusion got worse every moment
RIDGE (1)
A8   66:15   away: besides all this, there was generally a ridge or a furrow in the way wherever she wanted to send the
RIDGES (1)
A8   66: 2   croquet-ground in her life: it was all ridges and furrows: the croquet balls were live hedgehogs, and
RIDICULOUS (5)
T8   184:11   "It's too ridiculous!" cried Alice, losing all her patience this time.
T9   192:24   "Ridiculous!" cried the Queen. "Why, don't you see, child--"
A11   89: 2   pace," said the Dormouse: "not in that ridiculous fashion." And he got up very sulkily and crossed
T4   145:25   laughing through her tears, it all seemed so ridiculous--"I shouldn't be able to cry."
T9   201:26   "Make a remark," said the Red Queen: "it's ridiculous to leave all the conversation to the pudding!"
RIDING (3)
T8   184: 4   two or three of them. "The great art of riding, as I was saying is--to keep your balance properly.
T8   183: 3   "I'm afraid you've not had much practice in riding," she ventured to say, as she was helping him up from
T8   183:17   "The great art of riding," the Knight suddenly began in a loud voice, waving his
RIGHT (49)
A5   37: 4   your head--/ Do you think, at your age, it is right?"
T2   121:12   petals curled up a little more, she'd be all right."
T9   195: 7   "She's all right again now," said the Red Queen. "Do you know Languages?
T8   183:18   suddenly began in a loud voice, waving his right arm as he spoke, "is to keep--" Here the sentence ended
A9   71:14   "Right, as usual," said the Duchess: "what a clear way you have
A1   8:35   to say it over) "--yes, that's about the right distance--but then I wonder what Latitude or Longitude
A6   49:24   sort of knot, and then keep tight hold of its right ear and left foot, so as to prevent its undoing itself),
A8   62: 9   On which Seven looked up and said "That's right, Five! Always lay the blame on others!"
A2   15: 7   Alice's Right Foot, Esq.
T5   149:30   on one side," Alice said as she gently put it right for her; "and dear me, what a state your hair is in!"
T9   192:27   you mean by 'If you really are a Queen'? What right have you to call yourself so? You ca'n't be a Queen, you
T6   163:14   at it carefully. "That seems to be done right--" he began.
A9   70:27   and secondly, because she was exactly the right height to rest her chin on Alice's shoulder, and it was
A6   53:11   of the March Hare: she thought it must be the right house, because the chimneys were shaped like ears and
A5   41: 2   "Not quite right, I'm afraid," said Alice, timidly: "some of the words
A6   46:45   The door led right into a large kitchen, which was full of smoke from one
A7   60:39   that one of the trees had a door leading right into it. "That's very curious!" she thought. "But
A12   93: 7   move. She soon got it out again, and put it right; "not that it signifies much," she said to herself; "I
T8   190:26   as she stood watching him. "There he goes! Right on his head as usual! However, he gets on again pretty
A6   51:19   "In that direction," the Cat said, waving its right paw round, "lives a Hatter: and in that direction,"
T9   200:13   "I should never have known who were the right people to invite!"
A6   53: 4   "All right," said the Cat; and this time it vanished quite slowly,
A5   41: 1   "That is not said right," said the Caterpillar.
A9   72:27   "Just about as much right," said the Duchess, "as pigs have to fly; and the m----
T3   133: 3   "All right," said the Gnat. "Half way up that bush, you'll see a
T7   172:18   "Quite right," said the King: "this young lady saw him too. So of
T2   125: 3   "That's right," said the Queen, patting her on the head, which Alice
T2   122:18   "That's right!" said the Tiger-lily. "The daisies are worst of all.
A8   65:19   "That's right!" shouted the Queen. "Can you play croquet?"
A4   32:19   wandered about in the wood, "is to grow to my right size again; and the second thing is to find my way into
A1   12: 4   up at the thought that she was now the right size for going through the little door into that lovely
A5   43:37   so long since she had been anything near the right size, that it felt quite strange at first; but she got
A5   43:42   to another! However, I've got back to my right size: the next thing is, to get into that beautiful
A4   33:10   it tricks very much, if--if I'd only been the right size to do it! Oh dear! I'd nearly forgotten that I've
A12   95:38   "All right, so far," said the King; and he went on muttering over
A4   34: 2   could not see anything that looked like the right thing to eat or drink under the circumstances. There was
T6   163:18   queer. As I was saying, that seems to be done right--though I haven't time to look it over thoroughly just
A1   8:39   she began again. "I wonder if I shall fall right through the earth! How funny it'll seem to come out
T1   114: 2   which had been hurt by the fall. He had a right to be a little annoyed with the Queen, for he was
A11   88:42   "You've no right to grow here," said the Dormouse.
A9   72:25   "I've a right to think," said Alice sharply, for she was beginning to
T8   184: 7   and this time he fell flat on his back, right under the horse's feet.
T1   116:15   it up to a glass, the words will all go the right way again."
A2   19:15   O Mouse!" (Alice thought this must be the right way of speaking to a mouse: she had never done such a
T5   149:17   said "If your Majesty will only tell me the right way to begin, I'll do it as well as I can."
A6   50:19   just saying to herself "if one only knew the right way to change them--" when she was a little startled by
A1   8:43   this time, as it didn't sound at all the right word) "--but I shall have to ask them what the name of
A2   17:16   "I'm sure those are not the right words," said poor Alice, and her eyes filled with tears
RIGHT-HAND (3)
A5   44: 4   of their wits!" So she began nibbling at the right-hand bit again, and did not venture to go near the house
A5   41:39   said to herself, and nibbled a little of the right-hand bit to try the effect. The next moment she felt a
T8   189:17   / My fingers into glue, / Or madly squeeze a right-hand foot / Into a left-hand shoe, / Or if I drop upon
RIGHTLY (1)
A11   86:25   rather proud of it: for she thought, and rightly too, that very few little girls of her age knew the

RING (5)
A3   24:13   over at last, and they sat down again in a ring, and begged the Mouse to tell them something more.
T9   198: 6   then I'll ring the--the--which bell must I ring?" she went on, very much puzzled by the names. "I'm not a
T9   198: 5   song's over," thought Alice, "and then I'll ring the--the--which bell must I ring?" she went on, very much
T4   139:28   the next moment they were dancing round in a ring. This seemed quite natural (she remembered afterwards),
A3   21:16   They all sat down at once, in a large ring, with the Mouse in the middle. Alice kept her eyes
RINGING (1)
T4   138:16   could say; for the words of the old song kept ringing through her head like the ticking of a clock, and she
RINGLETS (5)
A2   16: 5   she said, "for her hair goes in such long ringlets, and mine doesn't go in ringlets at all; and I'm sure
A2   16: 5   in such long ringlets, and mine doesn't go in ringlets at all; and I'm sure I ca'n't be Mabel, for I know
T8W   18: 4   Wasp said. "When I was young, you know, my ringlets used to wave--"
T8W   18:13   "When I was young, my ringlets waved / And curled and crinkled on my head: / And
T8W   19: 8   plain: / But what was I to do, you know? / My ringlets would not grow again.
RIPER (1)
A12   99: 5   and how she would keep, through all her riper years, the simple and loving heart of her childhood; and
RIPPLING (1)
A12   98:37   be only rustling in the wind, and the pool rippling to the waving of the reeds--the rattling teacups
RISE (5)
T9   203: 4   thanks--" Alice began: and she really did rise as she spoke, several inches; but she got hold of the
A5   42:11   an immense length of neck, which seemed to rise like a stalk out of a sea of green leaves that lay far
T3   132:10   In another moment she felt the carriage rise straight up into the air, and in her fright she caught at
T9   203: 3   they nearly lifted her up into the air. "I rise to return thanks--" Alice began: and she really did rise
T7   178: 8   and the * * * * * * * * * * * * * * Unicorn rise to their feet, with angry looks at being interrupted in
RISES (1)
A10   82:28   tones of the Shark: / But, when the tide rises and sharks are around, / His voice has a timid and
RISING (2)
T5   153:28   "Oh, much better!" cried the Queen, her voice rising into a squeak as she went on. "Much be-etter! Be-etter!
A3   22:28   "In that case," said the Dodo solemnly, rising to its feet, "I move that the meeting adjourn, for the
RIVER (1)
T5   157:15   for the oars, and the boat, and the river, had vanished all in a moment, and she was back again in
RIVER-BANKS (1)
T5   156: 5   under trees, but always with the same tall river-banks frowning over their heads.
RIVERS (1)
T3   129: 4   able to see a little further. "Principal rivers--there are none. Principal mountains--I'm on the only
ROAD (12)
T4   140:21   could, "would you please tell me first which road--"
T7   170:14   both gone to the town. Just look along the road, and tell me if you can see either of them."
T8   190:30   watched the horse walking leisurely along the road, and the Knight tumbling off, first on one side and then
T8   190:13   reins, and turned his horse's head along the road by which they had come. "You've only a few yards to go,"
T3   137:21   went on and on, a long way, but wherever the road divided, there were sure to be two finger-posts pointing
T3   137:18   settle it," Alice said to herself, "when the road divides and they point different ways."
T8   190:19   handkerchief when I get to that turn in the road? I think it'll encourage me, you see."
T4   140:11   said doubtfully. "Would you tell me which road leads out of the wood?"
T7   170:16   "I see nobody on the road," said Alice.
T7   170:21   who was still looking intently along the road, shading her eyes with one hand. "I see somebody now!"
T7   172:15   "Who did you pass on the road?" the King went on, holding out his hand to the Messenger
T3   137:17   question to answer, as there was only one road through the wood, and the two finger-posts both pointed
-ROAR [See UPROAR]
ROARED (1)
A8   65:23   "Come on, then!" roared the Queen, and Alice joined the procession, wondering
ROAST (2)
T9   202:27   like kangaroos) scrambled into the dish of roast mutton, and began eagerly lapping up the gravy, "just
A1   11: 8   flavour of cherry-tart, custard, pine-apple, roast turkey, toffy, and hot buttered toast), she very soon
ROCK (2)
A9   74:17   sitting sad and lonely on a little ledge of rock, and, as they came nearer, Alice could hear him sighing
T4   142:15   on a mile or so, / And then they rested on a rock / Conveniently low: / And all the little Oysters stood /
ROCKED (1)
T8   190: 6   / Who seemed distracted with his woe, / Who rocked his body to and fro, / And muttered mumblingly and low,
-ROCKET [See SKY-ROCKET]
ROCKING-HORSE-FLY (2)
T3   133: 4   Gnat. "Half way up that bush, you'll see a Rocking-horse-fly, if you look. It's made entirely of wood,
T3   133: 8   Alice looked at the Rocking-horse-fly with great interest, and made up her mind
RODE (1)
T8   190:24   So they shook hands, and then the Knight rode slowly away into the forest. "It wo'n't take long to see
ROLL (1)
T1   113:17   just in time to see one of the White Pawns roll over and begin kicking: she watched it with great
ROLLED (5) [See also UNROLLED]
T9   197:13   as first one round head, and then the other, rolled down from her shoulder, and lay like a heavy lump in
T1   108:19   this led to a scramble, in which the ball rolled down upon the floor, and yards and yards of it got
T8   185:15   excitement as he said this, and instantly rolled out of the saddle, and fell headlong into a deep ditch
T5   156:17   And then the little sleeves were carefully rolled up, and the little arms were plunged in elbow-deep, to
T7   171:14   every moment, while the great eyes rolled wildly from side to side.
ROLLING (5)
T5   152:34   of her loneliness, two large tears came rolling down her cheeks.
T3   135:13   only sighed deeply while two large tears came rolling down its cheeks.
T1   107:16   had been trying to wind up, and had been rolling it up and down till it had all come undone again; and
T4   147: 4   couldn't quite succeed, and it ended in his rolling over, bundling up in the umbrella, with only his head
T9   196:14   and ever so much thunder got in--and it went rolling round the room in great lumps--and knocking over the

ROLLS (1)
    T8   188:41   'I sometimes dig for buttered rolls, / Or set limed twigs for crabs: / I sometimes search
ROME (2)
    A2   17: 2   capital of Paris, and Paris is the capital of Rome, and Rome--no, that's all wrong, I'm certain! I must have
    A2   17: 2   Paris, and Paris is the capital of Rome, and Rome--no, that's all wrong, I'm certain! I must have been
ROMPS (1)
    T1   107:15 the kitten had been having a grand game of romps with the ball of worsted Alice had been trying to wind
ROOF (7)
    A1   9:29   was lit up by a row of lamps hanging from the roof.
    A4   30:29   Here, Bill! Catch hold of this rope--Will the roof bear?--Mind that loose slate--Oh, it's coming down! Heads
    T9   196:13 know," said the Red Queen.) "And part of the roof came off, and ever so much thunder got in--and it went
    A12   93:15   sit with its mouth open, gazing up into the roof of the court.
    A2   15:12   at this moment her head struck against the roof of the hall: in fact she was now rather more than nine
    A4   31:36   next! If they had any sense, they'd take the roof off." After a minute or two they began moving about again
    A6   53:12   the chimneys were shaped like ears and the roof was thatched with fur. It was so large a house, that she
ROOFS (1)
    T3   129:15 next idea. "Something like cottages with the roofs taken off, and stalks put to them--and what quantities
ROOM (25) [See also DRAWING-ROOM, SCHOOL-ROOM]
    T1   110:42 glass, and then they hold up one in the other room.
    A4   28:26   sort of chance of her ever getting out of the room again, no wonder she felt unhappy.
    T2   120:16 the Looking-glass again--back into the old room--and there'd be an end of all my adventures!"
    A4   29:15   Why, there's hardly room for you, and no room at all for any lesson-books!"
    A11   88:38   to remain where she was as long as there was room for her.
    T3   130: 4 the chorus of voices went on. "There wasn't room for one where she came from. The land there is worth a
    A4   28:17   floor: in another minute there was not even room for this, and she tried the effect of lying down with one
    A4   29:14   learn lessons in here? Why, there's hardly room for you, and no room at all for any lesson-books!"
    T1   119: 2 look at the garden first!" She was out of the room in a moment, and ran down stairs--or, at least, it wasn't
    T9   196:14 thunder got in--and it went rolling round the room in great lumps--and knocking over the tables and things--
    A7   54: 8 all crowded together at one corner of it. "No room! No room!" they cried out when they saw Alice coming.
    A7   54: 9 they saw Alice coming. "There's plenty of room!" said Alice indignantly, and she sat down in a large
    T1   113: 3   "They don't keep this room so tidy as the other," Alice thought to herself, as she
    A6   49:13   with the Queen," and she hurried out of the room. The cook threw a frying-pan after her as she went, but
    T1   112: 2 jumped lightly down into the Looking-glass room. The very first thing she did was to look whether there
    A7   54: 8 together at one corner of it. "No room! No room!" they cried out when they saw Alice coming. "There's
    T1   112: 6 I shall be as warm here as I was in the old room," thought Alice: "warmer, in fact, because there'll be no
    A4   29: 8 in a sorrowful tone: "at least there's no room to grow up any more here."
    A5   42: 2 against her foot, that there was hardly room to open her mouth; but she did it at last, and managed to
    T1   115:17 at what she had done, and went round the room to see if she could find any water to throw over him.
    T1   110:37 fire smokes, and then smoke comes up in that room too--but that may be only pretence, just to make it look
    T1   112:11 noticed that what could be seen from the old room was quite common and uninteresting, but that all the rest
    A4   28: 1 the gloves, and was just going to leave the room, when her eye fell upon a little bottle that stood near
    A4   27:36   time she had found her way into a tidy little room with a table in the window, and on it (as she had hoped)
    T1   110:31 about Looking-glass House. First, there's the room you can see through the glass--that's just the same as
ROOTS (1) [See also TULIP-ROOTS]
    A5   42:33   "I've tried the roots of trees, and I've tried banks, and I've tried hedges,"
ROPE (1)
    A4   30:29   be particular--Here, Bill! Catch hold of this rope--Will the roof bear?--Mind that loose slate--Oh, it's
ROSE (13)
    T2   122: 4   "It could bark," said the Rose.
    T2   123:15   "But that's not your fault," the Rose added kindly. "You're beginning to fade, you know--and
    T2   121: 7 manners for us to begin, you know," said the Rose, "and I really was wondering when you'd speak! Said I to
    T2   123:38   "You ca'n't possibly do that," said the Rose: "I should advise you to walk the other way."
    T2   123: 6 that can move about like you," said the Rose. "I wonder how you do it--" ("You're always wondering,"
    T2   123:23 "Why, all round her head, of course," the Rose replied. "I was wondering you hadn't got some too. I
    T2   123:11 she has the same awkward shape as you," the Rose said: "but she's redder--and her petals are shorter, I
    T2   122:32 my opinion that you never think at all," the Rose said, in a rather severe tone.
    T2   123:20 "I daresay you'll see her soon," said the Rose. "She's one of the kind that has nine spikes, you know."
    T4   146:28 yesterday--my nice NEW RATTLE!" and his voice rose to a perfect scream.
    A12   97: 9   At this the whole pack rose up into the air, and came flying down upon her; she gave
    T2   122: 1 "There's the tree in the middle," said the Rose. "What else is it good for?"
    T2   123:33 "It's the fresh air that does it," said the Rose: "wonderfully fine air it is, out here."
ROSE'S (1)
    T2   123: 4 me?" Alice said, not choosing to notice the Rose's last remark.
ROSES (3)
    A8   63: 4 a little timidly, "why you are painting those roses?"
    A8   62: 1 stood near the entrance of the garden: the roses growing on it were white, but there were three gardeners
    A8   65: 9 Queen, who had meanwhile been examining the roses. "Off with their heads!" and the procession moved on,
ROSE-TREE (4)
    A8   63: 7 see, Miss, this here ought to have been a red rose-tree, and we put a white one in by mistake; and, if the
    A8   63:44   the three gardeners who were lying round the rose-tree; for, you see, as they were lying on their faces,
    A8   65: 4 "You make me giddy." And then, turning to the rose-tree, she went on "What have you been doing here?"
    A8   62: 1   A large rose-tree stood near the entrance of the garden: the roses
ROUGH (1)
    T8W   18: 2 "It's to comb hair with--your wig's so very rough, you know."
ROUGHLY (1)
    A6   48:36   "Speak roughly to your little boy, / And beat him when he sneezes: /
ROUND (100) [See also AROUND]
    A3   23:29   as prizes. There was exactly one a-piece, all round.
    A8   68: 7 with his head!" she said without even looking round.
    A9   70:33   'tis love, 'tis love, that makes the world go round!'"

ROUND (cont.)

A6	48:21	said, in a hoarse growl, "the world would go	round a deal faster than it does."
T6	165: 4	"And 'the wabe' is the grass-plot	round a sun-dial, I suppose?" said Alice, surprised at her own
T9	204:21	now on the table, merrily running round and	round after her own shawl, which was trailing behind her.
A10	79: 9	So they began solemnly dancing round and	round Alice, every now and then treading on her toes when they
A8	63: 2	checked himself suddenly: the others looked	round also, and all of them bowed low.
A4	29:28	Alice heard it say to itself "Then I'll go	round and get in at the window."
A8	66:11	a blow with its head, it would twist itself	round and look up in her face, with such a puzzled expression
T7	173:28	Hatta looked	round and nodded, and went on with his bread-and-butter.
T9	204:21	and was now on the table, merrily running	round and round after her own shawl, which was trailing behind
A10	79: 9	So they began solemnly dancing	round and round Alice, every now and then treading on her toes
T3	134:21	The Gnat amused itself meanwhile by humming	round and round her head: at last it settled again and
T6	165: 2	"To 'gyre' is to go	round and round like a gyroscope. To 'gimble' is to make holes
T2	128: 7	At the two-yard peg she faced	round, and said "A pawn goes two squares in its first move,
A2	20:16	them!" When the Mouse heard this, it turned	round and swam slowly back to her: its face was quite pale
T7	177:14	very obediently got up, and carried the dish	round, and the cake divided itself into three pieces as she
A3	23:28	had not got into it), and handed them	round as prizes. There was exactly one a-piece, all round.
T4	138: 4	other 'DEE.' "I suppose they've got 'TWEEDLE'	round at the back of the collar," she said to herself.
T4	140:12	I repeat to her?" said Tweedledee, looking	round at Tweedledum with great solemn eyes, and not noticing
T4	148: 8	be a tree left standing, for ever so far	round, by the time we've finished!"
A8	63:13	a sound of many footsteps, and Alice looked	round, eager to see the Queen.
T2	123:28	Alice looked	round eagerly and found that it was the Red Queen. "She's
A4	32:27	puppy was looking down at her with large	round eyes, and feebly stretching out one paw, trying to touch
A6	45: 6	opened by another footman in livery, with a	round face, and large eyes like a frog; and both footmen,
T7	177:12	cakes," the Unicorn remarked. "Hand it	round first, and cut it afterwards."
T6	163:17	Humpty Dumpty said gaily as she turned it	round for him. "I thought it looked a little queer. As I was
A7	57: 1	only have to whisper a hint to Time, and	round goes the clock in a twinkling! Half-past one, time for
T7	173:27	he went on, putting his arm affectionately	round Hatta's neck.
T8W	21: 2	on: "but the top of your head is nice and	round." He took off his own wig as he spoke, and stetched out
T9	197:13	about in great perplexity, as first one	round head, and then the other, rolled down from her shoulder,
A2	15:23	of tears, until there was a large pool	round her, about four inches deep, and reaching half down the
A4	33:14	certainly was "What?" Alice looked all	round her at the flowers and the blades of grass, but she
A3	23:24	finger; and the whole party at once crowded	round her, calling out, in a confused way, "Prizes! Prizes!"
T5	151: 9	it?" the Queen said, as she bound the plaster	round her finger with a bit of ribbon.
T3	134:21	amused itself meanwhile by humming round and	round her head: at last it settled again and remarked "I
T2	123:23	"Why, all	round her head, of course," the Rose replied. "I was wondering
A4	28:19	against the door, and the other arm curled	round her head. Still she went on growing, and, as a last
T2	127:12	Alice looked	round her in great surprise. "Why, I do believe we've been
A3	24: 1	Then they all crowded	round her once more, while the Dodo solemnly presented the
T4	148: 6	Tweedledum looked	round him with a satisfied smile. "I don't suppose," he said,
T8	182: 7	the reason the horse has all those anklets	round his feet."
T7	172: 2	great amusement, opened a bag that hung	round his neck, and handed a sandwich to the King, who
A7	58:14	"Then you keep moving	round, I suppose?" said Alice.
A3	22: 2	This is the driest thing I know. Silence all	round, if you please! 'William the Conqueror, whose cause was
T4	139:28	at once: the next moment they were dancing	round in a ring. This seemed quite natural (she remembered
T8	179:21	in "Ahoy! Ahoy! Check!" and Alice looked	round in some surprise for the new enemy.
T7	175:16	eye happened to fall upon Alice: he turned	round instantly, and stood for some time looking at her with
T4	139:14	fat, and very soon out of breath. "Four times	round is enough for one dance," Tweedledum panted out, and
A5	41:36	However, at last she stretched her arms	round it as far as they would go, and broke off a bit of the
A3	23:15	out "The race is over!" and they all crowded	round it, panting, and asking "But who has won?"
A8	68:29	to find quite a large crowd collected	round it: there was a dispute going on between the executioner
T6	162:34	one knee over the other and clasped his hands	round it, "they gave it me--for an un-birthday present."
A8	69: 3	no time, she'd have everybody executed, all	round. (It was this last remark that had made the whole party
T5	154:14	was always quite empty, though the others	round it were crowded as full as they could hold.
T6	165: 2	"To 'gyre' is to go round and	round like a gyroscope. To 'gimble' is to make holes like a
T5	155: 9	make me giddy soon, if you go on turning	round like that." She was now working with fourteen pairs at
A6	51:19	the Cat said, waving its right paw	round, "lives a Hatter: and in that direction," waving the
T5	154: 9	got: so she contented herself with turning	round, looking at the shelves as she came to them.
T5	154: 4	said very gently. "I should like to look all	round me first, if I might."
T6	164: 9	"Ah, you should see 'em come	round me of a Saturday night," Humpty Dumpty went on, wagging
A6	48:26	see the earth takes twenty-four hours to turn	round on its axis--"
T7	173:31	Hatta looked	round once more, and this time a tear or two trickled down his
T9	199: 2	Alice turned	round, ready to find fault with anybody. "Where's the servant
A1	9:39	open any of them. However, on the second time	round, she came upon a low curtain she had not noticed before,
A5	41:35	the two sides of it; and, as it was perfectly	round, she found this a very difficult question. However, at
T6	165:11	bird with its feathers sticking out all	round--something like a live mop."
T7	175: 1	doubt," the King said, without even looking	round. "That wood's full of them."
A11	87: 6	course, Alice could not stand, and she went	round the court and got behind him, and very soon found an
A12	96:25	words don't fit you," said the King looking	round the court with a smile. There was a dead silence.
A1	9:30	There were doors all	round the hall, but they were all locked; and when Alice had
T8	190:28	that comes of having so many things hung	round the horse--" So she went on talking to herself, as she
T8	184:15	a tone of great interest, clasping his arms	round the horse's neck as he spoke, just in time to save
T1	108:17	Alice wound two or three turns of the worsted	round the kitten's neck, just to see how it would look: this
T4	139:36	this), "to find myself singing 'Here we go round	the mulberry bush.' I don't know when I began it, but
A1	10:16	was not here before," said Alice), and tied	round the neck of the bottle was a paper label, with the words
T4	147:23	said to herself, as she arranged a bolster	round the neck of Tweedledee, "to keep his head from being cut
T4	138: 1	were standing under a tree, each with an arm	round the other's neck, and Alice knew which was which in a
T7	176: 9	"Then hand	round the plum-cake, Monster," the Lion said, lying down and
A11	86:10	get the trial done," she thought, "and hand	round the refreshments!" But there seemed to be no chance of
T9	196:14	so much thunder got in--and it went rolling	round the room in great lumps--and knocking over the tables

ROUND (cont.)
  T1   115:17   little alarmed at what she had done, and went round the room to see if she could find any water to throw
  A8   63:44   to the three gardeners who were lying round the rose-tree; for, you see, as they were lying on their
  T3   137: 4   wood, Alice with her arms clasped lovingly round the soft neck of the Fawn, till they came out into
  A7   54:14   Alice looked all round the table, but there was nothing on it but tea. "I don't
  A4   32:42   moment to be trampled under its feet, ran round the thistle again: then the puppy began a series of
  T7   176:24   nervous, and his voice quite quivered. "All round the town?" he said. "That's a good long way. Did you go
  T7   173: 2   the crown: / The Lion beat the Unicorn all round the town. / Some gave them white bread, some gave them
  T7   176:21   "Why, I beat you all round the town, you chicken!" the Lion replied angrily, half
  T8W 14:11   The Wasp took her arms, and let her help him round the tree, but when he got settled down again he only
  T2   126:19   was, that the trees and the other things round them never changed their places at all: however fast
  A11   86:36   put on his spectacles and looked anxiously round, to make out who was talking.
  A11   89:26   said--" the Hatter went on, looking anxiously round to see if he would deny it too; but the Dormouse denied
  T4   138: 7   they were alive, and she was just going round to see if the word 'TWEEDLE' was written at the back of
  T8W 14: 9   "Won't you let me help you round to the other side? You'll be out of the cold wind there
  T7   174:15   and Hatta set to work at once, carrying round trays of white and brown bread. Alice took a piece to
  T5   154: 6   said the Sheep; "but you ca'n't look all round you--unless you've got eyes at the back of your head."
  T8W 17: 7   it, just try tying a yellow handkerchief round your face. It'll cure you in no time!"
  A9   71: 5   say you're wondering why I don't put my arm round your waist," the Duchess said, after a pause: "the
ROUNDER (3)
  T10 205: 6   growing shorter--and fatter--and softer--and rounder--and--
  T1   115: 7   mouth went on getting larger and larger, and rounder and rounder, till her hand shook so with laughter that
  T1   115: 7   on getting larger and larger, and rounder and rounder, till her hand shook so with laughter that she nearly
ROW (5)
  T2   128: 6   tree, and then began slowly walking down the row.
  T4   142:18   the little Oysters stood / And waited in a row.
  A1   9:29   in a long, low hall, which was lit up by a row of lamps hanging from the roof.
  A2   18:24   in the sand with wooden spades, then a row of lodging-houses, and behind them a railway station.)
  T5   155:14   "Can you row?" the Sheep asked, handing her a pair of knitting-needles
ROWING (2)
  T5   156:13   stop it?" said the Sheep. "If you leave off rowing, it'll stop of itself."
  TI   103:16   that served to time / The rhythm of our rowing--/ Whose echoes live in memory yet, / Though envious
ROWLAND'S (1)
  T8   188:22   / And thence they make a stuff they call / Rowland's Macassar-Oil--/ Yet twopence-halfpenny is all / They
ROYAL (2)
  A8   65: 2   and began bowing to the King, the Queen, the royal children, and everybody else.
  A8   63:19   as the soldiers did. After these came the royal children: there were ten of them, and the little dears
RUB (1)
  T5   153:36   was sitting on the other side of the counter? Rub as she would, she could make nothing more of it: she was
RUBBED (4)
  T5   153:33   suddenly wrapped herself up in wool. Alice rubbed her eyes, and looked again. She couldn't make out what
  T9   199: 9   eyes for a minute: then he went nearer and rubbed it with his thumb, as if he were trying whether the
  A9   74: 7   The Gryphon sat up and rubbed its eyes: then it watched the Queen till she was out of
  T1   107: 8   with one paw, and then with the other paw she rubbed its face all over, the wrong way, beginning at the nose
RUBBING (5)
  T12 207: 1   Majesty shouldn't purr so loud," Alice said, rubbing her eyes, and addressing the kitten, respectfully, yet
  A12   95:22   of evidence we've heard yet," said the King, rubbing his hands; "so now let the jury--"
  T1   114: 1   "Imperial fiddlestick!" said the King, rubbing his nose, which had been hurt by the fall. He had a
  A7   60:15   to draw," the Dormouse went on, yawning and rubbing its eyes, for it was getting very sleepy; "and they
  T4   139:32   as she could make it out) by the branches rubbing one across the other, like fiddles and fiddle-sticks.
RUBBISH (1)
  T8W 19:12   wig from me and say / 'How can you put such rubbish on?'
RUDDY (1)
  TI   103:27   moody madness--/ Within, the firelight's ruddy glow, / And childhood's nest of gladness. / The magic
RUDE (3)
  A7   55:10   Alice said with some severity: "it's very rude."
  T4   140:33   there / After the day was done--/ 'It's very rude of him,' she said, / 'To come and spoil the fun!'
  A9   70:28   sharp chin. However, she did not like to be rude: so she bore it as well as she could.
RUDENESS (1)
  A7   60:29   This piece of rudeness was more than Alice could bear: she got up in great
RUG (1) [See also HEARTH-RUG]
  T12 207:33   comfortably down, with one elbow on the rug, and her chin in her hand, to watch the kittens. "Tell me,
RULE (17)
  T2   123:25   got some too. I thought it was the regular rule."
  T9   195:38   should be five times as cold, by the same rule--"
  T9   196:24   help saying foolish things as a general rule."
  A9   70:11   pleased at having found out a new kind of rule, "and vinegar that makes them sour--and camomile that
  A8   63:30   not remember ever having heard of such a rule at processions; "and besides, what would be the use of a
  A12   93:35   out "Silence!", and read out from his book, "Rule Forty-two. All persons more than a mile high to leave the
  A12   93:43   "It's the oldest rule in the book," said the King.
  T5   150: 6   it if you did want it," the Queen said. "The rule is, jam to-morrow and jam yesterday--but never jam to-day
  T8   180:10   Another Rule of Battle, that Alice had not noticed, seemed to be that
  T12 207: 8   only purr for 'yes,' and mew for 'no,' or any rule of that sort," she had said, "so that one could keep up a
  T9   192:20   "But if everybody obeyed that rule," said Alice, who was always ready for a little argument,
  T3   131: 7   of passengers altogether), and, as the rule seemed to be that they should all speak in turn, he went
  T8   180: 3   peeping out from her hiding-place. "One Rule seems to be, that if one Knight hits the other, he knocks
  T8   180: 5   misses, he tumbles off himself--and another Rule seems to be that they hold their clubs with their arms,
  T7   170: 1   now and then; and it seemed to be a regular rule that, whenever a horse stumbled, the rider fell off
  A12   93:42   said Alice; "besides, that's not a regular rule: you invented it just now."
  T5   152:31   Queen said. "Only I never can remember the rule. You must be very happy, living in this wood, and being

RULES (5)
 A1   10:14   another key on it, or at any rate a book of rules for shutting people up like telescopes: this time she
 A8   67:25   speak--and they don't seem to have any rules in particular: at least, if there are, nobody attends to
 T8   180: 1   "I wonder, now, what the Rules of Battle are," she said to herself, as she watched the
 T8   179:34   "You will observe the Rules of Battle, of course?" the White Knight remarked,
 A1   10:24   because they would not remember the simple rules their friends had taught them: such as, that a red-hot
RUMBLING (1)
 A4   30:23   without hearing anything more: at last came a rumbling of little cart-wheels; and the sound of a good many
RUN (16)
 T2   126:11   this moment, somehow or other, they began to run.
 T7   174:24   wood over yonder--How fast those Queens can run!"
 T7   175: 2   "But aren't you going to run and help her?" Alice asked, very much surprised at his
 T7   172:39   is, that it's my crown all the while! Let's run and see them." And they trotted off, Alice repeating to
 T2   127:21   If you want to get somewhere else, you must run at least twice as fast as that!"
 A6   46: 5   laughed so much at this, that she had to run back into the wood for fear of their hearing her; and,
 T8   190:34   encouraged him," she said, as she turned to run down the hill: "and now for the last brook, and to be a
 T3   129:18   checking herself just as she was beginning to run down the hill, and trying to find some excuse for turning
 T7   175:13   rather nervously. "You shouldn't have run him through with your horn, you know."
 A4   27:14   "Why, Mary Ann, what are you doing out here? Run home this moment, and fetch me a pair of gloves and a fan!
 A12   98:10   was a curious dream, dear, certainly; but now run in to your tea: it's getting late." So Alice got up and
 A4   32:37   a great thistle, to keep herself from being run over; and, the moment she appeared on the other side, the
 T7   169: 4   Alice got behind a tree, for fear of being run over, and watched them go by.
 T4   144: 8   said the Carpenter, / 'You've had a pleasant run! / Shall we be trotting home again?' / But answer came
 T2   128:30   she ran quickly into the wood ("and she can run very fast!" thought Alice), there was no way of guessing,
 T7   173: 6   she asked, as well as she could, for the run was putting her quite out of breath.
RUNNING (19)
 T7   173: 9   be good enough--" Alice panted out, after running a little further, "to stop a minute--just to get--
 A4   32:43   began a series of short charges at the stick, running a very little way forwards each time and a long way
 A8   65:42   Queen in a voice of thunder, and people began running about in all directions, tumbling up against each
 T7   174:22   pointing eagerly. "There's the White Queen running across the country! She came flying out of the wood
 T1   107:18   all knots and tangles, with the kitten running after its own tail in the middle.
 T8   182: 4   if they do come, I don't choose to have them running all about."
 T1   119: 3   down stairs--or, at least, it wasn't exactly running, but a new invention for getting down stairs quickly
 A10   78: 6   Turtle recovered his voice, and, with tears running down his cheeks, he went on again:--
 A3   23:13   race was over. However, when they had been running half an hour or so, and were quite dry again, the Dodo
 T2   126:14   began: all she remembers is, that they were running hand in hand, and the Queen went so fast that it was
 A12   92:10   could, for the accident of the gold-fish kept running in her head, and she had a vague sort of idea that
 A10   81:28   said Alice, whose thoughts were still running on the song, "I'd have said to the porpoise 'Keep back
 A6   45: 2   next, when suddenly a footman in livery came running out of the wood--(she considered him to be a footman
 T9   204:21   doll, and was now on the table, merrily running round and round after her own shawl, which was
 T2   125:21   There were a number of tiny little brooks running straight across it from side to side, and the ground
 T7   169: 1   The next moment soldiers came running through the wood, at first in twos and threes, then
 A3   23:11   "One, two, three, and away!", but they began running when they liked, and left off when they liked, so that
 T5   149: 2   owner: in another moment the White Queen came running wildly through the wood, with both arms stretched out
 T2   127:20   Queen. "Now, here, you see, it takes all the running you can do, to keep in the same place. If you want to
RUNS (1)
 T7   175: 4   "No use, no use!" said the King. "She runs so fearfully quick. You might as well try to catch a
RUSH (2)
 A4   32:15   it something out of a bottle. They all made a rush at Alice the moment she appeared; but she ran off as hard
 A4   32:38   on the other side, the puppy made another rush at the stick, and tumbled head over heels in its hurry to
RUSHED (2)
 A4   32:35   its feet at once, with a yelp of delight, and rushed at the stick, and made believe to worry it: then Alice
 T1   113:20   my child!" the White Queen cried out, as she rushed past the King, so violently that she knocked him over
RUSHES (10) [See also DREAM-RUSHES]
 T5   156:23   bunch after another of the darling scented rushes.
 T5   157: 1   off the seat, and down among the heap of rushes.
 T5   156:18   plunged in elbow-deep, to get hold of the rushes a good long way down before breaking them off--and for
 T5   156: 6   "Oh, please! There are some scented rushes!" Alice cried in a sudden transport of delight. "There
 T5   156:16   till it glided gently in among the waving rushes. And then the little sleeves were carefully rolled up,
 T5   156:28   she managed to pick plenty of beautiful rushes as the boat glided by, there was always a more lovely
 T5   156:34   What mattered it to her just then that the rushes had begun to fade, and to lose all their scent and
 T5   156:31   at last with a sigh at the obstinacy of the rushes in growing so far off, as, with flushed cheeks and
 T9   203:15   the ceiling, looking something like a bed of rushes with fireworks at the top. As to the bottles, they each
 T5   156:36   that she picked them? Even real scented rushes, you know, last only a very little while--and these,
RUST (1)
 T8   189: 9   my design / To keep the Menai bridge from rust / By boiling it in wine. / I thanked him much for telling
RUSTLED (1)
 A12   98:24   The long grass rustled at her feet as the White Rabbit hurried by--the
RUSTLING (1)
 A12   98:36   to dull reality--the grass would be only rustling in the wind, and the pool rippling to the waving of

-S-

SAD (5)
T8W   15: 7 china. While tasting the treacle, they had a sad accident: two of their party were engulphed--"
A9   74:17 saw the Mock Turtle in the distance, sitting sad and lonely on a little ledge of rock, and, as they came
A3   25: 2 at the Mouse's tail; "but why do you call it sad?" And she kept on puzzling about it while the mouse was
A3   24:17   "Mine is a long and sad tale!" said the Mouse, turning to Alice, and sighing.
T8   186:31   "You are sad," the Knight said in an anxious tone: "let me sing you a
SADDLE (7)
T8   185:15 he said this, and instantly rolled out of the saddle, and fell headlong into a deep ditch.
T8   179:32 as he took up his helmet (which hung from the saddle, and was something the shape of a horse's head) and put
T8   179:19 again. As soon as he was comfortably in the saddle, he began once more "You're my--" but here another
T8   183: 7 he asked, as he scrambled back into the saddle, keeping hold of Alice's hair with one hand, to save
T8   181:33   or something like one--fastened to the saddle," said Alice.
T8   182:20   in the bag." And he hung it to the saddle, which was already loaded with bunches of carrots, and
T8   184:42 proudly at his helmet, which hung from the saddle. "Yes," he said; "but I've invented a better one than
SADLY (8)
A3   23:33   "Only a thimble," said Alice sadly.
A10   79:12 the Mock Turtle sang this, very slowly and sadly:--
T6   166:22 so she sat down, and said "Thank you" rather sadly,
A10   79: 1 mad things all this time, sat down again very sadly and quietly, and looked at Alice.
T4   147:44   "Very well," the other said, rather sadly: "and she can watch us--only you'd better not come very
A12   95:36   The Knave shook his head sadly. "Do I look like it?" he said. (Which he certainly did
A1   9:32 up the other, trying every door, she walked sadly down the middle, wondering how she was ever to get out
T3   136:14 thought poor Alice. She answered, rather sadly, "Nothing, just now."
SAFE (3)
A4   32:17 as hard as she could, and soon found herself safe in a thick wood.
A9   74: 6 on the whole she thought it would be quite as safe to stay with it as to go after that savage Queen: so she
T8   181: 4 brook," said the White Knight. "I'll see you safe to the end of the wood--and then I must go back, you know
SAFELY (1)
T8W   21:13 getting very talkative, she thought she might safely leave him. "I think I must be going on now," she said.
SAFER (1)
T6   160:16   "Don't you think you'd be safer down on the ground?" Alice went on, not with any idea of
SAGE (1)
A5   38: 5   "In my youth," said the sage, as he shook his grey locks, / "I kept all my limbs very
SAID (968)
A3   21:12 to tell its age, there was no more to be said.
A8   65:34 "Did you say 'What a pity!'?" the Rabbit said.
A8   65:40 You see she came rather late, and the Queen said--"
A8   68:36 it very hard to make out exactly what they said.
A11   88:14 "Fourteenth of March, I think it was," he said.
A11   89:20 twinkled after that--only the March Hare said--"
T1   115:21 low, that Alice could hardly hear what they said.
T2   122:31 it. "I never thought of that before!" she said.
T4   147:24 "to keep his head from being cut off," as he said.
T4   148: 5 the trees pretty often, I should think," she said.
T6   163: 5 "I'd rather see that done on paper," she said.
T6   163:24 I don't know what you mean by 'glory,'" Alice said.
T9   199:14   "I don't know what you mean," she said.
T8W   16:13 the face is very good for the toothache," she said.
T9   192:33   "But she said a great deal more than that!" the White Queen moaned,
T3   134:24   "No, indeed," Alice said, a little anxiously.
T8W   15:13 "It's in this newspaper, though," Alice said a little timidly.
T2   128: 7 At the two-yard peg she faced round, and said "A pawn goes two squares in its first move, you know. So
T8   181:23   "I didn't know it," the Knight said, a shade of vexation passing over his face. "Then all the
A11   91:18   "Treacle," said a sleepy voice behind her.
T9   195:23 it," said the Red Queen: "when you've once said a thing, that fixes it, and you must take the
A8   65:25   "It's--it's a very fine day!" said a timid voice at her side. She was walking by the White
A10   79:13   "Will you walk a little faster?" said a whiting to a snail, / "There's a porpoise close behind
T6   161:25 Dumpty exclaimed triumphantly. "You never said a word like it!"
A10   78:22   "Of course," the Mock Turtle said: "advance twice, set to partners--"
T4   146:16   "It's only a rattle," Alice said, after a careful examination of the little white thing.
T6   159:17   "It's very provoking," Humpty Dumpty said after a long silence, looking away from Alice as he spoke
T3   129:25 "I think I'll go down the other way," she said after a pause; "and perhaps I may visit the elephants
A9   71: 6 put my arm round your waist," the Duchess said, after a pause: "the reason is, that I'm doubtful about
T5   149:35 "Come, you look rather better now!" she said, after altering most of the pins. "But really you should
T4   147:18   Alice said afterwards she had never seen such a fuss made about
T1   115: 3   She said afterwards that she had never seen in all her life such a
T4   139:34 "But it certainly was funny," (Alice said afterwards, when she was telling her sister the history
T9   202:38   ("And they did push so!" she said afterwards, when she was telling her sister the history
A5   42:32 the least idea what you're talking about," said Alice.
A6   46:41   "But what am I to do?" said Alice.
A6   51:11   "I don't much care where--" said Alice.
A6   51:25   "How do you know I'm mad?" said Alice.
A6   51:31   "I suppose so," said Alice.

SAID (cont.)
```
A6    51:35              "I call it purring, not growling,"  said Alice.
A7    55:18                                  "Exactly so,"  said Alice.
A7    56:37              "I don't know what you mean,"  said Alice.
A7    57:17              "I've heard something like it,"  said Alice.
A7    58:14   "Then you keep moving round, I suppose?"  said Alice.
A7    59:15              "Nobody asked your opinion,"  said Alice.
A7    60:17                            "Why with an M?"  said Alice.
A8    65:33                                "What for?"  said Alice.
A9    71:16              "It's a mineral, I think,"  said Alice.
A9    72:16   yourself to say it any longer than that,"  said Alice.
A9    73:15   "I never saw one, or heard of one,"  said Alice.
A9    74:10                        "What is the fun?"  said Alice.
A9    77: 1                      "What was that like?"  said Alice.
A10   79: 4                        "Very much indeed,"  said Alice.
A10   81:36            "Don't you mean 'purpose'?"  said Alice.
A12   93:18                                  "Nothing,"  said Alice.
A12   93:20                        "Nothing whatever,"  said Alice.
A12   93:38              "I'm not a mile high,"  said Alice.
A12   93:44      "Then it ought to be Number One,"  said Alice.
A12   96:10   goes on 'they all returned from him to you,'"  said Alice.
A12   97: 4                                  "I wo'n't!"  said Alice.
T4    145: 7              "Where I am now, of course,"  said Alice.
T5    151: 7   "Suppose he never commits the crime?"  said Alice.
T5    151:15              "Only for faults,"  said Alice.
T5    153: 8              "I ca'n't believe that!"  said Alice.
T5    157:11              "Are there many crabs here?"  said Alice.
T6    162:44              "Three hundred and sixty-five,"  said Alice.
T6    163:21                                "Certainly,"  said Alice.
T6    166:26              "I see you don't,"  said Alice.
T6    166:31              "Thank you very much,"  said Alice.
T6    166:36   "I will, if I can remember it so long,"  said Alice.
T6    167: 5   "I'm afraid I don't quite understand,"  said Alice.
T7    170:16              "I see nobody on the road,"  said Alice.
T7    171: 2              "I beg your pardon?"  said Alice.
T7    175:32              "Yes, if you like,"  said Alice.
T8    181:33   something like one--fastened to the saddle,"  said Alice.
T8    182:12              "It's meant for plum-cake,"  said Alice.
T8    184:25              "You were a little grave,"  said Alice.
T9    194:34              "To be sure I do,"  said Alice.
T8W   17: 1              "Oh, you mean stiff-neck,"  said Alice.
T8W   20:14              "I'm afraid not,"  said Alice.
A2    18:10              "That was a narrow escape!"  said Alice, a good deal frightened at the sudden change, but
A2    15:20   "You ought to be ashamed of yourself,"  said Alice, "a great girl like you," (she might well say this)
A10   81:41   my adventures--beginning from this morning,"  said Alice a little timidly; "but it's no use going back to
A6    47:12              "Please would you tell me,"  said Alice, a little timidly, for she was not quite sure
A8    63: 3   "Would you tell me, please,"  said Alice, a little timidly, "why you are painting those
T2    120:30              "O Tiger-lily!"  said Alice, addressing herself to one that was waving
A5    36: 7   perhaps your feelings may be different,"  said Alice: "all I know is, it would feel very queer to me."
A8    67:39   "It's a friend of mine--a Cheshire-Cat,"  said Alice: "allow me to introduce it."
A3    26:22   "I wish I had our Dinah here, I know I do!"  said Alice aloud, addressing nobody in particular. "She'd soon
A3    26: 6              "A knot!"  said Alice, always ready to make herself useful, and looking
T4    145:21              "I am real!"  said Alice, and began to cry.
A1    12:34   marked in currants. "Well, I'll eat it,"  said Alice, "and if it makes me grow larger, I can reach the
A10   78: 9   lived much under the sea--" ("I haven't,"  said Alice)--"and perhaps you were never even introduced to a
A8    65:12              "You sha'n't be beheaded!"  said Alice, and she put them into a large flower-pot that
A12   98: 6   "Oh, I've had such a curious dream!"  said Alice. And she told her sister, as well as she could
T6    164:29              "That'll do very well,"  said Alice: "and 'slithy'?"
T8    190:20              "Of course I'll wait,"  said Alice: "and thank you very much for coming so far--and
A1    10:16   on it ("which certainly was not here before,"  said Alice), and tied round the neck of the bottle was a paper
A5    42:13   "What can all that green stuff be?"  said Alice. "And where have my shoulders got to? And oh, my
A3    24:14   promised to tell me your history, you know,"  said Alice, "and why it is you hate--C and D," she added in a
A7    55: 1   it wasn't very civil of you to offer it,"  said Alice angrily.
A4    33: 7   "And yet what a dear little puppy it was!"  said Alice, as she leant against a buttercup to rest herself,
A7    60:35   "At any rate I'll never go there again!"  said Alice, as she picked her way through the wood. "It's the
T5    158:10   "Then I'll have one, please,"  said Alice, as she put the money down on the counter. For she
A2    19: 1   "I wish I hadn't cried so much!"  said Alice, as she swam about, trying to find her way out. "I
T9    196:38   "I haven't got a nightcap with me,"  said Alice, as she tried to obey the first direction: "and I
T3    137:25              "I do believe,"  said Alice at last, "that they live in the same house! I
T4    144:13              "I like the Walrus best,"  said Alice: "because he was a little sorry for the poor
A5    35:11   "I ca'n't explain myself, I'm afraid, Sir,"  said Alice, "because I'm not myself, you see."
A12   93:41   "Well, I sha'n't go, at any rate,"  said Alice; "besides, that's not a regular rule: you invented
T6    166:12              "I read it in a book,"  said Alice. "But I had some poetry repeated to me much easier
A6    52: 5   "I should like it very much,"  said Alice, "but I haven't been invited yet."
T9    193:17   "I didn't know I was to have a party at all,"  said Alice; "but, if there is to be one, I think I ought to
T3    132:37              "No use to them,"  said Alice; "but it's useful to the people that name them, I
A5    36: 2   "Well, perhaps you haven't found it so yet,"  said Alice; "but when you have to turn into a chrysalis--you
A6    46:43   "Oh, there's no use in talking to him,"  said Alice desperately: "he's perfectly idiotic!" And she
A9    76:29              "Yes,"  said Alice doubtfully: "it means--to--make--anything--prettier
A10   80:13   you, it's a very interesting dance to watch,"  said Alice, feeling very glad that it was over at last: "and I
```

SAID (cont.)

T8	186:38	"Or else what?"	said Alice, for the Knight had made a sudden pause.
T2	123:35	"I think I'll go and meet her,"	said Alice, for, though the flowers were interesting enough,
A5	43:25	"It matters a good deal to me,"	said Alice hastily; "but I'm not looking for eggs, as it
T9	196: 9	"I know what he came for,"	said Alice: "he wanted to punish the fish, because--"
A6	46:17	"Please, then,"	said Alice, "how am I to get in?"
A5	36:31	"I'm afraid I am, Sir,"	said Alice. "I ca'n't remember things as I used--and I don't
A9	73:12	"No,"	said Alice. "I don't even know what a Mock Turtle is."
A8	65:35	"No, I didn't,"	said Alice. "I don't think it's at all a pity. I said 'What
T9	193:27	"I don't know,"	said Alice. "I lost count."
A1	12: 1	"What a curious feeling!"	said Alice. "I must be shutting up like a telescope!"
T9	192: 1	"Well, this is grand!"	said Alice. "I never expected I should be a Queen so soon--and
A5	43: 5	"But I'm not a serpent, I tell you!"	said Alice. "I'm a--I'm a--"
T6	166: 1	"And then 'mome raths'?"	said Alice. "I'm afraid I'm giving you a great deal of trouble
T2	127:23	"I'd rather not try, please!"	said Alice. "I'm quite content to stay here--only I am so hot
T5	152:28	"The crow must have flown away, I think,"	said Alice. "I'm so glad it's gone. I thought it was the night
A4	32:29	trying to touch her. "Poor little thing!"	said Alice, in a coaxing tone, and she tried hard to whistle
A2	20: 1	"I wo'n't indeed!"	said Alice, in a great hurry to change the subject of
A9	77:10	And how many hours a day did you do lessons?"	said Alice, in a hurry to change the subject.
A3	22:26	"As wet as ever,"	said Alice in a melancholy tone: "it doesn't seem to dry me at
A2	19:32	"Well, perhaps not,"	said Alice in a soothing tone: "don't be angry about it. And
A5	42: 7	"Come, my head's free at last!"	said Alice in a tone of delight, which changed into alarm in
A10	81:32	"Wouldn't it, really?"	said Alice, in a tone of great surprise.
A9	76:12	"Certainly not!"	said Alice indignantly.
A7	54: 9	saw Alice coming. "There's plenty of room!"	said Alice indignantly, and she sat down in a large arm-chair
A5	42:28	"I'm not a serpent!"	said Alice indignantly. "Let me alone!"
T8	182: 1	I was wondering what the mouse-trap was for,"	said Alice. "It isn't very likely there would be any mice on
T5	150:10	"I don't understand you,"	said Alice. "It's dreadfully confusing!"
A7	55: 4	"I didn't know it was your table,"	said Alice: "it's laid for a great many more than three."
A10	81: 8	"Thank you,"	said Alice, "it's very interesting. I never knew so much about
A10	80:18	"Yes,"	said Alice, "I've often seen them at dinn----" she checked
A8	68: 1	"A cat may look at a king,"	said Alice. "I've read that in some book, but I don't remember
T9	193:22	"Manners are not taught in lessons,"	said Alice. "Lessons teach you to do sums, and things of that
A9	76:16	"You couldn't have wanted it much,"	said Alice; "living at the bottom of the sea."
T3	131:31	"Don't tease so,"	said Alice, looking about in vain to see where the voice came
A3	25: 1	"It is a long tail, certainly,"	said Alice, looking down with wonder at the Mouse's tail; "but
A12	97: 1	"Stuff and nonsense!"	said Alice loudly. "The idea of having the sentence first!"
T8	181: 6	"Thank you very much,"	said Alice. "May I help you off with your helmet?" It was
A11	88:43	"Don't talk nonsense,"	said Alice more boldly: "you know you're growing too."
A3	23: 2	"What is a Caucus-race?"	said Alice; not that she much wanted to know, but the Dodo had
T6	160:11	"Why do you sit out here all alone?"	said Alice, not wishing to begin an argument.
T2	127:37	"No, thank you,"	said Alice: "one's quite enough!"
T4	139:18	"Next Boy!"	said Alice, passing on to Tweedledee, though she felt quite
T5	157: 7	"Was it? I didn't see it,"	said Alice, peeping cautiously over the side of the boat into
A7	59:33	"What did they draw?"	said Alice, quite forgetting her promise.
T6	162:31	"It is really?"	said Alice, quite pleased to find that she had chosen a good
A7	58:21	"I'm afraid I don't know one,"	said Alice, rather alarmed at the proposal.
A5	43: 9	"I--I'm a little girl,"	said Alice, rather doubtfully, as she remembered the number of
A3	23:33	"Only a thimble,"	said Alice sadly.
A6	50: 4	If you're going to turn into a pig, my dear,"	said Alice, seriously, "I'll have nothing more to do with you.
T7	170: 9	"Yes, I did,"	said Alice: "several thousand, I should think."
A9	72:25	"I've a right to think,"	said Alice sharply, for she was beginning to feel a little
A12	95:23	"If any one of them can explain it,"	said Alice, (she had grown so large in the last few minutes
A12	97: 7	"Who cares for you?"	said Alice (she had grown to her full size by this time).
T6	164: 7	"Oh!"	said Alice. She was too much puzzled to make any other remark.
A8	67:32	"Not at all,"	said Alice: "she's so extremely--" Just then she noticed that
T4	148: 9	"And all about a rattle!"	said Alice, still hoping to make them a little ashamed of
T2	127:16	"Well, in our country,"	said Alice, still panting a little, "you'd generally get to
A8	64: 3	"How should I know?"	said Alice, surprised at her own courage. "It's no business of
T6	165: 5	the grass-plot round a sun-dial, I suppose?"	said Alice, surprised at her own ingenuity.
T2	125:10	"No, I shouldn't,"	said Alice, surprised into contradicting her at last: "a hill
A5	36:23	"Is that all?"	said Alice, swallowing down her anger as well as she could.
T5	151:18	I had done the things I was punished for,"	said Alice: "that makes all the difference."
A6	49:29	off sneezing by this time). "Don't grunt,"	said Alice; "that's not at all a proper way of expressing
T3	135: 5	"That would never do, I'm sure,"	said Alice: "the governess would never think of excusing me
T4	147:38	"Then you'd better not fight to-day,"	said Alice, thinking it a good opportunity to make peace.
A7	57: 5	"That would be grand, certainly,"	said Alice thoughtfully; "but then--I shouldn't be hungry for
A5	41:15	a little larger, Sir, if you wouldn't mind,"	said Alice: "three inches is such a wretched height to be."
A10	79: 2	"It must be a very pretty dance,"	said Alice timidly.
A5	41: 2	"Not quite right, I'm afraid,"	said Alice, timidly: "some of the words have got altered."
A4	32:18	"The first thing I've got to do,"	said Alice to herself, as she wandered about in the wood, "is
T2	120: 1	"I should see the garden far better,"	said Alice to herself, "if I could get to the top of that hill
A1	12: 8	about this; "for it might end, you know,"	said Alice to herself, "in my going out altogether, like a
A1	12:21	"Come, there's no use in crying like that!"	said Alice to herself rather sharply. "I advise you to leave
A4	30:35	Bill's got to come down the chimney, has he?"	said Alice to herself. "Why, they seem to put everything upon
A3	26: 3	"I beg your pardon,"	said Alice very humbly: "you had got to the fifth bend, I
A8	64: 8	"Nonsense!"	said Alice, very loudly and decidedly, and the Queen was
A11	88:41	"I ca'n't help it,"	said Alice very meekly: "I'm growing."
A7	60:26	"Really, now you ask me,"	said Alice, very much confused, "I don't think--"
A8	63:40	"My name is Alice, so please your Majesty,"	said Alice very politely; but she added, to herself, "Why,

SAID (cont.)

A9	76:10	"Yes," said Alice: "we learned French and music."
T8	186: 9	time to have it cooked for the next course?" said Alice. "Well, that was quick work, certainly!"
A10	78:13	"No, indeed," said Alice. "What sort of a dance is it?"
T6	163:42	"Would you tell me please," said Alice, "what that means?"
A8	65:28	"Very," said Alice. "Where's the Duchess?"
T6	163:33	"The question is," said Alice, "whether you can make words mean so many different
A9	70:34	"Somebody said," Alice whispered, "that it's done by everybody minding
A7	58:35	"What did they live on?" said Alice, who always took a great interest in questions of
A6	48:23	"Which would not be an advantage," said Alice, who felt very glad to get an opportunity of
T4	144:36	catch cold with lying on the damp grass," said Alice, who was a very thoughtful little girl.
A5	43:16	"I have tasted eggs, certainly," said Alice, who was a very truthful child; "but little girls
T9	192:20	"But if everybody obeyed that rule," said Alice, who was always ready for a little argument, "and
A5	42:41	"I'm very sorry you've been annoyed," said Alice, who was beginning to see its meaning.
T8	187: 8	"Well, what is the song, then?" said Alice, who was by this time completely bewildered.
A10	81:27	"If I'd been the whiting," said Alice, whose thoughts were still running on the song,
A10	81:12	"I never thought about it," said Alice. "Why?"
T7	171: 4	"I only meant that I didn't understand," said Alice. "Why one to come and one to go?"
A12	94:30	"It doesn't prove anything of the sort!" said Alice. "Why, you don't even know what they're about!"
T6	164:14	seem very clever at explaining words, Sir," said Alice. "Would you kindly tell me the meaning of the poem
A9	76: 7	"I've been to a day-school, too," said Alice. "You needn't be so proud as all that."
T5	155:32	"Indeed I did," said Alice: "you've said it very often--and very loud. Please,
A1	8:28	how many miles I've fallen by this time?" she said aloud. "I must be getting somewhere near the centre of
T6	159:14	"And how exactly like an egg he is!" she said aloud, standing with her hands ready to catch him, for
T4	148:20	on. "What a thick black cloud that is!" she said. "And how fast it comes! Why, I do believe it's got
T8	187:35	on a gate. / 'Who are you, aged man?' I said. / 'And how is it you live?' / And his answer trickled
T9	193:16	The White Queen smiled feebly, and said "And I invite you."
A1	10:20	that in a hurry. "No, I'll look first," she said, "and see whether it's marked 'poison' or not"; for she
A3	23: 9	circle, ("the exact shape doesn't matter," it said,) and then all the party were placed along the course,
T3	131:11	voice spoke next. "Change engines--" it said, and there it choked and was obliged to leave off.
A8	63:24	manner, smiling at everything that was said, and went by without noticing her. Then followed the
A12	93:26	of course, I meant," the King hastily said, and went on to himself in an undertone, "important--
A5	37: 1	"You are old, Father William," the young man said, / "And your hair has become very white; / And yet you
A1	12:38	She ate a little bit, and said anxiously to herself "Which way? Which way?", holding her
T8	182:25	"That's hardly enough," he said, anxiously. "You see the wind is so very strong here.
T6	159:25	like conversation, she thought, as he never said anything to her; in fact, his last remark was evidently
T8W	14:12	but when he got settled down again he only said, as before, "Worrity, worrity! Can't you leave a body
T6	168:20	her hand. "Good-bye, till we meet again!" she said as cheerfully as she could.
T9	194:23	Alice said, as gravely as she could, "They might go different ways."
T8	184: 3	"None to speak of," the Knight said, as if he didn't mind breaking two or three of them. "The
A7	56:21	English. "I don't quite understand you," she said, as politely as she could.
T4	140:20	to interrupt him. "If it's very long," she said, as politely as she could, "would you please tell me
T5	151: 8	be all the better, wouldn't it?" the Queen said, as she bound the plaster round her finger with a bit of
T5	149:30	know, if you pin it all on one side," Alice said as she gently put it right for her; "and dear me, what a
T3	136: 9	all frightened. "Here then! Here then!" Alice said, as she held out her hand and tried to stroke it; but it
T5	149: 5	very glad I happened to be in the way," Alice said, as she helped her to put on her shawl again.
T9	192: 9	to see her, "and if I really am a Queen," she said as she sat down again, "I shall be able to manage it
T3	135:39	"Well, at any rate it's a great comfort," she said as she stepped under the trees, "after being so hot, to
T5	155: 7	"Are you a child or a teetotum?" the Sheep said, as she took up another pair of needles. "You'll make me
T8	190:34	"I hope it encouraged him," she said, as she turned to run down the hill: "and now for the
T5	152: 8	"What is the matter?" she said, as soon as there was a chance of making herself heard.
T8	182:18	"It's rather a tight fit, you see," he said, as they got it in at last; "there are so many
A9	72:19	"I make you a present of everything I've said as yet."
T4	140: 6	"I hope you're not much tired?" she said at last.
T6	162:40	little. "I like birthday presents best," she said at last.
T7	175:18	"What--is--this?" he said at last.
T8	179:28	"She's my prisoner, you know!" the Red Knight said at last.
T5	154:16	"Things flow about so here!" she said at last in a plaintive tone, after she had spent a minute
T5	154: 1	"What is it you want to buy?" the Sheep said at last, looking up for a moment from her knitting.
T3	136:12	"What do you call yourself?" the Fawn said at last. Such a soft sweet voice it had!
T2	125:26	out just like a large chess-board!" Alice said at last. "There ought to be some men moving about
T6	162:25	"It is a--most--provoking--thing," he said at last, "when a person doesn't know a cravat from a
T5	156:30	"The prettiest are always further!" she said at last with a sigh at the obstinacy of the rushes in
T4	146: 5	up into it. "No, I don't think it is," he said: "at least--not under here. Nohow."
T1	110:25	the thing didn't succeed, principally, Alice said, because the kitten wouldn't fold its arms properly. So,
T7	176: 1	his eyes were half shut. "What's this!" he said, blinking lazily at Alice, and speaking in a deep hollow
T2	122:26	Alice did so. "It's very hard," she said; "but I don't see what that has to do with it."
T5	152:10	"I haven't pricked it yet," the Queen said, "but I soon shall--oh, oh, oh!"
T5	151:11	"Of course it would be all the better," she said: "but it wouldn't be all the better his being punished."
T2	125:14	"You may call it 'nonsense' if you like," she said, "but I've heard nonsense, compared with which that would
T8	184:42	helmet, which hung from the saddle. "Yes," he said; "but I've invented a better one than that--like a
A10	83: 7	"It's the first position in dancing," Alice said; but she was dreadfully puzzled by the whole thing, and
T2	123:11	has the same awkward shape as you," the Rose said: "but she's redder--and her petals are shorter, I think
A9	70:30	"The game's going on rather better now," she said, by way of keeping up the conversation a little.
T7	175:14	"It didn't hurt him," the Unicorn said carelessly, and he was going on, when his eye happened to
T1	110: 6	just as if you understood it: and when I said 'Check!' you purred! Well, it was a nice check, Kitty,
T8	184:39	"What a curious helmet you've got!" she said cheerfully. "Is that your invention too?"
A8	64:10	King laid his hand upon her arm, and timidly said "Consider, my dear: she is only a child!"
A3	25:39	our breath. 'I'll be judge, I'll be jury,' said cunning old Fury: 'I'll try the whole cause, and condemn
T4	143:17	to do!' / 'The night is fine,' the Walrus said. / 'Do you admire the view?

SAID (cont.)

T8	190:22	"I hope so," the Knight	said doubtfully: "but you didn't cry so much as I thought you
T8	181: 1	"I don't know," Alice	said doubtfully. "I don't want to be anybody's prisoner. I
T4	140:10	"Ye-es, pretty well--some poetry," Alice	said doubtfully. "Would you tell me which road leads out of
T8	190:14	had come. "You've only a few yards to go," he	said, "down the hill and over that little brook, and then
A3	23:21	the rest waited in silence. At last the Dodo	said "Everybody has won, and all must have prizes."
T5	152:12	"When do you expect to do it?" Alice	said, feeling very much inclined to laugh.
A8	62:15	"Yes, it is his business!"	said Five. "And I'll tell him--it was for bringing the cook
A8	62:11	"You'd better not talk!"	said Five. "I heard the Queen say only yesterday you deserved
A8	62: 7	"I couldn't help it,"	said Five, in a sulky tone. "Seven jogged my elbow."
A12	96:28	the jury consider their verdict," the King	said, for about the twentieth time that day.
A2	16: 4	"I'm sure I'm not Ada," she	said, "for her hair goes in such long ringlets, and mine
T9	202:30	thanks in a neat speech," the Red Queen	said, frowning at Alice as she spoke.
T6	163:16	"To be sure I was!" Humpty Dumpty	said gaily as she turned it round for him. "I thought it
T8W	21:14	him. "I think I must be going on now," she	said. "Good-bye."
T6	168:35	eyes or took any further notice of her, she	said "Good-bye!" once more, and, getting no answer to this,
T2	127:25	"I know what you'd like!" the Queen	said good-naturedly, taking a little box out of her pocket.
T8	184:36	"I haven't tried it yet," the Knight	said, gravely; "so I ca'n't tell for certain--but I'm afraid
T7	173:30	"Were you happy in prison, dear child?"	said Haigha.
T7	175:25	"It can talk,"	said Haigha solemnly.
T4	145:24	"If I wasn't real," Alice	said--half laughing through her tears, it all seemed so
T4	147:42	Tweedledee looked at his watch, and	said "Half-past four."
T7	174:10	"It's waiting for 'em now,"	said Hatta; "this is a bit of it as I'm eating."
T8	185:14	of fastness with me, I can assure you!" he	said. He raised his hands in some excitement as he said this,
A10	80: 4	far, too far!", and gave a look askance--/	Said he thanked the whiting kindly, but he would not join the
T9	196: 4	"He	said he would come in," the White Queen went on, "because he
T8W	20: 1	"I'm very sorry for you," Alice	said heartily: "and I think if your wig fitted a little better
A12	98: 4	"Wake up, Alice dear!"	said her sister. "Why, what a long sleep you've had!"
A5	40: 6	three questions, and that is enough," /	Said his father. "Don't give yourself airs! / Do you think I
A5	39: 5	"In my youth,"	said his father, "I took to the law, / And argued each case
T2	122:21	"How is it you can all talk so nicely?" Alice	said, hoping to get it into a better temper by a compliment.
T6	166:17	"Oh, it needn't come to that!" Alice hastily	said, hoping to keep him from beginning.
T9	194:40	again. "Can you answer useful questions?" she	said. "How is bread made?"
T6	161:27	"If I'd meant that, I'd have said it,"	said Humpty Dumpty.
T6	162:37	"I'm not offended,"	said Humpty Dumpty.
T6	164:38	"They are that,"	said Humpty Dumpty; "also they make their nests under
T6	161:18	"In that case we start afresh,"	said Humpty Dumpty, "and it's my turn to choose a subject--"
T6	162:11	"One ca'n't, perhaps,"	said Humpty Dumpty; "but two can. With proper assistance, you
T6	168:16	"That's all,"	said Humpty Dumpty. "Good-bye."
T6	164: 5	I make a word do a lot of work like that,"	said Humpty Dumpty. "I always pay it extra."
T6	164:17	"Let's hear it,"	said Humpty Dumpty. "I can explain all the poems that ever
T6	159:22	"Some people,"	said Humpty Dumpty, looking away from her as usual, "have no
T6	163:43	"Now you talk like a reasonable child,"	said Humpty Dumpty, looking very much pleased. "I meant by
T6	166:14	"As to poetry, you know,"	said Humpty Dumpty, stretching out one of his great hands, "I
T6	163:35	"The question is,"	said Humpty Dumpty, "which is to be master--that's all."
T6	168:26	"That's just what I complain of,"	said Humpty Dumpty. "Your face is the same as everybody has--
T3	137: 1	if you'll come a little further on," the Fawn	said. "I ca'n't remember here."
A12	94:42	to him: / She gave me a good character, / But	said I could not swim.
A12	95:34	to see some meaning in them, after all. '--said	I could not swim--' you ca'n't swim, can you?" he added,
T8	188:14	having no reply to give / To what the old man	said, / I cried 'Come, tell me how you live!' / And thumped
T4	144: 1	'I weep for you,' the Walrus	said: / 'I deeply sympathize.' / With sobs and tears he sorted
T8W	19: 3	/ And they had noticed the effect, / They	said I did not look so nice / As they had ventured to expect.
A9	76: 1	"I never	said I didn't!" interrupted Alice.
T5	150: 1	Alice couldn't help laughing, as she	said "I don't want you to hire me--and I don't care for jam."
T8	188:18	His accents mild took up the tale: / He	said 'I go my ways, / And when I find a mountain-rill, / I set
T8	188:33	He	said 'I hunt for haddocks' eyes / Among the heather bright, /
T8	188: 1	He	said 'I look for butterflies / That sleep among the wheat: / I
T5	158:14	the money, and put it away in a box: then she	said "I never put things into people's hands--that would never
T2	121: 8	"and I really was wondering when you'd speak! Said	I to myself, 'Her face has got some sense in it, though
T6	168: 7	And he was very proud and stiff: / He	said 'I'd go and wake them, if--'
T9	192:32	with a little shudder, "She says she only	said 'if'--"
T3	135:15	"You shouldn't make jokes," Alice	said, "if it makes you so unhappy."
T8W	17:13	"You could make your wig much neater," she	said, "if only you had a comb."
T9	192:30	"I only said 'if'!"	poor Alice pleaded in a piteous tone.
T3	132:35	the use of their having names," the Gnat	said, "if they wo'n't answer to them?"
T1	115:27	"You will, though," the Queen	said, "if you don't make a memorandum of it."
T9	194:31	and shut her eyes. "I can do Addition," she	said, "if you give me time--but I ca'n't do Subtraction under
T5	149:16	of their conversation, so she smiled and	said "If your Majesty will only tell me the right way to begin
A9	77: 2	ca'n't show it you, myself," the Mock Turtle	said: "I'm too stiff. And the Gryphon never learnt it."
T9	199:17	"Nothing!" Alice	said impatiently. "I've been knocking at it!"
T4	147: 8	you agree to have a battle?" Tweedledum	said in a calmer tone.
T6	160:36	write such things in a book," Humpty Dumpty	said in a calmer tone. "That's what you call a History of
T7	174: 6	"They're getting on very well," he	said in a choking voice: "each of them has been down about
T9	199: 1	"What is it, now?" the Frog	said in a deep hoarse whisper.
A11	91:15	till his eyes were nearly out of sight, he	said, in a deep voice, "What are tarts made of?"
T8	181:34	"Yes, it's a very good bee-hive," the Knight	said in a discontented tone, "one of the best kind. But not a
T8	181:17	you're admiring my little box," the Knight	said in a friendly tone. "It's my own invention--to keep
T3	130: 2	"I'm afraid I haven't got one," Alice	said in a frightened tone: "there wasn't a ticket-office where
A7	58:25	slowly opened its eyes. "I wasn't asleep," it	said in a hoarse, feeble voice, "I heard every word you
A6	48:20	minded their own business," the Duchess	said, in a hoarse growl, "the world would go round a deal

SAID (cont.)

T3	131: 4	to the gentleman in white, shut his eyes and said in a loud voice, "She ought to know her way to the
A2	20:18	pale (with passion, Alice thought), and it said, in a low trembling voice, "Let us get to the shore, and
A11	91:11	looked anxiously at the White Rabbit, who said, in a low voice, "Your Majesty must cross-examine this
T5	152:33	"Only it is so very lonely here!" Alice said in a melancholy voice; and, at the thought of her
T5	149:26	know what's the matter with it!" the Queen said, in a melancholy voice. "It's out of temper, I think.
T8W	16: 3	"It's all along of the wig," the Wasp said in a much gentler voice.
T8W	14: 3	"How you go on!" the Wasp said in a peevish tone. "Worrity, worrity! There never was
T5	153: 9	"Ca'n't you?" the Queen said in a pitying tone. "Try again: draw a long breath, and
A10	84:12	Alice replied, so eagerly that the Gryphon said, in a rather offended tone, "Hm! No accounting for
T2	122:32	that you never think at all," the Rose said, in a rather severe tone.
T2	122:13	"Never mind!" Alice said in a soothing tone, and, stooping down to the daisies,
T8W	16: 1	newspaper. "I'm afraid you're not well," she said in a soothing tone. "Can't I do anything for you?"
T4	146:24	Alice laid her hand upon his arm and said, in a soothing tone, "You needn't be so angry about an
T7	172:20	"I do my best," the Messenger said in a sullen tone. "I'm sure nobody walks much faster than
T5	158: 7	"Then two are cheaper than one?" Alice said in a surprised tone, taking out her purse.
T6	164: 3	a great deal to make one word mean," Alice said in a thoughtful tone.
T8	185: 7	"I'm afraid you must have hurt him," she said in a trembling voice, "being on the top of his head."
A12	93:24	your Majesty means, of course," he said, in a very respectful tone, but frowning and making faces
T4	146:13	"Do you see that?" he said, in a voice choking with passion, and his eyes grew large
T1	113: 8	are the Red King and the Red Queen," Alice said (in a whisper, for fear of frightening them), "and there
T8	184: 1	She was quite frightened this time, and said in an anxious tone, as she picked him up, "I hope no
T8	186:31	"You are sad," the Knight said in an anxious tone: "let me sing you a song to comfort
T9	195:17	"Don't let us quarrel," the White Queen said in an anxious tone. "What is the cause of lightning?"
A7	54:12	"Have some wine," the March Hare said in an encouraging tone.
T6	163:30	"When I use a word," Humpty Dumpty said, in rather a scornful tone, "it means just what I choose
T7	177: 8	with the knife. "It's very provoking!" she said, in reply to the Lion (she was getting quite used to
T8	186:11	"Well, not the next course," the Knight said in slow thoughtful tone: "no, certainly not the next
T6	162:27	"I know it's very ignorant of me," Alice said, in so humble a tone that Humpty Dumpty relented.
T6	162: 7	"I never ask advice about growing," Alice said indignantly.
T4	144:18	"That was mean!" Alice said indignantly. "Then I like the Carpenter best--if he
T7	171:11	young lady loves you with an H," the King said, introducing Alice in the hope of turning off the
T4	143: 7	'A loaf of bread,' the Walrus said, / 'Is what we chiefly need: / Pepper and vinegar besides
T8	183:14	nothing better to say than "Indeed?" but she said it as heartily as she could. They went on a little way in
T8W	19: 5	They said it did not fit, and so / It made me look extremely plain:
T5	149:13	yes, if you call that a-dressing," the Queen said. "It isn't my notion of the thing, at all."
T6	167:19	I said to him, I said it plain, / 'Then you must wake them up again.'
T6	161:27	"If I'd meant that, I'd have said it," said Humpty Dumpty.
A8	63:36	the Queen said, severely, "Who is this?" She said it to the Knave of Hearts, who only bowed and smiled in
T6	167:21	I said it very loud and clear: / I went and shouted in his ear."
T5	155:32	"Indeed I did," said Alice: "you've said it very often--and very loud. Please, where are the crabs
A12	98: 9	she had finished, her sister kissed her, and said "It was a curious dream, dear, certainly; but now run in
A7	59:23	a minute or two to think about it, and then said "It was a treacle-well."
T9	195:10	"Who ever said it was?" said the Red Queen.
T4	141: 6	/ 'If this were only cleared away,' / They said, 'it would be grand!'
T8	182:13	"We'd better take it with us," the Knight said. "It'll come in handy if we find any plum-cake. Help me
T3	132: 6	out of the window, quietly drew it in and said "It's only a brook we have to jump over." Everybody
T8W	16:17	The Wasp considered a little. "Well, no," he said: "it's when you hold up your head--so--without bending
T9	199:24	"To the Looking-Glass world it was Alice that said / 'I've a sceptre in hand, I've a crown on my head. / Let
T5	150:11	the effect of living backwards," the Queen said kindly: "it always makes one a little giddy at first--"
T2	127:10	The Queen propped her up against a tree, and said kindly, "You may rest a little, now."
T6	162: 5	age. Now if you'd asked my advice, I'd have said 'Leave off at seven'--but it's too late now."
T8	187: 1	"No, you don't understand," the Knight said, looking a little vexed. "That's what the name is called.
T6	160: 2	to yourself like that," Humpty Dumpty said, looking at her for the first time, "but tell me your
T2	124:18	"It's time for you to answer now," the Queen said looking at her watch: "open your mouth a little wider
T8W	17:14	"What, you're a Bee, are you?" the Wasp said, looking at her with more interest. "And you've got a
T9	195:25	"Which reminds me--" the White Queen said, looking down and nervously clasping and unclasping her
T7	176:17	we might have for the crown now!" the Unicorn said, looking slyly up at the crown, which the poor King was
T2	120:13	"It's no use talking about it," Alice said, looking up at the house and pretending it was arguing
T7	176: 9	hand round the plum-cake, Monster," the Lion said, lying down and putting his chin on his paws. "And sit
T3	135: 8	"Well, if she said 'Miss,' and didn't say anything more," the Gnat remarked,
T8	186: 3	it matter where my body happens to be?" he said. "My mind goes on working all the same. In fact, the more
T6	162:17	thoughts, "a beautiful cravat, I should have said--no, a belt, I mean--I beg your pardon!" she added in
T9	198:10	a long beak put its head out for a moment and said "No admittance till the week after next!" and shut the
T8W	15: 1	Alice hastily ran her eye down the paper and said "No. It says nothing about brown."
A10	78:11	tasted--" but checked herself hastily, and said "No never") "--so you can have no idea what a delightful"
A10	81:31	to have him with them," the Mock Turtle said. "No wise fish would go anywhere without a porpoise."
T4	145: 3	Alice said "Nobody can guess that."
T3	132:25	"I like them when they can talk," Alice said. "None of them ever talk, where I come from."
T2	123: 4	more people in the garden besides me?" Alice said, not choosing to notice the Rose's last remark.
A2	19:19	to wink with one of its little eyes, but it said nothing.
A9	74:24	at them with large eyes full of tears, but said nothing.
A9	74:39	must be more to come, so she sat still and said nothing.
T6	162: 1	didn't want to begin another argument, so she said nothing.
T4	143:21	/ And you are very nice!' / The Carpenter said nothing but / 'Cut us another slice. / I wish you were
A8	63: 5	Five and Seven said nothing, but looked at Two. Two began, in a low voice,
T5	155:24	a remark that needed any answer: so Alice said nothing, but pulled away. There was something very queer
T2	123:40	This sounded nonsense to Alice, so she said nothing, but set off at once towards the Red Queen. To
T4	143:29	And made them trot so quick!' / The Carpenter said nothing but / 'The butter's spread too thick!'
T6	162:22	Humpty Dumpty was very angry, though he said nothing for a minute or two. When he did speak again, it

SAID (cont.)
```
A5    41:11                                      Alice said nothing: she had never been so much contradicted in all
A10   82:34                                      Alice said nothing: she had sat down with her face in her hands,
A6    46:39   with variations. "I shall sit here," he said, "on and off, for days and days."
T5   153:11   Alice laughed. "There's no use trying," she said: "one ca'n't believe impossible things."
A12   94:11                             "Who is it directed to?" said one of the jurymen.
T5   152:30   "I wish I could manage to be glad!" the Queen said. "Only I never can remember the rule. You must be very
T7   173:11               "I'm good enough," the King said, "only I'm not strong enough. You see, a minute goes by
T7   172: 5   nothing but hay left now," the Messenger said, peeping into the bag.
A6    53: 2                             "I said 'pig'," replied Alice; "and I wish you wouldn't keep
T8   184:28             "Very much indeed," Alice said politely.
T4   139:10             "I was thinking," Alice said politely, "which is the best way out of this wood: it's
A2    17:16   "I'm sure those are not the right words," said poor Alice, and her eyes filled with tears again as she
T9   200:19   began. "You've missed the soup and fish," she said. "Put on the joint!" And the waiters set a leg of mutton
T2   127:35   "At the end of two yards," she said, putting in a peg to mark the distance, "I shall give you
T9   195:14   Red Queen drew herself up rather stiffly, and said "Queens never make bargains."
T9   201:10   be introduced to the pudding, please," Alice said rather hastily, "or we shall get no dinner at all. May I
T3   131:26             "Indeed I sha'n't!" Alice said rather impatiently. "I don't belong to this railway
T4   147:44             "Very well," the other said, rather sadly: "and she can watch us--only you'd better
T8W   14:17   may read it if you've a mind to," the Wasp said, rather sulkily. "Nobody's hindering you, that I know of
T7   170:11   and seven, that's the exact number," the King said, referring to his book. "I couldn't send all the horses,
A5    41: 1                             "That is not said right," said the Caterpillar.
T12  207: 1   Red Majesty shouldn't purr so loud," Alice said, rubbing her eyes, and addressing the kitten,
A8    62:14             "That's none of your business, Two!" said Seven.
T6   161:22       Alice made a short calculation, and said "Seven years and six months."
A8    63:35   all stopped and looked at her, and the Queen said, severely, "Who is this?" She said it to the Knave of
T3   131:16   Then a very gentle voice in the distance said, "She must be labeled 'Lass, with care,' you know--"
T1   107: 9   beginning at the nose: and just now, as I said, she was hard at work on the white kitten, which was
T8   182:24             "Only in the usual way," Alice said, smiling.
A12   93: 3   great emphasis, looking hard at Alice as he said so.
T2   122:34   saw anybody that looked stupider," a Violet said, so suddenly, that Alice quite jumped; for it hadn't
T12  207: 9   for 'no,' or any rule of that sort," she had said, "so that one could keep up a conversation! But how can
A5    36:29   took the hookah out of its mouth again, and said "So you think you're changed, do you?"
T3   131:35   very unhappy, evidently, and Alice would have said something pitying to comfort it, "if it would only sigh
T2   128:22   peg the Queen turned again, and this time she said "Speak in French when you ca'n't think of the English for
T9   201: 4             "May I give you a slice?" she said, taking up the knife and fork, and looking from one Queen
T7   175:26   The Unicorn looked dreamily at Alice, and said "Talk, child."
A7    56:33   might do something better with the time," she said, "than wasting it in asking riddles that have no answers
T6   166:22   ought to listen to it; so she sat down, and said "Thank you" rather sadly,
A12   94:27   the first really clever thing the King had said that day.
T6   162:10   indignant at this suggestion. "I mean," she said, "that one ca'n't help growing older."
T4   141: 9   half a year, / Do you suppose,' the Walrus said, / 'That they could get it clear?' / 'I doubt it,' said
T3   136:16             "Think again," it said: "that wo'n't do."
T5   151:20   "But if you hadn't done them," the Queen said, "that would have been better still; better, and better,
T7   176:25   quite quivered. "All round the town?" he said. "That's a good long way. Did you go by the old bridge,
T8W   17: 2                       The Wasp said "That's a new-fangled name. They called it conceit in my
T9   195:31                 The Red Queen said "That's a poor thing way of doing things. Now here, we
T2   126: 7   but her companion only smiled pleasantly, and said "That's easily managed. You can be the White Queen's Pawn
A8    62: 9       On which Seven looked up and said "That's right, Five! Always lay the blame on others!"
T3   137:13   suddenly. "However, I know my name now," she said: "that's some comfort. Alice--Alice--I won't forget it
A10   82: 8   then the Mock Turtle drew a long breath, and said "That's very curious!"
T8   187: 4             "Then I ought to have said 'That's what the song is called'?" Alice corrected
T4   141:11   they could get it clear?' / 'I doubt it,' said the Carpenter, / And shed a bitter tear.
T4   143: 5   / And all of us are fat!' / 'No hurry!' said the Carpenter. / They thanked him much for that.
T4   144: 7             'O Oysters,' said the Carpenter, / 'You've had a pleasant run! / Shall we
A6    51: 9   a good deal on where you want to get to," said the Cat.
A6    51:12   "Then it doesn't matter which way you go," said the Cat.
A6    53: 1             "Did you say 'pig', or 'fig'?" said the Cat.
A6    51:29             "To begin with," said the Cat, "a dog's not mad. You grant that?"
A6    53: 4             "All right," said the Cat; and this time it vanished quite slowly,
A6    52: 7             "You'll see me there," said the Cat, and vanished.
A6    52:21             "I thought it would," said the Cat, and vanished again.
A8    67:14             "How are you getting on?" said the Cat, as soon as there was mouth enough for it to
A6    52: 1             "Call it what you like," said the Cat. "Do you play croquet with the Queen to-day?"
A6    52:17   "By-the-bye, what became of the baby?" said the Cat. "I'd nearly forgotten to ask."
A6    51:15             "Oh, you're sure to do that," said the Cat, "if you only walk long enough."
A8    67:31             "How do you like the Queen?" said the Cat in a low voice.
A6    51:26             "You must be," said the Cat, "or you wouldn't have come here."
A6    51:23             "Oh, you ca'n't help that," said the Cat: "we're all mad here. I'm mad. You're mad."
A5    35: 4             "Who are you?" said the Caterpillar.
A5    35:13             "I don't see," said the Caterpillar.
A5    36: 1             "It isn't," said the Caterpillar.
A5    36: 6             "Not a bit," said the Caterpillar.
A5    36:14             "Why?" said the Caterpillar.
A5    36:22             "Keep your temper," said the Caterpillar.
A5    36:25             "No," said the Caterpillar.
A5    36:33             "Ca'n't remember what things?" said the Caterpillar.
A5    36:36   "Repeat 'You are old, Father William,'" said the Caterpillar.
A5    41: 1             "That is not said right," said the Caterpillar.
A5    41:10             "I don't know," said the Caterpillar.
```

SAID (cont.)

A5	41:13	"Are you content now?"	said the Caterpillar.
A5	41:21	"You'll get used to it in time,"	said the Caterpillar; and it put the hookah into its mouth,
A5	41:16	"It is a very good height indeed!"	said the Caterpillar angrily, rearing itself upright as it
A5	36: 9	"You!"	said the Caterpillar contemptuously. "Who are you?"
A5	41: 4	"It is wrong from beginning to end,"	said the Caterpillar, decidedly; and there was silence for
A5	41:31	"Of the mushroom,"	said the Caterpillar, just as if she had asked it aloud; and
A5	35: 9	"What do you mean by that?"	said the Caterpillar, sternly. "Explain yourself!"
A11	91:10	"Sha'n't,"	said the cook.
A11	91:17	"Pepper, mostly,"	said the cook.
A3	23:34	"Hand it over here,"	said the Dodo.
A3	22:35	"What I was going to say,"	said the Dodo in an offended tone, "was that the best thing to
A3	23:23	"Why, she, of course,"	said the Dodo, pointing to Alice with one finger; and the
A3	22:28	"In that case,"	said the Dodo solemnly, rising to its feet, "I move that the
A3	23: 5	"Why,"	said the Dodo, "the best way to explain it is to do it." (And,
A11	88:16	"Sixteenth,"	said the Dormouse.
A11	88:42	"You've no right to grow here,"	said the Dormouse.
A7	59: 1	"They lived on treacle,"	said the Dormouse, after thinking a minute or two.
A7	59:30	"One, indeed!"	said the Dormouse indignantly. However, he consented to go on.
A11	89: 1	"Yes, but I grow at a reasonable pace,"	said the Dormouse: "not in that ridiculous fashion." And he
A7	59: 5	"So they were,"	said the Dormouse; "very ill."
A7	60:11	"Of course they were,"	said the Dormouse: "well in."
A11	88:39	"I wish you wouldn't squeeze so,"	said the Dormouse, who was sitting next to her. "I can hardly
A7	59:34	"Treacle,"	said the Dormouse, without considering at all, this time.
A6	48: 3	"They all can,"	said the Duchess; "and most of 'em do."
A6	48: 6	"You don't know much,"	said the Duchess, "and that's a fact."
A6	47:15	"It's a Cheshire-Cat,"	said the Duchess, "and that's why. Pig!"
A9	70:32	"'Tis so,"	said the Duchess: "and the moral of that is--'Oh, 'tis love,
A9	72: 5	"I quite agree with you,"	said the Duchess; "and the moral of that is--'Be what you
A9	72:27	"Just about as much right,"	said the Duchess, "as pigs have to fly; and the m----"
A9	70: 2	I am to see you again, you dear old thing!"	said the Duchess, as she tucked her arm affectionately into
A6	48:27	"Talking of axes,"	said the Duchess, "chop off her head!"
A9	70:36	"Ah well! It means much the same thing,"	said the Duchess, digging her sharp little chin into Alice's
A9	70:22	"Tut, tut, child!"	said the Duchess. "Everything's got a moral, if only you can
A9	71:11	"Very true,"	said the Duchess: "flamingoes and mustard both bite. And the
A9	72:18	"Oh, don't talk about trouble!"	said the Duchess. "I make you a present of everything I've
A6	48:32	"Oh, don't bother me!"	said the Duchess. "I never could abide figures!" And with that
A9	71:14	"Right, as usual,"	said the Duchess: "what a clear way you have of putting
A9	71:17	"Of course it is,"	said the Duchess, who seemed ready to agree to everything that
A3	22:15	"Found what?"	said the Duck.
A3	22:18	'it' means well enough, when I find a thing,"	said the Duck: "it's generally a frog, or a worm. The question
A3	22:31	"Speak English!"	said the Eaglet. "I don't know the meaning of half those long
T4	140:20	Oyster looked at him, / But never a word he	said: / The eldest Oyster winked his eye, / And shook his
A6	46:42	"Anything you like,"	said the Footman, and began whistling.
A6	46:10	"There's no sort of use in knocking,"	said the Footman, "and that for two reasons. First, because
A6	46:33	"Are you to get in at all?"	said the Footman. "That's the first question, you know."
A7	55:39	Alice considered a little, and then	said "The fourth."
T9	199: 5	"Which door?"	said the Frog.
T3	130:21	window, and went away. "So young a child,"	said the gentleman sitting opposite to her, (he was dressed in
T3	134:19	"It always happens,"	said the Gnat.
T3	134: 9	"Crawling at your feet,"	said the Gnat (Alice drew her feet back in some alarm), "you
T3	133:12	"Look on the branch above your head,"	said the Gnat, "and there you'll find a Snap-dragon-fly. Its
T3	133: 7	"Sap and sawdust,"	said the Gnat. "Go on with the list."
T3	133: 3	"All right,"	said the Gnat. "Half way up that bush, you'll see a
A10	82:10	"It's all about as curious as it can be,"	said the Gryphon.
A10	82:15	and repeat ''Tis the voice of the sluggard,'"	said the Gryphon.
A10	82:31	from what I used to say when I was a child,"	said the Gryphon.
A10	84: 6	Yes, I think you'd better leave off,"	said the Gryphon, and Alice was only too glad to do so.
A10	78: 4	"Same as if he had a bone in his throat,"	said the Gryphon; and it set to work shaking him and punching
A10	81:10	"I can tell you more than that, if you like,"	said the Gryphon. "Do you know why it's called a whiting?"
A9	74: 9	out of sight: then it chuckled. "What fun!"	said the Gryphon, half to itself, half to Alice.
A10	83: 3	"She ca'n't explain it,"	said the Gryphon hastily. "Go on with the next verse."
A10	81:17	"Why, what are your shoes done with?"	said the Gryphon. "I mean, what makes them so shiny?"
A9	77: 4	"Hadn't time,"	said the Gryphon: "I went to the Classical master, though. He
A10	81:44	"No, no! The adventures first,"	said the Gryphon in an impatient tone: "explanations take such
A9	74:11	"Why, she,"	said the Gryphon. "It's all her fancy that: they never
A10	79: 8	"Oh, you sing,"	said the Gryphon. "I've forgotten the words."
A9	74:25	"This here young lady,"	said the Gryphon, "she wants for to know your history, she do
A9	77: 8	"So he did, so he did,"	said the Gryphon, sighing in his turn; and both creatures hid
A10	81: 4	"The reason is,"	said the Gryphon, "that they would go with the lobsters to the
A10	78:14	"Why,"	said the Gryphon, "you first form into a line along the
T3	129:33	"Tickets, please!"	said the Guard, putting his head in at the window. In a moment
T3	130: 6	"Don't make excuses,"	said the Guard: "you should have bought one from the
A7	56:18	"Which is just the case with mine,"	said the Hatter.
A7	56:30	"I haven't the slightest idea,"	said the Hatter.
A7	60:28	"Then you shouldn't talk,"	said the Hatter.
A11	88:21	"It isn't mine,"	said the Hatter.
A11	89:22	"You did!"	said the Hatter.
A11	90: 4	"That I ca'n't remember,"	said the Hatter.
A7	56:22	"The Dormouse is asleep again,"	said the Hatter, and he poured a little hot tea upon its nose

SAID (cont.)

A7	55:31	"It is the same thing with you," said the Hatter, and here the conversation dropped, and the
A7	58:15	"Exactly so," said the Hatter: "as the things get used up."
A7	57: 7	"Not at first, perhaps," said the Hatter: "but you could keep it to half-past one as
A7	55: 6	"Your hair wants cutting," said the Hatter. He had been looking at Alice for some time
A7	56:42	"Ah! That accounts for it," said the Hatter. "He wo'n't stand beating. Now, if you only
A11	90:23	"I ca'n't go no lower," said the Hatter: "I'm on the floor, as it is."
A7	59:13	"You mean you ca'n't take less," said the Hatter: "it's very easy to take more than nothing."
A7	60: 6	"You can draw water out of a water-well," said the Hatter; "so I should think you could draw treacle out
A11	89:25	"Well, at any rate, the Dormouse said--" the Hatter went on, looking anxiously round to see if
A7	58: 4	"Well, I'd hardly finished the first verse," said the Hatter, "when the Queen bawled out 'He's murdering
A7	55:23	"Not the same thing a bit!" said the Hatter. "Why, you might just as well say that 'I see
A7	58:12	"Yes, that's it," said the Hatter with a sigh: "it's always tea-time, and we've
A11	90:29	"I'd rather finish my tea," said the Hatter, with an anxious look at the Queen, who was
A7	56:35	"If you knew Time as well as I do," said the Hatter, "you wouldn't talk about wasting it. It's him
A11	87:13	"Herald, read the accusation!" said the King.
A11	89:15	"The twinkling of what?" said the King.
A11	90:10	"You're a very poor speaker," said the King.
A11	91: 4	"Call the next witness!" said the King.
A11	91: 9	"Give your evidence," said the King.
A12	93:39	"You are," said the King.
A12	93:43	"It's the oldest rule in the book," said the King.
A12	94:32	"Read them," said the King.
T7	171: 3	"It isn't respectable to beg," said the King.
T7	172: 4	"Another sandwich!" said the King.
T7	172:36	"Why the Lion and the Unicorn, of course," said the King.
A11	88:28	"Give your evidence," said the King: "and don't be nervous, or I'll have you
A8	67:44	"Don't be impertinent," said the King, "and don't look at me like that!" He got behind
A12	95:38	"All right, so far," said the King; and he went on muttering over the verses to
T7	172:38	"Yes, to be sure," said the King: "and the best of the joke is, that it's my
A11	90:31	"You may go," said the King, and the Hatter hurriedly left the court,
A11	88: 4	"Call the first witness," said the King; and the White Rabbit blew three blasts on the
A8	67:37	"Who are you talking to?" said the King, coming up to Alice, and looking at the Cat's
A8	68: 8	"I'll fetch the executioner myself," said the King eagerly, and he hurried off.
T7	170:26	"Not at all," said the King. "He's an Anglo-Saxon Messenger--and those are
A8	67:41	"I don't like the look of it at all," said the King: "however, it may kiss my hand, if it likes."
T7	171:16	"You alarm me!" said the King. "I feel faint--Give me a ham-sandwich!"
A12	93: 1	"The trial cannot proceed," said the King, in a very grave voice, "until all the jurymen
A11	89:24	"He denies it," said the King: "leave out that part."
A12	96:25	"Then the words don't fit you," said the King looking round the court with a smile. There was
T1	114:13	"What volcano?" said the King, looking up anxiously into the fire, as if he
T7	172:22	"He ca'n't do that," said the King, "or else he'd have been here first. However,
A12	95:22	important piece of evidence we've heard yet," said the King, rubbing his hands; "so now let the jury--"
T1	114: 1	"Imperial fiddlestick!" said the King, rubbing his nose, which had been hurt by the
A11	89:17	"Of course twinkling begins with a T!" said the King sharply. "Do you take me for a dunce? Go on!"
T7	175: 4	"No use, no use!" said the King. "She runs so fearfully quick. You might as well
A12	94:23	"If you didn't sign it," said the King, "that only makes the matter worse. You must
A12	95:30	"If there's no meaning in it," said the King, "that saves a world of trouble, you know, as we
A12	94:19	"He must have imitated somebody else's hand," said the King. (The jury all brightened up again.)
T7	172:18	"Quite right," said the King: "this young lady saw him too. So of course
A12	96:12	"Why, there they are!" said the King triumphantly, pointing to the tarts on the table
A12	94: 9	"It must have been that," said the King, "unless it was written to nobody, which isn't
A8	68: 3	"Well, it must be removed," said the King very decidedly; and he called to the Queen, who
T7	173: 7	"Dear me, no!" said the King. "What an idea!"
A11	88:10	"You ought to have finished," said the King. "When did you begin?"
A11	91:25	"Never mind!" said the King with an air of great relief. "Call the next
A12	94:21	"Please, your Majesty," said the Knave, "I didn't write it, and they ca'n't prove that
T8	182: 3	"Not very likely, perhaps," said the Knight; "but, if they do come, I don't choose to have
T8	186:35	"It's long," said the Knight, "but it's very, very beautiful. Everybody
T8	182:29	"Not yet," said the Knight. "But I've got a plan for keeping it from
T8	181: 9	"Now one can breathe more easily," said the Knight, putting back his shaggy hair with both hands,
T8	182:32	"First you take an upright stick," said the Knight. "Then you make your hair creep up it, like a
T8	184:29	"I'll tell you how I came to think of it," said the Knight. "You see, I said to myself 'The only
A6	47:16	She said the last word with such sudden violence that Alice quite
A6	49:27	it be murder to leave it behind?" She said the last words out loud, and the little thing grunted in
T7	176:19	"I should win easy," said the Lion.
T7	177:15	three pieces as she did so. "Now cut it up," said the Lion, as she returned to her place with the empty
T7	177:20	"She's kept none for herself, anyhow," said the Lion. "Do you like plum-cake, Monster?"
T6	167:17	Then some one came to me and said / 'The little fishes are in bed.'
T3	131:29	"You might make a joke on that," said the little voice close to her ear: "something about 'you
A3	26:24	if I might venture to ask the question?" said the Lory.
A3	22:10	"Not I!" said the Lory, hastily.
A3	22: 7	"Ugh!" said the Lory, with a shiver.
A7	54:16	"There isn't any," said the March Hare.
A7	55: 3	of you to sit down without being invited," said the March Hare.
A7	55:17	you think you can find out the answer to it?" said the March Hare.
A7	56:31	"Nor I," said the March Hare.
A7	58:28	"Tell us a story!" said the March Hare.
A7	60:18	"Why not?" said the March Hare.
A11	88:15	"Fifteenth," said the March Hare.

SAID (cont.)

A11	89:23	"I deny it!"	said the March Hare.
T7	172:17	"Nobody,"	said the Messenger.
T7	172:25	"I'll whisper it,"	said the Messenger, putting his hands to his mouth in the
A9	76: 2	"You did,"	said the Mock Turtle.
A9	76:11	"And washing?"	said the Mock Turtle.
A9	77:20	"Of course it was,"	said the Mock Turtle.
A10	79: 3	"Would you like to see a little of it?"	said the Mock Turtle.
A10	81:43	"Explain all that,"	said the Mock Turtle.
A10	83: 2	"I should like to have it explained,"	said the Mock Turtle.
A9	75: 2	We called him Tortoise because he taught us,"	said the Mock Turtle angrily. "Really you are very dull!"
A9	74:32	"Once,"	said the Mock Turtle at last, with a deep sigh, "I was a real
A10	80:20	"I don't know where Dinn may be,"	said the Mock Turtle; "but, if you've seen them so often, of
A10	82:32	"Well, I never heard it before,"	said the Mock Turtle; "but it sounds uncommon nonsense."
A10	80:24	"You're wrong about the crumbs,"	said the Mock Turtle: "crumbs would all wash off in the sea.
A9	74:27	"I'll tell it her,"	said the Mock Turtle in a deep, hollow tone. "Sit down, both
A9	76:13	"Ah! Then yours wasn't a really good school,"	said the Mock Turtle in a tone of great relief. "Now, at ours,
A9	77:12	"Ten hours the first day,"	said the Mock Turtle: "nine the next, and so on."
A10	78:35	again, and--that's all the first figure,"	said the Mock Turtle, suddenly dropping his voice; and the two
A10	80:16	"Oh, as to the whiting,"	said the Mock Turtle, "they--you've seen them, of course?"
A10	79: 5	"Come, let's try the first figure!"	said the Mock Turtle to the Gryphon. "We can do it without
A10	81:33	"Of course not,"	said the Mock Turtle. "Why, if a fish came to me, and told me
A9	76:18	"I couldn't afford to learn it,"	said the Mock Turtle with a sigh. "I only took the regular
A3	23:30	But she must have a prize herself, you know,"	said the Mouse.
A3	22: 8	"I beg your pardon!"	said the Mouse, frowning, but very politely. "Did you speak?"
A3	26: 8	"I shall do nothing of the sort,"	said the Mouse, getting up and walking away. "You insult me by
A3	22:11	"I thought you did,"	said the Mouse. "I proceed. 'Edwin and Morcar, the earls of
A3	26: 1	"You are not attending!"	said the Mouse to Alice, severely. "What are you thinking of
A3	25:23	For really this morning I've nothing to do.'	Said the mouse to the cur, Such a trial, dear sir, With no
A3	24:17	"Mine is a long and sad tale!"	said the Mouse, turning to Alice, and sighing.
A3	22: 1	"Ahem!"	said the Mouse with an important air. "Are you all ready? This
A8	62:13	"What for?"	said the one who had spoken first.
A4	31:26	"So you did, old fellow!"	said the others.
A5	42:38	it wasn't trouble enough hatching the eggs,"	said the Pigeon; "but I must be on the look-out for serpents,
A5	43:19	"I don't believe it,"	said the Pigeon; "but if they do, why, then they're a kind of
A5	43: 7	"Well! What are you?"	said the Pigeon. "I can see you're trying to invent something!
A5	43:28	"Well, be off, then!"	said the Pigeon in a sulky tone, as it settled down again into
A5	43:11	"A likely story indeed!"	said the Pigeon, in a tone of the deepest contempt. "I've seen
T9	201:22	"What impertinence!"	said the Pudding. "I wonder how you'd like it, if I were to
A9	73:13	the thing Mock Turtle Soup is made from,"	said the Queen.
A12	94: 6	"What's in it?"	said the Queen.
T2	127:38	"Thirst quenched, I hope?"	said the Queen.
T5	150: 3	"It's very good jam,"	said the Queen.
T9	196: 8	"Well, only on Thursdays,"	said the Queen.
T2	124:11	"I don't know what you mean by your way,"	said the Queen: "all the ways about here belong to me--but why
A9	73:16	"Come on, then,"	said the Queen, "and he shall tell you his history."
A9	74: 1	is, look at the picture.) "Up, lazy thing!"	said the Queen, "and take this young lady to see the Mock
A12	96:20	"Never!"	said the Queen, furiously, throwing an inkstand at the Lizard
T2	127:31	"While you're refreshing yourself,"	said the Queen, "I'll just take the measurements." And she
A8	64:15	"Get up!"	said the Queen in a shrill, loud voice, and the three
T5	150: 8	"No, it ca'n't,"	said the Queen. "It's jam every other day: to-day isn't any
T1	115:39	"What manner of things?"	said the Queen, looking over the book (in which Alice had put
T2	127:19	"A slow sort of country!"	said the Queen. "Now, here, you see, it takes all the running
T2	125: 3	"That's right,"	said the Queen, patting her on the head, which Alice didn't
A8	63:43	"And who are these?"	said the Queen, pointing to the three gardeners who were lying
A12	96:30	"No, no!"	said the Queen. "Sentence first--verdict afterwards."
A12	94:28	"That proves his guilt, of course,"	said the Queen, "so, off with--"
A8	63:38	"Idiot!"	said the Queen, tossing her head impatiently; and turning to
A12	97: 3	"Hold your tongue!"	said the Queen, turning purple.
T2	128:16	"You should have said,"	the Queen went on in a tone of grave reproof, "'It's
T5	151:13	"You're wrong there, at any rate,"	said the Queen. "Were you ever punished?"
T5	152:25	"Why, I've done all the screaming already,"	said the Queen. "What would be the good of having it all over
T2	127: 6	"Of course it is,"	said the Queen. "What would you have it?"
T5	153:13	"I daresay you haven't had much practice,"	said the Queen. "When I was your age, I always did it for
A8	65: 8	"I see!"	said the Queen, who had meanwhile been examining the roses.
A4	30: 4	"Digging for apples, indeed!"	said the Rabbit angrily. "Here! Come help me out of this!"
A8	65:29	"Hush! Hush!"	said the Rabbit in a low hurried tone. He looked anxiously
A4	31:28	"We must burn the house down!"	said the Rabbit's voice. And Alice called out, as loud as she
T8	179:36	"I always do,"	said the Red Knight, and they began banging away at each other
T8	179:31	"Well, we must fight for her, then,"	said the Red Knight, as he took up his helmet (which hung from
T9	194:13	"Then you think nothing would remain?"	said the Red Queen.
T9	194:33	"Of course you know your ABC?"	said the Red Queen.
T9	195:10	"Who ever said it was?"	said the Red Queen.
T9	196: 3	"What did he want?"	said the Red Queen.
T9	200:23	let me introduce you to that leg of mutton,"	said the Red Queen. "Alice--Mutton: Mutton--Alice." The leg of
T9	196:12	ca'n't think!" ("She never could, you know,"	said the Red Queen.) "And part of the roof came off, and ever
T9	197: 2	"I must do it myself, then,"	said the Red Queen, and she began:--
T2	124: 6	"Where do you come from?"	said the Red Queen. "And where are you going? Look up, speak
T9	195: 7	"She's all right again now,"	said the Red Queen. "Do you know Languages? What's the French
T9	193: 8	"Nobody said you did,"	said the Red Queen. "I said you couldn't if you tried."

SAID (cont.)

T9	201:26	"Make a remark,"	said the Red Queen: "it's ridiculous to leave all the
T9	202:19	a minute to think about it, and then guess,"	said the Red Queen. "Meanwhile, we'll drink your health--Queen
T9	196:36	"She's tired, poor thing!"	said the Red Queen. "Smoothe her hair--lend her your nightcap
T9	194:15	"Wrong, as usual,"	said the Red Queen: "the dog's temper would remain."
T9	195:22	"It's too late to correct it,"	said the Red Queen: "when you've once said a thing, that fixes
T2	122: 4	"It could bark,"	said the Rose.
T2	121: 7	"It isn't manners for us to begin, you know,"	said the Rose, "and I really was wondering when you'd speak!
T2	123:38	"You ca'n't possibly do that,"	said the Rose: "I should advise you to walk the other way."
T2	123: 6	in the garden that can move about like you,"	said the Rose. "I wonder how you do it--" ("You're always
T2	123:20	"I daresay you'll see her soon,"	said the Rose. "She's one of the kind that has nine spikes,
T2	122: 1	"There's the tree in the middle,"	said the Rose. "What else is it good for?"
T2	123:33	"It's the fresh air that does it,"	said the Rose: "wonderfully fine air it is, out here."
T5	150: 5	have it if you did want it," the Queen	said. "The rule is, jam to-morrow and jam yesterday--but never
A5	38: 5	"In my youth,"	said the sage, as he shook his grey locks, / "I kept all my
T2	128:18	tell me all this'--however, we'll suppose it	said--the Seventh Square is all forest--however, one of the
T5	158: 9	Only you must eat them both, if you buy two,"	said the Sheep.
T5	154: 6	of you, and on both sides, if you like,"	said the Sheep; "but you ca'n't look all round you--unless
T5	156:13	"How am I to stop it?"	said the Sheep. "If you leave off rowing, it'll stop of itself
T5	157:12	"Crabs, and all sorts of things,"	said the Sheep: "plenty of choice, only make up your mind. Now
T5	155:34	"In the water, of course!"	said the Sheep, sticking some of the needles into her hair, as
T5	155:38	"You are,"	said the Sheep: "you're a little goose."
T8	187:10	"I was coming to that," the Knight	said. "The song really is 'A-sitting On A Gate': and the
T2	121: 5	"As well as you can,"	said the Tiger-lily. "And a great deal louder."
T2	123: 7	how you do it--" ("You're always wondering,"	said the Tiger-lily), "but she's more bushy than you are."
T2	123:13	"They're done up close, like a dahlia,"	said the Tiger-lily: "not tumbled about, like yours."
T2	122:18	"That's right!"	said the Tiger-lily. "The daisies are worst of all. When one
T2	122:24	"Put your hand down, and feel the ground,"	said the Tiger-lily. "Then you'll know why."
T2	120:32	"We can talk,"	said the Tiger-lily, "when there's anybody worth talking to."
T7	176:20	"I'm not so sure of that,"	said the Unicorn.
T7	175:30	"Well, now that we have seen each other,"	said the Unicorn, "if you'll believe in me, I'll believe in
T7	175:23	always thought they were fabulous monsters!"	said the Unicorn. "Is it alive?"
A4	29:19	"Mary Ann! Mary Ann!"	said the voice. "Fetch me my gloves this moment!" Then came a
T8W	15:12	"There's no such word in the language!"	said the Wasp.
T8W	21:15	"Good-bye, and thank-ye,"	said the Wasp, and Alice tripped down the hill again, quite
T8W	15:15	"Let it stop there!"	said the Wasp, fretfully turning away his head.
T8W	18:10	"It aint what I'm used to,"	said the Wasp: "however I'll try; wait a bit." He was silent
T8W	17: 5	"It is, though,"	said the Wasp: "wait till you have it, and then you'll know."
T8	180:15	"It was a glorious victory, wasn't it?"	said the White Knight, as he came up panting.
T8	181: 3	will, when you've crossed the next brook,"	said the White Knight. "I'll see you safe to the end of the
T9	194: 5	"She ca'n't do Subtraction,"	said the White Queen. "Can you do Division? Divide a loaf by a
T9	193:10	"She's in that state of mind,"	said the White Queen, "that she wants to deny something--only
T9	195: 1	"How many acres of ground?"	said the White Queen. "You mustn't leave out so many things.
A12	94:17	"No, they're not,"	said the White Rabbit, "and that's the queerest thing about it
A12	94: 7	"I haven't opened it yet,"	said the White Rabbit; "but it seems to be a letter, written
A12	94:12	"It isn't directed at all,"	said the White Rabbit: "in fact, there's nothing written on
A12	94: 3	evidence to come yet, please your Majesty,"	said the White Rabbit, jumping up in a great hurry: "this
T5	152:15	will come undone directly. Oh, oh!" As she	said the words the brooch flew open, and the Queen clutched
A3	26:19	to lose your temper!" "Hold your tongue, Ma!"	said the young Crab, a little snappishly. "You're enough to
A5	39: 1	"You are old,"	said the youth, "and your jaws are too weak / For anything
A5	38: 1	"You are old,"	said the youth, "as I mentioned before, / And have grown most
A5	40: 1	"You are old,"	said the youth, "one would hardly suppose / That your eye was
T7	172:13	was nothing better," the King replied. "I	said there was nothing like it." Which Alice did not venture
T4	148: 7	with a satisfied smile. "I don't suppose," he	said, "there'll be a tree left standing, for ever so far round
A9	71:18	ready to agree to everything that Alice	said: "there's a large mustard-mine near here. And the moral
A2	18:17	As she	said these words her foot slipped, and in another moment,
T2	122:28	"In most gardens," the Tiger-lily	said, "they make the beds too soft--so that the flowers are
T6	166:38	on making remarks like that," Humpty Dumpty	said: "they're not sensible, and they put me out."
T8	185:15	He raised his hands in some excitement as he	said this, and instantly rolled out of the saddle, and fell
T2	126: 6	glanced rather shyly at the real Queen as she	said this, but her companion only smiled pleasantly, and said
A11	86:24	birds,) "I suppose they are the jurors." She	said this last word two or three times over to herself, being
A5	43:43	how is that to be done, I wonder?" As she	said this, she came suddenly upon an open place, with a little
A4	27:21	gloves--that is, if I can find them." As she	said this, she came upon a neat little house, on the door of
A2	18: 1	As she	said this she looked down at her hands, and was surprised to
A6	52:27	least not so mad as it was in March." As she	said this, she looked up, and there was the Cat again, sitting
A7	60:38	Just as she	said this, she noticed that one of the trees had a door
T1	111:11	She was up on the chimney-piece while she	said this, though she hardly knew how she had got there. And
T8	184:34	you'd be over when that was done," Alice	said thoughtfully: "but don't you think it would be rather
T3	135:27	"This must be the wood," she	said thoughtfully to herself, "where things have no names. I
T8	184:19	"I'll get one," the Knight	said thoughtfully to himself. "One or two--several."
T5	158: 3	"I should like to buy an egg, please," she	said timidly. "How do you sell them?"
T3	136:18	you tell me what you call yourself?" she	said timidly. "I think that might help a little."
A3	25: 5	"Fury	said to a mouse, That he met in the house, 'Let us both go to
A12	93:16	do you know about this business?" the King	said to Alice.
T8	181:28	on a tree. "Can you guess why I did that?" he	said to Alice.
T9	192:35	"So you did, you know," the Red Queen	said to Alice. "Always speak the truth--think before you speak
A9	72:40	"Let's go on with the game," the Queen	said to Alice; and Alice was too much frightened to say a word
A6	49:10	may nurse it a bit, if you like!" the Duchess	said to Alice, flinging the baby at her as she spoke. "I must
A9	73:10	the Queen left off, quite out of breath, and	said to Alice "Have you seen the Mock Turtle yet?"
T9	196:21	"Your Majesty must excuse her," the Red Queen	said to Alice, taking one of the White Queen's hands in her

SAID (cont.)

A7	59: 9	"Take some more tea," the March Hare said to Alice, very earnestly.
T5	152:21	That accounts for the bleeding, you see," she said to Alice with a smile. "Now you understand the way things
T4	140:33	day was done--/ 'It's very rude of him,' she said, / 'To come and spoil the fun!'
T7	174:17	they'll fight any more to-day," the King said to Hatta: "go and order the drums to begin." And Hatta
T1	116: 6	it's all in some language I don't know," she said to herself.
T4	138: 5	round at the back of the collar," she said to herself.
A2	18:20	in that case I can go back by railway," she said to herself. (Alice had been to the seaside once in her
A7	60:43	"Now, I'll manage better this time," she said to herself, and began by taking the little golden key,
A5	41:38	"And now which is which?" she said to herself, and nibbled a little of the right-hand bit to
T8W	13:18	"It's rheumatism, I should think," Alice said to herself, and she stooped over him, and said very
A4	32: 3	in the face. "I'll put a stop to this," she said to herself, and shouted out "You'd better not do that
T4	147:23	else, by the time they're ready!" she said to herself, as she arranged a bolster round the neck of
T8	191: 7	it have got there without my knowing it?" she said to herself, as she lifted it off, and set it on her lap
A4	27:18	"He took me for his housemaid," she said to herself as she ran. "How surprised he'll be when he
T8	190:25	take long to see him off, I expect," Alice said to herself, as she stood watching him. "There he goes!
T8	180: 1	now, what the Rules of Battle are," she said to herself, as she watched the fight, timidly peeping out
A6	47: 5	too much pepper in that soup!" Alice said to herself, as well as she could for sneezing.
A11	86:16	everything there. "That's the judge," she said to herself, "because of his great wig."
A9	73:20	pardoned." "Come, that's a good thing!" she said to herself, for she had felt quite unhappy at the number
A6	46:23	uncivil. "But perhaps he ca'n't help it," she said to herself; "his eyes are so very nearly at the top of
A12	93: 8	it right; "not that it signifies much," she said to herself; "I should think it would be quite as much use
T6	159: 5	himself. "It ca'n't be anybody else!" she said to herself. "I'm as certain of it, as if his name were
A11	91:31	for they haven't got much evidence yet," she said to herself. Imagine her surprise, when the White Rabbit
A3	26:37	"I wish I hadn't mentioned Dinah!" she said to herself in a melancholy tone. "Nobody seems to like
T3	132: 9	the Fourth Square, that's some comfort!" she said to herself. In another moment she felt the carriage rise
A6	50:15	into the wood. "If it had grown up," she said to herself, "it would have made a dreadfully ugly child:
T8	187:28	"But the tune isn't his own invention," she said to herself: "it's 'I give thee all, I can no more.'" She
A8	67:12	or two she made it out to be a grin, and she said to herself "It's the Cheshire-Cat: now I shall have
A9	70: 7	"When I'm a Duchess," she said to herself (not in a very hopeful tone, though), "I
A4	28:21	the window, and one foot up the chimney, and said to herself "Now I can do no more, whatever happens. What
T5	156:24	I only hope the boat wo'n't tipple over!" she said to herself. "Oh, what a lovely one! Only I couldn't quite
T1	119: 4	down stairs quickly and easily, as Alice said to herself. She just kept the tips of her fingers on the
A6	52:25	said to live. "I've seen hatters before," she said to herself: "the March Hare will be much the most
A4	27:27	"How queer it seems," Alice said to herself, "to be going messages for a rabbit! I suppose
T8	179: 7	"So I wasn't dreaming, after all," she said to herself, "unless--unless we're all part of the same
T4	140: 4	never do to say 'How d'ye do?' now," she said to herself: "we seem to have got beyond that, somehow!"
T3	137:18	pointed along it. "I'll settle it," Alice said to herself, "when the road divides and they point
A4	28: 5	something interesting is sure to happen," she said to herself, "whenever I eat or drink anything: so I'll
T6	167:19	I said to him, I said it plain, / 'Then you must wake them up
T8W	13:22	and turned his head away. "Ah, deary me!" he said to himself.
T4	148:14	There's only one sword, you know," Tweedledum said to his brother: "but you can have the umbrella--it's
A7	57: 3	("I only wish it was," the March Hare said to itself in a whisper.)
A6	52:24	in the direction in which the March Hare was said to live. "I've seen hatters before," she said to herself:
T12	208: 1	have enjoyed--I had such a quantity of poetry said to me, all about fishes! To-morrow morning you shall have
T8	184:30	to think of it," said the Knight. "You see, I said to myself 'The only difficulty is with the feet: the head
A11	89: 5	just as the Dormouse crossed the court, she said, to one of the officers of the court, "Bring me the list
T4	143:25	'It seems a shame,' the Walrus said, / 'To play them such a trick, / After we've brought them
T4	142:19	'The time has come,' the Walrus said, / 'To talk of many things. / Of shoes--and ships--and
A7	60: 9	"But they were in the well," Alice said to the Dormouse, not choosing to notice this last remark.
A8	69: 8	"She's in prison," the Queen said to the executioner: "fetch her here." And the executioner
A10	81: 2	"Tell her about the reason and all that," he said to the Gryphon.
A11	88:20	"Take off your hat," the King said to the Hatter.
A11	88: 1	"Consider your verdict," the King said to the jury.
A11	88:17	"Write that down," the King said to the jury; and the jury eagerly wrote down all three
A12	94: 2	hastily. "Consider your verdict," the King said to the jury, in a low trembling voice.
T7	175:10	pockets. "I had the best of it this time?" he said to the King, just glancing at him as he passed.
A8	64:12	The Queen turned angrily away from him, and said to the Knave "Turn them over!"
A9	75: 7	to sink into the earth. At last the Gryphon said to the Mock Turtle "Drive on, old fellow! Don't be all
A10	81:28	were still running on the song, "I'd have said to the porpoise 'Keep back, please! We don't want you
A12	96:19	you never had fits, my dear, I think?" he said to the Queen.
T3	129:38	angrily at Alice. And a great many voices all said together ("like the chorus of a song," thought Alice)
T9	194:26	"She ca'n't do sums a bit!" the Queens said together, with great emphasis.
A7	56:38	"Of course you don't!" the Hatter said, tossing his head contemptuously. "I dare say you never
T5	151:16	all the better for it, I know!" the Queen said triumphantly.
T8	186:42	that's the name of the song, is it?" Alice said, trying to feel interested.
T9	194:28	"Can you do sums?" Alice said, turning suddenly on the White Queen, for she didn't like
A7	56:27	"Have you guessed the riddle yet?" the Hatter said, turning to Alice again.
A7	55:36	silence. "What day of the month is it?" he said, turning to Alice: he had taken his watch out of his
A12	93:21	"That's very important," the King said, turning to the jury. They were just beginning to write
T4	144:27	"It's only the Red King snoring," said Tweedledee.
T4	148:17	"And darker," said Tweedledee.
T4	145: 1	"He's dreaming now," said Tweedledee: "and what do you think he's dreaming about?"
T4	138:20	/ Agreed to have a battle; / For Tweedledum said Tweedledee / Had spoiled his nice new rattle.
T4	140:12	"What shall I repeat to her?" said Tweedledee, looking round at Tweedledum with great solemn
T4	146: 8	"It may--if it chooses," said Tweedledee: "we've no objection. Contrariwise."
T4	147:36	"And I've got a toothache!" said Tweedledee, who had overheard the remark. "I'm far worse
T4	144:15	"He ate more than the Carpenter, though," said Tweedledee. "You see he held his handkerchief in front,
T4	140: 7	"Nohow. And thank you very much for asking," said Tweedledum.
T4	144:20	"But he ate as many as he could get," said Tweedledum.

SAID (cont.)

T4	144:31	"Isn't he a <u>lovely</u> sight?" said Tweedledum.
T4	145:14	"Ditto," said Tweedledum.
T4	147:43	"Let's fight till six, and then have dinner," said Tweedledum.
T4	139: 5	"I know what you're thinking about," said Tweedledum; "but it isn't so, nohow."
T4	147:30	"Do I look very pale?" said Tweedledum, coming up to have his helmet tied on. (He
T4	148:11	"I shouldn't have minded it so much," said Tweedledum, "if it hadn't been a new one."
T4	147:41	fight, but I don't care about going on long," said Tweedledum. "What's the time now?"
T4	145:18	it's no use <u>your</u> talking about waking him," said Tweedledum, "when you're only one of the things in his
A8	65: 6	"May it please your Majesty," said Two, in a very humble tone, going down on one knee as he
T5	149:38	sure I'll take <u>you</u> with pleasure!" the Queen said. "Two pence a week, and jam every other day."
T9	195:19	"The cause of lightning," Alice said very decidedly, for she felt quite certain about this,
T9	201: 6	"Certainly not," the Red Queen said, very decidedly: "it isn't etiquette to cut any one
T9	202:36	wouldn't be at all the thing," the Red Queen said very decidedly: so Alice tried to submit to it with good
T5	154: 3	"I don't <u>quite</u> know yet," Alice said very gently. "I should like to look all round me first,
T6	160:34	"I haven't indeed!" Alice said very gently. "It's in a book."
A12	94:35	"Begin at the beginning," the King said, very gravely, "and go on till you come to the end: then
A5	36:12	short remarks, and she drew herself up and said, very gravely, "I think you ought to tell me who <u>you</u> are,
T8	183:11	"I've had plenty of practice," the Knight said very gravely: "plenty of practice!"
A7	59:28	"No, please go on!" Alice said very humbly. "I wo'n't interrupt you again. I dare say
T8W	13:19	to herself, and she stooped over him, and said very kindly, "I hope you're not in much pain?"
T6	161:17	I'm afraid I ca'n't quite remember it," Alice said, very politely.
T9	201:41	"Please do," Alice said very politely.
T5	153:23	Then I hope your finger is better now?" Alice said very politely, as she crossed the little brook after the
A6	48: 4	"I don't know of any that do," Alice said very politely, feeling quite pleased to have got into a
A9	72:11	think I should understand that better," Alice said very politely, "if I had it written down: but I ca'n't
T8	185: 9	"I had to kick him, of course," the Knight said, very seriously. "And then he took the helmet off again--
T9	201:35	little wide of the mark. "As to fishes," she said, very slowly and solemnly, putting her mouth close to
T6	168:33	But Humpty Dumpty only shut his eyes, and said "Wait till you've tried."
A7	55:12	eyes very wide on hearing this; but all he <u>said</u> was "Why is a raven like a writing-desk?"
A6	51:19	"In <u>that</u> direction," the Cat said, waving its right paw round, "lives a Hatter: and in <u>that</u>
A9	76:34	it: so she turned to the Mock Turtle, and said "What else had you to learn?"
A8	65:36	Alice. "I don't think it's at all a pity. I said 'What for?'"
T9	199:12	"To answer the door?" he said. "What's it been asking of?" He was so hoarse that Alice
T8W	18: 3	tell you how I came to wear it," the Wasp said. "When I was young, you know, my ringlets used to wave--
T1	118:25	"It seems very pretty," she said when she had finished it, "but it's <u>rather</u> hard to
T12	207:18	("But it wouldn't look at it," she said, when she was explaining the thing afterwards to her
A12	95:36	shook his head sadly. "Do I look like it?" he said. (Which he certainly did <u>not</u>, being made entirely of
T8	188: 5	in the <u>street</u>. / I sell them <u>unto men</u>,' he <u>said</u>, / <u>Who sail on stormy seas</u>; / And <u>that's the way</u> I <u>get</u>
T1	114:19	up from bar to bar, till at last she said "Why, you'll be hours and hours getting to the table, at
T8	184:17	"Much more smoothly than a live horse," Alice said, with a little scream of laughter, in spite of all she
A11	91:13	"Well, if I must, I must," the King said with a melancholy air, and, after folding his arms and
T6	162:36	"I beg your pardon?" Alice said with a puzzled air.
T6	160: 8	"Of course it must," Humpty Dumpty said with a short laugh: "<u>my</u> name means the shape I am--and a
T5	149:32	The brush has got entangled in it!" the Queen said with a sigh. "And I lost the comb yesterday."
A9	77: 6	"I never went to him," the Mock Turtle said with a sigh. "He taught Laughing and Grief, they used to
T5	153: 1	"That's the way it's done," the Queen said with great decision: "nobody can do two things at once,
A7	55: 9	learn not to make personal remarks," Alice said with some severity: "it's very rude."
A8	68: 7	great or small. "Off with his head!" she said without even looking round.
T7	174:25	some enemy after her, no doubt," the King said, without even looking round. "That wood's full of them."
T5	156: 8	say 'please' to <u>me</u> about 'em," the Sheep said, without looking up from her knitting: "I didn't put 'em
A7	56:24	"The Dormouse shook its head impatiently, and said, without opening its eyes, "Of course, of course: just
T7	176: 6	Are you animal--or vegetable--or mineral?" he said, yawning at every other word.
T9	193: 8	"Nobody said you did," said the Red Queen. "I said you couldn't if you tried."
T9	193: 8	"Nobody said you did," said the Red Queen. "I said you couldn't if you
T6	159:19	"I said you <u>looked</u> like an egg, Sir," Alice gently explained.
T3	131:14	an extremely small voice, close to her ear, said "You might make a joke on that--something about 'horse'
T6	168: 5	"But he <u>was</u> <u>very</u> <u>stiff</u> and <u>proud</u>: / He <u>said</u>, '<u>You</u> <u>needn't</u> shout so <u>loud</u>!'
T4	138:10	"If you think we're wax-works," he said, "you ought to pay, you know. Wax-works weren't made to
T8W	18:15	and <u>crinkled</u> <u>on</u> <u>my</u> <u>head</u>: / And <u>then</u> <u>they</u> <u>said</u> '<u>You</u> <u>should</u> <u>be</u> shaved, / And <u>wear</u> a <u>yellow</u> <u>wig</u> instead.'
T3	130:20	and then through an opera-glass. At last he said "You're traveling the wrong way," and shut up the window,

SAIL (1)

T8	188: 6	/ I <u>sell</u> them <u>unto</u> <u>men</u>,' he <u>said</u>, / '<u>Who</u> <u>sail</u> <u>on</u> <u>stormy</u> <u>seas</u>; / And <u>that's</u> the <u>way</u> I <u>get</u> my <u>bread</u>--/ A

SALMON (1)

A10	78:16	cried the Mock Turtle. "Seals, turtles, salmon, and so on: then, when you've cleared all the

SALTWATER (2)

A3	23:27	and pulled out a box of comfits (luckily the saltwater had not got into it), and handed them round as
A2	18:18	moment, splash! she was up to her chin in saltwater. Her first idea was that she had somehow fallen into

SAL-VOLATILE (1)

T7	172:12	would be better," Alice suggested: "--or some sal-volatile."

SAME (44)

T5	158:29	it, and she quite expected the egg to do the same.
A2	16: 2	all the children she knew that were of the same age as herself, to see if she could have been changed for
T6	164:30	means 'lithe and slimy.' 'Lithe' is the same as 'active.' You see it's like a pormanteau--there are
T6	168:27	of," said Humpty Dumpty. "Your face is the same as everybody has--the two eyes, so--"(marking their
A10	78: 3	for a minute or two, sobs choked his voice. "Same as if he had a bone in his throat," said the Gryphon; and
T1	110:32	can see through the glass--that's just the same as our drawing-room, only the things go the other way. I
A8	64: 1	faces, and the pattern on their backs was the same as the rest of the pack, she could not tell whether they
A2	17: 6	and strange, and the words did not come the same as they used to do:--
T2	123:11	"Well, she has the same awkward shape as you," the Rose said: "but she's redder--

SAME (cont.)

T8	179: 8	"unless--unless we're all part of the same dream. Only I do hope it's my dream, and not the Red
T8W	21: 4	claw towards Alice, as if he wished to do the same for her, but she kept out of reach, and would not take
A4	34: 4	a large mushroom growing near her, about the same height as herself; and, when she had looked under it, and
T3	137:25	said Alice at last, "that they live in the same house! I wonder I never thought of that before--But I
T8	186: 4	he said. "My mind goes on working all the same. In fact, the more head-downwards I am, the more I keep
A12	99: 3	Lastly, she pictured to herself how this same little sister of hers would, in the after-time, be
T4	139:42	as they had begun: the music stopped at the same moment.
T6	168:29	in the middle, mouth under. It's always the same. Now if you had the two eyes on the same side of the nose
A10	78:24	"--change lobsters, and retire in same order," continued the Gryphon.
T2	127:20	all the running you can do, to keep in the same place. If you want to get somewhere else, you must run at
T9	195:38	But they should be five times as cold, by the same rule--"
A2	15:22	moment, I tell you!" But she went on all the same, shedding gallons of tears, until there was a large pool
T9	199:35	In a minute there was silence again, and the same shrill voice sang another verse:--
A6	46:11	for two reasons. First, because I'm on the same side of the door as you are: secondly, because they're
T6	168:30	the same. Now if you had the two eyes on the same side of the nose, for instance--or the mouth at the top--
T3	129:35	was holding out a ticket: they were about the same size as the people, and quite seemed to fill the carriage
A5	36:32	things as I used--and I don't keep the same size for ten minutes together!"
A1	12:41	quite surprised to find that she remained the same size. To be sure, this is what generally happens when one
A6	46: 1	croquet." The Frog-Footman repeated, in the same solemn tone, only changing the order of the words a
T5	156: 5	sometimes under trees, but always with the same tall river-banks frowning over their heads.
A2	15:41	a little different. But if I'm not the same, the next question is 'Who in the world am I?' Ah, that's
T12	207:10	you talk with a person if they always say the same thing?"
A7	55:23	"Not the same thing a bit!" said the Hatter. "Why, you might just as
A7	55:24	as well say that 'I see what I eat' is the same thing as 'I eat what I see'!"
A7	55:27	March Hare, "that 'I like what I get' is the same thing as 'I get what I like'!"
A7	55:30	sleep, "that 'I breathe when I sleep' is the same thing as 'I sleep when I breathe'!"
A9	70:36	"Ah well! It means much the same thing," said the Duchess, digging her sharp little chin
A7	55:31	"It is the same thing with you," said the Hatter, and here the
A7	55:22	least--at least I mean what I say--that's the same thing, you know."
A6	46:30	day, maybe," the Footman continued in the same tone, exactly as if nothing had happened.
T1	119: 8	have gone straight out at the door in the same way, if she hadn't caught hold of the door-post. She was
T3	137:22	were sure to be two finger-posts pointing the same way, one marked "TO TWEEDLEDUM'S HOUSE," and the other
A2	15:40	changed in the night? Let me think: was I the same when I got up this morning? I almost think I can remember
A9	74:21	And the Gryphon answered, very nearly in the same words as before, "It's all his fancy, that: he hasn't got
A7	56:17	readily: "but that's because it stays the same year for such a long time together."

SAND (3)

T4	141: 4	like anything to see / Such quantities of sand: / 'If this were only cleared away,' / They said, 'it
T9	200: 3	else that is pleasant to drink: / Mix sand with the cider, and wool with the wine--/ And welcome
A2	18:23	in the sea, some children digging in the sand with wooden spades, then a row of lodging-houses, and

SANDS (2)

| A10 | 82:26 | buttons, and turns out his toes. / When the sands are all dry, he is gay as a lark, / And will talk in |
| T4 | 140:36 | The sea was wet as wet could be, / The sands were dry as dry. / You could not see a cloud, because / |

SANDWICH (2) [See also HAM-SANDWICH]

| T7 | 172: 4 | "Another sandwich!" said the King. |
| T7 | 172: 2 | a bag that hung round his neck, and handed a sandwich to the King, who devoured it greedily. |

SANDWICHES (1)

| T8 | 181:18 | "It's my own invention--to keep clothes and sandwiches in. You see I carry it upside-down, so that the |

SANG (4)

T9	199:36	was silence again, and the same shrill voice sang another verse:--
T8	190:12	As the Knight sang the last words of the ballad, he gathered up the reins,
A6	49: 1	While the Duchess sang the second verse of the song, she kept tossing the baby
A10	79:12	to mark the time, while the Mock Turtle sang this, very slowly and sadly:--

SAP (1)

| T3 | 133: 7 | "Sap and sawdust," said the Gnat. "Go on with the list." |

SAT (30)

T8	179:25	then he got on again, and the two Knights sat and looked at each other for some time without speaking.
A4	33: 1	hoarsely all the while, till at last it sat down a good way off, panting, with its tongue hanging out
T2	128:21	and fun!" Alice got up and curtseyed, and sat down again.
T9	192: 9	"and if I really am a Queen," she said as she sat down again, "I shall be able to manage it quite well in
A3	24:12	back. However, it was over at last, and they sat down again in a ring, and begged the Mouse to tell them
A10	78:37	jumping about like mad things all this time, sat down again very sadly and quietly, and looked at Alice.
A2	15:18	get through was more hopeless than ever: she sat down and began to cry again.
A1	12:20	out with trying, the poor little thing sat down and cried.
A9	74:29	So they sat down, and nobody spoke for some minutes. Alice thought to
T6	166:22	case she really ought to listen to it; so she sat down, and said "Thank you" rather sadly,
A3	21:15	me! I'll soon make you dry enough!" They all sat down at once, in a large ring, with the Mouse in the
T8W	14:19	So Alice sat down by him, and spread out the paper on her knees, and
A7	54:10	of room!" said Alice indignantly, and she sat down in a large arm-chair at one end of the table.
T9	200:16	of them, but the middle one was empty. Alice sat down in it, rather uncomfortable at the silence, and
T4	146:22	Here he looked at Tweedledee, who immediately sat down on the ground, and tried to hide himself under the
T7	174:13	fight just then, and the Lion and the Unicorn sat down, panting, while the King called out "Ten minutes
T1	114: 8	The Queen gasped, and sat down: the rapid journey through the air had quite taken
A10	82:34	Alice said nothing: she had sat down with her face in her hands, wondering if anything
T6	159:28	Humpty Dumpty sat on a wall: / Humpty Dumpty had a great fall. / All the
A12	98:34	So she sat on, with closed eyes, and half believed herself in
A9	75: 5	added the Gryphon; and then they both sat silent and looked at poor Alice, who felt ready to sink
A7	55:32	here the conversation dropped, and the party sat silent for a minute, while Alice thought over all she
A9	74:39	thinking there must be more to come, so she sat still and said nothing.
A12	98:13	But her sister sat still just as she left her, leaning her head on her hand,

SAT (cont.)
T1   110:22 Red Queen, Kitty! Do you know, I think if you sat up and folded your arms, you'd look exactly like her. Now
A9   74: 7   The Gryphon sat up and rubbed its eyes: then it watched the Queen till she
A11   90:15 slipped the guinea-pig, head first, and then sat upon it.)
T1   108: 7 the kitten, and sometimes to herself. Kitty sat very demurely on her knee, pretending to watch the
T1   116: 1 lying near Alice on the table, and while she sat watching the White King (for she was still a little
T7   177:17 this isn't fair!" cried the Unicorn, as Alice sat with the knife in her hand, very much puzzled how to begin
-SATISFACTORY [See UNSATISFACTORY]
SATISFIED (2)
T4   148: 6   Tweedledum looked round him with a satisfied smile. "I don't suppose," he said, "there'll be a
T3   132: 7 brook we have to jump over." Everybody seemed satisfied with this, though Alice felt a little nervous at the
SATURDAY (1)
T6   164: 9 "Ah, you should see 'em come round me of a Saturday night," Humpty Dumpty went on, wagging his head
SAUCEPAN (2)
T4   147:32 though it certainly looked much more like a saucepan.)
A6   48:18 his precious nose!", as an unusually large saucepan flew close by it, and very nearly carried it off.
SAUCEPANS (1)
A6   48:12   came first; then followed a shower of saucepans, plates, and dishes. The Duchess took no notice of
SAUCER (2)
A1   9: 8 was the cat.) "I hope they'll remember her saucer of milk at tea-time. Dinah, my dear! I wish you were
T1   108:34 away by the tail just as I had put down the saucer of milk before her! What, you were thirsty, were you?
SAUNTERED (1)
T7   175: 9   At this moment the Unicorn sauntered by them, with his hands in his pockets. "I had the
SAVAGE (4)
A7   58: 7   "How dreadfully savage!" exclaimed Alice.
A2   15:30 The Duchess, the Duchess! Oh! Wo'n't she be savage if I've kept her waiting!" Alice felt so desperate that
A9   74: 6 as safe to stay with it as to go after that savage Queen: so she waited.
A9   70: 6 it was only the pepper that had made her so savage when they met in the kitchen.
SAVE (4)
A4   28:11 against the ceiling, and had to stoop to save her neck from being broken. She hastily put down the
A2   18: 8 and she dropped it hastily, just in time to save herself from shrinking away altogether.
T8   183: 8 hold of Alice's hair with one hand, to save himself from falling over on the other side.
T8   184:16 the horse's neck as he spoke, just in time to save himself from tumbling off again.
SAVED (1)
T1   109: 1   for Wednesday week--Suppose they had saved up all my punishments?" she went on, talking more to
SAVES (3)
A12   95:30 no meaning in it," said the King, "that saves a world of trouble, you know, as we needn't try to find
T2   124:14 Curtsey while you're thinking what to say. It saves time."
T12 207:23 you're thinking what to--what to purr. It saves time, remember!" And she caught it up and gave it one
SAVING (1)
T1   108:39 punished for any of them yet. You know I'm saving up all your punishments for Wednesday week--Suppose
SAW (28)
T9   195:11   Alice thought she saw a way out of the difficulty, this time. "If you'll tell me
A7   54: 9 "No room! No room!" they cried out when they saw Alice coming. "There's plenty of room!" said Alice
A6   51: 1   The Cat only grinned when it saw Alice. It looked good-natured, she thought: still it had
T1   108:22 they were comfortably settled again, "when I saw all the mischief you had been doing, I was very nearly
T8   187:33 I can: / There's little to relate. / I saw an aged aged man, / A-sitting on a gate. / 'Who are you,
T2   122:34   "I never saw anybody that looked stupider," a Violet said, so suddenly,
T2   122:36 cried the Tiger-lily. "As if you ever saw anybody! You keep your head under the leaves, and snore
T3   129: 7 down there? They ca'n't be bees--nobody ever saw bees a mile off, you know--" and for some time she stood
T6   159: 4 and, when she had come close to it, she saw clearly that it was HUMPTY DUMPTY himself. "It ca'n't be
A9   72:44 in the shade: however, the moment they saw her, they hurried back to the game, the Queen merely
T7   172:18 Quite right," said the King: "this young lady saw him too. So of course Nobody walks slower than you."
A1   10: 3 passage into the loveliest garden you ever saw. How she longed to get out of that dark hall, and wander
A6   53: 8 a cat! It's the most curious thing I ever saw in all my life!"
A6   47:17 violence that Alice quite jumped; but she saw in another moment that it was addressed to the baby, and
T8   187:16   Of all the strange things that Alice saw in her journey Through The Looking-Glass, this was the one
T9   195:44   "Humpty Dumpty saw it too," the White Queen went on in a low voice, more as
A1   8:17   and book-shelves: here and there she saw maps and pictures hung upon pegs. She took down a jar from
A8   67:30 hedgehog just now, only it ran away when it saw mine coming!"
T7   175:29 Unicorns were fabulous monsters, too? I never saw one alive before!"
A9   73:15   "I never saw one, or heard of one," said Alice.
A4   30: 8   "An arm, you goose! Who ever saw one that size? Why, it fills the whole window!"
T5   158:23 Well, this is the very queerest shop I ever saw!" * * * * * * * * * * * * * So she went on, wondering
T2   120:24 "Oh, it's too bad!" she cried. "I never saw such a house for getting in the way! Never!"
A12   93: 4   Alice looked at the jury-box, and saw that, in her haste, she had put the Lizard in head
T6   159: 2 she had come within a few yards of it, she saw that it had eyes and a nose and a mouth; and, when she had
A9   74:16   They had not gone far before they saw the Mock Turtle in the distance, sitting sad and lonely on
A10   82: 2 her adventures from the time when she first saw the White Rabbit. She was a little nervous about it, just
A7   60:33 they would call after her: the last time she saw them, they were trying to put the Dormouse into the teapot
SAWDUST (1)
T3   133: 7   "Sap and sawdust," said the Gnat. "Go on with the list."
SAWING (1)
T7   177: 7 with the great dish on her knees, and was sawing away diligently with the knife. "It's very provoking!"
SAY (114)
A1   8:38 but she thought they were nice grand words to say.)
A5   36:19 after her. "I've something important to say!"
A5   43:20 they're a kind of serpent: that's all I can say."
A9   77: 7 "He taught Laughing and Grief, they used to say."
T5   155:35 her hair, as her hands were full. "Feather, I say!"

SAY (cont.)

T6	163:41	lot of them! Impenetrability! That's what I	say!"
T7	173:32	down his cheek; but not a word would he	say.
A4	31:39	about again, and Alice heard the Rabbit	say "A barrowful will do, to begin with."
T7	171: 9	arrived: he was far too much out of breath to	say a word, and could only wave his hands about, and make the
A9	72:41	Alice; and Alice was too much frightened to	say a word, but slowly followed her back to the croquet-ground
A7	55:28	"You might just as well	say," added the Dormouse, which seemed to be talking in its
A7	55:26	"You might just as well	say," added the March Hare, "that 'I like what I get' is the
T3	136: 5	didn't help her much, and all she could	say, after a great deal of puzzling, was "L, I know it begins
A5	42:29	"Serpent, I	say again!" repeated the Pigeon, but in a more subdued tone,
A3	23: 4	to speak, and no one else seemed inclined to	say anything.
A1	8:25	they'll all think me at home! Why, I wouldn't	say anything about it, even if I fell off the top of the
T3	135: 8	"Well, if she said 'Miss,' and didn't	say anything more," the Gnat remarked, "of course you'd miss
T6	163:37	Alice was too much puzzled to	say anything; so after a minute Humpty Dumpty began again.
T9	192:23	for you to begin, you see nobody would ever	say anything, so that--"
A1	9:25	the wind, and was just in time to hear it	say, as it turned a corner, "Oh my ears and whiskers, how late
T8	183: 4	had much practice in riding," she ventured to	say, as she was helping him up from his fifth tumble.
T1	110:10	could tell you half the things Alice used to	say, beginning with her favourite phrase "Let's pretend." She
A8	69: 6	Alice could think of nothing else to	say but "It belongs to the Duchess: you'd better ask her about
A11	86:22	those twelve creatures," (she was obliged to	say "creatures," you see, because some of them were animals,
A1	10:19	It was all very well to	say "Drink me," but the wise little Alice was not going to do
T5	153: 5	"You needn't	say 'exactly,'" the Queen remarked. "I can believe it without
T5	155:36	"Why do you	say 'Feather' so often?" Alice asked at last, rather vexed.
T5	155:30	"Didn't you hear me	say 'Feather'?" the Sheep cried angrily, taking up quite a
T4	138:15	I'm sure I'm very sorry," was all Alice could	say; for the words of the old song kept ringing through her
T1	108:25	mischievous darling! What have you got to	say for yourself? Now don't interrupt me!" she went on,
TI	103:18	in memory yet, / Though envious years would	say "forget."
T2	125: 4	Alice didn't like at all: "though, when you	say 'garden'--I've seen gardens, compared with which this
T2	128: 3	forgetting them. At the end of four, I shall	say good-bye. And at the end of five, I shall go!"
T2	128:26	next peg, where she turned for a moment to	say "Good-bye," and then hurried on to the last.
T4	146:10	thought Alice, and she was just going to	say "Good-night" and leave them, when Tweedledum sprang out
T8W	20:11	as well as she could. At last she managed to	say gravely, "I can bite anything I want."
T4	140:23	eye, / And shook his heavy head--/ Meaning to	say he did not choose / To leave the oyster-bed.
T2	125: 8	"When you	say 'hill'," the Queen interrupted, "I could show you hills,
T4	144:32	Alice couldn't	say honestly that he was. He had a tall red night-cap on, with
T8W	19:11	nearly gone, / They take my wig from me and	say / 'How can you put such rubbish on?'
A2	17: 3	have been changed for Mabel! I'll try and	say 'How doth the little--'," and she crossed her hands on her
A5	36:34	"Well, I've tried to	say 'How doth the little busy bee,' but it all came different!
T3	137:27	I ca'n't stay there long. I'll just call and	say 'How d'ye do?' and ask them the way out of the wood. If I
T4	139:22	Tweedledum. "The first thing in a visit is to	say 'How d'ye do?' and shake hands!" And here the two brothers
T4	140: 4	just been dancing with. "It would never do to	say 'How d'ye do?' now," she said to herself: "we seem to have
A10	78:10	introduced to a lobster--" (Alice began to	say "I once tasted--" but checked herself hastily, and said
A9	72:14	"That's nothing to what I could	say if I chose," the Duchess replied, in a pleased tone.
A3	21: 9	who at last turned sulky, and would only	say, "I'm older than you, and must know better." And this
A9	73:18	walked off together, Alice heard the King	say in a low voice, to the company, generally, "You are all
T9	201:25	sort of voice, and Alice hadn't a word to	say in reply: she could only sit and look at it and gasp.
A9	72:13	down: but I ca'n't quite follow it as you	say it."
A9	72:16	"Pray don't trouble yourself to	say it any longer than that," said Alice.
A9	72:21	like that!" But she did not venture to	say it out loud.
T9	194:35	I," the White Queen whispered: "we'll often	say it over together, dear. And I'll tell you a secret--I can
A1	8:34	listen to her, still it was good practice to	say it over) "--yes, that's about the right distance--but then
T2	124:14	tone. "Curtsey while you're thinking what to	say. It saves time."
T6	167: 7	"I sent to them again to	say / 'It will be better to obey.'
A2	19:21	understand English," thought Alice. "I daresay it's a French mouse, come over with William the Conqueror
T6	162:29	a cravat, child, and a beautiful one, as you	say. It's a present from the White King and Queen. There now!
A8	62: 5	as she came up to them, she heard one of them	say "Look out now, Five! Don't go splashing paint over me like
T3	131:24	in her ear, "Never mind what they all	say, my dear, but take a return-ticket every time the train
T2	127:27	Alice thought it would not be civil to	say "No," though it wasn't at all what she wanted. She took it
T3	130:14	for I must confess that I don't) "Better	say nothing at all. Language is worth a thousand pounds a
T6	168:39	a great comfort to have such a long word to	say) "of all the unsatisfactory people I ever met--" She never
T3	129:22	when they ask me how I liked my walk. I shall	say 'Oh, I liked it well enough--' (here came the favourite
A11	90: 3	"But what did the Dormouse	say?" one of the jury asked.
A8	62:11	not talk!" said Five. "I heard the Queen	say only yesterday you deserved to be beheaded."
A6	53: 1	"Did you	say 'pig', or 'fig'?" said the Cat.
T5	156: 8	"You needn't	say 'please' to me about 'em," the Sheep said, without looking
T1	108:29	deny it, Kitty: I heard you! What's that you	say?" (pretending that the kitten was speaking). "Her paw went
A3	22:35	"What I was going to	say," said the Dodo in an offended tone, "was that the best
A3	24: 7	and, as she could not think of anything to	say, she simply bowed, and took the thimble, looking as solemn
T2	126:17	go faster, though she had no breath left to	say so.
T9	196:26	timidly at Alice, who felt she ought to	say something kind, but really couldn't think of anything at
A7	56: 9	but he could think of nothing better to	say than his first remark, "It was the best butter, you know
T8	183:13	Alice could think of nothing better to	say than "Indeed?" but she said it as heartily as she could.
T6	160:26	if you like! You didn't think I was going to	say that, did you? The King has promised me--with his very own
T8	183: 6	offended at the remark. "What makes you	say that?" he asked, as he scrambled back into the saddle,
A7	55:24	said the Hatter. "Why, you might just as well	say that 'I see what I eat' is the same thing as 'I eat what I
A7	55:22	replied; "at least--at least I mean what I	say--that's the same thing, you know."
T3	132:39	"I ca'n't	say," the Gnat replied. "Further on, in the wood down there,
A10	81:37	"I mean what I	say," the Mock Turtle replied, in an offended tone. And the
T12	207:10	how can you talk with a person if they always	say the same thing?"
A7	59:29	humbly. "I wo'n't interrupt you again. I dare	say there may be one."

SAY (cont.)

T7	172:13	"I didn't say there was nothing <u>better</u>," the King replied. "I said there
T5	152: 1	Alice was just beginning to say "There's a mistake somewhere--," when the Queen began
A7	60:24	moon, and memory, and muchness--you know you say things are 'much of a muchness'--did you ever see such a
T9	196:19	would be the use of it?" but she did not say this aloud, for fear of hurting the poor Queen's feelings
T7	177:17	"I say, this isn't fair!" cried the Unicorn, as Alice sat with
A2	15:21	"a great girl like you," (she might well say this), "to go on crying in this way! Stop this moment, I
A1	7:12	<u>very</u> much out of the way to hear the Rabbit say to itself "Oh dear! Oh dear! I shall be too late!" (when
A4	29:27	that attempt proved a failure. Alice heard it say to itself "Then I'll go round and get in at the window."
T12	207: 7	had once made the remark) that, whatever you say to them, they <u>always</u> purr. "If they would only purr for
T2	127:39	Alice did not know what to say to this, but luckily the Queen did not wait for an answer,
T6	159:24	Alice didn't know what to say to this: it wasn't at all like conversation, she thought,
A7	59:18	Alice did not quite know what to say to this: so she helped herself to some tea and
T1	110:16	them, and Alice had been reduced at last to say "Well, <u>you</u> can be one of them, then, and <u>I'll</u> be all the
A8	65:34	"Did you say 'What a pity!'?" the Rabbit said.
A9	76:24	heard of 'Uglification,'" Alice ventured to say. "What is it?"
A7	55:19	"Then you should say what you mean," the March Hare went on.
A10	82:30	"That's different from what <u>I</u> used to say when I was a child," said the Gryphon.
T5	155:17	not with needles--" Alice was beginning to say, when suddenly the needles turned into oars in her hands,
A6	48:15	much already, that it was quite impossible to say whether the blows hurt it or not.
A6	50: 6	again (or grunted, it was impossible to say which), and they went on for some while in silence.
A2	17:22	up again, dear!' I shall only look up and say 'Who am I, then? Tell me that first, and then, if I like
A10	81:34	and told me he was going a journey, I should say 'With what porpoise?'"
T5	153:13	"I daresay you haven't had much practice," said the Queen. "When I
A7	56:39	tossing his head contemptuously. "I dare say you never even spoke to Time!"
T8	184:22	a great hand at inventing things. Now, I daresay you noticed, the last time you picked me up, that I was
T6	161:21	So here's a question for you. How old did you say you were?"
T2	123:20	"I daresay you'll see her soon," said the Rose. "She's one of the
T2	124:20	a <u>little</u> wider when you speak, and always say 'your Majesty.'"
A9	71: 5	"I dare say you're wondering why I don't put my arm round your waist,"
T9	193:20	doing it," the Red Queen remarked: "but I dare say you've not had many lessons in manners yet."

SAYING (30)

A7	58:27	voice, "I heard every word you fellows were saying."
A10	82:21	that she hardly knew what she was saying; and the words came very queer indeed:--
T1	115:35	with the pencil for some time without saying anything; but Alice was too strong for him, and at last
A5	42:37	puzzled, but she thought there was no use in saying anything more till the Pigeon had finished.
A2	17:22	be no use their putting their heads down and saying 'Come up again, dear!' I shall only look up and say
T4	139:14	help pointing her finger at Tweedledum, and saying "First Boy!"
T9	196:23	it: "she means well, but she ca'n't help saying foolish things as a general rule."
T8	187:12	So saying, he stopped his horse and let the reins fall on its
T4	145:16	shouted this so loud that Alice couldn't help saying "Hush! You'll be waking him, I'm afraid, if you make so
T1	115:22	The King was saying "I assure you, my dear, I turned cold to the very ends
T2	120:21	minutes all went on well, and she was just saying "I really <u>shall</u> do it this time--" when the path gave a
A6	45:13	and this he handed over to the other, saying, in a solemn tone, "For the Duchess. An invitation from
T8	184: 4	of them. "The great art of riding, as I was saying is--to keep your balance properly. Like this, you know
T8W	18: 9	the Wasp couldn't do it too. "Would you mind saying it in rhyme?" she asked very politely.
A2	17: 5	crossed her hands on her lap as if she were saying lessons, and began to repeat it, but her voice sounded
T3	131:19	there are in the carriage!" thought Alice), saying "She must go by post, as she's got a head on her--"
T5	158:15	do--you must get it for yourself." And so saying, she went off to the other end of the shop, and set the
A9	74:37	Turtle. Alice was very nearly getting up and saying, "Thank you, Sir, for your interesting story," but she
T6	163:17	"I thought it looked a little queer. As I was saying, that <u>seems</u> to be done right--though I haven't time to
T4	138:17	ticking of a clock, and she could hardly help saying them out loud:--
A3	26:18	And an old Crab took the opportunity of saying to her daughter "Ah, my dear! Let this be a lesson to
A1	9:17	was walking hand in hand with Dinah, and was saying to her, very earnestly, "Now, Dinah, tell me the truth:
T6	168:37	quietly walked away: but she couldn't help saying to herself, as she went, "of all the unsatisfactory--"
A6	50:19	who might do very well as pigs, and was just saying to herself "if one only knew the right way to change
A1	9:12	Alice began to get rather sleepy, and went on saying to herself, in a dreamy sort of way, "Do cats eat bats?
A6	53:16	then she walked up towards it rather timidly, saying to herself "Suppose it should be raving mad after all!
A4	28:12	broken. She hastily put down the bottle, saying to herself "That's quite enough--I hope I sha'n't grow
A4	31: 1	about in the chimney close above her: then, saying to herself "This is Bill", she gave one sharp kick, and
T9	193:14	The Red Queen broke the silence by saying, to the White Queen, "I invite you to Alice's
A3	24: 2	the Dodo solemnly presented the thimble, saying "We beg your acceptance of this elegant thimble"; and,

SAYS (8)

T2	122: 5	"It says 'Boughwough!'" cried a Daisy. "That's why its branches
A9	74:13	"Everybody says 'come on!' here," thought Alice, as she went slowly after
T1	109:12	you know, with a white quilt; and perhaps it says 'Go to sleep, darlings, till the summer comes again.' And
A2	20: 9	so useful, it's worth a hundred pounds! He says it kills all the rats and--oh dear!" cried Alice in a
A2	20: 8	and it belongs to a farmer, you know, and he says it's so useful, it's worth a hundred pounds! He says it
T8W	15: 2	ran her eye down the paper and said "No. It says nothing about brown."
T9	192:32	Queen remarked, with a little shudder, "She <u>says</u> she only said 'if'--"
A4	30:33	Bill's got to go down--Here, Bill! The master says you've got to go down the chimney!"

SCALE (1)

A2	17:11	<u>pour the waters of the Nile / On every golden scale</u>!

SCALY (1)

A10	80: 7	"<u>What matters it how far we go</u>?" <u>his scaly friend replied</u>. / "<u>There is another shore, you know</u>,

SCARCELY (2)

T9	199:13	asking of?" He was so hoarse that Alice could scarcely hear him.
T4	144:11	/ <u>But answer came there none</u>--/ <u>And this was scarcely odd, because</u> / <u>They'd eaten every one</u>."

SCENE (1)

T8	187:18	Years afterwards she could bring the whole scene back again, as if it had been only yesterday--the mild

```
SCENT (1)
   T5   156:35   had  begun  to  fade,  and  to  lose  all  their  scent and beauty, from the very moment that she picked them?
SCENTED (3)
   T5   156:23   at  one  bunch  after  another of the darling scented rushes.
   T5   156: 6                        "Oh, please! There are some scented rushes!" Alice cried in a sudden transport of delight.
   T5   156:36   very  moment  that she picked them? Even real scented rushes, you know, last only a very little while--and
SCEPTRE (1)
   T9   199:25   world it was Alice that said / 'I've a sceptre in hand, I've a crown on my head. / Let the
SCHOOL (5) [See also DAY-SCHOOL]
   A10   82:18   thought Alice. "I might just as well be at school at once." However, she got up, and began to repeat it,
   A9    76: 5   the  best  of  educations--in fact, we went to school every day--"
   A9    74:42   sobbing  a  little  now and then, "we went to school in the sea. The master was an old Turtle--we used to
   A9    75: 9                        "Yes, we went to school in the sea, though you mayn't believe it--"
   A9    76:13   "Ah!  Then  yours  wasn't  a  really good school," said the Mock Turtle in a tone of great relief. "Now,
SCHOOLBOYS (1)
   T4   139:13   They looked so exactly like a couple of great schoolboys, that Alice couldn't help pointing her finger at
SCHOOL-ROOM (1)
   A1    8:32   things  of  this  sort  in her lessons in the school-room, and though this was not a very good opportunity
SCOLD (1)
   T1   112: 7   in  fact,  because there'll be no one here to scold me away from the fire. Oh, what fun it'll be, when they
SCOLDED (1)
   A1    12:24   very  seldom  followed it), and sometimes she scolded herself so severely as to bring tears into her eyes;
SCOLDING (1)
   T9   192: 3   a  severe tone (she was always rather fond of scolding herself), "It'll never do for you to be lolling about
-SCOPE [See GYROSCOPE, MICROSCOPE, TELESCOPE]
SCORNFUL (1)
   T6   163:30   use  a word," Humpty Dumpty said, in rather a scornful tone, "it means just what I choose it to mean--
SCORNFULLY (1)
   T5   157:10   home  with  me!"  But the Sheep only laughed scornfully, and went on with her knitting.
SCRAMBLE (1)
   T1   108:18   just  to  see how it would look: this led to a scramble, in which the ball rolled down upon the floor, and
SCRAMBLED (4)
   T5   156:32   cheeks  and  dripping  hair  and  hands, she scrambled back into her place, and began to arrange her
   T1   108: 12  a  voice  as  she could manage--and then she scrambled back into the arm-chair, taking the kitten and the
   T8   183: 6   "What  makes  you say that?" he asked, as he scrambled back into the saddle, keeping hold of Alice's hair
   T9   202:26  and three of them (who looked like kangaroos) scrambled into the dish of roast mutton, and began eagerly
SCRAMBLING (3)
   A4    30:41   guess  of  what  sort it was) scratching and scrambling about in the chimney close above her: then, saying
   T4   142:12   All hopping through the frothy waves, / And scrambling to the shore.
   T1   113:22   Lily! My imperial kitten!" and she began scrambling wildly up the side of the fender.
SCRATCHING (1)
   A4    30:41   (she  couldn't  guess of what sort it was) scratching and scrambling about in the chimney close above her
SCREAM (8)
   T4   146:28   NEW  RATTLE!"  and his voice rose to a perfect scream.
   T6   168: 1   Humpty  Dumpty  raised  his voice almost to a scream as he repeated this verse, and Alice thought, with a
   T3   132: 3   voice  began,  when it was drowned by a shrill scream from the engine, and everybody jumped up in alarm,
   A12   97:10   came  flying  down upon her; she gave a little scream, half of fright and half of anger, and tried to beat
   T5   152:23                        "But why don't you scream now?" Alice asked, holding her hands ready to put over
   T8   184:18   than a live horse," Alice said, with a little scream of laughter, in spite of all she could do to prevent it
   A8    65:38   ears--" the Rabbit began. Alice gave a little scream of laughter. "Oh, hush!" the Rabbit whispered in a
   T8W   20: 9                        Alice began with a little scream of laughter, which she turned into a cough as well as
SCREAMED (5)
   T9   202:21   drink your health--Queen Alice's health!" she screamed at the top of her voice, and all the guests began
   A10   78:30                        "Swim after them!" screamed the Gryphon.
   A5    42:27                        "Serpent!" screamed the Pigeon.
   A8    65: 3                        "Leave off that!" screamed the Queen. "You make me giddy." And then, turning to
   T9   203: 7   "Take care of yourself!" screamed the White Queen, seizing Alice's hair with both her
SCREAMING (5)
   T5   152:25                        "Why, I've done all the screaming already," said the Queen. "What would be the good of
   T1   114: 5   use,  and, as the poor little Lily was nearly screaming herself into a fit, she hastily picked up the Queen
   A8    64: 6   at  her for a moment like a wild beast, began screaming "Off with her head! Off with--"
   T5   152: 2   a  mistake somewhere--," when the Queen began screaming, so loud that she had to leave the sentence
   A8    68:12   she  heard the Queen's voice in the distance, screaming with passion. She had already heard her sentence
SCREAMS (1)
   T5   152: 6                        Her screams were so exactly like the whistle of a steam-engine,
-SCREW [See CORKSCREW]
SCROLL (1) [See also PARCHMENT-SCROLL]
   A11   86: 6   Rabbit,  with  a  trumpet  in one hand, and a scroll of parchment in the other. In the very middle of the
SCRUBBING (1)
   T12   207:30   in  my  dream--Dinah! Do you know that you're scrubbing a White Queen? Really, it's most disrespectful of
SCURRIED (1)
   A2    15:34   dropped the white kid-gloves and the fan, and scurried away into the darkness as hard as he could go.
SEA (17)
   A9    76:17   said  Alice;  "living  at  the  bottom of the sea."
   A2    18:19   idea  was that she had somehow fallen into the sea, "and in that case I can go back by railway," she said to
   A10   78:29                        "--as far out to sea as you can--"
   A10   80: 2   us up and throw us, with the lobsters, out to sea!" / But the snail replied "Too far, too far!", and gave a
   A10   80:25   Turtle:  "crumbs  would  all  wash off in the sea. But they have their tails in their mouths; and the reason
   A10   78:31                        "Turn a somersault in the sea!" cried the Mock Turtle, capering wildly about.
   A10   78: 8   "You  may  not  have  lived  much under the sea--" ("I haven't," said Alice)--"and perhaps you were never
```

SEA (cont.)

T4	142:23	wax--/ Of cabbages--and kings--/ And why the sea is boiling hot--/ And whether pigs have wings.'
A5	42:11	which seemed to rise like a stalk out of a sea of green leaves that lay far below her.
T4	140:23	"The sun was shining on the sea, / Shining with all his might: / He did his very best to
A10	81: 5	to the dance. So they got thrown out to sea. So they had to fall a long way. So they got their tails
A2	18:23	you find a number of bathing-machines in the sea, some children digging in the sand with wooden spades,
A10	81:21	"Boots and shoes under the sea," the Gryphon went on in a deep voice, "are done with
A9	74:42	now and then, "we went to school in the sea. The master was an old Turtle--we used to call him
T6	167: 1	The little fishes of the sea, / They sent an answer back to me.
A9	75: 9	"Yes, we went to school in the sea, though you mayn't believe it--"
T4	140:35	The sea was wet as wet could be, / The sands were dry as dry. /

SEALING (2)

T4	142:21	of many things: / Of shoes--and ships--and sealing wax--/ Of cabbages--and kings--/ And why the sea is
T8	186:28	it with other things--such as gunpowder and sealing-wax. And here I must leave you." They had just come to

SEALS (1)

A10	78:16	"Two lines!" cried the Mock Turtle. "Seals, turtles, salmon, and so on: then, when you've cleared

SEAOGRAPHY (1)

A9	76:38	flappers--"Mystery, ancient and modern, with Seaography: then Drawling--the Drawling-master was an old

SEARCH (2)

T8	189: 1	/ Or set limed twigs for crabs: / I sometimes search for grassy knolls / For wheels of Hansom-cabs. / And
A8	68:16	it was her turn or not. So she went off in search of her hedgehog.

SEAS (1)

T8	188: 6	unto men,' he said, / 'Who sail on stormy seas; / And that's the way I get my bread--/ A trifle, if you

SEA-SHORE (1)

A10	78:15	"you first form into a line along the sea-shore--"

SEASIDE (1)

A2	18:21	she said to herself. (Alice had been to the seaside once in her life, and had come to the general

SEAT (1)

T5	157: 1	poor Alice, it swept her straight off the seat, and down among the heap of rushes.

SEATED (3)

T7	177: 6	Alice had seated herself on the bank of a little brook, with the great
T7	170: 4	an open place, where she found the White King seated on the ground, busily writing in his memorandum-book.
A11	86: 1	The King and Queen of Hearts were seated on their throne when they arrived, with a great crowd

SEA-WEED (1)

T8W	17:12	all tangled and tumbled about like a heap of sea-weed. "You could make your wig much neater," she said, "if

SECOND (7)

T2	126: 9	Lily's too young to play: and you're in the Second Square to begin with: when you get to the Eighth Square
A4	32:20	"is to grow to my right size again; and the second thing is to find my way into that lovely garden. I
T6	162:16	now.) "At least," she corrected herself on second thoughts, "a beautiful cravat, I should have said--no,
A11	88:37	she would get up and leave the court; but on second thoughts she decided to remain where she was as long as
T3	135:24	little timid about going into it. However, on second thoughts, she made up her mind to go on: "for I
A1	9:39	would not open any of them. However, on the second time round, she came upon a low curtain she had not
A6	49: 1	While the Duchess sang the second verse of the song, she kept tossing the baby violently

SECONDLY (2)

A9	70:26	first because the Duchess was very ugly; and secondly, because she was exactly the right height to rest her
A6	46:12	I'm on the same side of the door as you are: secondly, because they're making such a noise inside, no one

SECRET (2)

T9	194:36	it over together, dear. And I'll tell you a secret--I can read words of one letter! Isn't that grand?
A12	95:19	liked them best, / For this must ever be / A secret, kept from all the rest, / Between yourself and me."

SECUNDA (1)

AI	3:15	/ Her edict "to begin it": / In gentler tones Secunda hopes / "There will be nonsense in it!" / While Tertia

SEE (152)

A5	35:12	said Alice, "because I'm not myself, you see."
A7	55:25	I eat' is the same thing as 'I eat what I see'!"
T8	184:33	are high enough, you see--then I'm over, you see."
T8	190:19	in the road? I think it'll encourage me, you see."
T4	140:37	/ The sands were dry as dry. / You could not see a cloud, because / No cloud was in the sky: / No birds
A6	51:32	"Well, then," the Cat went on, "you see a dog growls when it's angry, and wags its tail when it's
T3	129: 4	she stood on tiptoe in hopes of being able to see a little further. "Principal rivers--there are none.
A10	79: 3	"Would you like to see a little of it?" said the Mock Turtle.
T1	111: 2	now we come to the passage. You can just see a little peep of the passage in Looking-glass House, if
T7	173:12	King said, "only I'm not strong enough. You see, a minute goes by so fearfully quick. You might as well
T3	133: 3	said the Gnat. "Half way up that bush, you'll see a Rocking-horse-fly, if you look. It's made entirely of
A9	74: 2	and to hear his history. I must go back and see after some executions I have ordered;" and she walked off,
A1	8:31	thousand miles down, I think--" (for, you see, Alice had learnt several things of this sort in her
T1	110:33	only the things go the other way. I can see all of it when I get upon a chair--all but the bit just
A7	54:15	but there was nothing on it but tea. "I don't see any wine," she remarked.
A4	34: 1	and the blades of grass, but she could not see anything that looked like the right thing to eat or drink
A1	8:14	she was coming to, but it was too dark to see anything: then she looked at the sides of the well, and
T7	177: 4	lay down again. "There was too much dust to see anything. What a time the Monster is, cutting up that
A1	9:14	and sometimes "Do bats eat cats?" for, you see, as she couldn't answer either question, it didn't much
A8	63:44	who were lying round the rose-tree; for, you see, as they were lying on their faces, and the pattern on
A11	86:37	Alice could see, as well as if she were looking over their shoulders, that
A11	86:22	(she was obliged to say "creatures," you see, because some of them were animals, and some were birds,)
T8	185: 2	So I had a very little way to fall, you see--But there was the danger of falling into it, to be sure.
T9	192:24	Ridiculous!" cried the Queen. "Why, don't you see, child--" here she broke off with a frown, and, after
T7	170:15	look along the road, and tell me if you can see either of them."
T6	164: 9	"Ah, you should see 'em come round me of a Saturday night," Humpty Dumpty went
A2	16: 9	I know all the things I used to know. Let me see: four times five is twelve, and four times six is thirteen
T4	144:16	the Carpenter, though," said Tweedledee. "You see he held his handkerchief in front, so that the Carpenter

SEE (cont.)

T8	182:18	instead. "It's rather a tight fit, you see," he said, as they got it in at last; "there are so many
T8	182: 5	"You see," he went on after a pause, "it's as well to be provided
T1	114:22	clear that he could neither hear her nor see her.
A3	26:28	you ca'n't think! And oh, I wish you could see her after the birds! Why, she'll eat a little bird as soon
T9	192: 8	with the thought that there was nobody to see her, "and if I really am a Queen," she said as she sat
A2	19:34	you'd take a fancy to cats, if you could only see her. She is such a dear quiet thing," Alice went on, half
T2	123:20	"I daresay you'll see her soon," said the Rose. "She's one of the kind that has
T7	173:25	only give them oyster-shells in there--so you see he's very hungry and thirsty. How are you, dear child?" he
T8	190:25	away into the forest. "It wo'n't take long to see him off, I expect," Alice said to herself, as she stood
T9	194:17	"But I don't see how--
A10	79:15	behind us, and he's treading on my tail. / See how eagerly the lobsters and the turtles all advance! /
A9	74:30	minutes. Alice thought to herself "I don't see how he can ever finish, if he doesn't begin." But she
A11	86:18	wig (look at the frontispiece if you want to see how he did it), he did not look at all comfortable, and it
A4	33:11	that I've got to grow up again! Let me see--how is it to be managed? I suppose I ought to eat or
T1	108:18	the worsted round the kitten's neck, just to see how it would look: this led to a scramble, in which the
T9	196:30	she is! Pat her on the head, and see how pleased she'll be!" But this was more than Alice had
T1	110:27	it up to the Looking-glass, that it might see how sulky it was, "--and if you're not good directly," she
A8	68:10	Alice thought she might as well go back and see how the game was going on, as she heard the Queen's voice
T6	164:13	to ask what she paid them with; and so you see I ca'n't tell you.)
T8	181:23	to keep clothes and sandwiches in. You see I carry it upside-down, so that the rain ca'n't get in."
T8	184:30	I came to think of it," said the Knight. "You see, I said to myself 'The only difficulty is with the feet:
A11	89:26	Hatter went on, looking anxiously round to see if he would deny it too; but the Dormouse denied nothing,
T6	168:34	Alice waited a minute to see if he would speak again, but, as he never opened his eyes
T1	115:17	what she had done, and went round the room to see if she could find any water to throw over him. However,
A2	16: 2	knew that were of the same age as herself, to see if she could have been changed for any of them.
A6	48:28	glanced rather anxiously at the cook, to see if she meant to take the hint; but the cook was busily
A1	12: 6	however, she waited for a few minutes to see if she was going to shrink any further: she felt a little
T4	138: 7	were alive, and she was just going round to see if the word 'TWEEDLE' was written at the back of each
A6	50: 2	thought, and looked into its eyes again, to see if there were any tears.
A2	15: 2	they wo'n't walk the way I want to go! Let me see. I'll give them a new pair of boots every Christmas."
T5	158:20	away the more I walk towards it. Let me see, is this a chair? Why, it's got branches, I declare! How
A6	52:22	Alice waited a little, half expecting to see it again, but it did not appear, and after a minute or two
T12	207:20	it turned away its head, and pretended not to see it: but it looked a little ashamed of itself, so I think
T6	164:33	"I see it now," Alice remarked thoughtfully: "and what are
T4	148: 3	reach," cried Tweedledum, "whether I can see it or not!"
A1	8: 4	the field after it, and was just in time to see it pop down a large rabbit-hole under the hedge.
A1	12:17	she could not possibly reach it: she could see it quite plainly through the glass, and she tried her best
T5	157: 7	"Was it? I didn't see it," said Alice, peeping cautiously over the side of the
A8	63:32	down on their faces, so that they couldn't see it?" So she stood where she was, and waited.
T2	127:19	of country!" said the Queen. "Now, here, you see, it takes all the running you can do, to keep in the same
A6	50:14	creature down, and felt quite relieved to see it trot away quietly into the wood. "If it had grown up,"
A8	68:20	other side of the garden, where Alice could see it trying in a helpless sort of way to fly up into a tree
A1	9: 3	No, it'll never do to ask: perhaps I shall see it written up somewhere."
T6	164:31	slimy.' 'Lithe' is the same as 'active.' You see it's like a portmanteau--there are two meanings packed up
A5	42:42	annoyed," said Alice, who was beginning to see its meaning.
T12	208: 8	if Dinah hadn't washed you this morning! You see, Kitty, it must have been either me or the Red King. He
T9	199:38	quoth Alice, 'draw near! / 'Tis an honour to see me, a favour to hear: / 'Tis a privilege high to have
T1	113:13	closer down, "and I'm nearly sure they ca'n't see me. I feel somehow as if I was getting invisible--"
T8	190:16	then you'll be a Queen--But you'll stay and see me off first?" he added as Alice turned with an eager look
T5	153:21	cried in a triumphant tone. "Now you shall see me pin it on again, all by myself!"
A6	52: 7	"You'll see me there," said the Cat, and vanished.
T1	112: 8	the fire. Oh, what fun it'll be, when they see me through the glass in here, and ca'n't get at me!"
A8	63: 6	began, in a low voice, "Why, the fact is, you see, Miss, this here ought to have been a red rose-tree, and
A8	63: 9	all have our heads cut off, you know. So you see, Miss, we're doing our best, afore she comes, to--" At
T7	170:18	remarked in a fretful tone. "To be able to see Nobody! And at that distance too! Why, it's as much as I
T7	170:16	"I see nobody on the road," said Alice.
T9	192:23	person always waited for you to begin, you see nobody would ever say anything, so that--"
T8	185:20	was hurt this time. However, though she could see nothing but the soles of his feet, she was much relieved
T1	113:16	and made her turn her head just in time to see one of the White Pawns roll over and begin kicking: she
T1	111: 4	it's very like our passage as far as you can see, only you know it may be quite different on beyond. Oh,
T7	170:19	too! Why, it's as much as I can do to see real people, by this light!"
A5	35:13	"I don't see," said the Caterpillar.
A8	65: 8	"I see!" said the Queen, who had meanwhile been examining the
A3	23:19	forehead (the position in which you usually see Shakespeare, in the pictures of him), while the rest
A8	65:39	tone. "The Queen will hear you! You see she came rather late, and the Queen said--"
T1	118:26	"but it's rather hard to understand!" (You see she didn't like to confess, even to herself, that she
T5	152:21	"That accounts for the bleeding, you see," she said to Alice with a smile. "Now you understand the
A1	10: 9	could, if I only knew how to begin." For, you see, so many out-of-the-way things had happened lately, that
A12	95:33	and looking at them with one eye; "I seem to see some meaning in them, after all. '--said I could not swim
T7	170:21	the road, shading her eyes with one hand. "I see somebody now!" she exclaimed at last. "But he's coming
A7	60:25	things are 'much of a muchness'--did you ever see such a thing as a drawing of a muchness!"
T6	160:38	spoken to a King, I am: mayhap you'll never see such another: and, to show you I'm not proud, you may
T4	141: 3	close at hand: / They wept like anything to see / Such quantities of sand: / 'If this were only cleared
T1	109: 4	I suppose, when the day came. Or--let me see--suppose each punishment was to be going without a dinner.
T1	110:35	the fireplace. Oh! I do so wish I could see--that bit! I want so much to know whether they've a fire in
T6	163: 4	Humpty Dumpty looked doubtful. "I'd rather see that done on paper," he said.
T4	146:13	"Do you see that?" he said, in a voice choking with passion, and his
T1	107: 5	bearing it pretty well, considering): so you see that it couldn't have had any hand in the mischief.
T7	172: 8	Alice was glad to see that it revived him a good deal. "There's nothing like

SEE (cont.)

A12	98:20	could hear the very tones of her voice, and see that queer little toss of her head to keep back the
A2	18 2	down at her hands, and was surprised to see that she had put on one of the Rabbit's little white
A4	27:32	this mouse-hole till Dinah comes back and see that the mouse doesn't get out.' Only I don't think,"
A1	8:30	near the centre of the earth. Let me see: that would be four thousand miles down, I think--" (for
T1	112:14	on the chimney-piece (you know you can only see the back of it in the Looking-glass) had got the face of a
T1	108:16	had to leave off. Never mind, we'll go and see the bonfire to-morrow." Here Alice wound two or three
A6	48:26	it would make with the day and night! You see the earth takes twenty-four hours to turn round on its
T2	120: 1	"I should see the garden far better," said Alice to herself, "if I could
A6	53:17	mad after all! I almost wish I'd gone to see the Hatter instead!"
T7	178: 4	brook in her terror, and had just time to see the Lion and the * * * * * * * * * * * * * Unicorn rise
A9	74: 1	said the Queen, "and take this young lady to see the Mock Turtle, and to hear his history I must go back
A8	63:14	footsteps, and Alice looked round, eager to see the Queen.
T9	204: 6	and Alice turned again, just in time to see the Queen's broad good-natured face grinning at her for a
T8	182:25	hardly enough," he said, anxiously. "You see the wind is so _very_ strong here. It's as strong as soup."
T7	172:39	it's _my_ crown all the while! Let's run and see them." And they trotted off, Alice repeating to herself,
T8	184:33	my head--then the feet are high enough, you see--then I'm over, you see."
A12	93:31	and some "unimportant." Alice could see this, as she was near enough to look over their slates;
T1	110:32	House. First, there's the room you can see through the glass--that's just the same as our
T8	179:11	"I've a great mind to go and wake him, and see what happens!"
A7	55:24	"Why, you might just as well say that 'I see what I eat' is the same thing as 'I eat what I see'!"
T2	122:26	so. "It's very hard," she said; "but I don't see what that has to do with it."
T2	125: 1	"I only wanted to see what the garden was like, your Majesty--"
A11	91:30	over the list, feeling very curious to see what the next witness would be like, "--for they haven't
A4	28: 6	I eat or drink anything: so I'll just see what this bottle does. I do hope it'll make me grow large
A2	15:26	distance, and she hastily dried her eyes to see what was coming. It was the White Rabbit returning,
A4	34: 6	to her that she might as well look and see what was on top of it.
T8W	13: 4	she thought, looking anxiously back to see what was the matter. Something like a very old man (only
A6	49:32	Alice looked very anxiously into its face to see what was the matter with it. There could be no doubt that
T9	204: 3	a hoarse laugh at her side, and turned to see what was the matter with the White Queen; but, instead of
A4	31: 3	Bill", she gave one sharp kick, and waited to see what would happen next.
T1	113:18	she watched it with great curiosity to see what would happen next.
T4	148: 1	he added: "I generally hit every thing I can see--when I get really excited."
A5	42: 9	were nowhere to be found: all she could see, when she looked down, was an immense length of neck,
T3	131:31	so," said Alice, looking about in vain to see where the voice came from. "If you're so anxious to have a
T6	166:27	"If you can see whether I'm singing or not, you've sharper eyes than most
A1	10:21	hurry. "No, I'll look first," she said, "and see whether it's marked 'poison' or not"; for she had read
T3	131:10	Alice couldn't see who was sitting beyond the Beetle, but a hoarse voice
T9	201:15	However, she didn't see why the Red Queen should be the only one to give orders;
A9	70: 1	"You ca'n't think how glad I am to see you again, you dear old thing!" said the Duchess, as she
A3	26:40	Oh, my dear Dinah! I wonder if I shall ever see you any more!" And here poor Alice began to cry again, for
T6	166:26	"I see you don't," said Alice.
T8	181: 4	the next brook," said the White Knight. "I'll see you safe to the end of the wood--and then I must go back,
A5	42:14	to? And oh, my poor hands, how is it I ca'n't see you?" She was moving them about, as she spoke, but no
T8	181:17	"I see you're admiring my little box," the Knight said in a
A5	43: 7	"Well! _What_ are you?" said the Pigeon. "I can see you're trying to invent something!"

SEEING (2)

T7	170: 7	all!" the King cried in a tone of delight, on seeing Alice. "Did you happen to meet any soldiers, my dear,
A6	50:20	them--" when she was a little startled by seeing the Cheshire-Cat sitting on a bough of a tree a few

SEEM (13)

T5	156:26	quite reach it." And it certainly _did_ seem a little provoking ("almost as if it happened on purpose
T3	136: 8	Alice with its large gentle eyes, but didn't seem at all frightened. "Here then! Here then!" Alice said, as
T3	137:20	But this did not seem likely to happen. She went on and on, a long way, but
A2	15: 5	carrier," she thought; "and how funny it'll seem, sending presents to one's own feet! And how odd the
A9	72: 6	"and the moral of that is--'Be what you would seem to be'--or, if you'd like it put more simply--'Never
A1	8:40	fall right _through_ the earth! How funny it'll seem to come out among the people that walk with their heads
A3	22:27	said Alice in a melancholy tone: "it doesn't seem to dry me at all."
A11	88:30	This did not seem to encourage the witness at all: he kept shifting from
A8	67:25	one ca'n't hear oneself speak--and they don't seem to have any rules in particular: at least, if there are,
T4	140: 5	'How d'ye do?' _now_," she said to herself: "we seem to have got beyond that, somehow!"
A4	30:36	has he?" said Alice to herself. "Why, they seem to put everything upon Bill! I wouldn't be in Bill's
A12	95:33	knee, and looking at them with one eye; "I seem to see some meaning in them, after all. '--_said I could
T6	164:30	"You seem very clever at explaining words, Sir," said Alice. "Would

SEEMED (55)

T8	190: 5	/ With _eyes_, like _cinders_, _all_ _aglow_, / Who seemed distracted with his woe, / Who rocked his _body_ to and
T7	178: 2	came from, she couldn't make out: the air seemed full of it, and it rang through and through her head
T8	179: 1	After a while the noise seemed gradually to die away, till all was dead silence, and
A3	23: 4	that _somebody_ ought to speak, and no one else seemed inclined to say anything.
A6	48:29	the cook was busily stirring the soup, and seemed not to be listening, so she went on again: "Twenty-four
A1	13: 3	but out-of-the-way things to happen, that it seemed quite dull and stupid for life to go on in the common
T2	122: 8	all began shouting together, till the air seemed quite full of little shrill voices. "Silence, every one
T8	186:21	hoping to cheer him up, for the poor Knight seemed quite low-spirited about it.
A1	7:15	have wondered at this, but at the time it all seemed quite natural); but, when the Rabbit actually took _a_
T4	139:28	they were dancing round in a ring. This seemed quite natural (she remembered afterwards), and she was
A3	21: 6	about this, and after a few minutes it seemed quite natural to Alice to find herself talking
A9	71:17	"Of course it is," said the Duchess, who seemed ready to agree to everything that Alice said: "there's
T3	132: 7	only a brook we have to jump over." Everybody seemed satisfied with this, though Alice felt a little nervous
T4	145:25	said--half laughing through her tears, it all seemed so ridiculous--"I shouldn't be able to cry."
A4	33: 3	This seemed to Alice a good opportunity for making her escape: so
A8	68:18	in a fight with another hedgehog, which seemed to Alice an excellent opportunity for croqueting one of

SEEMED (cont.)
```
T5    149:21  It  would  have  been  all  the  better, as  it  seemed  to  Alice, if  she  had  got  some  one  else  to  dress  her,
A3     21:13                    At  last  the  Mouse, who  seemed  to be  a  person  of  some  authority  among  them, called  out
T7    170: 1  but  even  they  stumbled  now  and  then; and  it  seemed  to  be  a  regular  rule  that, whenever  a  horse  stumbled,
A1      8:10  before  she  found  herself  falling  down  what  seemed  to  be  a  very  deep  well.
T1    112:13    the  pictures  on  the  wall  next  the  fire  seemed  to  be  all  alive, and  the  very  clock  on  the
A2     14: 5  (for  when  she  looked  down  at  her  feet, they  seemed  to  be  almost  out  of  sight, they  were  getting  so  far
T5    154:11                       The  shop  seemed  to  be  full  of  all  manner  of  curious  things--but  the
A6     47: 3  the  fire, stirring  a  large  cauldron  which  seemed  to  be  full  of  soup.
A5     36:16  think  of  any  good  reason, and  the  Caterpillar  seemed  to  be  in  a  very  unpleasant  state  of  mind, she  turned
A5     42:18                    As  there  seemed  to  be  no  chance  of  getting  her  hands  up  to  her  head,
A11    86:10  "and  hand  round  the  refreshments!" But  there  seemed  to  be  no  chance  of  this; so  she  began  looking  at
A4     28:25  it  was  very  uncomfortable, and, as  there  seemed  to  be  no  sort  of  chance  of  her  ever  getting  out  of  the
A1     10:12                       There  seemed  to  be  no  use  in  waiting  by  the  little  door, so  she  went
A7     55:29  just  as  well  say," added  the  Dormouse, which  seemed  to  be  talking  in  its  sleep, "that  'I  breathe  when  I
T8    180:10  Rule  of  Battle, that  Alice  had  not  noticed, seemed  to  be  that  they  always  fell  on  their  heads; and  the
T3    131: 7  of  passengers  altogether), and, as  the  rule  seemed  to  be  that  they  should  all  speak  in  turn, he  went  on
T4    139:30  not  even  surprised  to  hear  music  playing: it  seemed  to  come  from  the  tree  under  which  they  were  dancing,
T8W    13: 2  over, when  she  heard  a  deep  sigh, which  seemed  to  come  from  the  wood  behind  her.
T3    129:35  about  the  same  size  as  the  people, and  quite  seemed  to  fill  the  carriage.
T7    169: 3     and  at  last  in  such  crowds  that  they  seemed  to  fill  the  whole  forest. Alice  got  behind  a  tree, for
T8    181:13        He  was  dressed  in  tin  armour, which  seemed  to  fit  him  very  badly, and  he  had  a  queer-shaped  little
A5     42:16  them  about, as  she  spoke, but  no  result  seemed  to  follow, except  a  little  shaking  among  the  distant
T2    126:22  thought  poor  puzzled  Alice. And  the  Queen  seemed  to  guess  her  thoughts, for  she  cried  "Faster! Don't  try
A4     27: 9  but  they  were  nowhere  to  be  seen--everything  seemed  to  have  changed  since  her  swim  in  the  pool; and  the
T3    135:18  sighs, and  this  time  the  poor  Gnat  really  seemed  to  have  sighed  itself  away, for, when  Alice  looked  up,
T5    153:32          She  looked  at  the  Queen, who  seemed  to  have  suddenly  wrapped  herself  up  in  wool. Alice
A7     56:19  felt  dreadfully  puzzled. The  Hatter's  remark  seemed  to  her  to  have  no  sort  of  meaning  in  it, and  yet  it  was
A2     19:19  mouse  looked  at  her  rather  inquisitively, and  seemed  to  her  to  wink  with  one  of  its  little  eyes, but  it  said
A12    98:22  into  her  eyes--and  still  as  she  listened, or  seemed  to  listen, the  whole  place  around  her  became  alive  with
T3    132:16                    But  the  beard  seemed  to  melt  away  as  she  touched  it, and  she  found  herself
T2    126:20  at  all: however  fast  they  went, they  never  seemed  to  pass  anything. "I  wonder  if  all  the  things  move
A2     19:27  gave  a  sudden  leap  out  of  the  water, and  seemed  to  quiver  all  over  with  fright. "Oh, I  beg  your  pardon!
A5     42:11  down, was  an  immense  length  of  neck, which  seemed  to  rise  like  a  stalk  out  of  a  sea  of  green  leaves  that
T2    127: 6  And  they  went  so  fast  that  at  last  they  seemed  to  skim  through  the  air, hardly  touching  the  ground
T8    181:27  it  into  the  bushes, when  a  sudden  thought  seemed  to  strike  him, and  he  hung  it  carefully  on  a  tree. "Can
T2    121: 2  she  couldn't  speak  for  a  minute: it  quite  seemed  to  take  her  breath  away. At  length, as  the  Tiger-lily
A8     67:21  she  had  some  one  to  listen  to  her. The  Cat  seemed  to  think  that  there  was  enough  of  it  now  in  sight, and
A6     46:38                   The  Footman  seemed  to  think  this  a  good  opportunity  for  repeating  his
A12    93:13  of  the  accident, all  except  the  Lizard, who  seemed  too  much  overcome  to  do  anything  but  sit  with  its  mouth
```
SEEMS (13)
```
T4    143:25                    'It  seems  a  shame,' the  Walrus  said, / 'To  play  them  such  a  trick,
A4     27:27             "How  queer  it  seems," Alice  said  to  herself, "to  be  going  messages  for  a
A12    94: 7   it  yet," said  the  White  Rabbit; "but  it  seems  to  be  a  letter, written  by  the  prisoner  to--to  somebody
T6    163:14  the  book  and  looked  at  it  carefully. "That  seems  to  be  done  right--" he  began.
T6    163:18  looked  a  little  queer. As  I  was  saying, that  seems  to  be  done  right--though  I  haven't  time  to  look  it  over
T8    180: 3  peeping  out  from  her  hiding-place. "One  Rule  seems  to  be, that  if  one  Knight  hits  the  other, he  knocks  him
T8    180: 5  he  tumbles  off  himself--and  another  Rule  seems  to  be  that  they  hold  their  clubs  with  their  arms, as  if
T1    118:28  she  couldn't  make  it  out  at  all.) "Somehow  it  seems  to  fill  my  head  with  ideas--only  I  don't  exactly  know
T5    158:19  shop  was  very  dark  towards  the  end. "The  egg  seems  to  get  further  away  the  more  I  walk  towards  it. Let  me
A2     17:12             "How  cheerfully  he  seems  to  grin, / How  neatly  spreads  his  claws, / And  welcomes
A3     26:38  said  to  herself  in  a  melancholy  tone. "Nobody  seems  to  like  her, down  here, and  I'm  sure  she's  the  best  cat
A5     42:31  of  sob, "I've  tried  every  way, but  nothing  seems  to  suit  them!"
T1    118:25             "It  seems  very  pretty," she  said  when  she  had  finished  it, "but
```
SEEN (28)
```
A6     53: 7          Well! I've  often  seen  a  cat  without  a  grin," thought  Alice; "but  a  grin  without
A5     43:12  in  a  tone  of  the  deepest  contempt. "I've  seen  a  good  many  little  girls  in  my  time, but  never  one  with
A1      8: 1  across  her  mind  that  she  had  never  before  seen  a  rabbit  with  either  a  waistcoat-pocket, or  a  watch  to
T8    179: 3  head  in  some  alarm. There  was  no  one  to  be  seen, and  her  first  thought  was  that  she  must  have  been
TC    209:12         / Alice  moving  under  skies / Never  seen  by  waking  eyes.
T7    175:30      "Well, now  that  we  have  seen  each  other," said  the  Unicorn, "if  you'll  believe  in  me,
A4     27: 8  about  for  them, but  they  were  nowhere  to  be  seen--everything  seemed  to  have  changed  since  her  swim  in  the
T1    112:11  looking  about, and  noticed  that  what  could  be  seen  from  the  old  room  was  quite  common  and  uninteresting, but
T2    125: 4  at  all: "though, when  you  say  'garden'--I've  seen  gardens, compared  with  which  this  would  be  a  wilderness
A6     52:24  which  the  March  Hare  was  said  to  live. "I've  seen  hatters  before," she  said  to  herself: "the  March  Hare
T1    115: 3    She  said  afterwards  that  she  had  never  seen  in  all  her  life  such  a  face  as  the  King  made, when  he
A2     19:16  a  thing  before, but  she  remembered  having  seen, in  her  brother's  Latin  Grammar, "A  mouse--of  a  mouse--to
T3    135:19  looked  up, there  was  nothing  whatever  to  be  seen  on  the  twig, and, as  she  was  getting  quite  chilly  with
A1      9:28  corner, but  the  Rabbit  was  no  longer  to  be  seen: she  found  herself  in  a  long, low  hall, which  was  lit  up
T8    188:12  use  so  large  a  fan / That  they  could  not  be  seen. / So, having  no  reply  to  give / To  what  the  old  man  said
T7    169: 5  thought  that  in  all  her  life  she  had  never  seen  soldiers  so  uncertain  on  their  feet: they  were  always
A8     66: 1             Alice  thought  she  had  never  seen  such  a  curious  croquet-ground  in  her  life: it  was  all
T4    147:18      Alice  said  afterwards  she  had  never  seen  such  a  fuss  made  about  anything  in  all  her  life--the  way
T8    181:11  mild  eyes  to  Alice. She  thought  she  had  never  seen  such  a  strange-looking  soldier  in  all  her  life.
A1     12:11  out, for  she  could  not  remember  ever  having  seen  such  a  thing.
A11    90:16             "I'm  glad  I've  seen  that  done," thought  Alice. "I've  so  often  read  in  the
A9     73:11  out  of  breath, and  said  to  Alice  "Have  you  seen  the  Mock  Turtle  yet?"
A10    80:18          "Yes," said  Alice, "I've  often  seen  them  at  dinn----" she  checked  herself  hastily.
A10    80:17  whiting," said  the  Mock  Turtle, "they--you've  seen  them, of  course?"
A10    80:21  be," said  the  Mock  Turtle; "but, if  you've  seen  them  so  often, of  course  you  know  what  they're  like?"
```

SEEN (cont.)
  TI   103: 7   I have not seen thy sunny face, / Nor heard thy silver laughter: / No
  T1   119: 1   back through the Looking-glass, before I've seen what the rest of the house is like! Let's have a look at
  A8   67: 9   whether she could get away without being seen, when she noticed a curious appearance in the air: it
SEIZED (2)
  T4 146:12   sprang out from under the umbrella, and seized her by the wrist.
  T9 204:14   any longer!" she cried, as she jumped up and seized the tablecloth with both hands: one good pull, and
SEIZING (1)
  T9 203: 7   care of yourself!" screamed the White Queen, seizing Alice's hair with both her hands. "Something's going
SELDOM (1)
  A1   12:23   herself very good advice (though she very seldom followed it), and sometimes she scolded herself so
SELFISH (1)
  T4 146:10   "Selfish things!" thought Alice, and she was just going to say
SELL (6)
  T8 188:37   / In the silent night. / And these I do not sell for gold / Or coin of silvery shine, / But for a copper
  A11 88:24   "I keep them to sell," the Hatter added as an explanation. "I've none of my
  T5 158: 4   egg, please," she said timidly. "How do you sell them?"
  T8 188: 4   wheat: / I make them into mutton-pies, / And sell them in the street. / I sell them unto men,' he said, /
  T8 188: 5   / And sell them in the street. / I sell them unto men,' he said, 'Who sail on stormy seas: /
  A5   38: 8   ointment--one shilling the box--/ Allow me to sell you a couple?"
SEND (3)
  T6 160:28   "To send all his horses and all his men," Alice interrupted,
  T7 170:11   King said, referring to his book. "I couldn't send all the horses, you know, because two of them are wanted
  A8   66:16   or a furrow in the way wherever she wanted to send the hedgehog to, and, as the doubled-up soldiers were
SENDING (2)
  A4   27:28   messages for a rabbit! I suppose Dinah'll be sending me on messages next!" And she began fancying the sort
  A2   15: 5   she thought; "and how funny it'll seem, sending presents to one's own feet! And how odd the directions
SENDS (1)
  A4t 27: 1   THE RABBIT SENDS IN A LITTLE BILL
SENSATION (2)
  A3   26:30   This speech caused a remarkable sensation among the party. Some of the birds hurried off at
  A11 88:34   Just at this moment Alice felt a very curious sensation, which puzzled her a good deal until she made out
SENSE (5) [See also NONSENSE]
  A9   71: 1   "and the moral of that is--'Take care of the sense, and the sounds will take care of themselves.'"
  T2 121: 9   Said I to myself, 'Her face has got some sense in it, though it's not a clever one!' Still, you're the
  A6   46:18   "There might be some sense in your knocking," the Footman went on, without
  T6 159:23   looking away from her as usual, "have no more sense than a baby!"
  A4   31:35   what they will do next! If they had any sense, they'd take the roof off." After a minute or two they
SENSIBLE (2)
  T6 166:38   like that," Humpty Dumpty said: "they're not sensible, and they put me out."
  T2 125:15   compared with which that would be as sensible as a dictionary!"
SENT (10)
  T6 166:39   "I sent a message to the fish: / I told them 'This is what I wish
  T6 167: 2   The little fishes of the sea, / They sent an answer back to me.
  T3 131:20   as she's got a head on her--" "She must be sent as a message by the telegraph--" "She must draw the train
  A11 88: 9   but I hadn't quite finished my tea when I was sent for."
  T7 173:24   and he hadn't finished his tea when he was sent in," Haigha whispered to Alice: "and they only give them
  T7 170:13   of them are wanted in the game. And I haven't sent the two Messengers, either. They're both gone to the town
  T7 170: 6   "I've sent them all!" the King cried in a tone of delight, on seeing
  A12 95: 1   He sent them word I had not gone / (We know it to be true): / If
  T1 109: 3   they do at the end of a year? I should be sent to prison, I suppose, when the day came. Or--let me see--
  T6 167: 7   "I sent to them again to say / 'It will be better to obey.'
SENTENCE (9)
  T8 183:19   arm as he spoke, "is to keep--" Here the sentence ended as suddenly as it had begun, as the Knight fell
  A12 97: 2   said Alice loudly. "The idea of having the sentence first!"
  A12 96:30   "No, no!" said the Queen. "Sentence first--verdict afterwards."
  T6 168:40   people I ever met--" She never finished the sentence, for at this moment a heavy crash shook the forest
  A2   19:25   "Ou est ma chatte?" which was the first sentence in her French lesson-book. The Mouse gave a sudden
  A8   65:32   close to her ear, and whispered "She's under sentence of execution."
  A9   73: 9   Queen, and Alice, were in custody and under sentence of execution.
  A8   68:12   with passion. She had already heard her sentence three of the players to be executed for having missed
  T5 152: 3   screaming, so loud that she had to leave the sentence unfinished. "Oh, oh, oh!" shouted the Queen, shaking
SENTENCED (1)
  A9   73: 5   head!" or "Off with her head!" Those whom she sentenced were taken into custody by the soldiers, who of
SERIES (2)
  T5 156:44   caught her under the chin, and, in spite of a series of little shrieks of "Oh, oh, oh!" from poor Alice, it
  A4   32:42   the thistle again: then the puppy began a series of short charges at the stick, running a very little
SERIOUS (2)
  T12 208: 6   who it was that dreamed it all. This is a serious question, my dear, and you should not go on licking
  T4 147:25   he added very gravely, "it's one of the most serious things that can possibly happen to one in a battle--to
SERIOUSLY (3)
  T8 185: 9   kick him, of course," the Knight said, very seriously. "And then he took the helmet off again--but it took
  T1 110: 5   Now, don't smile, my dear. I'm asking it seriously. Because, when we were playing just now, you watched
  A6   50: 4   to turn into a pig, my dear," said Alice, seriously, "I'll have nothing more to do with you. Mind now!"
SERPENT (9)
  A5   43: 4   needs come wriggling down from the sky! Ugh, Serpent!"
  A5   43:24   to me whether you're a little girl or a serpent?"
  A5   43:13   with such a neck as that! No, no! You're a serpent; and there's no use denying it. I suppose you'll be
  A5   42:29   "Serpent, I say again!" repeated the Pigeon, but in a more
  A5   43: 5   "But I'm not a serpent, I tell you!" said Alice. "I'm a--I'm a--"

SERPENT (cont.)
A5   42:28   "I'm not a serpent!" said Alice indignantly. "Let me alone!"
A5   42:27   "Serpent!" screamed the Pigeon.
A5   42:21   bend   about   easily   in any direction, like a serpent. She had just succeeded in curving it down into a
A5   43:20   "but if they do, why, then they're a kind of serpent: that's all I can say."
SERPENTS (3)
A5   43:17   "but little girls eat eggs quite as much as serpents do, you know."
A5   42:39   Pigeon; "but I must be on the look-out for serpents, night and day! Why, I haven't had a wink of sleep
A5   42:35   went on, without attending to her; "but those serpents! There's no pleasing them!"
SERVANT (2)
T9   198: 7   the names. "I'm not a visitor, and I'm not a servant. There ought to be one marked 'Queen,' you know--"
T9   199: 3   to find fault with anybody. "Where's the servant whose business it is to answer the door?" she began
SERVANTS' (1)
T9   198: 4   was marked "Visitors' Bell," and the other "Servants' Bell."
SERVANTS (1)
T3   135: 7   my name, she'd call me 'Miss,' as the servants do."
SERVED (1)
TI   103:15   suns were glowing--/ A simple chime, that served to time / The rhythm of our rowing--/ Whose echoes live
SET (31) [See also UPSET]
T9   200:19   she said. "Put on the joint!" And the waiters set a leg of mutton before Alice, who looked at it rather
A4   32:24   that she had not the smallest idea how to set about it; and, while she was peering about anxiously among
A4   31:31   out, as loud as she could, "If you do, I'll set Dinah at you!"
T1   114: 6   a fit, she hastily picked up the Queen and set her on the table by the side of her noisy little daughter
T1   115:13   she added, as she smoothed his hair, and set him upon the table near the Queen.
T8   188:20   ways, / And when I find a mountain-rill, / I set it in a blaze; / And thence they make a stuff they call /
T8   191: 7   said to herself, as she lifted it off, and set it on her lap to make out what it could possibly be.
T1   110:24   Alice got the Red Queen off the table, and set it up before the kitten as a model for it to imitate:
T8   188:42   'I sometimes dig for buttered rolls, / Or set limed twigs for crabs: / I sometimes search for grassy
T8   180: 7   they make when they tumble! Just like a whole set of fire-irons falling into the fender! And how quiet the
T9   195:27   last Tuesday--I mean one of the last set of Tuesdays, you know."
A12   94:14   added "It isn't a letter, after all: it's a set of verses."
T8   182:23   hair well fastened on?" he continued, as they set off.
A4   33: 4   opportunity for making her escape: so she set off at once, and ran till she was quite tired and out of
T2   123:40   nonsense to Alice, so she said nothing, but set off at once towards the Red Queen. To her surprise she
T2   120:18   turning her back upon the house, she set out once more down the path, determined to keep straight
A7   54: 1   There was a table set out under a tree in front of the house, and the March Hare
T9   202:12   'Bring it here! Let me sup!' / It is easy to set such a dish on the table. / 'Take the dish-cover up!' / Ah
T5   158:16   went off to the other end of the shop, and set the egg upright on a shelf.
A6   50:14   So she set the little creature down, and felt quite relieved to see
A12   95:11   in this affair, / He trusts to you to set them free, / Exactly as we were.
A10   78:22   the Mock Turtle said: "advance twice, set to partners--"
T9   195: 4   be feverish after so much thinking." So they set to work and fanned her with bunches of leaves, till she
A1   13: 5   So she set to work, and very soon finished off the cake. * * * * * *
T7   174:14   allowed for refreshments!" Haigha and Hatta set to work at once, carrying round trays of white and brown
A5   41:43   be lost, as she was shrinking rapidly: so she set to work at once to eat some of the other bit. Her chin was
A7   61: 2   the door that led into the garden. Then she set to work nibbling at the mushroom (she had kept a piece of
A10   78: 4   bone in his throat," said the Gryphon; and it set to work shaking him and punching him in the back. At last
A6   48:10   cauldron of soup off the fire, and at once set to work throwing everything within her reach at the
A5   43:33   the pieces of mushroom in her hands, and she set to work very carefully, nibbling first at one and then at
A12   93:12   had been found and handed back to them, they set to work very diligently to write out a history of the
SETTING (3) [See also UPSETTING]
AI   4: 2   home we steer, a merry crew, / Beneath the setting sun.
A12   98:14   leaning her head on her hand, watching the setting sun, and thinking of little Alice and all her
T8   187:20   blue eyes and kindly smile of the Knight--the setting sun gleaming through his hair, and shining on his
SETTLE (3)
T3   137:18   two finger-posts both pointed along it. "I'll settle it," Alice said to herself, "when the road divides and
T12   208:11   so you ought to know--Oh, Kitty, do help to settle it! I'm sure your paw can wait!" But the provoking
A8   68:34   appeared, she was appealed to by all three to settle the question, and they repeated their arguments to her,
SETTLED (7)
T3   134:22   humming round and round her head: at last it settled again and remarked "I suppose you don't want to lose
T1   108:22   went on, as soon as they were comfortably settled again, "when I saw all the mischief you had been doing
T12   207:33   turn to, I wonder?" she prattled on, as she settled comfortably down, with one elbow on the rug, and her
T8W   14:12   her help him round the tree, but when he got settled down again he only said, as before, "Worrity, worrity!
A5   43:28   then!" said the Pigeon in a sulky tone, as it settled down again into its nest. Alice crouched down among
A11   91:23   turned out, and, by the time they had settled down again, the cook had disappeared.
A8   65:43   up against each other: however, they got settled down in a minute or two, and the game began.
SETTLING (1)
A8   68: 6   The Queen had only one way of settling all difficulties, great or small. "Off with his head!
SEVEN (14)
A8   62:14   "That's none of your business, Two!" said Seven.
T6   162:12   proper assistance, you might have left off at seven."
T5   153: 4   "I'm seven and a half, exactly."
T6   162: 5   asked my advice, I'd have said 'Leave off at seven'--but it's too late now."
A8   62:17   Seven flung down his brush, and had just begun "Well, of all
A2   16:10   four times six is thirteen, and four times seven is--oh dear! I shall never get to twenty at that rate!
A8   62: 7   help it," said Five, in a sulky tone. "Seven jogged my elbow."
A8   62: 9   On which Seven looked up and said "That's right, Five! Always lay the
T4   141: 7   'If seven maids with seven mops / Swept it for half a year, / Do
T4   141: 7   'If seven maids with seven mops / Swept it for half a year, / Do you suppose,' the
A8   63: 5   Five and Seven said nothing, but looked at Two. Two began, in a low

SEVEN (cont.)
```
T7   170:10              "Four thousand two hundred and seven, that's the exact number," the King said, referring to
T6   161:22   Alice made  a  short  calculation, and said "Seven years and six months."
T6   162: 3                        "Seven years and six months!" Humpty Dumpty repeated
```
SEVENTH (1)
```
T2   128:18   this'--however,  we'll  suppose  it said--the Seventh Square is all forest--however, one of the Knights will
```
SEVERAL (13)
```
T8   184:20   said thoughtfully  to  himself. "One or two--several."
T9   203: 4   began:  and she really did rise as she spoke, several inches; but she got hold of the edge of the table, and
T7   169: 7      or  other,  and whenever  one  went down, several more always fell over him, so that the ground was soon
A1   10:21   marked  'poison'  or  not"; for she had read several nice little stories about children who had got burnt,
T1   113: 4   Alice thought to herself,  as  she noticed several of the chessmen down in the hearth among the cinders;
T9   204: 9   There was  not  a moment to be lost. Already several of the guests were lying down in the dishes, and the
T2   122:16            There was silence in a moment, and several of the pink daisies turned white.
A2   20:23   a Duck and a Dodo, a Lory and an Eaglet, and several other curious creatures. Alice led the way, and the
T2   120: 4   going a few yards along the path, and turning several sharp corners), "but I suppose it will at last. But
T7   177: 9   to  being  called  'the  Monster'). "I've cut several slices already, but they always join on again!"
A1    8:31   I think--"  (for,  you see, Alice had learnt several things of this sort in her lessons in the school-room,
T7   170: 9            "Yes, I did," said Alice: "several thousand, I should think."
A5   35: 8   morning, but I think I must have been changed several times since then."
```
SEVERE (2)
```
T2   122:33   think at all,"  the  Rose said, in a rather severe tone.
T9   192: 3   what it is, your Majesty," she went on, in a severe tone (she was always rather fond of scolding herself),
```
SEVERELY (5)
```
T6   166:28   eyes  than most," Humpty Dumpty remarked severely. Alice was silent.
A1   12:24   it), and sometimes she  scolded herself so severely as to bring tears into her eyes; and once she
A6   49: 4                     "I speak severely to my boy, / I beat him when he sneezes; / For he can
A3   26: 1   are not attending!" said the Mouse to Alice, severely. "What are you thinking of?"
A8   63:35    and  looked  at  her,  and  the Queen said, severely, "Who is this?" She said it to the Knave of Hearts,
```
SEVERITY (2)
```
A7   55:10   make  personal remarks," Alice said with some severity: "it's very rude."
T12  207: 3   the  kitten, respectfully,  yet  with some severity. "You woke me out of oh! such a nice dream! And
```
SH (2)
```
A7   59:25   but the Hatter and the March Hare went "Sh! Sh!" and the Dormouse sulkily remarked "If you ca'n't be civil
A7   59:25   but the Hatter and  the  March Hare went "Sh! Sh!" and the Dormouse sulkily remarked "If you ca'n't be
```
SHABBY-LOOKING (1)
```
T6   165:11      for  you). And a 'borogove' is a thin shabby-looking bird with its feathers sticking out all round--
```
SHADE (2)
```
A9   72:44   the Queen's absence, and were resting in the shade: however, the moment they saw her, they hurried back to
T8   181:23   "I didn't  know  it,"  the  Knight said, a shade of vexation passing over his face. "Then all the things
```
SHADING (2)
```
T8   187:25   she took in like a picture, as, with one hand shading her eyes, she leant against a tree, watching the
T7   170:21   was  still  looking  intently along the road, shading her eyes with one hand. "I see somebody now!" she
```
SHADOW (1)
```
TI   103:31                     And, though the shadow of a sigh / May tremble through the story, / For "happy
```
SHADOWS (1)
```
T8   187:24   cropping the grass at her feet--and the black shadows of the forest behind--all this she took in like a
```
SHADY (1)
```
T3   135:38   she reached the wood: it looked very cool and shady. "Well, at any rate it's a great comfort," she said as
```
SHAGGY (1)
```
T8   181:10   easily,"  said  the  Knight, putting back his shaggy hair with both hands, and turning his gentle face and
```
SHAKE (8)
```
A6   48:34   to it as she did so, and giving it a violent shake at the end of every line:--
T4   139:22   thing in a visit is to say 'How d'ye do?' and shake hands!" And here the two brothers gave each other a hug,
T4   139:24   held  out  the  two  hands that were free, to shake hands with her.
T6   160:39   and, to  show  you  I'm not proud, you may shake hands with me!" And he grinned almost from ear to ear,
T8   181: 8   manage by himself: however, she managed to shake him out of it at last.
T5   152: 4   shaking her hand  about as if she wanted to shake it off. "My finger's bleeding! Oh, oh, oh, oh!"
T9   204:27   which had just lighted upon the table, "I'll shake you into a kitten, that I will!"
T6   168:23    tone, giving her one of his fingers to shake: "you're so exactly like other people."
```
SHAKESPEARE (1)
```
A3   23:19   (the position  in  which you  usually see Shakespeare, in the pictures of him), while the rest waited in
```
SHAKING (9)
```
T10t 205: 1                              SHAKING
A5   42:16   no result  seemed to follow, except a little shaking among the distant green leaves.
T4   139:25            Alice did not like shaking hands with either of them first, for fear of hurting
T5   152: 4   unfinished. "Oh, oh, oh!" shouted the Queen, shaking her hand about as if she wanted to shake it off. "My
T10  205: 5   large and green: and still, as Alice went on shaking her, she kept on growing shorter--and fatter--and
A10  78: 4   throat," said the Gryphon; and it set to work shaking him and punching him in the back. At last the Mock
T7   172:31   whisper?" cried the poor King, jumping up and shaking himself. "If you do such a thing again, I'll have you
A7   55:37   his pocket,  and was looking at it uneasily, shaking it every now and then, and holding it to his ear.
T7   176:18   at  the crown, which the poor King was nearly shaking off his head, he trembled so much.
```
SHALL (50)
```
A2   14: 7   you now, dears? I'm sure I sha'n't be able! I shall be a great deal too far off to trouble myself about you:
T9   192: 9   a Queen," she said as she sat down again, "I shall be able to manage it quite well in time."
T1   112: 5      as  the  one  she  had  left behind. "So I shall be as warm here as I was in the old room," thought Alice
A2   19: 8   swam about, trying to find her way out. "I shall be punished for it now, I suppose, by being drowned in
T2   128:20   show you the way--and in the Eighth Square we shall be Queens together, and it's all feasting and fun!"
A1    7:13   the Rabbit say to itself "Oh dear! Oh dear! I shall be too late!" (when she thought it over afterwards it
T2   120:21   on well,  and  she was just saying "I really shall do it this time--" when the path gave a sudden twist and
```

SHALL (cont.)
A3   26: 8   "I shall do nothing of the sort," said the Mouse, getting up and
T3   130:16   "I shall dream about a thousand pounds to-night, I know I shall!"
A3   26:40   the world! Oh, my dear Dinah! I wonder if I shall ever see you any more!" And here poor Alice began to cry
A1   8:39   Presently she began again. "I wonder if I shall fall right through the earth! How funny it'll seem to
TI   103: 9   heard thy silver laughter: / No thought of me shall find a place / In thy young life's hereafter--/ Enough
T9   201:11   please," Alice said rather hastily, "or we shall get no dinner at all. May I give you some?"
A11   90:28   the guinea-pigs!" thought Alice. "Now we shall get on better."
T2   127:36   putting in a peg to mark the distance, "I shall give you your directions--have another biscuit?"
T2   128: 3   shall say good-bye. And at the end of five, I shall go!"
T12 208: 2   me, all about fishes! To-morrow morning you shall have a real treat. All the time you're eating your
A7   55:13   "Come, we shall have some fun now!" thought Alice. "I'm glad they've
A8   67:12   said to herself "It's the Cheshire-Cat: now I shall have somebody to talk to."
A1   8:43   didn't sound at all the right word) "--but I shall have to ask them what the name of the country is, you
A2   17:18   went on, "I must be Mabel after all, and I shall have to go and live in that poky little house, and have
T1   118:32   jumping up, "if I don't make haste, I shall have to go back through the Looking-glass, before I've
TI   103:29   nest of gladness. / The magic words shall hold thee fast: / Thou shalt not heed the raving blast.
A12   94:33   White Rabbit put on his spectacles. "Where shall I begin, please your Majesty?" he asked.
A4   29: 9   "But then," thought Alice, "shall I never get any older than I am now? That'll be a
T4   140:12   "What shall I repeat to her?" said Tweedledee, looking round at
A9   71: 7   doubtful about the temper of your flamingo. Shall I try the experiment'"
TC   209:15   hear, / Eager eye and willing ear, / Lovingly shall nestle near.
A2   16:10   thirteen, and four times seven is--oh dear! I shall never get to twenty at that rate! However, the
T1   115:25   horror of that moment," the King went on, "I shall never, never forget!"
TI   103:35   gone by, / And vanish'd summer glory--/ It shall not touch, with breath of bale, / The pleasance of our
T5   152:11   pricked it yet," the Queen said, "but I soon shall--oh, oh, oh!"
A2   17:22   down and saying 'Come up again, dear!' I shall only look up and say 'Who am I, then? Tell me that first
A9   70:19   you just now what the moral of that is, but I shall remember it in a bit."
T2   128: 2   but went on. "At the end of three yards I shall repeat them--for fear of your forgetting them. At the
T2   128: 3   your forgetting them. At the end of four, I shall say good-bye. And at the end of five, I shall go!"
T3   129:22   be when they ask me how I liked my walk. I shall say 'Oh, I liked it well enough--' (here came the
A1   9: 3   asking! No, it'll never do to ask: perhaps I shall see it written up somewhere."
T5   153:21   it!" she cried in a triumphant tone. "Now you shall see me pin it on again, all by myself!"
T9   201:37   riddle--all in poetry--all about fishes. Shall she repeat it?"
A10   79: 6   can do it without lobsters, you know. Which shall sing?"
A6   46:39   for repeating his remark, with variations. "I shall sit here," he said, "on and off, for days and days."
A6   46:26   "I shall sit here," the Footman remarked, "till to-morrow--"
TI   103:21   of dread, / With bitter tidings laden, / Shall summon to unwelcome bed / A melancholy maiden! / We are
A9   73:16   "Come on, then," said the Queen, "and he shall tell you his history."
A7   58:23   "Then the Dormouse shall!" they both cried. "Wake up, Dormouse!" And they pinched
A1   8:24   to herself. "After such a fall as this, I shall think nothing of tumbling down-stairs! How brave they'll
T3   130:17   about a thousand pounds to-night, I know I shall!" thought Alice.
T4   144: 9   Carpenter, / 'You've had a pleasant run! / Shall we be trotting home again?' / But answer came there none
A10   84: 8   "Shall we try another figure of the Lobster-Quadrille?" the
SHALT (1)
TI   103:30   The magic words shall hold thee fast: / Thou shalt not heed the raving blast.
SHAME (1)
T4   143:25   'It seems a shame,' the Walrus said, / 'To play them such a trick, / After
SHA'N'T (8)
T3   131:26   "Indeed I sha'n't!" Alice said rather impatiently. "I don't belong to
A2   14: 7   and stockings for you now, dears? I'm sure I sha'n't be able! I shall be a great deal too far off to
A8   65:12   "You sha'n't be beheaded!" said Alice, and she put them into a
T8   190:17   look in the direction to which he pointed. "I sha'n't be long. You'll wait and wave your handkerchief when I
A12   93:41   "Well, I sha'n't go, at any rate," said Alice; "besides, that's not a
A4   28:13   to herself "That's quite enough--I hope I sha'n't grow any more--As it is, I ca'n't get out at the door
A11   91:10   "Sha'n't," said the cook.
A4   30:32   fancy--Who's to go down the chimney?--Nay, I sha'n't! You do it!--That I wo'n't, then!--Bill's got to go
SHAPE (8)
T6   160:10   too. With a name like yours, you might be any shape, almost."
T2   123:11   "Well, she has the same awkward shape as you," the Rose said: "but she's redder--and her
A3   23: 9   race-course, in a sort of circle, ("the exact shape doesn't matter," it said,) and then all the party were
T6   160: 9   said with a short laugh: "my name means the shape I am--and a good handsome shape it is, too. With a name
T6   160: 9   means the shape I am--and a good handsome shape it is, too. With a name like yours, you might be any
T8   179:33   hung from the saddle, and was something the shape of a horse's head) and put it on.
T7   172:26   putting his hands to his mouth in the shape of a trumpet and stooping so as to get close to the
T8W   20: 5   with an expression of admiration: "it's the shape of your head as does it. Your jaws aint well shaped,
SHAPED (3) [See also QUEER-SHAPED]
A6   53:12   be the right house, because the chimneys were shaped like ears and the roof was thatched with fur. It was so
A8   63:15   ten soldiers carrying clubs: these were all shaped like the three gardeners, oblong and flat, with their
T8W   20: 6   of your head as does it. Your jaws aint well shaped, though--I should think you couldn't bite well?"
SHARE (1)
A10   83:17   and meat, / While the Owl had the dish as its share of the treat. / When the pie was all finished, the Owl,
SHARED (1)
A12   98:27   the teacups as the March Hare and his friends shared their never-ending meal, and the shrill voice of the
SHARING (1)
A10   83:15   one eye, / How the Owl and the Panther were sharing a pie: / The Panther took pie-crust, and gravy, and
SHARK (1)
A10   82:27   / And will talk in contemptuous tones of the Shark: / But, when the tide rises and sharks are around, / His
SHARKS (2)
A10   82:28   of the Shark: / But, when the tide rises and sharks are around, / His voice has a timid and tremulous sound

SHARKS (cont.)
  T8   182: 9   "To guard against the bites of sharks," the Knight replied. "It's an invention of my own. And
SHARP (9)
  A4   32:25   about anxiously among the trees, a little sharp bark just over her head made her look up in a great
  A9   70:28   Alice's shoulder, and it was an uncomfortably sharp chin. However, she did not like to be rude: so she bore
  T3   137:30   to herself as she went, till, on turning a sharp corner, she came upon two fat little men, so suddenly
  T2   120: 4   few yards along the path, and turning several sharp corners), "but I suppose it will at last. But how
  A5   42:24   under which she had been wandering, when a sharp hiss made her draw back in a hurry: a large pigeon had
  A4   31: 3   to herself "This is Bill", she gave one sharp kick, and waited to see what would happen next.
  A9   72:24   the Duchess asked, with another dig of her sharp little chin.
  A9   70:37   same thing," said the Duchess, digging her sharp little chin into Alice's shoulder as she added "and the
  T4   148:15   "but you can have the umbrella--it's quite as sharp. Only we must begin quick. It's getting as dark as it
SHARPER (1)
  T6   166:27   can see whether I'm singing or not, you've sharper eyes than most," Humpty Dumpty remarked severely.
SHARPLY (5)
  A3   26: 5   "I had not!" cried the Mouse, sharply and very angrily.
  A11   89:17   twinkling begins with a T!" said the King sharply. "Do you take me for a dunce? Go on!"
  A9   72:25   "I've a right to think," said Alice sharply, for she was beginning to feel a little worried.
  A1   12:22   like that!" said Alice to herself rather sharply. "I advise you to leave off this minute!" She
  T9   192:18   "Speak when you're spoken to!" the Queen sharply interrupted her.
SHAVED (1)
  T8W   18:15   my head: / And then they said 'You should be shaved, / And wear a yellow wig instead.'
SHAWL (9)
  T5   149: 4   Alice very civilly went to meet her with the shawl.
  T5   153:18   and a sudden gust of wind blew the Queen's shawl across a little brook. The Queen spread out her arms
  T5   149: 6   Alice said, as she helped her to put on her shawl again.
  T5   153:16   things before breakfast. There goes the shawl again!"
  T5   152:14   "When I fasten my shawl again," the poor Queen groaned out: "the brooch will
  T5   149: 1   She caught the shawl as she spoke, and looked about for the owner: in another
  T4   145:28   a hurricane in the wood--here's somebody's shawl being blown away!"
  T5   149:24   "and she's all over pins!--May I put your shawl straight for you?" she added aloud.
  T9   204:21   merrily running round and round after her own shawl, which was trailing behind her.
SHE (1098) [entries omitted]
SHE'D (4)
  T2   121:12   "If only her petals curled up a little more, she'd be all right."
  T3   135: 7   for that. If she couldn't remember my name, she'd call me 'Miss,' as the servants do."
  A8   69: 3   wasn't done about it in less than no time, she'd have everybody executed, all round. (It was this last
  A3   26:23   aloud, addressing nobody in particular. "She'd soon fetch it back!"
SHED (1)
  T4   141:12   / 'I doubt it,' said the Carpenter, / And shed a bitter tear.
SHEDDING (1)
  A2   15:22   I tell you!" But she went on all the same, shedding gallons of tears, until there was a large pool round
SHEEP (21)
  T5   158: 9   must eat them both, if you buy two," said the Sheep.
  T5   156:19   and for a while Alice forgot all about the Sheep and the knitting, as she bent over the side of the boat,
  T5   155:21   "Feather!" cried the Sheep, as she took up another pair of needles.
  T5   155:14   "Can you row?" the Sheep asked, handing her a pair of knitting-needles as she
  T5   154: 6   and on both sides, if you like," said the Sheep; "but you ca'n't look all round you--unless you've got
  T5   155:27   "Feather! Feather!" the Sheep cried again, taking more needles. "You'll be catching a
  T5   155:30   "Didn't you hear me say 'Feather'?" the Sheep cried angrily, taking up quite a bunch of needles.
  T5   156:13   "How am I to stop it?" said the Sheep. "If you leave off rowing, it'll stop of itself."
  T5   157: 9   a little crab to take home with me!" But the Sheep only laughed scornfully, and went on with her knitting.
  T5   157:12   "Crabs, and all sorts of things," said the Sheep: "plenty of choice, only make up your mind. Now, what do
  T5   158: 5   farthing for one--twopence for two," the Sheep replied.
  T5   155: 7   "Are you a child or a teetotum?" the Sheep said, as she took up another pair of needles. "You'll
  T5   154: 1   "What is it you want to buy?" the Sheep said at last, looking up for a moment from her knitting
  T5   156: 8   needn't say 'please' to me about 'em," the Sheep said, without looking up from her knitting: "I didn't
  T5   153:38   the counter, and opposite to her was an old Sheep, sitting in an arm-chair, knitting, and every now and
  T5   155:34   "In the water, of course!" said the Sheep, sticking some of the needles into her hair, as her
  T5   153:30   last word ended in a long bleat, so like a sheep that Alice quite started.
  T5   153:35   a shop? And was that really--was it really a sheep that was sitting on the other side of the counter? Rub
  T5   158:13   The Sheep took the money, and put it away in a box: then she said
  T5   157: 2   wasn't a bit hurt, and was soon up again: the Sheep went on with her knitting all the while, just as if
  T5   155:38   "You are," said the Sheep: "you're a little goose."
SHEEP-BELLS (1)
  A12   98:38   the rattling teacups would change to tinkling sheep-bells, and the Queen's shrill cries to the voice of the
SHELF (6)
  T5   158:16   end of the shop, and set the egg upright on a shelf.
  T6   168: 8   I took a corkscrew from the shelf: / I went to wake them up myself.
  T5   154:19   like a work-box, and was always in the shelf next above the one she was looking at. "And this one is
  T5   155: 3   her. "I'll follow it up to the very top shelf of all. It'll puzzle it to go through the ceiling, I
  T5   154:13   all was that, whenever she looked hard at any shelf, to make out exactly what it had on it, that particular
  T5   154:13   exactly what it had on it, that particular shelf was always quite empty, though the others round it were
SHE'LL (6)
  T9   196:30   is! Pat her on the head, and see how pleased she'll be!" But this was more than Alice had courage to do.
  T9   195: 3   head!" the Red Queen anxiously interrupted. "She'll be feverish after so much thinking." So they set to
  A3   26:29   wish you could see her after the birds! Why, she'll eat a little bird as soon as look at it!"
  A4   27: 4   Oh my dear paws! Oh my fur and whiskers! She'll get me executed, as sure as ferrets are ferrets! Where
  T3   131: 8   should all speak in turn, he went on with "She'll have to go back from here as luggage!"
  A1   9: 2   manage it?) "And what an ignorant little girl she'll think me for asking! No, it'll never do to ask: perhaps

-SHELLS [See OYSTER-SHELLS]
SHELVES (2) [See also BOOK-SHELVES]
    T5   154: 9 herself with turning round, looking at the shelves as she came to them.
    A1   8:18 pegs. She took down a jar from one of the shelves as she passed: it was labeled "ORANGE MARMALADE," but
SHEPHERD-BOY (1)
    A12   98:39 the Queen's shrill cries to the voice of the shepherd-boy--and the sneeze of the baby, the shriek of the
SHE'S (21)
    T7   175: 6 make a memorandum about her, if you like--She's a dear good creature," he repeated softly to himself, as
    T5   149:23 crooked," Alice thought to herself, "and she's all over pins!--May I put your shawl straight for you?"
    T9   195: 7   "She's all right again now," said the Red Queen. "Do you know
    T2   123:26   "She's coming!" cried the Larkspur. "I hear her footstep, thump
    T3   131: 1 in white paper), "ought to know which way she's going, even if she doesn't know her own name!"
    T3   131:20   Alice), saying "She must go by post, as she's got a head on her--" "She must be sent as a message by
    T2   123:29 eagerly and found that it was the Red Queen. "She's grown a good deal!" was her first remark. She had indeed
    A8   69: 8   "She's in prison," the Queen said to the executioner: "fetch
    T9   193:10   "She's in that state of mind," said the White Queen, "that she
    T7   177:20   "She's kept none for herself, anyhow," said the Lion. "Do you
    T2   123: 7 always wondering," said the Tiger-lily), "but she's more bushy than you are."
    T8   179:28   "She's my prisoner, you know!" the Red Knight said at last.
    T2   123:20 daresay you'll see her soon," said the Rose. "She's one of the kind that has nine spikes, you know."
    T2   123:12 awkward shape as you," the Rose said: "but she's redder--and her petals are shorter, I think."
    A2   16: 7 oh, she knows such a very little! Besides, she's she, and I'm I, and--oh dear, how puzzling it all is!
    A8   67:32   "Not at all," said Alice: "she's so extremely--" Just then she noticed that the Queen was
    A2   19:38 she is such a nice soft thing to nurse--and she's such a capital one for catching mice--oh, I beg your
    A3   26:27 to talk about her pet: "Dinah's our cat. And she's such a capital one for catching mice, you ca'n't think!
    A3   26:39 seems to like her, down here, and I'm sure she's the best cat in the world! Oh, my dear Dinah! I wonder
    T9   196:36   "She's tired, poor thing!" said the Red Queen. "Smoothe her
    A8   65:31 his mouth close to her ear, and whispered "She's under sentence of execution."
SHIFTING (1)
    A11   88:30 seem to encourage the witness at all: he kept shifting from one foot to the other, looking uneasily at the
SHILLING (1)
    A5   38: 7 supple / By the use of this ointment--one shilling the box--/ Allow me to sell you a couple?"
SHILLINGS (1)
    A11   88:19 then added them up, and reduced the answer to shillings and pence.
SHINE (1)
    T8   188:38 I do not sell for gold / Or coin of silvery shine, / But for a copper halfpenny, / And that will purchase
SHINGLE (1)
    A10   79:16 all advance! / They are waiting on the shingle--will you come and join the dance? / Will you, wo'n't
SHINING (6)
    T4   140:18   "The sun was shining--"
    T8   187:21 setting sun gleaming through his hair, and shining on his armour in a blaze of light that quite dazzled
    T4   140:23   "The sun was shining on the sea, / Shining with all his might: / He did his
    T4   140:29   The moon was shining sulkily, / Because she thought the sun / Had got no
    A2   17: 9 "How doth the little crocodile / Improve his shining tail, / And pour the waters of the Nile / On every
    T4   140:24   "The sun was shining on the sea, / Shining with all his might: / He did his very best to make /
SHINY (1)
    A10   81:18 said the Gryphon. "I mean, what makes them so shiny?"
SHIPS (1)
    T4   142:21 / 'To talk of many things: / Of shoes--and ships--and sealing wax--/ Of cabbages--and kings--/ And why
SHIVER (1)
    A3   22: 7   "Ugh!" said the Lory, with a shiver.
SHIVERING (1)
    T8W   13: 7 against a tree, all huddled up together, and shivering as if he were very cold.
SHOCK (1)
    A12   93:10 as the jury had a little recovered from the shock of being upset, and their slates and pencils had been
SHOE (1)
    T8   189:18 squeeze a right-hand foot / Into a left-hand shoe, / Or if I drop upon my toe / A very heavy weight, / I
SHOES (9)
    A11   89: 8 trembled so, that he shook off both his shoes.
    T4   142:21 Walrus said, / 'To talk of many things: / Of shoes--and ships--and sealing wax--/ Of cabbages--and kings--/
    A2   14: 6 little feet, I wonder who will put on your shoes and stockings for you now, dears? I'm sure I sha'n't be
    A10   81:17   "Why, what are your shoes done with?" said the Gryphon. "I mean, what makes them
    A11   90:32 the court, without even waiting to put his shoes on.
    A10   81:15 was thoroughly puzzled. "Does the boots and shoes!" she repeated in a wondering tone.
    A10   81:13   "It does the boots and shoes," the Gryphon replied very solemnly.
    A10   81:21   "Boots and shoes under the sea," the Gryphon went on in a deep voice,
    T4   142: 4 were brushed, their faces washed, / Their shoes were clean and neat--/ And this was odd, because, you
SHOOK (22)
    T8   190:24   So they shook hands, and then the Knight rode slowly away into the
    T8   180:13 side by side. When they got up again, they shook hands, and then the Red Knight mounted and galloped off.
    T10   205: 1 She took her off the table as she spoke, and shook her backwards and forwards with all her might.
    T8   181:29   Alice shook her head.
    T2   125:13   The Red Queen shook her head. "You may call it 'nonsense' if you like," she
    T8   188:29 day to day / Getting a little fatter. / I shook him well from side to side, / Until his face was blue: /
    A5   38: 5 "In my youth," said the sage, as he shook his grey locks, / "I kept all my limbs very supple / By
    T8   185:13   The Knight shook his head. "It was all kinds of fastness with me, I can
    A7   57:10   The Hatter shook his head mournfully. "Not I!" he replied. "We quarreled
    A12   95:36   The Knave shook his head sadly. "Do I look like it?" he said. (Which he
    T4   140:22 / The eldest Oyster winked his eye, / And shook his heavy head--/ Meaning to say he did not choose / To
    T8W   13:21   The Wasp only shook his shoulders, and turned his head away. "Ah, deary me!"

SHOOK (cont.)
A3   26:15   chorus "Yes, please do!" But the Mouse only shook its head impatiently, and walked a little quicker.
A7   56:24   "The Dormouse shook its head impatiently, and said, without opening its eyes
A7   58: 1   Here the Dormouse shook itself, and began singing in its sleep "Twinkle, twinkle
T2   120:22   time--" when the path gave a sudden twist and shook itself (as she described it afterwards), and the next
T3   137: 6   Fawn gave a sudden bound into the air, and shook itself free from Alice's arm. "I'm a Fawn!" it cried out
A5   41:25   of its mouth, and yawned once or twice, and shook itself. Then it got down off the mushroom, and crawled
A11   89: 7   the wretched Hatter trembled so, that he shook off both his shoes.
T1   115: 7   and rounder and rounder, till her hand shook so with laughter that she nearly let him drop upon the
T6   168:41   sentence, for at this moment a heavy crash shook the forest from end to end.
A4   29:22   to look for her, and she trembled till she shook the house, quite forgetting that she was now about a
SHOP (7)
T5   158: 2   and she was back again in the little dark shop.
T5   158:16   saying, she went off to the other end of the shop, and set the egg upright on a shelf.
T5   153:34   out what had happened at all. Was she in a shop? And was that really--was it really a sheep that was
T5   158:22   little brook! Well, this is the very queerest shop I ever saw!" * * * * * * * * * * * * * * So she went on,
T5   153:37   nothing more of it: she was in a little dark shop, leaning with her elbows on the counter, and opposite to
T5   154:11   The shop seemed to be full of all manner of curious things--but
T5   158:18   her way among the tables and chairs, for the shop was very dark towards the end. "The egg seems to get
SHORE (4) [See also SEA-SHORE]
A2   20:25   led the way, and the whole party swam to the shore.
T4   142:12   the frothy waves, / And scrambling to the shore.
A2   20:19   in a low trembling voice, "Let us get to the shore, and then I'll tell you my history, and you'll
A10   80: 8   his scaly friend replied. / "There is another shore, you know, upon the other side. / The further off from
SHORT (9)
T6   161:22   Alice made a short calculation, and said "Seven years and six months."
A4   32:43   again: then the puppy began a series of short charges at the stick, running a very little way forwards
T6   166: 4   'mome' I'm not certain about. I think it's short for 'from home'--meaning that they'd lost their way, you
T6   160: 8   Of course it must," Humpty Dumpty said with a short laugh: "my name means the shape I am--and a good
A5   36:12   at the Caterpillar's making such very short remarks, and she drew herself up and said, very gravely,
T8   184:21   There was a short silence after this, and then the Knight went on again.
A3   24: 3   thimble"; and, when it had finished this short speech, they all cheered.
T8W   21: 1   "Well, that's because your jaws are too short," the Wasp went on: "but the top of your head is nice
A8   66:22   and fighting for the hedgehogs; and in a very short time the Queen was in a furious passion, and went
SHORTER (4)
A5   41:28   taller, and the other side will make you grow shorter."
T10   205: 5   went on shaking her, she kept on growing shorter--and fatter--and softer--and rounder--and--
T2   123:12   said: "but she's redder--and her petals are shorter, I think."
A5   43:35   and growing sometimes taller, and sometimes shorter, until she had succeeded in bringing herself down to
SHOULD (63)
T2   123:38   ca'n't possibly do that," said the Rose: "I should advise you to walk the other way."
A8   63: 8   and, if the Queen was to find out, we should all have our heads cut off, you know. So you see, Miss,
T3   131: 8   and, as the rule seemed to be that they should all speak in turn, he went on with "She'll have to go
T9   192: 1   is grand!" said Alice. "I never expected I should be a Queen so soon--and I'll tell you what it is, your
T9   195:38   "But they should be five times as cold, by the same rule--"
A5   43: 3   to a shriek, "and just as I was thinking I should be free of them at last, they must needs come wriggling
A1   12: 9   altogether, like a candle. I wonder what I should be like then?" And she tried to fancy what the flame of
A6   53:17   rather timidly, saying to herself "Suppose it should be raving mad after all! I almost wish I'd gone to see
T1   109: 3   "What would they do at the end of a year? I should be sent to prison, I suppose, when the day came. Or--
T8W   18:15   on my head: / And then they said 'You should be shaved, / And wear a yellow wig instead.'
T9   201:15   However, she didn't see why the Red Queen should be the only one to give orders; so, as an experiment,
A12   95: 9   If I or she should chance to be / Involved in this affair, / He trusts to
A11   86:32   Gryphon whispered in reply, "for fear they should forget them before the end of the trial."
A5   44: 3   never do to come upon them this size: why, I should frighten them out of their wits!" So she began nibbling
T8   181:30   hopes some bees may make a nest in it--then I should get the honey."
T5   149:36   altering most of the pins. "But really you should have a lady's maid!"
T3   130: 6   "Don't make excuses," said the Guard: "you should have bought one from the engine-driver." And once more
A8   67:29   about at the other end of the ground--and I should have croqueted the Queen's hedgehog just now, only it
A4   33: 9   and fanned herself with one of the leaves. "I should have liked teaching it tricks very much, if--if I'd
T9   193: 2   "That's just what I complain of! You should have meant! What do you suppose is the use of a child
T6   162:17   on second thoughts, "a beautiful cravat, I should have said--no, a belt, I mean--I beg your pardon!" she
T2   128:16   "You should have said," the Queen went on in a tone of grave
T9   193: 4   of a child without any meaning? Even a joke should have some meaning--and a child's more important than a
T2   120:15   her. "I'm not going in again yet. I know I should have to get through the Looking-glass again--back into
T1   109: 6   dinner: then, when the miserable day came, I should have to go without fifty dinners at once! Well, I
A8   64: 3   "How should I know?" said Alice, surprised at her own courage.
A7   56:14   "Why should it?" muttered the Hatter. "Does your watch tell you
A7   55: 9   "You should learn not to make personal remarks," Alice said with
A6   52: 4   "I should like it very much," said Alice, "but I haven't been
T5   155:29   "A dear little crab!" thought Alice. "I should like that."
A5   41:14   "Well, I should like to be a little larger, Sir, if you wouldn't mind,"
T2   126: 4   if only I might join--though of course I should like to be a Queen, best."
T5   158: 3   "I should like to buy an egg, please," she said timidly. "How do
A10   83: 2   "I should like to have it explained," said the Mock Turtle.
A10   82:12   the Mock Turtle repeated thoughtfully. "I should like to hear her try and repeat something now. Tell her
T8   182:31   "I should like to hear it, very much."
T4   145:13   a sort of thing in his dream, what are you, I should like to know?"
T5   154: 3   quite know yet," Alice said very gently. "I should like to look all round me first, if I might."
A2   20: 4   is such a nice little dog, near our house, I should like to show you! A little bright-eyed terrier, you
A4   27:24   and hurried upstairs, in great fear lest she should meet the real Mary Ann, and be turned out of the house

SHOULD (cont.)
T9   200:12   without waiting to be asked," she thought: "I should never have known who were the right people to invite!"
T12   208: 6   This is a serious question, my dear, and you should not go on licking your paw like that--as if Dinah
A12   96: 1   be true'--that's the jury, of course--'If she should push the matter on'--that must be the Queen--'What
A12   95: 3   not gone / (We know it to be true): / If she should push the matter on, / What would become of you?
A7   55:19   "Then you should say what you mean," the March Hare went on.
A10   81:34   to me, and told me he was going a journey, I should say 'With what porpoise?'"
T6   164: 9   "Ah, you should see 'em come round me of a Saturday night," Humpty
T2   120: 1   "I should see the garden far better," said Alice to herself, "if
T5   157: 9   the dark water. "I wish it hadn't let go--I should so like a little crab to take home with me!" But the
T7   170: 9   Yes, I did," said Alice: "several thousand, I should think."
T8W   13:18   "It's rheumatism, I should think," Alice said to herself, and she stooped over him
T2   128: 9   through the Third Square--by railway, I should think--and you'll find yourself in the Fourth Square in
A1   9: 7   "Dinah'll miss me very much to-night, I should think!" (Dinah was the cat.) "I hope they'll remember
A12   93: 8   it signifies much," she said to herself; "I should think it would be quite as much use in the trial one
T4   148: 4   "You must hit the trees pretty often, I should think," she said.
T7   172:11   "I should think throwing cold water over you would be better,"
A2   19:11   is so out-of-the-way down here, that I should think very likely it can talk: at any rate, there's no
A7   60: 7   out of a water-well," said the Hatter; "so I should think you could draw treacle out of a treacle-well--eh,
T8W   20: 7   it. Your jaws aint well shaped, though--I should think you couldn't bite well?"
A5   36: 4   know--and then after that into a butterfly, I should think you'll feel it a little queer, wo'n't you?"
T9   196:17   Alice thought to herself "I never should try to remember my name in the middle of an accident!
A9   72:11   "I think I should understand that better," Alice said very politely, "if
T7   176:19   "I should win easy," said the Lion.
SHOULDER (9)
T1   115:32   of the pencil, which came some way over his shoulder, and began writing for him.
A9   70:27   the right height to rest her chin on Alice's shoulder, and it was an uncomfortably sharp chin. However, she
T9   197:14   and then the other, rolled down from her shoulder, and lay like a heavy lump in her lap. "I don't think
A8   65:30   hurried tone. He looked anxiously over his shoulder as he spoke, and then raised himself upon tiptoe, put
A9   70:37   digging her sharp little chin into Alice's shoulder as she added "and the moral of that is--'Take care of
T12   207:26   my pet!" she went on, looking over her shoulder at the White Kitten, which was still patiently
T9   196:35   a deep sigh, and laid her head on Alice's shoulder. "I am so sleepy!" she moaned.
T9   197: 9   as she put her head down on Alice's other shoulder, "just sing it through to me. I'm getting sleepy, too
A7   56:11   Alice had been looking over his shoulder with some curiosity. "What a funny watch!" she
SHOULDERS (6)
T8W   13:21   The Wasp only shook his shoulders, and turned his head away. "Ah, deary me!" he said
A5   42:14   stuff be?" said Alice. "And where have my shoulders got to? And oh, my poor hands, how is it I ca'n't
A1   10: 8   "it would be of very little use without my shoulders. Oh, how I wish I could shut up like a telescope! I
A11   86:37   as well as if she were looking over their shoulders, that all the jurors were writing down "Stupid
T8   181:15   little deal box fastened across his shoulders, upside-down, and with the lid hanging open. Alice
A5   42: 9   in another moment, when she found that her shoulders were nowhere to be found: all she could see, when
SHOULDN'T (18)
T4   145:12   "I shouldn't!" Alice exclaimed indignantly. "Besides, if I'm only
T4   145:25   her tears, it all seemed so ridiculous--"I shouldn't be able to cry."
A7   57: 6   said Alice thoughtfully; "but then--I shouldn't be hungry for it, you know."
T9   199:18   "Shouldn't do that--shouldn't do that--" the Frog muttered.
T9   199:18   "Shouldn't do that--shouldn't do that--" the Frog muttered. "Wexes it, you know."
T4   148:11   "I shouldn't have minded it so much," said Tweedledum, "if it
A7   56: 6   got in as well," the Hatter grumbled: "you shouldn't have put it in with the bread-knife."
T7   175:13   the King replied, rather nervously. "You shouldn't have run him through with your horn, you know."
T6   168:21   "I shouldn't know you again if we did meet," Humpty Dumpty
A4   29:11   then--always to have lessons to learn! Oh, I shouldn't like that!"
T3   135:29   what'll become of my name when I go in? I shouldn't like to lose it at all--because they'd have to give
T3   135:15   "You shouldn't make jokes," Alice said, "if it makes you so unhappy
T1   109: 7   to go without fifty dinners at once! Well, I shouldn't mind that much! I'd far rather go without them than
T12   207: 1   "Your Red Majesty shouldn't purr so loud," Alice said, rubbing her eyes, and
T9   194:12   it would come to bite me--and I'm sure I shouldn't remain!"
T2   125:10   "No, I shouldn't," said Alice, surprised into contradicting her at
A7   60:28   "Then you shouldn't talk," said the Hatter.
A5   43:26   for eggs, as it happens; and, if I was, I shouldn't want yours: I don't like them raw."
SHOUT (2)
T4   139:19   though she felt quite certain he would only shout out "Contrariwise!" and so he did.
T6   168: 5   very stiff and proud: / He said, 'You needn't shout so loud!'
SHOUTED (13)
A8   65:22   "Yes!" shouted Alice.
A12   97: 5   "Off with her head!" the Queen shouted at the top of her voice. Nobody moved.
T7   172:28   However, instead of whispering, he simply shouted, at the top of his voice, "They're at it again!"
T6   167:22   I said it very loud and clear: / I went and shouted in his ear."
A8   65:18   if it please your Majesty!" the soldiers shouted in reply.
A4   32: 3   put a stop to this," she said to herself, and shouted out "You'd better not do that again!", which produced
A10   78:28   "The lobsters!" shouted the Gryphon, with a bound into the air.
A8   65:16   "Are their heads off?" shouted the Queen.
A8   65:19   "That's right!" shouted the Queen. "Can you play croquet?"
A8   65:41   "Get to your places!" shouted the Queen in a voice of thunder, and people began
T5   152: 3   leave the sentence unfinished. "Oh, oh, oh!" shouted the Queen, shaking her hand about as if she wanted to
A9   72:36   "Now, I give you fair warning," shouted the Queen, stamping on the ground as she spoke.
T4   145:16   He shouted this so loud that Alice couldn't help saying "Hush!
SHOUTING (5)
T8   179:12   her thoughts were interrupted by a loud shouting of "Ahoy! Ahoy! Check!" and a Knight, dressed in
A8   67: 1   furious passion, and went stamping about, and shouting "Off with his head!" or "Off with her head!" about

SHOUTING (cont.)
A9   73: 4   off quarreling with the other players, and shouting "Off with his head!" or "Off with her head!" Those
T1   110:17   she had really frightened her old nurse by shouting suddenly in her ear, "Nurse! Do let's pretend that
T2   122: 8   cried another Daisy. And here they all began shouting together, till the air seemed quite full of little
SHOVEL (1)
T1   113:10   the White Queen sitting on the edge of the shovel--and here are two Castles walking arm in arm--I don't
SHOW (8)
T8   184: 6   bridle, and stretched out both his arms to show Alice what he meant, and this time he fell flat on his
A9   77: 2   "Well, I ca'n't show it you, myself," the Mock Turtle said: "I'm too stiff.
A2   20: 4   little dog, near our house, I should like to show you! A little bright-eyed terrier, you know, with oh,
T2   125: 8   say 'hill'," the Queen interrupted, "I could show you hills, in comparison with which you'd call that a
T6   160:39   mayhap you'll never see such another: and, to show you I'm not proud, you may shake hands with me!" And he
A2   19:33   be angry about it. And yet I wish I could show you our cat Dinah. I think you'd take a fancy to cats, if
T2   128:19   all forest--however, one of the Knights will show you the way--and in the Eighth Square we shall be Queens
T3   129:37   "Now then! Show your ticket, child!" the Guard went on, looking angrily
SHOWER (2)
A4   32: 1   had not long to doubt, for the next moment a shower of little pebbles came rattling in at the window, and
A6   48:12   the fire-irons came first; then followed a shower of saucepans, plates, and dishes. The Duchess took no
SHOWING (2)
A6   48:24   who felt very glad to get an opportunity of showing off a little of her knowledge. "Just think what work
A1   8:33   this was not a very good opportunity for showing off her knowledge, as there was no one to listen to
SHOWS (1)
T6   163:19   to look it over thoroughly just now--and that shows that there are three hundred and sixty-four days when
SHRIEK (5)
A4   29:37   get hold of anything, but she heard a little shriek and a fall, and a crash of broken glass, from which she
A5   43: 2   continued the Pigeon, raising its voice to a shriek, "and just as I was thinking I should be free of them
A7   60:22   by the Hatter, it woke up again with a little shriek, and went on: "--that begins with an M, such as
A12   98:40   shepherd-boy--and the sneeze of the baby, the shriek of the Gryphon, and all the other queer noises, would
A12   98:30   and dishes crashed around it--once more the shriek of the Gryphon, the squeaking of the Lizard's
SHRIEKED (1)
A11   91:19   "Collar that Dormouse!" the Queen shrieked out. "Behead that Dormouse! Turn that Dormouse out of
SHRIEKS (2)
A4   30:17   in the air. This time there were two little shrieks, and more sounds of broken glass. "What a number of
T5   156:45   the chin, and, in spite of a series of little shrieks of "Oh, oh, oh!" from poor Alice, it swept her
SHRILL (10)
A12   98:39   to tinkling sheep-bells, and the Queen's shrill cries to the voice of the shepherd-boy--and the sneeze
A11   91:33   the White Rabbit read out, at the top of his shrill little voice, the name "Alice!"
A8   64:15   "Get up!" said the Queen in a shrill, loud voice, and the three gardeners instantly jumped
A2   19:30   "Not like cats!" cried the Mouse in a shrill passionate voice. "Would you like cats, if you were me
T3   132: 3   little voice began, when it was drowned by a shrill scream from the engine, and everybody jumped up in
T4   148:21   "It's the crow!" Tweedledum cried out in a shrill voice of alarm; and the two brothers took to their
A12   98:27   shared their never-ending meal, and the shrill voice of the Queen ordering off her unfortunate guests
T9   199:35   minute there was silence again, and the same shrill voice sang another verse:--
T9   199:22   At this moment the door was flung open, and a shrill voice was heard singing:--
T2   122: 8   till the air seemed quite full of little shrill voices. "Silence, every one of you!" cried the
SHRIMP (1)
A10   81:26   the Gryphon replied, rather impatiently: "any shrimp could have told you that."
SHRINK (1)
A1   12: 6   for a few minutes to see if she was going to shrink any further: she felt a little nervous about this; "for
SHRINKING (4)
A2   18: 9   it hastily, just in time to save herself from shrinking away altogether.
A4   32:11   and was delighted to find that she began shrinking directly. As soon as she was small enough to get
A2   18: 7   was now about two feet high, and was going on shrinking rapidly: she soon found out that the cause of this
A5   41:42   that there was no time to be lost, as she was shrinking rapidly: so she set to work at once to eat some of
SHUDDER (2)
T6   168: 2   this verse, and Alice thought, with a shudder, "I wouldn't have been the messenger for anything!"
T9   192:32   and the Red Queen remarked, with a little shudder, "She says she only said 'if'--"
SHUN (1)
T1   118: 3   that catch! / Beware the Jubjub bird, and shun / The frumious Bandersnatch!"
SHUT (17)
A4   33: 2   out of its mouth, and its great eyes half shut.
A2   18:13   little door; but, alas! the little door was shut again, and the little golden key was lying on the glass
T9   194:30   The Queen gasped and shut her eyes. "I can do Addition," she said, "if you give me
T3   131: 3   was sitting next to the gentleman in white, shut his eyes and said in a loud voice, "She ought to know her
T6   168:33   nice," Alice objected. But Humpty Dumpty only shut his eyes, and said "Wait till you've tried."
A10   81: 2   reason is--" here the Mock Turtle yawned and shut his eyes. "Tell her about the reason and all that," he
T4   139:16   "Nohow!" Tweedledum cried out briskly, and shut his mouth up again with a snap.
A12   94: 1   The King turned pale, and shut his note-book hastily. "Consider your verdict," he said
T6   168:12   And when I found the door was shut, / I tried to turn the handle, but--"
T8   183:15   silence after this, the Knight with his eyes shut, muttering to himself, and Alice watching anxiously for
T7   178:10   put her hands over her ears, vainly trying to shut out the dreadful uproar.
T9   198:11   "No admittance till the week after next!" and shut the door again with a bang.
T1   108:31   fault, for keeping your eyes open--if you'd shut them tight up, it wouldn't have happened. Now don't make
A1   10: 8   without my shoulders. Oh, how I wish I could shut up like a telescope! I think I could, if I only knew how
T3   130:20   he said "You're traveling the wrong way," and shut up the window, and went away. "So young a child," said
T7   175:44   very tired and sleepy, and his eyes were half shut. "What's this!" he said, blinking lazily at Alice, and
T5   153:10   tone. "Try again: draw a long breath, and shut your eyes."
SHUTTING (3)
T4   147: 6   his head out: and there he lay, opening and shutting his mouth and his large eyes--"looking more like a
A1   10:14   key on it, or at any rate a book of rules for shutting people up like telescopes: this time she found a

SHUTTING (cont.)
  A1   12: 1 a curious feeling!" said Alice. "I must be shutting up like a telescope!"
SHY (3)
  T9   200:22   "You look a little shy: let me introduce you to that leg of mutton," said the Red
  T3   129:19 and trying to find some excuse for turning shy so suddenly. "It'll never do to go down among them without
  T9   201:19 large that she couldn't help feeling a little shy with it, as she had been with the mutton; however, she
SHYLY (2)
  T2   126: 6   She glanced rather shyly at the real Queen as she said this, but her companion
  A5   35: 6 for a conversation. Alice replied, rather shyly, "I--I hardly know, Sir, just at present--at least I
SHYNESS (1)
  T9   201:20 with the mutton; however, she conquered her shyness by a great effort, and cut a slice and handed it to
SIDE (50)
  T7   170:25 his great hands spread out like fans on each side.)
  T7   171:15 the great eyes rolled wildly from side to side.
  T8   183: 8 save himself from falling over on the other side.
  T6   165: 8   "And a long way beyond it on each side," Alice added.
  T5   149:29 straight, you know, if you pin it all on one side," Alice said as she gently put it right for her; "and
  A10   82: 3 creatures got so close to her, one on each side, and opened their eyes and mouths so very wide; but she
  T2   125:22 running straight across it from side to side, and the ground between was divided up into squares by a
  T8   190:30 and the Knight tumbling off, first on one side and then on the other. After the fourth or fifth tumble
  A4   29:16   And so she went on, taking first one side and then the other, and making quite a conversation of it
  T2   122:10 waving itself passionately from side to side, and trembling with excitement. "They know I ca'n't get
  T8   179:23 it was a White Knight. He drew up at Alice's side, and tumbled off his horse just as the Red Knight had
  T9   204: 2 this moment she heard a hoarse laugh at her side, and turned to see what was the matter with the White
  A1   9:31 and when Alice had been all the way down one side, and up the other, trying every door, she walked sadly
  A9   70:24 And she squeezed herself up closer to Alice's side as she spoke.
  T8   180:12 with their both falling off in this way, side by side. When they got up again, they shook hands, and
  T6   164:11 on, wagging his head gravely from side to side, "for to get their wages, you know."
  T1   114: 6 up the Queen and set her on the table by the side of her noisy little daughter.
  T3   135:23 to an open field, with a wood on the other side of it: it looked much darker than the last wood, and
  T9   198: 2 "QUEEN ALICE" in large letters, and on each side of the arch there was a bell-handle; one was marked
  T5   157: 8 it," said Alice, peeping cautiously over the side of the boat into the dark water. "I wish it hadn't let go
  T5   156:20 Sheep and the knitting, as she bent over the side of the boat, with just the ends of her tangled hair
  T5   153:36 really a sheep that was sitting on the other side of the counter? Rub as she would, she could make nothing
  A11   89: 3 up very sulkily and crossed over to the other side of the court.
  T8   185:17   Alice ran to the side of the ditch to look for him. She was rather startled by
  A6   46:11 two reasons. First, because I'm on the same side of the door as you are: secondly, because they're making
  T1   113:22   and she began scrambling wildly up the side of the fender.
  A8   68:20 that her flamingo was gone across the other side of the garden, where Alice could see it trying in a
  A8   68:25 Alice, "as all the arches are gone from this side of the ground." So she tucked it away under her arm, that
  T6   168:30 same. Now if you had the two eyes on the same side of the nose, for instance--or the mouth at the top--that
  A5   41:29   "One side of what? The other side of what?" thought Alice to
  A5   41:29   "One side of what? The other side of what?" thought Alice to herself.
  T8   182:44   and, as he generally did this on the side on which Alice was walking, she soon found that it was
  T9   204:19 mischief--but the Queen was no longer at her side--she had suddenly dwindled down to the size of a little
  A8   65:25 a very fine day!" said a timid voice at her side. She was walking by the White Rabbit, who was peeping
  T9   192:13 White Queen sitting close to her, one on each side: she would have liked very much to ask them how they came
  T9   203: 3 the two Queens pushed her so, one on each side, that they nearly lifted her up into the air. "I rise to
  A10   80: 8 is another shore, you know, upon the other side. / The further off from England the nearer is to France.
  A4   32:38 and, the moment she appeared on the other side, the puppy made another rush at the stick, and tumbled
  A11   86: 5 them, in chains, with a soldier on each side to guard him; and near the King was the White Rabbit,
  A2   15:17 as much as she could do, lying down on one side, to look through into the garden with one eye; but to get
  T7   171:15 while the great eyes rolled wildly from side to side.
  T2   125:22 little brooks running straight across it from side to side, and the ground between was divided up into
  T2   122:10 Tiger-lily, waving itself passionately from side to side, and trembling with excitement. "They know I
  T6   164:10 Dumpty went on, wagging his head gravely from side to side, "for to get their wages, you know."
  T8   188:29 a little fatter. / I shook him well from side to side, / Until his face was blue: / 'Come, tell me how
  T8   188:29 fatter. / I shook him well from side to side, / Until his face was blue: / 'Come, tell me how you live
  T8   180:12 their both falling off in this way, side by side. When they got up again, they shook hands, and then the
  A5   41:27 side will make you grow taller, and the other side will make you grow shorter."
  A5   41:27 the grass, merely remarking, as it went, "One side will make you grow taller, and the other side will make
  T8W   14: 9 "Won't you let me help you round to the other side? You'll be out of the cold wind there."
SIDES (5)
  A7   58:24 up, Dormouse!" And they pinched it on both sides at once.
  T5   154: 5 "You may look in front of you, and on both sides, if you like," said the Sheep; "but you ca'n't look all
  A5   41:34 minute, trying to make out which were the two sides of it; and, as it was perfectly round, she found this a
  A4   34: 5 when she had looked under it, and on both sides of it, and behind it, it occurred to her that she might
  A1   8:15 dark to see anything: then she looked at the sides of the well, and noticed that they were filled with
SIDEWAYS (1)
  T8   182:43 he had a habit of now and then falling off sideways; and, as he generally did this on the side on which
SIEVE (1)
  T8   187:38 through my head, / Like water through a sieve.
SIGH (11)
  T5   149:32 got entangled in it!" the Queen said with a sigh. "And I lost the comb yesterday."
  T9   196:34   The White Queen gave a deep sigh, and laid her head on Alice's shoulder. "I am so sleepy!"
  T5   156:30 are always further!" she said at last with a sigh at the obstinacy of the rushes in growing so far off, as,
  A9   77: 6 went to him," the Mock Turtle said with a sigh. "He taught Laughing and Grief, they used to say."
  A9   76:18 to learn it," said the Mock Turtle with a sigh. "I only took the regular course."
  A9   74:32 said the Mock Turtle at last, with a deep sigh, "I was a real Turtle."
  A7   58:12 "Yes, that's it," said the Hatter with a sigh: "it's always tea-time, and we've no time to wash the

SIGH (cont.)
    T3   131:36   pitying to comfort it, "if it would only sigh like other people!" she thought. But this was such a
    TI   103:31   And, though the shadow of a sigh / May tremble through the story, / For "happy summer days
    T3   131:37   But this was such a wonderfully small sigh, that she wouldn't have heard it at all, if it hadn't
    T8W   13: 2   going to spring over, when she heard a deep sigh, which seemed to come from the wood behind her.
SIGHED (9)
    T9   195:42   Alice sighed and gave it up. "It's exactly like the riddle with no
    A10   84:15   The Mock Turtle sighed deeply, and began, in a voice choked with sobs, to sing
    A10   78: 1   The Mock Turtle sighed deeply, and drew the back of one flapper across his
    T3   131:34   The little voice sighed deeply. It was very unhappy, evidently, and Alice would
    T3   135:13   But the Gnat only sighed deeply while two large tears came rolling down its
    T3   135:18   this time the poor Gnat really seemed to have sighed itself away, for, when Alice looked up, there was
    A7   56: 1   "Two days wrong!" sighed the Hatter. "I told you butter wouldn't suit the works!
    A3   26:16   "What a pity it wouldn't stay!" sighed the Lory, as soon as it was quite out of sight. And an
    A7   56:32   Alice sighed wearily. "I think you might do something better with
SIGHING (3)
    A3   24:18   tale!" said the Mouse, turning to Alice, and sighing.
    A9   74:18   as they came nearer, Alice could hear him sighing as if his heart would break. She pitied him deeply.
    A9   77: 8   "So he did, so he did," said the Gryphon, sighing in his turn; and both creatures hid their faces in
SIGHS (1)
    T3   135:17   Then came another of those melancholy little sighs, and this time the poor Gnat really seemed to have
SIGHT (17)
    A5   41:32   it aloud; and in another moment it was out of sight.
    T8   190:33   to him, and waited till he was out of sight.
    A3   26:17   the Lory, as soon as it was quite out of sight. And an old Crab took the opportunity of saying to her
    A8   67:21   to think that there was enough of it now in sight, and no more of it appeared.
    A11   91: 2   of the officers; but the Hatter was out of sight before the officer could get to the door.
    A8   68:23   was over, and both the hedgehogs were out of sight: "but it doesn't matter much," thought Alice, "as all
    A11   91:15   at the cook till his eyes were nearly out of sight, he said, in a deep voice, "What are tarts made of?"
    A1   9:23   passage, and the White Rabbit was still in sight, hurrying down it. There was not a moment to be lost:
    T4   148:22   brothers took to their heels and were out of sight in a moment.
    T7   173:15   trotted on in silence, till they came into sight of a great crowd, in the middle of which the Lion and
    T2   123:41   the Red Queen. To her surprise she lost sight of her in a moment, and found herself walking in at the
    T2   124: 5   face to face with the Red Queen, and full in sight of the hill she had been so long aiming at.
    A6   53:10   had not gone much farther before she came in sight of the house of the March Hare: she thought it must be
    T4   144:31   "Isn't he a lovely sight?" said Tweedledum.
    T2   120:26   However, there was the hill full in sight, so there was nothing to be done but start again. This
    A9   74: 8   then it watched the Queen till she was out of sight: then it chuckled. "What fun!" said the Gryphon, half to
    A2   14: 5   at her feet, they seemed to be almost out of sight, they were getting so far off). "Oh, my poor little feet
SIGN (1)
    A12   94:23   "If you didn't sign it," said the King, "that only makes the matter worse.
SIGNED (2)
    A12   94:22   they ca'n't prove that I did: there's no name signed at the end."
    A12   94:25   have meant some mischief, or else you'd have signed your name like an honest man."
SIGNIFIES (1)
    A12   93: 7   it out again, and put it right; "not that it signifies much," she said to herself; "I should think it would
SIGNIFY (1)
    A2   16:11   However, the Multiplication-Table doesn't signify: let's try Geography. London is the capital of Paris,
SILENCE (33)
    A4   32: 4   do that again!", which produced another dead silence.
    A6   50: 7   which), and they went on for some while in silence.
    A12   96:26   the court with a smile. There was a dead silence.
    A4   30:13   There was a long silence after this, and Alice could only hear whispers now and
    T8   184:21   There was a short silence after this, and then the Knight went on again. "I'm a
    T8   183:15   as she could. They went on a little way in silence after this, the Knight with his eyes shut, muttering
    T9   199:35   if any one's counting?" In a minute there was silence again, and the same shrill voice sang another verse:--
    A3   22: 2   all ready? This is the driest thing I know. Silence all round, if you please! 'William the Conqueror,
    T8   179: 2   gradually to die away, till all was dead silence, and Alice lifted up her head in some alarm. There was
    T9   201:30   moment she opened her lips, there was dead silence, and all eyes were fixed upon her; "and it's a very
    T9   200:17   sat down in it, rather uncomfortable at the silence, and longing for some one to speak.
    A12   93:34   busily writing in his note-book, called out "Silence!", and read out from his book, "Rule Forty-two. All
    A4   31: 9   alone--"Catch him, you by the hedge!" then silence, and then another confusion of voices--"Hold up his
    T1   114:10   could do nothing but hug the little Lily in silence. As soon as she had recovered her breath a little, she
    A5   35: 2   Alice looked at each other for some time in silence: at last the Caterpillar took the hookah out of its
    A3   23:20   pictures of him), while the rest waited in silence. At last the Dodo said "Everybody has won, and all
    A9   74:34   These words were followed by a very long silence, broken only by an occasional exclamation of "Hjckrrh!
    T9   193:14   The Red Queen broke the silence by saying, to the White Queen, "I invite you to
    T2   122: 9   seemed quite full of little shrill voices. "Silence, every one of you!" cried the Tiger-lily, waving
    T9   193:13   remarked; and then there was an uncomfortable silence for a minute or two.
    A5   41: 5   the Caterpillar, decidedly; and there was silence for some minutes.
    T2   122:16   There was silence in a moment, and several of the pink daisies turned
    A11   86:34   hastily, for the White Rabbit cried out "Silence in the court!", and the King put on his spectacles and
    A12   94:37   There was dead silence in the court, whilst the White Rabbit read out these
    A4   31:32   There was a dead silence instantly, and Alice thought to herself "I wonder what
    T6   159:17   provoking," Humpty Dumpty said after a long silence, looking away from Alice as he spoke, "to be called an
    T8   182:37   and for a few minutes she walked on in silence, puzzling over the idea, and every now and then
    T9   200: 7   once--" and in she went, and there was a dead silence the moment she appeared.
    T7   173:15   breath for talking; so they trotted on in silence, till they came into sight of a great crowd, in the
    T2   125:17   was a little offended: and they walked on in silence till they got to the top of the little hill.
    A7   55:35   The Hatter was the first to break the silence. "What day of the month is it?" he said, turning to

SILENCE (cont.)
```
  T2   127: 2  ago!  Faster!"  And they ran on for a time in  silence, with the wind whistling in Alice's ears, and almost
  AI     3:19                                    Anon, to sudden  silence won, / In fancy they pursue / The dream-child moving
```
SILENT (14)
```
  A7    60:19                                  Alice was silent.
  A8    64: 9  very  loudly  and decidedly, and the Queen was  silent.
  T6   166:28  Humpty  Dumpty  remarked severely. Alice was  silent.
  A8    65:20                      The soldiers were  silent, and looked at Alice, as the question was evidently
  A9    75: 5  added  the  Gryphon;  and  then they both sat  silent and looked at poor Alice, who felt ready to sink into
  A8    68:31   at  once,  while  all  the  rest were quite  silent, and looked very uncomfortable.
  T8W   18:11  Wasp: "however I'll try; wait a bit." He was  silent for a few moments, and then began again--
  T3   134:20                   After this, Alice was  silent for a minute or two, pondering. The Gnat amused itself
  A5    43:21  such  a new idea to Alice, that she was quite  silent for a minute or two, which gave the Pigeon the
  T3   136: 2                            She stood  silent for a minute, thinking: then she suddenly began again.
  A7    55:32  the  conversation  dropped, and the party sat  silent for a minute, while Alice thought over all she could
  T8   188:36  And work them into waistcoat-buttons / In the  silent night. / And these I do not sell for gold / Or coin of
  T7   174:20              For a minute or two Alice stood  silent, watching him. Suddenly she brightened up. "Look, look!
  T3   129: 8  off,  you know--" and for some time she stood  silent, watching one of them that was bustling about among the
```
SILVER (1)
```
  TI   103: 8  have not seen thy sunny face, / Nor heard thy  silver laughter: / No thought of me shall find a place / In
```
SILVERY (2)
```
  T1   111:13  beginning  to  melt  away, just like a bright  silvery mist.
  T8   188:38  And these I do not sell for gold / Or coin of  silvery shine, / But for a copper halfpenny, / And that will
```
SIMPLE (7)
```
  A12   99: 5  would  keep, through all her riper years, the  simple and loving heart of her childhood; and how she would
  TI   103:15  days,  /  When  summer suns were glowing--/ A  simple chime, that served to time / The rhythm of our rowing--
  A12   99:10  sorrows,  and  find  a pleasure in all their  simple joys, remembering her own child-life, and the happy
  A9    75: 4  to  be  ashamed of yourself for asking such a  simple question," added the Gryphon; and then they both sat
  A1    10:24   all  because  they  would  not  remember the  simple rules their friends had taught them: such as, that a
  A12   99: 9  ago;  and  how  she would feel with all their  simple sorrows, and find a pleasure in all their simple joys,
  TC   209: 6  /  Eager eye and willing ear, / Pleased a  simple tale to hear--
```
SIMPLETON (1)
```
  A9    76:32  you  don't  know what to uglify is, you are a simpleton."
```
SIMPLY (6)
```
  A4    32:23  excellent plan, no doubt, and very neatly and  simply arranged: the only difficulty was, that she had not the
  A3    24: 7  she  could  not think of anything to say, she  simply bowed, and took the thimble, looking as solemn as she
  T6   160:17  with  any  idea of making another riddle, but  simply in her good-natured anxiety for the queer creature.
  A9    72: 7  seem  to  be'--or, if you'd like it put more  simply--'Never imagine yourself not to be otherwise than what
  T7   172:28  news  too. However, instead of whispering, he  simply shouted, at the top of his voice, "They're at it again!
  T7   170:34  "He  lives  on  the  Hill," the King remarked  simply, without the least idea that he was joining in the game
```
SINCE (4)
```
  A4    27: 9  to be seen--everything seemed to have changed  since her swim in the pool; and the great hall, with the glass
  A5    43:37                      It was so long  since she had been anything near the right size, that it felt
  A7    58: 8                   "And ever  since that," the Hatter went on in a mournful tone, "he wo'n't
  A5    35: 8  think  I must have .been changed several times  since then."
```
SING (12)
```
  A7    57:13  given  by  the  Queen of Hearts, and I had to  sing
  A10   79: 7  do  it without lobsters, you know. Which shall  sing?"
  T9   196:37  Smoothe her hair--lend her your nightcap--and  sing her a soothing lullaby."
  A10   84:13  offended  tone, "Hm! No accounting for tastes!  Sing her 'Turtle Soup,' will you, old fellow?'"
  T8   186:36  very,  very beautiful. Everybody that hears me  sing it--either it brings the tears into their eyes, or else--
  T6   166:25                   only I don't  sing it," he added, as an explanation.
  T9   197: 9  head  down  on  Alice's other shoulder, "just  sing it through to me. I'm getting sleepy, too." In another
  A10   79: 8                       "Oh, you  sing," said the Gryphon. "I've forgotten the words."
  A10   84:16  and  began,  in  a voice choked with sobs, to  sing this:--
  T6   166:24  "In  winter,  when  the fields are white, / I  sing this song for your delight--
  T8   186:31  the  Knight  said in an anxious tone: "let me  sing you a song to comfort you."
  A10   84: 9  on.  "Or  would  you  like the Mock Turtle to  sing you another song?"
```
SINGERS (2)
```
  A11   90:30  at  the  Queen,  who  was reading the list of  singers.
  A11   89: 6   of  the  court, "Bring me  the list of the  singers in the last concert!" on which the wretched Hatter
```
SINGING (6)
```
  T9   199:23  was  flung open, and a shrill voice was heard  singing:--
  A6    48:33  with  that she began nursing her child again,  singing a sort of lullaby to it as she did so, and giving it a
  T4   139:35  the  history  of  all  this), "to find myself  singing 'Here we go round the mulberry bush.' I don't know
  A7    58: 1  Here  the  Dormouse shook itself, and began  singing in its sleep "Twinkle, twinkle, twinkle, twinkle--"
  T4   139:37  I began it, but somehow I felt as if I'd been  singing it a long long time!"
  T6   166:27  "If you can see whether I'm  singing or not, you've sharper eyes than most," Humpty Dumpty
```
SINGLE (2)
```
  T8   181:35   tone,  "one  of  the  best  kind. But not a  single bee has come near it yet. And the other thing is a
  T5   149:23  her,  she  was  so  dreadfully untidy. "Every  single thing's crooked," Alice thought to herself, "and she's
```
SINK (1)
```
  A9    75: 6  and  looked  at poor Alice, who felt ready to  sink into the earth. At last the Gryphon said to the Mock
```
SIR (10)
```
  T6   159:19              "I said you looked like an egg,  Sir," Alice gently explained. "And some eggs are very pretty,
  T6   167: 4  little fishes' answer was / 'We cannot do it,  Sir, because--'"
  A9    74:37  nearly  getting  up  and saying, "Thank you,  Sir, for your interesting story," but she could not help
  A5    41:14  "Well,  I  should like to be a little larger,  Sir, if you wouldn't mind," said Alice: "three inches is such
  A5    35: 6  replied,  rather shyly, "I--I hardly know,  Sir, just at present--at least I know who I was when I got up
  A5    35:11  "I  ca'n't  explain  myself,  I'm afraid,  Sir," said Alice, "because I'm not myself, you see."
```

SIR (cont.)
  A5   36:31   "I'm afraid I am, Sir," said Alice. "I ca'n't remember things as I used--and I
  T6   164:14   "You seem very clever at explaining words, Sir," said Alice. "Would you kindly tell me the meaning of the
  A2   15:33   began, in a low, timid voice, "If you please, Sir--" The Rabbit started violently, dropped the white
  A3   25:28   Said the mouse to the cur, Such a trial, dear sir, With no jury or judge, would be wasting our breath. 'I'll
SISTER (13)
  A12   98: 7   curious dream!" said Alice. And she told her sister, as well as she could remember them, all these strange
  T12 207:19   was explaining the thing afterwards to her sister: "it turned away its head, and pretended not to see it:
  A12   98: 9   reading about; when she had finished, her sister kissed her, and said "It was a curious dream, dear,
  A12   99: 3   she pictured to herself how this same little sister of hers would, in the after-time, be herself a grown
  A1   7: 1   beginning to get very tired of sitting by her on the bank and of having nothing to do: once or twice
  T1   110:12   She had had quite a long argument with her sister only the day before--all because Alice had begun with
  A12   98:13   But her sister sat still just as she left her, leaning her head on her
  T4   139:35   said afterwards, when she was telling her sister the history of all this), "to find myself singing 'Here
  T9   202:39   she said afterwards, when she was telling her sister the history of her feast. "You would have thought they
  A1   7: 3   or twice she had peeped into the book her sister was reading, but it had no pictures or conversations in
  T1   110:13   pretend we're kings and queens;" and her sister, who liked being very exact, had argued that they
  A12   98: 1   on the bank, with her head in the lap of her sister, who was gently brushing away some dead leaves that had
  A12   98: 4   "Wake up, Alice dear!" said her sister. "Why, what a long sleep you've had!"
SISTER'S (1)
  A12   98:23   with the strange creatures of her little sister's dream.
SISTERS (2)
  A7   58:32   "Once upon a time there were three little sisters," the Dormouse began in a great hurry; "and their
  A7   59:31   to go on. "And so these three little sisters--they were learning to draw, you know--"
SIT (13)
  T9   201:25   hadn't a word to say in reply: she could only sit and look at it and gasp.
  A3   21:14   of some authority among them, called out "Sit down, all of you, and listen to me! I'll soon make you dry
  T7   176:13   was evidently very uncomfortable at having to sit down between the two great creatures; but there was no
  A9   74:28   said the Mock Turtle in a deep, hollow tone. "Sit down, both of you, and don't speak a word till I've
  T7   176:10   down and putting his chin on his paws. "And sit down, both of you," (to the King and the Unicorn): "fair
  A11   90:25   "Then you may sit down," the King replied.
  A7   55: 2   "It wasn't very civil of you to sit down without being invited," said the March Hare.
  A6   46:39   his remark, with variations. "I shall sit here," he said, "on and off, for days and days."
  A6   46:26   "I shall sit here," the Footman remarked, "till to-morrow--"
  T6   160:11   "Why do you sit out here all alone?" said Alice, not wishing to begin an
  T12 207:22   "Sit up a little more stiffly, dear!" Alice cried with a merry
  A2   20: 6   fetch things when you throw them, and it'll sit up and beg for its dinner, and all sorts of things--I
  A12   93:14   seemed too much overcome to do anything but sit with its mouth open, gazing up into the roof of the court
SITS (1)
  A2   19:36   she swam lazily about in the pool, "and she sits purring so nicely by the fire, licking her paws and
SITTING (26) [See also A-SITTING]
  A7   54: 3   Hatter were having tea at it: a Dormouse was sitting between them, fast asleep, and the other two were
  T3   131:10   Alice couldn't see who was sitting beyond the Beetle, but a hoarse voice spoke next.
  A1   7: 1   Alice was beginning to get very tired of sitting by her sister on the bank and of having nothing to do:
  T9   192:12   at finding the Red Queen and the White Queen sitting close to her, one on each side: she would have liked
  T1   107:13   in the afternoon, and so, while Alice was sitting curled up in a corner of the great arm-chair, half
  T5   153:38   and opposite to her was an old Sheep, sitting in an arm-chair, knitting, and every now and then
  T9   204: 4   of the Queen, there was the leg of mutton sitting in the chair. "Here I am!" cried a voice from the
  T3   131: 6   There was a Beetle sitting next the Goat (it was a very queer carriage-full of
  A11   88:40   squeeze so," said the Dormouse, who was sitting next to her. "I can hardly breathe."
  T3   131: 3   A Goat, that was sitting next to the gentleman in white, shut his eyes and said
  A6   50:21   a little startled by seeing the Cheshire-Cat sitting on a bough of a tree a few yards off.
  A6   52:28   she looked up, and there was the Cat again, sitting on a branch of a tree.
  A6   47: 1   from one end to the other: the Duchess was sitting on a three-legged stool in the middle, nursing a baby:
  T1   113:10   there are the White King and the White Queen sitting on the edge of the shovel--and here are two Castles
  T2   127: 8   they stopped, and she found herself sitting on the ground, breathless and giddy.
  T8W   13: 6   (only that his face was more like a wasp) was sitting on the ground, leaning against a tree, all huddled up
  A6   46: 7   the Fish-Footman was gone, and the other was sitting on the ground near the door, staring stupidly up into
  T5   153:35   that really--was it really a sheep that was sitting on the other side of the counter? Rub as she would,
  A4   34: 9   those of a large blue caterpillar, that was sitting on the top, with its arms folded, quietly smoking a
  T3   130:22   away. "So young a child," said the gentleman sitting opposite to her, (he was dressed in white paper),
  T3   132:17   away as she touched it, and she found herself sitting quietly under a tree--while the Gnat (for that was the
  A9   74:17   they saw the Mock Turtle in the distance, sitting sad and lonely on a little ledge of rock, and, as they
  T3   135:20   and, as she was getting quite chilly with sitting still so long, she got up and walked on.
  T1   114:12   she called out to the White King, who was sitting sulkily among the ashes, "Mind the volcano!"
  T9   198:13   time; but at last a very old Frog, who was sitting under a tree, got up and hobbled slowly towards her:
  T6   159: 8   on that enormous face. Humpty Dumpty was sitting, with his legs crossed like a Turk, on the top of a
SIX (7)
  T4   147:43   "Let's fight till six, and then have dinner," said Tweedledum.
  T5   153:15   day. Why, sometimes I've believed as many as six impossible things before breakfast. There goes the shawl
  A2   16: 9   four times five is twelve, and four times six is thirteen, and four times seven is--oh dear! I shall
  T3   129:29   the hill, and jumped over the first of the six little brooks. * * * * * * * * * * * * * *
  T6   161:22   short calculation, and said "Seven years and six months."
  T6   162: 3   "Seven years and six months!" Humpty Dumpty repeated thoughtfully. "An
  A7   58: 9   "he wo'n't do a thing I ask! It's always six o'clock now."
SIXPENCE (1)
  A12   95:25   afraid of interrupting him,) "I'll give him sixpence. I don't believe there's an atom of meaning in it."
SIXTEENTH (1)
  A11   88:16   "Sixteenth," said the Dormouse.

SIXTH (1)
T2   128:12 Tweedledee--the Fifth is mostly water--the Sixth belongs to Humpty Dumpty--But you make no remark?"
SIXTY-FIVE (2)
T6   162:44   "Three hundred and sixty-five," said Alice.
T6   163: 1 "And if you take one from three hundred and sixty-five what remains?"
SIXTY-FOUR (2)
T6   163:20 that shows that there are three hundred and sixty-four days when you might get un-birthday presents--"
T6   163: 3   "Three hundred and sixty-four, of course."
SIZE (17)
A4   32:19 about in the wood, "is to grow to my right size again; and the second thing is to find my way into that
A5   41: 8   "Oh, I'm not particular as to size," Alice hastily replied; "only one doesn't like changing
A4   32: 8 thought, "it's sure to make some change in my size; and, as it ca'n't possibly make me larger, it must make
T3   129:35 out a ticket: they were about the same size as the people, and quite seemed to fill the carriage.
A12   97: 7 you?" said Alice (she had grown to her full size by this time). "You're nothing but a pack of cards!"
A5   41: 7   "What size do you want to be?" it asked.
A1   12: 4 up at the thought that she was now the right size for going through the little door into that lovely garden
A5   36:32 things as I used--and I don't keep the same size for ten minutes together!"
T4   144: 4 tears he sorted out / Those of the largest size, / Holding his pocket-handkerchief / Before his streaming
T3   132:20 certainly was a very large Gnat: "about the size of a chicken," Alice thought. Still, she couldn't feel
T9   204:20 side--she had suddenly dwindled down to the size of a little doll, and was now on the table, merrily
A5   43:37 since she had been anything near the right size, that it felt quite strange at first; but she got used to
A5   43:42 another! However, I've got back to my right size: the next thing is, to get into that beautiful garden--
A1   12:41 surprised to find that she remained the same size. To be sure, this is what generally happens when one eats
A4   33:10 very much, if--if I'd only been the right size to do it! Oh dear! I'd nearly forgotten that I've got to
A5   44: 3 Alice, "it'll never do to come upon them this size: why, I should frighten them out of their wits!" So she
A4   30: 8 "An arm, you goose! Who ever saw one that size? Why, it fills the whole window!"
SIZES (1)
A5   35:16 to begin with; and being so many different sizes in a day is very confusing."
SKIES (1)
TC   209:11 haunts me, phantomwise. / Alice moving under skies / Never seen by waking eyes.
SKILL (1)
AI   3: 3 we glide; / For both our oars, with little skill, / By little arms are plied, / While little hands make
SKIM (1)
T2   127: 6 they went so fast that at last they seemed to skim through the air, hardly touching the ground with their
SKIMMING (1)
A6   46:28 of the house opened, and a large plate came skimming out, straight at the Footman's head: it just grazed
SKIPPING (1)
T7   170:23 he goes into!" (For the Messenger kept skipping up and down, and wriggling like an eel, as he came
SKIRT (1)
A12   92: 4 tipped over the jury-box with the edge of her skirt, upsetting all the jurymen on to the heads of the crowd
SKY (7)
A6   46: 8 near the door, staring stupidly up into the sky.
A6   46:21 out, you know." He was looking up into the sky all the time he was speaking, and this Alice thought
TC   209: 7   Long has paled that sunny sky: / Echoes fade and memories die: / Autumn frosts have
TC   209: 1   A boat, beneath a sunny sky / Lingering onward dreamily / In an evening of July--
T4   140:38 see a cloud, because / No cloud was in the sky: / No birds were flying overhead--/ There were no birds to
A7   57:20 the world you fly, / Like a tea-tray in the sky. / Twinkle, twinkle--'"
A5   43: 4 they must needs come wriggling down from the sky! Ugh, Serpent!"
SKY-ROCKET (1)
A4   31:24 like a Jack-in-the-box, and up I goes like a sky-rocket!"
SLAIN (2)
TC   209: 9 fade and memories die: / Autumn frosts have slain July.
T1   118:17   "And, hast thou slain the Jabberwock? / Come to my arms, my beamish boy! / O
SLATE (3)
A11   87:12 of very little use, as it left no mark on the slate.
A4   30:30 rope--Will the roof bear?--Mind that loose slate--Oh, it's coming down! Heads below!" (a loud crash)--
A12   96:22 little Bill had left off writing on his slate with one finger, as he found it made no mark; but he now
SLATE-PENCIL (1)
A12   98:31 of the Gryphon, the squeaking of the Lizard's slate-pencil, and the choking of the suppressed guinea-pigs,
SLATES (7)
A12   93:11 from the shock of being upset, and their slates and pencils had been found and handed back to them,
A11   87: 1 were writing down "Stupid things!" on their slates, and she could even make out that one of them didn't
A11   88:18 eagerly wrote down all three dates on their slates, and then added them up, and reduced the answer to
A12   93:32 as she was near enough to look over their slates; "but it doesn't matter a bit," she thought to herself
A12   95:27   The jury all wrote down, on their slates, "She doesn't believe there's an atom of meaning in it
A11   86:28 twelve jurors were all writing very busily on slates. "What are they doing?" Alice whispered to the Gryphon.
A12   93:22 just beginning to write this down on their slates, when the White Rabbit interrupted: "Unimportant, your
SLATES'LL (1)
A11   87: 3 neighbour to tell him. "A nice muddle their slates'll be in, before the trial's over!" thought Alice.
SLEEP (8) [See also ASLEEP]
T8   188: 2 He said 'I look for butterflies / That sleep among the wheat: / I make them into mutton-pies, / And
T1   109:13 a white quilt; and perhaps it says 'Go to sleep, darlings, till the summer comes again.' And when they
A7   55:29 talking in its sleep, "that 'I breathe when I sleep' is the same thing as 'I sleep when I breathe'!"
A7   55:29 Dormouse, which seemed to be talking in its sleep, "that 'I breathe when I sleep' is the same thing as 'I
A5   42:40 night and day! Why, I haven't had a wink of sleep these three weeks!"
A7   58: 1 shook itself, and began singing in its sleep "Twinkle, twinkle, twinkle, twinkle--" and went on so
A7   55:30 breathe when I sleep' is the same thing as 'I sleep when I breathe'!"
A12   98: 4 dear!" said her sister. "Why, what a long sleep you've had!"
SLEEPING (1)
T4   144:29 hands, and led her up to where the King was sleeping.

SLEEPY (9)
T7   175:44   this was going on: he looked very tired and sleepy, and his eyes were half shut. "What's this!" he said,
A1   7: 7   she could, for the hot day made her feel very sleepy and stupid), whether the pleasure of making a
A7   60:15   and rubbing its eyes, for it was getting very sleepy; "and they drew all manner of things--everything that
A1   9:12   I wonder?" And here Alice began to get rather sleepy, and went on saying to herself, in a dreamy sort of way
T1   110: 2   so wish it was true! I'm sure the woods look sleepy in the autumn, when the leaves are getting brown.
T9   196:35   laid her head on Alice's shoulder. "I am so sleepy!" she moaned.
T9   197:10   "just sing it through to me. I'm getting sleepy, too." In another moment both Queens were fast asleep,
A5   35: 3   of its mouth, and addressed her in a languid, sleepy voice.
A11   91:18   "Treacle," said a sleepy voice behind her.
SLEEVES (1)
T5   156:17   among the waving rushes. And then the little sleeves were carefully rolled up, and the little arms were
SLICE (4)
T9   201:20   her shyness by a great effort, and cut a slice and handed it to the Red Queen.
T4   143:22   Carpenter said nothing but / 'Cut us another slice. / I wish you were not quite so deaf--/ I've had to ask
T9   201:23   wonder how you'd like it, if I were to cut a slice out of you, you creature!"
T9   201: 4   "May I give you a slice?" she said, taking up the knife and fork, and looking
SLICES (2)
T7   177:10   called 'the Monster'). "I've cut several slices already, but they always join on again!"
T3   134:11   a Bread-and-butter-fly. Its wings are thin slices of bread-and-butter, its body is a crust, and its head
SLIDING (1)
T1   115:40   (in which Alice had put 'The White Knight is sliding down the poker. He balances very badly'). "That's not
SLIGHTEST (2)
A7   56:30   "I haven't the slightest idea," said the Hatter.
A1   8:36   or Longitude I've got to?" (Alice had not the slightest idea what Latitude was, or Longitude either, but she
SLIMY (1)
T6   164:30   "Well, 'slithy' means 'lithe and slimy.' 'Lithe' is the same as 'active.' You see it's like a
SLIPPED (4)
A2   18:17   As she said these words her foot slipped, and in another moment, splash! she was up to her chin
T5   152:19   the brooch; but it was too late: the pin had slipped, and the Queen had pricked her finger.
A2   19: 9   made out that it was only a mouse, that had slipped in like herself.
A11   90:14   up at the mouth with strings: into this they slipped the guinea-pig, head first, and then sat upon it.)
SLIPPERY (1)
A1   12:19   one of the legs of the table, but it was too slippery; and when she had tired herself out with trying, the
SLITHY (6)
T6   164:29   "That'll do very well," said Alice: "and 'slithy'?"
T6   164:30   "Well, 'slithy' means 'lithe and slimy.' 'Lithe' is the same as
T1   116: 9   eht ni elbmig dna eryg diD / sevot yhtils eht dna ,gillirb sawT'
T1   116:18   'Twas brillig, and the slithy toves / Did gyre and gimble in the wabe: / All mimsy
T1   118:21   'Twas brillig, and the slithy toves / Did gyre and gimble in the wabe: / All mimsy
T6   164:21   "'Twas brillig, and the slithy toves / Did gyre and gimble in the wabe: / All mimsy
SLOW (4)
T9   199: 6   Alice almost stamped with irritation at the slow drawl in which he spoke. "This door, of course!"
T2   127:19   "A slow sort of country!" said the Queen. "Now, here, you see, it
T8   186:11   not the next course," the Knight said in slow thoughtful tone: "no, certainly not the next course."
T8   190: 1   know--/ Whose look was mild, whose speech was slow, / Whose hair was whiter than the snow, / Whose face was
SLOWER (1)
T7   172:19   lady saw him too. So of course Nobody walks slower than you."
SLOWLY (17)
A9   74:14   'come on!' here," thought Alice, as she went slowly after it: "I never was so ordered about before, in all
A10   79:12   time, while the Mock Turtle sang this, very slowly and sadly:--
T9   201:35   of the mark. "As to fishes," she said, very slowly and solemnly, putting her mouth close to Alice's ear,
T7   170:22   she exclaimed at last. "But he's coming very slowly--and what curious attitudes he goes into!" (For the
T8   190:24   So they shook hands, and then the Knight rode slowly away into the forest. "It wo'n't take long to see him
A4   27: 1   It was the White Rabbit, trotting slowly back again, and looking anxiously about as it went, as
A2   20:17   Mouse heard this, it turned round and swam slowly back to her: its face was quite pale (with passion,
T8   187:13   and let the reins fall on its neck: then, slowly beating time with one hand, and with a faint smile
A6   53: 4   said the Cat; and this time it vanished quite slowly, beginning with the end of the tail, and ending with
A9   72:41   was too much frightened to say a word, but slowly followed her back to the croquet-ground.
A1   8:11   the well was very deep, or she fell very slowly, for she had plenty of time as she went down to look
AI   3:32   Thus grew the tale of Wonderland: / Thus slowly, one by one, / Its quaint events were hammered out--/
A7   58:25   The Dormouse slowly opened its eyes. "I wasn't asleep," it said in a hoarse
T1   114:18   Alice watched the White King as he slowly struggled up from bar to bar, till at last she said
T1   114:24   up very gently, and lifted him across more slowly than she had lifted the Queen, that she mightn't take
T9   198:13   was sitting under a tree, got up and hobbled slowly towards her: he was dressed in bright yellow, and had
T2   128: 6   as she returned to the tree, and then began slowly walking down the row.
SLUGGARD (1)
A10   82:15   "Stand up and repeat ''Tis the voice of the sluggard,'" said the Gryphon.
SLYLY (1)
T7   176:17   for the crown now!" the Unicorn said, looking slyly up at the crown, which the poor King was nearly shaking
SMALL (15)
A2   18: 4   done that?" she thought. "I must be growing small again." She got up and went to the table to measure
T10   205: 4   resistance whatever: only her face grew very small, and her eyes got large and green: and still, as Alice
T8W   20:11   "Not with a mouth as small as that," the Wasp persisted. "If you was a-fighting,
A2   18:15   thought the poor child, "for I never was so small as this before, never! And I declare it's too bad, that
A1   9:38   the locks were too large, or the key was too small, but at any rate it would not open any of them. However,
A1   12:32   table: she opened it, and found in it a very small cake, on which the words "EAT ME" were beautifully
A4   32:11   began shrinking directly. As soon as she was small enough to get through the door, she ran out of the house
A6   49:34   nose: also its eyes were getting extremely small for a baby: altogether Alice did not like the look of
A8   68: 7   way of settling all difficulties, great or small. "Off with his head!" she said without even looking

SMALL (cont.)
A3   24:11   that they could not taste theirs, and the small ones choked and had to be patted on the back. However,
A1   10: 1   opened the door and found that it led into a small passage, not much larger than a rat-hole: she knelt down
A2   19: 8   or hippopotamus, but then she remembered how small she was now, and she soon made out that it was only a
T3   131:37   she thought. But this was such a wonderfully small sigh, that she wouldn't have heard it at all, if it
T3   131:14   Alice thought to herself. And an extremely small voice, close to her ear, said "You might make a joke on
T4   146:15   as he pointed with a trembling finger at a small white thing lying under the tree.
SMALLER (3)
A4   28:28   "when one wasn't always growing larger and smaller, and being ordered about by mice and rabbits. I almost
A1   12:35   I can reach the key; and if it makes me grow smaller, I can creep under the door: so either way I'll get
A4   32: 9   possibly make me larger, it must make me smaller, I suppose."
SMALLEST (2)
A4   32:23   the only difficulty was, that she had not the smallest idea how to set about it; and, while she was peering
A4   34:10   smoking a long hookah, and taking not the smallest notice of her or of anything else.
SMILE (9)
T7   175:27   could not help her lips curling up into a smile as she began: "Do you know, I always thought Unicorns
T4   148: 6   Tweedledum looked round him with a satisfied smile. "I don't suppose," he said, "there'll be a tree left
T8   187:13   beating time with one hand, and with a faint smile lighting up his gentle foolish face, as if he enjoyed
T1   110: 4   "Kitty, can you play chess? Now, don't smile, my dear. I'm asking it seriously. Because, when we were
T5   152:22   bleeding, you see," she said to Alice with a smile. "Now you understand the way things happen here."
T8   187:20   only yesterday--the mild blue eyes and kindly smile of the Knight--the setting sun gleaming through his hair
A3   22:33   And the Eaglet bent down its head to hide a smile: some of the other birds tittered audibly.
A12   96:26   said the King looking round the court with a smile. There was a dead silence.
TI   103: 5   thou / Are half a life asunder, / Thy loving smile will surely hail / The love-gift of a fairy-tale.
SMILED (8)
A8   67:36   The Queen smiled and passed on.
T5   149:16   very beginning of their conversation, so she smiled and said "If your Majesty will only tell me the right
T6   163:25   Humpty Dumpty smiled contemptuously. "Of course you don't--till I tell you.
T9   193:16   The White Queen smiled feebly, and said "And I invite you."
T4   140:22   Tweedledee smiled gently, and began again:
A8   63:36   it to the Knave of Hearts, who only bowed and smiled in reply.
T6   161: 6   him a little anxiously as she took it. "If he smiled much more the ends of his mouth might meet behind," she
T2   126: 7   as she said this, but her companion only smiled pleasantly, and said "That's easily managed. You can be
SMILING (4)
T8   182:24   "Only in the usual way," Alice said, smiling.
T6   163: 6   Alice couldn't help smiling as she took out her memorandum-book, and worked the
A8   63:23   it was talking in a hurried nervous manner, smiling at everything that was said, and went by without
A2   17:15   And welcomes little fishes in, / With gently smiling jaws!
SMOKE (3)
T3   130: 8   "The man that drives the engine. Why, the smoke alone is worth a thousand pounds a puff!"
T1   110:37   you know, unless our fire smokes, and then smoke comes up in that room too--but that may be only pretence
A6   46:45   right into a large kitchen, which was full of smoke from one end to the other: the Duchess was sitting on a
SMOKES (1)
T1   110:37   you never can tell, you know, unless our fire smokes, and then smoke comes up in that room too--but that may
SMOKING (2)
A4   34:10   on the top, with its arms folded, quietly smoking a long hookah, and taking not the smallest notice of
A5   41:22   it put the hookah into its mouth, and began smoking again.
SMOOTH (1)
T4   140:26   / He did his very best to make / The billows smooth and bright--/ And this was odd, because it was / The
SMOOTHE (1)
T9   196:36   tired, poor thing!" said the Red Queen. "Smoothe her hair--lend her your nightcap--and sing her a
SMOOTHED (1)
T1   115:13   think you're tidy enough!" she added, as she smoothed his hair, and set him upon the table near the Queen.
SMOOTHLY (2)
T8   184:17   "Much more smoothly than a live horse," Alice said, with a little scream
T8   184:14   "Does that kind go smoothly?" the Knight asked in a tone of great interest,
SNAIL (3)
A10   80:10   is to France. / Then turn not pale, beloved snail, but come and join the dance. / Will you, wo'n't you,
A10   80: 3   us, with the lobsters, out to sea!" / But the snail replied "Too far, too far!", and gave a look askance--/
A10   79:13   walk a little faster?" said a whiting to a snail, / "There's a porpoise close behind us, and he's
-SNAKE [See RATTLE-SNAKE]
SNAP (1)
T4   139:17   briskly, and shut his mouth up again with a snap.
SNAP-DRAGON-FLIES (1)
T3   134: 7   into candles--because they want to turn into Snap-dragon-flies!"
SNAP-DRAGON-FLY (1)
T3   133:13   said the Gnat, "and there you'll find a Snap-dragon-fly. Its body is made of plum-pudding, its wings
SNAPPISHLY (1)
A3   26:20   tongue, Ma!" said the young Crab, a little snappishly. "You're enough to try the patience of an oyster!"
SNATCH (2)
A4   29:35   she suddenly spread out her hand, and made a snatch in the air. She did not get hold of anything, but she
A4   30:16   spread out her hand again, and made another snatch in the air. This time there were two little shrieks,
SNEEZE (3)
T6   166: 8   bellowing and whistling, with a kind of sneeze in the middle: however, you'll hear it done, maybe--
A12   98:40   to the voice of the shepherd-boy--and the sneeze of the baby, the shriek of the Gryphon, and all the
A6   47:10   two creatures in the kitchen, that did not sneeze, were the cook, and a large cat, which was lying on the
SNEEZED (1)
A6   47: 8   too much of it in the air. Even the Duchess sneezed occasionally; and as for the baby, it was sneezing and
SNEEZES (2)
A6   49: 5   severely to my boy, / I beat him when he sneezes; / For he can thoroughly enjoy / The pepper when he

SNEEZES (cont.)
A6   48:37 to your little boy, / And beat him when he sneezes. / He only does it to annoy, / Because he knows it
SNEEZING (6)
A6   47: 6 said to herself, as well as she could for sneezing.
A11   91: 8 by the way the people near the door began sneezing all at once.
A6   46:15 noise going on within--a constant howling and sneezing, and every now and then a great crash, as if a dish
A6   47: 8 occasionally; and as for the baby, it was sneezing and howling alternately without a moment's pause. The
A6   49:29 thing grunted in reply (it had left off sneezing by this time). "Don't grunt," said Alice; "that's not
A12   98:29 to execution--once more the pig-baby was sneezing on the Duchess's knee, while plates and dishes
SNICKER-SNACK (1)
T1   118:14 through and through / The vorpal blade went snicker-snack! / He left it dead, and with its head / He went
SNORE (2)
T2   122:37 You keep your head under the leaves, and snore away there, till you know no more what's going on in the
T4   144:34 of untidy heap, and snoring loud--"fit to snore his head off!" as Tweedledum remarked.
SNORING (5)
T9   197:19 tone; but there was no answer but a gentle snoring.
T9   197:20   The snoring got more distinct every minute, and sounded more like
T9   197:11 moment both Queens were fast asleep, and snoring loud.
T4   144:34 crumpled up into a sort of untidy heap, and snoring loud--"fit to snore his head off!" as Tweedledum
T4   144:27   "It's only the Red King snoring," said Tweedledee.
SNORTED (1)
T8   190: 9 / As if his mouth were full of dough, / Who snorted like a buffalo--/ That summer evening long ago, /
SNORTING (1)
A6   49:18 thought Alice. The poor little thing was snorting like a steam-engine when she caught it, and kept
SNOUT (1)
A6   49:33 it had a very turn-up nose, much more like a snout than a real nose: also its eyes were getting extremely
SNOW (6)
T1   109: 9   "Do you hear the snow against the window-panes, Kitty? How nice and soft it
T1   108:24 the window, and putting you out into the snow! And you'd have deserved it, you little mischievous
T5   156:38 being dream-rushes, melted away almost like snow, as they lay in heaps at her feet--but Alice hardly
T1   109:10 How nice and soft it sounds! I wonder if the snow loves the trees and fields, that it kisses them so gently
TI   103:25   Without, the frost, the blinding snow, / The storm-wind's moody madness--/ Within, the
T8   190: 2 was slow, / Whose hair was whiter than the snow, / Whose face was very like a crow, / With eyes, like
SNOWDROP (2)
T1   108:33 excuses, but listen! Number two: you pulled Snowdrop away by the tail just as I had put down the saucer of
T12   207:26   "Snowdrop, my pet!" she went on, looking over her shoulder at
SNOWED (1)
T1   108:15 of sticks, Kitty! Only it got so cold, and it snowed so, they had to leave off. Never mind, we'll go and see
SNUG (1)
T1   109:12 them so gently? And then it covers them up snug, you know, with a white quilt; and perhaps it says 'Go to
SO (369)
A10   84: 7 Gryphon, and Alice was only too glad to do so.
A12   93: 3 emphasis, looking hard at Alice as he said so.
T2   126:17 faster, though she had no breath left to say so.
T3   129:24 so dusty and hot, and the elephants did tease so!'"
T9   195: 6 beg them to leave off, it blew her hair about so.
T6   163:37 Alice was too much puzzled to say anything; so after a minute Humpty Dumpty began again. "They've a temper
A11   87: 9 not make out at all what had become of it; so, after hunting all about for it, he was obliged to write
A10   82: 1   So Alice began telling them her adventures from the time when
T5   156:42 in the water and wouldn't come out again (so Alice explained it afterwards), and the consequence was
A12   98:11 now run in to your tea: it's getting late." So Alice got up and ran off, thinking while she ran, as well
T12   207:13   So Alice hunted among the chessmen on the table till she had
T1   114:23   So Alice picked him up very gently, and lifted him across more
T6   164:20   This sounded very hopeful, so Alice repeated the first verse:--
A10   80:22   "I believe so," Alice replied thoughtfully. "They have their tails in
T5   155:23 sound like a remark that needed any answer: so Alice said nothing, but pulled away. There was something
T8W   14:19   So Alice sat down by him, and spread out the paper on her
A1   9: 5 down, down. There was nothing else to do, so Alice soon began talking again. "Dinah'll miss me very much
T9   202:37 thing," the Red Queen said very decidedly: so Alice tried to submit to it with good grace.
A1   11: 6 However, this bottle was not marked "poison," so Alice ventured to taste it, and, finding it very nice (it
A2   20: 3 fond--of--of dogs?" The Mouse did not answer, so Alice went on eagerly: "There is such a nice little dog,
A6   48:34 singing a sort of lullaby to it as she did so, and giving it a violent shake at the end of every line:--
T6   161: 2 nearly as possible fell off the wall in doing so) and offered Alice his hand. She watched him a little
T4   142:14 and the Carpenter / Walked on a mile or so, / And then they rested on a rock / Conveniently low: / And
A3   23:13 when they had been running half an hour or so, and were quite dry again, the Dodo suddenly called out
A11   89:12 I hadn't begun my tea--not above a week or so--and what with the bread-and-butter getting so thin--and
T4   146:25 and said, in a soothing tone, "You needn't be so angry about an old rattle."
T1   108:21   "Do you know, I was so angry, Kitty," Alice went on, as soon as they were
T3   131:32 to see where the voice came from. "If you're so anxious to have a joke made, why don't you make one
T9   201:16 Queen should be the only one to give orders; so, as an experiment, she called out "Waiter! Bring back the
T4   139:26 for fear of hurting the other one's feelings; so, as the best way out of the difficulty, she took hold of
T7   172:26 mouth in the shape of a trumpet and stooping so as to get close to the King's ear. Alice was sorry for
A6   49:24 tight hold of its right ear and left foot, so as to prevent its undoing itself), she carried it out into
T7   170:28 happy. His name is Haigha." (He pronounced it so as to rhyme with 'mayor.')
T2   121: 1   Alice was so astonished that she couldn't speak for a minute: it quite
A5   40: 4 eel on the end of your nose--/ What made you so awfully clever?"
A4   30:35   "Oh! So Bill's got to come down the chimney, has he?" said Alice to
T3   133:10 it must have been just repainted, it looked so bright and sticky; and then she went on.
T8W   21: 9 done as well as two, if you must have them so close--"
A9   70:25   Alice did not much like her keeping so close to her: first because the Duchess was very ugly; and

SO (cont.)

A10	82: 3	it, just at first, the two creatures got	so close to her, one on each side, and opened their eyes and
A5	42: 1	some of the other bit. Her chin was pressed	so closely against her foot, that there was hardly room to
T1	108:15	it wants plenty of sticks, Kitty! Only it got	so cold, and it snowed so, they had to leave off. Never mind,
A7	60:12	This answer	so confused poor Alice, that she let the Dormouse go on for
T1	115: 2	she might as well dust him a little, he was	so covered with ashes.
T9	195:39	"Just	so!" cried the Red Queen. "Five times as warm, and five times
T8W	14: 7	"Perhaps it's only pain that makes him	so cross." So she tried once more."
T4	139:11	the best way out of this wood: it's getting	so dark. Would you tell me, please?"
T4	143:23	us another slice. / I wish you were not quite	so deaf--/ I've had to ask you twice!'
A2	15:31	savage if I've kept her waiting!" Alice felt	so desperate that she was ready to ask help of any one: so,
T9	194:35	"So do I," the White Queen whispered: "we'll often say it over
A8	67:24	a complaining tone, "and they all quarrel	so dreadfully one ca'n't hear oneself speak--and they don't
T5	149:22	had got some one else to dress her, she was	so dreadfully untidy. "Every single thing's crooked," Alice
T3	129:24	little toss of the head), 'only it was	so dusty and hot, and the elephants did tease so!'"
A10	84:12	Mock Turtle would be so kind," Alice replied,	so eagerly that the Gryphon said, in a rather offended tone,
T9	197:22	could even make out words, and she listened	so eagerly that, when the two great heads suddenly vanished
A5	41:19	to herself "I wish the creatures wouldn't be	so easily offended!"
A3	26:10	mean it!" pleaded poor Alice. "But you're	so easily offended, you know!"
A1	12:36	me grow smaller, I can creep under the door:	so either way I'll get into the garden, and I don't care which
T4	139:13	They looked	so exactly like a couple of great schoolboys, that Alice
T6	168:23	her one of his fingers to shake: "you're	so exactly like other people."
T5	152: 6	Her screams were	so exactly like the whistle of a steam-engine, that Alice had
A8	67:32	"Not at all," said Alice: "she's	so extremely--" Just then she noticed that the Queen was close
T8	190:21	Alice: "and thank you very much for coming	so far--and for the song--I liked it very much."
T4	143:27	such a trick, / After we've brought them out	so far, / And made them trot so quick!' / The Carpenter said
T5	156:31	at the obstinacy of the rushes in growing	so far off, as, with flushed cheeks and dripping hair and
A2	14: 5	to be almost out of sight, they were getting	so far off). "Oh, my poor little feet, I wonder who will put
T4	148: 7	"there'll be a tree left standing, for ever	so far round, by the time we've finished!"
A12	95:38	"All right,	so far," said the King; and he went on muttering over the
A6	51: 6	grinned a little wider. "Come, it's pleased	so far," thought Alice, and she went on. "Would you tell me,
T2	127: 6	the Queen. "Faster! Faster!" And they went	so fast that at last they seemed to skim through the air,
T2	126:14	were running hand in hand, and the Queen went	so fast that it was all she could do to keep up with her: and
T7	173:12	not strong enough. You see, a minute goes by	so fearfully quick. You might as well try to stop a
T7	175: 4	"No use, no use!" said the King. "She runs	so fearfully quick. You might as well try to catch a
T9	201:32	fishes in some way. Do you know why they're	so fond of fishes, all about here?"
T3	134: 6	"I wonder if that's the reason insects are	so fond of flying into candles--because they want to turn into
T9	196:15	over the tables and things--till I was	so frightened, I couldn't remember my own name!"
A10	82:19	up, and began to repeat it, but her head was	so full of the Lobster-Quadrille, that she hardly knew what
T1	109:11	the trees and fields, that it kisses them	so gently? And then it covers them up snug, you know, with a
T5	152:28	have flown away, I think," said Alice: "I'm	so glad it's gone. I thought it was the night coming on."
T8	188:27	of a way / To feed oneself on batter, / And	so go on from day to day / Getting a little fatter. / I shook
A11	86: 8	a large dish of tarts upon it: they looked	so good, that it made Alice quite hungry to look at them--"I
A8	69: 4	remark that had made the whole party look	so grave and anxious.)
A3	24: 5	whole thing very absurd, but they all looked	so grave that she did not dare to laugh; and, as she could not
T9	202:14	/ 'Take the dish-cover up!' / Ah, that is	so hard that I fear I'm unable!
T8	188:13	large a fan / That they could not be seen. /	So, having no reply to give / To what the old man said, / I
T4	139:19	he would only shout out "Contrariwise!" and	so he did.
A9	77: 8	"So he did,	so he did," said the Gryphon, sighing in his turn; and both
A9	77: 8	"So he did,	so he did," said the Gryphon, sighing in his turn;
T8W	21: 5	out of reach, and would not take the hint.	So he went on with his criticisms.
A10	82:24	sugar my hair.' / As a duck with his eyelids,	so he with his nose / Trims his belt and his buttons, and
T5	154:16	"Things flow about	so here!" she said at last in a plaintive tone, after she had
T6	161:20	just as if it was a game!" thought Alice.)	"So here's a question for you. How old did you say you were?"
T9	199:13	he said. "What's it been asking of?" He was	so hoarse that Alice could scarcely hear him.
T2	127:24	"I'm quite content to stay here--only I am	so hot and thirsty!"
T3	135:39	as she stepped under the trees, "after being	so hot, to get into the--into the--into what?" she went on,
T6	162:27	it's very ignorant of me," Alice said, in	so humble a tone that Humpty Dumpty relented.
A7	59:11	yet," Alice replied in an offended tone:	"so I ca'n't take more."
T8	184:36	tried it yet," the Knight said, gravely;	"so I ca'n't tell for certain--but I'm afraid it would be a
T8	185: 1	horse, it always touched the ground directly.	So I had a very little way to fall, you see--But there was the
T1	112: 5	as brightly as the one she had left behind.	"So I shall be as warm here as I was in the old room," thought
A7	60: 6	water out of a water-well," said the Hatter;	"so I should think you could draw treacle out of a treacle-well
T12	207:20	it: but it looked a little ashamed of itself,	so I think it must have been the Red Queen.")
T8	179: 6	on which she had tried to cut the plum-cake,	"So I wasn't dreaming, after all," she said to herself, "unless
A4	28: 6	herself, "whenever I eat or drink anything:	so I'll just see what this bottle does. I do hope it'll make
T5	154:17	tone, after she had spent a minute or	so in vainly pursuing a large bright thing that looked
A4	28: 9	It did	so indeed, and much sooner than she had expected: before she
T8W	19: 5	They said it did not fit, and	so / It made me look extremely plain: / But what was I to do,
T4	145:27	trees. But I wish it wouldn't flap its wings	so--it makes quite a hurricane in the wood--here's somebody's
T4	139: 7	continued Tweedledee, "if it was	so, it might be; and if it were so, it would be; but as
A1	12: 3	And	so it was indeed: she was now only ten inches high, and her
T4	139: 8	"if it was so, it might be; and if it were	so, it would be; but as it isn't, it ain't. That's logic."
A6	46:35	no doubt: only Alice did not like to be told	so. "It's really dreadful," she muttered to herself, "the way
T2	122:26	Alice did	so. "It's very hard," she said; "but I don't see what that has
A10	84:11	a song, please, if the Mock Turtle would be	so kind," Alice replied, so eagerly that the Gryphon said, in
T4	143:19	'It was	so kind of you to come! / And you are very nice!' / The
T8	188:11	To dye one's whiskers green, / And always use	so large a fan / That they could not be seen. / So, having no
A6	53:13	and the roof was thatched with fur. It was	so large a house, that she did not like to go nearer till she
A12	95:24	can explain it," said Alice, (she had grown	so large in the last few minutes that she wasn't a bit afraid

SO (cont.)

T9	201:18	in a moment, like a conjuring-trick. It was	so large that she couldn't help feeling a little shy with it,
T5	157: 9	water. "I wish it hadn't let go--I should	so like a little crab to take home with me!" But the Sheep
T5	153:30	The last word ended in a long bleat,	so like a sheep that Alice quite started.
A10	80:14	very glad that it was over at last: "and I do	so like that curious song about the whiting!"
T3	132:22	with it, after they had been talking together	so long.
T2	124: 5	and full in sight of the hill she had been	so long aiming at.
A6	51:13		"--so long as I get somewhere," Alice added as an explanation.
T6	166:36	"I will, if I can remember it	so long," said Alice.
T3	135:20	was getting quite chilly with sitting still	so long, she got up and walked on.
A5	43:37	It was	so long since she had been anything near the right size, that
A7	58: 2	twinkle, twinkle, twinkle--" and went on	so long that they had to pinch it to make it stop.
T6	168: 5	and proud: / He said, 'You needn't shout	so loud!'
T12	207: 1	"Your Red Majesty shouldn't purr	so loud," Alice said, rubbing her eyes, and addressing the
T4	145:16	He shouted this	so loud that Alice couldn't help saying "Hush! You'll be
T5	152: 2	somewhere--," when the Queen began screaming,	so loud that she had to leave the sentence unfinished. "Oh, oh
T1	115:20	talking together in a frightened whisper--so	so low, that Alice could hardly hear what they said.
A6	52:27	is May, it wo'n't be raving mad--at least not	so mad as it was in March." As she said this, she looked up,
A1	8:21	jar, for fear of killing somebody underneath,	so managed to put it into one of the cupboards as she fell
T4	144:19	I like the Carpenter best--if he didn't eat	so many as the Walrus."
T8	182:19	said, as they got it in at last; "there are	so many candlesticks in the bag." And he hung it to the saddle
A5	35:15	it myself, to begin with; and being	so many different sizes in a day is very confusing."
T6	163:34	said Alice, "whether you can make words mean	so many different things."
A2	17:19	next to no toys to play with, and oh, ever	so many lessons to learn! No, I've made up my mind about it:
T5	156:39	but Alice hardly noticed this, there were	so many other curious things to think about.
A1	10: 9	if I only knew how to begin." For, you see,	so many out-of-the-way things had happened lately, that Alice
T8W	21:10	Alice did not like having	so many personal remarks made on her, and as the Wasp had
A7	58:10	came into Alice's head. "Is that the reason	so many tea-things are put out here?" she asked.
T5	155:12	"How can she knit with	so many?" the puzzled child thought to herself. "She gets more
T9	195: 2	said the White Queen. "You mustn't leave out	so many things."
T8	190:28	on again pretty easily--that comes of having	so many things hung round the horse--" So she went on talking
T6	168:27	is the same as everybody has--the two eyes,	so--"(marking their places in the air with his thumb) "nose in
A4	28:14	at the door--I do wish I hadn't drunk quite	so much!"
T7	176:18	was nearly shaking off his head, he trembled	so much.
T9	194:29	for she didn't like being found fault with	so much.
T8W	20: 3	little better, they wouldn't tease you quite	so much."
A10	81: 8	Alice, "it's very interesting. I never knew	so much about a whiting before."
A6	48:14	when they hit her; and the baby was howling	so much already, that it was quite impossible to say whether
T8	190:22	Knight said doubtfully: "but you didn't cry	so much as I thought you would."
A6	46: 5	Alice laughed	so much at this, that she had to run back into the wood for
A5	41:11	Alice said nothing: she had never been	so much contradicted in all her life before, and she felt that
T1	119: 9	She was getting a little giddy with	so much floating in the air, and was rather glad to find
A4	27:15	gloves and a fan! Quick, now!" And Alice was	so much frightened that she ran off at once in the direction
T1	110:30	if you'll only attend, Kitty, and not talk	so much, I'll tell you all my ideas about Looking-glass House.
A1	13: 1	happens when one eats cake; but Alice had got	so much into the way of expecting nothing but out-of-the-way
T9	192:34	Queen moaned, wringing her hands. "Oh, ever	so much more than that!"
T4	145:17	You'll be waking him, I'm afraid, if you make	so much noise."
T4	140: 9	"So much obliged!" added Tweedledee. "You like poetry?"
T2	126:25	never be able to talk again, she was getting	so much out of breath: and still the Queen cried "Faster!
A2	19: 1	"I wish I hadn't cried	so much!" said Alice, as she swam about, trying to find her
T4	148:11	"I shouldn't have minded it	so much," said Tweedledum, "if it hadn't been a new one."
A2	14: 1	and curiouser!" cried Alice (she was	so much surprised, that for the moment she quite forgot how to
T9	195: 4	interrupted. "She'll be feverish after	so much thinking." So they set to work and fanned her with
T9	196:13	"And part of the roof came off, and ever	so much thunder got in--and it went rolling round the room in
T1	110:35	Oh! I do so wish I could see that bit! I want	so much to know whether they've a fire in the winter: you
T2	127:29	very dry: and she thought she had never been	so choked in all her life.
T8W	19: 3	the effect, / They said I did not look	so nice / As they had ventured to expect.
T2	122:21	"How is it you can all talk	so nicely?" Alice said, hoping to get it into a better temper
A2	19:36	about in the pool, "and she sits purring	so nicely by the fire, licking her paws and washing her face--
T4	139: 6	about," said Tweedledum; "but it isn't	so, nohow."
T7	177:15	divided itself into three pieces as she did	so. "Now cut it up," said the Lion, as she returned to her
A12	95:22	yet," said the King, rubbing his hands;	"so now let the jury--"
T8W	19: 9	So now that I am old and gray, / And all my hair is nearly
T9	192:11	Everything was happening	so oddly that she didn't feel a bit surprised at finding the
T7	172:18	said the King: "this young lady saw him too.	So of course Nobody walks slower than you."
T8	189:21	heavy weight, / I weep, for it reminds me	so / Of that old man I used to know--/ Whose look was mild,
A12	94:28	his guilt, of course," said the Queen,	"so, off with--"
T5	155:36	"Why do you say 'Feather'	so often?" Alice asked at last, rather vexed. "I'm not a bird!
A10	80:21	the Mock Turtle; "but, if you've seen them	so often, of course you know what they're like?"
A11	90:16	I've seen that done," thought Alice. "I've	so often read in the newspapers, at the end of trials, 'There
T8	183: 9	"Because people don't fall off quite	so often, when they've had much practice."
A5	41: 9	replied; "only one doesn't like changing	so often, you know."
A9	77:13	said the Mock Turtle: "nine the next, and	so on."
T3	131:22	the train herself the rest of the way--," and	so on.
A10	78:17	the Mock Turtle. "Seals, turtles, salmon, and	so on: then, when you've cleared all the jelly-fish out of the
T9	203: 3	made her speech: the two Queens pushed her	so, one on each side, that they nearly lifted her up into the
A9	74:14	as she went slowly after it: "I never was	so ordered about before, in all my life, never!"
A2	19:11	Alice, "to speak to this mouse? Everything is	so out-of-the-way down here, that I should think very likely
A8	63:40	"My name is Alice,	so please your Majesty," said Alice very politely; but she
A9	76: 7	day-school, too," said Alice. "You needn't be	so proud as all that."

SO (cont.)

```
T4   143:28   brought them out so far, / And made them trot  so quick!' / The Carpenter said nothing but / 'The butter's
T9   201:14   the pudding!" and the waiters took it away       so quickly that Alice couldn't return its bow.
A11   87: 8   an opportunity of taking it away. She did it     so quickly that the poor little juror (it was Bill, the
T7   175: 3   asked, very much surprised at his taking it      so quietly.
T8   185:24                "How can you go on talking          so quietly, head downwards?" Alice asked, as she dragged him
T2   120:18                                                    So, resolutely turning her back upon the house, she set out
T1   118: 7   / Long time the manxome foe he sought--/         So rested he by the Tumtum tree, / And stood awhile in thought
A10   84:17                "Beautiful Soup,                    so rich and green, / Waiting in a hot tureen! / Who for such
T4   145:25   laughing through her tears, it all seemed        so ridiculous--"I shouldn't be able to cry."
A6    51:31                "I suppose                          so," said Alice.
A7    55:18                "Exactly                            so," said Alice.
T3   131:31                "Don't tease                        so," said Alice, looking about in vain to see where the voice
A11   88:39   "I wish you wouldn't squeeze                      so," said the Dormouse, who was sitting next to her. "I can
A9    70:32                "'Tis                               so," said the Duchess: "and the moral of that is--'Oh, 'tis
A7    58:15                "Exactly                            so," said the Hatter: "as the things get used up."
A9    70: 6   it was only the pepper that had made her         so savage when they met in the kitchen.
T8   187:12                                                    So saying, he stopped his horse and let the reins fall on its
T5   158:15   never do--you must get it for yourself." And     so saying, she went off to the other end of the shop, and set
A1    12:24   it), and sometimes she scolded herself           so severely as to bring tears into her eyes; and once she
A2    19:24   notion how long ago anything had happened.)      So she began again: "Ou est ma chatte?" which was the first
T2   121:13           Alice didn't like being criticized,      so she began asking questions. "Aren't you sometimes
A11   86:11   But there seemed to be no chance of this;        so she began looking at everything about her to pass away the
A5    44: 4   I should frighten them out of their wits!"        So she began nibbling at the right-hand bit again, and did not
A2    19:13   at any rate, there's no harm in trying."         So she began: "O Mouse, do you know the way out of this pool?
T5   149:11        at all, she must manage it herself.         So she began rather timidly: "Am I addressing the White Queen
A7    60: 3   did not wish to offend the Dormouse again,       so she began very cautiously: "But I don't understand. Where
A9    70:28   chin. However, she did not like to be rude:      so she bore it as well as she could.
T4   145:29   herself: "and it's foolish to cry about it."     So she brushed away her tears, and went on, as cheerfully as
A2    20:14                                                    So she called softly after it, "Mouse dear! Do come back again
T5   154: 8   But these, as it happened, Alice had not got:    so she contented herself with turning round, looking at the
T2   120: 9                                            And     so she did: wandering up and down, and trying turn after turn,
A6    51: 2   had very long claws and a great many teeth,      so she felt that it ought to be treated with respect.
T6   168:19   felt that it would hardly be civil to stay.      So she got up, and held out her hand. "Good-bye, till we meet
T9   192: 6                                                    So she got up and walked about--rather stiffly just at first,
A7    59:18   Alice did not quite know what to say to this:    so she helped herself to some tea and bread-and-butter, and
T9   202:38                ("And they did push                 so!" she said afterwards, when she was telling her sister the
T6   162: 1   Alice didn't want to begin another argument,     so she said nothing.
T2   123:40            This sounded nonsense to Alice,         so she said nothing, but set off at once towards the Red Queen
T6   166:21   that case she really ought to listen to it;      so she sat down, and said "Thank you" rather sadly,
A12   98:34                                                    So she sat on, with closed eyes, and half believed herself in
A9    74:39   not help thinking there must be more to come,    so she sat still and said nothing.
A4    33: 4   a good opportunity for making her escape:        so she set off at once, and ran till she was quite tired and
A6    50:14                                                    So she set the little creature down, and felt quite relieved
A1    13: 5                                                    So she set to work, and very soon finished off the cake. * * *
A5    41:43   to be lost, as she was shrinking rapidly:        so she set to work at once to eat some of the other bit. Her
T5   149:16   at the very beginning of their conversation,     so she smiled and said "If your Majesty will only tell me the
T6   159:26   remark was evidently addressed to a tree--       so she stood and softly repeated to herself:--
A8    63:32   their faces, so that they couldn't see it?"      So she stood where she was, and waited.
A4    32:10                                                    So she swallowed one of the cakes, and was delighted to find
A6    47:18   it was addressed to the baby, and not to her,    so she took courage, and went on again:--
A6    51:17   Alice felt that this could not be denied,        so she tried another question. "What sort of people live about
T8W   14: 7   it's only pain that makes him so cross."         So she tried once more.
A8    68:25    are gone from this side of the ground."         So she tucked it away under her arm, that it might not escape
A9    76:34        to ask any more questions about it:         so she turned to the Mock Turtle, and said "What else had you
A9    74: 6   with it as to go after that savage Queen:        so she waited.
T3   137:29   to the Eighth Square before it gets dark!"       So she wandered on, talking to herself as she went, till, on
A1     7: 6                                                    So she was considering, in her own mind (as well as she could,
A1    10:12   to be no use in waiting by the little door,      so she went back to the table, half hoping she might find
T8W   13:14                                                    So she went back to the Wasp--rather unwillingly, for she was
A8    68:15   never knew whether it was her turn or not.       So she went off in search of her hedgehog.
A6    48:30   the soup, and seemed not to be listening,        so she went on again: "Twenty-four hours, I think; or is it
A7    59: 7   would be like, but it puzzled her too much:      so she went on: "But why did they live at the bottom of a well
A8    67:33   the Queen was close behind her, listening:       so she went on "--likely to win, that it's hardly worth while
A4    29:16                                            And     so she went on, taking first one side and then the other, and
T8   190:28   having so many things hung round the horse--"    So she went on talking to herself, as she watched the horse
T5   158:27   shop I ever saw!" * * * * * * * * * * * * *       So she went on, wondering more and more at every step, as
A10   81:18   said the Gryphon. "I mean, what makes them       so shiny?"
T9   196:35   and laid her head on Alice's shoulder. "I am     so sleepy!" she moaned.
A2    18:15   thought the poor child, "for I never was         so small as this before, never! And I declare it's too bad,
T8   185: 6   The Knight looked                                so solemn about it that Alice did not dare to laugh. "I'm
T6   160:23   did--" Here he pursed up his lips, and looked    so solemn and grand that Alice could hardly help laughing. "If
T9   192: 2   Alice. "I never expected I should be a Queen     so soon--and I'll tell you what it is, your Majesty," she went
T4   138: 6                                They stood          so still that she quite forgot they were alive, and she was
A9    70:14   wish people knew that: then they wouldn't be     so stingy about it, you know--"
T3   137:12   having lost her dear little fellow-traveler      so suddenly. "However, I know my name now," she said: "that's
T3   129:19   trying to find some excuse for turning shy       so suddenly. "It'll never do to go down among them without a
A1     8: 8   for some way, and then dipped suddenly down,     so suddenly that Alice had not a moment to think about
T2   122:34   anybody that looked stupider," a Violet said,    so suddenly, that Alice quite jumped; for it hadn't spoken
T4   148:18                          It was getting dark       so suddenly that Alice thought there must be a thunderstorm
```

SO (cont.)

T3	137:31	corner, she came upon two fat little men, so suddenly that she could not help starting back, but in
A6	53: 3	you wouldn't keep appearing and vanishing so suddenly; you make one quite giddy!"
T7	176:20	"I'm not so sure of that," said the Unicorn.
T9	192:23	you see nobody would ever say anything, so that-- "
A6	49: 3	up and down, and the poor little thing howled so, that Alice could hardly hear the words:--
A6	49:19	itself up and straightening itself out again, so that altogether, for the first minute or two, it was as
A9	73: 7	had to leave off being arches to do this, so that, by the end of half an hour or so, there were no
A11	89: 7	on which the wretched Hatter trembled so, that he shook off both his shoes.
A3	25: 3	about it while the mouse was speaking, so that her idea of the tale was something like this:--
T1	115:11	King couldn't hear her. "You make me laugh so that I can hardly hold you! And don't keep your mouth so
A3	23:12	they liked, and left off when they liked, so that it was not easy to know when the race was over.
T12	207: 9	or any rule of that sort," she had said, "so that one could keep up a conversation! But how can you talk
T4	144:16	"You see he held his handkerchief in front, so that the Carpenter couldn't count how many he took:
T2	122:29	said, "they make the beds too soft--so that the flowers are always asleep."
T7	169: 8	went down, several more always fell over him, so that the ground was soon covered with little heaps of men.
T8	181:19	in. You see I carry it upside-down, so that the rain ca'n't get in."
A8	63:32	if people had all to lie down on their faces, so that they couldn't see it?" So she stood where she was, and
T1	111: 9	the glass has got all soft like gauze, so that we can get through. Why, it's turning into a sort of
T5	156:15	So the boat was left to drift down the stream as it would,
A8	69:12	the Duchess, it had entirely disappeared: so the King and the executioner ran wildly up and down,
T8	190:22	"I hope so," the Knight said doubtfully: "but you didn't cry so much
T4	147:10	"I suppose so," the other sulkily replied, as he crawled out of the
T4	147:12	So the two brothers went off hand-in-hand into the wood, and
T2	125:27	to be some men moving about somewhere--and so there are!" she added in a tone of delight, and her heart
T5	156: 1	This offended Alice a little, so there was no more conversation for a minute or two, while
T5	155:19	a little boat, gliding along between banks: so there was nothing for it but to do her best.
T2	120:26	However, there was the hill full in sight, so there was nothing to be done but start again. This time she
A9	73: 7	this, so that, by the end of half an hour or so, there were no arches left, and all the players, except the
A7	59:31	However, he consented to go on. "And so these three little sisters--they were learning to draw, you
A10	79: 9	So they began solemnly dancing round and round Alice, every
A10	81: 6	So they got their tails fast in their mouths. So they couldn't get them out again. That's all."
A10	81: 6	out to sea. So they had to fall a long way. So they got their tails fast in their mouths. So they couldn't
A10	81: 5	they would go with the lobsters to the dance. So they got thrown out to sea. So they had to fall a long way.
A10	81: 5	to the dance. So they got thrown out to sea. So they had to fall a long way. So they got their tails fast
T1	108:15	Kitty! Only it got so cold, and it snowed so, they had to leave off. Never mind, we'll go and see the
T4	139: 3	/ Which frightened both the heroes so, / They quite forgot their quarrel."
A9	74:29	So they sat down, and nobody spoke for some minutes. Alice
T9	195: 4	"She'll be feverish after so much thinking." So they set to work and fanned her with bunches of leaves,
T8	190:24	So they shook hands, and then the Knight rode slowly away into
T7	173:14	Alice had no more breath for talking; so they trotted on in silence, till they came into sight of a
T3	137: 3	So they walked on together through the wood, Alice with her
A9	74:23	So they went up to the Mock Turtle, who looked at them with
A7	59: 5	"So they were," said the Dormouse; "very ill."
A11	89:13	and what with the bread-and-butter getting so thin--and the twinkling of the tea--"
T1	113: 3	"They don't keep this room so tidy as the other," Alice thought to herself, as she
T2	123:18	Alice didn't like this idea at all: so, to change the subject, she asked "Does she ever come out
T1	110:26	the kitten wouldn't fold its arms properly. So, to punish it, she held it up to the Looking-glass, that it
T7	169: 5	in all her life she had never seen soldiers so uncertain on their feet: they were always tripping over
T3	135:15	make jokes," Alice said, "if it makes you so unhappy."
T12	207:29	I wonder? That must be the reason you were so untidy in my dream--Dinah! Do you know that you're
A2	20: 8	to a farmer, you know, and he says it's so useful, it's worth a hundred pounds! He says it kills all
T8	182:16	open very carefully, because the Knight was so very awkward in putting in the dish: the first two or three
A8	64:14	The Knave did so, very carefully, with one foot.
T5	152:33	"Only it is so very lonely here!" Alice said in a melancholy voice; and,
A1	7:12	remarkable in that; nor did Alice think it so very much out of the way to hear the Rabbit say to itself
T6	160:18	anxiety for the queer creature. "That wall is so very narrow!"
A6	46:23	help it," she said to herself; "his eyes are so very nearly at the top of his head. But at any rate he
A1	7:11	There was nothing so very remarkable in that; nor did Alice think it so very
T8W	18: 2	"It's to comb hair with--your wig's so very rough, you know."
T8	182:26	he said, anxiously. "You see the wind is so very strong here. It's as strong as soup."
A2	17:26	do wish they would put their heads down! I am so very tired of being all alone here!"
A10	82: 4	each side, and opened their eyes and mouths so very wide; but she gained courage as she went on. Her
T8	184:38	He looked so vexed at the idea, that Alice changed the subject hastily.
T1	113:20	Queen cried out, as she rushed past the King, so violently that she knocked him over among the cinders. "My
A6	50:10	when I get it home?" when it grunted again, so violently, that she looked down into its face in some alarm
T3	129:26	visit the elephants later on. Besides, I do so want to get into the Third Square!"
T6	165: 9	"Exactly so. Well then, 'mimsy' is 'flimsy and miserable' (there's
A6	52:11	not much surprised at this, she was getting so well used to queer things happening. While she was still
A2	15:32	that she was ready to ask help of any one: so, when the Rabbit came near her, she began, in a low, timid
T1	107:13	finished with earlier in the afternoon, and so, while Alice was sitting curled up in a corner of the great
T6	160:21	Dumpty growled out. "Of course I don't think so! Why, if ever I did fall off--which there's no chance of--
T1	115:11	hardly hold you! And don't keep your mouth so wide open! All the ashes will get into it--there, now I
T1	110:35	the bit just behind the fireplace. Oh! I do so wish I could see that bit! I want so much to know whether
T1	110: 2	ball of worsted to clap her hands. "And I do so wish it was true! I'm sure the woods look sleepy in the
T9	203:19	which they hastily fitted on as wings, and so, with forks for legs, went fluttering about in all
T1	115: 7	and rounder and rounder, till her hand shook so with laughter that she nearly let him drop upon the floor.
T3	129:28	So, with this excuse, she ran down the hill, and jumped over
T8W	16:18	he said: "it's when you hold up your head--so--without bending your neck."
A5	36: 2	"Well, perhaps you haven't found it so yet," said Alice; "but when you have to turn into a

SO (cont.)

A10	78:11	herself hastily, and said "No never") "--so you can have no idea what a delightful thing a
T9	192:28	Queen'? What right have you to call yourself so? You ca'n't be a Queen, you know, till you've passed the
T1	108:13	with me--only Dinah was making you tidy, so you couldn't. I was watching the boys getting in sticks for
A4	31:25	"So you did, old fellow!" said the others.
T9	192:35	"So you did, you know," the Red Queen said to Alice. "Always
T12	208:10	Red King, Kitty? You were his wife, my dear, so you ought to know--Oh, Kitty, do help to settle it! I'm
T7	173:25	they only give them oyster-shells in there--so you see he's very hungry and thirsty. How are you, dear
T6	164:12	venture to ask what he paid them with; and so you see I ca'n't tell you.)
A8	63: 9	should all have our heads cut off, you know. So you see, Miss, we're doing our best, afore she comes, to--"
T1	107: 4	(and bearing it pretty well, considering): so you see that it couldn't have had any hand in the mischief
A5	36:30	the hookah out of its mouth again, and said "So you think you're changed, do you?"
T8	181: 3	"So you will, when you've crossed the next brook," said the
T2	128: 8	goes two squares in its first move, you know. So you'll go very quickly through the Third Square--by railway
T3	130:21	way," and shut up the window, and went away. "So young a child," said the gentleman sitting opposite to her,

SOB (2)

A5	42:30	more subdued tone, and added, with a kind of sob, "I've tried every way, but nothing seems to suit them!"
A12	98:33	filled the air, mixed up with the distant sob of the miserable Mock Turtle.

SOBBED (1)

A6	50: 5	do with you. Mind now!" The poor little thing sobbed again (or grunted, it was impossible to say which), and

SOBBING (3)

A9	74:41	went on at last, more calmly, though still sobbing a little now and then, "we went to school in the sea.
A9	74:36	from the Gryphon, and the constant heavy sobbing of the Mock Turtle. Alice was very nearly getting up
A6	50: 1	of the thing at all. "But perhaps it was only sobbing," she thought, and looked into its eyes again, to see

SOBS (4)

A12	99: 2	take the place of the Mock Turtle's heavy sobs.
T4	144: 3	Walrus said: / 'I deeply sympathize.' / With sobs and tears he sorted out / Those of the largest size, /
A10	78: 3	and tried to speak, but, for a minute or two, sobs choked his voice. "Same as if he had a bone in his throat
A10	84:16	deeply, and began, in a voice choked with sobs, to sing this:--

SOFT (7)

T8	191: 1	and threw herself down to rest on a lawn as soft as moss, with little flowerbeds dotted about it here and
T1	109:10	against the window-panes, Kitty? How nice and soft it sounds! I wonder if the snow loves the trees and
T1	111: 9	Kitty. Let's pretend the glass has got all soft like gauze, so that we can get through. Why, it's turning
T3	137: 4	with her arms clasped lovingly round the soft neck of the Fawn, till they came out into another open
T2	122:29	the Tiger-lily said, "they make the beds too soft--so that the flowers are always asleep."
T3	136:12	call yourself?" the Fawn said at last. Such a soft sweet voice it had!
A2	19:38	and washing her face--and she is such a nice soft thing to nurse--and she's such a capital one for catching

SOFTER (1)

T10	205: 6	she kept on growing shorter--and fatter--and softer--and rounder--and--

SOFTLY (3)

A2	20:14	So she called softly after it, "Mouse dear! Do come back again, and we
T6	159:27	addressed to a tree--so she stood and softly repeated to herself:--
T7	175: 7	She's a dear good creature," he repeated softly to himself, as he opened his memorandum-book. "Do you

SOLDIER (2)

T8	181:12	she had never seen such a strange-looking soldier in all her life.
A11	86: 4	was standing before them, in chains, with a soldier on each side to guard him; and near the King was the

SOLDIERS (13) [See also FOOT-SOLDIERS]

T7	169: 1	The next moment soldiers came running through the wood, at first in twos and
A8	63:15	First came ten soldiers carrying clubs: these were all shaped like the three
A8	63:18	with diamonds, and walked two and two, as the soldiers did. After these came the royal children: there were
A8	66: 3	and the mallets live flamingoes, and the soldiers had to double themselves up and stand on their hands
T7	170: 7	on seeing Alice. "Did you happen to meet any soldiers, my dear, as you came through the wood?"
A8	64: 2	not tell whether they were gardeners, or soldiers, or courtiers, or three of her own children.
A8	65:10	and the procession moved on, three of the soldiers remaining behind to execute the unfortunate gardeners
A8	65:17	are gone, if it please your Majesty!" the soldiers shouted in reply.
T7	169: 5	that in all her life she had never seen soldiers so uncertain on their feet: they were always tripping
A8	65:13	a large flower-pot that stood near. The three soldiers wandered about for a minute or two, looking for them,
A8	66:17	send the hedgehog to, and, as the doubled-up soldiers were always getting up and walking off to other parts
A8	65:20	The soldiers were silent, and looked at Alice, as the question was
A9	73: 6	she sentenced were taken into custody by the soldiers, who of course had to leave off being arches to do

SOLEMN (6)

T8	185: 6	The Knight looked so solemn about it that Alice did not dare to laugh. "I'm afraid
T6	160:23	Here he pursed up his lips, and looked so solemn and grand that Alice could. hardly help laughing. "If I
A3	24: 8	bowed, and took the thimble, looking as solemn as she could.
T4	140:13	looking round at Tweedledum with great solemn eyes, and not noticing Alice's question.
A6	45:13	he handed over to the other, saying, in a solemn tone, "For the Duchess. An invitation from the Queen to
A6	46: 1	The Frog-Footman repeated, in the same solemn tone, only changing the order of the words a little,

SOLEMNLY (6)

A10	81:13	boots and shoes," the Gryphon replied very solemnly.
T7	175:25	"It can talk," said Haigha solemnly.
A10	79: 9	So they began solemnly dancing round and round Alice, every now and then
A3	24: 1	crowded round her once more, while the Dodo solemnly presented the thimble, saying "We beg your acceptance
T9	201:35	"As to fishes," she said, very slowly and solemnly, putting her mouth close to Alice's ear, "her White
A3	22:28	"In that case," said the Dodo solemnly, rising to its feet, "I move that the meeting adjourn

SOLES (2)

A10	81:25	"Soles and eels, of course," the Gryphon replied, rather
T8	185:20	However, though she could see nothing but the soles of his feet, she was much relieved to hear that he was

SOLID (1)

A1	9:35	upon a little three-legged table, all made of solid glass: there was nothing on it but a tiny golden key,

SOME (107)

T9	201:11	we shall get no dinner at all. May I give you some?"
T4	144:23	characters--" Here she checked herself in some alarm, at hearing something that sounded to her like the
T8	179: 2	dead silence, and Alice lifted up her head in some alarm. There was no one to be seen, and her first thought
A6	50:10	that she looked down into its face in some alarm. This time there could be no mistake about it: it
T3	134:10	said the Gnat (Alice drew her feet back in some alarm), "you may observe a Bread-and-butter-fly. Its
T5	156:11	No, but I meant--please, may we wait and pick some?" Alice pleaded. "If you don't mind stopping the boat for
T8	179:18	herself at the moment, and watched him with some anxiety as he mounted again. As soon as he was
A11	90:17	newspapers, at the end of trials, 'There was some attempt at applause, which was immediately suppressed by
A3	21:13	last the Mouse, who seemed to be a person of some authority among them, called out "Sit down, all of you,
T8	181:30	"In hopes some bees may make a nest in it--then I should get the honey."
T8	179:27	Alice looked from one to the other in some bewilderment.
T9	200:10	guests, of all kinds: some were animals, some birds, and there were even a few flowers among them. "I'm
A8	68: 1	at a king," said Alice. "I've read that in some book, but I don't remember where."
A4	32: 8	these cakes," she thought, "it's sure to make some change in my size; and, as it ca'n't possibly make me
A2	18:23	find a number of bathing-machines in the sea, some children digging in the sand with wooden spades, then a
T3	137:13	I know my name now," she said: "that's some comfort. Alice--Alice--I won't forget it again. And now,
T3	132: 9	it'll take us into the Fourth Square, that's some comfort!" she said to herself. In another moment she felt
A7	56: 5	"Yes, but some crumbs must have got in as well," the Hatter grumbled:
T2	123:22	"Where does she wear them?" Alice asked with some curiosity.
A7	56:11	Alice had been looking over his shoulder with some curiosity. "What a funny watch!" she remarked. "It tells
A5	36: 3	you have to turn into a chrysalis--you will some day, you know--and then after that into a butterfly, I
A12	98: 2	of her sister, who was gently brushing away some dead leaves that had fluttered down from the trees upon
A6	49:15	Alice caught the baby with some difficulty, as it was a queer-shaped little creature, and
T6	159:20	an egg, Sir," Alice gently explained. "And some eggs are very pretty, you know," she added, hoping to
T7	174:25	"There's some enemy after her, no doubt," the King said, without even
T8	185:14	assure you!" he said. He raised his hands in some excitement as he said this, and instantly rolled out of
T3	129:19	to run down the hill, and trying to find some excuse for turning shy so suddenly. "It'll never do to go
A9	74: 3	his history. I must go back and see after some executions I have ordered;" and she walked off, leaving
T9	194:41	"I know that!" Alice cried eagerly. "You take some flour--"
A7	55:13	"Come, we shall have some fun now!" thought Alice. "I'm glad they've begun asking
T7	173: 3	round the town. / Some gave them white bread, some gave them brown: / Some gave them plum-cake and drummed
T7	173: 4	them white bread, some gave them brown: / Some gave them plum-cake and drummed them out of town."
T7	173: 3	Lion beat the Unicorn all round the town. / Some gave them white bread, some gave them brown: / Some gave
T7	172:16	on, holding out his hand to the Messenger for some hay.
T6	168:31	or the mouth at the top--that would be some help."
A10	82:14	looked at the Gryphon as if he thought it had some kind of authority over Alice.
T1	116: 5	part that she could read, "--for it's all in some language I don't know," she said to herself.
T9	193: 4	without any meaning? Even a joke should have some meaning--and a child's more important than a joke, I hope
A12	95:33	looking at them with one eye; "I seem to see some meaning in them, after all. '--said I could not swim--'
T2	125:26	Alice said at last. "There ought to be some men moving about somewhere--and so there are!" she added
A5	41: 5	decidedly; and there was silence for some minutes.
T2	125:19	For some minutes Alice stood without speaking, looking out in all
A9	74:29	So they sat down, and nobody spoke for some minutes. Alice thought to herself "I don't see how he can
A5	36:28	might tell her something worth hearing. For some minutes it puffed away without speaking; but at last it
A11	91:22	For some minutes the whole court was in confusion, getting the
A12	94:24	makes the matter worse. You must have eaten some mischief, or else you'd have signed your name like an
A11	90: 1	"After that," continued the Hatter, "I cut some more bread-and-butter--"
A6	53:14	not like to go nearer till she had nibbled some more of the left-hand bit of mushroom, and raised herself
T7	174: 2	But Hatta only munched away, and drank some more tea.
A7	59: 9	"Take some more tea," the March Hare said to Alice, very earnestly.
A3	24: 9	thing was to eat the comfits: this caused some noise and confusion, as the large birds complained that
A3	26:31	a remarkable sensation among the party. Some of the birds hurried off at once: one old Magpie began
A12	93:30	Some of the jury wrote it down "important," and some
T5	155:34	water, of course!" said the Sheep, sticking some of the needles into her hair, as her hands were full.
A3	22:33	Eaglet bent down its head to hide a smile: some of the other birds tittered audibly.
A5	41:43	rapidly: so she set to work at once to eat some of the other bit. Her chin was pressed so closely against
A5	41: 2	right, I'm afraid," said Alice, timidly: "some of the words have got altered."
T3	132:31	large kinds. But I can tell you the names of some of them."
A4	32: 2	pebbles came rattling in at the window, and some of them hit her in the face. "I'll put a stop to this,"
T6	163:38	Humpty Dumpty began again. "They've a temper, some of them--particularly verbs: they're the proudest--
T9	202:22	directly, and very queerly they managed it: some of them put their glasses upon their heads like
A11	86:22	obliged to say "creatures," you see, because some of them were animals, and some were birds,) "I suppose
T4	143: 3	cried, / 'Before we have our chat; / For some of us are out of breath, / And all of us are fat!' / 'No
A10	81:38	tone. And the Gryphon added "Come, let's hear some of your adventures."
T6	167:17	Then some one came to me and said / 'The little fishes are in bed.'
T5	149:22	better, as it seemed to Alice, if she had got some one else to dress her, she was so dreadfully untidy.
A8	67:20	of the game, feeling very glad she had some one to listen to her. The Cat seemed to think that there
T9	200:17	uncomfortable at the silence, and longing for some one to speak.
A6	48: 8	and thought it would be as well to introduce some other subject of conversation. While she was trying to
T1	116: 4	again), she turned over the leaves, to find some part that she could read, "--for it's all in some
T6	159:22	"Some people," said Humpty Dumpty, looking away from her as
T4	140:10	"Ye-es, pretty well--some poetry," Alice said doubtfully. "Would you tell me which
T6	166:12	"I read it in a book," said Alice. "But I had some poetry repeated to me much easier than that, by--
T7	172:12	you would be better," Alice suggested. "--or some sal-volatile."
T5	156: 6	"Oh, please! There are some scented rushes!" Alice cried in a sudden transport of
T2	121: 9	speak! Said I to myself, 'Her face has got some sense in it, though it's not a clever one!' Still, you're
A6	46:18	"There might be some sense in your knocking," the Footman went on, without
A7	55:10	to make personal remarks," Alice said with some severity: "it's very rude."
T12	207: 2	addressing the kitten, respectfully, yet with some severity. "You woke me out of oh! such a nice dream! And

SOME (cont.)
T8   179:21   Ahoy! Ahoy! Check!" and Alice looked round in some surprise for the new enemy.
A4   32: 5   Alice noticed, with some surprise, that the pebbles were all turning into little
A11   87:16   "The Queen of Hearts, she made some tarts, / All on a summer day: / The Knave of Hearts, he
A7   59:19   what to say to this: so she helped herself to some tea and bread-and-butter, and then turned to the Dormouse
A6   53: 6   and ending with the grin, which remained some time after the rest of it had gone.
A12   93:33   At this moment the King, who had been for some time busily writing in his note-book, called out
T1   116:13   She puzzled over this for some time, but at last a bright thought struck her. "Why, it's
T8   185:18   She was rather startled by the fall, as for some time he had kept on very well, and she was afraid that he
A5   35: 1   and Alice looked at each other for some time in silence: at last the Caterpillar took the hookah
A10   78:19   "That generally takes some time," interrupted the Gryphon.
T7   175:16   he turned round instantly, and stood for some time looking at her with an air of the deepest disgust.
T3   129: 8   ever saw bees a mile off, you know--" and for some time she stood silent, watching one of them that was
A7   55: 7   the Hatter. He had been looking at Alice for some time with great curiosity, and this was his first speech.
A4   30:22   She waited for some time without hearing anything more: at last came a
A7   60:13   Alice, that she let the Dormouse go on for some time without interrupting it.
T1   115:35   unhappy, and struggled with the pencil for some time without saying anything; but Alice was too strong
T8   179:26   two Knights sat and looked at each other for some time without speaking. Alice looked from one to the other
T2   123:24   Rose replied. "I was wondering you hadn't got some too. I thought it was the regular rule."
A12   93:30   of the jury wrote it down "important," and some "unimportant." Alice could see this, as she was near
A1   8: 7   went straight on like a tunnel for some way, and then dipped suddenly down, so suddenly that
T9   201:32   I think--every poem was about fishes in some way. Do you know why they're so fond of fishes, all about
A8   67: 8   She was looking about for some way of escape, and wondering whether she could get away
T1   115:32   hold of the end of the pencil, which came some way over his shoulder, and began writing for him.
T9   200:10   there were about fifty guests, of all kinds: some were animals, some birds, and there were even a few
A11   86:23   see, because some of them were animals, and some were birds,) "I suppose they are the jurors." She said
A6   50: 6   to say which), and they went on for some while in silence.
A7   54:12   "Have some wine," the March Hare said in an encouraging tone.
A3   23: 6   as you might like to try the thing yourself some winter-day, I will tell you how the Dodo managed it.)
SOMEBODY (10)
A12   94: 8   be a letter, written by the prisoner to--to somebody."
A2   17:24   come up: if not, I'll stay down here till I'm somebody else'--but, oh dear!" cried Alice, with a sudden
A12   94:19   He must have imitated somebody else's hand," said the King. (The jury all brightened
T1   118:29   I don't exactly know what they are! However, somebody killed something: that's clear, at any rate--"
T7   170:21   road, shading her eyes with one hand. "I see somebody now!" she exclaimed at last. "But he's coming very
A3   23: 3   but the Dodo had paused as if it thought that somebody ought to speak, and no one else seemed inclined to
A9   70:34   "Somebody said," Alice whispered, "that it's done by everybody
A8   67:12   "It's the Cheshire-Cat: now I shall have somebody to talk to."
A1   8:20   not like to drop the jar, for fear of killing somebody underneath, so managed to put it into one of the
T8W   13: 3   "There's somebody very unhappy there," she thought, looking anxiously
SOMEBODY'S (1)
T4   145:27   makes quite a hurricane in the wood--here's somebody's shawl being blown away!"
SOMEHOW (8)
T4   140: 5   to herself: "we seem to have got beyond that, somehow!"
T1   113:13   I'm nearly sure they ca'n't see me. I feel somehow as if I was getting invisible--"
A2   18:19   in saltwater. Her first idea was that she had somehow fallen into the sea, "and in that case I can go back
T4   139:37   bush.' I don't know when I began it, but somehow I felt as if I'd been singing it a long long time!"
T1   118:27   that she couldn't make it out at all.) "Somehow it seems to fill my head with ideas--only I don't
T1   111: 8   there's a way of getting through into it, somehow, Kitty. Let's pretend the glass has got all soft like
T4   147:17   "Every one of these things has got to go on, somehow or other."
T2   126:11   you'll be a Queen--"Just at this moment, somehow or other, they began to run.
SOMERSAULT (1)   [See also BACK-SOMERSAULT]
A10   78:31   "Turn a somersault in the sea!" cried the Mock Turtle, capering wildly
SOMETHING (44)
A5   43: 8   Pigeon. "I can see you're trying to invent something!"
T3   131:15   her ear, said "You might make a joke on that--something about 'horse' and 'hoarse,' you know."
A9   77:24   interrupted in a very decided tone. "Tell her something about the games now."
T3   131:30   said the little voice close to her ear: "something about 'you would if you could,' you know."
T6   160: 7   "Must a name mean something?" Alice asked doubtfully.
A4   27: 2   anxiously about as it went, as if it had lost something; and she heard it muttering to itself, "The Duchess!
T1   113:15   Here something began squeaking on the table behind Alice, and made
A7   56:32   Alice sighed wearily. "I think you might do something better with the time," she said, "than wasting it in
T6   166: 7   "Well, 'outgribing' is something between bellowing and whistling, with a kind of
A4   31:22   too flustered to tell you--all I know is, something comes at me like a Jack-in-the-box, and up I goes
A5   36:18   the Caterpillar called after her. "I've something important to say!"
T5   149: 8   frightened sort of way, and kept repeating something in a whisper to herself that sounded like
A4   28: 4   uncorked it and put it to her lips. "I know something interesting is sure to happen," she said to herself,
T9   196:26   timidly at Alice, who felt she ought to say something kind, but really couldn't think of anything at the
T9   203:14   candles all grew up to the ceiling, looking something like a bed of rushes with fireworks at the top. As
T6   165:12   with its feathers sticking out all round--something like a live mop."
T8W   13: 4   anxiously back to see what was the matter. Something like a very old man (only that his face was more
T6   164:35   "Well 'toves' are something like badgers--they're something like lizards--and
T6   164:36   they're something like lizards--and they're something like corkscrews."
T3   129:15   flowers they must be!" was her next idea. "Something like cottages with the roofs taken off, and stalks
A7   57:17   "I've heard something like it," said Alice.
T6   164:35   'toves' are something like badgers--they're something like lizards--and they're something like corkscrews
T8   181:32   "But you've got a bee-hive--or something like one--fastened to the saddle," said Alice.
T1   110:39   if they had a fire. Well then, the books are something like our books, only the words go the wrong way: I
A3   25: 4   speaking, so that her idea of the tale was something like this:--
A3   24:13   in a ring, and begged the Mouse to tell them something more.

SOMETHING (cont.)
```
A9    70:18   close  to  her  ear. "You're  thinking about  something, my dear, and that makes you forget to talk. I
A10   82:12   "I  should  like  to  hear her try and repeat  something now. Tell her to begin." He looked at the Gryphon as
A4    29:42   it  had  fallen  into  a cucumber-frame, or  something of the sort.
T9    193:11  said the White Queen, "that she wants to deny  something--only she doesn't know what to deny!"
T7    169: 6  on their feet: they were always tripping over  something or other, and whenever one went down, several more
A4    33:12   be managed? I suppose I ought to eat or drink  something or other; but the great question is 'What'?"
A4    32:15   up  by  two  guinea-pigs, who were giving it  something out of a bottle. They all made a rush at Alice the
A2    19: 5              Just then she heard  something splashing about in the pool a little way off, and
T4    144:23  she checked herself in some alarm, at hearing  something that sounded to her like the puffing of a large
T1    118:29  know  what they are! However, somebody killed  something: that's clear, at any rate--"
T8    179:32  helmet  (which  hung from the saddle, and was  something the shape of a horse's head) and put it on.
T5    153: 6  believe it  without  that. Now I'll give you  something to believe. I'm just one hundred and one, five
T8    191: 4  a  tone  of dismay, as she put her hands up to  something very heavy, that fitted tight all around her head.
T3    129: 2   she  was going  to  travel through. "It's  something very like learning geography," thought Alice, as she
T5    155:24  said  nothing, but  pulled away. There was  something very queer about the water, she thought, as every
A8    69: 2           The Queen's argument was that, if  something wasn't done about it in less than no time, she'd
A5    36:27   do,  and  perhaps after all it might tell her  something worth hearing. For some minutes it puffed away
```
SOMETHING'S (1)
```
T9    203: 8  seizing Alice's hair with both her hands. "Something's going to happen!"
```
SOMETIMES (16)
```
T5    156: 2  or  two,  while  the  boat  glided gently on,  sometimes among beds of weeds (which made the oars stick fast
T8    188:41                'I  sometimes  dig  for  buttered  rolls, / Or  set  limed  twigs  for
A1     9:13   "Do cats eat bats? Do cats eat bats?" for,  sometimes "Do bats eat cats?" for, you see, as she couldn't
T2    121:14  so  she  began  asking questions. "Aren't you  sometimes frightened at being planted out here, with nobody to
T9    195:33  days  and  nights two or three at a time, and  sometimes in the winter we take as many as five nights
T5    153:15  I  always did it for half-an-hour a day. Why,  sometimes I've believed as many as six impossible things
T5    154:18  pursuing  a  large bright thing that looked  sometimes like a doll and sometimes like a work-box, and was
T5    154:18  thing  that looked sometimes like a doll and  sometimes like a work-box, and was always in the shelf next
T8    189: 1  rolls, / Or  set  limed  twigs  for  crabs: / I  sometimes  search  for  grassy  knolls / For  wheels  of  Hansom-cabs
A1    12:24   (though  she  very  seldom  followed it), and  sometimes she scolded herself so severely as to bring tears
A5    43:35   the  other, and growing sometimes taller, and  sometimes shorter, until she had succeeded in bringing herself
A5    43:34   at  one  and  then at the other, and growing  sometimes taller, and sometimes shorter, until she had
T1    108: 6  all  the  time, sometimes to the kitten, and  sometimes to herself. Kitty sat very demurely on her knee,
T5    150: 7               "It must come  sometimes to 'jam to-day,'" Alice objected.
T1    108: 6  very  fast, as she was talking all the time,  sometimes to the kitten, and sometimes to herself. Kitty sat
T5    156: 4  fast  in  the  water, worse than ever), and  sometimes under trees, but always with the same tall
```
SOMEWHERE (8)
```
A1     9: 4   do to ask: perhaps I shall see it written up  somewhere."
T2    123:10  "There's  another  little girl in the garden,  somewhere!"
A6    51:13           "--so long as I get  somewhere," Alice added as an explanation.
T2    125:26  "There  ought  to  be  some men moving about  somewhere--and so there are!" she added in a tone of delight,
T2    127:17  panting  a  little, "you'd  generally get to  somewhere else--if you ran very fast for a long time as we've
T2    127:21  to  keep in the same place. If you want to get  somewhere else, you must run at least twice as fast as that!"
A1     8:29   time?"  she  said aloud. "I must be getting  somewhere near the centre of the earth. Let me see: that would
T5    152: 1  was  just beginning to say "There's a mistake  somewhere--," when the Queen began screaming, so loud that she
```
SON (2)
```
A5    37: 5   "In  my  youth," Father William replied to his  son, / "I feared it might injure the brain; / But, now that
T1    118: 1            "Beware  the  Jabberwock, my  son! / The  jaws  that  bite, the  claws  that  catch! / Beware  the
```
SONG (22)
```
A10   84:10  you  like the Mock Turtle to sing you another  song?"
A10   85: 5   off,  without  waiting  for  the  end of the  song.
T6    166:33  are  long, / Perhaps  you'll  understand  the  song:
T7    172:41  to  herself, as she ran, the words of the old  song:--
T8    187:27  a  half-dream, to the melancholy music of the  song.
A10   80:15  over  at last: "and I do so like that curious  song about the whiting!"
T6    166:24  when  the  fields  are  white, / I  sing this  song for  your delight--
T8    187:15   face,  as if he  enjoyed the music of his  song, he began.
T8    190:21  you  very much for coming so far--and for the  song--I liked it very much."
A10   81:28  whose  thoughts were still running on the  song, "I'd have said to the porpoise 'Keep back, please! We
T8    187: 4  "Then  I  ought to have said 'That's what the  song is called'?" Alice corrected herself.
T8    186:40  Or else it doesn't, you know. The name of the  song is called 'Haddocks' Eyes.'"
T8    187: 6  you  oughtn't: that's quite another thing! The  song is called 'Ways and Means': but that's only what it's
T8    186:42            "Oh, that's the name of the  song, is it?" Alice said, trying to feel interested.
T4    138:16  all Alice could say; for the words of the old  song kept ringing through her head like the ticking of a clock
A7    57:16               You know the  song, perhaps?"
A10   84:11              "Oh, a  song, please, if the Mock Turtle would be so kind," Alice
T8    187:10  "I was coming to that," the Knight said. "The  song really is 'A-sitting On A Gate': and the tune's my own
A6    49: 1   the  Duchess sang the second verse of the  song, she kept tossing the baby violently up and down, and the
T8    187: 8            "Well, what is the  song, then?" said Alice, who was by this time completely
T3    129:39  all  said together ("like the chorus of a  song," thought Alice) "Don't keep him waiting, child! Why, his
T8    186:32  said  in an anxious tone: "let me sing you a  song to comfort you."
```
SONG'S (1)
```
T9    198: 5            "I'll wait till the  song's over," thought Alice, "and then I'll ring the--the--
```
SOON (42)
```
A3    21:18   catch  a bad cold if she did not get dry very  soon.
T9    192: 2  "I  never  expected  I  should  be a Queen so  soon--and I'll tell you what it is, your Majesty," she went on
T8    179:19  him with some anxiety as he mounted again. As  soon as he was comfortably in the saddle, he began once more
A3    26:16   a pity it wouldn't stay!" sighed the Lory, as  soon as it was quite out of sight. And an old Crab took the
```

```
SOON (cont.)
  A3     26:29  the birds!  Why, she'll eat a little bird as soon as look at it!"
  A6     49:22                                            As soon as she had made out the proper way of nursing it (which
  T1    114:10    but hug the little Lily in silence. As soon as she had recovered her breath a little, she called out
  A4     32:11  to find that she began shrinking directly. As soon as she was small enough to get through the door, she ran
  A12    93:10                                            As soon as the jury had a little recovered from the shock of
  T5    152: 8         "What is the matter?" she said, as soon as there was a chance of making herself heard. "Have you
  A8     67:14  "How are you getting on?" said the Cat, as soon as there was mouth enough for it to speak with.
  T1    108:21  I was so angry, Kitty," Alice went on, as soon as they were comfortably settled again, "when I saw all
  T2    128:33     that she was a Pawn, and that it would soon be time for her to move.
  A1      9: 5  down.  There was nothing else to do, so Alice soon began talking again. "Dinah'll miss me very much to-night
  T7    174: 8                    "Then I suppose they'll soon bring the white bread and the brown?" Alice ventured to
  T3    135:22                                  She very soon came to an open field, with a wood on the other side of
  A8     66:18    off to other parts of the ground, Alice soon came to the conclusion that it was a very difficult game
  A9     73:22                          They very soon came upon a Gryphon, lying fast asleep in the sun. (If
  T7    169: 8  always fell over him, so that the ground was soon covered with little heaps of men.
  A3     26:23      addressing nobody in particular. "She'd soon fetch it back!"
  A1     11: 9  toffy, and hot buttered toast), she very soon finished it off. * * * * * * * * * *
  A1     13: 5          So she set to work, and very soon finished off the cake. * * * * * * * * * * *
  A11    87: 7  round the court and got behind him, and very soon found an opportunity of taking it away. She did it so
  A4     32:17  but she ran off as hard as she could, and soon found herself safe in a thick wood.
  A2     18: 7  high, and was going on shrinking rapidly: she soon found out that the cause of this was the fan she was
  T3    129:13  bee: in fact, it was an elephant--as Alice soon found out, though the idea quite took her breath away at
  T8    183: 1  on the side on which Alice was walking, she soon found that it was the best plan not to walk quite close
  A12    93: 7     way, being quite unable to move. She soon got it out again, and put it right; "not that it
  A4     28:16  She went on growing, and growing, and very soon had to kneel down on the floor: in another minute there
  A1     12:31                                  Soon her eye fell on a little glass box that was lying under
  T5    155: 8    pair of needles. "You'll make me giddy soon, if you go on turning round like that." She was now
  A3     26:36  pretexts they all moved off, and Alice was soon left alone.
  A2     19: 8  she remembered how small she was now, and she soon made out that it was only a mouse, that had slipped in
  A2     18:25  behind them a railway station.) However, she soon made out that she was in the pool of tears which she had
  A3     21:15  "Sit down, all of you, and listen to me! I'll soon make you dry enough!" They all sat down at once, in a
  T7    173:18  could not make out which was which; but she soon managed to distinguish the Unicorn by his horn.
  T4    139:39  The other two dancers were fat, and very soon out of breath. "Four times round is enough for one dance
  T2    123:20                  "I daresay you'll see her soon," said the Rose. "She's one of the kind that has nine
  T5    152:10    pricked it yet," the Queen said, "but I soon shall--oh, oh, oh!"
  A3     22: 4  whose cause was favoured by the pope, was soon submitted to by the English, who wanted leaders, and had
  A4     27:12                            Very soon the Rabbit noticed Alice, as she went hunting about, and
  T5    157: 2  However, she wasn't a bit hurt, and was soon up again: the Sheep went on with her knitting all the
SOONER (3)
  A1     11: 5  it is almost certain to disagree with you, sooner or later.
  A4     28: 9            It did so indeed, and much sooner than she had expected: before she had drunk half the
  T9    192:29  you've passed the proper examination. And the sooner we begin it, the better."
SOOTHING (6)
  T9    197: 1  the first direction: "and I don't know any soothing lullabies."
  T9    196:37  hair--lend her your nightcap--and sing her a soothing lullaby."
  T2    122:13                  "Never mind!" Alice said in a soothing tone, and, stooping down to the daisies, who were
  T8W    16: 1  "I'm afraid you're not well," she said in a soothing tone. "Can't I do anything for you?"
  A2     19:32      "Well, perhaps not," said Alice in a soothing tone: "don't be angry about it. And yet I wish I
  T4    146:24  laid her hand upon his arm and said, in a soothing tone, "You needn't be so angry about an old rattle."
SORROW (2)
  A9     74:19  break. She pitied him deeply. "What is his sorrow?" she asked the Gryphon. And the Gryphon answered, very
  A9     74:22  "It's all his fancy, that: he hasn't got no sorrow, you know. Come on!"
SORROWFUL (2)
  A4     29: 7  one--but I'm grown up now," she added in a sorrowful tone: "at least there's no room to grow up any more
  A2     20:10  all the rats and--oh dear!" cried Alice in a sorrowful tone. "I'm afraid I've offended it again!" For the
SORROWS (1)
  A12    99: 9  and how she would feel with all their simple sorrows, and find a pleasure in all their simple joys,
SORRY (5)
  T4    144:14  best," said Alice: "because he was a little sorry for the poor oysters."
  T7    172:27  as to get close to the King's ear. Alice was sorry for this, as she wanted to hear the news too. However,
  T8W    20: 1                  "I'm very sorry for you," Alice said heartily: "and I think if your wig
  T4    138:15              "I'm sure I'm very sorry," was all Alice could say; for the words of the old song
  A5     42:41          "I'm very sorry you've been annoyed," said Alice, who was beginning to
SORT (36)
  A4     29:42  into a cucumber-frame, or something of the sort.
  T9    193:23  teach you to do sums, and things of that sort."
  A1      8:31  see, Alice had learnt several things of this sort in her lessons in the school-room, and though this was
  A4     30:40  a little animal (she couldn't guess of what sort it was) scratching and scrambling about in the chimney
  A10    78:13              "No, indeed," said Alice. "What sort of a dance is it?"
  T6    162: 4     repeated thoughtfully. "An uncomfortable sort of age. Now if you'd asked my advice, I'd have said
  A4     28:25  uncomfortable, and, as there seemed to be no sort of chance of her ever getting out of the room again, no
  A3     23: 8  First it marked out a race-course, in a sort of circle, ("the exact shape doesn't matter," it said,)
  T6    159:21  she added, hoping to turn her remark into a sort of compliment.
  T2    127:19                  "A slow sort of country!" said the Queen. "Now, here, you see, it
  T6    166: 3              "Well, a 'rath' is a sort of green pig: but 'mome' I'm not certain about. I think
  A12    92:11  kept running in her head, and she had a vague sort of idea that they must be collected at once and put back
  T3    132:27              "What sort of insects do you rejoice in, where you come from?" the
  A6     49:23  nursing it (which was to twist it up into a sort of knot, and then keep tight hold of its right ear and
  A4     29: 3  and yet--it's rather curious, you know, this sort of life! I do wonder what can have happened to me! When I
```

SORT (cont.)
A6   48:34 she began nursing her child again, singing a sort of lullaby to it as she did so, and giving it a violent
A7   56:20 The Hatter's remark seemed to her to have no sort of meaning in it, and yet it was certainly English. "I
T5   150:19   "It's a poor sort of memory that only works backwards," the Queen remarked.
T1   111:10 we can get through. Why, it's turning into a sort of mist now, I declare! It'll be easy enough to get
A1   11: 7 and, finding it very nice (it had, in fact, a sort of mixed flavour of cherry-tart, custard, pine-apple,
A6   51:18 denied, so she tried another question. "What sort of people live about here?"
A9   72:20   "A cheap sort of present!" thought Alice. "I'm glad people don't give
T4   145: 9   "You'd be nowhere. Why, you're only a sort of thing in his dream!"
T4   145:13   indignantly. "Besides, if I'm only a sort of thing in his dream, what are you, I should like to
A4   27:29 on messages next!" And she began fancying the sort of thing that would happen: "'Miss Alice! Come here
T5   150:21   "What sort of things do you remember best?" Alice ventured to ask.
T4   144:34 a tassel, and he was lying crumpled up into a sort of untidy heap, and snoring loud--"fit to snore his head
A6   46:10   "There's no sort of use in knocking," said the Footman, "and that for two
T9   201:24   It spoke in a thick, suety sort of voice, and Alice hadn't a word to say in reply: she
T5   149: 8 only looked at her in a helpless frightened sort of way, and kept repeating something in a whisper to
A1   9:12 and went on saying to herself, in a dreamy sort of way, "Do cats eat bats? Do cats eat bats?" and
A8   68:21 where Alice could see it trying in a helpless sort of way to fly up into a tree.
A12   94:30   "It doesn't prove anything of the sort!" said Alice. "Why, you don't even know what they're
A3   26: 8   "I shall do nothing of the sort," said the Mouse, getting up and walking away. "You
T12 207: 9 'yes,' and mew for 'no,' or any rule of that sort," she had said, "so that one could keep up a
T8   186: 6   "Now the cleverest thing of the sort that I ever did," he went on after a pause, "was
SORTED (1)
T4   144: 3 deeply sympathize.' / With sobs and tears he sorted out / Those of the largest size, / Holding his
SORTS (5)
A11   86: 2 with a great crowd assembled about them--all sorts of little birds and beasts, as well as the whole pack of
A2   16: 6 I'm sure I ca'n't be Mabel, for I know all sorts of things, and she, oh, she knows such a very little!
T9   203:10 then (as Alice afterwards described it) all sorts of things happened in a moment. The candles all grew up
A2   20: 7 it'll sit up and beg for its dinner, and all sorts of things--I ca'n't remember half of them--and it
T5   157:12   "Crabs, and all sorts of things," said the Sheep: "plenty of choice, only make
SOUGHT (1)
T1   118: 6 sword in hand: / Long time the manxome foe he sought--/ So rested he by the Tumtum tree, / And stood awhile
SOUND (6)
A10   82:29 around, / His voice has a timid and tremulous sound."
T8   182:36   It didn't sound a comfortable plan, Alice thought, and for a few minutes
A1   8:43 was no one listening, this time, as it didn't sound at all the right word) "--but I shall have to ask them
T5   155:23   This didn't sound like a remark that needed any answer: so Alice said
A4   30:23 a rumbling of little cart-wheels, and the sound of a good many voices all talking together: she made out
A8   63:13 themselves flat upon their faces. There was a sound of many footsteps, and Alice looked round, eager to see
SOUNDED (13)
T2   122:30   This sounded a very good reason, and Alice was quite pleased to
A4   32:22   It sounded an excellent plan, no doubt, and very neatly and
A12   93:29 important--" as if he were trying which word sounded best.
A2   17: 5   and began to repeat it, but her voice sounded hoarse and strange, and the words did not come the
T5   149: 9   something in a whisper to herself that sounded like "Bread-and-butter, bread-and-butter," and Alice
T7   176: 2   and speaking in a deep hollow tone that sounded like the tolling of a great bell.
T9   197:20 snoring got more distinct every minute, and sounded more like a tune: at last she could even make out
T7   177:13   This sounded nonsense, but Alice very obediently got up, and
T2   123:40   This sounded nonsense to Alice, so she said nothing, but set off at
A5   36:20   This sounded promising, certainly. Alice turned and came back again
A4   33: 5 and out of breath, and till the puppy's bark sounded quite faint in the distance.
T4   144:23 in some alarm, at hearing something that sounded to her like the puffing of a large steam-engine in the
T6   164:20   This sounded very hopeful, so Alice repeated the first verse:--
SOUNDS (7)
T8   190:36 last brook, and to be a Queen! How grand it sounds!" A very few steps brought her to the edge of the brook
T1   109:10 the window-panes, Kitty? How nice and soft it sounds! I wonder if the snow loves the trees and fields, that
T3   131:13   "It sounds like a horse," Alice thought to herself. And an
A4   30:17 time there were two little shrieks, and more sounds of broken glass. "What a number of cucumber-frames
A4   30: 5 angrily. "Here! Come help me out of this!" (Sounds of more broken glass.)
A10   82:33 it before," said the Mock Turtle; "but it sounds uncommon nonsense."
A9   71: 1 of that is--'Take care of the sense, and the sounds will take care of themselves.'"
SOUP (29)
A6   47: 4 a large cauldron which seemed to be full of soup.
A10   84:25 of the e--e--evening, / Beautiful, beautiful Soup!
A10   84:34 the e--e--evening, / Beautiful, beauti--FUL SOUP!"
A10   85:11 of the e--e--evening, / Beautiful, beautiful Soup!"
T8   182:26 is so very strong here. It's as strong as soup."
T9   204: 8 the tureen, before she disappeared into the soup.
A6   47: 5 "There's certainly too much pepper in that soup!" Alice said to herself, as well as she could for
T9   200:18 last the Red Queen began. "You've missed the soup and fish," she said. "Put on the joint!" And the waiters
A6   48:29 hint; but the cook was busily stirring the soup, and seemed not to be listening, so she went on again:
A10   84:21 Soup! / Soup of the evening, beautiful Soup! / Beau--ootiful Soo--oop! / Beau--ootiful Soo--oop! /
A10   84:30   Soup? / Pennyworth only of beautiful soup. / Beau--ootiful Soo--oop! / Beau--ootiful Soo--oop! /
A10   84:22 the evening, beautiful Soup! / Beau--ootiful Soo--oop! / Beau--ootiful Soo--oop! / Soo--oop of the
A10   84:31 only of beautiful soup. / Beau--ootiful Soo--oop! / Beau--ootiful Soo--oop! / Soo--oop of the
A9   70: 9 wo'n't have any pepper in my kitchen at all. Soup does very well without--Maybe it's always pepper that
A9   73:13   "It's the thing Mock Turtle Soup is made from," said the Queen.
T9   204:10 guests were lying down in the dishes, and the soup ladle was walking up the table towards Alice's chair, and
A10   84:24   Soo--oop! / Beau--ootiful Soo--oop! / Soo--oop of the e--e--evening, / Beautiful, beautiful Soup!
A10   84:33   Soo--oop! / Beau--ootiful Soo--oop! / Soo--oop of the e--e--evening, / Beautiful, beauti--FUL SOUP!"

SOUP (cont.)

A10	85:10	"Soo--oop of the e--e--evening, / Beautiful, beautiful Soup!"
A10	84:20	/ Who for such dainties would not stoop? / Soup of the evening, beautiful Soup! / Soup of the evening,
A10	84:21	/ Soup of the evening, beautiful Soup! / Soup of the evening, beautiful Soup! / Beau--ootiful Soo--oop!
A6	48:10	to fix on one, the cook took the cauldron of soup off the fire, and at once set to work throwing everything
A10	84:29	else for two p / ennyworth only of beautiful Soup? / Pennyworth only of beautiful soup. / Beau--ootiful
A10	84:17	"Beautiful Soup, so rich and green, / Waiting in a hot tureen! / Who for
A10	84:20	not stoop? / Soup of the evening, beautiful Soup! / Soup of the evening, beautiful Soup! / Beau--ootiful
A10	84:23	/ Beau--ootiful Soo--oop! / Beau--ootiful Soo--oop! / Soo--oop of the e--e--evening, / Beautiful,
A10	84:32	/ Beau--ootiful Soo--oop! / Beau--ootiful Soo--oop! / Soo--oop of the e--e--evening, / Beautiful,
A10	84:26	"Beautiful Soup! Who cares for fish, / Game, or any other dish? / Who
A10	84:14	No accounting for tastes! Sing her 'Turtle Soup,' will you, old fellow?"

SOUP-TUREEN (1)

| T9 | 204: 5 | chair. "Here I am!" cried a voice from the soup-tureen, and Alice turned again, just in time to see the |

SOUR (1)

| A9 | 70:12 | kind of rule, "and vinegar that makes them sour--and camomile that makes them bitter--and--and |

SPADES (1)

| A2 | 18:24 | some children digging in the sand with wooden spades, then a row of lodging-houses, and behind them a |

SPEAK (31)

A3	22: 9	Mouse, frowning, but very politely. "Did you speak?"
A5	41: 6	The Caterpillar was the first to speak.
T4	138:14	"if you think we're alive, you ought to speak."
T9	200:17	at the silence, and longing for some one to speak.
A9	74:28	tone. "Sit down, both of you, and don't speak a word till I've finished."
T6	168:34	Alice waited a minute to see if he would speak again, but, as he never opened his eyes or took any
A5	41:23	time Alice waited patiently until it chose to speak again. In a minute or two the Caterpillar took the
T6	162:23	said nothing for a minute or two. When he did speak again, it was in a deep growl.
A9	76: 4	added the Gryphon, before Alice could speak again. The Mock Turtle went on.
T2	124:19	"open your mouth a little wider when you speak, and always say 'your Majesty.'"
A3	23: 4	as if it thought that somebody ought to speak, and no one else seemed inclined to say anything.
A8	67:25	quarrel so dreadfully one ca'n't hear oneself speak--and they don't seem to have any rules in particular: at
T9	192:36	"Always speak the truth--think before you speak--and write it down afterwards."
A10	78: 2	his eyes. He looked at Alice and tried to speak, but, for a minute or two, sobs choked his voice. "Same
T7	174: 1	"Speak, ca'n't you!" Haigha cried impatiently. But Hatta only
A3	22:31	"Speak English!" said the Eaglet. "I don't know the meaning of
A6	47:13	sure whether it was good manners for her to speak first, "why your cat grins like that?"
T2	121: 1	Alice was so astonished that she couldn't speak for a minute: it quite seemed to take her breath away.
A2	14: 2	that for the moment she quite forgot how to speak good English). "Now I'm opening out like the largest
T2	128:23	Queen turned again, and this time she said "Speak in French when you ca'n't think of the English for a
T3	131: 8	as the rule seemed to be that they should all speak in turn, he went on with "She'll have to go back from
T2	124: 7	Red Queen. "And where are you going? Look up, speak nicely, and don't twiddle your fingers all the time."
T8	184: 3	"None to speak of," the Knight said, as if he didn't mind breaking two
A6	48:36	"Speak roughly to your little boy, / And beat him when he
T2	121: 8	Rose, "and I really was wondering when you'd speak! Said I to myself, 'Her face has got some sense in it,
A6	49: 4	"I speak severely to my boy, / I beat him when he sneezes; / For
T9	192:36	know," the Red Queen said to Alice. "Always speak the truth--think before you speak--and write it down
A2	19:10	it be of any use, now," thought Alice, "to speak to this mouse? Everything is so out-of-the-way down here
T9	192:18	"Speak when you're spoken to!" the Queen sharply interrupted
A8	67:15	as soon as there was mouth enough for it to speak with.
T7	174: 3	"Speak, wo'n't you!" cried the King. "How are they getting on

SPEAKER (1)

| A11 | 90:10 | "You're a very poor speaker," said the King. |

SPEAKING (11)

T8	179:26	looked at each other for some time without speaking. Alice looked from one to the other in some
A6	46:22	looking up into the sky all the time he was speaking, and this Alice thought decidedly uncivil. "But
A5	36:28	For some minutes it puffed away without speaking; but at last it unfolded its arms, took the hookah
T1	108:30	you say?" (pretending that the kitten was speaking). "Her paw went into your eye? Well, that's your
T7	176: 1	this!" he said, blinking lazily at Alice, and speaking in a deep hollow tone that sounded like the tolling
T1	108: 2	looking reproachfully at the old cat, and speaking in as cross a voice as she could manage--and then she
T2	125:19	For some minutes Alice stood without speaking, looking out in all directions over the country--and
A3	25: 3	kept on puzzling about it while the mouse was speaking, so that her idea of the tale was something like this
T3	130:10	thought to herself "Then there's no use in speaking." The voices didn't join in, this time, as she hadn't
A2	19:15	(Alice thought this must be the right way of speaking to a mouse: she had never done such a thing before,
A8	67:17	eyes appeared, and then nodded. "It's no use speaking to it," she thought, "till its ears have come, or at

SPEAKS (2)

| T9 | 199:15 | "I speaks English, doesn't I?" the Frog went on. "Or are you deaf |
| T2 | 122:19 | "The daisies are worst of all. When one speaks, they all begin together, and it's enough to make one |

SPECTACLES (4)

T5	153:40	off to look at her through a great pair of spectacles.
A11	88:26	Here the Queen put on her spectacles, and began staring hard at the Hatter, who turned
A11	86:?5	in the court!", and the King put on his spectacles and looked anxiously round, to make out who was
A12	94:33	The White Rabbit put on his spectacles. "Where shall I begin, please your Majesty?" he

SPEECH (7)

A7	55: 8	with great curiosity, and this was his first speech.
A3	26:30	This speech caused a remarkable sensation among the party. Some of
T9	202:29	"You ought to return thanks in a neat speech," the Red Queen said, frowning at Alice as she spoke.
T9	203: 2	her to keep in her place while she made her speech: the two Queens pushed her so, one on each side, that
A3	24: 3	and, when it had finished this short speech, they all cheered.
T1	110:20	But this is taking us away from Alice's speech to the kitten. "Let's pretend that you're the Red Queen
T8	190: 1	I used to know--/ Whose look was mild, whose speech was slow, / Whose hair was whiter than the snow, /

SPEED (2)
  T3   137:10 in another moment it had darted away at full speed.
  A2   18:12 And now for the garden!" And she ran with all speed back to the little door; but, alas! the little door was
SPELL (2)
  T7   175: 8 as he opened his memorandum-book. "Do you spell 'creature' with a double 'e'?"
  A11   87: 2 make out that one of them didn't know how to spell "stupid," and that he had to ask his neighbour to tell
SPENT (1)
  T5   154:17 at last in a plaintive tone, after she had spent a minute or so in vainly pursuing a large bright thing
SPIED (1)
  T2   123:45 looking everywhere for the Queen (whom she spied out at last, a long way off), she thought she would try
SPIKES (1)
  T2   123:21 Rose. "She's one of the kind that has nine spikes, you know."
-SPIRITED [See LOW-SPIRITED]
SPIRITS (1)
  T8W   21:11 her, and as the Wasp had quite recovered his spirits, and was getting very talkative, she thought she might
SPITE (3)
  T5   156:44 of it caught her under the chin, and, in spite of a series of little shrieks of "Oh, oh, oh!" from poor
  A4   32:32 case it would be very likely to eat her up in spite of all her coaxing.
  T8   184:18 said, with a little scream of laughter, in spite of all she could do to prevent it.
SPLASH (1)
  A2   18:18 her foot slipped, and in another moment, splash! she was up to her chin in saltwater. Her first idea
SPLASHED (1)
  A12   98:25 White Rabbit hurried by--the frightened Mouse splashed his way through the neighbouring pool--she could hear
SPLASHING (2)
  A2   19: 5   Just then she heard something splashing about in the pool a little way off, and she swam
  A8   62: 6 one of them say "Look out now, Five! Don't go splashing paint over me like that!"
SPLENDIDLY (1)
  A2   15:27 coming. It was the White Rabbit returning, splendidly dressed, with a pair of white kid-gloves in one
SPOIL (1)
  T4   140:34 <u>very</u> <u>rude</u> <u>of</u> <u>him</u>,' <u>she</u> <u>said</u>, / 'To <u>come</u> <u>and</u> <u>spoil</u> <u>the</u> <u>fun</u>!'
SPOILED (1)
  T4   138:21 / For <u>Tweedledum</u> <u>said</u> <u>Tweedledee</u> / <u>Had</u> <u>spoiled</u> <u>his</u> <u>nice</u> <u>new</u> <u>rattle</u>.
SPOILT (1)
  T4   146:21 stamp about wildly and tear his hair. "It's spoilt, of course!" Here he looked at Tweedledee, who
SPOKE (37)
  A3   22:25 dear?" it continued, turning to Alice as it spoke.
  A8   67:45 at me like that!" He got behind Alice as he spoke.
  A9   70:24 herself up closer to Alice's side as she spoke.
  A12   93:25 but frowning and making faces at him as he spoke.
  T5   155:15 handing her a pair of knitting-needles as she spoke.
  T7   176:22 Lion replied angrily, half getting up as he spoke.
  T9   202:30 the Red Queen said, frowning at Alice as she spoke.
  T2   121: 3 the Tiger-lily only went on waving about, she spoke again, in a timid voice--almost in a whisper. "And can
  T5   153:17   The brooch had come undone as she spoke, and a sudden gust of wind blew the Queen's shawl across
  A12   94:14 on the <u>outside</u>." He unfolded the paper as he spoke, and added "It isn't a letter, after all: it's a set of
  T8W   17: 9   He untied the handkerchief as he spoke, and Alice looked at his wig in great surprise. It was
  T5   149: 1   She caught the shawl as she spoke, and looked about for the owner: in another moment the
  T10 205: 1   She took her off the table as she spoke, and shook her backwards and forwards with all her might
  T8W   21: 3 and round." He took off his own wig as he spoke, and stetched out one claw towards Alice, as if he
  A7   59:38   He moved on as he spoke, and the Dormouse followed him: the March Hare moved
  A8   65:30 He looked anxiously over his shoulder as he spoke, and then raised himself upon tiptoe, put his mouth
  T8   181:25 no use without them." He unfastened it as he spoke, and was just going to throw it into the bushes, when a
  A8   68:35 their arguments to her, though, as they all spoke at once, she found it very hard to make out exactly what
  A5   42:15 see you?" She was moving them about, as she spoke, but no result seemed to follow, except a little shaking
  A9   72:37 the Queen, stamping on the ground as she spoke; "either you or your head must be off, and that in about
  A1   8:45 Australia?" (and she tried to curtsey as she spoke--fancy, <u>curtseying</u> as you're falling through the air! Do
  A9   74:29   So they sat down, and nobody spoke for some minutes. Alice thought to herself "I don't see
  A6   49:11 to Alice, flinging the baby at her as she spoke. "I must go and get ready to play croquet with the Queen
  T9   201:24   It spoke in a thick, suety sort of voice, and Alice hadn't a word
  T8   183:18 in a loud voice, waving his right arm as he spoke, "is to keep--" Here the sentence ended as suddenly as
  A5   41:17   angrily, rearing itself upright as it spoke (it was exactly three inches high).
  T8   184:15 his arms round the horse's neck as he spoke, just in time to save himself from tumbling off again.
  T3   131:11 sitting beyond the Beetle, but a hoarse voice spoke next. "Change engines--" it said, and there it choked
  T9   203: 4 Alice began: and she really <u>did</u> rise as she spoke, several inches; but she got hold of the edge of the
  A12   96:21 throwing an inkstand at the Lizard as she spoke. (The unfortunate little Bill had left off writing on
  T5   150: 3 a large piece of plaster on her finger as she spoke, "there's the King's Messenger. He's in prison now,
  T9   199: 7 with irritation at the slow drawl in which he spoke. "<u>This</u> door, of course!"
  T6   159:18 a long silence, looking away from Alice as he spoke, "to be called an egg--<u>very</u>!"
  T9   201:34   She spoke to the Red Queen, whose answer was a little wide of the
  A7   56:39 contemptuously. "I dare say you never even spoke to Time!"
  A8   65: 7 humble tone, going down on one knee as he spoke, "we were trying--"
  T9   192:21 ready for a little argument, "and if you only spoke when you were spoken to, and the other person always
SPOKEN (6)
  T2   122:35 that Alice quite jumped; for it hadn't spoken before.
  T3   130:11 didn't join in, <u>this</u> time, as she hadn't spoken, but, to her great surprise, they all <u>thought</u> in chorus
  A8   62:13   "What <u>for</u>?" said the one who had spoken first.
  T6   160:38 Now, take a good look at me! I'm one that has spoken to a King, <u>I</u> am: mayhap you'll never see such another:
  T9   192:22   "and if you only spoke when you were spoken to, and the other person always waited for <u>you</u> to begin
  T9   192:18   "Speak when you're spoken to!" the Queen sharply interrupted her.

SPOON (1) [See also TEASPOON]
A10 83:19 <u>a</u> <u>boon</u>, / <u>Was</u> <u>kindly</u> <u>permitted</u> <u>to</u> <u>pocket</u> <u>the</u> <u>spoon</u>: / <u>While</u> <u>the</u> <u>Panther</u> <u>received</u> <u>knife</u> <u>and</u> <u>fork</u> <u>with</u> <u>a</u>
SPOT (1)
A11 88:29 be nervous, or I'll have you executed on the spot."
SPRANG (2)
T7 178: 3 quite deafened. She started to her feet and sprang across the little brook in her terror, and had just
T4 146:11 "Good-night" and leave them, when Tweedledum sprang out from under the umbrella, and seized her by the
SPRAWLING (1)
A12 92: 5 heads of the crowd below, and there they lay sprawling about, reminding her very much of a globe of
SPREAD (8)
T4 146: 4   Tweedledum spread a large umbrella over himself and his brother, and
T5 153:19   shawl across a little brook. The Queen spread out her arms again and went flying after it, and this
A4 30:15 as I tell you, you coward!", and at last she spread out her hand again, and made another snatch in the air.
A4 29:34 Rabbit just under the window, she suddenly spread out her hand, and made a snatch in the air. She did not
T7 170:25 eel, as he came along, with his great hands spread out like fans on each side.)
T8W 14:19   So Alice sat down by him, and spread out the paper on her knees, and began. "<u>Latest</u> <u>News</u>.
T1 107:17 had all come undone again; and there it was, spread over the hearth-rug, all knots and tangles, with the
T4 143:30 <u>Carpenter</u> <u>said</u> <u>nothing</u> <u>but</u> / '<u>The</u> <u>butter's</u> <u>spread</u> <u>too</u> <u>thick</u>!'
SPREADING (2)
T7 175:20   in front of Alice to introduce her, and spreading out both his hands towards her in an Anglo-Saxon
A12 95:32 find any. And yet I don't know," he went on, spreading out the verses on his knee, and looking at them with
SPREADS (1)
A2 17:13 <u>How</u> <u>cheerfully</u> <u>he</u> <u>seems</u> <u>to</u> <u>grin</u>, / <u>How</u> <u>neatly</u> <u>spreads</u> <u>his</u> <u>claws</u>, / <u>And</u> <u>welcomes</u> <u>little</u> <u>fishes</u> <u>in</u>, / <u>With</u>
SPRING (3)
T8W 13:10 was Alice's first thought, as she turned to spring over the brook:--but I'll just ask him what's the
T8W 13: 1   ...and she was just going to spring over, when she heard a deep sigh, which seemed to come
T6 166:29   "<u>In</u> <u>spring</u>, <u>when</u> <u>woods</u> <u>are</u> <u>getting</u> <u>green</u>, / <u>I'll</u> <u>try</u> <u>and</u> <u>tell</u> <u>you</u>
SPRINKLE (1)
T9 199:30 <u>up</u> <u>the</u> <u>glasses</u> <u>as</u> <u>quick</u> <u>as</u> <u>you</u> <u>can</u>, / <u>And</u> <u>sprinkle</u> <u>the</u> <u>table</u> <u>with</u> <u>buttons</u> <u>and</u> <u>bran</u>: / <u>Put</u> <u>cats</u> <u>in</u> <u>the</u>
SQUARE (12)
T3 129:27 Besides, I <u>do</u> so want to get into the Third Square!"
T3 135:26   and this was the only way to the Eighth Square.
T8 190:37 her to the edge of the brook. "The Eighth Square at last!" she cried as she bounded * * * * * * * * * *
T3 137:28 the wood. If I could only get to the Eighth Square before it gets dark!" So she wandered on, talking to
T2 128:10 in the Fourth Square in no time. Well, <u>that</u> square belongs to Tweedledum and Tweedledee--the Fifth is
T2 128: 9 So you'll go <u>very</u> quickly through the Third Square--by railway, I should think--and you'll find yourself
T2 128:10 think--and you'll find yourself in the Fourth Square in no time. Well, <u>that</u> square belongs to Tweedledum and
T2 128:18 however, we'll suppose it said--the Seventh Square is all forest--however, one of the Knights will show
T3 132: 9 all. "However, it'll take us into the Fourth Square, that's some comfort!" she said to herself. In another
T2 126: 9 too young to play: and you're in the Second Square to begin with: when you get to the Eighth Square you'll
T2 128:20 will show you the way--and in the Eighth Square we shall be Queens together, and it's all feasting and
T2 126:10 to begin with: when you get to the Eighth Square you'll be a Queen--"Just at this moment, somehow or
SQUARES (2)
T2 125:23 and the ground between was divided up into squares by a number of little green hedges, that reached from
T2 128: 8 she faced round, and said "A pawn goes two squares in its first move, you know. So you'll go <u>very</u> quickly
SQUEAK (2)
T5 153:29 cried the Queen, her voice rising into a squeak as she went on. "Much be-etter! Be-etter! Be-e-e-etter!
T5 151:22 with each "better," till it got quite to a squeak at last.
SQUEAKED (2)
A11 87: 5   One of the jurors had a pencil that squeaked. This, of course, Alice could <u>not</u> stand, and she went
T1 108:27 to tell you all your faults. Number one: you squeaked twice while Dinah was washing your face this morning.
SQUEAKING (3)
A12 98:31 it--once more the shriek of the Gryphon, the squeaking of the Lizard's slate-pencil, and the choking of the
T1 113:15   Here something began squeaking on the table behind Alice, and made her turn her
A4 31:17   Last came a little feeble, squeaking voice ("That's Bill," thought Alice), "Well, I
SQUEEZE (4)
T8 189:17 <u>I</u> <u>put</u> / <u>My</u> <u>fingers</u> <u>into</u> <u>glue</u>, / <u>Or</u> <u>madly</u> <u>squeeze</u> <u>a</u> <u>right-hand</u> <u>foot</u> / <u>Into</u> <u>a</u> <u>left-hand</u> <u>shoe</u>, / <u>Or</u> <u>if</u> <u>I</u>
T4 145:26 me here," she thought: "it's far too large to squeeze itself in among the trees. But I wish it wouldn't flap
T9 202:40 feast. "You would have thought they wanted to squeeze me flat!")
A11 88:39   "I wish you wouldn't squeeze so," said the Dormouse, who was sitting next to her.
SQUEEZED (1)
A9 70:23 a moral, if only you can find it." And she squeezed herself up closer to Alice's side as she spoke.
STAIRS (6) [See also UPSTAIRS]
A5 40: 8 <u>such</u> <u>stuff</u>? / <u>Be</u> <u>off</u>, <u>or</u> <u>I'll</u> <u>kick</u> <u>you</u> <u>down-stairs</u>!"
A4 29:20 Then came a little pattering of feet on the stairs. Alice knew it was the Rabbit coming to look for her,
A1   8:24 this, I shall think nothing of tumbling down-stairs! How brave they'll all think me at home! Why, I
T1 119: 3 was out of the room in a moment, and ran down stairs--or, at least, it wasn't exactly running, but a new
T1 119: 4 running, but a new invention for getting down stairs quickly and easily, as Alice said to herself. She just
T1 119: 6 floated gently down without even touching the stairs with her feet: then she floated on through the hall,
STALK (1)
A5 42:11 length of neck, which seemed to rise like a stalk out of a sea of green leaves that lay far below her.
STALKS (1)
T3 129:16 like cottages with the roofs taken off, and stalks put to them--and what quantities of honey they must
STAMP (1)
T4 146:20 knew it was!" cried Tweedledum, beginning to stamp about wildly and tear his hair. "It's spoilt, of course!
STAMPED (1)
T9 199: 6   Alice almost stamped with irritation at the slow drawl in which he spoke.
STAMPING (2)
A8 66:22 the Queen was in a furious passion, and went stamping about, and shouting "Off with his head!" or "Off with
A9 72:36 I give you fair warning," shouted the Queen, stamping on the ground as she spoke; "either you or your head

STAND (9) [See also INKSTAND]
A11   87: 6   squeaked. This, of course, Alice could <u>not</u> stand, and she went round the court and got behind him, and
A7   56:42   accounts for it," said the Hatter. "He wo'n't stand beating. Now, if you only kept on good terms with him,
T6   160: 1   "Don't stand chattering to yourself like that," Humpty Dumpty said,
A11   90:21   "If that's all you know about it, you may stand down," continued the King.
T8   184:32   the gate--then the head's high enough--then I stand on my head--then the feet are high enough, you see--then
A8   66: 4   the soldiers had to double themselves up and stand on their hands and feet, to make the arches.
A5   37: 3   <u>become very white;</u> / <u>And yet you incessantly stand on your head--/ Do you think, at your age, it is right</u>
T9   204:13   "I ca'n't stand this any longer!" she cried, as she jumped up and seized
A10   82:15   "Stand up and repeat ''Tis the voice of the sluggard,'" said
STANDING (6)
T9   198: 1   She was standing before an arched doorway, over which were the words
A11   86: 4   as the whole pack of cards: the Knave was standing before them, in chains, with a soldier on each side
T4   148: 7   suppose," he said, "there'll be a tree left standing, for ever so far round, by the time we've finished!"
T4   138: 1   They were standing under a tree, each with an arm round the other's neck
T7   173:21   to where Hatta, the other Messenger, was standing watching the fight, with a cup of tea in one hand and
T6   159:14   exactly like an egg he is!" she said aloud, standing with her hands ready to catch him, for she was every
STAR-FISH (1)
A6   49:17   arms and legs in all directions, "just like a star-fish," thought Alice. The poor little thing was snorting
STARING (3)
A11   89: 4   All this time the Queen had never left off staring at the Hatter, and, just as the Dormouse crossed the
A11   88:26   the Queen put on her spectacles, and began staring hard at the Hatter, who turned pale and fidgeted.
A6   46: 8   was sitting on the ground near the door, staring stupidly up into the sky.
START (2)
T6   161:18   "In that case we start afresh," said Humpty Dumpty, "and it's my turn to choose
T2   120:27   in sight, so there was nothing to be done but start again. This time she came upon a large flowerbed, with a
STARTED (5)
T5   153:31   long bleat, so like a sheep that Alice quite started.
T3   136:10   her hand and tried to stroke it; but it only started back a little, and then stood looking at her again.
T7   178: 3   her head till she felt quite deafened. She started to her feet and sprang across the little brook in her
A1   7:17   and looked at it, and then hurried on, Alice started to her feet, for it flashed across her mind that she
A2   15:33   voice, "If you please, Sir--" The Rabbit started violently, dropped the white kid-gloves and the fan,
STARTING (1)
T3   137:31   men, so suddenly that she could not help starting back, but in another moment she recovered herself,
STARTLED (5)
T8   179:17   Startled as she was, Alice was more frightened for him than
T4   138: 8   at the back of each collar, when she was startled by a voice coming from the one marked 'DUM.'
A6   50:20   way to change them--" when she was a little startled by seeing the Cheshire-Cat sitting on a bough of a
T8   185:18   of the ditch to look for him. She was rather startled by the fall, as for some time he had kept on very
A9   70:17   the Duchess by this time, and was a little startled when she heard her voice close to her ear. "You're
STATE (3)
T9   193:10   "She's in that state of mind," said the White Queen, "that she wants to deny
A5   36:17   Caterpillar seemed to be in a <u>very</u> unpleasant state of mind, she turned away.
T5   149:31   put it right for her; "and dear me, what a state your hair is in!"
STATION (1)
A2   18:25   of lodging-houses, and behind them a railway station.) However, she soon made out that she was in the pool
STAY (9)
T8   190:16   brook, and then you'll be a Queen--But you'll stay and see me off first?" he added as Alice turned with an
A2   17:21   made up my mind about it: if I'm Mabel, I'll stay down here. It'll be no use their putting their heads down
A2   17:24   being that person, I'll come up: if not, I'll stay down here till I'm somebody else'--but, oh dear!" cried
T2   127:23   please!" said Alice. "I'm quite content to stay here--only I <u>am</u> so hot and thirsty!"
A4   30:20   wish they <u>could</u>! I'm sure I don't want to stay in here any longer!"
A3   26:16   "What a pity it wouldn't stay!" sighed the Lory, as soon as it was quite out of sight.
T6   168:19   she felt that it would hardly be civil to stay. So she got up, and held out her hand. "Good-bye, till we
T3   137:26   I never thought of that before--But I ca'n't stay there long. I'll just call and say 'How d'ye do?' and ask
A9   74: 6   she thought it would be quite as safe to stay with it as to go after that savage Queen: so she waited.
STAYS (1)
A7   56:17   replied very readily: "but that's because it stays the same year for such a long time together."
STEADILY (1)
T6   159:11   could keep his balance--and, as his eyes were steadily fixed in the opposite direction, and he didn't take
STEADY (1)
A5   40: 2   <u>would hardly suppose</u> / <u>That your eye was as steady as ever;</u> / <u>Yet you balanced an eel on the end of your</u>
STEAM-ENGINE (3)
T4   144:24   sounded to her like the puffing of a large steam-engine in the wood near them, though she feared it was
T5   152: 6   screams were so exactly like the whistle of a steam-engine, that Alice had to hold both her hands over her
A6   49:18   The poor little thing was snorting like a steam-engine when she caught it, and kept doubling itself up
STEER (1)
AI   4: 1   <u>And now the tale is done,</u> / <u>And home we steer, a merry crew,</u> / <u>Beneath the setting sun.</u>
STEP (1) [See also FOOTSTEP]
T5   158:27   she went on, wondering more and more at every step, as everything turned into a tree the moment she came up
STEPPED (1)
T3   135:39   rate it's a great comfort," she said as she stepped under the trees, "after being so hot, to get into the
STEPS (1) [See also FOOTSTEPS]
T8   190:36   be a Queen! How grand it sounds!" A very few steps brought her to the edge of the brook. "The Eighth Square
STERNLY (1)
A5   35: 9   do you mean by that?" said the Caterpillar, sternly. "Explain yourself!"
STETCHED (1)
T8W   21: 3   He took off his own wig as he spoke, and stetched out one claw towards Alice, as if he wished to do the
STICK (6) [See also FIDDLESTICK]
A4   32:33   what she did, she picked up a little bit of stick, and held it out to the puppy: whereupon the puppy

STICK (cont.)
A4   32:36   with a yelp of delight, and rushed at the stick, and made believe to worry it: then Alice dodged behind
A4   32:39   side, the puppy made another rush at the stick, and tumbled head over heels in its hurry to get hold of
T5   156: 3 among beds of weeds (which made the oars stick fast in the water, worse than ever), and sometimes under
A4   32:43   puppy began a series of short charges at the stick, running a very little way forwards each time and a long
T8   182:32   "First you take an upright stick," said the Knight. "Then you make your hair creep up it,
STICKING (4)
T5   150: 2 tone. "For instance, now," she went on, sticking a large piece of plaster on her finger as she spoke,
T2   127:33 inches, and began measuring the ground, and sticking little pegs in here and there.
T6   165:11 a thin shabby-looking bird with its feathers sticking out all round--something like a live mop."
T5   155:34 "In the water, of course!" said the Sheep, sticking some of the needles into her hair, as her hands were
STICKS (3) [See also CANDLESTICKS, FIDDLE-STICKS]
A1   9:19   thump! thump! down she came upon a heap of sticks and dry leaves, and the fall was over.
T1   108:14 couldn't. I was watching the boys getting in sticks for the bonfire--and it wants plenty of sticks, Kitty!
T1   108:14 for the bonfire--and it wants plenty of sticks, Kitty! Only it got so cold, and it snowed so, they had
STICKY (1)
T3   133:10 been just repainted, it looked so bright and sticky; and then she went on.
STIFF (3)
T6   168: 4   "But he was very stiff and proud: / He said, 'You needn't shout so loud!'
A9   77: 3   you, myself," the Mock Turtle said: "I'm too stiff. And the Gryphon never learnt it."
T6   168: 6   And he was very proud and stiff: / He said 'I'd go and wake them, if--'
STIFFLY (3)
T9   195:14 But the Red Queen drew herself up rather stiffly, and said "Queens never make bargains."
T12   207:22   "Sit up a little more stiffly, dear!" Alice cried with a merry laugh. "And curtsey
T9   192: 6   So she got up and walked about--rather stiffly just at first, as she was afraid that the crown might
STIFF-NECK (1)
T8W   17: 1   "Oh, you mean stiff-neck," said Alice.
STIGAND (1)
A3   22:13   and Northumbria, declared for him; and even Stigand, the patriotic archbishop of Canterbury, found it
STILL (35)
T1   116: 2 she sat watching the White King (for she was still a little anxious about him, and had the ink all ready to
T1   114:15 "Blew--me--up," panted the Queen, who was still a little out of breath. "Mind you come up--the regular
T1   115:15 fell flat on his back, and lay perfectly still; and Alice was a little alarmed at what she had done,
A9   74:39   there must be more to come, so she sat still and said nothing.
T1   107:10 on the white kitten, which was lying quite still and trying to purr--no doubt feeling that it was all
T10   205: 4 small, and her eyes got large and green: and still, as Alice went on shaking her, she kept on growing
A12   98:15   hair that would always get into her eyes--and still as she listened, or seemed to listen, the whole place
T5   151:21 the Queen said, "that would have been better still; better, and better, and better!" Her voice went higher
A5   43:32   it. After a while she remembered that she still held the pieces of mushroom in her hands, and she set to
T7   170:35 he was joining in the game, while Alice was still hesitating for the name of a town beginning with H. "The
T4   148: 9   "And all about a rattle!" said Alice, still hoping to make them a little ashamed of themselves
A2   18:11   sudden change, but very glad to find herself still in existence. "And now for the garden!" And she ran with
A1   9:23   long passage, and the White Rabbit was still in sight, hurrying down it. There was not a moment to be
T5   157: 5 her place, very much relieved to find herself still in the boat.
A6   51: 2   Alice. It looked good-natured, she thought: still it had very long claws and a great many teeth, so she
A1   8:34   as there was no one to listen to her, still it was good practice to say it over) "--yes, that's
A4   28:24   had its full effect, and she grew no larger: still it was very uncomfortable, and, as there seemed to be no
A12   98:13   But her sister sat still just as she left her, leaning her head on her hand,
A9   74:40   "When we were still little," the Mock Turtle went on at last, more calmly,
A6   52:12   used to queer things happening. While she was still looking at the place where it had been, it suddenly
T7   170:20   All this was lost on Alice, who was still looking intently along the road, shading her eyes with
T8   179: 5 Messengers. However, there was the great dish still lying at her feet, on which she had tried to cut the
T2   127:16   "Well, in our country," said Alice, still panting a little, "you'd generally get to somewhere else
T12   207:27 her shoulder at the White Kitten, which was still patiently undergoing its toilet, "when will Dinah have
A10   81:27   the whiting," said Alice, whose thoughts were still running on the song, "I'd have said to the porpoise
T3   132:21 "about the size of a chicken," Alice thought. Still, she couldn't feel nervous with it, after they had been
TC   209:10   Still she haunts me, phantomwise. / Alice moving under skies /
A4   28:19   and the other arm curled round her head. Still she went on growing, and, as a last resource, she put
T3   135:20 as she was getting quite chilly with sitting still so long, she got up and walked on.
A9   74:41   Turtle went on at last, more calmly, though still sobbing a little now and then, "we went to school in the
T4   138: 6   They stood so still that she quite forgot they were alive, and she was just
T2   126:26 she was getting so much out of breath: and still the Queen cried "Faster! Faster!" and dragged her along.
T2   126:15 was all she could do to keep up with her: and still the Queen kept crying "Faster! Faster!" but Alice felt
T8W   19:13   And still, whenever I appear, / They hoot at me and call me 'Pig!'
T2   121:10 sense in it, though it's not a clever one!' Still, you're the right colour, and that goes a long way."
STING (1)
T3   131:44 really wanted to know was, whether it could sting or not, but she thought this wouldn't be quite a civil
STINGY (1)
A9   70:14   people knew that: then they wouldn't be so stingy about it, you know--"
STIR (1)
AI   3:10   / To beg a tale of breath too weak / To stir the tiniest feather! / Yet what can one poor voice avail
STIRRING (2)
A6   47: 3   a baby: the cook was leaning over the fire, stirring a large cauldron which seemed to be full of soup.
A6   48:29   to take the hint; but the cook was busily stirring the soup, and seemed not to be listening, so she went
STOCKINGS (1)
A2   14: 7   feet, I wonder who will put on your shoes and stockings for you now, dears? I'm sure I sha'n't be able! I
STOLE (2)
A11t   86: 1   WHO STOLE THE TARTS?
A11   87:18   on a summer day: / The Knave of Hearts, he stole those tarts / And took them quite away!"

STOLEN (1)
  A11   88:22   "Stolen!" the King exclaimed, turning to the jury, who
STOOD (24)
  T8   187:29   "it's 'I give thee all, I can no more.'" She stood and listened very attentively, but no tears came into
  T6   159:26   was evidently addressed to a tree--so she stood and softly repeated to herself:--
  T4   142:17   low: / And all the little Oysters stood / And waited in a row.
  T1   118: 8   So rested he by the Tumtum tree, / And stood awhile in thought.
  A3   23:18   without a great deal of thought, and it stood for a long time with one finger pressed upon its
  T7   175:16   upon Alice: he turned round instantly, and stood for some time looking at her with an air of the deepest
  T3   137:11   Alice stood looking after it, almost ready to cry with vexation at
  T3   136:10   but it only started back a little, and then stood looking at her again.
  T4   140: 1   Then they let go of Alice's hands, and stood looking at her for a minute: there was a rather awkward
  A6   45: 1   For a minute or two she stood looking at the house, and wondering what to do next,
  A8   62: 1   A large rose-tree stood near the entrance of the garden: the roses growing on it
  A4   28: 2   when her eye fell upon a little bottle that stood near the looking-glass. There was no label this time
  A8   65:13   and she put them into a large flower-pot that stood near. The three soldiers wandered about for a minute or
  T3   129: 3   learning geography," thought Alice, as she stood on tiptoe in hopes of being able to see a little further
  T3   136: 2   She stood silent for a minute, thinking: then she suddenly began
  T7   174:20   For a minute or two Alice stood silent, watching him. Suddenly she brightened up. "Look,
  T3   129: 8   a mile off, you know--" and for some time she stood silent, watching one of them that was bustling about
  T4   138: 6   They stood so still that she quite forgot they were alive, and she
  T1   118: 9   And, as in uffish thought he stood, / The Jabberwock, with eyes of flame, / Came whiffling
  A9   72:32   began to tremble. Alice looked up, and there stood the Queen in front of them, with her arms folded,
  T8   190:26   off, I expect," Alice said to herself, as she stood watching him. "There he goes! Right on his head as
  A8   63: 1   his eye chanced to fall upon Alice, as she stood watching them, and he checked himself suddenly: the
  A8   63:33   faces, so that they couldn't see it?" So she stood where she was, and waited.
  T2   125:19   For some minutes Alice stood without speaking, looking out in all directions over the
STOOL (1)
  A6   47: 2   the Duchess was sitting on a three-legged stool in the middle, nursing a baby: the cook was leaning over
STOOP (2)
  A10   84:19   hot tureen! / Who for such dainties would not stoop? / Soup of the evening, beautiful Soup! / Soup of the
  A4   28:11   head pressing against the ceiling, and had to stoop to save her neck from being broken. She hastily put down
STOOPED (1)
  T8W   13:19   should think," Alice said to herself, and she stooped over him, and said very kindly, "I hope you're not in
STOOPING (2)
  T2   122:13   mind!" Alice said in a soothing tone, and, stooping down to the daisies, who were just beginning again,
  T7   172:26   to his mouth in the shape of a trumpet and stooping so as to get close to the King's ear. Alice was sorry
STOP (13)
  A7   58: 3   so long that they had to pinch it to make it stop.
  A12   94:36   "and go on till you come to the end: then stop."
  T7   173:13   so fearfully quick. You might as well try to stop a Bandersnatch!"
  T7   173: 9   out, after running a little further, "to stop a minute--just to get--one's breath again?"
  A5   43:31   branches, and every now and then she had to stop and untwist it. After a while she remembered that she
  T6   164: 2   to do next, as I suppose you don't mean to stop here all the rest of your life."
  T2   120:12   usual, she ran against it before she could stop herself.
  A4   27:34   think," Alice went on, "that they'd let Dinah stop in the house if it began ordering people about like that!
  T5   156:13   "How am I to stop it?" said the Sheep. "If you leave off rowing, it'll stop
  T5   156:14   the Sheep. "If you leave off rowing, it'll stop of itself."
  T8W   15:15   "Let it stop there!" said the Wasp, fretfully turning away his head.
  A2   15:22   well say this), "to go on crying in this way! Stop this moment, I tell you!" But she went on all the same,
  A4   32: 3   some of them hit her in the face. "I'll put a stop to this," she said to herself, and shouted out "You'd
STOPPED (9)
  A8   63:34   procession came opposite to Alice, they all stopped and looked at her, and the Queen said, severely, "Who
  T2   127: 8   as Alice was getting quite exhausted, they stopped, and she found herself sitting on the ground,
  T4   139:42   as suddenly as they had begun: the music stopped at the same moment.
  A11   86:34   began in a loud indignant voice; but she stopped herself hastily, for the White Rabbit cried out
  T8   187:12   So saying, he stopped his horse and let the reins fall on its neck: then,
  T8   179:15   great club. Just as he reached her, the horse stopped suddenly: "You're my prisoner!" the Knight cried, as
  A4   29:18   a few minutes she heard a voice outside, and stopped to listen.
  T4   145:24   Alice ran a little way into the wood, and stopped under a large tree. "It can never get at me here," she
  T8   182:40   Whenever the horse stopped (which it did very often), he fell off in front; and,
STOPPING (3)
  A1   8: 9   that Alice had not a moment to think about stopping herself before she found herself falling down what
  T5   156:12   pick some?" Alice pleaded. "If you don't mind stopping the boat for a minute."
  T8   182:38   over the idea, and every now and then stopping to help the poor Knight, who certainly was not a good
STOPS (1)
  T3   131:25   but take a return-ticket every time the train stops."
STORIES (1)
  A1   10:22   or not"; for she had read several nice little stories about children who had got burnt, and eaten up by wild
-STORM [See THUNDERSTORM]
STORM-WIND'S (1)
  TI   103:26   Without, the frost, the blinding snow, / The storm-wind's moody madness--/ Within, the firelight's ruddy
STORMY (1)
  T8   188: 6   sell them unto men,' he said, / 'Who sail on stormy seas; / And that's the way I get my bread--/ A trifle,
STORY (11)
  A3   26:44   his mind, and was coming back to finish his story.
  A7   58:20   of this. I vote the young lady tells us a story."
  A9t   70: 1   THE MOCK TURTLE'S STORY
  A3   26:13   "Please come back, and finish your story!" Alice called after it. And the others all joined in
  A9   74:38   saying, "Thank you, Sir, for your interesting story," but she could not help thinking there must be more to

STORY (cont.)
```
AI     3:25                                   And ever, as the story drained / The wells of fancy dry, / And faintly strove
TI   103:32  shadow of a sigh / May tremble through the story, / For "happy summer days" gone by, / And vanish'd
A7    59:26  you ca'n't be civil, you'd better finish the story for yourself."
A5    43:11                                   "A likely story indeed!" said the Pigeon, in a tone of the deepest
A7    58:28                                   "Tell us a story!" said the March Hare.
AI     4: 3                            Alice! A childish story take, / And, with a gentle hand, / Lay it where
```
STRAIGHT (11)
```
T2   125:21  were a number of tiny little brooks running straight across it from side to side, and the ground between
A6    46:28  opened, and a large plate came skimming out, straight at the Footman's head: it just grazed his nose, and
T2   120: 7  hill, I suppose--no, it doesn't! This goes straight back to the house! Well then, I'll try it the other
T5   149:24  she's all over pins!--May I put your shawl straight for you?" she added aloud.
T5   156:45  "Oh, oh, oh!" from poor Alice, it swept her straight off the seat, and down among the heap of rushes.
A1     8: 7                         The rabbit-hole went straight on like a tunnel for some way, and then dipped
T2   120:19  once more down the path, determined to keep straight on till she got to the hill. For a few minutes all
T1   119: 7  on through the hall, and would have gone straight out at the door in the same way, if she hadn't caught
T2   120: 3  of that hill: and here's a path that leads straight to it--at least, no, it doesn't do that--" (after
T3   132:10  In another moment she felt the carriage rise straight up into the air, and in her fright she caught at the
T5   149:29                            "It ca'n't go straight, you know, if you pin it all on one side," Alice said
```
STRAIGHTEN᷃D (1)
```
A8    66: 9       just as she had got its neck nicely straightened out, and was going to give the hedgehog a blow
```
STRAIGHTENING (1)
```
A6    49:19  caught it, and kept doubling itself up and straightening itself out again, so that altogether, for the
```
STRANGE (7)
```
A12   98: 7  as well as she could remember them, all these strange Adventures of hers that you have just been reading
A2    17: 6  repeat it, but her voice sounded hoarse and strange, and the words did not come the same as they used to
A5    43:38   near the right size, that it felt quite strange at first; but she got used to it in a few minutes, and
A12   98:23  whole place around her became alive with the strange creatures of her little sister's dream.
T8   187:26  eyes, she leant against a tree, watching the strange pair, and listening, in a half-dream, to the
A12   99: 7  make their eyes bright and eager with many a strange tale, perhaps even with the dream of Wonderland of
T8   187:16                         Of all the strange things that Alice saw in her journey Through The
```
STRANGE-LOOKING (1)
```
T8   181:12  Alice. She thought she had never seen such a strange-looking soldier in all her life.
```
STREAM (2)
```
T5   156:15    So the boat was left to drift down the stream as it would, till it glided gently in among the waving
TC   209:19                    Ever drifting down the stream--/ Lingering in the golden gleam--/ Life, what is it
```
STREAMING (1)
```
T4   144: 6  Holding his pocket-handkerchief / Before his streaming eyes.
```
STREET (1)
```
T8   188: 4  them into mutton-pies, / And sell them in the street. / I sell them unto men,' he said, / 'Who sail on
```
STRENGTH (1)
```
A5    39: 7  each case with my wife; / And the muscular strength, which it gave to my jaw / Has lasted the rest of my
```
STRETCHED (4)
```
A5    41:36  very difficult question. However, at last she stretched her arms round it as far as they would go, and broke
A4    34: 7                         She stretched herself up on tiptoe, and peeped over the edge of
T8   184: 6  He let go the bridle, and stretched out both his arms to show Alice what he meant, and
T5   149: 3  wildly through the wood, with both arms stretched out wide, as if she were flying, and Alice very
```
STRETCHING (3)
```
A9    76:40  to come once a week: he taught us Drawling, Stretching, and Fainting in Coils."
T6   166:14  "As to poetry, you know," said Humpty Dumpty, stretching out one of his great hands, "I can repeat poetry as
A4    32:28  down at her with large round eyes, and feebly stretching out one paw, trying to touch her. "Poor little
```
STRIKE (1)
```
T8   181:27  the bushes, when a sudden thought seemed to strike him, and he hung it carefully on a tree. "Can you guess
```
STRINGS (3)
```
T4   147:21  on--and the trouble they gave her in tying strings and fastening buttons--"Really they'll be more like
A11   90:14  canvas bag, which tied up at the mouth with strings: into this they slipped the guinea-pig, head first,
T4   147:15  hope you're a good hand at pinning and tying strings?" Tweedledum remarked. "Every one of these things has
```
STROKE (1)
```
T3   136: 9  said, as she held out her hand and tried to stroke it; but it only started back a little, and then stood
```
STROKED (1)
```
T9   202: 1  The White Queen laughed with delight, and stroked Alice's cheek. Then she began:
```
STROKING (1)
```
T9   196:23  White Queen's hands in her own, and gently stroking it: "she means well, but she ca'n't help saying
```
STRONG (5)
```
T8   182:26  see the wind is so very strong here. It's as strong as soup."
T7   173:11  good enough," the King said, "only I'm not strong enough. You see, a minute goes by so fearfully quick.
T1   115:36  without saying anything; but Alice was too strong for him, and at last he panted out "My dear! I really
T8   182:26  said, anxiously. "You see the wind is so very strong here. It's as strong as soup."
T6   168:18  sudden, Alice thought: but, after such a very strong hint that she ought to be going, she felt that it would
```
STROVE (1)
```
AI     3:27  / The wells of fancy dry, / And faintly strove that weary one / To put the subject by, / "The rest
```
STRUCK (5)
```
A2    15:12                         Just at this moment her head struck against the roof of the hall: in fact she was now
T1   115:31  pocket, and began writing. A sudden thought struck her, and she took hold of the end of the pencil, which
A5    41:40  a violent blow underneath her chin: it had struck her foot!
T5   155: 2  you what--" she added, as a sudden thought struck her. "I'll follow it up to the very top shelf of all.
T1   116:14  for some time, but at last a bright thought struck her. "Why, it's a Looking-glass book, of course! And,
```
STRUGGLED (2)
```
T1   114:18  Alice watched the White King as he slowly struggled up from bar to bar, till at last she said "Why,
T1   115:34  The poor King looked puzzled and unhappy, and struggled with the pencil for some time without saying
```

STUFF (6)
A12   97: 1   "Stuff and nonsense!" said Alice loudly. "The idea of having
A5   40: 7   / Do you think I can listen all day to such stuff? / Be off, or I'll kick you down-stairs!"
A5   42:13   "What can all that green stuff be?" said Alice. "And where have my shoulders got to?
A10   84: 3   "What is the use of repeating all that stuff?" the Mock Turtle interrupted, "if you don't explain it
T8   188:21   I set it in a blaze; / And thence they make a stuff they call / Rowland's Macassar-Oil--/ Yet
T6   166:11   content. Who's been repeating all that hard stuff to you?"
STUFFED (1)
T6   159:12   least notice of her, she thought he must be a stuffed figure after all.
STUMBLED (2)
T7   169:11   better than the foot-soldiers; but even they stumbled now and then; and it seemed to be a regular rule that
T7   170: 2   to be a regular rule that, whenever a horse stumbled, the rider fell off instantly. The confusion got
STUPID (7)
A7   60: 8   could draw treacle out of a treacle-well--eh, stupid?"
A11   87: 2   that one of them didn't know how to spell "stupid," and that he had to ask his neighbour to tell him. "A
A1   13: 3   to happen, that it seemed quite dull and stupid for life to go on in the common way.
T6   160: 5   "It's a stupid name enough!" Humpty Dumpty interrupted impatiently.
A11   86:33   "Stupid things!" Alice began in a loud indignant voice; but she
A11   86:38   that all the jurors were writing down "Stupid things!" on their slates, and she could even make out
A1   7: 7   for the hot day made her feel very sleepy and stupid), whether the pleasure of making a daisy-chain would be
STUPIDER (1)
T2   122:34   "I never saw anybody that looked stupider," a Violet said, so suddenly, that Alice quite jumped
STUPIDEST (1)
A7   60:36   picked her way through the wood. "It's the stupidest tea-party I ever was at in all my life!"
STUPIDLY (1)
A6   46: 8   sitting on the ground near the door, staring stupidly up into the sky.
SUBDUED (1)
A5   42:29   again!" repeated the Pigeon, but in a more subdued tone, and added, with a kind of sob, "I've tried every
SUBJECT (15)
A9   77:11   said Alice, in a hurry to change the subject.
A10   83: 8   by the whole thing, and longed to change the subject.
T6   162:32   pleased to find that she had chosen a good subject after all.
T6   163:45   that we've had enough of that subject, and it would be just as well if you'd mention what
AI   3:28   faintly strove that weary one / To put the subject by, / "The rest next time--" "It is next time!" / The
T8   184:38   so vexed at the idea, that Alice changed the subject hastily. "What a curious helmet you've got!" she said
T6   161:19   Humpty Dumpty, "and it's my turn to choose a subject--" ("He talks about it just as if it was a game!"
T6   162:20   and she began to wish she hadn't chosen that subject. "If only I knew," she thought to herself, "which was
T6   162:14   remarked. (They had had quite enough of the subject of age, she thought: and, if they really were to take
A2   20: 1   said Alice, in a great hurry to change the subject of conversation. "Are you--are you fond--of--of dogs?"
A6   48: 8   it would be as well to introduce some other subject of conversation. While she was trying to fix on one,
T9   192:26   thinking for a minute, suddenly changed the subject of the conversation. "What do you mean by 'If you
A2   19:43   of its tail. "As if I would talk on such a subject! Our family always hated cats: nasty, low, vulgar
T2   123:18   like this idea at all: so, to change the subject, she asked "Does she ever come out here?"
A7   58:18   "Suppose we change the subject," the March Hare interrupted, yawning. "I'm getting
SUBJECTS (2)
T6   162:15   if they really were to take turns in choosing subjects, it was her turn now.) "At least," she corrected
A9   76:37   the Mock Turtle replied, counting off the subjects on his flappers--"Mystery, ancient and modern, with
SUBMIT (1)
T9   202:37   Queen said very decidedly: so Alice tried to submit to it with good grace.
SUBMITTED (1)
A3   22: 4   cause was favoured by the pope, was soon submitted to by the English, who wanted leaders, and had been
SUBTRACTION (4)
T9   194: 5   "She ca'n't do Subtraction," said the White Queen. "Can you do Division?
T9   194: 8   "Bread-and-butter, of course. Try another Subtraction sum. Take a bone from a dog: what remains?"
T9   194: 2   the Red Queen interrupted. "Can you do Subtraction? Take nine from eight."
T9   194:31   said, "if you give me time--but I ca'n't do Subtraction under any circumstances!"
SUCCEED (2)
T4   147: 4   from the angry brother. But he couldn't quite succeed, and it ended in his rolling over, bundling up in the
T1   110:25   for it to imitate: however, the thing didn't succeed, principally, Alice said, because the kitten wouldn't
SUCCEEDED (5)
T2   124: 3   It succeeded beautifully. She had not been walking a minute
A5   43:35   taller, and sometimes shorter, until she had succeeded in bringing herself down to her usual height.
T5   153:20   and went flying after it, and this time she succeeded in catching it herself. "I've got it!" she cried in
A5   42:21   any direction, like a serpent. She had just succeeded in curving it down into a graceful zigzag, and was
A8   66: 7   at first was in managing her flamingo: she succeeded in getting its body tucked away, comfortably enough,
SUCH (81)
A2   19:38   is such a nice soft thing to nurse--and she's such a capital one for catching mice--oh, I beg your pardon!"
A3   26:27   about her pet: "Dinah's our cat. And she's such a capital one for catching mice, you ca'n't think! And oh
T8W   14: 4   tone. "Worrity, worrity! There never was such a child!"
T7   173:16   Lion and Unicorn were fighting. They were in such a cloud of dust, that at first Alice could not make out
A8   66: 1   Alice thought she had never seen such a curious croquet-ground in her life: it was all ridges
A12   98: 6   "Oh, I've had such a curious dream!" said Alice. And she told her sister, as
A2   19:35   to cats, if you could only see her. She is such a dear quiet thing," Alice went on, half to herself, as
T9   202:12   it here! Let me sup!' / It is easy to set such a dish on the table. / 'Take the dish-cover up!' / Ah,
A10   81:45   in an impatient tone: "explanations take such a dreadful time."
T1   115: 3   that she had never seen in all her life such a face as the King made, when he found himself held in
A1   8:23   "Well!" thought Alice to herself. "After such a fall as this, I shall think nothing of tumbling
T4   147:18   Alice said afterwards she had never seen such a fuss made about anything in all her life--the way those
T2   120:24   "Oh, it's too bad!" she cried. "I never saw such a house for getting in the way! Never!"
A12   92: 3   in the last few minutes, and she jumped up in such a hurry that she tipped over the jury-box with the edge

SUCH (cont.)

A7	56:17	but that's because it stays the same year for such a long time together."
T6	168:39	this aloud, as it was a great comfort to have such a long word to say) "of all the unsatisfactory people I
T6	159: 9	like a Turk, on the top of a high wall--such a narrow one that Alice quite wondered how he could keep
A5	43:13	little girls in my time, but never one with such a neck as that! No, no! You're a serpent; and there's no
A5	43:21	This was such a new idea to Alice, that she was quite silent for a
T12	207: 3	with some severity. "You woke me out of oh! such a nice dream! And you've been along with me, Kitty--all
A2	20: 3	answer, so Alice went on eagerly: "There is such a nice little dog, near our house, I should like to show
A2	19:37	her paws and washing her face--and she is such a nice soft thing to nurse--and she's such a capital one
A6	46:12	as you are: secondly, because they're making such a noise inside, no one could possibly hear you." And
A9	70: 4	Alice was very glad to find her in such a pleasant temper, and thought to herself that perhaps it
A8	66:11	itself round and look up in her face, with such a puzzled expression that she could not help bursting out
T9	201:28	"Do you know, I've had such a quantity of poetry repeated to me to-day," Alice began,
T12	207:38	was one thing you would have enjoyed--I had such a quantity of poetry said to me, all about fishes!
A8	63:30	she could not remember ever having heard of such a rule at processions; "and besides, what would be the
A9	75: 4	ought to be ashamed of yourself for asking such a simple question," added the Gryphon; and then they both
T3	136:12	do you call yourself?" the Fawn said at last. Such a soft sweet voice it had!
T8	181:11	eyes to Alice. She thought she had never seen such a strange-looking soldier in all her life.
A2	19:43	the end of its tail. "As if I would talk on such a subject! Our family always hated cats: nasty, low,
A1	12:11	for she could not remember ever having seen such a thing.
T5	150:14	in great astonishment. "I never heard of such a thing!"
T7	172:31	jumping up and shaking himself. "If you do such a thing again, I'll have you buttered! It went through
A7	60:25	are 'much of a muchness'--did you ever see such a thing as a drawing of a muchness!"
A8	68:39	cut it off from: that he had never had to do such a thing before, and he wasn't going to begin at his time
A2	19:16	of speaking to a mouse: she had never done such a thing before, but she remembered having seen, in her
T9	196: 6	Now, as it happened, there wasn't such a thing in the house, that morning."
T9	195:26	clasping and unclasping her hands, "we had such a thunderstorm last Tuesday--I mean one of the last set
T9	196:11	Here the White Queen began again. "It was such a thunderstorm, you ca'n't think!" ("She never could, you
A4	28: 8	again, for really I'm quite tired of being such a tiny little thing!"
T9	201:40	like the cooing of a pigeon. "It would be such a treat! May I?"
A3	25:26	nothing to do.' Said the mouse to the cur, Such a trial, dear sir, With no jury or judge, would be
T4	143:26	a shame,' the Walrus said, / 'To play them such a trick, / After we've brought them out so far, / And
T4	148:10	to make them a little ashamed of fighting for such a trifle."
A2	16: 7	all sorts of things, and she, oh, she knows such a very little! Besides, she's she, and I'm I, and--oh
T6	168:17	was rather sudden, Alice thought: but, after such a very strong hint that she ought to be going, she felt
T3	131:36	like other people!" she thought. But this was such a wonderfully small sigh, that she wouldn't have heard it
A5	41:15	wouldn't mind," said Alice: "three inches is such a wretched height to be."
T4	147: 2	the umbrella, with himself in it: which was such an extraordinary thing to do, that it quite took off
A7	59: 6	Alice tried a little to fancy to herself what such an extraordinary way of living would be like, but it
AI	3: 7	Ah, cruel Three! In such an hour, / Beneath such dreamy weather, / To beg a tale
T6	160:38	to a King, I am: mayhap you'll never see such another: and, to show you I'm not proud, you may shake
T4	147:13	in a minute with their arms full of things--such as bolsters, blankets, hearth-rugs, table-cloths,
T8	186:28	it makes, mixing it with other things--such as gunpowder and sealing-wax. And here I must leave you."
A7	60:23	and went on: "--that begins with an M, such as mouse-traps, and the moon, and memory, and muchness--
A4	30:14	Alice could only hear whispers now and then; such as "Sure, I don't like it, yer honour, at all, at all!"
A1	11: 1	simple rules their friends had taught them: such as, that a red-hot poker will burn you if you hold it too
T5	156: 7	transport of delight. "There really are--and such beauties!"
T1	111: 7	Looking-glass House! I'm sure it's got, oh! such beautiful things in it! Let's pretend there's a way of
A8	68:14	the look of things at all, as the game was in such confusion that she never knew whether it was her turn or
T7	169: 3	then ten or twenty together, and at last in such crowds that they seemed to fill the whole forest. Alice
A10	84:19	green, / Waiting in a hot tureen! / Who for such dainties would not stoop? / Soup of the evening,
AI	3: 8	Ah, cruel Three! In such an hour, / Beneath such dreamy weather, / To beg a tale of breath too weak / To
T7	170:17	"I only wish I had such eyes," the King remarked in a fretful tone. "To be able
T1	115: 9	"Oh! please don't make such faces, my dear!" she cried out, quite forgetting that the
T8	179:37	they began banging away at each other with such fury that Alice got behind a tree to be out of the way of
T4	143:15	cried, / Turning a little blue. / 'After such kindness, that would be / A dismal thing to do!' / 'The
A2	20: 5	bright-eyed terrier, you know, with oh, such long curly brown hair! And it'll fetch things when you
A2	16: 4	I'm not Ada," she said, "for her hair goes in such long ringlets, and mine doesn't go in ringlets at all;
A3	26: 9	and walking away. "You insult me by talking such nonsense!"
T4	141: 4	at hand: / They wept like anything to see / Such quantities of sand: / 'If this were only cleared away,' /
T8W	19:12	my wig from me and say / 'How can you put such rubbish on?'
A5	40: 7	airs! / Do you think I can listen all day to such stuff? / Be off, or I'll kick you down-stairs!"
A6	47:16	She said the last word with such sudden violence that Alice quite jumped; but she saw in
A7	59:24	"There's no such thing!" Alice was beginning very angrily, but the Hatter
T6	160:35	"Ah, well! They may write such things in a book," Humpty Dumpty said in a calmer tone.
A9	70:13	makes them bitter--and--and barley-sugar and such things that make children sweet-tempered. I only wish
A5	36:11	little irritated at the Caterpillar's making such very short remarks, and she drew herself up and said,
T8W	15:12	"There's no such word in the language!" said the Wasp.

SUDDEN (17)

T6	168:17	This was rather sudden, Alice thought: but, after such a very strong hint that
T3	137: 5	another open field, and here the Fawn gave a sudden bound into the air, and shook itself free from Alice's
A2	17:25	else'--but, oh dear!" cried Alice, with a sudden burst of tears, "I do wish they would put their heads
A5	41:41	She was a good deal frightened by this very sudden change, but she felt that there was no time to be lost,
A2	18:11	said Alice, a good deal frightened at the sudden change, but very glad to find herself still in
T5	153:17	brooch had come undone as she spoke, and a sudden gust of wind blew the Queen's shawl across a little
A2	19:26	in her French lesson-book. The Mouse gave a sudden leap out of the water, and seemed to quiver all over
T3	137: 8	"And, dear me! you're a human child!" A sudden look of alarm came into its beautiful brown eyes, and
T6	160:31	bad!" Humpty Dumpty cried, breaking into a sudden passion. "You've been listening at doors--and behind
T8	186:38	what?" said Alice, for the Knight had made a sudden pause.
AI	3:19	Anon, to sudden silence won, / In fancy they pursue / The dream-child

SUDDEN (cont.)
```
  T8   181:26  going  to  throw  it  into the bushes, when a sudden thought seemed to strike him, and he hung it carefully
  T1   115:30  out  of  his  pocket,  and  began writing. A sudden thought struck her, and she took hold of the end of the
  T5   155: 2  but I'll tell you what--" she added, as a sudden thought struck her. "I'll follow it up to the very top
  T5   156: 7  are  some  scented  rushes!" Alice cried in a sudden transport of delight. "There really are--and such
  T2   120:22  shall do it this time--" when the path gave a sudden twist and shook itself (as she described it afterwards)
  A6    47:16              She said the last word with such sudden violence that Alice quite jumped; but she saw in
```
SUDDENLY (35)
```
  A6    45: 2  house,  and  wondering  what to do next, when suddenly a footman in livery came running out of the wood--
  A1     7: 9  of  getting  up and picking the daisies, when suddenly a White Rabbit with pink eyes ran close by her.
  A6    52:14  looking  at  the  place where it had been, it suddenly appeared again.
  T8   183:19  "is  to  keep--"  Here the sentence ended as suddenly as it had begun, as the Knight fell heavily on the
  T4   139:41  panted  out,  and  they  left  off dancing as suddenly as they had begun: the music stopped at the same
  T3   136: 2  stood silent for a minute, thinking: then she suddenly began again. "Then it really has happened, after all!
  T8   183:17    "The  great  art  of  riding," the Knight suddenly began in a loud voice, waving his right arm as he
  A3    23:14  or so, and were quite dry again, the Dodo suddenly called out "The race is over!" and they all crowded
  T9   192:26  a  frown,  and,  after thinking for a minute, suddenly changed the subject of the conversation. "What do you
  A1     8: 8  like  a  tunnel for some way, and then dipped suddenly down, so suddenly that Alice had not a moment to
  A10   78:36  all  the  first  figure," said the Mock Turtle, suddenly dropping his voice; and the two creatures, who had
  T9   204:19  the  Queen was no longer at her side--she had suddenly dwindled down to the size of a little doll, and was
  T8   182:42  went  on again (which it generally did rather suddenly), he fell off behind. Otherwise he kept on pretty
  T3   137:12   lost  her  dear  little  fellow-traveler  so suddenly. "However, I know my name now," she said: "that's
  T1   110:17  really  frightened  her old nurse by shouting suddenly in her ear, "Nurse! Do let's pretend that I'm a
  T3   129:19  trying to find some excuse for turning shy so suddenly. "It'll never do to go down among them without a good
  T1   118:31              "But oh!" thought Alice, suddenly jumping up, "if I don't make haste, I shall have to
  T2   127: 7  touching  the  ground  with  their feet, till suddenly, just as Alice was getting quite exhausted, they
  T9   194:28    "Can you do sums?" Alice said, turning suddenly on the White Queen, for she didn't like being found
  T6   162:13  "What a beautiful belt you've got on!" Alice suddenly remarked. (They had had quite enough of the subject
  T7   174:20  or  two  Alice  stood  silent,  watching him. Suddenly she brightened up. "Look, look!" she cried, pointing
  A1     9:34              Suddenly she came upon a little three-legged table, all made
  A4    29:33  heard  the  Rabbit just under the window, she suddenly spread out her hand, and made a snatch in the air.
  A1     8: 8  some  way,  and then dipped suddenly down, so suddenly that Alice had not a moment to think about stopping
  T2   122:34  that  looked  stupider," a Violet said, so suddenly, that Alice quite jumped; for it hadn't spoken before
  T4   148:18              It was getting dark so suddenly that Alice thought there must be a thunderstorm
  T3   137:31  corner, she came upon two fat little men, so suddenly that she could not help starting back, but in another
  T5   155:17  needles--" Alice  was beginning to say, when suddenly the needles turned into oars in her hands, and she
  A8    63: 1  stood watching them, and he checked himself suddenly: the others looked round also, and all of them bowed
  A1     9:18  me  the  truth: did you ever eat a bat?" when suddenly, thump! thump! down she came upon a heap of sticks
  A5    44: 1  done,  I  wonder?" As she said this, she came suddenly upon an open place, with a little house in it about
  T9   197:22  so  eagerly  that,  when the two great heads suddenly vanished from her lap, she hardly missed them.
  T5   153:32  She  looked  at  the  Queen, who seemed to have suddenly wrapped herself up in wool. Alice rubbed her eyes,
  A6    53: 3  you  wouldn't keep appearing and vanishing so suddenly; you make one quite giddy!"
  T8   179:15  Just  as  he  reached her, the horse stopped suddenly: "You're my prisoner!" the Knight cried, as he
```
SUET (1)
```
  A5    39: 2  jaws are too weak / For anything tougher than suet; / Yet you finished the goose, with the bones and the
```
SUETY (1)
```
  T9   201:24              It spoke in a thick, suety sort of voice, and Alice hadn't a word to say in reply:
```
SUGAR (5) [See also BARLEY-SUGAR]
```
  T3   134:12  body  is  a  crust, and its head is a lump of sugar."
  T8W   15: 3              "No brown sugar!" grumbled the Wasp. "A nice exploring party!"
  T8W   14:22  and  have  found  five  new  lumps of white sugar, large and in fine condition. In coming back--"
  A10   82:23  / 'You  have  baked  me  too brown, I must sugar my hair.' / As a duck with his eyelids, so he with his
  T8W   14:24              "Any brown sugar?" the Wasp interrupted.
```
SUGAR-LOAF (1)
```
  T8   184:43  I've  invented a better one than that--like a sugar-loaf. When I used to wear it, if I fell off the horse,
```
SUGGESTED (2)
```
  T3   134:16  head. "Supposing it couldn't find any?" she suggested.
  T7   172:12  cold  water  over you would be better," Alice suggested: "--or some sal-volatile."
```
SUGGESTION (1)
```
  T6   162: 9    Alice  felt  even  more  indignant at this suggestion. "I mean," she said, "that one ca'n't help growing
```
SUIT (3)
```
  A3    26:33  must  be  getting home: the night-air doesn't suit my throat!" And a Canary called out in a trembling voice,
  A7    56: 2  the  Hatter. "I told you butter wouldn't suit the works!" he added, looking angrily at the March Hare.
  A5    42:31  "I've  tried  every way, but nothing seems to suit them!"
```
SULKILY (6)
```
  T1   114:12  called out to the White King, who was sitting sulkily among the ashes, "Mind the volcano!"
  A11   89: 2  that  ridiculous fashion." And he got up very sulkily and crossed over to the other side of the court.
  T4   140:29              The moon was shining sulkily, / Because she thought the sun / Had got no business
  T8W   14:18  if  you've  a mind to," the Wasp said, rather sulkily. "Nobody's hindering you, that I know of."
  A7    59:26  March  Hare went "Sh! Sh!" and the Dormouse sulkily remarked "If you ca'n't be civil, you'd better finish
  T4   147:10              "I suppose so," the other sulkily replied, as he crawled out of the umbrella: "only she
```
SULKY (5)
```
  T9   201:12              But the Red Queen looked sulky, and growled "Pudding----Alice: Alice--Pudding. Remove
  A3    21: 9  argument  with  the Lory, who at last turned sulky, and would only say, "I'm older than you, and must know
  T1   110:27  to  the  Looking-glass, that it might see how sulky it was, "--and if you're not good directly," she added,
  A5    43:28  "Well,  be  off,  then!" said the Pigeon in a sulky tone, as it settled down again into its nest. Alice
  A8    62: 7    "I  couldn't  help it," said Five, in a sulky tone. "Seven jogged my elbow."
```
SULLEN (1)
```
  T7   172:20  "I  do  my  best," the Messenger said in a sullen tone. "I'm sure nobody walks much faster than I do!"
```

SUM (2)
```
  T6   163: 7   took  out  her memorandum-book, and worked the sum for him:
  T9   194: 9              of course. Try another Subtraction sum. Take a bone from a dog: what remains?"
```
SUMMER (9)
```
  T1   109:13   it says 'Go to  sleep,  darlings, till the summer comes again.' And when they wake up in the summer,
 A11    87:17   of Hearts, she made some tarts, / All on a summer day: / The Knave of Hearts, he stole those tarts / And
 A12    99:11   remembering her own child-life, and the happy summer days.
  TI   103:33   / May tremble through the story, / For "happy summer days" gone by, / And vanish'd summer glory--/ It shall
  T8   190:10   dough, / Who snorted like a buffalo--/ That summer evening long ago, / A-sitting on a gate."
  TI   103:34   "happy  summer  days" gone by, / And vanish'd summer glory--/ It shall not touch, with breath of bale, / The
  T1   109:14   comes again.' And  when they wake up in the summer, Kitty, they dress themselves all in green, and dance
  TI   103:14          A tale begun in other days, / When summer suns were glowing--/ A simple chime, that served to
  T6   166:32                  "In summer, when the days are long, / Perhaps you'll understand
```
SUMMERS (1)
```
  TC   209:18   Dreaming as the days go by, / Dreaming as the summers die:
```
SUMMON (1)
```
  TI   103:21   dread, / With bitter tidings laden, / Shall summon to unwelcome bed / A melancholy maiden! / We are but
```
SUMS (3)
```
  T9   194:26            "She ca'n't do sums a bit!" the Queens said together, with great emphasis.
  T9   194:28             "Can you do sums?" Alice said, turning suddenly on the White Queen, for
  T9   193:23     said Alice. "Lessons teach you to do sums, and things of that sort."
```
SUN (7)
```
  AI     4: 2   we steer, a merry crew, / Beneath the setting sun.
 A12    98:14   her head  on her hand, watching the setting sun, and thinking of little Alice and all her wonderful
  T8   187:20   and  kindly  smile of the Knight--the setting sun gleaming through his hair, and shining on his armour in a
  T4   140:30   shining sulkily, / Because she thought the sun / Had got no business to be there / After the day was done
  A9    73:23   came upon a Gryphon, lying fast asleep in the sun. (If you don't know what a Gryphon is, look at the picture
  T4   140:18                              "The sun was shining--"
  T4   140:23   "The sun was shining on the sea, / Shining with all his might: / He
```
SUN-DIAL (1)
```
  T6   165: 4   "And 'the wabe' is the grass-plot round a sun-dial, I suppose?" said Alice, surprised at her own
```
SUN-DIALS (1)
```
  T6   164:39   Dumpty; "also  they  make  their nests under sun-dials--also they live on cheese."
```
SUNNY (3)
```
  TI   103: 7            I have not seen thy sunny face, / Nor heard thy silver laughter: / No thought of
  TC   209: 7            Long has paled that sunny sky: / Echoes fade and memories die: / Autumn frosts
  TC   209: 1            A boat, beneath a sunny sky / Lingering onward dreamily / In an evening of July
```
SUNS (1)
```
  TI   103:14   A tale begun in other days, / When summer suns were glowing--/ A simple chime, that served to time / The
```
SUP (1)
```
  T9   202:11            'Bring it here! Let me sup!' / It is easy to set such a dish on the table. / 'Take
```
SUPPLE (1)
```
  A5    38: 6   his grey locks, / "I kept all my limbs very supple / By the use of this ointment--one shilling the box--/
```
SUPPORT (1)
```
  T9   202:31            "We must support you, you know," the White Queen whispered, as Alice
```
SUPPOSE (37)
```
  A4    32: 9   make me larger, it must make me smaller, I suppose."
  A9    76:27   exclaimed. "You  know what to beautify is, I suppose?"
  T9   194: 7                  "I suppose--" Alice was beginning, but the Red Queen answered for
  A2    19: 2   way out. "I shall be punished for it now, I suppose, by being drowned in my own tears! That will be a
  A4    27:28      "to  be  going  messages  for  a rabbit! I suppose Dinah'll be sending me on messages next!" And she
  T1   109: 4   I suppose, when the day came. Or--let me see--suppose each punishment was to be going without a dinner: then
  T5   151: 7                  "Suppose he never commits the crime?" said Alice.
  T4   148: 7   round him with a satisfied smile. "I don't suppose," he said, "there'll be a tree left standing, for ever
  A4    33:12   again! Let me see--how is it to be managed? I suppose I ought to eat or drink something or other; but the
  T3   132:38   it's useful  to the people that name them, I suppose. If not, why do things have names at all?"
  T9   193: 3   of! You should have meant! What do you suppose is the use of a child without any meaning? Even a joke
  A7    54: 6    thought Alice; "only as it's asleep, I suppose it doesn't mind."
  T2   128:18   of  you  to tell me all this'--however, we'll suppose it said--the Seventh Square is all forest--however,
  A6    53:16   towards it rather timidly, saying to herself "Suppose it should be raving mad after all! I almost wish I'd
  A7    56:44   you  liked  with  the  clock. For instance, suppose it were nine o'clock in the morning, just time to
  T2   120: 5   and turning  several  sharp corners), "but I suppose it will at last. But how curiously it twists! It's
  T2   120: 6   a path! Well this turn goes to the hill, I suppose--no, it doesn't! This goes straight back to the house!
  A7    58:14            "Then you keep moving round, I suppose?" said Alice.
  T6   165: 4   wabe' is the grass-plot round a sun-dial, I suppose?" said Alice, surprised at her own ingenuity.
  A6    51:31                  "I suppose so," said Alice.
  T4   147:10                  "I suppose so," the other sulkily replied, as he crawled out of
  A5    40: 1   are old," said the youth, "one would hardly suppose / That your eye was as steady as ever; / Yet you
  T8   181:36   yet. And the other thing is a mouse-trap. I suppose the mice keep the bees out--or the bees keep the mice
  T4   141: 9   mops / Swept it for half a year, / Do you suppose,' the Walrus said, / 'That they could get it clear?' /
 A11    86:23   them were animals, and some were birds,) "I suppose they are the jurors." She said this last word two or
  T1   109: 1   up  all  your punishments for Wednesday week--Suppose they had saved up all my punishments?" she went on,
  T7   174: 8                  "Then I suppose they'll soon bring the white bread and the brown?"
  T4   138: 4   on his collar, and the other 'DEE.' "I suppose they've got 'TWEEDLE' round at the back of the collar
  T4   145:26            "I hope you don't suppose those are real tears?" Tweedledum interrupted in a
  A7    58:18            "Suppose we change the subject," the March Hare interrupted,
  T1   109: 4   end of a year? I should be sent to prison, I suppose, when the day came. Or--let me see--suppose each
  T6   164: 1   you'd mention what you mean to do next, as I suppose you don't mean to stop here all the rest of your life
  T3   134:22   at  last  it settled again and remarked "I suppose you don't want to lose your name?"
  T8   186:13   "Then  it  would  have  to be the next day. I suppose you wouldn't have two pudding-courses in one dinner?"
```

SUPPOSE (cont.)
```
 T4    145: 6   he  left off dreaming about you, where do you suppose you'd be?"
 T8    184:34                                        "Yes, I suppose you'd be over when that was done," Alice said
 A5     43:14   a serpent;  and there's no use denying it. I suppose you'll be telling me next that you never tasted an
```
SUPPOSING (1)
```
 T3    134:15   A new difficulty came into Alice's head. "Supposing it couldn't find any?" she suggested.
```
SUPPRESS (1)
```
 A11    91:20   Dormouse! Turn that Dormouse out of court! Suppress him! Pinch him! Off with his whiskers!"
```
SUPPRESSED (4)
```
 A11    90:26   Here the other guinea-pig cheered, and was suppressed.
 A11    90:11   the guinea-pigs cheered, and was immediately suppressed by the officers of the court. (As that is rather a
 A11    90:18   attempt at applause, which was immediately suppressed by the officers of the court,' and I never
 A12    98:32   Lizard's slate-pencil, and the choking of the suppressed guinea-pigs, filled the air, mixed up with the
```
SURE (45)
```
 T12   207:36   it to your friends just yet, for I'm not sure.
 A4     27: 4   fur and whiskers! She'll get me executed, as sure as ferrets are ferrets! Where can I have dropped them, I
 A4     30:38   a good deal: this fireplace is narrow, to be sure; but I think I can kick a little!"
 A2     19: 4   own tears! That will be a queer thing, to be sure! However, everything is queer to-day."
 A2     16: 5   mine doesn't go in ringlets at all; and I'm sure I ca'n't be Mabel, for I know all sorts of things, and
 T9    192:38                                        "I'm sure I didn't mean--" Alice was beginning, but the Red Queen
 T9    194:34                                        "To be sure I do," said Alice.
 T7    177: 3                                        "I'm sure I don't know," the Lion growled out as he lay down again.
 A4     30:14   only hear whispers now and then; such as "Sure, I don't like it, yer honour, at all, at all!" "Do as I
 A4     30:20   of the window, I only wish they could! I'm sure I don't want to stay in here any longer!"
 A5     37: 7   the brain;  / But,  now that I'm perfectly sure I have none, / Why, I do it again and again."
 A2     14: 7   shoes and stockings for you now, dears? I'm sure I sha'n't be able! I shall be a great deal too far off to
 T9    194:12   remain: it would come to bite me--and I'm sure I shouldn't remain!"
 T6    163:16                                        "To be sure I was!" Humpty Dumpty said gaily as she turned it round
 T5    149:38   "I'm sure I'll take you with pleasure!" the Queen said.
 A2     16: 4                                        "I'm sure I'm not Ada," she said, "for her hair goes in such long
 T4    138:15                                        "I'm sure I'm very sorry," was all Alice could say; for the words
 A4     30:10                                        "Sure, it does, yer honour: but it's an arm for all that."
 T3    136: 1   I do believe it's got no name--why, to be sure it hasn't!"
 A10    83:12   did not dare to disobey, though she felt sure it would all come wrong, and she went on in a trembling
 A4     30: 7                                        "Sure, it's an arm, yer honour!" (He pronounced it "arrum.")
 T1    111: 6   get through into Looking-glass House! I'm sure it's got, oh! such beautiful things in it! Let's pretend
 T5    150:17                                        "I'm sure mine only works one way," Alice remarked. "I ca'n't
 T7    172:20   the Messenger said in a sullen tone. "I'm sure nobody walks much faster than I do!"
 T7    176:20                                        "I'm not so sure of that," said the Unicorn.
 T3    135: 5   "That would never do, I'm sure," said Alice: "the governess would never think of
 T7    172:38   "Yes, to be sure," said the King: "and the best of the joke is, that it's
 A8     67: 3   Alice began to feel very uneasy: to be sure, she had not as yet had any dispute with the Queen, but
 A3     21:17   her eyes anxiously fixed on it, for she felt sure she would catch a bad cold if she did not get dry very
 A3     26:38   "Nobody seems to like her, down here, and I'm sure she's the best cat in the world! Oh, my dear Dinah! I
 T8    185: 3   was the danger of falling into it, to be sure. That happened to me once--and the worst of it was,
 T3    137:32   another moment she recovered herself, feeling sure that they must be TWEEDLEDUM AND TWEEDLEDEE
 T1    110: 2   her hands. "And I do so wish it was true! I'm sure the woods look sleepy in the autumn, when the leaves are
 A4     30: 2   And then a voice she had never heard before, "Sure then I'm here! Digging for apples, yer honour!"
 T1    113:13   she put her head closer down, "and I'm nearly sure they ca'n't see me. I feel somehow as if I was getting
 A1     12:41   find that she remained the same size. To be sure, this is what generally happens when one eats cake; but
 A2     17:16                                        "I'm sure those are not the right words," said poor Alice, and her
 T3    137:21   but wherever the road divided, there were sure to be two finger-posts pointing the same way, one marked
 A6     51:15                                        "Oh, you're sure to do that," said the Cat, "if you only walk long enough
 A4     28: 5   to her lips. "I know something interesting is sure to happen," she said to herself, "whenever I eat or drink
 A6     49:26   child away with me," thought Alice, "they're sure to kill it in a day or two. Wouldn't it be murder to
 A4     32: 7   I eat one of these cakes," she thought, "it's sure to make some change in my size; and, as it ca'n't
 A5     43:41   How puzzling all these changes are! I'm never sure what I'm going to be, from one minute to another! However,
 A6     47:13   a little timidly, for she was not quite sure whether it was good manners for her to speak first, "why
 T12   208:11   to know--Oh, Kitty, do help to settle it! I'm sure your paw can wait!" But the provoking kitten only began
```
SURELY (1)
```
 TI    103: 5   half a life asunder, / Thy loving smile will surely hail / The love-gift of a fairy-tale.
```
SURPRISE (11)
```
 A10    81:32   it, really?" said Alice, in a tone of great surprise.
 T8    179:21   Ahoy! Check!" and Alice looked round in some surprise for the new enemy.
 T8W    17:10   spoke, and Alice looked at his wig in great surprise. It was bright yellow like the handkerchief, and all
 A9     76:26   The Gryphon lifted up both its paws in surprise. "Never heard of uglifying!" it exclaimed. "You know
 T2    123:41   set off at once towards the Red Queen. To her surprise she lost sight of her in a moment, and found herself
 T1    113: 6   but in another moment, with a little "Oh!" of surprise, she was down on her hands and knees watching them.
 A4     32: 5                   Alice noticed, with some surprise, that the pebbles were all turning into little cakes
 A9     72:29                   But here, to Alice's great surprise, the Duchess's voice died away, even in the middle of
 T3    130:12   time, as she hadn't spoken, but, to her great surprise, they all thought in chorus (I hope you understand
 A11    91:32   yet," she said to herself. Imagine her surprise, when the White Rabbit read out, at the top of his
 T2    127:12                   Alice looked round her in great surprise. "Why, I do believe we've been under this tree the
```
SURPRISED (18)
```
 T8    183: 5                   The Knight looked very much surprised, and a little offended at the remark. "What makes
 T9    204:24   this, but she was far too much excited to be surprised at anything now. "As for you," she repeated,
 T9    192:11   happening so oddly that she didn't feel a bit surprised at finding the Red Queen and the White Queen sitting
 A8     64: 3   "How should I know?" said Alice, surprised at her own courage. "It's no business of mine."
 T6    165: 5   round a sun-dial, I suppose?" said Alice, surprised at her own ingenuity.
 T7    175: 3   to run and help her?" Alice asked, very much surprised at his taking it so quietly.
```

SURPRISED (cont.)
```
  T3   135:40  into the--into what?" she went on, rather surprised at not being able to think of the word. "I mean to
  T8   186: 2                       The Knight looked surprised at the question. "What does it matter where my body
  T9   204:23  At any other time, Alice would have felt surprised at this, but she was far too much excited to be
  A6    52: 9                 Alice was not much surprised at this, she was getting so well used to queer
  A4    27:19      she said to herself as she ran. "How surprised he'll be when he finds out who I am! But I'd better
  T2   125:10              "No, I shouldn't," said Alice, surprised into contradicting her at last: "a hill ca'n't be a
  A2    14: 1  and curiouser!" cried Alice (she was so much surprised, that for the moment she quite forgot how to speak
  A8    68:28  she got back to the Cheshire-Cat, she was surprised to find quite a large crowd collected round it:
  A1    12:40  which way it was growing; and she was quite surprised to find that she remained the same size. To be sure,
  T4   139:29  remembered afterwards), and she was not even surprised to hear music playing: it seemed to come from the
  A2    18: 1  this she looked down at her hands, and was surprised to see that she had put on one of the Rabbit's
  T5   158: 7  two are cheaper than one?" Alice said in a surprised tone, taking out her purse.
```
SURVEY (1)
```
  T3   129: 1  the first thing to do was to make a grand survey of the country she was going to travel through. "It's
```
SWALLOW (1)
```
  A5    42: 3  mouth; but she did it at last, and managed to swallow a morsel of the left-hand bit. * * * * * * * * * * *
```
SWALLOWED (2)
```
  T7   174: 5              Hatta made a desperate effort, and swallowed a large piece of bread-and-butter. "They're getting
  A4    32:10                 So she swallowed one of the cakes, and was delighted to find that she
```
SWALLOWING (1)
```
  A5    36:23          "Is that all?" said Alice, swallowing down her anger as well as she could.
```
SWAM (5)
```
  A2    19: 1  I hadn't cried so much!" said Alice, as she swam about, trying to find her way out. "I shall be punished
  A2    19:36    Alice went on, half to herself, as she swam lazily about in the pool, "and she sits purring so nicely
  A2    19: 6  about in the pool a little way off, and she swam nearer to make out what it was: at first she thought it
  A2    20:16  the Mouse heard this, it turned round and swam slowly back to her: its face was quite pale (with passion
  A2    20:24    Alice led the way, and the whole party swam to the shore.
```
SWEET (1)
```
  T3   136:13  yourself?" the Fawn said at last. Such a soft sweet voice it had!
```
SWEET-TEMPERED (1)
```
  A9    70:13            and such things that make children sweet-tempered. I only wish people knew that: then they
```
SWEPT (2)
```
  T5   156:45  shrieks of "Oh, oh, oh!" from poor Alice, it swept her straight off the seat, and down among the heap of
  T4   141: 8          'If seven maids with seven mops / Swept it for half a year, / Do you suppose,' the Walrus said,
```
SWIM (5)
```
  A12   94:42  me a good character, / But said I could not swim. "Swim after them!" screamed the Gryphon.
  A10   78:30                         "Swim after them!" screamed the Gryphon.
  A12   95:34  all. '--said I could not swim--' you ca'n't swim, can you?" he added, turning to the Knave.
  A4    27: 9  everything seemed to have changed since her swim in the pool; and the great hall, with the glass table and
  A12   95:34   in them, after all. '--said I could not swim--' you ca'n't swim, can you?" he added, turning to the
```
SWIMMING (2)
```
  A2    19:14  the way out of this pool? I am very tired of swimming about here, O Mouse!" (Alice thought this must be the
  A2    20:11  I've offended it again!" For the Mouse was swimming away from her as hard as it could go, and making
```
SWINGING (1)
```
  T3   133: 5  It's made entirely of wood, and gets about by swinging itself from branch to branch."
```
SWORD (2)
```
  T1   118: 5                         He took his vorpal sword in hand: / Long time the manxome foe he sought--/ So
  T4   148:14              "There's only one sword, you know," Tweedledum said to his brother: "but you can
```
SYLLABLES (1)
```
  T8W   15:11    Alice repeated, dividing the word into syllables.
```
SYMPATHIZE (1)
```
  T4   144: 2  weep for you,' the Walrus said: / 'I deeply sympathize.' / With sobs and tears he sorted out / Those of
```

-T-

T (1)
   A11   89:17   "Of course twinkling begins with a T!" said the King sharply. "Do you take me for a dunce? Go on!
TABLE (35) [See also MULTIPLICATION-TABLE]
   A7   54:11   down in a large arm-chair at one end of the table.
   A1   9:34   Suddenly she came upon a little three-legged table, all made of solid glass: there was nothing on it but a
   T9   203: 5   inches; but she got hold of the edge of the table, and managed to pull herself down again.
   T1   110:24   a dear!" And Alice got the Red Queen off the table, and set it up before the kitten as a model for it to
   A4   27:10   the pool; and the great hall, with the glass table and the little door, had vanished completely.
   T9   202:25   drank the wine as it ran off the edges of the table--and three of them (who looked like kangaroos) scrambled
   T1   116: 1   There was a book lying near Alice on the table, and while she sat watching the White King (for she was
   A2   18:14   the little golden key was lying on the glass table as before, "and things are worse than ever," thought the
   T10   205: 1   She took her off the table as she spoke, and shook her backwards and forwards with
   T9   200: 8   Alice glanced nervously along the table, as she walked up the large hall, and noticed that there
   T1   114:20   Why, you'll be hours and hours getting to the table, at that rate. I'd far better help you, hadn't I?" But
   T1   113:15   Here something began squeaking on the table behind Alice, and made her turn her head just in time to
   A1   12:19   her best to climb up one of the legs of the table, but it was too slippery; and when she had tired herself
   A7   54:14   Alice looked all round the table, but there was nothing on it but tea. "I don't see any
   T1   114: 6   picked up the Queen and set her on the table by the side of her noisy little daughter.
   A1   12:16   golden key, and when she went back to the table for it, she found she could not possibly reach it: she
   A1   10:13   by the little door, so she went back to the table, half hoping she might find another key on it, or at any
   T9   204:27   over a bottle which had just lighted upon the table, "I'll shake you into a kitten, that I will!"
   A4   27:37   found her way into a tidy little room with a table in the window, and on it (as she had hoped) a fan and
   T9   204:20   the size of a little doll, and was now on the table, merrily running round and round after her own shawl,
   T1   115:14   she smoothed his hair, and set him upon the table near the Queen.
   A12   96:14   triumphantly, pointing to the tarts on the table. "Nothing can be clearer than that. Then again--'before
   A7   60:43   the long hall, and close to the little glass table. "Now, I'll manage better this time," she said to
   A7   55: 4   "I didn't know it was your table," said Alice: "it's laid for a great many more than
   A7   54: 1   There was a table set out under a tree in front of the house, and the
   A1   12:32   a little glass box that was lying under the table: she opened it, and found in it a very small cake, on
   T1   115: 1   breath away; but, before she put him on the table, she thought she might as well dust him a little, he was
   T9   202:12   sup!' / It is easy to set such a dish on the table. / 'Take the dish-cover up!' / Ah, that is so hard that
   T9   200:14   There were three chairs at the head of the table: the Red and White Queens had already taken two of them,
   T12   207:13   So Alice hunted among the chessmen on the table till she had found the Red Queen: then she went down on
   A2   18: 5   small again." She got up and went to the table to measure herself by it, and found that, as nearly as
   T9   204:11   dishes, and the soup ladle was walking up the table towards Alice's chair, and beckoning to her impatiently
   A7   54: 7   The table was a large one, but the three were all crowded together
   A11   86: 7   other. In the very middle of the court was a table, with a large dish of tarts upon it: they looked so good
   T9   199:30   as quick as you can, / And sprinkle the table with buttons and bran: / Put cats in the coffee, and
TABLECLOTH (1)
   T9   204:14   she cried, as she jumped up and seized the tablecloth with both hands: one good pull, and plates, dishes,
TABLE-CLOTHS (1)
   T4   147:14   such as bolsters, blankets, hearth-rugs, table-cloths, dish-covers, and coal-scuttles. "I hope you're a
TABLES (3)
   T8   180: 9   them get on and off them just as if they were tables!"
   T5   158:18   Alice, as she groped her way among the tables and chairs, for the shop was very dark towards the end.
   T9   196:15   room in great lumps--and knocking over the tables and things--till I was so frightened, I couldn't
TAIL (11)
   A12   93: 6   and the poor little thing was waving its tail about in a melancholy way, being quite unable to move.
   A6   53: 5   quite slowly, beginning with the end of the tail, and ending with the grin, which remained some time after
   A2   17: 9   the little crocodile / Improve his shining tail, / And pour the waters of the Nile / On every golden
   A2   19:43   who was trembling down to the end of its tail. "As if I would talk on such a subject! Our family always
   A3   25: 2   looking down with wonder at the Mouse's tail; "but why do you call it sad?" And she kept on puzzling
   A3   25: 1   "It is a long tail, certainly," said Alice, looking down with wonder at the
   T1   107:19   with the kitten running after its own tail in the middle.
   T1   108:34   Number two: you pulled Snowdrop away by the tail just as I had put down the saucer of milk before her!
   A10   79:14   close behind us, and he's treading on my tail. / See how eagerly the lobsters and the turtles all
   A6   51:34   Now I growl when I'm pleased, and wag my tail when I'm angry. Therefore I'm mad."
   A6   51:33   a dog growls when it's angry, and wags its tail when it's pleased. Now I growl when I'm pleased, and wag
TAILS (3)
   A10   81: 6   had to fall a long way. So they got their tails fast in their mouths. So they couldn't get them out
   A10   80:25   all wash off in the sea. But they have their tails in their mouths; and the reason is--" here the Mock
   A10   80:22   Alice replied thoughtfully. "They have their tails in their mouths--and they're all over crumbs."
TAKE (53)
   T9   194: 9   of course. Try another Subtraction sum. Take a bone from a dog: what remains?"
   A2   19:34   I could show you our cat Dinah. I think you'd take a fancy to cats, if you could only see her. She is such a
   T6   160:37   you call a History of England, that is. Now, take a good look at me! I'm one that has spoken to a King, I
   T9   202:19   "Take a minute to think about it, and then guess," said the Red
   T3   131:25   "Never mind what they all say, my dear, but take a return-ticket every time the train stops."
   AI   4: 3   Alice! A childish story take, / And, with a gentle hand, / Lay it where Childhood's
   T9   195:33   at a time, and sometimes in the winter we take as many as five nights together--for warmth, you know."
   T5   152:18   "Take care!" cried Alice. "You're holding it all crooked!" And
   A9   71: 1   as she added "and the moral of that is--'Take care of the sense, and the sounds will take care of

TAKE (cont.)

A9	71: 2	'Take care of the sense, and the sounds will take care of themselves.'"
T9	197:15	it ever happened before, that any one had to take care of two Queens asleep at once! No, not in all the
T2	121:15	at being planted out here, with nobody to take care of you?"
T9	203: 7	"Take care of yourself!" screamed the White Queen, seizing
T5	156:10	"I didn't put 'em there, and I'm not going to take 'em away."
T2	121: 2	speak for a minute: it quite seemed to take her breath away. At length, as the Tiger-lily only went
A4	27:20	be when he finds out who I am! But I'd better take him his fan and gloves--that is, if I can find them." As
T1	114:24	she had lifted the Queen, that she mightn't take his breath away; but, before she put him on the table,
A11	91: 1	"--and just take his head off outside," the Queen added to one of the
T5	157: 9	let go--I should so like a little crab to take home with me!" But the Sheep only laughed scornfully, and
A4	30:11	got no business there, at any rate: go and take it away!"
T8	182:13	"We'd better take it with us," the Knight said. "It'll come in handy if we
A7	59:13	"You mean you ca'n't take less," said the Hatter: "it's very easy to take more than
T8	190:25	rode slowly away into the forest. "It wo'n't take long to see him off, I expect," Alice said to herself, as
A11	89:18	with a T!" said the King sharply. "Do you take me for a dunce? Go on!"
A7	59:12	replied in an offended tone: "so I ca'n't take more."
T9	202: 8	me the fish! / That is easy, and will not take more than a minute. / 'Let it lie in a dish!' / That is
A7	59:14	less," said the Hatter: "it's very easy to take more than nothing."
T8W	19:11	/ And all my hair is nearly gone, / They take my wig from me and say / 'How can you put such rubbish on
T9	194: 2	Queen interrupted. "Can you do Subtraction? Take nine from eight."
A3	25:14	go to law: I will prosecute you.--Come, I'll take no denial: We must have the trial; For really this
A11	88:20	"Take off your hat," the King said to the Hatter.
T6	163: 1	"And if you take one from three hundred and sixty-five what remains?"
A1	8: 2	with either a waistcoat-pocket, or a watch to take out of it, and burning with curiosity, she ran across the
T6	166:35	In autumn, when the leaves are brown, / Take pen and ink, and write it down."
T9	194:41	"I know that!" Alice cried eagerly. "You take some flour--"
A7	59: 9	"Take some more tea," the March Hare said to Alice, very
A10	81:45	Gryphon in an impatient tone: "explanations take such a dreadful time."
T9	195:23	said a thing, that fixes it, and you must take the consequences."
T9	202:13	is easy to set such a dish on the table. / 'Take the dish-cover up!' / Ah, that is so hard that I fear I'm
A6	48:29	anxiously at the cook, to see if she meant to take the hint; but the cook was busily stirring the soup, and
T8W	21: 5	her, but she kept out of reach, and would not take the hint. So he went on with his criticisms.
T6	159:11	in the opposite direction, and he didn't take the least notice of her, she thought he must be a stuffed
T2	127:32	yourself," said the Queen, "I'll just take the measurements." And she took a ribbon out of her
A12	99: 2	lowing of the cattle in the distance would take the place of the Mock Turtle's heavy sobs.
A4	31:36	will do next! If they had any sense, they'd take the roof off." After a minute or two they began moving
A6	49:25	carried it out into the open air. "If I don't take this child away with me," thought Alice, "they're sure to
A9	74: 1	"Up, lazy thing!" said the Queen, "and take this young lady to see the Mock Turtle, and to hear his
T6	162:15	age, she thought: and, if they really were to take turns in choosing subjects, it was her turn now.) "At
T3	132: 8	of trains jumping at all. "However, it'll take us into the Fourth Square, that's some comfort!" she said
A10	80: 2	notion how delightful it will be / When they take us up and throw us, with the lobsters, out to sea!" / But
T5	149:38	"I'm sure I'll take you with pleasure!" the Queen said. "Two pence a week,
A9	72:38	must be off, and that in about half no time! Take your choice!"

TAKEN (8)

T3	134: 5	the Butterfly," Alice went on, after she had taken a good look at the insect with its head on fire, and had
A9	72:43	The other guests had taken advantage of the Queen's absence, and were resting in
T1	114: 9	the rapid journey through the air had quite taken away her breath, and for a minute or two she could do
A7	55:36	is it?" he said, turning to Alice: he had taken his watch out of his pocket, and was looking at it
A9	73: 5	with her head!" Those whom she sentenced were taken into custody by the soldiers, who of course had to leave
T3	129:15	idea. "Something like cottages with the roofs taken off, and stalks put to them--and what quantities of
A5	43: 1	"And just as I'd taken the highest tree in the wood," continued the Pigeon,
T9	200:15	table: the Red and White Queens had already taken two of them, but the middle one was empty. Alice sat

TAKES (3)

T2	127:20	said the Queen. "Now, here, you see, it takes all the running you can do, to keep in the same place.
A10	78:19	"That generally takes some time," interrupted the Gryphon.
A6	48:26	with the day and night! You see the earth takes twenty-four hours to turn round on its axis--"

TAKING (14)

T2	127:25	you'd like!" the Queen said good-naturedly, taking a little box out of her pocket. "Have a biscuit?"
A10	85: 4	"Come on!" cried the Gryphon, and, taking Alice by the hand, it hurried off, without waiting for
A4	29:16	And so she went on, taking first one side and then the other, and making quite a
A11	87: 7	him, and very soon found an opportunity of taking it away. She did it so quickly that the poor little
T7	175: 3	her?" Alice asked, very much surprised at his taking it so quietly.
T5	155:27	"Feather! Feather!" the Sheep cried again, taking more needles. "You'll be catching a crab directly."
A4	34:10	folded, quietly smoking a long hookah, and taking not the smallest notice of her or of anything else.
T9	196:22	excuse her," the Red Queen said to Alice, taking one of the White Queen's hands in her own, and gently
T5	158: 8	than one?" Alice said in a surprised tone, taking out her purse.
T1	108: 4	then she scrambled back into the arm-chair, taking the kitten and the worsted with her, and began winding
A7	61: 1	this time," she said to herself, and began by taking the little golden key, and unlocking the door that led
T5	155:31	me say 'Feather'?" the Sheep cried angrily, taking up quite a bunch of needles.
T9	201: 4	"May I give you a slice?" she said, taking up the knife and fork, and looking from one Queen to
T1	110:20	But this is taking us away from Alice's speech to the kitten. "Let's

TALE (15)

A3t	21: 1	A CAUCUS-RACE AND A LONG TALE
TI	103: 6	will surely hail / The love-gift of a fairy-tale.
TI	103:12	thou wilt not fail / To listen to my fairy-tale.
TI	103:36	breath of bale, / The pleasance of our fairy-tale.
TI	103:13	A tale begun in other days, / When summer suns were glowing--/ A
T8	188:17	His accents mild took up the tale: / He said 'I go my ways, / And when I find a
AI	3:34	events were hammered out--/ And now the tale is done, / And home we steer, a merry crew, / Beneath the

TALE (cont.)
```
  AI    3:17    in it!" / While Tertia interrupts the tale / Not more than once a minute.
  AI    3: 9    / Beneath such dreamy weather, / To beg a tale of breath too weak / To stir the tiniest feather! / Yet
  AI    3:31              Thus grew the tale of Wonderland: / Thus slowly, one by one, / Its quaint
  A12   99: 8    eyes bright and eager with many a strange tale, perhaps even with the dream of Wonderland of long ago;
  A3    24:17              "Mine is a long and sad tale!" said the Mouse, turning to Alice, and sighing.
  TC   209: 6    Eager eye and willing ear, / Pleased a simple tale to hear--
  TC   209:13              Children yet, the tale to hear, / Eager eye and willing ear, / Lovingly shall
  A3    25: 4    mouse was speaking, so that her idea of the tale was something like this:--
```
TALES (1)
```
  A4    29: 4    happened to me! When I used to read fairy tales, I fancied that kind of thing never happened, and now
```
TALK (31)
```
  T2   120:31        about in the wind, "I wish you could talk!"
  T2   121: 4    almost in a whisper. "And can all the flowers talk?"
  T2   122:23    gardens before, but none of the flowers could talk."
  T2   126:23    thoughts, for she cried "Faster! Don't try to talk!"
  A2    20:15    Mouse dear! Do come back again, and we wo'n't talk about cats, or dogs either, if you don't like them!" When
  A2    19:41    it must be really offended. "We wo'n't talk about her any more, if you'd rather not."
  A3    26:26    replied eagerly, for she was always ready to talk about her pet: "Dinah's our cat. And she's such a capital
  A9    72:18              "Oh, don't talk about trouble!" said the Duchess. "I make you a present
  A7    56:36    well as I do," said the Hatter, "you wouldn't talk about wasting it. It's him."
  T2   126:25    She felt as if she would never be able to talk again, she was getting so much out of breath: and still
  T3   132:25              "I like them when they can talk," Alice said. "None of them ever talk, where I come from
  T4   141:15    did beseech. / 'A pleasant walk, a pleasant talk, / Along the briny beach: / We cannot do with more than
  A2    19:12    here, that I should think very likely it can talk: at any rate, there's no harm in trying." So she began:
  T7   175:26    Unicorn looked dreamily at Alice, and said "Talk, child."
  A9    70:19    my dear, and that makes you forget to talk. I ca'n't tell you just now what the moral of that is,
  A10   82:27    are all dry, he is gay as a lark, / And will talk in contemptuous tones of the Shark: / But, when the tide
  T6   163:43              "Now you talk like a reasonable child," said Humpty Dumpty, looking
  A8    69: 1    could be beheaded, and that you weren't to talk nonsense.
  A11   88:43              "Don't talk nonsense," said Alice more boldly: "you know you're
  T4   142:20    'The time has come,' the Walrus said, / 'To talk of many things: / Of shoes--and ships--and sealing wax--/
  A2    19:43    down to the end of its tail. "As if I would talk on such a subject! Our family always hated cats: nasty,
  A8    62:11              "You'd better not talk!" said Five. "I heard the Queen say only yesterday you
  T7   175:25              "It can talk," said Haigha solemnly.
  A7    60:28              "Then you shouldn't talk," said the Hatter.
  T2   120:32              "We can talk," said the Tiger-lily, "when there's anybody worth
  T1   110:30    "Now, if you'll only attend, Kitty, and not talk so much, I'll tell you all my ideas about Looking-glass
  T2   122:21              "How is it you can all talk so nicely?" Alice said, hoping to get it into a better
  A8    67:13    Cheshire-Cat: now I shall have somebody to talk to."
  T3   132:26    can talk," Alice said. "None of them ever talk, where I come from."
  T12  207:10    could keep up a conversation! But how can you talk with a person if they always say the same thing?"
  T2   123:37    felt that it would be far grander to have a talk with a real Queen.
```
TALKATIVE (1)
```
  T8W   21:12    recovered his spirits, and was getting very talkative, she thought she might safely leave him. "I think I
```
TALKING (35)
```
  A2    15:11              Oh dear, what nonsense I'm talking!"
  A11   86:36    looked anxiously round, to make out who was talking.
  T9   194:25    to herself "What dreadful nonsense we are talking!"
  T6   162:42              "You don't know what you're talking about!" cried Humpty Dumpty. "How many days are there
  T2   120:13              "It's no use talking about it," Alice said, looking up at the house and
  A5    42:32    "I haven't the least idea what you're talking about," said Alice.
  T4   145:18              "Well, it's no use your talking about waking him," said Tweedledum, "when you're only
  A1     9: 6    was nothing else to do, so Alice soon began talking again. "Dinah'll miss me very much to-night, I should
  T1   108: 6    But she didn't get on very fast, as she was talking all the time, sometimes to the kitten, and sometimes
  A8    68:31    the King, and the Queen, who were all talking at once, while all the rest were quite silent, and
  A2    15:37    kept fanning herself all the time she went on talking. "Dear, dear! How queer everything is to-day! And
  A3    21: 7    seemed quite natural to Alice to find herself talking familiarly with them, as if she had known them all her
  A2    18: 3    little white kid-gloves while she was talking. "How can I have done that?" she thought. "I must be
  A8    63:23    Alice recognized the White Rabbit: it was talking in a hurried nervous manner, smiling at everything
  A7    55:29    say," added the Dormouse, which seemed to be talking in its sleep, "that 'I breathe when I sleep' is the
  T1   109: 2    saved up all my punishments?" she went on, talking more to herself than the kitten. "What would they do
  T4   145:28              "I know they're talking nonsense," Alice thought to herself: "and it's foolish
  A6    48:27              "Talking of axes," said the Duchess, "chop off her head!"
  T8   185:21    she was much relieved to hear that he was talking on in his usual tone. "All kinds of fastness," he
  A7    54: 4    as a cushion, resting their elbows on it, and talking over its head. "Very uncomfortable for the Dormouse,"
  T8   185:24    "How can you go on talking so quietly, head downwards?" Alice asked, as she
  T7   173:14    Alice had no more breath for talking; so they trotted on in silence, till they came into
  A3    26: 9    up and walking away. "You insult me by talking such nonsense!"
  T2   120:33    the Tiger-lily, "when there's anybody worth talking to."
  T1   107:14    up in a corner of the great arm-chair, half talking to herself and half asleep, the kitten had been having
  T8   190:29    things hung round the horse--" So she went on talking to herself, as she watched the horse walking
  T3   137:29    before it gets dark!" So she wandered on, talking to herself as she went, till, on turning a sharp
  A5    43:39    got used to it in a few minutes, and began talking to herself, as usual, "Come, there's half my plan done
  T9   196: 1    went on in a low voice, more as if she were talking to herself. "He came to the door with a corkscrew in
  A6    46:43              "Oh, there's no use in talking to him," said Alice desperately: "he's perfectly
  A8    67:37              "Who are you talking to?" said the King, coming up to Alice, and looking at
  T3   132:18    Gnat (for that was the insect she had been talking to) was balancing itself on a twig just over her head,
  T1   115:20    he had recovered, and he and the Queen were talking together in a frightened whisper--so low, that Alice
  A4    30:24    and the sound of a good many voices all talking together: she made out the words: "Where's the other
```

TALKING (cont.)
  T3   132:22 feel nervous with it, after they had been talking together so long.
TALKS (1)
  T6   161:19 "and it's my turn to choose a subject--" ("He talks about it just as if it was a game!" thought Alice.) "So
TALL (2)
  T4   144:32 couldn't say honestly that he was. He had a tall red night-cap on, with a tassel, and he was lying
  T5   156: 5   under trees, but always with the same tall river-banks frowning over their heads.
TALLER (3)
  A5   43:35   and then at the other, and growing sometimes taller, and sometimes shorter, until she had succeeded in
  A5   41:27   as it went, "One side will make you grow taller, and the other side will make you grow shorter."
  T2   123:31 inches high-- and here she was, half a head taller than Alice herself!
TANGLED (2) [See also ENTANGLED]
  T8W   17:11   bright yellow like the handkerchief, and all tangled and tumbled about like a heap of sea-weed. "You could
  T5   156:21 side of the boat, with just the ends of her tangled hair dipping into the water--while with bright eager
TANGLES (1)
  T1   107:18 spread over the hearth-rug, all knots and tangles, with the kitten running after its own tail in the
TAR-BARREL (1)
  T4   139: 2 flew down a monstrous crow, / As black as a tar-barrel; / Which frightened both the heroes so, / They
-TART [See CHERRY-TART]
TARTS (7)
  A11t 86: 1   WHO STOLE THE TARTS?
  A11   87:16   "The Queen of Hearts, she made some tarts, / All on a summer day: / The Knave of Hearts, he stole
  A11   87:18   day: / The Knave of Hearts, he stole those tarts / And took them quite away!"
  A11   91:15   of sight, he said, in a deep voice, "What are tarts made of?"
  A12   96:14   said the King triumphantly, pointing to the tarts on the table. "Nothing can be clearer than that. Then
  A11   86: 1   the court was a table, with a large dish of tarts upon it: they looked so good, that it made Alice quite
  A12   96: 7   two'--why, that must be what he did with the tarts, you know--"
TASSEL (1)
  T4   144:33 was. He had a tall red night-cap on, with a tassel, and he was lying crumpled up into a sort of untidy
TASTE (3)
  T7   174:16 white and brown bread. Alice took a piece to taste, but it was very dry.
  A1   11: 7   was not marked "poison," so Alice ventured to taste it, and, finding it very nice (it had, in fact, a sort
  A3   24:11   large birds complained that they could not taste theirs, and the small ones choked and had to be patted
TASTED (3)
  A5   43:15   you'll be telling me next that you never tasted an egg!"
  A10   78:10   to a lobster--" (Alice began to say "I once tasted--" but checked herself hastily, and said "No never")
  A5   43:16   "I have tasted eggs, certainly," said Alice, who was a very truthful
TASTES (1)
  A10   84:13   rather offended tone, "Hm! No accounting for tastes! Sing her 'Turtle Soup,' will you, old fellow?"
TASTING (1)
  T8W   15: 7   blue and white, and looked like china. While tasting the treacle, they had a sad accident: two of their
TAUGHT (6)
  T9   193:22   "Manners are not taught in lessons," said Alice. "Lessons teach you to do sums,
  A9   77: 7   him," the Mock Turtle said with a sigh. "He taught Laughing and Grief, they used to say."
  A1   10:24   remember the simple rules their friends had taught them: such as, that a red-hot poker will burn you if
  A9   76:39   conger-eel, that used to come once a week: he taught us Drawling, Stretching, and Fainting in Coils."
  A9   75: 2   "We called him Tortoise because he taught us," said the Mock Turtle angrily. "Really you are very
  T1   107:22 was in disgrace. "Really, Dinah ought to have taught you better manners! You ought, Dinah, you know you
TEA (18)
  A11   89:14   getting so thin--and the twinkling of the tea--"
  T7   174: 2 Hatta only munched away, and drank some more tea.
  T9   199:39   / 'Tis a privilege high to have dinner and tea / Along with the Red Queen, the White Queen, and me!"
  A7   59:19   to say to this: so she helped herself to some tea and bread-and-butter, and then turned to the Dormouse, and
  A7   56: 8   gloomily: then he dipped it into his cup of tea, and looked at it again: but he could think of nothing
  T9   199:31   / Put cats in the coffee, and mice in the tea--/ And welcome Queen Alice with thirty-times-three!"
  A7   54: 2   and the March Hare and the Hatter were having tea at it: a Dormouse was sitting between them, fast asleep,
  A7   54:15   the table, but there was nothing on it but tea. "I don't see any wine," she remarked.
  T7   173:21 standing watching the fight, with a cup of tea in one hand and a piece of bread-and-butter in the other.
  A12   98:10   dear, certainly; but now run in to your tea: it's getting late." So Alice got up and ran off, thinking
  A11   89:12   in a trembling voice, "and I hadn't begun my tea--not above a week or so--and what with the
  A11   90:29   "I'd rather finish my tea," said the Hatter, with an anxious look at the Queen, who
  A11   89:16   "It began with the tea," the Hatter replied.
  A7   59: 9   "Take some more tea," the March Hare said to Alice, very earnestly.
  A7   56:23   said the Hatter, and he poured a little hot tea upon its nose.
  T7   173:23 out of prison, and he hadn't finished his tea when he was sent in," Haigha whispered to Alice: "and they
  A11   88: 9   these in; but I hadn't quite finished my tea when I was sent for."
  T3   134:14   "Weak tea with cream in it."
TEACH (1)
  T9   193:22 not taught in lessons," said Alice. "Lessons teach you to do sums, and things of that sort."
TEACHING (1)
  A4   33: 9   with one of the leaves. "I should have liked teaching it tricks very much, if--if I'd only been the right
TEACUP (3)
  A11   90: 7   The miserable Hatter dropped his teacup and bread-and-butter and went down on one knee. "I'm a
  A11   88: 6   witness was the Hatter. He came in with a teacup in one hand and a piece of bread-and-butter in the
  A11   88:32   his confusion he bit a large piece out of his teacup instead of the bread-and-butter.
TEACUPS (2)
  A12   98:26   pool--she could hear the rattle of the teacups as the March Hare and his friends shared their
  A12   98:38   to the waving of the reeds--the rattling teacups would change to tinkling sheep-bells, and the Queen's
TEA-PARTY (2)
  A7t   54: 1   A MAD TEA-PARTY

TEA-PARTY (cont.)
A7   60:36 her way through the wood. "It's the stupidest tea-party I ever was at in all my life!"
TEAPOT (1)
A7   60:34 they were trying to put the Dormouse into the teapot.
TEAR (3)
T4   141:12 it,' said the Carpenter, / And shed a bitter tear.
T4   146:21 beginning to stamp about wildly and tear his hair. "It's spoilt, of course!" Here he looked at
T7   173:31 Hatta looked round once more, and this time a tear or two trickled down his cheek; but not a word would he
TEARS (20)
A2t   14: 1   THE POOL OF TEARS
A6   50: 2 into its eyes again, to see if there were any tears.
A2   17:17 said poor Alice, and her eyes filled with tears again as she went on, "I must be Mabel after all, and I
T4   145:29 to cry about it." So she brushed away her tears, and went on, as cheerfully as she could, "At any rate,
A9   74:24 who looked at them with large eyes full of tears, but said nothing.
T8   187:30 stood and listened very attentively, but no tears came into her eyes.
T5   152:34 at the thought of her loneliness, two large tears came rolling down her cheeks.
T3   135:13 the Gnat only sighed deeply while two large tears came rolling down its cheeks.
T5   152:41 laughing at this, even in the midst of her tears. "Can you keep from crying by considering things?" she
T4   144: 3 / 'I deeply sympathize.' / With sobs and tears he sorted out / Those of the largest size, / Holding his
A2   17:25 oh dear!" cried Alice, with a sudden burst of tears, "I do wish they would put their heads down! I am so
A6   50: 3   No, there were no tears. "If you're going to turn into a pig, my dear," said
A1   12:24 she scolded herself so severely as to bring tears into her eyes; and once she remembered trying to box her
T8   186:36 that hears me sing it--either it brings the tears into their eyes, or else--"
T4   145:24 real," Alice said--half laughing through her tears, it all seemed so ridiculous--"I shouldn't be able to
A10   78: 6 Mock Turtle recovered his voice, and, with tears running down his cheeks, he went on again:--
A2   19: 3 it now, I suppose, by being drowned in my own tears! That will be a queer thing, to be sure! However,
T4   145:26 "I hope you don't suppose those are real tears?" Tweedledum interrupted in a tone of great contempt.
A2   15:23 she went on all the same, shedding gallons of tears, until there was a large pool round her, about four
A2   18:26 she soon made out that she was in the pool of tears which she had wept when she was nine feet high.
TEASE (3)
T3   129:24 was so dusty and hot, and the elephants did tease so!'"
T3   131:31   "Don't tease so," said Alice, looking about in vain to see where the
T8W   20: 2 wig fitted a little better, they wouldn't tease you quite so much."
TEASES (1)
A6   48:39 only does it to annoy, / Because he knows it teases."
TEASPOON (1)
A7   57:12 before he went mad, you know--" (pointing his teaspoon at the March Hare,) "--it was at the great concert
TEA-THINGS (1)
A7   58:11 Alice's head. "Is that the reason so many tea-things are put out here?" she asked.
TEA-TIME (2)
A7   58:12 said the Hatter with a sigh: "it's always tea-time, and we've no time to wash the things between whiles
A1   9: 8 I hope they'll remember her saucer of milk at tea-time. Dinah, my dear! I wish you were down here with me!
TEA-TRAY (1)
A7   57:20 'Up above the world you fly, / Like a tea-tray in the sky. / Twinkle, twinkle--'"
TEETH (1)
A6   51: 2 still it had very long claws and a great many teeth, so she felt that it ought to be treated with respect.
TEETOTUM (1)
T5   155: 7   "Are you a child or a teetotum?" the Sheep said, as she took up another pair of
TELEGRAPH (1)
T3   131:21 her--" "She must be sent as a message by the telegraph--" "She must draw the train herself the rest of the
TELESCOPE (4)
A1   12: 2 said Alice. "I must be shutting up like a telescope!"
A1   10: 8 Oh, how I wish I could shut up like a telescope! I think I could, if I only knew how to begin. For,
A2   14: 3 "Now I'm opening out like the largest telescope that ever was! Good-bye, feet!" (for when she looked
T3   130:18 the Guard was looking at her, first through a telescope, then through a microscope, and then through an
TELESCOPES (1)
A1   10:14 a book of rules for shutting people up like telescopes: this time she found a little bottle on it ("which
TELL (67)
T8   184:36 yet," the Knight said, gravely; "so I ca'n't tell for certain--but I'm afraid it would be a little hard."
A10   81: 2 the Mock Turtle yawned and shut his eyes. "Tell her about the reason and all that," he said to the
A9   77:24 Gryphon interrupted in a very decided tone. "Tell her something about the games now."
A5   36:27 else to do, and perhaps after all it might tell her something worth hearing. For some minutes it puffed
A10   82:13 to hear her try and repeat something now. Tell her to begin." He looked at the Gryphon as if he thought
A11   87: 3 and that he had to ask his neighbour to tell him. "A nice muddle their slates'll be in, before the
A8   62:15 it is his business!" said Five. "And I'll tell him--it was for bringing the cook tulip-roots instead of
A9   74:27   "I'll tell it her," said the Mock Turtle in a deep, hollow tone.
A3   21:12 it was, and as the Lory positively refused to tell its age, there was no more to be said.
T2   128:17 reproof, "'It's extremely kind of you to tell me all this'--however, we'll suppose it said--the Seventh
T12   207:34 her chin in her hand, to watch the kittens. "Tell me, Dinah, did you turn to Humpty Dumpty? I think you did
T4   140:20 as politely as she could, "would you please tell me first which road--"
T8   188:15 / To what the old man said, / I cried 'Come, tell me how you live!' / And thumped him on the head.
T8   188:31 to side, / Until his face was blue: / 'Come, tell me how you live,' I cried, / 'And what it is you do!'
T7   170:14 to the town. Just look along the road, and tell me if you can see either of them."
A4   30: 6   "Now tell me, Pat, what's that in the window?"
T4   139:11 of this wood: it's getting so dark. Would you tell me, please?"
A8   63: 3   "Would you tell me, please," said Alice, a little timidly, "why you are
T6   163:42   "Would you tell me please," said Alice, "what that means?"
A6   51: 7 thought Alice, and she went on. "Would you tell me, please, which way I ought to go from here?"
A6   47:12   "Please would you tell me," said Alice, a little timidly, for she was not quite
T9   192:16 if the game was over. "Please, would you tell me--" she began, looking timidly at the Red Queen.

TELL (cont.)

A2	17:23	I shall only look up and say 'Who am I, then? Tell me that first, and then, if I like being that person,
T6	164:15	words, Sir," said Alice. "Would you kindly tell me the meaning of the poem called 'Jabberwocky'?"
T5	149:17	smiled and said "If your Majesty will only tell me the right way to begin, I'll do it as well as I can."
A1	9:18	saying to her, very earnestly, "Now, Dinah, tell me the truth: did you ever eat a bat?" when suddenly,
T9	195:12	out of the difficulty, this time. "If you'll tell me what language 'fiddle-de-dee' is, I'll tell you the
T3	136:17	but nothing came of it. "Please, would you tell me what you call yourself?" she said timidly. "I think
T4	140:11	poetry," Alice said doubtfully. "Would you tell me which road leads out of the wood?"
A5	36:13	and said, very gravely, "I think you ought to tell me who you are, first."
A3	24:14	"You promised to tell me your history, you know," said Alice, "and why it is
T6	160: 2	said, looking at her for the first time, "but tell me your name and your business."
T8	187:31	"I'll tell thee everything I can: / There's little to relate. / I
A3	24:13	down again in a ring, and begged the Mouse to tell them something more.
A7	58:28	"Tell us a story!" said the March Hare.
A4	31:14	How was it, old fellow? What happened to you? Tell us all about it!"
T7	172:23	However, now you've got your breath, you may tell us what's happened in the town."
A7	56:13	"It tells the day of the month, and doesn't tell what o'clock it is!"
A8	64: 1	same as the rest of the pack, she could not tell whether they were gardeners, or soldiers, or courtiers,
T6	164:13	he paid them with; and so you see I ca'n't tell you.)
T9	194:36	often say it over together, dear. And I'll tell you a secret--I can read words of one letter! Isn't that
A4	31:21	better now--but I'm a deal too flustered to tell you--all I know is, something comes at me like a
T1	110:30	attend, Kitty, and not talk so much, I'll tell you all my ideas about Looking-glass House. First,
T1	108:27	went on, holding up one finger. "I'm going to tell you all your faults. Number one: you squeaked twice while
A2	15:22	go on crying in this way! Stop this moment, I tell you!" But she went on all the same, shedding gallons of
T1	110:10	let's pretend--" And here I wish I could tell you half the things Alice used to say, beginning with her
A9	73:16	Come on, then," said the Queen, "and he shall tell you his history.
T8	184:29	"I'll tell you how I came to think of it," said the Knight. "You see
T8W	18: 3	"I'll tell you how I came to wear it," the Wasp said. "When I was
A3	23: 7	the thing yourself some winter-day, I will tell you how the Dodo managed it.)
T4	146:27	in a greater fury than ever. "It's new, I tell you--I bought it yesterday--my nice NEW RATTLE!" and his
T6	163:26	contemptuously. "Of course you don't--till I tell you. I meant 'there's a nice knock-down argument for
T3	137: 1	"I'll tell you, if you'll come a little further on," the Fawn said.
A9	70:19	and that makes you forget to talk. I ca'n't tell you just now what the moral of that is, but I shall
T1	110:36	they've a fire in the winter: you never can tell, you know, unless our fire smokes, and then smoke comes
A10	81:10	"I can tell you more than that, if you like," said the Gryphon. "Do
A10	81:40	"I could tell you my adventures--beginning from this morning," said
A2	20:19	"Let us get to the shore, and then I'll tell you my history, and you'll understand why it is I hate
A5	43: 5	"But I'm not a serpent, I tell you!" said Alice. "I'm a--I'm a--"
T9	195:12	me what language 'fiddle-de-dee' is, I'll tell you the French for it!" she exclaimed triumphantly.
T7	171: 6	"Don't I tell you?" the King repeated impatiently. "I must have two--to
T3	132:30	of them--at least the large kinds. But I can tell you the names of some of them."
T6	166:30	when woods are getting green, / I'll try and tell you what I mean:"
T9	192: 2	I should be a Queen so soon--and I'll tell you what it is, your Majesty," she went on, in a severe
T5	155: 1	one is the most provoking of all--but I'll tell you what--" she added, as a sudden thought struck her.
A7	56:14	it?" muttered the Hatter. "Does your watch tell you what year it is?"
A4	30:15	it, yer honour, at all, at all!" "Do as I tell you, you coward!", and at last she spread out her hand

TELLING (5)

T4	139:35	funny," (Alice said afterwards, when she was telling her sister the history of all this), "to find myself
T9	202:38	push so!" she said afterwards, when she was telling her sister the history of her feast. "You would have
A5	43:14	no use denying it. I suppose you'll be telling me next that you never tasted an egg!"
T8	189:11	boiling it in wine. / I thanked him much for telling me / The way he got his wealth, / But chiefly for his
A10	82: 1	So Alice began telling them her adventures from the time when she first saw

TELLS (2)

A7	56:12	"What a funny watch!" she remarked. "It tells the day of the month, and doesn't tell what o'clock it
A7	58:19	getting tired of this. I vote the young lady tells us a story."

TEMPER (14)

A5	41:12	before, and she felt that she was losing her temper.
T8W	16: 6	pleased to find that he was recovering his temper.
A9	70: 4	was very glad to find her in such a pleasant temper, and thought to herself that perhaps it was only the
T2	122:22	Alice said, hoping to get it into a better temper by a compliment. "I've been in many gardens before, but
A3	26:19	this be a lesson to you never to lose your temper!" "Hold your tongue, Ma!" said the young Crab, a little
T5	149:27	said, in a melancholy voice. "It's out of temper, I think. I've pinned it here, and I've pinned it there
A9	71: 7	"the reason is, that I'm doubtful about the temper of your flamingo. Shall I try the experiment'"
A5	36:22	"Keep your temper," said the Caterpillar.
T6	163:38	minute Humpty Dumpty began again. "They've a temper, some of them--particularly verbs: they're the proudest
T9	193:12	"A nasty, vicious temper," the Red Queen remarked; and then there was an
T9	194:15	as usual," said the Red Queen: "the dog's temper would remain."
T9	194:21	"Then if the dog went away, its temper would remain!" the Queen exclaimed triumphantly.
T9	194:19	the Red Queen cried. "The dog would lose its temper, wouldn't it?"
T6	167:10	fishes answered, with a grin, / 'Why, what a temper you are in!'

-TEMPERED [See GOOD-TEMPERED, HOT-TEMPERED, etc.]

TEN (9)

A8	63:17	their hands and feet at the corners: next the ten courtiers: these were ornamented all over with diamonds,
A9	77:12	"Ten hours the first day," said the Mock Turtle: "nine the next
A1	12: 3	And so it was indeed: she was now only ten inches high, and her face brightened up at the thought
T2	127: 1	the Queen repeated. "Why, we passed it ten minutes ago! Faster!" And they ran on for a time in
T7	174:13	sat down, panting, while the King called out "Ten minutes allowed for refreshments!" Haigha and Hatta set to
A5	36:32	as I used--and I don't keep the same size for ten minutes together!"
A8	63:19	these came the royal children: there were ten of them, and the little dears came jumping merrily along,
T7	169: 2	the wood, at first in twos and threes, then ten or twenty together, and at last in such crowds that they

TEN (cont.)
  A8   63:15   First came ten soldiers carrying clubs: these were all shaped like the
TERMS (1)
  A7   56:43 stand beating. Now, if you only kept on good terms with him, he'd do almost anything you liked with the
TERRIBLY (1)
  A4   32:30 she tried hard to whistle to it; but she was terribly frightened all the time at the thought that it might
TERRIER (1)
  A2   20: 5 should like to show you! A little bright-eyed terrier, you know, with oh, such long curly brown hair! And
TERROR (2)
  T7 178: 4 and sprang across the little brook in her terror, and had just time to see the Lion and the * * * * *
  A6   48:17 Alice, jumping up and down in an agony of terror. "Oh, there goes his precise nose!", as an unusually
TERTIA (1)
  AI   3:17 / "There will be nonsense in it!" / While Tertia interrupts the tale / Not more than once a minute.
THAN (61)
  T6 159:23 away from her as usual, "have no more sense than a baby!"
  T9 193: 5 some meaning--and a child's more important than a joke, I hope. You couldn't deny that, even if you tried
  T8 184:17   "Much more smoothly than a live horse," Alice said, with a little scream of
  A12 93:35 his book, "Rule Forty-two. All persons more than a mile high to leave the court."
  T9 202: 8 fish!' / That is easy, and will not take more than a minute. / 'Let it lie in a dish!' / That is easy,
  T2 120: 6   it twists! It's more like a corkscrew than a path! Well this turn goes to the hill, I suppose--no,
  A6   50:12   about it: it was neither more nor less than a pig, and she felt that it would be quite absurd for her
  A1   10: 2 it led into a small passage, not much larger than a rat-hole: she knelt down and looked along the passage
  A6   49:33 a very turn-up nose, much more like a snout than a real nose: also its eyes were getting extremely small
  A7   60:29   This piece of rudeness was more than Alice could bear: she got up in great disgust, and walked
  T9 196:30 see how pleased she'll be!" But this was more than Alice had courage to do.
  T2 123:31 high--and here she was, half a head taller than Alice herself!
  T4 147: 7 and his large eyes--"looking more like a fish than anything else," Alice thought.
  T4 147:22 they'll be more like bundles of old clothes than anything else, by the time they're ready!" she said to
  A7   60: 1 change; and Alice was a good deal worse off than before, as the March Hare had just upset the milk-jug
  T1 109: 8 that much! I'd far rather go without them than eat them!
  T5 156: 4 made the oars stick fast in the water, worse than ever), and sometimes under trees, but always with the
  T4 146:26 old!" Tweedledum cried, in a greater fury than ever. "It's new, I tell you--I bought it yesterday--my
  A2   15:18 one eye; but to get through was more hopeless than ever: she sat down and began to cry again.
  A2   18:15 glass table as before, "and things are worse than ever," thought the poor child, "for I never was so small
  T8 179:17 as she was, Alice was more frightened for him than for herself at the moment, and watched him with some
  T4 141:17 the briny beach: / We cannot do with more than four, / To give a hand to each.'
  T8 181: 7 off with your helmet?" It was evidently more than he could manage by himself: however, she managed to shake
  A7   56: 9 but he could think of nothing better to say than his first remark, "It was the best butter, you know."
  A4   29: 9 thought Alice, "shall I never get any older than I am now? That'll be a comfort, one way--never to be an
  T7 172:21 tone. "I'm sure nobody walks much faster than I do!"
  T2 123: 1 know no more what's going on in the world, than if you were a bud!"
  T8 183:13 Alice could think of nothing better to say than "Indeed?" but she said it as heartily as she could. They
  A6   48:21 "the world would go round a deal faster than it does."
  T6 166:28 I'm singing or not, you've sharper eyes than most," Humpty Dumpty remarked severely. Alice was silent.
  A2   15:13 of the hall: in fact she was now rather more than nine feet high, and she at once took up the little golden
  A8   69: 3 if something wasn't done about it in less than no time, she'd have everybody executed, all round. (It
  A7   59:14 said the Hatter: "it's very easy to take more than nothing."
  AI   3:18 / While Tertia interrupts the tale / Not more than once a minute.
  T5 158: 7   "Then two are cheaper than one?" Alice said in a surprised tone, taking out her
  T9 195:35   "Are five nights warmer than one night, then?" Alice ventured to ask.
  T9 197:17 you know, because there never was more than one Queen at a time. Do wake up, you heavy things!" she
  A4   28: 9   It did so indeed, and much sooner than she had expected: before she had drunk half the bottle,
  T1 114:24 gently, and lifted him across more slowly than she had lifted the Queen, that she mightn't take his
  A5   39: 2 your jaws are too weak / For anything tougher than suet; / Yet you finished the goose, with the bones and
  T9 192:34 wringing her hands. "Oh, ever so much more than that!"
  T6 166:13 I had some poetry repeated to me much easier than that, by--Tweedledee, I think it was."
  A10 81:10   "I can tell you more than that, if you like," said the Gryphon. "Do you know why
  T8 184:43 he said; "but I've invented a better one than that--like a sugar-loaf. When I used to wear it, if I
  A9   72:16 don't trouble yourself to say it any longer than that," said Alice.
  T9 192:33   "But she said a great deal more than that!" the White Queen moaned, wringing her hands. "Oh,
  A12 96:15 tarts on the table. "Nothing can be clearer than that. Then again--'before she had this fit'--you never
  T4 144:15   "He ate more than the Carpenter, though," said Tweedledee. "You see he held
  T7 169:11 Having four feet, these managed rather better than the foot-soldiers; but even they stumbled now and then;
  T1 109: 2   she went on, talking more to herself than the kitten. "What would they do at the end of a year? I
  T3 135:23 the other side of it: it looked much darker than the last wood, and Alice felt a little timid about going
  T8 190: 2 speech was slow, / Whose hair was whiter than the snow, / Whose face was very like a crow, / With eyes,
  A7   55: 5 said Alice: "it's laid for a great many more than three."
  T2 120:11 when she turned a corner rather more quickly than usual, she ran against it before she could stop herself.
  A7   56:33 something better with the time," she said, "than wasting it in asking riddles that have no answers."
  A9   72: 7 'Never imagine yourself not to be otherwise than what it might appear to others that what you were or
  A9   72: 9 you were or might have been was not otherwise than what you had been would have appeared to them to be
  T4 147:37 who had overheard the remark. "I'm far worse than you!"
  T7 172:19 saw him too. So of course Nobody walks slower than you."
  A3   21:10 turned sulky, and would only say, "I'm older than you, and must know better." And this Alice would not
  T2 123: 7 said the Tiger-lily), "but she's more bushy than you are."
THANK (12)
  A4   31:19   Alice), "Well, I hardly know--No more, thank ye; I'm better now--but I'm a deal too flustered to tell
  T8W 21:15   "Good-bye, and thank-ye," said the Wasp, and Alice tripped down the hill
  A10 80:13   "Thank you, it's a very interesting dance to watch," said Alice
  T6 166:22 to listen to it; so she sat down, and said "Thank you" rather sadly,

THANK (cont.)
```
A10    81: 8                                       "Thank you," said Alice, "it's very interesting. I never knew
T2    127:37                                      "No, thank you," said Alice: "one's quite enough!"
A9     74:37   Alice was very nearly getting up and saying, "Thank you, Sir, for your interesting story," but she could not
T4    140: 7                           "Nohow. And thank you very much for asking," said Tweedledum.
T8    190:20   "Of course I'll wait," said Alice: "and thank you very much for coming so far--and for the song--I
T6    166:31                                             "Thank you very much," said Alice.
T8    181: 6                                       "Thank you very much," said Alice. "May I help you off with
T9    202:34                                      "Thank you very much," she whispered in reply, "but I can do
```
THANKED (3)
```
T8    189:11   bridge from rust / By boiling it in wine. / I thanked him much for telling me / The way he got his wealth, /
T4    143: 6   / 'No hurry!' said the Carpenter. / They thanked him much for that.
A10    80: 4   too far!", and gave a look askance--/ Said he thanked the whiting kindly, but he would not join the dance. /
```
THANKS (2)
```
T9    203: 4   lifted her up into the air. "I rise to return thanks--" Alice began: and she really did rise as she spoke,
T9    202:29             "You ought to return thanks in a neat speech," the Red Queen said, frowning at
```
THAT (611) [entries omitted]
THATCHED (1)
```
A6     53:13    were shaped like ears and the roof was thatched with fur. It was so large a house, that she did not
```
THAT'LL (3)
```
A4     29:10   "shall I never get any older than I am now? That'll be a comfort, one way--never to be an old woman--but
T6    164:29                                       "That'll do very well," said Alice: "and 'slithy'?"
T9    200: 5   times nine!" Alice repeated in despair. "Oh, that'll never be done! I'd better go in at once--" and in she
```
THAT'S (81)
```
T8    185:12                                  "But that's a different kind of fastness," Alice objected.
A6     48: 6   "You don't know much," said the Duchess; "and that's a fact."
T7    176:25   quivered. "All round the town?" he said. "That's a good long way. Did you go by the old bridge, or the
A9     73:20   generally, "You are all pardoned." "Come, that's a good thing!" she said to herself, for she had felt
T6    164: 3                               "That's a great deal to make one word mean," Alice said in a
T3    135: 9   remarked, "of course you'd miss your lessons. That's a joke. I wish you had made it."
T8W    17: 2                        The Wasp said "That's a new-fangled name. They called it conceit in my time
T9    195:31                 The Red Queen said "That's a poor thin way of doing things. Now here, we mostly
A1     8:34   it was good practice to say it over) "--yes, that's about the right distance--but then I wonder what
A10    81: 7   mouths. So they couldn't get them out again. That's all."
T6    163:36   said Humpty Dumpty, "which is to be master--that's all."
A5     43:20   they do, why, then they're a kind of serpent: that's all I can say."
T6    168:16                                       "That's all," said Humpty Dumpty. "Good-bye."
A10    78:35          "Back to land again, and--that's all the first figure," said the Mock Turtle, suddenly
A2     17: 2   Paris is the capital of Rome, and Rome--no, that's all wrong, I'm certain! I must have been changed for
A11    90:21               "If that's all you know about it, you may stand down," continued
A7     56:16   course not," Alice replied very readily: "but that's because it stays the same year for such a long time
T8W    21: 1               "Well, that's because your jaws are too short," the Wasp went on:
T2    126: 1   she went on. "It's a great huge game of chess that's being played--all over the world--if this is the world
A4     31:17   Last came a little feeble, squeaking voice ("That's Bill," thought Alice), "Well, I hardly know--No more,
T1    118:29   they are! However, somebody killed something: that's clear, at any rate--"
A10    82:30               "That's different from what I used to say when I was a child,"
T2    126: 7   companion only smiled pleasantly, and said "That's easily managed. You can be the White Queen's Pawn, if
A9     77:23                  "That's enough about lessons," the Gryphon interrupted in a
T6    164:25                       "That's enough to begin with," Humpty Dumpty interrupted:
T7    175:38   the bag!" he whispered. "Quick! Not that one--that's full of hay!"
T8    182:25               "That's hardly enough," he said, anxiously. "You see the wind
A7     58:12          "Yes, that's it," said the Hatter with a sigh: "it's always tea-time
T3    135:32   find the creature that has got my old name! That's just like the advertisements, you know, when people
T1    110:32   the room you can see through the glass--that's just the same as our drawing-room, only the things go
T6    168:26                       "That's just what I complain of," said Humpty Dumpty. "Your
T9    193: 2                       "That's just what I complain of! You should have meant! What do
T4    139: 8   so, it would be; but as it isn't, it ain't. That's logic."
A8     62:14                       "That's none of your business, Two!" said Seven.
T1    115:41   down the poker. He balances very badly"). "That's not a memorandum of your feelings!"
A12    93:41   go, at any rate," said Alice; "besides, that's not a regular rule: you invented it just now."
A6     49:29   by this time). "Don't grunt," said Alice; "that's not at all a proper way of expressing yourself."
T2    123:15                       "But that's not your fault," the Rose added kindly. "You're
A9     72:14                       "That's nothing to what I could say if I chose," the Duchess
T8    187: 7   The song is called 'Ways and Means': but that's only what it's called, you know!"
T8    187: 6                 "No, you oughtn't: that's quite another thing! The song is called 'Ways and
A4     28:12   put down the bottle, saying to herself "That's quite enough--I hope I sha'n't grow any more--As it is,
A8     62: 9          On which Seven looked up and said "That's right, Five! Always lay the blame on others!"
T2    125: 3                       "That's right," said the Queen, patting her on the head, which
T2    122:18                       "That's right!" said the Tiger-lily. "The daisies are worst of
A8     65:19                       "That's right!" shouted the Queen. "Can you play croquet?"
T3    137:13   "However, I know my name now," she said: "that's some comfort. Alice--Alice--I won't forget it again.
T3    132: 9   it'll take us into the Fourth Square, that's some comfort!" she said to herself. In another moment
T9    194:14                       "I think that's the answer."
T5    150:11               "That's the effect of living backwards," the Queen said kindly:
T8    181: 5   the wood--and then I must go back, you know. That's the end of my move."
T7    170:10   "Four thousand two hundred and seven, that's the exact number," the King said, referring to his book
A6     46:33   Are you to get in at all?" said the Footman. "That's the first question, you know."
A2     15:42   next question is 'Who in the world am I?' Ah, that's the great puzzle!" And she began thinking over all the
A11    86:15   knew the name of nearly everything there. "That's the judge," she said to herself, "because of his great
A12    95:39   verses to himself: "'We know it to be true'--that's the jury, of course--'If she should push the matter on'
```

THAT'S (cont.)
```
 A11    86:21                                          "And that's the jury-box," thought Alice; "and those twelve
 A12    95:21                                    "That's the most important piece of evidence we've heard yet,"
 T8    186:42                                  "Oh, that's the name of the song, is it?" Alice said, trying to
 A12    94:17  No, they're not," said the White Rabbit, "and that's the queerest thing about it." (The jury all looked
 T3    134: 6  and had thought to herself, "I wonder if that's the reason insects are so fond of flying into candles--
 T8    182: 6  "it's as well to be provided for everything. That's the reason the horse has all those anklets round his
 A9    77:15                                    "That's the reason they're called lessons," the Gryphon
 A7    55:22    "at least--at least I mean what I say--that's the same thing, you know."
 T8    189: 3  knolls / For wheels of Hansom-cabs. / And that's the way' (he gave a wink) / 'By which I get my wealth--
 T8    188: 7    he said, / 'Who sail on stormy seas; / And that's the way I get my bread--/ A trifle, if you please.'
 T5    153: 1                                        "That's the way it's done," the Queen said with great decision:
 T1    108:38                                    "That's three faults, Kitty, and you've not been punished for
 T6    160:30            "Now I declare that's too bad!" Humpty Dumpty cried, breaking into a sudden
 A10    82: 8  the Mock Turtle drew a long breath, and said "That's very curious!"
 A7    60:39  the  trees had a door leading right into it. "That's very curious!" she thought. "But everything's curious
 A12    93:21                                        "That's very important," the King said, turning to the jury.
 A1     9:10  I'm afraid, but you might catch a bat, and that's very like a mouse, you know. But do cats eat bats, I
 T1    109:15  and dance about--whenever the wind blows--oh, that's very pretty!" cried Alice, dropping the ball of worsted
 T6    163:41    the  whole lot of them! Impenetrability! That's what I say!"
 T8    187: 2  the  Knight said, looking a little vexed. "That's what the name is called. The name really is 'The Aged
 T8    187: 4          "Then I ought to have said 'That's what the song is called'?" Alice corrected herself.
 T6    160:36  book," Humpty Dumpty said in a calmer tone. "That's what you call a History of England, that is. Now, take
 T2    122: 5  "It says 'Boughwough!'" cried a Daisy. "That's why its branches are called boughs!"
 A6     47:15  "It's a Cheshire-Cat," said the Duchess, "and that's why. Pig!"
 T1    108:31  speaking). "Her paw went into your eye? Well, that's your fault, for keeping your eyes open--if you'd shut
```
THE (3323) [entries omitted]
THEE (3)
```
 T8    187:29              she said to herself: "it's 'I give thee all, I can no more.'" She stood and listened very
 T8    187:31                          "I'll tell thee everything I can: / There's little to relate. / I saw an
 TI    103:29  of gladness. / The magic words shall hold thee fast: / Thou shalt not heed the raving blast.
```
THEIR (82) [entries omitted]
THEIRS (1) [entry omitted]
THEM (179) [entries omitted]
THEMSELVES (5) [entries omitted]
THEN (210) [entries omitted]
THENCE (1)
```
 T8    188:21  a mountain-rill, / I set it in a blaze; / And thence they make a stuff they call / Rowland's Macassar-Oil--/
```
THERE (185)
```
 T2    127:34  ground, and sticking little pegs in here and there.
 T3    131:28  a  wood just now--and I wish I could get back there!"
 T8W    14:10  other  side? You'll be out of the cold wind there."
 T4    140:31  thought the sun / Had got no business to be there / After the day was done--/ 'It's very rude of him,' she
 A7     60:35              "At any rate I'll never go there again!" said Alice, as she picked her way through the
 T2    126:27     and  dragged her along. "Are we nearly there?" Alice managed to pant out at last.
 T1    111:12  this,  though she hardly knew how she had got there. And certainly the glass was beginning to melt away,
 T5    156: 9   up from her knitting: "I didn't put 'em there, and I'm not going to take 'em away."
 T4    144:25  it was more likely to be a wild beast. "Are there any lions or tigers about here?" she asked timidly.
 T2    123: 3                      "Are there any more people in the garden besides me?" Alice said,
 T3    131:19  voices went on ("What a number of people there are in the carriage!" thought Alice), saying "She must
 A1     9: 9  my  dear! I wish you were down here with me! There are no mice in the air, I'm afraid, but you might catch
 A8     67:26  to have any lions in particular: at least, there's none, nobody attends to them--and you've no idea how
 T3    129: 4  to  see a little further. "Principal rivers--there are none. Principal mountains--I'm on the only one, but
 T6    164:26  to  begin with," Humpty Dumpty interrupted: "there are plenty of hard words there. 'Brillig' means four
 T2    125:27  to be some men moving about somewhere--and so there are!" she added in a tone of delight, and her heart
 T8    182:19  see,"  he said, as they got it in at last; "there are so many candlesticks in the bag." And he hung it to
 T5    156: 6                      "Oh, please! There are some scented rushes!" Alice cried in a sudden
 T1    113: 9  whisper,  for fear of frightening them), "and there are the White King and the White Queen sitting on the
 T6    163:19  over thoroughly just now--and that shows that there are three hundred and sixty-four days when you might get
 T6    164:31  as  'active.' You see it's like a portmanteau--there are two meanings packed up into one word."
 A4     30:11          "Well, it's got no business there, at any rate: go and take it away!"
 T5    151:13              "You're wrong there, at any rate," said the Queen. "Were you ever punished?"
 T6    164:26  interrupted:  "there are plenty of hard words there. 'Brillig' means four o'clock in the afternoon--the time
 T9    192:14  liked  very much to ask them how they came there, but she feared it would not be quite civil. However,
 T5    149:28  I've  pinned it here, and I've pinned it there, but there's no pleasing it!"
 A6     49:32  its  face to see what was the matter with it. There could be no doubt that it had a very turn-up nose, much
 A6     50:11  down  into its face in some alarm. This time there could be no mistake about it: it was neither more nor
 T9    196: 7                          "Is there generally?" Alice asked in an astonished tone.
 A4     31: 6  thing she heard was a general chorus of "There goes Bill!" then the Rabbit's voice alone--"Catch him,
 A6     48:17   up and down in an agony of terror. "Oh, there goes his precious nose!", as an unusually large saucepan
 T5    153:16  as  six impossible things before breakfast. There goes the shawl again!"
 T8    190:26  said  to herself, as she stood watching him. "There he goes! Right on his head as usual! However, he gets on
 T4    147: 6  in the umbrella, with only his head out: and there he lay, opening and shutting his mouth and his large
 T6    162:43   cried Humpty Dumpty. "How many days are there in a year?"
 A10    80: 8  how far we go?" his scaly friend replied. / "There is another shore, you know, upon the other side. / The
 A9     72: 1  here. And the moral of that is--'The more there is of mine, the less there is of yours.'"
 A9     72: 2  that  is--'The more there is of mine, the less there is of yours.'"
 A2     20: 3  did  not answer, so Alice went on eagerly: "There is such a nice little dog, near our house, I should like
 T9    193:18  to have a party at all," said Alice; "but, if there is to be one, I think I ought to invite the guests."
 T3    130: 5  room  for one where she came from. The land there is worth a thousand pounds an inch!"
```

THERE (cont.)

A7	54:16	"There isn't any," said the March Hare.
T3	131:11	spoke next. "Change engines--" it said, and there it choked and was obliged to leave off.
T9	201:17	out "Waiter! Bring back the pudding!" and there it was again in a moment, like a conjuring-trick. It was
T1	107:17	down till it had all come undone again; and there it was, spread over the hearth-rug, all knots and
T4	145:10	"If that there King was to wake," added Tweedledum, "you'd go out--
T3	137:27	thought of that before--But I ca'n't stay there long. I'll just call and say 'How d'ye do?' and ask them
T5	157:11	"Are there many crabs here?" said Alice.
A7	59:29	"I wo'n't interrupt you again. I dare say there may be one."
A6	46:18	"There might be some sense in your knocking," the Footman went
T4	148:18	getting dark so suddenly that Alice thought there must be a thunderstorm coming on. "What a thick black
A9	74:38	story," but she could not help thinking there must be more to come, so she sat still and said nothing.
A4	30:18	glass. "What a number of cucumber-frames there must be!" thought Alice. "I wonder what they'll do next!
T9	197:17	of England--it couldn't, you know, because there never was more than one Queen at a time. Do wake up, you
T8W	14: 4	said in a peevish tone. "Worrity, worrity! There never was such a child!"
T4	144:10	we be trotting home again?' / But answer came there none--/ And this was scarcely odd, because / They'd
T6	162:30	It's a present from the White King and Queen. There now!"
T1	115:12	so wide open! All the ashes will get into it--there, now I think you're tidy enough!" she added, as she
T8	191: 2	little flowerbeds dotted about it here and there. "Oh, how glad I am to get here! And what is this on my
A4	29: 6	ought to be a book written about me, that there ought! And when I grow up, I'll write one--but I'm grown
A4	29: 5	and now here I am in the middle of one! There ought to be a book written about me, that there ought!
T9	198: 7	"I'm not a visitor, and I'm not a servant. There ought to be one marked 'Queen,' you know--"
T2	125:26	a large chess-board!" Alice said at last. "There ought to be some men moving about somewhere--and so
T1	110:44	Kitty? I wonder if they'd give you milk in there? Perhaps Looking-glass milk isn't good to drink--but oh,
T5	156: 7	cried in a sudden transport of delight. "There really are--and such beauties!"
A6	52: 7	"You'll see me there," said the Cat, and vanished.
T8W	15:15	"Let it stop there!" said the Wasp, fretfully turning away his head.
A5	42:18	As there seemed to be no chance of getting her hands up to her
A11	86:10	"and hand round the refreshments!" But there seemed to be no chance of this; so she began looking at
A4	28:25	still it was very uncomfortable, and, as there seemed to be no sort of chance of her ever getting out
A1	10:12	There seemed to be no use in waiting by the little door, so
A1	8:16	with cupboards and book-shelves: here and there she saw maps and pictures hung upon pegs. She took down
T8W	13: 3	"There's somebody very unhappy there," she thought, looking anxiously back to see what was
T3	135: 2	she would call out 'Come here--,' and there she would have to leave off, because there wouldn't be
T7	173:25	"and they only give them oyster-shells in there--so you see he's very hungry and thirsty. How are you,
A9	72:31	hers began to tremble. Alice looked up, and there stood the Queen in front of them, with her arms folded,
A11	86:15	that she knew the name of nearly everything there. "That's the judge," she said to herself, "because of
T2	127: 1	"Nearly there!" the Queen repeated. "Why, we passed it ten minutes
A3	23:10	party were placed along the course, here and there. There was no "One, two, three, and away!", but they
A12	96:12	"Why, there they are!" said the King triumphantly, pointing to the
T3	129: 7	what are those creatures, making honey down there? They ca'n't be bees--nobody ever saw bees a mile off,
A12	92: 5	on to the heads of the crowd below, and there they lay sprawling about, reminding her very much of a
T3	132:40	Gnat replied. "Further on, in the wood down there, they've got no names--however, go on with your list of
A5	44: 2	in it about four feet high. "Whoever lives there," thought Alice, "it'll never do to come upon them this
T2	123: 1	your head under the leaves, and snore away there, till you know no more what's going on in the world,
T3	131: 6	There was a Beetle sitting next the Goat (it was a very queer
T9	198: 3	large letters, and on each side of the arch there was a bell-handle; one was marked "Visitors' Bell," and
A8	68:38	was, that you couldn't cut off a head unless there was a body to cut it off from: that he had never had to
T1	116: 1	There was a book lying near Alice on the table, and while she
T5	152: 8	"What is the matter?" she said, as soon as there was a chance of making herself heard. "Have you pricked
A12	96:26	King looking round the court with a smile. There was a dead silence.
A4	31:32	There was a dead silence instantly, and Alice thought to
T9	200: 7	better go in at once--" and in she went, and there was a dead silence the moment she appeared.
A8	68:29	find quite a large crowd collected round it: there was a dispute going on between the executioner, the King
A2	20:22	birds and animals that had fallen into it: there was a Duck and a Dodo, a Lory and an Eaglet, and several
T1	112: 3	very first thing she did was to look whether there was a fire in the fireplace, and she was quite pleased
A12	94:26	There was a general clapping of hands at this: it was the
A4	34: 3	to eat or drink under the circumstances. There was a large mushroom growing near her, about the same
A2	15:23	the same, shedding gallons of tears, until there was a large pool round her, about four inches deep, and
T6	168:14	There was a long pause.
A4	30:13	There was a long silence after this, and Alice could only hear
A6	46:13	one could possibly hear you." And certainly there was a most extraordinary noise going on within--a
T7	174:12	There was a pause in the fight just then, and the Lion and the
T4	140: 2	hands, and stood looking at her for a minute: there was a rather awkward pause, as Alice didn't know how to
T1	112: 4	and she was quite pleased to find that there was a real one, blazing away as brightly as the one she
T8	184:21	There was a short silence after this, and then the Knight went
A8	63:13	threw themselves flat upon their faces. There was a sound of many footsteps, and Alice looked round,
A7	54: 1	There was a table set out under a tree in front of the house,
T5	156:28	of beautiful rushes as the boat glided by, there was always a more lovely one that she couldn't reach.
T9	193:13	temper," the Red Queen remarked; and then there was an uncomfortable silence for a minute or two.
A6	47: 7	There was certainly too much of it in the air. Even the
T9	201:30	finding that, the moment she opened her lips, there was dead silence, and all eyes were fixed upon her; "and
A12	94:37	There was dead silence in the court, whilst the White Rabbit
A8	67:21	listen to her. The Cat seemed to think that there was enough of it now in sight, and no more of it
A3	23:28	into it), and handed them round as prizes. There was exactly one a-piece, all round.
A8	66:15	the act of crawling away: besides all this, there was generally a ridge or a furrow in the way wherever
A5	42: 1	was pressed so closely against her foot, that there was hardly room to open her mouth; but she did it at
A8	67:14	are you getting on?" said the Cat, as soon as there was mouth enough for it to speak with.
A9	76:36	"Well, there was Mystery," the Mock Turtle replied, counting off the
T9	197:19	she went on in an impatient tone; but there was no answer but a gentle snoring.

THERE (cont.)

T5	151:10		Alice felt there was no denying that. "Of course it would be all the
A4	28: 2	bottle that stood near the looking-glass.	There was no label this time with the words "DRINK ME," but
T5	156: 1	This offended Alice a little, so	there was no more conversation for a minute or two, while the
A3	21:12	the Lory positively refused to tell its age,	there was no more to be said.
A1	8:42	antipathies, I think--" (she was rather glad	there was no one listening, this time, as it didn't sound at
T8	179: 2	and Alice lifted up her head in some alarm.	There was no one to be seen, and her first thought was that
A1	8:33	opportunity for showing off her knowledge, as	there was no one to listen to her, still it was good practice
A3	23:10	were placed along the course, here and there.	There was no "One, two, three, and away!", but they began
T7	176:14	sit down between the two great creatures; but	there was no other place for him.
A5	41:42	by this very sudden change, but she felt that	there was no time to be lost, as she was shrinking rapidly: so
A5	42:36	was more and more puzzled, but she thought	there was no use in saying anything more till the Pigeon had
T2	128:31	("and she can run very fast!" thought Alice),	there was no way of guessing, but she was gone, and Alice
T9	192: 8	she comforted herself with the thought that	there was nobody to see her, "and if I really am a Queen," she
A1	9:24	Rabbit was still in sight, hurrying down it.	There was not a moment to be lost: away went Alice like the
T9	204: 9		There was not a moment to be lost. Already several of the
A4	28:17	to kneel down on the floor: in another minute	there was not even room for this, and she tried the effect of
T7	172:13		"I didn't say there was nothing better," the King replied. "I said there was
A1	9: 5	Down, down, down.	There was nothing else to do, so Alice soon began talking
T5	155:19	little boat, gliding along between banks: so	there was nothing for it but to do her best.
T7	172:14	nothing better," the King replied. "I said	there was nothing like it." Which Alice did not venture to
A1	9:35	three-legged table, all made of solid glass:	there was nothing on it but a tiny golden key, and Alice's
A7	54:14	Alice looked all round the table, but	there was nothing on it but tea. "I don't see any wine," she
A1	7:11		There was nothing so very remarkable in that; nor did Alice
T2	120:26	However, there was the hill full in sight, so	there was nothing to be done but start again. This time she
T3	135:19	itself away, for, when Alice looked up,	there was nothing whatever to be seen on the twig, and, as she
T12	207:38	only you'd been really with me in my dream,	there was one thing you would have enjoyed--I had such a
T3	137:16	not a very difficult question to answer, as	there was only one road through the wood, and the two
A11	88:38	decided to remain where she was as long as	there was room for her.
T9	199:35	I wonder if any one's counting?" In a minute	there was silence again, and the same shrill voice sang
A5	41: 5	to end," said the Caterpillar, decidedly; and	there was silence for some minutes.
T2	122:16		There was silence in a moment, and several of the pink daisies
A11	90:17	in the newspapers, at the end of trials,	'There was some attempt at applause, which was immediately
T5	155:24	so Alice said nothing, but pulled away.	There was something very queer about the water, she thought,
A6	52:28	March." As she said this, she looked up, and	there was the Cat again, sitting on a branch of a tree.
T8	185: 2	I had a very little way to fall, you see--But	there was the danger of falling into it, to be sure. That
T8	179: 5	those queer Anglo-Saxon Messengers. However,	there was the great dish still lying at her feet, on which she
T2	120:26		However, there was the hill full in sight, so there was nothing to
T9	204: 4	the White Queen; but, instead of the Queen,	there was the leg of mutton sitting in the chair. "Here I am!"
T5	149:10	bread-and-butter," and Alice felt that if	there was to be any conversation at all, she must manage it
T7	177: 4	the Lion growled out as he lay down again.	"There was too much dust to see anything. What a time the
T3	130: 3	got one," Alice said in a frightened tone:	"there wasn't a ticket-office where I came from." And again the
T3	130: 4	And again the chorus of voices went on.	"There wasn't room for one where she came from. The land there
T9	196: 6	for a hippopotamus. Now, as it happened,	there wasn't such a thing in the house, that morning."
T2	125:21	country--and a most curious country it was.	There were a number of tiny little brooks running straight
T9	200: 9	walked up the large hall, and noticed that	there were about fifty guests, of all kinds: some were animals
A6	50: 2	and looked into its eyes again, to see if	there were any tears.
A1	9:30		There were doors all round the hall, but they were all locked;
T9	200:10	all kinds: some were animals, some birds, and	there were even a few flowers among them. "I'm glad they've
A9	73: 7	so that, by the end of half an hour or so,	there were no arches left, and all the players, except the
T4	140:40	the sky: / No birds were flying overhead--/	There were no birds to fly.
A6	50: 3		No, there were no tears. "If you're going to turn into a pig, my
T1	110:15	exact, had argued that they couldn't, because	there were only two of them, and Alice had been reduced at
T5	156:39	at her feet--but Alice hardly noticed this,	there were so many other curious things to think about.
T3	137:21	a long way, but wherever the road divided,	there were sure to be two finger-posts pointing the same way,
A8	63:19	did. After these came the royal children:	there were ten of them, and the little dears came jumping
T9	200:14		There were three chairs at the head of the table: the Red and
A8	62: 2	the roses growing on it were white, but	there were three gardeners at it, busily painting them red.
A7	58:32	"Once upon a time there were	three little sisters," the Dormouse began in a
A4	30:17	and made another snatch in the air. This time	there were two little shrieks, and more sounds of broken glass
AI	3:16	it": / In gentler tones Secunda hopes /	"There will be nonsense in it!" / While Tertia interrupts the
T8	191: 6	"But how can it have got	there without my knowing it?" she said to herself, as she
T8	182: 2	was for," said Alice. "It isn't very likely	there would be any mice on the horse's back."
T9	192:15	feared it would not be quite civil. However,	there would be no harm, she thought, in asking if the game was
T3	135: 3	there she would have to leave off, because	there wouldn't be any name for her to call, and of course you
T3	133:13	branch above your head," said the Gnat, "and	there you'll find a Snap-dragon-fly. Its body is made of

THERE'D (1)

T2	120:16	again--back into the old room--and	there'd be an end of all my adventures!"

THEREFORE (1)

A6	51:34	I'm pleased, and wag my tail when I'm angry.	Therefore I'm mad."

THERE'LL (2)

T4	148: 7	satisfied smile. "I don't suppose," he said,	"there'll be a tree left standing, for ever so far round, by
T1	112: 7	thought Alice: "warmer, in fact, because	there'll be no one here to scold me away from the fire. Oh,

THERE'S (55)

T1	110:23	you'd look exactly like her. Now do try,	there's a dear!" And Alice got the Red Queen off the table,
A11	88: 2	not yet!" the Rabbit hastily interrupted.	"There's a great deal to come before that!"
A9	71:18	to agree to everything that Alice said:	"there's a large mustard-mine near here. And the moral of that
T5	152: 1	Alice was just beginning to say	"There's a mistake somewhere--," when the Queen began screaming
T6	163:26	course you don't--till I tell you. I meant	'there's a nice knock-down argument for you!'"
A10	79:14	little faster?" said a whiting to a snail, /	"There's a porpoise close behind us, and he's treading on my

THERE'S (cont.)

T1	111: 7	such beautiful things in it! Let's pretend there's a way of getting through into it, somehow, Kitty.
A12	95:25	"I'll give him sixpence. I don't believe there's an atom of meaning in it."
A12	95:28	down, on their slates, "She doesn't believe there's an atom of meaning in it," but none of them attempted
T2	123:10	eagerly, for the thought crossed her mind, "There's another little girl in the garden, somewhere!"
T6	165:10	Well then, 'mimsy' is 'flimsy and miserable' (there's another portmanteau for you). And a 'borogove' is a
A8	67: 7	people here: the great wonder is, that there's any one left alive!"
T2	120:32	"We can talk," said the Tiger-lily, "when there's anybody worth talking to."
A6	47: 5	"There's certainly too much pepper in that soup!" Alice said to
T6	163:22	And only one for birthday presents, you know. There's glory for you!"
A5	43:39	began talking to herself, as usual, "Come, there's half my plan done now! How puzzling all these changes
A1	12:29	Alice, "to pretend to be two people! Why, there's hardly enough of me left to make one respectable
A4	29:14	"How can you learn lessons in here? Why, there's hardly room for you, and no room at all for any
T8	187:32	"I'll tell thee everything I can: / There's little to relate. / I saw an aged aged man, /
A12	94: 3	"There's more evidence to come yet, please your Majesty," said
T6	160:22	think so! Why, if ever I did fall off--which there's no chance of--but if I did--" Here he pursed up his
A2	19:12	think very likely it can talk: at any rate, there's no harm in trying." So she began: "O Mouse, do you
A12	95:30	"If there's no meaning in it," said the King, "that saves a world
A12	94:22	write it, and they ca'n't prove that I did: there's no name signed at the end."
T5	149:28	pinned it here, and I've pinned it there, but there's no pleasing it!"
A5	42:35	attending to her; "but those serpents! There's no pleasing them!"
A4	29: 8	she added in a sorrowful tone: "at least there's no room to grow up any more here."
A6	46:10	"There's no sort of use in knocking," said the Footman, "and
A7	59:24	"There's no such thing!" Alice was beginning very angrily, but
T8W	15:12	"There's no such word in the language!" said the Wasp.
A5	43:13	a neck as that! No, no! You're a serpent; and there's no use denying it. I suppose you'll be telling me next
A1	12:21	"Come, there's no use in crying like that!" said Alice to herself
T3	130:10	Alice thought to herself "Then there's no use in speaking." The voices didn't join in, this
A6	46:43	"Oh, there's no use in talking to him," said Alice desperately:
T5	153:11	Alice laughed. "There's no use trying," she said: "one ca'n't believe
T6	160:13	"Why, because there's nobody with me!" cried Humpty Dumpty. "Did you think I
T7	172: 5	"There's nothing but hay left now," the Messenger said, peeping
T7	172: 8	glad to see that it revived him a good deal. "There's nothing like eating hay when you're faint," he
T4	145:23	bit realler by crying," Tweedledee remarked: "there's nothing to cry about."
A12	94:12	at all," said the White Rabbit: "in fact, there's nothing written on the outside." He unfolded the paper
T5	150:15	"--but there's one great advantage in it, that one's memory works
T2	123: 5	"There's one other flower in the garden that can move about
T9	195:29	was puzzled. "In our country," she remarked, "there's only one day at a time."
T4	148:14	"There's only one sword, you know," Tweedledum said to his
A7	54: 9	they cried out when they saw Alice coming. "There's plenty of room!" said Alice indignantly, and she sat
T7	174:25	"There's some enemy after her, no doubt," the King said,
T8W	13: 3	"There's somebody very unhappy there," she thought, looking
A8	67:27	is all the things being alive: for instance, there's the arch I've got to go through next walking about at
T3	134: 4	"And then there's the Butterfly," Alice went on, after she had taken a
T3	133:11	"And there's the Dragon-fly."
T3	133: 1	"Well, there's the Horse-fly," Alice began, counting off the names on
T5	150: 3	piece of plaster on her finger as she spoke, "there's the King's Messenger. He's in prison now, being
T1	110:31	my ideas about Looking-glass House. First, there's the room you can see through the glass--that's just
T2	122: 1	"There's the tree in the middle," said the Rose. "What else is
T7	174:22	"Look, look!" she cried, pointing eagerly. "There's the White Queen running across the country! She came

THESE (21) [entries omitted]

THEY (288) [entries omitted]

THEY'D (9)

T4	144:12	none--/ And this was scarcely odd, because / They'd eaten every one."
A11	86: 9	Alice quite hungry to look at them--"I wish they'd get the trial done," she thought, "and hand round the
T1	110:44	in Looking-glass House, Kitty? I wonder if they'd give you milk in there? Perhaps Looking-glass milk
A7	59: 4	done that, you know," Alice gently remarked. "They'd have been ill."
T3	135:30	I shouldn't like to lose it at all--because they'd have to give me another, and it would be almost certain
A4	27:33	Only I don't think," Alice went on, "that they'd let Dinah stop in the house if it began ordering people
T6	166: 4	it's short for 'from home'--meaning that they'd lost their way, you know."
T6	161:14	and all his men," Humpty Dumpty went on. "They'd pick me up again in a minute, they would! However, this
A4	31:36	they will do next! If they had any sense, they'd take the roof off." After a minute or two they began

THEY'LL (7)

A1	8:24	nothing of tumbling down-stairs! How brave they'll all think me at home! Why, I wouldn't say anything
T4	147:21	tying strings and fastening buttons--"Really they'll be more like bundles of old clothes than anything else
A4	30:19	there must be!" thought Alice. "I wonder what they'll do next! As for pulling me out of the window, I only
A4	30:28	they don't reach half high enough yet--Oh, they'll do well enough. Don't be particular--Here, Bill! Catch
T7	174:17	"I don't think they'll fight any more to-day," the King said to Hatta: "go
A1	9: 7	I should think!" (Dinah was the cat.) "I hope they'll remember her saucer of milk at tea-time. Dinah, my
T7	174: 8	"Then I suppose they'll soon bring the white bread and the brown?" Alice

THEY'RE (25)

A5	43:20	said the Pigeon; "but if they do, why, then they're a kind of serpent: that's all I can say."
A12	94:31	said Alice. "Why, you don't even know what they're about!"
A10	80:23	"They have their tails in their mouths--and they're all over crumbs."
T7	172:29	he simply shouted, at the top of his voice, "They're at it again!"
T7	170:13	I haven't sent the two Messengers, either. They're both gone to the town. Just look along the road, and
A6	51:21	"lives a March Hare. Visit either you like: they're both mad."
A9	77:15	"That's the reason they're called lessons," the Gryphon remarked: "because they
T2	123:13	"They're done up close, like a dahlia," said the Tiger-lily:
A10	81:20	a little before she gave her answer. "They're done with blacking, I believe."

THEY'RE (cont.)
  A8   67: 6   then," thought she, "what would become of me? They're dreadfully fond of beheading people here: the great
  T7   174: 6   swallowed a large piece of bread-and-butter. "They're getting on very well," he said in a choking voice:
  A10   80:21   seen them so often, of course you know what they're like?"
  A6   46:12   of the door as you are: secondly, because they're making such a noise inside, no one could possibly hear
  A12   94:17   "No, they're not," said the White Rabbit, "and that's the queerest
  T6   166:38   remarks like that," Humpty Dumpty said: "they're not sensible, and they put me out."
  A8   63:41   politely; but she added, to herself, "Why, they're only a pack of cards, after all. I needn't be afraid
  A11   86:31   "They're putting down their names," the Gryphon whispered in
  T4   147:22   old clothes than anything else, by the time they're ready!" she said to herself, as she arranged a bolster
  T9   201:32   was about fishes in some way. Do you know why they're so fond of fishes, all about here?"
  T6   164:36   badgers--they're something like lizards--and they're something like corkscrews."
  T6   164:35   "Well 'toves' are something like badgers--they're something like lizards--and they're something like
  A6   49:26   this child away with me," thought Alice, "they're sure to kill it in a day or two. Wouldn't it be murder
  T4   145:28   "I know they're talking nonsense," Alice thought to herself: "and it's
  T6   163:39   a temper, some of them--particularly verbs: they're the proudest--adjectives you can do anything with, but
  T8W   21: 7   "Then your eyes--they're too much in front, no doubt. One would have done as
THEY'VE (7)
  T1   110:36   see that bit! I want so much to know whether they've a fire in the winter: you never can tell, you know,
  T6   163:38   so after a minute Humpty Dumpty began again. "They've a temper, some of them--particularly verbs: they're
  A7   55:14   have some fun now!" thought Alice. "I'm glad they've begun asking riddles--I believe I can guess that," she
  T9   200:11   were even a few flowers among them. "I'm glad they've come without waiting to be asked," she thought: "I
  T3   132:40   replied. "Further on, in the wood down there, they've got no names--however, go on with your list of insects
  T4   138: 4   his collar, and the other 'DEE.' "I suppose they've got 'TWEEDLE' round at the back of the collar," she
  T8   183: 9   people don't fall off quite so often, when they've had much practice."
THICK (5)
  T4   143:30   said nothing but / 'The butter's spread too thick!'
  T4   142: 9   followed them, / And yet another four; / And thick and fast they came at last, / And more, and more, and
  T4   148:19   must be a thunderstorm coming on. "What a thick black cloud that is!" she said. "And how fast it comes!
  T9   201:24   It spoke in a thick, suety sort of voice, and Alice hadn't a word to say in
  A4   32:17   she could, and soon found herself safe in a thick wood.
THIMBLE (4)
  A3   24: 3   "We beg your acceptance of this elegant thimble"; and, when it had finished this short speech, they
  A3   24: 7   to say, she simply bowed, and took the thimble, looking as solemn as she could.
  A3   23:33   "Only a thimble," said Alice sadly.
  A3   24: 2   more, while the Dodo solemnly presented the thimble, saying "We beg your acceptance of this elegant
THIN (4)
  A11   89:13   and what with the bread-and-butter getting so thin--and the twinkling of the tea--"
  T6   165:10   portmanteau for you). And a 'borogove' is a thin shabby-looking bird with its feathers sticking out all
  T3   134:11   observe a Bread-and-butter-fly. Its wings are thin slices of bread-and-butter, its body is a crust, and its
  T9   195:31   The Red Queen said "That's a poor thin way of doing things. Now here, we mostly have days and
THING (84) [See also ANYTHING, SOMETHING, etc.]
  A1   12:12   could not remember ever having seen such a thing.
  A4   28: 8   I'm quite tired of being such a tiny little thing!"
  T5   150:14   great astonishment. "I never heard of such a thing!"
  T12   207:10   with a person if they always say the same thing?"
  A7   55:23   "Not the same thing a bit!" said the Hatter. "Why, you might just as well
  A10   78:12   "--so you can have no idea what a delightful thing a Lobster-Quadrille is!"
  A12   94:18   the White Rabbit, "and that's the queerest thing about it." (The jury all looked puzzled.)
  T12   207:19   at it," she said, when she was explaining the thing afterwards to her sister: "it turned away its head, and
  T7   172:31   up and shaking himself. "If you do such a thing again, I'll have you buttered! It went through and
  A7   59:24   "There's no such thing!" Alice was beginning very angrily, but the Hatter and
  A2   19:35   could only see her. She is such a dear quiet thing," Alice went on, half to herself, as she swam lazily
  A10   83: 8   but she was dreadfully puzzled by the whole thing, and longed to change the subject.
  A8   62: 3   them red. Alice thought this a very curious thing, and she went nearer to watch them, and, just as she
  A7   60:25   'much of a muchness'--did you ever see such a thing as a drawing of a muchness!"
  A7   55:24   well say that 'I see what I eat' is the same thing as 'I eat what I see'!"
  A7   55:27   Hare, "that 'I like what I get' is the same thing as 'I get what I like'!"
  A7   55:30   "that 'I breathe when I sleep' is the same thing as 'I sleep when I breathe'!"
  T5   149:14   the Queen said. "It isn't my notion of the thing, at all."
  A6   49:35   altogether Alice did not like the look of the thing at all. "But perhaps it was only sobbing," she thought,
  A8   68:39   off from: that he had never had to do such a thing before, and he wasn't going to begin at his time of life
  A2   19:16   to a mouse: she had never done such a thing before, but she remembered having seen, in her brother's
  T1   107:20   "Oh, you wicked, wicked little thing!" cried Alice, catching up the kitten, and giving it a
  T1   110:25   as a model for it to imitate: however, the thing didn't succeed, principally, Alice said, because the
  T1   107: 7   faces was this: first she held the poor thing down by its ear with one paw and then with the other
  A6   49:28   said the last words out loud, and the little thing grunted in reply (it had left off sneezing by this time)
  T6   162:25   "It is a--most--provoking--thing," he said at last, "when a person doesn't know a cravat
  A6   49: 2   violently up and down, and the poor little thing howled so, that Alice could hardly hear the words:--
  A7   58: 9   went on in a mournful tone, "he wo'n't do a thing I ask! It's always six o'clock now."
  T4   148: 1   very close," he added: "I generally hit every thing I can see--when I get really excited."
  A6   53: 8   a grin without a cat! It's the most curious thing I ever saw in all my life!"
  A3   22: 2   air. "Are you all ready? This is the driest thing I know. Silence all round, if you please! 'William the
  T9   201:31   were fixed upon her; "and it's a very curious thing, I think--every poem was about fishes in some way. Do
  T4   139:21   begun wrong!" cried Tweedledum. "The first thing in a visit is to say 'How d'ye do?' and shake hands!"
  T4   145: 9   "You'd be nowhere. Why, you're only a sort of thing in his dream!"
  T4   145:13   indignantly. "Besides, if I'm only a sort of thing in his dream, what are you, I should like to know?"
  T9   196: 6   Now, as it happened, there wasn't such a thing in the house, that morning."
  T8   181:36   bee has come near it yet. And the other thing is a mouse-trap. I suppose the mice keep the bees out--
  A4   32:20   grow to my right size again; and the second thing is to find my way into that lovely garden. I think that

THING (cont.)
```
A5     43:42   I've got back to my right size: the next thing is, to get into that beautiful garden--how is that to be
A4     32:18                           "The first thing I've got to do," said Alice to herself, as she wandered
T4    146:15   with a trembling finger at a small white thing lying under the tree.
A9     73:13                   "It's the thing Mock Turtle Soup is made from," said the Queen.
T3    132:11   the air, and in her fright she caught at the thing nearest to her hand, which happened to be the Goat's
A4     29: 4   to read fairy tales, I fancied that kind of thing never happened, and now here I am in the middle of one!
T4    146:17   a careful examination of the little white thing. "Not a rattle-snake, you know," she added hastily,
T8    186: 6               "Now the cleverest thing of the sort that I ever did," he went on after a pause,
A4     32:29   one paw, trying to touch her. "Poor little thing!" said Alice, in a coaxing tone, and she tried hard to
A9     70: 2   how glad I am to see you again, you dear old thing!" said the Duchess, as she tucked her arm affectionately
A9     70:36           "Ah well! It means much the same thing," said the Duchess, digging her sharp little chin into
A3     22:18   what 'it' means well enough, when I find a thing," said the Duck: "it's generally a frog, or a worm. The
A9     74: 1   a Gryphon is, look at the picture.) "Up, lazy thing!" said the Queen, "and take this young lady to see the
T9    196:36                   "She's tired, poor thing!" said the Red Queen. "Smoothe her hair--lend her your
A1     12:20   herself out with trying, the poor little thing sat down and cried.
T1    112: 2   into the Looking-glass room. The very first thing she did was to look whether there was a fire in the
A4     31: 5                           The first thing she heard was a general chorus of "There goes Bill!"
A9     73:20   "You are all pardoned." "Come, that's a good thing!" she said to herself, for she had felt quite unhappy at
A6     50: 5   to do with you. Mind now!" The poor little thing sobbed again (or grunted, it was impossible to say
T9    195:23   said the Red Queen: "when you've once said a thing, that fixes it, and you must take the consequences."
A10    84: 5   as you go on? It's by far the most confusing thing that I ever heard!"
T5    154:18   or so in vainly pursuing a large bright thing that looked sometimes like a doll and sometimes like a
A4     27:29   next!" And she began fancying the sort of thing that would happen: "'Miss Alice! Come here directly, and
A12    94:27   hands at this: it was the first really clever thing the King had said that day.
T9    202:36           "That wouldn't be at all the thing," the Red Queen said very decidedly: so Alice tried to
T8    187: 6   "No, you oughtn't: that's quite another thing! The song is called 'Ways and Means': but that's only
A2     19: 4   drowned in my own tears! That will be a queer thing, to be sure! However, everything is queer to-day."
T4    147: 3   in it: which was such an extraordinary thing to do, that it quite took off Alice's attention from the
T4    143:16   such kindness, that would be / A dismal thing to do!' / 'The night is fine,' the Walrus said. / 'Do
T3    129: 1                   Of course the first thing to do was to make a grand survey of the country she was
A4     34: 2   not see anything that looked like the right thing to eat or drink under the circumstances. There was a
A3     23: 1   Dodo in an offended tone, "was that the best thing to get us dry would be a Caucus-race."
A2     19:38   washing her face--and she is such a nice soft thing to nurse--and she's such a capital one for catching mice
T2    128:24   when you ca'n't think of the English for a thing--turn out your toes as you walk--and remember who you
A3     24: 5               Alice thought the whole thing very absurd, but they all looked so grave that she did
T1    107: 1                   One thing was certain, that the white kitten had had nothing to do
A6     49:17   a star-fish," thought Alice. The poor little thing was snorting like a steam-engine when she caught it, and
T2    126:18           The most curious part of the thing was, that the trees and the other things round them
A3     24: 9               The next thing was to eat the comfits: this caused some noise and
A12    93: 5   Lizard in head downwards, and the poor little thing was waving its tail about in a melancholy way, being
T5    155: 5           But even this plan failed: the 'thing' went through the ceiling as quietly as possible, as if
A7     55:31                   "It is the same thing with you," said the Hatter, and here the conversation
T4    148: 2           "And I hit every thing within reach," cried Tweedledum, "whether I can see it
A7     55:22   at least I mean what I say--that's the same thing, you know."
T12   207:38   really with me in my dream, there was one thing you would have enjoyed--I had such a quantity of poetry
A3     23: 6   to do it." (And, as you might like to try the thing yourself some winter-day, I will tell you how the Dodo
```
THING'S (1) [See also EVERYTHING'S, etc.]
```
T5    149:23   she was so dreadfully untidy. "Every single thing's crooked," Alice thought to herself, "and she's all
```
THINGS (79) [See also TEA-THINGS]
```
A9     71:15   "what a clear way you have of putting things!"
T5    153:12   she said: "one ca'n't believe impossible things."
T6    163:34   you can make words mean so many different things."
T8    182:21   of carrots, and fire-irons, and many other things.
T8    186: 5       I am, the more I keep inventing new things."
T9    195: 2   White Queen. "You mustn't leave out so many things."
A11    86:33               "Stupid things!" Alice began in a loud indignant voice; but she
A9     71: 3   "How fond she is of finding morals in things!" Alice thought to herself.
T1    110:10       And here I wish I could tell you half the things Alice used to say, beginning with her favourite phrase
A1     10:23   eaten up by wild beasts, and other unpleasant things, all because they would not remember the simple rules
A10    78:37   who had been jumping about like mad things all this time, sat down again very sadly and quietly,
A2     16: 6   I ca'n't be Mabel, for I know all sorts of things, and she, oh, she knows such a very little! Besides,
A7     60:24   and memory, and muchness--you know you say things are 'much of a muchness'--did you ever see such a thing
A2     18:14   was lying on the glass table as before, "and things are worse than ever," thought the poor child, "for I
T9    196:24   well, but she ca'n't help saying foolish things as a general rule."
A5     36:31   I am, Sir," said Alice. "I ca'n't remember things as I used--and I don't keep the same size for ten
A8     68:14   their turns, and she did not like the look of things at all, as the game was in such confusion that she
T5    153: 2   said with great decision: "nobody can do two things at once, you know. Let's consider your age to begin
T5    153:15   I've believed as many as six impossible things before breakfast. There goes the shawl again!"
T5    150:18   one way," Alice remarked. "I ca'n't remember things before they happen."
A8     67:27   you've no idea how confusing it is all the things being alive: for instance, there's the arch I've got to
A7     58:13   tea-time, and we've no time to wash the things between whiles."
T5    154:11   seemed to be full of all manner of curious things--but the oddest part of it all was that, whenever she
T8    181:21               "But the things can get out," Alice gently remarked. "Do you know the
T5    150:21               "What sort of things do you remember best?" Alice ventured to ask.
A2     19:44   family always hated cats: nasty, low, vulgar things! Don't let me hear the name again!"
A7     60:16   very sleepy; "and they drew all manner of things--everything that begins with an M--"
T5    154:16               "Things flow about so here!" she said at last in a plaintive
T6    164:27   afternoon--the time when you begin broiling things for dinner."
A7     58:15   "Exactly so," said the Hatter: "as the things get used up."
```

THINGS (cont.)
T1	110:33	just the same as our drawing-room, only the	things	go the other way. I can see all of it when I get upon a
A1	10:10	begin." For, you see, so many out-of-the-way	things	had happened lately, that Alice had begun to think that
T5	152:22	with a smile. "Now you understand the way	things	happen here."
T9	203:11	Alice afterwards described it) all sorts of	things	happened in a moment. The candles all grew up to the
A6	52:11	this, she was getting so well used to queer	things	happening. While she was still looking at the place
T4	147:16	Tweedledum remarked. "Every one of these	things	has got to go on, somehow or other."
T3	132:38	that name them, I suppose. If not, why do	things	have names at all?"
T3	135:28	she said thoughtfully to herself, "where	things	have no names. I wonder what'll become of my name when
T8	190:28	pretty easily--that comes of having so many	things	hung round the horse--" So she went on talking to
A2	20: 7	up and beg for its dinner, and all sorts of	things	--I ca'n't remember half of them--and it belongs to a
A2	16: 8	it all is! I'll try if I know all the	things	I used to know. Let me see: four times five is twelve,
T5	151:18	"Yes, but then I had done the	things	I was punished for," said Alice: "that makes all the
T6	160:35	"Ah, well! They may write such	things	in a book," Humpty Dumpty said in a calmer tone.
T4	145:19	said Tweedledum, "when you're only one of the	things	in his dream. You know very well you're not real."
T1	111: 7	House! I'm sure it's got, oh! such beautiful	things	in it! Let's pretend there's a way of getting through
A1	10:11	that Alice had begun to think that very few	things	indeed were really impossible.
T5	158:14	it away in a box: then she said "I never put	things	into people's hands--that would never do--you must get
T2	126:21	seemed to pass anything. "I wonder if all the	things	move along with us?" thought poor puzzled Alice. And
T8	181:24	vexation passing over his face. "Then all the	things	must have fallen out! And the box is no use without
T8	182:34	hair falls off is because it hangs down--things	never fall upwards, you know. It's a plan of my own
T9	195:31	Queen said "That's a poor thin way of doing	things	. Now here, we mostly have days and nights two or three
T8	184:22	went on again. "I'm a great hand at inventing	things	. Now, I daresay you noticed, the last time you picked
T4	142:20	come,' the Walrus said, / 'To talk of many	things	: / Of shoes--and ships--and sealing wax--/ Of cabbages
T9	193:23	Alice. "Lessons teach you to do sums, and	things	of that sort."
A1	8:31	(for, you see, Alice had learnt several	things	of this sort in her lessons in the school-room, and
A11	86:38	that all the jurors were writing down "Stupid	things	!" on their slates, and she could even make out that one
T2	126:19	the thing was, that the trees and the other	things	round them never changed their places at all: however
A5	36:33	"Ca'n't remember what	things	?" said the Caterpillar.
T1	115:39	"What manner of	things	?" said the Queen, looking over the book (in which Alice
T5	157:12	"Crabs, and all sorts of	things	," said the Sheep: "plenty of choice, only make up your
T5	152:41	"Can you keep from crying by considering	things	?" she asked.
T9	197:18	one Queen at a time. Do wake up, you heavy	things	!" she went on in an impatient tone; but there was no
T4	147:13	returned in a minute with their arms full of	things	--such as bolsters, blankets, hearth-rugs, table-cloths
T8	186:27	a difference it makes, mixing it with other	things	--such as gunpowder and sealing-wax. And here I must
T8	187:16	Of all the strange	things	that Alice saw in her journey Through The Looking-Glass
T4	147:26	very gravely, "it's one of the most serious	things	that can possibly happen to one in a battle--to get
T5	150: 1	"Oh,	things	that happened the week after next," the Queen replied
T1	115:38	this one a bit: it writes all manner of	things	that I don't intend--"
A9	70:13	them bitter--and--and barley-sugar and such	things	that make children sweet-tempered. I only wish people
T4	147:20	those two bustled about--and the quantity of	things	they put on--and the trouble they gave her in tying
T4	146:10	"Selfish	things	!" thought Alice, and she was just going to say
T9	196:15	great lumps--and knocking over the tables and	things	--till I was so frightened, I couldn't remember my own
A1	13: 2	way of expecting nothing but out-of-the-way	things	to happen, that it seemed quite dull and stupid for
T5	156:39	this, there were so many other curious	things	to think about.
A11	89:19	a poor man," the Hatter went on, "and most	things	twinkled after that--only the March Hare said--"
A2	15:38	How queer everything is to-day! And yesterday	things	went on just as usual. I wonder if I've changed in the
A8	62:18	and had just begun "Well, of all the unjust	things	--" when his eye chanced to fall upon Alice, as she
A2	20: 6	such long curly brown hair! And it'll fetch	things	when you throw them, and it'll sit up and beg for its
T9	193: 7	"I don't deny	things	with my hands," Alice objected.

THINK (110)
A3	26: 4	humbly: "you had got to the fifth bend, I	think	?"
A7	60:27	me," said Alice, very much confused, "I don't	think	--"
T2	123:12	she's redder--and her petals are shorter, I	think	."
T7	170: 9	did," said Alice: "several thousand, I should	think	."
T5	156:40	there were so many other curious things to	think	about.
T9	202:19	"Take a minute to	think	about it, and then guess," said the Red Queen.
A7	59:22	The Dormouse again took a minute or two to	think	about it, and then said "It was a treacle-well."
A1	8: 9	so suddenly that Alice had not a moment to	think	about stopping herself before she found herself falling
T3	136:16	"Think again," it said: "that wo'n't do."
T8W	13:18	"It's rheumatism, I should	think	," Alice said to herself, and she stooped over him, and
A4	27:33	that the mouse doesn't get out.' Only I don't	think	," Alice went on, "that they'd let Dinah stop in the
A3	26:28	a capital one for catching mice, you ca'n't	think	! And oh, I wish you could see her after the birds! Why,
A6	50:17	child: but it makes rather a handsome pig, I	think	." And she began thinking over other children she knew,
T2	128: 9	the Third Square--by railway, I should	think	--and you'll find yourself in the Fourth Square in no
T2	122:32	"It's my opinion that you never	think	at all," the Rose said, in a rather severe tone.
A5	37: 4	you incessantly stand on your head--/ Do you	think	, at your age, it is right?"
T9	192:36	Queen said to Alice. "Always speak the truth--think	before you speak--and write it down afterwards."
T9	202: 6	must be bought.' / That is easy: a penny, I	think	, could have bought it.
T9	202: 4	must be caught.' / That is easy: a baby, I	think	, could have caught it. / 'Next, the fish must be bought
A1	9: 7	Dinah'll miss me very much to-night, I should	think	!" (Dinah was the cat.) "I hope they'll remember her
T9	201:31	upon her; "and it's a very curious thing, I	think	--every poem was about fishes in some way. Do you know
A1	8:30	that would be four thousand miles down, I	think	--" (for, you see, Alice had learnt several things of
A12	96:18	had this fit'--you never had fits, my dear, I	think	?" he said to the Queen.
T4	145: 1	now," said Tweedledee: "and what do you	think	he's dreaming about?"
T3	134:26	the Gnat went on in a careless tone: "only	think	how convenient it would be if you could manage to go
A9	70: 1	"You ca'n't	think	how glad I am to see you again, you dear old thing!"
T8W	13: 9	"I don't	think	I can be of any use to him," was Alice's first thought,
A4	30:38	this fireplace is narrow, to be sure; but I	think	I can kick a little!"
A5	40: 7	father. "Don't give yourself airs! / Do you	think	I can listen all day to such stuff? / Be off, or I'll

THINK (cont.)

A2	15:40	the same when I got up this morning? I almost	think	I can remember feeling a little different. But if I'm
A1	10: 9	I wish I could shut up like a telescope! I	think	I could, if I only knew how to begin." For, you see, so
T6	160:14	with me!" cried Humpty Dumpty. "Did you	think	I didn't know the answer to <u>that</u>? Ask another."
A7	60:40	thought. "But everything's curious to-day. I	think	I may as well go in at once." And in she went.
T8W	21:13	she thought she might safely leave him. "I	think	I must be going on now," she said. "Good-bye."
A5	35: 7	who I <u>was</u> when I got up this morning, but I	think	I must have been changed several times since then."
T9	193:18	said Alice; "but, if there <u>is</u> to be one, I	think	<u>I</u> ought to invite the guests."
A9	72:11		"I think	I should understand that better," Alice said very
T6	160:25	you may turn pale, if you like! You didn't	think	I was going to say that, did you? <u>The King has promised</u>
T1	110:22	you're the Red Queen, Kitty! Do you know, I	think	if you sat up and folded your arms, you'd look exactly
T8W	20: 2	sorry for you," Alice said heartily: "and I	think	if your wig fitted a little better, they wouldn't tease
T2	123:35		"I think	I'll go and meet her," said Alice, for, though the
T3	129:17	what quantities of honey they must make! I	think	I'll go down and--no, I wo'n't go <u>just</u> yet," she went on
T3	129:25		"I think	I'll go down the other way," she said after a pause;
T9	197:15	lay like a heavy lump in her lap. "I don't	think	it <u>ever</u> happened before, that any one had to take care
T4	146: 5	brother, and looked up into it. "No, I don't	think	it <u>is</u>," he said: "at least--not under <u>here</u>. Nohow."
T12	207:21	it looked a <u>little</u> ashamed of itself, so I	think	it <u>must</u> have been the Red Queen.")
A1	7:12	so <u>very</u> remarkable in that; nor did Alice	think	it so <u>very</u> much out of the way to hear the Rabbit say to
T6	166:13	me much easier than that, by--Tweedledee, I	think	it was."
T12	208:14		Which do <u>you</u> think	it was?
A11	88:14	with the Dormouse. "Fourteenth of March, I	think	it was," he said.
A12	93: 8	much," she said to herself; "I should	think	it would be <u>quite</u> as much use in the trial one way up as
T8	184:35	Alice said thoughtfully: "but don't you	think	it would be rather hard?"
T8	190:19	when I get to that turn in the road? I	think	it'll encourage me, you see."
A8	65:35	"No, I didn't," said Alice. "I don't	think	it's at all a pity. I said 'What for?'"
T4	146: 3	for really it's coming on very dark. Do you	think	it's going to rain?"
T3	129: 5	mountains--I'm on the only one, but I don't	think	it's got any name. Principal towns--why, what <u>are</u> those
T6	166: 4	pig: but '<u>mome</u>' I'm not certain about. I	think	it's short for 'from home'--meaning that they'd lost
T5	149:27	in a melancholy voice. "It's out of temper, I	think.	I've pinned it here, and I've pinned it there, but
A1	8:25	tumbling down-stairs! How brave they'll all	think	me at home! Why, I wouldn't say anything about it, even
A1	9: 3	it?) "And what an ignorant little girl she'll	think	me for asking! No, it'll never do to ask: perhaps I
A1	8:24	herself. "After such a fall as this, I shall	think	nothing of tumbling down-stairs! How brave they'll all
T9	194:13		"Then you think	nothing would remain?" said the Red Queen.
A5	36:16	puzzling question; and, as Alice could not	think	of any good reason, and the Caterpillar seemed to be in
T9	196:26	to say something kind, but really couldn't	think	of anything at the moment.
A3	24: 6	did not dare to laugh; and, as she could not	think	of anything to say, she simply bowed, and took the
T3	135: 6	sure," said Alice: "the governess would never	think	of excusing me lessons for that. If she couldn't
T8	184:29	"I'll tell you how I came to	think	of it," said the Knight. "You see, I said to myself 'The
A7	56: 9	of tea, and looked at it again: but he could	think	of nothing better to say than his first remark, "It was
T8	183:13	Alice could	think	of nothing better to say than "Indeed?" but she said it
A8	69: 6	Alice could	think	of nothing else to say but "It belongs to the Duchess:
T2	128:23	she said "Speak in French when you ca'n't	think	of the English for a thing--turn out your toes as you
T3	135:41	on, rather surprised at not being able to	think	of the word. "I mean to get under the--under the--under
A6	48:31	so she went on again: "Twenty-four hours, I	think;	or is it twelve? I--"
A9	71:16	"It's a mineral, I	think,"	said Alice.
T5	152:28	light. "The crow must have flown away, I	think,"	said Alice: "I'm so glad it's gone. I thought it was
A9	72:25	"I've a right to	think,"	said Alice sharply, for she was beginning to feel a
T9	196:12	"It was <u>such</u> a thunderstorm, you ca'n't	think!"	("She <u>never</u> could, you know," said the Red Queen.)
T4	148: 5	You must hit the <u>trees</u> pretty often, I should	think,"	she said.
A1	8:41	their heads downwards! The antipathies, I	think--"	(she was rather glad there <u>was</u> no one listening, this
T6	160:21	Humpty Dumpty growled out. "Of course I don't	think	so! Why, if ever I <u>did</u> fall off--which there's no chance
T3	136:18	what <u>you</u> call yourself?" she said timidly. "I	think	that might help a little."
A6	51:27	Alice didn't	think	that proved it at all: however, she went on: "And how do
A8	67:21	some one to listen to her. The Cat seemed to	think	that there was enough of it now in sight, and no more of
A1	10:11	had happened lately, that Alice had begun to	think	that very few things indeed were really impossible.
A4	32:20	is to find my way into that lovely garden. I	think	that will be the best plan."
T9	194:14		"I think	that's the answer."
T1	113:11	are two Castles walking arm in arm--I don't	think	they can hear me," she went on, as she put her head
A8	67:23		"I don't think	they play at all fairly," Alice began, in rather a
T7	174:17		"I don't think	they'll fight any more to-day," the King said to Hatta:
A6	46:38	The Footman seemed to	think	this a good opportunity for repeating his remark, with
T7	172:11		"I should think	throwing cold water over you would be better," Alice
A6	50: 8	Alice was just beginning to	think	to herself, "Now, what am I to do with this creature,
A2	19:12	is so out-of-the-way down here, that I should	think	very likely it can talk: at any rate, there's no harm in
A2	15:40	I wonder if I've changed in the night? Let me	think:	was I the same when I got up this morning? I almost
T4	138:13	added the one marked 'DEE,' "if you	think	we're alive, you ought to speak."
T4	138:10	"If you	think	we're wax-works," he said, "you ought to pay, you know.
A6	48:25	showing off a little of her knowledge. "Just	think	what work it would make with the day and night! You see
A7	55:16	"Do you mean that you	think	you can find out the answer to it?" said the March Hare
A7	60: 7	a water-well," said the Hatter; "so I should	think	you could draw treacle out of a treacle-well--eh, stupid
A1	9: 1	as you're falling through the air! Do you	think	you could manage it?) "And what an ignorant little girl
T8W	20: 7	Your jaws aint well shaped, though--I should	think	you couldn't bite well?"
T12	207:35	me, Dinah, did you turn to Humpty Dumpty? I	think	you did--however, you'd better not mention it to your
A7	56:32	Alice sighed wearily. "I	think	you might do something better with the time," she said,
A5	36:13	drew herself up and said, very gravely, "I	think	you ought to tell me who <u>you</u> are, first."
T6	160:16		"Don't you think	you'd be safer down on the ground?" Alice went on, not
A10	84: 6	Yes, I	think	you'd better leave off," said the Gryphon, and Alice was
A2	19:34	yet I wish I could show you our cat Dinah. I	think	you'd take a fancy to cats, if you could only see her.
A5	36: 4	then after that into a butterfly, I should	think	you'll feel it a little queer, wo'n't you?"

THINK (cont.)
    A5   36:30 out of its mouth again, and said "So you think you're changed, do you?"
    T1   115:12 All the ashes will get into it--there, now I think you're tidy enough!" she added, as she smoothed his hair
THINKING (26)
    A7   59: 1 lived on treacle," said the Dormouse, after thinking a minute or two.
    T4   139: 5   "I know what you're thinking about," said Tweedledum; "but it isn't so, nohow."
    A9   70:18 she heard her voice close to her ear. "You're thinking about something, my dear, and that makes you forget
    A9   72:23   "Thinking again?" the Duchess asked, with another dig of her
    T4   139:10   "I was thinking," Alice said politely, "which is the best way out of
    T9   192:25 here she broke off with a frown, and, after thinking for a minute, suddenly changed the subject of the
    A5   43: 2 its voice to a shriek, "and just as I was thinking I should be free of them at last, they must needs
    T3   130:13 thought in chorus (I hope you understand what thinking in chorus means--for I must confess that I don't)
    T4   147:38 you'd better not fight to-day," said Alice, thinking it a good opportunity to make peace.
    T2   126:12   Alice never could quite make out, in thinking it over afterwards, how it was that they began: all
    A4   32:40 in its hurry to get hold of it: then Alice, thinking it was very like having a game of play with a
    A3   26: 2 the Mouse to Alice, severely. "What are you thinking of?"
    T8   188: 9   But I was thinking of a plan / To dye one's whiskers green, / And always
    T8   188:25   But I was thinking of a way / To feed oneself on batter, / And so go on
    A12   98:14 on her hand, watching the setting sun, and thinking of little Alice and all her wonderful Adventures,
    T8   186:30 Alice could only look puzzled: she was thinking of the pudding.
    A2   16: 1   Ah, that's the great puzzle!" And she began thinking over all the children she knew that were of the same
    A6   50:17 a handsome pig, I think." And she began thinking over other children she knew, who might do very well
    T9   195: 4   "She'll be feverish after so much thinking." So they set to work and fanned her with bunches of
    T4   146:18 a rattle-snake, you know," she added hastily, thinking that he was frightened: "only an old rattle--quite
    T3   136: 2   She stood silent for a minute, thinking: then she suddenly began again. "Then it really has
    A9   74:38 interesting story," but she could not help thinking there must be more to come, so she sat still and said
    T9   194:24 go different ways." But she couldn't help thinking to herself "What dreadful nonsense we are talking!"
    T2   124:14 added in a kinder tone. "Curtsey while you're thinking what to say. It saves time."
    T12 207:23 with a merry laugh. "And curtsey while you're thinking what to--what to purr. It saves time, remember!" And
    A12   98:11 getting late." So Alice got up and ran off, thinking while she ran, as well she might, what a wonderful
THINNER (1)
    T1   115:37 he panted out "My dear! I really must get a thinner pencil. I ca'n't manage this one a bit: it writes all
THIRD (2)
    T3   129:27 on. Besides, I do so want to get into the Third Square!"
    T2   128: 9 know. So you'll go very quickly through the Third Square--by railway, I should think--and you'll find
THIRST (1)
    T2   127:38   "Thirst quenched, I hope?" said the Queen.
THIRSTY (4)
    T2   127:24 content to stay here--only I am so hot and thirsty!"
    T7   173:26 in there--so you see he's very hungry and thirsty. How are you, dear child?" he went on, putting his arm
    T1   108:35 thirsty, were you? How do you know she wasn't thirsty too? Now for number three: you unwound every bit of
    T1   108:35 the saucer of milk before her! What, you were thirsty, were you? How do you know she wasn't thirsty too? Now
THIRTEEN (1)
    A2   16: 9 times five is twelve, and four times six is thirteen, and four times seven is--oh dear! I shall never get
THIRTY (2)
    T9   199:32 in the tea--/ And welcome Queen Alice with thirty-times-three!"
    T9   199:34 of cheering, and Alice thought to herself "Thirty times three makes ninety. I wonder if any one's
THIS (265) [entries omitted]
THISTLE (2)
    A4   32:42 to be trampled under its feet, ran round the thistle again: then the puppy began a series of short charges
    A4   32:37 to worry it: then Alice dodged behind a great thistle, to keep herself from being run over; and, the moment
THOROUGHLY (4)
    A6   49: 6 / I beat him when he sneezes; / For he can thoroughly enjoy / The pepper when he pleases!"
    T6   163:19 right--though I haven't time to look it over thoroughly just now--and that shows that there are three
    T6   162:19 she added in dismay, for Humpty Dumpty looked thoroughly offended, and she began to wish she hadn't chosen
    A10   81:15   Alice was thoroughly puzzled. "Does the boots and shoes!" she repeated
THOSE (19) [entries omitted]
THOU (4)
    TI   103: 3 of wonder! / Though time be fleet, and I and thou / Are half a life asunder, / Thy loving smile will surely
    TI   103:30 / The magic words shall hold thee fast: / Thou shalt not heed the raving blast.
    T1   118:17   "And, hast thou slain the Jabberwock? / Come to my arms, my beamish boy!
    TI   103:11 thy young life's hereafter--/ Enough that now thou wilt not fail / To listen to my fairy-tale.
THOUGH (38)
    T3   132: 7 over." Everybody seemed satisfied with this, though Alice felt a little nervous at the idea of trains
    T8   182:15   This took a long time to manage, though Alice held the bag open very carefully, because the
    T8W   15:13   "It's in this newspaper, though," Alice said a little timidly.
    A8   68:35 and they repeated their arguments to her, though, as they all spoke at once, she found it very hard to
    TI   103:18 rowing--/ Whose echoes live in memory yet, / Though envious years would say "forget."
    T6   162:22 Evidently Humpty Dumpty was very angry, though he said nothing for a minute or two. When he did speak
    A9   77: 5 the Gryphon: "I went to the Classical master, though. He was an old crab, he was."
    T3   131:42 and an old friend. And you wo'n't hurt me, though I am an insect."
    T6   163:18 As I was saying, that seems to be done right--though I haven't time to look it over thoroughly just now--and
    T8W   20: 6 head as does it. Your jaws aint well shaped, though--I should think you couldn't bite well?"
    A9   70: 8 said to herself (not in a very hopeful tone, though), "I wo'n't have any pepper in my kitchen at all. Soup
    T4   147:31 his helmet tied on. (He called it a helmet, though it certainly looked much more like a saucepan.)
    T2   127:27 thought it would not be civil to say "No," though it wasn't at all what she wanted. She took it, and ate
    T2   121: 9 myself, 'Her face has got some sense in it, though it's not a clever one!' Still, you're the right colour,
    T2   126: 4 mind being a Pawn, if only I might join--though of course I should like to be a Queen, best."
    T8W   17: 5   "It is, though," said the Wasp: "wait till you have it, and then
    T4   144:15   "He ate more than the Carpenter, though," said Tweedledee. "You see he held his handkerchief in

THOUGH (cont.)

T8	185:19	that he really <u>was</u> hurt this time. However, though she could see nothing but the soles of his feet, she
T4	144:24	a large steam-engine in the wood near them, though she feared it was more likely to be a wild beast. "Are
T4	139:18	Boy!" said Alice, passing on to Tweedledee, though she felt quite certain he would only shout out
A10	83:12	Alice did not dare to disobey, though she felt sure it would all come wrong, and she went on
T2	126:16	but Alice felt she <u>could</u> <u>not</u> go faster, though she had no breath left to say so.
T1	111:12	up on the chimney-piece while she said this, though she hardly knew how she had got there. And certainly
A12	98:35	and half believed herself in Wonderland, though she knew she had but to open them again, and all would
A7	60:32	others took the least notice of her going, though she looked back once or twice, half hoping that they
T5	156:27	it happened on purpose," she thought) that, though she managed to pick plenty of beautiful rushes as the
A1	12:23	She generally gave herself very good advice (though she very seldom followed it), and sometimes she scolded
A9	74:41	the Mock Turtle went on at last, more calmly, though still sobbing a little now and then, "we went to school
T2	123:35	think I'll go and meet her," said Alice, for, though the flowers were interesting enough, she felt that it
T3	129:13	it was an elephant--as Alice soon found out, though the idea quite took her breath away at first. "And what
T5	154:14	that particular shelf was always quite empty, though the others round it were crowded as full as they could
T1	115:27	"You will, though," the Queen said, "if you don't make a memorandum of it
TI	103:31	<u>And</u>, though <u>the</u> <u>shadow</u> <u>of</u> <u>a</u> <u>sigh</u> / <u>May</u> <u>tremble</u> <u>through</u> <u>the</u> <u>story</u>, /
A12	95: 8	<u>more</u>; / <u>They</u> <u>all</u> <u>returned</u> <u>from</u> <u>him</u> <u>to</u> <u>you</u>, / <u>Though</u> <u>they</u> <u>were</u> <u>mine</u> <u>before</u>.
A1	8:32	sort in her lessons in the school-room, and though this was not a <u>very</u> good opportunity for showing off
TI	103: 3	<u>brow</u> / <u>And</u> <u>dreaming</u> <u>eyes</u> <u>of</u> <u>wonder</u>! / <u>Though</u> <u>time</u> <u>be</u> <u>fleet</u>, <u>and</u> <u>I</u> <u>and</u> <u>thou</u> / <u>Are</u> <u>half</u> <u>a</u> <u>life</u> <u>asunder</u>
T2	125: 4	on the head, which Alice didn't like at all: "though, when you say 'garden'--I've seen gardens, compared
A9	75: 9	"Yes, we went to school in the sea, though you mayn't believe it--"

THOUGHT (166)

T1	118: 8	he <u>by</u> <u>the</u> <u>Tumtum</u> <u>tree</u>, / <u>And</u> <u>stood</u> <u>awhile</u> <u>in</u> thought.
T4	147: 7	more like a fish than anything else," Alice thought.
T7	175:42	It was just like a conjuring-trick, she thought.
T9	195:43	exactly like the riddle with no answer!" she thought.
A10	81:12	"I never thought about it," said Alice. "Why?"
A11	87: 4	slates'll be in, before the trial's over!" thought Alice.
T3	129:11	into them, "just as if it was a regular bee," thought Alice.
T3	130:17	a thousand pounds to-night, I know I shall!" thought Alice.
T4	148:13	"I wish the monstrous crow would come!" thought Alice.
T9	202:28	up the gravy, "just like pigs in a trough!" thought Alice.
A4	29:30	"<u>That</u> you wo'n't!" thought Alice, and after waiting till she fancied she heard
T4	146:10	"Selfish things!" thought Alice, and she was just going to say "Good-night" and
A6	51: 6	a little wider. "Come, it's pleased so far," thought Alice, and she went on. "Would you tell me, please,
T9	198: 5	"I'll wait till the song's over," thought Alice, "and then I'll ring the--the--which bell must I
A11	86:21	"And that's the jury-box," thought Alice, "and those twelve creatures," (she was obliged
A8	68:24	out of sight: "but it doesn't matter much," thought Alice, "as all the arches are gone from this side of
T5	158:17	"I wonder <u>why</u> it wouldn't do?" thought Alice, as she groped her way among the tables and
T3	129: 3	It's something very like learning geography," thought Alice, as she stood on tiptoe in hopes of being able
A9	74:13	"Everybody says 'come on!' here," thought Alice, as she went slowly after it: "I never was so
A6	53: 7	"Well! I've often seen a cat without a grin," thought Alice; "but a grin without a cat! It's the most
A4	31:42	"A barrowful of <u>what</u>?" thought Alice. But she had not long to doubt, for the next
T3	129:39	said together ("like the chorus of a song," thought Alice) "Don't keep him waiting, child! Why, his time
A2	19:21	"Perhaps it doesn't understand English," thought Alice. "I daresay it's a French mouse, come over with
A10	82:18	one about, and make one repeat lessons!" thought Alice. "I might just as well be at school at once."
T5	155:29	"A dear little crab!" thought Alice. "I should like that."
A4	30:18	a number of cucumber-frames there must be!" thought Alice. "I wonder what they'll do next! As for pulling
A9	72:20	"A cheap sort of present!" thought Alice. "I'm glad people don't give birthday-presents
A7	55:13	"Come, we shall have some fun now!" thought Alice. "I'm glad they've begun asking riddles--I
A5	44: 2	about four feet high. "Whoever lives there," thought Alice, "it'll never do to come upon them <u>this</u> size:
A11	90:16	"I'm glad I've seen that done," thought Alice. "I've so often read in the newspapers, at the
A11	90:27	"Come, that finishes the guinea-pigs!" thought Alice. "Now we shall get on better."
A7	54: 5	head. "Very uncomfortable for the Dormouse," thought Alice; "only as it's asleep, I suppose it doesn't mind
A2	15: 1	way you can--but I must be kind to them," thought Alice, "or perhaps they wo'n't walk the way I want to
T3	131:19	number of people there are in the carriage!" thought Alice), saying "She must go by post, as she's got a
A4	29: 9	"But then," thought Alice, "shall I <u>never</u> get any older than I am now?
T6	161:20	He talks about it just as if it was a game!" thought Alice.) "So here's a question for you. How old did you
T1	118:31	"But oh!" thought Alice, suddenly jumping up, "if I don't make haste, I
A6	49:17	in all directions, "just like a star-fish," thought Alice. The poor little thing was snorting like a
T2	128:31	into the wood ("and she <u>can</u> run very fast!" thought Alice), there was no way of guessing, but she was gone
A6	49:26	"If I don't take this <u>child</u> away with me," thought Alice, "they're sure to kill it in a day or two.
A5	41:29	"One side of <u>what</u>? The other side of <u>what</u>?" thought Alice to herself.
A1	8:23	"Well!" thought Alice to herself. "After such a fall as this, I shall
A2	19:10	"Would it be of any use, now," thought Alice, "to speak to this mouse? Everything is so
T1	112: 6	be as warm here as I was in the old room," thought Alice: "warmer, in fact, because there'll be no one
A4	31:18	feeble, squeaking voice ("That's Bill," thought Alice), "Well, I hardly know--No more, thank ye; I'm
T7	172:34	"It would have to be a very tiny earthquake!" thought Alice. "Who are at it again?" she ventured to ask.
A1	7: 4	in it, "and what is the use of a book," thought Alice, "without pictures or conversations?"
T8	182:36	It didn't sound a comfortable plan, Alice thought, and for a few minutes she walked on in silence,
A11	86: 9	them--"I wish they'd get the trial done," she thought, "and hand round the refreshments!" But there seemed
A2	15: 4	manage it. "They must go by the carrier," she thought; "and how funny it'll seem, sending presents to one's
T6	162:14	had quite enough of the subject of age, she thought: and, if they really were to take turns in choosing
A2	20:18	its face was quite pale (with passion, Alice thought), and it said, in a low trembling voice, "Let us get
A3	23:18	Dodo could not answer without a great deal of thought, and it stood for a long time with one finger pressed
A6	50: 1	all. "But perhaps it was only sobbing," she thought, and looked into its eyes again, to see if there were
A11	86:25	to herself, being rather proud of it: for she thought, and rightly too, that very few little girls of her
T6	161: 8	the ends of his mouth might meet behind," she thought: "And then I don't know <u>what</u> would happen to his head!
T5	155:25	was something very queer about the water, she thought, as every now and then the oars got fast in it, and

THOUGHT (cont.)

```
T6    159:25   this: it wasn't at all like conversation, she  thought, as he never said anything to her; in fact, his last
T8W    13:10   can be of any use to him," was Alice's first  thought, as she turned to spring over the brook:--but I'll
A11    88:36   was beginning to grow larger again, and she  thought at first she would get up and leave the court; but on
T6    168:17              This was rather sudden, Alice  thought: but, after such a very strong hint that she ought to
A7     60:39   right into it. "That's very curious!" she  thought. "But everything's curious to-day. I think I may as
T3    136:17                                      Alice  thought, but nothing came of it. "Please, would you tell me
T3    131:36   if it would only sigh like other people!" she  thought. But this was such a wonderfully small sigh, that she
T2    123: 9   Is she like me?" Alice asked eagerly, for the  thought crossed her mind, "There's another little girl in the
A6     46:22   all the time he was speaking, and this Alice  thought decidedly uncivil. "But perhaps he ca'n't help it,"
T6    159:12   he didn't take the least notice of her, she  thought he must be a stuffed figure after all.
T1    118: 9                   And, as in uffish thought he stood, / The Jabberwock, with eyes of flame, / Came
A2     18: 4   was talking. "How can I have done that?" she  thought. "I must be growing small again." She got up and went
T9    200:12     come without waiting to be asked," she  thought: "I should never have known who were the right people
T2    125: 7   to argue the point, but went on: "--and I  thought I'd try and find my way to the top of that hill--"
T9    192:15   civil. However, there would be no harm, she  thought, in asking if the game was over. "Please, would you
T3    130:12   spoken, but, to her great surprise, they all  thought in chorus (I hope you understand what thinking in
A10    82:13   to begin." He looked at the Gryphon as if he  thought it had some kind of authority over Alice.
T6    163:17   said gaily as she turned it round for him. "I  thought it looked a little queer. As I was saying, that seems
A2     19: 7   nearer to make out what it was: at first she  thought it must be a walrus or hippopotamus, but then she
A6     53:11   in sight of the house of the March Hare: she  thought it must be the right house, because the chimneys were
A9     77:17   This was quite a new idea to Alice, and she  thought it over a little before she made her next remark.
A1      7:13   Oh dear! I shall be too late!" (when she  thought it over afterwards it occurred to her that she ought
T8    185: 5   the other White Knight came and put it on. He  thought it was his own helmet."
T5    152:28   think," said Alice: "I'm so glad it's gone. I  thought it was the night coming on."
T2    123:24   "I was wondering you hadn't got some too. I  thought it was the regular rule."
A6     48: 7   not at all like the tone of this remark, and  thought it would be as well to introduce some other subject of
A9     74: 5   look of the creature, but on the whole she  thought it would be quite as safe to stay with it as to go
T5    149:15                                      Alice  thought it would never do to have an argument at the very
T2    127:27                                      Alice  thought it would not be civil to say "No," though it wasn't at
A6     52:21                        "I  thought it would," said the Cat, and vanished again.
T4    145:25   tree. "It can never get at me here," she  thought: "it's far too large to squeeze itself in among the
A4     32: 7   her head. "If I eat one of these cakes," she  thought, "it's sure to make some change in my size; and, as it
T8W    13: 3   "There's somebody very unhappy there," she  thought, looking anxiously back to see what was the matter.
T5    152:34   Alice said in a melancholy voice; and, at the  thought of her loneliness, two large tears came rolling down
TI    103: 9   face, / Nor heard thy silver laughter: / No  thought of me shall find a place / In thy young life's
T3    137:26   they live in the same house! I wonder I never  thought of that before--But I ca'n't stay there long. I'll
T2    122:31   Alice was quite pleased to know it. "I never  thought of that before!" she said.
A7     55:33   party sat silent for a minute, while Alice  thought over all she could remember about ravens and
A1     10: 7   "and even if my head would go through," thought poor Alice, "it would be of very little use without my
T3    136:14                     "I wish I knew!" thought poor Alice. She answered, rather sadly, "Nothing, just
A1     12:28   to be two people. "But it's no use now," thought poor Alice, "to pretend to be two people! Why, there's
A4     28:27                "It was much pleasanter at home," thought poor Alice, "when one wasn't always growing larger and
T2    126:21   wonder if all the things move along with us?" thought poor puzzled Alice. And the Queen seemed to guess her
T8    181:26   to throw it into the bushes, when a sudden  thought seemed to strike him, and he hung it carefully on a
T2    127:29   as she could: and it was very dry: and she  thought she had never been so nearly choked in all her life.
A8     66: 1                                      Alice  thought she had never seen such a curious croquet-ground in
T8    181:11   gentle face and large mild eyes to Alice. She  thought she had never seen such a strange-looking soldier in
A8     63:31   what would be the use of a procession," thought she, "if people had all to lie down on their faces, so
T1    115: 1   but, before she put him on the table, she  thought she might as well dust him a little, he was so covered
A8     68:10                                      Alice  thought she might as well go back and see how the game was
A5     36:26                                      Alice  thought she might as well wait, as she had nothing else to do,
T8W    21:12   spirits, and was getting very talkative, she  thought she might safely leave him. "I think I must be going
T9    195:11                                      Alice  thought she saw a way out of the difficulty, this time. "If
A8     67: 5   that it might happen any minute, "and then," thought she, "what would become of me? They're dreadfully fond
T8W    18: 7   had met had repeated poetry to her, and she  thought she would try if the Wasp couldn't do it too. "Would
T2    124: 1   she spied out at last, a long way off), she  thought she would try the plan, this time, of walking in the
A6     51: 2   it saw Alice. It looked good-natured, she  thought: still it had very long claws and a great many teeth,
T3    132:21   Gnat: "about the size of a chicken," Alice  thought. Still, she couldn't feel nervous with it, after they
T1    115:31   of his pocket, and began writing. A sudden  thought struck her, and she took hold of the end of the pencil
T5    155: 2   I'll tell you what--" she added, as a sudden  thought struck her. "I'll follow it up to the very top shelf
T1    116:13   over this for some time, but at last a bright  thought struck her. "Why, it's a Looking-glass book, of
T7    169: 5                                        She  thought that in all her life she had never seen soldiers so
A4     32:31   was terribly frightened all the time at the  thought that it might be hungry, in which case it would be
A1     12: 4   high, and her face brightened up at the  thought that she was now the right size for going through the
A3     23: 3   to know, but the Dodo had paused as if it  thought that somebody ought to speak, and no one else seemed
T9    192: 8   come off: but she comforted herself with the  thought that there was nobody to see her, "and if I really am
T5    156:27   ("almost as if it happened on purpose," she  thought) that, though she managed to pick plenty of beautiful
T1    114:14   looking up anxiously into the fire, as if he  thought that was the most likely place to find one.
A2     18:15   as before, "and things are worse than ever," thought the poor child, "for I never was so small as this
T4    140:30   The moon was shining sulkily, / Because she  thought the sun / Had got no business to be there / After the
A3     24: 5                                      Alice  thought the whole thing very absurd, but they all looked so
T4    148:18   It was getting dark so suddenly that Alice  thought there must be a thunderstorm coming on. "What a thick
A5     42:36   Alice was more and more puzzled, but she  thought there was no use in saying anything more till the
T9    202:39   the history of her feast. "You would have  thought they wanted to squeeze me flat!")
T7    175:23              "I always  thought they were fabulous monsters!" said the Unicorn. "Is it
A1      8:37   Latitude was, or Longitude either, but she  thought they were nice grand words to say.)
A8     62: 3   at it, busily painting them red. Alice  thought this a very curious thing, and she went nearer to
A2     19:14   of swimming about here, O Mouse!" (Alice  thought this must be the right way of speaking to a mouse: she
T3    132: 1   was, whether it could sting or not, but she  thought this wouldn't be quite a civil question to ask.
```

THOUGHT (cont.)

A8	67:17	nodded. "It's no use speaking to it," she thought, "till its ears have come, or at least one of them."
A9	71: 3	she is of finding morals in things!" Alice thought to herself.
A12	93:32	slates; "but it doesn't matter a bit," she thought to herself.
T9	195:16	"I wish Queens never asked questions," Alice thought to herself.
T3	131:13	"It sounds like a horse," Alice thought to herself. And an extremely small voice, close to her
T4	145:28	"I know they're talking nonsense," Alice thought to herself: "and it's foolish to cry about it." So she
T5	149:23	untidy. "Every single thing's crooked," Alice thought to herself, "and she's all over pins!--May I put your
T3	135:26	go on: "for I certainly won't go back," she thought to herself, and this was the only way to the Eighth
T1	113: 3	keep this room so tidy as the other," Alice thought to herself, as she noticed several of the chessmen
T9	203:23	"and very like birds they look," Alice thought to herself, as well as she could in the dreadful
A9	74:30	and nobody spoke for some minutes. Alice thought to herself "I don't see how he can ever finish, if he
T9	196:17	Alice thought to herself "I never should try to remember my name in
A5	41:19	pleaded poor Alice in a piteous tone. And she thought to herself "I wish the creatures wouldn't be so easily
T3	134: 6	at the insect with its head on fire, and had thought to herself, "I wonder if that's the reason insects are
A4	31:33	There was a dead silence instantly, and Alice thought to herself "I wonder what they will do next! If they
T7	178:11	If that doesn't 'drum them out of town,'" she thought to herself, "nothing ever will!"
T8W	14: 6	nearly walking on and leaving him, but she thought to herself "Perhaps it's only pain that makes him so
T5	155:12	can she knit with so many?" the puzzled child thought to herself. "She gets more and more like a porcupine
A9	70: 5	to find her in such a pleasant temper, and thought to herself that perhaps it was only the pepper that
T2	124:17	it. "I'll try it when I go home," she thought to herself, "the next time I'm a little late for
T3	130:10	Alice thought to herself "Then there's no use in speaking." The
T5	158:11	put the money down on the counter. For she thought to herself, "They mightn't be at all nice, you know."
T9	199:33	a confused noise of cheering, and Alice thought to herself "Thirty times three makes ninety. I wonder
T6	162:20	chosen that subject. "If only I knew," she thought to herself, "which was neck and which was waist!"
T7	175:28	a smile as she began: "Do you know, I always thought Unicorns were fabulous monsters, too? I never saw one
T8	179: 3	There was no one to be seen, and her first thought was that she must have been dreaming about the Lion
T6	168: 2	a scream as he repeated this verse, and Alice thought, with a shudder, "I wouldn't have been the messenger
A3	22:11	"I thought you did," said the Mouse. "I proceed. 'Edwin and
T6	161:26	"I thought you meant 'How old are you?'" Alice explained.
T8	190:23	doubtfully: "but you didn't cry so much as I thought you would."

THOUGHTFUL (5)

T8	184:24	you picked me up, that I was looking rather thoughtful?"
T4	144:37	the damp grass," said Alice, who was a very thoughtful little girl.
T6	164: 4	deal to make one word mean," Alice said in a thoughtful tone.
T6	168:25	one goes by, generally," Alice remarked in a thoughtful tone.
T8	186:11	not the next course," the Knight said in slow thoughtful tone: "no, certainly not the next course."

THOUGHTFULLY (11)

T3	134:18	that must happen very often," Alice remarked thoughtfully.
T6	162: 4	years and six months!" Humpty Dumpty repeated thoughtfully. "An uncomfortable sort of age. Now if you'd
T6	164:33	"I see it now," Alice remarked thoughtfully: "and what are 'toves'?"
T6	162:33	"They gave it me," Humpty Dumpty continued thoughtfully as he crossed one knee over the other and clasped
A5	41:33	Alice remained looking thoughtfully at the mushroom for a minute, trying to make out
T8	184:35	you'd be over when that was done," Alice said thoughtfully: "but don't you think it would be rather hard?"
A7	57: 5	"That would be grand, certainly," said Alice thoughtfully; "but then--I shouldn't be hungry for it, you
A10	82:11	all came different!" the Mock Turtle repeated thoughtfully. "I should like to hear her try and repeat
A10	80:22	"I believe so," Alice replied thoughtfully. "They have their tails in their mouths--and
T3	135:27	"This must be the wood," she said thoughtfully to herself, "where things have no names. I wonder
T8	184:19	"I'll get one," the Knight said thoughtfully to himself. "One or two--several."

THOUGHTS (7)

T6	162:16	"At least," she corrected herself on second thoughts, "a beautiful cravat, I should have said--no, a belt,
T2	126:22	Alice. And the Queen seemed to guess her thoughts, for she cried "Faster! Don't try to talk!"
T3	131:39	her ear very much, and quite took off her thoughts from the unhappiness of the poor little creature.
A11	88:37	get up and leave the court; but on second thoughts she decided to remain where she was as long as there
T3	135:24	timid about going into it. However, on second thoughts, she made up her mind to go on: "for I certainly
T8	179:12	At this moment her thoughts were interrupted by a loud shouting of "Ahoy! Ahoy!
A10	81:27	"If I'd been the whiting," said Alice, whose thoughts were still running on the song, "I'd have said to the

THOUSAND (9)

T7	170: 9	"Yes, I did," said Alice: "several thousand, I should think."
A1	8:30	of the earth. Let me see: that would be four thousand miles down, I think--" (for, you see, Alice had
T3	130: 1	him waiting, child! Why, his time is worth a thousand pounds a minute!"
T3	130: 9	the engine. Why, the smoke alone is worth a thousand pounds a puff!"
T3	130:14	say nothing at all. Language is worth a thousand pounds a word!"
T3	130: 5	she came from. The land there is worth a thousand pounds an inch!"
T3	130:16	"I shall dream about a thousand pounds to-night, I know I shall!" thought Alice.
A4	29:23	quite forgetting that she was now about a thousand times as large as the Rabbit, and had no reason to be
T7	170:10	"Four thousand two hundred and seven, that's the exact number," the

THREE (46)

A7	55: 5	Alice: "it's laid for a great many more than three."
T9	199:32	And welcome Queen Alice with thirty-times-three!"
A3	23:10	here and there. There was no "One, two, three, and away!", but they began running when they liked, and
T9	195:32	here, we mostly have days and nights two or three at a time, and sometimes in the winter we take as many
A11	87:14	On this the White Rabbit blew three blasts on the trumpet, and then unrolled the
A11	88: 5	said the King; and the White Rabbit blew three blasts on the trumpet, and called out "First witness!"
T9	200:14	There were three chairs at the head of the table: the Red and White
A11	88:18	the jury; and the jury eagerly wrote down all three dates on their slates, and then added them up, and
T1	108:38	"That's three faults, Kitty, and you've not been punished for any of
A8	62: 2	growing on it were white, but there were three gardeners at it, busily painting them red. Alice thought
A8	63:29	ought not to lie down on her face like the three gardeners, but she could not remember ever having heard
A8	64:15	the Queen in a shrill, loud voice, and the three gardeners instantly jumped up, and began bowing to the

THREE (cont.)
```
 A8    63:12   called  out  "The  Queen! The Queen!" and the  three gardeners instantly threw themselves flat upon their
 A8    63:16      clubs:  these  were  all  shaped  like the  three gardeners, oblong and flat, with their hands and feet at
 A8    63:43   are  these?" said the Queen, pointing to the  three gardeners who were lying round the rose-tree; for, you
 T6   162:44                                                  "Three hundred and sixty-five," said Alice.
 T6   163: 1         "And if you take one from three hundred and  sixty-five what remains?"
 T6   163:19   just  now--and  that  shows  that  there are  three hundred and sixty-four days when you might get
 T6   163: 3                                                  "Three hundred and sixty-four, of course."
 AI    3: 7                                     Ah, cruel  Three! In such an hour, / Beneath such dreamy weather, / To
 A5    41:17   itself  upright  as  it spoke (it was exactly  three inches high).
 T2   123:31   found  her  in  the  ashes,  she had been only  three inches high--and here she was, half a head taller than
 A5    41:15   Sir,  if  you  wouldn't  mind," said Alice: "three inches is such a wretched height to be."
 A7    58:32               "Once upon a time there were  three little sisters," the Dormouse began in a great hurry;
 A7    59:31   However, he consented to go on. "And so these  three little sisters--they were learning to draw, you know--"
 T9   199:34   and  Alice  thought  to herself "Thirty times  three makes ninety. I wonder if any one's counting?" In a
 A8    64: 2   were  gardeners,  or soldiers, or courtiers, or  three of her own children.
 A8    68:12   passion.  She  had already heard her sentence  three of the players to be executed for having missed their
 A8    65: 9   their  heads!"  and  the procession moved on,  three of the soldiers remaining behind to execute the
 T8   184: 4   said,  as  if  he didn't mind breaking two or  three of them. "The great art of riding, as I was saying is--
 T9   202:26   as  it  ran  off  the edges of the table--and  three of them (who looked like kangaroos) scrambled into the
A12    95: 6   her  one,  they  gave  him two, / You gave us  three or more; / They all returned from him to you, / Though
 A4    27:38   and on it (as she had hoped) a fan and two or  three pairs of tiny white kid-gloves: she took up the fan and
 T7   177:14   dish  round, and the cake divided itself into  three pieces as she did so. "Now cut it up," said the Lion, as
 A5    40: 5                    "I have answered  three questions, and that is enough," / Said his father.
 A8    65:13   into  a large flower-pot that stood near. The  three soldiers wandered about for a minute or two, looking for
 TC   209: 4                                    Children  three that nestle near, / Eager eye and willing ear, / Pleased
A11    86:24   the  jurors." She said this last word two or  three times over to herself, being rather proud of it: for she
 T8   182:17   in  putting  in  the  dish: the first two or  three times that he tried he fell in himself instead. "It's
 A8    68:33   Alice  appeared,  she  was appealed to by all  three to settle the question, and they repeated their
 AI    3:12   /  Yet what can one poor voice avail / Against  three tongues together?
 T1   108:17   bonfire  to-morrow."  Here Alice wound two or  three turns of the worsted round the kitten's neck, just to
 A5    42:40   day! Why, I haven't had a wink of sleep these  three weeks!"
 A7    54: 7               The table was a large one, but the  three were all crowded together at one corner of it. "No room!
 T2   128: 1   for  an  answer,  but went on. "At the end of  three yards I shall repeat them--for fear of your forgetting
 T1   108:36   know  she  wasn't thirsty too? Now for number  three: you unwound every bit of the worsted while I wasn't
```
THREE-LEGGED (2)
```
 A6    47: 1   to  the  other:  the Duchess was sitting on a  three-legged stool in the middle, nursing a baby: the cook was
 A1     9:34             Suddenly she came upon a little  three-legged table, all made of solid glass: there was nothing
```
THREES (1)
```
 T7   169: 2     through  the  wood,  at  first  in twos and  threes, then ten or twenty together, and at last in such
```
THREW (3)
```
 A6    49:13   and  she  hurried  out  of the room. The cook  threw a frying-pan after her as she went, but it just missed
 T8   191: 1   *  *  *  *  *  *  *  *  *  *  *  *  * across, and  threw herself down to rest on a lawn as soft as moss, with
 A8    63:12   The Queen!" and the three gardeners instantly  threw themselves flat upon their faces. There was a sound of
```
THROAT (2)
```
 A3    26:33   getting  home:  the night-air doesn't suit my  throat!" And a Canary called out in a trembling voice, to its
A10    78: 4   his  voice.  "Same as if he had a bone in his  throat," said the Gryphon; and it set to work shaking him and
```
THRONE (1)
```
A11    86: 1   King and Queen of Hearts were seated on their  throne when they arrived, with a great crowd assembled about
```
THROUGH (59)
```
 T5   153:40   every  now  and then leaving off to look at her  through a great pair of spectacles.
 AI     3:21   In  fancy they pursue / The dream-child moving  through a land / Of wonders wild and new, / In friendly chat
 T3   130:19   at  her,  first  through a telescope, then  through a microscope, and then through an opera-glass. At last
 T8   187:38   answer trickled through my head, / Like water  through a sieve.
 T3   130:18   this  time the Guard was looking at her, first  through a telescope, then through a microscope, and then
A12    99: 5     a  grown  woman;  and  how she would keep,  through all her riper years, the simple and loving heart of
 T3   130:19     then  through a microscope,  and  then  through an opera-glass. At last he said "You're traveling the
 T7   178: 2   out:  the  air seemed full of it, and it rang  through and through her head till she felt quite deafened. She
 T7   172:32   thing  again,  I'll have you buttered! It went  through and through my head like an earthquake!"
 T1   118:13               One, two! One, two! And  through and through / The vorpal blade went snicker-snack! /
 T4   138:16   for  the  words of the old song kept ringing  through her head like the ticking of a clock, and she could
 T7   178: 2   seemed  full  of  it, and it rang through and  through her head till she felt quite deafened. She started to
 T4   145:24   "If I wasn't real," Alice said--half laughing  through her tears, it all seemed so ridiculous--"I shouldn't
 T8   187:20   smile of the Knight--the setting sun gleaming  through his hair, and shining on his armour in a blaze of
 T1   111: 8   in it! Let's pretend there's a way of getting  through into it, somehow, Kitty. Let's pretend the glass has
 T1   110:29   not  good directly," she added, "I'll put you  through into Looking-glass House. How would you like that?
 T1   111: 1   how  nice  it  would  be if we could only get  through into Looking-glass House! I'm sure it's got, oh! such
 A2    15:17   she could do, lying down on one side, to look  through into the garden with one eye; but to get through was
 T3   129: 2   survey of the country she was going to travel  through. "It's something very like learning geography,"
 T7   172:32   I'll  have  you buttered! It went through and  through my head like an earthquake!"
 T8   187:37   is  it  you live?' / And his answer trickled  through my head, / Like water through a sieve.
 A8    67:28   for  instance,  there's the arch I've got to go  through next walking about at the other end of the ground--and
 T1   111:11   now,  I  declare! It'll be easy enough to get  through--" She was up on the chimney-piece while she said this
 A5    43:10   remembered  the number of changes she had gone  through, that day.
 A1     9: 1   spoke--fancy,  curtseying  as  you're falling  through the air! Do you think you could manage it?) "And what
 T1   114: 8   Queen gasped, and sat down: the rapid journey  through the air had quite taken away her breath, and for a
 T2   127: 6   went so fast that at last they seemed to skim  through the air, hardly touching the ground with their feet,
 T5   155: 5   But  even  this plan failed: the 'thing' went  through the ceiling as quietly as possible, as if it were
 T5   155: 3   very  top shelf of all. It'll puzzle it to go  through the ceiling, I expect!"
 A4    32:12     As  soon  as  she  was small enough to get  through the door, she ran out of the house, and found quite a
```

THROUGH (cont.)

A1	10: 6	but she could not even get her head	through the doorway; "and even if my head would go through,"
A1	8:39	began again. "I wonder if I shall fall right	through the earth! How funny it'll seem to come out among the
T4	142:11	/ And more, and more, and more--/ All hopping	through the frothy waves, / And scrambling to the shore.
T1	112: 1	In another moment Alice was	through the glass, and had jumped lightly down into the
A1	12:17	reach it: she could see it quite plainly	through the glass, and she tried her best to climb up one of
T1	112: 8	fire. Oh, what fun it'll be, when they see me	through the glass in here, and ca'n't get at me!"
T1	110:32	House. First, there's the room you can see	through the glass--that's just the same as our drawing-room,
T1	119: 7	the stairs with her feet: then she floated on	through the hall, and would have gone straight out at the door
A1	12: 5	that she was now the right size for going	through the little door into that lovely garden. First,
T2	120:15	in again yet. I know I should have to get	through the Looking-glass again--back into the old room--and
T1	118:32	I don't make haste, I shall have to go back	through the Looking-glass, before I've seen what the rest of
T8	187:16	strange things that Alice saw in her journey	Through The Looking-Glass, this was the one that she always
T12	207: 4	And you've been along with me, Kitty--all	through the Looking-glass world. Did you know it, dear?"
A12	98:25	by--the frightened Mouse splashed his way	through the neighbouring pool--she could hear the rattle of
TI	103:32	though the shadow of a sigh / May tremble	through the story, / For "happy summer days" gone by, / And
T2	128: 9	move, you know. So you'll go very quickly	through the Third Square--by railway, I should think--and
T1	118:11	with eyes of flame, / Came whiffling	through the tulgey wood, / And burbled as it came!
T1	118:13	One, two! One, two! And through and	through / The vorpal blade went snicker-snack! / He left it
T7	170: 8	to meet any soldiers, my dear, as you came	through the wood?"
T3	137: 3	So they walked on together	through the wood, Alice with her arms clasped lovingly round
T3	137:17	to answer, as there was only one road	through the wood, and the two finger-posts both pointed along
T7	169: 1	The next moment soldiers came running	through the wood, at first in twos and threes, then ten or
A7	60:36	again!" said Alice, as she picked her way	through the wood. "It's the stupidest tea-party I ever was at
T5	149: 3	moment the White Queen came running wildly	through the wood, with both arms stretched out wide, as if she
A1	10: 7	the doorway; "and even if my head would go	through," thought poor Alice, "it would be of very little use
T9	197: 9	down on Alice's other shoulder, "just sing it	through to me. I'm getting sleepy, too." In another moment
A2	15:18	into the garden with one eye; but to get	through was more hopeless than ever: she sat down and began to
T1	111: 9	got all soft like gauze, so that we can get	through. Why, it's turning into a sort of mist now, I declare!
T7	175:13	rather nervously. "You shouldn't have run him	through with your horn, you know."

THROW (6)

T8	181:26	it as he spoke, and was just going to	throw it into the bushes, when a sudden thought seemed to
T1	115:17	room to see if she could find any water to	throw over him. However, she could find nothing but a bottle
T1	116: 3	about him, and had the ink all ready to	throw over him, in case he fainted again), she turned over the
A10	78:26	you know," the Mock Turtle went on, "you	throw the--"
A2	20: 6	brown hair! And it'll fetch things when you	throw them, and it'll sit up and beg for its dinner, and all
A10	80: 2	it will be / When they take us up and	throw us, with the lobsters, out to sea!" / But the snail

THROWING (3)

A12	96:20	"Never!" said the Queen, furiously,	throwing an inkstand at the Lizard as she spoke. (The
T7	172:11	"I should think	throwing cold water over you would be better," Alice suggested
A6	48:10	of soup off the fire, and at once set to work	throwing everything within her reach at the Duchess and the

THROWN (1)

A10	81: 5	with the lobsters to the dance. So they got	thrown out to sea. So they had to fall a long way. So they got

THUMB (2)

T9	199: 9	then he went nearer and rubbed it with his	thumb, as if he were trying whether the paint would come off:
T6	168:28	"(marking their places in the air with his	thumb) "nose in the middle, mouth under. It's always the same.

THUMP (5)

T2	123:27	the Larkspur. "I hear her footstep, thump,	thump, along the gravel-walk!"
A1	9:19	you ever eat a bat?" when suddenly, thump!	thump! down she came upon a heap of sticks and dry leaves, and
T6	167:15	My heart went hop, my heart went	thump: / I filled the kettle at the pump.
T2	123:27	cried the Larkspur. "I hear her footstep,	thump, thump, along the gravel-walk!"
A1	9:18	did you ever eat a bat?" when suddenly,	thump! thump! down she came upon a heap of sticks and dry

THUMPED (1)

T8	188:16	/ I cried 'Come, tell me how you live!' / And	thumped him on the head.

THUNDER (3)

A8	65:41	your places!" shouted the Queen in a voice of	thunder, and people began running about in all directions,
T9	196:14	part of the roof came off, and ever so much	thunder got in--and it went rolling round the room in great
T9	195:20	she felt quite certain about this, "is the	thunder--no, no!" she hastily corrected herself. "I meant the

THUNDERSTORM (4)

A9	72:33	them, with her arms folded, frowning like a	thunderstorm.
T4	148:19	suddenly that Alice thought there must be a	thunderstorm coming on. "What a thick black cloud that is!"
T9	195:27	and unclasping her hands, "we had such a	thunderstorm last Tuesday--I mean one of the last set of
T9	196:11	the White Queen began again. "It was such a	thunderstorm, you ca'n't think!" ("She never could, you know,"

THURSDAYS (1)

T9	196: 8	"Well, only on Thursdays," said the Queen.

THUS (2)

AI	3:31	Thus grew the tale of Wonderland: / Thus slowly, one by one, /
AI	3:32	Thus grew the tale of Wonderland: / Thus slowly, one by one, / Its quaint events were hammered out

THY (4)

TI	103: 5	and I and thou / Are half a life asunder, /	Thy loving smile will surely hail / The love-gift of a
TI	103: 8	I have not seen thy sunny face, / Nor heard	thy silver laughter: / No thought of me shall find a place /
TI	103: 7	I have not seen	thy sunny face, / Nor heard thy silver laughter. / No thought
TI	103:10	/ No thought of me shall find a place / In	thy young life's hereafter--/ Enough that now thou wilt not

TICKET (2) [See also RETURN-TICKET]

T3	129:37	"Now then! Show your ticket, child!" the Guard went on, looking angrily at Alice.
T3	129:34	In a moment everybody was holding out a	ticket: they were about the same size as the people, and quite

TICKET-OFFICE (2)

T3	131: 5	loud voice, "She ought to know her way to the	ticket-office, even if she doesn't know her alphabet!"
T3	130: 3	said in a frightened tone: "there wasn't a	ticket-office where I came from." And again the chorus of

TICKETS (1)
    T3   129:33   "Tickets, please!" said the Guard, putting his head in at the
TICKING (1)
    T4   138:16   song kept ringing through her head like the ticking of a clock, and she could hardly help saying them out
TICKLED (1)
    T3   131:39   her ear. The consequence of this was that it tickled her ear very much, and quite took off her thoughts
TIDE (1)
    A10   82:28   tones of the Shark: / But, when the tide rises and sharks are around, / His voice has a timid and
TIDINGS (1)
    TI   103:20   then, ere voice of dread, / With bitter tidings laden, / Shall summon to unwelcome bed / A melancholy
TIDY (4) [See also UNTIDY]
    T1   113: 3   "They don't keep this room so tidy as the other," Alice thought to herself, as she noticed
    T1   115:13   will get into it--there, now I think you're tidy enough!" she added, as she smoothed his hair, and set him
    A4   27:36   By this time she had found her way into a tidy little room with a table in the window, and on it (as she
    T1   108:13   the window with me--only Dinah was making you tidy, so you couldn't. I was watching the boys getting in
TIE (1)
    A4   30:27   lad!--Here, put 'em up at this corner--No, tie 'em together first--they don't reach half high enough yet
TIED (3) [See also UNTIED]
    T4   147:31   said Tweedledum, coming up to have his helmet tied on. (He called it a helmet, though it certainly looked
    A1   10:16   was not here before," said Alice), and tied round the neck of the bottle was a paper label, with the
    A11   90:14   was done. They had a large canvas bag, which tied up at the mouth with strings: into this they slipped the
TIES (1)
    T8W   16:10   tree. And I gets a yellow handkerchief. And I ties up my face--as at the present."
TIGER-LILY (12)
    T2   121: 5   "As well as you can," said the Tiger-lily. "And a great deal louder."
    T2   122:36   "Hold your tongue!" cried the Tiger-lily. "As if you ever saw anybody! You keep your head
    T2   123: 7   do it--" ("You're always wondering," said the Tiger-lily), "but she's more bushy than you are."
    T2   123:13   done up close, like a dahlia," said the Tiger-lily: "not tumbled about, like yours."
    T2   121: 2   to take her breath away. At length, as the Tiger-lily only went on waving about, she spoke again, in a
    T2   121:11   "I don't care about the colour," the Tiger-lily remarked. "If only her petals curled up a little
    T2   120:30   "O Tiger-lily!" said Alice, addressing herself to one that was
    T2   122:28   "In most gardens," the Tiger-lily said, "they make the beds too soft--so that the
    T2   122:18   "That's right!" said the Tiger-lily. "The daisies are worst of all. When one speaks,
    T2   122:24   hand down, and feel the ground," said the Tiger-lily. "Then you'll know why."
    T2   122: 9   "Silence, every one of you!" cried the Tiger-lily, waving itself passionately from side to side, and
    T2   120:32   "We can talk," said the Tiger-lily, "when there's anybody worth talking to."
TIGERS (1)
    T4   144:26   to be a wild beast. "Are there any lions or tigers about here?" she asked timidly.
TIGHT (4)
    T8   191: 5   hands up to something very heavy, that fitted tight all around her head.
    T8   182:18   he fell in himself instead. "It's rather a tight fit, you see," he said, as they got it in at last;
    A6   49:23   it up into a sort of knot, and then keep tight hold of its right ear and left foot, so as to prevent
    T1   108:32   keeping your eyes open--if you'd shut them tight up, it wouldn't have happened. Now don't make any more
TILL (53)
    T8   179: 1   while the noise seemed gradually to die away, till all was dead silence, and Alice lifted up her head in
    A4   32:44   way back, and barking hoarsely all the while, till at last it sat down a good way off, panting, with its
    T1   114:19   as he slowly struggled up from bar to bar, till at last she said "Why, you'll be hours and hours getting
    A4   27:32   nurse! But I've got to watch this mouse-hole till Dinah comes back, and see that the mouse doesn't get out
    T8   190:32   she waved her handkerchief to him, and waited till he was out of sight.
    T1   115: 7   larger and larger, and rounder and rounder, till her hand shook so with laughter that she nearly let him
    A11   91:14   folding his arms and frowning at the cook till his eyes were nearly out of sight, he said, in a deep
    T6   163:26   smiled contemptuously. "Of course you don't--till I tell you. I meant 'there's a nice knock-down argument
    T9   196:15   and knocking over the tables and things--till I was so frightened, I couldn't remember my own name!"
    A2   17:24   I'll come up: if not, I'll stay down here till I'm somebody else'--but, oh dear!" cried Alice, with a
    T5   156:15   left to drift down the stream as it would, till it glided gently in among the waving rushes. And then the
    T5   151:22   Her voice went higher with each "better," till it got quite to a squeak at last.
    T1   107:17   wind up, and had been rolling it up and down till it had all come undone again; and there it was, spread
    A8   67:17   "It's no use speaking to it," she thought, "till its ears have come, or at least one of them." In another
    A9   74:28   Sit down, both of you, and don't speak a word till I've finished."
    T5   150: 5   punished: and the trial doesn't even begin till next Wednesday: and of course the crime comes last of all
    A11   90:19   court,' and I never understood what it meant till now."
    T3   137:30   wandered on, talking to herself as she went, till, on turning a sharp corner, she came upon two fat little
    T3   135:35   fancy calling everything you met 'Alice,' till one of them answered! Only they wouldn't answer at all,
    A4   29:31   you wo'n't!" thought Alice, and after waiting till she fancied she heard the Rabbit just under the window,
    T7   178: 2   it, and it rang through and through her head till she felt quite deafened. She started to her feet and
    T2   120:19   down the path, determined to keep straight on till she got to the hill. For a few minutes all went on well,
    A10   82: 5   went on. Her listeners were perfectly quiet till she got to the part about her repeating "You are old,
    A5   44: 5   and did not venture to go near the house till she had brought herself down to nine inches high.
    T12   207:13   Alice hunted among the chessmen on the table till she had found the Red Queen: then she went down on her
    A6   53:14   a house, that she did not like to go nearer till she had nibbled some more of the left-hand bit of
    T9   195: 5   work and fanned her with bunches of leaves, till she had to beg them to leave off, it blew her hair about
    A4   30:40   far down the chimney as she could, and waited till she heard a little animal (she couldn't guess of what
    A4   29:22   coming to look for her, and she trembled till she shook the house, quite forgetting that she was now
    A12   98:15   Alice and all her wonderful Adventures, till she too began dreaming after a fashion, and this was her
    A7   61: 3   (she had kept a piece of it in her pocket) till she was about a foot high; then she walked down the
    A9   74: 8   rubbed its eyes: then it watched the Queen till she was out of sight: then it chuckled. "What fun!" said
    A4   33: 4   her escape: so she set off at once, and ran till she was quite tired and out of breath, and till the
    T4   147:43   "Let's fight till six, and then have dinner," said Tweedledum.
    T2   127: 7   hardly touching the ground with their feet, till suddenly, just as Alice was getting quite exhausted, they
    T2   122: 8   And here they all began shouting together, till the air seemed quite full of little shrill voices.

TILL (cont.)
A8   67:16   Alice waited till the eyes appeared, and then nodded. "It's no use speaking
T9   197: 5   "Hush-a-by lady, in Alice's lap! / Till the feast's ready, we've time for a nap. / When the
A5   42:37 there was no use in saying anything more till the Pigeon had finished.
A4   33: 5 she was quite tired and out of breath, and till the puppy's bark sounded quite faint in the distance.
T9   198: 5   "I'll wait till the song's over," thought Alice, "and then I'll ring the
T1   109:13 and perhaps it says 'Go to sleep, darlings, till the summer comes again.' And when they wake up in the
T9   198:11 head out for a moment and said "No admittance till the week after next!" and shut the door again with a bang
T7   173:15 for talking; so they trotted on in silence, till they came into sight of a great crowd, in the middle of
T3   137: 4 lovingly round the soft neck of the Fawn, till they came out into another open field, and here the Fawn
T2   125:17 offended: and they walked on in silence till they got to the top of the little hill.
A6   46:26 "I shall sit here," the Footman remarked, "till to-morrow--"
T6   168:20 she got up, and held out her hand. "Good-bye, till we meet again!" she said as cheerfully as she could.
A12   94:36   the King said, very gravely, "and go on till you come to the end: then stop."
T8W   17: 5 "It is, though," said the Wasp: "wait till you have it, and then you'll know. And when you catches
T2   123: 1 head under the leaves, and snore away there, till you know no more what's going on in the world, than if
T9   192:28 yourself so? You ca'n't be a Queen, you know, till you've passed the proper examination. And the sooner we
T6   168:33 Dumpty only shut his eyes, and said "Wait till you've tried."
TILLIE (1)
A7   58:34 "and their names were Elsie, Lacie, and Tillie; and they lived at the bottom of a well--"
TIME (144) [See also AFTERTIME, BEDTIME, TEA-TIME]
A7   56:39   "I dare say you never even spoke to Time!"
A7   59:35 Dormouse, without considering at all, this time.
A10   81:45 tone: "explanations take such a dreadful time."
A11   86:12 at everything about her to pass away the time."
T2   124: 8   and don't twiddle your fingers all the time."
T2   124:14 while you're thinking what to say. It saves time."
T3   132:41 on with your list of insects: you're wasting time."
T4   139:38 I felt as if I'd been singing in a long long time!"
T9   192:10 "I shall be able to manage it quite well in time."
T9   194:38 don't be discouraged. You'll come to it in time."
T9   195:30 she remarked, "there's only one day at a time."
T8W   17: 3 name. They called it conceit in my time."
T8W   17: 8   round your face. It'll cure you in no time!"
T7   173:31 Hatta looked round once more, and this time a tear or two trickled down his cheek; but not a word
A6   53: 6 and ending with the grin, which remained some time after the rest of it had gone.
A5   41:23   This time Alice waited patiently until it chose to speak again. In
T9   204:23   At any other time, Alice would have felt surprised at this, but was far
A4   32:44 running a very little way forwards each time and a long way back, and barking hoarsely all the while,
T2   128: 4 She had got all the pegs put in by this time, and Alice looked on with great interest as she returned
A7   57: 1 lessons: you'd only have to whisper a hint to Time, and round goes the clock in a twinkling! Half-past one,
T8   184: 1 was walking. She was quite frightened this time, and said in an anxious tone, as she picked him up, "I
T9   195:32 mostly have days and nights two or three at a time, and sometimes in the winter we take as many as five
A9   70:16 She had quite forgotten the Duchess by this time, and was a little startled when she heard her voice close
A7   60:20 The Dormouse had closed its eyes by this time, and was going off into a doze; but, on being pinched by
A1   8:42 rather glad there was no one listening, this time, as it didn't sound at all the right word) "--but I shall
T3   130:11 in speaking." The voices didn't join in, this time, as she hadn't spoken, but, to her great surprise, they
A1   8:12 she fell very slowly, for she had plenty of time as she went down to look about her, and to wonder what
A7   56:35   "If you knew Time as well as I do," said the Hatter, "you wouldn't talk
T2   127:18   else--if you ran very fast for a long time as we've been doing."
A4   32:30 it; but she was terribly frightened all the time at the thought that it might be hungry, in which case it
TI   103: 3 brow / And dreaming eyes of wonder! / Though time be fleet, and I and thou / Are half a life asunder, / Thy
A12   93:33 this moment the King, who had been for some time busily writing in his note-book, called out "Silence!",
T1   116:13   She puzzled over this for some time, but at last a bright thought struck her. "Why, it's a
T9   198:12 Alice knocked and rang in vain for a long time; but at last a very old Frog, who was sitting under a
T9   194:31 I can do Addition," she said, "if you give me time--but I ca'n't do Subtraction under any circumstances!"
A5   43:12 "I've seen a good many little girls in my time, but never one with such a neck as that! No, no! You're a
T6   160: 2 Dumpty said, looking at her for the first time, "but tell me your name and your business."
T2   128:25 She did not wait for Alice to curtsey, this time, but walked on quickly to the next peg, where she turned
T8   187: 8 the song, then?" said Alice, who was by this time completely bewildered.
T9   197:18 there never was more than one Queen at a time. Do wake up, you heavy things!" she went on in an
A6   49:29 in reply (it had left off sneezing by this time). "Don't grunt," said Alice; "that's not at all a proper
T2   127:13 believe we've been under this tree the whole time! Everything's just as it was!"
T9   197: 5 Alice's lap! / Till the feast's ready, we've time for a nap. / When the feast's over, we'll go to the ball
A7   57: 2 goes the clock in a twinkling! Half-past one, time for dinner!"
T2   128:33 she was a Pawn, and that it would soon be time for her to move.
T2   124:18   "It's time for you to answer now," the Queen said looking at her
T4   142:19   'The time has come,' the Walrus said, / 'To talk of many things: /
T8   184: 7 arms to show Alice what he meant, and this time he fell flat on his back, right under the horse's feet.
A8   69:11 away the moment he was gone, and, by the time he had come back with the Duchess, it had entirely
T8   185:18 was rather startled by the fall, as for some time he had kept on very well, and she was afraid that he
T7   175:10 in his pockets. "I had the best of it this time?" he said to the King, just glancing at him as he passed
A6   46:21 know." He was looking up into the sky all the time he was speaking, and this Alice thought decidedly uncivil
T8   185:19 she was afraid that he really was hurt this time. However, though she could see nothing but the soles of
T9   195:11 she saw a way out of the difficulty, this time. "If you'll tell me what language 'fiddle-de-dee' is,
T2   124:17 I go home," she thought to herself, "the next time I'm a little late for dinner."
A5   35: 1 and Alice looked at each other for some time in silence: at last the Caterpillar took the hookah out
T2   127: 2 minutes ago! Faster!" And they ran on for a time in silence, with the wind whistling in Alice's ears, and
A10   78:19   "That generally takes some time," interrupted the Gryphon.
T3   130: 1 "Don't keep him waiting, child! Why, his time is worth a thousand pounds a minute!"

TIME (cont.)

A1	7:15	ought to have wondered at this, but at the time it all seemed quite natural); but, when the Rabbit
AI	3:29	one / To put the subject by, / "The rest next time--" "It is next time!" / The happy voices cry.
A6	53: 4	"All right," said the Cat; and this time it vanished quite slowly, beginning with the end of the
T8	179:23	This time it was a White Knight. He drew up at Alice's side, and
T5	152:27	By this time it was getting light. "The crow must have flown away, I
T7	175:16	he turned round instantly, and stood for some time looking at her with an air of the deepest disgust.
T4	147:41	going on long," said Tweedledum. "What's the time now?"
A8	68:39	before, and he wasn't going to begin at his time of life.
T2	124: 1	she thought she would try the plan, this time, of walking in the opposite direction.
A7	58: 5	when the Queen bawled out 'He's murdering the time! Off with his head!'"
T12	207:24	thinking what to--what to purr. It saves time, remember!" And she caught it up and gave it one little
A1	9:39	not open any of them. However, on the second time round, she came upon a low curtain she had not noticed
A5	41:21	"You'll get used to it in time," said the Caterpillar; and it put the hookah into its
A9	77: 4	"Hadn't time," said the Gryphon: "I went to the Classical master,
A10	78:37	been jumping about like mad things all this time, sat down again very sadly and quietly, and looked at
T2	120:27	was nothing to be done but start again. This time she came upon a large flowerbed, with a border of daisies
A1	10:15	for shutting people up like telescopes: this time she found a little bottle on it ("which certainly was not
A8	68:22	By the time she had caught the flamingo and brought it back, the
A4	27:36	By this time she had found her way into a tidy little room with a
A2	15.25	After a time she heard a little pattering of feet in the distance, and
A1	8:28	"I wonder how many miles I've fallen by this time?" she said aloud. "I must be getting somewhere near the
T2	128:22	the next peg the Queen turned again, and this time she said "Speak in French when you ca'n't think of the
A7	56:33	think you might do something better with the time," she said, "than wasting it in asking riddles that have
A7	60:43	glass table. "Now, I'll manage better this time," she said to herself, and began by taking the little
A7	60:33	that they would call after her: the last time she saw them, they were trying to put the Dormouse into
T3	129: 8	saw bees a mile off, you know--" and for some time she stood silent, watching one of them that was bustling
T5	153:19	arms again and went flying after it, and this time she succeeded in catching it herself. "I've got it!" she
A2	15:37	very hot, she kept fanning herself all the time she went on talking. "Dear, dear! How queer everything is
A8	69: 3	wasn't done about it in less than no time, she'd have everybody executed, all round. (It was this
T1	108: 6	get on very fast, as she was talking all the time, sometimes to the kitten, and sometimes to herself. Kitty
A9	72:38	head must be off, and that in about half no time! Take your choice!"
T8	184: 9	of practice!" he went on repeating, all the time that Alice was getting him on his feet again. "Plenty of
A12	96:29	the King said, for about the twentieth time that day.
T3	130:18	All this time the Guard was looking at her, first through a telescope,
AI	3:29	by, / "The rest next time--" "It is next time!" / The happy voices cry.
T1	118: 6	He took his vorpal sword in hand: / Long time the manxome foe he sought--/ So rested he by the Tumtum
T7	177: 4	was too much dust to see anything. What a time the Monster is, cutting up that cake!"
A2	19:19	beg your pardon!" cried Alice again, for this time the Mouse was bristling all over, and she felt certain it
T3	135:18	of those melancholy little sighs, and this time the poor Gnat really seemed to have sighed itself away,
A11	89: 4	All this time the Queen had never left off staring at the Hatter, and,
A8	66:22	for the hedgehogs; and in a very short time the Queen was in a furious passion, and went stamping
TI	103:15	glowing--/ A simple chime, that served to time / The rhythm of our rowing--/ Whose echoes live in memory
T3	131:25	say, my dear, but take a return-ticket every time the train stops."
A6	50:11	looked down into its face in some alarm. This time there could be no mistake about it: it was neither more
A7	58:32	"Once upon a time there were three little sisters," the Dormouse began in a
A4	30:16	and made another snatch in the air. This time there were two little shrieks, and more sounds of broken
A11	91:23	getting the Dormouse turned out, and, by the time they had settled down again, the cook had disappeared.
A9	73: 3	All the time they were playing the Queen never left off quarreling
T4	147:22	of old clothes than anything else, by the time they're ready!" she said to herself, as she arranged a
A5	41:42	sudden change, but she felt that there was no time to be lost, as she was shrinking rapidly: so she set to
A7	56:45	it were nine o'clock in the morning, just time to begin lessons: you'd only have to whisper a hint to
A2	20:21	It was high time to go, for the pool was getting quite crowded with the
T8	186: 9	"In time to have it cooked for the next course?" said Alice. "Well
A1	9:25	went Alice like the wind, and was just in time to hear it say, as it turned a corner, "Oh my ears and
T6	163:18	that seems to be done right--though I haven't time to look it over thoroughly just now--and that shows that
T8	182:15	This took a long time to manage, though Alice held the bag open very carefully,
A2	18: 8	holding, and she dropped it hastily, just in time to save herself from shrinking away altogether.
T8	184:16	round the horse's neck as he spoke, just in time to save himself from tumbling off again.
A1	8: 4	across the field after it, and was just in time to see it pop down a large rabbit-hole under the hedge.
T1	113:16	Alice, and made her turn her head just in time to see one of the White Pawns roll over and begin kicking
T7	178: 4	the little brook in her terror, and had just time to see the Lion and the * * * * * * * * * * * * * *
T9	204: 6	soup-tureen, and Alice turned again, just in time to see the Queen's broad good-natured face grinning at
A7	58:13	a sigh: "it's always tea-time, and we've no time to wash the things between whiles."
A7	56:17	it stays the same year for such a long time together."
T4	147: 1	All this time Tweedledee was trying his best to fold up the umbrella,
T2	128:10	find yourself in the Fourth Square in no time. Well, that square belongs to Tweedledum and Tweedledee--
T4	148: 8	left standing, for ever so far round, by the time we've finished!"
A7	56:41	replied; "but I know I have to beat time when I learn music."
A10	82: 1	began telling them her adventures from the time when she first saw the White Rabbit. She was a little
T2	120:21	was just saying "I really shall do it this time--" when the path gave a sudden twist and shook itself (as
T6	164:27	means four o'clock in the afternoon--the time when you begin broiling things for dinner."
A10	79:11	close, and waving their fore-paws to mark the time, while the Mock Turtle sang this, very slowly and sadly:
A7	55: 7	Hatter. He had been looking at Alice for some time with great curiosity, and this was his first speech.
A3	23:18	deal of thought, and it stood for a long time with one finger pressed upon its forehead (the position
T8	187:13	reins fall on its neck: then, slowly beating time with one hand, and with a faint smile lighting up his
A4	28: 3	the looking-glass. There was no label this time with the words "DRINK ME," but nevertheless she uncorked
A4	30:22	She waited for some time without hearing anything more: at last came a rumbling of
A7	60:13	that she let the Dormouse go on for some time without interrupting it.
T1	115:35	and struggled with the pencil for some time without saying anything; but Alice was too strong for him

TIME (cont.)
```
 T8    179:26  Knights sat and looked at each other for some time without speaking. Alice looked from one to the other in
 T8    184:12  cried Alice, losing all her patience this time. "You ought to have a wooden horse on wheels, that you
 T8    184:23  things. Now, I daresay you noticed, the last time you picked me up, that I was looking rather thoughtful?"
 A3     26:35  its children, "Come away, my dears! It's high time you were all in bed!" On various pretexts they all moved
T12    208: 2  morning you shall have a real treat. All the time you're eating your breakfast, I'll repeat 'The Walrus and
A12     97: 8  Alice (she had grown to her full size by this time). "You're nothing but a pack of cards!"
```
TIMES (20) [See also SOMETIMES]
```
 T7    174: 7  each of them has been down about eighty-seven times."
 T9    195:41  I'm five times as rich as you are, and five times as clever!"
 T9    195:38          "But they should be five times as cold, by the same rule--"
 T9    195:40  the Red Queen. "Five times as warm, and five times as cold--just as I'm five times as rich as you are, and
 A4     29:23  forgetting that she was now about a thousand times as large as the Rabbit, and had no reason to be afraid
 T9    195:40  and five times as cold--just as I'm five times as rich as you are, and five times as clever!"
 T9    195:39  "Just so!" cried the Red Queen. "Five times as warm, and five times as cold--just as I'm five times
 T9    195:37          "Five times as warm, of course."
 T6    159: 7      It might have been written a hundred times, easily, on that enormous face. Humpty Dumpty was
 A2     16: 9  the things I used to know. Let me see: four times five is twelve, and four times six is thirteen, and four
 T9    200: 4  wine--/ And welcome Queen Alice with ninety-times-nine!"
 T9    200: 5          "Ninety times nine!" Alice repeated in despair. "Oh, that'll never be
A11     86:24  jurors." She said this last word two or three times over to herself, being rather proud of it: for she
 T4    139:40  were fat, and very soon out of breath. "Four times round is enough for one dance," Tweedledum panted out,
 A2     16:10  and four times six is thirteen, and four times seven is--oh dear! I shall never get to twenty at that
 A5     35: 8  but I think I must have been changed several times since then."
 A2     16: 9  me see: four times five is twelve, and four times six is thirteen, and four times seven is--oh dear! I
 T8    182:17  putting in the dish: the first two or three times that he tried he fell in himself instead. "It's rather a
 T9    199:32  tea--/ And welcome Queen Alice with thirty-times-three!"
 T9    199:34      and Alice thought to herself "Thirty times three makes ninety. I wonder if any one's counting?" In
```
TIMID (5)
```
 T3    135:24  than the last wood, and Alice felt a little timid about going into it. However, on second thoughts, she
A10     82:29  and sharks are around, / His voice has a timid and tremulous sound."
 T2    121: 3  went on waving about, she spoke again, in a timid voice--almost in a whisper. "And can all the flowers
 A8     65:25      "It's--it's a very fine day!" said a timid voice at her side. She was walking by the White Rabbit,
 A2     15:33  Rabbit came near her, she began, in a low, timid voice, "If you please, Sir--" The Rabbit started
```
TIMIDLY (18)
```
A10     79: 2  "It must be a very pretty dance," said Alice timidly.
 T4    144:26  any lions or tigers about here?" she asked timidly.
 T8W    15:13  this newspaper, though," Alice said a little timidly.
 T5    149:11  must manage it herself. So she began rather timidly: "Am I addressing the White Queen?"
 A6     51: 4          "Cheshire-Puss," she began, rather timidly, as she did not at all know whether it would like the
 T6    168:15          "Is that all?" Alice timidly asked.
 T9    196:25          The White Queen looked timidly at Alice, who felt she ought to say something kind,
 T9    192:17  would you tell me--" she began, looking timidly at the Red Queen.
A10     81:41  from this morning," said Alice a little timidly; "but it's no use going back to yesterday, because I
 A6     47:12  would you tell me," said Alice, a little timidly, for she was not quite sure whether it was good
 T5    158: 3  should like to buy an egg, please," she said timidly. "How do you sell them?"
 T3    136:18  you tell me what you call yourself?" she said timidly. "I think that might help a little."
 T8    180: 2  said to herself, as she watched the fight, timidly peeping out from her hiding-place. "One Rule seems to
 A8     64:10  The King laid his hand upon her arm, and timidly said "Consider, my dear: she is only a child!"
 A6     53:16  even then she walked up towards it rather timidly, saying to herself "Suppose it should be raving mad
 A5     41: 2  "Not quite right, I'm afraid," said Alice, timidly: "some of the words have got altered."
 A6     46: 9          Alice went timidly up to the door, and knocked.
 A8     63: 3  you tell me, please," said Alice, a little timidly, "why you are painting those roses?"
```
TIN (1)
```
 T8    181:13          He was dressed in tin armour, which seemed to fit him very badly, and he had a
```
TINIEST (1)
```
 AI      3:10  beg a tale of breath too weak / To stir the tiniest feather! / Yet what can one poor voice avail / Against
```
TINKLING (1)
```
A12     98:38  reeds--the rattling teacups would change to tinkling sheep-bells, and the Queen's shrill cries to the
```
TINY (6)
```
 T7    172:34          "It would have to be a very tiny earthquake!" thought Alice. "Who are at it again?" she
 A1      9:35  of solid glass: there was nothing on it but a tiny golden key, and Alice's first idea was that this might
A12     98:17  about little Alice herself: once again the tiny hands were clasped upon her knee, and the bright eager
 T2    125:21  country it was. There were a number of tiny little brooks running straight across it from side to
 A4     28: 8  for really I'm quite tired of being such a tiny little thing!"
 A4     27:38  had hoped) a fan and two or three pairs of tiny white kid-gloves: she took up the fan and a pair of the
```
TIPPED (1)
```
A12     92: 3  and she jumped up in such a hurry that she tipped over the jury-box with the edge of her skirt, upsetting
```
TIPPLE (1)
```
 T5    156:24          "I only hope the boat wo'n't tipple over!" she said to herself. "Oh, what a lovely one!
```
TIPS (1)
```
 T1    119: 5  as Alice said to herself. She just kept the tips of her fingers on the hand-rail, and floated gently down
```
TIPTOE (3)
```
 A4     34: 7          She stretched herself up on tiptoe, and peeped over the edge of the mushroom, and her eyes
 T3    129: 3  geography," thought Alice, as she stood on tiptoe in hopes of being able to see a little further.
 A8     65:31  as he spoke, and then raised himself upon tiptoe, put his mouth close to her ear, and whispered "She's
```
TIRED (10)
```
 A4     33: 4  set off at once, and ran till she was quite tired and out of breath, and till the puppy's bark sounded
 T7    175:44  them while this was going on: he looked very tired and sleepy, and his eyes were half shut. "What's this!"
 A1     12:19  but it was too slippery; and when she had tired herself out with trying, the poor little thing sat down
```

TIRED (cont.)
```
A2    17:26   they would put their heads down! I am so very tired of being all alone here!"
A4    28: 7   me grow large again,  for really I'm quite tired of being such a tiny little thing!"
A1     7: 1              Alice was beginning to get very tired of sitting by her sister on the bank and of having
A2    19:14   you know the way out of this pool? I am very tired of swimming about here, O Mouse!" (Alice thought this
A7    58:19   March Hare interrupted, yawning. "I'm getting tired of this. I vote the young lady tells us a story."
T9   196:36                            "She's tired, poor thing!" said the Red Queen. "Smoothe her hair--
T4   140: 6                "I hope you're not much tired?" she said at last.
```
'TIS (7)
```
T9   199:39   'Tis an honour to see me, a favour to hear: / 'Tis a privilege high to have dinner and tea / Along with the
T9   199:38   creatures,'  quoth Alice,  'draw near! / 'Tis an honour to see me, a favour to hear: / 'Tis a privilege
A9    70:33   "and the moral of that is--'Oh, 'tis love, 'tis love, that makes the world go round!'"
A9    70:32   the Duchess: "and the moral of that is--'Oh, 'tis love, 'tis love, that makes the world go round!'"
A9    70:32                          "'Tis so," said the Duchess: "and the moral of that is--'Oh,
A10   82:22                    "'Tis the voice of the Lobster: I heard him declare / 'You have
A10   82:15   "Stand up and repeat ''Tis the voice of the sluggard,'" said the Gryphon.
```
TITTERED (1)
```
A3    22:34   head to hide a smile: some of the other birds tittered audibly.
```
TO (1484) [entries omitted]
TOAST (1)
```
A1    11: 9   roast turkey, toffy, and hot buttered toast), she very soon finished it off. * * * * * * * * * * *
```
TO-DAY (14)
```
A2    19: 4   to be sure! However, everything is queer to-day."
A6    52: 3   the Cat. "Do you play croquet with the Queen to-day?"
T5   150: 6   to-morrow and jam yesterday--but never jam to-day."
T9   201:29   had such a quantity of poetry repeated to me to-day," Alice began, a little frightened at finding that, the
T5   150: 7              "It must come sometimes to 'jam to-day,'" Alice objected.
A2    15:38   talking. "Dear, dear! How queer everything is to-day! And yesterday things went on just as usual. I wonder
T5   150: 4              "Well, I don't want any to-day, at any rate."
T5   152:38   you are. Consider what a long way you've come to-day. Consider what o'clock it is. Consider anything, only
T4   147:35   generally," he went on in a low voice: "only to-day I happen to have a headache."
A7    60:40   she thought. "But everything's curious to-day. I think I may as well go in at once." And in she went
T5   150: 8   said the Queen. "It's jam every other day: to-day isn't any other day, you know."
T7   175:21   in an Anglo-Saxon attitude. "We only found it to-day. It's as large as life, and twice as natural!"
T4   147:38           "Then you'd better not fight to-day," said Alice, thinking it a good opportunity to make
T7   174:17   "I don't think they'll fight any more to-day," the King said to Hatta: "go and order the drums to
```
TOE (1) [See also TIPTOE]
```
T8   189:19   Into a left-hand shoe, / Or if I drop upon my toe / A very heavy weight, / I weep, for it reminds me so / Of
```
TOES (4)
```
T2   128:24   of the English for a thing--turn out your toes as you walk--and remember who you are!" She did not wait
A10   83: 5              "But about his toes?" the Mock Turtle persisted. "How could he turn them out
A10   82:25   his belt and his buttons, and turns out his toes. / When the sands are all dry, he is gay as a lark, / And
A10   79:10   Alice, every now and then treading on her toes when they passed too close, and waving their fore-paws to
```
TOFFY (1)
```
A1    11: 8   custard, pine-apple, roast turkey, toffy, and hot buttered toast), she very soon finished it off.
```
TOGETHER (23)
```
AI     3:12   one poor voice avail / Against three tongues together?
A5    36:32   I don't keep the same size for ten minutes together!"
A6    46: 4   both bowed, and their curls got entangled together.
A7    56:17   it stays the same year for such a long time together."
A9    70: 3              into Alice's, and they walked off together.
A9    71:12   moral of that is--'Birds of a feather flock together.'"
A9    73:18              As they walked off together, Alice heard the King say in a low voice, to the
T7   169: 2   first in twos and threes, then ten or twenty together, and at last in such crowds that they seemed to fill
T2   128:20   and in the Eighth Square we shall be Queens together, and it's all feasting and fun!" Alice got up and
T2   122:19   worst of all. When one speaks, they all begin together, and it's enough to make one wither to hear the way
T8W   13: 7   leaning against a tree, all huddled up together, and shivering as if he were very cold.
A7    54: 8   a large one, but the three were all crowded together at one corner of it. "No room! No room!" they cried
T9   194:36   Queen whispered: "we'll often say it over together, dear. And I'll tell you a secret--I can read words
A4    30:27   Here, put 'em up at this corner--No, tie 'em together first--they don't reach half high enough yet--Oh,
T9   195:34   in the winter we take as many as five nights together--for warmth, you know."
T1   115:20   recovered, and he and the Queen were talking together in a frightened whisper--so low, that Alice could
T9   204:15   guests, and candles came crashing down together in a heap on the floor.
T3   129:38   at Alice. And a great many voices all said together ("like the chorus of a song," thought Alice) "Don't
A4    30:24   the sound of a good many voices all talking together: she made out the words: "Where's the other ladder?--
T3   132:22   nervous with it, after they had been talking together so long.
T3   137: 3              So they walked on together through the wood, Alice with her arms clasped
T2   122: 8   Daisy. And here they all began shouting together, till the air seemed quite full of little shrill
T9   194:26   "She can't do sums a bit!" the Queens said together, with great emphasis.
```
TOIL (1)
```
T8   188:24              is all / They give me for my toil.'
```
TOILET (1)
```
T12  207:27   which was still patiently undergoing its toilet, "when will Dinah have finished with your White Majesty
```
TOLD (9)
```
A12   98: 6   such a curious dream!" said Alice. And she told her sister, as well as she could remember them, all these
A10   81:34   Mock Turtle. "Why, if a fish came to me, and told me he was going a journey, I should say 'With what
A12   94:39              "They told me you had been to her, / And mentioned me to him: / She
A6    46:35   was, no doubt: only Alice did not like to be told so. "It's really dreadful," she muttered to herself, "the
T6   167:11              I told them once, I told them twice: / They would not listen to
T6   166:40   "I sent a message to the fish: / I told them 'This is what I wish.'
```

TOLD (cont.)
```
 T6   167:11                                 I told them once, I told them twice: / They would not listen to advice.
 A7    56: 1   "Two days wrong!" sighed the Hatter. "I told you butter wouldn't suit the works!" he added, looking
 A10   81:26   rather impatiently: "any shrimp could have told you that."
```
TOLLING (1)
```
 T7   176: 2   in a deep hollow tone that sounded like the tolling of a great bell.
```
TO-MORROW (5)
```
 A6    46:26   shall sit here," the Footman remarked, "till to-morrow--"
 T5   150: 6   want it," the Queen said. "The rule is, jam to-morrow and jam yesterday--but never jam to-day."
 T1   108:16   off. Never mind, we'll go and see the bonfire to-morrow." Here Alice wound two or three turns of the worsted
 T1   108:11                                 "Do you know what to-morrow is, Kitty?" Alice began. "You'd have guessed if
 T12  208: 1   of poetry said to me, all about fishes! To-morrow morning you shall have a real treat. All the time
```
TONE (84) [See also UNDERTONE]
```
 A6    46:32   I to get in?" asked Alice again, in a louder tone.
 A7    54:13   wine," the March Hare said in an encouraging tone.
 A9    72:15   I chose," the Duchess replied, in a pleased tone.
 A10   81:16   boots and shoes!" she repeated in a wondering tone.
 T2   122:33   at all," the Rose said, in a rather severe tone.
 T4   147: 9   have a battle?" Tweedledum said in a calmer tone.
 T6   164: 4   one word mean," Alice said in a thoughtful tone.
 T6   168:25   generally," Alice remarked in a thoughtful tone.
 T9   192:30   said 'if'!" poor Alice pleaded in a piteous tone.
 T9   196: 7   generally?" Alice asked in an astonished tone.
 T5   154:16   so here!" she said at last in a plaintive tone, after she had spent a minute or so in vainly pursuing a
 T8   185:21   to hear that he was talking on in his usual tone. "All kinds of fastness," he repeated: "but it was
 A5    42:30   repeated the Pigeon, but in a more subdued tone, and added, with a kind of sob, "I've tried every way,
 A12   96:27   "It's a pun!" the King added in an angry tone, and everybody laughed. "Let the jury consider their
 A5    41:18   used to it!" pleaded poor Alice in a piteous tone. And she thought to herself "I wish the creatures
 A4    32:29   "Poor little thing!" said Alice, in a coaxing tone, and she tried hard to whistle to it; but she was
 T2   122:13   "Never mind!" Alice said in a soothing tone, and, stooping down to the daisies, who were just
 A10   81:38   say," the Mock Turtle replied, in an offended tone. And the Gryphon added "Come, let's hear some of your
 A8    67:24   fairly," Alice began, in rather a complaining tone, "and they all quarrel so dreadfully one ca'n't hear
 A5    43:28   be off, then!" said the Pigeon in a sulky tone, as it settled down again into its nest. Alice crouched
 T8   184: 2   frightened this time, and said in an anxious tone, as she picked him up, "I hope no bones are broken?"
 A4    29: 8   I'm grown up now," she added in a sorrowful tone: "at least there's no room to grow up any more here."
 A12   93:24   of course," he said, in a very respectful tone, but frowning and making faces at him as he spoke.
 T9   197:19   heavy things!" she went on in an impatient tone; but there was no answer but a gentle snoring.
 T8W   16: 1   you're not well," she said in a soothing tone. "Can't I do anything for you?"
 T2   124:13   come out here at all?" she added in a kinder tone. "Curtsey while you're thinking what to say. It saves
 A2    19:32   "Well, perhaps not," said Alice in a soothing tone: "don't be angry about it. And yet I wish I could show
 A6    46:31   maybe," the Footman continued in the same tone, exactly as if nothing had happened.
 A10   81:45   first," said the Gryphon in an impatient tone: "explanations take such a dreadful time."
 T5   150: 2   after next," the Queen replied in a careless tone. "For instance, now," she went on, sticking a large piece
 A6    45:13   handed over to the other, saying, in a solemn tone, "For the Duchess. An invitation from the Queen to play
 T6   168:22   Humpty Dumpty replied in a discontented tone, giving her one of his fingers to shake: "you're so
 A8    65: 6   your Majesty," said Two, in a very humble tone, going down on one knee as he spoke, "we were trying--"
 A8    65:29   Hush! Hush!" said the Rabbit in a low hurried tone. He looked anxiously over his shoulder as he spoke, and
 A7    58: 8   since that," the Hatter went on in a mournful tone, "he wo'n't do a thing I ask! It's always six o'clock now
 A10   84:13   that the Gryphon said, in a rather offended tone, "Hm! No accounting for tastes! Sing her 'Turtle Soup,'
 A2    20:10   and--oh dear!" cried Alice in a sorrowful tone. "I'm afraid I've offended it again!" For the Mouse was
 T7   172:20   I do my best," the Messenger said in a sullen tone. "I'm sure nobody walks much faster than I do!"
 A3    22:26   "As wet as ever," said Alice in a melancholy tone: "it doesn't seem to dry me at all."
 T6   163:31   Humpty Dumpty said, in rather a scornful tone, "it means just what I choose it to mean--neither more
 T8   181:18   my little box," the Knight said in a friendly tone. "It's my own invention--to keep clothes and sandwiches
 T8   179:10   dream," she went on in a rather complaining tone: "I've a great mind to go and wake him, and see what
 T8   186:31   "You are sad," the Knight said in an anxious tone: "let me sing you a song to comfort you."
 T8   186:12   course," the Knight said in slow thoughtful tone: "no, certainly not the next course."
 A3    26:38   Dinah!" she said to herself in a melancholy tone. "Nobody seems to like her, down here, and I'm sure she's
 T5   153:21   "I've got it!" she cried in a triumphant tone. "Now you shall see me pin it on again, all by myself!"
 T2   125:27   somewhere--and so there are!" she added in a tone of delight, and her heart began to beat quick with
 T7   170: 6   "I've sent them all!" the King cried in a tone of delight, on seeing Alice. "Did you happen to meet any
 A5    42: 7   my head's free at last!" said Alice in a tone of delight, which changed into alarm in another moment,
 T8   191: 4   what is this on my head?" she exclaimed in a tone of dismay, as she put her hands up to something very
 T2   128:16   You should have said," the Queen went on in a tone of grave reproof, "'It's extremely kind of you to tell me
 T4   145:27   are real tears?" Tweedledum interrupted in a tone of great contempt.
 A10   81:23   "And what are they made of?" Alice asked in a tone of great curiosity.
 T8   182: 8   "But what are they for?" Alice asked in a tone of great curiosity.
 A12   92: 8   "Oh, I beg your pardon!" she exclaimed in a tone of great dismay, and began picking them up again as
 T8   184:14   that kind go smoothly?" the Knight asked in a tone of great interest, clasping his arms round the horse's
 A9    76:14   good school," said the Mock Turtle in a tone of great relief. "Now, at ours, they had, at the end of
 A10   81:32   "Wouldn't it, really?" said Alice, in a tone of great surprise.
 A5    43:11   A likely story indeed!" said the Pigeon, in a tone of the deepest contempt. "I've seen a good many little
 A6    48: 7                        Alice did not at all like the tone of this remark, and thought it would be as well to
 T8   181:35   bee-hive," the Knight said in a discontented tone, "one of the best kind. But not a single bee has come
 A6    46: 1   The Frog-Footman repeated, in the same solemn tone, only changing the order of the words a little, "From the
 T3   134:25   I don't know," the Gnat went on in a careless tone: "only think how convenient it would be if you could
 A8    62: 7   "I couldn't help it," said Five, in a sulky tone. "Seven jogged my elbow."
 T9   192: 3   is, your Majesty," she went on, in a severe tone (she was always rather fond of scolding herself), "It'll
 A9    74:27   her," said the Mock Turtle in a deep, hollow tone. "Sit down, both of you, and don't speak a word till I've
 A7    59:11   nothing yet," Alice replied in an offended tone: "so I ca'n't take more."
```

TONE (cont.)
T5   158: 7   cheaper than one?" Alice said in a surprised tone, taking out her purse.
A9   77:24   the Gryphon interrupted in a very decided tone. "Tell her something about the games now."
T6   162:28   ignorant of me," Alice said, in so humble a tone that Humpty Dumpty relented.
T2   125:16   again, as she was afraid from the Queen's tone that she was a little offended: and they walked on in
T7   176: 1   at Alice, and speaking in a deep hollow tone that sounded like the tolling of a great bell.
T5   157:14   "To buy!" Alice echoed in a tone that was half astonished and half frightened--for the
T6   160:36   in a book," Humpty Dumpty said in a calmer tone. "That's what you call a History of England, that is. Now
A8   65:39   hush!" the Rabbit whispered in a frightened tone. "The Queen will hear you! You see she came rather late,
T3   130: 2   haven't got one," Alice said in a frightened tone: "there wasn't a ticket-office where I came from." And
A9   70: 8   she said to herself (not in a very hopeful tone, though), "I wo'n't have any pepper in my kitchen at all.
T7   170:18   such eyes," the King remarked in a fretful tone. "To be able to see Nobody! And at that distance too! Why
T5   153: 9   "Ca'n't you?" the Queen said in a pitying tone. "Try again: draw a long breath, and shut your eyes."
A3   22:35   going to say," said the Dodo in an offended tone, "was that the best thing to get us dry would be a
T9   195:17   quarrel," the White Queen said in an anxious tone. "What is the cause of lightning?"
A4   27:13   about, and called out to her, in an angry tone, "Why, Mary Ann, what are you doing out here? Run home
T8W   14: 3   "How you go on!" the Wasp said in a peevish tone. "Worrity, worrity! There never was such a child!"
T4   146:24   her hand upon his arm and said, in a soothing tone, "You needn't be so angry about an old rattle."
TONES (3)
A12   98:19   looking up into hers--she could hear the very tones of her voice, and see that queer little toss of her head
A10   82:27   as a lark, / And will talk in contemptuous tones of the Shark: / But, when the tide rises and sharks are
AI   3:15   forth / Her edict "to begin it": / In gentler tones Secunda hopes / "There will be nonsense in it!" / While
TONGUE (5)
A9   76: 3   "Hold your tongue!" added the Gryphon, before Alice could speak again.
T2   122:36   "Hold your tongue!" cried the Tiger-lily. "As if you ever saw anybody!
A4   33: 1   it sat down a good way off, panting, with its tongue hanging out of its mouth, and its great eyes half shut
A3   26:19   to you never to lose your temper!" "Hold your tongue, Ma!" said the young Crab, a little snappishly. "You're
A12   97: 3   "Hold your tongue!" said the Queen, turning purple.
TONGUES (2)
T2   122:15   again, she whispered "If you don't hold your tongues, I'll pick you!"
AI   3:12   what can one poor voice avail / Against three tongues together?
TO-NIGHT (2)
T3   130:16   "I shall dream about a thousand pounds to-night, I know I shall!" thought Alice.
A1   9: 6   talking again. "Dinah'll miss me very much to-night, I should think!" (Dinah was the cat.) "I hope
TOO (67)
A11   88:44   Alice more boldly: "you know you're growing too."
T8   179:35   White Knight remarked, putting on his helmet too.
T8   184:40   she said cheerfully. "Is that your invention too?"
T8   185:23   another man's helmet on--with the man in it, too."
T6   160:30   "Now I declare that's too bad!" Humpty Dumpty cried, breaking into a sudden passion.
T2   120:24   "Oh, it's too bad!" she cried. "I never saw such a house for getting in
A2   18:16   as this before, never! And I declare it's too bad, that it is!"
A12   98:15   and all her wonderful Adventures, till she too began dreaming after a fashion, and this was her dream:--
A10   82:23   I heard him declare / 'You have baked me too brown, I must sugar my hair.' / As a duck with his eyelids
T1   110:38   smokes, and then smoke comes up in that room too--but that may be only pretence, just to make it look as if
A11   89:26   anxiously round to see if he would deny it too; but the Dormouse denied nothing, being fast asleep.
A10   79:10   then treading on her toes when they passed too close, and waving her fore-paws to mark the time, while
A1   8:14   make out what she was coming to, but it was too dark to see anything: then she looked at the sides of the
A10   80: 3   to sea!" / But the snail replied "Too far, too far!", and gave a look askance--/ Said he thanked the
A2   14: 8   I sha'n't be able! I shall be a great deal too far off to trouble myself about you: you must manage the
A10   80: 3   out to sea!" / But the snail replied "Too far, too far!", and gave a look askance--/ Said he thanked
T6   161:15   this conversation is going on a little too fast: let's go back to the last remark but one."
A4   31:20   thank ye; I'm better now--but I'm a deal too flustered to tell you--all I know is, something comes at
A10   84: 7   off," said the Gryphon, and Alice was only too glad to do so.
T7   172:28   for this, as she wanted to hear the news too. However, instead of whispering, he simply shouted, at the
T7   175:29   thought Unicorns were fabulous monsters, too? I never saw one alive before!"
T2   123:24   replied. "I was wondering you hadn't got some too. I thought it was the regular rule."
T8W   16: 7   "You'd be cross too, if you'd a wig like mine," the Wasp went on. "They jokes
T9   197:10   sing it through to me. I'm getting sleepy, too." In another moment both Queens were fast asleep, and
A1   9:37   of the hall; but, alas! either the locks were too large, or the key was too small, but at any rate it would
T4   145:25   never get at me here," she thought: "it's far too large to squeeze itself in among the trees. But I wish it
T6   162: 5   I'd have said 'Leave off at seven'--but it's too late now."
T5   152:19   And she caught at the brooch; but it was too late: the pin had slipped, and the Queen had pricked her
T9   195:22   "It's too late to correct it," said the Red Queen: "when you've once
A4   28:15   Alas! It was too late to wish that! She went on growing, and growing, and
A1   7:13   say to itself "Oh dear! Oh dear! I shall be too late!" (when she thought it over afterwards it occurred to
A1   11: 2   a red-hot poker will burn you if you hold it too long; and that, if you cut your finger very deeply with a
T6   159:32   "That last line is much too long for the poetry," she added, almost out loud,
T1   115: 5   invisible hand, and being dusted: he was far too much astonished to cry out, but his eyes and his mouth
T7   177: 4   growled out as he lay down again. "There was too much dust to see anything. What a time the Monster is,
T9   204:24   have felt surprised at this, but she was far too much excited to be surprised at anything now. "As for you
A9   72:41   game," the Queen said to Alice; and Alice was too much frightened to say a word, but slowly followed her
T2   124:15   Alice wondered a little at this, but she was too much in awe of the Queen to disbelieve it. "I'll try it
T8W   21: 7   "Then your eyes--they're too much in front, no doubt. One would have done as well as
A6   47: 7   There was certainly too much of it in the air. Even the Duchess sneezed
T7   171: 8   this moment the Messenger arrived: he was far too much out of breath to say a word, and could only wave his
A12   93:13   accident, all except the Lizard, who seemed too much overcome to do anything but sit with its mouth open,
A6   47: 5   "There's certainly too much pepper in that soup!" Alice said to herself, as well
T6   164: 7   "Oh!" said Alice. She was too much puzzled to make any other remark.
T6   163:37   Alice was too much puzzled to say anything; so after a minute Humpty

TOO (cont.)
```
A7     59: 7   of living would be like, but it puzzled her too much: so she went on: "But why did they live at the bottom
T1    108:36   were you? How do you know she wasn't thirsty too? Now for number three: you unwound every bit of the
T6    162: 8                                              "Too proud?" the other enquired.
T8    184:11                              "It's too ridiculous!" cried Alice, losing all her patience this
A9     76: 7          "I've been to a day-school, too," said Alice. "You needn't be so proud as all that."
T8W    21: 1      "Well, that's because your jaws are too short," the Wasp went on: "but the top of your head is
A1     12:19   up one of the legs of the table, but it was too slippery; and when she had tired herself out with trying,
A1      9:38   the locks were too large, or the key was too small, but at any rate it would not open any of them.
T7    172:18   said the King: "this young lady saw him too. So of course Nobody walks slower than you."
T2    122:28   the Tiger-lily said, "they make the beds too soft--so that the flowers are always asleep."
A9     77: 3   it you, myself," the Mock Turtle said: "I'm too stiff. And the Gryphon never learnt it."
T1    115:36   time without saying anything; but Alice was too strong for him, and at last he panted out "My dear! I
A11    86:25   proud of it: for she thought, and rightly too, that very few little girls of her age knew the meaning of
T9    195:44          "Humpty Dumpty saw it too," the White Queen went on in a low voice, more as if she
T4    143:30   said nothing but / 'The butter's spread too thick!'
T12   208:10   of course--but then I was part of his dream, too! Was it the Red King, Kitty? You were his wife, my dear,
A5     39: 1   are old," said the youth, "and your jaws are too weak / For anything tougher than suet; / Yet you finished
AI      3: 9   dreamy weather, / To beg a tale of breath too weak / To stir the tiniest feather! / Yet what can one
T7    170:18   be able to see Nobody! And at that distance too! Why, it's as much as I can do to see real people, by this
T6    160:10   shape I am--and a good handsome shape it is, too. With a name like yours, you might be any shape, almost."
T8W    18: 8   she would try if the Wasp couldn't do it too. "Would you mind saying it in rhyme?" she asked very
T2    126: 9   White Queen's Pawn, if you like, as Lily's too young to play: and you're in the Second Square to begin
```
TOOK (60)
```
T6    168: 8                         I took a corkscrew from the shelf: / I went to wake them up
A7     58:35   did they live on?" said Alice, who always took a great interest in questions of eating and drinking.
T6    167:13                         I took a kettle large and new, / Fit for the deed I had to do.
T7    175:39              Haigha took a large cake out of the bag, and gave it to Alice to hold
T8    182:15              This took a long time to manage, though Alice held the bag open
A7     59:22          The Dormouse again took a minute or two to think about it, and then said "It was
T9    203:17   at the top. As to the bottles, they each took a pair of plates, which they hastily fitted on as wings,
T7    174:15   round trays of white and brown bread. Alice took a piece to taste, but it was very dry.
T2    127:32   "I'll just take the measurements." And she took a ribbon out of her pocket, marked in inches, and began
A1      7:16   quite natural); but, when the Rabbit actually took a watch out of its waistcoat-pocket, and looked at it,
T1    115:29   looked on with great interest as the King took an enormous memorandum-book out of his pocket, and began
T6    168:35   again, but, as he never opened his eyes or took any further notice of her, she said "Good-bye!" once more
T4    144:17   that the Carpenter couldn't count how many he took: contrariwise.--
A6     47:18   addressed to the baby, and not to her, so she took courage, and went on again:--
A1      8:17   she saw maps and pictures hung upon pegs. She took down a jar from one of the shelves as she passed: it was
T8W    14:11                         The Wasp took her arms, and let her help him round the tree, but when
T3    129:13   Alice soon found out, though the idea quite took her breath away at first. "And what enormous flowers they
A9     72:39              The Duchess took her choice, and was gone in a moment.
T10   205: 1              She took her off the table as she spoke, and shook her backwards
T1    118: 5              He took his vorpal sword in hand: / Long time the manxome foe he
T4    139:27   as the best way out of the difficulty, she took hold of both hands at once: the next moment they were
T1    115:31   writing. A sudden thought struck her, and she took hold of the end of the pencil, which came some way over
T8    185:10   And then he took the helmet off again--but it took hours and hours to get me out. I was as fast as--as
T8    187:24   shadows of the forest behind--all this she took in like a picture, as, with one hand shading her eyes,
T2    127:28   though it wasn't at all what she wanted. She took it, and ate it as well as she could: and it was very dry:
T9    194:11   "The bone wouldn't remain, of course, if I took it--and the dog wouldn't remain: it would come to bite me
T9    201:14   Pudding. Remove the pudding!" and the waiters took it away so quickly that Alice couldn't return its bow.
T6    161: 5   She watched him a little anxiously as she took it. "If he smiled much more the ends of his mouth might
A4     27:18              "He took me for his housemaid," she said to herself as she ran.
T1    114:21   far better help you, hadn't I?" But the King took no notice of the question: it was quite clear that he
A6     48:13   of saucepans, plates, and dishes. The Duchess took no notice of them even when they hit her; and the baby
T4    147: 3   an extraordinary thing to do, that it quite took off Alice's attention from the angry brother. But he
T3    131:39   that it tickled her ear very much, and quite took off her thoughts from the unhappiness of the poor little
T8W    21: 3   the top of your head is nice and round." He took off his own wig as he spoke, and stetched out one claw
T4    144:28   at him!" the brothers cried, and they each took one of Alice's hands, and led her up to where the King
T6    163: 6   Alice couldn't help smiling as she took out her memorandum-book, and worked the sum for him:
A10    83:16   the Panther were sharing a pie: / The Panther took pie-crust, and gravy, and meat, / While the Owl had the
T6    163:13              Humpty Dumpty took the book and looked at it carefully. "That seems to be
A6     48: 9   While she was trying to fix on one, the cook took the cauldron of soup off the fire, and at once set to
T8    185:10   the Knight said, very seriously. "And then he took the helmet off again--but it took hours and hours to get
A5     35: 2   some time in silence: at last the Caterpillar took the hookah out of its mouth, and addressed her in a
A5     36:29   speaking; but at last it unfolded its arms, took the hookah out of its mouth again, and said "So you think
A5     41:24   again. In a minute or two the Caterpillar took the hookah out of its mouth, and yawned once or twice,
A7     60:31   asleep instantly, and neither of the others took the least notice of her going, though she looked back
T5    158:13              The Sheep took the money, and put it away in a box: then she said "I
A3     26:17   as it was quite out of sight. And an old Crab took the opportunity of saying to her daughter "Ah, my dear!
A7     59:40          place, and Alice rather unwillingly took the place of the March Hare. The Hatter was the only one
A9     76:19   said the Mock Turtle with a sigh. "I only took the regular course."
A3     24: 7   of anything to say, she simply bowed, and took the thimble, looking as solemn as she could.
A7     56: 7              The March Hare took the watch and looked at it gloomily: then he dipped it
A11    87:19   Knave of Hearts, he stole those tarts / And took them quite away!"
A5     39: 5          "In my youth," said his father, "I took to the law, / And argued each case with my wife; / And
T4    148:22   a shrill voice of alarm; and the two brothers took to their heels and were out of sight in a moment.
T5    155: 7   child or a teetotum?" the Sheep said, as she took up another pair of needles. "You'll make me giddy soon,
T5    155:21          "Feather!" cried the Sheep, as she took up another pair of needles.
T8    179:32   for her, then," said the Red Knight, as he took up his helmet (which hung from the saddle, and was
```

TOOK (cont.)
    A4   27:38   or three pairs of tiny white kid-gloves: she took up the fan and a pair of the gloves, and was just going
    A2   15:36   Alice took up the fan and gloves, and, as the hall was very hot, she
    A2   15:14   more than nine feet high, and she at once took up the little golden key and hurried off to the garden
    T8   188:17   His accents mild took up the tale: / He said 'I go my ways, / And when I find a
TOOTHACHE (3)
    T4   147:36   "And I've got a toothache!" said Tweedledee, who had overheard the remark.
    T8W   16:16   catch the word exactly. "Is it a kind of toothache?" she asked.
    T8W   16:13   him. "Tying up the face is very good for the toothache," she said.
TOP (21)
    T9   203:16   like a bed of rushes with fireworks at the top. As to the bottles, they each took a pair of plates, which
    T6   159: 9   with his legs crossed like a Turk, on the top of a high wall--such a narrow one that Alice quite
    A1   12:39   way? Which way?", holding her hand on the top of her head to feel which way it was growing; and she was
    T9   202:21   Queen Alice's health!" she screamed at the top of her voice, and all the guests began drinking it
    A12   97: 5   "Off with her head!" the Queen shouted at the top of her voice. Nobody moved.
    T8   185: 8   she said in a trembling voice, "being on the top of his head."
    A6   46:24   herself; "his eyes are so very nearly at the top of his head. But at any rate he might answer questions.--
    T8   183:20   had begun, as the White Knight fell heavily on the top of his head exactly in the path where Alice was walking.
    A11   91:32   when the White Rabbit read out, at the top of his shrill little voice, the name "Alice!"
    T7   172:29   of whispering, he simply shouted, at the top of his voice, "They're at it again!"
    A4   34: 6   she might as well look and see what was on top of it.
    A10   78:33   lobsters again!" yelled the Gryphon at the top of its voice.
    T2   125: 7   and I thought I'd try and find my way to the top of that hill--"
    T2   120: 2   said Alice to herself, "if I could get to the top of that hill: and here's a path that leads straight to it
    T8   184:31   already.' Now, first I put my head on the top of the gate--then the head's high enough--then I stand on
    A1   8:26   say anything about it, even if I fell off the top of the house!" (Which was very likely true.)
    T2   125:18   walked on in silence till they got to the top of the little hill.
    T8W   21: 2   are too short," the Wasp went on: "but the top of your head is nice and round." He took off his own wig
    T5   155: 3   struck her. "I'll follow it up to the very top shelf of all. It'll puzzle it to go through the ceiling, I
    T6   168:30   the nose, for instance--or the mouth at the top--that would be some help."
    A4   34: 9   blue caterpillar, that was sitting on the top, with its arms folded, quietly smoking a long hookah, and
TOPS (1)
    A5   42:23   leaves, which she found to be nothing but the tops of the trees under which she had been wandering, when a
TORTOISE (3)
    A9   74:43   master was an old Turtle--we used to call him Tortoise--"
    A9   75: 2   "We called him Tortoise because he taught us," said the Mock Turtle angrily.
    A9   75: 1   "Why did you call him Tortoise, if he wasn't one?" Alice asked.
TOSS (2)
    A12   98:20   tones of her voice, and see that queer little toss of her head to keep back the wandering hair that would
    T3   129:23   enough--' (here came the favourite little toss of the head), 'only it was so dusty and hot, and the
TOSSING (3)
    A8   63:38   "Idiot!" said the Queen, tossing her head impatiently; and turning to Alice, she went
    A7   56:38   "Of course you don't!" the Hatter said, tossing his head contemptuously. "I dare say you never even
    A6   49: 2   sang the second verse of the song, she kept tossing the baby violently up and down, and the poor little
TOUCH (2)
    A4   32:28   and feebly stretching out one paw, trying to touch her. "Poor little thing!" said Alice, in a coaxing tone,
    TI   103:35   / And vanish'd summer glory--/ It shall not touch, with breath of bale, / The pleasance of our fairy-tale
TOUCHED (2)
    T3   132:16   But the beard seemed to melt away as she touched it, and she found herself sitting quietly under a tree
    T8   185: 1   wear it, if I fell off the horse, it always touched the ground directly. So I had a very little way to
TOUCHING (3)
    T1   108: 9   now and then putting out one paw and gently touching the ball, as if it would be glad to help if it might
    T2   127: 7   they seemed to skim through the air, hardly touching the ground with their feet, till suddenly, just as
    T1   119: 6   and floated gently down without even touching the stairs with her feet: then she floated on through
TOUGHER (1)
    A5   39: 2   "and your jaws are too weak / For anything tougher than suet; / Yet you finished the goose, with the
TOUR (1)
    T8W   14:21   News. The Exploring Party have made another tour in the Pantry, and have found five new lumps of white
TOVES (6)
    T6   164:34   Alice remarked thoughtfully: "and what are 'toves'?"
    T6   164:35   "Well 'toves' are something like badgers--they're something like
    T1   116: 9   / :ebaw eht ni elbmig dna eryg diD / sevot yhtils eht dna ,gillirb sawT'
    T1   116:18   'Twas brillig, and the slithy toves / Did gyre and gimble in the wabe: / All mimsy were the
    T1   118:21   'Twas brillig, and the slithy toves / Did gyre and gimble in the wabe: / All mimsy were the
    T6   164:21   "'Twas brillig, and the slithy toves / Did gyre and gimble in the wabe: / All mimsy were the
TOWARDS (9)
    T8W   21: 4   wig as he spoke, and stetched out one claw towards Alice, as if he wished to do the same for her, but she
    T2   122:12   them!" it panted, bending its quivering head towards Alice, "or they wouldn't dare to do it!"
    T9   204:11   and the soup ladle was walking up the table towards Alice's chair, and beckoning to her impatiently to get
    T9   198:14   under a tree, got up and hobbled slowly towards her: he was dressed in bright yellow, and had enormous
    T7   175:20   her, and spreading out both his hands towards her in an Anglo-Saxon attitude. "We only found it
    T5   158:20   egg seems to get further away the more I walk towards it. Let me see, is this a chair? Why, it's got
    A6   53:16   about two feet high: even then she walked up towards it rather timidly, saying to herself "Suppose it
    T5   158:19   tables and chairs, for the shop was very dark towards the end. "The egg seems to get further away the more I
    T2   123:41   so she said nothing, but set off at once towards the Red Queen. To her surprise she lost sight of her
TOWN (8)
    T7   172:24   you may tell us what's happened in the town."
    T7   173: 4   gave them plum-cake and drummed them out of town."
    T7   170:36   Alice was still hesitating for the name of a town beginning with H. "The other Messenger's called Hatta. I
    T7   176:25   and his voice quite quivered. "All round the town?" he said. "That's a good long way. Did you go by the old

TOWN (cont.)
```
  T7    170:14  Messengers, either. They're both gone to the town. Just look along the road, and tell me if you can see
  T7    178:11              "If that doesn't 'drum them out of town,'" she thought to herself, "nothing ever will!"
  T7    173: 2  / The Lion beat the Unicorn all round the town. / Some gave them white bread, some gave them brown: /
  T7    176:21              "Why, I beat you all round the town, you chicken!" the Lion replied angrily, half getting up
```
TOWNS (1)
```
  T3    129: 6  I don't think it's got any name. Principal towns--why, what are those creatures, making honey down there?
```
TOYS (1)
```
  A2     17:19  that poky little house, and have next to no toys to play with, and oh, ever so many lessons to learn! No,
```
TRAILING (1)
```
  T9    204:21  and round after her own shawl, which was trailing behind her.
```
TRAIN (2)
```
  T3    131:21    by the telegraph--" "She must draw the train herself the rest of the way--," and so on.
  T3    131:25  dear, but take a return-ticket every time the train stops."
```
TRAINS (1)
```
  T3    132: 8  Alice felt a little nervous at the idea of trains jumping at all. "However, it'll take us into the Fourth
```
TRAMPLED (1)
```
  A4     32:41  cart-horse, and expecting every moment to be trampled under its feet, ran round the thistle again: then the
```
TRANSPORT (1)
```
  T5    156: 7  some scented rushes!" Alice cried in a sudden transport of delight. "There really are--and such beauties!"
```
TRAVEL (1)
```
  T3    129: 2  grand survey of the country she was going to travel through. "It's something very like learning geography,"
```
-TRAVELER [See FELLOW-TRAVELER]
TRAVELING (1)
```
  T3    130:20   an opera-glass. At last he said "You're traveling the wrong way," and shut up the window, and went
```
TRAYS (1)
```
  T7    174:15  and Hatta set to work at once, carrying round trays of white and brown bread. Alice took a piece to taste,
```
TREACLE (8)
```
  T9    200: 1            "Then fill up the glasses with treacle and ink, / Or anything else that is pleasant to drink.
  A7     60: 5  I don't understand. Where did they draw the treacle from?"
  A7     60: 7  the Hatter; "so I should think you could draw treacle out of a treacle-well--eh, stupid?"
  A11    91:18                       "Treacle," said a sleepy voice behind her.
  A7     59: 1              "They lived on treacle," said the Dormouse, after thinking a minute or two.
  A7     59:34              "Treacle," said the Dormouse, without considering at all, this
  T8W    15: 6  Alice went on reading, "they found a lake of treacle. The banks of the lake were blue and white, and looked
  T8W    15: 7  and looked like china. While tasting the treacle, they had a sad accident: two of their party were
```
TREACLE-WELL (2)
```
  A7     59:23  to think about it, and then said "It was a treacle-well."
  A7     60: 7  should think you could draw treacle out of a treacle-well--eh, stupid?"
```
TREADING (2)
```
  A10    79:10  round and round Alice, every now and then treading on her toes when they passed too close, and waving
  A10    79:14  "There's a porpoise close behind us, and he's treading on my tail. / See how eagerly the lobsters and the
```
TREASURES (1)
```
  T5    156:33  her place, and began to arrange her new-found treasures.
```
TREAT (4)
```
  T12   208: 2  To-morrow morning you shall have a real treat. All the time you're eating your breakfast, I'll repeat
  T9    201:40  the cooing of a pigeon. "It would be such a treat! May I?"
  T4    142: 2  young Oysters hurried up, / All eager for the treat: / Their coats were brushed, their faces washed, / Their
  A10    83:17  the Owl had the dish as its share of the treat. / When the pie was all finished, the Owl, as a boon, /
```
TREATED (1)
```
  A6     51: 3  many teeth, so she felt that it ought to be treated with respect.
```
TREE (28) [See also FRUIT-TREE, ROSE-TREE, WILLOW-TREE]
```
  A6     52:28  was the Cat again, sitting on a branch of a tree.
  A8     68:21  in a helpless sort of way to fly up into a tree.
  T4    146:15  finger at a small white thing lying under the tree.
  A6     50:21  the Cheshire-Cat sitting on a bough of a tree a few yards off.
  T8W    13: 6  was sitting on the ground, leaning against a tree, all huddled up together, and shivering as if he were
  T8W    16: 9  cross. And I gets cold. And I gets under a tree. And I gets a yellow handkerchief. And I ties up my face
  T9    199:21  he panted out, as he hobbled back to his tree, "and it'll let you alone, you know."
  T2    127:10            The Queen propped her up against a tree, and said kindly, "You may rest a little, now."
  T1    118: 7  foe he sought--/ So rested he by the Tumtum tree, / And stood awhile in thought.
  T2    128: 5  on with great interest as she returned to the tree, and then began slowly walking down the row.
  T8W    14:12  took her arms, and let her help him round the tree, but when he got settled down again he only said, as
  T8    181:27  to strike him, and he hung it carefully on a tree. "Can you guess why I did that?" he said to Alice.
  T4    138: 1              They were standing under a tree, each with an arm round the other's neck, and Alice knew
  T7    169: 4  to fill the whole forest. Alice got behind a tree, for fear of being run over, and watched them go by.
  T9    198:13  last a very old Frog, who was sitting under a tree, got up and hobbled slowly towards her: he was dressed in
  A7     54: 1            There was a table set out under a tree in front of the house, and the March Hare and the Hatter
  T2    122: 1              "There's the tree in the middle," said the Rose. "What else is it good for
  A5     43: 1  "And just as I'd taken the highest tree in the wood," continued the Pigeon, raising its voice to
  T4    145:25  way into the wood, and stopped under a large tree. "It can never get at me here," she thought: "it's far
  T4    148: 7  "I don't suppose," he said, "there'll be a tree left standing, for ever so far round, by the time we've
  T6    159:26  his last remark was evidently addressed to a tree--so she stood and softly repeated to herself:--
  T5    158:28  at every step, as everything turned into a tree the moment she came up to it, and she quite expected the
  T2    127:13  "Why, I do believe we've been under this tree the whole time! Everything's just as it was!"
  T8    179:37  other with such fury that Alice got behind a tree to be out of the way of the blows.
  T4    139:30  music playing: it seemed to come from the tree under which they were dancing, and it was done (as well
  T8    187:25  hand shading her eyes, she leant against a tree, watching the strange pair, and listening, in a
  T3    135:43  know!" putting her hand on the trunk of the tree. "What does it call itself, I wonder? I do believe it's
  T3    132:17  and she found herself sitting quietly under a tree--while the Gnat (for that was the insect she had been
```

TREES (15)
A4   32:25   she was peering about anxiously among the trees, a little sharp bark just over her head made her look up
T3   135:39   comfort," she said as she stepped under the trees, "after being so hot, to get into the--into the--into
T6   160:32   "You've been listening at doors--and behind trees--and down chimneys--or you couldn't have known it!"
T1   109:10   it sounds! I wonder if the snow <u>loves</u> the trees and fields, that it kisses them so gently? And then it
A5   42:33   "I've tried the roots of trees, and I've tried banks, and I've tried hedges," the
T2   126:18   most curious part of the thing was, that the trees and the other things round them never changed their
A5   43:29   into its nest. Alice crouched down among the trees as well as she could, for her neck kept getting
A6   46:29   nose, and broke to pieces against one of the trees behind him.
T5   156: 4   water, worse than ever), and sometimes under trees, but always with the same tall river-banks frowning over
T4   145:26   far too large to squeeze itself in among the trees. But I wish it wouldn't flap its wings so--it makes
T5   158:21   got branches, I declare! How very odd to find trees growing here! And actually here's a little brook! Well,
A7   60:38   as she said this, she noticed that one of the trees had a door leading right into it. "That's very curious!"
T4   148: 4   Alice laughed. "You must hit the <u>trees</u> pretty often, I should think," she said.
A5   42:23   she found to be nothing but the tops of the trees under which she had been wandering, when a sharp hiss
A12   98: 2   dead leaves that had fluttered down from the trees upon her face.
TREMBLE (2)
A9   72:31   the arm that was linked into hers began to tremble. Alice looked up, and there stood the Queen in front
TI   103:32   <u>And, though the shadow of a sigh</u> / <u>May tremble through the story</u>, / <u>For "happy summer days" gone by</u>,
TREMBLED (3)
T7   176:18   poor King was nearly shaking off his head, he trembled so much.
A11   89: 7   last concert!" on which the wretched Hatter trembled so, that he shook off both his shoes.
A4   29:21   the Rabbit coming to look for her, and she trembled till she shook the house, quite forgetting that she
TREMBLING (9)
A2   19:42   "We, indeed!" cried the Mouse, who was trembling down to the end of its tail. "As if <u>I</u> would talk on
T4   146:15   yellow all in a moment, as he pointed with a trembling finger at a small white thing lying under the tree.
A10   83:13   it would all come wrong, and she went on in a trembling voice:--
A12   94: 2   your verdict," he said to the jury, in a low trembling voice.
A11   89:11   man, your Majesty," the Hatter began, in a trembling voice, "and I hadn't begun my tea--not above a week
T8   185: 7   afraid you must have hurt him," she said in a trembling voice, "being on the top of his head."
A2   20:18   Alice thought), and it said, in a low trembling voice, "Let us get to the shore, and then I'll tell
A3   26:34   suit my throat!" And a Canary called out in a trembling voice, to its children, "Come away, my dears! It's
T2   122:10   itself passionately from side to side, and trembling with excitement. "They know I ca'n't get at them!"
TREMENDOUSLY (1)
T6   160:20   "What tremendously easy riddles you ask!" Humpty Dumpty growled out.
TREMULOUS (1)
A10   82:29   <u>are around,</u> / <u>His voice has a timid and tremulous sound</u>."
TRIAL (8)
A11   86:32   they should forget them before the end of the trial."
A12   93: 1   "The trial cannot proceed," said the King, in a very grave voice,
A3   25:27   to do.' Said the mouse to the cur, Such a trial, dear sir, With no jury or judge, would be wasting our
T5   150: 4   He's in prison now, being punished: and the trial doesn't even begin till next Wednesday: and of course
A11   86: 9   to look at them--"I wish they'd get the trial done," she thought, "and hand round the refreshments!"
A3   25:17   --Come, I'll take no denial: We must have the trial; For really this morning I've nothing to do.' Said the
A10   85: 6   "What trial is it?" Alice panted as she ran: but the Gryphon only
A12   93: 9   think it would be <u>quite</u> as much use in the trial one way up as the other."
TRIAL'S (3)
A10   85: 2   just begun to repeat it, when a cry of "The trial's beginning!" was heard in the distance.
A11   86:30   have anything to put down yet, before the trial's begun."
A11   87: 3   nice muddle their slates'll be in, before the trial's over!" thought Alice.
TRIALS (1)
A11   90:17   often read in the newspapers, at the end of trials, 'There was some attempt at applause, which was
TRICK (1) [See also CONJURING-TRICK]
T4   143:26   the Walrus said, / 'To play them such a trick, / After we've brought them out so far, / And made them
TRICKLED (3)
T7   173:31   round once more, and this time a tear or two trickled down his cheek; but not a word would he say.
T9   202:24   heads like extinguishers, and drank all that trickled down their faces--others upset the decanters, and
T8   187:37   / 'And how is it you live?' / And his answer trickled through my head, / Like water through a sieve.
TRICKLING (1)
A12   96:23   hastily began again, using the ink, that was trickling down his face, as long as it lasted.)
TRICKS (1)
A4   33: 9   the leaves. "I should have liked teaching it tricks very much, if--if I'd only been the right size to do
TRIED (32)
A9   71:10   feeling at all anxious to have the experiment tried.
T6   168:33   shut his eyes, and said "Wait till you've tried."
T9   193: 9   the Red Queen. "I said you couldn't if you tried."
A7   59: 6   Alice tried a little to fancy to herself what such an extraordinary
A6   51:17   felt that this could not be denied, so she tried another question. "What sort of people live about here?"
A5   42:33   "I've tried the roots of trees, and I've tried banks, and I've tried hedges," the Pigeon went on,
A5   42:30   tone, and added, with a kind of sob, "I've tried every way, but nothing seems to suit them!"
A4   32:29   said Alice, in a coaxing tone, and she tried hard to whistle to it; but she was terribly frightened
T8   182:17   dish: the first two or three times that he tried he fell in himself instead. "It's rather a tight fit,
A5   42:33   of trees, and I've tried banks, and I've tried hedges," the Pigeon went on, without attending to her;
A1   12:18   it quite plainly through the glass, and she tried her best to climb up one of the legs of the table, but
T8   184:36   "I haven't tried it yet," the Knight said, gravely; "so I ca'n't tell for
T8W   14: 8   only pain that makes him so cross." So she tried once more.
A4   28:17   there was not even room for this, and she tried the effect of lying down with one elbow against the door
A1   9:41   a little door about fifteen inches high: she tried the little golden key in the lock, and to her great
A5   42:33   "I've tried the roots of trees, and I've tried banks, and I've tried
A12   97:11   scream, half of fright and half of anger, and tried to beat them off, and found herself lying on the bank,

TRIED (cont.)
T5   152:17 and the Queen clutched wildly at it, and tried to clasp it again.
A1   8:45   is this New Zealand? Or Australia?" (and she tried to curtsey as she spoke--fancy, _curtseying_ as you're
T8   179: 6 still lying at her feet, on which she had tried to cut the plum-cake, "So I wasn't dreaming, after all,"
A1   12: 9   I wonder what I should be like then?" And she tried to fancy what the flame of a candle looks like after the
A5   42:19   of getting her hands up to her head, she tried to get her head down to _them_, and was delighted to find
A4   29:25   Presently the Rabbit came up to the door, and tried to open it; but, as the door opened inwards, and Alice's
A1   8:13   what was going to happen next. First, she tried to look down and make out what she was coming to, but it
T9   196:38 got a nightcap with me," said Alice, as she tried to obey the first direction: "and I don't know any
A4   29:25   Presently the Rabbit came up to the door, and tried to open it; but, as the door opened inwards, and Alice's
A5   36:34   "Well, I've tried to say 'How _doth_ _the_ _little_ _busy_ _bee_,' but it all came
A10   78: 2   across his eyes. He looked at Alice and tried to speak, but, for a minute or two, sobs choked his
T3   136: 9 Alice said, as she held out her hand and tried to stroke it; but it only started back a little, and
T9   202:37 the Red Queen said very decidedly: so Alice tried to submit to it with good grace.
T6   168:13 _And_ _when_ _I_ _found_ _the_ _door_ _was_ _shut_, / _I_ tried _to_ _turn_ _the_ _handle_, _but_--"
T9   193: 5 I hope. You couldn't deny that, even if you tried with both hands."
TRIFLE (2)
T4   148:10 them a _little_ ashamed of fighting for such a trifle.
T8   188: 8 / _And_ _that's_ _the_ _way_ _I_ _get_ _my_ _bread_--/ _A_ trifle, _if_ _you_ _please_.'
TRIMS (1)
A10   82:25   _duck_ _with_ _his_ _eyelids_, _so_ _he_ _with_ _his_ _nose_ / _Trims_ _his_ _belt_ _and_ _his_ _buttons_, _and_ _turns_ _out_ _his_ _toes_. / _When_
TRIPPED (1)
T8W   21:16   and thank-ye," said the Wasp, and Alice tripped down the hill again, quite pleased that she had gone
TRIPPING (1)
T7   169: 6 so uncertain on their feet: they were always tripping over something or other, and whenever one went down,
TRIUMPHANT (1)
T5   153:21 it herself. "I've got it!" she cried in a triumphant tone. "Now you shall see me pin it on again, all by
TRIUMPHANTLY (8)
A7   59:16   personal remarks now?" the Hatter asked triumphantly.
T5   151:17 the better for it, I know!" the Queen said triumphantly.
T9   194:22 its temper would remain!" the Queen exclaimed triumphantly.
T9   195:13 tell you the French for it!" she exclaimed triumphantly.
T4   145: 5 Tweedledee exclaimed, clapping his hands triumphantly. "And if he left off dreaming about you, where do
T12   207:16 "Now Kitty!" she cried, clapping her hands triumphantly. "Confess that was what you turned into!"
A12   96:13   "Why, there they are!" said the King triumphantly, pointing to the tarts on the table. "Nothing can
T6   161:24   "Wrong!" Humpty Dumpty exclaimed triumphantly. "You never said a word like it!"
TROT (2)
A6   50:15   down, and felt quite relieved to see it trot away quietly into the wood. "If it had grown up," she
T4   143:28 _brought_ _them_ _out_ _so_ _far_, / _And_ _made_ _them_ trot _so_ _quick_!' / _The_ _Carpenter_ _said_ _nothing_ _but_ / '_The_
TROTTED (2)
T7   172:40 the while! Let's run and see them." And they trotted off, Alice repeating to herself, as she ran, the words
T7   173:14 Alice had no more breath for talking; so they trotted on in silence, till they came into sight of a great
TROTTING (3)
A2   15:28   hand and a large fan in the other: he came trotting along in a great hurry, muttering to himself, as he
T4   144: 9 / '_You've_ _had_ _a_ _pleasant_ _run_! / _Shall_ _we_ _be_ trotting _home_ _again_?' / _But_ _answer_ _came_ _there_ _none_--/ _And_ _this_
A4   27: 1   It was the White Rabbit, trotting slowly back again, and looking anxiously about as it
TROUBLE (8)
T6   166: 2 "I'm afraid I'm giving you a great deal of trouble."
A5   42:38   "As if it wasn't trouble enough hatching the eggs," said the Pigeon; "but I
A2   14: 8   able! I shall be a great deal too far off to trouble myself about you: you must manage the best way you can
A1   7: 8   of making a daisy-chain would be worth the trouble of getting up and picking the daisies, when suddenly a
A9   72:18   "Oh, don't talk about trouble!" said the Duchess. "I make you a present of
T4   147:20 the quantity of things they put on--and the trouble they gave her in tying strings and fastening buttons--
A12   95:31   in it," said the King, "that saves a world of trouble, you know, as we needn't try to find any. And yet I
A9   72:16   "Pray don't trouble yourself to say it any longer than that," said Alice.
TROUGH (1)
T9   202:28 lapping up the gravy, "just like pigs in a trough!" thought Alice.
TRUE (6)
AI   3:24   _with_ _bird_ _or_ _beast_--/ _And_ _half_ _believe_ _it_ _true_.
A1   8:26   the top of the house!" (Which was very likely true.)
A12   95: 2   _them_ _word_ _I_ _had_ _not_ _gone_ / (_We_ _know_ _it_ _to_ _be_ _true_): / _If_ _she_ _should_ _push_ _the_ _matter_ _on_, / _What_ _would_ _become_
T1   110: 2 to clap her hands. "And I do so _wish_ it was true! I'm sure the woods look sleepy in the autumn, when the
A9   71:11   "Very true," said the Duchess: "flamingoes and mustard both bite.
A12   95:39   the verses to himself: "'_We_ _know_ _it_ _to_ _be_ _true_'--that's the jury, of course--'_If_ _she_ _should_ _push_ _the_
TRUMPET (4)
A11   88: 5   and the White Rabbit blew three blasts on the trumpet, and called out "First witness!"
T7   172:26 his hands to his mouth in the shape of a trumpet and stooping so as to get close to the King's ear·
A11   87:14   the White Rabbit blew three blasts on the trumpet, and then unrolled the parchment-scroll, and read as
A11   86: 6   near the King was the White Rabbit, with a trumpet in one hand, and a scroll of parchment in the other.
TRUNK (1)
T3   135:43 this, you know!" putting her hand on the trunk of the tree. "What _does_ it call itself, I wonder? I do
TRUSTS (1)
A12   95:11   _chance_ _to_ _be_ / _Involved_ _in_ _this_ _affair_, / _He_ _trusts_ _to_ _you_ _to_ _set_ _them_ _free_, / _Exactly_ _as_ _we_ _were_.
TRUTH (2)
A1   9:18   her, very earnestly, "Now, Dinah, tell me the truth: did you ever eat a bat?" when suddenly, thump! thump!
T9   192:36 Red Queen said to Alice. "Always speak the truth--think before you speak--and write it down afterwards."
TRUTHFUL (1)
A5   43:16   eggs, certainly," said Alice, who was a very truthful child; "but little girls eat eggs quite as much as
TRY (29)
T5   153: 9 you?" the Queen said in a pitying tone. "Try again: draw a long breath, and shut your eyes."

TRY (cont.)
T2   125: 7   the point, but went on: "--and I thought I'd try and find my way to the top of that hill--"
A10   82:12   thoughtfully. "I should like to hear her try and repeat something now. Tell her to begin." He looked at
A2   17: 3   I must have been changed for Mabel! I'll try and say 'How doth the little--'," and she crossed her
T6   166:30   spring, when woods are getting green, / I'll try and tell you what I mean:"
A10   84: 8   "Shall we try another figure of the Lobster-Quadrille?" the Gryphon went
T9   194: 8   for her. "Bread-and-butter, of course. Try another Subtraction sum. Take a bone from a dog: what
A2   17: 1   Multiplication-Table doesn't signify: let's try Geography. London is the capital of Paris, and Paris is
A2   16: 8   I, and--oh dear, how puzzling it all is! I'll try if I know all the things I used to know. Let me see: four
T8W   18: 8   poetry to her, and she thought she would try if the Wasp couldn't do it too. "Would you mind saying it
T8   182:35   It's a plan of my own invention. You may try it if you like."
T2   120: 8   straight back to the house! Well then, I'll try it the other way."
T2   124:16   in awe of the Queen to disbelieve it. "I'll try it when I go home," she thought to herself, "the next time
T2   127:23   "I'd rather not try, please!" said Alice. "I'm quite content to stay here--
A5   41:39   and nibbled a little of the right-hand bit to try the effect. The next moment she felt a violent blow
A9   71: 7   about the temper of your flamingo. Shall I try the experiment'"
A10   79: 5   "Come, let's try the first figure!" said the Mock Turtle to the Gryphon.
A3   26:20   Crab, a little snappishly. "You're enough to try the patience of an oyster!"
T2   124: 1   last, a long way off), she thought she would try the plan, this time, of walking in the opposite direction
A3   23: 6   it is to do it." (And, as you might like to try the thing yourself some winter-day, I will tell you how
A3   25:45   I'll be jury, said cunning old Fury: 'I'll try the whole cause, and condemn you to death.
T1   110:23   arms, you'd look exactly like her. Now do try, there's a dear!" And Alice got the Red Queen off the
T7   175: 5   runs so fearfully quick. You might as well try to catch a Bandersnatch! But I'll make a memorandum about
A12   95:31   a world of trouble, you know, as we needn't try to find any. And yet I don't know," he went on, spreading
T9   196:17   Alice thought to herself "I never should try to remember my name in the middle of an accident! Where
T7   173:12   goes by so fearfully quick. You might as well try to stop a Bandersnatch!"
T2   126:23   her thoughts, for she cried "Faster! Don't try to talk!"
T8W   17: 6   you'll know. And when you catches it, just try tying a yellow handkerchief round your face. It'll cure
T8W   18:11   I'm used to," said the Wasp: "however I'll try; wait a bit." He was silent for a few moments, and then
TRYING (24)
A8   65: 7   going down on one knee as he spoke, "we were trying--"
A1   9:32   all the way down one side and up the other, trying every door, she walked sadly down the middle, wondering
T4   147: 1   All this time Tweedledee was trying his best to fold up the umbrella, with himself in it:
A8   68:21   side of the garden, where Alice could see it trying in a helpless sort of way to fly up into a tree.
T5   153:11   Alice laughed. "There's no use trying," she said: "one ca'n't believe impossible things."
A2   19:12   it can talk: at any rate, there's no harm in trying." So she began: "O Mouse, do you know the way out of
A1   12:20   and when she had tired herself out with trying, the poor little thing sat down and cried.
A1   12:25   tears into her eyes, and once she remembered trying to box her own ears for having cheated herself in a
A4   27:17   once in the direction it pointed to, without trying to explain the mistake that it had made.
T8   186:42   the name of the song, is it?" Alice said, trying to feel interested.
A2   19: 2   so much!" said Alice, as she swam about, trying to find her way out. "I shall be punished for it now, I
T3   129:19   she was beginning to run down the hill, and trying to find some excuse for turning shy so suddenly. "It'll
T3   135:31   to be an ugly one. But then the fun would be, trying to find the creature that has got my old name! That's
A6   48: 9   other subject of conversation. While she was trying to fix on one, the cook took the cauldron of soup off
A5   43: 7   are you?" said the Pigeon. "I can see you're trying to invent something!"
A5   41:34   thoughtfully at the mushroom for a minute, trying to make out which were the two sides of it; and, as it
T1   107:10   white kitten, which was lying quite still and trying to purr--no doubt feeling that it was all meant for its
A7   60:33   her: the last time she saw them, they were trying to put the Dormouse into the teapot.
T7   178:10   and put her hands over her ears, vainly trying to shut out the dreadful uproar.
A4   32:28   eyes, and feebly stretching out one paw, trying to touch her. "Poor little thing!" said Alice, in a
T1   107:16   romps with the ball of worsted Alice had been trying to wind up, and had been rolling it up and down till it
T2   120: 9   And so she did: wandering up and down, and trying turn after turn, but always coming back to the house,
T9   199:10   and rubbed it with his thumb, as if he were trying whether the paint would come off: then he looked at
A12   93:28   unimportant--important--" as if he were trying which word sounded best.
TUCKED (3)
A8   66: 7   flamingo: she succeeded in getting its body tucked away, comfortably enough, under her arm, with its legs
A9   70: 2   you dear old thing!" said the Duchess, as she tucked her arm affectionately into Alice's, and they walked
A8   68:25   gone from this side of the ground." So she tucked it away under her arm, that it might not escape again,
TUESDAY (1)
T9   195:27   her hands, "we had such a thunderstorm last Tuesday--I mean one of the last set of Tuesdays, you know."
TUESDAYS (1)
T9   195:27   last Tuesday--I mean one of the last set of Tuesdays, you know."
TULGEY (1)
T1   118:11   eyes of flame, / Came whiffling through the tulgey wood, / And burbled as it came!
TULIP-ROOTS (1)
A8   62:16   I'll tell him--it was for bringing the cook tulip-roots instead of onions."
TUMBLE (4)
T8   183: 4   say, as she was helping him up from his fifth tumble.
T8   183:16   and Alice watching anxiously for the next tumble.
T8   190:31   then on the other. After the fourth or fifth tumble he reached the turn, and then she waved her
T8   180: 7   and Judy--What a noise they make when they tumble! Just like a whole set of fire-irons falling into the
TUMBLED (5)
T8W   17:11   like the handkerchief, and all tangled and tumbled about like a heap of sea-weed. "You could make your
T2   123:14   like a dahlia," said the Tiger-lily: "not tumbled about, like yours."
A4   32:39   the puppy made another rush at the stick, and tumbled head over heels in its hurry to get hold of it: then
T8   179:16   "You're my prisoner!" the Knight cried, as he tumbled off his horse.
T8   179:24   White Knight. He drew up at Alice's side, and tumbled off his horse just as the Red Knight had done: then he
TUMBLES (1)
T8   180: 4   him off his horse; and, if he misses, he tumbles off himself--and another Rule seems to be that they

TUMBLING (4)
```
  A1     8:24   such a fall as this, I shall think nothing of tumbling down-stairs! How brave they'll all think me at home!
  T8   184:16   he spoke, just in time to save himself from tumbling off again.
  T8   190:30   leisurely along the road, and the Knight tumbling off, first on one side and then on the other. After
  A8    65:42   people began running about in all directions, tumbling up against each other: however, they got settled down
```
TUMTUM (1)
```
  T1   118: 7   manxome foe he sought--/ So rested he by the Tumtum tree, / And stood awhile in thought.
```
TUNE (2)
```
  T9   197:21       every minute, and sounded more like a tune: at last she could even make out words, and she listened
  T8   187:28                       "But the tune isn't his own invention," she said to herself: "it's 'I
```
TUNE'S (1)
```
  T8   187:11   song really is 'A-sitting On A Gate': and the tune's my own invention."
```
TUNNEL (1)
```
  A1     8: 7   The rabbit-hole went straight on like a tunnel for some way, and then dipped suddenly down, so
```
TUREEN (2) [See also SOUP-TUREEN]
```
  T9   204: 7   at her for a moment over the edge of the tureen, before she disappeared into the soup.
 A10    84:18   Soup, so rich and green, / Waiting in a hot tureen! / Who for such dainties would not stoop? / Soup of the
```
TURK (1)
```
  T6   159: 9   was sitting, with his legs crossed like a Turk, on the top of a high wall--such a narrow one that Alice
```
TURKEY (1)
```
  A1    11: 8   of cherry-tart, custard, pine-apple, roast turkey, toffy, and hot buttered toast), she very soon finished
```
TURN (27)
```
 A10    78:31                                                 "Turn a somersault in the sea!" cried the Mock Turtle, capering
  T2   120: 9   so she did: wandering up and down, and trying turn after turn, but always coming back to the house, do what
  A9    77: 8   so he did," said the Gryphon, sighing in his turn; and both creatures hid their faces in their paws.
  T8   190:32   the fourth or fifth tumble he reached the turn, and then she waved her handkerchief to him, and waited
  T2   120:10   wandering up and down, and trying turn after turn, but always coming back to the house, do what she would.
  T2   120: 6   more like a corkscrew than a path! Well this turn goes to the hill, I suppose--no, it doesn't! This goes
  T3   131: 8   seemed to be that they should all speak in turn, he went on with "She'll have to go back from here as
  T1   113:16   on the table behind Alice, and made her turn her head just in time to see one of the White Pawns roll
  T6   159:20   very pretty, you know," she added, hoping to turn her remark into a sort of compliment.
  T8   190:18   and wave your handkerchief when I get to that turn in the road? I think it'll encourage me, you see."
  A5    36: 3   it so yet," said Alice; "but when you have to turn into a chrysalis--you will some day, you know--and then
  A6    50: 3   No, there were no tears. "If you're going to turn into a pig, my dear," said Alice, seriously, "I'll have
  T3   134: 7   of flying into candles--because they want to turn into Snap-dragon-flies!"
  T4   147:28   Alice laughed loud: but she managed to turn it into a cough, for fear of hurting his feelings.
 A10    80:10   from England the nearer is to France. / Then turn not pale, beloved snail, but come and join the dance. /
  T6   162:16   take turns in choosing subjects, it was her turn now.) "At least," she corrected herself on second
  A8    68:15   that she never knew whether it was her turn or not. So she went off in search of her hedgehog.
  T2   128:24   you ca'n't think of the English for a thing--turn out your toes as you walk--and remember who you are!" She
  T6   160:25   on, "the King has promised me--ah, you may turn pale, if you like! You didn't think I was going to say
  A6    48:26   You see the earth takes twenty-four hours to turn round on its axis--"
 A11    91:20   Queen shrieked out. "Behead that Dormouse! Turn that Dormouse out of court! Suppress him! Pinch him! Off
  T6   168:13   when I found the door was shut, / I tried to turn the handle, but--"
 A10    83: 6   the Mock Turtle persisted. "How could he turn them out with his nose, you know?"
  A8    64:13   angrily away from him, and said to the Knave "Turn them over!"
  T6   161:19   afresh," said Humpty Dumpty, "and it's my turn to choose a subject--" ("He talks about it just as if it
 T12   207:34   watch the kittens. "Tell me, Dinah, did you turn to Humpty Dumpty? I think you did--however, you'd better
 T12   207:32                       "And what did Dinah turn to, I wonder?" she prattled on, as she settled
```
TURNED (37)
```
  A5    38: 3   And have grown most uncommonly fat; / Yet you turned a back-somersault in at the door--/ Pray, what is the
  A1     9:25   and was just in time to hear it say, as it turned a corner, "Oh my ears and whiskers, how late it's
  T2   120:11   do what she would. Indeed, once, when she turned a corner rather more quickly than usual, she ran
  T2   128:22                   At the next peg the Queen turned again, and this time she said "Speak in French when you
  T9   204: 5   cried a voice from the soup-tureen, and Alice turned again, just in time to see the Queen's broad
  A5    36:20   This sounded promising, certainly. Alice turned and came back again.
  A8    64:12                             The Queen turned angrily away from him, and said to the Knave "Turn them
  A5    36:17   to be in a very unpleasant state of mind, she turned away.
 T12   207:19   the thing afterwards to her sister: "it turned away its head, and pretended not to see it: but it
  T1   115:22   The King was saying "I assure you, my dear, I turned cold to the very ends of my whiskers!"
  A8    64: 5                             The Queen turned crimson with fury, and, after glaring at her for a
  T2   128:26   walked on quickly to the next peg, where she turned for a moment to say "Good-bye," and then hurried on to
  T8W   13:21   The Wasp only shook his shoulders, and turned his head away. "Ah, deary me!" he said to himself.
  T8   190:13   of the ballad, he gathered up the reins, and turned his horse's head along the road by which they had come.
 T12   207:17   triumphantly. "Confess that was what you turned into!"
  T8W   20:10   with a little scream of laughter, which she turned into a cough as well as she could. At last she managed
  A6    52:19                       "It turned into a pig," Alice answered very quietly, just as if
  T5   158:28   more and more at every step, as everything turned into a tree the moment she came up to it, and she quite
  T5   155:17   beginning to say, when suddenly the needles turned into oars in her hands, and she found they were in a
  T6   163:16   sure I was!" Humpty Dumpty said gaily as he turned it round for him. "I thought it looked a little queer.
 A11    91:23   court was in confusion, getting the Dormouse turned out, and, by the time they had settled down again, the
  A4    27:25   she should meet the real Mary Ann, and be turned out of the house before she had found the fan and
  T1   116: 4   over him, in case he fainted again), she turned over the leaves, to find some part that she could read,
 A11    88:27   and began staring hard at the Hatter, who turned pale and fidgeted.
 A12    94: 1                       The King turned pale, and shut his note-book hastily. "Consider your
  A2    20:16   like them!" When the Mouse heard this, it turned round and swam slowly back to her: its face was quite
  T7   175:15   when his eye happened to fall upon Alice: he turned round instantly, and stood for some time looking at her
  T9   199: 2                       Alice turned round, ready to find fault with anybody. "Where's the
  A3    21: 9   a long argument with the Lory, who at last turned sulky, and would only say, "I'm older than you, and
  A1     9:27   getting!" She was close behind it when she turned the corner, but the Rabbit was no longer to be seen:
```

TURNED (cont.)
T8   190:34 "I hope it encouraged him," she said, as she turned to run down the hill: "and now for the last brook, and
T9   204: 2 she heard a hoarse laugh at her side, and turned to see what was the matter with the White Queen; but,
T8W   13:10   to him," was Alice's first thought, as she turned to spring over the brook:--but I'll just ask him what's
A7   59:19   to some tea and bread-and-butter, and then turned to the Dormouse, and repeated her question. "Why did
A9   76:34   to ask any more questions about it: so she turned to the Mock Turtle, and said "What else had you to
T2   122:17 in a moment, and several of the pink daisies turned white.
T8   190:16 stay and see me off first?" he added as Alice turned with an eager look in the direction to which he pointed

TURNING (26)
T4   143:14   'But not on us!' the Oysters cried, / Turning a little blue. / 'After such kindness, that would be /
T3   137:30 on, talking to herself as she went, till, on turning a sharp corner, she came upon two fat little men, so
T8W   15:15   "Let it stop there!" said the Wasp, fretfully turning away his head.
T9   204:17   "And as for you," she went on, turning fiercely upon the Red Queen, whom she considered as
T7   175:34 the plum-cake, old man!" the Unicorn went on, turning from her to the King. "None of your brown bread for
T2   120:18   So, resolutely turning her back upon the house, she set out once more down
T8   181:10 back his shaggy hair with both hands, and turning his gentle face and large mild eyes to Alice. She
T1   111: 9 gauze, so that we can get through. Why, it's turning into a sort of mist now, I declare! It'll be easy
A4   32: 5 with some surprise, that the pebbles were all turning into little cakes as they lay on the floor, and a
T7   171:12 King said, introducing Alice in the hope of turning off the Messenger's attention from himself--but it was
A12   97: 3   "Hold your tongue!" said the Queen, turning purple.
T5   155: 9 "You'll make me giddy soon, if you go on turning round like that." She was now working with fourteen
T5   154: 9 had not got: so she contented herself with turning round, looking at the shelves as she came to them.
T2   120: 4 (after going a few yards along the path, and turning several sharp corners), "but I suppose it will at last
T3   129:19 the hill, and trying to find some excuse for turning shy so suddenly. "It'll never do to go down among them
T9   194:28   "Can you do sums?" Alice said, turning suddenly on the White Queen, for she didn't like being
A3   23:32 have you got in your pocket?" it went on, turning to Alice.
A7   56:27 you guessed the riddle yet?" the Hatter said, turning to Alice again.
A3   24:17 Mine is a long and sad tale!" said the Mouse, turning to Alice, and sighing.
A3   22:25 you getting on now, my dear?" it continued, turning to Alice as it spoke.
A7   55:36 "What day of the month is it?" he said, turning to Alice: he had taken his watch out of his pocket,
A8   63:38 the Queen, tossing her head impatiently; and turning to Alice, she went on: "What's your name, child?"
A12   93:21   "That's very important," the King said, turning to the jury. They were just beginning to write this
A11   88:22   "Stolen!" the King exclaimed, turning to the jury, who instantly made a memorandum of the
A12   95:35 swim--' you ca'n't swim, can you?" he added, turning to the Knave.
A8   65: 4 the Queen. "You make me giddy." And then, turning to the rose-tree, she went on "What have you been

TURNS (5)
A8   68:13   to be executed for having missed their turns, and she did not like the look of things at all, as the
T6   162:15 she thought: and, if they really were to take turns in choosing subjects, it was her turn now.) "At least,"
T1   108:17 to-morrow." Here Alice wound two or three turns of the worsted round the kitten's neck, just to see how
A10   82:25 nose / Trims his belt and his buttons, and turns out his toes. / When the sands are all dry, he is gay as
A8   66:20 all played at once, without waiting for turns, quarreling all the while, and fighting for the

TURN-UP (1)
A6   49:33 There could be no doubt that it had a very turn-up nose, much more like a snout than a real nose: also

TURTLE (57)
A9   74:33 at last, with a deep sigh, "I was a real Turtle."
A9   76: 2   "You did," said the Mock Turtle.
A9   76:11   "And washing?" said the Mock Turtle.
A9   77:20   "Of course it was," said the Mock Turtle.
A10   79: 3 like to see a little of it?" said the Mock Turtle.
A10   81:43   "Explain all that," said the Mock Turtle.
A10   83: 2 like to have it explained," said the Mock Turtle.
A12   98:33 up with the distant sob of the miserable Mock Turtle.
A9   76: 9   "With extras?" asked the Mock Turtle, a little anxiously.
A9   74:36 and the constant heavy sobbing of the Mock Turtle. Alice was very nearly getting up and saying, "Thank
A9   76:34 questions about it: so she turned to the Mock Turtle, and said "What else had you to learn?"
A9   74: 2 "and take this young lady to see the Mock Turtle, and to hear his history. I must go back and see after
A9   75: 3 Tortoise because he taught us," said the Mock Turtle angrily. "Really you are very dull!"
A9   74:32   "Once," said the Mock Turtle at last, with a deep sigh, "I was a real Turtle."
A10   80:20 don't know where Dinn may be," said the Mock Turtle; "but, if you've seen them so often, of course you know
A10   82:32 Well, I never heard it before," said the Mock Turtle; "but it sounds uncommon nonsense."
A10   78:31 Turn a somersault in the sea!" cried the Mock Turtle, capering wildly about.
A10   80:24 You're wrong about the crumbs," said the Mock Turtle: "crumbs would all wash off in the sea. But they have
A10   82: 8 words all coming different, and then the Mock Turtle drew a long breath, and said "That's very curious!"
A9   75: 7 earth. At last the Gryphon said to the Mock Turtle "Drive on, old fellow! Don't be all day about it!" and
A10   85: 1 again!" cried the Gryphon, and the Mock Turtle had just begun to repeat it, when a cry of "The trial's
A9   74:27   "I'll tell it her," said the Mock Turtle in a deep, hollow tone. "Sit down, both of you, and
A9   76:14 wasn't a really good school," said the Mock Turtle in a tone of great relief. "Now, at ours, they had, at
A9   74:16 had not gone far before they saw the Mock Turtle in the distance, sitting sad and lonely on a little
A10   84: 3 use of repeating all that stuff?" the Mock Turtle interrupted, "if you don't explain it as you go on?
A9   73:12 said Alice. "I don't even know what a Mock Turtle is."
A9   77:12 "Ten hours the first day," said the Mock Turtle: "nine the next, and so on."
A10   83: 5   "But about his toes?" the Mock Turtle persisted. "How could he turn them out with his nose,
A10   78: 5 punching him in the back. At last the Mock Turtle recovered his voice, and, with tears running down his
A10   82:11   "It all came different!" the Mock Turtle repeated thoughtfully. "I should like to hear her try
A9   76:22 Writhing, of course, to begin with," the Mock Turtle replied; "and then the different branches of Arithmetic
A9   76:36 "Well, there was Mystery," the Mock Turtle replied, counting off the subjects on his flappers--
A10   81:37   "I mean what I say," the Mock Turtle replied, in an offended tone. And the Gryphon added
A10   78:22   "Of course," the Mock Turtle said: "advance twice, set to partners--"
A9   77: 2 Well, I ca'n't show it you, myself," the Mock Turtle said: "I'm too stiff. And the Gryphon never learnt it
A10   81:30 were obliged to have him with them," the Mock Turtle said. "No wise fish would go anywhere without a

TURTLE (cont.)
A9   77: 6   "I never went to him," the Mock Turtle said with a sigh. "He taught Laughing and Grief, they
A10   79:12   fore-paws to mark the time, while the Mock Turtle sang this, very slowly and sadly:--
A10   78:16   "Two lines!" cried the Mock Turtle. "Seals, turtles, salmon, and so on: then, when you've
A10   84:15   The Mock Turtle sighed deeply, and began, in a voice choked with sobs,
A10   78: 1   The Mock Turtle sighed deeply, and drew the back of one flapper across
A9   73:13   "It's the thing Mock Turtle Soup is made from," said the Queen.
A10   84:13   "Hm! No accounting for tastes! Sing her 'Turtle Soup,' will you, old fellow?"
A10   78:36   that's all the first figure," said the Mock Turtle, suddenly dropping his voice; and the two creatures,
A10   80:16   "Oh, as to the whiting," said the Mock Turtle, "they--you've seen them, of course?"
A10   84: 9   Gryphon went on. "Or would you like the Mock Turtle to sing you another song?"
A10   79: 5   let's try the first figure!" said the Mock Turtle to the Gryphon. "We can do it without lobsters, you
A9   74:42   to school in the sea. The master was an old Turtle--we used to call him Tortoise--"
A9   76: 4   before Alice could speak again. The Mock Turtle went on.
A9   74:40   "When we were still little," the Mock Turtle went on at last, more calmly, though still sobbing a
A10   78:26   "Then, you know," the Mock Turtle went on, "you throw the--"
A9   74:23   So they went up to the Mock Turtle, who looked at them with large eyes full of tears, but
A10   81:33   "Of course not," said the Mock Turtle. "Why, if a fish came to me, and told me he was going a
A9   76:18   I couldn't afford to learn it," said the Mock Turtle with a sigh. "I only took the regular course."
A10   84:11   "Oh, a song, please, if the Mock Turtle would be so kind," Alice replied, so eagerly that the
A10   81: 1   mouths; and the reason is--" here the Mock Turtle yawned and shut his eyes. "Tell her about the reason
A9   73:11   and said to Alice "Have you seen the Mock Turtle yet?"
TURTLE'S (2)
A12   99: 2   the distance would take the place of the Mock Turtle's heavy sobs.
A9t   70: 1   THE MOCK TURTLE'S STORY
TURTLES (2)
A10   79:15   tail. / See how eagerly the lobsters and the turtles all advance! / They are waiting on the shingle--will
A10   78:16   "Two lines!" cried the Mock Turtle. "Seals, turtles, salmon, and so on: then, when you've cleared all the
TUT (2)
A9   70:22   "Tut, tut, child!" said the Duchess. "Everything's got a moral, if
A9   70:22   "Tut, tut, child!" said the Duchess. "Everything's got a moral,
'TWAS (4)
T1   116: 9   diD / sevot yhtils eht dna ,gillirb sawT'
T1   116:18   'Twas brillig, and the slithy toves / Did gyre and gimble in
T1   118:21   'Twas brillig, and the slithy toves / Did gyre and gimble in
T6   164:21   "'Twas brillig, and the slithy toves / Did gyre and gimble in
TWEEDLE (2)
T4   138: 4   and the other 'DEE.' "I suppose they've got 'TWEEDLE' round at the back of the collar," she said to herself
T4   138: 7   she was just going round to see if the word 'TWEEDLE' was written at the back of each collar, when she was
TWEEDLEDEE (26)
T3   137:23   HOUSE," and the other "TO THE HOUSE OF TWEEDLEDEE."
T4t   138: 1   feeling sure that they must be TWEEDLEDUM AND TWEEDLEDEE
T4   144:27   "It's only the Red King snoring," said Tweedledee.
T4   145:15   "Ditto, ditto!" cried Tweedledee.
T4   148:17   "And darker," said Tweedledee.
T4   138:18   "Tweedledum and Tweedledee / Agreed to have a battle; / For Tweedledum said
T4   145: 1   "He's dreaming now," said Tweedledee: "and what do you think he's dreaming about?"
T4   140:17   Tweedledee began instantly:
T4   145: 4   "Why, about you!" Tweedledee exclaimed, clapping his hands triumphantly. "And if
T4   138:20   to have a battle; / For Tweedledum said Tweedledee / Had spoiled his nice new rattle.
T6   166:13   repeated to me much easier than that, by--Tweedledee, I think it was."
T4   139: 7   "Contrariwise," continued Tweedledee, "if it was so, it might be; and if it were so, it
T4   147:42   Tweedledee looked at his watch, and said "Half-past four."
T4   140:12   "What shall I repeat to her?" said Tweedledee, looking round at Tweedledum with great solemn eyes
T4   145:22   make yourself a bit realler by crying," Tweedledee remarked: "there's nothing to cry about."
T4   145: 8   "Not you!" Tweedledee retorted contemptuously. "You'd be nowhere. Why,
T4   140:22   Tweedledee smiled gently, and began again:
T2   128:11   Well, that square belongs to Tweedledum and Tweedledee--the Fifth is mostly water--the Sixth belongs to
T4   139:18   "Next Boy!" said Alice, passing on to Tweedledee, though she felt quite certain he would only shout
T4   147:24   as she arranged a bolster round the neck of Tweedledee, "to keep his head from being cut off," as he said
T4   147: 1   All this time Tweedledee was trying his best to fold up the umbrella, with
T4   147:36   "And I've got a toothache!" said Tweedledee, who had overheard the remark. "I'm far worse than
T4   146:22   "It's spoilt, of course!" Here he looked at Tweedledee, who immediately sat down on the ground, and tried
T4   140: 9   "So much obliged!" added Tweedledee. "You like poetry?"
T4   144:15   He ate more than the Carpenter, though," said Tweedledee. "You see he held his handkerchief in front, so
TWEEDLEDUM (33)
T4   140: 7   And thank you very much for asking," said Tweedledum.
T4   144:20   "But he ate as many as he could get," said Tweedledum.
T4   144:31   "Isn't he a lovely sight?" said Tweedledum.
T4   145:14   "Ditto," said Tweedledum.
T4   147:43   fight till six, and then have dinner," said Tweedledum.
T4   139:14   Alice couldn't help pointing her finger at Tweedledum, and saying "First Boy!"
T4t   138: 1   herself, feeling sure that they must be TWEEDLEDUM AND TWEEDLEDEE
T4   138:18   "Tweedledum and Tweedledee / Agreed to have a battle; / For
T2   128:11   in no time. Well, that square belongs to Tweedledum and Tweedledee--the Fifth is mostly water--the
T4   146:20   "I knew it was!" cried Tweedledum, beginning to stamp about wildly and tear his hair.
T4   139: 5   "I know what you're thinking about," said Tweedledum; "but it isn't so, nohow."
T4   147:30   "Do I look very pale?" said Tweedledum, coming up to have his helmet tied on. (He called
T4   146:26   "But it isn't old!" Tweedledum cried, in a greater fury than ever. "It's new, I

TWEEDLEDUM (cont.)

T4	139:16		"Nohow!" Tweedledum cried out briskly, and shut his mouth up again with
T4	148:21		"It's the crow!" Tweedledum cried out in a shrill voice of alarm; and the two
T4	148:11	"I shouldn't have minded it so much," said	Tweedledum, "if it hadn't been a new one."
T4	145:26	hope you don't suppose those are real tears?"	Tweedledum interrupted in a tone of great contempt.
T4	148: 6		Tweedledum looked round him with a satisfied smile. "I don't
T4	139:40	"Four times round is enough for one dance,"	Tweedledum panted out, and they left off dancing as suddenly
T4	144:35	snoring loud--"fit to snore his head off!" as	Tweedledum remarked.
T4	147:16	a good hand at pinning and tying strings?"	Tweedledum remarked. "Every one of these things has got to go
T4	140:15	Walrus and the Carpenter' is the longest,"	Tweedledum replied, giving his brother an affectionate hug.
T4	147: 8	"Of course you agree to have a battle?"	Tweedledum said in a calmer tone.
T4	148:14	"There's only one sword, you know,"	Tweedledum said to his brother: "but you can have the umbrella
T4	138:20	Tweedledee / Agreed to have a battle; / For	Tweedledum said Tweedledee / Had spoiled his nice new rattle.
T4	146:11	to say "Good-night" and leave them, when	Tweedledum sprang out from under the umbrella, and seized her
T4	146: 4		Tweedledum spread a large umbrella over himself and his
T4	139:21	"You've begun wrong!" cried	Tweedledum. "The first thing in a visit is to say 'How d'ye do
T4	147:41	but I don't care about going on long," said	Tweedledum. "What's the time now?"
T4	145:18	no use your talking about waking him," said	Tweedledum, "when you're only one of the things in his dream.
T4	148: 2	"And I hit every thing within reach," cried	Tweedledum, "whether I can see it or not!"
T4	140:13	to her?" said Tweedledee, looking round at	Tweedledum with great solemn eyes, and not noticing Alice's
T4	145:10	"If that there King was to wake," added	Tweedledum, "you'd go out--bang!--just like a candle!"

TWEEDLEDUM'S (1)

T3	137:22	pointing the same way, one marked "TO TWEEDLEDUM'S HOUSE," and the other "TO THE HOUSE OF TWEEDLEDEE

TWELFTH (1)

A9	77:21	"And how did you manage on the twelfth?" Alice went on eagerly.

TWELVE (4)

A2	16: 9	used to know. Let me see: four times five is twelve, and four times six is thirteen, and four times seven
A11	86:21	the jury-box," thought Alice; "and those twelve creatures," (she was obliged to say "creatures," you
A6	48:31	again: "Twenty-four hours, I think; or is it twelve? I--"
A11	86:28	The twelve jurors were all writing very busily on slates. "What

TWENTIETH (1)

A12	96:29	their verdict," the King said, for about the twentieth time that day.

TWENTY (2)

A2	16:10	times seven is--oh dear! I shall never get to twenty at that rate! However, the Multiplication-Table doesn't
T7	169: 2	at first in twos and threes, then ten or twenty together, and at last in such crowds that they seemed

TWENTY-FOUR (2)

A6	48:30	not to be listening, so she went on again: "Twenty-four hours, I think; or is it twelve? I--"
A6	48:26	the day and night! You see the earth takes twenty-four hours to turn round on its axis--"

TWICE (11)

A10	78:20	"--you advance twice--"
T4	143:24	were not quite so deaf--/ I've had to ask you twice!'
A5	41:25	hookah out of its mouth, and yawned once or twice, and shook itself. Then it got down off the mushroom,
T2	127:21	to get somewhere else, you must run at least twice as fast as that!"
T7	177:19	how to begin. "The Monster has given the Lion twice as much as me!"
T7	175:22	found it to-day. It's as large as life, and twice as natural!"
A7	60:32	of her going, though she looked back once or twice, half hoping that they would call after her: the last
A10	78:22	"Of course," the Mock Turtle said: "advance twice, set to partners--"
A1	7: 2	the bank and of having nothing to do: once or twice she had peeped into the book her sister was reading, but
T6	167:11	I told them once, I told them twice: / They would not listen to advice.
T1	108:27	you all your faults. Number one: you squeaked twice while Dinah was washing your face this morning. Now you

TWIDDLE (1)

T2	124: 7	you going? Look up, speak nicely, and don't twiddle your fingers all the time."

TWIG (2)

T3	135:20	there was nothing whatever to be seen on the twig, and, as she was getting quite chilly with sitting still
T3	132:19	been talking to) was balancing itself on a twig just over her head, and fanning her with its wings.

TWIGS (1)

T8	188:42	dig for buttered rolls, / Or set limed twigs for crabs: / I sometimes search for grassy knolls / For

TWINED (1)

AI	4: 5	hand, / Lay it where Childhood's dreams are twined / In Memory's mystic band. / Like pilgrim's wither'd

TWINKLE (8)

A7	57:21	fly, / Like a tea-tray in the sky. / Twinkle, twinkle--'"
A7	58: 2	in its sleep "Twinkle, twinkle, twinkle, twinkle--" and went on so long that they had to pinch it to
A7	57:14	'Twinkle, twinkle, little bat! / How I wonder what you're at!'
A7	57:21	you fly, / Like a tea-tray in the sky. / Twinkle, twinkle--'"
A7	58: 2	began singing in its sleep "Twinkle, twinkle, twinkle, twinkle--" and went on so long that they had to pinch
A7	57:14	'Twinkle, twinkle, little bat! / How I wonder what you're at!'
A7	58: 2	and began singing in its sleep "Twinkle, twinkle, twinkle, twinkle--" and went on so long that they had
A7	58: 2	shook itself, and began singing in its sleep "Twinkle, twinkle, twinkle, twinkle--" and went on so long that

TWINKLED (1)

A11	89:19	man," the Hatter went on, "and most things twinkled after that--only the March Hare said--"

TWINKLING (4)

A11	89:17	"Of course twinkling begins with a T!" said the King sharply. "Do you
A7	57: 2	a hint to Time, and round goes the clock in a twinkling! Half-past one, time for dinner!"
A11	89:14	the bread-and-butter getting so thin--and the twinkling of the tea--"
A11	89:15	"The twinkling of what?" said the King.

TWIST (3) [See also UNTWIST]

T2	120:22	it this time--" when the path gave a sudden twist and shook itself (as she described it afterwards), and
A6	49:23	the proper way of nursing it (which was to twist it up into a sort of knot, and then keep tight hold of
A8	66:10	the hedgehog a blow with its head, it would twist itself round and look up in her face, with such a

```
TWISTS (1)
T2    120: 5  suppose it will at last. But how curiously it twists! It's more like a corkscrew than a path! Well this turn
TWO (97)
A7     59: 2  said the Dormouse, after thinking a minute or two.
T1    113: 7  The chessmen were walking about, two and two!
T9    193:13  was an uncomfortable silence for a minute or two.
T7    174:20              For a minute or two Alice stood silent, watching him. Suddenly she brightened
A8     65:44  however, they got settled down in a minute or two, and the game began.
T1    118:13              One, two! One, two! And through and through / The vorpal blade went
T1    113: 7  them. The chessmen were walking about, two and two!
A8     63:18  ornamented all over with diamonds, and walked two and two, as the soldiers did. After these came the royal
T5    158: 7              "Then two are cheaper than one?" Alice said in a surprised tone,
A8     63:18  all over with diamonds, and walked two and two, as the soldiers did. After these came the royal children:
A8     63: 5  and Seven said nothing, but looked at Two. Two began, in a low voice, "Why, the fact is, you see, Miss,
T4    139:22  'How d'ye do?' and shake hands!" And here the two brothers gave each other a hug, and then they held out the
T4    148:22  cried out in a shrill voice of alarm; and the two brothers took to their heels and were out of sight in a
T4    147:12              So the two brothers went off hand-in-hand into the wood, and returned
T4    147:19  about anything in all her life--the way those two bustled about--and the quantity of things they put on--and
T6    162:11  ca'n't, perhaps," said Humpty Dumpty; "but two can. With proper assistance, you might have left off at
T1    113:11  on the edge of the shovel--and here are two Castles walking arm in arm--I don't think they can hear me
A10    82: 3  a little nervous about it, just at first, the two creatures got so close to her, one on each side, and
A6     47: 9           without a moment's pause. The only two creatures in the kitchen, that did not sneeze, were the
A10    78:36  Turtle, suddenly dropping his voice; and the two creatures, who had been jumping about like mad things all
T4    139:39              The other two dancers were fat, and very soon out of breath. "Four times
A7     56: 1              "Two days wrong!" sighed the Hatter. "I told you butter
T6    168:29  It's always the same. Now if you had the two eyes on the same side of the nose, for instance--or the
T6    168:27  "Your face is the same as everybody has--the two eyes, so--"(marking their places in the air with his
T3    137:30  on turning a sharp corner, she came upon two fat little men, so suddenly that she could not help
A2     18: 6  nearly as she could guess, she was now about two feet high, and was going on shrinking rapidly: she soon
A6     53:15  bit of mushroom, and raised herself to about two feet high: even then she walked up towards it rather
T3    137:17  was only one road through the wood, and the two finger-posts both pointed along it. "I'll settle it,"
T3    137:21  the road divided, there were sure to be two finger-posts pointing the same way, one marked "TO
T7    176:14              at having to sit down between the two great creatures; but there was no other place for him.
T9    197:22  and she listened so eagerly that, when the two great heads suddenly vanished from her lap, she hardly
A4     32:14  Bill, was in the middle, being held up by two guinea-pigs, who were giving it something out of a bottle.
T4    139:23  each other a hug, and then they held out the two hands that were free, to shake hands with her.
T5    149:20  "I've been a-dressing myself for the last two hours."
T7    170:10              "Four thousand two hundred and seven, that's the exact number," the King said
T8W    21: 8  no doubt. One would have done as well as two, if you must have them so close--"
A8     65: 6              "May it please your Majesty," said Two, in a very humble tone, going down on one knee as he spoke
A6     49:20  so that altogether, for the first minute or two, it was as much as she could do to hold it.
T8    179:25  had done: then he got on again, and the two Knights sat and looked at each other for some time without
T3    135:13  But the Gnat only sighed deeply while two large tears came rolling down its cheeks.
T5    152:34  voice; and, at the thought of her loneliness, two large tears came rolling down her cheeks.
A10    78:16              "Two lines!" cried the Mock Turtle. "Seals, turtles, salmon,
A4     30:17  snatch in the air. This time there were two little shrieks, and more sounds of broken glass. "What a
A8     65:14  three soldiers wandered about for a minute or two, looking for them, and then quietly marched off after the
T6    164:31  You see it's like a portmanteau--there are two meanings packed up into one word."
T7    170:13  wanted in the game. And I haven't sent the two Messengers, either. They're both gone to the town. Just
A12    93:40              "Nearly two miles high," added the Queen.
T8W    15: 8  tasting the treacle, they had a sad accident: two of their party were engulphed--"
T1    110:15  that they couldn't, because there were only two of them, and Alice had been reduced at last to say "Well,
T7    170:12  send all the horses, you know, because two of them are wanted in the game. And I haven't sent the two
T9    200:15  the Red and White Queens had already taken two of them, but the middle one was empty. Alice sat down in
T1    118:13              One, two! One, two! And through and through / The vorpal blade went
T9    195:32  Now here, we mostly have days and nights two or three at a time, and sometimes in the winter we take as
T8    184: 4  Knight said, as if he didn't mind breaking two or three of them. "The great art of riding, as I was
A4     27:37  and on it (as she had hoped) a fan and two or three pairs of tiny white kid-gloves: she took up the
A11    86:24  they are the jurors." She said this last word two or three times over to herself, being rather proud of it:
T8    182:17  awkward in putting in the dish: the first two or three times that he tried he fell in himself instead.
T1    108:17  see the bonfire to-morrow." Here Alice wound two or three turns of the worsted round the kitten's neck,
A10    84:28  other dish? / Who would not give all else for two p / ennyworth only of beautiful Soup? / Pennyworth only of
T5    149:38  take you with pleasure!" the Queen said. "Two pence a week, and jam every other day."
A1     12:28  child was very fond of pretending to be two people. "But it's no use now," thought poor Alice, "to
A1     12:29  now," thought poor Alice, "to pretend to be two people! Why, there's hardly enough of me left to make one
T3    134:20  After this, Alice was silent for a minute or two, pondering. The Gnat amused itself meanwhile by humming
T8    186:14  be the next day. I suppose you wouldn't have two pudding-courses in one dinner?"
T9    197:15  before, that any one had to take care of two Queens asleep at once! No, not in all the History of
T9    192:31              The two Queens looked at each other, and the Red Queen remarked,
T9    203: 2  in her place while she made her speech: the two Queens pushed her so, one on each side, that they nearly
A6     46:11  in knocking," said the Footman, "and that for two reasons. First, because I'm on the same side of the door
A8     62:14              "That's none of your business, Two!" said Seven.
T5    158: 9  "Only you must eat them both, if you buy two," said the Sheep.
T8    184:20  Knight said thoughtfully to himself. "One or two--several."
T1    114: 9  taken away her breath, and for a minute or two she could do nothing but hug the little Lily in silence.
A8     67:11  at first, but after watching it a minute or two she made it out to be a grin, and she said to herself
A6     45: 1              For a minute or two she stood looking at the house, and wondering what to do
A6     52:23  but it did not appear, and after a minute or two she walked on in the direction in which the March Hare was
A5     41:34  a minute, trying to make out which were the two sides of it; and, as it was perfectly round, she found
A10    78: 3  and tried to speak, but, for a minute or two, sobs choked his voice. "Same as if he had a bone in his
```

TWO (cont.)
```
  T2   128: 7   peg  she  faced  round, and said "A pawn goes two squares in its first move, you know. So you'll go very
  A5    41:24   until it chose to speak again. In a minute or two the Caterpillar took the hookah out of its mouth, and
  T5   158: 5   "Fivepence  farthing  for  one--twopence  for two," the Sheep replied.
  A4    31:37   they'd  take the roof off." After a minute or two they began moving about again, and Alice heard the Rabbit
  T5   153: 2   said  with  great  decision:  "nobody  can do two things at once, you know. Let's consider your age to begin
  A3    23:10   course,  here  and  there. There was no "One, two, three, and away!", but they began running when they liked
  T7   171: 7   the  King  repeated impatiently. "I must have two--to fetch and carry. One to fetch, and one to carry."
  A7    59:22        The  Dormouse  again  took  a minute or two to think about it, and then said "It was a treacle-well."
  T7   173:31   round  once  more,  and  this  time a tear or two trickled down his cheek; but not a word would he say.
  A8    63: 5   Five  and  Seven  said nothing, but looked at Two. Two began, in a low voice, "Why, the fact is, you see,
  A7    54: 3   between  them,  fast  asleep,  and  the other two were using it as a cushion, resting their elbows on it,
  T6   162:23   angry, though he said nothing for a minute or two. When he did speak again, it was in a deep growl.
  A5    43:22   that  she  was  quite  silent  for a minute or two, which gave the Pigeon the opportunity of adding "You're
  T5   156: 2   was  no  more  conversation  for  a minute or two, while the boat glided gently on, sometimes among beds of
  A12   96: 6   What, indeed!--'I gave her one, they gave him two'--why, that must be what he did with the tarts, you know--
  A6    49:27   Alice,  "they're  sure  to kill it in a day or two. Wouldn't it be murder to leave it behind?" She said the
  T2   127:35                          "At the end of two yards," she said, putting in a peg to mark the distance,
  A12   95: 5                I gave her one, they gave him two, / You gave us three or more; / They all returned from him
  T7   170:37   other  Messenger's  called Hatta. I must have two, you know--to come and go. One to come, and one to go."
  T1   108:33   make  any  more  excuses,  but listen! Number two: you pulled Snowdrop away by the tail just as I had put
```
TWOPENCE (1)
```
  T5   158: 5             "Fivepence farthing for one--twopence for two," the Sheep replied.
```
TWOPENCE-HALFPENNY (1)
```
  T8   188:23   they  call  /  Rowland's  Macassar-Oil--/ Yet twopence-halfpenny is all / They give me for my toil.'
```
TWOS (1)
```
  T7   169: 2   came  running  through  the  wood, at first in twos and threes, then ten or twenty together, and at last in
```
TWO-YARD (1)
```
  T2   128: 7                        At the two-yard peg she faced round, and said "A pawn goes two
```
TYING (4)
```
  T8W   17: 7   know.  And  when  you  catches  it, just try tying a yellow handkerchief round your face. It'll cure you in
  T4   147:21   they put on--and the trouble they gave her in tying strings and fastening buttons--"Really they'll be more
  T4   147:15   "I hope you're a good hand at pinning and tying strings?" Tweedledum remarked. "Every one of these
  T8W   16:12                Alice looked pityingly at him. "Tying up the face is very good for the toothache," she said.
```

-U-

UFFISH (1)
T1   118: 9   And, as in uffish thought he stood, / The Jabberwock, with eyes of flame,
UGH (2)
A3   22: 7   "Ugh!" said the Lory, with a shiver.
A5   43: 4   must needs come wriggling down from the sky! Ugh, Serpent!"
UGLIFICATION (2)
A9   76:24   "I never heard of 'Uglification,'" Alice ventured to say. "What is it?"
A9   76:23   of Arithmetic--Ambition, Distraction, Uglification, and Derision."
UGLIFY (1)
A9   76:32   Gryphon went on, "if you don't know what to uglify is, you are a simpleton."
UGLIFYING (1)
A9   76:27   up both its paws in surprise. "Never heard of uglifying!" it exclaimed. "You know what to beautify is, I
UGLY (3)
A9   70:26   to her: first because the Duchess was very ugly; and secondly, because she was exactly the right height
A6   50:16   to herself, "it would have made a dreadfully ugly child: but it makes rather a handsome pig, I think." And
T3   135:31   and it would be almost certain to be an ugly one. But then the fun would be, trying to find the
UMBRELLA (7)
T4   146:23   ground, and tried to hide himself under the umbrella.
T4   146:12   when Tweedledum sprang out from under the umbrella, and seized her by the wrist.
T4   148:15   said to his brother: "but you can have the umbrella--it's quite as sharp. Only we must begin quick. It's
T4   147:11   sulkily replied, as he crawled out of the umbrella: "only she must help us to dress up, you know."
T4   146: 4   Tweedledum spread a large umbrella over himself and his brother, and looked up into it.
T4   147: 2   Tweedledee was trying his best to fold up the umbrella, with himself in it: which was such an extraordinary
T4   147: 5   ended in his rolling over, bundling up in the umbrella, with only his head out: and there he lay, opening
UNABLE (2)
T9   202:14   up!' / Ah, that is so hard that I fear I'm unable!
A12   93: 6   tail about in a melancholy way, being quite unable to move. She soon got it out again, and put it right;
UN-BIRTHDAY (3)
T6   162:35   his hands round it, "they gave it me--for an un-birthday present."
T6   162:38   "I mean, what is an un-birthday present?"
T6   163:20   and sixty-four days when you might get un-birthday presents--"
UNCERTAIN (1)
T7   169: 6   all her life she had never seen soldiers so uncertain on their feet: they were always tripping over
UNCIVIL (1)
A6   46:22   speaking, and this Alice thought decidedly uncivil. "But perhaps he ca'n't help it," she said to herself;
UNCLASPING (1)
T9   195:26   said, looking down and nervously clasping and unclasping her hands, "we had such a thunderstorm last Tuesday
UNCLOUDED (1)
TI   103: 1   Child of the pure unclouded brow / And dreaming eyes of wonder! / Though time be
UNCOMFORTABLE (8)
A3   21: 3   to them, and all dripping wet, cross, and uncomfortable.
A8   68:32   the rest were quite silent, and looked very uncomfortable.
A4   28:24   and she grew no larger: still it was very uncomfortable, and, as there seemed to be no sort of chance of
T7   176:13   The King was evidently very uncomfortable at having to sit down between the two great
T9   200:16   one was empty. Alice sat down in it, rather uncomfortable at the silence, and longing for some one to
A7   54: 5   on it, and talking over its head. "Very uncomfortable for the Dormouse," thought Alice; "only as it's
T9   193:13   the Red Queen remarked; and then there was an uncomfortable silence for a minute or two.
T6   162: 4   Humpty Dumpty repeated thoughtfully. "An uncomfortable sort of age. Now if you'd asked my advice, I'd
UNCOMFORTABLY (1)
A9   70:28   her chin on Alice's shoulder, and it was an uncomfortably sharp chin. However, she did not like to be rude
UNCOMMON (1)
A10   82:33   before," said the Mock Turtle; "but it sounds uncommon nonsense."
UNCOMMONLY (1)
A5   38: 2   "as I mentioned before, / And have grown most uncommonly fat; / Yet you turned a back-somersault in at the
UNCORKED (1)
A4   28: 4   the words "DRINK ME," but nevertheless she uncorked it and put it to her lips. "I know something
UNDER (39)
T4   145:24   ran a little way into the wood, and stopped under a large tree. "It can never get at me here," she thought
T8W   16: 9   I gets cross. And I gets cold. And I gets under a tree. And I gets a yellow handkerchief. And I ties up
T4   138: 1   They were standing under a tree, each with an arm round the other's neck, and
T9   198:13   but at last a very old Frog, who was sitting under a tree, got up and hobbled slowly towards her: he was
A7   54: 1   There was a table set out under a tree in front of the house, and the March Hare and the
T3   132:17   it, and she found herself sitting quietly under a tree--while the Gnat (for that was the insect she had
T9   194:31   you give me time--but I ca'n't do Subtraction under any circumstances!"
A8   68:25   side of the ground." So she tucked it away under her arm, that it might not escape again, and went back
A8   66: 8   its body tucked away, comfortably enough, under her arm, with its legs hanging down, but generally, just
T4   146: 6   I don't think it is," he said: "at least--not under here. Nohow."
A6   45:11   The Fish-Footman began by producing from under his arm a great letter, nearly as large as himself, and
A4   34: 4   height as herself; and, when she had looked under it, and on both sides of it, and behind it, it occurred
T6   168:29   with his thumb) "nose in the middle, mouth under. It's always the same. Now if you had the two eyes on
A4   32:41   and expecting every moment to be trampled under its feet, ran round the thistle again: then the puppy
A8   65:32   mouth close to her ear, and whispered "She's under sentence of execution."
A9   73: 9   the Queen, and Alice, were in custody and under sentence of execution.

UNDER (cont.)
TC   209:11 she haunts me, phantomwise. / Alice moving under skies / Never seen by waking eyes.
T6   164:39 Humpty Dumpty; "also they make their nests under sun-dials--also they live on cheese."
T5   156:44   was that the handle of it caught her under the chin, and, in spite of a series of little shrieks of
A4   34: 2   looked like the right thing to eat or drink under the circumstances. There was a large mushroom growing
A1   12:35   and if it makes me grow smaller, I can creep under the door: so either way I'll get into the garden, and I
A1   8: 4   time to see it pop down a large rabbit-hole under the hedge.
T8   184: 8 and this time he fell flat on his back, right under the horse's feet.
T2   122:37 if you ever saw anybody! You keep your head under the leaves, and snore away there, till you know no more
A10   78: 8   "You may not have lived much under the sea--" ("I haven't," said Alice)--"and perhaps you
A10   81:21   "Boots and shoes under the sea," the Gryphon went on in a deep voice, "are done
A1   12:31   eye fell on a little glass box that was lying under the table: she opened it, and found in it a very small
T4   146:15 trembling finger at a small white thing lying under the tree.
T3   135:39 a great comfort," she said as she stepped under the trees, "after being so hot, to get into the--into
T4   146:23 down on the ground, and tried to hide himself under the umbrella.
T4   146:12 leave them, when Tweedledum sprang out from under the umbrella, and seized her by the wrist.
T3   135:41 able to think of the word. "I mean to get under the--under the--under this, you know!" putting her hand
T3   135:42 think of the word. "I mean to get under the--under the--under this, you know!" putting her hand on the
A4   29:33   till she fancied she heard the Rabbit just under the window, she suddenly spread out her hand, and made a
T2   127:13 great surprise. "Why, I do believe we've been under this tree the whole time! Everything's just as it was!"
T3   135:42 word. "I mean to get under the--under the--under this, you know!" putting her hand on the trunk of the
T5   156: 4 in the water, worse than ever), and sometimes under trees, but always with the same tall river-banks
A5   42:23   found to be nothing but the tops of the trees under which she had been wandering, when a sharp hiss made her
T4   139:30 playing: it seemed to come from the tree under which they were dancing, and it was done (as well as she
UNDERGOING (1)
T12   207:27 the White Kitten, which was still patiently undergoing its toilet, "when will Dinah have finished with
UNDERNEATH (2)
A5   41:40   The next moment she felt a violent blow underneath her chin: it had struck her foot!
A1   8:20   to drop the jar, for fear of killing somebody underneath, so managed to put it into one of the cupboards as
UNDERSTAND (15)
A2   19:21   "Perhaps it doesn't understand English," thought Alice. "I daresay it's a French
A5   35:15   Alice replied, very politely, "for I ca'n't understand it myself, to begin with; and being so many
T6   167: 5   "I'm afraid I don't quite understand," said Alice.
T7   171: 4   "I only meant that I didn't understand," said Alice. "Why one to come and one to go?"
A9   72:11   "I think I should understand that better," Alice said very politely, "if I had
T1   107:21   and giving it a little kiss to make it understand that it was in disgrace. "Really, Dinah ought to
T8   187: 1   "No, you don't understand," the Knight said, looking a little vexed. "That's
T6   166:33 when the days are long, / Perhaps you'll understand the song:
T5   152:22 she said to Alice with a smile. "Now you understand the way things happen here."
T3   130:12 they all thought in chorus (I hope you understand what thinking in chorus means--for I must confess
A7   60: 4   so she began very cautiously: "But I don't understand. Where did they draw the treacle from?"
A2   20:19   and then I'll tell you my history, and you'll understand why it is I hate cats and dogs."
T5   150:10   "I don't understand you," said Alice. "It's dreadfully confusing!"
T1   118:26 she had finished it, "but it's rather hard to understand!" (You see she didn't like to confess, even to
A7   56:21   yet it was certainly English. "I don't quite understand you," she said, as politely as she could.
UNDERSTOOD (2)
T1   110: 6 playing just now, you watched just as if you understood it: and when I said 'Check!' you purred! Well, it
A11   90:19   by the officers of the court,' and I never understood what it meant till now."
UNDERTONE (2)
A12   93:27   hastily said, and went on to himself in an undertone, "important--unimportant--unimportant--important--"
A11   91:26   "Call the next witness." And, he added, in an undertone to the Queen, "Really, my dear, you must
UN-DISH-COVER (1)
T9   202:18 in the middle: / Which is easiest to do, / Un-dish-cover the fish, or dishcover the riddle?"
UNDO (1)
A3   26: 7   anxiously about her. "Oh, do let me help to undo it!"
UNDOING (1)
A6   49:24   right ear and left foot, so as to prevent its undoing itself), she carried it out into the open air. "If I
UNDONE (3)
T1   107:17 rolling it up and down till it had all come undone again; and there it was, spread over the hearth-rug,
T5   153:17   The brooch had come undone as she spoke, and a sudden gust of wind blew the
T5   152:15 poor Queen groaned out: "the brooch will come undone directly. Oh, oh!" As she said the words the brooch
UNEASILY (2)
A11   88:31 shifting from one foot to the other, looking uneasily at the Queen, and in his confusion he bit a large
A7   55:37   out of his pocket, and was looking at it uneasily, shaking it every now and then, and holding it to his
UNEASY (1)
A8   67: 3   Alice began to feel very uneasy: to be sure, she had not as yet had any dispute with
UNFASTENED (1)
T8   181:25 out! And the box is no use without them." He unfastened it as he spoke, and was just going to throw it into
UNFINISHED (1)
T5   152: 3 so loud that she had to leave the sentence unfinished. "Oh, oh, oh!" shouted the Queen, shaking her hand
UNFOLDED (2)
A5   36:29   puffed away without speaking; but at last it unfolded its arms, took the hookah out of its mouth again, and
A12   94:13   there's nothing written on the outside." He unfolded the paper as he spoke, and added "It isn't a letter,
UNFORTUNATE (3)
A8   65:10   the soldiers remaining behind to execute the unfortunate gardeners, who ran to Alice for protection.
A12   98:28   shrill voice of the Queen ordering off her unfortunate guests to execution--once more the pig-baby was
A12   96:21   an inkstand at the Lizard as she spoke. (The unfortunate little Bill had left off writing on his slate with
UNHAPPINESS (1)
T3   131:40 and quite took off her thoughts from the unhappiness of the poor little creature.

UNHAPPY (6)
 A4   28:26 out of the room again, no wonder she felt unhappy.
 T3   135:16 make   jokes,"   Alice   said,   "if   it   makes   you   so   unhappy."
 T1   115:34   The poor King looked puzzled and unhappy, and struggled with the pencil for some time without
 A9   73:21 she said to herself, for she had felt quite unhappy at the number of executions the Queen had ordered.
 T3   131:34 The little voice sighed deeply. It was <u>very</u> unhappy, evidently, and Alice would have said something
 T8W   13: 3   "There's somebody <u>very</u> unhappy there," she thought, looking anxiously back to see
UNICORN (22)
 T7t 169: 1   THE LION AND THE UNICORN
 T7   176:20   "I'm not so sure of that," said the Unicorn.
 T7   173: 2 <u>fighting for the crown</u>: / The Lion <u>beat</u> the Unicorn <u>all round the town</u>. / <u>Some gave them white bread</u>, <u>some</u>
 T8   179: 4 have been dreaming about the Lion and the Unicorn and those queer Anglo-Saxon Messengers. However, there
 T7   177:17   "I say, this isn't fair!" cried the Unicorn, as Alice sat with the knife in her hand, very much
 T7   173:18 but she soon managed to distinguish the Unicorn by his horn.
 T7   176: 3   "Ah, what <u>is</u> it, now?" the Unicorn cried eagerly. "You'll never guess! I couldn't."
 T7   176: 7   "It's a fabulous monster!" the Unicorn cried out, before Alice could reply.
 T7   176:11 sit down, both of you," (to the King and the Unicorn): "fair play with the cake, you know!"
 T7   175:30 now that we <u>have</u> seen each other," said the Unicorn, "if you'll believe in me, I'll believe in you. Is
 T7   175:23   they were fabulous monsters!" said the Unicorn. "Is it alive?"
 T7   175:26   The Unicorn looked dreamily at Alice, and said "Talk, child."
 T7   172:36   "Why the Lion and the Unicorn, of course," said the King.
 T7   177:11 know how to manage Looking-glass cakes," the Unicorn remarked. "Hand it round first, and cut it afterwards
 T7   178: 8 the Lion and the * * * * * * * * * * * * Unicorn rise to their feet, with angry looks at being
 T7   175:14   "It didn't hurt him," the Unicorn said carelessly, and he was going on, when his eye
 T7   176:16 a fight we might have for the crown <u>now</u>!" the Unicorn said, looking slyly up at the crown, which the poor
 T7   174:13 in the fight just then, and the Lion and the Unicorn sat down, panting, while the King called out "Ten
 T7   175: 9   At this moment the Unicorn sauntered by them, with his hands in his pockets. "I
 T7   175:33 "Come, fetch out the plum-cake, old man!" the Unicorn went on, turning from her to the King. "None of your
 T7   173: 1   <u>The Lion and the Unicorn were fighting for the crown</u>: / The Lion <u>beat the</u>
 T7   173:16 crowd, in the middle of which the Lion and Unicorn were fighting. They were in such a cloud of dust, that
UNICORNS (1)
 T7   175:28 as she began: "Do you know, I always thought Unicorns were fabulous monsters, too? I never saw one alive
UNIMPORTANT (5)
 A12   93:30 the jury wrote it down "important," and some "unimportant." Alice could see this, as she was near enough to
 A12   93:28   in an undertone, "important--unimportant--unimportant--important--" as if he were trying which word
 A12   93:26   "<u>Un</u>important, of course, I meant," the King hastily said, and
 A12   93:27 on to himself in an undertone, "important--<u>un</u>important--unimportant--important--" as if he were trying
 A12   93:23 slates, when the White Rabbit interrupted: "<u>Un</u>important, your Majesty means, of course," he said, in a
UNINTERESTING (1)
 T1   112:11 seen from the old room was quite common and uninteresting, but that all the rest was as different as
UNJUST (1)
 A8   62:18 brush, and had just begun "Well, of all the unjust things--" when his eye chanced to fall upon Alice, as
UNLESS (6)
 A12   94: 9 "It must have been that," said the King, "unless it was written to nobody, which isn't usual, you know
 T1   110:37 in the winter: you never <u>can</u> tell, you know, unless our fire smokes, and then smoke comes up in that room
 A8   68:38   was, that you couldn't cut off a head unless there was a body to cut it off from: that he had never
 T8   179: 7 dreaming, after all," she said to herself, "unless--unless we're all part of the same dream. Only I do
 T8   179: 7 after all," she said to herself, "unless--unless we're all part of the same dream. Only I do hope it's
 T5   154: 6 Sheep; "but you ca'n't look <u>all</u> round you--unless you've got eyes at the back of your head."
UNLOCKING (1)
 A7   61: 1 began by taking the little golden key, and unlocking the door that led into the garden. Then she set to
UNPLEASANT (3)
 T4   144:22   Alice began, "Well! They were <u>both</u> very unpleasant characters--" Here she checked herself in some
 A5   36:17 and the Caterpillar seemed to be in a <u>very</u> unpleasant state of mind, she turned away.
 A1   10:23 burnt, and eaten up by wild beasts, and other unpleasant things, all because they <u>would</u> not remember the
UNROLLED (2)
 A8   66:14 very provoking to find that the hedgehog had unrolled itself, and was in the act of crawling away: besides
 A11   87:15 blew three blasts on the trumpet, and then unrolled the parchment-scroll, and read as follows:--
UNSATISFACTORY (2)
 T6   168:39 to have such a long word to say) "of all the unsatisfactory people I <u>ever</u> met--" She never finished the
 T6   168:38 saying to herself, as she went, "of all the unsatisfactory--" (she repeated this aloud, as it was a great
UNTIDY (4)
 T2   123:17 one ca'n't help one's petals getting a little untidy."
 T5   149:22 one else to dress her, she was so dreadfully untidy. "Every single thing's crooked," Alice thought to
 T4   144:34 and he was lying crumpled up into a sort of untidy heap, and snoring loud--"fit to snore his head off!" as
 T12 207:29 I wonder? That must be the reason you were so untidy in my dream--Dinah! Do you know that you're scrubbing a
UNTIED (1)
 T8W   17: 9   He untied the handkerchief as he spoke, and Alice looked at his
UNTIL (6)
 A12   93: 2   said the King, in a very grave voice, "until all the jurymen are back in their proper places--all,"
 T8   188:30 / <u>I shook him well from side to side</u>, / <u>Until his face was blue</u>: / '<u>Come, tell me how you live</u>,' <u>I</u>
 A5   41:23   This time Alice waited patiently until it chose to speak again. In a minute or two the
 A5   43:35 sometimes taller, and sometimes shorter, until she had succeeded in bringing herself down to her usual
 A11   88:35 sensation, which puzzled her a good deal until she made out what it was: she was beginning to grow
 A2   15:23 on all the same, shedding gallons of tears, until there was a large pool round her, about four inches deep
UNTO (1)
 T8   188: 5 / <u>And sell them in the street</u>. / <u>I sell them unto men</u>,' he said, / '<u>Who sail on stormy seas</u>; / <u>And that's</u>
UNTWIST (1)
 A5   43:31 and every now and then she had to stop and untwist it. After a while she remembered that she still held

UNUSUALLY (1)
    A6   48:18   "Oh, there goes his <u>precious</u> nose!", as an unusually large saucepan flew close by it, and very nearly
UNWELCOME (1)
    TI   103:21   With <u>bitter</u> <u>tidings</u> <u>laden</u>, / <u>Shall</u> <u>summon</u> <u>to</u> <u>unwelcome</u> <u>bed</u> / <u>A</u> <u>melancholy</u> <u>maiden</u>! / <u>We</u> <u>are</u> <u>but</u> <u>older</u>
UNWILLINGLY (2)
    T8W   13:14   So she went back to the Wasp--rather unwillingly, for she was <u>very</u> anxious to be a Queen.
    A7   59:40   into the Dormouse's place, and Alice rather unwillingly took the place of the March Hare. The Hatter was
UNWISELY (1)
    T6   160:29   and all his men," Alice interrupted, rather unwisely.
UNWOUND (2)
    T1   108:19   upon the floor, and yards and yards of it got unwound again.
    T1   108:36   wasn't thirsty too? Now for number three: you unwound every bit of the worsted while I wasn't looking!
UP (220) [entries omitted]
UPON (39)
    T1   110:34   the other way. I can see all of it when I get upon a chair--all but the bit just behind the fireplace. Oh! I
    A9   73:22   They very soon came upon a Gryphon, lying fast asleep in the sun. (If you don't
    A1   9:19   when suddenly, thump! thump! down she came upon a heap of sticks and dry leaves, and the fall was over.
    T2   120:27   be done but start again. This time she came upon a large flowerbed, with a border of daisies, and a
    A4   28: 2   going to leave the room, when her eye fell upon a little bottle that stood near the looking-glass. There
    A1   9:34   Suddenly she came upon a little three-legged table, all made of solid glass:
    A1   9:39   However, on the second time round, she came upon a low curtain she had not noticed before, and behind it
    A4   27:21   I can find them." As she said this, she came upon a neat little house, on the door of which was a bright
    A7   58:32   "Once upon a time there were three little sisters," the Dormouse
    A8   62:18   unjust things--" when his eye chanced to fall upon Alice, as she stood watching them, and he checked himself
    T7   175:15   was going on, when his eye happened to fall upon Alice: he turned round instantly, and stood for some time
    A5   44: 1   wonder?" As she said this, she came suddenly upon an open place, with a little house in it about four feet
    A4   30:36   to herself. "Why, they seem to put everything upon Bill! I wouldn't be in Bill's place for a good deal: this
    T9   201:31   was dead silence, and all eyes were fixed upon her; "and it's a very curious thing, I think--every poem
    A8   64:10   The King laid his hand upon her arm, and timidly said "Consider, my dear: she is only
    T8   179:14   in crimson armour, came galloping down upon her, brandishing a great club. Just as he reached her,
    A12   98: 3   leaves that had fluttered down from the trees upon her face.
    A12   98:18   once again the tiny hands were clasped upon her knee, and the bright eager eyes were looking up into
    A12   97:10   rose up into the air, and came flying down upon her; she gave a little scream, half of fright and half of
    T4   146:24   Alice laid her hand upon his arm and said, in a soothing tone, "You needn't be so
    A11   90:15   the guinea-pig, head first, and then sat upon it.)
    A4   27:23   plate with the name "W. RABBIT" engraved upon it. She went in without knocking, and hurried upstairs,
    A11   86: 8   court was a table, with a large dish of tarts upon it: they looked so good, that it made Alice quite hungry
    A3   23:18   stood for a long time with one finger pressed upon its forehead (the position in which you usually see
    A7   56:23   the Hatter, and he poured a little hot tea upon its nose.
    T8   189:19   <u>foot</u> / <u>Into</u> <u>a</u> <u>left-hand</u> <u>shoe</u>, / <u>Or</u> <u>if</u> <u>I</u> <u>drop</u> <u>upon</u> <u>my</u> <u>toe</u> / <u>A</u> <u>very</u> <u>heavy</u> <u>weight</u>, / <u>I</u> <u>weep</u>, <u>for</u> <u>it</u> <u>reminds</u> <u>me</u>
    A1   8:17   here and there she saw maps and pictures hung upon pegs. She took down a jar from one of the shelves as she
    T1   115: 8   so with laughter that she nearly let him drop upon the floor.
    T1   108:19   to a scramble, in which the ball rolled down upon the floor, and yards and yards of it got unwound again.
    T2   120:18   So, resolutely turning her back upon the house, she set out once more down the path,
    A10   80: 8   replied. / "<u>There</u> <u>is</u> <u>another</u> <u>shore</u>, <u>you</u> <u>know</u>, <u>upon</u> <u>the</u> <u>other</u> <u>side</u>. / <u>The</u> <u>further</u> <u>off</u> <u>from</u> <u>England</u> <u>the</u> <u>nearer</u>
    T9   204:17   as for <u>you</u>," she went on, turning fiercely upon the Red Queen, whom she considered as the cause of all
    T9   204:26   jumping over a bottle which had just lighted upon the table, "I'll shake you into a kitten, that I will!"
    T1   115:14   added, as she smoothed his hair, and set him upon the table near the Queen.
    A8   63:12   gardeners instantly threw themselves flat upon their faces. There was a sound of many footsteps, and
    T9   202:23   managed it: some of them put their glasses upon their heads like extinguishers, and drank all that
    A5   44: 3   thought Alice, "it'll never do to come upon them <u>this</u> size: why, I should frighten them out of their
    A8   65:31   shoulder as he spoke, and then raised himself upon tiptoe, put his mouth close to her ear, and whispered
    T3   137:30   till, on turning a sharp corner, she came upon two fat little men, so suddenly that she could not help
UPRIGHT (3)
    A5   41:17   said the Caterpillar angrily, rearing itself upright as it spoke (it was exactly three inches high).
    T5   158:16   to the other end of the shop, and set the egg upright on a shelf.
    T8   182:32   "First you take an upright stick," said the Knight. "Then you make your hair
UPROAR (1)
    T7   178:10   ears, vainly trying to shut out the dreadful uproar.
UPSET (4)
    A12   93:11   a little recovered from the shock of being upset, and their slates and pencils had been found and handed
    T9   202:24   all that trickled down their faces--others upset the decanters, and drank the wine as it ran off the
    A7   60: 1   off than before, as the March Hare had just upset the milk-jug into his plate.
    A12   92: 6   of a globe of gold-fish she had accidentally upset the week before.
UPSETTING (1)
    A12   92: 4   over the jury-box with the edge of her skirt, upsetting all the jurymen on to the heads of the crowd below,
UPSIDE-DOWN (3)
    T6   163:15   "You're holding it upside down!" Alice interrupted.
    T8   181:15   deal box fastened across his shoulders, upside-down, and with the lid hanging open. Alice looked at it
    T8   181:19   clothes and sandwiches in. You see I carry it upside-down, so that the rain ca'n't get in."
UPSTAIRS (1)
    A4   27:24   it. She went in without knocking, and hurried upstairs, in great fear lest she should meet the real Mary Ann
UPWARDS (1)
    T8   182:34   is because it hangs <u>down</u>--things never fall <u>upwards</u>, you know. It's a plan of my own invention. You may
US (28) [entries omitted]
USE (34)
    T6   163:30   "When <u>I</u> use a word," Humpty Dumpty said, in rather a scornful tone,
    T1   114: 4   Alice was very anxious to be of use, and, as the poor little Lily was nearly screaming herself
    A11   87:11   rest of the day; and this was of very little use, as it left no mark on the slate.
    A5   43:14   No, no! You're a serpent; and there's no use denying it. I suppose you'll be telling me next that you

USE (cont.)
```
A10   81:41   said Alice a little timidly; "but it's no use going back to yesterday, because I was a different person
A1    12:21                       "Come, there's no use in crying like that!" said Alice to herself rather sharply
A6    46:10                   "There's no sort of use in knocking," said the Footman, "and that for two reasons.
A5    42:37   more puzzled, but she thought there was no use in saying anything more till the Pigeon had finished.
T3   130:10   Alice thought to herself "Then there's no use in speaking." The voices didn't join in, this time, as she
A6    46:43                       "Oh, there's no use in talking to him," said Alice desperately: "he's
A12   93: 9   "I should think it would be quite as much use in the trial one way up as the other."
A1    10:12             There seemed to be no use in waiting by the little door, so she went back to the
T7   175: 4                           "No use, no use!" said the King. "She runs so fearfully quick. You
A2    19:10       "Would it be of any use, now," thought Alice, "to speak to this mouse? Everything
A1    12:28   of pretending to be two people. "But it's no use now," thought poor Alice, "to pretend to be two people!
A1     7: 4   or conversations in it, "and what is the use of a book," thought Alice, "without pictures or
T9   193: 3   should have meant! What do you suppose is the use of a child without any meaning? Even a joke should have
A8    63:31   processions; "and besides, what would be the use of a procession," thought she, "if people had all to lie
T9   196:18   the middle of an accident! Where would be the use of it?" but she did not say this aloud, for fear of
A10   84: 3                   "What is the use of repeating all that stuff?" the Mock Turtle interrupted,
T3   132:35                       "What's the use of their having names," the Gnat said, "if they wo'n't
A5    38: 7   / "I kept all my limbs very supple / By the use of this ointment--one shilling the box--/ Allow me to sell
T7   175: 4                           "No use, no use!" said the King. "She runs so fearfully quick. You might
T8   188:11   / To dye one's whiskers green, / And always use so large a fan / That they could not be seen. / So, having
A8    67:17   the eyes appeared, and then nodded. "It's no use speaking to it," she thought, "till its ears have come, or
T2   120:13                       "It's no use talking about it," Alice said, looking up at the house and
T7   171:13   attention from himself--but it was of no use--the Anglo-Saxon attitudes only got more extraordinary
A2    17:21   I'm Mabel, I'll stay down here. It'll be no use their putting their heads down and saying 'Come up again,
T8W   13: 9       "I don't think I can be of any use to him," was Alice's first thought, as she turned to
T3   132:37                   "No use to them," said Alice; "but it's useful to the people that
T5   153:11   Alice laughed. "There's no use trying," she said: "one ca'n't believe impossible things
A1    10: 7   poor Alice, "it would be of very little use without my shoulders. Oh, how I wish I could shut up like
T8   181:25   must have fallen out! And the box is no use without them." He unfastened it as he spoke, and was just
T4   145:18                   "Well, it's no use your talking about waking him," said Tweedledum, "when
```
USED (20)
```
A5    36:32   said Alice. "I ca'n't remember things as I used--and I don't keep the same size for ten minutes together!
T7   177: 9   in reply to the Lion (she was getting quite used to being called 'the Monster'). "I've cut several slices
A9    74:42   in the sea. The master was an old Turtle--we used to call him Tortoise--"
A9    76:39   Drawling-master was an old conger-eel, that used to come once a week: he taught us Drawling, Stretching,
A2    17: 6   and the words did not come the same as they used to do:--
T5   155: 6   as quietly as possible, as if it were quite used to do.
A5    43:38   it felt quite strange at first; but she got used to it in a few minutes, and began talking to herself, as
A5    41:21                       "You'll get used to it in time," said the Caterpillar; and it put the
A5    41:18                       "But I'm not used to it!" pleaded poor Alice in a piteous tone. And she
A2    16: 8   all is! I'll try if I know all the things I used to know. Let me see: four times five is twelve, and four
T8   189:22   for it reminds me so / Of that old man I used to know--/ Whose look was mild, whose speech was slow, /
A6    52:11   surprised at this, she was getting so well used to queer things happening. While she was still looking at
A4    29: 4   wonder what can have happened to me! When I used to read fairy tales, I fancied that kind of thing never
T8W   18:10                   "It aint what I'm used to," said the Wasp: "however I'll try; wait a bit." He
A9    77: 7   a sigh. "He taught Laughing and Grief, they used to say."
T1   110:10   I wish I could tell you half the things Alice used to say, beginning with her favourite phrase "Let's
A10   82:30           "That's different from what I used to say when I was a child," said the Gryphon.
T8W   18: 4   "When I was young, you know, my ringlets used to wave--"
T8   184:43   one than that--like a sugar-loaf. When I used to wear it, if I fell off the horse, it always touched
A7    58:15   so," said the Hatter: "as the things get used up."
```
USEFUL (4)
```
A3    26: 6   said Alice, always ready to make herself useful, and looking anxiously about her. "Oh, do let me help
A2    20: 9   to a farmer, you know, and he says it's so useful, it's worth a hundred pounds! He says it kills all the
T9   194:39   the Red Queen began again. "Can you answer useful questions?" she said. "How is bread made?"
T3   132:37   "No use to them," said Alice; "but it's useful to the people that name them, I suppose. If not, why do
```
USING (2)
```
A7    54: 4   them, fast asleep, and the other two were using it as a cushion, resting their elbows on it, and talking
A12   96:23   made no mark; but he now hastily began again, using the ink, that was trickling down his face, as long as it
```
USUAL (11)
```
A5    43:39   few minutes, and began talking to herself, as usual, "Come, there's half my plan done now! How puzzling all
T6   159:23   said Humpty Dumpty, looking away from her as usual, "have no more sense than a baby!"
A5    43:36   had succeeded in bringing herself down to her usual height.
T8   190:27   him. "There he goes! Right on his head as usual! However, he gets on again pretty easily--that comes of
A2    15:39   to-day! And yesterday things went on just as usual. I wonder if I've changed in the night? Let me think:
A9    71:14                       "Right, as usual," said the Duchess: "what a clear way you have of
T9   194:15                       "Wrong, as usual," said the Red Queen: "the dog's temper would remain."
T2   120:12   she turned a corner rather more quickly than usual, she ran against it before she could stop herself.
T8   185:21   to hear that he was talking on in his usual tone. "All kinds of fastness," he repeated: "but it was
T8   182:24                   "Only in the usual way," Alice said, smiling.
A12   94:10   "unless it was written to nobody, which isn't usual, you know."
```
USUALLY (2) [See also UNUSUALLY]
```
A1    11: 3   cut your finger very deeply with a knife, it usually bleeds; and she had never forgotten that, if you drink
A3    23:19   upon its forehead (the position in which you usually see Shakespeare, in the pictures of him), while the
```
USURPATION (1)
```
A3    22: 5   and had been of late much accustomed to usurpation and conquest. Edwin and Morcar, the earls of Mercia
```

-V-

VERY (307)

T6	159:18	from Alice as he spoke, "to be called an egg--very!"
A3	24: 5	Alice thought the whole thing very absurd, but they all looked so grave that she did not
T9	204:26	catching hold of the little creature in the act of jumping over a bottle which had just lighted upon
A3	26: 5	"I had not!" cried the Mouse, sharply and very angrily.
A7	59:24	"There's no such thing!" Alice was beginning very angrily, but the Hatter and the March Hare went "Sh! Sh!"
T6	162:22	Evidently Humpty Dumpty was very angry, though he said nothing for a minute or two. When
T8W	13:15	to the Wasp--rather unwillingly, for she was very anxious to be a Queen.
T1	114: 4	Alice was anxious to be of use, and, as the poor little Lily was
A6	49:31	The baby grunted again, and Alice looked very anxiously into its face to see what was the matter with
T8	187:29	all, I can no more.'" She stood and listened very attentively, but no tears came into her eyes.
T8	182:16	very carefully, because the Knight was so very awkward in putting in the dish: the first two or three
T3	135:11	you wish I had made it?" Alice asked. "It's a very bad one."
T8	181:13	in tin armour, which seemed to fit him very badly, and he had a queer-shaped little deal box fastened
T1	115:41	Knight is sliding down the poker. He balances very badly'). "That's not a memorandum of your feelings!"
T8	186:35	"It's long," said the Knight, "but it's very, very beautiful. Everybody that hears me sing it--either it
T5	149:15	it would never do to have an argument at the very beginning of their conversation, so she smiled and said
T4	140:25	/ Shining with all his might: / He did his very best to make / The billows smooth and bright--/ And this
T4	147:34	"I'm very brave, generally," he went on in a low voice: "only
A11	86:28	The twelve jurors were all writing very busily on slates. "What are they doing?" Alice whispered
T8	182:16	to manage, though Alice held the bag open very carefully, because the Knight was so very awkward in
A5	43:33	of mushroom in her hands, and she set to work very carefully, nibbling first at one and then at the other,
A3	26:32	once: one old Magpie began wrapping itself up very carefully, remarking "I really must be getting home: the
A8	64:14	The Knave did so, very carefully, with one foot.
A7	60: 4	to offend the Dormouse again, so she began very cautiously: "But I don't understand. Where did they draw
A7	55: 1	"Then it wasn't very civil of you to offer it," said Alice angrily.
A7	55: 2	"It wasn't very civil of you to sit down without being invited," said the
T5	149: 4	out wide, as if she were flying, and Alice very civilly went to meet her with the shawl.
A2	19:23	all her knowledge of history, Alice had no very clear notion how long ago anything had happened.) So she
T6	164:14	"You seem very clever at explaining words, Sir," said Alice. "Would you
T8	186:19	pudding ever will be cooked! And yet it was a very clever pudding to invent."
T1	112:13	next the fire seemed to be all alive, and the very clock on the chimney-piece (you know you can only see the
T4	147:45	she can watch us--only you'd better not come very close," he added: "I generally hit every thing I can see
T8W	13: 7	up together, and shivering as if he were very cold.
A5	35:16	and being so many different sizes in a day is very confusing."
T3	135:38	this way when she reached the wood: it looked very cool and shady. "Well, at any rate it's a great comfort,"
T8W	15: 9	"Were what?" the Wasp asked in a very cross voice.
A10	82: 8	Turtle drew a long breath, and said "That's very curious!"
A11	88:34	Just at this moment Alice felt a very curious sensation, which puzzled her a good deal until
A7	60:39	had a door leading right into it. "That's very curious!" she thought. "But everything's curious to-day.
A8	62: 3	painting them red. Alice thought this a very curious thing, and she went nearer to watch them, and,
T9	201:31	and all eyes were fixed upon her; "and it's a very curious thing, I think--every poem was about fishes in
A6	45: 8	that curled all over their heads. She felt very curious to know what it was all about, and crept a little
A11	91:30	Rabbit as he fumbled over the list, feeling very curious to see what the next witness would be like,
T6	164:37	"They must be very curious-looking creatures."
T4	146: 2	out of the wood, for really it's coming on very dark. Do you think it's going to rain?"
T5	158:18	among the tables and chairs, for the shop was very dark towards the end. "The egg seems to get further away
A9	77:24	about lessons," the Gryphon interrupted in a very decided tone. "Tell her something about the games now."
A8	68: 3	"Well, it must be removed," said the King very decidedly; and he called to the Queen, who was passing at
T9	195:19	"The cause of lightning," Alice said very decidedly, for she felt quite certain about this, "is the
T9	201: 6	"Certainly not," the Red Queen said, very decidedly: "it isn't etiquette to cut any one you've been
T9	202:36	be at all the thing," the Red Queen said very decidedly: so Alice tried to submit to it with good grace
A1	8:11	Either the well was very deep, or she fell very slowly, for she had plenty of time
A1	8:10	herself falling down what seemed to be a very deep well.
A1	11: 2	it too long; and that, if you cut your finger very deeply with a knife, it usually bleeds; and she had never
T1	108: 7	kitten, and sometimes to herself. Kitty sat very demurely on her knee, pretending to watch the progress of
A8	66:19	soon came to the conclusion that it was a very difficult game indeed.
A5	41:35	as it was perfectly round, she found this a very difficult question. However, at last she stretched her
T3	137:16	It was not a very difficult question to answer, as there was only one road
A12	93:12	and handed back to them, they set to work very diligently to write out a history of the accident, all
T7	174:16	Alice took a piece to taste, but it was very dry.
T2	127:29	and ate it as well as she could: and it was very dry: and she thought she had never been so nearly choked
A9	75: 3	said the Mock Turtle angrily. "Really you are very dull!"
A7	59: 9	some more tea," the March Hare said to Alice, very earnestly.
A1	9:17	in hand with Dinah, and was saying to her, very earnestly, "Now, Dinah, tell me the truth: did you ever
A7	59:13	you ca'n't take less," said the Hatter: "it's very easy to take more than nothing."
T8W	13:12	matter," she added, checking herself on the very edge. "If I once jump over, everything will change, and
T1	115:23	"I assure you, my dear, I turned cold to the very ends of my whiskers!"
T1	110:14	and queens;" and her sister, who liked being very exact, had argued that they couldn't, because there were
T1	108: 5	up the ball again. But she didn't get on very fast, as she was talking all the time, sometimes to the
T2	127:17	generally get to somewhere else--if you ran very fast for a long time as we've been doing."
T2	128:30	ran quickly into the wood ("and she can run very fast!" thought Alice), there was no way of guessing, but
A11	86:26	of it: for she thought, and rightly too, that very few little girls of her age knew the meaning of it at all
T8	190:36	and to be a Queen! How grand it sounds!" A very few steps brought her to the edge of the brook. "The
A1	10:11	lately, that Alice had begun to think that very few things indeed were really impossible.
A8	65:25	"It's--it's a very fine day!" said a timid voice at her side. She was
T1	112: 2	lightly down into the Looking-glass room. The very first thing she did was to look whether there was a fire
A1	12:27	against herself, for this curious child was very fond of pretending to be two people. "But it's no use now
T3	131:16	Then a very gentle voice in the distance said, "She must be labeled
T1	114:23	So Alice picked him up very gently, and lifted him across more slowly than she had

VERY (cont.)

T5	154: 3	"I don't <u>quite</u> know yet," Alice said very gently. "I should like to look all round me first, if I
T6	160:34	"I haven't indeed!" Alice said very gently. "It's in a book."
T5	149: 5	"I'm very glad I happened to be in the way," Alice said, as she
A8	67:20	and began an account of the game, feeling very glad she had some one to listen to her. The Cat seemed to
A10	80:14	dance to watch," said Alice, feeling very glad that it was over at last: "and I do so like that
A9	70: 4	Alice was very glad to find her in such a pleasant temper, and thought
A2	18:11	deal frightened at the sudden change, but very glad to find herself still in existence. "And now for the
A6	48:23	<u>not</u> be an advantage," said Alice, who felt very glad to get an opportunity of showing off a little of her
T7	170: 3	got worse every moment, and Alice was very glad to get out of the wood into an open place, where she
T8	189: 5	a wink) / 'By which I get my wealth--/ And very gladly will I drink / Your Honour's noble health.'
A1	12:23	off this minute!" She generally gave herself very good advice (though she very seldom followed it), and
T8	181:34	"Yes, it's a very good bee-hive," the Knight said in a discontented tone,
T8W	16:14	"And it's very good for the conceit," added the Wasp.
T8W	16:13	pityingly at him. "Tying up the face is very good for the toothache," she said.
A5	41:16	"It is a very good height indeed!" said the Caterpillar angrily,
T4	143:10	need: / Pepper and vinegar besides / Are very good indeed--/ Now, if you're ready, Oysters dear, / We
T5	150: 3	"It's very good jam," said the Queen.
A1	8:32	in the school-room, and though this was not a very good opportunity for showing off her knowledge, as there
T2	122:30	This sounded a very good reason, and Alice was quite pleased to know it. "I
A4	27: 7	fan and the pair of white kid-gloves, and she very good-naturedly began hunting about for them, but they
A12	93: 1	trial cannot proceed," said the King, in a very grave voice, "until all the jurymen are back in their
A12	94:35	"Begin at the beginning," the King said, very gravely, "and go on till you come to the end: then stop
A5	36:12	remarks, and she drew herself up and said, very gravely, "I think you ought to tell me who you are, first
T4	147:25	"You know," he added very gravely, "it's one of the most serious things that can
T8	183:11	I've had plenty of practice," the Knight said very gravely: "plenty of practice!"
A3	23:31	"Of course," the Dodo replied very gravely. "What else have you got in your pocket?" it went
T5	152:31	I never can remember the rule. You must be very happy, living in this wood, and being glad whenever you
T2	122:26	Alice did so. "It's very hard," she said; "but I don't see what that has to do
A8	68:35	as they all spoke at once, she found it very hard to make out exactly what they said.
T8	191: 4	dismay, as she put her hands up to something very heavy, that fitted tight all around her head.
T8	189:20	shoe, / Or if I drop upon my toe / A very heavy weight, / I weep, for it reminds me so / Of that
T6	164:20	This sounded very hopeful, so Alice repeated the first verse:
A9	70: 7	I'm a Duchess," she said to herself (not in a very hopeful tone, though), "I wo'n't have any pepper in my
A2	15:36	up the fan and gloves, and, as the hall was very hot, she kept fanning herself all the time she went on
A8	65: 6	"May it please your Majesty," said Two, in a very humble tone, going down on one knee as he spoke, "we were
A7	59:28	"No, please go on!" Alice said very humbly. "I wo'n't interrupt you again. I dare say there
A3	26: 3	"I beg your pardon," said Alice very humbly: "you had got to the fifth bend, I think?"
T7	173:25	them oyster-shells in there--so you see he's very hungry and thirsty. How are you, dear child?" he went on,
T6	162:27	"I know it's very ignorant of me," Alice said, in so humble a tone that
A7	59: 5	"So they were," said the Dormouse; "very ill."
A12	93:21	"That's very important," the King said, turning to the jury. They were
T12	207: 6	"it is a very inconvenient habit of kittens (Alice had once made the
A10	80:13	"Thank you, it's a very interesting dance to watch," said Alice, feeling very
A10	81: 8	"Thank you," said Alice, "it's very interesting. I never knew so much about a whiting before
T9	201:38	"Her Red Majesty's very kind to mention it," the White Queen murmured into
T8W	13:19	herself, and she stooped over him, and said very kindly, "I hope you're not in much pain?"
T3	132:20	It certainly was a <u>very</u> large Gnat: "about the size of a chicken," Alice thought.
T8	190: 3	was whiter than the snow, / Whose face was <u>very</u> like a crow, / With eyes, like cinders, all aglow, / Who
A1	9:10	afraid, but you might catch a bat, and that's very like a mouse, you know. But do cats eat bats, I wonder?"
T9	203:21	went fluttering about in all directions: "and very like birds they look," Alice thought to herself, as well
A4	32:40	get hold of it: then Alice, thinking it was very like having a game of play with a cart-horse, and
T3	129: 2	was going to travel through. "It's something very like learning geography," thought Alice, as she stood on
T1	111: 4	door of our drawing-room wide open: and it's very like our passage as far as you can see, only you know it
A2	19:12	out-of-the-way down here, that I should think very likely it can talk: at any rate, there's no harm in
T8	182: 3	"Not very likely, perhaps," said the Knight; "but, if they do come,
T8	182: 2	mouse-trap was for," said Alice. "It isn't very likely there would be any mice on the horse's back."
A4	32:31	it might be hungry, in which case it would be very likely to eat her up in spite of all her coaxing.
A1	8:26	I fell off the top of the house!" (Which was very likely true.)
A2	16: 7	of things, and she, oh, she knows such a very little! Besides, <u>she's</u> she, and <u>I'm</u> I, and--oh dear, how
A11	87:11	for the rest of the day; and this was of very little use, as it left no mark on the slate.
A1	10: 7	through," thought poor Alice, "it would be of very little use without my shoulders. Oh, how I wish I could
A4	32:43	of short charges at the stick, running a very little way forwards each time and a long way back, and
T8	185: 1	touched the ground directly. So I had a <u>very</u> little way to fall, you see--But there <u>was</u> the danger of
T5	156:37	real scented rushes, you know, last only a very little while--and these, being dream-rushes, melted away
A3	26:41	poor Alice began to cry again, for she felt very lonely and low-spirited. In a little while, however, she
T5	152:33	"Only it is so <u>very</u> lonely here!" Alice said in a melancholy voice; and, at
T8	186:33	"Is it very long?" Alice asked, for she had heard a good deal of
A6	51: 2	good-natured, she thought: still it had very long claws and a great many teeth, so she felt that it
T4	140:19	Alice ventured to interrupt him. "If it's <u>very</u> long," she said, as politely as she could, "would you
A9	74:34	These words were followed by a very long silence, broken only by an occasional exclamation of
T6	167:21	I said it <u>very</u> loud and clear: / I went and shouted in his ear."
T5	155:32	said Alice: "you've said it very often--and very loud. Please, where are the crabs?"
A8	64: 8	"Nonsense!" said Alice, very loudly and decidedly, and the Queen was silent.
A11	88:41	"I ca'n't help it," said Alice very meekly: "I'm growing."
A5	36:35	it all came different!" Alice replied in a very melancholy voice.
A11	86: 7	a scroll of parchment in the other. In the very middle of the court was a table, with a large dish of
T5	156:35	to lose all their scent and beauty, from the very moment that she picked them? Even real scented rushes,
T8	182:31	"I should like to hear it, very much."
T8	190:21	coming so far--and for the song--I liked it very much."

VERY (cont.)

T3	131:39	of this was that it tickled her ear very much, and quite took off her thoughts from the
A8	67:10	curious appearance in the air: it puzzled her very much at first, but after watching it a minute or two she
A7	60:26	"Really, now you ask me," said Alice, very much confused, "I don't think--"
T4	140: 7	"Nohow. And thank you very much for asking," said Tweedledum.
T8	190:20	course I'll wait," said Alice: "and thank you very much for coming so far--and for the song--I liked it very
A4	33: 9	"I should have liked teaching it tricks very much, if--if I'd only been the right size to do it! Oh
T5	152:12	do you expect to do it?" Alice said, feeling very much inclined to laugh.
T8	184:28	"Very much indeed," Alice said politely.
A10	79: 4	"Very much indeed," said Alice.
A12	92: 5	there they lay sprawling about, reminding her very much of a globe of gold-fish she had accidentally upset
A1	7:12	remarkable in that; nor did Alice think it so very much out of the way to hear the Rabbit say to itself "Oh
A9	70:10	that makes people hot-tempered," she went on, very much pleased at having found out a new kind of rule, "and
T6	163:44	child," said Humpty Dumpty, looking very much pleased. "I meant by 'impenetrability' that we've
T9	198: 6	the--which bell must I ring?" she went on, very much puzzled by the names. "I'm not a visitor, and I'm
T7	177:18	as Alice sat with the knife in her hand, very much puzzled how to begin. "The Monster has given the
T5	157: 5	remarked, as Alice got back into her place, very much relieved to find herself still in the boat.
T6	166:31	"Thank you very much," said Alice.
A6	52: 4	"I should like it very much," said Alice, "but I haven't been invited yet."
T8	181: 6	"Thank you very much," said Alice. "May I help you off with your helmet?"
T9	202:34	"Thank you very much," she whispered in reply, "but I can do quite well
T8	183: 5	The Knight looked very much surprised, and a little offended at the remark.
T7	175: 2	you going to run and help her?" Alice asked, very much surprised at his taking it so quietly.
T9	192:13	her, one on each side: she would have liked very much to ask them how they came there, but she feared it
A1	9: 6	soon began talking again. "Dinah'll miss me very much to-night, I should think!" (Dinah was the cat.) "I
A8	65:24	and Alice joined the procession, wondering very much what would happen next.
T6	160:19	for the queer creature. "That wall is so very narrow!"
A6	46:23	it," she said to herself; "his eyes are so very nearly at the top of his head. But at any rate he might
A6	48:18	large saucepan flew close by it, and very nearly carried it off.
A9	74:36	heavy sobbing of the Mock Turtle. Alice was very nearly getting up and saying, "Thank you, Sir, for your
A9	74:20	asked the Gryphon. And the Gryphon answered, very nearly in the same words as before, "It's all his fancy,
T1	108:23	all the mischief you had been doing, I was very nearly opening the window, and putting you out into the
T8W	14: 5	felt rather offended at this answer, and was very nearly walking on and leaving him, but she thought to
A4	32:22	It sounded an excellent plan, no doubt, and very neatly and simply arranged: the only difficulty was, that
T7	176:24	to prevent the quarrel going on: he was very nervous, and his voice quite quivered. "All round the
T8	186:26	"Not very nice alone," he interrupted, quite eagerly: "but you've
T8	186:25	"That wouldn't be very nice, I'm afraid--"
A1	11: 7	Alice ventured to taste it, and, finding it very nice (it had, in fact, a sort of mixed flavour of
T4	143:20	'It was so kind of you to come! / And you are very nice!' / The Carpenter said nothing but / 'Cut us another
T9	202:32	Queen whispered, as Alice got up to do it, very obediently, but a little frightened.
T7	177:13	This sounded nonsense, but Alice very obediently got up, and carried the dish round, and the
T5	158:21	chair? Why, it's got branches, I declare! How very odd to find trees growing here! And actually here's a
T3	134:18	"But that must happen very often," Alice remarked thoughtfully.
T5	155:32	"Indeed I did," said Alice: "you've said it very often--and very loud. Please, where are the crabs?"
T8	182:40	Whenever the horse stopped (which it did very often), he fell off in front; and, whenever it went on
T9	198:12	rang in vain for a long time; but at last a very old Frog, who was sitting under a tree, got up and
T8W	13: 5	to see what was the matter. Something like a very old man (only that his face was more like a wasp) was
T6	160:27	did you? The King has promised me--with his very own mouth--to--to--"
T4	147:30	"Do I look very pale?" said Tweedledum, coming up to have his helmet tied
T6	161:17	I ca'n't quite remember it," Alice said, very politely.
T9	201:41	"Please do," Alice said very politely.
T8W	18: 9	Would you mind saying it in rhyme?" she asked very politely.
T5	153:23	I hope your finger is better now?" Alice said very politely, as she crossed the little brook after the Queen
A8	63:40	is Alice, so please your Majesty," said Alice very politely; but she added, to herself, "Why, they're only a
A3	22: 8	your pardon!" said the Mouse, frowning, but very politely. "Did you speak?"
A6	48: 4	"I don't know of any that do," Alice said very politely, feeling quite pleased to have got into a
A5	35:14	I ca'n't put it more clearly," Alice replied, very politely, "for I ca'n't understand it myself, to begin
A9	72:11	I should understand that better," Alice said very politely, "if I had it written down: but I ca'n't quite
A11	90:10	"You're a very poor speaker," said the King.
T1	109:15	about--whenever the wind blows--oh, that's very pretty!" cried Alice, dropping the ball of worsted to
A10	79: 2	"It must be a very pretty dance," said Alice timidly.
T1	118:25	"It seems very pretty," she said when she had finished it, "but it's
T6	159:20	Alice gently explained. "And some eggs are very pretty, you know," she added, hoping to turn her remark
T6	168: 6	And he was very proud and stiff: / He said 'I'd go and wake them, if--'
T6	159:17	"It's very provoking," Humpty Dumpty said after a long silence,
T7	177: 8	sawing away diligently with the knife. "It's very provoking!" she said, in reply to the Lion (she was
A8	66:13	down, and was going to begin again, it was very provoking to find that the hedgehog had unrolled itself,
T5	155:24	nothing, but pulled away. There was something very queer about the water, she thought, as every now and then
T3	131: 6	was a Beetle sitting next the Goat (it was a very queer carriage-full of passengers altogether), and, as
A10	82:21	knew what she was saying; and the words came very queer indeed:--
A5	36: 8	said Alice: "all I know is, it would feel very queer to me."
T5	158:22	here's a little brook! Well, this is the very queerest shop I ever saw!" * * * * * * * * * * * * * So
T9	202:22	the guests began drinking it directly, and very queerly they managed it: some of them put their glasses
T2	128: 8	in its first move, you know. So you'll go very quickly through the Third Square--by railway, I should
A6	52:19	"It turned into a pig," Alice answered very quietly, just as if the Cat had come back in a natural
T9	194: 3	from eight I ca'n't, you know," Alice replied very readily: "but--"
A7	56:16	"Of course not," Alice replied very readily: "but that's because it stays the same year for
A1	7:11	There was nothing so very remarkable in that; nor did Alice think it so very much
A12	93:24	your Majesty means, of course," he said, in a very respectful tone, but frowning and making faces at him as
T8W	18: 2	"It's to comb hair with--your wig's so very rough, you know."

VERY (cont.)
```
A7     55:10        Alice said with some severity: "it's very rude."
T4    140:33   to be there / After the day was done--/ 'It's very rude of him,' she said, / 'To come and spoil the fun!'
A10    79: 1   like mad things all this time, sat down again very sadly and quietly, and looked at Alice.
A8     65:28                                 "Very," said Alice. "Where's the Duchess?"
A1     12:23   gave herself very good advice (though she very seldom followed it), and sometimes she scolded herself so
T8    185: 9   had to kick him, of course," the Knight said, very seriously. "And then he took the helmet off again--but it
A5     36:12   irritated at the Caterpillar's making such very short remarks, and she drew herself up and said, very
A8     66:21   and fighting for the hedgehogs; and in a very short time the Queen was in a furious passion, and went
A1      7: 7   as she could, for the hot day made her feel very sleepy and stupid), whether the pleasure of making a
A7     60:15   and rubbing its eyes, for it was getting very sleepy; "and they drew all manner of things--everything
A10    79:12   the time, while the Mock Turtle sang this, very slowly and sadly:--
T9    201:35   wide of the mark. "As to fishes," she said, very slowly and solemnly, putting her mouth close to Alice's
T7    170:22   now!" she exclaimed at last. "But he's coming very slowly--and what curious attitudes he goes into!" (For
A1      8:11   Either the well was very deep, or she fell very slowly, for she had plenty of time as she went down to
T10   205: 4   no resistance whatever: only her face grew very small, and her eyes got large and green: and still, as
A1     12:32   the table: she opened it, and found in it a very small cake, on which the words "EAT ME" were beautifully
A10    81:13   the boots and shoes," the Gryphon replied very solemnly.
A3     21:18   would catch a bad cold if she did not get dry soon.
T3    135:22                     She very soon came to an open field, with a wood on the other side
A9     73:22                     They very soon came upon a Gryphon, lying fast asleep in the sun.
A1     11: 9   turkey, toffy, and hot buttered toast), she very soon finished it off. * * * * * * * * * *
A1     13: 5         So she set to work, and very soon finished off the cake. * * * * * * * * * * *
A11    87: 7   went round the court and got behind him, and very soon found an opportunity of taking it away. She did it
A4     28:16   that! She went on growing, and growing, and very soon had to kneel down on the floor: in another minute
T4    139:39   The other two dancers were fat, and very soon out of breath. "Four times round is enough for one
A4     27:12                     Very soon the Rabbit noticed Alice, as she went hunting about,
T8W    20: 1               "I'm very sorry for you," Alice said heartily: "and I think if your
T4    138:15               "I'm sure I'm very sorry," was all Alice could say; for the words of the old
A5     42:41               "I'm very sorry you've been annoyed," said Alice, who was beginning
T6    168: 4         "But he was very stiff and proud: / He said, 'You needn't shout so loud!'
T8    182:26   he said, anxiously. "You see the wind is so very strong here. It's as strong as soup."
T6    168:17   sudden, Alice thought: but, after such a very strong hint that she ought to be going, she felt that it
A5     41:41   She was a good deal frightened by this very sudden change, but she felt that there was no time to be
A11    89: 2   in that ridiculous fashion." And he got up very sulkily and crossed over to the other side of the court.
A5     38: 6   shook his grey locks, / "I kept all my limbs very supple / By the use of this ointment--one shilling the
T8W    21:12   quite recovered his spirits, and was getting very talkative, she thought she might safely leave him. "I
T4    144:37   on the damp grass," said Alice, who was a very thoughtful little girl.
T7    172:34         "It would have to be a very tiny earthquake!" thought Alice. "Who are at it again?"
T7    175:44   them while this was going on: he looked very tired and sleepy, and his eyes were half shut. "What's
A2     17:26   wish they would put their heads down! I am so very tired of being all alone here!"
A1      7: 1         Alice was beginning to get very tired of sitting by her sister on the bank and of having
A2     19:14   do you know the way out of this pool? I am very tired of swimming about here, O Mouse!" (Alice thought
A12    98:19   were looking up into hers--she could hear the very tones of her voice, and see that queer little toss of her
T5    155: 3   thought struck her. "I'll follow it up to the very top shelf of all. It'll puzzle it to go through the
A9     71:11                     "Very true," said the Duchess: "flamingoes and mustard both
A5     43:16   eggs, certainly," said Alice, who was a very truthful child; "but little girls eat eggs quite as much
A6     49:33   it. There could be no doubt that it had a very turn-up nose, much more like a snout than a real nose:
A9     70:26   close to her: first because the Duchess was very ugly; and secondly, because she was exactly the right
A8     68:32   all the rest were quite silent, and looked very uncomfortable.
A4     28:24   effect, and she grew no larger: still it was very uncomfortable, and, as there seemed to be no sort of
T7    176:13                     The King was evidently very uncomfortable at having to sit down between the two great
A7     54: 5   elbows on it, and talking over its head. "Very uncomfortable for the Dormouse," thought Alice; "only as
A8     67: 3                     Alice began to feel very uneasy: to be sure, she had not as yet had any dispute
T3    131:34   The little voice sighed deeply. It was very unhappy, evidently, and Alice would have said something
T8W    13: 3         "There's somebody very unhappy there," she thought, looking anxiously back to
T4    144:22   a pause, Alice began, "Well! They were both very unpleasant characters--" Here she checked herself in some
A5     36:16   reason, and the Caterpillar seemed to be in a very unpleasant state of mind, she turned away.
T8    186:35   "It's long," said the Knight, "but it's very, very beautiful. Everybody that hears me sing it--either
T8    185:18   by the fall, as for some time he had kept on very well, and she was afraid that he really was hurt this
A6     50:18   over other children she knew, who might do very well as pigs, and was just saying to herself "if one only
T7    174: 6   of bread-and-butter. "They're getting on very well," he said in a choking voice: "each of them has been
T6    164:29                     "That'll do very well," said Alice: "and 'slithy'?"
T4    147:44                     "Very well," the other said, rather sadly: "and she can watch
T8W    20: 4         "Your wig fits very well," the Wasp murmured, looking at her with an
A1     10:19                     It was all very well to say "Drink me," but the wise little Alice was not
A9     70: 9   any pepper in my kitchen at all. Soup does very well without--Maybe it's always pepper that makes people
T4    145:20   only one of the things in his dream. You know very well you're not real."
A5     37: 2   young man said, / "And your hair has become very white; / And yet you incessantly stand on your head--/ Do
A10    82: 4   side, and opened their eyes and mouths so very wide; but she gained courage as she went on. Her
A7     55:11                     The Hatter opened his eyes very wide on hearing this; but all he said was "Why is a raven
```
VEXATION (2)
```
T3    137:11   looking after it, almost ready to cry with vexation at having lost her dear little fellow-traveler so
T8    181:23   didn't know it," the Knight said, a shade of vexation passing over his face. "Then all the things must have
```
VEXED (3)
```
T8    184:38                     He looked so vexed at the idea, that Alice changed the subject hastily.
T5    155:37   so often?" Alice asked at last, rather vexed. "I'm not a bird!"
T8    187: 2         the Knight said, looking a little vexed. "That's what the name is called. The name really is
```
VICIOUS (1)
```
T9    193:12                     "A nasty, vicious temper," the Red Queen remarked; and then there was an
```

VICTORY (1)
  T8   180:15   "It was a glorious victory, wasn't it?" said the White Knight, as he came up
VIEW (2)
  T4   143:18   fine,' the Walrus said. / 'Do you admire the view?
  T7   177: 1   bridge, or the market-place? You get the best view by the old bridge."
VINEGAR (2)
  T4   143: 9   / 'Is what we chiefly need: / Pepper and vinegar besides / Are very good indeed--/ Now, if you're ready
  A9   70:11   at having found out a new kind of rule, "and vinegar that makes them sour--and camomile that makes them
VIOLENCE (1)
  A6   47:16   She said the last word with such sudden violence that Alice quite jumped; but she saw in another
VIOLENT (2)
  A5   41:40   to try the effect. The next moment she felt a violent blow underneath her chin: it had struck her foot!
  A6   48:34   lullaby to it as she did so, and giving it a violent shake at the end of every line:--
VIOLENTLY (5)
  A2   15:34   "If you please, Sir--" The Rabbit started violently, dropped the white kid-gloves and the fan, and
  T1   113:20   cried out, as she rushed past the King, so violently that she knocked him over among the cinders. "My
  A6   50:10   I get it home?" when it grunted again, so violently, that she looked down into its face in some alarm.
  A6   49: 2   verse of the song, she kept tossing the baby violently up and down, and the poor little thing howled so,
  A5   42:25   had flown into her face, and was beating her violently with its wings.
VIOLET (1)
  T2   122:34   "I never saw anybody that looked stupider," a Violet said, so suddenly, that Alice quite jumped; for it
VISIT (3)
  A6   51:21   waving the other paw, "lives a March Hare. Visit either you like: they're both mad."
  T4   139:22   cried Tweedledum. "The first thing in a visit is to say 'How d'ye do?' and shake hands!" And here the
  T3   129:26   she said after a pause; "and perhaps I may visit the elephants later on. Besides, I do so want to get
VISITOR (1)
  T9   198: 7   very much puzzled by the names. "I'm not a visitor, and I'm not a servant. There ought to be one marked
VISITORS' (1)
  T9   198: 3   arch there was a bell-handle; one was marked "Visitors' Bell," and the other "Servants' Bell."
VOICE (90)
  A5   35: 3   mouth, and addressed her in a languid, sleepy voice.
  A5   36:35   Alice replied in a very melancholy voice.
  A8   67:31   do you like the Queen?" said the Cat in a low voice.
  A9   72:35   Majesty!" the Duchess began in a low, weak voice.
  A10   78:34   again!" yelled the Gryphon at the top of its voice.
  A10   83:13   come wrong, and she went on in a trembling voice:--
  A12   94: 2   he said to the jury, in a low trembling voice.
  T8W   15: 9   "Were what?" the Wasp asked in a very cross voice.
  T8W   16: 4   of the wig," the Wasp said in a much gentler voice.
  T2   121: 3   on waving about, she spoke again, in a timid voice--almost in a whisper. "And can all the flowers talk?"
  T6   168: 1   Humpty Dumpty raised his voice almost to a scream as he repeated this verse, and Alice
  A4   31: 7   of "There goes Bill!" then the Rabbit's voice alone--"Catch him, you by the hedge!" then silence, and
  A4   31:28   must burn the house down!" said the Rabbit's voice. And Alice called out, as loud as she could, "If you do,
  T9   201:24   It spoke in a thick, suety sort of voice, and Alice hadn't a word to say in reply: she could only
  T9   202:21   health!" she screamed at the top of her voice, and all the guests began drinking it directly, and very
  T5   152:33   very lonely here!" Alice said in a melancholy voice; and, at the thought of her loneliness, two large tears
  A11   89:12   Majesty," the Hatter began, in a trembling voice, "and I hadn't begun my tea--not above a week or so--and
  A12   98:19   hers--she could hear the very tones of her voice, and see that queer little toss of her head to keep back
  A8   64:15   "Get up!" said the Queen in a shrill, loud voice, and the three gardeners instantly jumped up, and began
  A10   78:36   said the Mock Turtle, suddenly dropping his voice; and the two creatures, who had been jumping about like
  A10   78: 6   back. At last the Mock Turtle recovered his voice, and, with tears running down his cheeks, he went on
  A10   81:22   under the sea," the Gryphon went on in a deep voice, "are done with whiting. Now you know."
  T1   108: 2   at the old cat, and speaking in as cross a voice as she could manage--and then she scrambled back into
  A8   65:25   "It's--it's a very fine day!" said a timid voice at her side. She was walking by the White Rabbit, who
  AI   3:11   the tiniest feather! / Yet what can one poor voice avail / Against three tongues together?
  T3   132: 2   "What, then you don't--" the little voice began, when it was drowned by a shrill scream from the
  A11   91:18   "Treacle," said a sleepy voice behind her.
  T8   185: 8   must have hurt him," she said in a trembling voice, "being on the top of his head."
  T8   179:20   once more "You're my--" but here another voice broke in "Ahoy! Ahoy! Check!" and Alice looked round in
  A11   86:33   things!" Alice began in a loud indignant voice; but she stopped herself hastily, for the White Rabbit
  T3   131:32   Alice, looking about in vain to see where the voice came from. "If you're so anxious to have a joke made,
  A10   84:15   Mock Turtle sighed deeply, and began, in a voice choked with sobs, to sing this:--
  T4   146:13   "Do you see that?" he said, in a voice choking with passion, and his eyes grew large and yellow
  T3   131:14   thought to herself. And an extremely small voice, close to her ear, said "You might make a joke on that--
  T3   131:31   might make a joke on that," said the little voice close to her ear: "something about 'you would if you
  A9   70:17   and was a little startled when she heard her voice close to her ear. "You're thinking about something, my
  T4   138: 8   of each collar, when she was startled by a voice coming from the one marked 'DUM.'
  A9   72:29   to Alice's great surprise, the Duchess's voice died away, even in the middle of her favourite word
  T7   174: 7   getting on very well," he said in a choking voice: "each of them has been down about eighty-seven times."
  A4   29:19   "Mary Ann! Mary Ann!" said the voice. "Fetch me my gloves this moment!" Then came a little
  T9   204: 5   sitting in the chair. "Here I am!" cried a voice from the soup-tureen, and Alice turned again, just in
  T8   186:17   he went on, holding his head down, and his voice getting lower and lower, "I don't believe that pudding
  A10   82:29   the tide rises and sharks are around / His voice has a timid and tremulous sound."
  A7   58:26   I wasn't asleep," it said in a hoarse, feeble voice, "I heard every word you fellows were saying."
  A2   15:33   came near her, she began, in a low, timid voice, "If you please, Sir--" The Rabbit started violently,
  T3   131:16   Then a very gentle voice in the distance said, "She must be labeled 'Lass, with
  A8   68:11   game was going on, as she heard the Queen's voice in the distance, screaming with passion. She had already
  T3   136:13   the Fawn said at last. Such a soft sweet voice it had!
  T5   149:27   with it!" the Queen said, in a melancholy voice. "It's out of temper, I think. I've pinned it here, and
  A2   20:18   thought), and it said, in a low trembling voice, "Let us get to the shore, and then I'll tell you my

VOICE (cont.)

T9	201:39	Queen murmured into Alice's other ear, in a voice like the cooing of a pigeon. "It would be such a treat!
T9	196: 1	saw it too," the White Queen went on in a low voice, more as if she were talking to herself. "He came to the
A12	97: 5	head!" the Queen shouted at the top of her voice. Nobody moved.
T4	148:21	the crow!" Tweedledum cried out in a shrill voice of alarm; and the two brothers took to their heels and
T3	137: 7	Alice's arm. "I'm a Fawn!" it cried out in a voice of delight. "And, dear me! you're a human child!" A
TI	103:19	Come, hearken then, ere voice of dread, / With bitter tidings laden, / Shall summon to
T1	113:19	"It is the voice of my child!" the White Queen cried out, as she rushed
A10	82:22	"'Tis the voice of the Lobster: I heard him declare / 'You have baked me
A12	98:28	their never-ending meal, and the shrill voice of the Queen ordering off her unfortunate guests to
A12	98:39	and the Queen's shrill cries to the voice of the shepherd-boy--and the sneeze of the baby, the
A10	82:15	"Stand up and repeat ''Tis the voice of the sluggard,'" said the Gryphon.
A8	65:41	"Get to your places!" shouted the Queen in a voice of thunder, and people began running about in all
T4	147:34	very brave, generally," he went on in a low voice: "only to-day I happen to have a headache."
A4	29:18	but after a few minutes she heard a voice outside, and stopped to listen.
T7	176:24	going on: he was very nervous, and his voice quite quivered. "All round the town?" he said. "That's a
T5	153:28	"Oh, much better!" cried the Queen, her voice rising into a squeak as she went on. "Much be-etter!
T4	146:28	it yesterday--my nice NEW RATTLE!" and his voice rose to a perfect scream.
A10	78: 3	but, for a minute or two, sobs choked his voice. "Same as if he had a bone in his throat," said the
T9	199:36	there was silence again, and the same shrill voice sang another verse:--
A4	30: 2	"Pat! Pat! Where are you?" And then a voice she had never heard before, "Sure then I'm here! Digging
T3	131: 4	in white, shut his eyes and said in a loud voice, "She ought to know her way to the ticket-office, even
T3	131:34	The little voice sighed deeply. It was very unhappy, evidently, and Alice
A2	17: 5	lessons, and began to repeat it, but her voice sounded hoarse and strange, and the words did not come
T3	131:11	was sitting beyond the Beetle, but a hoarse voice spoke next. "Change engines--" it said, and there it
A4	31:17	Last came a little feeble, squeaking voice ("That's Bill," thought Alice), "Well, I hardly know--No
A11	91:33	read out, at the top of his shrill little voice, the name "Alice!"
A4	30: 1	Next came an angry voice--the Rabbit's--"Pat! Pat! Where are you?" And then a
T7	172:29	he simply shouted, at the top of his voice, "They're at it again!"
A5	43: 2	the wood," continued the Pigeon, raising its voice to a shriek, "and just as I was thinking I should be
A3	26:34	And a Canary called out in a trembling voice, to its children, "Come away, my dears! It's high time
A9	73:19	together, Alice heard the King say in a low voice, to the company, generally, "You are all pardoned."
A12	93: 1	proceed," said the King, in a very grave voice, "until all the jurymen are back in their proper places
T9	199:22	moment the door was flung open, and a shrill voice was heard singing:--
T8	183:18	riding," the Knight suddenly began in a loud voice, waving his right arm as he spoke, "is to keep--" Here
T5	151:21	still; better, and better, and better!" Her voice went higher with each "better," till it got quite to a
T3	131:41	"I know you are a friend," the little voice went on: "a dear friend, and an old friend. And you
A11	91:15	were nearly out of sight, he said, in a deep voice, "What are tarts made of?"
A8	63: 6	but looked at Two. Two began, in a low voice, "Why, the fact is, you see, Miss, this here ought to
A2	19:30	cats!" cried the Mouse in a shrill passionate voice. "Would you like cats, if you were me?"
A11	91:12	at the White Rabbit, who said, in a low voice, "Your Majesty must cross-examine this witness."

VOICES (11)

T3	129:38	looking angrily at Alice. And a great many voices all said together ("like the chorus of a song," thought
A4	30:24	cart-wheels, and the sound of a good many voices all talking together: she made out the words: "Where's
A3	23:22	who is to give the prizes?" quite a chorus of voices asked.
AI	3:30	next time--" "It is next time!" / The happy voices cry.
T3	130:11	"Then there's no use in speaking." The voices didn't join in, this time, as she hadn't spoken, but,
A4	31:10	then silence, and then another confusion of voices--"Hold up his head--Brandy now--Don't choke him--How
T9	199:28	And hundreds of voices joined in the chorus:--
T2	122: 9	the air seemed quite full of little shrill voices. "Silence, every one of you!" cried the Tiger-lily,
T3	130: 4	where I came from." And again the chorus of voices went on. "There wasn't room for one where she came from
T3	131:18	And after that other voices went on ("What a number of people there are in the
T3	130: 7	engine-driver." And once more the chorus of voices went on with "The man that drives the engine. Why, the

VOLCANO (2)

T1	114:12	sitting sulkily among the ashes, "Mind the volcano!"
T1	114:13	"What volcano?" said the King, looking up anxiously into the fire

VORPAL (2)

T1	118:14	two! One, two! And through and through / The vorpal blade went snicker-snack! / He left it dead, and with
T1	118: 5	He took his vorpal sword in hand: / Long time the manxome foe he sought--/

VOTE (1)

A7	58:19	yawning. "I'm getting tired of this. I vote the young lady tells us a story."

VULGAR (1)

A2	19:44	Our family always hated cats: nasty, low, vulgar things! Don't let me hear the name again!"

-W-

W. (1)
  A4   27:22 which was a bright brass plate with the name "W. RABBIT" engraved upon it. She went in without knocking, and
WABE (6)
  T1   116:10 dnA / ,sevogorob eht erew ysmim llA / :ebaw eht ni elbmig dna eryg diD / sevot yhtils eht dna ,gillirb
  T1   116:19 the slithy toves / Did gyre and gimble in the wabe: / All mimsy were the borogoves, / And the mome raths
  T1   118:22 the slithy toves / Did gyre and gimble in the wabe: / All mimsy were the borogoves, / And the mome raths
  T6   164:22 the slithy toves / Did gyre and gimble in the wabe: / All mimsy were the borogoves, / And the mome raths
  T6   165: 4   "And 'the wabe' is the grass-plot round a sun-dial, I suppose?" said
  T6   165: 6   "Of course it is. It's called 'wabe' you know, because it goes a long way before it, and a
WAG (1)
  A6   51:34 pleased. Now I growl when I'm pleased, and wag my tail when I'm angry. Therefore I'm mad."
WAGES (1)
  T6   164:11 gravely from side to side, "for to get their wages, you know."
WAGGING (1)
  T6   164:10 of a Saturday night," Humpty Dumpty went on, wagging his head gravely from side to side, "for to get their
WAGS (1)
  A6   51:33 "you see a dog growls when it's angry, and wags its tail when it's pleased. Now I growl when I'm pleased,
WAIST (2)
  T6   162:21 to herself, "which was neck and which was waist!"
  A9   71: 6 wondering why I don't put my arm round your waist," the Duchess said, after a pause: "the reason is, that
WAISTCOAT-BUTTONS (1)
  T8   188:35 the heather bright, / And work them into waistcoat-buttons / In the silent night. / And these I do not
WAISTCOAT-POCKET (2)
  A1   7:16 the Rabbit actually took a watch out of its waistcoat-pocket, and looked at it, and then hurried on, Alice
  A1   8: 2 had never before seen a rabbit with either a waistcoat-pocket, or a watch to take out of it, and burning
WAIT (12)
  T8W   18:11 used to," said the Wasp: "however I'll try; wait a bit." He was silent for a few moments, and then began
  T4   143: 1   'But wait a bit,' the Oysters cried, / 'Before we have our chat; /
  T5   156:11   "No, but I meant--please, may we wait and pick some?" Alice pleaded. "If you don't mind
  T8   190:18 which he pointed. "I sha'n't be long. You'll wait and wave your handkerchief when I get to that turn in the
  A5   36:26   Alice thought she might as well wait, as she had nothing else to do, and perhaps after all it
  T12 208:12 do help to settle it! I'm sure your paw can wait!" But the provoking kitten only began on the other paw,
  T2   128:25 walk--and remember who you are!" She did not wait for Alice to curtsey, this time, but walked on quickly to
  T2   128: 1 to say to this, but luckily the Queen did not wait for an answer, but went on. "At the end of three yards I
  T8   190:20   "Of course I'll wait," said Alice: "and thank you very much for coming so far
  T9   198: 5   "I'll wait till the song's over," thought Alice, "and then I'll ring
  T8W   17: 5   "It is, though," said the Wasp: "wait till you have it, and then you'll know. And when you
  T6   168:33 Humpty Dumpty only shut his eyes, and said "Wait till you've tried."
WAITED (15)
  A8   63:33 see it?" So she stood where she was, and waited.
  A9   74: 6 it as to go after that savage Queen: so she waited.
  A6   52:22   Alice waited a little, half expecting to see it again, but it did
  T6   168:34   Alice waited a minute to see if he would speak again, but, as he
  A1   12: 6 into that lovely garden. First, however, she waited for a few minutes to see if she was going to shrink any
  A4   30:22   She waited for some time without hearing anything more: at last
  T9   192:22 were spoken to, and the other person always waited for you to begin, you see nobody would ever say
  T4   142:18 low: / And all the little Oysters stood / And waited in a row.
  A3   23:20 in the pictures of him), while the rest waited in silence. At last the Dodo said "Everybody has won,
  A9   74:31 ever finish, if he doesn't begin." But she waited patiently.
  A5   41:23   This time Alice waited patiently until it chose to speak again. In a minute or
  T8   190:32 then she waved her handkerchief to him, and waited till he was out of sight.
  A4   30:40 as far down the chimney as she could, and waited till she heard a little animal (she couldn't guess of
  A8   67:16   Alice waited till the eyes appeared, and then nodded. "It's no use
  A4   31: 3 "This is Bill", she gave one sharp kick, and waited to see what would happen next.
WAITER (1)
  T9   201:16 orders; so, as an experiment, she called out "Waiter! Bring back the pudding!" and there it was again in a
WAITERS (3)
  T9   201: 8 introduced to. Remove the joint!" And the waiters carried it off, and brought a large plum-pudding in
  T9   200:19 fish," she said. "Put on the joint!" And the waiters set a leg of mutton before Alice, who looked at it
  T9   201:14 Alice--Pudding. Remove the pudding!" and the waiters took it away so quickly that Alice couldn't return its
WAITING (12)
  A2   15:31 Oh! Won't she be savage if I've kept her waiting!" Alice felt so desperate that she was ready to ask
  A1   10:12   There seemed to be no use in waiting by the little door, so she went back to the table,
  T3   129:39 of a song," thought Alice) "Don't keep him waiting, child! Why, his time is worth a thousand pounds a
  T7   174:10   "It's waiting for 'em now," said Hatta; "this is a bit of it as I'm
  A10   85: 5 Alice by the hand, it hurried off, without waiting for the end of the song.
  A8   66:20 The players all played at once, without waiting for turns, quarreling all the while, and fighting for
  A10   84:18 "Beautiful Soup, so rich and green, / Waiting in a hot tureen! / Who for such dainties would not
  A10   79:16 and the turtles all advance! / They are waiting on the shingle--will you come and join the dance? /
  A4   32:13 quite a crowd of little animals and birds waiting outside. The poor little Lizard, Bill, was in the
  A4   29:31 "That you wo'n't!" thought Alice, and after waiting till she fancied she heard the Rabbit just under the
  T9   200:11 among them. "I'm glad they've come without waiting to be asked," she thought: "I should never have known
  A11   90:32 Hatter hurriedly left the court, without even waiting to put his shoes on.

WAKE (9)
T4	145:10	"If that there King was to wake," added Tweedledum, "you'd go out--bang!--just like a
T8	179:11	tone: "I've a great mind to go and wake him, and see what happens!"
T6	168: 7	very proud and stiff: / He said 'I'd go and wake them, if--'
T6	167:20	to him, I said it plain, / 'Then you must wake them up again.'
T6	168: 9	took a corkscrew from the shelf: / I went to wake them up myself.'
A12	98: 4	"Wake up, Alice dear!" said her sister. "Why, what a long sleep
A7	58:23	"Then the Dormouse shall!" they both cried. "Wake up, Dormouse!" And they pinched it on both sides at once.
T1	109:13	till the summer comes again.' And when they wake up in the summer, Kitty, they dress themselves all in
T9	197:18	never was more than one Queen at a time. Do wake up, you heavy things!" she went on in an impatient tone;

WAKING (4)
T11t	206: 1	WAKING
TC	209:12	/ Alice moving under skies / Never seen by waking eyes.
T4	145:17	Alice couldn't help saying "Hush! You'll be waking him, I'm afraid, if you make so much noise."
T4	145:18	"Well, it's no use your talking about waking him," said Tweedledum, "when you're only one of the

WALK (12) [See also GRAVEL-WALK]
A10	79:13	"Will you walk a little faster?" said a whiting to a snail / "There's a
T4	141:15	us!' / The Walrus did beseech. / 'A pleasant walk, a pleasant talk, / Along the briny beach: / We cannot do
T2	128:24	for a thing--turn out your toes as you walk--and remember who you are!" She did not wait for Alice to
A4	27:31	Come here directly, and get ready for your walk!' 'Coming in a minute, nurse! But I've got to watch this
T3	129:22	fun it'll be when they ask me how I liked my walk. I shall say 'Oh, I liked it well enough--' (here came
A6	51:15	sure to do that," said the Cat, "if you only walk long enough."
T8	183: 1	soon found that it was the best plan not to walk quite close to the horse.
T2	123:39	that," said the Rose: "I should advise you to walk the other way."
A2	15: 1	them," thought Alice, "or perhaps they wo'n't walk the way I want to go! Let me see. I'll give them a new
T5	158:20	"The egg seems to get further away the more I walk towards it. Let me see, is this a chair? Why, it's got
A1	8:41	it'll seem to come out among the people that walk with their heads downwards! The antipathies, I think--"
T4	141:13	'O Oysters, come and walk with us!' / The Walrus did beseech. / 'A pleasant walk, a

WALKED (19)
A3	26:15	Mouse only shook its head impatiently, and walked a little quicker.
T9	192: 6	So she got up and walked about--rather stiffly just at first, as she was afraid
T6	168:37	and, getting no answer to this, she quietly walked away: but she couldn't help saying to herself, as she
A7	61: 4	till she was about a foot high; then she walked down the little passage: and then--she found herself at
A9	74: 3	some executions I have ordered;" and she walked off, leaving Alice alone with the Gryphon. Alice did
A7	60:30	could bear: she got up in great disgust, and walked off: the Dormouse fell asleep instantly, and neither of
A9	70: 3	her arm affectionately into Alice's, and they walked off together.
A9	73:18	As they walked off together, Alice heard the King say in a low voice,
T3	135:21	with sitting still so long, she got up and walked on.
T4	142:14	The Walrus and the Carpenter / Walked on a mile or so, / And then they rested on a rock /
T8	182:37	Alice thought, and for a few minutes she walked on in silence, puzzling over the idea, and every now
T2	125:17	tone that she was a little offended: and they walked on in silence till they got to the top of the little
A6	52:23	did not appear, and after a minute or two she walked on in the direction in which the March Hare was said to
T2	128:25	not wait for Alice to curtsey, this time, but walked on quickly to the next peg, where she turned for a
T3	137: 3	So they walked on together through the wood, Alice with her arms
A1	9:32	side and up the other, trying every door, she walked sadly down the middle, wondering how she was ever to
A8	63:18	were ornamented all over with diamonds, and walked two and two, as the soldiers did. After these came the
T9	200: 8	glanced nervously along the table, as she walked up the large hall, and noticed that there were about
A6	53:16	herself to about two feet high: even then she walked up towards it rather timidly, saying to herself

WALKING (19)
T2	124: 3	It succeeded beautifully. She had not been walking a minute before she found herself face to face with
A8	67:28	there's the arch I've got to go through next walking about at the other end of the ground--and I should
T1	113: 7	and knees watching them. The chessmen were walking about, two and two!
T1	119:10	the air, and was rather glad to find herself walking again in the natural way.
T1	113:11	edge of the shovel--and here are two Castles walking arm in arm--I don't think they can hear me," she went
A3	26: 9	of the sort," said the Mouse, getting up and walking away. "You insult me by talking such nonsense!"
A8	65:26	day!" said a timid voice at her side. She was walking by the White Rabbit, who was peeping anxiously into
T4	141: 2	The Walrus and the Carpenter / Were walking close at hand: / They wept like anything to see / Such
T2	128: 6	returned to the tree, and then began slowly walking down the row.
A1	9:16	off, and had just begun to dream that she was walking hand in hand with Dinah, and was saying to her, very
T2	120:23	the next moment she found herself actually walking in at the door.
T2	123:42	sight of her in a moment, and found herself walking in at the front-door again.
T2	124: 1	thought she would try the plan, this time, of walking in the opposite direction.
T8	190:29	talking to herself, as she watched the horse walking leisurely along the road, and the Knight tumbling off,
A8	66:17	soldiers were always getting up and walking off to other parts of the ground, Alice soon came to
T8W	14: 6	offended at this answer, and was very nearly walking on and leaving him, but she thought to herself
T8	183: 1	did this on the side on which Alice was walking, she soon found that it was the best plan not to walk
T8	184: 1	his head exactly in the path where Alice was walking. She was quite frightened this time, and said in an
T9	204:10	down in the dishes, and the soup ladle was walking up the table towards Alice's chair, and beckoning to

WALKS (2)
| T7 | 172:21 | said in a sullen tone. "I'm sure nobody walks much faster than I do!" |
| T7 | 172:19 | young lady saw him too. So of course Nobody walks slower than you." |

WALL (5)
T6	159:28	"Humpty Dumpty sat on a wall: / Humpty Dumpty had a great fall. / All the King's
T6	161: 2	(and as nearly as possible fell off the wall in doing so) and offered Alice his hand. She watched him
T6	160:18	anxiety for the queer creature. "That wall is so very narrow!"
T1	112:13	possible. For instance, the pictures on the wall next the fire seemed to be all alive, and the very clock
T6	159: 9	crossed like a Turk, on the top of a high wall--such a narrow one that Alice quite wondered how he could

WALRUS (14)
| T4 | 144:19 | best--if he didn't eat so many as the Walrus." |
| T4 | 140:15 | "'The Walrus and the Carpenter' is the longest," Tweedledum replied, |

```
WALRUS (cont.)
  T12  208: 3  eating   your  breakfast,  I'll  repeat  'The Walrus and the Carpenter' to you; and then you can make
  T4   142:13                                          The Walrus and the Carpenter / Walked on a mile or so, / And then
  T4   141: 1                                          The Walrus and the Carpenter / Were walking close at hand: / They
  T4   144:13                           "I like the   Walrus best," said Alice: "because he was a little sorry for
  T4   141:14  'O Oysters, come and walk with us!' / The Walrus did beseech. / 'A pleasant walk, a pleasant talk, /
  A2    19: 7  it was: at first she thought it must be a walrus or hippopotamus, but then she remembered how small she
  T4   143:17  thing to do!' / 'The night is fine,' the Walrus said. / 'Do you admire the view?
  T4   144: 1              'I weep for you,' the  Walrus said: / 'I deeply sympathize.' / With sobs and tears he
  T4   143: 7              'A loaf of bread,' the  Walrus said, / 'Is what we chiefly need: / Pepper and vinegar
  T4   141: 9  it for half a year, / Do you suppose,' the Walrus said, / 'That they could get it clear?' / 'I doubt it,'
  T4   143:25          'It seems a shame,' the  Walrus said, / 'To play them such a trick, / After we've
  T4   142:19      'The time has come,' the  Walrus said, / 'To talk of many things: / Of shoes--and ships
WANDER (1)
  A1    10: 4  she longed to get out of that dark hall, and wander about among those beds of bright flowers and those cool
WANDERED (3)
  A8    65:13          that stood near. The three soldiers wandered about for a minute or two, looking for them, and then
  A4    32:18¯ got to do," said Alice to herself, as she wandered about in the wood, "is to grow to my right size again
  T3   137:29  Eighth Square before it gets dark!" So she wandered on, talking to herself as she went, till, on turning
WANDERING (4)
  T3   136: 7                  Just then a Fawn came wandering by: it looked at Alice with its large gentle eyes,
  A12   98:20  little toss of her head to keep back the wandering hair that would always get into her eyes--and still
  T2   120: 9              And so she did: wandering up and down, and trying turn after turn, but always
  A5    42:24  tops of the trees under which she had been wandering, when a sharp hiss made her draw back in a hurry: a
WANDERINGS (1)
  AI     3: 6  / While little hands make vain pretence / Our wanderings to guide.
WANT (25)
  T8W   20:11  to say gravely, "I can bite anything I want."
  A7    59:36                      "I want a clean cup," interrupted the Hatter: "let's all move one
  T5   150: 4                  "Well, I don't want any to-day, at any rate."
  T5   149:19                  "But I don't want it done at all!" groaned the poor Queen. "I've been
  T5   150: 5  "You couldn't have it if you did want it," the Queen said. "The rule is, jam to-morrow and jam
  T9   196: 3                  "What did he want?" said the Red Queen.
  T1   110:35  Oh! I do so wish I could see that bit! I want so much to know whether they've a fire in the winter: you
  T8   181: 2  "I don't want to be anybody's prisoner. I want to be a Queen."
  T8   181: 1  don't know," Alice said doubtfully. "I don't want to be anybody's prisoner. I want to be a Queen."
  A5    41: 7              "What size do you want to be?" it asked.
  T6   162: 1              Alice didn't want to begin another argument, so she said nothing.
  T5   157:13  only make up your mind. Now, what do you want to buy?"
  T5   154: 1              "What is it you want to buy?" the Sheep said at last, looking up for a moment
  T3   129:27  the elephants later on. Besides, I do so want to get into the Third Square!"
  T2   127:21  you can do, to keep in the same place. If you want to get somewhere else, you must run at least twice as
  A6    51: 9   "That depends a good deal on where you want to get to," said the Cat.
  A6    51:22              "But I don't want to go among mad people," Alice remarked.
  A2    15: 1  Alice, "or perhaps they wo'n't walk the way I want to go! Let me see. I'll give them a new pair of boots
  T3   134:23  again and remarked "I suppose you don't want to lose your name?"
  A11   86:18  over the wig (look at the frontispiece if you want to see how he did it), he did not look at all comfortable
  A4    30:20  I only wish they could! I'm sure I don't want to stay in here any longer!"
  T3   134: 7  so fond of flying into candles--because they want to turn into Snap-dragon-flies!"
  T5   150: 1  couldn't help laughing, as she said "I don't want you to hire me--and I don't care for jam."
  A10   81:29  to the porpoise 'Keep back, please! We don't want you with us!'"
  A5    43:26  as it happens; and, if I was, I shouldn't want yours: I don't like them raw."
WANTED (13)
  T7   170:12  the horses, you know, because two of them are wanted in the game. And I haven't sent the two Messengers,
  A9    76:16                  "You couldn't have wanted it much," said Alice; "living at the bottom of the sea
  A3    22: 4  was soon submitted to by the English, who wanted leaders, and had been of late much accustomed to
  T2   127:28  to say "No," though it wasn't at all what she wanted. She took it, and ate it as well as she could: and it
  T3   135: 1  without it! For instance, if the governess wanted to call you to your lessons, she would call out 'Come
  T7   172:27  King's ear. Alice was sorry for this, as she wanted to hear the news too. However, instead of whispering,
  A3    23: 2  a Caucus-race?" said Alice; not that she much wanted to know, but the Dodo had paused as if it thought that
  T3   131:44  inquired, a little anxiously. What she really wanted to know was, whether it could sting or not, but she
  T9   196: 9  "I know what he came for," said Alice: "he wanted to punish the fish, because--"
  T2   125: 1                  "I only wanted to see what the garden was like, your Majesty--"
  A8    66:16  a ridge or a furrow in the way wherever she wanted to send the hedgehog to, and, as the doubled-up
  T5   152: 4  the Queen, shaking her hand about as if she wanted to shake it off. "My finger's bleeding! Oh, oh, oh, oh!
  T9   202:40  of her feast. "You would have thought they wanted to squeeze me flat!")
WANTS (4)
  A7    55: 6                  "Your hair wants cutting," said the Hatter. He had been looking at Alice
  A9    74:25  This here young lady," said the Gryphon, "she wants for to know your history, she do."
  T1   108:14  getting in sticks for the bonfire--and it wants plenty of sticks, Kitty! Only it got so cold, and it
  T9   193:11  of mind," said the White Queen, "that she wants to deny something--only she doesn't know what to deny!"
WARM (3)
  T9   195:39  Just so!" cried the Red Queen. "Five times as warm, and five times as cold--just as I'm five times as rich
  T1   112: 5  one she had left behind. "So I shall be as warm here as I was in the old room," thought Alice: "warmer,
  T9   195:37                  "Five times as warm, of course."
WARMER (2)
  T1   112: 6  as I was in the old room," thought Alice: "warmer, in fact, because there'll be no one here to scold me
  T9   195:35                  "Are five nights warmer than one night, then?" Alice ventured to ask.
WARMTH (1)
  T9   195:34  we take as many as five nights together--for warmth, you know."
```

WARNING (1)
```
A9    72:36                                "Now, I give you fair warning," shouted the Queen, stamping on the ground as she
WAS (735)
A9    77: 5    master, though. He was an old crab, he was."
T2   127:14    tree the whole time! Everything's just as it was!"
T6   166:13    easier than that, by--Tweedledee, I think it was."
T12  208:14                                Which do you think it was?
T3   131: 6                             There was a Beetle sitting next the Goat (it was a very queer
T9   198: 3    letters, and on each side of the arch there was a bell-handle; one was marked "Visitors' Bell," and the
A8    68:38    that you couldn't cut off a head unless there was a body to cut it off from: that he had never had to do
T1   116: 1                             There was a book lying near Alice on the table, and while she sat
A4    27:22    a neat little house, on the door of which was a bright brass plate with the name "W. RABBIT" engraved
T5   152: 8    is the matter?" she said, as soon as there was a chance of making herself heard. "Have you pricked your
A10   82:30    different from what I used to say when I was a child," said the Gryphon.
A12   98: 9    finished, her sister kissed her, and said "It was a curious dream, dear, certainly; but now run in to your
A12   96:26    looking round the court with a smile. There was a dead silence.
A4    31:32                             There was a dead silence instantly, and Alice thought to herself "I
T9   200: 7    go in at once--" and in she went, and there was a dead silence the moment she appeared.
A10   81:42    no use going back to yesterday, because I was a different person then."
A8    68:29    quite a large crowd collected round it: there was a dispute going on between the executioner, the King, and
A2    20:22    and animals that had fallen into it: there was a Duck and a Dodo, a Lory and an Eaglet, and several other
T1   112: 3    first thing she did was to look whether there was a fire in the fireplace, and she was quite pleased to find
T6   161:20    subject--" ("He talks about it just as if it was a game!" thought Alice.) "So here's a question for you.
A4    31: 5          The first thing she heard was a general chorus of "There goes Bill!" then the Rabbit's
A12   94:26                             There was a general clapping of hands at this: it was the first
T8   180:15                                "It was a glorious victory, wasn't it?" said the White Knight, as
T8   191: 9                                 It was a golden crown.
A5    41:41                                She was a good deal frightened by this very sudden change, but she
A7    59:41    got any advantage from the change; and Alice was a good deal worse off than before, as the March Hare had
T6   168:38    " (she repeated this aloud, as it was a great comfort to have such a long word to say) "of all
T11  206: 1                    ..--it really was a kitten, after all.
A4    34: 3    eat or drink under the circumstances. There was a large mushroom growing near her, about the same height
A7    54: 7          The table was a large one, but the three were all crowded together at
A2    15:23    same, shedding gallons of tears, until there was a large pool round her, about four inches deep, and
T1   115:16    his back, and lay perfectly still; and Alice was a little alarmed at what she had done, and went round the
A1     9:40    she had not noticed before, and behind it was a little door about fifteen inches high: she tried the
A10   82: 2    time when she first saw the White Rabbit. She was a little nervous about it, just at first, the two
T2   125:17    she was afraid from the Queen's tone that she was a little offended: and they walked on in silence till they
T4   144:13    the Walrus best," said Alice: "because he was a little sorry for the poor oysters."
A6    50:20    knew the right way to change them--" when she was a little startled by seeing the Cheshire-Cat sitting on a
A9    70:16    quite forgotten the Duchess by this time, and was a little startled when she heard her voice close to her
T9   201:34    She spoke to the Red Queen, whose answer was a little wide of the mark. "As to fishes," she said, very
T6   168:14                             There was a long pause.
A4    30:13                             There was a long silence after this, and Alice could only hear
A6    46:13    could possibly hear you." And certainly there was a most extraordinary noise going on within--a constant
A2    18:10                                "That was a narrow escape!" said Alice, a good deal frightened at
T1   110: 7    and when I said 'Check!' you purred! Well, it was a nice check, Kitty, and really I might have won, if it
T5   157: 4    while, just as if nothing had happened. "That was a nice crab you caught!" she remarked, as Alice got back
A1    10:17    Alice), and tied round the neck of the bottle was a paper label, with the words "DRINK ME" beautifully
T7   174:12                             There was a pause in the fight just then, and the Lion and the
T2   128:32    gone, and Alice began to remember that she was a Pawn, and that it would soon be time for her to move.
T4   144:21                                This was a puzzler. After a pause, Alice began, "Well! They were
A6    49:15    caught the baby with some difficulty, as it was a queer-shaped little creature, and held out its arms and
T4   140: 2    and stood looking at her for a minute: there was a rather awkward pause, as Alice didn't know how to begin
T1   112: 4    and she was quite pleased to find that there was a real one, blazing away as brightly as the one she had
A9    74:32    the Mock Turtle at last, with a deep sigh, "I was a real Turtle.
T3   129:10    its proboscis into them, "just as if it was a regular bee," thought Alice.
T8   184:21                             There was a short silence after this, and then the Knight went on
A8    63:13    threw themselves flat upon their faces. There was a sound of many footsteps, and Alice looked round, eager
A7    54: 1                             There was a table set out under a tree in front of the house, and
A11   86: 7    in the other. In the very middle of the court was a table, with a large dish of tarts upon it: they looked
A7    59:23    or two to think about it, and then said "It was a treacle-well."
T8   186:19    that pudding ever will be cooked! And yet it was a very clever pudding to invent."
A8    66:19    Alice soon came to the conclusion that it was a very difficult game indeed.
T3   132:20                  It certainly was a very large Gnat: "about the size of a chicken," Alice
T3   131: 6    There was a Beetle sitting next the Goat it was a very queer carriage-full of passengers altogether), and,
T4   144:37    lying on the damp grass," said Alice, who was a very thoughtful little girl.
A5    43:16    have tasted eggs, certainly," said Alice, who was a very truthful child; "but little girls eat eggs quite as
T8   179:23                    This time it was a White Knight. He drew up at Alice's side, and tumbled
A7    61: 4    kept a piece of it in her pocket) till she was about a foot high; then she walked down the little passage
T9   201:32    a very curious thing, I think--every poem was about fishes in some way. Do you know why they're so fond
A6    47:17    jumped; but she saw in another moment that it was addressed to the baby, and not to her, so she took courage
T8W   20:12    small as that," the Wasp persisted. "If you was a-fighting, now--could you get hold of the other one by
T2   125:16                    Alice curtseyed again, as she was afraid from the Queen's tone that she was a little
T8   185:19    some time he had kept on very well, and she was afraid that he really was hurt this time. However, though
T9   192: 7    about--rather stiffly just at first, as she was afraid that the crown might come off: but she comforted
T9   201:17    Waiter! Bring back the pudding!" and there it was again in a moment, like a conjuring-trick. It was so large
T9   199:24          "To the Looking-Glass world it was Alice that said / 'I've a sceptre in hand, I've a crown on
T8   179:17                    Startled as she was, Alice was more frightened for him than for herself at the
T8W   13: 9    "I don't think I can be of any use to him," was Alice's first thought, as she turned to spring over the
```

WAS (cont.)

A6	45: 9	heads. She felt very curious to know what it was all about, and crept a little way out of the wood to
T4	138:15	"I'm sure I'm very sorry," was all Alice could say; for the words of the old song kept
A1	9:22	her feet in a moment: she looked up, but it was all dark overhead: before her was another long passage,
A10	83:18	as its share of the treat. / When the pie was all finished, the Owl, as a boon, / Was kindly permitted
T8	185:13	The Knight shook his head. "It was all kinds of fastness with me, I can assure you!" he said.
T1	107:11	and trying to purr--no doubt feeling that it was all meant for its good.
A8	66: 2	such a curious croquet-ground in her life: it was all ridges and furrows: the croquet balls were live
T2	126:14	in hand, and the Queen went so fast that it was all she could do to keep up with her: and still the Queen
A1	10:19	It was all very well to say "Drink me," but the wise little Alice
T8	182:20	the bag." And he hung it to the saddle, which was already loaded with bunches of carrots, and fire-irons,
T5	156:28	beautiful rushes as the boat glided by, there was always a more lovely one that she couldn't reach.
T5	154:19	a doll and sometimes like a work-box, and was always in the shelf next above the one she was looking at.
T5	154:14	what it had on it, that particular shelf was always quite empty, though the others round it were
T9	192: 3	Majesty," she went on, in a severe tone (she was always rather fond of scolding herself), "It'll never do
T9	192:20	everybody obeyed that rule," said Alice, who was always ready for a little argument, "and if you only spoke
A3	26:26	Alice replied eagerly, for she was always ready to talk about her pet: "Dinah's our cat. And
T3	129:12	was anything but a regular bee: in fact, it was an elephant--as Alice soon found out, though the idea
A5	42:10	all she could see, when she looked down, was an immense length of neck, which seemed to rise like a
A9	76:38	then Drawling--the Drawling-master was an old conger-eel, that used to come once a week: he
A9	77: 5	"I went to the Classical master, though. He was an old crab, he was."
T5	153:38	elbows on the counter, and opposite to her was an old Sheep, sitting in an arm-chair, knitting, and every
A9	74:42	"we went to school in the sea. The master was an old Turtle--used to call him Tortoise--"
T9	193:13	the Red Queen remarked; and then there was an uncomfortable silence for a minute or two.
A9	70:27	to rest her chin on Alice's shoulder, and it was an uncomfortably sharp chin. However, she did not like to
A3	21:11	would not allow, without knowing how old it was, and as the Lory positively refused to tell its age, there
T1	110:28	Looking-glass, that it might see how sulky it was, "--and if you're not good directly," she added, "I'll put
A8	63:33	they couldn't see it?" So she stood where she was, and waited.
A1	9:23	up, but it was all dark overhead: before her was another long passage, and the White Rabbit was still in
A5	36:15	Here was another puzzling question; and, as Alice could not think
T3	129:12	However, this was anything but a regular bee: in fact, it was an elephant--
A8	68:33	The moment Alice appeared, she was appealed to by all three to settle the question, and they
T2	120:14	looking up at the house and pretending it was arguing with her. "I'm not going in again yet. I know I
T1	112:12	and uninteresting, but that all the rest was as different as possible. For instance, the pictures on
T8	185:11	but it took hours and hours to get me out. I was as fast as--as lightning, you know."
A11	88:38	thoughts she decided to remain where she was as long as there was room for her.
A2	15:16	Poor Alice! It was as much as she could do, lying down on one side, to look
A6	49:20	altogether, for the first minute or two, it was as much as she could do to hold it.
A5	40: 2	"one would hardly suppose / That your eye was as steady as ever; / Yet you balanced an eel on the end of
A2	19: 6	off, and she swam nearer to make out what it was: at first she thought it must be a walrus or hippopotamus,
A7	60:36	wood. "It's the stupidest tea-party I ever was at in all my life!"
A7	57:12	his teaspoon at the March Hare,) "--it was at the great concert given by the Queen of Hearts, and I
T5	158: 1	river, had vanished all in a moment, and she was back again in the little dark shop.
T3	132:18	that was the insect she had been talking to) was balancing itself on a twig just over her head, and fanning
A5	42:25	a large pigeon had flown into her face, and was beating her violently with its wings.
T8	185: 3	That happened to me once--and the worst of it was, before I could get out again, the other White Knight came
T9	204: 1	as she could in the dreadful confusion that was beginning.
T9	192:38	"I'm sure I didn't mean--" Alice was beginning, but the Red Queen interrupted her impatiently.
T9	194: 7	"I suppose--" Alice was beginning, but the Red Queen answered for her.
A9	72:25	right to think," said Alice sharply, for she was beginning to feel a little worried.
A1	7: 1	Alice was beginning to get very tired of sitting by her sister on
A11	88:35	good deal until she made out what it was: she was beginning to grow larger again, and she thought at first
T1	111:13	she had got there. And certainly the glass was beginning to melt away, just like a bright silvery mist.
T3	129:18	she went on, checking herself just as she was beginning to run down the hill, and trying to find some
T5	155:17	not on land--and not with needles--" Alice was beginning to say, when suddenly the needles turned into
A5	42:41	sorry you've been annoyed," said Alice, who was beginning to see its meaning.
A7	59:24	"There's no such thing!" Alice was beginning very angrily, but the Hatter and the March Hare
A4	30:31	(a loud crash)--"Now, who did that?--It was Bill, I fancy--Who's to go down the chimney?--Nay, I
A11	87: 8	it so quickly that the poor little juror (it was Bill, the Lizard) could not make out at all what had
T8	188:30	him well from side to side, / Until his face was blue: / 'Come, tell me how you live,' I cried, / 'And what
T8W	17:10	Alice looked at his wig in great surprise. It was bright yellow like the handkerchief, and all tangled and
A2	19:40	cried Alice again, for this time the Mouse was bristling all over, and she felt certain it must be really
A6	48:29	if she meant to take the hint; but the cook was busily stirring the soup, and seemed not to be listening,
T3	129: 9	she stood silent, watching one of them that was bustling about among the flowers, poking its proboscis
T8	187: 8	what is the song, then?" said Alice, who was by this time completely bewildered.
T8	185:22	"All kinds of fastness," he repeated: "but it was careless of him to put another man's helmet on--with the
T1	107: 1	One thing was certain, that the white kitten had had nothing to do with
A7	56:20	to have no sort of meaning in it, and yet it was certainly English. "I don't quite understand you," she
A11	86:19	he did not look at all comfortable, and it was certainly not becoming.
A6	47: 7	There was certainly too much of it in the air. Even the Duchess
A8	67:33	Just then she noticed that the Queen was close behind her, listening: so she went on "--likely to
A1	9:26	and whiskers, how late it's getting!" She was close behind it when she turned the corner, but the Rabbit
T8	179:19	anxiety as he mounted again. As soon as he was comfortably in the saddle, he began once more "You're my--
A3	26:44	that the Mouse had changed his mind, and was coming back to finish his story.
A2	15:26	and she hastily dried her eyes to see what was coming. It was the White Rabbit returning, splendidly
A1	8:14	she tried to look down and make out what she was coming to, but it was too dark to see anything: then she
T8	187:10	"I was coming to that," the Knight said. "The song really is
A1	7: 6	So she was considering, in her own mind (as well as she could, for
T8	186:18	and lower, "I don't believe that pudding ever was cooked! In fact, I don't believe that pudding ever will be
T1	114: 3	to be a little annoyed with the Queen, for he was covered with ashes from head to foot.

WAS (cont.)

```
T4    146:20                                          "I knew it was!" cried Tweedledum, beginning to stamp about wildly and
T8    179: 1  noise  seemed gradually to die away, till all was dead silence, and Alice lifted up her head in some alarm.
T9    201:30  that,  the  moment she opened her lips, there was dead silence, and all eyes were fixed upon her; "and it's
A12    94:37                                        There was dead silence in the court, whilst the White Rabbit read
A5     42:19  she  tried  to get her head down to them, and was delighted to find that her neck would bend about easily in
A4     32:10     So  she  swallowed  one  of  the cakes, and was delighted to find that she began shrinking directly. As
T2    125:22  it  from side to side, and the ground between was divided up into squares by a number of little green hedges
T8    184:34  "Yes,  I  suppose  you'd  be  over when that was done," Alice said thoughtfully: "but don't you think it
T4    139:31  tree  under  which  they were dancing, and it was done (as well as she could make it out) by the branches
T4    140:32  got  no  business to be there / After the day was done--/ 'It's very rude of him,' she said, / 'To come and
A11    90:13  hard  word, I will just explain to you how it was done. They had a large canvas bag, which tied up at the
T1    113: 6  moment,  with a little "Oh!" of surprise, she was down on her hands and knees watching them. The chessmen
A1      9:15   which  way  she  put it. She felt that she was dozing off, and had just begun to dream that she was
A10    83: 7  position  in  dancing," Alice said; but she was dreadfully puzzled by the whole thing, and longed to
T9    198:14  got  up  and  hobbled  slowly towards her: he was dressed in bright yellow, and had enormous boots on.
T8    181:13                                           He was dressed in tin armour, which seemed to fit him very badly,
T3    130:22  the  gentleman  sitting  opposite to her, (he was dressed in white paper), "ought to know which way she's
T3    132: 2  you  don't--" the little voice began, when it was drowned by a shrill scream from the engine, and everybody
T9    200:16  already taken two of them, but the middle one was empty. Alice sat down in it, rather uncomfortable at the
A1      8:19               but to her great disappointment it was empty: she did not like to drop the jar, for fear of
A8     68:17                                  The hedgehog was engaged in a fight with another hedgehog, which seemed to
A8     67:21  to  her.  The Cat seemed to think that there was enough of it now in sight, and no more of it appeared.
A11    91: 6     in  her  hand,  and  Alice guessed who it was, even before she got into the court, by the way the people
A1      9:33  sadly  down  the  middle, wondering how she was ever to get out again.
T6    159:15  with  her  hands  ready to catch him, for she was every moment expecting him to fall.
T6    159:26  anything  to  her;  in  fact, his last remark was evidently addressed to a tree--so she stood and softly
A8     65:20  silent,  and  looked at Alice, as the question was evidently meant for her.
T8    181: 7  "May  I  help  you  off with your helmet?" It was evidently more than he could manage by himself: however,
T7    176:13                                      The King was evidently very uncomfortable at having to sit down between
A3     23:28  it),  and  handed them round as prizes. There was exactly one a-piece, all round.
A9     70:26  was  very  ugly;  and  secondly, because she was exactly the right height to rest her chin on Alice's
A5     41:17   rearing  itself  upright  as  it  spoke (it was exactly three inches high).
T12   207:18  it  wouldn't  look  at it," she said, when she was explaining the thing afterwards to her sister: "it turned
T1    115: 5  by  an  invisible  hand, and being dusted: he was far too much astonished to cry out, but his eyes and his
T9    204:24  would  have  felt  surprised at this, but she was far too much excited to be surprised at anything now. "As
T7    171: 8  At  this  moment  the  Messenger arrived: he was far too much out of breath to say a word, and could only
A3     22: 3  please!  'William  the Conqueror, whose cause was favoured by the pope, was soon submitted to by the English
T9    199:22              At  this  moment the door was flung open, and a shrill voice was heard singing:--
A8     62:15  business!"  said Five. "And I'll tell him--it was for bringing the cook tulip-roots instead of onions."
T8    182: 1     "I  was  wondering  what  the  mouse-trap was for," said Alice. "It isn't very likely there would be any
T4    146:18  know,"  she  added hastily, thinking that he was frightened: "only an old rattle--quite old and broken."
A6     46:45  door  led  right  into a large kitchen, which was full of smoke from one end to the other: the Duchess
T4    139:34                        "But it certainly was funny," (Alice said afterwards, when she was telling her
A8     66:15  act  of crawling away: besides all this, there was generally a ridge or a furrow in the way wherever she
A12    98: 1  with  her  head in the lap of her sister, who was gently brushing away some dead leaves that had fluttered
T1    119: 9  she  hadn't caught hold of the door-post. She was getting a little giddy with so much floating in the air,
T4    148:18                                           It was getting dark so suddenly that Alice thought there must be
T8    184:10  he went on repeating, all the time that Alice was getting him on his feet again. "Plenty of practice!"
T1    113:13  they  ca'n't  see  me.  I feel somehow as if I was getting invisible--"
T5    152:27                              By this time it was getting light. "The crow must have flown away, I think,"
T3    135:20  whatever  to  be seen on the twig, and, as she was getting quite chilly with sitting still so long, she got
A2     20:21     It  was  high time to go, for the pool was getting quite crowded with the birds and animals that had
T2    127: 7  with their feet, till suddenly, just as Alice was getting quite exhausted, they stopped, and she found
T7    177: 8        she  said,  in  reply to the Lion (she was getting quite used to being called 'the Monster'). "I've
T2    126:25  if  she  would never be able to talk again, she was getting so much out of breath: and still the Queen cried
A6     52:10  Alice  was  not  much surprised at this, she was getting so well used to queer things happening. While she
A7     60:15  went on, yawning and rubbing its eyes, for it was getting very sleepy; "and they drew all manner of things--
T8W    21:12  the  Wasp had quite recovered his spirits, and was getting very talkative, she thought she might safely leave
T7    172: 8                                        Alice was glad to see that it revived him a good deal. "There's
A10    81:34  "Why,  if  a  fish came to me, and told me he was going a journey, I should say 'With what porpoise?'"
A7     60:20     had  closed  its  eyes  by  this time, and was going off into a doze; but, on being pinched by the Hatter
A8     68:11  might  as  well  go back and see how the game was going on, as she heard the Queen's voice in the distance,
T7    175:43     The  Lion  had  joined them while this was going on: he looked very tired and sleepy, and his eyes
A2     18: 6  guess,  she  was now about two feet high, and was going on shrinking rapidly: she soon found out that the
T7    175:14  him,"  the  Unicorn  said carelessly, and he was going on, when his eye happened to fall upon Alice: he
A8     66:13  and,  when  she had got its head down, and was going to begin again, it was very provoking to find that
A5     42:22  curving  it  down into a graceful zigzag, and was going to dive in among the leaves, which she found to be
A8     66: 9  had  got its neck nicely straightened out, and was going to give the hedgehog a blow with its head, it would
A1      8:13  down  to  look  about her, and to wonder what was going to happen next. First, she tried to look down and
A7     56:25  its  eyes, "Of course, of course: just what I was going to remark myself."
A3     22:35             "What I was going to say," said the Dodo in an offended tone, "was
T6    160:26  turn  pale,  if  you like! You didn't think I was going to say that, did you? The King has promised me--with
A1     12: 6  she  waited  for  a few minutes to see if she was going to shrink any further: she felt a little nervous
T3    129: 2  was  to  make a grand survey of the country she was going to travel through. "It's something very like
A8     68:20  the  only  difficulty  was, that her flamingo was gone across the other side of the garden, where Alice
T2    128:31  Alice),  there  was no way of guessing, but she was gone, and Alice began to remember that she was a Pawn, and
A8     69:10  Cat's  head  began  fading away the moment he was gone, and, by the time he had come back with the Duchess,
A6     46: 7  when  she  next  peeped out, the Fish-Footman was gone, and the other was sitting on the ground near the
A9     72:39              The  Duchess took her choice, and was gone in a moment.
```

WAS (cont.)

T2	128:29	but exactly as she came to the last peg, she	was	gone. Whether she vanished into the air, or whether she
A6	47:13	for she was not quite sure whether it	was	good manners for her to speak first, "why your cat grins
A1	8:34	there was no one to listen to her, still it	was	good practice to say it over) "--yes, that's about the
A2	14: 4	out like the largest telescope that ever	was	! Good-bye, feet!" (for when she looked down at her feet,
A1	12:40	on the top of her head to feel which way it	was	growing; and she was quite surprised to find that she
T8W	13:16	"Oh, my old bones, my old bones!" he	was	grumbling on as Alice came up to him.
T2	123:31	had been only three inches high--and here she	was	, half a head taller than Alice herself!
T5	157:14	"To buy!" Alice echoed in a tone that	was	half astonished and half frightened--for the oars, and the
T9	192:11	Everything	was	happening so oddly that she didn't feel a bit surprised at
T1	107: 9	at the nose: and just now, as I said, she	was	hard at work on the white kitten, which was lying quite
A5	42: 1	so closely against her foot, that there	was	hardly room to open her mouth; but she did it at last, and
T4	144:32	Alice couldn't say honestly that he	was	. He had a tall red night-cap on, with a tassel, and he was
A11	88:14	Dormouse. "Fourteenth of March, I think it	was	," he said.
A10	85: 2	it, when a cry of "The trial's beginning!"	was	heard in the distance.
T9	199:22	the door was flung open, and a shrill voice	was	heard singing:--
T8	183: 4	in riding," she ventured to say, as she	was	helping him up from his fifth tumble.
A12	98:16	too began dreaming after a fashion, and this	was	her dream:--
T2	123:29	was the Red Queen. "She's grown a good deal!"	was	her first remark. She had indeed: when Alice first found
T3	129:15	"And what enormous flowers they must be!"	was	her next idea. "Something like cottages with the roofs
T6	162:15	were to take turns in choosing subjects, it	was	her turn now.) "At least," she corrected herself on second
A8	68:15	such confusion that she never knew whether it	was	her turn or not. So she went off in search of her hedgehog
A2	20:21	It	was	high time to go, for the pool was getting quite crowded
A7	55: 7	for some time with great curiosity, and this	was	his first speech.
T8	185: 5	Knight came and put it on. He thought it	was	his own helmet."
A2	18: 8	out that the cause of this was the fan she	was	holding, and she dropped it hastily, just in time to save
T3	129:34	head in at the window. In a moment everybody	was	holding out a ticket: they were about the same size as the
A3	21: 5	The first question of course	was	, how to get dry again: they had a consultation about this,
A6	48:14	of them even when they hit her; and the baby	was	howling so much already, that it was quite impossible to
T6	159: 4	had come close to it, she saw clearly that it	was	HUMPTY DUMPTY himself. "It ca'n't be anybody else!" she
T6	163:16	"To be sure I was!" Humpty Dumpty said gaily as she turned it round for him.
T8	185:19	very well, and she was afraid that he really	was	hurt this time. However, though she could see nothing but
A5	43:26	looking for eggs, as it happens; and, if I	was	, I shouldn't want yours: I don't like them raw."
A2	15:40	if I've changed in the night? Let me think:	was	I the same when I got up this morning? I almost think I
T8W	19: 7	/ It made me look extremely plain: / But what	was	I to do, you know? / My ringlets would not grow again.
A11	90:11	Here one of the guinea-pigs cheered, and	was	immediately suppressed by the officers of the court. (As
A11	90:18	'There was some attempt at applause, which	was	immediately suppressed by the officers of the court,' and
T12	207:11	this occasion the kitten only purred: and it	was	impossible to guess whether it meant "yes" or "no."
A6	50: 5	little thing sobbed again (or grunted, it	was	impossible to say which), and they went on for some while
T6	162:23	a minute or two. When he did speak again, it	was	in a deep growl.
A8	66:22	hedgehogs; and in a very short time the Queen	was	in a furious passion, and went stamping about, and
T5	153:37	would, she could make nothing more of it: she	was	in a little dark shop, leaning with her elbows on the
T3	131:27	belong to this railway journey at all--I	was	in a wood just now--and I wish I could get back there!"
A11	91:22	For some minutes the whole court	was	in confusion, getting the Dormouse turned out, and, by the
T1	107:22	a little kiss to make it understand that it	was	in disgrace. "Really, Dinah ought to have taught you
A6	45: 4	considered him to be a footman because he was	in	livery: otherwise, judging by his face only, she would
A8	66: 6	The chief difficulty Alice found at first	was	in managing her flamingo: she succeeded in getting its
A6	52:27	be raving mad--at least not so mad as it	was	in March." As she said this, she looked up, and there was
A8	68:14	like the look of things at all, as the game	was	in such confusion that she never knew whether it was her
A8	66:14	that the hedgehog had unrolled itself, and	was	in the act of crawling away: besides all this, there was
A4	32:14	outside. The poor little Lizard, Bill,	was	in the middle, being held up by two guinea-pigs, who were
T1	112: 6	left behind. "So I shall be as warm here as I	was	in the old room," thought Alice: "warmer, in fact, because
A2	18:25	station.) However, she soon made out that she	was	in the pool of tears which she had wept when she was nine
T4	140:38	You could not see a cloud, because / No cloud	was	in the sky: / No birds were flying overhead--/ There were
A1	12: 3	And so it	was	indeed: she was now only ten inches high, and her face
T8	186: 7	that I ever did," he went on after a pause, "	was	inventing a new pudding during the meat-course."
T8	184:26	"Well, just then I	was	inventing a new way of getting over a gate--would you like
T5	157: 7	"Was it? I didn't see it," said Alice, peeping cautiously over
A4	31:13	up his head--Brandy now--Don't choke him--How	was	it, old fellow? What happened to you? Tell us all about
T5	153:35	all. Was she in a shop? And was that really--	was	it really a sheep that was sitting on the other side of
T12	208:10	but then I was part of his dream, too! Was	it	the Red King, Kitty? You were his wife, my dear, so you
T7	170:35	simply, without the least idea that he was	joining	in the game, while Alice was still hesitating for
T5	152: 1	Alice	was	just beginning to say "There's a mistake somewhere--,"
A6	50: 8	Alice	was	just beginning to think to herself, "Now, what am I to do
T4	138:42	she quite forgot they were alive, and she	was	just going round to see if the word 'TWEEDLE' was written
A4	28: 1	took up the fan and a pair of the gloves, and	was	just going to leave the room, when her eye fell upon a
T4	146:10	"Selfish things!" thought Alice, and she	was	just going to say "Good-night" and leave them, when
T8W	13: 1	...and she	was	just going to spring over, when she heard a deep sigh,
T8	181:26	them." He unfastened it as he spoke, and	was	just going to throw it into the bushes, when a sudden
A1	9:25	be lost: away went Alice like the wind, and	was	just in time to hear it say, as it turned a corner, "Oh my
A1	8: 3	she ran across the field after it, and	was	just in time to see it pop down a large rabbit-hole under
T7	175:41	all came out of it Alice couldn't guess. It	was	just like a conjuring-trick, she thought.
A4	29:40	glass, from which she concluded that it	was	just possible it had fallen into a cucumber-frame, or
T2	120:27	For a few minutes all went on well, and she	was	just saying "I really shall do it this time--" when the
A6	50:19	she knew, who might do very well as pigs, and	was	just saying to herself "if one only knew the right way to
A10	83:19	pie was all finished, the Owl, as a boon, /	Was	kindly permitted to pocket the spoon. / While the Panther
T3	136: 6	could say, after a great deal of puzzling,	was	"L, I know it begins with L!"
A1	8:18	jar from one of the shelves as she passed: it	was	labeled "ORANGE MARMALADE," but to her great
A6	47: 2	stool in the middle, nursing a baby: the cook	was	leaning over the fire, stirring a large cauldron which
T5	156:15	So the boat	was	left to drift down the stream as it would, till it glided

WAS (cont.)

T1	116: 7		It was	like this.
T2	125: 1	"I only wanted to see what the garden was	like, your Majesty--"
A9	72:31	her favourite word "moral", and the arm that was	linked into hers began to tremble. Alice looked up, and
A1	9:28	she found herself in a long, low hall, which was	lit up by a row of lamps hanging from the roof.
T6	168:10	And when I found the door was	locked, / I pulled and pushed and kicked and knocked.
A8	67: 8	She was	looking about for some way of escape, and wondering
T5	154:19	always in the shelf next above the one she was	looking at. "And this one is the most provoking of all--
T3	130:18	All this time the Guard was	looking at her, first through a telescope, then through a
A7	55:37	he had taken his watch out of his pocket, and was	looking at it uneasily, shaking it every now and then, and
A4	32:27	An enormous puppy was	looking down at her with large round eyes, and feebly
T9	196: 5	in," the White Queen went on, "because he was	looking for a hippopotamus. Now, as it happened, there
A4	27: 6	I wonder?" Alice guessed in a moment that it was	looking for the fan and the pair of white kid-gloves, and
T8	184:23	the last time you picked me up, that I was	looking rather thoughtful?"
A6	46:21	knock, and I could let you out, you know." He was	looking up into the sky all the time he was speaking, and
A5	41:12	in all her life before, and she felt that she was	losing her temper.
T7	170:20	All this was	lost on Alice, who was still looking intently along the
T4	144:33	tall red night-cap on, with a tassel, and he was	lying crumpled up into a sort of untidy heap, and snoring
A2	18:14	was shut again, and the little golden key was	lying on the glass table as before, "and things are worse
A6	47:11	sneeze, were the cook, and a large cat, which was	lying on the hearth and grinning from ear to ear.
T1	107:10	was hard at work on the white kitten, which was	lying quite still and trying to purr--no doubt feeling
A1	12:31	Soon her eye fell on a little glass box that was	lying under the table: she opened it, and found in it a
T1	108:13	been up in the window with me--only Dinah was	making you tidy, so you couldn't. I was watching the boys
T9	198: 3	side of the arch there was a bell-handle; one was	marked "Visitors' Bell", and the other "Servants' Bell."
T4	144:18	"That was	mean!" Alice said indignantly. "Then I like the Carpenter
T8	190: 1	Of that old man I used to know--/ Whose look was	mild, whose speech was slow, / Whose hair was whiter than
A3	22:23	him the crown. William's conduct at first was	moderate. But the insolence of his Normans--' How are you
A5	42:36	Alice was	more and more puzzled, but she thought there was no use in
T8	179:17	Startled as she was, Alice was	more frightened for him than for herself at the moment,
A2	15:18	the garden with one eye; but to get through was	more hopeless than ever: she sat down and began to cry
T8W	13: 5	like a very old man (only that his face was	more like a wasp) was sitting on the ground, leaning
T4	144:25	in the wood near them, though she feared it was	more likely to be a wild beast. "Are there any lions or
A7	60:29	This piece of rudeness was	more than Alice could bear: she got up in great disgust,
T9	196:30	and see how pleased she'll be!" But this was	more than Alice had courage to do.
T9	197:17	it couldn't, you know, because there never was	more than one Queen at a time. Do wake up, you heavy
A8	67:14	getting on?" said the Cat, as soon as there was	mouth enough for it to speak with.
A5	42:15	poor hands, how is it I ca'n't see you?" She was	moving them about, as she spoke, but no result seemed to
A4	28:27	"It was	much pleasanter at home," thought poor Alice, "when one
T8	185:20	see nothing but the soles of his feet, she was	much relieved to hear that he was talking on in his usual
A9	76:36	"Well, there was	Mystery," the Mock Turtle replied, counting off the
A12	93:31	"unimportant." Alice could see this, as she was	near enough to look over their slates; "but it doesn't
T1	114: 5	to be of use, and, as the poor little Lily was	nearly screaming herself into a fit, she hastily picked up
T7	176:17	slyly up at the crown, which the poor King was	nearly shaking off his head, he trembled so much.
T6	162:20	only I knew," she thought to herself, "which was	neck and which was waist!"
A6	50:11	time there could be no mistake about it: it was	neither more nor less than a pig, and she felt that it
A2	18:26	the pool of tears which she had wept when she was	nine feet high.
T9	197:19	she went on in an impatient tone; but there was	no answer but a gentle snoring.
T5	151:10	Alice felt there was	no denying that. "Of course it would be all the better,"
A6	46:35	It was,	no doubt: only Alice did not like to be told so. "It's
A4	28: 3	that stood near the looking-glass. There was	no label this time with the words "DRINK ME," but
T9	204:19	the cause of all the mischief--but the Queen was	no longer at her side--she had suddenly dwindled down to
A1	9:27	it when she turned the corner, but the Rabbit was	no longer to be seen: she found herself in a long, low
T5	156: 1	This offended Alice a little, so there was	no more conversation for a minute or two, while the boat
A3	21:12	positively refused to tell its age, there was	no more to be said.
A1	8:42	I think--" (she was rather glad there was	no one listening, this time, as it didn't sound at all the
T8	179: 2	Alice lifted up her head in some alarm. There was	no one to be seen, and her first thought was that she must
A1	8:33	for showing off her knowledge, as there was	no one to listen to her, still it was good practice to say
A3	23:10	along the course, here and there. There was	no "One, two, three, and away!", but they began running
T7	176:14	between the two great creatures; but there was	no other place for him.
A5	41:42	very sudden change, but she felt that there was	no time to be lost, as she was shrinking rapidly: so she
A5	42:36	more and more puzzled, but she thought there was	no use in saying anything more till the Pigeon had
T2	128:31	she can run very fast!" thought Alice), there was	no way of guessing, but she was gone, and Alice began to
T9	192: 8	comforted herself with the thought that there was	nobody to see her, "and if I really am a Queen," she said
A1	9:21	Alice was	not a bit hurt, and she jumped up on to her feet in a
T8	182:38	to help the poor Knight, who certainly was	not a good rider.
T9	204: 9	There was	not a moment to be lost. Already several of the guests
A1	9:24	was still in sight, hurrying down it. There was	not a moment to be lost: away went Alice like the wind,
T3	137:16	It was	not a very difficult question to answer, as there was only
A1	8:32	lessons in the school-room, and though this was	not a very good opportunity for showing off her knowledge,
A5	35: 5	This was	not an encouraging opening for a conversation. Alice
A3	23:12	and left off when they liked, so that it was	not easy to know when the race was over. However, when
A4	28:17	down on the floor: in another minute there was	not even room for this, and she tried the effect of lying
T4	139:29	natural (she remembered afterwards), and she was	not even surprised to hear music playing: it seemed to
A1	10:20	to say "Drink me," but the wise little Alice was	not going to do that in a hurry. "No, I'll look first,"
A1	10:16	found a little bottle on it ("which certainly was	not here before," said Alice), and tied round the neck of
A1	11: 6	However, this bottle was	not marked "poison," so Alice ventured to taste it, and,
A6	52: 9	Alice was	not much surprised at this, she was getting so well used
A9	72: 9	others that what you were or might have been was	not otherwise than what you had been would have appeared
A6	47:13	me," said Alice, a little timidly, for she was	not quite sure whether it was good manners for her to
T7	172:13	"I didn't say there was	nothing better," the King replied. "I said there was

WAS (cont.)

A1	9: 5	Down, down, down. There was nothing else to do, so Alice soon began talking again.
T5	155:19	boat, gliding along between banks: so there was nothing for it but to do her best.
T7	172:14	better," the King replied. "I said there was nothing like it." Which Alice did not venture to deny.
A1	9:35	table, all made of solid glass: there was nothing on it but a tiny golden key, and Alice's first
A7	54:14	Alice looked all round the table, but there was nothing on it but tea. "I don't see any wine," she
A1	7:11	There was nothing so very remarkable in that; nor did Alice think it
T2	120:26	there was the hill full in sight, so there was nothing to be done but start again. This time she came
T3	135:19	itself away, for, when Alice looked up, there was nothing whatever to be seen on the twig, and, as she was
A4	29:22	shook the house, quite forgetting that she was now about a thousand times as large as the Rabbit, and had
A2	18: 6	found that, as nearly as she could guess, she was now about two feet high, and was going on shrinking
A2	19: 8	but then she remembered how small she was now, and she soon made out that it was only a mouse, that
T9	204:20	down to the size of a little doll, and was now on the table, merrily running round and round after
A1	12: 3	And so it was indeed: she was now only ten inches high, and her face brightened up at
A2	15:13	against the roof of the hall: in fact she was now rather more than nine feet high, and she at once took
A1	12: 4	face brightened up at the thought that she was now the right size for going through the little door into
T5	155: 9	if you go on turning round like that." She was now working with fourteen pairs at once, and Alice
T3	131:12	engines--" it said, and there it choked and was obliged to leave off.
A11	86:22	Alice; "and those twelve creatures," (she was obliged to say "creatures," you see, because some of them
A11	87:10	of it; so, after hunting all about for it, he was obliged to write with one finger for the rest of the day;
T4	140:27	/ The billows smooth and bright--/ And this was odd, because it was / The middle of the night.
T4	142: 5	/ Their shoes were clean and neat--/ And this was odd, because, you know, / They hadn't any feet.
T7	171:13	Messenger's attention from himself--but it was of no use--the Anglo-Saxon attitudes only got more
A11	87:11	one finger for the rest of the day; and this was of very little use, as it left no mark on the slate.
A4	34: 6	her that she might as well look and see what was on top of it.
T2	126: 3	you know. Oh, what fun it is! How I wish I was one of them! I wouldn't mind being a Pawn, if only I might
T12	207:38	you'd been really with me in my dream, there was one thing you would have enjoyed--I had such a quantity of
A2	19: 9	she was now, and she soon made out that it was only a mouse, that had slipped in like herself.
T3	137:16	a very difficult question to answer, as there was only one road through the wood, and the two finger-posts
A6	50: 1	the look of the thing at all. "But perhaps it was only sobbing," she thought, and looked into its eyes again
A9	70: 5	and thought to herself that perhaps it was only the pepper that had made her so savage when they met
A10	84: 7	leave off," said the Gryphon, and Alice was only too glad to do so.
A6	45: 6	loudly at the door with his knuckles. It was opened by another footman in livery, with a round face,
A1	8:36	had not the slightest idea what Latitude was, or Longitude either, but she thought they were nice grand
A5	41:32	had asked it aloud; and in another moment it was out of sight.
T8	190:33	her handkerchief to him, and waited till he was out of sight.
A11	91: 2	added to one of the officers; but the Hatter was out of sight before the officer could get to the door.
A9	74: 8	its eyes: then it watched the Queen till she was out of sight: then it chuckled. "What fun!" said the
T1	119: 2	Let's have a look at the garden first!" She was out of the room in a moment, and ran down stairs--or, at
A1	9:20	a heap of sticks and dry leaves, and the fall was over.
A8	68:23	the flamingo and brought it back, the fight was over, and both the hedgehogs were out of sight: "but it
A10	80:14	watch," said Alice, feeling very glad that it was over at last: "and I do so like that curious song about
A3	24:12	and had to be patted on the back. However, it was over at last, and they sat down again in a ring, and
A3	23:12	so that it was not easy to know when the race was over. However, when they had been running half an hour or
T9	192:16	no harm, she thought, in asking if the game was over. "Please, would you tell me--" she began, looking
T12	208: 9	was part of my dream, of course--but then I was part of his dream, too! Was it the Red King, Kitty? You
T12	208: 9	must have been either me or the Red King. He was part of my dream, of course--but then I was part of his
A8	68: 4	decidedly; and he called to the Queen, who was passing at the moment, "My dear! I wish you would have
A8	65:26	She was walking by the White Rabbit, who was peeping anxiously into her face.
A4	32:24	idea how to set about it; and, while she was peering about anxiously among the trees, a little sharp
A5	41:35	which were the two sides of it; and, as it was perfectly round, she found this a very difficult question.
A1	12:26	cheated herself in a game of croquet she was playing against herself, for this curious child was very
A4	29:26	as the door opened inwards, and Alice's elbow was pressed hard against it, that attempt proved a failure.
A5	42: 1	once to eat some of the other bit. Her chin was pressed so closely against her foot, that there was hardly
T5	151:18	"Yes, but then I had done the things I was punished for," said Alice: "that makes all the difference
T7	173: 6	she asked, as well as she could, for the run was putting her quite out of breath.
T9	195:29	Alice was puzzled. "In our country," she remarked, "there's only one
T8	186:10	for the next course?" said Alice. "Well, that was quick work, certainly!"
A9	77:17	This was quite a new idea to Alice, and she thought it over a
T1	114:21	the King took no notice of the question: it was quite clear that he could neither hear her nor see her.
T1	112:11	that what could be seen from the old room was quite common and uninteresting, but that all the rest was
T8	184: 1	in the path where Alice was walking. She was quite frightened this time, and said in an anxious tone,
A6	48:14	the baby was howling so much already, that it was quite impossible to say whether the blows hurt it or not.
A3	26:17	stay!" sighed the Lory, as soon as it was quite out of sight. And an old Crab took the opportunity
A2	20:17	round and swam slowly back to her: its face was quite pale (with passion, Alice thought), and it said, in
A11	86:14	but she had read about them in books, and she was quite pleased to find that she knew the name of nearly
T1	112: 4	there was a fire in the fireplace, and she was quite pleased to find that there was a real one, blazing
T2	122:30	This sounded a very good reason, and Alice was quite pleased to know it. "I never thought of that before!
A5	43:21	This was such a new idea to Alice, that she was quite silent for a minute or two, which gave the Pigeon
A1	12:40	to feel which way it was growing; and she was quite surprised to find that she remained the same size.
A4	33: 4	so she set off at once, and ran till she was quite tired and out of breath, and till the puppy's bark
T3	135:37	She was rambling on in this way when she reached the wood: it
T9	203: 1	In fact it was rather difficult for her to keep in her place while she
A8	63:28	Alice was rather doubtful whether she ought not to lie down on her
A1	8:42	downwards! The antipathies, I think--" (she was rather glad there was no one listening, this time, as it
T1	119:10	giddy with so much floating in the air, and was rather glad to find herself walking again in the natural
T8	185:17	to the side of the ditch to look for him. She was rather startled by the fall, as for some time he had kept
T6	168:17	This was rather sudden, Alice thought: but, after such a very
A1	7: 3	twice she had peeped into the book her sister was reading, but it had no pictures or conversations in it,
A11	90:30	with an anxious look at the Queen, who was reading the list of singers.

WAS (cont.)

A2	15:31	waiting!" Alice felt so desperate that she was ready to ask help of any one: so, when the Rabbit came
T9	196:28	"She never was really well brought up," the Red Queen went on: "but it's
T8W	16: 6	Alice repeated, quite pleased to find that he was recovering his temper.
A11	88:38	to remain where she was as long as there was room for her.
A4	33: 7	"And yet what a dear little puppy it was!" said Alice, as she leant against a buttercup to rest
A8	63:24	nervous manner, smiling at everything that was said, and went by without noticing her. Then followed the
A9	77:20	"Of course it was," said the Mock Turtle.
T9	195:10	"Who ever said it was?" said the Red Queen.
A6	52:24	on in the direction in which the March Hare was said to live. "I've seen hatters before," she said to
T7	177: 7	brook, with the great dish on her knees, and was sawing away diligently with the knife. "It's very
A10	82:20	that she hardly knew what she was saying; and the words came very queer indeed:--
T1	115:22	The King was saying "I assure you, my dear, I turned cold to the very
T8	184: 4	three of them. "The great art of riding, as I was saying is--to keep your balance properly. Like this, you
T6	163:17	"I thought it looked a little queer. As I was saying, that seems to be done right--though I haven't time
A1	9:17	she was walking hand in hand with Dinah, and was saying to her, very earnestly, "Now, Dinah, tell me the
T4	144:11	/ But answer came there none--/ And this was scarcely odd, because / They'd eaten every one."
A4	30:41	animal (she couldn't guess of what sort it was) scratching and scrambling about in the chimney close
A11	88: 9	in; but I hadn't quite finished my tea when I was sent for."
T7	173:24	and he hadn't finished his tea when he was sent in," Haigha whispered to Alice: "and they only give
T5	153:34	couldn't make out what had happened at all. Was she in a shop? And was that really--was it really a sheep
A11	88:35	her a good deal until she made out what it was: she was beginning to grow larger again, and she thought
T4	140:18	"The sun was shining--"
T4	140:23	"The sun was shining on the sea, / Shining with all his might: / He did
T4	140:29	The moon was shining sulkily, / Because she thought the sun / Had got
A5	41:42	that there was no time to be lost, as she was shrinking rapidly: so she set to work at once to eat some
A2	18:13	the little door; but, alas! the little door was shut again, and the little golden key was lying on the
T6	168:12	And when I found the door was shut, / I tried to turn the handle, but--"
T9	199:35	if any one's counting?" In a minute there was silence again, and the same shrill voice sang another
A5	41: 5	said the Caterpillar, decidedly; and there was silence for some minutes.
T2	122:16	There was silence in a moment, and several of the pink daisies
A7	60:19	Alice was silent.
A8	64: 9	very loudly and decidedly, and the Queen was silent.
T6	166:28	most," Humpty Dumpty remarked severely. Alice was silent.
T8W	18:11	the Wasp: "however I'll try; wait a bit." He was silent for a few moments, and then began again--
T3	134:20	After this, Alice was silent for a minute or two, pondering. The Gnat amused
A7	54: 3	the Hatter were having tea at it: a Dormouse was sitting between them, fast asleep, and the other two were
T3	131:10	Alice couldn't see who was sitting beyond the Beetle, but a hoarse voice spoke next.
T1	107:13	earlier in the afternoon, and so, while Alice was sitting curled up in a corner of the great arm-chair, half
A11	88:39	wouldn't squeeze so," said the Dormouse, who was sitting next to her. "I can hardly breathe."
T3	131: 3	A Goat, that was sitting next to the gentleman in white, shut his eyes and
A6	47: 1	smoke from one end to the other: the Duchess was sitting on a three-legged stool in the middle, nursing a
T8W	13: 6	man (only that his face was more like a wasp) was sitting on the ground, leaning against a tree, all huddled
A6	46: 7	out, the Fish-Footman was gone, and the other was sitting on the ground near the door, staring stupidly up
T5	153:35	was that really--was it really a sheep that was sitting on the other side of the counter? Rub as she would
A4	34: 9	met those of a large blue caterpillar, that was sitting on the top, with its arms folded, quietly smoking
T1	114:12	little, she called out to the White King, who was sitting sulkily among the ashes, "Mind the volcano!"
T9	198:13	a long time; but at last a very old Frog, who was sitting under a tree, got up and hobbled slowly towards
T6	159: 8	easily, on that enormous face. Humpty Dumpty was sitting, with his legs crossed like a Turk, on the top of
T4	144:29	hands, and led her up to where the King was sleeping.
T8	190: 1	to know--/ Whose look was mild, whose speech was slow, / Whose hair was whiter than the snow, / Whose face
A4	32:11	she began shrinking directly. As soon as she was small enough to get through the door, she ran out of the
A6	47: 8	sneezed occasionally; and as for the baby, it was sneezing and howling alternately without a moment's pause.
A12	98:29	guests to execution--once more the pig-baby was sneezing on the Duchess's knee, while plates and dishes
A6	49:18	thought Alice. The poor little thing was snorting like a steam-engine when she caught it, and kept
T1	108:21	"Do you know, I was so angry, Kitty," Alice went on, as soon as they were
T2	121: 1	Alice was so astonished that she couldn't speak for a minute: it
T1	115: 2	she might as well dust him a little, he was so covered with ashes.
T5	149:22	she had got some one else to dress her, she was so dreadfully untidy. "Every single thing's crooked,"
T3	129:24	favourite little toss of the head), 'only it was so dusty and hot, and the elephants did tease so!'"
T9	196:15	knocking over the tables and things--till I was so frightened, I couldn't remember my own name!"
A10	82:19	got up, and began to repeat it, but her head was so full of the Lobster-Quadrille, that she hardly knew
T9	199:13	he said. "What's it been asking of?" He was so hoarse that Alice could scarcely hear him.
T4	139: 7	"Contrariwise," continued Tweedledee, "if it was so, it might be; and if it were so, it would be; but as it
T4	143:19	'It was so kind of you to come! / And you are very nice!' / The
A6	53:13	ears and the roof was thatched with fur. It was so large a house, that she did not like to go nearer till
T9	201:18	again in a moment, like a conjuring-trick. It was so large that she couldn't help feeling a little shy with
A5	43:37	It was so long since she had been anything near the right size,
A4	27:15	of gloves and a fan! Quick, now!" And Alice was so much frightened that she ran off at once in the
A2	14: 1	"Curiouser and curiouser!" cried Alice (she was so much surprised, that for the moment she quite forgot
A9	74:14	Alice, as she went slowly after it: "I never was so ordered about before, in all my life, never!"
A2	18:15	ever," thought the poor child, "for I never was so small as this before, never! And I declare it's too bad
T8	182:16	bag open very carefully, because the Knight was so very awkward in putting in the dish: the first two or
A11	90:17	the newspapers, at the end of trials, 'There was some attempt at applause, which was immediately suppressed
A3	25: 4	was speaking, so that her idea of the tale was something like this:--
T8	179:32	his helmet (which hung from the saddle, and was something the shape of a horse's head) and put it on.
T5	155:24	so Alice said nothing, but pulled away. There was something very queer about the water, she thought, as
T7	169: 8	more always fell over him, so that the ground was soon covered with little heaps of men.
A3	26:36	pretexts they all moved off, and Alice was soon left alone.
A3	22: 4	whose cause was favoured by the pope, was soon submitted to by the English, who wanted leaders, and

WAS (cont.)

T5	157: 2	However, she wasn't a bit hurt, and	was soon up again: the Sheep went on with her knitting all the
T7	172:27	so as to get close to the King's ear. Alice	was sorry for this, as she wanted to hear the news too.
A6	46:22	was looking up into the sky all the time he	was speaking, and this Alice thought decidedly uncivil. "But
T1	108:30	that you say?" (pretending that the kitten	was speaking). "Her paw went into your eye? Well, that's your
A3	25: 3	she kept on puzzling about it while the mouse	was speaking, so that her idea of the tale was something like
T1	107:17	it had all come undone again; and there it	was, spread over the hearth-rug, all knots and tangles, with
T9	198: 1	She	was standing before an arched doorway, over which were the
A11	86: 4	as well as the whole pack of cards: the Knave	was standing before them, in chains, with a soldier on each
T7	173:21	close to where Hatta, the other Messenger,	was standing watching the fight, with a cup of tea in one hand
T4	138: 8	written at the back of each collar, when she	was startled by a voice coming from the one marked 'DUM.'
T1	116: 2	she sat watching the White King (for she	was still a little anxious about him, and had the ink all
T1	114:15	"Blew--me--up," panted the Queen, who	was still a little out of breath. "Mind you come up--the
T7	170:35	that he was joining in the game, while Alice	was still hesitating for the name of a town beginning with H.
A1	9:23	another long passage, and the White Rabbit	was still in sight, hurrying down it. There was not a moment
A6	52:12	used to queer things happening. While she	was still looking at the place where it had been, it suddenly
T7	170:20	All this was lost on Alice, who	was still looking intently along the road, shading her eyes
T12	207:27	over her shoulder at the White Kitten, which	was still patiently undergoing its toilet, "when will Dinah
T8W	14: 4	peevish tone. "Worrity, worrity! There never	was such a child!"
A5	43:21	This	was such a new idea to Alice, that she was quite silent for a
T9	196:11	Here the White Queen began again. "It	was such a thunderstorm, you ca'n't think!" ("She never could,
T3	131:36	like other people!" she thought. But this	was such a wonderfully small sigh, that she wouldn't have
T4	147: 2	up the umbrella, with himself in it: which	was such an extraordinary thing to do, that it quite took off
A11	90:26	Here the other guinea-pig cheered, and	was suppressed.
A8	68:28	When she got back to the Cheshire-Cat, she	was surprised to find quite a large crowd collected round it:
A2	18: 1	said this she looked down at her hands, and	was surprised to see that she had put on one of the Rabbit's
A2	20:11	afraid I've offended it again!" For the Mouse	was swimming away from her as hard as it could go, and making
A11	86:36	and looked anxiously round, to make out who	was talking.
T1	108: 5	But she didn't get on very fast, as she	was talking all the time, sometimes to the kitten, and
A2	18: 3	Rabbit's little white kid-gloves while she	was talking. "How can I have done that?" she thought. "I must
A8	63:23	them Alice recognized the White Rabbit: it	was talking in a hurried nervous manner, smiling at everything
T8	185:21	feet, she was much relieved to hear that he	was talking on in his usual tone. "All kinds of fastness," he
T4	139:35	was funny," (Alice said afterwards, when she	was telling her sister the history of all this), "to find
T9	202:38	did push so!" she said afterwards, when she	was telling her sister the history of her feast. "You would
A4	32:30	and she tried hard to whistle to it; but she	was terribly frightened all the time at the thought that it
A8	68:41	The King's argument	was that anything that had a head could be beheaded, and that
T12	208: 5	"Now, Kitty, let's consider who it	was that dreamed it all. This is a serious question, my dear,
A8	68:19	of them with the other: the only difficulty	was, that her flamingo was gone across the other side of the
A8	69: 2	The Queen's argument	was that, if something wasn't done about it in less than no
A9	76:20	"What	was that?" inquired Alice.
T3	131:38	close to her ear. The consequence of this	was that it tickled her ear very much, and quite took off her
A9	77: 1	"What	was that like?" said Alice.
T5	153:35	had happened at all. Was she in a shop? And	was that really--was it really a sheep that was sitting on the
A4	32:23	and simply arranged: the only difficulty	was, that she had not the smallest idea how to set about it;
A2	18:19	up to her chin in saltwater. Her first idea	was that she had somehow fallen into the sea, "and in that
T8	179: 3	was no one to be seen, and her first thought	was that she must have been dreaming about the Lion and the
A3	23: 1	to say," said the Dodo in an offended tone,	"was that the best thing to get us dry would be a Caucus-race
T5	156:43	explained it afterwards), and the consequence	was that the handle of it caught her under the chin, and, in
T2	126:18	The most curious part of the thing	was, that the trees and the other things round them never
T2	126:13	out, in thinking it over afterwards, how it	was that they began: all she remembers is, that they were
A1	9:36	but a tiny golden key, and Alice's first idea	was that this might belong to one of the doors of the hall;
T5	154:12	curious things--but the oddest part of it all	was that, whenever she looked hard at any shelf, to make out
A8	68:37	The executioner's argument	was, that you couldn't cut off a head unless there was a body
A12	95:13	My notion was that you had been / (Before she had this fit) / An
A6	53:12	chimneys were shaped like ears and the roof	was thatched with fur. It was so large a house, that she did
A7	56: 4	"It	was the best butter," the March Hare meekly replied.
A7	56: 9	better to say than his first remark, "It	was the best butter, you know."
T8	183: 1	Alice was walking, she soon found that it	was the best plan not to walk quite close to the horse.
T1	107: 2	kitten had had nothing to do with it--it	was the black kitten's fault entirely. For the white kitten
A6	52:28	As she said this, she looked up, and there	was the Cat again, sitting on a branch of a tree.
A1	9: 7	very much to-night, I should think!" (Dinah	was the cat.) "I hope they'll remember her saucer of milk at
T8	185: 2	a very little way to fall, you see--But there	was the danger of falling into it, to be sure. That happened
A11	91: 5	The next witness	was the Duchess's cook. She carried the pepper-box in her hand
A2	18: 7	she soon found out that the cause of this	was the fan she was holding, and she dropped it hastily, just
A12	94:26	was a general clapping of hands at this: it	was the first really clever thing the King had said that day.
A2	19:25	So she began again: "Ou est ma chatte?" which	was the first sentence in her French lesson-book. The Mouse
A7	55:35	The Hatter	was the first to break the silence. "What day of the month is
A5	41: 6	The Caterpillar	was the first to speak.
T8	179: 5	queer Anglo-Saxon Messengers. However, there	was the great dish still lying at her feet, on which she had
A11	88: 6	The first witness	was the Hatter. He came in with a teacup in one hand and a
T2	120:26	However, there	was the hill full in sight, so there was nothing to be done
T3	132:18	under a tree--while the Gnat (for that	was the insect she had been talking to) was balancing itself
A11	86:17	The judge, by the way,	was the King; and, as he wore his crown over the wig (look at
T9	204: 4	White Queen; but, instead of the Queen, there	was the leg of mutton sitting in the chair. "Here I am!" cried
A7	57: 3	("I only wish it	was," the March Hare said to itself in a whisper.
T8W	13: 4	thought, looking anxiously back to see what	was the matter. Something like a very old man (only that his
A6	49:32	very anxiously into its face to see what	was the matter with it. There could be no doubt that it had a
T9	204: 3	laugh at her side, and turned to see what	was the matter with the White Queen; but, instead of the Queen
T4	140:27	and bright--/ And this was odd, because it	was / The middle of the night.
T1	114:14	into the fire, as if he thought that	was the most likely place to find one.

WAS (cont.)

T5	152:28	Alice: "I'm so glad it's gone. I thought it was	the night coming on."
T8	187:17	her journey Through The Looking-Glass, this was	the one that she always remembered most clearly. Years
A7	59:40	took the place of the March Hare. The Hatter was	the only one who got any advantage from the change; and
T3	135:26	go back," she thought to herself, and this was	the only way to the Eighth Square.
T1	116:16	This was	the poem that Alice read
A4	29:21	of feet on the stairs. Alice knew it was	the Rabbit coming to look for her, and she trembled till
T2	123:28	Alice looked round eagerly and found that it was	the Red Queen. "She's grown a good deal!" was her first
T2	123:24	you hadn't got some too. I thought it was	the regular rule."
A8	63:45	their faces, and the pattern on their backs was	the same as the rest of the pack, she could not tell
A2	15:26	dried her eyes to see what was coming. It was	the White Rabbit returning, splendidly dressed, with a
A4	27: 1	It was	the White Rabbit, trotting slowly back again, and looking
A11	86: 5	on each side to guard him; and near the King was	the White Rabbit, with a trumpet in one hand, and a scroll
T2	125:20	the country--and a most curious country it was	There were a number of tiny little brooks running
T4	139:10	"I was	thinking," Alice said politely, "which is the best way out
A5	43: 2	raising its voice to a shriek, "and just as I was	thinking I should be free of them at last, they must needs
T8	188: 9	But I was	thinking of a plan / To dye one's whiskers green, / And
T8	188:25	But I was	thinking of a way / To feed oneself on batter, / And so go
T8	186:30	Alice could only look puzzled: she was	thinking of the pudding.
T1	107: 6	The way Dinah washed her children's faces was	this: first she held the poor thing down by its ear with
A8	69: 4	she'd have everybody executed, all round. (It was	this last remark that had made the whole party look so
A10	81:15	Alice was	thoroughly puzzled. "Does the boots and shoes!" she
T1	112: 1	In another moment Alice was	through the glass, and had jumped lightly down into the
T5	149:10	and Alice felt that if there was	to be any conversation at all, she must manage it herself.
T1	109: 5	came. Or--let me see--suppose each punishment was	to be going without a dinner: then, when the miserable day
A3	24: 9	The next thing was	to eat the comfits: this caused some noise and confusion,
A8	63: 8	a white one in by mistake; and, if the Queen was	to find out, we should all have our heads cut off, you
A1	8: 6	never once considering how in the world she was	to get out again.
T9	193:17	"I didn't know I was	to have a party at all," said Alice; "but, if there is to
T1	112: 3	room. The very first thing she did was	to look whether there was a fire in the fireplace, and she
T3	129: 1	Of course the first thing to do was	to make a grand survey of the country she was going to
A6	49:23	made out the proper way of nursing it (which was	to twist it up into a sort of knot, and then keep tight
T4	145:10	"If that there King was	to wake," added Tweedledum, "you'd go out--bang!--just
A1	8:14	and make out what she was coming to, but it was	too dark to see anything: then she looked at the sides of
T5	152:19	And she caught at the brooch; but it was	too late: the pin had slipped, and the Queen had pricked
A4	28:15	Alas! It was	too late to wish that! She went on growing, and growing,
T7	177: 4	Lion growled out as he lay down again. "There was	too much dust to see anything. What a time the Monster is,
A9	72:41	the game," the Queen said to Alice; and Alice was	too much frightened to say a word, but slowly followed her
T2	124:15	Alice wondered a little at this, but she was	too much in awe of the Queen to disbelieve it. "I'll try
T6	164: 7	"Oh!" said Alice. She was	too much puzzled to make any other remark.
T6	163:37	Alice was	too much puzzled to say anything; so after a minute Humpty
A1	12:19	climb up one of the legs of the table, but it was	too slippery; and when she had tired herself out with
A1	9:37	either the locks were too large, or the key was	too small, but at any rate it would not open any of them.
T1	115:35	some time without saying anything; but Alice was	too strong for him, and at last he panted out "My dear! I
T9	204:21	round and round after her own shawl, which was	trailing behind her.
A2	19:42	"We, indeed!" cried the Mouse, who was	trembling down to the end of its tail. "As if I would talk
A12	96:23	now hastily began again, using the ink, that was	trickling down his face, as long as it lasted.)
T1	110: 2	to clap her hands. "And I do so wish it was	true! I'm sure the woods look sleepy in the autumn, when
T4	147: 1	All this time Tweedledee was	trying his best to fold up the umbrella, with himself in
A6	48: 9	some other subject of conversation. While she was	trying to fix on one, the cook took the cauldron of soup
T1	111:11	It'll be easy enough to get through--" It was	up on the chimney-piece while she said this, though she
A2	18:18	slipped, and in another moment, splash! she was	up to her chin in saltwater. Her first idea was that she
T6	162:22	Evidently Humpty Dumpty was	very angry, though he said nothing for a minute or two.
T8W	13:15	back to the Wasp--rather unwillingly, for she was	very anxious to be a Queen.
T1	114: 4	Alice was	very anxious to be of use, and, as the poor little Lily
T5	158:18	way among the tables and chairs, for the shop was	very dark towards the end. "The egg seems to get further
A1	8:11	Either the well was	very deep, or she fell very slowly, for she had plenty of
T7	174:16	bread. Alice took a piece to taste, but it was	very dry.
T2	127:29	it, and ate it as well as she could: and it was	very dry: and she thought she had never been so nearly
A1	12:27	against herself, for this curious child was	very fond of pretending to be two people. "But it's no use
A9	70: 4	Alice was	very glad to find her in such a pleasant temper, and
T7	170: 3	confusion got worse every moment, and Alice was	very glad to get out of the wood into an open place, where
A2	15:36	took up the fan and gloves, and, as the hall was	very hot, she kept fanning herself all the time she went
T8	190: 3	hair was whiter than the snow, / Whose face was	very like a crow, / With eyes, like cinders, all aglow, /
A4	32:40	to get hold of it: then Alice, thinking it was	very like having a game of play with a cart-horse, and
A1	8:26	if I fell off the top of the house!" (Which was	very likely true.)
A9	74:36	heavy sobbing of the Mock Turtle. Alice was	very nearly getting up and saying, "Thank you, Sir, for
T1	108:23	I saw all the mischief you had been doing, I was	very nearly opening the window, and putting you out into
T8W	14: 5	felt rather offended at this answer, and was	very nearly walking on and leaving him, but she thought to
T7	176:24	to prevent the quarrel going on: he was	very nervous, and his voice quite quivered. "All round the
T6	168: 6	And he was	very proud and stiff: / He said 'I'd go and wake them, if
A8	66:13	head down, and was going to begin again, it was	very provoking to find that the hedgehog had unrolled
T6	168: 4	"But he was	very stiff and proud: / He said, 'You needn't shout so
A9	70:26	so close to her: first because the Duchess was	very ugly; and secondly, because she was exactly the right
A4	28:24	full effect, and she grew no larger: still it was	very uncomfortable, and, as there seemed to be no sort of
T3	131:34	The little voice sighed deeply. It was	very unhappy, evidently, and Alice would have said
T6	162:21	thought to herself, "which was neck and which was	waist!"
A8	65:26	day!" said a timid voice at her side. She was	walking by the White Rabbit, who was peeping anxiously
A1	9:16	off, and had just begun to dream that she was	walking hand in hand with Dinah, and was saying to her,
T8	182:44	generally did this on the side on which Alice was	walking, she soon found that it was the best plan not to

WAS (cont.)

T8	183:20	of his head exactly in the path where Alice was walking. She was quite frightened this time, and said in
T9	204:10	lying down in the dishes, and the soup ladle was walking up the table towards Alice's chair, and beckoning
T1	108:28	Number one: you squeaked twice while Dinah was washing your face this morning. Now you ca'n't deny it,
T1	108:13	Dinah was making you tidy, so you couldn't. I was watching the boys getting in sticks for the bonfire--and
T2	120:30	said Alice, addressing herself to one that was waving gracefully about in the wind, "I wish you could
A12	93: 5	in head downwards, and the poor little thing was waving its tail about in a melancholy way, being quite
T6	167: 3	The little fishes' answer was / 'We cannot do it, Sir, because--'"
T4	140:35	The sea was wet as wet could be, / The sands were dry as dry. / You
A4	33:14	The great question certainly was "What?" Alice looked all round her at the flowers and the
T12	207:17	her hands triumphantly. "Confess that was what you turned into!"
A5	35: 7	Sir, just at present--at least I know who I was when I got up this morning, but I think I must have been
T3	131:44	anxiously. What she really wanted to know was, whether it could sting or not, but she thought this
T7	173:17	that at first Alice could not make out which was which; but she soon managed to distinguish the Unicorn by
T4	138: 2	round the other's neck, and Alice knew which was which in a moment, because one of them had 'DUM'
T8	190: 2	was mild, whose speech was slow, / Whose hair was whiter than the snow, / Whose face was very like a crow, /
A7	55:12	very wide on hearing this; but all he said was "Why is a raven like a writing-desk?"
T8	182: 1	"I was wondering what the mouse-trap was for," said Alice. "It
T2	121: 8	you know," said the Rose, "and I really was wondering when you'd speak! Said I to myself, 'Her face
T2	123:23	her head, of course," the Rose replied. "I was wondering you hadn't got some too. I thought it was the
T4	138: 7	just going round to see if the word 'TWEEDLE' was written at the back of each collar, when she was startled
T6	166:20	he went on without noticing her remark, "was written entirely for your amusement."
A12	94: 9	have been that," said the King, "unless it was written to nobody, which isn't usual, you know."
T8W	18:13	"When I was young, my ringlets waved / And curled and crinkled on my
T8W	18: 4	I came to wear it," the Wasp said. "When I was young, you know, my ringlets used to wave--"
T5	153:14	had much practice," said the Queen. "When I was your age, I always did it for half-an-hour a day. Why,
A7	55: 4	"I didn't know it was your table," said Alice: "it's laid for a great many more

WASH (2)

A10	80:25	said the Mock Turtle: "crumbs would all wash off in the sea. But they have their tails in their mouths
A7	58:13	"it's always tea-time, and we've no time to wash the things between whiles."

WASHED (4)

T1	107: 3	For the white kitten had been having its face washed by the old cat for the last quarter of an hour (and
T1	107: 6	The way Dinah washed her children's faces was this: first she held the poor
T4	142: 3	/ Their coats were brushed, their faces washed, / Their shoes were clean and neat--/ And this was odd,
T12	208: 7	your paw like that--as if Dinah hadn't washed you this morning! You see, Kitty, it must have been

WASHING (4)

A9	76:15	at the end of the bill, 'French, music, and washing--extra.'"
A2	19:37	so nicely by the fire, licking her paws and washing her face--and she is such a nice soft thing to nurse--
A9	76:11	"And washing?" said the Mock Turtle.
T1	108:28	one: you squeaked twice while Dinah was washing your face this morning. Now you ca'n't deny it, Kitty:

WASN'T (23)

A12	95:24	so large in the last few minutes that she wasn't a bit afraid of interrupting him,) "I'll give him
T5	157: 2	However, she wasn't a bit hurt, and was soon up again: the Sheep went on
A9	76:13	"Ah! Then yours wasn't a really good school," said the Mock Turtle in a tone
T3	130: 3	one," Alice said in a frightened tone: "there wasn't a ticket-office where I came from." And again the
A4	28:28	at home," thought poor Alice, "when one wasn't always growing larger and smaller, and being ordered
A7	58:25	The Dormouse slowly opened its eyes. "I wasn't asleep," it said in a hoarse, feeble voice, "I heard
T6	159:24	Alice didn't know what to say to this: it wasn't at all like conversation, she thought, as he never said
T2	127:27	it would not be civil to say "No," though it wasn't at all what she wanted. She took it, and ate it as well
A8	69: 2	The Queen's argument was that, if something wasn't done about it in less than no time, she'd have
T8	179: 7	she had tried to cut the plum-cake, "So I wasn't dreaming, after all," she said to herself, "unless--
T1	119: 3	moment, and ran down stairs--or, at least, it wasn't exactly running, but a new invention for getting down
A8	68:39	never had to do such a thing before, and he wasn't going to begin at his time of life.
T8	180:15	"It was a glorious victory, wasn't it?" said the White Knight, as he came up panting.
T1	108:37	you unwound every bit of the worsted while I wasn't looking!
A7	55:34	about ravens and writing-desks, which wasn't much.
A9	75: 1	"Why did you call him Tortoise, if he wasn't one?" Alice asked.
T4	145:24	"If I wasn't real," Alice said--half laughing through her tears, it
T3	130: 4	again the chorus of voices went on. "There wasn't room for one where she came from. The land there is
T9	196: 6	a hippopotamus. Now, as it happened, there wasn't such a thing in the house, that morning."
T1	108:35	were thirsty, were you? How do you know she wasn't thirsty too? Now for number three: you unwound every
A5	42:38	"As if it wasn't trouble enough hatching the eggs," said the Pigeon,
A7	55: 1	"Then it wasn't very civil of you to offer it," said Alice angrily.
A7	55: 2	"It wasn't very civil of you to sit down without being invited,"

WASP (26)

T8W	15:12	no such word in the language!" said the Wasp.
T8W	16:14	it's very good for the conceit," added the Wasp.
T8W	15: 3	"No brown sugar!" grumbled the Wasp. "A nice exploring party!"
T8W	21:15	"Good-bye, and thank-ye," said the Wasp, and Alice tripped down the hill again, quite pleased
T8W	15: 9	"Were what?" the Wasp asked in a very cross voice.
T8W	16:17	The Wasp considered a little. "Well, no," he said: "it's when you
T8W	18: 8	to her, and she thought she would try if the Wasp couldn't do it too. "Would you mind saying it in rhyme?"
T8W	15:15	"Let it stop there!" said the Wasp, fretfully turning away his head.
T8W	21:11	many personal remarks made on her, and as the Wasp had quite recovered his spirits, and was getting very
T8W	18:10	"It aint what I'm used to," said the Wasp: "however I'll try; wait a bit." He was silent for a few
T8W	14:24	"Any brown sugar?" the Wasp interrupted.
T8W	20: 4	"Your wig fits very well," the Wasp murmured, looking at her with an expression of admiration
T8W	13:21	The Wasp only shook his shoulders, and turned his head away. "Ah,
T8W	20:11	"Not with a mouth as small as that," the Wasp persisted. "If you was a-fighting, now--could you get
T8W	13:14	So she went back to the Wasp--rather unwillingly, for she was very anxious to be a

WASP (cont.)
T8W   16: 3   "It's all along of the wig," the Wasp said in a much gentler voice.
T8W   14: 3   "How you go on!" the Wasp said in a peevish tone. "Worrity, worrity! There never
T8W   17:14   "What, you're a Bee, are you?" the Wasp said, looking at her with more interest. "And you've got
T8W   14:17 "You may read it if you've a mind to," the Wasp said, rather sulkily. "Nobody's hindering you, that I
T8W   17: 2   The Wasp said "That's a new-fangled name. They called it conceit
T8W   18: 3 "I'll tell you how I came to wear it," the Wasp said. "When I was young, you know, my ringlets used to
T8W   14:11   The Wasp took her arms, and let her help him round the tree, but
T8W   17: 5   "It is, though," said the Wasp: "wait till you have it, and then you'll know. And when
T8W   13: 6 old man (only that his face was more like a wasp) was sitting on the ground, leaning against a tree, all
T8W   21: 1 that's because your jaws are too short," the Wasp went on: "but the top of your head is nice and round." He
T8W   16: 7 be cross too, if you'd a wig like mine," the Wasp went on. "They jokes at one. And they worrits one. And
WASTING (4)
A7   56:33   better with the time," she said, "than wasting it in asking riddles that have no answers."
A7   56:36 said the Hatter, "you wouldn't talk about wasting it. It's him."
A3   25:32 dear sir, With no jury or judge, would be wasting our breath. 'I'll be judge, I'll be jury, said cunning
T3   132:41 go on with your list of insects: you're wasting time."
WATCH (14)
A7   56: 7   The March Hare took the watch and looked at it gloomily: then he dipped it into his
T4   147:42   Tweedledee looked at his watch, and said "Half-past four."
T2   124:19 to answer now," the Queen said looking at her watch: "open your mouth a little wider when you speak, and
A7   55:36 he said, turning to Alice: he had taken his watch out of his pocket, and was looking at it uneasily,
A1   7:16   but, when the Rabbit actually took a watch out of its waistcoat-pocket, and looked at it, and then
A10   80:13 "Thank you, it's a very interesting dance to watch," said Alice, feeling very glad that it was over at last
A7   56:12 shoulder with some curiosity. "What a funny watch!" she remarked. "It tells the day of the month, and
A7   56:14 should it?" muttered the Hatter. "Does your watch tell you what year it is?"
T12   207:34 on the rug, and her chin in her hand, to watch the kittens. "Tell me, Dinah, did you turn to Humpty
T1   108: 7 sat very demurely on her knee, pretending to watch the progress of the winding, and now and then putting
A8   62: 4 a very curious thing, and she went nearer to watch them, and, just as she came up to them, she heard one of
A4   27:31 'Coming in a minute, nurse! But I've got to watch this mouse-hole till Dinah comes back, and see that the
A1   8: 2 a rabbit with either a waistcoat-pocket, or a watch to take out of it, and burning with curiosity, she ran
T4   147:44 the other said, rather sadly: "and she can watch us--only you'd better not come very close," he added: "I
WATCHED (10)
T6   161: 4 in doing so) and offered Alice his hand. She watched him a little anxiously as she took it. "If he smiled
T8   179:18 for him than for herself at the moment, and watched him with some anxiety as he mounted again. As soon as
T1   113:17 White Pawns roll over and begin kicking: she watched it with great curiosity to see what would happen next
T1   110: 6 Because, when we were playing just now, you watched just as if you understood it: and when I said 'Check!'
T8   180: 2 of Battle are," she said to herself, as she watched the fight, timidly peeping out from her hiding-place.
T8   190:29   So she went on talking to herself, as she watched the horse walking leisurely along the road, and the
A9   74: 7 Gryphon sat up and rubbed its eyes: then it watched the Queen till she was out of sight: then it chuckled.
T1   114:18   Alice watched the White King as he slowly struggled up from bar to
A11   91:29   Alice watched the White Rabbit as he fumbled over the list, feeling
T7   169: 4 a tree, for fear of being run over, and watched them go by.
WATCHING (12)
T8   183:16 eyes shut, muttering to himself, and Alice watching anxiously for the next tumble.
T7   174:20   For a minute or two Alice stood silent, watching him. Suddenly she brightened up. "Look, look!" she
T8   190:26 expect," Alice said to herself, as she stood watching him. "There he goes! Right on his head as usual!
A8   67:11 it puzzled her very much at first, but after watching it a minute or two she made it out to be a grin, and
T3   129: 9 know--" and for some time she stood silent, watching one of them that was bustling about among the flowers
T1   108:13 was making you tidy, so you couldn't. I was watching the boys getting in sticks for the bonfire--and it
T7   173:21 Hatta, the other Messenger, was standing watching the fight, with a cup of tea in one hand and a piece
A12   98:14 she left her, leaning her head on her hand, watching the setting sun, and thinking of little Alice and all
T8   187:25 shading her eyes, she leant against a tree, watching the strange pair, and listening, in a half-dream, to
T1   116: 2 near Alice on the table, and while she sat watching the White King (for she was still a little anxious
A8   63: 1 eye chanced to fall upon Alice, as she stood watching them, and he checked himself suddenly: the others
T1   113: 6 surprise, she was down on her hands and knees watching them. The chessmen were walking about, two and two!
WATER (13) [See also SALTWATER]
T5t   149: 1   WOOL AND WATER
A2   19:26   The Mouse gave a sudden leap out of the water, and seemed to quiver all over with fright. "Oh, I beg
T5   156:42 the blade of one of the oars got fast in the water and wouldn't come out again (so Alice explained it
T5   157: 8 over the side of the boat into the dark water. "I wish it hadn't let go--I should so like a little
T5   155:34   "In the water, of course!" said the Sheep, sticking some of the
A7   60: 6   "You can draw water out of a water-well," said the Hatter; "so I should
T7   172:11 "I should think throwing cold water over you would be better," Alice suggested: "--or some
T5   155:25 There was something very queer about the water, she thought, as every now and then the oars got fast in
T2   128:12 and Tweedledee--the Fifth is mostly water--the Sixth belongs to Humpty Dumpty--But you make no
T8   187:38 his answer trickled through my head, / Like water through a sieve.
T1   115:17 round the room to see if she could find any water to throw over him. However, she could find nothing but a
T5   156:21 the ends of her tangled hair dipping into the water--while with bright eager eyes she caught at one bunch
T5   156: 3 weeds (which made the oars stick fast in the water, worse than ever), and sometimes under trees, but always
WATERS (1)
A2   17:10 / Improve his shining tail, / And pour the waters of the Nile / On every golden scale!
WATER-WELL (1)
A7   60: 6   "You can draw water out of a water-well," said the Hatter; "so I should think you could
WAVE (3)
T8W   18: 4 I was young, you know, my ringlets used to wave--"
T7   171: 9 out of breath to say a word, and could only wave his hands about, and make the most fearful faces at the
T8   190:18 pointed. "I sha'n't be long. You'll wait and wave your handkerchief when I get to that turn in the road? I
WAVED (2)
T8W   18:13   "When I was young, my ringlets waved / And curled and crinkled on my head: / And then they

WAVED (cont.)
T8   190:32   tumble he reached the turn, and then she waved her handkerchief to him, and waited till he was out of
WAVES (1)
T4   142:11   and more--/ All hopping through the frothy waves, / And scrambling to the shore.
WAVING (10)
T2   121: 3   At length, as the Tiger-lily only went on waving about, she spoke again, in a timid voice--almost in a
T2   120:31   Alice, addressing herself to one that was waving gracefully about in the wind, "I wish you could talk!"
T8   183:18   the Knight suddenly began in a loud voice, waving his right arm as he spoke, "is to keep--" Here the
A6   51:19   "In that direction," the Cat said, waving its right paw round, "lives a Hatter: and in that
A12   93: 6   head downwards, and the poor little thing was waving its tail about in a melancholy way, being quite unable
T2   122: 9   every one of you!" cried the Tiger-lily, waving itself passionately from side to side, and trembling
A12   98:37   in the wind, and the pool rippling to the waving of the reeds--the rattling teacups would change to
T5   156:16   it would, till it glided gently in among the waving rushes. And then the little sleeves were carefully
A6   51:20   "lives a Hatter: and in that direction," waving the other paw, "lives a March Hare. Visit either you
A10   79:11   on her toes when they passed too close, and waving their fore-paws to mark the time, while the Mock Turtle
WAX (2)
T8   186:28   other things--such as gunpowder and sealing-wax. And here I must leave you." They had just come to the end
T4   142:21   things: / Of shoes--and ships--and sealing wax--/ Of cabbages--and kings--/ And why the sea is boiling
WAX-WORKS (2)
T4   138:10   "If you think we're wax-works," he said, "you ought to pay, you know. Wax-works
T4   138:11   he said, "you ought to pay, you know. Wax-works weren't made to be looked at for nothing. Nohow!"
WAY (121) [See also OUT-OF-THE-WAY, etc.]
A1   13: 4   and stupid for life to go on in the common way.
A6   52:20   just as if the Cat had come back in a natural way.
A7   57:18   on, you know," the Hatter continued, "in this way:--
A10   78:17   you've cleared all the jelly-fish out of the way--"
T1   119:11   to find herself walking again in the natural way.
T2   120: 8   the house! Well then, I'll try it the other way."
T2   121:10   you're the right colour, and that goes a long way."
T2   123:39   Rose: "I should advise you to walk the other way."
T2   124:10   as well as she could, that she had lost her way.
T9   195:21   hastily corrected herself. "I meant the other way."
T9   204:12   to her impatiently to get out of its way.
A10   83: 1   if anything would ever happen in a natural way again.
T1   116:15   to a glass, the words will all go the right way again."
T5   150:17   "I'm sure mine only works one way," Alice remarked. "I ca'n't remember things before they
T5   149: 5   "I'm very glad I happened to be in the way," Alice said, as she helped her to put on her shawl again
T8   182:24   "Only in the usual way," Alice said, smiling.
A6   46:36   dreadful," she muttered to herself, "the way all the creatures argue. It's enough to drive one crazy!"
T5   158:18   do?" thought Alice, as she groped her way among the tables and chairs, for the shop was very dark
T9   198: 9   Just then the door opened a little way, and a creature with a long beak put its head out for a
T2   128:19   however, one of the Knights will show you the way--and in the Eighth Square we shall be Queens together, and
T5   149: 8   at her in a helpless frightened sort of way, and kept repeating something in a whisper to herself that
T3   130:20   At last he said "You're traveling the wrong way," and shut up the window, and went away. "So young a child
T3   131:22   must draw the train herself the rest of the way--," and so on.
A2   20:24   other curious creatures. Alice led the way, and the whole party swam to the shore.
A1   8: 7   went straight on like a tunnel for some way, and then dipped suddenly down, so suddenly that Alice had
A4   32:44   very little way forwards each time and a long way back, and barking hoarsely all the while, till at last it
T6   165: 7   'wabe' you know, because it goes a long way before it, and a long way behind it--"
T1   107: 8   paw she rubbed its face all over, the wrong way, beginning at the nose: and just now, as I said, she was
T6   165: 7   it goes a long way before it, and a long way behind it--"
A12   93: 6   was waving its tail about in a melancholy way, being quite unable to move. She soon got it out again,
T6   165: 8   "And a long way beyond it on each side," Alice added.
A5   42:30   added, with a kind of sob, "I've tried every way, but nothing seems to suit them!"
T3   137:21   likely to happen. She went on and on, a long way, but wherever the road divided, there were sure to be two
T7   176:25   round the town?" he said. "That's a good long way. Did you go by the old bridge, or the market-place? You
T1   107: 6   The way Dinah washed her children's faces was this: first she held
A1   9:12   on saying to herself, in a dreamy sort of way, "Do cats eat bats? Do cats eat bats?" and sometimes "Do
T9   201:32   I think--every poem was about fishes in some way. Do you know why they're so fond of fishes, all about here
T1   114:16   out of breath. "Mind you come up--the regular way--don't get blown up!"
T5   156:18   to get hold of the rushes a good long way down before breaking them off--and for a while Alice
A1   9:31   all locked; and when Alice had been all the way down one side and up the other, trying every door, she
A4   32:43   charges at the stick, running a very little way forwards each time and a long way back, and barking
T8   189: 3   / For wheels of Hansom-cabs. / And that's the way' (he gave a wink) / 'By which I get my wealth--/ And very
T8   189:12   / I thanked him much for telling me / The way he got his wealth, / But chiefly for his wish that he /
A1   12:39   said anxiously to herself "Which way? Which way?", holding her hand on the top of her head to feel which
T1   110:33   drawing-room, only the things go the other way. I can see all of it when I get upon a chair--all but the
T8   188: 7   / 'Who sail on stormy seas; / And that's the way I get my bread--/ A trifle, if you please.'
T1   110:40   like our books, only the words go the wrong way: I know that, because I've held up one of our books to the
A6   51: 7   went on. "Would you tell me, please, which way I ought to go from here?"
A2   15: 1   Alice, "or perhaps they wo'n't walk the way I want to go! Let me see. I'll give them a new pair of
T1   119: 8   gone straight out at the door in the same way, if she hadn't caught hold of the door-post. She was
A1   12:36   I can creep under the door: so either way I'll get into the garden, and I don't care which happens!
T8   183:14   heartily as she could. They went on a little way in silence after this, the Knight with his eyes shut,
A4   27:36   By this time she had found her way into a tidy little room with a table in the window, and on
A4   32:20   again; and the second thing is to find my way into that lovely garden. I think that will be the best
T4   145:24   Alice ran a little way into the wood, and stopped under a large tree. "It can
A1   12:40   her hand on the top of her head to feel which way it was growing; and she was quite surprised to find that
T5   153: 1   "That's the way it's done," the Queen said with great decision: "nobody
T12 207:37   "By the way, Kitty, if only you'd been really with me in my dream,

WAY (cont.)

T2	120:25	"I never saw such a house for getting in the way! Never!"
A4	29:10	than I am now? That'll be a comfort, one way--never to be an old woman--but then--always to have
T9	195:31	The Red Queen said "That's a poor thin way of doing things. Now here, we mostly have days and nights
A8	67: 8	She was looking about for some way of escape, and wondering whether she could get away
A1	13: 2	eats cake; but Alice had got so much into the way of expecting nothing but out-of-the-way things to happen,
A6	49:30	said Alice; "that's not at all a proper way of expressing yourself."
T8	184:26	"Well, just then I was inventing a new way of getting over a gate--would you like to hear it?"
T1	111: 7	things in it! Let's pretend there's a way of getting through into it, somehow, Kitty. Let's pretend
T2	128:31	run very fast!" thought Alice), there was no way of guessing, but she was gone, and Alice began to remember
A9	70:30	going on rather better now," she said, by way of keeping up the conversation a little.
A7	59: 7	fancy to herself what such an extraordinary way of living would be like, but it puzzled her too much: so
A6	49:22	As soon as she had made out the proper way of nursing it (which was to twist it up into a sort of
A8	68: 6	The Queen had only one way of settling all difficulties, great or small. "Off with
A2	19:15	Mouse!" (Alice thought this must be the right way of speaking to a mouse: she had never done such a thing
T8	179:38	that Alice got behind a tree to be out of the way of the blows.
A2	19: 6	splashing about in the pool a little way off, and she swam nearer to make out what it was: at first
A4	33: 1	the while, till at last it sat down a good way off, panting, with its tongue hanging out of its mouth,
T2	123:45	the Queen (whom she spied out at last, a long way off), she thought she would try the plan, this time, of
T3	137:22	sure to be two finger-posts pointing the same way, one marked "TO TWEEDLEDUM'S HOUSE," and the other "TO THE
A2	19: 2	Alice, as she swam about, trying to find her way out. "I shall be punished for it now, I suppose, by being
T4	139:26	the other one's feelings; so, as the best way out of the difficulty, she took hold of both hands at once
T9	195:11	Alice thought she saw a way out of the difficulty, this time. "If you'll tell me what
T3	137:28	call and say 'How d'ye do?' and ask them the way out of the wood. If I could only get to the Eighth Square
A6	45: 9	what it was all about, and crept a little way out of the wood to listen.
A2	19:13	So she began: "O Mouse, do you know the way out of this pool? I am very tired of swimming about here,
T4	139:10	Alice said politely, "which is the best way out of this wood: it's getting so dark. Would you tell me,
T1	115:32	of the end of the pencil, which came some way over his shoulder, and began writing for him.
A3	23:25	crowded round her, calling out, in a confused way, "Prizes! Prizes!"
T2	124:11	"I don't know what you mean by your way," said the Queen: "all the ways about here belong to me--
A1	9:15	either question, it didn't much matter which way she put it. She felt that she was dozing off, and had just
T3	129:25	"I think I'll go down the other way," she said after a pause; "and perhaps I may visit the
T3	131: 1	dressed in white paper), "ought to know which way she's going, even if she doesn't know her own name!"
T8	180:12	ended with their both falling off in this way, side by side. When they got up again, they shook hands,
A10	81: 6	thrown out to sea. So they had to fall a long way. So they got their tails fast in their mouths. So they
A2	15:21	well say this), "to go on crying in this way! Stop this moment, I tell you!" But she went on all the
A11	91: 7	even before she got into the court, by the way the people near the door began sneezing all at once.
T2	122:20	it's enough to make one wither to hear the way they go on!"
T5	152:22	Alice with a smile. "Now you understand the way things happen here."
T4	147:19	fuss made about anything in all her life--the way those two bustled about--and the quantity of things they
A12	98:25	hurried by--the frightened Mouse splashed his way through the neighbouring pool--she could hear the rattle
A7	60:36	there again!" said Alice, as she picked her way through the wood. "It's the stupidest tea-party I ever was
T5	149:17	"If your Majesty will only tell me the right way to begin, I'll do it as well as I can."
A6	50:19	saying to herself "if one only knew the right way to change them--" when she was a little startled by seeing
A3	23: 5	"Why," said the Dodo, "the best way to explain it is to do it." (And, as you might like to try
T8	185: 2	the ground directly. So I had a very little way to fall, you see--But there was the danger of falling into
T8	188:25	But I was thinking of a way / To feed oneself on batter, / And so go on from day to
A8	68:21	could see it trying in a helpless sort of way to fly up into a tree.
A1	7:12	did Alice think it so very much out of the way to hear the Rabbit say to itself "Oh dear! Oh dear! I
T3	135:26	she thought to herself, and this was the only way to the Eighth Square.
T3	131: 4	said in a loud voice, "She ought to know her way to the ticket-office, even if she doesn't know her
T2	125: 7	went on: "--and I thought I'd try and find my way to the top of that hill--"
A12	93: 9	would be quite as much use in the trial one way up as the other."
T3	133: 3	"All right," said the Gnat. "Half way up that bush, you'll see a Rocking-horse-fly, if you look.
A11	86:17	The judge, by the way, was the King; and, as he wore his crown over the wig
T3	135:37	She was rambling on in this way when she reached the wood: it looked very cool and shady.
A8	66:16	was generally a ridge or a furrow in the way wherever she wanted to send the hedgehog to, and, as the
A1	12:38	bit, and said anxiously to herself "Which way? Which way?", holding her hand on the top of her head to
A2	14: 9	myself about you: you must manage the best way you can--but I must be kind to them," thought Alice, "or
A6	51:12	"Then it doesn't matter which way you go," said the Cat.
A9	71:14	as usual," said the Duchess: "what a clear way you have of putting things!"
T6	166: 5	'from home'--meaning that they'd lost their way, you know."
A7	57: 9	"Is that the way you manage?" Alice asked.
T5	152:38	a great girl you are. Consider what a long way you've come to-day. Consider what o'clock it is. Consider

WAYS (6)

T3	137:19	the road divides and they point different ways."
T5	150:16	advantage in it, that one's memory works both ways."
T2	124:12	mean by your way," said the Queen: "all the ways about here belong to me--but why did you come out here at
T8	187: 7	quite another thing! The song is called 'Ways and Means': but that's only what it's called, you know!"
T8	188:18	mild took up the tale: / He said 'I go my ways, / And when I find a mountain-rill, / I set it in a blaze
T9	194:24	as she could, "They might go different ways." But she couldn't help thinking to herself "What

WE (69) [entries omitted]

WEAK (4)

A5	39: 1	old," said the youth, "and your jaws are too weak / For anything tougher than suet; / Yet you finished the
T3	134:14	"Weak tea with cream in it."
AI	3: 9	dreamy weather, / To beg a tale of breath too weak / To stir the tiniest feather! / Yet what can one poor
A9	72:34	your Majesty!" the Duchess began in a low, weak voice.

WEALTH (2)

| T8 | 189: 4 | way' (he gave a wink) / 'By which I get my wealth--/ And very gladly will I drink / Your Honour's noble |
| T8 | 189:12 | him much for telling me / The way he got his wealth, / But chiefly for his wish that he / Might drink my |

WEAR (5)
T8W   19:16   And that is why they do it, dear, / Because I wear a yellow wig."
T8W   18:16   then they said 'You should be shaved, / And wear a yellow wig instead.'
T8   184:43   than that--like a sugar-loaf. When I used to wear it, if I fell off the horse, it always touched the ground
T8W   18: 3   "I'll tell you how I came to wear it," the Wasp said. "When I was young, you know, my
T2   123:22   "Where does she wear them?" Alice asked with some curiosity.
WEARILY (2)
T7   176: 5   The Lion looked at Alice wearily. "Are you animal--or vegetable--or mineral?" he said,
A7   56:32   Alice sighed wearily. "I think you might do something better with the time
WEARY (1)
AI   3:27   wells of fancy dry, / And faintly strove that weary one / To put the subject by, / "The rest next time--"
WEATHER (1)
AI   3: 8   Three! In such an hour, / Beneath such dreamy weather, / To beg a tale of breath too weak / To stir the
WE'D (1)
T8   182:13   "We'd better take it with us," the Knight said. "It'll come in
WEDNESDAY (2)
T5   150: 5   and the trial doesn't even begin till next Wednesday: and of course the crime comes last of all."
T1   109: 1   know I'm saving up all your punishments for Wednesday week--Suppose they had saved up all my punishments?"
-WEED [See SEA-WEED]
WEEDS (1)
T5   156: 3   glided gently on, sometimes among beds of weeds (which made the oars stick fast in the water, worse than
WEEK (7)
T9   198:11   for a moment and said "No admittance till the week after next!" and shut the door again with a bang.
T5   150: 1   "Oh, things that happened the week after next," the Queen replied in a careless tone. "For
T5   149:39   with pleasure!" the Queen said. "Two pence a week, and jam every other day."
A12   92: 6   of gold-fish she had accidentally upset the week before.
A9   76:39   an old conger-eel, that used to come once a week: he taught us Drawling, Stretching, and Fainting in Coils
A11   89:12   "and I hadn't begun my tea--not above a week or so--and what with the bread-and-butter getting so thin
T1   109: 1   saving up all your punishments for Wednesday week--Suppose they had saved up all my punishments?" she went
WEEKS (1)
A5   42:40   I haven't had a wink of sleep these three weeks!"
WEEP (2)
T8   189:21   I drop upon my toe / A very heavy weight, / I weep, for it reminds me so / Of that old man I used to know--/
T4   144: 1   'I weep for you,' the Walrus said: / 'I deeply sympathize.' /
WEIGHT (1)
T8   189:20   / Or if I drop upon my toe / A very heavy weight, / I weep, for it reminds me so / Of that old man I
WELCOME (2)
T9   200: 4   with the cider, and wool with the wine--/ And welcome Queen Alice with ninety-times-nine!"
T9   199:32   in the coffee, and mice in the tea--/ And welcome Queen Alice with thirty-times-three!"
WELCOMES (1)
A2   17:14   grin, / How neatly spreads his claws, / And welcomes little fishes in, / With gently smiling jaws!
WE'LL (5)
T9   202:20   then guess," said the Red Queen. "Meanwhile, we'll drink your health--Queen Alice's health!" she screamed
T1   108:16   snowed so, they had to leave off. Never mind, we'll go and see the bonfire to-morrow." Here Alice wound two
T9   197: 6   time for a nap. / When the feast's over, we'll go to the ball--/ Red Queen, and White Queen, and Alice,
T9   194:35   "So do I," the White Queen whispered: "we'll often say it over together, dear. And I'll tell you a
T2   128:18   kind of you to tell me all this'--however, we'll suppose it said--the Seventh Square is all forest--
WELL (133) [See also TREACLE-WELL, WATER-WELL]
A1   8:10   falling down what seemed to be a very deep well.
A7   58:34   and Tillie; and they lived at the bottom of a well--"
A7   59: 8   on: "But why did they live at the bottom of a well?"
A7   59:21   "Why did they live at the bottom of a well?"
A11   86:27   However, "jurymen" would have done just as well.
T8W   20: 7   though--I should think you couldn't bite well?"
T6   166: 3   "Well, a 'rath' is a sort of green pig: but 'mome' I'm not
A7   60: 9   "But they were in the well," Alice said to the Dormouse, not choosing to notice this
A1   8:15   anything: then she looked at the sides of the well, and noticed that they were filled with cupboards and
T8   185:18   fall, as for some time he had kept on very well, and she was afraid that he really was hurt this time.
T2   120:20   to the hill. For a few minutes all went on well, and she was just saying "I really shall do it this time
T5   149:17   tell me the right way to begin, I'll do it as well as I can."
A7   56:35   "If you knew Time as well as I do," said the Hatter, "you wouldn't talk about
A11   86:37   Alice could see, as well as if she were looking over their shoulders, that all the
T6   166:15   of his great hands, "I can repeat poetry as well as other folk, if it comes to that--"
A6   50:18   other children she knew, who might do very well as pigs, and was just saying to herself "if one only knew
A5   36:23   said Alice, swallowing down her anger as well as she could.
A9   70:29   did not like to be rude: so she bore it as well as she could.
T2   127:28   what she wanted. She took it, and ate it as well as she could: and it was very dry: and she thought she
T8W   20:10   of laughter, which she turned into a cough as well as she could. At last she managed to say gravely, "I can
A5   43:30   nest. Alice crouched down among the trees as well as she could, for her neck kept getting entangled among
A6   47: 6   in that soup!" Alice said to herself, as well as she could for sneezing.
A1   7: 6   So she was considering, in her own mind (as well as she could, for the hot day made her feel very sleepy
T7   173: 6   one--that wins--get the crown?" she asked, as well as she could, for the run was putting her quite out of
T9   203:23   they look," Alice thought to herself, as well as she could in the dreadful confusion that was beginning
T4   139:31   which they were dancing, and it was done (as well as she could make it out) by the branches rubbing one
A12   98: 7   said Alice. And she told her sister, as well as she could remember them, all these strange Adventures
T2   124: 9   to all these directions, and explained, as well as she could, that she had lost her way.
A11   86: 3   all sorts of little birds and beasts, as well as the whole pack of cards: the Knave was standing before
T8W   21: 8   in front, no doubt. One would have done as well as two, if you must have them so close--"
T2   121: 5   "As well as you can," said the Tiger-lily. "And a great deal
T3   135:38   the wood: it looked very cool and shady. "Well, at any rate it's a great comfort," she said as she

WELL (cont.)

```
A11   89:25                                        "Well, at any rate, the Dormouse said--" the Hatter went on,
A10   82:18   lessons!" thought Alice. "I might just as well be at school at once." However, she got up, and began to
A5    43:28                                        "Well, be off, then!" said the Pigeon in a sulky tone, as it
T9   196:28            "She never was really well brought up," the Red Queen went on: "but it's amazing how
T9   196:23   her own, and gently stroking it: "she means well, but she ca'n't help saying foolish things as a general
T1   107: 4   quarter of an hour (and bearing it pretty well, considering): so you see that it couldn't have had any
T1   115: 2   him on the table, she thought she might as well dust him a little, he was so covered with ashes.
A5    43:23   adding "You're looking for eggs, I know that well enough; and what does it matter to me whether you're a
A4    30:28   reach half high enough yet--Oh, they'll do well enough. Don't be particular--Here, Bill! Catch hold of
T3   129:22   I liked my walk. I shall say 'Oh, I liked it well enough--' (here came the favourite little toss of the
A3    22:18                "I know what 'it' means well enough, when I find a thing," said the Duck: "it's
T8   182:43   fell off behind. Otherwise he kept on pretty well, except that he had a habit of now and then falling off
T8   182:22            "I hope you've got your hair well fastened on?" he continued, as they set off.
T8   188:29   day / Getting a little fatter. / I shook him well from side to side, / Until his face was blue: / 'Come,
A8    68:10           Alice thought she might as well go back and see how the game was going on, as she heard
A7    60:40   everything's curious to-day. I think I may as well go in at once." And in she went.
T7   174: 6   of bread-and-butter. "They're getting on very well," he said in a choking voice: "each of them has been down
A9    77: 2                                         "Well, I ca'n't show it you, myself," the Mock Turtle said:
T5   150: 4                                         "Well, I don't want any to-day, at any rate."
A4    31:18      voice ("That's Bill," thought Alice), "Well, I hardly know--No more, thank ye; I'm better now--but
A10   82:32                                         "Well, I never heard it before," said the Mock Turtle; "but it
A12   93:41                                         "Well, I sha'n't go, at any rate," said Alice; "besides, that's
A5    41:14                                         "Well, I should like to be a little larger, Sir, if you
T1   109: 7   have to go without fifty dinners at once! Well, I shouldn't mind that much! I'd far rather go without
A7    58: 4                                         "Well, I'd hardly finished the first verse," said the Hatter,
A11   91:13                                         "Well, if I must, I must," the King said with a melancholy air,
T3   135: 8                                         "Well, if she said 'Miss,' and didn't say anything more," the
T6   163:45   of that subject, and it would be just as well if you'd mention what you mean to do next, as I suppose
A1    12:33   EAT ME" were beautifully marked in currants. "Well, I'll eat it," said Alice, "and if it makes me grow
A7    60:11   "Of course they were," said the Dormouse: "well in."
T2   127:16                                         "Well, in our country," said Alice, still panting a little,
T9   192:10   again, "I shall be able to manage it quite well in time."
T9   194:44                                         "Well, it isn't picked at all," Alice explained: "it's ground--
A9    70:36                "Ah well! It means much the same thing," said the Duchess, digging
A8    68: 3                                         "Well, it must be removed," said the King very decidedly; and
T1   110: 7   it: and when I said 'Check!' you purred! Well, it was a nice check, Kitty, and really I might have won,
A4    30:11                                         "Well, it's got no business there, at any rate: go and take it
T4   145:18                                         "Well, it's no use your talking about waking him," said
A6    53: 7                                         "Well! I've often seen a cat without a grin," thought Alice;
A5    36:34                                         "Well, I've tried to say 'How doth the little busy bee,' but it
T8   184:26                                         "Well, just then I was inventing a new way of getting over a
A4    34: 6   it, it occurred to her that she might as well look and see what was on top of it.
T8W   16:17           The Wasp considered a little. "Well, no," he said: "it's when you hold up your head--so--
T8   186:11                                         "Well, not the next course," the Knight said in slow thoughtful
T8   186:15                                         "Well, not the next day," the Knight repeated as before: "not
T7   175:30                                         "Well, now that we have seen each other," said the Unicorn, "if
A8    62:17   flung down his brush, and had just begun "Well, of all the unjust things--" when his eye chanced to fall
T9   196: 8                                         "Well, only on Thursdays," said the Queen.
T6   166: 7                                         "Well, 'outgribing' is something between bellowing and
A2    19:32                                         "Well, perhaps not," said Alice in a soothing tone: "don't be
A5    36: 2                                         "Well, perhaps you haven't found it so yet," said Alice; "but
A5    36: 7                                         "Well, perhaps your feelings may be different," said Alice:
T6   164:29                "That'll do very well," said Alice: "and 'slithy'?"
A7    55:28          "You might just as well say," added the Dormouse, which seemed to be talking in
A7    55:26          "You might just as well say," added the March Hare, "that 'I like what I get' is
A7    55:24   said the Hatter. "Why, you might just as well say that 'I see what I eat' is the same thing as 'I eat
A2    15:21   Alice, "a great girl like you," (she might well say this), "to go on crying in this way! Stop this moment
T8W   20: 6   shape of your head as does it. Your jaws aint well shaped, though--I should think you couldn't bite well?"
T2   123:11                                         "Well, she has the same awkward shape as you," the Rose said:
A12   98:11   up and ran off, thinking while she ran, as well she might, what a wonderful dream it had been.
T8W   16: 1   down the newspaper. "I'm afraid you're not well," she said in a soothing tone. "Can't I do anything for
T6   164:30                "Well, 'slithy' means 'lithe and slimy.' 'Lithe' is the same as
T4   140:10          "Ye-es, pretty well--some poetry," Alice said doubtfully. "Would you tell me
T2   128:10   yourself in the Fourth Square in no time. Well, that square belongs to Tweedledum and Tweedledee--the
T8   186: 7   it cooked for the next course?" said Alice. "Well, that was quick work, certainly!"
T8W   21: 1                                         "Well, that's because your jaws are too short," the Wasp went
T1   108:30   was speaking). "Her paw went into your eye? Well, that's your fault, for keeping your eyes open--if you'd
A7    56: 5   "Yes, but some crumbs must have got in as well," the Hatter grumbled: "you shouldn't have put it in with
T4   147:44                "Very well," the other said, rather sadly: "and she can watch us--
T8W   20: 4          "Your wig fits very well," the Wasp murmured, looking at her with an expression of
T2   120: 7    This goes straight back to the house! Well then, I'll try it the other way."
T6   165: 9                "Exactly so. Well then, 'mimsy' is 'flimsy and miserable' (there's another
T1   110:39   just to make it look as if they had a fire. Well then, the books are something like our books, only the
A6    51:32                                         "Well, then," the Cat went on, "you see a dog growls when it's
A9    76:31                                         "Well, then," the Gryphon went on, "if you don't know what to
A9    76:36                                         "Well, there was Mystery," the Mock Turtle replied, counting
T3   133: 1                                         "Well, there's the Horse-fly," Alice began, counting off the
T6   160:35                "Ah, well! They may write such things in a book," Humpty Dumpty
T4   144:21   was a puzzler. After a pause, Alice began, "Well! They were both very unpleasant characters--" Here she
```

WELL (cont.)
```
T9   192: 1                                                   "Well, this is grand!" said Alice. "I never expected I should
T5   158:22   here! And  actually  here's  a  little  brook! Well, this is the very queerest shop I ever saw!" * * * * * *
T2   120: 6   It's  more  like  a  corkscrew  than  a  path! Well this turn goes to the hill, I suppose--no, it doesn't!
A1    8:23                                                   "Well!" thought Alice to herself. "After such a fall as this, I
T8   182: 5   "You see," he went on after a pause, "it's as well to be provided for everything. That's the reason the
A6   48: 8    of  this  remark,  and thought it would be as well to introduce some other subject of conversation. While
A1   10:19                                   It was all very well to say "Drink me," but the wise little Alice was not
T6   164:35                                                   "Well 'toves' are something like badgers--they're something
T7   175: 5    "She  runs so fearfully quick. You might as well try to catch a Bandersnatch! But I'll make a memorandum
T7   173:12   goes  by  so  fearfully  quick. You might as well try to stop a Bandersnatch!"
A6   52:11    much  surprised  at  this,  she was getting so well used to queer things happening. While she was still
A5   36:26                        Alice thought she might as well wait, as she had nothing else to do, and perhaps after
A1    8:11                                   Either the well was very deep, or she fell very slowly, for she had
T8   179:31                                                   "Well, we must fight for her, then," said the Red Knight, as he
A5   43: 7                                                   "Well! What are you?" said the Pigeon. "I can see you're trying
T8   187: 8                                                   "Well, what is the song, then?" said Alice, who was by this
T9   202:35   she  whispered  in reply, "but I can do quite well without."
A9   70: 9    pepper  in  my kitchen at all. Soup does very well without--Maybe it's always pepper that makes people
T4   147:33                                                   "Well--yes--a little," Alice replied gently.
T5   149:13                                                   "Well, yes, if you call that a-dressing," the Queen said. "It
T1   110:16   and  Alice  had  been reduced at last to say "Well, you can be one of them, then, and I'll be all the rest."
T4   145:20   one of the things in his dream. You know very well you're not real."
```
WELLS (1)
```
AI    3:26      And ever, as the story drained / The wells of fancy dry, / And faintly strove that weary one / To
```
WENT (179)
```
A2   20:13    making  quite  a  commotion in the pool as it went.
A7   60:41    I  may  as  well  go  in at once." And in she went.
A1    8: 5                      In another moment down went Alice after it, never once considering how in the world
A1    9:24    it.  There  was not a moment to be lost: away went Alice like the wind, and was just in time to hear it say,
T6   167:22     I said it very loud and clear: / I went and shouted in his ear."
T9   200: 6    done! I'd better go in at once--" and in she went, and there was a dead silence the moment she appeared.
A4   27: 2    back again, and looking anxiously about as it went, as if it had lost something; and she heard it muttering
T9   194:21                         "Then if the dog went away, its temper would remain!" the Queen exclaimed
T3   130:21   the  wrong  way," and shut up the window, and went away. "So young a child," said the gentleman sitting
A8   68:26    her  arm, that it might not escape again, and went back to have a little more conversation with her friend.
A8   69:13    looking  for  it, while the rest of the party went back to the game.
A1   12:16    forgotten  the little golden key, and when she went back to the table for it, she found she could not
A1   10:13    no  use  in waiting by the little door, so she went back to the table, half hoping she might find another key
T8W  13:14                             So she went back to the Wasp--rather unwillingly, for she was very
T7   174:18   "go  and order the drums to begin." And Hatta went bounding away like a grasshopper.
A6   49:13    The  cook  threw a frying-pan after her as she went, but it just missed her.
A8   63:24    smiling  at  everything  that  was said, and went by without noticing her. Then followed the Knave of
T12  207:14   till  she  had  found the Red Queen: then she went down on her knees on the hearth-rug, and put the kitten
A11   90: 8    dropped  his  teacup and bread-and-butter and went down on one knee. "I'm a poor man, your Majesty," he
T7   169: 7    over  something  or  other,  and whenever one went down, several more always fell over him, so that the
A1    8:12    slowly,  for she had plenty of time as she went down to look about her, and to wonder what was going to
T9   203:20   on  as  wings, and so, with forks for legs, went fluttering about in all directions: "and very like birds
T5   153:19   The  Queen  spread out her arms again and went flying after it, and this time she succeeded in catching
T1   118:16   / He left it dead, and with its head / He went galumphing back.
T5   151:22   better,  and  better, and better!" Her voice went higher with each "better," till it got quite to a squeak
T6   167:15               My heart went hop, my heart went thump: / I filled the kettle at the
A4   27:12    Very  soon the Rabbit noticed Alice, as she went hunting about, and called out to her, in an angry tone,
A6   46:44      idiotic!"  And  she  opened  the door and went in.
A4   27:23    the  name  "W. RABBIT" engraved upon it. She went in without knocking, and hurried upstairs, in great fear
T1   108:30   that  the  kitten  was speaking). "Her paw went into your eye? Well, that's your fault, for keeping your
A7   57:11    "We  quarreled  last  March--just  before he went mad, you know--" (pointing his teaspoon at the March Hare
T9   199: 9    his  large  dull  eyes for a minute: then he went nearer and rubbed it with his thumb, as if he were trying
A8   62: 4    thought  this  a  very curious thing, and she went nearer to watch them, and, just as she came up to them,
T6   168:37   she  couldn't  help saying to herself, as she went, "of all the unsatisfactory--" (she repeated this aloud,
T4   147:12                    So the two brothers went off hand-in-hand into the wood, and returned in a minute
A8   68:16    knew  whether  it was her turn or not. So she went off in search of her hedgehog.
A8   69: 9     "fetch her here." And the executioner went off like an arrow.
T5   158:15   must get it for yourself." And so saying, she went off to the other end of the shop, and set the egg upright
A7   55:19    you  should  say what you mean," the March Hare went on.
A9   76: 4    Alice  could  speak  again.  The Mock Turtle went on.
T3   133:10   it  looked  so bright and sticky; and then she went on.
T3   131:41   "I  know you are a friend," the little voice went on: "a dear friend, and an old friend. And you wo'n't
T8   183:14   she  said it as heartily as she could. They went on a little way in silence after this, the Knight with
T8   182: 5                    "You see," he went on after a pause, "it's as well to be provided for
T8   186: 6      thing  of  the  sort that I ever did," he went on after a pause, "was inventing a new pudding during the
T3   134: 4    "And  then  there's  the  Butterfly," Alice went on, after she had taken a good look at the insect with
A6   47:18    and  not  to her, so she took courage, and went on again:--
A10   78: 6    and,  with tears running down his cheeks, he went on again:--
T8   184:21   short  silence after this, and then the Knight went on again. "I'm a great hand at inventing things. Now, I
A6   48:30    soup,  and seemed not to be listening, so she went on again: "Twenty-four hours, I think; or is it twelve? I
T8   182:41   he  fell  off  in  front; and, whenever it went on again (which it generally did rather suddenly), he
A2   15:22    way!  Stop this moment, I tell you!" But she went on all the same, shedding gallons of tears, until there
A6   51:27    think  that  proved  it at all: however, she went on: "And how do you know that you're mad?"
T2   125: 6    Alice  didn't  dare  to argue the point, but went on: "--and I thought I'd try and find my way to the top
```

WENT (cont.)

A11	89:19	"I'm a poor man," the Hatter went on, "and most things twinkled after that--only the March
T3	137:20	But this did not seem likely to happen. She went on and on, a long way, but wherever the road divided,
T8W	14: 1	"Can I do anything for you?" Alice went on. "Aren't you rather cold here?"
T4	146: 1	about it." So she brushed away her tears, and went on, as cheerfully as she could, "At any rate, I'd better
T3	132:23	"--then you don't like all insects?" The Gnat went on, as quietly as if nothing had happened.
T8W	14:15	you like me to read you a bit of this?" Alice went on, as she picked up a newspaper which had been lying at
T1	113:12	in arm--I don't think they can hear me," she went on, as she put her head closer down, "and I'm nearly sure
T1	108:21	"Do you know, I was so angry, Kitty," Alice went on, as soon as they were comfortably settled again, "when
A9	74:40	"When we were still little," the Mock Turtle went on at last, more calmly, though still sobbing a little
T2	128: 1	the Queen did not wait for an answer, but went on. "At the end of three yards I shall repeat them--for
T9	196: 4	"He said he would come in," the White Queen went on, "because he was looking for a hippopotamus. Now, as
T9	196:28	was really well brought up," the Red Queen went on: "but it's amazing how good-tempered she is! Pat her
T8W	21: 2	because your jaws are too short," the Wasp went on: "but the top of your head is nice and round." He took
A7	59: 8	be like, but it puzzled her too much: so she went on: "But why did they live at the bottom of a well?"
T3	129:18	go down and--no, I wo'n't go just yet," she went on, checking herself just as she was beginning to run
A9	77:21	And how did you manage on the twelfth?" Alice went on eagerly.
A2	20: 3	of dogs?" The Mouse did not answer, so Alice went on eagerly: "There is such a nice little dog, near our
A6	50: 6	it was impossible to say which), and they went on for some while in silence.
A3	22:21	did not notice this question, but hurriedly went on, "--found it advisable to go with Edgar Atheling to
T1	115: 6	to cry out, but his eyes and his mouth went on getting larger and larger, and rounder and rounder,
A4	28:19	other arm curled round her head. Still she went on growing, and, as a last resource, she put one arm out
A4	28:15	Alas! It was too late to wish that! She went on growing, and growing, and very soon had to kneel down
A2	19:35	her. She is such a dear quiet thing," Alice went on, half to herself, as she swam lazily about in the pool
A10	82: 5	so very wide; but she gained courage as she went on. Her listeners were perfectly quiet till she got to
T8	186:16	as before: "not the next day. In fact," he went on, holding his head down, and his voice getting lower
T7	172:15	"Who did you pass on the road?" the King went on, holding out his hand to the Messenger for some hay.
T1	108:26	for yourself? Now don't interrupt me!" she went on, holding up one finger. "I'm going to tell you all
A2	17:17	and her eyes filled with tears again as she went on, "I must be Mabel after all, and I shall have to go
T1	115:25	"The horror of that moment," the King went on, "I shall never, never forget!"
A9	76:31	"Well, then," the Gryphon went on, "if you don't know what to uglify is, you are a
T3	134:25	"And yet I don't know," the Gnat went on in a careless tone: "only think how convenient it
A10	81:21	"Boots and shoes under the sea," the Gryphon went on in a deep voice, "are done with whiting. Now you know
T9	195:44	"Humpty Dumpty saw it too," the White Queen went on in a low voice, more as if she were talking to herself
T4	147:34	"I'm very brave, generally," he went on in a low voice: "only to-day I happen to have a
A7	58: 8	"And ever since that," the Hatter went on in a mournful tone, "he wo'n't do a thing I ask! It's
T8	179:10	belonging to another person's dream," she went on in a rather complaining tone: "I've a great mind to go
T9	192: 3	I'll tell you what it is, your Majesty," she went on, in a severe tone (she was always rather fond of
T2	128:16	"You should have said," the Queen went on in a tone of grave reproof, "'It's extremely kind of
A10	83:13	felt sure it would all come wrong, and she went on in a trembling voice:--
T9	197:18	at a time. Do wake up, you heavy things!" she went on in an impatient tone; but there was no answer but a
A9	75: 8	fellow! Don't be all day about it!" and he went on in these words:--
T2	125:28	began to beat quick with excitement as she went on. "It's a great huge game of chess that's being played
A2	15:38	everything is to-day! And yesterday things went on just as usual. I wonder if I've changed in the night?
A8	67:33	Queen was close behind her, listening: so she went on "--likely to win, that it's hardly worth while
T3	129:37	Now then! Show your ticket, child!" the Guard went on, looking angrily at Alice. And a great many voices all
A11	89:25	at any rate, the Dormouse said--" the Hatter went on, looking anxiously round to see if he would deny it
T12	207:26	"Snowdrop, my pet!" she went on, looking over her shoulder at the White Kitten, which
T5	153:29	Queen, her voice rising into a squeak as she went on. "Much be-etter! Be-etter! Be-e-e-etter! Be-e-ehh!"
A12	95:38	"All right, so far," said the King; and he went on muttering over the verses to himself: "'We know it to
T6	160:17	you'd be safer down on the ground?" Alice went on, not with any idea of making another riddle, but
T9	199:15	"I speaks English, doesn't I?" the Frog went on. "Or are you deaf? What did it ask you?"
A10	84: 9	figure of the Lobster-Quadrille?" the Gryphon went on. "Or would you like the Mock Turtle to sing you
A2	15: 3	And she went on planning to herself how she would manage it. "They
T7	173:26	and thirsty. How are you, dear child?" he went on, putting his arm affectionately round Hatta's neck.
T3	135:40	to get into the--into the--into what?" she went on, rather surprised at not being able to think of the
T8W	15: 5	"In coming back," Alice went on reading, "they found a lake of treacle. The banks of
T8	184: 9	"Plenty of practice!" he went on repeating, all the time that Alice was getting him on
A1	9:12	here Alice began to get rather sleepy, and went on saying to herself, in a dreamy sort of way, "Do cats
T10	205: 4	eyes got large and green: and still, as Alice went on shaking her, she kept on growing shorter--and fatter--
A7	58: 2	"Twinkle, twinkle, twinkle, twinkle--" and went on so long that they had to pinch it to make it stop.
A12	95:32	try to find any. And yet I don't know," he went on, spreading out the verses on his knee, and looking at
T5	150: 2	in a careless tone. "For instance, now," she went on, sticking a large piece of plaster on her finger as
A4	29:16	And so she went on, taking first one side and then the other, and making
A2	15:37	she kept fanning herself all the time she went on talking. "Dear, dear! How queer everything is to-day!
T1	109: 2	they had saved up all my punishments?" she went on, talking more to herself than the kitten. "What would
T8	190:28	so many things hung round the horse--" So she went on talking to herself, as she watched the horse walking
A7	60:22	it woke up again with a little shriek, and went on: "--that begins with an M, such as mouse-traps, and
A4	27:33	doesn't get out.' Only I don't think," Alice went on, "that they'd let Dinah stop in the house if it began
T6	160:24	hardly help laughing. "If I did fall," he went on, "the King has promised me--ah, you may turn pale, if
T3	130: 4	I came from." And again the chorus of voices went on. "There wasn't room for one where she came from. The
T8W	16: 8	too, if you'd a wig like mine," the Wasp went on. "They jokes at one. And they worrits one. And then I
T6	161:13	his horses and all his men," Humpty Dumpty went on. "They'd pick me up again in a minute, they would!
A12	93:27	course, I meant," the King hastily said, and went on to himself in an undertone, "important--unimportant--
T9	204:17	"And as for you," she went on, turning fiercely upon the Red Queen, whom she
T7	175:33	out the plum-cake, old man!" the Unicorn went on, turning from her to the King. "None of your brown
A3	23:32	"What else have you got in your pocket?" it went on, turning to Alice.
A9	70:10	pepper that makes people hot-tempered," she went on, very much pleased at having found out a new kind of
T9	198: 6	ring the--the--which bell must I ring?" she went on, very much puzzled by the names. "I'm not a visitor,
T6	164:10	round me of a Saturday night," Humpty Dumpty went on, wagging his head gravely from side to side, "for to

WENT (cont.)

T2	121: 3	away. At length, as the Tiger-lily only	went on waving about, she spoke again, in a timid voice--
T2	120:20	she got to the hill. For a few minutes all	went on well, and she was just saying "I really shall do it
T3	131:18	And after that other voices	went on ("What a number of people there are in the carriage!"
A8	65: 4	And then, turning to the rose-tree, she	went on "What have you been doing here?"
A8	63:39	head impatiently; and turning to Alice, she	went on: "What's your name, child?"
T5	157:10	But the Sheep only laughed scornfully, and	went on with her knitting.
T5	157: 3	a bit hurt, and was soon up again: the Sheep	went on with her knitting all the while, just as if nothing
T7	173:28	Hatta looked round and nodded, and	went on with his bread-and-butter.
T8W	21: 6	of reach, and would not take the hint. So he	went on .with his criticisms.
T3	131: 8	to be that they should all speak in turn, he	went on with "She'll have to go back from here as luggage!"
T3	130: 8	And once more the chorus of voices	went on with "The man that drives the engine. Why, the smoke
A5	42:34	banks, and I've tried hedges," the Pigeon	went on, without attending to her; "but those serpents!
A6	46:19	be some sense in your knocking," the Footman	went on, without attending to her, "if we had the door between
T6	166:19	"The piece I'm going to repeat," he	went on without noticing her remark, "was written entirely for
T5	158:27	ever saw!" * * * * * * * * * * * * * * So she	went on, wondering more and more at every step, as everything
A6	51: 7	it's pleased so far," thought Alice, and she	went on. "Would you tell me, please, which way I ought to go
A7	60:14	"They were learning to draw," the Dormouse	went on, yawning and rubbing its eyes, for it was getting very
A6	51:32	"Well, then," the Cat	went on, "you see a dog growls when it's angry, and wags its
A10	78:26	"Then, you know," the Mock Turtle	went on, "you throw the--"
A5	41:27	away into the grass, merely remarking, as it	went, "One side will make you grow taller, and the other side
T9	196:14	off, and ever so much thunder got in--and it	went rolling round the room in great lumps--and knocking over
A11	87: 6	of course, Alice could not stand, and she	went round the court and got behind him, and very soon found
T1	115:16	a little alarmed at what she had done, and	went round the room to see if she could find any water to
A7	59:25	angrily, but the Hatter and the March Hare	went "Sh! Sh!" and the Dormouse sulkily remarked "If you
A9	74:13	says 'come on!' here," thought Alice, as she	went slowly after it: "I never was so ordered about before, in
T1	118:14	And through and through / The vorpal blade	went snicker-snack! / He left it dead, and with its head / He
T2	127: 5	cried the Queen. "Faster! Faster!" And they	went so fast that at last they seemed to skim through the air,
T2	126:14	they were running hand in hand, and the Queen	went so fast that it was all she could do to keep up with her:
A8	66:22	time the Queen was in a furious passion, and	went stamping about, and shouting "Off with his head!" or "Off
A1	8: 7	The rabbit-hole	went straight on like a tunnel for some way, and then dipped
T2	126:20	their places at all: however fast they	went, they never seemed to pass anything. "I wonder if all the
T7	172:32	a thing again, I'll have you buttered! It	went through and through my head like an earthquake!"
T5	155: 5	But even this plan failed: the 'thing'	went through the ceiling as quietly as possible, as if it were
T6	167:15	My heart went hop, my heart	went thump: / I filled the kettle at the pump.
T3	137:30	So she wandered on, talking to herself as she	went, till, on turning a sharp corner, she came upon two fat
A6	46: 9	Alice	went timidly up to the door, and knocked.
A9	77: 6	"I never went to him," the Mock Turtle said with a sigh. "He taught
T5	149: 4	as if she were flying, and Alice very civilly	went to meet her with the shawl.
A9	76: 5	"We had the best of educations--in fact, we	went to school every day--"
A9	74:41	still sobbing a little now and then, "we	went to school in the sea. The master was an old Turtle--we
A9	75: 9	"Yes, we went to school in the sea, though you mayn't believe it--"
A9	77: 4	"Hadn't time," said the Gryphon: "I	went to the Classical master, though. He was an old crab, he
A2	18: 4	must be growing small again." She got up and	went to the table to measure herself by it, and found that, as
T6	168: 9	I took a corkscrew from the shelf: / I	went to wake them up myself.
T9	199:19	Frog muttered. "Wexes it, you know." Then he	went up and gave the door a kick with one of his great feet.
A9	74:23	So they	went up to the Mock Turtle, who looked at them with large eyes

WEPT (2)

T4	141: 3	/ Were walking close at hand: / They	wept like anything to see / Such quantities of sand: / 'If
A2	18:26	she was in the pool of tears which she had	wept when she was nine feet high.

WE'RE (6)

T4	138:14	added the one marked 'DEE,' "if you think	we're alive, you ought to speak."
A6	51:23	"Oh, you ca'n't help that," said the Cat:	"we're all mad here. I'm mad. You're mad."
T8	179: 8	all," she said to herself, "unless--unless	we're all part of the same dream. Only I do hope it's my dream
A8	63: 9	heads cut off, you know. So you see, Miss,	we're doing our best, afore she comes, to--" At this moment,
T1	110:13	because Alice had begun with "Let's pretend	we're kings and queens;" and her sister, who liked being very
T4	138:10	"If you think	we're wax-works," he said, "you ought to pay, you know."

WERE (169)

A12	95:12	to you to set them free, / Exactly as we	were.
T6	161:21	a question for you. How old did you say you	were?"
T2	123: 2	what's going on in the world, than if you	were a bud!"
T8	184:25	"You	were a little grave," said Alice.
T2	125:21	and a most curious country it was. There	were a number of tiny little brooks running straight across it
T9	200: 9	up the large hall, and noticed that there	were about fifty guests, of all kinds: some were animals, some
T3	129:35	everybody was holding out a ticket: they	were about the same size as the people, and quite seemed to
T4	138: 6	stood so still that she quite forgot they	were alive, and she was just going round to see if the word
A7	54: 7	The table was a large one, but the three	were all crowded together at one corner of it. "No room! No
A3	26:35	"Come away, my dears! It's high time you	were all in bed!" On various pretexts they all moved off, and
A1	9:30	There were doors all round the hall, but they	were all locked; and when Alice had been all the way down one
A8	63:21	merrily along, hand in hand, in couples: they	were all ornamented with hearts. Next came the guests, mostly
A8	63:15	First came ten soldiers carrying clubs: these	were all shaped like the three gardeners, oblong and flat,
A8	68:31	the executioner, the King, and the Queen, who	were all talking at once, while all the rest were quite silent
T5	151:16	"And you	were all the better for it, I know!" the Queen said
A4	32: 5	noticed, with some surprise, that the pebbles	were all turning into little cakes as they lay on the floor,
A11	86:28	The twelve jurors	were all writing very busily on slates. "What are they doing?"
A8	66:17	hedgehog to, and, as the doubled-up soldiers	were always getting up and walking off to other parts of the
T7	169: 6	soldiers so uncertain on their feet: they	were always tripping over something or other, and whenever one
A11	86:23	"creatures," you see, because some of them	were animals, and some were birds,) "I suppose they are the
T9	200:10	were about fifty guests, of all kinds: some	were animals, some birds, and there were even a few flowers
A6	50: 2	looked into its eyes again, to see if there	were any tears.

WERE (cont.)

A1	12:33	very small cake, on which the words "EAT ME" were	beautifully marked in currants. "Well, I'll eat it," said
A11	86:23	because some of them were animals, and some were	birds,) "I suppose they are the jurors." She said this
T8W	15: 6	a lake of treacle. The banks of the lake were	blue and white, and looked like china. While tasting the
T4	144:22	After a pause, Alice began, "Well! They were	both very unpleasant characters--" Here she checked
T4	142: 3	up, / All eager for the treat: / Their coats were	brushed, their faces washed, / Their shoes were clean and
T5	156:17	waving rushes. And then the little sleeves were	carefully rolled up, and the little arms were plunged in
A12	98:18	Alice herself: once again the tiny hands were	clasped upon her knee, and the bright eager eyes were
T4	142: 4	brushed, their faces washed, / Their shoes were	clean and neat--/ And this was odd, because, you know, /
T1	108:22	angry, Kitty," Alice went on, as soon as they were	comfortably settled again, "when I saw all the mischief
T5	154:14	quite empty, though the others round it were	crowded as full as they could hold.
T4	139:31	seemed to come from the tree under which they were	dancing, and it was done (as well as she could make it
T4	139:28	of both hands at once: the next moment they were	dancing round in a ring. This seemed quite natural (she
A1	9:30	There were	doors all round the hall, but they were all locked; and
A1	9: 8	milk at tea-time. Dinah, my dear! I wish you were	down here with me! There are no mice in the air, I'm
T4	140:36	The sea was wet as wet could be, / The sands were	dry as dry. / You could not see a cloud, because / No
A7	58:33	began in a great hurry; "and their names were	Elsie, Lacie, and Tillie; and they lived at the bottom of
T8W	15: 8	they had a sad accident: two of their party were	engulphed--"
T9	200:10	some were animals, some birds, and there were	even a few flowers among them. "I'm glad they've come
T7	175:23	"I always thought they were	fabulous monsters!" said the Unicorn. "Is it alive?"
T7	175:28	"Do you know, I always thought Unicorns were	fabulous monsters, too? I never saw one alive before!"
T9	197:10	sleepy, too." In another moment both Queens were	fast asleep, and snoring loud.
T4	139:39	The other two dancers were	fat, and very soon out of breath. "Four times round is
T7	173: 1	"The Lion and the Unicorn were	fighting for the crown: / The Lion beat the Unicorn all
T7	173:16	in the middle of which the Lion and Unicorn were	fighting. They were in such a cloud of dust, that at
A1	8:16	the sides of the well, and noticed that they were	filled with cupboards and book-shelves: here and there
T9	201:31	lips, there was dead silence, and all eyes were	fixed upon her; "and it's a very curious thing, I think--
T5	149: 4	with both arms stretched out wide, as if she were	flying, and Alice very civilly went to meet her with the
T4	140:39	because / No cloud was in the sky: / No birds were	flying overhead--/ There were no birds to fly.
A9	74:34	These words were	followed by a very long silence, broken only by an
T4	139:24	and then they held out the two hands that were	free, to shake hands with her.
T5	155:35	of the needles into her hair, as her hands were	full. "Feather, I say!"
T8	190: 8	mumblingly and low, / As if his mouth were	full of dough, / Who snorted like a buffalo--/ That
A8	64: 1	of the pack, she could not tell whether they were	gardeners, or soldiers, or courtiers, or three of her own
A6	49:34	like a snout than a real nose: also its eyes were	getting extremely small for a baby: altogether Alice did
A2	14: 5	they seemed to be almost out of sight, they were	getting so far off). "Oh, my poor little feet, I wonder
A4	32:15	middle, being held up by two guinea-pigs, who were	giving it something out of a bottle. They all made a rush
TI	103:14	tale begun in other days, / When summer suns were	glowing--/ A simple chime, that served to time / The
T7	175:44	he looked very tired and sleepy, and his eyes were	half shut. "What's this!" he said, blinking lazily at
AI	3:33	Thus slowly, one by one, / Its quaint events were	hammered out--/ And now the tale is done, / And home we
A7	54: 2	the house, and the March Hare and the Hatter were	having tea at it: a Dormouse was sitting between them,
T12	208:10	dream, too! Was it the Red King, Kitty? You were	his wife, my dear, so you ought to know--Oh, Kitty, do
T5	155:18	into oars in her hands, and she found they were	in a little boat, gliding along between banks: so there
A9	73: 9	except the King, the Queen, and Alice, were	in custody and under sentence of execution.
T7	173:16	the Lion and Unicorn were fighting. They were	in such a cloud of dust, that at first Alice could not
A7	60: 9	"But they were	in the well," Alice said to the Dormouse, not choosing to
A3	21: 1	They were	indeed a queer-looking party that assembled on the bank--
A6	46:20	had the door between us. For instance, if you were	inside, you might knock, and I could let you out, you
T2	123:36	her," said Alice, for, though the flowers were	interesting enough, she felt that it would be far grander
T8	179:12	At this moment her thoughts were	interrupted by a loud shouting of "Ahoy! Ahoy! Check!"
T6	164:18	"I can explain all the poems that ever were	invented--and a good many that haven't been invented just
T2	122:14	tone, and, stooping down to the daisies, who were	just beginning again, she whispered "If you don't hold
A12	93:22	the King said, turning to the jury. They were	just beginning to write this down on their slates, when
A7	60:14	"They were	learning to draw," the Dormouse went on, yawning and
A7	59:31	on. "And so these three little sisters--they were	learning to draw you know--"
A8	66: 2	was all ridges and furrows: the croquet balls were	live hedgehogs, and the mallets live flamingoes, and the
A11	86:37	Alice could see, as well as if she were	looking over their shoulders, that all the jurors were
A12	98:18	upon her knee, and the bright eager eyes were	looking up into hers--she could hear the very tones of
T9	204:10	to be lost. Already several of the guests were	lying down in the dishes, and the soup ladle was walking
A8	63:45	round the rose-tree; for, you see, as they were	lying on their faces, and the pattern on their backs was
A8	63:44	Queen, pointing to the three gardeners who were	lying round the rose-tree; for, you see, as they were
A2	19:31	voice. "Would you like cats, if you were	me?"
A12	95: 8	all returned from him to you, / Though they were	mine before.
A11	91:15	arms and frowning at the cook till his eyes were	nearly out of sight, he said, in a deep voice, "What are
A10	78: 9	("I haven't," said Alice)--"and perhaps you were	never even introduced to a lobster--" (Alice began to say
A1	8:37	or Longitude either, but she thought they were	nice grand words to say.)
A7	56:45	with the clock. For instance, suppose it were	nine o'clock in the morning, just time to begin lessons:
A9	73: 7	that, by the end of half an hour or so, there were	no arches left, and all the players, except the King, the
T4	140:40	sky: / No birds were flying overhead--/ There were	no birds to fly.
A6	50: 3	No, there were	no tears. "If you're going to turn into a pig, my dear,"
T4	143:23	but / 'Cut us another slice. / I wish you were	not quite so deaf--/ I've had to ask you twice!'
A5	42: 9	moment, when she found that her shoulders were	nowhere to be found: all she could see, when she looked
A4	27: 8	began hunting about for them, but they were	nowhere to be seen--everything seemed to have changed
A10	81:30	"They were	obliged to have him with them," the Mock Turtle said. "No
A2	16: 2	thinking over all the children she knew that were	of the same age as herself, to see if she could have been
T4	141: 5	to see / Such quantities of sand: / 'If this were	only cleared away,' / They said, 'it would be grand!'
T1	110:15	had argued that they couldn't, because there were	only two of them, and Alice had been reduced at last to
A9	72: 8	what it might appear to others that what you were	or might have been was not otherwise than what you had
A8	63:17	at the corners: next the ten courtiers: these were	ornamented all over with diamonds, and walked two and two
A8	68:23	the fight was over, and both the hedgehogs were	out of sight: "but it doesn't matter much," thought Alice

WERE (cont.)

T4	148:22	and the two brothers took to their heels and	were out of sight in a moment.
A10	82: 5	gained courage as she went on. Her listeners	were perfectly quiet till she got to the part about her
A3	23: 9	matter," it said,) and then all the party	were placed along the course, here and there. There was no
T1	110: 5	I'm asking it seriously. Because, when we	were playing just now, you watched just as if you understood
A9	73: 3	All the time they	were playing the Queen never left off quarreling with the
T5	156:17	were carefully rolled up, and the little arms	were plunged in elbow-deep, to get hold of the rushes a good
T8	180: 6	hold their clubs with their arms, as if they	were Punch and Judy--What a noise they make when they tumble!
A3	23:14	they had been running half an hour or so, and	were quite dry again, the Dodo suddenly called out "The race
A8	68:31	were all talking at once, while all the rest	were quite silent, and looked very uncomfortable.
T5	155: 6	the ceiling as quietly as possible, as if it	were quite used to it.
A1	10:11	begun to think that very few things indeed	were really impossible.
A9	72:44	taken advantage of the Queen's absence, and	were resting in the shade: however, the moment they saw her,
T2	126:13	they began: all she remembers is, that they	were running hand in hand, and the Queen went so fast that it
A7	59: 5	"So they were," said the Dormouse; "very ill."
A7	60:11	"Of course they were," said the Dormouse: "well in."
A7	58:26	feeble voice, "I heard every word you fellows	were saying."
A2	17: 4	she crossed her hands on her lap as if she	were saying lessons, and began to repeat it, but her voice
A11	86: 1	The King and Queen of Hearts	were seated on their throne when they arrived, with a great
A6	53:12	must be the right house, because the chimneys	were shaped like ears and the roof was thatched with fur. It
A10	83:15	with one eye, / How the Owl and the Panther	were sharing a pie: / The Panther took pie-crust, and gravy,
A8	65:20	The soldiers	were silent, and looked at Alice, as the question was
T5	152: 6	Her screams	were so exactly like the whistle of a steam-engine, that Alice
T4	139: 8	"if it was so, it might be; and if it	were so, it would be; but as it isn't, it ain't. That's logic
T5	156:39	feet--but Alice hardly noticed this, there	were so many other curious things to think about.
T12	207:29	I wonder? That must be the reason you	were so untidy in my dream--Dinah! Do you know that you're
T9	192:21	argument, "and if you only spoke when you	were spoken to, and the other person always waited for you to
T4	138: 1	They	were standing under a tree, each with an arm round the other's
T6	159:11	he could keep his balance--and, as his eyes	were steadily fixed in the opposite direction, and he didn't
A9	74:40	"When we	were still little," the Mock Turtle went on at last, more
A10	81:27	been the whiting," said Alice, whose thoughts	were still running on the song, "I'd have said to the porpoise
T3	137:21	way, but wherever the road divided, there	were sure to be two finger-posts pointing the same way, one
T8	180: 9	let them get on and off them just as if they	were tables!"
A9	73: 5	"Off with her head!" Those whom she sentenced	were taken into custody by the soldiers, who of course had to
T9	196: 1	Queen went on in a low voice, more as if she	were talking to herself. "He came to the door with a corkscrew
T1	115:20	found he had recovered, and he and the Queen	were talking together in a frightened whisper--so low, that
A8	63:19	After there came the royal children: there	were ten of them, and the little dears came jumping merrily
T1	116:11	shtar emom eht dnA / ,sevogorob eht erew	ysmim llA / :ebaw eht ni elbmig dna eryg diD / sevot yhtils
T1	116:20	Did gyre and gimble in the wabe: / All mimsy	were the borogoves, / And the mome raths outgrabe.
T1	118:23	Did gyre and gimble in the wabe: / All mimsy	were the borogoves, / And the mome raths outgrabe.
T6	164:23	Did gyre and gimble in the wabe: / All mimsy	were the borogoves, / And the mome raths outgrabe."
A6	47:10	in the kitchen, that did not sneeze,	were the cook, and a large cat, which was lying on the hearth
T9	200:12	she thought: "I should never have known who	were the right people to invite!"
A5	41:34	for a minute, trying to make out which	were the two sides of it; and, as it was perfectly round, she
T9	198: 1	standing before an arched doorway, over which	were the words "QUEEN ALICE" in large letters, and on each
T1	108:35	down the saucer of milk before her! What, you	were thirsty, were you? How do you know she wasn't thirsty too
T9	200:14	There	were three chairs at the head of the table: the Red and White
A8	62: 2	the roses growing on it were white, but there	were three gardeners at it, busily painting them red. Alice
A7	58:32	"Once upon a time there	were three little sisters," the Dormouse began in a great
T9	201:23	Pudding. "I wonder how you'd like it, if I	were to cut a slice out of you, you creature!"
T6	162:15	of age, she thought: and, if they really	were to take turns in choosing subjects, it was her turn now.)
A1	9:37	of the hall; but, alas! either the locks	were too large, or the key was too small, but at any rate it
A8	65: 7	tone, going down on one knee as he spoke, "we	were trying--"
A7	60:33	after her: the last time she saw them, they	were trying to put the Dormouse into the teapot.
T9	199:10	nearer and rubbed it with his thumb, as if he	were trying whether the paint would come off: then he looked
A12	93:28	unimportant--important--" as if he	were trying which word sounded best.
A4	30:17	another snatch in the air. This time there	were two little shrieks, and more sounds of broken glass.
A7	54: 3	between them, fast asleep, and the other two	were using it as a cushion, resting their elbows on it, and
T8W	13: 7	huddled up together, and shivering as if he	were very cold.
T1	113: 7	hands and knees watching them. The chessmen	were walking about, two and two!
T4	141: 2	The Walrus and the Carpenter / Were	walking close at hand: / They wept like anything to see /
T8W	15: 9	"Were	what?" the Wasp asked in a very cross voice.
A8	62: 2	of the garden: the roses growing on it were	white, but there were three gardeners at it, busily
T3	135:36	Only they wouldn't answer at all, if they	were wise."
A11	86:38	over their shoulders, that all the jurors	were writing down "Stupid things!" on their slates, and she
T6	159: 6	"I'm as certain of it, as if his name	were written all over his face!"
T5	151:13	wrong there, at any rate," said the Queen.	"Were you ever punished?"
T7	173:30	"Were you happy in prison, dear child?" said Haigha.
T1	108:35	of milk before her! What, you were thirsty,	were you? How do you know she wasn't thirsty too? Now for

WEREN'T (2)

T4	138:11	said, "you ought to pay, you know. Wax-works	weren't made to be looked at for nothing. Nohow!"
A8	69: 1	had a head could be beheaded, and that you	weren't to talk nonsense.

WET (4)

A3	22:26	"As wet as ever," said Alice in a melancholy tone: "it doesn't
T4	140:35	The sea was wet as wet could be, / The sands were dry as dry. / You could
T4	140:35	The sea was wet as wet could be, / The sands were dry as dry. / You could not see
A3	21: 3	fur clinging close to them, and all dripping	wet, cross, and uncomfortable.

WE'VE (9)

T2	127:18	else--if you ran very fast for a long time as	we've been doing."
T2	127:13	her in great surprise. "Why, I do believe	we've been under this tree the whole time! Everything's just

WE'VE (cont.)
```
T4    143:27  said, / 'To play them such a trick, / After we've brought them out so far, / And made them trot so quick!'
T4    148: 8  standing,  for ever so far round, by the time we've finished!"
T6    163:45  pleased. "I meant by 'impenetrability' that we've had enough of that subject, and it would be just as well
A12    95:21  "That's the most important piece of evidence we've heard yet," said the King, rubbing his hands; "so now
T4    146: 8  "It may--if it chooses," said Tweedledee: "we've no objection. Contrariwise."
A7     58:13  with a sigh: "it's always tea-time, and we've no time to wash the things between whiles."
T9    197: 5  in Alice's lap! / Till the feast's ready, we've time for a nap. / When the feast's over, we'll go to the
```
WEXES (1)
```
T9    199:19  shouldn't do that--" the Frog muttered. "Wexes it, you know." Then he went up and gave the door a kick
```
WHAT (279) [entries omitted]
WHATEVER (7)
```
A4     28:21  and said to herself "Now I can do no more, whatever happens. What will become of me?"
T10   205: 3  The Red Queen made no resistance whatever: only her face grew very small, and her eyes got
A12    93:19  "Nothing whatever?" persisted the King.
A12    93:20  "Nothing whatever," said Alice.
T9    199:26  my head. / Let the Looking-Glass creatures, whatever they be, / Come and dine with the Red Queen the
T3    135:19  for, when Alice looked up, there was nothing whatever to be seen on the twig, and, as she was getting quite
T12   207: 7  (Alice had once made the remark) that, whatever you say to them, they always purr. "If they would
```
WHAT'LL (1)
```
T3    135:28  "where things have no names. I wonder what'll become of my name when I go in? I shouldn't like to
```
WHAT'S (19)
```
T2    123: 1  and snore away there, till you know no more what's going on in the world, than if you were a bud!"
T7    172:23  now you've got your breath, you may tell us what's happened in the town."
A12    94: 6  "What's in it?" said the Queen.
T9    199:12  "To answer the door?" he said. "What's it been asking of?" He was so hoarse that Alice could
A3     22:32  the meaning of half those long words, and, what's more, I don't believe you do either!" And the Eaglet
T9    193:24  Can you do Addition?" the White Queen asked. "What's one and one and one and one and one and one and one and
T8    182:11  on. I'll go with you to the end of the wood--what's that dish for?"
A4     30: 6  "Now tell me, Pat, what's that in the window?"
T1    108:29  Now you ca'n't deny it, Kitty: I heard you! What's that you say?" (pretending that the kitten was
A7     56:29  "No, I give it up," Alice replied. "What's the answer?"
T9    194: 6  you do Division? Divide a loaf by a knife--what's the answer to that?"
T9    195: 8  said the Red Queen. "Do you know Languages? What's the French for fiddle-de-dee?"
T8W    13:11  spring over the brook:--but I'll just ask him what's the matter," she added, checking herself on the very
T5    149:26  "I don't know what's the matter with it!" the Queen said, in a melancholy
T4    147:41  care about going on long," said Tweedledum. "What's the time now?"
T3    132:35  "What's the use of their having names," the Gnat said, "if they
T7    175:44  and sleepy, and his eyes were half shut. "What's this!" he said, blinking lazily at Alice, and speaking
T6    165: 1  "And what's to 'gyre' and to 'gimble'?"
A8     63:39  and turning to Alice, she went on: "What's your name, child?"
```
WHEAT (1)
```
T8    188: 2  look for butterflies / That sleep among the wheat: / I make them into mutton-pies, / And sell them in the
```
WHEELS (2) [See also CART-WHEELS]
```
T8    189: 2  / I sometimes search for grassy knolls / For wheels of Hansom-cabs. / And that's the way' (he gave a wink)
T8    184:12  time. "You ought to have a wooden horse on wheels, that you ought!"
```
WHEN (167) [entries omitted]
WHENEVER (9)
```
T7    170: 1  and it seemed to be a regular rule that, whenever a horse stumbled, the rider fell off instantly. The
T8W    19:13  And still, whenever I appear, / They hoot at me and call me 'Pig!' / And
A4     28: 5  is sure to happen," she said to herself, "whenever I eat or drink anything: so I'll just see what this
T8    182:41  did very often), he fell off in front; and, whenever it went on again (which it generally did rather
T7    169: 7  always tripping over something or other, and whenever one went down, several more always fell over him, so
T5    154:12  but the oddest part of it all was that, whenever she looked hard at any shelf, to make out exactly
T8    182:40  Whenever the horse stopped (which it did very often), he fell
T1    109:15  themselves all in green, and dance about--whenever the wind blows--oh, that's very pretty!" cried Alice,
T5    152:32  happy, living in this wood, and being glad whenever you like!"
```
WHERE (35) [entries omitted]
WHERE'S (3)
```
A8     65:28  "Very," said Alice. "Where's the Duchess?"
A4     30:25  talking together: she made out the words: "Where's the other ladder?--Why, I hadn't to bring but one.
T9    199: 2  round, ready to find fault with anybody. "Where's the servant whose business it is to answer the door?"
```
WHEREUPON (1)
```
A4     32:34  bit of stick, and held it out to the puppy: whereupon the puppy jumped into the air off all its feet at
```
WHEREVER (3)
```
A8     66:16  was generally a ridge or a furrow in the way wherever she wanted to send the hedgehog to, and, as the
T3    137:21  happen. She went on and on, a long way, but wherever the road divided, there were sure to be two
A2     18:22  and had come to the general conclusion that wherever you go to on the English coast, you find a number of
```
WHETHER (23)
```
T4    148: 3  every thing within reach," cried Tweedledum, "whether I can see it or not!"
T6    166:27  "If you can see whether I'm singing or not, you've sharper eyes than most,"
T3    131:44  What she really wanted to know was, whether it could sting or not, but she thought this wouldn't
T12   207:12  only purred: and it was impossible to guess whether it meant "yes" or "no."
A6     47:13  a little timidly, for she was not quite sure whether it was good manners for her to speak first, "why your
A8     68:15  was in such confusion that she never knew whether it was her turn or not. So she went off in search of
A6     51: 5  rather timidly, as she did not at all know whether it would like the name: however, it only grinned a
A1     10:21  "No, I'll look first," she said, "and see whether it's marked 'poison' or not"; for she had read several
T4    142:24  And why the sea is boiling hot--/ And whether pigs have wings.'
A8     67: 9  about for some way of escape, and wondering whether she could get away without being seen, when she
A8     63:28  Alice was rather doubtful whether she ought not to lie down on her face like the three
```

WHETHER (cont.)

T2	128:30	gone. Whether she vanished into the air, or	whether	she ran quickly into the wood ("and she can run very
T2	128:29	as she came to the last peg, she was gone. Whether		she vanished into the air, or whether she ran quickly
A6	48:15	already, that it was quite impossible to say	whether	the blows hurt it or not.
T9	199:10	it with his thumb, as if he were trying	whether	the paint would come off: then he looked at Alice.
A1	7: 7	day made her feel very sleepy and stupid),	whether	the pleasure of making a daisy-chain would be worth
T1	112: 3	The very first thing she did was to look	whether	there was a fire in the fireplace, and she was quite
A8	64: 1	as the rest of the pack, she could not tell	whether	they were gardeners, or soldiers, or courtiers, or
T1	110:36	I could see that bit! I want so much to know	whether	they've a fire in the winter: you never can tell, you
T9	201: 2	and Alice returned the bow, not knowing	whether	to be frightened or amused.
A11	89:10	repeated angrily, "or I'll have you executed,	whether	you are nervous or not."
T6	163:33	"The question is," said Alice,	"whether	you can make words mean so many different things."
A5	43:24	well enough; and what does it matter to me	whether	you're a little girl or a serpent?"

WHICH (109) [entries omitted]

WHIFFLING (1)

| T1 | 118:11 | / The Jabberwock, with eyes of flame, / Came | whiffling | through the tulgey wood, / And burbled as it came! |

WHILE (52) [See also AWHILE, MEANWHILE]

T5	156:19	way down before breaking them off--and for a	while	Alice forgot all about the Sheep and the knitting, as
A7	55:32	and the party sat silent for a minute,	while	Alice thought over all she could remember about ravens
T1	107:13	with earlier in the afternoon, and so,	while	Alice was sitting curled up in a corner of the great
T7	170:35	least idea that he was joining in the game,	while	Alice was still hesitating for the name of a town
A8	68:31	and the Queen, who were all talking at once,	while	all the rest were quite silent, and looked very
A8	66:21	without waiting for turns, quarreling all the	while,	and fighting for the hedgehogs; and in a very short
T5	156:37	rushes, you know, last only a very little	while--and	these, being dream-rushes, melted away almost like
T1	108:28	your faults. Number one: you squeaked twice	while	Dinah was washing your face this morning. Now you ca'n't
A1	12:13	After a	while,	finding that nothing more happened, she decided on
A8	67:34	on "--likely to win, that it's hardly worth	while	finishing the game."
T7	175:40	out of the bag, and gave it to Alice to hold,	while	he got out a dish and carving-knife. How they all came
A3	26:41	very lonely and low-spirited. In a little	while,	however, she again heard a little pattering of
T1	108:37	three: you unwound every bit of the worsted	while	I wasn't looking!
A6	50: 6	to say which), and they went on for some	while	in silence.
T9	202:16	it like glue--/ Holds the lid to the dish,	while	it lies in the middle: / Which is easiest to do, /
T5	157: 3	the Sheep went on with her knitting all the	while,	just as if nothing had happened. "That was a nice crab
T7	172:39	of the joke is, that it's my crown all the	while!	Let's run and see them." And they trotted off, Alice
AI	3: 5	little skill, / By little arms are plied, /	While	little hands make vain pretence / Our wanderings to
A10	85: 7	only answered "Come on!" and ran the faster,	while	more and more faintly came, carried on the breeze that
A12	98:30	pig-baby was sneezing on the Duchess's knee,	while	plates and dishes crashed around it--once more the
T9	203: 1	rather difficult for her to keep in her place	while	she made her speech: the two Queens pushed her so, one
A12	98:11	late." So Alice got up and ran off, thinking	while	she ran, as well she might, what a wonderful dream it
A5	43:32	then she had to stop and untwist it. After a	while	she remembered that she still held the pieces of
T1	111:11	through--" She was up on the chimney-piece	while	she said this, though she hardly knew how she had got
T1	116: 1	was a book lying near Alice on the table, and	while	she sat watching the White King (for she was still a
A4	32:24	the smallest idea how to set about it; and,	while	she was peering about anxiously among the trees, a
A6	52:12	so well used to queer things happening. While		she was still looking at the place where it had been, it
A2	18: 3	one of the Rabbit's little white kid-gloves	while	she was talking. "How can I have done that?" she thought
A6	48: 9	introduce some other subject of conversation. While		she was trying to fix on one, the cook took the cauldron
T8W	15: 7	were blue and white, and looked like china.	While	tasting the treacle, they had a sad accident: two of
AI	3:17	hopes / "There will be nonsense in it!" /	While	Tertia interrupts the tale / Not more than once a minute
T5	156: 2	was no more conversation for a minute or two,	while	the boat glided gently on, sometimes among beds of weeds
A3	24: 1	Then they all crowded round her once more,	while	the Dodo solemnly presented the thimble, saying "We beg
A6	49: 1		While	the Duchess sang the second verse of the song, she kept
T3	132:17	found herself sitting quietly under a tree--while		the Gnat (for that was the insect she had been talking
T7	171:14	only got more extraordinary every moment,	while	the great eyes rolled wildly from side to side.
T7	174:13	the Lion and the Unicorn sat down, panting,	while	the King called out "Ten minutes allowed for
A12	99: 1	the confused clamour of the busy farm-yard--while		the lowing of the cattle in the distance would take the
A10	79:11	and waving their fore-paws to mark the time,	while	the Mock Turtle sang this, very slowly and sadly:--
A3	25: 3	it sad?" And she kept on puzzling about it	while	the mouse was speaking, so that her idea of the tale was
T8	179: 1	After a	while	the noise seemed gradually to die away, till all was
A10	83:17	took pie-crust, and gravy, and meat, /	While	the Owl had the dish as its share of the treat, / When
A10	84: 1	/ Was kindly permitted to pocket the spoon: /	While	the Panther received knife and fork with a growl, / And
A8	69:13	ran wildly up and down, looking for it,	while	the rest of the party went back to the game.
A3	23:20	see Shakespeare, in the pictures of him),	while	the rest waited in silence. At last the Dodo said
T7	175:43	The Lion had joined them	while	this was going on: he looked very tired and sleepy, and
A4	32:44	a long way back, and barking hoarsely all the	while,	till at last it sat down a good way off, panting, with
T3	135:13	But the Gnat only sighed deeply	while	two large tears came rolling down its cheeks.
T5	156:21	of her tangled hair dipping into the water--while		with bright eager eyes she caught at one bunch after
T2	127:31		"While	you're refreshing yourself," said the Queen, "I'll just
T2	124:13	at all?" she added in a kinder tone. "Curtsey	while	you're thinking what to say. It saves time."
T12	207:23	Alice cried with a merry laugh. "And curtsey	while	you're thinking what to--what to purr. It saves time,

WHILES (1)

| A7 | 58:13 | and we've no time to wash the things between | whiles." |

WHILST (1)

| A12 | 94:37 | There was dead silence in the court, | whilst | the White Rabbit read out these verses:-- |

WHISKERS (6)

A11	91:21	court! Suppress him! Pinch him! Off with his	whiskers!"
T1	115:23	my dear, I turned cold to the very ends of my	whiskers!"
T1	115:24	which the Queen replied "You haven't got any	whiskers."
T8	188:10	But I was thinking of a plan / To dye one's	whiskers	green, / And always use so large a fan / That they
A1	9:26	say, as it turned a corner, "Oh my ears and	whiskers,	how late it's getting!" She was close behind it when
A4	27: 4	The Duchess! Oh my dear paws! Oh my fur and	whiskers!	She'll get me executed, as sure as ferrets are

WHISPER (11)
A7   57: 3   it was," the March Hare said to itself in a whisper.)
T7   172: 7   "Hay, then," the King murmured in a faint whisper.
T9   199: 1   is it, now?" the Frog said in a deep hoarse whisper.
A7   57: 1   time to begin lessons: you'd only have to whisper a hint to Time, and round goes the clock in a
T2   121: 4   spoke again, in a timid voice--almost in a whisper. "And can all the flowers talk?"
T7   172:30   "Do you call that a whisper?" cried the poor King, jumping up and shaking himself
T1   113: 9   Red King and the Red Queen," Alice said (in a whisper, for fear of frightening them), "and there are the
A3   24:15   why it is you hate--C and D," she added in a whisper, half afraid that it would be offended again.
T7   172:25   "I'll whisper it," said the Messenger, putting his hands to his
T1   115:20   Queen were talking together in a frightened whisper--so low, that Alice could hardly hear what they said.
T5   149: 8   of way, and kept repeating something in a whisper to herself that sounded like "Bread-and-butter,
WHISPERED (12)
T9   202:31   must support you, you know," the White Queen whispered, as Alice got up to do it, very obediently, but a
T2   122:14   daisies, who were just beginning again, she whispered "If you don't hold your tongues, I'll pick you!"
A8   65:38   scream of laughter. "Oh, hush!" the Rabbit whispered in a frightened tone. "The Queen will hear you! You
T3   131:24   dressed in white paper leaned forwards and whispered in her ear, "Never mind what they all say, my dear,
T9   202:34   "Thank you very much," she whispered in reply, "but I can do quite well without."
A11   86:31   putting down their names," the Gryphon whispered in reply, "for fear they should forget them before
T7   175:37   and beckoned to Haigha. "Open the bag!" he whispered. "Quick! Not that one--that's full of hay!"
A8   65:31   tiptoe, put his mouth close to her ear, and whispered "She's under sentence of execution."
A9   70:34   "Somebody said," Alice whispered, "that it's done by everybody minding their own
T7   173:24   finished his tea when he was sent in," Haigha whispered to Alice: "and they only give them oyster-shells in
A11   86:29   on slates. "What are they doing?" Alice whispered to the Gryphon. "They ca'n't have anything to put
T9   194:35   "So do I," the White Queen whispered: "we'll often say it over together, dear. And I'll
WHISPERING (1)
T7   172:28   to hear the news too. However, instead of whispering, he simply shouted, at the top of his voice,
WHISPERS (1)
A4   30:14   silence after this, and Alice could only hear whispers now and then; such as "Sure, I don't like it, yer
WHISTLE (2)
T5   152: 6   Her screams were so exactly like the whistle of a steam-engine, that Alice had to hold both her
A4   32:30   in a coaxing tone, and she tried hard to whistle to it; but she was terribly frightened all the time at
WHISTLING (3)
A6   46:42   you like," said the Footman, and began whistling.
T2   127: 3   ran on for a time in silence, with the wind whistling in Alice's ears, and almost blowing her hair off her
T6   166: 7   is something between bellowing and whistling, with a kind of sneeze in the middle: however,
WHITE (99)
T2   122:17   and several of the pink daisies turned white.
T7   174:15   set to work at once, carrying round trays of white and brown bread. Alice took a piece to taste, but it was
T8W   15: 6   treacle. The banks of the lake were blue and white, and looked like china. While tasting the treacle, they
A5   37: 2   man said, / "And your hair has become very white; / And yet you incessantly stand on your head--/ Do you
T7   174: 8   "Then I suppose they'll soon bring the white bread and the brown?" Alice ventured to remark.
T7   173: 3   Unicorn all round the town. / Some gave them white bread, some gave them brown: / Some gave them plum-cake
A8   62: 2   of the garden: the roses growing on it were white, but there were three gardeners at it, busily painting
T6   166:23   "In winter, when the fields are white, / I sing this song for your delight--
A4   27: 7   it was looking for the fan and the pair of white kid-gloves, and she very good-naturedly began hunting
A2   15:34   the Rabbit started violently, dropped the white kid-gloves and the fan, and scurried away into the
A2   15:27   returning, splendidly dressed, with a pair of white kid-gloves in one hand and a large fan in the other: he
A4   27:38   hoped) a fan and two or three pairs of tiny white kid-gloves: she took up the fan and a pair of the gloves
A2   18: 2   she had put on one of the Rabbit's little white kid-gloves while she was talking. "How can I have done
T6   162:30   one, as you say. It's a present from the White King and Queen. There now!"
T1   113: 9   fear of frightening them), "and there are the White King and the White Queen sitting on the edge of the
T1   114:18   Alice watched the White King as he slowly struggled up from bar to bar, till at
T1   116: 2   on the table, and while she sat watching the White King (for she was still a little anxious about him, and
T7   170: 4   wood into an open place, where she found the White King seated on the ground, busily writing in his
T1   114:11   her breath a little, she called out to the White King, who was sitting sulkily among the ashes, "Mind the
T1   107: 2   the black kitten's fault entirely. For the white kitten had been having its face washed by the old cat
T1   107: 1   One thing was certain, that the white kitten had had nothing to do with it--it was the black
T1   107:10   now, as I said, she was hard at work on the white kitten, which was lying quite still and trying to purr--
T12   207:27   she went on, looking over her shoulder at the White Kitten, which was still patiently undergoing its toilet,
T8   180:15   was a glorious victory, wasn't it?" said the White Knight, as he came up panting.
T8   185: 4   was, before I could get out again, the other White Knight came and put it on. He thought it was his own
T8   179:23   This time it was a White Knight. He drew up at Alice's side, and tumbled off his
T8   181: 4   when you've crossed the next brook," said the White Knight. "I'll see you safe to the end of the wood--and
T1   115:40   over the book (in which Alice had put 'The White Knight is sliding down the poker. He balances very
T8   179:34   observe the Rules of Battle, of course?" the White Knight remarked, putting on his helmet too.
T8   179:29   "Yes, but then I came and rescued her!" the White Knight replied.
T12   207:28   "when will Dinah have finished with your White Majesty, I wonder? That must be the reason you were so
T9   201:36   putting her mouth close to Alice's ear, "her White Majesty knows a lovely riddle--all in poetry--all about
A8   63: 7   to have been a red rose-tree, and we put a white one in by mistake; and, if the Queen was to find out, we
T3   131:23   But the gentleman dressed in white paper leaned forwards and whispered in her ear, "Never
T3   130:22   sitting opposite to her, (he was dressed in white paper), "ought to know which way she's going, even if
T1   113:16   turn her head just in time to see one of the White Pawns roll over and begin kicking: she watched it with
T5   149:12   began rather timidly: "Am I addressing the White Queen?"
T9   197: 7   over, we'll go to the ball--/ Red Queen, and White Queen, and Alice and all!
T9   199:27   be, / Come and dine with the Red Queen, the White Queen, and me!'"
T9   199:40   and tea / Along with the Red Queen, the White Queen, and me!"
T9   194:42   "Where do you pick the flower?" the White Queen asked: "In a garden or in the hedges?"
T9   193:24   "Can you do Addition?" the White Queen asked. "What's one and one and one and one and one
T9   196:11   Here the White Queen began again. "It was such a thunderstorm, you

WHITE (cont.)
T9	204: 3	turned to see what was the matter with the	White	Queen; but, instead of the Queen, there was the leg of
T5	149: 2	about for the owner: in another moment the	White	Queen came running wildly through the wood, with both
T9	194: 5	"She can't do Subtraction," said the	White	Queen. "Can you do Division? Divide a loaf by a knife--
T1	113:19	"It is the voice of my child!" the	White	Queen cried out, as she rushed past the King, so
T9	194:28	do sums?" Alice said, turning suddenly on the	White	Queen, for she didn't like being found fault with so
T9	196:34	The	White	Queen gave a deep sigh, and laid her head on Alice's
T9	193:14	Red Queen broke the silence by saying, to the	White	Queen, "I invite you to Alice's dinner-party this
T9	202: 1	The	White	Queen laughed with delight, and stroked Alice's cheek.
T9	196:25	The	White	Queen looked timidly at Alice, who felt she ought to say
T9	192:33	she said a great deal more than that!" the	White	Queen moaned, wringing her hands. "Oh, ever so much more
T9	201:38	Red Majesty's very kind to mention it," the	White	Queen murmured into Alice's other ear, in a voice like
T5	149: 7	The	White	Queen only looked at her in a helpless frightened sort
T12	207:30	Dinah! Do you know that you're scrubbing a	White	Queen? Really, it's most disrespectful of you!
T7	174:22	she cried, pointing eagerly. "There's the	White	Queen running across the country! She came flying out of
T9	195:17	"Don't let us quarrel," the	White	Queen said in an anxious tone. "What is the cause of
T9	195:25	"Which reminds me--" the	White	Queen said, looking down and nervously clasping and
T9	203: 7	"Take care of yourself!" screamed the	White	Queen, seizing Alice's hair with both her hands.
T9	192:12	surprised at finding the Red Queen and the	White	Queen sitting close to her, one on each side: she would
T1	113:10	them), "and there are the White King and the	White	Queen sitting on the edge of the shovel--and here are
T9	193:16	The	White	Queen smiled feebly, and said "And I invite you."
T9	193:10	"She's in that state of mind," said the	White	Queen, "that she wants to deny something--only she
T9	196: 4	"He said he would come in," the	White	Queen went on, "because he was looking for a
T9	195:44	"Humpty Dumpty saw it too," the	White	Queen went on in a low voice, more as if she were
T9	202:31	"We must support you, you know," the	White	Queen whispered, as Alice got up to do it, very
T9	194:35	"So do I," the	White	Queen whispered: "we'll often say it over together, dear
T9	195: 1	"How many acres of ground?" said the	White	Queen. "You mustn't leave out so many things."
T9	196:22	Red Queen said to Alice, taking one of the	White	Queen's hands in her own, and gently stroking it: "she
T2	126: 8	said "That's easily managed. You can be the	White	Queen's Pawn, if you like, as Lily's too young to play:
T9	200:15	chairs at the head of the table: the Red and	White	Queens had already taken two of them, but the middle one
T1	109:12	then it covers them up snug, you know, with a	white	quilt; and perhaps it says 'Go to sleep, darlings, till
A12	94:17	"No, they're not," said the	White	Rabbit, "and that's the queerest thing about it." (The
A11	91:29	Alice watched the	White	Rabbit as he fumbled over the list, feeling very curious
A11	87:14	On this the	White	Rabbit blew three blasts on the trumpet, and then
A11	88: 4	the first witness," said the King; and the	White	Rabbit blew three blasts on the trumpet, and called out
A12	94: 7	"I haven't opened it yet," said the	White	Rabbit; "but it seems to be a letter, written by the
A11	86:34	but she stopped herself hastily, for the	White	Rabbit cried out "Silence in the court!", and the King
A12	98:24	The long grass rustled at her feet as the	White	Rabbit hurried by--the frightened Mouse splashed his way
A12	94:12	"It isn't directed at all," said the	White	Rabbit: "in fact, there's nothing written on the outside
A12	93:23	to write this down on their slates, when the	White	Rabbit interrupted: "Unimportant, your Majesty means, of
A8	63:22	Queens, and among them Alice recognized the	White	Rabbit: it was talking in a hurried nervous manner,
A12	94: 4	to come yet, please your Majesty," said the	White	Rabbit, jumping up in a great hurry: "this paper has
A12	94:33	The	White	Rabbit put on his spectacles. "Where shall I begin,
A11	91:32	to herself. Imagine her surprise, when the	White	Rabbit read out, at the top of his shrill little voice,
A12	94:37	was dead silence in the court, whilst the	White	Rabbit read out these verses:--
A2	15:27	her eyes to see what was coming. It was the	White	Rabbit returning, splendidly dressed, with a pair of
A10	82: 2	from the time when she first saw the	White	Rabbit. She was a little nervous about it, just at first
A4	27: 1	It was the	White	Rabbit, trotting slowly back again, and looking
A1	9:23	before her was another long passage, and the	White	Rabbit was still in sight, hurrying down it. There was
A11	91:11	The King looked anxiously at the	White	Rabbit, who said, in a low voice, "Your Majesty must
A8	65:26	voice at her side. She was walking by the	White	Rabbit, who was peeping anxiously into her face.
A11	86: 5	side to guard him; and near the King was the	White	Rabbit, with a trumpet in one hand, and a scroll of
A1	7: 9	up and picking the daisies, when suddenly a	White	Rabbit with pink eyes ran close by her.
T3	131: 3	that was sitting next to the gentleman in	white,	shut his eyes and said in a loud voice, "She ought to
T8W	14:22	the Pantry, and have found five new lumps of	white	sugar large and in fine condition. In coming back--"
T4	146:15	he pointed with a trembling finger at a small	white	thing lying under the tree.
T4	146:17	after a careful examination of the little	white	thing. "Not a rattle-snake you know," she added hastily

WHITER (1)
| T8 | 190: 2 | mild, whose speech was slow, / Whose hair was | whiter | than the snow, / Whose face was very like a crow, / |

WHITING (8)
A10	80:15	"and I do so like that curious song about the	whiting!"
A10	81:11	the Gryphon. "Do you know why it's called a	whiting?"
A10	81: 9	interesting. I never knew so much about a	whiting before."
A10	80: 4	gave a look askance--/ Said he thanked the	whiting	kindly, but he would not join the dance. / Would not,
A10	81:22	went on in a deep voice, "are done with	whiting. Now you know."
A10	81:27	"If I'd been the	whiting,"	said Alice, whose thoughts were still running on the
A10	80:16	"Oh, as to the	whiting,"	said the Mock Turtle, "they--you've seen them, of
A10	79:13	"Will you walk a little faster?" said a	whiting	to a snail, / "There's a porpoise close behind us, and

WHO (92) [entries omitted]
WHOEVER (1)
| A5 | 44: 2 | a little house in it about four feet high. " | Whoever | lives there," thought Alice, "it'll never do to come |

WHOLE (18)
A3	25:47	be jury, said cunning old Fury: 'I'll try the	whole	cause, and condemn you to death.'
A11	91:22	For some minutes the	whole	court was in confusion, getting the Dormouse turned out,
T7	169: 3	in such crowds that they seemed to fill the	whole	forest. Alice got behind a tree, for fear of being run
A8	67:18	at least one of them." In another minute the	whole	head appeared, and then Alice put down her flamingo, and
T6	163:40	but not verbs--however, I can manage the	whole	lot of them! Impenetrability! That's what I say!"
A11	86: 3	of little birds and beasts, as well as the	whole	pack of cards: the Knave was standing before them, in
A12	97: 9	At this the	whole	pack rose up into the air, and came flying down upon her
A3	23:24	pointing to Alice with one finger; and the	whole	party at once crowded round her, calling out, in a

WHOLE (cont.)
```
A8    69: 4  (It was this last remark that had made the whole party look so grave and anxious.)
A2    20:24  curious creatures. Alice led the way, and the whole party swam to the shore.
A12   98:22  as she listened, or seemed to listen, the whole place around her became alive with the strange creatures
T8   187:18  clearly. Years afterwards she could bring the whole scene back again, as if it had been only yesterday--the
T8   180: 7  noise they make when they tumble! Just like a whole set of fire-irons falling into the fender! And how quiet
A9    74: 5  like the look of the creature, but on the whole she thought it would be quite as safe to stay with it as
A10   83: 8  said; but she was dreadfully puzzled by the whole thing, and longed to change the subject.
A3    24: 5                             Alice thought the whole thing very absurd, but they all looked so grave that she
T2   127:13  I do believe we've been under this tree the whole time! Everything's just as it was!"
A4    30: 9  Who ever saw one that size? Why, it fills the whole window!"
```
WHOM (3) [entries omitted]
WHO'S (3)
```
T6   166:10  once heard it, you'll be quite content. Who's been repeating all that hard stuff to you?"
A7    59:16                             "Who's making personal remarks now?" the Hatter asked
A4    30:31  "Now, who did that?--It was Bill, I fancy--Who's to go down the chimney?--Nay, I sha'n't! You do it!--
```
WHOSE (9) [entries omitted]
WHY (82)
```
A10   81:12  "I never thought about it," said Alice. "Why?"
T2   122:25    said the Tiger-lily. "Then you'll know why."
T4   145: 4                         "Why, about you!" Tweedledee exclaimed, clapping his hands
T2   123:23                         "Why, all round her head, of course," the Rose replied. "I was
T6   160:13                         "Why, because there's nobody with me!" cried Humpty Dumpty.
A7    59: 8  it puzzled her too much: so she went on: "But why did they live at the bottom of a well?"
A7    59:20  to the Dormouse, and repeated her question. "Why did they live at the bottom of a well?"
A9    75: 1                         "Why did you call him Tortoise, if he wasn't one?" Alice asked.
T2   124:12  "all the ways about here belong to me--but why did you come out here at all?" she added in a kinder tone.
T3   132:38  the people that name them, I suppose. If not, why do things have names at all?"
A3    25: 2  down with wonder at the Mouse's tail; "but why do you call it sad?" And she kept on puzzling about it
T5   155:36                         "Why do you say 'Feather' so often?" Alice asked at last,
T6   160:11                         "Why do you sit out here all alone?" said Alice, not wishing to
T3   135:11                         "Why do you wish I had made it?" Alice asked. "It's a very bad
T3   131:33  "If you're so anxious to have a joke made, why don't you make one yourself?"
T5   152:23                         "But why don't you scream now?" Alice asked, holding her hands
T9   192:24        "Ridiculous!" cried the Queen. "Why, don't you see, child--" here she broke off with a frown,
T3   130: 1    Alice) "Don't keep him waiting, child! Why, his time is worth a thousand pounds a minute!"
T7   176:21                         "Why, I beat you all round the town, you chicken!" the Lion
T8   181:28  hung it carefully on a tree. "Can you guess why I did that?" he said to Alice.
T4   148:20  that is!" she said. "And how fast it comes! Why, I do believe it's got wings!"
T2   127:12  Alice looked round her in great surprise. "Why, I do believe we've been under this tree the whole time!
A5    37: 8  now that I'm perfectly sure I have none, / Why, I do it again and again."
A9    71: 5          "I dare say you're wondering why I don't put my arm round your waist," the Duchess said,
A4    30:25  out the words: "Where's the other ladder?--Why, I hadn't to bring but one. Bill's got the other--Bill!
A5    42:40  on the look-out for serpents, night and day! Why, I haven't had a wink of sleep these three weeks!"
A5    44: 3  "it'll never do to come upon them this size: why, I should frighten them out of their wits!" So she began
A1     8:25  How brave they'll all think me at home! Why, I wouldn't say anything about it, even if I fell off the
A10   81:33  "Of course not," said the Mock Turtle. "Why, if a fish came to me, and told me he was going a journey,
T6   160:21  growled out. "Of course I don't think so! Why, if ever I did fall off--which there's no chance of--but
A7    55:12  wide on hearing this; but all he said was "Why is a raven like a writing-desk?"
A4    30: 8  arm, you goose! Who ever saw one that size? Why, it fills the whole window!"
A2    20:19  tell you my history, and you'll understand why it is I hate cats and dogs."
A3    24:15  me your history, you know," said Alice, "and why it is you hate--C and D," she added in a whisper, half
T5   158:17                         "I wonder why it wouldn't do?" thought Alice, as she groped her way
T1   116:14  but at last a bright thought struck her. "Why, it's a Looking-glass book, of course! And, if I hold it
T7   170:18  able to see Nobody! And at that distance too! Why, it's as much as I can do to see real people, by this
A10   81:11  if you like," said the Gryphon. "Do you know why it's called a whiting?"
T5   158:20  walk towards it. Let me see, is this a chair? Why, it's got branches, I declare! How very odd to find trees
T1   111: 9  soft like gauze, so that we can get through. Why, it's turning into a sort of mist now, I declare! It'll be
T2   122: 5  It says 'Boughwough!'" cried a Daisy. "That's why its branches are called boughs!"
T5   152:25                         "Why, I've done all the screaming already," said the Queen.
T9   194:18                         "Why, look here!" the Red Queen cried. "The dog would lose its
A4    27:13  and called out to her, in an angry tone, "Why, Mary Ann, what are you doing out here? Run home this
A7    60:18                         "Why not?" said the March Hare.
T7   171: 4  meant that I didn't understand," said Alice. "Why one to come and one to go?"
A6    47:15  Cheshire-Cat," said the Duchess, "and that's why. Pig!"
A5    36:14                         "Why?" said the Caterpillar.
A3    23: 5                         "Why," said the Dodo, "the best way to explain it is to do it."
A10   78:14                         "Why," said the Gryphon, "you first form into a line along the
A3    23:23                         "Why, she, of course," said the Dodo, pointing to Alice with
A9    74:11                         "Why, she," said the Gryphon. "It's all her fancy that: they
A3    26:29  oh, I wish you could see her after the birds! Why, she'll eat a little bird as soon as look at it!"
A7    56:14                         "Why should it?" muttered the Hatter. "Does your watch tell you
T5   153:14  age, I always did it for half-an-hour a day. Why, sometimes I've believed as many as six impossible things
A12   96: 6  indeed!--'I gave her one, they gave him two'--why, that must be what he did with the tarts, you know--"
A8    63: 6  looked at Two. Two began, in a low voice, "Why, the fact is, you see, Miss, this here ought to have been
T7   172:36                         "Why the Lion and the Unicorn, of course," said the King.
T9   201:15        However, she didn't see why the Red Queen should be the only one to give orders; so,
T4   142:23  sealing wax--/ Of cabbages--and kings--/ And why the sea is boiling hot--/ And whether pigs have wings.'
T3   130: 8  went on with "The man that drives the engine. Why, the smoke alone is worth a thousand pounds a puff!"
A5    43:19    it," said the Pigeon; "but if they do, why, then they're a kind of serpent: that's all I can say."
```

WHY (cont.)
```
A12    96:12                                                    "Why, there they are!" said the King triumphantly, pointing to
A1     12:29   poor Alice, "to pretend to be two people! Why, there's hardly enough of me left to make one respectable
A4     29:14   herself. "How can you learn lessons in here? Why, there's hardly room for you, and no room at all for any
T8W    19:15   hoot at me and call me 'Pig!' / And that is why they do it, dear, / Because I wear a yellow wig."
A4     30:36   the chimney, has he?" said Alice to herself. "Why, they seem to put everything upon Bill! I wouldn't be in
A8     63:41   very politely; but she added, to herself, "Why, they're only a pack of cards, after all. I needn't be
T9    201:32   was about fishes in some way. Do you know why they're so fond of fishes, all about here?"
T3    136: 1   I wonder? I do believe it's got no name--why, to be sure it hasn't!"
T2    127: 1         "Nearly there!" the Queen repeated. "Why, we passed it ten minutes ago! Faster!" And they ran on
A12    98: 4   "Wake up, Alice dear!" said her sister. "Why, what a long sleep you've had!"
T6    167:10          The fishes answered, with a grin, / 'Why, what a temper you are in!'
T3    129: 6   think it's got any name. Principal towns--why, what are those creatures, making honey down there? They
A10    81:17                                                    "Why, what are your shoes done with?" said the Gryphon. "I mean
A7     60:17                                                    "Why with an M?" said Alice.
A8     63: 3   me, please," said Alice, a little timidly, "why you are painting those roses?"
A12    94:30   prove anything of the sort!" said Alice. "Why, you don't even know what they're about!"
A7     55:23   "Not the same thing a bit!" said the Hatter. "Why, you might just as well say that 'I see what I eat' is the
T1    114:19   up from bar to bar, till at last she said "Why, you'll be hours and hours getting to the table, at that
A6     47:14   it was good manners for her to speak first, "why your cat grins like that?"
T4    145: 9   retorted contemptuously. "You'd be nowhere. Why, you're only a sort of thing in his dream!"
```
WICKED (2)
```
T1    107:20                                                    "Oh, you wicked, wicked little thing!" cried Alice, catching up the kitten, and
T1    107:20                                                        "Oh, you wicked, wicked little thing!" cried Alice, catching up the
```
WIDE (6)
```
T5    149: 3     the wood, with both arms stretched out wide, as if she were flying, and Alice very civilly went to
A10    82: 4   and opened their eyes and mouths so very wide; but she gained courage as she went on. Her listeners
T9    201:34   to the Red Queen, whose answer was a little wide of the mark. "As to fishes," she said, very slowly and
A7     55:11          The Hatter opened his eyes very wide on hearing this; but all he said was "Why is a raven like
T1    115:12   hardly hold you! And don't keep your mouth so wide open! All the ashes will get into it--there, now I think
T1    111: 3   if you leave the door of our drawing-room wide open: and it's very like our passage as far as you can
```
WIDER (2)
```
A6     51: 6   the name: however, it only grinned a little wider. "Come, it's pleased so far," thought Alice, and she
T2    124:19    at her watch: "open your mouth a little wider when you speak, and always say 'your Majesty.'"
```
WIFE (2)
```
A5     39: 6   to the law, / And argued each case with my wife, / And the muscular strength, which it gave to my jaw /
T12   208:10   too! Was it the Red King, Kitty? You were his wife, my dear, so you ought to know--Oh, Kitty, do help to
```
WIG (13)
```
A11    86:16   she said to herself, "because of his great wig."
T8W    19:16   they do it, dear, / Because I wear a yellow wig."
T8W    16: 5                                     "Along of the wig?" Alice repeated, quite pleased to find that he was
T8W    21: 3   head is nice and round." He took off his own wig as he spoke, and stetched out one claw towards Alice, as
T8W    20: 4                                     "Your wig fits very well," the Wasp murmured, looking at her with an
T8W    20: 2   Alice said heartily: "and I think if your wig fitted a little better, they wouldn't tease you quite so
T8W    19:11   all my hair is nearly gone, / They take my wig from me and say / 'How can you put such rubbish on?'
T8W    17:10    as he spoke, and Alice looked at his wig in great surprise. It was bright yellow like the
T8W    18:16   'You should be shaved, / And wear a yellow wig instead.'
T8W    16: 7          "You'd be cross too, if you'd a wig like mine," the Wasp went on. "They jokes at one. And they
A11    86:18   the King; and, as he wore his crown over the wig (look at the frontispiece if you want to see how he did
T8W    17:12   like a heap of sea-weed. "You could make your wig much neater," she said, "if only you had a comb."
T8W    16: 3          "It's all along of the wig," the Wasp said in a much gentler voice.
```
WIG'S (1)
```
T8W    18: 2   explained. "It's to comb hair with--your wig's so very rough, you know."
```
WILD (4)
```
AI     3:22            moving through a land / Of wonders wild and new, / In friendly chat with bird or beast--/ And
T4    144:25   though she feared it was more likely to be a wild beast. "Are there any lions or tigers about here?" she
A8     64: 6   and, after glaring at her for a moment like a wild beast, began screaming "Off with her head! Off with--"
A1     10:23   children who had got burnt, and eaten up by wild beasts, and other unpleasant things, all because they
```
WILDERNESS (1)
```
T2    125: 5   gardens, compared with which this would be a wilderness."
```
WILDLY (7)
```
A10    78:32   in the sea!" cried the Mock Turtle, capering wildly about.
T4    146:21   cried Tweedledum, beginning to stamp about wildly and tear his hair. "It's spoilt, of course!" Here he
T5    152:16   the brooch flew open, and the Queen clutched wildly at it, and tried to clasp it again.
T7    171:14   every moment, while the great eyes rolled wildly from side to side.
T5    149: 2   another moment the White Queen came running wildly through the wood, with both arms stretched out wide, as
A8     69:12        so the King and the executioner ran wildly up and down, looking for it, while the rest of the
T1    113:22   My imperial kitten!" and she began scrambling wildly up the side of the fender.
```
WILL (55)
```
T7    178:12   town,'" she thought to herself, "nothing ever will!"
T9    204:27   table, "I'll shake you into a kitten, that I will!"
T1    116:15   And, if I hold it up to a glass, the words will all go the right way again."
T2    120: 5   several sharp corners), "but I suppose it will at last. But how curiously it twists! It's more like a
A2     19: 3    by being drowned in my own tears! That will be a queer thing, to be sure! However, everything is
T6    167: 8                 "I sent to them again to say / 'It will be better to obey.'
T8    186:18   In fact, I don't believe that pudding ever will be cooked! And yet it was a very clever pudding to invent
A6     52:25   before," she said to herself: "the March Hare will be much the most interesting, and perhaps, as this is May
AI     3:16   / In gentler tones Secunda hopes / "There will be nonsense in it!" / While Tertia interrupts the tale /
A4     32:21   my way into that lovely garden. I think that will be the best plan."
A10    80: 1   can really have no notion how delightful it will be / When they take us up and throw us, with the lobsters
```

WILL (cont.)
A4   28:22   "Now I can do no more, whatever happens. What will become of me?"
A1   11: 1   taught them: such as, that a red-hot poker will burn you if you hold it too long; and that, if you cut
T8W   13:13   very edge. "If I once jump over, everything will change, and then I can't help him."
T5   152:15   the poor Queen groaned out: "the brooch will come undone directly. Oh, oh!" As she said the words the
T12 207:28   still patiently undergoing its toilet, "when will Dinah have finished with your White Majesty, I wonder?
A4   31:34   Alice thought to herself "I wonder what they will do next! If they had any sense, they'd take the roof off
A4   31:40   and Alice heard the Rabbit say "A barrowful will do, to begin with."
T1   115:12   keep your mouth so wide open! All the ashes will get into it--there, now I think you're tidy enough!" she
A8   65:39   whispered in a frightened tone. "The Queen will hear you! You see she came rather late, and the Queen
T8   189: 5   'By which I get my wealth--/ And very gladly will I drink / Your Honour's noble health.'
T6   166:36   "I will, if I can remember it so long," said Alice.
A11   90:13   the court. (As that is rather a hard word, I will just explain to you how it was done. They had a large
A2   15: 6   to one's own feet! And how odd the directions will look!
A5   41:28   will make you grow taller, and the other side will make you grow shorter."
A5   41:27   merely remarking, as it went, "One side will make you grow taller, and the other side will make you
T9   202: 8   'Now cook me the fish!' / That is easy, and will not take more than a minute. / 'Let it lie in a dish!' /
T8   179:34   "You will observe the Rules of Battle, of course?" the White Knight
T5   149:17   so she smiled and said "If your Majesty will only tell me the right way to begin, I'll do it as well
A3   25:11   met in the house, 'Let us both go to law: I will prosecute you.--Come, I'll take no denial: We must have
T8   188:40   / But for a copper halfpenny, / And that will purchase nine.
A2   14: 6   off). "Oh, my poor little feet, I wonder who will put on your shoes and stockings for you now, dears? I'm
T3   136: 4   has happened, after all! And now, who am I? I will remember, if I can! I'm determined to do it!" But being
T2   128:19   is all forest--however, one of the Knights will show you the way--and in the Eighth Square we shall be
A5   36: 3   when you have to turn into a chrysalis--you will some day, you know--and then after that into a butterfly,
TI   103: 5   / Are half a life asunder, / Thy loving smile will surely hail / The love-gift of a fairy-tale.
A9   71: 1   is--'Take care of the sense, and the sounds will take care of themselves.'"
A10   82:27   sands are all dry, he is gay as a lark, / And will talk in contemptuous tones of the Shark / But, when the
A3   23: 7   to try the thing yourself some winter-day, I will tell you how the Dodo managed it.)
A4   30:29   Here, Bill! Catch hold of this rope--Will the roof bear?--Mind that loose slate--Oh, it's coming
T1   115:27   "You will, though," the Queen said, "if you don't make a memorandum
T8   181: 3   "So you will, when you've crossed the next brook," said the White
A10   79:16   advance! / They are waiting on the shingle--will you come and join the dance? / Will you, wo'n't you, will
A10   79:17   / Will you, wo'n't you, will you, wo'n't you, will you join the dance? / Will you, wo'n't you, will you,
A10   80:11   / Will you, wo'n't you, will you, wo'n't you, will you join the dance? / Will you, wo'n't you, will you,
A10   84:14   for tastes! Sing her 'Turtle Soup,' will you, old fellow?"
A10   79:13   "Will you walk a little faster?" said a whiting to a snail, /
A10   79:17   and join the dance? / Will you, wo'n't you, will you, wo'n't you, will you join the dance? / Will you,
A10   80:11   and join the dance. / Will you, wo'n't you, will you, wo'n't you, will you join the dance? / Will you,
A10   79:17   shingle--will you come and join the dance? / Will you, wo'n't you, will you, wo'n't you, will you join the
A10   79:18   you, wo'n't you, will you join the dance? / Will you, wo'n't you, will you, wo'n't you, wo'n't you join
A10   80:11   beloved snail, but come and join the dance. / Will you, wo'n't you, will you, wo'n't you, will you join the
A10   80:12   you, wo'n't you, will you join the dance? / Will you, wo'n't you, will you, wo'n't you, wo'n't you join
A10   79:18   you join the dance? / Will you, wo'n't you, will you, wo'n't you, wo'n't you join the dance?
A10   80:12   you join the dance? / Will you, wo'n't you, will you, wo'n't you, wo'n't you join the dance?"
WILLIAM (7)
A3   22:22   advisable to go with Edgar Atheling to meet William and offer him the crown. William's conduct at first
A5   37: 5   "In my youth," Father William replied to his son, / "I feared it might injure the
A5   36:36   "Repeat 'You are old, Father William,'" said the Caterpillar.
A2   19:22   I daresay it's a French mouse, come over with William the Conqueror." (For, with all her knowledge of
A3   22: 3   I know. Silence all round, if you please! 'William the Conqueror, whose cause was favoured by the pope,
A5   37: 1   "You are old, Father William," the young man said, / "And your hair has become very
A10   82: 6   part about her repeating "You are old Father William," to the Caterpillar, and the words all coming
WILLIAM'S (1)
A3   22:23   to meet William and offer him the crown. William's conduct at first was moderate. But the insolence of
WILLING (2)
TC   209:14   yet, the tale to hear, / Eager eye and willing ear, / Lovingly shall nestle near.
TC   209: 5   three that nestle near, / Eager eye and willing ear, / Pleased a simple tale to hear--
-WILLINGLY [See UNWILLINGLY]
WILLOW-TREE (1)
T2   120:28   flowerbed, with a border of daisies, and a willow-tree growing in the middle.
WILT (1)
TI   103:11   life's hereafter--/ Enough that now thou wilt not fail / To listen to my fairy-tale.
WIN (2)
T7   176:19   "I should win easy," said the Lion.
A8   67:34   her, listening: so she went on "--likely to win, that it's hardly worth while finishing the game."
WIND (9)
A12   98:37   the grass would be only rustling in the wind, and the pool rippling to the waving of the reeds--the
A1   9:25   a moment to be lost: away went Alice like the wind, and was just in time to hear it say, as it turned a
T5   153:18   undone as she spoke, and a sudden gust of wind blew the Queen's shawl across a little brook. The Queen
T1   109:15   all in green, and dance about--whenever the wind blows--oh, that's very pretty!" cried Alice, dropping the
T2   120:31   one that was waving gracefully about in the wind, "I wish you could talk!"
T8   182:25   enough," he said, anxiously. "You see the wind is so very strong here. It's as strong as soup."
T8W   14:10   to the other side? You'll be out of the cold wind there."
T1   107:16   the ball of worsted Alice had been trying to wind up, and had been rolling it up and down till it had all
T2   127: 3   they ran on for a time in silence, with the wind whistling in Alice's ears, and almost blowing her hair
WINDING (2)
T1   108: 8   knee, pretending to watch the progress of the winding, and now and then putting out one paw and gently
T1   108: 4   kitten and the worsted with her, and began winding up the ball again. But she didn't get on very fast, as

WINDOW (13)
```
A4    29:29  itself "Then I'll go round and get in at the window."
A4    30: 6    "Now tell me, Pat, what's that in the window?"
A4    30: 9  saw one that size? Why, it fills the whole window!"
A4    27:37  into a tidy little room with a table in the window, and on it (as she had hoped) a fan and two or three
A4    28:20  a last resource, she put one arm out of the window, and one foot up the chimney, and said to herself "Now
T1   108:23  had been doing, I was very nearly opening the window, and putting you out into the snow! And you'd have
A4    32: 2  of little pebbles came rattling in at the window, and some of them hit her in the face. "I'll put a stop
T3   130:21  traveling the wrong way," and shut up the window, and went away. "So young a child," said the gentleman
A4    30:20  they'll do next! As for pulling me out of the window I only wish they could! I'm sure I don't want to stay
T3   129:34  said the Guard, putting his head in at the window. In a moment everybody was holding out a ticket: they
T3   132: 5  The Horse, who had put his head out of the window, quietly drew it in and said "It's only a brook we have
A4    29:33  fancied she heard the Rabbit just under the window, she suddenly spread out her hand, and made a snatch in
T1   108:12  "You'd have guessed if you'd been up in the window with me--only Dinah was making you tidy, so you
```
WINDOW-PANES (1)
```
T1   109: 9           "Do you hear the snow against the window-panes, Kitty? How nice and soft it sounds! I wonder if
```
-WIND'S [See STORM-WIND'S]
WINE (5)
```
T9   200: 3  / Mix sand with the cider, and wool with the wine--/ And welcome Queen Alice with ninety-times-nine!"
T9   202:25  others upset the decanters, and drank the wine as it ran off the edges of the table--and three of them
T8   189:10  the Menai bridge from rust / By boiling it in wine. / I thanked him much for telling me / The way he got his
A7    54:15  was nothing on it but tea. "I don't see any wine," she remarked.
A7    54:12           "Have some wine," the March Hare said in an encouraging tone.
```
WINGS (8)
```
A5    42:26  face, and was beating her violently with its wings.
T3   132:19  just over her head, and fanning her with its wings.
T4   142:24  sea is boiling hot--/ And whether pigs have wings.'
T4   148:20  how fast it comes! Why, I do believe it's got wings!"
T9   203:19  of plates, which they hastily fitted on as wings, and so, with forks for legs, went fluttering about in
T3   134:10  "you may observe a Bread-and-butter-fly. Its wings are thin slices of bread-and-butter, its body is a crust
T3   133:14    Its body is made of plum-pudding, its wings of holly-leaves, and its head is a raisin burning in
T4   145:27  the trees. But I wish it wouldn't flap its wings so--it makes quite a hurricane in the wood--here's
```
WINK (3)
```
T8   189: 3  Hansom-cabs. / And that's the way' (he gave a wink) / 'By which I get my wealth--/ And very gladly will I
A5    42:40  serpents, night and day! Why, I haven't had a wink of sleep these three weeks!"
A2    19:19  rather inquisitively, and seemed to her to wink with one of its little eyes, but it said nothing.
```
WINKED (1)
```
T4   140:21  But never a word he said: / The eldest Oyster winked his eye, / And shook his heavy head--/ Meaning to say
```
WINS (1)
```
T7   173: 5           "Does--the one--that wins--get the crown?" she asked, as well as she could, for the
```
WINTER (3)
```
T9   195:33  two or three at a time, and sometimes in the winter we take as many as five nights together--for warmth,
T6   166:23           "In winter, when the fields are white, / I sing this song for your
T1   110:36  so much to know whether they've a fire in the winter: you never can tell, you know, unless our fire smokes,
```
WINTER-DAY (1)
```
A3    23: 6  you might like to try the thing yourself some winter-day, I will tell you how the Dodo managed it.)
```
WISE (3)
```
T3   135:36  they wouldn't answer at all, if they were wise."
A10   81:31  him with them," the Mock Turtle said. "No wise fish would go anywhere without a porpoise."
A1    10:19  was all very well to say "Drink me," but the wise little Alice was not going to do that in a hurry. "No,
```
-WISELY [See UNWISELY]
WISH (40)
```
T6   166:40  to the fish: / I told them 'This is what I wish.'
T3   131:28  at all--I was in a wood just now--and I wish I could get back there!"
T5   152:30           "I wish I could manage to be glad!" the Queen said. "Only I never
T1   110:35  bit just behind the fireplace. Oh! I do so wish I could see that bit! I want so much to know whether
A2    19:33  tone: "don't be angry about it. And yet I wish I could show you our cat Dinah. I think you'd take a
A1    10: 8  little use without my shoulders. Oh, how I wish I could shut up like a telescope! I think I could, if I
T1   110:10  Kitty dear, let's pretend--" And here I wish I could tell you half the things Alice used to say,
T3   135:11           "Why do you wish I had made it?" Alice asked. "It's a very bad one."
A3    26:22           "I wish I had our Dinah here, I know I do!" said Alice aloud,
T7   170:17           "I only wish I had such eyes," the King remarked in a fretful tone.
A2    19: 1           "I wish I hadn't cried so much!" said Alice, as she swam about,
A4    28:14  As it is, I ca'n't get out at the door--I do wish I hadn't drunk quite so much!"
A4    29: 1  ordered about by mice and rabbits. I almost wish I hadn't gone down that rabbit-hole--and yet--and yet--
A3    26:37           "I wish I hadn't mentioned Dinah!" she said to herself in a
T3   136:14           "I wish I knew!" thought poor Alice. She answered, rather sadly,
T2   126: 3  at all, you know. Oh, what fun it is! How I wish I was one of them! I wouldn't mind being a Pawn, if only
A6    53:17  it should be raving mad after all! I almost wish I'd gone to see the Hatter instead!"
T5   157: 8  the side of the boat into the dark water. "I wish it hadn't let go--I should so like a little crab to take
A7    57: 3           ("I only wish it was," the March Hare said to itself in a whisper.)
T1   110: 2  of worsted to clap her hands. "And I do so wish it was true! I'm sure the woods look sleepy in the autumn
T4   145:26  to squeeze itself in among the trees. But I wish it wouldn't flap its wings so--it makes quite a hurricane
A9    70:14  that make children sweet-tempered. I only wish people knew that: then they wouldn't be so stingy about
T9   195:16           "I wish Queens never asked questions," Alice thought to herself.
T6   162:19  looked thoroughly offended, and she began to wish she hadn't chosen that subject. "If only I knew," she
T8   189:13  way he got his wealth, / But chiefly for his wish that he / Might drink my noble health.
A4    28:15           Alas! It was too late to wish that! She went on growing, and growing, and very soon had
A5    41:19  a piteous tone. And she thought to herself "I wish the creatures wouldn't be so easily offended!"
T4   148:13           "I wish the monstrous crow would come!" thought Alice.
```

WISH (cont.)

A4	30:20	As for pulling me out of the window, I only wish they could! I'm sure I don't want to stay in here any
A2	17:26	Alice, with a sudden burst of tears, "I do wish they would put their heads down! I am so very tired of
A11	86: 9	made Alice quite hungry to look at them--"I wish they'd get the trial done," she thought, "and hand round
A7	60: 3	Alice did not wish to offend the Dormouse again, so she began very
A3	26:28	catching mice, you ca'n't think! And oh, I wish you could see her after the birds! Why, she'll eat a
T2	120:31	was waving gracefully about in the wind, "I wish you could talk!"
T3	135:10	you'd miss your lessons. That's a joke. I wish you had made it."
A1	9: 8	saucer of milk at tea-time. Dinah, my dear! I wish you were down here with me! There are no mice in the air,
T4	143:23	said nothing but / 'Cut us another slice. / I wish you were not quite so deaf--/ I've had to ask you twice!'
A8	68: 5	who was passing at the moment, "My dear! I wish you would have this cat removed!"
A6	53: 2	"I said 'pig'," replied Alice; "and I wish you wouldn't keep appearing and vanishing so suddenly;
A11	88:39	"I wish you wouldn't squeeze so," said the Dormouse, who was

WISHED (1)

T8W	21: 4	stetched out one claw towards Alice, as if he wished to do the same for her, but she kept out of reach, and

WISHING (1)

T6	160:11	you sit out here all alone?" said Alice, not wishing to begin an argument.

WITH (414) [entries omitted]

WITHER (1)

T2	122:20	begin together, and it's enough to make one wither to hear the way they go on!"

WITHER'D (1)

AI	4: 7	/ In Memory's mystic band. / Like pilgrim's wither'd wreath of flowers / Pluck'd in a far-off land.

WITHIN (5)

A6	46:14	there was a most extraordinary noise going on within--a constant howling and sneezing, and every now and
T6	159: 2	and more and more human: when she had come within a few yards of it, she saw that it had eyes and a nose
A6	48:11	and at once set to work throwing everything within her reach at the Duchess and the baby--the fire-irons
T4	148: 2	"And I hit every thing within reach," cried Tweedledum, "whether I can see it or not!
TI	103:27	snow, / The storm-wind's moody madness--/ Within, the firelight's ruddy glow, / And childhood's nest of

WITHOUT (47)

T9	202:35	whispered in reply, "but I can do quite well without."
A6	53: 8	without a grin," thought Alice; "but a grin without a cat! It's the most curious thing I ever saw in all
T1	109: 5	see--suppose each punishment was to be going without a dinner: then, when the miserable day came, I should
T3	129:20	"It'll never do to go down among them without a good long branch to brush them away--and what fun
A3	23:17	This question the Dodo could not answer without a great deal of thought, and it stood for a long time
A6	53: 7	"Well! I've often seen a cat without a grin," thought Alice; "but a grin without a cat!
A6	47: 9	baby, it was sneezing and howling alternately without a moment's pause. The only two creatures in the
A10	81:31	Turtle said. "No wise fish would go anywhere without a porpoise."
T9	193: 3	What do you suppose is the use of a child without any meaning? Even a joke should have some meaning--and
A5	42:34	and I've tried hedges," the Pigeon went on, without attending to her; "but those serpents! There's no
A6	46:19	sense in your knocking," the Footman went on, without attending to her, "if we had the door between us. For
A7	55: 2	"It wasn't very civil of you to sit down without being invited," said the March Hare.
A8	67: 9	and wondering whether she could get away without being seen, when she noticed a curious appearance in
T8W	16:18	said: "it's when you hold up your head--so--without bending your neck."
A7	59:34	"Treacle," said the Dormouse, without considering at all, this time.
A8	68: 7	great or small. "Off with his head!" she said without even looking round.
T7	174:25	enemy after her, no doubt," the King said, without even looking round. "That wood's full of them."
T1	119: 6	on the hand-rail, and floated gently down without even touching the stairs with her feet: then she
A11	90:32	and the Hatter hurriedly left the court, without even waiting to put his shoes on.
T1	109: 6	the miserable day came, I should have to go without fifty dinners at once! Well, I shouldn't mind that
A4	30:22	She waited for some time without hearing anything more: at last came a rumbling of
A7	60:13	that she let the Dormouse go on for some time without interrupting it.
T3	135: 1	it would be if you could manage to go home without it! For instance, if the governess wanted to call you
A4	27:23	"W. RABBIT" engraved upon it. She went in without knocking, and hurried upstairs, in great fear lest she
A3	21:11	know better." And this Alice would not allow, without knowing how old it was, and as the Lory positively
A10	79: 6	the Mock Turtle to the Gryphon. "We can do it without lobsters, you know. Which shall sing?"
T5	156: 9	'please' to me about 'em," the Sheep said, without looking up from her knitting: "I didn't put 'em there,
A9	70: 9	in my kitchen at all. Soup does very well without--Maybe it's always pepper that makes people
T8	191: 6	"But how can it have got there without my knowing it?" she said to herself, as she lifted it
A1	10: 7	poor Alice, "it would be of very little use without my shoulders. Oh, how I wish I could shut up like a
T6	166:19	"The piece I'm going to repeat," he went on without noticing her remark, "was written entirely for your
A8	63:24	at everything that was said, and went by without noticing her. Then followed the Knave of Hearts,
A7	56:24	shook its head impatiently, and said, without opening its eyes, "Of course, of course: just what I
A1	7: 5	what is the use of a book," thought Alice, "without pictures or conversations?"
T1	115:35	and struggled with the pencil for some time without saying anything; but Alice was too strong for him, and
T8	179:26	sat and looked at each other for some time without speaking. Alice looked from one to the other in some
A5	36:28	hearing. For some minutes it puffed away without speaking; but at last it unfolded its arms, took the
T2	125:19	For some minutes Alice stood without speaking, looking out in all directions over the
T5	153: 6	the Queen remarked. "I can believe it without that. Now I'll give you something to believe. I'm just
TI	103:25	Without, the frost, the blinding snow, / The storm-wind's
T7	170:34	lives on the Hill," the King remarked simply, without the least idea that he was joining in the game, while
T8	181:25	must have fallen out! And the box is no use without them." He unfastened it as he spoke, and was just
T1	109: 7	I shouldn't mind that much! I'd far rather go without them than eat them!
A4	27:17	off at once in the direction it pointed to, without trying to explain the mistake that it had made.
A10	85: 5	taking Alice by the hand, it hurried off, without waiting for the end of the song.
A8	66:20	The players all played at once, without waiting for turns, quarrelling all the while, and
T9	200:11	flowers among them. "I'm glad they've come without waiting to be asked," she thought: "I should never

WITNESS (10)

A11	88: 5	blasts on the trumpet, and called out "First witness!"
A11	91:12	voice, "Your Majesty must cross-examine this witness."
A11	91:26	with an air of great relief. "Call the next witness." And, he added, in an undertone to the Queen, "Really

WITNESS (cont.)
  A11   88:30   This did not seem to encourage the witness at all: he kept shifting from one foot to the other,
  A11   91:27 my dear, you must cross-examine the next witness. It quite makes my forehead ache!"
  A11   91: 4   "Call the next witness!" said the King.
  A11   88: 4   "Call the first witness," said the King; and the White Rabbit blew three
  A11   91: 5   The next witness was the Duchess's cook. She carried the pepper-box in
  A11   88: 6   The first witness was the Hatter. He came in with a teacup in one hand
  A11   91:30 feeling very curious to see what the next witness would be like, "--for they haven't got much evidence
WITS (1)
  A5   44: 4 why, I should frighten them out of their wits!" So she began nibbling at the right-hand bit again, and
WOE (1)
  T8   190: 5 all aglow, / Who seemed distracted with his woe, / Who rocked his body to and fro, / And muttered
WOKE (2)
  T12 207: 3 respectfully, yet with some severity. "You woke me out of oh! such a nice dream! And you've been along
  A7   60:21 doze; but, on being pinched by the Hatter, it woke up again with a little shriek, and went on: "--that
WOMAN (2)
  A12   99: 4 would, in the after-time, be herself a grown woman; and how she would keep, through all her riper years,
  A4   29:10 be a comfort, one way--never to be an old woman--but then--always to have lessons to learn! Oh, I
WON (4)
  A3   23:16 round it, panting, and asking "But who has won?"
  A3   23:21 silence. At last the Dodo said "Everybody has won, and all must have prizes."
  T1   110: 8 a nice check, Kitty, and really I might have won, if it hadn't been for that nasty Knight, that came
  AI   3:19   Anon, to sudden silence won, / In fancy they pursue / The dream-child moving through a
WONDER (34)
  T3   137:15 of these finger-posts ought I to follow, I wonder?"
  A4   27: 5 are ferrets! Where can I have dropped them, I wonder?" Alice guessed in a moment that it was looking for the
  A1   9:11 a mouse, you know. But do cats eat bats, I wonder?" And here Alice began to get rather sleepy, and went
  A5   43:43 beautiful garden--how is that to be done, I wonder?" As she said this, she came suddenly upon an open
  A3   25: 2 certainly," said Alice, looking down with wonder at the Mouse's tail; "but why do you call it sad?" And
  A1   8:28 down. Would the fall never come to an end? "I wonder how many miles I've fallen by this time?" she said
  T2   123: 6 can move about like you," said the Rose. "I wonder how you do it--" ("You're always wondering," said the
  T9   201:22 "What impertinence!" said the Pudding. "I wonder how you'd like it, if I were to cut a slice out of you,
  T3   135:43 of the tree. "What does it call itself, I wonder? I do believe it's got no name--why, to be sure it
  T3   137:26 at last, "that they live in the same house! I wonder I never thought of that before--But I ca'n't stay there
  T2   126:20 went, they never seemed to pass anything. "I wonder if all the things move along with us?" thought poor
  T9   199:34 herself "Thirty times three makes ninety. I wonder if any one's counting?" In a minute there was silence
  A3   26:39 best cat in the world! Oh, my dear Dinah! I wonder if I shall ever see you any more!" And here poor Alice
  A1   8:39   Presently she began again. "I wonder if I shall fall right through the earth! How funny
  A2   15:39 And yesterday things went on just as usual. I wonder if I've changed in the night? Let me think: was I the
  T3   134: 6 head on fire, and had thought to herself, "I wonder if that's the reason insects are so fond of flying into
  T1   109:10   Kitty? How nice and soft it sounds! I wonder if the snow loves the trees and fields, that it kisses
  T1   110:44 like to live in Looking-glass House, Kitty? I wonder if they'd give you milk in there? Perhaps Looking-glass
  A8   67: 7 fond of beheading people here: the great wonder is, that there's any one left alive!"
  T8   180: 1   "I wonder, now, what the Rules of Battle are," she said to
  A4   28:26 of her ever getting out of the room again, no wonder she felt unhappy.
  T12 207:32   "And what did Dinah turn to, I wonder?" she prattled on, as she settled comfortably down,
  T12 207:29 have finished with your White Majesty, I wonder? That must be the reason you were so untidy in my dream
  TI   103: 2 pure unclouded brow / And dreaming eyes of wonder! / Though time be fleet, and I and thou / Are half a
  A4   29: 3 curious, you know, this sort of life! I do wonder what can have happened to me! When I used to read fairy
  A1   12: 9 "in my going out altogether, like a candle. I wonder what I should be like then?" And she tried to fancy
  A1   8:35 that's about the right distance--but then I wonder what Latitude or Longitude I've got to?" (Alice had not
  A4   31:34 instantly, and Alice thought to herself "I wonder what they will do next! If they had any sense, they'd
  A4   30:19   there must be!" thought Alice. "I wonder what they'll do next! As for pulling me out of the
  A1   8:12 as she went down to look about her, and to wonder what was going to happen next. First, she tried to look
  A7   57:15   'Twinkle, twinkle, little bat! / How I wonder what you're at!'
  T3   135:28 to herself, "where things have no names. I wonder what'll become of my name when I go in? I shouldn't
  A2   14: 6 so far off). "Oh, my poor little feet, I wonder who will put on your shoes and stockings for you now,
  T5   158:17   "I wonder why it wouldn't do?" thought Alice, as she groped her
WONDERED (3)
  T2   124:15   Alice wondered a little at this, but she was too much in awe of the
  A1   7:14 it occurred to her that she ought to have wondered at this, but at the time it all seemed quite natural)
  T6   159:10 high wall--such a narrow one that Alice quite wondered how he could keep his balance--and, as his eyes were
WONDERFUL (2)
  A12   98:15 sun, and thinking of little Alice and all her wonderful Adventures, till she too began dreaming after a
  A12   98:12 while she ran, as well she might, what a wonderful dream it had been.
WONDERFULLY (2)
  T2   123:33 the fresh air that does it," said the Rose: "wonderfully fine air it is, out here."
  T3   131:37 people!" she thought. But this was such a wonderfully small sigh, that she wouldn't have heard it at all
WONDERING (12)
  A1   9:32 every door, she walked sadly down the middle, wondering how she was ever to get out again.
  A10   83: 1 she had sat down with her face in her hands, wondering if anything would ever happen in a natural way again
  T5   158:27 * * * * * * * * * * * * * So she went on, wondering more and more at every step, as everything turned
  T2   123: 7 "I wonder how you do it--" ("You're always wondering," said the Tiger-lily), "but she's more bushy than
  A10   81:16 "Does the boots and shoes!" she repeated in a wondering tone.
  A8   65:24 the Queen, and Alice joined the procession, wondering very much what would happen next.
  T8   182: 1   "I was wondering what the mouse-trap was for," said Alice. "It isn't
  A6   45: 1 or two she stood looking at the house, and wondering what to do next, when suddenly a footman in livery
  T2   121: 8 you know," said the Rose, "and I really was wondering when you'd speak! Said I to myself, 'Her face has
  A8   67: 8 was looking about for some way of escape, and wondering whether she could get away without being seen, when
  A9   71: 5   "I dare say you're wondering why I don't put my arm round your waist," the

WONDERING (cont.)
```
T2    123:24  head, of course," the Rose replied. "I was wondering you hadn't got some too. I thought it was the
```
WONDERLAND (4)
```
A12    99: 8  strange tale, perhaps even with the dream of Wonderland of long ago; and how she would feel with all their
TC    209:16                                          In a Wonderland they lie, / Dreaming as the days go by, / Dreaming
A12    98:35  closed eyes, and half believed herself in Wonderland, though she knew she had but to open them again,
AI     3:31                     Thus grew the tale of Wonderland: / Thus slowly, one by one, / Its quaint events
```
WONDERS (2)
```
AI     3:22  / The dream-child moving through a land / Of wonders wild and new, / In friendly chat with bird or beast--/
T9    196:33  and putting her hair in papers--would do wonders with her--"
```
WO'N'T [WON'T] (36)
```
T3    132:36  their having names," the Gnat said, "if they wo'n't answer to them?"
T9    201:10                                          "I won't be introduced to the pudding, please," Alice said rather
A6     52:26  interesting, and perhaps, as this is May, it wo'n't be raving mad--at least not so mad as it was in March."
T3    136:16            "Think again," it said: "that wo'n't do."
A7     58: 9  the Hatter went on in a mournful tone, "he wo'n't do a thing I ask! It's always six o'clock now."
T3    137:14  said: "that's some comfort. Alice--Alice--I won't forget it again. And now, which of these finger-posts
T3    135:25  made up her mind to go on: "for I certainly won't go back," she thought to herself, and this was the only
T3    129:17  must make! I think I'll go down and--no, I wo'n't go just yet," she went on, checking herself just as she
A9     70: 8  (not in a very hopeful tone, though), "I wo'n't have any pepper in my kitchen at all. Soup does very
T3    131:42  "a dear friend, and an old friend. And you wo'n't hurt me, though I am an insect."
A2     20: 1                                          "I wo'n't indeed!" said Alice, in a great hurry to change the
A7     59:28  No, please go on!" Alice said very humbly. "I wo'n't interrupt you again. I dare say there may be one."
T4    145:22                     "You wo'n't make yourself a bit realler by crying," Tweedledee
A12    97: 4                                          "I wo'n't!" said Alice.
A2     15:30  he came, "Oh! The Duchess, the Duchess! Oh! Wo'n't she be savage if I've kept her waiting!" Alice felt so
A7     56:42  That accounts for it," said the Hatter. "He wo'n't stand beating. Now, if you only kept on good terms with
T8    190:25  Knight rode slowly away into the forest. "It wo'n't take long to see him off, I expect," Alice said to
A2     20:15  it, "Mouse dear! Do come back again, and we wo'n't talk about cats, or dogs either, if you don't like
A2     19:41  felt certain it must be really offended. "We wo'n't talk about her any more, if you'd rather not."
A4     30:32  chimney?--Nay, I sha'n't! You do it!--That I wo'n't, then!--Bill's got to go down--Here, Bill! The master
A4     29:30                     "That you wo'n't!" thought Alice, and after waiting till she fancied she
T5    156:24           "I only hope the boat wo'n't tipple over!" she said to herself. "Oh, what a lovely
A2     15: 1  to them," thought Alice, "or perhaps they wo'n't walk the way I want to go! Let me see. I'll give them a
A5     36: 5  I should think you'll feel it a little queer, wo'n't you?"
T7    174: 3                     "Speak, wo'n't you!" cried the King. "How are they getting on with the
A10    79:18  / Will you, wo'n't you, will you, wo'n't you, wo'n't you join the dance?
A10    80:12  / Will you, wo'n't you, will you, wo'n't you, wo'n't you join the dance?"
T8W    14: 9                     "Won't you let me help you round to the other side? You'll be
A10    79:17  the dance? / Will you, wo'n't you, will you, wo'n't you, will you join the dance? / Will you, wo'n't you,
A10    80:11  the dance. / Will you, wo'n't you, will you, wo'n't you, will you join the dance? / Will you, wo'n't you,
A10    79:17  will you come and join the dance? / Will you, wo'n't you, will you, wo'n't you, will you join the dance? /
A10    79:18  you, will you join the dance? / Will you, wo'n't you, will you, wo'n't you, wo'n't you join the dance?
A10    80:11  but come and join the dance. / Will you, wo'n't you, will you, wo'n't you, will you join the dance? /
A10    80:12  you, will you join the dance? / Will you, wo'n't you, will you, wo'n't you, wo'n't you join the dance?"
A10    79:18  the dance? / Will you, wo'n't you, will you, wo'n't you, wo'n't you join the dance?
A10    80:12  the dance? / Will you, wo'n't you, will you wo'n't you, wo'n't you join the dance?"
```
WOOD (38)
```
A4     32:17  could, and soon found herself safe in a thick wood.
T4    140:11  Would you tell me which road leads out of the wood?"
T7    170: 8  soldiers, my dear, as you came through the wood?"
T8    186:29  you." They had just come to the end of the wood.
T3    137: 3    So they walked on together through the wood, Alice with her arms clasped lovingly round the soft neck
T3    135:23  of it: it looked much darker than the last wood, and Alice felt a little timid about going into it.
T5    152:32  rule. You must be very happy, living in this wood, and being glad whenever you like!"
T1    118:11  of flame, / Came whiffling through the tulgey wood, / And burbled as it came!
T3    133: 4            if you look. It's made entirely of wood, and gets about by swinging itself from branch to branch
T4    147:12  two brothers went off hand-in-hand into the wood, and returned in a minute with their arms full of things
T2    128:30  the air, or whether she ran quickly into the wood ("and she can run very fast!" thought Alice), there was
T4    145:24           Alice ran a little way into the wood, and stopped under a large tree. "It can never get at me
T3    137:17  as there was only one road through the wood, and the two finger-posts both pointed along it. "I'll
T8    181: 4  Knight. "I'll see you safe to the end of the wood--and then I must go back, you know. That's the end of my
T7    169: 1  next moment soldiers came running through the wood, at first in twos and threes, then ten or twenty together
T8W    13: 2  a deep sigh, which seemed to come from the wood behind her.
A5     43: 1  And just as I'd taken the highest tree in the wood," continued the Pigeon, raising its voice to a shriek,
T3    132:39  say," the Gnat replied. "Further on, in the wood down there, they've got no names--however, go on with
A6     46: 6  at this, that she had to run back into the wood for fear of their hearing her; and, when she next peeped
T4    146: 2  At any rate, I'd better be getting out of the wood, for really it's coming on very dark. Do you think it's
T4    145:27  wings so--it makes quite a hurricane in the wood--here's somebody's shawl being blown away!"
T3    137:28  d'ye do?' and ask them the way out of the wood. If I could only get to the Eighth Square before it gets
A6     50:15  relieved to see it trot away quietly into the wood. "If it had grown up," she said to herself, "it would
T7    170: 3  and Alice was very glad to get out of the wood into an open place, where she found the White King seated
A4     32:19  to herself, as she wandered about in the wood, "is to grow to my right size again; and the second thing
T3    135:37  rambling on in this way when she reached the wood: it looked very cool and shady. "Well, at any rate it's a
T4    139:11  politely, "which is the best way out of this wood: it's getting so dark. Would you tell me, please?"
A7     60:36  said Alice, as she picked her way through the wood. "It's the stupidest tea-party I ever was at in all my
T3    131:27  to this railway journey at all--I was in a wood just now--and I wish I could get back there!"
T4    144:24  the puffing of a large steam-engine in the wood near them, though she feared it was more likely to be a
T3    135:22  She very soon came to an open field, with a wood on the other side of it: it looked much darker than the
T7    174:23  the country! She came flying out of the wood over yonder--How fast those Queens can run!"
```

WOOD (cont.)
A6   45: 3   a footman in livery came running out of the wood--(she considered him to be a footman because he was in
T3   135:27   "This must be the wood," she said thoughtfully to herself, "where things have no
A6   45:10   all about, and crept a little way out of the wood to listen.
T8   182:11   me on. I'll go with you to the end of the wood--What's that dish for?"
T5   149: 3   White Queen came running wildly through the wood, with both arms stretched out wide, as if she were flying
T6   166: 9   you'll hear it done, maybe--down in the wood yonder--and, when you've once heard it, you'll be quite
WOODEN (2)
T8   184:12   her patience this time. "You ought to have a wooden horse on wheels, that you ought!"
A2   18:24   sea, some children digging in the sand with wooden spades, then a row of lodging-houses, and behind them a
WOOD'S (1)
T7   175: 1   King said, without even looking round. "That wood's full of them."
WOODS (2)
T6   166:29   "In spring, when woods are getting green, / I'll try and tell you what I mean
T1   110: 2   "And I do so wish it was true! I'm sure the woods look sleepy in the autumn, when the leaves are getting
WOOL (3)
T5   153:33   seemed to have suddenly wrapped herself up in wool. Alice rubbed her eyes, and looked again. She couldn't
T5t   149: 1   WOOL AND WATER
T9   200: 3   to drink: / Mix sand with the cider, and wool with the wine--/ And welcome Queen Alice with
WORD (28)
T3   130:15   at all. Language is worth a thousand pounds a word!"
T6   164:32   there are two meanings packed up into one word."
T7   176: 6   or mineral?" he said, yawning at every other word.
T7   171: 9   he was far too much out of breath to say a word, and could only wave his hands about, and make the most
A1   8:43   time, as it didn't sound at all the right word) "--but I shall have to ask them what the name of the
A9   72:41   and Alice was too much frightened to say a word, but slowly followed her back to the croquet-ground.
T6   164: 5   "When I make a word do a lot of work like that," said Humpty Dumpty, "I
T5   153:30   Be-etter! Be-e-e-etter! Be-e-ehh!" The last word ended in a long bleat, so like a sheep that Alice quite
T8W   16:15   Alice didn't catch the word exactly. "Is it a kind of toothache?" she asked.
T4   140:20   eldest Oyster looked at him, / But never a word he said: / The eldest Oyster winked his eye, / And shook
T6   163:30   "When I use a word," Humpty Dumpty said, in rather a scornful tone, "it
A12   95: 1   He sent them word I had not gone / (We know it to be true): / If she should
T3   135:41   surprised at not being able to think of the word. "I mean to get under the--under the--under this, you
A11   90:12   of the court. (As that is rather a hard word, I will just explain to you how it was done. They had a
T8W   15:12   "There's no such word in the language!" said the Wasp.
T8W   15:10   "En-gulph-ed," Alice repeated, dividing the word into syllables.
T6   161:25   exclaimed triumphantly. "You never said a word like it!"
T6   164: 3   "That's a great deal to make one word mean," Alice said in a thoughtful tone.
A9   72:30   away, even in the middle of her favourite word "moral", and the arm that was linked into hers began to
A12   93:28   important--" as if he were trying which word sounded best.
A9   74:28   "Sit down, both of you, and don't speak a word till I've finished."
T9   201:24   suety sort of voice, and Alice hadn't a word to say in reply: she could only sit and look at it and
T6   168:39   as it was a great comfort to have such a long word to say) "of all the unsatisfactory people I ever met--"
T4   138: 7   and she was just going round to see if the word 'TWEEDLE' was written at the back of each collar, when
A11   86:24   they are the jurors." She said this last word two or three times over to herself, being rather proud of
A6   47:16   She said the last word with such sudden violence that Alice quite jumped; but
T7   173:32   or two trickled down his cheek; but not a word would he say.
A7   58:26   in a hoarse, feeble voice, "I heard every word you fellows were saying."
WORDS (35)
A6   49: 3   howled so, that Alice could hardly hear the words:--
A9   75: 8   be all day about it!" and he went on in these words:--
A10   79: 8   sing," said the Gryphon. "I've forgotten the words."
A10   85: 9   the breeze that followed them, the melancholy words:--
A6   46: 2   solemn tone, only changing the order of the words a little, "From the Queen. An invitation for the Duchess
A10   82: 7   Father William," to the Caterpillar, and the words all coming different, and then the Mock Turtle drew a
T9   197:21   like a tune: at last she could even make out words, and she listened so eagerly that, when the two great
A3   22:32   "I don't know the meaning of half those long words, and, what's more, I don't believe you do either!" And
A9   74:21   the Gryphon answered, very nearly in the same words as before, "It's all his fancy, that: he hasn't got no
A10   82:21   she hardly knew what she was saying; and the words came very queer indeed:--
A2   17: 6   her voice sounded hoarse and strange, and the words did not come the same as they used to do:--
A12   96:25   "Then the words don't fit you," said the King looking round the court
A1   10:17   of the bottle was a paper label, with the words "DRINK ME" beautifully printed on it in large letters.
A4   28: 3   There was no label this time with the words "DRINK ME," but nevertheless she uncorked it and put it
A1   12:33   found in it a very small cake, on which the words "EAT ME" were beautifully marked in currants. "Well,
T1   110:40   books are something like our books, only the words go the wrong way: I know that, because I've held up one
A5   41: 3   afraid," said Alice, timidly: "some of the words have got altered."
A2   18:17   As she said these words her foot slipped, and in another moment, splash! she was
T6   163:33   is," said Alice, "whether you can make words mean so many different things."
T9   194:36   dear. And I'll tell you a secret--I can read words of one letter! Isn't that grand? However, don't be
T8   190:12   As the Knight sang the last words of the ballad, he gathered up the reins, and turned his
T7   172:40   Alice repeating to herself, as she ran, the words of the old song:--
T4   138:15   very sorry," was all Alice could say; for the words of the old song kept ringing through her head like the
A6   49:28   murder to leave it behind?" She said the last words out loud, and the little thing grunted in reply (it had
T9   198: 2   before an arched doorway, over which were the words "QUEEN ALICE" in large letters, and on each side of the
A2   17:16   "I'm sure those are not the right words," said poor Alice, and her eyes filled with tears again
TI   103:29   And childhood's nest of gladness. / The magic words shall hold thee fast: / Thou shalt not heed the raving
T9   197: 8   "And now you know the words," she added, as she put her head down on Alice's other
T6   164:14   "You seem very clever at explaining words, Sir," said Alice. "Would you kindly tell me the meaning
T5   152:16   undone directly. Oh, oh!" As she said the words the brooch flew open, and the Queen clutched wildly at
T6   164:26   Dumpty interrupted: "there are plenty of hard words there. 'Brillig' means four o'clock in the afternoon--

WORDS (cont.)
  A1   8:37   either, but she thought they were nice grand words to say.)
  A9   74:34   These words were followed by a very long silence, broken only by an
  A4   30:24   voices all talking together: she made out the words: "Where's the other ladder?--Why, I hadn't to bring but
  T1   116:15   course! And, if I hold it up to a glass, the words will all go the right way again."
WORE (1)
  A11   86:17   judge, by the way, was the King; and, as he wore his crown over the wig (look at the frontispiece if you
WORK (14)
  T9   195: 4   after so much thinking." So they set to work and fanned her with bunches of leaves, till she had to
  A1   13: 5   So she set to work, and very soon finished off the cake. * * * * * * * * * *
  T7   174:14   for refreshments!" Haigha and Hatta set to work at once, carrying round trays of white and brown bread.
  A5   41:43   as she was shrinking rapidly: so she set to work at once to eat some of the other bit. Her chin was
  T8   186:10   course?" said Alice. "Well, that was quick work, certainly!"
  A6   48:25   a little of her knowledge. "Just think what work it would make with the day and night! You see the earth
  T6   164: 5   "When I make a word do a lot of work like that," said Humpty Dumpty, "I always pay it extra."
  A7   61: 2   that led into the garden. Then she set to work nibbling at the mushroom (she had kept a piece of it in
  T1   107: 9   and just now, as I said, she was hard at work on the white kitten, which was lying quite still and
  A10   78: 4   his throat," said the Gryphon; and it set to work shaking him and punching him in the back. At last the
  T8   188:35   eyes / Among the heather bright, / And work them into waistcoat-buttons / In the silent night. / And
  A6   48:10   of soup off the fire, and at once set to work throwing everything within her reach at the Duchess and
  A5   43:33   of mushroom in her hands, and she set to work very carefully, nibbling first at one and then at the
  A12   93:12   found and handed back to them, they set to work very diligently to write out a history of the accident,
WORK-BOX (1)
  T5   154:19   sometimes like a doll and sometimes like a work-box, and was always in the shelf next above the one she
WORKED (1)
  T6   163: 7   as she took out her memorandum-book, and worked the sum for him:
WORKING (2)
  T8   186: 4   happens to be?" he said. "My mind goes on working all the same. In fact, the more head-downwards I am,
  T5   155: 9   go on turning round like that." She was now working with fourteen pairs at once, and Alice couldn't help
WORKS (4) [See also FIREWORKS, WAX-WORKS]
  T5   150:19   "It's a poor sort of memory that only works backwards," the Queen remarked.
  T5   150:16   one great advantage in it, that one's memory works both ways."
  A7   56: 2   Hatter. "I told you butter wouldn't suit the works!" he added, looking angrily at the March Hare.
  T5   150:17   "I'm sure mine only works one way," Alice remarked. "I ca'n't remember things
WORLD (12)
  A2   15:42   the same, the next question is 'Who in the world am I?' Ah, that's the great puzzle!" And she began
  T2   126: 2   played--all over the world--if this is the world at all, you know. Oh, what fun it is! How I wish I was
  T12   207: 4   with me, Kitty--all through the Looking-glass world. Did you know it, dear?"
  A9   70:33   is--'Oh, 'tis love, 'tis love, that makes the world go round!'"
  T2   126: 2   of chess that's being played--all over the world--if this is the world at all, you know. Oh, what fun it
  T9   199:24   "To the Looking-Glass world it was Alice that said / 'I've a sceptre in hand, I've a
  A12   95:30   meaning in it," said the King, "that saves a world of trouble, you know, as we needn't try to find any. And
  A3   26:39   here, and I'm sure she's the best cat in the world! Oh, my dear Dinah! I wonder if I shall ever see you any
  A1   8: 6   after it, never once considering how in the world she was to get out again.
  T2   123: 1   till you know no more what's going on in the world, than if you were a bud!"
  A6   48:21   the Duchess said, in a hoarse growl, "the world would go round a deal faster than it does."
  A7   57:19   'Up above the world you fly, / Like a tea-tray in the sky. / Twinkle,
WORM (1)
  A3   22:19   said the Duck: "it's generally a frog, or a worm. The question is, what did the archbishop find?"
WORRIED (1)
  A9   72:26   for she was beginning to feel a little worried.
WORRITS (1)
  T8W   16: 8   Wasp went on. "They jokes at one. And they worrits one. And then I gets cross. And I gets cold. And I
WORRITY (4)
  T8W   14:13   down again he only said, as before, "Worrity, worrity! Can't you leave a body alone?"
  T8W   14: 4   the Wasp said in a peevish tone. "Worrity, worrity! There never was such a child!"
  T8W   14:13   settled down again he only said, as before, "Worrity, worrity! Can't you leave a body alone?"
  T8W   14: 4   you go on!" the Wasp said in a peevish tone. "Worrity, worrity! There never was such a child!"
WORRY (1)
  A4   32:36   and rushed at the stick, and made believe to worry it: then Alice dodged behind a great thistle, to keep
WORSE (6)
  T7   170: 2   rider fell off instantly. The confusion got worse every moment, and Alice was very glad to get out of the
  A7   60: 1   from the change; and Alice was a good deal worse off than before, as the March Hare had just upset the
  T5   156: 4   (which made the oars stick fast in the water, worse than ever), and sometimes under trees, but always with
  A2   18:15   on the glass table as before, "and things are worse than ever," thought the poor child, "for I never was so
  T4   147:37   who had overheard the remark. "I'm far worse than you!"
  A12   94:24   said the King, "that only makes the matter worse. You must have meant some mischief, or else you'd have
WORST (2)
  T2   122:18   right!" said the Tiger-lily. "The daisies are worst of all. When one speaks, they all begin together, and
  T8   185: 3   to be sure. That happened to me once--and the worst of it was, before I could get out again, the other White
WORSTED (5)
  T1   107:15   having a grand game of romps with the ball of worsted Alice had been trying to wind up, and had been rolling
  T1   108:17   Here Alice wound two or three turns of the worsted round the kitten's neck, just to see how it would look
  T1   110: 1   pretty!" cried Alice, dropping the ball of worsted to clap her hands. "And I do so wish it was true! I'm
  T1   108:36   number three: you unwound every bit of the worsted while I wasn't looking!
  T1   108: 4   into the arm-chair, taking the kitten and the worsted with her, and began winding up the ball again. But she
WORTH (9) [See also PENNYWORTH]
  A2   20: 9   you know, and he says it's so useful, it's worth a hundred pounds! He says it kills all the rats and--oh
  T3   130: 1   keep him waiting, child! Why, his time is worth a thousand pounds a minute!"
  T3   130: 9   drives the engine. Why, the smoke alone is worth a thousand pounds a puff!"

WORTH (cont.)
T3   130:14   "Better say nothing at all. Language is worth a thousand pounds a word!"
T3   130: 5   one where she came from. The land there is worth a thousand pounds an inch!"
A5   36:27   perhaps after all it might tell her something worth hearing. For some minutes it puffed away without
T2   120:32   said the Tiger-lily, "when there's anybody worth talking to."
A1   7: 8   the pleasure of making a daisy-chain would be worth the trouble of getting up and picking the daisies, when
A8   67:34   went on "--likely to win, that it's hardly worth while finishing the game."

WOULD (180)
T8   190:23   "but you didn't cry so much as I thought you would."
T9   194:20   "Perhaps it would," Alice replied cautiously.
A10   83:12   not dare to disobey, though she felt sure it would all come wrong, and she went on in a trembling voice:--
A10   80:25   the crumbs," said the Mock Turtle: "crumbs would all wash off in the sea. But they have their tails in
A12   98:21   her head to keep back the wandering hair that would always get into her eyes--and still as she listened, or
A3   23: 1   tone, "was that the best thing to get us dry would be a Caucus-race."
T4   143:15   a little blue. / 'After such kindness, that would be / A dismal thing to do!' / 'The night is fine,' the
T8   184:37   I ca'n't tell for certain--but I'm afraid it would be a little hard."
T2   125: 5   I've seen gardens, compared with which this would be a wilderness."
T5   151:10   felt there was no denying that. "Of course it would be all the better," she said: "but it wouldn't be all
T5   151: 8   "That would be all the better, wouldn't it?" the Queen said, as she
T3   135:30   they'd have to give me another, and it would be almost certain to be an ugly one. But then the fun
T8   182: 2   for," said Alice. "It isn't very likely there would be any mice on the horse's back."
T2   125:15   I've heard nonsense, compared with which that would be as sensible as a dictionary!"
A6   48: 8   like the tone of this remark, and thought it would be as well to introduce some other subject of
T7   172:11   "I should think throwing cold water over you would be better," Alice suggested: "--or some sal-volatile."
T4   139: 8   it was so, it might be; and if it were so, it would be; but as it isn't, it ain't. That's logic."
T2   123:36   were interesting enough, she felt that it would be far grander to have a talk with a real Queen.
A1   8:30   the centre of the earth. Let me see: that would be four thousand miles down, I think--" (for, you see,
T1   108: 9   paw and gently touching the ball, as if it would be glad to help if it might.
T4   141: 6   were only cleared away,' / They said, 'it would be grand!'
A7   57: 5   "That would be grand, certainly," said Alice thoughtfully; "but then
T1   111: 5   different on beyond. Oh, Kitty, how nice it would be if we could only get through into Looking-glass
T3   134:26   careless tone: "only think how convenient it would be if you could manage to go home without it! For
T6   163:45   that we've had enough of that subject, and it would be just as well if you'd mention what you mean to do
A7   59: 7   what such an extraordinary way of living would be like, but it puzzled her too much: so she went on:
A11   91:30   very curious to see what the next witness would be like, "--for they haven't got much evidence yet," she
T9   192:15   it would not be quite civil. However, there would be no harm, she thought, in asking if the game was over.
T2   125:11   "a hill ca'n't be a valley, you know. That would be nonsense--"
A1   10: 7   would go through," thought poor Alice, "it would be of very little use without my shoulders. Oh, how I
A3   24:16   she added in a whisper, half afraid that it would be offended again.
A12   98:36   all would change to dull reality--the grass would be only rustling in the wind, and the pool rippling to
A6   50:12   nor less than a pig, and she felt that it would be quite absurd for her to carry it any further.
A12   93: 8   she said to herself; "I should think it would be quite as much use in the trial one way up as the
A9   74: 5   the creature, but on the whole she thought it would be quite as safe to stay with it as to go after that
T8   184:35   said thoughtfully: "but don't you think it would be rather hard?"
A10   84:11   "Oh, a song, please, if the Mock Turtle would be so kind," Alice replied, so eagerly that the Gryphon
T6   168:31   for instance--or the mouth at the top--that would be some help."
T9   201:40   in a voice like the cooing of a pigeon. "It would be such a treat! May I?"
T5   152:26   the screaming already," said the Queen. "What would be the good of having it all over again?"
A8   63:31   a rule at processions; "and besides, what would be the use of a procession," thought she, "if people had
T9   196:13   my name in the middle of an accident! Where would be the use of it?" but she did not say this aloud, for
T3   135:31   certain to be an ugly one. But then the fun would be, trying to find the creature that has got my old
A4   32:31   that it might be hungry, in which case it would be very likely to eat her up in spite of all her coaxing
A3   25:31   a trial, dear sir, With no jury or judge, would be wasting our breath. 'I'll be judge, I'll be jury,
A1   7: 8   whether the pleasure of making a daisy-chain would be worth the trouble of getting up and picking the
A8   67: 5   any minute, "and then," thought she, "what would become of me? They're dreadfully fond of beheading
A12   95: 4   / If she should push the matter on, / What would become of you?
A12   96: 3   the matter on'--that must be the Queen--'What would become of you?'--What, indeed!--'I gave her one, they
A5   42:20   them, and was delighted to find that her neck would bend about easily in any direction, like a serpent. She
A9   74:19   Alice could hear him sighing as if his heart would break. She pitied him deeply. "What is his sorrow?" she
A7   60:33   back once or twice, half hoping that they would call after her: the last time she saw them, they were
T3   135: 2   wanted to call you to your lessons, she would call out 'Come here--,' and there she would have to
A3   21:17   anxiously fixed on it, for she felt sure she would catch a bad cold if she did not get dry very soon.
A12   98:41   the Gryphon, and all the other queer noises, would change (she knew) to the confused clamour of the busy
A12   98:36   knew she had but to open them again, and all would change to dull reality--the grass would be only rustling
A12   98:38   the waving of the reeds--the rattling teacups would change to tinkling sheep-bells, and the Queen's shrill
T9   196: 4   "He said he would come in," the White Queen went on, "because he was
T6   161:11   what would happen to his head! I'm afraid it would come off!"
T9   199:10   thumb, as if he were trying whether the paint would come off: then he looked at Alice.
T4   148:13   "I wish the monstrous crow would come!" thought Alice.
T9   194:11   if I took it--and the dog wouldn't remain: it would come to bite me--and I'm sure I shouldn't remain!"
A9   73: 2   Queen merely remarking that a moment's delay would cost them their lives.
A11   89:26   went on, looking anxiously round to see if he would deny it too; but the Dormouse denied nothing, being fast
A12   92:12   once and put back into the jury-box, or they would die.
T3   134:17   "Then it would die, of course."
T9   196:32   kindness--and putting her hair in papers--would do wonders with her--"
A10   83: 1   her face in her hands, wondering if anything would ever happen in a natural way again.
T9   192:23   waited for you to begin, you see nobody would ever say anything, so that--"
A5   36: 8   be different," said Alice: "all I know is, it would feel very queer to me."
A12   99: 9   dream of Wonderland of long ago; and how she would feel with all their simple sorrows, and find a pleasure
A12   99: 6   loving heart of her childhood; and how she would gather about her other little children, and make their

WOULD (cont.)

```
A11   88:36  larger again, and she thought at first she would get up and leave the court; but on second thoughts she
A5    41:37  stretched her arms round it as far as they would go, and broke off a bit of the edge with each hand.
A10   81:31  them," the Mock Turtle said. "No wise fish would go anywhere without a porpoise."
A6    48:21  Duchess said, in a hoarse growl, "the world would go round a deal faster than it does."
A1    10: 6  through the doorway; "and even if my head would go through," thought poor Alice, "it would be of very
A10   81: 4  "The reason is," said the Gryphon, "that they would go with the lobsters to the dance. So they got thrown
A4    27:29  And she began fancying the sort of thing that would happen: "'Miss Alice! Come here directly, and get ready
A4    31: 4  gave one sharp kick, and waited to see what would happen next.
A8    65:24  the procession, wondering very much what would happen next.
T1   113:18  watched it with great curiosity to see what would happen next.
T6   161:10  she thought: "And then I don't know what would happen to his head! I'm afraid it would come off!"
T6   168:18  that she ought to be going, she felt that it would hardly be civil to stay. So she got up, and held out her
T5   155.26  now and then the oars got fast in it, and would hardly come out again.
A5    40: 1  "You are old," said the youth, "one would hardly suppose / That your eye was as steady as ever; /
A9    72: 9  been was not otherwise than what you had been would have appeared to them to be otherwise.'"
T5   149:21                                         It would have been all the better, as it seemed to Alice, if she
T5   151:20  you hadn't done them," the Queen said, "that would have been better still; better, and better, and better!"
A6    45: 4  otherwise, judging by his face only, she would have called him a fish)--and rapped loudly at the door
T8W   21: 8  they're too much in front, no doubt. One would have done as well as two, if you must have them so close
A11   86:27  the meaning of it at all. However, "jurymen" would have done just as well.
T12  207:38  with me in my dream, there was one thing you would have enjoyed--I had such a quantity of poetry said to me
T9   204:23                      At any other time, Alice would have felt surprised at this, but she was far too much
T1   119: 7  then she floated on through the hall, and would have gone straight out at the door in the same way, if
T9   192:13  sitting close to her, one on each side: she would have liked very much to ask them how they came there,
A6    50:16  If it had grown up," she said to herself, "it would have made a dreadfully ugly child: but it makes rather a
T3   131:35  It was very unhappy, evidently, and Alice would have said something pitying to comfort it, "if it would
A8    68: 5  passing at the moment, "My dear! I wish you would have this cat removed!"
T9   202:39  her sister the history of her feast. "You would have thought they wanted to squeeze me flat!")
T7   172:34                            "It would have to be a very tiny earthquake!" thought Alice. "Who
T8   186:13                  "Then it would have to be the next day. I suppose you wouldn't have two
T3   135: 3  would call out 'Come here--,' and there she would have to leave off, because there wouldn't be any name
T7   173:32  two trickled down his cheek; but not a word would he say.
T6   159:33  out loud, forgetting that Humpty Dumpty would hear her.
T6   161:14  "They'd pick me up again in a minute, they would! However, this conversation is going on a little too
T3   131:30  voice close to her ear: "something about 'you would if you could,' you know."
A12   99: 4  herself how this same little sister of hers would, in the after-time, be herself a grown woman; and how
T2   120:10  always coming back to the house, do what she would. Indeed, once, when she turned a corner rather more
A2    19:10                     "Would it be of any use, now," thought Alice, "to speak to this
A12   99: 5     be herself a grown woman; and how she would keep, through all her riper years, the simple and loving
A6    51: 5     as she did not at all know whether it would like the name: however, it only grinned a little wider.
T1   108:19  round the kitten's neck, just to see how it would look: this led to a scramble, in which the ball rolled
T9   194:18  look here!" the Red Queen cried. "The dog would lose its temper, wouldn't it?"
A6    48:25  of her knowledge. "Just think what work it would make with the day and night! You see the earth takes
A2    15: 3  And she went on planning to herself how she would manage it. "They must go by the carrier," she thought;
T2   126:25  any idea of doing that. She felt as if she would never be able to talk again, she was getting so much out
T3   135: 5                                   "That would never do, I'm sure," said Alice: "the governess would
T5   149:15                  Alice thought it would never do to have an argument at the very beginning of
T4   140: 4  people she had just been dancing with. "It would never do to say 'How d'ye do?' now," she said to herself
T5   158:14  "I never put things into people's hands--that would never do--you must get it for yourself." And so saying,
T3   135: 5  do, I'm sure," said Alice: "the governess would never think of excusing me lessons for that. If she
A3    21:10  you, and must know better." And this Alice would not allow, without knowing how old it was, and as the
A6    48:23                 "Which would not be an advantage," said Alice, who felt very glad to
T2   127:27         Alice thought it would not be civil to say "No," though it wasn't at all what
T9   192:14  them how they came there, but she feared it would not be quite civil. However, there would be no harm, she
A10   80: 5  not join the dance. / Would not, could not, would not, could not, could not join the dance. / Would not,
A10   80: 6  not join the dance. / Would not, could not, would not, could not, could not join the dance.
A10   80: 5  kindly, but he would not join the dance. / Would not, could not, would not, could not, could not join the
A10   80: 6  not, could not, could not join the dance. / Would not, could not, would not, could not, could not join the
A10   84:28  for fish, / Game, or any other dish? / Who would not give all else for two p / ennyworth only of
T8W   19: 8  But what was I to do, you know? / My ringlets would not grow again.
A10   80: 4     Said he thanked the whiting kindly, but he would not join the dance. / Would not, could not, would not,
T6   167:12  I told them once, I told them twice: / They would not listen to advice.
A1    9:38  or the key was too small, but at any rate it would not open any of them. However, on the second time round,
A1    10:24  and other unpleasant things, all because they would not remember the simple rules their friends had taught
A10   84:19  in a hot tureen! / Who for such dainties would not stoop? / Soup of the evening, beautiful Soup! / Soup
T8W   21: 5  same for her, but she kept out of reach, and would not take the hint. So he went on with his criticisms.
T12  207: 8  you say to them, they always purr. "If they would only purr for 'yes,' and mew for 'no,' or any rule of
A3    21: 9  with the Lory, who at last turned sulky, and would only say, "I'm older than you, and must know better."
T4   139:19  Tweedledee, though she felt quite certain he would only shout out "Contrariwise!" and so he did.
T3   131:36  said something pitying to comfort it, "if it would only sigh like other people!" she thought. But this was
A2    17:26  with a sudden burst of tears, "I do wish they would put their heads down! I am so very tired of being all
T9   194:16  usual," said the Red Queen: "the dog's temper would remain."
T9   194:13                "Then you think nothing would remain?" said the Red Queen.
T9   194:21  "Then if the dog went away, its temper would remain!" the Queen exclaimed triumphantly.
A6    52:21                      "I thought it would," said the Cat, and vanished again.
TI   103:18  live in memory yet, / Though envious years would say "forget."
A9    72: 6  "and the moral of that is--'Be what you would seem to be'--or, if you'd like it put more simply--
T5   153:36  on the other side of the counter? Rub as she would, she could make nothing more of it: she was in a little
T2   128:33  to remember that she was a Pawn, and that it would soon be time for her to move.
```

WOULD (cont.)
```
 T6   168:34              Alice waited a minute to see if he would speak again, but, as he never opened his eyes or took
A12    99: 2   the lowing of  the  cattle  in the distance would take the place of the Mock Turtle's heavy sobs.
 A2    19:43   down  to  the  end  of  its  tail. "As if I would talk on such a subject! Our family always hated cats:
 A1     8:27                         Down, down, down. "Would they do at the end of a year? I should be sent to prison
 T1   109: 3    more  to  herself  than  the  kitten. "What would they do at the end of a year? I should be sent to prison
 T5   156:15   boat  was  left to drift down the stream as it would, till it glided gently in among the waving rushes. And
T8W    18: 8   repeated  poetry  to  her, and she thought she would try if the Wasp couldn't do it too. "Would you mind
 T2   124: 1   out  at last, a long way off), she thought she would try the plan, this time, of walking in the opposite
 A8    66:10   to give the hedgehog a blow with its head, it would twist itself round and look up in her face, with such a
 T7   173: 8                                     "Would you--be good enough--" Alice panted out, after running a
 T2   127:15   "Of  course  it  is,"  said  the  Queen. "What would you have it?"
 T6   164:15    at  explaining  words,  Sir,"  said  Alice. "Would you kindly tell me the meaning of the poem called
 A2    19:31   the  Mouse  in  a  shrill  passionate voice. "Would you like cats, if you were me?"
T8W    14:14                                     "Would you like me to read you a bit of this?" Alice went on,
 T1   110:29   put you through into Looking-glass House. How would you like that?
A10    84: 9   Lobster-Quadrille?"  the  Gryphon went on. "Or would you like the Mock Turtle to sing you another song?"
 T8   184:27   inventing  a  new way of getting over a gate--would you like to hear it?"
 T1   110:43                "How would you like to live in Looking-glass House, Kitty? I wonder
A10    79: 3                                     "Would you like to see a little of it?" said the Mock Turtle.
T8W    18: 8   would  try  if  the Wasp couldn't do it too. "Would you mind saying it in rhyme?" she asked very politely.
 T4   140:20   long,"  she  said, as politely as she could, "would you please tell me first which road--"
 T4   139:11   way out of this wood: it's getting so dark. Would you tell me, please?"
 A8    63: 3                                     "Would you tell me, please," said Alice, a little timidly, "why
 T6   163:42                                     "Would you tell me please," said Alice, "what that means?"
 A6    51: 7   so  far,"  thought Alice,  and she went on. "Would you tell me, please, which way I ought to go from here?"
 A6    47:12                         "Please would you tell me," said Alice, a little timidly, for she was
 T9   192:16   in  asking  if  the game was over. "Please, would you tell me--" she began, looking timidly at the Red
 T3   136:17   thought,  but  nothing  came  of it. "Please, would you tell me what you call yourself?" she said timidly.
 T4   140:11   well--some  poetry,"  Alice said doubtfully. "Would you tell me which road leads out of the wood?"
```
WOULDN'T (37)
```
 T3   135:35   'Alice,' till one of them answered! Only they wouldn't answer at all, if they were wise."
 T5   151:11   would  be  all  the better," she said: "but it wouldn't be all the better his being punished."
 T3   135: 3   she  would  have  to leave off, because there wouldn't be any name for her to call, and of course you
 T9   202:36                 "That wouldn't be at all the thing," the Red Queen said very
 A4    30:37   Why, they seem to put everything upon Bill! I wouldn't be in Bill's place for a good deal: this fireplace is
 T3   132: 1   it  could  sting or not, but she thought this wouldn't be quite a civil question to ask.
 A5    41:19   she  thought to herself "I wish the creatures wouldn't be so easily offended!"
 A9    70:14    I  only  wish  people  knew that: then they wouldn't be so stingy about it, you know--"
 T8   186:25                      "That wouldn't be very nice, I'm afraid--"
 T5   156:42   of  one of the oars got fast in the water and wouldn't come out again (so Alice explained it afterwards),
 T2   122:12   its  quivering  head  towards Alice, "or they wouldn't dare to do it!"
 T5   158:17                 "I wonder why it wouldn't do?" thought Alice, as she groped her way among the
 T4   145:26   itself  in  among  the trees. But I wish it wouldn't flap its wings so--it makes quite a hurricane in the
 T1   110:26   principally, Alice said, because the kitten wouldn't fold its arms properly. So, to punish it, she held it
 T6   168: 2   verse,  and Alice thought, with a shudder, "I wouldn't have been the messenger for anything!"
 A6    51:26     "You must be," said  the  Cat, "or you wouldn't have come here."
 T1   108:32   eyes  open--if  you'd  shut them tight up, it wouldn't have happened. Now don't make any more excuses, but
 T3   131:37   was  such a wonderfully small sigh, that she wouldn't have heard it at all, if it hadn't come quite close
 T3   135: 4   any  name  for her to call, and of course you wouldn't have to go, you know."
 T8   186:13   would  have  to be the next day. I suppose you wouldn't have two pudding-courses in one dinner?"
 T9   194:19   Queen cried. "The dog would lose its temper, wouldn't it?"
 A6    49:27   "they're  sure  to  kill  it in a day or two. Wouldn't it be murder to leave it behind?" She said the last
A10    81:32                         "Wouldn't it, really?" said Alice, in a tone of great surprise.
 T5   151: 8   "That would be all the better, wouldn't it?" the Queen said, as she bound the plaster round
 A6    53: 2   I said 'pig'," replied Alice; "and I wish you wouldn't keep appearing and vanishing so suddenly; you make
T12   207:18                 ("But it wouldn't look at it," she said, when she was explaining the
 T6   168:32                 "It wouldn't look nice," Alice objected. But Humpty Dumpty only
 T2   126: 3   fun  it is! How I wish I was one of them! I wouldn't mind being a Pawn, if only I might join--though of
 A5    41:14    like  to  be a little larger, Sir, if you wouldn't mind," said Alice: "three inches is such a wretched
 T9   194:11   remain,  of course, if I took it--and the dog wouldn't remain: it would come to bite me--and I'm sure I
 T9   194:10           Alice considered. "The bone wouldn't remain, of course, if I took it--and the dog wouldn't
 A1     8:25   brave  they'll  all  think me at home! Why, I wouldn't say anything about it, even if I fell off the top of
A11    88:39                 "I wish you wouldn't squeeze so," said the Dormouse, who was sitting next
 A3    26:16                 "What a pity it wouldn't stay!" sighed the Lory, as soon as it was quite out
 A7    56: 2   wrong!"  sighed the Hatter. "I told you butter wouldn't suit the works!" he added, looking angrily at the
 A7    56:36   Time  as well as I do," said the Hatter, "you wouldn't talk about wasting it. It's him."
T8W    20: 2   if  your  wig  fitted  a  little better, they wouldn't tease you quite so much."
```
WOUND (1) [See also UNWOUND]
```
 T1   108:16   go and see the bonfire to-morrow." Here Alice wound two or three turns of the worsted round the kitten's
```
WOW (6)
```
 A6    48:42                         "Wow! wow! wow!"
 A6    49: 9                         "Wow! wow! wow!"
 A6    48:42                              "Wow! wow! wow!"
 A6    49: 9                              "Wow! wow! wow!"
 A6    48:42                                   "Wow! wow! wow!"
 A6    49: 9                                   "Wow! wow! wow!"
```
WRAPPED (1)
```
 T5   153:32   at  the  Queen,  who  seemed to have suddenly wrapped herself up in wool. Alice rubbed her eyes, and looked
```

WRAPPING (1)
A3   26:31   hurried off at once: one old Magpie began wrapping itself up very carefully, remarking "I really must be
WREATH (1)
AI   4: 7   mystic band. / Like pilgrim's wither'd wreath of flowers / Pluck'd in a far-off land.
WRETCHED (2)
A11   89: 7   singers in the last concert!" on which the wretched Hatter trembled so, that he shook off both his shoes
A5   41:15   mind," said Alice: "three inches is such a wretched height to be."
WRIGGLING (3)
T1   110: 8   hadn't been for that nasty Knight, that came wriggling down among my pieces. Kitty dear, let's pretend--"
A5   43: 3   be free of them at last, they must needs come wriggling down from the sky! Ugh, Serpent!"
T7   170:24   the Messenger kept skipping up and down, and wriggling like an eel, as he came along, with his great hands
WRINGING (2)
T5   152:36   don't go on like that!" cried the poor Queen, wringing her hands in despair. "Consider what a great girl you
T9   192:34   deal more than that!" the White Queen moaned, wringing her hands. "Oh, ever so much more than that!"
WRIST (1)
T4   146:12   under the umbrella, and seized her by the wrist.
WRITE (9)
A12   94:21   your Majesty," said the Knave, "I didn't write it, and they ca'n't prove that I did: there's no name
T6   166:35   the leaves are brown, / Take pen and ink, and write it down."
T9   192:36   speak the truth--think before you speak--and write it down afterwards."
A4   29: 7   that there ought! And when I grow up, I'll write one--but I'm grown up now," she added in a sorrowful
A12   93:12   to them, they set to work very diligently to write out a history of the accident, all except the Lizard,
T6   160:35   "Ah, well! They may write such things in a book," Humpty Dumpty said in a calmer
A11   88:17   "Write that down," the King said to the jury; and the jury
A12   93:22   to the jury. They were just beginning to write this down on their slates, when the White Rabbit
A11   87:10   hunting all about for it, he was obliged to write with one finger for the rest of the day; and this was of
WRITES (1)
T1   115:37   pencil. I ca'n't manage this one a bit: it writes all manner of things that I don't intend--"
WRITHING (1)
A9   76:21   "Reeling and Writhing, of course, to begin with," the Mock Turtle replied;
WRITING (7) [See also HANDWRITING]
T1   115:30   memorandum-book out of his pocket, and began writing. A sudden thought struck her, and she took hold of the
A11   86:38   their shoulders, that all the jurors were writing down "Stupid things!" on their slates, and she could
T1   115:32   came some way over his shoulder, and began writing for him.
T7   170: 5   the White King seated on the ground, busily writing in his memorandum-book.
A12   93:34   the King, who had been for some time busily writing in his note-book, called out "Silence!", and read out
A12   96:21   (The unfortunate little Bill had left off writing on his slate with one finger, as he found it made no
A11   86:28   The twelve jurors were all writing very busily on slates. "What are they doing?" Alice
WRITING-DESK (1)
A7   55:12   but all he said was "Why is a raven like a writing-desk?"
WRITING-DESKS (1)
A7   55:33   over all she could remember about ravens and writing-desks, which wasn't much.
WRITTEN (10)
T6   159: 7   It might have been written a hundred times, easily, on that enormous face. Humpty
A4   29: 6   the middle of one! There ought to be a book written about me, that there ought! And when I grow up, I'll
T6   159: 6   "I'm as certain of it, as if his name were written all over his face!"
T4   138: 7   going round to see if the word 'TWEEDLE' was written at the back of each collar, when she was startled by a
A12   94: 8   White Rabbit; "but it seems to be a letter, written by the prisoner to--to somebody."
A9   72:12   Alice said very politely, "if I had it written down: but I ca'n't quite follow it as you say it."
T6   166:20   he went on without noticing her remark, "was written entirely for your amusement."
A12   94:13   the White Rabbit: "in fact, there's nothing written on the outside." He unfolded the paper as he spoke,
A12   94: 9   been that," said the King, "unless it was written to nobody, which isn't usual, you know."
A1   9: 4   it'll never do to ask: perhaps I shall see it written up somewhere."
WRONG (12)
A10   80:24   "You're wrong about the crumbs," said the Mock Turtle: "crumbs would
A10   83:13   though she felt sure it would all come wrong, and she went on in a trembling voice:--
T9   194:15   "Wrong, as usual," said the Red Queen: "the dog's temper would
T4   139:21   "You've begun wrong!" cried Tweedledum. "The first thing in a visit is to
A5   41: 4   "It is wrong from beginning to end," said the Caterpillar, decidedly;
T6   161:24   "Wrong!" Humpty Dumpty exclaimed triumphantly. "You never said
A2   17: 2   the capital of Rome, and Rome--no, that's all wrong, I'm certain! I must have been changed for Mabel! I'll
A7   56: 1   "Two days wrong!" sighed the Hatter. "I told you butter wouldn't suit
T5   151:13   "You're wrong there, at any rate," said the Queen. "Were you ever
T3   130:20   At last he said "You're traveling the wrong way," and shut up the window, and went away. "So young a
T1   107: 8   other paw she rubbed its face all over, the wrong way, beginning at the nose: and just now, as I said, she
T1   110:40   like our books, only the words go the wrong way: I know that, because I've held up one of our books
WROTE (3)
A11   88:18   King said to the jury; and the jury eagerly wrote down all three dates on their slates, and then added
A12   95:27   The jury all wrote down, on their slates, "She doesn't believe there's an
A12   93:30   Some of the jury wrote it down "important," and some "unimportant." Alice could

-Y-

-YARD [See FARM-YARD, TWO-YARD]
YARDS (8)
  T2   120: 4 no, it doesn't do that--" (after going a few yards along the path, and turning several sharp corners), "but
  T1   108:19 the ball rolled down upon the floor, and yards and yards of it got unwound again.
  T2   128: 1 an answer, but went on. "At the end of three yards I shall repeat them--for fear of your forgetting them.
  T1   108:19 rolled down upon the floor, and yards and yards of it got unwound again.
  T6   159: 2 more human: when she had come within a few yards of it, she saw that it had eyes and a nose and a mouth;
  A6   50:21   sitting on a bough of a tree a few yards off.
  T2   127:35   "At the end of two yards," she said, putting in a peg to mark the distance, "I
  T8   190:14 by which they had come. "You've only a few yards to go," he said, "down the hill and over that little
YAWNED (2)
  A10   81: 1 and the reason is--" here the Mock Turtle yawned and shut his eyes. "Tell her about the reason and all
  A5   41:25   took the hookah out of its mouth, and yawned once or twice, and shook itself. Then it got down off
YAWNING (3)
  A7   60:14 were learning to draw," the Dormouse went on, yawning and rubbing its eyes, for it was getting very sleepy;
  T7   176: 6 animal--or vegetable--or mineral?" he said, yawning at every other word.
  A7   58:19 the subject," the March Hare interrupted, yawning. "I'm getting tired of this. I vote the young lady
YE (2) [See also D'YE]
  A4   31:19 Alice), "Well, I hardly know--No more, thank ye; I'm better now--but I'm a deal too flustered to tell you--
  T8W 21:15   "Good-bye, and thank-ye," said the Wasp, and Alice tripped down the hill again,
YEAR (5)
  T6   162:43 Humpty Dumpty. "How many days are there in a year?"
  T4   141: 8 maids with seven mops / Swept it for half a year, / Do you suppose,' the Walrus said, / 'That they could
  A7   56:17   "but that's because it stays the same year for such a long time together."
  T1   109: 3 kitten. "What would they do at the end of a year? I should be sent to prison, I suppose, when the day came
  A7   56:15 the Hatter. "Does your watch tell you what year it is?"
YEARS (5)
  T8   187:18 one that she always remembered most clearly. Years afterwards she could bring the whole scene back again,
  T6   161:22 made a short calculation, and said "Seven years and six months."
  T6   162: 3   "Seven years and six months!" Humpty Dumpty repeated thoughtfully.
  A12   99: 5 and how she would keep, through all her riper years, the simple and loving heart of her childhood; and how
  TI   103:18 echoes live in memory yet, / Though envious years would say "forget."
YELLED (1)
  A10   78:33   "Change lobsters again!" yelled the Gryphon at the top of its voice.
YELLOW (7)
  T4   146:14 with passion, and his eyes grew large and yellow all in a moment, as he pointed with a trembling finger
  T9   198:14 slowly towards her: he was dressed in bright yellow, and had enormous boots on.
  T8W 16:10 cold. And I gets under a tree. And I gets a yellow handkerchief. And I ties up my face--as at the present
  T8W 17: 7 And when you catches it, just try tying a yellow handkerchief round your face. It'll cure you in no
  T8W 17:10 at his wig in great surprise. It was bright yellow like the handkerchief, and all tangled and tumbled
  T8W 19:16 is why they do it, dear, / Because I wear a yellow wig."
  T8W 18:16 they said 'You should be shaved, / And wear a yellow wig instead.'
YELP (1)
  A4   32:35 into the air off all its feet at once, with a yelp of delight, and rushed at the stick, and made believe to
YER (4)
  A4   30: 3 "Sure then I'm here! Digging for apples, yer honour!"
  A4   30:14 now and then; such as "Sure, I don't like it, yer honour, at all, at all!" "Do as I tell you, you coward!",
  A4   30:10   "Sure, it does, yer honour: but it's an arm for all that."
  A4   30: 7   "Sure, it's an arm, yer honour!" (He pronounced it "arrum.")
YES [YE-ES] (28)
  T4   147:33   "Well--yes--a little," Alice replied gently.
  T5   155:16   "Yes, a little--but not on land--and not with needles--" Alice
  T6   161:13   "Yes, all his horses and all his men," Humpty Dumpty went on.
  T12 207: 8 always purr. "If they would only purr for 'yes,' and mew for 'no,' or any rule of that sort," she had
  A11   89: 1   "Yes, but I grow at a reasonable pace," said the Dormouse: "not
  A7   56: 5   "Yes, but some crumbs must have got in as well," the Hatter
  T8   179:29   "Yes, but then I came and rescued her!" the White Knight
  T5   151:18   "Yes, but then I had done the things I was punished for," said
  T8   184:42 at his helmet, which hung from the saddle. "Yes," he said; "but I've invented a better one than that--like
  T7   170: 9   "Yes, I did," said Alice: "several thousand, I should think."
  T8   184:34   "Yes, I suppose you'd be over when that was done," Alice said
  A10   84: 6   "Yes, I think you'd better leave off," said the Gryphon, and
  T5   149:13   "Well, yes, if you call that a-dressing," the Queen said. "It isn't
  T7   175:32   "Yes, if you like," said Alice.
  A8   62:15   "Yes, it is his business!" said Five. "And I'll tell him--it
  T8   181:34   "Yes, it's a very good bee-hive," the Knight said in a
  T12 207:12 it was impossible to guess whether it meant "yes" or "no."
  A3   26:14 it. And the others all joined in chorus "Yes, please do!" But the Mouse only shook its head impatiently
  A7   58:29   "Yes, please do!" pleaded Alice.
  T4   140:10   "Ye-es, pretty well--some poetry," Alice said doubtfully.
  A9   76:29   "Yes," said Alice doubtfully: "it means--to--make--anything--
  A10   80:18   "Yes," said Alice, "I've often seen them at dinn----" she
  A9   76:10   "Yes," said Alice: "we learned French and music."

YES (cont.)
```
 A8    65:22                                                        "Yes!" shouted Alice.
 A1     8:34   still it was good practice to say it over)  "--yes, that's about the right distance--but then I wonder what
 A7    58:12                                                        "Yes, that's it," said the Hatter with a sigh: "it's always
 T7   172:38                                                        "Yes, to be sure," said the King: "and the best of the joke is,
 A9    75: 9                                                        "Yes, we went to school in the sea, though you mayn't believe
```
YESTERDAY (7)
```
 T5   149:33   Queen  said with a sigh. "And I lost the comb yesterday."
 A10   81:41   timidly; "but it's no use going back to yesterday, because I was a different person then."
 T5   150: 6   said. "The rule is, jam to-morrow and jam yesterday--but never jam to-day."
 T4   146:27   than ever. "It's new, I tell you--I bought it yesterday--my nice NEW RATTLE!" and his voice rose to a
 T8   187:19   scene  back  again,  as  if  it had been only yesterday--the mild blue eyes and kindly smile of the Knight--
 A2    15:38   dear! How queer everything is to-day! And yesterday things went on just as usual. I wonder if I've
 A8    62:12   talk!" said Five. "I heard the Queen say only yesterday you deserved to be beheaded."
```
YET (44)
```
 A6    52: 6   said  Alice,  "but  I  haven't  been invited yet."
 A9    72:19   make you a present of everything I've said as yet."
 A9    73:11   said  to Alice "Have you seen the Mock Turtle yet?"
 T6   164:19   a  good  many  that haven't been invented just yet."
 T9   193:21   you've  not  had  many  lessons  in manners yet."
 A7    59:11                            "I've had nothing yet," Alice replied in an offended tone: "so I ca'n't take
 T5   154: 3                          "I don't quite know yet," Alice said very gently. "I should like to look all round
 T8   181:36   kind. But not a single bee has come near it yet. And the other thing is a mouse-trap. I suppose the mice
 A4    29: 2   wish I hadn't gone down that rabbit-hole--and yet--and yet--it's rather curious, you know, this sort of
 T4   142: 8   Four  other  Oysters  followed  them,  /  And yet another four; / And thick and fast they came at last, /
 A11   86:30   "They  ca'n't  have  anything  to  put down yet, before the trial's begun."
 T12  207:36   better  not  mention it to your friends just yet, for I'm not sure.
 A8    67: 3   feel  very  uneasy:  to be sure, she had not as yet had any dispute with the Queen, but she knew that it might
 A12   95:31   you  know,  as  we needn't try to find any. And yet I don't know," he went on, spreading out the verses on his
 T3   134:25                          "And yet I don't know," the Gnat went on in a careless tone: "only
 T2   120:15   was arguing with her. "I'm not going in again yet. I know I should have to get through the Looking-glass
 A2    19:33   soothing tone: "don't be angry about it. And yet I wish I could show you our cat Dinah. I think you'd take
 T8   186:19   believe that pudding ever will be cooked! And yet it was a very clever pudding to invent."
 A7    56:20   to her to have no sort of meaning in it, and yet it was certainly English. "I don't quite understand you,"
 A4    29: 2   gone  down  that  rabbit-hole--and yet--and yet--it's rather curious, you know, this sort of life! I do
 A11   88: 2                          "Not yet, not yet!" the Rabbit hastily interrupted. "There's a
 A4    30:28   first--they  don't  reach  half  high enough yet--Oh, they'll do well enough. Don't be particular--Here,
 A12   94: 3                  "There's more evidence to come yet, please your Majesty," said the White Rabbit, jumping up
 A5    36: 2   "Well,  perhaps  you  haven't  found  it so yet," said Alice; "but when you have to turn into a chrysalis
 A12   95:21   most  important  piece  of  evidence we've heard yet," said the King, rubbing his hands; "so now let the jury--
 T8   182:29                          "Not yet," said the Knight. "But I've got a plan for keeping it
 A12   94: 7                  "I haven't opened it yet," said the White Rabbit; "but it seems to be a letter,
 A11   91:31   like,  "--for  they  haven't  got much evidence yet," she said to herself. Imagine her surprise, when the
 T3   129:17   think  I'll go down and--no, I wo'n't go just yet," she went on, checking herself just as she was beginning
 A7    56:27                  "Have you guessed the riddle yet?" the Hatter said, turning to Alice again.
 T8   184:36                          "I haven't tried it yet," the Knight said, gravely; "so I ca'n't tell for certain
 T5   152:10                          "I haven't pricked it yet," the Queen said, "but I soon shall--oh, oh, oh!"
 A11   88: 2                          "Not yet, not yet!" the Rabbit hastily interrupted. "There's a great deal to
 TC   209:13                          Children yet, the tale to hear, / Eager eye and willing ear, / Lovingly
 TI   103:17   of  our  rowing--/ Whose echoes live in memory yet, / Though envious years would say "forget."
 T8   188:23   a  stuff  they  call  / Rowland's Macassar-Oil--/ Yet twopence-halfpenny is all / They give me for my toil.'
 A4    33: 7                          "And yet what a dear little puppy it was!" said Alice, as she leant
 AI     3:11   too  weak  /  To  stir  the tiniest feather! / Yet what can one poor voice avail / Against three tongues
 T12  207: 2   and  addressing  the  kitten, respectfully, yet with some severity. "You woke me out of oh! such a nice
 A5    40: 3   /  That  your  eye  was as steady as ever; / Yet you balanced an eel on the end of your nose--/ What made
 A5    39: 3   too  weak  /  For  anything tougher than suet; / Yet you finished the goose, with the bones and the beak--/
 A5    37: 3   /  "And your hair has become very white; / And yet you incessantly stand on your head--/ Do you think, at
 T1   108:39   and  you've not been punished for any of them yet. You know I'm saving up all your punishments for Wednesday
 A5    38: 3   /  And  have  grown  most  uncommonly fat; / Yet you turned a back-somersault in at the door--/ Pray, what
```
YONDER (2)
```
 T6   166: 9   you'll  hear  it  done, maybe--down in the wood yonder--and, when you've once heard it, you'll be quite
 T7   174:23   country! She came flying out of the wood over yonder--How fast those Queens can run!"
```
YOU (909) [entries omitted]
YOU'D (34)
```
 T8W   16: 7                          "You'd be cross too, if you'd a wig like mine," the Wasp went on. "They jokes at one.
 T6   162: 4   "An  uncomfortable  sort  of  age.  Now if you'd asked my advice, I'd have said 'Leave off at seven'--but
 T4   145: 6   off  dreaming about you, where do you suppose you'd be?"
 T8W   16: 7                          "You'd be cross too, if you'd a wig like mine," the Wasp went
 T4   145: 8   you!" Tweedledee retorted contemptuously. "You'd be nowhere. Why, you're only a sort of thing in his
 T8   184:34                          "Yes, I suppose you'd be over when that was done," Alice said thoughtfully:
 T6   160:16                          "Don't you think you'd be safer down on the ground?" Alice went on, not with
 T12  207:37                  "By the way, Kitty, if only you'd been really with me in my dream, there was one thing you
 T1   108:12   Kitty?" Alice began. "You'd have guessed if you'd been up in the window with me--only Dinah was making you
 A8    69: 7   else  to  say but "It belongs to the Duchess: you'd better ask her about it."
 A7    59:26   sulkily  remarked "If  you  ca'n't be civil, you'd better finish the story for yourself."
 A10   84: 6                          Yes, I think you'd better leave off," said the Gryphon, and Alice was only
 T4   147:45   rather  sadly: "and she can watch us--only you'd better not come very close," he added: "I generally hit
 A4    32: 3   this," she said to herself, and shouted out "You'd better not do that again!", which produced another dead
 T4   147:38                  "Then you'd better not fight to-day," said Alice, thinking it a good
 T12  207:35   to  Humpty  Dumpty? I think you did--however, you'd better not mention it to your friends just yet, for I'm
```

YOU'D (cont.)

A8	62:11	"You'd better not talk!" said Five. "I heard the Queen say only
T2	125: 9	show you hills, in comparison with which you'd call that a valley."
T2	127:16	said Alice, still panting a little, "you'd generally get to somewhere else--if you ran very fast
T4	145:10	there King was to wake," added Tweedledum, "you'd go out--bang!--just like a candle!"
T1	108:24	and putting you out into the snow! And you'd have deserved it, you little mischievous darling! What
T1	108:11	know what to-morrow is, Kitty?" Alice began. "You'd have guessed if you'd been up in the window with me--
A12	94:24	You must have meant some mischief, or else you'd have signed your name like an honest man."
T9	201:22	said the Pudding. "I wonder how you'd like it, if I were to cut a slice out of you, you
A9	72: 6	is--'Be what you would seem to be'--or, if you'd like it put more simply--'Never imagine yourself not to
T2	127:25	"I know what you'd like!" the Queen said good-naturedly, taking a little
T1	110:22	I think if you sat up and folded your arms, you'd look exactly like her. Now do try, there's a dear!" And
T6	164: 1	that subject, and it would be just as well if you'd mention what you mean to do next, as I suppose you don't
T3	135: 9	anything more," the Gnat remarked, "of course you'd miss your lessons. That's a joke. I wish you had made it
A7	56:45	in the morning, just time to begin lessons: you'd only have to whisper a hint to Time, and round goes the
A2	19:41	"We wo'n't talk about her any more, if you'd rather not."
T1	108:31	your fault, for keeping your eyes open--if you'd shut them tight up, it wouldn't have happened. Now don't
T2	121: 8	the Rose, "and I really was wondering when you'd speak! Said I to myself, 'Her face has got some sense in
A2	19:34	wish I could show you our cat Dinah. I think you'd take a fancy to cats, if you could only see her. She is

YOU'LL (32)

T8	190:15	the hill and over that little brook, and then you'll be a Queen--But you'll stay and see me off first?" he
T2	126:10	begin with: when you get to the Eighth Square you'll be a Queen--"Just at this moment, somehow or other,
A7	58:30	And be quick about it," added the Hatter, "or you'll be asleep again before it's done."
T5	155:28	the Sheep cried again, taking more needles. "You'll be catching a crab directly.
T1	114:19	from bar to bar, till at last she said "Why, you'll be hours and hours getting to the table, at that rate.
T8W	14:10	you let me help you round to the other side? You'll be out of the cold wind there."
T6	166:10	wood yonder--and, when you've once heard it, you'll be quite content. Who's been repeating all that hard
A5	43:14	and there's no use denying it. I suppose you'll be telling me next that you never tasted an egg!"
T4	145:17	loud that Alice couldn't help saying "Hush! You'll be waking him, I'm afraid, if you make so much noise."
T7	175:31	have seen each other," said the Unicorn, "if you'll believe in me, I'll believe in you. Is that a bargain?"
T3	137: 1	"I'll tell you, if you'll come a little further on," the Fawn said. "I ca'n't
T9	194:37	that grand? However, don't be discouraged. You'll come to it in time."
A5	36: 4	after that into a butterfly, I should think you'll feel it a little queer, wo'n't you?"
T3	133:13	above your head," said the Gnat, "and there you'll find a Snap-dragon-fly. Its body is made of
T2	128: 9	Third Square--by railway, I should think--and you'll find yourself in the Fourth Square in no time. Well,
A5	41:21	"You'll get used to it in time," said the Caterpillar; and it
T2	128: 8	two squares in its first move, you know. So you'll go very quickly through the Third Square--by railway, I
T6	166: 8	with a kind of sneeze in the middle: however, you'll hear it done, maybe--down in the wood yonder--and, when
T8W	17: 6	the Wasp: "wait till you have it, and then you'll know. And when you catches it, just try tying a yellow
T2	122:25	feel the ground," said the Tiger-lily. "Then you'll know why."
T5	155: 8	as she took up another pair of needles. "You'll make me giddy soon, if you go on turning round like
T7	176: 3	what is it, now?" the Unicorn cried eagerly. "You'll never guess! I couldn't."
T6	160:38	one that has spoken to a King, I am: mayhap you'll never see such another: and, to show you I'm not proud,
T1	110:30	"Now, if you'll only attend, Kitty, and not talk so much, I'll tell you
T3	133: 3	said the Gnat. "Half way up that bush, you'll see a Rocking-horse-fly, if you look. It's made
T2	123:20	"I daresay you'll see her soon," said the Rose. "She's one of the kind
A6	52: 7	"You'll see me there," said the Cat, and vanished.
T8	190:16	little brook, and then you'll be a Queen--But you'll stay and see me off first?" he added as Alice turned
T9	195:12	a way out of the difficulty, this time. "If you'll tell me what language 'fiddle-de-dee' is, I'll tell you
T6	166:33	"In summer, when the days are long, / Perhaps you'll understand the song:
A2	20:19	shore, and then I'll tell you my history, and you'll understand why it is I hate cats and dogs."
T8	190:18	to which he pointed. "I sha'n't be long. You'll wait and wave your handkerchief when I get to that turn

YOUNG (13)

T3	130:21	and shut up the window, and went away. "So young a child," said the gentleman sitting opposite to her,
A3	26:20	temper!" "Hold your tongue, Ma!" said the young Crab, a little snappishly. "You're enough to try the
T7	171:11	"This young lady loves you with an H," the King said, introducing
A9	74:25	"This here young lady," said the Gryphon, "she wants for to know your
T7	172:18	"Quite right," said the King: "this young lady saw him too. So of course Nobody walks slower than
A7	58:19	"I'm getting tired of this. I vote the young lady tells us a story."
A9	74: 1	lazy thing!" said the Queen, "and take this young lady to see the Mock Turtle, and to hear his history. I
TI	103:10	No thought of me shall find a place / In thy young life's hereafter--/ Enough that now thou wilt not fail /
A5	37: 1	"You are old, Father William," the young man said, / "And your hair has become very white; / And
T8W	18:13	"When I was young, my ringlets waved / And curled and crinkled on my head:
T4	142: 1	But four young Oysters hurried up, / All eager for the treat: / Their
T2	126: 9	Queen's Pawn, if you like, as Lily's too young to play: and you're in the Second Square to begin with:
T8W	18: 4	came to wear it," the Wasp said. "When I was young, you know, my ringlets used to wave--"

YOUR (145) [entries omitted]

YOU'RE (59)

T8W	17:14	"What, you're a Bee, are you?" the Wasp said, looking at her with
T1	110:19	Do let's pretend that I'm a hungry hyaena and you're a bone!"
T4	147:15	dish-covers, and coal-scuttles. "I hope you're a good hand at pinning and tying strings?" Tweedledum
T3	137: 7	out in a voice of delight. "And, dear me! you're a human child!" A sudden look of alarm came into its
A5	43:24	enough; and what does it matter to me whether you're a little girl or a serpent?"
T5	155:38	"You are," said the Sheep: "you're a little goose."
A5	43:13	never one with such a neck as that! No, no! You're a serpent; and there's no use denying it. I suppose
A11	90:10	"You're a very poor speaker," said the King.
T8	181:17	"I see you're admiring my little box," the Knight said in a friendly
T2	123: 6	said the Rose. "I wonder how you do it--" ("You're always wondering," said the Tiger-lily), "but she's
A7	57:15	twinkle, little bat! / How I wonder what you're at!'
T2	123:15	not your fault," the Rose added kindly. "You're beginning to fade, you know--and then one ca'n't help

YOU'RE (cont.)
A5   36:30   of its mouth again, and said "So you think you're changed, do you?"
A6   48:16   "Oh, please mind what you're doing!" cried Alice, jumping up and down in an agony of
T12   208: 2   you shall have a real treat. All the time you're eating your breakfast, I'll repeat 'The Walrus and the
A3   26:20   said the young Crab, a little snappishly. "You're enough to try the patience of an oyster!"
T7   172: 9   deal. "There's nothing like eating hay when you're faint," he remarked to her, as he munched away.
A1   9: 1   to curtsey as she spoke--fancy, curtseying as you're falling through the air! Do you think you could manage
A6   50: 3   No, there were no tears. "If you're going to turn into a pig, my dear," said Alice,
A11   88:43   nonsense," said Alice more boldly: "you know you're growing too."
T5   152:18   "Take care!" cried Alice. "You're holding it all crooked!" And she caught at the brooch;
T6   163:15   "You're holding it upside down!" Alice interrupted.
T2   126: 9   if you like, as Lily's too young to play: and you're in the Second Square to begin with: when you get to the
A5   43:23   gave the Pigeon the opportunity of adding "You're looking for eggs, I know that well enough; and what
A6   51:24   said the Cat: "we're all mad here. I'm mad. You're mad."
A6   51:28   she went on: "And how do you know that you're mad?"
T8   179:20   in the saddle, he began once more "You're my--" but here another voice broke in "Ahoy! Ahoy!
T8   179:15   he reached her, the horse stopped suddenly: "You're my prisoner!" the Knight cried, as he tumbled off his
T1   110:28   that it might see how sulky it was, "--and if you're not good directly," she added, "I'll put you through
T8W   13:20   over him, and said very kindly, "I hope you're not in much pain?"
T4   140: 6   "I hope you're not much tired?" she said at last.
T4   145:20   the things in his dream. You know very well you're not real."
T8W   15:17   Alice put down the newspaper. "I'm afraid you're not well," she said in a soothing tone. "Can't I do
A12   97: 8   had grown to her full size by this time). "You're nothing but a pack of cards!"
T4   145: 9   contemptuously. "You'd be nowhere. Why, you're only a sort of thing in his dream!"
T4   145:19   about waking him," said Tweedledum, "when you're only one of the things in his dream. You know very well
T4   143:11   besides / Are very good indeed--/ Now, if you're ready, Oysters dear, / We can begin to feed.'
T2   127:31   "While you're refreshing yourself," said the Queen, "I'll just take
T12   207:30   untidy in my dream--Dinah! Do you know that you're scrubbing a White Queen? Really, it's most
T3   131:32   in vain to see where the voice came from. "If you're so anxious to have a joke made, why don't you make one
A3   26:10   "I didn't mean it!" pleaded poor Alice. "But you're so easily offended, you know!"
T6   168:23   giving her one of his fingers to shake: "you're so exactly like other people."
T9   192:18   "Speak when you're spoken to!" the Queen sharply interrupted her.
A6   51:15   "Oh, you're sure to do that," said the Cat, "if you only walk long
T6   162:42   "You don't know what you're talking about!" cried Humpty Dumpty. "How many days are
A5   42:32   "I haven't the least idea what you're talking about," said Alice.
T1   110:21   speech to the kitten. "Let's pretend that you're the Red Queen, Kitty! Do you know, I think if you sat
T2   121:10   in it, though it's not a clever one!' Still, you're the right colour, and that goes a long way."
T4   139: 5   "I know what you're thinking about," said Tweedledum; "but it isn't so,
A9   70:17   when she heard her voice close to her ear. "You're thinking about something, my dear, and that makes you
T2   124:13   she added in a kinder tone. "Curtsey while you're thinking what to say. It saves time."
T12   207:23   cried with a merry laugh. "And curtsey while you're thinking what to--what to purr. It saves time,
T1   115:12   ashes will get into it--there, now I think you're tidy enough!" she added, as she smoothed his hair, and
T3   130:20   then through an opera-glass. At last he said "You're traveling the wrong way," and shut up the window, and
A5   43: 7   What are you?" said the Pigeon. "I can see you're trying to invent something!"
T3   132:41   however, go on with your list of insects: you're wasting time."
A9   71: 5   "I dare say you're wondering why I don't put my arm round your waist," the
A10   80:24   "You're wrong about the crumbs," said the Mock Turtle: "crumbs
T5   151:13   "You're wrong there, at any rate," said the Queen. "Were you

YOURS (5) [entries omitted]
YOURSELF (21) [entries omitted]
YOUTH (6)
A5   39: 1   "You are old," said the youth, "and your jaws are too weak / For anything tougher than
A5   38: 1   "You are old," said the youth, "as I mentioned before, / And have grown most
A5   37: 5   "In my youth," Father William replied to his son, / "I feared it
A5   40: 1   "You are old," said the youth, "one would hardly suppose / That your eye was as steady
A5   39: 5   "In my youth," said his father, "I took to the law, / And argued each
A5   38: 5   "In my youth," said the sage, as he shook his grey locks, / "I kept

YOU'VE (35)
T8W   14:17   "You may read it if you've a mind to," the Wasp said, rather sulkily. "Nobody's
T12   207: 3   You woke me out of oh! such a nice dream! And you've been along with me, Kitty--all through the
A5   42:41   "I'm very sorry you've been annoyed," said Alice, who was beginning to see its
T9   201: 7   decidedly: "it isn't etiquette to cut any one you've been introduced to. Remove the joint!" And the waiters
T6   160:31   cried, breaking into a sudden passion. "You've been listening at doors--and behind trees--and down
T4   139:21   "You've begun wrong!" cried Tweedledum. "The first thing in a
A10   78:17   Seals, turtles, salmon, and so on: then, when you've cleared all the jelly-fish out of the way--"
T5   152:38   great girl you are. Consider what a long way you've come to-day. Consider what o'clock it is. Consider
T8   181: 3   "So you will, when you've crossed the next brook," said the White Knight. "I'll
T8   181:32   "But you've got a bee-hive--or something like one--fastened to the
T8W   17:15   said, looking at her with more interest. "And you've got a comb. Much honey?"
T5   154: 6   "but you ca'n't look all round you--unless you've got eyes at the back of your head."
T6   162:13   "What a beautiful belt you've got on!" Alice suddenly remarked. (They had had quite
T8   184:39   the subject hastily. "What a curious helmet you've got!" she said cheerfully. "Is that your invention too
A4   30:33   got to go down--Here, Bill! The master says you've got to go down the chimney!"
T7   172:23   else he'd have been here first. However, now you've got your breath, you may tell us what's happened in the
T8   182:22   "I hope you've got your hair well fastened on?" he continued, as they
A12   98: 5   said her sister. "Why, what a long sleep you've had!"
T4   144: 8   'O Oysters,' said the Carpenter, / 'You've had a pleasant run! / Shall we be trotting home again?'
T9   200:18   At last the Red Queen began. "You've missed the soup and fish," she said. "Put on the joint!
A8   67:26   if there are, nobody attends to them--and you've no idea how confusing it is all the things being alive:
T8   186:26   alone," he interrupted, quite eagerly: "but you've no idea what a difference it makes, mixing it with

YOU'VE (cont.)

A11	88:42	"You've no right to grow here," said the Dormouse.
T1	108:38	"That's three faults, Kitty, and you've not been punished for any of them yet. You know I'm
T9	193:20	it," the Red Queen remarked: "but I daresay you've not had many lessons in manners yet."
T8	183: 3	"I'm afraid you've not had much practice in riding," she ventured to say,
T6	166: 9	maybe--down in the wood yonder--and, when you've once heard it, you'll be quite content. Who's been
T9	195:22	to correct it," said the Red Queen: "when you've once said a thing, that fixes it, and you must take the
T8	190:14	head along the road by which they had come. "You've only a few yards to go," he said, "down the hill and
T9	192:28	so? You ca'n't be a Queen, you know, till you've passed the proper examination. And the sooner we begin
T5	155:32	"Indeed I did," said Alice: "you've said it very often--and very loud. Please, where are
A10	80:16	to the whiting," said the Mock Turtle, "they--you've seen them, of course?"
A10	80:21	Dinn may be," said the Mock Turtle; "but, if you've seen them so often, of course you know what they're
T6	166:27	"If you can see whether I'm singing or not, you've sharper eyes than most," Humpty Dumpty remarked
T6	168:33	only shut his eyes, and said "Wait till you've tried."

-z-

ZEALAND (1)
   A1   8:45 is, you know. Please, Ma'am, is this New Zealand? Or Australia?" (and she tried to curtsey as she spoke
ZIGZAG (1)
   A5   42:22 succeeded in curving it down into a graceful zigzag, and was going to dive in among the leaves, which she

-numerals-

1 (1)
   T6   163: 9   365 / 1 /----/ 364 /----
364 (1)
   T6   163:11   365 / 1 /----/ 364 /----
365 (1)
   T6   163: 8   365 / 1 /----/ 364 /----

RANKING FREQUENCY LIST
(*ALICE'S ADVENTURES IN WONDERLAND*)

1.) 1653 (6.18%)
THE

2.) 870 (3.25%)
AND

3.) 734 (2.74%)
TO

4.) 636 (2.38%)
A

5.) 544 (2.03%)
SHE

6.) 535 (2.00%)
IT

7.) 515 (1.92%)
OF

8.) 463 (1.73%)
SAID

9.) 408 (1.52%)
I

10.) 387 (1.45%)
ALICE

11.) 374 (1.40%)
IN

12.) 368 (1.37%)
YOU

13.) 360 (1.35%)
WAS

14.) 285 (1.06%)
THAT

15.) 261 (0.975%)
AS

16.) 251 (0.938%)
HER

17.) 213 (0.796%)
AT

18.) 196 (0.732%)
ON

19.) 185 (0.691%)
WITH

20.) 184 (0.687%)
ALL

21.) 178 (0.665%)
HAD

22.) 172 (0.643%)
BUT

23.) 153 (0.572%)
FOR
SO

24.) 151 (0.564%)
BE

25.) 147 (0.549%)
NOT

26.) 146 (0.545%)
VERY

27.) 140 (0.523%)
WHAT

28.) 137 (0.512%)
THIS

29.) 132 (0.493%)
LITTLE

30.) 130 (0.486%)
THEY

31.) 118 (0.441%)
HE

32.) 114 (0.426%)
OUT

33.) 110 (0.411%)
IS

34.) 108 (0.404%)
ONE

35.) 100 (0.374%)
DOWN

36.) 97 (0.362%)
IF
UP

37.) 95 (0.355%)
ABOUT

38.) 94 (0.351%)
HIS

39.) 93 (0.347%)
THEN

40.) 89 (0.333%)
NO

41.) 88 (0.329%)
THEM

42.) 87 (0.325%)
KNOW

43.) 86 (0.321%)
LIKE

44.) 85 (0.318%)
HERSELF

45.) 84 (0.314%)
WERE

46.) 83 (0.310%)
AGAIN
WOULD

47.) 82 (0.306%)
WENT

48.) 81 (0.303%)
HAVE

49.) 80 (0.299%)
DO

50.) 79 (0.295%)
COULD
WHEN

51.) 78 (0.291%)
OR

52.) 77 (0.288%)
THERE

53.) 75 (0.280%)
OFF

54.) 73 (0.273%)
THOUGHT

55.) 70 (0.262%)
TIME

56.) 69 (0.258%)
QUEEN

57.) 68 (0.254%)
HOW
INTO
ME

58.) 67 (0.250%)
SEE

59.) 62 (0.232%)
DID
YOUR

60.) 61 (0.228%)
BY
DON'T
KING
NOW
WELL

61.) 60 (0.224%)
I'M
ITS
WHO

62.) 59 (0.220%)
BEGAN

63.) 58 (0.217%)
AN
MY

64.) 57 (0.213%)
ARE
IT'S
TURTLE

65.) 56 (0.209%)
MOCK

66.) 55 (0.205%)
GRYPHON
HATTER
QUITE

67.) 54 (0.202%)
WAY

68.) 53 (0.198%)
JUST
SOME
THINK

69.) 52 (0.194%)
THEIR

70.) 51 (0.191%)
FIRST
HERE
MUCH
SAY

71.) 50 (0.187%)
GO
MORE
ONLY
WHICH

72.) 49 (0.183%)
HEAD
THING
VOICE

73.) 47 (0.176%)
GOT
NEVER

74.) 46 (0.172%)
COME
GET

75.) 45 (0.168%)
LOOKED
MUST
OH

76.) 43 (0.161%)
HIM
RABBIT
SUCH

77.) 42 (0.157%)
AFTER
MOUSE
WHY

78.) 41 (0.153%)
ROUND

79.) 40 (0.149%)
ANY
CAME
OTHER
OVER
TONE
TWO

80.) 39 (0.146%)
BACK
BEFORE
DORMOUSE
DUCHESS
GREAT

81.) 37 (0.138%)
BEEN
FROM

82.) 36 (0.135%)
CAN

83.) 35 (0.131%)
ONCE

84.) 34 (0.127%)
I'VE
MARCH
THAT'S
WILL

85.) 33 (0.123%)
LARGE
LAST
NOTHING

86.) 32 (0.120%)
FOUND
LONG
NEXT
PUT
TELL
WE

87.) 31 (0.116%)
CAT
HARE
I'LL
RIGHT

88.) 30 (0.112%)
DOOR
HEARD
LOOKING
MADE
MOMENT
WHITE

89.) 29 (0.108%)
DEAR
EYES
REPLIED
THINGS

90.) 28 (0.105%)
CA'N'T
LOOK
MAKE
MIGHT
POOR
SEEMED
SHOULD
THREE
TOO

91.) 27 (0.101%)
CATERPILLAR
WHILE

92.) 26 (0.0971%)
COURSE
GOING
RATHER
WITHOUT
YET

93.) 25 (0.0934%)
AWAY
SHALL
SOON
SOUP
THAN

94.) 24 (0.0897%)
DAY
GOOD
SAME
SURE
THERE'S
TOOK
UPON
WO'N'T

95.) 23 (0.0859%)
ANOTHER
EVER
FELT
TAKE

96.) 22 (0.0822%)
ADDED
GETTING
HALF
MINUTE
TILL

97.) 21 (0.0785%)
ANYTHING
FIND
HAND
WISH
WORDS
YOU'RE

98.) 20 (0.0747%)
CRIED
HOWEVER
PLEASE
SORT

99.) 19 (0.0710%)
BEING
COURT
CURIOUS
FEET
OLD
TRIED

100.) 18 (0.0673%)
BEAUTIFUL
EAT
ENOUGH
EVEN
HOUSE
SOMETHING
USE
WONDER

101.) 17 (0.0635%)
DOESN'T
END
JURY
LET
PERHAPS
QUESTION
SIDE
SPOKE
TABLE
TALKING

102.) 16 (0.0598%)
ASKED
BIT
CALLED
DONE
GARDEN
HASTILY
HIGH
IDEA
INDEED
RAN
SAT
SILENCE
TURNED
UNDER

103.) 15 (0.0560%)
BECAUSE
BOTH
FACE
GAVE
KNEW
MAD
NEAR
SAYING
SEEN
SET
SPEAK
THROUGH

104.) 14 (0.0523%)
AIR
AM
ANXIOUSLY
BEGIN
BEGINNING
BETTER
CERTAINLY
CHANGE
DIDN'T
HEAR
ITSELF
LEFT
OUGHT
PEOPLE
REMEMBER
SAW
STILL
SUPPOSE
TALK

104.) 14 (cont.)
THESE
TRYING
US
WHERE

105.) 13 (0.0486%)
ALWAYS
BABY
BEHIND
BILL
CLOSE
COOK
DANCE
DODO
FAR
GONE
GROW
HANDS
KEPT
LOW
MAY
REALLY
ROOM
SEA
SIZE
SUDDENLY
THEY'RE
USED
WHOLE
WOULDN'T
YES

106.) 12 (0.0448%)
AFRAID
AMONG
ARM
BEST
CATS
DEAL
DINAH
EVERY
EVERYTHING
GAME
GIVE
HARDLY
MAJESTY
MANY
PIGEON
TEA
TRY
TURNING

107.) 11 (0.0411%)
ALICE'S
ASK
CREATURES
ELSE
FINISHED
GLAD
GROWING
HURRIED
HURRY
I'D
KEEP
LIFE
MAKES
MIND
MINUTES
NEARLY
POOL
READ
REST
TEARS
THINKING
THOUGH
WAITED
WASN'T
WHETHER

108.) 10 (0.0374%)
AGAINST
BELIEVE
BIRDS
BOTTLE
CHILD
CHILDREN
COMING
EITHER
EXPLAIN
FAN
FOOT
FOOTMAN
HAVING
HEADS
HOLD
LESSONS
MATTER
MEAN
MOUTH
NAME
OPENED
OUR
OWN
QUEER
REMARK
REMARKED
REPEATED
SIGHT
SMALL
SOLDIERS
STORY
THOSE
TOGETHER
TURN
WALKED
WITNESS
WORD
YOU'D
YOURSELF

109.) 9 (0.0336%)
ANGRILY
ANSWER
BEG
CALL
CONVERSATION
COULDN'T
DIFFERENT
DOES
DRY
FANCY
FEW
GLASS
HALL
HARD
HELP
INTERRUPTED
JOIN
KEY
KNAVE
LEAST
LEAVE
LYING
MINE
OFFENDED
PUZZLED
RATE
REASON
SERPENT
SHOOK
SHOUTED
SITTING
SLOWLY
TAIL
TIMIDLY
WAITING
WANT
WATCH

110.) 8 (0.0299%)
APPEARED
ASLEEP
CHANGED
DISTANCE
EACH
EAGERLY
EVERYBODY
EXACTLY
FACT
FEEL
FIVE
FOLLOWED
GARDENERS
GOLDEN
HADN'T
HAPPEN
HAVEN'T
HEARTS
IT'LL
LIVE
MAKING
MEANING
MORAL
MOST
MUSHROOM
NOBODY
NONSENSE
NOSE
NOTICED
OPPORTUNITY
PARTY
PIG
PLACE
PLAY
READY
RUNNING
SEEM
SISTER
SIT
STOOD
TALE
TOP
TWINKLE
WHITING
WINDOW
WOOD
WORK
YOU'VE

111.) 7 (0.0262%)
ARMS
BEGUN
BOOK
BRIGHT
BUSINESS
CHIN
CONTINUED
CROQUET
DEEP
DRAW
DREAM
DRINK
EVIDENCE
EYE
FALL
FEELING
FETCH
FRIGHTENED
FULL
GENERALLY
GOES
GROWN
HAIR
HAPPENED
HAS
HEDGEHOG
HISTORY
IMPORTANT
ISN'T

111.) 7 (cont.)
KIND
LARGER
LEARN
LISTEN
LOBSTERS
LORY
MANAGE
MIDDLE
MYSELF
NECK
OPEN
OTHERS
PEPPER
PLEASED
QUEEN'S
REPEAT
SHE'S
SHOES
SILENT
SIR
SLATES
SOMEBODY
SONG
SUBJECT
SURPRISED
TARTS
TIRED
TREES
TRIAL
WILLIAM
WONDERING
WORLD

112.) 6 (0.0224%)
ADVENTURES
AH
ALMOST
ANGRY
BECOME
BETWEEN
BREAD-AND-BUTTER
BROKEN
CHIMNEY
CHORUS
DREADFULLY
EAR
ENGLISH
EXCLAIMED
EXECUTED
FATHER
FELL
FORGOTTEN
FOUR
GLOVES
GRIN
HIMSELF
HOME
INCHES
LATE
LEAVES
LIKED
LOUD
MARKED
MELANCHOLY
NEW
NICE
PARDON
POLITELY
PUPPY
ROOF
SENTENCE
SEVEN
SHA'N'T
SHARP
SING
SLEEP
SNEEZING
STAND
STOP

112.) 6 (cont.)

STUPID
SUDDEN
TEN
TIMES
TOLD
TREMBLING
TROUBLE
UNDERSTAND
WOW
WRITE
WRITTEN
YOU'LL
YOUTH

113.) 5 (0.0187%)

ACROSS
ALONE
ALONG
ALOUD
ALTOGETHER
ANSWERED
ASKING
BREATH
CASE
CHESHIRE-CAT
CONFUSION
CROWDED
CURIOSITY
CUT
DARE
DEAD
DIRECTION
DOING
DREW
DROPPED
EARS
EGGS
EVENING
EXECUTIONER
FACES
FINGER
FINISH
FLAMINGO
GROUND
HAPPENS
HEIGHT
HOOKAH
HOT
INSTANTLY
INTERESTING
JUMPED
JURYMEN
KID-GLOVES
KNEE
LAY
LET'S
LIKELY
LIZARD
MAN
MEANS
MEANT
MORNING
MOVED
NEARER
NERVOUS
NINE
NOTICE
NUMBER
OFTEN
PACK
PAIR
PASSED
PIECE
POCKET
PRIZES
PROCESSION
QUIETLY
REMEMBERED
REPLY

113.) 5 (cont.)

RULE
SADLY
SCHOOL
SEEMS
SHOULDN'T
SHRIEK
SHRILL
SHUT
SIGHED
SIMPLE
SLEEPY
SOUNDED
SPEAKING
STAY
STRANGE
SURPRISE
SWAM
SWIM
TAKING
TEMPER
'TIS
TREACLE
TREE
TRUE
TWICE
UNIMPORTANT
UNTIL
USUAL
WALK
WALKING
WAVING
WHAT'S
WHISPERED
WRONG
YOUNG

114.) 4 (0.0149%)

AGE
ALAS
ANIMALS
ANN
ARCHES
ARGUMENT
BATS
BEAT
BEGINS
BESIDES
BILL'S
BOOTS
BOTTOM
BOWED
BOX
BUSILY
CAPITAL
CARE
CARRIED
CATCH
CHANCE
CONFUSED
CONSIDER
CORNER
CREATURE
CROWD
CRUMBS
CRY
DAYS
DECIDEDLY
DEEPLY
DIFFICULTY
DIGGING
DISH
DOUBT
DUCK
EARTH
ESCAPE
FALLEN
FAST
FEAR
FELLOW

114.) 4 (cont.)

FISH
FOND
FRENCH
FROWNING
GIRL
GRASS
GREEN
GRUNTED
GUINEA-PIGS
HEARING
HELD
HERS
HONOUR
HOURS
IMPATIENTLY
INDIGNANTLY
JUDGE
JUMPING
JURORS
JURY-BOX
KITCHEN
LED
LESS
LIVES
LOBSTER-QUADRILLE
MABEL
MANAGED
MARY
MICE
MISS
MOUTHS
MOVING
NATURAL
NONE
OFFICERS
ORDERED
OTHERWISE
OUTSIDE
PALE
PAPER
PARTICULAR
PASSAGE
PAWS
PERFECTLY
PERSON
PICTURES
PLAN
PLAYERS
POINTING
PORPOISE
PUZZLING
QUESTIONS
RABBIT-HOLE
RABBIT'S
REACH
ROSE-TREE
RUN
SAVAGE
SAYS
SECOND
SEVERAL
SEVERELY
SHARPLY
SHORT
SHOULDER
SHOULDERS
SHRINKING
SIDES
SIGH
SINCE
SKY
SOLEMNLY
SOMETIMES
SOUND
SOUNDS
STICK
STUFF
SUPPRESSED
TAKEN

TAUGHT
THANK
THEY'D
THEY'LL
THIMBLE
THOUGHTFULLY
TINY
TO-DAY
TONGUE
TWELVE
TWINKLING
UNCOMFORTABLE
VANISHED
VENTURED
VERDICT
VERSE
VERSES
VIOLENTLY
VOICES
WANTED
WORTH
WRITING
YER

115.) 3 (0.0112%)

ABOVE
ADVANCE
ADVANTAGE
ALIVE
ALLOW
ANXIOUS
AROUND
ATTENDING
BANK
BAT
BEHEADED
BELOW
BIRD
BREATHE
BRING
BRINGING
BROUGHT
BUTTER
CAKE
CAKES
CANDLE
CARDS
CAREFULLY
CAUCUS-RACE
CAUGHT
CAUSE
CAUTIOUSLY
CERTAIN
CHECKED
CHEERED
CHOKED
CIVIL
COMES
CONFUSING
CONSIDERED
CONSIDERING
COURAGE
CRAB
CRASH
CROQUET-GROUND
CROSSED
CROWN
DARK
DEARS
DECIDED
DELIGHT
DIRECTIONS
DOGS
DOTH
DUCHESS'S
DULL
EAGER
EAGLET
EASILY
EDGE

115.) 3 (cont.)

EFFECT
ELBOW
'EM
EXCEPT
EXECUTION
EXPECTING
FASTER
FIGURE
FILLED
FINDING
FIRE
FIT
FLOOR
FLOWERS
FLY
FOLDED
FORGETTING
FREE
FRIEND
FUN
FUNNY
FUR
FURTHER
FURY
GENERAL
GENTLY
GIRLS
GRAND
GRAVE
GRAVELY
GRINNED
GROWL
GUESS
GUESSED
GUESTS
HANDED
HANGING
HEDGEHOGS
HE'S
HOARSE
HOLDING
HOPE
HOPING
HOUR
HOWLING
HUNGRY
HUNTING
HURT
HUSH
IMMEDIATELY
IMPOSSIBLE
INSTANCE
INSTEAD
JOINED
KICK
KNOCKING
KNOWLEDGE
LADY
LAND
LEGS
LETTER
LIST
LISTENING
LIVED
LIVERY
LOBSTER
LONGER
LOST
LOUDLY
LOVE
M
MARK
MASTER
MENTIONED
MET
MILES
MISTAKE
MOVE
MUCHNESS

115.) 3 (cont.)	TONES	116.) 2 (cont.)	FISH-FOOTMAN	MOMENT'S
MUSIC	TORTOISE	CHOICE	FLAMINGOES	MONTH
MUTTERING	TOSSING	CHOSE	FLAT	MORCAR
NEEDN'T	TRIAL'S	CLAWS	FOLLOW	MOSTLY
NIBBLING	TRUMPET	CLEAR	FOOTSTEPS	MUSTARD
NIGHT	TUCKED	CLEVER	FOREHEAD	MUTTERED
NOISE	TURNS	CLOCK	FORGET	MYSTERY
NOR	UNFORTUNATE	CLOSED	FORGOT	NAMES
NOTION	UPSET	COAXING	FOUNTAINS	NARROW
NURSE	VENTURE	COLLECTED	FRIENDS	NEATLY
NURSING	WASHING	COMFITS	FRIGHT	NEITHER
O	WASTING	CONCERT	FROG	NIBBLED
OBLIGED	WATCHING	CONCLUDED	FRONT	NICELY
O'CLOCK	WEAK	CONCLUSION	GIDDY	NORTHUMBRIA
OPENING	WEEK	CONQUEROR	GIVING	NOTE-BOOK
ORDER	WHATEVER	CONSTANT	GOLD-FISH	NOWHERE
OUT-OF-THE-WAY	WHISKERS	CONTEMPTUOUSLY	GOOSE	OCCURRED
OWL	WHISPER	CONVERSATIONS	GREW	OFFER
PANTHER	WILD	COOL	GUINEA-PIG	OLDER
PASSION	WON	COURTIERS	HALF-PAST	ORDERING
PAT	WONDERLAND	CRIMSON	HAPPY	ORNAMENTED
PATTERING	WORSE	CROSS-EXAMINE	HASN'T	PAINTING
PAW	WROTE	CRYING	HATE	PANTING
PEEPED	YESTERDAY	CUP	HEART	PARIS
PICKED	YOURS	CUPBOARDS	HEAVY	PART
PIECES		CURIOUSER	HEDGE	PATIENTLY
PITY	116.) 2 (0.00747%)	CURLED	HINT	PAUSE
PLATE	ABSURD	CUSHION	HIT	PEBBLES
PLEADED	ACCIDENT	CUSTODY	HUMBLY	PERSISTED
POISON	ADDRESSED	DANCING	HURRIEDLY	PERSONAL
POSSIBLY	ADVICE	DECLARE	ILL	PICKING
PRAY	ADVISABLE	DELIGHTED	IMAGINE	PIE
PRESENT	AFTERWARDS	DELIGHTFUL	INSIDE	PIGS
PRESSED	AGO	DENIED	INTERRUPTING	PINCH
PROPER	AGREE	DENY	INTRODUCE	PINCHED
PUTTING	ALARM	DIFFICULT	INVITATION	PLACES
READING	ALREADY	DINAH'LL	INVITED	PLATES
REAL	ALSO	DINNER	JAR	PLAYING
REMAINED	ANGER	DIPPED	JAWS	PLEASURE
REMARKING	APPEAR	DIRECTED	KEEPING	PLENTY
REMARKS	APPLES	DIRECTLY	KINDLY	POSITION
REPEATING	ARCHBISHOP	DISAPPEARED	KING'S	PRESENTLY
ROSES	ASHAMED	DISHES	KNIFE	PROCEED
RULES	ASSEMBLED	DISPUTE	KNOT	PROUD
SAD	ATOM	DISTANT	KNOWING	PROVE
SCREAMED	ATTEMPT	DOG	KNOWS	PROVED
SENSE	AUTHORITY	DOORS	LABEL	PURRING
SERPENTS	BAD	DOUBTFUL	LAID	PUSH
SETTLED	BARK	DOUBTFULLY	LAP	QUARRELING
SHAKING	BARROWFUL	DOWN-STAIRS	LASTED	QUICK
SHE'LL	BEAR	DOWNWARDS	LATITUDE	QUICKLY
SHORE	BEAST	DRAWLING	LAUGHED	QUIET
SHOW	BEASTS	DREADFUL	LAUGHING	RACE
SIGHING	BEATING	DREAMY	LAW	RAILWAY
SIMPLY	BEAUTIFULLY	DRIVE	LEANING	RAISED
SLATE	BECAME	DRUNK	LEARNING	RAPIDLY
SLIPPED	BELONGS	EARLS	LEARNT	RATTLING
SMALLER	BEND	EARNESTLY	LEFT-HAND	RAVING
SNAIL	BENEATH	EASY	LIE	RECOVERED
SOBBING	BITE	EDWIN	LINE	RED
SOBS	BLASTS	ENCOURAGING	LIVING	REGULAR
SOLEMN	BLEW	ENTANGLED	LOCKS	RELIEF
SOMEWHERE	BLOW	ENTIRELY	LONELY	REMARKABLE
SORTS	BODY	EVERYTHING'S	LONGED	REMOVED
SPECTACLES	BOY	EXCELLENT	LONGITUDE	RESTING
SPEECH	BRANCHES	EXECUTIONS	LOVELY	RETURNED
STARING	BREAK	EXPERIMENT	LUCKILY	RIDDLES
STOPPED	BRIGHTENED	EXPLANATION	MA	RIGHT-HAND
SUCCEEDED	BROKE	EXTRAORDINARY	MANNER	RING
SUIT	BROWN	EXTREMELY	MATTERS	RINGLETS
SULKY	BURN	FAINTLY	MAYBE	ROME
SUN	BUSY	FALLING	MEEKLY	ROW
TAILS	CARES	FANCIED	MEET	ROYAL
TASTED	CARRYING	FASHION	MERCIA	RUBBING
TEACUP	CATCHING	FEATHER	MERELY	RUDE
TELESCOPE	CAT'S	FEEBLE	MESSAGES	RUSH
THEMSELVES	CAULDRON	FEELINGS	MILE	SAFE
THROW	CAUSED	FERRETS	MISERABLE	SALTWATER
TIMID	CHANGES	FIGHT	MISSED	SANG
TOES	CHANGING	FINE	MIXED	SAVE

116.) 2 (cont.)		117.) 1 (cont.)		
SCREAM	TWENTY-FOUR	ANCIENT	BORE	CLEARLY
SCREAMING	TWIST	ANIMAL	BOTHER	CLIMB
SECONDLY	UGH	ANIMAL'S	BOUGH	CLINGING
SELL	UGLIFICATION	ANNOY	BOUND	CLOSELY
SENDING	UGLY	ANNOYED	BOWING	CLOSER
SENSATION	UNDERNEATH	ANON	BOXED	CLUBS
SENT	UNDERTONE	ANSWERS	BRAIN	COAST
SETTING	UNEASILY	ANTIPATHIES	BRANCH	COILS
SH	UNFOLDED	ANYWHERE	BRANDY	COLD
SHAPED	UNHAPPY	A-PIECE	BRASS	COLLAR
SHE'D	UNLESS	APPEALED	BRAVE	COMFORT
SHORTER	UNPLEASANT	APPEARANCE	BREAD-KNIFE	COMFORTABLE
SHOUTING	UNROLLED	APPEARING	BREEZE	COMFORTABLY
SHOWER	USEFUL	APPLAUSE	BRIGHT-EYED	COMMON
SHOWING	USING	ARCH	BRISTLING	COMMOTION
SHUTTING	USUALLY	ARGUE	BROTHER'S	COMPANY
SIGNED	VIOLENT	ARGUED	BRUSH	COMPLAINED
SINGERS	WAISTCOAT-POCKET	ARGUMENTS	BRUSHING	COMPLAINING
SINGING	WAKE	ARITHMETIC	BURNING	COMPLETELY
SISTERS	WANDERED	ARM-CHAIR	BURNT	CONDEMN
SIX	WANDERING	ARM-IN-ARM	BURST	CONDUCT
SLIGHTEST	WANTS	ARRANGED	BURSTING	CONGER-EEL
SMALLEST	WASH	ARRIVED	BUTTERCUP	CONQUEST
SMILE	WATCHED	ARROW	BUTTERED	CONSENTED
SMILED	WATER	ARRUM	BUTTERFLY	CONSULTATION
SMILING	WE'RE	ASKANCE	BUTTONS	CONTEMPT
SMOKING	WET	ATE	BY-THE-BYE	CONTEMPTUOUS
SNATCH	WE'VE	ATHELING	C	CONTENT
SNEEZE	WHERE'S	ATTEMPTED	CALLING	CONTRADICTED
SNEEZES	WHEREVER	ATTENDED	CALMLY	CORNERS
SOB	WHO'S	ATTENDS	CAMOMILE	COST
SOONER	WHOSE	AUDIBLY	CANARY	COUNTING
SORROW	WIDE	AUSTRALIA	CANNOT	COUNTRY
SORROWFUL	WIG	AVAIL	CANTERBURY	COUPLE
SPLASHING	WILDLY	AWFULLY	CANVAS	COUPLES
SPREAD	WIND	AXES	CAPERING	COWARD
SQUEAKING	WINE	AXIS	CARDBOARD	CRASHED
STAMPING	WINK	BACKS	CARRIER	CRAWLED
STARTED	WISE	BACK-SOMERSAULT	CARRY	CRAWLING
STARTLED	WITHIN	BAG	CART-HORSE	CRAZY
STIRRING	WOMAN	BAKED	CART-WHEELS	CREEP
STOLE	WONDERFUL	BALANCED	CATERPILLAR'S	CREPT
STOOP	WRETCHED	BALLS	CATTLE	CREW
STRAIGHT	YAWNED	BAND	CEILING	CRIES
STRETCHED	YAWNING	BANKS	CENTRE	CROCODILE
STRETCHING	YEAR	BANQUET	CHAINS	CROQUETED
STRUCK		BARKING	CHANCED	CROQUETING
SULKILY	117.) 1 (0.00374%)	BARLEY-SUGAR	CHARACTER	CROSS
SUMMER	ABIDE	BATHING-MACHINES	CHARGES	CROSSLY
SWIMMING	ABLE	BAWLED	CHAT	CROUCHED
TAKES	ABSENCE	BEAK	CHATTE	CRUEL
TALLER	ACCEPTANCE	BEAUTIFY	CHEAP	CUCUMBER-FRAME
TASTE	ACCIDENTALLY	BECOMING	CHEATED	CUCUMBER-FRAMES
TEACUPS	ACCOUNT	BED	CHEEKS	CUNNING
TEA-PARTY	ACCOUNTING	BEDS	CHEERFULLY	CUR
TEA-TIME	ACCOUNTS	BEE	CHERRY-TART	CURLS
TELLING	ACCUSATION	BEGGED	CHESHIRE-CATS	CURLY
TELLS	ACCUSTOMED	BEHEAD	CHESHIRE-PUSS	CURRANTS
THISTLE	ACHE	BEHEADING	CHIEF	CURTAIN
THOROUGHLY	ACT	BELIEVED	CHILDHOOD	CURTSEY
THOUGHTS	ACTUALLY	BELONG	CHILDHOOD'S	CURTSEYING
THOUSAND	ADA	BELOVED	CHILDISH	CURVING
THREE-LEGGED	ADDING	BELT	CHILD-LIFE	CUSTARD
THREW	ADDRESSING	BENT	CHIMNEYS	CUTTING
THROAT	ADJOURN	BIRTHDAY-PRESENTS	CHOKE	D
THROWING	ADOPTION	BITTER	CHOKING	DAINTIES
THUMP	ADVISE	BLACKING	CHOOSING	DAISIES
THUS	AFFAIR	BLADES	CHOP	DAISY-CHAIN
TIED	AFFECTIONATELY	BLAME	CHRISTMAS	DARESAY
TIPTOE	AFFORD	BLEEDS	CHRYSALIS	DARKNESS
TREACLE-WELL	AFORE	BLOWN	CHUCKLED	DATES
TREADING	AFTERNOON	BLOWS	CIRCLE	DAUGHTER
TREMBLED	AFTER-TIME	BLUE	CIRCUMSTANCES	DAY-SCHOOL
TRIUMPHANTLY	AGONY	BOLDLY	CLAMOUR	DEATH
TROTTING	AHEM	BONE	CLAPPING	DECLARED
TUMBLING	AIRS	BONES	CLASPED	DEEPEST
TURTLES	ALARMED	BOOKS	CLASSICAL	DELAY
TURTLE'S	ALTERED	BOOK-SHELVES	CLEAN	DENIAL
TUT	ALTERNATELY	BOON	CLEARED	DENIES
	AMBITION		CLEARER	DENYING

117.) 1 (cont.)

DEPENDS	EVIDENTLY	FOOTMEN	HIGHEST	LATELY
DERISION	EXACT	FORE-PAWS	HIPPOPOTAMUS	LATER
DESERVED	EXAMINING	FORK	HISS	LATIN
DESPAIR	EXCLAMATION	FORM	HJCKRRH	LAUGH
DESPERATE	EXECUTE	FORTH	HM	LAUGHTER
DESPERATELY	EXECUTES	FORTY-TWO	HOARSELY	LAZILY
DIAMONDS	EXECUTIONER'S	FORWARDS	HOLIDAY	LAZY
DIE	EXISTENCE	FOURTEENTH	HOLLOW	LEADERS
DIED	EXPECTED	FOURTH	HONEST	LEADING
DIFFICULTIES	EXPLAINED	FRANCE	HOPED	LEANT
DIG	EXPLANATIONS	FRIENDLY	HOPEFUL	LEAP
DILIGENTLY	EXPRESSING	FRIGHTEN	HOPELESS	LEARNED
DINAH'S	EXPRESSION	FROG-FOOTMAN	HOPES	LEAVING
DINN	EXTRA	FRONTISPIECE	HOT-TEMPERED	LEDGE
DINN--	EXTRAS	FRYING-PAN	HOUSEMAID	LEISURELY
DISAGREE	EYELIDS	FUMBLED	HOWLED	LENGTH
DISAPPOINTMENT	FADING	FURIOUS	HUMBLE	LESSEN
DISGUST	FAILURE	FURIOUSLY	HUNDRED	LESSON
DISMAY	FAINT	FURROW	HUNG	LESSON-BOOK
DISOBEY	FAINTING	FURROWS	HURRYING	LESSON-BOOKS
DISTRACTION	FAIR	GAINED	IDIOT	LEST
DIVE	FAIRLY	GALLONS	IDIOTIC	LETTERS
DODGED	FAIRY	GAMES	IGNORANT	LICKING
DOG'S	FAMILIARLY	GAME'S	IMITATED	LIFTED
DOORWAY	FAMILY	GATHER	IMMEDIATE	LIKES
DORMOUSE'S	FANCYING	GAY	IMMENSE	LIMBS
DOUBLE	FANNED	GAZING	IMPATIENT	LINES
DOUBLED-UP	FANNING	GENTLE	IMPERIOUS	LINKED
DOUBLING	FARMER	GENTLER	IMPERTINENT	LIPS
DOZE	FARM-YARD	GEOGRAPHY	IMPROVE	LISTENED
DOZING	FAR-OFF	GIVEN	INCESSANTLY	LISTENERS
DRAGGLED	FARTHER	GLANCED	INCLINED	LIT
DRAINED	FAT	GLARING	INDIGNANT	LIZARD'S
DRAWING	FAVOURED	GLIDE	INJURE	LOCK
DRAWLING-MASTER	FAVOURITE	GLOBE	INK	LOCKED
DREAM-CHILD	FEARED	GLOOMILY	INKSTAND	LODGING-HOUSES
DREAMED	FEATHERS	GOOD-BYE	INQUIRED	LONDON
DREAMING	FEEBLY	GOOD-NATURED	INQUISITIVELY	LOOKING-GLASS
DREAMS	FELLOWS	GOOD-NATUREDLY	INSOLENCE	LOOK-OUT
DRESSED	FENDER	GRACEFUL	INSULT	LOOKS
DRIED	FIDGETED	GRAMMAR	INTEREST	LOOSE
DRIEST	FIELD	GRANT	INTERRUPT	LOSE
DRINKING	FIFTEEN	GRAVY	INTERRUPTS	LOSING
DRIPPING	FIFTEENTH	GRAZED	INTRODUCED	LOUDER
DROP	FIFTH	GREY	INVENT	LOVELIEST
DROPPING	FIG	GRIEF	INVENTED	LOVING
DROWNED	FIGHTING	GRINNING	INVOLVED	LOWER
DUNCE	FIGURES	GRINS	INWARDS	LOWING
EATEN	FILLS	GROWLED	IRRITATED	LOW-SPIRITED
EATING	FINDS	GROWLING	JACK-IN-THE-BOX	LULLABY
EATS	FINISHES	GROWLS	JAW	M--
EDGAR	FINISHING	GRUMBLED	JELLY-FISH	MA'AM
EDICT	FIRE-IRONS	GRUNT	JOGGED	MAGIC
EDUCATIONS	FIREPLACE	GUARD	JOURNEY	MAGPIE
EEL	FISHES	GUIDE	JOYS	MALLETS
EELS	FITS	GUILT	JUDGING	MANAGING
EGG	FITTED	HAMMERED	JUROR	MANNERS
EH	FIX	HANDSOME	JUSTICE	MAPS
ELBOWS	FIXED	HANDWRITING	KETTLE	MARCHED
ELEGANT	FLAME	HAPPENING	KILL	MARMALADE
ELEVENTH	FLAPPER	HARM	KILLING	MAYN'T
ELSE'S	FLAPPERS	HASTE	KILLS	MEAL
ELSIE	FLASHED	HAT	KINGS	MEANWHILE
EMPHASIS	FLASHES	HATCHING	KISS	MEASURE
EMPTY	FLAVOUR	HATED	KISSED	MEAT
ENCOURAGE	FLEW	HATTERS	KNEEL	MEETING
ENCOURAGED	FLINGING	HATTER'S	KNELT	MEMORANDUM
ENDING	FLOCK	HEAD'S	KNOCK	MEMORY
ENERGETIC	FLOWER-BEDS	HEAP	KNOCKED	MEMORY'S
ENGAGED	FLOWER-POT	HEARTH	KNOWN	MERRILY
ENGLAND	FLOWN	HEARTHRUG	KNUCKLES	MERRY
ENGRAVED	FLUNG	HE'D	LABELED	MILK
ENJOY	FLURRY	HEDGES	LACIE	MILK-JUG
ENNYWORTH	FLUSTERED	HEELS	LAD	MINDED
ENORMOUS	FLUTTERED	HE'LL	LADDER	MINDING
ENTRANCE	FLYING	HELPED	LAMPS	MINERAL
ESQ.	FOLDING	HELPLESS	LANGUID	MISCHIEF
EST	FOLLOWS	HERALD	LARGEST	MODERATE
EVENTS	FOOLISH	HID	LARK	MODERN
	FOOTMAN'S	HIDE	LASTLY	MOON

117.) 1 (cont.)

MORALS	PENNYWORTH	QUEEREST	SCROLL	SORRY
MORSEL	PEPPER-BOX	QUEER-LOOKING	SCURRIED	SOUR
MOURNFUL	PERMITTED	QUEER-SHAPED	SEALS	SPADES
MOURNFULLY	PERSONS	QUICKER	SEAOGRAPHY	SPEAKER
MOUSE-HOLE	PET	QUIVER	SEARCH	SPEED
MOUSE'S	PICTURE	RABBITS	SEA-SHORE	SPELL
MOUSE-TRAPS	PICTURED	RACE-COURSE	SEASIDE	SPITE
MUDDLE	PIE-CRUST	RAISING	SEATED	SPLASH
MULTIPLICATION-TABLE	PIG-BABY	RAPPED	SECRET	SPLASHED
MURDER	PILGRIM'S	RAT-HOLE	SECUNDA	SPLENDIDLY
MURDERING	PINE-APPLE	RATS	SEEING	SPOKEN
MUSCULAR	PINK	RATTLE	SELDOM	SPOON
MUSTARD-MINE	PITEOUS	RAVEN	SEND	SPOT
MYSTIC	PITIED	RAVENS	SENDS	SPRAWLING
NASTY	PLACED	RAW	SENTENCED	SPREADING
NAY	PLAINLY	REACHING	SERIES	SPREADS
NEAT	PLANNING	READILY	SERIOUSLY	SQUEAKED
NEEDS	PLAYED	REALITY	SETTLE	SQUEEZE
NEIGHBOUR	PLEASANT	REARING	SETTLING	SQUEEZED
NEIGHBOURING	PLEASANTER	REASONABLE	SEVERITY	STAIRS
NEST	PLEASES	REASONS	SHADE	STALK
NEVER-ENDING	PLEASING	RECEIVED	SHAKE	STANDING
NEVERTHELESS	PLIED	RECOGNIZED	SHAKESPEARE	STAR-FISH
NEWSPAPERS	PLUCK'D	RED-HOT	SHAPE	STATE
NIGHT-AIR	POINTED	REDUCED	SHARE	STATION
NILE	POKER	REEDS	SHARED	STAYS
NODDED	POKY	REELING	SHARING	STEADY
NOISES	POP	REFRESHMENTS	SHARK	STEAM-ENGINE
NORMANS	POPE	REFUSED	SHARKS	STEER
NOTICING	POSITIVELY	RELIEVED	SHEDDING	STERNLY
OARS	POSSIBLE	REMAIN	SHEEP-BELLS	STICKS
OBLONG	POUNDS	REMAINING	SHELVES	STIFF
OBSTACLE	POUR	REMEDIES	SHEPHERD-BOY	STIGAND
OCCASIONAL	POURED	REMEMBERING	SHIFTING	STINGY
OCCASIONALLY	POWDERED	REMINDING	SHILLING	STIR
ODD	PRACTICE	RESOURCE	SHILLINGS	STOCKINGS
OFFEND	PRECIOUS	RESPECT	SHINGLE	STOLEN
OFFICER	PRESENTED	RESPECTABLE	SHINING	STOOL
OINTMENT	PRESENTS	RESPECTFUL	SHINY	STOPPING
OLDEST	PRESSING	RESULT	SHIVER	STORIES
ONES	PRETENCE	RETIRE	SHOCK	STRAIGHTENED
ONE'S	PRETEND	RETURNING	SHRIEKED	STRAIGHTENING
ONESELF	PRETENDING	RICH	SHRIEKS	STRENGTH
ONIONS	PRETEXTS	RIDDLE	SHRIMP	STRINGS
OPINION	PRETTIER	RIDGE	SHRINK	STROVE
OPPOSITE	PRETTY	RIDGES	SHYLY	STUPIDEST
ORANGE	PREVENT	RIDICULOUS	SIGN	STUPIDLY
OU	PRIMA	RIGHTLY	SIGNIFIES	SUBDUED
OURS	PRINTED	RIPER	SIGNIFY	SUBJECTS
OURSELVES	PRISON	RIPPLING	SIMPLETON	SUBMITTED
OVERCOME	PRISONER	RISE	SINK	SUET
OVERHEAD	PRISONER'S	RISES	SISTER'S	SUGAR
OYSTER	PRIZE	RISING	SITS	SUPPLE
P	PROCESSIONS	ROARED	SIXPENCE	SUPPRESS
PACE	PRODUCED	ROAST	SIXTEENTH	SWALLOW
PAINT	PRODUCING	ROCK	SIZES	SWALLOWED
PAIRS	PROMISE	ROOTS	SKILL	SWALLOWING
PANTED	PROMISED	ROPE	SKIMMING	SWEET-TEMPERED
PARCHMENT	PROMISING	ROSE	SKIRT	T
PARCHMENT-SCROLL	PRONOUNCED	ROUGHLY	SKY-ROCKET	TALES
PARDONED	PROPOSAL	RUBBED	SLATE-PENCIL	TASTES
PARTNER	PROSECUTE	RUDENESS	SLATES'LL	TEACHING
PARTNERS	PROTECTION	RUMBLING	SLIPPERY	TEAPOT
PARTS	PROVES	RUSHED	SLUGGARD	TEASES
PASS	PROVOKING	RUSTLED	SMOKE	TEASPOON
PASSING	PUFFED	RUSTLING	SNAPPISHLY	TEA-THINGS
PASSIONATE	PULLED	SAGE	SNEEZED	TEA-TRAY
PAST	PULLING	SALMON	SNORTING	TEETH
PATIENCE	PUN	SAND	SNOUT	TELESCOPES
PATRIOTIC	PUNCHING	SANDS	SOBBED	TERMS
PATTED	PUNISHED	SAUCEPAN	SOFT	TERRIBLY
PATTERN	PUPPY'S	SAUCEPANS	SOFTLY	TERRIER
PAUSED	PURPLE	SAUCER	SOLDIER	TERROR
PEEPING	PURPOSE	SAVES	SOLES	TERTIA
PEERING	PURSUE	SCALE	SOLID	THANKED
PEGS	PUZZLE	SCALY	SOMEHOW	THATCHED
PENCE	QUAINT	SCHOOL-ROOM	SOMERSAULT	THAT'LL
PENCIL	QUARREL	SCOLDED	SON	THEIRS
PENCILS	QUARRELED	SCRAMBLING	SOOTHING	THEREFORE
	QUEENS	SCRATCHING	SORROWS	THEY'VE

117.) 1 (cont.)

THICK	VINEGAR
THIN	VIOLENCE
THIRTEEN	VISIT
THRONE	VOTE
THROWN	VULGAR
THUNDER	W
THUNDERSTORM	WAG
TIDE	WAGS
TIDY	WAIST
TIE	WAIT
TIGHT	WALRUS
TILLIE	WANDER
TINIEST	WANDERINGS
TINKLING	WARNING
TIPPED	WATERS
TITTERED	WATER-WELL
TOAST	WEARILY
TOFFY	WEARY
TO-MORROW	WEATHER
TONGUES	WEEKS
TO-NIGHT	WELCOMES
TOPS	WELLS
TOSS	WEPT
TOUCH	WEREN'T
TOUGHER	WHENEVER
TOWARDS	WHEREUPON
TOYS	WHILES
TRAMPLED	WHILST
TREAT	WHISPERS
TREATED	WHISTLE
TREMBLE	WHISTLING
TREMULOUS	WHOEVER
TRIALS	WHOM
TRICKLING	WIDER
TRICKS	WIFE
TRIMS	WILLIAM'S
TROT	WIN
TRUSTS	WINGS
TRUTH	WINTER-DAY
TRUTHFUL	WITHER'D
TULIP-ROOTS	WITS
TUMBLED	WOKE
TUNNEL	WONDERED
TUREEN	WONDERS
TURKEY	WOODEN
TURN-UP	WORE
TWELFTH	WORKS
TWENTIETH	WORM
TWENTY	WORRIED
TWINED	WORRY
TWINKLED	WRAPPING
UGLIFY	WREATH
UGLIFYING	WRIGGLING
UNABLE	WRITHING
UNCIVIL	WRITING-DESK
UNCOMFORTABLY	WRITING-DESKS
UNCOMMON	YARDS
UNCOMMONLY	YE
UNCORKED	YEARS
UNDERSTOOD	YELLED
UNDO	YELP
UNDOING	ZEALAND
UNEASY	ZIGZAG
UNJUST	
UNLOCKING	
UNTWIST	
UNUSUALLY	
UNWILLINGLY	
UPRIGHT	
UPSETTING	
UPSTAIRS	
USURPATION	
VAGUE	
VAIN	
VANISHING	
VARIATIONS	
VARIOUS	
VEGETABLE	
VELVET	

RANKING FREQUENCY LIST
(*THROUGH THE LOOKING-GLASS*)

1.) 1607 (5.42%) THE	28.) 149 (0.503%) HIS	53.) 76 (0.256%) ARE MY	72.) 53 (0.179%) DUMPTY HUMPTY	90.) 34 (cont.) TELL TOOK
2.) 907 (3.06%) AND	29.) 146 (0.492%) ONE VERY	54.) 75 (0.253%) HERSELF	73.) 52 (0.175%) THINK	91.) 33 (0.111%) BACK FIRST
3.) 760 (2.56%) A	30.) 144 (0.486%) THEY	55.) 74 (0.250%) INTO JUST	74.) 51 (0.172%) COME GET MAKE OVER	PUT TWEEDLEDUM
4.) 725 (2.45%) TO	31.) 135 (0.455%) HAD	56.) 72 (0.243%) TIME		92.) 32 (0.108%) ANOTHER BEFORE
5.) 566 (1.91%) IT	32.) 134 (0.452%) WHAT	57.) 71 (0.239%) COULD DOWN	75.) 50 (0.169%) GREAT LAST	SHOULD SIDE WHO
6.) 527 (1.78%) SHE	33.) 127 (0.428%) KNOW	YOUR	THINGS	93.) 30 (0.101%) ALWAYS
7.) 524 (1.77%) I	34.) 126 (0.425%) IS	58.) 70 (0.236%) CAN RED	76.) 49 (0.165%) CAME	BECAUSE HAND REALLY
8.) 509 (1.72%) YOU	35.) 125 (0.422%) THIS	59.) 69 (0.233%) NO	77.) 48 (0.162%) BEGAN	TILL
9.) 497 (1.68%) OF	36.) 123 (0.415%) LIKE	60.) 68 (0.229%) ABOUT	78.) 47 (0.159%) MUST	94.) 29 (0.0978%) GETTING HELP
10.) 477 (1.61%) SAID	37.) 122 (0.411%) DO	61.) 67 (0.226%) GOT WAY	79.) 45 (0.152%) BEEN THAT'S	NOTHING THERE'S WOOD
11.) 436 (1.47%) ALICE	38.) 117 (0.395%) LITTLE UP	WHITE	80.) 44 (0.148%) THROUGH	95.) 28 (0.0944%) ASKED
12.) 411 (1.39%) IN	39.) 116 (0.391%) OUT	62.) 65 (0.219%) FROM HIM I'M	81.) 43 (0.145%) AFTER MOMENT	GOOD HOWEVER TAKE THEIR
13.) 358 (1.21%) WAS	40.) 111 (0.374%) THEN	OFF	82.) 42 (0.142%) TONE	96.) 27 (0.0911%) LARGE
14.) 317 (1.07%) THAT	41.) 104 (0.351%) THERE	63.) 64 (0.216%) OTHER WELL	83.) 41 (0.138%) EYES	NAME NEXT
15.) 315 (1.06%) AS	42.) 99 (0.334%) HAVE	64.) 62 (0.209%) QUITE	OH	97.) 26 (0.0877%) MINUTE OLD
16.) 273 (0.921%) HER	43.) 97 (0.327%) ME NOT	65.) 61 (0.206%) HEAD	84.) 40 (0.135%) ANY HANDS	REMARKED SEEMED TWEEDLEDEE
17.) 251 (0.847%) ON	44.) 94 (0.317%) ONLY	KING MORE	85.) 39 (0.132%) LOOKING	98.) 25 (0.0843%) DEAR
18.) 232 (0.782%) AT	45.) 93 (0.314%) IT'S	66.) 60 (0.202%) BY GO	VOICE WHY	SHALL SOMETHING YOU'VE
19.) 223 (0.752%) WITH	46.) 91 (0.307%) WOULD	67.) 58 (0.196%) HERE	86.) 38 (0.128%) CA'N'T COULDN'T	99.) 24 (0.0809%) GOING
20.) 213 (0.718%) HE	47.) 90 (0.304%) THEM WENT	MUCH	LONG	KITTY THOUGH WHILE
21.) 204 (0.688%) BUT	48.) 88 (0.297%) THOUGHT	68.) 57 (0.192%) AN KNIGHT NEVER	87.) 37 (0.125%) AWAY DIDN'T I'LL	YOU'LL
22.) 203 (0.685%) SO	49.) 84 (0.283%) SEE		WE	100.) 23 (0.0776%) I'VE
23.) 200 (0.675%) FOR	50.) 82 (0.277%) NOW	69.) 56 (0.189%) CRIED HOW SAY	88.) 36 (0.121%) RATHER THAN	MIGHT SUPPOSE WOULDN'T
24.) 192 (0.648%) ALL	51.) 81 (0.273%) DON'T WERE	WHICH	89.) 35 (0.118%) COURSE	101.) 22 (0.0742%) ANSWER
25.) 180 (0.607%) QUEEN	WHEN	70.) 55 (0.186%) DID LOOKED	ITS LOOK SUCH	BEING EVER KITTEN
26.) 155 (0.523%) IF	52.) 78 (0.263%) AGAIN	ROUND TWO	THING TOO YOU'RE	MADE MAY MEAN
27.) 154 (0.519%) BE		71.) 54 (0.182%) OR SOME	90.) 34 (0.115%) BETTER	POOR SUDDENLY UNDER

101.) 22 (cont.)
UNICORN
YOU'D

102.) 21 (0.0708%)
ADDED
ALICE'S
EVERY
FIND
MANY
SHEEP
SURE
WHERE

103.) 20 (0.0675%)
EACH
FACE
FEET
HAIR
HEAR
KEEP
LOOKING-GLASS
ONCE
REPLIED
STILL
TREE
WILL
WITHOUT

104.) 19 (0.0641%)
BOTH
ENOUGH
HAS
OUGHT
SAME
WISH

105.) 18 (0.0607%)
ANYTHING
BEGIN
FOUND
GNAT
HORSE
LION
RIGHT
SPOKE
TABLE
TALKING
TURNED
YET

106.) 17 (0.0573%)
BEST
BREATH
DAY
DONE
FAST
FELT
HADN'T
HAPPENED
HOLD
PLEASE
SILENCE
SOON
TALK
THREE
TURN

107.) 16 (0.0540%)
AMONG
BEGINNING
CHILD
EVEN
GAVE
HOUSE
ISN'T
LET
MIND
SET
SITTING

107.) 16 (cont.)
SORT
SPEAK
STOOD
WONDER

108.) 15 (0.0506%)
AFRAID
AIR
ALONG
AM
CALL
CALLED
DOOR
EAR
END
FRIGHTENED
HIMSELF
REPEATED
SONG
THINKING
UPON
USE
WANT
WORD
YES

109.) 14 (0.0472%)
EXACTLY
FAR
GENTLY
GIVE
HILL
HOPE
INTERRUPTED
LET'S
LOUD
NICE
OWN
PUTTING
REMARK
SAW
SAYING
SHE'S
TRY
US
WORDS

110.) 13 (0.0438%)
AFTERWARDS
ASK
BELIEVE
CERTAINLY
DOES
DREAM
HALF
LEAVE
LIVE
MOUTH
NOBODY
OPEN
PEOPLE
REMEMBER
SAT
SEEN
SHOULDN'T
TURNING
WALKING
WALRUS
WHAT'S

111.) 12 (0.0405%)
BIT
BROOK
CARPENTER
CLOSE
DISH
ELSE
FELL
FULL

111.) 12 (cont.)
GROUND
HEARD
I'D
ITSELF
MEANT
MESSENGER
MOST
OUR
PUDDING
QUEENS
ROAD
ROOM
ROSE
RULE
RUN
SHOOK
SHUT
SOMETIMES
SQUARE
TIGER-LILY
TIMES
TOGETHER
TOP
TRIED
WASN'T
WHETHER

112.) 11 (0.0371%)
ALMOST
ARMS
BEHIND
BOAT
COMING
DOESN'T
FALL
GOES
HARDLY
IDEA
IT'LL
NEW
PLACE
PUZZLED
RUNNING
SUDDEN
SURPRISED
THEY'RE
WATER
YOURSELF

113.) 10 (0.0337%)
CAUGHT
CUT
DINAH
FASTER
FIGHT
FIVE
FOUR
GLAD
HAIGHA
HAPPEN
HATTA
HAVEN'T
HAVING
HELMET
KIND
MANAGE
MIDDLE
NEARLY
NECK
OYSTERS
POETRY
QUESTION
RAN
REAL
RUSHES
TO-DAY
TRYING

114.) 9 (0.0304%)
CONVERSATION
CROWN
DARK
DEAL
EAGERLY
GARDEN
HARD
HELD
INDEED
KEPT
LEFT
LIFE
MAN
MANAGED
READY
SEVERAL
SHAWL
STRAIGHT
TAKING
TEARS
THOSE
UNDERSTAND
WAIT
WALKED
WANTED
WATCHING

115.) 8 (0.0270%)
ACROSS
ANXIOUSLY
BOOK
BRIGHT
CARE
CREATURE
CRY
DREAMING
EASY
EGG
EXCLAIMED
FINGER
FIRE
FISH
FISHES
FLOWERS
FURTHER
HE'S
HOLDING
INVENTION
JAM
LEAST
LOST
LYING
MAJESTY
MAKES
MEANS
MEN
MUTTON
NAMES
NEAR
ONE'S
PAUSE
PLAN
PLENTY
PRETTY
QUICK
QUIETLY
REST
SEEMS
SENT
SEVEN
SLOWLY
SOUNDED
SUBJECT
TEMPER
TIMIDLY
TOWN
TREES
WATCHED
WHISPER

115.) 8 (cont.)
WO'N'T

116.) 7 (0.0236%)
ALARM
ALREADY
ARGUMENT
ARM
BAG
BATTLE
BEAUTIFUL
BREAD
BREAD-AND-BUTTER
BROWN
CERTAIN
CHORUS
COUNTRY
CURIOUS
DAYS
DINNER
FACT
FEAR
FEW
GENERALLY
GLASS
GONE
GUESS
HASTILY
HUNDRED
IMPATIENTLY
JOKE
KNEW
MARKED
MYSELF
NEEDLES
NONE
NONSENSE
NUMBER
OFTEN
PART
PAW
PERHAPS
PLUM-CAKE
PRACTICE
PRETEND
SADDLE
SHAKE
SHOP
SIGHT
SMILE
SOMEHOW
SUMMER
THANK
THESE
THOUGHTFULLY
THOUSAND
TOWARDS
UMBRELLA
VOICES
WAKE
WALK
WE'VE
WHENEVER
WHISPERED
WHOSE
WINGS
WRONG
YARDS

117.) 6 (0.0202%)
ABLE
ANXIOUS
BALL
BEGUN
COLD
COMES
COMFORT
CONSIDER
DELIGHT
DENY

117.) 6 (cont.)

DIFFERENT
DOING
EVERYBODY
EXPLAINED
FALLING
FAWN
FEATHER
FEEL
FINISHED
FROG
FUN
GAME
GIMBLE
GRAND
GRAVELY
GREEN
GROWING
GYRE
HAY
HEAVY
HIGH
HORSES
HUNG
HURT
INSECTS
KNITTING
LAUGH
LESSONS
MEET
MOME
MONSTER
NEEDN'T
NIGHT
NOTICED
PAIR
PANTED
PATH
PICKED
PLEASED
POLITELY
PROVOKING
QUEEN'S
QUICKLY
RATE
RATTLE
REMAIN
REPEAT
SHAKING
SHAPE
SHELF
SIGH
SILENT
SING
SLITHY
SMILED
SNOW
SOFT
SPEAKING
STOP
STOPPED
TEA
THEY'VE
TOVES
TRIUMPHANTLY
TWICE
USUAL
VENTURED
WABE
WAYS
WIND
WORK
YOUNG

118.) 5 (0.0169%)

AGAINST
AGED
AH
ALIVE
ALONE

118.) 5 (cont.)

ANGLO-SAXON
ANGRY
ANSWERED
ANYBODY
ASHES
ASKING
BEES
BEG
BLACK
BOX
BRILLIG
BUY
CAREFULLY
CONTRARIWISE
CREATURES
CROSSED
CROW
CURIOSITY
DEEP
DIRECTLY
DRESSED
DREW
DRINK
EAGER
EASILY
EIGHTH
EITHER
'EM
EVERYTHING
EVIDENTLY
EYE
FACES
FAULT
FILL
FINGERS
FIT
FLYING
FOREST
GATE
GENTLE
GETS
GOOD-BYE
GUARD
GUESTS
HAPPY
HOARSE
HOME
HOPING
HORSE'S
HOURS
JUMPED
KINDLY
KING'S
LAUGHED
LAY
LEAVES
LIFTED
LIKED
LIKELY
LOSE
LOW
MAKING
MEANING
MELANCHOLY
MIMSY
MINUTES
MOVE
NINE
NOHOW
NOISE
NOSE
O
OARS
OBJECTED
OFFENDED
OPENED
OUTGRABE
PEG
PICK

PIECE
POUNDS
PUNISHED
PURR
QUEER
RATHS
REASON
REGULAR
REPLY
ROLLED
ROLLING
SCREAM
SEEM
SHINING
SHOULDER
SHOW
SHRILL
SISTER
SIT
SIX
SNORING
SOMEWHERE
SPOKEN
SPREAD
STANDING
STRONG
SURPRISE
THEY'D
THOUGHTFUL
THOUGHTS
USED
WALL
WATCH
WAVING
WE'LL
WHOLE
WILDLY
WINDOW
WONDERING
WORLD
WORSTED
WORTH

119.) 4 (0.0135%)

AGE
AHOY
ALOUD
ANGRILY
ASLEEP
ASTONISHED
BACKWARDS
BELL
BESIDES
BETWEEN
BEYOND
BIRDS
BODY
BOROGOVES
BOUGHT
BRANCH
BRING
BROOCH
BROTHER
BROTHERS
BROUGHT
CAKE
CATCH
CATCHING
CHAIR
CHECK
CHOOSE
CIVIL
CLEAR
CLEVER
CLOUD
COLLAR
CRAB
CRABS
DAISIES
DANCING

119.) 4 (cont.)

DARESAY
DEAD
DECLARE
DIE
DIFFICULTY
DIRECTION
DIRECTIONS
DOG
DOUBTFULLY
DRY
EARS
EDGE
ENDED
ENORMOUS
FAINT
FAT
FEELING
FEELINGS
FIGHTING
FRONT
GIDDY
GIVING
GLORY
H
HEADS
HEALTH
HEAP
HERE'S
HISTORY
HOT
INK
INSECT
INSTANCE
INSTANTLY
INTEREST
INVENTED
INVENTING
INVITE
JUMPING
KEEPING
KINDS
KNEES
KNIFE
LAP
LARGER
LATE
LAUGHING
LEG
LISTEN
LOVELY
MANNERS
MATTER
MEMORANDUM-BOOK
MICE
MILD
MORNING
MUSIC
NOTICE
ODD
OPPOSITE
PAWN
PLAY
PLEASANT
PRESENT
PRISON
PROUD
REACHED
READ
REPEATING
RETURNED
RIDDLE
RIDICULOUS
RISE
SCRAMBLED
SEA
SELL
SHORT
SHOUTED
SIGHED

SINGING
SIZE
SLEEPY
SLICE
SLOW
SMALL
SOOTHING
SOUP
SPEECH
STAY
STICKING
SUBTRACTION
SUN
TAKEN
TALE
THICK
THIRSTY
THOU
THY
TO-MORROW
TUMBLE
'TWAS
UNCOMFORTABLE
UNLESS
UNTIDY
WAITED
WAKING
WASHED
WEEK
WE'RE
WHATEVER
WIDE
WRITTEN
YEARS
YESTERDAY

120.) 3 (0.0101%)

ADDITION
ADDRESSING
ADVICE
AFTERNOON
ARM-CHAIR
ARMOUR
A-SITTING
ATE
ATTITUDES
AUTUMN
AWKWARD
BAD
BANDERSNATCH
BEAT
BED
BEE
BELT
BIRD
BIRTHDAY
BLEW
BLOWN
BLUE
BONE
BOOKS
BOW
BOY
BRANCHES
BREAKING
BRIDGE
BROKE
BRUSH
BUSINESS
CANDLES
CARELESS
CARRIAGE
CARRY
CASE
CAUSE
CEILING
CHANCE
CHANGED
CHEEKS
CHEERFULLY

120.) 3 (cont.)

			121.) 2 (cont.)	
CHESSMEN	INSTEAD	SHY	BEDS	DISMAY
CHILDREN	JABBERWOCK	SIMPLY	BEE-HIVE	DITCH
CHIN	JABBERWOCKY	SIR	BEETLE	DOLL
CINDERS	JOIN	SKY	BELONG	DRAGGED
COMFORTABLY	JOINT	SOLDIERS	BELONGS	DRAWING-ROOM
CONFESS	JOURNEY	SOLEMN	BEWARE	DREADFULLY
CONSIDERED	KNOCKED	SORRY	BISCUIT	DREAMED
CONTINUED	LADY	SOUNDS	BITE	DREAMILY
COOKED	LAID	SQUEEZE	BITTER	DROP
CORKSCREW	LANGUAGE	STAIRS	BLADE	DRUMS
CORNER	LAUGHTER	STAND	BLAZE	DUM
CORRECTED	LIGHT	STARTED	BLEEDING	EARTHQUAKE
COUNTER	LIGHTNING	STARTLED	BLOWS	EASIER
COVERED	LILY	STIFFLY	BOILING	ECHOES
CRAVAT	LIPS	STRUCK	BONFIRE	EFFORT
CRYING	LIVING	SULKILY	BOTTLE	EIGHT
CURTSEY	MANNER	SUMS	BOUND	ELDEST
DARE	MEMORANDUM	SUNNY	BREAKFAST	ELEPHANTS
DECIDEDLY	MEMORY	TABLES	BROKEN	ENEMY
DEEPLY	MENTION	TEAR	BROOKS	ENGINE
DETERMINED	MILK	TELLING	BRUSHED	ENGLAND
DISTANCE	MISCHIEF	TEN	BUNCH	ENJOYED
DITTO	MISS	THEE	BUNCHES	ENQUIRED
DIVIDED	MONTHS	THEY'LL	BUSH	EVENING
DOUBT	MOVING	THIN	BUTTERED	EXACT
DRANK	MUTTERED	THROW	BUTTONS	EXAMINATION
DRAW	NATURAL	THUMP	CALMER	EXCITED
DREADFUL	NERVOUS	THUNDERSTORM	CANNOT	EXCUSES
DRESS	NERVOUSLY	TIDY	CARELESSLY	EXPECTED
DUST	NEST	TIGHT	CARRIED	EXPLAINING
D'YE	NIGHT-CAP	TIRED	CAT	EXTRAORDINARY
EAT	NIGHTS	TOLD	CAUTIOUSLY	EXTREMELY
EATING	NOR	TOUCHING	CHAIRS	FAIR
EMPTY	OYSTER	TREAT	CHANGE	FAN
ENDS	PANTING	TREMBLING	CHEEK	FATTER
ENGLISH	PAPER	TRICKLED	CHESS	FAVOURITE
ENTIRELY	PARDON	TUMBLED	CHICKEN	FEARED
EXCITEMENT	PASSAGE	UN-BIRTHDAY	CHIEFLY	FEARFULLY
EXCUSE	PASSED	UNDONE	CHIMNEY-PIECE	FEAST
EXPECT	PEEPING	UNHAPPY	CHOKED	FEAST'S
FABULOUS	PENCIL	VANISHED	CHOKING	FEED
FADE	PERSON	VERSE	CHOOSING	FENDER
FAIRY-TALE	PETALS	VEXED	CHOSEN	FIDDLE-DE-DEE
FASTENED	PIN	WAITERS	CLAPPING	FIELD
FASTNESS	POCKET	WAITING	CLASPED	FIELDS
FAULTS	POEM	WARM	CLASPING	FIFTY
FETCH	POINTED	WHISKERS	CLEARLY	FINDING
FIFTH	POINTING	WINE	CLOCK	FINE
FINGER-POSTS	POSSIBLE	WINTER	CLOTHES	FIRE-IRONS
FLAT	POSSIBLY	WITHIN	COLOUR	FIREPLACE
FLOOR	PRESENTS	WON'T	COMPARED	FITTED
FOND	PRETENDING	WOOL	COMPLAIN	FIXED
FOOLISH	PRICKED	WORKS	COMPLIMENT	FLEW
FORGET	PRINCIPAL	WORSE	CONFUSION	FLOATED
FORGETTING	PRISONER	WRITE	CONJURING-TRICK	FLOWER
FORGOT	PULLED	WRITING	CONSEQUENCE	FOLD
FORWARDS	QUANTITY	YEAR	CONSIDERING	FOLLOW
FOURTH	QUARREL		CONTEMPTUOUSLY	FOLLOWED
FRENCH	QUESTIONS	**121.) 2 (0.00675%)**	CONTENT	FOOT
FRIEND	RAIN	ABOVE	COUNT	FREE
GARDENS	REACH	ACTUALLY	COUNTING	FROWNING
GENTLEMAN	RECOVERED	A-DRESSING	CRIME	FURY
GIRL	REINS	AGO	CROOKED	GASPED
GLASSES	RETURN	ALSO	CURLED	GIVEN
GLIDED	RIDING	AMUSED	CURTSEYED	GLANCED
GRASS	RING	AMUSEMENT	DAISY	GLUE
GREW	ROUNDER	ANXIETY	DANCE	GOAT
GRINNED	ROW	AREN'T	DANGER	GOLDEN
GROWLED	RUBBED	ART	DARKER	GOOD-NATURED
HANDKERCHIEF	RUBBING	ASHAMED	DARLING	GOVERNESS
HAPPENS	SADLY	ASSURE	DEAF	GRAVE
HEART	SAYS	ASTONISHMENT	DEE	GROANED
HIT	SCENTED	ATTENTION	DESCRIBED	HABIT
HONEY	SCREAMING	BABY	DESPAIR	HADDOCKS'
HUG	SECOND	BADLY	DIFFERENCE	HALL
HURTING	SENTENCE	BALANCE	DIFFICULT	HANDED
IMPOSSIBLE	SETTLED	BANG	DISCONTENTED	HANDLE
INCHES	SHARP	BANK	DISH-COVER	HANGING
INDIGNANTLY	SHE'LL	BAR	DISHES	HEAPS
	SHOUTING	BEARD		HEARTH-RUG

121.) 2 (cont.)

				122.) 1 (cont.)
HEDGES	NEITHER	SETTLE	TWEEDLE	ANKLETS
HOBBLED	NESTLE	SEVERE	TWIG	ANNOYED
HOLDS	NICELY	SHADING	TYING	ANSWERS
HONOUR	NINETY	SHA'N'T	UNSATISFACTORY	ANYBODY'S
HOPES	NOBLE	SHE'D	UNWOUND	ANYHOW
HORN	NOTICING	SHOES	UPRIGHT	APPEARED
HUMAN	NURSE	SHORTER	UPSIDE-DOWN	ARCH
HUNGRY	OBEDIENTLY	SHOUT	USEFUL	ARCHED
HURRIED	OBEY	SHUDDER	VAIN	ARGUE
IDEAS	OBLIGED	SILVERY	VAINLY	ARGUED
IMMEDIATELY	OBSERVE	SIMPLE	VALLEY	ARGUING
IMPENETRABILITY	O'CLOCK	SINGLE	VENTURE	AROUND
IMPERIAL	OLDER	SIXTY-FIVE	VERBS	ARRANGE
INQUIRED	OPENING	SIXTY-FOUR	VEXATION	ARRANGED
INTERRUPT	OPPORTUNITY	SLAIN	VIEW	ARRIVED
INTRODUCE	ORDER	SLEEP	VISIT	ASSISTANCE
INTRODUCED	OTHERS	SLICES	VOLCANO	ASUNDER
INVISIBLE	PALE	SMILING	VORPAL	ATTEND
JOINED	PASS	SMOKE	WALKS	ATTENDED
JULY	PASSING	SMOOTHLY	WANDERING	ATTENTIVELY
KETTLE	PASSION	SNORE	WANTS	ATTITUDE
KICK	PAY	SNOWDROP	WARMER	AWE
KINDNESS	PEGS	SOFTLY	WAVE	AWHILE
KINGS	PIECES	SOLEMNLY	WAX-WORKS	BADGERS
KISS	PIGS	SOMEBODY	WEALTH	BALANCES
KITTENS	PINNED	SORTS	WEAR	BALANCING
KITTEN'S	PINS	SOUND	WEDNESDAY	BALE
KNEE	PITYING	SPEAKS	WEEP	BALLAD
KNIGHTS	PLACES	SPITE	WELCOME	BANGING
KNOCK-DOWN	PLASTER	SPRANG	WET	BANKS
KNOCKING	PLATES	SQUARES	WHEELS	BARGAIN
KNOWING	PLAYING	SQUEAK	WHISTLING	BARGAINS
KNOWN	PLEADED	START	WHOM	BARK
L	PLEASANCE	STATE	WICKED	BATTER
LAND	PLUM-PUDDING	STEAM-ENGINE	WILLING	BEACH
LEADS	POINT	STICK	WINDING	BEAK
LEANT	PRETENDED	STICKS	WONDERED	BEAMISH
LED	PREVENT	STIFF	WONDERFULLY	BEARING
LEGS	PROMISED	STOOPING	WOODS	BEAST
LID	PROPER	STOPPING	WORKING	BEATING
LIE	PROPERLY	STRANGE	WORST	BEAUTIES
LINGERING	PULL	STREAM	WRIGGLING	BEAUTIFULLY
LIST	PUNISH	STRETCHED	WRINGING	BEAUTY
LISTENED	PUNISHMENTS	STRINGS	YELLOW	BECKONED
LISTENING	PURRED	STRUGGLED	YONDER	BECKONING
LITHE	PUSHED	STUFF	YOURS	BECOME
LIVES	PUZZLING	STUMBLED		BEDTIME
LOAF	QUANTITIES	SUCCEED	**122.) 1 (0.00337%)**	BE-E-EHH
LONGER	RAILWAY	SUCCEEDED	ABC	BEGINS
LOT	RAISED	SUGGESTED	ACCENTS	BELIEVED
LOVE	RANG	SULKY	ACCIDENT	BELL-HANDLE
LOVES	REJOICE	SUM	ACCOUNTS	BELLOWING
LOVINGLY	RELIEVED	SWEPT	ACRES	BELONGING
LOWER	REMAINS	SWORD	ACT	BENDING
LUMP	REMEMBERED	TAIL	ACTIVE	BENEATH
MARK	REMINDS	TALL	ADDRESSED	BENT
MEANWHILE	REMOVE	TAUGHT	ADJECTIVES	BESEECH
MELT	RESTED	TEASE	ADMIRE	BEWILDERED
MESSAGE	RIBBON	THANKED	ADMIRING	BEWILDERMENT
MESSENGERS	RIDER	THANKS	ADMITTANCE	BILLOWS
MESSENGER'S	ROCKING-HORSE-FLY	THAT'LL	ADVANTAGE	BIRTHDAYS
MET	ROWING	THEMSELVES	ADVENTURES	BITES
MIGHTN'T	RULES	THERE'LL	ADVERTISEMENTS	BLANKETS
MILE	SAND	THIRD	ADVISE	BLAST
MISERABLE	SANDWICH	THOROUGHLY	AFFECTIONATE	BLAZING
MISSED	SANG	THUMB	AFFECTIONATELY	BLEAT
MIST	SATISFIED	THUNDER	AFRESH	BLINDING
MOANED	SAVE	TICKET	AGLOW	BLINKING
MONEY	SAVES	TICKET-OFFICE	AGREE	BLOTTING-PAPER
MONSTERS	SCARCELY	TIMID	AGREED	BLOWING
MONSTROUS	SCRAMBLING	TINY	AIMING	BOLSTER
MOSTLY	SCREAMED	'TIS	AIN'T	BOLSTERS
MOUNTED	SEATED	TOUCHED	ALARMED	BONES
MOUSE-TRAP	SEIZED	TRAIN	ALLOWED	BOOTS
MUNCHED	SEND	TRIFLE	ALPHABET	BORDER
MURMURED	SENSE	TROTTED	ALTERING	BOROGOVE
NARROW	SENSIBLE	TROUBLE	ALTOGETHER	BOTTLES
NASTY	SERIOUS	TUMBLING	AMAZING	BOUGHS
NEAT	SERIOUSLY	TUNE	ANIMAL	BOUGHWOUGH
	SERVANT	TURNS	ANIMALS	

122.) 1 (cont.)

BOUNDED	CLOSER	DIGNIFIED	EXPECTING	FRUMENTY
BOUNDING	CLUB	DILIGENTLY	EXPERIMENT	FRUMIOUS
BOYS	CLUBS	DINE	EXPLAIN	FUNNY
BRAN	CLUTCHED	DINNER-PARTY	EXPLANATION	FUSS
BRANDISHING	COAL-SCUTTLES	DINNERS	EXTINGUISHERS	GAILY
BRANDY	COATS	DIPPING	EXTRA	GALLOPED
BRASS	COFFEE	DISAPPEARED	FACED	GALLOPING
BRAVE	COIN	DISBELIEVE	FAIL	GALUMPHING
BREAD-AND-BUTTER-FLY	COMB	DISCOURAGED	FAILED	GASP
BREATHE	COMFORTABLE	DISGRACE	FAINTED	GATHERED
BREATHLESS	COMFORTED	DISGUST	FALLEN	GAUZE
BRIDLE	COMMITS	DISH-COVERS	FALLS	GENERAL
BRIGHTENED	COMMON	DISMAL	FALTERED	GEOGRAPHY
BRIGHTLY	COMPANION	DISRESPECTFUL	FANCIED	GIMLET
BRINGS	COMPARISON	DISTINCT	FANCY	GLADLY
BRINY	COMPLAINING	DISTINGUISH	FANNED	GLADNESS
BRISKLY	COMPLETED	DISTRACTED	FANNING	GLANCING
BROAD	COMPLETELY	DIVIDE	FANS	GLEAM
BROILING	CONFUSED	DIVIDES	FARTHER	GLEAMING
BROW	CONFUSING	DIVISION	FARTHING	GLIDING
BUD	CONQUERED	DOGS	FASTEN	GLORIOUS
BUFFALO	CONSEQUENCES	DOG'S	FASTENING	GLOW
BUNDLES	CONTEMPT	DOOR-POST	FAVOUR	GLOWING
BUNDLING	CONTENTED	DOORS	FEARFUL	GOAT'S
BURBLED	CONTRADICTING	DOORWAY	FEASTING	GOLD
BURNING	CONVENIENT	DOTTED	FEATHERS	GOOD-NATUREDLY
BUSHES	CONVENIENTLY	DOUBLE	FED	GOOD-NIGHT
BUSHY	COOING	DOUBTFUL	FEEBLY	GOOD-TEMPERED
BUSILY	COOK	DOUGH	FELLOW-TRAVELER	GOOSE
BUSTLED	COOL	DOWNWARDS	FEVERISH	GRACE
BUSTLING	COPPER	DRAGON-FLY	FIDDLE-DE-DEE'S	GRACEFULLY
BUTTERFLIES	CORKSCREWS	DRAWL	FIDDLES	GRADUALLY
BUTTERFLY	CORNERS	DREAD	FIDDLESTICK	GRAND'
BUTTER'S	CORRECT	DREAM-RUSHES	FIDDLE-STICKS	GRANDER
CABBAGES	COTTAGES	DRIFT	FIERCELY	GRASSHOPPER
CAKES	COUGH	DRIFTING	FIGURE	GRASS-PLOT
CALCULATION	COUPLE	DRINKING	FILLED	GRASSY
CALLAY	COURAGE	DRIPPING	FINGER'S	GRAVEL-WALK
CALLING	COVERS	DRIVES	FIRELIGHT'S	GRAVY
CALLOOH	CRASH	DROPPED	FIREWORKS	GREATER
CANDLE	CRASHING	DROPPING	FISHES'	GREEDILY
CANDLESTICKS	CRAWLED	DROWNED	FIVEPENCE	GRIN
CAREFUL	CRAWLING	DRUM	FIXES	GRINNING
CARRIAGE-FULL	CREAM	DRUMMED	FLAME	GROAN
CARROTS	CREEP	DULL	FLAP	GROPED
CARRYING	CRIMSON	DURING	FLEET	GROWL
CARVE	CRITICIZED	DUSTED	FLIMSY	GROWN
CARVING-KNIFE	CROPPING	DUSTY	FLOATING	GUESSED
CASTLES	CROSS	DWINDLED	FLOUR	GUESSING
CATS	CROWD	DYE	FLOW	GUNPOWDER
CHARACTERS	CROWDED	E	FLOWERBED	GUST
CHAT	CROWDS	EARLIER	FLOWERBEDS	GYROSCOPE
CHATTERING	CRUMPLED	EASIEST	FLOWN	HAIL
CHEAPER	CRUST	EATEN	FLUNG	HALF-AN-HOUR
CHECKED	CUP	ECHOED	FLUSHED	HALF-DREAM
CHECKING	CURIOUS-LOOKING	EDGES	FLUTTERING	HALF-PAST
CHEER	CURIOUSLY	EEL	FLY	HALFPENNY
CHEERING	CURLING	E'ER	FOE	HAM-SANDWICH
CHEESE	CUTTING	EFFECT	FOLDED	HAM-SANDWICHES
CHESS-BOARD	DAHLIA	EGGS	FOLK	HANDING
CHILDHOOD'S	DAMP	EIGHTY-SEVEN	FOOT-SOLDIERS	HAND-IN-HAND
CHILDREN'S	DANCERS	ELBOW	FOOTSTEP	HAND-RAIL
CHILD'S	DARLINGS	ELBOW-DEEP	FORK	HANDSOME
CHILLY	DARTED	ELBOWS	FORKS	HANDY
CHIME	DASH	ELEPHANT	FOURTEEN	HANGS
CHIMNEYS	DAUGHTER	EMBROIDERED	FRABJOUS	HANSOM-CABS
CHOICE	DAZZLED	EMPHASIS	FRESH	HAPPENING
CHOOSES	DEAFENED	ENCOURAGE	FRET	HARM
CHORTLED	DECANTERS	ENCOURAGED	FRETFUL	HASN'T
CHRISTMAS-BOX	DECISION	ENGINE-DRIVER	FRIENDLY	HAST
CIDER	DEED	ENGINES	FRIENDS	HASTE
CIRCUMSTANCES	DEEPEST	ENTANGLED	FRIGHT	HATE
CIVILLY	DEMURELY	ENVIOUS	FRIGHTENING	HATTA'S
CLAP	DENYING	ERE	FRO	HAUNTS
CLASP	DESERVED	ETIQUETTE	FRONT-DOOR	HEADACHE
CLAWS	DESIGN	EVERYTHING'S	FROST	HEAD-DOWNWARDS
CLEAN	DESPERATE	EVERYWHERE	FROSTS	HEADLONG
CLEARED	DEVOURED	EXCEPT	FROTHY	HEAD'S
CLEVEREST	DICTIONARY	EXCUSING	FROWN	HEARING
	DIG	EXHAUSTED	FRUIT-TREE	HEARKEN

122.) 1 (cont.)

HEARS	KNOCKS	MEAT-COURSE	PATIENCE	QUILT
HEARTH	KNOLLS	MELTED	PATIENTLY	QUIVERED
HEARTH-RUGS	KNOTS	MEMORIES	PATTING	QUIVERING
HEARTILY	KNOWS	MENAI	PAWNS	QUOTH
HEATHER	LABELED	MERRILY	PAWS	RAISIN
HEAVILY	LADEN	MERRY	PEACE	RAMBLING
HE'D	LADLE	MEW	PEEP	RAPID
HEED	LADY'S	MICROSCOPE	PEN	RATH
HEELS	LANGUAGES	MIDST	PENCE	RATTLE-SNAKE
HE'LL	LAPPING	MINCE-PIE	PENNY	RAVING
HELPED	LARGEST	MINDED	PEOPLE'S	READILY
HELPING	LARKSPUR	MINE	PEPPER	REALLER
HELPLESS	LASS	MINERAL	PERFECT	REASONABLE
HEREAFTER	LATER	MISCHIEVOUS	PERFECTLY	REDDER
HEROES	LAWN	MISSES	PERPLEXITY	REDUCED
HESITATING	LAZILY	MISTAKE	PERSON'S	REFERRING
HIDE	LEANED	MIX	PET	REFRESHING
HIDEOUS	LEANING	MIXING	PHANTOMWISE	REFRESHMENTS
HIDING-PLACE	LEARNING	MODEL	PHRASE	RELATE
HIGHER	LEAVING	MOODY	PICTURE	RELEASED
HILLS	LEFT-HAND	MOON	PICTURES	RELENTED
HINT	LEISURELY	MOP	PIG	REMARKS
HIPPOPOTAMUS	LEND	MOPS	PIGEON	REMEMBERS
HIRE	LENGTH	MOSS	PINK	REPAINTED
HITS	LESS	MOUNTAIN-RILL	PINNING	REPROACHFULLY
HOLES	LETTER	MOUNTAINS	PITEOUS	REPROOF
HOLLOW	LETTERS	MULBERRY	PLACED	RESCUED
HOLLY-LEAVES	LICKING	MUMBLINGLY	PLAIN	RESISTANCE
HONESTLY	LIDDELL	MUSTN'T	PLAINTIVE	RESOLUTELY
HONOUR'S	LID'S	MUTTERING	PLANTED	RESPECTABLE
HOP	LIES	MUTTON-PIES	PLAYED	RESPECTFULLY
HOPEFUL	LIFE'S	NAP	PLEASANTLY	RETORTED
HOPPING	LIGHTED	NEARER	PLEASING	RETURN-TICKET
HORROR	LIGHTING	NEAREST	PLEASURE	REVIVED
HORSE-FLY	LIGHTLY	NEED	PLUNGED	RHYME
HOUR	LILY'S	NEEDED	POCKET-HANDKERCHIEF	RHYTHM
HUGE	LIMED	NESTS	POCKETS	RICH
HUMBLE	LINE	NEW-FOUND	POEMS	RIDDLES
HUMMING	LIONS	NEWS	POKER	RIGHT-HAND
HUNDREDS	LIZARDS	NINETY-TIMES-NINE	POKING	RINGING
HUNT	LOADED	NODDED	PONDERING	RISING
HUNTED	LOCKED	NOISY	PORCUPINE	RIVER
HURRICANE	LOGIC	NOTION	PORMANTEAU	RIVER-BANKS
HURRY	LOLLING	NOWHERE	PORTMANTEAU	RIVERS
HUSH	LONELINESS	OBEYED	POST	ROAST
HUSH-A-BY	LONELY	OBJECTION	PRATTLED	ROCK
HYAENA	LONGEST	OBSTINACY	PRECIOUS	ROCKED
IGNORANT	LONGING	OCCASION	PRETENCE	RODE
IMITATE	LOOKS	ODDEST	PRETTIEST	ROLL
IMPATIENT	LOOSE	ODDLY	PRINCIPALLY	ROLLS
IMPERTINENCE	LOSING	OFFERED	PRIVILEGE	ROMPS
IMPORTANT	LOUDER	ONESELF	PROBOSCIS	ROOF
INCH	LOVE-GIFT	ONWARD	PROGRESS	ROOFS
INCLINED	LOVING	OPERA-GLASS	PRONOUNCED	ROSE'S
INCONVENIENT	LOW-SPIRITED	OPINION	PROPPED	ROWLAND'S
INDIGNANT	LUCKILY	ORDERS	PROUDEST	RUB
INGENUITY	LUGGAGE	OTHER'S	PROUDLY	RUDDY
INTEND	LULLABIES	OTHERWISE	PROVIDED	RUDE
INTENTLY	LULLABY	OUGHTN'T	PROVOKED	RUG
INTERESTED	LUMPS	OUTGRIBING	PUDDING-COURSES	RUNS
INTERESTING	MACASSAR-OIL	OUTSIDE	PUFF	RUSHED
INTRODUCING	MADLY	OVERHEAD	PUFFING	RUST
INVENT	MADNESS	OVERHEARD	PUMP	SAD
IRRITATION	MAGIC	OWNER	PUNCH	SAFE
JAWS	MAID	OYSTER-BED	PUNISHMENT	SAFER
JOINING	MAIDEN	OYSTER-SHELLS	PURCHASE	SAIL
JOKES	MAIDS	PACKED	PURE	SAL-VOLATILE
JOY	MAJESTY'S	PAID	PURPOSE	SANDS
JUBJUB	MAN'S	PAINT	PURSE	SANDWICHES
JUDY	MANXOME	PAIRS	PURSED	SAP
JUMP	MARKET-PLACE	PALED	PURSUING	SATURDAY
KANGAROOS	MARKING	PANT	PUSH	SAUCEPAN
KICKED	MASTER	PAPERS	PUZZLE	SAUCER
KICKING	MATTERED	PARTICULAR	PUZZLER	SAUNTERED
KILLED	MAYBE	PARTICULARLY	QUARTER	SAVED
KINDER	MAYHAP	PARTY	QUEEREST	SAVING
KISSES	MAYOR	PASSENGERS	QUEERLY	SAWDUST
KNIT	MEANINGS	PASSIONATELY	QUEER-SHAPED	SAWING
KNITTING-NEEDLES	MEASUREMENTS	PAST	QUENCHED	SCENE
	MEASURING	PAT	QUIET	SCENT

122.) 1 (cont.)

SCEPTRE
SCHOOLBOYS
SCOLD
SCOLDING
SCORNFUL
SCORNFULLY
SCRAMBLE
SCREAMS
SCRUBBING
SEALING
SEALING-WAX
SEARCH
SEAS
SEAT
SECRET
SEEING
SEIZING
SELFISH
SERIES
SERVANTS
SERVANTS'
SERVED
SETTING
SEVENTH
SEVERELY
SEVERITY
SHABBY-LOOKING
SHADE
SHADOW
SHADOWS
SHADY
SHAGGY
SHALT
SHAME
SHARKS
SHARPER
SHARPLY
SHED
SHELVES
SHINE
SHIPS
SHOE
SHORE
SHOULDERS
SHOVEL
SHOWS
SHRIEKS
SHUN
SHUTTING
SHYLY
SHYNESS
SIDES
SIDEWAYS
SIEVE
SIGHS
SILVER
SIXTH
SKIES
SKIM
SKIPPING
SLEEPING
SLEEVES
SLIDING
SLIMY
SLIPPED
SLOWER
SLYLY
SMOKES
SMOOTH
SMOOTHE
SMOOTHED
SNAP
SNAP-DRAGON-FLIES
SNAP-DRAGON-FLY
SNEEZE
SNICKER-SNACK
SNORTED
SNOWED
SNUG

SOBS
SOFTER
SOLDIER
SOLES
SOMEBODY'S
SOMETHING'S
SON
SONG'S
SOONER
SORTED
SOUGHT
SOUP-TUREEN
SPECTACLES
SPEED
SPELL
SPENT
SPIED
SPIKES
SPOIL
SPOILED
SPOILT
SPREADING
SPRING
SPRINKLE
SQUEAKED
SQUEAKING
STALKS
STAMP
STAMPED
STARTING
STEADILY
STEP
STEPPED
STEPS
STICKY
STING
STOPS
STORM-WIND'S
STORMY
STORY
STRANGE-LOOKING
STREAMING
STREET
STRETCHING
STRIKE
STROKE
STROKED
STROKING
STUFFED
STUPID
STUPIDER
SUBJECTS
SUBMIT
SUETY
SUGAR
SUGAR-LOAF
SUGGESTION
SULLEN
SUMMERS
SUMMON
SUN-DIAL
SUN-DIALS
SUNS
SUP
SUPPORT
SUPPOSING
SURELY
SURVEY
SWALLOWED
SWEET
SWINGING
SYMPATHIZE
TABLECLOTH
TABLE-CLOTHS
TAKES
TALKS
TALLER
TANGLED
TANGLES
TAR-BARREL

TASSEL
TASTE
TEACH
TEETOTUM
TELEGRAPH
TELESCOPE
TERROR
THENCE
THERE'D
THING'S
THINNER
THIRST
THIRTY
THIRTY-TIMES-THREE
THREES
THREW
THROWING
THUMPED
THURSDAYS
TICKETS
TICKING
TICKLED
TIDINGS
TIED
TIGERS
TIN
TIPPLE
TIPS
TIPTOE
TOE
TOES
TOIL
TOILET
TOLLING
TONGUE
TONGUES
TO-NIGHT
TOOTHACHE
TOSS
TOUCH
TOWNS
TRAILING
TRAINS
TRANSPORT
TRAVEL
TRAVELING
TRAYS
TREACLE
TREASURES
TREMBLE
TREMBLED
TREMENDOUSLY
TRIAL
TRICK
TRIPPING
TRIUMPHANT
TROT
TROTTING
TROUGH
TRUE
TRUMPET
TRUNK
TRUTH
TUESDAY
TUESDAYS
TULGEY
TUMBLES
TUMTUM
TUNE'S
TUREEN
TURK
TWEEDLEDUM'S
TWENTY
TWIDDLE
TWIGS
TWIST
TWISTS
TWOPENCE
TWOPENCE-HALFPENNY
TWOS

TWO-YARD
UFFISH
UGLY
UNABLE
UNCERTAIN
UNCLASPING
UNCLOUDED
UNDERGOING
UNDERSTOOD
UN-DISH-COVER
UNFASTENED
UNFINISHED
UNHAPPINESS
UNICORNS
UNINTERESTING
UNPLEASANT
UNTIL
UNTO
UNWELCOME
UNWISELY
UPROAR
UPSET
UPSIDE
UPWARDS
VANISH'D
VEGETABLE
VICIOUS
VICTORY
VINEGAR
VIOLENTLY
VIOLET
VISITOR
VISITORS'
WAGES
WAGGING
WAIST
WAISTCOAT-BUTTONS
WAITER
WANDERED
WARMTH
WASHING
WASTING
WAVED
WAVES
WAX
WEAK
WEARILY
WE'D
WEEDS
WEIGHT
WEPT
WEREN'T
WEXES
WHAT'LL
WHEAT
WHERE'S
WHEREVER
WHIFFLING
WHISPERING
WHISTLE
WHITER
WHO'S
WIDER
WIFE
WILD
WILDERNESS
WILLOW-TREE
WILT
WIN
WINDOW-PANES
WINK
WINKED
WINS
WISE
WISHING
WITHER
WOE
WOKE
WON
WONDERLAND

WONDERS
WOODEN
WOOD'S
WORK-BOX
WORKED
WOUND
WRAPPED
WRIST
WRITES
YAWNING
1
364
365

REVERSE INDEX

PAUSED	WAVED	WONDERLAND	HIDING-PLACE	LATITUDE
REFUSED	BELIEVED	GRAND	MARKET-PLACE	ATTITUDE
CONFUSED	RELIEVED	SAND	PACE	BEE
AMUSED	RECEIVED	THOUSAND	RACE	DEE
CHEATED	LIVED	STAND	GRACE	FIDDLE-DE-DEE
REPEATED	ARRIVED	INKSTAND	DISGRACE	TWEEDLEDEE
TREATED	REVIVED	UNDERSTAND	CAUCUS-RACE	COFFEE
SEATED	INVOLVED	END	PIECE	THEE
HATED	BELOVED	BEND	A-PIECE	KNEE
FLOATED	MOVED	OFFEND	FRONTISPIECE	FREE
IMITATED	REMOVED	FRIEND	CHIMNEY-PIECE	AGREE
IRRITATED	PROVED	LEND	TICKET-OFFICE	DISAGREE
DISTRACTED	SERVED	SEND	ALICE	THREE
OBJECTED	DESERVED	PRETEND	SLICE	TREE
COLLECTED	WE'D	INTEND	MICE	ROSE-TREE
EXPECTED	BOWED	ATTEND	NICE	FRUIT-TREE
DIRECTED	ALLOWED	FIND	CHOICE	WILLOW-TREE
CORRECTED	SWALLOWED	BEHIND	REJOICE	SEE
CONTRADICTED	FOLLOWED	KIND	VOICE	SAFE
FIDGETED	SNOWED	MIND	PRACTICE	LIFE
COMPLETED	VEXED	WIND	NOTICE	CHILD-LIFE
CROQUETED	FIXED	SECOND	JUSTICE	KNIFE
LIFTED	MIXED	FOND	ADVICE	BREAD-KNIFE
LIGHTED	BOXED	BEYOND	TWICE	CARVING-KNIFE
DELIGHTED	PLAYED	BOUND	DANCE	WIFE
WAITED	OBEYED	FOUND	CHANCE	AGE
EXCITED	CURTSEYED	NEW-FOUND	ASKANCE	LUGGAGE
LOW-SPIRITED	BRIGHT-EYED	ROUND	BALANCE	CARRIAGE
INVITED	ENJOYED	AROUND	APPEARANCE	MANAGE
MELTED	ANNOYED	GROUND	FRANCE	COURAGE
PLANTED	GRAZED	CROQUET-GROUND	ENTRANCE	ENCOURAGE
PANTED	SNEEZED	SOUND	PLEASANCE	SAGE
WANTED	SQUEEZED	WOUND	ACCEPTANCE	PASSAGE
SCENTED	CRITICIZED	UNWOUND	DISTANCE	MESSAGE
RELENTED	SEIZED	GOOD	RESISTANCE	ADVANTAGE
ORNAMENTED	RECOGNIZED	CHILDHOOD	ASSISTANCE	LANGUAGE
PRESENTED	VANISH'D	STOOD	INSTANCE	SAVAGE
CONSENTED	I'D	UNDERSTOOD	ADMITTANCE	EDGE
CONTENTED	LAID	WOOD	ADVANCE	HEDGE
DISCONTENTED	MAID	BEARD	EVIDENCE	LEDGE
INVENTED	HOUSEMAID	HEARD	THENCE	KNOWLEDGE
FAINTED	PAID	OVERHEARD	PATIENCE	RIDGE
REPAINTED	AFRAID	SLUGGARD	SILENCE	BRIDGE
POINTED	SAID	HARD	VIOLENCE	JUDGE
PRINTED	DID	CARDBOARD	INSOLENCE	PRIVILEGE
HUNTED	HID	CHESS-BOARD	IMPERTINENCE	CHANGE
MOUNTED	LID	CUSTARD	PENCE	ORANGE
GRUNTED	SOLID	MUSTARD	FIVEPENCE	ARRANGE
ATTEMPTED	TIMID	GUARD	TWOPENCE	STRANGE
INTERRUPTED	RAPID	AWKWARD	SIXPENCE	LARGE
DARTED	STUPID	ONWARD	DIFFERENCE	HUGE
STARTED	LANGUID	COWARD	ABSENCE	HE
COMFORTED	PLUCK'D	FARM-YARD	PRETENCE	ACHE
SNORTED	HERALD	TWO-YARD	SENTENCE	HEADACHE
SORTED	HELD	LIZARD	EXISTENCE	TOOTHACHE
RETORTED	FIELD	WITHER'D	CONSEQUENCE	SHE
LASTED	CHILD	THIRD	SINCE	THE
TASTED	DREAM-CHILD	THIRD	ONCE	BREATHE
SUGGESTED	MILD	AFFORD	DUNCE	LITHE
RESTED	WILD	WORD	RESOURCE	SMOOTHE
INTERESTED	OLD	SWORD	INTRODUCE	LACIE
PERSISTED	COLD	ABSURD	FADE	DIE
WORSTED	SCOLD	BUD	SHADE	LIE
EXHAUSTED	FOLD	LOUD	MARMALADE	TILLIE
DUSTED	GOLD	ALOUD	BLADE	PIE
PATTED	HOLD	CLOUD	MADE	MINCE-PIE
FITTED	TOLD	PROUD	ABIDE	MAGPIE
SUBMITTED	WORLD	YOU'D	HIDE	ELSIE
PERMITTED	COULD	CROWD	GLIDE	TIE
DOTTED	SHOULD	THEY'D	SIDE	CAKE
TROTTED	WOULD	E	SEASIDE	PLUM-CAKE
EXECUTED	AND	BE	INSIDE	SHAKE
SHOUTED	BAND	OUTGRABE	OUTSIDE	LAKE
RESCUED	STIGAND	WABE	TIDE	MAKE
SUBDUED	HAND	GLOBE	GUIDE	RATTLE-SNAKE
ARGUED	LEFT-HAND	MAYBE	DIVIDE	TAKE
CONTINUED	RIGHT-HAND	PEACE	WIDE	MISTAKE
SHAVED	LAND	FACE	RODE	EARTHQUAKE
ENGRAVED	ZEALAND	PLACE	RUDE	WAKE
SAVED	ENGLAND	FIREPLACE	LONGITUDE	LIKE

WIG
TWIG
BANG
RANG
SPRANG
SANG
SOBBING
RUBBING
SCRUBBING
OUTGRIBING
NOTICING
DANCING
BALANCING
GLANCING
PRODUCING
INTRODUCING
BEHEADING
LEADING
READING
SPREADING
TREADING
FADING
SHADING
ADDING
SHEDDING
PUDDING
PLUM-PUDDING
BLEEDING
GLIDING
SLIDING
RIDING
DIVIDING
SCOLDING
FOLDING
HOLDING
HANDING
STANDING
ENDING
BENDING
NEVER-ENDING
SENDING
PRETENDING
ATTENDING
FINDING
BLINDING
MINDING
REMINDING
WINDING
BOUNDING
BEING
SEEING
PUFFING
MANAGING
ENCOURAGING
JUDGING
WAGGING
DIGGING
BANGING
HANGING
CHANGING
CLINGING
FLINGING
RINGING
BRINGING
WRINGING
SINGING
SWINGING
LONGING
BELONGING
REACHING
TEACHING
PUNCHING
CATCHING
HATCHING
SCRATCHING
WATCHING
STRETCHING
TOUCHING
SIGHING
LAUGHING

GALUMPHING
SPLASHING
CRASHING
WASHING
REFRESHING
BRANDISHING
VANISHING
FINISHING
WISHING
BRUSHING
THING
SOMETHING
WRITHING
NOTHING
SOOTHING
FARTHING
ANYTHING
EVERYTHING
KING
SPEAKING
BREAKING
SQUEAKING
SHAKING
MAKING
TAKING
WAKING
BLACKING
CHECKING
KICKING
LICKING
PICKING
TICKING
STICKING
UNLOCKING
KNOCKING
TALKING
WALKING
THINKING
BLINKING
DRINKING
SHRINKING
CHOKING
SMOKING
LOOKING
STRANGE-LOOKING
QUEER-LOOKING
CURIOUS-LOOKING
SHABBY-LOOKING
POKING
STROKING
PROVOKING
BARKING
MARKING
REMARKING
WORKING
ASKING
SEALING
NIBBLING
RAMBLING
SCRAMBLING
TREMBLING
RUMBLING
GRUMBLING
TUMBLING
DOUBLING
BUNDLING
FEELING
REELING
ATHELING
QUARRELING
TRAVELING
WHIFFLING
WRIGGLING
TRAILING
CEILING
SMILING
BOILING
BROILING
TRICKLING
TINKLING

TWINKLING
CALLING
FALLING
TELLING
SHILLING
KILLING
WILLING
LOLLING
ROLLING
TOLLING
PULLING
RIPPLING
DARLING
CURLING
WHISTLING
BRISTLING
BUSTLING
RUSTLING
RATTLING
SETTLING
CRAWLING
DRAWLING
SPRAWLING
HOWLING
GROWLING
PUZZLING
GLEAMING
SCREAMING
DREAMING
STREAMING
AIMING
SKIMMING
SWIMMING
HUMMING
COMING
BECOMING
LEANING
MEANING
OPENING
HAPPENING
STRAIGHTENING
FRIGHTENING
FASTENING
LISTENING
EVENING
COMPLAINING
EXPLAINING
REMAINING
SHINING
EXAMINING
JOINING
FANNING
PLANNING
BEGINNING
PINNING
GRINNING
CUNNING
RUNNING
BECKONING
LEARNING
WARNING
MORNING
BURNING
TURNING
RETURNING
LIGHTNING
YAWNING
FROWNING
DOING
UNDOING
GOING
UNDERGOING
COOING
KEEPING
SLEEPING
PEEPING
HELPING
STAMPING
JUMPING
HOPING

GALLOPING
STOOPING
LAPPING
CLAPPING
WRAPPING
DIPPING
SKIPPING
DRIPPING
TRIPPING
HOPPING
CROPPING
DROPPING
STOPPING
CLASPING
UNCLASPING
RING
BEARING
HEARING
APPEARING
REARING
SHARING
GLARING
STARING
BRING
REMEMBERING
CONSIDERING
WANDERING
HINDERING
PONDERING
WONDERING
ORDERING
MURDERING
CHEERING
PEERING
LINGERING
CAPERING
WHISPERING
ALTERING
CHATTERING
PATTERING
FLUTTERING
MUTTERING
SHIVERING
QUIVERING
RECOVERING
ADMIRING
EXPLORING
SNORING
SPRING
REFERRING
STIRRING
PURRING
DURING
NEIGHBOURING
MEASURING
SING
PLEASING
RAISING
PROMISING
RISING
LOSING
CHOOSING
SUPPOSING
NURSING
PASSING
A-DRESSING
ADDRESSING
PRESSING
EXPRESSING
GUESSING
TOSSING
USING
EXCUSING
CONFUSING
EATING
BEATING
REPEATING
FLOATING
HESITATING
EXPECTING

CONTRADICTING
MEETING
CROQUETING
SHIFTING
DRIFTING
FIGHTING
A-FIGHTING
LIGHTING
WAITING
WHITING
WRITING
HANDWRITING
PANTING
INVENTING
FAINTING
PAINTING
POINTING
HUNTING
COUNTING
ACCOUNTING
INTERRUPTING
STARTING
SNORTING
HURTING
STING
FEASTING
TASTING
WASTING
RESTING
INTERESTING
UNINTERESTING
BURSTING
PATTING
GETTING
FORGETTING
SETTING
UPSETTING
KNITTING
SITTING
A-SITTING
TROTTING
CUTTING
SHUTTING
PUTTING
SHOUTING
ARGUING
PURSUING
LEAVING
HAVING
RAVING
SAVING
WAVING
GIVING
LIVING
LOVING
MOVING
CURVING
DRAWING
SAWING
BOWING
SHOWING
LOWING
BLOWING
GLOWING
SWALLOWING
BELLOWING
KNOWING
ROWING
GROWING
THROWING
COAXING
MIXING
PLAYING
SAYING
FANCYING
CURTSEYING
UGLIFYING
LYING
FLYING
DENYING

WORM	GIVEN	ADDITION	TOO	FAR
RHEUMATISM	SIGN	CONDITION	FRO	EDGAR
DUM	DESIGN	POSITION	SO	VINEGAR
TWEEDLEDUM	IN	MENTION	ALSO	VULGAR
MEMORANDUM	AGAIN	ATTENTION	TO	SUGAR
DRUM	BARGAIN	INVENTION	INTO	BARLEY-SUGAR
ARRUM	DAISY-CHAIN	COMMOTION	UNTO	JAR
SUM	PLAIN	NOTION	DITTO	CATERPILLAR
TUMTUM	COMPLAIN	ADOPTION	TWO	COLLAR
TEETOTUM	EXPLAIN	SUGGESTION	FORTY-TWO	PARTICULAR
AN	SLAIN	QUESTION	NIGHT-CAP	MUSCULAR
CAN	REMAIN	EXECUTION	NIGHTCAP	REGULAR
CLEAN	PAIN	SALMON	HEAP	GRAMMAR
MEAN	RAIN	COMMON	CHEAP	UPROAR
FAN	BRAIN	UNCOMMON	LEAP	REMEMBER
BEGAN	TRAIN	SUMMON	MAYHAP	NUMBER
THAN	CERTAIN	ANON	LAP	OFFICER
PLAN	UNCERTAIN	BOON	CLAP	SAUCER
MAN	CURTAIN	MOON	FLAP	LADDER
GENTLEMAN	VAIN	AFTERNOON	NAP	REDDER
WOMAN	BEGIN	SPOON	SNAP	SHUDDER
FOOTMAN	CHIN	TEASPOON	MOUSE-TRAP	CIDER
FROG-FOOTMAN	THIN	SOON	SAP	STUPIDER
FISH-FOOTMAN	WITHIN	UPON	DEEP	RIDER
HUMAN	COIN	WHEREUPON	ELBOW-DEEP	CONSIDER
GROAN	JOIN	CAULDRON	SHEEP	WIDER
SAUCEPAN	PIN	SON	KEEP	OLDER
FRYING-PAN	GRIN	REASON	SLEEP	SHOULDER
RAN	RAISIN	POISON	ASLEEP	GRANDER
BRAN	TIN	COMPARISON	PEEP	WANDER
LADEN	LATIN	PRISON	CREEP	FENDER
SUDDEN	WIN	CRIMSON	WEEP	KINDER
MAIDEN	EDWIN	PERSON	STEP	WONDER
GOLDEN	CONDEMN	LESSON	FOOTSTEP	YONDER
WOODEN	SOLEMN	SIMPLETON	HELP	UNDER
GARDEN	AUTUMN	MUTTON	YELP	THUNDER
BEEN	ANN	ANGLO-SAXON	DAMP	ROUNDER
GREEN	DINN	LEARN	STAMP	ASUNDER
TUREEN	DINN--	MODERN	SHRIMP	ORDER
SOUP-TUREEN	ON	PATTERN	THUMP	BORDER
SEEN	RIBBON	UNICORN	JUMP	MURDER
FIFTEEN	LONDON	HORN	LUMP	LOUDER
THIRTEEN	PARDON	BURN	PUMP	GUNPOWDER
FOURTEEN	PIGEON	ADJOURN	HOP	E'ER
QUEEN	GRYPHON	TURN	CHOP	CHEER
BETWEEN	FASHION	RETURN	SHOP	STEER
KITCHEN	CUSHION	FUN	ARCHBISHOP	QUEER
THEN	LION	BEGUN	MOP	SAFER
WHEN	COMPANION	SHUN	STOOP	OFFER
TAKEN	OPINION	PUN	POP	EAGER
CHICKEN	OCCASION	RUN	DROP	ANGER
SPOKEN	DECISION	SUN	SNOWDROP	DANGER
BROKEN	DERISION	FAWN	TOP	MESSENGER
HEARKEN	DIVISION	LAWN	STOP	FINGER
FALLEN	PASSION	PAWN	SHARP	LONGER
SULLEN	PROCESSION	OWN	GASP	LARGER
STOLEN	EXPRESSION	DOWN	CLASP	HER
MEN	CONFUSION	UPSIDE-DOWN	WASP	HIGHER
CHESSMEN	CONCLUSION	KNOCK-DOWN	UP	TOUGHER
FOOTMEN	UGLIFICATION	BLOWN	CUP	FEATHER
JURYMEN	CALCULATION	FLOWN	TEACUP	HEATHER
PEN	EXCLAMATION	KNOWN	BUTTERCUP	WEATHER
OPEN	EXPLANATION	BROWN	DOUBLED-UP	FATHER
HAPPEN	EXAMINATION	CROWN	TURN-UP	GATHER
CHILDREN	USURPATION	FROWN	SOUP	RATHER
CHOSEN	ADMIRATION	GROWN	SUP	TOGETHER
LESSEN	SENSATION	THROWN	ESQ.	ALTOGETHER
TEN	CONVERSATION	TOWN	BAR	WHETHER
EATEN	ACCUSATION	O	MORCAR	EITHER
OFTEN	IRRITATION	DO	EAR	NEITHER
FRIGHTEN	INVITATION	UNDO	BEAR	WITHER
FASTEN	CONSULTATION	DODO	DEAR	PANTHER
LISTEN	STATION	GO	FEAR	OTHER
KITTEN	VEXATION	AGO	HEAR	BOTHER
WRITTEN	SUBTRACTION	FLAMINGO	CLEAR	ANOTHER
FORGOTTEN	DISTRACTION	WHO	NEAR	BROTHER
RAVEN	OBJECTION	BUFFALO	APPEAR	FARTHER
EVEN	DIRECTION	NO	TEAR	FURTHER
SEVEN	PROTECTION	VOLCANO	WEAR	SOLDIER
EIGHTY-SEVEN	AMBITION		YEAR	EARLIER

CARRIER	BREAD-AND-BUTTER	HANSOM-CABS	CABBAGES	BOTTLES
TERRIER	EVER	CRABS	MESSAGES	COAL-SCUTTLES
EASIER	CLEVER	LIMBS	COTTAGES	RULES
PRETTIER	NEVER	CRUMBS	LANGUAGES	GAME'S
SPEAKER	WHENEVER	SOBS	WAGES	GAMES
QUICKER	WHOEVER	VERBS	EDGES	NAMES
POKER	WHEREVER	CLUBS	HEDGES	CUCUMBER-FRAMES
DARKER	WHATEVER	HEAD'S	RIDGES	TIMES
FELLOW-TRAVELER	HOWEVER	HEADS	CHANGES	SOMETIMES
REALLER	SHIVER	LEADS	CHARGES	COMES
SMALLER	RIVER	SPREADS	HE'S	WELCOMES
TALLER	ENGINE-DRIVER	BEDS	SANDWICHES	WINDOW-PANES
GENTLER	QUIVER	FLOWERBEDS	HAM-SANDWICHES	ENGINES
PUZZLER	SILVER	FLOWER-BEDS	BRANCHES	BATHING-MACHINES
CALMER	OVER	BLEEDS	INCHES	LINES
SUMMER	DISH-COVER	NEEDS	BUNCHES	ONE'S
FARMER	UN-DISH-COVER	REEDS	ARCHES	ONES
WARMER	SHOWER	WEEDS	CATCHES	BONES
MANNER	LOWER	HUNDREDS	SHE'S	TONES
DINNER	FLOWER	MAIDS	ASHES	TUNE'S
THINNER	SLOWER	LID'S	FLASHES	DOES
EXECUTIONER	ANSWER	EYELIDS	DISHES	GOES
SOONER	YER	FIELDS	FISHES	FLAMINGOES
PRISONER	AIR	CHILD'S	FISHES'	ECHOES
CORNER	FAIR	HOLDS	FINISHES	SHOES
PARTNER	AFFAIR	HANDS	BUSHES	HEROES
OWNER	HAIR	ROWLAND'S	RUSHES	TOES
CHEAPER	CHAIR	SANDS	DREAM-RUSHES	TELESCOPES
PAPER	ARM-CHAIR	ENDS	CLOTHES	HOPES
BLOTTING-PAPER	PAIR	FRIENDS	LULLABIES	CARES
NEWSPAPER	DESPAIR	DEPENDS	REMEDIES	SQUARES
RIPER	NIGHT-AIR	SENDS	SIGNIFIES	ACRES
TEMPER	THEIR	ATTENDS	ANTIPATHIES	HERE'S
PROPER	SIR	FINDS	SKIES	THERE'S
FLAPPER	STIR	KINDS	LIES	WHERE'S
PEPPER	OR	REMINDS	SNAP-DRAGON-FLIES	FIGURES
COPPER	FOR	STORM-WIND'S	BUTTERFLIES	TREASURES
GRASSHOPPER	NOR	DIAMONDS	DENIES	CREATURES
SHARPER	DOOR	POUNDS	MUTTON-PIES	PICTURES
WHISPER	FRONT-DOOR	SOUNDS	CRIES	ADVENTURES
CLEARER	FLOOR	CHILDHOOD'S	SERIES	PLEASES
NEARER	POOR	WOOD'S	MEMORIES	TEASES
CLOSER	CONQUEROR	WOODS	STORIES	NOISES
CURIOUSER	TERROR	CARDS	DAISIES	RISES
NEATER	HORROR	CUPBOARDS	TIES	ELSE'S
GREATER	JUROR	BACKWARDS	QUANTITIES	CHOOSES
LATER	VISITOR	INWARDS	DIFFICULTIES	ROSE'S
WATER	MAYOR	DOWNWARDS	DAINTIES	ROSES
SALTWATER	PURR	TOWARDS	BEAUTIES	VERSES
CHARACTER	CUR	UPWARDS	CAKES	HORSE'S
AFTER	FUR	AFTERWARDS	MAKES	HORSES
HEREAFTER	OUR	FORWARDS	TAKES	PUDDING-COURSES
SOFTER	NEIGHBOUR	YARDS	LIKES	GLASSES
DAUGHTER	FOUR	LIZARD'S	SPIKES	KISSES
LAUGHTER	TWENTY-FOUR	LIZARDS	JOKES	MISSES
WAITER	SIXTY-FOUR	BIRDS	SMOKES	EXCUSES
WHITER	HOUR	WORDS	TALES	LODGING-HOUSES
PLEASANTER	FLOUR	CROWDS	SYLLABLES	MOUSE'S
CARPENTER	COLOUR	FACES	TABLES	DORMOUSE'S
WINTER	CLAMOUR	PLACES	PEBBLES	DATES
COUNTER	ARMOUR	PIECES	TUMBLES	PLATES
QUARTER	HONOUR	ALICE'S	SPECTACLES	SLATES
SHORTER	POUR	SLICES	FIDDLES	BITES
FASTER	SOUR	VOICES	RIDDLES	WRITES
PLASTER	TOUR	BALANCES	NEEDLES	TASTES
MASTER	FAVOUR	CIRCUMSTANCES	KNITTING-NEEDLES	EXECUTES
DRAWLING-MASTER	FLAVOUR	CONSEQUENCES	CANDLES	MINUTES
LOBSTER	YOUR	BLADES	BUNDLES	TONGUES
SISTER	LARKSPUR	SPADES	TANGLES	LEAVES
BOLSTER	AS	SIDES	WHILES	HOLLY-LEAVES
MONSTER	IDEAS	BESIDES	MILES	SAVES
OYSTER	SEAS	DIVIDES	KNUCKLES	WAVES
BATTER	HAS	ATTITUDES	HOLES	SLEEVES
FATTER	ALAS	BEES	SOLES	LIVES
HATTER	CHRISTMAS	FIDDLE-DE-DEE'S	PEOPLE'S	DRIVES
MATTER	EXTRAS	KNEES	APPLES	ADJECTIVES
BETTER	HATTA'S	THREES	COUPLES	SHELVES
LETTER	CANVAS	TREES	TURTLE'S	BOOK-SHELVES
BITTER	WAS	YE-ES	TURTLES	THEMSELVES
BUTTER	'TWAS	LIFE'S	CASTLES	OURSELVES

BOROGOVES	THANKS	WINS	LISTENERS	HISS
LOVES	BOOKS	LIONS	MANNERS	KISS
GLOVES	LESSON-BOOKS	ONIONS	DINNERS	MISS
KID-GLOVES	LOOKS	PROCESSIONS	EXECUTIONER'S	MOSS
PROVES	BROOKS	EDUCATIONS	PRISONER'S	CROSS
TOVES	SHARKS	VARIATIONS	CORNERS	ACROSS
AXES	REMARKS	EXPLANATIONS	PARTNERS	TOSS
WEXES	FORKS	CONVERSATIONS	PAPERS	DUCHESS'S
FIXES	WORKS	DIRECTIONS	NEWSPAPERS	FUSS
YES	FIREWORKS	QUESTIONS	FLAPPERS	CHESHIRE-PUSS
EYES	WAX-WORKS	EXECUTIONS	WHISPERS	BATS
SNEEZES	WRITING-DESKS	GALLONS	WATERS	CAT'S
PRIZES	SEALS	FIRE-IRONS	CHARACTERS	CATS
SIZES	SUN-DIALS	REASONS	WAITERS	CHESHIRE-CATS
ROOFS	TRIAL'S	PERSON'S	DECANTERS	EATS
WAGS	TRIALS	PERSONS	LOBSTERS	THAT'S
LEGS	ANIMAL'S	LESSONS	SISTER'S	WHAT'S
PEGS	ANIMALS	BUTTONS	SISTERS	COATS
EGGS	MORALS	WAISTCOAT-BUTTONS	BOLSTERS	GOAT'S
PIGS	PETALS	UNICORNS	MONSTERS	RATS
GUINEA-PIGS	EELS	TURNS	OYSTERS	SUBJECTS
WIG'S	HEELS	RUNS	HATTER'S	INSECTS
TWIGS	WHEELS	SUNS	HATTERS	GETS
HANGS	CART-WHEELS	PAWNS	MATTERS	TICKETS
TIDINGS	TAILS	TOWNS	LETTERS	POCKETS
THING'S	PENCILS	WHO'S	BUTTER'S	BLANKETS
THINGS	COILS	KANGAROOS	RIVERS	LET'S
TEA-THINGS	BALLS	TWOS	COVERS	RINGLETS
SOMETHING'S	FALLS	HEAPS	DISH-COVERS	ANKLETS
EVERYTHING'S	SHEEP-BELLS	PERHAPS	FLOWERS	MALLETS
KING'S	OYSTER-SHELLS	MAPS	ANSWERS	FERRETS
KINGS	TELLS	MOUSE-TRAPS	PLAYERS	FIRELIGHT'S
STOCKINGS	WELLS	STEPS	AIRS	NIGHTS
FEELINGS	BILL'S	FOOTSTEPS	CHAIRS	KNIGHTS
SHILLINGS	FILLS	SHIPS	PAIRS	THOUGHTS
DARLINGS	HILLS	LIPS	STAIRS	IT'S
MEANINGS	KILLS	TIPS	UPSTAIRS	ITS
BRINGS	KNOLLS	LAMPS	THEIRS	RABBIT'S
WANDERINGS	ROLLS	ROMPS	DOORS	RABBITS
STRINGS	EARLS	LUMPS	JURORS	FITS
WINGS	GIRLS	MOPS	VISITORS'	COMFITS
BELONGS	CURLS	TOPS	OURS	HITS
SONG'S	GROWLS	STOPS	HOURS	COMMITS
DOG'S	SCREAMS	TEACUPS	HONOUR'S	SPIRITS
DOGS	DREAMS	EARS	YOURS	WORRITS
HEDGEHOGS	WILLIAM'S	DEARS	LASS	SITS
HEARTH-RUGS	SEEMS	HEARS	GLASS	WITS
DINAH'S	POEMS	TEARS	OPERA-GLASS	FAULTS
SIGHS	PILGRIM'S	YEARS	LOOKING-GLASS	ELEPHANTS
BOUGHS	TRIMS	CATERPILLAR'S	PASS	CURRANTS
RATHS	ARMS	OARS	BRASS	SERVANTS'
MONTHS	TERMS	REMEMBERS	GRASS	SERVANTS
TABLE-CLOTHS	CRITICISMS	OFFICERS	CONFESS	WANTS
MOUTHS	TWEEDLEDUM'S	DANCERS	CHESS	ACCENTS
IS	DRUMS	LEADERS	DUCHESS	MEASUREMENTS
PROBOSCIS	SUMS	SHOULDERS	LESS	ADVERTISEMENTS
HIS	MEANS	CINDERS	NEVERTHELESS	REFRESHMENTS
THIS	FANS	WONDERS	HOPELESS	PUNISHMENTS
CHRYSALIS	MAN'S	ORDERS	CARELESS	MOMENT'S
PARIS	NORMANS	BADGERS	BREATHLESS	MOMENTS
EMPHASIS	FOOTMAN'S	TIGERS	UNLESS	ARGUMENTS
'TIS	SAUCEPANS	PASSENGERS	HELPLESS	SERPENTS
AXIS	GARDENS	MESSENGER'S	GLADNESS	PRESENTS
SPEAKS	QUEEN'S	MESSENGERS	MADNESS	EVENTS
BACKS	QUEENS	FINGER'S	KINDNESS	HAUNTS
TRICKS	HAPPENS	FINGERS	RUDENESS	ACCOUNTS
STICKS	CHILDREN'S	SINGERS	MUCHNESS	KNOTS
FIDDLE-STICKS	KITTEN'S	HERS	LONELINESS	BOOTS
CANDLESTICKS	KITTENS	EXTINGUISHERS	UNHAPPINESS	ROOTS
HADDOCKS'	RAVENS	FEATHERS	BUSINESS	TULIP-ROOTS
LOCKS	BARGAINS	OTHER'S	DARKNESS	CARROTS
KNOCKS	CHAINS	OTHERS	WILDERNESS	INTERRUPTS
CHEEKS	REMAINS	BROTHER'S	GOVERNESS	HEARTS
WEEKS	TRAINS	BROTHERS	WITNESS	PARTS
SHRIEKS	FOUNTAINS	SOLDIERS	FASTNESS	TARTS
TALKS	MOUNTAINS	FOOT-SOLDIERS	SHYNESS	SORTS
STALKS	REINS	COURTIERS	DRESS	BEASTS
WALKS	BEGINS	WHISKERS	PROGRESS	FEAST'S
BANKS	PINS	SUMMERS	SUPPRESS	BLASTS
RIVER-BANKS	GRINS	GARDENERS	GUESS	NESTS

UNJUST	SIX	BEAUTIFY	SNAP-DRAGON-FLY	QUEERLY
MUST	BOX	SHAGGY	BUTTERFLY	EAGERLY
RUST	JACK-IN-THE-BOX	STINGY	BREAD-AND-BUTTER-FLY	PROPERLY
CRUST	WORK-BOX	SEAOGRAPHY	MUMBLINGLY	FAIRLY
PIE-CRUST	PEPPER-BOX	GEOGRAPHY	UNWILLINGLY	CURLY
BUT	CHRISTMAS-BOX	SHY	LOVINGLY	CARELESSLY
CUT	JURY-BOX	BUSHY	PITYINGLY	CROSSLY
SHUT	DAY	THY	UGLY	TREMENDOUSLY
OUT	BIRTHDAY	SLITHY	ROUGHLY	SERIOUSLY
ABOUT	UN-BIRTHDAY	FROTHY	THOROUGHLY	CURIOUSLY
SHOUT	HOLIDAY	WHY	SNAPPISHLY	FURIOUSLY
WITHOUT	TO-DAY	STICKY	SMOOTHLY	CAUTIOUSLY
LOOK-OUT	WINTER-DAY	JABBERWOCKY	GAILY	ANXIOUSLY
SNOUT	YESTERDAY	SULKY	READILY	CONTEMPTUOUSLY
PUT	SATURDAY	POKY	STEADILY	NERVOUSLY
TUT	WEDNESDAY	SKY	GREEDILY	NEATLY
NEXT	TUESDAY	SCALY	LUCKILY	EXACTLY
PORTMANTEAU	GAY	COMFORTABLY	SULKILY	PERFECTLY
OU	HAY	UNCOMFORTABLY	LILY	DIRECTLY
THOU	LAY	FEEBLY	TIGER-LILY	QUIETLY
YOU	DELAY	AUDIBLY	DREAMILY	SOFTLY
W.	CALLAY	TERRIBLY	FAMILY	LIGHTLY
JAW	PLAY	POSSIBLY	GLOOMILY	RIGHTLY
LAW	MAY	HUMBLY	WEARILY	BRIGHTLY
CLAW	DISMAY	BADLY	ANGRILY	TRIUMPHANTLY
PAW	NAY	GLADLY	MERRILY	INDIGNANTLY
RAW	PAY	MADLY	EASILY	PLEASANTLY
DRAW	GRAY	SADLY	UNEASILY	INCESSANTLY
SAW	PRAY	ODDLY	BUSILY	INSTANTLY
FEW	TEA-TRAY	DECIDEDLY	HEARTILY	EVIDENTLY
VIEW	SAY	HURRIEDLY	HASTILY	GENTLY
BLEW	STAY	GOOD-NATUREDLY	HEAVILY	DILIGENTLY
FLEW	WAY	SPLENDIDLY	LAZILY	OBEDIENTLY
MEW	AWAY	TIMIDLY	QUICKLY	CONVENIENTLY
NEW	OUT-OF-THE-WAY	RAPIDLY	MEEKLY	PATIENTLY
KNEW	RAILWAY	STUPIDLY	BRISKLY	IMPATIENTLY
CREW	DOORWAY	WILDLY	REALLY	VIOLENTLY
CORKSCREW	BY	BOLDLY	OCCASIONALLY	PRESENTLY
DREW	BABY	FRIENDLY	PRINCIPALLY	INTENTLY
GREW	PIG-BABY	KINDLY	GENERALLY	FAINTLY
THREW	HUSH-A-BY	SECONDLY	ACCIDENTALLY	LASTLY
BOW	LULLABY	HARDLY	GRADUALLY	HONESTLY
ELBOW	OBSTINACY	LOUDLY	USUALLY	EARNESTLY
SHADOW	FANCY	PROUDLY	UNUSUALLY	MOSTLY
WINDOW	READY	NICELY	ACTUALLY	JULY
HOW	ALREADY	SCARCELY	CHILLY	SLOWLY
SOMEHOW	STEADY	FIERCELY	CIVILLY	SHYLY
NOHOW	SHADY	SAFELY	DREADFULLY	SLYLY
SHOW	LADY	LIKELY	GRACEFULLY	MY
ANYHOW	GIDDY	EXTREMELY	CAREFULLY	DREAMY
LOW	RUDDY	LONELY	REPROACHFULLY	ENEMY
BLOW	TIDY	MERELY	BEAUTIFULLY	SLIMY
BELOW	UNTIDY	SEVERELY	SCORNFULLY	STORMY
FLOW	HANDY	ENTIRELY	MOURNFULLY	ANY
GLOW	BRANDY	DEMURELY	FEARFULLY	MANY
AGLOW	BODY	SURELY	WONDERFULLY	COMPANY
ALLOW	SOMEBODY	LEISURELY	CHEERFULLY	DENY
SWALLOW	NOBODY	UNWISELY	DOUBTFULLY	SHINY
FELLOW	ANYBODY	CLOSELY	RESPECTFULLY	BRINY
YELLOW	EVERYBODY	HOARSELY	FRETFULLY	TINY
FOLLOW	MOODY	IMMEDIATELY	THOUGHTFULLY	PENNY
HOLLOW	CUSTODY	LATELY	AWFULLY	HALFPENNY
SLOW	JUDY	PASSIONATELY	CALMLY	TWOPENCE-HALFPENNY
NOW	OBEY	AFFECTIONATELY	SUDDENLY	FUNNY
KNOW	DISOBEY	ALTERNATELY	PLAINLY	SUNNY
SNOW	TULGEY	DESPERATELY	CERTAINLY	AGONY
ROW	THEY	COMPLETELY	VAINLY	BOY
BROW	KEY	POLITELY	SOLEMNLY	SHEPHERD-BOY
CROW	TURKEY	RESOLUTELY	ONLY	AHOY
GROW	VALLEY	GRAVELY	UNCOMMONLY	JOY
THROW	CHIMNEY	INQUISITIVELY	STERNLY	ENJOY
ARROW	HONEY	POSITIVELY	MELANCHOLY	ANNOY
NARROW	MONEY	ATTENTIVELY	DEEPLY	SLEEPY
TO-MORROW	JOURNEY	LOVELY	REPLY	HAPPY
SORROW	GREY	FLY	SIMPLY	UNHAPPY
FURROW	CURTSEY	CHIEFLY	SHARPLY	PUPPY
WOW	SURVEY	HORSE-FLY	CLEARLY	DEARY
WAX	TOFFY	ROCKING-HORSE-FLY	NEARLY	WEARY
FIX	UGLIFY	STIFFLY	FAMILIARLY	MARY
MIX	SIGNIFY	DRAGON-FLY	PARTICULARLY	CANARY

EXTRAORDINARY
DICTIONARY   1
CRY   364
DRY   365
SLIPPERY
MYSTERY
VERY
EVERY
LIVERY
SILVERY
ANGRY
HUNGRY
FAIRY
LORY
GLORY
MEMORY
UNSATISFACTORY
VICTORY
STORY
HISTORY
CARRY
MULBERRY
MERRY
SORRY
WORRY
HURRY
FLURRY
TRY
POETRY
PANTRY
COUNTRY
CANTERBURY
FURY
JURY
EASY
UNEASY
DAISY
NOISY
FLIMSY
MIMSY
GRASSY
BUSY
ANXIETY
NINETY
SUETY
FIFTY
REALITY
IMPENETRABILITY
OPPORTUNITY
PITY
SEVERITY
AUTHORITY
WORRITY
CURIOSITY
QUANTITY
INGENUITY
PERPLEXITY
DIFFICULTY
PLENTY
FRUMENTY
TWENTY
EMPTY
DUMPTY
HUMPTY
PARTY
TEA-PARTY
DINNER-PARTY
THIRTY
NASTY
MAJESTY
THIRSTY
DUSTY
PRETTY
KITTY
BEAUTY
BUY
HEAVY
GRAVY
LAZY
CRAZY

A REVERSE KWIC CONCORDANCE
("ALICE")

ALICE (847)

AI	4: 3	Alice! A childish story take, / And, with a gentle hand, /
A1	7: 1	Alice was beginning to get very tired of sitting by her
A1	9:21	Alice was not a bit hurt, and she jumped up on to her feet
A1	10: 1	Alice opened the door and found that it led into a small
A2	15:36	Alice took up the fan and gloves, and, as the hall was very
A3	23:26	Alice had no idea what to do, and in despair she put her
A3	24: 5	Alice thought the whole thing very absurd, but they all
A3	26:26	Alice replied eagerly, for she was always ready to talk
A4	32: 5	Alice noticed, with some surprise, that the pebbles were all
A5	36:26	Alice thought she might as well wait, as she had nothing
A5	36:37	Alice folded her hands, and began:--
A5	41:11	Alice said nothing: she had never been so much contradicted
A5	41:33	Alice remained looking thoughtfully at the mushroom for a
A5	42:36	Alice was more and more puzzled, but she thought there was
A6	46: 5	Alice laughed so much at this, that she had to run back into
A6	46: 9	Alice went timidly up to the door, and knocked.
A6	48: 7	Alice did not at all like the tone of this remark, and
A6	48:28	Alice glanced rather anxiously at the cook, to see if she
A6	49:15	Alice caught the baby with some difficulty, as it was a
A6	50: 8	Alice was just beginning to think to herself, "Now, what am
A6	51:17	Alice felt that this could not be denied, so she tried
A6	51:27	Alice didn't think that proved it at all: however, she went
A6	52: 9	Alice was not much surprised at this, she was getting so
A6	52:22	Alice waited a little, half expecting to see it again, but
A7	54:14	Alice looked all round the table, but there was nothing on
A7	55:39	Alice considered a little, and then said "The fourth."
A7	56:11	Alice had been looking over his shoulder with some curiosity
A7	56:19	Alice felt dreadfully puzzled. The Hatter's remark seemed to
A7	56:32	Alice sighed wearily. "I think you might do something better
A7	59: 6	Alice tried a little to fancy to herself what such an
A7	59:18	Alice did not quite know what to say to this: so she helped
A7	60: 3	Alice did not wish to offend the Dormouse again, so she
A7	60:19	Alice was silent.
A8	63:28	Alice was rather doubtful whether she ought not to lie down
A8	66: 1	Alice thought she had never seen such a curious
A8	67: 3	Alice began to feel very uneasy: to be sure, she had not as
A8	67:16	Alice waited till the eyes appeared, and then nodded. "It's
A8	68:10	Alice thought she might as well go back and see how the game
A8	69: 6	Alice could think of nothing else to say but "It belongs to
A9	70: 4	Alice was very glad to find her in such a pleasant temper,
A9	70:25	Alice did not much like her keeping so close to her: first
A9	76:33	Alice did not feel encouraged to ask any more questions
A10	81:15	Alice was thoroughly puzzled. "Does the boots and shoes!"
A10	81:19	Alice looked down at them, and considered a little before
A10	82:34	Alice said nothing: she had sat down with her face in her
A10	83:12	Alice did not dare to disobey though she felt sure it would
A11	86:13	Alice had never been in a court of justice before, but she
A11	86:37	Alice could see, as well as if she were looking over their
A11	91:29	Alice watched the White Rabbit as he fumbled over the list,
A12	93: 4	Alice looked at the jury-box, and saw that, in her haste,
T1	114: 4	Alice was very anxious to be of use, and, as the poor little
T1	114:18	Alice watched the White King as he slowly struggled up from
T1	115:29	Alice looked on with great interest as the King took an
T2	121: 1	Alice was so astonished that she couldn't speak for a minute
T2	121:13	Alice didn't like being criticized, so she began asking
T2	122:26	Alice did so. "It's very hard," she said; "but I don't see
T2	123:18	Alice didn't like this idea at all: so, to change the
T2	123:28	Alice looked round eagerly and found that it was the Red
T2	124: 9	Alice attended to all these directions, and explained, as
T2	124:15	Alice wondered a little at this, but she was too much in awe
T2	125: 6	Alice didn't dare to argue the point, but went on: "--and I
T2	125:16	Alice curtseyed again, as she was afraid from the Queen's
T2	126:12	Alice never could quite make out, in thinking it over
T2	127:12	Alice looked round her in great surprise. "Why I do believe
T2	127:27	Alice thought it would not be civil to say "No," though it
T2	127:39	Alice did not know what to say to this, but luckily the
T3	130:10	Alice thought to herself "Then there's no use in speaking."
T3	131:10	Alice couldn't see who was sitting beyond the Beetle, but a
T3	133: 8	Alice looked at the Rocking-horse-fly with great interest,
T3	136:17	Alice thought, but nothing came of it. "Please, would you
T3	137:11	Alice stood looking after it, almost ready to cry with
T4	139:25	Alice did not like shaking hands with either of them first,
T4	144:32	Alice couldn't say honestly that he was. He had a tall red
T4	145: 3	Alice said "Nobody can guess that."
T4	146:24	Alice laid her hand upon his arm and said, in a soothing
T4	147:18	Alice said afterwards she had never seen such a fuss made
T4	147:28	Alice laughed loud: but she managed to turn it into a cough,
T4	148: 4	Alice laughed. "You must hit the trees pretty often, I
T4	145:24	Alice ran a little way into the wood, and stopped under a

ALICE (cont.)

T5	149:15	Alice thought it would never do to have an argument at the
T5	149:34	Alice carefully released the brush, and did her best to get
T5	150: 1	Alice couldn't help laughing, as she said "I don't want you
T5	151:10	Alice felt there was no denying that. "Of course it would be
T5	152: 1	Alice was just beginning to say "There's a mistake somewhere
T5	152:40	Alice could not help laughing at this, even in the midst of
T5	153:11	Alice laughed. "There's no use trying," she said: "one
T6	159:24	Alice didn't know what to say to this: it wasn't at all like
T6	161:22	Alice made a short calculation, and said "Seven years and
T6	162: 1	Alice didn't want to begin another argument, so she said
T6	162: 9	Alice felt even more indignant at this suggestion. "I mean,"
T6	162:40	Alice considered a little. "I like birthday presents best,"
T6	163: 6	Alice couldn't help smiling as she took out her
T6	163:37	Alice was too much puzzled to say anything; so after a
T6	164:12	(Alice didn't venture to ask what he paid them with; and so
T6	166:21	Alice felt that in that case she really ought to listen to
T6	168:34	Alice waited a minute to see if he would speak again, but,
T7	172: 8	Alice was glad to see that it revived him a good deal.
T7	173:14	Alice had no more breath for talking; so they trotted on in
T7	175:27	Alice could not help her lips curling up into a smile as she
T7	177: 6	Alice had seated herself on the bank of a little brook, with
T8	181:29	Alice shook her head.
T8	183:13	Alice could think of nothing better to say than "Indeed?"
T8	185:17	Alice ran to the side of the ditch to look for him. She was
T8	186:30	Alice could only look puzzled: she was thinking of the
T9	194:10	Alice considered. "The bone wouldn't remain, of course, if I
T9	194:23	Alice said, as gravely as she could, "They might go
T9	195:11	Alice thought she saw a way out of the difficulty, this time
T9	195:29	Alice was puzzled. "In our country," she remarked, "there's
T9	195:42	Alice sighed and gave it up. "It's exactly like the riddle
T9	196:17	Alice thought to herself "I never should try to remember my
T9	198:12	Alice knocked and rang in vain for a long time; but at last
T9	199: 2	Alice turned round, ready to find fault with anybody.
T9	199: 6	Alice almost stamped with irritation at the slow drawl in
T9	200: 8	Alice glanced nervously along the table, as she walked up
TC	209: 0	Alice Pleasance Liddell
T8W	14: 5	Alice felt rather offended at this answer, and was very
T8W	15: 1	Alice hastily ran her eye down the paper and said "No. It
T8W	15:17	Alice put down the newspaper. "I'm afraid you're not well,"
T8W	16:12	Alice looked pityingly at him. "Tying up the face is very
T8W	16:15	Alice didn't catch the word exactly. "Is it a kind of
T8W	20: 9	Alice began with a little scream of laughter, which she
T8W	21:10	Alice did not like having so many personal remarks made on
T7	174:15	carrying round trays of white and brown bread. Alice took a piece to taste, but it was very dry.
A4	27:12	Very soon the Rabbit noticed Alice, as she went hunting about, and called out to her, in
A7	58:29	"Yes, please do!" pleaded Alice.
T5	156: 1	This offended Alice a little, so there was no more conversation for a
T8	184:28	"Very much indeed," Alice said politely.
T3	134:24	"No, indeed," Alice said, a little anxiously.
T6	160:34	"I haven't indeed!" Alice said very gently. "It's in a book."
T8W	15:10	"En-gulph-ed," Alice repeated, dividing the word into syllables.
A6	53: 2	"I said 'pig'," replied Alice; "and I wish you wouldn't keep appearing and vanishing
T5	152:18	"Take care!" cried Alice. "You're holding it all crooked!" And she caught at
A12	92: 1	"Here!" cried Alice, quite forgetting in the flurry of the moment how
T1	107:20	"Oh, you wicked, wicked little thing!" cried Alice, catching up the kitten, and giving it a little kiss
A6	48:16	"Oh, please mind what you're doing!" cried Alice, jumping up and down in an agony of terror. "Oh, there
A2	19:28	with fright. "Oh, I beg your pardon!" cried Alice hastily, afraid that she had hurt the poor animal's
A2	19:39	catching mice--oh, I beg your pardon!" cried Alice again, for this time the Mouse was bristling all over,
A2	20:10	says it kills all the rats and--oh dear!" cried Alice in a sorrowful tone. "I'm afraid I've offended it
A2	17:25	till I'm somebody else'--but, oh dear!" cried Alice, with a sudden burst of tears, "I do wish they would
A2	14: 1	"Curiouser and curiouser!" cried Alice (she was so much surprised, that for the moment she
T8	184:11	"It's too ridiculous!" cried Alice, losing all her patience this time. "You ought to have
T1	110: 1	the wind blows--oh, that's very pretty!" cried Alice, dropping the ball of worsted to clap her hands. "And
T5	149:23	untidy. "Every single thing's crooked," Alice thought to herself, "and she's all over pins!--May I
A6	46:32	"How am I to get in?" asked Alice again, in a louder tone.
T8	187: 5	to have said 'That's what the song is called'?" Alice corrected herself.
T2	126:21	move along with us?" thought poor puzzled Alice. And the Queen seemed to guess her thoughts, for she
A7	58: 7	"How dreadfully savage!" exclaimed Alice.
A9	77:14	"What a curious plan!" exclaimed Alice.
T9	197:12	"What am I to do?" exclaimed Alice, looking about in great perplexity, as first one round
A9	72: 3	"Oh, I know!" exclaimed Alice, who had not attended to this last remark. "It's a
T5	154: 8	But these, as it happened, Alice had not got: so she contented herself with turning
T2	128:28	How it happened, Alice never knew, but exactly as she came to the last peg,
A8	62: 3	gardeners at it, busily painting them red. Alice thought this a very curious thing, and she went nearer
T6	161: 3	fell off the wall in doing so) and offered Alice his hand. She watched him a little anxiously as she
A9	76:20	"What was that?" inquired Alice.
A9	76: 1	"I never said I didn't!" interrupted Alice.
T1	107:16	a grand game of romps with the ball of worsted Alice had been trying to wind up, and had been rolling it up
A8	65:22	"Yes!" shouted Alice.

ALICE (cont.)

A6	51:25	"How do you know I'm mad?"	said Alice.
T7	170:16	"I see nobody on the road,"	said Alice.
A8	65:12	"You sha'n't be beheaded!"	said Alice, and she put them into a large flower-pot that stood
A10	79: 4	"Very much indeed,"	said Alice.
A10	78:13	"No, indeed,"	said Alice. "What sort of a dance is it?"
A2	20: 1	"I wo'n't indeed!"	said Alice, in a great hurry to change the subject of
A5	42:41	"I'm very sorry you've been annoyed,"	said Alice, who was beginning to see its meaning.
A5	41: 2	"Not quite right, I'm afraid,"	said Alice, timidly: "some of the words have got altered."
T5	155:32	"Indeed I did,"	said Alice: "you've said it very often--and very loud. Please,
T7	170: 9	"Yes, I did,"	said Alice: "several thousand, I should think."
T9	192: 1	"Well, this is grand!"	said Alice. "I never expected I should be a Queen so soon--and
T6	167: 5	"I'm afraid I don't quite understand,"	said Alice.
T7	171: 4	"I only meant that I didn't understand,"	said Alice. "Why one to come and one to go?"
A5	41:15	little larger, Sir, if you wouldn't mind,"	said Alice: "three inches is such a wretched height to be."
A5	42:13	"What can all that green stuff be?"	said Alice. "And where have my shoulders got to? And oh, my poor
A3	23: 2	"What is a Caucus-race?"	said Alice; not that she much wanted to know, but the Dodo had
A10	79: 2	"It must be a very pretty dance,"	said Alice timidly.
A6	48:23	"Which would not be an advantage,"	said Alice, who felt very glad to get an opportunity of showing
A4	30:36	got to come down the chimney, has he?"	said Alice to herself. "Why, they seem to put everything upon
T8	182:12	"It's meant for plum-cake,"	said Alice.
A9	77: 1	"What was that like?"	said Alice.
T7	175:32	"Yes, if you like,"	said Alice: "it's laid for a great many more than three."
A7	55: 4	"I didn't know it was your table,"	said Alice sadly.
A3	23:33	"Only a thimble,"	said Alice.
T8	181:33	like one--fastened to the saddle,"	said Alice, still hoping to make them a little ashamed of
T4	148: 9	"And all about a rattle!"	said Alice, who was always ready for a little argument, "and if
T9	192:20	"But if everybody obeyed that rule,"	said Alice, as she tried to obey the first direction: "and I
T9	196:38	"I haven't got a nightcap with me,"	said Alice, very much confused, "I don't think--"
A7	60:26	"Really, now you ask me,"	said Alice, a little timidly, for she was not quite sure whether
A6	47:12	"Please would you tell me,"	said Alice hastily; "but I'm not looking for eggs, as it happens;
A5	43:25	"It matters a good deal to me,"	said Alice.
T5	151: 7	"Suppose he never commits the crime?"	said Alice.
A9	73:15	"I never saw one, or heard of one,"	said Alice.
A12	93:44	"Then it ought to be Number One,"	said Alice, rather alarmed at the proposal.
A7	58:21	"I'm afraid I don't know one,"	said Alice, not wishing to begin an argument.
T6	160:11	"Why do you sit out here all alone?"	said Alice, a good deal frightened at the sudden change, but very
A2	18:10	"That was a narrow escape!"	said Alice.
T5	157:11	"Are there many crabs here?"	said Alice.
A6	51:11	"I don't much care where--"	said Alice), and tied round the neck of the bottle was a paper
A1	10:16	it ("which certainly was not here before,"	said Alice: "the governess would never think of excusing me
T3	135: 5	"That would never do, I'm sure,"	said Alice, a little timidly, "why you are painting those roses
A8	63: 3	"Would you tell me, please,"	said Alice, "what that means?"
T6	163:42	"Would you tell me please,"	said Alice, as she put the money down on the counter. For she
T5	158:10	"Then I'll have one, please,"	said Alice. "I'm quite content to stay here--only I am so hot and
T2	127:23	"I'd rather not try, please!"	said Alice, very loudly and decidedly, and the Queen was silent.
A8	64: 8	"Nonsense!"	said Alice loudly. "The idea of having the sentence first!"
A12	97: 1	"Stuff and nonsense!"	said Alice more boldly: "you know you're growing too."
A11	88:43	"Don't talk nonsense,"	said Alice.
A7	58:14	"Then you keep moving round, I suppose?"	said Alice, surprised at her own ingenuity.
T6	165: 5	grass-plot round a sun-dial, I suppose?"	said Alice.
A10	81:36	"Don't you mean 'purpose'?"	said Alice. "Well, that was quick work, certainly!"
T4	145: 7	"Where I am now, of course,"	said Alice; "besides, that's not a regular rule: you invented it
T8	186: 9	to have it cooked for the next course?"	said Alice.
A12	93:41	"Well, I sha'n't go, at any rate,"	said Alice at last, "that they live in the same house! I wonder I
T8	184:25	"You were a little grave,"	said Alice, "a great girl like you," (she might well say this),
T3	137:25	"I do believe,"	said Alice, in a coaxing tone, and she tried hard to whistle to
T6	162:44	"Three hundred and sixty-five,"	said Alice.
A2	15:20	"You ought to be ashamed of yourself,"	said Alice. "I've read that in some book, but I don't remember
A4	32:29	trying to touch her. "Poor little thing!"	said Alice. "I must be shutting up like a telescope!"
A12	93:18	"Nothing,"	said Alice a little timidly; "but it's no use going back to
A8	68: 1	"A cat may look at a king,"	said Alice, whose thoughts were still running on the song, "I'd
A1	12: 1	"What a curious feeling!"	said Alice.
A6	51:35	"I call it purring, not growling,"	said Alice, feeling very glad that it was over at last: "and I do
A10	81:41	adventures--beginning from this morning,"	said Alice, as she swam about, trying to find her way out. "I
A10	81:27	"If I'd been the whiting,"	said Alice; "living at the bottom of the sea."
T6	166:36	"I will, if I can remember it so long,"	said Alice, "but I haven't been invited yet."
A10	80:13	it's a very interesting dance to watch,"	said Alice.
A2	19: 1	"I wish I hadn't cried so much!"	said Alice. "May I help you off with your helmet?" It was
A9	76:16	"You couldn't have wanted it much,"	said Alice.
A6	52: 5	"I should like it very much,"	said Alice. She was too much puzzled to make any other remark.
T6	166:31	"Thank you very much,"	said Alice.
T8	181: 6	"Thank you very much,"	said Alice.
A12	93:38	"I'm not a mile high,"	said Alice: "I'm so glad it's gone. I thought it was the night
T6	164: 7	"Oh!"	said Alice sharply, for she was beginning to feel a little
T8W	17: 1	"Oh, you mean stiff-neck,"	said Alice. "But I had some poetry repeated to me much easier
A9	71:16	"It's a mineral, I think,"	
T5	152:28	"The crow must have flown away, I think,"	
A9	72:25	"I've a right to think,"	
T6	166:12	"I read it in a book,"	

ALICE (cont.)

T4	145:21	"I am real!"	said Alice, and began to cry.
A8	67:32	"Not at all,"	said Alice: "she's so extremely--" Just then she noticed that the
T9	193:17	didn't know I was to have a party at all,"	said Alice; "but, if there is to be one, I think I ought to
A5	36:23	"Is that all?"	said Alice, swallowing down her anger as well as she could.
T6	164:29	"That'll do very well,"	said Alice: "and 'slithy'?"
A5	43: 9	"I--I'm a little girl,"	said Alice, rather doubtfully, as she remembered the number of
A7	60:17	"Why with an M?"	said Alice.
A12	98: 6	"Oh, I've had such a curious dream!"	said Alice. And she told her sister, as well as she could
T3	132:37	"No use to them,"	said Alice; "but it's useful to the people that name them, I
A6	46:43	"Oh, there's no use in talking to him,"	said Alice desperately: "he's perfectly idiotic!" And she opened
A7	54: 9	Alice coming. "There's plenty of room!"	said Alice indignantly, and she sat down in a large arm-chair at
A7	56:37	"I don't know what you mean,"	said Alice.
A6	46:17	"Please, then,"	said Alice, "how am I to get in?"
T8	187: 8	"Well, what is the song, then?"	said Alice, who was by this time completely bewildered.
A7	60:35	"At any rate I'll never go there again!"	said Alice, as she picked her way through the wood. "It's the
A7	58:35	"What did they live on?"	said Alice, who always took a great interest in questions of
A3	26: 3	"I beg your pardon,"	said Alice very humbly: "you had got to the fifth bend, I think
T7	171: 2	"I beg your pardon?"	said Alice.
A7	59:15	"Nobody asked your opinion,"	said Alice.
A9	74:10	"What is the fun?"	said Alice.
T9	194:34	"To be sure I do,"	said Alice.
A3	26:22	I wish I had our Dinah here, I know I do!"	said Alice aloud, addressing nobody in particular. "She'd soon
A6	46:41	"But what am I to do?"	said Alice.
A4	32:18	"The first thing I've got to do,"	said Alice to herself, as she wandered about in the wood, "is to
A9	73:12	"No,"	said Alice. "I don't even know what a Mock Turtle is."
A9	76: 7	"I've been to a day-school, too,"	said Alice. "You needn't be so proud as all that."
T3	131:31	"Don't tease so,"	said Alice, looking about in vain to see where the voice came
A6	51:31	"I suppose so,"	said Alice.
A7	55:18	"Exactly so,"	said Alice.
A6	50: 4	you're going to turn into a pig, my dear,"	said Alice, seriously, "I'll have nothing more to do with you."
T2	123:35	"I think I'll go and meet her,"	said Alice, for, though the flowers were interesting enough, she
T2	120: 1	"I should see the garden far better,"	said Alice to herself, "if I could get to the top of that hill:
A3	22:26	"As wet as ever,"	said Alice in a melancholy tone: "it doesn't seem to dry me at
A12	93:20	"Nothing whatever,"	said Alice.
A5	35:11	I ca'n't explain myself, I'm afraid, Sir,"	said Alice, "because I'm not myself, you see."
A5	36:31	"I'm afraid I am, Sir,"	said Alice. "I ca'n't remember things as I used--and I don't keep
T6	164:14	very clever at explaining words, Sir,"	said Alice. "Would you kindly tell me the meaning of the poem
T5	151:19	I had done the things I was punished for,"	said Alice: "that makes all the difference."
T9	196: 9	"I know what he came for,"	said Alice. "he wanted to punish the fish, because--"
T8	182: 1	wondering what the mouse-trap was for,"	said Alice. "It isn't very likely there would be any mice on the
A8	65:33	"What for?"	said Alice.
A4	33: 7	"And yet what a dear little puppy it was!"	said Alice, as she leant against a buttercup to rest herself, and
A9	76:10	"Yes,"	said Alice: "we learned French and music."
A9	76:29	"Yes,"	said Alice doubtfully: "it means--to--make--anything--prettier."
A10	80:18	"Yes,"	said Alice, "I've often seen them at dinn----" she checked
T6	166: 1	"And then 'mome raths'?"	said Alice. "I'm afraid I'm giving you a great deal of trouble."
T6	163:33	"The question is,"	said Alice, "whether you can make words mean so many different
T9	193:22	"Manners are not taught in lessons,"	said Alice. "Lessons teach you to do sums, and things of that
A9	77:10	how many hours a day did you do lessons?"	said Alice, in a hurry to change the subject.
T4	144:37	catch cold with lying on the damp grass,"	said Alice, who was a very thoughtful little girl.
T5	151:15	"Only for faults,"	said Alice.
A8	67:39	"It's a friend of mine--a Cheshire-Cat,"	said Alice: "allow me to introduce it."
A1	12:21	Come, there's no use in crying like that!"	said Alice to herself rather sharply. "I advise you to leave off
T5	153: 8	"I ca'n't believe that!"	said Alice.
A9	72:17	yourself to say it any longer than that,"	said Alice.
T8	186:38	"Or else what?"	said Alice, for the Knight had made a sudden pause.
A5	36: 2	perhaps you haven't found it so yet,"	said Alice; "but when you have to turn into a chrysalis--you will
T5	157: 7	"Was it? I didn't see it,"	said Alice, peeping cautiously over the side of the boat into the
A7	57:17	"I've heard something like it,"	said Alice.
A12	95:23	"If any one of them can explain it,"	said Alice, (she had grown so large in the last few minutes that
A11	88:41	"I ca'n't help it,"	said Alice very meekly: "I'm growing."
A7	55: 1	it wasn't very civil of you to offer it,"	said Alice angrily.
A1	12:34	marked in currants. "Well, I'll eat it,"	said Alice, "and if it makes me grow larger, I can reach the key;
A10	81:12	"I never thought about it,"	said Alice. "Why?"
T8	190:20	"Of course I'll wait,"	said Alice, "and thank you very much for coming so far--and for
A8	65:35	"No, I didn't,"	said Alice. "I don't think it's at all a pity. I said 'What for?'
T2	125:10	"No, I shouldn't,"	said Alice, surprised into contradicting her at last: "a hill
A5	42:28	"I'm not a serpent!"	said Alice indignantly. "Let me alone!"
A5	36: 7	perhaps your feelings may be different,"	said Alice: "all I know is, it would feel very queer to me."
A10	78: 9	lived much under the sea--" ("I haven't,"	said Alice)--"and perhaps you were never even introduced to a
T6	166:26	"I see you don't,"	said Alice.
A12	97: 4	"I wo'n't!"	said Alice.
A6	49:29	off sneezing by this time). "Don't grunt,"	said Alice; "that's not at all a proper way of expressing
T8W	20:14	"I'm afraid not,"	said Alice.
A2	19:32	"Well, perhaps not,"	said Alice in a soothing tone: "don't be angry about it. And yet
A9	76:12	"Certainly not!"	said Alice indignantly.
A3	26: 6	"A knot!"	said Alice, always ready to make herself useful, and looking
A12	94:30	"It doesn't prove anything of the sort!"	said Alice. "Why, you don't even know what they're about!"
A5	42: 7	"Come, my head's free at last!"	said Alice in a tone of delight, which changed into alarm in

ALICE (cont.)

T4	144:13	"I like the Walrus best," said Alice: "because he was a <u>little</u> sorry for the poor oysters
A5	42:32	the least idea what you're talking about," said Alice.
T5	150:10	"I don't understand you," said Alice. "It's dreadfully confusing!"
A10	81: 8	"Thank you," said Alice, "it's very interesting. I never knew so much about a
T2	127:37	"No, thank you," said Alice: "one's <u>quite</u> enough!"
A5	43: 5	"But I'm <u>not</u> a serpent, I tell you!" said Alice. "I'm a--I'm a--"
A12	96:11	on '<u>they all returned from him to you</u>,'" said Alice.
A12	97: 7	"Who cares for <u>you</u>?" said Alice (she had grown to her full size by this time). "You're
A7	59:33	"What did they draw?" said Alice, quite forgetting her promise.
A8	64: 3	"How should <u>I</u> know?" said Alice, surprised at her own courage. "It's no business of
T9	193:27	"I don't know," said Alice. "I lost count."
A1	12: 8	about this; "for it might end, you know," said Alice to herself, "in my going out altogether, like a candle
A3	24:14	to tell me your history, you know," said Alice, "and why it is you hate--C and D," she added in a
T4	147:38	"Then you'd better not fight to-day," said Alice, thinking it a good opportunity to make peace.
A9	70:34	"Somebody said," Alice whispered, "that it's done by everybody minding their
T2	120:30	"O Tiger-lily!" said Alice, addressing herself to one that was waving gracefully
T6	162:31	"It is really?" said Alice, quite pleased to find that she <u>had</u> chosen a good
A10	81:32	"Wouldn't it, really?" said Alice, in a tone of great surprise.
T6	163:21	"Certainly," said Alice.
A7	57: 5	"That would be grand, certainly," said Alice thoughtfully; "but then--I shouldn't be hungry for it,
A3	25: 1	"It <u>is</u> a long tail, certainly," said Alice, looking down with wonder at the Mouse's tail; "but
A5	43:16	"I <u>have</u> tasted eggs, certainly," said Alice, who was a very truthful child; "but little girls eat
T4	139:18	"Next Boy!" said Alice, passing on to Tweedledee, though she felt quite
A8	65:28	"Very," said Alice. "Where's the Duchess?"
T2	127:16	"Well, in <u>our</u> country," said Alice, still panting a little, "you'd generally get to
A8	63:40	My name is Alice, so please your Majesty," said Alice very politely; but she added, to herself, "Why,
A1	7:11	was nothing so <u>very</u> remarkable in that; nor did Alice think it so <u>very</u> much out of the way to hear the
T9	194:20	"Perhaps it would," Alice replied cautiously.
A11	91: 6	She carried the pepper-box in her hand, and Alice guessed who it was, even before she got into the court
T3	135:23	it looked much darker than the last wood, and Alice felt a little timid about going into it. However, on
A7	59:39	March Hare moved into the Dormouse's place, and Alice rather unwillingly took the place of the March Hare.
A9	72:40	on with the game," the Queen said to Alice; and Alice was too much frightened to say a word, but slowly
T9	201: 2	in the dish and made a little bow to Alice; and Alice returned the bow, not knowing whether to be frightened
T9	201:24	It spoke in a thick, suety sort of voice, and Alice hadn't a word to say in reply: she could only sit and
A4	31:29	the house down!" said the Rabbit's voice. And Alice called out, as loud as she could, "If you do, I'll set
T8	179: 2	to die away, till all was dead silence, and Alice lifted up her head in some alarm. There was no one to
T5	155:10	now working with fourteen pairs at once, and Alice couldn't help looking at her in great astonishment.
A7	59:41	one who got any advantage from the change; and Alice was a good deal worse off than before, as the March
T8W	17: 9	He untied the handkerchief as he spoke, and Alice looked at his wig in great surprise. It was bright
T2	128: 4	had got all the pegs put in by this time, and Alice looked on with great interest as she returned to the
T2	128:32	was no way of guessing, but she was gone, and Alice began to remember that she was a Pawn, and that it
T6	168: 2	to a scream as he repeated this verse, and Alice thought, with a shudder, "I wouldn't have been the
A3	26:36	On various pretexts they all moved off, and Alice was soon left alone.
T8	183:16	with his eyes shut, muttering to himself, and Alice watching anxiously for the next tumble.
T9	199:33	Then followed a confused noise of cheering, and Alice thought to herself "Thirty times three makes ninety. I
T5	149: 4	stretched out wide, as if she were flying, and Alice very civilly went to meet her with the shawl.
T8	179:21	another voice broke in "Ahoy! Ahoy! Check!" and Alice looked round in some surprise for the new enemy.
T4	138: 2	each with an arm round the other's neck, and Alice knew which was which in a moment, because one of them
T1	115:16	flat on his back, and lay perfectly still; and Alice was a little alarmed at what she had done, and went
T1	110:15	because there were only two of them, and Alice had been reduced at last to say "Well, <u>you</u> can be one
T9	204: 5	I am!" cried a voice from the soup-tureen, and Alice turned again, just in time to see the Queen's broad
A8	65:23	"Come on, then!" roared the Queen, and Alice joined the procession, wondering very much what would
A9	73: 9	the players, except the King, the Queen, and Alice, were in custody and under sentence of execution.
T9	197: 7	to the ball--/ <u>Red Queen</u>, and <u>White Queen</u>, <u>and Alice</u>, and all!
A6	49:31	The baby grunted again, and Alice looked very anxiously into its face to see what was
A4	31:38	or two they began moving about again, and Alice heard the Rabbit say "A barrowful will do, to begin
A10	84: 7	you'd better leave off," said the Gryphon, and Alice was only too glad to do so.
T2	122:30	This sounded a very good reason, and Alice was quite pleased to know it. "I never thought of that
T8W	21:15	"Good-bye, and thank-ye," said the Wasp, and Alice tripped down the hill again, quite pleased that she
T1	110:23	like her. Now do try, there's a dear!" And Alice got the Red Queen off the table, and set it up before
A5	35: 1	The Caterpillar and Alice looked at each other for some time in silence: at last
T5	149: 9	like "Bread-and-butter, bread-and-butter," and Alice felt that if there was to be any conversation at all,
A4	30:13	There was a long silence after this, and Alice could only hear whispers now and then; such as "Sure,
A8	63:13	faces. There was a sound of many footsteps, and Alice looked round, eager to see the Queen.
T7	170: 3	The confusion got worse every moment, and Alice was very glad to get out of the wood into an open
A4	27:15	me a pair of gloves and a fan! Quick, now!" And Alice was so much frightened that she ran off at once in the
A4	31:33	There was a dead silence instantly, and Alice thought to herself "I wonder what they <u>will</u> do next!
T3	131:35	deeply. It was <u>very</u> unhappy, evidently, and Alice would have said something pitying to comfort it, "if
T1	113:15	something began squeaking on the table behind Alice, and made her turn her head just in time to see one of
A8	67:45	"and don't look at me like that!" He got behind Alice as he spoke.
A10	84:12	please, if the Mock Turtle would be so kind," Alice replied, so eagerly that the Gryphon said, in a rather
T8W	18: 1	"It isn't that kind," Alice hastily explained. "It's to comb hair with--your wig's
T2	122:13	"Never mind!" Alice said in a soothing tone, and, stooping down to the
A10	79: 9	So they began solemnly dancing round and round Alice, every now and then treading on her toes when they
A8	66:18	and walking off to other parts of the ground, Alice soon came to the conclusion that it was a very
T6	160:16	you think you'd be safer down on the ground?" Alice went on, not with any idea of making another riddle,
T3	137: 3	So they walked on together through the wood, Alice with her arms clasped lovingly round the soft neck of
T2	125:25	it's marked out just like a large chess-board!" Alice said at last. "There ought to be some men moving about
A9	71:13	"Only mustard isn't a bird," Alice remarked.

ALICE (cont.)

T12	207: 1	"Your Red Majesty shouldn't purr so loud,"	Alice said, rubbing her eyes, and addressing the kitten,
T9	201:13	looked sulky, and growled "Pudding----Alice: Alice--Pudding. Remove the pudding!" and the waiters took it
T3	137:14	now," she said: "that's some comfort. Alice--Alice--I won't forget it again. And now, which of these
T6	168:32	"It wouldn't look nice,"	Alice objected. But Humpty Dumpty only shut his eyes, and
A11	86: 8	upon it: they looked so good, that it made	Alice quite hungry to look at them--"I wish they'd get the
T5	149:30	you know, if you pin it all on one side,"	Alice said as she gently put it right for her; "and dear me,
T6	165: 8	"And a long way beyond it on each side,"	Alice added.
A1	8:31	thousand miles down, I think--" (for, you see,	Alice had learnt several things of this sort in her lessons
A7	57: 9	"Is that the way you manage?"	Alice asked.
A9	72:31	arm that was linked into hers began to tremble.	Alice looked up, and there stood the Queen in front of them,
A3	21:16	in a large ring, with the Mouse in the middle.	Alice kept her eyes anxiously fixed on it, for she felt sure
T5	156:19	down before breaking them off--and for a while	Alice forgot all about the Sheep and the knitting, as she
T7	170:35	idea that he was joining in the game, while	Alice was still hesitating for the name of a town beginning
A7	55:33	and the party sat silent for a minute, while	Alice thought over all she could remember about ravens and
T1	107:13	with earlier in the afternoon, and so, while	Alice was sitting curled up in a corner of the great
A6	51:22	"But I don't want to go among mad people,"	Alice remarked.
A9	74:36	the constant heavy sobbing of the Mock Turtle.	Alice was very nearly getting up and saying, "Thank you, Sir
T4	146:16	"It's only a rattle,"	Alice said, after a careful examination of the little white
T4	147:33	"Well--yes--a little,"	Alice replied gently.
A1	10:19	well to say "Drink me," but the wise little	Alice was not going to do that in a hurry. "No, I'll look
A12	98:14	the setting sun, and thinking of little	Alice and all her wonderful Adventures, till she too began
A12	98:17	First, she dreamed about little	Alice herself: once again the tiny hands were clasped upon
T2	123: 9	"Is she like me?"	Alice asked eagerly, for the thought crossed her mind,
T6	162:27	"I know it's very ignorant of me,"	Alice said, in so humble a tone that Humpty Dumpty relented
T2	123: 3	any more people in the garden besides me?"	Alice said, not choosing to notice the Rose's last remark.
T2	122: 3	"But what could it do, if any danger came?"	Alice asked.
A11	91:33	the top of his shrill little voice, the name "Alice!"
T9	204:23	At any other time,	Alice would have felt surprised at this, but she was far too
A5	41:23	This time	Alice waited patiently until it chose to speak again. In a
T5	156:11	I meant--please, may we wait and pick some?"	Alice pleaded. "If you don't mind stopping the boat for a
T9	200: 5	"Ninety times nine!"	Alice repeated in despair. "Oh, that'll never be done! I'd
T5	158: 7	"Then two are cheaper than one?"	Alice said in a surprised tone, taking out her purse.
A9	70:21	"Perhaps it hasn't one,"	Alice ventured to remark.
A9	75: 1	did you call him Tortoise, if he wasn't one?"	Alice asked.
T3	130: 2	"I'm afraid I haven't got one,"	Alice said in a frightened tone: "there wasn't a
T8	184:34	I suppose you'd be over when that was done,"	Alice said thoughtfully: "but don't you think it would be
T4	140:19	Here	Alice ventured to interrupt him. "If it's very long," she
A1	9:11	know. But do cats eat bats, I wonder?" And here	Alice began to get rather sleepy, and went on saying to
T1	108:16	we'll go and see the bonfire to-morrow." Here	Alice wound two or three turns of the worsted round the
T5	152:33	"Only it is so very lonely here!"	Alice said in a melancholy voice; and, at the thought of her
T2	126:27	and dragged her along. "Are we nearly there?"	Alice managed to pant out at last.
T8	183:20	the top of his head exactly in the path where	Alice was walking. She was quite frightened this time, and
A8	68:20	gone across the other side of the garden, where	Alice could see it trying in a helpless sort of way to fly
A6	51:13	"--so long as I get somewhere,"	Alice added as an explanation.
A9	76: 3	"Hold your tongue!" added the Gryphon, before	Alice could speak again. The Mock Turtle went on.
T9	200:20	And the waiters set a leg of mutton before	Alice, who looked at it rather anxiously, as she had never
T7	177:22	But before	Alice could answer him, the drums began.
T7	176: 7	monster!" the Unicorn cried out, before	Alice could reply.
A4	29:27	hard against it, that attempt proved a failure.	Alice heard it say to itself "Then I'll go round and get in
T9	201:10	"I won't be introduced to the pudding, please,"	Alice said rather hastily, "or we shall get no dinner at all
TC	209:11	Still she haunts me, phantomwise. / Alice moving under skies / Never seen by waking eyes.
T4	147: 7	"looking more like a fish than anything else,"	Alice thought.
T4	145:28	"I know they're talking nonsense,"	Alice thought to herself: "and it's foolish to cry about it
T9	194: 7	"I suppose--"	Alice was beginning, but the Red Queen answered for her.
T3	131:13	"It sounds like a horse,"	Alice thought to herself. And an extremely small voice,
T8	184:17	"Much more smoothly than a live horse,"	Alice said, with a little scream of laughter, in spite of
A11	87: 6	had a pencil that squeaked. This, of course,	Alice could not stand, and she went round the court and got
T1	110:12	her sister only the day before--all because	Alice had begun with "Let's pretend we're kings and queens;"
T4	144:21	This was a puzzler. After a pause,	Alice began, "Well! They were both very unpleasant
A2	19:14	very tired of swimming about here, O Mouse!" (Alice thought this must be the right way of speaking to a
A9	71: 9	"He might bite,"	Alice cautiously replied, not feeling at all anxious to have
A5	41: 8	"Oh, I'm not particular as to size,"	Alice hastily replied; "only one doesn't like changing so
T7	172:40	Let's run and see them." And they trotted off,	Alice repeating to herself, as she ran, the words of the old
T8	182:28	for keeping the hair from being blown off?"	Alice enquired.
A2	18:20	can go back by railway," she said to herself. (Alice had been to the seaside once in her life, and had come
T8	186:20	"What did you mean it to be made of?"	Alice asked, hoping to cheer him up, for the poor Knight
A10	81:23	"And what are they made of?"	Alice asked in a tone of great curiosity.
T7	175:20	Haigha replied eagerly, coming in front of	Alice to introduce her, and spreading out both his hands
A6	52:19	"It turned into a pig,"	Alice answered very quietly, just as if the Cat had come
T8W	16: 5	"Along of the wig?"	Alice repeated, quite pleased to find that he was recovering
A10	83: 7	"It's the first position in dancing,"	Alice said; but she was dreadfully puzzled by the whole
T7	171:12	you with an H," the King said, introducing	Alice in the hope of turning off the Messenger's attention
T9	201:13	Red Queen looked sulky, and growled "Pudding----Alice: Alice--Pudding. Remove the pudding!" and the waiters
T7	170: 7	the King cried in a tone of delight, on seeing	Alice. "Did you happen to meet any soldiers, my dear, as you
A7	59:24	"There's no such thing!"	Alice was beginning very angrily, but the Hatter and the
A2	19:35	only see her. She is such a dear quiet thing,"	Alice went on, half to herself, as she swam lazily about in
T6	160: 7	"Must a name mean something?"	Alice asked doubtfully.
T9	199:17	"Nothing!"	Alice said impatiently. "I've been knocking at it!"
T8	179:26	at each other for some time without speaking.	Alice looked from one to the other in some bewilderment.

ALICE (cont.)

A10	85: 4	"Come on!" cried the Gryphon, and, taking	Alice by the hand, it hurried off, without waiting for the
T4	139:10	"I was thinking,"	Alice said politely, "which is the best way out of this wood
T9	195:19	"The cause of lightning,"	Alice said very decidedly, for she felt quite certain about
A11	86:29	very busily on slates. "What are they doing?"	Alice whispered to the Gryphon. "They ca'n't have anything
A2	15:31	Wo'n't she be savage if I've kept her waiting!"	Alice felt so desperate that she was ready to ask help of
A9	74: 4	I have ordered;" and she walked off, leaving	Alice alone with the Gryphon. Alice did not quite like the
T6	162: 7	"I never ask advice about growing,"	Alice said indignantly.
T8	186:33	"Is it very long?"	Alice asked, for she had heard a good deal of poetry that
T7	170:30	"I love my love with an H,"	Alice couldn't help beginning, "because he is Happy. I hate
T2	125: 4	said the Queen, patting her on the head, which	Alice didn't like at all: "though, when you say 'garden'--
T1	115:40	said the Queen, looking over the book (in which	Alice had put 'The White Knight is sliding down the poker,
T8	182:44	as he generally did this on the side on which	Alice was walking, she soon found that it was the best plan
T7	172:14	"I said there was nothing like it." Which	Alice did not venture to deny.
T8	182:15	This took a long time to manage, though	Alice held the bag open very carefully, because the Knight
T8W	15:13	"It's in this newspaper, though,"	Alice said a little timidly.
T3	132: 7	Everybody seemed satisfied with this, though	Alice felt a little nervous at the idea of trains jumping at
T7	173: 8	"Would you--be good enough--"	Alice panted out, after running a little further, "to stop a
T9	195: 9	"Fiddle-de-dee's not English,"	Alice replied gravely.
A4	29:13	"Oh, you foolish	Alice!" she answered herself. "How can you learn lessons in
A9	77:21	"And how did you manage on the twelfth?"	Alice went on eagerly.
T9	199:37	"'O Looking-Glass creatures,' quoth	Alice, 'draw near! / 'Tis an honour to see me, a favour to
T8W	15: 5	"In coming back,"	Alice went on reading, "they found a lake of treacle. The
T3	132:25	"I like them when they can talk,"	Alice said. "None of them ever talk, where I come from."
T8W	13:18	"It's rheumatism, I should think,"	Alice said to herself, and she stooped over him, and said
A4	27:33	mouse doesn't get out.' Only I don't think,"	Alice went on, "that they'd let Dinah stop in the house if
T9	203:22	directions: "and very like birds they look,"	Alice thought to herself, as well as she could in the
T4	145:24	"If I wasn't real,"	Alice said--half laughing through her tears, it all seemed
T4	138:15	"I'm sure I'm very sorry," was all	Alice could say; for the words of the old song kept ringing
T9	194:44	"Well, it isn't picked at all,"	Alice explained: "it's ground--"
T8W	17: 4	"Conceit isn't a disease at all,"	Alice remarked.
T3	132:29	"I don't rejoice in insects at all,"	Alice explained, "because I'm rather afraid of them--at
T6	168:15	"Is that all?"	Alice timidly asked.
A7	60: 9	"But they were in the well,"	Alice said to the Dormouse, not choosing to notice this last
T5	153:33	to have suddenly wrapped herself up in wool.	Alice rubbed her eyes, and looked again. She couldn't make
A8	63:22	guests, mostly Kings and Queens, and among them	Alice recognized the White Rabbit: it was talking in a
T2	123:22	"Where does she wear them?"	Alice asked with some curiosity.
T6	159:18	said after a long silence, looking away from	Alice as he spoke, "to be called an egg--very!"
T3	132: 4	the engine, and everybody jumped up in alarm,	Alice among the rest.
T6	164: 3	"That's a great deal to make one word mean,"	Alice said in a thoughtful tone.
T4	144:18	"That was mean!"	Alice said indignantly. "Then I like the Carpenter best--if
T9	192:38	"I'm sure I didn't mean--"	Alice was beginning, but the Red Queen interrupted her
A8	65:37	She boxed the Queen's ears--" the Rabbit began.	Alice gave a little scream of laughter. "Oh, hush!" the
T9	196:30	how pleased she'll be!" But this was more than	Alice had courage to do.
A7	60:29	This piece of rudeness was more than	Alice could bear: she got up in great disgust, and walked
T2	123:31	high--and here she was, half a head taller than	Alice herself!
T8	182:36	It didn't sound a comfortable plan,	Alice thought, and for a few minutes she walked on in
T6	168:17	This was rather sudden,	Alice thought: but, after such a very strong hint that she
T9t	192: 1	QUEEN	ALICe
T9	200:23	to that leg of mutton," said the Red Queen.	"Alice--Mutton: Mutton--Alice." The leg of mutton got up in
T1	113: 8	"Here are the Red King and the Red Queen,"	Alice said (in a whisper, for fear of frightening them),
T9	199:32	and mice in the tea--/ And welcome Queen	Alice with thirty-times-three!"
T9	200: 4	and wool with the wine--/ And welcome Queen	Alice with ninety-times-nine!"
T9	198: 2	doorway, over which were the words "QUEEN	ALICe" in large letters, and on each side of the arch there
A8	67:19	minute the whole head appeared, and then	Alice put down her flamingo, and began an account of the
T3	136: 9	seem at all frightened. "Here then! Here then!"	Alice said, as she held out her hand and tried to stroke it;
T9	195:35	"Are five nights warmer than one night, then?"	Alice ventured to ask.
A4	32:40	over heels in its hurry to get hold of it: then	Alice, thinking it was very like having a game of play with
A4	32:36	the stick, and made believe to worry it: then	Alice dodged behind a great thistle, to keep herself from
T2	128:14	I--I didn't know I had to make one--just then,"	Alice faltered out.
T2	123:30	was her first remark. She had indeed: when	Alice first found her in the ashes, she had been only three
A1	9:31	the hall, but they were all locked; and when	Alice had been all the way down one side and up the other,
T3	135:19	seemed to have sighed itself away, for, when	Alice looked up, there was nothing whatever to be seen on
T3	132:21	very large Gnat: "about the size of a chicken,"	Alice thought. Still, she couldn't feel nervous with it,
T6	160:28	"To send all his horses and all his men,"	Alice interrupted, rather unwisely.
A6	45: 7	and large eyes like a frog; and both footmen,	Alice noticed, had powdered hair that curled all over their
T8	181:15	upside-down, and with the lid hanging open.	Alice looked at it with great curiosity.
T5	155:36	"Why do you say 'Feather' so often?"	Alice asked at last, rather vexed. "I'm not a bird!"
T3	134:18	"But that must happen very often,"	Alice remarked thoughtfully.
A7	58:17	happens when you come to the beginning again?"	Alice ventured to ask.
A1	7:17	and looked at it, and then hurried on,	Alice started to her feet, for it flashed across her mind
T3	133: 6	"What does it live on?"	Alice asked, with great curiosity.
T3	134: 1	"And what does it live on?"	Alice asked, as before.
A7	59:28	"No, please go on!"	Alice said very humbly. "I wo'n't interrupt you again. I
T6	162:13	"What a beautiful belt you've got on!"	Alice suddenly remarked. (They had had quite enough of the
T7	170:20	All this was lost on	Alice, who was still looking intently along the road,
T6	162:36	"I beg your pardon?"	Alice said with a puzzled air.
A9	74: 4	off, leaving Alice alone with the Gryphon.	Alice did not quite like the look of the creature, but on
A2	20:17	to her: its face was quite pale (with passion,	Alice thought), and it said, in a low trembling voice, "Let
A9	76:24	"I never heard of 'Uglification,'"	Alice ventured to say. "What is it?"

ALICE (cont.)

A5	35: 5	not an encouraging opening for a conversation. Alice replied, rather shyly, "I--I hardly know, Sir, just at
A5	36:11	again to the beginning of the conversation. Alice felt a little irritated at the Caterpillar's making
A8	62:18	things--" when his eye chanced to fall upon Alice, as she stood watching them, and he checked himself
T7	175:15	going on, when his eye happened to fall upon Alice: he turned round instantly, and stood for some time
T9	201: 1	said the Red Queen. "Alice--Mutton: Mutton--Alice." The leg of mutton got up in the dish and made a
T2	128:21	together, and it's all feasting and fun!" Alice got up and curtseyed, and sat down again.
T6	163:15	"You're holding it upside down!" Alice interrupted.
T7	174: 9	soon bring the white bread and the brown?" Alice ventured to remark.
T9	201:41	"Please do," Alice said very politely.
A7	55:21	"I do," Alice hastily replied; "at least--at least I mean what I say
A6	48: 4	"I don't know of any that do," Alice said very politely, feeling quite pleased to have got
A10	82: 1	So Alice began telling them her adventures from the time when
T1	114:23	So Alice picked him up very gently, and lifted him across more
T12	207:13	So Alice hunted among the chessmen on the table till she had
T8W	14:19	So Alice sat down by him, and spread out the paper on her knees
A12	98:11	now run in to your tea: it's getting late." So Alice got up and ran off, thinking while she ran, as well
A10	80:22	"I believe so," Alice replied thoughtfully. "They have their tails in their
T6	164:20	This sounded very hopeful, so Alice repeated the first verse:--
T5	156:42	in the water and wouldn't come out again (so Alice explained it afterwards), and the consequence was that
A1	11: 6	this bottle was not marked "poison," so Alice ventured to taste it, and, finding it very nice (it
A1	9: 5	down, down. There was nothing else to do, so Alice soon began talking again. "Dinah'll miss me very much
A2	20: 3	of--of dogs?" The Mouse did not answer, so Alice went on eagerly: "There is such a nice little dog,
T5	155:23	sound like a remark that needed any answer: so Alice said nothing, but pulled away. There was something
T9	202:37	thing," the Red Queen said very decidedly: so Alice tried to submit to it with good grace.
A9	77:17	This was quite a new idea to Alice, and she thought it over a little before she made her
A5	43:21	This was such a new idea to Alice, that she was quite silent for a minute or two, which
A8	68:18	a fight with another hedgehog, which seemed to Alice an excellent opportunity for croqueting one of them
A4	33: 3	This seemed to Alice a good opportunity for making her escape: so she set
T5	149:21	would have been all the better, as it seemed to Alice, if she had got some one else to dress her, she was so
T7	173:24	tea when he was sent in," Haigha whispered to Alice: "and they only give them oyster-shells in there--so
A9	73:10	left off, quite out of breath, and said to Alice "Have you seen the Mock Turtle yet?"
T8	181:28	"Can you guess why I did that?" he said to Alice.
T5	152:21	for the bleeding, you see," she said to Alice with a smile. "Now you understand the way things
A7	59: 9	"Take some more tea," the March Hare said to Alice, very earnestly.
A12	93:17	you know about this business?" the King said to Alice.
T9	196:21	Majesty must excuse her," the Red Queen said to Alice, taking one of the White Queen's hands in her own, and
T9	192:35	"So you did, you know," the Red Queen said to Alice. "Always speak the truth--think before you speak--and
A9	72:40	"Let's go on with the game," the Queen said to Alice; and Alice was too much frightened to say a word, but
A6	49:11	it a bit, if you like!" the Duchess said to Alice, flinging the baby at her as she spoke. "I must go and
T2	123:40	This sounded nonsense to Alice, so she said nothing, but set off at once towards the
A3	26: 1	"You are not attending!" said the Mouse to Alice, severely. "What are you thinking of?"
A8	63:34	When the procession came opposite to Alice, they all stopped and looked at her, and the Queen
A9	74: 9	fun!" said the Gryphon, half to itself, half to Alice.
A3	22:25	on now, my dear?" it continued, turning to Alice as it spoke.
A7	55:36	day of the month is it?" he said, turning to Alice: he had taken his watch out of his pocket, and was
A7	56:28	the riddle yet?" the Hatter said, turning to Alice again.
A8	63:39	tossing her head impatiently; and turning to Alice, she went on: "What's your name, child?"
A3	24:17	long and sad tale!" said the Mouse to Alice, and sighing.
A3	23:32	you got in your pocket?" it went on, turning to Alice.
A3	23:23	she, of course," said the Dodo, pointing to Alice with one finger; and the whole party at once crowded
A3	21: 7	after a few minutes it seemed quite natural to Alice to find herself talking familiarly with them, as if
A8	65:11	execute the unfortunate gardeners, who ran to Alice for protection.
A8	67:37	you talking to?" said the King, coming up to Alice, and looking at the Cat's head with great curiosity.
T8	181:11	turning his gentle face and large mild eyes to Alice. She thought she had never seen such a strange-looking
T7	175:39	a large cake out of the bag, and gave it to Alice to hold, while he got out a dish and carving-knife.
A1	8:36	what Latitude or Longitude I've got to?" (Alice had not the slightest idea what Latitude was, or
T9	201: 2	got up in the dish and made a little bow to Alice; and Alice returned the bow, not knowing whether to be
T7	174:20	For a minute or two Alice stood silent, watching him. Suddenly she brightened up
A12	98: 4	"Wake up, Alice dear!" said her sister. "Why, what a long sleep you've
A7	56:29	"No, I give it up," Alice replied. "What's the answer?"
A6	47: 5	certainly too much pepper in that soup!" Alice said to herself, as well as she could for sneezing.
T7	172:27	stooping so as to get close to the King's ear. Alice was sorry for this, as she wanted to hear the news too
T12	207:22	"Sit up a little more stiffly, dear!" Alice cried with a merry laugh. "And curtsey while you're
T1	116: 1	There was a book lying near Alice on the table, and while she sat watching the White
A4	27: 6	Where can I have dropped them, I wonder?" Alice guessed in a moment that it was looking for the fan
T7	175: 2	"But aren't you going to run and help her?" Alice asked, very much surprised at his taking it so quietly
A9	73:18	As they walked off together, Alice heard the King say in a low voice, to the company,
A6	49:35	getting extremely small for a baby: altogether Alice did not like the look of the thing at all. "But
T1	113: 3	don't keep this room so tidy as the other," Alice thought to herself, as she noticed several of the
A9	74:18	little ledge of rock, and, as they came nearer, Alice could hear him sighing as if his heart would break.
A10	78:10	you were never even introduced to a lobster--" (Alice began to say "I once tasted--" but checked herself
T7	172:12	throwing cold water over you would be better," Alice suggested: "--or some sal-volatile."
A9	72:11	"I think I should understand that better," Alice said very politely, "if I had it written down: but I
A10	82:14	he thought it had some kind of authority over Alice.
T6	159:19	"I said you looked like an egg, Sir," Alice gently explained. "And some eggs are very pretty, you
T2	128:25	and remember who you are!" She did not wait for Alice to curtsey, this time, but walked on quickly to the
T8	182: 8	"But what are they for?" Alice asked in a tone of great curiosity.
A4	28:23	Luckily for Alice, the little magic bottle had now had its full effect,
A2	15:16	Poor Alice! It was as much as she could do, lying down on one

ALICE (cont.)

A3	26:10	"I didn't mean it!" pleaded poor	Alice. "But you're so easily offended, you know!"
A5	41:18	"But I'm not used to it!" pleaded poor	Alice in a piteous tone. And she thought to herself "I wish
A7	60:12	This answer so confused poor	Alice, that she let the Dormouse go on for some time without
A2	17:16	sure those are not the right words," said poor	Alice, and her eyes filled with tears again as she went on,
A3	26:40	I shall ever see you any more!" And here poor	Alice began to cry again, for she felt very lonely and
T9	192:30	"I only said 'if'!" poor	Alice pleaded in a piteous tone.
T5	156:45	of little shrieks of "Oh, oh, oh!" from poor	Alice, it swept her straight off the seat, and down among
A1	12:14	into the garden at once; but, alas for poor	Alice! when she got to the door, she found she had forgotten
A9	75: 6	then they both sat silent and looked at poor	Alice, who felt ready to sink into the earth. At last the
A4	28:27	"It was much pleasanter at home," thought poor	Alice, "when one wasn't always growing larger and smaller,
A1	10: 7	even if my head would go through," thought poor	Alice, "it would be of very little use without my shoulders.
T3	136:14	"I wish I knew!" thought poor	Alice. She answered, rather sadly, "Nothing, just now."
A1	12:28	two people. "But it's no use now," thought poor	Alice, "to pretend to be two people! Why, there's hardly
T8	190:16	you'll stay and see me off first?" he added as	Alice turned with an eager look in the direction to which he
T5	157: 4	was a nice crab you caught!" she remarked, as	Alice got back into her place, very much relieved to find
T9	202:32	you, you know," the White Queen whispered, as	Alice got up to do it, very obediently, but a little
A5	36:15	Here was another puzzling question; and, as	Alice could not think of any good reason, and the
T4	140: 2	a minute: there was a rather awkward pause, as	Alice didn't know how to begin a conversation with people
T10	205: 4	and her eyes got large and green: and still, as	Alice went on shaking her, she kept on growing shorter--and
T9	203: 9	And then (as	Alice afterwards described it) all sorts of things happened
T8W	13:17	bones, my old bones!" he was grumbling on as	Alice came up to him.
T7	177:17	"I say, this isn't fair!" cried the Unicorn, as	Alice sat with the knife in her hand, very much puzzled how
T3	129:13	a regular bee: in fact, it was an elephant--as	Alice soon found out, though the idea quite took her breath
T2	127: 7	ground with their feet, till suddenly, just as	Alice was getting quite exhausted, they stopped, and she
T1	119: 4	for getting down stairs quickly and easily, as	Alice said to herself. She just kept the tips of her fingers
T8	179:17	Startled as she was,	Alice was more frightened for him than for herself at the
T9	199:24	"To the Looking-Glass world it was	Alice that said / 'I've a sceptre in hand, I've a crown on
T9	193: 7	"I don't deny things with my hands,"	Alice objected.
T5	150:13	"Living backwards!"	Alice repeated in great astonishment. "I never heard of such
T8	185:24	you go on talking so quietly, head downwards?"	Alice asked, as she dragged him out by the feet, and laid
T2	122:12	it panted, bending its quivering head towards	Alice, "or they wouldn't dare to do it!"
T8W	21: 4	as he spoke, and stetched out one claw towards	Alice, as if he wished to do the same for her, but she kept
T5	156: 6	"Oh, please! There are some scented rushes!"	Alice cried in a sudden transport of delight. "There really
T3	135:15	"You shouldn't make jokes,"	Alice said, "if it makes you so unhappy."
T5	155:17	but not on land--and not with needles--"	Alice was beginning to say, when suddenly the needles turned
A2	20:24	an Eaglet, and several other curious creatures.	Alice led the way, and the whole party swam to the shore.
T2	125:19	For some minutes	Alice stood without speaking, looking out in all directions
A9	74:29	sat down, and nobody spoke for some minutes.	Alice thought to herself "I don't see how she can ever finish
A11	86:33	"Stupid things!"	Alice began in a loud indignant voice; but she stopped
T1	110:10	here I wish I could tell you half the things	Alice used to say, beginning with her favourite phrase
A9	71: 3	"How fond she is of finding morals in things!"	Alice thought to herself.
A8	63:40	"My name is Alice, so please your Majesty," said	Alice very politely;
T6	160: 4	"My name is	Alice, but--"
A6	46:22	the sky all the time he was speaking, and this	Alice thought decidedly uncivil. "But perhaps he ca'n't help
A3	21:10	older than you, and must know better." And this	Alice would not allow, without knowing how old it was, and
T8W	14:14	"Would you like me to read you a bit of this?"	Alice went on, as she picked up a newspaper which had been
T3	134:20	After this,	Alice was silent for a minute or two, pondering. The Gnat
T9	203: 4	up into the air. "I rise to return thanks--"	Alice began: and she really did rise as she spoke, several
A7	55: 9	You should learn not to make personal remarks,"	Alice said with some severity: "it's very rude."
A4	27:27	"How queer it seems,"	Alice said to herself, "to be going messages for a rabbit! I
T9	194:28	"Can you do sums?"	Alice said, turning suddenly on the White Queen, for she
T12	207: 6	"it is a very inconvenient habit of kittens (Alice	had once made the remark) that, whatever you say to
T9	195:16	"I wish Queens never asked questions,"	Alice thought to herself.
A4	29:21	came a little pattering of feet on the stairs.	Alice knew it was the Rabbit coming to look for her, and she
T8	185:12	"But that's a different kind of fastness,"	Alice objected.
A4	27:30	the sort of thing that would happen: "'Miss	Alice! Come here directly, and get ready for your walk!'
A8	65:20	The soldiers were silent, and looked at	Alice, as the question was evidently meant for her.
A10	79: 1	again very sadly and quietly, and looked at	Alice.
T9	199:11	the paint would come off: then he looked at	Alice.
A10	78: 2	of one flapper across his eyes. He looked at	Alice and tried to speak, but, for a minute or two, sobs
T7	176: 5	The Lion looked at	Alice wearily. "Are you animal--or vegetable--or mineral?"
T3	136: 7	then a Fawn came wandering by: it looked at	Alice with its large gentle eyes, but didn't seem at all
A12	93:37	Everybody looked at	Alice.
A12	93: 3	repeated with great emphasis, looking hard at	Alice as he said so.
A7	55: 7	said the Hatter. He had been looking at	Alice for some time with great curiosity, and this was his
T9	202:30	a neat speech," the Red Queen said, frowning at	Alice as she spoke.
A4	32:16	out of a bottle. They all made a rush at	Alice the moment she appeared; but she ran off as hard as
T9	196:25	The White Queen looked timidly at	Alice, who felt she ought to say something kind, but really
T7	175:26	The Unicorn looked dreamily at	Alice, and said "Talk, child."
T3	129:38	child!" the Guard went on, looking angrily at	Alice. And a great many voices all said together ("like the
T7	176: 1	"What's this!" he said, blinking lazily at	Alice, and speaking in a deep hollow tone that sounded like
T8	184:38	He looked so vexed at the idea, that	Alice changed the subject hastily. "What a curious helmet
T6	160:23	his lips, and looked so solemn and grand that	Alice could hardly help laughing. "If I did fall," he went
T4	145:16	He shouted this so loud that	Alice couldn't help saying "Hush! You'll be waking him, I'm
A6	47:16	the last word with such sudden violence that	Alice quite jumped; but she saw in another moment that it
T8	180:10	Another Rule of Battle, that	Alice had not noticed, seemed to be that they always fell on
T8	184:10	he went on repeating, all the time that	Alice was getting him on his feet again. "Plenty of
T5	152: 7	like the whistle of a steam-engine, that	Alice had to hold both her hands over her ears.
T6	159: 9	the top of a high wall--such a narrow one that	Alice quite wondered how he could keep his balance--and, as

ALICE (cont.)

T9	199:13	it been asking of?" He was so hoarse that	Alice	could scarcely hear him.
A9	71:18	who seemed ready to agree to everything that	Alice	said: "there's a large mustard-mine near here. And the
T1	116:16	This was the poem that	Alice	read
A6	49: 3	down, and the poor little thing howled so, that	Alice	could hardly hear the words:--
T6	166:17	"Oh, it needn't come to that!"	Alice	hastily said, hoping to keep him from beginning.
T5	153:31	ended in a long bleat, so like a sheep that	Alice	quite started.
T8	187:16	Of all the strange things that	Alice	saw in her journey Through The Looking-Glass, this was
T4	139:14	exactly like a couple of great schoolboys, that	Alice	couldn't help pointing her finger at Tweedledum, and
T8	185: 6	The Knight looked so solemn about it that	Alice	did not dare to laugh. "I'm afraid you must have hurt
T2	126:24	Not that	Alice	had any idea of doing that. She felt as if she would
T1	115:21	together in a frightened whisper--so low, that	Alice	could hardly hear what they said.
T9	194:41	"I know that!"	Alice	cried eagerly. "You take some flour--"
A1	10:10	out-of-the-way things had happened lately, that	Alice	had begun to think that very few things indeed were
T9	201:14	and the waiters took it away so quickly that	Alice	couldn't return its bow.
T2	122:35	stupider," a Violet said, so suddenly, that	Alice	quite jumped; for it hadn't spoken before.
T4	148:18	It was getting dark so suddenly that	Alice	thought there must be a thunderstorm coming on. "What
A1	8: 8	and then dipped suddenly down, so suddenly that	Alice	had not a moment to think about stopping herself
T8	179:37	banging away at each other with such fury that	Alice	got behind a tree to be out of the way of the blows.
A4	33:14	The great question certainly was "What"	Alice	looked all round her at the flowers and the blades of
T3	134: 9	"Crawling at your feet," said the Gnat (Alice drew her feet back in some alarm), "you may observe a
T8	190:25	"It wo'n't take long to see him off, I expect,"	Alice	said to herself, as she stood watching him. "There he
T3	131:43	"What kind of insect?"	Alice	inquired, a little anxiously. What she really wanted
T3	135:35	collar'--just fancy calling everything you met 'Alice,' till one of them answered! Only they wouldn't answer
A7	59:11	"I've had nothing yet,"	Alice	replied in an offended tone: "so I ca'n't take more."
T5	154: 3	"I don't quite know yet,"	Alice	said very gently. "I should like to look all round me
T5	155:29	"A dear little crab!" thought	Alice.	"I should like that."
A4	30:19	of cucumber-frames there must be!" thought	Alice.	"I wonder what they'll do next! As for pulling me out
T3	129:11	"just as if it was a regular bee," thought	Alice.	
T3	131:19	of people there are in the carriage!" thought	Alice.	
T7	172:34	have to be a very tiny earthquake!" thought	Alice.	"Who are at it again?" she ventured to ask.
A6	49:26	I don't take this child away with me," thought	Alice,	"they're sure to kill it in a day or two. Wouldn't it
T6	161:20	about it just as if it was a game!" thought	Alice.)	"So here's a question for you. How old did you say
T4	148:13	"I wish the monstrous crow would come!" thought	Alice.	
A11	90:16	"I'm glad I've seen that done," thought	Alice.	"I've so often read in the newspapers, at the end of
A9	74:13	"Everybody says 'come on!' here," thought	Alice,	as she went slowly after it: "I never was so ordered
A5	44: 2	four feet high. "Whoever lives there," thought	Alice,	"it'll never do to come upon them this size: why, I
A7	54: 5	"Very uncomfortable for the Dormouse," thought	Alice;	"only as it's asleep, I suppose it doesn't mind."
T3	129:39	together ("like the chorus of a song," thought | Alice)	"Don't keep him waiting, child! Why, his time is
A8	68:24	of sight: "but it doesn't matter much," thought	Alice,	"as all the arches are gone from this side of the
T9	202:28	gravy, "just like pigs in a trough!" thought	Alice.	
T1	118:31	"But oh!" thought	Alice,	suddenly jumping up, "if I don't make haste, I shall
A6	49:17	directions, "just like a star-fish," thought	Alice.	The poor little thing was snorting like a
A2	19:21	Perhaps it doesn't understand English," thought	Alice.	"I daresay it's a French mouse, come over with
A1	7: 5	in it, "and what is the use of a book," thought	Alice,	"without pictures or conversations?"
T3	130:17	pounds to-night, I know I shall!" thought	Alice.	
A1	8:23	"Well!" thought	Alice	to herself. "After such a fall as this, I shall think
A4	31:18	feeble, squeaking voice ("That's Bill," thought | Alice),	"Well, I hardly know--No more, thank ye; I'm better
A2	15: 1	you can--but I must be kind to them," thought	Alice,	"or perhaps they wo'n't walk the way I want to go!
T1	112: 6	as warm here as I was in the old room," thought	Alice:	"warmer, in fact, because there'll be no one here to
A4	29: 9	"But then," thought	Alice,	"shall I never get any older than I am now? That'll
A6	53: 7	I've often seen a cat without a grin," thought	Alice;	"but a grin without a cat! It's the most curious
T5	158:17	"I wonder why it wouldn't do?" thought	Alice,	as she groped her way among the tables and chairs,
A6	51: 6	wider. "Come, it's pleased so far," thought	Alice,	and she went on. "Would you tell me, please, which
T9	198: 5	"I'll wait till the song's over," thought	Alice,	"and then I'll ring the--the--which bell must I ring
A11	87: 4	be in, before the trial's over!" thought	Alice.	
A11	90:27	"Come, that finishes the guinea-pigs!" thought	Alice.	"Now we shall get on better."
T4	146:10	"Selfish things!" thought	Alice,	and she was just going to say "Good-night" and leave
A10	82:18	about, and make one repeat lessons!" thought	Alice.	"I might just as well be at school at once." However,
A5	41:29	side of what? The other side of what?" thought	Alice	to herself.
A4	31:42	"A barrowful of what?" thought	Alice.	But she had not long to doubt, for the next moment a
A9	72:20	"A cheap sort of present!" thought	Alice.	"I'm glad people don't give birthday-presents like
A4	29:31	"That you wo'n't!" thought	Alice,	and after waiting till she fancied she heard the
T2	128:31	the wood ("and she can run very fast!" thought | Alice),	there was no way of guessing, but she was gone, and
A2	19:10	"Would it be of any use, now," thought	Alice,	"to speak to this mouse? Everything is so
A7	55:13	"Come, we shall have some fun now!" thought	Alice.	"I'm glad they've begun asking riddles--I believe I
A11	86:21	"And that's the jury-box," thought	Alice;	"and those twelve creatures," (she was obliged to say
T3	129: 3	very like learning geography," thought	Alice,	as she stood on tiptoe in hopes of being able to see
T3	135:11	"Why do you wish I had made it?"	Alice	asked. "It's a very bad one."
T3	137:18	both pointed along it. "I'll settle it,"	Alice	said to herself, "when the road divides and they point
T7	175:41	and carving-knife. How they all came out of it	Alice	couldn't guess. It was just like a conjuring-trick,
T5	152:12	"When do you expect to do it?"	Alice	said, feeling very much inclined to laugh.
T6	161:17	"I'm afraid I ca'n't quite remember it,"	Alice	said, very politely.
T8	186:42	"Oh, that's the name of the song, is it?"	Alice	said, trying to feel interested.
A10	85: 6	"What trial is it?"	Alice	panted as she ran: but the Gryphon only answered "Come
T2	120:13	"It's no use talking about it,"	Alice	said, looking up at the house and pretending it was
T3	131:26	"Indeed I sha'n't!"	Alice	said rather impatiently. "I don't belong to this
A12	93:31	it down "important," and some "unimportant."	Alice	could see this, as she was near enough to look over
T4	145:12	"I shouldn't!"	Alice	exclaimed indignantly. "Besides, if I'm only a sort of
A8	68:33	The moment	Alice	appeared, she was appealed to by all three to settle

ALICE (cont.)

T1	112: 1	In another moment	Alice was through the glass, and had jumped lightly down
A11	88:34	Just at this moment	Alice felt a very curious sensation, which puzzled her a
T6	163:28	doesn't mean 'a nice knock-down argument,'"	Alice objected.
A5	36:35	little busy bee,' but it all came different!"	Alice replied in a very melancholy voice.
A1	8: 5	In another moment down went	Alice after it, never once considering how in the world she
A1	9:25	There was not a moment to be lost: away went	Alice like the wind, and was just in time to hear it say, as
A7	56:16	"Of course not,"	Alice replied very readily: "but that's because it stays the
A7	56:40	"Perhaps not,"	Alice cautiously replied; "but I know I have to beat time
T3	137:13	my name now," she said: "that's some comfort.	Alice--Alice--I won't forget it again. And now, which of
T5	150:21	"What sort of things do you remember best?"	Alice ventured to ask.
A5	43:29	tone, as it settled down again into its nest.	Alice got behind a tree, for fear of being run over, and
T7	169: 3	that they seemed to fill the whole forest.	Alice could not make out which was which; but she soon
T7	173:17	were in such a cloud of dust, that at first	Alice had got so much into the way of expecting nothing but
A1	13: 1	what generally happens when one eats cake; but	Alice very obediently got up, and carried the dish round,
T7	177:13	This sounded nonsense, but	Alice was too strong for him, and at last he panted out "My
T1	115:35	for some time without saying anything; but	Alice felt she could not go faster, though she had no breath
T2	126:16	the Queen kept crying "Faster! Faster!" but	Alice hardly noticed this, there were so many other curious
T5	156:38	snow, as they lay in heaps at her feet--but	Alice gently remarked. "Do you know the lid's open?"
T8	181:21	"But the things can get out,"	Alice explained.
T6	161:26	"I thought you meant 'How old are you?'"	Alice went on. "Aren't you rather cold here?"
T8W	14: 1	"Can I do anything for you?"	Alice said heartily: "and I think if your wig fitted a
T8W	20: 1	"I'm very sorry for you,"	Alice. It looked good-natured, she thought: still it had
A6	51: 1	The Cat only grinned when it saw	Alice coming. "There's plenty of room!" said Alice
A7	54: 9	No room! No room!" they cried out when they saw	Alice what he meant, and this time he fell flat on his back,
T8	184: 7	bridle, and stretched out both his arms to show	Alice asked, holding her hands ready to put over her ears
T5	152:23	"But why don't you scream now?"	Alice said very politely, as she crossed the little brook
T5	153:23	"Then I hope your finger is better now?"	Alice remarked thoughtfully: "and what are 'toves'?"
T6	164:33	"I see it now,"	Alice said doubtfully. "I don't want to be anybody's
T8	181: 1	"I don't know,"	Alice gently remarked. "They'd have been ill."
A7	59: 3	"They couldn't have done that, you know,"	Alice replied very readily: "but--"
T9	194: 3	"Nine from eight I ca'n't, you know,"	Alice began, a little frightened at finding that, the moment
T9	201:29	a quantity of poetry repeated to me to-day,"	Alice objected.
T5	150: 7	"It must come sometimes to 'jam to-day,'"	Alice said, as she helped her to put on her shawl again.
T5	149: 5	"I'm very glad I happened to be in the way,"	Alice remarked. "I ca'n't remember things before they happen
T8	182:24	"I'm sure mine only works one way,"	Alice said, smiling.
T2	122:21	"Only in the usual way,"	Alice said, hoping to get it into a better temper by a
T6	166:28	"How is it you can all talk so nicely?"	Alice was silent.
T3	133: 1	than most," Humpty Dumpty remarked severely.	Alice began, counting off the names on her fingers.
T3	134: 4	"Well, there's the Horse-fly,"	Alice went on, after she had taken a good look at the insect
T1	110:25	"And then there's the Butterfly,"	Alice said, because the kitten wouldn't fold its arms
T9	196: 7	however, the thing didn't succeed, principally,	Alice asked in an astonished tone.
T6	168:24	"Is there generally?"	Alice remarked in a thoughtful tone.
A5	36:20	"The face is what one goes by, generally,"	Alice turned and came back again.
A6	46:35	This sounded promising, certainly.	Alice did not like to be told so. "It's really dreadful,"
A5	35:14	It was, no doubt: only	Alice replied, very politely, "for I ca'n't understand it
A8	67:23	"I'm afraid I ca'n't put it more clearly,"	Alice began, in rather a complaining tone, "and they all
T4	139:34	"I don't think they play at all fairly,"	(Alice said afterwards, when she was telling her sister the
T6	163:24	"But it certainly was funny,"	Alice said.
A3	26:13	"I don't know what you mean by 'glory,'"	Alice called after it. And the others all joined in chorus
A2	19:23	"Please come back, and finish your story!"	Alice had no very clear notion how long ago anything had
T4	140:10	(For, with all her knowledge of history,	Alice said doubtfully. "Would you tell me which road leads
A8	66: 6	"Ye-es, pretty well--some poetry,"	Alice found at first was in managing her flamingo: she
T9	200:16	The chief difficulty	Alice sat down in it, rather uncomfortable at the silence,
T1	108:11	two of them, but the middle one was empty.	Alice began. "You'd have guessed if you'd been up in the
T1	108:21	"Do you know what to-morrow is, Kitty?"	Alice went on, as soon as they were comfortably settled
T5	157:14	"Do you know, I was so angry, Kitty,"	Alice echoed in a tone that was half astonished and half
		"To buy!"	

A MULTI-WORD KWIC CONCORDANCE

```
AFRAID SIR SAID ALICE (2)
  A5    35:11            "I ca'n't explain myself, I'm afraid, Sir," said Alice, "because I'm not myself, you see."
  A5    36:31                             "I'm afraid I am, Sir," said Alice. "I ca'n't remember things as I
AFTERWARDS TELLING SISTER (2)
  T4   139:34  "But it certainly was funny," (Alice said afterwards, when she was telling her sister the history of all
  T9   202:38            ("And they did push so!" she said afterwards, when she was telling her sister the history of her
ALICE ASKED TONE GREAT (2)
  A10   81:23            "And what are they made of?" Alice asked in a tone of great curiosity.
  T8   182: 8            "But what are they for?" Alice asked in a tone of great curiosity.
ALICE BEGINNING RED QUEEN (2)
  T9   192:38            "I'm sure I didn't mean--" Alice was beginning, but the Red Queen interrupted her
  T9   194: 7            "I suppose--" Alice was beginning, but the Red Queen answered for her.
ALICE CAUTIOUSLY REPLIED (2)
  A7    56:40            "Perhaps not," Alice cautiously replied; "but I know I have to beat time when
  A9    71: 9            "He might bite," Alice cautiously replied, not feeling at all anxious to have
ALICE CONSIDERED LITTLE (2)
  A7    55:39                                         Alice considered a little, and then said "The fourth."
  T6   162:40                                         Alice considered a little. "I like birthday presents best,"
ALICE COULDN'T HELP (5)
  T4   139:14  like a couple of great schoolboys, that Alice couldn't help pointing her finger at Tweedledum, and
  T5   150: 1                                         Alice couldn't help laughing, as she said "I don't want you to
  T5   155:10  now working with fourteen pairs at once, and Alice couldn't help looking at her in great astonishment.
  T6   163: 6                                         Alice couldn't help smiling as she took out her
  T7   170:30            "I love my love with an H," Alice couldn't help beginning, "because he is Happy. I hate
ALICE DON'T EVEN KNOW (2)
  A9    73:12                             "No," said Alice. "I don't even know what a Mock Turtle is."
  A12   94:30  "It doesn't prove anything of the sort!" said Alice. "Why, you don't even know what they're about!"
ALICE HASTILY REPLIED (2)
  A5    41: 8            "Oh, I'm not particular as to size," Alice hastily replied; "only one doesn't like changing so
  A7    55:21            "I do," Alice hastily replied; "at least--at least I mean what I say--
ALICE LOOKED GREAT (3)
  T1   115:29                                         Alice looked on with great interest as the King took an
  T2   128: 4  had got all the pegs put in by this time, and Alice looked on with great interest as she returned to the
  T8   181:15  upside-down, and with the lid hanging open. Alice looked at it with great curiosity.
ALICE MUCH SURPRISED (2)
  A2    14: 1            "Curiouser and curiouser!" cried Alice (she was so much surprised, that for the moment she
  A6    52: 9                                         Alice was not much surprised at this, she was getting so well
ALICE QUITE FORGETTING (2)
  A7    59:33            "What did they draw?" said Alice, quite forgetting her promise.
  A12   92: 1            "Here!" cried Alice, quite forgetting in the flurry of the moment how large
ALICE REMARKED THOUGHTFULLY (2)
  T3   134:18            "But that must happen very often," Alice remarked thoughtfully.
  T6   164:33            "I see it now," Alice remarked thoughtfully: "and what are 'toves'?"
ALICE REPLIED EAGERLY (2)
  A3    26:26                                         Alice replied eagerly, for she was always ready to talk about
  A10   84:12  please, if the Mock Turtle would be so kind," Alice replied, so eagerly that the Gryphon said, in a rather
ALICE SAID AFTERWARDS (2)
  T4   139:34            "But it certainly was funny," (Alice said afterwards, when she was telling her sister the
  T4   147:18                                         Alice said afterwards she had never seen such a fuss made
ALICE SAID DOUBTFULLY (2)
  T4   140:10            "Ye-es, pretty well--some poetry," Alice said doubtfully. "Would you tell me which road leads out
  T8   181: 1            "I don't know," Alice said doubtfully. "I don't want to be anybody's prisoner.
ALICE SAID POLITELY (3)
  A6    48: 4            "I don't know of any that do," Alice said very politely, feeling quite pleased to have got
  A9    72:11  "I think I should understand that better," Alice said very politely, "if I had it written down: but I
  T5   153:23  "Then I hope your finger is better now?" Alice said very politely, as she crossed the little brook
ALICE SURPRISED OWN (2)
  A8    64: 3            "How should I know?" said Alice, surprised at her own courage. "It's no business of mine
  T6   165: 5  grass-plot round a sun-dial, I suppose?" said Alice, surprised at her own ingenuity.
ALICE THOUGHT MIGHT WELL (2)
  A5    36:26                                         Alice thought she might as well wait, as she had nothing else
  A8    68:10                                         Alice thought she might as well go back and see how the game
ALICE THOUGHT NEVER SEEN (2)
  A8    66: 1                                         Alice thought she had never seen such a curious croquet-ground
  T8   181:11  his gentle face and large mild eyes to Alice. She thought she had never seen such a strange-looking
ASKED TONE GREAT CURIOSITY (2)
  A10   81:23            "And what are they made of?" Alice asked in a tone of great curiosity.
  T8   182: 8            "But what are they for?" Alice asked in a tone of great curiosity.
BATTLE TWEEDLEDUM SAID (2)
  T4   138:19  Tweedledum and Tweedledee / Agreed to have a battle; / For Tweedledum said Tweedledee / Had spoiled his
  T4   147: 8            "Of course you agree to have a battle?" Tweedledum said in a calmer tone.
BEAUTIFUL SOUP (2)
  A10   84:21            beautiful Soup! / Soup of the evening, beautiful Soup! / Beau--ootiful Soo--oop! / Beau--ootiful
  A10   84:30  only of beautiful Soup? / Pennyworth only of beautiful soup. / Beau--ootiful Soo--oop! / Beau--ootiful
BEG PARDON CRIED ALICE (2)
  A2    19:27  seemed to quiver all over with fright. "Oh, I beg your pardon!" cried Alice hastily, afraid that she had
  A2    19:39  such a capital one for catching mice--oh, I beg your pardon!" cried Alice again, for this time the Mouse
BEG PARDON SAID ALICE (2)
  A3    26: 3            "I beg your pardon," said Alice very humbly: "you had got to the
  T7   171: 2            "I beg your pardon?" said Alice.
```

BEGAN THINKING CHILDREN (2)
A2   16: 1 am I?' Ah, that's the great puzzle!" And she began thinking over all the children she knew that were of the
A6   50:17 rather a handsome pig, I think." And she began thinking over other children she knew, who might do very
BEGINNING CONVERSATION (2)
A5   36:10 Which brought them back again to the beginning of the conversation. Alice felt a little irritated
T5   149:16 never do to have an argument at the very beginning of their conversation, so she smiled and said "If
BEGINNING RED QUEEN (2)
T9   192:38   "I'm sure I didn't mean--" Alice was beginning, but the Red Queen interrupted her impatiently.
T9   194: 7   "I suppose--" Alice was beginning, but the Red Queen answered for her.
BELIEVE THERE'S ATOM (2)
A12   95:25 him,) "I'll give him sixpence. I don't believe there's an atom of meaning in it."
A12   95:27 all wrote down, on their slates, "She doesn't believe there's an atom of meaning in it," but none of them
BETTER ALICE SAID POLITELY (2)
A9   72:11   "I think I should understand that better," Alice said very politely, "if I had it written down:
T5   153:23   "Then I hope your finger is better now?" Alice said very politely, as she crossed the
BLEW THREE BLASTS TRUMPET (2)
A11   87:14   On this the White Rabbit blew three blasts on the trumpet, and then unrolled the
A11   88: 5 witness," said the King; and the White Rabbit blew three blasts on the trumpet, and called out "First
BOROGOVES MOME RATHS (4)
T1   116:11 .ebargtuo shtar emom eht dnA / ,sevogorob eht erew ysmim llA / :ebaw eht ni elbmig dna eryg diD / sevot
T1   116:20 and gimble in the wabe: / All mimsy were the borogoves, / And the mome raths outgrabe.
T1   118:23 and gimble in the wabe: / All mimsy were the borogoves, / And the mome raths outgrabe.
T6   164:23 and gimble in the wabe: / All mimsy were the borogoves, / And the mome raths outgrabe."
BRILLIG SLITHY TOVES GYRE (4)
T1   116: 9 dna eryg diD / sevot yhtils eht dna ,gillirb sawT'
T1   116:18   'Twas brillig, and the slithy toves / Did gyre and gimble in the
T1   118:21   'Twas brillig, and the slithy toves / Did gyre and gimble in the
T6   164:21   "'Twas brillig, and the slithy toves / Did gyre and gimble in the
CAME ROLLING DOWN CHEEKS (2)
T3   135:13 Gnat only sighed deeply while two large tears came rolling down its cheeks.
T5   152:34 thought of her loneliness, two large tears came rolling down her cheeks.
CA'N'T REMEMBER THINGS (3)
A5   36:31 "I'm afraid I am, Sir," said Alice. "I ca'n't remember things as I used--and I don't keep the same
A5   36:33   "Ca'n't remember what things?" said the Caterpillar.
T5   150:17 mine only works one way," Alice remarked. "I ca'n't remember things before they happen."
CATERPILLAR TOOK HOOKAH (2)
A5   35: 2 other for some time in silence: at last the Caterpillar took the hookah out of its mouth, and addressed
A5   41:24 chose to speak again. In a minute or two the Caterpillar took the hookah out of its mouth, and yawned once
CERTAINLY SAID ALICE (4)
A3   25: 1   "It is a long tail, certainly," said Alice, looking down with wonder at the
A5   43:16   "I have tasted eggs, certainly," said Alice, who was a very truthful child; "but
A7   57: 5   "That would be grand, certainly," said Alice thoughtfully; "but then--I shouldn't be
A9   76:12   "Certainly not!" said Alice indignantly.
CHIN ALICE'S SHOULDER (2)
A9   70:27 she was exactly the right height to rest her chin on Alice's shoulder, and it was an uncomfortably sharp
A9   70:37 said the Duchess, digging her sharp little chin into Alice's shoulder as she added "and the moral of that
CLAPPING HANDS TRIUMPHANTLY (2)
T4   145: 4 "Why, about you!" Tweedledee exclaimed, clapping his hands triumphantly. "And if he left off dreaming
T12   207:16 look at each other. "Now Kitty!" she cried, clapping her hands triumphantly. "Confess that was what you
COME JOIN DANCE WILL (2)
A10   79:16 They are waiting on the shingle--will you come and join the dance? / Will you, wo'n't you, will you,
A10   80:10 / Then turn not pale, beloved snail, but come and join the dance. / Will you, wo'n't you, will you,
CONSIDER VERDICT KING SAID (2)
A11   88: 1   "Consider your verdict," the King said to the jury.
A12   96:28 tone, and everybody laughed. "Let the jury consider their verdict," the King said, for about the
COURSE SAID MOCK TURTLE (2)
A9   77:20   "Of course it was," said the Mock Turtle.
A10   81:33   "Of course not," said the Mock Turtle. "Why, if a fish came to me,
CURTSEY WHILE YOU'RE (2)
T2   124:13 here at all?" she added in a kinder tone. "Curtsey while you're thinking what to say. It saves time."
T12   207:23 dear!" Alice cried with a merry laugh. "And curtsey while you're thinking what to--what to purr. It saves
DEAL FRIGHTENED SUDDEN (2)
A2   18:10 That was a narrow escape!" said Alice, a good deal frightened at the sudden change, but very glad to find
A5   41:41   She was a good deal frightened by this very sudden change, but she felt that
DON'T BELIEVE PUDDING EVER (2)
T8   186:17 and his voice getting lower and lower, "I don't believe that pudding ever was cooked! In fact, I don't
T8   186:18 that pudding ever was cooked! In fact, I don't believe that pudding ever will be cooked! And yet it was
DON'T KNOW ALICE SAID (2)
A6   48: 4   "I don't know of any that do," Alice said very politely, feeling
T8   181: 1   "I don't know," Alice said doubtfully. "I don't want to be
DON'T KNOW MEAN SAID (2)
A7   56:37   "I don't know what you mean," said Alice.
T9   199:14   "I don't know what you mean," she said.
DON'T KNOW SAID ALICE (2)
A7   58:21   "I'm afraid I don't know one," said Alice, rather alarmed at the proposal.
T9   193:27   "I don't know," said Alice. "I lost count."
DON'T QUITE UNDERSTAND (2)
A7   56:21 in it, and yet it was certainly English. "I don't quite understand you," she said, as politely as she
T6   167: 5   "I'm afraid I don't quite understand," said Alice.

EAGER EYE WILLING EAR (2)
  TC   209: 5   Children three that nestle near, / Eager eye and willing ear, / Pleased a simple tale to hear--
  TC   209:14   Children yet, the tale to hear, / Eager eye and willing ear, / Lovingly shall nestle near.
EDWIN MORCAR EARLS MERCIA (2)
  A3   22: 6 much accustomed to usurpation and conquest. Edwin and Morcar, the earls of Mercia and Northumbria--'"
  A3   22:11   you did," said the Mouse. "I proceed. 'Edwin and Morcar, the earls of Mercia and Northumbria,
FEARFULLY QUICK MIGHT WELL (2)
  T7   173:12 strong enough. You see, a minute goes by so fearfully quick. You might as well try to stop a Bandersnatch!
  T7   175: 4 "No use, no use!" said the King. "She runs so fearfully quick. You might as well try to catch a
FIGURE SAID MOCK TURTLE (2)
  A10   78:35 Back to land again, and--that's all the first figure," said the Mock Turtle, suddenly dropping his voice;
  A10   79: 5   "Come, let's try the first figure!" said the Mock Turtle to the Gryphon. "We can do it
FIRST FIGURE SAID MOCK (2)
  A10   78:35 "Back to land again, and--that's all the first figure," said the Mock Turtle, suddenly dropping his
  A10   79: 5   "Come, let's try the first figure!" said the Mock Turtle to the Gryphon. "We can do
FRIGHTENED SUDDEN CHANGE (2)
  A2   18:10 was a narrow escape!" said Alice, a good deal frightened at the sudden change, but very glad to find herself
  A5   41:41   She was a good deal frightened by this very sudden change, but she felt that there
GIMBLE WABE MIMSY (4)
  T1   116:10 eht erew ysmim llA / :ebaw eht ni elbmig dna eryg diD / sevot yhtils eht dna ,gillirb sawT'
  T1   116:19 brillig, and the slithy toves / Did gyre and gimble in the wabe: / All mimsy were the borogoves, / And the
  T1   118:22 brillig, and the slithy toves / Did gyre and gimble in the wabe: / All mimsy were the borogoves, / And the
  T6   164:22 brillig, and the slithy toves / Did gyre and gimble in the wabe: / All mimsy were the borogoves, / And the
GIVE EVIDENCE SAID KING (2)
  A11   88:28   "Give your evidence," said the King: "and don't be nervous, or
  A11   91: 9   "Give your evidence," said the King.
GOOD DEAL FRIGHTENED (2)
  A2   18:10 "That was a narrow escape!" said Alice, a good deal frightened at the sudden change, but very glad to
  A5   41:41   She was a good deal frightened by this very sudden change, but she felt
GYRE GIMBLE WABE MIMSY (4)
  T1   116:10 erew ysmim llA / :ebaw eht ni elbmig dna eryg diD / sevot yhtils eht dna ,gillirb sawT'
  T1   116:19 'Twas brillig, and the slithy toves / Did gyre and gimble in the wabe: / All mimsy were the borogoves, /
  T1   118:22 'Twas brillig, and the slithy toves / Did gyre and gimble in the wabe: / All mimsy were the borogoves, /
  T6   164:22 "'Twas brillig, and the slithy toves / Did gyre and gimble in the wabe: / All mimsy were the borogoves, /
HAND PIECE BREAD-AND-BUTTER (2)
  A11   88: 7 the Hatter. He came in with a teacup in one hand and a piece of bread-and-butter in the other. "I beg
  T7   173:22 watching the fight, with a cup of tea in one hand and a piece of bread-and-butter in the other.
HEARD LITTLE PATTERING (2)
  A2   15:25   After a time she heard a little pattering of feet in the distance, and she
  A3   26:42   In a little while, however, she again heard a little pattering of footsteps in the distance, and she
HUMPTY DUMPTY INTERRUPTED (2)
  T6   160: 5   "It's a stupid name enough!" Humpty Dumpty interrupted impatiently. "What does it mean?"
  T6   164:25   "That's enough to begin with," Humpty Dumpty interrupted: "there are plenty of hard words
HUMPTY DUMPTY LOOKED (2)
  T6   162:18 I beg your pardon!" she added in dismay, for Humpty Dumpty looked thoroughly offended, and she began to
  T6   163: 4   Humpty Dumpty looked doubtful. "I'd rather see that done on
IDEA CAME ALICE'S HEAD (2)
  A7   58:10   A bright idea came into Alice's head. "Is that the reason so many
  T8W   18: 6   A curious idea came into Alice's head. Almost every one she had met had
I'M AFRAID SAID ALICE (2)
  A5   41: 2   "Not quite right, I'm afraid," said Alice, timidly: "some of the words have got
  T8W   20:14   "I'm afraid not," said Alice.
I'M AFRAID SIR SAID (2)
  A5   35:11   "I ca'n't explain myself, I'm afraid, Sir," said Alice, "because I'm not myself, you see
  A5   36:31   "I'm afraid I am, Sir," said Alice. "I ca'n't remember things
I'M POOR MAN MAJESTY (2)
  A11   89:11   "I'm a poor man, your Majesty," the Hatter began, in a
  A11   90: 8 bread-and-butter and went down on one knee. "I'm a poor man, your Majesty," he began.
IMMEDIATELY SUPPRESSED (2)
  A11   90:11 Here one of the guinea-pigs cheered, and was immediately suppressed by the officers of the court. (As that
  A11   90:18   was some attempt at applause, which was immediately suppressed by the officers of the court,' and I
JUST WELL SAY ADDED (2)
  A7   55:26   "You might just as well say," added the March Hare, "that 'I like what I
  A7   55:28   "You might just as well say," added the Dormouse, which seemed to be
LARGE TEARS CAME ROLLING (2)
  T3   135:13 But the Gnat only sighed deeply while two large tears came rolling down its cheeks.
  T5   152:34 and, at the thought of her loneliness, two large tears came rolling down her cheeks.
LIKE HUMPTY DUMPTY SAID (2)
  T6   160: 1 "Don't stand chattering to yourself like that," Humpty Dumpty said, looking at her for the first
  T6   166:37 "You needn't go on making remarks like that," Humpty Dumpty said: "they're not sensible, and
LIKE THREE GARDENERS (2)
  A8   63:15   carrying clubs: these were all shaped like the three gardeners, oblong and flat, with their hands
  A8   63:29 whether she ought not to lie down on her face like the three gardeners, but she could not remember ever
LION UNICORN FIGHTING (2)
  T7   173: 1   "The Lion and the Unicorn were fighting for the crown: / The Lion
  T7   173:16 of a great crowd, in the middle of which the Lion and Unicorn were fighting. They were in such a cloud of
LITTLE MORE CONVERSATION (2)
  A8   68:26 not escape again, and went back to have a little more conversation with her friend.
  T5   156: 1   This offended Alice a little, so there was no more conversation for a minute or two,

LITTLE PATTERING FEET (2)
    A2   15:25   After a time she heard a little pattering of feet in the distance, and she hastily
    A4   29:20   "Fetch me my gloves this moment!" Then came a little pattering of feet on the stairs. Alice knew it was the
LITTLE SCREAM LAUGHTER (3)
    A8   65:38   ears--" the Rabbit began. Alice gave a little scream of laughter. "Oh, hush!" the Rabbit whispered in
    T8   184:17   than a live horse," Alice said, with a little scream of laughter, in spite of all she could do to
    T8W   20: 9   Alice began with a little scream of laughter, which she turned into a cough as
LOOKING-GLASS CREATURES (2)
    T9   199:26   in hand, I've a crown on my head. / Let the Looking-Glass creatures, whatever they be, / Come and dine
    T9   199:37   "'O Looking-Glass creatures,' quoth Alice, 'draw near! / 'Tis an
MARCH HARE INTERRUPTED (2)
    A7   58:18   "Suppose we change the subject," the March Hare interrupted, yawning. "I'm getting tired of this. I
    A11   89:21   "I didn't!" the March Hare interrupted in a great hurry.
MIGHT JUST WELL SAY (3)
    A7   55:23   same thing a bit!" said the Hatter. "Why, you might just as well say that 'I see what I eat' is the same
    A7   55:26   "You might just as well say," added the March Hare, "that 'I like
    A7   55:28   "You might just as well say," added the Dormouse, which seemed to
MIMSY BOROGOVES MOME RATHS (4)
    T1   116:11   emom eht dnA / ,sevogorob eht erew ysmim llA / :ebaw eht ni elbmig dna eryg diD / sevot yhtils eht dna
    T1   116:20   / Did gyre and gimble in the wabe: / All mimsy were the borogoves, / And the mome raths outgrabe.
    T1   118:23   / Did gyre and gimble in the wabe: / All mimsy were the borogoves, / And the mome raths outgrabe.
    T6   164:23   / Did gyre and gimble in the wabe: / All mimsy were the borogoves, / And the mome raths outgrabe."
MOCK TURTLE REPLIED (3)
    A9   76:21   and Writhing, of course, to begin with," the Mock Turtle replied; "and then the different branches of
    A9   76:36   "Well, there was Mystery," the Mock Turtle replied, counting off the subjects on his flappers
    A10   81:37   "I mean what I say," the Mock Turtle replied, in an offended tone. And the Gryphon
MOCK TURTLE SIGHED DEEPLY (2)
    A10   78: 1   The Mock Turtle sighed deeply, and drew the back of one flapper
    A10   84:15   The Mock Turtle sighed deeply, and began, in a voice choked with
MOCK TURTLE YOU'VE SEEN (2)
    A10   80:16   "Oh, as to the whiting," said the Mock Turtle, "they--you've seen them, of course?"
    A10   80:20   "I don't know where Dinn may be," said the Mock Turtle; "but, if you've seen them so often, of course you
MORCAR EARLS MERCIA (2)
    A3   22: 6   to usurpation and conquest. Edwin and Morcar, the earls of Mercia and Northumbria--'"
    A3   22:12   did," said the Mouse. "I proceed. 'Edwin and Morcar, the earls of Mercia and Northumbria, declared for him;
NICE KNOCK-DOWN ARGUMENT (2)
    T6   163:26   don't--till I tell you. I meant 'there's a nice knock-down argument for you!'"
    T6   163:28   "But 'glory' doesn't mean 'a nice knock-down argument,'" Alice objected.
NONSENSE SAID ALICE LOUDLY (2)
    A8   64: 8   "Nonsense!" said Alice, very loudly and decidedly, and the
    A12   97: 1   "Stuff and nonsense!" said Alice loudly. "The idea of having the sentence
OUT-OF-THE-WAY THINGS (2)
    A1   10:10   knew how to begin." For, you see, so many out-of-the-way things had happened lately, that Alice had
    A1   13: 2   so much into the way of expecting nothing but out-of-the-way things to happen, that it seemed quite dull and
PIECE BREAD-AND-BUTTER (3)
    A11   88: 7   He came in with a teacup in one hand and a piece of bread-and-butter in the other. "I beg pardon, your
    T7   173:22   fight, with a cup of tea in one hand and a piece of bread-and-butter in the other.
    T7   174: 5   a desperate effort, and swallowed a large piece of bread-and-butter. "They're getting on very well," he
QUICK MIGHT WELL TRY (2)
    T7   173:12   You see, a minute goes by so fearfully quick. You might as well try to stop a Bandersnatch!"
    T7   175: 4   use!" said the King. "She runs so fearfully quick. You might as well try to catch a Bandersnatch! But I'll
QUITE UNDERSTAND SAID (2)
    A7   56:21   and yet it was certainly English. "I don't quite understand you," she said, as politely as she could.
    T6   167: 5   "I'm afraid I don't quite understand," said Alice.
RABBIT BLEW THREE BLASTS (2)
    A11   87:14   On this the White Rabbit blew three blasts on the trumpet, and then unrolled the
    A11   88: 4   first witness," said the King; and the White Rabbit blew three blasts on the trumpet, and called out "First
RATHER COMPLAINING TONE (2)
    A8   67:23   they play at all fairly," Alice began, in rather a complaining tone, "and they all quarrel so dreadfully
    T8   179:10   to another person's dream," she went on in a rather complaining tone: "I've a great mind to go and wake him
RED QUEEN SAID ALICE (2)
    T9   192:35   "So you did, you know," the Red Queen said to Alice. "Always speak the truth--think before
    T9   196:21   "Your Majesty must excuse her," the Red Queen said to Alice, taking one of the White Queen's hands
RED QUEEN SAID DECIDEDLY (2)
    T9   201: 6   "Certainly not," the Red Queen said, very decidedly: "it isn't etiquette to cut any
    T9   202:36   "That wouldn't be at all the thing," the Red Queen said very decidedly: so Alice tried to submit to it
RED QUEEN WHITE QUEEN (4)
    T9   192:12   didn't feel a bit surprised at finding the Red Queen and the White Queen sitting close to her, one on
    T9   197: 7   the feast's over, we'll go to the ball--/ Red Queen, and White Queen, and Alice, and all!
    T9   199:27   whatever they be, / Come and dine with the Red Queen, the White Queen, and me!'"
    T9   199:40   high to have dinner and tea / Along with the Red Queen, the White Queen, and me!"
REPEATED THOUGHTFULLY (2)
    A10   82:11   "It all came different!" the Mock Turtle repeated thoughtfully. "I should like to hear her try and
    T6   162: 3   "Seven years and six months!" Humpty Dumpty repeated thoughtfully. "An uncomfortable sort of age. Now if
REPLIED OFFENDED TONE (2)
    A7   59:11   "I've had nothing yet," Alice replied in an offended tone: "so I ca'n't take more."
    A10   81:37   "I mean what I say," the Mock Turtle replied, in an offended tone. And the Gryphon added "Come,
SAID AFTERWARDS NEVER SEEN (2)
    T1   115: 3   She said afterwards that she had never seen in all her life such a
    T4   147:18   Alice said afterwards she had never seen such a fuss made about

```
SAID AFTERWARDS TELLING (2)
  T4   139:34      "But  it  certainly  was  funny,"  (Alice said afterwards, when she was telling her sister the history
  T9   202:38                    ("And they did push so!" she said afterwards, when she was telling her sister the history
SAID ALICE ALWAYS READY (2)
  A3    26: 6                              "A knot!" said Alice, always ready to make herself useful, and looking
  T9   192:20   "But if everybody obeyed that rule," said Alice, who was always ready for a little argument, "and
SAID ALICE DON'T EVEN (2)
  A9    73:12                               "No," said Alice. "I don't even know what a Mock Turtle is."
  A12   94:30  "It doesn't prove anything of the sort!" said Alice. "Why, you don't even know what they're about!"
SAID ALICE LITTLE TIMIDLY (3)
  A6    47:12                "Please would you tell me," said Alice, a little timidly, for she was not quite sure
  A8    63: 3               "Would you tell me, please," said Alice, a little timidly, "why you are painting those
  A10   81:41  my adventures--beginning from this morning," said Alice a little timidly; "but it's no use going back to
SAID ALICE SURPRISED OWN (2)
  A8    64: 3                       "How should I know?" said Alice, surprised at her own courage. "It's no business of
  T6   165: 5  the grass-plot round a sun-dial, I suppose?" said Alice, surprised at her own ingenuity.
SAID EVEN LOOKING ROUND (2)
  A8    68: 7  great or small. "Off with his head!" she said without even looking round.
  T7   174:25  some enemy after her, no doubt," the King said, without even looking round. "That wood's full of them."
SAID HUMPTY DUMPTY (2)
  T6   166:14               "As to poetry, you know," said Humpty Dumpty, stretching out one of his great hands, "I
  T6   168:16                      "That's all," said Humpty Dumpty. "Good-bye."
SAID HUMPTY DUMPTY LOOKING (2)
  T6   159:22                        "Some people," said Humpty Dumpty, looking away from her as usual, "have no
  T6   163:43  "Now you talk like a reasonable child," said Humpty Dumpty, looking very much pleased. "I meant by
SAID MOCK TURTLE YOU'VE (2)
  A10   80:16            "Oh, as to the whiting," said the Mock Turtle, "they--you've seen them, of course?"
  A10   80:20        "I don't know where Dinn may be," said the Mock Turtle; "but, if you've seen them so often, of
SAID SAID RED QUEEN (2)
  T9   193: 8                  "Nobody said you did," said the Red Queen. "I said you couldn't if you
  T9   195:10       "Who ever said it was?" said the Red Queen.
SEEMED QUITE NATURAL (2)
  A1    7:15  have wondered at this, but at the time it all seemed quite natural); but, when the Rabbit actually took a
  T4   139:28  they were dancing round in a ring. This seemed quite natural (she remembered afterwards), and she was
SEVEN YEARS SIX MONTHS (2)
  T6   161:22  Alice made a short calculation, and said "Seven years and six months."
  T6   162: 3                  "Seven years and six months!" Humpty Dumpty repeated
SHE'S CAPITAL CATCHING (2)
  A2    19:38  she is such a nice soft thing to nurse--and she's such a capital one for catching mice--oh, I beg your
  A3    26:27  to talk about her pet: "Dinah's our cat. And she's such a capital one for catching mice, you ca'n't think!
SHOOK HEAD IMPATIENTLY (2)
  A3    26:15  chorus "Yes, please do!" But the Mouse only shook its head impatiently, and walked a little quicker.
  A7    56:24            "The Dormouse shook its head impatiently, and said, without opening its eyes
SIDE WILL MAKE GROW (2)
  A5    41:27  the grass, merely remarking, as it went, "One side will make you grow taller, and the other side will make
  A5    41:27  side will make you grow taller, and the other side will make you grow shorter."
SLITHY TOVES GYRE GIMBLE (4)
  T1   116: 9  eht ni elbmig dna eryg diD / sevot yhtils eht dna ,gillirb sawT'
  T1   116:18       'Twas brillig, and the slithy toves / Did gyre and gimble in the wabe: / All mimsy
  T1   118:21       'Twas brillig, and the slithy toves / Did gyre and gimble in the wabe: / All mimsy
  T6   164:21      "'Twas brillig, and the slithy toves / Did gyre and gimble in the wabe: / All mimsy
SOUNDED NONSENSE ALICE (2)
  T2   123:40           This sounded nonsense to Alice, so she said nothing, but set off at
  T7   177:13           This sounded nonsense, but Alice very obediently got up, and
SOUP BEAU--OOTIFUL (2)
  A10   84:21  Soup! / Soup of the evening, beautiful Soup! / Beau--ootiful Soo--oop! / Beau--ootiful Soo--oop! /
  A10   84:30  Soup? / Pennyworth only of beautiful soup. / Beau--ootiful Soo--oop! / Beau--ootiful Soo--oop! /
STOOD SILENT WATCHING (2)
  T3   129: 8  a mile off, you know--" and for some time she stood silent, watching one of them that was bustling about
  T7   174:20           For a minute or two Alice stood silent, watching him. Suddenly she brightened up. "Look,
SUPPRESSED OFFICERS COURT (2)
  A11   90:11  the guinea-pigs cheered, and was immediately suppressed by the officers of the court. (As that is rather a
  A11   90:18  attempt at applause, which was immediately suppressed by the officers of the court,' and I never
TEARS CAME ROLLING DOWN (2)
  T3   135:13  the Gnat only sighed deeply while two large tears came rolling down its cheeks.
  T5   152:34  at the thought of her loneliness, two large tears came rolling down her cheeks.
TELL PLEASE SAID ALICE (2)
  A8    63: 3              "Would you tell me, please," said Alice, a little timidly, "why you are
  T6   163:42              "Would you tell me please," said Alice, "what that means?"
TELLING SISTER HISTORY (2)
  T4   139:35  funny," (Alice said afterwards, when she was telling her sister the history of all this), "to find myself
  T9   202:38  push so!" she said afterwards, when she was telling her sister the history of her feast. "You would have
THANK MUCH SAID ALICE (2)
  T6   166:31                  "Thank you very much," said Alice.
  T8   181: 6                  "Thank you very much," said Alice. "May I help you off with
THINK I'LL GO DOWN (2)
  T3   129:17  what quantities of honey they must make! I think I'll go down and--no, I wo'n't go just yet," she went on
  T3   129:25                  "I think I'll go down the other way," she said after a pause;
THINK NOTHING BETTER SAY (2)
  A7    56: 9  of tea, and looked at it again: but he could think of nothing better to say than his first remark, "It was
```

THINK (cont.)
    T8   183:13   Alice could think of nothing better to say than "Indeed?" but she said it
THINKING CHILDREN KNEW (2)
    A2   16: 1   Ah, that's the great puzzle!" And she began thinking over all the children she knew that were of the same
    A6   50:17   a handsome pig, I think." And she began thinking over other children she knew, who might do very well
THOUGHT ALICE I'M GLAD (2)
    A7   55:13   "Come, we shall have some fun now!" thought Alice. "I'm glad they've begun asking riddles--I
    A9   72:20   "A cheap sort of present!" thought Alice. "I'm glad people don't give birthday-presents
THREE BLASTS TRUMPET (2)
    A11   87:14   On this the White Rabbit blew three blasts on the trumpet, and then unrolled the
    A11   88: 5   said the King; and the White Rabbit blew three blasts on the trumpet, and called out "First witness!"
THREE GARDENERS INSTANTLY (2)
    A8   63:12   called out "The Queen! The Queen!" and the three gardeners instantly threw themselves flat upon their
    A8   64:15   the Queen in a shrill, loud voice, and the three gardeners instantly jumped up, and began bowing to the
THREE HUNDRED SIXTY-FIVE (2)
    T6   162:44   "Three hundred and sixty-five," said Alice.
    T6   163: 1   "And if you take one from three hundred and sixty-five what remains?"
THREE HUNDRED SIXTY-FOUR (2)
    T6   163: 3   "Three hundred and sixty-four, of course."
    T6   163:19   just now--and that shows that there are three hundred and sixty-four days when you might get
THREE LITTLE SISTERS (2)
    A7   58:32   "Once upon a time there were three little sisters," the Dormouse began in a great hurry;
    A7   59:31 However, he consented to go on. "And so these three little sisters--they were learning to draw, you know--"
TOVES GYRE GIMBLE WABE (4)
    T1   116: 9   / :ebaw eht ni elbmig dna eryg diD / sevot yhtils eht dna ,gillirb sawT'
    T1   116:18   'Twas brillig, and the slithy toves / Did gyre and gimble in the wabe: / All mimsy were the
    T1   118:21   'Twas brillig, and the slithy toves / Did gyre and gimble in the wabe: / All mimsy were the
    T6   164:21   "'Twas brillig, and the slithy toves / Did gyre and gimble in the wabe: / All mimsy were the
TREACLE SAID DORMOUSE (2)
    A7   59: 1   "They lived on treacle," said the Dormouse, after thinking a minute or two.
    A7   59:34   "Treacle," said the Dormouse, without considering at all, this
TURTLE YOU'VE SEEN COURSE (2)
    A10   80:16   "Oh, as to the whiting," said the Mock Turtle, "they--you've seen them, of course?"
    A10   80:20   don't know where Dinn may be," said the Mock Turtle; "but, if you've seen them so often, of course you know
'TWAS BRILLIG SLITHY TOVES (4)
    T1   116: 9   diD / sevot yhtils eht dna ,gillirb sawT'
    T1   116:18   'Twas brillig, and the slithy toves / Did gyre and gimble in
    T1   118:21   'Twas brillig, and the slithy toves / Did gyre and gimble in
    T6   164:21   "'Twas brillig, and the slithy toves / Did gyre and gimble in
TWO LARGE TEARS CAME (2)
    T3   135:13   But the Gnat only sighed deeply while two large tears came rolling down its cheeks.
    T5   152:34   voice; and, at the thought of her loneliness, two large tears came rolling down her cheeks.
UNCOMFORTABLE SILENCE (2)
    T9   193:13   the Red Queen remarked; and then there was an uncomfortable silence for a minute or two.
    T9   200:16   one was empty. Alice sat down in it, rather uncomfortable at the silence, and longing for some one to
WABE MIMSY BOROGOVES MOME (4)
    T1   116:10   dnA / ,sevogorob eht erew ysmim llA / :ebaw eht ni elbmig dna eryg diD / sevot yhtils eht dna ,gillirb
    T1   116:19   the slithy toves / Did gyre and gimble in the wabe: / All mimsy were the borogoves, / And the mome raths
    T1   118:22   the slithy toves / Did gyre and gimble in the wabe: / All mimsy were the borogoves, / And the mome raths
    T6   164:22   the slithy toves / Did gyre and gimble in the wabe: / All mimsy were the borogoves, / And the mome raths
WHITE QUEEN WHISPERED (2)
    T9   194:35   "So do I," the White Queen whispered: "we'll often say it over together, dear
    T9   202:31   "We must support you, you know," the White Queen whispered, as Alice got up to do it, very
WHITE RABBIT BLEW THREE (2)
    A11   87:14   On this the White Rabbit blew three blasts on the trumpet, and then
    A11   88: 4   the first witness," said the King; and the White Rabbit blew three blasts on the trumpet, and called out

A TEXT-ORDERED KWIC CONCORDANCE
(COMPOSITE ENTRIES)

RABBIT (52)
```
A1t     7: 1                                       DOWN THE RABBIT-HOLE
A1      7: 9    picking   the   daisies,   when suddenly a White Rabbit with pink eyes ran close by her.
A1      7:12    it so _very_  much out of the way to hear the Rabbit say to itself "Oh dear! Oh dear! I shall be too late!"
A1      7:16    it  all  seemed quite natural); but, when the Rabbit actually _took_ _a_ _watch_ _out_ _of_ _its_ _waistcoat-pocket_, and
A1      8: 1    her  mind  that  she  had never before seen a rabbit with either a waistcoat-pocket, or a watch to take out
A1      8: 4    was   just  in time to see it pop down a large rabbit-hole under the hedge.
A1      8: 7                                       The rabbit-hole went straight on like a tunnel for some way, and
A1      9:23    her  was  another long passage, and the White Rabbit was still in sight, hurrying down it. There was not a
A1      9:27    behind it when she turned the corner, but the Rabbit was no longer to be seen: she found herself in a long,
A2     15:27    eyes to see what was coming. It was the White Rabbit returning, splendidly dressed, with a pair of white
A2     15:32    ready  to  ask  help of any one: so, when the Rabbit came near her, she began, in a low, timid voice, "If
A2     15:33    low, timid voice, "If you please, Sir--" The Rabbit started violently, dropped the white kid-gloves and the
A2     18: 2       to see that she had  put on one of the Rabbit's little white kid-gloves while she was talking. "How
A4t    27: 1                                  THE RABBIT SENDS IN A LITTLE BILL
A4     27: 1                        It was the White Rabbit, trotting slowly back again, and looking anxiously
A4     27:12                       Very soon the Rabbit noticed Alice, as she went hunting about, and called
A4     27:22    was  a  bright  brass plate with the name "W. RABBIT" engraved upon it. She went in without knocking, and
A4     27:28    said  to herself, "to be going messages for a rabbit! I suppose Dinah'll be sending me on messages next!"
A4     29: 1    smaller,  and being ordered about by mice and rabbits. I almost wish I hadn't gone down that rabbit-hole--
A4     29: 2      I almost wish I hadn't gone down that rabbit-hole--and yet--and yet--it's rather curious, you know,
A4     29:21    of  feet on the stairs. Alice knew it was the Rabbit coming to look for her, and she trembled till she shook
A4     29:23    now  about  a  thousand times as large as the Rabbit, and had no reason to be afraid of it.
A4     29:25                      Presently the Rabbit came up to the door, and tried to open it; but, as the
A4     29:32    after  waiting till she fancied she heard the Rabbit just under the window, she suddenly spread out her hand
A4     30: 1                   Next came an angry voice--the Rabbit's--"Pat! Pat! Where are you?" And then a voice she had
A4     30: 4    "Digging  for  apples,  indeed!"  said  the Rabbit angrily. "Here! Come help me out of _this_!" (Sounds of
A4     31: 7    general chorus of "There goes Bill!" then the Rabbit's voice alone--"Catch him, you by the hedge!" then
A4     31:28    "We  must  burn  the  house  down!" said the Rabbit's voice. And Alice called out, as loud as she could,
A4     31:39    began moving about again, and Alice heard the Rabbit say "A barrowful will do, to begin with."
A8     63:23    and  among  them  Alice recognized the White Rabbit: it was talking in a hurried nervous manner, smiling at
A8     65:26    at  her  side.  She  was walking by the White Rabbit, who was peeping anxiously into her face.
A8     65:29                 "Hush! Hush!" said the Rabbit in a low hurried tone. He looked anxiously over his
A8     65:34             "Did you say 'What a pity!'?" the Rabbit said.
A8     65:37            "She boxed the Queen's ears--" the Rabbit began. Alice gave a little scream of laughter. "Oh,
A8     65:38    a  little scream of laughter. "Oh, hush!" the Rabbit whispered in a frightened tone. "The Queen will hear
A10    82: 2    from  the  time when she first saw the White Rabbit. She was a little nervous about it, just at first, the
A11    86: 5    to guard him; and near the King was the White Rabbit, with a trumpet in one hand, and a scroll of parchment
A11    86:34    she  stopped  herself  hastily, for the White Rabbit cried out "Silence in the court!", and the King put on
A11    87:14                 On this the White Rabbit blew three blasts on the trumpet, and then unrolled the
A11    88: 2               "Not yet, not yet!" the Rabbit hastily interrupted. "There's a great deal to come
A11    88: 4    first  witness," said the King; and the White Rabbit blew three blasts on the trumpet, and called out "First
A11    91:11    The  King  looked  anxiously  at  the White Rabbit, who said, in a low voice, "Your Majesty must
A11    91:29               Alice watched the White Rabbit as he fumbled over the list, feeling very curious to
A11    91:32    herself. Imagine her surprise, when the White Rabbit read out, at the top of his shrill little voice, the
A12    93:23    this  down  on  their slates, when the White Rabbit interrupted: "_Unimportant_, your Majesty means, of
A12    94: 4    yet,  please  your  Majesty," said the White Rabbit, jumping up in a great hurry: "this paper has just been
A12    94: 7    "I  haven't  opened  it  yet," said the White Rabbit; "but it seems to be a letter, written by the prisoner
A12    94:12    "It  isn't  directed at all," said the White Rabbit: "in fact, there's nothing written on the _outside_." He
A12    94:17             "No, they're not," said the White Rabbit, "and that's the queerest thing about it." (The jury
A12    94:33                      The White Rabbit put on his spectacles. "Where shall I begin, please
A12    94:37    dead  silence  in the court, whilst the White Rabbit read out these verses:--
A12    98:24    long  grass  rustled at her feet as the White Rabbit hurried by--the frightened Mouse splashed his way
```

DINAH (25)
```
A1      9: 6    to  do,  so Alice soon began talking again. "Dinah'll miss me very much to-night, I should think!" (Dinah
A1      9: 7    miss  me  very much to-night, I should think!" (Dinah was the cat.) "I hope they'll remember her saucer of
A1      9: 8    remember  her  saucer of milk at tea-time. Dinah, my dear! I wish you were down here with me! There are
A1      9:17    dream  that she was walking hand in hand with Dinah, and was saying to her, very earnestly, "Now, Dinah,
A1      9:17    and  was  saying to her, very earnestly, "Now, Dinah, tell me the truth: did you ever eat a bat?" when
A2     19:33    it.  And  yet I wish I could show you our cat Dinah. I think you'd take a fancy to cats, if you could only
A3     26:22                 "I wish I had our Dinah here, I know I do!" said Alice aloud, addressing nobody
A3     26:24             "And who is Dinah, if I might venture to ask the question?" said the Lory.
A3     26:27    she  was always ready to talk about her pet: "Dinah's our cat. And she's such a capital one for catching
A3     26:37           "I  wish  I hadn't mentioned Dinah!" she said to herself in a melancholy tone. "Nobody
A3     26:39    she's  the  best cat in the world! Oh, my dear Dinah! I wonder if I shall ever see you any more!" And here
A4     27:28    "to be going messages for a rabbit! I suppose Dinah'll be sending me on messages next!" And she began
A4     27:32    But  I've  got  to watch this mouse-hole till Dinah comes back, and see that the mouse doesn't get out.'
A4     27:34    don't think," Alice went on, "that they'd let Dinah stop in the house if it began ordering people about like
A4     31:31    as  loud  as  she could, "If you do, I'll set Dinah at you!"
T1    107: 6                      The way Dinah washed her children's faces was this: first she held the
T1    107:22    understand  that  it was in disgrace. "Really, Dinah ought to have taught you better manners! You _ought_,
T1    108: 1    to have taught you better manners! You _ought_, Dinah, you know you ought!" she added, looking reproachfully
T1    108:12    if  you'd  been up in the window with me--only Dinah was making you tidy, so you couldn't. I was watching the
T1    108:28    faults. Number one: you squeaked twice while Dinah was washing your face this morning. Now you ca'n't deny
T12   207:28    patiently  undergoing  its toilet, "when _will_ Dinah have finished with your White Majesty? That
T12   207:30    be the reason you were so untidy in my dream--Dinah! Do you know that you're scrubbing a White Queen? Really
T12   207:32           "And what did Dinah turn to, I wonder?" she prattled on, as she settled
T12   207:34    in her hand, to watch the kittens. "Tell me, Dinah, did you turn to Humpty Dumpty? I _think_ you did--however
T12   208: 7    _not_ go on licking your paw like that--as if Dinah hadn't washed you this morning! You see, Kitty, it _must_
```

KITTY (24)

T1	108: 7	to the kitten, and sometimes to herself. Kitty sat very demurely on her knee, pretending to watch the
T1	108:11	"Do you know what to-morrow is, Kitty?" Alice began. "You'd have guessed if you'd been up in
T1	108:14	the bonfire--and it wants plenty of sticks, Kitty! Only it got so cold, and it snowed so, they had to
T1	108:21	"Do you know, I was so angry, Kitty, when I saw all the mischief you had been doing
T1	108:29	face this morning. Now you ca'n't deny it, Kitty: I heard you! What's that you say?" (pretending that the
T1	108:38	"That's three faults, Kitty, and you've not been punished for any of them yet. You
T1	109: 9	you hear the snow against the window-panes, Kitty? How nice and soft it sounds! I wonder if the snow loves
T1	109:14	again.' And when they wake up in the summer, Kitty, they dress themselves all in green, and dance about--
T1	110: 4	"Kitty, can you play chess? Now, don't smile, my dear. I'm
T1	110: 7	you purred! Well, it was a nice check, Kitty, and really I might have won, if it hadn't been for that
T1	110: 9	that came wriggling down among my pieces. Kitty dear, let's pretend--" And here I wish I could tell you
T1	110:21	"Let's pretend that you're the Red Queen, Kitty! Do you know, I think if you sat up and folded your arms
T1	110:30	"Now, if you'll only attend, Kitty, and not talk so much, I'll tell you all my ideas about
T1	110:43	you like to live in Looking-glass House, Kitty? I wonder if they'd give you milk in there? Perhaps
T1	111: 1	milk isn't good to drink--but oh, Kitty! now we come to the passage. You can just see a little
T1	111: 5	know it may be quite different on beyond. Oh, Kitty, how nice it would be if we could only get through into
T1	111: 8	a way of getting through into it, somehow, Kitty. Let's pretend the glass has got all soft like gauze, so
T12	207: 4	a nice dream! And you've been along with me, Kitty--all through the Looking-glass world. Did you know it,
T12	207:16	and the Queen to look at each other. "Now Kitty!" she cried, clapping her hands triumphantly. "Confess
T12	207:37	"By the way, Kitty, if only you'd been really with me in my dream, there
T12	208: 5	"Now, Kitty, let's consider who it was that dreamed it all. This is
T12	208: 8	hadn't washed you this morning! You see, Kitty, it must have been either me or the Red King. He was
T12	208:10	part of his dream, too! Was it the Red King, Kitty? You were his wife, my dear, so you ought to know--Oh,
T12	208:11	his wife, my dear, so you ought to know--Oh, Kitty, do help to settle it! I'm sure your paw can wait!" But

CURIOSITY (41)

A1	8: 3	a watch to take out of it, and burning with curiosity, she ran across the field after it, and was just in
A1	12: 1	"What a curious feeling!" said Alice. "I must be shutting up like a
A1	12:27	she was playing against herself, for this curious child was very fond of pretending to be two people.
A2	14: 1	"Curiouser and curiouser!" cried Alice (she was so much
A2	14: 1	"Curiouser and curiouser!" cried Alice (she was so much surprised, that for
A2	20:23	Dodo, a Lory and an Eaglet, and several other curious creatures. Alice led the way, and the whole party swam
A4	29: 2	rabbit-hole--and yet--and yet--it's rather curious, you know, this sort of life! I do wonder what can
A6	45: 8	curled all over their heads. She felt very curious to know what it was all about, and crept a little way
A6	53: 8	"but a grin without a cat! It's the most curious thing I ever saw in all my life!"
A7	55: 7	looking at Alice for some time with great curiosity, and this was his first speech.
A7	56:11	had been looking over his shoulder with some curiosity. "What a funny watch!" she remarked. "It tells the
A7	60:39	a door leading right into it. "That's very curious!" she thought. "But everything's curious to-day. I
A7	60:40	very curious!" she thought. "But everything's curious to-day. I think I may as well go in at once." And in
A8	62: 3	painting them red. Alice thought this a very curious thing, and she went nearer to watch them, and, just as
A8	66: 1	Alice thought she had never seen such a curious croquet-ground in her life: it was all ridges and
A8	67:10	away without being seen, when she noticed a curious appearance in the air: it puzzled her very much at
A8	67:38	and looking at the Cat's head with great curiosity.
A9	77:14	"What a curious plan!" exclaimed Alice.
A10	80:15	it was over at last: "and I do so like that curious song about the whiting!"
A10	81:24	they made of?" Alice asked in a tone of great curiosity.
A10	82: 9	drew a long breath, and said "That's very curious!"
A10	82:10	"It's all about as curious as it can be," said the Gryphon.
A11	88:34	Just at this moment Alice felt a very curious sensation, which puzzled her a good deal until she
A11	91:30	as he fumbled over the list, feeling very curious to see what the next witness would be like, "--for
A12	98: 6	"Oh, I've had such a curious dream!" said Alice. And she told her sister, as well
A12	98: 9	her sister kissed her, and said "It was a curious dream, dear, certainly; but now run in to your tea:
T1	113:17	and begin kicking: she watched it with great curiosity to see what would happen next.
T2	120: 5	"but I suppose it will at last. But how curiously it twists! It's more like a corkscrew than a path!
T2	123:22	does she wear them?" Alice asked with some curiosity.
T2	125:20	all directions over the country--and a most curious country it was. There were a number of tiny little
T2	126:18	The most curious part of the thing was, that the trees and the other
T3	133: 6	does it live on?" Alice asked, with great curiosity.
T5	154:11	The shop seemed to be full of all manner of curious things--but the oddest part of it all was, that,
T5	156:39	hardly noticed this, there were so many other curious things to think about.
T6	164:37	"They must be very curious-looking creatures."
T7	170:23	last. "But he's coming very slowly--and what curious attitudes he goes into!" (For the Messenger kept
T8	181:16	hanging open. Alice looked at it with great curiosity.
T8	182: 8	are they for?" Alice asked in a tone of great curiosity.
T8	184:39	Alice changed the subject hastily. "What a curious helmet you've got!" she said cheerfully. "Is that your
T9	201:31	eyes were fixed upon her; "and it's a very curious thing, I think--every poem was about fishes in some
T8W	18: 6	A curious idea came into Alice's head. Almost every one she had

CROQUET (12)

A1	12:26	ears for having cheated herself in a game of croquet she was playing against herself, for this curious
A6	45:14	Duchess. An invitation from the Queen to play croquet." The Frog-Footman repeated, in the same solemn tone,
A6	46: 3	Queen. An invitation for the Duchess to play croquet."
A6	49:12	she spoke. "I must go and get ready to play croquet with the Queen," and she hurried out of the room. The
A6	52: 2	it what you like," said the Cat. "Do you play croquet with the Queen to-day?"
A8t	62: 2	THE QUEEN'S CROQUET-GROUND
A8	65:19	right!" shouted the Queen. "Can you play croquet?"
A8	66: 1	thought she had never seen such a curious croquet-ground in her life: it was all ridges and furrows: the
A8	66: 2	her life: it was all ridges and furrows: the croquet balls were live hedgehogs, and the mallets live
A8	67:29	other end of the ground--and I should have croqueted the Queen's hedgehog just now, only it ran away when
A8	68:18	seemed to Alice an excellent opportunity for croqueting one of them with the other: the only difficulty was
A9	72:42	a word, but slowly followed her back to the croquet-ground.

BABY (15)
```
A6     47: 2   a three-legged stool in the middle, nursing a baby: the cook was leaning over the fire, stirring a large
A6     47: 8   Duchess  sneezed occasionally; and as for the baby, it was sneezing and howling alternately without a
A6     47:18   another  moment  that it was addressed to the baby, and not to her, so she took courage, and went on again:
A6     48:11   within  her  reach  at  the  Duchess and the baby--the fire-irons came first; then followed a shower of
A6     48:14   of  them  even  when  they  hit her; and the baby was howling so much already, that it was quite impossible
A6     48:41              CHORUS (in which the cook and the baby joined):--
A6     49: 2   verse  of  the  song,  she  kept tossing the baby violently up and down, and the poor little thing howled
A6     49:11   the  Duchess  said  to Alice, flinging the baby at her as she spoke. "I must go and get ready to play
A6     49:15              Alice caught the baby with some difficulty, as it was a queer-shaped little
A6     49:31              The baby grunted again, and Alice looked very anxiously into its
A6     49:34   its  eyes  were getting extremely small for a baby: altogether Alice did not like the look of the thing at
A6     52:17   "By-the-bye,  what became of the baby?" said the Cat. "I'd nearly forgotten to ask."
A12    98:40   of the shepherd-boy--and  the  sneeze of the baby, the shriek of the Gryphon, and all the other queer
T6    159:23   from her as usual, "have no more sense than a baby!"
T9    202: 4   the  fish  must be caught.' / That is easy: a baby, I think, could have caught it. / 'Next, the fish must be
```
BILL (17)
```
A4t    27: 1              THE RABBIT SENDS IN A LITTLE BILL
A4     30:26   ladder?--Why, I  hadn't to  bring  but one. Bill's got the other--Bill! Fetch it here, lad!--Here, put 'em
A4     30:26    to  bring  but  one.  Bill's got the other--Bill! Fetch it here, lad!--Here, put 'em up at this corner--No
A4     30:29   do  well  enough.  Don't be particular--Here, Bill! Catch hold of this rope--Will the roof bear?--Mind that
A4     30:31   (a  loud  crash)--"Now, who did that?--It was Bill, I fancy--Who's to go down the chimney?--Nay, I sha'n't!
A4     30:33   I  sha'n't! You do it!--That I wo'n't, then!--Bill's got to go down--Here, Bill! The master says you've got
A4     30:33   I wo'n't, then!--Bill's got to go down--Here, Bill! The master says you've got to go down the chimney!"
A4     30:35              "Oh! So Bill's got to come down the chimney, has he?" said Alice to
A4     30:36   "Why,  they  seem  to  put  everything upon Bill! I wouldn't be in Bill's place for a good deal: this
A4     30:37   to put everything upon Bill! I wouldn't be in Bill's place for a good deal: this fireplace is narrow, to be
A4     31: 2   above her:  then, saying to herself "This is Bill", she gave one sharp kick, and waited to see what would
A4     31: 7   she heard was a general chorus of "There goes Bill!" then the Rabbit's voice alone--"Catch him, you by the
A4     31:17   a  little  feeble,  squeaking  voice ("That's Bill," thought Alice), "Well, I hardly know--No more, thank ye
A4     32:14   waiting  outside.  The  poor  little Lizard, Bill, was in the middle, being held up by two guinea-pigs, who
A9     76:15   "Now,  at  ours,  they had, at the end of the bill, 'French, music, and washing--extra.'"
A11    87: 8   so quickly that the poor little juror (it was Bill, the Lizard) could not make out at all what had become of
A12    96:21   Lizard as she spoke. (The unfortunate little Bill had left off writing on his slate with one finger, as he
```
COOK (14)
```
A6     47: 2   stool  in  the  middle,  nursing  a baby: the cook was leaning over the fire, stirring a large cauldron
A6     47:10   in the kitchen, that did not sneeze, were the cook, and a large cat, which was lying on the hearth and
A6     48: 9   While  she  was  trying  to  fix on one, the cook took the cauldron of soup off the fire, and at once set
A6     48:28   Alice  glanced  rather  anxiously at  the cook, to see if she meant to take the hint; but the cook was
A6     48:29   to see if she meant to take the hint; but the cook was busily stirring the soup, and seemed not to be
A6     48:41              CHORUS (in which the cook and the baby joined):--
A6     49:13   Queen," and she hurried out of the room. The cook threw a frying-pan after her as she went, but it just
A8     62:16   "And I'll tell him--it was for bringing the cook tulip-roots instead of onions."
A11    91: 5              The next witness was the Duchess's cook. She carried the pepper-box in her hand, and Alice
A11    91:10              "Sha'n't," said the cook.
A11    91:14   after  folding  his  arms and frowning at the cook till his eyes were nearly out of sight, he said, in a
A11    91:17              "Pepper, mostly," said the cook.
A11    91:24   by  the time they had settled down again, the cook had disappeared.
T9    202: 7              'Now cook me the fish!' / That is easy, and will not take more than
```
BROOK (15)
```
T2    125:21   it  was.  There  were a number of tiny little brooks running straight across it from side to side, and the
T2    125:23   of  little  green  hedges,  that reached from brook to brook.
T2    125:24   green  hedges,  that  reached  from brook to brook.
T3    129:29   and  jumped  over the first of the six little brooks. * * * * * * * * * * * * *
T3    132: 6   quietly  drew  it  in  and  said "It's only a brook we have to jump over." Everybody seemed satisfied with
T5    153:18   wind  blew  the Queen's shawl across a little brook. The Queen spread out her arms again and went flying
T5    153:24   said very politely, as she crossed the little brook after the Queen. * * * * * * * * * * * * * *
T5    158:22   growing here! And  actually here's a little brook! Well, this is the very queerest shop I ever saw!" * * *
T7    177: 6   had  seated  herself  on the bank of a little brook, with the great dish on her knees, and was sawing away
T7    178: 4   to  her  feet  and  sprang across the little brook in her terror, and had just time to see the Lion and the
T8    181: 3   "So  you  will,  when you've crossed the next brook," said the White Knight. "I'll see you safe to the end
T8    190:15   he  said,  "down the hill and over that little brook, and then you'll be a Queen--But you'll stay and see me
T8    190:35   to  run  down the hill: "and now for the last brook, and to be a Queen! How grand it sounds!" A very few
T8    190:37   very few steps brought her to the edge of the brook. "The Eighth Square at last!" she cried as she bounded *
T8W    13:10   thought,  as  she  turned  to spring over the brook:--but I'll just ask him what's the matter," she added,
```
SQUARE (14)
```
T2    125:23   and  the  ground  between was divided up into squares by a number of little green hedges, that reached from
T2    126: 9   too  young  to play: and you're in the Second Square to begin with: when you get to the Eighth Square you'll
T2    126:10   to  begin  with:  when  you get to the Eighth Square you'll be a Queen--"Just at this moment, somehow or
T2    128: 8   she  faced  round,  and said "A pawn goes two squares in its first move, you know. So you'll go very quickly
T2    128: 9   So  you'll  go  very  quickly through the Third Square--by railway, I should think--and you'll find yourself
T2    128:10   think--and you'll find yourself in the Fourth Square in no time. Well, that square belongs to Tweedledum and
T2    128:10   in  the  Fourth Square in no time. Well, that square belongs to Tweedledum and Tweedledee--the Fifth is
T2    128:18   however,  we'll  suppose it said--the Seventh Square is all forest--however, one of the Knights will show
T2    128:20   will  show  you  the  way--and in the Eighth Square we shall be Queens together, and it's all feasting and
T3    129:27   Besides,  I  do  so want to get into the Third Square!"
T3    132: 6   all.  "However,  it'll take us into the Fourth Square, that's some comfort!" she said to herself. In another
T3    135:26   and  this  was  the  only way to the Eighth Square.
T3    137:28   the  wood.  If I could only get to the Eighth Square before it gets dark!" So she wandered on, talking to
T8    190:37   her  to  the  edge  of the brook. "The Eighth Square at last!" she cried as she bounded * * * * * * * * * *
```

DUCHESS (42)

A2	15:30	muttering to himself, as he came, "Oh! The Duchess, the Duchess! Oh! Wo'n't she be savage if I've kept
A2	15:30	to himself, as he came, "Oh! The Duchess, the Duchess!. Oh! Wo'n't she be savage if I've kept her waiting!"
A4	27: 3	and she heard it muttering to itself, "The Duchess! The Duchess! Oh my dear paws! Oh my fur and whiskers!
A4	27: 3	it muttering to itself, "The Duchess! The Duchess! Oh my dear paws! Oh my fur and whiskers! She'll get
A6	45:13	the other, saying, in a solemn tone, "For the Duchess. An invitation from the Queen to play croquet." The
A6	46: 2	"From the Queen. An invitation for the Duchess to play croquet."
A6	47: 1	full of smoke from one end to the other: the Duchess was sitting on a three-legged stool in the middle,
A6	47: 7	certainly too much of it in the air. Even the Duchess sneezed occasionally; and as for the baby, it was
A6	47:15	"It's a Cheshire-Cat," said the Duchess, "and that's why. Pig!"
A6	48: 3	"They all can," said the Duchess; "and most of 'em do."
A6	48: 6	"You don't know much," said the Duchess; "and that's a fact."
A6	48:11	throwing everything within her reach at the Duchess and the baby--the fire-irons came first; then followed
A6	48:13	shower of saucepans, plates, and dishes. The Duchess took no notice of them even when they hit her; and the
A6	48:20	"If everybody minded their own business," the Duchess said, in a hoarse growl, "the world would go round a
A6	48:27	"Talking of axes," said the Duchess, "chop off her head!"
A6	48:32	"Oh, don't bother me!" said the Duchess. "I never could abide figures!" And with that she
A6	49: 1	While the Duchess sang the second verse of the song, she kept tossing
A6	49:10	You may nurse it a bit, if you like!" the Duchess said to Alice, flinging the baby at her as she spoke.
A8	65:28	"Very," said Alice. "Where's the Duchess?"
A8	69: 7	of nothing else to say but "It belongs to the Duchess: you'd better ask her about it."
A8	69:11	and, by the time he had come back with the Duchess, it had entirely disappeared: so the King and the
A9	70: 2	see you again, you dear old thing!" said the Duchess, as she tucked her arm affectionately into Alice's,
A9	70: 7	"When I'm a Duchess," she said to herself (not in a very hopeful tone,
A9	70:16	She had quite forgotten the Duchess by this time, and was a little startled when she heard
A9	70:22	"Tut, tut, child!" said the Duchess. "Everything's got a moral, if only you can find it."
A9	70:26	keeping so close to her: first because the Duchess was very ugly; and secondly, because she was exactly
A9	70:32	"'Tis so," said the Duchess: "and the moral of that is--'Oh, 'tis love, 'tis love,
A9	70:36	well! It means much the same thing," said the Duchess, digging her sharp little chin into Alice's shoulder
A9	71: 6	why I don't put my arm round your waist," the Duchess said, after a pause: "the reason is, that I'm doubtful
A9	71:11	"Very true," said the Duchess: "flamingoes and mustard both bite. And the moral of
A9	71:14	"Right, as usual," said the Duchess: "what a clear way you have of putting things!"
A9	71:17	"Of course it is," said the Duchess, who seemed ready to agree to everything that Alice
A9	72: 5	"I quite agree with you," said the Duchess; "and the moral of that is--'Be what you would seem to
A9	72:14	nothing to what I could say if I chose," the Duchess replied, in a pleased tone.
A9	72:18	"Oh, don't talk about trouble!" said the Duchess. "I make you a present of everything I've said as yet
A9	72:23	"Thinking again?" the Duchess asked, with another dig of her sharp little chin.
A9	72:27	"Just about as much right," said the Duchess, "as pigs have to fly; and the m----"
A9	72:29	But here, to Alice's great surprise, the Duchess's voice died away, even in the middle of her favourite
A9	72:34	"A fine day, your Majesty!" the Duchess began in a low, weak voice.
A9	72:39	The Duchess took her choice, and was gone in a moment.
A11	91: 5	The next witness was the Duchess's cook. She carried the pepper-box in her hand, and
A12	98:29	once more the pig-baby was sneezing on the Duchess's knee, while plates and dishes crashed around it--

SISTER (16)

A1	7: 1	beginning to get very tired of sitting by her sister on the bank and of having nothing to do: once or twice
A1	7: 3	or twice she had peeped into the book her sister was reading, but it had no pictures or conversations in
A7	58:32	"Once upon a time there were three little sisters," the Dormouse began in a great hurry; "and their
A7	59:31	to go on. "And so these three little sisters--they were learning to draw, you know--"
A12	98: 1	on the bank, with her head in the lap of her sister, who was gently brushing away some dead leaves that had
A12	98: 4	"Wake up, Alice dear!" said her sister. "Why, what a long sleep you've had!"
A12	98: 7	curious dream!" said Alice. And she told her sister, as well as she could remember them, all these strange
A12	98: 9	reading about; when she had finished, her sister kissed her, and said "It was a curious dream, dear,
A12	98:13	But her sister sat still just as she left her, leaning her head on her
A12	98:23	with the strange creatures of her little sister's dream.
A12	99: 3	she pictured to herself how this same little sister of hers would, in the after-time, be herself a grown
T1	110:12	She had had quite a long argument with her sister only the day before--all because Alice had begun with
T1	110:13	pretend we're kings and queens;" and her sister, who liked being very exact, had argued that they
T4	139:35	said afterwards, when she was telling her sister the history of all this), "to find myself singing 'Here
T9	202:39	she said afterwards, when she was telling her sister the history of her feast. "You would have thought they
T12	207:19	was explaining the thing afterwards to her sister: "it turned away its head, and pretended not to see it:

A KWIC CONCORDANCE
(ITALICS AS EMPHASIS)

```
UNIMPORTANT (2)
  A12    93:26                                              "Unimportant, of course, I meant," the King hastily said, and
  A12    93:23   slates, when the White Rabbit interrupted: "Unimportant, your Majesty means, of course," he said, in a
AIR (1)
  A6     47: 7   There was certainly too much of it in the air. Even the Duchess sneezed occasionally; and as for the
ALL (7)
  A12    93: 2   the jurymen are back in their proper places--all," he repeated with great emphasis, looking hard at Alice
  T3    132:23                                "--then you don't like all insects?" the Gnat went on, as quietly as if nothing had
  A3     23:21   At last the Dodo said "Everybody has won, and all must have prizes."
  T5    154: 6   like," said the Sheep; "but you ca'n't look all round you--unless you've got eyes at the back of your head
  A9     70: 8   "I wo'n't have any pepper in my kitchen at all. Soup does very well without--Maybe it's always pepper
  T2    121: 4   a timid voice--almost in a whisper. "And can all the flowers talk?"
  T2    122:32   "It's my opinion that you never think at all," the Rose said, in a rather severe tone.
ALONE (1)
  T8    186:26                                              "Not very nice alone," he interrupted, quite eagerly: "but you've no idea
ALWAYS (2)
  T12   207: 7   remark) that, whatever you say to them, they always purr. "If they would only purr for 'yes,' and mew for
  T12   207:10   But how can you talk with a person if they always say the same thing?"
AM (5)
  T3    131:42   old friend. And you wo'n't hurt me, though I am an insect."
  T9    197:12                                      "What am I to do?" exclaimed Alice, looking about in great
  T4    145:21                                          "I am real!" said Alice, and began to cry.
  T2    127:24   "I'm quite content to stay here--only I am so hot and thirsty!"
  T9    196:35   and laid her head on Alice's shoulder. "I am so sleepy!" she moaned.
AND (2)
  T9    195:40   just as I'm five times as rich as you are, and five times as clever!"
  T9    195:39   cried the Red Queen. "Five times as warm, and five times as cold--just as I'm five times as rich as you
ANY (1)
  T9    194:31   me time--but I ca'n't do Subtraction under any circumstances!"
ANYTHING (1)
  T6    168: 3   "I wouldn't have been the messenger for anything!"
ARE (9)
  A9     76:32   on, "if you don't know what to uglify is, you are a simpleton."
  T3    129: 4   a little further. "Principal rivers--there are none. Principal mountains--I'm on the only one, but I
  T9    194:25     to herself "What dreadful nonsense we are talking!"
  T5    155:33   it very often--and very loud. Please, where are the crabs?"
  T3    129: 6   it's got any name. Principal towns--why, what are those creatures, making honey down there? They ca'n't be
  T6    161:26              "I thought you meant 'How old are you?'" Alice explained.
  A4     27:14   her, in an angry tone, "Why, Mary Ann, what are you doing out here? Run home this moment, and fetch me a
  A8     67:37                          "Who are you talking to?" said the King, coming up to Alice, and
  A6     46:33                       "Are you to get in at all?" said the Footman. "That's the first
AT (2)
  A9     70: 8   "I wo'n't have any pepper in my kitchen at all. Soup does very well without--Maybe it's always pepper
  T2    122:32   "It's my opinion that you never think at all," the Rose said, in a rather severe tone.
BACK (1)
  T3    135:25   her mind to go on: "for I certainly won't go back," she thought to herself, and this was the only way to
BEG (1)
  A12    92: 8                                "Oh, I beg your pardon!" she exclaimed in a tone of great dismay, and
BEGAN (1)
  A11    89:16                                          "It began with the tea," the Hatter replied.
BEGINS (1)
  A11    89:17                        "Of course twinkling begins with a T!" said the King sharply. "Do you take me for a
BEST (2)
  A7     56: 4                              "It was the best butter," the March Hare meekly replied.
  A7     56:10   to say than his first remark, "It was the best butter, you know."
BETTER (1)
  T7    172:13             "I didn't say there was nothing better," the King replied. "I said there was nothing like it."
BIT (1)
  T9    194:26                      "She ca'n't do sums a bit!" the Queens said together, with great emphasis.
BOOK (1)
  T6    160:35   "Ah, well! They may write such things in a book," Humpty Dumpty said in a calmer tone. "That's what you
BOROGOVE (1)
  T6    165:10   (there's another portmanteau for you). And a 'borogove' is a thin shabby-looking bird with its feathers
BOTH (1)
  T4    144:22   After a pause, Alice began, "Well! They were both very unpleasant characters--" Here she checked herself in
BRILLIG (1)
  T6    164:26   "there are plenty of hard words there. 'Brillig' means four o'clock in the afternoon--the time when
BROILING (1)
  T6    164:27   in the afternoon--the time when you begin broiling things for dinner."
CALLED (2)
  T4    147:31   coming up to have his helmet tied on. (He called it a helmet, though it certainly looked much more like
  T8    187: 7   'Ways and Means': but that's only what it's called, you know!"
CAN (13)
  A5     42:13                                  "What can all that green stuff be?" said Alice. "And where have my
  A4     29: 3   you know, this sort of life! I do wonder what can have happened to me! When I used to read fairy tales, I
  A2     18: 3   white kid-gloves while she was talking. "How can I have done that?" she thought. "I must be growing small
  A4     27: 5     as sure as ferrets are ferrets! Where can I have dropped them, I wonder?" Alice guessed in a moment
  T8    191: 6                              "But how can it have got there without my knowing it?" she said to
  T6    163:33   "The question is," said Alice, "whether you can make words mean so many different things."
  T7    174:23   the wood over yonder--How fast those Queens can run!"
```

CAN (cont.)
  T2   128:30   she ran quickly into the wood ("and she <u>can</u> run very fast!" thought Alice), there was no way of
  T5   155:12   "How <u>can</u> she knit with so many?" the puzzled child thought to
  T2   120:32   "We <u>can</u> talk," said the Tiger-lily, "when there's anybody worth
  T1   110:36   they've a fire in the winter: you never <u>can</u> tell, you know, unless our fire smokes, and then smoke
  T8   185:24   "How <u>can</u> you go on talking so quietly, head downwards?" Alice asked
  T12 207:10 one could keep up a conversation! But how <u>can</u> you talk with a person if they <u>always</u> say the same thing
CA'N'T (3)
  T2   125:11   into contradicting her at last: "a hill <u>ca'n't</u> be a valley, you know. That would be nonsense--"
  T5   153:11   "There's no use trying," she said: "one <u>ca'n't</u> believe impossible things."
  T5   149:29   "It <u>ca'n't</u> go straight, you know, if you pin it all on one side,"
COLD (1)
  T9   195:38   "But they should be five times as <u>cold</u>, by the same rule--"
COULD (4)
  A6   48: 2   grinned; in fact, I didn't know that cats <u>could</u> grin."
  A10   83: 5   his toes?" the Mock Turtle persisted. "How <u>could</u> he turn them out with his nose, you know?"
  A4   30:20   me out of the window, I only wish they <u>could</u>! I'm sure I don't want to stay in here any longer!"
  T2   126:16   crying "Faster! Faster!" but Alice felt she <u>could</u> <u>not</u> go faster, though she had no breath left to say so.
COULDN'T (1)
  T1   107: 5   pretty well, considering): so you see that it <u>couldn't</u> have had any hand in the mischief.
COURSE (1)
  T8   186:12   thoughtful tone: "no, certainly not the next <u>course</u>."
CURTSEYING (1)
  A1   9: 1   she tried to curtsey as she spoke--fancy, <u>curtseying</u> as you're falling through the air! Do you think you
DAY (1)
  T8   186:16   the Knight repeated as before: "not the next <u>day</u>. In fact," he went on, holding his head down, and his
DID (9)
  T6   160:24   that Alice could hardly help laughing. "If I <u>did</u> fall," he went on, "<u>the King has promised</u> me--ah, you may
  T6   160:21   "Of course I don't think so! Why, if ever I <u>did</u> fall off--which there's no chance of--but if I did--" Here
  T6   168:21   "I shouldn't know you again if we <u>did</u> meet," Humpty Dumpty replied in a discontented tone,
  T9   202:38   ("And they <u>did</u> push so!" she said afterwards, when she was telling her
  T9   203: 4   return thanks--" Alice began: and she really <u>did</u> rise as she spoke, several inches; but she got hold of the
  T5   156:26   I couldn't quite reach it." And it certainly <u>did</u> seem a little provoking ("almost as if it happened on
  T6   162:23   he said nothing for a minute or two. When he <u>did</u> speak again, it was in a deep growl.
  T3   129:24   it <u>was</u> so dusty and hot, and the elephants <u>did</u> tease so!'"
  T5   150: 5   "You couldn't have it if you <u>did</u> want it," the Queen said. "The rule is, jam to-morrow and
DINAH (1)
  T12 207:32   "And what did <u>Dinah</u> turn to, I wonder?" she prattled on, as she settled
DO (4)
  T8   182: 3   perhaps," said the Knight; "but, if they <u>do</u> come, I don't choose to have them running all about."
  T12 208:11 my dear, so you ought to know--Oh, Kitty, <u>do</u> help to settle it! I'm sure your paw can wait!" But the
  T3   129:26   may visit the elephants later on. Besides, I <u>do</u> so want to get into the Third Square!"
  T5   157:13   of choice, only make up your mind. Now, what <u>do</u> you want to buy?"
DOES (1)
  T3   135:43   her hand on the trunk of the tree. "What <u>does</u> it call itself, I wonder? I do believe it's got no name--
DON'T (1)
  A5   41:10   "I <u>don't</u> know," said the Caterpillar.
DOWN (1)
  T8   182:34   the reason hair falls off is because it hangs <u>down</u>--things never fall <u>upwards</u>, you know. It's a plan of my
EVER (4)
  A9   74:30   thought to herself "I don't see how he can <u>ever</u> finish, if he doesn't begin." But she waited patiently.
  A10   83: 1   in her hands, wondering if anything would <u>ever</u> happen in a natural way again.
  T9   197:15   a heavy lump in her lap. "I don't think it <u>ever</u> happened before, that any one had to take care of two
  T6   168:40   to say) "of all the unsatisfactory people I <u>ever</u> met--" She never finished the sentence, for at this
EVERYBODY (1)
  A3   23:21   waited in silence. At last the Dodo said "<u>Everybody</u> has won, and <u>all</u> must have prizes."
EVERYTHING (1)
  T8   182: 6   a pause, "it's as well to be provided for <u>everything</u>. That's the reason the horse has all those anklets
FALLING (1)
  T8   182:30   "But I've got a plan for keeping it from <u>falling</u> off."
FIT (1)
  A12   96:25   "Then the words don't <u>fit</u> you," said the King looking round the court with a smile.
FITS (1)
  A12   96:17   '<u>before</u> <u>she</u> <u>had</u> <u>this</u> <u>fit</u>'--you never had <u>fits</u>, my dear, I think?" he said to the Queen.
FIVE (1)
  T2   128: 3   <u>four</u>, I shall say good-bye. And at the end of <u>five</u>, I shall go!"
FOUR (1)
  T2   128: 3   fear of your forgetting them. At the end of <u>four</u>, I shall say good-bye. And at the end of <u>five</u>, I shall
GIMBLE (2)
  T6   165: 1   "And what's to '<u>gyre</u>' and to '<u>gimble</u>'?"
  T6   165: 2   to go round and round like a gyroscope. To '<u>gimble</u>' is to make holes like a gimlet."
GOOD (1)
  T7   173:11   "I'm <u>good</u> enough," the King said, "only I'm not <u>strong</u> enough. You
GROUND (1)
  T9   194:44   isn't <u>picked</u> at all," Alice explained: "it's <u>ground</u>--"
GYRE (2)
  T6   165: 1   "And what's to '<u>gyre</u>' and to '<u>gimble</u>'?"
  T6   165: 2   "To '<u>gyre</u>' is to go round and round like a gyroscope. To '<u>gimble</u>'
HAD (3)
  T6   162:31   said Alice, quite pleased to find that she <u>had</u> chosen a good subject after all.

```
HAD (cont.)
  T5    151:18                              "Yes, but then I had done the things I was punished for," said Alice: "that
  T6    166:12   "I read it in a book," said Alice. "But I had some poetry repeated to me much easier than that, by--
HADN'T (1)
  T5    151:20                      "But if you hadn't done them," the Queen said, "that would have been
HANDS (1)
  T9    193: 7           "I don't deny things with my hands," Alice objected.
HATED (1)
  A2     19:44   talk on such a subject! Our family always hated cats: nasty, low, vulgar things! Don't let me hear the
HAVE (5)
  A5     42:13   that green stuff be?" said Alice. "And where have my shoulders got to? And oh, my poor hands, how is it I
  T7    175:30                "Well, now that we have seen each other," said the Unicorn, "if you'll believe in
  A5     43:16                      "I have tasted eggs, certainly," said Alice, who was a very
  A10    80:25   would all wash off in the sea. But they have their tails in their mouths; and the reason is--" here
  A8     65: 4   turning to the rose-tree, she went on "What have you been doing here?"
HE (4)
  A9     76:39   conger-eel, that used to come once a week: he taught us Drawling, Stretching, and Fainting in Coils."
  A9     77: 5   Classical master, though. He was an old crab, he was."
  A7     57:11       "We quarreled last March--just before he went mad, you know--" (pointing his teaspoon at the March
  T3    131: 8   to be that they should all speak in turn, he went on with "She'll have to go back from here as luggage!
HEAD (1)
  T8    184:30   'The only difficulty is with the feet: the head is high enough already.' Now, first I put my head on the
HER (3)
  A8     69: 7   "It belongs to the Duchess: you'd better ask her about it."
  T6    159:25   she thought, as he never said anything to her; in fact, his last remark was evidently addressed to a
  T6    162:16   to take turns in choosing subjects, it was her turn now.) "At least," she corrected herself on second
HERE (7)
  A4     29: 8   "at least there's no room to grow up any more here."
  T3    137: 2     on," the Fawn said. "I ca'n't remember here."
  T4    146: 6   think it is," he said: "at least--not under here. Nohow."
  A11    88:42                      "You've no right to grow here," said the Dormouse.
  T4    145:25   under a large tree. "It can never get at me here," she thought: "it's far too large to squeeze itself in
  T9    195:32   "That's a poor thin way of doing things. Now here, we mostly have days and nights two or three at a time,
  T2    127:19   slow sort of country!" said the Queen. "Now, here, you see, it takes all the running you can do, to keep in
HIM (1)
  A7     56:36   "you wouldn't talk about wasting it. It's him."
HIS (1)
  A8     68:39   thing before, and he wasn't going to begin at his time of life.
I (33)
  T6    160:38   at me! I'm one that has spoken to a King, I am: mayhap you'll never see such another: and, to show you
  A6     51:35                              "I call it purring, not growling," said Alice.
  T8    179:29                  "Yes, but then I came and rescued her!" the White Knight replied.
  T7    170:19   at that distance too! Why, it's as much as I can do to see real people, by this light!"
  T6    163:40   can do anything with, but not verbs--however, I can manage the whole lot of them! Impenetrability! That's
  T6    166:15   stretching out one of his great hands, "I can repeat poetry as well as other folk, if it comes to that
  T3    132:26   Alice said. "None of them ever talk, where I come from."
  T5    152:30                      "I wish I could manage to be glad!" the Queen said. "Only I never can
  T2    125: 8   When you say 'hill'," the Queen interrupted, "I could show you hills, in comparison with which you'd call
  T7    176: 4   Unicorn cried eagerly. "You'll never guess! I couldn't."
  A12    95:25   interrupting him,) "I'll give him sixpence. I don't believe there's an atom of meaning in it."
  T3    130:13   in chorus means--for I must confess that I don't) "Better say nothing at all. Language is worth a
  A10    84: 5   on? It's by far the most confusing thing that I ever heard!"
  A3     22:18   "I know what 'it' means well enough, when I find a thing," said the Duck: "it's generally a frog, or a
  A11    89: 1                      "Yes, but I grow at a reasonable pace," said the Dormouse: "not in that
  A6     51:33   and wags its tail when it's pleased. Now I growl when I'm pleased, and wag my tail when I'm angry.
  T3    135:11                  "Why do you wish I had made it?" Alice asked. "It's a very bad one."
  T7    170:17   "I only wish I had such eyes," the King remarked in a fretful tone. "To be
  T4    148: 2                      "And I hit every thing within reach," cried Tweedledum, "whether I
  A8     64: 3                  "How should I know?" said Alice, surprised at her own courage. "It's no
  A10    82:32                  "Well, I never heard it before," said the Mock Turtle; "but it sounds
  T9    193:18   Alice; "but, if there is to be one, I think I ought to invite the guests."
  T6    163:41   lot of them! Impenetrability! That's what I say!"
  A8     65: 8                      "I see!" said the Queen, who had meanwhile been examining the
  A2     14: 7   and stockings for you now, dears? I'm sure I sha'n't be able! I shall be a great deal too far off to
  T2    123:38   You ca'n't possibly do that," said the Rose: "I should advise you to walk the other way."
  T9    194:12   it would come to bite me--and I'm sure I shouldn't remain!"
  A6     46:41                      "But what am I to do?" said Alice.
  T5    156:13                      "How am I to stop it?" said the Sheep. "If you leave off rowing, it'll
  T6    163:30                      "When I use a word," Humpty Dumpty said, in rather a scornful tone,
  A10    82:30   "That's different from what I used to say when I was a child," said the Gryphon.
  A3     25:10   he met in the house, 'Let us both go to law: I will prosecute you.--Come, I'll take no denial: We must have
  A2     19:43   trembling down to the end of its tail. "As if I would talk on such a subject! Our family always hated cats:
IF (2)
  T6    160:22   did fall off--which there's no chance of--but if I did--" Here he pursed up his lips, and looked so solemn
  T6    160:24   grand that Alice could hardly help laughing. "If I did fall," he went on, "the King has promised me--ah, you
I'LL (2)
  T1    110:16   say "Well, you can be one of them, then, and I'll be all the rest." And once she had really frightened her
  A3     21:14   out "Sit down, all of you, and listen to me! I'll soon make you dry enough!" They all sat down at once, in
I'M (4)
  A9     70: 7                      "When I'm a Duchess," she said to herself (not in a very hopeful
```

I'M (cont.)
     A2   16: 7   such a very little! Besides, she's she, and I'm I, and--oh dear, how puzzling it all is! I'll try if I
     A12   93:38   "I'm not a mile high," said Alice.
     T4   145:12   Alice exclaimed indignantly. "Besides, if I'm only a sort of thing in his dream, what are you, I should
IN (1)
     A7   60: 9   "But they were in the well," Alice said to the Dormouse, not choosing to
INSIDE (1)
     A6   46:20   door between us. For instance, if you were inside, you might knock, and I could let you out, you know."
INTO (1)
     T8   185: 2   you see--But there was the danger of falling into it, to be sure. That happened to me once--and the worst
IS (19)
     A3   23: 2   "What is a Caucus-race?" said Alice; not that she much wanted to
     A3   25: 1   "It is a long tail, certainly," said Alice, looking down with
     T8   187:10   to that," the Knight said. "The song really is 'A-sitting On A Gate': and the tune's my own invention."
     T6   162:38   "I mean, what is an un-birthday present?"
     T9   192: 1   "Well, this is grand!" said Alice. "I never expected I should be a Queen
     A8   62:15   "Yes, it is his business!" said Five. "And I'll tell him--it was for
     T7   176: 3   "Ah, what is it, now?" the Unicorn cried eagerly. "You'll never guess! I
     A4   33:11   I've got to grow up again! Let me see--how is it to be managed? I suppose I ought to eat or drink
     AI   3:29   the subject by, / "The rest next time--" "It is next time!" / The happy voices cry.
     A5   43:43   is, to get into that beautiful garden--how is that to be done, I wonder?" As she said this, she came
     T8   187: 2   what the name is called. The name really is 'The Aged Aged Man.'"
     A9   74:10   "What is the fun?" said Alice.
     T5   152: 8   "What is the matter?" she said, as soon as there was a chance of
     A7   55:31   "It is the same thing with you," said the Hatter, and here the
     T8   187: 8   "Well, what is the song, then?" said Alice, who was by this time
     A10   84: 3   "What is the use of repeating all that stuff?" the Mock Turtle
     T2   126: 2   being played--all over the world--if this is the world at all, you know. Oh, what fun it is! How I wish
     T8   191: 3   "Oh, how glad I am to get here! And what is this on my head?" she exclaimed in a tone of dismay, as she
     T9   193:18   a party at all," said Alice; "but, if there is to be one, I think I ought to invite the guests."
ISN'T (2)
     T8   187:28   "But the tune isn't his own invention," she said to herself: "it's 'I give
     T4   146:26   "But it isn't old!" Tweedledum cried, in a greater fury than ever.
IT (4)
     T9   199:20   a kick with one of his great feet. "You let it alone," he panted out, as he hobbled back to his tree, "and
     A7   56:36   the Hatter, "you wouldn't talk about wasting it. It's him."
     T3   134:13   "And what does it live on?"
     A3   22:16   "Found it," the Mouse replied rather crossly: "of course you know
I'VE (4)
     A9   76: 7   "I've been to a day-school, too," said Alice. "You needn't be
     T4   147:36   "And I've got a toothache!" said Tweedledee, who had overheard the
     T2   125:14   it 'nonsense' if you like," she said, "but I've heard nonsense, compared with which that would be as
     T2   125: 4   like at all: "though, when you say 'garden'--I've seen gardens, compared with which this would be a
JUST (1)
     T3   129:17   I think I'll go down and--no, I wo'n't go just yet," she went on, checking herself just as she was
KNOW (1)
     T3   136: 6   after a great deal of puzzling, was "L, I know it begins with L!"
LESS (1)
     A7   59:13   "You mean you ca'n't take less," said the Hatter: "it's very easy to take more than
LIKE (2)
     T7   172:14   the King replied. "I said there was nothing like it." Which Alice did not venture to deny.
     T2   126: 4   only I might join--though of course I should like to be a Queen, best."
LITTLE (9)
     T4   147:33   "Well--yes--a little," Alice replied gently.
     T1   114: 2   been hurt by the fall. He had a right to be a little annoyed with the Queen, for he was covered with ashes
     T4   148:10   said Alice, still hoping to make them a little ashamed of fighting for such a trifle.
     T12   207:20   and pretended not to see it: but it looked a little ashamed of itself, so I think it must have been the Red
     A5   41:14   "Well, I should like to be a little larger, Sir, if you wouldn't mind," said Alice: "three
     T2   125:17   afraid from the Queen's tone that she was a little offended: and they walked on in silence till they got
     T9   201:19   was so large that she couldn't help feeling a little shy with it, as she had been with the mutton; however,
     T4   144:13   Walrus best," said Alice: "because he was a little sorry for the poor oysters."
     T2   124:19   said looking at her watch: "open your mouth a little wider when you speak, and always say 'your Majesty.'"
LOOKED (1)
     T6   159:19   "I said you looked like an egg, Sir," Alice gently explained. "And some
LOVELY (1)
     T4   144:31   "Isn't he a lovely sight?" said Tweedledum.
LOVES (1)
     T1   109:10   nice and soft it sounds! I wonder if the snow loves the trees and fields, that it kisses them so gently? And
ME (8)
     A5   36: 8   "all I know is, it would feel very queer to me."
     T5   156: 8   "You needn't say 'please' to me about 'em," the Sheep said, without looking up from her
     T5   150: 2   as she said "I don't want you to hire me--and I don't care for jam."
     A10   81:34   said the Mock Turtle. "Why, if a fish came to me, and told me he was going a journey, I should say 'With
     T2   124:12   the Queen: "all the ways about here belong to me--but why did you come out here at all?" she added in a
     T9   197: 9   other shoulder, "just sing it through to me. I'm getting sleepy, too." In another moment both Queens
     A5   43:25   "It matters a good deal to me," said Alice hastily; "but I'm not looking for eggs, as it
     A6   48:32   "Oh, don't bother me!" said the Duchess. "I never could abide figures!" And with
MIMSY (1)
     T6   165: 9   "Exactly so. Well then, 'mimsy' is 'flimsy and miserable' (there's another portmanteau

```
MINE (3)
  A8     64: 4   at her own courage. "It's no business of mine."
  T5    150:17                          "I'm sure mine only works one way," Alice remarked. "I ca'n't remember
  A7     56:18              "Which is just the case with mine," said the Hatter.
MOME (2)
  T6    166: 3   "Well, a 'rath' is a sort of green pig: but 'mome' I'm not certain about. I think it's short for 'from
  T6    166: 1                    "And then 'mome raths'?" said Alice. "I'm afraid I'm giving you a great
MORE (2)
  A7     59:14   said the Hatter: "it's very easy to take more than nothing."
  AI      3:18   it!" / While Tertia interrupts the tale / Not more than once a minute.
MOST (1)
  T6    162:25                    "It is a--most--provoking--thing," he said at last, "when a person
MUCH (1)
  T4    140: 9              "So much obliged!" added Tweedledee. "You like poetry?"
MUST (10)
  T6    160: 7                      "Must a name mean something?" Alice asked doubtfully.
  A9     74:38   story," but she could not help thinking there must be more to come, so she sat still and said nothing.
  T5    150: 7                      "It must come sometimes to 'jam to-day,'" Alice objected.
  T5    158: 9              "Only you must eat them both, if you buy two," said the Sheep.
  T1    115:37   and at last he panted out "My dear! I really must get a thinner pencil. I ca'n't manage this one a bit: it
  T4    147:40                    "We must have a bit of a fight, but I don't care about going on
  T12   208: 8   washed you this morning! You see, Kitty, it must have been either me or the Red King. He was part of my
  T12   207:21   a little ashamed of itself, so I think it must have been the Red Queen.")
  A12    94:24   King, "that only makes the matter worse. You must have meant some mischief, or else you'd have signed your
  A11    90: 5                    "You must remember," remarked the King, "or I'll have you executed
MY (9)
  T6    162: 5   uncomfortable sort of age. Now if you'd asked my advice, I'd have said 'Leave off at seven'--but it's too
  T7    172:39   King: "and the best of the joke is, that it's my crown all the while! Let's run and see them." And they
  T8    179: 8   part of the same dream. Only I do hope it's my dream, and not the Red King's! I don't like belonging to
  T6    160: 9    Humpty Dumpty said with a short laugh: "my name means the shape I am--and a good handsome shape it is,
  T3    135:28   have no names. I wonder what'll become of my name when I go in? I shouldn't like to lose it at all--
  T5    149:14   that a-dressing," the Queen said. "It isn't my notion of the thing, at all."
  T2    122:32                      "It's my opinion that you never think at all," the Rose said, in a
  T8    179:28              "She's my prisoner, you know!" the Red Knight said at last.
  T1    109: 1   Wednesday week--Suppose they had saved up all my punishments?" she went on, talking more to herself than the
MYSELF (1)
  A5     35:11                  "I ca'n't explain myself, I'm afraid, Sir," said Alice, "because I'm not myself,
NAME (1)
  T6    160: 4                    "My name is Alice, but--"
NEVER (4)
  A1      8:27              Down, down, down. Would the fall never come to an end? "I wonder how many miles I've fallen by
  T9    196:12   such a thunderstorm, you ca'n't think!" ("She never could, you know," said the Red Queen.) "And part of the
  T1    115:26   moment," the King went on, "I shall never, never forget!"
  A4     29: 9        "But then," thought Alice, "shall I never get any older than I am now? That'll be a comfort, one
NEW (1)
  T4    146:27   cried, in a greater fury than ever. "It's new, I tell you--I bought it yesterday--my nice NEW RATTLE!"
NEXT (2)
  T8    186:11                    "Well, not the next course," the Knight said in slow thoughtful tone: "no,
  T8    186:15                    "Well, not the next day," the Knight repeated as before: "not the next day.
NO (1)
  A6     50:11   face in some alarm. This time there could be no mistake about it: it was neither more nor less than a pig,
NOT (13)
  T8    182:39   to help the poor Knight, who certainly was not a good rider.
  A5     43: 5                    "But I'm not a serpent, I tell you!" said Alice. "I'm a--I'm a--"
  A5     42:28                    "I'm not a serpent!" said Alice indignantly. "Let me alone!"
  A6     48:23              "Which would not be an advantage," said Alice, who felt very glad to get an
  A12    95:37   like it?" he said. (Which he certainly did not, being made entirely of cardboard.)
  A3     26: 5                    "I had not!" cried the Mouse, sharply and very angrily.
  T2    126:16   "Faster! Faster!" but Alice felt she could not go faster, though she had no breath left to say so.
  T12   208: 6   a serious question, my dear, and you should not go on licking your paw like that--as if Dinah hadn't
  T2    120:14   and pretending it was arguing with her. "I'm not going in again yet. I know I should have to get through
  T5    154: 8        But these, as it happened, Alice had not got: so she contented herself with turning round, looking
  A1     11: 6              However, this bottle was not marked "poison," so Alice ventured to taste it, and,
  A6     47:10   only two creatures in the kitchen, that did not sneeze, were the cook, and a large cat, which was lying on
  A11    87: 6   that squeaked. This, of course, Alice could not stand, and she went round the court and got behind him,
NOW (5)
  T5    152:23                    "But why don't you scream now?" Alice asked, holding her hands ready to put over her
  T9    204:24   too much excited to be surprised at anything now. "As for you," she repeated, catching hold of the little
  T7    177:15   itself into three pieces as she did so. "Now cut it up," said the Lion, as she returned to her place
  T4    140: 4   "It would never do to say 'How d'ye do?' now," she said to herself: "we seem to have got beyond that,
  T7    176:16   "What a fight we might have for the crown now!" the Unicorn said, looking slyly up at the crown, which
OFF (1)
  T8    190:25   the forest. "It wo'n't take long to see him off, I expect," Alice said to herself, as she stood watching
ONE (6)
  A7     59:29   interrupt you again. I dare say there may be one."
  T6    162:11                    "One ca'n't, perhaps," said Humpty Dumpty; "but two can. With
  T6    163:22              "And only one for birthday presents, you know. There's glory for you!"
  T5    158:10              "Then I'll have one, please," said Alice, as she put the money down on the
  A1     12:30   Why, there's hardly enough of me left to make one respectable person!"
  A5     43:13   good many little girls in my time, but never one with such a neck as that! No, no! You're a serpent; and
```

OTHER (1)
  T5   150: 8 it ca'n't," said the Queen. "It's jam every <u>other</u> day: to-day isn't any other day, you know."
OUGHT (4)
  T1   108: 1 ought to have taught you better manners! You <u>ought</u>, Dinah, you know you ought!" she added, looking
  T9   198: 8 not a visitor, and I'm not a servant. There <u>ought</u> to be one marked 'Queen,' you know--"
  T6   166:21 Alice felt that in that case she really <u>ought</u> to listen to it; so she sat down, and said "Thank you"
  T9   196:25 Queen looked timidly at Alice, who felt she <u>ought</u> to·say something kind, but really couldn't think of
OUR (2)
  T2   127:16   "Well, in <u>our</u> country," said Alice, still panting a little, "you'd
  T9   195:29   Alice was puzzled. "In <u>our</u> country," she remarked, "there's only one day at a time."
OURS (1)
  A9   76:14 Turtle in a tone of great relief. "Now, at <u>ours</u>, they had, at the end of the bill, 'French, music, <u>and</u>
OUT (1)
  T8   181:21   "But the things can get <u>out</u>," Alice gently remarked. "Do you know the lid's open?"
OUTGRABE (1)
  T6   166: 6   "And what does '<u>outgrabe</u>' mean?"
OUTGRIBING (1)
  T6   166: 7   "Well, '<u>outgribing</u>' is something between·bellowing and whistling, with
OUTSIDE (2)
  T4   146: 7   "But it may rain <u>outside</u>?"
  A12 94:13 "in fact, there's nothing written on the <u>outside</u>." He unfolded the paper as he spoke, and added "It
PEEP (1)
  T1   111: 2 to the passage. You can just see a little <u>peep</u> of the passage in Looking-glass House, if you leave the
PICKED (1)
  T9   194:44   "Well, it isn't <u>picked</u> at all," Alice explained: "it's <u>ground</u>--"
PLEASE (2)
  T1   115: 9   "Oh! <u>please</u> don't make such faces, my dear!" she cried out, quite
  A6   48:16   "Oh, <u>please</u> mind what you're doing!" cried Alice, jumping up and
PLENTY (1)
  A7   54: 9 out when they saw Alice coming. "There's <u>plenty</u> of room!" said Alice indignantly, and she sat down in a
POISON (1)
  A1   10:21 she said, "and see whether it's marked '<u>poison</u>' or not"; for she had read several nice little stories
PRECIOUS (1)
  A6   48:17 in an agony of terror. "Oh, there goes his <u>precious</u> nose!", as an unusually large saucepan flew close by
PROVES (1)
  A12 94:28   "That <u>proves</u> his guilt, of course," said the Queen, "so, off with--"
PROVOKING (1)
  T6   162:25   "It is a--most--<u>provoking</u>--thing," he said at last, "when a person doesn't
QUITE (7)
  A12 93: 8 said to herself; "I should think it would be <u>quite</u> as much use in the trial one way up as the other."
  T3   131:38 have heard it at all, if it hadn't come <u>quite</u> close to her ear. The consequence of this was that it
  T8   183: 2 found that it was the best plan not to walk <u>quite</u> close to the horse.
  T6   166:10 and, when you've once heard it, you'll be <u>quite</u> content. Who's been repeating all that hard stuff to you
  T2   127:37   "No, thank you," said Alice: "one's <u>quite</u> enough!"
  T5   154: 3   "I don't <u>quite</u> know yet," Alice said very gently. "I should like to
  A5   41: 2   "Not <u>quite</u> right, I'm afraid," said Alice, timidly: "some of the
RATH (1)
  T6   166: 3   "Well, a '<u>rath</u>' is a sort of green pig: but '<u>mome</u>' I'm not certain about
RATHER (1)
  T1   118:26 she said when she had finished it, "but it's <u>rather</u> hard to understand!" (You see she didn't like to
RATHS (1)
  T6   166: 1   "And then '<u>mome raths</u>'?" said Alice. "I'm afraid I'm giving you a great deal
REAL (1)
  T4   145:26   "I hope you don't suppose those are <u>real</u> tears?" Tweedledum interrupted in a tone of great
RED (1)
  A8   63: 7 you see, Miss, this here ought to have been a <u>red</u> rose-tree, and we put a white one in by mistake; and, if
REJOICE (1)
  T3   132:29   "I don't <u>rejoice</u> in insects at all," Alice explained, "because I'm
SAID (1)
  A7   55:12 eyes very wide on hearing this; but all he <u>said</u> was "Why is a raven like a writing-desk?"
SAME (1)
  T3   137:25 said Alice at last, "that they live in the <u>same</u> house! I wonder I never thought of that before--But I
SAYS (1)
  T9   192:32 Queen remarked, with a little shudder, "She <u>says</u> she only said 'if'--"
SEE (1)
  T6   166:27   "If you can <u>see</u> whether I'm singing or not, you've sharper eyes than most
SEEMS (1)
  T6   163:18 looked a little queer. As I was saying, that <u>seems</u> to be done right--though I haven't time to look it over
SHALL (1)
  T2   120:21 on well, and she was just saying "I really <u>shall</u> do it this time--" when the path gave a sudden twist and
SHE (5)
  T4   147:44 well," the other said, rather sadly: "and <u>she</u> can watch us--only you'd better not come <u>very</u> close," he
  A12 95:27 The jury all wrote down, on their slates, "<u>She</u> doesn't believe there's an atom of meaning in it," but
  T4   147:11 as he crawled out of the umbrella: "only <u>she</u> must help us to dress up, you know."
  A3   23:23   "Why, <u>she</u>, of course," said the Dodo, pointing to Alice with one
  A9   74:11   "Why, <u>she</u>," said the Gryphon. "It's all her fancy that: they never
SHE'D (1)
  A3   26:23 aloud, addressing nobody in particular. "<u>She'd</u> soon fetch it back!"
SHEEP (1)
  T5   153:35 a shop? And was that really--was it really a <u>sheep</u> that was sitting on the other side of the counter? Rub

```
SHE'S (1)
  A2    16: 7   oh, she  knows  such a very little! Besides, she's she, and I'm I, and--oh dear, how puzzling it all is!
SHOULD (2)
  T9   193: 2        "That's just what I complain of! You should have meant! What do you suppose is the use of a child
  T2   128:16                              "You should have said," the Queen went on in a tone of grave
SIT (1)
  A11   90:25                          "Then you may sit down," the King replied.
SLITHY (2)
  T6   164:29   "That'll do very well," said Alice: "and 'slithy'?"
  T6   164:30                     "Well, 'slithy' means 'lithe and slimy.' 'Lithe' is the same as
SOME (5)
  A4    32: 8   these cakes," she thought, "it's sure to make some change in my size; and, as it ca'n't possibly make me
  T3   137:13      I know my name now," she said: "that's some comfort. Alice--Alice--I won't forget it again. And now,
  T6   168:31   or the mouth at the top--that would be some help."
  T4   140:10                "Ye-es, pretty well--some poetry," Alice said doubtfully. "Would you tell me which
  T2   121: 9   speak! Said I to myself, 'Her face has got some sense in it, though it's not a clever one!' Still, you're
SOMEBODY (2)
  T1   118:29   I don't exactly know what they are! However, somebody killed something: that's clear, at any rate--"
  A3    23: 3   but the Dodo had paused as if it thought that somebody ought to speak, and no one else seemed inclined to
SOMETHING (3)
  A4    28: 4   uncorked it and put it to her lips. "I know something interesting is sure to happen," she said to herself,
  T9   193:11   said the White Queen, "that she wants to deny something--only she doesn't know what to deny!"
  T1   118:29   know what they are! However, somebody killed something: that's clear, at any rate--"
SOMEWHERE (1)
  A6    51:13                "--so long as I get somewhere," Alice added as an explanation.
SONG (2)
  T8   187: 4   "Then I ought to have said 'That's what the song is called'?" Alice corrected herself.
  T8   187: 6   you oughtn't: that's quite another thing! The song is called 'Ways and Means': but that's only what it's
SPEAKER (1)
  A11   90:10                "You're a very poor speaker," said the King.
STOLEN (1)
  A11   88:22                       "Stolen!" the King exclaimed, turning to the jury, who
STRONG (1)
  T7   173:11   good enough," the King said, "only I'm not strong enough. You see, a minute goes by so fearfully quick.
SUCH (4)
  T9   195:26   clasping and unclasping her hands, "we had such a thunderstorm last Tuesday--I mean one of the last set
  T9   196:11   Here the White Queen began again. "It was such a thunderstorm, you ca'n't think!" ("She never could, you
  T9   201:40   like the cooing of a pigeon. "It would be such a treat! May I?"
  T5   156: 7   transport of delight. "There really are--and such beauties!"
TEARS (1)
  T8   186:36   that hears me sing it--either it brings the tears into their eyes, or else--"
THAT (30)
  A4    29:12   have lessons to learn! Oh, I shouldn't like that!"
  T1   110:29   into Looking-glass House. How would you like that?
  T9   194: 6   a loaf by a knife--what's the answer to that?"
  T7   172:30                  "Do you call that a whisper?" cried the poor King, jumping up and shaking
  T2   120: 3   straight to it--at least, no, it doesn't do that--" (after going a few yards along the path, and turning
  T9   194:41               "I know that!" Alice cried eagerly. "You take some flour--"
  T6   160:14   "Did you think I didn't know the answer to that? Ask another."
  T1   110:40   only the words go the wrong way: I know that, because I've held up one of our books to the glass, and
  T1   110:35   the fireplace. Oh! I do so wish I could see that bit! I want so much to know whether they've a fire in the
  T2   122: 7               "Didn't you know that?" cried another Daisy. And here they all began shouting
  A6    51:19                 "In that direction," the Cat said, waving its right paw round,
  A6    51:20   its right paw round, "lives a Hatter: and in that direction," waving the other paw, "lives a March Hare.
  T7   178:11             "If that doesn't 'drum them out of town,'" she thought to herself,
  A10   78:19             "That generally takes some time," interrupted the Gryphon.
  T9   194:37   secret--I can read words of one letter! Isn't that grand? However, don't be discouraged. You'll come to it
  T4   146:13              "Do you see that?" he said, in a voice choking with passion, and his eyes
  A4    30:32   the chimney?--Nay, I sha'n't! You do it!--That I wo'n't, then!--Bill's got to go down--Here, Bill! The
  A1    10:20   but the wise little Alice was not going to do that in a hurry. "No, I'll look first," she said, "and see
  A9    71: 1   shoulder as she added "and the moral of that is--'Take care of the sense, and the sounds will take
  A9    77: 1               "What was that like?" said Alice.
  T1   109: 7   fifty dinners at once! Well, I shouldn't mind that much! I'd far rather go without them than eat them!
  T5   151:10        Alice felt there was no denying that. "Of course it would be all the better," she said: "but
  T5   153: 8         "I ca'n't believe that!" said Alice.
  T3   131:29        "You might make a joke on that," said the little voice close to her ear: "something
  T2   126:24      Not that Alice had any idea of doing that. She felt as if she would never be able to talk again,
  T2   128:10   in the Fourth Square in no time. Well, that square belongs to Tweedledum and Tweedledee--the Fifth is
  A12   96:15   on the table. "Nothing can be clearer than that. Then again--'before she had this fit'--you never had
  A9    70:14   sweet-tempered. I only wish people knew that: then they wouldn't be so stingy about it, you know--"
  A5    43:23   of adding "You're looking for eggs, I know that well enough; and what does it matter to me whether you're
  A4    29:30                "That you wo'n't!" thought Alice, and after waiting till she
THAT'S (3)
  A9    73:20   generally, "You are all pardoned." "Come, that's a good thing!" she said to herself, for she had felt
  A2    17: 2   Paris is the capital of Rome, and Rome--no, that's all wrong, I'm certain! I must have been changed for
  A2    15:42   next question is 'Who in the world am I?' Ah, that's the great puzzle!" And she began thinking over all the
THEIR (1)
  A12   99: 7   about her other little children, and make their eyes bright and eager with many a strange tale, perhaps
THEM (2)
  A5    42:19   her head, she tried to get her head down to them, and was delighted to find that her neck would bend about
```

THEM (cont.)
T3   132:37   "No use to them," said Alice; "but it's useful to the people that name
THEN (1)
A7   61: 5   then she walked down the little passage: and then--she found herself at last in the beautiful garden, among
THERE (2)
A7   60:35   "At any rate I'll never go there again!" said Alice, as she picked her way through the
T5   151:13   "You're wrong there, at any rate," said the Queen. "Were you ever punished?"
THESE (1)
A8   63:43   "And who are these?" said the Queen, pointing to the three gardeners who
THEY (2)
T7   169:11   better than the foot-soldiers; but even they stumbled now and then; and it seemed to be a regular rule
T6   161:14   on. "They'd pick me up again in a minute, they would! However, this conversation is going on a little
THINK (5)
A4   30:38   this fireplace is narrow, to be sure; but I think I can kick a little!"
A11   88:14   with the Dormouse. "Fourteenth of March, I think it was," he said.
A6   48:31   so she went on again: "Twenty-four hours, I think; or is it twelve? I--"
A9   71:16   "It's a mineral, I think," said Alice.
T12 207:35   me, Dinah, did you turn to Humpty Dumpty? I think you did--however, you'd better not mention it to your
THIS (7)
T9   199: 7   at the slow drawl in which he spoke. "This door, of course!"
A5   44: 3   Alice, "it'll never do to come upon them this size: why, I should frighten them out of their wits!" So
A4   30: 5   Rabbit angrily. "Here! Come help me out of this!" (Sounds of more broken glass.)
T3   130:11   use in speaking." The voices didn't join in, this time, as she hadn't spoken, but, to her great surprise,
T2   120: 6   It's more like a corkscrew than a path! Well this turn goes to the hill, I suppose--no, it doesn't! This
A11   91:12   a low voice, "Your Majesty must cross-examine this witness."
T3   135:42   "I mean to get under the--under the--under this, you know!" putting her hand on the trunk of the tree.
THOUGHT (1)
T3   130:12   spoken, but, to her great surprise, they all thought in chorus (I hope you understand what thinking in
THREE (1)
T2   128: 1   for an answer, but went on. "At the end of three yards I shall repeat them--for fear of your forgetting
THROUGH (1)
A1   8:39   began again. "I wonder if I shall fall right through the earth! How funny it'll seem to come out among the
TO-DAY (2)
T5   150: 6   to-morrow and jam yesterday--but never jam to-day."
T5   150: 4   "Well, I don't want any to-day, at any rate."
TOVES (2)
T6   164:34   Alice remarked thoughtfully: "and what are 'toves'?"
T6   164:35   "Well 'toves' are something like badgers--they're something like
TREES (1)
T4   148: 4   Alice laughed. "You must hit the trees pretty often, I should think," she said.
TRY (1)
T9   196:17   Alice thought to herself "I never should try to remember my name in the middle of an accident! Where
TWO (5)
T6   162:11   ca'n't, perhaps," said Humpty Dumpty; "but two can. With proper assistance, you might have left off at
A4   30:17   snatch in the air. This time there were two little shrieks, and more sounds of broken glass. "What a
T7   171: 7   the King repeated impatiently. "I must have two--to fetch and carry. One to fetch, and one to carry."
A12   96: 6   What, indeed!--'I gave her one, they gave him two'--why, that must be what he did with the tarts, you know--
T7   170:37   other Messenger's called Hatta. I must have two, you know--to come and go. One to come, and one to go."
UPWARDS (1)
T8   182:34   is because it hangs down--things never fall upwards, you know. It's a plan of my own invention. You may
VERY (31)
T6   159:18   from Alice as he spoke, "to be called an egg--very!"
T8   182:16   very carefully, because the Knight was so very awkward in putting in the dish: the first two or three
T8   186:35   "It's long," said the Knight, "but it's very, very beautiful. Everybody that hears me sing it--either it
T4   147:45   she can watch us--only you'd better not come very close," he added: "I generally hit every thing I can see
A1   11: 2   it too long; and that, if you cut your finger very deeply with a knife, it usually bleeds, and she had never
T7   174:16   Alice took a piece to taste, but it was very dry.
T2   127:29   and ate it as well as she could: and it was very dry: and she thought she had never been so nearly choked
A1   8:32   in the school-room, and though this was not a very good opportunity for showing off her knowledge, as there
A7   59: 5   "So they were," said the Dormouse; "very ill."
T3   132:20   It certainly was a very large Gnat: "about the size of a chicken," Alice thought.
T8   185: 1   touched the ground directly. So I had a very little way to fall, you see--But there was the danger of
T5   152:33   "Only it is so very lonely here!" Alice said in a melancholy voice; and, at
A6   51: 2   good-natured, she thought: still it had a very long claws and a great many teeth, so she felt that it
T4   140:19   Alice ventured to interrupt him. "If it's very long," she said, as politely as she could, "would you
T4   140: 7   "Nohow. And thank you very much for asking," said Tweedledum.
A1   7:12   remarkable in that; nor did Alice think it so very much out of the way to hear the Rabbit say to itself "Oh
T6   160:19   for the queer creature. "That wall is so very narrow!"
A6   46:23   it," she said to herself; "his eyes are so very nearly at the top of his head. But at any rate he might
A11   90:10   "You're a very poor speaker," said the King.
T6   159:17   "It's very provoking," Humpty Dumpty said after a long silence,
T2   128: 8   in its first move, you know. So you'll go very quickly through the Third Square--by railway, I should
A1   7:11   There was nothing so very remarkable in that; nor did Alice think it so very much
A5   36:12   irritated at the Caterpillar's making such very short remarks, and she drew herself up and said, very
T8   182:26   he said, anxiously. "You see the wind is so very strong here. It's as strong as soup."
T6   168:17   sudden, Alice thought: but, after such a very strong hint that she ought to be going, she felt that it
A2   17:26   wish they would put their heads down! I am so very tired of being all alone here!"
A6   49:33   it. There could be no doubt that it had a very turn-up nose, much more like a snout than a real nose:
A9   70:26   close to her: first because the Duchess was very ugly; and secondly, because she was exactly the right
T3   131:34   The little voice sighed deeply. It was very unhappy, evidently, and Alice would have said something

VERY (cont.)
A5   36:16   reason, and the Caterpillar seemed to be in a very unpleasant state of mind, she turned away.
A10   82: 4   side, and opened their eyes and mouths so very wide; but she gained courage as she went on. Her
WABE (2)
T6   165: 4   "And 'the wabe' is the grass-plot round a sun-dial, I suppose?" said
T6   165: 6   "Of course it is. It's called 'wabe' you know, because it goes a long way before it, and a
WAS (15)
A12   98: 9   finished, her sister kissed her, and said "It was a curious dream, dear, certainly; but now run in to your
T11 206: 1   ..--it really was a kitten, after all.
A6   46:13   could possibly hear you." And certainly there was a most extraordinary noise going on within--a constant
A2   18:10   "That was a narrow escape!" said Alice, a good deal frightened at
T1   110: 7   and when I said 'Check!' you purred! Well, it was a nice check, Kitty, and really I might have won, if it
T1   111:13   she had got there. And certainly the glass was beginning to melt away, just like a bright silvery mist.
T8   186:18   and lower, "I don't believe that pudding ever was cooked! In fact, I don't believe that pudding ever will be
T4   139:34   "But it certainly was funny," (Alice said afterwards, when she was telling her
T8   185:19   very well, and she was afraid that he really was hurt this time. However, though she could see nothing but
T12 208:10   but then I was part of his dream, too! Was it the Red King, Kitty? You were his wife, my dear, so you
A1   8:42   I think--" (she was rather glad there was no one listening, this time, as it didn't sound at all the
T8   186:10   for the next course?" said Alice. "Well, that was quick work, certainly!"
T3   129:24   favourite little toss of the head), 'only it was so dusty and hot, and the elephants did tease so!'"
T8   185: 2   a very little way to fall, you see--But there was the danger of falling into it, to be sure. That happened
A5   35: 7   Sir, just at present--at least I know who I was when I got up this morning, but I think I must have been
WASHING (1)
A9   76:15   at the end of the bill, 'French, music, and washing--extra.'"
WERE (1)
T8   184:25   "You were a little grave," said Alice.
WHAT (10)
T5   156:25   tipple over!" she said to herself. "Oh, what a lovely one! Only I couldn't quite reach it." And it
A5   43: 7   "Well! What are you?" said the Pigeon. "I can see you're trying to
A3   22:15   "Found what?" said the Duck.
A11   89:15   "The twinkling of what?" said the King.
T3   135:40   being so hot, to get into the--into the--into what?" she went on, rather surprised at not being able to
A5   41:29   "One side of what? The other side of what?" thought Alice to herself.
A5   36:33   "Ca'n't remember what things?" said the Caterpillar.
A4   31:41   "A barrowful of what?" thought Alice. But she had not long to doubt, for the
A5   41:29   "One side of what? The other side of what?" thought Alice to herself.
T6   161: 9   behind," she thought: "And then I don't know what would happen to his head! I'm afraid it would come off!"
WHATEVER (1)
A12   93:19   "Nothing whatever?" persisted the King.
WHICH (1)
T9   198: 6   thought Alice, "and then I'll ring the--the--which bell must I ring?" she went on, very much puzzled by the
WHITE (1)
T1   107: 1   One thing was certain, that the white kitten had had nothing to do with it--it was the black
WHY (2)
T5   155:36   "Why do you say 'Feather' so often?" Alice asked at last,
T5   158:17   "I wonder why it wouldn't do?" thought Alice, as she groped her way
WILL (6)
A2   19: 3   by being drowned in my own tears! That will be a queer thing, to be sure! However, everything is
T8   186:18   In fact, I don't believe that pudding ever will be cooked! And yet it was a very clever pudding to invent
A4   28:22   "Now I can do no more, whatever happens. What will become of me?"
T12 207:28   still patiently undergoing its toilet, "when will Dinah have finished with your White Majesty, I wonder?
A4   31:34   Alice thought to herself "I wonder what they will do next! If they had any sense, they'd take the roof off
T3   136: 4   has happened, after all! And now, who am I? I will remember, if I can! I'm determined to do it!" But being
WISH (3)
T2   126: 3   at all, you know. Oh, what fun it is! How I wish I was one of them! I wouldn't mind being a Pawn, if only
T1   110: 2   of worsted to clap her hands. "And I do so wish it was true! I'm sure the woods look sleepy in the autumn
T2   120:31   was waving gracefully about in the wind, "I wish you could talk!"
WO'N'T (1)
A2   15:30   he came, "Oh! The Duchess, the Duchess! Oh! Wo'n't she be savage if I've kept her waiting!" Alice felt so
WOULD (12)
A12   98:21   her head to keep back the wandering hair that would always get into her eyes--and still as she listened, or
T8   184:37   I ca'n't tell for certain--but I'm afraid it would be a little hard."
T4   141: 6   were only cleared away,' / They said, 'it would be grand!'
T9   196: 4   "He said he would come in," the White Queen went on, "because he was
A1   10: 6   through the doorway; "and even if my head would go through," thought poor Alice, "it would be of very
A10   81: 4   "The reason is," said the Gryphon, "that they would go with the lobsters to the dance. So they got thrown
T12 207:38   with me in my dream, there was one thing you would have enjoyed--I had such a quantity of poetry said to me
T3   131:30   voice close to her ear: "something about 'you would if you could,' you know."
A1   10:24   and other unpleasant things, all because they would not remember the simple rules their friends had taught
A2   17:26   with a sudden burst of tears, "I do wish they would put their heads down! I am so very tired of being all
T1   109: 3   more to herself than the kitten. "What would they do at the end of a year? I should be sent to prison
A8   66:10   to give the hedgehog a blow with its head, it would twist itself round and look up in her face, with such a
WOULDN'T (1)
T5   156:42   of one of the oars got fast in the water and wouldn't come out again (so Alice explained it afterwards),
YET (2)
A11   91:31   like, "--for they haven't got much evidence yet," she said to herself. Imagine her surprise, when the
T5   152:10   "I haven't pricked it yet," the Queen said, "but I soon shall--oh, oh, oh!"
YOU (37)
A5   36: 9   said the Caterpillar contemptuously. "Who are you?"
T6   164:13   paid them with; and so you see I ca'n't tell you.)

YOU (cont.)
```
 T9    193:16   Queen  smiled  feebly, and said "And I invite you."
 T9    199:21   he  hobbled  back to his tree, "and it'll let you alone, you know."
 A4     29:14   lessons in here? Why, there's hardly room for you, and no room at all for any lesson-books!"
 A5     36:13   gravely, "I  think  you ought to tell me who you are, first."
 T3    136:18   came  of  it. "Please, would you tell me what you call yourself?" she said timidly. "I think that might help
 T1    110:16   Alice  had been reduced at last to say "Well, you can be one of them, then, and I'll be all the rest." And
 T2    127:20   "Now, here, you see, it takes all the running you can do, to keep in the same place. If you want to get
 T4    148:15   know," Tweedledum  said to his brother: "but you can have the umbrella--it's quite as sharp. Only we must
 T2    121: 5                       "As well as you can," said the Tiger-lily. "And a great deal louder."
 T3    132:27   What sort of insects do you rejoice in, where you come from?" the Gnat inquired.
 A3     25:12   'Let  us  both go  to  law: I will prosecute you?--Come, I'll take no denial: We must have the trial; For
 A4     30:32   to go  down  the  chimney?--Nay,  I  sha'n't! You do it!--That I wo'n't, then!--Bill's got to go down--Here,
 T9    194:28                       "Can you do sums?" Alice said, turning suddenly on the White Queen,
 T5    151:13   there,  at  any  rate," said the Queen. "Were you ever punished?"
 T2    122:36   your  tongue!"  cried  the Tiger-lily. "As if you ever saw anybody! You keep your head under the leaves, and
 T3    135:10   miss  your  lessons.  That's a joke. I wish you had made it."
 T2    123:24   course,"  the  Rose replied. "I was wondering you hadn't got some too. I thought it was the regular rule."
 T4    145:13   only  a  sort  of thing in his dream, what are you, I should like to know?"
 T5    152:41   at this, even in the midst of her tears. "Can you keep from crying by considering things?" she asked.
 A2     19:31   Mouse  in  a  shrill passionate voice. "Would you like cats, if you were me?"
 A7     57: 9                       "Is that the way you manage?" Alice asked.
 A11    91:27   an  undertone to the Queen, "Really, my dear, you must cross-examine the next witness. It quite makes my
 T5    150:21                 "What sort of things do you remember best?" Alice ventured to ask.
 A12    97: 7                 "Who cares for you?" said Alice (she had grown to her full size by this time)
 A5     35: 4                       "Who are you?" said the Caterpillar.
 T9    204:25   to  be  surprised  at  anything  now. "As for you," she repeated, catching hold of the little creature in
 T9    204:17                 "And as for you," she went on, turning fiercely upon the Red Queen, whom
 A10    79: 8                 "Oh, you sing," said the Gryphon. "I've forgotten the words."
 T5    153: 6   "I can believe it without that. Now I'll give you something to believe. I'm just one hundred and one, five
 T12   208:14                       Which do you think it was?
 T9    192:22   to,  and  the  other person always waited for you to begin, you see nobody would ever say anything, so that
 T4    145: 4                 "Why, about you!" Tweedledee exclaimed, clapping his hands triumphantly.
 T5    149:38             "I'm sure I'll take you with pleasure!" the Queen said. "Two pence a week, and jam
 A10    81:29   porpoise  'Keep  back,  please! We don't want you with us!'"
 T9    201:23   like  it,  if  I  were  to cut a slice out of you, you creature!"
```
YOU'D (2)
```
 A8     62:11                       "You'd better not talk!" said Five. "I heard the Queen say only
 T2    127:25             "I know what you'd like!" the Queen said good-naturedly, taking a little
```
YOUR (14)
```
 A10    81:38   the  Gryphon  added "Come, let's hear some of your adventures."
 A8     62:14                 "That's none of your business, Two!" said Seven.
 T1    108:31   "Her  paw went  into  your eye! Well, that's your fault, for keeping your eyes open--if you'd shut them
 T2    123:15                 "But that's not your fault," the Rose added kindly. "You're beginning to fade,
 T1    115:42   very  badly'). "That's  not  a memorandum of your feelings!"
 A5     36: 7                 "Well, perhaps your feelings may be different," said Alice: "all I know is,
 A7     59:15                 "Nobody asked your opinion," said Alice.
 A10    81:17                 "Why, what are your shoes done with?" said the Gryphon. "I mean, what makes
 A7     55: 4             "I didn't know it was your table," said Alice: "it's laid for a great many more than
 T4    145:18             "Well, it's no use your talking about waking him," said Tweedledum, "when you're
 A3     26:19   Let  this  be  a  lesson to you never to lose your temper!" "Hold your tongue, Ma!" said the young Crab, a
 T2    122:36                 "Hold your tongue!" cried the Tiger-lily. "As if you ever saw
 A7     56:14   "Why  should  it?" muttered the Hatter. "Does your watch tell you what year it is?"
 T2    124:11             "I don't know what you mean by your way," said the Queen: "all the ways about here belong to
```
YOURS (1)
```
 A5     43:27   it  happens;  and, if I was, I shouldn't want yours: I don't like them raw."
```

A REVERSE KWIC CONCORDANCE
(SAMPLE ENTRIES)

ANXIOUSLY (23)

A11	86:36	the King put on his spectacles and looked anxiously round, to make out who was talking.
A8	65:30	Rabbit in a low hurried tone. He looked anxiously over his shoulder as he spoke, and then raised himself
A11	91:11	The King looked anxiously at the White Rabbit, who said, in a low voice, "Your
A1	12:38	She ate a little bit, and said anxiously to herself "Which way? Which way?", holding her hand on
T8	182:25	"That's hardly enough," he said, anxiously. "You see the wind is so very strong here. It's as
T3	131:43	kind of insect?" Alice inquired, a little anxiously. What she really wanted to know was, whether it could
T3	134:24	"No, indeed," Alice said, a little anxiously.
A9	76: 9	extras?" asked the Mock Turtle, a little anxiously.
T6	161: 4	Alice his hand. She watched him a little anxiously as she took it. "If he smiled much more the ends of his
T8	183:16	muttering to himself, and Alice watching anxiously for the next tumble.
A3	26: 7	ready to make herself useful, and looking anxiously about her. "Oh, do let me help to undo it!"
A4	27: 2	trotting slowly back again, and looking anxiously about as it went, as if it had lost something; and she
A11	89:26	said--" the Hatter went on, looking anxiously round to see if he would deny it too; but the Dormouse
T8W	13: 4	very unhappy there," she thought, looking anxiously back to see what was the matter. Something like a very
A8	65:26	by the White Rabbit, who was peeping anxiously into her face.
A8	63:10	to--" At this moment, Five, who had been anxiously looking across the garden, called out "The Queen! The
T9	195: 3	"Fan her head!" the Red Queen anxiously interrupted. "She'll be feverish after so much thinking
T1	114:13	"What volcano?" said the King, looking up anxiously into the fire, as if he thought that was the most
A6	48:28	Alice glanced rather anxiously at the cook, to see if she meant to take the hint; but
T9	200:20	before Alice, who looked at it rather anxiously, as she had never had to carve a joint before.
A3	21:16	Mouse in the middle. Alice kept her eyes anxiously fixed on it, for she felt sure she would catch a bad
A4	32:24	about it; and, while she was peering about anxiously among the trees, a little sharp bark just over her head
A6	49:31	baby grunted again, and Alice looked very anxiously into its face to see what was the matter with it. There

ASK (25)

T3	137:27	long. I'll just call and say 'How d'ye do?' and ask them the way out of the wood. If I could only get to
A7	58: 9	on in a mournful tone, "he wo'n't do a thing I ask! It's always six o'clock now."
A11	87: 2	know how to spell "stupid," and that he had to ask his neighbour to tell him. "A nice muddle their
T4	143:24	I wish you were not quite so deaf--/ I've had to ask you twice!'
A9	76:33	Alice did not feel encouraged to ask any more questions about it: so she turned to the Mock
T9	195:36	warmer than one night, then?" Alice ventured to ask.
A7	58:17	come to the beginning again?" Alice ventured to ask.
T5	150:22	things do you remember best?" Alice ventured to ask.
T7	172:35	Alice. "Who are at it again?" she ventured to ask.
A3	26:24	"And who is Dinah, if I might venture to ask the question?" said the Lory.
T6	164:12	(Alice didn't venture to ask what he paid them with; and so you see I ca'n't tell
A1	8:43	at all the right word) "--but I shall have to ask them what the name of the country is, you know. Please,
T9	192:14	on each side: she would have liked very much to ask them how they came there, but she feared it would not
A6	52:18	baby?" said the Cat. "I'd nearly forgotten to ask."
T3	132: 1	this wouldn't be quite a civil question to ask.
A1	9: 3	think me for asking! No, it'll never do to ask: perhaps I shall see it written up somewhere."
A2	15:31	Alice felt so desperate that she was ready to ask help of any one: so, when the Rabbit came near her, she
A8	69: 7	say but "It belongs to the Duchess: you'd better ask her about it."
T6	162: 7	"I never ask advice about growing," Alice said indignantly.
T6	160:14	"Did you think I didn't know the answer to that? Ask another."
T9	199:16	the Frog went on. "Or are you deaf? What did it ask you?"
T8W	13:11	turned to spring over the brook:--but I'll just ask him what's the matter," she added, checking herself on
T6	160:20	"What tremendously easy riddles you ask!" Humpty Dumpty growled out. "Of course I don't think
A7	60:26	"Really, now you ask me," said Alice, very much confused, "I don't think--"
T3	129:21	brush them away--and what fun it'll be when they ask me how I liked my walk. I shall say 'Oh, I liked it

CURIOSITY (10)

T2	123:22	does she wear them?" Alice asked with some curiosity.
A7	56:11	been looking over his shoulder with some curiosity. "What a funny watch!" she remarked. "It tells the day
A1	8: 3	watch to take out of it, and burning with curiosity, she ran across the field after it, and was just in
A10	81:24	made of?" Alice asked in a tone of great curiosity.
T8	182: 8	they for?" Alice asked in a tone of great curiosity.
A8	67:38	and looking at the Cat's head with great curiosity.
T3	133: 6	does it live on?" Alice asked, with great curiosity.
A7	55: 7	looking at Alice for some time with great curiosity, and this was his first speech.
T1	113:17	begin kicking: she watched it with great curiosity to see what would happen next.
T8	181:16	open. Alice looked at it with great curiosity.

DEAL (21)

A6	48:21	in a hoarse growl, "the world would go round a deal faster than it does."
A4	31:20	No more, thank ye; I'm better now--but I'm a deal too flustered to tell you--all I know is, something
T8	186:33	long?" Alice asked, for she had heard a good deal of poetry that day.
A2	18:10	"That was a narrow escape!" said Alice, a good deal frightened at the sudden change, but very glad to find
T7	172: 8	was glad to see that it revived him a good deal. "There's nothing like eating hay when you're faint,"
T2	123:29	that it was the Red Queen. "She's grown a good deal!" was her first remark. She had indeed: when Alice
A11	88:35	curious sensation, which puzzled her a good deal until she made out what it was: she was beginning to
A4	30:37	Bill! I wouldn't be in Bill's place for a good deal: this fireplace is narrow, to be sure; but I think I
A7	60: 1	advantage from the change; and Alice was a good deal worse off than before, as the March Hare had just upset
A5	41:41	She was a good deal frightened by this very sudden change, but she felt
A6	51: 9	"That depends a good deal on where you want to get to," said the Cat.
A5	43:25	"It matters a good deal to me," said Alice hastily; "but I'm not looking for
T8	181:14	very badly, and he had a queer-shaped little deal box fastened across his shoulders, upside-down, and
T9	192:33	"But she said a great deal more than that!" the White Queen moaned, wringing her
T2	121: 5	as you can," said the Tiger-lily. "And a great deal louder."
A2	14: 8	I'm sure I sha'n't be able! I shall be a great deal too far off to trouble myself about you: you must
T3	136: 6	her much, and all she could say, after a great deal of puzzling, was "L, I know it begins with L!"
A11	88: 3	Rabbit hastily interrupted. "There's a great deal to come before that!"

DEAL (cont.)
T6	164: 3	"That's a great deal to make one word mean," Alice said in a thoughtful tone
A3	23:17	the Dodo could not answer without a great deal of thought, and it stood for a long time with one
T6	166: 2	said Alice. "I'm afraid I'm giving you a great deal of trouble."

DEAR (55)
T7	173: 7	"Dear me, no!" said the King. "What an idea!"
T5	155:29	"A dear little crab!" thought Alice. "I should like that."
A2	19:35	cats, if you could only see her. She is such a dear quiet thing," Alice went on, half to herself, as she
T3	131:41	you are a friend," the little voice went on: "a dear friend, and an old friend. And you wo'n't hurt me,
T7	175: 6	a memorandum about her, if you like--She's a dear good creature," he repeated softly to himself, as he
T1	110:23	look exactly like her. Now do try, there's a dear!" And Alice got the Red Queen off the table, and set it
A4	33: 7	"And yet what a dear little puppy it was!" said Alice, as she leant against
T5	149:30	said as she gently put it right for her; "and dear me, what a state your hair is in!"
T3	137: 7	it cried out in a voice of delight. "And, dear me! you're a human child!" A sudden look of alarm came
A12	98: 4	"Wake up, Alice dear!" said her sister. "Why, what a long sleep you've had!"
A2	20:14	So she called softly after it, "Mouse dear! Do come back again, and we wo'n't talk about cats, or
A2	15:37	herself all the time she went on talking. "Dear, dear! How queer everything is to-day! And yesterday
A2	15:11	Oh dear, what nonsense I'm talking!"
A2	16: 7	little! Besides, she's she, and I'm I, and--oh dear, how puzzling it all is! I'll try if I know all the
A2	20:10	pounds! He says it kills all the rats and--oh dear!" cried Alice in a sorrowful tone. "I'm afraid I've
A1	7:13	of the way to hear the Rabbit say to itself "Oh dear! Oh dear! I shall be too late!" (when she thought it
A1	7:13	to hear the Rabbit say to itself "Oh dear! Oh dear! I shall be too late!" (when she thought it over
A2	16:10	six is thirteen, and four times seven is--oh dear! I shall never get to twenty at that rate! However, the
A4	33:10	if I'd only been the right size to do it! Oh dear! I'd nearly forgotten that I've got to grow up again!
A2	17:25	stay down here till I'm somebody else'--but, oh dear!" cried Alice, with a sudden burst of tears, "I do wish
A3	25:27	do.' Said the mouse to the cur, Such a trial, dear sir, With no jury or judge, would be wasting our breath
A12	98:10	kissed her, and said "It was a curious dream, dear, certainly; but now run in to your tea: it's getting
TI	103:23	melancholy maiden! / We are but older children, dear, / Who fret to find our bedtime near.
A2	17:22	their heads down and saying 'Come up again, dear!' I shall only look up and say 'Who am I, then? Tell me
T7	173:30	"Were you happy in prison, dear child?" said Haigha.
A2	15:38	all the time she went on talking. "Dear, dear! How queer everything is to-day! And yesterday things
T3	137:12	ready to cry with vexation at having lost her dear little fellow-traveler so suddenly. "However, I know my
T9	194:36	whispered: "we'll often say it over together, dear. And I'll tell you a secret--I can read words of one
T12	208: 4	and then you can make believe it's oysters, dear!
T4	143:11	good indeed--/ Now, if you're ready, Oysters dear, / We can begin to feed.'
T8W	19:15	call me 'Pig!' / And that is why they do it, dear, / Because I wear a yellow wig."
T12	207: 5	the Looking-glass world. Did you know it, dear?"
T7	173:26	see he's very hungry and thirsty. How are you, dear child?" he went on, putting his arm affectionately
A9	70: 1	think how glad I am to see you again, you dear old thing!" said the Duchess, as she tucked her arm
T12	207:22	"Sit up a little more stiffly, dear!" Alice cried with a merry laugh. "And curtsey while
T12	208:10	it the Red King, Kitty? You were his wife, my dear, so you ought to know--Oh, Kitty, do help to settle it!
T1	110: 4	Kitty, can you play chess? Now, don't smile, my dear. I'm asking it seriously. Because, when we were playing
A6	50: 4	tears. "If you're going to turn into a pig, my dear," said Alice, seriously, "I'll have nothing more to do
A9	70:18	her ear. "You're thinking about something, my dear, and that makes you forget to talk. I ca'n't tell you
A3	26:18	opportunity of saying to her daughter "Ah, my dear! Let this be a lesson to you never to lose your temper!
A1	9: 8	her saucer of milk at tea-time. Dinah, my dear! I wish you were down here with me! There are no mice
A3	26:39	sure she's the best cat in the world! Oh, my dear Dinah! I wonder if I shall ever see you any more!" And
A4	27: 4	to itself, "The Duchess! The Duchess! Oh my dear paws! Oh my fur and whiskers! She'll get me executed,
T12	208: 6	dreamed it all. This is a serious question, my dear, and you should not go on licking your paw like that--
A8	64:11	upon her arm, and timidly said "Consider, my dear: she is only a child!"
T1	115: 9	"Oh! please don't make such faces, my dear!" she cried out, quite forgetting that the King
T7	170: 7	Alice. "Did you happen to meet any soldiers, my dear, as you came through the wood?"
A12	96:18	she had this fit'--you never had fits, my dear, I think?" he said to the Queen.
A8	68: 4	the Queen, who was passing at the moment, "My dear! I wish you would have this cat removed!"
T1	115:36	strong for him, and at last he panted out "My dear! I really must get a thinner pencil. I ca'n't manage
T1	115:22	The King was saying "I assure you, my dear, I turned cold to the very ends of my whiskers!"
A3	22:25	his Normans--' How are you getting on now, my dear?" it continued, turning to Alice as it spoke.
T3	131:24	in her ear, "Never mind what they all say, my dear, but take a return-ticket every time the train stops."
A11	91:27	in an undertone to the Queen, "Really, my dear, you must cross-examine the next witness. It quite
T1	110: 9	that came wriggling down among my pieces. Kitty dear, let's pretend--" And here I wish I could tell you half

DELIGHT (9)
T3	137: 7	"I'm a Fawn!" it cried out in a voice of delight. "And, dear me! you're a human child!" A sudden look of
T2	125:27	and so there are!" she added in a tone of delight, and her heart began to beat quick with excitement as
T7	170: 6	sent them all!" the King cried in a tone of delight, on seeing Alice. "Did you happen to meet any soldiers,
A5	42: 7	free at last!" said Alice in a tone of delight, which changed into alarm in another moment, when she
A4	32:35	air off all its feet at once, with a yelp of delight, and rushed at the stick, and made believe to worry it:
T5	156: 7	Alice cried in a sudden transport of delight. "There really are--and such beauties!"
T9	202: 1	The White Queen laughed with delight, and stroked Alice's cheek. Then she began:
T6	166:24	are white, / I sing this song for your delight--
A1	9:42	golden key in the lock, and to her great delight it fitted!

DISTANCE (11)
T2	127:36	she said, putting in a peg to mark the distance, "I shall give you your directions--have another
A10	85: 3	"The trial's beginning!" was heard in the distance.
T3	131:16	Then a very gentle voice in the distance said, "She must be labeled 'Lass, with care,' you know
A8	68:11	on, as she heard the Queen's voice in the distance, screaming with passion. She had already heard her
A9	74:17	far before they saw the Mock Turtle in the distance, sitting sad and lonely on a little ledge of rock, and,
A12	99: 2	while the lowing of the cattle in the distance would take the place of the Mock Turtle's heavy sobs.
A3	26:42	a little pattering of footsteps in the distance, and she looked up eagerly, half hoping that the Mouse
A2	15:25	she heard a little pattering of feet in the distance, and she hastily dried her eyes to see what was coming.
A4	33: 5	the puppy's bark sounded quite faint in the distance.

DISTANCE (cont.)
```
T7   170:18        "To  be  able  to see Nobody! And at that distance too! Why, it's as much as I can do to see real people,
A1     8:35   say it over) "--yes, that's about the right distance--but then I wonder what Latitude or Longitude I've got
```
FACT (15)
```
A6    48: 6     know  much,"  said the Duchess; "and that's a fact."
A11   88:23   jury,  who  instantly made a memorandum of the fact.
A8    63: 6     at Two. Two began, in a low voice, "Why, the fact is, you see, Miss, this here ought to have been a red
T9   203: 1                                                In fact it was rather difficult for her to keep in her place
A1    11: 7   taste it, and, finding it very nice (it had, in fact, a sort of mixed flavour of cherry-tart, custard,
T8   186:18   don't believe that pudding ever was cooked! In fact, I don't believe that pudding ever will be cooked! And
A6    48: 1     know that Cheshire-Cats always grinned; in fact, I didn't know that cats could grin."
T3   129:12        this was anything but a regular bee: in fact, it was an elephant--as Alice soon found out, though
T8   186: 4   said. "My mind goes on working all the same. In fact, the more head-downwards I am, the more I keep
A2    15:13   head struck against the roof of the hall: in fact she was now rather more than nine feet high, and she at
T6   159:25   thought, as he never said anything to her; in fact, his last remark was evidently addressed to a tree--so
T1   112: 6   in the old room," thought Alice: "warmer, in fact, because there'll be no one here to scold me away from
A9    76: 5             "We had the best of educations--in fact, we went to school every day--"
A12   94:12   directed at all," said the White Rabbit: "in fact, there's nothing written on the outside." He unfolded
T8   186:16   repeated as before: "not the next day. In fact," he went on, holding his head down, and his voice
```
GRAVELY (10)
```
T6   164:10     Humpty Dumpty went on, wagging his head gravely from side to side, "for to get their wages, you know."
T9   195: 9   "Fiddle-de-dee's not English," Alice replied gravely.
T8   184:36   "I haven't tried it yet," the Knight said, gravely; "so I ca'n't tell for certain--but I'm afraid it would
T9   194:23                     Alice said, as gravely as she could, "They might go different ways." But she
T8W   20:11     as she could. At last she managed to say gravely, "I can bite anything I want."
T4   147:25             "You know," he added very gravely, "it's one of the most serious things that can possibly
A3    23:31         "Of course," the Dodo replied very gravely. "What else have you got in your pocket?" it went on,
A5    36:12     and she drew herself up and said, very gravely, "I think you ought to tell me who you are, first."
A12   94:35   Begin at the beginning," the King said, very gravely, "and go on till you come to the end: then stop."
T8   183:11   plenty of practice," the Knight said very gravely: "plenty of practice!"
```
HANDS (53)
```
T5   156:32   as, with flushed cheeks and dripping hair and hands, she scrambled back into her place, and began to
T4   139:22   in a visit is to say 'How d'ye do?' and shake hands!" And here the two brothers gave each other a hug, and
T4   139:24   out the two hands that were free, to shake hands with her.
T6   160:39   and, to show you I'm not proud, you may shake hands with me!" And he grinned almost from ear to ear, as he
AI     3: 5   / By little arms are plied, / While little hands make vain pretence / Our wanderings to guide.
A12   94:26             There was a general clapping of hands at this: it was the first really clever thing the King
T4   139:25             Alice did not like shaking hands with either of them first, for fear of hurting the
T4   139:27   out of the difficulty, she took hold of both hands at once: the next moment they were dancing round in a
T9   193: 6             deny that, even if you tried with both hands."
T9   204:14   jumped up and seized the tablecloth with both hands: one good pull, and plates, dishes, guests, and candles
T8   181:10   Knight, putting back his shaggy hair with both hands, and turning his gentle face and large mild eyes to
T8   180:13   by side. When they got up again, they shook hands, and then the Red Knight mounted and galloped off.
T8   190:24                     So they shook hands, and then the Knight rode slowly away into the forest.
T4   139:24   other a hug, and then they held out the two hands that were free, to shake hands with her.
A5    36:37                     Alice folded her hands, and began:--
A2    17: 4   'How doth the little--'," and she crossed her hands on her lap as if she were saying lessons, and began to
T5   152:24       you scream now?" Alice asked, holding her hands ready to put over her ears again.
T9   192:34   that!" the White Queen moaned, wringing her hands. "Oh, ever so much more than that!"
T5   152:37   like that!" cried the poor Queen, wringing her hands in despair. "Consider what a great girl you are.
T12  207:16   other. "Now Kitty!" she cried, clapping her hands triumphantly. "Confess that was what you turned into!"
T9   195:26   down and nervously clasping and unclasping her hands, "we had such a thunderstorm last Tuesday--I mean one
A5    42:18   As there seemed to be no chance of getting her hands up to her head, she tried to get her head down to them,
T6   159:15   egg he is!" she said aloud, standing with her hands ready to catch him, for she was every moment expecting
T5   152: 7   steam-engine, that Alice had to hold both her hands over her ears.
T9   203: 8   Queen, seizing Alice's hair with both her hands. "Something's going to happen!"
A10   82:34   nothing: she had sat down with her face in her hands, wondering if anything would ever happen in a natural
A5    43:33   she still held the pieces of mushroom in her hands, and she set to work very carefully, nibbling first at
T5   155:18   suddenly the needles turned into oars in her hands, and she found they were in a little boat, gliding
T1   113: 6   little "Oh!" of surprise, she was down on her hands and knees watching them. The chessmen were walking
T1   110: 1       dropping the ball of worsted to clap her hands. "And I do so wish it was true! I'm sure the woods look
T5   155:35   some of the needles into her hair, as her hands were full. "Feather, I say!"
A2    18: 1       As she said this she looked down at her hands, and was surprised to see that she had put on one of
T7   178: 9   before she dropped to her knees, and put her hands over her ears, vainly trying to shut out the dreadful
T8   191: 4   exclaimed in a tone of dismay, as she put her hands up to something very heavy, that fitted tight all
A8    63:16   three gardeners, oblong and flat, with their hands and feet at the corners: next the ten courtiers: these
A8    66: 4   had to double themselves up and stand on their hands and feet, to make the arches.
A5    42:14     have my shoulders got to? And oh, my poor hands, how is it I ca'n't see you?" She was moving them about
T4   144:29     cried, and they each took one of Alice's hands, and led her up to where the King was sleeping.
T4   140: 1             Then they let go of Alice's hands, and stood looking at her for a minute: there was a
T5   158:14     she said "I never put things into people's hands--that would never do--you must get it for yourself."
T6   162:34     one knee over the other and clasped his hands round it, "they gave it me--for an un-birthday present
T8   185:14   me, I can assure you!" he said. He raised his hands in some excitement as he said this, and instantly
T7   171: 9   breath to say a word, and could only wave his hands about, and make the most fearful faces at the poor King
A12   95:22   we've heard yet," said the King, rubbing his hands; "so now let the jury--"
T4   145: 4   about you!" Tweedledee exclaimed, clapping his hands triumphantly. "And if he left off dreaming about you,
T7   172:25   whisper it," said the Messenger, putting his hands to his mouth in the shape of a trumpet and stooping so
T7   175: 9   moment the Unicorn sauntered by them, with his hands in his pockets. "I had the best of it this time?" he
T7   175:20   to introduce her, and spreading out both his hands towards her in an Anglo-Saxon attitude. "We only found
T9   196:22   said to Alice, taking one of the White Queen's hands in her own, and gently stroking it: "she means well,
```

HANDS (cont.)

T6	166:15	Humpty Dumpty, stretching out one of his great hands, "I can repeat poetry as well as other folk, if it
T7	170:25	like an eel, as he came along, with his great hands spread out like fans on each side.)
T9	193: 7	"I don't deny things with my hands," Alice objected.
A12	98:18	little Alice herself: once again the tiny hands were clasped upon her knee, and the bright eager eyes

HERSELF (163)

A1	12:24	followed it), and sometimes she scolded herself so severely as to bring tears into her eyes; and once
A4	34: 7	She stretched herself up on tiptoe, and peeped over the edge of the mushroom,
T4	144:22	unpleasant characters--" Here she checked herself in some alarm, at hearing something that sounded to her
A10	80:19	often seen them at dinn----" she checked herself hastily.
A10	78:11	began to say "I once tasted--" but checked herself hastily, and said "No never") "--so you can have no
A4	33: 8	a buttercup to rest herself, and fanned herself with one of the leaves. "I should have liked teaching
A7	59:18	know what to say to this: so she helped herself to some tea and bread-and-butter, and then turned to
T5	153:33	Queen, who seemed to have suddenly wrapped herself up in wool. Alice rubbed her eyes, and looked again.
A11	86:34	in a loud indignant voice; but she stopped herself hastily, for the White Rabbit cried out "Silence in the
T3	137:32	back, but in another moment she recovered herself, feeling sure that they must be TWEEDLEDUM AND
A4	29:13	"Oh, you foolish Alice!" she answered herself. "How can you learn lessons in here? Why, there's
A1	12:19	it was too slippery; and when she had tired herself out with trying, the poor little thing sat down and
A6	53:15	of the left-hand bit of mushroom, and raised herself to about two feet high: even then she walked up towards
A1	12:26	to box her own ears for having cheated herself in a game of croquet she was playing against herself,
T7	177: 6	Alice had seated herself on the bank of a little brook, with the great dish on
T8	187: 5	what the song is called'?" Alice corrected herself.
T6	162:16	was her turn now.) "At least," she corrected herself on second thoughts, "a beautiful cravat, I should have
T9	195:21	the thunder--no, no!" she hastily corrected herself. "I meant the other way."
T5	154: 9	Alice had not got: so she contented herself with turning round, looking at the shelves as she came
T9	192: 7	the crown might come off: but she comforted herself with the thought that there was nobody to see her, "and
A12	98:34	sat on, with closed eyes, and half believed herself in Wonderland, though she knew she had but to open them
A9	70:23	if only you can find it." And she squeezed herself up closer to Alice's side as she spoke.
T1	119:10	in the air, and was rather glad to find herself walking again in the natural way.
A2	18:11	at the sudden change, but very glad to find herself still in existence. "And now for the garden!" And she
T5	157: 5	into her place, very much relieved to find herself still in the boat.
A3	21: 7	it seemed quite natural to Alice to find herself talking familiarly with them, as if she had known them
A12	97:11	anger, and tried to beat them off, and found herself lying on the bank, with her head in the lap of her
T2	123:42	she lost sight of her in a moment, and found herself walking in at the front-door again.
T2	127: 8	quite exhausted, they stopped, and she found herself sitting on the ground, breathless and giddy.
T3	132:17	melt away as she touched it, and she found herself sitting quietly under a tree--while the Gnat (for that
T2	124: 4	not been walking a minute before she found herself face to face with the Red Queen, and full in sight of
A1	8: 9	about stopping herself before she found herself falling down what seemed to be a very deep well.
A7	60:42	Once more she found herself in the long hall, and close to the little glass table.
A1	9:28	Rabbit was no longer to be seen: she found herself in a long, low hall, which was lit up by a row of lamps
A7	61: 5	down the little passage: and then--she found herself at last in the beautiful garden, among the bright
T2	120:23	afterwards), and the next moment she found herself actually walking in at the door.
A4	32:17	ran off as hard as she could, and soon found herself safe in a thick wood.
A12	99: 4	sister of hers would, in the after-time, be herself a grown woman; and how she would keep, through all her
A12	98:17	First, she dreamed about little Alice herself: once again the tiny hands were clasped upon her knee,
T2	123:32	here she was, half a head taller than Alice herself!
A3	26: 6	"A knot!" said Alice, always ready to make herself useful, and looking anxiously about her. "Oh, do let me
A2	19: 9	was only a mouse, that had slipped in like herself.
A2	18: 5	She got up and went to the table to measure herself by it, and found that, as nearly as she could guess,
A1	12:23	leave off this minute!" She generally gave herself very good advice (though she very seldom followed it),
A2	18: 9	she dropped it hastily, just in time to save herself from shrinking away altogether.
A3	23:30	"But she must have a prize herself, you know," said the Mouse.
T9	192: 4	tone (she was always rather fond of scolding herself), "It'll never do for you to be lolling about on the
A5	43:36	shorter, until she had succeeded in bringing herself down to her usual height.
T5	152: 9	as soon as there was a chance of making herself heard. "Have you pricked your finger?"
T8W	13:12	him what's the matter," she added, checking herself on the very edge. "If I once jump over, everything will
T3	129:18	I wo'n't go just yet," she went on, checking herself just as she was beginning to run down the hill, and
T1	114: 5	as the poor little Lily was nearly screaming herself into a fit, she hastily picked up the Queen and set her
A2	15:37	as the hall was very hot, she kept fanning herself all the time she went on talking. "Dear, dear! How
A1	8: 9	had not a moment to think about stopping herself before she found herself falling down what seemed to be
T2	120:30	"O Tiger-lily!" said Alice, addressing herself to one that was waving gracefully about in the wind, "I
T9	203: 6	the edge of the table, and managed to pull herself down again.
T3	131:21	by the telegraph--" "She must draw the train herself the rest of the way--," and so on.
A8	63:41	said Alice very politely; but she added, to herself, "Why, they're only a pack of cards, after all. I
A6	46:36	so. "It's really dreadful," she muttered to herself, "the way all the creatures argue. It's enough to drive
A12	99: 3	Lastly, she pictured to herself how this same little sister of hers would, in the
T6	159:27	a tree--so she stood and softly repeated to herself:--
A4	28:21	and one foot up the chimney, and said to herself "Now I can do no more, whatever happens. What will
T8W	13:18	rheumatism, I should think," Alice said to herself, and she stooped over him, and said very kindly, "I
A6	47: 6	too much pepper in that soup!" Alice said to herself, as well as she could for sneezing.
T1	119: 4	stairs quickly and easily, as Alice said to herself. She just kept the tips of her fingers on the hand-rail
A4	27:27	"How queer it seems," Alice said to herself, "to be going messages for a rabbit! I suppose Dinah'll
T8	190:26	to see him off, I expect," Alice said to herself, as she stood watching him. "There he goes! Right on
T3	137:18	along it. "I'll settle it," Alice said to herself, "when the road divides and they point different ways
A4	27:18	"He took me for his housemaid," she said to herself as she ran. "How surprised he'll be when he finds out
A8	67:12	made it out to be a grin, and she said to herself "It's the Cheshire-Cat: now I shall have somebody to
A11	86:16	there. "That's the judge," she said to herself, "because of his great wig."
A7	61: 1	I'll manage better this time," she said to herself, and began by taking the little golden key, and
T8	180: 1	what the Rules of Battle are," she said to herself, as she watched the fight, timidly peeping out from her
A6	52:25	"I've seen hatters before," she said to herself: "the March Hare will be much the most interesting, and

HERSELF (cont.)

```
T6   159: 5        "It ca'n't be anybody else!" she said to herself. "I'm as certain of it, as if his name were written all
A9    73:20          "Come, that's a good thing!" she said to herself, for she had felt quite unhappy at the number of
A3    26:37   wish I hadn't mentioned Dinah!" she said to herself in a melancholy tone. "Nobody seems to like her, down
A5    41:38        "And now which is which?" she said to herself, and nibbled a little of the right-hand bit to try the
A12   93: 8       "not that it signifies much," she said to herself; "I should think it would be quite as much use in the
T8   179: 7   I wasn't dreaming, after all," she said to herself, "unless--unless we're all part of the same dream. Only
A4    28: 5   interesting is sure to happen," she said to herself, "whenever I eat or drink anything: so I'll just see
T8   187:28   tune isn't his own invention," she said to herself: "it's 'I give thee all, I can no more.'" She stood and
A6    50:16   the wood. "If it had grown up," she said to herself, "it would have made a dreadfully ugly child: but it
T4   138: 5      at the back of the collar," she said to herself.
T5   156:24   the boat wo'n't tipple over!" she said to herself. "Oh, what a lovely one! Only I couldn't quite reach it
A4    32: 3   face. "I'll put a stop to this," she said to herself, and shouted out "You'd better not do that again!",
A9    70: 7          "When I'm a Duchess," she said to herself (not in a very hopeful tone, though), "I wo'n't have
A11   91:31   haven't got much evidence yet," she said to herself. Imagine her surprise, when the White Rabbit read out,
T8   191: 7     there without my knowing it?" she said to herself, as she lifted it off, and set it on her lap to make
A6    46:23   "But perhaps he ca'n't help it," she said to herself; "his eyes are so very nearly at the top of his head.
T3   132: 9   Square, that's some comfort!" she said to herself. In another moment she felt the carriage rise straight
T4   140: 5   do to say 'How d'ye do?' now," she said to herself: "we seem to have got beyond that, somehow!"
T1   116: 6   in some language I don't know," she said to herself.
A2    18:20   case I can go back by railway," she said to herself. (Alice had been to the seaside once in her life, and
T4   147:23      by the time they're ready!" she said to herself, as she arranged a bolster round the neck of Tweedledee
A4    30:36   down the chimney, has he?" said Alice to herself. "Why, they seem to put everything upon Bill! I
A4    32:18   first thing I've got to do," said Alice to herself, as she wandered about in the wood, "is to grow to my
T2   120: 1   see the garden far better," said Alice to herself, "if I could get to the top of that hill: and here's a
A1    12:21   no use in crying like that!" said Alice to herself rather sharply. "I advise you to leave off this minute!
A1    12: 8   "for it might end, you know," said Alice to herself, "in my going out altogether, like a candle. I wonder
A1     8:23                    "Well!" thought Alice to herself. "After such a fall as this, I shall think nothing of
A5    41:30   The other side of what?" thought Alice to herself.
T1   109: 2   punishments?" she went on, talking more to herself than the kitten. "What would they do at the end of a
A2    19:35   a dear quiet thing," Alice went on, half to herself, as she swam lazily about in the pool, "and she sits
T9   196: 1   a low voice, more as if she were talking to herself. "He came to the door with a corkscrew in his hand--"
T1   107:14   of the great arm-chair, half talking to herself and half asleep, the kitten had been having a grand
A5    43:39   to it in a few minutes, and began talking to herself, as usual, "Come, there's half my plan done now! How
T3   137:29   gets dark!" So she wandered on, talking to herself as she went, till, on turning a sharp corner, she came
T8   190:29   round the horse--" So she went on talking to herself, as she watched the horse walking leisurely along the
T9   194:24   ways." But she couldn't help thinking to herself "What dreadful nonsense we are talking!"
A2    15: 3              And she went on planning to herself how she would manage it. "They must go by the carrier,"
T7   172:40   And they trotted off, Alice repeating to herself, as she ran, the words of the old song:--
A4    28:12   She hastily put down the bottle, saying to herself "That's quite enough--I hope I sha'n't grow any more--
A4    31: 1   the chimney close above her: then, saying to herself "This is Bill", she gave one sharp kick, and waited to
A1     9:12   to get rather sleepy, and went on saying to herself, in a dreamy sort of way, "Do cats eat bats? Do cats
T6   168:37   walked away: but she couldn't help saying to herself, as she went, "of all the unsatisfactory--" (she
A6    50:19   do very well as pigs, and was just saying to herself "if one only knew the right way to change them--" when
A6    53:16   up towards it rather timidly, saying to herself "Suppose it should be raving mad after all! I almost
A6    50: 8       Alice was just beginning to think to herself, "Now, what am I to do with this creature, when I get
T1   118:27   (You see she didn't like to confess, even to herself, that she couldn't make it out at all.) "Somehow it
T5   149: 1   and kept repeating something in a whisper to herself that sounded like "Bread-and-butter, bread-and-butter,"
A11   86:24   this last word two or three times over to herself, being rather proud of it: for she thought, and rightly
T1   108: 6   sometimes to the kitten, and sometimes to herself. Kitty sat very demurely on her knee, pretending to
T3   134: 6   with its head on fire, and had thought to herself, "I wonder if that's the reason insects are so fond of
T5   155:13   with so many?" the puzzled child thought to herself. "She gets more and more like a porcupine every minute!
A9    70: 5   in such a pleasant temper, and thought to herself that perhaps it was only the pepper that had made her
T3   130:10                           Alice thought to herself "Then there's no use in speaking." The voices didn't
T9   196:17                           Alice thought to herself "I never should try to remember my name in the middle
T5   149:23   single thing's crooked," Alice thought to herself, "and she's all over pins!--May I put your shawl
T9   199:34   noise of cheering, and Alice thought to herself "Thirty times three makes ninety. I wonder if any one's
A4    31:34   dead silence instantly, and Alice thought to herself "I wonder what they will do next! If they had any sense
T4   145:28   they're talking nonsense," Alice thought to herself: "and it's foolish to cry about it." So she brushed
T3   131:13   "It sounds like a horse," Alice thought to herself. And an extremely small voice, close to her ear, said
T9   203:23   very like birds they look," Alice thought to herself, as well as she could in the dreadful confusion that
T1   113: 4   room so tidy as the other," Alice thought to herself, as she noticed several of the chessmen down in the
A9    74:30   spoke for some minutes. Alice thought to herself "I don't see how he can ever finish, if he doesn't
A9    71: 4   finding morals in things!" Alice thought to herself.
T9   195:16   never asked questions," Alice thought to herself.
A5    41:19   Alice in a piteous tone. And she thought to herself "I wish the creatures wouldn't be so easily offended!"
T2   124:17   "I'll try it when I go home," she thought to herself, "the next time I'm a little late for dinner."
T3   135:26   I certainly won't go back," she thought to herself, and this was the only way to the Eighth Square.
T7   178:11   'drum them out of town,'" she thought to herself, "nothing ever will!"
T5   158:11   down on the counter. For she thought to herself, "They mightn't be at all nice, you know."
A12   93:32   but it doesn't matter a bit," she thought to herself.
T8W   14: 6   on and leaving him, but she thought to herself "Perhaps it's only pain that makes him so cross." So
T6   162:20   subject. "If only I knew," she thought to herself, "which was neck and which was waist!"
A7    59: 6              Alice tried a little to fancy to herself what such an extraordinary way of living would be like,
T3   135:27   must be the wood," she said thoughtfully to herself, "where things have no names. I wonder what'll become
A1    12:38   She ate a little bit, and said anxiously to herself "Which way? Which way?", holding her hand on the top of
A4    32:37   Alice dodged behind a great thistle, to keep herself from being run over; and, the moment she appeared on
T2   120:12   she ran against it before she could stop herself.
T7   177:20               "She's kept none for herself, anyhow," said the Lion. "Do you like plum-cake,
T8   179:18   Alice was more frightened for him than for herself at the moment, and watched him with some anxiety as he
```

HERSELF (cont.)

A2	16: 2	she knew that were of the same age as herself, to see if she could have been changed for any of them
A4	34: 4	growing near her, about the same height as herself; and, when she had looked under it, and on both sides
A5	44: 6	to go near the house till she had brought herself down to nine inches high.
T5	149:11	any conversation at all, she must manage it herself. So she began rather timidly: "Am I addressing the
T5	153:20	and this time she succeeded in catching it herself. "I've got it!" she cried in a triumphant tone. "Now
A4	33: 8	as she leant against a buttercup to rest herself., and fanned herself with one of the leaves. "I should
A1	12:27	in a game of croquet she was playing against herself, for this curious child was very fond of pretending to
A5	36:12	making such very short remarks, and she drew herself up and said, very gravely, "I think you ought to tell
T9	195:14	But the Red Queen drew herself up rather stiffly, and said "Queens never make bargains
T8	191: 1	* * * * * * * * * * * * across, and threw herself down to rest on a lawn as soft as moss, with little

HURRY (12)

A12	92: 3	last few minutes, and she jumped up in such a hurry that she tipped over the jury-box with the edge of her
A9	77:11	a day did you do lessons?" said Alice, in a hurry to change the subject.
A5	42:24	when a sharp hiss made her draw back in a hurry: a large pigeon had flown into her face, and was
A1	10:20	little Alice was not going to do that in a hurry. "No, I'll look first," she said, "and see whether it's
T4	143: 5	out of breath, / And all of us are fat!' / 'No hurry!' said the Carpenter. / They thanked him much for that.
A4	32:39	the stick, and tumbled head over heels in its hurry to get hold of it: then Alice, thinking it was very
A11	89:21	didn't!" the March Hare interrupted in a great hurry.
A2	20: 1	"I wo'n't indeed!" said Alice, in a great hurry to change the subject of conversation. "Are you--are
A2	15:29	the other: he came trotting along in a great hurry, muttering to himself, as he came, "Oh! The Duchess,
A7	58:33	little sisters," the Dormouse began in a great hurry; "and their names were Elsie, Lacie, and Tillie; and
A12	94: 4	said the White Rabbit, jumping up in a great hurry: "this paper has just been picked up."
A4	32:26	just over her head made her look up in a great hurry.

IDEA (28)

T3	129:13	elephant--as Alice soon found out, though the idea quite took her breath away at first. "And what enormous
T8	182:37	she walked on in silence, puzzling over the idea, and every now and then stopping to help the poor
T8	184:38	He looked so vexed at the idea, that Alice changed the subject hastily. "What a
T3	132: 8	this, though Alice felt a little nervous at the idea of trains jumping at all. "However, it'll take us into
A12	97: 1	"Stuff and nonsense!" said Alice loudly. "The idea of having the sentence first!"
A12	92:11	in her head, and she had a vague sort of idea that they must be collected at once and put back into
T7	173: 7	"Dear me, no!" said the King. "What an idea!"
A3	23:26	Alice had no idea what to do, and in despair she put her hand in her
A10	78:11	and said "No never") "--so you can have no idea what a delightful thing a Lobster-Quadrille is!"
A8	67:26	are, nobody attends to them--and you've no idea how confusing it is all the things being alive: for
T8	186:27	he interrupted, quite eagerly: "but you've no idea what a difference it makes, mixing it with other things
A3	25: 4	it while the mouse was speaking, so that her idea of the tale was something like this:--
T2	123:18	Alice didn't like this idea at all: so, to change the subject, she asked "Does she
T8W	18: 6	A curious idea came into Alice's head. Almost every one she had met
A7	58:10	A bright idea came into Alice's head. "Is that the reason so many
A4	32: 6	cakes as they lay on the floor, and a bright idea came into her head. "If I eat one of these cakes," she
A5	42:32	"I haven't the least idea what you're talking about," said Alice.
T7	170:35	the King remarked simply, without the least idea that he was joining in the game, while Alice was still
A4	32:24	difficulty was, that she had not the smallest idea how to set about it; and, while she was peering about
A7	56:30	"I haven't the slightest idea," said the Hatter.
A1	8:36	I've got to?" (Alice had not the slightest idea what Latitude was, or Longitude either, but she thought
A2	18:18	she was up to her chin in saltwater. Her first idea was that she had somehow fallen into the sea, "and in
A1	9:36	on it but a tiny golden key, and Alice's first idea was that this might belong to one of the doors of the
T3	129:15	enormous flowers they must be!" was her next idea. "Something like cottages with the roofs taken off, and
A9	77:17	This was quite a new idea to Alice, and she thought it over a little before she
A5	43:21	This was such a new idea to Alice, that she was quite silent for a minute or two
T2	126:24	Not that Alice had any idea of doing that. She felt as if she would never be able
T6	160:17	on the ground?" Alice went on, not with any idea of making another riddle, but simply in her

IMPATIENTLY (11)

A8	63:38	Idiot!" said the Queen, tossing her head impatiently; and turning to Alice, she went on: "What's your name,
A7	56:24	"The Dormouse shook its head impatiently, and said, without opening its eyes, "Of course, of
A3	26:15	do!" But the Mouse only shook its head impatiently, and walked a little quicker.
T7	174: 1	"Speak, ca'n't you!" Haigha cried impatiently. But Hatta only munched away, and drank some more tea.
T7	171: 6	"Don't I tell you?" the King repeated impatiently. "I must have two--to fetch and carry. One to fetch,
T6	160: 6	name enough!" Humpty Dumpty interrupted impatiently. "What does it mean?"
T9	199:17	"Nothing!" Alice said impatiently. "I've been knocking at it!"
T9	193: 1	but the Red Queen interrupted her impatiently.
T9	204:11	Alice's chair, and beckoning to her impatiently to get out of its way.
A10	81:25	of course," the Gryphon replied, rather impatiently: "any shrimp could have told you that."
T3	131:26	"Indeed I sha'n't!" Alice said rather impatiently. "I don't belong to this railway journey at all--I was

KEY (9)

A1	12:35	"and if it makes me grow larger, I can reach the key; and if it makes me grow smaller, I can creep under the
A1	9:37	alas! either the locks were too large, or the key was too small, but at any rate it would not open any of
A1	9:41	fifteen inches high: she tried the little golden key in the lock, and to her great delight it fitted!
A2	18:14	door was shut again, and the little golden key was lying on the glass table as before, "and things are
A7	61: 1	herself, and began by taking the little golden key, and unlocking the door that led into the garden. Then
A1	12:15	she found she had forgotten the little golden key, and when she went back to the table for it, she found
A2	15:14	high, and she at once took up the little golden key and hurried off to the garden door.
A1	9:35	glass: there was nothing on it but a tiny golden key, and Alice's first idea was that this might belong to
A1	10:13	to the table, half hoping she might find another key on it, or at any rate a book of rules for shutting

KNOW (219)

T5	154: 3	"I don't quite know yet," Alice said very gently. "I should like to look
A7	59:18	Alice did not quite know what to say to this: so she helped herself to some tea
A12	95: 2	He sent them word I had not gone / (We know it to be true): / If she should push the matter on, /
A12	95:39	on muttering over the verses to himself: "'We know it to be true'--that's the jury, of course--'If she

KNOW (cont.)

A3	22:18	"I know what 'it' means well enough, when I find a thing," said
T2	127:25	"I know what you'd like!" the Queen said good-naturedly, taking
T3	131:41	"I know you are a friend," the little voice went on: "a dear
T4	139: 5	"I know what you're thinking about," said Tweedledum; "but it
T4	145:28	"I know they're talking nonsense," Alice thought to herself:
T6	162:27	"I know it's very ignorant of me," Alice said, in so humble a
T9	194:41	"I know that!" Alice cried eagerly. "You take some flour--"
T9	196: 9	"I know what he came for," said Alice: "he wanted to punish the
A8	64: 3	"How should I know?" said Alice, surprised at her own courage. "It's no
A3	26:22	"I wish I had our Dinah here, I know I do!" said Alice aloud, addressing nobody in
A2	16: 8	oh dear, how puzzling it all is! I'll try if I know all the things I used to know. Let me see: four times
A3	22: 2	"Are you all ready? This is the driest thing I know. Silence all round, if you please! 'William the
A9	72: 3	"Oh, I know!" exclaimed Alice, who had not attended to this last
T3	136: 6	say, after a great deal of puzzling, was "L, I know it begins with L!"
A5	36: 8	feelings may be different," said Alice: "all I know is, it would feel very queer to me."
A4	31:21	but I'm a deal too flustered to tell you--all I know is, something comes at me like a Jack-in-the-box, and
T3	137:13	little fellow-traveler so suddenly. "However, I know my name now," she said: "that's some comfort. Alice--
A2	16: 6	at all; and I'm sure I ca'n't be Mabel, for I know all sorts of things, and she, oh, she knows such a very
A5	43:23	of adding "You're looking for eggs, I know that well enough; and what does it matter to me whether
A4	28: 4	she uncorked it and put it to her lips. "I know something interesting is sure to happen," she said to
T8W	14:18	rather sulkily. "Nobody's hindering you, that I know of."
T2	120:15	with her. "I'm not going in again yet. I know I should have to get through the Looking-glass again--
T3	130:16	shall dream about a thousand pounds to-night, I know I shall!" thought Alice.
T5	151:16	"And you were all the better for it, I know!" the Queen said triumphantly.
A5	35: 7	I hardly know, Sir, just at present--at least I know who I was when I got up this morning, but I think I
A7	56:40	"Perhaps not," Alice cautiously replied; "but I know I have to beat time when I learn music."
T1	110:40	our books, only the words go the wrong way: I know that, because I've held up one of our books to the
A6	51: 5	began, rather timidly, as she did not at all know whether it would like the name: however, it only
T8W	17: 6	Wasp: "wait till you have it, and then you'll know. And when you catches it, just try tying a yellow
T2	122:25	the ground," said the Tiger-lily. "Then you'll know why."
A12	95:17	Don't let him know she liked them best, / For this must ever be / A secret
A9	73:12	"No," said Alice. "I don't even know what a Mock Turtle is."
A12	94:31	of the sort!" said Alice. "Why, you don't even know what they're about!"
T2	122:31	good reason, and Alice was quite pleased to know it. "I never thought of that before!" she said.
T8	189:22	it reminds me so / Of that old man I used to know--/ Whose look was mild, whose speech was slow, / Whose
A2	16: 8	is! I'll try if I know all the things I used to know. Let me see: four times five is twelve, and four times
A3	23: 3	said Alice; not that she much wanted to know, but the Dodo had paused as if it thought that somebody
T3	131:44	a little anxiously. What she really wanted to know was, whether it could sting or not, but she thought
T4	145:13	in his dream, what are you, I should like to know?"
T1	110:35	so wish I could see that bit! I want so much to know whether they've a fire in the winter: you never can
A9	74:26	lady," said the Gryphon, "she wants for to know your history, she do."
A6	45: 9	all over their heads. She felt very curious to know what it was all about, and crept a little way out of
T3	131: 4	eyes and said in a loud voice, "She ought to know her way to the ticket-office, even if she doesn't know
T3	131: 1	her, (he was dressed in white paper), "ought to know which way she's going, even if she doesn't know her own
T12	208:11	You were his wife, my dear, so you ought to know--Oh, Kitty, do help to settle it! I'm sure your paw can
A3	23:12	off when they liked, so that it was not easy to know when the race was over. However, when they had been
T6	159:24	Alice didn't know what to say to this: it wasn't at all like conversation
T4	140: 2	was a rather awkward pause, as Alice didn't know how to begin a conversation with people she had just
A6	48: 1	"I didn't know that Cheshire-Cats always grinned; in fact, I didn't
A7	55: 4	"I didn't know it was your table," said Alice: "it's laid for a great
T8	181:23	"I didn't know it," the Knight said, a shade of vexation passing over
T9	193:17	"I didn't know I was to have a party at all," said Alice; "but, if
T2	128:14	"I--I had to make one--just then," Alice faltered out.
T6	160:14	cried Humpty Dumpty. "Did you think I didn't know the answer to that? Ask another."
A6	48: 2	Cheshire-Cats always grinned; in fact, I didn't know that cats could grin."
A11	87: 2	she could even make out that one of them didn't know how to spell "stupid," and that he had to ask his
T6	168:21	"I shouldn't know you again if we did meet," Humpty Dumpty replied in a
A5	41:10	"I don't know," said the Caterpillar.
A6	48: 4	"I don't know of any that do," Alice said very politely, feeling
A7	56:37	"I don't know what you mean," said Alice.
A10	80:20	"I don't know where Dinn may be," said the Mock Turtle; "but, if
T2	124:11	"I don't know what you mean by your way," said the Queen: "all the
T5	149:26	"I don't know what's the matter with it!" the Queen said, in a
T6	163:24	"I don't know what you mean by 'glory,'" Alice said.
T8	181: 1	"I don't know," Alice said doubtfully. "I don't want to be anybody's
T9	193:27	"I don't know," said Alice. "I lost count."
T9	199:14	"I don't know what you mean," she said.
A7	58:21	"I'm afraid I don't know one," said Alice, rather alarmed at the proposal.
T9	197: 1	tried to obey the first direction: "and I don't know any soothing lullabies."
T1	116: 5	read, "--for it's all in some language I don't know," she said to herself.
T7	177: 3	"I'm sure I don't know," the Lion growled out as he lay down again. "There was
T4	139:36	'Here we go round the mulberry bush.' I don't know when I began it, but somehow I felt as if I'd been
T6	161: 9	meet behind," she thought: "And then I don't know what would happen to his head! I'm afraid it would come
A3	22:31	"Speak English!" said the Eaglet. "I don't know the meaning of half those long words, and, what's more,
T3	134:25	"And yet I don't know," the Gnat went on in a careless tone: "only think how
A12	95:32	as we needn't try to find any. And yet I don't know," he went on, spreading out the verses on his knee, and
T8	181:37	out--or the bees keep the mice out, I don't know which."
A6	48: 6	"You don't know much," said the Duchess; "and that's a fact."
T6	162:42	"You don't know what you're talking about!" cried Humpty Dumpty. "How

KNOW (cont.)

T7	177:11	"You don't know how to manage Looking-glass cakes," the Unicorn
A9	76:31	Well, then," the Gryphon went on, "if you don't know what to uglify is, you <u>are</u> a simpleton."
A9	73:23	lying fast asleep in the sun. (If you don't know what a Gryphon is, look at the picture.) "Up, lazy
T3	131: 5	way to the ticket-office, even if she doesn't know her alphabet!"
T3	131: 1	know which way she's going, even if she doesn't know her own name!"
T9	193:11	she wants to deny <u>something</u>--only she doesn't know what to deny!"
T6	162:26	thing," he said at last, "when a person doesn't know a cravat from a belt!"
T2	127:39	Alice did not know what to say to this, but luckily the Queen did not wait
A3	21:10	would only say, "I'm older than you, and must know better." And this Alice would not allow, without
A7	57:16	You know the song, perhaps?"
T4	147:25	"You know," he added very gravely, "it's one of the most serious
A7	57:11	last March--just before <u>he</u> went mad, you know--" (pointing his teaspoon at the March Hare,) "--it was
A3	26:11	poor Alice. "But you're so easily offended, you know!"
T9	192: 5	like that! Queens have to be dignified, you know!"
T8	187: 7	Means': but that's only what it's <u>called</u>, you know!"
A9	76:27	"Never heard of uglifying!" it exclaimed. "You know what to beautify is, I suppose?"
T12	207: 5	all through the Looking-glass world. Did you know it, dear?"
T9	192:35	"So you did, you know," the Red Queen said to Alice. "Always speak the truth
T9	196:12	you ca'n't think!" ("She <u>never</u> could, you know," said the Red Queen.) "And part of the roof came off,
T3	131:30	"something about 'you <u>would</u> if <u>you</u> could,' you know."
A1	12: 8	nervous about this; "for it might end, you know," said Alice to herself, "in my going out altogether,
T4	148:14	"There's only one sword, you know," Tweedledum said to his brother: "but <u>you</u> can have the
T6	165: 6	"Of course it is. It's called 'wabe' you know, because it goes a long way before it, and a long way
T1	112:14	and the very clock on the chimney-piece (you know you can only see the back of it in the Looking-glass)
T5	158:12	to herself, "They mightn't be at all nice, you know."
T5	153: 2	"nobody can do two things at once, you know. Let's consider your age to begin with--how old are you
T2	123:16	added kindly. "You're beginning to fade, you know--and then one ca'n't help one's petals getting a little
T7	176:12	and the Unicorn): "fair play with the cake, you know!"
T4	146:17	little white thing. "Not a rattle-<u>snake</u>, you know," she added hastily, thinking that he was frightened:
A12	95:31	the King, "that saves a world of trouble, you know, as we needn't try to find any. And yet I don't know,"
T9	199:21	back to his tree, "and it'll let <u>you</u> alone, you know."
T3	131:17	"She must be labeled 'Lass, with care,' you know--"
A10	80: 8	friend <u>replied</u>. / <u>There is another shore</u>, <u>you know</u>, <u>upon the other side</u>. / <u>The further off from England</u>
A10	83: 6	"How <u>could</u> he turn them out with his nose, you know?"
T3	131:15	that--something about 'horse' and 'hoarse,' you know."
T9	194:33	"Of course you know your ABC?" said the Red Queen.
A10	80:21	if you've seen them so often, of course you know what they're like?"
A3	22:17	Mouse replied rather crossly: "of course you know what 'it' means."
T4	142: 5	and <u>neat</u>--/ And <u>this was</u> odd, <u>because</u>, <u>you know</u>, / They <u>hadn't any feet</u>.
A1	9:10	catch a bat, and that's very like a mouse, you know. But do cats eat bats, I wonder?" And here Alice began
T2	128: 8	"A pawn goes two squares in its first move, you know. So you'll go <u>very</u> quickly through the Third Square--by
T3	129: 8	be bees--nobody ever saw bees a mile off, you know--" and for some time she stood silent, watching one of
A8	63: 9	out, we should all have our heads cut off, you know. So you see, Miss, we're doing our best, afore she
A3	23:30	"But she must have a prize herself, you know," said the Mouse.
A7	55:22	I mean what I say--that's the same thing, you know."
T8	185:11	get me out. I was as fast as--as lightning, you know."
T8W	18: 4	wear it," the Wasp said. "When I was young, you know, my ringlets used to wave--"
T1	109:12	so gently? And then it covers them up snug, you know, with a white quilt; and perhaps it says 'Go to sleep,
T1	108: 1	you better manners! You <u>ought</u> to, Dinah, you know you ought!" she added, looking reproachfully at the old
T8W	18: 2	comb hair with--your wig's so <u>very</u> rough, you know."
T9	195:34	many as five nights together--for warmth, you know."
T8	181: 5	end of the wood--and then I must go back, you know. That's the end of my move."
A12	94:10	was written to nobody, which isn't usual, you know."
A11	90:21	"If that's all you know about it, you may stand down," continued the King.
T2	126: 2	the world--if this <u>is</u> the world at all, you know. Oh, what fun it is! How I <u>wish</u> I was one of them! I
T1	110:36	a fire in the winter: you never <u>can</u> tell, you know, unless our fire smokes, and then smoke comes up in
T2	123: 1	the leaves, and snore away there, till you know no more what's going on in the world, than if you were
T4	145:19	you're only one of the things in his dream. You know very well you're not real."
T9	192:38	to call yourself so? You ca'n't be a Queen, you know, till you've passed the proper examination. And the
T9	198: 8	There <u>ought</u> to be one marked 'Queen,' you know--"
A10	78:26	"Then, you know," the Mock Turtle went on, "you throw the--"
A5	41: 9	"only one doesn't like changing so often, you know."
T2	121: 7	"It isn't manners for us to begin, you know," said the Rose, "and I really was wondering when you'd
A7	57:18	"It goes on, you know," the Hatter continued, "in this way:--
A6	46:34	the Footman. "That's the first question, you know."
T7	175:13	have run him through with your horn, you know."
T1	108:11	"Do you know what to-morrow is, Kitty?" Alice began. "You'd have
T1	108:21	"Do you know, I was so angry, Kitty," Alice went on, as soon as they
T9	201:28	"Do you know, I've had such a quantity of poetry repeated to me
T8	181:22	can get <u>out</u>," Alice gently remarked. "Do you know the lid's open?"
A2	19:13	harm in trying." So she began: "O Mouse, do you know the way out of this pool? I am very tired of swimming
T12	207:30	you were so untidy in my dream--Dinah! Do you know that you're scrubbing a White Queen? Really, it's most
T7	175:28	curling up into a smile as she began: "Do you know, I always thought Unicorns were fabulous monsters, too?
T9	195: 7	right again now," said the Red Queen. "Do you know Languages? What's the French for fiddle-de-dee?"
A10	81:11	that, if you like," said the Gryphon. "Do you know why it's called a whiting?"
T8W	19: 7	<u>extremely plain</u>: / But <u>what was</u> <u>I</u> to <u>do</u>, <u>you know?</u> / <u>My ringlets would</u> <u>not grow again</u>.
A5	43:18	eat eggs quite as much as serpents do, you know."
A12	93:16	"What do you know about this business?" the King said to Alice.
A6	51:25	"How do you know I'm mad?" said Alice.

KNOW (cont.)

A6	51:28	at all: however, she went on: "And how do you know that you're mad?"
T1	108:35	What, you were thirsty, were you? How do you know she wasn't thirsty too? Now for number three: you
T9	201:32	every poem was about fishes in some way. Do you know why they're so fond of fishes, all about here?"
T1	110:21	that you're the Red Queen, Kitty! Do you know, I think if you sat up and folded your arms, you'd look
T3	135: 4	and of course you wouldn't have to go, you know."
T7	170:37	Messenger's called Hatta. I must have two, you know--to come and go. One to come, and one to go."
T4	147:11	"only she must help us to dress up, you know."
A2	20: 5	to show you! A little bright-eyed terrier, you know, with oh, such long curly brown hair! And it'll fetch
A2	20: 8	half of them--and it belongs to a farmer, you know, and he says it's so useful, it's worth a hundred
T8	179:28	"She's my prisoner, you know!" the Red Knight said at last.
A7	56:10	his first remark, "It was the best butter, you know."
T8	182:35	it hangs down--things never fall upwards, you know. It's a plan of my own invention. You may try it if you
T6	164:11	from side to side, "for to get their wages, you know."
T5	156:36	she picked them? Even real scented rushes, you know, last only a very little while--and these, being
T2	123:21	She's one of the kind that has nine spikes, you know."
T7	170:12	his book. "I couldn't send all the horses, you know, because two of them are wanted in the game. And I
A1	8:44	ask them what the name of the country is, you know. Please, Ma'am, is this New Zealand? Or Australia?"
T8	184: 5	to keep your balance properly. Like this, you know--"
T3	135:42	to get under the--under the--under this, you know!" putting her hand on the trunk of the tree. "What does
A10	79: 6	Gryphon. "We can do it without lobsters, you know. Which shall sing?"
A7	60:24	and the moon, and memory, and muchness--you know you say things are 'much of a muchness'--did you ever
T3	135:33	name! That's just like the advertisements, you know, when people lose dogs--'answers to the name of "Dash":
T6	163:22	"And only one for birthday presents, you know. There's glory for you!"
A12	96: 8	that must be what he did with the tarts, you know--"
A4	29: 2	and yet--and yet--it's rather curious, you know, this sort of life! I do wonder what can have happened
T9	195:28	I mean one of the last set of Tuesdays, you know."
A7	59: 3	"They couldn't have done that, you know," Alice gently remarked. "They'd have been ill."
T1	108:39	not been punished for any of them yet. You know I'm saving up all your punishments for Wednesday week--
T5	149:29	"It ca'n't go straight, you know, if you pin it all on one side," Alice said as she
A7	57: 6	"but then--I shouldn't be hungry for it, you know."
T9	199:19	do that--" the Frog muttered. "Wexes it, you know." Then he went up and gave the door a kick with one of
A9	70:15	then they wouldn't be so stingy about it, you know--"
T9	194: 3	"Nine from eight I ca'n't, you know," Alice replied very readily: "but--"
T2	122: 7	"Didn't you know that?" cried another Daisy. And here they all began
T9	197:17	in all the History of England--it couldn't, you know, because there never was more than one Queen at a time.
T8	186:40	"Or else it doesn't, you know. The name of the song is called 'Haddocks' Eyes.'"
A6	46:21	you might knock, and I could let you out, you know." He was looking up into the sky all the time he was
T9	202:31	"We must support you, you know," the White Queen whispered, as Alice got up to do it,
A7	59:32	little sisters--they were learning to draw, you know--"
T9	197: 8	"And now you know the words," she added, as she put her head down on
A10	81:22	a deep voice, "are done with whiting. Now you know."
A9	74:22	his fancy, that: he hasn't got no sorrow, you know. Come on!"
A5	36: 4	turn into a chrysalis--you will some day, you know--and then after that into a butterfly, I should think
T5	150: 9	other day: to-day isn't any other day, you know."
T4	138:11	wax-works," he said, "you ought to pay, you know. Wax-works weren't made to be looked at for nothing.
T6	166: 5	home'--meaning that they'd lost their way, you know."
A9	74:12	her fancy that: they never executes nobody, you know. Come on!"
T2	125:11	her at last: "a hill ca'n't be a valley, you know. That would be nonsense--"
A11	88:43	talk nonsense," said Alice more boldly: "you know you're growing too."
T1	111: 4	our passage as far as you can see, only you know it may be quite different on beyond. Oh, Kitty, how
A3	24:14	"You promised to tell me your history, you know," said Alice, "and why it is you hate--C and D," she
T6	166:14	"As to poetry, you know," said Humpty Dumpty, stretching out one of his great
T6	159:20	explained. "And some eggs are very pretty, you know," she added, hoping to turn her remark into a sort of
T2	122:11	to side, and trembling with excitement. "They know I ca'n't get at them!" it panted, bending its quivering
A5	35: 6	Alice replied, rather shyly, "I--I hardly know, Sir, just at present--at least I know who I was when I
A4	31:19	("That's Bill," thought Alice), "Well, I hardly know--No more, thank ye; I'm better now--but I'm a deal too
T1	118:28	fill my head with ideas--only I don't exactly know what they are! However, somebody killed something:

LAST (84)

A4	31:16	Last came a little feeble, squeaking voice ("That's Bill,"
A4	28:19	her head. Still she went on growing, and, as a last resource, she put one arm out of the window, and one
A7	57:11	mournfully. "Not I!" he replied. "We quarreled last March--just before he went mad, you know--" (pointing
A8	63:26	King's crown on a crimson velvet cushion; and, last of all this grand procession, came THE KING AND THE
T8	184:23	things. Now, I daresay you noticed, the last time you picked me up, that I was looking rather
A6	47:16	She said the last word with such sudden violence that Alice quite jumped;
A6	49:28	it be murder to leave it behind?" She said the last words out loud, and the little thing grunted in reply
T9	195:27	a thunderstorm last Tuesday--I mean one of the last set of Tuesdays, you know."
T8	190:12	As the Knight sang the last words of the ballad, he gathered up the reins, and
T5	153:30	Be-etter! Be-e-e-etter! Be-e-ehh!" The last word ended in a long bleat, so like a sheep that Alice
T3	135:23	side of it: it looked much darker than the last wood, and Alice felt a little timid about going into it
A12	95:24	it," said Alice, (she had grown so large in the last few minutes that she wasn't a bit afraid of
A12	92: 2	of the moment how large she had grown in the last few minutes, and she jumped up in such a hurry that she
A11	89: 6	court, "Bring me the list of the singers in the last concert!" on which the wretched Hatter trembled so,
T2	128:29	never knew, but exactly as she came to the last peg, she was gone. Whether she vanished into the air,
T6	161:15	on a little too fast: let's go back to the last remark but one."
T2	128:27	to say "Good-bye," and then hurried on to the last.
A7	60:33	half hoping that they would call after her: the last time she saw them, they were trying to put the Dormouse
T5	149:20	Queen. "I've been a-dressing myself for the last two hours."
T1	107: 3	having its face washed by the old cat for the last quarter of an hour (and bearing it pretty well,
T8	190:35	turned to run down the hill: "and now for the last brook, and to be a Queen! How grand it sounds!" A very

LAST (cont.)

T9	195:27	her hands, "we had such a thunderstorm last Tuesday--I mean one of the last set of Tuesdays, you
T5	150: 6	next Wednesday: and of course the crime comes last of all."
T2	1__: 4	Alice said, not choosing to notice the Rose's last remark.
T6	159:26	as he never said anything to her; in fact, his last remark was evidently addressed to a tree--so she stood
A11	86:24	"I suppose they are the jurors." She said this last word two or three times over to herself, being rather
A7	60:10	to the Dormouse, not choosing to notice this last remark.
A9	72: 4	exclaimed Alice, who had not attended to this last remark. "It's a vegetable. It doesn't look like one,
A8	69: 4	everybody executed, all round. (It was this last remark that had made the whole party look so grave and
A3	21:13	At last the Mouse, who seemed to be a person of some authority
T9	200:18	At last the Red Queen began. "You've missed the soup and fish,"
T3	134:22	by humming round and round her head: at last it settled again and remarked "I suppose you don't want
T1	110:15	only two of them, and Alice had been reduced at last to say "Well, you can be one of them, then, and I'll be
T5	155:36	do you say 'Feather' so often?" Alice asked at last, rather vexed. "I'm not a bird!"
T7	170:22	hand. "I see somebody now!" she exclaimed at last. "But he's coming very slowly--and what curious
T2	125:26	just like a large chess-board!" Alice said at last. "There ought to be some men moving about somewhere--
T6	162:25	"It is a--most--provoking--thing," he said at last, "when a person doesn't know a cravat from a belt!"
T7	175:18	"What--is--this?" he said at last.
T4	140: 6	"I hope you're not much tired?" she said at last.
T5	154:16	"Things flow about so here!" she said at last in a plaintive tone, after she had spent a minute or so
T5	156:30	"The prettiest are always further!" she said at last with a sigh at the obstinacy of the rushes in growing
T6	162:41	"I like birthday presents best," she said at last.
T3	136:12	"What do you call yourself?" the Fawn said at last. Such a soft sweet voice it had!
T5	154: 1	"What is it you want to buy?" the Sheep said at last, looking up for a moment from her knitting.
T8	179:28	my prisoner, you know!" the Red Knight said at last.
T8W	20:10	turned into a cough as well as she could. At last she managed to say gravely, "I can bite anything I want
A4	30:15	all!" "Do as I tell you, you coward!", and at last she spread out her hand again, and made another snatch
T1	115:36	but Alice was too strong for him, and at last he panted out "My dear! I really must get a thinner
T7	169: 2	and threes, then ten or twenty together, and at last in such crowds that they seemed to fill the whole
T3	137:25	"I do believe," said Alice at last, "that they live in the same house! I wonder I never
A3	23:20	of him), while the rest waited in silence. At last the Dodo said "Everybody has won, and all must have
A5	35: 2	at each other for some time in silence: at last the Caterpillar took the hookah out of its mouth, and
A5	42: 7	"Come, my head's free at last!" said Alice in a tone of delight, which changed into
A9	74:32	"Once," said the Mock Turtle at last, with a deep sigh, "I was a real Turtle."
T4	142: 9	another four; / And thick and fast they came at last, / And more, and more, and more--/ All hopping through
T9	197:21	every minute, and sounded more like a tune: at last she could even make out words, and she listened so
T8	190:37	to the edge of the brook. "The Eighth Square at last!" she cried as she bounded * * * * * * * * * * * * * *
A4	30:22	for some time without hearing anything more: at last came a rumbling of little cart-wheels, and the sound of
A7	61: 5	little passage: and then--she found herself at last in the beautiful garden, among the bright flower-beds
A9	75: 6	who felt ready to sink into the earth. At last the Gryphon said to the Mock Turtle "Drive on, old
T5	151:22	each "better," till it got quite to a squeak at last.
A10	78: 5	shaking him and punching him in the back. At last the Mock Turtle recovered his voice, and, with tears
A4	33: 1	and barking hoarsely all the while, till at last it sat down a good way off, panting, with its tongue
T1	114:19	he slowly struggled up from bar to bar, till at last she said "Why, you'll be hours and hours getting to the
T2	120: 5	sharp corners), "but I suppose it will at last. But how curiously it twists! It's more like a
A5	43: 3	as I was thinking I should be free of them at last, they must needs come wriggling down from the sky! Ugh,
T8	182:19	fit, you see," he said, as they got it in at last; "there are so many candlesticks in the bag." And he
A9	74:40	were still little," the Mock Turtle went on at last, more calmly, though still sobbing a little now and
A3	21: 9	had quite a long argument with the Lory, who at last turned sulky, and would only say, "I'm older than you,
T2	125:11	said Alice, surprised into contradicting her at last: "a hill ca'n't be a valley, you know. That would be
A5	41:36	this a very difficult question. However, at last she stretched her arms round it as far as they would go
A3	24:12	be patted on the back. However, it was over at last, and they sat down again in a ring, and begged the
A10	80:14	Alice, feeling very glad that it was over at last: "and I do so like that curious song about the whiting!
T3	130:20	microscope, and then through an opera-glass. At last he said "You're traveling the wrong way," and shut up
T2	127: 6	"Faster! Faster!" And they went so fast that at last they seemed to skim through the air, hardly touching
A5	42: 2	room to open her mouth; but she did it at last, and managed to swallow a morsel of the left-hand bit.
T8	181: 8	however, she managed to shake him out of it at last.
T1	116:13	She puzzled over this for some time, but at last a bright thought struck her. "Why, it's a Looking-glass
T9	198:12	and rang in vain for a long time; but at last a very old Frog, who was sitting under a tree, got up
A5	36:28	minutes it puffed away without speaking; but at last it unfolded its arms, took the hookah out of its mouth
T2	123:45	everywhere for the Queen (whom she spied out at last, a long way off), she thought she would try the plan,
T2	126:27	we nearly there?" Alice managed to pant out at last.
T6	159:32	"That last line is much too long for the poetry," she added,
T5	156:36	them? Even real scented rushes, you know, last only a very little while--and these, being dream-rushes

LEAST (17)

T6	159:12	the opposite direction, and he didn't take the least notice of her, she thought he must be a stuffed figure
A7	60:31	instantly, and neither of the others took the least notice of her going, though she looked back once or
A5	42:32	"I haven't the least idea what you're talking about," said Alice.
T7	170:35	Hill," the King remarked simply, without the least idea that he was joining in the game, while Alice was
A6	52:27	as this is May, it wo'n't be raving mad--at least not so mad as it was in March." As she said this, she
A7	55:21	"I do," Alice hastily replied; "at least--at least I mean what I say--that's the same thing, you
T4	146: 6	it. "No, I don't think it is," he said: "at least--not under here. Nohow."
A4	29: 8	up now," she added in a sorrowful tone: "at least there's no room to grow up any more here."
T3	132:30	"because I'm rather afraid of them--at least the large kinds. But I can tell you the names of some
T2	127:21	want to get somewhere else, you must run at least twice as fast as that!"
A8	67:26	don't seem to have any rules in particular: at least, if there are, nobody attends to them--and you've no
A8	67:17	she thought, "till its ears have come, or at least one of them." In another minute the whole head appeared
T1	119: 3	room in a moment, and ran down stairs--or, at least, it wasn't exactly running, but a new invention for
T2	120: 3	here's a path that leads straight to it--at least, no, it doesn't do that--" (after going a few yards
A5	35: 7	"I--I hardly know, Sir, just at present--at least I know who I was when I got up this morning, but I

LEAST (cont.)
A7   55:21   "I do," Alice hastily replied; "at least--at least I mean what I say--that's the same thing, you know."
T6   162:16   choosing subjects, it was her turn now.) "At least," she corrected herself on second thoughts, "a
LITTLE (253)
T2   123:44   A little provoked, she drew back, and, after looking everywhere
T7   175:12   "A little--a little," the King replied, rather nervously. "You
T9   196:32   "A little kindness--and putting her hair in papers--would do
A3   26:20   Hold your tongue, Ma!" said the young Crab, a little snappishly. "You're enough to try the patience of an
A12   93:10   As soon as the jury had a little recovered from the shock of being upset, and their
A7   59: 6   Alice tried a little to fancy to herself what such an extraordinary way of
A3   26:15   only shook its head impatiently, and walked a little quicker.
T6   163:17   it round for him. "I thought it looked a little queer. As I was saying, that seems to be done right--
T12 207:20   and pretended not to see it: but it looked a little ashamed of itself, so I think it must have been the Red
A5   41:39   is which?" she said to herself, and nibbled a little of the right-hand bit to try the effect. The next
T9   198: 9   Just then the door opened a little way, and a creature with a long beak put its head out
A6   51: 6   like the name: however, it only grinned a little wider. "Come, it's pleased so far," thought Alice, and
A10   81:19   Alice looked down at them, and considered a little before she gave her answer. "They're done with blacking
A7   55:39   Alice considered a little, and then said "The fourth."
T6   162:40   Alice considered a little. "I like birthday presents best," she said at last.
T8W   16:17   The Wasp considered a little. "Well, no," he said: "it's when you hold up your head
T2   124:15   Alice wondered a little at this, but she was too much in awe of the Queen to
T3   131:43   "What kind of insect?" Alice inquired, a little anxiously. What she really wanted to know was, whether
A7   56:23   again," said the Hatter, and he poured a little hot tea upon its nose.
A6   52:22   Alice waited a little, half expecting to see it again, but it did not appear,
T8W   20: 2   heartily: "and I think if your wig fitted a little better, they wouldn't tease you quite so much."
T3   134:24   "No, indeed," Alice said, a little anxiously.
T8W   15:13   It's in this newspaper, though," Alice said a little timidly.
T8   183: 5   The Knight looked very much surprised, and a little offended at the remark. "What makes you say that?" he
A1   10:15   up like telescopes: this time she found a little bottle on it ("which certainly was not here before,"
A2   15:25   After a time she heard a little pattering of feet in the distance, and she hastily
A4   30:40   as she could, and waited till she heard a little animal (she couldn't guess of what sort it was)
A4   29:37   did not get hold of anything, but she heard a little shriek and a fall, and a crash of broken glass, from
A3   26:42   In a little while, however, she again heard a little pattering of footsteps in the distance, and she looked
T8   184:37   for certain--but I'm afraid it would be a little hard."
A5   41:14   "Well, I should like to be a little larger, Sir, if you wouldn't mind," said Alice: "three
T1   114: 2   been hurt by the fall. He had a right to be a little annoyed with the Queen, for he was covered with ashes
T5   156: 1   This offended Alice a little, so there was no more conversation for a minute or two,
A6   47:12   "Please would you tell me," said Alice, a little timidly, for she was not quite sure whether it was good
A8   63: 3   "Would you tell me, please," said Alice, a little timidly, "why you are painting those roses?"
A10   81:41   beginning from this morning," said Alice a little timidly; "but it's no use going back to yesterday,
T9   201: 1   leg of mutton got up in the dish and made a little bow to Alice; and Alice returned the bow, not knowing
A10   79: 3   "Would you like to see a little of it?" said the Mock Turtle.
T3   129: 4   on tiptoe in hopes of being able to see a little further. "Principal rivers--there are none. Principal
T1   111: 2   we come to the passage. You can just see a little peep of the passage in Looking-glass House, if you
T5   157: 9   "I wish it hadn't let go--I should so like a little crab to take home with me!" But the Sheep only laughed
A9   76: 9   "With extras?" asked the Mock Turtle, a little anxiously.
T7   175:12   "A little--a little," the King replied, rather nervously. "You shouldn't
A4   29:20   "Fetch me my gloves this moment!" Then came a little pattering of feet on the stairs. Alice knew it was the
A4   31:16   Last came a little feeble, squeaking voice ("That's Bill," thought Alice),
T3   137: 1   "I'll tell you, if you'll come a little further on," the Fawn said. "I ca'n't remember here."
T5   150:12   the Queen said kindly: "it always makes one a little giddy at first--"
T8   184:25   "You were a little grave," said Alice.
T5   155:38   "You are," said the Sheep: "you're a little goose."
A5   43:24   what does it matter to me whether you're a little girl or a serpent?"
A1   12:38   She ate a little bit, and said anxiously to herself "Which way? Which
A8   65:38   ears--" the Rabbit began. Alice gave a little scream of laughter. "Oh, hush!" the Rabbit whispered in
A12   97:10   and came flying down upon her; she gave a little scream, half of fright and half of anger, and tried to
A8   68:26   not escape again, and went back to have a little more conversation with her friend.
A6   48:24   glad to get an opportunity of showing off a little of her knowledge. "Just think what work it would make
T1   113: 1   in the Looking-glass) had got the face of a little old man, and grinned at her.
T9   204:20   had suddenly dwindled down to the size of a little doll, and was now on the table, merrily running round
T7   177: 6   Alice had seated herself on the bank of a little brook, with the great dish on her knees, and was sawing
A9   74:41   at last, more calmly, though still sobbing a little now and then, "we went to school in the sea. The master
T2   127:26   the Queen said good-naturedly, taking a little box out of her pocket. "Have a biscuit?"
T8   187: 1   don't understand," the Knight said, looking a little vexed. "That's what the name is called. The name really
T9   201:19   was so large that she couldn't help feeling a little shy with it, as she had been with the mutton; however,
A2   15:41   I almost think I can remember feeling a little different. But if I'm not the same, the next question
T7   173: 9   enough--" Alice panted out, after running a little further, "to stop a minute--just to get--one's breath
T4   143:14   not on us!' the Oysters cried, / Turning a little blue. / 'After such kindness, that would be / A dismal
T2   127:16   in our country," said Alice, still panting a little, "you'd generally get to somewhere else--if you ran
T1   119: 9   hold of the door-post. She was getting a little giddy with so much floating in the air, and was rather
T2   123:17   then one ca'n't help one's petals getting a little untidy."
T8   188:28   / And so go on from day to day / Getting a little fatter. / I shook him well from side to side, / Until
T1   114:11   As soon as she had recovered her breath a little, she called out to the White King, who was sitting
T9   192:32   other, and the Red Queen remarked, with a little shudder, "She says she only said 'if'--"
T8   184:17   than a live horse," Alice said, with a little scream of laughter, in spite of all she could do to
A5   44: 1   she came suddenly upon an open place, with a little house in it about four feet high. "Whoever lives there
T8W   20: 9   Alice began with a little scream of laughter, which she turned into a cough, as
A7   60:22   by the Hatter, it woke up again with a little shriek, and went on: "--that begins with an M, such as
T1   113: 5   the cinders; but in another moment, with a little "Oh!" of surprise, she was down on her hands and knees

LITTLE (cont.)

```
T2    124:19  said looking at her watch: "open your mouth a little wider when you speak, and always say 'your Majesty.'"
T3    136:10      to  stroke  it; but it only started back a little, and then stood looking at her again.
A4     30:38  narrow,  to be sure; but I think I can kick a little!"
A10    79:13                "Will you walk a little faster?" said a whiting to a snail, / "There's a
T9    200:22            "You look a little shy: let me introduce you to that leg of mutton," said
A9     72:26      sharply,  for  she was beginning to feel a little worried.
T1    116: 2  watching  the White King (for she was still a little anxious about him, and had the ink all ready to throw
T1    114:15  me--up," panted the Queen, who was still a little out of breath. "Mind you come up--the regular way--
A2     19: 6  heard something splashing about in the pool a little way off, and she swam nearer to make out what it was:
T5    156:26  quite  reach it." And it certainly did seem a little provoking ("almost as if it happened on purpose," she
T4    148:10      said Alice,  still hoping to make them a little ashamed of fighting for such a trifle.
T2    124:17  she  thought to herself, "the next time I'm a little late for dinner."
A5     43: 9                "I--I'm a little girl," said Alice, rather doubtfully, as she remembered
T6    161: 4  and offered Alice his hand. She watched him a little anxiously as she took it. "If he smiled much more the
T1    115: 2      she  thought  she might as well dust him a little, he was so covered with ashes.
T9    201:29  poetry repeated to me to-day," Alice began, a little frightened at finding that, the moment she opened her
T4    145:24            Alice ran a little way into the wood, and stopped under a large tree. "It
A3     26:41  she  felt  very lonely and low-spirited. In a little while, however, she again heard a little pattering of
T5    155:18  in her  hands, and she found they were in a little boat, gliding along between banks: so there was nothing
T5    153:37  could  make  nothing more of it: she was in a little dark shop, leaning with her elbows on the counter, and
A4t    27: 1                THE RABBIT SENDS IN A LITTLE BILL
T6    161:15      However,  this  conversation is going on a little too fast: let's go back to the last remark but one."
A1     12:31                Soon her eye fell on a little glass box that was lying under the table: she opened it
T8    183:14  it as  heartily as she could. They went on a little way in silence after this, the Knight with his eyes
A9     74:17  in the  distance, sitting sad and lonely on a little ledge of rock, and, as they came nearer, Alice could
A9     70:31  said, by way of keeping up the conversation a little.
A1      9:34            Suddenly she came upon a little three-legged table, all made of solid glass: there was
A4     28: 2  to  leave the room, when her eye fell upon a little bottle that stood near the looking-glass. There was no
T3    136:19  she  said timidly. "I think that might help a little."
A4     32:33  Hardly  knowing what she did, she picked up a little bit of stick, and held it out to the puppy: whereupon
T2    121:12      remarked.  "If only her petals curled up a little more, she'd be all right."
T12   207:22                "Sit up a little more stiffly, dear!" Alice cried with a merry laugh.
A9     77:18  new  idea to Alice, and she thought it over a little before she made her next remark. "Then the eleventh day
T9    192:21  rule," said Alice, who was always ready for a little argument, "and if you only spoke when you were spoken
A9     70:17  forgotten the Duchess by this time, and was a little startled when she heard her voice close to her ear.
T1    115:16      and  lay perfectly still; and Alice was a little alarmed at what she had done, and went round the room
T4    144:13  Walrus  best,"  said Alice: "because he was a little sorry for the poor oysters."
A6     50:20  right  way to change them--" when she was a little startled by seeing the Cheshire-Cat sitting on a bough
T2    125:17  afraid  from  the Queen's tone that she was a little offended: and they walked on in silence till they got
A10    82: 2  she  first  saw the White Rabbit. She was a little nervous about it, just at first, the two creatures got
T9    201:34  spoke  to  the Red Queen, whose answer was a little wide of the mark. "As to fishes," she said, very slowly
A1      9:40  had  not  noticed before, and behind it was a little door about fifteen inches high: she tried the little
A6     46: 2  tone,  only changing the order of the words a little, "From the Queen. An invitation for the Duchess to play
A4     32:25  peering  about  anxiously among the trees, a little sharp bark just over her head made her look up in a
T5    158:22  trees  growing  here! And actually here's a little brook! Well, this is the very queerest shop I ever saw!
T5    155:16                "Yes, a little--but not on land--and not with needles--" Alice was
T4    147:33            "Well--yes--a little," Alice replied gently.
T5    153:18  gust of wind blew the Queen's shawl across a little brook. The Queen spread out her arms again and went
A3     26:29  see  her after the birds! Why, she'll eat a little bird as soon as look at it!"
T1    107:21      catching  up  the kitten, and giving it a little kiss to make it understand that it was in disgrace.
A5     36: 5  a butterfly, I should think you'll feel it a little queer, wo'n't you?"
T3    135:24  darker  than  the last wood, and Alice felt a little timid about going into it. However, on second thoughts,
T3    132: 7      satisfied  with  this, though Alice felt a little nervous at the idea of trains jumping at all. "However,
A5     36:11  beginning  of the conversation. Alice felt a little irritated at the Caterpillar's making such very short
A1     12: 7  was  going  to shrink any further: she felt a little nervous about this; "for it might end, you know," said
A5     42:16      but  no  result seemed to follow, except a little shaking among the distant green leaves.
A6     45: 9  to  know  what it was all about, and crept a little way out of the wood to listen.
T2    127:11      a  tree,  and said kindly, "You may rest a little, now."
T9    202:32  Alice got up to do it, very obediently, but a little frightened.
A2     20: 4  near our house, I should like to show you! A little bright-eyed terrier, you know, with oh, such long curly
T1    107:20            "Oh, you wicked, wicked little thing!" cried Alice, catching up the kitten, and giving
T8    181:14  fit him very badly, and he had a queer-shaped little deal box fastened across his shoulders, upside-down,
A6     49:16  some  difficulty,  as it was a queer-shaped little creature, and held out its arms and legs in all
A2     20: 4  Alice went on eagerly: "There is such a nice little dog, near our house, I should like to show you! A
A1     10:22      or  not";  for she had read several nice little stories about children who had got burnt, and eaten up
A7     58:32            "Once upon a time there were three little sisters," the Dormouse began in a great hurry; "and
A7     59:31  he  consented  to go on. "And so these three little sisters--they were learning to draw, you know--"
T3    131:34                The little voice sighed deeply. It was very unhappy, evidently,
T6    167: 1                The little fishes of the sea, / They sent an answer back to me.
T6    167: 3                The little fishes' answer was / 'We cannot do it, Sir, because--'"
A1      9:41  door about fifteen inches high: she tried the little golden key in the lock, and to her great delight it
T5    153:24  Alice  said very politely, as she crossed the little brook after the Queen. * * * * * * * * * * * *
T6    167:18      Then  some  one came to me and said / 'The little fishes are in bed.'
T3    131:29  "You  might  make a joke on that," said the little voice close to her ear: "something about 'you would if
A6     49:28      She  said  the last words out loud, and the little thing grunted in reply (it had left off sneezing by
A4     27:10  the  great hall, with the glass table and the little door, had vanished completely.
A8     63:20  children:  there  were ten of them, and the little dears came jumping merrily along, hand in hand, in
A2     18:13  alas! the little door was shut again, and the little golden key was lying on the glass table as before, "and
T5    156:17      sleeves  were  carefully rolled up, and the little arms were plunged in elbow-deep, to get hold of the
```

LITTLE (cont.)

```
T3   131:41          "I know you are a friend," the little voice went on: "a dear friend, and an old friend. And
A4    28:23               Luckily for Alice, the little magic bottle had now had its full effect, and she grew
T9   204:25  for you," she repeated, catching hold of the little creature in the very act of jumping over a bottle which
T4   146:17       said, after a careful examination of the little white thing. "Not a rattle-snake, you know," she added
T2   125:18  on in silence till they got to the top of the little hill.
A7    61: 1  she said to herself, and began by taking the little golden key, and unlocking the door that led into the
T1   114:10      or two she could do nothing but hug the little Lily in silence. As soon as she had recovered her
A1    12: 5  was now the right size for going through the little door into that lovely garden. First, however, she
A2    17: 8               "How doth the little crocodile / Improve his shining tail, / And pour the
A2    17: 4       for Mabel! I'll try and say 'How doth the little--'," and she crossed her hands on her lap as if she
A5    36:34       "Well, I've tried to say 'How doth the little busy bee,' but it all came different!" Alice replied in
T4   142:17  on a rock / Conveniently low: / And all the little Oysters stood / And waited in a row.
T5   156:16      in among the waving rushes. And then the little sleeves were carefully rolled up, and the little arms
A1    12:15  to the door, she found she had forgotten the little golden key, and when she went back to the table for it,
T5   158: 1  in a moment, and she was back again in the little dark shop.
A7    61: 4  about a foot high; then she walked down the little passage: and then--she found herself at last in the
A7    60:43  herself in the long hall, and close to the little glass table. "Now, I'll manage better this time," she
A2    18:13       And she ran with all speed back to the little door; but, alas! the little door was shut again, and
A2    15:14  nine feet high, and she at once took up the little golden key and hurried off to the garden door.
A2    18:13  speed back to the little door; but, alas! the little door was shut again, and the little golden key was
T7   178: 4  She started to her feet and sprang across the little brook in her terror, and had just time to see the Lion
A6    50:14               So she set the little creature down, and felt quite relieved to see it trot
T3   132: 2            "What, then you don't--" the little voice began, when it was drowned by a shrill scream
A1    10:12  There seemed to be no use in waiting by the little door, so she went back to the table, half hoping she
AI     3: 5  skill, / By little arms are plied, / While little hands make vain pretence / Our wanderings to guide.
A7    57:14               'Twinkle, twinkle, little bat! / How I wonder what you're at!'
A12   99: 3  Lastly, she pictured to herself how this same little sister of hers would, in the after-time, be herself a
T12  207:24      And she caught it up and gave it one little kiss, "just in honour of its having been a Red Queen."
A1    10:19  all very well to say "Drink me," but the wise little Alice was not going to do that in a hurry. "No, I'll
A12   96:21  at the Lizard as she spoke. (The unfortunate little Bill had left off writing on his slate with one finger,
T3   129:23  it well enough--' (here came the favourite little toss of the head), 'only it was so dusty and hot, and
A4    32:13  out of the house, and found quite a crowd of little animals and birds waiting outside. The poor little
A12   98:14  watching the setting sun, and thinking of little Alice and all her wonderful Adventures, till she too
A4    30:23  anything more: at last came a rumbling of little cart-wheels, and the sound of a good many voices all
T2   122: 8  together, till the air seemed quite full of little shrill voices. "Silence, every one of you!" cried the
T2   125:23  was divided up into squares by a number of little green hedges, that reached from brook to brook.
A4    32: 1  to doubt, for the next moment a shower of little pebbles came rattling in at the window, and some of
T5   156:44  under the chin, and, in spite of a series of little shrieks of "Oh, oh, oh!" from poor Alice, it swept her
A11   86: 3  crowd assembled about them--all sorts of little birds and beasts, as well as the whole pack of cards:
T2   127:34  and began measuring the ground, and sticking little pegs in here and there.
T7   169: 8  him, so that the ground was soon covered with little heaps of men.
AI     3: 3  leisurely we glide; / For both our oars, with little skill, / By little arms are plied, / While little hands
T8   191: 2  down to rest on a lawn as soft as moss, with little flowerbeds dotted about it here and there. "Oh, how
A11   91:33  Rabbit read out, at the top of his shrill little voice, the name "Alice!"
A9    74:40             "When we were still little," the Mock Turtle went on at last, more calmly, though
T4   144:37  grass," said Alice, who was a very thoughtful little girl.
A4    32: 6       that the pebbles were all turning into little cakes as they lay on the floor, and a bright idea came
A4    30:17  snatch in the air. This time there were two little shrieks, and more sounds of broken glass. "What a
A9    72:24  Duchess asked, with another dig of her sharp little chin.
A9    70:37  thing," said the Duchess, digging her sharp little chin into Alice's shoulder as she added "and the moral
T5   155:29             "A dear little crab!" thought Alice. "I should like that."
A4    33: 7             "And yet what a dear little puppy it was!" said Alice, as she leant against a
T3   137:12  to cry with vexation at having lost her dear little fellow-traveler so suddenly. "However, I know my name
A12   98:20  very tones of her voice, and see that queer little toss of her head to keep back the wandering hair that
A12   98:23       alive with the strange creatures of her little sister's dream.
A12   99: 6  and how she would gather about her other little children, and make their eyes bright and eager with
T2   123:10  thought crossed her mind, "There's another little girl in the garden, somewhere!"
A6    49: 2  the baby violently up and down, and the poor little thing howled so, that Alice could hardly hear the words
A12   93: 5  the Lizard in head downwards, and the poor little thing was waving its tail about in a melancholy way,
A6    49:17  like a star-fish," thought Alice. The poor little thing was snorting like a steam-engine when she caught
A4    32:13  animals and birds waiting outside. The poor little Lizard, Bill, was in the middle, being held up by two
T3   131:40  her thoughts from the unhappiness of the poor little creature.
A1    12:20  had tired herself out with trying, the poor little thing sat down and cried.
T1   114: 4  very anxious to be of use, and, as the poor little Lily was nearly screaming herself into a fit, she
A11   87: 8  it away. She did it so quickly that the poor little juror (it was Bill, the Lizard) could not make out at
A6    50: 5  more to do with you. Mind now!" The poor little thing sobbed again (or grunted, it was impossible to
A4    32:29       out one paw, trying to touch her. "Poor little thing!" said Alice, in a coaxing tone, and she tried
A2    14: 6  they were getting so far off). "Oh, my poor little feet, I wonder who will put on your shoes and stockings
A6    48:36               "Speak roughly to your little boy, / And beat him when he sneezes: / He only does it
A2    17:14  How neatly spreads his claws, / And welcomes little fishes in, / With gently smiling jaws!
T8   187:32  "I'll tell thee everything I can: / There's little to relate. / I saw an aged aged man, / A-sitting on a
A2    19:19  and seemed to her to wink with one of its little eyes, but it said nothing.
A2    18: 2  see that she had put on one of the Rabbit's little white kid-gloves while she was talking. "How can I have
A4    27:21  them." As she said this, she came upon a neat little house, on the door of which was a bright brass plate
T4   139:12             But the fat little men only looked at each other and grinned.
T3   137:30  turning a sharp corner, she came upon two fat little men, so suddenly that she could not help starting back,
T8   190:15  to go," he said, "down the hill and over that little brook, and then you'll be a Queen--But you'll stay and
A1     9: 2  you could manage it?) "And what an ignorant little girl she'll think me for asking! No, it'll never do to
A5    43:17       Alice, who was a very truthful child; "but little girls eat eggs quite as much as serpents do, you know
```

LITTLE (cont.)
A12   98:17   First, she dreamed about little Alice herself: once again the tiny hands were clasped
T1   108:25   the snow! And you'd have deserved it, you little mischievous darling! What have you got to say for
A11   86:26   she thought, and rightly too that very few little girls of her age knew the meaning of it at all. However
T3   129:29   hill, and jumped over the first of the six little brooks. * * * * * * * * * * * * * *
AI   3: 4   / For both our oars, with little skill, / By little arms are plied, / While little hands make vain pretence
A4   27:36   this time she had found her way into a tidy little room with a table in the window and on it (as she had
A2   17:18   and I shall have to go and live in that poky little house, and have next to no toys to play with, and oh,
T3 135:17   Then came another of those melancholy little sighs, and this time the poor Gnat really seemed to
T8 181:17   "I see you're admiring my little box," the Knight said in a friendly tone. "It's my own
A5   43:12   the deepest contempt. "I've seen a good many little girls in my time, but never one with such a neck as
A4   28: 8   really I'm quite tired of being such a tiny little thing!"
T2 125:21   country it was. There were a number of tiny little brooks running straight across it from side to side,
T8 185: 2   touched the ground directly. So I had a very little way to fall, you see--But there was the danger of
A4   32:43   of short charges at the stick, running a very little way forwards each time and a long way back, and barking
A2   16: 7   of things, and she, oh, she knows such a very little! Besides, she's she, and I'm I, and--oh dear, how
T5 156:37   scented rushes, you know, last only a very little while--and these, being dream-rushes, melted away
A1   10: 7   thought poor Alice, "it would be of very little use without my shoulders. Oh, how I wish I could shut
A11   87:11   for the rest of the day; and this was of very little use, as it left no mark on the slate.
T1 114: 6   set her on the table by the side of her noisy little daughter.

LOW (18)
A11   91:12   anxiously at the White Rabbit, who said, in a low voice, "Your Majesty must cross-examine this witness."
A2   20:18   (with passion, Alice thought), and it said, in a low trembling voice, "Let us get to the shore, and then
A2   15:33   when the Rabbit came near her, she began, in a low, timid voice, "If you please, Sir--" The Rabbit started
A8   63: 6   said nothing, but looked at Two. Two began, in a low voice, "Why, the fact is, you see, Miss, this here
A9   72:34   fine day, your Majesty!" the Duchess began in a low, weak voice.
T4 147:34   "I'm very brave, generally," he went on in a low voice: "only to-day I happen to have a headache."
T9 196: 1   Dumpty saw it too," the White Queen went on in a low voice, more as if she were talking to herself. "He came
A8   67:31   "How do you like the Queen?" said the Cat in a low voice.
A8   65:29   "Hush! Hush!" said the Rabbit in a low hurried tone. He looked anxiously over his shoulder as
A9   73:18   off together, Alice heard the King say in a low voice, to the company, generally, "You are all pardoned
A12   94: 2   your verdict," he said to the jury, in a low trembling voice.
A1   9:39   on the second time round, she came upon a low curtain she had not noticed before, and behind it was a
A8   63: 2   others looked round also, and all of them bowed low.
T8 190: 7   body to and fro, / And muttered mumblingly and low, / As if his mouth were full of dough, / Who snorted
A1   9:28   longer to be seen: she found herself in a long, low hall, which was lit up by a row of lamps hanging from
T1 115:20   talking together in a frightened whisper--so low, that Alice could hardly hear what they said.
T4 142:16   / And then they rested on a rock / Conveniently low: / And all the little Oysters stood / And waited in a
A2   19:44   a subject! Our family always hated cats: nasty, low, vulgar things! Don't let me hear the name again!"

MATTER (16)
A12   95: 3   know it to be true): / If she should push the matter on, / What would become of you?
A12   96: 2   the jury, of course--'If she should push the matter on'--that must be the Queen--'What would become of you
T9 204: 1   at her side, and turned to see what was the matter with the White Queen; but, instead of the Queen, there
A6   49:32   anxiously into its face to see what was the matter with it. There could be no doubt that it had a very
T8W 13: 4   looking anxiously back to see what was the matter. Something like a very old man (only that his face was
A12   94:24   sign it," said the King, "that only makes the matter worse. You must have meant some mischief, or else you'd
T5 152: 8   "What is the matter?" she said, as soon as there was a chance of making
T8W 13:11   the brook:--but I'll just ask him what's the matter," she added, checking herself on the very edge. "If I
T5 149:26   "I don't know what's the matter with it!" the Queen said, in a melancholy voice. "It's
A1   9:15   answer either question, it didn't much matter which way she put it. She felt that she was dozing off,
A5   43:24   I know that well enough; and what does it matter to me whether you're a little girl or a serpent?"
T8 186: 3   surprised at the question. "What does it matter where my body happens to be?" he said. "My mind goes on
A3   23: 9   a sort of circle, ("the exact shape doesn't matter," it said,) and then all the party were placed along
A6   51:12   "Then it doesn't matter which way you go," said the Cat.
A12   93:32   to look over their slates; "but it doesn't matter a bit," she thought to herself.
A8   68:24   hedgehogs were out of sight: "but it doesn't matter much," thought Alice, "as all the arches are gone from

MEAN (33)
T6 164: 3   "That's a great deal to make one word mean," Alice said in a thoughtful tone.
T6 166: 6   "And what does 'outgrabe' mean?"
T6 160: 7   "Must a name mean something?" Alice asked doubtfully.
A10   81:37   "I mean what I say," the Mock Turtle replied, in an offended
T6 162:38   "I mean, what is an un-birthday present?"
T3 135:41   at not being able to think of the word. "I mean to get under the--under the--under this, you know!"
A10   81:18   are your shoes done with?" said the Gryphon. "I mean, what makes them so shiny?"
T6 162: 9   felt even more indignant at this suggestion. "I mean," she said, "that one ca'n't help growing older."
T6 166:30   getting green, / I'll try and tell you what I mean:"
T6 162:17   cravat, I should have said--no, a belt, I mean--I beg your pardon!" she added in dismay, for Humpty
A7   55:21   Alice hastily replied; "at least--at least I mean what I say--that's the same thing, you know."
T9 195:27   "we had such a thunderstorm last Tuesday--I mean one of the last set of Tuesdays, you know."
T6 163:31   tone, "it means just what I choose it to mean--neither more nor less."
T4 144:18   "That was mean!" Alice said indignantly. "Then I like the Carpenter
T6 163:34   is," said Alice, "whether you can make words mean so many different things."
T6 160: 6   Dumpty interrupted impatiently. "What does it mean?"
A3   26:10   "I didn't mean it!" pleaded poor Alice. "But you're so easily offended
T9 192:38   "I'm sure I didn't mean--" Alice was beginning, but the Red Queen interrupted
T6 164: 2   you mean to do next, as I suppose you don't mean to stop here all the rest of your life."
T6 163:28   "But 'glory' doesn't mean 'a nice knock-down argument,'" Alice objected.
A7   59:13   "You mean you ca'n't take less," said the Hatter: "it's very easy
T8 186:20   "What did you mean it to be made of?" Alice asked, hoping to cheer him up,
T8W 17: 1   "Oh, you mean stiff-neck," said Alice.

MEAN (cont.)

A7	55:16	"Do you mean that you think you can find out the answer to it?" said
A5	35: 9	"What do you mean by that?" said the Caterpillar, sternly. "Explain
T9	192:27	the subject of the conversation. "What do you mean by 'If you really are a Queen'? What right have you to
T6	164: 1	would be just as well if you'd mention what you mean to do next, as I suppose you don't mean to stop here
A7	56:37	"I don't know what you mean," said Alice.
T2	124:11	"I don't know what you mean by your way," said the Queen: "all the ways about here
T6	163:24	"I don't know what you mean by 'glory,'" Alice said.
T9	199:14	"Then you should say what you mean," she said.
A7	55:19	"Then you should say what you mean," the March Hare went on.
A10	81:36	"Don't you mean 'purpose'?" said Alice.

MELANCHOLY (11)

TI	103:22	/ Shall summon to unwelcome bed / A melancholy maiden! / We are but older children, dear, / Who fret
A11	91:13	if I must, I must," the King said with a melancholy air, and, after folding his arms and frowning at the
T5	152:33	is so very lonely here!" Alice said in a melancholy voice; and, at the thought of her loneliness, two large
T5	149:27	the matter with it!" the Queen said, in a melancholy voice. "It's out of temper, I think. I've pinned it
A3	22:26	"As wet as ever," said Alice in a melancholy tone: "it doesn't seem to dry me at all."
A3	26:37	Dinah!" she said to herself in a melancholy tone. "Nobody seems to like her, down here, and I'm
A12	93: 6	thing was waving its tail about in a melancholy way, being quite unable to move. She soon got it out
A10	85: 9	on the breeze that followed them, the melancholy words:--
T8	187:26	and listening, in a half-dream, to the melancholy music of the song.
T3	135:17	Then came another of those melancholy little sighs, and this time the poor Gnat really seemed
A5	36:35	came different!" Alice replied in a very melancholy voice.

MOMENT (73)

T9	203:11	it) all sorts of things happened in a moment. The candles all grew up to the ceiling, looking
A4	27: 6	dropped them, I wonder?" Alice guessed in a moment that it was looking for the fan and the pair of white
T2	122:16	There was silence in a moment, and several of the pink daisies turned white.
A9	72:39	Duchess took her choice, and was gone in a moment.
T4	138: 2	neck, and Alice knew which was which in a moment, because one of them had 'DUM' embroidered on his
T5	158: 1	boat, and the river, had vanished all in a moment, and she was back again in the little dark shop.
T4	146:14	and his eyes grew large and yellow all in a moment, as he pointed with a trembling finger at a small white
T1	119: 2	garden first!" She was out of the room in a moment, and ran down stairs--or, at least, it wasn't exactly
T9	201:17	the pudding!" and there it was again in a moment, like a conjuring-trick. It was so large that she
T2	123:42	To her surprise she lost sight of her in a moment, and found herself walking in at the front-door again.
A1	9:22	hurt, and she jumped up on to her feet in a moment: she looked up, but it was all dark overhead: before
T4	148:23	to their heels and were out of sight in a moment.
T3	129:34	putting his head in at the window. In a moment everybody was holding out a ticket: they were about the
T2	128:26	to the next peg, where she turned for a moment to say "Good-bye," and then hurried on to the last.
T5	154: 2	the Sheep said at last, looking up for a moment from her knitting.
T9	204: 7	broad good-natured face grinning at her for a moment over the edge of the tureen, before she disappeared
A8	64: 6	with fury, and, after glaring at her for a moment like a wild beast, began screaming "Off with her head!
T9	198:10	with a long beak put its head out for a moment and said "No admittance till the week after next!" and
A1	8: 9	down, so suddenly that Alice had not a moment to think about stopping herself before she found
T9	204: 9	There was not a moment to be lost. Already several of the guests were lying
A1	9:24	in sight, hurrying down it. There was not a moment to be lost: away went Alice like the wind, and was just
A8	68:33	The moment Alice appeared, she was appealed to by all three to
A4	32:37	to keep herself from being run over; and, the moment she appeared on the other side, the puppy made another
A4	32:16	a bottle. They all made a rush at Alice the moment she appeared; but she ran off as hard as she could, and
T9	200: 7	in she went, and there was a dead silence the moment she appeared.
T5	158:28	step, as everything turned into a tree the moment she came up to it, and she quite expected the egg to do
A12	92: 1	Alice, quite forgetting in the flurry of the moment how large she had grown in the last few minutes, and
A9	72:44	and were resting in the shade: however, the moment they saw her, they hurried back to the game, the Queen
A2	14: 2	(she was so much surprised, that for the moment she quite forgot how to speak good English). "Now I'm
T8	179:18	frightened for him than for herself at the moment, and watched him with some anxiety as he mounted again.
T9	196:27	but really couldn't think of anything at the moment.
A8	68: 4	called to the Queen, who was passing at the moment, "My dear! I wish you would have this cat removed!"
T9	201:30	a little frightened at finding that, the moment she opened her lips, there was dead silence, and all
A8	69:10	The Cat's head began fading away the moment he was gone, and, by the time he had come back with the
T4	139:42	they had begun: the music stopped at the same moment.
A1	8: 5	In another moment down went Alice after it, never once considering how in
T1	112: 1	In another moment Alice was through the glass, and had jumped lightly
A2	18:18	these words her foot slipped, and in another moment, splash! she was up to her chin in saltwater. Her first
A5	41:32	as if she had asked it aloud; and in another moment it was out of sight.
T3	137: 9	into its beautiful brown eyes, and in another moment it had darted away at full speed.
T3	132:10	comfort!" she said to herself. In another moment she felt the carriage rise straight up into the air,
A5	42: 8	delight, which changed into alarm in another moment, when she found that her shoulders were nowhere to be
T9	197:10	to me. I'm getting sleepy, too." In another moment both Queens were fast asleep, and snoring loud.
T5	149: 2	and looked about for the owner: in another moment the White Queen came running wildly through the wood,
T3	137:32	could not help starting back, but in another moment she recovered herself, feeling sure that they must be
T1	113: 5	the hearth among the cinders; but in another moment, with a little "Oh!" of surprise, she was down on her
A6	47:17	Alice quite jumped; but she saw in another moment that it was addressed to the baby, and not to her, so
A4	27:14	what are you doing out here? Run home this moment, and fetch me a pair of gloves and a fan! Quick, now!"
A2	15:22	"to go on crying in this way! Stop this moment, I tell you!" But she went on all the same, shedding
A4	29:20	said the voice. "Fetch me my gloves this moment!" Then came a little pattering of feet on the stairs.
A6	46:27	At this moment the door of the house opened, and a large plate came
A12	93:33	At this moment the King, who had been for some time busily writing in
T7	171: 8	At this moment the Messenger arrived: he was far too much out of
T7	175: 9	At this moment the Unicorn sauntered by them, with his hands in his
T8	179:12	At this moment her thoughts were interrupted by a loud shouting of
T9	199:22	At this moment the door·was flung open, and a shrill voice was heard

MOMENT (cont.)
T9   204: 2   At this moment she heard a hoarse laugh at her side, and turned to see
A8   63:10   our best, afore she comes, to--" At this moment, Five, who had been anxiously looking across the garden
T6   168:41   She never finished the sentence, for at this moment a heavy crash shook the forest from end to end.
A2   15:12   Just at this moment her head struck against the roof of the hall: in fact
A11   88:34   Just at this moment Alice felt a very curious sensation, which puzzled her
T2   126:11   Square you'll be a Queen--"Just at this moment, somehow or other, they began to run.
T1   115:25   "The horror of that moment," the King went on, "I shall never, never forget!"
T7   169: 1   The next moment soldiers came running through the wood, at first in
T2   120:23   she described it afterwards), and the next moment she found herself actually walking in at the door.
T4   139:28   she took hold of both hands at once: the next moment they were dancing round in a ring. This seemed quite
A4   32: 1   But she had not long to doubt, for the next moment a shower of little pebbles came rattling in at the
A5   41:39   right-hand bit to try the effect. The next moment she felt a violent blow underneath her chin: it had
T5   156:35   all their scent and beauty, from the very moment that she picked them? Even real scented rushes, you
T7   170: 3   off instantly. The confusion got worse every moment, and Alice was very glad to get out of the wood into an
A4   32:41   play with a cart-horse, and expecting every moment to be trampled under its feet, ran round the thistle
T6   159:15   hands ready to catch him, for she was every moment expecting him to fall.
T7   171:14   attitudes only got more extraordinary every moment, while the great eyes rolled wildly from side to side.

NEXT (59)
A4   30: 1   Next came an angry voice--the Rabbit's--"Pat! Pat! Where are
T4   139:18   "Next Boy!" said Alice, passing on to Tweedledee, though she
A6   46: 6   for fear of their hearing her; and, when she next peeped out, the Fish-Footman was gone, and the other
A3   24: 9   The next thing was to eat the comfits: this caused some noise
A11   91: 5   The next witness was the Duchess's cook. She carried the
T7   169: 1   The next moment soldiers came running through the wood, at first
T8   181: 3   "So you will, when you've crossed the next brook," said the White Knight. "I'll see you safe to
T2   120:23   (as she described it afterwards), and the next moment she found herself actually walking in at the
T8   186:13   "Then it would have to be the next day. I suppose you wouldn't have two pudding-courses in
T4   139:27   she took hold of both hands at once: the next moment they were dancing round in a ring. This seemed
A2   15:42   little different. But if I'm not the same, the next question is 'Who in the world am I?' Ah, that's the
A11   91:27   "Really, my dear, you must cross-examine the next witness. It quite makes my forehead ache!"
A9   77:12   the first day," said the Mock Turtle: "nine the next, and so on."
A5   43:42   However, I've got back to my right size: the next thing is, to get into that beautiful garden--how is
T2   124:17   when I go home," she thought to herself, "the next time I'm a little late for dinner."
A10   83:10   "Go on with the next verse," the Gryphon repeated: "it begins 'I passed by
A10   83: 4   it," said the Gryphon hastily. "Go on with the next verse."
A11   91: 4   "Call the next witness!" said the King.
A11   91:26   the King with an air of great relief. "Call the next witness." And, he added, in an undertone to the Queen,
T2   128:26   this time, but walked on quickly to the next peg, where she turned for a moment to say "Good-bye,"
T8   186: 9   "In time to have it cooked for the next course?" said Alice. "Well, that was quick work,
A4   32: 1   Alice. But she had not long to doubt, for the next moment a shower of little pebbles came rattling in at
T8   183:16   himself, and Alice watching anxiously for the next tumble.
T2   128:22   At the next peg the Queen turned again, and this time she said
A11   91:30   the list, feeling very curious to see what the next witness would be like, "--for they haven't got much
A5   41:39   of the right-hand bit to try the effect. The next moment she felt a violent blow underneath her chin: it
T8   186:16   day," the Knight repeated as before: "not the next day. In fact," he went on, holding his head down, and
T8   186:11   "Well, not the next course," the Knight said in slow thoughtful tone: "no,
T8   186:15   "Well, not the next day," the Knight repeated as before: "not the next day.
T8   186:12   in slow thoughtful tone: "no, certainly not the next course."
T3   131:11   beyond the Beetle, but a hoarse voice spoke next. "Change engines--" it said, and there it choked and
A5   43:14   use denying it. I suppose you'll be telling me next that you never tasted an egg!"
A2   17:19   go and live in that poky little house, and have next to no toys to play with, and oh, ever so many lessons
T5   154:19   like a work-box, and was always in the shelf next above the one she was looking at. "And this one is the
T3   131: 6   There was a Beetle sitting next the Goat (it was a very queer carriage-full of
A11   88:40   squeeze so," said the Dormouse, who was sitting next to her. "I can hardly breathe."
T3   131: 3   A Goat, that was sitting next to the gentleman in white, shut his eyes and said in a
A8   67:28   there's the arch I've got to go through next walking about at the other end of the ground--and I
T1   112:13   For instance, the pictures on the wall next the fire seemed to be all alive, and the very clock on
T5   150: 5   punished: and the trial doesn't even begin till next Wednesday: and of course the crime comes last of all."
A4   31: 4   sharp kick, and waited to see what would happen next.
T1   113:18   with great curiosity to see what would happen next.
A8   65:24   wondering very much what would happen next.
A1   8:13   her, and to wonder what was going to happen next. First, she tried to look down and make out what she
A4   31:35   thought to herself "I wonder what they will do next! If they had any sense, they'd take the roof off."
A4   30:19   be!" thought Alice. "I wonder what they'll do next! As for pulling me out of the window, I only wish they
T6   164: 1   as well if you'd mention what you mean to do next, as I suppose you don't mean to stop here all the rest
A6   45: 2   looking at the house, and wondering what to do next, when suddenly a footman in livery came running out of
A9   77:18   thought it over a little before she made her next remark. "Then the eleventh day must have been a holiday
T3   129:15   what enormous flowers they must be!" was her next idea. "Something like cottages with the roofs taken off
T5   150: 1   "Oh, things that happened the week after next," the Queen replied in a careless tone. "For instance,
T9   198:11   and said "No admittance till the week after next!" and shut the door again with a bang.
A6   46:30   "--or next day, maybe," the Footman continued in the same tone,
A4   27:29   I suppose Dinah'll be sending me on messages next!" And she began fancying the sort of thing that would
AI   3:29   the subject by, / "The rest next time--" "It is next time!" / The happy voices cry.
A8   63:17   flat, with their hands and feet at the corners: next the ten courtiers: these were ornamented all over with
A8   63:21   couples: they were all ornamented with hearts. Next came the guests, mostly Kings and Queens, and among
T9   202: 5   easy: a baby, I think, could have caught it. / 'Next, the fish must be bought.' / That is easy: a penny, I
AI   3:29   weary one / To put the subject by, / "The rest next time--" "It is next time!" / The happy voices cry.

NONSENSE (15)
A8   64: 8   "Nonsense!" said Alice, very loudly and decidedly, and the Queen

NONSENSE (cont.)

T2	123:40	This sounded nonsense to Alice, so she said nothing, but set off at once
T7	177:13	This sounded nonsense, but Alice very obediently got up, and carried the dish
A12	97: 1	"Stuff and nonsense!" said Alice loudly. "The idea of having the sentence
T2	125:14	if you like," she said, "but I've heard nonsense, compared with which that would be as sensible as a
T2	125:11	ca'n't be a valley, you know. That would be nonsense--"
AI	3:16	tones Secunda hopes / "There will be nonsense in it!" / While Tertia interrupts the tale / Not more
T4	145:28	"I know they're talking nonsense," Alice thought to herself: "and it's foolish to cry
A3	26: 9	away. "You insult me by talking such nonsense!"
A8	69: 1	be beheaded, and that you weren't to talk nonsense.
A11	88:43	"Don't talk nonsense," said Alice more boldly: "you know you're growing too
T9	194:25	help thinking to herself "What dreadful nonsense we are talking!"
A10	82:33	the Mock Turtle; "but it sounds uncommon nonsense.
A2	15:11	Oh dear, what nonsense I'm talking!"
T2	125:13	Red Queen shook her head. "You may call it 'nonsense' if you like," she said, "but I've heard nonsense,

NOTHING (63)

A12	93:18	"Nothing," said Alice.
A12	93:19	"Nothing whatever?" persisted the King.
A12	93:20	"Nothing whatever," said Alice.
T9	199:17	"Nothing!" Alice said impatiently. "I've been knocking at it!"
T1	107: 1	was certain, that the white kitten had had nothing to do with it--it was the black kitten's fault entirely
A5	36:26	thought she might as well wait, as she had nothing else to do, and perhaps after all it might tell her
A7	59:11	"I've had nothing yet," Alice replied in an offended tone: "so I ca'n't
A11	89:27	would deny it too; but the Dormouse denied nothing, being fast asleep.
A9	74:39	be more to come, so she sat still and said nothing.
A5	41:11	Alice said nothing: she had never been so much contradicted in all her
A10	82:34	Alice said nothing: she had sat down with her face in her hands, wondering
T5	155:24	remark that needed any answer: so Alice said nothing, but pulled away. There was something very queer about
T6	162:22	Humpty Dumpty was very angry, though he said nothing for a minute or two. When he did speak again, it was in
T2	123:40	This sounded nonsense to Alice, so she said nothing, but set off at once towards the Red Queen. To her
T6	162: 1	want to begin another argument, so she said nothing.
A8	63: 5	Five and Seven said nothing, but looked at Two. Two began, in a low voice, "Why,
T4	143:21	And you are very nice!' / The Carpenter said nothing but / 'Cut us another slice. / I wish you were not
T4	143:29	them trot so quick!' / The Carpenter said nothing but / 'The butter's spread too thick!'
A2	19:20	with one of its little eyes, but it said nothing.
A9	74:24	them with large eyes full of tears, but said nothing.
T1	115:18	to throw over him. However, she could find nothing but a bottle of ink, and when she got back with it she
A5	42:23	in among the leaves, which she found to be nothing but the tops of the trees under which she had been
T8	185:20	this time. However, though she could see nothing but the soles of his feet, she was much relieved to
T5	153:36	counter? Rub as she would, she could make nothing more of it: she was in a little dark shop, leaning with
A12	96:14	pointing to the tarts on the table. "Nothing can be clearer than that. Then again--'before she had
A12	97: 8	to her full size by this time). "You're nothing but a pack of cards!"
A6	50: 4	my dear," said Alice, seriously, "I'll have nothing more to do with you. Mind now!" The poor little thing
A3	25:21	have the trial; For really this morning I've nothing to do.' Said the mouse to the cur, Such a trial, dear
T5	157: 3	with her knitting all the while, just as if nothing had happened. "That was a nice crab you caught!" she
A6	46:31	continued in the same tone, exactly as if nothing had happened.
T3	132:24	insects?" the Gnat went on, as quietly as if nothing had happened.
T7	178:12	them out of town,'" she thought to herself, "nothing ever will!"
A8	69: 6	Alice could think of nothing else to say but "It belongs to the Duchess: you'd
T8	183:13	Alice could think of nothing better to say than "Indeed?" but she said it as
A7	56: 9	looked at it again: but he could think of nothing better to say than his first remark, "It was the best
A1	13: 2	had got so much into the way of expecting nothing but out-of-the-way things to happen, that it seemed
A1	7: 2	by her sister on the bank and of having nothing to do: once or twice she had peeped into the book her
A1	8:24	"After such a fall as this, I shall think nothing of tumbling down-stairs! How brave they'll all think me
T9	194:13	"Then you think nothing would remain?" said the Red Queen.
A7	59:14	Hatter: "it's very easy to take more than nothing."
T1	114:10	breath, and for a minute or two she could do nothing but hug the little Lily in silence. As soon as she had
A3	26: 8	"I shall do nothing of the sort," said the Mouse, getting up and walking
T4	138:11	Wax-works weren't made to be looked at for nothing. Nohow!"
A1	7:11	There was nothing so very remarkable in that; nor did Alice think it so
T7	172:14	better," the King replied. "I said there was nothing like it." Which Alice did not venture to deny.
A1	9: 5	Down, down, down. There was nothing else to do, so Alice soon began talking again.
T5	155:19	gliding along between banks: so there was nothing for it but to do her best.
T2	120:26	was the hill full in sight, so there was nothing to be done but start again. This time she came upon a
T3	135:19	away, for, when Alice looked up, there was nothing whatever to be seen on the twig, and, as she was
A1	9:35	table, all made of solid glass: there was nothing on it but a tiny golden key, and Alice's first idea was
A7	54:14	looked all round the table, but there was nothing on it but tea. "I don't see any wine," she remarked.
T7	172:13	"I didn't say there was nothing better," the King replied. "I said there was nothing
T7	172: 5	"There's nothing but hay left now," the Messenger said, peeping into the
T4	145:23	by crying," Tweedledee remarked: "there's nothing to cry about."
T7	172: 9	that it revived him a good deal. "There's nothing like eating hay when you're faint," he remarked to her,
A12	94:13	said the White Rabbit: "in fact, there's nothing written on the outside." He unfolded the paper as he
A9	72:14	"That's nothing to what I could say if I chose," the Duchess replied,
A1	12:13	After a while, finding that nothing more happened, she decided on going into the garden at
T3	136:17	Alice thought, but nothing came of it. "Please, would you tell me what you call
A5	42:31	a kind of sob, "I've tried every way, but nothing seems to suit them!"
T3	130:14	for I must confess that I don't) "Better say nothing at all. Language is worth a thousand pounds a word!"
T3	136:15	poor Alice. She answered, rather sadly, "Nothing, just now."

OFF (141)

```
                                                        "Off with her head!" the Queen shouted at the top of her
A12    97: 5
A8     64: 7   wild  beast, began screaming "Off with her head! Off with--"
A11    91: 1                   "--and just take his head outside," the Queen added to one of the officers; but
T4    144:35   heap,  and  snoring loud--"fit to snore his head off!" as Tweedledum remarked.
A8     65:15   two,  looking for them, and then quietly marched off after the others.
A1     13: 5       So she  set to work, and very soon finished off the cake. * * * * * * * * * *
A2     15:14   once  took  up the little golden key and hurried off to the garden door.
A8     68: 9   myself,"  said  the King eagerly, and he hurried off.
A3     26:31          among  the  party. Some of the birds hurried off at once: one old Magpie began wrapping itself up very
A10    85: 5   and,  taking  Alice by the hand, it hurried off, without waiting for the end of the song.
A7     60:30   bear:  she  got up in great disgust, and walked off: the Dormouse fell asleep instantly, and neither of the
A9     74: 3   some  executions I have ordered;" and she walked off, leaving Alice alone with the Gryphon. Alice did not
A9     70: 3   arm affectionately into Alice's, and they walked off together.
A9     73:18                       As they walked off together, Alice heard the King say in a low voice, to
T8    179:24   Knight.  He drew up at Alice's side, and tumbled off his horse just as the Red Knight had done: then he got
T8    179:16   my  prisoner!"  the Knight cried, as he tumbled off his horse.
T8    180:14   and  then  the Red Knight mounted and galloped off.
T7    172:40   while!  Let's run and see them." And they trotted off, Alice repeating to herself, as she ran, the words of
A3     26:36   all  in bed!" On various pretexts they all moved off, and Alice was soon left alone.
A6     46:40   variations.  "I shall sit here," he said, "on and off, for days and days."
T8    180: 9   quiet  the  horses are! They let them get on and off them just as if they were tables!"
A5     40: 8   think I  can listen all day to such stuff? / Be off, or I'll kick you down-stairs!"
A5     43:28                       "Well, be off, then!" said the Pigeon in a sulky tone, as it settled
A9     72:37   as she  spoke; "either you or your head must be off, and that in about half no time! Take your choice!"
A11    88:20                       "Take off your hat," the King said to the Hatter.
A5     41:37   arms round it as far as they would go, and broke off a bit of the edge with each hand.
T9    192:25       "Why,  don't  you see, child--" here she broke off with a frown, and, after thinking for a minute,
T3    129: 8   They ca'n't be bees--nobody ever saw bees a mile off, you know--" and for some time she stood silent,
T8    190:16   you'll  be  a Queen--But you'll stay and see me off first?" he added as Alice turned with an eager look in
T9    196:13   said  the Red Queen.) "And part of the roof came off, and ever so much thunder got in--and it went rolling
A7     58: 5   the  Queen bawled out 'He's murdering the time! Off with his head!'"
T6    161:12   happen  to  his head! I'm afraid it would come off!"
T9    199:10   if  he  were trying whether the paint would come off: then he looked at Alice.
T9    192: 7       as  she  was afraid that the crown might come off: but she comforted herself with the thought that there
A7     60: 1   from the change; and Alice was a good deal worse off than before, as the March Hare had just upset the
A8     65: 3                       "Leave off that!" screamed the Queen. "You make me giddy." And
T6    162: 5   if  you'd  asked my advice, I'd have said 'Leave off at seven'--but it's too late now."
A9     73: 6       by  the  soldiers, who of course had to leave off being arches to do this, so that, by the end of half an
T1    108:15   got so cold, and it snowed so, they had to leave off. Never mind, we'll go and see the bonfire to-morrow."
T3    131:12   and  there  it choked and was obliged to leave off.
T3    135: 3   'Come here--,' and there she would have to leave off, because there wouldn't be any name for her to call,
T9    195: 6   of  leaves,  till she had to beg them to leave off, it blew her hair about so.
A1     12:22   herself  rather  sharply. "I advise you to leave off this minute!" She generally gave herself very good
A10    84: 6                       Yes, I think you'd better leave off," said the Gryphon, and Alice was only too glad to do
T5    156:13   am  I  to stop it?" said the Sheep. "If you leave off rowing, it'll stop of itself."
A4     31:36       If  they  had any sense, they'd take the roof off." After a minute or two they began moving about again,
T7    176:18   crown,  which  the poor King was nearly shaking off his head, he trembled so much.
A8     66:18       soldiers  were  always getting up and walking off to other parts of the ground, Alice soon came to the
T8    184:16       just  in  time to save himself from tumbling off again.
T8    190:30       along  the  road, and the Knight tumbling off, first on one side and then on the other. After the
T8    180:12   and  the  battle ended with their both falling off in this way, side by side. When they got up again, they
T8    182:30   "But I've got a plan for keeping it from falling off."
T8    182:43       that  he  had a habit of now and then falling off sideways; and, as he generally did this on the side on
A8     64: 6   for a moment like a wild beast, began screaming "Off with her head! Off with--"
T7    171:12   said,  introducing  Alice in the hope of turning off the Messenger's attention from himself--but it was of
A7     60:21   had  closed its eyes by this time, and was going off into a doze; but, on being pinched by the Hatter, it
A12    98:28   meal, and the shrill voice of the Queen ordering off her unfortunate guests to execution--once more the
A9     76:37   was  Mystery,"  the Mock Turtle replied, counting off the subjects on his flappers--"Mystery, ancient and
T3    133: 1   there's  the  Horse-fly," Alice began, counting off the names on her fingers.
A9     73: 6   quarreling with the other players, and shouting "Off with his head!" or "Off with her head!" Those whom she
A8     67: 1   passion,  and went stamping about, and shouting "Off with his head!" or "Off with her head!" about once in a
T5    153:39       knitting, and every now and then leaving off to look at her through a great pair of spectacles.
A6     48:24   felt  very glad to get an opportunity of showing off a little of her knowledge. "Just think what work it
A1      8:33   this was not a very good opportunity for showing off her knowledge, as there was no one to listen to her,
A1      9:15   way  she  put it. She felt that she was dozing off, and had just begun to dream that she was walking hand
A10    80:25       said  the Mock Turtle: "crumbs would all wash off in the sea. But they have their tails in their mouths;
A11    89: 8   the  wretched Hatter trembled so, that he shook off both his shoes.
T8W    21: 3   the  top of your head is nice and round." He took off his own wig as he spoke, and stetched out one claw
T3    131:39   it  tickled  her ear very much, and quite took off her thoughts from the unhappiness of the poor little
T4    147: 3   an  extraordinary thing to do, that it quite took off Alice's attention from the angry brother. But he
T6    160:22   course I don't think so! Why, if ever I did fall off--which there's no chance of--but if I did--" Here he
T8    183: 9       "Because people don't fall off quite so often, when they've had much practice."
A8     68: 7   of  settling all difficulties, great or small. "Off with his head!" she said without even looking round.
T8    182:41   horse stopped (which it did very often), he fell off in front; and, whenever it went on again (which it
T8    182:42       it  generally did rather suddenly), he fell off behind. Otherwise he kept on pretty well, except that
T6    161: 1   leant  forwards (and as nearly as possible fell off the wall in doing so) and offered Alice his hand. She
A1      8:26   I wouldn't say anything about it, even if I fell off the top of the house!" (Which was very likely true.)
T8    184:43   a  sugar-loaf. When I used to wear it, if I fell off the horse, it always touched the ground directly. So I
T7    170: 2   that,  whenever a horse stumbled, the rider fell off instantly. The confusion got worse every moment, and
```

OFF (cont.)

```
T5    156:19  rushes a good long way down before breaking them off--and for a while Alice forgot all about the Sheep and
A12    97:11  fright and half of anger, and tried to beat them off, and found herself lying on the bank, with her head in
T8    190:25  into the forest. "It wo'n't take long to see him off, I expect," Alice said to herself, as she stood
A11    91:21  Dormouse out of court! Suppress him! Pinch him! Off with his whiskers!"
T8    180: 4  that if one Knight hits the other, he knocks him off his horse; and, if he misses, he tumbles off himself--
A12    98:11  tea: it's getting late." So Alice got up and ran off, thinking while she ran, as well she might, what a
A4     27:16  And Alice was so much frightened that she ran off at once in the direction it pointed to, without trying
A4     32:16  at Alice the moment she appeared; but she ran off as hard as she could, and soon found herself safe in a
T9    202:25  the decanters, and drank the wine as it ran off the edges of the table--and three of them (who looked
T1    110:23  there's a dear!" And Alice got the Red Queen off the table, and set it up before the kitten as a model
T3    129:16  "Something like cottages with the roofs taken off, and stalks put to them--and what quantities of honey
A5     41:25  or twice, and shook itself. Then it got down off the mushroom, and crawled away into the grass, merely
T8    182:28  a plan for keeping the hair from being blown off?" Alice enquired.
A12    94:28  his guilt, of course," said the Queen, "so, off with--"
A6     48:27  "Talking of axes," said the Duchess, "chop off her head!"
A6     48:10  fix on one, the cook took the cauldron of soup off the fire, and at once set to work throwing everything
A2     14: 8  sha'n't be able! I shall be a great deal too far off to trouble myself about you: you must manage the best
A2     14: 5  be almost out of sight, they were getting so far off). "Oh, my poor little feet, I wonder who will put on
T5    156:31  at the obstinacy of the rushes in growing so far off, as, with flushed cheeks and dripping hair and hands,
T10   205: 1                    She took her off the table as she spoke, and shook her backwards and
A10    80: 9  you know, upon the other side. / The further off from England the nearer is to France. / Then turn not
A4     32:35  puppy: whereupon the puppy jumped into the air off all its feet at once, with a yelp of delight, and
T2    127: 3  in Alice's ears, and almost blowing her hair off her head, she fancied.
A8     67: 1  about, and shouting "Off with his head!" or "Off with her head!" about once in a minute.
A9     73: 5  players, and shouting "Off with his head!" or "Off with her head!" Those whom she sentenced were taken
A8     65:16                "Are their heads off?" shouted the Queen.
A6     50:21       sitting on a bough of a tree a few yards off.
T8    180: 4  him off his horse; and, if he misses, he tumbles off himself--and another Rule seems to be that they hold
A8     65: 9  who had meanwhile been examining the roses. "Off with their heads!" and the procession moved on, three
T8    182:34  it, like a fruit-tree. Now the reason hair falls off is because it hangs down--things never fall upwards,
T8    185:10  very seriously. "And then he took the helmet off again--but it took hours and hours to get me out. I was
A4     33: 4  opportunity for making her escape: so she set off at once, and ran till she was quite tired and out of
T2    123:40  nonsense to Alice, so she said nothing, but set off at once towards the Red Queen. To her surprise she lost
T8    182:23  well fastened on?" he continued, as they set off.
A12    96:21  she spoke. (The unfortunate little Bill had left off writing on his slate with one finger, as he found it
A6     49:29  the little thing grunted in reply (it had left off sneezing by this time). "Don't grunt," said Alice;
A3     23:11  but they began running when they liked, and left off when they liked, so that it was not easy to know when
T4    145: 5  clapping his hands triumphantly. "And if he left off dreaming about you, where do you suppose you'd be?"
T6    162:12  can. With proper assistance, you might have left off at seven."
A9     73:10                Then the Queen left off, quite out of breath, and said to Alice "Have you seen
A11    89: 4       All this time the Queen never left off staring at the Hatter, and, just as the Dormouse
A9     73: 3  the time they were playing the Queen never left off quarreling with the other players, and shouting "Off
T4    139:41  one dance," Tweedledum panted out, and they left off dancing as suddenly as they had begun: the music
T5    156:45  oh, oh!" from poor Alice, it swept her straight off the seat, and down among the heap of rushes.
A1     11: 9  hot buttered toast), she very soon finished it off. * * * * * * * * * *
T9    201: 8  Remove the joint!" And the waiters carried it off, and brought a large plum-pudding in its place.
A6     48:19  flew close by it, and very nearly carried it off.
T8    191: 7  it?" she said to herself, as she lifted it off, and set it on her lap to make out what it could
T5    152: 4  her hand about as if she wanted to shake it off. "My finger's bleeding! Oh, oh, oh, oh!"
A8     68:38  cut off a head unless there was a body to cut it off from: that he had never had to do such a thing before,
T5    158:15  get it for yourself." And so saying, she went off to the other end of the shop, and set the egg upright
A8     68:16  knew whether it was her turn or not. So she went off in search of her hedgehog.
A8     69: 9  "fetch her here." And the executioner went off like an arrow.
T4    147:12             So the two brothers went off hand-in-hand into the wood, and returned in a minute
T4    147:27  happen to one in a battle--to get one's head cut off."
T4    147:24  of Tweedledee, "to keep his head from being cut off," as he said.
A8     63: 9  to find out, we should all have our heads cut off, you know. So you see, Miss, we're doing our best,
A8     68:37        argument was, that you couldn't cut off a head unless there was a body to cut it off from: that
T8    181: 6  you very much," said Alice. "May I help you off with your helmet?" It was evidently more than he could
A4     33: 1  the while, till at last it sat down a good way off, panting, with its tongue hanging out of its mouth, and
A2     19: 6       splashing about in the pool a little way off, and she swam nearer to make out what it was: at first
T2    123:45  Queen (whom she spied out at last, a long way off), she thought she would try the plan, this time, of
```

OFFENDED (15)

```
A3     24:16  in a whisper, half afraid that it would be offended again.
T8    183: 5  looked very much surprised, and a little offended at the remark. "What makes you say that?" he asked, as
T2    125:17  from the Queen's tone that she was a little offended: and they walked on in silence till they got to the top
A2     20:11  Alice in a sorrowful tone. "I'm afraid I've offended it again!" For the Mouse was swimming away from her as
A7     59:11  "I've had nothing yet," Alice replied in an offended tone: "so I ca'n't take more."
A10    81:37  what I say," the Mock Turtle replied, in an offended tone. And the Gryphon added "Come, let's hear some of
A3     22:35  I was going to say," said the Dodo in an offended tone, "was that the best thing to get us dry would be a
A10    84:13  eagerly that the Gryphon said, in a rather offended tone, "Hm! No accounting for tastes! Sing her 'Turtle
T8W    14: 5            Alice felt rather offended at this answer, and was very nearly walking on and
T5    156: 1            This offended Alice a little, so there was no more conversation for a
T6    162:37       "I'm not offended," said Humpty Dumpty.
T6    162:19  dismay, for Humpty Dumpty looked thoroughly offended, and she began to wish she hadn't chosen that subject.
A5     41:20  "I wish the creatures wouldn't be so easily offended!"
A3     26:11  pleaded poor Alice. "But you're so easily offended, you know!"
A2     19:41       and she felt certain it must be really offended. "We wo'n't talk about her any more, if you'd rather
```

OPPORTUNITY (10)
A4   33: 3   This seemed to Alice a good opportunity for making her escape: so she set off at once, and ran
A6   46:38   The - Footman seemed to think this a good opportunity for repeating his remark, with variations. "I shall sit
T4   147:39   to-day," said Alice, thinking it a good opportunity to make peace.
A1   8:32   and though this was not a very good opportunity for showing off her knowledge, as there was no one to
A3   26:17   out of sight. And an old Crab took the opportunity of saying to her daughter "Ah, my dear! Let this be a
A5   43:22   minute or two, which gave the Pigeon the opportunity of adding "You're looking for eggs, I know that well
T9   193:19   "We gave you the opportunity of doing it," the Red Queen remarked: "but I daresay
A11   87: 7   got behind him, and very soon found an opportunity of taking it away. She did it so quickly that the poor
A6   48:24   said Alice, who felt very glad to get an opportunity of showing off a little of her knowledge. "Just think
A8   68:18   which seemed to Alice an excellent opportunity for croqueting one of them with the other: the only

POLITELY (13)
T8   184:28   "Very much indeed," Alice said politely.
T4   139:10   "I was thinking," Alice said politely, "which is the best way out of this wood: it's getting
T4   140:20   him. "If it's very long," she said, as politely as she could, "would you please tell me first which
A7   56:21   I don't quite understand you," she said, as politely as she could.
A5   35:14   put it more clearly," Alice replied, very politely, "for I ca'n't understand it myself, to begin with; and
T8W   18: 9   mind saying it in rhyme?" she asked very politely.
T9   201:41   "Please do," Alice said very politely.
A6   48: 4   don't know of any that do," Alice said very politely, feeling quite pleased to have got into a conversation
A9   72:11   understand that better," Alice said very politely, "if I had it written down: but I ca'n't quite follow
T6   161:17   ca'n't quite remember it," Alice said, very politely.
T5   153:23   your finger is better now?" Alice said very politely, as she crossed the little brook after the Queen. * * *
A8   63:40   so please your Majesty," said Alice very politely; but she added, to herself, "Why, they're only a pack
A3   22: 8   pardon!" said the Mouse, frowning, but very politely. "Did you speak?"

POOR (51)
A2   15:16   Poor Alice! It was as much as she could do, lying down on
A11   89:11   "I'm a poor man, your Majesty," the Hatter began, in a trembling
A11   89:19   "I'm a poor man," the Hatter went on, "and most things twinkled
A11   90: 8   and went down on one knee. "I'm a poor man, your Majesty," he began.
T9   195:31   The Red Queen said "That's a poor thin way of doing things. Now here, we mostly have days
T5   150:19   "It's a poor sort of memory that only works backwards," the Queen
A3   26:10   "I didn't mean it!" pleaded poor Alice. "But you're so easily offended, you know!"
A5   41:18   "But I'm not used to it!" pleaded poor Alice in a piteous tone. And she thought to herself "I
T9   196:36   "She's tired, poor thing!" said the Red Queen. "Smoothe her hair--lend her
A7   60:12   This answer so confused poor Alice, that she let the Dormouse go on for some time
A2   17:16   "I'm sure those are not the right words," said poor Alice, and her eyes filled with tears again as she went
T1   115:34   The poor King looked puzzled and unhappy, and struggled with the
T7   172:30   "Do you call that a whisper?" cried the poor King, jumping up and shaking himself. "If you do such a
T5   152:36   "Oh, don't go on like that!" cried the poor Queen, wringing her hands in despair. "Consider what a
T5   149:19   "But I don't want it done at all!" groaned the poor Queen. "I've been a-dressing myself for the last two
T1   107: 7   children's faces was this: first she held the poor thing down by its ear with one paw, and then with the
A6   49: 2   tossing the baby violently up and down, and the poor little thing howled so, that Alice could hardly hear
A12   93: 5   had put the Lizard in head downwards, and the poor little thing was waving its tail about in a melancholy
A6   49:17   "just like a star-fish," thought Alice. The poor little thing was snorting like a steam-engine when she
A4   32:13   little animals and birds waiting outside. The poor little Lizard, Bill, was in the middle, being held up
T3   135:18   melancholy little sighs, and this time the poor Gnat really seemed to have sighed itself away, for,
T3   131:40   off her thoughts from the unhappiness of the poor little creature.
T8W   21:17   gone back and given a few minutes to making the poor old creature comfortable.
T9   196:19   did not say this aloud, for fear of hurting the poor Queen's feelings.
A1   12:20   when she had tired herself out with trying, the poor little thing sat down and cried.
T7   176:17   said, looking slyly up at the crown, which the poor King was nearly shaking off his head, he trembled so
T5   152:14   "When I fasten my shawl again," the poor Queen groaned out: "the brooch will come undone
T8   182:38   and every now and then stopping to help the poor Knight, who certainly was not a good rider.
T8   186:21   Alice asked, hoping to cheer him up, for the poor Knight seemed quite low-spirited about it.
T4   144:14   Alice: "because he was a little sorry for the poor oysters."
T1   114: 4   was very anxious to be of use, and, as the poor little Lily was nearly screaming herself into a fit,
T7   171:10   about, and make the most fearful faces at the poor King.
A11   87: 8   taking it away. She did it so quickly that the poor little juror (it was Bill, the Lizard) could not make
A2   18:15   "and things are worse than ever," thought the poor child, "for I never was so small as this before, never!
A2   19:28   Alice hastily, afraid that she had hurt the poor animal's feelings. "I quite forgot you didn't like cats
A6   50: 5   nothing more to do with you. Mind now!" The poor little thing sobbed again (or grunted, it was
AI   3:11   To stir the tiniest feather! / Yet what can one poor voice avail / Against three tongues together?
A3   26:40   if I shall ever see you any more!" And here poor Alice began to cry again, for she felt very lonely and
T9   192:30   "I only said 'if'!" poor Alice pleaded in a piteous tone.
T5   156:45   series of little shrieks of "Oh, oh, oh!" from poor Alice, it swept her straight off the seat, and down
A4   32:28   stretching out one paw, trying to touch her. "Poor little thing!" said Alice, in a coaxing tone, and she
A1   12:14   on going into the garden at once; but, alas for poor Alice! when she got to the door, she found she had
A9   75: 6   and then they both sat silent and looked at poor Alice, who felt ready to sink into the earth. At last
A4   28:27   "It was much pleasanter at home," thought poor Alice, "when one wasn't always growing larger and
A1   10: 7   "and even if my head would go through," thought poor Alice, "it would be of very little use without my
T2   126:21   if all the things move along with us?" thought poor puzzled Alice. And the Queen seemed to guess her
T3   136:14   "I wish I knew!" thought poor Alice. She answered, rather sadly, "Nothing, just now
A1   12:28   be two people. "But it's no use now," thought poor Alice, "to pretend to be two people! Why, there's
A5   42:14   "And where have my shoulders got to? And oh, my poor hands, how is it I ca'n't see you?" She was moving them
A2   14: 6   sight, they were getting so far off). "Oh, my poor little feet, I wonder who will put on your shoes and
A11   90:10   "You're a very poor speaker," said the King.

PRETEND (8)
A1   12:28   it's no use now," thought poor Alice, "to pretend to be two people! Why, there's hardly enough of me left
T1   110:11   beginning with her favourite phrase "Let's pretend." She had had quite a long argument with her sister

PRETEND (cont.)
    T1   110:13   all because Alice had begun with "Let's pretend we're kings and queens;" and her sister, who liked
    T1   110:21   from Alice's speech to the kitten. "Let's pretend that you're the Red Queen, Kitty! Do you know, I think
    T1   110:18   suddenly in her ear, "Nurse! Do let's pretend that I'm a hungry hyaena and you're a bone!"
    T1   110: 9   down among my pieces. Kitty dear, let's pretend--" And here I wish I could tell you half the things
    T1   111: 7   got, oh! such beautiful things in it! Let's pretend there's a way of getting through into it, somehow,
    T1   111: 8   through into it, somehow, Kitty. Let's pretend the glass has got all soft like gauze, so that we can
RATE (15)
    T1   114:20   hours and hours getting to the table, at that rate. I'd far better help you, hadn't I?" But the King took
    A2   16:11   oh dear! I shall never get to twenty at that rate! However, the Multiplication-Table doesn't signify:
    A7   60:35   "At any rate I'll never go there again!" said Alice, as she picked
    T4   146: 1   went on, as cheerfully as she could, "At any rate, I'd better be getting out of the wood, for really it's
    T5   151:13   "You're wrong there, at any rate," said the Queen. "Were you ever punished?"
    A4   30:11   "Well, it's got no business there, at any rate: go and take it away!"
    A2   19:12   I should think very likely it can talk: at any rate, there's no harm in trying." So she began: "O Mouse, do
    A11   89:25   "Well, at any rate, the Dormouse said--" the Hatter went on, looking
    T3   135:38   it looked very cool and shady. "Well, at any rate it's a great comfort," she said as she stepped under
    A12   93:41   "Well, I sha'n't go, at any rate," said Alice; "besides, that's not a regular rule: you
    T1   118:30   somebody killed something: that's clear, at any rate--"
    A1   10:14   she might find another key on it, or at any rate a book of rules for shutting people up like telescopes:
    A6   46:24   very nearly at the top of his head. But at any rate he might answer questions.--How am I to get in?" she
    A1   9:38   too large, or the key was too small, but at any rate it would not open any of them. However, on the second
    T5   150: 4   "Well, I don't want any to-day, at any rate."
REMEMBER (27)
    A7   55:33   while Alice thought over all she could remember about ravens and writing-desks, which wasn't much.
    A12   98: 7   she told her sister, as well as she could remember them, all these strange Adventures of hers that you
    T2   128:24   thing--turn out your toes as you walk--and remember who you are!" She did not wait for Alice to curtsey,
    T12 207:24   what to--what to purr. It saves time, remember!" And she caught it up and gave it one little kiss,
    T6   161:17   "I'm afraid I ca'n't quite remember it," Alice said, very politely.
    A9   70:20   now what the moral of that is, but I shall remember it in a bit."
    T3   136: 4   after all! And now, who am I? I will remember, if I can! I'm determined to do it!" But being
    A1   9: 7   (Dinah was the cat.) "I hope they'll remember her saucer of milk at tea-time. Dinah, my dear! I wish
    T6   166:36   "I will, if I can remember it so long," said Alice.
    A2   15:41   I got up this morning? I almost think I can remember feeling a little different. But if I'm not the same,
    T5   152:31   be glad!" the Queen said. "Only I never can remember the rule. You must be very happy, living in this wood,
    T2   128:32   but she was gone, and Alice began to remember that she was a Pawn, and that it would soon be time for
    T9   196:17   thought to herself "I never should try to remember my name in the middle of an accident! Where would be
    A5   36:33   "Ca'n't remember what things?" said the Caterpillar.
    T5   150:18   works one way," Alice remarked. "I ca'n't remember things before they happen."
    T3   137: 2   further on," the Fawn said. "I ca'n't remember here."
    A5   36:31   afraid I am, Sir," said Alice. "I ca'n't remember things as I used--and I don't keep the same size for
    A2   20: 7   dinner, and all sorts of things--I ca'n't remember half of them--and it belongs to a farmer, you know, and
    A11   90: 4   "That I ca'n't remember," said the Hatter.
    T3   135: 7   me lessons for that. If she couldn't remember my name, she'd call me 'Miss,' as the servants do."
    T9   196:16   till I was so frightened, I couldn't remember my own name!"
    A8   68: 2   "I've read that in some book, but I don't remember where."
    A1   12:11   the candle is blown out, for she could not remember ever having seen such a thing.
    A8   63:29   like the three gardeners, but she could not remember ever having heard of such a rule at processions; "and
    A1   10:24   things, all because they would not remember the simple rules their friends had taught them: such as
    A11   90: 5   "You must remember," remarked the King, "or I'll have you executed."
    T5   150:21   "What sort of things do you remember best?" Alice ventured to ask.
REPLY (10)
    T7   176: 8   the Unicorn cried out, before Alice could reply.
    A8   63:37   Knave of Hearts, who only bowed and smiled in reply.
    A3   26:12   The Mouse only growled in reply.
    T9   202:34   "Thank you very much," she whispered in reply, "but I can do quite well without."
    A11   86:32   down their names," the Gryphon whispered in reply "for fear they should forget them before the end of
    A6   49:28   out loud, and the little thing grunted in reply (it had left off sneezing by this time). "Don't grunt,"
    A8   65:18   please your Majesty!" the soldiers shouted in reply.
    T7   177: 8   the knife. "It's very provoking!" she said, in reply to the Lion (she was getting quite used to being called
    T9   201:25   of voice, and Alice hadn't a word to say in reply: she could only sit and look at it and gasp.
    T8   188:13   / That they could not be seen. / So, having no reply to give / To what the old man said, / I cried 'Come,
SIDE (50)
    T8   182:44   sideways; and, as he generally did this on the side on which Alice was walking, she soon found that it was
    T8   185:17   Alice ran to the side of the ditch to look for him. She was rather startled
    T1   113:22   kitten!" and she began scrambling wildly up the side of the fender.
    T5   156:20   Sheep and the knitting, as she bent over the side of the boat, with just the ends of her tangled hair
    T5   157: 8   it," said Alice, peeping cautiously over the side of the boat into the dark water. "I wish it hadn't let
    T1   114: 6   up the Queen and set her on the table by the side of her noisy little daughter.
    A6   46:11   for two reasons. First, because I'm on the same side of the door as you are: secondly, because they're
    T6   168:30   same. Now if you had the two eyes on the same side of the nose, for instance--or the mouth at the top--
    A5   41:29   "One side of what? The other side of what?" thought Alice to
    T5   149:29   go straight, you know, if you pin it all on one side," Alice said as she gently put it right for her; "and
    A2   15:17   was as much as she could do, lying down on one side, to look through into the garden with one eye; but to
    T8   190:30   road, and the Knight tumbling off, first on one side and then on the other. After the fourth or fifth tumble
    A1   9:31   and when Alice had been all the way down one side and up the other, trying every door, she walked sadly
    A5   41:29   the grass, merely remarking, as it went, "One side will make you grow taller, and the other side will make
    A4   29:16   And so she went on, taking first one side and then the other, and making quite a conversation of
    T9   198: 2   "QUEEN ALICE" in large letters, and on each side of the arch there was a bell-handle; one was marked
    T9   203: 3   the two Queens pushed her so, one on each side, that they nearly lifted her up into the air. "I rise

SIDE (cont.)
A10	82: 3	two creatures got so close to her, one on each side, and opened their eyes and mouths so <u>very</u> wide; but she
T9	192:13	White Queen sitting close to her, one on each side: she would have liked very much to ask them how they
A11	86: 5	before them, in chains, with a soldier on each side to guard him; and near the King was the White Rabbit,
T7	170:25	his great hands spread out like fans on each side.)
T6	165: 8	"And a long way beyond it on each side," Alice added.
T8	188:29	<u>a little fatter</u>. / I shook <u>him well from side</u> to <u>side</u>, / <u>Until his face was</u> blue: / '<u>Come</u>, <u>tell me</u>
T2	125:22	little brooks running straight across it from side to side, and the ground between was divided up into
T7	171:15	moment, while the great eyes rolled wildly from side to side.
T2	122:10	the Tiger-lily, waving itself passionately from side to side, and trembling with excitement. "They know I
T6	164:10	Dumpty went on, wagging his head gravely from side to side, "for to get their wages, you know."
T8	188:29	<u>little fatter</u>. / I shook <u>him well from side</u> to <u>side</u>, / <u>Until his face was</u> blue: / <u>'Come</u>, <u>tell me how you</u>
T2	125:22	brooks running straight across it from side to side, and the ground between was divided up into squares by
T7	171:15	while the great eyes rolled wildly from side to side.
T2	122:10	waving itself passionately from side to side, and trembling with excitement. "They know I ca'n't get
T6	164:11	went on, wagging his head gravely from side to side, "for to get their wages, you know."
A8	65:25	a very fine day!" said a timid voice at her side. She was walking by the White Rabbit, who was peeping
T9	204: 2	At this moment she heard a hoarse laugh at her side, and turned to see what was the matter with the White
T9	204:19	mischief--but the Queen was no longer at her side--she had suddenly dwindled down to the size of a little
A5	41:27	side will make you grow taller, and the other side will make you grow shorter."
A4	32:38	over; and, the moment she appeared on the other side, the puppy made another rush at the stick, and tumbled
T3	135:23	came to an open field, with a wood on the other side of it: it looked much darker than the last wood, and
T5	153:36	it really a <u>sheep</u> that was sitting on the other side of the counter? Rub as she would, she could make
T8	183: 8	to save himself from falling over on the other side.
A10	80: 8	is <u>another shore, you know</u>, <u>upon the other side</u>. / <u>The further off from England the nearer is to France</u>
T8W	14:·9	"Won't you let me help you round to the other side? You'll be out of the cold wind there."
A11	89: 3	up very sulkily and crossed over to the other side of the court.
A8	68:20	that her flamingo was gone across the other side of the garden, where Alice could see it trying in a
A5	41:29	"One side of <u>what</u>? The other side of <u>what</u>?" thought Alice to herself.
A9	70:24	And she squeezed herself up closer to Alice's side as she spoke.
T8	179:23	it was a White Knight. He drew up at Alice's side, and tumbled off his horse just as the Red Knight had
A8	68:25	Alice, "as all the arches are gone from this side of the ground." So she tucked it away under her arm,
T8	180:12	ended with their both falling off in this way, side by side. When they got up again, they shook hands, and
T8	180:12	their both falling off in this way, side by side. When they got up again, they shook hands, and then the

SIGHT (17)
T4	148:22	brothers took to their heels and were out of sight in a moment.
A8	68:23	was over, and both the hedgehogs were out of sight: "but it doesn't matter much," thought Alice, "as all
A3	26:17	the Lory, as soon as it was quite out of sight. And an old Crab took the opportunity of saying to her
T8	190:33	to him, and waited till he was out of sight.
A9	74: 8	then it watched the Queen till she was out of sight: then it chuckled. "What fun!" said the Gryphon, half
A11	91: 2	one of the officers; but the Hatter was out of sight before the officer could get to the door.
A5	41:32	it aloud; and in another moment it was out of sight.
A2	14: 5	at her feet, they seemed to be almost out of sight, they were getting so far off). "Oh, my poor little
A11	91:15	at the cook till his eyes were nearly out of sight, he said, in a deep voice, "What are tarts made of?"
A6	53:10	had not gone much farther before she came in sight of the house of the March Hare: she thought it must be
A1	9:23	passage, and the White Rabbit was still in sight, hurrying down it. There was not a moment to be lost:
T2	124: 5	face to face with the Red Queen, and full in sight of the hill she had been so long aiming at.
T2	120:26	However, there was the hill full in sight, so there was nothing to be done but start again. This
A8	67:21	to think that there was enough of it now in sight, and no more of it appeared.
T7	173:15	trotted on in silence, till they came into sight of a great crowd, in the middle of which the Lion and
T2	123:41	the Red Queen. To her surprise she lost sight of her in a moment, and found herself walking in at the
T4	144:31	"Isn't he a <u>lovely</u> sight?" said Tweedledum.

SILENCE (33)
A4	31:32	There was a dead silence instantly, and Alice thought to herself "I wonder what
T9	200: 7	and in she went, and there was a dead silence the moment she appeared.
A12	96:26	the court with a smile. There was a dead silence.
A4	32: 4	do that again!", which produced another dead silence.
A12	94:37	There was dead silence in the court, whilst the White Rabbit read out these
T9	201:30	moment she opened her lips, there was dead silence, and all eyes were fixed upon her; "and it's a very
T8	179: 2	gradually to die away, till all was dead silence, and Alice lifted up her head in some alarm. There was
T9	193:14	The Red Queen broke the silence by saying, to the White Queen, "I invite you to Alice's
A7	55:35	The Hatter was the first to break the silence. "What day of the month is it?" he said, turning to
T9	200:17	sat down in it, rather uncomfortable at the silence, and longing for some one to speak.
T9	193:13	and then there was an uncomfortable silence for a minute or two.
T6	159:17	provoking," Humpty Dumpty said after a long silence, looking away from Alice as he spoke, "to be called an
A4	30:13	There was a long silence after this, and Alice could only hear whispers now and
A9	74:34	These words were followed by a very long silence, broken only by an occasional exclamation of "Hjckrrh!"
AI	3:19	<u>Anon</u>, <u>to sudden silence won</u>, / <u>In fancy they pursue</u> / <u>The dream-child moving</u>
A4	31: 9	alone--"Catch him, you by the hedge!" then silence, and then another confusion of voices--"Hold up his
A3	23:20	pictures of him), while the rest waited in silence. At last the Dodo said "<u>Everybody</u> has won, and <u>all</u> must
A6	50: 7	which), and they went on for some while in silence.
T2	127: 2	ago! Faster!" And they ran on for a time in silence, with the wind whistling in Alice's ears, and almost
A5	35: 2	Alice looked at each other for some time in silence: at last the Caterpillar took the hookah out of its
T8	182:37	and for a few minutes she walked on in silence, puzzling over the idea, and every now and then
T2	125:17	was a <u>little</u> offended: and they walked on in silence till they got to the top of the little hill.
T7	173:15	breath for talking; so they trotted on in silence, till they came into sight of a great crowd, in the
T8	183:15	as she could. They went on a little way in silence after this, the Knight with his eyes shut, muttering to
T1	114:10	could do nothing but hug the little Lily in silence. As soon as she had recovered her breath a little, she
T2	122:16	There was silence in a moment, and several of the pink daisies turned
A5	41: 5	the Caterpillar, decidedly; and there was silence for some minutes.

SILENCE (cont.)
```
T9   199:35   any one's counting?" In a minute there was silence again, and the same shrill voice sang another verse:--
T2   122: 9   seemed  quite full of little shrill voices. "Silence, every one of you!" cried the Tiger-lily, waving itself
T8   184:21               There was a short silence after this, and then the Knight went on again. "I'm a
A11  86:34    hastily,  for  the White Rabbit cried out "Silence in the court!", and the King put on his spectacles and
A12  93:34    busily writing in his note-book, called out "Silence!", and read out from his book, "Rule Forty-two. All
A3   22: 2    all  ready? This is the driest thing I know. Silence all round, if you please! 'William the Conqueror, whose
```
SUBJECT (15)
```
T6   161:19   Humpty Dumpty, "and it's my turn to choose a subject--" ("He talks about it just as if it was a game!"
A2   19:43    of  its tail. "As if I would talk on such a subject! Our family always hated cats: nasty, low, vulgar
T6   162:32   pleased  to  find that she had chosen a good subject after all.
T8   184:38   so vexed at the idea, that Alice changed the subject hastily. "What a curious helmet you've got!" she said
T9   192:26   thinking  for a minute, suddenly changed the subject of the conversation. "What do you mean by 'If you
A7   58:18               "Suppose we change the subject," the March Hare interrupted, yawning. "I'm getting
A10  83: 8    by the whole thing, and longed to change the subject.
T2   123:18   like  this  idea at all: so, to change the subject, she asked "Does she ever come out here?"
A9   77:11          said Alice, in a hurry to change the subject.
A2   20: 1    said  Alice, in a great hurry to change the subject of conversation. "Are you--are you fond--of--of dogs?"
T6   162:14   remarked. (They had had quite enough of the subject of age, she thought: and, if they really were to take
AI   3:28     faintly  strove  that weary one / To put the subject by, / "The rest next time--" "It is next time!" / The
A6   48: 8    it  would be as well to introduce some other subject of conversation. While she was trying to fix on one,
T6   163:45          that we've had enough of that subject, and it would be just as well if you'd mention what you
T6   162:20   and she began to wish she hadn't chosen that subject. "If only I knew," she thought to herself, "which was
```
SURE (45)
```
A4   30: 7                        "Sure, it's an arm, yer honour!" (He pronounced it "arrum.")
A4   30:10                        "Sure, it does, yer honour: but it's an arm for all that."
T6   163:16         "To be sure I was!" Humpty Dumpty said gaily as she turned it round
T9   194:34                     "To be sure I do," said Alice.
A1   12:41    to  find that she remained the same size. To be sure, this is what generally happens when one eats cake; but
A2   19: 4    my own tears! That will be a queer thing, to be sure! However, everything is queer to-day."
T7   172:38             "Yes, to be sure," said the King: "and the best of the joke is, that
T8   185: 3    there was the danger of falling into it, to be sure. That happened to me once--and the worst of it was,
A4   30:38    a  good  deal: this fireplace is narrow, to be sure; but I think I can kick a little!"
T3   136: 1    I  do  believe it's got no name--why, to be sure it hasn't!"
A8   67: 3         Alice began to feel very uneasy: to be sure, she had not as yet had any dispute with the Queen, but
T3   137:21   way,  but wherever the road divided, there were sure to be two finger-posts pointing the same way, one
A4   30: 2    And  then  a voice she had never heard before, "Sure I'm here! Digging for apples, yer honour!"
A6   51:15              "Oh, you're sure to do that," said the Cat, "if you only walk long
A6   49:26    child  away  with me," thought Alice, "they're sure to kill it in a day or two. Wouldn't it be murder to
A6   47:13    Alice,  a little timidly, for she was not quite sure whether it was good manners for her to speak first,
T3   137:32   another  moment  she recovered herself, feeling sure that they must be TWEEDLEDUM AND TWEEDLEDEE
A2   16: 4                        "I'm not Ada," she said, "for her hair goes in such long
A2   17:16                        "I'm sure those are not the right words," said poor Alice, and
T4   138:15                        "I'm sure I'm very sorry," was all Alice could say; for the words
T5   149:38                        "I'm sure I'll take you with pleasure!" the Queen said. "Two
T5   150:17                        "I'm sure mine only works one way," Alice remarked. "I ca'n't
T7   177: 3                        "I'm sure I don't know," the Lion growled out as he lay down
T9   192:38                        "I'm sure I didn't mean--" Alice was beginning, but the Red Queen
A4   30:20    out  of the window, I only wish they could! I'm sure I don't want to stay in here any longer!"
T9   194:12       remain:  it  would come to bite me--and I'm sure I shouldn't remain!"
A3   26:38    "Nobody seems to like her, down here, and I'm sure she's the best cat in the world! Oh, my dear Dinah! I
A2   16: 5    and mine doesn't go in ringlets at all; and I'm sure I ca'n't be Mabel, for I know all sorts of things, and
T7   172:20       the  Messenger  said in a sullen tone. "I'm sure nobody walks much faster than I do!"
T1   111: 6    only  get through into Looking-glass House! I'm sure it's got, oh! such beautiful things in it! Let's
T1   110: 2    her hands. "And I do so wish it was true! I'm sure the woods look sleepy in the autumn, when the leaves
T3   135: 5         "That would never do, I'm sure," said Alice: "the governess would never think of
A2   14: 7    shoes  and  stockings for you now, dears? I'm sure I sha'n't be able! I shall be a great deal too far off
T12  208:11   to  know--Oh,  Kitty, do help to settle it! I'm sure your paw can wait!" But the provoking kitten only began
T7   176:20                        "I'm not so sure of that," said the Unicorn.
A5   43:41    How  puzzling  all these changes are! I'm never sure what I'm going to be, from one minute to another!
A4   27: 4    my fur and whiskers! She'll get me executed, as sure as ferrets are ferrets! Where can I have dropped them,
A4   30:14    could only hear whispers now and then; such as "Sure, I don't like it, yer honour, at all, at all!" "Do as I
A4   28: 5    to  her  lips. "I know something interesting is sure to happen," she said to herself, "whenever I eat or
A4   32: 7    I  eat  one of these cakes," she thought, "it's sure to make some change in my size; and, as it ca'n't
A10  83:12    Alice  did not dare to disobey, though she felt sure it would all come wrong, and she went on in a trembling
A3   21:17    her  eyes  anxiously fixed on it, for she felt sure she would catch a bad cold if she did not get dry very
T12  207:36       it  to  your friends just yet, for I'm not sure.
T1   113:13   she  put  her head closer down, "and I'm nearly sure they ca'n't see me. I feel somehow as if I was getting
A5   37: 7    injure the brain; / But, now that I'm perfectly sure I have none, / Why, I do it again and again."
```
THING (84)
```
T9   195:23   said  the  Red Queen: "when you've once said a thing, that fixes it, and you must take the consequences."
A3   22:18     what  'it' means well enough, when I find a thing," said the Duck: "it's generally a frog, or a worm. The
A7   60:25    'much  of a muchness'--did you ever see such a thing as a drawing of a muchness!"
A2   19:16    speaking to a mouse: she had never done such a thing before, but she remembered having seen, in her
T5   150:14    great  astonishment. "I never heard of such a thing!"
A1   12:12    she could not remember ever having seen such a thing.
A8   68:39    off  from: that he had never had to do such a thing before, and he wasn't going to begin at his time of
T7   172:31       up  and shaking himself. "If you do such a thing again, I'll have you buttered! It went through and
T9   196: 6        Now,  as it happened, there wasn't such a thing in the house, that morning."
A7   58: 9    went on in a mournful tone, "he wo'n't do a thing I ask! It's always six o'clock now."
```

THING (cont.)

T2	128:24	when you ca'n't think of the English for a thing--turn out your toes as you walk--and remember who you
A9	70: 2	how glad I am to see you again, you dear old thing!" said the Duchess, as she tucked her arm
A4	32:20	to grow to my right size again; and the second thing is to find my way into that lovely garden. I think that
A9	73:20	"You are all pardoned." "Come, that's a good thing," she said to herself, for she had felt quite unhappy
T5	155: 5	But even this plan failed: the 'thing' went through the ceiling as quietly as possible, as if
A6	49:35	altogether Alice did not like the look of the thing at all. "But perhaps it was only sobbing," she thought,
T5	149:14	the Queen said. "It isn't my notion of the thing, at all."
T2	126:18	The most curious part of the thing was, that the trees and the other things round them
T12	207:19	at it," she said, when she was explaining the thing afterwards to her sister: "it turned away its head, and
T9	202:36	"That wouldn't be at all the thing," the Red Queen said very decidedly: so Alice tried to
T1	110:25	as a model for it to imitate: however, the thing didn't succeed, principally, Alice said, because the
A9	73:13	"It's the thing Mock Turtle Soup is made from," said the Queen.
T3	132:11	the air, and in her fright she caught at the thing nearest to her hand, which happened to be the Goat's
A3	23: 6	to do it." (And, as you might like to try the thing yourself some winter-day, I will tell you how the Dodo
A3	24: 5	Alice thought the whole thing very absurd, but they all looked so grave that she did
A10	83: 8	but she was dreadfully puzzled by the whole thing, and longed to change the subject.
T1	107:20	"Oh, you wicked, wicked little thing!" cried Alice, catching up the kitten, and giving it a
A6	49:28	said the last words out loud, and the little thing grunted in reply (it had left off sneezing by this
A6	49: 2	violently up and down, and the poor little thing howled so, that Alice could hardly hear the words:--
A12	93: 5	Lizard in head downwards, and the poor little thing was waving its tail about in a melancholy way, being
A6	49:17	a star-fish," thought Alice. The poor little thing was snorting like a steam-engine when she caught it,
A1	12:20	tired herself out with trying, the poor little thing sat down and cried.
A6	50: 5	to do with you. Mind now!" The poor little thing sobbed again (or grunted, it was impossible to say
A4	32:29	out one paw, trying to touch her. "Poor little thing!" said Alice, in a coaxing tone, and she tried hard to
A4	28: 8	I'm quite tired of being such a tiny little thing!"
A9	70:36	"Ah well! It means much the same thing," said the Duchess, digging her sharp little chin into
A7	55:30	"that 'I breathe when I sleep' is the same thing as 'I sleep when I breathe'!"
A7	55:24	well say that 'I see what I eat' is the same thing as 'I eat what I see'!"
A7	55:27	Hare, "that 'I like what I get' is the same thing as 'I get what I like'!"
A7	55:31	"It is the same thing with you," said the Hatter, and here the conversation
A7	55:22	at least I mean what I say--that's the same thing, you know."
A7	55:23	"Not the same thing a bit!" said the Hatter. "Why, you might just as well
T12	207:10	talk with a person if they always say the same thing?"
T1	107: 1	One thing was certain, that the white kitten had had nothing to
T12	207:38	been really with me in my dream, there was one thing you would have enjoyed--I had such a quantity of poetry
T4	146:17	a careful examination of the little white thing. "Not a rattle-snake, you know," she added hastily,
T4	146:15	with a trembling finger at a small white thing lying under the tree.
A4	29: 4	to read fairy tales, I fancied that kind of thing never happened, and now here I am in the middle of one!
T4	145: 9	"You'd be nowhere. Why, you're only a sort of thing in his dream!"
T4	145:13	indignantly. "Besides, if I'm only a sort of thing in his dream, what are you, I should like to know?"
A4	27:29	next!" And she began fancying the sort of thing that would happen: "'Miss Alice! Come here directly,
T6	162:25	"It is a--most--provoking--thing," he said at last, "when a person doesn't know a cravat
A10	84: 5	as you go on? It's by far the most confusing thing that I ever heard!"
A7	59:24	"There's no such thing!" Alice was beginning very angrily, but the Hatter and
T4	143:16	'After such kindness, that would be / A dismal thing to do!' / 'The night is fine,' the Walrus said. / 'Do
A10	78:12	"--so you can have no idea what a delightful thing a Lobster-Quadrille is!"
A2	19: 4	drowned in my own tears! That will be a queer thing, to be sure! However, everything is queer to-day."
T8	181:36	single bee has come near it yet. And the other thing is a mouse-trap. I suppose the mice keep the bees out--
T8	187: 6	"No, you oughtn't: that's quite another thing! The song is called 'Ways and Means': but that's only
A12	94:27	hands at this: it was the first really clever thing the King had said that day.
T9	196:36	"She's tired, poor thing!" said the Red Queen. "Smoothe her hair--lend her your
T1	107: 7	faces was this: first she held the poor thing down by its ear with one paw, and then with the other
A6	53: 8	a grin without a cat! It's the most curious thing I ever saw in all my life!"
A8	62: 3	them red. Alice thought this a very curious thing, and she went nearer to watch them, and, just as she
T9	201:31	were fixed upon her; "and it's a very curious thing, I think--every poem was about fishes in some way. Do
A2	19:35	could only see her. She is such a dear quiet thing," Alice went on, half to herself, as she swam lazily
A2	19:38	washing her face--and she is such a nice soft thing to nurse--and she's such a capital one for catching
A4	34: 2	not see anything that looked like the right thing to eat or drink under the circumstances. There was a
T5	154:18	minute or so in vainly pursuing a large bright thing that looked sometimes like a doll and sometimes like a
A3	23: 1	Dodo in an offended tone, "was that the best thing to get us dry would be a Caucus-race."
A3	22: 2	air. "Are you all ready? This is the driest thing I know. Silence all round, if you please! 'William the
A12	94:18	the White Rabbit, "and that's the queerest thing about it." (The jury all looked puzzled.)
T8	186: 6	"Now the cleverest thing of the sort that I ever did," he went on after a pause,
A4	31: 5	The first thing she heard was a general chorus of "There goes Bill!"
A4	32:18	"The first thing I've got to do," said Alice to herself, as she wandered
T3	129: 1	Of course the first thing to do was to make a grand survey of the country she was
T4	139:21	begun wrong!" cried Tweedledum. "The first thing in a visit is to say 'How d'ye do?' and shake hands!"
T1	112: 2	into the Looking-glass room. The very first thing she did was to look whether there was a fire in the
A3	24: 9	The next thing was to eat the comfits: this caused some noise and
A5	43:42	I've got back to my right size: the next thing is, to get into that beautiful garden--how is that to
T4	147: 3	himself in it: which was such an extraordinary thing to do, that it quite took off Alice's attention from
T4	148: 2	"And I hit every thing within reach," cried Tweedledum, "whether I can see it
T4	148: 1	very close," he added: "I generally hit every thing I can see--when I get really excited."
A9	74: 1	a Gryphon is, look at the picture.) "Up, lazy thing!" said the Queen, "and take this young lady to see the

THINGS (79)

T5	154:16	"Things flow about so here!" she said at last in a plaintive
A10	78:37	who had been jumping about like mad things all this time, sat down again very sadly and quietly,
A11	86:33	"Stupid things!" Alice began in a loud indignant voice; but she
A11	86:38	that all the jurors were writing down "Stupid things!" on their slates, and she could even make out that one

THINGS (cont.)

A2	18:14	was lying on the glass table as before, "and things are worse than ever," thought the poor child, "for I
T9	196:15	great lumps--and knocking over the tables and things--till I was so frightened, I couldn't remember my own
T9	193:23	Alice. "Lessons teach you to do sums, and things of that sort."
T8	187:16	Of all the strange things that Alice saw in her journey Through The Looking-Glass
T5	151:18	"Yes, but then I had done the things I was punished for," said Alice: "that makes all the
T1	110:10	And here I wish I could tell you half the things Alice used to say, beginning with her favourite phrase
T4	145:19	said Tweedledum, "when you're only one of the things in his dream. You know very well you're not real."
A7	58:13	tea-time, and we've no time to wash the things between whiles."
T2	126:21	seemed to pass anything. "I wonder if all the things move along with us?" thought poor puzzled Alice. And
T8	181:24	vexation passing over his face. "Then all the things must have fallen out! And the box is no use without
A8	67:27	you've no idea how confusing it is all the things being alive: for instance, there's the arch I've got to
A2	16: 8	it all is! I'll try if I know all the things I used to know. Let me see: four times five is twelve,
A7	58:15	"Exactly so," said the Hatter: "as the things get used up."
T8	181:21	"But the things can get out," Alice gently remarked. "Do you know the
T1	110:33	just the same as our drawing-room, only the things go the other way. I can see all of it when I get upon a
T5	153:12	she said: "one ca'n't believe impossible things."
T5	153:15	I've believed as many as six impossible things before breakfast. There goes the shawl again!"
T3	135:28	she said thoughtfully to herself, "where things have no names. I wonder what'll become of my name when
T4	147:16	Tweedledum remarked. "Every one of these things has got to go on, somehow or other."
A8	68:14	their turns, and she did not like the look of things at all, as the game was in such confusion that she
T4	147:13	returned in a minute with their arms full of things--such as bolsters, blankets, hearth-rugs, table-cloths,
T1	115:38	this one a bit: it writes all manner of things that I don't intend--"
A7	60:16	very sleepy; "and they drew all manner of things--everything that begins with an M--"
T1	115:39	"What manner of things?" said the Queen, looking over the book (in which Alice
A2	20: 7	up and beg for its dinner, and all sorts of things--I ca'n't remember half of them--and it belongs to a
T5	157:12	"Crabs, and all sorts of things," said the Sheep: "plenty of choice, only make up your
T9	203:11	Alice afterwards described it) all sorts of things happened in a moment. The candles all grew up to the
A2	16: 6	I ca'n't be Mabel, for I know all sorts of things, and she, oh, she knows such a very little! Besides,
T5	150:21	"What sort of things do you remember best?" Alice ventured to ask.
T4	147:20	those two bustled about--and the quantity of things they put on--and the trouble they gave her in tying
T6	164:27	afternoon--the time when you begin broiling things for dinner--"
T9	195:31	Queen said "That's a poor thin way of doing things. Now here, we mostly have days and nights two or three
T5	152:41	"Can you keep from crying by considering things?" she asked.
T8	184:22	went on again. "I'm a great hand at inventing things. Now, I daresay you noticed, the last time you picked
A9	71:15	"what a clear way you have of putting things!"
A2	20: 6	such long curly brown hair! And it'll fetch things when you throw them, and it'll sit up and beg for its
A9	70:13	them bitter--and--and barley-sugar and such things that make children sweet-tempered. I only wish people
T6	160:35	"Ah, well! They may write such things in a book," Humpty Dumpty said in a calmer tone.
T5	150: 1	"Oh, things that happened the week after next," the Queen replied
T4	146:10	"Selfish things!" thought Alice, and she was just going to say
T9	196:24	well, but she ca'n't help saying foolish things as a general rule."
A1	8:31	(for, you see, Alice had learnt several things of this sort in her lessons in the school-room, and
T1	111: 7	House! I'm sure it's got, oh! such beautiful things in it! Let's pretend there's a way of getting through
A9	71: 3	"How fond she is of finding morals in things!" Alice thought to herself.
T8	182:34	hair falls off is because it hangs down--things never fall upwards, you know. It's a plan of my own
T3	132:38	that name them, I suppose. If not, why do things have names at all?"
T5	153: 2	said with great decision: "nobody can do two things at once, you know. Let's consider your age to begin
A2	19:44	family always hated cats: nasty, low, vulgar things! Don't let me hear the name again!"
T5	150:18	one way," Alice remarked. "I ca'n't remember things before they happen."
A5	36:31	I am, Sir," said Alice. "I ca'n't remember things as I used--and I don't keep the same size for ten
A6	52:11	this, she was getting so well used to queer things happening. While she was still looking at the place
T2	126:19	the thing was, that the trees and the other things round them never changed their places at all: however
T8	186:27	a difference it makes, mixing it with other things--such as gunpowder and sealing-wax. And here I must
T8	182:21	of carrots, and fire-irons, and many other things.
T4	147:26	very gravely, "it's one of the most serious things that can possibly happen to one in a battle--to get
T5	154:11	seemed to be full of all manner of curious things--but the oddest part of it all was that, whenever she
T5	156:39	this, there were so many other curious things to think about.
A5	36:33	"Ca'n't remember what things?" said the Caterpillar.
A1	10:23	eaten up by wild beasts, and other unpleasant things, all because they would not remember the simple rules
T6	163:34	you can make words mean so many different things."
A11	89:19	a poor man," the Hatter went on, "and most things twinkled after that--only the March Hare said--"
A8	62:18	and had just begun "Well, of all the unjust things--" when his eye chanced to fall upon Alice, as she
T5	158:14	it away in a box: then she said "I never put things into people's hands--that would never do--you must get
A1	10:11	that Alice had begun to think that very few things indeed were really impossible.
T8	186: 5	I am, the more I keep inventing new things."
A2	15:38	How queer everything is to-day! And yesterday things went on just as usual. I wonder if I've changed in the
A7	60:24	and memory, and muchness--you know you say things are 'much of a muchness'--did you ever see such a thing
T5	152:22	with a smile. "Now you understand the way things happen here."
A1	13: 2	way of expecting nothing but out-of-the-way things to happen, that it seemed quite dull and stupid for
A1	10:10	begin." For, you see, so many out-of-the-way things had happened lately, that Alice had begun to think that
T4	142:20	come,' the Walrus said, / 'To talk of many things: / Of shoes--and ships--and sealing wax--/ Of cabbages
T8	190:28	pretty easily--that comes of having so many things hung round the horse--" So she went on talking to
T9	195: 2	White Queen. "You mustn't leave out so many things."
T9	193: 7	"I don't deny things with my hands," Alice objected.
T9	197:18	one Queen at a time. Do wake up, you heavy things!" she went on in an impatient tone; but there was no

THINK (110)

T3	136:16	"Think again," it said: "that wo'n't do."
A8	69: 6	Alice could think of nothing else to say but "It belongs to the Duchess:
T8	183:13	Alice could think of nothing better to say than "Indeed?" but she said it

```
THINK (cont.)
  A7    56: 9   of  tea,  and looked at it again: but he could  think of nothing better to say than his first remark, "It was
  T7   172:11                                    "I should  think throwing cold water over you would be better," Alice
  T7   170: 9   did," said Alice: "several thousand, I should  think."
 A12    93: 8             much," she said to herself; "I should  think it would be quite as much use in the trial one way up
 T8W    20: 7   Your  jaws  aint well shaped, though--I should  think you couldn't bite well?"
 T8W    13:18                     "It's rheumatism, I should  think,".Alice said to herself, and she stooped over him, and
  T4   148: 5   "You must hit the trees pretty often, I should  think," she said.
  A7    60: 7   a  water-well,"  said the Hatter; "so I should  think you could draw treacle out of a treacle-well--eh,
  A2    19:12   is  so out-of-the-way down here, that I should  think very likely it can talk: at any rate, there's no harm
  A1     9: 7   "Dinah'll miss me very much to-night, I should  think!" (Dinah was the cat.) "I hope they'll remember her
  T2   128: 9   through the Third Square--by railway, I should  think--and you'll find yourself in the Fourth Square in no
  A5    36: 4   and then after that into a butterfly, I should  think you'll feel it a little queer, wo'n't you?"
  A1     7:12     so very remarkable in that; nor did Alice  think it so very much out of the way to hear the Rabbit say
  A2    15:40   I wonder if I've changed in the night? Let me  think: was I the same when I got up this morning? I almost
  T9   192:36   Queen  said to Alice. "Always speak the truth--  think before you speak--and write it down afterwards."
  A9    72:11                               "I think I should understand that better," Alice said very
  T2   123:35                               "I think I'll go and meet her," said Alice, for, though the
  T3   129:25                               "I think I'll go down the other way," she said after a pause;
  T9   194:14                               "I think that's the answer."
  T8   190:19        when I get to that turn in the road? I think it'll encourage me, you see."
 T8W    20: 2   sorry  for  you," Alice said heartily: "and I think if your wig fitted a little better, they wouldn't tease
  A3    26: 4   very humbly: "you had got to the fifth bend, I think?"
  T6   166:13   to me much easier than that, by--Tweedledee, I think it was."
  T3   129:17   and what quantities of honey they must make! I think I'll go down and--no, I wo'n't go just yet," she went
  T9   193:18     said Alice; "but, if there is to be one, I think I ought to invite the guests."
  A1    10: 9   how I wish I could shut up like a telescope! I think I could, if I only knew how to begin." For, you see, so
  A6    50:17   child:  but  it makes rather a handsome pig, I think." And she began thinking over other children she knew,
  T9   201:31   upon  her;  "and it's a very curious thing, I think--every poem was about fishes in some way. Do you know
  A2    19:34   yet  I  wish I could show you our cat Dinah. I think you'd take a fancy to cats, if you could only see her.
 A11    88:14   with  the  Dormouse. "Fourteenth of March, I think it was," he said.
  A9    71:16                       "It's a mineral, I think," said Alice.
 T8W    21:13   she  thought  she might safely leave him. "I think I must be going on now," she said. "Good-bye."
  A4    32:20   is  to  find my way into that lovely garden. I think that will be the best plan."
  A1     8:30   see: that would be four thousand miles down, I think--" (for, you see, Alice had learnt several things of
 T12   207:21   but it looked a little ashamed of itself, so I think it must have been the Red Queen.")
 A12    96:18   had  this fit'--you never had fits, my dear, I think?" he said to the Queen.
  T5   149:27   in a melancholy voice. "It's out of temper, I think. I've pinned it here, and I've pinned it there, but
  T2   123:12   she's  redder--and  her petals are shorter, I think."
  A1     8:41   with their heads downwards! The antipathies, I think--" (she was rather glad there was no one listening,
 A10    84: 6                           Yes, I think you'd better leave off," said the Gryphon, and Alice
  A6    48:31   so  she  went on again: "Twenty-four hours, I think; or is it twelve? I--"
  A4    30:38   this  fireplace  is narrow, to be sure; but I think I can kick a little!"
  A5    35: 7   who  I  was when I got up this morning, but I think I must have been changed several times since then."
  T6   166: 4   green pig: but 'mome' I'm not certain about. I think it's short for 'from home'--meaning that they'd lost
  T1   115:12   All  the  ashes will get into it--there, now I think you're tidy enough!" she added, as she smoothed his
  T1   110:22   you're  the  Red Queen, Kitty! Do you know, I think if you sat up and folded your arms, you'd look exactly
  A7    60:40   thought.  "But  everything's curious to-day. I think I may as well go in at once." And in she went.
  T5   152:28      light.  "The  crow must have flown away, I think," said Alice: "I'm so glad it's gone. I thought it was
  T9   202: 4   must  be  caught.' / That is easy: a baby, I think, could have caught it. / 'Next, the fish must be bought
  T3   136:18   what  you call yourself?" she said timidly. "I think that might help a little."
  A5    36:13   she drew herself up and said, very gravely, "I think you ought to tell me who you are, first."
  A7    56:32                   Alice sighed wearily. "I think you might do something better with the time," she said,
  T9   202: 6   must  be  bought.' / That is easy: a penny, I think, could have bought it.
 T12   207:35   me,  Dinah, did you turn to Humpty Dumpty? I think you did--however, you'd better not mention it to your
  A1     8:25   of tumbling down-stairs! How brave they'll all  think me at home! Why, I wouldn't say anything about it, even
  A1     8:24   herself.  "After  such a fall as this, I shall  think nothing of tumbling down-stairs! How brave they'll all
  A1     9: 3   it?)  "And what an ignorant little girl she'll  think me for asking! No, it'll never do to ask: perhaps I
  A6    46:38                 The Footman seemed to  think this a good opportunity for repeating his remark, with
  A8    67:21   some  one  to listen to her. The Cat seemed to  think that there was enough of it now in sight, and no more
  T3   135:41   went on, rather surprised at not being able to  think of the word. "I mean to get under the--under the--under
  T8   184:29               "I'll tell you how I came to  think of it," said the Knight. "You see, I said to myself,
  T9   202:19                "Take a minute to  think about it, and then guess," said the Red Queen.
  A6    50: 8        Alice was just beginning to  think to herself, "Now, what am I to do with this creature,
  A1    10:11   had  happened  lately, that Alice had begun to  think that very few things indeed were really impossible.
  A7    59:22   The  Dormouse  again took a minute or two to  think about it, and then said "It was a treacle-well."
  T5   156:40   there  were  so many other curious things to  think about.
  A9    72:25                "I've a right to  think," said Alice sharply, for she was beginning to feel a
  A1     8: 9   so  suddenly  that Alice had not a moment to  think about stopping herself before she found herself falling
  T3   135: 6   sure,"  said Alice: "the governess would never  think of excusing me lessons for that. If she couldn't
  T2   122:32           "It's my opinion that you never  think at all," the Rose said, in a rather severe tone.
  A9    70: 1                 "You ca'n't  think how glad I am to see you again, you dear old thing!"
  A3    26:28   a  capital  one for catching mice, you ca'n't  think! And oh, I wish you could see her after the birds! Why,
  T9   196:12   again. "It was such a thunderstorm, you ca'n't  think!" ("She never could, you know," said the Red Queen.)
  T2   128:23   time she said "Speak in French when you ca'n't  think of the English for a thing--turn out your toes as you
  A6    51:27                 Alice didn't  think that proved it at all: however, she went on: "And how
  T6   160:25   ah, you may turn pale, if you like! You didn't  think I was going to say that, did you? The King has promised
  T9   196:26     to  say something kind, but really couldn't  think of anything at the moment.
  A8    67:23                   "I don't  think they play at all fairly," Alice began, in rather a
  T7   174:17                   "I don't  think they'll fight any more to-day," the King said to Hatta:
```

THINK (cont.)

T8W	13: 9	"I don't think I can be of any use to him," was Alice's first thought,
A7	60:27	me," said Alice, very much confused, "I don't think--"
A8	65:35	"No, I didn't," said Alice. "I don't think it's at all a pity. I said 'What for?'"
T6	160:21	Humpty Dumpty growled out. "Of course I don't think so! Why, if ever I did fall off--which there's no
T1	113:11	are two Castles walking arm in arm--I don't think they can hear me," she went on, as she put her head
T4	146: 5	brother, and looked up into it. "No, I don't think it is," he said: "at least--not under here. Nohow."
T9	197:15	and lay like a heavy lump in her lap. "I don't think it ever happened before, that any one had to take care
T3	129: 5	mountains--I'm on the only one, but I don't think it's got any name. Principal towns--why, what are those
A4	27:33	that the mouse doesn't get out.' Only I don't think," Alice went on, "that they'd let Dinah stop in the
A5	36:16	puzzling question; and, as Alice could not think of any good reason, and the Caterpillar seemed to be in
A3	24: 6	did not dare to laugh; and, as she could not think of anything to say, she simply bowed, and took the
A2	15:40	the same when I got up this morning? I almost think I can remember feeling a little different. But if I'm
A6	48:25	showing off a little of her knowledge. "Just think what work it would make with the day and night! You see
T6	160:14	nobody with me!" cried Humpty Dumpty. "Did you think I didn't know the answer to that? Ask another."
T4	138:10	"If you think we're wax-works," he said, "you ought to pay, you know.
T4	138:13	added the one marked 'DEE,' "if you think we're alive, you ought to speak."
T9	194:13	"Then you think nothing would remain?" said the Red Queen.
A5	37: 4	you incessantly stand on your head--/ Do you think, at your age, it is right?"
T12	208:14	Which do you think it was?
T4	146: 3	for really it's coming on very dark. Do you think it's going to rain?"
A1	9: 1	as you're falling through the air! Do you think you could manage it?) "And what an ignorant little girl
A5	40: 7	father. "Don't give yourself airs! / Do you think I can listen all day to such stuff? / Be off, or I'll
T4	145: 1	now," said Tweedledee: "and what do you think he's dreaming about?"
A5	36:30	out of its mouth again, and said "So you think you're changed, do you?"
A7	55:16	"Do you mean that you think you can find out the answer to it?" said the March Hare
T6	160:16	"Don't you think you'd be safer down on the ground?" Alice went on, not
T8	184:35	done," Alice said thoughtfully: "but don't you think it would be rather hard?"
T3	134:26	the Gnat went on in a careless tone: "only think how convenient it would be if you could manage to go

THINKING (26)

A9	72:23	"Thinking again?" the Duchess asked, with another dig of her
A12	98:14	on her hand, watching the setting sun, and thinking of little Alice and all her wonderful Adventures, till
T4	147:38	you'd better not fight to-day," said Alice, thinking it a good opportunity to make peace.
A4	32:40	in its hurry to get hold of it: then Alice, thinking it was very like having a game of play with a
T2	124:14	in a kinder tone. "Curtsey while you're thinking what to say. It saves time."
T12	207:23	a merry laugh. "And curtsey while you're thinking what to--what to purr. It saves time, remember!" And
A9	70:18	heard her voice close to her ear. "You're thinking about something, my dear, and that makes you forget to
T4	139: 5	"I know what you're thinking about," said Tweedledum; "but it isn't so, nohow."
T3	136: 2	She stood silent for a minute, thinking: then she suddenly began again. "Then it really has
A12	98:11	getting late." So Alice got up and ran off, thinking while she ran, as well she might, what a wonderful
T9	195: 4	"She'll be feverish after so much thinking." So they set to work and fanned her with bunches of
A2	16: 1	Ah, that's the great puzzle!" And she began thinking over all the children she knew that were of the same
A6	50:17	a handsome pig, I think." And she began thinking over other children she knew, who might do very well as
T2	126:12	Alice never could quite make out, in thinking it over afterwards, how it was that they began: all she
T9	194:24	go different ways." But she couldn't help thinking to herself "What dreadful nonsense we are talking!"
A9	74:38	interesting story," but she could not help thinking there must be more to come, so she sat still and said
T9	192:25	here she broke off with a frown, and, after thinking for a minute, suddenly changed the subject of the
A7	59: 1	lived on treacle," said the Dormouse, after thinking a minute or two.
T8	186:30	Alice could only look puzzled: she was thinking of the pudding.
T4	139:10	"I was thinking," Alice said politely, "which is the best way out of
A5	43: 2	its voice to a shriek, "and just as I was thinking I should be free of them at last, they must needs come
T8	188: 9	But I was thinking of a plan / To dye one's whiskers green, / And always
T8	188:25	But I was thinking of a way / To feed oneself on batter, / And so go on
T3	130:13	in chorus (I hope you understand what thinking in chorus means--for I must confess that I don't)
A3	26: 2	the Mouse to Alice, severely. "What are you thinking of?"
T4	146:18	rattle-snake, you know," she added hastily, thinking that he was frightened: "only an old rattle--quite old

TIME (144)

A7	58:32	"Once upon a time there were three little sisters," the Dormouse began in
A2	15:25	After a time she heard a little pattering of feet in the distance,
T2	127: 2	ten minutes ago! Faster!" And they ran on for a time in silence, with the wind whistling in Alice's ears,
T9	195:32	mostly have days and nights two or three at a time, and sometimes in the winter we take as many as five
T9	197:18	there never was more than one Queen at a time. Do wake up, you heavy things!" she went on in an
T9	195:30	she remarked, "there's only one day at a time."
T7	177: 4	There was too much dust to see anything. What a time the Monster is, cutting up that cake!"
A1	9:39	not open any of them. However, on the second time round, she came upon a low curtain she had not noticed
T2	128:33	that she was a Pawn, and that it would soon be time for her to move.
T4	142:19	'The time has come,' the Walrus said, / 'To talk of many things:
A7	58: 5	"when the Queen bawled out 'He's murdering the time! Off with his head!'"
A7	56:33	"I think you might do something better with the time," she said, "than wasting it in asking riddles that
A10	79:11	close, and waving their fore-paws to mark the time, while the Mock Turtle sang this, very slowly and sadly
A9	73: 3	All the time they were playing the Queen never left off quarreling
A4	32:30	to it; but she was terribly frightened all the time at the thought that it might be hungry, in which case
A2	15:37	was very hot, she kept fanning herself all the time she went on talking. "Dear, dear! How queer everything
T1	108: 6	get on very fast, as she was talking all the time, sometimes to the kitten, and sometimes to herself.
T8	184: 9	of practice!" he went on repeating, all the time that Alice was getting him on his feet again. "Plenty
T2	124: 8	nicely, and don't twiddle your fingers all the time."
T12	208: 2	morning you shall have a real treat. All the time you're eating your breakfast, I'll repeat 'The Walrus
A6	46:21	know." He was looking up into the sky all the time he was speaking, and this Alice thought decidedly
A10	82: 1	began telling them her adventures from the time when she first saw the White Rabbit. She was a little
T6	164:27	means four o'clock in the afternoon--the time when you begin broiling things for dinner."

TIME (cont.)

```
T4   147:41   going   on   long," said Tweedledum. "What's the time now?"
A1     7:15   she ought to have wondered at this, but at the time it all seemed quite natural); but, when the Rabbit
A11   86:12       at everything  about her to pass away the time.
A8    68:22                             By the time she had caught the flamingo and brought it back, the
A8    69:11   fading away the moment he was gone, and, by the time he had come back with the Duchess, it had entirely
A11   91:23   getting  the Dormouse turned out, and, by the time they had settled down again, the cook had disappeared.
T4   148: 8   left  standing,  for ever so far round, by the time we've finished!"
T4   147:22       of old  clothes than anything else, by the time they're ready!" she said to herself, as she arranged a
T2   127:13   do believe we've been under this tree the whole time! Everything's just as it was!"
T9   194:31   "I can do Addition," she said, "if you give me time--but I ca'n't do Subtraction under any circumstances!"
A6    53: 6   and  ending  with the grin, which remained some time after the rest of it had gone.
A4    30:22                       She waited for some time without hearing anything more: at last came a rumbling
T3   129: 8   saw  bees  a mile off, you know--" and for some time she stood silent, watching one of them that was
T7   175:16   he  turned round instantly, and stood for some time looking at her with an air of the deepest disgust.
A7    55: 7   Hatter.  He had been looking at Alice for some time with great curiosity, and this was his first speech.
T1   115:35   unhappy, and struggled with the pencil for some time without saying anything; but Alice was too strong for
A12   93:33   At  this moment the King, who had been for some time busily writing in his note-book, called out "Silence!",
A7    60:13   Alice, that she let the Dormouse go on for some time without interrupting it.
A5    35: 1   and Alice looked at each other for some time in silence: at last the Caterpillar took the hookah out
T8   179:26   Knights sat  and looked at each other for some time without speaking. Alice looked from one to the other in
T8   185:18   was  rather startled by the fall, as for some time he had kept on very well, and she was afraid that he
T1   116:13                   She puzzled over this for some time, but at last a bright thought struck her. "Why, it's a
A10   78:19       "That generally takes some time," interrupted the Gryphon.
A7    57: 2   goes  the  clock in a twinkling! Half-past one, time for dinner!"
T9   197: 5   in Alice's lap! / Till the feast's ready, we've time for a nap. / When the feast's over, we'll go to the
A1     8:12   or  she fell very slowly, for she had plenty of time as she went down to look about her, and to wonder what
T8   187:13   reins  fall  on its neck: then, slowly beating time with one hand, and with a faint smile lighting up his
T3   132:41   go on with your list of insects: you're wasting time."
A7    56:17   because  it stays the same year for such a long time together."
T8   182:15                   This took a long time to manage, though Alice held the bag open very
A3    23:18   great  deal of thought, and it stood for a long time with one finger pressed upon its forehead (the position
T9   198:12       Alice  knocked and rang in vain for a long time; but at last a very old Frog, who was sitting under a
T2   127:18   somewhere  else--if you ran very fast for a long time as we've been doing."
T1   118: 6       He took his vorpal sword in hand: / Long time the manxome foe he sought--/ So rested he by the Tumtum
T4   139:38   I  felt  as if I'd been singing it a long long time!"
A4    32:44   stick,  running a very little way forwards each time and a long way back, and barking hoarsely all the while
A2    20:21                             It was high time to go, for the pool was getting quite crowded with the
A3    26:35   its  children, "Come away, my dears! It's high time you were all in bed!" On various pretexts they all
TI   103: 3   brow  /  And dreaming eyes of wonder! / Though time be fleet, and I and thou / Are half a life asunder, /
A12   96:29       the King said, for about the twentieth time that day.
A10   81:45   tone:  "explanations  take such a dreadful time."
T8   186: 9                       "In time to have it cooked for the next course?" said Alice.
T9   192:10   "I  shall  be able to manage it quite well in time."
A5    41:21           "You'll get used to it in time," said the Caterpillar; and it put the hookah into its
T9   194:38   don't  be  discouraged. You'll come to it in time."
T1   113:16   Alice,  and made her turn her head just in time to see one of the White Pawns roll over and begin
T8   184:16   round  the  horse's neck as he spoke, just in time to save himself from tumbling off again.
T9   204: 6   soup-tureen,  and  Alice turned again, just in time to see the Queen's broad good-natured face grinning at
A1     9:25   away  went Alice like the wind, and was just in time to hear it say, as it turned a corner, "Oh my ears and
A1     8: 4   ran  across the field after it, and was just in time to see it pop down a large rabbit-hole under the hedge
A2    18: 8   holding,  and  she dropped it hastily, just in time to save herself from shrinking away altogether.
A7    58:13   a  sigh:  "it's always tea-time, and we've no time to wash the things between whiles."
A9    72:38   head  must  be off, and that in about half no time! Take your choice!"
A8    69: 3   something  wasn't done about it in less than no time, she'd have everybody executed, all round. (It was this
T2   128:10   you'll find yourself in the Fourth Square in no time. Well, that square belongs to Tweedledum and Tweedledee
T8W   17: 8           round your face. It'll cure you in no time!"
A5    41:42   sudden  change,  but she felt that there was no time to be lost, as she was shrinking rapidly: so she set to
TI   103:15   were  glowing--/ A simple chime, that served to time / The rhythm of our rowing--/ Whose echoes live in
A7    56:39           "I dare say you never even spoke to Time!"
A7    57: 1   lessons:  you'd  only have to whisper a hint to Time, and round goes the clock in a twinkling! Half-past one
T9   204:23                   At any other time, Alice would have felt surprised at this, but she was
T12  207:24   you're thinking what to--what to purr. It saves time, remember!" And she caught it up and gave it one little
T2   124:14   while  you're  thinking what to say. It saves time."
A8    68:39   before,  and  he wasn't going to begin at his time of life.
T3   130: 1   Alice) "Don't keep him waiting, child! Why, his time is worth a thousand pounds a minute!"
A5    41:23                       This time Alice waited patiently until it chose to speak again.
T8   179:23                       This time it was a White Knight. He drew up at Alice's side, and
T8   184: 1   was  walking.  She was quite frightened this time, and said in an anxious tone, as she picked him up, "I
T7   173:31           Hatta looked round once more, and this time a tear or two trickled down his cheek; but not a word
T2   128:22   the  next  peg the Queen turned again, and this time she said "Speak in French when you ca'n't think of the
T3   135:18   of  those  melancholy little sighs, and this time the poor Gnat really seemed to have sighed itself away,
A6    53: 4       "All right," said the Cat; and this time it vanished quite slowly, beginning with the end of the
T5   153:19   arms  again and went flying after it, and this time she succeeded in catching it herself. "I've got it!"
T8   184: 7   his  arms to show Alice what he meant, and this time he fell flat on his back, right under the horse's feet
T8   184:12   cried  Alice,  losing all her patience this time. "You ought to have a wooden horse on wheels, that you
A1     8:42   rather  glad there was no one listening, this time, as it didn't sound at all the right word) "--but I
A4    28: 3   near the looking-glass. There was no label this time with the words "DRINK ME," but nevertheless she
A11   89: 4                   All this time the Queen had never left off staring at the Hatter, and
T3   130:18                   All this time the Guard was looking at her, first through a telescope
```

TIME (cont.)

T4	147: 1		All this time Tweedledee was trying his best to fold up the umbrella,
A10	78:37	had been jumping about like mad things all	this time, sat down again very sadly and quietly, and looked at
A7	59:35	the Dormouse, without considering at all,	this time.
A6	50:11	looked down into its face in some alarm. This	time there could be no mistake about it: it was neither more
T2	124: 1	off), she thought she would try the plan,	this time, of walking in the opposite direction.
T3	130:11	in speaking." The voices didn't join in,	this time, as she hadn't spoken, but, to her great surprise, they
T2	120:27	was nothing to be done but start again. This	time she came upon a large flowerbed, with a border of
A7	60:43	glass table. "Now, I'll manage better	this time," she said to herself, and began by taking the little
A4	30:16	again, and made another snatch in the air. This	time there were two little shrieks, and more sounds of
A2	19:39	I beg your pardon!" cried Alice again, for	this time the Mouse was bristling all over, and she felt certain
A1	10:15	for shutting people up like telescopes:	this time she found a little bottle on it ("which certainly was
T7	175:10	in his pockets. "I had the best of it	this time?" he said to the King, just glancing at him as he
T2	120:21	she was just saying "I really shall do it	this time--" when the path gave a sudden twist and shook itself
T8	185:19	and she was afraid that he really was hurt	this time. However, though she could see nothing but the soles of
A4	27:36		By this time she had found her way into a tidy little room with a
T5	152:27		By this time it was getting light. "The crow must have flown away, I
A12	97: 8	Alice (she had grown to her full size by	this time). "You're nothing but a pack of cards!"
A6	49:29	in reply (it had left off sneezing by	this time). "Don't grunt," said Alice; "that's not at all a
A1	8:28	"I wonder how many miles I've fallen by	this time?" she said aloud. "I must be getting somewhere near the
T2	128: 4	She had got all the pegs put in by	this time, and Alice looked on with great interest as she
T8	187: 8	is the song, then?" said Alice, who was by	this time completely bewildered.
A7	60:20	The Dormouse had closed its eyes by	this time, and was going off into a doze; but, on being pinched
A9	70:16	She had quite forgotten the Duchess by	this time, and was a little startled when she heard her voice
T2	128:25	She did not wait for Alice to curtsey,	this time, but walked on quickly to the next peg, where she
T9	195:11	she saw a way out of the difficulty,	this time. "If you'll tell me what language 'fiddle-de-dee' is,
T2	124:18		"It's for you to answer now," the Queen said looking at her
A7	56:41	cautiously replied; "but I know I have to beat	time when I learn music."
A9	77: 4		"Hadn't time," said the Gryphon: "I went to the Classical master,
T6	163:18	that seems to be done right--though I haven't	time to look it over thoroughly just now--and that shows
A8	66:22	fighting for the hedgehogs; and in a very short	time the Queen was in a furious passion, and went stamping
T8	184:23	things. Now, I daresay you noticed, the last	time you picked me up, that I was looking rather thoughtful
A7	60:33	hoping that they would call after her: the last	time she saw them, they were trying to put the Dormouse into
T6	160: 2	Dumpty said, looking at her for the first	time, "but tell me your name and your business."
T7	178: 4	the little brook in her terror, and had just	time to see the Lion and the * * * * * * * * * * * * *
A7	56:45	it were nine o'clock in the morning, just	time to begin lessons: you'd only have to whisper a hint to
T2	124:17	I go home," she thought to herself, "the next	time I'm a little late for dinner."
AI	3:29	by, / "The rest next time--" "It is next	time!" / The happy voices cry.
AI	3:29	one / To put the subject by, / "The rest next	time--" "It is next time!" / The happy voices cry.
A5	43:12	"I've seen a good many little girls in my	time, but never one with such a neck as that! No, no! You're
T8W	17: 3	new-fangled name. They called it conceit in my	time."
T3	131:25	say, my dear, but take a return-ticket every	time the train stops."

TIMIDLY (18)

T9	196:25		The White Queen looked timidly at Alice, who felt she ought to say something kind, but
T4	144:26	any lions or tigers about here?" she asked	timidly.
T5	158: 3	should like to buy an egg, please," she said	timidly. "How do you sell them?"
T3	136:18	tell me what you call yourself?" she said	timidly. "I think that might help a little."
A8	64:10	The King laid his hand upon her arm, and	timidly said "Consider, my dear: she is only a child!"
A5	41: 2	"Not quite right, I'm afraid," said Alice,	timidly: "some of the words have got altered."
A10	79: 2	"It must be a very pretty dance," said Alice	timidly.
T6	168:15	"Is that all?" Alice	timidly asked.
T8W	15:13	this newspaper, though," Alice said a little	timidly.
A6	47:12	would you tell me," said Alice, a little	timidly, for she was not quite sure whether it was good manners
A8	63: 3	you tell me, please," said Alice, a little	timidly, "why you are painting those roses?"
A10	81:41	from this morning," said Alice a little	timidly; "but it's no use going back to yesterday, because I
T9	192:17	would you tell me--" she began, looking	timidly at the Red Queen.
T5	149:11	must manage it herself. So she began rather	timidly: "Am I addressing the White Queen?"
A6	51: 4	"Cheshire-Puss," she began, rather	timidly, as she did not at all know whether it would like the
A6	53:16	even then she walked up towards it rather	timidly, saying to herself "Suppose it should be raving mad
T8	180: 2	said to herself, as she watched the fight,	timidly peeping out from her hiding-place. "One Rule seems to
A6	46: 9		Alice went timidly up to the door, and knocked.

TONE (84)

T6	162:28	ignorant of me," Alice said, in so humble a	tone that Humpty Dumpty relented.
T2	125:27	somewhere--and so there are!" she added in a	tone of delight, and her heart began to beat quick with
T7	170: 6	"I've sent them all!" the King cried in a	tone of delight, on seeing Alice. "Did you happen to meet
A10	81:23	"And what are they made of?" Alice asked in a	tone of great curiosity.
T8	182: 8	"But what are they for?" Alice asked in a	tone of great curiosity.
T8	184:14	that kind go smoothly?" the Knight asked in a	tone of great interest, clasping his arms round the horse's
T8	191: 4	what is this on my head?" she exclaimed in a	tone of dismay, as she put her hands up to something very
A12	92: 8	"Oh, I beg your pardon!" she exclaimed in a	tone of great dismay, and began picking them up again as
T5	157:14	"To buy!" Alice echoed in a	tone that was half astonished and half frightened--for the
T4	145:27	are real tears?" Tweedledum interrupted in a	tone of great contempt.
A5	42: 7	"Come, my head's free at last!" said Alice in a	tone of delight, which changed into alarm in another moment,
A10	81:32	"Wouldn't it, really?" said Alice, in a	tone of great surprise.
A9	76:14	really good school," said the Mock Turtle in a	tone of great relief. "Now, at ours, they had, at the end of
T2	128:16	"You should have said," the Queen went on in a	tone of grave reproof, "'It's extremely kind of you to tell
A5	43:11	"A likely story indeed!" said the Pigeon, in a	tone of the deepest contempt. "I've seen a good many little
A9	77:24	the Gryphon interrupted in a very decided	tone. "Tell her something about the games now."
A7	59:11	had nothing yet," Alice replied in an offended	tone: "so I ca'n't take more."

TONE (cont.)

A10	81:38	I say," the Mock Turtle replied, in an offended tone.	And the Gryphon added "Come, let's hear some of your
A3	22:35	was going to say," said the Dodo in an offended tone,	"was that the best thing to get us dry would be a
A10	84:13	that the Gryphon said, in a rather offended tone,	"Hm! No accounting for tastes! Sing her 'Turtle Soup,'
T9	196: 7	there generally?" Alice asked in an astonished tone.	
A8	65:29	"Hush! Hush!" said the Rabbit in a low hurried tone.	He looked anxiously over his shoulder as he spoke, and
A8	65:39	Oh, hush!" the Rabbit whispered in a frightened tone.	"The Queen will hear you! You see she came rather late
T3	130: 2	I haven't got one," Alice said in a frightened tone:	"there wasn't a ticket-office where I came from." And
A9	72:15	if I chose," the Duchess replied, in a pleased tone.	
T5	158: 7	cheaper than one?" Alice said in a surprised tone,	taking out her purse.
T6	168:22	Humpty Dumpty replied in a discontented tone,	giving her one of his fingers to shake: "you're so
T8	181:35	bee-hive," the Knight said in a discontented tone,	"one of the best kind. But not a single bee has come
A5	42:30	repeated the Pigeon, but in a more subdued tone,	and added, with a kind of sob, "I've tried every way,
A6	48: 7	Alice did not at all like the tone of this remark, and thought it would be as well to
A8	65: 6	your Majesty," said Two, in a very humble tone,	going down on one knee as he spoke, "we were trying--
A6	46:31	day, maybe," the Footman continued in the same tone,	exactly as if nothing had happened.
T9	192: 3	it is, your Majesty," she went on, in a severe tone (she was always rather fond of scolding herself),
T2	122:33	at all," the Rose said, in a rather severe tone.	
T5	154:16	about so here!" she said at last in a plaintive tone.	after she had spent a minute or so in vainly pursuing
A7	54:13	wine," the March Hare said in an encouraging tone.	"You needn't be so angry about an old rattle."
T4	146:24	her hand upon his arm and said, in a soothing tone,	and, stooping down to the daisies, who were just
T2	122:13	"Never mind!" Alice said in a soothing tone,	"Can't I do anything for you?"
T8W	16: 1	afraid you're not well," she said in a soothing tone:	"don't be angry about it. And yet I wish I could show
A2	19:32	"Well, perhaps not," said Alice in a soothing tone:	"and they all quarrel so dreadfully one ca'n't hear
A8	67:24	fairly," Alice began, in rather a complaining tone,	"I've a great mind to go and wake him, and see what
T8	179:10	dream," she went on in a rather complaining tone.	
A10	81:16	boots and shoes!" she repeated in a wondering tone.	and she tried hard to whistle to it; but she was
A4	32:29	"Poor little thing!" said Alice, in a coaxing tone,	"Try again: draw a long breath, and shut your eyes."
T5	153: 9	"Ca'n't you?" the Queen said in a pitying tone.	"Worrity, worrity! There never was such a child!"
T8W	14: 3	"How you go on!" the Wasp said in a peevish tone.	"All kinds of fastness," he repeated: "but it was
T8	185:21	to hear that he was talking on in his usual tone.	though), "I wo'n't have any pepper in my kitchen at
A9	70: 8	she said to herself (not in a very hopeful tone,	"it means just what I choose it to mean--neither more
T6	163:31	word," Humpty Dumpty said, in rather a scornful tone,	"he wo'n't do a thing I ask! It's always six o'clock
A7	58: 8	since that," the Hatter went on in a mournful tone,	but frowning and making faces at him as he spoke.
A12	93:24	of course," he said, in a very respectful tone,	"To be able to see Nobody! And at that distance too!
T7	170:18	had such eyes," the King remarked in a fretful tone.	
T6	168:25	by, generally," Alice remarked in a thoughtful tone.	
T6	164: 4	make one word mean," Alice said in a thoughtful tone.	
T8	186:12	course," the Knight said in slow thoughtful tone:	"no, certainly not the next course."
A4	29: 8	but I'm grown up now," she added in a sorrowful tone:	"at least there's no room to grow up any more here."
A2	20:10	rats and--oh dear!" cried Alice in a sorrowful tone.	"I'm afraid I've offended it again!" For the Mouse was
T7	172:20	"I do my best," the Messenger said in a sullen tone.	"I'm sure nobody walks much faster than I do!"
A6	45:13	handed over to the other, saying, in a solemn tone,	"For the Duchess. An invitation from the Queen to play
A6	46: 1	The Frog-Footman repeated, in the same solemn tone,	only changing the order of the words a little, "From
T2	124:13	come out here at all?" she added in a kinder tone.	"Curtsey while you're thinking what to say. It saves
A6	46:32	am I to get in?" asked Alice again, in a louder tone.	
T4	147: 9	to have a battle?" Tweedledum said in a calmer tone.	"That's what you call a History of England, that is.
T6	160:36	in a book," Humpty Dumpty said in a calmer tone.	that she was a little offended: and they walked on in
T2	125:16	again, as she was afraid from the Queen's tone	"For instance, now," she went on, sticking a large
T5	150: 2	after next," the Queen replied in a careless tone.	"only think how convenient it would be if you could
T3	134:25	I don't know," the Gnat went on in a careless tone:	
T9	192:30	said 'if'!" poor Alice pleaded in a piteous tone.	And she thought to herself "I wish the creatures
A5	41:18	used to it!" pleaded poor Alice in a piteous tone.	as she picked him up, "I hope no bones are broken?"
T8	184: 2	frightened this time, and said in an anxious tone,	"What is the cause of lightning?"
T9	195:17	us quarrel," the White Queen said in an anxious tone.	"let me sing you a song to comfort you."
T8	186:31	"You are sad," the Knight said in an anxious tone:	"Now you shall see me pin it on again, all by myself!
T5	153:21	"I've got it!" she cried in a triumphant tone.	but there was no answer but a gentle snoring.
T9	197:19	you heavy things!" she went on in an impatient tone;	"explanations take such a dreadful time."
A10	81:45	first," said the Gryphon in an impatient tone:	"Sit down, both of you, and don't speak a word till
A9	74:27	it her," said the Mock Turtle in a deep, hollow tone.	"Seven jogged my elbow."
T7	176: 1	lazily at Alice, and speaking in a deep hollow tone that sounded like the tolling of a great bell.
A8	62: 7	"I couldn't help it," said Five, in a sulky tone.	"Seven jogged my elbow."
A5	43:28	Well, be off, then!" said the Pigeon in a sulky tone,	as it settled down again into its nest. Alice crouched
T8	181:18	my little box," the Knight said in a friendly tone:	"It's my own invention--to keep clothes and sandwiches
A3	22:26	"As wet as ever," said Alice in a melancholy tone:	"it doesn't seem to dry me at all."
A3	26:38	Dinah!" she said to herself in a melancholy tone.	"Nobody seems to like her, down here, and I'm sure
A12	96:27	"It's a pun!" the King added in an angry tone,	and everybody laughed. "Let the jury consider their
A4	27:13	about, and called out to her, in an angry tone,	"Why, Mary Ann, what are you doing out here? Run home

UNDERSTAND (15)

A9	72:11	"I think I should understand that better," Alice said very politely, "if I had it
T6	167: 5	"I'm afraid I don't quite understand," said Alice.
A7	56:21	it was certainly English. "I don't quite understand you," she said, as politely as she could.
A2	20:19	then I'll tell you my history, and you'll understand why it is I hate cats and dogs."
T6	166:33	when the days are long, / Perhaps you'll understand the song."
T1	118:26	had finished it, "but it's rather hard to understand!" (You see she didn't like to confess, even to herself,
T1	107:21	and giving it a little kiss to make it understand that it was in disgrace. "Really, Dinah ought to have
A5	35:15	replied, very politely, "for I ca'n't understand it myself, to begin with; and being so many different
T7	171: 4	"I only meant that I didn't understand," said Alice. "Why one to come and one to go?"
T5	150:10	"I don't understand you," said Alice. "It's dreadfully confusing!"
A7	60: 4	she began very cautiously: "But I don't understand. Where did they draw the treacle from?"

UNDERSTAND (cont.)
T8   187: 1   "No, you don't understand," the Knight said, looking a little vexed. "That's what
A2   19:21   "Perhaps it doesn't understand English," thought Alice. "I daresay it's a French mouse
T3   130:12   they all thought in chorus (I hope you understand what thinking in chorus means--for I must confess that
T5   152:22   she said to Alice with a smile. "Now you understand the way things happen here."
USE (34)
T9   196:18   in the middle of an accident! Where would be the use of it?" but she did not say this aloud, for fear of
A8   63:31   at processions; "and besides, what would be the use of a procession," thought she, "if people had all to
T9   193: 3   should have meant! What do you suppose is the use of a child without any meaning? Even a joke should have
A10   84: 3   "What is the use of repeating all that stuff?" the Mock Turtle
A1   7: 4   or conversations in it, "and what is the use of a book," thought Alice, "without pictures or
T3   132:35   "What's the use of their having names," the Gnat said, "if they wo'n't
A5   38: 7   / "I kept all my limbs very supple / By the use of this ointment--one shilling the box--/ Allow me to
A1   10: 7   thought poor Alice, "it would be of very little use without my shoulders. Oh, how I wish I could shut up
A11   87:11   the rest of the day; and this was of very little use, as it left no mark on the slate.
T1   114: 4   Alice was very anxious to be of use, and, as the poor little Lily was nearly screaming
A6   46:10   "There's no sort of use in knocking," said the Footman, "and that for two
A12   93: 9   "I should think it would be quite as much use in the trial one way up as the other."
T6   163:30   "When I use a word," Humpty Dumpty said, in rather a scornful tone,
T3   132:37   "No use to them," said Alice; "but it's useful to the people
T7   175: 4   "No use, no use!" said the King. "She runs so fearfully quick.
A2   17:21   if I'm Mabel, I'll stay down here. It'll be no use their putting their heads down and saying 'Come up
A1   10:12   There seemed to be no use in waiting by the little door, so she went back to the
T7   175: 4   "No use, no use!" said the King. "She runs so fearfully quick. You
T7   171:13   attention from himself--but it was of no use--the Anglo-Saxon attitudes only got more extraordinary
A5   42:37   and more puzzled, but she thought there was no use in saying anything more till the Pigeon had finished.
T5   153:11   Alice laughed. "There's no use trying," she said: "one ca'n't believe impossible
A5   43:14   that! No, no! You're a serpent; and there's no use denying it. I suppose you'll be telling me next that
A1   12:21   "Come, there's no use in crying like that!" said Alice to herself rather
A6   46:43   "Oh, there's no use in talking to him," said Alice desperately: "he's
T3   130:10   Alice thought to herself "Then there's no use in speaking." The voices didn't join in, this time, as
T8   181:25   things must have fallen out! And the box is no use without them." He unfastened it as he spoke, and was
T2   120:13   "It's no use talking about it," Alice said, looking up at the house
A8   67:17   the eyes appeared, and then nodded. "It's no use speaking to it," she thought, "till its ears have come,
T4   145:18   "Well, it's no use your talking about waking him," said Tweedledum, "when
A1   12:28   of pretending to be two people. "But it's no use now," thought poor Alice, "to pretend to be two people!
A10   81:41   said Alice a little timidly; "but it's no use going back to yesterday, because I was a different
T8   188:11   plan / To dye one's whiskers green, / And always use so large a fan / That they could not be seen. / So,
T8W   13: 9   "I don't think I can be of any use to him," was Alice's first thought, as she turned to
A2   19:10   "Would it be of any use, now," thought Alice, "to speak to this mouse?
VOICE (90)
T9   204: 5   sitting in the chair. "Here I am!" cried a voice from the soup-tureen, and Alice turned again, just in
A4   29:18   but after a few minutes she heard a voice outside, and stopped to listen.
A4   30: 2   "Pat! Pat! Where are you?" And then a voice she had never heard before, "Sure then I'm here!
T4   146:13   "Do you see that?" he said, in a voice choking with passion, and his eyes grew large and
A10   84:15   The Mock Turtle sighed deeply, and began, in a voice choked with sobs, to sing this:--
A8   65:41   "Get to your places!" shouted the Queen in a voice of thunder, and people began running about in all
T9   201:39   Queen murmured into Alice's other ear, in a voice like the cooing of a pigeon. "It would be such a treat!
T3   137: 7   Alice's arm. "I'm a Fawn!" it cried out in a voice of delight. "And, dear me! you're a human child!" A
T1   108: 2   at the old cat, and speaking in as cross a voice as she could manage--and then she scrambled back into
T4   138: 8   of each collar, when she was startled by a voice coming from the one marked 'DUM.'
A8   65:25   "It's--it's a very fine day!" said a timid voice at her side. She was walking by the White Rabbit, who
T2   121: 3   on waving about, she spoke again, in a timid voice--almost in a whisper. "And can all the flowers talk?"
A2   15:33   came near her, she began, in a low, timid voice, "If you please, Sir--" The Rabbit started violently,
T3   131: 4   in white, shut his eyes and said in a loud voice, "She ought to know her way to the ticket-office, even
T8   183:18   riding," the Knight suddenly began in a loud voice, waving his right arm as he spoke, "is to keep--" Here
A8   64:15   "Get up!" said the Queen in a shrill, loud voice, and the three gardeners instantly jumped up, and began
A4   29:19   "Mary Ann! Mary Ann!" said the voice. "Fetch me my gloves this moment!" Then came a little
T3   131:32   Alice, looking about in vain to see where the voice came from. "If you're so anxious to have a joke made,
A12   98:39   and the Queen's shrill cries to the voice of the shepherd-boy--and the sneeze of the baby, the
T1   113:19   "It is the voice of my child!" the White Queen cried out, as she rushed
A10   82:22   "'Tis the voice of the Lobster: I heard him declare / 'You have baked
A10   82:15   "Stand up and repeat ''Tis the voice of the sluggard,'" said the Gryphon.
A7   58:26   "I wasn't asleep," it said in a hoarse, feeble voice, "I heard every word you fellows were saying."
T3   131:16   Then a very gentle voice in the distance said, "She must be labeled 'Lass, with
T3   131:34   The little voice sighed deeply. It was very unhappy, evidently, and
T3   131:29   might make a joke on that," said the little voice close to her ear: "something about 'you would if you
T3   131:41   "I know you are a friend," the little voice went on: "a dear friend, and an old friend. And you
T3   132: 2   "What, then you don't--" the little voice began, when it was drowned by a shrill scream from the
A11   91:33   read out, at the top of his shrill little voice, the name "Alice!"
TI   103:19   Come, hearken then, ere voice of dread, / With bitter tidings laden, / Shall summon
T3   131:11   was sitting beyond the Beetle, but a hoarse voice spoke next. "Change engines--" it said, and there it
A2   19:30   cats!" cried the Mouse in a shrill passionate voice. "Would you like cats, if you were me?"
A12   93: 1   proceed," said the King, in a very grave voice, "until all the jurymen are back in their proper places
T9   201:24   It spoke in a thick, suety sort of voice, and Alice hadn't a word to say in reply: she could
A4   31:17   Last came a little feeble, squeaking voice ("That's Bill," thought Alice), "Well, I hardly know--
T7   174: 7   getting on very well," he said in a choking voice: "each of them has been down about eighty-seven times
T8   185: 8   must have hurt him," she said in a trembling voice, "being on the top of his head."
A11   89:12   Majesty," the Hatter began, in a trembling voice, "and I hadn't begun my tea--not above a week or so--
A10   83:13   all come wrong, and she went on in a trembling voice:--

VOICE (cont.)

A3	26:34	And a Canary called out in a trembling voice, to its children, "Come away, my dears! It's high time
A2	20:18	thought), and it said, in a low trembling voice, "Let us get to the shore, and then I'll tell you my
A12	94: 2	he said to the jury, in a low trembling voice.
A9	72:35	Majesty!" the Duchess began in a low, weak voice.
T3	131:14	thought to herself. And an extremely small voice, close to her ear, said "You might make a joke on that
T9	199:22	moment the door was flung open, and a shrill voice was heard singing:--
T4	148:21	the crow!" Tweedledum cried out in a shrill voice of alarm; and the two brothers took to their heels and
A12	98:28	shared their never-ending meal, and the shrill voice of the Queen ordering off her unfortunate guests to
T9	199:36	there was silence again, and the same shrill voice sang another verse:--
A11	91:15	were nearly out of sight, he said, in a deep voice, "What are tarts made of?"
A10	81:22	under the sea," the Gryphon went on in a deep voice, "are done with whiting. Now you know."
A9	70:17	and was a little startled when she heard her voice close to her ear. "You're thinking about something, my
T9	202:21	health!" she screamed at the top of her voice, and all the guests began drinking it directly, and
A12	97: 5	her head!" the Queen shouted at the top of her voice. Nobody moved.
A12	98:19	hers--she could hear the very tones of her voice, and see that queer little toss of her head to keep
T5	153:28	"Oh, much better!" cried the Queen, her voice rising into a squeak as she went on. "Much be-etter!
T5	151:21	still; better, and better, and better!" Her voice went higher with each "better," till it got quite to a
A2	17: 5	lessons, and began to repeat it, but her voice sounded hoarse and strange, and the words did not come
T8	179:20	began once more "You're my--" but here another voice broke in "Ahoy! Ahoy! Check!" and Alice looked round in
T8W	16: 4	of the wig," the Wasp said in a much gentler voice.
AI	3:11	the tiniest feather! / Yet what can one poor voice avail / Against three tongues together?
A10	78: 3	but, for a minute or two, sobs choked his voice. "Same as if he had a bone in his throat," said the
A10	78: 6	back. At last the Mock Turtle recovered his voice, and, with tears running down his cheeks, he went on
T6	168: 1	Humpty Dumpty raised his voice almost to a scream as he repeated this verse, and Alice
T4	146:28	it yesterday--my nice NEW RATTLE!" and his voice rose to a perfect scream.
T8	186:17	he went on, holding his head down, and his voice getting lower and lower, "I don't believe that pudding
T7	176:24	quarrel going on: he was very nervous, and his voice quite quivered. "All round the town?" he said. "That's
A10	82:29	the tide rises and sharks are around, / His voice has a timid and tremulous sound."
T7	172:29	he simply shouted, at the top of his voice, "They're at it again!"
A10	78:36	said the Mock Turtle, suddenly dropping his voice; and the two creatures, who had been jumping about like
A8	68:11	game was going on, as she heard the Queen's voice in the distance, screaming with passion. She had
T8W	15: 9	"Were what?" the Wasp asked in a very cross voice.
A9	72:29	here, to Alice's great surprise, the Duchess's voice died away, even in the middle of her favourite word
A10	78:34	again!" yelled the Gryphon at the top of its voice.
A5	43: 2	the wood," continued the Pigeon, raising its voice to a shriek, "and just as I was thinking I should be
A4	31:28	must burn the house down!" said the Rabbit's voice. And Alice called out, as loud as she could, "If you do
A4	31: 7	chorus of "There goes Bill!" then the Rabbit's voice alone--"Catch him, you by the hedge!" then silence, and
T3	136:13	the Fawn said at last. Such a soft sweet voice it had!
A11	86:33	things!" Alice began in a loud indignant voice; but she stopped herself hastily, for the White Rabbit
A11	91:12	at the White Rabbit, who said, in a low voice, "Your Majesty must cross-examine this witness."
A8	63: 6	but looked at Two. Two began, in a low voice, "Why, the fact is, you see, Miss, this here ought to
T4	147:34	very brave, generally," he went on in a low voice: "only to-day I happen to have a headache."
T9	196: 1	saw it too," the White Queen went on in a low voice, more as if she were talking to herself. "He came to
A8	67:31	do you like the Queen?" said the Cat in a low voice.
A9	73:19	together, Alice heard the King say in a low voice, to the company, generally, "You are all pardoned."
T5	152:33	very lonely here!" Alice said in a melancholy voice; and, at the thought of her loneliness, two large tears
T5	149:27	with it!" the Queen said, in a melancholy voice. "It's out of temper, I think. I've pinned it here, and
A5	36:35	different!" Alice replied in a very melancholy voice.
A11	91:18	"Treacle," said a sleepy voice behind her.
A5	35: 3	mouth, and addressed her in a languid, sleepy voice.
A4	30: 1	Next came an angry voice--the Rabbit's--"Pat! Pat! Where are you?" And then a

WAY (121)

T8	188:25	But I was thinking of a way / To feed oneself on batter, / And so go on from day to
T1	111: 7	beautiful things in it! Let's pretend there's a way of getting through into it, somehow, Kitty. Let's
T9	195:11	Alice thought she saw a way out of the difficulty, this time. "If you'll tell me
A3	23:25	crowded round her, calling out, in a confused way, "Prizes! Prizes!"
A4	33: 1	all the while, till at last it sat down a good way off, panting, with its tongue hanging out of its mouth,
T1	107: 6	The way Dinah washed her children's faces was this: first she
A2	20:24	several other curious creatures. Alice led the way, and the whole party swam to the shore.
T5	152:22	to Alice with a smile. "Now you understand the way things happen here."
T4	147:19	a fuss made about anything in all her life--the way those two bustled about--and the quantity of things
T8	189:12	wine. / I thanked him much for telling me / The way he got his wealth, / But chiefly for his wish that he /
A6	46:36	really dreadful," she muttered to herself, "the way all the creatures argue. It's enough to drive one
T3	131:22	"She must draw the train herself the rest of the way--," and so on.
T8	179:38	that Alice got behind a tree to be out of the way of the blows.
A1	7:12	nor did Alice think it so very much out of the way to hear the Rabbit say to itself "Oh dear! Oh dear! I
A10	78:17	you've cleared all the jelly-fish out of the way--"
A2	15: 1	thought Alice, "or perhaps they wo'n't walk the way I want to go! Let me see. I'll give them a new pair of
A1	9:31	were all locked; and when Alice had been all the way down one side and up the other, trying every door, she
T3	137:28	call and say 'How d'ye do?' and ask them the way out of the wood. If I could only get to the Eighth
T5	149: 5	"I'm very glad I happened to be in the way," Alice said, as she helped her to put on her shawl
T2	120:25	"I never saw such a house for getting in the way! Never!"
A8	66:16	there was generally a ridge or a furrow in the way wherever she wanted to send the hedgehog to, and, as
A1	13: 2	eats cake; but Alice had got so much into the way of expecting nothing but out-of-the-way things to
T2	122:20	and it's enough to make one wither to hear the way they go on!"
T5	153: 1	"That's the way it's done," the Queen said with great decision: "nobody
T8	188: 7	/ 'Who sail on stormy seas; / And that's the way I get my bread--/ A trifle, if you please.'
T8	189: 3	/ For wheels of Hansom-cabs. / And that's the way' (he gave a wink) / 'By which I get my wealth--/ And
A7	57: 9	"Is that the way you manage?" Alice asked.

WAY (cont.)

T2	128:19	however, one of the Knights will show you the	way--and in the Eighth Square we shall be Queens together,
A2	19:13	trying." So she began: "O Mouse, do you know the	way out of this pool? I am very tired of swimming about
T12	207:37	"By the	way, Kitty, if only you'd been really with me in my dream,
A11	86:17	The judge, by the	way, was the King; and, as he wore his crown over the wig
A11	91: 7	was, even before she got into the court, by the	way the people near the door began sneezing all at once.
T9	198: 9	Just then the door opened a little	way, and a creature with a long beak put its head out for a
A2	19: 6	something splashing about in the pool a little	way off, and she swam nearer to make out what it was: at
T4	145:24	Alice ran a little	way into the wood, and stopped under a large tree. "It can
T8	183:14	as heartily as she could. They went on a little	way in silence after this, the Knight with his eyes shut,
A6	45: 9	know what it was all about, and crept a little	way out of the wood to listen.
T8	185: 2	the ground directly. So I had a <u>very</u> little	way to fall, you see--But there <u>was</u> the danger of falling
A4	32:43	charges at the stick, running a very little	way forwards each time and a long way back, and barking
T3	137:22	sure to be two finger-posts pointing the same	way, one marked "TO TWEEDLEDUM'S HOUSE," and the other "TO
T1	119: 8	have gone straight out at the door in the same	way, if she hadn't caught hold of the door-post. She was
T1	115:32	hold of the end of the pencil, which came some	way over his shoulder, and began writing for him.
T9	201:32	I think--every poem was about fishes in some	way. Do you know why they're so fond of fishes, all about
A1	8: 7	went straight on like a tunnel for some	way, and then dipped suddenly down, so suddenly that Alice
A8	67: 8	She was looking about for some	way of escape, and wondering whether she could get away
A12	93: 9	it would be <u>quite</u> as much use in the trial one	way up as the other."
T5	150:17	"I'm sure <u>mine</u> only works one	way," Alice remarked. "I ca'n't remember things before they
A4	29:10	older than I am now? That'll be a comfort, one	way--never to be an old woman--but then--always to have
A8	68: 6	The Queen had only one	way of settling all difficulties, great or small. "Off with
T3	133: 3	"All right," said the Gnat. "Half	way up that bush, you'll see a Rocking-horse-fly, if you
T5	149: 8	looked at her in a helpless frightened sort of	way, and kept repeating something in a whisper to herself
A8	68:21	Alice could see it trying in a helpless sort of	way to fly up into a tree.
A1	9:12	went on saying to herself, in a dreamy sort of	way, "Do cats eat bats? Do cats eat bats?" and sometimes
T6	165: 8	"And a long	way beyond it on each side," Alice added.
A4	32:44	a very little way forwards each time and a long	way back, and barking hoarsely all the while, till at last
T6	165: 7	because it goes a long way before it, and a long	way behind it--"
A10	81: 6	thrown out to sea. So they had to fall a long	way. So they got their tails fast in their mouths. So they
T3	137:21	likely to happen. She went on and on, a long	way, but wherever the road divided, there were sure to be
T2	121:10	you're the right colour, and that goes a long	way."
T6	165: 7	called 'wabe' you know, because it goes a long	way before it, and a long way behind it--"
T5	152:38	what a great girl you are. Consider what a long	way you've come to-day. Consider what o'clock it is.
T2	123:45	the Queen (whom she spied out at last, a long	way off), she thought she would try the plan, this time, of
T5	156:18	to get hold of the rushes a good long	way down before breaking them off--and for a while Alice
T7	176:25	round the town?" he said. "That's a good long	way. Did you go by the old bridge, or the market-place? You
T3	130:20	At last he said "You're traveling the wrong	way," and shut up the window, and went away. "So young a
T1	110:40	like our books, only the words go the wrong	way: I know <u>that</u>, because I've held up one of our books to
T1	107: 8	paw she rubbed its face all over, the wrong	way, beginning at the nose: and just now, as I said, she
A6	51: 7	she went on. "Would you tell me, please, which	way I ought to go from here?"
A1	12:38	little bit, and said anxiously to herself "Which	way? Which way?", holding her hand on the top of her head
A1	12:40	her hand on the top of her head to feel which	way it was growing; and she was quite surprised to find
A1	9:15	either question, it didn't much matter which	way she put it. She felt that she was dozing off, and had
A6	51:12	"Then it doesn't matter which	way you go," said the Cat.
T3	131: 1	dressed in white paper), "ought to know which	way she's going, even if she doesn't know her own name!"
A1	12:39	and said anxiously to herself "Which way? Which	way?", holding her hand on the top of her head to feel
A6	52:20	just as if the Cat had come back in a natural	way.
A10	83: 1	if anything would <u>ever</u> happen in a natural	way again.
T1	119:11	to find herself walking again in the natural	way.
T8	182:24	"Only in the usual	way," Alice said, smiling.
T9	195:31	The Red Queen said "That's a poor thin	way of doing things. Now <u>here</u>, we mostly have days and
A1	13: 4	dull and stupid for life to go on in the common	way.
T2	128:31	<u>can</u> run very fast!" thought Alice), there was no	way of guessing, but she was gone, and Alice began to
A9	71:14	as usual," said the Duchess: "what a clear	way you have of putting things!"
T1	114:16	out of breath. "Mind you come up--the regular	way--don't get blown up!"
A7	60:36	go <u>there</u> again!" said Alice, as she picked her	way through the wood. "It's the stupidest tea-party I ever
T5	158:18	wouldn't do?" thought Alice, as she groped her	way among the tables and chairs, for the shop was very dark
A2	19: 2	Alice, as she swam about, trying to find her	way out. "I shall be punished for it now, I suppose, by
A4	27:36	By this time she had found her	way into a tidy little room with a table in the window, and
T2	124:10	as well as she could, that she had lost her	way.
T3	131: 4	and said in a loud voice, "She ought to know her	way to the ticket-office, even if she doesn't know her
A1	12:36	smaller, I can creep under the door: so either	way I'll get into the garden, and I don't care which
T2	123:39	the Rose: "<u>I</u> should advise you to walk the other	way."
T3	129:25	"I think I'll go down the other	way," she said after a pause; "and perhaps I may visit the
T1	110:33	our drawing-room, only the things go the other	way. I can see all of it when I get upon a chair--all but
T2	120: 8	to the house! Well then, I'll try it the other	way."
T9	195:21	hastily corrected herself. "I meant the other	way."
A6	49:30	grunt," said Alice; "that's not at all a proper	way of expressing yourself."
A6	49:22	As soon as she had made out the proper	way of nursing it (which was to twist it up into a sort of
T6	166: 5	for 'from home'--meaning that they'd lost their	way, you know."
T2	124:11	"I don't know what you mean by <u>your</u>	way," said the Queen: "all the ways about here belong to <u>me</u>
A12	98:25	hurried by--the frightened Mouse splashed his	way through the neighbouring pool--she could hear the
A7	57:18	on, you know," the Hatter continued, "in this	way:--
T8	180:12	battle ended with their both falling off in this	way, side by side. When they got up again, they shook hands
A2	15:21	might well say this), "to go on crying in this	way! Stop this moment, I tell you!" But she went on all the
T3	135:37	She was rambling on in this	way when she reached the wood: it looked very cool and
T9	204:12	beckoning to her impatiently to get out of its	way.
A2	19:15	O Mouse!" (Alice thought this must be the right	way of speaking to a mouse: she had never done such a thing

WAY (cont.)

T5	149:17	"If your Majesty will only tell me the right way to begin, I'll do it as well as I can."
T1	116:15	up to a glass, the words will all go the right way again."
A6	50:19	saying to herself "if one only knew the right way to change them--" when she was a little startled by
A2	14: 9	myself about you: you must manage the best way you can--but I must be kind to them," thought Alice,
A3	23: 5	"Why," said the Dodo, "the best way to explain it is to do it." (And, as you might like to
T4	139:26	the other one's feelings; so, as the best way out of the difficulty, she took hold of both hands at
T4	139:10	Alice said politely, "which is the best way out of this wood. it's getting so dark. Would you tell
T8	184:26	"Well, just then I was inventing a new way of getting over a gate--would you like to hear it?"
A9	70:30	game's going on rather better now," she said, by way of keeping up the conversation a little.
T3	135:26	she thought to herself, and this was the only way to the Eighth Square.
A12	93: 6	thing was waving its tail about in a melancholy way, being quite unable to move. She soon got it out again,
T2	125: 7	went on: "--and I thought I'd try and find my way to the top of that hill--"
A4	32:20	size again; and the second thing is to find my way into that lovely garden. I think that will be the best
A7	59: 7	to fancy to herself what such an extraordinary way of living would be like, but it puzzled her too much:
A5	42:30	and added, with a kind of sob, "I've tried every way, but nothing seems to suit them!"

WOOD (38)

T3	135:22	She very soon came to an open field, with a wood on the other side of it: it looked much darker than the
T3	131:27	to this railway journey at all--I was in a wood just now--and I wish I could get back there!"
T3	135:37	rambling on in this way when she reached the wood: it looked very cool and shady. "Well, at any rate it's
T3	135:27	"This must be the wood," she said thoughtfully to herself, "where things have
T8	181: 4	Knight. "I'll see you safe to the end of the wood--and then I must go back, you know. That's the end of
T8	186:29	you." They had just come to the end of the wood.
T8	182:11	help me on. I'll go with you to the end of the wood--What's that dish for?"
A6	45: 3	a footman in livery came running out of the wood--(she considered him to be a footman because he was in
T4	146: 2	"At any rate, I'd better be getting out of the wood, for really it's coming on very dark. Do you think it's
T7	174:23	across the country! She came flying out of the wood over yonder--How fast those Queens can run!"
T4	140:11	"Would you tell me which road leads out of the wood?"
T7	170: 3	and Alice was very glad to get out of the wood into an open place, where she found the White King
T3	137:28	'How d'ye do?' and ask them the way out of the wood. If I could only get to the Eighth Square before it
A6	45:10	all about, and crept a little way out of the wood to listen.
T3	137:17	answer, as there was only one road through the wood, and the two finger-posts both pointed along it. "I'll
T7	170: 8	any soldiers, my dear, as you came through the wood?"
T7	169: 1	next moment soldiers came running through the wood, at first in twos and threes, then ten or twenty
T3	137: 3	So they walked on together through the wood, Alice with her arms clasped lovingly round the soft
A7	60:36	said Alice, as she picked her way through the wood. "It's the stupidest tea-party I ever was at in all my
T5	149: 3	the White Queen came running wildly through the wood, with both arms stretched out wide, as if she were
T8W	13: 2	a deep sigh, which seemed to come from the wood behind her.
A5	43: 1	"And just as I'd taken the highest tree in the wood," continued the Pigeon, raising its voice to a shriek,
T4	145:27	its wings so--it makes quite a hurricane in the wood--here's somebody's shawl being blown away!"
T4	144:24	like the puffing of a large steam-engine in the wood near them, though she feared it was more likely to be a
T3	132:39	say," the Gnat replied. "Further on, in the wood down there, they've got no names--however, go on with
T6	166: 9	you'll hear it done, maybe--down in the wood yonder--and, when you've once heard it, you'll be quite
A4	32:19	Alice to herself, as she wandered about in the wood, "is to grow to my right size again; and the second
T4	147:12	the two brothers went off hand-in-hand into the wood, and returned in a minute with their arms full of
A6	46: 6	much at this, that she had to run back into the wood for fear of their hearing her; and, when she next
T4	145:24	Alice ran a little way into the wood, and stopped under a large tree. "It can never get at
T2	128:30	the air, or whether she ran quickly into the wood ("and she can run very fast!" thought Alice), there was
A6	50:15	relieved to see it trot away quietly into the wood. "If it had grown up," she said to herself, "it would
T3	133: 4	if you look. It's made entirely of wood, and gets about by swinging itself from branch to
A4	32:17	could, and soon found herself safe in a thick wood.
T4	139:11	politely, "which is the best way out of this wood: it's getting so dark. Would you tell me, please?"
T5	152:32	rule. You must be very happy, living in this wood, and being glad whenever you like!"
T3	135:23	side of it: it looked much darker than the last wood, and Alice felt a little timid about going into it.
T1	118:11	of flame, / Came whiffling through the tulgey wood, / And burbled as it came!

WORK (14)

T8	188:35	eyes / Among the heather bright, / And work them into waistcoat-buttons / In the silent night. /
T6	164: 5	"When I make a word do a lot of work like that," said Humpty Dumpty, "I always pay it extra
T8	186:10	next course?" said Alice. "Well, that was quick work, certainly!"
T7	174:14	for refreshments!" Haigha and Hatta set to work at once, carrying round trays of white and brown bread.
A6	48:10	of soup off the fire, and at once set to work throwing everything within her reach at the Duchess and
A5	43:33	pieces of mushroom in her hands, and she set to work very carefully, nibbling first at one and then at the
A7	61: 2	door that led into the garden. Then she set to work nibbling at the mushroom (she had kept a piece of it in
A1	13: 5	So she set to work, and very soon finished off the cake. * * * * * * * * *
A5	41:43	as she was shrinking rapidly: so she set to work at once to eat some of the other bit. Her chin was
A10	78: 4	in his throat," said the Gryphon; and it set to work shaking him and punching him in the back. At last the
A12	93:12	been found and handed back to them, they set to work very diligently to write out a history of the accident,
T9	195: 4	after so much thinking." So they set to work and fanned her with bunches of leaves, till she had to
T1	107: 9	nose: and just now, as I said, she was hard at work on the white kitten, which was lying quite still and
A6	48:25	off a little of her knowledge. "Just think what work it would make with the day and night! You see the earth